Holy Bible

Complete Authorized King James Version in KWIKSCAN™

Berean
Bible Publishers
P.O. Box 91617
Louisville, Kentucky 40291
www.bereanbiblepublishers.com

ISBN: 978-0-9798641-3-1

HOLY BIBLE

Complete Authorized King James Version
In
KWIKSCAN™

KWIKSCAN™ EDITORIAL STAFF

Editor In Chief: M.F. Morris, D.D.
Editor: Nila Vae L. Morris
Executive Editor:
Scott M. Morris
Managing Editor:
Scott P. Jones
Statistical Editor:
Julianne Morris
Senior Scan Editor:
Karl David, Ph.D.
Warren Humphrey, Ph.D.
Scan Review Editor:
George Overby, Ph.D.
Editor of Introductions:
Scott M. Morris
Business Manager:
Kenneth Nichols

Scan Editorial Staff:
Senior Coordinator:
Grace Taylor
Proof Editors:
Ronald C. Hunt
Beverly C. Hunt
Elven Fairchild
Molly Ann Fairchild
Jean Gibson
Mitchell Riggs
Carolyn A. Boltin
Computer Scan Editor:
Scott P. Jones
Typesetting Editor:
Alfred Rodriquez
Computer Systems:
Wayne Doege

HOW **KWIKSCAN**™ BENEFITS YOU

Try a simple experiment and immediately you will see the tremendous benefits of **KWIKSCAN**™. First, read every word in the text below. Secondly, go back through the text reading only those words in bold type. Once you read a couple of columns, you will never want to read anything printed the traditional way again.

- **KWIKSCAN™ words** (The words printed in bold type)
- **comprise about 50% of a** total
- **Text,** and often much less.
- **And,** as you are about to find out,
- **by reading the**
- **bold words**
- **only, you** will
- **reduce reading time by up**
- **to Two Thirds!** (Much less time for some people and a little more for others.)
- **This is true because** of two reasons. The first is obvious.
- **You simply eliminate** the necessity of
- **reading about half the**
- **words** – words that can be left out without changing the overall meaning of the text.
- **Secondly,** and less obvious until you think about it,
- **you eliminate left to right**
- **head and or eyemovement**
- **– a big problem** many have
- **in reading and** also
- **a consumer of** large chunks of your valuable

- **time.**
- **Besides** the benefits of
- **saving** huge amounts of
- **time, KWIKSCAN**™ also
- **increases** the
- **understanding** of most readers
- **by making the text** less complicated and
- **easier to follow.**
- **It helps retention too.** (You will remember more of what you read!)
- **If right now, you are**
- **reading just the bold words** when you finish,
- **you will read only**
- **119 out of** a total of
- **256 words,** and you will do it
- **in about one-third the time**
- **required to read the entire**
- **text. Yes, after** reading the exciting new
- **KWIKSCAN**™ way,
- **you will never want to go**
- **back to the old** and ordinary
- **ways of reading** and you will know why KWIKSCAN™ is called "The greatest step forward in reading since the invention of the printing press."

Statistical Information

The Old Testament

Verses: **23,137**
Chapters: **929**
Books: **39**
Total Words: **610,362**
Scan Words: **260,139**

STATISTICS FOR:
The New Testament

Verses: **7,957**
Chapters: **260**
Books: **27**
Total Words: **180,551**
Scan Words: **87,700**

STATISTICS FOR:
The Complete Bible

Verses: **31,094**
Chapters: **1,189**
Books: **66**
Total Words: **790,913**
Scan Words: **347,839**

AVERAGE **SCAN** FOR THE OLD TESTAMENT: 43%

AVERAGE **SCAN** FOR THE NEW TESTAMENT: 46%

AVERAGE **SCAN** FOR THE HOLY BIBLE: 44.5%

12-3-12
CHRISTIAN GROWTH, WITNESSING, AND MINISTRY PLAN

12-3-12 was developed and launched in the great First Baptist Church of Van Nuys, California under the leadership of Dr. Jess Moody, Senior Pastor.

The Plan is designed to involve every member of the church in active ministry:

1. Consistently Reading and Studying the Bible.
2. Witnessing and Winning the Lost.
3. Personally Discipling those Won and Leading Them Into Their Own Ministry.

Benefits in spiritual and numerical growth derived from 12-3-12 have been tremendous, involving hundreds of church members in active ministry for the first time and winning hundreds more to Christ. The Plan utilizes the New Testament and the Holy Bible in KWIKSCAN™ as its basic text. For more information write or call:

SUGGESTED PLANS
FOR BIBLE READING AND STUDY

Thy Word have I hid in mine heart that I might not sin against Thee.

Psalm 119:11

Thy Word is a lamp unto my feet and a light unto my pathway.

Psalm 119:105

Introduction

The time requirements to read scriptural passages printed in KWIKSCAN™ are based on definitive research studies. These studies show that average slow readers can read 250 words per minute (more skilled readers may read much faster). However, the time requirements of the PLANS presented here, are based on a reading level of 250 words per minute.

Furthermore, the time requirements relate to reading the SCAN (words printed in larger, bold-faced type). The publisher encourages readers to study every word of the complete text as time permits. "All scripture is given by inspiration of God..." (II Timothy 3:16) and "all scripture" is profitable for Christian growth. On the other hand, KWIKSCAN™ is a marvelous breakthrough for rapid review and learning enhancement, as proved by research studies.

Why should Bibles be printed any other way? Through KWIKSCAN™, the reader has every word of a traditional text plus enormous benefits for rapid review, greater understanding and retention.

PLAN A
READING THE NEW TESTAMENT IN ONE MONTH OR TWELVE TIMES IN ONE YEAR

(Reading Time — 8 - 12 Minutes Each Day)

Reading Schedule

Day	Check √	Day	Check √	Day	Check √
1. Matt. 1:1 - 9:27	_	11. 19:44 - **John** 1:31	_	21. 5:3 - 15:9	_
2. 9:28 - 16:4	_	12. 1:32 - 7:36	_	22. 15:10 - **II Cor.** 12:4	_
3. 16:5 - 23:4	_	13. 7:37 - 13:33	_	23. 12:5 - **Eph.** 5:19	_
4. 23:5 - 28:20	_	14. 13:34 - 21:17	_	24. 5:20 - **I Thes.** 4:16	_
5. **Mark** 1:1 - 7:31	_	15. 21:18 - **Acts** 7:57	_	25. 4:17 - **Titus** 2:13	_
6. 7:32 - 13:31	_	16. 7:58 - 14:13	_	26. 2:14 - **Heb.** 11:8	_
7. 13:32 - **Luke** 3:15	_	17. 14:14 - 21:14	_	27. 11:9 - **I Pt.** 3:22	_
8. 3:16 - 8:39	_	18. 21:15 - 28:17	_	28. 4:1 - **Jude** 1:25	_
9. 8:40 - 13:11	_	19. 28:18 - **Rom.** 9:19	_	29. **Rev.** 1:1 - 12:17	_
10. 13:12 - 19:43	_	20. 9:20 - **I Cor.** 5:2	_	30. 13:1 - 22:21	_

Simplified Reading Schedule — *Just read 13 pages of the New Testament*

PLAN B
READING THE COMPLETE BIBLE
IN ONE YEAR

(Reading Time — 5 Minutes Each Day)

Reading Schedule

Day	Check √	Day	Check √	Day	Check √
1. **Gen.** 1:1 - 3:19	_	45. 26:21 - **Num.** 1:28	_	89. 13:1 - 15:6	_
2. 3:20 - 5:32	_	46. 1:29 - 4:7	_	90. 15:7 - 17:27	_
3. 6:1 - 7:24	_	47. 4:8 - 6:13	_	91. 17:28 - 19:17	_
4. 8:1 - 12:6	_	48. 6:14 - 9:13	_	92. 19:18 - 21:15	_
5. 12:7 - 16:8	_	49. 9:14 - 11:31	_	93. 22:1 - 24:10	_
6. 16:9 - 19:15	_	50. 11:32 - 14:45	_	94. 24:11 - 26:14	_
7. 19:16 - 21:34	_	51. 15:1 - 16:50	_	95. 26:15 - 30:7	_
8. 22:1 - 24:48	_	52. 17:1 - 19:17	_	96. 30:8 - **II Sam.** 2:12	_
9. 24:49 - 27:10	_	53. 19:18 - 22:11	_	97. 2:13 - 14:12	_
10. 27:11 - 29:6	_	54. 22:12 - 24:13	_	98. 5:11 - 9:6	_
11. 29:7 - 31:27	_	55. 24:14 - 28:10	_	99. 9:7 - 12:12	_
12. 31:28 - 34:6	_	56. 28:11 - 31:21	_	100. 12:13 - 14:12	_
13. 34:7 - 37:31	_	57. 31:22 - 34:7	_	101. 14:13 - 16:14	_
14. 37:32 - 40:11	_	58. 34:8 - **Deut.** 1:27	_	102. 16:15 - 18:33	_
15. 40:12 - 42:24	_	59. 1:28 - 4:5	_	103. 19:1 - 20:26	_
16. 42:25 - 45:15	_	60. 4:6 - 6:9	_	104. 21:1 - 24:11	_
17. 45:16 - 49:12	_	61. 6:10 - 10:8	_	105. 24:12 - **I Kgs.** 1:53	_
18. 49:13 - **Ex.** 2:25	_	62. 10:9 - 14:7	_	106. 2:1 - 3:24	_
19. 3:1 - 5:12	_	63. 14:8 - 18:5	_	107. 3:25 - 6:38	_
20. 5:13 - 8:18	_	64. 18:6 - 21:13	_	108. 7:1 - 8:63	_
21. 8:19 - 10:16	_	65. 21:14 - 23:25	_	109. 8:64 - 11:14	_
22. 10:17 - 12:38	_	66. 24:1 - 27:26	_	110. 11:15 - 13:4	_
23. 12:39 - 14:31	_	67. 28:1 - 29:21	_	111. 13:5 - 15:7	_
24. 15:1 - 17:5	_	68. 29:22 - 32:43	_	112. 15:8 - 17:20	_
25. 17:6 - 20:12	_	69. 32:44 - **Josh.** 3:5	_	113. 17:21 - 19:6	_
26. 20:13 - 22:19	_	70. 3:6 - 6:18	_	114. 19:7 - 20:35	_
27. 22:20 - 25:19	_	71. 6:19 - 9:4	_	115. 20:36 - 22:26	_
28. 25:20 - 27:15	_	72. 9:5 - 11:11	_	116. 22:27 - **II Kgs.** 2:7	_
29. 27:16 - 29:16	_	73. 11:12 - 18:4	_	117. 2:18 - 4:30	_
30. 29:17 - 30:38	_	74. 18:5 - 22:31	_	118. 4:31 - 6:12	_
31. 31:1 - 33:10	_	75. 22:32 - **Jud.** 1:11	_	119. 6:13 - 8:13	_
32. 33:11 - 35:24	_	76. 1:12 - 3:24	_	120. 8:14 - 10:11	_
33. 35:25 - 39:43	_	77. 3:25 - 6:16	_	121. 10:12 - 13:5	_
34. 40:1 - **Lev.** 2:16	_	78. 6:17 - 8:17	_	122. 13:6 - 15:25	_
35. 3:1 - 5:19	_	79. 8:18 - 10:13	_	123. 15:26 - 18:4	_
36. 6:1 - 8:8	_	80. 10:14 - 13:8	_	124. 18:5 - 19:34	_
37. 8:9 - 10:15	_	81. 13:9 - 15:20	_	125. 19:35 - 22:20	_
38. 10:16 - 13:22	_	82. 16:1 - 20:10	_	126. 23:1 - 25:4	_
39. 13:23 - 14:21	_	83. 20:11 - **Ruth** 1:13	_	127. 25:5 - **I Chr.** 6:47	_
40. 14:22 - 16:16	_	84. 1:14 - 4:22	_	128. 6:48 - 11:8	_
41. 16:17 - 19:26	_	85. **I Sam.** 1:1 - 3:8	_	129. 11:9 - 14:17	_
42. 19:27 - 22:26	_	86. 3:9 - 7:4	_	130. 15:1 - 18:7	_
43. 22:27 - 24:23	_	87. 7:5 - 10:8	_	131. 18:8 - 21:30	_
44. 25:1 - 26:20	_	88. 10:9 - 12:25	_	132. 22:1 - 28:8	_

133. 28:9 - **II Chr.** 3:3		**184.** 130:1 - 139:8		**235.** 51:56 - **Lam.** 1:15	
134. 3:4 - 6:36		**185.** 139:9 - 145:21		**236.** 1:16 - 3:66	
135. 6:37 - 9:29		**186.** 146:1 - **Pro.** 2:11		**237.** 4:1 - **Ez.** 3:7	
136. 9:30 - 14:3		**187.** 2:12 - 6:29		**238.** 3:8 - 6:4	
137. 14:4 - 18:12		**188.** 6:30 - 10:27		**239.** 6:5 - 9:11	
138. 18:13 - 20:30		**189.** 10:28 - 13:6		**240.** 10:1 - 12:20	
139. 20:31 - 24:4		**190.** 13:7 - 15:12		**241.** 12:21 - 16:8	
140. 24:5 - 26:6		**191.** 15:13 - 17:5		**242.** 16:9 - 17:18	
141. 26:7 - 29:16		**192.** 17:6 - 19:14		**243.** 17:19 - 20:27	
142. 29:17 - 32:4		**193.** 19:15 - 21:16		**244.** 20:28 - 22:19	
143. 32:5 - 34:11		**194.** 21:17 - 23:27		**245.** 22:20 - 24:9	
144. 34:12 - 36:23		**195.** 23:28 - 25:28		**246.** 24:10 - 27:18	
145. Ezra 1:1 - 5:2		**196.** 26:1 - 28:9		**247.** 27:19 - 30:6	
146. 5:3 - 8:2		**197.** 28:10 - 30:17		**248.** 30:7 - 33:6	
147. 8:3 - 10:44		**198.** 30:18 - **Ecc.** 2:17		**249.** 33:7 - 35:6	
148. Neh. 1:1 - 4:12		**199.** 2:18 - 7:3		**250.** 35:7 - 37:22	
149. 4:13 - 7:50		**200.** 7:4 - 11:6		**251.** 37:23 - 40:9	
150. 7:51 - 9:35		**201.** 11:7 - **Song** 5:7		**252.** 40:10 - 42:12	
151. 9:36 - 13:14		**202.** 5:8 - **Isa.** 2:9		**253.** 42:13 - 44:18	
152. 13:15 - **Est.** 3:8		**203.** 2:10 - 5:30		**254.** 44:19 - 46:16	
153. 3:9 - 7:2		**204.** 6:1 - 9:17		**255.** 46:17 - 48:35	
154. 7:3 - 10:3		**205.** 9:18 - 14:6		**256. Dan.** 1:1 - 2:49	
155. Job 1:1 - 5:19		**206.** 14:7 - 19:20		**257.** 3:1 - 5:6	
156. 5:20 - 10:8		**207.** 19:20 - 25:9		**258.** 5:7 - 7:10	
157. 10:9 - 15:12		**208.** 25:10 - 30:4		**259.** 7:11 - 9:24	
158. 15:13 - 20:21		**209.** 30:5 - 34:11		**260.** 9:25 - 11:37	
159. 20:22 - 24:22		**210.** 34:12 - 38:5		**261.** 11:38 - **Hos.** 4:5	
160. 24:23 - 31:27		**211.** 38:6 - 42:3		**262.** 4:6 - 10:11	
161. 31:28 - 34:26		**212.** 42:4 - 45:18		**263.** 10:12 - **Joel** 2:18	
162. 34:27 - 39:10		**213.** 45:19 - 49:17		**264.** 2:19 - **Amos** 3:15	
163. 39:11 - **Ps.** 2:10		**214.** 49:18 - 53:3		**265.** 4:1 - 8:6	
164. 2:11 - 10:11		**215.** 53:4 - 57:14		**266.** 8:7 - **Jon.** 2:10	
165. 10:12 - 18:36		**216.** 57:15 - 60:22		**267.** 3:1 - **Micah** 4:10	
166. 18:37 - 24:10		**217.** 61:1 - 65:20		**268.** 4:11 - **Nahum** 2:13	
167. 25:1 - 31:8		**218.** 65:21 - **Jer.** 2:37		**269.** 3:1 - **Zeph.** 1:8	
168. 31:9 - 37:23		**219.** 3:1 - 5:26		**270.** 1:9 - **Hag.** 2:13	
169. 37:24 - 44:4		**220.** 5:27 - 8:22		**271.** 2:14 - **Zech.** 5:8	
170. 44:5 - 50:23		**221.** 9:1 - 12:5		**272.** 5:9 - 10:4	
171. 51:1 - 59:10		**222.** 12:6 - 16:4		**273.** 10:5 - 14:21	
172. 59:11 - 67:7		**223.** 16:5 - 19:10		**274. Mal.** 1:1 - 4:6	
173. 68:1 - 72:16		**224.** 19:11 - 23:8		**275. Matt.** 1:1 - 5:2	
174. 72:17 - 78:28		**225.** 28:9 - 26:10		**276.** 5:3 - 6:34	
175. 78:29 - 84:9		**226.** 26:11 - 29:10		**277.** 7:1 - 9:21	
176. 84:10 - 89:52		**227.** 29:11 - 31:24		**278.** 9:22 - 12:1	
177. 90:1 - 97:7		**228.** 31:25 - 33:18		**279.** 12:2 - 13:32	
178. 97:8 - 104:23		**229.** 33:19 - 36:18		**280.** 13:33 - 15:31	
179. 104:24 - 107:21		**230.** 36:19 - 39:3		**281.** 15:32 - 18:13	
180. 107:22 - 114:8		**231.** 39:4 - 42:11		**282.** 18:14 - 20:23	
181. 115:1 - 119:49		**232.** 42:12 - 46:12		**283.** 20:24 - 22:23	
182. 119:50 - 119:151		**233.** 46:13 - 49:25		**284.** 22:24 - 24:39	
183. 119:152 - 129:8		**234.** 49:26 - 51:55		**285.** 24:40 - 26:36	

Day	Check √	Day	Check √	Day	Check √
286. 26:37 - 27:51	_	**313.** 10:3 - 12:11	_	**340.** 3:17 - 8:18	_
287. 27:52 - **Mk.** 2:15	_	**314.** 12:12 - 14:21	_	**341.** 8:19 - 12:18	_
288. 2:16 - 5:2	_	**315.** 14:22 - 17:22	_	**342.** 12:19 - **Gal.** 3:24	_
289. 5:3 - 6:48	_	**316.** 17:23 - 19:31	_	**343.** 3:25 - **Eph.** 1:23	_
290. 6:49 - 9:9	_	**317.** 19:32 - **Acts** 1:8	_	**344.** 2:1 - 6:4	_
291. 9:10 - 10:43	_	**318.** 1:9 - 3:26	_	**345.** 6:5 - **Phil.** 3:14	_
292. 10:44 - 12:39	_	**319.** 4:1 - 5:41	_	**346.** 3:15 - **Col.** 3:25	_
293. 12:40 - 14:42	_	**320.** 5:42 - 8:29	_	**347.** 4:1 - **I Thes.** 2:28	_
294. 14:43 - 16:20	_	**321.** 8:30 - 10:27	_	**348.** **II Thes.** 1:1 -	_
295. **Lk.** 1:1 - 2:26	_	**322.** 10:28 - 13:7	_	**ITimothy.** 4:2	
296. 2:27 - 4:34	_	**323.** 13:8 - 15:9	_	**349.** 4:3 - **II Tm.** 2:19	_
297. 4:35 - 6:25	_	**324.** 15:10 - 17:13	_	**350.** 2:20 - **Phlm.** 1:25	_
298. 6:26 - 7:50	_	**325.** 17:14 - 19:25	_	**351.** **Heb.** 1:1 - 5:14	_
299. 8:1 - 9:18	_	**326.** 19:26 - 21:27	_	**352.** 6:1 - 9:20	_
300. 9:19 - 10:31	_	**327.** 21:28 - 23:32		**353.** 9:21 - 12:5	
301. 10:32 - 12:14	_	**328.** 23:33 - 26:22		**354.** 12:6 - **James** 2:17	
302. 12:15 - 14:3	_	**329.** 26:23 - 28:31		**355.** 2:18 - **I Pet.** 1:25	
303. 14:4 - 16:16		**330.** **Rom.** 1:1 - 4:5		**356.** 2:1 - 5:14	
304. 16:17 - 18:31		**331.** 4:6 - 7:25		**357.** **II Pet.** 1:1 - 5:14	
305. 18:32 - 20:31		**332.** 8:1 - 11:10		**358.** **I Jn.** 1:6 - 5:13	
306. 20:32 - 22:46		**333.** 11:11 - 13:14		**359.** 5:14 - **Rev.** 2:2	
307. 22:47 - 24:19		**334.** 14:1 - **I Cor.** 1:18		**360.** 2:3 - 5:8	
308. 24:20 - **Jn.** 2:15		**335.** 1:19 - 6:3		**361.** 5:9 - 9:15	
309. 2:16 - 4:49		**336.** 6:4 - 9:15		**362.** 9:16 - 13:10	
310. 4:50 - 6:42		**337.** 9:16 - 12:23		**363.** 13:11 - 17:4	
311. 6:43 - 8:15		**338.** 12:24 - 15:24		**364.** 17:5 - 20:3	
312. 8:16 - 10:2		**339.** 15:25 - **II Cor.** 3:16		**365.** 20:4 - 22:21	

Simplified Reading Schedule — *Just read 4 1/2 pages of the Bible text each day for 365 days.*

PLAN C
READING THE NEW TESTAMENT IN ONE MONTH (OR TWELVE TIMES IN ONE YEAR) AND THE OLD TESTAMENT ONCE DURING THE YEAR.

New Testament Daily Reading Schedule
(The Same as Plan A)

Old Testament
(Reading Time — 3 Minutes Each Day)

Reading Schedule

Day	Check √	Day	Check √	Day	Check √
1. Gen. 1:1 - 3:5	_	**7.** 18:10 - 19:32	_	**13.** 29:9 - 30:43	_
2. 3:6 - 4:26	_	**8.** 19:33 - 21:34	_	**14.** 31:1 - 32:21	_
3. 5:1 - 8:22	_	**9.** 22:1 - 24:14	_	**15.** 32:22 - 34:31	_
4. 9:1 - 12:5	_	**10.** 24:15 - 25:34	_	**16.** 35:1 - 37:34	_
5. 12:6 - 15:7		**11.** 26:1 - 27:29		**17.** 37:35 - 40:12	
6. 15:8 - 18:9		**12.** 27:30 - 29:8		**18.** 40:13 - 41:37	

Day	Check √	Day	Check √	Day	Check √	Day	Check √
19. 41:38 - 43:25		**70.** 21:9 - 22:34		**121.** 17:18 - 18:16			
20. 43:26 - 45:28		**71.** 22:35 - 25:3		**122.** 18:17 - 20:10			
21. 46:1 - 48:22		**72.** 25:4 - 27:23		**123.** 20:11 - 21:15			
22. 49:1 - 50:26		**73.** 28:1 - 31:7		**124.** 22:1 - 23:23			
23. Ex. 1:1 - 3:9		**74.** 31:8 - 32:7		**125.** 23:24 - 25:25			
24. 3:10 - 5:3		**75.** 32:8 - 35:5		**126.** 25:26 - 27:7			
25. 5:4 - 7:17		**76.** 35:6 - **Deut.** 1:21		**127.** 27:6 - 30:7			
26. 7:18 - 9:9		**77.** 1:22 - 3:7		**128.** 30:8 - **II Sam.** 1:18			
27. 9:10 - 11:7		**78.** 3:8 - 4:32		**129.** 1:19 - 3:24			
28. 11:8 - 12:42		**79.** 4:33 - 6:25		**130.** 3:25 - 6:7			
29. 12:43 - 14:20		**80.** 7:1 - 9:29		**131.** 6:8 - 9:6			
30. 14:21 - 16:11		**81.** 10:1 - 12:17		**132.** 9:7 - 11:27			
31. 16:12 - 18:15		**82.** 12:18 - 15:9		**133.** 12:1 - 13:17			
32. 18:16 - 20:20		**83.** 15:10 - 18:14		**134.** 13:18 - 14:33			
33. 20:21 - 22:8		**84.** 18:15 - 21:3		**135.** 15:1 - 16:19			
34. 22:9 - 24:3		**85.** 21:4 - 22:30		**136.** 16:20 - 18:22			
35. 23:4 - 26:5		**86.** 23:1 - 25:5		**137.** 18:23 - 19:40			
36. 26:6 - 27:20		**87.** 25:6 - 28:17		**138.** 19:41 - 22:4			
37. 27:21 - 29:3		**88.** 28:18 - 29:17		**139.** 22:5 - 24:15			
38. 29:4 - 30:4		**89.** 29:18 - 31:30		**140.** 24:16 - **I Kgs.** 1:47			
39. 30:5 - 32:4		**90.** 32:1 - 33:22		**141.** 1:48 - 2:46			
40. 32:5 - 33:14		**91.** 33:23 - **Josh.** 2:24		**142.** 3:1 - 4:34			
41. 33:15 - 35:2		**92.** 3:1 - 6:4		**143.** 5:1 - 7:39			
42. 35:3 - 38:22		**93.** 6:5 - 7:26		**144.** 7:40 - 8:50			
43. 38:23 - 40:22		**94.** 8:1 - 9:27		**145.** 8:51 - 10:10			
44. 40:23 - **Lev.** 2:14		**95.** 10:1 - 11:18		**146.** 10:11 - 11:35			
45. 2:15 - 5:3		**96.** 11:19 - 17:13		**147.** 11:36 - 13:9			
46. 5:4 - 6:30		**97.** 17:14 - 22:8		**148.** 13:10 - 14:23			
47. 7:1 - 8:18		**98.** 22:9 - 23:14		**149.** 14:24 - 16:23			
48. 8:19 - 10:9		**99.** 23:15 - **Jud.** 1:13		**150.** 16:24 - 18:16			
49. 10:10 - 12:8		**100.** 1:14 - 3:7		**151.** 18:17 - 19:10			
50. 13:1 - 13:46		**101.** 3:8 - 5:8		**152.** 19:11 - 20:28			
51. 13:47 - 14:31		**102.** 5:9 - 6:34		**153.** 20:29 - 21:29			
52. 14:32 - 16:12		**103.** 6:35 - 8:24		**154.** 22:1 - 22:53			
53. 16:13 - 18:30		**104.** 8:25 - 9:48		**155. II Kgs.** 1:1 - 2:25			
54. 19:1 - 20:20		**105.** 9:49 - 11:30		**156.** 3:1 - 4:22			
55. 20:21 - 23:6		**106.** 11:31 - 13:25		**157.** 4:23 - 5:17			
56. 23:7 - 24:13		**107.** 14:1 - 15:20		**158.** 5:18 - 6:33			
57. 24:14 - 25:44		**108.** 16:1 - 17:5		**159.** 7:1 - 8:24			
58. 25:45 - 27:4		**109.** 17:6 - 19:10		**160.** 8:25 - 10:5			
59. 27:5 - **Num.** 1:50		**110.** 19:11 - 20:27		**161.** 10:6 - 11:18			
60. 1:51 - 3:48		**111.** 20:28 - **Ruth** 1:12		**162.** 11:19 - 14:7			
61. 3:49 - 5:18		**112.** 1:13 - 3:18		**163.** 14:8 - 15:34			
62. 5:19 - 7:59		**113.** 4:1 - **I Sam.** 2:11		**164.** 15:35 - 17:28			
63. 7:60 - 9:23		**114.** 2:12 - 4:5		**165.** 17:29 - 19:6			
64. 10:1 - 11:22		**115.** 4:6 - 7:3		**167.** 19:7 - 20:21			
65. 11:23 - 14:10		**116.** 7:4 - 10:2		**168.** 23:8 - 24:20			
66. 14:11 - 15:41		**117.** 10:3 - 11:15		**169.** 25:1 - **I Chr.** 4:43			
67. 16:1 - 17:11		**118.** 12:1 - 14:11		**170.** 5:1 - 8:40			
68. 17:12 - 19:12		**119.** 14:12 - 15:18		**171.** 9:1 - 11:47			
69. 19:13 - 21:8		**120.** 15:19 - 17:17		**172.** 12:1 - 14:17			

Day	Check √	Day	Check √	Day	Check √
173. 15:1 - 17:8	_	**224.** 31:13 - 35:23	_	**275.** 17:4 - 21:10	_
174. 17:9 - 20:8	_	**225.** 35:24 - 39:13	_	**276.** 21:11 - 25:12	_
175. 21:1 - 23:4	_	**226.** 40:1 - 44:26	_	**277.** 26:1 - 29:9	_
176. 23:5 - 28:11	_	**227.** 45:1 - 50:13	_	**278.** 29:10 - 32:7	_
177. 28:12 - **II Chr.** 2:5	_	**228.** 50:14 - 56:6	_	**279.** 32:8 - 36:7	_
178. 2:6 - 5:14	_	**229.** 56:7 - 62:12	_	**280.** 36:8 - 38:9	_
179. 6:1 - 7:13	_	**230.** 63:1 - 68:17	_	**281.** 38:10 - 41:15	_
180. 7:14 - 9:31	_	**231.** 68:18 - 71:24	_	**282.** 41:16 - 43:28	_
181. 10:1 - 13:6	_	**232.** 72:1 - 76:12	_	**283.** 44:1 - 47:3	_
182. 13:7 - 16:8	_	**233.** 77:1 - 79:7	_	**284.** 47:4 - 49:19	_
183. 16:9 - 18:18	_	**234.** 79:8 - 85:8	_	**285.** 49:20 - 52:6	_
184. 18:19 - 20:22	_	**235.** 85:9 - 89:37	_	**286.** 52:7 - 55:5	_
185. 20:23 - 22:5	_	**236.** 89:38 - 94:12	_	**287.** 55:6 - 58:10	_
186. 22:6 - 24:14	_	**237.** 94:13 - 102:14	_	**288.** 58:11 - 61:2	_
187. 24:15 - 25:28	_	**238.** 102:15 - 105:6	_	**289.** 61:3 - 65:6	_
188. 26:1 - 28:20	_	**239.** 105:7 - 107:6	_	**290.** 65:7 - **Jer.** 1:13	_
189. 28:21 - 30:9	_	**240.** 107: - 110:7	_	**291.** 1:14 - 3:25	_
190. 30:10 - 32:15	_	**241.** 111:1 - 118:9	_	**292.** 4:1 - 6:6	_
191. 32:16 - 34:8	_	**242.** 118:10 - 119:70	_	**293.** 6:7 - 8:10	_
192. 34:9 - 35:27	_	**243.** 119:71 - 119:143	_	**294.** 8:11 - 10:25	_
193. 36:1 - **Ezra** 2:62	_	**244.** 119:144 - 125:5	_	**295.** 11:1 - 13:20	_
194. 2:63 - 5:7	_	**245.** 126:1 - 134:13	_	**296.** 13:21 - 16:11	_
195. 5:8 - 7:19	_	**246.** 134:14 - 140:6	_	**297.** 16:12 - 18:23	_
196. 7:20 - 9:7	_	**247.** 140:7 - 145:17	_	**298.** 19:1 - 22:5	_
197. 9:8 - **Neh.** 2:5	_	**248.** 145:18 - 150:6	_	**299.** 22:6 - 24:2	_
198. 2:6 - 4:13	_	**249. Prov.** 1:1 - 4:9	_	**300.** 24:3 - 26:17	_
199. 4:14 - 6:19	_	**250.** 4:10 - 7:12	_	**301.** 26:18 - 28:17	_
200. 7:1 - 8:18	_	**251.** 7:13 - 10:22	_	**302.** 29:1 - 30:19	_
201. 9:1 - 10:36	_	**252.** 10:23 - 12:12	_	**303.** 30:20 - 32:11	_
202. 10:37 - 13:12	_	**253.** 12:13 - 14:10	_	**304.** 32:12 - 34:2	_
203. 13:13 - **Est.** 2:13	_	**254.** 14:11 - 15:23	_	**305.** 34:3 - 36:6	_
204. 2:14 - 5:2	_	**255.** 15:24 - 17:3		**306.** 36:7 - 38:6	
205. 5:3 - 8:4		**256.** 17:4 - 18:21		**307.** 38:7 - 40:5	
206. 8:5 - 10:3		**257.** 18:22 - 20:14		**308.** 40:6 - 42:17	
207. Job 1:1 - 4:13		**258.** 20:15 - 21:31		**309.** 42:18 - 45:3	
208. 4:14 - 7:21		**259.** 22:1 - 23:24		**310.** 45:4 - 48:32	
209. 8:1 - 11:16		**260.** 23:25 - 25:11		**311.** 48:33 - 50:13	
210. 11:17 - 15:14		**261.** 25:12 - 27:11		**312.** 50:14 - 51:46	
211. 15:15 - 19:21		**262.** 27:12 - 29:3		**313.** 51:47 - 52:34	
212. 19:22 - 22:18		**263.** 29:4 - 30:26		**314. Lam.** 1:1 - 2:18	
213. 22:19 - 27:8		**264.** 30:26 - **Ecc.** 2:12		**315.** 2:19 - 4:17	
214. 27:9 - 30:31		**265.** 2:13 - 5:7		**316.** 4:18 - **Eze.** 2:7	
215. 31:1 - 33:33		**266.** 5:8 - 8:17		**317.** 2:8 - 5:3	
216. 34:1 - 37:18		**267.** 9:1 - 12:14		**318.** 5:4 7:27	
217. 37:14 - 40:24		**268. Songs** 1:1 - 5:7		**319.** 8:1 - 10:13	
218. 41:1 - **Psalm** 3:8		**269.** 5:8 - **Isa.** 1:15		**320.** 10:14 - 12:18	
219. 4:1 - 9:20		**270.** 1:16 - 4:4		**321.** 12:19 - 14:21	
220. 10:1 - 17:7		**271.** 4:5 - 6:13		**322.** 14:22 - 16:46	
221. 17:8 - 20:9		**272.** 7:1 - 9:15		**323.** 16:47 - 18:20	
222. 21:1 - 25:14		**273.** 9:16 - 13:5		**324.** 18:21 - 20:30	
223. 25:15 - 31:12		**274.** 13:6 - 17:3		**325.** 20:31 - 22:10	

Day	Check √	Day	Check √	Day	Check √
326. 22:11 - 23:36	_	**340.** 48:13 - **Dan.** 2:15	_	**354.** 9:1 - **Jonah** 1:15	_
327. 23:37 - 25:9	_	**341.** 2:16 - 3:20	_	**355.** 1:16 - **Micah** 2:13	_
328. 25:10 - 27:29	_	**342.** 3:21 - 5:5	_	**356.** 3:1 - 6:16	_
329. 27:30 - 29:21	_	**343.** 5:6 - 6:23	_	**357.** 7:1 - **Nahum** 3:19	_
330. 30:1 - 32:20	_	**344.** 6:24 - 8:12	_	**358. Hub.** 1:1 - 3:19	_
331. 32:21 - 33:33	_	**345.** 8:13 - 10:8	_	**359. Zeph.** 1:1 - 3:20	_
332. 34:1 - 36:12	_	**346.** 10:9 - 11:29	_	**360. Hg.** 1:1 - **Zec.** 1:12	
333. 36:13 - 37:24	_	**347.** 11:30 - **Hos.** 2:11	_	**361.**1:13 - 5:6	
334. 37:25 - 39:29	_	**348.** 2:12 - 7:6	_	**362.** 5:7 - 9:6	
335. 40:1 - 41:4		**349.** 7:7 - 12:9		**363.** 9:7 - 13:3	
336. 41:5 - 43:12		**350.** 12:10 - **Joel** 2:8		**364.** 13:4 - **Mal.** 2:7	
337. 43:13 - 44:25		**351.** 2:19 - **Amos** 1:12		**365.** 2:8 - 4:6	
338. 44:26 - 46:11		**352.** 1:13 - 5:18		CONGRATULATIONS!	
339. 46:12 - 48 12		**353.** 5:19 - 8:14		God Bless You!	

Simplified Reading Schedule — Just read 3 1/2 pages of the Old Testament text each day for 365 days.

ALTERNATE PLANS
TWELVE HOURS ALONE WITH THE LORD AND HIS WORD.

Many Christians have received unusual spiritual growth and knowledge by setting aside twelve hours to be alone with the Lord to fast, pray, and feed on His word. One may read the Complete New Testament in KWIKSCAN™ in six hours, leaving six additional hours for prayer.

FORTY-EIGHT HOURS ALONE WITH THE LORD AND HIS WORD.

The Complete Bible in KWIKSCAN™ can be read in 31 hours. One may set aside a 48 hour period, using 31 hours to read the complete Bible, and having 17 additional hours for prayer and rest.

Contents

THE BOOKS OF
The Old Testament

THE BOOKS OF
The New Testament

THE BOOK OF GENESIS

BACKGROUND INFORMATION

Author: Moses according to tradition

Date Written: Usually considered to be **between 1491-1451 B.C.**

Number of:
Verses—1,533
Chapters—50
Total Words— 38,267
Scan Words—15,588
Scan Words Represent Approximately 40% of Total Words

Theme: The Book on Beginnings— the Created Order, Life, Man, Sin, Redemption, and the Setting apart of God's Chosen People

OUTLINE OF THE BOOK

I. **The Creation**
    1:1 — 2:25
II. **The Fall** of Adam and Eve
    3:1 — 4:7
III. **History Between the Fall and** the Great **Flood**
    4:8 —7:24
IV. **History Between the Flood and** the Tower of **Babel**
    8:1 — 11:9
V. **The Call of Abram Until the Death of Joseph**
    11:10 — 50:26

1

CHAPTER 1

■ ■ ■ ■ 1. **In the beginning God created the heaven and the earth.** 2. **And the earth was without form,** and void; **and darkness was upon the face of the deep.** And the Spirit of God moved upon the face of the waters.

■ 3. **And God said, Let there be light: and there was** light.

■ 4. **And God saw** the light, **that it was good: and God divided the light from the darkness.**

■ 5. **And God called the light Day, and the darkness** he called **Night. And the evening and the morning were the first day.**

6. And God said, Let there be a firmament in the midst of the waters, and let it divide the waters from the waters.

■ 7. **And God made the firmament, and** divided the waters which *were* under the firmament from the waters which *were* above the firmament: and it was so.

8. And God **called the firmament Heaven. And the evening and the morning were the second day.** 9. **And God said,** Let the waters under the heaven be gathered together unto one place, and **let the dry land appear:** and it was so.

■ 10. **And God called the dry land Earth; and** the gathering together of **the waters called he Seas:** and God saw that *it was* good.

■ 11. **And God said, Let the earth bring forth grass,** the **herb** yielding seed, **and the fruit tree** yielding fruit **after his kind,** whose seed *is* in itself, upon the earth: and it was so.

12. And the earth brought forth grass, *and* herb yielding seed after his kind, and the tree yielding fruit, whose seed *was* in itself, after his kind: **and God saw that it was good.**

■ 13. **And the evening and the morning were the third day.**

■ 14. **And God said, Let there be lights in the firmament** of the heaven **to divide the day from the night;** and let them be for signs, and for seasons, and for days, and years:

15. And let them be for lights in the firmament of the heaven to give light upon the earth: and it was so.

■ 16. **And God made two great lights; the greater** light **to rule the day, and the lesser** light to rule **the night: he made the stars also.**

17. And God set them in the firmament of the heaven to give light upon the earth,

■ 18. **And** to rule over the day and over the night, and to divide the light from the darkness: and God saw that **it was** good.

19. And the evening and the morning were **the fourth day.**

■ 20. **And God said, Let the waters bring forth** abundantly **the moving creature** that hath life, **and fowl that** may **fly** above the earth in the open firmament of heaven.

■ 21. **And God created** great **whales, and every** living **creature** that moveth, which the waters brought forth abundantly, **after their kind,** and every winged fowl after his kind: **and God saw** that **it was good.**

■ 22. **And God blessed them, saying, Be fruitful, and multiply,** and fill the waters

2

in the seas, and let fowl multiply in the earth. 23. **And the evening and the morning were the fifth day.** 24. **And God said, Let the earth bring forth the** living **creature after his kind,** cattle, and creeping thing, and beast of the earth after his kind: **and it was so.** 25. **And God made the beast** of the earth after his kind, **and cattle** after their kind, **and every thing that creepeth** upon the earth **after his kind: and God saw that it was good.** 26. **And God said, Let us make man in our image,** after our likeness: **and let them have dominion** over the fish of the sea, and over the fowl of the air, and over the cattle, and over all the earth, and over every creeping thing that creepeth upon the earth. 27. **So God created man in his** *own* **image,** in the image of God created he him; **male and female** created he them. 28. **And** God blessed them, and God **said unto them, Be fruitful,** and **multiply, and replenish the earth,** and subdue it: **and have dominion** over the fish of the sea, and over the fowl of the air, and over every living thing that moveth upon the earth. 29. **And God said,** Behold, **I have given you every herb** bearing seed, which *is* upon the face of all the earth, **and** every tree, in the which *is* **the fruit of a tree** yielding seed; to you it shall be **for meat.**

30. **And to every beast** of the earth, **and** to every **fowl** of the air, and to every thing that creepeth upon the earth, wherein *there is* life, **I have given** every green herb **for meat:** and it was so. 31. **And God saw every thing that he** had **made,** and, behold, *it* **was** very **good. And the evening and the morning were the sixth day.**

CHAPTER 2

1. Thus the heavens and the earth were finished, and all the host of them. 2. **And on the seventh day God** ended his work which he had made; and he **rested** on the seventh day **from all his work** which he had made. 3. **And God blessed the seventh day, and sanctified it: because** that **in it he** had **rested from** all **his work** which God created and made. 4. These *are* the generations of the heavens and of the earth when they were created, in the day that the LORD God made the earth and the heavens, 5. **And** every plant of the field before it was in the earth, and every herb of the field before it grew: for the LORD **God had not caused it to rain** upon the earth, and *there* **was** not a man to till the ground. 6. **But there went up a mist** from the earth, **and watered** the whole face of **the ground.** 7. **And** the LORD **God formed man of the dust** of the ground, **and breathed into his nostrils the breath of**

3

■ life; and man became
■ a living soul.
■ 8. And the LORD God
■ planted a garden eastward
■ in Eden; and
■ there he put the
■ man whom he had formed.
■ 9. And out of the ground
■ made the LORD God
■ to grow every tree that
■ is pleasant to the sight,
■ and good for
■ food; the tree of life
■ also in the midst of the garden, and
■ the tree of knowledge
■ of good and evil.
■ 10. And a river went out of
■ Eden to water the garden;
and from thence it was parted,
and became into four heads.
11. The name of the first *is* Pison:
that *is* it which compasseth the whole
land of Havilah, where *there is* gold;
12. And the gold of that land *is* good:
there *is* bdellium and the onyx stone.
13. And the name of the second
river *is* Gihon: the same *is* it
that compasseth the whole
land of Ethiopia.
14. And the name of the third river
is Hiddekel: that *is* it which goeth
toward the east of Assyria. And
the fourth river *is* Euphrates.
■ 15. And the LORD
■ God took the man, and put him
■ into the garden of Eden
■ to dress it
■ and to
■ keep it.
■ 16. And the LORD God
■ commanded the man,
■ saying, Of every tree
of the garden thou mayest
■ freely eat:
■ 17. But of the tree of the
■ knowledge of good and
■ evil, thou shalt not eat of it:
■ for in the day that
■ thou eatest thereof
■ thou shalt surely
■ die.
■ 18. And the LORD
■ God said, It is not

■ good that the
■ man should
■ be alone; I will make
■ him an help meet for him.
■ 19. And out of the ground the LORD
■ God formed every
■ beast of the field,
■ and every
■ fowl of the air;
■ and brought them
■ unto Adam to see what
he would call them:
■ and whatsoever Adam
■ called every living
■ creature, that was
■ the name thereof.
20. And Adam gave names to all
cattle, and to the fowl of the air,
and to every beast of the field;
but for Adam there was not
found an help meet for him.
■ 21. And the LORD
■ God caused a deep
■ sleep to fall upon
■ Adam, and he slept:
■ and he took one of his
■ ribs, and closed up the flesh
instead thereof;
■ 22. And the rib, which the
LORD God had taken from man,
■ made he
■ a woman, and brought
her unto the man.
■ 23. And Adam
■ said, This is now
■ bone of my bones, and
■ flesh of my flesh: she
■ shall be called Woman,
because she was taken out of Man.
■ 24. Therefore shall a man
■ leave his father and his
■ mother, and shall
■ cleave unto his wife: and
■ they shall be one flesh.
■ 25. And they were both
■ naked, the man and his wife,
■ and were not ashamed.

CHAPTER 3

■ 1. Now the serpent was
■ more subtil than any
■ beast of the field which the
LORD God had made.

And he said unto the woman, Yea, hath God said, Ye shall not eat of every tree of the garden?

2. And the woman said unto the serpent, We may eat of the fruit of the trees of the garden:

3. But of the fruit of the tree which is in the midst of the garden, God hath said, Ye shall not eat of it, neither shall ye touch it, lest ye die.

4. And the serpent said unto the woman, Ye shall not surely die:

5. For God doth know that in the day ye eat thereof, then your eyes shall be opened, and ye shall be as gods, knowing good and evil.

6. And when the woman saw that the tree was good for food, and that it was pleasant to the eyes, and a tree to be desired to make one wise, she took of the fruit thereof, and did eat, and gave also unto her husband with her; and he did eat.

7. And the eyes of them both were opened, and they knew that they were naked; and they sewed fig leaves together, and made themselves aprons.

8. And they heard the voice of the LORD God walking in the garden in the cool of the day: and Adam and his wife hid themselves from the presence of the LORD God amongst the trees of the garden.

9. And the LORD God called unto Adam, and said unto him, Where art thou?

10. And he said, I heard thy voice in the garden, and I was afraid, because I was naked; and I hid myself.

11. And he said, Who told thee that thou wast naked? Hast thou eaten of the tree, whereof I commanded thee that thou shouldest not eat?

12. And the man said, The woman whom thou gavest to be with me, she gave me of the tree, and I did eat.

13. And the LORD God said unto the woman, What is this that thou hast done? And the woman said, The serpent beguiled me, and I did eat.

14. And the LORD God said unto the serpent, Because thou hast done this, thou art cursed above all cattle, and above every beast of the field; upon thy belly shalt thou go, and dust shalt thou eat all the days of thy life:

15. And I will put enmity between thee and the woman, and between thy seed and her seed; it shall bruise thy head, and thou shalt bruise his heel.

16. Unto the woman he said, I will greatly multiply thy sorrow and thy conception; in sorrow thou shalt bring forth children; and thy desire shall be to thy husband, and he shall rule over thee.

17. And unto Adam he said, Because thou hast hearkened unto the voice of thy wife, and hast eaten of the tree, of which I commanded thee, saying, Thou shalt not eat of it: cursed is the ground for thy sake; in sorrow shalt thou eat of it all the days of thy life;

18. Thorns also and thistles shall it bring forth to thee;

and thou shalt eat
the herb of the field;
19. In the sweat of thy
face shalt thou eat bread,
till thou return unto the ground;
for out of it wast thou taken: for
dust thou *art,* and unto
dust shalt thou return.
20. And Adam called
his wife's name Eve;
because she was the
mother of all living.
21. Unto Adam also
and to
his wife did the LORD
God make coats of
skins, and clothed them.
22. And the LORD
God said, Behold, the
man is become as one
of us, to know good
and evil: and now,
lest he put forth his hand, and
take also
of the tree of life, and eat, and
live for ever:
23. Therefore the LORD
God sent him forth
from the garden of Eden,
to till the ground from
whence he was taken.
24. So he drove out
the man; and he
placed at the east
of the garden of Eden
Cherubims, and a flaming
sword which turned every way,
to keep the way of
the tree of life.

CHAPTER 4

1. And Adam
knew Eve his wife;
and she conceived, and
bare Cain, and said, I have
gotten a man from the LORD.
2. And she again bare his brother
Abel. And Abel was a
keeper of sheep, but Cain
was a tiller of the ground.
3. And in process of time
it came to pass, that
Cain brought of the

fruit of the ground
an offering unto the LORD.
4. And Abel, he also
brought of
the firstlings of his
flock and of the fat thereof.
And the LORD had
respect unto Abel and to
his offering:
5. But unto Cain
and to his offering
he had not respect.
And Cain was very
wroth, and his countenance fell.
6. And the LORD said unto
Cain, Why art thou wroth?
and why is thy countenance fallen?
7. If thou doest well, shalt
thou not be accepted?
and if thou doest
not well,
sin lieth at the door. And
unto thee *shall be* his desire,
and thou shalt rule over him.
8. And Cain talked with Abel
his brother: and it came to pass,
when they were in the field, that
Cain rose up against
Abel his brother,
and slew him.
9. And the LORD
said unto Cain,
Where is Abel thy brother?
And he said, I know not:
Am I my brother's keeper?
10. And he said,
What hast thou done?
the voice of thy
brother's blood crieth
unto me from the ground.
11. And now art thou
cursed from the earth, which hath
opened her mouth to receive thy
brother's blood from thy hand;
12. When thou tillest the
ground, it shall not henceforth
yield unto thee
her strength; a fugitive
and a vagabond
shalt thou be in the earth.
13. And Cain said
unto the LORD,
My punishment is

greater than I can bear. 14. Behold, thou hast driven me out this day from the face of the earth; and from thy face shall I be hid; and I shall be a fugitive and a vagabond in the earth; and it shall come to pass, *that* every one that findeth me shall slay me. 15. And the LORD said unto him, Therefore whosoever slayeth Cain, vengeance shall be taken on him sevenfold. And the LORD set a mark upon Cain, lest any finding him should kill him. 16. And Cain went out from the presence of the LORD, and dwelt in the land of Nod, on the east of Eden. 17. And Cain knew his wife; and she conceived, and bare Enoch: and he builded a city, and called the name of the city, after the name of his son, Enoch. 18. And unto Enoch was born Irad: and Irad begat Mehujael: and Mehujael begat Methusael: and Methusael begat Lamech. 19. And Lamech took unto him two wives: the name of the one *was* Adah, and the name of the other Zillah. 20. And Adah bare Jabal: he was the father of such as dwell in tents, and *of such as have* cattle. 21. And his brother's name *was* Jubal: he was the father of all such as handle the harp and organ. 22. And Zillah, she also bare Tubal-cain, an instructor of every

artificer in brass and iron: and the sister of Tubal-cain *was* Naamah. 23. And Lamech said unto his wives, Adah and Zillah, Hear my voice; ye wives of Lamech, hearken unto my speech: for I have slain a man to my wounding, and a young man to my hurt. 24. If Cain shall be avenged sevenfold, truly Lamech seventy and sevenfold. 25. And Adam knew his wife again; and she bare a son, and called his name Seth: For God, said she, hath appointed me another seed instead of Abel, whom Cain slew. 26. And to Seth, to him also there was born a son; and he called his name Enos: then began men to call upon the name of the LORD.

CHAPTER 5

1. This *is* the book of the generations of Adam. In the day that God created man, in the likeness of God made he him;
2. Male and female created he them; and blessed them, and called their name Adam, in the day when they were created.
3. And Adam lived an hundred and thirty years, and begat *a son* in his own likeness, after his image; and called his name Seth:
4. And the days of Adam after he had begotten Seth were eight hundred years: and he begat sons and daughters:
5. And all the days that Adam lived were nine hundred and thirty years: and he died.
6. And Seth lived an hundred and five years, and begat Enos:
7. And Seth lived after he begat Enos eight hundred and seven years,

and begat sons and daughters:

8. And all the days of Seth were nine hundred and twelve years: and he died.

■ 9. **And Enos** lived ninety years, and **begat Cainan:**

10. And Enos lived after he begat Cainan eight hundred and fifteen years, and begat sons and daughters:

11. And all the days of Enos were nine hundred and five years: and he died.

■ 12. **And Cainan** lived seventy years and **begat Mahalaleel:**

13. And Cainan lived after he begat Mahalaleel eight hundred and forty years, and begat sons and daughters:

14. And all the days of Cainan were nine hundred and ten years: and he died.

■ 15. **And Mahalaleel** lived sixty and five years, and **begat Jared:**

16. And Mahalaleel lived after he begat Jared eight hundred and thirty years, and begat sons and daughters:

17. And all the days of Mahalaleel were eight hundred ninety and five years: and he died.

■ 18. **And Jared** lived an hundred sixty and two years, and he **begat Enoch:**

19. And Jared lived after he begat Enoch eight hundred years, and begat sons and daughters:

20. And all the days of Jared were nine hundred sixty and two years: and he died.

■ 21. **And Enoch** lived sixty and five years, and **begat Methuselah:**

22. And Enoch walked with God after he begat Methuselah three hundred years, and begat sons and daughters:

23. And all the days of Enoch were three hundred sixty and five years:

■ 24. **And Enoch walked with God: and he was not; for God took him.**

25. **And Methuselah** lived an hundred eighty and seven years, and **begat Lamech:**

26. And Methuselah lived after he begat Lamech seven hundred eighty and two years, and begat sons and daughters:

■ 27. **And all the days of Methuselah were nine hundred sixty and nine years:** and he died.

■ 28. **And Lamech** lived an hundred eighty and two years, and **begat** a son:

29. And he called his name **Noah, saying, This same shall comfort us concerning our work and toil** of our hands, because of the ground which the LORD hath cursed.

30. And Lamech lived after he begat Noah five hundred ninety and five years, and begat sons and daughters:

31. And all the days of Lamech were seven hundred seventy and seven years: and he died.

■ 32. **And Noah** was five hundred years old: and Noah **begat Shem, Ham, and Japheth.**

CHAPTER 6

■ 1. **And it came to pass, when men began to multiply** on the face of the earth, **and daughters were born unto them,**

■ 2. **That the sons of God saw the daughters of men** that they *were* fair; **and they took** them **wives of all** which **they chose.**

■ 3. **And the LORD said, My spirit shall not always strive with man,** for that he also *is* flesh: yet his days shall be an hundred and twenty years.

■ 4. **There were giants** in the earth **in those days; and** also after that, **when the sons of God came in unto the daughters of men, and they bare**

8

■ children to them,
■ the same became mighty
■ men which *were* of old, men
■ of renown.
■ 5. And God saw that
■ the wickedness of
■ man was great in the earth,
■ and *that*
■ every imagination
of the thoughts
■ of his heart was only
■ evil continually.
■ 6. And it repented the LORD
■ that he had made man
on the earth, and it grieved him at his heart.
■ 7. And the LORD said, I
■ will destroy man whom I have
created from the face of the earth;
■ both man, and
■ beast, and
■ the creeping thing, and the
■ fowls of the air; for it repenteth
me that I have made them.
■ 8. But Noah found grace
■ in the eyes of the LORD.
9. These *are* the generations of Noah:
■ Noah was a
■ just man
■ and perfect in his
generations, *and* Noah
■ walked with God.
10. And Noah begat three sons,
Shem, Ham, and Japheth.
■ 11. The earth also
■ was corrupt before God,
■ and the earth was
■ filled with violence.
12. And God looked upon the
earth, and, behold, it was corrupt;
■ for all flesh had corrupted
■ his way upon the earth.
■ 13. And God said unto
■ Noah, The end of all
■ flesh is come before me;
for the earth is filled with violence
through them; and, behold,
■ I will destroy them
with the earth.
■ 14. Make thee
■ an ark of gopher wood; rooms shalt
thou make in the ark, and shalt pitch
it within and without with pitch.

■ 15. And this is the fashion
■ which thou shalt make it *of:*
■ The length of the ark *shall be*
■ three hundred cubits,
■ the breadth of it
■ fifty cubits, and the
■ height of it
■ thirty cubits.
■ 16. A window shalt thou
■ make to the ark, and in a cubit
shalt thou finish it above;
■ and the door of the ark
■ shalt thou set in
■ the side thereof;
■ with lower, second, and
■ third stories shalt thou make it.
■ 17. And, behold, I, even I, do
■ bring a flood
of waters upon the earth,
■ to destroy all flesh, wherein *is*
the breath of life, from under heaven;
■ and every thing
that *is* in the earth
■ shall die.
■ 18. But with thee will I
■ establish my covenant;
■ and thou shalt come
■ into the ark, thou, and
■ thy sons, and
■ thy wife, and thy
■ sons' wives with thee.
■ 19. And of every
■ living thing of all flesh,
■ two of every sort shalt
■ thou bring into the ark, to
keep *them* alive with thee;
■ they shall be male
■ and female.
20. Of fowls after their kind, and of
cattle after their kind, of every
creeping thing of the earth after his
kind, two of every *sort* shall come
unto thee, to keep *them* alive.
■ 21. And take thou unto thee of all
■ food that is eaten, and thou
shalt gather *it* to thee; and it
shall be for food
■ for thee, and for them.
■ 22. Thus did Noah; according to
■ all that God commanded
him, so did he.

CHAPTER 7

| |

9

1. And the LORD said unto Noah, Come thou and all thy house into the ark; for thee have I seen righteous before me in this generation.

2. Of every clean beast thou shalt take to thee by sevens, the male and his female: and of beasts that *are* not clean by two, the male and his female.

3. Of fowls also of the air by sevens, the male and the female; to keep seed alive upon the face of all the earth.

4. For yet seven days, and I will cause it to rain upon the earth forty days and forty nights; and every living substance that I have made will I destroy from off the face of the earth.

5. And Noah did according unto all that the LORD commanded him.

6. And Noah *was* six hundred years old when the flood of waters was upon the earth.

7. And Noah went in, and his sons, and his wife, and his sons' wives with him, into the ark, because of the waters of the flood.

8. Of clean beasts, and of beasts that *are* not clean, and of fowls, and of every thing that creepeth upon the earth,

9. There went in two and two unto Noah into the ark, the male and the female, as God had commanded Noah.

10. And it came to pass after seven days, that the waters of the flood were upon the earth.

11. In the six hundredth year of Noah's life, in the second month, the seventeenth day of the month, the same day were all the fountains of the great deep broken up, and the windows of heaven were opened.

12. And the rain was upon the earth forty days and forty nights.

13. In the selfsame day entered Noah, and Shem, and Ham, and Japheth, the sons of Noah, and Noah's wife, and the three wives of his sons with them, into the ark;

14. They, and every beast after his kind, and all the cattle after their kind, and every creeping thing that creepeth upon the earth after his kind, and every fowl after his kind, every bird of every sort.

15. And they went in unto Noah into the ark, two and two of all flesh, wherein *is* the breath of life.

16. And they that went in, went in male and female of all flesh, as God had commanded him: and the LORD shut him in.

17. And the flood was forty days upon the earth; and the waters increased, and bare up the ark, and it was lift up above the earth.

18. And the waters prevailed, and were increased greatly upon the earth; and the ark went upon the face of the waters.

19. And the waters prevailed exceedingly upon the earth; and all the high hills, that *were* under the whole heaven, were covered.

20. Fifteen cubits upward did the waters prevail; and the mountains were covered.

21. And all flesh died that moved upon the earth, both of fowl, and of cattle, and of beast, and of every creeping thing that creepeth upon the earth, and every man:

22. All in whose nostrils *was* the breath of life, of all that *was* in the dry *land*, died.

23. And every living substance was destroyed which was upon the face of the ground, both man, and cattle, and the

creeping things, and the fowl of the heaven; and they were destroyed from the earth: and Noah only remained *alive*, and they that *were* with him in the ark.

24. **And the waters prevailed upon the earth an hundred and fifty days.**

CHAPTER 8

1. **And God remembered Noah,** and every living thing, **and** all the cattle that *was* with him in the ark: and God **made a wind to pass over the earth, and the waters assuaged;**

2. The fountains also of the deep and the windows of heaven were stopped, and the rain from heaven was restrained;

3. And the waters returned from off the earth continually: and **after the end of the hundred and fifty days the waters were abated.**

4. **And the ark rested in the seventh month,** on the seventeenth day of the month, **upon the mountains of Ararat.**

5. **And** the waters decreased continually until **the tenth month:** in the tenth *month,* on the first *day* of the month, **were the tops of the mountains seen.**

6. **And** it came to pass **at the end of forty days,** that **Noah opened the window** of the ark which he had made:

7. **And** he **sent** forth **a raven,** which went forth to and fro, until the waters were dried up from off the earth.

8. **Also** he sent forth **a dove** from him, to see if the waters were abated from off the face of the ground;

9. **But the dove found no rest** for the sole of her foot, **and** she

returned unto him into **the ark,** for the waters *were* on the face of the whole earth: then he put forth his hand, and took her, and pulled her in unto him into the ark.

10. **And he stayed yet other seven days; and again he sent forth the dove** out of the ark;

11. **And the dove came in** to him in the evening; **and,** lo, **in her mouth was an olive leaf** plucked off: **so Noah knew that the waters were abated** from off the earth.

12. **And he stayed yet other seven days; and sent forth the dove; which returned not again** unto him any more.

13. **And** it came to pass in the six hundredth and first year, in the first *month,* the first *day* of the month, **the waters were dried up** from off the earth: and Noah removed the covering of the ark, and looked, and, behold, the face of the ground was dry.

14. And in the second month, on the seven and twentieth day of the month, was the earth dried.

15. **And God spake unto Noah,** saying,

16. **Go forth** of the ark, thou, and thy wife, and thy sons, and thy sons' wives with thee.

17. Bring forth with thee every living thing that *is* with thee, of all flesh, *both* of fowl, and of cattle, and of every creeping thing that creepeth upon the earth; that they may breed abundantly in the earth, and be fruitful, and multiply upon the earth.

18. **And Noah went** forth, and his sons, and his wife, and his sons' wives with him:

19. Every beast, every creeping thing, and every fowl, *and* whatsoever creepeth upon the earth, after their kinds, went forth out of the ark.

20. **And** Noah **builded an altar unto**

■ the LORD; and took of
■ every clean beast,
■ and of every clean
■ fowl, and offered burnt
■ offerings on the altar.
■ 21. And the LORD smelled a
■ sweet savour; and the LORD
■ said in his heart,
■ I will not again curse
■ the ground any more for man's
sake; for the imagination of man's
heart *is* evil from his youth;
■ neither will I again
■ smite any more
■ everything living, as I have
done.
■ 22. While the earth
■ remaineth, seedtime and
■ harvest, and cold and heat,
■ and Summer and Winter,
■ and day and night shall not
■ cease.

CHAPTER 9

■ 1. And God blessed
Noah and his sons, and
■ said unto them, Be fruitful, and
multiply, and replenish the earth.
2. And
■ the fear of you and
the dread of you
■ shall be upon every beast
of the earth, and upon every
fowl of the air, upon
■ all that moveth upon the
■ earth, and upon all the fishes
of the sea; into your hand
are they delivered.
■ 3. Every moving
■ thing that liveth
■ shall be meat
■ for you; even as
■ the green herb have
I given you all things.
■ 4. But flesh with
■ the life thereof, which
■ is the blood thereof,
■ shall ye not eat.
5. And surely your blood of your lives
will I require; at the hand of every
beast will I require it, and at the hand
of man; at the hand of every man's

brother will I require the life of man.
■ 6. Whoso sheddeth man's
■ blood, by man shall
■ his blood be shed: for
■ in the image of God
■ made he man.
■ 7. And you, be ye fruitful,
and multiply; bring forth
abundantly in the earth,
■ and multiply therein.
■ 8. And God spake
■ unto Noah, and to his
■ sons with him, saying,
9. And I, behold,
■ I establish my covenant
■ with you, and with your
■ seed after you;
■ 10. And with every living
■ creature that *is* with you, of
■ the fowl, of the
■ cattle, and of every
■ beast of the earth with you;
from all that go out of the ark,
to every beast of the earth.
11. And I will establish my
covenant with you,
■ neither shall all flesh
■ be cut off any more
■ by the waters of
■ a flood; neither shall there any
more be a flood to destroy the earth.
■ 12. And God said, This is the
■ token of the covenant which I
make between me and you
and every living creature that *is*
with you, for perpetual generations:
■ 13. I do set my bow in
■ the cloud, and it shall
be for a token of a covenant
between me and the earth.
14. And it shall come to pass,
■ when I bring a cloud
over the earth, that
■ the bow shall be
■ seen in the cloud:
15. And I will remember my covenant,
which *is* between me and you and
every living creature of all flesh;
and the waters shall no more
become a flood to destroy all flesh.
16. And the bow shall be in the cloud;
■ and I will look upon it, that
■■ I may remember the

everlasting covenant between God and every living creature of all flesh that *is* upon the earth.

17. And God said unto Noah, This *is* the token of the covenant, which I have established between me and all flesh that *is* upon the earth.

18. **And the sons of Noah,** that went forth of the ark, **were Shem, and Ham, and Japheth: and Ham is the father of Canaan.**

19. These *are* the three sons of Noah: and **of them was the whole earth overspread.**

20. **And Noah** began *to be* an husbandman, and he **planted a vineyard:**

21. **And he drank of the wine, and was drunken; and he was uncovered within his tent.**

22. **And Ham, the** father of Canaan, **saw the nakedness** of his father, **and told his** two **brethren** without.

23. **And Shem and Japheth took a garment, and laid** *it* upon both their shoulders, **and went backward, and covered** the nakedness of **their father;** and their faces *were* backward, and they saw not their father's nakedness.

24. **And Noah awoke** from his wine, **and knew what his younger son had done** unto him.

25. **And** he **said, Cursed be Canaan;** a servant of servants shall he be unto his brethren.

26. **And** he said, **Blessed be the LORD** God **of Shem;** and **Canaan shall be his servant.**

27. **God shall enlarge**

Japheth, and he shall dwell in the tents of Shem; and **Canaan shall be his servant.**

28. **And Noah lived after the flood three hundred and fifty years.**

29. **And all the days of Noah were nine hundred and fifty years:** and he died.

CHAPTER 10

1. **Now these are the generations of the sons of Noah, Shem, Ham, and Japheth: and unto them were sons born after the flood.**

2. **The sons of Japheth;** Gomer, and Magog, and Madai, and Javan, and Tubal, and Meshech, and Tiras.

3. And the sons of Gomer; Ashkenaz, and Riphath, and Togarmah.

4. And the sons of Javan; Elishah, and Tarshish, Kittim, and Dodanim.

5. By these **were the isles of the Gentiles divided** in their lands; every one after his tongue, after their families, in their nations.

6. **And the sons of Ham; Cush, and Mizraim, and Phut, and Canaan.**

7. And the sons of Cush; Seba, and Havilah, and Sabtah, and Raamah, and Sabtechah: and the sons of Raamah; Sheba, and Dedan.

8. **And Cush begat Nimrod:** he began to be a mighty one in the earth.

9. **He was a mighty hunter before the LORD:** wherefore it is said, Even as Nimrod the mighty hunter before the LORD.

10. **And the beginning of his kingdom was Babel, and Erech, and Accad, and Calneh, in the land of Shinar.**

11. **Out of that land went forth Asshur, and builded Nineveh, and** the city

■ **Rehoboth, and**
■ **Calah,**
■ 12. **And Resen** between
Nineveh and Calah: the same
■ **is a great city.**
13. And Mizraim begat Ludim,
and Anamim, and Lehabim,
and Naphtuhim,
14. And Pathrusim, and Casluhim,
(out of whom came Philistim,)
and Caphtorim.
■ 15. **And Canaan begat**
■ **Sidon** his first born,
■ **and Heth,**
■ 16. **And the Jebusite,** and the
■ **Amorite,** and the
■ **Girgasite,**
17. And the
■ **Hivite,** and the
■ **Arkite,** and the
■ **Sinite,**
18. And the
■ **Arvadite,** and the
■ **Zemarite, and the**
■ **Hamathite: and**
■ **afterward** were the families of
■ **the Canaanites**
■ **spread abroad.**
19. And the border of the Canaanites
was from Sidon, as thou comest to
Gerar, unto Gaza; as thou goest, unto
Sodom, and Gomorrah, and Admah,
and Zeboim, even unto Lasha.
20. These *are* the sons of Ham, after
their families, after their tongues, in
their countries, *and* in their nations.
■ 21. **Unto Shem** also, the father of
all the children of Eber, the brother of
Japheth the elder, even to him
■ **were** *children*
■ **born.**
22. The children of Shem;
■ **Elam,** and
■ **Asshur,** and
■ **Arphaxad,** and
■ **Lud, and Aram.**
■ 23. **And the children**
■ **of Aram; Uz,** and
■ **Hul,** and
■ **Gether, and Mash.**
■ 24. **And Arphaxad**
■ **begat Salah; and**
■ **Salah begat Eber.**

■ 25. **And unto Eber were**
■ **born two sons:** the name of
■ **one was Peleg; for in**
■ **his days was the earth**
■ **divided; and his brother's**
■ **name was Joktan.**
26. And Joktan begat Almodad,
and Sheleph, and Hazarmaveth,
and Jerah,
27. And Hadoram, and Uzal,
and Diklah,
28. And Obal, and Abimael,
and Sheba,
29. And Ophir, and Havilah,
and Jobab: all these *were* the
sons of Joktan.
30. And their dwelling was from
Mesha, as thou goest unto
Sephar a mount of the east.
31. These *are* the sons of Shem,
after their families, after their tongues,
in their lands, after their nations.
■ 32. **These are the families of**
■ **the sons of Noah,** after their
generations, in their nations: and
■ **by these were the nations**
■ **divided** in the earth after the flood.

CHAPTER 11

■ 1. **And the whole earth**
■ **was of one language,**
and of one speech.
■ 2. **And it came to pass,**
as they journeyed from the east,
■ **that they found a plain in**
■ **the land of Shinar; and** they
■ **dwelt there.**
3. And they said one to another, Go
to, let us make brick, and burn them
throughly. And they had brick for
stone, and slime had they for morter.
■ 4. **And they said,** Go to,
■ **let us build** us
■ **a city and a tower, whose**
■ **top may reach** unto
■ **heaven; and let us make** us
■ **a name, lest we be**
■ **scattered** abroad upon
the face of the whole earth.
■ 5. **And the LORD came**
■ **down to see the city**
■ **and the tower,** which the
children of men builded.

14

6. **And the LORD said,**
Behold, the people is one.
and they have all one language;
and this they begin to do:
and now nothing will
be restrained from them,
which they have
imagined to do.
7. Go to,
let us go down, and there
confound their language,
that they may not understand
one another's speech.
8. **So the LORD scattered**
them abroad from thence
upon the face of all the earth:
and they left off to build the city.
9. **Therefore is the**
name of it called
Babel; because the LORD
did there confound the
language of all the earth:
and from thence did the LORD
scatter them abroad upon
the face of all the earth.
10. **These are the**
generations of Shem: Shem
was an hundred years old, and begat
Arphaxad two years after the flood:
11. And Shem lived after he begat
Arphaxad five hundred years, and
begat sons and daughters.
12. And Arphaxad lived five
and thirty years, and begat
Salah:
13. And Arphaxad lived after he
begat Salah four hundred and three
years, and begat sons and daughters.
14. And Salah lived thirty
years, and begat
Eber:
15. And Salah lived after he begat
Eber four hundred and three years,
and begat sons and daughters.
16. And Eber lived four
and thirty years, and begat
Peleg:
17. And Eber lived after he
begat Peleg four hundred and
thirty years, and begat sons
and daughters.
18. And Peleg lived thirty
years, and begat

Reu:
19. And Peleg lived after he begat
Reu two hundred and nine years,
and begat sons and daughters.
20. And Reu lived two
and thirty years, and begat
Serug:
21. And Reu lived after he begat
Serug two hundred and seven years,
and begat sons and daughters.
22. And Serug lived thirty
years, and begat
Nahor:
23. And Serug lived after he begat
Nahor two hundred years, and begat
sons and daughters.
24. And Nahor lived nine
and twenty years, and begat
Terah:
25. And Nahor lived after he begat
Terah an hundred and nineteen
years, and begat sons and daughters.
26. **And Terah** lived
seventy years, and
begat Abram, Nahor,
and Haran.
27. Now these *are* the generations of
Terah: Terah begat Abram, Nahor,
and Haran; and Haran begat Lot.
28. **And Haran died before**
his father Terah
in the land of his nativity,
in Ur of the Chaldees.
29. **And Abram and**
Nahor took them
wives: the name of
Abram's wife was
Sarai; and the name of
Nahor's wife, Milcah, the
daughter of Haran, the father of
Milcah, and the father of Iscah.
30. **But Sarai was**
barren; she *had* no child.
31. **And Terah took**
Abram his son,
and Lot the son of Haran
his son's son, and Sarai his
daughter in law, his son Abram's wife;
and they went forth with them
from Ur of the Chaldees, to go
into the land of
Canaan; and they came
unto Haran, and dwelt there.

32. And the days of Terah were two hundred and five years: and Terah died in Haran.

CHAPTER 12

1. **Now the LORD had said unto Abram, Get thee out of thy country,** and from thy kindred, and from thy father's house, **unto a land** that **I will shew thee:** 2. **And I will make of thee a great nation,** and I will bless thee, and make thy name great; and thou shalt be a blessing: 3. And I will bless them that bless thee, and curse him that curseth thee: and **in thee shall all families of the earth be blessed.** 4. So Abram departed, as the LORD had spoken unto him; and Lot went with him: and Abram *was* seventy and five years old when he departed out of Haran. 5. **And Abram took Sarai** his wife, and **Lot** his brother's son, **and all their substance** that they had gathered, and the souls that they had gotten in Haran; **and they went** forth to go into the land of Canaan; and **into** the land of **Canaan they came.** 6. **And Abram passed through** the land unto the place of Sichem, **unto the plain of Moreh.** And the Canaanite *was* then in the land. 7. **And the LORD appeared unto Abram, and said, Unto thy seed will I give this land: and there builded he an altar unto the LORD,** who appeared unto him. 8. **And he removed** from thence **unto a mountain** on the **east of Bethel, and pitched** his tent, *having* Bethel on the west, and Hai on the east: **and there** he **builded an altar** unto the LORD, **and called upon** the name of **the LORD.** 9. **And Abram journeyed,** going on still **toward the south.** 10. **And there was a famine in the land: and Abram went** down **into Egypt** to sojourn there; for the famine *was* grievous in the land. 11. **And** it came to pass, **when he was come near** to enter into Egypt, that **he said unto Sarai** his wife, Behold now, **I know that thou art** a **fair** woman **to look upon:** 12. **Therefore** it shall come to pass, **when the Egyptians** shall **see thee,** that **they shall say, This is his wife: and they will kill me,** but they will save thee alive. 13. **Say,** I pray thee, **thou art my sister:** that it may be well with me for thy sake; and my soul shall live because of thee. 14. **And** it came to pass, that, when Abram was come into Egypt, **the Egyptians beheld** the woman **that she was very fair.** 15. The princes also of Pharaoh saw her, and commended her before Pharaoh: **and the woman was taken into Pharaoh's house.** 16. **And he entreated Abram well for her sake:** and he had sheep, and oxen, and he asses, and menservants, and maidservants, and she asses, and camels. 17. **And the LORD plagued Pharaoh** and his house with great plagues **because of Sarai** Abram's wife. 18. **And Pharaoh called Abram and said, What is this** *that*

thou hast done unto me? why didst thou not tell me that she *was* thy wife? 19. Why saidst thou, She is my sister? so I might have taken her to me to wife: now therefore behold thy wife, take her, and go thy way. 20. And Pharaoh commanded *his* men concerning him: and they sent him away, and his wife, and all that he had.

CHAPTER 13

1. And Abram went up out of Egypt, he, and his wife, and all that he had, and Lot with him, into the south. 2. And Abram was very rich in cattle, in silver, and in gold. 3. And he went on his journeys from the south even to Beth-el, unto the place where his tent had been at the beginning, between Bethel and Hai; 4. Unto the place of the altar, which he had made there at the first: and there Abram called on the name of the LORD. 5. And Lot also, which went with Abram, had flocks, and herds, and tents. 6. And the land was not able to bear them, that they might dwell together: for their substance was great, so that they could not dwell together. 7. And there was a strife between the herdmen of Abram's cattle and the herdmen of Lot's cattle: and the Canaanite and the Perizzite dwelled then in the land. 8. And Abram said unto Lot, Let there be no strife, I pray thee, between me and thee, and between my herdmen and thy herdmen; for we be brethren. 9. *Is* not the whole land before thee? separate thyself, I pray thee, from me: if thou wilt take the left hand, then I will go to the right; or if thou depart to the right hand, then I will go to the left. 10. And Lot lifted up his eyes, and beheld all the plain of Jordan, that it was well watered every where, before the LORD destroyed Sodom and Gomorrah, even as the garden of the LORD, like the land of Egypt, as thou comest unto Zoar. 11. Then Lot chose him all the plain of Jordan; and Lot journeyed east: and they separated themselves the one from the other. 12. Abram dwelled in the land of Canaan, and Lot dwelled in the cities of the plain, and pitched his tent toward Sodom. 13. But the men of Sodom were wicked and sinners before the LORD exceedingly. 14. And the LORD said unto Abram, after that Lot was separated from him, Lift up now thine eyes, and look from the place where thou art northward, and southward, and eastward, and westward: 15. For all the land which thou seest, to thee will I give it, and to thy seed for ever. 16. And I will make thy seed as the dust of the earth: so that if a man can number the dust of the earth, *then* shall thy seed also be numbered. 17. Arise, walk through the land in the length of it and in the breadth of it; for I will give it unto thee. 18. Then Abram removed

his tent, and came and
**dwelt in the plain
of Mamre,** which *is*
in Hebron, and built there
an altar unto the LORD.

CHAPTER 14

1. And it came to pass
**in the days of Amraphel
king of Shinar, Arioch king
of Ellasar, Chedorlaomer
king of Elam, and Tidal
king of nations;**
2. *That these*
**made war with Bera
king of Sodom,** and with
**Birsha king of Gomorrah,
Shinab king of Admah,
and Shemeber king of
Zeboiim, and the king
of Bela, which is Zoar.**
3. All these were joined together
in the vale of Siddim, which
is the salt sea.
4. Twelve years they served
Chedorlaomer, and in the
thirteenth year they rebelled.
5. And in the fourteenth year came
Chedorlaomer, and the kings that *were*
with him, and smote the Rephaims in
Ashteroth Karnaim, and the Zuzims
in Ham, and the Emins in
Shaveh Kiriathaim,
6. And the Horites in their mount
Seir, unto Elparan, which *is* by
the wilderness.
7. And they returned, and came to
Enmishpat, which *is* Kadesh, and
smote all the country of the
Amalekites, and also the Amorites,
that dwelt in Hazezontamar.
8. And there went out the king
of Sodom, and the king of
Gomorrah, and the king of Admah,
and the king of Zeboiim, and the
king of Bela (the same *is* Zoar;)
and they joined battle
with them in the vale of Siddim;
9. **With Chedorlaomer**
the king of Elam, and with
Tidal king of nations, and
Amraphel king of Shinar,
and Arioch king of

Ellasar; four kings with five.
10. **And** the vale of
**Siddim was full of slimepits;
and the kings of Sodom
and Gomorrah fled, and
fell there;** and they that remained
fled to the mountain.
11. **And they took all the
goods of Sodom and
Gomorrah,** and all their
victuals, and went their way.
12. **And they took Lot,** Abram's
brother's son, who dwelt in Sodom,
and his goods, and departed.
13. **And** there came
one that had
escaped, and told Abram
the Hebrew; for he dwelt in the plain
of Mamre the Amorite, brother of
Eshcol, and brother of Aner: and
these *were* confederate with Abram.
14. **And when Abram heard**
that his brother was taken captive,
**he armed his trained
servants,** born in his own
house, three hundred and eighteen,
and pursued *them* unto Dan.
15. **And** he
divided himself
against them, he and
his servants, by night,
and smote them, and pursued
them unto Hobah, which *is* on
the left hand of Damascus.
16. **And he brought
back all the goods,** and
also brought again
his brother Lot, and
his goods, and
the women also,
and the people.
17. And the king of Sodom went out
to meet him after his return from the
slaughter of Chedorlaomer, and of the
kings that *were* with him, at the valley
of Shaveh, which *is* the king's dale.
18. **And Melchizedek king of
Salem brought forth bread
and wine: and he was the
priest of the most high God.**
19. **And he** blessed him, and
**said, Blessed be Abram
of the most high God,**

possessor of heaven and earth:

20. **And blessed be** the most high **God, which hath delivered thine enemies into thy hand. And he gave him tithes of all.**

21. **And the king of Sodom said** unto Abram, **Give me the persons, and take the goods** to thyself.

22. **And Abram said** to the king of Sodom, I have lift up mine hand unto the LORD, the most high God, the possessor of heaven and earth,

23. That I will not *take* from a thread even to a shoelatchet, and that **I will not take any thing that is thine,** lest thou shouldest say, I have made Abram rich:

24. Save only that which the young men have eaten, and the portion of the men which went with me, Aner, Eshcol, and Mamre; let them take their portion.

CHAPTER 15

1. **After these things the word of the LORD came unto Abram in a vision, saying, Fear not, Abram: I am thy shield, and thy exceeding great reward.**

2. **And Abram said,** LORD God, **what wilt thou give me, seeing I go childless,** and the steward of my house *is* this Eliezer of Damascus?

3. And Abram said, Behold, to me thou hast given no seed: and, lo, one born in my house is mine heir.

4. And, behold, the word of the LORD *came* unto him, saying, This shall not be thine heir; but he that shall come forth out of thine own bowels shall be thine heir.

5. **And he brought him forth abroad, and said, Look now toward heaven, and tell the stars, if thou be able to number them:** **and he said** unto him,

So shall thy seed be.

6. **And he believed in the LORD; and he counted it to him for righteousness.**

7. **And he said** unto him, **I am the LORD that brought thee out of Ur** of the Chaldees, **to give thee this land** to inherit it.

8. **And he said, LORD** God, **whereby shall I know that I shall inherit it?**

9. **And he said** unto him, **Take** me **an heifer** of three years old, and **a she goat** of three years old, and **a ram** of three years old, and **a turtledove, and a young pigeon.**

10. **And he took** unto him all **these, and divided them** in the midst, and laid each piece one against another: **but the birds divided he not.**

11. **And when the fowls came down upon the carcases, Abram drove them away.**

12. **And** when the sun was going down, **a deep sleep fell upon Abram; and,** lo, an horror `of **great darkness** fell upon him.

13. **And he said unto Abram,** Know of a surety that **thy seed shall be a stranger in a land** *that is* not theirs, **and shall serve them;** and they shall afflict them **four hundred years;**

14. **And also that nation,** whom they shall serve, **will I judge: and afterward shall they come out with great substance.**

15. And thou shalt go to thy fathers in peace; thou shalt be buried in a good old age.

16. But in the fourth generation they shall come hither again: for the iniquity of the Amorites *is* not yet full.

17. And it came to pass, that, when the sun went down, and it was dark, behold a smoking furnace, and a burning lamp that passed between those pieces.

18. **In the same day the LORD made a covenant with Abram, saying, Unto thy seed have I given this land, from the river of Egypt unto** the great river, **the river Euphrates:**

19. The Kenites, and the Kenizzites, and the Kadmonites,

20. And the Hittites, and the Perizzites, and the Rephaims,

21. And the Amorites, and the Canaanites, and the Girgashites, and the Jebusites.

CHAPTER 16

1. **Now Sarai** Abram's wife bare him no children: and she **had an handmaid,** an Egyptian, **whose name was Hagar.**

2. **And Sarai said** unto Abram, Behold now, **the LORD hath restrained me from bearing: I pray thee, go in unto my maid;** it may be **that I may obtain children by her.** And Abram hearkened to the voice of Sarai.

3. **And Sarai** Abram's wife **took Hagar** her maid the Egyptian, after Abram had dwelt ten years in the land of Canaan, **and gave her to** her husband **Abram** to be his wife.

4. **And** he went in unto **Hagar, and she conceived: and** when she saw that she had conceived, **her mistress was despised in her eyes.**

5. **And Sarai said unto Abram, My wrong be upon thee: I have given my maid** into thy bosom; **and when she** saw that she had conceived, **I was despised in her eyes:** the LORD

judge between me and thee.

6. **But Abram said unto Sarai,** Behold, thy maid *is* in thine hand; **do to her as it pleaseth thee. And when Sarai dealt hardly with her, she fled from her face.**

7. **And the angel of the LORD found her by a fountain** of water **in the wilderness,** by the fountain in the way to Shur.

8. **And he said, Hagar,** Sarai's maid, whence camest thou? and **whither wilt thou go? And she said, I flee from** the face of my mistress **Sarai.**

9. **And the angel of the LORD said** unto her, **Return** to thy mistress, **and submit thyself under her** hands.

10. And the angel of the LORD said unto her, **I will multiply thy seed exceedingly,** that it shall not be numbered for multitude.

11. And the angel of the LORD said unto her, Behold, **thou** *art* with child and **shalt bear a son, and shalt call his name Ishmael;** because the LORD hath heard thy affliction.

12. **And he will be a wild man**; his hand *will be* against every man, and every man's hand against him; and he shall dwell in the presence of all his brethren.

13. **And she called the name of the LORD** that spake unto her, **Thou God seest me:** for she said, Have I also here looked after him that seeth me?

14. **Wherefore the well was called Beerlahairoi;** behold, *it is* between Kadesh and Bered.

15. **And Hagar bare Abram a son; and** Abram **called** his son's

name, which Hagar bare,
■ **Ishmael.**
16. And Abram *was* fourscore and six years old, when Hagar bare Ishmael to Abram.

CHAPTER 17

■ 1. **And when Abram**
■ **was ninety** years old and
■ **nine, the LORD**
■ **appeared** to Abram,
■ **and said** unto him,
■ **I am the Almighty God;**
■ **walk before me, and be**
■ **thou perfect.**
■ 2. **And I will make my**
■ **covenant** between me and thee,
■ **and will multiply**
■ **thee exceedingly.**
■ 3. **And Abram fell on his**
■ **face: and God talked**
■ **with him, saying,**
4. As for me, behold, my covenant *is* with thee, and thou shalt be a father of many nations.
5. Neither shall thy name any more be called Abram, but
■ **thy name shall be**
■ **Abraham; for a father**
■ **of many nations have**
■ **I made thee.**
6. And I will make thee exceeding fruitful, and I will make nations of thee,
■ **and kings shall**
■ **come out of thee.**
■ 7. **And I will establish my**
■ **covenant between me and**
■ **thee and thy seed after**
■ **thee** in their generations for an everlasting covenant, to be a God unto thee, and to thy seed after thee.
■ 8. **And I will give unto thee,**
■ **and to thy seed** after thee, the land wherein thou art a stranger, all
■ **the land of Canaan, for an**
■ **everlasting possession;** and I will be their God.
9. And God said unto Abraham, Thou shalt keep my covenant therefore, thou, and thy seed after thee in their generations.
■ 10. **This is my covenant,**

■ **which ye shall keep,** between me and you and thy seed after thee;
■ **Every man child among**
■ **you shall be circumcised.**
11. And ye shall circumcise the flesh of your foreskin; and
■ **it shall be a token of**
■ **the covenant betwixt**
■ **me and you.**
12. And he that is eight days old shall be circumcised among you, every man child in your generations, he that is born in the house, or bought with money of any stranger, which *is* not of thy seed.
■ 13. **He that is born in thy**
■ **house, and he that is**
■ **bought with thy money,**
■ **must needs be**
■ **circumcised:** and my covenant shall be in your flesh for an everlasting covenant.
■ 14. **And the uncircumcised**
■ **man child** whose flesh of his foreskin is not circumcised, that soul
■ **shall be cut off** from his people; he hath broken my covenant.
■ 15. **And God**
■ **said** unto Abraham,
■ **As for Sarai** thy wife,
■ **thou shalt not call her**
■ **name Sarai, but Sarah**
shall her name *be*.
■ 16. **And I will bless her,**
■ **and give thee a son** also
■ **of her:** yea, I will bless her,
■ **and she shall be a**
■ **mother of nations;**
kings of people shall be of her.
■ 17. **Then Abraham fell**
■ **upon his face, and**
■ **laughed, and said** in his heart,
■ **Shall a child be born unto**
■ **him that is an hundred**
■ **years old? and** shall
■ **Sarah, that is ninety**
years old, bear?
18. And Abraham said unto God, O that Ishmael might live before thee!
■ 19. **And God said,**
■ **Sarah** thy wife
■ **shall bear thee a son** indeed;
■ **and thou shalt call his**

■ **name Isaac:** and I will establish
my covenant with him for an
everlasting covenant, *and*
with his seed after him.

■ 20. **And as for Ishmael,**
I have heard thee: Behold,

■ **I have blessed him, and**
will make him fruitful, and will
multiply him exceedingly;

■ **twelve princes shall he**
■ **beget, and I will make**
■ **him a great nation.**

■ 21. **But my covenant will I**
■ **establish with Isaac,** which
Sarah shall bear unto thee at
this set time in the next year.
22. And he left off talking with him,
and God went up from Abraham.

■ 23. **And Abraham**
■ **took Ishmael** his son,
■ **and** all that were born in his
house, and all that were
bought with his money,

■ **every male** among the
men of Abraham's house;

■ **and circumcised** the flesh of
■ **their foreskin**
in the self same day,

■ **as God had said** unto him.
24. And Abraham *was* ninety years
old and nine, when he was
circumcised in the flesh of his foreskin.
25. And Ishmael his son *was* thirteen
years old, when he was circumcised
in the flesh of his foreskin.
26. In the selfsame day was Abraham
circumcised, and Ishmael his son.
27. And all the men of his house,
born in the house, and bought with
money of the stranger, were
circumcised with him.

CHAPTER 18

■ 1. **And the LORD appeared**
■ **unto him** in the plains of Mamre:
■ **and he sat in the tent** door
in the heat of the day;

■ 2. **And he** lift up his eyes and
■ **looked, and,** lo,
■ **three men stood by**
■ **him: and when he**
■ **saw them, he ran to**
■ **meet them** from the tent door,

■ **and bowed** himself
toward the ground,

■ 3. **And said, My LORD,** if
now I have found favour in thy sight,

■ **pass not away,** I pray thee,
■ **from thy servant:**

■ 4. **Let a little water,** I pray you,
■ **be fetched, and wash**
■ **your feet, and rest**
yourselves under the tree:

■ 5. **And I will fetch** a morsel of
■ **bread,** and comfort ye your
hearts; after that ye shall pass
on: for therefore are ye come
to your servant.

■ **And they said,**
■ **So do,** as thou hast said.

■ 6. **And Abraham hastened**
■ **into the tent unto Sarah,**
■ **and said, Make ready**
quickly three measures of
fine meal, knead *it*, and make

■ **cakes** upon the hearth.

■ 7. **And Abraham**
ran unto the herd, and

■ **fetched a calf** tender and good,
and gave *it* unto a young man;

■ **and** he
■ **hasted to dress it.**

■ 8. **And he took butter,** and
■ **milk, and the calf**
which he had dressed,

■ **and set it before them;** and
he stood by them under the tree,

■ **and they did eat.**

■ 9. **And they said** unto him,
■ **Where is Sarah** thy wife? And
■ **he said,** Behold,
■ **in the tent.**

■ 10. **And he said,** I will
certainly return unto thee
according to the time of life; and,

■ **lo, Sarah** thy wife
■ **shall have a son. And Sarah**
■ **heard it** in the tent
door, which *was* behind him.
11. Now Abraham and Sarah *were*
old *and* well stricken in age; *and*
it ceased to be with Sarah after
the manner of women.

■ 12. **Therefore Sarah**
■ **laughed** within herself,
■ **saying, After I am** waxed

old shall I have pleasure, my lord being old also? 13. And the LORD said unto Abraham, Wherefore did Sarah laugh, saying, Shall I of a surety bear a child, which am old? 14. Is any thing too hard for the LORD? At the time appointed I will return unto thee, according to the time of life, and Sarah shall have a son. 15. Then Sarah denied, saying, I laughed not; for she was afraid. And he said, Nay; but thou didst laugh. 16. And the men rose up from thence, and looked toward Sodom: and Abraham went with them to bring them on the way.

17. And the LORD said, Shall I hide from Abraham that thing which I do; 18. Seeing that Abraham shall surely become a great and mighty nation, and all the nations of the earth shall be blessed in him? 19. For I know him, that he will command his children and his household after him, and they shall keep the way of the LORD, to do justice and judgment; that the LORD may bring upon Abraham that which he hath spoken of him. 20. And the LORD said, Because the cry of Sodom and Gomorrah is great, and because their sin is very grievous; 21. I will go down now, and see whether they have done altogether according to the cry of it, which is come unto me; and if not, I will know. 22. And the men turned their faces from thence, and went toward Sodom: but Abraham stood yet before the LORD.

23. And Abraham drew near, and said, Wilt thou also destroy the righteous with the wicked? 24. Peradventure there be fifty righteous within the city: wilt thou also destroy and not spare the place for the fifty righteous that *are* therein? 25. That be far from thee to do after this manner, to slay the righteous with the wicked: and that the righteous should be as the wicked, that be far from thee: Shall not the Judge of all the earth do right? 26. And the LORD said, If I find in Sodom fifty righteous within the city, then I will spare all the place for their sakes. 27. And Abraham answered and said, Behold now, I have taken upon me to speak unto the LORD, which *am but* dust and ashes: 28. Peradventure there shall lack five of the fifty righteous: wilt thou destroy all the city for *lack of* five? And he said, If I find there forty and five, I will not destroy it. 29. And he spake unto him yet again, and said, Peradventure there shall be forty found there. And he said, I will not do *it* for forty's sake. 30. And he said *unto him*, Oh let not the LORD be angry, and I will speak: Peradventure there shall thirty be found there. And he said, I will not do it, if I find thirty there. 31. And he said, Behold now, I have taken upon me to speak unto the LORD: Peradventure there shall be twenty found there. And he said, I will not destroy it for twenty's sake. 32. And he said, Oh let

23

not the LORD be angry, and I will speak yet but this once: **Peradventure ten shall be found** there. **And he said, I will not destroy it for ten's sake.** 33. **And the LORD went his way,** as soon as he had left communing with Abraham: and Abraham returned unto his place.

CHAPTER 19

1. **And there came two angels to Sodom** at even; **and Lot sat in the gate** of Sodom: **and** Lot **seeing them rose up to meet them; and** he **bowed** himself with his face toward the ground; 2. **And** he **said,** Behold now, **my lords, turn** in, I pray you, **into your servant's house, and tarry all night,** and wash your feet, and ye shall rise up early, and go on your ways. **And they said, Nay;** but **we will abide in the street** all night. 3. **And he pressed** upon **them greatly; and they** turned in unto him, and **entered into his house; and he made them a feast,** and did bake unleavened bread, and they did eat. 4. **But** before they lay down, the men of the city, *even* **the men of Sodom, compassed the house** round, both old and young, all the people from every quarter: 5. **And they called** unto Lot, and said unto him, **Where are the men** which came in to thee this night? **bring them out** unto us, **that we may know them.** 6. **And Lot went out** at the door unto them, and shut the door after him,

7. **And said,** I pray you, brethren, **do not so wickedly.** 8. Behold now, **I have two daughters** which have not known man; let me, I pray you, bring them out unto you, and **do** ye **to them as is good in your eyes:** only unto these men do nothing; for therefore came they under the shadow of my roof. 9. **And they said, Stand back.** And they said *again*, This one *fellow* came in to sojourn, and he will needs be a judge: **now will we deal worse with thee, than with them. And they** pressed sore upon the man, *even* Lot, and **came near to break the door.** 10. **But the men** put forth their hand, and **pulled Lot into the house** to them, **and shut** to **the door.** 11. **And they smote the men** that *were* at the door of the house **with blindness,** both small and great: so that they wearied themselves to find the door. 12. **And the men said** unto Lot, **Hast thou here any besides?** son in law, and thy sons, and thy daughters, and whatsoever thou hast in the city, **bring them out of this place:** 13. **For we will destroy this place, because** the cry of them is waxen great before the face of the LORD; and **the LORD hath sent us to destroy it.** 14. **And Lot** went out, and **spake unto his sons in law,** which married his daughters, **and said,** Up, **get** you **out of this place; for the LORD will destroy this city. But he seemed**

24

as one that mocked
unto his sons in law.
15. **And when the
morning arose,** then
**the angels hastened
Lot, saying, Arise, take
thy wife, and** thy two
daughters, which are here;
**lest thou be consumed
in the iniquity of the city.**
16. And while he lingered, the men
laid hold upon his hand, and upon
the hand of his wife, and upon
the hand of his two daughters;
**the LORD being
merciful** unto him: and they
**brought him forth, and
set him without the city.**
17. **And** it came to pass, when they
had brought them forth abroad, that
he said, Escape for thy life;
look not behind thee,
neither stay thou in all the
plain; escape to the mountain,
lest thou be consumed.
18. **And Lot said** unto them,
Oh, not so, my LORD:
19. Behold now, thy servant
hath found grace in thy sight, and
**thou hast magnified
thy mercy,** which thou
hast shewed unto me
in saving my life; and
**I cannot escape to the
mountain, lest some
evil take me,** and I die:
20. **Behold now, this
city is near** to flee unto,
**and it is a little one: Oh, let
me escape thither,** (*is* it not a
little one?) and my soul shall live.
21. **And he said** unto him, See,
**I have accepted thee
concerning this thing also,
that I will not overthrow this
city,** for the which thou hast spoken.
22. **Haste thee, escape
thither;** for I cannot do anything
till thou be come thither.
Therefore the name of
the city was called Zoar.
23. The sun was risen upon the earth
when Lot entered into

Zoar.
24. **Then the LORD rained
upon Sodom and** upon
**Gomorrah brimstone and
fire** from the LORD out of heaven;
25. **And he overthrew
those cities,** and all the
plain, and all the inhabitants
of the cities, and that which
grew upon the ground.
26. **But his wife looked
back** from behind him,
and she
became a pillar of salt.
27. **And Abraham gat up
early** in the morning to the place
where he stood before the LORD:
28. **And** he
**looked toward Sodom
and Gomorrah,** and toward
all the land of the plain, and beheld,
and, lo,
**the smoke of the
country went up as the
smoke of a furnace.**
29. And it came to pass, when God
destroyed the cities of the plain,
that God remembered Abraham,
and sent Lot out of the midst of
the overthrow, when he overthrew
the cities in the which Lot dwelt.
30. **And Lot went up out of
Zoar,** and dwelt in the mountain,
**and his two daughters with
him;** for he feared to dwell in Zoar:
and he
dwelt in a cave, he
and his two daughters.
31. **And the firstborn
said** unto the younger,
**Our father is old, and there
is not a man** in the earth
to come in unto us after
the manner of all the earth:
32. **Come, let us make
our father drink wine,
and we will lie with him,
that we may preserve
seed** of our father.
33. And they made their
father drink wine that night:
**and the firstborn
went in,**

and lay with her father; and he perceived not when she lay down, nor when she arose. 34. **And** it came to pass on the morrow, that **the firstborn said** unto the younger, Behold, **I lay** yesternight **with my father: let us make him drink wine this night also; and go thou** in, **and lie with him,** that we may preserve seed of our father. 35. And they made their father drink wine that night also: **and the younger arose, and lay with him; and he perceived not** when she lay down, nor when she arose. 36. Thus were both the daughters of Lot with child by their father. 37. **And the first born bare a son, and called his name Moab:** the same *is* **the father of the Moabites** unto this day. 38. **And the younger,** she also **bare** a son, and called his name **Benammi:** the same *is* **the father of the children of Ammon** unto this day.

CHAPTER 20

1. **And Abraham journeyed** from thence toward the **south** country, and dwelled between Kadesh and Shur, **and sojourned in Gerar.** 2. **And Abraham said of Sarah** his wife, **She is my sister: and Abimelech king of Gerar** sent, and **took Sarah.** 3. **But God came to Abimelech in a dream** by night, **and said** to him, Behold, **thou art** *but* **a dead man,for the woman** which thou hast taken; for she **is a man's wife.** 4. **But Abimelech had not** **come near her: and he said, LORD,** wilt thou slay also a righteous nation? 5. **Said he not unto me, She is my sister?** and she, even she herself said, He *is* my brother: **in** the integrity of my heart and **innocency** of my hands **have I done this.** 6. **And God said** unto him in a dream, **Yea, I know** that thou didst this in the integrity of thy heart; **for I also withheld thee from sinning against me:** therefore suffered I thee not to touch her. 7. **Now therefore restore the man his wife; for he is a prophet, and he shall pray for thee, and thou shalt live:** and if thou restore *her* not, know thou that thou shalt surely die, thou, and all that *are* thine. 8. Therefore Abimelech rose early in the morning, and called all his servants, and told all these things in their ears: and the men were sore afraid. 9. **Then Abimelech called Abraham, and said** unto him, **What hast thou done unto us?** and what have I offended thee, that thou hast brought on me and on my kingdom a great sin? thou hast done deeds unto me that ought not to be done. 10. And Abimelech said unto Abraham, What sawest thou, that thou hast done this thing? 11. **And Abraham said,** Because **I thought, Surely the fear of God is not in this place; and they will slay me for my wife's sake.** 12. **And** yet indeed **she is my sister;** she *is* **the daughter of my father, but not** the daughter of **my mother;** and she became my wife. 13. **And it came to pass,**

when God caused me to
wander from my father's house,
that I said unto her,
This *is* thy kindness which
thou shalt shew unto me;
at every place
whither we shall come,
say of me, He is
my brother.

14. And Abimelech took
sheep, and oxen, and menservants,
and womenservants, and
gave *them* unto
Abraham, and restored him
Sarah his wife.

15. And Abimelech said, Behold,
my land *is* before thee: dwell
where it pleaseth thee.

16. And unto Sarah he said, Behold,
I have given thy brother a thousand
pieces of silver: behold, he *is* to thee
a covering of the eyes, unto all that
are with thee, and with all *other*:
thus she was reproved.

17. So Abraham
prayed unto God:
and God healed
Abimelech, and his wife, and
his maidservants; and
they bare children.

18. For the LORD had fast
closed up all
the wombs of the house
of Abimelech, because
of Sarah Abraham's wife.

CHAPTER 21

1. And the LORD visited Sarah
as he had said, and the LORD
did unto Sarah as he
had spoken.

2. For Sarah conceived,
and bare Abraham
a son in his old age,
at the set time of which
God had spoken to him.

3. And Abraham
called the name of
his son that was born unto
him, whom Sarah bare to him,
Isaac.

4. And Abraham circumcised his son
Isaac being eight days old, as God
had commanded him.

5. And Abraham was
an hundred years
old, when his son
Isaac was born unto him.

6. And Sarah said, God
hath made me to laugh, *so that*
all that hear will laugh with me.

7. And she said,
Who would have
said unto Abraham,
that Sarah should have
given children suck? for I
have born *him* a son in his old age.

8. And the child grew,
and was weaned: and
Abraham made a great feast the
same day that Isaac was weaned.

9. And Sarah saw the son
of Hagar the Egyptian, which
she had born unto Abraham,
mocking.

10. Wherefore she said unto
Abraham, Cast out this
bondwoman and her son:
for the son of this bondwoman
shall not be heir with
my son, *even*
with Isaac.

11. And the thing was very
grievous in Abraham's sight
because of his son.

12. And God
said unto Abraham,
Let it not be grievous in thy
sight because of the lad, and
because of thy bondwoman;
in all that
Sarah hath said unto thee,
hearken unto her voice;
for in Isaac shall thy
seed be called.

13. And also of the son of
the bondwoman will I make
a nation, because he *is* thy seed.

14. And Abraham rose up
early in the morning, and
took bread, and a bottle of
water, and gave it unto
Hagar, putting *it* on her
shoulder, and the child,
and sent her away:
and she departed, and

27

wandered in the wilderness of Beersheba. 15. And the water was spent in the bottle, and she cast the child under one of the shrubs. 16. And she went, and sat her down over against *him* a good way off, as it were a bow shot: for she said, Let me not see the death of the child. And she sat over against *him*, and lift up her voice, and wept. 17. And God heard the voice of the lad; and the angel of God called to Hagar out of heaven, and said unto her, What aileth thee, Hagar? fear not; for God hath heard the voice of the lad where he *is*. 18. Arise, lift up the lad, and hold him in thine hand; for I will make him a great nation. 19. And God opened her eyes, and she saw a well of water; and she went, and filled the bottle with water, and gave the lad drink. 20. And God was with the lad; and he grew, and dwelt in the wilderness, and became an archer. 21. And he dwelt in the wilderness of Paran: and his mother took him a wife out of the land of Egypt. 22. And it came to pass at that time, that Abimelech and Phichol the chief captain of his host spake unto Abraham, saying, God is with thee in all that thou doest: 23. Now therefore swear unto me here by God that thou wilt not deal falsely with me, nor with my son, nor with my son's son: *but* according to the kindness that I have done unto thee, thou shalt do unto me, and to the land wherein thou hast sojourned. 24. And Abraham said, I will swear. 25. And Abraham reproved Abimelech because of a well of water, which Abimelech's servants had violently taken away. 26. And Abimelech said, I wot not who hath done this thing; neither didst thou tell me, neither yet heard I *of it*, but to-day. 27. And Abraham took sheep and oxen, and gave them unto Abimelech; and both of them made a covenant. 28. And Abraham set seven ewe lambs of the flock by themselves. 29. And Abimelech said unto Abraham, What mean these seven ewe lambs which thou hast set by themselves? 30. And he said, For these seven ewe lambs shalt thou take of my hand, that they may be a witness unto me, that I have digged this well. 31. Wherefore he called that place Beersheba; because there they sware both of them. 32. Thus they made a covenant at Beersheba: then Abimelech rose up, and Phichol the chief captain of his host, and they returned into the land of the Philistines. 33. And Abraham planted a grove in Beersheba, and called there on the name of the LORD, the everlasting God. 34. And Abraham sojourned in the Philistines' land many days.

CHAPTER 22

1. And it came to pass after these things, that God did tempt Abraham, and said unto him, Abraham: and he said, Behold, *here* I *am.*

2. And he said, Take now thy son, thine only *son* Isaac, whom thou lovest, and get thee into the land of Moriah; and offer him there for a burnt offering upon one of the mountains which I will tell thee of.

3. And Abraham rose up early in the morning, and saddled his ass, and took two of his young men with him, and Isaac his son, and clave the wood for the burnt offering, and rose up, and went unto the place of which God had told him.

4. Then on the third day Abraham lifted up his eyes, and saw the place afar off.

5. And Abraham said unto his young men, Abide ye here with the ass; and I and the lad will go yonder and worship, and come again to you.

6. And Abraham took the wood of the burnt offering, and laid it upon Isaac his son; and he took the fire in his hand, and a knife; and they went both of them together.

7. And Isaac spake unto Abraham his father, and said, My father: and he said, Here *am* I, my son. And he said, Behold the fire and the wood: but where is the lamb for a burnt offering?

8. And Abraham said, My son, God will provide himself a lamb for a burnt offering: so they went both of them together.

9. And they came to the place which God had told him of; and Abraham built an altar there, and laid the wood in order, and bound Isaac his son, and laid him on the altar upon the wood.

10. And Abraham stretched forth his hand, and took the knife to slay his son.

11. And the angel of the LORD called unto him out of heaven, and said, Abraham, Abraham: and he said, Here *am* I.

12. And he said, Lay not thine hand upon the lad, neither do thou any thing unto him: for now I know that thou fearest God, seeing thou hast not withheld thy son, thine only *son* from me.

13. And Abraham lifted up his eyes, and looked, and behold behind him a ram caught in a thicket by his horns: and Abraham went and took the ram, and offered him up for a burnt offering in the stead of his son.

14. And Abraham called the name of that place Jehovahjireh: as it is said *to* this day, In the mount of the LORD it shall be seen.

15. And the angel of the LORD called unto Abraham out of heaven the second time,

16. And said, By myself have I sworn, saith the LORD, for because thou hast done this thing, and hast not withheld thy son, thine only *son*:

17. That in blessing I will bless thee,

■ **and** in multiplying I will
■ **multiply thy seed as**
■ **the stars** of the heaven,
■ **and as the sand** which *is*
■ **upon the sea shore;**
and thy seed shall possess
the gate of his enemies;
■ 18. **And in thy seed shall**
■ **all the nations** of the earth
■ **be blessed; because thou**
■ **hast obeyed** my voice.
■ 19. **So Abraham returned**
unto his young men, and they rose
up and went together to Beersheba;
■ **and** Abraham
■ **dwelt at Beersheba.**
20. And it came to pass after these
things, that it was told Abraham,
saying, Behold, Milcah, she hath also
born children unto thy brother Nahor;
21. Huz his firstborn, and Buz
his brother, and Kemuel the
father of Aram,
22. And Chesed, and Hazo, and
Pildash, and Jidlaph, and Bethuel.
23. And Bethuel begat Rebekah:
these eight Milcah did bear to
Nahor, Abraham's brother.
24. And his concubine, whose
name *was* Reumah, she bare
also Tebah, and Gaham, and
Thahash, and Maachah.

CHAPTER 23

1. And Sarah was an hundred and
seven and twenty years old: *these*
were the years of the life of Sarah.
■ 2. **And Sarah died in**
Kirjatharba; the same *is*
■ **Hebron in the land of**
■ **Canaan: and Abraham**
■ **came** to mourn for Sarah, and
■ **to weep for her.**
■ 3. **And Abraham**
■ **stood** up from
■ **before his dead, and**
■ **spake unto the sons**
■ **of Heth, saying,**
■ 4. **I am a stranger and**
■ **a sojourner** with you:
■ **give me a** possession of a
■ **burying place** with you,
■ **that I may bury my**

■ **dead** out of my sight.
■ 5. **And the children of**
■ **Heth answered** Abraham,
saying unto him,
6. Hear us, my lord:
■ **thou art a mighty**
■ **prince** among us:
■ **in the choice of our**
■ **sepulchres bury thy**
■ **dead;** none of us shall withhold
from thee his sepulchre, but that
thou mayest bury thy dead.
7. And Abraham stood up, and bowed
himself to the people of the land,
even to the children of Heth.
■ 8. **And he communed with**
■ **them, saying,** If it be your mind
that I should bury my dead out of
my sight; hear me, and
■ **entreat for me to**
■ **Ephron** the son of Zohar,
■ 9. **That he may give me the**
■ **cave of Machpelah,** which he
hath, which *is* in the end of his field;
for as much money as it is worth he
shall give it me for a possession of
a buryingplace amongst you.
10. And Ephron dwelt among
the children of Heth:
■ **and Ephron the Hittite**
■ **answered** Abraham in the
audience of the children of Heth,
even of all that went in at the
gate of his city, saying,
11. Nay, my lord, hear me:
■ **the field give I thee, and the**
■ **cave** that *is* therein, I give it thee;
in the presence of the sons of my
people give I it thee:
■ **bury thy dead.**
■ 12. **And Abraham**
■ **bowed** down himself
before the people of the land.
■ 13. **And** he
■ **spake unto Ephron** in the
audience of the people of the land,
■ **saying,** But if thou *wilt give*
it, I pray thee, hear me:
■ **I will give thee money for**
■ **the field;** take *it* of me, and I
will bury my dead there.
■ 14. **And Ephron answered**
Abraham, saying unto him,

15. My lord, hearken unto me: **the land is worth four hundred shekels of silver; what is that betwixt me and thee?** bury therefore thy dead. 16. And Abraham hearkened unto Ephron; **and Abraham weighed** to Ephron the silver, which he had named in the audience of the sons of Heth, **four hundred shekels of silver,** current *money* with the merchant. 17. **And the field of Ephron** which *was* in Machpelah, which *was* before Mamre, the field, and **the cave** which *was* therein, **and all the trees** that *were* in the field, that *were* in all the borders round about, **were made sure** 18. Unto Abraham for a possession in the presence of the children of Heth, before all that went in at the gate of his city. 19. **And** after this, **Abraham buried Sarah his wife in the cave** of the field of Machpelah before Mamre: **the same is Hebron in** the land of **Canaan.** 20. And the field, and the cave that *is* therein, were made sure unto Abraham for a possession of a buryingplace by the sons of Heth.

CHAPTER 24

1. **And Abraham was old, and** well stricken in age: and **the LORD had blessed Abraham in all things.** 2. **And Abraham said unto his eldest servant** of his house, that ruled over all that he had, **Put,** I pray thee, **thy hand under my thigh**: 3. **And** I will make thee **swear by the LORD,** the God of heaven, and the God of the earth, **that thou shalt not take a wife unto my son of the daughters of the Canaanites,** among whom I dwell: 4. **But thou shalt go unto my country,** and to my kindred, **and take a wife unto** my son **Isaac.** 5. **And the servant said** unto him, **Peradventure the woman will not be willing to follow** me unto this land: **must I needs bring thy son again unto the land from whence thou camest?** 6. **And Abraham said** unto him, **Beware thou that thou bring not my son thither again.** 7. **The LORD** God of heaven, which took me from my father's house, and from the and ofmy kindred, and which **spake unto me,** and that sware unto me, **saying, Unto thy seed will I give this land; he shall send his angel** before thee, **and thou shalt take a wife unto my son** from thence. 8. **And if the woman will not** be willing to **follow thee,** then **thou shalt be clear from** this **my oath:** only bring not my son thither again. 9. **And the servant** put his hand under the thigh of Abraham his master, and **sware** to him **concerning that matter.** 10. **And the servant took ten camels** of the camels of his master, and departed; **for all the goods of his master** were in his hand: and he arose, **and went to Mesopotamia, unto the city of Nahor.** 11. **And he made his camels to kneel** down without the city **by a well** of water

■ **at the time** of the evening, *even* the time that ■ **women go out to** ■ **draw water.**

■ 12. **And he said, O LORD** ■ **God** of my master Abraham, I pray thee, send me good speed this day, and ■ **shew kindness unto my** ■ **master Abraham.**

13. Behold, I stand *here* by the well of water; and the daughters of the men of the city come out to draw water:

■ 14. **And let it come to pass,** ■ **that the damsel to whom** ■ **I shall say, Let down** ■ **thy pitcher,** I pray thee, ■ **that I may drink; and** ■ **she shall say, Drink, and** ■ **I will give thy camels** drink ■ **also: let the same be** ■ **she that thou hast** ■ **appointed for** thy servant ■ **Isaac**; and thereby shall I know that thou hast shewed kindness unto my master.

■ 15. **And it came to pass,** before he had done speaking, ■ **that,** behold, ■ **Rebekah came out, who** ■ **was born to Bethuel, son of** ■ **Milcah, the wife of Nahor,** ■ **Abraham's brother, with her** ■ **pitcher** upon her shoulder.

■ 16. **And the damsel was** very ■ **fair to look upon, a virgin,** neither had any man known her: and she went down to the well, and filled her pitcher, and came up.

■ 17. **And the servant** ran to meet her, and ■ **said, Let me,** I pray thee, ■ **drink a little** ■ **water** of thy pitcher.

■ 18. **And she said, Drink,** my lord: and she hasted, and let down her pitcher upon her hand, and gave him drink.

■ 19. **And** when she had done giving him drink, she said, ■ **I will draw water for thy** ■ **camels also,** until they have done drinking.

20. And she hasted, and emptied her pitcher into the trough, and ran again unto the well to draw *water*, and drew for all his camels.

21. And the man wondering at her held his peace, to wit whether the LORD had made his journey prosperous or not.

■ 22. **And** it came to pass, ■ **as the camels had** ■ **done drinking,** that ■ **the man took a golden** ■ **earring** of half a shekel weight, ■ **and two bracelets** for her hands of ten *shekels* weight ■ **of gold;**

■ 23. **And said, Whose** ■ **daughter art thou?** tell me, I pray thee: ■ **is there room in thy father's** ■ **house for us to lodge** in?

■ 24. **And she said** unto him, ■ **I am the daughter of** ■ **Bethuel** the son of Milcah, which she bare unto Nahor.

■ 25. **She said** ■ **moreover** unto him, ■ **We have** both straw and provender enough, and ■ **room to lodge** in.

■ 26. **And the man** bowed down his head, and ■ **worshipped the LORD.**

■ 27. **And he said,** ■ **Blessed be the LORD** God of my master Abraham, ■ **who** hath not left destitute my master of his mercy and his truth: I *being* in the way, the LORD ■ **led me to the house of** ■ **my master's brethren.**

■ 28. **And the damsel** ■ **ran, and told** *them of* ■ **her mother's house** ■ **these things.**

■ 29. **And Rebekah had a** ■ **brother,** and his name *was* ■ **Laban: and Laban** ■ **ran** out unto the man, ■ **unto the well.**

30. And it came to pass, when ■ **he saw the earring and** ■ **bracelets upon his sister's**

32

■ **hands, and** when he
■ **heard** the words of
■ **Rebekah his sister,** saying, Thus
spake the man unto me; that he came
unto the man; and, behold, he stood
by the camels at the well.
■ 31. **And he said, Come**
■ **in**, thou blessed of the LORD;
wherefore standest thou without?
■ **for I have prepared the**
■ **house**, and room for the camels.
32. And the man came into the
house: and he ungirded his camels,
and gave straw and provender for the
camels, and water to wash his feet,
and the men's feet that *were* with him.
■ 33. **And there was set**
■ **meat before him** to eat:
■ **but he said, I will not eat,**
■ **until I have told mine**
■ **errand**. And he said, Speak on.
34. And he said,
■ **I am Abraham's servant.**
■ 35. **And** the LORD hath blessed
■ **my master** greatly; and he
■ **is become great:** and he
hath given him flocks, and
herds, and silver, and gold, and
menservants, and maidservants,
and camels, and asses.
■ 36. **And Sarah my master's**
■ **wife bare a son** to my
master when she was old:
■ **and unto him hath he**
■ **given all** that
■ **he hath.**
■ 37. **And my master made**
■ **me swear, saying,** Thou
shalt not take a wife to my son of
the daughters of the Canaanites,
in whose land I dwell:
38. But thou shalt
■ **go unto my father's house,**
■ **and to my kindred, and**
■ **take a wife unto my son.**
39. And I said unto my master,
Peradventure the woman will
not follow me.
40. And he said unto me, The LORD,
before whom I walk, will sendhisangel
with thee, and prosper thy way; and
thou shalt take a wife for my son of
my kindred, and of my father's house:

41. Then shalt thou be clear from *this*
my oath, when thou comest to my
kindred; and if they give not thee *one,*
thou shalt be clear from my oath.
42. And I came this day unto the
well, and said, O LORD God of
my master Abraham, if now thou
do prosper my way which I go:
43. Behold, I stand by the well of
water; and it shall come to pass,
that when the virgin cometh forth to
draw *water*, and I say to her, Give
me, I pray thee, a little water of
thy pitcher to drink;
44. And she say to me, Both drink
thou, and I will also draw for thy
camels: *let* the same *be* the woman
whom the LORD hath appointed
out for my master's son.
45. And before I had done speaking
in mine heart, behold, Rebekah came
forth with her pitcher on her shoulder;
and she went down unto the well,
and drew *water*: and I said unto her,
Let me drink, I pray thee.
46. And she made haste, and let
down her pitcher from her *shoulder*,
and said, Drink, and I will give thy
camels drink also: so I drank, and
she made the camels drink also.
47. And I asked her, and said, Whose
daughter *art* thou? And she said, the
daughter of Bethuel, Nahor's son,
whom Milcah bare unto him: and I
put the earring upon her face, and
the bracelets upon her hands.
48. And I bowed down my head, and
worshipped the LORD, and blessed
theLORD God ofmy master Abraham,
which had led me in the right way
to take my master's brother's
daughter unto his son.
■ 49. **And now if ye will**
■ **deal kindly** and truly
■ **with my master, tell me:**
and if not, tell me; that I may turn
to the right hand, or to the left.
■ 50. **Then Laban and**
■ **Bethuel answered** and said,
■ **The thing proceedeth**
■ **from the LORD:** we cannot
speak unto thee bad or good.
■ 51. **Behold, Rebekah is**

before thee, take her, and go, and let her be thy master's son's wife, as the LORD hath spoken.

52. And it came to pass, that, when Abraham's servant heard their words, he worshipped the LORD, *bowing himself* to the earth.

53. And the servant brought forth jewels of silver, and jewels of gold, and raiment, and gave them to Rebekah: he gave also to her brother and to her mother precious things.

54. And they did eat and drink, he and the men that *were* with him, and tarried all night; and they rose up in the morning, and he said, Send me away unto my master.

55. And her brother and her mother said, Let the damsel abide with us a few days, at the least ten; after that she shall go.

56. And he said unto them, Hinder me not, seeing the LORD hath prospered my way; send me away that I may go to my master.

57. And they said, We will call the damsel, and inquire at her mouth.

58. And they called Rebekah, and said unto her, Wilt thou go with this man? And she said, I will go.

59. And they sent away Rebekah their sister, and her nurse, and Abraham's servant, and his men.

60. And they blessed Rebekah, and said unto her, Thou art our sister, be thou the mother of thousands of millions, and let thy seed possess the gate of those which hate them.

61. And Rebekah arose, and her damsels, and they rode upon the camels, and followed the man: and the servant took Rebekah, and went his way.

62. And Isaac came from the way of the well Lahairoi; for he dwelt in the south country.

63. And Isaac went out to meditate in the field at the eventide: and he lifted up his eyes, and saw, and, behold, the camels *were* coming.

64. And Rebekah lifted up her eyes, and when she saw Isaac, she lighted off the camel.

65. For she had said unto the servant, What man *is* this that walketh in the field to meet us? And the servant *had* said, It is my master:therefore she took a vail, and covered herself.

66. And the servant told Isaac all things that he had done.

67. And Isaac brought her into his mother Sarah's tent, and took Rebekah, and she became his wife; and he loved her: and Isaac was comforted after his mother's death.

CHAPTER 25

1. Then again Abraham took a wife, and her name *was* Keturah.

2. And she bare him Zimran, and Jokshan, and Medan, and Midian, and Ishbak, and Shuah.

3. And Jokshan begat Sheba, and Dedan. And the sons of Dedan were Asshurim, and Letushim, and Leummim.

4. And the sons of Midian; Ephah, and Epher, and Hanoch, and Abidah, and Eldaah. All these *were* the children of Keturah.

5. And Abraham gave all that he had unto Isaac.

6. But unto the sons of the concubines, which Abraham had, Abraham gave gifts, and sent them away from Isaac his son, while he yet lived, eastward,

34

unto the east country.

7. And these *are* the days of the years of Abraham's life which he lived, an hundred threescore and fifteen years.

8. **Then Abraham** gave up the ghost, and **died** in a good old age, an old man, and full *of years;* **and was gathered to his people.**

9. **And** his sons **Isaac and Ishmael buried him in the cave of Machpelah,** in the field of Ephron the son of Zohar the Hittite, which *is* before Mamre;

10. The field which Abraham purchased of the sons of Heth: there was Abraham buried, and Sarah his wife.

11. **And** it came to pass after the death of Abraham, that **God blessed** his son **Isaac;** and Isaac dwelt by the well Lahairoi.

12. Now these *are* the generations of Ishmael, Abraham's son, whom Hagar the Egyptian, Sarah's handmaid, bare unto Abraham:

13. And these *are* the names of the sons of Ishmael, by their names, according to their generations: the firstborn of Ishmael, Nebajoth; and Kedar, and Adbeel, and Mibsam,

14. And Mishma, and Dumah, and Massa,

15. Hadar, and Tema, Jetur, Naphish, and Kedemah:

16. These *are* the sons of Ishmael, and these *are* their names, by their towns, and by their castles; twelve princes according to their nations.

17. And these *are* the years of the life of Ishmael, an hundred and thirty and seven years: and he gave up the ghost and died; and was gathered unto his people.

18. And they dwelt from Havilah unto Shur, that *is* before Egypt, as thou goest toward Assyria: *and* he died in the presence of all his brethren.

19. And these *are* the generations of Isaac, Abraham's son: Abraham begat Isaac:

20. **And Isaac was forty years old when he took Rebekah to wife,** the daughter of Bethuel the Syrian of Padanaram, the sister to Laban the Syrian.

21. **And Isaac entreated the LORD for his wife, because she was barren**: and the LORD was intreated of him, **and Rebekah** his wife **conceived.**

22. **And the children struggled** together **within her; and she said,** if *it be* so, **why am I thus?** And she went to enquire of the LORD.

23. **And the LORD said** unto her, **Two nations are in thy womb**, and two manner of people shall be separated from thy bowels; and *the one* people shall be stronger than *the other* people; **and the elder shall serve the younger.**

24. **And** when her days to be delivered were fulfilled, behold, **there were twins in her womb.**

25. **And the first came out red**, all over **like an hairy garment; and they called his name Esau.**

26. **And after that came his brother out, and his hand took hold on Esau's heel; and his name was called Jacob:** and Isaac *was* threescore years old when she bare them.

27. And the boys grew: and **Esau was a cunning hunter**, a man of the field; **and Jacob was a plain man**, dwelling in tents.

28. **And Isaac loved Esau**, because he did eat of *his* venison: **but Rebekah loved Jacob.**

29. **And Jacob sod pottage: and Esau came from the field,**

■ and he was faint:
■ 30. **And Esau said to Jacob,**
■ **Feed me,** I pray thee, with
■ **that** same red
■ **pottage; for I am faint:**
■ **therefore was his**
■ **name called Edom.**
■ 31. **And Jacob said,**
■ **Sell me** this day
■ **thy birthright.**
■ 32. **And Esau said,** Behold,
■ **I am at the point to die:** and
■ **what profit shall this**
■ **birthright do** to
■ **me?**

33. And Jacob said, Swear to
me this day; and he sware unto him:

■ **and he sold his birthright**
■ **unto Jacob.**
■ 34. **Then Jacob**
■ **gave Esau** bread and
■ **pottage** of lentiles; and

he did eat and drink, and
rose up, and went his way:

■ **thus Esau despised**
■ **his birthright.**

CHAPTER 26

■ 1. **And there was a famine** in
the land, beside the first famine that
was in the days of Abraham.

■ **And Isaac went unto**
■ **Abimelech king of the**
■ **Philistines** unto Gerar.
■ 2. **And the LORD**
appeared unto him, and
■ **said, Go not down into**
■ **Egypt;** dwell in the land which
I shall tell thee of:

3. Sojourn in this land, and

■ **I will be with thee, and will**
■ **bless thee;** for unto thee, and unto
thy seed, I will give all these
countries, and I will perform the
oath which I sware unto Abraham
thy father;

■ 4. **And I will** make thy
seed to multiply as the
stars of heaven, and will

■ **give unto thy seed all**
■ **these countries; and in**
■ **thy seed shall all the**
■ **nations** of the earth

■ **be blessed;**

5. Because that Abraham obeyed
my voice, and kept my charge,
my commandments, my statutes,
and my laws.

■ 6. **And Isaac dwelt**
■ **in Gerar:**
■ 7. **And the men** of the place
■ **asked** him
■ **of his wife; and he said,**
■ **She is my sister:** for he feared
to say, *She is* my wife; lest, *said
he*, the men of the place should
kill me for Rebekah; because
she *was* fair to look upon.

■ 8. **And it came to pass,**
when he had been there a long time,
■ **that Abimelech** king
of the Philistines
■ **looked out** at
■ **a window, and**
■ **saw,** and, behold,
■ **Isaac** *was*
■ **sporting with**
■ **Rebekah** his wife.
■ 9. **And Abimelech**
■ **called Isaac, and**
■ **said,** Behold, of a surety
■ **she is thy wife;** and how saidst
thou, She *is* my sister? And Isaac
said unto him, Because I said,
Lest I die for her.

■ 10. **And Abimelech said,**
■ **What is this thou hast**
■ **done** unto us? one of the
people might lightly have lien with
thy wife, and thou shouldest have
brought guiltiness upon us.

■ 11. **And Abimelech charged**
■ **all his people, saying, He**
■ **that toucheth this man**
■ **or his wife shall** surely
■ **be put to death.**
■ 12. **Then Isaac sowed**
■ **in that land, and**
■ **received** in the same year
■ **an hundredfold:** and
the LORD blessed him.
■ 13. **And the man** waxed great,
and went forward, and grew until he
■ **became very great:**

14. For he had possession of
flocks, and possession of herds,

and great store of servants:

■ **and the Philistines**
■ **envied him.**

15. For all the wells which his father's servants had digged in the days of Abraham his father, the Philistines had stopped them, and filled them with earth.

■ 16. **And Abimelech**
■ **said unto Isaac, Go**
■ **from us; for thou art** much
■ **mightier than we.**
■ 17. **And Isaac**
■ **departed** thence,
■ **and pitched his tent**
■ **in** the valley of
■ **Gerar,** and dwelt there.
■ 18. **And Isaac digged**
■ **again the wells**
of water, which they had
■ **digged in the days**
■ **of Abraham** his father;
■ **for the Philistines had**
■ **stopped them** after the death
of Abraham: and he called their names after the names by which his father had called them.
■ 19. **And Isaac's servants**
■ **digged** in the valley,
■ **and found** there
■ **a well of springing water.**
■ 20. **And the herdmen**
■ **of Gerar did strive**
with Isaac's herdmen,
■ **saying, The water is ours:** and he called the name of the well Esek; because they strove with him.
■ 21. **And they digged**
■ **another well, and strove**
■ **for that also**: and he called the name of it Sitnah.
■ 22. **And he** removed
from thence, and
■ **digged another well; and**
■ **for that they strove not: and**
■ **he called the name of it**
■ **Rehoboth;** and he said, For now the LORD hath made room for us, and we shall be fruitful in the land.
■ 23. **And he went** up from thence
■ **to Beersheba.**
■ 24. **And the LORD appeared**
■ **unto him** the same night,

■ **and said, I am the God**
■ **of Abraham** thy father:
■ **fear not, for I am with thee,**
and will bless thee, and multiply thy seed for my servant Abraham's sake.
■ 25. **And he builded an**
■ **altar there, and called**
■ **upon** the name of
■ **the LORD,** and
pitched his tent there:
■ **and** there
■ **Isaac's servants**
■ **digged a well.**
■ 26. **Then Abimelech**
■ **went to him** from Gerar,
and Ahuzzath one of his friends, and Phichol the chief captain of his army.
■ 27. **And Isaac said** unto them,
■ **Wherefore come ye to me,**
■ **seeing ye hate me,** and
have sent me away from you?
28. And they said,
■ **We saw** certainly
■ **that the LORD was with**
■ **thee:** and we said, Let there be now an oath betwixt us, *even* betwixt us and thee, and let us make a covenant with thee;
29. That thou wilt do us no hurt, as we have not touched thee, and as we have done unto thee nothing but good, and have sent thee away in peace: thou *art* now the blessed of the LORD.
■ 30. **And he made them a**
■ **feast**, and they did eat and drink.
■ 31. **And they rose up** betimes
■ **in the morning, and sware**
■ **one to another: and**
Isaac sent them away, and they
■ **departed** from him
■ **in peace.**
■ 32. **And** it came to pass
■ **the same day,** that
■ **Isaac's servants** came, and
■ **told him** concerning the well which they had digged, and said unto him,
■ **We have found water.**
■ 33. **And he called it**
■ **Shebah: therefore** the name of
■ **the city is Beersheba**
■ **unto this day.**
■ 34. **And Esau** was

forty years old when he
took to wife Judith
the daughter of Beeri
the Hittite, and Bashemath
the daughter of Elon the Hittite:
35. **Which were a grief** of mind
unto Isaac and to
Rebekah.

CHAPTER 27

1. **And** it came to pass, that
when Isaac was old,
and his eyes were dim,
so that he could not see,
he called Esau his eldest son,
and said unto him, My son: and
he said unto him, Behold, *here am* I.
2. And he said, Behold now, I am old,
I know not the day
of my death:
3. Now therefore take, I
pray thee, thy weapons,
thy quiver and thy bow, and
go out to the field, and
take me some venison;
4. **And make me savoury**
meat, such as I love,
and bring *it* to me,
that I may eat; that my
soul may bless thee
before I die.
5. **And Rebekah heard** when
Isaac spake to Esau his son. And
Esau went to the field to hunt *for*
venison, *and* to bring *it.*
6. **And** Rebekah
spake unto Jacob her son,
saying, Behold, I heard thy father
speak unto Esau thy brother, saying,
7. Bring me venison, and make me
savoury meat, that I may eat, and
bless thee before the LORD
before my death.
8. Now therefore,
my son, obey my
voice according to that
which I command thee.
9. **Go** now to the flock, and
fetch me from thence
two good kids of the
goats; and I will make them
savoury meat for thy father,
such as he loveth:

10. **And** thou shalt
bring it to thy father,
that he may eat,
and that he may
bless thee before his death.
11. **And Jacob said** to
Rebekah his mother, Behold,
Esau my brother
is a hairy man, and
I am a smooth man:
12. **My father** peradventure
will feel me, and I shall
seem to him as a deceiver;
and I shall bring a curse
upon me, and not a blessing.
13. **And his mother**
said unto him, Upon me
be thy curse, my son: only
obey my voice,
and go fetch me *them.*
14. **And he** went, and fetched, and
brought them to his mother:
and his mother made
savoury meat,
such as his father loved.
15. **And Rebekah took** goodly
raiment of her eldest son
Esau, which *were*
with her in the house,
and put them upon
Jacob her younger son:
16. **And she put the**
skins of the kids
of the goats upon
his hands, and
upon the smooth of his
neck:
17. And she gave the savoury
meat and the bread, which she
had prepared, into the hand
of her son Jacob.
18. **And he came unto**
his father, and said, My
father: and he said, Here *am* I;
who art thou, my son?
19. **And Jacob**
said unto his father,
I am Esau thy first born;
I have done according
as thou badest me:
arise, I pray thee, sit
and eat of my venison, that
thy soul may bless me.

20. **And Isaac said** unto his son, **How is it that thou hast found it so quickly**, my son? **And he said, Because the LORD** thy God **brought it to me.**

21. **And Isaac said** unto Jacob, **Come near,** I pray thee, **that I may feel thee,** my son, whether thou *be* my very son Esau or not.

22. **And Jacob went near** unto Isaac his father; **and he felt him, and said, The voice is Jacob's** voice, **but the hands are** the hands **of Esau.**

23. **And he discerned him not,** because his hands were hairy, as his brother Esau's hands: **so he blessed him.**

24. And he said, *Art* thou my very son Esau? And he said, I *am.*

25. **And he said, Bring it near** to me, **and I will eat** of my son's venison, that my soul may bless thee. **And he brought it** near to him, **and he did eat:** and he brought him wine and he drank.

26. **And** his father **Isaac said** unto him, **Come near now, and kiss me,** my son.

27. **And he** came near, and **kissed him: and he smelled** the smell of **his raiment, and blessed him, and said,** See, the smell of my son *is* as the smell of a field which the LORD hath blessed:

28. **Therefore God give thee of the dew of heaven, and the fatness of the earth, and plenty of corn and wine:**

29. **Let people serve thee, and nations bow down to thee**: be lord over thy brethren, **and let thy mother's sons bow down to thee: cursed be every one that curseth**

thee, and blessed be he that blesseth thee.

30. **And it came to pass**, as soon as Isaac had made an end of blessing Jacob, and Jacob was yet scarce gone out from the presence of Isaac his father, **that Esau** his brother **came in from his hunting.**

31. **And** he also had **made savoury meat, and brought it unto his father,** and said unto his father, Let my father arise, and eat of his son's venison, that thy soul may bless me.

32. **And Isaac** his father **said** unto him, **Who art thou? And he said, I am** thy son, thy firstborn **Esau.**

33. **And Isaac trembled** very exceedingly, **and said, Who?** where *is* he that **hath taken venison, and brought it me, and I** have eaten of all before thou camest, and **have blessed him? yea, and he shall be blessed.**

34. **And when Esau heard** the words of his father, **he cried** with **a** great and exceeding **bitter cry, and said** unto his father, **Bless me,** *even* me **also,** O **my father.**

35. **And he said, Thy brother** came with subtilty, and **hath taken away thy blessing.**

36. **And he said, Is not he rightly named Jacob? for he hath supplanted me** these **two times: he took away my birthright; and,** behold, now he **hath taken away my blessing. And he said, Hast thou not reserved a blessing for me?**

37. **And Isaac** answered and **said** unto Esau, Behold,

I have made him thy lord, and all his brethren have I given to him for servants; and with corn and wine have I sustained him: and what shall I do now unto thee, my son? 38. And Esau said unto his father, Hast thou but one blessing, my father? bless me, *even* me also, O my father. And Esau lifted up his voice, and wept. 39. And Isaac his father answered and said unto him, Behold, thy dwelling shall be the fatness of the earth, and of the dew of heaven from above; 40. And by thy sword shalt thou live, and shalt serve thy brother; and it shall come to pass when thou shalt have the dominion, that thou shalt break his yoke from off thy neck. 41. And Esau hated Jacob because of the blessing wherewith his father blessed him: and Esau said in his heart, The days of mourning for my father are at hand; then will I slay my brother Jacob. 42. And these words of Esau her elder son were told to Rebekah: and she sent and called Jacob her younger son, and said unto him, Behold, thy brother Esau, as touching thee, doth comfort himself, purposing to kill thee. 43. Now therefore, my son, obey my voice; arise, flee thou to Laban my brother to Haran; 44. And tarry with him a few days, until thy brother's fury turn away; 45. Until thy brother's anger turn away from thee, and he forget *that* which thou hast done to him:

then I will send, and fetch thee from thence: why should I be deprived also of you both in one day? 46. And Rebekah said to Isaac, I am weary of my life because of the daughters of Heth: if Jacob take a wife of the daughters of Heth, such as these *which are* of the daughters of the land, what good shall my life do me?

CHAPTER 28

1. And Isaac called Jacob, and blessed him, and charged him, and said unto him, Thou shalt not take a wife of the daughters of Canaan. 2. Arise, go to Padanaram, to the house of Bethuel thy mother's father; and take thee a wife from thence of the daughters of Laban thy mother's brother. 3. And God Almighty bless thee, and make thee fruitful, and multiply thee, that thou mayest be a multitude of people; 4. And give thee the blessing of Abraham, to thee, and to thy seed with thee; that thou mayest inherit the land wherein thou art a stranger, which God gave unto Abraham. 5. And Isaac sent away Jacob: and he went to Padanaram unto Laban, son of Bethuel the Syrian, the brother of Rebekah, Jacob's and Esau's mother. 6. When Esau saw that Isaac had blessed Jacob, and sent him away to Padanaram, to take him a wife from thence; and that as he blessed him he gave him a charge, saying, Thou shalt not take a wife of the daughers of

Canaan;

7. **And that Jacob obeyed** his father and his mother, **and was gone to Padanaram;**

8. **And Esau seeing that the daughters of Canaan pleased not Isaac** his father;

9. **Then went Esau unto Ishmael, and took** unto the wives which he had **Mahalath the daughter of Ishmael Abraham's son,** the sister of Nebajoth, **to be his wife.**

10. **And Jacob** went out from Beersheba, and **went toward Haran.**

11. **And he lighted upon a certain place, and tarried** there all night, **because the sun was set; and he took** of the **stones** of that place, **and put them for his pillows, and lay down** in that place **to sleep.**

12. **And he dreamed,** and behold **a ladder** set up on the earth, and the top of it **reached to heaven: and** behold the **angels** of God **ascending and descending on it.**

13. **And**, behold, **the LORD stood above it, and said, I am the** LORD **God of Abraham** thy father, **and** the God of **Isaac**: the land whereon thou liest, to thee will I give it, and to thy seed;

14. **And thy seed shall be as the dust** of the earth, **and thou shalt spread** abroad **to the west,** and to the **east**, and to the **north, and** to the **south: and in thee** and in thy seed

shall all the families of the **earth be blessed.**

15. **And, behold,** I *am* with thee, and **will keep thee** in all *places* whither thou goest, **and** will bring thee again into this land; for **I will not leave thee**, until I have done *that* which I have spoken to thee of.

16. **And Jacob awaked** out of his sleep, **and** he **said**, Surely **the LORD is in this place; and I knew it not.**

17. **And he was afraid, and said, How dreadful is** this place! this *is* none other but **the house of God, and this is the gate of heaven.**

18. **And Jacob** rose up early in the morning, and **took the stone** that he had put *for* his pillows, **and set it up for a pillar, and poured oil upon** the top of **it.**

19. **And he called the** name of that **place Bethel:** but the name of that city *was called* Luz at the first.

20. **And Jacob vowed a vow, saying, If God will be with me, and** will **keep me** in this way that I go, **and will give me bread** to eat, **and raiment** to put on,

21. So that I come again to my father's house in peace; **then shall the LORD be my God:**

22. **And this stone**, which I have set *for* a pillar, **shall be God's house: and** of **all** that **thou shalt give me I will** surely **give the tenth unto thee.**

41

CHAPTER 29

■ 1. **Then Jacob went on his**
■ **journey,** and came into the
land of the people of the east.
■ 2. **And he looked, and**
■ **behold a well** in the field,
■ **and,** lo, there *were*
■ **three flocks of sheep**
■ **lying by it;** for out of that
well they watered the flocks:
■ **and a great stone was**
■ **upon the well's mouth.**
3. And thither were all
the flocks gathered:
■ **and they rolled the stone**
■ **from the well's mouth, and**
■ **watered the sheep**, and
put the stone again upon the
well's mouth in his place.
■ 4. **And Jacob said**
unto them, My brethren,
■ **whence be ye? And**
■ **they said, Of Haran** *are* we.
■ 5. **And he said** unto them,
■ **Know ye Laban**
the son of Nahor?
■ **And they said,**
■ **We know him.**
■ 6. **And he said** unto them,
■ **Is he well? And they said,**
■ **He is well: and, behold,**
■ **Rachel his daughter**
■ **cometh** with the sheep.
■ 7. **And he said, Lo, it is yet**
■ **high day, neither is it time**
■ **that the cattle should be**
■ **gathered** together: water ye
the sheep, and go *and* feed *them*.
■ 8. **And they said, We**
■ **cannot**, until all the flocks
be gathered together, and
■ **till they roll the stone**
■ **from the well's mouth;**
■ **then we water the sheep.**
■ 9.**And** while he yet spake with them,
■ **Rachel came with her**
■ **father's sheep:**
for she kept them.
■ 10. **And** it came to pass, when
■ **Jacob saw Rachel** the
daughter of Laban his
mother's brother,
■ **and** the sheep of Laban his

mother's brother, that Jacob
■ **went near,** and rolled the stone
from the well's mouth, and watered the
flock of Laban his mother's brother.
■ 11. **And Jacob kissed**
■ **Rachel,** and lifted up his voice,
■ **and wept.**
■ 12. **And Jacob told**
■ **Rachel that he was** her
father's brother, and that he *was*
■ **Rebekah's son: and she**
■ **ran and told her father.**
13. And it came to pass,
■ **when Laban heard** the tidings
of Jacob his sister's son, that
■ **he ran to meet him,** and
embraced him, and kissed him,
■ **and brought him to his**
■ **house.** And he told Laban
all these things.
14. And Laban said to him, Surely
thou *art* my bone and my flesh.
■ **And he abode with him**
■ **the space of a month.**
15. And Laban said unto Jacob,
Because thou *art* my brother,
shouldest thou therefore serve
me for nought? tell me, what
shall thy wages *be*?
■ 16. **And Laban had two**
■ **daughters:** the name of
■ **the elder was Leah,**
■ **and** the name of
■ **the younger was Rachel.**
17. Leah *was* tender eyed; but
■ **Rachel was beautiful**
and well favoured.
■ 18. **And Jacob loved**
■ **Rachel; and said, I will**
■ **serve thee seven years for**
■ **Rachel** thy younger daughter.
19. And Laban said, *It is* better
that I give her to thee, than that
I should give her to another
man: abide with me.
■ 20. **And Jacob served**
■ **seven years for Rachel; and**
■ **they seemed** unto him
■ **but a few days,** for the
love he had to her.
■ 21. **And Jacob said unto**
■ **Laban, Give me my**
■ **wife**, for my days are fulfilled,

that I may go in unto her.

22. And Laban gathered together all the men of the place, and made a feast.

23. And it came to pass in the evening, that he took Leah his daughter, and brought her to him; and he went in unto her.

24. And Laban gave unto his daughter Leah Zilpah his maid *for* an handmaid.

25. And it came to pass, that in the morning, behold, it *was* Leah: and he said to Laban, What is this thou hast done unto me? did not I serve with thee for Rachel? wherefore then hast thou beguiled me?

26. And Laban said, It must not be so done in our country, to give the younger before the firstborn.

27. Fulfil her week, and we will give thee this also for the service which thou shalt serve with me yet seven other years.

28. And Jacob did so, and fulfilled her week: and he gave him Rachel his daughter to wife also.

29. And Laban gave to Rachel his daughter Bilhah his handmaid to be her maid.

30. And he went in also unto Rachel, and he loved also Rachel more than Leah, and served with him yet seven other years.

31. And when the LORD saw that Leah was hated, he opened her womb: but Rachel was barren.

32. And Leah conceived, and bare a son, and she called his name Reuben: for she said, Surely the LORD hath looked upon my affliction; now therefore my husband will love me.

33. And she conceived again, and bare a son; and said, Because the LORD hath heard I *was* hated, he hath therefore given me this *son* also: and she called his name Simeon.

34. And she conceived again, and bare a son; and said, Now this time will my husband be joined unto me, because I have born him three sons: therefore was his name called Levi.

35. And she conceived again, and bare a son: and she said, Now will I praise the LORD: therefore she called his name Judah; and left bearing.

CHAPTER 30

1. And when Rachel saw that she bare Jacob no children, Rachel envied her sister; and said unto Jacob, Give me children, or else I die.

2. And Jacob's anger was kindled against Rachel: and he said, Am I in God's stead, who hath withheld from thee the fruit of the womb?

3. And she said, Behold my maid Bilhah, go in unto her; and she shall bear upon my knees, that I may also have children by her.

4. And she gave him Bilhah her handmaid to wife: and Jacob went in unto her.

5. And Bilhah conceived, and bare Jacob a son.

6. And Rachel said, God hath judged me, and hath also heard my voice, and hath given me a son: therefore called she his name Dan.

7. And Bilhah Rachel's maid conceived again, and bare Jacob a second son.

8. And Rachel said, With great wrestlings have I wrestled with my sister, and I have prevailed: and she called his name Naphtali.

9. **When Leah** saw that she had **left bearing, she took Zilpah her maid, and gave her Jacob to wife.**

10. **And Zilpah** Leah's maid **bare** Jacob a son.

11. And Leah said, A troop cometh: and she called his name **Gad.**

12. And Zilpah Leah's maid bare Jacob a second son.

13. **And** Leah said, Happy am I, for the daughters will call me blessed: and she called his name **Asher.**

14. **And Reuben** went in the days of wheat harvest, and **found mandrakes** in the field, **and brought them unto** his mother **Leah. Then Rachel said to Leah, Give me,** I pray thee, **of thy son's mandrakes.**

15. **And she said** unto her, *Is it* a small matter that **thou hast taken my husband? and wouldest thou take away my son's mandrakes also? And Rachel said, Therefore he shall lie with thee tonight for thy son's mandrakes.**

16. **And Jacob came out of the field** in the evening, **and Leah** went out to meet him, and **said, Thou must come in unto me; for surely I have hired thee** with my son's mandrakes. **And he lay with her** that night.

17. **And** God hearkened unto **Leah,** and she **conceived, and bare** Jacob the fifth son.

18. And Leah said, God hath given me my hire, because I have given my maiden to my husband: and she called his name **Issachar.**

19. **And Leah conceived again, and bare** Jacob the sixth son.

20. And Leah said, God hath endued me *with* a good dowry; now will my husband dwell with me, because I have born him six sons: and she called his name **Zebulun**.

21. **And afterwards she bare a daughter,** and called her name **Dinah.**

22. **And God remembered Rachel,** and God hearkened to her, **and opened her womb.**

23. **And she** conceived, and **bare a son**; and said, God hath taken away my reproach:

24. **And she called his name Joseph; and said, The LORD shall add to me another son.**

25. **And** it came to pass, **when Rachel had born Joseph,** that **Jacob said unto Laban, Send me** away, that I may go **unto mine own** place, and to my **country.**

26. Give *me* my wives and my children, for whom I have served thee, and let me go: for thou knowest my service which I have done thee.

27. **And Laban said** unto him, I pray thee, if I have found favour in thine eyes, *tarry:for* **I have learned** by experience **that the LORD hath blessed me for thy sake.**

28. And he said, **Appoint me thy wages,** and I will give *it.*

29. And he said unto him, Thou knowest how I have served thee, and how thy cattle was with me.

30. For *it was* little which thou hadst before I *came*, and it is *now* increased unto a multitude; and the LORD hath blessed thee since my coming: and now when shall I provide for mine own house also?

31. **And he said, What shall I give thee? And Jacob said, Thou shalt not give me any thing**: if thou wilt do

this thing for me, I will again feed *and* keep thy flock.

32. **I will pass through all thy flock to-day, removing** from thence **all the speckled and spotted cattle, and all the brown** cattle among the **sheep, and the spotted and speckled** among the **goats: and of such shall be my hire.**

33. **So** shall my righteousness answer for me in time to come, when it shall come for my hire before thy face: **every one that is not speckled and spotted among the goats, and brown among the sheep, that shall be counted stolen with me.**

34. **And Laban said**, Behold, **I would it** might **be according to thy word.**

35. And he removed that day the he goats that were ringstraked and spotted, and all the she goats that were speckled and spotted, *and* every one that had *some* white in it, and all the brown among the sheep, and gave *them* into the hand of his sons.

36. **And he set three days' journey betwixt himself and Jacob:** and Jacob fed the rest of Laban's flocks.

37. **And Jacob took** him **rods of green poplar, and of the hazel and chestnut tree; and pilled white strakes in them, and made** the white appear which *was* in the **rods.**

38. **And he set the rods** which he had pilled **before the flocks** in the gutters **in the watering troughs** when the flocks came to drink, **that they should conceive when they came to drink.**

39. **And the flocks** conceived before the rods, and **brought forth cattle ringstraked, speckled,**

and spotted.

40. **And** Jacob did separate the lambs, and set the faces of the flocks toward the ringstraked, and all the brown in the flock of Laban; and **he put his own flocks by themselves, and put them not unto Laban's cattle.**

41. And it came to pass, **whensoever the stronger cattle did conceive,** that **Jacob laid the rods before** the eyes of **the cattle** in the gutters, **that they might conceive among the rods.**

42. **But when the cattle were feeble, he put them not in:** so the feebler were Laban's, and the stronger Jacob's.

43. **And the man increased exceedingly,** and had much cattle, and maidservants, and menservants, and camels, and asses.

CHAPTER 31

1. **And he heard** the words of **Laban's sons, saying, Jacob hath taken away all that was our father's;** and of *that* which *was* our father's hath he gotten all this glory.

2. And Jacob beheld the countenance of Laban, and, behold, it *was* not toward him as before.

3. **And the LORD said unto Jacob, Return unto the land of thy fathers, and** to thy kindred; and **I will be with thee.**

4. **And Jacob** sent and **called Rachel and Leah** to the field unto his flock,

5. **And said** unto them, I see **your father's countenance, that it is not toward me as before;** but the God of my father hath been with me.

6. And ye know that with all my power I have served your father.

7. And your father hath deceived me,

and changed my wages ten times; but God suffered him not to hurt me.

8. If he said thus, The speckled shall be thy wages; then all the cattle bare speckled: and if he said thus, The ringstraked shall be thy hire; then bare all the cattle ringstraked.

9. Thus God hath taken away the cattle of your father, and given *them* to me.

10. And it came to pass at the time that the cattle conceived, that I lifted up mine eyes, and saw in a dream, and, behold, the rams which leaped upon the cattle *were* ringstraked, speckled, and grisled.

11. **And the angel of God spake unto me** in a dream, **saying,** Jacob: And I said, Here *am* I.

12. And he said, Lift up now thine eyes, and see, all the rams which leap upon the cattle *are* ringstraked, speckled, and grisled: for I have seen all that Laban doeth unto thee.

13. I *am* the God of Bethel, where thou anointedst the pillar, *and* where thou vowedst a vow unto me: now arise, get thee out from this land, and **return unto the land of thy kindred.**

14. **And Rachel and Leah answered** and said unto him, **Is there yet any portion or inheritance for us in our father's house?**

15. Are we not counted of him strangers? **for he hath sold us,** and hath quite devoured also our money.

16. For all the riches which God hath taken from our father, that *is* ours, and our children's: **now then, whatsoever God hath said unto thee, do.**

17. **Then Jacob** rose up, and **set his sons and his wives upon camels;**

18. **And he carried away all his cattle, and** all his **goods** which he had gotten, the cattle of his getting, which he had gotten in Padanaram, for **to go to Isaac his father** in the land of Canaan.

19. **And** Laban went to shear his sheep: and **Rachel had stolen the images that were her father's.**

20. **And Jacob stole away unawares** to Laban the Syrian, in that he told him not that he fled.

21. So he fled with all that he had; and he rose up, **and passed over the river,** and set his face *toward* the mount Gilead.

22. **And it was told Laban** on the third day **that Jacob was fled.**

23. **And he** took his brethren with him, and **pursued after him seven days'** journey; **and** they **overtook him in the mount Gilead.**

24. **And God came to Laban** the Syrian **in a dream** by night, **and said** unto him, Take heed that thou **speak not to Jacob either good or bad.**

25. Then Laban overtook Jacob. Now Jacob had pitched his tent in the mount: and Laban with his brethren pitched in the mount of Gilead.

26. **And Laban said to Jacob, What hast thou done,** that thou hast stolen away unawares to me, and carried away my daughters, as captives *taken* with the sword?

27. **Wherefore didst thou flee away secretly, and steal** away **from me;** and didst not tell me, that I might have sent thee away with mirth, and with songs, with tabret, and with harp?

28. **And hast not suffered me to kiss my sons and** my **daughters**? thou hast now

done foolishly in *so* doing.

29. It is in the power of my hand to do you hurt: but the **God** of your father **spake unto me** yesternight, **saying,** Take thou heed that thou **speak not to Jacob either good or bad.**

30. And now, *though* thou wouldest needs be gone, because thou sore longedst after thy father's house, **yet wherefore hast thou stolen my gods?**

31. And Jacob answered and said to Laban, Because I was afraid: for I said, Peradventure thou wouldest take by force thy daughters from me.

32. With whomsoever thou findest thy gods, let him not live: before our brethren discern thou what *is* thine with me, and take *it* to thee. **For Jacob knew not that Rachel had stolen them.**

33. And Laban went into Jacob's tent, and into Leah's tent, and into the two maidservants' tents; but he found *them* not. Then went he out of Leah's tent, and **entered** into **Rachel's tent.**

34. **Now Rachel had** taken the images, and **put them in the camel's furniture, and sat upon them. And Laban** searched all the tent, but **found them not.**

35. And she said to her father, Let it not displease my lord that I cannot rise up before thee; for the custom of women *is* upon me. And he searched but found not the images.

36. **And Jacob was wroth**, and chode **with Laban:** and Jacob answered **and said** to Laban, What *is* my trespass? **what is my sin, that thou hast so hotly pursued after me?**

37. Whereas thou hast searched all my stuff, **what hast thou found** of all thy household stuff? set *it* here before my brethren and thy brethren, that they may judge betwixt us both.

38. **This twenty years have I been with thee;** thy ewes and thy she goats have not cast their young, and the rams of thy flock have I not eaten.

39. That which was torn *of beasts* I brought not unto thee; I bare the loss of it; of my hand didst thou require it, *whether* stolen by day, or stolen by night.

40. *Thus* I was; in the day the drought consumed me, and the frost by night; and my sleep departed from mine eyes.

41. Thus have I been twenty years in thy house; **I served thee fourteen years for thy two daughters, and six years for thy cattle: and thou hast changed my wages ten times.**

42. **Except the God of my father,** the God of Abraham, and the fear of Isaac, **had been with me, surely thou hadst sent me away** now **empty. God hath seen mine affliction and** the labour of my hands, and **rebuked thee** yesternight.

43. And Laban answered and said unto Jacob, **These** daughters **are my daughters, and** *these* children *are* **my children, and** *these* cattle *are* **my cattle,** and all that thou seest *is* mine: **and what can I do** this day unto these my daughters, or unto their children which they have born?

44. Now therefore come thou, **let us make a covenant,** I and thou; and let it be for a witness between me and thee.

45. And Jacob took a stone, and set it up for a pillar.
46. And Jacob said unto his brethren, Gather stones; and they took stones, and made an heap: and they did eat there upon the heap.
47. And Laban called it Jegarsahadutha: but Jacob called it Galeed.
48. And Laban said, This heap is a witness between me and thee this day. Therefore was the name of it called Galeed;
49. And Mizpah; for he said, The LORD watch between me and thee, when we are absent one fromanother.
50. If thou shalt afflict my daughters, or if thou shalt take*other* wives beside my daughters, no man *is* with us; see, God *is* witness betwixt me and thee.
51. And Laban said to Jacob, Behold this heap, and behold *this* pillar, which I have cast betwixt me and thee:
52. This heap *be* witness, and *this* pillar *be* witness, that I will not pass over this heap to thee, and that thou shalt not pass over this heap and this pillar unto me, for harm.
53. The God of Abraham, and the God of Nahor, the God of their father, judge betwixt us. And Jacob sware by the fear of his father Isaac.
54. Then Jacob offered sacrifice upon the mount, and called his brethren to eat bread: and they did eat bread, and tarried all night in the mount.
55. And early in the morning Laban rose up, and kissed his sons and his daughters, and blessed them: and Laban departed, and returned unto his place.

CHAPTER 32

1. And Jacob went on his way, and the angels of God met him.
2. And when Jacob saw them, he said, This is God's host: and he called the name of that place Mahanaim.
3. And Jacob sent messengers before him to Esau his brother unto the land of Seir, the country of Edom.
4. And he commanded them, saying, Thus shall ye speak unto my lord Esau; Thy servant Jacob saith thus, I have sojourned with Laban, and stayed there until now:
5. And I have oxen, and asses, flocks, and menservants, and womenservants: and I have sent to tell my lord, that I may find grace in thy sight.
6. And the messengers returned to Jacob, saying, We came to thy brother Esau, and also he cometh to meet thee, and four hundred men with him.
7. Then Jacob was greatly afraid and distressed: and he divided the people that *was* with him, and the flocks, and herds, and the camels, into two bands;
8. And said, If Esau come to the one company, and smite it, then the other company which is left shall escape.
9. And Jacob said, O God of my father Abraham, and God of my father Isaac, the LORD which saidst unto me, Return unto thy country, and to thy kindred, and I will deal well with thee:
10. I am not worthy of the least of all the mercies, and of all the truth,

which thou hast shewed unto thy servant; for with my staff I passed over this Jordan; and now I am become two bands.

11. **Deliver me,** I pray thee, **from the hand of** my brother, from the hand of **Esau**: for I fear him, **lest he** will come and **smite me,** *and* the mother with the children.

12. And thou saidst, I will surely do thee good, and make thy seed as the sand of the sea, which cannot be numbered for multitude.

13. **And he lodged there that** same **night; and took** of that which came to his hand **a present for Esau** his brother;

14. **Two hundred she goats,** and **twenty he goats, two hundred ewes,** and **twenty rams,**

15. **Thirty milch camels** with their colts, **forty kine,** and **ten bulls, twenty she asses, and ten foals.**

16. **And he** delivered *them* into the hand of his servants, every drove by themselves; and **said unto his servants,** Pass over before me, and put a space betwixt drove and drove.

17. And he commanded the foremost, saying, **When Esau** my brother **meeteth thee, and asketh** thee, saying, **Whose art thou**? and whither goest thou? **and whose are these before thee?**

18. **Then thou shalt say, They be** thy servant **Jacob's; it is a present sent unto** my lord **Esau:** and, behold, also he *is* behind us.

19. And so commanded he the second, and the third, and all that followed the droves, saying, On this manner shall ye speak unto Esau, when ye find him.

20. **And say** ye moreover, Behold, thy servant **Jacob is behind us. For** he said, **I will appease him with the present** that goeth before me, and afterward I will see his face; peradventure he will accept of me.

21. **So went the present** over **before him**: and himself lodged that night in the company.

22. **And he rose** up **that night, and took his** two **wives,** and **his** two women **servants, and his** eleven **sons,** and passed over the ford Jabbok.

23. And he took them, **and sent them over the brook,** and sent over that he had.

24. **And Jacob was left alone; and there wrestled a man with him** until the breaking of the day.

25. **And when he saw that he prevailed not** against him, **he touched the hollow of his thigh; and** the hollow of **Jacob's thigh was out of joint,** as he wrestled with him.

26. **And he said, Let me go, for the day breaketh. And he said, I will not** let thee go, **except thou bless me.**

27. **And he said** unto him, **What is thy name**? And he said, Jacob.

28. **And he said, Thy name shall be** called no more Jacob, but **Israel:** for as a prince hast thou power with God and with men, and hast prevailed.

29. **And Jacob asked him**, and said, **Tell me,** I pray thee, **thy name. And he said, Wherefore is it that thou dost ask** after my name? **And he blessed him** there.

30. **And Jacob called** the name of **the place Peniel: for I have seen God** face to face, and my life is preserved. 31. And as he passed over Peniel the sun rose upon him, and he halted upon his thigh. 32. **Therefore the children of Israel eat not of the sinew** which shrank, **which is upon the hollow of the thigh, unto this day**: because he touched the hollow of Jacob's thigh in the sinew that shrank.

CHAPTER 33

1. **And Jacob** lifted up his eyes, and **looked, and, behold, Esau came,** and with him four hundred men. And he divided the children unto Leah, and unto Rachel, and unto the two handmaids. 2. And he put the handmaids and their children foremost, and Leah and her children after, and Rachel and Joseph hindermost. 3. **And he** passed over before them, and **bowed** himself to the ground **seven times, until he came near to his brother.** 4. **And Esau ran** to meet him, **and embraced him,** and fell on his neck, **and kissed him: and they wept.** 5. **And he** lifted up his eyes, and **saw the women and the children; and said, Who are those** with thee? **And he said, The children which God hath** graciously **given thy servant.** 6. Then the handmaidens came near, they and their children, and they bowed themselves. 7. And Leah also with her children came near, and bowed themselves: and after came Joseph near and Rachel, and they bowed themselves.

8. **And he said, What meanest thou by all this drove** which I met? **And he said, These are to find grace in the sight of my lord.** 9. **And Esau said, I have enough,** my brother; keep that thou hast unto thyself. 10. **And Jacob said,** Nay, I pray thee, **if** now **I have found grace** in thy sight, **then receive my present** at my hand: for therefore I have seen thy face, as though I had seen the face of God, and thou wast pleased with me. 11. **Take,** I pray thee, **my blessing that is brought to thee**; because God hath dealt graciously with me, and because I have enough. **And he urged him, and he took it.** 12. **And he said, Let us take our journey,** and let us go, and I will go before thee. 13. **And he said** unto him, **My** lord knoweth that the **children are tender, and the flocks** and herds **with young are with me: and if men should overdrive them** one day, **all** the flock **will die.** 14. **Let my lord,** I pray thee, **pass over before his servant: and I will lead on softly,** according as the cattle that goeth before me and the children be able to endure, until I come unto my lord unto Seir. 15. **And Esau said, Let me** now **leave with thee some** of the folk **that are with me. And he said, What needeth it?** let me find grace in the sight of my lord. 16. **So Esau returned** that day on his way **unto Seir.**

50

17. **And Jacob journeyed to Succoth, and built** him **an house, and** made **booths for his cattle:** therefore the name of the place is called Succoth.

18. **And Jacob came to Shalem,** a city of Shechem, which *is* **in** the land of **Canaan,** when he came from Padanaram; **and pitched his tent** before the city.

19. **And he bought** a parcel of **a field,** where he had spread his tent, at the hand of the children of Hamor, Shechem's father, **for an hundred pieces of money.**

20. **And he erected there an altar,** and called it El-elohe-Israel.

CHAPTER 34

1. **And Dinah the daughter of** Leah, which she bare unto **Jacob, went** out **to see the daughters of the land.**

2. **And when Shechem the son of Hamor** the Hivite, **prince of the country, saw her, he took her, and** lay with her, and **defiled her.**

3. **And** his soul clave unto Dinah the daughter of Jacob, and **he loved the damsel, and** spake kindly unto the damsel.

4. **And Shechem spake unto his father** Hamor, saying, **Get me this damsel to wife.**

5. **And Jacob heard that** he had defiled Dinah his daughter: **now his sons were with his cattle in the field:** and Jacob held his peace until they were come.

6. **And Hamor the** father of Shechem **went out unto Jacob** to commune with him.

7. **And the sons of Jacob came out of the field**

when they heard it: and the men were grieved, **and they were very wroth,** because he had wrought folly in Israel in lying with Jacob's daughter: which thing ought not to be done.

8. **And Hamor communed** with them, **saying,** The soul of **my son** Shechem **longeth for your daughter:** I pray you **give her him to wife.**

9. **And make ye marriages with us,** and give your daughters unto us, and take our daughters unto you.

10. **And ye shall dwell with us**: and the land shall be before you; dwell and trade ye therein, and get you possessions therein.

11. **And Shechem said** unto her father and unto her brethren, Let me find grace in your eyes, and what ye shall say unto me I will give.

12. Ask me never so much dowry and gift, and **I will give according as ye shall say** unto me: **but give me the damsel to wife.**

13. **And the sons of Jacob answered** Shechem and Hamor his father **deceitfully,** and said, **because he had defiled** Dinah **their sister:**

14. **And they said** unto them, **We cannot** do this thing, to **give our sister to one that is uncircumcised;** for that *were* a reproach unto us:

15. But in this will we consent unto you: **If** ye will be as we *be,* that **every male** of you **be circumcised;**

16. **Then will we give our daughters unto you,** and we will take your daughters to us, **and we will dwell with you,** and we will become one people.

17. **But if ye will not** hearken unto us, to **be circumcised; then will we take our daughter,** and we will be gone. 18. **And their words pleased Hamor, and Shechem** Hamor's son. 19. And the young man deferred not to do the thing, because he had delight in Jacob's daughter: and he *was* more honourable than all the house of his father. 20. **And Hamor and Shechem** his son came unto the gate of their city, and **communed with the men of their city, saying,** 21. These men *are* peaceable with us; therefore let them dwell in the land, and trade therein; for **the land,** behold, *it* **is large enough for them; let us take their daughters** to us for wives, **and** let us **give them our daughters.** 22. **Only herein will the men consent** unto us for **to dwell with us,** to be one people, **if every male** among us **be circumcised,** as they *are* circumcised. 23. *Shall* not their cattle and their substance and every beast of theirs *be* ours? only let us consent unto them, and they will dwell with us. 24. **And** unto Hamor and unto Shechem his son hearkened all that went out of the gate of his city; and **every male was circumcised,** all that went out of the gate of his city. 25. **And** it came to pass **on the third day, when they were sore,** that two of the sons of Jacob, **Simeon and Levi, Dinah's brethren, took each** man **his sword,** and came upon the city boldly, **and slew all the males.**

26. **And they slew Hamor and Shechem** his son with the edge of the sword, **and took Dinah out of Shechem's house,** and went out. 27. **The sons of Jacob** came upon the slain, and **spoiled the city,** because they had defiled their sister. 28. **They took** their **sheep,** and their **oxen,** and their **asses, and that which was in the city, and** that which *was* in the **field,** 29. **And all their wealth,** and all **their little ones, and their wives** took they captive, and spoiled even all that *was* in the house. 30. **And Jacob said to Simeon and Levi, Ye** have troubled me to **make me to stink among** the inhabitants of the land, among **the Canaanites and the Perizzites:** and I *being* few in number, **they shall gather themselves** together against me, **and slay me;** and I shall be destroyed, I and my house. 31. **And they said, Should he deal with our sister as with an harlot?**

CHAPTER 35

1. **And God said unto Jacob, Arise, go up to Beth-el**, and dwell there: **and make** there **an altar unto God,** that appeared unto thee when thou fleddest from the face of Esau thy brother. 2. **Then Jacob said** unto his household, and **to all** that *were* **with him, Put away the strange gods**

that *are* among you, and
be clean, and change
your garments:
3. **And let us** arise, and
go up
to Beth-el; and
I will make there
an altar unto God, who
answered me in the day of
my distress, and was with
me in the way which I went.
4. **And they gave**
unto Jacob all
the strange gods
which *were* in their hand,
and all their earrings
which *were* in their ears;
and Jacob hid them
under the oak which
was by Shechem.
5. And they journeyed:
and the terror of God
was upon the cities
that *were* round about them,
and they did not
pursue after the sons of
Jacob.
6. **So Jacob came to** Luz,
which *is* in the land of Canaan, that *is*,
Beth-el, he and all the people
that *were* with him.
7. **And he built** there
an altar, and called the
place El-beth-el: because
there God appeared
unto him, when he fled from
the face of his brother.
8. **But Deborah Rebekah's**
nurse died, and she was
buried beneath Beth-el
under an oak: and the name
of it was called Allonbachuth.
9. **And God appeared**
unto Jacob again, when
he came out of Padan-aram,
and blessed him.
10. **And God said** unto
him, Thy name *is* Jacob:
thy name shall not be
called any more Jacob,
but Israel shall be thy name:
and he called his name Israel.
11. And God said unto

him, I *am* God Almighty:
be fruitful and multiply;
a nation and a company
of nations shall be of
thee, and kings shall
come out of thy loins;
12. And the land which I gave
Abraham and Isaac, to thee I
will give it, and to thy seed
after thee will I give the land.
13. And God went up from him in
the place where he talked with him.
14. **And Jacob set**
up a pillar in the place
where he talked with
him, even a pillar of
stone: and he poured
a drink offering thereon,
and he poured
oil thereon.
15. **And Jacob**
called the name of
the place where
God spake with him,
Beth-el.
16. **And they journeyed**
from Beth-el; and there was
but a little way to come
to Ephrath: and
Rachel travailed, and she
had hard labour.
17. **And** it came to pass, when
she was in hard labour, that
the midwife said unto her,
Fear not; thou shalt
have this son also.
18. **And** it came to pass,
as her soul was in
departing, (for she died) that
she called his name
Ben-oni: but his father
called him Benjamin.
19. **And Rachel died,**
and was buried in the
way to Ephrath, which *is*
Beth-lehem.
20. And Jacob set a pillar upon
her grave: that *is* the pillar of
Rachel's grave unto this day.
21. And Israel journeyed, and spread
his tent beyond the tower of Edar.
22. **And it came to pass,**
when Israel dwelt in that land,

■ **that Reuben** went and
■ **lay with Bilhah his father's**
■ **concubine: and Israel**
■ **heard it.** Now the sons
of Jacob were twelve:
23. The sons of Leah; Reuben,
Jacob's firstborn, and Simeon,
and Levi, and Judah, and
Issachar, and Zebulun:
24. The sons of Rachel;
Joseph, and Benjamin:
25. And the sons of Bilhah, Rachel's
handmaid; Dan, and Naphtali:
26. And the sons of Zilpah, Leah's
handmaid: Gad, and Asher: these
are the sons of Jacob, which were
born to him in Padanaram.
■ 27. **And Jacob came unto**
■ **Isaac** his father unto Mamre, unto
the city of Arbah, which *is* Hebron,
where Abraham and Isaac sojourned.
28. And the days of Isaac were an
hundred and fourscore years.
■ 29. **And Isaac** gave
up the ghost, and
■ **died**, and was gathered
unto his people,
■ **being old and full of**
■ **days: and his sons Esau**
■ **and Jacob buried him**.

CHAPTER 36

1. Now these *are* the generations
of Esau, who *is* Edom.
2. Esau took his wives of the
daughters of Canaan; Adah the
daughter of Elon the Hittite, and
Aholibamah the daughter of Anah
the daughter of Zibeon the Hivite;
3. And Bashemath Ishmael's
daughter, sister of Nebajoth.
4. And Adah bare to Esau Eliphaz;
and Bashemath bare Reuel;
5. And Aholibamah bare Jeush,
and Jaalam, and Korah: these *are*
the sons of Esau, which were born
unto him in the land of Canaan.
■ 6. **And Esau took**
■ **his wives,** and
■ **his sons, and** his
■ **daughters,** and all
■ **the persons of**
■ **his house,** and

■ **his cattle, and** all his
■ **beasts, and all his**
■ **substance,** which he
had got in the land of Canaan;
■ **and went** into the country
■ **from the face of** his brother
■ **Jacob.**
■ 7. **For their riches**
■ **were more than** that
they might dwell together; and
■ **the land** wherein
they were strangers
■ **could** not
■ **bear** them
■ **because of their cattle.**
■ 8. **Thus dwelt Esau in**
■ **mount Seir: Esau is Edom.**
9. And these *are* the generations
of Esau the father of the
Edomites in mount Seir:
10. These *are* the names of Esau's
sons; Eliphaz the son of Adah the
wife of Esau, Reuel the son of
Bashemath the wife of Esau.
11. And the sons of Eliphaz
were Teman, Omar, Zepho,
and Gatam, and Kenaz.
12. And Timna was concubine to
Eliphaz Esau's son; and she bare
to Eliphaz Amalek: these *were* the
sons of Adah Esau's wife.
13. And these *are* the sons of Reuel;
Nahath, and Zerah, Shammah, and
Mizzah: these were the sons of
Bashemath Esau's wife.
14. And these were the sons of
Aholibamah, the daughter of Anah
the daughter of Zibeon, Esau's
wife: and she bare to Esau Jeush,
and Jaalam, and Korah.
15. These *were* dukes of the sons
of Esau: the sons of Eliphaz the
firstborn *son* of Esau; duke Teman,
duke Omar, duke Zepho, duke Kenaz,
16. Duke Korah, duke Gatam, *and*
duke Amalek: these *are* the dukes
that came of Eliphaz in the land of
Edom; these *were* the sons of Adah.
17. And these *are* the sons of Reuel
Esau's son; duke Nahath, duke Zerah,
duke Shammah, duke Mizzah: these
are the dukes *that came* of Reuel in
the land of Edom; these *are* the sons

of Bashemath Esau's wife.

18. And these *are* the sons of Aholibamah Esau's wife; duke Jeush, duke Jaalam, duke Korah: these *were* the dukes *that came* of Aholibamah the daughter of Anah, Esau's wife.

19. These *are* the sons of Esau, who *is* Edom, and these *are* their dukes.

20. These *are* the sons of Seir the Horite, who inhabited the land; Lotan, and Shobal, and Zibeon, and Anah,

21. And Dishon, and Ezer, and Dishan: these *are* the dukes of the Horites, the children of Seir in the land of Edom.

22. And the children of Lotan were Hori and Hemam; and Lotan's sister *was* Timna.

23. And the children of Shobal *were* these; Alvan, and Manahath, and Ebal, Shepho, and Onam.

24. And these *are* the children of Zibeon; both Ajah, and Anah: this *was that* Anah that found the mules in the wilderness, as he fed the asses of Zibeon his father.

25. And the children of Anah *were* these; Dishon, and Aholibamah the daughter of Anah.

26. And these *are* the children of Dishon; Hemdan, and Eshban, and Ithran, and Cheran.

27. The children of Ezer *are* these; Bilhan, and Zaavan, and Akan.

28. The children of Dishan *are* these; Uz, and Aran.

29. These *are* the dukes *that came* of the Horites; duke Lotan, duke Shobal, duke Zibeon, duke Anah,

30. Duke Dishon, duke Ezer, duke Dishan: these *are* the dukes *that came* of Hori, among their dukes in the land of Seir.

31. And these *are* the kings that reigned in the land of Edom, before there reigned any king over the children of Israel.

32. And Bela the son of Beor reigned in Edom: and the name of his city *was* Dinhabah.

33. And Bela died, and Jobab the son of Zerah of Bozrah reigned in his stead.

34. And Jobab died, and Husham of the land of Temani reigned in his stead.

35. And Husham died, and Hadad the son of Bedad, who smote Midian in the field of Moab, reigned in his stead: and the name of his city *was* Avith.

36. And Hadad died, and Samlah of Masrekah reigned in his stead.

37. And Samlah died, and Saul of Rehoboth *by* the river reigned in his stead.

38. And Saul died, and Baal-hanan the son of Achbor reigned in his stead.

39. And Baal-hanan the son of Achbor died, and Hadar reigned in his stead: and the name of his city *was* Pau;
and his wife's name *was* Mehetabel, the daughter of Matred, the daughter of Mezahab.

40. And these *are* the names of the dukes *that came* of Esau, according to their families, after their places, by their names; duke Timnah, duke Alvah, duke Jetheth,

41. Duke Aholibamah, duke Elah, duke Pinon,

42. Duke Kenaz, duke Teman, duke Mibzar,

43. Duke Magdiel, duke Iram: these *be* the dukes of Edom, according to their habitations in the land of their possession: he *is* Esau the father of the Edomites.

CHAPTER 37

■ 1. **And Jacob dwelt** in the land wherein his father was a stranger, **in the land of Canaan.**

2. These *are* the generations of Jacob.
■ **Joseph, being**
■ **seventeen** years old,
■ **was feeding the flock with**
■ **his brethren;** and the lad *was* with the sons of Bilhah, and with the sons of Zilpah, his father's wives:
■ **and Joseph brought unto**
■ **his father their evil report.**
■ 3. **Now Israel loved**
■ **Joseph more than all**

■ **his children,** because he
was the son of his old age:
■ **and** he
■ **made him a coat**
■ **of many colours.**
■ 4. **And** when his brethren saw that
their father loved him more than all
■ **his brethren,** they
■ **hated him,** and could not
speak peaceably unto him.
■ 5. **And Joseph**
■ **dreamed** a dream,
■ **and he told it his brethren:**
and they hated him yet the more.
6. And he said unto them,
■ **Hear,** I pray you,
■ **this dream** which I have dreamed:
■ 7. **For, behold, we were**
■ **binding sheaves** in the field,
■ **and, lo, my sheaf arose,**
■ **and** also stood upright; and, behold,
■ **your sheaves** stood
round about, and
■ **made obeisance**
■ **to my sheaf.**
■ 8. **And his brethren**
■ **said** to him,
■ **Shalt thou** indeed
■ **reign over us?** or shalt thou
indeed have dominion over us?
■ **And they hated him yet**
■ **the more** for his dreams,
and for his words.
■ 9. **And he dreamed** yet
■ **another dream, and**
told it his brethren, and
■ **said,** Behold,
■ **I have dreamed** a
dream more; and, behold,
the sun and the moon and
■ **the eleven stars made**
■ **obeisance to me.**
■ 10. **And** he told *it* to his
father, and to his brethren: and
■ **his father rebuked him,**
■ **and said** unto him, What *is* this
dream that thou hast dreamed?
■ **Shall I and thy mother and**
■ **thy brethren** indeed come to
■ **bow down ourselves**
■ **to thee** to the earth?
■ 11. **And his brethren**
■ **envied him;** but his

father observed the saying.
12. And his brethren went to feed
their father's flock in Shechem.
■ 13. **And Israel said**
■ **unto Joseph, Do not**
■ **thy brethren feed the**
■ **flock** in Shechem? come,
and I will send thee unto them.
And he said to him, Here *am I.*
14. And he said to him,
■ **Go,** I pray thee,
■ **see whether it be well with**
■ **thy brethren, and** well with
■ **the flocks; and bring**
■ **me word** again. So he sent
him out of the vale of Hebron,
and he came to Shechem.
■ 15. **And a certain**
■ **man found him,**
and, behold, *he was*
■ **wandering** in the field:
■ **and the man**
■ **asked** him, saying,
■ **What seekest thou?**
■ 16. **And he said, I seek my**
■ **brethren: tell me,** I pray thee,
■ **where they feed**
■ **their flocks.**
■ 17. **And the man said,**
They are departed hence; for
■ **I heard them say, Let us**
■ **go to Dothan. And Joseph**
went after his brethren, and
■ **found them in Dothan.**
■ 18. **And when they saw**
■ **him** afar off, even before
he came near unto them,
■ **they conspired** against him
■ **to slay him.**
19. And they said one to another,
Behold, this dreamer cometh.
20. Come now therefore, and let us
slay him, and cast him into some pit,
and we will say, Some evil beast hath
devoured him: and we shall see what
will become of his dreams.
■ 21. **And Reuben** heard *it,* and he
delivered him out of their hands; and
■ **said, Let us not kill him.**
22. And Reuben said
unto them, Shed no blood,
■ **but cast him into this**
■ **pit** that *is* in the wilderness,

56

and lay no hand upon him;
that he might rid him
out of their hands, to
deliver him to his
father again.
23. **And** it came to pass,
when Joseph was come
unto his brethren, that
they stripped Joseph out
of his coat, *his coat of many*
colours that *was* on him;
24. **And** they took him, and
cast him into a pit: and the pit
was empty, *there was* no water in it.
25. **And they sat**
down to eat bread:
and they lifted up their eyes and
looked, and, behold, a
company of Ishmeelites
came from Gilead
with their camels bearing
spicery and balm and myrrh,
going to carry *it* down
to Egypt.
26. **And Judah**
said unto his brethren,
What profit is it if
we slay our brother,
and conceal his blood?
27. Come, and
let us sell him to the
Ishmeelites, and let not our
hand be upon him; for he *is* our
brother *and* our flesh. And his
brethren were content.
28. Then there passed by
Midianites merchantmen;
and they drew and lifted
up Joseph out of the pit, and
sold Joseph to the Ishmeelites
for twenty pieces of silver:
and they brought Joseph into Egypt.
29. **And Reuben returned**
unto the pit; and, behold,
Joseph was not in the pit;
and he rent his clothes.
30. And he returned unto his
brethren, and said, The child *is*
not; and I, whither shall I go?
31. **And they took**
Joseph's coat, and
killed a kid of the goats,
and dipped the coat

in the blood;
32. **And** they sent the coat
of *many* colours, and they
brought it to their father;
and said, This have we
found: know now whether it
be thy son's coat or no.
33. **And he** knew it, and
said, It is my son's coat;
an evil beast hath
devoured him; Joseph is
without doubt rent in pieces.
34. **And Jacob** rent his clothes,
and put sackcloth upon his loins, and
mourned for his son
many days.
35. **And** all his sons and
all his daughters rose up
to comfort him; but he
refused to be
comforted; and he said,
For I will go down into
the grave unto my son
mourning. Thus his father
wept for him.
36. **And the Midianites**
sold him into Egypt
unto Potiphar, an
officer of Pharaoh's,
and captain of the
guard.

CHAPTER 38

1. **And** it came to pass
at that time, that
Judah went down
from his brethren, and
turned in to a certain
Adullamite, whose
name was Hirah.
2. **And Judah saw** there
a daughter of a certain
Canaanite, whose name
was Shuah; and he took
her, and went in unto her.
3. **And she conceived, and**
bare a son; and he called his name
Er.
4. **And she conceived**
again, and bare a son;
and she called his name
Onan.
5. **And she yet again**

conceived, and bare a son; and called his name Shelah: and he was at Chezib, when she bare him.

6. And Judah took a wife for Er his firstborn, whose name was Tamar.

7. And Er, Judah's firstborn, was wicked in the sight of the LORD; and the LORD slew him.

8. And Judah said unto Onan, Go in unto thy brother's wife, and marry her, and raise up seed to thy brother.

9. And Onan knew that the seed should not be his; and it came to pass, when he went in unto his brother's wife, that he spilled it on the ground, lest that he should give seed to his brother.

10. And the thing which he did displeased the LORD: wherefore he slew him also.

11. Then said Judah to Tamar his daughter in law, Remain a widow at thy father's house, till Shelah my son be grown: for he said, Lest peradventure he die also, as his brethren did. And Tamar went and dwelt in her father's house.

12. And in process of time the daughter of Shuah Judah's wife died; and Judah was comforted, and went up unto his sheepshearers to Timnath, he and his friend Hirah the Adullamite.

13. And it was told Tamar, saying, Behold thy father in law goeth up to Timnath to shear his sheep.

14. And she put her widow's garments off from her, and covered her with a veil, and wrapped herself, and sat in an open place, which is by the way to Timnath;

for she saw that Shelah was grown, and she was not given unto him to wife.

15. When Judah saw her, he thought her to be an harlot; because she had covered her face.

16. And he turned unto her by the way, and said, Go to, I pray thee, let me come in unto thee; (for he knew not that she was his daughter in law.) And she said, What wilt thou give me, that thou mayest come in unto me?

17. And he said, I will send thee a kid from the flock. And she said, Wilt thou give me a pledge, till thou send it?

18. And he said, What pledge shall I give thee? And she said, Thy signet, and thy bracelets, and thy staff that is in thine hand. And he gave it her, and came in unto her, and she conceived by him.

19. And she arose, and went away, and laid by her vail from her, and put on the garments of her widowhood.

20. And Judah sent the kid by the hand of his friend the Adullamite, to receive his pledge from the woman's hand: but he found her not.

21. Then he asked the men of that place, saying, Where is the harlot, that was openly by the way side? And they said, There was no harlot in this place.

22. And he returned to Judah, and said, I cannot find her; and also the men of the place said, that there was no harlot in this place.

23. And Judah said, Let her take it to her, lest we be shamed: behold, I sent this kid, and thou hast not found her.

24. **And** it came to pass about **three months after,** that **it was told Judah,** saying, **Tamar** thy daughter in law **hath played the harlot; and** also, behold, **she is with child by whoredom. And Judah said,** Bring her forth, and **let her be burnt.** 25. **When she was brought** forth, **she sent to her father in law, saying, By the man, whose these are, am I with child:** and she said, Discern, I pray thee, **whose are these, the signet, and bracelets, and staff.** 26. **And Judah** acknowledged *them,* and **said, She hath been more righteous than I;** because that I gave her not to Shelah my son. And he knew her again no more. 27. **And** it came to pass **in the time of her travail,** that, behold, **twins were in her womb.** 28. **And** it came to pass, when she travailed, that *the* **one put out his hand: and the midwife** took and **bound upon his hand a scarlet thread, saying, This came out first.** 29. **And** it came to pass, **as he drew back his hand,** that, behold, **his brother came out:** and she said, How hast thou broken forth? *this* breach *be* upon thee: **therefore his name was called Pharez.** 30. **And afterward came out his brother,** that had the scarlet **thread** upon his hand: **and his name was called Zarah.**

CHAPTER 39

1. **And Joseph was brought down to Egypt; and Potiphar, an officer of Pharaoh,** captain of the guard, an Egyptian, **bought him** of the hands of the Ishmeelites, which had brought him down thither. 2. **And the LORD was with Joseph, and he was** a **prosperous** man; and he was in the house of his master the Egyptian. 3. **And his master saw that the LORD** *was* with him, and that the LORD **made all that he did to prosper** in his hand. 4. **And** Joseph found grace in his sight, and he served him: and **he made him overseer over his house,** and all *that* he had he put into his hand. 5. **And** it came to pass from the time *that* he had made him overseer in his house, and over all that he had, that **the LORD blessed the Egyptian's house for Joseph's sake;** and the blessing of the LORD was upon all that he had in the house, and in the field. 6. And he left all that he had in Joseph's hand; and he knew not ought he had, save the bread which he did eat. **And Joseph was a goodly person, and well favoured.** 7. **And** it came to pass after these things, that **his master's wife cast her eyes upon Joseph; and** she **said, Lie with me.** 8. **But he refused, and said** unto his master's wife, Behold, **my master** wotteth not what *is* with me in the house, and he **hath committed all** that he hath **to my hand;** 9. *There is* none greater in this house than I; neither hath he kept back any thing from me but thee, because

59

■ thou art his wife: how
■ then can I do this great
■ wickedness, and
■ sin against God?
■ 10. And it came to pass, as
■ she spake to Joseph day
■ by day, that he hearkened not
unto her, to lie by her, *or*
■ to be with her.
■ 11. And it came to pass
about this time, that
■ Joseph went into the
■ house to do his business;
■ and there was none of
■ the men of the house
■ there within.
■ 12. And she caught him by
■ his garment, saying, Lie
■ with me: and he left his
■ garment in her hand,
■ and fled, and got him out.
■ 13. And it came to pass,
when she saw that he had left
his garment in her hand, and
was fled forth,
■ 14. That she called
■ unto the men of her
■ house, and spake unto them,
■ saying, See, he hath brought in
an Hebrew unto us to mock us;
■ he came in unto me to
■ lie with me, and I cried
■ with a loud voice:
15. And it came to pass,
■ when he heard that I lifted
up my voice and cried, that
■ he left his garment with me,
■ and fled, and got him out.
■ 16. And she laid up
■ his garment by her,
■ until his lord came home.
■ 17. And she spake unto
him according to these words,
■ saying, The Hebrew servant,
which thou hast brought unto us,
■ came in unto me to
■ mock me:
18. And it came to pass, as I lifted
up my voice and cried, that he left
his garment with me, and fled out.
19. And it came to pass,
■ when his master heard
■ the words of his wife, which she

spake unto him, saying, After this
manner did thy servant to me; that
■ his wrath was kindled.
■ 20. And Joseph's
■ master took him, and
■ put him into the prison, a
place where the king's prisoners *were*
bound: and he was there in the prison.
■ 21. But the LORD was with
■ Joseph, and shewed him mercy,
■ and gave him favour in
■ the sight of the keeper
■ of the prison.
■ 22. And the keeper of
■ the prison committed
■ to Joseph's hand all
■ the prisoners that *were* in
the prison; and whatsoever they
did there, he was the doer *of it.*
23. The keeper of the prison looked
not to any thing *that was* under his
hand; because the LORD was
with him, and *that* which he did,
the LORD made *it* to prosper.

CHAPTER 40

■ 1. And it came to pass
after these things, *that*
■ the butler of the king of
■ Egypt and his baker
■ had offended their lord
■ the king of Egypt.
2. And Pharaoh was wroth against
two *of* his officers, against the
chief of the butlers, and against
the chief of the bakers.
■ 3. And he put them in ward in
the house of the captain of the guard,
■ into the prison, the place
■ where Joseph was bound.
4. And the captain of the guard
charged Joseph with them, and
he served them: and they
continued a season in ward.
■ 5. And they dreamed
■ a dream both of them,
■ each man his dream
■ in one night, each man according
to the interpretation of his dream, the
butler and the baker of the king of
Egypt,which *were* bound in the prison.
■ 6. And Joseph
■ came in unto them

in the morning, and looked upon them, and, behold, they were sad.

7. **And he asked** Pharaoh's officers that *were* with him in the ward of his lord's house, saying, **Wherefore look ye so sadly to day?**

8. **And they said** unto him, **We have dreamed** a dream, **and there is no interpreter** of it. And **Joseph said** unto them, **Do not interpretations belong to God? tell me them,** I pray you.

9. **And the chief butler** told his dream to Joseph, and **said** to him, **In my dream,** behold, **a vine was before me;**

10. **And in the vine were three branches: and it** *was* as though it **budded, and** her **blossoms shot forth; and** the clusters thereof brought forth **ripe grapes:**

11. **And Pharaoh's cup was in my hand: and I took the grapes, and pressed them** into Pharaoh's cup, **and** I **gave the cup into Pharaoh's hand.**

12. **And Joseph said** unto him, This *is* the interpretation of it: **The three branches are three days:**

13. **Yet within three days shall Pharaoh** lift up thine head, and **restore thee unto thy place:** and thou shalt deliver Pharaoh's cup into his hand, after the former manner when thou wast his butler.

14. **But think on me when it shall be well with thee,** and shew kindness, I pray thee, unto me, and make mention of me unto Pharaoh, and bring me out of this house:

15. For indeed I was stolen away out of the land of the Hebrews: and here also have I done nothing that they should put me into the dungeon.

16. **When the chief baker saw that the interpretation was good, he said** unto Joseph, I also *was* **in my dream,** and, behold, **I had three white baskets on my head:**

17. **And in the uppermost basket there was** of all manner of **bakemeats for Pharaoh; and the birds did eat them** out of the basket upon my head.

18. **And Joseph** answered and **said,** This *is* the interpretation thereof: **The three baskets are three days:**

19. **Yet within three days shall Pharaoh lift up thy head from off thee, and** shall **hang thee on a tree; and the birds shall eat thy flesh** from off thee.

20. **And** it came to pass **the third day, which was Pharaoh's birthday,** that **he made a feast** unto all his servants: and he lifted up the head of the chief butler and of the chief baker among his servants.

21. **And he restored the chief butler** unto his butlership again; and he gave the cup into Pharaoh's hand:

22. **But he hanged the chief baker:** as Joseph had interpreted to them.

23. **Yet did not the chief butler remember Joseph,** but forgat him.

CHAPTER 41

1. **And** it came to pass **at the end of two** full **years,** that **Pharaoh dreamed:**

and, behold,
he stood by the river.
2. And, behold,
there came up
out of the river seven
well favoured kine and
fatfleshed; and they
fed in a meadow.
3. And, behold,
seven other kine came
up after them out of the river,
ill favoured and
leanfleshed; and stood by the
other kine upon the brink of the river.
4. And the ill
favoured and leanfleshed kine
did eat up
the seven well favoured
and fat kine. So Pharaoh awoke.
5. And he slept and
dreamed the second
time: and, behold,
seven ears of corn came up
upon one stalk, rank and good.
6. And, behold,
seven thin ears and
blasted with the east wind
sprung up after them.
7. And the seven thin ears
devoured the seven rank and
full ears. And
Pharaoh awoke,
and, behold, *it was* a dream.
8. And it came to pass
in the morning that
his spirit was troubled;
and he sent and
called for all
the magicians of Egypt,
and all
the wise men thereof:
and Pharaoh
told them his
dream; but *there was*
none that
could interpret
them unto Pharaoh.
9. Then spake the
chief butler unto Pharaoh,
saying, I do remember
my faults this day:
10. Pharaoh was wroth
with his servants, and

put me in ward in the captain of
the guard's house,
both me and the
chief baker:
11. And we dreamed a dream
in one night, I and he; we dreamed
each man according to the
interpretation of his dream.
12. And there was there
with us a young man,
an Hebrew, servant to the captain
of the guard; and we told him,
and he interpreted to us
our dreams; to each
man according to his
dream he did interpret.
13. And it came to pass,
as he interpreted to us,
so it was; me he restored unto
mine office, and him he hanged.
14. Then Pharaoh sent and
called Joseph, and they brought
him hastily out of the dungeon: and
he shaved *himself*,
and changed his raiment, and
came in unto Pharaoh.
15. And Pharaoh
said unto Joseph,
I have dreamed a dream,
and *there is*
none that
can interpret it: and I
have heard say of thee, *that*
thou canst understand a dream to
interpret it.
16. And Joseph
answered Pharaoh, saying,
It is not in
me: God shall give Pharaoh
an answer of peace.
17. And Pharaoh said unto Joseph,
In my dream, behold, I stood upon
the bank of the river:
18. And, behold, there came up out
of the river seven kine, fatfleshed
and well favoured; and they fed
in a meadow:
19. And, behold, seven other kine
came up after them, poor and very
ill favoured and leanfleshed, such
as I never saw in all the land of
Egypt for badness:
20. And the lean and the ill

favoured kine did eat up
the first seven fat kine:
21. And when they had eaten them
up, it could not be known that they
had eaten them; but they *were* still
ill favoured, as at the
beginning. So I awoke.
22. And I saw in my dream, and,
behold, seven ears came up in
one stalk, full and good:
23. And, behold, seven ears,
withered, thin, *and* blasted with the
east wind, sprung up after them:
24. And the thin ears devoured the
seven good ears: and I told *this* unto
the magicians; but *there was* none
that could declare *it* to me.
25. **And Joseph said** unto Pharaoh, The
dream of Pharaoh *is* one:
**God hath shewed Pharaoh
what he is about to do.**
26. **The seven good kine
are seven years; and the
seven good ears are
seven years:** the dream *is* one.
27. **And the seven thin and
ill favoured kine** that came
up after them *are* seven years;
**and the seven empty
ears** blasted with the east wind
**shall be seven years
of famine.**
28. This *is* the thing which I have
spoken unto Pharaoh: What God *is*
about to do he sheweth untoPharaoh.
29. **Behold, there come
seven years of** great
plenty throughout all the landof
Egypt:
30. **And** there shall arise
**after them seven years of
famine**; and all the plenty shall
be forgotten in the land of Egypt;
**and the famine shall
consume the land;**
31. And the plenty shall not be
known in the land by reason of
that famine following;
**for it shall be
very grievous.**
32. And for that the dream was
doubled unto Pharaoh twice;

it is because the thing *is*
established by God,
**and God will shortly
bring it to pass.**
33. **Now** therefore
**let Pharaoh look out a man
discreet and wise, and set
him over the land** of Egypt.
34. Let Pharaoh do *this*,
**and let him appoint
officers** over the land,
and take up
the fifth part of the land of
Egypt in the seven plenteous years.
35. And let them gather
**all the food of those good
years** that come, and lay up corn
under the hand of Pharaoh, and
let them keep food in the cities.
36. **And that food shall
be for store** to the land
**against the seven years
of famine,** which shall be in the
land of Egypt; that the land perish
not through the famine.
37. **And the thing was good
in the eyes of Pharaoh,**
and in the eyes of all his servants.
38. **And Pharaoh
said** unto his servants,
**Can we find such a
one as this** *is*, a man
**in whom the Spirit
of God is?**
39. **And Pharaoh said
unto Joseph,** Forasmuch
as God hath shewed thee all this,
**there is none so discreet
and wise as thou art:**
40. Thou shalt be over my house, and
**according unto thy word
shall all my people be
ruled: only in the throne
will I be greater** than thou.
41. And Pharaoh said unto Joseph,
**See, I have set thee
over all** the land of
Egypt.
42. **And Pharaoh took** off
his ring from his hand,
**and put it upon
Joseph's hand, and
arrayed him in** vestures of

fine linen, and put a gold chain about his neck; 43. And he made him to ride in the second chariot which he had; and they cried before him, Bow the knee: and he made him *ruler* over all the land of Egypt. 44. And Pharaoh said unto Joseph, I *am* Pharaoh, and without thee shall no man lift up his hand or foot in all the land of Egypt. 45. And Pharaoh called Joseph's name Zaphnath-paaneah; and he gave him to wife Asenath the daughter of Poti-pherah priest of On. And Joseph went out over *all* the land of Egypt. 46. And Joseph was thirty years old when he stood before Pharaoh king of Egypt. And Joseph went out from the presence of Pharaoh, and went throughout all the land of Egypt. 47. And in the seven plenteous years the earth brought forth by handfuls. 48. And he gathered up all the food of the seven years, which were in the land of Egypt, and laid up the food in the cities: the food of the field, which *was* round about every city, laid he up in the same. 49. And Joseph gathered corn as the sand of the sea, very much, until he left numbering; for *it was* without number. 50. And unto Joseph were born two sons before the years of famine came, which Asenath the daughter of Poti-pherah priest of On bare unto him. 51. And Joseph called the name of the firstborn Manasseh: For God, *said he,* hath made me forget all my toil, and all my father's house. 52. And the name of the second called he Ephraim:

For God hath caused me to be fruitful in the land of my affliction. 53. And the seven years of plenteousness, that was in the land of Egypt, were ended. 54. And the seven years of dearth began to come, according as Joseph had said: and the dearth was in all lands; but in all the land of Egypt there was bread. 55. And when all the land of Egypt was famished, the people cried to Pharaoh for bread: and Pharaoh said unto all the Egyptians, Go unto Joseph; what he saith to you, do. 56. And the famine was over all the face of the earth: and Joseph opened all the storehouses, and sold unto the Egyptians; and the famine waxed sore in the land of Egypt. 57. And all countries came into Egypt to Joseph for to buy corn; because that the famine was *so* sore in all lands.

CHAPTER 42

1. Now when Jacob saw that there was corn in Egypt, Jacob said unto his sons, Why do ye look one upon another? 2. And he said, Behold, I have heard that there is corn in Egypt: get you down thither, and buy for us from thence; that we may live, and not die. 3. And Joseph's ten brethren went down to buy corn in Egypt. 4. But Benjamin, Joseph's brother, Jacob sent not with his brethren; for he said, Lest peradventure mischief befall him.

64

5. And the sons of Israel came to buy *corn* among those that came: for the famine was in the land of Canaan.

6. And Joseph *was* the governor over the land, *and* he *it was* that sold to all the people of the land: **and Joseph's brethren came,** and bowed down themselves before him **with their faces to the earth.**

7. **And Joseph saw his brethren,** and he knew them, **but made himself strange** unto them, **and spake roughly** unto them; **and** he **said** unto them, **Whence come ye? And they said, From** the land of **Canaan** to buy food.

8. **And Joseph knew his brethren, but they knew not him.**

9. **And Joseph** remembered the dreams which he dreamed of them, and **said unto them, Ye are spies**; to see the nakedness of the land ye are come.

10. **And they said** unto him, **Nay,** my lord, **but to buy food** are **thy servants come.**

11. We *are* all one man's sons; we *are* true *men*, thy servants are no spies.

12. And he said unto them, Nay, but to see the nakedness of the land ye are come.

13. And they said, **Thy servants are twelve brethren,** the sons of one man in the land of Canaan; **and,** behold, **the youngest is** this day **with our father,** and one *is* not.

14. **And Joseph said** unto them, That *is it* that I spake unto you, saying, Ye *are* spies:

15. **Hereby ye shall be proved**: By the life of Pharaoh **ye shall not go forth** hence, **except your youngest brother come hither.**

16. **Send one** of you, **and let him fetch your brother,** and ye shall be kept in prison, that your words may be proved, whether *there be any* truth in you: or else by the life of Pharaoh surely ye *are* spies.

17. **And he put them** all together **into ward three days.**

18. **And Joseph said** unto them the third day, **This do, and live;** *for* I fear God:

19. **If ye be true men, let one of your brethren be bound in** the house of your **prison: go ye, carry corn for** the famine of **your houses:**

20. **But bring your youngest brother** unto me; so shall your words be verified, and ye shall not die. And they did so.

21. **And they said** one to another, **We are** verily **guilty concerning our brother,** in that we saw the anguish of his soul, **when he besought us,** and **we would not hear; therefore is this distress come upon us.**

22. **And Reuben answered** them, saying, **Spake I not** unto you, **saying, Do not sin against the child;** and ye would not hear? **therefore,** behold, also **his blood is required.**

23. **And they knew not that Joseph understood them; for he spake** unto them **by an interpreter.**

24. **And he turned** himself about from them, **and wept**; and returned to them again, and communed with them, **and took from them Simeon,** and bound him before their eyes.

25. **Then Joseph commanded to** fill their sacks

with corn, and to restore every man's money into his sack, and to **give them provision** for the way: and thus did he unto them. 26. **And they** laded their asses with the corn, and **departed** thence. 27. **And as one of them opened his sack** to give his ass provender in the inn, **he espied his money;** for, behold, it *was* in his sack's mouth. 28. **And he said** unto his brethren, **My money is restored;** and, lo, *it is* even in my sack: and their heart failed *them,* **and they were afraid,** saying one to another, What *is* this *that* God hath done unto us? 29. **And they came unto Jacob** their father unto the land of Canaan, **and told him** all that befell unto them; **saying,** 30. The man, *who is* **the lord of the land,** spake roughly to us, and **took us for spies** of the country. 31. **And we said** unto him, We *are* true *men*; we are no spies: 32. **We be twelve brethren,** sons of our father; one *is* not, and the youngest *is* this day with our father in the land of Canaan. 33. **And** the man, **the lord** of the country, **said** unto us, Hereby shall I know that ye *are* true *men*; **leave one of your brethren here** with me, and take *food for* the famine of your households, and be gone: 34. **And bring your youngest brother** unto me: **then shall I know that ye are no spies,** but *that* ye *are* true *men: so* will I deliver you your brother, and ye shall traffick in the land. 35. **And** it came to pass **as they emptied**

their sacks, that, behold, **every man's** bundle of **money was in his sack: and** when *both* they and their father saw the bundles of money, **they were afraid.** 36. **And Jacob** their father **said** unto them, Me have ye bereaved *of my children*: **Joseph is not, and Simeon is not, and ye will take Benjamin away:** all these things are against me. 37. **And Reuben spake** unto his father, saying, **Slay my two sons, if I bring him not** to thee: deliver him into my hand, and I will bring him **to thee again.** 38. **And he said, My son shall not go** down with you; for his brother is dead, and he is left alone: **if mischief befall him** by the way in the which ye go, **then shall ye bring down my** gray hairs with **sorrow to the grave.**

CHAPTER 43

1. And the famine *was* sore in the land. 2. **And** it came to pass, **when they had eaten up the corn** which they had brought out of Egypt, **their father said** unto them, **Go** again, **buy** us a little **food.** 3. **And Judah spake** unto him, saying, **The man did solemnly protest** unto us, **saying, Ye shall not see my face, except your brother be with you.** 4. **If thou wilt send our brother** with us, **we will go** down and buy thee food: 5. **But if thou wilt not** send *him,* **we will not go** down: for the man

said unto us, Ye shall not see my face, except your brother *be* with you.

6. **And Israel said, Wherefore dealt ye so ill with me,** *as* to tell the man whether ye had yet a brother?

7. And they said, The man asked us straitly of our state, and of our kindred, saying, *Is* your father yet alive? have ye *another* brother? and we told him according to the tenor of these words: could we certainly know that he would say, Bring your brother down?

8. **And Judah said** unto Israel his father, **Send the lad with me,** and we will arise and go; **that we may live,** and not die, both we, and thou, *and* also our little ones.

9. **I will be surety for him;** of my hand shalt thou require him: **if I bring him not unto thee,** and set him before thee, then **let me bear the blame** for ever:

10. For except we had lingered, surely now we had returned this second time.

11. **And their father Israel said** unto them, **If it must be so** now, do this; take of the best fruits in the land in your vessels, and **carry** down **the man a present,** a little balm, and a little honey, spices, and myrrh, nuts, and almonds:

12. **And take double money** in your hand; and the money that was brought again in the mouth of your sacks, carry *it* again in your hand; peradventure it *was* an oversight:

13. **Take also your brother,** and arise, go again unto the man:

14. **And God** Almighty **give you mercy before the man,** that he may send away your other brother, and Benjamin. If I be bereaved *of my children,* I am bereaved.

15. **And the men** took that present, and they took double money in their hand and Benjamin; and rose up, and **went** down **to Egypt,** and stood before Joseph.

16. **And when Joseph saw Benjamin** with them, **he said** to the ruler of his house, **Bring these men home,** and slay, and make ready; **for these men shall dine with me** at noon.

17. And the man did as Joseph bade; and the man brought the men into Joseph's house.

18. **And the men were afraid,** because they were brought into Joseph's house; and they said, Because of the money that was returned in our sacks at the first time are we brought in; that he may seek occasion against us, and fall upon us, and take us for bondmen, and our asses.

19. **And they came near to** the steward of **Joseph's house,** and they communed with him at the door of the house,

20. And said, O sir, we came indeed down at the first time to buy food:

21. And it came to pass, when we came to the inn, that we opened our sacks, and, behold, *every* man's money *was* in the mouth of his sack, our money in full weight: and we have brought it again in our hand.

22. And other money have we brought down in our hands to buy food: we cannot tell who put our money in our sacks.

23. And he said, Peace *be* to you, fear not: your God, and the God of your father, hath given you treasure in your sacks: I had your money. And he brought Simeon out unto them.

24. And the man brought the men into Joseph's house, and gave *them* water, and they washed their feet; and he gave their asses provender.

25. **And they made ready the present** against Joseph

came at noon: for they heard that they should eat bread there.

26. **And when Joseph came home, they brought** him **the present** which *was* in their hand into the house, **and bowed** themselves to him to the earth.

27. **And he asked** them of *their* welfare, and said, **Is your father well,** the old man of whom ye spake? *Is* he yet alive?

28. **And they answered,** Thy servant **our father is in good health,** he *is* yet alive. And they bowed down their heads, and made obeisance.

29. **And he** lifted up his eyes, and **saw his brother Benjamin,** his mother's son, **and said, Is this your younger brother,** of whom ye spake unto me? And he said, God be gracious unto thee, my son.

30. **And Joseph made haste; for his bowels did yearn upon his brother:** and he sought *where* to weep; **and he entered** into **his chamber, and wept** there.

31. **And he** washed his face, and went out, and **refrained himself, and said, Set on bread.**

32. **And they set** on for **him by himself,** and for them by themselves, and for the Egyptians, which did eat with him, by themselves: **because the Egyptians might not eat bread with the Hebrews**; for that *is* an abomination unto the Egyptians.

33. **And they sat** before him, the firstborn **according to his birthright,** and the youngest according to his youth: and the men marvelled one at another.

34. **And he** took *and* **sent messes unto them** from before him: **but Benjamin's mess**

was five times so much as **any of theirs.** And they drank, and were merry with him.

CHAPTER 44

1. **And he commanded the steward** of his house, **saying, Fill the men's sacks with food,** as much as they can carry, **and put every man's money in his sack's mouth.**

2. **And put my** cup, the **silver cup, in the sack's mouth of the youngest,** and his corn money. **And** he did according to the word that Joseph had spoken.

3. As soon as the morning was light, **the men were sent away,** they and their asses.

4. **And when they were gone** out of the city, *and* not *yet* far off, **Joseph said unto his steward,** Up, **follow after the men; and** when thou dost overtake them, **say** unto them, **Wherefore have ye rewarded evil for good?**

5. *Is* not this *it* in which my lord drinketh, and whereby indeed he divineth? ye have done evil in so doing.

6. **And he overtook them, and** he **spake** unto them **these** same **words.**

7. **And they said** unto him, Wherefore saith my lord these words? **God forbid that thy servants should do according to this thing:**

8. **Behold, the money,** which **we found** in our sacks' mouths, **we brought again** unto thee out of the land of Canaan: **how then should we steal** out of thy lord's house silver or gold?

9. **With whomsoever of thy servants it be found,** both **let him die, and we** also

will be my lord's **bondmen.**

10. And he said, Now also *let it be* according unto your words: he with whom it is found shall be my servant; and ye shall be blameless. 11. **Then they** speedily took down every man his sack to the ground, and **opened every man his sack.** 12. **And he searched,** *and* began at the eldest, and left at the youngest: **and the cup was found in Benjamin's sack.** 13. **Then they rent their clothes,** and laded every man his ass, and returned to the city. 14. **And** Judah and his brethren **came to Joseph's house;** for he *was* yet there: and they fell before him on the ground. 15. **And Joseph said** unto them, **What deed is this that ye have done?** wot ye not that such a man as I can certainly divine? 16. **And Judah said, What shall we say** unto my lord? what shall we speak? or how shall we clear ourselves? **God hath found** out **the iniquity of thy servants:** behold, **we are my lord's servants,** both we, and *he* also with whom the cup is found. 17. **And he said, God forbid** that I should do so: **but the man in whose hand the cup is found, he shall be my servant;** and as for you, get you up in peace unto your father. 18. **Then Judah** came near unto him, and **said,** Oh **my lord, let thy servant,** I pray thee, **speak a word** in my lord's ears, and let not thine anger burn against thy servant: for thou *art* even as Pharaoh. 19. **My lord asked** his servants, saying, **Have ye a father, or a brother?** 20. **And we said** unto my lord, **We have a father,** an old man, **and a child of his old age,** a little one; **and his brother is dead,** and he alone is left of his mother, and his father loveth him. 21. **And thou saidst** unto thy servants, **Bring him** down **unto me,** that I may set mine eyes upon him. 22. **And we said** unto my lord, **The lad cannot leave his father:** for *if* he should leave his father, *his father* would die. 23. **And thou saidst** unto thy servants, **Except your youngest brother come** down with you, **ye shall see my face no more.** 24. **And** it came to pass **when we came** up **unto** thy servant **my father,** we told him the words of my lord. 25. **And our father said,** Go again, *and* **buy** us a little **food.** 26. **And we said,** We cannot go down: **if our youngest brother be with us, then will we go** down: for we may not see the man's face, except our youngest brother *be* with us. 27. **And** thy servant **my father said** unto us, Ye know that **my wife bare** me **two sons:** 28. **And the one** went out from me, and I said, Surely he **is torn in pieces;** and I saw him not since: 29. **And if ye take this also** from me, and mischief befall him, **ye shall bring down**

■ **my** gray hairs with
■ **sorrow to the grave.**
■ 30. **Now therefore when**
■ **I come to** thy servant
■ **my father, and the lad be**
■ **not with us;** seeing that his
life is bound up in the lad's life;
■ 31. **It shall come to**
■ **pass,** when he seeth that
the lad *is* not *with us,*
■ **that he will die**: and thy servants
shall bring down the gray hairs
of thy servant our father with
sorrow to the grave.
■ 32. **For thy servant**
■ **became surety for the**
■ **lad** unto my father, saying,
■ **If I bring him not** unto thee, then
■ **I shall bear the blame**
to my father for ever.
■ 33. **Now therefore,** I pray thee,
■ **let thy servant abide**
■ **instead of the lad** a bondman
to my lord; and let the lad go up
with his brethren.
34. For how shall I go up to my
father, and the lad *be* not with me?
lest peradventure I see the evil that
shall come on my father.

CHAPTER 45

■ 1. **Then Joseph could**
■ **not refrain himself** before
all them that stood by him;
■ **and he cried, Cause every**
■ **man to go out from me.And**
■ **there stood no man** with him,
■ **while Joseph made himself**
■ **known unto his brethren.**
■ 2. **And he wept aloud:**
and the Egyptians and the
house of Pharaoh heard.
■ 3. **And Joseph said** unto
his brethren, I *am* Joseph; doth my
father yet live? And his brethren
could not answer him; for they
were troubled at his presence.
4. And Joseph said unto his brethren,
Come near to me, I pray you. And
they came near. And he said,
■ **I am Joseph your brother,**
whom ye sold into Egypt.
5. Now therefore

■ **be not grieved,**
nor angry with yourselves,
■ **that ye sold me** hither:
for God did send me before
you to preserve life.
6. For these two years *hath* the
famine *been* in the land: and yet *there*
are five years, in the which *there*
shall neither *be* earing nor harvest.
7. And
■ **God sent me before**
■ **you to preserve you**
a posterity in the earth,
■ **and to save your lives**
by a great deliverance.
■ 8. **So** now
■ **it was not you**
that sent me hither,
■ **but God: and he hath**
■ **made me** a father to Pharaoh,
and lord of all his house, and
■ **a ruler throughout**
all the land of
■ **Egypt.**
9. Haste ye, and
■ **go up to my father, and**
■ **say** unto him, Thus saith
■ **thy son Joseph, God**
■ **hath made** me
■ **lord of all Egypt: come**
■ **down** unto me, tarry not:
■ 10. **And** thou shalt
■ **dwell in** the land of
■ **Goshen, and** thou shalt
■ **be near unto me, thou, and**
■ **thy children,** and thy children's
children, and thy flocks, and thy
herds, and all that thou hast:
■ 11. **And there will I nourish**
■ **thee;** for yet *there are* five years
of famine; lest thou, and thy
household, and all that thou
hast, come to poverty.
12. And, behold, your eyes see, and
the eyes of my brother Benjamin, that
it is my mouth that speaketh unto you.
■ 13. **And ye shall tell my**
■ **father of all my glory in**
■ **Egypt,** and of all that ye have
seen; and ye shall haste and
■ **bring down my father** hither.
■ 14. **And he fell upon** his brother
■ **Benjamin's neck, and wept;**

and Benjamin wept upon his neck.

15. **Moreover he kissed all his brethren,** and wept upon them: and after that his brethren talked with him.

16. **And the fame thereof was heard in Pharaoh's house,** saying, Joseph's brethren are come: **and it pleased Pharaoh** well, and his servants.

17. **And Pharaoh said unto Joseph, Say unto thy brethren,** This do ye; lade your beasts, and **go,** get you **unto** the land of **Canaan;**

18. **And take your father** and your households, **and come** unto me: **and I will give you the good** of the land **of Egypt,** and ye shall eat the fat of the land.

19. Now thou art commanded, this do ye; take you wagons out of the land of Egypt for your little ones, and for your wives, and bring your father, and come.

20. Also regard not your stuff; for the good of all the land of Egypt *is* your's.

21. **And the children of Israel did so:** and Joseph gave them wagons, according to the commandment of Pharaoh, and gave them provision for the way.

22. To all of them he gave each man changes of raiment; but to Benjamin he gave three hundred *pieces* of silver, and five changes of raiment.

23. And to his father he sent after this *manner;* ten asses laden with the good things of Egypt, and ten she asses laden with corn and bread and meat for his father by the way.

24. **So he sent his brethren away,** and they departed: and he said unto them, See that ye fall not out by the way.

25. **And they** went up out of Egypt, and **came** into the land of Canaan

unto Jacob their father,

26. **And told him, saying, Joseph is yet alive, and he is governor** over all the land of Egypt. **And Jacob's heart fainted, for he believed them not.**

27. **And** they told him all the words of Joseph, which he had said unto them: and **when he saw the wagons** which Joseph had **sent to carry him,** the spirit of **Jacob** their father **revived:**

28. **And Israel said,** *It is* enough; Joseph **my son is yet alive: I will** go and **see him before I die.**

CHAPTER 46

1. **And Israel took his journey** with all that he had, **and came to Beer-sheba, and offered sacrifices unto the God** of his father Isaac.

2. **And God spake unto Israel in the visions of the night,** and said, Jacob, Jacob. And he said, Here *am* I.

3. And he said, I *am* God, the God of thy father: **fear not to go** down **into Egypt; for I will** there **make of thee a great nation:**

4. I will go down with thee into Egypt; **and I will also surely bring thee up again:** and Joseph shall put his hand upon thine eyes.

5. **And Jacob rose** up from Beer-sheba: **and the sons of Israel** carried Jacob their father, and their little ones, and their wives, in the wagons which Pharaoh had sent to carry him.

6. And they took their cattle, and their goods, which they had gotten in the land of Canaan, and **came into Egypt, Jacob,**

■ **and all his seed with him:**

7. His sons, and his sons' sons with him, his daughters, and his sons' daughters, and all his seed brought he with him into Egypt.
8. And these *are* the names of the children of Israel, which came into Egypt, Jacob and his sons: Reuben, Jacob's firstborn.
9. And the sons of Reuben; Hanoch, and Phallu, and Hezron, and Carmi.
10. And the sons of Simeon; Jemuel, and Jamin, and Ohad, and Jachin, and Zohar, and Shaul the son of a Canaanitish woman.
11. And the sons of Levi; Gershon, Kohath, and Merari.
12. And the sons of Judah; Er, and Onan, and Shelah, and Pharez, and Zarah: but Er and Onan died in the land of Canaan. And the sons of Pharez were Hezron and Hamul.
13. And the sons of Issachar; Tola, and Phuvah, and Job, and Shimron.
14. And the sons of Zebulun; Sered, and Elon, and Jahleel.
15. These *be* the sons of Leah, which she bare unto Jacob in Padan-aram, with his daughter Dinah: all the souls of his sons and his daughters *were* thirty and three.
16. And the sons of Gad; Ziphion, and Haggi, Shuni, and Ezbon, Eri, and Arodi, and Areli.
17. And the sons of Asher; Jimnah, and Ishuah, and Isui, and Beriah, and Serah their sister: and the sons of Beriah; Heber, and Malchiel.
18. These *are* the sons of Zilpah, whom Laban gave to Leah his daughter, and these she bare unto Jacob, *even* sixteen souls.
19. The sons of Rachel Jacob's wife; Joseph, and Benjamin.
20. And unto Joseph in the land of Egypt were born Manasseh and Ephraim, which Asenath the daughter of Potipherah priest of On bare unto him.
21. And the sons of Benjamin *were* Belah, and Becher, and Ashbel, Gera, and Naaman, Ehi, and Rosh, Muppim, and Huppim, and Ard.

22. These *are* the sons of Rachel, which were born to Jacob: all the souls *were* fourteen.
23. And the sons of Dan; Hushim.
24. And the sons of Naphtali; Jahzeel, and Guni, and Jezer, and Shillem.
25. These *are* the sons of Bilhah, which Laban gave unto Rachel his daughter, and she bare these unto Jacob: all the souls *were* seven.
26. All the souls that came with Jacob into Egypt, which came out of his loins, besides Jacob's sons' wives, all the souls *were* threescore and six;
27. And the sons of Joseph, which were born him in Egypt, *were* two souls: all the souls of the house of Jacob, which came into Egypt, *were* threescore and ten.
28. And he sent Judah before him unto Joseph, to direct his face unto Goshen; and they came into the land of Goshen.
■ 29. **And Joseph made**
■ **ready his chariot, and**
■ **went up to meet Israel**
■ **his father,** to Goshen, and presented himself unto him;
■ **and he fell on his neck,**
■ **and wept on his neck**
■ **a good while.**
■ 30. **And Israel**
■ **said** unto Joseph,
■ **Now let me die,** since I have seen thy face,
■ **because thou art yet alive.**
■ 31. **And Joseph said** unto his brethren, and unto his father's house,
■ **I will go up, and shew**
■ **Pharaoh, and say** unto him,
■ **My brethren,** and my father's house, which *were* in the land of Canaan, are come unto me;
32. And the men
■ **are shepherds,** for their trade hath been to feed cattle;
■ **and they have brought**
■ **their flocks,** and their herds, and all that they have.
■ 33. **And** it shall come to pass,
■ **when Pharaoh** shall call you, and

shall say, What is
your occupation?
34. **That ye shall say,**
Thy servants' trade
hath been about cattle
from our youth even until now,
both we, *and* also our fathers:
that ye may dwell in the
land of Goshen; for
every shepherd is
an abomination
unto the Egyptians.

CHAPTER 47

1. **Then Joseph** came and
told Pharaoh, and said,
My father and my
brethren, and their flocks,
and their herds, and all that they
have, are come out of the land of
Canaan; and, behold, they
are in the land of Goshen.
2. And he took some of his
brethren, *even* five men, and
presented them unto Pharaoh.
3. **And Pharaoh said**
unto his brethren, What
is your occupation?
And they said unto Pharaoh,
Thy servants are
shepherds, both we,
and also our fathers.
4. They said morever unto Pharaoh,
For to sojourn in the land arewecome;
for thy servants have no pasture for
their flocks; for the famine *is* sore in
the land of Canaan: now therefore,
we pray thee, let thy servants
dwell in the land of Goshen.
5. **And Pharaoh spake**
unto Joseph,
saying, Thy father and thy
brethren are come unto thee:
6. The land of
Egypt is before thee; in the
best of the land make thy
father and brethren to dwell;
in the land of
Goshen let them dwell: and
if thou knowest *any* men of activity
among them, then make them rulers
over my cattle.
7. **And Joseph**

brought in Jacob
his father, and set him
before Pharaoh: and
Jacob blessed Pharaoh.
8. **And Pharaoh**
said unto Jacob,
How old art thou?
9. **And Jacob said** unto
Pharaoh, The days of the
years of my pilgrimage *are*
an hundred and thirty
years: few and evil have the days of
the years of my life been, and have
not attained unto the days of the
years of the life of my fathers
in the days of their pilgrimage.
10. **And Jacob**
blessed Pharaoh, and
went out from
before Pharaoh.
11. **And Joseph** placed
his father and his brethren, and
gave them a possession
in the land of Egypt, in
the best of the land, in
the land of Rameses, as
Pharaoh had commanded.
12. And Joseph nourished his
father, and his brethren, and
all his father's household, with
bread, according to *their* families.
13. And *there was* no bread in all the
land; for the famine *was* very sore,
so that the land of Egypt and *all*
the land of Canaan fainted by
reason of the famine.
14. **And Joseph gathered**
up all the money that was
found in the land of
Egypt, and in the land of
Canaan, for the corn which
they bought: and Joseph
brought the money
into Pharaoh's house.
15. **And when money failed**
in the land of Egypt, and
in the land of Canaan,
all the Egyptians came unto
Joseph, and said, Give us
bread: for why should we die in thy
presence? for the money faileth.
16. **And Joseph said, Give**
your cattle; and I will give

you for your cattle, if money fail.
17. **And they brought**
their cattle unto Joseph:
and Joseph gave them
bread in exchange for horses,
and for the flocks, and for the cattle
of the herds, and for the asses:
and he fed them with bread
for all their cattle for that year.
18. When that year was ended,
they came unto him
the second year, and
said unto him, We will not
hide *it* from my lord, how that
our money is spent; my
lord also hath our herds of cattle;
there is not ought
left in the sight of my lord,
but our bodies,
and our lands:
19. Wherefore shall we die before
thine eyes, both we and our land?
buy us and our land for
bread, and we and our land
will be servants unto
Pharaoh: and give *us* seed,
that we may live, and not die,
that the land be not desolate.
20. **And Joseph**
bought all the land
of Egypt for Pharaoh;
for the Egyptians sold every
man his field, because
the famine prevailed over them:
so the land became Pharaoh's.
21. And as for the people, he
removed them to cities from *one*
end of the borders of Egypt
even to the *other* end thereof.
22. **Only the land of the**
priests bought he not; for the
priests had a portion *assigned them*
of Pharaoh, and did eat their portion
which Pharaoh gave them:
wherefore they sold not their lands.
23. **Then Joseph said**
unto the people,
Behold, I have bought you this
day and your land for Pharaoh: lo,
here is seed for you, and
ye shall sow the land.
24. **And** it shall come to pass
in the increase, that ye shall

give the fifth part unto
Pharaoh, and four parts shall be
your own, for seed of the field, and
for your food, and for them of your
households, and for food for your
little ones.
25. **And they said, Thou hast**
saved our lives: let us find grace
in the sight of my lord,
and we will be Pharaoh's servants.
26. **And Joseph made** it
a law over the land of
Egypt unto this day,
that Pharaoh should
have the fifth part, except
the land of the priests only, *which*
became not Pharaoh's.
27. **And Israel dwelt in** the
land of Egypt, in the country of
Goshen; and they had
possessions therein,
and grew, and
multiplied exceedingly.
28. And Jacob lived in the land of
Egypt seventeen years: so the
whole age of Jacob was an
hundred forty and seven years.
29. **And the time drew**
nigh that Israel must
die: and he called his son
Joseph, and said unto him, If
now I have found grace in thy sight,
put, I pray thee,
thy hand under my thigh,
and deal kindly and truly with me;
bury me not, I pray thee,
in Egypt:
30. **But I will lie with my**
fathers, and thou shalt carry
me out of Egypt, and bury me
in their buryingplace.
And he said, I will do
as thou hast said.
31. **And he said, Swear**
unto me. And he sware
unto him. And Israel bowed
himself upon the bed's head.

CHAPTER 48

1. **And it came to**
pass after these things,
that one told Joseph, Behold,
thy father is sick: and

he took with him his two
sons, Manasseh and Ephraim.
2. And one told
Jacob, and said, Behold,
thy son Joseph cometh
unto thee: and Israel strengthened
himself, and sat upon the bed.
3. And Jacob said unto
Joseph, God Almighty
appeared unto me at Luz in
the land of Canaan, and blessed me,
4. And said unto me, Behold,
I will make thee fruitful,
and multiply thee, and I will make
of thee a multitude of people;
and will give this land
to thy seed after thee
for an everlasting
possession.
5. And now thy two sons,
Ephraim and Manasseh, which were
born unto thee in the land of Egypt
before I came unto thee into Egypt,
are mine; as Reuben and
Simeon, they shall be mine.
6. And thy issue, which
thou begettest after them,
shall be thine, and shall be
called after the name of their
brethren in their inheritance.
7. And as for me, when I came from
Padan, Rachel died by me in the land
of Canaan in the way, when yet *there*
was but a little way to come unto
Ephrath: and I buried her there
in the way of Ephrath; the
same *is* Bethlehem.
8. And Israel beheld
Joseph's sons, and
said, Who are these?
9. And Joseph
said unto his father,
They are my sons, whom
God hath given me in this *place*.
And he said, Bring
them, I pray thee, unto me,
and I will bless them.
10. Now the eyes of Israel were dim
for age, *so that* he could not see. And
he brought them near unto him;
and he kissed them,
and embraced them.
11. And Israel said unto Joseph,

I had not thought to see thy face:
and, lo, God hath shewed me
also thy seed.
12. And Joseph brought them
out from between his knees,
and he bowed himself with his
face to the earth.
13. And Joseph
took them both,
Ephraim in his right hand
toward Israel's left hand,
and Manasseh in his left hand
toward Israel's right hand,
and brought *them* near unto him.
14. And Israel stretched
out his right hand, and
laid it upon Ephraim's
head, who *was* the younger,
and his left hand upon
Manasseh's head,
guiding his hands
wittingly; for Manasseh
was the firstborn.
15. And he blessed Joseph, and
said, God, before whom my
fathers Abraham and Isaac did
walk, the God which fed me all
my life long unto this day,
16. The Angel which
redeemed me from all evil,
bless the lads; and let
my name be named
on them, and the name of
my fathers Abraham
and Isaac; and let them
grow into a multitude
in the midst of the earth.
17. And when Joseph
saw that his father laid his
right hand upon the head of
Ephraim, it displeased him:
and he held up his father's
hand, to remove it from Ephraim's
head unto Manasseh's head.
18. And Joseph said unto
his father, Not so, my father: for
this is the firstborn; put thy
right hand upon his head.
19. And his father refused,
and said, I know it, my son,
I know *it*: he also shall become a
people, and he also shall be great:
but truly his younger

75

brother shall be greater
than he, and his seed shall
become a multitude of nations.
20. And he blessed them that day,
saying, In thee shall Israel bless,
saying, God make thee as
Ephraim and as Manasseh:
and he set Ephraim
before Manasseh.
21. And Israel
said unto Joseph,
Behold, I die: but God
shall be with you, and bring
you again unto
the land of your fathers.
22. Moreover I have given to thee
one portion above thy brethren, which
I took out of the hand of the Amorite
with my sword and with my bow.

CHAPTER 49

1. And Jacob called
unto his sons, and said,
Gather yourselves together, that I
may tell you *that* which shall befall
you in the last days.
2. Gather yourselves together,
and hear, ye sons of Jacob; and
hearken unto Israel
your father.
3. Reuben, thou *art*
my firstborn, my might,
and the beginning of my
strength, the excellency of dignity,
and the excellency of power:
4. Unstable as water,
thou shalt not excel;
because thou wentest up to thy
father's bed; then defiledst thou
it: he went up to my couch.
5. Simeon and
Levi are brethren;
instruments of cruelty
are in their habitations.
6. O my soul, come not thou into
their secret; unto their assembly,
mine honour, be not thou united:
for in their anger they slew
a man, and in their selfwill they
digged down a wall.
7. Cursed be their
anger, for *it was* fierce;
and their wrath, for it was cruel:

I will divide them in Jacob,
and scatter them in Israel.
8. Judah, thou art he
whom thy brethren
shall praise: thy hand *shall
be* in the neck of thine enemies;
thy father's children shall
bow down before thee.
9. Judah *is* a lion's whelp: from
the prey, my son, thou art gone
up: he stooped down, he couched
as a lion, and as an old lion;
who shall rouse him up?
10. The sceptre shall not
depart from Judah, nor
a lawgiver from between his feet,
until Shiloh come; and
unto him shall the gathering
of the people be.
11. Binding his foal unto the vine,
and his ass's colt unto the choice
vine; he washed his garments in wine,
and his clothes in the blood of grapes:
12. His eyes *shall be* red with wine,
and his teeth white with milk.
13. Zebulun shall
dwell at the haven of
the sea; and he *shall
be* for an haven of ships;
and his border shall
be unto Zidon.
14. Issachar is a
strong ass couching down
between two burdens:
15. And he saw that rest *was* good,
and the land that *it was* pleasant;
and bowed his shoulder to bear, and
became a servant
unto tribute.
16. Dan shall judge
his people, as one of the tribes of
Israel.
17. Dan shall be a serpent by the
way, an adder in the path, that
biteth the horse heels, so that
his rider shall fall backward.
18. I have waited for thy
salvation, O LORD.
19. Gad, a troop
shall overcome him: but he
shall overcome at the last.
20. Out of Asher his bread
shall be fat, and he shall yield

■ **royal dainties.**
■ 21. **Naphtali** *is* a hind let loose: he
■ **giveth goodly words.**
■ 22. **Joseph is a fruitful**
■ **bough**, *even* a fruitful bough
by a well; *whose* branches
run over the wall:
23. The archers have sorely grieved
him, and shot *at him*, and hated him:
24. But his bow abode in
strength, and the arms of
■ **his hands were made**
■ **strong by** the hands of
■ **the mighty God of Jacob**;
(from thence *is* the shepherd,
the stone of Israel:)
25. *Even* by the God of thy father,
who shall help thee; and by the
Almighty, who shall bless thee with
blessings of heaven above, blessings
of the deep that lieth under, blessings
of the breasts, and of the womb:
26. The blessings of thy father have
prevailed above the blessings of my
progenitors unto the utmost bound
of the everlasting hills: they shall be
on the head of Joseph, and on the
crown of the head of him that was
separate from his brethren.
■ 27. **Benjamin shall ravin**
■ **as a wolf**: in the morning he
shall devour the prey, and at night
he shall divide the spoil.
■ 28. **All these are the**
■ **twelve tribes** of Israel:
■ **and this is it that their**
■ **father spake** unto them,
■ **and blessed them;** every
one according to his blessing
he blessed them.
■ 29. **And he charged them,**
■ **and said** unto them, I am to
be gathered unto my people:
■ **bury me with my fathers**
in the cave that *is* in the field of
Ephron the Hittite,
30. In the cave that *is* in the field of
Machpelah, which *is* before Mamre,
in the land of Canaan, which
Abraham bought with the field
of Ephron the Hittite for a
possession of a buryingplace.
31. There they buried Abraham and

Sarah his wife; there they buried
Isaac and Rebekah his wife;
and there I buried Leah.
32. The purchase of the field and
of the cave that *is* therein *was*
from the children of Heth.
■ 33. **And when Jacob**
■ **had made an end of**
■ **commanding his sons, he**
gathered up his feet into the bed, and
■ **yielded up the ghost,** and
was gathered unto his people.

CHAPTER 50

■ 1. **And Joseph** fell
upon his father's face, and
■ **wept upon him, and**
■ **kissed him.**
■ 2. **And** Joseph commanded
his servants the physicians
to embalm his father: and
■ **the physicians**
■ **embalmed Israel.**
3. And forty days were fulfilled for
him; for so are fulfilled the days
of those which are embalmed:
and the Egyptians mourned for
him threescore and ten days.
■ 4. **And when the days**
■ **of his mourning were**
■ **past, Joseph spake**
■ **unto** the house of
■ **Pharaoh, saying,** If now
I have found grace in your eyes,
speak, I pray you, in the ears
of Pharaoh, saying,
5. My father made me swear, saying,
Lo, I die: in my grave which I have
digged for me in the land of Canaan,
there shalt thou bury me.
■ **Now therefore let me**
■ **go** up, I pray thee, and
■ **bury my father,**
and I will come again.
■ 6. **And Pharaoh said, Go** up,
■ **and bury thy father,**
according as he made thee swear.
7. And Joseph went up to bury
his father: and with him went up
all the servants of Pharaoh, the
elders of his house, and all the
elders of the land of Egypt,
8. And all the house of Joseph,

and his brethren, and his father's house: only their little ones, and their flocks, and their herds, they left in the land of Goshen.

9. **And there went up with him both chariots and horsemen: and** it was **a very great company.**

10. **And they came** to the threshingfloor of Atad, which *is* **beyond Jordan, and there they mourned** with a great and very sore lamentation: and he made a mourning for his father seven days.

11. And when the inhabitants of the land, the Canaanites, saw the mourning in the floor of Atad, they said, This *is* a grievous mourning to the Egyptians: wherefore the name of it was called Abelmizraim, which *is* beyond Jo-rdan.

12. **And his sons did** unto him according **as he commanded** them:

13. **For his sons carried him into** the land of **Canaan, and buried him in the cave of the field of Machpelah, which Abraham bought** with the field for a possession of a buryingplace of Ephron the Hittite, before Mamre.

14. **And Joseph returned into Egypt, he, and his brethren,** and all that went up with him to bury his father, **after he had buried his father.**

15. **And when Joseph's brethren saw that their father was dead, they said, Joseph will** peradventure **hate us,** and will certainly requite us all the evil which we did unto him.

16. **And they sent a messenger unto Joseph, saying, Thy father did command** before he died, **saying,**

17. So shall ye say unto Joseph, **Forgive,** I pray thee now, **the trespass of thy**

brethren, and their sin; for they did unto thee evil: **and** now, we pray thee, **forgive the trespass of the servants of the God of thy father. And Joseph wept** when they spake unto him.

18. And his brethren also went and fell down before his face; and they said, Behold, we *be* thy servants.

19. **And Joseph said** unto them, **Fear not: for am I in the place of God?**

20. But as for you, **ye thought evil against me; but God meant it unto good,** to bring to pass, as *it is* this day, to save much people alive.

21. **Now** therefore fear ye not: **I will nourish you,** and your little ones. **And he** comforted them, and **spake kindly** unto them.

22. **And** Joseph dwelt in Egypt, he, and his father's house: and **Joseph lived an hundred and ten years.**

23. And Joseph saw Ephraim's children of the third *generation*: the children also of Machir the son of Manasseh were brought up upon Joseph's knees.

24. **And Joseph said** unto his brethren, **I die: and God will** surely visit you, and **bring you out of this land unto the land** which **he sware to Abraham,** to Isaac, and to Jacob.

25. **And Joseph took an oath of the children of Israel, saying,** God will surely visit you, and **ye shall carry up my bones from hence.**

26. **So Joseph died, being an hundred and ten years old:** and they embalmed him, **and he was put in a coffin in Egypt.**

THE BOOK OF EXODUS

BACKGROUND INFORMATION

Author: Moses according to tradition
Date Written: Usually considered to be **between 1491 — 1451 B.C.**

Number of:
Verses—1,213
Chapters—40
Total Words—32,692
Scan Words—15,281
Scan Words Represent Approximately 46% of Total Words

Theme: Israel, God's Chosen Nation,
Delivered from Bondage and Set apart for Divine Service

OUTLINE OF THE BOOK

I.   God's Chosen People **Under Egyptian Bondage** 1:1 — 12:36
II.   **The Exodus** from Egypt **Under** the Leadership of **Moses,** God's Anointed 12:37 — 18:27
III. The Lord's Dealings with His People **at Mount Sinai** 19:1 — 40:38

CHAPTER 1

1. **Now** these *are* the names of **the children of Israel, which came into Egypt;** every man and his household came **with Jacob.**
2. Reuben, Simeon, Levi, and Judah,
3. Issachar, Zebulun, and Benjamin,
4. Dan, and Naphtali, Gad, and Asher.
5. And all the souls that came out of the loins of Jacob **were seventy souls:** for Joseph was in Egypt *already.*
6. **And Joseph died, and all his brethren,** and all that generation.
7. **And the children of Israel** were fruitful, and **increased** abundantly, and multiplied, and waxed exceeding mighty; **and the land was filled with them.**
8. **Now there arose** up **a new king over Egypt, which knew not Joseph.**
9. **And he said** unto his people, Behold, the people of **the children of Israel are more** and mightier **than we:**
10. Come on, **let us deal wisely with them; lest they** multiply, and it come to pass, that, when there falleth out any war, they **join** also unto **our enemies, and fight against us,** and *so* get them up out of the land.
11. **Therefore they** did **set over them taskmasters to** afflict them with their burdens. And they **built for Pharaoh treasure cities,** Pithom and Raamses.
12. **But the more they afflicted them, the more they multiplied** and grew. And they were grieved because of the children of Israel.
13. **And the Egyptians** made the children of Israel to serve with rigour:
14. And they **made their lives bitter with hard bondage,** in morter, and in brick, and in all manner of service in the field: all their service, wherein they made them serve, *was* with rigour.
15. **And the king of Egypt spake to the Hebrew midwives,** of which the name of the one *was* Shiphrah, and the name of the other Puah:
16. **And he said, When ye do the office of a midwife to the Hebrew women,** and see *them* upon the stools; **if it be a son,** then ye shall **kill him: but** if it *be* **a daughter,** then she **shall live.**
17. **But the midwives feared God, and** did not as the king of Egypt commanded them, but **saved the men children alive.**
18. **And the king** of Egypt called for the midwives, and **said unto them, Why have ye done this** thing, and have saved the men children alive?
19. **And the midwives said** unto Pharaoh, Because **the Hebrew women are** not as the Egyptian women; for they *are* **lively, and are delivered ere the midwives come** in unto them.
20. **Therefore God dealt well with the midwives:** and the people multiplied, and waxed very mighty.
21. **And** it came to pass, because the midwives feared God, that he **made them houses.**
22. **And Pharaoh charged** all **his people,** saying, **Every son** that is **born ye shall cast into the river,** and every daughter ye shall save alive.

CHAPTER 2

■ 1. **And** there went
■ **a man** of the house of Levi, and
■ **took to wife a**
■ **daughter of Levi.**
■ 2. **And the woman**
conceived, and
■ **bare a son: and** when she saw
him that he *was* a goodly *child,* she
■ **hid him three months.**
■ 3. **And when she could**
■ **not longer hide him,**
■ **she took** for him
■ **an ark** of bulrushes, and
daubed it with slime and with pitch,
■ **and put the child**
■ **therein; and** she
■ **laid it** in the flags
■ **by the river's brink.**
■ 4. **And his sister stood afar**
■ **off,** to wit what would be done tohim.
■ 5. **And the daughter of**
■ **Pharaoh came** down
■ **to wash herself at**
■ **the river;** and her maidens
walked along by the river's
side; and when she saw
the ark among the flags,
she sent her maid to fetch it.
■ 6. **And when she**
had opened *it,* she
■ **saw the child:** and,
behold, the babe wept. And
■ **she had compassion** on him,
■ **and said, This is one**
■ **of the Hebrews' children.**
■ 7. **Then said his sister**
to Pharaoh's daughter,
■ **Shall I** go and
■ **call** to thee
■ **a nurse** of the Hebrew women,
that she may nurse the child
■ **for thee?**
■ 8. And Pharaoh's
daughter said to her, Go.
■ **And the maid** went and
■ **called the child's mother.**
■ 9. **And Pharaoh's**
■ **daughter said** unto her,
■ **Take this child** away,
■ **and nurse it for me,** and
I will give *thee* thy wages. And the

■ woman took the child, and nursed it.
■ 10. **And the child grew,**
■ **and** she brought him unto
■ **Pharaoh's daughter,**
and he became her son. And she
■ **called his name**
■ **Moses: and she said,**
■ **Because I drew him**
■ **out of the water.**
■ 11. **And it came to**
■ **pass** in those days,
■ **when Moses**
■ **was grown,** that
■ **he went out unto**
■ **his brethren,**
and looked on their burdens:
■ **and** he
■ **spied an Egyptian**
■ **smiting an Hebrew,**
one of his brethren.
12. And he looked
this way and that way,
■ **and when he**
■ **saw** that *there was*
■ **no man, he slew**
■ **the Egyptian, and**
■ **hid him** in the sand.
13. **And** when he went out
■ **the second day,** behold,
■ **two** men of the
■ **Hebrews strove**
■ **together: and he said**
to him that did the wrong,
■ **Wherefore smitest**
■ **thou thy fellow?**
14. **And he said, Who**
■ **made thee** a prince and
■ **a judge** over us?
■ **intendest thou to**
■ **kill me, as** thou killedst
■ **the Egyptian? And**
■ **Moses feared,** and said,
Surely this thing is known.
■ 15. **Now when**
■ **Pharaoh heard** this thing,
■ **he sought to slay**
■ **Moses. But Moses fled**
from the face of Pharaoh,
■ **and dwelt in** the land of
■ **Midian: and he sat**
■ **down by a well.**
■ 16. **Now the priest of**
■ **Midian had seven**

81

daughters: and they came
and drew *water*, and filled the troughs
to water their father's
flock.
17. And the
shepherds came and
drove them away:
but Moses stood up and
helped them, and
watered their flock.
18. And when they came to Reuel
their father, he
said, How is it that ye
are come so soon to day?
19. And they said, An
Egyptian delivered us out
of the hand of the shepherds, and
also drew *water* enough for us,
and watered the flock.
20. And he
said unto his daughters, And
where is he? why *is*
it *that* ye have left the man?
call him, that he may eat bread.
21. And Moses was content
to dwell with the man:
and he gave Moses
Zipporah his daughter.
22. And she bare
him a son, and he
called his name
Gershom: for he said, I have
been a stranger in a strange land.
23. And it came to
pass in process of time,
that the king of Egypt
died: and the children
of Israel sighed by reason
of the bondage, and they
cried, and their cry came up
unto God by reason
of the bondage.
24. And God heard
their groaning, and God
remembered his
covenant with Abraham,
with Isaac, and with Jacob.
25. And God looked upon the
children of Israel, and God
had respect unto *them*.

CHAPTER 3
1. Now Moses kept the

flock of Jethro his father
in law, the priest of Midian:
and he led the flock to the
backside of the desert, and came
to the mountain of
God, *even* to Horeb.
2. And the angel of the
LORD appeared unto him
in a flame of fire
out of the midst of
a bush: and he looked,
and, behold,
the bush burned with fire,
and the bush
was not consumed.
3. And Moses said, I will now
turn aside, and
see this great sight,
why the bush is not burnt.
4. And when
the LORD saw that he
turned aside to see, God
called unto him out of
the midst of the bush,
and said, Moses, Moses.
And he said, Here *am* I.
5. And he
said, Draw not nigh hither:
put off thy shoes
from off thy feet,
for the place
whereon thou standest
is holy ground.
6. Moreover he said,
I am the God of
thy father, the God of
Abraham, the God of
Isaac, and the God of Jacob.
And Moses hid his face; for
he was afraid to look upon God.
7. And the LORD said,
I have surely seen
the affliction of my
people which *are*
in Egypt, and have heard their
cry by reason of their taskmasters; for
I know their sorrows;
8. And I am come
down to deliver them
out of the hand of the
Egyptians, and to
bring them up out of that land
unto a good

■ **land** and a large, unto a land
■ **flowing with milk and**
■ **honey;** unto the place of the
Canaanites, and the Hittites, and
the Amorites, and the Perizzites,
and the Hivites, and the Jebusites.
9. Now therefore, behold,
■ **the cry of the children of**
■ **Israel is come unto me:**
and I have also seen the
oppression wherewith the
Egyptians oppress them.
10. Come now
■ **therefore,** and
■ **I will send thee unto**
■ **Pharaoh, that thou mayest**
■ **bring** forth my people the children of
■ **Israel out of Egypt**.
11. **And Moses said** unto God,
■ **Who am I, that I should**
go unto Pharaoh, and that I should
■ **bring** forth the children of
■ **Israel out of Egypt?**
12. **And he said**, Certainly
■ **I will be with thee;**
■ **and** this *shall be* a token
unto thee, that I have sent thee:
■ **When thou hast brought** forth
■ **the people out of Egypt,**
■ **ye shall serve God**
■ **upon this mountain.**
13. **And Moses said**
unto God, Behold,
■ **when I come unto**
the children of
■ **Israel, and** shall
■ **say** unto them, The
■ **God** of your fathers
■ **hath sent me** unto you;
■ **and they shall say** to me,
■ **What is his name? what**
■ **shall I say** unto them?
14. **And God said** unto Moses,
■ **I AM THAT I AM:** and he said,
■ **Thus shalt thou say**
unto the children of Israel,
■ **I AM hath sent me** unto you.
15. And God said moreover
unto Moses, Thus shalt thou
say unto the children of Israel,
■ **the LORD God of your**
■ **fathers,** the God of Abraham, the
God of Isaac, and the God of Jacob,

■ **hath sent me** unto you:
■ **this is my name for ever,**
■ **and this is my memorial**
■ **unto all generations.**
16. **Go, and gather the**
■ **elders of Israel** together,
■ **and say** unto them,
■ **The LORD God** of your
fathers, the God of Abraham,
of Isaac, and of Jacob,
■ **appeared unto me, saying,**
■ **I have** surely visited you, and
■ **seen that which is**
■ **done to you in Egypt:**
17. **And** I have said,
■ **I will bring you** up
■ **out of** the affliction of
■ **Egypt** unto the land of the
Canaanites, and the Hittites, and the
Amorites, and the Perizzites, and the
Hivites, and the Jebusites, unto a
land flowing with milk and honey.
18. And they shall
hearken to thy voice:
■ **and thou shalt come,**
thou and the elders of Israel,
■ **unto the king** of Egypt,
■ **and** ye shall
■ **say** unto him,
■ **The LORD** God of the Hebrews
■ **hath met with us:** and
■ **now let us go,** we beseech
thee, three days' journey
■ **into the wilderness,**
■ **that we may sacrifice**
■ **to the LORD** our God.
19. **And** I am sure that
■ **the king** of Egypt
■ **will not let you go,**
no, not by a mighty hand.
20. **And I will** stretch
out my hand, and
■ **smite Egypt** with all my wonders
which I will do in the midst thereof:
■ **and after that he**
■ **will let you go.**
21. **And** I will give this people
favour in the sight of the Egyptians:
and it shall come to pass, that,
■ **when ye go, ye**
■ **shall not go empty.**
22. **But** every woman shall borrow
of her neighbour, and of her that

sojourneth in her house, jewels of silver, and jewels of gold, and raiment: and ye shall put *them* upon your sons, and upon your daughters; and

ye shall spoil the Egyptians.

CHAPTER 4

1. **And Moses** answered and **said, But**, behold, **they will not believe me,** nor hearken unto my voice: **for they will say, The LORD hath not appeared unto thee.**

2. **And the LORD said** unto him, **What is that in thine hand? And he said, A rod.**

3. And he said, **Cast it on the ground.** And he cast it on the ground, **and it became a serpent; and Moses fled** from before it.

4. **And the LORD said** unto Moses, Put forth thine hand, and **take it by the tail. And he** put forth his hand, and **caught it, and it became a rod** in his hand:

5. **That they may believe that the LORD** God of their fathers, the God of Abraham, the God of Isaac, and the God of Jacob, hath **appeared unto thee.**

6. **And the LORD said** furthermore unto him, **Put now thine hand into thy bosom**. And he put his hand into his bosom: **and when he took it out**, behold, **his hand was leprous** as snow.

7. And he said, Put thine hand into thy bosom again. **And he put his hand into his bosom again; and** plucked it out of his bosom, and, behold, **it** was **turned again as his other flesh.**

8. And it shall come to pass, if they will not believe thee, neither hearken to the voice of the first sign, that they will believe the voice of the latter sign.

9. And it shall come to pass, **if they will not believe** also **these two signs,** neither hearken unto thy voice, that **thou shalt take** of the **water of the river, and pour it upon the dry land: and the** water which thou takest out of the **river shall become blood** upon the dry *land.*

10. **And Moses said** unto the LORD, **O my LORD, I am not eloquent,** neither heretofore, nor since thou hast spoken unto thy servant: **but I am slow of speech**, and of a slow tongue.

11. **And the LORD said** unto him, **Who hath made man's mouth?** or who maketh the dumb, or deaf, or the seeing, or the blind? **have not I the LORD?**

12. Now therefore go, and **I will** be with thy mouth, and **teach thee what thou shalt say.**

13. **And he said, O my LORD, send,** I pray thee, by the hand *of* **him whom thou wilt** send.

14. **And the anger of the LORD was kindled against Moses, and he said, Is not Aaron** the Levite **thy brother? I know that he can speak well. And** also, behold, **he cometh** forth **to meet thee: and** when he seeth thee, **he will be glad** in his heart.

15. **And thou shalt** speak unto him, and **put words in his mouth:**

■ and I will be with thy mouth, and with his mouth, and will
■ teach you what
■ ye shall do.
16. And he shall be thy
■ spokesman unto the people: and he shall be, *even* he shall be to thee instead of a mouth, and thou shalt be to him instead of God.
17. And thou shalt take this rod in thine hand, wherewith thou shalt do signs.
18. And Moses
■ went and returned
■ to Jethro his father in law,
■ and said unto him,
■ Let me go, I pray thee, and return
■ unto my brethren which *are*
■ in Egypt, and see whether they be yet alive.
■ And Jethro said to Moses,
■ Go in peace.
19. And the LORD
■ said unto Moses in Midian,
■ Go, return
■ into Egypt: for all
■ the men are dead
■ which sought thy life.
20. And Moses took his
■ wife and his sons, and set them upon an ass, and he
■ returned to the land of
■ Egypt: and Moses took
■ the rod of God in his hand.
21. And the LORD said unto Moses, When thou goest to return into Egypt, see that thou
■ do all those wonders before
■ Pharaoh, which I have put in thine hand:
■ but I will harden his
■ heart, that he shall
■ not let the people go.
22. And thou shalt
■ say unto Pharaoh,
■ Thus saith the LORD,
■ Israel is my son, *even* my
■ firstborn:
23. And I say unto thee,
■ Let my son go,
that he may serve me:
■ and if thou refuse
to let him go, behold,

■ I will slay thy son, *even*
■ thy firstborn.
24. And it came to pass by the way
■ in the inn, that
■ the LORD met him, and
■ sought to kill him.
25. Then Zipporah
took a sharp stone, and
■ cut off the foreskin of her
■ son, and cast *it* at his feet,
■ and said, Surely a bloody husband *art* thou to me.
26. So he let him go: then she said,
■ A bloody husband
■ thou art, because
■ of the circumcision.
27. And the LORD said to
■ Aaron, Go into the wilderness to
■ meet Moses. And he went, and met him in the mount of God, and kissed him.
28. And Moses told
■ Aaron all the words of
■ the LORD who had sent him, and all the signs which he had
■ commanded him.
29. And Moses
■ and Aaron went and
■ gathered together
■ all the elders of the children
■ of Israel:
30. And Aaron spake all
■ the words which the LORD
■ had spoken unto Moses, and did the signs in the sight of the people.
31. And the people
■ believed: and when they heard that the LORD had visited the children of Israel, and that he had looked upon their affliction, then they
■ bowed their heads
■ and worshipped.

CHAPTER 5

■ 1. And afterward
■ Moses and Aaron went in, and
■ told Pharaoh, Thus saith the
■ LORD God of Israel,
■ Let my people go, that
■ they may hold a feast
■ unto me in the wilderness.
2. And Pharaoh said,
Who *is* the LORD, that I should obey

his voice to let Israel go?
I know not the LORD,
neither will I let Israel go.
3. **And they said,** The
God of the Hebrews hath
met with us: let us go,
we pray thee, three days' journey
into the desert,
and sacrifice unto
the LORD our God;
lest he fall upon us
with pestilence, or with
the sword.
4. **And the king** of Egypt
said unto them, Wherefore
do ye, Moses and Aaron, let
the people from their works?
get you
unto your burdens.
5. And Pharaoh said, Behold,
the people of the land now
are many, and ye make
them rest from their burdens.
6. **And Pharaoh**
commanded the same day
the taskmasters of the
people, and their officers,
saying,
7. **Ye shall no more give**
the people straw to make
brick, as heretofore: let them go
and gather straw for themselves.
8. **And the tale of** the
bricks, which they did make
heretofore, ye shall lay upon them; ye
shall not diminish
aught thereof:
for they be idle; therefore
they cry, saying, Let us go *and*
sacrifice to our God.
9. **Let** there more work be laid upon
the men, that they may
labour therein;
and let them
not regard vain words.
10. **And the taskmasters**
of the people went out, and
their officers, and they
spake to the people,
saying, Thus saith Pharaoh,
I will not give you straw.
11. **Go** ye,
get you

straw where ye can
find it: yet not ought of your
work shall be diminished.
12. **So the people** were
scattered abroad
throughout all the land of
Egypt to gather stubble
instead of straw.
13. **And the taskmasters**
hasted them, saying,
Fulfil your works, *your*
daily tasks, as when
there was straw.
14. **And the officers**
of the children
of Israel, which Pharaoh's
taskmasters had set over them,
were beaten, and
demanded, Wherefore
have ye not fulfilled your
task in making brick both
yesterday and to day, as heretofore?
15. **Then the officers**
of the children of Israel
came and cried
unto Pharaoh, saying,
Wherefore dealest thou
thus with thy servants?
16. **There is no straw**
given unto thy servants,
and they say to us,
Make brick: and, behold,
thy servants are beaten;
but the fault is in
thine own people.
17. **But he said, Ye are**
idle, *ye are* idle: therefore
ye say, Let us go and do
sacrifice to the LORD.
18. **Go** therefore now,
and work; for
there shall no straw be
given you, yet shall ye
deliver the tale of bricks.
19. And the officers of the children
of Israel did see *that* they *were* in
evil *case*, after it was said, Ye
shall not minish *aught* from your
bricks of your daily task.
20. **And they met Moses**
and Aaron, who stood in the way,
as they came forth from Pharaoh:
21. **And** they

said unto them,
The LORD look upon
you, and judge; because
ye have made
our savour to be
abhorred in the eyes of
Pharaoh, and in the eyes of
his servants, to put a
sword in their hand to slay us.
22. And Moses returned
unto the LORD, and said,
LORD, wherefore hast thou so
evil entreated this people?
why is it that thou
hast sent me?
23. For since I came to
Pharaoh to speak in thy name,
he hath done evil to this
people; neither hast thou
delivered thy people at all.

CHAPTER 6

1. Then the LORD said
unto Moses, Now shalt thou
see what I will do to Pharaoh: for
with a strong hand shall
he let them go, and with
a strong hand shall he
drive them out of his land.
2. And God spake unto
Moses, and said unto him,
I am the LORD:
3. And I appeared
unto Abraham, unto
Isaac, and unto
Jacob, by the name of God
Almighty, but by my name
JEHOVAH was I not
known to them.
4. And I have also
established my
covenant with them,
to give them the land of
Canaan, the land of their
pilgrimage, wherein they
were strangers.
5. And I have also
heard the groaning
of the children of Israel,
whom the Egyptians keep
in bondage; and I have
remembered my covenant.
6. Wherefore say

unto the children of Israel,
I am the LORD, and
I will bring you out from
under the burdens of the
Egyptians, and I will rid you
out of their
bondage, and I will
redeem you with a
stretched out arm, and
with great judgments:
7. And I will take you to me
for a people, and I
will be to you a God: and
ye shall know that I am the LORD
your God, which bringeth
you out from under the
burdens of the Egyptians.
8. And I will bring you in
unto the land, concerning the
which I did
swear to give it to
Abraham, to
Isaac, and to
Jacob; and I will give it you
for an heritage: I am the LORD.
9. And Moses spake
so unto the children of
Israel: but they
hearkened not unto
Moses for anguish
of spirit, and for
cruel bondage.
10. And the LORD
spake unto Moses, saying,
11. Go in, speak
unto Pharaoh king of Egypt,
that he let the children
of Israel go out of his land.
12. And Moses spake
before the LORD,
saying, Behold,
the children of Israel
have not hearkened unto me;
how then
shall Pharaoh hear me,
who am of uncircumcised lips?
13. And the LORD spake
unto Moses and unto Aaron, and
gave them a charge
unto the children of Israel,
and unto Pharaoh king of Egypt,
to bring the children
of Israel out of the

■ **land of Egypt.**

14. These *be* the heads of their fathers' houses: The sons of Reuben the firstborn of Israel; Hanoch, and Pallu, Hezron, and Carmi: these *be* the families of Reuben.

15. And the sons of Simeon; Jemuel, and Jamin, and Ohad, and Jachin, and Zohar, and Shaul the son of a Canaanitish woman: these *are* the families of Simeon.

16. And these *are* the names of the sons of Levi according to their generations; Gershon, and Kohath, and Merari: and the years of the life of Levi *were* an hundred thirty and seven years.

17. The sons of Gershon; Libni, and Shimi, according to their families.

18. And the sons of Kohath; Amram, and Izhar, and Hebron, and Uzziel: and the years of the life of Kohath *were* an hundred thirty and three years.

19. And the sons of Merari; Mahali and Mushi: these *are* the families of Levi according to their generations.

20. And Amram took him Jochebed his father's sister to wife; and she bare him Aaron and Moses: and the years of the life of Amram *were* an hundred and thirty and seven years.

21. And the sons of Izhar; Korah, and Nepheg, and Zichri.

22. And the sons of Uzziel; Mishael, and Elzaphan, and Zithri.

23. And Aaron took him Elisheba, daughter of Amminadab, sister of Naashon, to wife; and she bare him Nadab, and Abihu, Eleazar, and Ithamar.

24. And the sons of Korah; Assir, and Elkanah, and Abiasaph: these *are* the families of the Korhites.

25. And Eleazar Aaron's son took him one of the daughters of Putiel to wife; and she bare him Phinehas: these *are* the heads of the fathers of the Levites according to their families.

26. These *are* that Aaron and Moses, to whom the LORD said, Bring out the children of Israel from the land of Egypt according to their armies.

27. These *are* they which spake to Pharaoh king of Egypt, to bring out the children of Israel from Egypt: these *are* that Moses and Aaron.

28. And it came to pass on the day *when* the LORD spake unto Moses in the land of Egypt,

29. That the LORD spake unto Moses, saying, I *am* the LORD: speak thou unto Pharaoh king of Egypt all that I say unto thee.

30. And Moses said before the LORD, Behold, I *am* of uncircumcised lips, and how shall Pharaoh hearken unto me?

CHAPTER 7

■ 1. **And the LORD said unto Moses,** See, **I have made thee a god to Pharaoh: and Aaron** thy brother **shall be thy prophet.**

■ 2. **Thou shalt speak all that I command thee: and Aaron** thy brother **shall speak unto Pharaoh,** that he send the children of Israel out of his land.

■ 3. **And I will harden Pharaoh's heart, and multiply my signs** and my wonders **in the land** of Egypt.

■ 4. **But Pharaoh shall not hearken** unto you, **that I may lay my hand upon Egypt, and bring** forth mine armies, *and* my people **the children of Israel, out** of the land **of Egypt by great judgments.**

■ 5. **And the Egyptians shall know that I am the LORD,** when I stretch forth mine hand upon Egypt, and bring out the children of Israel from among them.

6. And Moses and Aaron did as the LORD commanded them, so did they.

■ 7. **And Moses was fourscore years old, and Aaron fourscore and three**

years old, when they
spake unto Pharaoh.

8. And the LORD spake
unto Moses and unto Aaron,
saying,

9. When Pharaoh
shall speak unto you,
saying, Shew a miracle
for you: then thou shalt
say unto Aaron,
Take thy rod, and cast
it before Pharaoh, and it
shall become a serpent.

10. And Moses and Aaron
went in unto Pharaoh, and they
did so
as the LORD had
commanded:
and Aaron cast down
his rod before Pharaoh, and
before his servants, and it
became a serpent.

11. Then Pharaoh also
called the wise men and the
sorcerers: now
the magicians of Egypt,
they also did in like manner
with their enchantments.

12. For they
cast down every man
his rod, and they became
serpents: but Aaron's rod
swallowed up their rods.

13. And he hardened Pharaoh's
heart, that he hearkened not unto
them; as the LORD had said.

14. And the LORD said unto
Moses, Pharaoh's heart
is hardened, he refuseth
to let the people go.

15. Get thee unto Pharaoh
in the morning; lo, he goeth out
unto the water; and thou shalt stand
by the river's brink
against he come;
and the rod which
was turned to a serpent
shalt thou take in thine hand.

16. And thou shalt
say unto him, The
LORD God of the Hebrews
hath sent me unto thee,
saying, Let my people

go, that they may
serve me in the wilderness:
and, behold, hitherto
thou wouldest not hear.

17. Thus saith the LORD,
In this thou shalt know that
I am the LORD: behold,
I will smite with the rod
that is in mine hand upon
the waters which are in the river,
and they shall be
turned to blood.

18. And the fish that is in the river
shall die, and the river
shall stink; and the
Egyptians shall
lothe to drink of
the water of the river.

19. And the LORD spake unto Moses,
Say unto Aaron, Take thy
rod, and stretch out thine
hand upon the waters of
Egypt, upon their streams, upon their
rivers, and upon their ponds, and
upon all their pools of water,
that they may become
blood; and that there may be blood
throughout all the land of
Egypt, both in vessels of
wood, and in vessels of
stone.

20. And Moses and Aaron did so,
as the LORD commanded; and
he lifted up the rod, and
smote the waters that were in
the river, in the sight of Pharaoh,
and in the sight of his servants;
and all the waters
that were in the river were
turned to blood.

21. And the fish
that was in the river
died; and the river
stank, and the Egyptians
could not drink of
the water of the river;
and there was blood
throughout all the land of Egypt.

22. And the
magicians of Egypt
did so with their
enchantments: and
Pharaoh's heart was

hardened, neither did he hearken unto them; as the LORD had said.

23. And Pharaoh turned and went into his house, neither did he set his heart to this also.

24. And all the Egyptians digged round about the river for water to drink; for they could not drink of the water of the river.

25. And seven days were fulfilled, after that the LORD had smitten the river.

CHAPTER 8

1. And the LORD spake unto Moses, Go unto Pharaoh, and say unto him, Thus saith the LORD, Let my people go, that they may serve me.

2. And if thou refuse to let *them* go, behold, I will smite all thy borders with frogs:

3. And the river shall bring forth frogs abundantly, which shall go up and come into thine house, and into thy bedchamber, and upon thy bed, and into the house of thy servants, and upon thy people, and into thine ovens, and into thy kneadingtroughs:

4. And the frogs shall come up both on thee, and upon thy people, and upon all thy servants.

5. And the LORD spake unto Moses, Say unto Aaron, Stretch forth thine hand with thy rod over the streams, over the rivers, and over the ponds, and cause frogs to come up upon the land of Egypt.

6. And Aaron stretched out his hand over the waters of Egypt; and the frogs came up, and covered the land of Egypt.

7. And the magicians did so with their enchantments, and brought up frogs upon the land of Egypt.

8. Then Pharaoh called for Moses and Aaron, and said, Entreat the LORD, that he may take away the frogs from me, and from my people; and I will let the people go, that they may do sacrifice unto the LORD.

9. And Moses said unto Pharaoh, Glory over me: when shall I entreat for thee, and for thy servants, and for thy people, to destroy the frogs from thee and thy houses, *that* they may remain in the river only?

10. And he said, Tomorrow. And he said, *Be it* according to thy word: that thou mayest know that *there is* none like unto the LORD our God.

11. And the frogs shall depart from thee, and from thy houses, and from thy servants, and from thy people; they shall remain in the river only.

12. And Moses and Aaron went out from Pharaoh: and Moses cried unto the LORD because of the frogs which he had brought against Pharaoh.

13. And the LORD did according to the word of Moses; and the frogs died out of the houses, out of the villages, and out of the fields.

14. And they gathered them together upon heaps: and the land stank.

15. But when Pharaoh saw that there was respite, he hardened his heart, and hearkened not unto them; as the LORD had said.

16. And the LORD said unto Moses, Say unto Aaron, Stretch out thy rod, and smite the dust of the land,

that it may become lice throughout all the land of Egypt. 17. **And they did so;** for Aaron stretched out his hand with his rod, and smote the dust of the earth, **and it became lice in man, and in beast;** all the dust of the land became lice throughout all the land of Egypt. 18. **And the magicians did** so with **their enchantments to bring forth lice, but they could not:** so there were lice upon man, and upon beast. 19. **Then the magicians said unto Pharaoh, This is the finger of God: and Pharaoh's heart was hardened,** and he hearkened not unto them; as the LORD had said. 20. **And the LORD said unto Moses, Rise up early** in the morning, **and stand before Pharaoh;** lo, he cometh forth to the water; **and say** unto him, Thus saith the LORD, **Let my people go,** that they may serve me. 21. **Else,** if thou wilt not let my people go, behold, **I will send swarms of flies upon thee,** and upon thy servants, **and upon thy people,** and into thy houses: **and the houses** of the Egyptians **shall be full** of swarms **of flies,** and also the ground whereon they *are.* 22. **And I will sever** in that day **the land of Goshen, in which my people dwell, that no** swarms *of* **flies shall be there;** to the end thou mayest know that I *am* the LORD in the midst of the earth. 23. And I will put a division between my people and thy people: tomorrow shall this sign be. 24. **And the LORD did so; and there came a**

grievous swarm of flies into the house of Pharaoh, and *into* his servants' houses, and **into all the land of Egypt: the land was corrupted by** reason of **the** swarm *of* **flies**. 25. **And Pharaoh** called for Moses and for Aaron, and **said, Go** ye, **sacrifice to your God in the land.** 26. **And Moses said, It is not meet so to do;** for we shall sacrifice the abomination of the Egyptians to the LORD our God: lo, **shall we sacrifice the abomination of the Egyptians** before their eyes, and will they not stone us? 27. **We will go** three days' journey **into the wilderness, and sacrifice to the LORD** our God, **as he shall command us**. 28. **And Pharaoh said, I will let you go,** that ye may sacrifice to the LORD your God in the wilderness; **only ye shall not go very far away:** entreat for me. 29. **And Moses said,** Behold, I go out from thee, and **I will entreat the LORD that the** swarms *of* **flies may depart** from Pharaoh, from his servants, and from his people, tomorrow: **but let not Pharaoh deal deceitfully** any more **in not letting the people go** to sacrifice to the LORD. 30. **And Moses went** out from Pharaoh, **and entreated the LORD**. 31. **And the LORD did according to the word of Moses; and** he **removed the** swarms *of* **flies from Pharaoh**, from his servants, **and** from

■ his people; there
remained not one.
■ 32. And Pharaoh
■ hardened his heart at
■ this time also, neither would
■ he let the people go.

CHAPTER 9

■ 1. Then the LORD said
■ unto Moses, Go in unto
■ Pharaoh, and tell him, Thus
saith the LORD God of the Hebrews,
■ Let my people go, that
■ they may serve me.
■ 2. For if thou refuse to let
them go, and wilt hold them still,
■ 3. Behold, the hand of
■ the LORD is upon thy cattle
which *is* in the field, upon the
■ horses, upon the
■ asses, upon the
■ camels, upon the
■ oxen, and upon the
■ sheep: there shall be a
■ very grievous murrain.
■ 4. And the LORD shall
■ sever between the cattle of
■ Israel and the cattle of
■ Egypt: and there
■ shall nothing die
of all *that is* the children's
■ of Israel.
5. And the LORD appointed a set
time, saying, Tomorrow the LORD
shall do this thing in the land.
■ 6. And the LORD did that
■ thing on the morrow, and
■ all the cattle of Egypt
■ died: but of the cattle of the
children of Israel died not one.
■ 7. And Pharaoh sent, and, behold,
■ there was not one of the
■ cattle of the Israelites
■ dead. And the heart
■ of Pharaoh was
■ hardened, and he did
■ not let the people go.
■ 8. And the LORD said
unto Moses and unto Aaron,
■ Take to you handfuls of
■ ashes of the furnace,
■ and let Moses
■ sprinkle it toward the

■ heaven in the sight of Pharaoh.
■ 9. And it shall become small
■ dust in all the land of
■ Egypt, and shall be
■ a boil breaking forth
■ with blains upon
■ man, and upon
■ beast, throughout
all the land of Egypt.
■ 10. And they took
ashes of the furnace, and
■ stood before Pharaoh;
■ and Moses sprinkled
■ it up toward heaven;
■ and it became a boil
■ breaking forth with
■ blains upon man, and upon
■ beast.
■ 11. And the magicians
■ could not stand before
■ Moses because of
■ the boils; for the boil was
upon the magicians, and
upon all the Egyptians.
■ 12. And the LORD hardened
■ the heart of Pharaoh, and
■ he hearkened not unto them;
as the LORD had spoken untoMoses.
■ 13. And the LORD
■ said unto Moses, Rise up
early in the morning, and
■ stand before Pharaoh,
■ and say unto him, Thus saith
the LORD God of the Hebrews,
■ Let my people go, that
■ they may serve me.
■ 14. For I will at this time
■ send all my plagues
upon thine heart, and upon
thy servants, and
■ upon thy people; that thou
■ mayest know that there is
■ none like me in all the earth.
15. For now I will stretch out my
hand, that I may smite thee and thy
people with pestilence; and thou
shalt be cut off from the earth.
16. And in very deed
■ for this cause have I
■ raised thee up, for
■ to shew in thee my
■ power; and that my
■ name may be declared

throughout all the earth.

17. As yet exaltest thou thyself against my people, that thou wilt not let them go?

18. **Behold, tomorrow** about this time **I will cause** it to rain a very grievous **hail, such as hath not been in Egypt** since the foundation thereof even until now.

19. Send therefore now, *and* **gather thy cattle, and** all that thou hast in the field; **for upon every man and beast** which shall be found in the field, and shall not be brought home, **the hail shall come** down upon them, **and they shall die.**

20. **He that feared the** word of the **LORD among the servants of Pharaoh made his servants and his cattle flee into the houses:**

21. And he that regarded not the word of the LORD left his servants and his cattle in the field.

22. And the LORD said unto Moses, Stretch forth thine hand toward heaven, that there may be hail in all the land of Egypt, upon man, and upon beast, and upon every herb of the field, throughout the land of Egypt.

23. **And Moses stretched forth his rod** toward heaven: **and the LORD sent thunder and hail,** and the fire ran along upon the ground; and the LORD rained hail upon the land of Egypt.

24. **So there was** hail, and **fire mingled with the hail,** very grievous, such as **there was none like it in** all the land of **Egypt since it became a nation.**

25. **And the hail smote** throughout all the land of Egypt **all that was in the field, both**

man and beast; and the hail smote **every herb** of the field, **and brake every tree** of the field.

26. **Only in** the land of **Goshen,** where the children of Israel *were,* **was there no hail.**

27. **And Pharaoh** sent, and **called for Moses and Aaron, and said** unto them, **I have sinned** this time: **the LORD is righteous,** and I and my people *are* wicked.

28. **Entreat the LORD** (for *it is* enough) **that there be no more** mighty thunderings and **hail; and I will let you go,** and ye shall stay no longer.

29. **And Moses said** unto him, **As soon as I am gone** out of the city, **I will spread** abroad **my hands unto the LORD; and the thunder shall cease, neither shall there be any more hail; that thou mayest know** how that **the earth is the LORD's.**

30. **But** as for thee and thy servants, **I know that ye will not** yet **fear the LORD** God.

31. And the flax and the barley was smitten: for the barley *was* in the ear, and the flax *was* bolled.

32. But the wheat and the rie were not smitten: for they *were* not grown up.

33. **And Moses** went out of the city from Pharaoh, and **spread** abroad **his hands unto the LORD: and the thunders and hail ceased,** and the rain was not poured upon the earth.

34. **And** when **Pharaoh** saw that the rain and the hail and the thunders were ceased,he **sinned yet more, and hardened his heart,** he and his servants.

35. And the heart of

EXODUS 10

Plague of Locusts

Pharaoh was hardened,
■ **neither would he**
■ **let** the children of
■ **Israel go;** as the LORD
had spoken by Moses.

CHAPTER 10

■ 1. **And the LORD**
■ **said** unto Moses,
■ **Go in unto Pharaoh: for I**
■ **have hardened his heart,**
and the heart of his servants,
■ **that I might shew** these
■ **my signs before him:**
■ 2. **And that thou**
■ **mayest tell** in the ears of
■ **thy son,** and of thy son's son,
■ **what things I have wrought**
■ **in Egypt,** and my signs which I
have done among them;
■ **that ye may know** how that
■ **I am the LORD.**
■ 3. **And Moses and Aaron**
■ **came in unto Pharaoh,**
■ **and said** unto him, Thus saith
the LORD God of the Hebrews,
■ **How long wilt thou refuse**
■ **to humble thyself** before me?
■ **let my people go,** that
they may serve me.
■ 4. **Else,** if thou refuse to let my
people go, behold, tomorrow
■ **will I bring the**
■ **locusts** into thy coast:
■ 5. **And they shall cover**
■ **the face of the earth,** that
one cannot be able to see the earth:
■ **and they shall eat the**
■ **residue** of that which is escaped,
■ **which remaineth unto**
■ **you from the hail,** and
shall eat every tree which
groweth for you out of the field:
■ 6. **And they shall fill**
thy houses, and the houses
of all thy servants, and
■ **the houses of all the**
■ **Egyptians;** which neither thy
fathers, nor thy fathers' fathers
have seen, since the day that
they were upon the earth unto
this day. And he turned himself,
and went out from Pharaoh.

■ 7. **And Pharaoh's servants**
■ **said** unto him, How long shall this
man be a snare unto us?
■ **let the men go, that they**
■ **may serve the LORD** their
God: knowest thou not yet
that Egypt is destroyed?
■ 8. **And** Moses and Aaron
were brought again unto
■ **Pharaoh:** and he
■ **said** unto them, Go, serve
the LORD your God: *but*
■ **who are they that shall go?**
■ 9. **And Moses said,**
■ **We will go with our**
■ **young and** with our
■ **old,** with our sons and
with our daughters,
■ **with our flocks and** with our
■ **herds** will we go;
■ **for we must hold a**
■ **feast unto the LORD.**
■ 10. **And he said** unto them,
Let the LORD be so with you, as
I will let you go, and your little ones:
look *to it*; for evil *is* before you.
■ 11. **Not so:** go now ye *that*
are men, and serve the LORD;
for that ye did desire.
■ **And they were driven out**
■ **from Pharaoh's presence.**
■ 12. **And the LORD**
■ **said** unto Moses,
■ **Stretch out thine**
■ **hand** over the land of Egypt
■ **for the locusts,**
■ **that they may come**
up upon the land of Egypt,
■ **and eat every**
■ **herb** of the land, *even* all that
■ **the hail** hath
■ **left.**
13. And Moses stretched forth
his rod over the land of Egypt,
■ **and the LORD brought**
■ **an east wind** upon the land
all that day, and all *that* night;
■ **and when it was**
■ **morning, the east wind**
■ **brought the locusts.**
■ 14. **And the locusts** went
up over all the land of Egypt, and
rested in all the coasts of Egypt:

very grievous *were they;*
before them there were no
such locusts as they, neither
after them shall be such.

15. For they
**covered the face of the
whole earth,** so that the
land was darkened;
**and they did eat
every herb** of the land,
**and all the fruit of the trees
which the hail had left: and
there remained not any
green thing** in the trees,
or in the herbs of the field,
through all the land of Egypt.

16. **Then Pharaoh called
for Moses and Aaron in
haste; and he said, I have
sinned against** the LORD your
God, and against you.

17. Now therefore
forgive, I pray thee,
my sin only this once,
**and entreat the
LORD** your God,
**that he may
take away** from me
this death only.

18. **And he went out
from Pharaoh, and
entreated the LORD.**

19. **And the LORD
turned a** mighty strong
west wind, which took away
the locusts, and cast them
into the Red sea; there
remained not one locust in
all the coasts of Egypt.

20. **But the LORD hardened
Pharaoh's heart, so that
he would not let** the children of
Israel go.

21. **And the LORD
said** unto Moses,
**Stretch out thine
hand** toward heaven,
**that there may be darkness
over the land** of Egypt, even
darkness *which* may be felt.

22. And Moses stretched forth
his hand toward heaven; and
there was a thick darkness in
all the land of Egypt three days:

23. **They saw not
one another,** neither
rose any from his place
**for three days:
but** all the children of
**Israel had light
in their dwellings.**

24. **And Pharaoh**
called unto Moses, and
said, Go ye,
**serve the LORD; only let
your flocks and your
herds be stayed:** let
your little ones also go with you.

25. **And Moses said,
Thou must give us also
sacrifices** and burnt offerings,
**that we may sacrifice
unto the LORD** our God.

26. **Our cattle also
shall go with us;** there
shall not an hoof be left behind;
for thereof must we take to
serve the LORD our God; and
**we know not with what
we must serve the LORD,
until we come thither.**

27. **But the LORD hardened
Pharaoh's heart, and he
would not let them go.**

28. **And Pharaoh
said** unto him, Get thee
from me, take heed to thyself,
**see my face no more; for
in that day** thou seest my face
thou shalt die.

29. **And Moses said,**
Thou hast spoken well,
**I will see thy face
again no more.**

CHAPTER 11

1. **And the LORD
said** unto Moses,
**Yet will I bring
one plague** *more*
upon Pharaoh, and upon
**Egypt; afterwards he
will let you go** hence: when
he shall let *you* go, he shall surely
thrust you out hence altogether.

2. Speak now in the ears

of the people, and
let every man borrow of
his neighbour, and every
woman of her neighbour,
jewels of silver and jewels of
gold.
3. And the LORD gave
the people favour in
the sight of the Egyptians.
Moreover the man
Moses was very great
in the land of Egypt, in the
sight of Pharaoh's servants,
and in the sight
of the people.
4. And Moses said,
Thus saith the LORD,
About midnight will I go
out into the midst of Egypt:
5. And all the firstborn
in the land of Egypt
shall die, from the first born of
Pharaoh that sitteth
upon his throne, even
unto the firstborn of
the maidservant
that is behind the mill;
and all the
firstborn of beasts.
6. And there shall
be a great cry
throughout all the land of
Egypt, such as there was none
like it, nor shall be like it any more.
7. But against any of
the children of Israel
shall not a dog move his
tongue, against man or beast:
that ye may know how
that the LORD doth
put a difference between
the Egyptians and Israel.
8. And all these
thy servants
shall come down unto me, and
bow down themselves
unto me,
saying, Get thee
out, and all the people
that follow thee: and
after that I will go out. And
he went out from
Pharaoh in a great anger.

9. And the LORD
said unto Moses,
Pharaoh shall not
hearken unto you; that my
wonders may be multiplied
in the land of Egypt.
10. And Moses and Aaron did all
these wonders before Pharaoh: and
the LORD hardened Pharaoh's heart,
so that he would not let the children
of Israel go out of his land.

CHAPTER 12

1. And the LORD spake
unto Moses and Aaron
in the land of Egypt, saying,
2. This month
shall be unto you the
beginning of months: it shall be
the first month of
the year to you.
3. Speak ye unto all
the congregation of
Israel, saying, In the tenth
day of this month they
shall take to them every man
a lamb, according to the house
of their fathers, a lamb for an house:
4. And if the household
be too little for the lamb,
let him and his
neighbour next unto his house
take it according to
the number of the
souls; every man according
to his eating shall make your
count for the lamb.
5. Your lamb shall be
without blemish, a male of
the first year: ye shall take it out
from the sheep, or from the goats:
6. And ye shall
keep it up
until the fourteenth day
of the same month:
and the whole assembly of
the congregation of Israel
shall kill it in the evening.
7. And they shall take of
the blood, and strike it
on the two side posts and
on the upper door post of
the houses, wherein

they shall eat it.

■ 8. **And they shall**
■ **eat the flesh** in
■ **that night,** roast with fire,
and unleavened bread; *and*
with bitter *herbs* they shall eat it.

■ 9. **Eat not of it raw,**
■ **nor sodden** at all
■ **with water, but roast**
■ **with fire;** his head with his legs,
and with the purtenance thereof.

■ 10. **And** ye shall
let nothing of it remain
until the morning; and
■ **that which**
■ **remaineth** of it until the morning
■ **ye shall burn with fire.**
11. And thus shall ye
■ **eat it; with your loins**
■ **girded,** your shoes on your
feet, and your staff in your hand;
■ **and** ye shall
■ **eat** it
■ **in haste: it is the**
■ **LORD's passover.**
■ 12. **For I will pass through**
■ **the land** of Egypt this night,
■ **and will smite all the**
■ **firstborn** in the land of Egypt,
■ **both man and beast; and**
■ **against all the gods of**
■ **Egypt I will execute**
■ **judgment:** I *am* the LORD.
■ 13. **And the blood**
■ **shall be** to you for
■ **a token** upon the
houses where ye *are*: and
■ **when I see the blood, I will**
■ **pass over you,** and the plague
shall not be upon you to destroy *you,*
■ **when I smite** the land of
■ **Egypt.**
■ 14. **And this day shall**
■ **be unto you for a**
■ **memorial;** and ye shall keep it
■ **a feast to the LORD**
throughout your generations;
ye shall keep it a feast
■ **by an ordinance for ever.**
■ 15. **Seven days shall ye**
■ **eat unleavened bread;**
even the first day ye shall put
away leaven out of your houses:

■ **for whosoever eateth**
■ **leavened bread from the**
■ **first day until the seventh**
■ **day, that soul shall be**
■ **cut off from Israel.**
■ 16. **And in the first day** *there*
shall be an holy convocation,
■ **and in the seventh day**
■ **there shall be an holy**
■ **convocation** to you;
■ **no manner of work**
■ **shall be done** in them,
■ **save that which**
■ **every man must eat,**
that only may be done of you.
■ 17. **And ye shall**
■ **observe the feast of**
■ **unleavened bread;**
■ **for** in this selfsame day have
■ **I brought your armies**
■ **out of** the land of
■ **Egypt: therefore** shall ye
observe this day in your generations
by an ordinance for ever.
■ 18. **In the first month,**
■ **on the fourteenth**
■ **day** of the month at even,
■ **ye shall eat unleavened**
■ **bread, until the**
■ **one and twentieth**
■ **day** of the month at even.
■ 19. **Seven days shall**
■ **there be no leaven**
■ **found in your houses:**
for whosoever eateth that which
is leavened, even that soul shall
be cut off from the congregation
of Israel, whether he be a stranger,
or born in the land.
20. Ye shall eat nothing leavened;
in all your habitations shall
ye eat unleavened bread.
■ 21. **Then Moses called** for all
■ **the elders of Israel, and**
■ **said** unto them, Draw out and
■ **take** you
■ **a lamb** according to your families,
■ **and kill the passover.**
■ 22. **And ye shall**
■ **take** a bunch of
■ **hyssop, and dip it in the**
■ **blood** that *is* in the bason,
■ **and strike the lintel and the**

- two side posts with the
- blood that *is* in the bason;
- and none of you
- shall go out at the

door of his house
- until the
- morning.
- 23. For the LORD
- will pass through to
- smite the Egyptians;
- and when he seeth
- the blood upon the lintel,

and on the two side posts,
- the LORD will pass

over the door, and
- will not suffer the destroyer
- to come in unto your
- houses to smite *you.*

24. And ye shall observe this
thing for an ordinance to thee
and to thy sons for ever.
- 25. And it shall come to pass,
- when ye be
- come to the land which
- the LORD will give you,

according as he hath promised, that
- ye shall keep this service.

26. And it shall come to pass,
- when your children
- shall say unto you,
- What mean ye by
- this service?

27. That ye shall say,
- It is the sacrifice of the
- LORD's passover, who

passed over the houses of
the children of Israel in Egypt,
- when he smote the
- Egyptians, and delivered
- our houses. And the
- people bowed the head
- and worshipped.

28. And the children
- of Israel went away, and
- did as the LORD had
- commanded Moses

and Aaron, so did they.

29. And it came to pass, that
- at midnight the LORD
- smote all the
- firstborn in the land of Egypt,
- from the firstborn of
- Pharaoh that sat on his throne

- unto the firstborn of
- the captive that *was*
- in the dungeon; and all
- the firstborn of cattle.

30. And Pharaoh rose up
- in the night, he, and all his

servants, and all the Egyptians;
- and there was a great cry
- in Egypt; for *there was* not a house

where *there was* not one dead.

31. And he called for Moses
- and Aaron by night, and
- said, Rise up, *and* get you forth

from among my people, both ye
and the children of Israel; and
- go, serve the LORD,
- as ye have said.

32. Also take your flocks and
your herds, as ye have said,
and be gone; and bless me also.

33. And the Egyptians
- were urgent upon the people,
- that they might send
- them out of the land in
- haste; for they said,
- We be all dead men.

34. And the people took their
dough before it was leavened, their
kneadingtroughs being bound up in
their clothes upon their shoulders.

35. And the children of
- Israel did according to the

word of Moses; and they
- borrowed of the Egyptians
- jewels of silver, and jewels of
- gold, and raiment:

36. And the LORD gave the people
favour in the sight of the Egyptians,
so that they lent unto them *such*
things as they required.
- And they spoiled
- the Egyptians.

37. And the children of Israel
- journeyed from
- Rameses to Succoth,
- about six hundred
- thousand on foot *that were*
- men, beside children.

38. And a mixed
- multitude went up also
- with them; and flocks, and

herds, *even* very much cattle.

39. And they baked

unleavened cakes of the dough which they brought forth out of Egypt, for it was not leavened; because they were thrust out of Egypt, and could not tarry, neither had they prepared for themselves any victual.

40. Now the sojourning of the children of Israel, who dwelt in Egypt, was four hundred and thirty years.

41. And it came to pass at the end of the four hundred and thirty years, even the selfsame day it came to pass, that all the hosts of the LORD went out from the land of Egypt.

42. It is a night to be much observed unto the LORD for bringing them out from the land of Egypt: this *is* that night of the LORD to be observed of all the children of Israel in their generations.

43. And the LORD said unto Moses and Aaron, This is the ordinance of the passover: There shall no stranger eat thereof:

44. But every man's servant that is bought for money, when thou hast circumcised him, then shall he eat thereof.

45. A foreigner and an hired servant shall not eat thereof.

46. In one house shall it be eaten; thou shalt not carry forth aught of the flesh abroad out of the house; neither shall ye break a bone thereof.

47. All the congregation of Israel shall keep it.

48. And when a stranger shall sojourn with thee, and will keep the passover to the LORD, let all his males be circumcised, and then let him come near and keep it; and he shall be as one that is born in the land: for no uncircumcised person shall eat thereof.

49. One law shall be to him that is homeborn, and unto the stranger that sojourneth among you.

50. Thus did all the children of Israel; as the LORD commanded Moses and Aaron, so did they.

51. And it came to pass the selfsame day,*that* the LORD did bring the children of Israel out of the land of Egypt by their armies.

CHAPTER 13

1. And the LORD spake unto Moses, saying,

2. Sanctify unto me all the firstborn, whatsoever openeth the womb among the children of Israel, both of man and of beast: it is mine.

3. And Moses said unto the people, Remember this day, in which ye came out from Egypt, out of the house of bondage; for by strength of hand the LORD brought you out from this *place*: there shall no leavened bread be eaten.

4. This day came ye out in the month Abib.

5. And it shall be when the LORD shall bring thee into the land of the Canaanites, and the Hittites, and the Amorites, and the Hivites, and the Jebusites, which he sware unto thy fathers to give thee, a land flowing with milk and honey, that thou shalt keep this service in this month.

6. Seven days thou shalt eat unleavened bread, and in the seventh day shall be a feast to the LORD. 7. Unleavened bread shall be eaten seven days; and there shall no leavened bread be seen with thee, neither shall there be leaven seen with thee in all thy quarters. 8. And thou shalt shew thy son in that day, saying, This is done because of that which the LORD did unto me when I came forth out of Egypt. 9. And it shall be for a sign unto thee upon thine hand, and for a memorial between thine eyes, that the LORD's law may be in thy mouth: for with a strong hand hath the LORD brought thee out of Egypt. 10. Thou shalt therefore keep this ordinance in his season from year to year. 11. And it shall be when the LORD shall bring thee into the land of the Canaanites, as he sware unto thee and to thy fathers, and shall give it thee, 12. That thou shalt set apart unto the LORD all that openeth the matrix, and every firstling that cometh of a beast which thou hast; the males shall be the LORD's. 13. And every firstling of an ass thou shalt redeem with a lamb; and if thou wilt not redeem it, then thou shalt break his neck: and all the firstborn of man among thy children shalt thou redeem. 14. And it shall be when thy son asketh thee in time to come, saying, What is this? that thou shalt say unto him, By strength of hand the LORD brought us out from Egypt, from the house of bondage: 15. And it came to pass, when Pharaoh would hardly let us go, that the LORD slew all the firstborn in the land of Egypt, both the firstborn of man, and the firstborn of beast: therefore I sacrifice to the LORD all that openeth the matrix, being males; but all the firstborn of my children I redeem. 16. And it shall be for a token upon thine hand, and for frontlets between thine eyes: for by strength of hand the LORD brought us forth out of Egypt. 17. And it came to pass, when Pharaoh had let the people go, that God led them not through the way of the land of the Philistines, although that was near; for God said, Lest peradventure the people repent when they see war, and they return to Egypt: 18. But God led the people about, through the way of the wilderness of the Red sea: and the children of Israel went up harnessed out of the land of Egypt. 19. And Moses took the bones of Joseph with him: for he had straitly sworn the children of Israel, saying, God will surely visit you; and ye shall carry up my bones away hence with you. 20. And they took their journey from Succoth, and encamped in Etham, in the edge of the wilderness.

21. **And the LORD went before them by day in a pillar of a cloud,** to lead them the way; **and by night in a pillar of fire,** to give them light; to go by day and night:

22. **He took not away the pillar** of the cloud by day, nor the pillar of fire by night, **from before the people.**

CHAPTER 14

1. **And the LORD spake unto Moses, saying,**

2. **Speak unto the children of Israel, that they turn and encamp** before Pi-hahiroth, between Migdol and the sea, over against Baal-zephon: before it shall ye encamp **by the sea.**

3. **For Pharaoh will say** of the children of Israel, They *are* entangled in the land, **the wilderness hath shut them in.**

4. **And I will harden Pharaoh's heart, that he** shall **follow after them; and I will be honoured upon Pharaoh,** and upon all his host; **that the Egyptians may know** that **I am the LORD.** And they did so.

5. **And it was told the king** of Egypt **that the people fled**: and the heart of Pharaoh and of his servants was turned against the people, **and they said, Why have we** done this, that we have **let Israel go from serving us?**

6. And he made ready his chariot, and took his people with him:

7. **And he took six hundred** chosen **chariots,** and all the chariots of Egypt, and captains over every one of them.

8. And the LORD hardened the heart of Pharaoh king of Egypt,

and he **pursued after the children of Israel: and** the children of **Israel went out with an high hand.**

9. **But the Egyptians** pursued after them, all the horses *and* chariots of Pharaoh, and his horsemen, and his army, and **overtook them encamping by the sea,** beside Pi-hahiroth, before Baal-zephon.

10. **And** when Pharaoh drew nigh, the children of **Israel lifted up their eyes,** and, behold, the Egyptians marched after them; **and** they **were sore afraid: and** the children of Israel **cried out unto the LORD.**

11. **And they said** unto Moses, Because *there were* no graves in Egypt, **hast thou taken us** away **to die in the wilderness?** wherefore hast thou dealt thus with us, to carry us forth out of Egypt?

12. *Is* not this the word that we did tell thee in Egypt, saying, Let us alone, that we may serve the Egyptians? For **it had been better** for us **to serve the Egyptians, than** that we should **die in the wilderness.**

13. **And Moses said** unto the people, **Fear ye not, stand still, and see the salvation of the LORD,** which he will shew to you to-day: **for the Egyptians** whom ye have seen to-day, **ye shall see** them again **no more for ever.**

14. **The LORD shall fight for you,** and ye shall hold your peace.

15. **And the LORD said** unto Moses, **Wherefore criest thou unto me?** speak unto the children of Israel, that they **go forward:**

■ 16. **But lift** thou up
■ **thy rod,** and stretch out thine hand
■ **over the sea, and divide it:**
■ **and** the children of Israel shall
■ **go on dry ground**
■ **through** the midst of
■ **the sea.**
■ 17. **And** I, behold, I will harden
■ **the** hearts of
■ **Egyptians,** and they
■ **shall follow** them:
■ **and I will get me**
■ **honour upon Pharaoh,**
and upon all his host, upon his
chariots, and upon his horsemen.
18.And the Egyptians shall know that I
am the LORD, when I have gotten me
honour upon Pharaoh, upon his
chariots, and upon his horsemen.
■ 19. **And the angel of**
■ **God,** which went before the
camp of Israel, removed and
■ **went behind them; and**
■ **the pillar of the cloud**
went from before their face, and
■ **stood behind them:**
20. And it came
■ **between** the camp of
■ **the Egyptians and** the camp of
■ **Israel; and it was** a cloud and
■ **darkness to them, but** it gave
■ **light by night**
■ **to these: so** that
■ **the one came not**
■ **near the other all** the
■ **night.**
21. And Moses stretched
out his hand over the sea;
■ **and the LORD**
■ **caused** the sea to go *back* by
■ **a strong east wind all**
■ **that night, and made the**
■ **sea dry land, and the**
■ **waters were divided.**
■ 22. **And** the children of
■ **Israel went into the midst of**
■ **the sea** upon the dry *ground*: and
■ **the waters were**
■ **a wall** unto them
■ **on their right** hand,
■ **and** on their
■ **left.**
■ 23. **And the Egyptians**

■ **pursued,** and went in
■ **after them** to the midst of
the sea, *even* all Pharaoh's horses,
his chariots, and his horsemen.
■ 24. **And** it came to pass,
that in the morning watch
■ **the LORD looked**
unto the host of the Egyptians
■ **through the pillar of**
■ **fire and of the cloud,**
■ **and troubled** the host of
■ **the Egyptians,**
■ 25. **And** took off their
chariot wheels, that they
drave them heavily: so that
■ **the Egyptians said, Let**
■ **us flee** from the face of Israel;
■ **for the LORD fighteth** for them
■ **against the Egyptians.**
■ 26. **And the LORD said unto**
■ **Moses, Stretch out thine**
■ **hand over the sea, that the**
■ **waters may come again**
■ **upon the Egyptians,** upon their
chariots, and upon their horsemen.
27. And Moses stretched
forth his hand over the sea,
■ **and the sea returned to**
■ **his strength** when the morning
appeared; and the Egyptians fled
against it; and the LORD overthrew
the Egyptians in the midst of the sea.
■ 28. **And the waters**
■ **returned, and covered**
the chariots, and the horsemen, *and*
■ **all the host of Pharaoh that**
came into the sea after them; there
■ **remained not so much**
■ **as one of them.**
29. But the children of Israel walked
upon dry *land* in the midst of the sea;
and the waters *were* a wall unto them
on their right hand, and on their left.
■ 30. **Thus the LORD**
■ **saved Israel** that day
out of the hand of the Egyptians;
■ **and Israel saw the**
■ **Egyptians dead**
■ **upon the sea shore.**
■ 31. **And Israel** saw that great
work which the LORD did upon
the Egyptians: and the people
■ **feared the LORD,**

and believed the LORD,
and his servant Moses.

CHAPTER 15

1. **Then sang Moses and** the children of **Israel this song unto the LORD,** and spake, saying, **I will sing unto the LORD, for he hath triumphed** gloriously: **the horse and** his **rider hath he thrown into the sea.**

2. **The LORD is my strength and song, and he is become my salvation: he is my God,** and I will prepare him an habitation; my father's God, **and I will exalt him.**

3. **The LORD is a man of war:** the LORD *is* his name.

4. **Pharaoh's** chariots and his **host hath he cast into the sea:** his chosen captains also are drowned in the Red sea.

5. **The depths have covered them:** they sank into the bottom as a stone.

6. **Thy right hand,** O LORD, is become glorious in power: thy right hand, O LORD, **hath dashed** in pieces **the enemy.**

7. **And** in the greatness of thine excellency thou **hast overthrown them that rose up against thee:** thou sentest forth **thy wrath,** *which* **consumed them as stubble.**

8. **And with the blast of thy nostrils the waters were gathered together,** the floods stood upright as an heap, *and* the depths were congealed in the heart of the sea.

9. **The enemy said,** I will pursue, **I will overtake,** I will divide the spoil; **my lust shall be satisfied** upon them; I will draw my sword,

my hand shall destroy them.

10. **Thou didst blow with thy wind, the sea covered them:** they sank as lead in the mighty waters.

11. **Who is like unto thee, O LORD,** among the gods? who *is* like thee, **glorious in holiness,** fearful *in* praises, **doing wonders?**

12. **Thou stretchedst out thy right hand, the earth swallowed them.**

13. **Thou in thy mercy hast led forth the people which thou hast redeemed:** thou hast guided *them* in thy strength unto thy holy habitation.

14. **The people shall hear, and be afraid:** sorrow shall take hold on the inhabitants of Palestina.

15. Then the dukes of Edom shall be amazed; the mighty men of Moab, trembling shall take hold upon them; all the inhabitants of Canaan shall melt away.

16. **Fear and dread shall fall upon them; by the greatness of thine arm** they **shall** be *as* still as a stone; till **thy people pass over,** O LORD, till the people pass over, **which thou hast purchased.**

17. **Thou shalt** bring them in, and **plant them in the mountain of thine inheritance,** *in* the place, O LORD, **which thou hast made for thee to dwell in,** *in* **the Sanctuary,** O LORD, **which thy hands have established.**

18. **The LORD shall reign for ever** and ever.

19. **For** the horse of **Pharaoh went** in with his chariots and with his horsemen **into the sea, and the LORD brought again**

the waters of the sea
upon them; but the children of
Israel went on dry
land in the midst of the sea.
20. And Miriam the prophetess,
the sister of Aaron, took
a timbrel in her hand;
and all the women went out
after her with timbrels
and with dances.
21. And Miriam answered
them, Sing ye to the LORD,
for he hath triumphed
gloriously; the horse and his
rider hath he thrown into the sea.
22. So Moses brought
Israel from the Red
sea, and they went out
into the wilderness of
Shur; and they went
three days in the wilderness,
and found no water.
23. And when they came
to Marah, they could not
drink of the waters of Marah,
for they were bitter: therefore
the name of it was called Marah.
24. And the people
murmured against
Moses, saying,
What shall we drink?
25. And he cried unto the LORD;
and the LORD shewed him
a tree, which when he had
cast into the waters,
the waters were made
sweet: there he made for
them a statute and an ordinance,
and there he proved them,
26. And said, If thou wilt diligently
hearken to the
voice of the LORD thy God,
and wilt
do that which is
right in his sight, and
wilt give ear to his commandments,
and keep all his statutes,
I will put none of these
diseases upon thee, which
I have brought upon the Egyptians:
for I am the LORD
that healeth thee.
27. And they came to Elim,

where *were* twelve wells of water, and
threescore and ten palm trees:
and they
encamped there by the waters.

CHAPTER 16

1. And they took their journey
from Elim, and all the
congregation of the children of
Israel came unto the
wilderness of Sin,
which *is* between Elim and
Sinai, on the fifteenth day of
the second month after their
departing out of the land of Egypt.
2. And the whole
congregation of
the children of Israel
murmured against Moses
and Aaron in the wilderness:
3. And the children
of Israel said unto them,
Would to God we had
died by the hand of the LORD
in the land of
Egypt, when we sat by
the flesh pots, *and* when
we did eat bread to the full;
for ye have brought us
forth into this wilderness, to
kill this whole
assembly with hunger.
4. Then said the
LORD unto Moses, Behold,
I will rain bread from
heaven for you; and the
people shall go out and
gather a certain rate
every day, that I may
prove them, whether they
will walk in my law, or no.
5. And it shall come to pass, that
on the sixth day they
shall prepare *that* which they
bring in; and it shall be
twice as much
as they gather daily.
6. And Moses and Aaron
said unto all the children of Israel,
At even, then
ye shall know that
the LORD hath
brought you out from the land

104

of Egypt:

7. **And in the morning,** then **ye shall see the glory of the LORD;** for that he heareth your murmurings against the LORD: and what *are* we, that ye murmur against us?

8. And Moses said, *This shall be,* when the LORD shall give you in the evening flesh to eat, and in the morning bread to the full; for that the LORDheareth your murmurings which ye murmur against him: and what *are* we? your murmurings *are* not against us, but against the LORD.

9. And Moses spake unto Aaron, Say unto all the congregation of the children of Israel, Come near before the LORD: for he hath heard your murmurings.

10. **And it came to pass, as Aaron spake unto the** whole **congregation** of the children of Israel, that they looked toward the wilderness, and, behold, **the glory of the LORD appeared in the cloud.**

11. **And the LORD spake unto Moses, saying,**

12. **I have heard the murmurings** of the children **of Israel: speak unto them, saying, At even ye shall eat flesh, and in the morning ye shall be filled with bread; and ye shall know** that **I am the LORD your God.**

13. **And** it came to pass, that **at even the quails** came up, and **covered the camp: and in the morning** the dew lay round about the host.

14. **And when the dew** that lay **was gone** up, behold, upon the face of the wilderness **there lay a small round thing,** *as* small *as* the hoar frost on the ground.

15. **And when the children of Israel saw it, they said** one to another, **It is manna:** for they

wist not what it *was.*

And Moses said unto them, **This is the bread which the LORD hath given you to eat.**

16. This *is* the thing which the LORD hath commanded, **Gather** of it every man according to his eating, **an omer for every man, according to the number of your persons;** take ye every man for *them* which *are* in his tents.

17. And the children of Israel did so, and gathered, some more, some less.

18. And when they did mete *it* with an omer, he that gathered much had nothing over, and **he that gathered little had no lack;** they gathered every man according to his eating.

19. **And Moses said, Let no man leave of it till the morning.**

20. Notwithstanding they hearkened not unto Moses; **but some** of them **left** of **it until the morning, and it bred worms, and stank:** and Moses was wroth with them.

21. And they gathered it every morning, every man according to his eating: and when the sun waxed hot, it melted.

22. **And** it came to pass, *that* **on the sixth day they gathered twice as much** bread, two omers for one *man:* **and** all **the rulers** of the congregation came and **told Moses.**

23. **And he said** unto them, This *is that* which the LORD hath said, **Tomorrow is the rest of the** holy **sabbath unto the LORD: bake that which ye will bake today,** and seethe that ye will seethe; **and that which remaineth over lay up for you to be kept until the morning.**

24. And they laid it up till the morning, as Moses bade:

■ **and it did not stink,**
■ **neither was there**
■ **any worm therein.**

25. And Moses said, Eat that today; for today *is* a sabbath unto the LORD: today ye shall not find it in the field.

■ 26. **Six days ye shall gather**
■ **it; but on the seventh day,**
■ **which is the sabbath,** in it
■ **there shall be none.**

■ 27. **And** it came to pass, *that*
■ **there went out**
■ **some** of the people
■ **on the seventh**
■ **day for to gather,**
■ **and they found none.**

■ 28. **And the LORD**
■ **said** unto Moses,
■ **How long refuse ye**
■ **to keep my**
■ **commandments** and my laws?

29. See, for that

■ **the LORD hath given you the**
■ **sabbath, therefore** he giveth

you on the sixth day the bread of two days; abide ye every man in his place,

■ **let no man go out of his**
■ **place on the seventh day.**

■ 30. **So the people rested**
■ **on the seventh day.**

■ 31. **And** the house of
■ **Israel called**
■ **the name** thereof
■ **Manna: and it was like**
■ **coriander seed,** white;
■ **and the taste** of it
■ **was like wafers**
■ **made with honey.**

■ 32. **And Moses said,** This *is*
■ **the thing which the LORD**
■ **commandeth, Fill an omer**
■ **of it to** be kept for your generations;

that they may see the bread wherewith I have fed you in the wilderness, when I brought you forth from the land of Egypt.

33. And Moses said unto Aaron, Take a pot, and put an omer full of manna therein, and

■ **lay it up before the**
■ **LORD, to be kept for**

■ **your generations.**

34. As the LORD commanded Moses, so Aaron laid it up before the Testimony, to be kept.

■ 35. **And the children of**
■ **Israel did eat manna forty**
■ **years,** until they came to a land

inhabited; they did eat manna,

■ **until they came unto**
■ **the borders of the**
■ **land of Canaan.**

36. Now an omer *is* the tenth *part* of an ephah.

CHAPTER 17

■ 1. **And all the congregation**
of the children of Israel

■ **journeyed from the**
■ **wilderness of Sin,** after

their journeys, according to the commandment of the LORD,

■ **and pitched in Rephidim:**
■ **and there was no**
■ **water** for the people to drink.

■ 2. **Wherefore the people**
■ **did chide with Moses,**
■ **and said, Give us water** that

we may drink. And Moses said unto them, Why chide ye with me? wherefore do ye tempt the LORD?

3. And the people thirsted there for water; and the people murmured against Moses, and said, Wherefore *is* this *that*

■ **thou hast brought us** up
■ **out of Egypt, to kill us**

and our children and our cattle

■ **with thirst?**

■ 4. **And Moses cried**
■ **unto the LORD,** saying,
■ **What shall I do** unto this people?
■ **they be** almost
■ **ready to stone me.**

■ 5. **And the LORD**
■ **said** unto Moses,
■ **Go on before the**
■ **people, and take** with thee of
■ **the elders** of Israel;
■ **and thy rod,** where

with thou smotest the river, take in thine hand, and go.

■ 6. **Behold, I will stand**
■ **before thee there**

upon the rock in Horeb;

■ **and thou shalt smite the**
■ **rock, and there shall**
■ **come water out of it,**
that the people may drink.
■ **And Moses did so** in
the sight of the elders of Israel.
■ 7. **And he called**
■ **the** name of the
■ **place Massah, and**
■ **Meribah,** because of the chiding
of the children of Israel, and
■ **because they tempted**
■ **the LORD, saying, Is the**
■ **LORD among us, or not?**
8. Then came Amalek, and
fought with Israel in Rephidim.
■ 9. **And Moses**
■ **said** unto Joshua,
■ **Choose** us out
■ **men, and go** out,
■ **fight with Amalek:** tomorrow
I will stand on the top of the hill
with the rod of God in mine hand.
■ 10. **So Joshua did**
■ **as Moses** had
■ **said** to him, and fought with Amalek:
■ **and Moses, Aaron,**
■ **and Hur went up to**
■ **the top of the hill.**
■ 11. **And** it came to pass,
■ **when Moses held**
■ **up his hand,** that
■ **Israel prevailed: and**
■ **when he let down his**
■ **hand, Amalek prevailed.**
12. But Moses hands *were* heavy;
■ **and they took a**
■ **stone,** and put *it* under him,
■ **and he sat thereon; and**
■ **Aaron and Hur stayed up**
■ **his hands,** the one on the one
side, and the other on the other side;
and his hands were steady
■ **until the going**
■ **down of the sun.**
■ 13. **And Joshua**
■ **discomfited**
■ **Amalek** and his people
■ **with the** edge of the
■ **sword.**
■ 14. **And the**
■ **LORD said** unto Moses,

■ **Write** this *for*
■ **a memorial** in a book, and
rehearse *it* in the ears of Joshua:
■ **for I will** utterly
■ **put out the remembrance**
■ **of Amalek** from under heaven.
■ 15. **And Moses built an**
■ **altar, and called** the name of
■ **it Jehovah–nissi:**
16. For he said,
■ **Because the LORD**
hath sworn *that* the LORD
■ **will have war with Amalek**
from generation to generation.

CHAPTER 18

■ 1. **When Jethro,**
the priest of Midian,
■ **Moses' father in law,**
■ **heard of all that God had**
■ **done** for Moses, and for Israel
his people, *and* that the LORD
had brought Israel out of Egypt;
■ 2. **Then Jethro,**
Moses' father in law,
■ **took Zipporah,** Moses'
wife, after he had sent her back,
■ 3. **And her two sons;** of which
the name of the one *was* Gershom;
for he said, I have been an
alien in a strange land:
4. And the name of the other *was*
Eliezer; for the God of my father, *said*
he, was mine help, and delivered me
from the sword of Pharaoh:
■ 5. **And** Jethro, Moses' father in law,
■ **came** with his sons and his wife
■ **unto Moses into the**
■ **wilderness,** where he encamped
■ **at the mount of God:**
6. And he said unto Moses, I
thy father in law Jethro am come
unto thee, and thy wife, and her
two sons with her.
■ 7. **And Moses went out to**
■ **meet his father in law,** and
did obeisance, and kissed him; and
they asked each other of *their*
welfare; and they came into the tent.
■ 8. **And Moses told his father**
■ **in law all that the LORD had**
■ **done** unto Pharaoh and to the
Egyptians for Israel's

sake, *and* all the travail that had come upon them by the way,

■ ■ **and how the LORD delivered them.**

9. And Jethro rejoiced for all the goodness which the LORD had done to Israel, whom he had delivered out of the hand of the Egyptians.

■ ■ ■ **10. And Jethro said, Blessed be the LORD, who hath delivered you**

out of the hand of the Egyptians, and out of the hand of Pharaoh, who hath delivered the people from under the hand of the Egyptians.

■ ■ ■ **11. Now I know that the LORD is greater than all gods:** for in the thing wherein they dealt proudly *he was* above them.

■ **12. And Jethro,** Moses' father in law,

■ ■ ■ ■ ■ **took a burnt offering and sacrifices for God: and Aaron came, and all the elders** of Israel, **to eat bread** with Moses' father in law **before God.**

■ ■ ■ ■ ■ ■ ■ **13. And** it came to pass **on the morrow,** that **Moses sat to judge the people: and the people stood** by Moses **from the morning unto the evening.**

■ **14. And** when **Moses' father in law** saw all that he did to the people, he ■ **said, What is this** thing **that thou doest** to the people? why sittest thou thyself alone, and all the people stand by thee from morning unto even?

■ **15. And Moses said** unto his father in law, Because ■ ■ **the people come** unto me **to inquire of God:**

16. When they have a matter, they come unto me; ■ **and I judge** between one and another, ■ **and** I do ■ **make them know the**

■ **statutes of God,** and his laws.

■ **17. And Moses' father in law** said unto him, ■ **The thing** that thou doest ■ **is not good.**

■ **18. Thou wilt** surely ■ **wear away,** both thou, and this people that *is* with thee: for this thing *is* too heavy for thee; thou art not able to perform it thyself alone.

■ **19. Hearken** now ■ **unto my** voice, I will give thee ■ **counsel,** and God shall be with thee: ■ **Be thou for the people** ■ **to God-ward,** that thou mayest bring the causes unto God:

■ **20. And thou shalt teach them ordinances and laws,** and shalt shew them the way wherein they must walk, ■ ■ **and the work** that **they must do.**

■ ■ **21. Moreover** thou shalt **provide** out of all the people ■ **able men,** such as fear God, men of truth, hating covetousness; ■ **and place** such over ■ **them, to be rulers of thousands,** *and* rulers of **hundreds**, rulers of **fifties, and** rulers of **tens:**

■ **22. And let them judge the people** at all seasons: **and** it shall be, *that* **every great matter they shall bring unto thee,** but every small matter **they shall judge:** so shall it be easier for thyself, ■ ■ **and they shall bear the burden with thee.**

23. If thou shalt do this thing, and God command thee *so,* then thoushalt be able to endure, and all this people shall also go to their place in peace.

■ **24. So Moses** hearkened to the voice of his father in law, and ■ **did all that he had said.**

25. And Moses chose able men out of all Israel, and made them heads over the people, rulers of thousands,

rulers of hundreds, rulers of fifties, and rulers of tens. 26. **And they judged the people** at all seasons: **the hard causes they brought unto Moses,** but every small matter **they judged themselves.** 27. **And Moses** let his **father in law** depart; and he **went his way into his own land.**

CHAPTER 19

1. **In the third month,** when the children of Israel were gone forth out of the land of Egypt, the same day **came they into the wilderness of Sinai.** 2. For they were departed from Rephidim, and were come *to* the desert of Sinai, and had pitched in the wilderness; **and there Israel camped before the mount.** 3. **And Moses went up unto God, and the LORD called unto him out of the mountain, saying,** Thus shalt thou say to the house of Jacob, and **tell the children of Israel;** 4. **Ye have seen** what I did unto the Egyptians, and **how I** bare you on eagles' wings, and **brought you unto myself.** 5. **Now therefore,** if ye will **obey my voice** indeed, **and keep my covenant, then ye shall be a peculiar treasure unto me** above all people: for all the earth *is* mine: 6. **And** ye shall be unto me **a kingdom of priests, and an holy nation.** These *are* the words which thou shalt speak unto the children of Israel. 7. **And Moses** came and called for the elders of the people, and **laid before their faces all these words which the LORD commanded him.** 8. **And all the people**

answered together, and said, **All that the LORD hath spoken we will do. And Moses returned the words** of the people **unto the LORD.** 9. **And the LORD said** unto Moses, Lo, **I come** unto thee **in a thick cloud, that the people may hear when I speak with thee,** and believe thee for ever. And Moses told the words of the people unto the LORD. 10. **And the LORD said** unto Moses, **Go unto the people, and sanctify them** to-day and to-morrow, **and let them wash their clothes,** 11. **And** be ready against the third day: for **the third day the LORD will come down in the sight of all the people** upon mount Sinai. 12. **And** thou shalt **set bounds** unto the people round about, saying, Take heed to yourselves, **that ye go not up into the mount,** or touch the border of it: **whosoever toucheth the mount shall be surely put to death:** 13. There shall not an hand touch it, but he shall surely be stoned, or shot through; whether *it be* beast or man, it shall not live: **when the trumpet soundeth long, they shall come up to the mount.** 14. **And Moses went down** from the mount unto the people, **and sanctified the people; and they washed their clothes.** 15. And he said unto the people, Be ready against the third day: come not at *your* wives. 16. **And** it came to pass **on the third day** in the morning, that

109

■ there were thunders
■ and lightnings, and a
■ thick cloud upon the
■ mount, and the voice of
■ the trumpet exceeding
■ loud; so that all
■ the people that *was* in the camp
■ trembled.
■ 17. And Moses brought forth
■ the people out of the camp
■ to meet with God; and they
stood at the nether part of the mount.
■ 18. And mount Sinai
■ was altogether on a
■ smoke, because the LORD
■ descended upon it in fire:
and the smoke thereof ascended
as the smoke of a furnace,
■ and the whole mount
■ quaked greatly.
■ 19. And when the voice of
■ the trumpet
■ sounded long, and waxed
■ louder and louder,
■ Moses spake, and God
■ answered him by a voice.
20. And the LORD came down upon
mount Sinai, on the top of the mount:
■ and the LORD called
■ Moses up to the top of
■ the mount; and Moses went up.
■ 21. And the LORD
■ said unto Moses, Go down,
■ charge the people, lest
■ they break through
■ unto the LORD to
■ gaze, and many of them
■ perish.
■ 22. And let the priests also,
■ which come near to the LORD,
■ sanctify themselves, lest
the LORD break forth upon them.
■ 23. And Moses
■ said unto the LORD,
■ The people cannot
■ come up to mount Sinai:
■ for thou chargedst us, saying,
■ Set bounds about the
■ mount, and sanctify it.
■ 24. And the LORD
■ said unto him, Away,
get thee down, and thou shalt
■ come up, thou,

■ and Aaron with thee: but let not
the priests and the people break
through to come up unto the LORD,
lest he break forth upon them.
■ 25. So Moses went
■ down unto the
■ people, and spake unto them.

CHAPTER 20

■ 1. And God spake all
■ these words, saying,
■ 2. I am the LORD thy
■ God, which have
■ brought thee out of the land of
■ Egypt, out of the house of bondage.
■ 3. Thou shalt have no
■ other gods before me.
■ 4. Thou shalt not
■ make unto thee
■ any graven image, or any
■ likeness of any thing that *is*
■ in heaven above,
■ or that *is* in the
■ earth beneath,
■ or that *is*
■ in the water under the earth.
■ 5. Thou shalt not
■ bow down thyself
■ to them, nor serve
■ them: for I the LORD thy God
■ am a jealous God, visiting
■ the iniquity of the fathers
■ upon the children unto
the third and fourth *generation*
■ of them that hate me;
■ 6. And shewing mercy
■ unto thousands of
■ them that love me,
and keep my commandments.
■ 7. Thou shalt not take the
■ name of the LORD thy God
■ in vain; for the LORD will
■ not hold him guiltless
that taketh his name in vain.
■ 8. Remember the sabbath
■ day, to keep it holy.
■ 9. Six days shalt thou
■ labour, and do all thy work:
■ 10. But the seventh
■ day is the sabbath
■ of the LORD thy God:
■ in it thou shalt not do any
■ work, thou, nor thy son, nor thy

daughter, thy manservant, nor thy maidservant, nor thy cattle, nor thy stranger that *is* within thy gates:

11. **For in six days the LORD made heaven and earth,** the sea, and all that in them *is,* **and rested the seventh day:** wherefore the LORD blessed the sabbath day, **and hallowed it.**

12. **Honour thy father and thy mother:** that thy days may be long upon the land which the LORD thy God giveth thee.

13. **Thou shalt not kill.**

14. **Thou shalt not commit adultery.**

15. **Thou shalt not steal.**

16. **Thou shalt not bear false witness** against thy neighbour.

17. **Thou shalt not covet** thy neighbour's house, thou shalt not covet thy neighbour's wife, nor his manservant, nor his maidservant, nor his ox, nor his ass, nor **any thing that is thy neighbour's.**

18. **And all the people saw the thunderings, and the lightnings,** and the noise of the trumpet, **and the mountain smoking:** and when the people saw *it,* they removed, and stood afar off.

19. **And they said** unto Moses, Speak thou with us, and we will hear: but **let not God speak with us, lest we die.**

20. **And Moses said** unto the people, **Fear not: for God is come to prove you,** and that his fear may be before your faces, **that ye sin not.**

21. And the people stood afar off, **and Moses drew near unto** the thick darkness where **God** *was.*

22. **And the LORD said** unto Moses, Thus thou shalt **say unto the children of Israel,** Ye have seen that **I have talked with you from heaven.**

23. **Ye shall not make** with me **gods of silver, neither** shall ye make unto you gods **of gold.**

24. **An altar of earth** thou shalt **make unto me, and** shalt **sacrifice** thereon **thy burnt offerings,** and thy peace offerings, thy sheep, and thine oxen: in all places where I record my name I will come unto thee, **and I will bless thee.**

25. **And if thou** wilt **make** me **an altar of stone, thou shalt not build it of hewn stone: for** if thou lift up **thy tool** upon it, thou **hast polluted it.**

26. **Neither** shalt thou **go up by steps unto mine altar, that thy nakedness be not discovered** thereon.

CHAPTER 21

1. **Now these** *are* the **judgments** which thou shalt **set before them.**

2. **If thou buy an Hebrew servant, six years he shall serve: and** in **the seventh he shall go** out **free** for nothing.

3. **If he came** in **by himself, he shall go** out **by himself:** if he were **married,** then **his wife shall go** out **with him.**

4. **If his master have given him a wife, and she have born him sons or daughters; the wife and her children shall be her master's,** and he shall go out by himself.

5. **And if the servant** shall plainly **say, I love my master,**

my wife, and my children;

I will not go out free:

6. Then his master shall bring him unto the judges; he shall also bring him to the door, or unto the door post; and his master shall bore his ear through with an aul; and he shall serve him for ever.

7. And if a man sell his daughter to be a maidservant, she shall not go out as the menservants do.

8. If she please not her master, who hath betrothed her to himself, then shall he let her be redeemed: to sell her unto a strange nation he shall have no power, seeing he hath dealt deceitfully with her.

9. And if he have betrothed her unto his son, he shall deal with her after the manner of daughters.

10. If he take him another wife; her food, her raiment, and her duty of marriage, shall he not diminish.

11. And if he do not these three unto her, then shall she go out free without money.

12. He that smiteth a man, so that he die, shall be surely put to death.

13. And if a man lie not in wait, but God deliver him into his hand; then I will appoint thee a place whither he shall flee.

14. But if a man come presumptuously upon his neighbour, to slay him with guile; thou shalt take him from mine altar, that he may die.

15. And he that smiteth his father, or his mother, shall be surely put to death.

16. And he that stealeth a man, and selleth him, or if he be found in his hand, he shall surely be put to death.

17. And he that curseth his father, or his mother, shall surely be put to death.

18. And if men strive together, and one smite another with a stone, or with his fist, and he die not, but keepeth his bed:

19. If he rise again, and walk abroad upon his staff, then shall he that smote him be quit: only he shall pay for the loss of his time, and shall cause him to be thoroughly healed.

20. And if a man smite his servant, or his maid, with a rod, and he die under his hand; he shall be surely punished.

21. Notwithstanding, if he continue a day or two, he shall not be punished: for he is his money.

22. If men strive, and hurt a woman with child, so that her fruit depart from her, and yet no mischief follow: he shall be surely punished, according as the woman's husband will lay upon him; and he shall pay as the judges determine.

23. And if any mischief follow, then thou shalt give life for life,

24. Eye for eye, tooth for tooth, hand for hand, foot for foot,

25. Burning for burning, wound for wound, stripe for stripe.

26. And if a man smite the eye of his servant, or the eye of his maid, that it perish; he shall let him go free for his eye's sake.

27. And if he smite out his manservant's tooth, or his maidservant's tooth; he shall let him go

112

■ **free** for his tooth's sake.

■ 28. **If an ox gore a man**
or a woman, that they die:
■ **then the ox shall be** surely
■ **stoned,** and his flesh
shall not be eaten;
■ **but the owner** of the ox
■ **shall be quit.**
■ 29. **But if the ox were wont to**
■ **push with his horn** in time past,
and it hath been testified to his owner,
■ **and** he hath not kept him in, but that
■ **he hath killed**
■ **a man** or a woman;
■ **the ox** shall be stoned,
■ **and his owner** also
■ **shall be put to death.**
■ 30. **If there be laid on**
■ **him a sum of money,** then
■ **he shall give** for
■ **the ransom of his life**
whatsoever is laid upon him.
31. Whether he have gored a
son, or have gored a daughter,
according to this judgment
shall it be done unto him.
■ 32. **If the ox shall push a**
■ **manservant** or a maidservant;
■ **he shall give unto their**
■ **master thirty shekels** of silver,
and the ox shall be stoned.
■ 33. **And if a man** shall
open a pit, or if a man shall
■ **dig a pit, and not cover**
■ **it, and an ox or** an
■ **ass fall therein;**
■ 34. **The owner of the**
■ **pit shall** make *it* good, *and*
■ **give money unto**
■ **the owner** of them;
■ **and the dead beast**
■ **shall be his.**
■ 35. **And if one man's ox hurt**
■ **another's, that he die;** then
■ **they shall sell the live ox,**
■ **and divide the money** of it;
■ **and the dead ox**
■ **also** they shall divide.
36. Or if it be known that the ox
hath used to push in time past,
and his owner hath not kept him
in; he shall surely pay ox for ox;
and the dead shall be his own.

CHAPTER 22

■ 1. **If a man shall steal an ox,**
or a sheep, and kill it, or sell it;
■ **he shall restore five oxen** for
an ox, and four sheep for a sheep.
■ 2. **If a thief be found**
■ **breaking up, and be**
■ **smitten that he die,**
■ **there shall no blood**
■ **be shed for him.**
■ 3. **If the sun be risen**
■ **upon him,** *there shall*
be blood *shed for* him; *for*
■ **he should make**
■ **full restitution; if**
■ **he have nothing,** then
■ **he shall be sold**
■ **for his theft.**
4. If the theft be certainly found in his
hand alive, whether it be ox, or ass,
or sheep; he shall restore double.
■ 5. **If a man shall cause a**
■ **field or vineyard to be**
■ **eaten,** and shall put in his beast,
and shall feed in another man's field;
of the best of his own field, and
■ **of** the best of
■ **his own vineyard, shall**
■ **he make restitution.**
6. **If fire break out,**
and catch in thorns,
■ **so that** the stacks of corn,
or the standing corn, or
■ **the field, be**
■ **consumed** *therewith;*
■ **he that kindled the**
■ **fire shall** surely
■ **make restitution.**
■ 7. **If a man shall deliver**
■ **unto his neighbour**
■ **money** or stuff to keep,
■ **and it be stolen**
out of the man's house;
■ **if the thief be found,**
■ **let him pay double.**
■ 8. **If** the thief be
■ **not** found, then
■ **the master** of the house
■ **shall be brought**
unto the judges,
■ **to see whether**
■ **he have** put his hand unto
■ **his neighbour's goods.**

113

9. **For all manner of trespass,** *whether it be* for ox, for ass, for sheep, for raiment, *or* for any manner of lost thing **which another challengeth to be his,** the cause of both parties **shall come before the judges; and whom the judges** shall **condemn, he shall pay double unto his neighbour.** 10. **If a man deliver unto his neighbour** an ass, or an ox, or a sheep, or **any beast, to keep; and it die, or be hurt, or driven away,** no man seeing *it.* 11. **Then shall an oath of the LORD be between them** both, that he hath not put his hand unto his neighbour's goods; and the owner of it shall accep*t thereof,* **and he shall not make it good.** 12. **And if it be stolen** from him, **he shall make restitution** unto the owner thereof. 13. **If it be torn in pieces,** *then* let him bring it *for* witness, *and* **he shall not make good** that which was torn. 14. **And if a man borrow aught** of his neighbour, **and it be hurt, or die,** the owner thereof *being* not with it, **he shall** surely **make it good.** 15. **But if the owner** thereof **be with it, he shall not make it good: if it be** an **hired** *thing,* it came for his hire. 16. **And if a man entice a maid** that is not betrothed, and lie with her, **he shall** surely **endow her to be his wife.** 17. **If her father** utterly **refuse to give her** unto him, **he shall pay money** according to the dowry of virgins. 18. **Thou shalt not suffer a witch to live.** 19. **Whosoever lieth with a beast shall** surely **be put to death.** 20. **He that sacrificeth unto any god, save** unto **the LORD** only, he **shall be** utterly **destroyed.** 21. Thou shalt neither vex a stranger, nor oppress him: for ye were strangers in the land of Egypt. 22. **Ye shall not afflict any widow, or fatherless child.** 23. If thou afflict them in any wise, and they cry at all unto me, **I will** surely **hear their cry;** 24. **And** my wrath shall wax hot, and **I will kill you with the sword;** and your wives shall be widows, and your children fatherless. 25. **If thou lend money to any of my people** *that is* poor by thee, **thou shalt not** be to him as an usurer, neither shalt thou **lay upon him usury.** 26. **If thou** at all **take thy neighbour's raiment** to pledge, **thou shalt deliver it unto him by that the sun goeth down:** 27. **For that is his covering** only, it *is* his raiment for his skin: **wherein shall he sleep?** and it shall come to pass, when he crieth unto me, that I will hear; for I *am* gracious. 28. **Thou shalt not revile the gods, nor curse the ruler** of thy people. 29. **Thou shalt not delay to offer the first** of thy ripe **fruits, and** of thy liquors: **the firstborn of thy sons shalt thou give unto me.** 30. **Likewise** shalt thou do with **thine oxen, and** with thy **sheep:** seven days it shall be with his dam; **on the eighth day thou shalt give it me.** 31. **And ye shall**

■ **be holy** men unto me:
■ **neither** shall ye
■ **eat any flesh** *that is*
■ **torn of beasts** in the field;
ye shall cast it to the dogs.

CHAPTER 23

■ 1. **Thou shalt not raise**
■ **a false report: put not**
■ **thine hand** with the wicked
■ **to be an**
■ **unrighteous witness.**
■ 2. **Thou shalt not follow a**
■ **multitude to do evil;** neither
shalt thou speak in a cause to decline
after many to wrest *judgment:*
■ 3. **Neither** shalt thou
■ **countenance a**
■ **poor man** in his cause.
■ 4. **If thou meet thine**
■ **enemy's ox or his ass going**
■ **astray, thou shalt** surely
■ **bring it back** to him again.
■ 5. **If thou see the**
■ **ass** of him that hateth thee
■ **lying under his burden,**
and wouldest forbear to help him,
■ **thou shalt** surely
■ **help** with
■ **him.**
■ 6. **Thou shalt not**
■ **wrest the judgment**
■ **of thy poor** in his cause.
■ 7. **Keep** thee
■ **far from a false matter;**
■ **and the innocent and**
■ **righteous slay** thou
■ **not:** for I will not justify the wicked.
■ 8. **And thou shalt**
■ **take no gift: for the gift**
■ **blindeth the wise, and**
■ **perverteth** the words of
■ **the righteous.**
■ 9. **Also thou shalt not**
■ **oppress a stranger:**
for ye know the heart of a
stranger, seeing ye were
strangers in the land of Egypt.
■ 10. **And six years** thou shalt
■ **sow thy land, and** shalt
■ **gather** in
■ **the fruits** thereof:
■ 11. **But the seventh**

■ **year** thou shalt
■ **let it rest** and lie still;
■ **that the poor** of thy people
■ **may eat: and** what they leave
■ **the beasts of the**
■ **field** shall eat.
■ **In like manner**
thou shalt deal with
■ **thy vineyard, and** with thy
■ **oliveyard.**
■ 12. **Six days** thou shalt do thy
■ **work, and on the**
■ **seventh day** thou shalt
■ **rest:** that thine ox
and thine ass may rest,
■ **and** the son of thy handmaid,
and the stranger, may
■ **be refreshed.**
■ 13. **And** in all *things*
that I have said unto you
■ **be circumspect: and**
■ **make no mention** of the name
■ **of other gods,** neither
let it be heard out of thy mouth.
■ 14. **Three times** thou shalt
■ **keep a feast** unto me
■ **in the year.**
■ 15. Thou shalt keep
■ **the feast of unleavened**
■ **bread:** (thou shalt eat unleavened
bread seven days, as I commanded
thee, in the time appointed of the
month Abib; for in it thou camest
out from Egypt: and none shall
appear before me empty:)
■ 16. **And the feast of harvest,**
the firstfruits of thy labours,
which thou hast sown in the field:
■ **and the feast of**
■ **ingathering,** *which is* in the end
of the year, when thou hast gathered
in thy labours out of the field.
■ 17. **Three times in the year**
■ **all thy males shall appear**
■ **before the LORD God.**
■ 18. **Thou shalt not offer**
■ **the blood** of my sacrifice
■ **with leavened**
■ **bread; neither shall**
■ **the fat** of my sacrifice
■ **remain until the morning.**
■ 19. **The** first of the
■ **firstfruits** of thy land

115

thou shalt bring into the house of the LORD thy God. Thou shalt not seethe a kid in his mother's milk.

20. Behold, I send an Angel before thee, to keep thee in the way, and to bring thee into the place which I have prepared.

21. Beware of him, and obey his voice, provoke him not; for he will not pardon your transgressions: for my name is in him.

22. But if thou shalt indeed obey his voice, and do all that I speak; then I will be an enemy unto thine enemies, and an adversary unto thine adversaries.

23. For mine Angel shall go before thee, and bring thee in unto the Amorites, and the Hittites, and the Perizzites, and the Canaanites, the Hivites, and the Jebusites: and I will cut them off.

24. Thou shalt not bow down to their gods, nor serve them, nor do after their works: but thou shalt utterly overthrow them, and quite break down their images.

25. And ye shall serve the LORD your God, and he shall bless thy bread, and thy water; and I will take sickness away from the midst of thee.

26. There shall nothing cast their young, nor be barren, in thy land: the number of thy days I will fulfil.

27. I will send my fear before thee, and will destroy all the people to whom thou shalt come, and I will make all thine enemies turn their backs unto thee.

28. And I will send hornets before thee, which shall drive out the Hivite, the Canaanite, and the Hittite, from before thee.

29. I will not drive them out from before thee in one year; lest the land become desolate, and the beast of the field multiply against thee.

30. By little and little I will drive them out from before thee, until thou be increased, and inherit the land.

31. And I will set thy bounds from the Red sea even unto the sea of the Philistines, and from the desert unto the river: for I will deliver the inhabitants of the land into your hand; and thou shalt drive them out before thee.

32. Thou shalt make no covenant with them, nor with their gods.

33. They shall not dwell in thy land, lest they make thee sin against me: for if thou serve their gods, it will surely be a snare unto thee.

CHAPTER 24

1. And he said unto Moses, Come up unto the LORD, thou, and Aaron, Nadab, and Abihu, and seventy of the elders of Israel; and worship ye afar off.

2. And Moses alone shall come near the LORD: but they shall not come nigh; neither shall the people go up with him.

3. And Moses came and told the people all the words of the LORD, and all the judgments: and all the people answered with one voice, and said, All the words which the LORD hath said will we do.

4. And Moses wrote all the words of the LORD, and rose up early in the morning, and builded an altar under

the hill, and twelve pillars, according to the twelve tribes of Israel.

5. **And he sent young men** of the children of Israel, **which offered burnt offerings, and** sacrificed **peace offerings** of oxen **unto the LORD.**

6. **And Moses took half of the blood, and put** *it* **in basins; and half** of the blood **he sprinkled on the altar.**

7. **And he took the book of the covenant, and read in the audience of the people: and they said, All that the LORD hath said will we do,** and be obedient.

8. **And Moses took the blood, and sprinkled it on the people, and said,** Behold **the blood of the covenant,** which the LORD hath made with you concerning all these words.

9. **Then went up Moses,** and Aaron, Nadab, and Abihu, **and** seventy of **the elders of Israel:**

10. **And they saw** the **God** of Israel: **and there was under his feet** as it were **a paved work of a sapphire stone, and as** it were **the** body of **heaven in** *his* **clearness.**

11. And upon the nobles of the children of Israel he laid not his hand: also they saw God, and did eat and drink.

12. **And the LORD said unto Moses, Come up** to me into the mount, and be there: **and I will give thee tables of stone, and a law, and commandments which I have written; that thou mayest teach them.**

13. **And Moses** rose up, **and** his minister

Joshua: and Moses **went up into the mount of God.**

14. **And he said unto the elders, Tarry** ye **here** for us, **until we come again** unto you: and, behold, **Aaron and Hur are with you: if any man have any matters** to do, **let him come unto them.**

15. **And Moses went up into** the mount, and **a cloud** covered the mount.

16. **And the glory of the LORD abode upon mount Sinai,** and the cloud covered it **six days: and the seventh day he called** unto **Moses** out of the midst of the cloud.

17. **And the sight** of the glory of the LORD **was like devouring fire** on the top of the mount in the eyes of the children of Israel.

18. **And Moses** went into the midst of the cloud, and gat him up into the mount: and Moses **was in the mount forty days and forty nights.**

CHAPTER 25

1. **And the Lord spake unto Moses** saying,

2. **Speak unto** the children of **Israel, that they bring** me an offering: of every man that giveth it **willingly** with his heart ye shall take **my offering.**

3. **And this** *is* the **offering** which **ye shall take of** them; **gold, and silver, and brass,**

4. **And blue, and purple, and scarlet,** and fine **linen, and goats' hair,**

5. **And rams'**

skins dyed red, and badgers' skins, and shittim wood,

6. Oil for the light, spices for anointing oil, and for sweet incense,

7. Onyx stones, and stones to be set in the ephod, and in the breastplate.

8. And let them make me a sanctuary; that I may dwell among them.

9. According to all that I shew thee, *after* the pattern of the tabernacle, and the pattern of all the instruments thereof, even so shall ye make it.

10. And they shall make an ark of shittim wood: two cubits and a half *shall be* the length thereof, and a cubit and a half the breadth thereof, and a cubit and a half the height thereof.

11. And thou shalt overlay it with pure gold, within and without shalt thou overlay it, and shalt make upon it a crown of gold round about.

12. And thou shalt cast four rings of gold for it, and put them in the four corners thereof; and two rings *shall be* in the one side of it, and two rings in the other side of it.

13. And thou shalt make staves of shittim wood, and overlay them with gold.

14. And thou shalt put the staves into the rings by the sides of the ark, that the ark may be borne with them.

15. The staves shall be in the rings of the ark: they shall not be taken from it.

16. And thou shalt put into the ark the testimony which I shall give thee.

17. And thou shalt make a mercy seat of pure gold: two cubits and a half *shall be* the length thereof, and a cubit and a half the breadth thereof.

18. And thou shalt make two cherubims of gold, *of* beaten work shalt thou make them, in the two ends of the mercy seat.

19. And make one cherub on the one end, and the other cherub on the other end: *even of* the mercy seat shall ye make the cherubims on the two ends thereof.

20. And the cherubims shall stretch forth their wings on high, covering the mercy seat with their wings, and their faces shall look one to another; toward the mercy seat shall the faces of the cherubims be.

21. And thou shalt put the mercy seat above upon the ark; and in the ark thou shalt put the testimony that I shall give thee.

22. And there I will meet with thee, and I will commune with thee from above the mercy seat, from between the two cherubims which *are* upon the ark of the testimony, of all *things* which I will give thee in commandment unto the children of Israel.

23. Thou shalt also make a table of shittim wood: two cubits *shall be* the length thereof, and a cubit the breadth thereof, and a cubit and a half the height thereof.

24. And thou shalt overlay it with pure gold, and make thereto a crown of gold round about.

25. And thou shalt make unto it a border of an hand breadth

round about, and thou shalt make a golden crown **to the border thereof round about.** 26. **And** thou shalt make for it **four rings** of gold, and put the rings **in the four corners** that *are* on the four feet thereof. 27. Over against the border shall the rings be for places of the staves to bear the table. 28. **And** thou shalt **make** the **staves of shittim wood, and overlay them with gold, that the table may be borne** with them. 29. **And** thou shalt **make** the **dishes** thereof, **and spoons** thereof, **and covers** thereof, **and bowls** thereof, to cover withal: **of pure gold** shalt thou make them. 30. **And** thou shalt **set upon the table shewbread before me alway.** 31. **And** thou shalt **make a candlestick of pure gold:** *of* beaten work shall the candlestick be made: his shaft, and his branches, his bowls, his knops, and his flowers, shall be of the same. 32. **And six branches shall come out of the sides** of it; **three** branches of the candlestick **out of the one side, and three** branches of the candlestick **out of the other side:** 33. **Three bowls** made **like** unto **almonds, with a knop and a flower in one branch;** and three bowls made like almonds in the other branch, *with* a knop and a flower: **so in the six branches** that come out of the candlestick. 34. **And** in the candle sticks *shall be* four **bowls made like** unto **almonds, with** their **knops and** their **flowers.** 35. **And there shall be a knop under two branches of the same,** and a knop under two branches of the same, and a knop under two branches of the same, **according to the six branches that proceed out of the candlestick.** 36. **Their knops and** their **branches shall** be of the same: all it *shall* **be one beaten work of pure gold.** 37. **And** thou shalt make the **seven lamps** thereof: and they shall light the lamps thereof, **that** they may **give light** over against it. 38. **And the tongs** thereof, **and** the **snuffdishes** thereof, **shall be** *of* **pure gold.** 39. **Of a talent of** pure **gold shall he make** it, with all **these vessels.** 40. And look that thou **make them after their pattern, which was shewed thee in the mount.**

CHAPTER 26

1. **Moreover** thou shalt **make** the tabernacle **with ten curtains of** fine twined **linen, and blue, and purple, and scarlet: with cherubims of cunning work** shalt thou make them. 2. **The length** of one curtain *shall be* eight and twenty cubits, **and the breadth of** one curtain four cubits: and **every** one of the **curtains shall have one measure.** 3. **The five curtains shall be coupled together** one to another;

and other five curtains
shall be coupled
one to another.

4. And thou shalt
make loops of blue upon
the edge of the one curtain from
the selvedge in the coupling; and
likewise shalt thou make in the
uttermost edge of *another* curtain,
in the coupling
of the second.

5. Fifty loops shalt thou make
in the
one curtain, and fifty
loops shalt thou make in
the edge of the curtain that *is*
in the coupling of the
second; that the loops may
take hold one of another.

6. And thou shalt
make fifty taches of gold,
and couple the curtains
together with the taches:
and it shall be
one tabernacle.

7. And thou shalt
make curtains of goats'
hair to be a covering upon
the tabernacle: eleven
curtains shalt thou make.

8. The length of one curtain
shall be thirty cubits, and the
breadth of one curtain four
cubits: and the eleven curtains
shall be all of
one measure.

9. And thou shalt
couple five curtains
by themselves, and
six curtains by
themselves, and shalt
double the sixth
curtain in the forefront
of the tabernacle.

10. And thou shalt
make fifty loops on the
edge of the one curtain
that is outmost in the coupling,
and fifty loops in the edge
of the curtain which coupleth
the second.

11. And thou shalt make
fifty taches of brass,
and put the taches into the loops,
and couple the tent
together, that it may be one.

12. And the remnant that
remaineth of the curtains of the tent,
the half curtain that
remaineth, shall hang
over the backside
of the tabernacle.

13. And a cubit on the one side, and
a cubit on the other side of that which
remaineth in the length of the curtains
of the tent, it shall hang over the sides
of the tabernacle on this side and on
that side, to cover it.

14. And thou shalt
make a covering for the
tent of rams' skins dyed red,
and a covering
above of badgers' skins.

15. And thou shalt
make boards for the tabernacle
of shittim wood
standing up.

16. Ten cubits *shall be*
the length of a board,
and a cubit and
a half *shall be*
the breadth of one board.

17. Two tenons shall
there be in one board,
set in order one
against another: thus
shalt thou make for all the
boards of the tabernacle.

18. And thou shalt
make the boards for the tabernacle,
twenty boards on
the south side southward.

19. And thou shalt
make forty sockets of
silver under the twenty boards;
two sockets under
one board for his
two tenons, and two
sockets under another
board for his two tenons.

20. And for the second
side of the tabernacle
on the north side there
shall be twenty boards:

21. And their
forty sockets of silver; two

sockets under one board, and two sockets under another board.

22. **And for the sides** of the tabernacle westward thou shalt **make six boards.**

23. **And two boards** shalt thou make **for the corners** of the tabernacle in the two sides.

24. **And they shall be coupled together beneath, and** they shall be coupled together **above** the head of it **unto one ring:** thus shall it be for them both; they shall be for the two corners.

25. And they shall be eight boards, and their sockets *of* silver, sixteen sockets; two sockets under one board, and two sockets under another board.

26. **And** thou shalt **make bars of shittim wood; five for the boards of the one side** of the tabernacle,

27. **And five bars for the boards of the other side** of the tabernacle, **and five bars** for the boards of the side of the tabernacle, **for the two sides westward.**

28. **And the middle bar** in the midst of the boards **shall reach from end to end.**

29. **And** thou shalt **overlay the boards with gold, and make their rings of gold for places for the bars: and** thou shalt **overlay the bars with gold.**

30. **And** thou shalt **rear up the tabernacle according to the fashion** thereof which was **shewed thee in the mount.**

31. **And** thou shalt **make a veil of blue, and purple, and scarlet, and fine** twined **linen of cunning work: with cherubims** shall it be made:

32. **And** thou shalt **hang it upon four pillars of shittim wood overlaid with gold: their hooks** *shall be* **of gold, upon** the **four sockets of silver.**

33. **And** thou shalt **hang** up **the veil under the taches, that thou mayest bring in** thither within the veil **the ark of the testimony: and the veil shall divide** unto you **between the holy place and the most holy.**

34. **And** thou shalt **put the mercy seat upon the ark** of the testimony **in the most holy place.**

35. **And** thou shalt **set the table without the veil, and the candlestick** over against the table **on the side** of the tabernacle **toward the south: and** thou shalt **put the table on the north side.**

36. **And** thou shalt **make an hanging** for the **door** of the tent, **of blue, and purple, and scarlet, and** fine twined **linen, wrought with needlework.**

37. **And** thou shalt **make for the hanging five pillars of shittim wood, and overlay them with gold, and their hooks** *shall be* **of gold: and** thou shalt **cast five sockets of brass for them.**

CHAPTER 27

1. **And** thou shalt **make an altar of shittim wood,** five cubits long, and five cubits broad; the altar *shall be* **foursquare:** and the height thereof shall be three cubits.

2. **And** thou shalt **make the horns** of it

upon the four corners thereof: his horns shall be of the same: and thou shalt overlay it with brass. 3. And thou shalt make his pans to receive his ashes, and his shovels, and his basins, and his fleshhooks, and his firepans: all the vessels thereof thou shalt make of brass. 4. And thou shalt make for it a grate of network of brass; and upon the net shalt thou make four brasen rings in the four corners thereof. 5. And thou shalt put it under the compass of the altar beneath, that the net may be even to the midst of the altar. 6. And thou shalt make staves for the altar, staves of shittim wood, and overlay them with brass. 7. And the staves shall be put into the rings, and the staves shall be upon the two sides of the altar, to bear it. 8. Hollow with boards shalt thou make it: as it was shewed thee in the mount, so shall they make *it*. 9. And thou shalt make the court of the tabernacle: for the south side southward *there* shall be hangings for the court of fine twined linen of an hundred cubits long for one side: 10. And the twenty pillars thereof and their twenty sockets *shall be* of brass; the hooks of the pillars and their fillets shall be of silver. 11. And likewise for the north side in length *there shall be* hangings of an hundred *cubits* long, and his twenty pillars and their twenty sockets *of* brass; the hooks of the pillars and their fillets *of* silver. 12. And *for* the breadth of the court on the west side shall be hangings of fifty cubits: their pillars ten, and their sockets ten. 13. And the breadth of the court on the east side eastward shall be fifty cubits. 14. The hangings of one side of the gate shall be fifteen cubits: their pillars three, and their sockets three. 15. And on the other side *shall be* hangings fifteen cubits: their pillars three, and their sockets three. 16. And for the gate of the court shall be an hanging of twenty cubits, of blue, and purple, and scarlet, and fine twined linen, wrought with needlework: and their pillars *shall be* four, and their sockets four. 17. All the pillars round about the court shall be filleted with silver; their hooks *shall be* of silver, and their sockets of brass. 18. The length of the court shall be an hundred cubits, and the breadth fifty every where, and the height five cubits of fine twined

- linen, and their
- sockets of brass.
- 19. **All the vessels** of the
tabernacle in all the service thereof,
- **and all the pins** thereof,
and all the pins of the court,
- **shall be of brass.**
- 20. **And** thou shalt
- **command** the children of
- **Israel, that they bring** thee
- **pure oil** olive beaten
- **for** the light, to cause
- **the lamp to burn always.**
- 21. **In the tabernacle**
of the congregation
- **without the veil,** which
is before the testimony,
- **Aaron and his sons shall**
- **order it from evening to**
- **morning before the LORD:**
- **it shall be a statute**
- **for ever** unto their generations
- **on** the
- **behalf of** the children
- **of Israel.**

CHAPTER 28

- 1. **And take** thou unto thee
- **Aaron** thy brother,
- **and his sons** with him, from
among the children of Israel,
- **that he may minister unto**
- **me in the priest's office,**
even Aaron, Nadab and Abihu,
Eleazar and Ithamar, Aaron's sons.
- 2. And thou shalt
- **make holy garments**
- **for Aaron** thy brother
- **for glory and for beauty.**
- 3. And thou shalt
- **speak unto all that**
- **are** wise hearted, whom I have
- **filled with the spirit of**
- **wisdom, that they may**
- **make Aaron's garments to**
- **consecrate him,** that he may
minister unto me in the priest's office.
- 4. And these *are* the garments
which they shall make;
- **a breastplate, and an**
- **ephod, and a robe, and**
- **a broidered coat, a mitre,**
- **and a girdle:** and they shall make

- **holy garments for**
- **Aaron** thy brother,
- **and his sons,** that he
may minister unto me in
the priest's office.
- 5. And they shall
- **take gold, and blue,**
- **and purple, and**
- **scarlet, and** fine
- **linen.**
- 6. **And** they shall
- **make the ephod of**
- **gold, of blue,** and *of*
- **purple,** of
- **scarlet, and** fine twined
- **linen, with cunning work.**
- 7. **It shall have the two**
- **shoulderpieces** thereof
joined at the two edges thereof;
and *so* it shall be
- **joined together.**
- 8. **And the** curious
- **girdle of the ephod,**
which *is* upon it,
- **shall be** of
- **the same,** according to
the work thereof; *even of*
gold, *of* blue, and purple, and
scarlet, and fine twined linen.
- 9. **And** thou shalt
- **take two onyx stones,**
- **and grave** on them
- **the names of the**
- **children of Israel:**
- 10. **Six** of their
- **names on one**
- **stone, and** the other
- **six** names of the rest
- **on the other** stone,
- **according to their birth.**
- 11. With the work of an engraver in
stone, *like* the engravings of a signet,
shalt thou engrave the two stones
with the names of the children of
Israel: thou shalt make them to be
- **set in ouches of gold.**
- 12. **And** thou shalt
- **put the two stones upon**
- **the shoulders of the**
- **ephod** for stones of memorial
unto the children of Israel:
- **and Aaron shall bear**
- **their names before the**

123

LORD upon his two shoulders for a memorial.

13. And thou shalt make ouches of gold;

14. And two chains *of* pure gold at the ends; *of* wreathen work shalt thou make them, and fasten the wreathen chains to the ouches.

15. And thou shalt make the breastplate of judgment with cunning work; after the work of the ephod thou shalt make it; of gold, of blue, and *of* purple, and *of* scarlet, and *of* fine twined linen, shalt thou make it.

16. Foursquare it shall be being doubled; a span *shall be* the length thereof, and a span *shall be* the breadth thereof.

17. And thou shalt set in it settings of stones, *even* four rows of stones: the first row shall be a sardius, a topaz, and a carbuncle: *this shall be* the first row.

18. And the second row *shall be* an emerald, a sapphire, and a diamond.

19. And the third row a ligure, an agate, and an amethyst.

20. And the fourth row a beryl, and an onyx, and a jasper: they shall be set in gold in their enclosings.

21. And the stones shall be with the names of the children of Israel, twelve, according to their names, like the engravings of a signet; every one with his name shall they be according to the twelve tribes.

22. And thou shalt make upon the breastplate chains at the ends of wreathen work of pure gold.

23. And thou shalt make upon the breastplate two rings of gold, and shalt put the two rings on the two ends of the breastplate.

24. And thou shalt put the two wreathen chains of gold in the two rings *which are* on the ends of the breastplate.

25. And the other two ends of the two wreathen chains thou shalt fasten in the two ouches, and put *them* on the shoulderpieces of the ephod before it.

26. And thou shalt make two rings of gold, and thou shalt put them upon the two ends of the breastplate in the border thereof, which *is* in the side of the ephod inward.

27. And two other rings of gold thou shalt make, and shalt put them on the two sides of the ephod underneath, toward the forepart thereof, over against the *other* coupling thereof, above the curious girdle of the ephod.

28. And they shall bind the breastplate by the rings thereof unto the rings of the ephod with a lace of blue, that *it* may be above the curious girdle of the ephod, and that the breastplate be not loosed from the ephod.

29. And Aaron shall bear the names of the children of Israel in the breastplate of judgment upon his heart, when he goeth in unto the holy *place,* for a memorial before the LORD continually.

30. And thou shalt put in the breastplate of judgment the Urim and the

Thummim; and they shall be upon Aaron's heart, when he goeth in before the LORD: and Aaron shall bear the judgment of the children of Israel upon his heart before the LORD continually.

31. And thou shalt make the robe of the ephod all of blue.

32. And there shall be an hole in the top of it, in the midst thereof: it shall have a binding of woven work round about the hole of it, as it were the hole of an habergeon, that it be not rent.

33. And beneath upon the hem of it thou shalt make pomegranates of blue, and of purple, and of scarlet, round about the hem thereof; and bells of gold between them round about:

34. A golden bell and a pomegranate, a golden bell and a pomegranate, upon the hem of the robe roundabout.

35. And it shall be upon Aaron to minister: and his sound shall be heard when he goeth in unto the holy place before the LORD, and when he cometh out, that he die not.

36. And thou shalt make a plate of pure gold, and grave upon it, *like* the engravings of a signet, HOLINESS TO THE LORD.

37. And thou shalt put it on a blue lace, that it may be upon the mitre; upon the forefront of the mitre it shall be.

38. And it shall be upon Aaron's forehead, that Aaron may bear the iniquity of the holy things, which the children of Israel shall hallow in all their holy gifts; and it shall be always upon his forehead, that they may be accepted before the LORD.

39. And thou shalt embroider the coat of fine linen, and thou shalt make the mitre of fine linen, and thou shalt make the girdle of needlework.

40. And for Aaron's sons thou shalt make coats, and thou shalt make for them girdles, and bonnets shalt thou make for them, for glory and for beauty.

41. And thou shalt put them upon Aaron thy brother, and his sons with him; and shalt anoint them, and consecrate them, and sanctify them, that they may minister unto me in the priest's office.

42. And thou shalt make them linen breeches to cover their nakedness; from the loins even unto the thighs they shall reach:

43. And they shall be upon Aaron, and upon his sons, when they come in unto the tabernacle of the congregation, or when they come near unto the altar to minister in the holy place; that they bear not iniquity, and die: it shall be a statute for ever unto him and his seed after him.

CHAPTER 29

1. And this *is* the thing that thou shalt do unto them to hallow them, to minister unto me in the priest's office:

Take one young
bullock, and two
rams without blemish,
2. And unleavened
bread, and cakes
unleavened tempered
with oil, and wafers
unleavened anointed with oil:
of wheaten flour
shalt thou make them.
3. And thou shalt
put them into one basket,
and bring them in the basket,
with the bullock and
the two rams.
4. And Aaron and his
sons thou shalt bring
unto the door of the
tabernacle of the congregation,
and shalt wash them with water.
5. And thou shalt
take the garments, and put
upon Aaron the coat, and the
robe of the ephod, and the ephod,
and the breastplate, and gird him
with the curious girdle of the ephod:
6. And thou shalt put the mitre
upon his head, and put the
holy crown upon the mitre.
7. Then shalt thou
take the anointing oil,
and pour it upon his
head, and anoint him.
8. And thou shalt
bring his sons,
and put coats upon them.
9. And thou shalt
gird them with girdles,
Aaron and his sons, and
put the bonnets on them:
and the priest's office shall
be theirs for a perpetual
statute: and thou shalt
consecrate Aaron
and his sons.
10. And thou shalt
cause a bullock to
be brought before the
tabernacle of the congregation:
and Aaron and his sons shall put their
hands upon the head of the bullock.
11. And thou shalt
kill the bullock before

the LORD, *by* the door of the
tabernacle of the congregation.
12. And thou shalt
take of
the blood of the bullock,
and put it upon the horns
of the altar with thy finger,
and pour all the blood
beside the bottom of
the altar.
13. And thou shalt
take all
the fat that covereth the
inwards, and the caul *that is* above
the liver, and the two kidneys, and the
fat that *is* upon them,
and burn them
upon the altar.
14. But the flesh of the bullock,
and his skin, and
his dung, shalt thou
burn with fire without the
camp: it is a sin offering.
15. Thou shalt also
take one ram; and Aaron
and his sons shall put their
hands upon the head of the ram.
16. And thou shalt
slay the ram, and thou shalt
take his blood, and
sprinkle it round about upon
the altar.
17. And thou shalt
cut the ram in pieces,
and wash the inwards of him,
and his legs,
and put *them* unto
his pieces, and
unto his head.
18. And thou shalt
burn the whole ram upon
the altar: it is a burnt
offering unto the LORD: it *is*
a sweet savour, an
offering made by fire
unto the LORD.
19. And thou shalt
take the other ram; and Aaron
and his sons shall put their hands
upon the head of the ram.
20. Then shalt thou kill the ram,
and take of
his blood, and put

it upon the tip of the right ear of Aaron, and upon the tip of the right ear of his sons, and upon the thumb of their right hand, and upon the great toe of their right foot, and sprinkle the blood upon the altar round about. 21. **And** thou shalt **take of the blood** that *is* **upon the altar, and of the anointing oil, and sprinkle** *it* **upon Aaron, and** upon his garments, and upon **his sons,** and upon the garments of his sons with him: **and he shall be hallowed, and his garments, and his sons,** and his sons' garments **with him.** 22. **Also** thou shalt **take** of the ram **the fat and the rump, and the fat that covereth the inwards,** and the caul *above* the liver, and the two kidneys, and the fat that *is* upon them, **and the right shoulder; for it is a ram of consecration:** 23. **And** one loaf of **bread,** and one **cake** of oiled bread, **and one wafer out of the basket** of the unleavened bread **that is before the LORD:** 24. **And** thou shalt **put all in the hands of Aaron, and** in the hands of **his sons;** and shalt wave them **for a wave offering before the LORD.** 25. And thou shalt receive *them* of their hands, **and burn them upon the altar for a burnt offering, for a sweet savour before the LORD:** it *is* an offering made by fire unto the LORD. 26. **And** thou shalt **take the breast of**

the ram of Aaron's consecration, and wave it for a wave offering before the LORD: and it shall be thy part. 27. **And** thou shalt **sanctify the breast** of the wave offering, **and the shoulder of the heave offering,** which is waved, **and which is heaved up,** of the ram of the consecration, *even* of *that* which *is* for Aaron, and of *that* which is for his sons: 28. **And it shall be Aaron's and his sons' by a statute for ever** from the children of Israel: for it *is* an heave offering: and it shall be an heave offering from the children of Israel of the sacrifice of their peace offerings, *even* their heave offering unto the LORD. 29. **And the holy garments of Aaron shall be his sons' after him,** to be anointed therein, and to be consecrated in them. 30. **And that son that is priest in his stead shall put them on seven days, when he cometh into** the tabernacle of the congregation to minister in **the holy place.** 31. **And thou shalt take the ram** of the consecration, **and seethe his flesh in the holy place.** 32. **And Aaron and his sons shall eat the flesh** of the ram, **and the bread** that *is* in the basket **by the door of the tabernacle** of the congregation. 33. And they shall eat those things wherewith the atonement was made, to consecrate *and* to sanctify them: **but a stranger shall not eat thereof, because they are holy.** 34. **And if aught of the flesh** of the consecrations, **or** of the **bread, remain unto the morning, then** thou shalt **burn the remainder**

with fire: it shall not be
eaten, because it is holy.
35. And thus shalt thou
do unto Aaron, and to
his sons, according to all *things*
which I have commanded thee:
seven days shalt
thou consecrate them.
36. And thou shalt
offer every day a bullock
for a sin offering for
atonement: and thou shalt
cleanse the altar,
when thou hast made
an atonement for it, and
thou shalt anoint it, to sanctify it.
37. Seven days thou shalt
make an atonement for
the altar, and sanctify it;
and it shall be an altar
most holy: whatsoever
toucheth the altar
shall be holy.
38. Now this *is that* which thou shalt
offer upon the altar; two
lambs of the first year
day by day continually.
39. The one
lamb thou shalt offer
in the morning; and the
other lamb thou shalt offer
at even:
40. And with the one
lamb a tenth deal of
flour mingled with the
fourth part of an hin of beaten
oil; and the fourth part of an hin of
wine for a drink offering.
41. And the other
lamb thou shalt offer
at even, and shalt do thereto
according to the meat offering of the
morning, and according to the drink
offering thereof, for a sweet savour,
an offering made by
fire unto the LORD.
42. This shall be a
continual burnt offering
throughout your generations
at the door of the
tabernacle of the
congregation before the LORD:
where I will meet you,

to speak there unto thee.
43. And there I will meet with
the children of Israel, and
the tabernacle shall be
sanctified by my glory.
44. And I will sanctify the
tabernacle of the congregation,
and the altar: I will
sanctify also both
Aaron and his sons, to minister
to me in the priest's office.
45. And I will dwell
among the children of
Israel, and will be their God.
46. And they shall know
that I *am* the LORD their God, that
brought them forth
out of the land of
Egypt, that I may dwell
among them: I am
the LORD their God.

CHAPTER 30

1. And thou shalt
make an altar to
burn incense upon:
of shittim wood
shalt thou make it.
2. A cubit *shall be* the length thereof,
and a cubit the breadth thereof;
foursquare shall it be: and two
cubits *shall be* the height thereof: the
horns thereof *shall be* of the same.
3. And thou shalt
overlay it with pure gold, the
top thereof, and the sides thereof
round about, and the horns thereof;
and thou shalt
make unto it
a crown of gold
round about.
4. And two golden
rings shalt thou make to *it*
under the crown of it,
by the two
corners thereof, upon
the two sides of it shalt thou
make it; and they shall be
for places for the
staves to bear it withal.
5. And thou shalt
make the
staves of shittim

wood, and overlay them with gold.

6. **And** thou shalt **put it before the veil that is by the ark of the testimony,** before the mercy seat that *is* over the testimony, where I will meet with thee.

7. **And Aaron shall burn** thereon **sweet incense every morning: when he dresseth the lamps,** he shall burn incense upon it.

8. **And when Aaron lighteth the lamps at even, he shall burn incense upon it,** a perpetual incense before the LORD throughout your generations.

9. **Ye shall offer no strange incense thereon,** nor burnt sacrifice, nor meat offering; neither shall ye pour drink offering thereon.

10. **And Aaron shall make an atonement upon the horns** of it **once in a year with the blood of the sin offering** of atonements: once in the year shall he make atonement upon it throughout your generations: **it is** most **holy unto the LORD.**

11. **And the LORD spake unto Moses,** saying,

12. **When thou takest the sum of the children of Israel** after their number, **then shall they give every man a ransom for his soul unto the LORD,** when *thou* numberest them; **that there be no plague among them,** when thou numberest them.

13. **This they shall give,** every one that passeth among them that are numbered, half a shekel after the shekel of the sanctuary: (a shekel *is* twenty gerahs:) **an half shekel** *shall be* the **offering of the LORD.**

14. **Every one** that passeth among them that are numbered,

from twenty years old and above, shall give an offering unto the LORD.

15. **The rich shall not give more, and the poor shall not give less** than half a shekel, when *they* give an offering unto the LORD, **to make an atonement for your souls.**

16. **And** thou shalt **take the atonement money** of the children of Israel, **and** shalt **appoint it for the service of the tabernacle** of the congregation; that it may be a memorial unto the children of Israel before the LORD, to make an atonement for your souls.

17. **And the LORD spake unto Moses,** saying,

18. Thou shalt also **make a laver of brass, and** his **foot also of brass, to wash withal: and** thou shalt **put it between the tabernacle** of the congregation **and the altar, and** thou shalt **put water therein.**

19. **For Aaron and his sons shall wash their hands and their feet thereat:**

20. **When they go into the tabernacle** of the congregation, they shall wash with water, **that they die not;** or when they come near to the altar to minister, to burn offering made by fire unto the LORD:

21. So they shall wash their hands and their feet, that they die not: **and it shall be a statute for ever to them,** *even* to him and to his seed throughout their generations.

22. **Moreover the LORD spake unto Moses, saying,**

23. **Take** thou also unto thee principal **spices, of pure myrrh** five hundred *shekels,*

■ **and** of sweet
■ **cinnamon** half so much,
even two hundred
■ **and** fifty *shekels*, and of sweet
■ **calamus** two hundred
and fifty *shekels*,
■ 24. **And** of
■ **cassia** five hundred *shekels*,
after the shekel of the sanctuary,
■ **and** of
■ **oil** olive an hin:
■ 25. **And** thou shalt
■ **make** it an oil of holy ointment,
an ointment compound after the
art of the apothecary: it shall be
■ **an holy anointing oil.**
■ 26. **And** thou shalt
■ **anoint the tabernacle**
of the congregation therewith,
■ **and the ark** of the testimony,
■ 27. **And the table**
and all his vessels,
■ **and the candlestick**
and his vessels,
■ **and the altar of incense,**
■ 28. **And the altar of**
■ **burnt offering with all** his
■ **vessels, and the**
■ **laver** and his foot.
■ 29. **And** thou shalt
■ **sanctify them, that**
■ **they may be** most
■ **holy:** whatsoever
toucheth them shall be holy.
■ 30. **And** thou shalt
■ **anoint Aaron and his**
■ **sons, and consecrate**
■ **them**, that *they* may minister
unto me in the priest's office.
■ 31. **And** thou shalt
■ **speak unto** the children of
■ **Israel, saying, This shall**
■ **be an holy anointing oil** unto
me throughout your generations.
■ 32. **Upon man's flesh shall**
■ **it not be poured, neither**
■ **shall ye make any other**
■ **like it,** after the composition of it:
■ **it is holy,** *and* it shall
be holy unto you.
■ 33. **Whosoever**
■ **compoundeth any**
■ **like it, or** whosoever

■ **putteth** *any* of
■ **it upon a**
■ **stranger, shall** even
■ **be cut off from his people.**
■ 34. **And the LORD said unto**
■ **Moses, Take** unto thee sweet
■ **spices, stacte,**
■ **and onycha, and**
■ **galbanum;** *these* sweet spices
■ **with pure frankincense:** of
each shall there be a like *weight:*
■ 35. **And** thou shalt
■ **make** it
■ **a perfume,** a confection after
the art of the apothecary,
tempered together, pure *and* holy:
■ 36. **And** thou shalt
■ **beat** *some* of
■ **it very small, and put** of
■ **it before the testimony**
■ **in the tabernacle**
of the congregation,
■ **where I will meet with thee:**
it shall be unto you most holy.
■ 37. **And** *as for* the perfume
which thou shalt make,
■ **ye shall not make to**
■ **yourselves** according to
■ **the composition thereof:**
■ **it shall be** unto thee
■ **holy for the LORD.**
38. Whosoever shall make like
unto that, to smell thereto, shall
even be cut off from his people.

CHAPTER 31

■ 1. **And the LORD spake**
■ **unto Moses, saying,**
■ 2. **See, I have called** by name
■ **Bezaleel** the son of Uri, the
son of Hur, of the tribe of Judah:
■ 3. **And** I have
■ **filled him with the spirit of**
■ **God, in wisdom, and in**
■ **understanding, and in**
■ **knowledge, and in all**
■ **manner of workmanship,**
4. To devise cunning works, to work
in gold, and in silver, and in brass,
5. And in cutting of stones, to set
them, and in carving of timber, to
work in all manner of workmanship.
■ 6. **And I,** behold, I

have given with
him Aholiab, the son of
Ahisamach, of the tribe of Dan:
and in the hearts of all
that are wise hearted
I have put wisdom,
that they may make all that
I have commanded thee;
7. The tabernacle
of the congregation, and
the ark of the testimony, and
the mercy seat that *is*thereupon,
and all the furniture of the tabernacle,
8. And the table
and his furniture, and
the pure
candlestick with all his furniture,
and the altar of incense,
9. And the altar of burnt
offering with all his furniture,
and the laver and his foot,
10. And the cloths
of service, and
the holy garments
for Aaron the priest,
and the garments of
his sons, to minister
in the priest's office,
11. And the anointing oil,
and sweet incense for
the holy *place:* according to
all that I have commanded
thee shall they do.
12. And the LORD
spake unto Moses, saying,
13. Speak thou also
unto the children of
Israel, saying, Verily my
sabbaths ye shall keep: for
it is a sign between me and you
throughout your generations;
that ye may know that
I am the LORD that
doth sanctify you.
14. Ye shall keep
the sabbath therefore;
for it is holy unto you:
every one that
defileth it shall surely
be put to death: for whosoever
doeth *any* work therein, that soul shall
be cut off from among his people.
15. Six days may work be

done; but in the seventh is
the sabbath of rest, holy
to the LORD: whosoever doeth
any work in the sabbath day, he
shall surely be put to death.
16. Wherefore the children of
Israel shall keep the
sabbath, to observe the sabbath
throughout their generations,
for a perpetual covenant.
17. It is a sign between me
and the children of Israel for ever:
for in six days the LORD
made heaven and earth,
and on the seventh day he
rested, and was refreshed.
18. And he gave unto
Moses, when he had
made an end of communing
with him upon mount Sinai,
two tables of
testimony, tables of stone,
written with the
finger of God.

CHAPTER 32

1. And when the people saw that
Moses delayed to
come down out of the mount,
the people gathered
themselves together unto Aaron,
and said unto him, Up,
make us gods, which
shall go before us; for
as for this Moses, the man that
brought us up out of the land of Egypt,
we wot not what is
become of him.
2. And Aaron said unto them,
Break off the golden
earrings, which *are* in the
ears of your wives, of your
sons, and of your daughters,
and bring them unto me.
3. And all
the people brake off the golden
earrings which *were* in their ears, and
brought them unto Aaron.
4. And he received *them* at their
hand, and fashioned it with a
graving tool, after he had
made it
a molten calf: and they

said, These be
thy gods, O Israel,
which brought thee up
out of the land of
Egypt.
5. And when
Aaron saw *it,* he
built an altar
before it; and Aaron
made
proclamation, and said,
To-morrow is a
feast to the LORD.
6. And they rose up
early on the morrow, and
offered burnt
offerings, and brought
peace offerings;
and the people sat
down to eat and to
drink, and rose up to play.
7. And the LORD said
unto Moses, Go, get thee
down; for thy
people, which thou
broughtest out of the land of Egypt,
have corrupted
themselves:
8. They have turned aside
quickly out of the way which I
commanded them:
they have made them
a molten calf, and have
worshipped it, and have
sacrificed thereunto, and said,
These *be* thy gods, O Israel,
which have brought thee up
out of the land of Egypt.
9. And the LORD said
unto Moses, I have seen
this people, and, behold,
it is a stiffnecked people:
10. Now therefore
let me alone, that my wrath
may wax hot against them, and
that I may consume
them: and I will make
of thee a great nation.
11. And Moses besought
the LORD his God,
and said, LORD, why doth
thy wrath wax hot against thy
people, which thou hast brought forth
out of the land of Egypt with great
power, and with a mighty hand?
12. Wherefore should the
Egyptians speak, and
say, for mischief did he
bring them out to slay them
in the mountains, and to consume
them from the face of the earth?
Turn from thy fierce
wrath, and repent of this
evil against thy people.
13. Remember
Abraham, Isaac,
and Israel, thy servants,
to whom thou swarest by
thine own self, and saidst unto them,
I will multiply your seed
as the stars of heaven,
and all this land
that I have spoken of
will I give unto your seed,
and they shall inherit *it* for ever.
14. And the LORD
repented of the evil which
he thought to do unto his people.
15. And Moses turned, and
went down from the mount,
and the two tables of
the testimony were in his
hand: the tables *were* written on
both their sides; on the one side and
on the other *were* they written.
16. And the tables *were*
the work of God,
and the writing was the writing
of God, graven upon the tables.
17. And when Joshua
heard the noise of the
people as they shouted,
he said unto Moses,
There is a noise
of war in the camp.
18. And he said, It is
not the voice of *them that*
shout for mastery,
neither *is it*
the voice of *them that*
cry for being overcome:
but the noise of them
that sing do I hear.
19. And it came to pass, as soon
as he came nigh
unto the camp, that

he saw the
calf, and the dancing:
and Moses' anger
waxed hot, and he cast
the tables out of his hands,
and brake them
beneath the mount.
20. And he took the
calf which they had made,
and burnt it in the fire,
and ground it to
powder, and strawed
it upon the water,
and made the children of
Israel drink of it.
21. And Moses said unto Aaron,
What did this people unto thee,
that thou hast brought so great
a sin upon them?
22. And Aaron said, Let not
the anger of my lord wax
hot: thou knowest the people, that
they are set on mischief.
23. For they said unto me,
Make us gods, which shall
go before us: for *as for* this
Moses, the man that brought
us up out of the land of Egypt,
we wot not what is become of him.
24. And I said unto them,
Whosoever hath
any gold, let them
break it off. So they gave *it* me:
then I cast it into the
fire, and there came
out this calf.
25. And when Moses saw that
the people were naked; (for
Aaron had made them naked unto
their shame among *their* enemies:)
26. Then Moses stood
in the gate of the camp, and
said, Who is on the
LORD's side? *let him*
come unto me. And
all the sons of Levi
gathered themselves
together unto him.
27. And he said unto them,
Thus saith the
LORD God of Israel,
Put every man his
sword by his side,

and go in and out from gate to
gate throughout the camp,
and slay every man
his brother, and every man
his companion, and every
man his neighbour.
28. And the children of Levi
did according to the word of Moses:
and there fell of the people
that day about three
thousand men.
29. For Moses had
said, Consecrate
yourselves today to the
LORD, even every man upon
his son, and upon his brother;
that he may bestow upon you
a blessing this day.
30. And it came to pass
on the morrow, that
Moses said unto the people,
Ye have sinned a
great sin: and now
I will go up unto the LORD;
peradventure I shall make
an atonement for your sin.
31. And Moses
returned unto the
LORD, and said, Oh,
this people have
sinned a great sin,
and have made them
gods of gold.
32. Yet now, if thou wilt
forgive their sin—; and
if not, blot me, I pray thee,
out of thy book which
thou hast written.
33. And the LORD
said unto Moses,
Whosoever hath
sinned against me,
him will I blot out
of my book.
34. Therefore now
go, lead the people unto
the place of which I have
spoken unto thee: behold,
mine Angel shall go before thee:
nevertheless in the day when I visit
I will visit their sin upon them.
35. And the LORD
plagued the people,

because they made
the calf, which Aaron made.

CHAPTER 33

1. And the LORD said
unto Moses, Depart, *and*
go up hence,
thou and the people
which thou hast brought up
out of the land of Egypt,
unto the land which I
sware unto Abraham, to
Isaac, and to
Jacob, saying, Unto
thy seed will I give it:
2. And I will send an angel
before thee; and I will drive out
the Canaanite, the Amorite, and the
Hittite, and the Perizzite, the Hivite,
and the Jebusite:
3. Unto a land flowing
with milk and honey:
for I will not go up in the
midst of thee; for thou *art*
a stiffnecked people: lest I
consume thee in the way.
4. And when
the people heard
these evil tidings, they
mourned: and no man did
put on him his ornaments.
5. For the LORD had
said unto Moses, Say
unto the children of Israel,
Ye are a stiffnecked
people: I will come up into
the midst of thee in a moment,
and consume thee:
therefore now
put off thy
ornaments from thee,
that I may know
what to do unto thee.
6. And the children of
Israel stripped themselves
of their ornaments
by the mount Horeb.
7. And Moses took
the tabernacle, and
pitched it without the camp,
afar off from the
camp, and called it the
Tabernacle of the congregation.

And it came to pass, *that*
every one which sought
the LORD went out unto the
tabernacle of the congregation,
which *was* without the camp.
8. And it came to pass,
when Moses went out
unto the tabernacle, *that* all
the people rose up, and stood
every man *at* his tent door, and
looked after Moses,
until he was gone into
the tabernacle.
9. And it came to pass,
as Moses entered into the
tabernacle, the cloudy
pillar descended, and stood
at the door of the tabernacle,
and the Lord
talked with Moses.
10. And all the people
saw the cloudy pillar
stand *at* the tabernacle door:
and all the people rose up
and worshipped, every
man in his tent door.
11. And the LORD spake
unto Moses face to face,
as a man speaketh
unto his friend. And he
turned again into the
camp: but his servant
Joshua, the son of
Nun, a young man,
departed not out
of the tabernacle.
12. And Moses said
unto the LORD, See,
thou sayest unto me,
Bring up this people: and thou
hast not let me know whom thou wilt
send with me. Yet thou hast said, I
know thee by name, and thou hast
also found grace in my sight.
13. Now therefore,
I pray thee, if I have
found grace in thy sight;
shew me now thy way, that
I may know thee, that I may find
grace in thy sight: and consider
that this nation *is* thy people.
14. And he said, My
presence shall go with

134

CHAPTER 34

thee, and I will give thee rest.

15. **And he said unto him, If thy presence go not with me, carry us not up hence.**

16. **For wherein shall it be known** here **that I and thy people have found grace in thy sight?** *is it* not in that thou goest with us? **so shall we be separated,** I and thy people, **from all the people** that *are* **upon** the face of **the earth.**

17. **And the LORD said** unto Moses, **I will do this thing** also that thou hast spoken: **for thou hast found grace in my sight,** and I know thee by name.

18. **And he said,** I beseech thee, **shew me thy glory.**

19. **And he said, I will make all my goodness pass before thee,** and I will proclaim the name of the LORD before thee; **and will be gracious** to whom I will be gracious, **and** will **shew mercy on whom I will** shew mercy.

20. **And he said, Thou canst not see my face: for there shall no man see me, and live.**

21. **And the LORD said,** Behold, **there is a place by me,** and thou shalt stand upon a rock:

22. **And** it shall come to pass, **while my glory passeth by,** that **I will put thee in a clift of the rock, and** will **cover thee with my hand while I pass by:**

23. And I will take away mine hand, **and thou shalt see my back parts:** but my face shall not be seen.

1. **And the LORD said unto Moses, Hew** thee **two tables of stone** like unto the first: **and I will write upon these** tables **the words that were in the first tables,** which thou brakest.

2. And be ready in the morning, and **come up in the morning** unto mount Sinai, **and present thyself** there **to me** in the top of the mount.

3. **And no man shall come up with thee,** neither let any man be seen throughout all the mount; neither let the flocks nor herds feed before that mount.

4. **And he hewed two tables of stone** like unto the first; and Moses rose up early in the morning, **and went up unto mount Sinai,** as the LORD had commanded him, and took in his hand the two tables of stone.

5. **And the LORD descended in the cloud, and stood with him** there, and proclaimed the name of the LORD.

6. **And the LORD passed** by **before him, and proclaimed,** The LORD, **The LORD God, merciful and gracious, longsuffering, and abundant in goodness and truth,**

7. **Keeping mercy** for thousands, **forgiving iniquity and** transgression and sin, and that **will by no means clear the guilty; visiting the iniquity of the fathers upon** the children, and upon the children's children, unto **the third and** to the **fourth generation.**

8. **And Moses** made haste, and **bowed his head** toward the earth,

135

and worshipped.

9. And he said, If now I have found grace in thy sight, O LORD, let my LORD, I pray thee, go among us; for it is a stiffnecked people; and pardon our iniquity and our sin, and take us for thine inheritance.

10. And he said, Behold, I make a covenant: before all thy people I will do marvels, such as have not been done in all the earth, nor in any nation: and all the people among which thou art shall see the work of the LORD: for it is a terrible thing that I will do with thee. 11. Observe thou that which I command thee this day: behold, I drive out before thee the Amorite, and the Canaanite, and the Hittite, and the Perizzite, and the Hivite, and the Jebusite. 12. Take heed to thyself, lest thou make a covenant with the inhabitants of the land whither thou goest, lest it be for a snare in the midst of thee: 13. But ye shall destroy their altars, break their images, and cut down their groves: 14. For thou shalt worship no other god: for the LORD, whose name is Jealous, is a jealous God: 15. Lest thou make a covenant with the inhabitants of the land, and they go a whoring after their gods, and do sacrifice unto their gods, and one call thee, and thou eat of his sacrifice; 16. And thou take of their daughters unto thy sons, and their daughters go a whoring after their gods, and make thy sons go a whoring after their gods. 17. Thou shalt make thee no molten gods.

18. The feast of unleavened bread shalt thou keep. Seven days thou shalt eat unleavened bread, as I commanded thee, in the time of the month Abib: for in the month Abib thou camest out from Egypt.

19. All that openeth the matrix is mine; and every firstling among thy cattle, whether ox or sheep, that is male.

20. But the firstling of an ass thou shalt redeem with a lamb: and if thou redeem him not, then shalt thou break his neck. All the firstborn of thy sons thou shalt redeem. And none shall appear before me empty.

21. Six days thou shalt work, but on the seventh day thou shalt rest: in earing time and in harvest thou shalt rest.

22. And thou shalt observe the feast of weeks, of the firstfruits of wheat harvest, and the feast of ingathering at the year's end.

23. Thrice in the year shall all your men children appear before the LORD God, the God of Israel.

24. For I will cast out the nations before thee, and enlarge thy borders: neither shall any man desire thy land, when thou shalt go up to appear before the LORD thy God thrice in the year.

25. Thou shalt not offer the blood of my sacrifice with leaven; neither shall the sacrifice of the feast of the passover be left unto the morning.

26. The first of the firstfruits of thy land thou shalt bring unto the house of the LORD thy God. Thou shalt not seethe a kid in his mother's milk.

27. **And the LORD said unto Moses, Write** thou these words: **for** after the tenor of these words **I have made a covenant with thee and with Israel.** 28. **And he was there with the LORD forty days and** forty **nights; he did neither eat** bread, **nor drink** water. **And he wrote** upon the tables **the words of the covenant, the ten commandments.** 29. **And** it came to pass, **when Moses came down** from mount Sinai **with the two tables of testimony** in Moses' hand, when **he** came down from the mount, that Moses **wist not that the skin of his face shone** while he talked with him. 30. **And** when **Aaron and all** the children of **Israel** saw Moses, behold, the skin of his face shone; and they **were afraid to come nigh him.** 31. **And Moses** called unto them; and Aaron and all the rulers of the congregation returned unto him: and Moses **talked with them.** 32. And afterward all the children of Israel came nigh: **and he gave them in commandment all that the LORD had spoken with him** in mount Sinai. 33. **And till Moses had done speaking with them, he put a veil on his face.** 34. **But** when Moses went in **before the LORD** to speak with him, **he took the veil off, until he came out.** And he came out, and spake unto the children of Israel *that* which he was commanded. 35. **And** the children of Israel saw **the face of Moses,** that the skin of Moses' face **shone: and Moses put the veil upon his face** again, **until he went in to speak with him.**

CHAPTER 35

1. **And Moses gathered all the congregation** of the children of Israel **together, and said** unto them, **These are the words** which **the LORD** hath **commanded,** that *ye* should do them. 2. **Six days shall work be done, but** on **the seventh day** there **shall be** to you an **holy** day, **a sabbath of rest to the LORD: whosoever doeth work therein shall be put to death.** 3. **Ye shall kindle no fire** throughout your habitations **upon the sabbath day.** 4. And Moses spake unto all the congregation of the children of Israel, saying, This *is* the thing which the LORD commanded, saying, 5. **Take** ye from among you **an offering unto the LORD: whosoever is** of a **willing** heart, **let him bring** it, **an offering of** the LORD; **gold, and silver, and brass,** 6. **And blue, and purple, and scarlet, and fine** linen, and goats' hair, 7. **And rams' skins dyed red, and badgers' skins, and shittim wood,** 8. **And oil** for the light, **and spices** for anointing oil, and for the sweet incense, 9. **And onyx stones, and stones** to be set **for the ephod, and** for the

137

breastplate.

10. **And every wise hearted among you shall come, and make all that the LORD hath commanded;**

11. **The tabernacle,** his tent, and his covering, his taches, and his boards, his bars, his pillars, and his sockets,

12. **The ark,** and the staves thereof, *with* the mercy seat, and the veil of the covering,

13. **The table,** and his staves, and all his vessels, and the shewbread,

14. **The candlestick** also for the light, and his furniture, and his lamps, with the oil for the light,

15. **And the incense altar,** and his staves, and the anointing oil, and the sweet incense, and the hanging for the door at the entering in of the tabernacle,

16. **The altar of burnt offering,** with his brasen grate, his staves, and all his vessels, the laver and his foot,

17. **The hangings of the court,** his pillars, and their sockets, **and** the hanging **for the door** of the court,

18. **The pins** of the tabernacle, and the pins of the court, and **their cords,**

19. **The cloths of service,** to do service in the holy *place,* **the holy garments for Aaron** the priest, **and** the garments of **his sons,** to minister in the priest's office.

20. **And all the congregation of** the children of Israel **departed from** the presence of **Moses.**

21. **And** they came, **every one whose heart stirred him** up, **and** every one whom **his spirit made willing, and they brought the LORD's offering** to the work of the tabernacle of the congregation, and for all his service, and for the holy garments.

22. **And they came, both men and women, as many as were willing hearted, and brought** bracelets, and earrings, and rings, and tablets, all jewels of gold: and every man that offered *offered* **an offering** of gold **unto the LORD.**

23. And every man, with whom was found blue, and purple, and scarlet, and fine linen, and goats' *hair,* and red skins of rams, and badgers' skins, brought *them.*

24. Every one that did offer an offering of silver and brass brought the LORD's offering: and every man, with whom was found shittim wood for any work of the service, brought *it.*

25. **And** all **the women** that were wise-hearted **did spin with their hands, and brought** that which they had spun, **both** of **blue,** and of **purple,** *and* of **scarlet, and** of **fine linen.**

26. **And** all the women whose heart stirred them up in wisdom spun **goats' hair.**

27. **And the rulers brought** onyx **stones,** and stones to be set, **for the ephod, and** for the **breastplate;**

28. **And spice, and oil** for the light, and for the anointing oil, and for the sweet incense.

29. **The children of Israel brought a willing offering** unto the LORD, every man and woman, whose heart made them willing to bring **for all manner of work, which the LORD** had **commanded to be made** by the hand of Moses.

30. **And Moses said**

unto the children of Israel, See,
■ **the LORD hath called** by name
■ **Bezaleel** the son of Uri, the
son of Hur, of the tribe of Judah;
■ 31. **And** he hath
■ **filled him with the spirit**
■ **of God,** in wisdom, in
understanding, and in knowledge,
and in all manner of workmanship;
32. And to devise curious works,
to work in gold, and in silver,
and in brass,
33. And in the cutting of stones, to
set *them*, and in carving of wood, to
make any manner of cunning work.
■ 34. **And he hath put in his**
■ **heart that he may teach,**
■ **both he, and Aholiab,** the son
of Ahisamach, of the tribe of Dan.
■ 35. **Them hath he filled**
■ **with wisdom** of heart,
■ **to work all manner of work,**
of the engraver, and of the cunning
workman, and of the embroiderer,
in blue, and in purple, in scarlet,
and in fine linen, and of the weaver,
■ **even of them that do any**
■ **work, and of those that**
■ **devise cunning work.**

CHAPTER 36

1. Then wrought Bezaleel and
Aholiab, and every wise hearted man,
in whom the LORD put wisdom and
understanding to know how to work
all manner of work for the service of
the sanctuary, according to all that
the LORD had commanded.
■ 2. **And Moses called**
■ **Bezaleel and Aholiab,**
■ **and every wise hearted**
■ **man,** in whose heart the LORD
had put wisdom, *even* every one
whose heart stirred him up
■ **to come unto the**
■ **work to do it:**
■ 3. **And they**
■ **received** of Moses all
■ **the offering,**
■ **which** the children of
■ **Israel had brought**
■ **for** the work of the service of
■ **the sanctuary,**

■ **to make it** *withal.*
■ **And they**
■ **brought** yet unto him free
■ **offerings every morning.**
■ 4. **And all the wise**
■ **men, that wrought** all
■ **the work of the**
■ **sanctuary, came** every man
from his work which they made;
■ 5. **And** they
■ **spake unto Moses,** saying,
■ **The people bring** much
■ **more than enough** for the
service of the work, which
the LORD commanded to make.
■ 6. **And Moses gave**
■ **commandment,** and they
caused it to be proclaimed
throughout the camp, saying,
■ **Let neither man nor woman**
■ **make any more** work
■ **for the offering** of the sanctuary.
■ **So the people were**
■ **restrained from bringing.**
■ 7. **For** the stuff
■ **they had** was
■ **sufficient for all the**
■ **work** to make it, and too much.
■ 8. **And** every
wise-hearted man among
■ **them that wrought the work**
■ **of the tabernacle** made ten
curtains *of* fine twined linen, and
blue, and purple, and scarlet:
with cherubims of cunning
work made he them.
9. The length of one curtain *was*
twenty and eight cubits, and the
breadth of one curtain four cubits:
the curtains *were* all of one size.
10. And he coupled the five curtains
one unto another: and the *other* five
curtains he coupled one unto another.
11. And he made loops of blue on
the edge of one curtain from the
selvedge in the coupling: likewise he
made in the uttermost side of *another*
curtain, in the coupling of the second.
12. Fifty loops made he in one
curtain, and fifty loops made he in
the edge of the curtain which *was* in
the coupling of the second: the
loops held one *curtain* to another.

13. And he made fifty taches of gold, and coupled the curtains one unto another with the taches: so it became one tabernacle.

14. And he **made curtains** of goats' *hair* **for the tent over the tabernacle:** eleven curtains he made them.

15. The length of one curtain *was* thirty cubits, and four cubits *was* the breadth of one curtain: the eleven curtains *were* of one size.

16. And he coupled five curtains by themselves, and six curtains by themselves.

17. And he made fifty loops upon the uttermost edge of the curtain in the coupling, and fifty loops made he upon the edge of the curtain which coupleth the second.

18. And he made fifty taches *of* brass to couple the tent together, that it might be one.

19. **And he made a covering for the tent** *of* rams' skins dyed red, and a covering *of* badgers' skins above *that.*

20. **And he made boards for the tabernacle** *of* shittim wood, standing up.

21. The length of a board *was* ten cubits, and the breadth of a board one cubit and a half.

22. One board had two tenons, equally distant one from another: thus did he make for all the boards of the tabernacle.

23. And he made boards for the tabernacle; twenty boards for the south side southward:

24. And forty sockets of silver he made under the twenty boards; two sockets under one board for his two tenons, and two sockets under another board for his two tenons.

25. And for the other side of the tabernacle, *which is* toward the north corner, he made twenty boards,

26. And their forty sockets of silver; two sockets under one board, and two sockets under another board.

27. And for the sides of the tabernacle westward he made six boards.

28. And two boards made he for the corners of the tabernacle in the two sides.

29. And they were coupled beneath, and coupled together at the head thereof, to one ring: thus he did to both of them in both the corners.

30. And there were eight boards; and their sockets *were* sixteen sockets of silver, under every board two sockets.

31. **And he made bars** of shittim wood; five **for the boards of** the one side of the tabernacle,

32. And five bars for the boards of the other side of the tabernacle, and five bars for the boards of the tabernacle for the sides westward.

33. And he made the middle bar to shoot through the boards from the one end to the other.

34. **And he overlaid the boards with gold, and made their rings of gold** *to be* places for the bars, **and overlaid the bars with gold.**

35. **And he made a veil** *of* blue, and purple, and scarlet, and fine twined linen: *with* cherubims made he it of cunning work.

36. **And** he made thereunto four **pillars** *of* shittim *wood,* and overlaid them with gold: their hooks *were of* gold; and he cast for them four sockets of silver.

37. **And he made an hanging for the tabernacle door** *of* blue, and purple, and scarlet, and fine twined linen, of needlework;

38. And the five pillars of it with their hooks: and he overlaid their chapiters and their fillets with gold: but their five sockets *were of* brass.

CHAPTER 37

1. **And Bezaleel made the ark** *of* shittim wood: two cubits and a half *was* the length of it, and a

cubit and a half the breadth of it, and a cubit and a half the height of it:

■ 2. **And he overlaid it with** ■ **pure gold** within and without, and made a crown of gold to it round about.

■ 3. **And he cast for it four** ■ **rings of gold,** *to be set* by the four corners of it; even two rings upon the one side of it, and two rings upon the other side of it.

■ 4. **And he made staves** *of* shittim wood, and overlaid them with gold.

■ 5. **And he put the staves** ■ **into the rings by the sides** ■ **of the ark,** to bear the ark.

■ 6. **And he made the** ■ **mercy seat of pure gold:** two cubits and a half *was* the length thereof, and one cubit and a half the breadth thereof.

■ 7. **And he made two** ■ **cherubims of gold, beaten** ■ **out of one piece** made he them, on the two ends of the mercy seat;

8. One cherub on the end on this side, and another cherub on the *other* end on that side: out of the mercy seat made he the cherubims on the two ends thereof.

9. And the cherubims spread out *their* wings on high, *and* covered with their wings over the mercy seat, with their faces one to another; *even* to the mercy seatward were the faces of the cherubims.

■ 10. **And he made the table** *of* shittim wood: two cubits *was* the length thereof, and a cubit the breadth thereof, and a cubit and a half the height thereof:

■ 11. **And he overlaid it with** ■ **pure gold,** and made thereunto a crown of gold round about.

12. Also he made thereunto a border of an handbreadth round about; and made a crown of gold for the border thereof round about.

13. And he cast for it four rings of gold, and put the rings upon the four corners that *were* in the four feet thereof.

14. Over against the border were the rings, the places for the staves to bear the table.

■ 15. **And he made the** ■ **staves** *of* shittim wood, and ■ **overlaid** them ■ **with gold, to bear the** ■ **table.**

■ 16. **And the made the vessels** ■ **which were upon the table,** his dishes, and his spoons, and his bowls, and his covers to cover withal, *of* pure gold.

■ 17. **And he made the** ■ **candlestick of pure** ■ **gold:** *of* beaten work made he the candlestick; his shaft, and his branch, his bowls, his knops, and his flowers, were of the same:

18. And six branches going out of the sides thereof; three branches of the candlestick out of the one side thereof, and three branches of the candlestick out of the other side thereof:

19. Three bowls made after the fashion of almonds in one branch, a knop and a flower; and three bowls made like almonds in another branch, a knop and a flower: so throughout the six branches going out of the candlestick.

20. And in the candlestick *were* four bowls made like almonds, his knops, and his flowers:

21. And a knop under two branches of the same, and a knop under two branches of the same, and a knop under two branches of the same, according to the six branches going out of it.

22. Their knops and their branches were of the same: all of it *was* one beaten work *of* pure gold.

■ 23. **And he made** his even ■ **lamps, and** his ■ **snuffers, and** his ■ **snuffdishes, of pure gold.**

■ 24. **Of a talent of pure** ■ **gold made he it, and** ■ **all the vessels** thereof.

■ 25. **And he made the** ■ **incense altar** *of* shittim wood:

the length of it *was* a cubit, and the breadth of it a cubit; *it was* foursquare; and two cubits *was* the height of it; the horns thereof were of the same.

26. **And he overlaid it with pure gold,** *both* the top of it, and the sides thereof round about, and the horns of it: also he made unto it a crown of gold round about.

27. And he made two rings of gold for it under the crown thereof, by the two corners of it, upon the two sides thereof, to be places for the staves to bear it withal.

28. And he made the staves *of* shittim wood, and overlaid them with gold.

29. **And he made the holy anointing oil, and** the pure **incense of sweet spices,** according to the work of the apothecary

CHAPTER 38

1. **And he made the altar of burnt offering** of shittim wood: five cubits *was* the length thereof, and five cubits the breadth thereof; *it was* foursquare; and three cubits the height thereof.

2. **And he made the horns** thereof on the four corners of it; the horns thereof were of the same: and he **overlaid** it **with brass.**

3. **And** he made **all the vessels of the altar,** the pots, and the shovels, and the basins, *and* the fleshhooks, and the firepans: all the vessels thereof **made he of brass.**

4. And he made for the altar a brasen grate of network under the compass thereof beneath unto the midst of it.

5. **And he cast four rings** for the four ends of the grate **of brass,** *to be* places for the staves.

6. **And he made the staves** *of* shittim wood, and **overlaid** them **with brass.**

7. **And he put the staves into the rings** on the sides of the altar, **to bear it** withal; he made the altar hollow with boards.

8. **And he made the laver of brass, and the foot** of it of brass, of the looking glasses of *the women* assembling, which assembled *at* the door of the tabernacle of the congregation.

9. **And he made** the court: on the south side southward the **hangings of the court** *were of* fine twined linen, an hundred cubits:

10. **Their pillars** *were* twenty, **and** their brasen **sockets** twenty; the hooks of the pillars and their fillets *were* of silver.

11. And for the north side *the hangings were* an hundred cubits, their pillars *were* twenty, and their sockets of brass twenty; the hooks of the pillars and their fillets *of* silver.

12. And for the west side *were* hangings of fifty cubits, their pillars ten, and their sockets ten; the hooks of the pillars and their fillets *of* silver.

13. And for the east side eastward fifty cubits.

14. The hangings of the one side *of the gate were* fifteen cubits; their pillars three, and their sockets three.

15. And for the other side of the court gate, on this hand and that hand, *were* hangings of fifteen cubits; their pillars three, and their sockets three.

16. All the hangings of the court round about *were* of fine twined linen.

17. And the sockets for the pillars *were of* brass; the hooks of the pillars and their fillets *of* silver; and the overlaying of their chapiters *of* silver; and all the pillars of the court *were* filleted with silver.

18. **And the hanging for the gate** of the court *was* needlework, *of* blue, and purple, and scarlet, and fine twined linen: and twenty cubits *was* the length, and the height in the breadth *was* five cubits, answerable to the hangings of the court.

19. **And their pillars** *were* four, and their sockets *of* brass

four; their hooks *of* silver, and the overlaying of their chapiters and their fillets *of* silver.

20. **And all the pins of the tabernacle,** and of the court round about, *were of* brass.

21. **This is the sum** of the tabernacle, *even* **of the tabernacle of testimony, as it was counted,** according to the commandment of Moses, **for the service of the Levites, by** the hand of **Ithamar, son to Aaron** the priest.

22. **And Bezaleel** the son Uri, the son of Hur, of the tribe of Judah, **made all that the LORD commanded Moses.**

23. **And with him was Aholiab**, son of Ahisamach, of the tribe of Dan, **an engraver, and a cunning workman,** and an embroiderer in blue, and in purple, and in scarlet, and fine linen.

24. **All the gold** that was occupied **for the work** in all the work **of the holy place,** even the gold of the offering, **was twenty** and **nine talents, and seven hundred** and **thirty shekels,** after the shekel of the sanctuary.

25. **And the silver** of them that were numbered of the congregation **was an hundred talents, and a thousand seven hundred** and **threescore and fifteen shekels,** after the shekel of the sanctuary:

26. A bekah for every man, *that is,* **half a shekel,** after the shekel of the sanctuary, **for every one** that went to be **numbered, from twenty years old and upward,** for **six hundred** thousand **and three thousand** and **five hundred and fifty men.**

27. **And of the hundred talents of silver were cast the sockets of the sanctuary, and** the sockets of **the veil; an hundred sockets of the hundred talents,** a talent for a socket.

28. **And** of the **thousand seven hundred seventy** and **five shekels he made hooks for the pillars, and overlaid their chapiters, and filleted them.**

29. **And the brass of the offering was seventy talents, and two thousand** and **four hundred shekels.**

30. **And** therewith **he made the sockets to the door** of the tabernacle of the congregation, and **the brasen altar, and the** brasen **grate for it, and all the vessels of the altar,**

31. **And the sockets of the court** round about, **and** the sockets of **the court gate, and all the pins of the tabernacle, and** all the pins of **the court round about.**

CHAPTER 39

1. **And** of the blue, and purple, and scarlet, **they made cloths** of service, **to do service in the holy place, and** made the **holy garments for Aaron;** as the LORD commanded Moses.

2. **And he made the ephod** *of* gold, blue, and purple, and scarlet, and fine twined linen.

3. **And they** did **beat the gold into thin plates, and cut it into wires, to**

■ **work it in the blue,** and in the
■ **purple, and** in the
■ **scarlet,** and in the fine
linen, *with* cunning work.

4. They made shoulderpieces for it, to couple *it* together: by the two edges was it coupled together.

5. And the curious girdle of his ephod, that *was* upon it, *was* of the same, according to the work thereof; *of* gold, blue, and purple, and scarlet, and fine twined linen; as the LORD commanded Moses.

■ 6. **And they wrought onyx**
■ **stones** inclosed in ouches of gold, graven, as signets are graven,
■ **with the names of the**
■ **children of Israel.**

7. And he put them on the shoulders of the ephod, *that they should be* stones for a memorial to the children of Israel; as the LORD commanded Moses.

■ 8. **And he made the**
■ **breastplate of cunning**
■ **work,** like the work of the ephod; of gold, blue, and purple, and scarlet, and fine twined linen.

9. It was foursquare; they made the breastplate double: a span *was* the length thereof, and a span the breadth thereof, *being* doubled.

■ 10. **And they set in it four**
■ **rows of stones:** *the first* row *was* a sardius, a topaz, and a carbuncle: this *was* the first row.

11. And the second row, an emerald, a sapphire, and a diamond.

12. And the third row, a ligure, an agate, and an amethyst.

13. And the fourth row, a beryl, an onyx, and a jasper: *they were* enclosed in ouches of gold in their enclosings.

■ 14. **And the stones were** according to the names of the children of Israel, twelve, according to their names, *like* the engravings of a signet, every one with his name,
■ **according to the**
■ **twelve tribes.**
■ 15. **And they made** upon the breastplate

■ **chains** at the ends,
of wreathen work
■ **of pure gold.**
■ 16. **And** they made two ouches of gold, and two
■ **gold rings;** and put the two rings in the two ends of the breastplate.
■ 17. **And they**
■ **put the** two wreathen
■ **chains** of gold
■ **in the** two
■ **rings on the** ends of the
■ **breastplate.**

18. And the two ends of the two wreathen chains they fastened in the two ouches, and put them on the shoulderpieces of the ephod, before it.

19. And they made two rings of gold, and put *them* on the two ends of the breastplate, upon the border of it, which *was* on the side of the ephod inward.

■ 20. **And they made** two *other*
■ **golden rings, and put**
■ **them on** the two sides of
■ **the ephod** underneath, toward the forepart of it, over against the *other* coupling thereof, above the curious girdle of the ephod.

21. And they did bind the breastplate by his rings unto the rings of the ephod with a lace of blue, that it might be above the curious girdle of the ephod, and that the breastplate might not be loosed from the ephod; as the LORD commanded Moses.

■ 22. **And he made the**
■ **robe of the ephod** of woven work, all *of* blue.

23. And *there was* an hole in the midst of the robe, as the hole of an habergeon, *with* a band round about the hole, that it should not rend.

■ 24. **And** they made
■ **upon the hems of the robe**
■ **pomegranates** *of* blue, and purple, and scarlet, *and* twined *linen.*
■ 25. **And** they made
■ **bells of pure gold, and**
■ **put the bells between the**
■ **pomegranates upon the**
■ **hem of the robe,** round

about between the pomegranates;

26. A bell and a pomegranate, a bell and a pomegranate, round about the hem of the robe to minister *in*; as the LORD commanded Moses.

27. **And they made coats** of fine linen *of* woven work for Aaron, and for his sons,

28. **And a mitre** *of* fine linen, and goodly **bonnets** *of* fine linen, **and** linen **breeches** *of* fine twined linen,

29. **And a girdle** *of* fine twined linen, and blue, and purple, and scarlet, *of* needlework; **as the LORD commanded Moses.**

30. **And they made the plate of the holy crown** *of* pure gold, **and wrote upon it** a writing, *like to* the engravings of a signet, **HOLINESS TO THE LORD.**

31. And they tied unto it a lace of blue, to fasten *it* on high upon the mitre; as the LORD commanded Moses.

32. **Thus was** all **the work of the tabernacle** of the tent of the congregation **finished: and the children of Israel did** according to **all that the LORD commanded Moses:** so did they.

33. **And they brought the tabernacle unto Moses, the tent:** and all his furniture, his taches, his boards, his bars, and his pillars, and his sockets,

34. **And the covering** of rams' skins dyed red, and the covering of badgers' skins, and the veil of the covering,

35. **The ark** of the testimony, and the staves thereof, and the mercy seat,

36. **The table,** *and* all the vessels thereof, and the shewbread,

37. **The** pure **candlestick,** *with* the lamps thereof, *even with* the lamps to be set in order, and all the vessels

thereof, and the oil for light,

38. **And the golden altar,** and the anointing oil, and the sweet incense, and the hanging for the tabernacle door,

39. **The brasen altar,** and his grate of brass, his staves, and all his vessels, the laver and his foot,

40. **The hangings of the court,** his pillars, and his sockets, and the hanging for the court gate, his cords, and his pins, and all the vessels of the service of the tabernacle, for the tent of the congregation,

41. **The cloths of service** to do service in the holy *place,* **and the holy garments** for Aaron the priest, and his sons' garments, to minister in the priest's office.

42. According to all that the LORD commanded Moses, so the children of Israel made all the work.

43. **And Moses did look upon** all **the work,** and, behold, **they had done** it **as the LORD** had **commanded,** even so had they done it: **and Moses blessed them.**

CHAPTER 40

1. **And the LORD spake unto Moses, saying,**

2. **On the first day of the first month** shalt thou **set up the tabernacle** of the tent of the congregation.

3. **And** thou shalt **put therein the ark** of the testimony, **and cover the ark with the veil.**

4. **And** thou shalt **bring in the table, and set in order the things** that are to be set in order **upon it; and** thou shalt **bring in the candlestick, and light the lamps** thereof.

5. **And** thou shalt

set the altar of gold for the
incense before
the ark of the testimony,
and put the hanging of the
door to the tabernacle.
6. And thou shalt
set the altar of the
burnt offering before
the door of the tabernacle
of the tent of the congregation.
7. And thou shalt
set the laver between
the tent of the congregation
and the altar, and shalt
put water therein.
8. And thou shalt
set up the court round about,
and hang up the hanging
at the court gate.
9. And thou shalt
take the anointing oil,
and anoint the tabernacle,
and all that is therein, and shalt
hallow it, and all
the vessels thereof:
and it shall be holy.
10. And thou shalt
anoint the altar of the burnt offering,
and all his vessels,
and sanctify the altar:
and it shall be an altar most
holy.
11. And thou shalt
anoint the laver and his foot,
and sanctify it.
12. And thou shalt
bring Aaron and his
sons unto the door of the
tabernacle of the congregation,
and wash them with water.
13. And thou shalt
put upon Aaron the holy
garments, and anoint him,
and sanctify him; that he may
minister unto me in the priest's office.
14. And thou shalt
bring his sons,
and clothe them with coats:
15. And thou shalt
anoint them, as thou didst anoint
their father, that they may minister
unto me in the priest's office:
for their anointing

shall surely
be an
everlasting priesthood throughout
their generations.
16. Thus did Moses:
according to all that the LORD
commanded him, so did he.
17. And it came to pass
in the first month in
the second year, on the
first day of the month, that
the tabernacle
was reared up.
18. And Moses reared up the
tabernacle, and fastened his
sockets, and set up the boards
thereof, and put in the bars thereof,
and reared up his pillars.
19. And he spread abroad the tent
over the tabernacle, and put the
covering of the tent above upon it;
as the LORD
commanded Moses.
20. And he took and
put the testimony into
the ark, and set the staves
on the ark, and put the mercy
seat above upon the ark:
21. And he brought the ark
into the tabernacle, and
set up the veil of the covering,
and covered the ark
of the testimony; as the
LORD commanded Moses.
22. And he put the table in
the tent of the congregation, upon the
side of the tabernacle northward,
without the veil.
23. And he set the bread in
order upon it before the LORD;
as the LORDhad commanded Moses.
24. And he put the
candlestick in the tent
of the congregation, over
against the table, on the side
of the tabernacle southward.
25. And he lighted the
lamps before the LORD; as
the LORD commanded Moses.
26. And he put the golden
altar in the tent of the congregation
before the veil:
27. And he burnt sweet

■ incense thereon; as
the LORD commanded Moses.
■ 28. **And he set up the**
■ **hanging at the door**
■ **of the tabernacle.**
■ 29. **And he put the altar**
■ **of burnt offering by the**
■ **door** of the tabernacle of
the tent of the congregation,
■ **and offered** upon it the
■ **burnt offering and the**
■ **meat offering; as the**
■ **LORD commanded** Moses.
■ 30. **And he set the**
■ **laver between the**
■ **tent** of the congregation
■ **and the altar, and put**
■ **water there, to wash** withal.
■ 31. **And Moses and Aaron**
■ **and his sons washed**
■ **their hands and** their
■ **feet** thereat:
■ 32. **When they went into**
■ **the tent** of the congregation,
■ **and** when they
■ **came near** unto
■ **the altar,** they washed;
as the LORD commanded Moses.
■ 33. **And he reared up the**
■ **court round** about

■ **the tabernacle**and the altar, and
set up the hanging of the court gate.
■ **So Moses finished**
■ **the work.**
■ 34. **Then a cloud covered**
■ **the tent** of the congregation,
■ **and the glory of the LORD**
■ **filled the tabernacle**.
■ 35. **And Moses was**
■ **not able to enter** into
the tent of the congregation,
■ **because the cloud**
■ **abode thereon,** and the glory
of the LORD filled the tabernacle.
■ 36. **And when the cloud was**
■ **taken up** from over the tabernacle,
■ **the children of Israel**
■ **went onward in** all
■ **their journeys:**
■ 37. **But if the cloud**
■ **were not taken up,** then
■ **they journeyed**
■ **not** till the day that it was taken up.
■ 38. **For the cloud** of the LORD
■ **was upon the tabernacle by**
■ **day, and fire** was on it
■ **by night, in**
■ **the sight** of all the house
■ **of Israel, throughout**
■ **all their journeys.**

THE
TEN COMMANDMENTS

1. *Thou Shalt Have No Other gods Before Me.*

2. *Thou Shalt Not Make Unto Thee Any Graven Image.*

3. *Thou Shalt Not Take the Name of the Lord Thy God in Vain.*

4. *Remember the Sabbath Day, to Keep it Holy.*

5. *Honor Thy Father and Thy Mother.*

6. *Thou Shalt Not Kill.*

7. *Thou Shalt Not Commit Adultery.*

8. *Thou Shalt Not Steal.*

9. *Thou Shalt Not Bear False Witness Against Thy Neighbor.*

10. *Thou Shalt Not Covet.*

THE BOOK OF LEVITICUS

BACKGROUND INFORMATION

Author: Moses according to tradition

Date Written: Usually considered to be **between 1491 — 1451 B.C.**

Number of:
Verses—851
Chapters —27
Total Words—24,546
Scan Words—11,018
Scan Words Represent Approximately 44% of Total Words

Theme: How the Lord Sets Apart Israel by Giving Specific Standards of Morality, Conduct, and Worship.

OUTLINE OF THE BOOK

CHAPTER 1

1. **And the LORD called** unto **Moses,** and spake unto him out of the tabernacle of the congregation, **saying,**

2. **Speak unto** the children of **Israel, and say** unto them, **If any man** of you **bring an offering unto the LORD, ye shall bring your offering of the cattle,** *even* of the herd, and of the flock.

3. If his offering *be* a burnt sacrifice of the herd, **let him offer a male without blemish:** he shall offer it **of his own** voluntary **will at the door of the tabernacle** of the congregation before the LORD.

4. And he shall put his hand upon the head of the burnt offering; **and it shall be accepted** for him **to make atonement for him.**

5. **And he shall kill the bullock** before the LORD: **and the priests,** Aaron's sons, **shall** bring the blood, and **sprinkle the blood** round about **upon the altar** that *is by* the door of the tabernacle of the congregation.

6. **And he shall** flay the burnt offering, and **cut it into his pieces.**

7. **And** the sons of Aaron **the priest shall put fire upon the altar,** and lay the wood in order upon the fire:

8. **And** the priests, Aaron's sons, shall **lay the parts,** the head, and the fat, in order **upon the wood** that *is* on the fire which *is* upon the altar:

9. **But his inwards and** his **legs shall he wash** in water: **and the priest shall burn all on the altar, to be** a burnt sacrifice, **an offering** made by fire, **of a sweet savour unto the LORD.**

10. **And if his offering be** of the flocks, *namely*, of the **sheep, or** of the **goats,** for a burnt sacrifice; **he shall bring** it **a male without blemish.**

11. **And** he shall **kill it on the side of the altar northward** before the LORD: **and the priests,** Aaron's sons, **shall sprinkle his blood** round **about** upon **the altar.**

12. **And** he shall **cut it into** his **pieces,** with his head and his fat: **and** the priest shall **lay them** in order **on the wood** that *is* **on the fire** which *is* **upon the altar:**

13. **But he shall wash the inwards and the legs** with water: and the priest shall bring *it* all, **and burn it upon the altar:** it *is* a burnt sacrifice, an offering made by fire, of a sweet savour unto the LORD.

14. **And if** the burnt sacrifice for **his offering** to the LORD **be** of **fowls,** then **he shall bring** his offering of **turtledoves, or** of **young pigeons.**

15. **And the priest shall** bring it unto the altar, and **wring off his head, and burn it on the altar;** and **the blood** thereof **shall be wrung out at the side** of the altar:

16. **And he shall pluck** away his crop with **his feathers, and cast it** beside the altar **on the east part, by** the place of **the ashes:**

17. **And he shall cleave it with the wings** thereof,

- but shall not divide it
- asunder: and the priest
- shall burn it upon the altar,
upon the wood that *is* upon the fire:
- it is a burnt sacrifice, an
offering made by fire, of
- a sweet savour
- unto the LORD.

CHAPTER 2

1. And when any will offer
- a meat offering
unto the LORD, his offering
- shall be of fine
- flour; and he shall
- pour oil upon it,
- and put
- frankincense thereon:
2. And he shall
- bring it to Aaron's sons
- the priests: and he shall take
thereout his handful of the flour
thereof, and of the oil thereof, with
all the frankincense thereof;
- and the priest shall
- burn the memorial of
- it upon the altar,
to be an offering made by fire, of
a sweet savour unto the LORD:
3. And the remnant
of the meat offering
- shall be Aaron's and his
- sons': *it is* a thing most holy of the
offerings of the LORD made by fire.
4. And if thou bring
- an oblation of a meat
- offering baken in the oven,*it*
- shall be unleavened
- cakes of fine flour mingled
- with oil, or unleavened
- wafers anointed with oil.
5. And if thy oblation be
- a meat offering baken
- in a pan, it shall be *of*
- fine flour unleavened,
- mingled with oil.
6. Thou shalt part it in pieces, and
pour oil thereon: it *is* a meat offering.
7. And if thy oblation
- be a meat offering
- baken in the fryingpan,
- it shall be made *of*
- fine flour with oil.

8. And thou shalt bring the meat
offering that is made of these
things unto the LORD: and when
it is presented unto the priest,
he shall bring it unto the altar.
9. And the priest shall
take from the meat offering
a memorial thereof, and shall
- burn it upon the altar:
it is an offering made by fire, of
a sweet savour unto the LORD.
10. And that which is
- left of the meat offering
- shall be Aaron's and his
- sons': *it is* a thing most holy of the
offerings of the LORD made by fire.
11. No meat offering,
which ye shall bring unto the LORD,
- shall be made with
- leaven: for ye shall
- burn no leaven, nor any
- honey, in any offering
of the LORD made by fire.
12. As for the oblation
of the firstfruits, ye shall
offer them unto the LORD: but
- they shall not be burnt
- on the altar for a sweet savour.
13. And every oblation of
- thy meat offering shalt thou
- season with salt; neither shalt
thou suffer the salt of the covenant
of thy God to be lacking from thy
meat offering: with all thine
offerings thou shalt offer salt.
14. And if thou offer a
- meat offering of thy
- firstfruits unto the LORD,
- thou shalt offer for the
meat offering of thy firstfruits
- green ears of corn
- dried by the fire,
even corn beaten out of full ears.
15. And thou shalt
- put oil upon it,
- and lay
- frankincense thereon:
it *is* a meat offering.
16. And the priest
- shall burn the memorial of
- it, *part* of the beaten corn thereof,
and *part* of the oil thereof, with
all the frankincense thereof:

■ it is an offering made
■ by fire unto the LORD.

CHAPTER 3

■ 1. And if his oblation
■ be a sacrifice of
■ peace offering,
if he offer *it* of the herd;
whether *it be* a male or female,
■ he shall offer it without
■ blemish before the LORD.
■ 2. And he shall
■ lay his hand upon
■ the head of his offering,
■ and kill it at the door
■ of the tabernacle of the
congregation: and Aaron's sons
■ the priests shall
■ sprinkle the blood
■ upon the altar round about.
■ 3. And he shall
■ offer of the sacrifice of
■ the peace offering an
offering made by fire unto the LORD;
■ the fat that covereth
■ the inwards, and all the
fat that *is* upon the inwards,
■ 4. And the two kidneys, and
■ the fat that *is* on them,
which *is* by the flanks,
■ and the caul above the
■ liver, with the kidneys, it
■ shall he take away.
■ 5. And Aaron's sons shall
■ burn it on the altar
upon the burnt sacrifice, which *is*
upon the wood that *is* on the fire:
it is an offering made by fire, of
a sweet savour unto the LORD.
■ 6. And if his
offering for a sacrifice of
■ peace offering unto the LORD
■ be of the flock; male or female,
■ he shall offer it
■ without blemish.
■ 7. If he offer a lamb
for his offering, then shall he
offer it before the LORD.
■ 8. And he shall lay his
■ hand upon the head
■ of his offering, and kill it
■ before the tabernacle
of the congregation:

■ and Aaron's sons
■ shall sprinkle the
■ blood thereof round about
■ upon the altar.
■ 9. And he shall
■ offer of the sacrifice of
■ the peace offering
an offering made
■ by fire unto the
■ LORD; the fat thereof,
■ and the whole
■ rump, it shall he take off hard
by the backbone; and the fat
that covereth the inwards, and
all the fat that *is* upon the inwards,
■ 10. And the two kidneys,
and the fat that *is* upon them,
which *is* by the flanks,
■ and the caul above
the liver, with the kidneys, it
■ shall he take away.
■ 11. And the priest shall
■ burn it upon the altar:
it is the food of the offering
made by fire unto the LORD.
■ 12. And if his offering
■ be a goat, then he shall
offer it before the LORD.
■ 13. And he shall lay his
■ hand upon the head of it,
■ and kill it before the
■ tabernacle of the congregation:
■ and the sons of
■ Aaron shall sprinkle
■ the blood thereof
■ upon the altar round about.
■ 14. And he shall offer thereof
his offering, *even* an offering
made by fire unto the LORD;
■ the fat that covereth
■ the inwards, and all the
fat that *is* upon the inwards,
■ 15. And the two kidneys,
and the fat that *is* upon them, which
is by the flanks, and the caul
above the liver, with the kidneys, it
■ shall he take away.
■ 16. And the priest shall
■ burn them upon the altar:
it is the food of the offering made
by fire for a sweet savour: all
the fat *is* the LORD's.
■ 17. It shall be a perpetual

■ statute for your
■ generations throughout
■ all your dwellings, that ye
■ eat neither fat nor blood.

CHAPTER 4

1. And the LORD spake
unto Moses, saying
2. Speak unto the children of Israel,
saying, If a soul shall sin through
ignorance against any of the
commandments of the LORD
concerning things which ought
not to be done, and shall do
against any of them:
■ 3. **If the priest** that is anointed do
■ **sin** according to the
sin of the people; then
■ **let him bring for his**
■ **sin,** which he hath sinned,
■ **a young bullock**
■ **without blemish** unto
the LORD for a sin offering.
4. And he shall bring the bullock
■ **unto the door of the**
■ **tabernacle** of the
congregation before the LORD;
■ **and** shall
■ **lay his hand**
■ **upon the** bullock's
■ **head, and kill the**
■ **bullock** before the LORD.
■ 5. **And** the priest
that is anointed shall
■ **take of the** bullock's
■ **blood, and bring it to the**
■ **tabernacle** of the congregation:
■ 6. **And** the priest shall
■ **dip his finger in the blood,**
■ **and sprinkle** of the blood
■ **seven times** before the LORD,
■ **before the veil** of the sanctuary.
■ 7. **And** the priest shall
■ **put** some of the
■ **blood upon the horns**
■ **of the altar of** sweet
■ **incense** before the LORD, which is
in the tabernacle of the congregation;
■ **and** shall
■ **pour all the**
■ **blood** of the bullock
■ **at the bottom of**
■ **the altar of** the

■ **burnt offering,** which is
at the door of the tabernacle
of the congregation.
■ 8. **And he shall**
■ **take** off from it all
■ **the fat** of the bullock
■ **for the sin offering;**
the fat that covereth the inwards, and
all the fat that *is* upon the inwards,
■ 9. **And the two kidneys,**
and the fat that *is* upon them,
which *is* by the flanks,
■ **and the caul** above the
liver, with the kidneys, it
■ **shall he take away,**
10. As it was taken off from
the bullock of the sacrifice
of the peace offerings: and
■ **the priest shall burn**
■ **them upon the altar**
of the burnt offering.
■ 11. **And the skin** of the bullock,
■ **and** all his
■ **flesh, with his head,** and with
■ **his legs,** and
■ **his inwards, and his dung,**
12. Even the whole bullock
■ **shall he carry** forth
■ **without the camp**
unto a clean place, where
the ashes are poured out,
■ **and burn him on the**
■ **wood** with fire: where the ashes
are poured out shall he be burnt.
■ 13. **And if the whole**
■ **congregation** of Israel
■ **sin through ignorance,**
■ **and the thing be hid**
■ **from the** eyes of the
■ **assembly,**
and they have done *somewhat*
against any of the commandments of
the LORD *concerning things* which
should not be done, and are guilty;
■ 14. **When the sin,** which
they have sinned against it,
■ **is known,** then
■ **the congregation shall offer**
■ **a young bullock for the sin,**
and bring him before the tabernacle
of the congregation.
■ 15. **And the elders**
of the congregation

shall lay their hands
upon the head of the
bullock before the LORD:
and the bullock shall
be killed before the LORD.
16. **And the priest**
that is anointed
shall bring of the bullock's
blood to the
tabernacle of the congregation:
17. **And** the priest shall
dip his finger in *some* of
the blood, and
sprinkle it seven times
before the LORD, *even*
before the veil.
18. **And he shall**
put some of the
blood upon the
horns of the altar which *is*
before the LORD, that *is* in the
tabernacle of the congregation,
and shall pour out all
the blood at the bottom
of the altar of the burnt
offering, which *is at* the door of
the tabernacle of the congregation.
19. **And** he shall
take all his fat from him,
and burn it upon the altar.
20. And he shall do with the bullock
as he did with the bullock for a sin
offering, so shall he do with this: and
the priest shall make an
atonement for them, and
it shall be forgiven them.
21. **And he shall carry** forth
the bullock without the
camp, and burn him
as he burned the first bullock:
it is a sin offering
for the congregation.
22. **When a ruler hath**
sinned, and done *somewhat*
through ignorance *against* any
of the commandments of the LORD
his God *concerning things* which
should not be done, and is guilty;
23. Or if his sin, wherein he hath
sinned, come to his knowledge;
he shall bring his offering,
a kid of the goats,
a male without blemish:

24. **And** he shall
lay his hand upon
the head of the goat,
and kill it in the place
where they kill the burnt
offering before the LORD:
it is a sin offering.
25. And the priest shall take of the
blood of the sin offering with his
finger, and put *it* upon the horns of
the altar of burnt offering, and
shall pour out his blood at the
bottom of the altar of burnt offering.
26. And he shall burn all his fat
upon the altar, as the fat of the
sacrifice of peace offerings:
and the priest shall
make an atonement
for him as concerning his sin,
and it shall be
forgiven him.
27. **And if any one of the**
common people sin
through ignorance, while
he doeth *somewhat against* any
of the commandments of the LORD
concerning things which ought
not to be done, and be guilty;
28. Or if his sin, which he hath
sinned, come to his knowledge: then
he shall bring his offering,
a kid of the goats, a
female without blemish,
for his sin which he hath sinned.
29. **And** he shall
lay his hand upon
the head of the sin offering,
and slay the sin offering
in the place of the
burnt offering.
30. And the priest shall take of
the blood thereof with his finger,
and put *it* upon the horns of the
altar of burnt offering, and shall
pour out all the blood thereof
at the bottom of the altar.
31. And he shall take away all the
fat thereof, as the fat is taken away
from off the sacrifice of peace
offerings; and the priest shall
burn *it* upon the altar for a sweet
savour unto the LORD;
and the priest shall make

■ an atonement for him, and
■ it shall be forgiven him.
■ 32. And if he bring a
■ lamb for a sin offering,
■ he shall bring it
■ a female without blemish.
33. And he shall lay his hand upon the head of the sin offering, and slay it for a sin offering in the place where they kill the burnt offering.
34. And the priest shall take of the blood of the sin offering with his finger, and put it upon the horns of the altar of burnt offering, and shall pour out all the blood thereof at the bottom of the altar:
35. And he shall take away all the fat thereof, as the fat of the lamb is taken away from the sacrifice of the peace offerings; and the priest shall burn them upon the altar, according to the offerings made by fire unto the LORD:
■ and the priest shall make
■ an atonement for his sin
that he hath committed,
■ and it shall be
■ forgiven him.

CHAPTER 5

■ 1. And if a soul sin,
■ and hear the voice of
■ swearing, and is a witness,
whether he hath seen or known of it;
■ if he do not utter it, then
■ he shall bear his iniquity.
■ 2. Or if a soul touch any
■ unclean thing, whether it be a
carcase of an unclean beast, or a carcase of unclean cattle, or the carcase of unclean creeping things,
■ and if it be hidden from him;
■ he also shall be
■ unclean, and guilty.
■ 3. Or if he touch the
■ uncleanness of man,
whatsoever uncleanness it be that a man shall be defiled withal,
■ and it be hid from him;
■ when he knoweth of it, then
■ he shall be guilty.
■ 4. Or if a soul swear,
■ pronouncing with his lips
■ to do evil, or to do good,

■ whatsoever it be that
■ a man shall pronounce
■ with an oath, and
■ it be hid from him;
■ when he knoweth of it, then
■ he shall be guilty
in one of these.
5. And it shall be,
■ when he shall be guilty
in one of these things, that
■ he shall confess that
■ he hath sinned in that thing:
■ 6. And he shall bring
■ his trespass offering
unto the LORD for his sin which he hath sinned,
■ a female from the flock, a
■ lamb or a kid of the
■ goats, for a sin offering;
■ and the priest shall make
■ an atonement for him
concerning his sin.
■ 7. And if he be not able
■ to bring a lamb, then
■ he shall bring for his trespass,
which he hath committed,
■ two turtledoves, or two
■ young pigeons, unto the LORD;
■ one for a sin offering,
■ and the other for a
■ burnt offering.
■ 8. And he shall bring them unto
■ the priest, who
■ shall offer that which is for
■ the sin offering first,
and wring off his head from his neck, but shall not divide it asunder:
■ 9. And he shall sprinkle of
■ the blood of the sin offering
■ upon the side of the altar;
■ and the rest of the blood
■ shall be wrung out at
■ the bottom of the altar:
it is a sin offering.
■ 10. And he shall offer the
■ second for a burnt offering,
according to the manner: and the priest shall make an atonement for him for his sin which he hath sinned, and it shall be forgiven him.
■ 11. But if he be not able to
■ bring two turtledoves, or
■ two young pigeons, then

- **he** that sinned
- **shall bring** for his offering
- **the tenth part of an**
- **ephah of fine flour** for a sin offering; he shall put no oil upon it, neither shall he put *any* frankincense thereon: for it *is* a sin offering. 12. Then shall he bring it to the priest, and
- **the priest shall take**
- **his handful of it,** *even* a memorial thereof,
- **and burn it on the altar,** according to the offerings made by fire unto the LORD: it *is* a sin offering.
- 13. **And the priest shall**
- **make an atonement for**
- **him** as touching his sin that he hath sinned in one of these,
- **and it shall be forgiven**
- **him:** and *the remnant* shall be the priest's, as a meat offering. 14. And the LORD spake unto Moses, saying,
- 15. **If a soul** commit a trespass, and
- **sin through ignorance,**
- **in the holy things of the**
- **LORD; then he shall bring** for his trespass unto the LORD
- **a ram without**
- **blemish** out of the flocks,
- **with thy estimation by**
- **shekels of silver,** after the shekel of the sanctuary, for a trespass offering:
- 16. **And he shall make**
- **amends for the harm that**
- **he hath done** in the holy thing,
- **and shall add the fifth part**
- **thereto,** and give it unto the priest:
- **and the priest shall make**
- **an atonement** for him with the ram of the trespass offering,
- **and it shall be**
- **forgiven him.**
- 17. **And if a soul** sin, and
- **commit any** of these
- **things** which are
- **forbidden** to be done
- **by the commandments** of the LORD;
- **though he wist it not,**

- **yet is he guilty,** and shall bear his iniquity.
- 18. **And he shall bring a**
- **ram without blemish** out of the flock, with thy estimation,
- **for a trespass offering,**
- **unto the priest: and the**
- **priest shall make an**
- **atonement for him** concerning his ignorance wherein he erred and wist *it* not, and it shall be forgiven him. 19. It *is* a trespass offering: he hath certainly trespassed against the LORD.

CHAPTER 6

1. And the LORD spake unto Moses, saying,
- 2. **If a soul** sin, and commit a trespass against the LORD, and
- **lie unto his neighbour** in that which was delivered him to keep, or in fellowship, or in a thing taken away by violence,
- **or hath deceived**
- **his neighbour;**
- 3. **Or have found that which**
- **was lost,** and lieth concerning it,
- **and sweareth falsely;** in any of all these that a man doeth, sinning therein: 4. Then it shall be, because he hath sinned, and is guilty, that
- **he shall restore that which**
- **he took** violently away,
- **or the thing which he**
- **hath deceitfully gotten,**
- **or that** which was
- **delivered him to keep, or**
- **the lost thing** which he found,
- 5. **Or all that about**
- **which he hath sworn**
- **falsely; he shall** even
- **restore** it in
- **the principal, and**
- **shall add the fifth**
- **part more** thereto,
- **and give it** unto him
- **to whom it appertaineth,**
- **in the day of his**
- **trespass offering.**
- 6. **And he shall bring** his trespass offering unto the LORD,

a ram without
blemish out of the flock,
with thy estimation, for a
trespass offering, unto the priest:
7. And the priest shall
make an atonement
for him before the LORD:
and it shall be forgiven
him for any thing of all that he
hath done in trespassing therein.
8. And the LORD spake
unto Moses, saying,
9. Command Aaron
and his sons, saying,
This is the law of the burnt
offering: It *is* the burnt offering,
because of the burning
upon the altar all night
unto the morning, and the fire
of the altar shall be burning in it.
10. And the priest
shall put on his
linen garment, and his linen
breeches shall he put upon his flesh,
and take up the ashes
which the fire hath consumed
with the burnt offering on the altar,
and he shall
put them beside the altar.
11. And he shall put off his
garments, and put on other
garments, and carry forth
the ashes without the
camp unto a clean place.
12. And the fire upon the altar
shall be burning in it; it shall not be
put out: and the priest shall burn
wood on it every morning, and
lay the burnt offering in order
upon it; and he shall burn thereon
the fat of the peace offerings.
13. The fire shall ever be burning
upon the altar; it
shall never go out.
14. And this is the law of
the meat offering: the
sons of Aaron shall offer it
before the LORD, before the altar.
15. And he
shall take of it
his handful, of the
flour of the meat offering,
and of the

oil thereof,
and all
the frankincense
which *is* upon the meat offering,
and shall
burn it upon the altar
for a sweet savour, *even* the
memorial of it, unto the LORD.
16. And the remainder
thereof shall Aaron and his
sons eat: with unleavened
bread shall it be eaten
in the holy place;
in the court of the tabernacle of
the congregation they shall eat it.
17. It shall not be
baken with leaven.
I have given it *unto them for* their
portion of my offerings made by fire;
it is most holy, as is the
sin offering, and as the
trespass offering.
18. All the males among
the children of Aaron shall
eat of it. It shall be a statute
for ever in your generations
concerning the offerings of the LORD
made by fire: every
one that toucheth
them shall be holy.
19. And the LORD spake
unto Moses, saying,
20. This is the offering
of Aaron and of his
sons, which they shall offer
unto the LORD in the day
when he is anointed; the
tenth part of an ephah
of fine flour for a meat
offering perpetual, half of
it in the morning,
and half thereof
at night.
21. In a pan
it shall be made
with oil; and *when it is*
baken, thou shalt bring it in:
and the baken
pieces of the meat offering
shalt thou offer
for a sweet savour
unto the LORD.
22. And the priest of his sons that is

157

anointed in his stead shall offer it: *it is* a statute for ever unto the LORD; it shall be wholly burnt.

23. For every meat offering for the priest shall be wholly burnt: it shall not be eaten.

24. And the LORD spake unto Moses, saying,

25. Speak unto Aaron and to his sons, saying,

This is the law of the sin offering: In the place **where the burnt offering is killed shall the sin offering be killed** before the LORD: **it is most holy.**

26. **The priest that offereth it for sin shall eat it: in the holy place** shall it be eaten, in the court of the tabernacle of the congregation.

27. **Whatsoever shall touch the flesh thereof shall be holy: and when there is** sprinkled of the **blood** thereof **upon any garment,** thou shalt **wash that** whereon it was sprinkled **in the holy place.**

28. **But the earthen vessel wherein it is sodden shall be broken: and** if it be sodden in **a brasen pot, it shall be both scoured, and rinsed in water.**

29. **All the males among the priests shall eat thereof: it is most holy.**

30. **And no sin offering,** whereof *any* of the blood is brought into the tabernacle of the congregation to reconcile *withal* in the holy *place,* **shall be eaten: it shall be burnt** in the fire.

CHAPTER 7

1. **Likewise this is the law of the trespass offering:** it *is* most holy.

2. **In the place where they kill the burnt offering shall they kill the trespass offering: and the blood** thereof **shall he sprinkle** round about **upon the altar.**

3. And he shall offer of it all the fat thereof; the rump, and the fat that covereth the inwards,

4. And the two kidneys, and the fat that *is* on them, which *is* by the flanks, and the caul *that is* above the liver, with the kidneys, it shall he take away:

5. And the priest shall burn them upon the altar *for* an offering made by fire unto the LORD: it *is* a trespass offering.

6. **Every male among the priests shall eat thereof:** it shall be eaten in the holy place: it *is* most holy.

7. **As the sin offering is, so is the trespass offering: there is one law for them: the priest that maketh atonement therewith shall have it.**

8. **And the priest that offereth any man's burnt offering,** *even* the priest **shall have** to himself **the skin** of the burnt offering which he hath offered.

9. **And all the meat offering** that is baken in the oven, and all that is dressed in the fryingpan, and in the pan, **shall be the priest's that offereth it.**

10. **And every meat offering,** mingled with oil, and dry, **shall all the sons of Aaron have, one as much as another.**

11. **And this is the law of the** sacrifice of **peace offerings,** which he shall offer unto the LORD.

12. If he offer it for a thanksgiving, then **he shall offer with the sacrifice of thanksgiving unleavened cakes mingled**

with oil, and unleavened
wafers anointed with oil,
and cakes mingled with
oil, of fine flour, fried.
13. **Besides** the cakes,
he shall offer *for* his offering
leavened bread
with the sacrifice of thanksgiving
of his peace offerings.
14. **And of it he shall offer
one out of the whole
oblation for an heave
offering** unto the LORD,
**and it shall be the priest's
that sprinkleth the blood**
of the peace offerings.
15. **And the flesh**
of the sacrifice of his peace
offerings for thanksgiving
**shall be eaten the same
day** that it is offered; he shall not
leave any of it until the morning.
16. **But if** the sacrifice of
**his offering be a vow, or a
voluntary offering, it shall
be eaten the same day**
that he offereth his sacrifice:
**and on the morrow
also the remainder
of it shall be eaten:**
17. **But the remainder**
of the flesh of the sacrifice
**on the third day shall
be burnt with fire.**
18. **And if any of the flesh**
of the sacrifice of his peace offerings
be eaten at all
on the third day, it shall not
be accepted, neither shall it be
imputed unto him that offereth it:
**it shall be an
abomination,** and the soul that
eateth of it shall bear his iniquity.
19. **And the flesh that
toucheth any unclean
thing shall not be eaten;**
it shall be burnt with fire: and
as for the flesh, all that be
clean shall eat thereof.
20. **But the soul that
eateth** *of* the flesh of the sacrifice
of peace offerings,
that *pertain* unto the LORD,

having his
uncleanness
upon him, even that soul
shall be cut off from his people.
21. **Moreover the soul that
shall touch any unclean
thing,** *as* the uncleanness of man,
or *any* unclean beast, or any
abominable unclean *thing,* and eat
of the flesh of the sacrifice of peace
offerings, which *pertain* unto the
LORD, even that soul
shall be cut off from his people.
22. And the LORD spake
unto Moses, saying,
23. Speak unto the
children of Israel, saying,
Ye shall eat no manner of
fat, of ox, or of sheep, or of goat.
24. And the fat of the beast
that dieth of itself, and
the fat of that which is
torn with beasts,
**may be used in any
other use: but ye
shall in no wise eat of it.**
25. **For whosoever eateth
the fat** of the beast, of which men
offer an offering made by fire unto the
LORD, even the soul that eateth *it*
shall be cut off from his people.
26. **Moreover** ye shall eat no
manner of blood, *whether it be* of fowl
or of beast, in any of your dwelling.
27. **Whatsoever soul** *it be*
that eateth any manner of
blood, even that soul
shall be cut off from his people.
28. And the LORD spake
unto Moses, saying,
29. Speak unto the
children of Israel, saying,
He that offereth the sacrifice of
his peace offerings
unto the LORD
shall bring his oblation
unto the LORD of the sacrifice
of his peace offerings.
30. His own hands shall bring the
offerings of the LORD made by fire,
the fat with the breast, it
**shall he bring, that the
breast may be** waved

■ for a wave offering
before the LORD.
31. And the priest shall burn
the fat upon the altar: but
■ the breast shall be
■ Aaron's and his sons'.
■ 32. And the right shoulder
■ shall ye give unto the priest
■ for an heave offering of the
sacrifices of your peace offerings.
■ 33. He among the
■ sons of Aaron, that
■ offereth the blood of
■ the peace offerings,
and the fat,
■ shall have the right
■ shoulder for *his* part.
34. For the wave breast and the
heave shoulder have I taken of the
children of Israel from off the
sacrifices of their peace offerings, and
have given them unto Aaron
the priest and unto his sons
by a statute for ever from among
the children of Israel.
■ 35. This is the portion of
■ the anointing of Aaron,
■ and of the anointing of
■ his sons, out of the
■ offerings of the LORD
■ made by fire,
in the day *when* he presented
them to minister unto the LORD
in the priest's office;
■ 36. Which the LORD
■ commanded to be given
them of the children of Israel,
■ in the day that he anointed
■ them, *by* a statute for ever
throughout their generations.
37. This *is* the law of the burnt
offering, of the meat offering,
and of the sin offering, and of the
trespass offering, and of the
consecrations, and of the sacrifice
of the peace offerings;
38. Which the LORD
commanded Moses
■ in mount Sinai,
in the day that he commanded
the children of Israel to offer
their oblations unto the LORD,
in the wilderness of Sinai.

CHAPTER 8
■ 1. And the LORD spake
■ unto Moses, saying,
■ 2. Take Aaron and
■ his sons with him,
■ and the garments, and
■ the anointing oil, and
■ a bullock for the sin
■ offering, and
■ two rams, and a basket
■ of unleavened bread;
■ 3. And gather thou
■ all the congregation together
■ unto the door of the
■ tabernacle of the congregation.
■ 4. And Moses did as the
■ LORD commanded him;
and the assembly was gathered
together unto the door of the
tabernacle of the congregation.
5. And Moses said unto the
congregation, This *is* the thing which
the LORD commanded to be done.
■ 6. And Moses brought
■ Aaron and his sons, and
■ washed them with water.
■ 7. And he put upon him
■ the coat, and girded him with
■ the girdle, and clothed him with
■ the robe, and put
■ the ephod upon him,
■ and he girded him with
■ the curious girdle
■ of the ephod, and
bound *it* unto him therewith.
■ 8. And he put the
■ breastplate upon him: also
■ he put in the breastplate
■ the Urim and the Thummim.
■ 9. And he put the mitre
■ upon his head; also upon
■ the mitre, *even* upon his forefront,
■ did he put the golden plate, the
■ holy crown; as the LORD
commanded Moses.
■ 10. And Moses
took the anointing oil, and
■ anointed the tabernacle
■ and all that was therein,
■ and sanctified them.
■ 11. And he sprinkled thereof
■ upon the altar seven times,
■ and anointed the altar and

all his vessels, both the laver and his foot, to sanctify them.

12. **And he poured of the anointing oil upon Aaron's head,** and anointed him, **to sanctify him.**

13. **And Moses brought Aaron's sons,** and **put coats upon them,** and **girded them with girdles, and put bonnets upon them; as the LORD commanded** Moses.

14. **And he brought the bullock for the sin offering: and Aaron** and his sons laid their hands upon the head of the bullock for the sin offering.

15. And he **slew it; and Moses took the blood, and put it upon the horns of the altar** round about with his finger, **and purified the altar, and poured the blood at the bottom of the altar,** and sanctified it, **to make reconciliation** upon it.

16. **And he took all the fat** that *was* upon the inwards, **and the caul** *above* the liver, **and the two kidneys,** and their fat, **and** Moses **burned it upon the altar.**

17. **But the bullock,** and **his hide, his flesh, and his dung, he burnt** with fire **without the camp;** as the LORD commanded Moses.

18. **And he brought the ram for the burnt offering: and Aaron and his sons laid their hands upon the head** of the ram.

19. **And he killed it; and Moses sprinkled the blood upon the altar** round about.

20. **And he cut the ram into pieces; and Moses burnt the head,** and the pieces, and the fat.

21. And he washed the inwards and the legs in water; **and Moses burnt the whole ram upon the altar:** it *was* a burnt sacrifice for a sweet savour, *and* an offering made by fire unto the LORD; as the LORD commanded Moses.

22. **And he brought** the other ram, **the ram of consecration:** and Aaron and his sons laid their hands upon the head of the ram.

23. And he slew *it;* **and Moses took** of **the blood** of it, **and put it upon the tip of Aaron's right ear,** and **upon the thumb of his right hand, and upon the great toe of his right foot.**

24. **And he brought Aaron's sons, and** Moses **put** of the **blood upon the tip of their right ear,** and **upon the thumbs of their right hands, and upon the great toes of their right feet: and** Moses **sprinkled the blood upon the altar** round about.

25. **And he took the fat,** and **the rump,** and all the fat that *was* upon the inwards, and **the caul** *above* the liver, and **the two kidneys, and their fat, and the right shoulder:**

26. **And out of the basket of unleavened bread,** that *was* before the LORD, **he took one unleavened cake,** and **a cake of oiled bread,** and **one wafer, and put them on the fat, and** upon **the right shoulder:**

27. **And he put all upon Aaron's hands, and upon his sons' hands,** and waved them **for a wave**

■ **offering** before the LORD:
■ 28. **And Moses took**
■ **them from off their**
■ **hands, and burnt them**
■ **on the altar** upon the burnt
offering: they *were* consecrations
■ **for a sweet savour:**
it *is* an offering made by fire
■ **unto the LORD.**
■ 29. **And Moses took**
■ **the breast,** and waved it
■ **for a wave offering**
before the LORD:
■ **for of the ram of**
■ **consecration it was**
■ **Moses' part; as the**
■ **LORD commanded** Moses.
■ 30. **And Moses took**
■ **of the anointing oil, and** of
■ **the blood** which *was*
■ **upon the altar, and**
■ **sprinkled it upon**
■ **Aaron,** *and* upon his garments,
■ **and upon his sons,** and
upon his sons' garments with him;
■ **and sanctified**
■ **Aaron,** *and* his garments,
■ **and his sons,**
and his sons' garments with him.
■ 31. **And Moses said**
unto Aaron and to his sons,
■ **Boil the flesh** *at* the door of the
tabernacle of the congregation:
■ **and** there
■ **eat it with the bread** that *is*
■ **in the basket of**
■ **consecrations,**
as I commanded, saying,
Aaron and his sons shall eat it.
■ 32. **And that which**
■ **remaineth** of the flesh
and of the bread shall ye
■ **burn with fire.**
■ 33. **And ye shall not**
■ **go out** of the door
■ **of the tabernacle**
of the congregation
■ **in seven days, until the**
■ **days of your consecration**
■ **be at an end:** for seven
days shall he consecrate you.
34. As he hath done this day, so
the LORD hath commanded to do,

to make an atonement for you.
35. Therefore shall ye abide *at*
the door of the tabernacle of the
congregation day and night
seven days, and keep the
charge of the LORD, that ye
die not: for so I am commanded.
■ 36. **So Aaron and his**
■ **sons did all things which**
■ **the LORD commanded**
by the hand of Moses.

CHAPTER 9

1. And it came to pass
■ **on the eighth day,** *that*
■ **Moses** called Aaron and his
sons, and the elders of Israel;
2. And he
■ **said unto Aaron, Take** thee
■ **a young calf for a**
■ **sin offering,** and
■ **a ram for a burnt offering,**
■ **without blemish, and offer**
■ **them before the LORD.**
■ 3. **And unto** the children of
■ **Israel** thou shalt
■ **speak,** saying,
■ **Take ye a kid of the**
■ **goats for a sin offering;** and
■ **a calf and a lamb,**
■ **both of the first year,**
■ **without blemish, for**
■ **a burnt offering;**
■ 4. **Also a bullock and a**
■ **ram for peace offerings,**
to sacrifice before the LORD;
■ **and a meat offering**
■ **mingled with oil: for**
■ **to day the LORD will**
■ **appear unto you.**
■ 5. **And they brought**
■ **that which Moses**
■ **commanded** before the
tabernacle of the congregation:
■ **and all the congregation**
■ **drew near** and stood
before the LORD.
6. And Moses said, This *is* the
thing which the LORD commanded
that ye should do: and the glory
of the LORD shall appear unto you.
■ 7. **And Moses said**
■ **unto Aaron, Go unto**

■ **the altar,** and offer thy sin offering, and thy burnt offering,

■ **and make an atonement** for thyself, and for the people: and offer the offering of the people, and make an atonement for them; as the LORD commanded.

■ 8. **Aaron** therefore

■ **went unto the altar,**

■ **and slew the calf of**

■ **the sin offering,** which *was*

■ **for himself.**

9. And the sons of Aaron brought the blood unto him: and he dipped his finger in the blood, and put *it* upon the horns of the altar, and poured out the blood at the bottom of the altar:

10. But the fat, and the kidneys, and the caul above the liver of the sin offering, he burnt upon the altar; as the LORD commanded Moses.

11. And the flesh and the hide he burnt with fire without the camp.

12. And he slew the burnt offering; and Aaron's sons presented unto him the blood, which he sprinkled round about upon the altar.

13. And they presented the burnt offering unto him, with the pieces thereof, and the head: and he burnt *them* upon the altar.

14. And he did wash the inwards and the legs, and burnt *them* upon the burnt offering on the altar.

■ 15. **And he brought the**

■ **people's offering,** and took the goat, which *was* the sin offering for the people, and slew it,

■ **and offered it**

■ **for sin,** as the first.

16. And he brought the burnt offering, and offered it according to the manner.

■ 17. **And he brought**

■ **the meat offering,** and took an handful thereof, and burnt *it* upon the altar, beside the burnt sacrifice of the morning.

■ 18. **He slew also the bullock**

■ **and the ram for a sacrifice**

■ **of peace offerings,** which *was* for the people: and Aaron's sons presented unto

him the blood, which he sprinkled upon the altar round about,

19. And the fat of the bullock and of the ram, the rump, and that which covereth *the inwards,* and the kidneys, and the caul *above* the liver:

20. And they put the fat upon the breasts, and he burnt the fat upon the altar:

■ 21. **And the breasts and**

■ **the right shoulder Aaron**

■ **waved for a wave**

■ **offering before the**

■ **LORD;** as Moses commanded.

■ 22. **And Aaron lifted up his**

■ **hand toward the people,**

■ **and blessed them, and**

■ **came down from offering** of the sin offering, and the burnt offering, and peace offerings.

■ 23. **And Moses and Aaron**

■ **went into the tabernacle** of the congregation,

■ **and came out, and**

■ **blessed the people: and**

■ **the glory of the LORD**

■ **appeared** unto all the people.

■ 24. **And there came a fire**

■ **out from before the LORD,**

■ **and consumed** upon the altar

■ **the burnt offering**

■ **and the fat:** which

■ **when all the people**

■ **saw, they shouted,**

■ **and fell on their faces.**

CHAPTER 10

■ 1. **And Nadab and**

■ **Abihu,** the sons of Aaron,

■ **took either of them**

■ **his censer,** and put fire therein, and put incense thereon,

■ **and offered strange**

■ **fire before the LORD,**

■ **which he commanded**

■ **them not.**

■ 2. **And there went out**

■ **fire from the LORD,**

■ **and devoured them,** and they died before the LORD.

■ 3. **Then Moses said unto**

■ **Aaron, This is it that**

■ **the LORD spake,** saying,

■ I will be sanctified in
■ them that come nigh me,
■ and before all the
■ people I will be glorified.
And Aaron held his peace.
■ 4. And Moses called
Mishael and Elzaphan,
■ the sons of Uzziel
the uncle of Aaron,
■ and said unto them, Come near,
■ carry your brethren
from before the sanctuary
■ out of the camp.
5. So they went near, and carried
them in their coats out of the
camp; as Moses had said.
■ 6. And Moses said
■ unto Aaron, and unto
■ Eleazar and unto
■ Ithamar, his sons,
■ Uncover not your
■ heads, neither rend your clothes;
■ lest ye die, and lest
wrath come upon all the people:
■ but let your brethren,
the whole house of
■ Israel, bewail the
■ burning which
■ the LORD hath kindled.
■ 7. And ye shall not
■ go out from the door
■ of the tabernacle
of the congregation,
■ lest ye die: for the anointing
oil of the LORD *is* upon you.
■ And they did according
■ to the word of Moses.
■ 8. And the LORD spake
■ unto Aaron, saying,
■ 9. Do not drink wine
■ nor strong drink,
thou, nor thy sons with thee,
■ when ye go into the
■ tabernacle of the congregation,
■ lest ye die: it shall be
■ a statute for ever
throughout your generations:
■ 10. And that ye may
■ put difference between
■ holy and unholy, and
between unclean and clean;
■ 11. And that ye may
■ teach the children of

■ Israel all the statutes which
■ the LORD hath spoken
unto them by the hand of Moses.
■ 12. And Moses spake unto
■ Aaron, and unto Eleazar and unto
Ithamar, his sons that were left,
■ Take the meat offering
■ that remaineth of the offerings
of the LORD made by fire,
■ and eat it without leaven
beside the altar: for it *is* most holy:
13. And ye shall eat it in the holy
place, because it *is* thy due, and
thy sons' due, of the sacrifices
of the LORD made by fire: for
so I am commanded.
■ 14. And the wave breast
■ and heave shoulder
■ shall ye eat in a clean
■ place; thou, and
■ thy sons, and thy
■ daughters with thee: for *they be*
thy due, and thy sons' due, *which* are
given out of the sacrifices of peace
offerings of the children of Israel.
■ 15. The heave shoulder and
■ the wave breast shall they bring
with the offerings made by fire of the
fat, to wave *it for* a wave offering
before the LORD; and it
■ shall be thine, and thy
■ sons' with thee, by a statute
■ for ever; as the LORD
hath commanded.
■ 16. And Moses diligently
■ sought the goat of the
■ sin offering, and, behold,
■ it was burnt: and he
■ was angry with Eleazar
■ and Ithamar, the sons of
Aaron *which were* left *alive,*
■ saying,
■ 17. Wherefore have ye not
■ eaten the sin offering in the
■ holy place, seeing it is most
■ holy, and *God* hath given it you to
bear the iniquity of the congregation,
■ to make atonement
for them before the LORD?
■ 18. Behold, the blood
■ of it was not brought in
■ within the holy place:
■ ye should indeed have

- **eaten it** in the holy *place,*
- **as I commanded.**
- 19. **And Aaron said** unto Moses, Behold, this day have
- **they offered their sin**
- **offering and their burnt**
- **offering** before the LORD; and such things have befallen me:
- **and if I had eaten the sin**
- **offering to day, should**
- **it have been accepted** in the sight of the LORD?
- 20. **And when Moses**
- **heard that, he was content.**

CHAPTER 11

- 1. **And the LORD spake** unto Moses and to Aaron,
- **saying** unto them,
- 2. Speak unto the children of Israel, saying,
- **These are the beasts**
- **which ye shall eat** among all the beasts that *are* on the earth.
- 3. **Whatsoever parteth**
- **the hoof,** and is clovenfooted,
- **and cheweth the cud,** among the beasts, that
- **shall ye eat.**
- 4. **Nevertheless these shall**
- **ye not eat** of them that chew the cud, or of them that divide the hoof: *as*
- **the camel,** because he cheweth the cud, but divideth not the hoof;
- **he is unclean unto you.**
- 5. **And the coney,** because he cheweth the cud, but divideth not the hoof; he *is* unclean unto you.
- 6. **And the hare,** because he cheweth the cud, but divideth not the hoof; he *is* unclean unto you.
- 7. **And the swine, though**
- **he divide the hoof,** and be clovenfooted,
- **yet he cheweth not the**
- **cud; he is unclean** to you.
- 8. Of their flesh shall ye not eat, and their carcase shall ye not touch; they *are* unclean to you.
- 9. **These shall ye eat of**
- **all that are in the waters:**
- **whatsoever hath fins and**

- **scales** in the waters, in the seas, and in the rivers, them shall ye eat.
- 10. **And all that have**
- **not fins and scales** in the seas, and in the rivers, of all that move in the waters, and of any living thing which *is* in the waters, they
- **shall be an abomination**
- **unto you:**
- 11. They shall be even an abomination unto you; ye shall not eat of their flesh, but ye shall have their carcases in abomination.
- 12. Whatsoever hath no fins nor scales in the waters, that *shall be* an abomination unto you.
- 13. **And these are** they which ye shall have
- **in abomination among**
- **the fowls;** they shall not be eaten, they *are* an abomination:
- **the eagle,** and
- **the ossifrage,** and
- **the ospray,**
- 14. **And the vulture,** and
- **the kite** after his kind;
- 15. **Every raven** after his kind;
- 16. **And the owl,** and the night hawk, and
- **the cuckoo,** and
- **the hawk** after his kind,
- 17. And the little owl, and
- **the cormorant,** and the great owl,
- 18. **And the swan,** and
- **the pelican,** and
- **the gier eagle,**
- 19. **And the stork, the**
- **heron** after her kind, and
- **the lapwing, and the bat.**
- 20. **All fowls that creep,** going
- **upon all four, shall be an**
- **abomination** unto you:
- 21. **Yet these may ye eat**
- **of every flying creeping**
- **thing** that goeth upon *all* four,
- **which have legs above**
- **their feet, to leap** withal upon the earth;
- 22. **Even these** of them
- **ye may eat; the locust** after his kind, and the bald locust after his kind, and

■ **the beetle** after his kind,
■ **and the grasshopper**
after his kind.
23. But all *other* flying creeping
things, which have four feet,
shall be an abomination unto you.
24. And for these ye shall be unclean:
whosoever toucheth the carcase of
them shall be unclean until the even.
25. And whosoever beareth
aught of the carcase of them
shall wash his clothes, and be
unclean until the even.
26. *The carcases* of every beast
which divideth the hoof, and *is* not
clovenfooted, nor cheweth the cud,
are unclean unto you: every one that
toucheth them shall be unclean.
■ 27. **And whatsoever goeth**
■ **upon his paws,** among all
manner of beasts that go on *all* four,
■ **those are unclean** unto you:
whoso toucheth their carcase
shall be unclean until the even.
28. And he that beareth the carcase
of them shall wash his clothes,
and be unclean until the even:
they *are* unclean unto you.
■ 29. **These also**
■ **shall be unclean**
unto you among the creeping
things that creep upon the earth;
■ **the weasel,** and
■ **the mouse,** and
■ **the tortoise** after his kind,
■ 30. **And the ferret,** and
■ **the chameleon,** and
■ **the lizard,** and
■ **the snail, and the mole.**
31. These *are* unclean to
you among all that creep:
■ **whosoever doth touch**
■ **them, when they be**
■ **dead, shall be**
■ **unclean until the even.**
32. And upon whatsoever *any* of
them, when they are dead, doth fall,
it shall be unclean; whether *it be* any
vessel of wood, or raiment, or skin,
or sack, whatsoever vessel *it be,*
wherein *any* work is done, it must be
put into water, and it shall be unclean
until the even; so it shall be cleansed.

■ 33. **And every earthen**
■ **vessel, whereinto any of**
■ **them falleth, whatsoever**
■ **is in it shall be unclean; and**
■ **ye shall break it.**
34. Of all meat which may be eaten,
that on which *such* water cometh
shall be unclean: and all drink that
may be drunk in every *such*
vessel shall be unclean.
■ 35. **And every thing**
■ **whereupon any part of their**
■ **carcase falleth shall be**
■ **unclean;** *whether it be* oven, or
ranges for pots, they shall be broken
down: *for* they *are* unclean
and shall be unclean unto you.
■ 36. **Nevertheless a fountain**
■ **or pit, wherein there is**
■ **plenty of water, shall be**
■ **clean:** but that which toucheth
their carcase shall be unclean.
■ 37. **And if any part of their**
■ **carcase fall upon any**
■ **sowing seed** which is to be sown,
■ **it shall be clean.**
■ 38. **But if any water be**
■ **put upon the seed, and**
■ **any part of their carcase**
■ **fall thereon, it shall be**
■ **unclean** unto you.
■ 39. **And if any beast,**
■ **of which ye may eat,**
■ **die; he that toucheth**
■ **the carcase** thereof
■ **shall be unclean**
■ **until the even.**
40. And he that eateth of the
carcase of it shall wash his clothes,
and be unclean until the even: he
also that beareth the carcase
of it shall wash his clothes,
and be unclean until the even.
■ 41. **And every creeping**
■ **thing** that creepeth upon the
earth *shall be* an abomination; it
■ **shall not be eaten.**
■ 42. **Whatsoever goeth upon**
■ **the belly, and whatsoever**
■ **goeth upon all four, or**
■ **whatsoever hath more feet**
■ **among all creeping**
■ **things** that creep upon the earth,

them ye shall not eat;
for they *are* an abomination.
43. Ye shall not make yourselves
abominable with any creeping thing
that creepeth, neither shall ye make
yourselves unclean with them,
that ye should be defiled thereby.
44. **For I am the
LORD** your God:
**ye shall therefore sanctify
yourselves, and ye shall
be holy; for I am holy:**
neither shall ye defile yourselves
with any manner of creeping thing
that creepeth upon the earth.
45. **For I am the LORD
that bringeth you up
out of the land of Egypt,
to be your God:** ye shall
therefore be holy, for I *am* holy.
46. This *is* the law of the beasts,
and of the fowl, and of every
living creature that moveth in
the waters, and of every creature
that creepeth upon the earth:
47. To make a difference between
the unclean and the clean, and
between the beast that may be eaten
and the beast that may not be eaten.

CHAPTER 12

1. **And the LORD
spake** unto Moses, saying,
2. Speak unto the
children of Israel, saying,
If a woman have
conceived seed, and
born a man child: then
**she shall be unclean
seven days;** according to
the days of the separation for her
infirmity shall she be unclean.
3. **And in the eighth
day** the flesh of
**his foreskin shall
be circumcised.**
4. **And she shall then
continue in** the blood of
**her purifying three and
thirty days;** she shall touch
no hallowed thing, nor come into
the sanctuary, until the days
of her purifying be fulfilled.

5. **But if she bear a
maid child, then she
shall be unclean two
weeks,** as in her separation:
and she shall
continue in the blood of
**her purifying threescore
and six days.**
6. **And when the days of
her purifying are fulfilled,**
for a son, or for a daughter,
**she shall bring a
lamb** of the first year
**for a burnt offering,
and a young pigeon,
or a turtledove,
for a sin offering,**
unto the door of the tabernacle of
the congregation, unto the priest:
7. Who shall offer it before the LORD,
and make an atonement for her;
**and she shall be cleansed
from the issue of her
blood.** This *is* the law for her
that hath borne a male or a female.
8. **And if she be not able
to bring a lamb, then she
shall bring two turtles, or
two young pigeons;** the
one for the burnt offering, and
the other for a sin offering:
and the priest shall
make an atonement
for her, and she shall be clean.

CHAPTER 13

1. **And the LORD spake**
unto Moses and Aaron, saying,
2. **When a man shall
have** in the skin of his flesh
**a rising, a scab, or
bright spot, and it be**
in the skin of his flesh
**like the plague
of leprosy;** then
he shall be brought
unto Aaron the priest, or
unto one of his sons
the priests:
3. **And the priest shall look**
on the plague in the skin of the flesh:
and when the hair in the plague
is turned white, and

167

■ the plague in sight
■ be deeper than
■ the skin of his flesh,
■ it is a plague of
■ leprosy: and the
■ priest shall look on him, and
■ pronounce him unclean.
■ 4. If the bright spot be
■ white in the skin of his flesh,
■ and in sight *be*
■ not deeper than the
■ skin, and the hair thereof
■ be not turned white; then
■ the priest shall shut
■ up him *that hath* the plague
■ seven days:
5. And the priest shall look on him
■ the seventh day: and, behold,
■ if the plague in his sight
be at a stay, *and* the plague
■ spread not in the skin; then
■ the priest shall shut him
■ up seven days more:
6. And the priest shall look
■ on him again
■ the seventh day: and, behold,
■ if the plague be somewhat
■ dark, and the plague
■ spread not in the skin, the
■ priest shall pronounce him
■ clean: it *is but* a scab: and he shall
wash his clothes, and be clean.
■ 7. But if the scab spread
■ much abroad in the skin,
after that he hath been seen of the
priest for his cleansing,
■ he shall be seen of
■ the priest again:
■ 8. And if the priest see that, behold,
■ the scab spreadeth
in the skin, then
■ the priest shall pronounce
■ him unclean: it *is* a leprosy.
■ 9. When the plague of
■ leprosy is in a man, then he
shall be brought unto the priest;
10. And the priest shall
see *him:* and, behold,
■ if the rising be
■ white in the skin,
■ and it have turned the hair
■ white, and there be quick
■ raw flesh in the rising;

■ 11. It is an old leprosy
in the skin of his flesh,
■ and the priest shall
■ pronounce him
■ unclean, and shall not
shut him up: for he *is* unclean.
■ 12. And if a leprosy break
■ out abroad in the skin,
■ and the leprosy cover all
■ the skin of *him that hath* the plague
■ from his head even
■ to his foot,
wheresoever the priest looketh;
■ 13. Then the priest
shall consider: and, behold, *if* the
leprosy have covered all his flesh, he
■ shall pronounce him
■ clean *that hath* the plague: it
is all turned white: he *is* clean.
■ 14. But when raw flesh
■ appeareth in him,
he shall be unclean.
■ 15. And the priest
■ shall see the raw flesh, and
■ pronounce him to be
■ unclean: for the
■ raw flesh *is* unclean: it
■ is a leprosy.
■ 16. Or if the raw flesh turn
■ again, and be changed unto white,
he shall come unto the priest;
17. And the priest shall see
him: and, behold, *if* the plague
be turned into white; then
■ the priest shall
■ pronounce him clean
that hath the plague: he *is* clean.
■ 18. The flesh also, in
which, *even* in the skin thereof,
■ was a boil, and is healed,
■ 19. And in the place of the
■ boil there be a white
■ rising, or a bright spot, white,
■ and somewhat reddish,
and it be shewed to the priest;
■ 20. And if, when the
■ priest seeth it, behold,
■ it be in sight
■ lower than the skin,
and the hair thereof be turned white;
■ the priest shall pronounce
■ him unclean: it *is* a plague of
leprosy broken out of the boil.

21. **But if** the priest look on it, and, behold, **there be no white hairs** therein, **and if it be not lower than the skin, but** *be* **somewhat dark;** then **the priest shall shut him up seven days:**

22. **And if it spread** much abroad in the skin, then **the priest shall pronounce him unclean:** it *is* a plague.

23. **But if the bright spot** stay in his place, *and* **spread not, it is a burning boil; and the priest shall pronounce him clean.**

24. **Or if there be any flesh,** in the skin **whereof there is a hot burning, and** the quick *flesh* that burneth have **a white bright spot, somewhat reddish, or** white;

25. Then the priest shall look upon it: and, behold, **if the hair in the bright spot** be **turned white, and** it *be in* sight **deeper than the skin; it is a leprosy** broken out of the burning: **wherefore the priest shall pronounce him unclean:** it *is* the plague of leprosy.

26. **But if** the priest look on it, and, behold, **there be no white hair** in the bright spot, **and** it *be* **no lower than the other skin, but** *be* **somewhat dark;** then **the priest shall shut him up seven days:**

27. And the priest shall look **upon** him **the seventh day:** *and* **if it be spread** much abroad in the skin, then **the priest shall pronounce him unclean:** it *is* the plague of leprosy.

28. **And if the bright spot** stay in his place, *and* **spread not** in the skin, but it *be* somewhat dark; **it is a rising** of the burning, **and the priest shall pronounce him clean: for it is an inflammation** of the burning.

29. **If a man or woman have a plague upon the head or the beard;**

30. Then the priest shall see the plague: and, behold, **if it be** in sight **deeper than the skin; and** *there be* **in it a yellow thin hair; then the priest shall pronounce him unclean:** it *is* a dry scall, *even* a leprosy upon the head or beard.

31. **And if the priest look** on the plague of the scall, **and,** behold, **it be not** in sight **deeper than the skin, and** *that* **there is no black hair in it; then the priest shall shut up him** *that hath* the plague of the scall **seven days:**

32. **And in the seventh day** the priest shall look on the plague: and, behold, **if the scall spread not, and there be in it no yellow hair, and the scall be not** in sight **deeper** than the skin;

33. **He shall be shaven,** but the scall shall he not shave; **and** the priest shall **shut up** *him that hath* the scall **seven days more:**

34. **And in the seventh day** the priest shall look on the scall: and, behold, **if the scall be not spread** in the skin, **nor** *be* in sight **deeper** than the skin; **then the priest shall**

pronounce him clean: and he shall wash his clothes, and be clean.

35. **But if the scall spread** much in the skin **after his cleansing;**

36. Then the priest shall look on him: and, behold, if the scall be spread in the skin, **the priest shall not seek for yellow hair; he is unclean.**

37. **But if the scall be** in his sight **at a stay, and** *that* **there is black hair** grown up therein; the scall is healed, he *is* clean: and **the priest shall pronounce him clean.**

38. **If a man** also **or a woman have** in the skin of their flesh bright spots, *even* **white bright spots;**

39. Then the priest shall look: and, behold, **if the bright spots** in the skin of their flesh **be darkish white; it is a freckled spot** *that* groweth in the skin; **he is clean.**

40. **And the man whose** hair is fallen off his **head,** he **is bald;** *yet* **is** he **clean.**

41. And he that hath his hair fallen off from the part of his head toward his face, he *is* forehead bald: *yet is* he clean.

42. **And if there be in the bald head,** or bald forehead, **a white reddish sore; it is a leprosy sprung up** in his bald head, or his bald forehead.

43. Then the priest shall look upon it: and, behold, **if the rising of the sore be white reddish** in his bald head, or in his bald forehead, as the leprosy appeareth in the skin of the flesh;

44. **He is a leprous man, he is unclean:** the priest

shall pronounce him utterly unclean; his plague *is* in his head.

45. **And** the leper in whom the plague *is,* **his clothes shall be rent, and his head bare, and he shall put a covering upon his upper lip, and shall cry, Unclean, unclean.**

46. **All the days wherein the plague shall be in him** he shall be defiled; he *is* unclean: **he shall dwell alone; without the camp** *shall* his habitation *be.*

47. **The garment also that the plague of leprosy is in,** *whether it be* a woollen garment, or a linen garment;

48. Whether *it be* in the warp, or woof; of linen, or of woollen; whether in a skin, or in any thing made of skin;

49. **And if the plague be greenish or reddish in the garment,** or in the skin, either in the warp, or in the woof, or in any thing of skin; **it** *is* a plague of leprosy, and **shall be shewed unto the priest:**

50. And the priest shall look upon the plague, **and shut up** *it that hath* the plague **seven days:**

51. **And** he shall look on the plague **on the seventh day: if the plague be spread in the garment,** either in the warp, or in the woof, or in a skin, *or* in any work that is made of skin; **the plague is a fretting leprosy; it is unclean.**

52. **He shall therefore burn that garment,** whether warp or woof, in woollen or in linen, or any thing of skin, wherein the plague is: for it *is* a fretting leprosy; it shall be burnt in the fire.

53. **And if** the priest shall look, and, behold, **the plague be not spread** in the garment, either in the warp, or in

the woof, or in any thing of skin;

54. **Then the priest shall command that they wash the thing** wherein the plague *is,* **and** he **shall shut it up seven days** more:

55. **And** the priest shall look on the plague, **after** that **it is washed:** and, behold, **if the plague have not changed his colour, and the plague be not spread; it is unclean; thou shalt burn it** in the fire; it *is* fret inward, *whether* it *be* bare within or without.

56. **And if** the priest look, and, behold, **the plague be somewhat dark after the washing** of it; **then he shall rend it out of the garment,** or out of the skin, or out of the warp, or out of the woof:

57. **And if it appear still in the garment,** either in the warp, or in the woof, or in any thing of skin; it *is* a spreading *plague:* **thou shalt burn that wherein the plague is with fire.**

58. **And the garment,** either warp, or woof, or whatsoever thing of skin *it be,* **which thou shalt wash, if the plague be departed** from them, **then it shall be washed the second time, and shall be clean.**

59. This *is* the law of the plague of leprosy in a garment of woollen or linen, either in the warp, or woof, or any thing of skins, to pronounce it clean, or to pronounce it unclean.

CHAPTER 14

1. And the LORD spake unto Moses, saying,

2. **This shall be the law of the leper in** the day of **his cleansing: He shall be brought unto the priest:**

3. **And** the priest shall go forth out of the camp; and the priest shall look, and, behold, **if the plague of leprosy be healed** in the leper;

4. **Then shall the priest command to take for him** that is to be cleansed **two birds alive and clean,** and **cedar wood,** and **scarlet, and hyssop:**

5. **And** the priest **shall** command that **one** of the birds **be killed** in an earthen vessel over running water:

6. **As for the living bird,** he shall **take it, and the cedar wood,** and the **scarlet,** and the **hyssop, and** shall **dip them** and the living bird **in the blood of the bird that was killed** over the running water:

7. **And** he shall **sprinkle upon him** that is to be cleansed from the leprosy **seven times, and** shall **pronounce him clean, and** shall **let the living bird loose** into the open field.

8. **And he that is to be cleansed shall wash his clothes,** and **shave** off all his hair, **and wash himself** in water, that he may be clean: **and after that he shall come into the camp, and** shall **tarry** abroad **out of his tent seven days.**

9. But it shall be **on the seventh day,** that **he shall shave all his hair off his head and his beard and his eyebrows,** even all his hair he shall shave off; **and** he shall **wash his clothes, also he**

171

shall wash his flesh in water, and he shall be clean. 10. And on the eighth day he shall take two he lambs without blemish, and one ewe lamb of the first year without blemish, and three tenth deals of fine flour for a meat offering, mingled with oil, and one log of oil. 11. And the priest that maketh *him* clean shall present the man that is to be made clean, and those things, before the LORD, *at* the door of the tabernacle of the congregation: 12. And the priest shall take one he lamb, and offer him for a trespass offering, and the log of oil, and wave them *for* a wave offering before the LORD: 13. And he shall slay the lamb in the place where he shall kill the sin offering and the burnt offering, in the holy place: for as the sin offering *is* the priest's, *so is* the trespass offering: it *is* most holy: 14. And the priest shall take *some* of the blood of the trespass offering, and the priest shall put it upon the tip of the right ear of him that is to be cleansed, and upon the thumb of his right hand, and upon the great toe of his right foot: 15. And the priest shall take *some* of the log of oil, and pour *it* into the palm of his own left hand: 16. And the priest shall dip his right finger in the oil that *is* in his left hand, and shall sprinkle of the oil with his finger seven times before the LORD: 17. And of the rest of the oil that is in his hand

shall the priest put upon the tip of the right ear of him that is to be cleansed, and upon the thumb of his right hand, and upon the great toe of his right foot, upon the blood of the trespass offering: 18. And the remnant of the oil that *is* in the priest's hand he shall pour upon the head of him that is to be cleansed: and the priest shall make an atonement for him before the LORD. 19. And the priest shall offer the sin offering, and make an atonement for him that is to be cleansed from his uncleanness; and afterward he shall kill the burnt offering: 20. And the priest shall offer the burnt offering and the meat offering upon the altar: and the priest shall make an atonement for him, and he shall be clean. 21. And if he be poor, and cannot get so much; then he shall take one lamb for a trespass offering to be waved, to make an atonement for him, and one tenth deal of fine flour mingled with oil for a meat offering, and a log of oil; 22. And two turtledoves, or two young pigeons, such as he is able to get; and the one shall be a sin offering, and the other a burnt offering. 23. And he shall bring them on the eighth day for his cleansing unto the priest, unto the door of the tabernacle of the congregation, before the LORD. 24. And the priest shall take the lamb of the

■ **trespass offering,**
■ **and the log of oil,**
and the priest shall wave them
■ **for a wave offering**
before the LORD:
■ 25. **And he shall**
■ **kill the lamb of the**
■ **trespass offering,**
and the priest shall take *some* of the
blood of the trespass offering, and put
it upon the tip of the right ear of him
that is to be cleansed, and upon the
thumb of his right hand, and upon
the great toe of his right foot:
■ 26. **And the priest shall**
■ **pour of the oil into** the palm of
■ **his own left hand:**
■ 27. **And** the priest shall
■ **sprinkle** with his right finger
■ **some of the oil**
that *is* in his left hand
■ **seven times**
■ **before the LORD:**
■ 28. **And the priest shall put**
■ **of the oil** that *is* in his hand
■ **upon** the tip of the right ear of
■ **him that is to be cleansed,**
and upon the thumb of his right hand,
and upon the great toe of his right
foot, upon the place of the blood
of the trespass offering:
■ 29. And the rest of the oil that *is* in
the priest's hand he shall put upon the
head of him that is to be cleansed,
■ **to make an atonement**
■ **for him** before the LORD.
■ 30. **And he shall offer** the
■ **one of the turtledoves,**
■ **or** of the
■ **young pigeons,**
such as he can get;
■ 31. *Even* such as he is
able to get, the one
■ **for a sin offering, and the**
■ **other for a burnt offering,**
■ **with the meat offering: and**
■ **the priest shall make an**
■ **atonement for him** that is to
be cleansed before the LORD.
■ 32. **This is the law of him**
in whom *is* the plague of leprosy,
■ **whose hand is not able to**
■ **get that which pertaineth**

■ **to his cleansing.**
■ 33. **And the LORD spake**
unto Moses and unto Aaron,
■ **saying,**
■ 34. **When ye be**
■ **come into** the land of
■ **Canaan,** which I give
to you for a possession,
■ **and I put** the plague of
■ **leprosy in a house**
of the land of your possession;
35. And he that owneth the house
shall come and tell the priest,
saying, It seemeth to me *there*
is as it were a plague in the house:
■ 36. **Then the priest shall**
■ **command that they empty**
■ **the house,** before the priest go
into it to see the plague, that all that
is in the house be not made unclean:
and afterward the priest shall go
in to see the house:
■ 37. **And** he shall look on
the plague, and, behold,
■ **if the plague be in**
■ **the walls** of the house
■ **with hollow strakes,**
■ **greenish or reddish,**
■ **which** in sight
■ **are lower than the wall;**
■ 38. **Then the priest**
■ **shall** go out of the house
to the door of the house, and
■ **shut up the house**
■ **seven days:**
■ 39. **And** the priest shall
■ **come again the**
■ **seventh day,** and shall look:
■ **and,** behold,
■ **if the plague be spread**
■ **in the walls** of the house;
■ 40. **Then the priest shall**
■ **command that they take**
■ **away the stones in which**
■ **the plague is, and** they shall
■ **cast them** into an unclean place
■ **without the city:**
■ 41. **And he shall cause the**
■ **house to be scraped within**
round about, and they shall pour out
the dust that they scrape off without
the city into an unclean place:
■ 42. **And they shall take**

other stones, and put *them* in the place of those stones; and he shall take other morter, and shall plaster the house. 43. And if the plague come again, and break out in the house, after that he hath taken away the stones, and after he hath scraped the house, and after it is plastered; 44. Then the priest shall come and look, and, behold, *if* the plague be spread in the house, it is a fretting leprosy in the house: it *is* unclean. 45. And he shall break down the house, the stones of it, and the timber thereof, and all the morter of the house; and he shall carry them forth out of the city into an unclean place. 46. Moreover he that goeth into the house all the while that it is shut up shall be unclean until the even. 47. And he that lieth in the house shall wash his clothes; and he that eateth in the house shall wash his clothes. 48. And if the priest shall come in, and look *upon it,* and, behold, the plague hath not spread in the house, after the house was plastered: then the priest shall pronounce the house clean, because the plague is healed. 49. And he shall take to cleanse the house two birds, and cedar wood, and scarlet, and hyssop: 50. And he shall kill the one of the birds in an earthen vessel over running water: 51. And he shall take the

cedar wood, and the hyssop, and the scarlet, and the living bird, and dip them in the blood of the slain bird, and in the running water, and sprinkle the house seven times: 52. And he shall cleanse the house with the blood of the bird, and with the running water, and with the living bird, and with the cedar wood, and with the hyssop, and with the scarlet: 53. But he shall let go the living bird out of the city into the open fields, and make an atonement for the house: and it shall be clean. 54. This is the law for all manner of plague of leprosy, and scall, 55. And for the leprosy of a garment, and of a house, 56. And for a rising, and for a scab, and for a bright spot: 57. To teach when it is unclean, and when it is clean: this *is* the law of leprosy.

CHAPTER 15

1. And the LORD spake unto Moses and to Aaron, saying, 2. Speak unto the children of Israel, and say unto them, When any man hath a running issue out of his flesh, *because of* his issue he is unclean. 3. And this shall be his uncleanness in his issue: whether his flesh run with his issue, or his flesh be stopped from his issue, it *is* his uncleanness. 4. Every bed, whereon he lieth that hath the issue, is unclean: and every thing, whereon he sitteth, shall be unclean.

5. And whosoever toucheth his bed shall wash his clothes, and bathe *himself* in water, and be unclean until the even.

6. And he that sitteth on *any* thing whereon he sat that hath the issue shall wash his clothes, and bathe *himself* in water, and be unclean until the even.

7. And he that toucheth the flesh of **him** that hath the issue **shall wash his clothes, and bathe** *himself* in water, **and be unclean until the even.**

8. And if he that hath the issue spit upon him that is clean; then he shall wash his clothes, and bathe *himself* in water, and be unclean until the even.

9. And what saddle soever he rideth upon that hath the issue shall be unclean.

10. And whosoever toucheth any thing that was under him shall be unclean until the even: and he that beareth *any of* those things shall wash his clothes, and bathe *himself* in water, and be unclean until the even.

11. And whomsoever he toucheth that hath the issue, and hath not rinsed his hands in water, he shall wash his clothes, and bathe *himself* in water, and be unclean until the even.

12. And the vessel of earth, that he toucheth which hath the issue, shall be broken: and every vessel of wood shall be rinsed in water.

13. And when he that hath an issue is cleansed of his issue; **then he shall number** to himself **seven days for his cleansing,** and wash his clothes, and bathe his flesh in running water, and shall be clean.

14. And on the eighth day he shall take to him **two turtledoves, or two young pigeons, and come** before the LORD **unto** the door of

the tabernacle of the congregation, and give them unto the priest:

15. And the priest shall offer them, the one *for* a sin offering, and the other *for* a burnt offering; and the priest shall make an atonement **for him before the LORD** for his issue.

16. And if any man's seed of copulation go out from him, then **he shall wash** all his flesh in water, **and be unclean until the even.**

17. And every garment, and every skin, whereon is the seed of copulation, shall be washed with water, and be unclean until the even.

18. The woman also with whom man shall lie with seed of copulation, they shall *both* **bathe** *themselves* in water, **and be unclean until the even.**

19. And if a woman have an issue, *and* her issue in her flesh be blood, **she shall be put apart seven days: and whosoever toucheth her shall be unclean until the even.**

20. And every thing that she lieth upon in her separation shall be unclean: every thing also that she sitteth upon shall be unclean.

21. And whosoever toucheth her bed shall wash his clothes, and bathe *himself* in water, and be unclean until the even.

22. And whosoever toucheth any thing that she sat upon shall wash his clothes, and bathe *himself* in water, and be unclean until the even.

23. And if it *be* on *her* bed, or on any thing whereon she sitteth, when he toucheth it, he shall be unclean until the even.

24. And if any man lie with her at all,

■ and her flowers be
■ upon him, he shall be
■ unclean seven days;
and all the bed whereon
he lieth shall be unclean.
■ 25. **And if a woman**
■ **have an issue of her blood**
many days out of the time of her
separation, or if it run beyond the time
of her separation; all the days of the
issue of her uncleanness shall be
as the days of her separation:
■ **she shall be unclean.**
26. Every bed whereon she lieth all
the days of her issue shall be unto
her as the bed of her separation:
and whatsoever she sitteth upon
shall be unclean, as the
uncleanness of her separation.
27. And whosoever toucheth those
things shall be unclean, and shall
wash his clothes, and bathe *himself* in
water, and be unclean until the even.
■ 28. **But if she be**
■ **cleansed** of her issue, then
■ **she shall number** to herself
■ **seven days, and**
after that she shall
■ **be clean.**
29. And on the eighth day she shall
take unto her two turtles, or two young
pigeons, and bring them unto the
priest, to the door of the tabernacle
of the congregation.
30. And the priest shall offer the
one *for* a sin offering, and the other
for a burnt offering; and the priest
shall make an atonement for her
before the LORD for the issue
of her uncleanness.
■ 31. **Thus shall ye separate**
■ **the children of Israel from**
■ **their uncleanness; that**
■ **they die not in their**
■ **uncleanness, when they**
■ **defile my tabernacle**
■ **that is among them.**
32. This *is* the law of him that hath an
issue, and *of him* whose seed goeth
from him, and is defiled therewith;
33. And of her that is sick of her
flowers, and of him that hath an issue,
of the man, and of the woman, and of

| him that lieth with her that is unclean.

CHAPTER 16

1. And the LORD spake unto
Moses after the death of the two
sons of Aaron, when they offered
before the LORD, and died;
■ 2. **And the LORD said**
■ **unto Moses, Speak**
■ **unto Aaron** thy brother,
■ **that he come not at**
■ **all times into the holy**
■ **place** within the vail before the
mercy seat, which *is* upon the ark;
■ **that he die not: for I will**
■ **appear** in the cloud
■ **upon the mercy seat.**
■ 3. **Thus shall Aaron**
■ **come** into the holy *place:*
■ **with a young bullock**
■ **for a sin offering, and a**
■ **ram for a burnt offering.**
4. He shall put on the holy linen coat,
and he shall have the linen breeches
upon his flesh, and shall be girded
with a linen girdle, and with the linen
mitre shall he be attired: these
are holy garments; therefore
shall he wash his flesh in water,
and *so* put them on.
■ 5. **And he shall take**
■ **of the congregation**
of the children of Israel
■ **two kids of the goats for**
■ **a sin offering, and one**
■ **ram for a burnt offering.**
■ 6. **And** Aaron shall
■ **offer his bullock of**
■ **the sin offering,** which *is*
■ **for himself, and make**
■ **an atonement for himself,**
■ **and for his house.**
7. And he shall take the two goats,
and present them before the
LORD *at* the door of the
tabernacle of the congregation.
■ 8. **And Aaron shall cast lots**
■ **upon the two goats; one** lot
■ **for the LORD, and the**
■ **other lot for the scapegoat.**
■ 9. **And Aaron shall bring**
■ **the goat upon which the**
■ **LORD's lot fell, and offer him**

for a sin offering.

10. **But** the goat, on which the lot fell to be **the scapegoat, shall be presented alive** before the LORD, **to make an atonement with him,** *and* **to let him go** for a scapegoat **into the wilderness.**

11. And Aaron shall bring the bullock of the sin offering, which *is* for himself, and shall make an atonement for himself, and for his house, and shall kill the bullock of the sin offering which *is* for himself:

12. **And he shall take a censer** full **of burning coals** of fire from **off the altar** before the LORD, **and his hands full of sweet incense** beaten small, **and bring it within the veil:**

13. **And he shall put the incense upon the fire before the LORD,** that the cloud of the incense may cover the mercy seat that *is* upon the testimony, **that he die not:**

14. **And he shall take of the blood of the bullock, and sprinkle it with his finger upon the mercy seat eastward; and before the mercy seat** shall he sprinkle of the blood with his finger **seven times.**

15. **Then shall he kill the goat** of the sin offering, that *is* for the people, **and bring his blood within the veil, and do** with that blood **as he did with the blood of the bullock,** and sprinkle it upon the mercy seat, and before the mercy seat:

16. **And he shall make an atonement for the holy place, because of the uncleanness of** the children of **Israel, and** because of their transgressions in **all their sins:** and so shall

he do for the tabernacle of the congregation, that remaineth among them in the midst of their uncleanness.

17. **And there shall be no man in the tabernacle** of the congregation **when he goeth in to make an atonement in the holy place, until he come out,** and have made an atonement for himself, and for his household, and for all the congregation of Israel.

18. And he shall go out unto the altar that *is* before the LORD, and make an atonement for it; and shall take of the blood of the bullock, and of the blood of the goat, and put *it* upon the horns of the altar round about.

19. And he shall sprinkle of the blood upon it with his finger seven times, and cleanse it, and hallow it from the uncleanness of the children of Israel.

20. **And when he hath made an end of reconciling the holy place, and the tabernacle** of the congregation, **and the altar, he shall bring the live goat:**

21. **And Aaron shall lay both** his **hands upon the head** of the live goat, **and confess over him all the iniquities of** the children of **Israel,** and all their transgressions in all their sins, **putting them upon thehead of the goat, and shall send him away by the hand of a fit man into the wilderness:**

22. **And the goat shall bear** upon him **all their iniquities** unto a land not inhabited: and he shall let go the goat in the wilderness.

23. And Aaron shall come into the tabernacle of the congregation, and shall put off the linen garments, which he put on when he went into the holy *place,* and shall leave them there:

24. And he shall wash his flesh with

water in the holy place, and put on his garments, and come forth, and offer his burnt offering, and the burnt offering of the people, and make an atonement for himself, and for the people.

25. And the fat of the sin offering shall he burn upon the altar.

26. And he that let go the goat for the scapegoat shall wash his clothes, and bathe his flesh in water, and afterward come into the camp.

27. And the bullock *for* the sin offering, and the goat *for* the sin offering, whose blood was brought in to make atonement in the holy *place,* shall *one* carry forth without thecamp; and they shall burn in the fire their skins, and their flesh, and their dung.

28. And he that burneth them shall wash his clothes, and bathe his flesh in water, and afterward he shall come into the camp.

29. And this shall be a statute for ever unto you: *that* **in the seventh month, on the tenth day** of the month, **ye shall afflict your souls, and do no work at all, whether it be one of your own country, or a stranger** that sojourneth **among you:**

30. For on that day shall the priest make an atonement for you, to cleanse you, *that* ye may be clean from all your sins before the LORD.

31. It shall be a sabbath of rest unto you, and ye shall afflict your souls, by a statute for ever.

32. And the priest, whom he shall anoint, and whom he shall consecrate to minister in the priest's office in his father's stead, shall make the atonement, and shall put on the linen clothes, *even* the holy garments:

33. And he shall make an atonement for the holy sanctuary, and he shall makean atonement for the tabernacle of the congregation, and for the altar, and he shall make an

atonement for the priests, and for all the people of the congregation.

34. And this shall be an everlasting statute unto you, to make an atonement for the children of Israel for all their sins once a year. And he did as the LORD commanded Moses.

CHAPTER 17

1. And the LORD spake unto Moses, saying,

2. Speak unto Aaron, and unto his sons, and unto all the children of Israel, and say unto them;

This is the thing which **the LORD hath commanded,** saying,

3. What man soever *there be* **of** the house of **Israel, that killeth an ox, or lamb, or goat,** in the camp, or that killeth *it* out of the camp,

4. And bringeth it not unto the door of **the tabernacle** of the congregation, to offer an offering **unto the LORD** before the tabernacle of the LORD;

blood shall be imputed unto that man;he hath shed blood; and that man shall be cut off from among his people:

5. To the end that the children of Israel may bring their sacrifices, which they offer in the open field, even that they may bring them unto the LORD, unto the door of the tabernacle of the congregation, unto the priest, and offer them

for peace offerings unto the LORD.

6. And the priest shall sprinkle the blood upon the altar of the LORD *at* the door of the tabernacle of the congregation, and burn the fat for a sweet savour unto the LORD.

7. And they shall no more offer their sacrifices unto devils, after whom they have gone a-whoring.

This shall be a

■ **statute for ever** unto them
throughout their generations.
8. And thou shalt say unto them,
■ **Whatsoever man** *there be*
■ **of** the house of
■ **Israel, or of** the
■ **strangers** which sojourn
■ **among you, that offereth a**
■ **burnt offering or sacrifice,**
9. **And bringeth it not**
■ **unto the** door of the
■ **tabernacle** of the
congregation, to offer it unto
the LORD; even that man
■ **shall be cut off**
from among his people.
■ 10. **And whatsoever**
■ **man** *there be* of the house
■ **of Israel, or of** the
■ **strangers** that sojourn
■ **among you, that**
■ **eateth** any manner of
■ **blood; I will** even set
my face against that soul
that eateth blood, and will
■ **cut him off** from among his people.
■ 11. **For the life of the flesh**
■ **is in the blood:** and I
have given it to you upon the altar
■ **to make an atonement for**
■ **your souls:** for *is* the blood *that*
maketh an atonement for the soul.
■ 12. **Therefore I said**
unto the children of Israel,
■ **No soul** of you
■ **shall eat blood,**
neither shall any stranger that
sojourneth among you eat blood.
■ 13. **And whatsoever man**
there be of the children of Israel, or of
the strangers that sojourn among you,
■ **which hunteth** and catcheth
■ **any beast or fowl that**
■ **may be eaten; he shall**
■ **even pour out the blood**
■ **thereof,** and cover it with dust.
■ 14. **For** *it is* the life of all flesh;
■ **the blood** of it
■ **is** for
■ **the life thereof:**
therefore I said unto the children of
Israel, Ye shall eat the blood of no
manner of flesh: for the life of all flesh

is the blood thereof: whosoever
eateth it shall be cut off.
■ 15. **And every soul that**
■ **eateth that which died**
■ **of itself, or** that which
■ **was torn with beasts,**
whether it be one of your own
country, or a stranger, he
■ **shall** both
■ **wash his clothes,**
■ **and bathe** *himself* in water,
■ **and be unclean until the**
■ **even:** then shall he be clean.
16. But if he wash *them* not,
nor bathe his flesh; then he
shall bear his iniquity.

CHAPTER 18
■ 1. **And the LORD spake**
■ **unto Moses, saying,**
■ 2. **Speak unto** the children of
■ **Israel, and say** unto
them, I am the LORD your God.
■ 3. **After the doings** of the land
■ **of Egypt,** wherein ye
dwelt, shall ye not do:
■ **and** after the doings of the land of
■ **Canaan,** whither I bring you,
■ **shall ye not do:** neither
shall ye walk in their ordinances.
■ 4. **Ye shall do my**
■ **judgments, and keep**
■ **mine ordinances,** to walk
therein: I *am* the LORD your God.
5. Ye shall therefore keep my
statutes, and my judgments:
which if a man do, he shall
live in them: I *am* the LORD.
■ 6. **None** of you
■ **shall approach** to any that is
■ **near of kin** to him,
■ **to uncover their**
■ **nakedness:** I *am* the LORD.
■ 7. **The nakedness of**
■ **thy father, or**
the nakedness of thy
■ **mother,** shalt thou not uncover:
she *is* thy mother; thou shalt not
uncover her nakedness.
■ 8. **The nakedness of**
■ **thy father's wife** shalt thou not
uncover: it *is* thy father's nakedness.
9. The nakedness of

thy sister, the daughter of
thy father, or daughter of
thy mother, *whether she be* born
at home, or born abroad, *even* their
nakedness thou shalt not uncover.
10. The nakedness of
thy son's daughter, or of
thy daughter's daughter,
even their nakedness thou
shalt not uncover: for theirs
is thine own nakedness.
11. The nakedness of
thy father's wife's
daughter, begotten of thy
father, she *is* thy sister, thou
shalt not uncover her nakedness.
12. Thou shalt not
uncover the nakedness of
thy father's sister:
she *is* thy father's near kinswoman.
13. Thou shalt not
uncover the nakedness of
thy mother's sister: for she
is thy mother's near kinswoman.
14. Thou shalt not
uncover the nakedness of
thy father's brother,
thou shalt not approach to
his wife: she *is* thine aunt.
15. Thou shalt not
uncover the nakedness of
thy daughter in law:
she *is* thy son's wife; thou shalt
not uncover her nakedness.
16. Thou shalt not
uncover the nakedness of
thy brother's wife:
it *is* thy brother's nakedness.
17. Thou shalt not
uncover the nakedness of
a woman and her
daughter, neither
shalt thou take
her son's daughter, or
her daughter's daughter,
to uncover her nakedness;
for they *are* her near
kinswomen: it *is* wickedness.
18. Neither shalt thou
take a wife to her
sister, to vex her, to
uncover her nakedness,
beside the other in

her life time.
19. Also thou shalt
not approach unto
a woman to
uncover her nakedness,
as long as she is put
apart for her uncleanness.
20. Moreover thou
shalt not lie carnally
with thy neighbour's
wife, to defile thyself with her.
21. And thou shalt not let
any of thy seed pass
through the fire to
Molech, neither shalt
thou profane the name
of thy God: I *am* the LORD.
22. Thou shalt not lie
with mankind, as
with womankind:
it is abomination.
23. Neither shalt thou
lie with any beast
to defile thyself therewith:
neither shall any woman
stand before a beast to
lie down thereto: it *is* confusion.
24. Defile not ye
yourselves in *any* of
these things: for in all these
the nations are defiled
which I cast out before you:
25. And the land is defiled:
therefore I do visit
the iniquity thereof
upon it, and
the land itself vomiteth
out her inhabitants.
26. Ye shall therefore
keep my statutes and my
judgments, and shall not commit
any of these abominations; *neither*
any of your own nation, nor any
stranger that sojourneth among you:
27. (For all these abominations have
the men of the land done, which *were*
before you, and the land is defiled;)
28. That the land spue
not you out also,
when ye defile it, as it spued out
the nations that *were* before you.
29. For whosoever
shall commit any of

■ **these abominations,**
even the souls that commit *them*
■ **shall be cut off**
from among their people.
30. Therefore shall ye keep mine
ordinance, that *ye* commit not *any one*
of these abominable customs, which
were committed before you, and that
ye defile not yourselves therein: I
am the LORD your God.

CHAPTER 19

1. And the LORD spake
unto Moses, saying,
2. Speak unto all the congregation
of the children of Israel, and
say unto them,
■ **Ye shall be holy:**
■ **for I the LORD your**
■ **God am holy.**
■ 3. **Ye shall fear every man**
■ **his mother, and his father,**
■ **and keep my sabbaths:**
I *am* the LORD your God.
■ 4. **Turn ye not unto idols,**
nor make to yourselves molten
gods: I *am* the LORD your God.
5. And if ye offer a sacrifice of
peace offerings unto the LORD,
ye shall offer it at your own will.
6. It shall be eaten the same day ye
offer it, and on the morrow: and if
aught remain until the third day, it
shall be burnt in the fire.
7. And if it be eaten at all on the
third day, it *is* abominable; it
shall not be accepted.
8. Therefore *every one* that eateth it
shall bear his iniquity, because he
hath profaned the hallowed thing of
the LORD: and that soul shall be
cut off from among his people.
■ 9. **And when ye reap**
the harvest of your land,
■ **thou shalt not wholly**
■ **reap the corners of thy**
■ **field, neither** shalt thou
■ **gather the gleanings**
of thy harvest.
■ 10. **And thou shalt not**
■ **glean thy vineyard,**
■ **neither** shalt thou
■ **gather every grape**

of thy vineyard;
■ **thou shalt leave them for**
■ **the poor and stranger:**
I *am* the LORD your God.
■ 11. **Ye shall not steal,**
■ **neither deal falsely,**
■ **neither lie one to another.**
■ 12. **And ye shall**
■ **not swear by my name**
■ **falsely, neither** shalt thou
■ **profane the name**
■ **of thy God:** I *am* the LORD.
■ 13. **Thou shalt not defraud**
■ **thy neighbour, neither**
■ **rob him: the wages of**
■ **him that is hired shall**
■ **not abide with thee**
■ **all night** until the morning.
■ 14. **Thou shalt not curse**
■ **the deaf, nor put a**
■ **stumblingblock before**
■ **the blind,** but shalt fear
thy God: I *am* the LORD.
15. Ye shall do no
unrighteousness in judgment:
■ **thou shalt not**
■ **respect** the person of
■ **the poor, nor**
■ **honor** the person of
■ **the mighty: but in**
■ **righteousness shalt thou**
■ **judge thy neighbour.**
■ 16. **Thou shalt not**
■ **go** up and down
■ **as a talebearer**
among thy people:
■ **neither** shalt thou
■ **stand against the blood of**
■ **thy neighbour;** I *am* the LORD.
■ 17. **Thou shalt not hate**
■ **thy brother** in thine heart:
■ **thou shalt in any wise**
■ **rebuke thy neighbour,**
and not suffer sin upon him.
■ 18. **Thou shalt not avenge,**
■ **nor bear any grudge**
against the children of thy people,
■ **but** thou shalt
■ **love thy neighbour**
■ **as thyself:** I *am* the LORD.
■ 19. **Ye shall keep my**
■ **statutes. Thou shalt not**
■ **let thy cattle gender with**

a diverse kind: thou shalt not sow thy field with mingled seed: neither shall a garment mingled of linen and woollen come upon thee. 20. And whosoever lieth carnally with a woman, that is a bondmaid, betrothed to an husband, and not at all redeemed, nor freedom givenher; she shall be scourged; they shall not be put to death, because she was not free. 21. And he shall bring his trespass offering unto the LORD, unto the door of the tabernacle of the congregation, even a ram for a trespass offering. 22. And the priest shall make an atonement for him with the ram of the trespass offering before the LORD for his sin which he hath done: and the sin which he hath done shall be forgiven him. 23. And when ye shall come into the land, and shall have planted all manner of trees for food, then ye shall count the fruit thereof as uncircumcised: three years shall it be as uncircumcised unto you: it shall not be eaten of. 24. But in the fourth year all the fruit thereof shall be holy to praise the LORD withal. 25. And in the fifth year shall ye eat of the fruit thereof, that it may yield unto you the increase thereof: I am the LORD your God. 26. Ye shall not eat any thing with the blood: neither shall ye use enchantment, nor observe times. 27. Ye shall not round the corners of your heads, neither shalt thou mar the corners of thy beard. 28. Ye shall not make any cuttings in your flesh for the dead, nor print any marks upon you: I am the LORD. 29. Do not prostitute thy daughter, to cause her to be a whore; lest the land fall to whoredom, and the land become full of wickedness. 30. Ye shall keep my sabbaths, and reverence my sanctuary: I am the LORD. 31. Regard not them that have familiar spirits, neither seek after wizards, to be defiled by them: I am the LORD your God. 32. Thou shalt rise up before the hoary head, and honour the face of the old man, and fear thy God: I am the LORD. 33. And if a stranger sojourn with thee in your land, ye shall not vex him. 34. But the stranger that dwelleth with you shall be unto you as one born among you, and thou shalt love him as thyself; for ye were strangers in the land of Egypt: I am the LORD your God. 35. Ye shall do no unrighteousness in judgment, in meteyard, in weight, or in measure. 36. Just balances, just weights, a just ephah, and a just hin, shall ye have: I am the LORD your God, which brought you out of the land of Egypt. 37. Therefore shall ye observe all my statutes, and all my judgments, and do them: I am the LORD.

CHAPTER 20

1. And the LORD spake unto Moses, saying,

2. Again, thou shalt say to the children of Israel, **Whosoever he be Of** the children of **Israel, or of the strangers** that sojourn **in Israel, that giveth** any of **his seed unto Molech;** he shall surely be put to death: **the people** of the land **shall stone him** with stones.

3. And I will set my face against that man, and will cut him off from among his people; **because he hath given of his seed unto Molech,** to defile my sanctuary, and **to profane my holy name.**

4. **And if the people** of the land do any ways hide their eyes from the man, when he giveth of his seed unto Molech, and **kill him not:**

5. **Then I will set my face against that man,** and against **his family, and will cut him off,** and all that go a-whoring after him, to commit whoredom with Molech, from among their people.

6. **And the soul that turneth after such as have familiar spirits, and** after **wizards,** to go a-whoring after them, **I will** even set my face against that soul, and will **cut him off** from amonghis people.

7. **Sanctify yourselves** therefore, **and be ye holy:** for I *am* the LORD your God.

8. And ye shall keep my statutes, and do them: I *am* the LORD which sanctify you.

9. **For every one that curseth** his **father or** his **mother shall be** surely **put to death:** he hath cursed his father or his mother; his blood *shall be* upon him.

10. **And the man that committeth adultery with another man's wife,** *even he* that committeth adultery with his neighbour's wife, **the adulterer and the adulteress shall** surely **be put to death.**

11. **And the man that lieth with his father's wife** hath uncovered his father's nakedness: **both** of them **shall** surely **be put to death;** their blood *shall be* upon them.

12. **And if a man lie with his daughter in law, both** of them **shall** surely **be put to death:** they have wrought confusion; their blood *shall be* upon them.

13. **If a man also lie with mankind, as** he lieth **with a woman, both** of them have committed an abomination: they **shall** surely **be put to death;** their blood *shall be* upon them.

14. **And if a man take a wife and her mother, it is wickedness:** they shall be burnt with fire, both he and they; that there be no wickedness among you.

15. **And if a man lie with a beast, he shall** surely **be put to death:** and ye shall slay the beast.

16. **And if a woman approach** unto **any beast, and lie down thereto, thou shalt kill the woman, and the beast:** they shall surely be put to death; their blood *shall be* upon them.

17. **And if a man shall take his sister, his father's daughter, or his mother's daughter, and see her nakedness,** and she see his nakedness;

it is a wicked thing; and they shall be cut off in the sight of their people: he hath uncovered his sister's nakedness; he shall bear his iniquity.

18. **And if a man shall lie with a woman having her sickness,** and shall uncover her nakedness; he hath discovered her fountain, and she hath uncovered the fountain of her blood: and **both of them shall be cut off** from among their people.

19. **And thou shalt not uncover the nakedness of** thy mother's sister, nor of thy father's sister: for he uncovereth his **near kin:** they shall bear their iniquity.

20. **And if a man shall lie with his uncle's wife,** he hath uncovered his uncle's nakedness: they shall bear their sin; **they shall die childless.**

21. **And if a man shall take his brother's wife, it is an unclean thing:** he hath uncovered his brother's nakedness; they shall be childless.

22. **Ye shall therefore keep all my statutes, and** all my judgments, and **do them:** that the land, whither I bring you to dwell therein, spue you not out.

23. **And ye shall not walk in the manners of the nation, which I cast out** before you: **for** they committed all these things, and therefore **I abhorred them.**

24. But I have said unto you, **Ye shall inherit** their land, and I will give it unto you to possess it, **a land that floweth with milk and honey: I** am the LORD your God, which **have separated you from other people.**

25. Ye shall therefore put difference between clean beasts and unclean,

and between unclean fowls andclean: and ye shall not make your souls abominable by beast, or by fowl, or by any manner of living thing that creepeth on the ground, which I have separated from you as unclean.

26. And ye shall be holy unto me: for **I the LORD am holy, and have severed you** from *other* people, **that ye should be mine.**

27. **A man** also **or woman that hath a familiar spirit, or that is a wizard, shall** surely **be put to death:** they shall stone them with stones: their blood *shall be* upon them.

CHAPTER 21

1. **And the LORD said unto Moses, Speak unto the priests** the sons of Aaron, **and say** unto them, **There shall none be defiled for the dead** among his people:

2. **But for his kin,** that is near unto him, *that is,* for his mother, and for his father, and for his son, and for his daughter, and for his brother.

3. And for his sister a virgin, that is nigh unto him, which hath had no husband; for her **may he be defiled.**

4. **But he shall not** defile himself, *being* a chief man among his people, to **profane himself.**

5. **They shall not make baldness** upon their head, **neither** shall they **shave off the corner of their beard, nor** make any **cuttings in their flesh.**

6. **They shall be holy** unto their God, and not profane the name of their God: for the offerings of the LORD made by fire, *and* the bread of their God, they do offer: therefore they shall be holy.

7. **They shall not take a wife that is a whore, or profane; neither** shall they take

a woman put away from her husband: for he is holy unto his God. 8. **Thou shalt sanctify him therefore;** for he offereth the bread of thy God: he shall be holy unto thee: for I the LORD, which sanctify you, *am* holy. 9. **And the daughter of any priest, if she profane herself by playing the whore, she** profaneth her father: she **shall be burnt with fire.** 10. **And** *he that is* **the high priest** among his brethren, **upon whose head the anointing oil was poured,** and that is consecrated to put on the garments, **shall not uncover his head, nor rend his clothes;** 11. **Neither shall he go in to any dead body, nor defile himself** for his father, or for his mother; 12. **Neither shall he go out of the sanctuary, nor profane the sanctuary** of his God; for the crown of the anointing oil ofhis God *is* upon him: I *am* theLORD. 13. **And he shall take a wife in her virginity.** 14. A widow, or a divorced woman, or profane, *or* an harlot, these shall he not take: but he shall take a virgin of his own people to wife. 15. **Neither shall he profane his seed among his people:** for I the LORD do sanctify him. 16. And the LORD spake unto Moses, saying, 17. **Speak unto Aaron,** saying, **Whosoever** *he be* of thy seed in their generations **that hath any blemish, let him not approach to offer the bread of his God.** 18. For whatsoever man *he be* that hath a blemish, he shall notapproach: a blind man, or a lame, or he thathath

a flat nose, or any thing superfluous, 19. Or a man that is brokenfooted, or brokenhanded, 20. Or crookbackt, or a dwarf, or that hath a blemish in his eye, or be scurvy, or scabbed, or hath his stones broken; 21. **No man that hath a blemish of the seed of Aaron** the priest **shall come nigh to offer the offerings** of the LORD made by fire: he hath a blemish; he shall not come nigh to offer the bread of his God. 22. **He shall eat the bread of his God,** *both* of the most holy, and of the holy. 23. **Only he shall not go in unto the veil, nor** come nigh unto the **altar,** because he hath a blemish; that he profane not my sanctuaries: for I the LORD do sanctify them. 24. And Moses told *it* unto Aaron, and to his sons, and unto all the children of Israel.

CHAPTER 22

1. And the LORD spake unto Moses, saying, 2. **Speak unto Aaron and to his sons,** that they separate themselves from the holy things of the children of Israel, **and** that they profane not my holy name *in those things* which they hallow unto me: I *am* the LORD. 3. **Say** unto them, **Whosoever** *he be* of all your seed among your generations, that **goeth unto the holy things,** which the children of Israel hallow unto the LORD, **having** his **uncleanness** upon him, that soul **shall be cut off** from my presence: I *am* the LORD. 4. What man soever of the seed of Aaron *is* a leper, or hath a running issue; he shall not eat of the holy things, until he be clean. And whoso toucheth any thing *that*

is unclean *by* the dead, or a man whose seed goeth from him;

5. Or whosoever toucheth any creeping thing, whereby he may be made unclean, or a man of whom he may take uncleanness, whatsoever uncleanness he hath;

6. The soul which hath touched any such shall be unclean until even, and shall not eat of the holy things, unless he wash his flesh with water.

7. And when the sun is down, he shall be clean, and shall afterward eat of the holy things; because it *is* his food.

8. That which dieth of itself, or is torn *with beasts,* he shall not eat to defile himself therewith; I *am* the LORD.

9. They shall therefore keep mine ordinance, lest they bear sin for it, and die therefore, if they profane it: I the LORD do sanctify them.

10. There shall no stranger eat *of* the holy thing: a sojourner of the priest, **or** an **hired servant,** shall not **eat of the holy thing.**

11. But if the priest buy any soul with his money, he shall eat of it, **and he that is born in his house: they shall eat of his meat.**

12. If the priest's **daughter** also **be married unto a stranger, she may not eat** of an offering **of the holy things.**

13. But if the priest's **daughter be a widow, or divorced, and have no child, and is returned unto her father's house,** as in her youth, **she shall eat of her father's meat:** but there shall be no stranger eat thereof.

14. And if a man eat of the holy thing unwittingly, then **he shall put the fifth part thereof** unto it,

and shall **give it unto the priest with the holy thing.**

15. And they shall not profane the holy things of the children of Israel, which they offer unto the LORD;

16. Or suffer them to bear the iniquity of trespass, when they eat their holy things: for I the LORD do sanctify them.

17. And the LORD spake unto Moses, saying,

18. Speak unto Aaron, and to his sons, and unto all the children of Israel, and say unto them,

Whatsoever he be of the house **of Israel, or of the strangers in Israel, that will offer his oblation for all his vows, and** for all his **freewill offerings,** which **they will offer** unto the LORD **for a burnt offering;**

19. *Ye shall offer* at your own will **a male without blemish, of the beeves,** of the **sheep, or** of the **goats.**

20. **But whatsoever hath a blemish, that shall ye not offer:** for it shall not be acceptable for you.

21. **And whosoever offereth** a sacrifice of **peace offerings** unto the LORD to accomplish *his* vow, or a freewill offering in beeves or sheep, it shall be perfect to be accepted; **there shall be no blemish therein.**

22. Blind, or broken, or maimed, or having a wen, or scurvy, or scabbed, ye shall not offer these unto the LORD, nor make an offering by fire of them upon the altar unto the LORD.

23. Either a bullock or a lamb that hath any thing superfluous or lacking in his parts, that mayest thou offer *for* a freewill offering; but for a vow it shall not be accepted.

24. **Ye shall not offer unto the LORD that which is bruised, or crushed,**

or broken, or cut;
neither shall ye make *any*
offering thereof in your land.
25. **Neither from a**
stranger's hand
shall ye offer the bread
of your God of any of these;
because their
corruption is in them,
and blemishes *be* in them:
they shall not be
accepted for you.
26. And the LORD spake
unto Moses, saying,
27. **When a bullock,** or a
sheep, or a goat,
is brought forth, then
it shall be seven days
under the dam; and from
the eighth day and thenceforth
it shall be accepted
for an offering
made by fire unto the LORD.
28. **And whether it be**
cow or ewe, ye shall not
kill it and her young both
in one day.
29. **And when ye** will
offer a sacrifice of
thanksgiving unto the LORD,
offer it at your own will.
30. On the same day it shall be
eaten up; ye shall leave none of it
until the morrow: I *am* the LORD.
31. **Therefore** shall ye
keep my commandments,
and do them: I *am* the LORD.
32. **Neither** shall ye
profane my holy name; but
I will be hallowed among
the children of Israel:
I *am* the LORD which hallow you,
33. That brought you out of
the land of Egypt, to be your
God: I *am* the LORD.

CHAPTER 23

1. And the LORD spake
unto Moses, saying,
2. **Speak unto** the children of
Israel, and say unto them,
Concerning the feasts
of the LORD, which ye shall

proclaim *to be* holy convocations,
even these *are* my feasts.
3. **Six days shall work be**
done: but the seventh day
is the sabbath of rest,
an holy convocation;
ye shall do no work
therein: it *is* the sabbath of
the LORD in all your dwellings.
4. **These are the feasts**
of the LORD, *even* holy convocations,
which ye shall proclaim
in their seasons.
5. **In the fourteenth day**
of the first month at even
is the LORD's passover.
6. **And on the fifteenth**
day of the same month is
the feast of unleavened
bread unto the LORD:
seven days ye must
eat unleavened bread.
7. **In the first day ye**
shall have an holy
convocation: ye shall
do no servile work therein.
8. **But ye shall offer an**
offering made by fire
unto the LORD
seven days: in the
seventh day is an
holy convocation:
ye shall do no servile work *therein*.
9. And the LORD spake
unto Moses, saying,
10. Speak unto the children of
Israel, and say unto them,
When ye be come into
the land which I give unto you,
and shall
reap the harvest thereof, then
ye shall bring a sheaf of
the firstfruits of your harvest
unto the priest:
11. **And he shall wave**
the sheaf before the
LORD, to be accepted for you,
on the morrow after the
sabbath the priest shall wave it.
12. **And ye shall offer**
that day when ye wave the sheaf
an he lamb without
blemish of the first year

for a burnt offering unto the LORD.

13. **And the meat offering** thereof **shall be** two tenth deals of **fine flour mingled with oil,** an offering made by fire unto the LORD *for* a sweet savour: **and the drink offering** thereof *shall be* **of wine,** the fourth *part* of an hin.

14. And ye shall **eat neither bread,** nor **parched corn, nor green ears, until the selfsame day that ye have brought an offering** unto your God: *it shall be* a statute for ever throughout your generations in all your dwellings.

15. **And** ye shall **count** unto you **from the morrow after the sabbath,** from **the day** that **ye brought the sheaf** of the wave offering; **seven sabbaths** shall be complete:

16. Even unto **the morrow after the seventh sabbath shall ye number fifty days; and** ye shall **offer a new meat offering** unto the LORD.

17. **Ye shall bring** out of your habitations **two wave loaves of** two tenth deals: they shall be **of fine flour;** they shall be **baken with leaven; they are the firstfruits unto the LORD.**

18. And ye shall **offer with the bread seven lambs without blemish of the first year,** and **one young bullock, and two rams: they shall be for a burnt offering** unto the LORD, with their meat offering, and their drink offerings, *even* an offering made by fire, of sweet savour unto the LORD.

19. **Then** ye shall **sacrifice one kid of the goats for a sin offering, and two lambs** of the first year **for** a sacrifice of **peace offerings.**

20. And the priest shall wave them with the bread of the firstfruits *for* a wave offering before the LORD, with the two lambs: **they shall be** holy to the LORD **for the priest.**

21. **And** ye shall **proclaim on the selfsame day,** *that* it may be **an holy convocation** unto you: **ye shall do no servile work** *therein:* **it shall be a statute for ever** in all your dwellings throughout your generations.

22. **And when ye reap the harvest** of your land, **thou shalt not make clean riddance of the corners of thy field** when thou reapest, **neither** shalt thou **gather** any **gleaning** of thy harvest: thou shalt **leave them unto the poor, and** to the **stranger:** I *am* the LORD your God.

23. And the LORD spake unto Moses, saying,

24. Speak unto the children of Israel, saying, In **the seventh month,** in **the first day** of the month, **shall ye have a sabbath, a memorial of blowing of trumpets,** an holy convocation.

25. Ye shall do no servile work *therein:* but **ye shall offer an offering** made by fire **unto the LORD.**

26. And the LORD spake unto Moses, saying,

27. **Also on the tenth day of this seventh month there shall be a day of atonement:** it shall be

an holy convocation unto you;
and ye shall afflict your souls, and offer an offering made by fire **unto the LORD.**
28. And ye shall do no work in that same day: for it *is* a day of atonement, to make an atonement for you before the LORD your God.
29. **For whatsoever soul it be that shall not be afflicted** in that same day, he **shall be cut off** from among his people.
30. **And whatsoever soul** *it be* **that doeth any work** in **that** same **day,** the same soul **will I destroy** from among his people.
31. Ye shall do no manner of work: *it shall be* a statute for ever throughout your generations in all your dwellings.
32. It *shall be* unto you a sabbath of rest, and ye shall afflict your souls: **in the ninth day of the month** at even, **from even unto even, shall ye celebrate your sabbath.**
33. And the LORD spake unto Moses, saying,
34. Speak unto the children of Israel, saying, **The fifteenth day of this seventh month shall be the feast of tabernacles for seven days** unto the LORD.
35. **On the first day** *shall be* an holy convocation: **ye shall do no servile work** *therein.*
36. **Seven days ye shall offer an offering** made by fire **unto the LORD: on the eighth day shall be an holy convocation** unto you; **and ye shall offer an offering** made by fire **unto the LORD: it is a solemn assembly;** *and* ye shall do no servile work *therein.*

37. **These are the feasts of the LORD, which ye shall proclaim to be holy convocations,** to offer an offering made by fire unto the LORD, **a burnt offering,** and a **meat offering, a sacrifice, and drink offerings, every thing upon his day:**
38. **Beside the sabbaths of the LORD,** and beside your **gifts,** and beside all your **vows, and** beside all your **freewill offerings, which ye give unto the LORD.**
39. **Also in the fifteenth day of the seventh month, when ye have gathered in the fruit** of the land, **ye shall keep a feast** unto the LORD **seven days: on the first day shall be a sabbath, and on the eighth day shall be a sabbath.**
40. **And ye shall take** you on the first day the boughs of goodly trees, **branches of palm trees, and the boughs of** thick trees, and **willows** of the brook; **and ye shall rejoice** before the LORD your God seven days.
41. **And** ye shall keep it a **feast unto the LORD seven days** in the year. *It shall be* a statute for ever in your generations: ye shall celebrate it in the seventh month.
42. Ye shall dwell in booths seven days; **all that are Israelites** born **shall dwell in booths:**
43. **That your generations may know that I made** the children of **Israel to dwell in booths, when I brought them out of** the land of **Egypt:** I *am* the LORD your God.
44. **And Moses declared**

unto the children of
Israel the feasts
of the LORD.

CHAPTER 24

1. And the LORD spake
unto Moses, saying,
2. Command the children of
Israel, that they
bring unto thee
pure oil olive beaten for the light,
to cause the lamps
to burn continually.
3. Without the
veil of the testimony,
in the tabernacle
of the congregation,
shall Aaron order it
from the evening unto
the morning before the LORD
continually: *it shall be* a statute
for ever in your generations.
4. He shall order the lamps
upon the pure candlestick
before the LORD continually.
5. And thou shalt take
fine flour, and bake
twelve cakes thereof: two
tenth deals shall be in one cake.
6. And thou shalt
set them in two
rows, six on a row,
upon the pure table
before the LORD.
7. And thou shalt
put pure
frankincense upon each
row, that it may be on the bread
for a memorial, *even* an
offering made by fire unto the LORD.
8. Every sabbath he
shall set it in order before
the LORD continually, *being taken*
from the children of Israel
by an everlasting
covenant.
9. And it shall be
Aaron's and his
sons'; and they shall
eat it in the holy place:
for it *is* most holy unto him of the
offerings of the LORD made
by fire by a perpetual statute.

10. And the son of an
Israelitish woman, whose
father was an Egyptian, went
out among the children of Israel: and
this son of the Israelitish *woman*
and a man of Israel
strove together in the camp;
11. And the Israelitish
woman's son blasphemed
the name of the Lord, and
cursed. And they brought
him unto Moses: (and his
mother's name *was* Shelomith, the
daughter of Dibri, of the tribe of Dan:)
12. And they put him in ward,
that the mind of the LORD
might be shewed them.
13. And the LORD spake
unto Moses, saying,
14. Bring forth him that
hath cursed without the camp;
and let all that heard *him* lay their
hands upon his head,
and let all the
congregation stone him.
15. And thou shalt speak unto
the children of Israel, saying,
Whosoever curseth
his God shall bear his sin.
16. And he that
blasphemeth the
name of the LORD, he
shall surely
be put to death, and all
the congregation
shall certainly
stone him: as well
the stranger, as he
that is born in the land, when he
blasphemeth the name *of
the Lord,* shall be put to death.
17. And he that killeth
any man shall surely
be put to death.
18. And he that killeth
a beast shall make
it good; beast for beast.
19. And if a man cause
a blemish in his
neighbour; as he hath done,
so shall it be done to him;
20. Breach for breach,
eye for eye, tooth for tooth:

as he hath caused a blemish in a man, so shall it be done to him *again*.

21. And he that killeth a beast, he shall restore it: and he that killeth a man, he shall be put to death.

22. **Ye shall have one manner of law,** as well **for the stranger, as for** one of **your own country:** for I *am* the LORD your God.

23. And Moses spake to the children of Israel, that they should bring forth him that had cursed out of the camp, and stone him with stones. And the children of Israel did as the LORD commanded Moses.

CHAPTER 25

1. **And the LORD spake unto Moses in mount Sinai, saying,**

2. Speak unto the children of Israel, and say unto them, **When ye come into the land** which I give you, **then shall the land keep a sabbath** unto the LORD.

3. **Six years** thou shalt **sow** thy field, **and** six years thou shalt **prune thy vineyard, and gather** in the **fruit** thereof;

4. **But** in **the seventh year shall be a sabbath of rest unto the land,** a sabbath for the LORD: thou shalt **neither sow** thy field, **nor prune** thy vineyard.

5. **That which groweth of its own accord** of thy harvest **thou shalt not reap, neither gather the grapes** of thy vine undressed: *for* it is a year of rest unto the land.

6. **And the sabbath of the land shall be meat for you;** for thee, and for thy servant, and for thy maid, and for thy hired servant, and for thy stranger that sojourneth with thee.

7. **And for thy cattle, and** for the **beast** that *are* in thy land, **shall all the increase thereof be meat.**

8. **And thou shalt number seven sabbaths of years** unto thee, **seven times seven years; and the space** of the seven sabbaths of years **shall be** unto thee **forty and nine years.**

9. **Then** shalt thou **cause the trumpet of the jubile to sound on the tenth day of the seventh month,** in the day of atonement shall ye make the trumpet sound throughout all your land.

10. **And ye shall hallow the fiftieth year, and proclaim liberty throughout all the land** unto all the inhabitants thereof: it shall be a jubile unto you; **and ye shall return every man unto his possession, and** ye shall return **every man unto his family.**

11. A jubile shall that fiftieth year be unto you: **ye shall not sow, neither reap** that which groweth of itself in it, **nor gather the grapes** in it of thy vine undressed.

12. For it *is* **the jubile; it shall be holy** unto you: **ye shall eat the increase** thereof out **of the field.**

13. In the year of this jubile ye shall return every man unto his possession.

14. **And if thou sell** aught **unto thy neighbour, or buyest** *aught* of thy neighbour's hand, **ye shall not oppress one another:**

15. According to the number of years after the jubile thou shalt buy of thy

neighbour, *and* according unto the number of years of the fruits he shall sell unto thee:

16. According to the multitude of years thou shalt increase the price thereof, and according to the fewness of years thou shalt diminish the price of it: for *according* to the number *of the years* of the fruits doth he sell unto thee.

17. Ye shall not therefore oppress one another; **but thou shalt fear thy God:** for I *am* the LORD your God.

18. Wherefore ye shall **do my statutes, and keep my judgments,** and do them; **and** ye shall **dwell** in the land **in safety.**

19. And the land shall yield her fruit, and ye shall eat your fill, and dwell therein in safety.

20. **And if ye** shall **say, What shall we eat the seventh year?** behold, we shall not sow, nor gather in our increase:

21. **Then I will command my blessing** upon you **in the sixth year, and it shall bring forth fruit for three years.**

22. **And ye shall sow the eighth year, and eat yet of old fruit until the ninth year;** until her fruits come in ye shall eat *of* the old *store.*

23. **The land shall not be sold** for ever: **for the land is mine; for ye are strangers and sojourners with me.**

24. **And in** all the land of **your possession ye shall grant a redemption for the land.**

25. **If thy brother be** waxen **poor, and hath sold** away *some* of **his possession, and if** any of **his kin come to redeem it, then shall he redeem that which his brother sold.**

26. And if the man have none to redeem it, and himself be able to redeem it;

27. Then let him count the years of the sale thereof, and restore the overplus unto the man to whom he sold it; that he may return unto his possession.

28. **But if he be not able to restore it** to him, **then that which is sold shall remain in the hand of him that hath bought it until the year of jubile: and** in the jubile it shall go out, and **he shall return unto his possession.**

29. **And if a man sell a** dwelling **house in a walled city,** then **he may redeem it within a whole year after it is sold;** *within* a full year may he redeem it.

30. **And if it be not redeemed within** the space of **a full year, then the house** that *is* in the walled city **shall be established for ever to him that bought it** throughout his generations: **it shall not go out in the jubile.**

31. **But the houses of the villages which have no wall round about them shall be counted as the fields of the country: they may be redeemed,** and they shall go out in the jubile.

32. **Notwithstanding the cities of the Levites, and the houses of the cities** of their possession, **may the Levites redeem at any time.**

33. **And if a man purchase of the Levites, then** the house that was sold, and the city of **his possession, shall go out in the year of jubile:** for the houses of the cities of the Levites *are* their possession among the children of Israel.

34. **But the field of the**

suburbs of their cities
may not be sold; for it *is*
their perpetual possession.

35. And if thy brother
be waxen poor, and
fallen in decay with thee; then
thou shalt relieve him: *yea,*
though *he be*
a stranger, or a sojourner;
that he may live with thee.

36. Take thou no usury
of him, or increase:
but fear thy God; that
thy brother may live with thee.

37. Thou shalt
not give him thy
money upon usury,
nor lend him thy
victuals for increase.

38. I *am* the LORD your God, which
brought you forth out of the land of
Egypt, to give you the land of
Canaan, *and* to be your God.

39. And if thy
brother *that dwelleth* by thee
be waxen poor, and be
sold unto thee; thou shalt
not compel him to serve
as a bondservant:

40. But as an hired
servant, *and* as a sojourner,
he shall be with thee, *and* shall
serve thee unto the
year of jubile.

41. And then shall he
depart from thee, *both*
he and his children with him,
and shall
return unto his own
family, and unto the
possession of his
fathers shall he return.

42. For they are my
servants, which
I brought forth
out of the land of
Egypt: they shall not
be sold as bondmen.

43. Thou shalt not rule
over him with rigour;
but shalt fear thy God.

44. Both thy bondmen,
and thy bondmaids,
which thou shalt have,
shall be of the heathen that
are round about you; of them shall
ye buy bondmen and bondmaids.

45. Moreover of the children
of the strangers that do sojourn
among you, of them
shall ye buy, and of their
families that *are* with you,
which they begat in your land:
and they shall be
your possession.

46. And ye shall take them
as an inheritance for your
children after you, to inherit *them*
for a possession; they shall be your
bondmen for ever:
but over your
brethren the children of Israel,
ye shall not rule one
over another with rigour.

47. And if a sojourner
or stranger wax rich
by thee, and thy
brother *that dwelleth* by him
wax poor, and sell
himself unto the stranger
or sojourner by thee,
or to the stock of
the stranger's family:

48. After that he is sold
he may be redeemed
again; one of his
brethren may redeem him:

49. Either his uncle, or his uncle's
son, may redeem him, or
any that is nigh
of kin unto him of his family
may redeem him; or
if he be able,
he may redeem himself.

50. And he shall reckon with him that
bought him from the year that he was
sold to him unto the year of jubile:
and the price of his sale shall be
according unto the number of years,
according to the time of an hired
servant shall it be with him.

51. If *there be* yet many years *behind,*
according unto them he shall give
again the price of his redemption out
of the money that he was bought for.

52. And if there remain but few years

unto the year of jubile, then he shall count with him, *and* according unto his years shall he give him again the price of his redemption.

53. *And* as a yearly hired servant shall he be with him: *and the other* shall not rule with rigour over him in thy sight.

54. **And if he be not redeemed** in these *years,* **then he shall go out in the year of jubile, both he, and his children** with him.

55. **For** unto me **the children of Israel** *are* servants; they **are my servants** whom I brought forth out of the land of Egypt: I *am* the LORD your God.

CHAPTER 26

1. **Ye shall make you no idols nor graven image,** neither rear you up a standing image, neither shall ye set up *any* image of stone in your land, to bow down unto it: for I *am* the LORD your God.

2. **Ye shall keep my sabbaths, and reverence my sanctuary:** I *am* the LORD.

3. **If ye walk in my statutes,** and keep my commandments, and do them;

4. **Then I will give you rain** in due season, **and the land shall yield her increase, and the trees** of the field shall yield their **fruit.**

5. And your threshing shall reach unto the vintage, and the vintage shall reach unto the sowing time: **and ye shall eat your bread to the full, and dwell in your land safely.**

6. **And I will give peace** in the land, **and ye shall lie down, and none shall make you afraid: and I will rid evil beasts out of the land, neither shall the sword go through your land.**

7. **And** ye shall chase **your enemies,** and they **shall fall before you** by the sword.

8. **And five of you shall chase an hundred, and an hundred of you shall put ten thousand to flight:** and your enemies shall fall before you by the sword.

9. **For I will** have respect unto you, and make you fruitful, and **multiply you, and establish my covenant with you.**

10. And ye shall eat old store, and bring forth the old because of the new.

11. **And I will set my tabernacle among you:** and my soul shall not abhor you.

12. **And I will** walk among you, and will **be your God, and ye shall be my people.**

13. I *am* the LORD your God, which brought you forth out of the land of Egypt, that ye should not be their bondmen; and I have broken the bands of your yoke, and made you go upright.

14. **But if ye will not hearken unto me,** and will not do all these commandments;

15. And if ye shall despise my statutes, or if your soul abhor my judgments, so that ye will not do all my commandments, *but* that ye break my covenant:

16. I also will do this unto you; **I will** even **appoint over you terror, consumption, and the burning ague, that shall consume the eyes,** and cause sorrow of heart: **and ye shall sow your seed in vain, for your enemies shall eat it.**

17. And I will set my face against you, **and ye shall be slain before your enemies:** they that hate you shall reign over you; **and** ye shall

■ flee when none
■ pursueth you.
■ 18. And if ye will
■ not yet for all this
■ hearken unto me, then
■ I will punish you seven
■ times more for your sins.
19. And I will break the
pride of your power;
■ and I will make your
■ heaven as iron, and
■ your earth as brass:
20. And your strength
shall be spent in vain: for
■ your land shall not yield
■ her increase, neither
■ shall the trees of the land
■ yield their fruits.
21. And if ye walk
contrary unto me, and
■ will not hearken unto me;
■ I will bring seven times
■ more plagues upon
you according to your sins.
22. I will also send
■ wild beasts among you,
■ which shall rob you of your
■ children, and destroy your
■ cattle, and make you
few in number; and
■ your high ways
■ shall be desolate.
■ 23. And if ye will not be
■ reformed by me by these
things, but will walk contrary unto me;
■ 24. Then will I also walk
contrary unto you, and will
■ punish you yet
■ seven times for your sins.
25. And I will bring a sword
upon you, that shall avenge the
quarrel of *my* covenant: and
■ when ye are gathered together
■ within your cities, I
■ will send the
■ pestilence among you;
■ and ye shall be delivered
■ into the hand of the enemy.
26. *And* when I have broken the
staff of your bread, ten women
shall bake your bread in one oven,
and they shall deliver *you* your
bread again by weight:

■ and ye shall eat,
■ and not be satisfied.
■ 27. And if ye will not for all this
■ hearken unto me, but
walk contrary unto me;
■ 28. Then I will walk contrary unto
you also in fury; and I, even I, will
■ chastise you seven
■ times for your sins.
29. And ye shall eat
■ the flesh of your sons,
■ and the flesh of your
■ daughters shall ye eat.
■ 30. And I will destroy
your high places, and
■ cut down your images,
■ and cast your carcases
■ upon the carcases of
■ your idols, and my
soul shall abhor you.
31. And I will make your
■ cities waste, and bring your
sanctuaries unto desolation,
■ and I will not smell
■ the savour of your
■ sweet odours.
32. And I will bring the land into
desolation: and your enemies which
dwell therein shall be astonished at it.
■ 33. And I will scatter you
■ among the heathen, and
will draw out a sword after you:
■ and your land shall be
■ desolate, and your cities waste.
34. Then shall the land
enjoy her sabbaths, as long
as it lieth desolate, and ye
be in your enemies' land;
■ *even* then shall the land
rest, and enjoy her sabbaths.
35. As long as it lieth desolate it shall
rest; because it did not rest in your
sabbaths, when ye dwelt upon it.
■ 36. And upon them that
■ are left *alive* of you
■ I will send a faintness
into their hearts in the lands
of their enemies;
■ and the sound of a shaken
■ leaf shall chase them;
■ and they shall flee, as fleeing
from a sword; and they shall fall
■ when none pursueth.

37. **And** they shall fall one upon another, as it were before a sword, when none pursueth: and **ye shall have no power to stand before your enemies.**

38. **And ye shall perish** among the heathen, **and** the land of **your enemies shall eat you up.**

39. **And they that are left** of you **shall pine away in their iniquity in your enemies' lands;** and also in the iniquities of their fathers shall they pine away with them.

40. **If they shall confess their iniquity, and** the iniquity of their fathers, with their trespass which they trespassed against me, and that also they have walked contrary unto me;

41. And *that* I also have walked contrary unto them, and have brought them into the land of their enemies; **if** then **their uncircumcised hearts be humbled, and** they then **accept of the punishment of their iniquity:**

42. **Then will I remember my covenant with Jacob,** and also my covenant with **Isaac, and** also my covenant with **Abraham** will I remember; **and I will remember the land.**

43. The land also shall be left of them, and shall enjoy her sabbaths, while she lieth desolate without them: and they shall accept of the punishment of their iniquity: because, even because they despised my judgments, and because their soul abhorred my statutes.

44. **And** yet for all that, **when they be in the land of their enemies, I will not** cast them away, neither will I abhor them, to **destroy them utterly, and** to **break my covenant** with them: **for I am the LORD** their God.

45. But I will for their sakes remember the covenant of their ancestors, whom I brought forth outof the land of Egypt n the sight of the heathen, that I might be their God: I *am* the LORD.

46. These *are* the statutes and judgments and laws, which the LORD made between him and the children of Israel in mount Sinai by the hand of Moses.

CHAPTER 27

1. **And the LORD spake unto Moses, saying,**

2. **Speak unto** the children of **Israel, and say** unto them, **When a man shall make a singular vow, the persons shall be for the LORD by thy estimation.**

3. **And thy estimation shall be of the male from twenty years old** even **unto sixty** years old, **even thy estimation shall be fifty shekels of silver,** after the shekel of the sanctuary.

4. **And if** it *be* **a female,** then **thy estimation shall be thirty shekels.**

5. **And if it be from five years** old even unto twenty years old, then **thy estimation shall be of the male twenty shekels, and for the female ten shekels.**

6. **And if it be from a month** old even **unto five years** old, then **thy estimation shall be of the male five shekels** of silver, **and for the female thy** estimation *shall b* **three shekels** o silver.

7. **And** if *it be* **from sixty** years old and **above; if** *it be* **a male, then thy estimation shall be fifteen shekels, and**

196

■ for the female
■ ten shekels.
■ 8. But if he be poorer
■ than thy estimation,
■ then he shall present himself
before the priest, and
■ the priest shall value him;
■ according to his ability that
vowed shall the priest value him.
■ 9. And if it be a beast, whereof
men bring an offering unto the LORD,
■ all that any man giveth
of such unto the LORD
■ shall be holy.
■ 10. He shall not alter it, nor
■ change it, a good for a
bad, or a bad for a good:
■ and if he shall at all
■ change beast for
■ beast, then it and
■ the exchange thereof
■ shall be holy.
■ 11. And if it be any unclean
■ beast, of which they do not
offer a sacrifice unto the LORD,
■ then he shall present the
■ beast before the priest:
■ 12. And the priest shall
■ value it, whether it be good
or bad: as thou valuest it, *who
art* the priest, so shall it be.
■ 13. But if he will at all
■ redeem it, then
■ he shall add a fifth part
■ thereof unto thy estimation.
■ 14. And when a man shall
■ sanctify his house to be
■ holy unto the LORD, then the
priest shall estimate it,
whether it be good or bad: as
■ the priest shall estimate
■ it, so shall it stand.
■ 15. And if he that sanctified it
■ will redeem his house, then
■ he shall add the fifth
■ part of the money of
■ thy estimation unto it,
■ and it shall be his.
■ 16. And if a man shall
■ sanctify unto the LORD *some*
■ part of a field of
his possession, then
■ thy estimation shall be

■ according to the seed
■ thereof: an homer of
barley seed *shall be valued* at
fifty shekels of silver.
■ 17. If he sanctify his
■ field from the year of
■ jubile, according to thy
■ estimation it shall stand.
■ 18. But if he sanctify his field
■ after the
■ jubile, then
■ the priest shall
■ reckon unto him the money
■ according to the years
■ that remain, even
■ unto the year of the jubile,
■ and it shall be abated
■ from thy estimation.
■ 19. And if he that
sanctified the field
■ will in any wise
■ redeem it, then he shall
■ add the fifth part of the
money of thy estimation unto it,
and it shall be assured to him.
■ 20. And if he will not redeem
the field, or if he have
■ sold the field to another man,
■ it shall not be
■ redeemed any more.
■ 21. But the field,
■ when it goeth out in
■ the jubile, shall be holy unto
the LORD, as a field devoted;
■ the possession thereof
■ shall be the priest's.
■ 22. And if a man
■ sanctify unto the LORD
■ a field which he hath
■ bought, which *is* not of the
fields of his possession;
■ 23. Then the priest
■ shall reckon unto him
■ the worth of thy
■ estimation, *even*
■ unto the year of
■ the jubile: and he shall give
■ thine estimation in that day,
■ as a holy thing
■ unto the LORD.
■ 24. In the year of the
■ jubile the field shall return
■ unto him of whom it was

■ **bought,** *even* to him to whom the possession of the land *did belong.*

■ 25. **And** all thy ■ **estimations shall be** ■ **according to the shekel** ■ **of the sanctuary:** twenty gerahs shall be the shekel.

■ 26. **Only the firstling of the** ■ **beasts, which should** ■ **be the LORD's** firstling, ■ **no man shall** ■ **sanctify it;** whether *it be* ox, or sheep: it *is* the LORD's.

■ 27. **And if it be** of ■ **an unclean beast, then he** ■ **shall redeem it according** ■ **to thine estimation,** and shall add a fifth *part* of it thereto: ■ **or if it be not redeemed,** ■ **then it shall be sold** according to thy estimation.

■ 28. **Notwithstanding no** ■ **devoted thing,** that a man shall devote unto the LORD of all that he hath, *both* of man and beast, and of the field of his possession, ■ **shall be sold or** ■ **redeemed:** every devoted thing *is* most holy unto the LORD.

■ 29. **None devoted,** which shall be devoted ■ **of men, shall be** ■ **redeemed; but shall** surely ■ **be put to death.**

■ 30. **And all the tithe of** ■ **the land,** *whether* of the seed of the land, *or* of the fruit of the tree, *is* the LORD's: *it* ■ **is holy unto the LORD.**

■ 31. **And if a man will** at all ■ **redeem** *aught* of ■ **his tithes, he** ■ **shall add** thereto ■ **the fifth part** thereof.

■ 32. **And** concerning ■ **the tithe of the herd, or** of ■ **the flock,** *even* of whatsoever passeth under the rod, the tenth ■ **shall be holy** ■ **unto the LORD.**

33. He shall not search whether it be good or bad, neither shall he change it: and if he change it at all, then both it and the change thereof shall be holy; it shall not be redeemed.

■ 34. **These are the** ■ **commandments, which** ■ **the LORD commanded** ■ **Moses for** the children of ■ **Israel in mount Sinai.**

198

THE BOOK OF NUMBERS

BACKGROUND
INFORMATION

Author: Moses according to tradition
Date Written: Usually considered to be
between 1491 — 1451 B.C.

Number of:
Verses—1,288
Chapters—36
Total Words—32,902
Scan Words—11,934
Scan Words Represent Approximately 36% of Total Words

Theme: The Story of **Israel Wandering in the Wilderness and the Numbering of the** Twelve **Tribes**

OUTLINE OF
THE BOOK

I. **The Departure from Sinai**
1:1 — 10:10
II. **The Journey** from Sinai **to Moab**
10:11 — 21:35
III. **The Prophecies of Balaam**
22:1 — 25:18
IV. **The Preparation for** Entering **the Promised Land**
26:1 — 36:13

CHAPTER 1

1. **And the LORD spake unto Moses in** the wilderness of Sinai, in the tabernacle of the congregation, **on the first day of the second month, in the second year after they were come out of** the land of **Egypt, saying,**

2. **Take ye the sum** of all the congregation **of the children of Israel,** after their families, by the house of their fathers, with the number of *their* names, every male by their polls;

3. **From twenty years old and upward, all that are able to go** forth **to war** in Israel: thou and Aaron shall **number them by their armies.**

4. And with you there shall be a man of every tribe; every one head of the house of his fathers.

5. And these *are* the names of the men that shall stand with you: of *the tribe of* Reuben; Elizur the son of Shedeur.

6. Of Simeon; Shelumiel the son of Zurishaddai.

7. Of Judah; Nahshon the son of Amminadab.

8. Of Issachar; Nethaneel the son of Zuar.

9. Of Zebulun; Eliab the son of Helon.

10. Of the children of Joseph: of Ephraim; Elishama the son of Ammihud: of Manasseh; Gamaliel the son of Pedahzur.

11. Of Benjamin; Abidan the son of Gideoni.

12. Of Dan; Ahiezer the son of Ammishaddai.

13. Of Asher; Pagiel the son of Ocran.

14. Of Gad; Eliasaph the son of Deuel.

15. Of Naphtali; Ahira the son of Enan.

16. These *were* the renowned of the congregation, princes of the tribes of their fathers, heads of thousands in Israel.

17. And Moses and Aaron took these men which are expressed by *their* names:

18. **And they assembled** all the congregation together on the first *day* of the second month, and they declared their pedigrees **after their families,** by the house of their fathers, according to the number of the names, from twenty years old and upward, by their polls.

19. **As the LORD commanded** Moses, so he numbered **them in the wilderness** of Sinai.

20. **And the children of Reuben,** Israel's eldest son, by their generations, after their families, by the house of their fathers, according to the number of the names, by their polls, every male from twenty years old and upward, all that were able to go forth to war;

21. Those that were **numbered** of them, *even* of the tribe of Reuben, *were* **forty and six thousand and five hundred.**

22. **Of the children of Simeon,** by their generations, after their families, by the house of their fathers, those that were numbered of them, according to the number of the names, by their polls, every male from twenty years old and upward, all that were able to go forth to war;

23. **Those** that were **numbered** of them, *even* of the tribe of Simeon, **were fifty and nine thousand and three hundred.**

24. **Of the children of Gad,** by their generations, after their families, by the house of their fathers, according to the number of the names, from twenty years old and upward, all that were

able to go forth to war;

25. **Those** that were **numbered** of them, *even* of the tribe of Gad, **were forty** and **five thousand six hundred and fifty.**

26. **Of the children of Judah,** by their generations, after their families, by the house of their fathers, according to the number of the names, from twenty years old and upward, all that were able to go forth to war;

27. **Those** that were **numbered** of them, *even* of the tribe of Judah, **were threescore** and **fourteen thousand** and **six hundred.**

28. **Of the children of Issachar,** by their generations, after their families, by the house of their fathers, according to the number of the names, from twenty years old and upward, all that were able to go forth to war;

29. **Those** that were **numbered** of them, *even* of the tribe of Issachar, **were fifty** and **four thousand** and **four hundred.**

30. **Of the children of Zebulun,** by their generations, after their families, by the house of their fathers, according to the number of the names, from twenty years old and upward, all that were able to go forth to war;

31. **Those** that were **numbered** of them, *even* of the tribe of Zebulun, **were fifty** and **seven thousand** and **four hundred**

32. **Of the children of Joseph, namely,** of the children of **Ephraim,** by their generations, after their families, by the house of their fathers, according to the number of the names, from twenty

years old and upward, all that were able to go forth to war;

33. Those that were **numbered** of them, *even* of the tribe of Ephraim, *were* **forty thousand** and **five hundred.**

34. Of the children **of Manasseh,** by their generations, after their families, by the house of their fathers, according to the number of the names, from twenty years old and upward, all that were able to go forth to war;

35. **Those** that were **numbered** of them, *even* of the tribe of Manasseh, **were thirty** and **two thousand** and **two hundred.**

36. **Of the children of Benjamin,** by their generations, after their families, by the house of their fathers, according to the number of the names, from twenty years old and upward, all that were able to go forth to war;

37. **Those** that were **numbered** of them, *even* of the tribe of Benjamin, **were thirty** and **five thousand** and **four hundred.**

38. Of the children **of Dan,** by their generations, after their families, by the house of their fathers, according to the number of the names, from twenty years old and upward, all that were able to go forth to war;

39. Those that were numbered of them, *even* of the tribe of Dan, *were* **threescore** and **two thousand and seven hundred.**

40. Of the children **of Asher,** by their generations, after their families, by the house of their fathers, according to the number of the names, from twenty years old and upward, all that were able to go forth to war;

41. Those that were numbered of

them, *even* of the tribe of Asher, *were*
■ **forty** and
■ **one thousand** and
■ **five hundred.**
42. Of the children
■ **of Naphtali,** throughout their
generations, after their families, by the
house of their fathers, according to
the number of the names, from twenty
years old and upward, all
that were able to go forth to war;
43. Those that were
numbered of them, *even* of
the tribe of Naphtali, *were*
■ **fifty** and
■ **three thousand** and
■ **four hundred.**
44. These *are*
■ **those** that were numbered,
which Moses and Aaron
numbered, and the princes of
Israel, *being* twelve men: each
one was for the house of his fathers.
45. So were all those that were
numbered of the children of Israel, by
the house of their fathers, from twenty
years old and upward, all that were
■ **able to go forth to**
■ **war in Israel;**
46. Even all they that were numbered
■ **were six hundred** thousand and
■ **three thousand** and
■ **five hundred and fifty.**
47. **But the Levites** after
the tribe of their fathers
■ **were not numbered**
■ **among them.**
48. **For the LORD**
■ **had spoken unto**
■ **Moses, saying,**
49. Only thou shalt not number the
tribe of Levi, neither take the sum of
them among the children of Israel:
50. But
■ **thou shalt appoint**
■ **the Levites over the**
■ **tabernacle** of testimony, and over
all the vessels thereof,
■ **and** over all things that *belong* to it:
■ **they shall bear the**
■ **tabernacle,** and all the
vessels thereof; and they shall
minister unto it, and shall encamp

round about the tabernacle.
■ 51. **And** when the tabernacle
setteth forward, the Levites
■ **shall take it down: and**
when the tabernacle is to be
pitched, the Levites shall
■ **set it up: and the stranger**
■ **that cometh nigh shall**
■ **be put to death.**
■ 52. **And** the children of
■ **Israel shall pitch**
■ **their tents,** every man by his
own camp, and every man
■ **by his own standard,**
throughout their hosts.
■ 53. **But the Levites**
■ **shall pitch round** about
■ **the tabernacle** of testimony,
that there be no wrath upon the
congregation of the children of Israel:
■ **and** the Levites shall
■ **keep the charge of the**
■ **tabernacle** of testimony.
■ 54. **And** the children of
■ **Israel did** according to
■ **all that the LORD**
■ **commanded** Moses,so did they.

CHAPTER 2

■ 1. **And the LORD spake** unto
Moses and unto Aaron, saying,
■ 2. **Every man** of the
children of Israel
■ **shall pitch by his own**
■ **standard, with the ensign**
■ **of their father's house:** far off
■ **about the tabernacle** of
the congregation shall they pitch.
■ 3. **And on the east side**
toward the rising of the sun shall
■ **they of the**
■ **standard** of the camp
■ **of Judah pitch**
throughout their armies:
■ **and Nahshon the**
son of Amminadab
■ **shall be captain**
of the children of Judah.
4. And his host, and those
that were numbered of them,
were threescore and fourteen
thousand and six hundred.
■ 5. **And those** that do pitch

■ next unto him shall be the
■ tribe of Issachar: and
■ Nethaneel the son of Zuar
■ shall be captain
of the children of Issachar.

6. And his host, and those that were numbered thereof, *were* fifty and four thousand and four hundred.

■ 7. Then the tribe of Zebulun:
■ and Eliab the son of Helon
■ shall be captain of
the children of Zebulun.

■ 8. And his host, and those that were numbered thereof, *were* fifty and seven thousand and four hundred.

9. All that were numbered in the camp of Judah *were* an hundred thousand and fourscore thousand and six thousand and four hundred, throughout their armies.

■ These shall first set forth.
■ 10. On the south side shall
■ be the standard of the camp of
■ Reuben according to their armies:
■ and the captain of
the children of Reuben
■ shall be Elizur
the son of Shedeur.

11. And his host, and those that were numbered thereof, were forty and six thousand and five hundred.

■ 12. And those which pitch
■ by him shall be the tribe of
■ Simeon: and the captain
of the children of Simeon
■ shall be Shelumiel
the son of Zurishaddai.

13. And his host, and those that were numbered of them, *were* fifty and nine thousand and three hundred.

■ 14. Then the tribe
■ of Gad: and the
■ captain of the sons of Gad
■ shall be Eliasaph
the son of Reuel.

15. And his host, and those that were numbered of them, *were* forty and five thousand and six hundred and fifty.

16. All that were numbered in the camp of Reuben *were* an hundred thousand and fifty and one thousand and four hundred and fifty, throughout their armies. And they shall set forth

in the second rank.

17. Then the tabernacle of the congregation shall set forward with the camp of the Levites in the midst of the camp: as they encamp, so shall they set forward, every man in his place by their standards.

■ 18. On the west side shall
■ be the standard of the camp
■ of Ephraim according
to their armies:
■ and the captain
of the sons of Ephraim
■ shall be Elishama
the son of Ammihud.

19. And his host, and those that were numbered of them, *were* forty thousand and five hundred.

■ 20. And by him
shall be the tribe of
■ Manasseh: and
■ the captain of the
children of Manasseh
■ shall be Gamaliel
the son of Pedahzur.

21. And his host, and those that were numbered of them, *were* thirty and two thousand and two hundred.

■ 22. Then the tribe of
■ Benjamin: and the
■ captain of the sons of Benjamin
■ shall be Abidan
the son of Gideoni.

23. And his host, and those that were numbered of them, *were* thirty and five thousand and four hundred.

24. All that were numbered of the camp of Ephraim *were* an hundred thousand and eight thousand and an hundred, throughout their armies. And they shall go forward in the third rank.

■ 25. The standard of the camp
■ of Dan shall be on the
■ north side by their armies:
■ and the captain of
the children of Dan
■ shall be Ahiezer the
son of Ammishaddai.

26. And his host, and those that were numbered of them, *were* threescore and two thousand and sevenhundred.

27. **And those that encamp by him shall be the tribe of Asher: and the captain** of the children of Asher **shall be Pagiel** the son of Ocran. 28. And his host, and those that were numbered of them, *were* forty and one thousand and five hundred. 29. **Then** the tribe of **Naphtali: and the captain** of the children of Naphtali **shall be Ahira** the son of Enan. 30. And his host, and those that were numbered of them, *were* fifty and three thousand and four hundred. 31. All they that were numbered in the camp of Dan *were* an hundred thousand and fifty and seven thousand and six hundred. They shall go hindmost with their standards. 32. These *are* those which were numbered of the children of Israel by the house of their fathers: **all those that were numbered of the camps** throughout their hosts **were six hundred** thousand and **three thousand** and **five hundred and fifty.** 33. **But the Levites were not numbered** among the children of Israel; **as the LORD commanded Moses.** 34. And the children of Israel did according to all that the LORD commanded Moses: **so they pitched by their standards, and** so they **set forward,** every one after their families, **according to the house of their fathers.**

CHAPTER 3

1. These also *are* the generations of Aaron and Moses in the day *that* the LORD spake with Moses in mount Sinai. 2. **And these are the** names of the **sons of Aaron; Nadab the firstborn, and Abihu, Eleazar, and Ithamar.** 3. These *are* the names of the sons of Aaron, the priests which were anointed, whom he consecrated to minister in the priest's office. 4. **And Nadab and Abihu died before the LORD, when they offered strange fire before the LORD,** in the wilderness of Sinai, and they had no children: **and Eleazar and Ithamar ministered in the priest's office** in the sight of Aaron their father. 5. **And the LORD spake unto Moses, saying,** 6. **Bring the tribe of Levi near, and present them before Aaron the priest, that they may minister unto him.** 7. **And they shall keep** his **charge,** and the charge **of** the whole congregation before the tabernacle of the congregation, to do the service of the tabernacle. 8. **And** they shall keep all the instruments of the tabernacle of the congregation, and the charge of the children of Israel, to **do the service of the tabernacle.** 9. **And thou shalt give the Levites unto Aaron and to his sons:** they *are* wholly given unto him out of the children of Israel. 10. And thou shalt appoint Aaron and his sons, **and they shall wait on their priest's office:** and the stranger that cometh nigh shall be put to death. 11. **And the LORD spake** unto Moses, **saying,** 12. And I, behold, **I have taken the Levites** from among the children of Israel **instead of all the firstborn**

that openeth the matrix among
the children of Israel:
therefore the Levites
shall be mine;
13. **Because** all the
firstborn *are* mine; *for* on
the day that
I smote all the
firstborn in the land of
Egypt I hallowed unto
me all the firstborn in
Israel, both man and beast: mine
shall they be: I *am* the LORD.
14. And the LORD spake unto Moses
in the wilderness of Sinai, saying,
15. **Number the children**
of Levi after the house of
their fathers, by their families:
every male from a
month old and upward
shalt thou number them.
16. **And Moses**
numbered them according
to the word of the LORD,
as he was commanded.
17. And these were the sons
of Levi by their names; Gershon,
and Kohath, and Merari.
18. And these *are* the names
of the sons of Gershon by their
families; Libni, and Shimei.
19. And the sons of Kohath
by their families; Amram, and
Izehar, Hebron, and Uzziel.
20. And the sons of Merari by their
families; Mahli, and Mushi. These *are*
the families of the Levites according
to the house of their fathers.
21. Of Gershon *was* the family of
the Libnites, and the family of the
Shimites: these *are* the families
of the Gershonites.
22. Those that were numbered of
them, according to the number of
all the males, from a month old
and upward, *even* those that were
numbered of them *were* seven
thousand and five hundred.
23. **The families of the**
Gershonites shall pitch
behind the tabernacle
westward.
24. And the chief of the house of

the father of the Gershonites
shall be Eliasaph the son of Lael.
25. **And the charge** of the sons
of Gershon in the
tabernacle of the congregation
shall be the tabernacle, and
the tent, the covering thereof,
and the
hanging for the door of the
tabernacle of the congregation,
26. **And the hangings of**
the court, and the curtain
for the door of the court,
which *is* by the tabernacle,
and by the altar round about,
and the cords of it
for all the service thereof.
27. And of Kohath *was* the family
of the Amramites, and the family
of the Izeharites, and the family
of the Hebronites, and the family
of the Uzzielites: these *are*
the families of
the Kohathites.
28. In the number of all the males,
from a month old and upward, *were*
eight thousand and six hundred,
keeping the charge of the sanctuary.
29. The families of the sons of Kohath
shall pitch on the side of the
tabernacle southward.
30. And the chief of the house of the
father of the families of the Kohathites
shall be Elizaphan the son of Uzziel.
31. **And their charge**
shall be the ark, and the
table, and the
candlestick, and
the altars, and the vessels
of the sanctuary wherewith
they minister, and the hanging,
and all the service thereof.
32. **And Eleazar** the
son of Aaron the priest
shall be chief over the chief of
the Levites, *and have* the oversight of
them that keep the
charge of the sanctuary.
33. Of Merari *was* the family
of the Mahlites, and the family
of the Mushites: these *are*
the families of Merari.
34. And those that were numbered

of them, according to the number of all the males, from a month old and upward, *were* six thousand and two hundred.

35. And the chief of the house of the father of the families of Merari *was* Zuriel the son of Abihail: *these* **shall pitch on the side of the tabernacle northward.**

36. **And under the** custody and **charge** of the sons **of Merari shall be the boards of the tabernacle, and the bars** thereof, and the **pillars** thereof, and the **sockets** thereof, **and all the vessels** thereof, and all that serveth thereto,

37. **And the pillars of the court** round about, and **their sockets, and their pins, and** their **cords.**

38. **But those that encamp** before the tabernacle **toward the east,** *even* **before the tabernacle** of the congregation eastward, **shall be Moses, and Aaron and his sons, keeping the charge of the sanctuary** for the charge of the children of Israel; and the stranger that cometh nigh shall be put to death.

39. **All that were numbered of the Levites,** which Moses and Aaron numbered at the commandment of the LORD, throughout their families, all the males from a month old and upward, **were twenty** and **two thousand.**

40. **And the LORD said unto Moses, Number all the firstborn** of the **males** of the children of Israel **from a month old** and upward, and take the number of their names.

41. **And thou shalt take the Levites for me** (I *am* the LORD) **instead of all the firstborn** among the children of Israel; **and the cattle of the**

Levites instead of all **the firstlings among the cattle of** the children of **Israel.**

42. And Moses numbered, as the LORD commanded him, all the firstborn among the children of Israel.

43. **And all the firstborn males** by the number of names, from a month old and upward, of those that were numbered of them, **were twenty** and **two thousand two hundred** and **threescore and thirteen.**

44. **And the LORD spake** unto Moses, **saying,**

45. Take the Levites instead of all the firstborn among the children of Israel, and the cattle of the Levites instead of their cattle; and the Levites shall be mine: I *am* the LORD

46. **And for those that are to be redeemed** of the two hundred and threescore and thirteen **of the firstborn** of the children **of Israel,** which are more than the Levites;

47. Thou shalt even **take five shekels apiece** by the poll, after the shekel of the sanctuary shalt thou take *them:* (the shekel *is* twenty gerahs:)

48. **And** thou shalt **give the money,** wherewith the odd number of them is to be redeemed, **unto Aaron and to his sons.**

49. **And Moses took the redemption money of** them that were over and above them that were redeemed by the Levites:

50. Of the firstborn of the children of Israel took he the money; **a thousand three hundred and threescore and five shekels,** after the shekel of the sanctuary:

51. **And** Moses

■ **gave the money** of
them that were redeemed
■ **unto Aaron and to**
■ **his sons,** according to
the word of the LORD,
■ **as the LORD**
■ **commanded** Moses.

CHAPTER 4

■ 1. **And the LORD spake**
■ **unto Moses and** unto
■ **Aaron, saying,**
■ 2. **Take the sum of the**
■ **sons of Kohath** from among
the sons of Levi, after their families,
by the house of their fathers,
■ 3. **From thirty** years
old and upward even
■ **until fifty years old,**
all that enter into the host,
■ **to do the work in the**
■ **tabernacle** of the congregation.
4. This *shall be* the service of the
sons of Kohath in the tabernacle
of the congregation,
■ **about the most holy things:**
■ 5. **And when the camp**
■ **setteth forward,**
■ **Aaron** shall come,
■ **and his sons,** and they
■ **shall take down the**
■ **covering vail, and cover**
■ **the ark** of testimony with it:
■ 6. **And shall put**
■ **thereon the** covering of
■ **badgers skins, and** shall
■ **spread over it a cloth** wholly
■ **of blue,** and shall put
in the staves thereof.
■ 7. **And upon the table**
■ **of shewbread they**
■ **shall spread a cloth**
■ **of blue, and put** thereon
■ **the dishes,** and the spoons,
■ **and the** bowls, and covers
to cover withal: and the
■ **continual bread** shall be
■ **thereon:**
■ 8. **And they shall spread**
■ **upon them a cloth of**
■ **scarlet, and cover** the same
■ **with** a covering of
■ **badgers' skins,** and

shall put in the staves thereof.
■ 9. **And they shall take a**
■ **cloth of blue, and cover**
■ **the candlestick** of the light,
■ **and** his
■ **lamps,** and his
■ **tongs, and** his
■ **snuffdishes, and all**
■ **the oil vessels** thereof,
wherewith they minister unto it:
■ 10. **And** they shall
■ **put it** and all the vessels thereof
■ **within a covering of**
■ **badgers' skins,** and
shall put *it* upon a bar.
■ 11. **And upon the golden**
■ **altar they shall spread**
■ **a cloth of blue, and**
■ **cover it with** a covering of
■ **badgers' skins,** and shall
put to the staves thereof:
■ 12. **And they shall take**
■ **all the instruments** of
ministry, wherewith they minister
■ **in the sanctuary, and put**
■ **them in a cloth of blue, and**
■ **cover them with** a covering of
■ **badgers' skins,** and
shall put *them* on a bar:
■ 13. **And they shall take**
■ **away the ashes from**
■ **the altar, and spread**
■ **a purple cloth thereon:**
■ 14. **And they shall put**
■ **upon it** all the vessels thereof,
wherewith they minister about it,
even the censers, the fleshhooks,
and the shovels, and the basons,
■ **all the vessels of the altar;**
■ **and** they shall spread upon it
■ **a covering of badgers'**
■ **skins,** and put to the staves of it.
■ 15. **And when Aaron and**
■ **his sons have made**
■ **an end of covering**
■ **the sanctuary,** and all the
vessels of the sanctuary, as the
camp is to set forward; after that,
■ **the sons of Kohath shall**
■ **come to bear it: but they**
■ **shall not touch any holy**
■ **thing, lest they die.** These
things are the burden of the sons

207

of Kohath in the tabernacle of the congregation.

16. **And to** the office of **Eleazar** the son of Aaron the priest **pertaineth the oil for the light, and** the sweet **incense, and** the **daily meat offering, and** the **anointing oil,** *and* the oversight of all the tabernacle, **and of all that therein is,** in the sanctuary, and in the vessels thereof.

17. **And the LORD spake unto Moses and** unto **Aaron saying,**

18. **Cut ye not off the tribe of** the families of **the Kohathites** from among the Levites:

19. **But** thus do unto them, that they may live, and not die, **when they approach** unto **the most holy things: Aaron and his sons shall go in, and appoint** them **every one to his service** and to his burden:

20. **But they shall not** go in to **see when the holy things are covered, lest they die.**

21. And the LORD spake unto Moses, saying,

22. **Take also the sum of the sons of Gershon,** throughout the houses of their fathers, by their families;

23. **From thirty years old** and upward **until fifty years old** shalt thou number them; all that enter in to perform the service, to do the work in the tabernacle of the congregation.

24. This *is* the service of the families of the Gershonites, to serve, and for burdens:

25. **And they shall bear the curtains of the tabernacle,** and the tabernacle of the congregation, his covering, and **the covering of** the **badgers' skins** that *is* above upon it, and

the hanging for the door of the tabernacle of the congregation,

26. **And** the hangings of **the court,** and the hanging for the door of **the gate of the court,** which is by the tabernacle and by the altar round about, and **their cords, and all the instruments of their service,** and all that is made for them: so shall they serve.

27. At the appointment of Aaron and his sons shall be all the service of the sons of the Gershonites, in all their burdens, and in all their service: and ye shall appoint unto them in charge all their burdens.

28. This is the service of the families of **the sons of Gershon** in the tabernacle of the congregation: and their charge **shall be under the hand of Ithamar the son of Aaron** the priest.

29. **As for the sons of Merari,** thou shalt number them after their families, by the house of their fathers;

30. **From thirty years old and upward even unto fifty** years old **shalt thou number** them, every one that entereth into the service, to do the work of the tabernacle of the congregation.

31. **And this is** the charge of **their burden,** according to all their service in the tabernacle of the congregation; **the boards of the tabernacle, and the bars** thereof, and the **pillars** thereof, **and sockets thereof,**

32. **And the pillars of the court** round about, and **their sockets, and** their **pins, and their cords, with all their instruments,** and with all their service: and by name ye

shall reckon the instruments of the charge of their burden.

33. This *is* the service of the families of the sons of Merari, according to all their service, in the tabernacle of the congregation, under the hand of Ithamar the son of Aaron the priest.

34. **And** Moses and Aaron and the chief of the congregation numbered **the sons of the Kohathites** after their families, and after the house of their fathers,

35. From thirty years old and upward even unto fifty years old, every one that entereth into the service, for the work in the tabernacle of the congregation:

36. And those that were **numbered** of them by their families were **two thousand seven hundred and fifty.**

37. These *were* they that were numbered of the families of the Kohathites, all that might do service in the tabernacle of the congregation, which Moses and Aaron did number according to the commandment of the LORD by the hand of Moses.

38. **And** those that were numbered of **the sons of Gershon,** throughout their families, and by the house of their fathers,

39. From thirty years old and upward even unto fifty years old, every one that entereth into the service, for the work in the tabernacle of the congregation,

40. Even those that were **numbered** of them, throughout their families, by the house of their fathers, were **two thousand** and **six hundred and thirty.**

41. These *are* they that were numbered of the families of the sons of Gershon, of all that might do service in the tabernacle of the congregation, whom Moses and Aaron did number according to the commandment of the LORD.

42. **And** those that were numbered of the families of **the sons of Merari,** throughout their families, by the house of their fathers,

43. From thirty years old and upward even unto fifty years old, every one that entereth into the service, for the work in the tabernacle of the congregation,

44. Even those that were **numbered** of them after their families, were **three thousand** and **two hundred.**

45. These *be* those that were numbered of the families of the sons of Merari, whom Moses and Aaron numbered according to the word of the LORD by the hand of Moses.

46. **All those that were numbered of the Levites,** whom Moses and Aaron and the chief of Israel numbered, after their families, and after the house of their fathers,

47. **From thirty** years old and upward even **unto fifty years old,** every one **that came to do the service** of the ministry, and the service of the burden in the tabernacle of the congregation.

48. Even those that were numbered of them, **were eight thousand** and **five hundred and fourscore,**

49. According to the commandment of the LORD they were numbered by the hand of Moses, every one according to his service, and according to his burden: thus were they numbered of him, as the LORD commanded Moses.

CHAPTER 5

1. **And the LORD spake unto Moses, saying,**

2. **Command** the children of Israel, **that they put out of the camp every leper, and every one that hath an**

issue, and whosoever is
defiled by the dead:
3. **Both male and female**shall
ye put out, without the camp shall ye
put them; that they defile not their
camps, in the midst whereof I dwell.
4. And the children of Israel did so,
and put them out without the camp:
as the LORD spake unto Moses,
so did the children of Israel.
5. **And** the LORD spake
unto Moses, saying,
6. Speak unto the children of Israel,
**When a man or woman
shall commit any sin** that men
commit, to do a trespass against the
LORD, and that person be guilty;
7. **Then they shall confess
their sin** which they have done:
**and he shall recompense
his trespass** with
the principal thereof,
and add unto it
**the fifth part thereof, and
give it unto him** against
whom he hath trespassed.
8. **But if the man
have no kinsman** to
recompense the trespass unto,
**let the trespass be
recompensed unto the
LORD, even** to the priest; beside
the ram of the
atonement, whereby
an atonement
shall be made for him.
9. And every offering of all the
holy things of the children of
Israel, which they bring unto
the priest, shall be his.
10. **And** every man's
hallowed things shall be his:
**whatsoever any
man giveth the priest,
it shall be his.**
11. **And the LORD spake
unto Moses,** saying,
12. **Speak unto** the children of
Israel, and say unto them,
If any man's wife go aside, and
**commit a trespass
against him,**
13. And a man lie with her carnally,

and it be hid from the eyes of her
husband, and be kept close,
**and she be defiled,
and there be no witness
against her,** neither
she be taken *with the manner;*
14. And the spirit of jealousy come
upon him, and he be jealous of his
wife, and she be defiled: or if the
spirit of jealousy come upon
him, and he be jealous of his
wife, and she be not defiled:
15. **Then shall the man bring
his wife unto the priest, and**
he shall bring her offering for her,
**the tenth part of an ephah
of barley meal;** he shall pour
no oil upon it, nor put frankincense
thereon; for it *is* an offering of
jealousy, an offering of memorial,
bringing iniquity to remembrance.
16. **And the priest
shall** bring her near, and
set her before the LORD:
17. **And the priest shall take
holy water** in an earthen vessel;
and of
the dust that is
**in the floor of the
tabernacle** the priest shall take,
and put it into the water:
18. **And the priest shall** set the
woman before the LORD, and
**uncover the woman's
head, and put the
offering** of memorial
in her hands, which
is the jealousy offering:
and the priest
**shall have in his hand
the bitter water that
causeth the curse:**
19. **And the priest shall
charge her by an oath,**
and say unto the woman,
**If no man have lain with
thee,** and if thou hast not gone
aside to uncleanness *with another*
**instead of thy husband, be
thou free from this bitter
water** that causeth the curse:
20. **But** if thou hast gone aside *to*
another instead of thy husband, and

if thou be defiled, and some man have lain with thee beside thine husband:

21. **Then** the priest shall charge the woman with an oath of cursing, and the priest shall say unto the woman, **The LORD make thee a curse and** an oath among thy people, when the LORD doth **make thy thigh to rot, and thy belly to swell;**

22. **And this water that causeth the curse shall go into thy bowels,** to make *thy* belly to swell, and *thy* thigh to rot: **And the woman shall say, Amen,** amen.

23. **And the priest shall write these curses in a book, and** he shall **blot them out with the bitter water:**

24. And he shall cause the woman to drink the bitter water that causeth the curse: and the water that causeth the curse shall enter into her, *and become* bitter.

25. **Then the priest shall take the** jealousy **offering out of the woman's hand, and shall wave the offering before the LORD,** and offer it upon the altar:

26. And the priest shall take an handful of the offering, *even* the memorial thereof, **and burn it upon the altar, and** afterward **shall cause the woman to drink the water.**

27. **And** when he hath made her to drink the water, then it shall come to pass, *that,* **if she be defiled,** and have done trespass against her husband, that **the water** that causeth the curse **shall enter into** her, *and become* bitter, **and her belly shall swell, and her thigh shall rot:** and the woman shall be a curse among her people.

28. **And if the woman be**

not defiled, but be clean; then **she shall be free,** and shall conceive seed.

29. This *is* the law of jealousies, when a wife goeth aside *to another* instead of her husband, and is defiled;

30. Or when the spirit of jealousy cometh upon him, and he be jealous over his wife, and shall set the woman before the LORD, and the priest shall execute upon her all this law.

31. Then shall the man be guiltless from iniquity, and this woman shall bear her iniquity.

CHAPTER 6

1. **And the LORD spake unto Moses, saying,**

2. Speak unto the children of Israel, and say unto them, **When either man or woman shall separate themselves** to vow a vow of a Nazarite, to separate *themselves* **unto the LORD:**

3. **He shall separate himself from wine and strong drink, and** shall drink no vinegar of wine, or vinegar of strong drink, neither shall he drink any liquor of grapes, nor eat moist grapes, or dried.

4. All the days of his separation **shall** he **eat nothing that is made of the vine tree,** from the kernels even to the husk.

5. All the days of the vow of his separation **there shall no razor come upon his head:** until the days be fulfilled, in the which he separateth *himself* unto the LORD, **he shall be holy, and shall let the locks of the hair** of his head **grow.**

6. All the days that he separateth *himself* unto the LORD **he shall come at no dead body.**

7. He shall not make himself unclean for his father, or for

his mother, for his brother, or for his sister, when they die:

because the consecration of his God is upon his head.

8. **All the days of his separation he is holy unto the LORD.**

9. **And if any man die** very **suddenly by him,** and he hath defiled the head of his consecration; **then he shall shave his head** in the day of his cleansing, **on the seventh day** shall he shave it.

10. **And on the eighth day he shall bring two turtles, or** two **young pigeons, to the priest, to** the door of the tabernacle of the congregation:

11. And the priest shall **offer the one for a sin offering, and the other for a burnt offering,** and make an atonement for him, for that he sinned by the dead, and shall hallow his head that same day.

12. **And he shall consecrate unto the LORD the days of his separation,** and shall bring a lamb of the first year for a trespass offering: **but the days that were before shall be lost, because his separation was defiled.**

13. **And** this *is* the law of the Nazarite, **when the days of his separation are fulfilled: he shall be brought unto the door of the tabernacle** of the congregation:

14. **And he shall offer** his offering unto the LORD, **one he lamb** of the first year **without blemish for a burnt offering, and one ewe lamb** of the first year without blemish **for a sin offering, and**

one ram without blemish **for peace offerings,**

15. **And a basket of unleavened bread, cakes** of fine flour mingled with oil, **and wafers** of unleavened bread **anointed with oil, and their meat** offering, **and** their **drink offerings.**

16. **And the priest shall bring them before the LORD,** and shall offer his sin offering, and his burnt offering:

17. And he shall offer the ram *for* a sacrifice of peace offerings unto the LORD, with the basket of unleavened bread: the priest shall offer also his meat offering, and his drink offering.

18. **And the Nazarite shall shave the head** of his separation **at the door of the tabernacle** of the congregation, **and shall take the hair** of the head of his separation, **and put it in the fire which is under the sacrifice of the peace offerings.**

19. **And the priest shall take the sodden shoulder of the ram, and one unleavened cake** out of the basket, **and one unleavened wafer, and** shall **put them upon the hands of the Nazarite,** after *the hair of* his separation is shaven:

20. **And the priest shall wave them for a wave offering before the LORD:** this *is* holy for the priest, with the wave breast and heave shoulder: **and after that the Nazarite may drink wine.**

21. **This is the law of the Nazarite** who hath vowed, *and of* his offering unto the LORD for his separation, beside *that* that his hand shall get: according to the vow which he vowed, so he must do after the law of his separation.

22. **And the LORD spake**

unto Moses, saying,

23. Speak unto Aaron and unto his sons, saying, On this wise ye shall **bless the children of Israel, saying** unto them,

24. **The LORD bless thee, and keep thee:**

25. **The LORD make his face shine upon thee, and be gracious unto thee:**

26. **The LORD lift up his countenance upon thee, and give thee peace.**

27. And they shall put my name upon the children of Israel, and I will bless them.

CHAPTER 7

1. **And** it came to pass on **the day that Moses had fully set up the tabernacle, and had anointed it, and sanctified it,** and all the instruments thereof, both the altar and all the vessels thereof, and had anointed them, and sanctified them;

2. That the princes of Israel, heads of the house of their fathers, who *were* **the princes of the tribes,** and were over them that were numbered, **offered:**

3. And they brought **their offering before the LORD, six covered wagons, and twelve oxen;** a wagon for two of the princes, and for each one an ox: and they brought them before the tabernacle.

4. **And the LORD spake unto Moses, saying,**

5. Take *it* of them, that they may be to do the service of the tabernacle of the congregation; and thou shalt **give them unto the Levites,** to every man according to his service.

6. And Moses took the wagons and the oxen, and gave them unto the Levites.

7. **Two wagons and four oxen he gave unto the sons of Gershon,** according to their service:

8. **And four wagons and eight oxen he gave unto the sons of Merari,** according unto their service, under the hand of Ithamar the son of Aaron the priest.

9. **But unto the sons of Kohath he gave none: because the service of the sanctuary belonging unto them was that they should bear upon their shoulders.**

10. **And the princes offered for dedicating of the altar** in the day that it was anointed, even the princes offered **their offering before the altar.**

11. **And the LORD said** unto Moses, **They shall offer their offering, each prince on his day, for the dedicating of the altar.**

12. **And** he that offered his offering **the first day** was Nahshon the son of Amminadab, of the tribe of **Judah:**

13. And his offering *was* one silver charger, the weight thereof *was* an hundred and thirty *shekels,* one silver bowl of seventy shekels, after the shekel of the sanctuary; both of them *were* full of fine flour mingled with oil for a meat offering:

14. One spoon of ten *shekels* of gold, full of incense:

15. One young bullock, one ram, one lamb of the first year, for a burnt offering:

16. One kid of the goats for a sin offering:

17. And for a sacrifice of peace offerings, two oxen, five rams, five he goats, five lambs of the first year: this *was* the offering of Nahshon the son of Amminadab.

18. **On the second day** Nethaneel the son of Zuar, prince of **Issachar,** did offer:

19. He offered *for* his offering one silver charger, the weight whereof *was* an hundred and thirty *shekels,* one silver bowl of seventy shekels,

after the shekel of the sanctuary; both of them full of fine flour mingled with oil for a meat offering:

20. One spoon of gold of ten *shekels,* full of incense:

21. One young bullock, one ram, one lamb of the first year, for a burnt offering:

22. One kid of the goats for a sin offering:

23. And for a sacrifice of peace offerings, two oxen, five rams, five he goats, five lambs of the first ear: this *was* the offering of Nethaneel the son of Zuar.

■ 24. **On the third day** Eliab the son of Helon, prince of the children of ■ **Zebulun,** *did offer:*

25. His offering *was* one silver charger, the weight whereof *was* an hundred and thirty *shekels,* one silver bowl of seventy shekels, after the shekel of the sanctuary; both of them full of fine flour mingled with oil for a meat offering:

26. One golden spoon of ten *shekels,* full of incense:

27. One young bullock, one ram, one lamb of the first year, for a burnt offering:

28. One kid of the goats for a sin offering:

29. And for a sacrifice of peace offerings, two oxen, five rams, five he goats, five lambs of the first year: this *was* the offering of Eliab the son of Helon.

■ 30. **On the fourth day** Elizur the son of Shedeur, prince of the children of ■ **Reuben,** *did offer:*

31. His offering *was* one silver charger of the weight of an hundred and thirty *shekels,* one silver bowl of seventy shekels, after the shekel of the sanctuary; both of them full of fine flour mingled with oil for a meat offering:

32. One golden spoon of ten *shekels,* full of incense:

33. One young bullock, one ram, one lamb of the first year, for a burnt offering:

34. One kid of the goats for a sin offering:

35. And for a sacrifice of peace offerings, two oxen, five rams, five he goats, five lambs of the first year: this *was* the offering of Elizur the son of Shedeur.

■ 36. **On the fifth day** Shelumiel the son of Zurishaddai, prince of the children of ■ **Simeon,** *did offer:*

37. His offering *was* one silver charger, the weight whereof *was* an hundred and thirty *shekels,* one silver bowl of seventy shekels, after the shekel of the sanctuary; both of them full of fine flour mingled with oil for a meat offering:

38. One golden spoon of ten *shekels,* full of incense:

39. One young bullock, one ram, one lamb of the first year, for a burnt offering:

40. One kid of the goats for a sin offering:

41. And for a sacrifice of peace offerings, two oxen, five rams, five he goats, five lambs of the first year: this *was* the offering of Shelumiel the son of Zurishaddai.

■ 42. **On the sixth day** Eliasaph the son of Deuel, prince of the children of ■ **Gad,** *offered:*

43. His offering *was* one silver charger of the weight of an hundred and thirty *shekels,* a silver bowl of seventy shekels, after the shekel of the sanctuary; both of them full of fine flour mingled with oil for a meat offering:

44. One golden spoon of ten *shekels,* full of incense:

45. One young bullock, one ram, one lamb of the first year, for a burnt offering:

46. One kid of the goats for a sin offering:

47. And for a sacrifice of peace offerings, two oxen, five rams, five he goats, five lambs of the first year: this *was* the offering of Eliasaph the son of Deuel.

■ 48. **On the seventh day**
Elishama the son of Ammihud,
prince of the children of

■ **Ephraim,** *offered:*
49. His offering *was* one silver
charger, the weight whereof *was* an
hundred and thirty *shekels,* one silver
bowl of seventy shekels, after the
shekel of the sanctuary; both of
them full of fine flour mingled
with oil for a meat offering:
50. One golden spoon of ten
shekels, full of incense:
51. One young bullock, one
ram, one lamb of the first
year, for a burnt offering:
52. One kid of the goats
for a sin offering:
53. And for a sacrifice of peace
offerings, two oxen, five rams,
five he goats, five lambs of the
first year: this *was* the offering
of Elishama the son of Ammihud.

■ 54. **On the eighth day**
offered Gamaliel the son of
Pedahzur, prince of the children of

■ **Manasseh:**
55. His offering *was* one silver
charger of the weight of an hundred
and thirty *shekels,* one silver bowl
of seventy shekels, after the
shekel of the sanctuary; both
of them full offine flour mingled
with oil for a meat offering:
56. One golden spoon of ten
shekels, full of incense:
57. One young bullock, one
ram, one lamb of the first
year, for a burnt offering:
58. One kid of the goats
for a sin offering:
59. And for a sacrifice of peace
offerings, two oxen, five rams, five
he goats, five lambs of the first
year: this *was* the offering of
Gamaliel the son of Pedahzur.

■ 60. **On the ninth day**
Abidan the son of Gideoni,
prince of the children of

■ **Benjamin,** *offered:*
61. His offering *was* one silver
charger, the weight whereof *was* an
hundred and thirty *shekels,* one

silver bowl of seventy shekels,
after the shekel of the sanctuary; both
of them full of fine flour
mingled with oil for a meat offering:
62. One golden spoon of ten
shekels, full of incense:
63. One young bullock, one
ram, one lamb of the first
year, for a burnt offering:
64. One kid of the goats
for a sin offering:
65. And for a sacrifice of peace
offerings, two oxen, five rams, five
he goats, five lambs of the first
year: this *was* the offering of
Abidan the son of Gideoni.

■ 66. **On the tenth day**
Ahiezer the son of Ammishaddai,
prince of the children of

■ **Dan,** *offered:*
67. His offering *was* one silver
charger, the weight whereof *was* an
hundred and thirty *shekels,* one
silver bowl of seventy shekels,
after the shekel of the sanctuary; both
of them full of fine flour
mingled with oil for a meat offering:
68. One golden spoon of ten
shekels, full of incense:
69. One young bullock, one
ram, one lamb of the first
year, for a burnt offering:
70. One kid of the goats
for a sin offering:
71. And for a sacrifice of peace
offerings, two oxen, five rams, five
he goats, five lambs of the first
year: this *was* the offering of
Ahiezer the son of Ammishaddai.

■ 72. **On the eleventh**
■ **day** Pagiel the son of Ocran,
prince of the children of

■ **Asher,** *offered:*
73. His offering *was* one silver
charger, the weight whereof *was* an
hundred and thirty *shekels,* one silver
bowl of seventy shekels, after the
shekel of the sanctuary; both of
them full of fine flour mingled
with oil for a meat offering:
74. One golden spoon of ten
shekels, full of incense:
75. One young bullock, one

ram, one lamb of the first year, for a burnt offering:

76. One kid of the goats for a sin offering:

77. And for a sacrifice of peace offerings, two oxen, five rams, five he goats, five lambs of the first year: this *was* the offering of Pagiel the son of Ocran.

78. **On the twelfth day** Ahira the son of Enan, prince of the children of **Naphtali,** *offered:*

79. His offering *was* one silver charger, the weight whereof *was* an hundred and thirty *shekels,* one silver bowl of seventy shekels, after the shekel of the sanctuary; both of them full of fine flour mingled with oil for a meat offering:

80. One golden spoon of ten *shekels,* full of incense:

81. One young bullock, one ram, one lamb of the first year, for a burnt offering:

82. One kid of the goats for a sin offering:

83. And for a sacrifice of peace offerings, two oxen, five rams, five he goats, five lambs of the first year: this *was* the offering of Ahira the son of Enan.

84. **This was the dedication of the altar,** in the day when it was anointed, **by the princes of Israel: twelve chargers of silver, twelve silver bowls, twelve spoons of gold:**

85. Each charger of silver *weighing* an hundred and thirty *shekels,* each bowl seventy: **all the silver vessels weighed two thousand** and **four hundred shekels,** after the shekel of the sanctuary:

86. **The golden spoons** *were* twelve, full of incense, **weighing** ten *shekels* apiece, after the shekel of the sanctuary: all the gold of the spoons *was* **an hundred** and **twenty shekels.**

87. **All the oxen for the burnt offering were twelve bullocks, the rams twelve, the lambs of the first year twelve, with their meat offering: and the kids of the goats for sin offering twelve.**

88. **And all the oxen for** the sacrifice of **the peace offerings were twenty** and **four bullocks, the rams sixty, the he goats sixty, the lambs** of the first year **sixty. This was the dedication of the altar, after that it was anointed.**

89. **And when Moses was gone into the tabernacle** of the congregation to speak with him, then **he heard the voice of one speaking** unto him **from off the mercy seat** that *was* upon the ark of testimony, from between the two cherubims: and he spake unto him.

CHAPTER 8

1. And the LORD spake unto Moses, **saying,**

2. **Speak unto Aaron and say** unto him, When thou **lightest** the lamps, **the seven lamps** shall give light **over against the candlestick.**

3. **And Aaron did so;** he lighted the lamps thereof over against the candlestick, as the LORD commanded Moses.

4. **And** this work of **the candlestick was of beaten gold,** unto **the shaft** thereof, unto **the flowers** thereof, **was beaten work: according unto the pattern** which the LORD had **shewed Moses,** so he made the candlestick.

5. **And the LORD**

spake unto Moses,

saying,

6. **Take the Levites** from among the children of Israel, **and cleanse them.**

7. And thus shalt thou do unto them, to cleanse them: **Sprinkle water of purifying upon them,** and **let them shave all their flesh, and** let them **wash their clothes, and so make themselves clean.**

8. **Then** let them **take a young bullock with his meat offering, even** fine **flour mingled with oil, and another young bullock** shalt thou take **for a sin offering.**

9. **And** thou shalt **bring the Levites before the tabernacle** of the congregation: **and** thou shalt gather **the whole assembly of** the children of **Israel** together:

10. And thou shalt bring the Levites before the LORD: and the children of Israel shall put their hands upon the Levites:

11. **And Aaron shall offer the Levites before the LORD** for an offering of the children of Israel, **that they may execute the service of the LORD.**

12. **And the Levites shall lay their hands upon the heads of the bullocks:** and thou shalt offer the **one for a sin offering, and the other for a burnt offering,** unto the LORD, **to make an atonement for the Levites.**

13. And thou shalt set the Levites before Aaron, and before his sons, and offer them for an offering unto the LORD.

14. Thus shalt thou separate the Levites from among the children of Israel: **and the Levites**

shall be mine.

15. **And after that shall the Levites go in to do the service of the tabernacle** of the congregation: and thou shalt cleanse them, and offer them for an offering.

16. For they are wholly given unto me from among the children of Israel; instead of such as open every womb, even instead of the firstborn of all the children of Israel, have I taken them unto me.

17. For all the firstborn of the children of Israel are mine, both man and beast: on the day that I smote every firstborn in the land of Egypt I sanctified them for myself.

18. **And I have taken the Levites for all the firstborn of the children of Israel.**

19. **And I have given the Levites** as a gift **to Aaron and to his sons** from among the children of Israel, **to do the service of the children of Israel in the tabernacle** of the congregation, and to make an atonement for the children of Israel: **that there be no plague among** the children of **Israel, when** the children of **Israel come nigh unto the sanctuary.**

20. And Moses, and Aaron, and all the congregation of the children of Israel, did to the Levites according unto all that the LORD commanded Moses concerning the Levites, so did the children of Israel unto them.

21. **And the Levites were purified,** and they washed their clothes; and Aaron offered them as an offering before the LORD; and Aaron made an atonement for them to cleanse them.

22. **And** after that **went** the Levites in **to do their service in the tabernacle** of the congregation before Aaron, and before his sons: as the LORD had

commanded Moses concerning the Levites, so did they unto them.

23. **And** the LORD spake unto Moses, saying,

24. This *is it* that *belongeth* unto the Levites: **from twenty and five years old and upward they shall** go in to wait upon the **service** of **the tabernacle** of the congregation:

25. **And from the age of fifty** years **they** shall cease waiting upon the service *thereof*, and **shall serve no more:**

26. **But shall minister with their brethren** in the tabernacle of the congregation, **to keep the charge, and shall do no service.** Thus shalt thou do unto the Levites touching their charge.

CHAPTER 9

1. **And the LORD spake unto Moses** in the wilderness of Sinai, in the first month of the second year after they were come out of the land of Egypt, **saying,**

2. **Let the children of Israel also keep the passover** at his appointed season.

3. **In the fourteenth day of this month,** at even, ye shall keep it in his appointed season: **according to** all **the rites** of it, **and** according to all the **ceremonies thereof,** shall ye keep it.

4. And Moses spake unto the children of Israel, that they should keep the passover.

5. **And they kept the passover** on the fourteenth day of the first month at even in the wilderness of Sinai: **according to all that the LORD commanded Moses,** so did the children of Israel.

6. **And there were certain men,** who were **defiled by the dead body of a man, that** they **could not keep the passover** on that day: **and they came before Moses and** before Aaron on that day:

7. **And** those men **said** unto him, **We are defiled by** the dead body of a man: **wherefore** are we kept back, that **we may not offer an offering of the LORD in his appointed season** among the children of Israel?

8. **And Moses said** unto them, **Stand still, and I will hear what the LORD will command** concerning you.

9. **And the LORD spake** unto Moses, **saying,**

10. Speak unto the children of Israel, saying, **If any man** of you or of your posterity shall **be unclean by reason of a dead body, or be in a journey** afar off, yet **he shall keep the passover** unto the LORD.

11. **The fourteenth day of the second month at even they shall keep it,** *and* eat it with unleavened bread and bitter *herbs.*

12. They shall leave none of it unto the morning, nor break any bone of it: **according to all the ordinances of the passover** they shall keep it.

13. **But the man that is clean, and is not in a journey, and forbeareth to keep the passover,** even the same soul **shall be cut off from** among **his people:** because he brought not the offering of the LORD in his appointed season, that man shall bear his sin.

218

■ 14. **And if a stranger shall**
sojourn among you, and will
■ **keep the passover**
unto the LORD;
■ **according to the**
■ **ordinance** of the passover,
■ **and** according to the
■ **manner thereof, so shall**
■ **he do: ye shall have one**
■ **ordinance,** both for the stranger,
and for him that was born in the land.
■ 15. **And on the day that the**
■ **tabernacle was reared**
■ **up the cloud covered**
■ **the tabernacle,** *namely,*
the tent of the testimony:
■ **and at even there was**
upon the tabernacle as it were
■ **the appearance of**
■ **fire, until the morning.**
16. So it was alway: the cloud
covered it *by day,* and the
appearance of fire by night.
■ 17. **And when the cloud**
■ **was taken up** from the
tabernacle, then after that
■ **the children of Israel**
■ **journeyed: and** in
■ **the place where the cloud**
■ **abode,** there the children of
■ **Israel pitched their tents.**
18. At the commandment of the
LORD the children of Israel journeyed,
and at the commandment of the
LORD they pitched: as long as the
cloud abode upon the tabernacle
they rested in their tents.
19. And when the cloud tarried long
upon the tabernacle many days, then
the children of Israel kept the charge
of the LORD, and journeyed not.
20. And *so* it was, when the cloud
was a few days upon the tabernacle;
according to the commandment of
the LORD they abode in their tents,
and according to the commandment
of the LORD they journeyed.
■ 21. **And** *so* it was, when the cloud
abode from even unto the morning,
and *that* the cloud was taken up in
the morning, then they journeyed:
■ **whether** *it was*
■ **by day or by night that**

■ **the cloud was taken**
■ **up, they journeyed.**
■ 22. **Or whether** *it were*
■ **two days,** or a month,
■ **or a year, that the**
■ **cloud tarried upon the**
■ **tabernacle,** remaining thereon,
■ **the children of Israel**
■ **abode in their tents, and**
■ **journeyed not:** but when it
was taken up, they journeyed.
23. At the commandment of the
LORD they rested in the tents, and at
the commandment of the LORD they
journeyed: they kept the charge of
the LORD, at the commandment
of the LORD by the hand of Moses.

CHAPTER 10

■ 1. **And the LORD spake**
■ **unto Moses,** saying,
■ 2. **Make** thee
■ **two trumpets of silver;**
of a whole piece shalt thou
make them: that thou mayest
■ **use them for the calling**
■ **of the assembly,** and
for the journeying of the camps.
■ 3. **And when they**
■ **shall blow** with
■ **them, all the assembly**
■ **shall assemble**
themselves to thee
■ **at the door of the**
■ **tabernacle** of the congregation.
■ 4. **And if they blow** *but* with
■ **one trumpet, then the**
■ **princes,** *which are* heads
of the thousands of Israel,
■ **shall gather** themselves
■ **unto thee.**
■ 5. **When ye blow an alarm,**
■ **then the camps** that lie
■ **on the east** parts
■ **shall go forward.**
■ 6. **When ye blow** an alarm
■ **the second time,**
■ **then the camps** that lie
■ **on the south side shall**
■ **take their journey:** they shall
blow an alarm for their journeys.
■ 7. **But when the**
■ **congregation is to be**

gathered together,
ye shall blow, but
ye shall not
sound an alarm.
8. **And** the sons of Aaron,
the priests, shall blow
with the trumpets;
and they shall be to you
for an ordinance for ever
throughout your
generations.
9. **And if ye go to war**
in your land against the
enemy that oppresseth you,
then ye shall blow
an alarm with the trumpets;
and ye shall be
remembered before
the LORD your God,
and ye
shall be saved
from your enemies.
10. **Also** in the day of your
gladness, and in your solemn days,
and in the beginnings of your months,
ye shall blow with
the trumpets over your
burnt offerings, and
over the sacrifices of your
peace offerings; that
they may be to you
for a memorial before your
God: I *am* the LORD your God.
11. **And** it came to pass
on the twentieth day of
the second month, in
the second year, that
the cloud was taken up from
off the tabernacle of the testimony.
12. **And the children of**
Israel took their journeys
out of the wilderness of
Sinai; and the cloud rested
in the wilderness of Paran.
13. And they first took their journey
according to the commandment of
the LORD by the hand of Moses.
14. **In the first place**
went the standard
of the camp of the children
of Judah according to their
armies: and over his host *was*
Nahshon the son of Amminadab.

15. **And** over the host of
the tribe of the children
of Issachar *was*
Nethaneel the son of Zuar.
16. **And** over the host of
the tribe of the children
of Zebulun *was*
Eliab the son of Helon.
17. **And** the tabernacle
was taken down; and
the sons of Gershon
and the sons of Merari
set forward, bearing
the tabernacle.
18. **And the standard of**
the camp of Reuben set
forward according to their
armies: and over his host *was*
Elizur the son of Shedeur.
19. **And** over the host of
the tribe of the children
of Simeon *was* Shelumiel
the son of Zurishaddai.
20. **And** over the host of
the tribe of the children of
Gad *was* Eliasaph the son of Deuel.
21. **And the Kohathites set**
forward, bearing the
sanctuary: and *the other* did set
up the tabernacle against they came.
22. **And the standard**
of the camp of the children
of Ephraim set forward
according to their armies: and
over his host *was* Elishama
the son of Ammihud.
23. **And** over the host of
the tribe of the children of
Manasseh *was* Gamaliel
the son of Pedahzur.
24. **And** over the host of
the tribe of the children of
Benjamin *was* Abidan
the son of Gideoni.
25. **And the standard**
of the camp of the children
of Dan set forward, which
was the rereward of all
the camps throughout their
hosts: and over his host *was*
Ahiezer the son of Ammishaddai.
26. **And** over the host of
the tribe of the children

of Asher *was* Pagiel the son of Ocran.

27. **And** over the host of the tribe of the children of **Naphtali** *was* Ahira the son of Enan.

28. **Thus were the journeyings** of the children **of Israel** according to their armies, **when they set forward.**

29. **And Moses said unto Hobab,** the son of Raguel the Midianite, **Moses' father in law, We are journeying unto the place** of **which the LORD said, I will give it you: come** thou **with us,** and we will do thee good: for the LORD hath spoken good concerning Israel.

30. **And he said** unto him, **I will not go; but I will depart to mine own land,** and to my kindred.

31. **And he said, Leave us not,** I pray thee; forasmuch as thou knowest how we are to encamp in the wilderness, **and** thou mayest **be to us** instead of **eyes.**

32. **And** it shall be, if thou go with us, yea, it shall be, that **what** goodness **the LORD shall do unto us,** the same **will we do unto thee.**

33. **And they departed** from the mount of the LORD **three days' journey: and the ark of the covenant** of the LORD **went before them** in the three days' journey, **to search out a resting place** for them.

34. **And the cloud** of the LORD **was upon them by day,** when they went out of the camp.

35. **And** it came to pass, **when the ark set forward,** that

Moses said, Rise up, LORD, and let thine enemies be scattered; and let them that hate thee flee before thee.

36. **And when it rested,** he said, Return, O LORD, **unto** the many thousands of **Israel.**

CHAPTER 11

1. **And when the people complained,** it displeased the LORD: **and the LORD heard it;** and **his anger was kindled; and the fire of the LORD** burnt among them, and **consumed them** *that were* **in the uttermost parts of the camp.**

2. **And the people cried unto Moses; and when Moses prayed** unto the LORD, **the fire was quenched.**

3. And he called the name of the place Taberah: because the fire of the LORD burnt among them.

4. **And the mixed multitude** that *was* **among them fell a lusting: and** the children of **Israel also** wept again, and **said, Who shall give us flesh to eat?**

5. **We remember the fish,** which we did eat **in Egypt** freely; **the cucumbers,** and the **melons,** and the **leeks,** and the **onions, and the garlick:**

6. **But now** our soul *is* dried away: **there is nothing** at all, **beside this manna,** *before* our eyes.

7. And the manna *was* as coriander seed, and the colour thereof as the colour of bdellium.

8. **And the people** went about, and **gathered it, and ground it in mills, or beat it** in a mortar,

■ **and baked it** in pans,
and made cakes of it:
■ **and the taste** of it
■ **was** as the taste
■ **of fresh oil.**
9. And when the dew fell
upon the camp in the night,
the manna fell upon it.
■ 10. **Then Moses heard**
■ **the people weep** throughout
their families, every man in
the door of his tent:
■ **and the anger of the**
■ **LORD was kindled**
■ **greatly; Moses also**
■ **was displeased.**
■ 11. **And Moses said**
■ **unto the LORD,**
Wherefore hast thou afflicted
thy servant? and wherefore
■ **have I not found**
■ **favour in thy sight, that thou**
■ **layest the burden of all**
■ **this people upon me?**
12. Have I conceived all this people?
have I begotten them, that thou
shouldest say unto me, Carry
them in thy bosom, as a nursing
father beareth the sucking child,
unto the land which thou swarest
unto their fathers?
■ 13. **Whence should I**
■ **have flesh to give** unto all
■ **this people? for they weep**
■ **unto me, saying, Give us**
■ **flesh, that we may eat.**
■ 14. **I am not able to bear** all
■ **this** people
■ **alone,**
because *it is* too heavy for me.
15. And if thou deal thus with me, kill
me, I pray thee, out of hand, if I have
found favour in thy sight; and let me
not see my wretchedness.
■ 16. **And the LORD said**
■ **unto Moses, Gather unto**
■ **me seventy men of the**
■ **elders of Israel,** whom thou
knowest to be the elders of the
people, and officers over them;
■ **and bring them unto the**
■ **tabernacle** of the congregation,
■ **that they may stand** there

■ **with thee.**
■ 17. **And I will** come down and
talk with thee there: and I will
■ **take of the spirit which**
■ **is upon thee, and** will
■ **put it upon them; and**
■ **they shall bear the burden**
■ **of the people with thee,**
that thou bear *it* not thyself alone.
■ 18. **And say** thou
■ **unto the people, Sanctify**
■ **yourselves against to-**
■ **morrow, and** ye shall eat
flesh: for ye have wept in the
ears of the LORD, saying, Who
shall give us flesh to eat? for *it*
was well with us in Egypt: therefore
■ **the LORD will give**
■ **you flesh,** and ye shall eat.
19. Ye shall not eat one day,
nor two days, nor five days,
neither ten days, nor twenty days;
20. *But* even
■ **a whole month, until** it
come out at your nostrils, and
■ **it be loathsome unto**
■ **you: because** that
■ **ye** have despised the
LORD which *is* among you, and have
■ **wept** before him,
■ **saying, Why came we** forth
■ **out of Egypt?**
■ 21. **And Moses said, The**
■ **people,** among whom I *am,*
■ **are six hundred thousand**
footmen; and thou hast said,
I will give them flesh, that
they may eat a whole month.
■ 22. **Shall the flocks and**
■ **the herds be slain** for them,
■ **to suffice them?**
■ **or shall** all the
■ **fish** of the sea
■ **be gathered** together
■ **for them,** to suffice them?
■ 23. **And the LORD**
■ **said** unto Moses,
■ **Is the LORD'S hand**
■ **waxed short?**
thou shalt see now whether my word
shall come to pass unto thee or not.
■ 24. **And Moses**
went out, and told the people

the words of the LORD, and ■ **gathered the seventy men** of the elders of the people, and set them ■ **round** about ■ **the tabernacle.** ■ 25. **And the LORD came** ■ **down in a cloud,** and spake unto him, ■ **and took of the** ■ **spirit** that *was* upon him, ■ **and gave it unto the** ■ **seventy elders: and** it came to pass, *that,* ■ **when the spirit rested** ■ **upon them, they** ■ **prophesied,** and did not cease. ■ 26. **But** there remained ■ **two of the men** in the camp, the name of the one *was* ■ **Eldad, and** the name of the other ■ **Medad:** and the spirit rested upon them; and they *were* of them that were written, but ■ **went not** out ■ **unto the tabernacle:** ■ **and they prophesied** ■ **in the camp.** ■ 27. **And** there ran ■ **a young man,** and ■ **said, Eldad and Medad** ■ **do prophesy in the camp.** 28. **And** Joshua the son of Nun, the servant of Moses, *one* of his young men, answered and said, My lord Moses, forbid them. ■ 29. **And Moses said** unto him, ■ **Enviest thou for my** ■ **sake? would God that** ■ **all the LORD'S people** ■ **were prophets,** *and* that the LORD would put his spirit upon them! 30. **And** Moses gat him into the camp, he and the elders of Israel. ■ 31. **And** there went forth ■ **a wind from the LORD,** and ■ **brought quails from the sea,** ■ **and let them fall by the** ■ **camp, as it were a day's** ■ **journey on this side, and** as it were a day's journey on ■ **the other side, round about** ■ **the camp, and** as it were ■ **two cubits high**

upon the face of the earth. ■ 32. **And the people stood** ■ **up all that day,** and all ■ **that night, and** all ■ **the next day, and** they ■ **gathered the quails:** he that gathered least gathered ten homers: and they spread *them* all abroad for themselves round about the camp. ■ 33. **And while the flesh** ■ **was yet between their** ■ **teeth,** ere it was chewed, ■ **the wrath of the LORD** ■ **was kindled against** ■ **the people, and the** ■ **LORD smote the people** ■ **with a** very great ■ **plague.** 34. **And** he called the name of that place Kibrothhattaavah: because there ■ **they buried the** ■ **people that lusted.** 35. *And* the people journeyed from Kibrothhattaavah unto Hazeroth; and abode at Hazeroth.

CHAPTER 12

■ 1. **And Miriam and Aaron** ■ **spake against Moses** ■ **because** of the Ethiopian woman whom he had married: for ■ **he had married an** ■ **Ethiopian woman.** 2. **And** they said, Hath the LORD indeed spoken only by Moses? hath he not spoken also by us? ■ **And the LORD heard it.** ■ 3. **(Now** the man ■ **Moses was very meek,** above all the men which *were* upon the face of the earth.) ■ 4. **And the LORD** ■ **spake suddenly** ■ **unto Moses,** and unto ■ **Aaron, and** unto ■ **Miriam, Come** out ye three ■ **unto the tabernacle** of the congregation. And they three came out. ■ 5. **And the LORD came** down ■ **in** the pillar of ■ **the cloud,** and stood

in the door of the tabernacle,
■ **and called Aaron and**
■ **Miriam:** and they both came forth.
■ 6. **And he said,**
Hear now my words:
■ **If there be a prophet**
■ **among you,I** the LORD will make myself known unto him in a vision,*and*
■ **will speak unto**
■ **him in a dream.**
■ 7. **My servant Moses is not**
■ **so,** who *is* faithful in all mine house.
■ 8. **With him will I speak**
■ **mouth to mouth,** even apparently, and not in dark speeches; and the similitude of the LORD shall he behold:
■ **wherefore then were**
■ **ye not afraid to speak**
■ **against** my servant
■ **Moses?**
■ 9. **And the anger of the**
■ **LORD was kindled**
■ **against them;** and he departed.
■ 10. **And the cloud**
■ **departed** from off the tabernacle;
■ **and,** behold,
■ **Miriam became**
■ **leprous, white as snow:**
and Aaron looked upon Miriam, and, behold, *she was* leprous.
■ 11. **And Aaron said unto**
■ **Moses,** Alas, my lord, I beseech thee,say not the sin upon us, wherein
■ **we have done foolishly,** and
■ **wherein we have sinned.**
■ 12. **Let her not be as one**
■ **dead,** of whom the flesh is half consumed when he cometh out of his mother's womb.
■ 13. **And Moses cried**
■ **unto the LORD,** saying,
■ **Heal her now, O**
■ **God,** I beseech thee.
■ 14. **And the LORD said**
unto Moses, If her father had but spit in her face, should she not be ashamed seven days?
■ **let her be shut out from the**
■ **camp seven days,** and after that let her be received in *again*.
15. And Miriam was shut out from the camp seven days:

■ **and the people journeyed**
■ **not till Miriam was**
■ **brought in again.**
■ 16. **And** afterward
■ **the people removed from**
■ **Hazeroth, and pitched in**
■ **the wilderness of Paran.**

CHAPTER 13
■ 1. **And the LORD spake**
■ **unto Moses, saying,**
■ 2. **Send** thou
■ **men, that they may search**
■ **the land of Canaan,** which I give unto the children of Israel:
■ **of every tribe**
of their fathers shall ye
■ **send a man,**
every one a ruler among them.
■ 3. **And Moses by the**
■ **commandment of the**
■ **LORD sent them from**
■ **the wilderness of Paran:**
all those men *were* heads of the children of Israel.
■ 4. **And these were their**
■ **names:** of the tribe of Reuben,
■ **Shammua** the son of Zaccur.
5. Of the tribe of Simeon,
■ **Shaphat** the son of Hori.
6. Of the tribe of Judah,
■ **Caleb** the son of Jephunneh.
7. Of the tribe of Issachar,
■ **Igal** the son of Joseph.
8. Of the tribe of Ephraim,
■ **Oshea** the son of Nun.
9. Of the tribe of Benjamin,
■ **Palti** the son of Raphu.
10. Of the tribe of Zebulun,
■ **Gaddiel** the son of Sodi.
11. Of the tribe of Joseph,
namely, of the tribe of Manasseh,
■ **Gaddi** the son of Susi.
12. Of the tribe of Dan,
■ **Ammiel** the son of Gemalli.
13. Of the tribe of Asher,
■ **Sethur** the son of Michael.
14. Of the tribe of Naphtali,
■ **Nahbi** the son of Vophsi.
15. Of the tribe of Gad,
■ **Geuel** the son of Machi.
16. These *are* the names of the men which Moses sent to spy out

the land. And Moses called Oshea
the son of Nun Jehoshua.

**17. And Moses sent
them to spy out the
land of Canaan,
and said unto them,** Get
you up this *way* southward, and
go up
into the mountain:
18. And see the land, what it *is,*
and the people
that dwelleth therein,
**whether they be strong
or weak,** few or many;
**19. And what the land
is** that they dwell in,
whether it *be*
good or bad; and what cities
they be that they dwell in, whether
in tents, or in strong holds;
20. And what the land *is,* whether it *be*
fat or lean,
whether there be wood therein, or
not. And be ye of good courage,
**and bring of the fruit of
the land.** Now the time *was*
the time of the firstripe grapes.
**21. So they went up, and
searched the land** from
the wilderness of Zin unto
Rehob, as men come to Hamath.
22. And they ascended by the
south, and came unto Hebron;
where Ahiman, Sheshai, and
Talmai, the children of Anak,
were. (Now Hebron was built seven
years before Zoan in Egypt.)
**23. And they came unto the
brook of Eshcol, and cut**
down from thence a branch with
**one cluster of
grapes, and** they
bare it between two
**upon a staff; and
they brought** of the
pomegranates, and of the
figs.
24. The place was called the brook
Eshcol, because of the cluster of
grapes which the children of Israel
cut down from thence.
25. And they returned
from searching of the land

after forty days.
26. **And they** went and
came to Moses, and to Aaron,
and to all the congregation of
the children of Israel, unto
the wilderness of Paran, to Kadesh;
and brought back
word unto them,
and unto all the congregation,
**and shewed them
the fruit** of the land.
27. And they told him,
**and said, We came unto
the land** whither thou sentest us,
and surely
**it floweth with milk and
honey;** and this *is* the fruit of it.
28. **Nevertheless the people
be strong** that dwell in the land,
and the cities are walled,
and very great: and moreover we
saw the children of Anak there.
29. The Amalekites dwell in
the land of the south: and the
Hittites, and the Jebusites, and
the Amorites, dwell in the mountains:
and the Canaanites dwell by
the sea, and by the coast of Jordan.
30. **And Caleb**
stilled the people before Moses, and
**said, Let us go up at
once, and possess it;**
for we are well able to overcome it.
31. **But the men that
went up with him said,**
We be not able to go up against
the people; for they
are stronger than we.
32. **And they brought** up
an evil report of the land which
they had searched unto the children
of Israel, saying, The land, through
which we have gone to search it, *is* a
land that eateth up the inhabitants
thereof; and all the people that we
saw in it *are* men of a great stature.
33. **And there we saw** the
giants, the sons of Anak,
which come of the giants:
and we were in our own sight
as grasshoppers,
and so we were
in their sight.

CHAPTER 14

1. **And all the congregation** lifted up their voice, and cried; and the people **wept that night.**

2. **And all** the children of **Israel murmured against Moses and** against Aaron: and the whole congregation **said** unto them, **Would God that we had died in** the land of **Egypt!** or would God we had died in this wilderness!

3. **And** wherefore **hath the LORD brought us unto this land, to fall by the sword,** that our wives and our children should be a prey? were it not better for us to return into Egypt?

4. **And they said** one to another, Let us make a captain, and **let us return into Egypt.**

5. **Then Moses and Aaron fell on their faces before all the assembly** of the congregation of the children of Israel.

6. **And Joshua** the son of Nun, **and Caleb** the son of Jephunneh, *which were* of them that searched the land, **rent their clothes:**

7. **And they spake** unto all the company of the children of Israel, **saying, The land, which we passed through** to search it, **is an exceeding good land.**

8. **If the LORD delight in us,** then **he will bring us into this land,** and give it us; a land which floweth with milk and honey.

9. **Only rebel not** ye **against the LORD,** neither fear ye the people of the land; for they *are* bread for us: their defence is departed from them, and the LORD *is* with us: fear them not.

10. **But all the congregation bade stone them** with stones. **And the glory of the LORD appeared in the tabernacle** of the congregation before all the children of Israel.

11. **And the LORD said** unto Moses, **How long will this people provoke me?** and how long will it be ere they believe me, for all the signs which I have shewed among them?

12. **I will smite them** with the pestilence, **and disinherit them, and will make of thee a greater nation** and mightier than they.

13. **And Moses said** unto the LORD, **Then the Egyptians shall hear it,** (for thou broughtest up this people in thy might from among them;)

14. **And they will tell** *it* to the inhabitants of this land: *for* they have heard **that** thou LORD *art* among this people, that thou LORD art seen face to face, and *that* thy cloud standeth over them, and *that* thou goest before them, by day time in a pillar of a cloud, and in a pillar of fire by night.

15. Now *if* thou shalt kill *all* this people as one man, then the nations which have heard the fame of thee will speak, saying,

16. Because **the LORD was not able to bring this people into the land which he sware unto them,** therefore **he hath slain them in the wilderness.**

17. And now, I beseech thee, let the power of my LORD be great, according as thou hast spoken, saying,

18. **The LORD is longsuffering, and of great mercy,** forgiving iniquity and transgression, and by no means clearing *the guilty,* visiting the iniquity of the fathers upon the children unto the third and fourth *generation.*

19. **Pardon,** I beseech thee, **the iniquity of this people according**

■ **unto** the greatness of
■ **thy mercy,** and as thou
hast forgiven this people,
from Egypt even until now.
■ 20. **And the LORD**
■ **said, I have pardoned**
■ **according to thy word:**
■ 21. **But** as
■ **truly** as I live, all
■ **the earth shall be filled**
■ **with the glory of the LORD.**
■ 22. **Because all those men**
■ **which have seen my glory,**
and my miracles, which I did in
Egypt and in the wilderness,
■ **and have tempted me**
■ **now these ten times,** and
have not hearkened to my voice;
23. Surely they
■ **shall not see the land**
■ **which I sware unto**
■ **their fathers,** neither shall
any of them that provoked me see it:
■ 24. **But my servant Caleb,**
because he had another
spirit with him, and
■ **hath followed me fully,**
■ **him will I bring into the**
■ **land** whereinto he went; and
his seed shall possess it.
25. (Now the Amalekites and the
Canaanites dwelt in the valley.)
■ **Tomorrow** turn you, and
■ **get** you
■ **into the wilderness by**
■ **the way of the Red sea.**
■ 26. **And the LORD**
■ **spake unto Moses**
and unto Aaron,
■ **saying,**
■ 27. **How long shall I**
■ **bear with this evil**
■ **congregation,** which murmur
against me? I have heard the
murmurings of the children of Israel,
which they murmur against me.
■ 28. **Say unto them,**
As *truly* as I live, saith the
LORD, as ye have spoken in
mine ears, so will I do to you:
■ 29. **Your carcases shall fall**
■ **in this wilderness; and all** that
were numbered of you, according to

your whole number,
■ **from twenty years old**
■ **and upward** which have
murmured against me.
30. Doubtless ye
■ **shall not come into**
■ **the land,** *concerning* which
I sware to make you dwell therein,
■ **save Caleb**
the son of Jephunneh,
■ **and Joshua** the son of Nun.
■ 31. **But your little ones,**
■ **which ye said should**
■ **be a prey,** them will I bring in, and
■ **they shall know the land**
which ye have despised.
■ 32. **But** *as for* you,
■ **your carcases,** they
■ **shall fall in this wilderness.**
■ 33. **And your children shall**
■ **wander in the wilderness**
■ **forty years,** and bear your
whoredoms, until your carcases
be wasted in the wilderness.
■ 34. **After the number of** the
■ **days** in which
■ **ye searched the land,** *even*
■ **forty days, each day**
■ **for a year,** shall ye bear your
iniquities, *even* forty years, and ye
shall know my breach of promise.
35. I the LORD have said, I will surely
do it unto all this evil congregation,
that are gathered together against
me: in this wilderness they shall be
consumed, and there they shall die.
■ 36. **And the men,** which
■ **Moses sent to search**
■ **the land, who** returned, and
■ **made** all
■ **the congregation**
■ **to murmur** against him, by
bringing up a slander upon the land,
37. Even those men that did bring up
the evil report upon the land,
■ **died by the plague**
■ **before the LORD.**
■ 38. **But Joshua** the son of Nun,
■ **and Caleb** the son of
Jephunneh, *which were* of the men
that went to search the land,
■ **lived** *still.*
39. And Moses told these sayings

unto all the children of Israel:

■ **and the people**
■ **mourned greatly.**
■ 40. **And they rose up**
■ **early** in the morning, and gat them up into the top of the mountain,
■ **saying,** Lo,
■ **we** *be here,* and
■ **will go** up
■ **unto the place which the**
■ **LORD hath promised:**
■ **for we have sinned.**
■ 41. **And Moses said,**
Wherefore now do ye transgress the commandment of the LORD? but it shall not prosper.
■ 42. **Go not up, for the LORD**
■ **is not among you;** that ye be not smitten before your enemies.
43. For the Amalekites and the Canaanites *are* there before you,
■ **and ye shall fall by**
■ **the sword:** because ye are turned away from the LORD,therefore the LORD will not be with you.
■ 44. **But they presumed**
■ **to go up** unto the hill top:
■ **nevertheless the ark**
of the covenant of the LORD,
■ **and Moses, departed**
■ **not out of the camp.**
■ 45. **Then the**
■ **Amalekites** came down,
■ **and the Canaanites**
which dwelt in that hill, and
■ **smote them, and**
■ **discomfited them,**
■ **even unto Hormah.**

CHAPTER 15

■ 1. **And the LORD**
■ **spake** unto Moses,
■ **saying,**
2. Speak unto the children of Israel, and say unto them,
■ **When ye** be
■ **come into the land** of your habitations, which I give unto you,
■ 3. **And will make**
an offering by fire unto the LORD,
■ **a burnt offering, or a**
■ **sacrifice in performing**
■ **a vow, or in a**

■ **freewill offering,**
or in your solemn feasts, to make a sweet savour
■ **unto the LORD,**
of the herd or of the flock:
■ 4. **Then** shall he that offereth his offering unto the LORD
■ **bring a meat**
■ **offering** of a tenth deal
■ **of flour mingled with**
the fourth *part* of an hin of
■ **oil.**
■ 5. **And** the fourth *part* of an hin of
■ **wine for a drink**
■ **offering** shalt thou prepare
■ **with the burnt offering**
■ **or sacrifice,** for one lamb.
6. Or for a ram, thou shalt prepare *for* a meat offering two tenth deals of flour mingled with the third *part* of an hin of oil.
7. And for a drink offering thou shalt offer the third *part* of an hin of wine, *for* a sweet savour unto the LORD.
8. And when thou preparest a bullock *for* a burnt offering, or *for* a sacrifice in performing a vow, or peace offerings unto the LORD:
9. Then shall he bring with a bullock a meat offering of three tenth deals of flour mingled with half an hin of oil.
10. And thou shalt bring for a drink offering half an hin of wine, *for* an offering made by fire, of a sweet savour unto the LORD.
■ 11. **Thus shall it be done**
■ **for one bullock, or for**
■ **one ram, or for a**
■ **lamb, or a kid.**
12. According to the number that ye shall prepare, so shall ye do to every one according to their number.
■ 13. **All** that are
■ **born of the country**
■ **shall do these things**
after this manner, in offering an offering made by fire, of a sweet savour unto the LORD.
■ 14. **And** if
■ **a stranger** sojourn with you, or whosoever *be* among you in your generations, and
■ **will offer an offering**

228

made by fire, of a sweet savour **unto the LORD; as ye do,** so he shall do.

15. One ordinance *shall be both* for you of the congregation, and also for the stranger that sojourneth *with you,* an ordinance for ever in your generations: as ye *are,* so shall the stranger be before the LORD.

16. **One law and one manner shall be for you, and** for **the stranger** that sojourneth with you.

17. **And the LORD spake unto Moses, saying,**

18. **Speak unto** the children of **Israel, and say** unto them, **When ye come into the land** whither I bring you,

19. Then it shall be, that, **when ye eat of the bread of the land,** ye shall offer up an heave offering unto the LORD.

20. **Ye shall offer up a cake of the first of your dough for an heave offering:** as *ye do* the heave offering of the threshingfloor, so shall ye heave it.

21. Of the first of your dough ye shall give unto the LORD an heave offering in your generations.

22. **And if ye have erred, and not observed** all **these commandments,** which the LORD hath spoken unto Moses,

23. *Even* all that the LORD hath commanded you by the hand of Moses, from the day that the LORD commanded *Moses,* and henceforward among your generations;

24. Then it shall be**, if aught be committed by ignorance without the knowledge of the congregation,** that all **the congregation shall offer one young bullock for a burnt offering,** for a sweet savour unto the LORD, **with his meat offering, and his drink offering,** according to the manner, **and one kid of the goats for a sin offering.**

25. And the priest shall make an atonement for all the congregation of the children of Israel, and it shall be forgiven them; for it *is* ignorance: and they shall bring their offering, a sacrifice made by fire unto the LORD, and their sin offering before the LORD, for their ignorance:

26. **And it shall be forgiven all the congregation** of the children of Israel, and the stranger that sojourneth among them; **seeing** all **the people were in ignorance.**

27. **And if any soul sin through ignorance,** then he shall **bring a she goat** of the first year **for a sin offering.**

28. **And the priest shall make an atonement** for the soul that sinneth ignorantly, when he sinneth by ignorance **before the LORD,** to make an atonement for him; **and it shall be forgiven him.**

29. Ye shall have one law for him that sinneth through ignorance, *both for* him that is born among the children of Israel, and for the stranger that sojourneth among them.

30. **But the soul that doeth aught presumptuously,** *whether he be* born in the land, or a stranger, the same reproacheth the LORD; and that soul **shall be cut off** from among his people.

31. **Because he hath despised the word of the LORD,** and hath broken his commandment, that soul shall utterly be cut off; his iniquity *shall be* upon him.

32. **And while** the children of Israel were **in the wilderness, they found a man that**

gathered sticks upon
the sabbath day.
33. And they
that found him gathering sticks
brought him unto Moses and
Aaron, and unto all the congregation.
34. And they put him in ward,
because it was not
declared what should
be done to him.
35. And the LORD
said unto Moses,
The man shall be surely
put to death:
all the congregation shall stone
him with stones without the camp.
36. And all
the congregation
brought him without the
camp, and stoned him
with stones, and he died; as
the LORD commanded Moses.
37. And the LORD spake
unto Moses, saying,
38. Speak unto the children
of Israel, and bid them that they
make them
fringes in the borders
of their garments
throughout their generations,
and that they
put upon the
fringe of the borders
a ribband of blue:
39. And it shall be unto
you for a fringe, that ye may
look upon it, and
remember all the
commandments
of the LORD, and
do them; and that ye
seek not after your
own heart and your own
eyes, after
which ye use
to go a-whoring:
40. That ye may remember,
and do all my commandments,
and be holy unto your God.
41. I *am* the LORD your God,
which brought you out of the
land of Egypt, to be your
God: I *am* the LORD your God.

CHAPTER 16

1. Now Korah, the son of Izhar,
the son of Kohath, the son of Levi,
and Dathan and
Abiram, the sons of Eliab,
and On, the son
of Peleth, sons of Reuben,
took men:
2. And they rose up
before Moses, with certain
of the children of Israel,
two hundred and fifty
princes of the assembly,
famous in the congregation,
men of renown:
3. And they gathered
themselves together
against Moses and against
Aaron, and said unto them,
Ye take too much upon
you, seeing all the
congregation are
holy, every one of them,
and the LORD is among
them: wherefore then lift ye
up yourselves above the
congregation of the LORD?
4. And when
Moses heard *it,* he
fell upon his face:
5. And he spake unto
Korah and unto all his company,
saying, Even
tomorrow the LORD will
shew who are his, and who
is holy; and will cause
him to come near unto him: even
him whom he hath
chosen will he cause
to come near unto him.
6. This do; Take you
censers,
Korah, and all his company;
7. And put fire therein,
and put incense in
them before the LORD
to morrow: and it
shall be *that* the man
whom the LORD
doth choose, he
shall be holy: ye *take* too
much upon you, ye sons of Levi.
8. And Moses said unto

Korah, Hear, I pray you, ye sons of Levi:

9. **Seemeth it** *but* **a small thing** unto you, **that** the **God** of Israel **hath separated you** from the congregation of Israel, to bring you near to himself **to do the service of the tabernacle** of the LORD, and to stand before the congregation to minister unto them?

10. And he hath brought thee near *to him,* and all thy brethren the sons of Levi with thee: **and seek ye the priesthood also?**

11. **For** which cause *both* **thou** and all thy company **are gathered** together **against the LORD: and what is Aaron, that ye murmur against him?**

12. **And Moses sent to call Dathan and Abiram,** the sons of Eliab: **which said, We will not come up:**

13. **Is it a small thing that thou hast brought us up** out of a land that floweth with milk and honey, **to kill us in the wilderness,** except thou make thyself altogether a prince over us?

14. **Moreover thou hast not** brought us into a land that floweth with milk and honey, or **given us inheritance of fields and vineyards:** wilt thou put out the eyes of these men? **we will not come up.**

15. **And Moses was very wroth, and said** unto the LORD, Respect not thou their offering: I have not taken one ass from them, neither have I hurt one of them.

16. And Moses said **unto Korah, Be thou and all thy company before the LORD,** thou, and they, and Aaron, **to morrow:**

17. **And take every man his censer,** and put incense in them, and bring ye before the LORD every man his censer, two hundred and fifty censers; thou also, and Aaron, each *of you* his censer.

18. **And they** took every man his censer, and **put fire in them, and laid incense thereon, and stood in the door of the tabernacle** of the congregation with Moses and Aaron.

19. And Korah gathered all the congregation against them unto the door of the tabernacle of the congregation: **and the glory of the LORD appeared** unto all the congregation.

20. **And the LORD spake unto Moses and** unto **Aaron, saying,**

21. **Separate yourselves from** among **this congregation, that I may consume them** in a moment.

22. **And they fell upon their faces, and said, O God,** the God of the spirits of all flesh, **shall one man sin, and wilt thou be wroth with all the congregation?**

23. **And the LORD spake** unto Moses, **saying,**

24. Speak unto the congregation, saying, **Get you up from about the tabernacle of Korah, Dathan, and Abiram.**

25. **And Moses** rose up and went unto Dathan and Abiram; and the elders of Israel followed him.

26. And he **spake unto the congregation, saying, Depart,** I pray you, **from the tents of these wicked men, and touch nothing of theirs,** lest ye be consumed in all their sins.

27. So they gat up from the tabernacle of Korah, Dathan, and Abiram, on every side: and Dathan and Abiram came out, and stood in the door of their tents, and their wives, and their sons, and their little children. 28. And Moses said,

Hereby ye shall know that the LORD hath sent me to do all these works; for *I have* not *done them* of mine own mind. 29. If these men die the common death of all men, or if they be visited after the visitation of all men; *then* the LORD hath not sent me. 30. But if the LORD make a new thing, and the earth open her mouth, and swallow them up, with all that *appertain* unto them, and they go down quick into the pit; then ye shall understand that these men have provoked the LORD. 31. And it came to pass, as he had made an end of speaking all these words, that the ground clave asunder that *was* under them:

32. And the earth opened her mouth, and swallowed them up, and their houses, and all the men that *appertained* unto Korah, **and all their goods.** 33. They, and all that *appertained* to them, went down alive into the pit, and the earth closed upon them: and they perished from among the congregation. 34. And all Israel that *were* round about them fled at the cry of them: for they said, Lest the earth swallow us up *also*.

35. And there came out a fire from the LORD, and consumed the two hundred and fifty men that offered incense. 36. And the LORD spake unto Moses, saying, 37. Speak unto Eleazar the son of Aaron the priest, **that he take up the censers** out of the burning, **and scatter** thou

the fire yonder; for they are hallowed. 38. The censers of these sinners against their own souls, let them make them broad plates *for* a covering of the altar: for they offered them before the LORD, therefore they are hallowed: and they shall be a sign unto the children of Israel. **39. And Eleazar** the priest **took the brasen censers,** wherewith they that were burnt had offered; **and** they were **made broad plates for a covering of the altar: 40. To be a memorial unto** the children of **Israel, that no stranger,** which *is* not of the seed of Aaron, come near to **offer incense before the LORD;** that he be not **as Korah, and** as **his company:** as the LORD said to him by the hand of Moses.

41. But on the morrow all the congregation of the children of Israel **murmured against Moses and** against **Aaron, saying, Ye have killed the people of the LORD.** **42. And** it came to pass, when **the congregation** was gathered against Moses and against Aaron, that they **looked toward the tabernacle** of the congregation: **and,** behold, **the cloud covered it, and the glory of the LORD appeared.** 43. And Moses and Aaron came before the tabernacle of the congregation. **44. And the LORD spake unto Moses, saying, 45. Get** you **up from** among **this congregation, that I may consume them**

as in a moment. And they fell upon their faces. 46. **And Moses said unto Aaron, Take a censer, and put fire** therein **from off the altar, and** put on **incense, and go** quickly **unto the congregation, and make an atonement for them: for** there is wrath gone out from the LORD; **the plague is begun.** 47. **And Aaron** took as Moses commanded, and **ran into the midst of the congregation;** and, behold, the plague was begun among the people: and he put on incense, **and made an atonement for the people.** 48. **And he stood between the dead and the living; and the plague was stayed.** 49. **Now they that died** in the plague **were fourteen thousand** and **seven hundred,** beside them that died about the matter of Korah. 50. **And Aaron returned unto** Moses unto **the door of the tabernacle** of the congregation: and the plague was stayed.

CHAPTER 17

1. **And the LORD spake unto Moses, saying,** 2. Speak unto the children of Israel, and **take** of **every one** of them **a rod according to the house of their fathers,** of all their princes according to the house of their fathers **twelve rods: write** thou **every man's name upon his rod.** 3. **And** thou shalt **write Aaron's name upon the rod of Levi:** for one rod *shall be* for the head of the house of their fathers. 4. **And** thou shalt **lay them up in the tabernacle** of the congregation before the testimony, where I will meet with you. 5. **And** it shall come to pass, *that* **the man's rod, whom I shall choose, shall blossom: and I will make to cease** from me **the murmurings of** the children of **Israel,** whereby they murmur against you. 6. And Moses spake unto the children of Israel, and every one of their princes gave him a rod apiece, for each prince one, according to their fathers' houses, *even* twelve rods: and the rod of Aaron *was* among their rods. 7. **And Moses laid up the rods before the LORD in the tabernacle** of witness. 8. **And** it came to pass, that **on the morrow Moses went into the tabernacle** of witness; **and,** behold, **the rod of Aaron** for the house of Levi **was budded,** and brought forth buds, **and bloomed** blossoms, **and yielded almonds.** 9. **And Moses brought out all the rods** from before the LORD unto all the children of Israel: and they looked, **and took every man his rod.** 10. **And the LORD said** unto Moses, **Bring Aaron's rod** again before the testimony, **to be kept for a token against the rebels;** and thou shalt quite take away their murmurings from me, **that they die not.** 11. **And Moses did** *so:* **as the LORD**

233

■ commanded him, so did he.
■ 12. **And the children**
■ **of Israel spake unto**
■ **Moses,** saying, Behold,
we die, we perish, we all perish.
■ 13. **Whosoever**
■ **cometh** any thing
■ **near** unto
■ **the tabernacle of the LORD**
■ **shall die: shall we be**
■ **consumed with dying?**

CHAPTER 18

■ 1. **And the LORD said unto**
■ **Aaron, Thou and thy sons**
and thy father's house with thee
■ **shall bear the iniquity**
■ **of the sanctuary: and**
thou and thy sons with thee
shall bear the iniquity of
■ **your priesthood.**
■ 2. **And thy brethren** also of the
tribe of Levi, the tribe of thy father,
■ **bring** thou
■ **with thee, that they**
■ **may** be joined unto thee, and
■ **minister unto thee: but**
■ **thou and thy sons** with thee
■ **shall minister before**
■ **the tabernacle** of witness.
■ 3. **And they shall keep**
■ **thy charge,** and the charge
of all the tabernacle:
■ **only they shall not come**
■ **nigh the vessels of the**
■ **sanctuary and the altar,**
that neither they, nor ye also, die.
4. And they shall be joined unto thee,
and keep the charge of the tabernacle
of the congregation, for all the
service of the tabernacle:
■ **and a stranger shall not**
■ **come nigh unto you.**
■ 5. **And ye shall keep**
■ **the charge of the**
■ **sanctuary, and** the charge of
■ **the altar: that there**
■ **be no wrath any**
■ **more upon** the children of
■ **Israel.**
6. And I, behold,
■ **I have taken** your brethren
■ **the Levites** from among the

children of Israel: to you *they are*
given *as* a gift for the LORD,
■ **to do the service of the**
■ **tabernacle** of the congregation.
■ 7. **Therefore thou**
■ **and thy sons** with thee
■ **shall keep your priest's**
■ **office for everything of**
■ **the altar, and within the**
■ **veil;** and ye shall serve:
■ **I have given your priest's**
■ **office unto you as a** service of
■ **gift: and the stranger**
■ **that cometh nigh shall**
■ **be put to death.**
■ 8. **And the LORD spake**
■ **unto Aaron,** Behold,
■ **I** also
■ **have given thee** the
■ **charge of mine heave**
■ **offerings of all the hallowed**
■ **things** of the children of Israel;
unto thee have I given them
■ **by reason of the**
■ **anointing,** and to thy sons,
by an ordinance for ever.
■ 9. **This shall be thine**
of the most holy things,
■ **reserved from the fire:**
every oblation of theirs,
■ **every meat offering**
of theirs, and every
■ **sin offering** of theirs,
■ **and** every
■ **trespass offering** of theirs
■ **which they shall render**
■ **unto me, shall be** most holy
■ **for thee and for thy sons.**
■ 10. **In the most holy**
■ **place** shalt thou eat it;
■ **every male shall eat**
■ **it:** it shall be holy unto thee.
11. And this *is* thine; the heave
offering of their gift, with all the wave
offerings of the children of Israel: I
have given them unto thee, and to thy
sons and to thy daughters with thee,
by a statute for ever: every one that
is clean in thy house shall eat of it.
■ 12. **All the best of the**
■ **oil,** and all the best of
■ **the wine, and** of
■ **the wheat,** the firstfruits of them

which they shall offer unto the LORD, them have I given thee.

13. And whatsoever is first ripe in the land, which they shall bring unto the LORD, shall be thine; every one that is clean in thine house shall eat of it.

14. Every thing devoted in Israel shall be thine.

15. Every thing that openeth the matrix in all flesh, which they bring unto the LORD, *whether it be* of men or beasts, shall be thine: nevertheless the firstborn of man shalt thou surely redeem, and the firstling of unclean beasts shalt thou redeem.

16. And those that are to be redeemed from a month old shalt thou redeem, according to thine estimation, for the money of five shekels, after the shekel of the sanctuary, which *is* twenty gerahs.

17. But the firstling of a cow, or the firstling of a sheep, or the firstling of a goat, thou shalt not redeem; they are holy: thou shalt sprinkle their blood upon the altar, and shalt burn their fat for an offering made by fire, for a sweet savour unto the LORD.

18. And the flesh of them shall be thine, as the wave breast and as the right shoulder are thine.

19. All the heave offerings of the holy things, which the children of Israel offer unto the LORD, have I given thee, and thy sons and thy daughters with thee, by a statute for ever: it is a covenant of salt for ever before the LORD unto thee and to thy seed with thee.

20. And the LORD spake unto Aaron, Thou shalt have no inheritance in their land, neither shalt thou have any part among them: I am thy part and thine inheritance among the children of Israel.

21. And, behold, I have given the children of Levi all the tenth in Israel for an inheritance, for their service which they serve, *even* the service of the tabernacle of the congregation.

22. Neither must the children of Israel henceforth come nigh the tabernacle of the congregation, lest they bear sin, and die.

23. But the Levites shall do the service of the tabernacle of the congregation, and they shall bear their iniquity: *it shall be* a statute for ever throughout your generations, that among the children of Israel they have no inheritance.

24. But the tithes of the children of Israel, which they offer *as* an heave offering unto the LORD, I have given to the Levites to inherit: therefore I have said unto them, Among the children of Israel they shall have no inheritance.

25. And the LORD spake unto Moses, saying,

26. Thus speak unto the Levites, and say unto them, When ye take of the children of Israel the tithes which I have given you from them for your inheritance, then ye shall offer up an heave offering of it for the LORD, even a tenth part

of the tithe.

27. **And this** your heave offering **shall be reckoned unto you, as** though *it were* **the corn** of the threshingfloor, **and** as **the fulness of the winepress.**

28. **Thus ye also shall offer** an heave offering unto the LORD **of** all **your tithes,** which ye receive of the children of Israel; **and** ye **shall give** thereof the LORD's heave offering **to Aaron the priest.**

29. **Out of all your gifts ye shall offer every heave offering of the LORD,** of all the best thereof, *even* the hallowed part thereof out of it.

30. Therefore thou shalt say unto them, When ye have heaved the best thereof from it, then it shall be counted unto the Levites as the increase of the threshingfloor, and as the increase of the winepress.

31. **And ye shall eat it** in every place, ye and your households: **for it is your reward for your service** in the tabernacle of the congregation.

32. **And ye shall bear no sin** by reason of it, **when ye have heaved** from it **the best of it: neither shall ye pollute the holy things** of the children of Israel, **lest ye die.**

CHAPTER 19

1. And the LORD spake unto Moses and unto Aaron, saying,

2. **This is the ordinance** of the law **which the LORD** hath **commanded, saying, Speak unto the children of Israel, that they bring** thee **a red heifer without** spot, wherein *is* no **blemish, and upon which never came yoke:**

3. **And** ye shall **give her unto Eleazar** the priest, **that he may bring her** forth **without the camp, and** *one* shall **slay her** before his face:

4. **And Eleazar** the priest **shall take** of **her blood with his finger, and sprinkle** of her blood directly **before the tabernacle** of the congregation **seven times:**

5. **And** *one* shall **burn** the heifer in his sight; **her skin,** and her **flesh, and** her **blood, with her dung,** hall he burn:

6. **And** the priest shall **take cedar wood, and hyssop, and scarlet, and cast it into** the midst of **the burning of the heifer.**

7. **Then the priest shall wash his clothes, and** he shall **bathe** his flesh in water, **and afterward** he shall **come into the camp, and** the priest **shall be unclean until the even.**

8. **And he that burneth her shall wash his clothes** in water, **and bathe** his flesh in water, **and** shall **be unclean until the even.**

9. **And a man that is clean shall gather up the ashes** of the heifer, and lay *them* up **without the camp** in a clean place, **and it shall be kept for** the congregation of the children of Israel for a **water of separation: it is a purification for sin.**

10. And he that gathereth the ashes of the heifer shall wash his clothes,

and be unclean until the even: and it shall be unto the children of Israel, and unto the stranger that sojourneth among them, for a statute for ever.

11. **He that toucheth the dead** body of any man **shall be unclean** seven days.

12. **He shall purify himself with it on the third day, and on the seventh day he shall be clean: but if he purify not himself** the third day, then the seventh day **he shall not be clean.**

13. Whosoever toucheth the dead body of any man that is dead, **and** purifieth not himself, **defileth the tabernacle of the LORD;** and that soul shall be cut off from Israel: **because the water of separation was not sprinkled upon him,** he shall be unclean; his uncleanness *is* yet upon him.

14. **This is the law, when a man dieth in a tent:** all that come into the tent, and **all that is in the tent,** shall be unclean seven days.

15. And every open vessel, which hath no covering bound upon it, **is unclean.**

16. **And whosoever toucheth** one that is slain with a sword in the open fields, or **a dead body, or a bone of a man, or a grave, shall be unclean seven days.**

17. And for an unclean *person* **they shall take of the ashes of the burnt heifer** of purification for sin, **and running water** shall be put thereto in a vessel:

18. **And a clean person shall take hyssop, and dip it in the water, and sprinkle** *it* upon **the tent, and** upon all the **vessels, and** upon **the persons that were there, and upon him that touched** **a bone,** or one slain, **or one dead, or a grave:**

19. And the clean *person* shall sprinkle upon the unclean **on the third day, and on the seventh day: and** on the seventh day he **shall purify himself, and wash his clothes, and bathe** himself in water, **and shall be clean at even.**

20. **But the man that** shall be unclean, and **shall not purify himself,** that soul **shall be cut off** from among the congregation, **because he hath defiled the sanctuary of the LORD:** the water of separation hath not been sprinkled upon him; he *is* unclean.

21. **And it shall be a perpetual statute** unto them, **that he that** sprinkleth the water of separation shall wash his clothes; and he that **toucheth the water of separation shall be unclean** until even.

22. And whatsoever the unclean *person* toucheth shall be unclean; and the soul that toucheth *it* shall be unclean until even.

CHAPTER 20

1. **Then came the** children of **Israel,** *even* the whole congregation, **into the desert of Zin** in the first month: and the people abode **in Kadesh; and Miriam died** there, **and was buried there.**

2. **And there was no water** for the congregation: **and they gathered** themselves **together against Moses and** against **Aaron.**

3. And the people chode with Moses, and spake, **saying, Would God**

that we had died when
our brethren died
before the LORD!
4. And why have
ye brought up
the congregation of the
LORD into this wilderness, that
we and our cattle should die there?
5. And wherefore have ye made us
to come up out of Egypt, to bring us in
unto this evil place? it is
no place of seed, or of figs, or of
vines, or of pomegranates;
neither is there any water to drink.
6. And Moses and
Aaron went from the
presence of the assembly
unto the door of the
tabernacle of the congregation,
and they
fell upon their
faces: and the glory of
the LORD appeared
unto them.
7. And the LORD spake unto Moses,
saying,
8. Take the rod, and gather
thou the assembly together,
thou, and Aaron thy brother,
and speak ye unto the
rock before their eyes;
and it shall give forth his water,
and thou shalt
bring forth to them
water out of the rock:
so thou shalt give the congregation
and their beasts drink.
9. And Moses took the
rod from before the LORD,
as he commanded him.
10. And Moses and Aaron
gathered the
congregation together
before the rock, and he
said unto them,
Hear now, ye rebels; must
we fetch you water
out of this rock?
11. And Moses
lifted up his hand, and
with his rod he smote the
rock twice: and the water
came out abundantly,

and the congregation
drank, and their beasts also.
12. And the LORD spake
unto Moses and Aaron,
Because ye believed
me not, to sanctify me
in the eyes of the children of
Israel, therefore
ye shall not bring this
congregation into the
land which I have given them.
13. This is the water of
Meribah; because
the children of
Israel strove with the LORD,
and he was sanctified in them.
14. And Moses sent
messengers from Kadesh
unto the king of Edom,
Thus saith thy brother
Israel, Thou knowest all
the travail that hath
befallen us:
15. How our fathers went down
into Egypt, and we have dwelt
in Egypt a long time; and the
Egyptians vexed us, and our fathers:
16. And when we cried
unto the LORD, he
heard our voice, and
sent an angel, and hath
brought us forth
out of Egypt: and, behold,
we are in Kadesh, a city
in the uttermost of thy border:
17. Let us pass, I pray thee,
through thy country: we will
not pass through the fields, or through
the vineyards, neither will we drink of
the water of the wells: we will go by
the king's high way, we will not turn
to the right hand nor to the left, until
we have passed thy borders.
18. And Edom said unto him,
Thou shalt not pass
by me, lest I come out
against thee with the sword.
19. And the children of
Israel said unto him,
We will go by the high
way: and if I and my
cattle drink of thy water,
then I will pay for it: I will

only, without *doing* anything
else, go through on my feet.
20. And he said, Thou
shalt not go through.
■ **And Edom came out**
■ **against him with much**
■ **people, and** with a strong hand.
21. Thus Edom
■ **refused to give Israel**
■ **passage through his**
■ **border: wherefore Israel**
■ **turned away** from him.
22. **And** the children of Israel,
even the whole congregation,
■ **journeyed** from
Kadesh, and came
■ **unto mount Hor.**
23. **And the LORD**
■ **spake unto Moses**
■ **and Aaron** in mount Hor,
by the coast of the land of Edom,
■ **saying,**
24. **Aaron** shall be gathered
unto his people: for he
■ **shall not enter into the**
■ **land** which I have given
unto the children of Israel,
■ **because ye rebelled**
■ **against my word at the**
■ **water of Meribah.**
25. **Take Aaron and Eleazar**
his son, and bring them up
■ **unto mount Hor:**
26. **And strip Aaron of his**
■ **garments, and put them**
■ **upon Eleazar his son:**
and Aaron shall be gathered *unto*
his people, and shall die there.
27. And Moses did as the
LORD commanded: and they
went up into mount Hor in the
sight of all the congregation.
28. **And Moses**
■ **stripped Aaron of his**
■ **garments, and put them**
■ **upon Eleazar** his son;
■ **and Aaron died**
■ **there in the** top of the
■ **mount:** and Moses and Eleazar
came down from the mount.
29. **And when** all
■ **the congregation saw**
■ **that Aaron was dead,**

■ **they mourned** for Aaron
■ **thirty days,** *even*
all the house of Israel.

CHAPTER 21

■ 1. **And when king Arad**
■ **the Canaanite,**
which dwelt in the south,
■ **heard** tell
■ **that Israel came** by
the way of the spies; then
■ **he fought against Israel,**
■ **and took** *some* of them
■ **prisoners.**
2. **And Israel vowed** a vow
■ **unto the LORD,** and said,
■ **If thou** wilt indeed
■ **deliver this people into**
■ **my hand, then I will utterly**
■ **destroy their cities.**
3. **And the LORD**
■ **hearkened** to the voice of Israel,
■ **and delivered** up
■ **the Canaanites;**
■ **and they** utterly
■ **destroyed them** and their cities:
■ **and he called** the name of
■ **the place Hormah.**
4. **And they**
■ **journeyed** from mount Hor
■ **by** the way of
■ **the Red sea, to compass**
■ **the land of Edom:**
■ **and** the soul of
■ **the people was** much
■ **discouraged because**
■ **of the way.**
5. **And** the people
■ **spake against**
■ **God, and** against
■ **Moses,** Wherefore have
■ **ye brought us** up
■ **out of Egypt to die**
in the wilderness? for
■ **there is no bread,**
■ **neither** *is there any*
■ **water; and our soul loatheth**
■ **this light bread.**
6. **And the LORD sent fiery**
■ **serpents** among the people,
■ **and they bit the**
■ **people; and much**
■ **people of Israel died.**

7. **Therefore the people came to Moses, and said, We have sinned,** for we have spoken against the LORD, and against thee; **pray unto the LORD, that he take away the serpents** from us. **And Moses prayed** for the people.

8. **And the LORD said** unto Moses, **Make thee a fiery serpent, and set it upon a pole: and** it shall come to pass, that **every one that is bitten, when he looketh upon it, shall live.**

9. **And Moses made a serpent of brass,** and put it upon a pole, **and** it came to pass, that if a serpent had bitten **any man, when he beheld the serpent of brass,** he **lived.**

10. **And** the children of **Israel set forward, and pitched in Oboth.**

11. **And they journeyed from** Oboth, and pitched at **Ijeabarim,** in the wilderness which *is* before Moab, **toward** the sunrising.

12. From thence they removed, and pitched in the valley of **Zared.**

13. From thence they removed, and pitched on the other side of Arnon, which *is* in the wilderness that cometh out of the coasts of the Amorites: for Arnon *is* the border of Moab, between Moab and the Amorites.

14. Wherefore it is said in the book of the wars of the LORD, What he did in the Red sea, and in the brooks of Arnon,

15. And at the stream of the brooks that goeth down to the dwelling of Ar, and lieth upon the border of Moab.

16. **And** from thence **they went to Beer: that is the well whereof the LORD** **spake** unto Moses, Gather the people together, and I will give them water.

17. **Then Israel sang this song, Spring up, O well;** sing ye unto it:

18. **The princes digged the well,** the nobles of the people digged it, **by the direction of the lawgiver,** with their staves. **And from the wilderness they went to Mattanah:**

19. And from Mattanah to **Nahaliel: and** from Nahaliel to **Bamoth:**

20. And from Bamoth *in* the valley, that *is* **in the country of Moab, to the top of Pisgah,** which looketh **toward Jeshimon.**

21. **And Israel sent messengers unto Sihon king of the Amorites, saying,**

22. **Let me pass through thy land: we will not turn into the fields, or** into the vineyards; we will not **drink** *of* **the waters** of the well: **but we will go** along **by the king's high way,** until we be past thy borders.

23. **And Sihon would not suffer Israel to pass** through his border: **but** Sihon **gathered all his people** together, and went out against Israel into the wilderness: and he came to Jahaz, **and fought against Israel.**

24. **And Israel smote him with** the edge of **the sword, and possessed his land** from Arnon unto Jabbok, even unto the children of Ammon: for the border of the children of Ammon *was* strong.

25. **And Israel** took all these cities: and Israel **dwelt in all the cities**

Balaam Refuses to Curse Israel

of the Amorites, in Heshbon, and in all the villages thereof.

26. For Heshbon *was* the city of Sihon the king of the Amorites, who had fought against the former king of Moab, and taken all his land out of his hand,

even unto Arnon.

27. Wherefore they that speak in proverbs say, Come into Heshbon, let the city of Sihon be built and prepared:

28. For there is a fire gone out of Heshbon, a flame from the city of Sihon: it hath consumed Ar of Moab, *and* the lords of the high places of Arnon.

29. Woe to thee, Moab! thou art undone, O people of Chemosh: he hath given his sons that escaped, and his daughters, into captivity unto Sihon king of the Amorites.

30. We have shot at them; Heshbon is perished even unto Dibon, and we have laid them waste even unto Nophah, which *reacheth* unto Medeba.

31. Thus Israel dwelt in the land of the Amorites.

32. **And Moses sent to spy out Jaazer, and** they took the villages thereof, and **drove out the Amorites** that *were* there.

33. **And they** turned and **went** up **by** the way of **Bashan: and Og the king of Bashan went out against them,** he, and all his people, **to the battle** at Edrei.

34. **And the LORD said** unto Moses, **Fear him not: for I have delivered him into thy hand,** and all his people, and his land; and thou shalt do to him as thou didst unto Sihon king of the Amorites, which dwelt at Heshbon.

35. **So they smote him, and** his sons, and all his people, until there was none left him alive: and they **possessed his land.**

CHAPTER 22

1. **And** the children of **Israel set forward,** and pitched **in the plains of Moab** on this side Jordan **by Jericho.**

2. **And Balak** the son of Zippor **saw all that Israel had done to the Amorites.**

3. **And** Moab **was** sore **afraid** of the people, because they *were* many: and Moab was distressed because of the children of Israel.

4. And Moab said unto the elders of Midian, Now shall this company lick up all *that are* round about us, as the ox licketh up the grass of the field. And **Balak** the son of Zippor **was king of the Moabites** at that time.

5. **He sent messengers** therefore **unto Balaam** the son of Beor to Pethor, which *is* by the river of the land of the children of his people, to call him, **saying, Behold, there is a people** come out **from Egypt:** behold, they cover the face of the earth, **and they abide** over **against me:**

6. **Come** now therefore, I pray thee, **curse** me **this people;** for they *are* too mighty for me: peradventure I shall prevail, **that we may smite them, and** *that* I may **drive them out of the land: for** I wot that he whom thou blessest *is* blessed, and he **whom thou cursest is cursed.**

7. **And the elders of Moab and** the elders of **Midian departed with the rewards of divination** in their hand; and they came **unto Balaam, and spake** unto him

the words of Balak.

8. **And he said** unto them, **Lodge here this night, and I will bring you word** again, **as the LORD shall speak unto me:** and the princes of Moab abode with Balaam.

9. And God came unto Balaam, and said, What men *are* these with thee?

10. And Balaam said unto God, Balak the son of Zippor, king of Moab, hath sent unto me, *saying,*

11. Behold, *there is* a people come out of Egypt, which covereth the face of the earth: come now, curse me them; peradventure I shall be able to overcome them, and drive them out.

12. **And God said unto Balaam, Thou shalt not go with them; thou shalt not curse the people: for they are blessed.**

13. **And Balaam rose** up in the morning, and **said unto the princes of Balak,** Get you into your land: for **the LORD refuseth to give me leave to go with you.**

14. **And the princes** of Moab rose up, and they **went unto Balak, and said, Balaam refuseth to come with us.**

15. **And Balak sent** yet again **princes,** more, and **more honourable** than they.

16. **And they** came to Balaam, and **said** to him, Thus saith Balak the son of Zippor, **Let nothing,** I pray thee, **hinder thee from coming** unto me:

17. **For I will promote thee unto very great honour,** and I will do whatsoever thou sayest unto me: **come therefore,** I pray thee, **curse** me **this people.**

18. **And Balaam answered** and said unto the servants of Balak, **If Balak would give me his house full of silver and gold, I cannot go beyond the word of the LORD** my God, to do less or more.

19. Now therefore, I pray you, **tarry ye also here this night, that I may know what the LORD will say** unto me more.

20. **And God** came unto Balaam at night, and **said unto him,** If the men come to call thee, **rise up, and go with them; but** yet **the word which I** shall **say** unto thee, **that shalt thou do.**

21. **And Balaam** rose up in the morning, and **saddled his ass, and went** with the princes of Moab.

22. **And God's anger was kindled because he went: and the angel of the LORD stood in the way** for an adversary against him. Now he was riding upon his ass, and his two servants *were* with him.

23. **And the ass saw the angel** of the LORD standing in the way, and his sword drawn in his hand: **and** the ass **turned aside** out of the way, and went **into the field: and Balaam smote the ass, to turn her into the way.**

24. But the angel of the LORD stood in a path of the vineyards, **a wall being on this side, and** a wall on **that** side.

25. **And** when **the ass** saw the angel of the LORD, she **thrust herself unto the wall, and crushed Balaam's foot** against the wall: **and he smote her again.**

26. **And the angel** of the LORD **went further, and stood in**

242

a narrow place, where was no way to turn either to the right hand or to the left. 27. **And** when the ass saw the angel of the LORD, she fell down under Balaam: and Balaam's anger was kindled, and he smote the ass with a staff. 28. And the LORD opened the mouth of the ass, and she said unto Balaam, What have I done unto thee, that thou hast smitten me these three times? 29. **And Balaam said** unto the ass, Because thou hast mocked me: I would there were a sword in mine hand, for now would I kill thee. 30. **And the ass** said unto Balaam, Am not I thine ass, upon which thou hast ridden ever since *I was* thine unto this day? was I ever wont to do so unto thee? And he said, Nay. 31. Then the LORD opened the eyes of Balaam, and he saw the angel of the LORD standing in the way, and his sword drawn in his hand: and he bowed down his head, and fell flat on his face. 32. **And the angel** of the LORD said unto him, Wherefore hast thou smitten thine ass these three times? behold, I went out to withstand thee, because thy way is perverse before me: 33. And the ass saw me, and turned from me these three times: unless she had turned from me, surely now also I had slain thee, and saved her alive. 34. **And Balaam said** unto the angel of the LORD, I have sinned; for I knew not that thou stoodest in the way against me: now therefore, if it displease thee, I will get me back again. 35. And the angel of the LORD said unto Balaam, Go with the men: but only the word that I shall speak unto thee, that thou shalt speak. So Balaam went with the princes of Balak. 36. And when Balak heard that Balaam was come, he went out to meet him unto a city of Moab, which *is* in the border of Arnon, which *is* in the utmost coast. 37. **And** Balak said unto Balaam, Did I not earnestly send unto thee to call thee? wherefore camest thou not unto me? am I not able indeed to promote thee to honour? 38. And Balaam said unto Balak, Lo, I am come unto thee: have I now any power at all to say any thing? the word that God putteth in my mouth, that shall I speak. 39. And Balaam went with Balak, and they came unto Kirjath-huzoth. 40. And Balak offered oxen and sheep, and sent to Balaam, and to the princes that *were* with him. 41. And it came to pass on the morrow, that Balak took Balaam, and brought him up into the high places of Baal, that thence he might see the utmost *part* of the people.

CHAPTER 23

1. And Balaam said unto Balak, Build me here seven altars, and prepare me here

243

■ seven oxen and
■ seven rams.
■ 2. **And Balak** did as Balaam
had spoken; and Balak
■ **and Balaam offered**
■ **on every altar a**
■ **bullock and a ram.**
■ 3. **And Balaam**
■ **said** unto Balak,
■ **Stand by thy burnt offering,**
■ **and I will go:** peradventure
■ **the LORD will come**
■ **to meet me:** and whatsoever
he sheweth me I will tell thee.
And he went to an high place.
■ 4. **And God met Balaam:**
and he said unto him, I have prepared
seven altars, and I have offered upon
every altar a bullock and a ram.
■ 5. **And** the LORD
■ **put a word in**
■ **Balaam's mouth, and**
■ **said,** Return unto Balak, and
■ **thus thou shalt speak.**
■ 6. **And he returned** unto him,
■ **and,** lo, he
■ **stood by his** burnt
■ **sacrifice,** he, and all the
princes of Moab.
■ 7. **And** he took up his parable, and
■ **said, Balak** the king of Moab
■ **hath brought me**
■ **from Aram,** out of the
mountains of the east,
■ **saying, Come, curse** me
■ **Jacob, and** come,
■ **defy Israel.**
■ 8. **How shall I curse,**
■ **whom God hath not**
■ **cursed?** or how shall I defy,
whom the LORD hath not defied?
■ 9. **For from the** top of the
■ **rocks** I see him,
■ **and** from the
■ **hills I behold him:** lo, the
people shall dwell alone, and shall
not be reckoned among the nations.
■ 10. **Who can count**
the dust of Jacob, and
■ **the number** of the fourth *part*
■ **of Israel? Let me**
■ **die** the death of the
■ **righteous,** and let

my last end be like his!
■ 11. **And Balak**
■ **said** unto Balaam,
■ **What hast thou done** unto
■ **me? I took thee to curse**
■ **mine enemies, and,** behold,
■ **thou hast blessed**
■ **them** altogether.
■ 12. **And he answered** and said,
■ **Must I not** take heed to
■ **speak that which the LORD**
■ **hath put in my mouth?**
■ 13. **And Balak** said unto him,
Come, I pray thee, with me unto
another place, from whence
thou mayest see them: thou
shalt see but the utmost part
of them, and shalt not see them
all: and curse me them from thence.
14. And he
■ **brought him**
into the field of Zophim,
■ **to the top of Pisgah, and**
■ **built seven altars, and**
■ **offered a bullock and**
■ **a ram on every altar.**
■ 15. **And he said unto Balak,**
■ **Stand here** by thy burnt offering,
■ **while I meet the**
■ **LORD yonder.**
■ 16. **And the LORD**
■ **met Balaam,** and
put a word in his mouth,
■ **and said, Go again**
■ **unto Balak, and say** thus.
17. And when he came to him,
behold, he stood by his burnt offering,
and the princes of Moab with him.
And Balak said unto him,
What hath the LORD spoken?
18. And he took up his
parable, and said,
■ **Rise up, Balak, and** hear;
■ **hearken unto me,**
thou son of Zippor.
19. **God is not a man, that**
■ **he should lie; neither the**
■ **son of man, that he should**
■ **repent:** hath he said, and shall
he not do *it?* or hath he spoken,
and shall he not make it good?
20. **Behold, I have**
■ **received commandment**

■ **to bless** and he hath blessed;
■ **and I cannot reverse it.**
■ 21. **He hath not** beheld
iniquity in Jacob, neither hath he
■ **seen perverseness**
■ **in Israel:** the LORD his
■ **God is with him,** and the
shout of a king is among them.
■ 22. **God brought them**
■ **out of Egypt;** he hath as it
were the strength of an unicorn.
■ 23. **Surely there is no**
■ **enchantment against**
■ **Jacob,** neither *is there* any
divination against Israel: according to
this time it shall be said of Jacob and
of Israel, What hath God wrought!
■ 24. **Behold, the people shall**
■ **rise up as a great lion, and**
lift up himself as a young lion: he
■ **shall not lie down until**
■ **he eat of the prey,** and
drink the blood of the slain.
■ 25. **And Balak**
■ **said** unto Balaam,
■ **Neither curse them** at all,
■ **nor bless them** at all.
■ 26. **But Balaam**
■ **answered** and said unto
Balak, Told not I thee, saying,
■ **All that the LORD**
■ **speaketh,** that
■ **I must do?**
■ 27. **And Balak said**
unto Balaam, Come, I pray thee,
■ **I will bring thee unto**
■ **another place;**
peradventure it will please
God that thou mayest curse
me them from thence.
■ 28. **And Balak brought**
■ **Balaam unto the top**
■ **of Peor,** that looketh
toward Jeshimon.
■ 29. **And Balaam**
■ **said** unto Balak,
■ **Build** me here
■ **seven altars, and**
■ **prepare** me here
■ **seven bullocks**
■ **and seven rams.**
■ 30. **And Balak did**
■ **as Balaam** had

■ **said,** and offered a bullock
and a ram on *every* altar.

CHAPTER 24

■ 1. **And when**
■ **Balaam saw** that
■ **it pleased the LORD**
■ **to bless Israel, he**
■ **went not,** as at other times,
■ **to seek** for
■ **enchantments, but** he
■ **set his face**
■ **toward** the wilderness.
2. And Balaam lifted up
his eyes, and he saw
■ **Israel** abiding *in his tents*
according to their tribes;
■ **and the spirit of God**
■ **came upon him.**
3. **And he** took up his parable, and
■ **said,** Balaam the son of
Beor hath said, and the man
whose eyes are open hath said:
4. He hath said, which heard the
words of God, which saw the vision
of the Almighty, falling *into a*
trance, but having his eyes open:
■ 5. **How goodly are**
■ **thy tents,** O Jacob,
■ **and** thy
■ **tabernacles, O Israel!**
6. As the valleys are they spread
forth, as gardens by the river's
side, as the trees of lign aloes
which the LORD hath planted, *and*
as cedar trees beside the waters.
7. He shall pour the water out
of his buckets, and his seed
shall be in many waters, and
■ **his king** shall be higher than Agag,
■ **and his kingdom**
■ **shall be exalted.**
■ 8. **God brought him** forth
■ **out of Egypt;** he hath as it
were the strength of an unicorn:
■ **he shall eat up** the nations
■ **his enemies,** and
shall break their bones,
■ **and pierce them** through
■ **with his arrows.**
9. He couched, he lay down
as a lion, and as a great lion:
who shall stir him up?

Blessed is he that blesseth thee, and cursed is he that curseth thee. 10. And Balak's anger was kindled against Balaam, and he smote his hands together: and Balak said unto Balaam, I called thee to curse mine enemies, and, behold, thou hast altogether blessed them these three times. 11. Therefore now flee thou to thy place: I thought to promote thee unto great honour; but, lo, the LORD hath kept thee back from honour. 12. And Balaam said unto Balak, Spake I not also to thy messengers which thou sentest unto me, saying, 13. If Balak would give me his house full of silver and gold, I cannot go beyond the commandment of the LORD, to do *either* good or bad of mine own mind; *but* what the LORD saith, that will I speak? 14. And now, behold, I go unto my people: come *therefore, and* I will advertise thee what this people shall do to thy people in the latter days. 15. And he took up his parable, and said, Balaam the son of Beor hath said, and the man whose eyes are open hath said: 16. He hath said, which heard the words of God, and knew the knowledge of the most High, *which* saw the vision of the Almighty, falling *into a trance,* but having his eyes open: 17. I shall see him, but not now: I shall behold him, but not nigh: there shall come a Star out of Jacob, and a Sceptre shall rise out of Israel, and shall smite the corners of Moab, and destroy all the children of Sheth. 18. And Edom shall be a possession, Seir also shall be a possession for his enemies; and Israel shall do valiantly. 19. Out of Jacob shall come he that shall have dominion, and shall destroy him that remaineth of the city. 20. And when he looked on Amalek, he took up his parable, and said, Amalek was the first of the nations; but his latter end shall be that he perish for ever. 21. And he looked on the Kenites, and took up his parable, and said, Strong is thy dwellingplace, and thou puttest thy nest in a rock. 22. Nevertheless the Kenite shall be wasted, until Asshur shall carry thee away captive. 23. And he took up his parable, and said, Alas, who shall live when God doeth this! 24. And ships shall come from the coast of Chittim, and shall afflict Asshur, and shall afflict Eber, and he also shall perish for ever. 25. And Balaam rose up, and went and returned to his place: and Balak also went his way.

CHAPTER 25

1. And Israel abode in Shittim, and the people began to commit whoredom with the daughters of Moab. 2. And they called the people unto the sacrifices of their gods: and the people did eat, and bowed

down to their gods.
3. **And Israel**
joined himself unto
Baal-peor: and the
anger of the LORD was
kindled against Israel.
4. **And the LORD**
said unto Moses,
Take all the heads of the
people, and hang them up
before the LORD against the sun,
that the fierce
anger of the LORD may be
turned away from Israel.
5. **And Moses said**
unto the judges of Israel,
Slay ye
every one his men that were
joined unto Baal-peor.
6. **And,** behold,
one of the children
of Israel came and
brought unto his brethren
a Midianitish woman in
the sight of Moses, and in the
sight of all the congregation of the
children of Israel, who *were* weeping
before the door of the
tabernacle of the congregation.
7. **And** when
Phinehas, the son of
Eleazar, the son of Aaron
the priest, saw *it*, he rose up
from among the congregation, and
took a javelin in his hand;
8. **And** he
went after the
man of Israel into the tent,
and thrust both
of them through,
the man of Israel,
and the
woman through her belly.
So the plague was
stayed from the children of Israel.
9. **And those that**
died in the plague
were twenty and
four thousand.
10. **And the LORD**
spake unto Moses,
saying,
11. **Phinehas,** the son of

Eleazar, the son of Aaron the priest,
hath turned my wrath
away from the children of
Israel, while he was zealous
for my sake among them, that
I consumed not the children
of Israel in my jealousy.
12. **Wherefore** say, Behold,
I give unto him my
covenant of peace:
13. And he shall have it,
and his seed after him,
even the covenant of
an everlasting priesthood;
because he was zealous
for his God, and made an
atonement for the children of
Israel.
14. **Now** the name of
the Israelite that was
slain, *even* that was slain
with the Midianitish woman,
was Zimri, the son of Salu,
a prince of a chief house among
the Simeonites.
15. **And the** name of the
Midianitish
woman that was slain
was Cozbi, the daughter of
Zur; he *was* head over a people,
and of a chief house in Midian.
16. **And the LORD**
spake unto Moses,
saying,
17. **Vex the Midianites,**
and smite them:
18. **For** they vex you with
their wiles, wherewith
they have beguiled
you in the matter of
Peor, and in the matter of
Cozbi, the daughter of a
prince of Midian, their sister,
which was slain in the
day of the plague
for Peor's sake.

CHAPTER 26

1. **And** it came to pass
after the plague, that
the LORD spake
unto Moses and unto
Eleazar the son of Aaron

the priest, saying,

■ 2. **Take the sum of all**
■ **the congregation**
of the children of Israel,
■ **from twenty years old**
■ **and upward,** throughout
their fathers' house, all
■ **that are able to**
■ **go to war** in Israel.

3. And Moses and Eleazar the priest spake with them in the plains of Moab by Jordan *near* Jericho, saying,

4. *Take the sum of the people,* from twenty years old and upward; as the LORD commanded Moses and the children of Israel, which went forth out of the land of Egypt.

5. Reuben, the eldest son of Israel:
■ **the children of**
■ **Reuben;** Hanoch, *of whom cometh*
the family of the Hanochites: of Pallu, the family of the Palluites:

6. Of Hezron, the family of the Hezronites: of Carmi, the family of the Carmites.

7. These *are* the families of the Reubenites: and they that were
■ **numbered** of them were
■ **forty** and
■ **three thousand** and
■ **seven hundred and thirty.**

8. And the sons of Pallu; Eliab.

9. And the sons of Eliab; Nemuel, and Dathan, and Abiram. This *is that* Dathan and Abiram, *which were* famous in the congregation, who strove against Moses and against Aaron in the company of Korah, when they strove against the LORD:

10. And the earth opened her mouth, and swallowed them up together with Korah, when that company died, what time the fire devoured twohundredand fifty men: and they became a sign.

11. Notwithstanding the children of Korah died not.

12. The sons of Simeon after their families: of Nemuel, the family of the Nemuelites: of Jamin, the family of the Jaminites: of Jachin, the family of the Jachinites:

13. Of Zerah, the family of the Zarhites: of Shaul, the

family of the Shaulites.

■ 14. **These are the families of**
■ **the Simeonites, twenty** and
■ **two thousand** and
■ **two hundred.**

15. The children of Gad after their families: of Zephon, the family of the Zephonites: of Haggi, the family of the Haggites: of Shuni, the family of the Shunites:

16. Of Ozni, the family of the Oznites: of Eri, the family of the Erites:

17. Of Arod, the family of the Arodites: of Areli, the family of the Arelites.

18. These *are* the families of
■ **the children of Gad**
according to those that were
■ **numbered** of them,
■ **forty thousand** and
■ **five hundred.**

19. The sons of Judah *were* Er and Onan: and Er and Onan died in the land of Canaan.

20. And the sons of Judah after their families were; of Shelah, the family of the Shelanites: of Pharez, the family of the Pharzites: of Zerah, the family of the Zarhites.

21. And the sons of Pharez were; of Hezron, the family of the Hezronites: of Hamul, the family of the Hamulites.

22. These *are*
■ **the families of Judah**
according to those that were
■ **numbered** of them,
■ **threescore** and
■ **sixteen thousand** and
■ **five hundred.**

23. *Of* the sons of Issachar after their families: *of* Tola, the family of the Tolaites: of Pua, the family of the Punites:

24. Of Jashub, the family of the Jashubites: of Shimron, the family of the Shimronites.

25. These *are*
■ **the families of Issachar**
according to those that were
■ **numbered** of them,
■ **threescore** and
■ **four thousand** and

three hundred.

26. *Of* the sons of Zebulun after their families: of Sered, the family of the Sardites: of Elon, the family of the Elonites: of Jahleel, the family of the Jahleelites.

27. These *are* **the families of the Zebulunites** according to those that were **numbered** of them, **threescore thousand** and **five hundred.**

28. **The sons of Joseph** after their families **were Manasseh and Ephraim.**

29. Of the sons of Manasseh: of Machir, the family of the Machirites: and Machir begat Gilead: of Gilead *come* the family of the Gileadites.

30. These *are* the sons of Gilead: *of* Jeezer, the family of the Jeezerites: of Helek, the family of the Helekites:

31. And *of* Asriel, the family of the Asrielites: and *of* Shechem, the family of the Shechemites:

32. And *of* Shemida, the family of the Shemidaites: and *of* Hepher, the family of the Hepherites.

33. And Zelophehad the son of Hepher had no sons, but daughters: and the names of the daughters of Zelophehad *were* Mahlah, and Noah, Hoglah, Milcah, and Tirzah.

34. These *are* **the families of Manasseh,** and those that were **numbered** of them, **fifty** and **two thousand** and **seven hundred.**

35. These *are* the sons of Ephraim after their families: of Shuthelah, the family of the Shuthalhites: of Becher, the family of the Bachrites: of Tahan, the family of the Tahanites.

36. And these *are* the sons of Shuthelah: of Eran, the family of the Eranites.

37. These *are* **the families of** the sons of **Ephraim** according to

those that were **numbered** of them, **thirty** and **two thousand** and **five hundred.** These *are* the sons of Joseph after their families.

38. The sons of Benjamin after their families: of Bela, the family of the Belaites: of Ashbel, the family of the Ashbelites: of Ahiram, the family of the Ahiramites:

39. Of Shupham, the family of the Shuphamites: of Hupham, the family of the Huphamites.

40. And the sons of Bela were Ard and Naaman: *of Ard,* the family of the Ardites: *and* of Naaman, the family of the Naamites.

41. These *are* the sons of **Benjamin** after their families: and they that were **numbered** of them *were* **forty** and **five thousand** and **six hundred.**

42. These *are* the sons of Dan after their families: of Shuham, the family of the Shuhamites. These *are* **the families of Dan** after their families.

43. All the families of the Shuhamites, according to those that were **numbered** of them, *were* **threescore** and **four thousand** and **four hundred.**

44. *Of* the children of Asher after their families: of Jimna, the family of the Jimnites: of Jesui, the family of the Jesuites: of Beriah, the family of the Beriites.

45. Of the sons of Beriah: of Heber, the family of the Heberites: of Malchiel, the family of the Malchielites.

46. And the name of the daughter of Asher *was* Sarah.

47. These *are* the families of the sons of **Asher** according to those that were **numbered** of them; *who were* **fifty** and **three thousand** and

■ four hundred.

48. *Of* the sons of Naphtali after their families: of Jahzeel, the family of the Jahzeelites: of Guni, the family of the Gunites:

49. Of Jezer, the family of the Jezerites: of Shillem, the family of the Shillemites.

50. These *are* the families of

■ **Naphtali** according to their families: and they that were

■ **numbered** of them *were*

■ **forty** and

■ **five thousand** and

■ **four hundred.**

51. **These were the**

■ **numbered of the children**

■ **of Israel, six hundred**

■ **thousand and a thousand**

■ **seven hundred and thirty.**

52. **And the LORD spake**

■ **unto Moses, saying,**

53. Unto these the land shall be divided for an inheritance according to the number of names.

54. To many thou shalt give the more inheritance, and to few thou shalt give the less inheritance: to every one shall his inheritance be given according to those that were numbered of him.

55. Notwithstanding

■ **the land shall be divided**

■ **by lot: according to the**

■ **names of the tribes of**

■ **their fathers** they shall inherit.

56. According to the lot shall the possession thereof be divided between many and few.

57. **And these** *are* they that

■ **were** numbered of

■ **the Levites after their**

■ **families:** of

■ **Gershon,** the family of the Gershonites: of

■ **Kohath,** the family of the Kohathites: of

■ **Merari,** the family of the Merarites.

58. These *are* the families of the Levites: the family of the Libnites, the family of the Hebronites, the family of the Mahlites, the family of the Mushites, the family of theKorathites.

■ **And Kohath begat Amram.**

■ 59. **And** the name of

■ **Amram's wife was**

■ **Jochebed, the daughter**

■ **of Levi,** whom *her mother* bare to Levi in Egypt:

■ **and she bare unto**

■ **Amram Aaron and Moses,**

■ **and Miriam** their sister.

60. And unto Aaron was born Nadab, and Abihu, Eleazar, and Ithamar.

61. And Nadab and Abihu died, when they offered strange fire before the LORD.

■ 62. **And those** that were

■ **numbered** of them

■ **were twenty** and

■ **three thousand, all males**

■ **from a month old** and upward: for they were not numbered among the children of Israel, because there was no inheritance given them among the children of Israel.

■ 63. **These** *are* they that were numbered by

■ **Moses and**

■ **Eleazar** the priest, who

■ **numbered** the children of Israel

■ **in the plains of Moab**

■ **by Jordan** *near* Jericho.

■ 64. **But among these** there

■ **was not a man** of them whom Moses and Aaron the priest

■ **numbered, when they**

■ **numbered the children**

■ **of Israel in the wilderness**

■ **of Sinai.**

■ 65. **For the LORD had**

■ **said** of them,

■ **They shall** surely

■ **die in the wilderness.**

■ **And there was not**

■ **left a man** of them,

■ **save Caleb** the son of Jephunneh,

■ **and Joshua** the son of Nun.

CHAPTER 27

■ 1. **Then came the daughters**

■ **of Zelophehad,** the son of Hepher, the son of Gilead, the son of Machir, the son of Manasseh, of the families of Manasseh the son of

Joseph: and these *are* the names of his daughters; Mahlah, Noah, and Hoglah, and Milcah, and Tirzah.

2. **And they stood** before Moses, and before Eleazar the priest, and before the princes and all the congregation, **by the door of the tabernacle** of the congregation, **saying,**

3. **Our father died in the wilderness,** and he was **not in the company** of them that gathered themselves together against the LORD in the company **of Korah; but died in his own sin, and had no sons.**

4. Why should the name of our father be done away from among his family, because he hath no son? **Give** unto **us** *therefore* **a possession among the brethren of our father.**

5. And Moses brought their cause before the LORD.

6. **And the LORD spake unto Moses, saying,**

7. **The daughters of Zelophehad speak right:** thou shalt surely give them a possession of an inheritance among their father's brethren; and **thou shalt cause the inheritance of their father to pass unto them.**

8. **And** thou shalt **speak unto** the children of **Israel, saying, If a man die, and have no son, then** ye **shall** cause **his inheritance** to **pass unto his daughter.**

9. And if he have no **daughter,** then ye shall give his inheritance unto his brethren.

10. And if he have no brethren, then ye shall give his inheritance unto his father's brethren.

11. And if his father have no brethren, **then ye shall give his inheritance unto his kinsman** that is next to him of his family, and he shall possess it: and **it shall be** unto the children of Israel **a statute of judgment, as the LORD commanded** Moses.

12. **And the LORD said unto Moses, Get** thee **up into** this **mount Abarim, and see the land which I have given unto** the children of **Israel.**

13. **And** when **thou** hast seen it, thou also **shalt be gathered unto thy people,** **as Aaron** thy brother **was** gathered.

14. **For ye rebelled against my commandment** in the desert of Zin, in the strife of the congregation, **to sanctify me at the water** before their eyes: that *is* the water **of Meribah** in Kadesh in the wilderness of Zin.

15. **And Moses spake** unto the LORD, saying,

16. **Let the LORD, the** God of the spirits of all flesh, **set a man over the congregation,**

17. Which may go out before them, and which may go in before them, and which may lead them out, and which may bring them in; **that the congregation of the LORD be not as sheep which have no shepherd.**

18. **And the LORD said** unto Moses, **Take** thee **Joshua** the son of Nun, a man in whom *is* the spirit, **and lay thine hand upon him;**

19. **And set him before Eleazar** the priest, **and** before all **the congregation; and give**

251

■ him a charge in their sight.
■ 20. **And** thou shalt
■ **put some of thine honour**
■ **upon him, that** all the
congregation of the children of
■ **Israel may be obedient.**
■ 21. **And** he shall stand before
■ **Eleazar** the priest, who
■ **shall ask counsel for him**
■ **after the judgment of Urim**
■ **before the LORD: at his**
■ **word shall they go out,**
■ **and** at his word they shall
■ **come in, both he, and** all
the children of Israel with him, even
■ **all the congregation.**
■ 22. **And Moses did as the**
■ **LORD commanded** him:
and he took Joshua, and set him
before Eleazar the priest, and
before all the congregation:
23. And he laid his hands upon him,
and gave him a charge, as the LORD
commanded by the hand of Moses.

CHAPTER 28

■ 1. **And the LORD spake**
■ **unto Moses,** saying,
■ 2. **Command** the children of
■ **Israel, and say** unto them,
■ **My offering, and**
my bread for my
■ **sacrifices** made by fire,
for a sweet savour unto me,
■ **shall ye observe**
to offer unto me
■ **in their** due
■ **season.**
3. And thou shalt say unto them,
■ **This** *is* the offering
made by fire which
■ **ye shall offer unto**
■ **the LORD; two lambs**
of the first year without spot
■ **day by day,** *for* a
continual burnt offering.
■ 4. **The one lamb** shalt thou offer
■ **in the morning, and the**
■ **other** lamb shalt thou offer
■ **at even;**
5. **And** a tenth *part* of an ephah of
■ **flour for a meat offering,**
■ **mingled with** the fourth

part of an hin of beaten
■ **oil.**
■ 6. **It is a continual burnt**
■ **offering,** which was
■ **ordained in mount Sinai** for a
sweet savour, a sacrifice made by fire
■ **unto the LORD.**
7. And the drink offering thereof *shall
be* the fourth *part* of an hin for the one
lamb: in the holy *place* shalt thou
cause the strong wine to be poured
unto the LORD *for* a drink offering.
8. And the other lamb shalt thou offer
at even: as the meat offering of the
morning, and as the drink offering
thereof, thou shalt offer *it,* a
sacrifice made by fire, of a sweet
savour unto the LORD.
■ 9. **And on the sabbath day**
■ **two lambs** of the first year without
spot, and two tenth deals of flour
■ **for a meat offering,**
mingled with oil,
■ **and the drink**
■ **offering** thereof:
10. *This is* the burnt offering of every
sabbath, beside the continual burnt
offering, and his drink offering.
■ 11. **And in the beginnings of**
■ **your months ye shall offer**
a burnt offering unto the LORD;
■ **two young bullocks, and**
■ **one ram, seven lambs of**
■ **the first year without spot;**
■ 12. **And** three tenth deals of
■ **flour** *for* a meat offering,
■ **mingled with oil,** for one
bullock; and two tenth deals of flour
■ **for a meat offering,**
mingled with oil, for one ram;
13. And a several tenth deal of flour
mingled with oil *for* a meat offering
unto one lamb; *for* a burnt offering
of a sweet savour, a sacrifice
made by fire unto the LORD.
■ 14. **And their drink offerings**
shall be half an hin of wine unto
a bullock, and the third *part* of
an hin unto a ram, and a fourth
part of an hin unto a lamb: this
■ **is the burnt offering**
■ **of every month**
■ **throughout** the months of

■ the year.

■ 15. And one kid of the

■ goats for a sin offering

unto the LORD shall be offered,

■ beside the continual burnt

■ offering, and his drink offering.

■ 16. And in

■ the fourteenth day

■ of the first month is the

■ passover of the LORD.

■ 17. And in

■ the fifteenth day of this month

■ is the feast: seven days

■ shall unleavened

■ bread be eaten.

■ 18. In the first day

shall be an holy convocation;

■ ye shall do no manner of servile

■ work *therein:*

■ 19. But ye

■ shall offer a sacrifice

made by fire *for* a burnt offering

■ unto the LORD; two

■ young bullocks, and

■ one ram, and seven lambs

of the first year: they shall be

unto you without blemish:

■ 20. And their meat offering

■ shall be of flour mingled

■ with oil: three tenth deals

shall ye offer for a bullock,

and two tenth deals for a ram;

21. A several tenth deal shalt

thou offer for every lamb,

throughout the seven lambs:

■ 22. And one goat for a

■ sin offering, to make

■ an atonement for you.

■ 23. Ye shall offer these

■ beside the burnt offering

in the morning, which *is* for a

continual burnt offering.

24. After this manner ye

shall offer daily,

■ throughout the seven days,

the meat of the sacrifice made by fire,

of a sweet savour unto the LORD: it

shall be offered beside the continual

burnt offering, and his drink offering.

■ 25. And on the seventh

■ day ye shall have an

holy convocation; ye shall

■ do no servile work.

■ 26. Also in the day of the

■ firstfruits, when ye bring a new

meat offering unto the LORD,

■ after your weeks be out,

■ ye shall have an holy

■ convocation;

ye shall do no servile work:

27. But ye shall offer the burnt

offering for a sweet savour unto

the LORD; two young bullocks, one

ram, seven lambs of the first year;

28. And their meat offering of

flour mingled with oil, three tenth

deals unto one bullock, two

tenth deals unto one ram,

29. A several tenth deal unto one

lamb, throughout the seven lambs;

30. *And* one kid of the goats, to

make an atonement for you.

31. Ye shall offer *them* beside

the continual burnt offering, and

his meat offering, (they shall

be unto you without blemish)

and their drink offerings.

CHAPTER 29

■ 1. And in the seventh

■ month, on the first

■ day of the month, ye

shall have an holy convocation;

■ ye shall do no servile

■ work: it is a day of blowing

■ the trumpets unto you.

■ 2. And ye shall offer

a burnt offering for a sweet

savour unto the LORD;

■ one young bullock, one

■ ram, and seven lambs

of the first year without blemish:

3. And their meat offering *shall*

be of flour mingled with oil, three

tenth deals for a bullock, *and*

two tenth deals for a ram,

4. And one tenth deal for one lamb,

throughout the seven lambs:

■ 5. And one kid of the goats

■ for a sin offering, to make

■ an atonement for you:

6. Beside the burnt offering of the

month, and his meat offering, and

the daily burnt offering, and his meat

offering, and their drink offerings,

according unto their manner, for a

sweet savour, a sacrifice made by fire unto the LORD.

7. **And** ye shall have **on the tenth day of this seventh month** an holy convocation; and **ye shall afflict your souls: ye shall not** do any **work** *therein:*

8. **But ye shall offer a burnt offering unto the LORD** *for* a sweet savour; one young bullock, one ram, *and* seven lambs of the first year; they shall be unto you without blemish:

9. And their meat offering *shall be of* flour mingled with oil, three tenth deals to a bullock, *and* two tenth deals to one ram,

10. A several tenth deal for one lamb, throughout the seven lambs:

11. One kid of the goats *for* a sin offering; beside the sin offering of atonement, and the continual burnt offering, and the meat offering of it, and their drink offerings.

12. **And on the fifteenth day of the seventh month** ye shall have an holy convocation; ye shall do no servile work, and **ye shall keep a feast unto the LORD seven days:**

13. **And ye shall offer** a burnt offering, a sacrifice made by fire, of a sweet savour unto the LORD; **thirteen young bullocks, two rams, and fourteen lambs** of the first year; they shall be without blemish:

14. **And their meat offering shall be of flour mingled with oil,** three tenth deals unto every bullock of the thirteen bullocks, two tenth deals to each ram of the two rams,

15. And a several tenth deal to each lamb of the fourteen lambs:

16. **And one kid of the goats for a sin offering;** beside the continual burnt offering, his meat offering, and his drink offering.

17. **And on the second day** ye shall offer **twelve young bullocks, two rams, fourteen lambs** of the first year without spot:

18. **And their meat** offering **and their drink offerings** for the bullocks, for the rams, and for the lambs, **shall be according to their number,** after the manner:

19. **And one kid** of the goats **for a sin offering;** beside the continual burnt offering, and the meat offering thereof, and their drink offerings.

20. **And on the third day eleven bullocks, two rams, fourteen lambs** of the first year without blemish;

21. **And their meat** offering **and their drink offerings** for the bullocks, for the rams, and for the lambs, *shall be* according to their number, after the manner:

22. **And one goat for a sin offering;** beside the continual burnt offering, and his meat offering, and his drink offering.

23. **And on the fourth day ten bullocks, two rams, and fourteen lambs** of the first year without blemish:

24. **Their meat** offering **and their drink offerings** for the bullocks, for the rams, and for the lambs, *shall be* according to their number, after the manner:

25. **And one kid** of the goats **for a sin offering;** beside the continual burnt offering, his meat offering, and his drink offering.

26. **And on the fifth day nine bullocks, two rams, and fourteen lambs** of the first year without spot:

27. **And their meat** offering **and their drink offerings** for the bullocks, for the rams, and for the lambs, *shall be* according to their number, after the manner:

28. **And one goat for a sin offering;** beside the continual burnt offering, and his meat offering, and his drink offering.

29. **And on the sixth day eight bullocks, two rams, and fourteen lambs** of the first year without blemish:

30. **And their meat** offering **and** their **drink offerings** for the bullocks, for the rams, and for the lambs, *shall be* according to their number, after the manner:

31. **And one goat for a sin offering;** beside the continual burnt offering, his meat offering, and his drink offering.

32. **And on the seventh day seven bullocks, two rams, and fourteen lambs** of the first year without blemish:

33. **And their meat** offering **and** their **drink offerings** for the bullocks, for the rams, and for the lambs, *shall be* according to their number, after the manner:

34. **And one goat for a sin offering;** beside the continual burnt offering, his meat offering, and his drink offering.

35. **On the eighth day ye shall have a solemn assembly: ye shall do no** servile **work** *therein:*

36. **But ye shall offer a burnt offering,** a sacrifice made by fire, **of a sweet savour unto the LORD: one bullock, one ram, seven lambs** of the first year without blemish:

37. **Their meat** offering **and** their **drink offerings** for the bullock, for the ram, and for the lambs, *shall be* according to their number, after the manner:

38. **And one goat for a sin offering;** beside the continual burnt offering, and his meat offering, and his drink offering.

39. **These things** ye shall **do unto the LORD** in your set feasts, **beside your vows, and your freewill offerings,** for your burnt offerings, and for your meat offerings, and for your drink offerings, and for your peace offerings.

40. **And Moses told** the children of **Israel** according to **all that the LORD commanded** Moses.

CHAPTER 30

1. **And Moses spake unto the heads of the tribes** concerning the children of Israel, **saying, This** *is* the thing which **the LORD hath commanded.**

2. **If a man vow** a vow unto the LORD, **or swear an oath** to bind his soul with a bond; **he shall not break his word,** he shall do according to all that proceedeth out of his mouth.

3. **If a woman also vow** a vow **unto the LORD,** and bind *herself* by a bond, **being in her father's house** in her youth;

4. **And her father hear her** vow, and her bond wherewith she hath bound her soul, **and** her father **shall hold his peace** at her; **then all her vows shall stand,** and every bond wherewith she hath bound her soul shall stand.

5. **But if her father disallow her** in the day that he heareth; **not any of her vows,** or of her bonds wherewith she hath bound her soul, **shall stand: and the LORD shall forgive her,** because her father disallowed her.

6. **And if she had** at all **an husband, when she**

vowed, or uttered aught out of her lips, wherewith she bound her soul;

7. **And her husband heard it, and held his peace** at her in the day that he heard *it:* **then her vows shall stand,** and her bonds wherewith she bound her soul shall stand.

8. **But if her husband disallowed her** on the day that he heard *it;* **then he shall make her vow** which she vowed, and that which she uttered with her lips, wherewith she bound her soul, **of none effect: and the LORD shall forgive her.**

9. **But every vow of a widow, and of her that is divorced,** wherewith they have bound their souls, **shall stand** against her.

10. And if she vowed in her husband's house, or bound her soul by a bond with an oath;

11. And her husband heard *it,* and held his peace at her, *and* disallowed her not: then all her vows shall stand, and every bond wherewith she bound her soul shall stand.

12. But if her husband hath utterly made them void on the day he heard *them; then* whatsoever proceeded out of her lips concerning her vows, or concerning the bond of her soul, shall not stand: her husband hath made them void; and the LORD shall forgive her.

13. **Every vow,** and every binding oath **to afflict the soul, her husband may establish it, or** her husband may **make it void.**

14. **But if her husband** altogether **hold his peace** at her from day to day; then he establisheth all her vows, or all her bonds, which *are* upon her: **he confirmeth them,** because he held his peace at

her in the day that he heard *them.*

15. **But if he shall** any ways **make them void after that he hath heard them; then he shall bear her iniquity.**

16. **These are the statutes,** which the LORD commanded Moses, **between a man and his wife, between the father and his daughter, being yet** in her youth **in her father's house.**

CHAPTER 31

1. **And the LORD spake unto Moses, saying,**

2. **Avenge** the children of **Israel of the Midianites: afterward shalt thou be gathered unto thy people.**

3. **And Moses spake unto the people, saying, Arm** some of **yourselves** unto the war, **and** let them **go against the Midianites, and avenge the LORD** of Midian.

4. **Of every tribe a thousand,** throughout all the tribes of Israel, **shall ye send to the war.**

5. **So there were** delivered out of the thousands of Israel, a thousand of *every* tribe, **twelve thousand armed for war.**

6. **And Moses sent them to the war,** a thousand of *every* tribe, them **and Phinehas** the son of Eleazar **the priest,** to the war, **with the holy instruments, and the trumpets to blow in his hand.**

7. **And they warred against the Midianites,** as the LORD commanded Moses; **and they slew all the males.**

8. **And** they slew **the kings of Midian,** beside the

rest of them that were slain; *namely,* Evi, and Rekem, and Zur, and Hur, and Reba, five kings of Midian: Balaam also the son of Beor they slew with the sword.

9. **And** the children of **Israel took all the women** of Midian **captives, and their little ones, and** took the spoil of all their **cattle, and all their flocks, and** all their **goods.**

10. **And they burnt** all their **cities** wherein they dwelt, **and** all their goodly **castles,** with fire.

11. And they took all the spoil, and all the prey, *both* of men and of beasts.

12. **And they brought the captives, and the prey, and the spoil, unto Moses, and Eleazar** the priest, and unto the congregation of the children of Israel, unto the camp at the plains of Moab, which *are* by Jordan *near* Jericho.

13. And Moses, and Eleazar the priest, and all the princes of the congregation, went forth to meet them without the camp.

14. **And Moses was wroth with the officers** of the host, *with* the captains over thousands, and captains over hundreds, which came from the battle.

15. **And** Moses **said** unto them, **Have ye saved all the women alive?**

16. **Behold, these caused** the children of **Israel,** through the counsel of Balaam, **to commit trespass against the LORD in the matter of Peor, and there was a plague** among the congregation of the LORD.

17. Now therefore **kill every male among the little ones, and** kill

every woman that hath known man by lying with him.

18. **But all the women children,** that have not known a man by lying with him, **keep alive for yourselves.**

19. **And** do ye **abide without the camp seven days:** whosoever hath killed any person, and whosoever hath touched any slain, **purify both yourselves and your captives on the third** day, **and** on the **seventh day.**

20. **And purify all your raiment,** and all that is made **of skins, and** all work of goats' *hair,* and all **things made of wood.**

21. **And Eleazar** the priest **said** unto the men of war which went to the battle, This *is* the ordinance of the law which the LORD commanded Moses;

22. **Only the gold,** and the **silver, the brass, the iron, the tin, and** the **lead,**

23. Every thing that may abide the fire, ye **shall** make *it* **go through the fire, and it shall be clean: nevertheless it shall be purified with the water of separation:** and all that abideth not the fire ye shall make go through the water.

24. **And** ye shall **wash your clothes on the seventh day, and** ye shall **be clean, and afterward** ye shall **come into the camp.**

25. **And the LORD spake unto Moses, saying,**

26. **Take the sum of the**

■ **prey** that was taken, *both* of
man and of beast, thou, and
Eleazar the priest, and the chief
fathers of the congregation:
■ 27. **And divide** the prey
■ **into two parts; between**
■ **them** that took the war upon them,
■ **who went out to**
■ **battle, and** between all
■ **the congregation:**
■ 28. **And levy a tribute unto**
■ **the Lord of the men** of war
■ **which went out to**
■ **battle: one** soul
■ **of five hundred,** *both* of the
persons, and of the beeves, and
of the asses, and of the sheep:
■ 29. **Take it** of their half,
■ **and give it unto**
■ **Eleazar** the priest,
■ **for an heave offering**
■ **of the LORD.**
■ 30. **And** of the children
■ **of Israel's half,** thou shalt
■ **take one portion of fifty,**
of the persons, of the beeves,
of the asses, and of the flocks,
of all manner of beasts,
■ **and give** them
■ **unto the Levites,** which keep the
charge of the tabernacle of theLORD.
■ 31. **And Moses and**
■ **Eleazar** the priest
■ **did as the LORD**
■ **commanded** Moses.
■ 32. **And the booty,**
being the rest of the prey
which the men of war had caught,
■ **was six hundred** thousand and
■ **seventy** thousand and
■ **five thousand sheep,**
■ 33. **And threescore and**
■ **twelve thousand beeves,**
■ 34. **And threescore and**
■ **one thousand asses,**
■ 35. **And thirty** and
■ **two thousand** persons in all, of
■ **women that had not known**
■ **man by lying with him.**
36. And the half, *which was* the
portion of them that went out to war,
was in number three hundred
thousand and seven and thirty

thousand and five hundred sheep:
■ 37. **And the LORD'S**
■ **tribute of the sheep**
■ **was six hundred** and
■ **threescore and fifteen.**
■ 38. **And the beeves** *were*
thirty and six thousand; of
which the LORD'S tribute *was*
■ **threescore and twelve.**
■ 39. **And the asses** *were* thirty
thousand and five hundred; of
which the LORD'S tribute *was*
■ **threescore and one.**
■ 40. **And** the persons *were*
sixteen thousand; of which
the LORD'S tribute *was*
■ **thirty** and
■ **two persons.**
■ 41. **And Moses gave the**
tribute, *which was* the LORD'S
■ **heave offering, unto**
■ **Eleazar** the priest,
■ **as the LORD**
■ **commanded** Moses.
42. And of the children of
Israel's half, which Moses
divided from the men that warred,
■ 43. **(Now the half that**
■ **pertained unto the**
■ **congregation** was three
hundred thousand and
thirty thousand *and* seven
thousand and five hundred sheep,
44. And thirty and six
thousand beeves,
45. And thirty thousand
asses and five hundred,
46. And sixteen thousand persons;)
47. Even of the children
of Israel's half,
■ **Moses took one portion**
■ **of fifty,** *both* of man and of beast,
■ **and gave** them
■ **unto the Levites,**
■ **which kept** the charge of
■ **the tabernacle** of the LORD;
as the LORD commanded Moses.
■ 48. **And the officers** which
were over thousands of the host,
the captains of thousands,
and captains of hundreds,
■ **came** near
■ **unto Moses:**

49. **And** they **said** unto Moses, **Thy servants have taken the sum of the men of war** which *are* **under our charge, and there lacketh not one man of us.** 50. **We have** therefore **brought an oblation for the LORD,** what every man hath gotten, of jewels of gold, chains, and bracelets, rings, earrings, and tablets, **to make an atonement for our souls** before the LORD. 51. **And** Moses and Eleazar the priest took **the gold** of them, *even* all wrought jewels. 52. And all the gold of the offering that **they offered up to the LORD,** of the captains of thousands, and of the captains of hundreds, **was sixteen thousand seven hundred and fifty shekels.** 53. (*For* the men of war had taken spoil, every man for himself.) 54. **And Moses** and Eleazar the priest took the gold of the captains of thousands and of hundreds, and **brought it into the tabernacle** of the congregation, **for a memorial for** the children of Israel **before the LORD.**

CHAPTER 32

1. **Now the children of Reuben and** the children of **Gad had a** very great **multitude of cattle: and** when **they saw the land of Jazer, and** the land of **Gilead,** that, behold, the place **was a place for cattle;** 2. **The children of Gad and** the children of **Reuben** came and **spake unto Moses, and** to **Eleazar** the priest, and unto the princes of the congregation, **saying,** 3. Ataroth, and Dibon, and Jazer, and Nimrah, and Heshbon, and Elealeh, and Shebam, and Nebo, and Beon, 4. *Even* the country which the LORD smote before the congregation of Israel, *is* a land for cattle, and thy servants have cattle: 5. Wherefore, said they, **if we have found grace in thy sight, let this land be given unto thy servants** for a possession, **and bring us not over Jordan.** 6. **And Moses said** unto the children of Gad and to the children of Reuben, **Shall your brethren go to war, and shall ye sit here?** 7. **And** wherefore **discourage** ye **the heart** of the children **of Israel from going** over **into the land** which the LORD hath given them? 8. **Thus did your fathers, when I sent them** from Kadesh-barnea **to see the land.** 9. **For** when they went up unto the valley of Eshcol, and saw the land, **they discouraged** the heart of the children of **Israel, that they should not go into the land** which the LORD had given them. 10. **And the LORD'S anger was kindled** the same time, **and he sware, saying,** 11. **Surely none of the men that came up out of Egypt,** from twenty years old and upward, **shall see the land** which I sware unto Abraham, unto Isaac, and unto Jacob; because they have not wholly followed me: 12. **Save Caleb** the son of Jephunneh the Kenezite, **and Joshua** the son of Nun: for they have wholly followed the LORD.

13. **And the LORD'S anger was kindled against Israel, and he made them wander** in the wilderness **forty years, until all the generation,** that had done evil in the sight of the LORD, **was consumed.**

14. And, behold, ye are risen up in your fathers' stead, an increase of sinful men, to augment yet the fierce anger of the LORD toward Israel.

15. **For if ye turn away** from after him, **he will** yet again **leave them in the wilderness;** and ye shall destroy all this people.

16. **And they** came near unto him, and **said, We will build sheepfolds here for our cattle, and cities for our little ones:**

17. **But we** ourselves **will go** ready armed **before** the children of **Israel, until we have brought them unto their place: and** our little ones shall dwell in the fenced cities because of the inhabitants of the land.

18. **We will not return** unto our houses, **until the children of Israel have inherited every man his inheritance.**

19. For we will not inherit with them on yonder side Jordan, or forward; because our inheritance is fallen to us on this side Jordan eastward.

20. **And Moses said** untothem, **If ye will do this thing,** if ye will go armed before the LORD to war,

21. And will go all of you armed over Jordan before the LORD, until he hath driven out his enemies from before him,

22. And the land be subdued before the LORD: then afterward ye shall return, and be guiltless before the LORD, and before Israel; and **this land shall be your possession before the LORD.**

23. **But if ye will not do so,** behold, ye have sinned against the LORD: and **be sure your sin will find you out.**

24. **Build you cities** for your little ones, **and folds** for your sheep; **and** do **that which** hath **proceeded out of your mouth.**

25. And the children of Gad and the children of Reuben spake unto Moses, saying, Thy servants will do as my lord commandeth.

26. Our little ones, our wives, our flocks, and all our cattle, shall be there in the cities of Gilead:

27. But thy servants will pass over, every man armed for war, before the LORD to battle, as my lord saith.

28. **So concerning them Moses commanded Eleazar** the priest, and **Joshua** the son of Nun, **and the chief fathers** of the tribes of the children **of Israel:**

29. And Moses said unto them, **If the children of Gad and** the children of **Reuben will pass** with you **over Jordan,** every man **armed to battle,** before the LORD, **and the land shall be subdued** before you; then **ye shall give them the land of Gilead** for a possession:

30. **But if they will not** pass over with you armed, **they shall have possessions among you in** the land of **Canaan.**

31. **And the children of Gad and** the children of **Reuben answered, saying,** As the LORD hath said unto thy servants, so will we do.

32. **We will pass over** armed before the LORD **into** the land of **Canaan, that** the possession of our inheritance on **this side Jordan may be ours.** 33. **And Moses gave** unto **them,** *even* to the children of Gad, and to the children of Reuben, and unto half the tribe of Manasseh the son of Joseph, **the kingdom** of Sihon king **of the Amorites, and** the kingdom of Og king of **Bashan,** the land, with the cities thereof in the coasts, *even* the cities of the country round about.

34. **And the children of Gad** built Dibon, and Ataroth, and Aroer, 35. And Atroth, Shophan, and Jaazer, and Jogbehah, 36. And Beth-nimrah, and Beth-haran, fenced cities: and folds for sheep. 37. **And** the children of **Reuben** built Heshbon, and Elealeh, and Kirjathaim, 38. And Nebo, and Baal-meon, (their names being changed,) and Shibmah: and gave other names unto the cities which they builded. 39. **And** the children of **Machir the son of Manasseh** went to Gilead, and **took it, and dispossessed the Amorite which was in it.** 40. And Moses gave Gilead unto Machir the son of Manasseh; and he dwelt therein. 41. And Jair the son of Manasseh went and took the small towns thereof, and called them Havoth-jair. 42. And Nobah went and tookKenath, and the villages thereof, and called it Nobah, after his own name.

CHAPTER 33

1. **These are the journeys** of the children **of Israel, which went forth out** of the land **of Egypt** with their armies under

the hand of Moses and Aaron. 2. **And Moses wrote their goings out** according to their journeys **by the commandment of the LORD: and these are their journeys** according to their goings out. 3. **And they departed from Rameses in the first month, on the fifteenth day of** the first month; on the morrow **after the passover** the children of Israel went out with an high hand in the sight of all the Egyptians. 4. For the Egyptians buried all *their* firstborn, which the LORD hadsmitten among them: upon their gods also the LORD executed judgments. 5. And the children of Israel removed from Rameses, and pitched in Succoth. 6. And they departed from Succoth, and pitched in Etham, which *is* in the edge of the wilderness. 7. And they removed from Etham, and turned again unto Pihahiroth, which *is* before Baalz-ephon: and they pitched before Migdol. 8. And they departed from before Pihahiroth, **and passed through the midst of the sea** into the wilderness, and went three days' journey in the wilderness of Etham, and pitched in Marah. 9. And they removed from Marah, and came unto Elim: and in Elim *were* twelve fountains of water, and threescore and ten palm trees; and they pitched there. 10. And they removed from Elim, and encamped by the Red sea. 11. And they removed from the Red sea, and encamped in the wilderness of Sin. 12. And they took their journey out of the wilderness of Sin, and encamped in Dophkah. 13. And they departed from Dophkah, and encamped in Alush. 14. And they removed from Alush, and encamped at Rephidim, where

was no water for the people to drink.
15. And they departed from Rephidim,
■ **and pitched in the**
■ **wilderness of Sinai.**
■ 16. **And they removed**
■ **from the desert of Sinai,**
and pitched at Kibroth-hattaavah.
17. And they departed from
Kibroth-hattaavah, and
encamped at Hazeroth.
18. And they departed from
Hazeroth, and pitched in Rithmah.
19. And they departed from Rithmah,
and pitched at Rimmon-parez.
20. And they departed from
Rimmon-parez, and pitched in Libnah.
21. And they removed from Libnah,
and pitched at Rissah.
22. And they journeyed from Rissah,
and pitched in Kehelathah.
23. And they went from Kehelathah,
and pitched in mount Shapher.
24. And they removed from mount
Shapher, and encamped in Haradah.
25. And they removed from Haradah,
and pitched in Makheloth.
26. And they removed from
Makheloth, and encamped at Tahath.
27. And they departed from
Tahath, and pitched at Tarah.
28. And they removed from
Tarah, and pitched in Mithcah.
29. And they went from Mithcah,
and pitched in Hashmonah.
30. And they departed from
Hashmonah, and encamped
at Moseroth.
31. And they departed from
Moseroth, and pitched in
Bene-jaakan.
32. And they removed from
Bene-jaakan, and encamped
at Hor-hagidgad.
33. And they went from Hor-hagidgad,
and pitched in Jotbathah.
34. And they removed from
Jotbathah, and encamped
at Ebronah.
35. And they departed from Ebronah,
and encamped at Ezion-gaber.
36. And they removed from
Ezion-gaber, and pitched in the
wilderness of Zin, which *is* Kadesh.

37. And they removed from Kadesh,
■ **and pitched in mount Hor,**
in the edge of the land of Edom.
■ 38. **And Aaron** the priest
■ **went up into mount Hor**
at the commandment of the LORD,
■ **and died there, in the**
■ **fortieth year after the**
■ **children of Israel were**
■ **come out of** the land of
■ **Egypt, in the first day**
■ **of the fifth month.**
■ 39. **And Aaron was an**
■ **hundred and twenty** and
■ **three years old when**
■ **he died** in mount Hor.
40. And king Arad the Canaanite,
which dwelt in the south in the land
of Canaan, heard of the coming
of the children of Israel.
■ 41. **And they departed**
■ **from mount Hor,** and
pitched in Zalmonah.
42. And they departed from
Zalmonah, and pitched in Punon.
43. And they departed from
Punon, and pitched in Oboth.
44. And they departed from
Oboth, and pitched in Ije-abarim,
in the border of Moab.
45. And they departed from Iim,
and pitched in Dibon-gad.
46. And they removed from
Dibon-gad, and encamped in
Almon-diblathaim.
47. And they removed from
Almon-diblathaim, and pitched in the
mountains of Abarim, before Nebo.
48. And they departed from
the mountains of Abarim,
■ **and pitched in the**
■ **plains of Moab** by Jordan
■ **near Jericho.**
49. And they pitched by Jordan, from
Beth-jesimoth *even* unto Abel-shittim
in the plains of Moab.
■ 50. **And the LORD**
■ **spake unto Moses**
in the plains of Moab by
Jordan *near* Jericho,
■ **saying,**
51. Speak unto the children
of Israel, and say unto them,

■ **When ye are passed over**
■ **Jordan** into the land of Canaan;
■ 52. **Then ye shall drive**
■ **out all the inhabitants**
of the land from before you,
■ **and destroy all their**
■ **pictures, and** destroy all
■ **their molten**
■ **images, and** quite
■ **pluck down** all
■ **their high places:**
■ 53. **And** ye shall
■ **dispossess the inhabitants**
of the land, and dwell therein: for I
have given you the land to possess it.
■ 54. **And ye shall**
■ **divide the land** by lot
■ **for an inheritance** among your
families: *and* to the more ye shall give
the more inheritance, and to the fewer
ye shall give the less inheritance:
every man's *inheritance* shall be
in the place where his lot falleth;
■ **according to the tribes**
■ **of your fathers** ye shall inherit.
■ 55. **But if ye will not drive**
■ **out the inhabitants** of
the land from before you;
■ **then** it shall come to pass, that
■ **those which** ye let
■ **remain** of them
■ **shall be pricks in your eyes,**
■ **and thorns in your sides,**
■ **and shall vex you**
in the land wherein ye dwell.
■ 56. **Moreover** it shall
come to pass, *that*
■ **I shall do unto you, as I**
■ **thought to do unto them.**

CHAPTER 34

■ 1. **And the LORD spake**
■ **unto Moses, saying,**
2. Command the children of
Israel, and say unto them, When
ye come into the land of Canaan;
■ **(this is the land that shall**
■ **fall unto you for an**
■ **inheritance, even** the land of
■ **Canaan with the**
■ **coasts thereof:)**
3. Then your south quarter
shall be from the wilderness of

Zin along by the coast of Edom,
■ **and your south border shall**
■ **be the outmost coast of the**
■ **salt sea eastward:**
4. And your border shall turn from the
south to the ascent of Akrabbim, and
pass on to Zin: and the going forth
thereof shall be from the south to
Kadesh-barnea, and shall go on to
Hazar-addar, and pass on to Azmon:
5. And the border shall
fetch a compass from Azmon
■ **unto the river of Egypt,** and
the goings out of it shall be at the sea.
■ 6. **And** *as for* the western
border, ye shall even have
■ **the great sea** for a border: this
■ **shall be your west border.**
■ 7. **And** this shall be your north
border: from the great sea ye shall
point out for you mount Hor:
■ 8. **From mount Hor** ye
shall point out *your border*
■ **unto the entrance**
■ **of Hamath;** and the goings forth
of the border shall be to Zedad:
9. And the border shall go on to
Ziphron, and the goings out of
it shall be at Hazar-enan: this
■ **shall be your north border.**
■ 10. **And** ye shall point
out your east border
■ **from Hazar-enan** to Shepham:
11. And the coast shall go down
from Shepham to Riblah,
on the east side of Ain; and
■ **the border shall**
■ **descend,** and shall reach
■ **unto** the side of
■ **the sea of Chinnereth**
■ **eastward:**
12. And the border shall go down
■ **to Jordan,** and the goings
out of it shall be at the salt sea:
■ **this shall be your land** with
the coasts thereof round about.
13. **And Moses**
■ **commanded**
the children of Israel,
■ **saying, This is the land**
■ **which ye shall** inherit by lot,
which the LORD commanded to
■ **give unto the nine tribes,**

■ **and to the half tribe:**
■ 14. **For** the tribe of the children of
■ **Reuben** according to
the house of their fathers,
■ **and** the tribe of the children of
■ **Gad** according to the
house of their fathers, have
received *their inheritance;*
■ **and half the tribe of**
■ **Manasseh have received**
■ **their inheritance:**
15. The two tribes and the half tribe
have received their inheritance
■ **on this side Jordan**
near Jericho eastward,
toward the sunrising.
16. And the LORD spake
unto Moses, saying,
■ 17. **These are** the names of
■ **the men which shall**
■ **divide the land** unto you:
■ **Eleazar** the priest,
■ **and Joshua** the son of Nun.
■ 18. **And** ye shall take
■ **one prince of every tribe,**
to divide the land by inheritance.
19. And the names of the men
are these: Of the tribe of Judah,
Calebthe son of Jephunneh.
20. And of the tribe of the
children of Simeon, Shemuel
the son of Ammihud.
21. Of the tribe of Benjamin,
Elidad the son of Chislon.
22. And the prince of the tribe
of the children of Dan, Bukki
the son of Jogli.
23. The prince of the children
of Joseph, for the tribe of the
children of Manasseh, Hanniel
the son of Ephod.
24. And the prince of the tribe
of the children of Ephraim,
Kemuel the son of Shiphtan.
25. And the prince of the tribe
of the children of Zebulun,
Elizaphan the son of Parnach.
26. And the prince of the tribe
of the children of Issachar,
Paltiel the son of Azzan.
27. And the prince of the tribe of
the children of Asher, Ahihud the
son of Shelomi.

28. And the prince of the tribe of
the children of Naphtali, Pedahel
the son of Ammihud.
29. These *are they* whom the
LORD commanded to divide the
inheritance unto the children of
Israel in the land of Canaan.

CHAPTER 35

■ 1. **And the LORD spake**
■ **unto Moses** in the plains of
Moab by Jordan *near* Jericho,
■ **saying,**
■ 2. **Command** the children of
■ **Israel, that they give unto**
■ **the Levites** of the inheritance
of their possession
■ **cities to dwell in; and** ye shall
give *also* unto the Levites suburbs
for the cities round about them.
3. And the cities shall they
have to dwell in; and the
■ **suburbs** of them shall be
■ **for their cattle,** and for their
goods, and for all their beasts.
■ 4. **And the suburbs**
of the cities, which ye
shall give unto the Levites,
■ **shall reach from the wall**
■ **of the city and outward a**
■ **thousand cubits** round about.
5. And ye shall measure from without
the city on the east side two thousand
cubits, and on the south side two
thousand cubits, and on the west side
two thousand cubits, and on the north
side two thousand cubits; and the city
shall be in the midst: this *shall be* to
them the suburbs of the cities.
■ 6. **And among the cities**
■ **which ye shall give unto**
■ **the Levites there shall**
■ **be six cities for refuge,**
which ye shall appoint
■ **for the manslayer, that**
■ **he may flee thither:**
■ **and to them** ye shall
■ **add forty** and
■ **two cities.**
■ 7. **So** all the cities which
■ **ye shall give to**
■ **the Levites** *shall be*
■ **forty** and

eight cities: them *shall ye give* with their suburbs.

8. **And the cities** which ye **shall** give *shall* **be of the possession of** the children of **Israel:** from *them that have* many ye shall give many; but from *them that have* few ye shall give few: **every one shall give of his cities unto the Levites** according to his inheritance which he inheriteth.

9. **And the LORD spake unto Moses, saying,** 10. Speak unto the children of Israel, and say unto them, **When ye** be **come over Jordan into** the land of **Canaan;** 11. **Then ye shall appoint** you cities to be **cities of refuge** for you; **that the slayer may flee thither,** which killeth any person at unawares. 12. **And they shall be** unto you **cities for refuge from the avenger;** that the manslayer die not, **until he stand** before the congregation **in judgment.**

13. **And of these cities** which ye shall give six cities shall ye have for refuge. 14. Ye shall give **three cities on this side Jordan, and three** cities shall ye give **in** the land of **Canaan,** *which* shall be cities of refuge. 15. These six cities **shall be a refuge, both for** the children of **Israel, and for the stranger,** and for the sojourner among them: **that every one that killeth any person unawares may flee thither.**

16. **And if he smite him with an instrument of iron,** so that he die, he *is* a murderer: the murderer shall surely be put to death. 17. And if he smite him **with throwing a stone,** wherewith he may die, and he die, he *is* a murderer: the murderer shall surely be put to death. 18. **Or** *if* he smite him **with an hand weapon of wood,** wherewith he may die, and he die, he *is* a murderer: the murderer shall surely be put to death. 19. The revenger of blood himself shall slay the murderer: when he meeteth him, he shall slay him. 20. But if he thrust him of hatred, or hurl at him by laying of wait, that he die; 21. **Or in enmity smite him with his hand, that he die: he** that smote *him* **shall** surely **be put to death; for he is a murderer:** the revenger of blood shall slay the murderer, when he meeteth him.

22. **But if he thrust him suddenly without enmity,** or have cast upon him any thing without laying of wait, 23. Or with any stone, wherewith a man may die, seeing *him* not, and cast *it* upon him, **that he die, and was not his enemy, neither sought his harm:** 24. **Then the congregation shall judge** between the slayer and the revenger of blood according to these judgments: 25. **And the congregation shall** deliver the slayer out of the hand of the revenger of blood, and the congregation shall **restore him to the city of his refuge,** whither he was fled: **and he shall abide in it unto the death of the high priest,** which was anointed with the holy oil. 26. **But if the slayer**

shall at any time
come without the border of
the city of his refuge,
whither he was fled;
27. And the revenger of
blood find him without the
borders of the city of his refuge,
and the revenger of blood
kill the slayer; he shall
not be guilty of blood:
28. Because he should
have remained in the
city of his refuge until the
death of the high priest:
but after the death of the
high priest the slayer
shall return into the land
of his possession.
29. So these things shall be
for a statute of judgment
unto you throughout your
generations in all your dwellings.
30. Whoso killeth any person,
the murderer shall be
put to death by the mouth
of witnesses: but one
witness shall not
testify against any person *to*
cause him to die.
31. Moreover ye shall
take no satisfaction for
the life of a murderer,
which *is* guilty of death: but
he shall be surely
put to death.
32. And ye shall
take no satisfaction for
him that is fled to the
city of his refuge, that he
should come again to
dwell in the land, until
the death of the priest.
33. So ye shall not pollute
the land wherein ye *are;* for
blood it defileth the land: and
the land cannot be cleansed of
the blood that is shed therein,
but by the blood of him that shed it.
34. Defile not therefore
the land which ye
shall inhabit, wherein I dwell:
for I the LORD dwell among
the children of Israel.

CHAPTER 36

1. And the chief fathers
of the families of the children of
Gilead, the son of Machir, the son
of Manasseh, of the families of
the sons of Joseph, came near, and
spake before Moses, and
before the princes, the chief
fathers of the children of Israel:
2. And they said, The LORD
commanded my lord to give the
land for an inheritance by lot to the
children of Israel: and my lord was
commanded by the LORD
to give the inheritance
of Zelophehad our brother
unto his daughters.
3. And if they be married to
any of the sons of the other
tribes of the children of Israel,
then shall their inheritance
be taken from the inheritance of our
fathers, and shall be put to the
inheritance of the tribe whereunto
they are received: so shall it
be taken from the lot
of our inheritance.
4. And when the jubile of the children
of Israel shall be, then shall their
inheritance be put unto the
inheritance of the tribe whereunto
they are received: so shall their
inheritance be taken away from the
inheritance of the tribe of our fathers.
5. And Moses commanded
the children of Israel according
to the word of the LORD,
saying, The tribe of the
sons of Joseph hath
said well.
6. This *is* the thing which
the LORD doth command
concerning the daughters
of Zelophehad, saying,
Let them marry
to whom they think best;
only to the family of the tribe
of their father shall they marry.
7. So shall not the
inheritance of the
children of Israel
remove from tribe to tribe:
for every one of the children of Israel

shall keep himself to the inheritance of the tribe of his fathers.

8. **And every daughter, that possesseth an inheritance** in any tribe of the children of Israel, **shall be wife unto one of the family of the tribe of her father,** that the children of Israel may enjoy every man the inheritance of his fathers.

9. Neither shall the inheritance remove from *one* tribe to another tribe; but **every one of the tribes** of the children of Israel **shall keep** himself to **his own inheritance.**

10. Even as the LORD commanded Moses, **so** did **the daughters of Zelophehad:**

11. For Mahlah, Tirzah, and Hoglah, and Milcah, and Noah, the daughters of Zelophehad, were married unto their father's brothers' sons:

12. *And* they were **married** into the families of **the sons of Manasseh** the son of Joseph, **and their inheritance remained in the tribe** of the family of their father.

13. **These are the commandments and the judgments, which the LORD commanded** by the hand of Moses unto the children of **Israel** in the plains of Moab by Jordan *near* Jericho.

DEUTERONOMY

■ **Deuteronomy is the last of**
■ **the five books which form**
■ **the Pentateuch.**
■ **The events** which
■ **it relates took place**
during a forty day period just prior
to the death of Moses and
■ **just before the children**
■ **of Israel entered into the**
■ **Promised Land**
under the leadership of Joshua.
One of the unique features of
the book is that it
■ **gives a clear portrait of**
■ **the heart of Moses** as he
speaks to the children of Israel.
■ **The discourses of Moses are**
■ **eloquent.** He reminds the people
of how the Lord has entered into a
covenant relationship with them, has
separated them for Himself, and has
guided and protected them through
His miraculous power. Finally, **he**
■ **pleas compassion-ately,**
■ **urging** and warning

■ **Israel not to turn from**
■ **the Lord.** Interestingly,
■ **Deuteronomy is a**
■ **pre-eminent source for**
■ **the New Testament.**
■ **Jesus used passages**
■ **from it** when He was tempted by
Satan. It was also the source Jesus
utilized when speaking about the
greatest commandment.
■ **Deuteronomy serves**
■ **as the conclusion to**
■ **a significant period**
■ **of history.** The children of
Israel have wandered in the
wilderness for forty years.
■ **A new generation**
■ **had been born.**
■ **Moses,** the great deliverer
and lawgiver,
■ **has died, and Joshua**
■ **makes preparation**
■ **to cross** the Jordan River
■ **into that long-sought**
■ **Land of Promise.**

THE BOOK OF DEUTERONOMY

BACKGROUND INFORMATION

Author: Moses according to most traditions
Date Written: Usually considered to be **between 1491 — 1451 B.C.**

Number of:
Verses—959
Chapters —34
Total Worlds—28,461
Scan Words—9,688
Scan Words Represent Approximately 37% of Total Words

Theme: The Law Given through Moses **is** carefully **Reviewed, closing with a Song, Blessings, and the Death of Moses**

OUTLINE OF THE BOOK

I. **The History of Israel Reviewed**
   1:1 — 4:49
II. **The Law Reviewed**
   5:1 — 26:19
III. **The Results of Obedience**
   27:1 — 28:68
IV. **The Covenant is Given Anew**
   31:1 — 34:12

269

CHAPTER 1

■ 1. **These be the words** which
■ **Moses spake unto**
■ **all Israel** on this side
Jordan in the wilderness,
■ **in the plain over against the**
■ **Red sea,** between Paran,
and Tophel, and Laban,
and Hazeroth, and Dizahab.
2. (*There are* eleven days' *journey*
from Horeb by the way of mount
Seir unto Kadesh–barnea.)
3. And it came to pass in the
fortieth year, in the eleventh month,
on the first *day* of the month, *that*
■ **Moses spake** unto the
children of Israel, according unto
■ **all that the LORD**
■ **had given** him
■ **in commandment** unto them;
4. After he had slain Sihon the king
of the Amorites, which dwelt in
Heshbon, and Og the king of Bashan,
which dwelt at Astaroth in Edrei:
5. On this side Jordan, in the
land of Moab, began Moses
to declare this law,
■ **saying,**
6. The LORD our
■ **God spake unto**
■ **us in Horeb, saying,**
■ **Ye have dwelt long**
■ **enough in this mount:**
7. Turn you, and take
your journey, and
■ **go to the mount of**
■ **the Amorites,** and unto all *the*
places nigh thereunto, in the plain,
in the hills, and in the vale, and in
the south, and by the sea side,
■ **to the land of the**
■ **Canaanites, and unto**
■ **Lebanon, unto** the great river,
■ **the river Euphrates.**
8. Behold, I have set
the land before you:
■ **go in and possess the land**
■ **which the LORD sware unto**
■ **your fathers,** Abraham, Isaac,
and Jacob, to give unto them
■ **and to their seed** after them.
9. And I spake unto you at that
time, saying, I am not able to

bear you myself alone:
10. The LORD your
■ **God hath multiplied you,**
and, behold, ye *are* this day
■ **as the stars of**
■ **heaven** for multitude.
11. (The LORD God of your fathers
make you a thousand times so
many more as ye *are,* and bless
you, as he hath promised you!)
■ 12. **How can I** myself
■ **alone bear** your cumbrance, and
■ **your burden,** and your strife?
■ 13. **Take** you
■ **wise men,** and understanding,
and known among your tribes,
■ **and I will make**
■ **them rulers** over you.
■ 14. **And ye answered me,**
■ **and said, The thing**
which thou hast spoken
■ **is good** for us to do.
■ 15. **So I took the**
■ **chief of your tribes,**
wise men, and known,
■ **and made them**
heads over you,
■ **captains** over thousands, and
captains over hundreds, and captains
over fifties, and captains over tens,
and officers among your tribes.
■ 16. **And I charged your**
■ **judges** at that time,
■ **saying, Hear the causes**
■ **between your brethren,**
■ **and judge righteously**
between *every* man and his brother,
and the stranger *that is* with him.
17. Ye shall not respect
persons in judgment; *but*
■ **ye shall hear the small as**
■ **well as the great; ye shall**
■ **not be afraid of** the face of
■ **man; for the judgment**
■ **is God's: and the cause that**
■ **is too hard** for you,
■ **bring it unto**
■ **me,** and I will hear it.
18. And I commanded you at that
time all the things which ye should do.
■ 19. **And when we departed**
■ **from Horeb, we went**
■ **through all that**

great and terrible
wilderness, which ye saw by the
way of the mountain of the Amorites,
as the LORD our God commanded us;
and we came to
Kadesh–barnea.
20. **And I said** unto you, Ye
are come unto the mountain of
the Amorites, which the LORD
our God doth give unto us.
21. **Behold, the LORD thy**
God hath set the land
before thee: go up and
possess it, as the LORD God
of thy fathers hath said unto thee; fear
not, neither be discouraged.
22. **And ye** came near unto
me every one of you, and
said, We will send
men before us,
and they shall search us
out the land, and bring us word
again by what way we must go up,
and into what cities we shall come.
23. **And** the saying
pleased me well: and
I took twelve men of you,
one of a tribe:
24. And they turned and went up into
the mountain, and came unto the
valley of Eshcol, and searched it out.
25. **And they took of the**
fruit of the land in their hands,
and brought it down
unto us, and brought us wordagain,
and said, It is a good land
which the LORD our God doth giveus.
26. **Notwithstanding ye**
would not go up, but
rebelled against the
commandment of the LORD yourGod:
27. **And ye**
murmured in your tents,
and said, Because the
LORD hated us, he
hath brought us forth
out of the land
of Egypt, to deliver us
into the hand of the
Amorites, to destroy us.
28. Whither shall we go up?
our brethren have
discouraged our heart,

saying, The people is
greater and taller than we;
the cities are great and
walled up to heaven; and
moreover we have seen the
sons of the Anakims there.
29. **Then I said** unto you, Dread
not, neither be afraid of them.
30. **The LORD** your God
which goeth before you, he
shall fight for you,
according to all that
he did for you
in Egypt before your eyes;
31. **And in the wilderness,**
where thou hast seen how that the
LORD thy God bare thee, as a man
doth bear his son, in all the way that
ye went, until ye came into this place.
32. **Yet** in this thing
ye did not believe
the LORD your God,
33. **Who went** in the way
before you, to search you
out a place to pitch
your tents *in,*
in fire by night, to shew
you by what way ye should go,
and in a cloud by day.
34. **And the LORD**
heard the voice of
your words, and was
wroth, and sware, saying,
35. Surely
there shall not
one of these men
of this evil generation
see that good
land, which I sware to
give unto your fathers.
36. **Save Caleb** the son
of Jephunneh; he shall see it,
and to him will I give the land
that he hath trodden upon,
and to his children, because he
hath wholly followed the LORD.
37. Also the LORD was angry with
me for your sakes, saying, Thou
also shalt not go in thither.
38. *But*
Joshua the son of Nun, which
standeth before thee, he shall go
in thither: encourage him: for he

271

shall cause Israel to inherit it.

39. **Moreover** your little ones, which ye said should be a prey, and **your children,** which in that day had no knowledge between good and evil, they **shall go in** thither, and unto them will I give it, **and** they shall **possess it.**

40. **But as for you,** turn you, and **take your journey into the wilderness by** the way of **the Red sea.**

41. **Then ye answered** and said unto me, **We have sinned** against the LORD, **we will** go up and **fight, according to all** that the LORD our **God commanded** us. And when ye had girded on every man his weapons of war, ye were ready to go up into the hill.

42. **And the LORD said** unto me, Say unto them. **Go not up,** neither fight; **for I am not among you; lest ye be smitten** before your enemies.

43. **So** I spake unto you; and **ye** would not hear, but **rebelled against** the commandment of **the LORD, and went** presumptuously **up** into the hill.

44. **And the Amorites,** which dwelt in that mountain, came out against you, and **chased you,** as bees do, **and destroyed you** in Seir, *even* unto Hormah.

45. **And ye** returned and **wept before the LORD; but the LORD would not hearken** to your voice, nor give ear unto you.

46. **So ye abode in Kadesh** many days, according unto the days that ye abode *there.*

CHAPTER 2

1. **Then we** turned, and **took our journey into the wilderness** by the way of the Red sea, as the LORD spake unto me: and we compassed mount Seir many days.

2. **And the LORD spake unto me, saying,**

3. Ye have compassed **this mountain long enough: turn** you **northward.**

4. **And command** thou **the people, saying, Ye are to pass through the coast of** your brethren **the children of Esau,** which dwell **in Seir; and they shall be afraid of you**: take ye good heed unto yourselves therefore:

5. **Meddle not with them;** for I will not give you of their land, no, not so much as a foot breadth; **because I have given mount Seir unto Esau** *for* a possession.

6. **Ye shall buy meat of them** for money, that ye may eat; **and** ye shall also buy **water** of them for money, that ye may drink.

7. **For** the LORD thy **God hath blessed thee** in all the works of thy hand: he knoweth thy walking through this great wilderness: **these forty years the LORD** thy God **hath been with thee;** thou hast lacked nothing.

8. **And when we passed by** from our brethren **the children of Esau,** which dwelt in Seir, through the way of the plain from Elath, and from Ezion–gaber, we turned and passed **by** the way of **the wilderness of Moab.**

9. **And the LORD said** unto me, **Distress not the Moabites,** neither contend with them in battle:

for I will not give thee of
their land *for* a possession;
because I have given
Ar unto the children
of Lot *for* a possession.
10. **The Emims dwelt therein**
in times past, a people great, and
many, and tall, as the Anakims;
11. **Which also**
were accounted
giants, as the Anakims; but the
Moabites called them Emims.
12. **The Horims** also
dwelt in Seir beforetime;
but the children of Esau
succeeded them, when they
had destroyed them from beforethem,
and dwelt in their stead; as Israel
did unto the land of his possession,
which the LORD gave unto them.
13. **Now rise up, said I,**
and get you over the
brook Zered. And we
went over the brook Zered.
14. **And the space**
in which we came
from Kadesh–barnea,
until we were come over the brook
Zered, was thirty and
eight years; until all the
generation of the men of
war were wasted
out from among the host, as
the LORD sware unto them.
15. For indeed the hand of the
LORD was against them, to
destroy them from among the
host, until they were consumed.
16. **So** it came to pass,
when all the men of
war were consumed and
dead from among the people,
17. That
the LORD spake unto me,
saying,
18. Thou art to
pass over through
Ar, the coast of Moab,
this day:
19. **And when thou**
comest nigh over against
the children of Ammon,
distress them not,

nor meddle with them:
for I will not give thee of
the land of the children of
Ammon *any* possession; because
I have given it unto the
children of Lot *for* a possession.
20. (That also was ac-counted
a land of giants: giants dwelt
therein in old time; and the
Ammonites call them Zamzummims;
21. **A people great,** and many,
and tall, as the Anakims;
but the LORD destroyed
them before them; and
they succeeded them,
and dwelt in their stead:
22. As he did to the children of
Esau, which dwelt in Seir, when
he destroyed the Horims from
before them; and they succeeded
them, and dwelt in their stead
even unto this day:
23. And the Avims which dwelt
in Hazerim, *even* unto Azzah, the
Caphtorims, which came forth
out of Caphtor, destroyed them,
and dwelt in their stead.)
24. **Rise** ye
up, take your journey, and
pass over the
river Arnon: behold,
I have given into thine hand
Sihon the Amorite, king of Heshbon,
and his land: begin to
possess it, and contend
with him in battle.
25. **This day will I begin**
to put the dread of thee and
the fear of thee upon
the nations *that are* under the
whole heaven, who shall hear report
of thee, and shall tremble, and be
in anguish because of thee.
26. **And I sent messengers**
out of the wilderness of Kedemoth
unto Sihon king of Heshbon
with words of
peace, saying,
27. **Let me pass through thy**
land: I will go along by the high
way, **I will neither turn**
unto the right hand
nor to the left.

28. Thou shalt sell me meat for money, that I may eat; and give me water for money, that I may drink: only I will pass through on my feet;

29. (As the children of Esau which dwell in Seir, and the Moabites which dwell in Ar, did unto me;) until I shall pass over Jordan into the land which the LORD our God giveth us.

30. **But Sihon** king of Heshbon **would not let us pass by him: for** the LORD thy **God hardened his spirit,** and made his heart obstinate, that he might deliver him into thy hand, as *appeareth* this day.

31. **And the LORD said** unto me, Behold, **I have begun to give Sihon and his land before thee:** begin to possess, that thou mayest inherit his land.

32. **Then Sihon came out against us,** he and all his people, to fight at Jahaz.

33. **And** the LORD our **God delivered him before us;** and we smote him, and his sons, and all his people.

34. **And we took all his cities** at that time, **and** utterly **destroyed the men,** and the **women, and** the **little ones,** of every city, we left none to remain:

35. **Only the cattle we took** for a prey unto ourselves, **and the spoil of the cities** which we took.

36. From Aroer, which *is* by the brink of the river of Arnon, and *from* the city that *is* by the river, even unto Gilead, there was not one city too strong for us: the LORD our God delivered all unto us:

37. **Only unto the land of the children of Ammon thou camest not,** *nor* unto any place of the river Jabbok, nor unto the cities in the mountains, **nor unto whatsoever** the LORD our **| ■ | God forbad** us.

CHAPTER 3

1. **Then we** turned, and **went up** the way **to Bashan: and Og the king of Bashan came out against us,** he and all his people, to battle at Edrei.

2. **And the LORD said** unto me, **Fear him not: for I will deliver him,** and all his people, **and his land,** into thy hand; and thou shalt do unto him as thou didst unto Sihon king of the Amorites, which dwelt at Heshbon.

3. **So** the LORD our **God delivered** into our hands **Og** also, the king of Bashan, and all his people: and we smote him until none was left to him remaining.

4. **And we took all his cities** at that time, there was not a city which we took not from them, threescore cities, all the region of Argob, the kingdom of Og in Bashan.

5. **All these cities were fenced with high walls,** gates, and bars; beside unwalled towns a great many.

6. **And we** utterly **destroyed** them, as we did unto Sihon king of Heshbon, utterly destroying **the men, women, and children,** of every city.

7. **But** all **the cattle, and the spoil** of the cities, **we took** for a prey to ourselves.

8. **And we took** at that time out of the hand of **the two kings of the Amorites** the land that *was* **on this side Jordan, from the river** of **Arnon unto mount Hermon;**

9. (*Which* Hermon the Sidonians call Sirion; and the Amorites call it Shenir;)

10. All the cities of the plain, and all Gilead, and all Bashan, unto Salchah and Edrei, cities

of the kingdom of Og in Bashan.

11. **For only Og king of Bashan remained of the** remnant of **giants;** behold **his bedstead was** a bedstead **of iron;** *is* it not in Rabbath of the children of Ammon? **nine cubits was the length** thereof, **and four cubits the breadth** of it, after the cubit of a man.

12. **And this land,** *which* we possessed at that time, from Aroer, which *is* by the river Arnon, and half mount Gilead, and the cities thereof, **gave I unto the Reubenites and to the Gadites.**

13. **And the rest of Gilead,** and all Bashan, *being* the kingdom of Og, **gave I unto the half tribe of Manasseh;** all the region of Argob, with all Bashan, which was called the land of giants.

14. Jair the son of Manasseh took all the country of Argob unto the coasts of Geshuri and Maachathi; and called them after his own name, Bashan–havoth–jair, unto this day.

15. And I gave Gilead unto Machir.

16. **And unto the Reubenites and** unto **the Gadites I gave from Gilead** even **unto the river Arnon half the valley, and the border** even **unto the river Jabbok,** *which is* the border of the children of Ammon;

17. **The plain also, and Jordan,** and the coast *thereof,* **from Chinnereth** even **unto** the sea of the plain, *even* **the salt sea,** under Ashdoth–pisgah eastward.

18. **And I commanded you** at that time, **saying, The LORD** your God **hath given you this land** to possess it: **ye shall pass over armed before your brethren** the children of Israel, *all that* are meet for the war.

19. **But your wives,** and your **little ones, and your cattle,** (*for* I know that ye have much cattle,) **shall abide in your cities** which I have given you;

20. **Until the LORD have given rest unto your brethren,** as well as unto you, **and** *until* **they also possess the land which** the LORD your **God hath given them beyond Jordan:** and *then* shall ye return every man unto his possession, which I have given you.

21. **And I commanded Joshua** at that time, **saying, Thine eyes have seen all** that **the LORD** your God **hath done unto these two kings: so shall the LORD do unto all the kingdoms whither thou passest.**

22. **Ye shall not fear them: for the LORD** your God he **shall fight for you.**

23. **And I besought the LORD** at that time, **saying,**

24. **O Lord GOD,** thou hast begun to shew thy servant thy greatness, and thy mighty hand: for what God *is there* in heaven or in earth, that can do according to thy works, and according to thy might?

25. I pray thee, **let me go over, and see the** good **land** that *is* **beyond Jordan,** that goodly mountain, and Lebanon.

26. **But the LORD was wroth with me** for your sakes, **and would not hear me: and** the LORD **said** unto me, Let it suffice thee; **speak no more unto me of this matter.**

27. **Get thee up into the top of Pisgah,** and lift up thine eyes

westward, and northward, and
southward, and eastward,
and behold it with thine eyes:
for thou shalt not
go over this
Jordan.
28. **But charge Joshua,** and
encourage him, and strengthen him:
for he shall go over
before this people,
and he shall
cause them to inherit
the land which thou shalt see.
29. So we abode in the valley
over against Beth–peor.

CHAPTER 4

1. **Now** therefore
hearken, O Israel, unto the
statutes and unto the judgments,
which I teach
you, for to do *them,*
that ye may live,and go in and
possess the land which the
LORD God of your fathers giveth you.
2. **Ye shall not add unto the**
word which I command
you, neither shall ye
diminish *aught* from
it, that ye may keep the
commandments of the LORD
your God which I command you.
3. **Your eyes have seen**
what the LORD did because
of Baal–peor: for all the
men that followed Baal–peor, the
LORD thy God hath destroyed
them from among you.
4. **But ye that did cleave**
unto the LORD your God
are alive every one
of you this day.
5. **Behold, I have taught**
you statutes and judgments, even
as the LORD my God
commanded me, that
ye should do so in the land
whither ye go to possess it.
6. **Keep** therefore and do
them; for
this is your wisdom
and your understanding
in the sight of the

nations, which shall
hear all these statutes,
and say, Surely this great
nation is a
wise and understanding people.
7. **For what nation is**
there so great, who
hath God so nigh unto
them, as the LORD our God *is* in
all things that we call upon him *for?*
8. **And** what nation *is*
there so great, that
hath statutes and
judgments so righteous
as all this law, which I set
before you this day?
9. **Only take heed** to thyself,
and keep thy soul
diligently, lest thou forget the
things which thine eyes have seen,
and lest they depart from thy heart
all the days of thy life: but
teach them
thy sons, and
thy sons' sons;
10. **Specially the day**
that thou stoodest before
the LORD thy God in Horeb,
when the LORD said
unto me, Gather me
the people together,
and I will make them hear
my words, that they may
learn to fear me all the days
that they shall
live upon the earth,
and *that* they may
teach their children.
11. **And ye came**
near and stood under
the mountain; and
the mountain burned
with fire unto the midst of
heaven, with darkness, clouds,
and thick darkness.
12. **And the LORD spake**
unto you out of the midst
of the fire: ye heard the voice
of the words, but saw no
similitude; only *ye heard* a voice.
13. **And** he
declared unto you
his covenant, which he

commanded you to perform, *even*
ten commandments;
and he wrote them upon
two tables of stone.
14. And the LORD
commanded me at that time
to teach you statutes and
judgments, that ye might
do them in the land whither
ye go over to possess it.
15. Take ye therefore good
heed unto yourselves; for ye
saw no manner of similitude on the
day *that* the LORD spake unto you
in Horeb out of the midst of the fire:
16. Lest ye corrupt *yourselves,* and
make you
a graven image, the
similitude of any figure, the
likeness of male or female,
17. The likeness of any beast that
is on the earth, the likeness of any
winged fowl that flieth in the air,
18. The likeness of any thing that
creepeth on the ground, the likeness
of any fish that *is* in the waters
beneath the earth:
19. And lest thou lift up thine
eyes unto heaven, and when thou
seest the sun, and the moon,
and the stars, *even* all
the host of heaven,
shouldest be driven to worship them,
and serve them, which the
LORD thy God hath divided unto all
nations under the whole heaven.
20. But the LORD hath
taken you, and brought you
forth out of the iron furnace, *even*
out of Egypt, to be unto him
a people of inheritance,
as *ye are* this day.
21. Furthermore the LORD
was angry with me
for your sakes,
and sware that I should
not go over Jordan,
and that I should not go in unto that
good land, which the LORD thy God
giveth thee *for* an inheritance:
22. But I must die in this
land, I must not go over Jordan:
but ye shall go over, and

possess that good land.
23. Take heed unto yourselves,
lest ye forget the covenant
of the LORD your God,
which he made with you,
and make you
a graven image, *or* the likeness
of any *thing,* which the LORD
thy God hath forbidden thee.
24. For the LORD thy God
is a consuming fire,
even a jealous God.
25. When thou shalt beget
children, and children's children, and
ye shall have remained
long in the land, and shall
corrupt yourselves, and
make a graven image,
or the likeness of any *thing,*
and shall
do evil in the sight
of the LORD thy God, to
provoke him to anger:
26. I call heaven and
earth to witness
against you this day, that
ye shall soon utterly perish
from off the land whereunto ye
go over Jordan to possess it; ye
shall not prolong *your* days upon it,
but shall utterly be destroyed.
27. And the LORD shall
scatter you among the
nations, and ye shall be left
few in number among
the heathen, whither the
LORD shall lead you.
28. And there ye shall
serve gods, the work of
men's hands, wood and
stone, which neither see, nor
hear, nor eat, nor smell.
29. But if from thence
thou shalt seek
the LORD thy God,
thou shalt find him, if
thou seek him with all thy
heart and with all thy soul.
30. When thou art in
tribulation, and all
these things are
come upon thee,
even in the latter days,

■ **if thou turn to** the LORD thy
■ **God, and shalt**
■ **be obedient** unto his voice;
31. (For the LORD thy
God is a merciful God;)
■ **he will not forsake**
■ **thee,** neither destroy thee,
nor forget the covenant of thy
fathers which he sware unto them.
■ 32. **For ask now of the days**
that are past, which were before thee,
■ **since** the day that
■ **God created man**
upon the earth, and ask from the
one side of heaven unto the other,
■ **whether there hath been**
■ **any such thing as this great**
■ **thing** *is*, or hath been heard like it?
■ 33. **Did ever people**
■ **hear** the voice of
■ **God speaking**
■ **out of** the midst of
■ **the fire,** as thou hast heard,
■ **and live?**
■ 34. **Or hath God**
■ **assayed to** go *and*
■ **take him a nation from the**
■ **midst of another** nation, by
temptations, by signs, and by
wonders, and by war, and by a mighty
hand, and by a stretched out arm,
and by great terrors, according to all
that the LORD your God did for you in
Egypt before your eyes?
■ 35. **Unto thee it was**
■ **shewed, that thou mightest**
■ **know that the LORD** he
■ **is God; there is**
■ **none else** beside him.
36. Out of heaven he made thee to
hear his voice, that he might instruct
thee: and upon earth he shewed thee
his great fire; and thou heardest his
words out of the midst of the fire.
37. And because he loved thy
fathers, therefore he chose their
seed after them, and brought
thee out in his sight with his
mighty power out of Egypt;
38. To drive out nations from
before thee greater and mightier
than thou *art*, to bring thee in,
to give thee their land for an

inheritance, as it *is* this day.
39. Know therefore this day, and
consider *it* in thine heart, that the
LORD he *is* God in heaven
above,and upon the earth
beneath: *there is* none else.
■ 40. **Thou shalt keep**
■ **therefore his statutes,**
■ **and his commandments,**
which I command thee this day, that
it may go well with thee, and with
thy children after thee, and
■ **that thou mayest prolong**
■ **thy days** upon the earth, which the
LORD thy God giveth thee, for ever.
■ 41. **Then Moses severed**
■ **three cities on this side**
■ **Jordan** toward the sun rising;
■ 42. **That the slayer**
■ **might flee thither, which**
■ **should kill his neighbour**
■ **unawares,** and hated him not
in times past; and that fleeing unto
one of these cities he might live:
■ 43. **Namely, Bezer** in
the wilderness, in the plain
country, of the Reubenites; and
■ **Ramoth** in Gilead, of the Gadites;
■ **and Golan** in Bashan,
of the Manassites.
■ 44. **And this is the**
■ **law which Moses**
■ **set before** the children of
■ **Israel:**
45. These *are* the testimonies,
and the statutes, and the judgments,
which Moses spake unto the
children of Israel, after they
came forth out of Egypt.
46. On this side Jordan, in the valley
over against Beth–peor, in the land of
Sihon king of the Amorites, who dwelt
at Heshbon, whom Moses and the
children of Israel smote, after they
were come forth out of Egypt:
47. And they possessed his land,and
the land of Og king of Bashan, two
kings of the Amorites, which *were* on
this side Jordan toward the sun rising;
48. From Aroer, which *is* by the bank
of the river Arnon, even unto mount
Sion, which *is* Hermon,
49. And all the plain on this

side Jordan eastward, even
unto the sea of the plain, under
the springs of Pisgah.

CHAPTER 5

1. **And Moses called all Israel, and said** unto them, **Hear, O Israel, the statutes** and judgments **which I speak** in your ears this day, **that ye may learn them, and** keep, and **do them.**

2. The LORD our God made a covenant with us in Horeb.

3. **The LORD made not this covenant with our fathers, but with us**, *even* us, **who are** all of us here **alive** this day.

4. **The LORD talked with you face to face** in the mount **out of the midst of the fire,**

5. (I stood between the LORD and you at that time, to shew you the word of the LORD: for ye were afraid by reason of the fire, and went not up into the mount;)

saying,

6. **I am the LORD thy God,** which brought thee out of the land of Egypt, from the house of bondage.

7. **Thou shalt have none other gods before me.**

8. **Thou shalt not make** thee **any graven image,** *or* any likeness *of any thing* that *is* in heaven above, or that *is* in the earth beneath, or that *is* in the waters beneath the earth:

9. **Thou shalt not bow down** thyself **unto them, nor serve them: for I** the LORD thy God **am a jealous God, visiting the iniquity of the fathers upon the children** unto the third and fourth *generation* **of them that hate me,**

10. **And shewing mercy unto** thousands of **them that love me and keep my commandments.**

11. **Thou shalt not takethe name of the LORD** thy God **in vain**: for the LORD will not hold *him* guiltless that taketh his name in vain.

12. **Keep the sabbath** day to sanctify it, as the LORD thy God hath commanded thee.

13. **Six days thou shalt labour,** and do all thy work:

14. **But the seventh day is the sabbath of the LORD** thy God: **in it thou shalt not** do any **work,** thou, nor thy son, nor thy daughter, nor thy manservant, nor thy maidservant, nor thine ox, nor thine ass, nor any of thy cattle, nor thy stranger that *is* within thy gates; that thy manservant and thy maidservant may rest as well as thou.

15. And remember that thou wast a servant in the land of Egypt, and *that* the LORD thy God brought thee out thence through a mighty hand and by a stretched out arm: therefore the LORD thy God commanded thee to keep the sabbath day.

16. **Honour thy father and** thy **mother,** as the LORD thy God hath commanded thee; **that thy days may be prolonged, and that it may go well with thee,** in the land which the LORD thy God giveth thee.

17. **Thou shalt not kill.**

18. **Neither shalt thou commit adultery.**

19. **Neither shalt thou steal.**

20. **Neither shalt thou bear false witness against** thy neighbour.

21. **Neither shalt thou desire thy neighbour's wife,** neither shalt thou covet thy neighbour's house, **his field,** or his manservant, or his maidservant, his ox, or his ass, **or any thing that is thy neighbour's.**

22. These words the LORD spake

unto all your assembly in the mount out of the midst of the fire, of the cloud, and of the thick darkness, with a great voice: and he added no more. And he wrote them in two tables of stone, and delivered them unto me.

23. **And** it came to pass, **when ye heard the voice out of the midst of the darkness,** (for the mountain did burn with fire,) that ye came near unto me, *even* all the heads of your tribes, and your elders;

24. **And ye said,** Behold, the LORD our **God hath shewed us his glory and his greatness,** and we have heard his voice out of the midst of the fire: **we have seen this day that God doth talk with man, and he liveth.**

25. **Now therefore why should we die?** for this great fire will consume us: **if we hear the voice of** the LORD our **God any more, then we shall die.**

26. **For who is** there of all flesh, that **hath heard the voice of** the living **God** speaking out of the midst of the fire, as we have, **and lived?**

27. **Go thou near, and hear all** that the LORD our **God shall say: and speak** thou unto us **all that** the LORD our **God shall speak** unto thee; **and we will** hear it, and **do it.**

28. **And the LORD heard** the voice of **your words,** when ye spake unto me; **and** the LORD **said unto me, I have heard** the voice of the words of **this people,** which they have spoken unto thee: they have well said all that they have spoken.

29. **O that there were such an heart in them, that they would fear me, and keep all my commandments** always, that it might be well with them, and with their children for ever!

30. **Go say to them, Get you into your tents again.**

31. **But as for thee, stand** thou here **by me, and I will speak unto thee all the commandments,** and the statutes, and the judgments, **which thou shalt teach** them, that they may do *them* in the land which I give them to possess it.

32. Ye shall observe to do therefore as the LORD your God hath commanded you: ye shall not turn asideto the right hand or to the left.

33. **Ye shall walk in all the ways** which the LORD your **God hath commanded you, that ye may live, and that it may be well with you, and that ye may prolong your days** in the land which ye shall possess.

CHAPTER 6

1. **Now these are the commandments,** the statutes, and the judgments, which the LORD your God commanded to teach you, that ye might do *them* in the land whither ye go to possess it:

2. That thou mightest fear the LORD thy God, to keep all his statutes and his commandments,which I command thee, thou, and thy son, and thy son's son, all the days of thy life; and that thy days may be prolonged.

3. Hear therefore, O Israel, and observe to do *it;* that it may be well with thee, and that ye may increase mightily, as the LORD God of thy fathers hath promised thee, in the land that floweth with milk and honey.

4. **Hear, O Israel: The LORD our God is one LORD:**

5. **And thou shalt love the**

280

■ LORD thy God with all
■ thine heart, and with all thy
■ soul, and with all thy
■ might.
■ 6. And these words,
which I command thee this day,
■ shall be in thine heart:
7. And thou shalt
■ teach them diligently unto
■ thy children, and shalt
■ talk of them when thou
■ sittest in thine house,
■ and when thou walkest
■ by the way, and when
■ thou liest down, and
■ when thou risest up.
■ 8. And thou shalt
■ bind them for a sign
■ upon thine hand, and
■ they shall be as frontlets
■ between thine eyes.
■ 9. And thou shalt
■ write them upon the
■ posts of thy house,
■ and on thy gates.
10. And it shall be,
when the LORD thy
■ God shall have brought
■ thee into the land which
he sware unto thy fathers, to
Abraham, to Isaac, and to Jacob,
■ to give thee great and goodly
■ cities, which thou buildedst not,
■ 11. And houses full of all
■ good things, which thou filledst
not, and wells digged, which thou
diggedst not, vineyards and olive
trees, which thou plantedst not; when
thou shalt have eaten and be full;
■ 12. Then beware lest thou
■ forget the LORD, which brought
thee forth out of the land of Egypt,
from the house of bondage.
■ 13. Thou shalt fear
■ the LORD thy God,
■ and serve him, and
shalt swear by his name.
■ 14. Ye shall not go after
■ other gods, of the gods of the
people which *are* round about you;
15.(For the LORD thy God *is* a jealous
God among you) lest the anger of the
LORD thy God be kindled against

thee, and destroy thee from
off the face of the earth.
■ 16. Ye shall not tempt
■ the LORD your God, as
ye tempted *him* in Massah.
17. Ye shall diligently keep the
commandments of the LORD
your God, and his testimonies,
and his statutes, which he
hath commanded thee.
■ 18. And thou shalt do
■ that which is right and good
■ in the sight of the LORD: that
it may be well with thee, and that
thou mayest go in and possess
the good land which the LORD
sware unto thy fathers.
19. To cast out all thine
enemies from before thee,
as the LORD hath spoken.
■ 20. And when thy
■ son asketh thee in
■ time to come, saying,
■ What mean the testimonies,
and the statutes, and the
judgments, which the LORD
our God hath commanded you?
■ 21. Then thou shalt
■ say unto thy son,
■ We were Pharaoh's bondmen
■ in Egypt; and the LORD
■ brought us out of Egypt
with a mighty hand:
22. And the LORD shewed
signs and wonders, great
and sore, upon Egypt, upon
Pharaoh, and upon all his
household, before our eyes:
23. And he brought us out from
thence, that he might bring us in,
to give us the land which he
sware unto our fathers.
■ 24. And the LORD
■ commanded us to do all
■ these statutes, to fear the
LORD our God, for our good
always, that he might preserve
us alive, as *it is* at this day.
25. And it shall be our
righteousness, if we observe
to do all these commandments
before the LORD our God, as
he hath commanded us.

CHAPTER 7

1. **When the LORD thy God shall bring thee into the land** whither thou goest to possess it, **and hath cast out many nations before thee,** the Hittites, and the Girgashites, and the Amorites, and the Canaanites, and the Perizzites, and the Hivites, and the Jebusites, seven nations greater and mightier than thou;

2. **And when the LORD thy God shall deliver them before thee; thou shalt smite them, and utterly destroy them; thou shalt make no covenant with them, nor shew mercy unto them:**

3. **Neither shalt thou make marriages with them;** thy daughter thou shalt not give unto his son, nor his daughter shalt thou take unto thy son.

4. **For they will turn away thy son from following me, that they may serve other gods: so will** the anger of **the LORD** be kindled against you, and **destroy thee** suddenly.

5. **But** thus shall ye deal with them; **ye shall destroy their altars,** and break down their images, and cut down their groves, and burn their graven images with fire.

6. **For thou art an holy people** unto the LORD thy God: the LORD thy God hath chosen thee to be a special people unto himself, above all people that *are* upon the face of the earth.

7. **The LORD did not** set his love upon you, nor **choose you, because ye were more in number** than any people; for ye *were* the fewest of all people:

8. **But because the LORD loved you, and** because he **would keep the oath** which he had sworn unto your **fathers,** hath the LORD brought you out with a mighty hand, and redeemed you out of the house of bondmen, from the hand of Pharaoh king of Egypt.

9. **Know therefore that** the LORD thy **God,** he *is* God, the faithful God, which **keepeth covenant and mercy with them that love him** and keep his commandments to a thousand generations;

10. And repayeth them that hate him to their face, to destroy them: he will not be slack to him that hateth him, he will repay him to his face.

11. Thou shalt therefore keep the commandments, and the statutes, and the judgments, which I command thee this day, to do them.

12. **Wherefore** it shall come to pass, **if ye hearken to these judgments,** and keep, and do them, that the LORD thy **God shall keep** unto thee **the covenant** and the mercy which **he sware unto thy fathers:**

13. And he will love thee, and bless thee, and multiply thee: he will also bless the fruit of thy womb, and the fruit of thy land, thy corn, and thy wine, and thine oil, the increase of thy kine, and the flocks of thy sheep, in the land which he sware unto thy fathers to give thee.

14. **Thou shalt be blessed above all people:** there shall not be male or female barren among you, or among your cattle.

15. **And the LORD will take away from thee all sickness,** and will put none of the evil diseases of Egypt, which thou knowest, upon thee; but will lay them upon all *them* that hate thee.

16. **And thou shalt consume all the people** which the LORD thy **God shall deliver** thee; thine eye shall

■ **have no pity upon**
■ **them: neither** shalt thou
■ **serve their gods;** for
that *will be* a snare unto thee.
■ 17. **If thou** shalt
■ **say** in thine heart,
■ **These nations are**
■ **more than I; how can**
■ **I dispossess them?**
■ 18. **Thou shalt not**
■ **be afraid** of them:
■ **but** shalt well
■ **remember what** the LORD thy
■ **God did unto Pharaoh,**
and unto all Egypt;
19. The great temptations
which thine eyes saw, and the signs,
and the wonders, and the mighty
hand, and the stretched out arm,
whereby the LORD thy God
brought thee out:
■ **so shall the LORD** thy God
■ **do unto all the people**
■ **of whom thou art afraid.**
20. Moreover the LORD thy God
will send the hornet among them,
until they that are left, and hide
themselves from thee, be destroyed.
21. Thou shalt not be affrighted at
them: for the LORD thy God *is* among
you, a mighty God and terrible.
■ 22. **And the LORD** thy God
■ **will put out those**
■ **nations** before thee
■ **by little and little:** thou
mayest not consume them at
once, lest the beasts of the
field increase upon thee.
23. But the LORD thy God shall
deliver them unto thee, and shall
destroy them with a mighty
destruction, until they be destroyed.
24. And he shall deliver their
kings into thine hand, and
thou shalt destroy their name
from under heaven: there shall
no man be able to stand
before thee, until thou have
destroyed them.
■ 25. **The graven**
■ **images of their gods**
■ **shall ye burn** with fire:
■ **thou shalt not desire**

■ **the silver or gold** *that is*
■ **on them,** nor take *it* unto thee, lest
thou be snared therin: for it *is* an
abomination to the LORD thy God.
■ 26. **Neither shalt thou**
■ **bring an abomination into**
■ **thine house,** lest thou be a
cursed thing like it: *but* thou shalt
utterly detest it, and thou shalt
utterly abhor it; for it *is* a cursed thing.

CHAPTER 8

1. All the commandments which I
command thee this day shall ye
observe to do, that ye may live,
and multiply, and go in and possess
the land which the LORD sware
unto your fathers.
■ 2. **And thou shalt remember**
all the way which the LORD thy
■ **God led thee** these
■ **forty years in the**
■ **wilderness,** to humble thee,
and to prove thee, to know what *was*
in thine heart, whether thou wouldest
keep his commandments, or no.
■ 3. **And he humbled thee,**
■ **and suffered thee to**
■ **hunger, and fed thee with**
■ **manna,** which thou knewest
not, neither did thy fathers know;
■ **that he might make**
■ **thee know that man**
■ **doth not live by bread**
■ **only, but by every**
■ **word that proceedeth**
■ **out of the mouth of**
■ **the LORD** doth man live.
■ 4. **Thy raiment waxed**
■ **not old** upon thee,
■ **neither did thy foot**
■ **swell,** these forty years.
■ 5. **Thou shalt also**
■ **consider** in thine heart,
■ **that, as a man**
■ **chasteneth his son,**
■ **so the LORD** thy God
■ **chasteneth thee.**
6. Therefore thou shalt keep the
commandments of the LORD thy God,
to walk in his ways, and to fear him.
■ 7. **For** the LORD thy
■ **God bringeth thee into a**

■ **good land,** a land of brooks of water, of fountains and depths that spring out of valleys and hills;

8. A land of wheat, and barley, and vines, and fig trees, and pomegranates; a land of oil olive, and honey;

9. ■ **A land wherein** thou shalt eat bread without scarceness, ■ **thou shalt not lack** ■ **any thing** in it; a land whose stones *are* iron, and out of whose hills thou mayest dig brass.

10. ■ **When thou hast** ■ **eaten** and art full, ■ **then thou shalt bless** ■ **the LORD** thy God for the good land which he hath given thee.

11. ■ **Beware that thou forget** ■ **not the LORD** thy God, in not keeping his commandments, and his judgments, and his statutes, which I command thee this day:

12. Lest *when* thou hast eaten and art full, and hast built goodly houses, and dwelt *therein;*

13. And *when* thy herds and thy flocks multiply, and thy silver and thy gold is multiplied, and all that thou hast is multiplied;

14. Then thine heart be lifted up, and thou forget the LORD thy God, which brought thee forth out of the land of Egypt, from the house of bondage;

15. Who led thee through that great and terrible wilderness, *wherein were* fiery serpents, and scorpions, and drought, where *there was* no water; who brought thee forth water out of the rock of flint;

16. Who fed thee in the wilderness with manna, which thy fathers knew not, that he might humble thee, and that he might prove thee, to do thee good at thy latter end;

17. ■ **And** thou ■ **say in thine heart, My** ■ **power and the might** ■ **of mine hand hath** ■ **gotten me this wealth.**

18. ■ **But** thou shalt ■ **remember the LORD** thy God: for *it is* he that

■ **giveth thee power** ■ **to get wealth,** that he may establish his covenant which he sware unto thy fathers, as *it is* this day.

19. ■ **And it shall be,** ■ **if thou** do at all ■ **forget** the LORD thy ■ **God, and walk after** ■ **other gods,** and serve them, and worship them, ■ **I testify** against you this day ■ **that ye shall surely perish.**

20. As the nations which the LORD destroyeth before your face, so shall ye perish; because ye would not be obedient unto the voice of the LORD your God.

CHAPTER 9

1. ■ **Hear, O Israel:** Thou *art* to ■ **pass over Jordan** ■ **this day, to** go in to ■ **possess nations** ■ **greater** and mightier ■ **than thyself,** cities great and fenced up to heaven,

2. ■ **A people great and** ■ **tall,** the children of the Anakims, whom thou knowest, and ■ **of whom thou hast heard** ■ **say, Who can stand before** ■ **the children of Anak!**

3. ■ **Understand** therefore ■ **this day,** that the LORD thy ■ **God** *is* he which goeth over before thee; *as* a consuming fire he ■ **shall destroy them,** and he shall bring them down before thy face: so shalt thou drive them out, and destroy them quickly, as the LORD hath said unto thee.

4. ■ **Speak not thou in** ■ **thine heart,** after that the LORD thy God hath cast them out from before thee, saying, For ■ **my righteousness** the LORD ■ **hath brought me in to** ■ **possess this land:** but for the wickedness of these nations the LORD doth drive them out from before thee.

5. ■ **Not for thy**

■ **righteousness,** or for the
uprightness of thine heart, dost
thou go to possess their land:
■ **but for the wickedness of**
■ **these nations** the LORD thy
■ **God doth drive them out**
from before thee, and that he
may perform the word which the
LORD sware unto thy fathers,
Abraham, Isaac, and Jacob.
6. Understand therefore,
that the LORD thy
■ **God giveth thee not**
■ **this good land** to possess it
■ **for thy righteousness;**
■ **for thou art a**
■ **stiffnecked people.**
■ 7. **Remember,** *and*
forget not, how
■ **thou provokedst** the LORD thy
■ **God to wrath in the**
■ **wilderness:** from the day
that thou didst depart out of the
land of Egypt, until ye came unto
this place, ye have been
rebellious against the LORD.
■ 8. **Also in Horeb ye**
■ **provoked the LORD to**
■ **wrath,** so that the LORD was angry
with you to have destroyed you.
9. When I was gone up into the mount
to receive the tables of stone, *even*
the tables of the covenant which the
LORD made with you, then I abode in
the mount forty days and forty nights,
I neither did eat bread nor drinkwater:
10. And the LORD delivered unto me
two tables of stone written with the
finger of God;and on them *waswritten*
according to all the words, which the
LORD spake with you in the mount
out of the midst of the fire in the
day of the assembly.
■ 11. **And** it came to pass
■ **at the end of forty**
■ **days and** forty
■ **nights,** *that*
■ **the LORD gave me** the two
■ **tables of stone,**
■ **even** the tables of
■ **the covenant.**
■ 12. **And** the LORD
■ **said** unto me, Arise,

■ **get** thee
■ **down quickly** from hence;
■ **for thy people** which
thou hast brought forth out of Egypt
■ **have corrupted**
■ **themselves;** they are quickly
turned aside out of the way
which I commanded them;
■ **they have made them**
■ **a molten image.**
13. Furthermore the LORD
spake unto me, saying, I
have seen this people, and,
■ **behold, it is a**
■ **stiffnecked people:**
■ 14. **Let me** alone, that I may
■ **destroy them, and**
blot out their name from
under heaven: and I will
■ **make of thee a**
■ **nation mightier and**
■ **greater than they.**
15. **So I** turned and
■ **came down** from the mount,
and the mount burned with fire:
■ **and the two**
■ **tables** of the covenant
■ **were in my** two
■ **hands.**
16. And I looked, and, behold,
■ **ye had** sinned against the
LORD your God, *and* had
■ **made** you
■ **a molten calf:** ye had turned
aside quickly out of the way which
the LORD had commanded you.
■ 17. **And I took the** two
■ **tables, and** cast them
out of my two hands, and
■ **brake them** before your eyes.
18. **And** I fell down before
the LORD, as at the first,
forty days and forty nights: I
■ **did neither eat** bread,
■ **nor drink** water,
■ **because of** all
■ **your sins** which ye sinned, in doing
wickedly in the sight of the
LORD, to provoke him to anger.
■ 19. **For I was afraid of**
■ **the anger** and hot displeasure,
■ **wherewith the LORD**
■ **was wroth against**

■ **you** to destroy you.
■ **But the LORD**
■ **hearkened unto me** at
■ **that time also.**
■ 20. **And the LORD was**
■ **very angry with Aaron**
■ **to have destroyed him:**
■ **and I prayed for**
■ **Aaron** also the same time.
■ 21. **And I took** your sin,
■ **the calf** which ye had made,
■ **and burnt it** with
fire, and stamped it,
■ **and ground it** very small, *even*
■ **until it was** as small as
■ **dust: and** I
■ **cast the dust** thereof
■ **into the brook** that
descended out of the mount.
22. And at Taberah, and at
Massah, and at Kibroth–hattaavah,
ye provoked the LORD to wrath.
■ 23. **Likewise when the**
■ **LORD sent you from**
■ **Kadesh–barnea,**
■ **saying, Go** up and
■ **possess the land**
which I have given you; then
■ **ye rebelled** against the
commandment of the LORD your
God, and ye believed him not,
nor hearkened to his voice.
■ 24. **Ye have been**
■ **rebellious** against the LORD
■ **from the day** that
■ **I knew you.**
25. Thus I fell down before
the LORD forty days and forty
nights, as I fell down *at the first;*
because the LORD had said
he would destroy you.
■ 26. **I prayed** therefore
unto the LORD, and said,
■ **O Lord GOD, destroy not**
■ **thy people** and thine inheritance,
which thou hast redeemed throughthy
greatness, which thou hast brought
forth out of Egypt with a mighty hand.
27. Remember thy servants,
Abraham, Isaac, and Jacob;
look not unto the stubbornness
of this people, nor to their
wickedness, nor to their sin:

■ 28. **Lest the land whence**
■ **thou broughtest us**
■ **out say, Because the**
■ **LORD was not able to**
■ **bring them into the land**
which he promised them, and
because he hated them,
■ **he hath brought them out**
■ **to slay them** in the wilderness.
29. Yet they *are* thy people and
thine inheritance, which thou
broughtest out by thy mighty
power and by thy stretched out arm.

CHAPTER 10

■ 1. **At that time the**
■ **LORD said** unto me,
■ **Hew** thee
■ **two tables of stone like** unto
■ **the first, and come**
■ **up unto me** into the mount,
■ **and make** thee
■ **an ark of wood.**
■ 2. **And I will write on**
■ **the tables the words**
■ **that were in the first**
■ **tables which thou brakest,**
and thou shalt put them in the ark.
■ 3. **And I made an ark** of
shittim wood, and hewed two
tables of stone like unto the first,
and went up into the mount, having
the two tables in mine hand.
■ 4. **And he wrote on the**
■ **tables,** according to the first writing,
the ten commandments,
which the LORD spake unto you
in the mount out of the midst of
the fire in the day of the assembly;
and the LORD gave them unto me.
■ 5. **And I** turned myself and
■ **came down** from the mount,
■ **and put the tables in the**
■ **ark** which I had made; and therethey
be, as the LORD commanded me.
■ 6. **And** the children of
■ **Israel took their journey**
from Beeroth of the children of Jaakan
■ **to Mosera: there Aaron**
■ **died,** and there he was buried;
■ **and Eleazar his son**
■ **ministered in the priest's**
■ **office** in his stead.

7. **From thence they journeyed** unto Gudgodah; and from Gudgodah **to Jotbath,** a land of rivers of waters.

8. **At that time the LORD separated the tribe of Levi, to bear the ark** of the covenant of the LORD, **to stand before the LORD to minister unto him,** and to bless in his name, unto this day.

9. **Wherefore Levi hath no** part nor **inheritance with his brethren; the LORD is his inheritance,** according as the LORD thy God promised him.

10. And I stayed in the mount, according to the first time, forty days and forty nights; **and the LORD hearkened unto me** at that time also, **and** the LORD **would not destroy thee.**

11. **And the LORD said** unto me, Arise, **take thy journey before the people, that they may** go in and **possess the land,** which I sware unto their fathers to give unto them.

12. **And now, Israel, what doth the LORD** thy God **require of thee, but to fear** the LORD thy **God, to walk in all his ways, and to love him, and to serve the LORD thy God with all thy heart and with all thy soul,**

13. To keep the commandments of the LORD, and his statutes, which I command thee this day for thy good?

14. **Behold,** the heaven and **the heaven of heavens is the LORD's** thy God, **the earth also,** with all that therein *is.*

15. **Only the LORD had a delight in thy fathers** to love them,

and he chose their seed after them, *even* you **above all people,** as *it is* this day.

16. **Circumcise** therefore the foreskin of **your heart, and be no more stiffnecked.**

17. **For the LORD** your God **is God of gods, and Lord of lords, a great God, a mighty, and** a **terrible, which regardeth not persons, nor taketh reward:**

18. **He doth execute the judgment of the fatherless and widow, and loveth the stranger,** in giving him food and raiment.

19. **Love** ye therefore **the stranger: for ye were strangers in** the land of **Egypt.**

20. **Thou shalt fear the LORD** thy God; him shalt thou serve, and to him shalt thou cleave, and swear by his name.

21. **He is thy praise,** and he *is* thy God, that hath done for thee these great and terrible things, which thine eyes have seen.

22. Thy fathers went down into Egypt with threescore and ten persons; **and now** the LORD thy **God hath made thee as the stars of heaven** for multitude.

CHAPTER 11

1. Therefore thou shalt love theLORD thy God, and keep his charge, and his statutes, and his judgments, and his commandments, alway.

2. **And know ye this day:** for *I speak* not with your children which have not known, and which have not seenthe chastisement of the LORD your God, **his greatness,** his mighty hand, **and his stretched out arm,**

3. **And his miracles, and** his **acts,** which he did in the midst

of Egypt unto Pharaoh the king
of Egypt, and unto all his land;
4. And what he did unto the army of
Egypt, unto their horses, and to their
chariots; how he made the water of
the Red sea to overflow them as
they pursued after you, and
how the LORD hath destroyed
them unto this day;
5. And what he did unto
you in the wilderness, until
ye came into this place;
6. And what he did unto Dathan and
Abiram, the sons of Eliab, the son of
Reuben: how the earth opened her
mouth, and swallowed them up, and
their households, and their tents, and
all the substance that *was* in their
possession, in the midst of all Israel:
■ 7. **But your eyes have**
■ **seen all the great acts**
■ **of the LORD** which he did.
■ 8. **Therefore** shall ye
■ **keep** all
■ **the commandments** which I
command you this day, that ye may
be strong, and go in and possess the
land, whither ye go to possess it;
9. And that ye may prolong *your* days
in the land, which the LORD sware
unto your fathers to give unto them
and to their seed, a land that
floweth with milk and honey.
■ 10. **For the land, whither**
■ **thou goest** in to possess it,
■ **is not as** the land of
■ **Egypt,** from whence ye came out,
where thou sowedst thy seed, and
wateredst *it* with thy foot, as
■ **a garden of herbs:**
■ 11. **But the land, whither**
■ **ye go** to possess it,
■ **is a land of hills and**
■ **valleys, and drinketh water**
■ **of the rain of heaven:**
■ 12. **A land which**
■ **the LORD** thy God
■ **careth for:** the eyes of the
LORD thy God *are* always upon it,
from the beginning of the year
even unto the end of the year.
13. And it shall come to pass,
■ **if ye shall hearken** diligently

■ **unto my commandments**
which I command you this day,
to love the LORD your God,
and to serve him with all your
heart and with all your soul,
14. That
■ **I will give you** the
■ **rain** of your land
■ **in** his
■ **due season,**
the first rain and the latter rain,
■ **that thou mayest**
■ **gather in thy corn,**
and thy wine, and thine oil.
15. And I will send grass in thy
fields for thy cattle, that thou
mayest eat and be full.
■ 16. **Take heed** to yourselves,
■ **that your heart be not**
■ **deceived, and ye turn**
■ **aside, and serve other**
■ **gods,** and worship them;
■ 17. **And** *then*
■ **the LORD's wrath**
■ **be kindled** against you,
■ **and he shut up the heaven,**
■ **that there be no rain,**
and that the land yield not her fruit;
■ **and** *lest*
■ **ye perish** quickly from off the good
land which the LORD giveth you.
■ 18. **Therefore shall ye lay**
■ **up these my words in**
■ **your heart** and in your soul,
and bind them for a sign upon
your hand, that they may be
as frontlets between your eyes.
■ 19. **And ye shall teach**
■ **them your children,** speaking
of them when thou sittest in thine
house, and when thou walkest
by the way, when thou liest
down, and when thou risest up.
20. And thou shalt write them
upon the door posts of thine
house, and upon thy gates:
21. That your days may be multiplied,
and the days of your children,
in the land which the LORD sware
unto your fathers to give them,
as the days of heaven upon the earth.
■ 22. **For if ye shall diligently**
■ **keep all these**

commandments which I command you, to do them, to love the LORD your God, to walk in all his ways, and to cleave unto him;

23. Then will the LORD drive out all these nations from before you, and ye shall possess greater nations and mightier than yourselves.

24. **Every place whereon the soles of your feet shall tread shall be yours:** from the wilderness and Lebanon, from the river, the river Euphrates, even unto the uttermost sea shall your coastbe.

25. **There shall no man be able to stand before you:** *for* the LORD your God shall lay the fear of you and the dread of you upon all the land that ye shall tread upon, as he hath said unto you.

26. **Behold, I set before you this day a blessing and a curse;**

27. **A blessing, if ye obey** the commandments of the LORD your God, which I command you this day:

28. **And a curse, if ye will not obey** the commandments of the LORD your God, but turn aside out of the way which I command you this day, to go after other gods, which ye have not known.

29. And it shall come to pass, when the LORD thy God hath brought thee in unto the land whither thou goest to possess it, that thou shalt put the blessing upon mount Gerizim, and the curse upon mount Ebal.

30. *Are* they not on the other side Jordan, by the way where the sun goeth down, in the land of the Canaanites, which dwell in the champaign over against Gilgal, beside the plains of Moreh?

31. For ye shall pass over Jordan to go in to possess the land which the LORD your God giveth you, and ye shall possess it, and dwell therein.

32. And ye shall observe to do all the statutes and judgments which I set before you this day.

CHAPTER 12

1. **These are the statutes** and judgments, which **ye shall observe** to do in the land, whichthe LORD God of thy fathers giveth thee to possess it, all the days that ye live upon the earth.

2. **Ye shall** utterly **destroy all the places, wherein the nations** which ye shall possess **served their gods,** upon the high mountains, and upon the hills, and under every green tree:

3. **And ye shall** overthrow their altars, and break their pillars, and **burn their** groves with fire; and ye shall hew down the **graven images** of their gods, and destroy the names of them out of that place.

4. **Ye shall not do so unto the LORD** your God.

5. **But unto the place which** the LORD your **God shall choose out of all your tribes to put his name there,** *even* unto his habitation shall ye seek, **and thither thou shalt come:**

6. **And** thither ye shall **bring your burnt offerings,** and your **sacrifices,** and your **tithes,** and **heave offerings** of your hand, and your **vows,** and your **freewill offerings, and the firstlings of your herds and** of your **flocks:**

7. And there ye shall eat before the LORD your God, and ye shall rejoice in all that ye put your hand unto, ye and your households, wherein the LORD thy God hath blessed thee.

8. **Ye shall not do after all the things that we do here this day, every man whatsoever is right in his own eyes.**

9. **For ye are not as yet come to the rest** and to the inheritance, which the LORD your **God giveth you.**
10. **But when ye go over Jordan,** and dwell in the land which the LORD your God giveth you to inherit, and *when* he giveth you rest from all your enemies round about, so that ye dwell in safety;
11. **Then there shall be a place which** the LORD your **God shall choose to cause his name to dwell there;** thither shall ye bring all that I command you; your burnt offerings, and your sacrifices, your tithes, and the heave offering of your hand, and all your choice vows which ye vow unto the LORD:
12. **And ye shall rejoice before the LORD** your God, ye, and your sons, and your daughters, and your menservants, and your maidservants, and the Levite that *is* within your gates; forasmuch as he hath no part nor inheritance with you.
13. **Take heed to thyself that thou offer not thy burnt offerings in every place that thou seest:**
14. But in the place which the LORD shall choose in one of thy tribes, there thou shalt offer thy burnt offerings, and there thou shalt do all that I command thee.
15. **Notwithstanding thou mayest kill and eat flesh in all thy gates,** whatsoever thy soul lusteth after, according to the blessing of the LORD thy God which he hath given thee: the unclean and the clean may eat thereof, as of the roebuck, and as of the hart.
16. **Only ye shall not eat the blood;** ye shall pour it upon the earth as water.
17. **Thou mayest not eat within thy gates the tithe of thy corn, or** of thy **wine, or** of thy **oil, or the firstlings of thy herds or** of thy **flock, nor any** of thy **vows** which thou vowest, **nor** thy freewill offerings, or heave **offering** of thine hand:
18. **But thou must eat them before the LORD** thy God **in the place** which the LORD thy **God shall choose,** thou, and thy son, and thy daughter, and thy manservant, and thy maidservant, and the Levite that *is* within thy gates: and thou shalt rejoice before the LORD thy God in all that thou puttest thine hands unto.
19. Take heed to thyself that thou **forsake not the Levite** as long as thou livest upon the earth.
20. When the LORD thy God shall enlarge thy border, as he hath promised thee, and thou shalt say, I will eat flesh, because thy soul longeth to eat flesh; thou mayest eat flesh, whatsoever thy soul lusteth after.
21. **If the place which the LORD** thy God **hath chosen to put his name** there **be too far from thee, then thou shalt kill of thy herd** and of thy flock, which the LORD hath given thee, as I have commanded thee, **and** thou shalt **eat** in thy gates **whatsoever thy soul lusteth after.**
22. Even as the roebuck and the hart is eaten, so thou shalt eat them: the unclean and the clean shall eat *of* them alike.
23. **Only** be sure that thou **eat not the blood:** for the blood *is* the life; and thou mayest not eat the life with the flesh.
24. Thou shalt not eat it; thou shalt pour it upon the earth as water.
25. Thou shalt not eat it; that it may go well with thee, and with thy children after thee, when thou shalt do *that which is* right in the sight of the LORD.
26. **Only thy holy things** which thou hast, and thy vows, thou shalt

take, and go
unto the place which
the LORD shall choose:
27. **And** thou shalt
offer thy burnt offerings,
the flesh and the blood,
upon the altar of the
LORD thy God: and the
blood of thy sacrifices
shall be poured out upon the
altar of the LORD thy God,
and thou shalt eat the flesh.
28. **Observe and** hear all these
words which I command thee, that it
may go well with thee, and with thy
children after thee for ever, when thou
doest that which is
good and right in the
sight of the LORD thy God.
29. When the LORD thy God
shall cut off the nations from
before thee, whither thou goest to
possess them, and thou succeedest
them, and dwellest in their land;
30. Take heed to thyself that thou be
not snared by following them, after
that they be destroyed from before
thee; and that thou enquire not
after their gods, saying, How did
these nations serve their gods?
even so will I do likewise.
31. Thou shalt not do so unto the
LORD thy God: for every abomination
to the LORD, which he hateth, have
they done unto their gods; for even
their sons and their daughters they
have burnt in the fire to their gods.
32. **What thing soever**
I command you,
observe to do it: thou
shalt not add thereto,
nor diminish from it.

CHAPTER 13

1. **If** there arise among you
a prophet, or a
dreamer of dreams, and
giveth thee a sign or a wonder,
2. **And the sign** or the wonder
come to pass, whereof
he spake unto thee,
saying, Let us go after
other gods, which thou hast not

known, and let us serve them;
3. **Thou shalt not hearken**
unto the words of that prophet, or
that dreamer of dreams:
for the LORD your God
proveth you, to know
whether ye love the
LORD your God with all your
heart and with all your soul.
4. Ye shall walk after the LORD your
God, and fear him, and keep his
commandments, and obey his
voice, and ye shall serve him,
and cleave unto him.
5. **And that prophet,**
or that dreamer of dreams,
shall be put to death;
because he hath spoken to turn
you away from the LORD your God,
which brought you out of the land
of Egypt, and redeemed you out
of the house of bondage, to thrust
thee out of the way which the
LORD thy God commanded
thee to walk in. So shalt thou put
the evil away from the midst of thee.
6. **If thy brother,**
the son of thy mother, or
thy son, or thy
daughter, or the wife
of thy bosom, or thy friend,
which *is* as thine own soul,
entice thee secretly,
saying, Let us go and
serve other gods, which thou
hast not known, thou, nor thy fathers;
7. *Namely,* of the gods of the people
which *are* round about you, nigh unto
thee, or far off from thee, from the
one end of the earth even unto
the *other* end of the earth;
8. **Thou shalt not consent**
unto him, nor hearken unto him;
neither shall thine eye
pity him, neither shalt thou spare,
neither shalt thou
conceal him:
9. **But thou shalt surely kill**
him; thine hand shall be first
upon him to put him
to death, and afterwards the
hand of all the people.
10. **And thou shalt stone**

■ **him** with stones, that he die;
because he hath sought to thrust
thee away from the LORD thy God,
which brought thee out of the land of
Egypt, from the house of bondage.

■ 11. **And all Israel**
■ **shall** hear, and
■ **fear, and** shall
■ **do no more** any such
■ **wickedness** as
this is among you.

■ 12. **If thou shalt hear** *say*
■ **in one of thy cities,** which
the LORD thy God hath given
thee to dwell there, saying,

■ 13. **Certain men,**
the children of Belial,
■ **are gone out from among**
■ **you, and have withdrawn**
■ **the inhabitants of their**
■ **city, saying, Let us** go and
■ **serve other gods,** which
ye have not known;

■ 14. **Then shalt thou**
■ **inquire,** and make search,
and ask diligently; and, behold,
■ **if it be truth,** *and* the thing
certain, *that* such abomination
is wrought among you;

■ 15. **Thou shalt** surely
■ **smite the inhabitants**
■ **of that city** with the edge of the
sword, destroying it utterly, and all
that is therein, and the cattle there
of, with the edge of the sword.

■ 16. **And** thou shalt
■ **gather** all
■ **the spoil** of it into the
midst of the street thereof,
■ **and** shalt
■ **burn** with fire
■ **the city, and all the**
■ **spoil** thereof every whit, for the
LORDthy God:and it shall be an heap
for ever; t shall not be built again.

■ 17. **And there shall cleave**
■ **nought of the cursed thing**
■ **to thine hand:** that the LORD
may turn from the fierceness of his
anger, and shew thee mercy,
and have compassion upon thee,
and multiply thee, as he hath
sworn unto thy fathers;

18. When thou shalt hearken to the
voice of the LORD thy God, to keepall
his commandments which I command
thee this day, to do *that which is* right
in the eyes of the LORD thy God.

CHAPTER 14

■ 1. **Ye are the children**
■ **of** the LORD your
■ **God: ye shall not cut**
■ **yourselves, nor make**
■ **any baldness between**
■ **your eyes for the dead.**
■ 2. **For thou art an holy**
■ **people** unto the LORD thy God,
and the LORD hath chosen thee
to\be a peculiar people unto
himself, above all the nations
that *are* upon the earth.
3. Thou shalt not eat
any abominable thing.
4. These *are* the beasts which
■ **ye shall eat: the ox,** the
■ **sheep, and** the
■ **goat,**
5. The hart, and the roebuck,
and the fallow deer, and the wild
goat, and the pygarg, and the
wild ox, and the chamois.
■ 6. **And every beast**
■ **that parteth the hoof,**
and cleaveth the cleft
into two claws,
■ **and cheweth the**
■ **cud** among the beasts,
■ **that ye shall eat.**
7. Nevertheless these
■ **ye shall not eat of them that**
■ **chew the cud, or** of them that
■ **divide the cloven hoof;**
■ **as the camel,** and the
■ **hare, and the coney:** for they
chew the cud, but divide not the hoof;
therefore they *are* unclean unto you.
■ 8. **And the swine,**
■ **because it divideth the**
■ **hoof, yet cheweth not**
■ **the cud,** it *is* unclean unto you:
■ **ye shall not eat** of their flesh,
■ **nor touch their**
■ **dead carcase.**
9. These ye shall eat of all that *are*
■ **in the waters: all that**

have fins and scales shall ye eat:

10. **And whatsoever hath not fins and scales ye may not eat;** it *is* unclean unto you.

11. Of all clean birds ye shall eat.

12. But these *are they* of which **ye shall not eat: the eagle,** and the **ossifrage,** and the **ospray,**

13. And the **glede,** and the **kite,** and the **vulture** after his kind,

14. And every **raven** after his kind,

15. And the **owl,** and the **night hawk,** and the **cuckow,** and the **hawk** after his kind,

16. The little owl, and the great **owl,** and the **swan,**

17. And the **pelican,** and the **gier eagle,** and the **cormorant,**

18. And the **stork,** and the **heron** after her kind, and the **lapwing, and** the **bat.**

19. **And every creeping thing that flieth is unclean** unto you: they shall not be eaten.

20. **But of all clean fowls ye may eat.**

21. **Ye shall not eat of anything that dieth of itself: thou shalt give it unto the stranger** that *is* in thy gates, that he may eat it; **or** thou mayest **sell it unto an alien:** for thou *art* an holy people unto the LORD thy God. **Thou shalt not seethe a kid in his mother's milk.**

22. **Thou shalt** truly **tithe all** the increase of **thy seed,** that the field bringeth forth year by year.

23. And thou shalt eat before the LORD thy God, in the place which he shall choose to place his name there, the tithe of thy **corn,** of thy wine, and of thine **oil,** and the firstlings of thy **herds and** of thy **flocks; that thou mayest learn to fear the LORD** thy God **always.**

24. **And if the way be too long** for thee, so **that thou art not able to carry it;** or if the place be too far from thee, which the LORD thy God shall choose to set his name there, when the LORD thy God hath blessed thee:

25. Then shalt thou **turn it into money,** and bind up the money in thine hand, and shalt go unto the place which the LORD thy God shall choose:

26. **And** thou shalt **bestow that money for** whatsoever thy soul lusteth after, for oxen, or for sheep, or for wine, or for strong drink, or for **whatsoever thy soul desireth: and** thou shalt **eat there before the LORD** thy God, and thou shalt rejoice, thou, and thine household,

27. **And the Levite** that *is* within thy gates; **thou shalt not forsake** him; **for he hath no** part nor **inheritance** with thee.

28. **At the end of three years** thou shalt **bring forth all the tithe** of thine increase the same year, **and** shalt **lay it up** within thy gates:

29. **And the Levite,** (because he hath no part nor inheritance with thee,) **and the stranger, and the fatherless, and the widow,** which *are* within thy gates, shall come, and

■ **shall eat** and be satisfied; that the LORD thy God may bless thee in all the work of thine hand which thou doest.

CHAPTER 15

■ 1. **At the end of**
■ **every seven years**
■ **thou shalt** make a
■ **release.**
2. And this *is* the manner of the release:
■ **Every creditor** that lendeth *aught* unto his neighbour shall release *it;* he shall not exact *it* of his neighbour, or of his brother; because it is called the LORD's release.
■ 3. **Of a foreigner thou**
■ **mayest exact it again:**
■ **but that which is thine with**
■ **thy brother** thine hand shall
■ **release;**
■ 4. **Save when there shall be**
■ **no poor among you;** for the LORD shall greatly bless thee in the land which the LORD thy God giveth thee *for* an inheritance to possess it:
5. Only if thou carefully hearken unto the voice of the LORD thy God, to observe to
■ **do all these**
■ **commandments**
which I command thee this day.
■ 6. **For the LORD** thy God
■ **blesseth thee,**
as he promised thee:
■ **and thou shalt lend unto**
■ **many nations, but thou**
■ **shalt not borrow; and thou**
■ **shalt reign over many**
■ **nations, but they shall**
■ **not reign over thee.**
■ 7. **If there be among you a**
■ **poor man** of one of thy brethren within any of thy gates in thy land which the LORD thy God giveth thee,
■ **thou shalt not harden**
■ **thine heart,** nor shut thine hand from thy poor brother:
■ 8. **But** thou
■ **shalt open thine**
■ **hand** wide unto him,
■ **and** shalt surely

■ **lend him sufficient for his**
■ **need,** *in that* which he wanteth.
■ 9. **Beware that there be**
■ **not a thought in thy**
■ **wicked heart, saying,**
■ **The seventh year, the year**
■ **of release, is at hand;**
■ **and** thine eye be evil against
■ **thy poor brother,** and
■ **thou givest him nought;**
■ **and he cry unto the**
■ **LORD** against thee,
■ **and it be sin unto thee.**
10. Thou shalt surely give him, and thine heart shall not be grieved when thou givest unto him: because that for this thing the LORD thy God shall bless thee in all thy works, and in all that thou puttest thine hand unto.
■ 11. **For the poor shall never**
■ **cease out of the land:**
therefore I command thee, saying, Thou shalt open thine hand wide unto thy brother, to thy poor, and to thy needy, in thy land.
■ 12. **And if** thy brother,
■ **an Hebrew** man, or an Hebrew woman,
■ **be sold unto thee,**
■ **and serve** thee
■ **six years;** then in
■ **the seventh year** thou shalt
■ **let him go free** from thee.
■ 13. **And** when thou sendest him out free from thee,
■ **thou shalt not let**
■ **him go** away
■ **empty:**
14. Thou shalt furnish him liberally out of thy flock, and out of thy floor, and out of thy winepress: *of that* wherewith the LORD thy God hath blessed thee thou shalt give untohim.
15. And thou shalt remember that thou wast a bondman in the land of Egypt, and the LORD thy God redeemed thee: therefore I command thee this thing to day.
■ 16. **And** it shall be,
■ **if he** say unto thee, I
■ **will not go away** from thee;
■ **because he loveth thee**
and thine house, because he

is well with thee;

17. **Then** thou shalt **take an aul, and thrust it through his ear** unto the door, **and he shall be thy servant for ever.** And also unto thy maidservant thou shalt do likewise. 18. It shall not seem hard unto thee, when thou sendesthim away freefrom thee; for he hath been worth a double hired servant *to thee,* in serving thee six years: and the LORD thy God shall bless thee in all that thou doest.

19. **All the firstling males** that come **of thy herd** and of thy flock thou shalt **sanctify unto the LORD** thy God: thou shalt do no work with the firstling of thy bullock, nor shear the firstling of thy sheep.

20. **Thou shalt eat it before the LORD** thy God year by year in the place which the LORD shall choose, thou and thy household.

21. **And if there be any blemish therein,** *as if it be* lame, or blind, *or have* any ill blemish, **thou shalt not sacrifice it unto the LORD** thy God. 22. Thou shalt eat it within thy gates: the unclean and the clean *person shall eat it* alike, as the roebuck, and as the hart. 23. Only thou shalt not eat the blood thereof; thou shalt pour it upon the ground as water.

CHAPTER 16

1. **Observe the month of Abib, and keep the passover** unto the LORD thy God: for in the month of Abib the LORD thy God brought thee forth out of Egypt by night. 2. Thou shalt therefore sacrifice the passover unto the LORD thy God, of the flock and the herd, in the place which the LORD shall choose to place his name there.

3. **Thou shalt eat no leavened bread** with it; **seven days shalt thou eat** **unleavened bread** therewith, **even the bread of affliction; for thou camest forth out of** the land of **Egypt in haste:** that thou mayest remember the day when thou camest forth out of the land of Egypt all the days of thy life.

4. And there shall be no leavened bread seen with thee in all thy coast seven days; **neither shall** there **any** *thing* of the **flesh, which thou sacrificedst** the first day at even, **remain all night** until the morning.

5. **Thou mayest not sacrifice the passover within any of thy gates,** which the LORD thy God giveth thee:

6. **But at the place** which the LORD thy **God shall choose** to place his name in, there thou shalt sacrifice the passover at even, at the going down of the sun, at the season that thou camest forth out of Egypt.

7. And thou shalt roast and eat *it* in the place which the LORD thy God shall choose: and thou shalt turn in the morning, and go unto thy tents.

8. Six days thou shalt eat unleavened bread: and **on the seventh day shall be a solemn assembly** to the LORD thy God: **thou shalt do no work** *therein.*

9. Seven weeks shalt thou number unto thee: begin to **number** the **seven weeks from such time as thou beginnest to** *put* the **sickle** to **the corn.**

10. **And** thou shalt **keep the feast of weeks** unto the LORD thy God **with a** tribute of a **freewill offering** of thine hand, which thou shalt give *unto the LORD*

thy God, according as the LORD thy God hath blessed thee:

11. **And** thou shalt **rejoice before the LORD** thy God, thou, and thy son, and thy daughter, and thy manservant, and thy maidservant, and the Levite that *is* within thy gates, and the stranger, and the fatherless, and the widow, that *are* among you, in the place which the LORD thy God hath chosen to place his name there.

12. And thou shalt remember that thou wast a bondman in Egypt: and thou shalt observe and do these statutes.

13. **Thou shalt observe the feast of tabernacles seven days, after** that **thou hast gathered** in thy **corn and** thy **wine:**

14. And thou shalt rejoice in thy feast, thou, and thy son, and thy daughter, and thy manservant, and thy maidservant, and the Levite, the stranger, and the fatherless, and the widow, that *are* within thy gates.

15. **Seven days shalt thou keep a solemn feast** unto the LORD thy God **in the place which the LORD shall choose:** because the LORD thy God shall bless thee in all thine increase, and in all the works of thine hands, therefore thou shalt surely rejoice.

16. **Three times** in **a year shall all** thy **males appear before the LORD** thy God **in the place which he shall choose; in the feast of unleavened bread, and in the feast of weeks, and in the feast of tabernacles: and they shall not appear** before the LORD **empty:**

17. Every man *shall give* as he is able, according to the blessing of the LORD thy God which he hath given thee.

18. **Judges and officers shalt thou make** thee **in all thy gates,** which the LORD thy God giveth thee, throughout thy tribes: **and they shall judge the people with just judgment.**

19. **Thou shalt not wrest judgment; thou shalt not respect persons, neither take a gift:** for a gift doth blind the eyes of the wise, and pervert the words of the righteous.

20. That which is altogether just shalt thou follow, that thou mayest live, and inherit the land which the LORD thy God giveth thee.

21. **Thou shalt not plant thee a grove** of any trees **near** unto **the altar of** the LORD thy **God,** which thou shalt make thee.

22. **Neither** shalt thou **set** thee **up any image;** which the LORD thy God hateth.

CHAPTER 17

1. **Thou shalt not sacrifice** unto the LORD thy God **any bullock, or sheep, wherein is blemish,** *or* any evilfavouredness: for that *is* an abomination unto the LORD thy God.

2. **If there be** found among you, within any of thy gates which the LORD thy God giveth thee, **man or woman, that hath** wrought wickedness in the sight of the LORD thy God, in transgressing his covenant,

3. And hath gone and **served other gods, and worshipped them,** either the sun, or moon, or any of the host of heaven, which I have not commanded;

4. And it be told thee, and thou hast heard *of it,* and inquired diligently, and, behold, *it be* true, *and* the thing certain, that such abomination is wrought in Israel:

5. **Then shalt thou** bring forth

that man or that woman, which have committed that wicked thing, unto thy gates, *even* that man or that woman, and shalt **stone them** with stones, **till they die.** 6. **At the mouth of two** witnesses, **or three witnesses, shall he** that is worthy of death **be put to death;** *but* at the mouth of one witness he shall not be put to death. 7. The hands of the witnesses shall be first upon him to put him to death, and afterward the hands of all the people. So thou shalt put the evil away from among you. 8. **If there arise a matter too hard for thee in judgment,** between blood and blood, between plea and plea, and between stroke and stroke, *being* matters of controversy within thy gates: **then** shalt thou arise, and **get** thee up **into the place which the LORD** thy God **shall choose;** 9. **And** thou shalt **come unto the priests** the Levites, **and** unto **the judge** that shall be in those days, and inquire; **and they shall shew thee the sentence** of judgment: 10. **And thou shalt do according to the sentence,** which they of that place which the LORD shall choose shall shew thee; and thou shalt observe to do according to all that they inform thee: 11. According to the sentence of the law which they shall teach thee, and according to the judgment which they shall tell thee, thou shalt do: **thou shalt not decline from the sentence** which they shall shew thee, *to the* right hand, nor *to* the left. 12. **And the man that will do presumptuously, and will**

not hearken unto the priest that standeth to minister there before the LORD thy God, or unto the judge, even that man **shall die:** and thou shalt put away the evil from Israel. 13. And all the people shall hear, and fear, and do no more presumptuously. 14. **When thou art come unto the land** which the LORD thy God giveth thee, and shalt possess it, and shalt dwell therein, **and shalt say, I will set a king over me, like as all the nations** that *are* about me; 15. **Thou shalt** in any wise **set him king over thee, whom** the LORD thy **God shall choose:** *one* **from among thy brethren** shalt thou set king over thee: **thou mayest not set a stranger over thee,** which *is* not thy brother. 16. **But he shall not multiply horses to himself, nor cause** the **people to return to Egypt,** to the end that he should multiply horses: forasmuch as the LORD hath said unto you, Ye shall henceforth return no more that way. 17. **Neither shall he multiply wives to himself,** that his heart turn not away: **neither** shall he greatly multiply to himself **silver and gold.** 18. And it shall be, **when he sitteth upon the throne** of his kingdom, that **he shall write him a copy of this law in a book** out of that which is before the priests the Levites: 19. And it shall be with him, and he shall read therein all the days of his life: that he may learn to fear the LORD his God, to keep all the words of this law and these statutes, to do them: 20. **That his heart be not lifted up above his**

297

■ **brethren,** and that he turn not aside from the commandment, *to* the right hand, or *to* the left: to the end that he may prolong *his* days in his kingdom, he, and his children, in the midst of Israel.

CHAPTER 18

1. The priests the Levites, *and* ■ **all the tribe of Levi,** ■ **shall have no** part nor ■ **inheritance with Israel:** they shall eat the offerings of the LORD made by fire, and his inheritance.
2. Therefore shall they have no inheritance among their brethren: the LORD *is* their inheritance, as he hath said unto them.
3. ■ **And this shall be the** ■ **priest's due from the** ■ **people,** from them that offer a sacrifice, whether *it be* ox or sheep; and ■ **they shall give unto the** ■ **priest the shoulder,** and ■ **the two cheeks,** ■ **and the maw.**
4. ■ **The firstfruit** *also* ■ **of thy corn,** of thy ■ **wine,** and of thine ■ **oil, and** the first of ■ **the fleece of thy sheep,** shalt thou give him.
5. ■ **For** the LORD thy ■ **God hath chosen him** out of all thy tribes, ■ **to stand to minister in** ■ **the name of the LORD,** him and his sons for ever.
6. ■ **And if a Levite come** from any of thy gates out of all Israel, where he sojourned, and come ■ **with** all the ■ **desire** of his mind ■ **unto the place which** ■ **the LORD** shall ■ **choose;**
7. Then he shall minister in the name of the LORD his God, ■ **as all** his brethren ■ **the Levites** *do,* ■ **which stand** there ■ **before the LORD.**

8. ■ **They shall have** ■ **like portions** to eat, ■ **beside that which** ■ **cometh of the sale** ■ **of his patrimony.**
9. ■ **When thou art come** ■ **into the land** which the LORD thy God giveth thee, thou shalt not learn to do after the abominations of those nations.
10. ■ **There shall not be found** ■ **among you any one that** ■ **maketh his son or** his ■ **daughter to pass through** ■ **the fire, or that useth** ■ **divination, or an** ■ **observer of times,** or an ■ **enchanter, or a witch.**
11. ■ **Or a charmer,** or ■ **a consulter with** ■ **familiar spirits, or** a ■ **wizard, or a necromancer.**
12. ■ **For** all that do ■ **these** things ■ **are an abomination unto** ■ **the LORD:** and because of these abominations the LORD thy God doth drive them out from before thee.
13. Thou shalt be perfect with the LORD thy God.
14. For these nations, which thou shalt possess, hearkened unto observers of times, and unto diviners: but as for thee, the LORD thy God hath not suffered thee so *to do.*
15. ■ **The LORD** thy God ■ **will raise up unto thee** ■ **a Prophet from the** ■ **midst of thee,** of thy brethren, ■ **like unto me; unto him** ■ **ye shall hearken;**
16. ■ **According to all that** ■ **thou desiredst of** the LORD thy ■ **God in Horeb** in the day of the assembly, ■ **saying, Let me not** ■ **hear again the voice** ■ **of the LORD** my God, ■ **neither let me see** ■ **this great fire** any more, ■ **that I die not.**
17. ■ **And the LORD said** ■ **unto me,** They have well *spoken*

that which they have spoken.
18. **I will raise** them **up a Prophet** from among their brethren, **like** unto **thee, and will put my words in his mouth;** and he shall speak unto them all that I shall command him.
19. And it shall come to pass, *that* **whosoever will not hearken unto my words which he shall speak in my name, I will require it of him.**
20. **But the prophet, which shall presume to speak** a word **in my name, which I have not commanded** him to speak, **or** that **shall speak in the name of other gods,** even **that prophet shall die.**
21. **And if thou say** in thine heart, **How shall we know the word which the LORD hath not spoken?**
22. **When a prophet speaketh in the name of the LORD, if the thing follow not,** nor come to pass, that *is* the thing which **the LORD hath not spoken, but the prophet hath spoken** it **presumptuously:** thou shalt not be afraid of him.

CHAPTER 19

1. **When** the LORD thy **God hath cut off the nations,** whose land the LORD thy God giveth thee, and thou succeedest them, and dwellest in their cities, and in their houses;
2. **Thou shalt separate three cities** for thee in the midst of thy land, which the LORD thy God giveth thee to possess it.
3. **Thou shalt prepare thee a way, and divide the coasts of thy land,** which the LORD thy God giveth thee to inherit, **into three parts, that every slayer may flee thither.**
4. And this *is* the case of the slayer, which shall flee thither, that he may live: **Whoso killeth his neighbour ignorantly,** whom he hated not in time past;
5. As when a man goeth into the wood with his neighbour to hew wood, and his hand fetcheth a stroke with the axe to cut down the tree, and the head slippeth from the helve, and lighteth upon his neighbour, that he die; **he shall flee unto one of those cities,** and live:
6. **Lest the avenger** of the blood **pursue the slayer,** while his heart is hot, and overtake him, because the way is long, **and slay him; whereas he was not worthy of death,** inasmuch as he hated him not in time past.
7. Wherefore I command thee, saying, Thou shalt separate three cities for thee.
8. **And if the LORD thy God enlarge thy coast,** as he hath sworn unto thy fathers, and give thee all the land which he promised to give unto thy fathers;
9. **If thou shalt keep all these commandments** to do them, which I command thee this day, to love the LORD thy God, and to walk ever in his ways; **then shalt thou add three cities more for thee, beside these three:**
10. That innocent blood be not shed in thy land, which the LORD thy God giveth thee *for* an inheritance, and *so* blood be upon thee.
11. **But if any man hate his neighbour,** and lie in wait for him, and rise up against him, **and smite him mortally** that he die, **and fleeth into one**

299

of these cities:

12. **Then the elders** of his city **shall** send and fetch him thence, and **deliver him into the hand of the avenger** of blood, **that he may die.**

13. Thine eye shall not pity him, but thou shalt put away *the guilt of* innocent blood from Israel, that it may go well with thee.

14. **Thou shalt not remove thy neighbour's landmark,** which they of old time have set in thine inheritance, which thou shalt inherit in the land that the LORD thy God giveth thee to possess it.

15. **One witness shall not rise up against a man** for any iniquity, or **for any sin,** in any sin that he sinneth: **at the mouth of two** witnesses, **or** at the mouth of **three witnesses, shall the matter be established.**

16. **If a false witness rise up against any man** to testify against him *that which is* wrong;

17. **Then both** the **men,** between whom the controversy is, **shall stand before the LORD, before the priests and the judges,** which shall be in those days;

18. **And the judges shall make** diligent **inquisition: and,** behold, **if the witness be a false witness,** *and* hath testified falsely against his brother;

19. **Then shall ye do unto him, as he had thought to have done unto his brother:** so shalt thou put the evil away from among you.

20. And those which remain shall hear, and fear, and shall henceforth commit no more any such evil among you.

21. **And thine eye** shall not pity; **but life shall go for life, eye for eye, tooth for tooth, hand for hand, foot for foot.**

CHAPTER 20

1. When thou goest out to battle against thine enemies, and seest horses, and chariots, *and* a people more than thou, be not afraid of them: for the LORD thy God *is* with thee, which brought thee up out of the land of Egypt.

2. And it shall be, **when ye are come nigh unto the battle,** that **the priest shall** approach and **speak unto the people,**

3. And shall say unto them, Hear, O Israel, ye approach this day unto battle against your enemies: **let not your hearts faint,** fear not, and do not tremble, neither be ye terrified because of them;

4. **For** the LORD your **God** *is* he that **goeth with you,** to fight for you against your enemies, to save you.

5. **And the officers shall speak unto the people, saying, What man** *is there* that **hath built a new house, and hath not dedicated it? let him** go and **return to his house,** lest he die in the battle, and another man dedicate it.

6. **And what man** *is he* that **hath planted a vineyard, and hath not** yet **eaten of it? let him also** go and **return** unto his house, lest he die in the battle, and another man eat of it.

7. **And what man is there that hath betrothed a wife, and hath not taken her? let him** go and **return** unto his house, **lest he die in the battle,**

and another man take her.

8. **And the officers** shall speak further unto the people, and they **shall say, What man** *is there that* **is fearful and fainthearted?** **let him** go and **return unto his house,** lest his brethren's heart faint as well as his heart.

9. **And** it shall be, **when the officers have made an end of speaking** unto the people that **they shall make captains of the armies** to lead the people.

10. **When thou comest** nigh **unto a city to fight against it, then proclaim peace** unto it.

11. And it shall be, **if it make thee answer of peace,** and open unto thee, then it shall be, *that* **all the people** *that is* found **therein shall be tributaries unto thee,** and they shall serve thee.

12. **And if it will make no peace** with thee, but will make war against thee, **then** thou shalt **besiege it:**

13. **And when the LORD** thy God **hath delivered it into thine hands, thou shalt smite every male** thereof with the edge of the sword:

14. **But the women,** and **the little ones,** and **the cattle, and** all that is in the city, *even all* **the spoil** thereof, **shalt thou take** unto thyself; and thou shalt eat the spoil of thine enemies, which the LORD thy God hath given thee.

15. **Thus shalt thou do unto** all the **cities** *which are* very **far off** from thee, which *are* not of the cities of these nations.

16. **But of the cities** of these people, **which** the LORD thy **God doth give thee for an inheritance, thou shalt save alive nothing that breatheth:**

17. **But thou shalt utterly destroy them;** *namely,* the Hittites, and the Amorites, the Canaanites, and the Perizzites, the Hivites, and the Jebusites; as the LORD thy God hath commanded thee:

18. **That they teach you not to do after all their abominations,** which they have done unto their gods; so should ye sin against the LORD your God.

19. **When thou shalt besiege a city a long time,** in making war against it to take it, **thou shalt not destroy the trees** thereof by forcing an axe against them: **for thou mayest eat of them,** and thou shalt not cut them down (for the tree of the field *is* man's *life*) to employ *them* in the siege:

20. **Only** the **trees which** thou knowest that they **be not trees for meat, thou shalt destroy** and cut them down; and thou shalt build bulwarks against the city that maketh war with thee, until it be subdued.

CHAPTER 21

1. **If one be found slain in** the land which the LORD thy God giveth thee to possess it, lying **in the field, and it be not known who hath slain him:**

2. **Then thy elders and thy judges** shall come forth, and they **shall measure unto the cities which are round about him** that is slain:

3. **And** it shall be, *that* **the city** *which is* **next unto the slain man,**

even the elders of that
city shall take an heifer,
which hath not been wrought with,
and which hath not drawn in the yoke;
4. **And** the elders of that city shall
bring down
the heifer unto a
rough valley, which is
neither eared nor
sown, and shall
strike off the heifer's
neck there in the valley:
5. **And the priests**
the sons of Levi
shall come near; for them
the LORD thy God hath chosen to
minister unto him, and to bless
in the name of the LORD;
and by their word shall
every controversy
and every stroke
be tried:
6. **And** all
the elders of that city,
that are next unto the slain *man,*
shall wash their hands over
the heifer that is
beheaded in the valley:
7. And they shall answer
and say, Our hands have
not shed this blood,
neither have our eyes seen *it.*
8. **Be merciful, O LORD,**
unto thy people Israel, whom
thou hast redeemed,
and lay not innocent
blood unto thy people of
Israel's charge. And the
blood shall be forgiven them.
9. **So shalt thou put**
away the guilt of innocent
blood from among you, when
thou shalt do *that which is* right
in the sight of the LORD.
10. **When thou goest** forth
to war against thine
enemies, and the LORD
thy God hath delivered them
into thine hands, and thou
hast taken them captive,
11. **And seest**
among the captives
a beautiful woman, and

hast a desire unto her,
that thou wouldest have her
to thy wife;
12. **Then thou shalt**
bring her home
to thine house, and she shall
shave her head, and pare her nails;
13. **And she shall** put theraiment
of her captivity from off her, and shall
remain in thine house, and
bewail her father and her
mother a full month: and
after that thou shalt
go in unto her, and
be her husband, and
she shall be thy wife.
14. And it shall be,
if thou have no delight
in her, then thou shalt
let her go whither she will;
but thou shalt not sell her
at all for money, thou shalt not
make merchandise of her,
because thou hast
humbled her.
15. **If a man have two**
wives, one beloved, and
another hated, and they
have born him children, *both*
the beloved and the hated;
and if the firstborn son
be hers that was hated:
16. **Then it shall be, when**
he maketh his sons to
inherit *that* which he hath, *that*
he may not make the son
of the beloved firstborn
before the son of the
hated, which is indeed
the firstborn:
17. **But he shall**
acknowledge the son of
the hated for the firstborn,
by giving him a double
portion of all that he hath: for
he *is* the beginning of his strength;
the right of the firstborn is his.
18. **If** a man have
a stubborn and
rebellious son, which will
not obey the voice of his father,
or the voice of his mother, and *that,*
when they have chastened

him, will not
hearken unto them:
19. **Then shall his**
father and his
mother lay hold on him, and
bring him out
unto the elders of his city,
and unto the gate of his place;
20. **And they shall say**
unto the elders of his city, This
our son is stubborn and
rebellious, he will
not obey our voice;
he is a glutton,
and a drunkard.
21. **And** all
the men of his city
shall stone him with stones, that
he die: so shalt thou put evil
away from among you; and all
Israel shall hear, and fear.
22. **And if a man have**
committed a sin worthy of
death, and hebe to be put to death,
and thou hang him on a tree:
23. **His body shall**
not remain all night
upon the tree, but
thou shalt in any wise
bury him that day; (for he
that is hanged *is* accursed of God;)
that thy land be not defiled,
which the LORD thy God giveth
thee *for* an inheritance.

CHAPTER 22

1. **Thou shalt not see**
thy brother's ox or his
sheep go astray, and
hide thyself from them:
thou shalt in any case
bring them again
unto thy brother.
2. **And if thy brother**
be not nigh unto thee,
or if thou know him
not, then thou shalt
bring it unto thine own
house, and it shall be with thee
until thy brother seek
after it, and thou shalt
restore it to him again.
3. **In like manner shalt**

thou do with his ass; and so
shalt thou do with his raiment; and
with all lost thing of
thy brother's, which he
hath lost, and thou hast found,
shalt thou do likewise: thou
mayest not hide thyself.
4. Thou shalt not see thy brother's
ass or his oxfall down by the way,
and hide thyself from them: thou shalt
surely help him to lift *them* up again.
5. **The woman shall not**
wear that which pertaineth
unto a man, neither shall a
man put on a woman's
garment: for all that do so *are*
abomination unto the LORD thy God.
6. **If a bird's nest** chance to
be before thee in the way
in any tree, or on the ground,
whether they be young
ones, or eggs, and the
dam sitting upon the
young, or upon the
eggs, thou shalt not take
the dam with the young:
7. *But* thou shalt in any wise
let the dam go, and take
the young to thee; that it may
be well with thee, and *that* thou
mayest prolong *thy* days.
8. **When thou buildest a** new
house, then thou shalt
make a battlement for
thy roof, that thou bring
not blood upon thine
house, if any man fall from thence.
9. **Thou shalt not sow**
thy vineyard with divers
seeds: lest the fruit of thy
seed which thou hast sown, and
the fruit of thy vineyard,
be defiled.
10. **Thou shalt not plow** with
an ox and an ass together.
11. **Thou shalt not wear**
a garment of divers
sorts, *as of*
woollen and linen together.
12. **Thou shalt make** thee
fringes upon the four
quarters of thy vesture,
wherewith thou coverest *thyself.*

13. **If any man take a wife,** and go in unto her, **and hate her,**

14. And give occasions of speech against her, and bring up an evil name upon her, **and say, I took this woman, and** when I came to her, I **found her not a maid:**

15. **Then shall the father** of the damsel, **and** her **mother, take** and bring forth *the* **tokens of the damsel's virginity unto the elders** of the city in the gate:

16. **And the** damsel's **father shall say** unto the elders, **I gave my daughter unto this man** to wife, **and he hateth her;**

17. **And,** lo, he **hath given occasions of speech against her,** saying, I found not thy daughter a maid; and yet these *are the tokens of* my daughter's virginity. **And they shall spread the cloth before the elders** of the city.

18. **And the elders** of that city **shall take that man and chastise him;**

19. **And** they shall **amerce him in an hundred shekels of silver, and give them unto the father** of the damsel, because he hath brought up an evil name upon a virgin of Israel: and she shall be his wife; **he may not put her away** all his days.

20. **But if this thing be true,** *and the tokens of* virginity be not found for the damsel:

21. **Then they shall bring** out **the damsel to the door of her father's house, and the men of her city shall stone her** with stones that she die: because she hath wrought folly in Israel, to play the whore in her father's house: so shalt thou put evil away from among you.

22. **If a man be found lying with a woman married to an husband, then they shall both** of them **die,** *both* the man that lay with the woman, and the woman: so shalt thou put away evil from Israel.

23. **If** a damsel *that is* **a virgin be betrothed unto an husband, and a man** find her in the city, and **lie with her;**

24. **Then ye shall** bring them both out unto the gate of that city, and ye shall **stone them** with stones that they die; the damsel, because she cried not, *being* in the city; and the man, because he hath humbled his neighbour's wife: so thou shalt put away evil from among you.

25. **But if a man find a betrothed damsel in the field, and** the man **force her,** and lie with her: **then the man only** that lay with her **shall die.**

26. **But unto the damsel** thou shalt **do nothing;** *there is* in the damsel no sin *worthy* of death: for as when a man riseth against his neighbour, and slayeth him, even so *is* this matter:

27. For he found her in the field, *and* the betrothed damsel cried, and *there was* none to save her.

28. **If a man find** a damsel *that is* **a virgin, which is not betrothed, and lay hold on her, and lie with her,** and they be found;

29. **Then the man** that lay with her **shall give** unto **the** damsel's **father fifty shekels of silver, and she shall be his wife;** because he hath humbled her, he may not put her away all his days.

30. **A man shall not take his father's wife,** nor

| | discover his father's skirt.

CHAPTER 23

■ 1. **He that is wounded in**
■ **the stones, or hath**
■ **his privy member cut**
■ **off, shall not enter** into
■ **the congregation**
■ **of the LORD.**
■ 2. **A bastard shall not enter**
into the congregation of the LORD;
■ **even to his tenth**
■ **generation** shall he not enter
into the congregation of the LORD.
■ 3. **An Ammonite or Moabite**
■ **shall not enter** into the
congregation of the LORD;
even to their tenth generation
shall they not enter into the
congregation of the LORD for ever:
■ 4. **Because they met you**
■ **not with bread and** with
■ **water** in the way,
■ **when ye came** forth
■ **out of Egypt; and because**
■ **they hired** against thee
■ **Balaam** the son of Beor
of Pethor of Mesopotamia,
■ **to curse thee.**
5. Nevertheless the LORD thy God
would not hearken unto Balaam; but
the LORD thy God turned the curse
into a blessing unto thee, because
the LORD thy God loved thee.
6. Thou shalt not seek their peacenor
their prosperity all thy days for ever.
■ 7. **Thou shalt not abhor**
■ **an Edomite; for he is thy**
■ **brother:** thou shalt not abhor an
Egyptian; because thou wast a
stranger in his land.
8. The children that are begotten of
them shall enter into the congregation
of the LORD in their third generation.
■ 9. **When the host goeth** forth
■ **against thine enemies,** then
■ **keep** thee
■ **from every wicked thing.**
10. If there be among you
■ **any man, that is not clean**
■ **by reason of uncleanness**
■ **that chanceth him by night,**
■ **then shall he go** abroad

■ **out of the camp,** he
shall not come within the camp:
■ 11. But it shall be,
■ **when evening cometh** on,
■ **he shall wash** himself with water:
■ **and when the sun is**
■ **down, he shall come**
■ **into the camp again.**
■ 12. **Thou shalt have a place**
■ **also without the camp,**
whither thou shalt go forth abroad:
■ 13. **And thou shalt have**
■ **a paddle upon thy**
■ **weapon; and** it shall be,
■ **when thou wilt ease**
■ **thyself abroad, thou**
■ **shalt dig therewith,**
■ **and** shalt turn back and
■ **cover that which**
■ **cometh from thee:**
■ 14. **For the LORD** thy God
■ **walketh in** the midst of
■ **thy camp,** to deliver thee, and to
give up thine enemies before thee;
■ **therefore shall thy camp**
■ **be holy:** that he see no unclean
thing in thee, and turn away fromthee.
■ 15. **Thou shalt not**
■ **deliver unto his master**
■ **the servant which** is
■ **escaped** from his master
■ **unto thee:**
■ 16. **He shall dwell with thee,**
even among you, in that place which
he shall choose in one of thy gates,
where it liketh him best:
■ **thou shalt not**
■ **oppress him.**
■ 17. **There shall be no**
■ **whore of the daughters**
■ **of Israel, nor a sodomite**
■ **of the sons of Israel.**
■ 18. **Thou shalt not bring the**
■ **hire of a whore, or the price**
■ **of a dog, into the house**
■ **of the LORD** thy God
■ **for any vow:** for even
both these *are* abomination
unto the LORD thy God.
■ 19. **Thou shalt not lend upon**
■ **usury to thy**
■ **brother;** usury of money,
usury of victuals, usury of

any thing that is lent upon usury:

20. **Unto a stranger thou mayest lend upon usury;** but unto thy brother thou shalt not lend upon usury: that the LORD thy God may bless thee in all that thou settest thine hand to in the land whither thou goest to possess it.

21. **When thou shalt vow** a vow **unto** the LORD thy **God, thou shalt not slack to pay it:** for the LORD thy God will surely require it of thee; and it would be sin in thee.

22. **But if thou shalt forbear to vow, it shall be no sin in thee.**

23. **That which is gone out of thy lips thou shalt keep** and perform; *even* a freewill offering, according as thou hast vowed unto the LORD thy God, which thou hast promised with thy mouth.

24. **When thou comest into thy neighbour's vineyard,** then **thou mayest eat grapes** thy fill at thine own pleasure; **but** thou **shalt not put any in thy vessel.**

25. **When thou comest into the** standing **corn of thy neighbour,** then **thou mayest pluck the ears** with thine hand; **but** thou **shalt not move a sickle** unto thy neighbour's standing corn.

CHAPTER 24

1. **When a man hath taken a wife,** and married her, **and** it come to pass that **she find no favour in his eyes, because he** hath **found some uncleanness** in her: **then let him write** her **a bill of divorcement,** and give *it* in her hand, and send her out of his house.

2. **And when she is departed** out of his house, **she may** go and **be another man's wife.**

3. **And if the latter husband hate her, and write** her **a bill of divorcement,** and giveth *it* in her hand, and sendeth her out of his house; **or if the latter husband die,** which took her *to be* his wife;

4. **Her former husband,** which sent her away, **may not take her again** to be his wife, after that **she is defiled;** for that *is* abomination before the LORD: and thou shalt not cause the land to sin, which the LORD thy God giveth thee *for* an inheritance.

5. **When a man hath taken a** new **wife, he shall not go** out **to war, neither** shall he **be charged with any business: but** he **shall be free** at home **one year, and shall cheer** up **his wife** which he hath taken.

6. **No man shall take the** nether or the upper **millstone to pledge:** for he taketh *a man's* life to pledge.

7. **If a man be found stealing** any of **his brethren** of the children of Israel, **and** maketh merchandise of him, or **selleth him; then that thief shall die;** and thou shalt put evil away from among you.

8. **Take heed in the plague of leprosy,** that thou observe diligently, **and do according to all that the priests** the Levites shall **teach you:** as I commanded them, so ye shall observe to do.

9. Remember what the LORD thy God did unto Miriam by the way, after that ye were come forth out of Egypt.

10. **When thou** dost **lend thy brother any thing, thou shalt not go into his house to fetch his pledge.** 11. Thou shalt stand abroad, and **the man** to whom thou dost lend **shall bring** out **the pledge** abroad **unto thee.** 12. **And if the man be poor, thou shalt not sleep with his pledge:** 13. In any case **thou shalt deliver him the pledge** again **when the sun goeth down, that he may sleep in his** own **raiment,** and bless thee: and it shall be righteousness unto thee before the LORD thy God. 14. **Thou shalt not oppress an hired servant that is poor** and needy, **whether** he be **of thy brethren, or** of thy **strangers** that are in thy land within thy gates: 15. At his day **thou shalt give him his hire, neither shall the sun go down upon it;** for he is poor, and setteth his heart upon it: lest he cry against thee unto the LORD, and it be sin unto thee. 16. **The fathers shall not be put to death for the children, neither shall the children be put to death for the fathers:** every man shall be put to death for his own sin. 17. **Thou shalt not pervert** the **judgment of the stranger,** nor of **the fatherless; nor take a widow's raiment to pledge:** 18. But thou shalt remember that thou wast a bondman in Egypt, and the LORD thy God redeemed thee thence: therefore I command thee to do this thing. 19. **When thou cuttest** down **thine harvest** in thy field,

and hast forgot a sheaf in the field, **thou shalt not** go again to **fetch it:** it shall be for the stranger, for the fatherless, and for the widow: that the LORD thy God may bless thee in all the work of thine hands. 20. **When thou beatest thine olive tree, thou shalt not go over the boughs again:** it shall be for the stranger, for the fatherless, and for the widow. 21. **When thou gatherest the grapes** of thy vineyard, **thou shalt not glean it** afterward: **it shall be for the stranger,** for the **fatherless, and** for the **widow.** 22. And thou shalt remember that thou wast a bondman in the land of Egypt: therefore I command thee to do this thing.

CHAPTER 25

1. **If there be a controversy** between men, and they come unto judgment, that **the judges** may judge them; then they **shall justify the righteous, and condemn the wicked.** 2. And it shall be, **if the wicked man be worthy to be beaten,** that the judge shall cause him to lie down, and to be beaten before his face, according to his fault, by a certain number. 3. **Forty stripes he may give him, and not exceed:** lest, if he should exceed, and beat him above these with many stripes, then thy brother should seem vile unto thee. 4. **Thou shalt not muzzle the ox when he treadeth out the corn.** 5. **If brethren dwell together, and one** of them **die, and have no child, the wife** of the dead

■ **shall not marry** without unto
■ **a stranger: her husband's**
■ **brother shall** go in unto her, and
■ **take her** to him
■ **to wife, and perform the**
■ **duty of an husband's**
■ **brother** unto her.
■ 6. And it shall be,
■ **that the firstborn**
which she beareth
■ **shall succeed in the name**
■ **of his brother** which is dead, that
his name be not put out of Israel.
■ 7. **And if the man like not to**
■ **take his brother's wife,** then
■ **let his brother's wife**
■ **go** up to the gate
■ **unto the elders, and say,**
My husband's brother
refuseth to raise up unto his
brother a name in Israel, he
■ **will not perform the duty of**
■ **my husband's brother.**
■ 8. **Then the elders** of his city
■ **shall** call him, and
■ **speak unto him: and**
■ **if he** stand to it, and
■ **say, I like not to take her;**
■ 9. **Then shall his brother's**
■ **wife** come unto him in the
presence of the elders, and
■ **loose his shoe** from off his foot,
■ **and spit in his face,**
and shall answer
■ **and say, So shall it be**
done unto that man that will
not build up his brother's house.
■ 10. **And his name shall**
■ **be called** in Israel,
■ **The house of him that**
■ **hath his shoe loosed.**
■ 11. **When men strive** together
■ **one with another,**
■ **and the wife of** the
■ **one** draweth near for to
■ **deliver her husband**
■ **out of the hand of**
■ **him that smiteth him,**
and putteth forth her hand,
■ **and taketh him**
■ **by the secrets:**
■ 12. **Then thou shalt**
■ **cut off her hand,** thine

eye shall not pity her.
■ 13. **Thou shalt not**
■ **have** in thy bag
■ **divers weights, a**
great and a small.
■ 14. **Thou shalt not**
■ **have** in thine house
■ **divers measures,**
a great and a small.
■ 15. **But** thou shalt have
■ **a perfect and**
■ **just weight,** a perfect
■ **and** just
■ **measure** shalt thou have: that thy
days may be lengthened in the land
which the LORD thy God giveth thee.
16. For all that do such things, and
all that do unrighteously, are an
abomination unto the LORD thy God.
17. Remember what Amalek did
unto thee by the way, when ye
were come forth out of Egypt;
18. How he met thee by the way,
and smote the hindmost of thee,
even all that were feeble behind
thee, when thou wast faint and
weary; and he feared not God.
19. Therefore it shall be, when the
LORD thy God hath given thee rest
from all thine enemies round about,
in the land which the LORD thy God
giveth thee for an inheritance to
possess it, that thou shalt blot out the
remembrance of Amalek from under
heaven; thou shalt not forget it.

CHAPTER 26
■ 1. And it shall be,
■ **when thou art come in** unto
■ **the land** which the LORD thy God
giveth thee for an inheritance, and
possessest it, and dwellest therein;
2. That thou shalt
■ **take of the first** of all the
■ **fruit** of the earth, which thou
shalt bring of thy land that the
LORD thy God giveth thee,
■ **and** shalt
■ **put it in a basket,** and
shalt go unto the place which
the LORD thy God shall choose
to place his name there.
■ 3. **And** thou shalt

■ **go unto the priest** that
shall be in those days,
■ **and say** unto him,
■ **I profess** this day
■ **unto the LORD** thy God,
■ **that I am come unto the**
■ **country** which the LORD sware
unto our fathers for to give us.
■ 4. **And the priest shall** take the
basket out of thine hand, and
■ **set it** down
■ **before the altar** of the
LORD thy God.
5. And thou shalt speak and say
before the LORD thy God, A Syrian
ready to perish *was* my father, and he
went down into Egypt, and sojourned
there with a few, and became there a
nation, great, mighty, and populous:
6. And the Egyptians evil entreated
us, and afflicted us, and laid
upon us hard bondage:
7. And when we cried unto the LORD
God of our fathers, the LORD heard
our voice, and looked on ouraffliction,
and our labour, and our oppression:
8. And the LORD brought us forth
out of Egypt with a mighty hand,
and with an outstretched arm,
and with great terribleness, and
with signs, and with wonders:
9. And he hath brought us into
this place, and hath given us this
land, *even* a land that floweth
with milk and honey.
10. And now, behold, I have brought
the firstfruits of the land, which thou,
O LORD, hast given me. And thou
shalt set it before the LORD thy
God, and worship before the
LORD thy God:
11. And thou shalt rejoice in every
good *thing* which the LORD thy God
hath given unto thee, and unto thine
house, thou, and the Levite, and
the stranger that *is* among you.
■ 12. **When thou hast made**
■ **an end of tithing** all
the tithes of thine increase
■ **the third year,** *which*
is the year of tithing,
■ **and hast given it unto the**
■ **Levite, the stranger, the**

■ **fatherless, and** the
■ **widow,** that they may eat
within thy gates, and be filled;
■ 13. **Then thou shalt say**
■ **before the LORD** thy God,
■ **I have brought away the**
■ **hallowed things out of**
■ **mine house, and** also have
■ **given them** unto the Levite, and
unto the stranger, to the fatherless,
and to the widow, according to all
thy commandments which thou
hast commanded me:
■ **I have not transgressed**
■ **thy commandments,**
neither have I forgotten *them.*
■ 14. **I have not eaten thereof**
■ **in my mourning, neither**
■ **have I taken** away
■ **aught** thereof
■ **for any unclean use,**
■ **nor given aught** thereof
■ **for the dead:** *but* I have
hearkened to the voice of the LORD
my God, *and* have done according to
all that thou hast commanded me.
■ 15. **Look down** from
thy holy habitation,
■ **from heaven, and**
■ **bless** thy people
■ **Israel,** and the land which thou
hast given us, as thou swarest
unto our fathers, a land that
floweth with milk and honey.
16. This day the LORD thy God
hath commanded thee to do these
statutes and judgments: thou shalt
therefore keep and do them with all
thine heart, and with all thy soul.
■ 17. **Thou hast avouched the**
■ **LORD** this day to be thy God, and
■ **to walk in his ways,** and to
keep his statutes, and his
commandments, and his judgments,
and to hearken unto his voice:
■ 18. **And the LORD hath**
■ **avouched thee** this day
■ **to be his peculiar people,**
as he hath promised thee,
and that *thou* shouldest keep
all his commandments;
■ 19. **And to make thee high**
■ **above all nations** which he

hath made, in praise, and in name, and in honour; and that thou mayest be an holy people unto the LORD thy God, as he hath spoken.

CHAPTER 27

1. And Moses with the elders of Israel commanded the people, saying, Keep all the commandments which I command you this day.

2. **And it shall be on the day** when **ye** shall **pass over Jordan** unto the land which the LORD thy God giveth thee, that **thou shalt set** thee **up great stones, and plaster them** with plaster:

3. **And** thou shalt **write upon them** all **the words of this law,** when thou art passed over, that thou mayest go in unto the land which the LORD thy God giveth thee, a land that floweth with milk and honey; as the LORD God of thy fathers hath promised thee.

4. Therefore it shall be when ye be gone over Jordan, *that* **ye shall set up these stones,** which I command you this day, **in mount Ebal,** and thou shalt plaster them with plaster.

5. **And there shalt thou build** an altar unto the LORD thy God, **an altar of stones: thou shalt not lift up any iron tool upon them.**

6. Thou shalt build the altar of the LORD thy God of whole stones: **and thou shalt offer burnt offerings thereon** unto the LORD thy God:

7. **And** thou shalt offer **peace offerings, and** shalt **eat there, and rejoice before the LORD** thy God.

8. **And** thou shalt **write upon the stones** all the words of **this law very plainly.**

9. And Moses and the priests the Levites spake unto all Israel, saying, Take heed, and hearken, O Israel; this day thou art become the people of the LORD thy God.

10. Thou shalt therefore obey the voice of the LORD thy God, and do his commandments and his statutes, which I command thee this day.

11. **And Moses charged the people** the same day, **saying,**

12. **These shall stand upon mount Gerizim to bless the people,** when ye are come over Jordan; **Simeon, and Levi, and Judah, and Issachar, and Joseph, and Benjamin:**

13. **And these shall stand upon mount Ebal to curse; Reuben, Gad, and Asher, and Zebulun, Dan, and Naphtali.**

14. **And the Levites shall** speak, and **say unto** all the men of **Israel** with a loud voice,

15. **Cursed be the man that maketh any graven or molten image,** an abomination unto the LORD, the work of the hands of the craftsman, and putteth *it* in a secret *place*. And all the people shall answer and say, Amen.

16. **Cursed be he that setteth light by his father or** his **mother.** And all the people shall say, Amen.

17. **Cursed be he that removeth his neighbour's landmark.** And all the people shall say, Amen.

18. **Cursed be he that maketh the blind to wander** out of the way. And all the people shall say, Amen.

19. **Cursed be he that**

perverteth the **judgment** of the stranger, fatherless, and widow. And all the people shall say, Amen.

20. **Cursed be he that lieth with his father's wife;** because he uncovereth his father's skirt. And all the people shall say, Amen.

21. **Cursed be he that lieth with any** manner of **beast.** And all the people shall say, Amen.

22. **Cursed be he that lieth with his sister,** the daughter of his father, **or** the daughter of his mother. And all the people shall say, Amen.

23. Cursed *be* he that lieth with **his mother in law.** And all the people shall say, Amen.

24. **Cursed be he that smiteth his neighbour secretly.** And all the people shall say, Amen.

25. **Cursed be he that taketh reward to slay an innocent person.** And all the people shall say, Amen.

26. **Cursed be he that confirmeth not** all **the words of this law to do them. And all the people shall say, Amen.**

CHAPTER 28

1. And it shall come to pass, **if thou** shalt **hearken** diligently **unto the voice of the LORD** thy God, to observe *and* to do all his commandments which I command thee this day, that the LORD thy God will set thee on high above all nations of the earth:

2. And all **these blessings shall come on thee,** and overtake thee, if thou shalt hearken unto the voice of the LORD thy God.

3. **Blessed shalt thou be in the city, and** blessed *shalt* thou *be* in the **field.**

4. **Blessed shall be the fruit of thy body,** and the fruit of **thy ground,** and the fruit of **thy cattle,** the increase of thy **kine, and** the flocks of thy **sheep,**

5. Blessed *shall be* **thy basket and** thy **store.**

6. **Blessed shalt thou be when thou comest in, and** blessed *shalt* thou *be* when thou **goest out.**

7. **The LORD shall cause thine enemies** that rise up against thee **to be smitten before thy face: they shall come out against thee one way, and flee before thee seven ways.**

8. **The LORD shall command the blessing upon** thee in **thy storehouses, and in all** that **thou settest thine hand unto;** and he shall bless thee in the land which the LORD thy God giveth thee.

9. **The LORD shall establish thee an holy people** unto himself, as he hath sworn unto thee, if thou shalt keep the commandments of the LORD thy God, and walk in his ways.

10. **And all people of the earth shall see** that thou art called by the name of the LORD; **and** they shall **be afraid of thee.**

11. **And the LORD shall make thee plenteous in goods, in the fruit of thy body,** and in the fruit of **thy cattle, and** in the fruit of **thy ground,** in the land which the LORD sware unto thy fathers to give thee.

12. **The LORD shall open unto thee his good**

311

■ **treasure,** the heaven to give the rain unto thy land in his season, and to bless all the work of thinehand: and

■ **thou shalt lend** unto many nations,

■ **and** thou shalt

■ **not borrow.**

■ 13. **And** the LORD shall

■ **make thee the head, and not the tail; and thou shalt be above only, and** thou shalt **not be beneath; if that thou hearken** unto the commandments of the LORD thy God, which I command thee this day, to observe and to do *them:*

■ 14. **And** thou shalt

■ **not go aside from any of the words which I command** thee this day, *to* the right hand, or *to* the left, to go after other gods to serve them.

■ 15. **But** it shall come to pass,

■ **if thou wilt not hearken** unto the voice of the LORD thy God, to observe to do all his commandments and his statutes which I command thee this day; that all these curses shall come upon thee, and overtake thee:

■ 16. **Cursed shalt thou be in the city, and** cursed *shalt* thou *be* in the

■ **field.**

■ 17. **Cursed shall be thy basket and** thy **store.**

■ 18. Cursed shall be

■ **the fruit of thy body,** and the fruit of thy

■ **land,** the increase of thy

■ **kine, and** the flocks of thy **sheep.**

■ 19. **Cursed shalt thou be when thou comest in, and** cursed *shalt* thou *be* when thou

■ **goest out.**

■ 20. **The LORD shall send** upon thee

■ **cursing, vexation, and rebuke,** in all that thou settest thine hand unto for to do, until thou be destroyed, and until

thou perish quickly; because of the wickedness of thy doings, whereby thou hast forsaken me.

■ 21. **The LORD shall make the pestilence cleave unto thee,** until he have consumed thee from off the land, whither thou goest to possess it.

■ 22. **The LORD shall smite thee with** a **consumption,** and with a fever, and with an inflammation, and with an extreme burning, and with the sword, and with blasting, and with mildew; and they shall pursue thee until thou perish.

■ 23. **And thy heaven** that *is* over thy head **shall be brass, and the earth** that is under thee *shall* be **iron.**

■ 24. **The LORD shall make the rain of thy land powder and dust:** from heaven shall it come down upon thee, until thou be destroyed.

■ 25. **The LORD shall cause thee to be smitten before thine enemies:** thou shalt go out one way against them, and flee seven ways before them: and shalt be removed into all the kingdoms of the earth.

■ 26. **And thy carcase shall be meat unto all fowls** of the air, **and** unto the **beasts** of the earth, and no man shall fray *them* away.

■ 27. **The LORD will smite thee with the botch of Egypt,** and with the **emerods,** and with the **scab, and** with the **itch,** whereof thou canst not be healed.

■ 28. **The LORD shall smite thee with madness, and blindness, and astonishment of heart:**

■ 29. **And thou shalt grope at noonday, as** the blind gropeth **in darkness, and thou**

■ **shalt not prosper** in thy
ways: and thou shalt be only
oppressed and spoiled evermore,
and no man shall save *thee.*
■ 30. **Thou shalt betroth**
■ **a wife, and another** man
■ **shall lie with her: thou**
■ **shalt build an house,**
■ **and** thou shalt
■ **not dwell therein:** thou shalt
■ **plant a vineyard, and** shalt
■ **not gather the**
■ **grapes** thereof.
■ 31. **Thine ox shall be**
■ **slain** before thine eyes,
and thou shalt not eat thereof:
■ **thine ass** *shall be* violently
■ **taken away** from before thy face,
and shall not be restored to thee:
■ **thy sheep** *shall be*
■ **given unto thine**
■ **enemies,** and thou shalt
have none to rescue *them.*
■ 32. **Thy sons and** thy
■ **daughters** *shall be*
■ **given unto another**
■ **people,** and thine eyes shall
look, and fail *with longing* for them
all the day long; and *there*
shall be no might in thine hand.
■ 33. **The fruit of thy**
■ **land,** and all thy labours,
■ **shall a nation which thou**
■ **knowest not eat up;**
and thou shalt be only oppressed
and crushed alway:
34. So that thou shalt be mad
for the sight of thine eyes
which thou shalt see.
■ 35. **The LORD shall smite**
■ **thee in the knees, and** in the
■ **legs, with a** sore
■ **botch that cannot be**
■ **healed,** from the sole of thy
foot unto the top of thy head.
■ 36. **The LORD shall bring**
■ **thee, and thy king** which
thou shalt set over thee,
■ **unto a nation which neither**
■ **thou nor thy fathers have**
■ **known; and there shalt**
■ **thou serve other gods,**
wood and stone.

■ 37. **And thou shalt**
■ **become** an astonishment,
■ **a proverb,** and a byword,
■ **among all nations** whither
the LORD shall lead thee.
■ 38. **Thou shalt carry**
■ **much seed** out
■ **into the field, and**
shalt gather *but* little in; for
■ **the locust shall consume it.**
■ 39. **Thou shalt plant**
■ **vineyards,** and dress *them,*
■ **but** shalt
■ **neither drink of the**
■ **wine, nor gather** *the*
■ **grapes;** for the worms
shall eat them.
■ 40. **Thou shalt**
■ **have olive trees**
throughout all thy coasts,
■ **but** thou
■ **shalt not anoint thyself**
■ **with the oil;** for thine olive
shall cast *his fruit.*
■ 41. **Thou shalt beget**
■ **sons and daughters, but**
thou shalt not enjoy them; for
■ **they shall go into captivity.**
42. All thy trees and fruit of thy
land shall the locust consume.
43. The stranger that *is* within thee
shall get up above thee very high;
and thou shalt come down very low.
44. He shall lend to thee, and thou
shalt not lend to him: he shall be the
head, and thou shalt be the tail.
■ 45. **Moreover all these**
■ **curses shall come upon**
■ **thee,** and shall pursue thee, and
overtake thee, till thou be destroyed;
■ **because thou hearkenedst**
■ **not unto** the voice of the LORD thy
■ **God,** to keep his commandments
and his statutes which he
commanded thee:
■ 46. **And they shall be upon**
■ **thee for a sign** and for a wonder,
and upon thy seed for ever.
■ 47. **Because thou servedst**
■ **not the LORD** thy God with
joyfulness, and with gladness of
heart, for the abundance of all *things;*
■ 48. **Therefore shalt thou**

serve thine enemies which the LORD shall send against thee, in hunger, and in thirst, and in nakedness, and in want of all *things:* and he shall put a yoke of iron upon thy neck, until he have destroyed thee.

49. **The LORD shall bring a nation against thee from far,** from the end of the earth, *as swift* as the eagle flieth; a nation whose tongue thou shalt not understand;

50. **A nation of fierce countenance, which shall not regard the person of the old, nor shew favour to the young:**

51. **And** he **shall eat the fruit** of thy cattle, and the fruit **of thy land, until thou be destroyed:** which *also* shall not leave thee *either* corn, wine, or oil, *or* the increase of thy kine, or flocks of thy sheep, until he have destroyed thee.

52. **And he shall besiege thee** in all thy gates, **until thy high** and fenced **walls come down,** wherein thou trustedst, throughout all thy land: and he shall besiege thee in all thy gates throughout all thy land, which the LORD thy God hath given thee.

53. **And thou shalt eat** the fruit of thine own body, **the flesh of thy sons and** of **thy daughters,** which the LORD thy God hath given thee, in the siege, and in the straitness, wherewith thine enemies shall distress thee:

54. *So that* **the man that is tender among you,** and very delicate, **his eye shall be evil toward his brother, and** toward the **wife** of his bosom, **and** toward the remnant of **his children** which he shall leave:

55. **So that he will not give** to any of **them** of **the flesh of his children whom he shall eat:** because he hath nothing left him in the siege, and in the straitness, wherewith thine enemies shall distress thee in all thy gates.

56. **The tender** and delicate **woman** among you, which would not adventure to set the sole of her foot upon the ground for delicateness and tenderness, her eye **shall be evil toward the husband of her bosom, and** toward **her son, and** toward her **daughter,**

57. And toward her young one that cometh out from between her feet, and toward her children which she shall bear: **for she shall eat them** for want of all *things* secretly in the siege and straitness, wherewith thine enemy shall distress thee in thy gates.

58. **If thou wilt not** observe to **do** all the words of **this law** that are written in this book, **that thou mayest fear** this glorious and fearful name, **THE LORD THY GOD;**

59. **Then the LORD will make thy plagues** wonderful, and the plagues of thy seed, *even* great plagues, and **of long continuance,** and sore sicknesses, and of long continuance.

60. **Moreover he will bring upon thee all the diseases of Egypt,** which thou wast afraid of; and they shall cleave unto thee.

61. **Also every sickness,** and every plague, which *is* not written in the book of this law, them will the LORD bring upon thee, **until thou be destroyed.**

62. **And ye shall be left few in number,** whereas ye were as the stars of heaven for multitude; because thou wouldest not obey the voice of the LORD thy God.

63. And it shall come to pass, *that*

as the LORD rejoiced over you to do you **good,** and to multiply you; **so the LORD will destroy you**, and to bring you to nought; and ye shall be plucked from off the land whither thou goest to possess it.

64. And the LORD shall scatter thee among all people, from the one end of the earth even unto the other; and there thou shalt serve other gods, which neither thou nor thy fathers have known, *even* wood and stone.

65. And among these nations shalt thou find no ease, neither shall the sole of thy foot have rest: but the LORD shall give thee there a trembling heart, and failing of eyes, and sorrow of mind:

66. And thy life shall hang in doubt before thee; and thou shalt fear day and night, and shalt have none assurance of thy life:

67. In the morning thou shalt say, Would God it were even! and at even thou shalt say, Would God it were morning! for the fear of thine heart wherewith thou shalt fear, and for the sight of thine eyes which thou shalt see.

68. And the LORD shall bring thee into Egypt again with ships, by the way whereof I spake unto thee, Thou shalt see it no more again: and there ye shall be sold unto your enemies for bondmen and bondwomen, and no man shall buy *you.*

CHAPTER 29

1. These are the words of the covenant, which the LORD commanded Moses to make with the children of Israel **in** the land of **Moab, beside the covenant** which **he made** with them **in Horeb.**

2. And Moses called unto all Israel, and said unto them, **Ye have seen all that the LORD did** before your eyes in the land of Egypt unto Pharaoh, and unto all his servants, and unto all his land;

3. The great temptations which thine eyes have seen, the signs, and those great miracles:

4. Yet the LORD hath not given you an heart to perceive, and eyes to see, and ears to hear, unto this day.

5. And I have led you forty years in the wilderness: your clothes are not waxen old upon you, and thy shoe is not waxen old upon thy foot.

6. Ye have not eaten bread, neither have ye drunk wine or strong drink: that ye might know that I *am* the LORD your God.

7. And when ye came unto this place, Sihon the king of Heshbon, **and Og** the king of Bashan, **came out against us** unto battle, **and we smote them:**

8. And we took their land, and gave it for an inheritance **unto the Reubenites, and to the Gadites,** and to the half tribe of Manasseh.

9. Keep therefore the words of **this covenant,** and do them, **that ye may prosper** in all that ye do.

10. Ye stand this day all of you before the LORD your God; your captains of your tribes, your elders, and your officers, *with* all the men of Israel,

11. Your little ones, your wives, and thy stranger that *is* in thy camp, from the hewer of thy wood unto the drawer of thy water:

12. That thou shouldest enter into covenant with the LORD thy God, and into his oath, which the LORD thy God maketh with thee this day:

13. That he may establish

thee to day for a people unto himself, and *that* he may be unto thee a God, as he hath said unto thee, and as he hath sworn unto thy fathers, to Abraham, to Isaac, and to Jacob.
14. Neither with you only do I make this covenant and this oath;
15. But with *him* that standeth here with us this day before the LORD our God, and also with *him* that *is* not here with us this day:
16. (For ye know how we have dwelt in the land of Egypt; and how we came through the nations which ye passed by;
17. And ye have seen their abominations, and their idols, wood and stone, silver and gold, which *were* among them:)
18. Lest there should be among you man, or woman, or family, or tribe, whose heart turneth away this day from the LORD our God, to go *and* serve the gods of these nations; lest there should be among you a root that beareth gall and wormwood;
19. And it come to pass, when he heareth the words of this curse, that he bless himself in his heart, saying, I shall have peace, though I walk in the imagination of mine heart, to add drunkenness to thirst:
20. The LORD will not spare him, but then the anger of the LORD and his jealousy shall smoke against that man, and all the curses that are written in this book shall lie upon him, and the LORD shall blot out his name from under heaven.
21. And the LORD shall separate him unto evil out of all the tribes of Israel, according to all the curses of the covenant that are written in this book of the law:
22. So that the generation to come of your children that shall rise up after you, and the stranger that shall come from a far land, shall say, when they see the plagues of that land, and the sicknesses which the LORD hath laid upon it;
23. And that the whole land thereof is brimstone, and salt, *and* burning, that it is not sown, nor beareth, nor any grass groweth therein, like the overthrow of Sodom, and Gomorrah, Admah, and Zeboim, which the LORD overthrew in his anger, and in his wrath:
24. Even all nations shall say, Wherefore hath the LORD done thus unto this land? what *meaneth* the heat of this great anger?
25. Then men shall say, Because they have forsaken the covenant of the LORD God of their fathers, which he made with them when he brought them forth out of the land of Egypt:
26. For they went and served other gods, and worshipped them, gods whom they knew not, and *whom* he had not given unto them:
27. And the anger of the LORD was kindled against this land, to bring upon it all the curses that are written in this book:
28. And the LORD rooted them out of their land in anger, and in wrath, and in great indignation, and cast them into another land, as it is this day.
29. The secret things belong unto the LORD our God: but those things *which are* revealed belong unto us and to our children for ever, that we may do all the words of this law.

CHAPTER 30

1. And it shall come to pass, when all these things are come upon thee, the blessing and the curse, which I have set before thee, and thou shalt call them

■ **to mind among** all
■ **the nations,** whither the
LORD thy God hath driven thee,
■ 2. **And shalt return**
■ **unto the LORD** thy God,
■ **and** shalt
■ **obey his voice** according to
all that I command thee this day,
thou and thy children, with all thine
heart, and with all thy soul;
3. That
■ **then the LORD** thy God
■ **will** turn thy captivity,
and have compassion upon
thee, and will return and
■ **gather thee from all**
■ **the nations,** whither the
LORD thy God hath scattered thee.
4. If *any* of thine be driven out unto
the outmost *parts of* heaven, from
thence will the LORD thy God
gather thee, and from thence
will he fetch thee:
■ 5. **And** the LORD thy God will
■ **bring thee into the land**
■ **which thy fathers**
■ **possessed,** and thou shalt
possess it; and he will do thee good,
and multiply thee above thy fathers.
■ 6. **And the LORD** thy God
■ **will circumcise thine heart,**
and the heart of thy seed, to love the
LORD thy God with all thineheart, and
with all thy soul, that thou mayestlive.
■ 7. **And** the LORD thy God
■ **will put all these curses**
■ **upon thine enemies,** and
on them that hate thee, which
persecuted thee.
■ 8. **And thou shalt return**
■ **and obey** the voice of
■ **the LORD,** and do all his
commandments which I
command thee this day.
■ 9. **And the LORD** thy God
■ **will make thee plenteous in**
■ **every work of thine hand,**
in the fruit of thy body, and in the fruit
of thy cattle, and in the fruit of thy
land, for good: for the LORD will
again rejoice over thee for good,
as he rejoiced over thy fathers:
10. If thou shalt hearken unto the

voice of the LORD thy God, to
keep his commandments and his
statutes which are written in this
book of the law, *and* if thou turn
unto the LORD thy God with all
thine heart, and with all thy soul.
■ 11. **For this commandment**
which I command thee this day, it
■ **is not hidden** from thee,
neither is it far off.
12. It *is* not in heaven, that thou
shouldest say, Who shall go up for
us to heaven, and bring it unto us,
that we may hear it, and do it?
13. Neither *is* it beyond the sea, that
thou shouldest say, Who shall go
over the sea for us, and bring it unto
us, that we may hear it, and do it?
■ 14. **But the word is**
■ **very nigh unto** thee, in
■ **thy mouth, and** in thy
■ **heart,** that thou mayest do it.
■ 15. **See, I have set before**
■ **thee this day life and good,**
■ **and death and evil;**
16. In that I command thee this dayto
love the LORD thy God, to walk in his
ways, and to keep hiscommandments
and his statutes and his judgments,
that thou mayest live and multiply:
and the LORD thy God shall bless
thee in the land whither thou
goest to possess it.
■ 17. **But if thine heart turn**
■ **away,** so that thou wilt not
hear, but shalt be drawn away,
■ **and worship other**
■ **gods,** and serve them;
■ 18. **I denounce** unto
■ **you this day,**
■ **that ye shall** surely
■ **perish,** *and that* ye shall
not prolong *your* days upon
the land, whither thou passest
over Jordan to go to possess it.
19. I call heaven and earth to record
this day against you, *that* I have set
before you life and death, blessing
and cursing: therefore choose life,
that both thou and thy seed may live:
■ 20. **That thou mayest love**
■ **the LORD** thy God, *and* that
thou mayest obey his voice, and

that thou mayest cleave unto him:
■ **for he is thy life, and the**
■ **length of thy days:** that
thou mayest dwell in the land
which the LORD sware unto thy
fathers, to Abraham, to Isaac,
and to Jacob, to give them.

CHAPTER 31

■ 1. **And Moses** went and
■ **spake** these words
■ **unto all Israel.**
2. And he
■ **said** unto them,
■ **I am an hundred and**
■ **twenty years old this day;**
I can no more go out and come in:
■ **also the LORD** hath
■ **said unto me, Thou**
■ **shalt not go over** this
■ **Jordan.**
3. **The LORD** thy God, he
■ **will go over before**
■ **thee, and** he will
■ **destroy these nations**
■ **from before thee,**
and thou shalt possess them:
■ **and Joshua,** he
■ **shall go** over
■ **before thee, as**
■ **the LORD** hath
■ **said.**
4. And the LORD shall do unto them
as he did to Sihon and to Og, kings of
the Amorites, and unto the land
of them, whom he destroyed.
5. And the LORD shall give them
up before your face, that ye may
do unto them according unto
all the commandments which
I have commanded you.
■ 6. **Be strong and of a**
■ **good courage, fear**
■ **not,** nor be afraid of them:
■ **for the LORD** thy God, he *it is* that
■ **doth go with thee;**
■ **he will not fail thee,**
■ **nor forsake thee.**
■ 7. **And Moses called unto**
■ **Joshua,and said** unto
him in the sight of all Israel,
■ **Be strong** and of a good courage:
■ **for thou must go with this**

■ **people unto the land which**
■ **the LORD hath sworn**
unto their fathers to give them;
■ **and thou shalt cause**
■ **them to inherit it.**
8. And the LORD, he *it is* that doth
go before thee; he will be with thee,
he will not fail thee, neither forsake
thee: fear not, neither be dismayed.
■ 9. **And Moses wrote this**
■ **law, and delivered it unto**
■ **the priests** the sons of Levi,
which bare the ark of the
covenant of the LORD, and
unto all the elders of Israel.
■ 10. **And Moses**
■ **commanded them, saying,**
■ **At the end of every seven**
■ **years,** in the solemnity of the year
of release, in the feast oftabernacles,
11. When all Israel is come to
appear before the LORD thy God
in the place which he shall choose,
■ **thou shalt read this**
■ **law before all Israel**
in their hearing.
12. Gather the people together, men
and women, and children, and thy
stranger that *is* within thy gates,
that they may hear, and that they
may learn, and fear the LORD
your God, and observe to do
all the words of this law:
13. And *that* their children, which
have not known *any thing,* may hear,
and learn to fear the LORD your God,
as long as ye live in the land whither
ye go over Jordan to possess it.
■ 14. **And the LORD said unto**
■ **Moses, Behold, thy days**
■ **approach that thou must**
■ **die: call Joshua, and**
■ **present yourselves in the**
■ **tabernacle** of the congregation,
■ **that I may give him a**
■ **charge.** And Moses and Joshua
went, and presented themselves in
the tabernacle of the congregation.
■ 15. **And the LORD appeared**
■ **in the tabernacle in a pillar**
■ **of a cloud:** and the pillar of
the cloud stood over the door
of the tabernacle.

16. **And** the LORD **said unto Moses, Behold, thou shalt sleep with thy fathers; and this people** will rise up, and go a whoring after the gods of the strangers of the land, whither they go *to be* among them, and **will forsake me, and break my covenant** which I have made with them. 17. **Then my anger shall be kindled against them** in that day, and I will forsake them, and I will hide my face from them, and they shall be devoured, and many evils and troubles shall befall them; so that they will say in that day, Are not these evils come upon us, because our God *is* not among us? 18. And I will surely hide my face in that day for all the evils which they shall have wrought, in that they are turned unto other gods. 19. **Now** therefore **write** ye **this song** for you, **and** teach it the children of Israel: **put it in their mouths, that this song may be a witness for me against** the children of **Israel.** 20. **For when I shall have brought them into the land** which I sware unto their fathers, **that floweth with milk and honey;** and they shall have eaten and filled themselves, and waxen fat; **then will they turn unto other gods,** and serve them, and provoke me, **and break my covenant.** 21. **And** it shall come to pass, when many evils and troubles are befallen them, that **this song shall testify against them** as a witness; for it shall not be forgotten out of the mouths of their seed: **for I know their imagination** which they go about, even now, **before I have brought them into the land** which I sware.

22. **Moses** therefore **wrote this song** the same day, **and taught** it the children of **Israel.** 23. **And he gave Joshua** the son of Nun **a charge, and said, Be strong and of a good courage: for thou shalt bring** the children of **Israel into the land** which I sware unto them: and I will be with thee. 24. **And it came to pass, when Moses had made an end of writing the** words of this **law** in a book, until they were finished, 25. **That Moses commanded the Levites,** which bare the ark of the covenant of the LORD, saying, 26. **Take this book** of the law, **and put it in the** side of the **ark** of the covenant of the LORD your God, that it may be there for a witness against thee. 27. **For I know thy rebellion,** and thy stiff neck: behold, while I am yet alive with you this day, ye have been rebellious against the LORD; and how much more after my death? 28. **Gather** unto me all **the elders** of your tribes, **and** your **officers, that I may speak these words in their ears,** and call heaven and earth to record against them. 29. For I know that after my death **ye will utterly corrupt yourselves,** and turn aside from the way which I have commanded you; **and evil will befall you** in the latter days; **because ye will do evil in the sight of the LORD,** to provoke him to anger through the work of your hands. 30. **And Moses spake** in the ears of all the congregation of Israel

■| the words of this song,
until they were ended.

CHAPTER 32

■ 1. Give ear, O ye
■ heavens, and I will speak;
and hear, O earth, the
words of my mouth.
■ 2. My doctrine shall drop as
■ the rain, my speech shall distil as
the dew, as the small rain upon the
tender herb, and as the showers
upon the grass:
■ 3. Because I will publish
■ the name of the LORD:
ascribe ye greatness unto our God.
4. *He is* the Rock,
■ his work is perfect: for all his
ways *are* judgment:a God of truth and
without iniquity, just and right is he.
■ 5. They have corrupted
■ themselves, their spot *is* not the
spot of his children: *they are* a
perverse and crooked generation.
■ 6. Do ye thus requite the
■ LORD, O foolish people
and unwise? *is* not he thy father
that hath bought thee?
■ hath he not made thee,
and established thee?
■ 7. Remember the days
■ of old, consider the years of
many generations: ask thy father, and
he will shew thee; thy elders,
and they will tell thee.
■ 8. When the Most High
■ divided to the nations
■ their inheritance, when he
separated the sons of Adam,
■ he set the
■ bounds of the people
■ according to the
■ number of the children of
■ Israel.
■ 9. For the LORD'S portion
■ is his people; Jacob is
the lot of his inheritance.
■ 10. He found him in a desert
■ land, and in the waste howling
wilderness; he led him about, he
■ instructed him, he kept him
as the apple of his eye.
11. As an eagle stirreth up her nest,

fluttereth over her young, spreadeth
abroad her wings, taketh them,
beareth them on her wings:
■ 12. So the LORD alone did
■ lead him, and there was
■ no strange god with him.
13. He made him ride on the high
places of the earth, that he might eat
the increase of the fields; and he
made him to suck honey out of the
rock, and oil out of the flinty rock;
14. Butter of kine, and milk of sheep,
with fat of lambs, and rams of the
breed of Bashan, and goats, with the
fat of kidneys of wheat; and thoudidst
drink the pure blood of the grape.
■ 15. But Jeshurun waxed fat,
and kicked: thou art waxen fat,
thou art grown thick, thou art
covered *with fatness;*
■ then he forsook
■ God *which* made him,
■ and lightly esteemed the
■ Rock of his salvation.
■ 16. They provoked him
■ to jealousy with strange
■ gods, with abominations
provoked they him to anger.
■ 17. They sacrificed unto
■ devils, not to God; to gods
whom they knew not, to new *gods*
that came newly up, whom
your fathers feared not.
18. Of the Rock *that* begat thee thou
art unmindful, and hast forgotten
God that formed thee.
■ 19. And when
■ the LORD saw *it,* he
■ abhorred them, because
of the provoking of his sons,
and of his daughters.
■ 20. And he
■ said, I will hide my face
■ from them, I will see what their
end *shall be:* for they *are* a very
froward generation, children in
whom *is* no faith.
■ 21. They have moved me to
■ jealousy with *that which* is not
God; they have provoked me to anger
with their vanities: and I will move
them to jealousy with *those which*
are not a people; I will provoke them

to anger with a foolish nation.

22. For a fire is kindled in mine anger, and shall burn unto the lowest hell, and shall consume the earth with her increase, and set on fire the foundations of the mountains.

23. **I will heap mischiefs upon them;** I will spend mine arrows upon them.

24. *They shall be* burnt with hunger, and devoured with burning heat, and with bitter destruction: I will also send the teeth of beasts upon them, with the poison of serpents of the dust.

25. The sword without, and terror within, shall destroy both the young man and the virgin, the suckling *also* with the man of gray hairs.

26. **I said, I would scatter them into corners, I would make the remembrance of them to cease** from among men:

27. **Were it not that I feared the wrath of the enemy,** lest their adversaries should behave themselves strangely, *and* **lest they should say, Our hand is high, and the LORD hath not done all this.**

28. For they *are* a nation void of counsel, neither *is there any* understanding in them.

29. **O that they were wise, that they understood this,** *that* they would consider their latter end!

30. **How should one chase a thousand, and two put ten thousand to flight, except their Rock had sold them,** and the LORD had shut them up?

31. **For their rock is not as our Rock,** even our enemies themselves *being* judges.

32. **For their vine is of the vine of Sodom, and** of the fields of **Gomorrah:** their grapes *are* grapes of gall, their clusters *are* bitter:

33. **Their wine is the poison of dragons,** and the cruel venom of asps.

34. *Is* not this laid up in store with me, *and* sealed up among my treasures?

35. **To me belongeth vengeance** and recompence; their foot shall slide in *due* time: for **the day of their calamity is at hand,** and the things that shall come upon them make haste.

36. **For the LORD shall judge his people,** and repent himself for his servants, when he seeth that *their* power is gone, and *there is* none shut up, or left.

37. And he shall say, **Where are their gods,** *their* rock **in whom they trusted,**

38. Which did eat the fat of their sacrifices, *and* drank the wine of their drink offerings? let them rise up and help you, *and* be your protection.

39. **See now that I,** *even* I, **am he, and there is no god with me:** I kill, and I make alive; I wound, and I heal: neither *is there any* that can deliver out of my hand.

40. For I lift up my hand to heaven, and say, **I live for ever.**

41. If I whet my glittering sword, and mine hand take hold on judgment; **I will render vengeance to mine enemies,** and will reward them that hate me.

42. I will make mine arrows drunk with blood, and my sword shall devour flesh; *and that* with the blood of the slain and of the captives, from the beginning of revenges upon the enemy.

43. **Rejoice, O ye nations, with his people: for he will avenge the blood of his servants,** and will render vengeance to his adversaries, and will be merciful unto his land, *and* to his people.

44. **And Moses** came and **spake** all the words of **this song in the ears of the people,** he, and Hoshea

the son of Nun.

45. And Moses made an end of speaking all these words to all Israel:

■ 46. **And** he
■ **said** unto them,
■ **Set your hearts unto** all the words which I testify among you this day, which ye shall command your children to observe to do,
■ **all the words of this law.**
■ 47. **For it is not a vain thing** for you; because
■ **it is your life:** and through this thing ye shall prolong *your* days in the land, whither ye go over Jordan to possess it.
■ 48. **And the LORD spake**
■ **unto Moses** that self same day, saying,
■ 49. **Get thee up** into this mountain Abarim,
■ **unto mount Nebo,** which is in the land of Moab, that *is* over against Jericho;
■ **and behold** the land of
■ **Canaan, which I give**
■ **unto** the children of
■ **Israel** for a possession:
■ 50. **And die in the mount** whither thou goest up, and be gathered unto thy people; as Aaron thy brother died in mount Hor, and was gathered unto his people:
■ 51. **Because ye trespassed** against me among the children of Israel
■ **at the waters of**
■ **Meribah-Kadesh,** in the wilderness of Zin; because ye sanctified me not in the midst of the children of Israel.
■ 52. **Yet thou shalt see**
■ **the land** before *thee;*
■ **but** thou
■ **shalt not go thither** unto the land which I give the children of Israel.

CHAPTER 33

■ 1. **And** this *is* the blessing, wherewith
■ **Moses** the man of God
■ **blessed** the children of

■ **Israel before his death.**
■ 2. **And** he
■ **said, The LORD came from**
■ **Sinai,** and rose up from Seir unto them; he shined forth from mount Paran, and he came
■ **with ten thousands of saints:**
■ **from his right hand went a**
■ **fiery law** for them.
■ 3. **Yea, he loved the**
■ **people;** all his saints *are* in thy hand: and they sat down at thy feet; *every one* shall receive of thy words.
■ 4. **Moses commanded us**
■ **a law, even the inheritance** of the congregation of Jacob.
5. And he was king in Jeshurun, when the heads of the people *and* the tribes of Israel were gathered together.
■ 6. **Let Reuben live,** and not die;
■ **and let not his men be few.**
7. And this *is the blessing* of Judah: and he said,
■ **Hear, LORD, the voice**
■ **of Judah,** and bring him unto his people:
■ **let his hands be sufficient**
■ **for him; and be thou**
■ **an help** to *him*
■ **from his enemies.**
■ 8. **And of Levi** he said,
■ **Let thy Thummim and** thy
■ **Urim be with thy holy**
■ **one,** whom thou didst prove at Massah, *and with* whom thou didst strive at the waters of Meribah;
9. Who said unto his father and to his mother, I have not seen him; neither did he acknowledge his brethren, nor knew his own children: for they have observed thy word, and kept thy covenant.
■ 10. **They shall teach** Jacob thy judgments, and
■ **Israel thy law:** they shall put incense before thee,
■ **and** whole burnt
■ **sacrifice upon thine altar.**
11. Bless, LORD, his substance, and accept the work of his hands; smite through the loins of them that rise against him, and of them that hate him, that they rise not again.

12. **And of Benjamin he said, The beloved of the LORD shall dwell in safety** by him; **and the Lord shall cover him all the day long,** and he shall dwell between his shoulders.

13. **And of Joseph he said, Blessed** of the LORD **be his land,** for the precious things of heaven, for the dew, and for the deep that coucheth beneath,

14. And for the precious fruits *brought forth* by the sun, and for the precious things put forth by the moon,

15. And for the chief things of the ancient mountains, and for the precious things of the lasting hills,

16. And for the precious things of the earth and fulness thereof, and *for* the good will of him that dwelt in the bush: let *the blessing* come upon the head of Joseph, and upon the top of the head of him *that was* separated from his brethren.

17. His glory *is like* the firstling of his bullock, and his horns *are like* the horns of unicorns: with them **he shall push the people together to the ends of the earth: and they are the ten thousands of Ephraim, and** they *are* **the thousands of Manasseh.**

18. **And of Zebulun he said, Rejoice,** Zebulun, in thy going out; **and, Issachar,** in thy tents.

19. **They shall call the people unto the mountain; there they shall offer sacrifices of righteousness:** for they shall suck *of* the abundance of the seas, and *of* treasures hid in the sand.

20. **And** of Gad he said, **Blessed be he that enlargeth Gad: he dwelleth as a lion,** and teareth the arm with the crown of the head.

21. And he provided the first part for himself, because there, *in* a portion of the lawgiver, *was he* seated; and he came with the heads of the people, he executed the justice of the LORD, and his judgments with Israel.

22. **And** of Dan he said, **Dan is a lion's whelp: he shall leap from Bashan.**

23. **And of Naphtali he said, O Naphtali, satisfied with favour,** and full with the blessing of the LORD: **possess thou the west and the south.**

24. **And of Asher he said, Let Asher be blessed with children;** let him be acceptable to his brethren, and let him dip his foot in oil.

25. Thy shoes *shall be* iron and brass; and as thy days, so shall thy strength *be.*

26. **There is none like unto the God of Jeshurun,** who rideth upon the heaven in thy help, and in his excellency on the sky.

27. **The eternal God is thy refuge, and underneath are the everlasting arms:** and he shall thrust out the enemy from before thee; and shall say, Destroy *them.*

28. **Israel then shall dwell in safety alone:** the fountain of Jacob *shall be* upon a land of corn and wine; also his heavens shall drop down dew.

29. **Happy art thou, O Israel:** who *is* like unto thee, O people saved by the LORD, the shield of thy help, and who *is* the sword of thy excellency! and thine enemies shall be found liars unto thee; and thou shalt tread upon their high places.

CHAPTER 34

1. **And Moses went** up from the plains of Moab **unto the mountain of Nebo, to the top of Pisgah,** that *is* over against Jericho. **And the LORD shewed him all the land of Gilead,** unto Dan,

2. **And** all

323

■ **Naphtali, and** the land of
■ **Ephraim, and Manasseh,**
■ **and** all the land of
■ **Judah,** unto the utmost sea,
■ 3. **And the south,** and the
plain of the valley of Jericho,
the city of palm trees,
■ **unto Zoar.**
■ 4. **And the LORD said** unto him,
■ **This is the land which I**
■ **sware unto Abraham,**
unto Isaac, and unto Jacob, saying,
■ **I will give it unto thy seed:**
■ **I have caused thee to**
■ **see it** with thine eyes,
■ **but thou shalt not go** over
■ **thither.**
■ 5. **So Moses** the
servant of the LORD
■ **died** there in the land of Moab,
according to the word of the LORD.
■ 6. **And he buried him**
■ **in** a valley in the land of
■ **Moab,** over against Beth–peor:
■ **but no man knoweth of**
■ **his sepulchre** unto this day.
7. And Moses *was* an hundred
and twenty years old

■ **when he died: his eye was**
■ **not dim, nor his natural**
■ **force abated.**
■ 8. **And** the children of
■ **Israel wept for Moses**
in the plains of Moab
■ **thirty days:**
so the days of weeping
and mourning for
Moses were ended.
■ 9. **And Joshua** the son of Nun
■ **was full of the spirit of**
■ **wisdom; for Moses had laid**
■ **his hands upon him:** and the
children of Israel hearkened unto him,
and did as the LORD commanded
Moses.
■ 10. **And there arose not a**
■ **prophet since in Israel like**
■ **unto Moses, whom the**
■ **LORD knew face to face,**
11. In all the signs and the wonders,
which the LORD sent him to do in
the land of Egypt to Pharaoh, and
to all his servants, and to all his land,
12. And in all that mighty hand, and
in all the great terror which Moses
shewed in the sight of all Israel.

THE BOOK OF JOSHUA

BACKGROUND INFORMATION

Author : Joshua the successor of Moses
Date Written: Between 1491 — 1451 B.C.

Number of:
Verses—658
Chapters—24
Total Worlds—18,858
Scan Words—6,002
Scan Words Represent Approximately 31% of Total Words

Theme: Entering into the Land of Promise, and the Conquering and Dividing of the land

OUTLINE OF THE BOOK

I.   **Entering Canaan,** the Promised Land
     1:1 — 5:15
II. **The Conquest** of Canaan
     6:1 — 12:24
III. **The Division of the Land** Between the Twelve Tribes
     13:1 — 22:24
IV. **The Death of Joshua**
     23:1 — 24:33

CHAPTER 1

■ 1. **Now after the death**
■ **of Moses** the servant of
the LORD it came to pass, that
■ **the LORD spake unto**
■ **Joshua** the son of Nun,
Moses' minister,
■ **saying,**
2. Moses my servant is
dead; now therefore arise,
■ **go over** this
■ **Jordan,** thou, and all this people,
■ **unto the land which**
■ **I do give** to them, *even*
■ **to** the children of
■ **Israel.**
3. **Every place** that the sole of
■ **your foot shall**
■ **tread** upon, that
■ **have I given unto you,**
as I said unto Moses.
■ 4. **From the wilderness**
and this Lebanon even
■ **unto** the great river,
■ **the river Euphrates,**
all the land of the Hittites,
■ **and unto the great sea**
toward the going down of the sun,
■ **shall be your coast.**
■ 5. **There shall not any man**
■ **be able to stand before**
■ **thee** all the days of thy life:
■ **as I was with Moses,**
■ **so I will be with thee:**
I will not fail thee, nor forsake thee.
6. Be strong and of a good courage:
for unto this people shalt thou divide
for an inheritance the land, which I
sware unto their fathers to give them.
■ 7. **Only be** thou
■ **strong and** very
■ **courageous,** that thou
mayest observe to
■ **do according to all**
■ **the law,** which Moses my
servant commanded thee:
■ **turn not from it** *to* the
right hand or *to* the left,
■ **that thou mayest prosper**
withersoever thou goest.
■ 8. **This book of the law**
■ **shall not depart out of**
■ **thy mouth;** but thou shalt
■ **meditate therein day and**
■ **night,** that thou mayest observe to
■ **do** according to
■ **all that is written therein:**
■ **for then thou shalt make**
■ **thy way prosperous,**
■ **and then thou shalt**
■ **have good success.**
9. Have not I commanded thee?
Be strong and of a good courage;
■ **be not afraid, neither** be thou
■ **dismayed: for the**
■ **LORD** thy God
■ **is with thee** whithersoever
thou goest.
■ 10. **Then Joshua**
■ **commanded the**
■ **officers** of the people,
■ **saying,**
11. Pass through the host, and
■ **command the people,**
■ **saying, Prepare** you
■ **victuals; for within three**
■ **days ye shall pass over** this
■ **Jordan,** to go in
■ **to possess the land,**
which the LORD your God
giveth you to possess it.
■ 12. **And to the**
■ **Reubenites, and** to the
■ **Gadites, and** to
■ **half the tribe of Manasseh,**
■ **spake Joshua, saying,**
■ 13. **Remember the word** which
■ **Moses** the servant of the LORD
■ **commanded you,**
saying, The LORD your
■ **God** hath given you rest, and
■ **hath given you this land.**
14. Your wives, your little ones,
and your cattle, shall remain in
the land which Moses gave you
on this side Jordan; but
■ **ye shall pass before your**
■ **brethren armed,** all the mighty
men of valour, and help them;
■ 15. **Until the LORD have**
■ **given your brethren rest,** as
he hath given you, and they also have
possessed the land which the LORD
your God giveth them: then ye
shall return unto the land of your
possession, and enjoy it, which

Moses the LORD's servant gave you on this side Jordan toward the sunrising.

16. **And they answered Joshua, saying, All that thou commandest us we will do,** and whithersoever thou sendest us, we will go.

17. According as we hearkened unto Moses in all things,so will we hearken unto thee: only the LORD thy God be with thee, as he was with Moses.

18. **Whosoever** *he be* that **doth rebel against thy commandment,** and will not hearken unto thy words in all that thou commandest him, he **shall be put to death:** only be strong and of a good courage.

CHAPTER 2

1. **And Joshua** the son of Nun **sent** out of Shittim **two men to spy** secretly, **saying, Go view** the land, even **Jericho. And they** went, and **came into an harlot's house, named Rahab,** and lodged there.

2. **And it was told the king of Jericho,** saying, Behold, **there came men** in hither to-night of the children of Israel **to search out the country.**

3. **And the king** of Jericho **sent unto Rahab, saying, Bring forth the men** that are come to thee, which are entered into thine house: for they be come to search out all the country.

4. **And the woman** took the two men, and **hid them, and said** thus, **There came men** unto me, **but** I wist not whence they *were:*

5. And it came to pass *about the time* of shutting of the gate, **when it was dark, that the men went out:** whither the men went I wot not: pursue after them quickly; for ye shall overtake them.

6. **But she had brought them** up **to the roof** of the house, **and hid them** with the stalks of flax, which she had laid in order upon the roof.

7. And the men pursued after them the way to Jordan unto the fords: and as soon as they which pursued after them were gone out, they shut the gate.

8. And before they were laid down, she came up unto them upon theroof;

9. **And she said unto the men, I know** that **the LORD hath given you the land, and** that **your terror is fallen upon us,** and that all the inhabitants of the land faint because of you.

10. **For we** have **heard how the LORD dried up** the water of **the Red sea** for you, when ye came out of Egypt; **and what ye did unto the two kings of the Amorites,** that *were* on the other side Jordan, Sihon and Og, whom ye utterly destroyed.

11. **And** as soon as we had heard *these things,* **our hearts did melt,** neither did there remain any more courage in any man, because of you: **for the LORD your God, he is God** in heaven above, and in earth beneath.

12. Now therefore, **I pray you,** swear unto me by the LORD, **since I have shewed you kindness,** that **ye will also shew kindness unto my father's house,** and give me a true token:

13. And *that* ye will save alive my father, and my mother, and my brethren, and my sisters, and all that they have, and deliver our lives from death.

14. **And the men answered** her, Our life for yours, if ye utter not this our business. And it shall be,

■ **when the LORD hath**
■ **given us the land,** that
■ **we will deal kindly** and truly
■ **with thee.**
■ 15. **Then she let them**
■ **down by a cord**
■ **through the window: for** her
house *was* upon the town wall, and
■ **she dwelt upon the wall.**
16. And she said unto them, Get
you to the mountain, lest the
pursuers meet you; and hide
yourselves there three days,
until the pursuers be returned: and
afterward may ye go your way.
■ 17. **And the men**
■ **said unto her,** We *will be*
blameless of this thine oath
which thou hast made us swear.
■ 18. **Behold, when we come**
■ **into the land,** thou shalt
■ **bind this** line of
■ **scarlet thread in the**
■ **window** which thou didst let us
down by: and thou shalt bring thy
father, and thy mother, and thy
brethren, and all thy father's
household, home unto thee.
19. And it shall be, *that* whosoever
shall go out of the doors of thy house
into the street, his blood *shall be* upon
his head, and we *will be* guiltless:
■ **and whosoever**
■ **shall be** with thee
■ **in the house, his blood**
■ **shall be on our head, if**
■ **any hand be upon him.**
20. And if thou utter this our
business, then we will be quit
of thine oath which thou hast
made us to swear.
■ 21. **And she said,**
■ **According unto**
■ **your words, so be it.**
■ **And she** sent them away,
and they departed: and she
■ **bound the scarlet line**
■ **in the window.**
22. And they went, and came unto
the mountain, and abode there three
days, until the pursuers were
returned: and the pursuers sought
them throughout all the way,

but found *them* not.
■ 23. **So the two men**
■ **returned,** and descended from the
mountain, and passed over, and
came to Joshua the son of Nun, and
told him all *things* that befell them:
■ 24. **And they said unto**
■ **Joshua, Truly the LORD**
■ **hath delivered into**
■ **our hands all the**
■ **land; for** even
■ **all the inhabitants**
of the country do
■ **faint because of us.**

CHAPTER 3

■ 1. **And Joshua**
rose early in the morning; and
they removed from Shittim, and
■ **came to Jordan,** he
■ **and all** the children of
■ **Israel,** and
■ **lodged there** before
they passed over.
■ 2. **And** it came to pass
after three days, that
■ **the officers went**
■ **through the host;**
3. And they commanded the people,
■ **saying, When ye see**
■ **the ark** of the covenant of the
LORD your God, and the priests
the Levites bearing it, then
■ **ye shall** remove
from your place, and
■ **go after it.**
4. Yet there shall be a space between
you and it, about two thousand cubits
by measure: come not near unto it,
that ye may know the way by which
ye must go: for ye have not passed
this way heretofore.
■ 5. **And Joshua said**
unto the people,
■ **Sanctify yourselves: for**
■ **to-morrow the LORD will**
■ **do wonders** among you.
■ 6. **And Joshua spake unto**
■ **the priests, saying, Take** up
■ **the ark** of the covenant,
■ **and pass over before**
■ **the people.** And they took
up the ark of the covenant, and

went before the people.

7. And the LORD said unto Joshua, This day will I begin to magnify thee in the sight of all Israel, that they may know that,

as I was with Moses, so I will be with thee.

8. And thou shalt **command the priests that bear the ark** of the covenant, **saying, When ye are come to the** brink of the water of **Jordan,** ye shall **stand still** in Jordan.

9. And Joshua said unto the children of Israel, **Come hither, and hear the words of the LORD** your God.

10. And Joshua said, **Hereby ye shall know** that the living **God is among you,** and *that* he will without fail drive out from before you the Canaanites, and the Hittites, and the Hivites, and the Perizzites, and the Girgashites, and the Amorites, and the Jebusites.

11. Behold, the ark of the covenant of the LORD of all the earth **passeth over before you into Jordan.**

12. Now therefore take you twelve men out of the tribes of Israel, out of every tribe a man.

13. And it shall come to pass, **as soon as** the soles of **the feet of the priests** that bear the ark of the LORD, the LORD of all the earth, **shall rest in the waters** of Jordan, *that* **the waters** of Jordan **shall be cut off** *from* the waters that come down from above; **and** they shall **stand upon an heap.**

14. And it came to pass, when the people removed from their tents, to pass over Jordan, and the priests bearing the ark of the covenant before the people;

15. And as they that bare the ark were come unto Jordan, and

the feet of the priests that bare the ark **were dipped in** the brim of **the water,** (for Jordan overfloweth all his banks all the time of harvest,)

16. That **the waters** which came down from above stood *and* **rose up upon an heap** very far from the city Adam, that *is* beside Zaretan: and those that came down toward the sea of the plain, *even* the salt sea, failed, **and were cut off: and the people passed over** right against Jericho.

17. And the priests that bare the ark of the covenant of the LORD **stood** firm **on dry ground in the midst of Jordan, and all the Israelites passed over on dry ground,** until all the people were passed clean over Jordan.

CHAPTER 4

1. **And** it came to pass, when all the people were clean passed over Jordan, that **the LORD spake unto Joshua, saying,**

2. **Take** you twelve men out of the people, **out of every tribe a man,**

3. **And command** ye **them, saying, Take** you hence **out of the** midst of **Jordan,** out of the place where the priests' feet stood firm, **twelve stones,** and ye shall carry them over with you, **and leave them** in the lodging place, **where ye shall lodge this night.**

4. **Then Joshua called** the twelve men, whom he had prepared of the children of Israel, **out of every tribe a man:**

5. **And Joshua said** unto them, **Pass** over **before the ark** of the LORD your

God into the midst of Jordan,
■ **and take** you
■ **up** every man of you
■ **a stone** upon his shoulder,
according unto the number of the
tribes of the children of Israel:
■ 6. **That this may be**
■ **a sign** among you,
■ **that when your**
■ **children ask** *their fathers*
in time to come, saying,
■ **What mean ye by**
■ **these stones?**
7. Then ye shall
■ **answer them, That the**
■ **waters of Jordan were**
■ **cut off** before the ark of the
covenant of the LORD; when it
passed over Jordan, the waters
of Jordan were cut off:
■ **and these stones shall**
■ **be for a memorial**
unto the children of Israel for ever.
■ 8. **And** the children of
■ **Israel did** so
■ **as Joshua commanded,** and
took up twelve stones out of the midst
of Jordan, as the LORD spake unto
Joshua, according to the
number of the tribes of the children
of Israel, and carried them over with
them unto the place where they
lodged, and laid them down there.
■ 9. **And Joshua set up twelve**
■ **stones in the midst of**
■ **Jordan,** in the place
■ **where the feet of the priests**
which bare the ark of the covenant
■ **stood:** and they are there
unto this day.
10. For the priests which bare the ark
stood in the midst of Jordan, until
every thing was finished that the
LORD commanded Joshua to speak
unto the people, according to all that
Moses commanded Joshua: and the
people hasted and passed over.
■ 11. **And** it came to pass,
■ **when all the**
■ **people** were clean
■ **passed over,** that
■ **the ark** of the LORD
■ **passed over, and**

■ **the priests,**
in the presence of the people.
■ 12. **And** the children of Reuben,
and the children of Gad, and half
the tribe of Manasseh, passed over
armed before the children of Israel,
as Moses spake unto them:
■ 13. **About forty thousand**
■ **prepared for war**
■ **passed over** before the LORD
■ **unto battle,** to the
plains of Jericho.
14. On that day the LORD magnified
Joshua in the sight of all Israel; and
they feared him, as they feared
Moses, all the days of his life.
15. And the LORD spake
unto Joshua, saying,
16. Command the priests that
bear the ark of the testimony,
that they come up out of Jordan.
17. Joshua therefore commanded
the priests, saying, Come ye
up out of Jordan.
■ 18. **And it came to pass,**
■ **when the priests** that bare
the ark of the covenant of the LORD
■ **were come** up
■ **out** of the midst
■ **of Jordan,** *and* the soles of
the priests' feet were lifted up
■ **unto the dry land, that**
■ **the waters of Jordan**
■ **returned** unto their place,
and flowed over all his banks,
as *they did* before.
■ 19. **And the people**
came up out of Jordan on the
tenth *day* of the first month, and
■ **encamped in Gilgal,**
in the east border of Jericho.
■ 20. **And those twelve**
■ **stones,** which
■ **they took out of Jordan,**
■ **did Joshua pitch in Gilgal.**
■ 21. **And he spake**
unto the children of Israel,
■ **saying, When your**
■ **children shall ask** their
fathers in time to come, saying,
■ **What mean these stones?**
■ 22. **Then** ye shall
■ **let your children know,**

■ **saying, Israel came over**
■ **this Jordan on dry land.**
23. For the LORD your God dried up the waters of Jordan from before you, until ye were passed over, as the LORD your God did to the Red sea, which he dried up from before us, until we were gone over:
■ 24. **That all the people of**
■ **the earth might know the**
■ **hand of the LORD,** that it
■ **is mighty:** that ye might fear the LORD your God for ever.

CHAPTER 5
■ 1. **And** it came to pass,
■ **when** all
■ **the kings of the**
■ **Amorites,** which *were* on the side of Jordan westward,
■ **and** all the kings of the
■ **Canaanites,** which *were* by the sea,
■ **heard that the LORD** had
■ **dried up** the waters of
■ **Jordan** from before the children of Israel, until we were passed over, that
■ **their heart melted,** neither was there spirit in them any more, because of the children of Israel.
■ 2. **At that time the LORD**
■ **said** unto Joshua, Make thee sharp knives, and
■ **circumcise again the**
■ **children of Israel** the second time.
■ 3. **And Joshua** made him sharp knives, and
■ **circumcised the children of**
■ **Israel** at the hill of the foreskins.
■ 4. **And this is** the cause
■ **why Joshua did**
■ **circumcise:**
■ **All** the people
■ **that came out of**
■ **Egypt,** *that were* males,
■ **even all the men of war,**
■ **died in the wilderness** by the way, after they came out of Egypt.
5. Now all the people that came out were circumcised:
■ **but all** the people *that were*
■ **born in the wilderness** by the

way as they came forth out of Egypt,
■ **them they had not**
■ **circumcised.**
6. **For** the children of
■ **Israel walked forty years**
■ **in the wilderness, till**
■ **all the** people *that were*
■ **men of war, which**
■ **came out of Egypt, were**
■ **consumed, because they**
■ **obeyed not** the voice of
■ **the LORD:** unto whom the LORD sware that he would not shew them the land, which the LORD sware unto their fathers that he would give us, a land that floweth with milk and honey.
■ 7. **And their children,** *whom* he raised up in their stead, them
■ **Joshua circumcised:** for they were uncircumcised, because they had not circumcised them by the way.
■ 8. **And** it came to pass,
■ **when they had done**
■ **circumcising** all the people, that
■ **they abode** in their places
■ **in the camp, till they**
■ **were whole.**
■ 9. **And the LORD said** unto Joshua, This day have
■ **I rolled away the reproach**
■ **of Egypt** from off you.
■ **Wherefore the name**
■ **of the place is called**
■ **Gilgal** unto this day.
■ 10. **And** the children of
■ **Israel** encamped in Gilgal, and
■ **kept the passover on the**
■ **fourteenth day of the month** at even in the plains of Jericho.
11. And they did eat of the old corn of the land on the morrow after the passover, unleavened cakes, and parched *corn* in the selfsame day.
■ 12. **And the manna ceased** on the morrow after they had eaten of the old corn of the land; neither had the children of Israel manna anymore;
■ **but they did eat of the**
■ **fruit of the land of**
■ **Canaan** that year.
■ 13. **And it came to pass,** when
■ **Joshua** was by Jericho, that he lifted up his eyes and

■ looked, and, behold,
■ there stood a man
over against him
■ with his sword
■ drawn in his hand:
■ and Joshua went unto him, and
■ said unto him,
■ Art thou for us, or for
■ our adversaries?
■ 14. And he said, Nay; but as
■ captain of the host of the
■ LORD am I now come.
■ And Joshua fell on his
face to the earth, and
■ did worship, and
■ said unto him,
■ What saith my Lord
■ unto his servant?
■ 15. And the captain
■ of the LORD's host
■ said unto Joshua,
■ Loose thy shoe
from off thy foot;
■ for the place whereon
■ thou standest is holy.
And Joshua did so.

CHAPTER 6

■ 1. Now Jericho was straitly
■ shut up because
■ of the children of
■ Israel: none went out,
and none came in.
■ 2. And the LORD said
■ unto Joshua, See, I
■ have given into thine
■ hand Jericho, and the king
thereof, *and* the mighty men of valour.
3. And ye shall
■ compass the city,
all *ye* men of war,
■ and go round about
■ the city once. Thus shalt
■ thou do six days.
■ 4. And seven priests
■ shall bear before the ark
■ seven trumpets of rams' horns:
■ and the seventh day ye shall
■ compass the city seven
■ times, and the priests shall
■ blow with
■ the trumpets.
5. And it shall come to pass, that

■ when they make a long
■ blast with the ram's horn,
■ and when ye hear
■ the sound of the
■ trumpet, all the people
■ shall shout with a great shout;
■ and the wall of the city
■ shall fall down flat, and
the people shall ascend up
every man straight before him.
6. And Joshua the son of Nun called
the priests, and said unto them,
Take up the ark of the covenant,
and let seven priests bear seven
trumpets of rams' horns before
the ark of the LORD.
7. And he said unto the people,
Pass on, and compass the city,
and let him that is armed pass
on before the ark of the LORD.
■ 8. And it came to pass,
when Joshua had spoken
unto the people, that
■ the seven priests
■ bearing the seven
■ trumpets of rams' horns
■ passed on
■ before the LORD,
■ and blew with
■ the trumpets: and the ark
of the covenant of the LORD
■ followed them.
■ 9. And the armed men went
■ before the priests that blew with
the trumpets, and the rereward came
after the ark, *the priests* going on, and
blowing with the trumpets.
■ 10. And Joshua had
■ commanded the people,
■ saying, Ye shall not shout, nor
■ make any noise
with your voice,
■ neither shall any word
■ proceed out of your
■ mouth, until the day I bid
■ you shout; then shall ye shout.
■ 11. So the ark of the LORD
■ compassed the city,
going about *it*
■ once: and they
came into the camp, and
■ lodged in the camp.
12. And Joshua rose early

in the morning, and the priests took up the ark of the LORD.

13. And seven priests bearing seven trumpets of rams' horns before the ark of the LORD went on continually, and blew with the trumpets: and the armed men went before them; but the rereward came after the ark of the LORD, *the priests* going on, and blowing with the trumpets.

14. **And the second day they compassed the city once,** and returned into the camp: **so they did six days.**

15. And it came to pass **on the seventh day, that they** rose early about the dawning of the day, and **compassed the city after the same manner seven times:** only on that day they compassed the city seven times.

16. **And** it came to pass at the seventh time, when **the priests blew with the trumpets, Joshua said unto the people, Shout;** for the LORD hath given you the city.

17. **And the city shall be accursed,** *even* it, and all that *are* therein, to the LORD: **only Rahab the harlot shall live, she and all that are with her in the house,** because she hid the messengers that we sent.

18. **And** ye, in any wise **keep** *yourselves* **from the accursed thing, lest ye make yourselves accursed,** when ye take of the accursed thing, and make the camp of Israel a curse, and trouble it.

19. **But all the silver,** and **gold, and vessels of brass and iron, are consecrated** unto the LORD: **they shall come into the treasury of the LORD.**

20. So the people shouted when *the priests* blew with the trumpets: **and it came to pass, when the people heard the sound of the trumpet, and the people shouted** with a great shout, that **the wall fell down flat, so that the people went up into the city,** every man straight before him, and they took the city.

21. **And they utterly destroyed** all that *was* in **the city, both man and woman, young and old,** and **ox, and sheep, and ass, with the edge of the sword.**

22. But Joshua had said unto the two men that had spied out the country, Go into the harlot's house, and bring out thence the woman, and all that she hath, as ye sware unto her.

23. **And the young men that were spies** went in, and **brought out Rahab, and** her **mother, and** her brethren, **and all that she had; and** they brought out **all her kindred, and left them without the camp** of Israel.

24. **And they burnt the city with fire,** and all that *was* therein: **only the silver, and the gold, and the vessels of brass and** of **iron, they put into the treasury** of the house of the LORD.

25. **And Joshua saved Rahab** the harlot alive, and her father's household, and all that she had; and she dwelleth in Israel *even* unto this day; because she hid the messengers, which Joshua sent to spy out Jericho.

26. **And Joshua adjured** them at that time, **saying, Cursed be the man** before the LORD, **that** riseth up and

buildeth this city Jericho: he shall lay the foundation thereof in his firstborn, and in his youngest *son* shall he set up the gates of it.

27. **So the LORD was with Joshua: and his fame was noised throughout** all **the country.**

CHAPTER 7

1. **But** the children of Israel committed a trespass in the accursed thing: for **Achan,** the son of Carmi, the son of Zabdi, the son of Zerah, of the tribe of Judah, **took of the accursed thing: and the anger of the LORD was kindled against** the children of **Israel.**

2. **And Joshua sent men from Jericho to Ai,** which *is* beside Beth-aven, on the east of Beth-el, and spake unto them, **saying,** Go up and **view the country.** And the men went up and viewed Ai.

3. **And they returned to Joshua, and said** unto him, **Let not all the people go** up; **but let about two or three thousand men go up and smite Ai;** *and* make not all the people to labour thither; **for they are but few.**

4. **So there went up** thither of the people **about three thousand men: and they fled before the men of Ai.**

5. **And the men of Ai smote** of them **about thirty** and **six men:** for they chased them *from* before the gate *even* unto Shebarim, and smote them in the going down: **wherefore the hearts of the people melted,** and became as water.

6. **And Joshua rent his clothes, and fell** to the earth **upon his face before the ark** of the LORD **until the eventide, he and the elders of Israel,** and put dust upon their heads.

7. **And Joshua said, Alas, O LORD** God, wherefore **hast thou** at all **brought this people over Jordan,** to deliver us into the hand of the Amorites, **to destroy us?** would to God we had been content, and dwelt on the other side Jordan!

8. **O LORD, what shall I say, when Israel turneth their backs before their enemies!**

9. For the Canaanites and all the inhabitants of the land shall hear *of it,* and shall environ us round, and cut off our name from the earth: and what wilt thou do unto thy great name?

10. **And the LORD said** unto Joshua, **Get thee up;** wherefore liest thou thus upon thy face?

11. **Israel hath sinned,** and they have also transgressed my covenant which I commanded them: **for they have** even **taken of the accursed thing,** and have also stolen, and dissembled also, **and** they **have put it** even **among their own stuff.**

12. **Therefore** the children of **Israel could not stand** before their enemies, *but* turned *their* backs before their enemies, **because they were accursed:** neither will I be with you any more, except ye destroy the accursed from among you.

13. **Up, sanctify the people,** and say, Sanctify yourselves **against to-morrow: for** thus saith the LORD God of Israel, **There is an accursed thing in the midst of thee,** O Israel: **thou canst not stand before thine enemies, until**

■ ye take away the accursed
■ thing from among you.

14. In the morning therefore ye shall be brought according to your tribes: and it shall be, *that* the tribe which the LORD taketh shall come according to the families *thereof;* and the family which the LORD shall take shall come by households; and the household which the LORD shall take shall come man by man.

■ 15. **And it shall be, that he**
■ **that is taken with the**
■ **accursed thing shall**
■ **be burnt with fire,** he

and all that he hath:
■ **because he hath**
■ **transgressed the**
■ **covenant** of the LORD,
■ **and because he hath**
■ **wrought folly in Israel.**

■ 16. **So Joshua** rose up

early in the morning, and
■ **brought Israel by**
■ **their tribes;** and the

tribe of Judah was taken:

17. And he brought the family of Judah; and he took the family of the Zarhites: and he brought the family of the Zarhites man by man; and Zabdi was taken:

18. And he brought his household man by man;

■ **and Achan,** the son of Carmi,

the son of Zabdi, the son of Zerah,
■ **of the tribe of Judah,**
■ **was taken.**

■ 19. **And Joshua said unto**
■ **Achan,** My son, give, I pray thee,

glory to the LORD God of Israel, and
■ **make confession** unto him;
■ **and tell me** now
■ **what thou hast done;**

hide *it* not from me.
■ 20. **And Achan**
■ **answered** Joshua,

and said, Indeed
■ **I have sinned** against the

LORD God of Israel, and thus and thus have I done:
■ 21. **When I saw among**
■ **the spoils a** goodly
■ **Babylonish garment, and**

■ **two hundred shekels of**
■ **silver, and a wedge of**
■ **gold** of fifty shekels weight, then
■ **I coveted them, and**
■ **took them;** and, behold,
■ **they are hid in the**
■ **earth in** the midst of
■ **my tent,** and the silver under it.

■ 22. **So Joshua sent**
■ **messengers,** and they ran unto

the tent; and, behold, *it was* hid in his tent, and the silver under it.

■ 23. **And they took them**

out of the midst of the tent,
■ **and brought them**
■ **unto Joshua,**

and unto all the children of Israel, and laid them out before the LORD.

24. And Joshua,
■ **and all Israel** with him,
■ **took Achan** the son of Zerah,

and the silver, and the garment, and the wedge of gold, and
■ **his sons, and** his
■ **daughters,** and his

oxen, and his asses, and his sheep, and his tent,
■ **and all that he had: and** they
■ **brought them unto**
■ **the valley of Achor.**

25. And Joshua said, Why hast thou troubled us? the LORD shall trouble thee this day.
■ **And all Israel stoned**
■ **him** with stones,
■ **and burned them**
■ **with fire,** after they had

stoned them with stones.
26. **And** they
■ **raised over him a great**
■ **heap of stones** unto this day.
■ **So the LORD turned**
■ **from** the fierceness of
■ **his anger.** Wherefore the

name of that place was called, The valley of Achor, unto this day.

CHAPTER 8

■ 1. **And the LORD said**
■ **unto Joshua,** Fear not,

neither be thou dismayed:
■ **take all the people**
■ **of war** with thee,

■ **and** arise,

■ **go** up

■ **to Ai:** see, I have given into thy
hand the king of Ai, and his people,
and his city, and his land:

■ 2. **And** thou shalt

■ **do to Ai** and her king

■ **as thou didst unto Jericho**
and her king: only the spoil thereof,
and the cattle thereof, shall ye take
for a prey unto yourselves: lay thee
an ambush for the city behind it.
3. So Joshua arose, and all the
people of war, to go up against Ai:

■ **and Joshua chose** out

■ **thirty thousand**

■ **mighty men** of valour,

■ **and sent them** away

■ **by night.**
4. And he commanded them,

■ **saying,** Behold,

■ **ye shall lie in**

■ **wait** against the city, *even*

■ **behind the city:** go not very
far from the city, but be ye all ready:

■ 5. **And I, and all the**

■ **people** that *are* with me,

■ **will approach** unto

■ **the city: and** it shall
come to pass,

■ **when they come out**

■ **against us,** as at the first, that

■ **we will flee before them,**
6. (For they will come out after us)
till we have drawn them from the
city; for they will say, They flee
before us, as at the first: therefore
we will flee before them.

■ 7. **Then ye shall rise**

■ **up** from the ambush,

■ **and seize** upon

■ **the city:** for the LORD your
God will deliver it into your hand.

■ 8. **And** it shall be,

■ **when ye have taken**

■ **the city,** that ye shall

■ **set the city on fire:** according to
the commandment of the LORD shall
ye do. See, I have commanded you.
9. Joshua therefore sent them forth:
and they went to lie in ambush, and
abode between Beth-el and Ai, on the
west side of Ai: but Joshua lodged

that night among the people.

■ 10. **And Joshua** rose up
early in the morning, and
numbered the people, and went
up, he and the elders of Israel,
before the people to Ai.

■ 11. **And all the people,**
even the people

■ **of war** that *were* with him,
went up, and drew nigh, and

■ **came before the city, and**

■ **pitched on the north side**
of Ai: now *there was* a valley
between them and Ai.

■ 12. **And he took about five**

■ **thousand men,** and set them

■ **to lie in ambush** between Beth-
el and Ai, on the west side of the city.
13. And when they had set the
people, *even* all the host that
was on the north of the city, and
their liers in wait on the west of
the city, Joshua went that night
into the midst of the valley.
14. And it came to pass,

■ **when the king of Ai**

■ **saw it,** that they hasted
and rose up early, and

■ **the men of the city went out**

■ **against Israel to battle,** he
and all his people, at a timeappointed,
before the plain; but he wist not
that *there were* liers in ambush
against him behind the city.

■ 15. **And Joshua and all**

■ **Israel made as if they were**

■ **beaten** before them, and fled by
the way of the wilderness.
16. And all the people that *were* in Ai
were called together to pursue after
them: and they pursued after Joshua,
and were drawn away from the city.

■ 17. **And there was not a**

■ **man left in Ai or Beth-el,**

■ **that went not out after**

■ **Israel:** and they left the city
open, and pursued after Israel.

■ 18. **And the LORD said**

■ **unto Joshua, Stretch out**

■ **the spear** that *is* in thy hand

■ **toward Ai; for I will give**

■ **it into thine hand. And**

■ **Joshua stretched out the**

■ **spear** that *he had* in his hand
■ **toward the city.**
■ 19. **And the ambush** arose
quickly out of their place, and they ran
as soon as he had stretched
out his hand: and they
■ **entered into the city,**
■ **and took it,** and hasted
■ **and set the city on fire.**
■ 20. **And** when
■ **the men of Ai** looked
behind them, they
■ **saw,** and, behold,
■ **the smoke of the city**
ascended up to heaven,
■ **and they had no power to**
■ **flee** this way or that way: and the
people that fled to the wilderness
turned back upon the pursuers.
■ 21. **And when Joshua and**
■ **all Israel saw that the**
■ **ambush had taken the**
■ **city,** and that the smoke
of the city ascended, then
■ **they turned again,**
■ **and slew the men of Ai.**
22. And the other issued out of the
city against them; so they were in
the midst of Israel, some on this
side, and some on that side:
■ **and** they smote them, so that
■ **they let none** of them
■ **remain or escape.**
23. **And the king of Ai**
■ **they took alive, and**
■ **brought him to Joshua.**
24. And it came to pass, when Israel
had made an end of slaying all the
inhabitants of Ai in the field, in the
wilderness wherein they chased
them, and when they were all fallen
on the edge of the sword, until they
were consumed, that all the Israelites
returned unto Ai, and smote it
with the edge of the sword.
■ 25. **And** *so* it was, *that*
■ **all that fell** that day, both
■ **of men and women,**
■ **were twelve thousand,**
even all the men of Ai.
26. For Joshua drew not his hand
back, wherewith he stretched out
the spear, until he had utterly

destroyed all the inhabitants of Ai.
27. Only the cattle and the spoil of
that city Israel took for a prey unto
themselves, according unto the word
of the LORD which he
commanded Joshua.
■ 28. **And Joshua burnt Ai,**
and made it an heap for ever,
even a desolation unto this day.
■ 29. **And the king of Ai**
■ **he hanged on a tree**
■ **until** eventide: and as soon as
■ **the sun was down, Joshua**
■ **commanded that they** should
■ **take his carcase** down from
the tree, and cast it at the
entering of the gate of the city,
■ **and raise thereon a**
■ **great heap of stones,**
that remaineth unto this day.
■ 30. **Then Joshua**
■ **built an altar unto**
■ **the LORD** God of Israel
■ **in mount Ebal,**
31. As Moses the servant of the
LORD commanded the children of
Israel, as it is written in the book of
the law of Moses, an altar of whole
stones, over which no man hath lift up
any iron: and they offered thereon
burnt offerings unto the LORD, and
sacrificed peace offerings.
■ 32. **And he wrote** there
■ **upon the stones a copy**
■ **of the law of Moses,**
which he wrote in the presence
of the children of Israel.
■ 33. **And all Israel,** and
■ **their elders,** and
■ **officers, and their**
■ **judges, stood on this**
■ **side the ark and** on
■ **that side before the**
■ **priests** the Levites,
■ **which bare the**
■ **ark** of the covenant of
the LORD, as well
the stranger, as he that was
born among them; half of them
over against mount Gerizim,
and half of them over against mount
Ebal; as Moses the servant of the
LORD had commanded before,

that they should bless
the people of Israel.

34. **And** afterward
**he read all the words of the
law,** the blessings and cursings,
according to all that is
**written in the
book of the law.**
35. **There was not a word**
of all that Moses commanded,
**which Joshua read not
before all** the congregation of
Israel, with the women, and the
little ones, and the strangers that
were conversant among them.

CHAPTER 9

1. **And it came to pass,
when all the kings** which *were*
on this side Jordan, in the hills,
and in the valleys, and in all
the coasts of the great sea over
against Lebanon, the Hittite, and the
Amorite, the Canaanite, the Perizzite,
the Hivite, and the Jebusite,
heard *thereof;*
2. That
they gathered
themselves together,
to fight with Joshua and with
Israel, with one accord.
3. **And when the inhabitants
of Gibeon heard what
Joshua had done
unto Jericho and to Ai,**
4. **They** did work wilily,
and went and
**made as if they had been
ambassadors, and took
old sacks upon their
asses,** and wine bottles,
old, and rent, and bound up;
5. **And old shoes** and
clouted upon their feet,
and old garments upon them;
**and all the
bread** of their provision
was dry and mouldy.
6. **And they went to
Joshua** unto the camp at Gilgal,
and said unto him, and
to the men of Israel,
We be

**come from a far
country: now** therefore
make ye
a league with us.
7. **And the men of Israel
said** unto the Hivites, Peradventure
ye dwell among us; and
**how shall we make
a league with you?**
8. **And they said** unto Joshua,
**We are thy servants.
And Joshua said** unto them,
**Who are ye? and from
whence come ye?**
9. **And they said** unto him,
**From a very far country
thy servants are come
because of** the name of
the LORD thy God:
for we have heard
the fame of him, and
all that he did in Egypt,
10. **And all that he did to the
two kings of the Amorites,**
that *were* beyond Jordan, to Sihon
king of Heshbon, and to Og king of
Bashan, which *was* at Ashtaroth.
11. **Wherefore our elders**
and all the inhabitants of our country
spake to us,
saying, Take victuals with
you for the journey, and
**go to meet them, and
say** unto them, We *are*
your servants: therefore now
make ye a league with us.
12. **This our bread we
took hot** *for* our provision out
of our houses on the day we
came forth to go unto you;
but now, behold,
it is dry, and it is
mouldy:
13. **And these bottles
of wine,** which we filled,
were new; and, behold,
they be rent: and these
**our garments and our
shoes are become old
by reason of the very
long journey.**
14. **And the men**
took of their victuals, and

asked not
counsel at the mouth
of the LORD.
15. **And Joshua made
peace with them, and
made a league** with them,
to let them live: and the princes
of the congregation sware unto them.
16. **And** it came to pass
**at the end of three
days** after they had made a
league with them, that
**they heard that they
were their neighbours,
and** *that* they
dwelt among them.
17. **And** the children of
Israel journeyed, and
**came unto their cities on
the third day.** Now their cities
were Gibeon, and Chephirah, and
Beeroth, and Kirjath-jearim.
18. **And** the children of Israel
smote them not, because the
princes of the congregation had sworn
unto them by the LORD God of Israel.
**And all the
congregation murmured
against the princes.**
19. **But all the princes
said** unto all the congregation,
We have sworn unto them
by the LORD God of Israel: now
**therefore we may
not touch them.**
20. This we will do to them; we will
even let them live, lest wrath be
upon us, because of the oath
which we sware unto them.
21. And the princes said
unto them, Let them live;
**but let them be hewers
of wood and drawers
of water unto all the
congregation;** as the
princes had promised them.
22. **And Joshua**
called for them, and he
spake unto them, saying,
**Wherefore have ye
beguiled us,** saying, We
are very far from you; when
ye dwell among us?

23. **Now therefore ye are
cursed,** and there shall none of
you be freed from being bondmen,
and hewers of wood and drawers
of water for the house of my God.
24. **And they
answered** Joshua, and said,
**Because it was certainly
told thy servants,** how that
the LORD thy God
commanded his servant
**Moses to give you
all the land, and** to
destroy all
the inhabitants
of the land from before you,
therefore we were sore
afraid of our lives because of
you, and have done this thing.
25. **And now,** behold,
**we are in thine hand:
as it seemeth good
and right unto thee
to do** unto us, do.
26. And so did he unto them,
and delivered them out of the
hand of the children of Israel,
that they slew them not.
27. **And Joshua
made them** that day
**hewers of wood and
drawers of water for the
congregation,** and for the altar
of the LORD, even unto this day, in
the place which he should choose.

CHAPTER 10

1. Now it came to pass,
**when Adoni–zedec
king of Jerusalem** had
**heard how Joshua had
taken Ai, and** had utterly
destroyed it; as he had done
to Jericho and her king, so he
had done to Ai and her king;
**and how the inhabitants
of Gibeon had made
peace with Israel,**
and were among them;
2. That
they feared greatly,
**because Gibeon was
a great city,** as one of the

royal cities, and because it *was* greater than Ai, and all the men thereof *were* mighty.

3. **Wherefore Adoni-zedec** king of Jerusalem, **sent unto Hoham king of Hebron,** and unto **Piram king of Jarmuth,** and unto **Japhia king of Lachish, and** unto **Debir king of Eglon, saying,**

4. **Come** up unto me, **and help me, that we may smite Gibeon: for it hath made peace with** Joshua and with the children of **Israel.**

5. **Therefore the five kings** of the Amorites, the king of Jerusalem, the king of Hebron, the king of Jarmuth, the king of Lachish, the king of Eglon, gathered themselves together, and went up, they and all their hosts, and **encamped before Gibeon, and made war** against it.

6. **And the men of Gibeon sent unto Joshua** to the camp to Gilgal, **saying,** Slack not thy hand from thy servants; **come** up to us quickly, **and save us,** and help us: for all the kings of the Amorites that dwell in the mountains are gathered together against us.

7. **So Joshua ascended** from Gilgal, he, **and all the people of war** with him, and all the mighty men of valour.

8. **And the LORD said** unto Joshua, **Fear them not: for I have delivered them into thine hand;** there shall not a man of them stand before thee.

9. **Joshua therefore** came unto them suddenly, *and* **went up from Gilgal all night.**

10. **And the LORD** discomfited them before Israel, and **slew them** with a great slaughter **at Gibeon,** and chased them along the way that goeth up to Beth-horon, and smote them to Azekah, and unto Makkedah.

11. **And** it came to pass, **as they fled** from before Israel, *and* were in the going down to Beth-horon, that **the LORD cast down great stones** from heaven upon them unto Azekah, **and** they died: **they were more which died with hailstones than they whom** the children of **Israel slew** with the sword.

12. **Then spake Joshua to the LORD** in the day when the LORD delivered up the Amorites before the children of Israel, **and** he **said** in the sight of Israel, **Sun, stand** thou **still upon Gibeon; and** thou, **Moon, in the valley of Ajalon.**

13. **And the sun stood still, and the moon stayed, until the people had avenged themselves upon their enemies.** *Is* not this written in the book of Jasher? So the sun stood still in the midst of heaven, and hasted not to go down about a whole day.

14. **And there was no day like that before it or after it,** that the LORD hearkened unto the voice of a man: for the LORD fought for Israel.

15. **And Joshua returned,** and all Israel with him, **unto** the camp to **Gilgal.**

16. **But these five kings fled, and hid** themselves **in a cave** at Makkedah.

17. **And it was told Joshua,** saying, The five kings are found hid in a cave at Makkedah.

18. **And Joshua said, Roll great stones upon the**

mouth of the cave, and set
men by it for to keep them:
19. **And** stay ye not, *but*
pursue after
your enemies,
and smite the hindmost of them;
suffer them not to enter
into their cities: for the
LORD your God hath delivered
them into your hand.
20. And it came to pass,
when Joshua
and the children of
Israel had made an
end of slaying them with
a very great slaughter, till
they were consumed, that
the rest which
remained of them
entered into fenced cities.
21. **And** all the people
returned to the camp to
Joshua at Makkedah in peace:
none moved his tongue
against any of the children of
Israel.
22. **Then said Joshua,**
Open the mouth of the
cave, and bring out those five
kings unto me out of the cave.
23. And they did so, and broughtforth
those five kings unto him out of the
cave, the king of Jerusalem, the king
of Hebron, the king of Jarmuth, the
king of Lachish, *and* the king ofEglon.
24. **And** it came to pass,
when they brought
out those kings
unto Joshua, that
Joshua called for all
the men of Israel, and
said unto the captains of
the men of war which went with him,
Come near,
put your feet upon the
necks of these kings. And they
came near, and put their feet upon
the necks of them.
25. **And Joshua said** unto
them, Fear not, nor be dismayed,
be strong and of good courage: for
thus shall the LORD do
to all your enemies

against whom ye fight.
26. **And** afterward
Joshua smote them, and
slew them, and hanged
them on five trees: and
they were hanging upon the
trees until the evening.
27. **And** it came to pass
at the time of the going
down of the sun, *that*
Joshua commanded, and
they took them down
off the trees, and cast
them into the cave
wherein they had been hid,
and laid great stones
in the cave's mouth,
which remain until this very day.
28. **And that day Joshua**
took Makkedah, and
smote it with the
edge of the sword, and
the king thereof he
utterly destroyed, them,
and all the souls that *were*
therein; he let none remain:
and he did to the king of Makkedah
as he did unto the king of Jericho.
29. **Then** Joshua passed
from Makkedah, and all
Israel with him, unto Libnah, and
fought against Libnah:
30. **And the LORD delivered**
it also, and the king thereof,
into the hand of Israel; and
he smote it with the edge of the
sword, and all the souls that *were*
therein; he let none remain in it;
but did unto the king thereof as
he did unto the king of Jericho.
31. And Joshua passed from
Libnah, and all Israel with him,
unto Lachish, and encamped
against it, and fought against it:
32. **And the LORD delivered**
Lachish into the hand of
Israel, which took it on the
second day, and smote it with the
edge of the sword, and all the souls
that *were* therein, according to
all that he had done to Libnah.
33. **Then Horam king of**
Gezer came up to help

Lachish; and Joshua smote him and his people, until he had left him none remaining.

34. And from Lachish Joshua passed unto Eglon, and all Israel with him; and they encamped against it, and fought against it:

35. And they took it on that day, and smote it with the edge of the sword, and all the souls that *were* therein he utterly destroyed that day, according to all that he had done to Lachish.

36. And Joshua went up from Eglon, and all Israel with him, unto Hebron; and they fought against it:

37. And they took it, and smote it with the edge of the sword, and the king thereof, and all the cities thereof, and all the souls that *were* therein; he left none remaining, according to all that he had done to Eglon; but destroyed it utterly, and all the souls that *were* therein.

38. And Joshua returned, and all Israel with him, to Debir; and fought against it:

39. And he took it, and the king thereof, and all the cities thereof; and they smote them with the edge of the sword, and utterly destroyed all the souls that *were* therein; he left none remaining: as he had done to Hebron, so he did to Debir, and to the king thereof; as he had done also to Libnah, and to her king.

40. So Joshua smote all the country of the hills, and of the south, and of the vale, and of the springs, and all their kings: he left none remaining, but utterly destroyed all that breathed, as the LORD God of Israel commanded.

41. And Joshua smote them from Kadesh-barnea even unto Gaza, and all the country of Goshen, even unto Gibeon.

42. And all these kings and their land did Joshua take at one time, because the LORD God of Israel fought for Israel.

43. And Joshua returned, and all Israel with him, unto the camp to Gilgal.

CHAPTER 11

1. And it came to pass, when Jabin king of Hazor had heard those things, that he sent to Jobab king of Madon, and to the king of Shimron, and to the king of Achshaph,

2. And to the kings that *were* on the north of the mountains, and of the plains south of Chinneroth, and in the valley, and in the borders of Dor on the west,

3. And to the Canaanite on the east and on the west, and *to* the Amorite, and the Hittite, and the Perizzite, and the Jebusite in the mountains, and *to* the Hivite under Hermon in the land of Mizpeh.

4. And they went out, they and all their hosts with them, much people, even as the sand that is upon the sea shore in multitude, with horses and chariots very many.

5. And when all these kings were met together, they came and pitched together at the waters of Merom, to fight against Israel.

6. And the LORD said unto Joshua, Be not afraid because of them: for to-morrow about this time will I deliver them up all slain before Israel: thou shalt hough their horses, and burn their chariots with fire.

7. So Joshua came,

and all the people of war with him,
■ **against them** by the
waters of Merom
■ **suddenly; and they**
■ **fell upon them.**
■ 8. **And the LORD delivered**
■ **them into the hand of**
■ **Israel,** who smote them, and
chased them unto great Zidon, and
unto Misrephoth-maim, and unto the
valley of Mizpeh eastward; and
they smote them, until they
left them none remaining.
9. And Joshua did unto them
as the LORD bade him: he
hocked their horses, and
burnt their chariots with fire.
■ 10. **And Joshua** at that time
■ **turned back, and took**
■ **Hazor**, and smote the king thereof
with the sword: for Hazor beforetime
was the head of all those kingdoms.
■ 11. **And they smote**
■ **all the souls** that *were*
■ **therein** with the edge of the
sword, utterly destroying *them*:
there was not any left to breathe:
■ **and** he
■ **burnt Hazor with fire.**
■ 12. **And all the**
■ **cities** of those kings,
■ **and all the kings** of them,
■ **did Joshua take,** and smote
them with the edge of the sword, *and*
he utterly destroyed them, as Moses
the servant of the LORD commanded.
■ 13. **But** *as for*
■ **the cities that stood still**
■ **in their strength, Israel**
■ **burned none of them, save**
■ **Hazor** only; *that* did Joshua burn.
■ 14. **And all the spoil**
■ **of these cities**, and the
cattle, the children of
■ **Israel took** for a
prey unto themselves;
■ **but every man they smote**
with the edge of the sword, until
they had destroyed them, neither
left they any to breathe.
■ 15. **As the LORD**
■ **commanded** Moses his
servant, so did Moses command

Joshua, and so did
■ **Joshua;** he
■ **left nothing undone** of all
that the LORD commanded Moses.
■ 16. **So Joshua took all**
■ **that land**, the hills, and all
the south country, and all the
land of Goshen, and the valley,
and the plain, and the mountain of
Israel, and the valley of the same;
17. *Even* from the mount Halak,
that goeth up to Seir, even unto
Baal-gad in the valley of Lebanon
under mount Hermon:
■ **and all their kings**
■ **he took,** and smote them,
■ **and slew them.**
■ 18. **Joshua made war**
■ **a long time with all**
■ **those kings.**
■ 19. **There was not a city**
■ **that made peace** with
the children of Israel,
■ **save** the Hivites the inhabitants of
■ **Gibeon:** all *other* they
took in battle.
■ 20. **For it was of the LORD to**
■ **harden their hearts,** that they
should come against Israel in battle,
■ **that he might destroy them**
■ **utterly, and that they might**
■ **have no favour, but that he**
■ **might destroy them,** as the
LORD commanded Moses.
■ 21. **And** at that time came
■ **Joshua,** and
■ **cut off the Anakims**
from the mountains,
■ **from Hebron,** from
■ **Debir,** from
■ **Anab,** and from all the mountains of
■ **Judah, and from**
all the mountains of
■ **Israel: Joshua**
■ **destroyed them** utterly
■ **with their cities.**
■ 22. **There was none**
■ **of the Anakims left** in the
land of the children of Israel:
■ **only in Gaza,** in
■ **Gath, and in**
■ **Ashdod,** there remained.
■ 23. **So Joshua took the**

■ **whole land,** according to all
that the LORD said unto Moses;
■ **and** Joshua
■ **gave it for an inheritance**
■ **unto Israel according to**
■ **their divisions by their tribes.**
■ **And the land**
■ **rested from war.**

CHAPTER 12

■ 1. **Now** these *are*
■ **the kings** of the land,
■ **which the children of**
■ **Israel smote, and**
■ **possessed their land**
on the other side Jordan toward
the rising of the sun, from the
river Arnon unto mount Hermon,
and all the plain on the east:
2. Sihon king of the Amorites, who
dwelt in Heshbon, *and* ruled from
Aroer, which *is* upon the bank of the
river Arnon, and from the middle of
the river, and from half Gilead, even
unto the river Jabbok, *which is* the
border of the children of Ammon;
3. And from the plain to the sea of
Chinneroth on the east, and unto the
sea of the plain, *even* the salt sea on
the east, the way to Beth-jeshimoth;
and from the south, under
Ashdoth–pisgah:
4. And the coast of Og king of
Bashan, *which was* of the remnant
of the giants, that dwelt at
Ashtaroth and at Edrei,
5. And reigned in mount Hermon,
and in Salcah, and in all Bashan, unto
the border of the Geshurites and the
Maachathites, and half Gilead, the
border of Sihon king of Heshbon.
6. Them did Moses the servant of the
LORD and the children of Israel
smite: and Moses the servant of the
LORD gave it *for* a possession unto
the Reubenites, and the Gadites, and
the half tribe of Manasseh.
7. And these *are* the kings of the
country which Joshua and the
children of Israel smote on this side
Jordan on the west, from Baal-gad in
the valley of Lebanon even unto the
mount Halak, that goeth up to Seir;

which Joshua gave unto the tribes
of Israel *for* a possession
according to their divisions;
8. In the mountains, and in the
valleys, and in the plains, and in the
springs, and in the wilderness,
and in the south country; the Hittites,
the Amorites, and the Canaanites,
the Perizzites, the Hivites,
and the Jebusites:
9. The king of Jericho, one; the king
of Ai, which *is* beside Beth-el, one;
10. The king of Jerusalem, one;
the king of Hebron, one;
11. The king of Jarmuth, one;
the king of Lachish, one;
12. The king of Eglon, one;
the king of Gezer, one;
13. The king of Debir, one;
the king of Geder, one;
14. The king of Hormah, one;
the king of Arad, one;
15. The king of Libnah, one;
the king of Adullam, one;
16. The king of Makkedah, one;
the king of Beth-el, one;
17. The king of Tappuah, one;
the king of Hepher, one;
18. The king of Aphek, one;
the king of Lasharon, one;
19. The king of Madon, one;
the king of Hazor, one;
20. The king of Shimron–meron,
one; the king of Achshaph, one;
21. The king of Taanach, one;
the king of Megiddo, one;
22. The king of Kedesh, one; the
king of Jokneam of Carmel, one;
23. The king of Dor in the coast
of Dor, one; the king of the
nations of Gilgal, one;
24. The king of Tirzah, one:
■ **all the kings thirty and one.**

CHAPTER 13

■ 1. **Now Joshua was old and**
■ **stricken in years; and the**
■ **LORD said** unto him, Thou
art old *and* stricken in years, and
■ **there remaineth yet**
■ **very much land to**
■ **be possessed.**
2. **This is the land that**

344

yet remaineth: all the
borders of the Philistines,
and all Geshuri,
3. **From Sihor**, which *is*
before Egypt, even
unto the borders of
Ekron northward, which is
counted to the Canaanite:
five lords of the Philistines; the
Gazathites, and the
Ashdothites, the
Eshkalonites, the
Gittites, and the Ekronites;
also the Avites:
4. **From the south,** all the land of
the Canaanites, and
Mearah that *is*
beside the Sidonians
unto Aphek, to the borders
of the Amorites:
5. **And** the land of
the Giblites, and all
Lebanon, toward the sunrising,
from Baal–gad
under mount Hermon
unto the entering
into Hamath.
6. **All the inhabitants**
of the hill country
from Lebanon unto
Misrephoth-maim, and
all the Sidonians, them
will I drive out from
before the children of Israel:
only divide thou it by
lot unto the Israelites
for an inheritance,
as I have commanded thee.
7. **Now** therefore
divide this land
for an inheritance
unto the nine tribes, and
the half tribe of Manasseh,
8. **With whom the**
Reubenites and the Gadites
have received their
inheritance, which
Moses gave them,
beyond Jordan eastward,
even as Moses the servant
of the LORD gave them;
9. From Aroer, that *is* upon the bank
of the river Arnon, and the city that

is in the midst of the river, and all
the plain of Medeba unto Dibon;
10. And all the cities of Sihon king
of the Amorites, which reigned in
Heshbon, unto the border of the
children of Ammon;
11. And Gilead, and the border of
the Geshurites and Maachathites,
and all mount Hermon, and all
Bashan unto Salcah;
12. All the kingdom of Og in Bashan,
which reigned in Ashtaroth and in
Edrei, who remained of the remnant
of the giants: for these did Moses
smite, and cast them out.
13. **Nevertheless the**
children of Israel expelled
not the Geshurites, nor
the Maachathites: but
the Geshurites and the
Maachathites dwell among
the Israelites until this day.
14. **Only unto** the tribes of
Levi he gave none
inheritance; the sacrifices
of the LORD God of
Israel made by fire
are their inheritance,
as he said unto them.
15. And Moses gave unto the tribe of
the children of Reuben *inheritance*
according to their families.
16. And their coast was from Aroer,
that *is* on the bank of the river Arnon,
and the city that *is* in the midst of the
river, and all the plain by Medeba;
17. Heshbon, and all her cities
that *are* in the plain; Dibon, and
Bamoth-baal, and Beth-baal-meon,
18. And Jahaza, and
Kedemoth, and Mephaath,
19. And Kirjathaim, and Sibmah,
and Zareth-shahar in the
mount of the valley,
20. And Beth-peor, and
Ashdoth-pisgah, and Beth-jeshimoth,
21. And all the cities of the plain, and
all the kingdom of Sihon king of the
Amorites, which reigned in Heshbon,
whom Moses smote with the princes
of Midian, Evi, and Rekem, and Zur,
and Hur, and Reba,*which were* dukes
of Sihon, dwelling in the country.

■ 22. **Balaam also the son**
■ **of Beor, the soothsayer,**
■ **did the children of Israel**
■ **slay** with the sword among
them that were slain by them.
23. And the border of the children of
Reuben was Jordan, and the border
thereof. This *was* the inheritance
of the children of Reuben after
their families, the cities and
the villages thereof.
24. And Moses gave *inheritance*
unto the tribe of Gad, *even* unto
the children of Gad according
to their families.
25. And their coast was Jazer, and
all the cities of Gilead, and half
the land of the children of Ammon,
unto Aroer that *is* before Rabbah;
26. And from Heshbon unto
Ramath-mizpeh, and Betonim;
and from Mahanaim unto
the border of Debir;
27. And in the valley, Beth-aram,
and Beth-nimrah, and Succoth, and
Zaphon, the rest of the kingdom of
Sihon king of Heshbon, Jordan and
his border, *even* unto the edge of
the sea of Chinnereth on the
other side Jordan eastward.
28. This *is* the inheritance of the
children of Gad after their families,
the cities, and their villages.
29. And Moses gave *inheritance* unto
the half tribe of Manasseh: and *this*
was *the possession* of the half tribe
of the children of Manasseh
by their families.
30. And their coast was from
Mahanaim, all Bashan, all the
kingdom of Og king of Bashan,
and all the towns of Jair, which
are in Bashan, threescore cities:
31. And half Gilead, and Ashtaroth,
and Edrei, cities of the kingdom of Og
in Bashan, *were pertaining* unto the
children of Machir the son of
Manasseh, *even* to the one half of the
children of Machir by their families.
32. These *are the countries* which
Moses did distribute for inheritance in
the plains of Moab, on the other side
Jordan, by Jericho, eastward.

33. But unto the tribe of Levi Moses
gave not *any* inheritance: the LORD
God of Israel *was* their inheritance,
as he said unto them.

CHAPTER 14

1. And these *are the countries* which
the children of Israel inherited in the
land of Canaan, which Eleazar the
priest, and Joshua the son of Nun,
and the heads of the fathers of the
tribes of the children of Israel,
distributed for inheritance to them.
2. By lot *was* their inheritance,
as the LORD commanded by the
hand of Moses, for the nine
tribes, and *for* the half tribe.
3. For Moses had given the
inheritance of two tribes and an
half tribe on the other side Jordan:
but unto the Levites he gave
none inheritance among them.
4. For the children of Joseph were
two tribes, Manasseh and Ephraim:
therefore they gave no part unto the
Levites in the land, save cities to
dwell *in*, with their suburbs for their
cattle and for their substance.
■ 5. **As the LORD**
■ **commanded Moses, so the**
■ **children of Israel did, and**
■ **they divided the land.**
■ 6. **Then the children of**
■ **Judah came unto Joshua**
■ **in Gilgal: and Caleb** the
son of Jephunneh the Kenezite
■ **said unto him, Thou**
■ **knowest the thing** that
■ **the LORD said unto**
■ **Moses** the man of God
■ **concerning me and thee**
■ **in Kadesh-barnea.**
■ 7. **Forty years old was**
■ **I when Moses** the
servant of the LORD
■ **sent me from**
■ **Kadesh-barnea to espy out**
■ **the land;** and I brought him word
again as *it was* in mine heart.
■ 8. **Nevertheless my**
■ **brethren that went up with**
■ **me made the heart of the**
■ **people melt: but I wholly**

CHAPTER 15

followed the LORD my God.

9. **And Moses sware** on that day, saying, Surely **the land whereon thy feet have trodden shall be thine inheritance,** and thy children's for ever, **because thou hast wholly followed the LORD** my God. 10. **And** now, behold, **the LORD hath kept me alive,** as he said, **these forty** and **five years,** even since the LORD spake this word unto Moses, while *the children of* Israel wandered in the wilderness: **and now,** lo, **I am** this day **fourscore and five years old.** 11. **As yet I am as strong this day as I was in the day that Moses sent me:** as my strength *was* then, even so *is* my strength now, for war, both to go out, and to come in. 12. **Now therefore give me this mountain,** whereof the LORD spake in that day; **for thou heardest** in that day how the Anakims *were* there, and **that the cities were great and fenced: if so be the LORD will be with me, then I shall be able to drive them out, as the LORD said.** 13. **And Joshua blessed him, and gave unto Caleb** the son of Jephunneh **Hebron for an inheritance.** 14. Hebron therefore became the inheritance of Caleb the son of Jephunneh the Kenezite unto this day, **because that he wholly followed the LORD** God of Israel. 15. And the name of Hebron before *was* Kirjath-arba; *which* Arba *was* a great man among the Anakims. **And the land had rest from war.**

1. *This* then was the lot of the tribe of the children of Judah by their families; *even* to the border of Edom the wilderness of Zin southward *was* the uttermost part of the south coast. 2. And their south border was from the shore of the salt sea, from the bay that looketh southward: 3. And it went out to the south side to Maaleh-acrabbim, and passed along to Zin, and ascended up on the south side unto Kadesh-barnea, andpassed along to Hezron, and went up to Adar, and fetched a compass to Karkaa: 4. *From thence* it passed toward Azmon, and went out unto the river of Egypt; and the goings out of that coast were at the sea: this shall be your south coast. 5. And the east border *was* the salt sea, *even* unto the end of Jordan. And *their* border in the north quarter *was* from the bay of the sea at the uttermost part of Jordan: 6. And the border went up to Beth-hogla, and passed along by the north of Beth-arabah; and the border went up to the stone of Bohan the son of Reuben: 7. And the border went up toward Debir from the valley of Achor, and so northward, looking toward Gilgal, that *is* before the going up to Adummim, which *is* on the south side of the river: and the border passed toward the waters of En-shemesh, and the goings out thereof were at En-rogel: 8. And the border went up by the valley of the son of Hinnom unto the south side of the Jebusite; the same *is* Jerusalem: and the border went up to the top of the mountain that *lieth* before the valley ofHinnom westward, which *is* at the end of the valley of the giants northward: 9. And the border was drawn from the top of the hill unto the fountain of the water of Nephtoah, and went out to the cities of mount Ephron; and the border was drawn to Baalah, which *is* Kirjath-jearim:

10. And the border compassed from Baalah westward unto mount Seir, and passed along unto the side of mount Jearim, which *is* Chesalon, on the north side, and went down to Beth-shemesh, and passed on to Timnah:

11. And the border went out unto the side of Ekron northward: and the border was drawn to Shicron, and passed along to mount Baalah, and went out unto Jabneel;and the goings out of the border were at the sea.

12. And the west border *was* to the great sea, and the coast *thereof*. This *is* the coast of the children of Judah round about according to their families.

13. And unto Caleb the son of Jephunneh he gave a part among the children of Judah, according to the commandment of the LORD to Joshua, *even* the city of Arba the father of Anak, which *city is* Hebron.

14. **And Caleb** drove thence the three sons of Anak, Sheshai, and Ahiman, and Talmai, the children of Anak.

15. And he **went** up thence **to the inhabitants of Debir: and the name of Debir before was Kirjath-sepher.**

16. **And Caleb said, He that smiteth Kirjath-sepher,** and taketh it, **to him will I give Achsah my daughter to wife.**

17. **And Othniel the son of** Kenaz, **the brother of Caleb, took it: and he gave him Achsah his daughter to wife.**

18. **And** it came to pass, **as she came unto him,** that **she moved him to ask of her father a field:** and she lighted off *her* ass; **and Caleb said unto her, What wouldest thou?**

19. **Who answered,** Give me a blessing; for **thou hast given me a south land; give me also springs of water. And he gave her the upper springs, and the nether springs.**

20. This *is* the inheritance of the tribe of the children of Judah according to their families.

21. And the uttermost cities of the tribe of the children of Judah toward the coast of Edom southward were Kabzeel, and Eder, and Jagur,

22. And Kinah, and Dimonah, and Adadah,

23. And Kedesh, and Hazor, and Ithnan,

24. Ziph, and Telem, and Bealoth,

25. And Hazor, Hadattah, and Kerioth, *and* Hezron, which *is* Hazor,

26. Amam, and Shema, and Moladah,

27. And Hazar-gaddah, and Heshmon, and Beth-palet,

28. And Hazar-shual, and Beer-sheba, and Bizjothjah,

29. Baalah, and Iim, and Azem,

30. And Eltolad, and Chesil, and Hormah,

31. And Ziklag, and Madmannah, and Sansannah,

32. And Lebaoth, and Shilhim, and Ain, and Rimmon: all the cities *are* twenty and nine, with their villages:

33. *And* in the valley, Eshtaol, and Zoreah, and Ashnah,

34. And Zanoah, and En–gannim, Tappuah, and Enam,

35. Jarmuth, and Adullam, Socoh, and Azekah,

36. And Sharaim, and Adithaim, and Gederah, and Gederothaim; fourteen cities with their villages:

37. Zenan, and Hadashah, and Migdal-gad,

38. And Dilean, and Mizpeh, and Joktheel,

39. Lachish, and Bozkath, andEglon,

40. And Cabbon, and Lahmam, and Kithlish,

41. And Gederoth, Beth-dagon, and Naamah, and Makkedah; sixteen cities with their villages:

42. Libnah, and Ether, and Ashan,

43. And Jiphtah, and Ashnah, and Nezib,

44. And Keilah, and Achzib, and Mareshah; nine cities with their villages:

45. Ekron, with her towns and her villages:

46. From Ekron even unto the sea, all that *lay* near Ashdod, with their villages:

47. Ashdod with her towns and her villages, Gaza with her towns and her villages, unto the river of Egypt, and the great sea, and the border *thereof:*

48. And in the mountains, Shamir, and Jattir, and Socoh,

49. And Dannah, and Kirjath-sannah, which *is* Debir,

50. And Anab, and Eshtemoh, and Anim,

51. And Goshen, and Holon, and Giloh; eleven cities with their villages:

52. Arab, and Dumah, and Eshean,

53. And Janum, and Beth-tappuah, and Aphekah,

54. And Humtah, and Kirjath-arba, which *is* Hebron, and Zior; nine cities with their villages:

55. Maon, Carmel, and Ziph, and Juttah,

56. And Jezreel, and Jokdeam, and Zanoah,

57. Cain, Gibeah, and Timnah; ten cities with their villages:

58. Halhul, Beth-zur, and Gedor,

59. And Maarath, and Beth-anoth, and Eltekon; six cities with their villages:

60. Kirjath-baal, which *is* Kirjath-jearim, and Rabbah; two cities with their villages:

61. In the wilderness, Beth-arabah, Middin, and Secacah,

62. And Nibshan, and the city of Salt, and Engedi; six cities with their villages.

63. **As for the Jebusites the inhabitants of Jerusalem, the children of Judah could not drive them out; but the Jebusites dwell with the children of Judah at Jerusalem unto this day.**

CHAPTER 16

1. And the lot of the children of Joseph fell from Jordan by Jericho, unto the water of Jericho on the east, to the wilderness that goeth up from Jericho throughout mount Beth-el,

2. And goeth out from Beth-el to Luz, and passeth along unto the borders of Archi to Ataroth,

3. And goeth down westward to the coast of Japhleti, unto the coast of Beth-horon the nether, and to Gezer; and the goings out thereof are at the sea.

4. So the children of Joseph, Manasseh and Ephraim, took their inheritance.

5. And the border of the children of Ephraim according to their families was *thus:* even the border of their inheritance on the east side was Ataroth-addar, unto Beth-horon the upper;

6. And the border went out toward the sea to Michmethah on the north side; and the border went about eastward unto Taanath-shiloh, and passed by it on the east to Janohah;

7. And it went down from Janohah to Ataroth, and to Naarath, and came to Jericho, and went out at Jordan.

8. The border went out from Tappuah westward unto the river Kanah; and the goings out thereof were at the sea. This *is* the inheritance of the tribe of the children of Ephraim by their families.

9. And the separate cities for the children of Ephraim *were* among the inheritance of the children of Manasseh, all the cities with their villages.

10. And they drave not out the Canaanites that dwelt in Gezer: but the Canaanites dwell among the Ephraimites unto this day, and serve under tribute.

CHAPTER 17

1. **There was also a lot for the tribe of Manasseh;** for he *was* the firstborn of Joseph; *to wit,* for Machir the firstborn of Manasseh, the

father of Gilead: because he
was a man of war, therefore
he had Gilead and Bashan.

2. There was also *a lot* for the rest of
the children of Manasseh by their
families; for the children of Abiezer,
and for the children of Helek, and for
the children of Asriel, and for the
children of Shechem, and for the
children of Hepher, and for the
children of Shemida: these *were* the
male children of Manasseh the son
of Joseph by their families.

3. But Zelophehad, the son of
Hepher, the son of Gilead, the son of
Machir, the son of Manasseh, had no
sons, but daughters: and these *are*
the names of his daughters, Mahlah,
and Noah, Hoglah, Milcah, andTirzah.

4. And they came near beforeEleazar
the priest, and before Joshua the son
of Nun, and before the princes,
saying, The LORD commanded
Moses to give us an inheritance
among our brethren. Therefore
according to the commandment of the
LORD he gave them an inheritance
among the brethren of their father.

5. And there fell ten portions to
Manasseh, beside the land of
Gilead and Bashan, which *were*
on the other side Jordan;

6. Because the daughters of
Manasseh had an inheritance among
his sons: and the rest of Manasseh's
sons had the land of Gilead.

7. And the coast of Manasseh was
from Asher to Michmethah, that *lieth*
before Shechem; and the border went
along on the right hand unto the
inhabitants of En-tappuah.

8. *Now* Manasseh had the land of
Tappuah: but Tappuah on the border
of Manasseh *belonged* to the
children of Ephraim;

9. And the coast descended unto the
river Kanah, southward of the river:
these cities of Ephraim *are* among
the cities of Manasseh: the coast
of Manasseh also *was* on the north
side of the river, and the outgoings
of it were at the sea:

10. Southward *it was* Ephraim's,
and northward *it was* Manasseh's,
and the sea is his border; and they
met together in Asher on the north,
and in Issachar on the east.

11. And Manasseh had in Issachar
and in Asher Beth-shean and her
towns, and Ibleam and her towns,
and the inhabitants of Dor and her
towns, and the inhabitants of En-dor
and her towns, and the inhabitants of
Taanach and her towns, and the
inhabitants of Megiddo and her
towns, *even* three countries.

12. **Yet the children of
Manasseh could not
drive out the inhabitants
of those cities; but the
Canaanites** would
dwell in that land.

13. **Yet** it came to pass,
when the children of
Israel were waxen strong, that they
**put the Canaanites to
tribute; but did not** utterly
drive them out.

14. **And the children of
Joseph spake unto Joshua,
saying, Why hast thou
given me but one lot
and one portion** to inherit,
seeing I am a great people,
forasmuch as the LORD hath
blessed me hitherto?

15. **And Joshua
answered** them,
**If thou be a great people,
then get thee up to the
wood country, and cut
down for thyself there in
the land of the Perizzites
and of the giants,** if mount
Ephraim be too narrow for thee.

16. **And the children of
Joseph said, The hill is
not enough for us: and
all the Canaanites** that dwell
in the land of the valley
have chariots of iron, *both*
they who *are* of Beth-shean and
her towns, and *they* who *are* of
the valley of Jezreel.

17. **And Joshua spake
unto the house of Joseph,**

even to Ephraim and to Manasseh, **saying, Thou art a great people,** and hast great power: **thou shalt not have one lot only:** **18. But the mountain shall be thine;** for it *is* a wood, and thou shalt cut it down: and the outgoings of it shall be thine: **for thou shalt drive out the Canaanites,** though they have iron chariots, *and* **though they be strong.**

CHAPTER 18

1. And the whole congregation of the children of **Israel assembled** together **at Shiloh, and set up the tabernacle** of the congregation there. **And the land was subdued before them.** **2. And there remained** among the children of Israel **seven tribes, which had not yet received their inheritance.** **3. And Joshua said** unto the children of Israel, **How long are ye slack to go to possess the land,** which the LORD God of your fathers hath given you? **4. Give out from among you three men for each tribe: and I will send them,** and they shall rise, and go **through the land,** and describe it according to the inheritance of them; and **they shall come again to me.** **5. And they shall divide it into seven parts:** Judah shall abide in their coast on the south, and the house of Joseph shall abide in their coasts on the north. 6. Ye shall therefore describe the land *into* seven parts, and bring *the description* hither to me, that I may cast lots for you here before the LORD our God.

7. But the Levites have no part among you; for the priesthood of the LORD *is* their inheritance: and Gad, and Reuben, and half the tribe of Manasseh, have received their inheritance beyond Jordan on the east, which Moses the servant of the LORD gave them. **8. And the men arose, and went away: and Joshua charged them** that went to describe the land, saying, **Go and walk through the land, and describe it, and come again to me, that I may** here **cast lots for you before the LORD** in Shiloh. **9. And the men went** and passed through the land, and described it by cities into seven parts in a book, **and came again to Joshua** to the host at Shiloh. **10. And Joshua cast lots for them in Shiloh** before the LORD: **and there** Joshua **divided the land unto the children of Israel according to their divisions.**
11. And the lot of the tribe of the children of Benjamin came up according to their families: and the coast of their lot came forth between the children of Judah and the children of Joseph.
12. And their border on the north side was from Jordan; and the border went up to the side of Jericho on the north side, and went up through the mountains westward; and the goings out thereof were at the wilderness of Beth-aven.
13. And the border went over from thence toward Luz, to the side of Luz, which *is* Beth-el, southward; and the border descended to Ataroth-adar, near the hill that *lieth* on the south side of the nether Beth-horon.
14. And the border was drawn *thence,* and compassed the corner of

the sea southward, from the hill that
lieth before Beth-horon southward;
and the goings out thereof were at
Kirjath-baal, which *is* Kirjath-jearim,
a city of the children of Judah:
this *was* the west quarter.

15. And the south quarter *was* from
the end of Kirjath-jearim, and the
border went out on the west, andwent
out to the well of waters of Nephtoah:

16. And the border came down to the
end of the mountain that *lieth* before
the valley of the son of Hinnom, *and*
which *is* in the valley of the giants on
the north, and descended to the
valley of Hinnom, to the side of
Jebusi on the south, and
descended to En-rogel,

17. And was drawn from the north,
and went forth to En-shemesh, and
went forth toward Geliloth, which *is*
over against the going up of
Adummim, and descended to the
stone of Bohan the son of Reuben,

18. And passed along toward the
side over against Arabah northward,
and went down unto Arabah:

19. And the border passed along to
the side of Beth-hoglah northward:
and the outgoings of the border
were at the north bay of the salt
sea at the south end of Jordan:
this *was* the south coast.

20. And Jordan was the border
of it on the east side. This *was*
the inheritance of the children of
Benjamin, by the coasts thereofround
about, according to their families.

21. Now the cities of the tribe of the
children of Benjamin according to
their families were Jericho, and
Beth-hoglah, and the valley of Keziz,

22. And Beth-arabah, and
Zemaraim, and Beth-el,

23. And Avim, and Pharah,
and Ophrah,

24. And Chephar-haammonai,
and Ophni, and Gaba; twelve
cities with their villages:

25. Gibeon, and Ramah, andBeeroth,

26. And Mizpeh, and Chephirah,
and Mozah,

27. And Rekem, and Irpeel,

and Taralah,

28. And Zelah, Eleph, and Jebusi,
which *is* Jerusalem, Gibeath, *and*
Kirjath; fourteen cities with their
villages. This *is* the inheritance
of the children of Benjamin
according to their families.

CHAPTER 19

1. And the second lot came forth to
Simeon, *even* for the tribe of the
children of Simeon according to their
families: and their inheritance was
within the inheritance of the
children of Judah.

2. And they had in their
inheritance Beer-sheba,
and Sheba, and Moladah,

3. And Hazar-shual, and
Balah, and Azem,

4. And Eltolad, and
Bethul, and Hormah,

5. And Ziklag, and Beth-
marcaboth, and Hazar-suan,

6. And Beth-lebaoth, and Sharuhen;
thirteen cities and their villages:

7. Ain, Remmon, and Ether, and
Ashan; four cities and their villages:

8. And all the villages that *were* round
about these cities to Baalath–beer,
Ramath of the south. This *is* the
inheritance of the tribe of the children
of Simeon according to their families.

9. Out of the portion of the children
of Judah *was* the inheritance of the
children of Simeon: for the part of the
children of Judah was too much for
them: therefore the children of
Simeon had their inheritance within
the inheritance of them.

10. And the third lot came up for
the children of Zebulun according
to their families: and the border of
their inheritance was unto Sarid:

11. And their border went up toward
the sea, and Maralah, and reached
to Dabbasheth, and reached to the
river that *is* before Jokneam;

12. And turned from Sarid eastward
toward the sunrising unto the border
of Chisloth-tabor, and then goeth out
to Daberath, and goeth up to Japhia,

13. And from thence passeth on

along on the east to Gittah-hepher,
to Ittah-kazin, and goeth out to
Remmon-methoar to Neah;

14. And the border compasseth it on
the north side to Hannathon: and the
outgoings thereof are in the valley
of Jiphthah-el:

15. And Kattath, and Nahallal, and
Shimron, and Idalah, and Beth-lehem:
twelve cities with their villages.

16. This *is* the inheritance of the
children of Zebulun according to
their families, these cities with
their villages.

17. *And* the fourth lot came out to
Issachar, for the children of Issachar
according to their families.

18. And their border was
toward Jezreel, and
Chesulloth, and Shunem,

19. And Haphraim, and
Shihon, and Anaharath,

20. And Rabbith, and
Kishion, and Abez,

21. And Remeth, and En-gannim,
and En-haddah, and Beth-pazzez;

22. And the coast reacheth to Tabor,
and Shahazimah, and Beth-shemesh;
and the outgoings of their border
were at Jordan: sixteen cities
with their villages.

23. This *is* the inheritance of the
tribe of the children of Issachar
according to their families, the
cities and their villages.

24. And the fifth lot came out for
the tribe of the children of Asher
according to their families.

25. And their border was Helkath,
and Hali, and Beten, and Achshaph,

26. And Alammelech, and Amad, and
Misheal; and reacheth to Carmel
westward, and to Shihor-libnath;

27. And turneth toward the sunrising
to Beth-dagon, and reacheth to
Zebulun, and to the valley of
Jiphthah–el toward the north side of
Beth-emek, and Neiel, and goeth
out to Cabul on the left hand,

28. And Hebron, and Rehob,
and Hammon, and Kanah,
even unto great Zidon;

29. And *then* the coast turneth to

Ramah, and to the strong city Tyre;
and the coast turneth to Hosah; and
the outgoings thereof are at the sea
from the coast to Achzib:

30. Ummah also, and Aphek,
and Rehob: twenty and two
cities with their villages.

31. This *is* the inheritance of the
tribe of the children of Asher
according to their families, these
cities with their villages.

32. The sixth lot came out to
the children of Naphtali, *even*
for the children of Naphtali
according to their families.

33. And their coast was from Heleph,
from Allon to Zaanannim, and Adami,
Nekeb,and Jabneel, unto Lakum; and
the outgoings thereof were at Jordan:

34. And *then* the coast turneth
westward to Aznoth-tabor, and goeth
out from thence to Hukkok, and
reacheth to Zebulun on the south
side, and reacheth to Asher on the
west side, and to Judah upon
Jordan toward the sunrising.

35. And the fenced cities *are*
Ziddim, Zer, and Hammath,
Rakkath, and Chinnereth,

36. And Adamah, and
Ramah, and Hazor,

37. And Kedesh, and
Edrei, and En-hazor,

38. And Iron, and Migdal-el, Horem,
and Beth-anath, and Beth-shemesh;
nineteen cities with their villages.

39. This *is* the inheritance of the
tribe of the children of Naphtali
according to their families, the
cities and their villages.

40. *And* the seventh lot came out
for the tribe of the children of Dan
according to their families.

41. And the coast of their
inheritance was Zorah, and
Eshtaol, and Ir-shemesh,

42. And Shaalabbin,
and Ajalon, and Jethlah,

43. And Elon, and
Thimnathah, and Ekron,

44. And Eltekeh, and
Gibbethon, and Baalath,

45. And Jehud, and Bene–berak,

and Gath-rimmon,

46. And Me-jarkon, and Rakkon, with the border before Japho.

47. And the coast of the children of Dan went out *too little* for them: therefore the children of Dan went up to fight against Leshem, and took it, and smote it with the edge of the sword, and possessed it, and dwelt therein, and called Leshem, Dan, after the name of Dan their father.

48. This *is* the inheritance of the tribe of the children of Dan according to their families, these cities with their villages.

49. **When they had made an end of dividing the land** for inheritance by their coasts, **the children of Israel gave an inheritance to Joshua** the son of Nun among them:

50. **According to the word of the LORD they gave him** the city which he asked, *even* **Timnath-serah in mount Ephraim: and he built the city, and dwelt therein.**

51. These *are* the inheritances, which Eleazar the priest, and Joshua the son of Nun, and the heads of the fathers of the tribes of the children of Israel, divided for an inheritance by lot in Shiloh before the LORD, at the door of the tabernacle of the congregation. **So they made an end of dividing the country.**

CHAPTER 20

1. **The LORD also spake unto Joshua, saying,**

2. **Speak to** the children of **Israel, saying, Appoint out for you cities of refuge,** whereof I spake unto you by the hand of Moses:

3. **That the slayer that killeth any person unawares and unwittingly may flee thither: and they shall be your refuge from the avenger of blood.**

4. **And when he that doth flee unto one of those** **cities** shall stand at the entering of the gate of the city, **and shall declare his cause in the ears of the elders** of that city, **they shall take him** into the city unto them, **and** give him a place, that **he may dwell among them.**

5. **And if the avenger** of blood **pursue after him,** then **they shall not deliver the slayer** up into his hand; **because he smote his neighbour unwittingly, and hated him not beforetime.**

6. **And he shall** dwell in that city, until he **stand before the congregation for judgment, and until the death of the high priest that shall be in those days: then shall the slayer return,** and come unto his own city, and unto his own house, **unto the city from whence he fled.**

7. **And they appointed Kedesh** in Galilee in mount Naphtali, and **Shechem** in mount Ephraim, **and** Kirjath-arba, which *is* **Hebron,** in the mountain of Judah.

8. **And** on the other side **Jordan** by Jericho eastward, they assigned **Bezer** in the wilderness upon the plain out of the tribe of Reuben, and **Ramoth** in Gilead out of the tribe of Gad, **and Golan** in Bashan out of the tribe of Manasseh.

9. **These were the cities appointed for all** the children of **Israel, and for the stranger that sojourneth among them, that whosoever killeth** *any* person at unawares **might flee thither,** and not die by the hand of the avenger of blood, until he stood before

354

|■| the congregation.

CHAPTER 21

■ 1. **Then came near the**
■ **heads** of the fathers
■ **of the Levites unto Eleazar**
■ **the priest, and unto**
■ **Joshua** the son of Nun,
■ **and unto the heads**
of the fathers
■ **of the tribes** of the
children of Israel;
■ 2. **And they spake** unto them
at Shiloh in the land of Canaan,
■ **saying, The LORD**
■ **commanded**
by the hand of Moses
■ **to give us cities to dwell**
■ **in, with the suburbs**
■ **thereof for our cattle.**
■ 3. **And the children of Israel**
■ **gave unto the Levites out**
■ **of their inheritance, at**
■ **the commandment of**
■ **the LORD,** these cities
and their suburbs.

4. And the lot came out for the families of the Kohathites: and the children of Aaron the priest, *which were* of the Levites, had by lot out of the tribe of Judah, and out of the tribe of Simeon, and out of the tribe of Benjamin, thirteen cities.

5. And the rest of the children of Kohath *had* by lot out of the families of the tribe of Ephraim, and out of the tribe of Dan, and out of the half tribe of Manasseh, ten cities.

6. And the children of Gershon *had* by lot out of the families of the tribe of Issachar, and out of the tribe of Asher, and out of the tribe of Naphtali, and out of the half tribe of Manasseh in Bashan, thirteen cities.

7. The children of Merari by their families had out of the tribe of Reuben, and out of the tribe of Gad, and out of the tribe of Zebulun, twelve cities.

8. And the children of Israel gave by lot unto the Levites these cities with their suburbs, as the LORD commanded by the hand of Moses.

9. And they gave out of the tribe of the children of Judah, and out of the tribe of the children of Simeon, these cities which are *here* mentioned by name.

10. Which the children of Aaron, *being* of the families of the Kohathites, *who were* of the children of Levi, had: for theirs was the first lot.

11. And they gave them the city of Arba the father of Anak, which *city is* Hebron, in the hill *country* of Judah, with the suburbs thereof round about it.

12. But the fields of the city, and the villages thereof, gave they to Caleb the son of Jephunneh for his possession.

13. Thus they gave to the children of Aaron the priest Hebron with her suburbs, *to be* a city of refuge for the slayer; and Libnah with her suburbs,

14. And Jattir with her suburbs, and Eshtemoa with her suburbs,

15. And Holon with her suburbs, and Debir with her suburbs,

16. And Ain with her suburbs, and Juttah with her suburbs, *and* Beth-shemesh with her suburbs; nine cities out of those two tribes.

17. And out of the tribe of Benjamin, Gibeon with her suburbs, Geba with her suburbs,

18. Anathoth with her suburbs, and Almon with her suburbs; four cities.

19. All the cities of the children of Aaron, the priests, *were* thirteen cities with their suburbs.

20. And the families of the children of Kohath, the Levites which remained of the children of Kohath, even they had the cities of their lot out of the tribe of Ephraim.

21. For they gave them Shechem with her suburbs in mount Ephraim, *to be* a city of refuge for the slayer; and Gezer with her suburbs,

22. And Kibzaim with her suburbs, and Beth-horon with her suburbs; four cities.

23. And out of the tribe of Dan, Eltekeh with her suburbs, Gibbethon with her suburbs,

24. Aijalon with her suburbs, Gath-rimmon with her suburbs; four cities.

25. And out of the half tribe of Manasseh, Tanach with her suburbs, and Gath-rimmon with her suburbs; two cities.

26. All the cities *were* ten with their suburbs for the families of the children of Kohath that remained.

27. And unto the children of Gershon, of the families of the Levites, out of the *other* half tribe of Manasseh *they gave* Golan in Bashan with her suburbs, *to be* a city of refuge for the slayer; and Beeshterah with her suburbs; two cities.

28. And out of the tribe of Issachar, Kishon with her suburbs, Dabareh with her suburbs,

29. Jarmuth with her suburbs,En-gannim with her suburbs; four cities.

30. And out of the tribe of Asher, Mishal with her suburbs, Abdon with her suburbs,

31. Helkath with her suburbs, and Rehob with her suburbs; four cities.

32. And out of the tribe of Naphtali, Kedesh in Galilee with her suburbs, *to be* a city of refuge for the slayer; and Hammoth-dor with her suburbs, and Kartan with her suburbs; three cities.

33. All the cities of the Gershonites according to their families *were* thirteen cities with their suburbs.

34. And unto the families of the children of Merari, the rest of the Levites, out of the tribe of Zebulun, Jokneam with her suburbs, and Kartah with her suburbs,

35. Dimnah with her suburbs, Nahalal with her suburbs; four cities.

36. And out of the tribe of Reuben, Bezer with her suburbs, and Jahazah with her suburbs,

37. Kedemoth with her suburbs, and Mephaath with her suburbs; four cities.

38. And out of the tribe of Gad, Ramoth in Gilead with her suburbs, *to be* a city of refuge for the slayer; and Mahanaim with her suburbs,

39. Heshbon with her suburbs, Jazer with her suburbs; four cities in all.

40. So all the cities for the children of Merari by their families, which were remaining of the families of the Levites, were *by* their lot twelve cities.

41. **All the cities of the Levites** within the possession of the children of Israel **were forty and eight cities with their suburbs.**

42. These cities were every one with their suburbs round about them: thus *were* all these cities.

43. **And the LORD gave unto Israel all the land which he sware to give unto their fathers;** and they possessed it, and dwelt therein.

44. **And the LORD gave them rest** round about, according to all that he sware unto their fathers: **and there stood not a man of all their enemies before them;** the LORD delivered all their enemies into their hand.

45. **There failed not aught of any good thing which the LORD had spoken unto** the house of **Israel; all came to pass.**

CHAPTER 22

1. **Then Joshua called the Reubenites, and the Gadites, and the half tribe of Manasseh,**

2. **And said** unto them, **Ye have kept all that Moses** the servant of the LORD **commanded you, and have obeyed my voice** in all that I commanded you:

3. Ye have not left your brethren these many days unto this day, but have kept the charge of the commandment of the LORD yourGod.

4. **And now** the LORD your **God hath given rest unto your brethren,** as he promised them: **therefore** now

return ye, and get you unto your tents, *and* **unto the land of your possession,** which Moses the servant of the LORD gave you on the other side Jordan.

5. **But take diligent heed to do** the commandment and **the law,** which Moses the servant of the LORD charged you, **to love the LORD** your God, and to walk in all his ways, **and to keep his commandments,** and to cleave unto him, **and** to **serve him with all your heart and** with all your **soul.**

6. **So Joshua blessed them, and sent them away:** and they went unto their tents.

7. **Now to the one half of the tribe of Manasseh Moses had given** *possession* in **Bashan: but unto the other half** thereof **gave Joshua** among their brethren **on this side Jordan westward.** And when Joshua sent them away also unto their tents, then he blessed them,

8. **And he spake** unto them, **saying, Return with much riches unto your tents, and with** very much **cattle,** with **silver,** and with **gold,** and with **brass,** and with **iron, and with very much raiment: divide the spoil of your enemies** with your brethren.

9. **And the children of Reuben and** the children of **Gad and the half tribe of Manasseh returned,** and departed from the children of Israel out of Shiloh, which *is* in the land of Canaan, **to** go unto the country of **Gilead,** to

the land of their possession, whereof they were possessed, according to the word of the LORD by the hand of Moses.

10. **And** when **they** came unto the borders of Jordan, that *are* in the land of Canaan, the children of Reuben and the children of Gad and the half tribe of Manasseh **built** there an altar **by Jordan, a great altar** to see to.

11. **And the children of Israel heard** say, Behold, the children of **Reuben and** the children of **Gad and the half tribe of Manasseh have built an altar** over against the land of Canaan, in the borders of Jordan, **at the passage of the children of Israel.**

12. **And when** the children of **Israel heard of it, the whole congregation** of the children of Israel **gathered** themselves together at Shiloh, **to go up to war against them.**

13. **And** the children of **Israel sent** unto the children of Reuben, and to the children of Gad, and to the half tribe of Manasseh, into the land of Gilead, **Phinehas the son of Eleazar the priest,**

14. **And with him ten princes,** of each chief house a prince throughout all the tribes of Israel; **and each one was an head of the house of their fathers** among the thousands of Israel.

15. **And they came unto** the children of **Reuben,** and to the children of **Gad, and** to **the half tribe of Manasseh,** unto the land of Gilead, **and they**

■ spake with them, saying,
■ 16. **Thus saith the whole**
■ **congregation** of the LORD,
■ **What trespass is this** that
■ **ye have committed**
against the God of Israel,
■ **to turn away** this day
■ **from following the LORD,**
■ **in that ye have builded**
■ **you an altar,**
that ye might rebel this day
against the LORD?
17. *Is* the iniquity of Peor too little
for us, from which we are not
cleansed until this day, although
there was a plague in the
congregation of the LORD,
18. But that ye must turn away
this day from following the LORD?
and it will be, *seeing* ye
rebel to day against
■ **the LORD**, that to-morrow he
■ **will be wroth with the**
■ **whole congregation** of Israel.
■ 19. **Notwithstanding, if the**
■ **land of your possession**
■ **be unclean, then pass** ye
■ **over unto the** land of the
■ **possession of the LORD,**
■ **wherein the LORD's**
■ **tabernacle dwelleth, and**
■ **take possession among**
■ **us: but rebel not** against
the LORD, nor rebel against us,
■ **in building you an**
■ **altar beside the altar**
■ **of the LORD** our God.
20. Did not Achan the son of Zerah
commit a trespass in the accursed
thing, and wrath fell on all the
congregation of Israel? and that man
perished not alone in his iniquity.
■ 21. **Then** the children of
■ **Reuben** and the children of
■ **Gad and the half tribe of**
■ **Manasseh** answered, and
■ **said unto the heads of**
■ **the thousands of Israel,**
■ 22. **The LORD God** of gods,
the LORD God of gods, he
■ **knoweth, and Israel** he
■ **shall know; if it be in**
■ **rebellion, or** if in

■ **transgression against the**
■ **LORD,** (save us not this day,)
■ 23. **That we have built us an**
■ **altar to turn from following**
■ **the LORD,** or if to offer thereon
burnt offering or meat offering, or if
to offer peace offerings thereon,
■ **let the LORD himself**
■ **require it;**
■ 24. **And if we have not** *rather*
■ **done it** for fear of *this* thing,
■ **saying, In time to come**
■ **your children might speak**
■ **unto our children, saying,**
■ **What have ye to do with**
■ **the LORD God of Israel?**
■ 25. **For the LORD hath made**
■ **Jordan a border between**
■ **us and you,** ye children
of Reuben and children of Gad;
ye have no part in the LORD:
so shall your children make our
children cease from fearing the LORD.
■ 26. **Therefore we said,**
■ **Let us** now prepare to
■ **build** us
■ **an altar, not for burnt**
■ **offering, nor for sacrifice:**
■ 27. **But that it may be a**
■ **witness between us, and**
■ **you,** and our generations after us,
■ **that we might do the**
■ **service of the LORD** before
him with our burnt offerings,
and with our sacrifices, and
with our peace offerings;
■ **that your children**
■ **may not say to our**
■ **children** in time to come,
■ **Ye have no part**
■ **in the LORD.**
28. Therefore said we, that it shall
be, when they should *so* say to us or
to our generations in time to
come, that we may say *again,*
■ **Behold the pattern of**
■ **the altar** of the LORD,
■ **which our fathers made,**
not for burnt offerings,
nor for sacrifices; but
■ **it is a witness between**
■ **us and you.**
■ 29. **God forbid that we**

should rebel against
the LORD, and turn this day
from following the LORD,
to build an altar for burnt
offerings, for meat offerings,
or for sacrifices,
beside the altar of
the LORD our God
that is before his
tabernacle.
30. And when
Phinehas the priest,
and the princes of the
congregation and heads
of the thousands of Israel
which *were* with him,
heard the words that the
children of Reuben and the
children of Gad and the
children of Manasseh spake,
it pleased them.
31. And Phinehas the
son of Eleazar the priest
said unto the children of Reuben,
and to the children of Gad, and
to the children of Manasseh,
This day we perceive that the
LORD *is* among us, because
ye have not committed
this trespass against
the LORD: now ye have
delivered the children of
Israel out of the hand
of the LORD.
32. And Phinehas the
son of Eleazar the priest,
and the princes, returned
from the children of Reuben, and
from the children of Gad,
out of the land of Gilead,
unto the land of
Canaan, to the children of Israel,
and brought them word again.
33. And the thing
pleased the children of
Israel; and the children of
Israel blessed God, and
did not intend to go up
against them in battle,
to destroy the land wherein the
children of Reuben and Gad dwelt.
34. And the children of
Reuben and the children of

Gad called the altar Ed:
for it shall be a witness
between us that the
LORD is God.

CHAPTER 23

1. And it came to pass
a long time after that
the LORD had given
rest unto Israel from all
their enemies round about, that
Joshua waxed old
and stricken in age.
2. And Joshua called for
all Israel, *and* for their elders,
and for their heads, and for their
judges, and for their officers,
and said unto them,
I am old *and* stricken in age:
3. And ye have seen all
that the LORD your God
hath done unto all these
nations because of
you; for the LORD your
God *is* he that hath
fought for you.
4. Behold, I have
divided unto you
by lot these nations
that remain, to be an
inheritance for your tribes,
from Jordan, with all the nations
that I have cut off, even unto
the great sea westward.
5. And the LORD your
God, he
shall expel them
from before you, and
drive them from out of your sight;
and ye shall possess
their land, as the LORD your
God hath promised unto you.
6. Be ye therefore
very courageous to keep and
to do all that is
written in the book
of the law of Moses,
that ye turn not
aside therefrom *to* the
right hand or *to* the left;
7. That ye come not
among these nations,
these that remain among you;

■ **neither** make
■ **mention** of
■ **the name of their gods,**
■ **nor** cause to swear *by them,* neither
■ **serve them,**
■ **nor bow** yourselves
■ **unto them:**
■ 8. **But cleave unto the**
■ **LORD** your God, as ye have
done unto this day.
■ 9. **For the LORD hath**
■ **driven out** from before you
■ **great nations** and
strong: but *as for* you,
■ **no man hath been**
■ **able to stand before**
■ **you unto this day.**
■ 10. **One man of you shall**
■ **chase a thousand: for the**
■ **LORD** your God, he *it is* that
■ **fighteth for you,** as
he hath promised you.
■ 11. **Take good heed**
■ **therefore** unto yourselves,
■ **that ye love the**
■ **LORD** your God.
■ 12. **Else if ye** do in any wise
■ **go back, and cleave**
■ **unto the remnant of**
■ **these nations,** *even*
these that remain among you,
■ **and** shall
■ **make marriages with them,**
and go in unto them, and they to you:
13. Know for a certainty
that the LORD your
■ **God will no more**
■ **drive out** *any of*
■ **these nations** from before you;
■ **but they shall be snares**
■ **and traps** unto you, and scourges
in your sides, and thorns in your eyes,
■ **until ye perish** from off this
good land which the LORD your
God hath given you.
14. And, behold, this day
■ **I am going the way**
■ **of all the earth: and**
■ **ye know** in all your hearts
and in all your souls, that
■ **not one thing hath**
■ **failed** of all the good things
■ **which the LORD** your God

■ **spake** concerning you; all are
come to pass unto you, *and* not
one thing hath failed thereof.
■ 15. **Therefore** it shall
come to pass, *that*
■ **as all good things are**
■ **come** upon you, which the
LORD your God promised you;
■ **so shall the LORD**
■ **bring upon you** all
■ **evil** things,
■ **until he have destroyed**
■ **you** from off this good land which
the LORD your God hath given you.
■ 16. **When ye have**
■ **transgressed the**
■ **covenant of the LORD** your
God, which he commanded you,
■ **and have** gone and
■ **served other gods,**
and bowed yourselves to them;
■ **then shall the anger of the**
■ **LORD be kindled against**
■ **you, and ye shall perish**
■ **quickly** from off the good land
which he hath given unto you.

CHAPTER 24

■ 1. **And Joshua gathered**
■ **all the tribes** of Israel
■ **to Shechem,** and called for the
elders of Israel, and for their heads,
and for their judges, and for their
officers; and they presented
themselves before God.
■ 2. **And** Joshua
■ **said** unto all the people,
■ **Thus saith the**
■ **LORD** God of Israel,
■ **Your fathers dwelt on**
■ **the other side of the**
■ **flood** in old time, *even* Terah,
the father of Abraham, and the
father of Nachor:
■ **and they served**
■ **other gods.**
■ 3. **And I took** your father
■ **Abraham** from the
other side of the flood,
■ **and led him throughout**
all the land of
■ **Canaan,** and
■ **multiplied his seed,**

and gave him Isaac.

4. And I gave unto Isaac Jacob and Esau: and I gave unto Esau mount Seir, to possess it; but Jacob and his children went down into Egypt.

5. I sent Moses also and Aaron, and I plagued Egypt, according to that which I did among them: and afterward I brought you out.

6. And I brought your fathers out of Egypt: and ye came unto the sea; and the Egyptians pursued after your fathers with chariots and horsemen unto the Red sea.

7. And when they cried unto the LORD, he put darkness between you and the Egyptians, and brought the sea upon them, and covered them; and your eyes have seen what I have done in Egypt: and ye dwelt in the wilderness a long season.

8. And I brought you into the land of the Amorites, which dwelt on the other side Jordan; and they fought with you: and I gave them into your hand, that ye might possess their land; and I destroyed them from before you.

9. Then Balak the son of Zippor, king of Moab, arose and warred against Israel, and sent and called Balaam the son of Beor to curse you:

10. But I would not hearken unto Balaam; therefore he blessed you still: so I delivered you out of his hand.

11. And you went over Jordan, and came unto Jericho: and the men of Jericho fought against

you, the Amorites, and the Perizzites, and the Canaanites, and the Hittites, and the Girgashites, the Hivites, and the Jebusites; and I delivered them into your hand.

12. And I sent the hornet before you, which drave them out from before you, *even* the two kings of the Amorites; but not with thy sword, nor with thy bow.

13. And I have given you a land for which ye did not labour, and cities which ye built not, and ye dwell in them; of the vineyards and oliveyards which ye planted not do ye eat.

14. Now therefore fear the LORD, and serve him in sincerity and in truth: and put away the gods which your fathers served on the other side of the flood, and in Egypt; and serve ye the LORD.

15. And if it seem evil unto you to serve the LORD, choose you this day whom ye will serve; whether the gods which your fathers served that *were* on the other side of the flood, or the gods of the Amorites, in whose land ye dwell: but as for me and my house, we will serve the LORD.

16. And the people answered and said, God forbid that we should forsake the LORD, to serve other gods;

17. For the LORD our God, he *it is* that brought us up and our fathers out of the land of Egypt, from the house of bondage, and which did those great signs in our sight, and preserved us in all the way wherein we went, and among all

the people through whom we passed:

■ 18. **And the LORD drave out**
■ **from before us all the**
■ **people,** even the Amorites which
dwelt in the land:*therefore* will we also
serve the LORD; for he *is* our God.
■ 19. **And Joshua said**
unto the people,
■ **Ye cannot serve the LORD:**
for he *is* an holy God; he *is* a jealous
God; he will not forgive your
transgressions nor your sins.
■ 20. **If ye forsake the LORD,**
■ **and serve strange gods,** then
he will turn and do you hurt,
and consume you, after that he
hath done you good.
■ 21. **And the people**
■ **said** unto Joshua,
■ **Nay; but we will**
■ **serve the LORD.**
■ 22. **And Joshua**
■ **said** unto the people,
■ **Ye are witnesses**
against yourselves
■ **that ye have chosen** you
■ **the LORD,** to serve him.
■ **And they said, We**
■ **are witnesses.**
23. Now therefore put away, *said he,*
the strange gods which *are* among
you, and incline your heart unto the
LORD God of Israel.
■ 24. **And the people**
■ **said** unto Joshua,
■ **The LORD our God will**
■ **we serve, and his voice**
■ **will we obey.**
25. So Joshua made a covenant with
the people that day, and set them a
statute and an ordinance in Shechem.
■ 26. **And Joshua wrote**
■ **these words in the**
■ **book of the law** of God,
■ **and took a great stone,**
■ **and set it** up there

■ **under an oak**, that *was*
by the sanctuary of the LORD.
■ 27. **And Joshua said**
unto all the people, Behold,
■ **this stone shall be a**
■ **witness unto us;** for it hath
heard all the words of the LORD
which he spake unto us: it shall
be therefore a witness unto you,
lest ye deny your God.
■ 28. **So Joshua let the**
■ **people depart, every**
■ **man unto his inheritance.**
■ 29. **And** it came to pass
■ **after these things,** that
■ **Joshua** the son of Nun,
the servant of the LORD,
■ **died, being an hundred**
■ **and ten years old.**
■ 30. **And they buried him**
in the border of his inheritance
in Timnath-serah, which *is* in
mount Ephraim, on the north
side of the hill of Gaash.
■ 31. **And Israel served**
■ **the LORD all the days of**
■ **Joshua, and all the days of**
■ **the elders that overlived**
■ **Joshua,** and which had known
all the works of the LORD, that
he had done for Israel.
■ 32. **And the bones of**
■ **Joseph,** which the children of
Israel brought up out of Egypt,
■ **buried they in Shechem,** in a
parcel of ground which Jacob bought
of the sons of Hamor the father of
Shechem for an hundred pieces of
silver: and it became the inheritance
of the children of Joseph.
■ 33. **And Eleazar the son**
■ **of Aaron died; and they**
■ **buried him** in a hill *that*
pertained to Phinehas his son,
which was given him
■ **in mount Ephraim.**

THE BOOK OF JUDGES

BACKGROUND INFORMATION

Author: Unknown
Date Written: possibly
between 1050 — 1000 B.C.

Number of:
Verses —618
Chapters—21
Total Words—18,976
Scan Words—8,780
Scan Words Represent
Approximately 46% of
Total Words

Theme: The History of
the Judges of Israel

OUTLINE OF THE BOOK

I.   **The Past Reviewed**
     1:1 — 3:4
II. **The First Five Judges** of
     Israel
     3:5 — 5:31
III. **The Life** and Victories
     of Gideon
     6:1 — 9:57
IV. **The Next Six Judges** of
     Israel
     10:1 — 12:15
V.   **The Life,** Victories,
     Defeat, and Restoration
     of Samson
     13:1 — 16:31
VI. **The Lawlessness**
     of Israel
     17:1 — 21:25

CHAPTER 1

1. Now after the death of Joshua it came to pass, that the children of Israel asked the LORD, saying, Who shall go up for us against the Canaanites first, to fight against them? 2. And the LORD said, Judah shall go up: behold, I have delivered the land into his hand. 3. And Judah said unto Simeon his brother, Come up with me into my lot, that we may fight against the Canaanites; and I likewise will go with thee into thy lot. So Simeon went with him. 4. And Judah went up; and the LORD delivered the Canaanites and the Perizzites into their hand: and they slew of them in Bezek ten thousand men. 5. And they found Adoni-bezek in Bezek: and they fought against him, and they slew the Canaanites and the Perizzites. 6. But Adoni-bezek fled; and they pursued after him, and caught him, and cut off his thumbs and his great toes. 7. And Adoni-bezek said, Threescore and ten kings, having their thumbs and their great toes cut off, gathered *their meat* under my table: as I have done, so God hath requited me. And they brought him to Jerusalem, and there he died. 8. Now the children of Judah had fought against Jerusalem, and had taken it, and smitten it with the edge of the sword, and set the city on fire. 9. And afterward the children of Judah went down to fight against the Canaanites, that dwelt in the mountain, and in the south, and in the valley. 10. And Judah went against the Canaanites that dwelt in Hebron: (now the name of Hebron before *was* Kirjath-arba:) and they slew Sheshai, and Ahiman, and Talmai. 11. And from thence he went against the inhabitants of Debir: and the name of Debir before *was* Kirjath-sepher: 12. And Caleb said, He that smiteth Kirjath-sepher, and taketh it, to him will I give Achsah my daughter to wife. 13. And Othniel the son of Kenaz, Caleb's younger brother, took it: and he gave him Achsah his daughter to wife. 14. And it came to pass, when she came to him, that she moved him to ask of her father a field: and she lighted from off *her* ass; and Caleb said unto her, What wilt thou? 15. And she said unto him, Give me a blessing: for thou hast given me a south land; give me also springs of water. And Caleb gave her the upper springs and the nether springs. 16. And the children of the Kenite, Moses' father in law, went up out of the city of palm trees with the children of Judah into the wilderness of Judah, which *lieth* in the south of Arad; and they went and dwelt among the people. 17. And Judah went with Simeon his brother, and they slew the Canaanites that inhabited Zephath, and utterly destroyed it. And the name of

the city was called Hormah. 18. **Also Judah took Gaza** with the coast thereof, **and Askelon** with the coast thereof, **and Ekron** with the coast thereof. 19. **And the LORD was with Judah; and** he **drave out the inhabitants of the mountain; but could not drive out the inhabitants of the valley, because they had chariots of iron.** 20. **And they gave Hebron unto Caleb, as Moses said:** and he expelled thence the three sons of Anak. 21. **And the children of Benjamin did not drive out the Jebusites that inhabited Jerusalem;** but the Jebusites dwell with the children of Benjamin in Jerusalem unto this day. 22. **And the house of Joseph,** they also **went up against Beth-el: and the LORD was with them.** 23. And the house of Joseph sent to descry Beth–el. (Now the name of the city before *was* Luz.) 24. **And** the **spies saw a man come** forth **out of the city, and they said** unto him, **Shew us,** we pray thee, **the entrance into the city, and we will shew thee mercy.** 25. **And when he shewed them the entrance** into the city, **they smote the city with** the edge of the sword; **but** they **let go the man and** all **his family.** 26. **And the man went into the land of the Hittites, and built a city,** and **called** the name thereof **Luz:** which *is* the name thereof unto this day.

27. **Neither did Manasseh drive out the inhabitants of Beth-shean** and her towns, nor **Taanach** and her towns, nor the inhabitants of **Dor** and her towns, nor the inhabitants of **Ibleam** and her towns, **nor the inhabitants of Megiddo** and her towns: **but the Canaanites would dwell in that land.** 28. **And** it came to pass, when **Israel** was strong, that they **put the Canaanites to tribute, and did not** utterly **drive them out.** 29. **Neither did Ephraim drive out the Canaanites that dwelt in Gezer;** but the Canaanites dwelt in Gezer among them. 30. **Neither did Zebulun drive out the inhabitants of Kitron, nor** the inhabitants of **Nahalol;** but the Canaanites dwelt among them, and became tributaries. 31. **Neither did Asher drive out the inhabitants of Accho,** nor the inhabitants of **Zidon,** nor of **Ahlab,** nor of **Achzib,** nor of **Helbah,** nor of **Aphik, nor of Rehob:** 32. **But the Asherites dwelt among the Canaanites,** the inhabitants of the land: for they did not drive them out. 33. **Neither did Naphtali drive out the inhabitants of Beth-shemesh, nor** the inhabitants of **Beth-anath; but he dwelt among the Canaanites,** the inhabitants of the land: nevertheless the inhabitants of Beth-shemesh and of Beth-anath became tributaries unto them. 34. **And the Amorites forced the children of Dan into the mountain:** for they would not suffer them

35. **But the Amorites would dwell in mount Heres** in Aijalon, **and** in **Shaalbim: yet** the hand of **the house of Joseph prevailed, so that they became tributaries.**

36. And the coast of the Amorites *was* from the going up to Akrabbim, from the rock, and upward.

CHAPTER 2

1. **And an angel of the LORD came** up from Gilgal **to Bochim, and said, I made you to go up out of Egypt,** and have brought you **unto the land** which **I sware unto your fathers; and** I said, **I will never break my covenant** with you.

2. **And ye shall make no league with the inhabitants of this land; ye shall throw down their altars: but ye have not obeyed my voice:** why have ye done this?

3. **Wherefore** I also said, **I will not drive them out** from before you; **but they shall be as thorns in your sides, and their gods shall be a snare unto you.**

4. **And** it came to pass, **when the angel** of the LORD **spake these words** unto all the children of **Israel,** that the people lifted up their voice, and **wept.**

5. **And they called the** name of that **place Bochim: and they sacrificed** there **unto the LORD.**

6. **And when Joshua** had **let the people go,** the children of **Israel went every man unto his inheritance** to possess the land.

7. **And the people served the LORD all the days of Joshua, and** all the days of **the elders** that outlived Joshua, **who had seen** all **the** great **works of the LORD,** that he did for Israel.

8. **And Joshua** the son of Nun, the servant of the LORD, **died, being an hundred and ten years old.**

9. **And they buried him in** the border of his inheritance in **Timnath-heres, in** the **mount** of **Ephraim,** on the north side of the hill Gaash.

10. **And** also **all that generation were gathered unto their fathers: and there arose another generation** after them, **which knew not the LORD, nor** yet **the works which he had done for Israel.**

11. **And** the children of **Israel did evil in the sight of the LORD, and served Baalim:**

12. And they forsook the LORD God of their fathers, which brought them out of the land of Egypt, and followed other gods, of the gods of the people that *were* round about them, and bowed themselves unto them, and provoked the LORD to anger.

13. And they forsook the LORD, and served Baal and Ashtaroth.

14. **And the anger of the LORD was hot against Israel, and he delivered them into the hands of** spoilers that spoiled them, and he sold them into the hands of **their enemies** round about, so that they could not any longer stand before their enemies.

15. **Whithersoever**

they went out,
the hand of the LORD was
against them for evil, as the
LORD had said, and as the
LORD had sworn unto them:
and they were
greatly distressed.
16. **Nevertheless the LORD**
raised up judges, which
delivered them out of the hand
of those that spoiled them.
17. And yet they would not hearken
unto their judges, but they went
a-whoring after other gods, and
bowed themselves unto them: they
turned quickly out of the way which
their fathers walked in, obeying the
commandments of the LORD;
but they did not so.
18. **And** when the LORD
raised them up judges, then
the LORD was with the
judge, and delivered them
out of the hand of their
enemies all the days of the judge:
for it repented the LORD
because of their groanings
by reason of them that oppressed
them and vexed them.
19. **And** it came to pass,
when the judge
was dead, *that*
they returned, and corrupted
themselves more than their fathers,
in following other gods to
serve them, and to bow down unto
them; they ceased not from their own
doings, nor from their stubborn way.
20. **And the anger of the**
LORD was hot against
Israel; and he said, Because
that this people hath transgressed
my covenant which I commanded
their fathers, and have not
hearkened unto my voice;
21. **I** also
will not henceforth
drive out any from before
them of the nations which
Joshua left when he died:
22. **That through them I may**
prove Israel, whether they
will keep the way of the

LORD to walk therein, as
their fathers did keep *it*, or not.
23. Therefore the LORD left those
nations, without driving them out
hastily; neither delivered he
them into the hand of Joshua.

CHAPTER 3

1. **Now these are the**
nations which the LORD
left, to prove Israel by them,
even as many *of Israel* as had not
known all the wars of Canaan;
2. Only that the generations of
the children of Israel might know, to
teach them war, at the least such
as before knew nothing thereof;
3. **Namely, five lords**
of the Philistines, and all
the Canaanites, and
the Sidonians, and
the Hivites that dwelt
in mount Lebanon, from
mount Baal–hermon unto the
entering in of Hamath.
4. And they were to prove Israel by
them, to know whether they would
hearken unto the commandments
of the LORD, which he commanded
their fathers by the hand of Moses.
5. **And** the children of
Israel dwelt among the
Canaanites, Hittites, and
Amorites, and
Perizzites, and
Hivites, and Jebusites:
6. **And** they
took their daughters to
be their wives, and gave
their daughters to their sons,
and served their gods.
7. **And** the children of
Israel did evil in the sight of the
LORD,and forgat the LORD their God,
and served Baalim
and the groves.
8. **Therefore** the anger of
the LORD was hot
against Israel, and he
sold them into the hand
of Chushan–rishathaim
king of Mesopotamia:
and the children of

Israel served Chushan–rishathaim eight years.

9. And when the children of Israel cried unto the LORD, the LORD raised up a deliverer to the children of Israel, who delivered them, even Othniel the son of Kenaz, Caleb's younger brother.

10. And the spirit of the LORD came upon him, and he judged Israel, and went out to war: and the LORD delivered Chushan–rishathaim king of Mesopotamia into his hand; and his hand prevailed against Chushan–rishathaim.

11. And the land had rest forty years. And Othniel the son of Kenaz died.

12. And the children of Israel did evil again in the sight of the LORD: and the LORD strengthened Eglon the king of Moab against Israel, because they had done evil in the sight of theLORD.

13. And he gathered unto him the children of Ammon and Amalek, and went and smote Israel, and possessed the city of palm trees.

14. So the children of Israel served Eglon the king of Moab eighteen years.

15. But when the children of Israel cried unto the LORD, the LORD raised them up a deliverer, Ehud the son of Gera, a Benjamite, a man lefthanded: and by him the children of Israel sent a present unto Eglon the king of Moab.

16. But Ehud made him a dagger which had two edges, of a cubit length; and he did gird it under his raiment upon his right thigh.

17. And he brought the present unto Eglon king of Moab: and Eglon was a very fat man.

18. And when he had made an end to offer the present, he sent away the people that bare the present.

19. But he himself turned again from the quarries that were by Gilgal, and said, I have a secret errand unto thee, O king: who said, Keep silence. And all that stood by him went out from him.

20. And Ehud came unto him; and he was sitting in a summer parlour, which he had for himself alone. And Ehud said, I have a message from God unto thee. And he arose out of his seat.

21. And Ehud put forth his left hand, and took the dagger from his right thigh, and thrust it into his belly:

22. And the haft also went in after the blade; and the fat closed upon the blade, so that he could not draw the dagger out of his belly; and the dirt came out.

23. Then Ehud went forth through the porch, and shut the doors of the parlour upon him, and locked them.

24. When he was gone out, his servants came; and when they saw that, behold, the doors of the parlour were locked, they said, Surely he covereth his feet in his summer chamber.

25. And they tarried till they were ashamed: and, behold, he opened not the doors of the parlour; therefore they took a key, and opened them: and, behold, their lord was fallen down dead on the earth.

26. And Ehud escaped while they tarried, and passed beyond the quarries, and escaped

unto Seirath.

27. **And** it came to pass, when he was come, that **he blew a trumpet in the mountain of Ephraim, and** the children of **Israel went down with him from the mount,** and he before them.

28. **And he said** unto them, **Follow after me: for the LORD hath delivered** your enemies **the Moabites into your hand. And they** went down after him, and **took the fords of Jordan toward Moab,** and suffered not a man to pass over.

29. **And they slew** of Moab at that time **about ten thousand** men, all lusty, and all **men of valour;** and there escaped not a man.

30. **So Moab was subdued** that day under the hand of Israel. **And the land had rest fourscore years.**

31. **And after him was Shamgar** the son of Anath, **which slew of the Philistines six hundred men with an ox goad:** and he also delivered Israel.

CHAPTER 4

1. **And** the children of **Israel again did evil** in the sight of the LORD, **when Ehud was dead.**

2. **And the LORD sold them into the hand of Jabin king of Canaan,** that reigned in Hazor; **the captain of whose host was Sisera,** which dwelt in Harosheth of the Gentiles.

3. **And** the children of **Israel cried** unto the LORD: **for he had nine hundred chariots** of iron; **and twenty years he mightily oppressed** the children of **Israel.**

4. **And Deborah, a prophetess,** the wife of Lapidoth, she **judged Israel** at that time.

5. And she dwelt under the palm tree of Deborah between Ramah and Beth-el in mount Ephraim: and the children of Israel came up to her for judgment.

6. **And she** sent and **called Barak** the son of Abinoam out of Kedesh–naphtali, **and said** unto him, **Hath not the LORD** God of Israel **commanded,** *saying,* **Go** and draw **toward mount Tabor, and take** with thee **ten thousand men** of the children **of Naphtali and of** the children of **Zebulun?**

7. **And I will draw unto thee** to the river Kishon Sisera, **the captain of Jabin's army,** with his chariots and his multitude; **and I will deliver him** into thine hand.

8. **And Barak said** unto her, **If thou wilt go** with me, **then I will go:** but if thou wilt not go with me, *then* I will not go.

9. **And she said, I will surely go** with thee: notwithstanding the journey that thou takest shall not be for thine honour; **for the LORD shall sell Sisera into the hand of a woman. And Deborah** arose, and **went with Barak to Kedesh.**

10. And Barak called Zebulun and Naphtali to Kedesh; and he went up with ten thousand men at his feet: and Deborah went up with him.

11. **Now Heber** the Kenite, **which was of the children of Hobab the father in law of Moses,** had severed

himself from the Kenites, and
pitched his tent unto
the plain of Zaanaim,
which *is* by Kedesh.
12. **And they shewed Sisera**
that Barak the son of Abinoam
was gone up to
mount Tabor.
13. **And Sisera gathered**
together all his chariots,
even nine hundred chariots of iron,
and all the people that *were*
with him, from Harosheth of the
Gentiles unto the river of Kishon.
14. **And Deborah said**
unto Barak, Up; for
this is the day in which
the LORD hath delivered
Sisera into thine hand: is not
the LORD gone out before thee?
So Barak went
down from mount Tabor,
and ten thousand
men after him.
15. **And the LORD**
discomfited Sisera, and all
his chariots, and all
his host, with the edge of the
sword before Barak;
so that Sisera lighted
down off *his* chariot, and
fled away on his feet.
16. **But Barak pursued**
after the chariots, and after the host,
unto Harosheth of the Gentiles:
and all the host of Sisera
fell upon the edge of the sword;
and there was not a man left.
17. **Howbeit Sisera**
fled away on his feet
to the tent of Jael the wife
of Heber the Kenite: for *there*
was peace between Jabin the
king of Hazor and the house
of Heber the Kenite.
18. **And Jael went out**
to meet Sisera, and
said unto him, Turn in, my lord,
turn in to me; fear not.
And when he had turned in
unto her into the tent,
she covered him
with a mantle.

19. **And he said** unto her,
Give me, I pray thee,
a little water to drink;
for I am thirsty.
And she opened
a bottle of milk, and
gave him drink,
and covered him.
20. **Again he said** unto her,
Stand in the door of the tent,
and it shall be,
when any man doth
come and inquire of thee,
and say, Is there any
man here? that thou shalt
say, No.
21. **Then Jael** Heber's wife
took a nail of the tent,
and took an
hammer in her hand,
and went softly unto him,
and smote the nail into his
temples, and fastened it
into the ground: for he was
fast asleep and weary. So he died.
22. **And**, behold,
as Barak pursued Sisera,
Jael came out to meet him, and
said unto him, Come, and I will shew
thee the man whom thou seekest.
And when he came
into her *tent*, behold,
Sisera lay dead, and
the nail *was* in his temples.
23. **So God**
subdued on that day
Jabin the king of Canaan
before the children of
Israel.
24. **And** the hand of the children of
Israel prospered, and
prevailed against Jabin
the king of Canaan, until they had
destroyed Jabin king of Canaan.

CHAPTER 5

1. **Then sang Deborah**
and Barak the son of
Abinoam on that day,
saying,
2. **Praise ye the LORD for**
the avenging of Israel,
when the people willingly

■ offered themselves.
■ 3. **Hear, O** ye
■ **kings;** give ear, O ye
■ princes; I, *even*
■ **I, will sing unto**
■ **the LORD**; I will sing *praise*
to the LORD God of Israel.
■ 4. **LORD, when thou**
■ **wentest out** of Seir, when
thou marchedst out of the field
■ **of Edom, the earth**
■ **trembled,** and the
heavens dropped, the clouds
also dropped water.
■ 5. **The mountains melted**
from before the LORD,
■ **even** that
■ **Sinai** from before the
LORD God of Israel.
■ 6. **In the days of**
■ **Shamgar** the son of Anath,
■ **in the days of Jael,**
■ **the highways were**
■ **unoccupied,** and the
travellers walked through byways.
■ 7. **The inhabitants** *of*
the villages ceased, they
■ **ceased in Israel, until** that
■ **I Deborah arose,** that
I arose a mother in Israel.
■ 8. **They chose new gods;**
■ **then was war** in the gates:
was there a shield or spear seen
among forty thousand in Israel?
■ 9. **My heart is toward**
■ **the governors** of Israel,
■ **that offered themselves**
■ **willingly among the**
■ **people.** Bless ye the LORD.
■ 10. **Speak, ye that ride**
■ **on white asses,** ye
■ **that sit in judgment,**
■ **and walk by the way.**
■ 11. **They that are**
■ **delivered from the** noise of
■ **archers in the places of**
■ **drawing water, there**
■ **shall they rehearse the**
■ **righteous acts of the**
■ **LORD,** *even* the righteous acts
toward the inhabitants of his villages
in Israel: then shall the people of
the LORD go down to the gates.

■ 12. **Awake**, awake,
■ **Deborah:** awake, awake,
■ **utter a song: arise, Barak,**
■ **and lead thy captivity**
■ **captive,** thou son of Abinoam.
■ 13. **Then he made him that**
■ **remaineth have dominion**
■ **over the nobles** among
the people: the LORD made me
have dominion over the mighty.
14. Out of Ephraim *was there* a root
of them against Amalek; after thee,
Benjamin, among thy people; out
of Machir came down governors,
and out of Zebulun they that
handle the pen of the writer.
■ 15. **And the princes**
■ **of Issachar were**
■ **with Deborah**; even
■ **Issachar, and** also
■ **Barak:** he was sent on foot into the
valley. For the divisions of Reuben
there were great thoughts of heart.
16. Why abodest thou among the
sheepfolds, to hear the bleatings
of the flocks? For the divisions
of Reuben *there were* great
searchings of heart.
17. Gilead abode beyond Jordan:
and why did Dan remain in ships?
Asher continued on the sea shore,
and abode in his breaches.
18. Zebulun and Naphtali *were* a
people *that* jeoparded their lives
unto the death in the high places
of the field.
19. The kings came *and* fought, then
■ **fought the kings of**
■ **Canaan in Taanach**
by the waters of Megiddo;
■ **they took no gain**
■ **of money.**
■ 20. **They fought from**
■ **heaven;** the stars in
their courses fought
■ **against Sisera.**
■ 21. **The river of Kishon**
■ **swept them away,** that
ancient river, the river Kishon.
■ **O my soul, thou hast**
■ **trodden down strength.**
22. Then were
■ **the horsehoofs broken**

by the means of the
prancings, the prancings
of their mighty ones.
23. **Curse ye Meroz, said
the angel of the LORD,** curse
ye bitterly the inhabitants thereof;
**because they came not to
the help of the LORD,** to the
help of the LORD against the mighty.
24. **Blessed above
women shall Jael** the
wife of Heber the Kenite
be, blessed shall she be
above women in the tent.
25. He asked water, *and* she
gave *him* milk; she brought
forth butter in a lordly dish.
26. She put her hand to the
nail, and her right hand to the
workmen's hammer; and
**with the hammer she
smote Sisera,** she smote off
his head, when she had pierced
and stricken through his temples.
27. **At her feet he** bowed, he
fell, he lay down: at her feet hebowed,
he fell: where he bowed, there he
fell down
dead.
28. **The mother of Sisera**
looked out at a window, and
cried through the lattice,
**Why is his chariot so
long in coming?** why tarry
the wheels of his chariots?
29. Her wise ladies answered her,
yea, she returned answer to herself,
30. Have they not sped?
**have they not divided the
prey;** to every man a damsel
or two; to Sisera a prey of divers
colours, a prey of divers colours
of needlework, of divers colours
of needlework on both sides,
meet for the necks of *them*
that take the spoil?
31. **So let all thine enemies
perish, O LORD: but
let them that love him
be as the sun when he
goeth forth in his might.
And the land had rest
forty years.**

CHAPTER 6

1. **And** the children of
Israel did evil in the
sight of the LORD:
**and the LORD delivered
them into the hand of
Midian seven years.**
2. And the hand of Midian
prevailed against Israel:
and because of the
Midianites the children of
Israel made them the
dens which *are*
in the mountains, and
caves, and strong holds.
3. **And** *so* it was,
when Israel had sown, that
the Midianites came up, and
**the Amalekites, and the
children of the east,** even they
came up against them;
4. And they encamped against them,
**and destroyed the
increase of the earth,**
till thou come unto Gaza,
and left no sustenance for
Israel, neither sheep, nor ox, nor ass.
5. **For they came up with
their cattle and their
tents,** and they came as
grasshoppers for multitude; *for*
both they and their camels were
without number: and they entered
into the land to destroy it.
6. **And Israel was
greatly impoverished**
because of the Midianites;
and the children of Israel
cried unto the LORD.
7. **And** it came to pass, when
the children of Israel cried unto the
LORD because of the Midianites,
8. That
the LORD sent a prophet
unto the children of Israel,
which said unto them,
**Thus saith the
LORD** God of Israel,
**I brought you up from
Egypt,** and brought you forth
out of the house of bondage;
9. **And I delivered you
out of the hand** of the

Egyptians, and out of the hand **of all that oppressed you,** and drave them out from before you, **and gave you their land;** 10. **And I said** unto you, **I am the LORD** your God; **fear not the gods of the Amorites,** in whose land ye dwell: **but ye have not obeyed my voice.** 11. **And there came an angel** of the LORD, **and sat under an oak** which *was* in Ophrah, **that pertained unto Joash** the Abiezrite: **and his son Gideon threshed wheat by the winepress, to hide it from the Midianites.** 12. **And the angel** of the LORD **appeared unto him, and said** unto him, **The LORD is with thee,** thou mighty man of valour. 13. **And Gideon said** unto him, Oh my Lord, **if the LORD be with us, why then is all this befallen us? and where be all his miracles which our fathers told us** of, saying, Did not the LORD bring us up from Egypt? but now the LORD hath forsaken us, and delivered us into the hands of the Midianites. 14. **And the LORD** looked upon him, and **said, Go** in this thy might, and **thou shalt save Israel** from the hand of the Midianites: have not I sent thee? 15. **And he said** unto him, Oh my Lord, wherewith shall I save Israel? behold, **my family is poor** in Manasseh, **and I am the least in my father's house.** 16. **And the LORD said** unto him, **Surely I will be with thee,** and thou shalt smite the Midianites as one man.

17. **And he said** unto him, If now I have found grace in thy sight, then shew me **a sign** that thou talkest with me. 18. **Depart not hence,** I pray thee, **until I come** unto thee, **and bring** forth **my present, and** set *it* before thee. **And he said, I will tarry** until thou come again. 19. **And Gideon** went in, and **made ready a kid, and unleavened cakes** of an ephah of flour: the flesh he put in a basket, and he put the broth in a pot, **and brought it out unto him** under the oak, and presented *it*. 20. And the angel of God said unto him, Take the flesh and the unleavened cakes, and lay *them* upon this rock, and pour out the broth. And he did so. 21. **Then the angel** of the LORD **put forth the end of the staff** that *was* in his hand, **and touched the flesh and** the unleavened **cakes; and there rose up fire** out of the rock, **and consumed the flesh and** the unleavened **cakes. Then the angel** of the LORD **departed** out of his sight. 22. **And** when **Gideon perceived that he was an angel** of the LORD, Gideon said, Alas, O LORD God! for because I have seen an angel of the LORD face to face. 23. **And the LORD said** unto him, **Peace be unto thee; fear not: thou shalt not die.** 24. **Then Gideon built an altar** there unto the LORD, **and called it Jehovah-shalom:** unto this day it *is* yet in Ophrah of the Abiezrites. 25. **And** it came to pass **the same night,** that

■ the LORD said unto him,
Take thy father's young bullock,
even the second bullock of
seven years old, and
■ throw down the altar of
■ Baal that thy father hath,
and cut down the grove that *is* by it:
■ 26. And build an altar unto
■ the LORD thy God upon the top
of this rock, in the ordered place,
and take the second bullock,
■ and offer a burnt sacrifice
■ with the wood of the grove
■ which thou shalt cut down.
■ 27. Then Gideon took
ten men of his servants, and
■ did as the LORD had
■ said unto him: and *so* it was,
because he feared his father's
household, and the men of the
city, that he could not do *it* by
day, that he did *it* by night.
■ 28. And when
■ the men of the city arose
■ early in the morning, behold,
the altar of Baal was cast down, and
the grove was cut down that *was* by
it, and the second bullock was
offered upon the altar *that was* built.
■ 29. And they
■ said one to another,
■ Who hath done this
■ thing? And when they
■ inquired and asked,
■ they said, Gideon
the son of Joash
hath done this thing.
■ 30. Then the men of the city
■ said unto Joash, Bring out
■ thy son, that he may die:
because he hath cast down the altar
of Baal, and because he hath cut
down the grove that *was* by it.
■ 31. And Joash said unto
all that stood against him,
■ Will ye plead for
■ Baal? will ye save him?
■ he that will plead for him,
■ let him be put to death
whilst *it is yet* morning:
■ if he be a god, let him
■ plead for himself, because
one hath cast down his altar.

■ 32. Therefore on that day he
■ called him Jerubbaal, saying,
Let Baal plead against
him, because he hath thrown
down his altar.
■ 33. Then all the Midianites
■ and the Amalekites and
■ the children of the east
■ were gathered together,
and went over, and pitched in
the valley of Jezreel.
■ 34. But the Spirit of the
■ LORD came upon Gideon,
■ and he blew a trumpet;
■ and Abiezer was
■ gathered after him.
■ 35. And he sent messengers
■ throughout all Manasseh;
who also was gathered after him:
■ and he sent messengers
■ unto Asher, and unto
■ Zebulun, and unto
■ Naphtali; and they came
up to meet them.
■ 36. And Gideon said
■ unto God, If thou wilt
■ save Israel by mine
■ hand, as thou hast said,
37. Behold,
■ I will put a fleece of wool
■ in the floor; and if the dew
■ be on the fleece only, and *it*
be dry upon all the earth *beside*,
■ then shall I know that
■ thou wilt save Israel by
■ mine hand, as thou hast said.
■ 38. And it was so: for he
■ rose up early on the morrow,
and thrust the fleece together,
■ and wringed the dew
■ out of the fleece, a
■ bowl full of water.
■ 39. And Gideon
■ said unto God,
■ Let not thine anger
■ be hot against me, and I
will speak but this once:
■ let me prove, I pray thee,
■ but this once with the
■ fleece; let it now be dry
■ only upon the fleece, and
upon all the ground let there be dew.
■ 40. And God did so that

night: for it was dry upon the fleece only, and there was dew on all the ground.

CHAPTER 7

1. **Then** Jerubbaal, who *is* **Gideon, and all the people** that *were* with him, rose up early, and **pitched beside the well of Harod: so that the host of the Midianites were on the north** side of them, by the hill of Moreh, in the valley.

2. **And the LORD said** unto Gideon, **The people** that *are* **with thee are too many for me to give the Midianites** into their hands, **lest Israel vaunt** themselves against me, **saying, Mine own hand hath saved me.**

3. **Now** therefore go to, **proclaim** in the ears of the people, saying, **Whosoever is** fearful and **afraid, let him return** and depart early from mount Gilead. **And there returned** of the people **twenty** and **two thousand; and there remained ten thousand.**

4. **And the LORD said** unto Gideon, **The people are yet too many; bring them down unto the water, and** I will try them for thee there: and it shall be, *that* of whom I say unto thee, This shall go with thee, the same shall go with thee; and of whomsoever I say unto thee, This shall not go with thee, the same shall not go.

5. So he brought down the people unto the water: and the LORD said unto Gideon, **Every one that lappeth of the water** with his tongue, **as a dog** lappeth, **him shalt thou set by himself;** likewise every one that boweth down upon his knees to drink.

6. **And the number** of them **that lapped,** *putting* their hand to their mouth, **were three hundred men:** but all the rest of the people bowed down upon their knees to drink water.

7. **And the LORD said** unto Gideon, **By the three hundred men that lapped will I** save you, and **deliver the Midianites** into thine hand: and let all the *other* people go every man unto his place.

8. **So the people took victuals** in their hand, **and their trumpets: and he sent all the rest** *of* Israel every man **unto his tent, and** retained those three hundred men: and the host of Midian was beneath him in the valley.

9. And it came to pass the same night, that **the LORD said** unto him, **Arise,** get thee down unto the host; **for I have delivered it into thine hand.**

10. **But if thou fear** to go down, **go** thou **with Phurah** thy servant **down to the host:**

11. **And thou shalt hear what they say; and afterward shall thine hands be strengthened** to go down unto the host. Then went he down with Phurah his servant unto the outside of the armed men that *were* in the host.

12. **And the Midianites and** the **Amalekites and** all **the children of the east** lay along in the valley like grasshoppers for multitude; and their camels **were without number,** as the sand by the sea side **for multitude.**

13. **And when Gideon was come,** behold, *there was*

375

■ **a man** that
■ **told a dream** unto his fellow,
■ **and said,** Behold, I
dreamed a dream, and, lo,
■ **a cake of barley bread**
■ **tumbled into the host of**
■ **Midian, and came unto**
■ **a tent,** and smote it that it fell,
■ **and overturned it,**
that the tent lay along.
■ 14. **And his fellow**
■ **answered** and said,
■ **This is** nothing else save
■ **the sword of Gideon** the
son of Joash, a man of Israel:
for into his hand hath God delivered
Midian, and all the host.
15. And it was *so,*
■ **when Gideon**
■ **heard** the telling of
■ **the dream, and the**
■ **interpretation** thereof, that
■ **he worshipped,** and
returned into the host of Israel,
■ **and said, Arise; for the**
■ **LORD hath delivered**
into your hand
■ **the host of Midian.**
■ 16. **And he divided**
■ **the** three hundred
■ **men into three**
■ **companies, and he put**
■ **a trumpet** in every man's hand,
■ **with empty pitchers, and**
■ **lamps within the pitchers.**
17. **And he said** unto them,
■ **Look on me, and do**
■ **likewise:** and, behold, when I come
to the outside of the camp, it shall be
that, as I do, so shall ye do.
■ 18. **When I blow with**
■ **a trumpet,** I and all that
are with me, then
■ **blow ye the trumpets**
also on every side of all the camp,
■ **and say, The sword of**
■ **the LORD, and of Gideon.**
19. **So Gideon,** and the hundred
men that*were* with him, came untothe
outside of the camp in the beginning
of the middle watch; and they had
but newly set the watch: and they
blew the trumpets, and brake the

pitchers that *were* in their hands.
■ 20. **And the three**
■ **companies blew the**
■ **trumpets, and brake**
■ **the pitchers, and held**
■ **the lamps** in their left hands,
and the trumpets in their right
hands to blow *withal:*
■ **and they cried, The**
■ **sword of the LORD,**
■ **and of Gideon.**
■ 21. **And they** stood every
man in his place round
about the camp: and all the
host ran, and cried, and fled.
22. And the three hundred
■ **blew the trumpets,**
■ **and the LORD set**
■ **every man's sword**
■ **against his fellow,**
even throughout all the host:
■ **and the host fled** to Beth-shittah
in Zererath, *and* to the border of
Abel–meholah, unto Tabbath.
■ 23. **And the men of Israel**
gathered themselves together
out of Naphtali, and out of Asher,
and out of all Manasseh, and
■ **pursued after the**
■ **Midianites.**
24. **And Gideon**
■ **sent messengers**
■ **throughout** all mount
■ **Ephraim, saying,**
■ **come** down
■ **against the Midianites,**
■ **and** take before them the waters
unto Beth-barah and Jordan. Then all
■ **the men of Ephraim** gathered
themselves together, and took the
waters unto Beth-barah and Jordan.
25. And they
■ **took two princes**
■ **of the Midianites,**
■ **Oreb and Zeeb;** and
they slew Oreb upon the rock
Oreb, and Zeeb they slew at
the winepress of Zeeb, and
pursued Midian,
■ **and brought the**
■ **heads** of Oreb and Zeeb
■ **to Gideon** on the
other side Jordan.

CHAPTER 8

■ 1. **And the men of**
■ **Ephraim said** unto him,
Why hast thou served us thus, that
■ **thou calledst us**
■ **not,** when thou wentest
■ **to fight with the Midianites?**
And they did chide with him sharply.
■ 2. **And he said** unto them, What
have I done now in comparison of
you? *Is* not the gleaning of the
grapes of Ephraim better than
the vintage of Abiezer?
■ 3. **God hath delivered**
■ **into your hands the**
■ **princes** of Midian, Oreb and Zeeb:
■ **and what was I able**
■ **to do** in comparison of you?
■ **Then their anger was**
■ **abated** toward him,
when he had said that.
■ 4. **And Gideon came to**
■ **Jordan,** *and* passed over, he, and
the three hundred men that *were* with
him, faint, yet pursuing *them.*
■ 5. **And he said unto**
■ **the men of Succoth,**
■ **Give,** I pray you, loaves of
■ **bread unto the people that**
■ **follow me; for** they *be* faint, and
■ **I am pursuing after Zebah**
■ **and Zalmunna,** kings of Midian.
■ 6. **And the princes** of Succoth
■ **said, Are** the hands of
■ **Zebah and Zalmunna now**
■ **in thine hand,** that we should
give bread unto thine army?
■ 7. **And Gideon said,** Therefore
■ **when the LORD hath**
■ **delivered Zebah and**
■ **Zalmunna** into mine hand, then
■ **I will tear your flesh** with
the thorns of the wilderness
and with briers.
■ 8. **And he went** up thence
■ **to Penuel,** and spake
unto them likewise:
■ **and the men** of Penuel
■ **answered him as the men**
■ **of Succoth** had answered *him.*
9. And he spake also unto the men of
Penuel, saying, When I come again in
peace, I will break down this tower.

■ 10. **Now Zebah and**
■ **Zalmunna were in**
■ **Karkor, and** their hosts
■ **with them, about fifteen**
■ **thousand men,** all that were
left of all the hosts of the children
of the east: for there fell an
hundred and twenty thousand
men that drew sword.
■ 11. **And Gideon** went up by
the way of them that dwelt in tents
on the east of Nobah and
Jogbehah, and smote the host:
for the host was secure.
12. And when Zebah and
Zalmunna fled, he
■ **pursued after** them, and took
■ **the two kings** of Midian,
Zebah and Zalmunna,
■ **and discomfited**
■ **all the host.**
■ 13. **And Gideon** the son of Joash
■ **returned from battle**
before the sun *was up,*
14. And caught a young man of the
men of Succoth, and inquired of him:
and he described unto him theprinces
of Succoth, and the elders thereof,
even threescore and seventeen men.
■ 15. **And he came**
■ **unto** the men of
■ **Succoth, and**
■ **said,** Behold Zebah and
Zalmunna, with whom ye
did upbraid me, saying,
■ **Are** the hands of
■ **Zebah and**
■ **Zalmunna now in**
■ **thine hand,** that we should
■ **give bread unto**
■ **thy men** *that are* weary?
■ 16. **And he took the**
■ **elders** of the city,
■ **and thorns** of the wilderness
■ **and briers, and with**
■ **them he taught the**
■ **men of Succoth.**
■ 17. **And he beat down the**
■ **tower of Penuel, and slew**
■ **the men** of the city.
■ 18. **Then said he unto Zebah**
■ **and Zalmunna, What**
■ **manner of men were they**

■ whom ye slew at Tabor?
■ And they answered, As
■ thou art, so *were* they; each one
resembled the children of a king.
■ 19. And he said, They were
■ my brethren, *even* the sons of
my mother: *as* the LORD liveth,
■ if ye had saved them
■ alive, I would not slay you.
■ 20. And he said unto Jether
■ his firstborn, Up, *and*
■ slay them. But the
■ youth drew not his
■ sword: for he feared,
because he *was* yet a youth.
■ 21. Then Zebah and Zalmunna said,
Rise thou, and fall upon us: for as
the man *is, so is* his strength. And
■ Gideon arose, and
■ slew Zebah and Zalmunna,
and took away the ornaments that
were on their camels' necks.
■ 22. Then the men of Israel
■ said unto Gideon, Rule thou
■ over us, both thou, and
thy son, and thy son's son also:
■ for thou hast delivered
■ us from the hand of
■ Midian.
■ 23. And Gideon
■ said unto them,
■ I will not rule over you,
■ neither shall my
■ son rule over you:
■ the LORD shall
■ rule over you.
■ 24. And Gideon
■ said unto them,
■ I would desire a
■ request of you,
■ that ye would give me
■ every man the earrings
■ of his prey. (For they had
golden earrings, because
they *were* Ishmaelites.)
25. And they answered,
We will willingly give *them*.
■ And they spread a garment, and
■ did cast therein every man
the earrings of his prey.
■ 26. And the weight of
the golden earrings that he
■ requested was

■ a thousand and
■ seven hundred shekels
■ of gold; beside ornaments,
and collars, and purple raiment
that *was* on the kings of Midian,
and beside the chains that *were*
about their camels' necks.
■ 27. And Gideon made
■ an ephod thereof,
■ and put it in his
■ city, *even* in Ophrah:
■ and all Israel went thither
■ a-whoring after it: which
■ thing became a snare unto
■ Gideon, and to his house.
28. Thus was Midian subdued before
the children of Israel, so that they
lifted up their heads no more. And
the country was in quietness
forty years in the days of Gideon.
29. And Jerubbaal the son of Joash
went and dwelt in his own house.
■ 30. And Gideon
■ had threescore and
■ ten sons of his body begotten:
for he had many wives.
■ 31. And his concubine
that *was* in Shechem, she also
■ bare him a son, whose name he
■ called Abimelech.
32. And Gideon the son of Joash
■ died in a good old age,
■ and was buried in the
■ sepulchre of Joash his
■ father, in Ophrah of the Abi–ezrites.
33. And it came to pass,
■ as soon as Gideon
■ was dead, that the children of
■ Israel turned again, and
went a-whoring after Baalim,
■ and made Baal–berith
■ their god.
34. And the children of
■ Israel remembered not
■ the LORD their God, who had
delivered them out of the hands
of all their enemies on every side:
■ 35. Neither shewed they
■ kindness to the house
■ of Jerubbaal, *namely,*
■ Gideon, according to all
the goodness which he had
shewed unto Israel.

CHAPTER 9

1. **And Abimelech** the son of Jerubbaal **went to Shechem** unto his mother's brethren, **and communed** with them, and **with all the family** of the house of his mother's father, **saying,**

2. **Speak,** I pray you, **in the ears of** all the men of **Shechem, Whether** *is* better for you, either that all **the sons of Jerubbaal,** *which are* threescore and ten persons, **reign over you, or that one reign over you?** remember also that I *am* your bone and your flesh.

3. **And his mother's brethren** spake of him in the ears of all the men of Shechem all these words: and their hearts **inclined to follow Abimelech; for they** said, He is our brother.

4. **And they gave him** threescore and ten *pieces* of **silver** out of the house of Baal—berith, **wherewith Abimelech hired vain and light persons,** which followed him.

5. **And he went unto** his father's house at **Ophrah, and slew his brethren** the sons of Jerubbaal, *being* threescore and ten persons, upon one stone: notwithstanding **yet Jotham the youngest** son of Jerubbaal was left; for he **hid himself.**

6. **And all the men of Shechem** gathered together, **and** all the house of **Millo,** and went, and **made Abimelech king,** by the plain of the pillar that *was* in Shechem.

7. **And when they told it to Jotham, he** went and stood in the top of mount Gerizim, and lifted up his voice, and cried, and **said** unto them, **Hearken unto me,** ye men of Shechem, **that God may hearken unto you.**

8. **The trees went forth** *on a time* **to anoint a king** over them; **and they said unto the olive tree, Reign thou over us.**

9. **But the olive tree said** unto them, **Should I leave my fatness,** wherewith by me they honour God and man, and go to be promoted over the trees?

10. **And the trees said to the fig tree,** Come thou, *and* **reign over us.**

11. **But the fig tree said** unto them, **Should I forsake** my sweetness, and **my good fruit,** and go to be promoted over the trees?

12. **Then said the trees unto the vine,** Come thou, *and* **reign over us.**

13. **And the vine said** unto them, **Should I leave my wine,** which cheereth God and man, and go to be promoted over the trees?

14. **Then said all the trees unto the bramble,** Come thou, *and* **reign over us.**

15. **And the bramble said** unto the trees, **If in truth ye anoint me king** over you, **then** come *and* **put your trust in my shadow: and if not, let fire** come out of the bramble, and **devour the cedars of Lebanon.**

16. **Now** therefore, **if ye have** done **truly** and sincerely, in that ye have **made Abimelech king, and** if ye **have dealt well with**

■ **Jerubbaal and his house,**
and have done unto him according
to the deserving of his hands;
17. (For my father fought for you, and
adventured his life far, and delivered
you out of the hand of Midian:
18. And ye are risen up against my
father's house this day, and have
slain his sons, threescore and ten
persons, upon one stone, and
have made Abimelech, the son
of his maidservant, king over the
men of Shechem, because he
is your brother;)
19. If ye then have dealt truly
and sincerely with Jerubbaal and
with his house this day,
■ **then rejoice** ye in Abimelech,
and let him also rejoice in you:
20. **But if not, let fire** come
out from Abimelech, and
■ **devour** the men of
■ **Shechem,** and the house of
■ **Millo; and** let fire come out
from the men of Shechem, and from
the house of Millo, and devour
■ **Abimelech.**
21. **And Jotham** ran away, and
■ **fled,** and went
■ **to Beer,** and dwelt there,
■ **for fear of Abimelech**
■ **his brother.**
22. When Abimelech had
reigned three years over Israel,
■ **23. Then God sent**
■ **an evil spirit**
■ **between Abimelech**
■ **and** the men of
■ **Shechem;** and the men
of Shechem dealt treacherously
with Abimelech:
■ **24. That the cruelty done**
■ **to the** threescore and ten
■ **sons of Jerubbaal might**
■ **come, and their blood be**
■ **laid upon Abimelech their**
■ **brother,** which slew them;
■ **and upon** the men of
■ **Shechem, which**
■ **aided him in** the
■ **killing** of
■ **his brethren.**
25. **And** the men of

■ **Shechem set** liers
■ **in wait for him in** the top of
■ **the mountains, and** they
■ **robbed all that**
■ **came** along that way
■ **by** them:
■ **and it was told Abimelech.**
26. **And Gaal** the son of Ebed
■ **came with his**
■ **brethren,** and went over
■ **to Shechem: and**
the men of Shechem
■ **put their confidence in him.**
27. **And they** went out into
the fields, and gathered their
vineyards, and trode *the grapes,*
and made merry, and
■ **went into the house of their**
■ **god, and did eat and drink,**
■ **and cursed Abimelech.**
28. **And Gaal** the son of Ebed
■ **said, Who is Abimelech,** and
■ **who is Shechem, that we**
■ **should serve him?** *is* not *he*
the son of Jerubbaal? and Zebul
his officer? serve the men of
Hamor the father of Shechem:
for why should we serve him?
■ **29. And would to God this**
■ **people were under my**
■ **hand! then would I**
■ **remove Abimelech.** And
he said to Abimelech, Increase
thine army, and come out.
■ **30. And when Zebul**
■ **the ruler** of the city
■ **heard the words of**
■ **Gaal** the son of Ebed,
■ **his anger was kindled.**
■ **31. And he sent messengers**
■ **unto Abimelech** privily,
■ **saying,** Behold,
■ **Gaal** the son of Ebed
■ **and his brethren be**
■ **come to Shechem;**
and, behold, they fortify
the city against thee.
■ **32. Now** therefore up
■ **by night, thou and the**
■ **people** that *is* with thee, and
■ **lie in wait in the field:**
33. **And** it shall be, *that*
■ **in the morning,** as soon as the

sun is up, thou shalt rise early, and set upon the city: and, behold, **when he** and the people tha*t* **is** with him **come out against thee,** then mayest thou **do to them as thou shalt find occasion.** 34. **And Abimelech** rose up, **and all the people** that *were* with him, by night, and they **laid wait against Shechem** in four companies. 35. **And Gaal** the son of Ebed went out, and **stood in the entering of the gate of the city:** and Abimelech rose up, and the people that *were* with him, from lying in wait. 36. **And** when Gaal saw the people, he **said to Zebul,** Behold, **there come people down from** the top of **the mountains. And Zebul said** unto him, **Thou seest the shadow** of the mountains **as if they were men.** 37. **And Gaal spake again,** and said, **See there come people** down by the middle of the land, and another company come along **by the plain of Meonenim.** 38. **Then said Zebul** unto him, Where *is* now thy mouth, wherewith thou saidst, Who *is* Abimelech, that we should serve him? **is not this the people that thou hast despised?** go out, I pray now, **and fight with them.** 39. **And Gaal** went out before the men of Shechem, and **fought with Abimelech.** 40. **And Abimelech chased him, and he fled** before him, **and many were** overthrown *and* **wounded,** *even* unto the entering of the gate. 41. **And Abimelech dwelt at Arumah: and Zebul**

thrust out Gaal and his brethren, that they should not dwell in Shechem. 42. **And** it came to pass on the morrow, that **the people went** out into the field; **and** they **told Abimelech.** 43. **And he took the people, and divided them into three companies,** and laid wait in the field, and looked, and, behold, the people *were* come forth out of the city; and he rose up against them, and smote them. 44. And Abimelech, and the company that *was* with him, rushed forward, and stood in the entering of the gate of the city: and the two *other* companies ran upon all *the people* that *were* in the fields, and slew them. 45. **And Abimelech fought against the city** all that day; and he took the city, and slew the people that *was* therein, **and beat down the city, and sowed it with salt.** 46. **And** when all **the men** of the tower **of Shechem** heard *that,* they **entered** into an hold of **the house of the god Berith.** 47. **And it was told Abimelech,** that all the men of the tower of Shechem were gathered together. 48. And Abimelech gat him up to mount Zalmon, he and all the people that *were* with him; **and Abimelech took an axe** in his hand, **and cut down a bough from the trees,** and took it, **and laid it on his shoulder, and said** unto the people that *were* with him, What ye have seen me do, make haste, *and* **do as I have done.** 49. **And** all **the people** likewise **cut down every man his bough,**

and followed Abimelech, and
put them to the hold, and
set the hold on fire upon them;
so that all the men of the tower
of Shechem died also, about
a thousand men and women.
50. Then went
Abimelech to Thebez,
and encamped against Thebez,
and took it.
51. But there was a
strong tower within the city,
and thither fled all the men
and women, and all they
of the city, and shut it to them, and
gat them up to the top of the tower.
52. And Abimelech
came unto the tower, and
fought against it, and went hard
unto the door of the tower
to burn it with fire.
53. And a certain
woman cast a piece
of a millstone upon
Abimelech's head, and all
to brake his skull.
54. Then he called
hastily unto the young man
his armour-bearer, and
said unto him, Draw thy sword, and
slay me, that men say
not of me, A women slew
him. And his young man thrust
him through, and he died.
55. And when the men of
Israel saw that Abimelech
was dead, they departed
every man unto his place.
56. Thus God rendered the
wickedness of Abimelech,
which he did unto his father,
in slaying his
seventy brethren:
57. And all the
evil of the men of
Shechem did God
render upon their heads: and
upon them came
the curse of Jotham
the son of Jerubbaal.

CHAPTER 10
1. And after Abimelech

there arose to defend Israel
Tola the son of Puah, the son of
Dodo, a man of Issachar, and he
dwelt in Shamir in mount Ephraim.
2. And he judged
Israel twenty and
three years, and died,
and was buried in Shamir.
3. And after him arose
Jair, a Gileadite, and
judged Israel twenty and
two years.
4. And he had thirty
sons that rode on
thirty ass colts, and they
had thirty cities, which are
called Havoth-jair unto this
day, which are in the land of Gilead.
5. And Jair died, and was
buried in Camon.
6. And the children of
Israel did evil again
in the sight of the LORD,
and served Baalim,
and Ashtaroth, and
the gods of Syria,
and the gods of
Zidon, and the gods of
Moab, and the gods of
the children of
Ammon, and the gods
of the Philistines, and forsook
the LORD, and served not him.
7. And the anger of
the LORD was hot
against Israel, and he
sold them into the hands
of the Philistines, and
into the hands of the children of
Ammon.
8. And that year
they vexed and
oppressed the children of
Israel: eighteen years, all the
children of Israel that were on the
other side Jordan in the land of the
Amorites, which is in Gilead.
9. Moreover the children of
Ammon passed over
Jordan to fight also against
Judah, and against
Benjamin, and
against the house of

Ephraim; so that Israel was sore distressed.

10. **And** the children of **Israel cried unto the LORD, saying, We have sinned against thee,** both because we have forsaken our God, and also served Baalim.

11. **And the LORD said** unto the children of Israel, **Did not I deliver you** from the Egyptians, and from the Amorites, from the children of Ammon, and from the Philistines?

12. The Zidonians also, and the Amalekites, and the Maonites, did oppress you; and ye cried to me, and I delivered you out of their hand.

13. **Yet ye have forsaken me,** and served other gods: **wherefore I will deliver you no more.**

14. **Go and cry unto the gods which ye have chosen; let them deliver you** in the time of your tribulation.

15. **And** the children of **Israel said unto the LORD**, We have sinned: **do thou unto us whatsoever seemeth good** unto thee; **deliver us only, we pray thee,** this day.

16. **And they put away the strange gods** from among them, **and served the LORD:** and his soul was grieved for the misery of Israel.

17. **Then** the children of **Ammon** were gathered together, and **encamped in Gilead. And** the children of **Israel** assembled themselves together, and **encamped in Mizpeh.**

18. **And the people** *and* princes **of Gilead said** one to another, **What man** *is he* that **will** begin to **fight against** the children of **Ammon? he shall be**

head over all the inhabitants **of Gilead.**

CHAPTER 11

1. **Now Jephthah** the Gileadite **was a mighty man** of valour, **and** he *was* **the son of an harlot:** and Gilead begat Jephthah.

2. **And Gilead's** wife bare him sons; and his wife's **sons** grew up, and they **thrust out Jephthah, and said** unto him, **Thou shalt not inherit in our father's house; for thou art the son of a strange woman.**

3. **Then Jephthah fled** from his brethren, **and dwelt in** the land of **Tob: and** there were gathered **vain men** to Jephthah, and **went out with him.**

4. **And** it came to pass in process of time, that the children of **Ammon made war against Israel.**

5. **And** it was so, that when the children of Ammon made war against Israel, **the elders of Gilead went to** fetch **Jephthah** out of the land of Tob:

6. **And** they **said** unto Jephthah, Come, and **be our captain,** that we may fight with the children of Ammon.

7. **And Jephthah said** unto the elders of Gilead, **Did not ye** hate me, and **expel me** out of my father's house? and why are ye come unto me now when ye are in distress?

8. **And the elders** of Gilead **said** unto Jephthah, Therefore **we turn again to thee now, that thou mayest** go with us, and fight against the children of Ammon, and **be our head** over all the inhabitants of Gilead.

9. **And Jephthah**

383

■ **said** unto the elders of Gilead,
■ **If ye bring me** home again
■ **to fight against** the children of
■ **Ammon, and the LORD**
■ **deliver them** before me,
■ **shall I be your head?**
10. **And the elders** of Gilead
■ **said** unto Jephthah,
■ **The LORD be witness**
■ **between us,** if we do not
so according to thy words.
11. Then Jephthah went with the
elders ofGilead, and the people made
him head and captain over them:
■ **and Jephthah uttered**
■ **all his words before**
■ **the LORD** in Mizpeh.
12. **And Jephthah sent**
■ **messengers unto the**
■ **king** of the children
■ **of Ammon, saying,**
■ **What hast thou to do**
■ **with me,** that thou art come
against me to fight in my land?
13. **And the king** of the
children of Ammon
■ **answered** unto the
messengers of Jephthah,
■ **Because Israel took**
■ **away my land, when they**
•■ **came up out of Egypt,**
from Arnon even unto Jabbok, and
unto Jordan: now therefore restore
those *lands* again peaceably.
14. **And Jephthah** sent
messengers again unto the
king of the children of Ammon:
15. And
■ **said** unto him, Thus saith Jephthah,
■ **Israel took not away the**
■ **land** of Moab, nor the land
of the children of Ammon:
16. **But when Israel came**
■ **up from Egypt**, and walked
through the wilderness unto the
Red sea, and came to Kadesh;
17. Then Israel sent messengers
■ **unto the king of Edom,**
■ **saying, Let me,** I pray thee,
■ **pass through thy land:**
■ **but the king of Edom**
would not hearken *thereto*.
■ **And** in like manner they sent unto

■ **the king of Moab:** but he
■ **would not consent:** and
Israel abode in Kadesh.
■ 18. **Then they went along**
■ **through the wilderness**,
and compassed the land of Edom,
and the land of Moab, and came by
the east side of the land of Moab,
■ **and pitched on the other**
■ **side of Arnon**, but came not
within the border of Moab: for
Arnon *was* the border of Moab.
■ 19. **And Israel sent**
■ **messengers unto**
■ **Sihon king of the**
■ **Amorites,** the king of Heshbon;
■ **and** Israel
■ **said** unto him,
■ **Let us pass,** we pray thee,
■ **through thy land** into my place.
■ 20. **But Sihon trusted not**
■ **Israel to pass** through his
coast: but Sihon gathered all his
people together, and pitched in
Jahaz, and fought against Israel.
■ 21. **And the LORD** God of Israel
■ **delivered Sihon and all his**
■ **people into the hand of**
■ **Israel,** and they smote them:
■ **so Israel possessed all**
■ **the land** of the Amorites, the
inhabitants of that country.
■ 22. **And** they possessed
■ **all the coasts of the**
■ **Amorites**, from Arnon even
unto Jabbok, and from the
wilderness even unto Jordan.
23. So now the LORD God of Israel
hath dispossessed the Amorites
from before his people Israel,
and shouldest thou possess it?
24. Wilt not thou possess
that which Chemosh thy god
giveth thee to possess?
■ **So whomsoever the**
■ **LORD our God shall**
■ **drive out from before us,**
■ **them will we possess.**
■ 25. **And now art thou** any thing
■ **better than Balak** the
son of Zippor, king of Moab?
■ **did he ever strive**
■ **against Israel,** or did

384

he ever fight against them,

26. While Israel dwelt **in Heshbon** and her towns, **and** in **Aroer** and her towns, **and in all the cities that be along by the coasts of Arnon, three hundred years? why** therefore **did ye not recover them within that time?**

27. **Wherefore I have not sinned against thee, but thou doest me wrong to war against me:** **the LORD** the Judge **be judge** this day **between** the children of **Israel and** the children of **Ammon.**

28. **Howbeit the king** of the children **of Ammon hearkened not unto** the words of **Jephthah** which he sent him.

29. **Then the spirit of the LORD came upon Jephthah**, and he passed over Gilead, and Manasseh, and passed over Mizpeh of Gilead, and from Mizpeh of Gilead he passed over *unto* the children of Ammon.

30. **And Jephthah vowed a vow unto the LORD, and said, If thou shalt** without fail **deliver** the children of **Ammon into mine hands,**

31. **Then** it shall be, that **whatsoever cometh forth of the doors of my house to meet me,** when I return in peace from the children of Ammon, **shall** surely **be the LORD's, and I will offer it** up **for a burnt offering.**

32. **So Jephthah passed over unto** the children of **Ammon to fight against them;** and **the LORD delivered them into his hands.**

33. And he smote them from Aroer, even till thou come to Minnith, *even* twenty cities, and unto the plain of the vineyards, with a very great slaughter. Thus the children of Ammon were subdued before the children of Israel.

34. **And Jephthah came to Mizpeh unto his house, and,** behold, **his daughter came out to meet him** with timbrels and with dances: and she *was* *his* only child; beside her he had neither son nor daughter.

35. **And** it came to pass, when he saw her, that **he rent his clothes, and said,** Alas, my daughter! thou hast brought me very low, and thou art one of them that trouble me: for **I have opened my mouth unto the LORD, and I cannot go back.**

36. **And she said** unto him, My father, *if* thou hast opened thy mouth unto the LORD, **do to me according to that which hath proceeded out of thy mouth;** forasmuch as the LORD hath taken vengeance for thee of thine enemies, *even* of the children of Ammon.

37. **And she said** unto her father, **Let this thing be done for me: let me alone two months, that I may go up and down upon the mountains, and bewail my virginity,** I and my fellows.

38. **And he said, Go.** And he sent her away *for* two months: and she went with her companions, and bewailed her virginity upon the mountains.

39. **And** it came to pass **at the end of two months,** that **she returned unto her father, who did with her according to his vow** which he had vowed: and she knew no man. **And it was a custom** in Israel,

40. **That the daughters of Israel went yearly to lament the daughter of Jephthah** the Gileadite **four days in a year.**

CHAPTER 12

1. **And the men of Ephraim** gathered themselves together, and **went northward, and said unto Jephthah, Wherefore passedst thou over to fight** against the children of **Ammon, and didst not call us** to go with thee? we will burn thine house upon thee with fire.

2. **And Jephthah said** unto them, **I and my people were at great strife with** the children of **Ammon; and when I called you, ye delivered me not out of their hands.**

3. And when I saw that ye delivered *me* not, I put my life in my hands, and passed over against the children of Ammon, and the LORD delivered them into my hand: **wherefore then are ye come** up unto me this day, **to fight against me?**

4. **Then Jephthah gathered** together all **the men of Gilead, and** fought with Ephraim: and the men of Gilead **smote Ephraim, because they said, Ye Gileadites are fugitives of Ephraim** among the Ephraimites, *and* among the Manassites.

5. **And the Gileadites took the passages of Jordan** before the Ephraimites: **and** it was *so* that when **those Ephraimites which were escaped said, Let me go over;** that **the men of Gilead said** unto him, **Art thou an Ephraimite?** If he said, Nay;

6. **Then said they** unto him, **Say** now

Shibboleth: and he said Sibboleth: for he could not frame to **pronounce it right. Then they** took him, and **slew him at the passages of Jordan: and there fell** at that time **of the Ephraimites forty and two thousand.**

7. **And Jephthah judged Israel six years.** Then died Jephthah the Gileadite, and was buried in *one of* the cities of Gilead.

8. **And after him Ibzan** of Beth–lehem **judged Israel.**

9. **And he had thirty sons, and thirty daughters, whom he sent abroad, and took in thirty daughters from abroad for his sons. And he judged Israel seven years.**

10. Then died Ibzan, and was buried at Beth-lehem.

11. **And after him Elon,** a Zebulonite, **judged Israel;** and he judged Israel **ten years.**

12. And Elon the Zebulonite died, and was buried in Aijalon in the country of Zebulun.

13. **And after him Abdon** the son of Hillel, a Pirathonite, judged Israel.

14. And he had forty sons and thirty nephews, that rode on threescore and ten ass colts: and he **judged Israel eight years.**

15. And Abdon the son of Hillel the Pirathonite died, and was buried in Pirathon in the land of Ephraim, in the mount of the Amalekites.

CHAPTER 13

1. **And** the children of **Israel did evil again** in the sight of the LORD; **and the LORD delivered**

- them into the hand of the
- Philistines forty years.
- 2. **And there was a**
- **certain man** of Zorah, of
the family of the Danites,
- **whose name was**
- **Manoah; and his wife**
- **was barren,** and bare not.
- 3. **And the angel of theLORD**
- **appeared unto the woman,**
- **and said** unto her, Behold now,
thou *art* barren, and bearest not: but
- **thou shalt conceive,**
and bear a son.
- 4. **Now therefore** beware,
I pray thee, and
- **drink not wine** nor strong drink,
- **and eat not any**
- **unclean thing:**
- 5. **For,** lo,
- **thou shalt** conceive, and
- **bear a son; and no razor**
- **shall come on his head:**
- **for the child shall be a**
- **Nazarite unto God from the**
- **womb: and he shall begin**
- **to deliver Israel out of the**
- **hand of the Philistines.**
- 6. **Then the woman came**
- **and told her husband,** saying,
A man of God came unto me, and his
countenance *was* like the
countenance of an angel of God, very
terrible: but I asked him not whence
he *was,* neither told he me his name:
7. But he said unto me, Behold, thou
shalt conceive, and bear a son; and
now drink no wine nor strong drink,
neither eat any unclean *thing:* for the
child shall be a Nazarite to God from
the womb to the day of his death.
- 8. **Then Manoah entreated**
- **the LORD, and said, O**
- **my Lord, let the man of**
- **God** which thou didst send
- **come again** unto us,
- **and teach us what we shall**
- **do** unto the child that shall be born.
- 9. **And God hearkened**
to the voice of Manoah;
- **and the angel** of God
- **came again unto the**
- **woman** as she sat in the field:

- **but Manoah** her husband
- **was not with her.**
- 10. **And the**
- **woman** made haste, and
- **ran, and shewed her**
- **husband,** and said unto him,
Behold, the man hath appeared unto
me, that came unto me the *other* day.
- 11. **And Manoah** arose,
and went after his wife, and
- **came to the man,**and said unto
him, *Art* thou the man that spakest
unto the woman? And he said, I *am.*
- 12. **And** Manoah
- **said,** Now let thy
words come to pass.
- **How shall we order the**
- **child,**and *how* shall we do untohim?
- 13. **And the angel** of the LORD
- **said** unto Manoah,
- **Of all that I said unto the**
- **woman let her beware.**
- 14. **She may not** eat of any *thing*
that cometh of the vine, neither let her
- **drink wine** or strong drink,
- **nor eat any unclean**
- **thing:** all that I commanded
her let her observe.
- 15. **And Manoah said** unto
the angel of the LORD, I pray thee,
- **let us detain thee, until**
- **we shall have made**
- **ready a kid for thee.**
- 16. **And the angel** of the LORD
- **said** unto Manoah, Though
thou detain me, I will not eat
of thy bread: and
- **if thou wilt offer a burnt**
- **offering, thou must offer it**
- **unto the LORD.**For Manoah knew
not that he*was* an angel of the LORD.
17. And Manoah said unto the angel
of the LORD, What *is* thy name,
that when thy sayings come to
pass we may do thee honour?
18. And the angel of the LORD said
unto him, Why askest thou thus after
my name, seeing it *is* secret?
- 19. **So Manoah took a**
- **kid** with a meat offering,
- **and offered it** upon a rock
- **unto the LORD: and** *the*
angel did wonderously; and

387

Manoah and his wife looked on.
20. For it came to pass,
when the flame went up
toward heaven from
off the altar, that
the angel of the LORD
ascended in the
flame of the altar.
And Manoah and his
wife looked on *it*, and
fell on their faces
to the ground.
21. But the angel of the LORD did no
more appear to Manoah and to his
wife. Then Manoah knew that he
was an angel of the LORD.
22. **And Manoah**
said unto his wife,
We shall surely
die, because we
have seen God.
23. **But his wife said** unto him,
If the LORD were pleased to
kill us, he would not have
received a burnt offering
and a meat offering at our hands,
neither would he have shewed us all
these *things*, nor would as at this time
have told us *such things* as these.
24. **And the woman bare a**
son, and called his name
Samson: and the child grew,
and the LORD blessed him.
25. **And the Spirit of the**
LORD began to move him
at times in the camp of
Dan between Zorah and Eshtaol.

CHAPTER 14

1. **And Samson** went
down to Timnath, and
saw a woman in Timnath
of the daughters
of the Philistines.
2. **And he** came up, and
told his father and his
mother, and said, I have
seen a woman in Timnath of the
daughters of the Philistines: now
therefore get her for me to wife.
3. **Then his father** and his mother
said unto him,
Is there never a woman
among the daughters of thy
brethren, or among all my people,
that thou goest to take a wife of
the uncircumcised Philistines?
And Samson
said unto his father,
Get her for me; for
she pleaseth me well.
4. **But his father and** his
mother knew not that it was
of the LORD, that he sought
an occasion against the
Philistines: for at that time the
Philistines had dominion over Israel.
5. **Then went Samson** down,
and his father and his
mother, to Timnath,
and came to the vineyards
of Timnath: and, behold,
a young
lion roared against him.
6. **And** the spirit of
the LORD came mightily
upon him, and he rent
him as he would have rent
a kid, and he had nothing
in his hand: but he told not his
father or his mother what hehaddone.
7. **And he** went down, and
talked with the woman;and
she pleased Samson well.
8. **And** after a time
he returned to take her,
and he turned aside to
see the carcase of
the lion: and, behold,
there was a swarm of bees and
honey in the
carcase of the lion.
9. **And he took thereof**
in his hands, and went on eating,
and came to his father
and mother, and he gave
them, and they did eat: but he
told not them that he had taken the
honey out of the carcase of the lion.
10. **So his father went**
down unto the woman:
and Samson made there
a feast; for so used
the young men to do.
11. **And** it came to pass,
when they saw him, that

388

they brought thirty
companions
to be with him.
12. And Samson
said unto them,
I will now put forth
a riddle unto you:
if ye can certainly
declare it me
within the seven days
of the feast, and find it out,
then I will give you thirty
sheets and thirty change
of garments:
13. But if ye
cannot declare it me,
then shall ye give me thirty
sheets and thirty change ofgarments.
And they said unto him, Put forth
thy riddle, that we may hear it.
14. And he said unto them,
Out of the eater came forth
meat, and out of the strong
came forth sweetness.
And they could not in three
days expound the riddle.
15. And it came to pass
on the seventh day, that
they said unto Samson's
wife, Entice thy husband,
that he may declare unto
us the riddle, lest we burn
thee and thy father's
house with fire: have ye called
us to take that we have? is it not so?
16. And Samson's wife
wept before him, and
said, Thou dost but hate me, and
lovest me not: thou hast
put forth a riddle unto
the children of my people,
and hast not told it me.
And he said unto her, Behold,
I have not told it my
father nor my mother,
and shall I tell it thee?
17. And she wept
before him the seven days,
while their feast
lasted: and it came to pass
on the seventh day, that
he told her, because she
lay sore upon him:

and she told the
riddle to the children of
her people.
18. And the men of the city
said unto him on the seventh
day before the sun went down,
What is sweeter than
honey? and what is
stronger than a lion?
And he said unto them,
If ye had not plowed with
my heifer, ye had not
found out my riddle.
19. And the Spirit of the
LORD came upon him, and
he went down to Ashkelon, and
slew thirty men of them,
and took their spoil, and
gave change of garments
unto them which
expounded the riddle.
And his anger was kindled,
and he
went up to his
father's house.
20. But Samson's wife
was given to his companion,
whom he had used as
his friend.

CHAPTER 15

1. But it came to pass within
a while after, in the
time of wheat harvest, that
Samson visited his wife
with a kid; and he said, I will
go in to my wife into the chamber.
But her father would
not suffer him to go in.
2. And her father said,
I verily thought that thou hadst
utterly hated her; therefore I
gave her to thy companion:
is not her younger sister
fairer than she? take her,
I pray thee, instead of her.
3. And Samson
said concerning them,
Now shall I be more
blameless than the
Philistines, though I do
them a displeasure.
4. And Samson went and

caught three hundred
foxes, and took firebrands,
and turned tail to tail, and
put a firebrand in the midst
between two tails.
5. And when he had set the
brands on fire, he let them
go into the standing corn of
the Philistines, and burnt up both
the shocks, and also the standing
corn, with the vineyards *and* olives.
6. Then the Philistines said,
Who hath done this? And
they answered, Samson,
the son in law of the Timnite,
because he had taken
his wife, and given her to
his companion. And the
Philistines came up, and
burnt her and her
father with fire.
7. And Samson said unto
them, Though ye have done
this, yet will I be avenged of
you, and after that I will cease.
8. And he
smote them hip and thigh
with a great slaughter:
and he went down and dwelt
in the top of the rock Etam.
9. Then the
Philistines went up, and
pitched in Judah, and
spread themselves in Lehi.
10. And the men of
Judah said, Why are
ye come up against us?
And they answered, To
bind Samson are we come up,
to do to him as he hath done to us.
11. Then three thousand
men of Judah went to
the top of the rock Etam,
and said to Samson,
Knowest thou not that the
Philistines *are* rulers over us?
what is this *that*
thou hast done unto
us? And he said unto them,
As they did unto me, so
have I done unto them.
12. And they said unto him,
We are come down

to bind thee, that we may
deliver thee into the hand
of the Philistines. And
Samson said unto them,
Swear unto me,
that ye will not fall
upon me yourselves.
13. And they
spake unto him, saying,
No; but we will bind thee
fast, and deliver thee into their hand:
but surely
we will not kill thee.
And they bound him
with two new cords, and
brought him up from the rock.
14. And when he
came unto Lehi,
the Philistines shouted
against him: and the Spirit
of the LORD came mightily
upon him, and the
cords that *were* upon his arms
became as flax that was
burnt with fire, and his
bands loosed from off his hands.
15. And he found a new
jawbone of an ass,
and put forth his hand, and took it,
and slew a thousand
men therewith.
16. And Samson said, With the
jawbone of an ass, heaps upon
heaps, with the jaw of an ass
have I slain a thousand men.
17. And it came to pass, when he
had made an end of speaking, that
he cast away the
jawbone out of his hand,
and called that
place Ramath-lehi.
18. And he was sore
athirst, and called
on the LORD, and said,
Thou hast given this
great deliverance
into the hand of thy servant:
and now shall I die for
thirst, and fall into the hand
of the uncircumcised?
19. But God clave an
hollow place that *was*
in the jaw, and there came

■ **water thereout;** and when
he had drunk, his spirit came again,
■ **and he revived:** wherefore he
called the name thereof En–hakkore,
which *is* in Lehi unto this day.
■ 20. **And he judged Israel**
in the days of the Philistines
■ **twenty years.**

CHAPTER 16

■ 1. **Then went Samson**
■ **to Gaza, and saw** there
■ **an harlot, and went**
■ **in unto her.**
■ 2. **And** *it was told*
■ **the Gazites,** saying,
Samson is come hither.
And they compassed *him* in, and
■ **laid wait for him** all
night in the gate of the city,
and were quiet all the night,
■ **saying, In the**
■ **morning,** when it is day,
■ **we shall kill him.**
■ 3. **And Samson**
lay till midnight, and
■ **arose at midnight,**
■ **and took** the doors of
■ **the gate of the**
■ **city,** and the two posts,
■ **and went away**
■ **with them, bar and all,**
and put *them* upon his shoulders,
■ **and carried them** up
■ **to the top of an hill**
that *is* before Hebron.
■ 4. **And** it came to pass
■ **afterward,** that
■ **he loved a woman**
■ **in** the valley of
■ **Sorek, whose**
■ **name was Delilah.**
■ 5. **And** the lords of
■ **the Philistines came** up
■ **unto her, and said** unto her,
■ **Entice him, and see**
■ **wherein his** great
■ **strength lieth,** and by what
means we may prevail against him,
■ **that we may bind**
■ **him** to afflict him;
■ **and we will give**
■ **thee** every one of us

■ **eleven hundred**
■ **pieces of silver.**
■ 6. **And Delilah said to**
■ **Samson, Tell me,** I pray thee,
■ **wherein thy** great
■ **strength lieth,** and wherewith
thou mightest be bound to afflictthee.
■ 7. **And Samson**
■ **said** unto her, If they
■ **bind me with seven green**
■ **withs** that were never dried,
■ **then shall I be**
■ **weak,** and be as another man.
■ 8. **Then the** lords of the
■ **Philistines brought** up to her
■ **seven green withs**
which had not been dried,
■ **and she bound him** with them.
■ 9. **Now there were**
■ **men** lying in wait,
■ **abiding with her**
■ **in the chamber.**
■ **And she said** unto him,
■ **The Philistines be upon**
■ **thee, Samson. And he**
■ **brake the withs, as**
■ **a thread** of tow is broken
when it toucheth the fire.
■ **So his strength**
■ **was not known.**
■ 10. **And Delilah**
■ **said** unto Samson, Behold,
■ **thou hast mocked**
■ **me,** and told me lies:
■ **now tell me,** I pray thee,
■ **wherewith thou**
■ **mightest be bound.**
■ 11. **And he said** unto her,
■ **If they bind me** fast
■ **with new ropes** that
never were occupied,
■ **then shall I be weak,**
and be as another man.
■ 12. **Delilah therefore**
■ **took new ropes, and**
■ **bound him** therewith,
■ **and said** unto him,
■ **The Philistines be upon**
■ **thee,** Samson. And *there were*
liers in wait abiding in the chamber.
■ **And he brake**
■ **them** from off his arms
■ **like a thread.**

13. **And Delilah said** unto Samson, Hitherto **thou hast mocked me,** and told me lies: **tell me wherewith thou mightest be bound. And he said** unto her, If thou **weavest** the **seven locks of my head with the web.** 14. **And she fastened it with the pin, and said** unto him, **The Philistines be upon thee, Samson. And he awaked** out of his sleep, **and went away with the pin** of the beam, **and** with the **web.** 15. **And she said** unto him, **How canst thou say, I love thee, when** thine heart *is* not with me? **thou hast mocked me these three times,** and hast not told me wherein thy great strength *lieth.* 16. **And** it came to pass, **when she pressed him daily** with her words, and urged him, **so that his soul was vexed unto death;** 17. **That he told her** all his heart, and said unto her, **There hath not come a razor upon mine head; for I have been a Nazarite unto God from my mother's womb: if I be shaven,** then my strength will go from me, and **I shall become weak,** and be like any *other* man. 18. **And** when **Delilah** saw that he had told her all his heart, she sent and **called** for the lords of **the Philistines, saying,** Come up this once, for **he hath shewed me all his heart. Then the** lords of the **Philistines came up** unto her, **and brought money** in their hand.

19. **And she made him sleep upon her knees; and she** called for a man, and she caused him to **shave off the seven locks of his head;** and she began to afflict him, **and his strength went from him.** 20. **And she said, The Philistines be upon thee, Samson. And he awoke** out of his sleep, **and said, I will go out as at other times** before, and shake myself. **And he wist not that the LORD** was **departed from him.** 21. **But the Philistines took him, and put out his eyes, and brought him** down **to Gaza, and bound him** with fetters of brass; **and he did grind in the prison house.** 22. Howbeit the hair of his head began to grow again after he was shaven. 23. **Then the lords of the Philistines gathered** them together for **to offer** a great **sacrifice unto Dagon their god, and** to rejoice: for **they said, Our god hath delivered Samson** our enemy **into our hand.** 24. **And** when **the people** saw him, they **praised their god:** for they said, Our god hath delivered into our hands our enemy, and the destroyer of our country, which slew many of us. 25. **And** it came to pass, **when their hearts were merry,** that they said, Call for Samson, that he may make us sport. And **they called for Samson out of the prison house;** and he made them sport: **and they set him**

■ **between the pillars.**

■ 26. **And Samson said** unto
the lad that held him by the hand,

■ **Suffer me that I may feel**

■ **the pillars whereupon**

■ **the house standeth,**
that I may lean upon them.

■ 27. **Now the** house was full
of men and women; and all the

■ **lords of the Philistines**

■ **were there; and** *there*
were upon the roof

■ **about three thousand**

■ **men and women,** that
beheld while Samson made sport.

■ 28. **And Samson**

■ **called unto the LORD,**

■ **and said, O Lord**
God, remember me, I pray thee, and

■ **strengthen me,** I pray thee,
only this once, O God,

■ **that I may be** at once

■ **avenged of the**

■ **Philistines** for my two eyes.

■ 29. **And Samson took**

■ **hold of the** two middle

■ **pillars upon which the**

■ **house stood,** and on which it was
borne up, of the one with his right
hand, and of the other with his left.

■ 30. **And** Samson

■ **said, Let me die**

■ **with the Philistines.**

■ **And he bowed** himself

■ **with all his might;**

■ **and the house fell**
upon the lords, and upon all
the people that *were* therein.

■ **So the dead** which
he slew at his death

■ **were more than**

■ **they which he**

■ **slew in his life.**

■ 31. **Then his brethren**
and all the house of his
father came down, and

■ **took him, and**
brought *him* up, and

■ **buried him** between
Zorah and Eshtaol

■ **in the burying**

■ **place of** Manoah

■ **his father.** And he

| | judged Israel twenty years.

CHAPTER 17

■ 1. **And** there was

■ **a man of** mount

■ **Ephraim, whose**

■ **name was Micah.**

2. And he

■ **said unto his mother,**

■ **The eleven hundred**

■ **shekels of silver** that were

■ **taken from thee,**
about which thou cursedst,
and spakest of also in mine
ears, behold, the silver

■ **is with me; I took it. And his**

■ **mother said, Blessed be**

■ **thou of the LORD,** my son.

■ 3. **And when he**

■ **had restored the**
eleven hundred *shekels* of

■ **silver to his mother, his**

■ **mother said, I** had wholly

■ **dedicated the silver unto**

■ **the LORD** from my hand for myson,

■ **to make a graven**

■ **image** and a molten image:

■ **now** therefore

■ **I will restore it unto thee.**

■ 4. **Yet** he restored the
money unto his mother; and

■ **his mother took two**

■ **hundred shekels of silver,**

■ **and** gave them to the founder, who

■ **made** thereof

■ **a graven image**

■ **and** a molten image: and

■ **they were in the**

■ **house of Micah.**

■ 5. **And** the man

■ **Micah had an house**

■ **of gods, and made an**

■ **ephod, and teraphim,**

■ **and consecrated one**

■ **of his sons, who**

■ **became his priest.**

6. In those days *there was* no king
in Israel, *but* every man did *that*
which was right in his own eyes.

■ 7. **And there was a**

■ **young man** out of
Beth-lehem-judah of the family

■ **of Judah, who was a**

393

■ **Levite,** and he sojourned there.

8. And the man departed out of the city from Beth-lehem-judah to sojourn where he could find *a place:*

■ **and he came to** mount
■ **Ephraim to the house**
■ **of Micah,** as he journeyed.
■ 9. **And Micah said** unto him,
■ **Whence comest thou?**
■ **And he said** unto him,
■ **I am a Levite** of Beth-lehem-judah, and I go to sojourn where I may find *a place.*
■ 10. **And Micah said** unto him,
■ **Dwell with me, and be**
■ **unto me** a father and
■ **a priest, and I will**
■ **give thee** ten *shekels* of
■ **silver** by the year,
■ **and a suit of**
■ **apparel, and** thy
■ **victuals. So the**
■ **Levite went in.**

11. And the Levite was content to dwell with the man; and the young man was unto him as one of his sons.

■ 12. **And Micah consecrated**
■ **the Levite; and the young**
■ **man became his priest,**
and was in the house of Micah.
■ 13. **Then said**
■ **Micah, Now** know I that
■ **the LORD will do me**
■ **good, seeing I have**
■ **a Levite to my priest.**

CHAPTER 18

■ 1. **In those days there**
■ **was no king in Israel:**
■ **and** in those days the tribe of
■ **the Danites sought** them
■ **an inheritance to**
■ **dwell in; for** unto that day *all*
■ **their inheritance had**
■ **not fallen unto them**
among the tribes of Israel.
■ 2. **And the children of**
■ **Dan sent** of their family
■ **five men** from their coasts, men of
valour, from Zorah, and from Eshtaol,
■ **to spy out the land, and**
to search it; and they said unto them, Go, search the land: who

■ **when they came to** mount
■ **Ephraim, to the house of**
■ **Micah, they lodged there.**
3. When they *were* by the house of Micah,
■ **they knew the voice**
■ **of** the young man
■ **the Levite:** and they
turned in thither,
■ **and said unto him, Who**
■ **brought thee hither?** and
what makest thou in this *place*? and what hast thou here?
■ 4. **And he said** unto them,
Thus and thus dealeth
■ **Micah** with me, and
■ **hath hired me, and**
■ **I am his priest.**
■ 5. **And they said** unto him,
■ **Ask counsel,** we pray thee,
■ **of God, that we may know**
■ **whether our way** which we go
■ **shall be prosperous.**
■ 6. **And the priest**
■ **said** unto them,
■ **Go in peace:** before the
LORD *is* your way wherein ye go.
■ 7. **Then the five men**
■ **departed, and came to**
■ **Laish, and saw the people**
that *were* therein, how they
■ **dwelt** careless,
■ **after the manner of the**
■ **Zidonians, quiet and**
■ **secure; and there**
■ **was no magistrate** in the
land, that might put *them* to shame in *any* thing; and they *were* far from the Zidonians, and had no business with *any* man.
■ 8. **And they came unto**
■ **their brethren to Zorah** and
■ **Eshtaol: and** their brethren
■ **said** unto them, What *say* ye?
9. And they said, Arise, that we may
■ **go up against them:**
■ **for** we have seen
■ **the land,** and, behold, it
■ **is very good:** and *are* ye
still? be not slothful to
■ **go, and** to
■ **enter** to possess
■ **the land.**

10. When ye go, ye shall come unto a people secure, and to a large land: **for God hath given it into your hands; a place where there is no want** of any thing that is in the earth. 11. **And there went** from thence of the family **of the Danites,** out of Zorah and out of Eshtaol, **six hundred men** appointed with weapons **of war.** 12. And they went up, and pitched in Kirjath-jearim, in Judah: wherefore they called that place Mahaneh–dan unto this day: behold, it is behind Kirjath-jearim. 13. **And they passed** thence **unto** mount **Ephraim, and came unto the house of Micah.** 14. **Then** answered **the five** men **that went to spy out the country** of Laish, and **said** unto their brethren, Do ye know that **there is in these houses an ephod,** and **teraphim,** and **a graven image, and a molten image?** now therefore **consider what ye have to do.** 15. **And they** turned thitherward, and **came to** the house of the young man **the Levite,** even unto the house of Micah, **and saluted him.** 16. **And the six hundred men**appointed with their weapons of war, whichwere of the children ofDan, **stood by the entering of the gate.** 17. **And the five men** that went to spy out the land went up,and came in thither, and took the graven image, and the ephod, and the teraphim, and the molten image: and the prieststood in the entering of the gate with the six

hundred men that were appointed with weapons of war. 18. And these **went into Micah's house, and fetched the carved image, the ephod,** and **the teraphim, and the molten image. Then said the priest** unto them, **What do ye?** 19. **And they said** unto him, **Hold thy peace,** lay thine hand upon thy mouth, **and go with us, and be** to us a father and a priest: is it better for thee to be **a priest unto** the house of one man, or that thou be a priest unto a tribe and a family in **Israel?** 20. **And the priest's heart was glad, and he took the ephod, and the teraphim, and the graven image, and went in the midst of the people.** 21. **So they** turned and **departed,** and put the little ones and the cattle and the carriage before them. 22. **And** when they were a good way from the house of Micah, **the men** that were in the houses **near** to **Micah's house** were **gathered together, and overtook the children of Dan.** 23. **And** they cried unto **the children of Dan.** And they turned their faces, and **said unto Micah, What aileth thee, that thou comest with such a company?** 24. **And he said, Ye have taken** away **my gods** which I made, **and the priest,** and ye are gone away: and what have I more? and what is this that ye say unto me, What aileth thee? 25. **And the children**

■ **of Dan said** unto him,
■ **Let not thy voice**
■ **be heard** among us,
■ **lest** angry fellows run upon thee, and
■ **thou lose thy life, with the**
■ **lives of thy household.**
26. And the children of
Dan went their way:
■ **and when Micah saw that**
■ **they were too strong for**
■ **him, he turned** and went
■ **back unto his house.**
27. **And they took the**
■ **things** which Micah had made,
■ **and the priest** which he had,
■ **and came unto Laish,** unto a
people *that were* at quiet and secure:
■ **and** they
■ **smote them** with
the edge of the sword,
■ **and burnt the city** with fire.
28. **And there was no**
■ **deliverer, because it was**
■ **far from Zidon,** and they had no
business with *any* man; and it was in
the valley that *lieth* by Beth-rehob.
■ **And they built a city,**
and dwelt therein.
29. **And** they
■ **called** the name of
■ **the city Dan,** after the name
of Dan their father, who was born
unto Israel: howbeit the name
of the city *was* Laish at the first.
30. **And the children of Dan**
■ **set up the graven image:**
■ **and Jonathan,** the son of
Gershom, the son of Manasseh, he
■ **and his sons were priests**
to the tribe of Dan until the
day of the captivity of the land.
31. **And they set** them
■ **up Micah's graven**
■ **image,** which he made,
■ **all the time that the house**
■ **of God was in Shiloh.**

CHAPTER 19

1. **And** it came to pass
■ **in those days,** when
■ **there was no king in**
■ **Israel,** that there was
■ **a certain Levite** sojourning

on the side of mount Ephraim, who
■ **took** to him
■ **a concubine** out
of Beth-lehem-judah.
2. **And his concubine**
■ **played the whore against**
■ **him, and went** away from him
■ **unto her father's**
■ **house** to Beth-lehem-judah,
■ **and was there four** whole
■ **months.**
3. **And her husband** arose, and
■ **went after her,** to speak
friendly unto her, *and*
■ **to bring her again,**
having his servant with him,
and a couple of asses:
■ **and she brought him into**
■ **her father's house: and** when
the father of the damsel saw him,
■ **he rejoiced to meet him.**
4. And his father in law, the
damsel's father, retained him;
■ **and he abode with him**
■ **three days:** so they did eat
and drink, and lodged there.
5. **And** it came to pass
■ **on the fourth day,** when they
arose early in the morning, that
■ **he rose up to depart: and**
■ **the damsel's father said** unto
his son in law, Comfort thine heart
with a morsel of bread,
and afterward go your way.
6. And they sat down, and did
eat and drink both of them
together: for the damsel's
father had said unto the man,
■ **Be content,** I pray thee,
■ **and tarry all night,**
and let thine heart be merry.
7. And when the man rose up to
depart, his father in law urged him:
■ **therefore he lodged**
■ **there again.**
8. **And he arose**
early in the morning
■ **on the fifth day to depart:**
and the damsel's father said,
Comfort thine heart, I pray thee.
■ **And they tarried until**
■ **afternoon,** and they
did eat both of them.

9. **And when the man rose up to depart,** he, and his concubine, and his servant, his father in law, **the damsel's father, said unto him,** Behold, now **the day draweth toward evening,** I pray you **tarry all night:** behold, the day groweth to an end, lodge here, that thine heart may be merry; and tomorrow get you early on your way, that thou mayest go home. 10. **But the man would not tarry** that night, **but he** rose up and **departed, and came over against Jebus, which is Jerusalem; and** *there were* with him two asses saddled, **his concubine** also *was* **with him.** 11. *And* when they *were* by Jebus, the day was far spent; **and the servant said** unto his master, Come, I pray thee, and **let us turn in into this city** of the Jebusites, **and lodge** in it. 12. **And his master said** unto him, **We will not turn** aside hither **into the city of a stranger,** that *is* not of the children of Israel; **we will pass over to Gibeah.** 13. And he said unto his servant, Come, and let us draw near to one of these places to lodge all night, in Gibeah, or in Ramah. 14. And they passed on and went their way; and the sun went down upon them *when they were* by Gibeah, which *belongeth* to Benjamin. 15. **And they turned** aside thither, **to go in and** to **lodge in Gibeah: and** when he went in, **he sat him down in** a **street** of the city: **for** *there was* **no man** that **took them into his house to lodging.** 16. **And,** behold, there came **an old man** from his work out of the field at even, **which was also of** mount **Ephraim;** and he **sojourned in Gibeah:** but the men of the place *were* Benjamites. 17. **And when he** had lifted up his eyes, he **saw a wayfaring man in the street** of the city: and **the old man said, Whither goest thou?** and whence comest thou? 18. **And he said** unto him, We *are* passing from Beth-lehem-judah **toward** the side of **mount Ephraim;** from thence *am* I: and I went to Beth-lehem-judah, but I *am now* going **to the house of the LORD; and** there *is* **no man** that **receiveth me** to house. 19. **Yet there is both straw** and provender **for our asses; and** there is **bread** and wine also **for me,** and for thy handmaid, and for the young man *which is* with thy servants: *there is* no want of any thing. 20. **And the old man said,** Peace *be* with thee; howsoever **let all thy wants lie upon me; only lodge not in the street.** 21. **So he brought him into his house,** and gave provender unto the asses: **and they washed their feet, and did eat and drink.** 22. **Now as they were making their hearts merry,** behold, the men of the city, **certain sons of Belial,** beset the house round about, *and* **beat at the door,** and spake to the master of the house, the old man, **saying, Bring forth the man that came into thine house,**

that we may know him.

23. **And** the man,
the master of the house,
went out unto them,
and said unto them,
Nay, my brethren, *nay,* I pray you,
do not so wickedly;
seeing that this man is come
into mine house, do not this folly.
24. **Behold, here is**
my daughter a maiden,
and his concubine;
them I will bring out now, and
humble ye them,
and do with them what
seemeth good unto you:
but unto this man do
not so vile a thing.
25. **But the men would**
not hearken to him:
so the man took his
concubine, and
brought her forth
unto them; and they knew
her, and abused her all the
nightuntil the morning: and whenthe
day began to spring, they let her go.
26. Then came the woman in the
dawning of the day, and fell down
at the door of the man's house
where her lord *was*, till it was light.
27. **And her lord rose**
up in the morning, and
opened the doors of the house,
and went out to go his
way: and, behold, the woman
his concubine was
fallen down at the door
of the house, and her
hands *were* upon the threshold.
28. **And he said**
unto her, Up, and
let us be going. But
none answered. Then
the man took her up
upon an ass, and the man
rose up, and gat him unto his place.
29. **And when he was**
come into his house,
he took a knife, and
laid hold on his concubine,
and divided her,
together with her bones,

into twelve pieces,
and sent her into all
the coasts of Israel.
30. **And** it was so, that
all that saw it said,
There was no such deed
done nor seen from the
day that the children of
Israel came up
out of the land of
Egypt unto this day: consider of it,
take advice, and speak *your minds.*

CHAPTER 20

1. **Then all the children**
of Israel went out, and
the congregation was
gathered together
as one man, from Dan even to
Beer-sheba, with the land of Gilead,
unto the LORD in Mizpeh.
2. **And the chief** of all
the people, *even*
of all the tribes of Israel,
presented themselves
in the assembly
of the people of God,
four hundred thousand
footmen that drew sword.
3. **(Now the children**
of Benjamin heard
that the children of
Israel were gone up to
Mizpeh.) Then said the
children of Israel, Tell *us,*
how was this wickedness?
4. **And the Levite, the**
husband of the woman
that was slain, answered and
said, I came into Gibeah
that belongeth to
Benjamin, I and my concubine,
to lodge.
5. **And the men** of Gibeah
rose against me, and beset
the house round about upon
me by night, *and* thought
to have slain me:
and my concubine have
they forced, that
she is dead.
6. **And I took my**
concubine, and cut

398

her in pieces, and
sent her throughout all
the country of the inheritance of
Israel: for they have
committed lewdness and folly
in Israel.

7. Behold, ye *are* all children of Israel;
give here your advice and counsel.

8. And all the people arose as one
man, saying, We will not any *of us*
go to his tent, neither will we any
of us turn into his house.

9. But now this
shall be the thing which
we will do to Gibeah; we
will go up by lot against it;

10. And we will take ten
men of an hundred
throughout all the tribes of
Israel, and an hundred of a
thousand, and a thousand out
of ten thousand, to fetch victual
for the people, that they may do,
when they come to
Gibeah of Benjamin,
according to all the folly that
they have wrought in Israel.

11. So all the men of Israel
were gathered against
the city, knit together
as one man.

12. And the tribes of Israel sent men
through all the tribe of Benjamin,
saying, What wickedness *is*
this that is done among you?

13. Now therefore
deliver us the men, the children
of Belial, which *are*
in Gibeah, that we may
put them to death, and
put away evil from Israel,
But the children of Benjamin
would not hearken to the voice
of their brethren the children of Israel.

14. But the children of Benjamin
gathered themselves together
out of the cities unto Gibeah, to go out
to battle against the children of
Israel.

15. And the children of
Benjamin were numbered
at that time out of the cities
twenty and

six thousand
men that drew sword,
beside the inhabitants of
Gibeah, which werenumbered
seven hundred chosen
men.

16. Among all this people *there*
were seven hundred chosen
men lefthanded; every
one could sling stones
at an hair breadth,
and not miss.

17. And the men of
Israel, beside Benjamin, were
numbered four hundred
thousand men that drew
sword: all these *were* men of war.

18. And the children
of Israel arose, and
went up to the house of
God, and asked counsel of God,
and said, Which of us shall
go up first to the battle
against the children of Benjamin?
And the LORD said,
Judah shall go up first.

19. And the children of Israel rose
up in the morning, and encamped
against Gibeah.

20. And the men of Israel went
out to battle against Benjamin;
and the men of
Israel put themselves in
array to fight against them at
Gibeah.

21. And the children
of Benjamin came forth
out of Gibeah, and
destroyed down to the ground
of the Israelites that day
twenty and
two thousand men.

22. And the people the men of
Israel encouraged themselves,
and set their battle again in array
in the place where they put
themselves in array the first day.

23. (And the children of
Israel went up and wept
before the LORD until even,
and asked counsel of the
LORD, saying, Shall I go up
again to battle against the

children of Benjamin my brother?
■ **And the LORD said,**
■ **Go up against him.)**
24. And the children of Israel came near against the children of Benjamin the second day.
25. ■ **And Benjamin**
■ **went** forth against them
■ **out** of Gibeah
■ **the second day, and**
■ **destroyed** down to the ground of the children
■ **of Israel** again
■ **eighteen thousand**
■ **men;** all these drew the sword.
26. ■ **Then** all the children of
■ **Israel,** and all the people,
■ **went up,** and came
■ **unto the house of**
■ **God, and wept,** and sat there before the LORD,
■ **and fasted** that day until even,
■ **and offered** burnt offerings and peace
■ **offerings before the LORD.**
27. ■ **And** the children of
■ **Israel inquired of the LORD,** (for the ark of the covenant of God *was* there in those days,
28. And Phinehas, the son of Eleazar, the son of Aaron, stood before it in those days,) saying,
■ **Shall I** yet again
■ **go out to battle**
■ **against** the children of
■ **Benjamin** my brother,
■ **or shall I cease? And**
■ **the LORD said, Go up;**
■ **for to morrow I will deliver**
■ **them into thine hand.**
29. ■ **And Israel set liers**
■ **in wait round** about
■ **Gibeah.**
30. And the children of Israel went up against the children of Benjamin on the third day, and put themselves in array against Gibeah, as at other times.
31. ■ **And** the children of
■ **Benjamin went out against**
■ **the people, and were**
■ **drawn away from the city;**
and they began to smite of the people, *and* kill, as at other times, in the highways, of which one goeth up to the house of God, and the other to Gibeah in the field, about thirty men of Israel.
32. And the children of Benjamin said, They *are* smitten down before us, as at the first. But the children of Israel said, Let us flee, and draw them from the city unto the highways.
33. ■ **And all the men of Israel**
■ **rose** up out of their place, and put themselves in array at Baal–tamar:
■ **and the liers in wait** of Israel
■ **came forth** out of their places, *even* out of the meadows of Gibeah.
34. ■ **And there came against**
■ **Gibeah ten thousand**
■ **chosen men** out of all Israel, and the battle was sore: but they knew not that evil *was* near them.
35. ■ **And the LORD smote**
■ **Benjamin** before Israel:
■ **and** the children of Israel
■ **destroyed** of the Benjamites that day
■ **twenty** and
■ **five thousand** and an hundred
■ **men:** all these drew the sword.
36. ■ **So** the children of
■ **Benjamin saw that they**
■ **were smitten: for** the men of
■ **Israel** gave place to the Benjamites, because they
■ **trusted** unto
■ **the liers in wait** which they had set beside Gibeah.
37. And the liers in wait hasted, and rushed upon Gibeah; and the liers in wait drew *themselves* along, and smote all the city with the edge of the sword.
38. ■ **Now there was**
■ **an appointed sign**
■ **between** the men of
■ **Israel and the liers in wait,**
■ **that they should make a**
■ **great flame with smoke**
■ **rise up out of the city.**
39. And when the men of Israel retired in the battle, Benjamin began to smite *and* kill of the men of Israel about thirty persons: for they said,

Surely they are smitten down before us, as *in* the first battle.

40. **But when the flame began to arise** up out of the city with a pillar of smoke, **the Benjamites looked** behind them, **and,** behold, **the flame** of the city **ascended** up **to heaven.**

41. **And when** the men of **Israel turned again, the men of Benjamin were amazed:** for they saw that evil was come upon them.

42. **Therefore they turned** *their backs* before the men of Israel **unto the way of the wilderness; but the battle overtook them;** and them which *came* out of the cities they destroyed in the midst of them.

43. *Thus* they enclosed the Benjamites round about, *and* chased them, *and* trode them down with ease over against Gibeah toward the sunrising.

44. **And there fell of Benjamin** eighteen thousand men; all these *were* men of valour.

45. And they turned and fled toward the wilderness unto the rock of Rimmon: and they gleaned of them in the highways five thousand men; and pursued hard after them unto Gidom, and slew two thousand men of them.

46. So that all which fell **that day** of Benjamin were **twenty** and **five thousand men** that drew the sword; all these *were* men of valour.

47. **But six hundred** men turned and **fled to** the wilderness unto **the rock Rimmon, and abode** in the rock Rimmon **four months.**

48. **And** the men of **Israel turned again upon the children of Benjamin, and smote them**

with the edge of **the sword,** as well the men of *every* city, as the beast, and all that came to hand: **also they set on fire all the cities that they came to.**

CHAPTER 21

1. Now the men of Israel had sworn in Mizpeh, saying, There shall not any of us give his daughter unto Benjamin to wife.

2. **And the people came to the house of God,** and abode there till even before God, **and lifted up their voices, and wept** sore;

3. **And said, O LORD** God of Israel, **why is this come to pass** in Israel, **that there should be** today **one tribe lacking in Israel?**

4. **And** it came to pass **on the morrow, that the people** rose early, and **built** there **an altar, and offered** burnt offerings and peace **offerings.**

5. **And** the children of Israel **said, Who** is there **among** all **the tribes** of Israel that **came not** up with the congregation **unto the LORD? For they** had **made a great oath concerning him that came not** up to the LORD to Mizpeh, **saying, He shall** surely **be put to death.**

6. **And** the children of **Israel repented** them **for Benjamin** their brother, **and said, There is one tribe cut off from Israel** this day.

7. **How shall we do for wives for them that remain, seeing we have sworn** by the LORD **that we will not give them of our daughters to wives?**

■ 8. **And they said,**
■ **What** one *is there* of the
■ **tribes** of Israel that
■ **came not up to Mizpeh**
■ **to the LORD? And,** behold,
■ **there came none** to the camp
■ **from Jabesh-gilead**
to the assembly.
9. For the people were numbered,
and, behold, *there were* none of the
inhabitants of Jabesh-gilead there.
■ 10. **And the congregation**
■ **sent** thither
■ **twelve thousand**
■ **men** of the valiantest,
■ **and commanded**
■ **them,** saying,
■ **Go and smite the**
■ **inhabitants of**
■ **Jabesh-gilead** with the
edge of the sword, with the
women and the children.
11. And this *is* the
thing that ye shall do,
■ **Ye shall** utterly
■ **destroy every male,**
■ **and every woman**
■ **that hath lain by man.**
■ 12. **And they found** among
the inhabitants of Jabesh-gilead
■ **four hundred young**
■ **virgins,** that had known no
man by lying with any male:
■ **and they brought**
■ **them** unto the camp
■ **to Shiloh,** which *is*
■ **in** the land of
■ **Canaan.**
13. **And the** whole
■ **congregation sent some**
■ **to speak to the children**
■ **of Benjamin that were in**
■ **the rock Rimmon,** and
to call peaceably unto them.
14. And Benjamin
came again at that time;
■ **and they gave them**
■ **wives** which they had saved alive
■ **of the women of**
■ **Jabesh-gilead: and yet** so
■ **they sufficed them not.**
15. And the people repented them for
Benjamin, because that the LORDhad

made a breach in the tribes of Israel.
■ 16. **Then the elders**
of the congregation
■ **said, How shall we do**
■ **for wives for them that**
■ **remain,** seeing the women
are destroyed out of Benjamin?
17. And they said, *There must
be* an inheritance for them that be
escaped of Benjamin, that a tribe
be not destroyed out of Israel.
18. Howbeit we may not give
them wives of our daughters:
for the children of Israel have
sworn, saying, Cursed *be* he
that giveth a wife to Benjamin.
■ 19. **Then they said,** Behold,
■ **there is a feast of the LORD**
■ **in Shiloh yearly** *in a place*
which *is* on the north side of Beth-el,
on the east side of the highway that
goeth up from Beth-el to Shechem,
and on the south of Lebonah.
■ 20. **Therefore they**
■ **commanded the children**
■ **of Benjamin,** saying, Go and
■ **lie in wait in the vineyards;**
■ 21. **And** see, and, behold,
■ **if the daughters of Shiloh**
■ **come out to dance** in dances,
■ **then come ye out of**
■ **the vineyards, and**
■ **catch** you
■ **every man his wife**
of the daughters of Shiloh,
■ **and go to the**
■ **land of Benjamin.**
22. **And** it shall be,
■ **when their**
■ **fathers** or their brethren
■ **come** unto us
■ **to complain,** that
■ **we will say** unto them,
■ **Be favourable unto them**
■ **for our sakes: because**
■ **we reserved not to each**
■ **man his wife** in the war: for
ye did not give unto them at this
time, *that* ye should be guilty.
■ 23. **And the children of**
■ **Benjamin did so,** and took *them*
wives, according to their number, of
them that danced, whom they caught:

■ **and they went and returned**
■ **unto their inheritance,**
■ **and repaired the cities,**
■ **and dwelt in them.**
■ 24. **And** the children of
■ **Israel departed** thence
at that time, every man to his tribe

and to his family, and they went
out from thence every man
■ **to his inheritance.**
■ 25. **In those days there**
■ **was no king in Israel: every**
■ **man did that which was**
■ **right in his own eyes.**

A CONFESSION OF LOVE

Entreat me not to leave thee, or to return from following after thee: for whither thou goest, I will go; and where thou lodgest, I will lodge: thy people shall be my people, and thy God my God.

Ruth 1:16

THE BOOK OF RUTH

BACKGROUND INFORMATION

Author: Unknown
Date Written: Possibly around 400 B.C.

Number of:
Verses—85
Chapters—4
Total Words—2,578
Scan Words—1,121
Scan Words Represent Approximately 43% of Total Words

Theme: A Story of Love and Devotion as seen through Ruth, her Mother-in-law, and Boaz, the Ancestors of David

OUTLINE OF THE BOOK

I. **The Migration of** Elimelech **to Moab**
   1:1 — 5

II. **The Mourning of Naomi and Ruth,** her Daughter-in-Law
   1:6 — 1:18

III. **The Return to Bethlehem**
   1:19 — 1:22

IV. **The Relationship between Ruth and Boaz**
   2:1 — 4:22

CHAPTER 1

1. Now it came to pass in the days when the judges ruled, that there was a famine in the land. And **a** certain **man of Beth-lehem-judah went to** sojourn in the country of **Moab,** he, and his wife, and his two sons. 2. And the name of **the man was Elimelech, and** the name of **his wife Naomi, and** the name of **his two sons Mahlon and Chilion,** Ephrathites of Beth-lehem-judah. **And they** came into the country of Moab, and **continued there.** 3. **And Elimelech** Naomi's husband **died; and she was left, and her two sons.** 4. **And they took them wives** of the women of Moab; the name of the **one was Orpah, and** the name of **the other Ruth:** and they dwelled there about ten years. 5. **And Mahlon and Chilion died** also both of them; **and the woman was left** of her two sons and her husband. 6. Then she arose **with her daughters in law,** that she might return from the country of Moab: for she had heard in the country of Moab how that the LORD had visited his people in giving them bread. 7. **Wherefore she** went forth out of the place where she was, **and her two daughters in law** with her; and they **went** on the way to return **unto** the land of **Judah.** 8. **And Naomi said** unto her two daughters in law, **Go, return each to her mother's house:** the LORD deal kindly with you, as ye have dealt with the dead, and with me. 9. **The LORD grant you that ye may find rest,** each *of you* in the house of her husband. **Then she kissed them; and they** lifted up their voice, and **wept.** 10. **And they said** unto her, Surely **we will return with thee unto thy people.** 11. **And Naomi said,** Turn again, my daughters: **why will ye go with me?** *are* there yet *any more* sons in my womb, that they may be your husbands? 12. **Turn again,** my daughters, **go your way;** for **I am too old to have an husband.** If I should say, I have hope, **if I should have an husband** also **to-night, and** should also **bear sons;** 13. **Would ye tarry** for them **till they were grown?** would ye stay for them from having husbands? nay, my daughters; **for it grieveth me much for your sakes that the** hand of the **LORD is** gone out **against me.** 14. And they lifted up their voice, and wept again: **and Orpah kissed her mother in law; but Ruth clave unto her.** 15. **And she said,** Behold, **thy sister in law is gone back** unto her people, and unto her gods: return thou after thy sister in law. 16. **And Ruth said, Entreat me not to leave thee,** *or to* return from following after thee: **for whither thou goest, I will go; and** where thou lodgest, I will lodge: **thy people shall be my**

people, and thy
God my God:

17. **Where thou diest,
will I die,** and there will I be
buried: the LORD do so to me,
and more also, *if aught* but
death part thee and me.

18. When she saw that she was
stedfastly minded to go with her,
then she left speaking unto her.

19. **So they** two went until they
came to Beth-lehem. And
it came to pass, when they
were come to Beth-lehem, that
**all the city was moved
about them, and they
said, Is this Naomi?**

20. **And she said** unto them,
**Call me not Naomi, call
me Mara: for** the Almighty
hath dealt very bitterly with me.

21. **I went out full and
the LORD hath brought
me home** again
**empty: why then call ye
me Naomi, seeing the
LORD hath** testified against
me, and the Almighty hath
afflicted me?

22. **So Naomi** returned,
and Ruth the Moabitess,
her daughter in law, with her,
which returned out of the
country of Moab: and they
**came to Beth-lehem
in the beginning of
barley harvest.**

CHAPTER 2

1. **And Naomi had a
kinsman** of her husband's,
a mighty man of wealth,
of the family of Elimelech; and
his name was Boaz.

2. **And Ruth** the Moabitess
**said unto Naomi, Let
me now go** to the field,
and glean ears of corn
after *him* in whose sight I shall
find grace. And she said unto
her, Go, my daughter.

3. **And she** went, and came, and
gleaned in the field after the

reapers: and her hap was to light
**on a part of the field
belonging unto Boaz,** who
was of the kindred of Elimelech.

4. **And,** behold,
Boaz came from Beth-lehem, and
said unto the reapers,
The LORD *be* with you. And they
answered him, The LORD bless thee.

5. Then said Boaz unto his servant
that was set over the reapers,
Whose damsel is this?

6. **And the servant** that
was set over the reapers
answered and said,
**It is the Moabitish damsel
that came back with
Naomi** out of the country of Moab:

7. **And she said,** I pray you,
**let me glean and
gather after the
reapers** among the sheaves:
so she came, and hath
continued even
from the morning until now,
that she tarried a little in the house.

8. **Then said Boaz unto Ruth,**
Hearest thou not, my daughter?
**Go not to glean in another
field,** neither go from hence,
but abide here fast
by my maidens:

9. *Let* thine eyes *be* on the field that
they do reap, and go thou after them:
have I not charged the young men
that they shall not touch thee?
and when thou art athirst, go
unto the vessels, and drink of *that*
which the young men have drawn.

10. **Then she** fell on her face, and
bowed herself to the ground,
and said unto him,
**Why have I found
grace in thine eyes,**
that thou shouldest take knowledge
of me, seeing I *am* a stranger?

11. **And Boaz
answered** and said unto her,
It hath fully
been shewed me, all that
**thou hast done unto
thy mother in law** since
the death of thine husband:

and how thou hast left
thy father and thy mother, and
the land of thy
nativity, and art
come unto a people which
thou knewest not heretofore.
12. The LORD recompense thy work,
and a full reward be
given thee of the LORD
God of Israel, under whose
wings thou art come to trust.
13. Then she said,
Let me find favour
in thy sight, my lord;
for that
thou hast comforted
me, and for that thou hast
spoken friendly unto thine
handmaid, though I be not like
unto one of thine handmaidens.
14. And Boaz said unto her,
At mealtime come thou hither,
and eat of the bread, and dip
thy morsel in the vinegar. And she
sat beside the reapers: and he
reached her parched *corn,*
and she did eat, and
was sufficed, and left.
15. And when she was
risen up to glean,
Boaz commanded
his young men,
saying, Let her glean
even among the sheaves,
and reproach her not:
16. And let fall also *some* of the
handfuls of purpose for her, and
leave *them,* that she may glean
them, and rebuke her not.
17. So she gleaned
in the field until even, and
beat out that she had gleaned:
and it was about an
ephah of barley.
18. And she took *it* up, and
went into the city:
and her mother in law saw
what she had gleaned:
and she brought forth, and
gave to
her that she had
reserved after she was sufficed.
19. And her mother in

law said unto her,
Where hast thou gleaned
to day? and where wroughtest
thou? blessed be he that did
take knowledge of thee.
And she shewed her mother in law
with whom she had wrought, and
said, The man's name
with whom I wrought to-day
is Boaz.
20. And Naomi said
unto her daughter in law,
Blessed be he of the LORD,
who hath not left off his kindness
to the living and to the dead.
And Naomi said unto her,
The man is near of
kin unto us, one of
our next kinsmen.
21. And Ruth the Moabitess
said, He said unto me also,
Thou shalt keep fast by my
young men, until they have
ended all my harvest.
22. And Naomi said
unto Ruth her daughter in law,
It is good, my daughter, that thou
go out with his maidens, that they
meet thee not in any other field.
23. So she kept fast
by the maidens of Boaz to
glean unto the end of barley
harvest and of wheat harvest;
and dwelt with her
mother in law.

CHAPTER 3

1. Then Naomi her mother in law
said unto her,
My daughter, shall I not
seek rest for thee,
that it may be well with thee?
2. And now *is* not
Boaz of our kindred, with whose
maidens thou wast? Behold, he
winnoweth barley to night
in the threshingfloor.
3. Wash thyself
therefore, and anoint thee, and
put thy raiment upon thee,
and get thee down to the
floor: but make not thy self
known unto the man,

■ until he shall have
■ done eating and drinking.
4. And it shall be,
■ when he lieth
■ down, that thou shalt
■ mark the place
where he shall lie,
■ and thou shalt
■ go in, and uncover
■ his feet, and lay thee
■ down; and he will tell
■ thee what thou shalt do.
5. And she said unto her, All that
thou sayest unto me I will do.
6. And she went down unto the
floor, and did according to all
that her mother in law bade her.
■ 7. And when Boaz
■ had eaten and drunk,
and his heart was merry,
■ he went to
■ lie down at the end
of the heap of corn:
■ and she came softly, and
■ uncovered his feet,
■ and laid her
■ down.
8. And it came to pass
■ at midnight, that
■ the man was afraid, and
■ turned himself: and,
■ behold, a woman
■ lay at his feet.
■ 9. And he said, Who
■ art thou? And she answered,
■ I am Ruth thine handmaid:
spread therefore thy skirt over
thine handmaid; for thou *art* a
near kinsman.
■ 10. And he said, Blessed be
■ thou of the LORD, my daughter:
for thou hast shewed more kindness
in the latter end than at the beginning,
inasmuch as thou followedst not
young men, whether poor or rich.
■ 11. And now, my daughter,
■ fear not; I will do to thee
■ all that thou requirest:
for all the city of my people
■ doth know that thou art
■ a virtuous woman.
12. And now
■ it is true that I *am thy*

near kinsman: howbeit
■ there is a kinsman
■ nearer than I.
13. Tarry this night, and it
shall be in the morning, *that*
■ if he will perform unto thee
■ the part of a kinsman, well;
■ let him do the kinsman's part:
■ but if he will not do the
part of a kinsman to thee,
■ then will I do the part of a
kinsman to thee, *as* the LORD
liveth: lie down until the morning.
■ 14. And she lay at his feet
■ until the morning: and she
■ rose up
■ before one could know
■ another. And he said,
Let it not be known that a
■ woman came into the floor.
■ 15. Also he said, Bring the
veil that *thou hast* upon thee,
and hold it. And when she held it,
■ he measured six measures
■ of barley, and laid it on
■ her: and she went into the city.
16. And when she came to
■ her mother in law, she said,
Who *art* thou, my daughter? And
■ she told her
■ all that the man
■ had done to her.
17. And she said, These six
measures of barley gave he me;
for he said to me, Go not empty
unto thy mother in law.
■ 18. Then said she,
■ Sit still, my daughter,
■ until thou know how the
■ matter will fall: for the man
will not be in rest, until he have
finished the thing this day.

CHAPTER 4

■ 1. Then went Boaz up
■ to the gate, and sat him
down there: and, behold,
■ the kinsman of whom Boaz spake
came by; unto whom he said, Ho,
such a one! turn aside, sit down here.
And he turned aside, and sat down.
■ 2. And he took
■ ten men of the elders

■ of the city,
■ and said, Sit ye down
■ here. And they sat down.
■ 3. And he said unto the
■ kinsman, Naomi, that is come
again out of the country of Moab,
■ selleth a parcel of land,
■ which was our brother
■ Elimelech's:
4. And I thought to advertise thee,
saying, Buy *it* before the inhabitants,
and before the elders of my people.
■ If thou wilt redeem it,
■ redeem it: but if thou wilt
■ not redeem *it, then*
■ tell me, that I may know:
■ for *there is* none to redeem
it beside thee; and I *am* after thee.
And he said,
■ I will redeem it.
■ 5. Then said Boaz,
What day thou buyest the
field of the hand of Naomi,
■ thou must buy it also
■ of Ruth the Moabitess,
■ the wife of the dead,
■ to raise up the
■ name of the dead upon
■ his inheritance.
■ 6. And the kinsman said,
■ I cannot redeem *it* for myself,
■ lest I mar mine own
■ inheritance: redeem
■ thou my right to thyself;
■ for I cannot redeem *it.*
7. Now this *was the manner* in former
time in Israel concerning redeeming
and concerning changing, for to
confirm all things; a man plucked off
his shoe, and gave *it* to his neighbour:
and this *was* a testimony in Israel.
■ 8. Therefore the
■ kinsman said unto
■ Boaz, Buy it for thee.
■ So he drew off his shoe.
■ 9. And Boaz said
unto the elders, and
■ unto all the people,
■ Ye are witnesses this day, that I
■ have bought all that was
■ Elimelech's, and all that *was*
■ Chilion's and Mahlon's,
of the hand of Naomi.

■ 10. Moreover Ruth
the Moabitess, the wife of Mahlon,
■ have I purchased to be my
■ wife, to raise up the name
■ of the dead upon his
■ inheritance, that the name of the
dead be not cut off from among his
brethren, and from the gate of his
place: ye *are* witnesses this day.
■ 11. And all the people that
were in the gate, and the elders,
■ said, *We are* witnesses.
■ The LORD make the
■ woman that is come into
■ thine house like Rachel and
like Leah, which two did build the
house of Israel: and do thou
worthily in Ephratah, and be
■ famous in Beth-lehem:
12. And let thy house be like
the house of Pharez, whom
Tamar bare unto Judah, of the
seed which the LORD shall
give thee of this young woman.
■ 13. So Boaz took Ruth,
and she was his wife: and when
he went in unto her, the LORD
gave her conception,
■ and she bare a son.
■ 14. And the women said
■ unto Naomi, Blessed *be*
■ the LORD, which
■ hath not left thee this day
■ without a kinsman, that his
name may be famous in Israel.
■ 15. And he shall be unto thee
■ a restorer of thy life,
and a nourisher of thine old age:
■ for thy daughter in law,
■ which loveth thee, which
■ is better to thee than
■ seven sons, hath born him.
16. And Naomi took the child,
and laid it in her bosom, and
became nurse unto it.
■ 17. And the
■ women her neighbours
■ gave it a name, saying,
■ There is a son born
■ to Naomi; and they
■ called his name
■ Obed: he is the father of
■ Jesse, the father of David.

18. Now these *are* the generations of Pharez: Pharez begat Hezron,
19. And Hezron begat Ram, and Ram begat Amminadab,
20. And Amminadab begat Nahshon,
and Nahshon begat Salmon,
21. And Salmon begat Boaz, and Boaz begat Obed,
22. And Obed begat Jesse, and Jesse begat David.

THE HISTORICAL BOOKS

Included in the historical books of the Bible are: I and II Samuel, I and II Kings, I and II Chronicles, Ezra, and Nehemiah.

■ **The History began just**
■ **after the Judges** *of Israel*
■ **and continued through** *the period of the Kings, Saul, David and Solomon, the Divided Kingdoms, the downfall of the Northern Kingdom,*
■ **the destruction of**
■ **Jerusalem, the captivity,**
■ **and the return of a remnant** *to rebuild the walls of Jerusalem and the Temple.*
■ **During Israel's** *long*
■ **journey in the wilderness,** *under the leadership of Moses,*
■ **God had revealed that**
■ **the new nation he**
■ **would establish** *in the Promised Land*
■ **would be unique.** *The children of Israel were to be a PeculiarPeople, and a living witness to the heathen nations that would surround them.*
■ **In Israel there would not**
■ **be an earthly king,** *as in heathen nations.*
■ **Rather, God**
■ **would govern**

His people directly
■ **through His Prophets,**
■ **Priests, and Judges.** *While in the wilderness*
■ **God established** *the law,*
■ **a code of conduct** *for the family, society, commerce, and government.*
■ **Israel came into the**
■ **Promised Land** *through God's miraculous power,*
■ **and quickly rebelled** *against God's will,*
■ **demanding an**
■ **earthly king.**
■ **God instructed Samuel**
■ **to anoint Saul king,** *and as God had warned*
■ **the abuses of**
■ **monarchy began**
■ **almost immediately.**
■ **There were brief**
■ **periods of** *glory and*
■ **prosperity during**
■ **the reigns of David**
■ **and Solomon.**
■ **Thereafter, came** *deterioration,*
■ **decay, and the final**
■ **destruction of God's**
■ **chosen people**
■ **as a nation.**

THE BOOK OF FIRST SAMUEL

BACKGROUND INFORMATION

Author: Unknown
Date Written: Probably
around 1000 B.C.

Number of:
Verses—810
Chapters —31
Total Words —25,061
Scan Words —11,197
Scan Words Represent
Approximately 44% of
Total Words

**Theme: The End of the
Judges, and the Beginning
of the Monarchy** through
Saul and David

OUTLINE OF
THE BOOK

I. The Life of
   Samuel
   1:1 — 8:22
II. The Reign of
   King Saul
   9:1 — 15:35
III. **The Conflict** Between
   Saul and David
   **and the Triumph of
   David**
   16:1 — 31:13

CHAPTER 1

1. **Now** there was a certain man of Ramathaim-zophim, of mount Ephraim, and his name *was* **Elkanah,** the son of Jeroham, the son of Elihu, the son of Tohu, the son of Zuph, an Ephrathite:

2. And he **had two wives;** the name of the one *was* **Hannah, and** the name of the other **Peninnah: and Peninnah had children, but Hannah had no children.**

3. **And this man went** up out of his city yearly **to worship and** to **sacrifice unto the LORD** of hosts in Shiloh. And the two sons of Eli, Hophni and Phinehas, the priests of the LORD, *were* there.

4. **And** when the time was that Elkanah offered, **he gave to Peninnah his wife, and** to all **her sons and** her **daughters, portions:**

5. **But unto Hannah he gave a worthy portion; for he loved Hannah: but the LORD had shut up her womb.**

6. And her adversary also provoked her sore, for to make her fret, because the LORD had shut up her womb.

7. **And as** he did so year by year, when **she went** up **to the house of the LORD,** so she provoked her; therefore **she wept,** and did not eat.

8. **Then said Elkanah** her husband to her, Hannah, **why weepest thou?** and why eatest thou not? and why is thy heart grieved? **am not I better to thee than ten sons?**

9. **So Hannah rose** up **after they had eaten** in Shiloh, **and** after they had

drunk. Now Eli the priest sat upon a seat **by** a post of **the temple** of the LORD.

10. **And she** *was* **in bitterness** of soul, and **prayed unto the LORD,** and wept sore.

11. **And she vowed** a vow, and said, O LORD of hosts, **if thou wilt** indeed look on the affliction of thine handmaid, and remember me, and not forget thine handmaid, but wilt **give** unto **thine handmaid a man child, then I will give him unto the LORD all** the days of **his life, and there shall no razor come upon his head.**

12. **And** it came to pass, **as she continued praying** before the LORD, that **Eli marked her mouth.**

13. Now Hannah, she spake in her heart; **only her lips moved,** but her voice was not heard: **therefore Eli thought she had been drunken.**

14. **And Eli said** unto her, How long wilt thou be drunken? **put away thy wine** from thee.

15. **And Hannah** answered and **said,** No, my lord, **I am a woman of a sorrowful spirit:** I have drunk neither wine nor strong drink, buthave poured out my soul before the LORD.

16. Count **not** thine handmaid for a daughter **of Belial: for out** of the abundance **of** my complaint and **grief have I spoken** hitherto.

17. **Then Eli** answered and **said, Go in peace: and** the **God** of Israel **grant thee thy petition** that thou hast asked of him.

18. And she said, Let thine handmaid find grace in thy sight.

So the woman went her way, **and did eat, and** her countenance **was no more sad.** 19. **And they rose up** in the morning early, **and worshipped** before **the LORD, and returned,** and came **to their house** to Ramah: **and Elkanah knew** Hannah **his wife; and** the LORD remembered her. 20. Wherefore it came to pass, when the time was come about after Hannah had conceived, that **she bare a son, and called his name Samuel,** *saying,* Because I have asked him of the LORD. 21. **And** the man **Elkanah,** and all his house, **went up to offer** unto the LORD **the yearly sacrifice, and his vow.** 22. **But Hannah** went not up; for she **said** unto her husband, **I will not go up until the child be weaned, and then I will bring him,** that he may appear **before the LORD,** and there abide for ever. 23. And Elkanah her husband said unto her, Do what seemeth thee good; tarry until thou have weaned him; only the LORD establish his word. So the woman abode, and gave her son suck until she weaned him. 24. **And when she had weaned him, she took** him up with her, with **three bullocks,** and one ephah of **flour, and** a bottle of **wine,** and brought him **unto the house of the LORD in Shiloh:** and the child *was* young. 25. **And they slew a bullock, and brought the child to Eli.** 26. **And she said,** Oh my lord, *as* thy soul liveth, my lord, I *am* the woman that stood by thee here, praying unto the LORD. 27. **For this child I prayed; and the LORD hath given me my petition** which I asked of him: 28. **Therefore** also I have lent him to the LORD; **as long as he liveth he shall be lent to the LORD.** And he worshipped the LORD there.

CHAPTER 2

1. **And Hannah prayed,** and said, **My heart rejoiceth** in the LORD, mine horn is exalted in the LORD: my mouth is enlarged over mine enemies; because I rejoice **in thy salvation.** 2. **There is none** holy as the LORD: for *there is* none beside thee: neither *is there* any rock **like our God.** 3. Talk no more so exceeding proudly; **let not arrogancy come out of your mouth: for the LORD is a God of knowledge, and by him** actions are weighed. 4. **The** bows of the **mighty men are broken, and they that stumbled are girded with strength.** 5. *They that were* full have hired out themselves for bread; and *they that were* hungry ceased: so that the barren hath born seven; and she that hath many children is waxed feeble. 6. **The LORD killeth, and maketh alive:** he bringeth down to the grave, and bringeth up. 7. **The LORD maketh poor, and** maketh **rich:** he bringeth low, and lifteth up. 8. He raiseth up the poor out of the dust, *and* lifteth up the beggar from the dunghill, to set *them* among princes, and to make them inherit the throne of glory: **for the pillars of the earth are the LORD's, and he hath**

set the world upon them.

9. **He will keep the feet of his saints,** and the wicked shall be silent in darkness; **for by strength shall no man prevail.**

10. **The adversaries of the LORD shall be broken** to pieces; out of heaven shall he thunder upon them: the LORD shall judge the ends of the earth; **and he shall** give strength unto his king, and **exalt the horn of his anointed.**

11. **And Elkanah went to** Ramah to **his house. And the child did minister unto the LORD before Eli the priest.**

12. **Now the sons of Eli** *were* sons of Belial; they **knew not the LORD.**

13. **And** the priest's custom with the people *was, that,* **when any man offered sacrifice, the priest's servant came,** while the flesh was in seething, **with a fleshhook** of three teeth in his hand;

14. **And he struck it into the pan,** or kettle, or caldron, or pot; **all** that **the fleshhook brought up the priest took** for himself. So they did in Shiloh, unto all the Israelites that came thither.

15. Also before they burnt the fat, the priest's servant came, and said to the man that sacrificed, Give flesh to roast for the priest; for he will not have sodden flesh of thee, but raw.

16. **And if any man said** unto him, Let them not fail to **burn the fat presently, and then take as much as thy soul desireth;** then he would **answer him, Nay;** **but** thou shalt **give it me now:** and **if not,** I will

take it by force.

17. **Wherefore the sin** of the young men **was very great** before the LORD: **for men abhorred the offering of the LORD.**

18. **But Samuel ministered before the LORD,** *being* a child, girded with a linen ephod.

19. **Moreover his mother made** him **a little coat, and brought it** to him from year to year, **when she came** up with her husband **to offer the yearly sacrifice.**

20. **And Eli** blessed Elkanah and his wife, and **said, The LORD give thee seed** of this woman for the loan which is lent **to the LORD.** And they went unto their own home.

21. **And** the LORD visited **Hannah,** so that she **conceived, and bare three sons and two daughters. And** the child **Samuel grew before the LORD.**

22. **Now Eli was very old, and** heard all that **his sons** did unto all Israel; and how they **lay with the women that assembled at the door of the tabernacle** of the congregation.

23. **And he said** unto them, Why do ye such things? for **I hear of your evil dealings** by all this people.

24. Nay, my sons; for *it is* no good report that I hear: **ye make the LORD's people to transgress.**

25. If one man sin against another, the judge shall judge him: **but if a man sin against the LORD, who shall entreat for him?** Notwithstanding

they hearkened
not unto the voice of
their father, because
the LORD would slay them.
26. And the child
Samuel grew on,
and was in favour both
with the LORD, and also with
men.
27. And there came
a man of God unto
Eli, and said unto him,
Thus saith the LORD,
Did I plainly
appear unto the house of
thy father, when they were
in Egypt in Pharaoh's house?
28. And did I
choose him out of
all the tribes of Israel
to be my priest, to offer
upon mine altar, to burn incense,
to wear an ephod before me?
and did I give unto the house of
thy father all
the offerings made by
fire of the children of Israel?
29. Wherefore kick ye
at my sacrifice and
at mine offering, which I
have commanded in my habitation;
and honourest thy sons
above me, to make
yourselves fat with
the chiefest of all
the offerings of
Israel my people?
30. Wherefore
the LORD God of Israel saith,
I said indeed that thy house, and
the house of thy father,
should walk before me for
ever: but now the LORD saith,
Be it far from me; for them that
honour me I will honour, and they that
despise me shall be lightly esteemed.
31. Behold, the days come, that
I will cut off
thine arm, and the arm of
thy father's house, that there
shall not be an old manin thine house.
32. And thou shalt see an enemy
in my habitation, in all the wealth

which God shall give Israel:
and there shall not
be an old man in thine
house for ever.
33. And the man of thine, whom I
shall not cut off from mine altar,
shall be to consume thine eyes,
and to grieve thine heart: and all
the increase of thine
house shall die in the
flower of their age.
34. And this shall be
a sign unto thee,
that shall come upon
thy two sons,
on Hophni and Phinehas;
in one day they
shall die both of them.
35. And I will raise me
up a faithful priest,
that shall do according to that which
is in mine heart and in my mind: and
I will build him a sure house;
and he shall walk before
mine anointed for ever.
36. And it shall come to pass, that
every one that is
left in thine house shall come
and crouch to him for a piece of
silver and a morsel of bread, and
shall say, Put
me, I pray thee,
into one of the priests'
offices, that I may
eat a piece of bread.

CHAPTER 3

1. And the child
Samuel ministered
unto the LORD
before Eli. And the
word of the LORD
was precious in those days;
there was no open vision.
2. And it came to pass at that time,
when Eli was
laid down in his place, and
his eyes began to wax dim,
that he could not see;
3. And ere the lamp of God went
out in the temple of the LORD,
where the ark of God was,
and Samuel was

laid down to sleep;

4. That the LORD called Samuel: and he answered, Here *am* I.

5. And he ran unto Eli, and said, Here am I. for thou calledst me. And he said, I called not; lie down again. And he went and lay down.

6. And the LORD called yet again, Samuel. And Samuel arose and went to Eli, and said, Here *am* I; for thou didst call me. And he answered, I called not, my son; lie down again.

7. Now Samuel did not yet know the LORD, neither was the word of the LORD yet revealed unto him.

8. And the LORD called Samuel again the third time. And he arose and went to Eli, and said, Here *am* I; for thou didst call me. And Eli perceived that the LORD had called the child.

9. Therefore Eli said unto Samuel, Go, lie down: and it shall be, if he call thee, that thou shalt say, Speak, LORD; for thy servant heareth. So Samuel went and lay down in his place.

10. And the LORD came, and stood, and called as at other times, Samuel, Samuel. Then Samuel answered, Speak; for thy servant heareth.

11. And the LORD said to Samuel, Behold, I will do a thing in Israel, at which both the ears of every one that heareth it shall tingle.

12. In that day I will perform against Eli all things which I have spoken concerning his house:

when I begin, I will also make an end.

13. For I have told him that I will judge his house for ever for the iniquity which he knoweth; because his sons made themselves vile, and he restrained them not.

14. And therefore I have sworn unto the house of Eli, that the iniquity of Eli's house shall not be purged with sacrifice nor offering for ever.

15. And Samuel lay until the morning, and opened the doors of the house of the LORD. And Samuel feared to shew Eli the vision.

16. Then Eli called Samuel, and said, Samuel, my son. And he answered, Here *am* I.

17. And he said, What is the thing that the LORD hath said unto thee? I pray thee hide *it* not from me: God do so to thee, and more also, if thou hide *any* thing from me of all the things that he said unto thee.

18. And Samuel told him every whit, and hid nothing from him. And he said, It is the LORD: let him do what seemeth him good.

19. And Samuel grew, and the LORD was with him, and did let none of his words fall to the ground.

20. And all Israel from Dan even to Beer-sheba knew that Samuel was established *to be* a prophet of the LORD.

21. And the LORD appeared again in Shiloh: for the LORD revealed himself to Samuel in Shiloh by the word of the LORD.

CHAPTER 4

1. And the word of

418

Samuel came to all Israel.
Now Israel went out
against the Philistines
to battle, and pitched beside
Eben-ezer: and the Philistines
pitched in Aphek.
2. **And** the Philistines put
themselves in array against Israel:
and when they joined battle,
Israel was smitten before
the Philistines: and they
slew of the army in the field
about four thousand men.
3. **And** when the people
were come into the camp,
the elders of Israel
said, Wherefore hath
the LORD smitten us
to-day before the Philistines?
Let us fetch the ark of
the covenant of the
LORD out of Shiloh unto us,
that, when it cometh among us,
it may save us out of the
hand of our enemies.
4. **So the people sent to**
Shiloh, that they might bring from
thence the ark of the covenant of
the LORD of hosts, which dwelleth
between the cherubims:
and the two sons of
Eli, Hophni and Phinehas,
were there with the
ark of the covenant of God.
5. **And when the ark**
of the covenant of the LORD
came into the camp,
all Israel shouted
with a great shout,
so that the earth rang again.
6. **And when the Philistines**
heard the noise of the
shout, they said, What *meaneth*
the noise of this great shout in
the camp of the Hebrews? And
they understood
that the ark of the LORD
was come into the camp.
7. **And the Philistines**
were afraid, for they said,
God is come into the camp.
And they said,
Woe unto us! for there hath not

been such a thing heretofore.
8. **Woe unto us!**
who shall deliver us out of the
hand of these mighty Gods?
these are the Gods that
smote the Egyptians with
all the plagues in the wilderness.
9. **Be strong** and quit yourselves
like men, O ye Philistines, that ye
be not servants unto the
Hebrews, as they
have been to you: quit
yourselves like men,
and fight.
10. And the Philistines fought,
and Israel was smitten,
and they fled every man into his tent:
and there was a very
great slaughter; for
there fell of Israel thirty
thousand footmen.
11. **And the ark of God was**
taken; and the two sons
of Eli, Hophni and Phinehas,
were slain.
12. **And there ran a**
man of Benjamin
out of the army, and came
to Shiloh the same day
with his clothes rent, and
with earth upon his head.
13. **And** when he came, lo,
Eli sat upon a seat by
the wayside watching: for
his heart trembled for
the ark of God.
And when the man came into the city,
and told *it,* all the city cried out.
14. And when Eli heard the noise of
the crying, he said, What *meaneth* the
noise of this tumult? And the man
came in hastily, and told Eli.
15. **Now Eli was ninety** and
eight years old; and his eyes
were dim, that he could not see.
16. **And the man**
said unto Eli, I *am* he
that came out of the army, and
I fled to-day out of the
army. And he said, What
is there done, my son?
17. And the messenger
answered and said,

Israel is fled before
the Philistines, and
there hath been also
a great slaughter
among the people,
and thy two sons
also, Hophni and Phinehas,
are dead, and the
ark of God is taken.
18. And it came to pass,
when he made mention
of the ark of God, that
he fell from off the seat
backward by the side of the gate,
and his neck brake,
and he died: for he was
an old man, and heavy. And
he had judged
Israel forty years.
19. And his daughter
in law, Phinehas' wife,
was with child, near
to be delivered: and
when she heard the tidings
that the ark of God
was taken, and that her
father in law and her
husband were dead, she
bowed herself and travailed; for
her pains came upon her.
20. And about the time
of her death the women
that stood by her
said unto her, Fear not; for
thou hast born a son.
But she answered not,
neither did she regard it.
21. And she named the
child Ichabod, saying, The
glory is departed from Israel:
because the ark of God was
taken, and because of her father
in law and her husband.
22. And she said, The glory is
departed from Israel: for
the ark of God is taken.

CHAPTER 5

1. And the Philistines
took the ark of God, and
brought it from Eben-ezer
unto Ashdod.
2. When the Philistines took
the ark of God, they brought it
into the house of
Dagon, and set it by Dagon.
3. And when they of
Ashdod arose early
on the morrow, behold,
Dagon was fallen upon
his face to the earth
before the ark of the LORD.
And they took Dagon, and
set him in his place again.
4. And when they arose
early on the morrow
morning, behold,
Dagon was fallen
upon his face to the ground
before the ark of the LORD;
and the head of Dagon
and both the palms of
his hands were cut off
upon the threshold; only the
stump of Dagon was left to him.
5. Therefore neither
the priests of Dagon,
nor any that come into
Dagon's house, tread
on the threshold
of Dagon in Ashdod unto this day.
6. But the hand of
the LORD was heavy upon
them of Ashdod, and he
destroyed them, and smote
them with emerods, even
Ashdod and the coasts thereof.
7. And when
the men of Ashdod
saw that it was so, they
said, The ark of the God
of Israel shall not abide
with us: for his hand is sore
upon us, and upon Dagon our god.
8. They sent therefore and
gathered all the lords
of the Philistines unto them,
and said, What shall we
do with the ark of the God
of Israel? And they answered,
Let the ark of the God of Israel
be carried about
unto Gath. And they carried
the ark of the God of Israel about
thither.
9. And it was so, that, after

they had carried it about,
- **the hand of the LORD was**
- **against the city with** a very
- **great destruction:**

and he smote the men of the city, both small and great, and they had emerods in their secret parts.
- 10. **Therefore they**
- **sent the ark** of God
- **to Ekron. And** it came to pass, as

the ark of God came to Ekron, that
- **the Ekronites cried** out, saying,
- **They have brought** about
- **the ark** of the God of Israel to us,
- **to slay us** and our people.
- 11. **So they** sent and
- **gathered** together all
- **the lords of the Philistines,**
- **and said, Send** away
- **the ark** of the God of

Israel, and let it go again
- **to his own place, that it slay**
- **us not,** and our people: for there

was a deadly destruction throughout all the city; the hand of God was very heavy there.
- 12. **And the men that**
- **died not were smitten**
- **with the emerods:** and the

cry of the city went up to heaven.

CHAPTER 6

- 1. **And the ark** of the LORD
- **was in the country**

of the Philistines
- **seven months.**
- 2. **And the Philistines called**
- **for the priests** and the diviners,
- **saying, What shall we**
- **do** to the ark of the LORD?

tell us wherewith we shall send it to his place.
- 3. **And they said,** If ye
- **send away the ark**

of the God of Israel, send it
- **not empty; but** in any wise
- **return** him
- **a trespass offering: then**
- **ye shall be healed,** and it

shall be known to you why his hand is not removed from you.

4. Then said they, What *shall be* the trespass offering which we shall

return to him? They answered, Five golden emerods, and five golden mice, *according to* the number of the lords of the Philistines: for one plague *was* on you all, and on your lords.

5. Wherefore ye shall make images of your emerods, and images of your mice that mar the land; and ye shall
- **give glory unto the God of**
- **Israel: peradventure he**
- **will lighten his hand from**
- **off you,** and from off
- **your gods, and** from off
- **your land.**

6. Wherefore then do ye harden your hearts, as the Egyptians and Pharaoh hardened their hearts? when he had wrought wonderfully among them, did they not let the people go, and they departed?
- 7. **Now** therefore
- **make a new cart, and**
- **take two milch kine,**

on which there hath come no yoke,
- **and tie** the kine
- **to the cart, and bring**
- **their calves** home
- **from them:**
- 8. **And take the**
- **ark** of the LORD,
- **and lay it upon the**
- **cart; and put** the jewels of

gold, which ye return him *for*
- **a trespass offering, in**
- **a coffer** by the side thereof;
- **and send it away,**

that it may go.

9. And see, if it goeth up by the way of his own coast to Beth-shemesh, *then* he hath done us this great evil: but if not, then we shall know that *it is* not his hand *that* smote us: it *was* a chance *that* happened to us.
- 10. **And the men did so;**

and took two milch kine, and tied them to the cart, and shut up their calves at home:

11. And they laid the ark of the LORD upon the cart, and the coffer with the mice of gold and the images of their emerods.

12. And the kine took the straightway to the way of Beth-shemesh, *and*

went along the highway, lowing as they went, and turned not aside *to* the right hand or *to* the left; and the lords of the Philistines went after them unto the border of Beth-shemesh.

13. **And they of Beth-shemesh were reaping** their **wheat** harvest in the valley: **and they** lifted up their eyes, and **saw the ark, and rejoiced** to see *it.*

14. **And the cart came into the field of Joshua,** a Beth-shemite, and stood there, **where there was a great stone: and they clave the** wood of the **cart, and offered the kine a burnt offering unto the LORD.**

15. **And the Levites took** down **the ark** of the LORD, **and the coffer** that *was* with it, wherein the jewels of gold *were,* **and put them on the great stone: and** the men of Beth-shemesh **offered burnt offerings and** sacrificed **sacrifices** the same day **unto the LORD.**

16. **And when** the five lords of **the Philistines had seen it, they returned to Ekron** the same day.

17. And these *are* the golden emerods which the Philistines returned *for* a trespass offering unto the LORD; for Ashdod one, for Gaza one, for Askelon one, for Gath one, for Ekron one;

18. And the golden mice, *according to* the number of all the cities of the Philistines *belonging* to the five lords, *both* of fenced cities, and of country villages, even unto the great *stone of* Abel, whereon they set down the ark of the LORD: *which stone remaineth* unto this day in the field of Joshua, the Bethshemite.

19. **And he smote the men of Beth-shemesh, because** **they had looked into the ark of the LORD, even he smote** of the people **fifty thousand** and **threescore and ten men:** and the people lamented, because the LORD had smitten *many* of the people with a great slaughter.

20. And the men of Beth-shemesh said, Who is able to stand before this holy LORD God? and to whom shall he go up from us?

21. **And they sent messengers to** the inhabitants of **Kirjath-jearim, saying, The Philistines have brought** again **the ark** of the LORD; **come** ye down, **and fetch it** up to you.

CHAPTER 7

1. **And the men** of Kirjath-jearim **came,** and fetched up the ark of the LORD, **and brought it into the house of Abinadab** in the hill, **and sanctified Eleazar his son to keep the ark** of the LORD.

2. **And** it came to pass, while **the ark abode in Kirjath-jearim,** that the time was long; for it was **twenty years: and** all the house of **Israel lamented after the LORD.**

3. **And Samuel spake unto** all the house of **Israel, saying, If ye** do return unto the LORD with all your hearts, *then* **put away the strange gods** and Ashtaroth from among you, **and prepare your hearts unto the LORD, and serve him only: and he will deliver you out of the hand of the Philistines.**

4. Then the children of Israel did put away Baalim and Ashtaroth, and

served the LORD only.

■ 5. **And Samuel said,**
■ **Gather all Israel to Mizpeh,**
and I will pray for you unto the LORD.

■ 6. **And they**
gathered together to Mizpeh, and
■ **drew water, and poured**
■ **it out before the LORD,**
■ **and fasted on that day,**
■ **and said** there,
■ **We have sinned**
against the LORD.
■ **And Samuel**
■ **judged** the children of
■ **Israel** in Mizpeh.
■ 7. **And** when the Philistines
heard that the children of I
srael were gathered together
to Mizpeh, the lords of
■ **the Philistines went up**
■ **against Israel. And**
when the children of Israel heard *it,*
■ **they were afraid**
of the Philistines.
■ 8. **And** the children of Israel
■ **said to Samuel, Cease**
■ **not to cry unto the**
■ **LORD** our God for us,
■ **that he will save us**
out of the hand of the Philistines.
■ 9. **And Samuel took**
■ **a sucking lamb,**
■ **and offered** it for
■ **a burnt offering** wholly
■ **unto the LORD:** and Samuel
cried unto the LORD for Israel;
and the LORD heard him.
■ 10. **And** as Samuel was
offering up the burnt offering,
■ **the Philistines drew**
■ **near to battle** against Israel:
■ **but the LORD thundered** with
■ **a great thunder** on that day
upon the Philistines,
■ **and discomfited them;**
■ **and they were smitten**
■ **before Israel.**
11. And the men of Israel went
out of Mizpeh, and pursued the
Philistines, and smote them,
until *they came* under Bethcar.
■ 12. **Then Samuel**
■ **took a stone,**

and set *it* between Mizpeh and Shen,
■ **and called the name of it**
■ **Ebenezer, saying, Hitherto**
■ **hath the LORD helped us.**
■ 13. **So the Philistines**
were subdued, and they
■ **came no more into the**
■ **coast of Israel:** and the hand of
the LORD was against the Philistines
■ **all the days of Samuel.**
■ 14. **And the cities** which
■ **the Philistines**
■ **had taken** from Israel
■ **were restored to Israel,**
from Ekron even unto Gath;
and the coasts thereof did
Israel deliver out of the hands
of the Philistines. And there
was peace between Israel
and the Amorites.
■ 15. **And Samuel**
■ **judged Israel all** the days of
■ **his life.**
■ 16. **And he went**
from year to year
■ **in circuit** to Bethel,
and Gilgal, and Mizpeh,
■ **and judged Israel**
in all those places.
■ 17. **And his return was**
■ **to Ramah;** for there was his
house; and there he judged Israel;
■ **and there he built**
■ **an altar unto the LORD.**

CHAPTER 8

■ 1. **And** it came to pass,
■ **when Samuel was old,** that
■ **he made his sons**
■ **judges over Israel.**
2. Now the name of his firstborn
was Joel; and the name of his
second, Abiah: *they were* judges
in Beer-sheba.
■ 3. **And his sons walked**
■ **not in his ways, but**
turned aside after lucre, and
■ **took bribes, and**
■ **perverted judgment.**
■ 4. **Then** all
■ **the elders**
of Israel gathered
themselves together, and

came to Samuel unto Ramah,
5. And said unto him,
Behold, thou art old, and thy
sons walk not in thy ways: now
make us a king to judge
us like all the nations.
6. But the thing displeased
Samuel, when they said, Give
us a king to judge us. And Samuel
prayed unto the LORD.
7. And the LORD
said unto Samuel,
Hearken unto the voice of the
people
in all that they say unto thee:
for they have not rejected
thee, but they have rejected
me, that I should not
reign over them.
8. According to all the works which
they have done since the day that I
brought them up out of Egypt even
unto this day, wherewith they have
forsaken me, and served other gods,
so do they also unto thee.
9. Now therefore hearken unto
their voice: howbeit yet protest
solemnly unto them, and
shew them the manner
of the king that shall
reign over them.
10. And Samuel told
all the words of the LORD unto
the people that asked
of him a king.
11. And he said, This will be
the manner of the king that
shall reign over you:
He will take your
sons, and appoint them
for himself, for his
chariots, and to be his
horsemen; and some
shall run before his chariots.
12. And he will
appoint him
captains over thousands, and
captains over fifties; and will set
them to ear his
ground, and to
reap his harvest, and to
make his
instruments of war,

and instruments of his chariots.
13. And he will take
your daughters to be
confectionaries, and to be
cooks, and to be bakers.
14. And he will take your
fields, and your vineyards, and your
oliveyards, even the best of them,
and give them to his servants.
15. And he will take
the tenth of your
seed, and of
your vineyards, and give
to his officers, and to his
servants.
16. And he will take your
menservants, and your maidservants,
and your goodliest young men, and
your asses, and put them to his work.
17. He will take the tenth
of your sheep:
and ye shall be
his servants.
18. And ye shall
cry out in that day
because of your king
which ye shall have chosen you;
and the LORD will not
hear you in that day.
19. Nevertheless the people
refused to obey the voice of
Samuel; and they
said, Nay; but
we will have a king over us;
20. That we also may be like all the
nations; and that our king may judge
us, and go out before us,
and fight our battles.
21. And Samuel heard all the words
of the people, and he rehearsed
them in the ears of the LORD.
22. And the LORD
said to Samuel,
Hearken unto their voice,
and make them a king.
And Samuel said unto the men of
Israel, Go ye every man unto his city.

CHAPTER 9

1. Now there was a
man of Benjamin, whose
name was
Kish, the son of Abiel, the

son of Zeror, the son of Bechorath, the son of Aphiah,

a Benjamite, a mighty **man of power.** 2. **And he had a son,** whose name *was* **Saul, a choice** young man, **and a goodly:** and *there was* not among the children of Israel a goodlier **person** than he: **from his shoulders and upward** *he was* **higher than any of the people.** 3. **And the asses of Kish** Saul's father **were lost. And Kish said to Saul** his son, Take now one of the servants with thee, and arise, **go seek the asses.** 4. **And he passed through** mount **Ephraim, and** passed through the land of **Shalisha,** but they found *them* not: then they passed through the land of **Shalim, and** *there they were* not: and he passed through **the land of the Benjamites, but they found them not.** 5. **And when they were come to** the land of **Zuph, Saul said to his servant** that *was* with him, Come, and **let us return; lest my father** leave *caring* for the asses, and **take thought for us.** 6. **And he said** unto him, Behold now, **there is in this city a man of God,** and *he is* an honourable man; all that he saith cometh surely to pass: now let us go thither; **peradventure he can shew us our way** that we should go. 7. **Then said Saul** to his servant, But, behold, *if* we go, **what shall we bring the man?** for the bread is spent in our vessels, and *there is* not a present to bring to the man of God: what have we?

8. **And the servant answered** Saul again, and said, Behold, **I have here** at hand the fourth part of a shekel of **silver: that will I give to the man of God, to tell us our way.** 9. **(Beforetime in Israel,** when a man went to inquire of God, thus he spake, Come, and let us go to the seer: for **he that is now called a Prophet was** beforetime **called a Seer.)** 10. Then said Saul to his servant, Well said; come, let us go. So they went unto the city where the man of God *was.* 11. **And as they went** up the hill to the city, **they found young maidens going out to draw water,** and said unto them, **Is the seer here?** 12. **And they answered** them, and said, He is; behold, *he is* before you: make haste now, for **he came to-day to** the city; for *there is* a **sacrifice** of the people to-day **in the high place:** 13. As soon as ye be come into the city, ye shall straightway find him, before he go up to the high place to eat: for the people will not eat until he come, because he doth bless the sacrifice; *and* afterwards they eat that be bidden. Now therefore get you up; for about this time ye shall find him. 14. **And they went** up **into the city:** *and* when they were come into the city, behold, **Samuel came** out **against them, for** **to go up to the high place.** 15. **Now the LORD had told Samuel** in his ear **a day before** Saul came, saying, 16. To-morrow about this time **I will send thee a man** out of the land of Benjamin, **and thou shalt**

anoint him *io be*
captain over my people
Israel, that he may save my people
out of the hand of the Philistines:
for I have looked upon my people,
because their cry is come unto me.
17. And when Samuel saw
Saul, the LORD said unto him,
Behold the man
whom I spake to thee of! this same
shall reign over my people.
18. Then Saul drew near to
Samuel in the gate, and said,
Tell me, I pray thee,
where the seer's house is.
19. And Samuel
answered Saul, and said,
I am the seer: go up before me
unto the high
place; for ye shall
eat with me to-day,
and to-morrow I
will let thee go, and will
tell thee all that is
in thine heart.
20. And as for thine
asses that were lost three days
ago, set not thy mind on them; for
they are found. And on whom *is*
all the desire of
Israel? Is *it* not
on thee,
and on all thy father's house?
21. And Saul answered
and said, *Am* not I a Benjamite, of
the smallest of the tribes of Israel?
and my family the least of all the
families of the tribe of Benjamin?
wherefore then
speakest thou so to me?
22. And Samuel took
Saul and his
servant, and brought them
into the parlour, and
made them sit in the
chiefest place among
them that were bidden, which *were*
about thirty persons.
23. And Samuel said
unto the cook, Bring the
portion which I gave thee,
of which I said unto thee,
Set it by thee.

24. And the cook took up
the shoulder, and
that which *was* upon it, and
set it before Saul. And *Samuel*
said, Behold that which is left! set it
before thee, *and* eat: for unto this
time hath it been kept for thee since I
said, I have invited the people.
So Saul did eat with
Samuel that day.
25. And when they were
come down from the high place
into the city, Samuel
communed with Saul
upon the top of the house.
26. And they arose early:
and it came to pass about
the spring of the day, that
Samuel called Saul
to the top of the house,
saying, Up, that I may
send thee away. And Saul
arose, and they went out both of
them, he and Samuel, abroad.
27. And as they were going
down to the end of the
city, Samuel said to Saul,
Bid the servant pass on
before us, (and he passed on.)
but stand thou still a while,
that I may shew thee
the word of God.

CHAPTER 10

1. Then Samuel took a vial
of oil, and poured it upon
his head, and kissed him,
and said, *Is it* not because
the LORD hath anointed
thee to be captain
over his inheritance?
2. When thou art
departed from me to day, then
thou shalt find two men
by Rachel's sepulchre in the
border of Benjamin at Zelzah;
and they will say unto thee,
The asses
which thou wentest to seek
are found: and, lo,
thy father hath left the care of
the asses, and
sorroweth for you, saying, What

shall I do for my son?

3. **Then shalt thou go** on forward from thence, and thou shalt come **to the plain of Tabor, and** there shall **meet** thee **three men going up to God to Beth-el,** one carrying three kids, and another carrying three loaves of bread, and another carrying a bottle of wine:

4. **And they will salute thee, and give thee two loaves of bread;** which thou shalt receive of their hands.

5. **After that** thou shalt come to the hill of God, where *is* the garrison of the Philistines: and it shall come to pass, **when thou art come thither to the city,** that **thou shalt meet** a company of **prophets** coming down from the high place with a psaltery, and a tabret, and a pipe, and a harp, before them; **and they shall prophesy:**

6. **And the Spirit of the LORD will come upon thee, and thou shalt prophesy** with them, **and shalt be turned into another man.**

7. And let it be, when these signs are come unto thee, *that* thou do as occasion serve thee; **for God is with thee.**

8. **And** thou shalt **go** down before me **to Gilgal; and,** behold, I will come down unto thee, to **offer burnt offerings, and** to sacrifice sacrifices of **peace offerings: seven days** shalt thou tarry, **till I come** to thee, **and shew thee what thou shalt do.**

9. **And** it was *so,* that **when he** had **turned** his back **to go from Samuel, God gave him another heart:**

and all those signs came to pass that day.

10. **And** when they came thither to **the** hill, behold, a company of **prophets met him; and the Spirit of God came upon him, and he prophesied** among them.

11. And it came to pass, when all that knew him beforetime saw that, behold, he prophesied among the prophets, **then the people said** one to another, What *is* this *that* is come unto the son of Kish? **Is Saul also among the prophets?**

12. And one of the same place answered and said, But who *is* their father? **Therefore it became a proverb,** *Is* Saul also among the prophets?

13. **And when he** had **made an end of prophesying, he came to the high place.**

14. **And Saul's uncle said** unto him and to his servant, **Whither went ye? And** he said, To seek the **asses: and** when we saw that *they were* no where, **we came to Samuel.**

15. **And Saul's uncle said, Tell me,** I pray thee, **what Samuel said** unto you.

16. **And Saul said** unto his uncle, **He told us** plainly that **the asses were found. But of the matter of the kingdom,** whereof Samuel spake, **he told him not.**

17. **And Samuel called the people together unto the LORD to Mizpeh;**

18. **And said** unto the children of Israel, **Thus saith the LORD** God of Israel, **I brought up Israel out of Egypt, and delivered you out of the**

■ **hand** of the Egyptians, and out
of the hand of all kingdoms, *and*
■ **of them that**
■ **oppressed you:**
■ 19. **And ye have** this day
■ **rejected your God,** who
himself saved you out of all your
adversities and your tribulations;
■ **and** ye have
■ **said** unto him, *Nay,* but
■ **set a king over**
■ **us. Now** therefore
■ **present yourselves**
before the LORD
■ **by your tribes,**
and by your thousands.
■ 20. **And** when
■ **Samuel** had
■ **caused** all
■ **the tribes** of Israel
■ **to come near,** the tribe
of Benjamin was taken.
■ 21. **When he had caused**
■ **the tribe of Benjamin to**
■ **come** near by their families,
■ **the family of Matri was**
■ **taken, and Saul the son**
■ **of Kish** was taken:
■ **and when they sought him,**
■ **he could not be found.**
22. Therefore they inquired of
the LORD further, if the man
should yet come thither. And
the LORD answered, Behold,
■ **he** hath
■ **hid himself** among the stuff.
■ 23. **And they** ran and
■ **fetched him** thence:
■ **and** when
■ **he stood** among
the people, he was
■ **higher than** any of
■ **the people from his**
■ **shoulders and upward.**
■ 24. **And Samuel**
■ **said** to all the people,
■ **See** ye him
■ **whom the LORD hath**
■ **chosen,** that *there is* none
like him among all the people?
■ **And all the people**
■ **shouted,** and said,
■ **God save the king.**

25. Then Samuel told the
people the manner of the
kingdom, and wrote it in a book,
and laid it up before the LORD.
■ **And Samuel sent** all
■ **the people away,**
every man to his house.
■ 26. **And Saul also**
■ **went home** to Gibeah;
■ **and** there went
■ **with him a band of**
■ **men, whose hearts**
■ **God had touched.**
■ 27. **But the children of**
■ **Belial** said, How shall this
man save us? And they
■ **despised him,**
■ **and brought** him
■ **no presents. But**
■ **he held his peace.**

CHAPTER 11

■ 1. **Then Nahash the**
■ **Ammonite came**
up, and encamped
■ **against Jabesh-**
■ **gilead: and** all
■ **the men of Jabesh**
■ **said** unto Nahash,
■ **Make a covenant** with us,
■ **and we will serve thee.**
■ 2. **And Nahash** the Ammonite
■ **answered** them,
■ **On this condition**
will I make *a covenant* with you,
■ **that I may thrust out** all
■ **your right eyes,** and lay it
■ **for a reproach upon** all
■ **Israel.**
■ 3. **And the elders of**
■ **Jabesh said** unto him,
■ **Give us seven days'** respite,
■ **that we may send**
■ **messengers unto**
all the coasts of
■ **Israel: and** then,
■ **if there be no man to**
■ **save us, we will come** out
■ **to thee.**
■ 4. **Then came the**
■ **messengers**
to Gibeah of Saul,
■ **and told the** tidings

in the ears of the **people: and** all **the people** lifted up their voices, and **wept.**

5. **And,** behold, **Saul came** after the herd **out of the field; and** Saul **said, What aileth the people** that they weep? **And they told him** the tidings of the men of Jabesh.

6. **And the Spirit of God came upon Saul** when he heard those tidings, **and his anger was kindled** greatly.

7. **And he took** a yoke of **oxen, and hewed them in pieces, and sent them throughout** all the coasts of **Israel** by the hands of messengers, **saying, Whosoever cometh not forth** after Saul and after Samuel, **so shall it be done unto his oxen. And the fear of the LORD fell on the people, and they came** out with one consent.

8. **And** when **he numbered** them in Bezek, the children of **Israel** were **three hundred thousand, and** the men of **Judah thirty thousand.**

9. **And they said unto the messengers that came,** Thus shall ye say **unto** the men of **Jabesh-gilead, To-morrow,** by *that time* the sun be hot, **ye shall have help. And** the messengers came and shewed *it* to **the men of Jabesh;** and they **were glad.**

10. **Therefore the men** of Jabesh **said, To morrow we will come** out unto you, **and ye shall do with us all that seemeth good** unto you.

11. **And** it was *so* on the morrow, that **Saul put the people in three companies; and they came** into the midst of the host **in the morning watch, and slew the Ammonites** until the heat of the day: and it came to pass, that they which remained were scattered, so that two of them were not left together.

12. **And the people said unto Samuel, Who** *is* he that **said, Shall Saul reign over us? bring the men, that we may put them to death.**

13. **And Saul said, There shall not a man be put to death** this day: **for** to-day **the LORD hath wrought salvation in Israel.**

14. **Then said Samuel** to the people, Come, and **let us go to Gilgal, and renew the kingdom** there.

15. **And all the people went** to Gilgal; **and** there **they made Saul king** before the LORD in Gilgal; and **there they sacrificed** sacrifices of peace offerings **before the LORD;** and there Saul **and all** the men of **Israel rejoiced** greatly.

CHAPTER 12

1. **And Samuel said** unto all Israel, Behold, **I have hearkened unto your voice** in all that ye said unto me, **and have made a king over you.**

2. **And now,** behold, **the king walketh before you: and I am old** and grayheaded; and, behold, my sons *are* with you: **and I have walked before you from my**

childhood unto this day.
3. **Behold,** here I *am:*
witness against me before the
LORD, and before his anointed:
whose ox have I taken? or whose ass
have I taken? or whom have I
defrauded? whom have I
oppressed? or of whose hand
have I received *any* bribe to
blind mine eyes therewith?
and I will restore it you.
4. And they said, Thou hast not
defrauded us, nor oppressed us,
neither hast thou taken ought
of any man's hand.
5. And he said unto them,
The LORD is witness
against you, and his anointed
is witness this day, that
ye have not found
aught in my hand.
And they answered, *He is* witness.
6. **And Samuel said**
unto the people, *It is*
the LORD that advanced
Moses and Aaron, and that
brought your fathers up
out of the land of
Egypt.
7. **Now** therefore
stand still, that I may
reason with you
before the LORD
of all the righteous acts
of the LORD, which he did
to you and to your fathers.
8. **When** Jacob was come into
Egypt, and your fathers cried unto
the LORD, then the LORD
sent Moses and Aaron, which
brought forth
your fathers out of
Egypt, and made them
dwell in this place.
9. **And** when
they forgat the
LORD their God,
he sold them into
the hand of Sisera,
captain of the host of Hazor,
and into the hand of
the Philistines, and
into the hand of the king of

Moab, and they fought
against them.
10. **And they cried**
unto the LORD, and said,
We have sinned,
because we have forsaken
the LORD, and have served
Baalim and Ashtaroth: but
now deliver us out of the
hand of our enemies,
and we will serve thee.
11. **And the LORD**
sent Jerubbaal, and Bedan, and
Jephthah, and Samuel, and
delivered you out of the hand
of your enemies on every side,
and ye dwelled safe.
12. **And when** ye saw thatNahash
the king of the children of
Ammon came against you,
ye said unto me, Nay; but
a king shall reign over us:
when the LORD your God
was your king.
13. **Now** therefore
behold the king
whom ye have chosen, *and*
whom ye have desired!
and, behold, the LORD hath
set a king over you.
14. **If ye will fear the**
LORD, and serve him, and obey
his voice, and not rebel against the
commandment of the LORD,
then shall both ye and also
the king that reigneth over you
continue following
the LORD your God:
15. **But if ye will**
not obey the voice of
the LORD, but rebel against
the commandment of the LORD,
then shall the hand of the
LORD be against you,
as *it was* against your fathers.
16. **Now** therefore stand and
see this great thing,
which the LORD will
do before your eyes.
17. *Is it* not wheat harvest to day?
I will call unto the LORD,
and he shall send thunder
and rain; that ye may

- perceive and see
- that your wickedness
- is great, which ye have done

in the sight of the LORD,

- in asking you a king.

18. So Samuel called unto the LORD; and the LORD sent thunder and rain that day:

- and all the people
- greatly feared the
- LORD and Samuel.
- 19. And all
- the people said unto Samuel,
- Pray for thy servants

unto the LORD thy God,

- that we die not: for we have
- added unto all our sins this
- evil, to ask us a king.
- 20. And Samuel
- said unto the people,
- Fear not:

ye have done all this wickedness: yet

- turn not aside
- from following the LORD, but

serve the LORD with all your heart;
21. And turn ye not aside: for *then should ye go* after vain *things,* which cannot profit nor deliver; for they *are* vain.

- 22. For the LORD
- will not forsake his
- people for his great
- name's sake:

because it hath pleased the LORD to make you his people.

- 23. Moreover as for me,
- God forbid that I should
- sin against the LORD
- in ceasing to pray for
- you: but I will teach you the

good and the right way:

- 24. Only fear the LORD,
- and serve him in truth with all

your heart: for consider how great *things* he hath done for you.

- 25. But if ye shall still
- do wickedly, ye shall
- be consumed, both
- ye and your king.

CHAPTER 13

- 1. Saul reigned one year;

and when he had

- reigned two years
- over Israel,
- 2. Saul chose him
- three thousand men of Israel;
- whereof two thousand
- were with Saul

in Michmash and in mount Beth-el,

- and a thousand were
- with Jonathan in Gibeah
- of Benjamin:

and the rest of the people he sent every man to his tent.

- 3. And Jonathan
- smote the garrison of the
- Philistines that *was*
- in Geba, and the
- Philistines heard *of it.*
- And Saul blew the
- trumpet throughout all the land,
- saying, Let the
- Hebrews hear.
- 4. And all
- Israel heard say
- that Saul had
- smitten a garrison of
- the Philistines, and *that*

Israel also was had in abomination with the Philistines. And the people

- were called together
- after Saul to Gilgal.
- 5. And the Philistines
- gathered themselves
- together to fight with
- Israel, thirty thousand chariots,

and six thousand horsemen, and people as the sand which is on the sea shore in multitude: and they came up, and pitched

- in Michmash,

eastward from Beth-aven.

- 6. When the men of
- Israel saw that
- they were in a strait,

(for the people were distressed,) then

- the people did hide
- themselves in caves, and

in thickets, and in rocks, and in high places, and in pits.

- 7. And *some of* the Hebrews

went over Jordan to the land of Gad and Gilead. As for

- Saul, he
- was yet

431

in Gilgal, and all the people followed him trembling.

8. And he tarried seven days, according to the set time that Samuel had appointed: but Samuel came not to Gilgal; and the people were scattered from him.

9. And Saul said, Bring hither a burnt offering to me, and peace offerings. And he offered the burnt offering.

10. And it came to pass, that as soon as he had made an end of offering the burnt offering, behold, Samuel came; and Saul went out to meet him, that he might salute him.

11. And Samuel said, What hast thou done? And Saul said, Because I saw that the people were scattered from me, and that thou camest not within the days appointed, and that the Philistines gathered themselves together at Michmash;

12. Therefore said I, The Philistines will come down now upon me to Gilgal, and I have not made supplication unto the LORD: I forced myself therefore, and offered a burnt offering.

13. And Samuel said to Saul, Thou hast done foolishly: thou hast not kept the commandment of the LORD thy God, which he commanded thee: for now would the LORD have established thy kingdom upon Israel for ever.

14. But now thy kingdom shall not continue: the LORD hath sought him a man after his own heart, and the LORD hath commanded him to be captain over his people, because thou hast not kept that which the LORD commanded thee.

15. And Samuel arose, and gat him up from Gilgal unto Gibeah of Benjamin. And Saul numbered the people that were present with him, about six hundred men.

16. And Saul, and Jonathan his son, and the people that were present with them, abode in Gibeah of Benjamin: but the Philistines encamped in Michmash.

17. And the spoilers came out of the camp of the Philistines in three companies: one company turned unto the way that leadeth to Ophrah, unto the land of Shual:

18. And another company turned the way to Beth-horon: and another company turned to the way of the border that looketh to the valley of Zeboim toward the wilderness.

19. Now there was no smith found throughout all the land of Israel: for the Philistines said, Lest the Hebrews make them swords or spears:

20. But all the Israelites went down to the Philistines, to sharpen every man his share, and his coulter, and his axe, and his mattock.

21. Yet they had a file for the mattocks, and for the coulters, and for the forks, and for the axes, and to sharpen the goads.

22. So it came to pass in the day of battle, that there was neither sword nor spear found in the hand of any of the people that were with Saul and Jonathan: but with Saul and with Jonathan his son was there found.

23. And the garrison of the Philistines went out to the passage of Michmash.

CHAPTER 14

■ 1. **Now** it came to
pass upon a day, that
■ **Jonathan the son of**
■ **Saul said unto the**
■ **young man that bare**
■ **his armour,** Come, and
■ **let us go over to**
■ **the Philistines'**
garrison, that *is* on the other side.
■ **But he told not his father.**
2. And Saul tarried in the uttermost
part of Gibeah under a pomegranate
tree which *is* in Migron: and the
people that *were* with him *were*
about six hundred men;
3. And Ahiah, the son of Ahitub,
I-chabod's brother, the son of
Phinehas, the son of Eli, the LORD'S
priest in Shiloh, wearing an ephod.
■ **And the people knew not**
■ **that Jonathan was gone.**
4. And between the passages, by
which Jonathan sought to go over
unto the Philistines' garrison, *there*
was a sharp rock on the one side,
and a sharp rock on the other side:
and the name of the one *was* Bozez,
and the name of the other Seneh.
5. The forefront of the one *was* situate
northward over against Michmash,
and the other southward over
against Gibeah.
■ 6. **And Jonathan**
■ **said** to the young man that
bare his armour, Come, and
■ **let us go over**
■ **unto the garrison**
of these uncircumcised: it may be
that the LORD will work for us:
■ **for there is no restraint**
■ **to the LORD to save by**
■ **many or by few.**
7. And his armour-bearer said
unto him, Do all that *is* in thine heart:
turn thee; behold, I *am* with thee
according to thy heart.
8. Then said Jonathan, Behold,
■ **we will pass over unto**
■ **these men, and** we will
■ **discover ourselves**
■ **unto them.**
■ 9. **If they say** thus unto us,

■ **Tarry until we come** to you;
■ **then we will stand** still
■ **in our place,**
and will not go up unto them.
■ 10. **But if they say** thus,
■ **Come up unto us;**
■ **then** we will go up: for
■ **the LORD hath delivered**
■ **them into our hand: and**
■ **this shall be a sign** unto us.
■ 11. **And both of them**
■ **discovered themselves**
■ **unto** the garrison of
■ **the Philistines:**
and the Philistines said, Behold, the
Hebrews come forth out of the holes
where they had hid themselves.
■ 12. **And the men**
of the garrison answered Jonathan
and his armour-bearer, and
■ **said, Come up to us,**
and we will shew you a thing.
■ **And Jonathan said** unto his
armour-bearer, Come up after me: for
■ **the LORD hath delivered**
■ **them** into the hand of Israel.
13. And Jonathan climbed up
upon his hands and upon his feet,
and his armour-bearer after him:
■ **and they fell**
■ **before Jonathan;**
and his armour-bearer slew after him.
■ 14. **And that first slaughter,**
which Jonathan and his
armour-bearer made,
■ **was about twenty men,**
within as it were an half acre of land,
which a yoke *of oxen might plow.*
■ 15. **And there was trembling**
in the host, in the field, and
■ **among all the people:**
the garrison, and the spoilers, they
also trembled, and the earth quaked:
so it was a very great trembling.
■ 16. **And the watchmen**
■ **of Saul** in Gibeah of Benjamin
■ **looked; and,** behold,
■ **the multitude melted**
■ **away, and they went**
■ **on beating** down
■ **one another.**
■ 17. **Then said Saul**
unto the people that *were* with

him, Number now, and

■ **see who is gone** from us.
■ **And when they had**
■ **numbered,** behold,
■ **Jonathan and his armour-**
■ **bearer were not there.**
■ 18. **And Saul said** unto Ahiah,
■ **Bring hither the ark of**
■ **God.** For the ark of God was at
that time with the children of Israel.
■ 19. **And** it came to pass,
■ **while Saul talked**
■ **unto the priest,** that
■ **the noise** that *was* in the host
■ **of the Philistines** went on and
■ **increased:** and Saul said unto
the priest, Withdraw thine hand.
■ 20. **And** Saul and all
■ **the people** that *were* with him
■ **assembled themselves,**
■ **and** they
■ **came to** the
■ **battle: and,** behold,
■ **every man's sword**
■ **was against his fellow,**
and there was a very
great discomfiture.
■ 21. **Moreover the**
■ **Hebrews that were**
■ **with the Philistines**
before that time, which went up
with them into the camp *from the*
country round about, even they also
■ **turned to be with the**
■ **Israelites** that *were* with
Saul and Jonathan.
■ 22. **Likewise all**
■ **the men** of Israel
■ **which** had
■ **hid themselves**
in mount Ephraim, *when* they
heard that the Philistines
fled, even they also
■ **followed hard after**
■ **them in the battle.**
■ 23. **So the LORD saved Israel**
■ **that day:** and the battle passed
over unto Beth-aven.
■ 24. **And the men** of Israel
■ **were distressed** that day:
■ **for Saul** had adjured the people,
■ **saying, Cursed be**
■ **the man that eateth** *any*

■ **food until evening,**
that I may be avenged
on mine enemies.
■ **So none** of the people
■ **tasted** *any*
■ **food.**
■ 25. **And** *all*
■ **they** of the land
■ **came to a wood; and there**
■ **was honey** upon the ground.
26. And when the people were
come into the wood, behold,
the honey dropped;
■ **but no man put his**
■ **hand to his mouth:**
■ **for the** people feared the
■ **oath.**
■ 27. **But Jonathan**
■ **heard not** when his
father charged the people with
■ **the oath: wherefore**
■ **he put** forth the end of
■ **the rod** that *was* in
his hand, and dipped it
■ **in an honeycomb,**
■ **and** put his hand
■ **to his mouth;** and his
eyes were enlightened.
■ 28. **Then** answered
■ **one of the people,** and
■ **said, Thy father** straitly
■ **charged the people**
with an oath, saying,
■ **Cursed be the man**
■ **that eateth** *any* food
■ **this day. And the**
■ **people were faint.**
■ 29. **Then said Jonathan,**
My father hath troubled the land:
■ **see,** I pray you,
■ **how mine eyes** have been
■ **enlightened, because**
■ **I tasted** a little of
■ **this honey.**
30. How much more,
■ **if** haply
■ **the people had eaten**
freely to day of the spoil of their
enemies which they found? for
■ **had there not been** now
■ **a much greater slaughter**
■ **among the Philistines?**
31. And they smote the Philistines

that day from Michmash to Aijalon: and the people were very faint.

32. **And the people** flew upon the spoil, and **took sheep, and** oxen, and **calves, and slew them** on the ground: **and** the people **did eat them with the blood.**

33. **Then** they told **Saul,** saying, Behold, the people sin against the LORD, in that they eat with the blood. And he **said, Ye have transgressed:** roll a great stone unto me this day.

34. And Saul said, **Disperse** yourselves **among the people, and say** unto them, **Bring me** hither every man **his ox, and** every man his **sheep, and slay them here, and eat; and sin not against the LORD in eating** with the **blood.** And all the people brought every man his ox with him that night, and slew *them* there.

35. **And Saul built an altar unto the LORD:** the same was the first altar that he built unto the LORD.

36. **And** Saul **said, Let us go** down **after the Philistines** by night, **and spoil them** until the morning light, **and** let us **not leave a man** of them. And they said, Do whatsoever seemeth good unto thee. **Then said the priest, Let us draw near** hither **unto God.**

37. **And Saul asked** counsel of God, Shall I go down after the Philistines? **wilt thou deliver them** into the hand of Israel? **But he answered him not** that day.

38. **And Saul said, Draw ye near** hither, all the chief of the people: and know **and see wherein this sin hath been** this day.

39. **For,** *as* the LORD liveth, which saveth Israel, **though it be in Jonathan my son, he shall** surely **die.** But *there was* not a man among all the people *that* answered him.

40. **Then said he unto all Israel, Be ye on one side, and I and Jonathan** my son **will be on the other side.** And the people said unto Saul, Do what seemeth good unto thee.

41. **Therefore Saul said unto the LORD** God of Israel, **Give a perfect lot. And Saul and Jonathan were taken: but the people escaped.**

42. **And Saul said, Cast lots between me and Jonathan** my son. **And Jonathan was taken.**

43. **Then Saul said** to Jonathan, **Tell me what thou hast done. And Jonathan told him,** and said, **I did but taste a little honey** with the end of the rod that *was* in mine hand, **and,** lo, **I must die.**

44. **And Saul answered,** God do so and more also: for **thou shalt surely die,** Jonathan.

45. **And the people** said unto Saul, **Shall Jonathan die, who** hath **wrought** this great **salvation in Israel? God forbid:** as the LORD liveth, there shall not one hair of his head fall to the ground; for he hath wrought with God this day. **So the people rescued Jonathan,** that he died not.

46. Then Saul went up from following the Philistines: and the Philistines went to their own place.

47. **So Saul took** the kingdom over **Israel, and fought against** all **his enemies** on every side, against Moab, and against the children of Ammon, and against Edom, and against the kings of Zobah, and against the Philistines: **and** whithersoever he turned himself, he **vexed them.**

48. And he gathered an host, and smote the Amalekites, and delivered Israel out of the hands of them that spoiled them.

49. Now the sons of Saul were Jonathan, and Ishui, and Melchi-shua: and the names of his two daughters *were these;* the name of the firstborn Merab, and the name of the younger Michal:

50. And the name of Saul's wife was Ahinoam, the daughter of Ahimaaz: and the name of the captain of his host *was* Abner, the son of Ner, Saul's uncle.

51. And Kish *was* the father of Saul; and Ner the father of Abner *was* the son of Abiel.

52. **And there was** sore **war against the Philistines all the days of Saul: and** when Saul saw **any strong man, or** any **valiant man, he took** him **unto him.**

CHAPTER 15

1. **Samuel also said unto Saul, The LORD sent me to anoint thee** *to be* **king** over his people, over Israel: **now** therefore **hearken** thou **unto** the voice of the words of **the LORD.**

2. Thus saith the LORD of hosts, **I remember that which Amalek did to Israel,** how he laid *wait* for him in the way, **when he came up from Egypt.**

3. **Now go and** smite Amalek, and utterly **destroy all that they have, and spare them not;** but slay both man and woman, infant and suckling, ox and sheep, camel and ass.

4. **And Saul gathered the people** together, and numbered them in Telaim, two hundred thousand footmen, and ten thousand men of Judah.

5. **And** Saul **came to a city of Amalek,** and laid wait in the valley.

6. **And** Saul **said unto the Kenites, Go,** depart, get you down **from among the Amalekites,** lest I destroy you with them: **for ye shewed kindness to** all the children of **Israel,** when they came up out of Egypt. So the Kenites departed from among the Amalekites.

7. **And Saul smote the Amalekites** from Havilah *until* thou comest to Shur, that is over against Egypt.

8. **And he took Agag the king** of the Amalekites **alive, and utterly destroyed all the people** with the edge of the sword.

9. **But** Saul and the people **spared Agag, and the best** of the **sheep,** and of the oxen, and of the fatlings, and the lambs, **and all that was good,** and would not utterly destroy them: but every thing *that was* vile and refuse, that they destroyed utterly.

10. **Then came the word of the LORD unto Samuel, saying,**

11. It repenteth me that I have set up **Saul** *to be* king: for he is **turned back from**

following me, and hath not performed my commandments. And it grieved Samuel; and he cried unto the LORD all night.

12. And when Samuel rose early to meet Saul in the morning, it was told Samuel, saying, Saul came to Carmel, and, behold, he set him up a place, and is gone about, and passed on, and gone down to Gilgal.

13. And Samuel came to Saul: and Saul said unto him, Blessed be thou of the LORD: I have performed the commandment of the LORD.

14. And Samuel said, What meaneth then this bleating of the sheep in mine ears, and the lowing of the oxen which I hear?

15. And Saul said, They have brought them from the Amalekites: for the people spared the best of the sheep and of the oxen, to sacrifice unto the LORD thy God; and the rest we have utterly destroyed.

16. Then Samuel said unto Saul, Stay, and I will tell thee what the LORD hath said to me this night. And he said unto him, Say on.

17. And Samuel said, When thou wast little in thine own sight, wast thou not made the head of the tribes of Israel, and the LORD anointed thee king over Israel?

18. And the LORD sent thee on a journey, and said, Go and utterly destroy the sinners the Amalekites, and fight against them until they be consumed.

19. Wherefore then didst thou not obey the voice of the LORD, but didst fly upon the spoil, and didst evil in the sight of the LORD?

20. And Saul said unto Samuel, Yea, I have obeyed the voice of the LORD, and have gone the way which the LORD sent me, and have brought Agag the king of Amalek, and have utterly destroyed the Amalekites.

21. But the people took of the spoil, sheep and oxen, the chief of the things which should have been utterly destroyed, to sacrifice unto the LORD thy God in Gilgal.

22. And Samuel said, Hath the LORD as great delight in burnt offerings and sacrifices, as in obeying the voice of the LORD? Behold, to obey is better than sacrifice, and to hearken than the fat of rams.

23. For rebellion is as the sin of witchcraft, and stubbornness is as iniquity and idolatry. Because thou hast rejected the word of the LORD, he hath also rejected thee from being king.

24. And Saul said unto Samuel, I have sinned: for I have transgressed the commandment of the LORD, and thy words: because I feared the people, and obeyed their voice.

25. Now therefore, I pray thee, pardon my sin, and turn again with me, that I may worship the LORD.

26. And Samuel said unto Saul, I will not return with thee: for thou hast rejected the word of the LORD, and the LORD hath rejected thee from being king over Israel.

27. And as Samuel turned about to go away, he laid hold upon the skirt of his mantle,

28. And Samuel said unto him, The LORD hath rent the kingdom of Israel from thee this day, and hath given it to a neighbour of thine, *that is* better than thou. 29. And also the Strength of Israel will not lie nor repent: for he *is* not a man, that he should repent. 30. Then he said, I have sinned: yet honour me now, I pray thee, before the elders of my people, and before Israel, and turn again with me, that I may worship the LORD thy God. 31. So Samuel turned again after Saul; and Saul worshipped the LORD. 32. Then said Samuel, Bring ye hither to me Agag the king of the Amalekites. And Agag came unto him delicately. And Agag said, Surely the bitterness of death is past. 33. And Samuel said, As the sword hath made women childless, so shall thy mother be childless among women. And Samuel hewed Agag in pieces before the LORD in Gilgal. 34. Then Samuel went to Ramah; and Saul went up to his house to Gibeah of Saul. 35. And Samuel came no more to see Saul until the day of his death: nevertheless Samuel mourned for Saul: and the LORD repented that he had made Saul king over Israel.

CHAPTER 16

1. And the LORD said unto Samuel, How long wilt thou mourn for Saul, seeing I have rejected him from reigning over Israel? fill thine horn with oil, and go, I will send thee to Jesse the Beth-lehemite: for I have provided me a king among his sons. 2. And Samuel said, How can I go? if Saul hear *it,* he will kill me. And the LORD said, Take an heifer with thee, and say, I am come to sacrifice to the LORD. 3. And call Jesse to the sacrifice, and I will shew thee what thou shalt do: and thou shalt anoint unto me *him* whom I name unto thee. 4. And Samuel did that which the LORD spake, and came to Beth-lehem. And the elders of the town trembled at his coming, and said, Comest thou peaceably? 5. And he said, Peaceably: I am come to sacrifice unto the LORD: sanctify yourselves, and come with me to the sacrifice. And he sanctified Jesse and his sons, and called them to the sacrifice. 6. And it came to pass, when they were come, that he looked on Eliab, and said, Surely the LORD's anointed *is* before him. 7. But the LORD said unto Samuel, Look not on his countenance, or on the height of his stature; because I have refused him: for *the LORD seeth* not as man seeth; for man looketh on the outward appearance, but the LORD looketh on the heart. 8. Then Jesse called Abinadab, and made him pass before Samuel. And he said, Neither hath the LORD chosen this. 9. Then Jesse made Shammah to pass by. And he said, Neither

hath the LORD chosen this.

10. Again, Jesse made **seven of his sons to pass before Samuel. And Samuel said** unto Jesse, **The LORD hath not chosen these.**

11. And Samuel said unto Jesse, **Are here all thy children? And he said, There remaineth** yet **the youngest,** and, behold, he keepeth the sheep. **And Samuel said** unto Jesse, Send and **fetch him:** for we will not sit down till he come hither.

12. **And he sent, and brought him in. Now** he was ruddy, and withal of a **beautiful** countenance, and goodly to look to. **And the LORD said, Arise, anoint him: for this is he.**

13. **Then Samuel took the** horn of **oil, and anointed him** in the midst of his brethren: **and the Spirit of the LORD came upon David** from that day forward. **So Samuel** rose up, and **went to Ramah.**

14. **But the Spirit of the LORD departed from Saul, and an evil spirit** from the LORD **troubled him.**

15. **And Saul's servants said** unto him, Behold now, an evil spirit from God troubleth thee.

16. **Let** our lord now command **thy servants,** which are before thee, to **seek out a man,** who is **a cunning player on an harp: and** it shall come to pass, **when the evil spirit** from God **is upon thee,** that **he shall play** with his hand, **and thou shalt be well.**

17. And Saul said unto his servants, Provide me now a man that can play well, and bring him to me.

18. **Then answered** one of **the servants,** and said, Behold, I have seen **a son of Jesse the** Beth-lehemite, that **is cunning in playing, and a** mighty **valiant man,** and a man **of war, and** prudent in matters, **and a comely person, and the LORD is with him.**

19. **Wherefore Saul sent** messengers **unto Jesse, and said, Send me David** thy son, which is with the sheep.

20. **And Jesse took** an ass laden with **bread, and** a bottle of **wine, and a kid, and sent them** by David his son **unto Saul.**

21. **And David came to Saul,** and stood before him: **and he loved him greatly; and he became his armourbearer.**

22. And Saul sent to Jesse, saying, Let David, I pray thee, stand before me; for he hath found favour in my sight.

23. **And** it came to pass, **when the evil spirit** from God **was upon Saul, that David took an harp, and played** with his hand: **so Saul was refreshed,** and was well, **and the evil spirit departed** from him.

CHAPTER 17

1. **Now the Philistines gathered together** their armies **to battle,** and were gathered together **at Shochoh,** which belongeth to Judah, and pitched between Shochoh and Azekah, in Ephes-dammim.

2. **And Saul and** the men of **Israel** were **gathered** together, and pitched

■ **by the valley of Elah,**
and set the battle in array
against the Philistines.
3. And the Philistines stood on a
mountain on the one side, and Israel
stood on amountain on the other side:
■ **and there was a valley**
■ **between them.**
■ 4. **And there went out**
■ **a champion** out
■ **of the camp of the**
■ **Philistines, named**
■ **Goliath,** of Gath,
■ **whose height was six**
■ **cubits and a span.**
5. And *he had* an helmet of brass
upon his head, and he *was* armed
with a coat of mail; and the weight
of the coat *was* five
thousand shekels of brass.
6. And *he had* greaves of brass
upon his legs, and a target of brass
between his shoulders.
7. And the staff of his spear *was*
like a weaver's beam; and his spear's
head *weighed* six hundred shekels
of iron: and one bearing a shield
went before him.
■ 8. **And he** stood and
■ **cried unto** the armies of
■ **Israel, and said** unto them,
Why are ye come out to set *your*
battle in array? *am* not I a Philistine,
and ye servants to Saul?
■ **choose** you
■ **a man** for you,
■ **and let him come** down
■ **to me.**
■ 9. **If he** be able to
fight with me, and to
■ **kill me, then will we be**
■ **your servants: but if I**
prevail against him, and
■ **kill him, then shall**
■ **ye** be our servants, and
■ **serve us.**
■ 10. **And the Philistine**
■ **said, I defy** the armies of
■ **Israel** this day;
■ **give me a man, that**
■ **we may fight together.**
■ 11. **When Saul and** all
■ **Israel heard those**

■ **words** of the Philistine,
■ **they were** dismayed, and greatly
■ **afraid.**
■ 12. **Now** David *was* the son
of that Ephrathite of Bethlehem-judah,
whose name *was*
■ **Jesse;** and he
■ **had eight sons:**
and the man went among men
for an old man in the days of Saul.
■ 13. **And the three eldest**
sons of Jesse went *and*
■ **followed Saul to the battle:**
and the names of his three sons that
went to the battle *were* Eliab the
firstborn, and next unto him
Abinadab, and the third Shammah.
■ 14. **And David** *was*
■ **the youngest:** and the
three eldest followed Saul.
15. But David went and
■ **returned from Saul**
■ **to feed his father's**
■ **sheep** at Beth-lehem.
16. And the Philistine drew
near morning and evening, and
presented himself forty days.
■ 17. **And Jesse said**
■ **unto David** his son,
■ **Take** now for thy
brethren an ephah of
■ **this** parched
■ **corn, and these** ten
■ **loaves,** and run
■ **to the camp** of thy brethren;
18. And carry these ten cheeses unto
the captain of *their* thousand,
■ **and look how thy brethren**
■ **fare,** and take their pledge.
19. Now Saul, and they, and all the
men of Israel, *were* in the valley of
Elah, fighting with the Philistines.
■ 20. **And David rose** up
■ **early** in the morning,
and left the sheep with a keeper,
and took, and went, as Jesse
had commanded him;
■ **and** he
■ **came to the trench, as the**
■ **host was going forth to** the
■ **fight,** and shouted for the battle.
21. For Israel and the Philistines
had put the battle in array,

army against army.

22. **And David** left his carriage in the hand of the keeper of the carriage, and **ran into the army,** and came **and saluted his brethren.**

23. **And as he talked with them,** behold, there came up the champion, the Philistine of Gath, **Goliath** by name, out of the armies of the Philistines, and **spake** according to **the same words: and David heard them.**

24. **And** all the men of **Israel,** when they saw the man, **fled from him,** and were sore afraid.

25. **And the men of Israel said,** Have ye seen this man that is come up? surely to defy Israel is he come up: and it shall be, *that* **the man who killeth him, the king will enrich** him with great riches, **and will give him his daughter, and make his father's house free in Israel.**

26. **And David spake** to the men that stood by him, saying, What shall be done to the man that killeth this Philistine, and taketh away the reproach from Israel? for **who is this** uncircumcised **Philistine, that he should defy the armies of the living God?**

27. And the people answered him after this manner, saying, So shall it be done to the man that killeth him.

28. **And** Eliab **his eldest brother heard** when he spake unto the men; and Eliab's anger was kindled against **David, and** he **said, Why camest thou** down hither? and with whom hast thou left those few sheep in the wilderness? **I know thy pride,** and the naughtiness of thine heart;

for thou art come down **that thou mightest see the battle.**

29. **And David said, What have I** now **done? Is there not a cause?**

30. And he turned from him toward another, and spake after the same manner: and the people answered him again after the former manner.

31. And when the words were heard which David spake, they rehearsed *them* before Saul: and he sent for him.

32. **And David said to Saul,** Let no man's heart fail because of him; **thy servant will** go and **fight** with **this Philistine.**

33. **And Saul said** to David, Thou art not able to go against this Philistine to fight with him: for **thou art but a youth, and he** **a man of war** from his youth.

34. **And David said** unto Saul, **Thy servant kept** his father's **sheep, and there came a lion, and a bear, and took a lamb** out of the flock:

35. **And I went out** after him, **and** smote him, and delivered *it* out of his mouth: and when he arose against me, I caught *him* by his beard, and smote him, and slew him.

36. Thy servant **slew both the lion and the bear: and this uncircumcised Philistine shall be as one of them, seeing he hath defied** the armies of the living **God.**

37. **David said moreover, The LORD** that delivered me out of the paw of the lion, and out of the paw of the bear, he **will deliver me** out of the hand of this Philistine. **And Saul said** unto David, **Go, and the LORD be with thee.**

38. **And Saul armed David**

441

with his armour, and he put an helmet of brass upon his head; also he armed him with a coat of mail. 39. And David girded his sword upon his armour, and he assayed to go; for he had not proved *it.* **And David said** unto Saul, **I cannot go with these; for I have not proved them. And David put them off him.** 40. **And he took his staff** in his hand, **and chose** him **five smooth stones out of the brook,** and put them in a shepherd's bag which he had, even in a scrip; **and his sling was in his hand:** and he drew near to the Philistine. 41. And the Philistine came on and drew near unto David; and the man that bare the shield *went* before him. 42. **And when the Philistine** looked about, and **saw David, he disdained him: for he was but a youth,** and ruddy, and of a fair countenance. 43. **And the Philistine said** unto David, **Am I a dog, that thou comest** to me **with staves?** And the Philistine cursed David by his gods. 44. And the Philistine said to David, **Come to me, and I will give thy flesh unto the fowls** of the air, **and to the beasts** of the field. 45. **Then said David** to the Philistine, **Thou comest** to me **with a sword, and** with a **spear, and** with a **shield: but I come** to thee **in the name of the LORD of hosts,** the God of the armies of Israel, **whom thou hast defied.** 46. **This day will the LORD deliver thee** into mine hand; **and I will** smite thee, and **take thine head from thee;**

and I will give the carcases of the host of the Philistines this day unto the fowls of the air, and to the wild beasts of the earth; **that all the earth may know that there is a God in Israel.** 47. And all this assembly shall know that the LORD saveth not with sword and spear: for the battle is the LORD's, and he will give you into our hands. 48. **And** it came to pass, when the Philistine arose, and came, and drew nigh to meet **David,** that David hasted, and **ran toward the army to meet the Philistine.** 49. **And** David put his hand in his bag, and **took** thence **a stone, and slang it, and smote the Philistine in his forehead,** that the stone sunk into his forehead; **and he fell upon his face to the earth.** 50. So David prevailed over the Philistine with a sling and with a stone, and smote the Philistine, and slew him; **but there was no sword in the hand of David.** 51. **Therefore David** ran, and **stood upon the Philistine, and took his sword,** and drew it out of the sheath thereof, and slew him, **and cut off his head** therewith. **And when the Philistines saw their champion was dead, they fled.** 52. **And** the men of **Israel and of Judah arose, and** shouted, and **pursued the Philistines,** until thou come to the valley, and to the gates of Ekron. And the wounded of the Philistines fell down by the way to Shaaraim, even unto Gath, and unto Ekron. 53. **And** the children of

Israel returned from chasing after the Philistines, and they spoiled their tents.

54. And David took the head of the Philistine, and brought it to Jerusalem; but he put his armour in his tent.

55. And when Saul saw David go forth against the Philistine, he said unto Abner, the captain of the host, Abner, whose son is this youth? And Abner said, *As* thy soul liveth, O king, I cannot tell.

56. And the king said, Enquire thou whose son the stripling is.

57. And as David returned from the slaughter of the Philistine, Abner took him, and brought him before Saul with the head of the Philistine in his hand.

58. And Saul said to him, Whose son art thou, *thou* young man? And David answered, I am the son of thy servant Jesse the Bethlehemite.

CHAPTER 18

1. And it came to pass, when he had made an end of speaking unto Saul, that the soul of Jonathan was knit with the soul of David, and Jonathan loved him as his own soul.

2. And Saul took him that day, and would let him go no more home to his father's house.

3. Then Jonathan and David made a covenant, because he loved him as his own soul.

4. And Jonathan stripped himself of the robe that was upon him, and gave it to David, and his garments, even to his sword, and to his bow, and to his girdle.

5. And David went out whithersoever Saul sent him, *and* behaved himself wisely: and Saul set him over the men of war, and he was accepted in the sight of all the people, and also in the sight of Saul's servants.

6. And it came to pass as they came, when David was returned from the slaughter of the Philistine, that the women came out of all cities of Israel, singing and dancing, to meet king Saul, with tabrets, with joy, and with instruments of music.

7. And the women answered one another as they played, and said, Saul hath slain his thousands, and David his ten thousands.

8. And Saul was very wroth, and the saying displeased him; and he said, They have ascribed unto David ten thousands, and to me they have ascribed *but* thousands: and *what* can he have more but the kingdom?

9. And Saul eyed David from that day and forward.

10. And it came to pass on the morrow, that the evil spirit from God came upon Saul, and he prophesied in the midst of the house: and David played with his hand, as at other times: and there was a javelin in Saul's hand.

11. And Saul cast the javelin; for he said, I will smite David even to the wall with it. And David avoided out of his presence twice.

12. And Saul was afraid of David,

because the LORD was with him, and was departed from Saul.

13. **Therefore Saul removed him** from him, **and made him his captain** over a thousand; **and he went** out and came in **before the people.**

14. **And David behaved** himself **wisely** in all his ways; **and the LORD was with him.**

15. **Wherefore** when **Saul** saw that he behaved himself very wisely, he **was afraid of him.**

16. **But all Israel and Judah loved David,** because he went out and came in before them.

17. **And Saul said to David,** Behold **my elder daughter Merab,** her **will I give thee** to wife: **only be thou valiant for me, and fight the LORD's battles.** For Saul said, Let not mine hand be upon him, but let the hand of the Philistines be upon him.

18. **And David said** unto Saul, **Who am I?** and what *is* my life, or my father's family in Israel, **that I should be son in law to the king?**

19. **But** it came to pass at the time **when Merab** Saul's daughter **should have been given to David,** that **she was given unto Adriel** the Meholathite **to wife.**

20. **And Michal Saul's daughter loved David:** and they told Saul, and the thing pleased him.

21. **And Saul said, I will give** him **her, that she may be a snare to him,** and that the hand of the Philistines may be against him. Wherefore Saul said to David, Thou shalt this day be my son in law in *the one of* the twain.

22. **And Saul commanded his servants,** *saying,* **Commune with David secretly, and say,** Behold, **the king hath delight in thee,** and all his servants love thee: now **therefore be the king's son in law.**

23. And Saul's servants spake those words in the ears of David. **And David said, Seemeth it** to you **a light thing to be a king's son in law, seeing that I am a poor man,** and lightly esteemed?

24. **And the servants** of Saul **told him,** saying, On this manner spake David.

25. **And Saul said,** Thus shall ye **say to David, The king desireth not any dowry, but an hundred foreskins of the Philistines,** to be avenged of the king's enemies. **But Saul thought to make David fall by** the hand of **the Philistines.**

26. **And** when his servants told David these words, **it pleased David** well **to be the king's son in law:** and the days were not expired.

27. **Wherefore David** arose and went, he **and his men,** and **slew** of the Philistines **two hundred men; and** David **brought their foreskins,** and they gave them in full tale **to the king,** that he might be the king's son in law. **And Saul gave him Michal** his daughter **to wife.**

28. **And Saul saw** and knew **that the LORD was with David, and that Michal** Saul's daughter **loved him.**

29. **And Saul was** yet the **more afraid of David; and** Saul

444

became David's enemy continually.

30. Then the princes of the Philistines went forth: and it came to pass, after they went forth, *that* David behaved himself more wisely than all the servants of Saul; so that his name was much set by.

CHAPTER 19

1. **And Saul spake to Jonathan** his son, **and** to all **his servants, that they should kill David.**

2. **But Jonathan** Saul's son **delighted** much **in David: and** Jonathan **told David, saying,** Saul my father seeketh to kill thee: now therefore, I pray thee, **take heed** to thyself until the morning, and abide in a secret *place,* **and hide thyself:**

3. **And I will** go out and stand beside my father in the field where thou *art,* and I will **commune with my father of thee;** and what I see, that I will tell thee.

4. **And Jonathan spake good of David** unto Saul his father, and said unto him, **Let not the king sin against** his servant, against **David; because he hath not sinned against thee,** and because his works *have been* to thee-ward very good:

5. **For he** did put his life in his hand, and **slew the Philistine, and the LORD wrought** a great **salvation for** all **Israel:** thou sawest *it,* and didst rejoice: **wherefore then wilt thou** sin against innocent blood, to **slay David without a cause?**

6. **And Saul hearkened unto** the voice of **Jonathan:** and Saul sware,

As the LORD liveth, he shall not be slain.

7. **And Jonathan** called David, and Jonathan shewed him all those things. And Jonathan **brought David to Saul, and he was in his presence, as in times past.**

8. **And there was war** again: **and David** went out, and **fought** with **the Philistines,** and slew them **with a great slaughter; and they fled** from him.

9. **And the evil spirit** from the LORD **was upon Saul, as he sat** in his house **with his javelin in his hand: and David played** with *his* hand.

10. **And Saul sought to smite David** even to the wall **with the javelin: but he** slipped away out of Saul's presence, and he smote the javelin into the wall: and David fled, and **escaped** that night.

11. **Saul also sent messengers unto David's house,** to watch him, and **to slay him** in the morning: **and Michal** David's wife **told him,** saying, If thou save not thy life to-night, to-morrow thou shalt be slain.

12. So Michal let David down through a window: **and he** went, and fled, and **escaped.**

13. **And Michal took an image, and laid it in the bed,** and put a pillow of goats' *hair* for his bolster, **and covered it with a cloth.**

14. **And** when Saul sent messengers to take David, **she said, He is sick.**

15. **And Saul sent** the messengers *again* to see David, **saying, Bring him up** to me **in the bed, that I**

■ may slay him.
■ 16. And when the
■ messengers were
■ come in, behold,
■ there was an image
■ in the bed, with a pillow
of goats' hair *for* his bolster.
■ 17. And Saul said unto
■ Michal, Why hast thou
■ deceived me so, and sent away
mine enemy, that he is escaped? And
Michal answered Saul, He said unto
me, Let me go; why should I kill thee?
■ 18. So David fled,
and escaped, and came
■ to Samuel to Ramah,
■ and told him all that
■ Saul had done to him.
■ And he and Samuel went and
■ dwelt in Naioth.
19. And it was told Saul, saying,
Behold, David *is* at Naioth in Ramah.
■ 20. And Saul sent
■ messengers to take David:
■ and when they saw
the company of
■ the prophets prophesying,
■ and Samuel standing *as*
appointed over them,
■ the Spirit of God was upon
■ the messengers of Saul,
■ and they also prophesied.
■ 21. And when it was told
■ Saul, he
■ sent other
■ messengers, and
they prophesied likewise.
And Saul sent messengers
■ again the third time, and
■ they prophesied also.
■ 22. Then went he also
to Ramah, and came to a great
well that *is* in Sechu: and he asked
and said, Where *are* Samuel and
David? And *one* said, Behold,
they be at Naioth in Ramah.
23. And he went thither
■ to Naioth in Ramah:
■ and the Spirit of God
■ was upon him also,
■ and he went on, and
■ prophesied, until he
came to Naioth in Ramah.

■ 24. And he stripped off his
■ clothes also, and prophesied
before Samuel in like manner,
■ and lay down
■ naked all that
■ day and all that
■ night. Wherefore
■ they say, Is Saul
■ also among
■ the prophets?

CHAPTER 20

■ 1. And David fled
from Naioth in Ramah,
■ and came and said before
■ Jonathan, What have I done?
what *is* mine iniquity? and
■ what is my sin before
■ thy father, that he
■ seeketh my life?
■ 2. And he said
unto him, God forbid;
■ thou shalt not die: behold,
■ my father will do
■ nothing either great or small,
■ but that he will shew it me:
and why should my father hide this
thing from me? it is not so.
■ 3. And David sware
moreover, and said,
■ Thy father certainly
■ knoweth that I have found
■ grace in thine eyes; and he
■ saith, Let not Jonathan
■ know this, lest he be grieved:
■ but truly as the LORD
■ liveth, and *as* thy soul liveth,
■ there is but a step
■ between me and death.
4. Then said Jonathan unto David,
Whatsoever thy soul desireth,
I will even do *it* for thee.
■ 5. And David said
unto Jonathan, Behold,
■ to-morrow *is* the new moon, and
■ I should not fail to
■ sit with the king at meat:
■ but let me go, that I may
■ hide myself
■ in the field unto
■ the third day at even.
■ 6. If thy father at all
■ miss me, then

446

say, David earnestly
asked leave of me
that he might run to
Beth-lehem his city:
for there is
a yearly sacrifice
there for all the family.
7. If he say thus,
It is well; thy servant shall
have peace: but if he bevery
wroth, then be sure that
evil is determined by him.
8. Therefore thou shalt
deal kindly with thy
servant; for thou hast brought thy
servant into a covenant of the LORD
with thee: notwithstanding,
if there be in me iniquity,
slay me thyself; for why
shouldest thou bring me to thy father?
9. And Jonathan said,
Far be it from thee: for
if I knew certainly that
evil were determined
by my father to come upon thee,
then would not I tell it thee?
10. Then said David to Jonathan,
Who shall tell me? or what if thy
father answer thee roughly?
11. And Jonathan said unto David,
Come, and let us go out into the field.
And they went out both of them
into the field.
12. And Jonathan said
unto David, O LORD God of Israel,
when I have sounded
my father about
tomorrow any time,
or the third day, and,
behold, if there be good toward
David, and I then send not
unto thee, and shew it thee;
13. The LORD do so
and much more to Jonathan: but if
it please my father to do
thee evil, then I will shew it
thee, and send thee away,
that thou mayest go in peace: and
the LORD be with thee, as he
hath been with my father.
14. And thou shalt
not only while yet I live
shew me the kindness

of the LORD, that I die not:
15. But also
thou shalt not
cut off thy kindness from
my house for ever: no, not
when the LORD hath cut
off the enemies of David
every one from the face of the earth.
16. So Jonathan made a
covenant with the house of
David, saying, Let the LORD
even require it at the hand of
David's enemies.
17. And Jonathan caused
David to swear again, because
he loved him: for he loved him
as he loved his own soul.
18. Then Jonathan
said to David,
To-morrow is the new moon: and
thou shalt be missed,
because thy seat
will be empty.
19. And when thou hast
stayed three days,
then thou shalt
go down
quickly, and come
to the place where
thou didst hide
thyself when the business
was in hand, and shalt remain
by the stone Ezel.
20. And I will shoot three
arrows on the side thereof, as
though I shot at a mark.
21. And, behold,
I will send a lad, saying,
Go, find out the arrows.
If I expressly
say unto the lad, Behold,
the arrows are on
this side of thee, take them;
then come thou:
for there is peace to thee,
and no hurt; as the LORD liveth.
22. But if I say thus unto
the young man, Behold,
the arrows are beyond
thee; go thy way: for
the LORD hath sent
thee away.
23. And as touching the

matter which thou and I have spoken of, behold,

the LORD be between thee and me for ever.

24. **So David hid** himself **in the field: and when the new moon was come, the king sat** him **down to eat** meat.

25. And the king sat upon his seat, as at other times, *even* upon a seat by the wall: and Jonathan arose, and Abner sat by Saul's side,

and David's place was empty.

26. **Nevertheless Saul** spake not any thing that day: for he **thought, Something hath befallen him,** he *is* not clean; surely he *is* not clean.

27. **And** it came to pass **on the** morrow, *which was* the **second day** of the month, that **David's place was empty: and Saul said** unto Jonathan his son, **Wherefore cometh not the son of Jesse to meat,** neither yesterday, nor to-day?

28. **And Jonathan answered** Saul, **David** earnestly **asked leave** of me **to go to Beth-lehem:**

29. And he said, Let me go, I pray thee; **for** our family hath **a sacrifice** in the city; and my brother,he hath commanded me *to be there:* and now, if I have found favour in thine eyes, let me get away, I pray thee, and see my brethren. Therefore he cometh not unto the king's table.

30. **Then Saul's anger was kindled against Jonathan, and he said** unto him, **Thou son of the perverse rebellious woman,** do not **I know that thou hast chosen the son of Jesse to thine own confusion,** and unto the confusion of thy mother's nakedness?

31. **For as long as the son of Jesse liveth** upon the ground, **thou shalt not be established, nor thy kingdom.** Wherefore **now** send and **fetch him unto me, for he shall surely die.**

32. **And Jonathan answered** Saul his father, and said unto him, **Wherefore shall he be slain? what hath he done?**

33. **And Saul cast a javelin at him** to smite him: whereby Jonathan knew that it was determined of his father to slay David.

34. **So Jonathan arose** from the table **in** fierce **anger, and** did eat no meat the second day of the month: for he **was grieved for David,** because his father had done him shame.

35. **And** it came to pass **in the morning,** that **Jonathan went out into the field** at the time appointed with David, **and a** little **lad with him.**

36. **And he said unto his lad, Run, find** out now **the arrows which I shoot.** *And* as the lad ran, he shot an arrow beyond him.

37. **And when the lad was come to** the place of **the arrow** which Jonathan had shot, **Jonathan cried** after the lad, and said, **Is not the arrow beyond thee?**

38. **And** Jonathan cried after **the** lad, Make speed, haste, stay not. And Jonathan's **lad gathered up the arrows, and came to his master.**

39. **But** the lad knew not any thing: **only Jonathan and**

David knew the matter.
40. **And Jonathan gave
his artillery unto his
lad, and said** unto him,
Go, carry *them*
to the city.
41. **And** as soon as
the lad was gone,
**David arose out of
a place** toward the south,
and fell on his face
to the ground, and
bowed himself
**three times: and they
kissed** one another,
and wept one with another,
until David exceeded.
42. **And Jonathan
said** to David,
Go in peace, forasmuch as
we have sworn both of us
in the name of the LORD,
**saying, The LORD be
between me and thee,** and
between my seed and thy seed
for ever. And he arose and
departed: and Jonathan
went into the city.

CHAPTER 21

1. **Then came David to** Nob to
**Ahimelech the priest: and
Ahimelech was afraid**
at the meeting of David,
and said unto him,
Why art thou alone,
and no man with thee?
2. **And David said**
unto Ahimelech the priest,
**The king hath commanded
me a business, and** hath
said unto me,
Let no man know
any thing of the business
**whereabout I send
thee, and what I have
commanded thee:**
and I have appointed *my* servants
to such and such a place.
3. **Now** therefore what
is under thine hand?
**give me five loaves
of bread** in mine hand,

or what there is present.
4. **And the priest
answered** David, and said,
**There is no common
bread** under mine hand,
**but there is hallowed
bread; if the young
men have kept
themselves** at least
from women.
5. **And David answered** the
priest, and said unto him, Of a truth
**women have been
kept from us** about
these three days,
since I came out,
**and the vessels of the
young men are holy,**
and *the bread is* in a manner
common, yea, though it were
sanctified this day in the vessel.
6. **So the priest gave
him** hallowed *bread:* for there
was no bread there but the
shewbread, that was
**taken from before
the LORD, to put hot
bread** in the day
when it was taken away.
7. **Now a** certain
**man of the servants of
Saul was there** that day,
**detained before the
LORD;** and his name *was* Doeg,
an Edomite, the chiefest of the
herdmen that *belonged* to Saul.
8. **And David said**
unto Ahimelech, And
is there not here under thine hand
**spear or sword? for I
have neither** brought my
sword nor my weapons with me,
**because the king's business
required haste.**
9. **And the priest said,
The sword of Goliath** the
Philistine, whom thou slewest
in the valley of Elah, behold, it
is here wrapped in a cloth behind
the ephod: if thou wilt take that,
**take it: for there is no
other** save that here.
And David said, There is

■ none like that; give it me.
■ 10. **And David** arose and
■ **fled** that day
■ **for fear of Saul, and**
■ **went to** Achish the king of
■ **Gath.**
■ 11. **And the servants**
■ **of Achish said** unto him,
■ **Is not this David**
■ **the king** of the land?
■ **did they not sing** one to
another of him in dances, saying,
■ **Saul hath slain his**
■ **thousands, and David** his
■ **ten thousands?**
■ 12. **And David** laid up
these words in his heart, and
■ **was** sore
■ **afraid of Achish**
■ **the king** of Gath.
■ 13. **And he changed his**
■ **behaviour before them,**
■ **and feigned himself**
■ **mad** in their hands,
■ **and scrabbled on**
■ **the doors** of the gate,
■ **and let his spittle fall**
■ **down upon his beard.**
■ 14. **Then said Achish**
unto his servants, Lo, ye see
■ **the man is mad:** wherefore *then*
have ye brought him to me?
15. Have I need of mad men, that ye
have brought this *fellow* to play the
mad man in my presence?
■ **shall this fellow come**
■ **into my house?**

CHAPTER 22

■ 1. **David therefore**
departed thence, and
■ **escaped to the cave**
■ **Adullam: and**
when his brethren and
■ **all his father's**
■ **house** heard *it*, they
■ **went** down thither
■ **to him.**
■ 2. **And every one** *that was*
■ **in distress, and**
every one that *was*
■ **in debt, and** every one *that was*
■ **discontented,**

■ **gathered** themselves
■ **unto him; and he became**
■ **a captain over them:**
■ **and there were** with him
■ **about four hundred men.**
■ 3. **And David went** thence
■ **to** Mizpeh of
■ **Moab: and** he
■ **said unto the king** of Moab,
■ **Let my father and** my
■ **mother,** I pray thee,
■ **come** forth,
■ **and be with you, till I know**
■ **what God will do for me.**
4. And he brought them before the
king of Moab: and they dwelt with him
all the while that David was in the hold.
■ 5. **And the prophet Gad**
■ **said unto David,**
Abide not in the hold;
■ **depart, and get** thee
■ **into the land of Judah.**
■ **Then David** departed, and
■ **came into the forest**
■ **of Hareth.**
■ 6. **When Saul heard that**
■ **David was discovered,**
and the men that *were* with him,
(now Saul abode in Gibeah under
a tree in Ramah, having his spear
in his hand, and all his servants
were standing about him;)
■ 7. **Then Saul said** unto his
servants that stood about him,
Hear now, ye Benjamites;
■ **will the son of**
■ **Jesse give** every one of
■ **you fields and vineyards,**
■ **and make you** all
■ **captains** of thousands,
and captains of hundreds;
8. That all of
■ **you have conspired**
■ **against me, and** *there*
is none that sheweth me that
■ **my son hath made a**
■ **league with the son**
■ **of Jesse, and there**
■ **is none** of you
■ **that is sorry for me,**
or sheweth unto me that my son hath
stirred up my servant against me, to
lie in wait, as at this day?

450

9. **Then answered Doeg** the Edomite, which was set over the servants of Saul,

and said, I saw the son of Jesse coming to Nob, **to Ahimelech** the son of Ahitub. 10. **And he inquired of the LORD for him, and gave him victuals, and** gave him **the sword of Goliath** the Philistine. 11. **Then the king sent to call Ahimelech** the priest, the son of Ahitub, **and all** his father's house, **the priests** that *were* **in Nob: and they came** all of them **to the king.** 12. And Saul said, Hear now, thou son of Ahitub. And he answered, Here I *am,* my lord. 13. **And Saul said** unto him, **Why have ye conspired against me, thou and the son of Jesse,** in that **thou hast given him bread, and a sword, and** hast **inquired of God for him, that he should rise against me,** to lie in wait, as at this day? 14. **Then Ahimelech answered** the king, and said, And **who is so faithful among all thy servants as David,** which is the king's son in law, and goeth at thy bidding, and is honourable in thine house? 15. Did I then begin to inquire of God for him? be it far from me: **let not the king impute any thing unto his servant,** *nor* to all the house of my father: **for thy servant knew nothing of all this,** less or more. 16. **And the king said, Thou shalt surely die, Ahimelech,** thou, **and all thy father's house.** 17. **And the king said unto the footmen** that stood about him, Turn, and **slay the priests** of the LORD:

because their hand also *is* with David, and because they knew when he fled, and did not shew it to me. **But the servants** of the king **would not put forth their hand** to fall **upon the priests of the LORD.** 18. **And the king said to Doeg,** Turn thou, and **fall upon the priests.** And Doeg the Edomite turned, **and he** fell upon the priests, and **slew** on that day **fourscore and five persons** that did wear a linen ephod. 19. **And Nob, the city** of the priests, **smote he with** the edge of **the sword,** both men and women, children and sucklings, and oxen, and asses, and sheep, with the edge of the sword. 20. **And one of the sons of Ahimelech** the son of Ahitub, named Abiathar, **escaped, and fled after David.** 21. **And Abiathar shewed David that Saul had slain the LORD's priests.** 22. **And David said** unto Abiathar, **I knew** *it* **that** day, when **Doeg** the Edomite *was* there, that he **would** surely **tell Saul: I have occasioned the death** of all the persons **of thy father's house.** 23. **Abide** thou **with me,** fear not: **for** he that seeketh my life seeketh thy life: but **with me thou shalt be in safeguard.**

CHAPTER 23

1. **Then they told David, saying,** Behold, **the Philistines fight against Keilah,** and they rob the

threshingfloors.

2. **Therefore David inquired of the LORD,** saying, **Shall I** go and **smite these Philistines? And the LORD said** unto David, **Go,** and smite the Philistines, **and save Keilah.**

3. **And David's men said** unto him, Behold, **we be afraid here in Judah: how much more** then **if we come** to Keilah **against** the armies of **the Philistines?**

4. **Then David inquired of the LORD yet again. And the LORD** answered him and **said, Arise, go** down to Keilah; for **I will deliver the Philistines** into thine hand.

5. **So David and his men went** to Keilah, **and fought** with **the Philistines,** and brought away their cattle, **and smote them with a great slaughter.** So David saved the inhabitants of Keilah.

6. **And** it came to pass, **when Abiathar** the son of Ahimelech **fled to David** to Keilah, *that* **he came** down **with an ephod** in his hand.

7. **And it was told Saul that David was come to Keilah. And Saul said, God hath delivered him into mine hand; for he is shut in,** by entering into a town that hath gates and bars.

8. **And Saul called all the people** together **to war,** to go down to Keilah, **to besiege David and his men.**

9. **And David** knew that Saul secretly practised mischief against him; and he **said to Abiathar** the priest, **Bring** hither **the ephod.**

10. **Then said David, O LORD God of Israel, thy servant hath** certainly **heard that Saul seeketh** to come to Keilah, **to destroy the city for my sake.**

11. **Will the men of Keilah deliver me up** into his hand? **will Saul come down, as thy servant hath heard?** O LORD God of Israel, I beseech thee, tell thy servant. **And the LORD said, He will come down.**

12. Then said David, Will the men of Keilah deliver me **and** my men into the hand of Saul? And the LORD said, **They will deliver thee up.**

13. **Then David and his men,** *which were* about six hundred, arose and **departed out of Keilah,** and went whithersoever they could go. **And it was told Saul that David** was **escaped** from Keilah; **and he forbare to go forth.**

14. **And David abode** in the wilderness in strong holds, and remained in a mountain **in the wilderness of Ziph. And Saul sought him every day, but God delivered him** not into his hand.

15. **And David saw that Saul was come out to seek his life:** and David *was* in the wilderness of Ziph in a wood.

16. **And Jonathan** Saul's son arose, and **went to David into the wood,** and strengthened his hand in God.

17. **And** he **said** unto him, **Fear not:** for the hand of Saul **my father shall not find thee; and thou shalt be king over Israel, and I** shall be

452

■ **next unto thee;** and that also Saul my father knoweth.

■ 18. **And they** two **made a covenant before the LORD:** and David abode in the wood, and Jonathan went to his house.

■ 19. **Then came up the Ziphites to Saul** to Gibeah, **saying, Doth not David hide himself with us in** strong holds in **the wood,** in the hill of Hachilah, which *is* on the south of Jeshimon?

■ 20. **Now** therefore, O king, **come down** according to all the desire of thy soul to come down; **and our part shall be to deliver him** into the king's hand.

■ 21. **And Saul said,** Blessed *be* ye of the LORD; for ye have compassion on me.

■ 22. **Go,** I pray you, prepare yet, and know **and see** his place where his haunt is, *and* who hath seen him there: for it is told me *that* he dealeth very subtilly.

23. See therefore, and take knowledge of all the lurking places **where he hideth** himself, **and come** ye again **to me** with the certainty, **and I will go with you: and** it shall come to pass, if he be in the land, that I will **search him out** throughout all the thousands of Judah.

■ 24. **And they** arose, and **went to Ziph** before Saul: **but David and his men were in the wilderness of Maon,** in the plain on the south of Jeshimon.

25. Saul also and his men went to seek *him*. And they told David; wherefore he came down into a rock, and abode in the wilderness of Maon. **And when Saul heard that, he pursued after David** in the wilderness of Maon.

■ 26. **And Saul went on this side of the mountain, and David** and his men

■ **on that side** of the mountain: and David made haste to get away for fear of Saul; **for Saul** and his men **compassed David and his men** round about **to take them.**

■ 27. **But there came a messenger** unto Saul, **saying,** Haste thee, and **come; for the Philistines have invaded the land.**

■ 28. **Wherefore Saul returned** from pursuing after David, **and went against the Philistines:** therefore they called that place Sela-hammahlekoth.

■ 29. **And David** went up from thence, and **dwelt in strong holds at En-gedi.**

CHAPTER 24

■ 1. **And** it came to pass, when **Saul** was **returned from following the Philistines,** that it was told him, saying, Behold, David is in the wilderness of En-gedi.

■ 2. **Then Saul took three thousand** chosen **men** out of all Israel, **and went to seek David and his men** upon the rocks of the wild goats.

■ 3. **And he came to the sheepcotes** by the way, where *was* a cave; **and** Saul **went in to cover his feet: and David and his men remained in the sides of the cave.**

■ 4. **And the men** of David **said** unto him, Behold the day of which **the LORD said unto thee,** Behold, **I will deliver thine enemy into thine hand,** that thou mayest do to him as it shall seem good unto thee. **Then David arose,**

and cut off the skirt
of Saul's robe privily.
5. **And** it came to pass
afterward, that
David's heart smote him,
because he had cut off Saul's skirt.
6. **And he said** unto his men,
**The LORD forbid that I
should do this** thing
unto my master,
the LORD's anointed, to stretch
forth mine hand against him, seeing
he *is* the anointed of the LORD.
7. **So David stayed his
servants** with these words,
**and suffered them not
to rise against Saul.
But Saul rose** up out of the cave,
and went on his way.
8. **David also**
rose afterward, and
**went out of the cave,
and cried after Saul,** saying,
My lord the king.
And when Saul looked behind him,
David stooped with his face to
the earth, and bowed himself.
9. And David said to Saul, Wherefore
hearest thou men's words, saying,
Behold, David seeketh thy hurt?
10. Behold,
this day thine eyes
have seen how that
**the LORD had
delivered thee** to-day
**into mine hand in the
cave: and some bade
me kill thee: but**
mine eye spared thee; and I said,
**I will not put forth mine
hand against** my lord; for he *is*
the LORD's anointed.
11. Moreover, my father,
see, yea, see the skirt of thy
robe in my hand: for in that
**I cut off the skirt of thy
robe, and killed thee
not,** know thou and see that
**there is neither evil
nor transgression in
mine hand,** and I have not
sinned against thee;
yet thou huntest my

soul to take it.
12. The LORD judge between me
and thee, and the LORD avenge
me of thee: but mine hand shall
not be upon thee.
13. **As saith the
proverb** of the ancients,
**Wickedness proceedeth
from the wicked:**
but mine hand shall not be upon thee.
14. **After whom** is the king of
Israel come out? after whom
**dost thou pursue? after
a dead dog, after a flea.**
15. **The LORD therefore**
be judge, and judge between
me and thee, and see, and
**plead my cause,
and deliver me out
of thine hand.**
16. **And** it came to pass, when
David had made an end of speaking
these words unto Saul, that
**Saul said, Is this
thy voice,** my son
David? And Saul
lifted up his voice, and
wept.
17. **And he said** to David,
**Thou art more righteous
than I:** for thou hast rewarded
me good, whereas I have
rewarded thee evil.
18. **And** thou hast shewed
this day how that thou
**hast dealt well with
me:** forasmuch as
when the LORD had
delivered me into thine hand,
thou killedst me not.
19. For if a man find his enemy,
will he let him go well away?
**wherefore the LORD
reward thee good** for that
thou hast done unto me this day.
20. **And now,** behold,
I know well
that thou shalt surely
be king, and that the kingdom of
**Israel shall be
established in thine hand.**
21. **Swear** now therefore unto me
by the LORD, that thou wilt

■ **not cut off my seed** after me,
■ **and** that thou
■ **wilt not destroy my name**
out of my father's house.
■ 22. **And David**
■ **sware** unto Saul.
■ **And Saul went home;**
but David and his men gat
them up unto the hold.

CHAPTER 25

■ 1. **And Samuel died;**
■ **and all the Israelites**
were gathered together, and
■ **lamented him, and**
■ **buried him** in his house
■ **at Ramah. And**
■ **David** arose, and
■ **went** down
■ **to the wilderness of Paran.**
■ 2. **And there was**
■ **a man in Maon,**
whose possessions *were* in Carmel;
■ **and the man was very**
■ **great,** and he had three thousand
sheep, and a thousand goats: and he
was shearing his sheep in Carmel.
■ 3.**Now the name of the man**
■ **was Nabal; and** the name of
■ **his wife Abigail: and she**
■ **was a woman of good**
■ **understanding, and** of a
■ **beautiful** countenance:
■ **but the man was** churlish and
■ **evil** in his doings; and he *was* of the
house of Caleb.
■ 4. **And**
David heard in the wilderness that
■ **Nabal did shear his sheep.**
■ 5. **And David sent** out
■ **ten young men,** and David
said unto the young men, Get
you up to Carmel, and go
■ **to Nabal,** and greet
him in my name:
■ 6. **And thus** shall ye
■ **say to him** that liveth *in prosperity,*
■ **Peace** *be* both
■ **to thee, and** peace *be* to
■ **thine house,**
and peace *be* unto all that thou hast.
■ 7. And now I have heard that thou
hast shearers: now

■ **thy shepherds** which
■ **were with us, we hurt**
■ **them not, neither was there**
■ **ought missing** unto them, all the
■ **while they were in Carmel.**
8. Ask thy young men, and
they will shew thee.
■ **Wherefore** let the young men
find favour in thine eyes: for we
come in a good day:
■ **give,** I pray thee,
■ **whatsoever cometh**
■ **to thine hand unto thy**
■ **servants,** and to thy son David.
■ 9. **And** when David's
young men came,
■ **they spake to**
■ **Nabal** according to all
■ **those words in the name**
■ **of David,** and ceased.
■ 10. **And Nabal answered**
David's servants, and said,
■ **Who is David?** and
who *is* the son of Jesse?
■ **there be many**
■ **servants** now a days
■ **that break away** every man
■ **from his master.**
■ 11. **Shall I then take**
■ **my bread, and** my
■ **water,** and my flesh that I
have killed for my shearers,
■ **and give it unto men,**
whom I know not whence they *be?*
■ 12. **So David's young men**
turned their way, and went again, and
■ **came and told**
■ **him** all those sayings.
■ 13. **And David**
■ **said** unto his men,
■ **Gird** ye
■ **on every man his**
■ **sword.** And they girded on
every man his sword; and David
also girded on his sword:
■ **and there went** up
■ **after David about four**
■ **hundred men;** and two
hundred abode by the stuff.
■ 14. **But one of the**
■ **young men told**
■ **Abigail,** Nabal's wife,
■ **saying,** Behold,

455

David sent messengers out of the wilderness to salute our master; and he railed on them. 15. But the men *were* very good unto us, and we were not hurt, neither missed we any thing, as long as we were conversant with them, when we were in the fields: 16. They were a wall unto us both by night and day, all the while we were with them keeping the sheep. 17. Now therefore know and consider what thou wilt do; for evil is determined against our master, and against all his household: for he *is* such a son of Belial, that *a man* cannot speak to him. 18. Then Abigail made haste, and took two hundred loaves, and two bottles of wine, and five sheep ready dressed, and five measures of parched corn, and an hundred clusters of raisins, and two hundred cakes of figs, and laid them on asses. 19. And she said unto her servants, Go on before me; behold, I come after you. But she told not her husband Nabal. 20. And it was so, *as* she rode on the ass, that she came down by the covert on the hill, and, behold, David and his men came down against her; and she met them. 21. Now David had said, Surely in vain have I kept all that this *fellow* hath in the wilderness, so that nothing was missed of all that pertained unto him: and he hath requited me evil for good. 22. So andmore also do God unto the enemies of David, if I leave of all that *pertain* to him by the morning light any that pisseth against the wall. 23. And when Abigail saw David, she hasted, and lighted off the ass, and fell before David on her face, and bowed herself to the ground, 24. And fell at his feet, and said, Upon me, my lord, *upon* me *let* this iniquity *be*: and let thine handmaid, I pray thee, speak in thine audience, and hear the words of thine handmaid. 25. Let not my lord, I pray thee, regard this man of Belial, *even* Nabal: for as his name *is,* so *is* he; Nabal *is* his name, and folly *is* with him: but I thine handmaid saw not the young men of my lord, whom thou didst send. 26. Now therefore, my lord, *as* the LORD liveth, and *as* thy soul liveth, seeing the LORD hath withholden thee from coming to shed blood, and from avenging thyself with thine own hand, now let thine enemies, and they that seek evil to my lord, be as Nabal. 27. And now this blessing which thine handmaid hath brought unto my lord, let it even be given unto the young men that follow my lord. 28. I pray thee, forgive the trespass of thine handmaid: for the LORD will certainly make my lord a sure house; because my lord fighteth the battles of the LORD, and evil hath not been found in thee *all* thy days. 29. Yet a man is

risen to pursue thee, and **to seek thy soul: but the soul of my lord shall be bound in** the bundle of **life** with the LORD thy God; **and the souls of thine enemies,** them **shall he sling out,** *as out* of the middle of a sling.

30. **And** it shall come to pass, **when the LORD shall have done** to my lord according to **all the good** that he hath **spoken concerning thee, and** shall have **appointed thee ruler over Israel;**

31. That this shall be no grief unto thee, nor offence of heart unto my lord, either that thou hast shed blood causeless, or that my lord hath avenged himself: but when the LORD shall have dealt well with my lord, **then remember thine handmaid.**

32. **And David said** to Abigail, **Blessed be the LORD** God of Israel, **which sent thee** this day to meet me:

33. **And** blessed *be* thy advice, and blessed *be* thou, which hast **kept me** this day **from coming to shed blood, and** from **avenging myself** with mine own hand.

34. **For in** very **deed,** *as* **the LORD** God of Israel liveth, which **hath kept me** back **from hurting thee, except thou hadst** hasted and **come** to meet me, surely **there had not been left unto Nabal** by the morning light **any** that pisseth against the wall.

35. **So David received** of her hand **that which she had brought** him, **and said** unto her,

Go up **in peace** to thine house; see, I have hearkened to thy voice, and have accepted thy person.

36. **And** Abigail came to **Nabal;** and, behold, he **held a feast in his house,** like the feast of a king; **and** Nabal's heart *w as* merry within him, for **he was very drunken: wherefore she told him nothing,** less or more, until the morning light.

37. **But** it came to pass **in the morning, when the wine was gone out of Nabal, and his wife had told him** these things, that **his heart died** within him, **and he became as a stone.**

38. **And** it came to pass about **ten days after,** that **the LORD smote Nabal, that he died.**

39. **And when David heard** that Nabal was dead, **he said, Blessed be the LORD, that hath** pleaded the cause of my reproach from the hand of Nabal, and hath **kept his servant from evil:** for the LORD hath returned the wickedness of Nabal upon his own head. **And David** sent and **communed with Abigail, to take her** to him **to wife.**

40. And when the servants of David were come to Abigail to Carmel, they spake unto her, saying, David sent us unto thee, to take thee to him to wife.

41. **And she** arose, and **bowed** herself on *her* face to the earth, **and said,** Behold, **let thine handmaid be a servant to** wash the feet of **the servants of my lord.**

42. **And Abigail hasted,** and arose **and rode** upon an ass,

■ **with five damsels** of hers
■ **that went after her;** and she
went after the messengers of David,
■ **and became his wife.**
■ 43. **David also took**
■ **Ahinoam** of Jezreel;
■ **and they were** also
■ **both** of them
■ **his wives.**
■ 44. **But Saul had given**
■ **Michal** his daughter,
■ **David's wife, to**
■ **Phalti** the son of Laish,
■ **which was**
■ **of Gallim.**

CHAPTER 26

■ 1. **And the Ziphites**
■ **came** unto Saul to Gibeah,
■ **saying, Doth not David**
■ **hide himself in** the hill of
■ **Hachilah,** *which is*
before Jeshimon?
■ 2. **Then Saul** arose, and
■ **went** down
■ **to** the wilderness of
■ **Ziph, having three**
■ **thousand** chosen
■ **men** of Israel with him,
■ **to seek David**
in the wilderness of Ziph.
3. And Saul pitched in the
hill of Hachilah, which *is*
before Jeshimon, by the way.
■ **But David** abode in the
wilderness, and he
■ **saw that Saul came**
■ **after him** into the wilderness.
4. David therefore sent out spies,
■ **and understood** that
■ **Saul** was come
■ **in very deed.**
5. **And David** arose, and
■ **came to the place**
■ **where** Saul had pitched:
and David beheld the place where
■ **Saul lay, and Abner**
the son of Ner, the captain of his host:
■ **and Saul lay in the trench,**
■ **and the people** pitched
■ **round about him.**
6. Then answered David and said to
Ahimelech the Hittite, and to Abishai

the son of Zeruiah, brother to Joab,
saying, Who will go down with me to
Saul to the camp? And Abishai said, I
will go down with thee.
■ 7. **So David and**
■ **Abishai came** to the people
■ **by night: and,** behold,
■ **Saul lay sleeping**
within the trench,
■ **and his spear**
stuck in the ground
■ **at his bolster:** but Abner and
the people lay round about him.
■ 8. **Then said Abishai** to David,
■ **God hath delivered thine**
■ **enemy into thine hand**
this day: now therefore
■ **let me smite him,** I pray
thee, with the spear even to the
earth at once, and I will not *smite*
him the second time.
■ 9. **And David said** to Abishai,
■ **Destroy him not: for who**
■ **can stretch forth his**
■ **hand against the**
■ **LORD's anointed,**
■ **and be guiltless?**
10. David said furthermore,
As the LORD liveth,
■ **the LORD shall smite him;**
or his day shall come to die; or he
shall descend into battle, and perish.
11. The LORD forbid that I
should stretch forth mine hand
against the LORD's anointed:
■ **but,** I pray thee,
■ **take** thou now
■ **the spear** that *is* at his bolster,
■ **and the cruse of**
■ **water, and let us go.**
12. **So** David took the spear
and the cruse of water from
Saul's bolster; and
■ **they gat them away, and**
■ **no man saw it,** nor knew *it,* neither
awaked for they were all asleep;
■ **because a deep sleep**
■ **from the LORD was** fallen
■ **upon them.**
13. **Then David** went
over to the other side, and
■ **stood on** the top of
■ **an hill afar off;**

a great space *being* between them:

14. **And** David **cried to the people,** and to Abner the son of Ner, saying, Answerest thou not, Abner? Then Abner answered and said, Who *art* thou *that* criest to the king?

15. **And** David **said to Abner, Art not thou a valiant man?** and who *is* like to thee in Israel? **wherefore** then **hast thou not kept** thy lord **the king? for there came one** of the people in **to destroy the king** thy lord.

16. This thing *is* not good that thou hast done. *As* the LORD liveth, **ye are worthy to die, because ye have not kept your master,** the LORD's anointed. And now **see where the king's spear is,** and the cruse of water that *was* at his bolster.

17. **And Saul** knew David's voice, and **said, Is this** thy voice, **my son David? And David said,** *It is* my voice, my lord, O king.

18. And he said, **Wherefore doth my lord** thus **pursue** after **his servant?** for what have I done? or what evil *is* in mine hand?

19. Now therefore, I pray thee, let my lord the king hear the words of his servant. **If the LORD** have **stirred thee** up **against me, let him accept an offering: but if** *they be* the children of **men, cursed be they** before the LORD; **for they have driven me out** this day **from** abiding in **the inheritance of the LORD,** saying, Go, serve other gods.

20. **Now** therefore, **let not my blood fall to the earth before the** face of the **LORD:** for the king of Israel is come out to seek a flea, as when one doth hunt a partridge in the mountains.

21. **Then said Saul, I have sinned: return,** my son David: **for I will no more do thee harm,** because my soul was precious in thine eyes this day: behold, I have played the fool, and have erred exceedingly.

22. **And David** answered and **said,** Behold **the king's spear!** and **let one of the young men come over and fetch it.**

23. **The LORD render** to every man **his righteousness and** his **faithfulness; for the LORD delivered thee** into *my* hand to-day, **but I would not stretch forth mine hand against the LORD's anointed.**

24. And, behold, as thy life was much set by this day in mine eyes, so let my life be much set by in the eyes of the LORD, and let him deliver me out of all tribulation.

25. **Then Saul said** to David, **Blessed be thou,** my son **David: thou shalt both do great things, and** also shalt still **prevail. So David went** on **his way, and Saul** returned **to his place.**

CHAPTER 27

1. **And David said in his heart, I shall** now **perish one day by the hand of Saul:** *there is* nothing better for me than that **I should** speedily **escape into the land of the Philistines;** and Saul shall despair of me, to seek me any more in any coast of Israel: so shall I escape out of his hand.

2. **And David** arose, and he **passed over with the** six hundred **men that were with him**

■ unto Achish, the son of Maoch,
■ king of Gath.

3. And David dwelt with Achish at Gath, he and his men, every man with his household, *even* David with his two wives, Ahinoam the Jezreelitess, and Abigail the Carmelitess, Nabal's wife.

■ 4. And it was told Saul

that David was fled to Gath:

■ and he sought no more again
■ for him.
■ 5. And David said unto
■ Achish, If I have now found

grace in thine eyes, let them

■ give me a place

in some town in the country,

■ that I may dwell there:

for why should thy servant dwell in the royal city with thee?

■ 6. Then Achish gave him
■ Ziklag that day: wherefore

Ziklag pertaineth unto the kings of Judah unto this day.

■ 7. And the time that
■ David dwelt in the country
■ of the Philistines was
■ a full year and four months.
■ 8. And David and
■ his men went up, and
■ invaded the Geshurites,
■ and the Gezrites, and the
■ Amalekites: for those *nations*

were of old the inhabitants of the land, as thou goest to Shur, even unto the land of Egypt.

■ 9. And David
■ smote the land, and
■ left neither man nor
■ woman alive, and took
■ away the sheep, and the
■ oxen, and the
■ asses, and the
■ camels, and the apparel,
■ and returned, and came
■ to Achish.

10. And Achish said, Whither have ye made a road to-day? And David said, Against the south of Judah, and against the south of the Jerahmeelites, and against the south of the Kenites.

■ 11. And David saved
■ neither man nor woman

■ alive, to bring tidings to
■ Gath, saying, Lest they should

tell on us, saying, So did David, and so *will be* his manner all the while he dwelleth in the country of the Philistines.

■ 12. And Achish believed
■ David, saying, He hath
■ made his people
■ Israel utterly to
■ abhor him; therefore
■ he shall be my
■ servant for ever.

CHAPTER 28

■ 1. And it came to pass

in those days, that

■ the Philistines gathered
■ their armies together
■ for warfare, to fight
■ with Israel. And Achish
■ said unto David,

Know thou assuredly, that

■ thou shalt go out
■ with me to battle,

thou and thy men.

2. And David said to Achish, Surely thou shalt know what thy servant can do. And Achish said to David, Therefore will I make thee keeper of mine head for ever.

■ 3. Now Samuel was dead,

and all Israel had lamented him, and buried him in Ramah, even in his own city.

■ And Saul had put away
■ those that had familiar
■ spirits, and the wizards,
■ out of the land.

4. And the Philistines gathered themselves together, and came and pitched in Shunem: and Saul gathered all Israel together, and they pitched in Gilboa.

■ 5. And when Saul saw
■ the host of the Philistines,
■ he was afraid,

and his heart greatly trembled.

■ 6. And when Saul inquired
■ of the LORD, the LORD
■ answered him not, neither by

dreams, nor by Urim, nor by prophets.

■ 7. Then said

Saul unto his servants,
Seek me a woman that
hath a familiar spirit, that
I may go to her, and
inquire of her. And his
servants said to him, Behold,
there is a woman
that hath a familiar spirit
at En-dor.
8. **And Saul disguised**
himself, and put on
other raiment, and he
went, and two men
with him, and they came
to the woman
by night: and he
said, I pray thee,
divine unto me by
the familiar spirit,
and bring me *him*
up, whom I shall
name unto thee.
9. **And the woman said**
unto him, Behold, thou knowest what
Saul hath done, how he hath
cut off those that have
familiar spirits, and
the wizards, out of the
land: wherefore then
layest thou a snare for
my life, to cause me to die?
10. **And Saul sware**
to her by the LORD,
saying, *As* the LORD liveth,
there shall no punishment
happen to thee for this thing.
11. Then said the woman,
Whom shall I bring up unto
thee? And he said, Bring me up
Samuel.
12. **And when the woman**
saw Samuel, she cried
with a loud voice: and the
woman spake to Saul, saying,
Why hast thou deceived
me? for thou art Saul.
13. **And the king said** unto her,
Be not afraid: for what
sawest thou? And the woman
said unto Saul, I saw gods
ascending out of the earth.
14. And he said unto her,
What form *is* he of?

And she said,
An old man cometh up;
and he is covered with
a mantle. And Saul
perceived that it was
Samuel, and he stooped
with *his* face to the ground, and
bowed himself.
15. **And Samuel said to**
Saul, Why hast thou
disquieted me, to bring
me up? And Saul
answered, I am sore distressed;
for the Philistines
make war against me,
and God is departed from
me, and answereth me no more,
neither by prophets, nor by dreams:
therefore I have called
thee, that thou mayest
make known unto
me what I shall do.
16. **Then said Samuel,**
Wherefore then
dost thou ask of me,
seeing the LORD
is departed from thee, and
is become thine enemy?
17. And the LORD hath done
to him, as he spake by me:
for the LORD hath rent
the kingdom out of
thine hand, and given
it to thy neighbour, *even* to
David:
18. **Because thou**
obeyedst not the voice of
the LORD, nor executedst his
fierce wrath upon Amalek, therefore
hath the LORD done this thing unto
thee this day.
19. **Moreover the**
LORD will also
deliver Israel with thee
into the hand of the
Philistines: and to morrow
shalt thou and thy sons be
with me: the LORD also shall
deliver the host of Israel into
the hand of the Philistines.
20. **Then Saul fell**
straightway all along
on the earth, and was soreafraid,

461

because of the words of Samuel:
**and there was no strength
in him; for he had eaten
no bread all** the
day, nor all the night.
21. **And the woman**
came unto Saul, and
saw that he was sore
troubled, and said unto him,
Behold, thine handmaid hath obeyed
thy voice, and I have put my life in my
hand, and have hearkened unto thy
words which thou spakest unto me.
22. Now therefore, I pray thee,
hearken thou also unto the voice
of thine handmaid, and
let me set a morsel of
bread before thee; and eat,
**that thou mayest
have strength, when
thou goest** on thy way.
23. **But he refused,**
and said, I will not eat.
But his servants,
together with the woman,
compelled him;
and he hearkened unto their
voice. So he arose from the earth,
and sat upon the bed.
24. **And the woman had a** fat
calf in the house;
and she hasted, and
killed it, and took
flour, and kneaded *it,*
**and did bake
unleavened bread** thereof:
25. **And** she
brought it before Saul,
and before his servants;
and they did eat.
Then they rose up,
and went away that night.

CHAPTER 29

1. **Now the Philistines
gathered together** all
their armies to Aphek: and
the Israelites pitched by a fountain
which *is* in Jezreel.
2. And the lords of the Philistines
passed on by hundreds, and
**by thousands: but David
and his men passed** on

**in the rereward
with Achish.**
3. **Then said the princes of
the Philistines, What do
these Hebrews here?** And
Achish said unto the princes of the
Philistines, *Is* not this David, the
servant of Saul the king of Israel,
which hath been with me these
days, or these years, and I have
found no fault in him since he fell
unto me unto this day?
4. **And the** princes of the
**Philistines were
wroth** with him;
and the princes
of the Philistines
said unto him,
Make this fellow return,
that he may go again to his place
which thou hast appointed him,
and let him not go down
with us to battle,
lest in the battle
he be an adversary to us:
for wherewith should he reconcile
himself unto his master? *should it* not
be with the heads of these men?
5. *Is* not this David, of whom they
sang one to another in dances,
saying, Saul slew his thousands,
and David his ten thousands?
6. **Then Achish called
David, and said** unto him,
Surely, as the LORD liveth, thou hast
been upright, and thy going out and
thy coming in with me in the host *is*
good in my sight: for
**I have not found
evil in thee** since the day of
thy coming unto me unto this day:
**nevertheless the lords
favour thee not.**
7. **Wherefore now** return, and
go in peace,
**that thou displease not the
lords of the Philistines.**
8. **And David said** unto Achish,
But what have I done?
and what hast thou found in thy
servant so long as I have been
with thee unto this day,
that I may not go fight against

the enemies of my lord
the king?
9. And Achish answered and
said to David,
I know that
thou art good in my sight,
as an angel of God:
notwithstanding the
princes of the Philistines
have said, He shall
not go up with us
to the battle.
10. Wherefore now rise
up early in the morning
with thy master's servants
that are come with thee:
and as soon as ye be up
early in the morning, and have light,
depart.
11. So David and his men
rose up early to depart
in the morning, to return
into the land of the
Philistines. And the
Philistines went up to Jezreel.

CHAPTER 30

1. And it came to pass,
when David and his men
were come to Ziklag
on the third day, that
the Amalekites had
invaded the south, and
Ziklag, and smitten Ziklag,
and burned it with fire;
2. And had taken the
women captives, that *were*
therein: they slew not any, either
great or small, but carried *them*
away, and went on their way.
3. So David and his men came to
the city, and, behold, *it was* burned
with fire; and their wives, and their
sons, and their daughters, were
taken captives.
4. Then David and
the people that *were*
with him lifted up their voice and
wept, until they had no
more power to weep.
5. And David's two wives
were taken captives, Ahinoam
the Jezreelitess, and Abigail

the wife of Nabal the Carmelite.
6. And David was greatly
distressed; for the people
spake of stoning him,
because the soul of all the
people was grieved,
every man for his sons and
for his daughters:
but David encouraged
himself in the LORD his God.
7. And David
said to Abiathar the priest,
Ahimelech's son, I pray thee,
bring me hither
the ephod. And Abiathar
brought thither the ephod to David.
8. And David inquired
at the LORD, saying,
Shall I pursue after this
troop? shall I overtake them?
And he answered him,
Pursue: for thou shalt surely
overtake them, and without fail
recover all.
9. So David went, he
and the six hundred
men that *were* with him, and
came to the brook
Besor, where those that
were left behind stayed.
10. But David pursued, he
and four hundred men: for
two hundred abode
behind, which were so
faint that they could not
go over the brook Besor.
11. And they found
an Egyptian in the field,
and brought him to David,
and gave him bread,
and he did eat; and they
made him drink water;
12. And they gave him a piece of
a cake of figs, and two clusters
of raisins: and when he had
eaten, his spirit came again to him:
for he had eaten
no bread, nor drunk *any*
water, three
days and three nights.
13. And David said unto him,
To whom belongest thou?
and whence *art* thou?

And he said, I am a young man of Egypt, servant to an Amalekite; and my master left me, because three days agone I fell sick. 14. We made an invasion upon the south of the Cherethites, and upon the coast which belongeth to Judah, and upon the south of Caleb; and we burned Ziklag with fire. 15. And David said to him, Canst thou bring me down to this company? And he said, Swear unto me by God, that thou wilt neither kill me, nor deliver me into the hands of my master, and I will bring thee down to this company. 16. And when he had brought him down, behold, they were spread abroad upon all the earth, eating and drinking, and dancing, because of all the great spoil that they had taken out of the land of the Philistines, and out of the land of Judah. 17. And David smote them from the twilight even unto the evening of the next day: and there escaped not a man of them, save four hundred young men, which rode upon camels, and fled. 18. And David recovered all that the Amalekites had carried away: and David rescued his two wives. 19. And there was nothing lacking to them, neither small nor great, neither sons nor daughters, neither spoil, nor any thing that they had taken to them: David recovered all. 20. And David took all the flocks and the herds, which they drave before those other cattle, and said,

This is David's spoil. 21. And David came to the two hundred men, which were so faint that they could not follow David, whom they had made also to abide at the brook Besor: and they went forth to meet David, and to meet the people that were with him: and when David came near to the people, he saluted them. 22. Then answered all the wicked men and men of Belial, of those that went with David, and said, Because they went not with us, we will not give them aught of the spoil that we have recovered, save to every man his wife and his children, that they may lead them away, and depart. 23. Then said David, Ye shall not do so, my brethren, with that which the LORD hath given us, who hath preserved us, and delivered the company that came against us into our hand. 24. For who will hearken unto you in this matter? but as his part is that goeth down to the battle, so shall his part be that tarrieth by the stuff: they shall part alike. 25. And it was so from that day forward, that he made it a statute and an ordinance for Israel unto this day. 26. And when David came to Ziklag, he sent of the spoil unto the elders of Judah, even to his friends, saying, Behold a present for you of the spoil of the enemies of the LORD;

27. To *them* which *were* in Beth-el, and to *them* which *were* in south Ramoth, and to *them* which *were* in Jattir,

28. And to *them* which *were* in Aroer, and to *them* which *were* in Siphmoth, and to *them* which *were* in Eshtemoa,

29. And to *them* which *were* in Rachal, and to *them* which *were* in the cities of the Jerahmeelites, and to *them* which *were* in the cities of the Kenites,

30. And to *them* which *were* in Hormah, and to *them* which *were* in Chorashan, and to *them* which *were* in Athach,

31. And to *them* which *were* in Hebron, and to all the places where David himself and his men were wont to haunt.

CHAPTER 31

1. Now the Philistines fought against Israel: and the men of Israel fled from before the Philistines, and fell down slain in mount Gilboa.

2. And the Philistines followed hard upon Saul and upon his sons; and the Philistines slew Jonathan, and Abinadab, and Melchishua, Saul's sons.

3. And the battle went sore against Saul, and the archers hit him; and he was sore wounded of the archers.

4. Then said Saul unto his armour-bearer, Draw thy sword, and thrust me through therewith; lest these uncircumcised come and thrust me through, and abuse me. But his armour-bearer would not; for he was sore afraid. Therefore Saul took a sword, and fell upon it.

5. And when his armour-bearer saw that Saul was dead, he fell likewise upon his sword, and died with him.

6. So Saul died, and his three sons, and his armour-bearer, and all his men, that same day together.

7. And when the men of Israel that *were* on the other side of the valley, and *they* that *were* on the other side Jordan, saw that the men of Israel fled, and that Saul and his sons were dead, they forsook the cities, and fled; and the Philistines came and dwelt in them.

8. And it came to pass on the morrow, when the Philistines came to strip the slain, that they found Saul and his three sons fallen in mount Gilboa.

9. And they cut off his head, and stripped off his armour, and sent into the land of the Philistines round about, to publish it *in* the house of their idols, and among the people.

10. And they put his armour in the house of Ashtaroth: and they fastened his body to the wall of Beth-shan.

11. And when the inhabitants of Jabesh-gilead heard of that which the Philistines had done to Saul;

12. All the valiant men arose, and went all night, and took the body of Saul and the bodies of his sons from the wall of Beth-shan, and came to Jabesh, and burnt them there.

13. And they took their bones, and buried them under a tree at Jabesh, and fasted seven days.

THE WAY
OF SALVATION

1. *All Have Sinned*
   Romans 3:23

2. *Sin Brings Death*
   Romans 6:23

3. *Eternal Life Through
   Jesus Christ*
   Romans 6:23b

4. *Confess and Believe*
   Romans 10:9, 10

5. *Ask Jesus to Save You*
   Romans 10:13

THE BOOK OF SECOND SAMUEL

BACKGROUND INFORMATION

Author: Unknown
Date Written: probably around 1000 B.C.

Number of:
Verses—695
Chapters—24
Total Words—20,612
Scan Words—8,400
Scan Words Represent Approximately 40% of Total Words

Theme: The Establishment of David as king

OUTLINE OF THE BOOK

I. **The Death of Saul, and the Anointing of David** as King.
    1:1 — 4:12
II. **The Reign of David Until the Rebellion of Absalom**
    5:1 — 14:33
III. **The Rebellion Until the Census** of Israel.
    15:1 — 24:25

CHAPTER 1

1. **Now** it came to pass **after the death of Saul,** when **David** was **returned** from the slaughter of the Amalekites, **and** David had **abode two days in Ziklag;** 2. It came even to pass on the third day, that, behold, **a man came** out of the camp from Saul **with his clothes rent, and earth upon his head:** and *so* it was, when he came to David, that he fell to the earth, and did obeisance. 3. **And David said** unto him, **From whence comest thou? And he said** unto him, **Out of the camp of Israel am I escaped.** 4. And David said unto him, How went the matter? I pray thee, tell me. And he answered, That **the people** are **fled from the battle, and many** of the people also **are** fallen and **dead; and Saul and Jonathan** his son **are dead also.** 5. **And David said** unto the young man that told him, **How knowest thou that Saul and Jonathan** his son **be dead?** 6. **And the young man** that told him **said, As I happened by** chance upon mount **Gilboa,** behold, **Saul leaned upon his spear; and,** lo, **the chariots** and horsemen **followed** hard after **him.** 7. **And** when he looked behind him, **he saw me,** and called unto me. And I answered, Here *am* I. 8. **And he said** unto me, **Who art thou? And I answered** him, **I am an Amalekite.** 9. **He said** unto me again, Stand, I pray thee, upon me, and **slay me:** for anguish is come upon me, because my life *is* yet whole in me. 10. **So I** stood upon him, and **slew him, because I was sure** that **he could not live** after that he was fallen: **and I took the crown** that *was* upon his head, **and the bracelet** that *was* on his arm, **and have brought them** hither **unto my lord.** 11. **Then David took** hold on **his clothes, and rent them; and likewise all the men** that *were* with him: 12. **And they mourned,** and wept, **and fasted until even,** for Saul, and for Jonathan his son, and for the people of the LORD, and for the house of Israel; because they were fallen by the sword. 13. **And David said unto the young man** that told him, **Whence art thou? And he answered, I am** the son of a stranger, **an Amalekite.** 14. **And David said** unto him, **How wast thou not afraid to** stretch forth thine hand to **destroy the LORD's anointed?** 15. **And David called one of the young men, and said,** Go near, *and* **fall upon him. And he smote him that he died.** 16. **And David said** unto him, **Thy blood be upon thy head;** for **thy mouth** hath **testified against thee,** saying, I have slain the LORD's anointed. 17. **And David lamented**

with this lamentation
over Saul and over
Jonathan his son:
18. (Also he bade them teach the
children of Judah *the use of* the
bow: behold, *it is* written in the
book of Jasher.)
19. **The beauty of Israel**
is slain upon thy high places:
how are the mighty fallen!
20. Tell *it* not in Gath,
publish it not in the
streets of Askelon;
lest the daughters of the
Philistines rejoice,
lest the daughters of the
uncircumcised triumph.
21. Ye mountains of Gilboa,
let there be no dew,
neither *let there be*
rain, upon you, nor
fields of offerings:
for there
the shield of the
mighty is vilely
cast away, the shield of Saul,
as though he had not
been anointed with oil.
22. From the blood of the slain, from
the fat of the mighty, the bow of
Jonathan turned not back, and the
sword of Saul returned not empty.
23. **Saul and Jonathan**
were lovely and pleasant in
their lives, and in their death they
were not divided: they were
swifter than eagles, they were
stronger than lions.
24. **Ye daughters of Israel,**
weep over Saul, who clothed you in
scarlet, with *other* delights, who put on
ornaments of gold upon your apparel.
25. How are the mighty fallen in the
midst of the battle! O Jonathan, *thou*
wast slain in thine high places.
26. **I am distressed for thee,**
my brother Jonathan: very
pleasant hast thou been unto me:
thy love to me was
wonderful, passing
the love of women.
27. **How are the mighty**
fallen, and the weapons

|■| **of war perished!**

CHAPTER 2

1. **And** it came to pass
after this, that
David inquired of
the LORD, saying,
Shall I go up into any
of the cities of
Judah? And the
LORD said unto him,
Go up. And David said,
Whither shall I go up? And he said,
Unto Hebron.
2. **So David went** up thither,
and his two wives also,
Ahinoam the Jezreelitess, and
Abigail Nabal's wife the Carmelite.
3. **And his men** that *were* with him
did David bring up, every
man with his household:
and they dwelt in the cities of
Hebron.
4. **And the men of**
Judah came, and there they
anointed David king
over the house of Judah.
And they told David, saying,
That the men of
Jabesh-gilead were
they that buried Saul.
5. **And David sent**
messengers unto
the men of Jabesh-gilead,
and said unto them,
Blessed be ye of the
LORD, that ye have
shewed this
kindness unto
your lord, *even* unto
Saul, and have buried him.
6. **And now the LORD**
shew kindness and
truth unto you: and I also
will requite you this kindness,
because ye have done this thing.
7. **Therefore** now let your hands
be strengthened, and be ye
valiant: for your master
Saul is dead, and
also the house of
Judah have
anointed me king over them.

8. **But Abner** the son of Ner, **captain of Saul's host, took Ish-bosheth the son of Saul,** and brought him over to Mahanaim; 9. **And made him king** over Gilead, and over the Ashurites, and over Jezreel, and over Ephraim, and over Benjamin, and **over all Israel.** 10. **Ish-bosheth** Saul's son **was forty years old** when he began to reign over Israel, **and reigned two years. But** the house of **Judah followed David.** 11. **And** the time that **David was king** in Hebron **over** the house of **Judah** was **seven years and six months.** 12. **And Abner** the son of Ner, **and the servants of Ish-bosheth** the son of Saul, went out from Mahanaim to Gibeon. 13. **And Joab** the son of Zeruiah, **and the servants of David,** went out, and **met together by the pool of Gibeon**: and they sat down, the one on the one side of the pool, and the other on the other side of thepool. 14. **And Abner said to Joab, Let the young men** now arise, and **play before us.** And Joab said, Let them arise. 15. **Then there** arose and **went** over by number **twelve of Benjamin,** which *pertained* to Ish-bosheth the son of Saul, **and twelve of the servants of David.** 16. **And** they caught **every one** his fellow by the head, and **thrust his sword in his fellow's side; so they fell down together:** wherefore that place was called Helkath-hazzurim,

which is in Gibeon. 17. **And there was a very sore battle** that day; **and Abner was beaten,** and the men of Israel, before the servants of David. 18. **And there were three sons** of Zeruiah **there, Joab, and Abishai, and Asahel:** and Asahel *was as* light of foot as a wild roe. 19. **And Asahel pursued after Abner; and** in going he **turned not to the right** hand **nor to the left from following Abner.** 20. Then Abner looked behind him, and said, *Art* thou Asahel? And he answered, I am. 21. **And Abner said to him, Turn** thee **aside** to thy right hand or to thy left, and lay thee hold on one of the young men, and take thee his armour. **But Asahel would not** turn aside from following of him. 22. **And Abner said again** to Asahel, **Turn** thee **aside** from following me: **wherefore should I smite thee** to the ground? **how** then **should I** hold up my **face** to **Joab thy brother?** 23. **Howbeit he refused to turn aside: wherefore Abner with the hinder end of the spear smote him** under the fifth *rib,* that the spear came out behind him; **and he fell** down **there, and died** in the same place: and it came to pass, *that* as many as came to the place where Asahel fell down and died stood still. 24. **Joab also and Abishai pursued** after **Abner: and** the sun went down when

they were come to the hill of
Ammah, that *lieth* before Giah by
the way of the wilderness of Gibeon.
25. And the children of Benjamin
gathered themselves together after
Abner, and became one troop, and
stood on the top of an hill.
26. **Then Abner called
to Joab,** and said,
**Shall the sword devour
for ever?** knowest thou not that
**it will be bitterness
in the** latter
end? how long shall it be then,
ere thou bid the people return
from following their brethren?
27. And Joab said, *As* God
liveth, unless thou hadst spoken,
surely then in the morning the
people had gone up every one
from following his brother.
28. **So Joab** blew a trumpet,
and all the people
stood still, and
pursued after
**Israel no more,
neither fought** they
any more.
29. And Abner and his men
walked all that night through
the plain, and passed over
Jordan, and went through
all Bithron, and they came
to Mahanaim.
30. **And** Joab returned from
following Abner: and when he had
gathered all the people together,
**there lacked of David's
servants nineteen men
and Asahel.**
31. **But** the servants of David
had smitten of Benjamin, and
of Abner's men, *so that*
**three hundred and
threescore men died.**
32. **And they took up
Asahel, and buried him**
in the sepulchre of his father,
which *was in* Bethlehem. And Joab
and his men went all night,
and they
came to Hebron
at break of day.

CHAPTER 3

1. **Now there was long
war between the house
of Saul and** the house of
**David: but David
waxed stronger**
and stronger, and the house of
Saul waxed weaker and weaker.
2. **And unto David were
sons born in Hebron:**
and his firstborn was Amnon,
of Ahinoam the Jezreelitess;
3. And his second, Chileab, of
Abigail the wife of Nabal the
Carmelite; and the third, Absalom
the son of Maacah the daughter
of Talmai king of Geshur;
4. And the fourth, Adonijah the
son of Haggith; and the fifth,
Shephatiah the son of Abital;
5. And the sixth, Ithream, by
Eglah David's wife. These were
born to David in Hebron.
6. **And** it came to pass,
while there was war
between the house of Saul
and the house of David, that
**Abner made himself strong
for the house of Saul.**
7. **And Saul had a
concubine,** whose name *was*
Rizpah, the daughter of Aiah:
**and Ish-bosheth said to
Abner, Wherefore hast
thou gone in unto my
father's concubine?**
8. **Then was Abner very
wroth** for the words of
Ish–bosheth, and said,
**Am I a dog's head,
which** against Judah do
shew kindness this day
**unto the house of
Saul** thy father, to his
brethren, and to his friends,
**and have not delivered
thee into the hand of David,**
that thou chargest me to–day with
a fault concerning this woman?
9. So do God to Abner, and more
also, except, as the LORD hath
sworn to David, even so I do to him;
10. To translate the kingdom from

the house of Saul, and to set up the throne of David over Israel and over Judah, from Dan even to Beer–sheba. 11. **And he could not answer Abner** a word again, **because he feared him.** 12. **And Abner sent messengers to David** on his behalf, **saying,** Whose is the land? saying also, **Make thy league with me,** and, behold, my hand *shall be* with thee, **to bring** about **all Israel unto thee.** 13. **And he said,** Well; **I will** make a league with thee: **but** one thing I require of thee, that is, Thou shalt not see my face, except thou first **bring Michal** Saul's daughter, **when thou comest** to see my face. 14. **And David sent messengers to Ish–bosheth** Saul's son, saying, **Deliver me my wife Michal,** which I espoused to *me* for an hundred foreskins of the Philistines. 15. **And Ish–bosheth** sent, and **took her from her husband,** *even* from Phaltiel the son of Laish. 16. **And her husband went** with her along **weeping behind her to Bahurim.** Then said Abner unto him, Go, return. And he returned. 17. **And Abner had communication with the elders of Israel,** saying, Ye sought for David in times past **to be king over you:** 18. **Now then do it: for the LORD hath spoken of David, saying, By the hand of** my servant **David I will save** my people **Israel** out of the hand of the Philistines, and out of the hand of all their enemies. 19. And Abner also spake in the ears of Benjamin: and Abner went also to speak in the ears of David in Hebron all that seemed good to Israel, and that seemed good to the whole house of Benjamin. 20. **So Abner came to David** to Hebron, and twenty men with him. **And David made** Abner and the men that *were* with him **a feast.** 21. **And Abner said** unto David, **I will** arise and go, and will **gather all Israel unto** my lord **the king,** that they may make a league with thee, and that thou mayest reign over all that thine heart desireth. **And David sent Abner away;** and he went **in peace.** 22. And, behold, the servants of David **and Joab came from pursuing a troop, and brought in a great spoil** with them: but Abner *was* not with David in Hebron; for he had sent him away, and he was gone in peace. 23. When Joab **and** all the host that *was* with him were come, **they told Joab,** saying, **Abner** the son of Ner **came to the king, and he** hath **sent him away,** and he is gone **in peace.** 24. **Then Joab came to the king,** and said, **What hast thou done?** behold, Abner came unto thee; why *is* it *that* **thou** hast **sent him away,** and he is quite gone? 25. **Thou knowest Abner** the son of Ner, that he **came to deceive thee,** and to know thy going out and thy coming in, and to know all that thou doest.

26. **And** when **Joab** was come out from David, he **sent messengers after Abner,** which brought him again from the well of Sirah: **but David knew it not.**
27. **And when Abner** was **returned** to Hebron, **Joab took him aside** in the gate to speak with him **quietly, and smote him** there under the fifth *rib*, that he died, **for the blood of Asahel his brother.**
28. **And** afterward **when David heard** *it*, **he said, I and my kingdom are guiltless before the LORD for** ever from **the blood of Abner** the son of Ner:
29. **Let it rest on the head of Joab,** and on all his father's house; and let there not fail from the house of Joab one that hath an issue, or that is a leper, or that leaneth on a staff, or that falleth on the sword, or that lacketh bread.
30. **So Joab, and Abishai** his brother **slew Abner, because he had slain their brother Asahel** at Gibeon in the battle.
31. **And David said** to Joab, and **to all the people** that *were* with him, Rend your clothes, and gird you with sackcloth, and **mourn before Abner.** And king David *himself* followed the bier.
32. **And they buried Abner in Hebron: and the king** lifted up his voice, and **wept at the grave of Abner;** and all the people wept.
33. And the king lamented over Abner, and said, Died Abner as a fool dieth?
34. Thy hands *were* not bound, nor thy feet put into fetters: as a man falleth before wicked men, *so* fellest thou. And all the people wept again over him.

35. **And** when all **the people came to cause David to eat** meat while it was yet day, **David sware,** saying, **So do God to me,** and more also, **if I taste bread,** or ought else, **till the sun be down.**
36. **And** all the people took notice *of it*, and it pleased them: as **whatsoever the king did pleased all the people.**
37. **For all the people** and all Israel **understood** that day **that it was not of the king to slay Abner** the son of Ner.
38. **And the king said** unto his servants, **Know** ye not that **there is** a prince and **a great man fallen this day** in Israel?
39. **And** I *am* this day weak, though anointed king; and these men the sons of Zeruiah *be* too hard for me: **the LORD shall reward the doer of evil according to his wickedness.**

CHAPTER 4

1. **And when Saul's son heard that Abner was dead** in Hebron, **his hands were feeble,** and all the Israelites were troubled.
2. And Saul's son had two men *that were* captains of bands: the name of the one *was* Baanah, and the name of the other Rechab, the sons of Rimmon a Beerothite, of the children of Benjamin: (for Beeroth also was reckoned to Benjamin.
3. And the Beerothites fled to Gittaim, and were sojourners there until this day.)
4. **And Jonathan, Saul's son, had a son that was lame of his feet. He was five years old when** the tidings came of Saul and Jonathan out of Jezreel, and his nurse took him up, and fled:

and it came to pass, as she made haste to flee, that **he fell, and became lame. And his name was Mephibosheth.**

5. **And the sons of Rimmon** the Beerothite, Rechab and Baanah, went, and **came** about the heat of the day **to the house of Ish–bosheth, who lay on a bed at noon.**

6. **And they came** thither into the midst of the house, **as though they would have fetched wheat;** and they smote him under the fifth *rib*: and Rechab and Baanah his brother escaped.

7. For when they came into the house, he lay on his bed in his bedchamber, **and they** smote him, and **slew him, and beheaded him, and took his head,** and gat them away through the plain all night.

8. **And they brought the head** of Ishbosheth **unto David** to Hebron, **and said** to the king, **Behold the head of** Ishbosheth the son of Saul **thine enemy,** which sought thy life; and the LORD hath avenged my lord the king this day of Saul, and of his seed.

9. **And David answered** Rechab and Baanah his brother, the sons of Rimmon the Beerothite, and said unto them, As the LORD liveth, who hath redeemed my soul out of all adversity,

10. **When one told me,** saying, Behold, **Saul is dead, thinking to have brought good tidings,** I took hold of him, and **slew him** in Ziklag, **who thought** that **I would have given him a reward for his tidings:**

11. How much more, when **wicked men have slain a** **righteous person** in his own house upon his bed? shall I not therefore now require his blood of your hand, and take you away from the earth?

12. And David commanded his young men, **and they slew them, and cut off their hands and** their **feet, and hanged them** up over the pool **in Hebron. But they took the head of Ish–bosheth, and buried it in the sepulchre of Abner** in Hebron.

CHAPTER 5

1. **Then came all the tribes of Israel to David** unto Hebron, and spake, **saying,** Behold, **we are thy bone and** thy **flesh.**

2. Also in time past, when Saul was king over us, thou wast he that leddest out and broughtest in Israel: and the LORD said to thee, Thou shalt feed my people Israel, and thou shalt be a captain over Israel.

3. So all the elders of Israel came to the king to Hebron; **and king David made a league with them** in Hebron before the LORD: **and they anointed David king over Israel.**

4. **David was thirty years old** when he began to reign, **and he reigned forty years.**

5. In Hebron he reigned **over Judah seven years and six months: and** in Jerusalem he reigned **thirty** and **three years over all Israel and Judah.**

6. **And the king and his men went to Jerusalem unto the Jebusites,** the inhabitants of the land: **which spake unto David,** **saying, Except thou take away the blind and the**

474

lame, thou shalt not come in hither: thinking, David cannot come in hither. 7. **Nevertheless David took** the strong hold of **Zion:** the same is the city of David. 8. **And David said** on that day, **Whosoever** getteth up to the gutter, and **smiteth the Jebusites,** and the lame and the blind *that are* hated of David's soul, *he* **shall be chief and captain. Wherefore they said, The blind and** the **lame shall not come into the house.** 9. **So David dwelt in the fort, and called it the city of David.** And David built round about from Millo and inward. 10. **And David** went on, and **grew great, and the LORD** God of hosts **was with him.** 11. **And Hiram king of Tyre sent** messengers to David, and cedar **trees, and carpenters, and** masons: and they **built David an house.** 12. And David perceived that the LORD had established him king over Israel, and that he had exalted his kingdom for his people Israel's sake. 13. **And David took him more concubines and wives** out of Jerusalem, after he was come from Hebron: **and there were** yet **sons and daughters born to David.** 14. And these *be* the names of those that were born unto him in Jerusalem; Shammuah, and Shobab, and Nathan, and Solomon, 15. Ibhar also, and Elishua, and Nepheg, and Japhia, 16. And Elishama, and Eliada, and Eliphalet. 17. **But when the Philistines heard that they had anointed David king over Israel,** all the Philistines came up to seek David; and David heard *of it,* and went down to the hold. 18. **The Philistines** also **came and spread themselves in the valley of Rephaim.** 19. **And David inquired of the LORD,** saying, Shall I go up to the Philistines? **wilt thou deliver them into mine hand? And the LORD said** unto David, Go up: for **I will doubtless deliver the Philistines** into thine hand. 20. **And David** came to Baal–perazim, and David **smote them there, and** said, The LORD hath broken forth upon mine enemies before me, as the breach of waters. Therefore **he called the** name of that **place Baal-perazim.** 21. **And** there **they left their images, and David** and his men **burned them.** 22. **And the Philistines came** up yet **again,** and spread themselves in the valley of Rephaim. 23. **And when David inquired of the LORD, he said,** Thou shalt not go up; *but* fetch a compass behind them, and **come upon them over against the mulberry trees.** 24. And let it be, **when thou hearest the sound** of a going **in the tops of the mulberry trees,** that then thou shalt bestir thyself: for **then shall the LORD go** out **before thee, to smite** the host of **the Philistines.** 25. **And David did** so, **as the LORD** had **commanded him; and smote the Philistines** from Geba until thou come to Gazer.

CHAPTER 6

■ 1. **Again, David**
■ **gathered** together all
■ **the chosen men of**
■ **Israel, thirty thousand.**
2. And David arose,
■ **and went** with all the people that
were with him from Baale of Judah,
■ **to bring up** from thence
■ **the ark of God,** whose
name is called by the name of
the LORD of hosts that dwelleth
between the cherubims.
■ 3. **And they set the ark of**
■ **God upon a new cart, and**
■ **brought it out of the house**
■ **of Abinadab** that *was* in Gibeah:
and Uzzah and Ahio, the sons of
Abinadab, drave the new cart.
■ 4. **And they** brought it out of the
house of Abinadab which *was* at
Gibeah, accompanying the ark of
God: and Ahio went before the ark.
5. And David and all the house
of Israel
■ **played** before the LORD on
■ **all manner of instruments**
made of fir wood, even on harps,
and on psalteries, and on timbrels,
and on cornets, and on cymbals.
■ 6. **And when they came to**
■ **Nachon's threshingfloor,**
■ **Uzzah put forth his hand**
■ **to the ark** of God,
■ **and took hold of it;**
■ **for the oxen shook it.**
■ 7. **And the anger of**
■ **the LORD was** kindled
■ **against Uzzah; and**
■ **God smote him** there
■ **for his error;** and there
he died by the ark of God.
■ 8. **And David was**
■ **displeased,** because the
LORD had made a breach upon
Uzzah: and he called the name of
the place Perezuzzah to this day.
■ 9. **And** David
■ **was afraid of the**
■ **LORD** that day,
■ **and said, How shall**
■ **the ark** of the LORD
■ **come to me?**

■ 10. **So David** would not remo
ve the ark of the LORD unto him
into the city of David: but David
■ **carried it aside**
■ **into the house of**
■ **Obed-edom** the Gittite.
■ 11. **And the ark** of the LORD
■ **continued in the house**
■ **of Obed-edom** the Gittite
■ **three months: and the LORD**
■ **blessed Obed-edom,**
and all his household.
■ 12. **And it was told** king
■ **David,** saying,
■ **The LORD hath**
■ **blessed** the house of
■ **Obed-edom,** and all that
pertaineth unto him, because
of the ark of God.
■ **So David** went and
■ **brought up the ark** of
God from the house of Obed-edom
■ **into the city of David**
■ **with gladness.**
■ 13. **And** it was *so*, that
■ **when they** that bare
the ark of the LORD
■ **had gone six paces,**
■ **he sacrificed oxen**
■ **and fatlings.**
■ 14. **And David**
■ **danced before**
■ **the LORD** with all *his* might;
■ **and** David
■ **was girded with**
■ **a linen ephod.**
15. So David and all the house
of Israel brought up the ark of
the LORD with shouting, and
with the sound of the trumpet.
■ 16. **And as the ark** of the LORD
■ **came into the city** of David,
■ **Michal** Saul's daughter looked
through a window, and
■ **saw** king
■ **David leaping**
■ **and dancing** before the LORD;
■ **and she despised him**
■ **in her heart.**
■ 17. **And they brought** in
■ **the ark** of the LORD, and
set it in his place,
■ **in the midst of the**

476

tabernacle that David had pitched for it:

and David offered burnt offerings and peace offerings before the LORD.

18. And as soon as David had made an end of offering burnt offerings and peace offerings, he blessed the people in the name of the LORD of hosts.

19. And he dealt among all the people, *even* among the whole multitude of Israel, as well to the women as men, to every one a cakeof bread, and a good piece *of flesh,* and a flagon *of wine.* So all the people departed every one to his house.

20. **Then David returned to** bless **his household.** **And Michal** the daughter of Saul **came** out **to meet David, and** said, How glorious was **the king** of Israel to-day, **who uncovered himself to-day in the eyes of the handmaids** of his servants, as one of the vain fellows shamelessly uncovereth himself!

21. **And David said** unto Michal, **It was before the LORD,** which chose me before thy father, and before all his house, to appoint me ruler over the people of the LORD, over Israel: therefore will I play before the LORD.

22. **And I will yet be more vile** than thus, **and** will be **base in mine own sight: and** of the maidservants which thou hast spoken of, **of them shall I be had in honour.**

23. **Therefore Michal** the daughter of Saul **had no child unto the day of her death.**

CHAPTER 7

1. **And it came to pass,** **when** the king sat in his house, and **the LORD had given him rest** round about **from all his enemies;**

2. **That the king said unto Nathan** the prophet, See now, **I dwell in an house of cedar, but the ark of God dwelleth within curtains.**

3. And Nathan said to the king, Go, do all that *is* in thine heart; for the LORD *is* with thee.

4. **And** it came to pass **that night,** that the word of **the LORD came unto Nathan, saying,**

5. **Go** and **tell** my servant **David, Thus saith the LORD, Shalt thou build me an house for me to dwell in?**

6. **Whereas I have not dwelt in any house since** the time that **I brought** up the children of **Israel out of Egypt,** even to this day, but have walked in a tent and in a tabernacle.

7. In all *the places* wherein I have walked with all the children of Israel spake I a word with any of the tribes of Israel, whom I commanded to feed my people Israel, saying, Why build ye not me an house of cedar?

8. **Now therefore** so shalt thou **say unto** my servant **David,** Thus saith the LORD of hosts, **I took thee from** the sheepcote, from **following** the **sheep, to be ruler over** my people, over **Israel:**

9. **And I was with thee** whithersoever thou wentest, and have cut off all thine enemies out of thy sight, **and have made thee a great name,** like unto the name of the great *men* that *are* in the earth.

10. **Moreover I will appoint**

477

a place for my people
Israel, and will plant them, that
they may dwell in a place of their
own, and move no more;
neither shall the children
of wickedness afflict them
any more, as beforetime,
11. And as since the time that I
commanded judges *to be* over
my people Israel, and have caused
thee to rest from all thine enemies.
Also the LORD telleth thee that he
will make thee an house.
12. **And when** thy
days be fulfilled, and
thou shalt sleep with
thy fathers, I will set
up thy seed after thee, which
shall proceed out of thy bowels,
and I will establish
his kingdom.
13. **He shall build an house**
for my name, and I will stablish
the throne of his kingdom for ever.
14. I will be his father, and
he shall be my son.
If he commit iniquity,
I will chasten him with
the rod of men, and with the
stripes of the children of men:
15. **But my mercy shall not**
depart away from him,
as I took it from Saul,
whom I put away before thee.
16. **And thine house and**
thy kingdom shall be established
for ever before thee:
thy throne shall be
established for ever.
17. **According to all**
these words, and
according to all this vision, so
did Nathan speak
unto David.
18. **Then** went king
David in, and
sat before the LORD, and he
said, Who am I, O Lord
GOD? and what *is* my house,
that thou hast brought
me hitherto?
19. And this was yet a small thing in
thy sight, O Lord GOD; but thou hast

spoken also of thy servant's house for
a great while to come. And is this the
manner of man, O Lord GOD?
20. And what can David say more
unto thee? for thou, Lord GOD,
knowest thy servant.
21. **For thy word's sake,**
and according to thine own heart,
hast thou done all these
great things, to make
thy servant know *them.*
22. **Wherefore thou art**
great, O LORD God:
for *there is* none like thee,
neither is there any God
beside thee, according to all
that we have heard with our ears.
23. **And what** one
nation in the earth
is like thy people, *even* like
Israel, whom God went
to redeem for a people to
himself, and to make him a name,
and to do for you great things and
terrible, for thy land, before thy
people, which thou redeemedst
to thee from Egypt, *from* the
nations and their gods?
24. For thou hast confirmed to
thyself thy people Israel *to be* a
people unto thee for ever: and
thou, LORD, art become their God.
25. **And now, O LORD** God,
the word that thou hast spoken
concerning thy servant, and
concerning his house,
establish it for ever, and do
as thou hast said.
26. **And let thy name be**
magnified for ever, saying, The
LORD of hosts *is* the God over Israel:
and let the house of thy servant
David be established before thee.
27. **For thou,** O LORD
of hosts, God of Israel,
hast revealed to thy
servant, saying, I will
build thee an house: therefore
hath thy servant found in his heart
to pray this prayer unto thee.
28. And now, O Lord GOD, thou
art that God, and thy words be true,
and thou hast promised this

goodness unto thy servant:

29. **Therefore** now let it please thee to **bless the house of thy servant,** that it may continue for ever before thee: **for thou**, O Lord GOD, **hast spoken it: and** with thy blessing **let the house of thy servant be blessed for ever.**

CHAPTER 8

1. **And after this** it came to pass that **David smote the Philistines, and subdued them:** and David took Metheg–ammah out of the hand of the Philistines.

2. **And he smote Moab,** and measured them with a line, casting them down to the ground; even with two lines measured he to put todeath, and with one full line to keep alive. **And so the Moabites became David's servants,** *and* brought gifts.

3. David smote also Hadadezer, the son of Rehob, king of Zobah, as he went to recover his border at the river Euphrates.

4. **And David took** from him **a thousand chariots, and seven hundred horsemen, and twenty thousand footmen: and David houghed all the** chariot **horses, but reserved** of them *for* **an hundred** chariots.

5. **And** when the Syrians of Damascus came to succour Hadadezer king of Zobah, **David slew of the Syrians two and twenty thousand** men.

6. **Then** David put garrisons in Syria of Damascus: *and* **the Syrians became servants to David, and brought gifts.** And the LORD preserved David

whithersoever he went.

7. **And David took** the shields of gold that were on the servants of Hadadezer, and brought them to Jerusalem.

8. And from Betah, and fromBerothai, cities of Hadadezer, king David took exceeding much brass.

9. When Toi king of Hamath heard that David had smitten all the host of Hadadezer,

10. Then Toi sent Joram his son unto king David, to salute him, and to bless him, because he had fought against Hadadezer, and smitten him: for Hadadezer had wars with Toi. And *Joram* brought with him **vessels of silver,** and vessels of **gold, and** vessels of **brass:**

11. **Which** also king **David did dedicate unto the LORD,** with the silver and gold that he had dedicated of all nations which he subdued;

12. Of Syria, and of Moab, and of the children of Ammon, and of the Philistines, and of Amalek, and of the spoil of Hadadezer, son of Rehob, king of Zobah.

13. And David gat *him* a name when he returned from smiting of the Syrians in the valley of salt, *being* eighteen thousand *men.*

14. **And he put garrisons in Edom;** throughout all Edom put he garrisons, and all they of Edom became David's servants. **And the LORD preserved David** whithersoever he went.

15. **And David reigned over all Israel; and** David **executed judgment and justice unto all his people.**

16. **And Joab** the son of Zeruiah **was over the host; and Jehoshaphat** the son of Ahilud **was recorder;**

17. **And Zadok** the son of Ahitub, **and Ahimelech** the son of Abiathar,

■ were the priests; and
■ Seraiah was the scribe;
18. And Benaiah the son of Jehoiada
was over both the Cherethites
and the Pelethites;
■ and David's sons
■ were chief rulers.

CHAPTER 9

■ 1. And David said,
■ Is there yet
■ any that is
■ left of the house of Saul,
■ that I may shew him
■ kindness for
■ Jonathan's sake?
■ 2. And *there was* of
■ the house of Saul a
■ servant whose name *was*
■ Ziba. And when they had called
him unto David, the king
■ said unto him, *Art* thou Ziba?
And he said, Thy servant *is* he.
3. And the king said, *Is* there not yet
any of the house of Saul, that I may
shew the kindness of God unto him?
And Ziba said unto the king,
■ Jonathan hath yet a son,
■ which is lame on his feet.
4. And the king said unto him,
Where *is* he? And Ziba said
unto the king, Behold,
■ he is in the house of Machir,
the son of Ammiel, in Lo–debar.
■ 5. Then king David
■ sent, and fetched him
out of the house of Machir, the
son of Ammiel, from Lo–debar.
■ 6. Now when
■ Mephibosheth, the son
of Jonathan, the son of Saul,
■ was come unto David,
■ he fell on his face, and
■ did reverence. And David
said, Mephibosheth. And he
answered, Behold thy servant!
■ 7. And David said unto him,
■ Fear not: for I will surely
■ shew thee kindness for
■ Jonathan thy father's sake,
■ and will restore thee all
■ the land of Saul thy father;
■ and thou shalt eat bread

■ at my table continually.
8. And he bowed himself, and
said, What *is* thy servant, that
thou shouldest look upon such a
dead dog as I *am*?
■ 9. Then the king called to
■ Ziba, Saul's servant, and
■ said unto him, I have given unto
thy master's son all that pertained
to Saul and to all his house.
■ 10. Thou therefore,
■ and thy sons, and thy
■ servants, shall till the
■ land for him, and thou
shalt bring in *the fruits*, that thy
master's son may have food to eat:
■ but Mephibosheth
thy master's son
■ shall eat bread alway
■ at my table. Now Ziba
■ had fifteen sons and
■ twenty servants.
11. Then said Ziba unto the king,
According to all that my lord the king
hath commanded his servant, so shall
thy servant do. As for Mephibosheth,
said the king, he shall eat at my table,
as one of the king's sons.
12. And Mephibosheth had a
young son, whose name *was* Micha.
■ And all that dwelt in the
house of Ziba
■ were servants
■ unto Mephibosheth.
■ 13. So Mephibosheth
dwelt in Jerusalem: for he
■ did eat continually
■ at the king's table; and
■ was lame on both his feet.

CHAPTER 10

■ 1. And it came to pass
after this, that
■ the king of the children
■ of Ammon died,
■ and Hanun his son
■ reigned in his stead.
■ 2. Then said David, I
■ will shew kindness unto
■ Hanun the son of Nahash,
■ as his father shewed
■ kindness unto me. And
■ David sent to comfort

480

him by the hand of
his servants for his father.
And David's servants came into
the land of the children of Ammon.
3. **And the princes**
of the children
of Ammon said unto
Hanun their lord,
Thinkest thou that David
doth honour thy father, that he
hath sent comforters unto
thee? hath not David rather
sent his servants unto thee,
to search the city,
and to spy it out, and to
overthrow it?
4. **Wherefore Hanun**
took David's servants,
and shaved off the one
half of
their beards, and cut off
their garments in the
middle, *even* to their buttocks,
and sent them away.
5. When they told *it* unto
David, he
sent to meet them, because
the men were greatly
ashamed: and the king
said, Tarry at Jericho
until your beards be
grown, and *then* return.
6. **And** when the children of
Ammon saw that they stank before
David, the children of Ammon
sent and hired the Syrians of
Beth–rehob and the Syrians of Zoba,
twenty thousand footmen, and of king
Maacah a thousand men, and of
Ish–tob twelve thousand men.
7. **And when David**
heard of *it,*
he sent Joab, and all
the host of the mighty men.
8. And the children of
Ammon came out,
and put the battle in array
at the entering in of the
gate: and the Syrians of Zoba, and
of Rehob, and Ish–tob, and Maacah,
were by themselves in the field.
9. **When Joab saw**
that the front of the

battle was against
him before and behind,
he chose of all the
choice men of Israel,
and put them in array
against the Syrians:
10. **And the rest** of the people
he delivered into the hand of
Abishai his brother,
that he might
put *them* in array
against the children of
Ammon.
11. **And he said, If the**
Syrians be too strong
for me, then thou shalt
help me: but if the children of
Ammon be too strong for
thee, then I will come and
help thee.
12. Be of good courage, and let us
play the men for our people, and for
the cities of our God: and the LORD
do that which seemeth him good.
13. **And Joab drew nigh,**
and the people that *were* with him,
unto the battle against
the Syrians: and they
fled before him.
14. **And when** the children of
Ammon saw that
the Syrians were
fled, then fled they
also before Abishai, and
entered into the city.
So Joab returned
from the children of
Ammon, and came
to Jerusalem.
15. **And when the**
Syrians saw that they
were smitten before Israel,
they gathered themselves
together.
16. And Hadarezer sent, and brought
out the Syrians that *were* beyond
the river: and they came to Helam;
and Shobach the captain
of the host of Hadarezer
went before them.
17. And when it was told David,
he gathered all Israel together,
and passed over Jordan,

and came to Helam. **And** the Syrians set themselves in array against **David, and fought with him.** 18. **And** the Syrians fled before Israel; and David **slew the men of seven hundred chariots** of the Syrians, **and forty thousand horsemen, and** smote Shobach **the captain of their host,** who died there. 19. **And** when all **the kings that were servants to Hadarezer** saw that they were smitten before Israel, they **made peace with Israel, and served them. So the Syrians feared to help** the children of **Ammon any more.**

CHAPTER 11

1. **And** it came to pass, **after the year was expired,** at the time when kings go forth *to battle,* that **David sent Joab, and his** servants with him, and all Israel; **and they destroyed** the children of **Ammon, and besieged Rabbah. But David tarried** still **at Jerusalem.** 2. **And** it came to pass **in an eveningtide,** that **David arose from** off **his bed, and walked upon the roof** of the king's house: **and** from the roof **he saw a woman washing herself; and the woman was very beautiful** to look upon. 3. **And David** sent and **inquired after the woman. And one said, Is not this Bath-sheba,** the daughter of Eliam, **the wife of Uriah** the Hittite?

4. **And David sent messengers, and took her;** and she came in unto him, **and he lay with her;** for she was purified from her uncleanness: and she returned unto her house. 5. **And the woman conceived,** and sent **and told David, and said, I am with child.** 6. **And David sent to Joab, saying, Send me Uriah** the Hittite. And Joab sent Uriah to David. 7. **And** when Uriah was come unto him, **David demanded of him how Joab did,** and how the people did, and **how the war prospered.** 8. **And David said to Uriah, Go** down **to thy house,** and wash thy feet. And Uriah departed out of the king's house, and there followed him a mess *of meat* from the king. 9. **But Uriah slept at** the door of **the king's house with all the servants** of his lord, and went not down to his house. 10. **And** when **they** had **told David,** saying, Uriah went not down unto his house, **David said unto Uriah,** Camest thou not from *thy* journey? **why** *then* **didst thou not go** down **unto thine house?** 11. **And Uriah said** unto David, **The ark, and Israel,** and Judah, **abide in tents;** and my lord Joab, and the servants of my lord, are encamped in the open fields; **shall I then go into mine house, to eat and** to drink, and to **lie with my wife?** *as* thou livest, and *as* thy soul liveth, I will not do this thing. 12. **And David said** to Uriah, **Tarry here to-day** also, **and** to-morrow

482

I will let thee depart.
So Uriah abode in Jerusalem
that day, and the morrow.
13. **And** when
David had called him, he did
eat and drink before him; and he
made him drunk: and
at even he went out to
lie on his bed with the
servants of his lord,
but went not down
to his house.
14. **And** it came to pass
in the morning, that
David wrote a letter
to Joab, and sent
it by the hand of
Uriah.
15. And he wrote in the letter, saying,
Set ye
Uriah in the forefront of
the hottest battle,
and retire ye from him,
that he may be smitten, and
die.
16. **And** it came to pass, when
Joab observed the city, that he
assigned Uriah unto
a place where he knew
that valiant men were.
17. And the men of the
city went out, and
fought with Joab: and there
fell some of the people of
the servants of David;
and Uriah the Hittite
died also.
18. **Then Joab sent and**
told David all the things
concerning the war;
19. **And charged the**
messenger, saying,
When thou hast made
an end of telling the matters
of the war unto the king,
20. **And if** so be that
the king's wrath arise, and he
say unto thee, Wherefore approached
ye so nigh unto the city when ye
did fight? knew ye not that they
would shoot from the wall?
21. Who smote Abimelech the son
of Jerubbesheth? did not a woman

cast a piece of a millstone upon him
from the wall, that he died in
Thebez? why went ye nigh the wall?
then say thou,
Thy servant Uriah the Hittite
is dead also.
22. **So the messenger**
went, and came and
shewed David all that Joab
had sent him for.
23. And the messenger said unto
David, Surely the men prevailed
against us, and came out unto us
into the field, and we were upon them
even unto the entering of the gate.
24. And the shooters shot from off
the wall upon thy servants; and
some of the king's servants be
dead, and thy servant Uriah
the Hittite is dead also.
25. **Then David said**
unto the messenger, Thus shalt thou
say unto Joab, Let not
this thing displease
thee, for the sword devoureth
one as well as another:
make thy battle more
strong against the city,
and overthrow it: and
encourage thou him.
26. **And when the wife of**
Uriah heard that Uriah
her husband was dead,
she mourned for her husband.
27. **And when the mourning**
was past, David sent and
fetched her to his house,
and she became his wife,
and bare him a son.
But the thing that David had done
displeased the LORD.

CHAPTER 12

1. **And the LORD sent**
Nathan unto David.
And he came unto him,
and said unto him,
There were two
men in one city; the
one rich, and the
other poor.
2. **The rich man had** exceeding
many flocks and herds:

483

3. But the poor man had nothing, save one little ewe lamb, which he had bought and nourished up: and it grew up together with him, and with his children; it did eat of his own meat, and drank of his own cup, and lay in his bosom, and was unto him as a daughter. 4. And there came a traveller unto the rich man, and he spared to take of his own flock and of his own herd, to dress for the wayfaring man that was come unto him; but took the poor man's lamb, and dressed it for the man that was come to him. 5. And David's anger was greatly kindled against the man; and he said to Nathan, As the LORD liveth, the man that hath done this thing shall surely die: 6. And he shall restore the lamb fourfold, because he did this thing, and because he had no pity. 7. And Nathan said to David, Thou art the man. Thus saith the LORD God of Israel, I anointed thee king over Israel, and I delivered thee out of the hand of Saul; 8. And I gave thee thy master's house, and thy master's wives into thy bosom, and gave thee the house of Israel and of Judah; and if that had been too little, I would moreover have given unto thee such and such things. 9. Wherefore hast thou despised the commandment of the LORD, to do evil in his sight? thou hast killed Uriah the Hittite with the sword, and hast taken his wife to be thy wife, and hast slain him with the sword of the children of Ammon. 10. Now therefore the sword shall never depart from thine house; because thou hast despised me, and hast taken the wife of Uriah the Hittite to be thy wife. 11. Thus saith the LORD, Behold, I will raise up evil against thee out of thine own house, and I will take thy wives before thine eyes, and give them unto thy neighbour, and he shall lie with thy wives in the sight of this sun. 12. For thou didst *it* secretly: but I will do this thing before all Israel, and before the sun. 13. And David said unto Nathan, I have sinned against the LORD. And Nathan said unto David, The LORD also hath put away thy sin; thou shalt not die. 14. Howbeit, because by this deed thou hast given great occasion to the enemies of the LORD to blaspheme, the child also *that is* born unto thee shall surely die. 15. And Nathan departed unto his house.

And the LORD struck the child that Uriah's wife bare unto David, and it was very sick. 16. David therefore besought God for the child; and David fasted, and went in, and lay all night upon the earth. 17. And the elders of his house arose, *and went* to him, to raise him up from the earth: but he would not, neither did he eat bread with them. 18. And it came to pass on the seventh day, that the child died. And the servants of David feared to tell him

that the child was dead:
■ **for** they said, Behold,
■ **while the child was yet**
■ **alive,** we spake unto him, and
■ **he would not hearken**
unto our voice:
■ **how will he** then
■ **vex himself if we tell him** that
■ **the child is dead?**
■ 19. **But** when David saw
that his servants whispered,
■ **David perceived that the**
■ **child was dead:** therefore
David said unto his servants,
Is the child dead? And they
said, He is dead.
■ 20. **Then David**
■ **arose** from the earth,
■ **and washed, and anointed**
■ **himself,** and changed his apparel,
■ **and came into the house of**
■ **the LORD, and worshipped:**
■ **then** he came to his own house;
and when he required, they set
bread before him, and
■ **he did eat.**
■ 21. **Then said his**
■ **servants** unto him, What thing
is this that thou hast done?
■ **thou didst fast**
■ **and weep** for the child,
■ **while it was alive; but when**
■ **the child was dead, thou**
■ **didst rise and eat** bread.
■ 22. **And he said,** While the
child was yet alive, I fasted
and wept: for I said,
■ **Who can tell whether**
■ **GOD will be gracious** to me,
■ **that the child may live?**
■ 23. **But now he is dead,**
wherefore should I fast?
■ **can I bring him back** again?
■ **I shall go to him, but he**
■ **shall not return** to me.
■ 24. **And David comforted**
■ **Bath-sheba** his wife, and went
in unto her, and lay with her:
■ **and she bare a son, and he**
■ **called his name Solomon:**
■ **and the LORD loved him.**
■ 25. **And** he sent by the hand of
■ **Nathan** the prophet; and he

■ **called his name Jedidiah,**
■ **because of the LORD.**
■ 26. **And Joab fought**
■ **against** Rabbah of the children of
■ **Ammon, and took**
■ **the royal city.**
■ 27. **And Joab sent**
■ **messengers to David, and**
■ **said,** I have fought against Rabbah,
and have taken the city of waters.
28. Now therefore
■ **gather the** rest of the
■ **people** together,
■ **and encamp against the**
■ **city, and take it: lest I**
■ **take the city, and it be**
■ **called after my name.**
■ 29. **And David** gathered
all the people together, and
went to Rabbah, and
■ **fought against it,**
■ **and took it.**
■ 30. **And he took their**
■ **king's crown** from off his head,
the weight whereof *was* a talent of
gold with the precious stones:
■ **and it was set on David's**
■ **head. And he brought** forth
■ **the spoil** of the city
■ **in great abundance.**
■ 31. **And he brought** forth
■ **the people** that *were* therein,
■ **and put them under**
■ **saws, and** under harrows
of iron, and under
■ **axes** of iron,
■ **and made them pass**
■ **through the brickkiln:**
and thus did he unto all the
cities of the children of Ammon.
■ **So David and** all
■ **the people returned**
■ **unto Jerusalem.**

CHAPTER 13

■ 1. **And** it came to
pass after this, that
■ **Absalom the son of David**
■ **had a fair sister, whose**
■ **name was Tamar; and**
■ **Amnon the son of**
■ **David loved her.**
■ 2. **And Amnon was so**

■ **vexed, that he fell sick**
■ **for his sister Tamar;** for she
was a virgin; and Amnon thought it
hard for him to do anything to her.
3. But Amnon had a friend,
whose name *was*
■ **Jonadab, the son of** Shimeah
■ **David's brother:**
and Jonadab *was* a very subtil man.
4. And he
■ **said** unto him,
■ **Why art thou,**
being the king's son,
■ **lean** from day to day?
wilt thou not tell me?
■ **And Amnon said** unto him,
■ **I love Tamar, my brother**
■ **Absalom's sister.**
5. **And Jonadab said** unto
him, Lay thee down on thy bed, and
■ **make thyself sick: and**
■ **when thy father cometh**
■ **to see thee, say**
unto him, I pray thee,
■ **let my sister Tamar**
■ **come, and give me meat,**
and dress the meat in my sight, that
I may see *it,* and eat *it* at her hand.
6. So Amnon lay down, and made
himself sick: and when the king was
come to see him, Amnon said unto the
king, I pray thee, let Tamar my sister
come, and make me a couple of cakes
in my sight, that I may eat at her hand.
7. **Then David sent** home to
■ **Tamar,** saying, Go now
■ **to** thy brother
■ **Amnon's house,**
and dress him meat.
8. **So Tamar went**
to her brother Amnon's house;
and he was laid down.
■ **And** she took flour, and
kneaded *it,* and
■ **made cakes in his sight,**
and did bake the cakes.
9. And she took a pan, and
poured *them* out before him;
■ **but he refused to eat.**
And Amnon said, Have out
all men from me. And they went
out every man from him.
10. **And Amnon**

■ **said** unto Tamar,
■ **Bring the meat into the**
■ **chamber,** that I may eat of
thine hand. And Tamar took the
cakes which she had made,
and brought them into the
chamber to Amnon her brother.
11. **And when she had**
■ **brought them** unto him to eat,
■ **he took hold of her,**
■ **and said** unto her,
■ **Come lie with me,** my sister.
12. **And she answered** him,
■ **Nay,** my brother,
■ **do not force me;** for no
such thing ought to be done in
Israel: do not thou this folly.
13. **And** I, whither shall I cause my
shame to go? and as for thee, thou
shalt be as one of the fools in Israel.
Now therefore, I pray thee,
■ **speak unto the king;**
■ **for he will not withhold**
■ **me from thee.**
14. **Howbeit he would**
■ **not hearken unto her** voice:
■ **but,** being stronger than she,
■ **forced her, and lay**
■ **with her.**
15. **Then Amnon hated**
■ **her** exceedingly;
■ **so that the hatred**
wherewith he hated her
■ **was greater than the**
■ **love wherewith he had**
■ **loved her. And Amnon**
■ **said** unto her, Arise,
■ **be gone.**
16. **And she said** unto him,
■ **There is no cause: this**
■ **evil in sending me away**
■ **is greater than the other**
that thou didst unto me. But he
would not hearken unto her.
17. **Then he called**
■ **his servant**
that ministered unto him,
■ **and said, Put now**
■ **this woman out** from me,
and bolt the door after her.
18. **And she had a garment**
■ **of divers colours upon**
■ **her: for** with

such robes were the king's daughters *that were* virgins apparelled. Then his servant brought her out, and bolted the door after her.

19. And Tamar put ashes on her head, and rent her garment of divers colours that *was* on her, and laid her hand on her head, and went on crying.

20. And Absalom her brother said unto her, Hath Amnon thy brother been with thee? but hold now thy peace, my sister: he is thy brother; regard not this thing. So Tamar remained desolate in her brother Absalom's house.

21. But when king David heard of all these things, he was very wroth.

22. And Absalom spake unto his brother Amnon neither good nor bad: for Absalom hated Amnon, because he had forced his sister Tamar.

23. And it came to pass after two full years, that Absalom had sheepshearers in Baal-hazor, which is beside Ephraim: and Absalom invited all the king's sons.

24. And Absalom came to the king, and said, Behold now, thy servant hath sheepshearers; let the king, I beseech thee, and his servants go with thy servant.

25. And the king said to Absalom, Nay, my son, let us not all now go, lest we be chargeable unto thee. And he pressed him: howbeit he would not go, but blessed him.

26. Then said Absalom, If not, I pray thee, let my brother Amnon go with us. And the king said unto him, Why should he go with thee?

27. But Absalom pressed him, that he let Amnon and all the king's sons go with him.

28. Now Absalom had commanded his servants, saying, Mark ye now when Amnon's heart is merry with wine, and when I say unto you, Smite Amnon; then kill him, fear not: have not I commanded you? be courageous, and be valiant.

29. And the servants of Absalom did unto Amnon as Absalom had commanded. Then all the king's sons arose, and every man gat him up upon his mule, and fled.

30. And it came to pass, while they were in the way, that tidings came to David, saying, Absalom hath slain all the king's sons, and there is not one of them left.

31. Then the king arose, and tare his garments, and lay on the earth; and all his servants stood by with their clothes rent.

32. And Jonadab, the son of Shimeah David's brother, answered and said, Let not my lord suppose *that* they have slain all the young men the king's sons; for Amnon only is dead: for by the appointment of Absalom this hath been determined from the day that he forced his sister Tamar.

33. Now therefore let not my lord

the king take the thing to his heart, to think that all the king's sons are dead: for Amnon only is dead. 34. But Absalom fled. And the young man that kept the watch lifted up his eyes, and looked, and, behold, there came much people by the way of the hill side behind him. 35. And Jonadab said unto the king, Behold, the king's sons come: as thy servant said, so it is.

36. **And** it came to pass, **as soon as he** had **made an end of speaking,** that, behold, **the king's sons came, and lifted up their voice and wept: and the king also** and all his servants **wept** very sore. 37. But Absalom fled, and went to Talmai, the son of Ammihud, king of Geshur. And *David* mourned for his son every day.

38. **So Absalom fled, and went to Geshur, and was there three years.** 39. **And** *the soul of* king **David longed to go** forth **unto Absalom: for he was comforted concerning Amnon,** **seeing he was dead.**

CHAPTER 14

1. **Now Joab** the son of Zeruiah **perceived that the king's heart was toward Absalom.** 2. **And Joab** sent to Tekoah, and **fetched** thence **a wise woman, and said** unto her, I pray thee, **feign thyself to be** a mourner, and put on now mourning apparel, and anoint not thyself with oil, but be **as a woman that had a long time mourned for the dead:** 3. **And come to the king, and speak** on **this** manner **unto him. So Joab put**

the words in her mouth. 4. **And when the woman** of Tekoah **spake to the king, she** fell on her face to the ground, and did obeisance, and **said,** Help, O king. 5. And the king said unto her, What aileth thee? And she answered, **I am** indeed **a widow** woman, and mine husband is dead. 6. **And** thy handmaid **had two sons, and they** two **strove together** in the field, **and** *there was* none to part them, but the **one smote the other, and slew him.** 7. **And,** behold, **the** whole **family** is risen against thine handmaid, and they **said, Deliver him that smote his brother, that we may kill him,** for the life of his brother whom he slew; and we will destroy the heir also: and so they shall quench my coal which is left, **and** shall not **leave** to my husband **neither name nor remainder upon the earth.** 8. **And the king said** unto the woman, Go to thine house, **and I will give charge concerning thee.** 9. **And the woman** of Tekoah **said** unto the king, My lord, O king, **the iniquity be on me,** and on my father's house: **and the king and his throne be guiltless.** 10. And the king said, Whoever saith *ought* unto thee, bring him to me, and he shall not touch thee any more. 11. Then said she, I pray thee, let the king **remember the LORD** thy God, **that thou wouldest not**

suffer the revengers of
blood to destroy any
more, lest they destroy my son.
And he said, *As* the LORD liveth,
there shall not one hair of
thy son fall to the earth.
12. Then the woman said, Let
thine handmaid, I pray thee,
speak *one* word unto my lord
the king. And he said, Say on.
13. And the woman said,
Wherefore then hast thou
thought such a thing against
the people of God? for
the king doth speak this thing
as one which is faulty, in
that the king doth not fetch
home again his banished.
14. For we must needs die, and
are as water spilt
on the ground,
which cannot be gathered up again;
neither doth God respect
any person: yet doth
he devise means, that
his banished be not
expelled from him.
15. Now therefore that
I am come to
speak of this thing
unto my lord
the king, *it is* because
the people have made
me afraid: and thy handmaid
said, I will now speak unto the
king; it may be that the king will
perform the request of his handmaid.
16. For the king will hear, to
deliver his handmaid out of the
hand of the man *that would* destroy
me and my son together out
of the inheritance of God.
17. Then thine handmaid said,
The word of my lord the king
shall now be comfortable:
for as an angel of
God, so is my lord
the king to discern
good and bad: therefore
the LORD thy God
will be with thee.
18. Then the king answered and said
unto the woman, Hide not from me, I

pray thee, the thing that I shall ask
thee. And the woman said, Let
my lord the king now speak.
19. And the king said,
Is not the hand of
Joab with thee in all this?
And the woman answered
and said, As thy soul liveth, my
lord the king, none can turn to
the right hand or to the left
from ought that my lord the king
hath spoken: for thy servant
Joab, he bade me, and he
put all these words in the
mouth of thine handmaid:
20. To fetch about this form of
speech hath thy servant Joab
done this thing: and
my lord is wise, according
to the wisdom of an angel of God,
to know all things that
are in the earth.
21. And the king said
unto Joab, Behold now,
I have done this thing:
go therefore,
bring the young man
Absalom again.
22. And Joab fell to the
ground on his face, and
bowed himself, and
thanked the king: and Joab
said, To-day thy servant
knoweth that
I have found grace
in thy sight, my lord,
O king, in that the king hath
fulfilled the request of his servant.
23. So Joab arose and
went to Geshur, and
brought Absalom
to Jerusalem.
24. And the king said, Let
him turn to his own house,
and let him not see my
face. So Absalom returned
to his own house, and saw
not the king's face.
25. But in all Israel
there was none to be so much
praised as Absalom for
his beauty: from the sole of his
foot even to the crown of his head

there was no blemish in him.
26. **And when he polled his head,** (for it was **at** every **year's end** that he polled it: because **the hair** was heavy on him, therefore he polled it:) he **weighed** the hair of his head at **two hundred shekels** after the king's weight.
27. **And unto Absalom there were born three sons, and one daughter,** whose name *was* Tamar: she was a woman of a fair countenance.
28. **So Absalom dwelt two** full **years in Jerusalem, and saw not the king's face.**
29. **Therefore Absalom sent for Joab,** to have sent him to the king; **but he would not come** to him: and when he sent again the second time, he would not come.
30. **Therefore he said unto his servants, See, Joab's field is near mine,** and he hath barley there; go and **set it on fire.** And Absalom's servants set the field on fire.
31. **Then Joab** arose, and **came to Absalom** unto *his* house, **and said** unto him, **Wherefore have thy servants set my field on fire?**
32. **And Absalom answered** Joab, Behold, **I sent unto thee,** saying, Come hither, **that I may** send thee to the king, to say, Wherefore am I come from Geshur? *it had been* good for me *to have been* there still: now therefore let me **see the king's face; and if there be any iniquity in me, let him kill me.**
33. **So** Joab came to **the king,** and told him:

and when he had **called for Absalom, he came** to the king, **and bowed** himself on his face to the ground **before the king: and the king kissed Absalom.**

CHAPTER 15

1. **And** it came to pass **after this,** that **Absalom prepared** him **chariots and horses, and fifty men to run before him.**
2. **And Absalom** rose up early, and **stood beside the** way of the **gate: and** it was *so,* that **when any man** that had a controversy **came to the king for judgment,** then **Absalom** called unto him, and **said,** Of what city *art* thou? And he said, Thy servant *is* of one of the tribes of Israel.
3. And Absalom said unto him, See, **thy matters are good** and right; **but there is no man deputed of the king to hear thee.**
4. Absalom said moreover, **Oh that I were made judge** in the land, that every man which hath any suit or cause might come unto me, and **I would do him justice!**
5. **And** it was *so,* that **when any man came nigh** *to him* to do him obeisance, **he** put forth his hand, and **took him, and kissed him.**
6. **And on this manner** did **Absalom** to all Israel that came to the king for judgment: so Absalom **stole the hearts of the men of Israel.**
7. **And** it came to pass **after forty years,** that **Absalom said unto the king,** I pray thee, **let me go and pay my**

vow, which I have vowed **unto the LORD,** in Hebron.

8. **For thy servant vowed** a vow **while** I abode **at Geshur** in Syria, saying, **If the LORD shall bring me** again indeed **to Jerusalem, then I will serve the LORD.**

9. **And the king said** unto him, **Go in peace. So he** arose, and **went to Hebron.**

10. **But Absalom sent spies throughout** all the tribes of **Israel, saying, As** soon as **ye hear** the sound of **the trumpet,** then ye shall say, **Absalom reigneth in Hebron.**

11. And with Absalom went two hundred men out of Jerusalem, *that were* called; and they went in their simplicity, and they knew not any thing.

12. **And Absalom sent for Ahithophel** the Gilonite, **David's counsellor,** from his city, *even* from Giloh, while he offered sacrifices. **And the conspiracy was strong; for the people increased** continually **with Absalom.**

13. **And there came a messenger to David,** saying, **The hearts of the men of Israel are after Absalom.**

14. **And David said** unto all his servants that *were* with him at Jerusalem, Arise, and **let us flee;** for we shall not *else* escape from Absalom: make speed to depart, **lest he** overtake us suddenly, and bring evil upon us, and **smite the city with the edge of the sword.**

15. And the king's servants said unto the king, Behold, thy servants *are ready to do* whatsoever my lord the king shall appoint.

16. **And the king** went forth, **and** all **his household** after him. And the king left ten women, *which were* concubines, to keep the house.

17. And the king went forth, and all the people after him, and **tarried in a place that was far off.**

18. **And** all his servants passed on beside him; and all the Cherethites, and all the Pelethites, and all the Gittites, **six hundred men which came after him from Gath, passed on before the king.**

19. **Then said the king to Ittai the Gittite,** Wherefore goest thou also with us? **return to thy place,** and abide with the king: for thou *art* a stranger, and also an exile.

20. Whereas thou camest *but* yesterday, should I this day make thee go up and down with us? seeing I go whither I may, return thou, **and take back thy brethren: mercy and truth be with thee.**

21. **And Ittai answered** the king, and said, As the LORD liveth, and *as* my lord the king liveth, **surely in what place** my lord **the king shall be, whether in death or life,** even **there** also **will thy servant be.**

22. **And David said** to Ittai, **Go and pass over.** And Ittai the Gittite passed over, and all his men, and all the little ones that *were* with him.

23. And all the country wept with a loud voice, **and all the people passed over:** the king also himself passed over **the brook Kidron, and** all the people passed over, **toward** the way of **the wilderness.**

24. **And** lo **Zadok** also, **and all the Levites**

491

were with him,
bearing the ark of the covenant
of God: and they set down the
ark of God; and Abiathar went up,
until all the people had done
passing out of the city.
25. **And the king said**
unto Zadok, Carry
back the ark of God
into the city: if I shall find
favour in the eyes of the
LORD, he will bring me
again, and shew me *both* it,
and his habitation:
26. **But if** he thus say,
I have no delight
in thee; behold,
here am I, let him do to me
as seemeth good unto him.
27. The king said also unto Zadok
the priest, *Art not* thou a seer? return
into the city in peace, and your two
sons with you, Ahimaaz thy son, and
Jonathan the son of Abiathar.
28. See, I will tarry in the plain of
the wilderness, until there come
word from you to certify me.
29. **Zadok therefore**
and Abiathar
carried the ark of God again
to Jerusalem: and they
tarried there.
30. **And David went** up
by the ascent of
mount Olivet, and wept
as he went up, and had his head
covered, and he went barefoot:
and all the people
that *was* with him
covered every man
his head, and they went up,
weeping as they went up.
31. **And one**
told David, saying,
Ahithophel is
among the conspirators
with Absalom. And David
said, O LORD, I pray thee,
turn the counsel of
Ahithophel into
foolishness.
32. **And** it came to pass, that
when David was

come to the top *of the*
mount, where he
worshipped God, behold,
Hushai the Archite
came to meet him
with his coat rent, and
earth upon his head:
33. Unto whom
David said, If thou
passest on with me, then
thou shalt be a
burden unto me:
34. **But** if thou
return to the city, and say unto
Absalom, I will be thy servant,
O king; *as I have been* thy father's
servant hitherto, so *will* I now
also *be* thy servant:
then mayest thou for me
defeat the counsel
of Ahithophel.
35. **And** *hast thou* not there with
thee Zadok and Abiathar the priests?
therefore it shall be, *that*
what thing soever
thou shalt hear out
of the king's house, thou shalt
tell it to Zadok and Abiathar
the priests.
36. Behold, *they have* there with
them their two sons, Ahimaaz Zadok's
son, and Jonathan Abiathar's *son; and*
by them ye shall
send unto me
every thing that
ye can hear.
37. **So Hushai David's**
friend came into the city,
and Absalom came
into Jerusalem.

CHAPTER 16

1. **And when**
David was a little
past the top of the
hill, behold, Ziba
the servant of Mephibosheth
met him, with a couple of
asses saddled, and upon
them two hundred *loaves* of
bread, and
an hundred bunches of
raisins, and an hundred of summer

fruits, and a bottle of
wine.
2. And the king said unto Ziba, What
meanest thou by these? And Ziba
said, The asses *be* for the king's
household to ride on; and the bread
and summer fruit for the young men
to eat; and the wine, that such as be
faint in the wilderness may drink.
3. And the king said, And where is
thy master's son? And Ziba said unto
the king, Behold, he abideth at
Jerusalem: for he said, To-day shall
the house of Israel restore me the
kingdom of my father.
4. Then said the king to Ziba, Behold,
thine *are* all that *pertained* unto
Mephibosheth. And Ziba said, I
humbly beseech thee *that* I may find
grace in thy sight, my lord, O king.
5. **And when** king
David came to Bahurim,
behold, thence came out
a man of the family
of the house of Saul,
whose name was
Shimei, the son of Gera: he
came forth,
and cursed still as he came.
6. **And** he
cast stones at David, and
at all the servants of king David: and
all the people and all the mighty men
were on his right hand and on his left.
7. **And** thus
said Shimei when he cursed,
Come out, come out,
thou bloody man,
and thou man of Belial:
8. **The LORD hath returned**
upon thee all the blood
of the house of Saul,
in whose stead thou hast reigned;
and the LORD
hath delivered the kingdom
into the hand of Absalom
thy son: and, behold, thou *art*
taken in thy mischief because
thou art a bloody man.
9. **Then said Abishai**
the son of Zeruiah
unto the king, Why should
this dead dog curse my lord

the king? let me
go over, I pray thee,
and take off his head.
10. **And the king said,**
What have I to do with you,
ye sons of Zeruiah? so
let him curse,
because the LORD hath said unto
him, Curse David. Who shall then
say, Wherefore hast thou done so?
11. And David said to Abishai,
and to all his servants,
Behold, my son, which
came forth of my bowels,
seeketh my life: how
much more now
may this Benjamite do *it?*
let him alone, and let him curse;
for the LORD hath
bidden him.
12. **It may be that the**
LORD will look on mine
affliction, and that the LORD will
requite me good
for his cursing this day.
13. And as David and his men went
by the way, Shimei went along on
the hill's side over against him, and
cursed as he went, and threw
stones at him, and cast dust.
14. And the king, and all the people
that *were* with him, came weary,
and refreshed themselves there.
15. **And Absalom,**
and all the people
the men of Israel, came
to Jerusalem, and
Ahithophel with him.
16. **And** it came to pass, when
Hushai the Archite,
David's friend, was come
unto Absalom, that Hushai
said unto Absalom,
God save the king,
God save the king.
17. **And Absalom**
said to Hushai, *Is* this thy
kindness to thy friend?
why wentest thou not
with thy friend?
18. **And Hushai said**
unto Absalom, Nay; but
whom the LORD,

493

and this people,
and all the men of Israel,
choose, his will I be, and
with him will I abide.
19. And again, whom should I
serve? *should I* not *serve* in
the presence of his son?
as I have served in thy
father's presence, so
will I be in thy presence.
20. **Then said Absalom**
to Ahithophel, Give
counsel among you
what we shall do.
21. **And Ahithophel**
said unto Absalom,
Go in unto thy father's
concubines, which he
hath left to keep the house;
and all Israel shall hear
that thou art abhorred
of thy father: then shall
the hands of all that are
with thee be strong.
22. So they spread Absalom a
tent upon the top of the house;
and Absalom went in unto
his father's concubines in
the sight of all Israel.
23. **And the counsel**
of Ahithophel, which he
counselled in those days,
was as if a man had
inquired at the oracle
of God: so *was* all the
counsel of Ahithophel both
with David and with Absalom.

CHAPTER 17

1. **Moreover Ahithophel**
said unto Absalom,
Let me now
choose out
twelve thousand
men, and I will arise and
pursue after
David this night:
2. **And I** will come upon him while
he is weary and weak handed, and
will make him afraid: and all
the people that *are*
with him shall flee; and
I will smite the king only:

3. **And I will bring back** all
the people unto thee: the
man whom thou seekest *is* as
if all returned: *so* all the people
shall be in peace.
4. **And the saying**
pleased Absalom well,
and all the elders of Israel.
5. **Then said**
Absalom, Call now
Hushai the Archite also,
and let us
hear likewise
what he saith.
6. And when Hushai was come to
Absalom, Absalom spake unto him,
saying, Ahithophel hath spoken
after this manner: shall we do after
his saying? if not; speak thou.
7. **And Hushai**
said unto Absalom,
The counsel that
Ahithophel hath given
is not good at this time.
8. **For,** said Hushai, thou knowest
thy father and his
men, that they
be mighty men, and they be
chafed in their minds, as a bear
robbed of her whelps in the field:
and thy father is a man
of war, and will not
lodge with the people.
9. Behold, he is hid now in some pit,
or in some *other* place: and it will
come to pass, when some of them
be overthrown at the first, that
whosoever heareth it will say,
There is a slaughter among the
people that follow Absalom.
10. And he also *that is* valiant, whose
heart *is* as the heart of a lion, shall
utterly melt: for all Israel knoweth that
thy father *is* a mighty man, and *they*
which *be* with him *are* valiant men.
11. **Therefore I counsel**
that all Israel be generally
gathered unto thee, from Dan
even to Beer-sheba, as the sand
that *is* by the sea for multitude;
and that thou go to
battle in thine own person.
12. **So shall we come upon**

494

him in some place where he shall be found, and we will light upon him as the dew falleth on the ground: **and** of him and of all the men that *are* with him **there shall not be left so much as one.**

13. Moreover, if he be gotten into a city, then shall all Israel bring ropes to that city, and we will draw it into the river, until there be not one small stone found there.

14. **And Absalom** and all the men of Israel **said, The counsel of Hushai** the Archite **is better than** the counsel of **Ahithophel. For the LORD had appointed to defeat the** good **counsel of Ahithophel,** to the intent that the LORD might bring evil upon Absalom.

15. **Then said Hushai unto** Zadok and to Abiathar **the priests, Thus and thus did Ahithophel counsel** Absalom and the elders of Israel; and thus **and thus have I counselled.**

16. **Now** therefore send quickly, and **tell David,** saying, **Lodge not** this night **in the** plains of the **wilderness,** but speedily pass over; lest the king be swallowed up, and all the people that *are* with him.

17. Now Jonathan and Ahimaaz stayed by En-rogel; for they might not be seen to come into the city: and a wench went and told them; **and they went and told king David.**

18. **Nevertheless a lad saw them, and told Absalom: but they** went both of them away quickly, and **came to a man's house** in Bahurim, **which had a well** in his court; **whither they went down.**

19. And the woman took and spread a covering over the well's mouth, and spread ground corn thereon; and the thing was not known.

20. **And when Absalom's servants came** to the woman to the house, they said, Where *is* Ahimaaz and Jonathan? And the woman said unto them, They be gone over the brook of water. And when **they** had **sought and could not find them,** they returned to Jerusalem.

21. **And** it came to pass, after they were departed, that **they** came up out of the well, and **went and told** king **David,** and said unto David, Arise, and pass quickly over the water: for thus hath Ahithophel counselled against you.

22. **Then David arose, and** all the people that *were* with him, and they **passed over Jordan:** by the morning light there lacked not one of them that was not gone over Jordan.

23. **And when Ahithophel saw that his counsel was not followed, he** saddled *his* ass, and arose, and **gat** him home **to his house,** to his city, **and put his household in order, and hanged himself,** and died, and was buried in the sepulchre of his father.

24. Then David came to Mahanaim. **And Absalom passed over Jordan,** he and all the men of Israel with him.

25. **And** Absalom **made Amasa captain of the host instead of Joab:** which **Amasa** *was* a man's son, whose name *was* Ithra an Israelite, that **went in to Abigail the daughter of Nahash,** sister to Zeruiah Joab's mother.

26. So Israel and Absalom pitched in the land of Gilead.

27. **And it came to pass,**

■ when David was come
■ to Mahanaim, that
■ Shobi the son of Nahash of
Rabbah of the children of Ammon,
■ and Machir
the son of Ammiel of Lo–debar,
■ and Barzillai
the Gileadite of Rogelim,
■ 28. Brought beds, and
■ basins, and earthen
■ vessels, and
■ wheat, and
■ barley, and flour, and parched
■ corn, and beans,
and lentiles, and parched *pulse*,
■ 29. And honey, and butter,
■ and sheep, and
■ cheese of kine,
■ for David, and for
■ the people that *were*
■ with him, to eat:
■ for they said,
The people is hungry,
and weary, and thirsty,
in the wilderness.

CHAPTER 18

■ 1. And David numbered
■ the people that *were* with him,
■ and set captains of
thousands, and captains of hundreds
■ over them.
■ 2. And David sent forth
■ a third part of the people
■ under the hand of
■ Joab, and a third part
■ under the hand of
■ Abishai the son of
Zeruiah, Joab's brother,
■ and a third part
■ under the hand of
■ Ittai the Gittite.
■ And the king
■ said unto the people,
■ I will surely go forth
■ with you myself also.
■ 3. But the people answered,
■ Thou shalt not go forth:
for if we flee away, they will not care
■ for us; neither if half of us
die, will they care for us: but now
■ thou art worth ten
■ thousand of us: therefore

now *it is* better that thou
■ succour us out of the city.
4. And the king said unto them,
What seemeth you best I will do.
■ And the king stood by
■ the gate side,
■ and all the people came
■ out by hundreds and by thousands.
■ 5. And the king
■ commanded Joab and
Abishai and Ittai, saying,
■ Deal gently for my sake
with the young man, *even*
■ with Absalom. And all
■ the people heard when the
king gave all the captains charge
concerning Absalom.
■ 6. So the people
■ went out into the field
■ against Israel:
and the battle was
■ in the wood of Ephraim;
7. Where the people of Israel were
slain before the servants of David,
■ and there was there a
■ great slaughter that day
■ of twenty thousand men.
8. For the battle was there scattered
over the face of all the country:
■ and the wood devoured
■ more people that day
■ than the sword devoured.
■ 9. And Absalom met the
■ servants of David. And
■ Absalom rode upon
■ a mule, and the mule went
■ under the thick boughs of
■ a great oak, and his
■ head caught hold of the oak,
■ and he was taken up
between the heaven and the earth;
■ and the mule that *was* under him
■ went away.
■ 10. And a certain man
■ saw it, and told Joab,
and said, Behold, I saw
Absalom hanged in an oak.
■ 11. And Joab said unto
the man that told him, And,
behold, thou sawest *him*, and
■ why didst thou not
■ smite him there to the ground?
and I would have given thee ten

496

shekels of silver, and a girdle.

12. **And the man said** unto Joab, **Though I** should **receive a thousand shekels** of silver in mine hand, **yet would I not put forth mine hand against the king's son: for** in our hearing **the king charged thee** and Abishai and Ittai, saying, **Beware that none touch** the young man **Absalom.**

13. Otherwise I should have wrought falsehood against mine own life: for there is no matter hid from the king, and thou thyself wouldest have set thyself against *me.*

14. **Then** said **Joab,** I may not tarry thus with thee. And he **took three darts** in his hand, **and thrust them through the heart of Absalom,** while he *was* yet alive in the midst of the oak.

15. **And ten young men that bare Joab's armour compassed** about and smote **Absalom, and slew him.**

16. And Joab blew the trumpet, and the people returned from pursuing after Israel: for Joab held back the people.

17. **And they took Absalom, and cast him into a great pit** in the wood, **and laid** a very great heap of **stones upon him: and all Israel fled** every one to his tent.

18. Now **Absalom** in his lifetime **had** taken and **reared up for himself a pillar,** which *is* in the king's dale: **for he said, I have no son to keep my name** in remembrance: and he called the pillar after his own name: **and it is called** unto this day, **Absalom's place.**

19. **Then said Ahimaaz** the son of Zadok, **Let me** now run, and

bear the king tidings, how that the LORD hath avenged him of his enemies.

20. **And Joab said** unto him, Thou shalt **not** bear tidings **this day, but** thou shalt bear tidings **another** day: but this day thou shalt bear no tidings, **because the king's son is dead.**

21. **Then said Joab to Cushi, Go tell the king what thou hast seen.** And Cushi bowed himself unto Joab, and ran.

22. **Then said Ahimaaz** the son of Zadok yet **again to Joab,** But howsoever, **let me,** I pray thee, **also run after Cushi.** And Joab said, Wherefore wilt thou run, my son, seeing that thou hast no tidings ready?

23. But howsoever, *said he,* let me run. And he said unto him, Run. **Then Ahimaaz** ran by the way of the plain, and **overran Cushi.**

24. And David sat between the two gates: **and the watchman** went up to the roof **over the gate** unto the wall, and lifted up his eyes, and **looked,** and behold a man running alone.

25. **And** the watchman cried, and **told the king. And the king said, If he be alone, there is tidings in his mouth.** And he came apace, and drew near.

26. **And the watchman saw another man** running: and the watchman called unto the porter, and said, Behold *another* man **running alone. And the king said, He also bringeth tidings.**

27. **And the watchman said,** Me thinketh **the running of the foremost is** like the running of

Ahimaaz the son of Zadok. And the king said, He *is* a good man, and cometh with good tidings.

28. And Ahimaaz called, and said unto the king, All is well. And he fell down to the earth upon his face before the king, and said, Blessed *be* the LORD thy God, which hath delivered up the men that lifted up their hand against my lord the king.

29. And the king said, Is the young man Absalom safe? And Ahimaaz answered, When Joab sent the king's servant, and me thy servant, I saw a great tumult, but I knew not what it was.

30. And the king said unto him, Turn aside, *and* stand here. And he turned aside, and stood still.

31. And, behold, Cushi came; and Cushi said, Tidings, my lord the king: for the LORD hath avenged thee this day of all them that rose up against thee.

32. And the king said unto Cushi, Is the young man Absalom safe? And Cushi answered, The enemies of my lord the king, and all that rise against thee to do *thee* hurt, be as that young man is.

33. And the king was much moved, and went up to the chamber over the gate, and wept: and as he went, thus he said, O my son Absalom, my son, my son Absalom! would God I had died for thee, O Absalom, my son, my son!

CHAPTER 19

1. And it was told Joab, Behold, the king weepeth and mourneth for Absalom.

2. And the victory that day was turned into mourning unto all the people: for the people heard say that day how the king was grieved for his son.

3. And the people gat them by stealth that day into the city, as people being ashamed steal away when they flee in battle.

4. But the king covered his face, and the king cried with a loud voice, O my son Absalom, O Absalom, my son, my son!

5. And Joab came into the house to the king, and said, Thou hast shamed this day the faces of all thy servants, which this day have saved thy life, and the lives of thy sons and of thy daughters, and the lives of thy wives, and the lives of thy concubines;

6. In that thou lovest thine enemies, and hatest thy friends. For thou hast declared this day, that thou regardest neither princes nor servants: for this day I perceive, that if Absalom had lived, and all we had died this day, then it had pleased thee well.

7. Now therefore arise, go forth, and speak comfortably unto thy servants: for I swear by the LORD, if thou go not forth, there will not tarry one with thee this night: and that will be worse unto thee than all the evil that befell thee from thy youth until now.

8. Then the king arose, and

■ **sat in the gate.** And they told unto all the people, saying, Behold, the king doth sit in the gate.

■ **And all the people came**
■ **before the king:** for Israel had fled every man to his tent.

■ 9. **And all the people**
■ **were at strife** throughout all the tribes of Israel,

■ **saying, The king saved**
■ **us out of the hand of**
■ **our enemies,** and he delivered us out of the hand of the Philistines;

■ **and now he is fled out of**
■ **the land for Absalom.**

■ 10. **And Absalom,** whom we anointed over us,

■ **is dead** in battle.

■ **Now** therefore why

■ **speak** ye not a word

■ **of bringing the king back?**

■ 11. **And king David sent** to Zadok and to Abiathar

■ **the priests,** saying, Speak

■ **unto the elders of Judah,**

■ **saying, Why are ye the**

■ **last to bring the king**

■ **back** to his house?

■ **seeing** the speech of

■ **all Israel is come to**

■ **the king,** *even* to his house.

■ 12. **Ye are my brethren,** ye *are* my bones and my flesh: wherefore then are ye the last to bring back the king?

■ 13. **And say** ye

■ **to Amasa,** *Art* thou not of my bone, and of my flesh? God do so to me, and more also, if thou

■ **be** not

■ **captain of the host**

■ **before me** continually

■ **in the room of Joab.**

14. And he bowed *the heart* of all the men of Judah, even as the heart of one man;

■ **so** that

■ **they sent this word unto**

■ **the king, Return thou,**

■ **and all thy servants.**

■ 15. **So the king** returned, and

■ **came to Jordan. And**

■ **Judah came** to Gilgal, to go

■ **to meet the king,** to conduct the king over Jordan.

■ 16. **And Shimei** the son of Gera, a Benjamite, which *was* of Bahurim, hasted and

■ **came** down

■ **with** the men of

■ **Judah** to meet king David.

■ 17. **And there were a**

■ **thousand men of**

■ **Benjamin with him,** and Ziba the servant of the house of Saul, and his fifteen sons and his twenty servants with him; and they went over Jordan before the king.

18. And there went over a ferry boat to carry over the king's household, and to do what he thought good.

■ **And Shimei** the son of Gera

■ **fell down before the king,** as he was come over Jordan;

■ 19. **And said** unto the king,

■ **Let not my lord impute**

■ **iniquity unto me,** neither do thou remember that which thy servant did perversely the day that my lord the king went out of Jerusalem, that the king should take it to his heart.

20. **For** thy servant doth know that

■ **I have sinned:**

■ **therefore,** behold,

■ **I** am

■ **come** the

■ **first** this day of all the house of Joseph to go down

■ **to meet** my lord

■ **the king.**

■ 21. **But Abishai** the son of Zeruiah

■ **answered** and said,

■ **Shall not Shimei be**

■ **put to death** for this,

■ **because he cursed**

■ **the LORD's anointed?**

■ 22. **And David said,** What have I to do with you, ye sons of Zeruiah, that ye should this day be adversaries unto me?

■ **shall there any man be**

■ **put to death** this day in Israel?

■ **for** do not

■ **I know that I am** this day

■ **king over Israel?**

23. **Therefore the king said unto Shimei, Thou shalt not die**. And the king sware unto him.

24. **And Mephibosheth the son of Saul came** down to meet the king, **and had neither dressed his feet, nor trimmed his beard, nor washed his clothes, from the day the king departed** until the day he came *again* in peace.

25. **And** it came to pass, when he was come to Jerusalem to meet **the king,** that the king **said unto him, Wherefore wentest not thou with me,** Mephibosheth?

26. **And he answered**, My lord, O king, **my servant deceived me:**for thy servant said, I will saddle me an ass, that I may ride thereon, and go to the king; because thy servant *is*lame.

27. **And** he hath **slandered thy servant** unto my lord the king; but my lord the king is as an angel of God: **do therefore what is good in thine eyes.**

28. **For** all of **my father's house were but dead men** before mylord the king: **yet didst thou set thy servant** among them that did eat **at thine own table. What right** therefore **have I** yet **to cry** any more **unto the king?**

29. **And the king said** unto him, **Why speakest thou any more** of thy matters? I have said, **Thou and Ziba divide the land.**

30. **And Mephibosheth said** unto the king, Yea, **let him take all, forasmuch as** my lord **the king is come again in peace** unto his own house.

31. **And Barzillai** the Gileadite came down from Rogelim, and **went over Jordan with the king,** to conduct him over Jordan.

32. **Now Barzillai** was a very aged man, *even* fourscore years old: and he had **provided the king** of **sustenance while he lay at Mahanaim;** for he *was* a very great man.

33. **And the king said** unto Barzillai, **Come** thou over **with me,** and I will feed thee with me in Jerusalem.

34. **And Barzillai said** unto the king, **How long have I to live,** that I should go up with the king unto Jerusalem?

35. **I am** this day **fourscore years old:** *and* can I discern between good and evil? can thy servant taste what I eat or what I drink? can I hear any more the voice of singing men and singing women? **wherefore** then **should thy servant be yet a burden unto** my lord **the king?**

36. Thy servant will go a little way over Jordan with the king: and why should the king recompense it me with such a reward?

37. **Let thy servant,** I pray thee, **turn back again, that I may die in mine own city,** *and be buried* by the grave of my father and of my mother. **But** behold thy servant **Chimham; let him go** over **with** my lord **the king; and do to him what shall seem good** unto thee.

38. And the king answered, Chimham shall go over with me, and I will do to him that which shall seem good unto thee: and whatsoever thou shalt require of me, *that* will I do for thee.

39. And all the people went over Jordan. And when the king was come over, the king kissed Barzillai, and blessed him; and

he returned unto his own place.

40. Then the king went on to Gilgal, and Chimham went on **with him:** and all the people of Judah conducted the king, and also half the people of Israel.

41. **And,** behold, all **the men of Israel came to the king, and said** unto the king, **Why have** our brethren **the men of Judah stolen thee away, and** have **brought the king, and his** household, and all David's **men** with him, **over Jordan?**

42. **And** all the men of **Judah answered** the men of Israel, **Because the king is near of kin to us: wherefore then be ye angry** for this matter? have we eaten at all of the king's *cost*? or **hath he given us any gift?**

43. **And** the men of **Israel answered** the men of Judah, and said, We have ten parts in the king, and **we have also more right in David than ye:** why then did ye despise us, that our advice should not be first had in bringing back our king? **And the words** of the men **of Judah were fiercer than the words** of the men **of Israel.**

CHAPTER 20

1. **And** there happened to be there **a man** of Belial, **whose name was Sheba,** the son of Bichri, **a Benjamite:** and he **blew a trumpet, and said, We have no part in David,** neither have we inheritance in the son of Jesse: **every man to his tents,** O Israel.

2. **So** every man of **Israel** went up from after David, *and* **followed Sheba** the son of Bichri: **but** the men of **Judah clave unto their king,** from Jordan even to Jerusalem.

3. **And David came to** his house at **Jerusalem; and** the king **took the ten** women *his* **concubines, whom he** had **left to keep the house, and put them in ward, and** fed them, but **went not in unto them.** So they were shut up unto the day of their **death,** living in widowhood.

4. **Then said the king to Amasa, Assemble** me **the men of Judah within three days,** and be thou here present.

5. **So Amasa went** to assemble *the men* of Judah: **but** he **tarried longer than the** set **time** which he had **appointed** him.

6. **And David said** to Abishai, **Now shall Sheba** the son of Bichri **do us more harm than** did **Absalom: take** thou **thy lord's servants, and pursue** after **him, lest he** get him fenced cities, and **escape** us.

7. **And there went** out after him **Joab's men,** and the Cherethites, and the Pelethites, **and all the mighty men: and** they went out of Jerusalem, to pursue after Sheba the son of Bichri.

8. When they *were* at the great stone which *is* in Gibeon, **Amasa went before them. And Joab's** garment that he had put on was girded unto him, and upon it a girdle *with* a **sword** fastened upon

his loins in the sheath thereof; and as he went forth it

fell out.

9. **And Joab said to Amasa, Art thou in health,** my brother? **And Joab took Amasa by the beard** with the right hand **to kiss him.**

10. **But Amasa took no heed to the sword** that *was* **in Joab's hand: so he smote him** therewith **in the fifth rib,** and shed out his bowels to the ground, and struck him not again;

and he died. So Joab and Abishai his brother pursued after Sheba the son of Bichri.

11. **And one of Joab's men** stood by him, and **said, He that favoureth Joab, and he that is for David, let him go after Joab.**

12. **And Amasa wallowed in blood** in the midst of the highway.

And when the man saw that all the people stood still,

he removed Amasa out of the highway into the field, **and cast a cloth upon him, when he saw that every one that came by him stood still.**

13. **When he was removed** out of the highway, all **the people went** on after Joab, to pursue **after Sheba** the son of Bichri.

14. And he went through all the tribes of Israel unto Abel, and to Beth–maachah, and all the Berites: and they were gathered together, and went also after him.

15. **And they** came and **besieged him in Abel** of Beth–maachah, and they cast up a bank against the city, and it stood in the trench: **and** all the people that *were* with Joab

battered the wall, to throw it down.

16. **Then cried a wise woman out of the city,** Hear, hear; say, I pray you, **unto Joab, Come near** hither, **that I may speak with thee.**

17. And when he was come near unto her, the woman said, *Art* thou Joab? And he answered, I *am* he. Then she said unto him, Hear the words of thine handmaid. And he answered, I do hear.

18. Then she spake, saying, They were wont to speak in old time, saying, They shall surely ask *counsel* at Abel: and so they ended *the*matter.

19. **I am** *one of them that are* **peaceable and faithful in Israel: thou seekest to destroy a city** and a mother in Israel: why wilt thou swallow up the inheritance of the LORD?

20. **And Joab answered** and said, Far be it, **far be it from me, that I should** swallow up or **destroy**.

21. The matter *is* not so: but a man of mount Ephraim, **Sheba** the son of Bichri by name, **hath lifted up his hand against the king,** *even* against David: **deliver him** only, **and I will depart** from the city. **And the woman said** unto Joab, Behold, **his head shall be thrown to thee over the wall.**

22. **Then the woman went unto** all **the people** in her wisdom. **And they cut off the head of Sheba** the son of Bichri, **and cast it out to Joab.** And he blew a trumpet, and they retired from the city, every man to his tent. **And Joab returned to Jerusalem** unto the king.

23. Now Joab *was* over all the host

502

of Israel: and Benaiah the son of
Jehoiada *was* over the Cherethites
and over the Pelethites:
24. And Adoram *was* over the
tribute: and Jehoshaphat the
son of Ahilud *was* recorder:
25. And Sheva *was* scribe: and
Zadok and Abiathar *were* the priests:
26. And Ira also the Jairite
was a chief ruler about David.

CHAPTER 21

1. **Then there was a famine** in the days of David **three years,** year after year; **and David inquired of the LORD. And the LORD answered, It is for Saul,** and for *his* bloody house, **because he slew the Gibeonites.**

2. And the king called the Gibeonites, and said unto them; (now the Gibeonites *were* not of the children of Israel, but of the remnant of the Amorites; and the children of Israel had sworn unto them: and Saul sought to slay them in his zeal to the children of Israel and Judah.)

3. **Wherefore David said unto the Gibeonites, What shall I do for you?** and wherewith shall I make theatonement, **that ye may bless the inheritance of the LORD?**

4. And the Gibeonites said unto him, We will have no silver nor gold of Saul, nor of his house; neither for us shalt thou kill any man in Israel. And he said, **What ye shall say, that will I do for you.**

5. **And they answered** the king, **The man that** consumed us, and that **devised** against us **that we should be destroyed** from remaining in any of the coasts of Israel,

6. **Let seven men of his sons be delivered** unto us, **and we will hang them** up

unto the LORD in Gibeah of Saul, *whom* the LORD did choose. **And the king said, I will give them.**

7. **But the king spared Mephibosheth, the son of Jonathan** the son of Saul, **because of the LORD's oath** that *was* **between them**, between David and Jonathan the son of Saul.

8. **But the king took the two sons of Rizpah** the daughter of Aiah, whom she bare unto Saul, Armoni and Mephibosheth; **and the five sons of Michal** the daughter of Saul, whom she brought up for Adriel the son of Barzillai the Meholathite:

9. **And he delivered them** into the hands of the Gibeonites, **and they hanged them** in the hill before the LORD: and they fell *all* seven together, and were put to death in the *days* of harvest, in the first days, in the beginning of barley harvest.

10. And Rizpah the daughter of Aiah took sackcloth, and spread it for her upon the rock, from the beginning of harvest until water dropped upon them out of heaven, and suffered neither the birds of the air to rest on them by day, nor the beasts of the field by night.

11. And it was told David what Rizpah the daughter of Aiah, the concubine of Saul, had done.

12. **And David** went and **took the bones of Saul and** the bones of **Jonathan** his son **from the men of Jabesh-gilead, which had stolen them** from the street of Beth-shan, where the Philistines had hanged them, when the Philistines had slain Saul in Gilboa:

13. And he brought up from thence the bones of Saul and the bones of Jonathan his son; and they gathered the bones of them that were hanged.

14. **And the bones** of

Saul and Jonathan his son
■ **buried they in the**
■ **country of Benjamin** in
Zelah, in the sepulchre of Kish
his father: and they performed
all that the king commanded.
■ **And after that God was**
■ **entreated for the land.**
■ 15. **Moreover the**
■ **Philistines had** yet
■ **war again with Israel;**
■ **and David** went down,
■ **and his servants** with him, and
■ **fought against the**
■ **Philistines: and**
■ **David waxed faint.**
■ 16. **And Ishbi-benob,**
which *was* of the sons of
■ **the giant,** the *weight* of
■ **whose spear weighed**
■ **three hundred shekels**
of brass in weight, he being
girded with a new *sword*,
■ **thought to have**
■ **slain David.**
■ 17. **But Abishai**
the son of Zeruiah
■ **succoured him,** and
smote the Philistine,
■ **and killed him. Then**
■ **the men of David**
■ **sware** unto him, saying,
■ **Thou shalt go no**
■ **more out** with us
■ **to battle, that thou quench**
■ **not the light of Israel.**
18. **And** it came to pass after
this, that there was again a battle
with the Philistines at Gob: then
Sibbechai the Hushathite slew
■ **Saph,** which *was* of
the sons of the giant.
19. **And** there was again a battle
in Gob with the Philistines, where
■ **Elhanan** the son of
Jaare–oregim, a Beth–lehemite, slew
■ **the brother of Goliath**
the Gittite, the staff of whose
spear *was* like a weaver's beam.
20. **And** there was yet a
battle in Gath, where was
■ **a man of great stature,**
■ **that had** on every hand

■ **six fingers, and** on every foot
■ **six toes,** four and twenty in
number; and he also was
born to the giant.
21. And when he defied Israel,
Jonathan the son of Shimeah
the brother of David slew him.
■ 22. **These four were born**
■ **to the giant in Gath,**
■ **and fell by the hand**
■ **of David, and** by the hand of
■ **his servants.**

CHAPTER 22

■ 1. **And David spake unto**
■ **the LORD the words of this**
■ **song** in the day *that* the LORD had
delivered him out of the hand of all his
enemies, and out of the hand of Saul:
2. And he said,
■ **The LORD is my rock,**
■ **and my fortress, and** my
■ **deliverer;**
3. The God of my rock;
■ **in him will I trust: he is**
■ **my shield, and** the horn of my
■ **salvation,** my high tower, and
■ **my refuge, my saviour;**
thou savest me from violence.
4. **I will call on the**
■ **LORD, who is worthy**
■ **to be praised:** so shall I
be saved from mine enemies.
5. **When** the waves of
■ **death compassed**
■ **me,** the floods of ungodly
men made me afraid;
6. The sorrows of hell compassed
me about; the snares of death
prevented me;
7. In my distress
■ **I called upon the LORD,**
and cried to my God:
■ **and he did hear my**
■ **voice** out of his temple,
and my cry *did enter* into his ears.
8. **Then the earth shook**
and trembled; the foundations
of heaven moved and shook,
■ **because he was wroth.**
9. There went up a smoke out of his
nostrils, and fire out of his mouth
devoured: coals were kindled by it.

10. **He bowed the heavens** also, **and came down;** and darkness *was* under his feet.

11. **And** he rode upon a cherub, and did fly: and he **was seen upon the wings of the wind.**

12. **And he made darkness** pavilions round **about him,** dark waters, *and* thick clouds of the skies.

13. Through the brightness before him were coals of fire kindled.

14. **The LORD** thundered from heaven, and the most High **uttered his voice.**

15. And he sent out arrows, **and scattered them;** lightning, and discomfited them.

16. And the channels of the sea appeared, **the foundations of the world were discovered, at the rebuking of the LORD,** at the blast of the breath of his nostrils.

17. He sent from above, he took me; he drew me out of many waters;

18. **He delivered me from my** strong **enemy,** *and* from them that hated me: for they were too strong for me.

19. They prevented me in the day of my calamity: but the LORD was my stay.

20. He brought me forth also into a large place: he delivered me, because he delighted in me.

21. **The LORD rewarded me** according to my righteousness: according to the cleanness of my hands hath he recompensed me.

22. **For I have kept the ways of the LORD,** and have not wickedly departed from my God.

23. **For** all **his judgments** *were* before me: **and** *as for* his **statutes, I did not depart from them.**

24. **I** was also upright before him, and **have kept myself from** mine **iniquity.**

25. **Therefore the LORD** hath **recompensed me** according to my righteousness; according to my cleanness in his eye sight.

26. With the merciful **thou wilt shew thyself merciful, and** with the upright man thou wilt shew thyself **upright.**

27. With the pure thou wilt shew thyself pure; and with the froward thou wilt shew thyself unsavoury.

28. **And the afflicted** people **thou wilt save:** but thine eyes *are* upon the haughty, *that* thou mayest bring *them* down.

29. **For thou art my lamp,** O LORD: and the LORD will lighten my darkness.

30. For by thee I have run through a troop: by my God have I leaped over a wall.

31. **As for God, his way is perfect; the word of the LORD is tried:** he *is* a buckler to all them that **trust in him.**

32. For who *is* God, save the LORD? and who *is* a rock, save our God?

33. God *is* my strength *and* power: and **he maketh my way perfect.**

34. **He maketh my feet like hinds' feet:** and setteth me upon my high places.

35. He teacheth my hands to war; so that a bow of steel is broken by mine arms.

36. **Thou hast also given me the shield of thy salvation: and** thy gentleness hath **made me great.**

37. Thou hast enlarged my steps under me; so that my feet did not slip.

38. I have pursued mine enemies, and destroyed them; and turned not again until I had consumed them.

39. And I have consumed them, and wounded them, that they could not arise: yea, they are fallen under my feet.

40. **For thou** hast

■ girded me with strength
■ to battle: them that rose up
against me hast thou subdued
under me.
41. Thou hast also given me the
necks of mine enemies, that I
might destroy them that hate me.
42. They looked, but *there was*
none to save; *even* unto the LORD,
but he answered them not.
43. Then did I beat them as
small as the dust of the earth,
I did stamp them as the mire
of the street, *and* did spread
them abroad.
■ 44. **Thou** also
■ hast delivered me from
■ the strivings of my people,
thou hast kept me *to be* head of
the heathen: a people *which* I
knew not shall serve me.
■ 45. **Strangers** shall submit
themselves unto me: as soon
as they hear, they
■ shall be obedient unto me.
46. Strangers shall fade away,
and they shall be afraid out of
their close places.
■ 47. **The LORD liveth;**
and blessed *be* my rock;
■ and exalted be the God of
■ the rock of my salvation.
■ 48. It is God that avengeth
■ me, and that bringeth
down the people under me.
■ 49. **And** that
■ bringeth me forth
■ from mine enemies:
thou also hast lifted me up
on high above them that rose up
against me: thou hast delivered
me from the violent man.
■ 50. **Therefore I will give**
■ thanks unto thee, O
■ LORD, among the heathen,
■ and I will sing praises
■ unto thy name.
■ 51. He is the tower of
■ salvation for his king:
■ and sheweth mercy
■ to his anointed,
unto David, and to his
seed for evermore.

CHAPTER 23

■ 1. **Now these be the last**
■ **words of David.** David the
son of Jesse said, and the
man *who was* raised up on high,
■ the anointed of the
■ God of Jacob, and
■ the sweet psalmist
of Israel, said,
■ 2. **The Spirit of the**
■ **LORD spake by me,**
and his word *was* in my tongue.
3. The God of Israel said, the
Rock of Israel spake to me,
■ He that ruleth over
■ men must be just, ruling
■ in the fear of God.
4. And *he shall be* as the light of the
morning, *when* the sun riseth, *even* a
morning without clouds; *as* the
tender grass *springing* out of the
earth by clear shining after rain.
5. Although my house *be* not
so with God; yet
■ he hath made with me
■ an everlasting covenant,
ordered in all *things,* and sure: for
■ this is all
■ my salvation, and all *my* desire,
although he make *it* not to grow.
■ 6. **But the sons of Belial**
shall be all of them as thorns
thrust away, because they
cannot be taken with hands:
7. But the man *that* shall touch
them must be fenced with iron
and the staff of a spear; and they
■ shall be utterly burned
■ with fire in the *same* place.
■ 8. These be the names of
■ the mighty men whom
■ David had: The Tachmonite
that sat in the seat, chief among
the captains; the same *was*
■ Adino the Eznite:
■ he lift up his spear against
■ eight hundred, whom
■ he slew at one time.
■ 9. **And** after him *was*
■ Eleazar the son of Dodo the
Ahohite, *one* of the three mighty men
with David, when they defied the
Philistines *that* were there gathered

together to battle, and the men
of Israel were gone away:

10. He arose, and
smote the Philistines
until his hand was
weary, and his hand clave
unto the sword: and the LORD
wrought a great victory that day;
and the people returned
after him only to spoil.

11. And after him was
Shammah the son of
Agee the Hararite. And
the Philistines
were gathered
together into a troop, where was
a piece of ground full of lentiles:
and the people fled
from the Philistines.

12. But he stood in the midst
of the ground, and defended it,
and slew the Philistines:
and the LORD wrought
a great victory.

13. And three of the thirty chief went
down, and came to David in the
harvest time unto the cave of
Adullam: and the troop of the
Philistines pitched in the
valley of Rephaim.

14. And David was then in an hold,
and the garrison of the Philistines
was then in Beth–lehem.

15. And David longed, and said,
Oh that one would give me drink
of the water of the well of
Beth–lehem, which is by the gate!

16. And the three mighty
men brake through the
host of the Philistines,
and drew water out of
the well of Beth–lehem,
that was by the gate, and took it,
and brought it to David:
nevertheless he would not
drink thereof, but poured
it out unto the LORD.

17. And he said, Be it far
from me, O LORD, that
I should do this: is
not this the blood of
the men that
went in jeopardy of

their lives? therefore he
would not drink it. These things
did these three mighty men.

18. And Abishai, the brother
of Joab, the son of Zeruiah,
was chief among three. And he
lifted up his spear
against three hundred,
and slew them, and
had the name among three.

19. Was he not most honourable
of three? therefore he was their
captain: howbeit he attained
not unto the *first* three.

20. And Benaiah the
son of Jehoiada, the son
of a valiant man, of Kabzeel,
who had done many acts, he
slew two lionlike men
of Moab: he went down also
and slew
a lion in the midst of a pit in
time of snow:

21. And he slew an
Egyptian, a goodly man: and the
Egyptian had a spear in his hand;
but he went down to him with a staff,
and plucked the spear out of the
Egyptian's hand, and slew him
with his own spear.

22. These *things* did Benaiah the
son of Jehoiada, and had the
name among three mighty men.

23. He was more honourable
than the thirty, but he
attained not to the *first* three.
And David set him
over his guard.

24. Asahel the brother of Joab
was one of the thirty; Elhanan
the son of Dodo of Beth–lehem,

25. Shammah the Harodite,
Elika the Harodite,

26. Helez the Paltite, Ira the
son of Ikkesh the Tekoite,

27. Abiezer the Anethothite,
Mebunnai the Hushathite,

28. Zalmon the Ahohite,
Maharai the Netophathite,

29. Heleb the son of Baanah, a
Netophathite, Ittai the son of Ribai out
of Gibeah of the children of Benjamin,

30. Benaiah the Pirathonite, Hiddai

of the brooks of Gaash,

31. Abi–albon the Arbathite,
Azmaveth the Barhumite,

32. Eliahba the Shaalbonite, of
the sons of Jashen, Jonathan,

33. Shammah the Hararite, Ahiam
the son of Sharar the Hararite,

34. Eliphelet the son of Ahasbai,
the son of the Maachathite, Eliam
the son of Ahithophel the Gilonite,

35. Hezrai the Carmelite,
Paarai the Arbite,

36. Igal the son of Nathan
of Zobah, Bani the Gadite,

37. Zelek the Ammonite, Nahari
the Beerothite, armour-bearer
to Joab the son of Zeruiah,

38. Ira an Ithrite, Gareb an Ithrite,

39. Uriah the Hittite: thirty and
seven in all.

CHAPTER 24

1. **And again the anger of
the LORD was kindled
against Israel,** and he moved
David against them to say, Go,
number Israel and Judah.

2. **For the king said to
Joab** the captain of the
host, which *was* with him,
Go now through all the
tribes of Israel, from
Dan even to Beer–sheba, and
number ye
the people, that I may
know the number of the people.

3. **And Joab said** unto the
king, Now the LORD thy God add
unto the people,howmany soeverthey
be, an hundredfold, and that the eyes
of my lord the king may see *it*: but
why doth my lord
**the king delight
in this thing?**

4. **Notwithstanding the
king's word prevailed** against
Joab, and against
the captains of the host.
And Joab and the
captains of the host
went out from the
presence of the king,
to number the

people of Israel.

5. And they passed over Jordan, and
pitched in Aroer, on the right side of
the city that *lieth* in the midst
of the river of Gad, and toward Jazer:

6. **Then they came to
Gilead, and** to the land of
Tahtim–hodshi; and they came
to Dan-jaan, and about to Zidon,

7. **And** came to the strong hold of
Tyre, and to all
**the cities of the
Hivites, and** of the
Canaanites: and they went
out to the south of Judah, *even*
to Beer–sheba.

8. **So when they had gone
through all the land, they
came to Jerusalem at
the end of nine months
and twenty days.**

9. And Joab gave up the sum of the
number of the people unto the king:
and there were in Israel
**eight hundred thousand
valiant men that drew
the sword; and the men of
Judah were five hundred
thousand men.**

10. **And David's heart
smote him after** that
he had
**numbered the people.
And David said** unto the LORD,
I have sinned greatly
in that I have done: and now, I
beseech thee, O LORD, take
away the iniquity of thy servant;
**for I have done
very foolishly.**

11. **For** when David was up
**in the morning, the word
of the LORD came unto
the prophet Gad,** David's seer,
saying,

12. **Go and say unto
David,** Thus saith the LORD,
**I offer thee three
things; choose** thee
one of them,
that I may do it unto thee.

13. So Gad came to David, and
told him, and said unto him,

Shall seven years of famine come unto thee in thy land? or wilt thou flee three months before thine enemies, while they pursue thee? or that there be three days' pestilence in thy land? now advise, and see what answer I shall return to him that sent me.

14. And David said unto Gad, I am in a great strait: let us fall now into the hand of the LORD; for his mercies are great: and let me not fall into the hand of man.

15. So the LORD sent a pestilence upon Israel from the morning even to the time appointed: and there died of the people from Dan even to Beer-sheba seventy thousand men.

16. And when the angel stretched out his hand upon Jerusalem to destroy it, the LORD repented him of the evil, and said to the angel that destroyed the people, It is enough: stay now thine hand. And the angel of the LORD was by the threshingplace of Araunah the Jebusite.

17. And David spake unto the LORD when he saw the angel that smote the people, and said, Lo, I have sinned, and I have done wickedly: but these sheep, what have they done? let thine hand, I pray thee, be against me, and against my father's house.

18. And Gad came that day to David, and said unto him, Go up, rear an altar unto the LORD in the threshingfloor of Araunah the Jebusite.

19. And David, according to the saying of Gad, went up as the LORD commanded.

20. And Araunah looked, and saw the king and his servants coming on toward him: and Araunah went out, and bowed himself before the king on his face upon the ground.

21. And Araunah said, Wherefore is my lord the king come to his servant? And David said, To buy the threshingfloor of thee, to build an altar unto the LORD, that the plague may be stayed from the people.

22. And Araunah said unto David, Let my lord the king take and offer up what *seemeth* good unto him: behold, here be oxen for burnt sacrifice, and threshing instruments and *other* instruments of the oxen for wood.

23. All these things did Araunah, *as* a king, give unto the king. And Araunah said unto the king, The LORD thy God accept thee.

24. And the king said unto Araunah, Nay; but I will surely buy it of thee at a price: neither will I offer burnt offerings unto the LORD my God of that which doth cost me nothing. So David bought the threshingfloor and the oxen for fifty shekels of silver.

25. And David built there an altar unto the LORD, and offered burnt offerings and peace offerings. So the LORD was entreated for the land, and the plague was stayed from Israel.

DAVID'S CHARGE
TO SOLOMON

Be Thou Strong
Therefore,
and Shew Thyself a Man;
and Keep the Charge
of the Lord Thy God,
to Keep His Statutes,
and His Commandments,
and His Testimonies,
as it is Written in the Law
of Moses, That Thou
Mayest Prosper in All
That Thou doest...

I Kings 2:2,3

THE BOOK OF FIRST KINGS

BACKGROUND
INFORMATION

Author: Unknown although
some scholars have
designated Jeremiah as the
author
**Date Written: Between
562 — 536 B.C.**

Number of:
Verses—816
Chapters—22
Total Words—24,524
Scan Words—10,263
Scan Words Represent
Approximately 41% of
Total Words

Theme: Events during
the Reign
of Solomon, the Prophet
Elijah, and the Reign of
Ahab

OUTLINE OF
THE BOOK

I. **The Final Acts of David**
    1:1 — 2:11
II. **The Reign of** King
    Solomon
    2:12 — 11:43
III. **The Kingdom is
    Divided**
    12:1 —14:31
IV. **The Reign of Ahab and
    His Contending with
    Elijah**
    15:1 — 22:39
V. **The Reign of
    Jehoshaphat and
    Ahaziah**
    22:40 — 53

CHAPTER 1

1. Now king
David was old
and stricken in years;
and they covered him
with clothes,
but he gat no heat.
2. **Wherefore his servants**
said unto him,
Let there be sought for
my lord the king
a young virgin:
and let her stand before the king, and
let her cherish him, and let her
lie in thy bosom, that my lord
the king may get heat.
3. **So they**
sought for a fair damsel throughout
all the coasts of Israel, and
found Abishag a Shunammite,
and brought her to the king.
4. **And the damsel was very**
fair, and cherished the king,
and ministered to him: but
the king knew her not.
5. **Then Adonijah**
the son of Haggith
exalted himself, saying,
I will be king: and he prepared
him chariots and horsemen, and fifty
men to run before him.
6. And his father had not displeased
him at any time in saying, Why hast
thou done so? and he also was a very
goodly man; and his mother bare him
after Absalom.
7. **And he conferred with**
Joab the son of Zeruiah,
and with
Abiathar the priest:
and they following Adonijah
helped him.
8. **But Zadok the priest,** and
Benaiah the son of Jehoiada, and
Nathan the prophet, and
Shimei, and
Rei, and the mighty men
which belonged to David,
were not with Adonijah.
9. **And Adonijah**
slew sheep and
oxen and fat cattle
by the stone of Zoheleth,

which is by En-rogel,
and called all
his brethren the king's sons,
and all
the men of Judah
the king's servants:
10. **But Nathan the prophet,**
and Benaiah, and
the mighty men, and
Solomon his brother,
he called not.
11. **Wherefore Nathan**
spake unto Bath-sheba
the mother of Solomon,
saying, Hast thou not heard that
Adonijah the son of Haggith
doth reign, and David our lord
knoweth it not?
12. Now therefore come,
let me, I pray thee,
give thee counsel,
that thou mayest
save thine own life, and the
life of thy son Solomon.
13. **Go** and get thee in
unto king
David, and say unto him,
Didst not thou, my lord, O king,
swear unto thine handmaid,
saying, Assuredly
Solomon thy son
shall reign after me, and he shall
sit upon my throne?
why then doth
Adonijah reign?
14. **Behold, while thou yet**
talkest there with the king,
I also
will come in after thee, and
confirm thy words.
15. **And Bath-sheba went**
in unto the king into the
chamber: and the king was very old;
and Abishag the Shunammite
ministered unto the king.
16. And Bath-sheba bowed, and did
obeisance unto the king.
And the king said, What
wouldest thou?
17. **And she said**
unto him, My lord,
thou swarest by the LORD thy
God unto thine handmaid,

saying, Assuredly **Solomon** thy son **shall reign after me,** and he shall sit upon my throne.

18. **And now,** behold, **Adonijah reigneth; and** now, my lord the king, **thou knowest it not:**

19. And he hath slain oxen and fat cattle and sheep in abundance, and hath called all the sons of the king, and Abiathar the priest, and Joab the captain of the host: but Solomon thy servant hath he not called.

20. And thou, my lord, **O king, the eyes of all Israel are upon thee,** that thou shouldest **tell them who shall sit on the throne** of my lord the king after him.

21. **Otherwise** it shall come to pass, **when** my lord **the king shall sleep** with his fathers, that **I and** my son **Solomon shall be counted offenders.**

22. And, lo, **while she** yet **talked** with the king, **Nathan** the prophet also **came in.**

23. And they told the king, saying, Behold Nathan the prophet. **And** when he was come in before the king, he **bowed** himself **before the king** with his face to the ground.

24. **And Nathan said,** My lord, O king, **hast thou said, Adonijah shall reign** after me, and he shall sit upon my throne?

25. **For he** is gone down this day, and hath slain oxen and fat cattle and sheep in abundance, and **hath called** all **the king's sons,** and **the captains** of the host, **and Abiathar the priest;**

and, behold, **they eat and drink** before him, **and say, God save king Adonijah.**

26. **But me,** even me thy servant, **and Zadok the priest,** and **Benaiah** the son of Jehoiada, **and** thy servant **Solomon, hath he not called.**

27. Is this thing done by my lord the king, and thou hast not shewed it unto thy servant, who should sit on the throne of my lord the king after him?

28. **Then king David answered** and said, **Call me Bath-sheba. And she came** into the king's presence, and stood before the king.

29. **And the king sware,** and said, As the LORD liveth, that hath redeemed my soul out of all distress,

30. **Even as I sware unto** thee by **the LORD** God of Israel, **saying,** Assuredly **Solomon** thy son **shall reign** after me, and he shall sit **upon my throne** in my stead; even so will I certainly do this day.

31. **Then Bath-sheba bowed** with her face to the earth, and did reverence to the king, **and said, Let** my lord **king David live for ever.**

32. **And** king **David said, Call** me **Zadok** the priest, and **Nathan** the prophet, **and Benaiah** the son of Jehoiada. And they came before the king.

33. **The king** also **said unto them, Take** with you the **servants** of your lord, **and cause Solomon** my son **to ride upon mine own mule, and bring him down to Gihon:**

34. **And let Zadok the priest**

and Nathan the prophet
anoint him there
king over Israel:
and blow ye with
the trumpet, and say, God
save king Solomon.
35. Then ye shall come up after him, that he may come and sit upon my throne;
for he shall be king in my stead: and I have appointed him to be ruler over Israel and over Judah.
36. And Benaiah the son of Jehoiada answered the king, and
said, Amen: the LORD God of my lord the king say so too.
37. As the LORD hath been with my lord the king,
even so be he with Solomon,
and make his throne greater than the throne of my lord king David.
38. So Zadok the priest, and Nathan the prophet,
and Benaiah the son of Jehoiada, and the Cherethites, and the Pelethites,
went down, and caused Solomon to ride upon king David's mule, and brought him to Gihon.
39. And Zadok the priest took an horn of oil out of the tabernacle, and anointed Solomon. And they blew the trumpet; and all the people said, God save king Solomon.
40. And all the people came up after him, and the people piped with pipes, and
rejoiced with great joy, so that the earth rent with the sound of them.
41. And Adonijah and all the guests that were with him heard it as they had made an end of eating.
And when
Joab heard the sound of the trumpet, he
said, Wherefore is this noise of the city being in an uproar?
42. And while he yet

spake, behold,
Jonathan
the son of Abiathar the priest
came: and Adonijah said unto him, Come in; for thou art a valiant man, and bringest good tidings.
43. And Jonathan answered
and said to Adonijah, Verily our lord king
David hath made
Solomon king.
44. And the king hath sent with him Zadok the priest, and Nathan the prophet, and Benaiah the son of Jehoiada, and the Cherethites, and the Pelethites, and they have caused him to ride upon the king's mule:
45. And Zadok the priest
and Nathan the prophet
have anointed
him king in Gihon:
and they are
come up from thence
rejoicing,
so that the city rang again.
This is the noise that
ye have heard.
46. And also Solomon sitteth on the throne of the kingdom.
47. And moreover the king's servants came to
bless our lord king
David, saying, God make
the name of Solomon better
than thy name, and make
his throne greater than thy
throne. And the king bowed himself upon the bed.
48. And also thus said the
king, Blessed be the LORD
God of Israel,
which hath given one
to sit on my throne this day,
mine eyes even seeing it.
49. And all the
guests that were
with Adonijah
were afraid, and rose up,
and went every
man his way.
50. And Adonijah feared
because of Solomon, and arose,
and went, and caught hold

on the horns of the altar.
51. And it was told
Solomon, saying,
Behold, Adonijah
feareth king Solomon: for, lo, he
hath caught hold on
the horns of the altar,
saying, Let king
Solomon swear unto me to-day
that he will not slay his
servant with the sword.
52. And Solomon said,
If he will shew himself a
worthy man,
there shall not an hair
of him fall to the earth:
but if wickedness shall be
found in him, he shall die.
53. So king Solomon sent, and
they brought him
down from the altar.
And he came and
bowed himself
to king
Solomon: and Solomon
said unto him,
Go to thine house.

CHAPTER 2

1. Now the days of David
drew nigh that he should
die; and he charged
Solomon his son,
saying,
2. I go the way of all the earth:
be thou
strong therefore,
and shew thyself a man;
3. And keep the charge
of the LORD thy
God, to walk in his ways,
to keep his statutes,
and his commandments,
and his judgments,
and his testimonies,
as it is written in
the law of Moses,
that thou mayest prosper
in all that thou doest, and
whithersoever thou turnest thyself:
4. That the LORD may
continue his word which he
spake concerning me,

saying, If thy children
take heed to their way, to
walk before me in truth with
all their heart and with all their soul,
there shall not
fail thee (said he)
a man on the throne
of Israel.
5. Moreover thou knowest
also what Joab
the son of Zeruiah
did to me, and what he did to
the two captains of the hosts of Israel,
unto Abner the son of Ner,
and unto Amasa
the son of Jether,
whom he slew,
and shed the blood of war in peace,
and put the blood of war upon his
girdle that was about his loins, and in
his shoes that were on his feet.
6. Do therefore according to thy
wisdom, and
let not his hoar
head go down to
the grave in peace.
7. But shew kindness unto
the sons of Barzillai
the Gileadite,
and let them be of those that
eat at thy table: for so
they came to me when
I fled because of
Absalom thy brother.
8. And, behold, thou hast with thee
Shimei the son of Gera, a
Benjamite of Bahurim, which
cursed me
with a grievous curse in the day
when I went to Mahanaim:
but he came down
to meet me at Jordan, and
I sware to him by the LORD,
saying, I will not put thee
to death with the sword.
9. Now therefore
hold him not guiltless:
for thou art a wise man, and knowest
what thou oughtest to do unto him;
but his hoar
head bring thou down
to the grave with blood.
10. So David slept

with his fathers,

and was buried
in the city of David.
11. And the days that
David reigned over Israel were
forty years: seven years reigned
he in Hebron, and thirty and three
years reigned he in Jerusalem.
12. **Then sat Solomon upon**
the throne of David his father;
and his kingdom was
established greatly.
13. **And Adonijah**
the son of Haggith
came to Bath-sheba
the mother of Solomon. And she
said, Comest thou peaceably?
And he said, Peaceably.
14. He said moreover, I have
somewhat to say unto thee.
And she said, Say on.
15. **And he said,**
Thou knowest that
the kingdom was mine,
and that all Israel set their faces
on me, that I should reign:
howbeit the kingdom
is turned about,
and is become
my brother's:
for it was his from the LORD.
16. **And now I ask one**
petition of thee, deny me not.
And she said unto him, Say on.
17. And he said,
Speak, I pray thee,
unto Solomon the king, (for he
will not say thee nay,)
that he give me Abishag
the Shunammite to wife.
18. And Bath-sheba said, Well; I will
speak for thee unto the king.
19. **Bath-sheba** therefore
went unto king
Solomon, to speak
unto him for Adonijah.
And the king rose up to
meet her, and bowed himself
unto her, and sat down on his throne,
and caused a seat to be set for the
king's mother;
and she sat on
his right hand.

20. **Then she said, I**
desire one small
petition of thee; I pray thee, say
me not nay. And the king said unto
her, Ask on, my mother: for I will not
say thee nay.
21. And she said,
Let Abishag the Shunammite
be given to Adonijah
thy brother
to wife.
22. **And king Solomon**
answered and said
unto his mother, And
why dost thou ask Abishag the
Shunammite for Adonijah?
ask for him the kingdom
also; for he is mine elder brother;
even for him, and for Abiathar the
priest, and for Joab the son of
Zeruiah.
23. **Then king Solomon**
sware by the LORD,
saying, God do so
to me, and more also,
if Adonijah have not
spoken this word
against his own life.
24. **Now therefore, as the**
LORD liveth, which hath
established me, and set me
on the throne of David my father,
and who hath made me an house,
as he promised,
Adonijah shall be put to
death this day.
25. **And** king
Solomon sent by the hand of
Benaiah the son of Jehoiada;
and he fell upon him
that he died.
26. **And unto Abiathar**
the priest
said the king, Get thee to
Anathoth, unto thine own fields; for
thou art worthy of death:
but I will not at this time put
thee to death, because
thou barest the ark of the
LORD God before David my father,
and because thou hast been afflicted
in all wherein my father was afflicted.
27. **So Solomon thrust out**

Abiathar from being priest unto the LORD; that he might fulfil the word of the LORD, which he spake concerning the house of Eli in Shiloh.

28. **Then tidings came to Joab:** for Joab had turned after Adonijah, though he turned not after Absalom. **And Joab fled unto the tabernacle** of the LORD, **and caught hold on the horns of the altar.**

29. **And it was told king Solomon** that Joab was fled unto the tabernacle of the LORD; **and, behold, he** is by the altar. Then Solomon **sent Benaiah** the son of Jehoiada, **saying, Go, fall upon him.**

30. **And Benaiah came** to the tabernacle of the LORD, **and said** unto him, Thus saith the king, **Come forth. And he said, Nay; but I will die here. And Benaiah brought the king word again,** saying, Thus said Joab, and thus he answered me.

31. **And the king said** unto him, **Do as he hath said, and fall upon him, and bury him;** that thou mayest take away the innocent blood, which Joab shed, from me, and from the house of my father.

32. **And the LORD shall return his blood upon his own head, who fell upon two men more righteous and better than he, and slew** them with the sword, my father David not knowing thereof, to wit, **Abner** the son of Ner, captain of the host of Israel, **and Amasa** the son of Jether, captain of the host of Judah.

33. **Their blood shall therefore return upon the head of Joab,** and upon the head of his seed for ever: but upon David, and upon his seed, and upon his house, and upon his throne, shall

there be peace for ever from the LORD.

34. **So Benaiah** the son of Jehoiada went up, and **fell upon him, and slew him:** and he was buried in his own house in the wilderness.

35. **And the king put Benaiah** the son of Jehoiada **in his room over the host: and Zadok** the priest **did the king put in the room of Abiathar.**

36. **And the king sent** and called **for Shimei, and said** unto him, **Build thee an house in Jerusalem,** and dwell there, **and go not forth thence** any whither.

37. **For** it shall be, that **on the day thou goest out,** and passest over the brook Kidron, **thou shalt** know for certain that thou shalt surely **die:** thy blood shall be upon thine own head.

38. And Shimei said unto the king, The saying is good: as my lord the king hath said, so will thy servant do. **And Shimei dwelt in Jerusalem many days.**

39. **And** it came to pass **at the end of three years,** that **two** of the **servants of Shimei ran away unto Achish** son of Maachah **king of Gath.** And they told Shimei, saying, Behold, thy servants be in Gath.

40. **And Shimei arose,** and saddled his ass, **and went to Gath** to Achish to seek his servants: and Shimei went, **and brought his servants from Gath.**

41. **And it was told Solomon** that Shimei had gone from Jerusalem to Gath, and was come again.

42. **And the king** sent and **called** for

Shimei, and said unto him,
Did I not make thee to
swear by the LORD,
and protested unto thee,
saying, Know for a certain,
on the day thou goest out,
and walkest abroad any whither, that
thou shalt surely die? and
thou saidst unto me, The word
that I have heard is good.
43. Why then hast thou
not kept the oath of the
LORD, and the commandment
that I have charged thee with?
44. The king said moreover to Shimei,
Thou knowest all
the wickedness
which thine heart is privy to,
that thou didst to
David my father:
therefore the Lord shall
return thy wickedness
upon thine own head;
45. And king Solomon shall be
blessed, and the throne of David
shall be established before the
LORD for ever.
46. So the king commanded
Benaiah the son of Jehoiada;
which went out, and
fell upon him, that he
died. And the kingdom was
established in the hand of Solomon.

CHAPTER 3

1. And Solomon made
affinity with Pharaoh king of
Egypt, and took Pharaoh's
daughter, and brought her
into the city of David,
until he had made an end
of building his own
house, and the house
of the LORD, and the wall of
Jerusalem round about.
2. Only the people
sacrificed in high places,
because there was no house built
unto the name of the LORD, until
those days.
3. And Solomon loved the
LORD, walking in the
statutes of David his father:

only he sacrificed
and burnt incense
in high places.
4. And the king went to
Gibeon to sacrifice there; for
that was the great high place: a
thousand burnt offerings did Solomon
offer upon that altar.
5. In Gibeon the LORD
appeared to Solomon
in a dream by night:
and God
said, Ask what I
shall give thee.
6. And Solomon said,
Thou hast shewed unto thy servant
David my father great mercy,
according as he walked before
thee in truth, and in righteousness,
and in uprightness of heart with
thee; and thou hast kept for him
this great kindness, that thou hast
given him a son to sit on his throne,
as it is this day.
7. And now, O LORD my God,
thou hast made thy servant
king instead of David my
father: and I am but a little
child: I know not how to go
out or come in.
8. And thy servant is in the midst of
thy people which thou hast chosen, a
great people, that cannot be
numbered nor counted for multitude.
9. Give therefore thy
servant an understanding
heart to judge thy people,
that I may discern between
good and bad: for who is able
to judge this thy so great a people?
10. And the speech
pleased the LORD, that
Solomon had asked this thing.
11. And God said unto him,
Because thou hast
asked this thing,
and hast not
asked for thyself
long life; neither hast asked
riches for thyself,
nor hast asked the life of
thine enemies; but hast
asked for thyself

understanding to
discern judgment;

12. **Behold,** I have done
according to thy words: lo,
**I have given thee a wise
and an understanding
heart; so that there was
none like thee before** thee,
neither after thee
**shall any arise
like unto thee.**

13. **And I have also given
thee that which thou hast
not asked, both riches, and
honour:** so that there shall not be
any among the kings like unto
thee all thy days.

14. **And if thou wilt walk in
my ways,** to keep my statutes and
my commandments, as thy father
David did walk, then
I will lengthen thy days.

15. **And Solomon** awoke; and,
behold, it was a dream. And he
came to Jerusalem,
and stood before the ark of the
covenant of the LORD,
**and offered up
burnt offerings,**
and offered peace offerings,
and made a feast
to all his servants.

16. **Then came** there
two women, that were
harlots, unto the king,
and stood before him.

17. **And the one** woman
said, O my lord,
**I and this woman dwell
in one house; and I was
delivered of a child**
with her in the house.

18. **And** it came to pass
the third day after that
I was delivered, that
this woman was delivered
also: and we were together; there
was no stranger with us in the house,
save we two in the house.

19. **And this woman's child
died** in the night;
because she overlaid it.

20. **And she** arose at midnight, and

took my son from beside me,
**while thine handmaid
slept,** and laid it in her bosom,
**and laid her dead
child in my bosom.**

21. **And when I rose**
in the morning
to give my child suck, behold,
it was dead: but when
I had considered it
in the morning,
behold, it was not my son,
which I did bear.

22. **And the other woman
said, Nay; but the living is
my son,** and the dead is thy son.
And this said, No; but the dead is thy
son, and the living is my son.
**Thus they spake
before the king.**

23. Then said the king, The one
saith, This is my son that liveth,
and thy son is the dead: and the
other saith, Nay; but thy son is the
dead, and my son is the living.

24. **And the king said, Bring
me a sword.** And they brought a
sword before the king.

25. **And the king said,
Divide the living child in
two, and give half to the
one, and half to the other.**

26. **Then spake the woman
whose the living child was**
unto the king, for her bowels
yearned upon her son,
and she said, O my lord,
**give her the living child,
and in no wise slay it. But
the other said,** Let it be neither
mine nor thine, but
divide it.

27. **Then the king
answered** and said,
Give her the living child,
and in no wise slay it:
she is the mother thereof.

28. **And all Israel heard** of the
judgment which the king had judged;
and they feared the king:
**for they saw that the
wisdom of God
was in him,**

| | to do judgment.

CHAPTER 4

1. **So king Solomon was king** over all Israel. 2. **And these were the princes** which he had; **Azariah** the son of Zadok the priest, 3. **Elihoreph** and **Ahiah,** the sons of Shisha, scribes; **Jehoshaphat** the son of Ahilud, the recorder. 4. **And Benaiah** the son of Jehoiada **was over the host: and Zadok and Abiathar were the priests:** 5. **And Azariah** the son of Nathan **was over the officers: and Zabud** the son of Nathan **was principal officer, and the king's friend:** 6. **And Ahishar was over the household: and Adoniram** the son of Abda **was over the tribute.** 7. **And Solomon had twelve officers** over all Israel, **which provided victuals for the king** and his household: **each man his month in a year** made provision.

8. And these are their names: The son of Hur, in mount Ephraim:

9. The son of Dekar, in Makaz, and in Shaalbim, and Beth-shemesh, and Elon-beth-hanan:

10. The son of Hesed, in Aruboth; to him pertained Sochoh, and all the land of Hepher:

11. The son of Abinadab, in all the region of Dor; which had Taphath the daughter of Solomon to wife:

12. Baana the son of Ahilud; to him pertained Taanach and Megiddo, and all Beth-shean, which is by Zartanah beneath Jezreel, from Beth-shean to Abel-meholah, even unto the place that is beyond Jokneam:

13. The son of Geber, in Ramoth-gilead; to him pertained the towns of Jair the son of Manasseh, which are in Gilead; to him also pertained the region of Argob, which is in Bashan,threescore great cities with walls and brasen bars:

14. Ahinadab the son of Iddo had Mahanaim:

15. Ahimaaz was in Naphtali; he also took Basmath the daughter of Solomon to wife:

16. Baanah the son of Hushai was in Asher and in Aloth:

17. Jehoshaphat the son of Paruah, in Issachar:

18. Shimei the son of Elah, in Benjamin:

19. Geber the son of Uri was in the country of Gilead, in the country of Sihon king of the Amorites, and of Og king of Bashan; and he was the only officer which was in the land.

20. **Judah and Israel were many, as the sand** which is **by the sea** in multitude, **eating and drinking, and making merry.** 21. **And Solomon reigned over all kingdoms from the river unto the land of the Philistines, and unto the border of Egypt: they brought presents, and served Solomon all the days of his life.**

22. And Solomon's provision for one day was thirty measures of fine flour, and threescore measures of meal,

23. Ten fat oxen, and twenty oxen out of the pastures, and an hundred sheep, beside harts, and roebucks, and fallowdeer, and fatted fowl.

24. For he had dominion over all the region on this side the river, from Tiphsah even to Azzah, over all the kings on this side the river: **and he had peace on all sides round about him.** 25. **And Judah and Israel dwelt safely, every man under his vine and under his fig tree, from Dan even to Beer-sheba,** all the days of Solomon. 26. **And Solomon had forty**

■ thousand stalls of
■ horses for his chariots,
■ and twelve thousand
■ horsemen.
■ 27. And those officers
■ provided victual for king
■ Solomon, and for all that
■ came unto king
■ Solomon's table, every man in
his month: they lacked nothing.
■ 28. Barley also and straw
for the horses and dromedaries
brought they unto the place where
the officers were, every man
according to his charge.
■ 29. And God gave Solomon
■ wisdom and
■ understanding exceedingmuch,
■ and largeness of heart, even
as the sand that is on the sea shore.
■ 30. And Solomon's wisdom
■ excelled the wisdom of
all the children of
■ the east country,
■ and all the wisdom of
■ Egypt.
■ 31. For he was wiser than
■ all men; than Ethan the Ezrahite,
and Heman, and Chalcol, and Darda,
the sons of Mahol:
■ and his fame was in
■ all nations round about.
■ 32. And he spake three
■ thousand proverbs:
■ and his songs were a
■ thousand and five.
■ 33. And he spake of trees,
from the cedar tree that is in Lebanon
even unto the hyssop that springeth
out of the wall: he spake also of
■ beasts, and of
■ fowl, and of
■ creeping things, and of
■ fishes.
■ 34. And there came of all
■ people to hear the
■ wisdom of Solomon,
■ from all kings of the earth,
which had heard of his wisdom.

CHAPTER 5
■| 1. And Hiram king of Tyre
■| sent his servants unto

■ Solomon; for he had heard
that they had anointed him
king in the room of his father:
■ for Hiram was ever
■ a lover of David.
■ 2. And Solomon sent
to Hiram, saying,
■ 3. Thou knowest
■ how that David
■ my father could not
■ build an house unto
the name of the LORD his
■ God for the wars which were
■ about him on every side,
until the LORD put them under
the soles of his feet.
■ 4. But now the LORD my
■ God hath given me
■ rest on every side,
■ so that there is neither
■ adversary nor evil occurrent.
5. And, behold,
■ I purpose to build
■ an house unto
the name of the LORD my
■ God, as the LORD spake untoDavid
my father, saying, Thy son, whom I
will set upon thy throne in thy room,he
shall build an house unto my name.
■ 6. Now therefore command
■ thou that they hew me
■ cedar trees out of
■ Lebanon; and my servants shall
be with thy servants:
■ and unto thee will I give
■ hire for thy servants according
to all that thou shalt appoint:
■ for thou knowest that
■ there is not among us
■ any that can skill to hew
■ timber like unto the
■ Sidonians.
7. And it came to pass,
■ when Hiram heard
the words of Solomon, that
■ he rejoiced greatly, and said,
Blessed be the LORD this day, which
hath given unto David a wise son
over this great people.
■ 8. And Hiram sent to
■ Solomon, saying, I have
considered the things which thou
sentest to me for: and

I will do all thy desire concerning timber of cedar, and concerning timber of fir.

9. My servants shall bring them down from Lebanon unto the sea: and I will convey them by sea in floats unto the place that thou shalt appoint me, and will cause them to be discharged there, and thou shalt receive them:

and thou shalt accomplish my desire, in giving food for my household.

10. So Hiram gave Solomon cedar trees and fir trees according to all his desire.

11. And Solomon gave Hiram twenty thousand measures of wheat for food to his household, and twenty measures of pure oil: thus gave Solomon to Hiram year by year.

12. And the LORD gave Solomon wisdom, as he promised him:

and there was peace between Hiram and Solomon; and they two made a league together.

13. And king Solomon raised a levy out of all Israel; and the levy was thirty thousand men.

14. And he sent them to Lebanon, ten thousand a month by courses: a month they were in Lebanon, and two months at home: and Adoniram was over the levy.

15. And Solomon had threescore and ten thousand that bare burdens, and fourscore thousand hewers in the mountains;

16. Beside the chief of Solomon's officers which were over the work, three thousand and three hundred, which ruled over the people that wrought in the work.

17. And the king commanded, and they brought great stones, costly stones, and hewed stones, to lay the foundation of the house.

18. And Solomon's builders and Hiram's builders did hew them, and the stonesquarers: so they prepared timber and stones to build the house.

CHAPTER 6

1. And it came to pass in the four hundred and eightieth year after the children of Israel were come out of the land of Egypt, in the fourth year of Solomon's reign over Israel, in the month Zif, which is the second month, that he began to build the house of the LORD.

2. And the house which king Solomon built for the LORD, 'the length thereof was threescore cubits, and the breadth thereof twenty cubits, and the height thereof thirty cubits.

3. And the porch before the temple of the house, twenty cubits was the length thereof, according to the breadth of the house; and ten cubits was the breadth thereof before the house.

4. And for the house he made windows of narrow lights.

5. And against the wall of the house he built chambers round about, against the walls of the house round about, both of the temple and of the oracle: and he made chambers round about:

6. The nethermost chamber was five cubits broad, and the middle was six cubits broad, and the third was seven cubits broad: for without in the wall of the house

he made narrowed
rests round about,
that the beams should
not be fastened in the
walls of the house.
7. **And the house,**
when it was in building,
was built of stone made
ready before it was
brought thither:
so that there was
neither hammer nor
axe nor any tool of iron
heard in the house,
while it was in building.
8. **The door for the middle**
chamber was in the right
side of the house:
and they went up
with winding stairs
into the middle chamber, and
out of the middle into the third.
9. **So he built the house,**
and finished it;
and covered the house with
beams and boards of cedar.
10. And then he built chambers
against all the house, five cubits
high: and they rested on the
house with timber of cedar.
11. **And the word of**
the LORD came to
Solomon, saying,
12. **Concerning this**
house which thou art in building,
if thou wilt walk in my
statutes, and execute my
judgments, and keep all my
commandments to walk in them;
then will I perform my word
with thee, which I spake
unto David thy father:
13. **And I will dwell among**
the children of Israel,
and will not forsake my people Israel.
14. So Solomon built the house,
and finished it.
15. And he built the walls of the house
within with boards of cedar, both the
floor of the house, and the walls of
the ceiling: and he covered them on
the inside with wood, and covered the
floor of the house with planks of fir.

16. And he built twenty cubits on the
sides of the house, both the floor and
the walls with boards of cedar:
he even built *them* for it within,
even for the oracle, *even* for the
most holy *place.*
17. **And** the house, that is,
the temple before it,
was forty cubits long.
18. And the cedar of the house
within was carved with knops and
open flowers: all *was* cedar; there
was no stone seen.
19. **And the oracle he**
prepared in the house within,
to set there the ark of the
covenant of the LORD.
20. And the oracle in the forepart
was twenty cubits in length, and
twenty cubits in breadth, and twenty
cubits in the height thereof:
and he overlaid it with pure
gold; and so covered the
altar *which* was of cedar.
21. So Solomon overlaid the house
within with pure gold:
and he made a partition
by the chains of gold
before the oracle;
and he overlaid it with gold.
22. **And the whole house**
he overlaid with gold,
until he had finished all the house:
also the whole altar
that was by the oracle
he overlaid with gold.
23. **And within the oracle**
he made two cherubims
of olive tree, each ten
cubits high.
24. And five cubits *was* the one wing
of the cherub, and five cubits the
other wing of the cherub: from the
uttermost part of the one wing unto
the uttermost part of the other *were*
ten cubits.
25. And the other cherub *was* ten
cubits: both the cherubims *were* of
one measure and one size.
26. The height of the one cherub *was*
ten cubits, and so *was it* of the other
cherub.
27. **And he set the**

cherubims within the inner house: and they stretched forth the wings of the cherubims, so that the wing of the one touched the one wall, and the wing of the other cherub touched the other wall; and their wings touched one another in the midst of the house. 28. And he overlaid the cherubims with gold. 29. And he carved all the walls of the house round about with carved figures of cherubims and palm trees and open flowers, within and without. 30. And the floors of the house he overlaid with gold, within and without. 31. And for the entering of the oracle he made doors of olive tree: the lintel and side posts were a fifth part of the wall. 32. The two doors also were of olive tree; and he carved upon them carvings of cherubims and palm trees and open flowers, and overlaid them with gold, and spread gold upon the cherubims, and upon the palm trees. 33. So also made he for the door of the temple posts of olive tree, a fourth part of the wall. 34. And the two doors were of fir tree: the two leaves of the one door were folding, and the two leaves of the other door were folding. 35. And he carved thereon cherubims and palm trees and open flowers: and covered them with gold fitted upon the carved work. 36. And he built the inner court with three rows of hewed stone, and a row of cedar beams. 37. In the fourth year was the foundation of the house of the LORD laid, in the month Zif: 38. And in the eleventh year, in the month Bul, which is the eighth month, was the house finished throughout all the parts thereof, and according to all the fashion of it. So was he seven years in building it.

CHAPTER 7

1. But Solomon was building his own house thirteen years, and he finished all his house. 2. He built also the house of the forest of Lebanon; the length thereof was an hundred cubits, and the breadth thereof fifty cubits, and the height thereof thirty cubits, upon four rows of cedar pillars, with cedar beams upon the pillars. 3. And it was covered with cedar above upon the beams, that lay on forty five pillars, fifteen in a row. 4. And there were windows in three rows, and light was against light in three ranks. 5. And all the doors and posts were square, with the windows: and light was against light in three ranks. 6. And he made a porch of pillars; the length thereof was fifty cubits, and the breadth thereof thirty cubits: and the porch was before them: and the other pillars and the thick beam were before them. 7. Then he made a porch for the throne where he might judge, even the porch of judgment: and it was covered with cedar from one side of the floor to the other. 8. And his house where he dwelt had another court within the porch, which was of the like work. Solomon made also an house for Pharaoh's daughter, whom he had taken to wife,

like unto this porch.

9. All these were of costly stones, according to the measures of hewed stones, sawed with saws, within and without, even from the foundation unto the coping, and so on the outside toward the great court.

10. And the foundation was of costly stones, even great stones, stones of ten cubits, and stones of eight cubits.

11. And above were costly stones, after the measures of hewed stones, and cedars.

12. And the great court round about was with three rows of hewed stones, and a row of cedar beams, both forthe inner court of the house of the LORD, and for the porch of the house.

■ 13. **And king**
■ **Solomon** sent and
■ **fetched Hiram out of Tyre.**
■ 14. **He was a widow's son**
of the tribe of Naphtali, and his father was a man of Tyre,
■ **a worker in brass:**
■ **and** he was
■ **filled with wisdom, and**
■ **understanding,** and cunning to
work all works in brass.
■ **And he came to king**
■ **Solomon, and wrought**
■ **all his work.**

15. For he cast two pillars of brass, of eighteen cubits high apiece: and a line of twelve cubits did compass either of them about.

16. And he made two chapiters of molten brass, to set upon the tops of the pillars: the height of the one chapiter was five cubits, and the height of the other chapiter was five cubits:

17. And nets of checker work, and wreaths of chain work, for the chapiters which were upon the top of the pillars; seven for the one chapiter, and seven for the other chapiter.

18. And he made the pillars, and two rows round about upon the one network, to cover the chapiters that were upon the top, with pomegranates: and so did he for the other chapiter.

19. And the chapiters that were upon the top of the pillars were of lily work in the porch, four cubits.

20. And the chapiters upon the two pillars had pomegranates also above, over against the belly which was by the network: and the pomegranates were two hundred in rows round about upon the other chapiter.

21. And he set up the pillars in the porch of the temple: and he set up the right pillar, and called the name thereof Jachin: and he set up the left pillar, and called the name thereof Boaz.

22. And upon the top of the pillars was lily work: so was the work of the pillars finished.

23. And he made a molten sea, ten cubits from the one brim to the other: it was round all about, and his height was five cubits: and a line of thirty cubits did compass it round about.

24. And under the brim of it round about there were knops compassing it, ten in a cubit, compassing the sea round about: the knops were cast in two rows, when it was cast.

25. It stood upon twelve oxen, three looking toward the north, and three looking toward the west, and three looking toward the south, and three looking toward the east: and the sea was set above upon them, and all their hinder parts were inward.

26. And it was an hand breadth thick, and the brim thereof was wrought like the brim of a cup, with flowers of lilies: it contained two thousand baths.

27. And he made ten bases of brass; four cubits was the length of one base, and four cubits the breadth thereof, and three cubits the height of it.

28. And the work of the bases was on this manner: they had borders, and the borders were between the ledges:

29. And on the borders that were between the ledges were lions, oxen, and cherubims: and upon the ledges there was a base above: and beneath the lions and oxen were certain additions made of thin work.

30. And every base had four brasen wheels, and plates of brass: and the four corners thereof had undersetters: under the laver were undersetters molten, at the side of every addition.

31. And the mouth of it within the chapiter and above was a cubit: but the mouth thereof was round after the work of the base, a cubit and an half: and also upon the mouth of it were gravings with their borders, foursquare, not round.

32. And under the borders were four wheels; and the axletrees of the wheels were joined to the base: and the height of a wheel was a cubit and half a cubit.

33. And the work of the wheels was like the work of a chariot wheel: their axletrees, and their naves, and their felloes, and their spokes, were all molten.

34. And there were four undersetters to the four corners of one base: and the undersetters were of the very base itself.

35. And in the top of the base was there a round compass of half a cubit high: and on the top of the base the ledges thereof and the borders thereof were of the same.

36. For on the plates of the ledges thereof, and on the borders thereof, he graved cherubims, lions, and palm trees, according to the proportion of every one, and additions roundabout.

37. After this manner he made the ten bases: all of them had one casting, one measure, and one size.

38. Then made he ten lavers ofbrass: one laver contained forty baths: and every laver was four cubits: and upon every one of the ten bases one laver.

39. And he put five bases on the right side of the house, and five on the left side of the house: and he set the sea on the right side of the house eastward over against the south.

40. And Hiram made the lavers, and the shovels, and the basons.

So Hiram made an end of doing all the work that he made king Solomon for the house of the LORD:

41. The two pillars, and the two bowls of the chapiters that were on the top of the two pillars; and the two networks, to cover the two bowls of the chapiters which were upon the top of the pillars;

42. And four hundred pomegranates for the two networks, even two rows of pomegranates for one network, to cover the two bowls of the chapiters that were upon the pillars;

43. And the ten bases, and ten lavers on the bases;

44. And one sea, and twelve oxen under the sea;

45. And the pots, and the shovels, and the basons: and all these vessels, which Hiram made to king Solomon for the house of the LORD, were of bright brass.

46. In the plain of Jordan did the king cast them, in the clay ground between Succoth and Zarthan.

47. And Solomon left all the vessels unweighed, because they were exceeding many: neither was the weight of the brass found out.

48. **And Solomon made all the vessels that pertained unto the house of the LORD: the altar of gold, and the table of gold, whereupon the shewbread was,**

49. **And the candlesticks of pure gold,** five on the right side, and five on the left,

before the oracle, with the **flowers,** and the **lamps,** and the **tongs of gold,**

50. **And the bowls,** and the **snuffers,** and the **basins,** and the **spoons, and** the **censers** of pure gold; and the hinges of gold, both for the doors of the inner house, the most holy place, and for the doors of the house, to wit, of the temple.

51. **So was ended all the work that king Solomon**

made for the house of the LORD.
**And Solomon brought
in the things which
David** his father
had dedicated;
even the silver, and the gold,
and the vessels, did
**he put among the treasures
of the house of the LORD.**

CHAPTER 8

1. **Then Solomon assembled**
the elders of Israel, and all the heads
of the tribes, the chief of the fathers of
the children of
Israel, unto king Solomon
**in Jerusalem, that
they might bring** up
**the ark of the
covenant** of the LORD
out of the city of David, which is
Zion.
2. And all the men of Israel
assembled themselves unto king
Solomon at the feast in the month
Ethanim, which is the seventh month.
3. And all the elders of
Israel came, and
the priests took up the ark.
4. And they
brought up the ark
of the LORD,
and the tabernacle
of the congregation,
and all the holy vessels that
were in the tabernacle, even those did
the priests and the Levites bring up.
5. **And king Solomon,
and all** the congregation of
Israel, that were
assembled unto him,
were with him before the ark,
**sacrificing sheep and oxen,
that could not be**
told nor
numbered for multitude.
6. **And the priests brought** in
the ark of the covenant of the
LORD unto his place, into the
oracle of the house,
to the most holy place, even
under the wings of the cherubims.
7. For the cherubims spread forth

their two wings over the place of the
ark, and the cherubims covered the
ark and the staves thereof above.
8. And they drew out the staves, that
the ends of the staves were seen out
in the holy place before the oracle,
and they were not seen without: and
there they are unto this day.
9. **There was nothing in the
ark save the two tables of
stone,** which Moses put there
at Horeb, when the LORD made a
covenant with the children of Israel,
when they came out of the land
of Egypt.
10. **And it came to pass,
when the priests were
come out of the holy place,
that the cloud filled the
house** of the LORD,
11. **So that the priests could
not stand to minister**
because of the cloud:
**for the glory of the LORD
had filled the house**
of the LORD.
12. **Then spake Solomon,** The
LORD said that he would dwell in the
thick darkness.
13. **I have surely built thee
an house to dwell in,** a settled
place for thee to abide in for ever.
14. **And the king turned**
his face about,
and blessed all
the congregation of
Israel: (and all the congregation
of Israel stood;)
15. **And he said, Blessed
be the LORD** God of Israel,
which spake with his mouth
unto David my father,
and hath with his hand
fulfilled it, saying,
16. Since the day that I brought forth
my people Israel out of Egypt,
**I chose no city out
of all** the tribes of
Israel to build an house,
that my name might be therein;
but I chose David
to be over my people Israel.
17. **And it was in the heart**

527

of David my father
to build an house
for the name of the
LORD God of Israel.
18. And the LORD said
unto David my father,
Whereas it was in
thine heart to build
an house unto my name,
thou didst well
that it was in thine heart.
19. Nevertheless thou
shalt not build the house;
but thy son that shall come
forth out of thy loins, he
shall build the house
unto my name.
20. And the LORD hath
performed his word
that he spake, and
I am risen up in the room of David my
father, and sit on the throne of Israel,
as the LORD promised, and
have built an house
for the name of the LORD
God of Israel.
21. And I have
set there
a place for the ark, wherein is
the covenant of the LORD, which he
made with our fathers, when he
brought them out of the land of Egypt.
22. And Solomon stood
before the altar
of the LORD in the presence of
all the congregation of Israel,
and spread forth his
hands toward heaven:
23. And he said, LORD
God of Israel,
there is no God like thee, in
heaven above, or on earth beneath,
who keepest covenant and
mercy with thy servants that
walk before thee
with all their heart:
24. Who hast kept with
thy servant
David my father
that thou promisedst him:
thou spakest also with thy mouth,
and hast fulfilled it with thine
hand, as it is this day.

25. Therefore now,
LORD God of Israel,
keep with thy servant
David my father
that thou
promisedst him, saying,
There shall not fail thee
a man in my sight
to sit on the throne of Israel;
so that thy children take
heed to their way, that they
walk before me
as thou hast walked before me.
26. And now, O God of Israel,
let thy word, I pray thee,
be verified, which thou spakest
unto thy servant David my father.
27. But will God indeed
dwell on the earth? behold, the
heaven and heaven of heavens
cannot contain thee; how
much less this house
that I have builded?
28. Yet have thou respect
unto the prayer of thy
servant, and to his supplication, O
LORD my God, to hearken unto the
cry and to the prayer, which thy
servant prayeth before thee to-day:
29. That thine eyes may be
open toward this house
night and day, even toward the
place of which thou hast said, My
name shall be there: that thou mayest
hearken unto the prayer which thy
servant shall make toward this place.
30. And hearken thou
to the supplication of thy
servant, and of thy people
Israel, when they shall
pray toward this place:
and hear thou in heaven
thy dwelling place:
and when thou
hearest, forgive.
31. If any man trespass
against his neighbour,
and an oath be laid
upon him to cause him to swear,
and the oath come before
thine altar in this house:
32. Then hear thou
in heaven, and do,

■ and judge thy servants,
■ condemning the wicked,
to bring his way upon his head;
■ and justifying the righteous,
■ to give him according to his
righteousness.
■ 33. When thy people
■ Israel be smitten down
■ before the enemy, because
■ they have sinned against thee,
■ and shall turn again to thee,
■ and confess thy name,
and pray, and make supplication
unto thee in this house:
■ 34. Then hear thou in heaven,
■ and forgive the sin of
thy people Israel,
■ and bring them again
■ unto the land which thou
gavest unto their fathers.
■ 35. When heaven is shut up, and
■ there is no rain, because
■ they have sinned against thee;
■ if they pray toward this
■ place, and confess thy name,
■ and turn from their
sin, when thou afflictest them:
■ 36. Then hear thou in heaven,
■ and forgive the sin
of thy servants, and of thy
people Israel, that thou
■ teach them the good
■ way wherein they should walk,
■ and give rain upon thy land,
which thou hast given to thy people
for an inheritance.
■ 37. If there be in the land
■ famine, if there be
■ pestilence, blasting,
■ mildew, locust, or if there be
■ caterpiller; if their enemy besiege
them in the land of their cities;
■ whatsoever plague,
■ whatsoever sickness
■ there be;
38. What prayer and supplication
soever be made by any man, or by all
thy people Israel, which shall know
every man the plague of his own
heart, and spread forth his hands
toward this house:
■ 39. Then hear thou in
heaven thy dwelling place,

■ and forgive, and do,
■ and give to every man
■ according to his ways, whose
heart thou knowest; (for thou, even
thou only, knowest the hearts of all
the children of men;)
■ 40. That they may fear thee
all the days that they live in the land
which thou gavest unto our fathers.
41. Moreover concerning a stranger,
that is not of thy people Israel, but
cometh out of a far country for thy
name's sake;
42. (For they shall hear of thy great
name, and of thy strong hand, and of
thy stretched out arm;) when he shall
come and pray toward this house;
■ 43. Hear thou in heaven
thy dwelling place,
■ and do according to
■ all that the stranger
■ calleth to thee for: that
■ all people of the earth
■ may know thy name, to
■ fear thee, as do thy
■ people Israel; and
■ that they may know that
■ this house, which I have builded,
■ is called by thy name.
44. If thy people go out
■ to battle against their
■ enemy, whithersoever thou
shalt send them,
■ and shall pray
unto the LORD toward the city
which thou hast chosen, and
■ toward the house
that I have built for thy name:
■ 45. Then hear thou in heaven
their prayer and their supplication,
■ and maintain their cause.
46. If they sin against thee,
■ (for there is
■ no man that
■ sinneth not,) and thou
■ be angry with them,
■ and deliver them to the
■ enemy, so that they carry them
away captives unto the land of the
enemy, far or near;
47. Yet if they shall bethink
themselves in the land whither they
were carried captives, and

■ **repent,** and make supplication unto thee in the land of them that carried them captives,

■ **saying, We have sinned,** and have done perversely, we have committed wickedness;

■ 48. **And so return unto thee**
■ **with all their heart,** and with all their soul, in the land of their enemies, which led them away captive,

■ **and pray** unto thee toward their land, which thou gavest unto their fathers, the city which thou hast chosen, and the house which I have built for thy name:

■ 49. **Then hear** thou
■ **their prayer** and their supplication in heaven thy dwelling place, and maintain their cause,

■ 50. **And forgive** thy people that have sinned against thee, and all their transgressions wherein they have transgressed against thee, and give them compassion before them who carried them captive, that they may have compassion on them:

■ 51. **For they be thy people,** and thine inheritance, which thou broughtest forth out of Egypt, from the midst of the furnace of iron:

■ 52. **That thine eyes may be**
■ **open unto the supplication**
■ **of thy servant, and** unto the supplication of thy people

■ **Israel,** to hearken unto them in all that they call for unto thee.

■ 53. **For thou didst separate**
■ **them from among all the**
■ **people of the earth, to be**
■ **thine inheritance,** as thou spakest by the hand of Moses thy servant, when thou broughtest our fathers out of Egypt, O LORD God.

■ 54. **And** it was so, that
■ **when Solomon had made**
■ **an end of praying** all this prayer and supplication unto the LORD,

■ **he arose** from before the altar of the LORD, from kneeling on his knees with his hands spread up to heaven.

■ 55. **And he stood, and**
■ **blessed all** the congregation of

■ **Israel** with a loud voice,
■ **saying,**
■ 56. **Blessed be the LORD,**
■ **that hath given rest** unto his people Israel,

■ **according to all that he**
■ **promised:** there hath not failed one word of all his good promise, which he promised by the hand of Moses his servant.

■ 57. The LORD our
■ **God be with us,** as he was with our fathers:
■ **let him not** leave us, nor
■ **forsake us:**
■ 58. **That he may incline**
■ **our hearts** unto him, to walk in all his ways, and
■ **to keep his**
■ **commandments,** and his statutes, and his judgments, which he commanded our fathers.

■ 59. **And let** these
■ **my words,** wherewith I have made supplication before the LORD,
■ **be nigh unto** the LORD our
■ **God day and night, that he**
■ **maintain the cause of his**
■ **servant, and the cause of** his people
■ **Israel at all times,** as the matter shall require:

■ 60. **That all the people**
■ **of the earth may know**
■ **that the LORD is God,** and that there is none else.

■ 61. **Let your heart** therefore
■ **be perfect** with the LORD our God, to walk in his statutes, and
■ **to keep his**
■ **commandments,** as at this day.

■ 62. **And the king, and**
■ **all Israel** with him,
■ **offered sacrifice** before the LORD.

63. And Solomon offered a sacrifice of peace offerings, which he offered unto the LORD, two and twenty thousand oxen, and an hundred and twenty thousand sheep.

■ **So the king and**
■ **all** the children of

Israel dedicated the house of the LORD. 64. **The same day did the king hallow the middle of the court** that was before the house of the LORD: **for there he offered burnt offerings, and meat offerings, and** the fat of the **peace offerings:** because the brasen altar that was before the LORD was too little to receive the burnt offerings, and meat offerings, and the fat of the peace offerings. 65. **And at that time Solomon held a feast;** and all Israel with him, a great congregation, from the entering in of Hamath unto the river of Egypt, before the LORD our God, seven days and seven days, even **fourteen days.** 66. **On the eighth day he sent the people away: and they** blessed the king, and **went unto their tents joyful and glad** of heart **for** all **the goodness** that **the LORD had done for David** his servant, **and for Israel** his people.

CHAPTER 9

1. **And it came to pass,** when Solomon had finished the building of the house of the LORD, and the king's house, and all Solomon's desire which he was pleased to do, 2. **That the LORD appeared to Solomon the second time,** as he had appeared unto him at Gibeon. 3. **And the LORD said** unto him, **I have heard thy prayer and** thy supplication, that thou hast made before me: **I have hallowed this house,** which thou hast built, **to put my name there for ever;** and mine eyes and mine heart shall be there perpetually.

4. **And if thou wilt walk before me, as David thy father walked,** in integrity of heart, and in uprightness, **to do** according to **all that I have commanded** thee, and wilt keep my statutes and my judgments: 5. **Then I will establish** the throne of **thy kingdom** upon Israel for ever, **as I promised** to David thy father, saying, There shall not fail thee a man upon the throne of Israel. 6. **But if ye** shall at all turn from following me, ye or your children, and **will not keep my commandments** and my statutes which I have set before you, **but** go and **serve other gods,** and worship them: 7. **Then will I cut off Israel** out of the land which I have given them; **and this house,** which I have hallowed for my name, **will I cast out of my sight; and Israel shall be** a proverb and **a byword among all people:** 8. **And at this house,** which is high, **every one** that passeth by it shall be astonished, and shall hiss; and they **shall say, Why hath the LORD done thus unto this land, and to this house?** 9. **And they shall answer, Because they forsook the LORD** their God, who brought forth their fathers out of the land of Egypt, and have taken hold upon other gods, and have worshipped them, and served them: therefore hath the LORD brought upon them all this evil. 10. **And** it came to pass **at the end of twenty years,** when Solomon had built the two houses, the house of the LORD, and the king's house, 11. (Now Hiram the king of Tyre had

furnished Solomon with cedar trees and fir trees, and with gold, according to all his desire,) that then **king Solomon gave Hiram twenty cities in** the land of **Galilee.** 12. **And Hiram came** out from Tyre **to see the cities** which Solomon had given him; **and they pleased him not.** 13. And he said, What cities *are* these which thou hast given me, my brother? **And he called them the land of Cabul unto this day.** 14. **And Hiram sent** to **the king sixscore talents of gold.** 15. **And this is the reason of the levy** which king **Solomon raised; for to build the house of the LORD,** and **his own house,** and **Millo,** and **the wall of Jerusalem,** and Hazor, and **Megiddo, and Gezer.** 16. **For Pharaoh** king of Egypt **had gone up, and taken Gezer,** and burnt it with fire, **and slain the Canaanites** that dwelt in the city, **and given it** *for* a present **unto his daughter, Solomon's wife.** 17. **And Solomon built Gezer,** and **Beth-horon** the nether, 18. **And Baalath,** and **Tadmor** in the wilderness, in the land, 19. **And all the cities of store** that Solomon had, and **cities for** his **chariots, and cities for his horsemen,** and that which Solomon desired to build in Jerusalem, and in Lebanon, and in all the land of his dominion. 20. **And all the people** *that were* **left** of the Amorites, Hittites, Perizzites, Hivites, and Jebusites, **which were not of the children of Israel,** 21. **Their children** that were left after them in the land, **whom** the children of **Israel** also **were not able** utterly **to destroy, upon those did Solomon levy a tribute of bondservice** unto this day. 22. **But** of the children **of Israel did Solomon make no bondmen: but they were men of war, and** his **servants,** and his **princes,** and his **captains, and rulers of his chariots, and his horsemen.** 23. **These were the chief** of the **officers** that *were* **over Solomon's work, five hundred and fifty, which bare rule over the people** that wrought in the work. 24. **But Pharaoh's daughter came up** out of the city of David **unto her house which Solomon had built** for her: **then did he build Millo.** 25. **And three times in a year did Solomon offer** burnt **offerings** and peace offerings upon the altar which he built unto the LORD, **and he burnt incense upon the altar** that *was* before the LORD. So he finished the house. 26. **And king Solomon made a navy** of ships in Ezion-geber, which *is* beside Eloth, **on the** shore of the **Red sea,** in the land of Edom. 27. **And Hiram sent in the navy** his servants, **shipmen that had knowledge of the sea, with** the servants of Solomon.

28. **And they came to Ophir, and fetched** from thence **gold, four hundred and twenty talents,** and brought *it* to king Solomon.

CHAPTER 10

1. **And when the queen of Sheba heard of the fame of Solomon** concerning the name of the LORD, **she came to prove him with hard questions.**

2. And she came to Jerusalem with a very great train, with camels that bare spices, and very much gold, and precious stones: **and** when she was come to Solomon, **she communed with him** of all that was in her heart.

3. **And Solomon told her all her questions:** there was not *any* thing hid from the king, which he told her not.

4. And when the queen of Sheba had seen all Solomon's wisdom, and the house that he had built,

5. And the meat of his table, and the sitting of his servants, and the attendance of his ministers, and their apparel, and his cupbearers, and his ascent by which he went up unto the house of the LORD; there was no more spirit in her.

6. **And she said to the king, It was a true report that I heard** in mine own land of thy acts and of thy wisdom.

7. **Howbeit I believed not** the words, **until I came,** and mine eyes had seen *it:* **and, behold, the half was not told me: thy wisdom and prosperity exceedeth the fame which I heard.**

8. Happy *are* thy men, happy *are* these thy servants, which stand continually before thee, *and* that hear thy wisdom.

9. **Blessed be** the LORD **thy God, which delighted in thee,** to set thee on the throne of Israel: because the LORD loved Israel for ever, therefore made he thee king, to do judgment and justice.

10. **And she gave the king an hundred and twenty talents of gold,** and of **spices** very great store, **and precious stones:** there came no more such abundance of spices as these which the queen of Sheba gave to king Solomon.

11. **And the navy also of Hiram,** that brought gold from Ophir, **brought in from Ophir** great plenty of **almug trees, and precious stones.**

12. And the king made of the almug trees pillars for the house of the LORD, and for the king's house, harps also and psalteries for singers: there came no such almug trees, nor were seen unto this day.

13. **And king Solomon gave unto the queen of Sheba** all her desire, **whatsoever she asked,** beside *that* which Solomon gave her of his royal bounty. **So she** turned and **went to her own country,** she and her servants.

14. **Now the weight of gold that came to Solomon in one year was six hundred threescore and six talents** of gold,

15. **Beside that he had** of the merchantmen, and of **the traffic of** the **spice merchants,** and of all **the kings of Arabia, and** of **the governors of the country.**

16. **And king Solomon made two hundred targets of** beaten **gold:** six hundred *shekels* of gold went to one target.

17. **And** *he made*

■ three hundred
■ shields of beaten
■ gold; three pound of gold went to
one shield: and the king put them in
the house of the forest of Lebanon.
■ 18. Moreover the
■ king made a great
■ throne of ivory, and
■ overlaid it
■ with the best
■ gold.
■ 19. The throne had
■ six steps, and the top of the
throne *was* round behind:
■ and there were stays
■ on either side on the place
■ of the seat,
■ and two lions stood
■ beside the stays.
■ 20. And twelve
■ lions stood there
■ on the
■ one side and on the other
■ upon the six steps: there was
not the like made in any kingdom.
■ 21. And all king Solomon's
■ drinking vessels were *of*
■ gold, and all the vessels
of the house of the forest
of Lebanon *were of* pure gold; none
were of silver: it was nothing
accounted of in the days of Solomon.
■ 22. For the king had at sea
■ a navy of Tharshish with the navy
of Hiram: once in three years came
the navy of Tharshish,
■ bringing gold, and
■ silver, ivory, and
■ apes, and peacocks.
■ 23. So king Solomon
■ exceeded all the kings of
■ the earth for riches and for
■ wisdom.
■ 24. And all the earth
■ sought to Solomon,
■ to hear his wisdom, which
■ God had put in his heart.
■ 25. And they brought every
man his present, vessels of
■ silver, and vessels of
■ gold, and
■ garments, and
■ armour, and

■ spices, horses, and
■ mules, a rate year by year.
■ 26. And Solomon
gathered together chariots
and horsemen: and he
■ had a thousand and
■ four hundred chariots,
■ and twelve thousand
■ horsemen, whom he bestowed
in the cities for chariots, and with
the king at Jerusalem.
■ 27. And the king
■ made silver *to be*
■ in Jerusalem as stones,
■ and cedars made he *to be*
■ as the sycomore trees that
are in the vale, for abundance.
28. And Solomon had horses brought
out of Egypt, and linen yarn: the
king's merchants received the linen
yarn at a price.
29. And a chariot came up and went
out of Egypt for six hundred *shekels*
of silver, and an horse for an hundred
and fifty: and so for all the kings of the
Hittites, and for the kings of Syria, did
they bring *them* out by their means.

CHAPTER 11

■ 1. But king Solomon loved
■ many strange women,
together with the daughter of
Pharaoh, women of the Moabites,
Ammonites, Edomites, Zidonians,
and Hittites:
■ 2. Of the nations
■ concerning which the LORD
■ said unto the children of Israel,
■ Ye shall not go in to them,
neither shall they come in unto you:
■ for surely
■ they will turn away your
■ heart after their gods:
Solomon clave unto these in love.
■ 3. And he had seven
■ hundred wives, princesses,
■ and three hundred
■ concubines: and his wives
turned away his heart.
4. For it came to pass,
■ when Solomon was old, *that*
■ his wives turned away his
■ heart after other gods: and

his heart was not perfect with the LORD his God, as *was* the heart of David his father.

5. **For Solomon went after Ashtoreth the goddess of the Zidonians, and** after **Milcom** the abomination **of the Ammonites.**

6. **And Solomon** did evil in the sight of the LORD, and **went not fully after the LORD, as did David his father.**

7. **Then did Solomon build an high place for Chemosh,** the abomination **of Moab,** in the hill that *is* before Jerusalem, **and for Molech, the** abomination of the children **of Ammon.**

8. **And likewise** did he **for all his strange wives, which** burnt incense and **sacrificed unto their gods.**

9. **And the LORD was angry with Solomon,** because his heart was turned from the LORD God of Israel, which had appeared unto him twice,

10. And had commanded him concerning this thing, that he should not go after other gods: but he kept not thatwhich the LORD commanded.

11. **Wherefore the LORD said** unto Solomon, **Forasmuch as** this is done of thee, and **thou hast not kept my covenant** and my statutes, which I have commanded thee, **I will** surely **rend the kingdom from thee,** and will give it to thy servant.

12. **Notwithstanding in thy days I will not do it for David thy father's sake:** but I will rend it out of the hand of thy son.

13. **Howbeit I will not rend** away **all the kingdom; but will give one tribe to thy son** for David my servant's sake,

and for Jerusalem's sake which I have chosen.

14. **And the LORD stirred up an adversary** unto Solomon, **Hadad the Edomite:** he *was* of the king's seed in Edom.

15. **For** it came to pass, **when David was in Edom, and Joab** the captain of the host **was gone up to bury the slain, after he had smitten every male in Edom;**

16. (For six months did Joab remain there with all Israel, until he had cut off every male in Edom:)

17. **That Hadad fled,** he and certain Edomites of his father's servants with him, to go **into Egypt; Hadad being yet a little child.**

18. **And they** arose out of Midian, and came to Paran: and they took men with them out of Paran, and they **came to Egypt, unto Pharaoh** king of Egypt; **which gave him an house,** and appointed him **victuals, and** gave him **land.**

19. **And Hadad found great favour in the sight of Pharaoh, so that he gave him to wife** the sister of his own wife, **the sister of Tahpenes the queen.**

20. **And the sister** of Tahpenes **bare him Genubath his son,** whom Tahpenes weaned in Pharaoh's house: and Genubath was in Pharaoh's household among the sons of Pharaoh.

21. **And when Hadad heard** in Egypt **that David slept with his fathers,** and that Joab the captain of the host was dead, **Hadad said to Pharaoh, Let me depart,** that I may go **to mine own country.**

22. **Then Pharaoh said** unto him, But **what hast thou lacked with**

me, that, behold, thou seekest to go to thine own country?

And he answered, Nothing: howbeit let me go in any wise.

23. **And God stirred him up another adversary, Rezon the son of Eliadah,** which fled from his lord Hadadezer king of Zobah:

24. **And he gathered men** unto him, and became captain over a band, when David slew them *of Zobah:* **and they went to Damascus, and** dwelt therein, and **reigned** in Damascus.

25. **And he was an adversary to Israel all the days of Solomon,** beside the mischief that Hadad *did:* and he abhorred Israel, and reigned over Syria.

26. **And Jeroboam the son of Nebat,** an Ephrathite of Zereda, **Solomon's servant,** whose mother's name *was* Zeruah, a widow woman, even he **lifted up his hand against the king.**

27. **And this was the cause that he lifted up his hand against the king:** **Solomon built Millo, and repaired the breaches of the city of David** his father.

28. **And** the man **Jeroboam was a mighty man** of valour: **and Solomon seeing** the young man **that he was industrious,** he **made him ruler over all** the charge of **the house of Joseph.**

29. **And** it came to pass at that time **when Jeroboam went out of Jerusalem,** that **the prophet Ahijah** the Shilonite **found him** in the way; and he had **clad** himself **with a new garment;** and they two *were* alone in the field:

30. **And Ahijah caught the** new **garment that** *was* on him, and **rent it in twelve pieces:**

31. **And he said** to Jeroboam, **Take thee ten pieces: for thus saith the LORD,** the God of Israel, Behold, **I will rend the kingdom out of the hand of Solomon, and will give ten tribes to thee:**

32. (But he shall have one tribe for my servant David's sake, and for Jerusalem's sake, the city which I have chosen out of all the tribes of Israel:)

33. **Because** that **they have** forsaken me, and have **worshipped Ashtoreth** the goddess of the Zidonians, **Chemosh** the god of the Moabites, **and Milcom** the god of the children of Ammon, **and have not walked in my ways,** to do *that which is* right in mine eyes, and *to keep* my statutes and my judgments, as *did* David his father.

34. **Howbeit I will not take the whole kingdom** out of his hand: **but I will make him prince all** the days of **his life for David my servant's sake,** whom I chose, because he kept my commandments and my statutes:

35. **But I will take the kingdom out of his son's hand, and** will **give** it unto **thee,** *even* **ten tribes.**

36. **And unto his son will I give one tribe, that David** my servant **may have a light alway** before me **in Jerusalem,** the city which I have chosen me to put my name there.

37. **And I will take thee,**

■ **and thou** shalt reign according
to all that thy soul desireth, and
■ **shalt be king over Israel.**
38. And it shall be,
■ **if thou wilt hearken unto all**
■ **that I command** thee, and wilt
walk in my ways, and do *that is* right
in my sight, to keep my statutes
and my commandments, as David
my servant did; that
■ **I will be with thee,**
■ **and build thee a** sure
■ **house, as I built for David,**
and will give Israel unto thee.
■ 39. **And I will** for this
■ **afflict the seed of David,**
■ **but not for ever.**
■ 40. **Solomon sought** therefore
■ **to kill Jeroboam. And**
■ **Jeroboam** arose, and
■ **fled into Egypt,** unto Shishak
king of Egypt, and was in Egypt
■ **until the death of Solomon.**
■ 41. **And the rest of the**
■ **acts of Solomon,**
and all that he did, and his wisdom,
■ **are they not**
■ **written in the book of**
■ **the acts of Solomon?**
42. And the time that
■ **Solomon reigned**
in Jerusalem over all Israel *was*
■ **forty years.**
■ 43. **And Solomon slept** with
his fathers, and was buried in
the city of David his father:
■ **and Rehoboam his son**
■ **reigned in his stead.**

CHAPTER 12

■ 1. **And Rehoboam went**
■ **to Shechem: for all Israel**
■ **were come** to Shechem
■ **to make him king.**
2. And it came to pass,
■ **when Jeroboam** the son of
Nebat, who was yet in Egypt,
■ **heard of it,** (for he was fled from
the presence of king Solomon, and
Jeroboam dwelt in Egypt;)
3. That they sent and called him. And
■ **Jeroboam and all the**
■ **congregation** of Israel

■ **came, and spake unto**
■ **Rehoboam, saying,**
■ 4. **Thy father made our**
■ **yoke grievous: now** therefore
■ **make** thou the grievous
service of thy father, and
■ **his heavy yoke**
which he put upon us,
■ **lighter, and we**
■ **will serve thee.**
■ 5. **And he said** unto them,
■ **Depart yet for three days,**
■ **then come again** to me.
And the people departed.
■ 6. **And king Rehoboam**
■ **consulted with the old**
■ **men,** that stood before Solomon
his father while he yet lived,
■ **and said, How do ye**
■ **advise that I may**
■ **answer** this people?
7. **And they spake** unto him,
■ **saying, If thou wilt be**
■ **a servant unto this**
■ **people this day,**
and wilt serve them, and answerthem,
and speak good words to them,
■ **then they will be thy**
■ **servants for ever.**
■ 8. **But he** forsook the counsel
of the old men, which they had
given him, and
■ **consulted with the young**
■ **men** that were grown up with him,
and which stood before him:
■ 9. **And he said** unto them,
■ **What counsel give ye**
that we may answer this people,
who have spoken to me, saying,
Make the yoke which thy father
did put upon us lighter?
■ 10. **And the young men**
that were grown up with him
■ **spake** unto him,
■ **saying, Thus shalt**
■ **thou speak** unto this people
that spake unto thee, saying, Thy
father made our yoke heavy, but
make thou *it* lighter unto us; thus
shalt thou say unto them,
■ **My little finger shall**
■ **be thicker than my**
■ **father's loins.**

11. And now whereas my father did lade you with a heavy yoke, I will add to your yoke: **my father hath chastised you with whips, but I will chastise you with scorpions.** 12. **So Jeroboam and all the people came** to Rehoboam **the third day,** as the king had appointed, saying, Come to me again the third day. 13. **And the king answered** the people **roughly, and forsook the old men's counsel** that they gave him; 14. **And spake** to them after the counsel of the young men, **saying,** My father made your yoke heavy, and **I will add to your yoke:** my father *also* chastised you with whips, but I will chastise you with scorpions. 15. Wherefore the king hearkened not unto the people; for the cause was from the LORD, that he might perform his saying, which the LORD spake by Ahijah the Shilonite unto Jeroboam the son of Nebat. 16. **So when all Israel saw that the king hearkened not unto them, the people answered** the king, **saying, What portion have we in David?** neither *have we* inheritance in the son of Jesse: to your tents, O Israel: now see to thine own house, David. **So Israel departed** unto their tents. 17. But *as for* the children of Israel which dwelt in the cities of Judah, Rehoboam reigned over them. 18. **Then king Rehoboam sent Adoram, who was over the tribute; and all Israel stoned him** with stones, **that he died. Therefore** king **Rehoboam made speed** to get him up to his chariot, **to flee to Jerusalem.** 19. So Israel rebelled against the house of David unto this day. 20. **And** it came to pass, **when all Israel heard that Jeroboam was come again,** that **they** sent and called him unto the congregation, and **made him king over all Israel:** there was none that followed the house of David, but the tribe of Judah only. 21. **And** when **Rehoboam** was come to Jerusalem, he **assembled** all the house of **Judah, with the tribe of Benjamin,** an hundred and fourscore thousand chosen men, which were warriors, **to fight against** the house of **Israel, to bring the kingdom again to Rehoboam** the son of Solomon. 22. **But the word of God came unto Shemaiah** the man of God, **saying,** 23. **Speak unto Rehoboam,** the son of Solomon, king of Judah, **and** unto all the house of **Judah and Benjamin,** and to the remnant of the people, saying, 24. Thus saith the LORD, **Ye shall not** go up, nor **fight against your brethren** the children of Israel: return every man to his house; for this thing is from me. **They hearkened** therefore **to the word of the LORD, and returned** to depart, according to the word of the LORD. 25. **Then Jeroboam built Shechem in mount Ephraim, and dwelt therein;** and went out from thence, **and built Penuel.** 26. **And Jeroboam said in his heart, Now shall the kingdom return to the house of David:** 27. **If this people go up to do sacrifice in**

the house of the LORD at
Jerusalem, then
shall the heart of
this people turn again
unto their lord, *even* unto
Rehoboam king of Judah,
and they shall kill me, and go
again to Rehoboam king of Judah.
28. **Whereupon the**
king took counsel, and
made two calves of gold,
and said unto them, It is too much
for you to go up to Jerusalem:
behold thy gods,
O Israel, which brought thee
up out of the land of Egypt.
29. And he set the one in Beth-el,
and the other put he in Dan.
30. **And this thing became**
a sin: for the people went
to worship before the
one, *even* unto Dan.
31. **And he made an**
house of high places,
and made priests of the
lowest of the people, which were
not of the sons
of Levi.
32. **And Jeroboam**
ordained a feast
in the eighth month, on the
fifteenth day of the month,
like unto
the feast that *is*
in Judah,
and he offered upon the altar.
So did he in Beth-el,
sacrificing unto the calves
that he had made: and he
placed in Beth-el the priests of the
high places which he had made.
33. So he offered upon the altarwhich
he had made in Beth-el the fifteenth
day of the eighth month, *even* in the
month which he had devised of his
own heart; and ordained a feast unto
the children of Israel: and he offered
upon the altar, and burnt incense.

CHAPTER 13

1. **And, behold, there came**
a man of God out of Judah
by the word of the LORD
unto Beth-el: and
Jeroboam stood by
the altar to burn incense.
2. **And he cried**
against the altar in
the word of the LORD,
and said, O altar, altar,
thus saith the LORD; Behold,
a child shall be born unto
the house of David, Josiah
by name; and upon thee
shall he offer the priests
of the high places
that burn incense upon thee,
and men's bones shall
be burnt upon thee.
3. And he gave a sign the
same day, saying,
This is the sign which
the LORD hath spoken;
Behold, the altar shall be
rent, and the ashes
that *are* upon it shall be
poured out.
4. And it came to pass,
when king
Jeroboam heard the saying of
the man of God, which had cried
against the altar in Beth-el, that
he put forth his hand from
the altar, saying, Lay hold
on him. And his hand,
which he put forth against him,
dried up, so that he could
not pull it in again to him.
5. **The altar also was rent,**
and the ashes poured out
from the altar,
according to the sign which
the man of God had given by
the word of the LORD.
6. **And the king** answered and
said unto the man of God,
Entreat now the face of the LORD
thy God, and
pray for me, that my hand
may be restored me again.
And the man of God
besought the LORD, and
the king's hand was
restored him again, and
became as *it was* before.
7. **And the king said**

unto the man of God,

Come home with me, and refresh thyself, and I will give thee a reward. 8. And the man of God said unto the king, If thou wilt give me half thine house, I will not go in with thee, neither will I eat bread nor drink water in this place: 9. For so was it charged me by the word of the LORD, saying, Eat no bread, nor drink water, nor turn again by the same way that thou camest. 10. So he went another way, and returned not by the way that he came to Beth-el. 11. Now there dwelt an old prophet in Beth-el; and his sons came and told him all the works that the man of God had done that day in Beth-el: the words which he had spoken unto the king, them they told also to their father. 12. And their father said unto them, What way went he? For his sons had seen what way the man of God went, which came from Judah. 13. And he said unto his sons, Saddle me the ass. So they saddled him the ass: and he rode thereon, 14. And went after the man of God, and found him sitting under an oak: and he said unto him, Art thou the man of God that camest from Judah? And he said, I am. 15. Then he said unto him, Come home with me, and eat bread. 16. And he said, I may not return with thee, nor go in with thee: neither will I eat bread nor drink water with thee in this place: 17. For it was said to me by the word of the LORD, Thou shalt eat no bread nor drink water there, nor turn again to go by the way that thou camest. 18. He said unto him, I am a prophet also as thou *art;* and an angel spake unto me by the word of the LORD, saying, Bring him back with thee into thine house, that he may eat bread and drink water. But he lied unto him. 19. So he went back with him, and did eat bread in his house, and drank water. 20. And it came to pass, as they sat at the table, that the word of the LORD came unto the prophet that brought him back: 21. And he cried unto the man of God that came from Judah, saying, Thus saith the LORD, Forasmuch as thou hast disobeyed the mouth of the LORD, and hast not kept the commandment which the LORD thy God commanded thee, 22. But camest back, and hast eaten bread and drunk water in the place, of the which *the LORD* did say to thee, Eat no bread, and drink no water; thy carcase shall not come unto the sepulchre of thy fathers. 23. And it came to pass, after he had eaten bread, and after he had drunk, that he saddled for him the ass, *to wit,* for the prophet whom he had brought back. 24. And when he was gone, a lion met him by the way, and slew him: and his carcase was cast in the way, and the ass stood by it, the lion also stood by the carcase. 25. And, behold, men passed by, and saw the carcase cast in the way, and the lion standing

by the carcase: **and they** came and **told it in the city where the old prophet dwelt.** 26. **And when the prophet that brought him back** from the way **heard** *thereof,* **he said, It is the man of God, who was disobedient** unto the word of the LORD: therefore the LORD hath delivered him unto the lion, which hath torn him, and slain him, according to the word of the LORD, which he spake unto him. 27. And he spake to his sons, saying, Saddle me the ass. And they saddled *him.* 28. **And he went and found his carcase** cast in the way, and the ass **and** the lion standing by the carcase: **the lion had not eaten the carcase,** nor torn the ass. 29. **And the prophet took up the carcase** of the man of God, and laid it upon the ass, **and brought it back:** and the old prophet came to the city, to mourn and to bury him. 30. **And he laid his carcase in his own grave;** and they mourned over him, *saying,* Alas, my brother! 31. And it came to pass, **after he had buried him,** that **he spake** to his sons, **saying, When I am dead,** then **bury me** in the sepulchre **wherein the man of God is buried;** lay my bones beside his bones: 32. **For the saying which he cried** by the word of the LORD **against the altar in Beth-el, and** against all the houses of **the high places** which *are* in the cities of Samaria, **shall surely come to pass.** 33. **After this** thing **Jeroboam returned not from his evil** way, but made again of the lowest of the people priests of the high places: whosoever would, he consecrated him, and he became *one* of the priests of the high places. 34. **And this thing became sin unto the house of Jeroboam, even to cut it off,** and to destroy *it* **from** off the face of **the earth.**

CHAPTER 14

1. **At that time Abijah the son of Jeroboam fell sick.** 2. **And Jeroboam said to his wife, Arise,** I pray thee, and **disguise thyself,** that thou be not known to be the wife of Jeroboam; and **get thee to Shiloh:** behold, **there is Ahijah the prophet,** which told me that *I should be* king over this people. 3. And take with thee ten loaves, and cracknels, and a cruse of honey, and go to him: **he shall tell thee what shall become of the child.** 4. **And Jeroboam's wife did so,** and arose, and went to Shiloh, and came to the house of Ahijah. **But Ahijah could not see; for his eyes were set by** reason of his **age.** 5. **And the LORD said unto Ahijah,** Behold, **the wife of Jeroboam cometh** to ask a thing of thee for her son; for he *is* sick: thus and thus shalt thou say unto her: for it shall be, **when she cometh in, that she shall feign** herself **to be another woman.** 6. **And** it was *so,* when Ahijah heard the sound of her feet, **as she came in** at the door, that **he said, Come in, thou wife of Jeroboam;** why feignest thou thyself *to be* another? **for I am sent to thee**

with heavy tidings.

7. Go, tell Jeroboam, Thus saith the LORD God of Israel, Forasmuch as I exalted thee from among the people, and made thee prince over my people Israel,

8. And rent the kingdom away from the house of David, and gave it thee: and yet thou hast not been as my servant David, who kept my commandments, and who followed me with all his heart, to do *that* only *which was* right in mine eyes;

9. But hast done evil above all that were before thee: for thou hast gone and made thee other gods and molten images, to provoke me to anger, and hast cast me behind thy back:

10. Therefore, behold, I will bring evil upon the house of Jeroboam, and will cut off from Jeroboam him that pisseth against the wall, *and* him that is shut up and left in Israel, and will take away the remnant of the house of Jeroboam, as a man taketh away dung, till it be all gone.

11. Him that dieth of Jeroboam in the city shall the dogs eat; and him that dieth in the field shall the fowls of the air eat: for the LORD hath spoken *it*.

12. Arise thou therefore, get thee to thine own house: *and* when thy feet enter into the city, the child shall die.

13. And all Israel shall mourn for him, and bury him: for he only of Jeroboam shall come to the grave, because in him there is found some good thing toward the LORD God of Israel in the house of Jeroboam.

14. Moreover the LORD shall raise him

up a king over Israel, who shall cut off the house of Jeroboam that day: but what? even now.

15. For the LORD shall smite Israel, as a reed is shaken in the water, and he shall root up Israel out of this good land, which he gave to their fathers, and shall scatter them beyond the river, because they have made their groves, provoking the LORD to anger.

16. And he shall give Israel up because of the sins of Jeroboam, who did sin, and who made Israel to sin.

17. And Jeroboam's wife arose, and departed, and came to Tirzah: and when she came to the threshold of the door, the child died;

18. And they buried him; and all Israel mourned for him, according to the word of the LORD, which he spake by the hand of his servant Ahijah the prophet.

19. And the rest of the acts of Jeroboam, how he warred, and how he reigned, behold, they are written in the book of the chronicles of the kings of Israel.

20. And the days which Jeroboam reigned *were* two and twenty years: and he slept with his fathers, and Nadab his son reigned in his stead.

21. And Rehoboam the son of Solomon reigned in Judah. Rehoboam *was* forty and one years old when he began to reign, and he reigned seventeen years in Jerusalem, the city which the LORD did choose out of all the tribes of Israel, to put his name there. And his mother's name

was Naamah an Ammonitess.

22. **And Judah did evil in the sight of the LORD,** and they provoked him to jealousy with their sins which they had committed, above all that their fathers had done.

23. **For they also built** them **high places, and images, and groves,** on every high hill, and under every green tree.

24. **And there were** also **sodomites in the land: and they did according to all the abominations of the nations** which **the LORD cast out** before the children of Israel.

25. **And** it came to pass **in the fifth year of** king **Rehoboam,** that **Shishak king of Egypt came up against Jerusalem:**

26. **And he took away the treasures of the house of the LORD,** and the treasures of the king's house; he even took away all: **and** he took away **all the shields of gold** which Solomon had made.

27. **And king Rehoboam made in their stead brasen shields,** and committed them unto the hands of the chief of the guard, which kept the door of the king's house.

28. **And** it was so, **when the king went into the house of the LORD,** that **the guard bare them,** and brought them back into the guard chamber.

29. **Now the rest of the acts of Rehoboam,** and all that he did, **are** they not **written in** the book of **the chronicles of the kings of Judah?**

30. And there was war between Rehoboam and Jeroboam all their days.

31. **And Rehoboam** slept with his fathers, and

was buried with his fathers **in the city of David.** And his mother's name was Naamah an Ammonitess. **And Abijam his son reigned in his stead.**

CHAPTER 15

1. Now in the eighteenth year of king Jeroboam the son of Nebat reigned Abijam over Judah.

2. **Three years reigned he in Jerusalem.** and his mother's name was Maachah, the daughter of Abishalom.

3. **And he walked in all the sins of his father,** which he had done before him: and his heart was not perfect with the LORD his God, as the heart of David his father.

4. **Nevertheless for David's sake** did the LORD his **God give him a lamp in Jerusalem, to set up his son** after him, and to establish Jerusalem:

5. Because David did that which was right in the eyes of the LORD, and turned not aside from any thing that he commanded him all the days of his life, save only in the matter of Uriah the Hittite.

6. **And there was war between Rehoboam and Jeroboam all the days of his life.**

7. **Now the rest of the acts of Abijam,** and all that he did, **are** they not **written in the** book of the **chronicles** of the kings of Judah? And there was war between Abijam and Jeroboam.

8. **And Abijam slept** with his fathers; and they buried him in the city of David: **and Asa his son reigned** in his stead.

9. And in the twentieth year of Jeroboam king of Israel reigned Asa over Judah.

10. **And forty** and **one years reigned he**

in Jerusalem. And his mother's name *was* Maachah, the daughter of Abishalom.

11. **And Asa did** *that which was* **right in the eyes of the LORD, as did David** his father.

12. **And he took away the sodomites** out of the land, **and removed all the idols** that his fathers had made.

13. **And also Maachah his mother,** even her **he removed** from *being* queen, **because she** had **made an idol** in a grove; **and Asa destroyed her idol,** and burnt *it* by the brook Kidron.

14. **But the high places were not removed: nevertheless Asa's heart was perfect with the LORD** all his days.

15. And he brought in the things which his father had dedicated, and the things which himself had dedicated, into the house of the LORD, silver, and gold, and vessels.

16. **And there was war between Asa and Baasha king of Israel all their days.**

17. **And Baasha** king of Israel went up against Judah, and **built Ramah, that he might not suffer any to go out or come in to Asa** king of Judah.

18. **Then Asa took all the silver and** the **gold** *that were* **left in the treasures** of the house of the LORD, and the treasures of the king's house, **and delivered them** into the hand of his servants: and king Asa sent them **to Ben-hadad,** the son of Tabrimon, the son of Hezion, **king of Syria,** that dwelt at Damascus, **saying,**

19. **There is a league between me and thee,** *and* between my father and thy father: behold, I have sent unto thee a present of silver and gold; come and **break thy league with Baasha king of Israel,** that he may depart from me.

20. **So Ben-hadad** hearkened unto king Asa, and **sent the captains of the hosts** which he had **against** the cities of **Israel,** and smote Ijon, and Dan, and Abel-beth-maachah, and all Cinneroth, with all the land of Naphtali.

21. **And** it came to pass, **when Baasha heard** *thereof,* that **he left off building of Ramah,** and dwelt in Tirzah.

22. **Then king Asa made a proclamation** throughout all Judah; none *was* exempted: **and they took away the stones of Ramah, and the timber thereof,** wherewith Baasha had builded; **and king Asa built with them Geba** of Benjamin, **and Mizpah.**

23. **The rest of all the acts of Asa,** and all his might, and all that he did, and the cities which he built, **are** they not **written in** the book of **the chronicles** of the kings of Judah? Nevertheless in the time of his old age he was diseased in his feet.

24. **And Asa slept** with his fathers, **and was buried** with his fathers **in the city of David** his father: **and Jehoshaphat his son reigned** in his stead.

25. **And Nadab** the son of Jeroboam **began to reign over Israel** in the second year of Asa king of Judah, **and reigned** over Israel **two years.**

26. **And he did evil** in the sight of the LORD, and walked in the way of his father, **and** in his sin wherewith

he made Israel to sin.

27. **And Baasha the son of Ahijah,** of the house of Issachar, conspired against him; and Baasha **smote him** at Gibbethon, which *belonged* to the Philistines; for Nadab and all Israel laid siege to Gibbethon.

28. **Even in the third year of Asa** king of Judah **did Baasha slay him, and reigned in his stead.**

29. **And** it came to pass, when he reigned, *that* **he smote all the house of Jeroboam; he left not** to Jeroboam **any that breathed,** until he had destroyed him, **according unto the saying of the LORD,** which he spake by his servant Ahijah the Shilonite:

30. Because of the sins of Jeroboam which he sinned, and which he made Israel sin, by his provocation wherewith he provoked the LORD God of Israel to anger.

31. **Now the rest of the acts of Nadab,** and all that he did, **are** they not **written in** the book of **the chronicles** of the kings of Israel?

32. And there was war between Asa and Baasha king of Israel all their days.

33. **In the third year of Asa king of Judah began Baasha** the son of Ahijah **to reign** over all Israel in Tirzah, **twenty and four years.**

34. **And he did evil** in the sight of the LORD, **and** walked in the way of Jeroboam, and in his sin wherewith he **made Israel to sin.**

CHAPTER 16

1. **Then the word of the LORD came to Jehu** the son of Hanani **against Baasha, saying,**

2. Forasmuch as I exalted thee out of the dust, and made thee prince over my people Israel; and **thou hast walked in the way of Jeroboam, and hast made** my people **Israel to sin,** to provoke me to anger with their sins;

3. **Behold, I will take away the posterity of Baasha,** and the posterity of his house; and will make thy house like the house of Jeroboam the son of Nebat.

4. Him that dieth of Baasha in the city shall the dogs eat; and him that dieth of his in the fields shall the fowls of the air eat.

5. **Now the rest of the acts of Baasha,** and what he did, and his might, **are** they not **written in the** book of the **chronicles** of the kings of Israel?

6. **So Baasha slept** with his fathers, and was buried in Tirzah: **and Elah his son reigned** in his stead.

7. And also by the hand of the prophet Jehu the son of Hanani came the word of the LORD against Baasha, and against his house, even for all the evil that he did in the sight of the LORD, in provoking him to anger with the work of his hands, in being like the house of Jeroboam; and because he killed him.

8. **In the twenty and sixth year of Asa** king of Judah **began Elah** the son of Baasha **to reign over Israel** in Tirzah, **two years.**

9. **And** his servant **Zimri, captain of half his chariots, conspired against him, as he was** in Tirzah, drinking himself **drunk** in the house of Arza steward of *his* house in Tirzah.

10. **And Zimri** went in and smote him, and **killed him,** in the twenty and seventh year of Asa king of Judah, **and reigned in his stead.**

11. **And** it came to pass,

when he began to reign, as soon as he sat on his throne, *that* **he slew all the house of Baasha:** he left him not one that pisseth against a wall, neither of his kinsfolks, nor of his friends. 12. Thus did Zimri destroy all the house of Baasha, according to the word of the LORD, which he spake against Baasha by Jehu the prophet, 13. For all the sins of Baasha, andthe sins of Elah his son, by which they sinned, and by which they madeIsrael to sin, in provoking the LORD God of Israel to anger with their vanities. 14. Now the rest of the acts of Elah, and all that he did, *are* they not written in the book of the chronicles of the kings of Israel? 15. **In the twenty** and **seventh year of Asa** king of Judah **did Zimri reign seven days** in Tirzah. **And the people were encamped against Gibbethon,** which *belonged* to the Philistines. 16. **And the people** *that were* encamped **heard say, Zimri hath** conspired, and hath also **slain the king: wherefore all Israel made Omri,** the captain of the host, **king** over Israel **that day** in the camp. 17. **And Omri** went up from Gibbethon, **and all Israel** with him, and they **besieged Tirzah.** 18. **And** it came to pass, **when Zimri saw that the city was taken,** that **he** went into the palace of the king's house, and **burnt the king's house over him** with fire, **and died.** 19. For his sins which he sinned in doing evil in the sight of the LORD, in walking in the way of Jeroboam, and in his sin which he did, to make Israel to sin. 20. **Now the rest of the acts of Zimri, and his treason** that he wrought, **are** they not **written in the book of** the **chronicles** of the kings of Israel? 21. **Then were the people of Israel divided into two parts: half** of the people **followed Tibni** the son of Ginath, to make him king; **and half followed Omri.** 22. **But** the people that followed **Omri prevailed against** the people that followed **Tibni** the son of Ginath: **so Tibni died,** and Omri reigned. 23. **In the thirty** and **first year of Asa** king of Judah **began Omri to reign** over Israel, **twelve years:** six years reigned he in Tirzah. 24. **And he bought the hill Samaria** of Shemer for two talents of silver, **and built** on the hill, and called the name of **the city** which he built, after the name of Shemer, owner of the hill, **Samaria.** 25. **But Omri wrought evil in the eyes of the LORD,** and did **worse than all** that *were* **before him.** 26. For he walked in all the way of Jeroboam the son of Nebat, and in his sin wherewith he made Israel to sin, to provoke the LORD God of Israel to anger with their vanities. 27. Now the rest of the acts of Omri which he did, and his might that he shewed, *are* they not written in the book of the chronicles of the kings of Israel? 28. **So Omri slept** with his fathers, **and was buried in Samaria: and Ahab his son reigned** in his stead. 29. **And in the thirty** and **eighth year of**

Asa king of Judah **began Ahab** the son of Omri **to reign** over Israel: **and Ahab** the son of Omri **reigned** over Israel in Samaria **twenty** and **two years.** 30. **And Ahab** the son of Omri **did evil** in the sight of the LORD **above all** that *were* **before him.** 31. **And** it came to pass, as if it had been a light thing for him to walk in the sins of Jeroboam the son of Nebat, that **he took to wife Jezebel the daughter of Ethbaal king of the Zidonians,** and went **and served Baal,** and worshipped him. 32. **And he reared up an altar for Baal** in the house of Baal, which he had built **in Samaria.** 33. **And Ahab** made a grove; and Ahab **did more to provoke the LORD** God of Israel to anger **than all the kings** of Israel that were **before him.** 34. **In his days did Hiel the Beth-elite build Jericho:** he laid the foundation thereof in Abiram his firstborn, and set up the gates thereof in his youngest *son* Segub, according to the word of the LORD, which he spake by Joshua the son of Nun.

CHAPTER 17

1. **And Elijah the Tishbite,** *who was* of the inhabitants of Gilead, **said unto Ahab, As the LORD** God of Israel **liveth,** before whom I stand, **there shall not be dew nor rain these years, but according to my word.** 2. **And the word of the LORD came unto him, saying,** 3. Get thee hence, and **turn** thee **eastward, and hide** thyself **by the brook Cherith,** that *is* before Jordan. 4. And it shall be, *that* **thou shalt drink of the brook; and I have commanded the ravens to feed thee** there. 5. **So he went** and did according unto the word of the LORD: for he went and dwelt by the brook Cherith, that *is* before Jordan. 6. **And the ravens brought him bread and flesh** in the morning, and bread and flesh in the evening; and he drank of the brook. 7. **And** it came to pass after a while, that **the brook dried up,** because there had been no rain in the land. 8. **And the word of the LORD came unto him, saying,** 9. **Arise, get thee to Zarephath,** which *belongeth* to Zidon, **and dwell there:** behold, **I have commanded a widow woman** there **to sustain thee.** 10. So he arose and went to Zarephath. **And when he came to** the gate of **the city,** behold, **the widow woman was** there **gathering of sticks: and he** called to her, and **said, Fetch me,** I pray thee, **a little water** in a vessel, that I may drink. 11. **And as she was going** to fetch *it,* **he** called to her, and **said, Bring me,** I pray thee, **a morsel of bread** in thine hand. 12. **And she said,** *As* the LORD thy God liveth, **I have not a cake, but an handful of meal** in a barrel, **and a little oil** in a cruse: and, behold, **I am gathering two sticks,**

that I may go in and
dress it for me and my
son, that we may eat it,
and die.

13. And Elijah said
unto her, Fear not; go *and*
do as thou hast said:
but make me thereof
a little cake first, and bring
it unto me, and after make for
thee and for thy son.

14. For thus saith the
LORD God of Israel,
The barrel of meal shall
not waste, neither shall
the cruse of
oil fail, until the day *that*
the LORD sendeth
rain upon the earth.

15. And she went and
did according to the
saying of Elijah:
and she, and he, and her
house, did eat *many* days.

16. And the barrel of
meal wasted not, neither
did the cruse of
oil fail, according to the word of the
LORD, which he spake by Elijah.

17. And it came to pass
after these things, *that*
the son of the woman,
the mistress of the house,
fell sick; and his sickness
was so sore, that
there was no breath left
in him.

18. And she said unto
Elijah, What have I to do with
thee, O thou man of God?
art thou come unto me to call
my sin to remembrance, and
to slay my son?

19. And he said unto her,
Give me thy son.
And he took him
out of her bosom, and carried him
up into a loft, where he abode,
and laid him upon
his own bed.

20. And he cried unto the
LORD, and said, O LORD my God,
hast thou also

brought evil upon the
widow with whom I sojourn,
by slaying her son?

21. And he stretched
himself upon the child
three times, and cried
unto the LORD, and said,
O LORD my God, I pray thee,
let this child's soul
come into him again.

22. And the LORD
heard the voice of
Elijah; and the soul of the
child came into him again,
and he revived.

23. And Elijah took the child,
and brought him down out of the
chamber into the house, and
delivered him unto his
mother: and Elijah
said, See, thy son liveth.

24. And the woman
said to Elijah,
Now by this
I know that
thou art a man of God, and
that the word of the LORD
in thy mouth is truth.

CHAPTER 18

1. And it came to pass
after many days, that
the word of the LORD came
to Elijah in the third year,
saying, Go, shew thyself
unto Ahab; and I will send
rain upon the earth.

2. And Elijah went to shew himself
unto Ahab. And *there was* a sore
famine in Samaria.

3. And Ahab called
Obadiah, which *was*
the governor of his house.
(Now Obadiah feared
the LORD greatly:

4. For it was *so,*
when Jezebel cut off the
prophets of the LORD, that
Obadiah took an
hundred prophets, and
hid them by fifty in a
cave, and fed them
with bread and water.)

5. **And Ahab said unto Obadiah, Go** into the land, **unto all fountains** of water, **and** unto **all brooks: peradventure we may find grass to save the horses and mules** alive, that we lose not all the beasts. 6. **So they divided the land** between them **to pass throughout it: Ahab went one way** by himself, **and Obadiah went another** way by himself. 7. **And as Obadiah was in the way,** behold, **Elijah met him: and he** knew him, and fell on his face, and **said, Art thou** that my lord **Elijah?** 8. **And he answered** him, **I am: go, tell thy lord,** Behold, **Elijah is here.** 9. **And he said, What have I sinned, that thou wouldest deliver thy servant into the hand of Ahab, to slay me?** 10. *As* the LORD thy God liveth, **there is no nation** or kingdom, **whither my lord hath not sent to seek thee:** and when they said, *He is* not *there;* he took an oath of the kingdom and nation, that they found thee not. 11. **And now thou sayest, Go, tell thy lord,** Behold, **Elijah is here.** 12. **And** it shall come to pass, **as soon as I am gone** from thee, that **the spirit of the LORD shall carry thee whither I know not; and** *so* **when** I come and tell **Ahab,** and he **cannot find thee, he shall slay me:** but I thy servant fear the LORD from my youth. 13. **Was it not told** my lord what I did when Jezebel slew the prophets of the LORD, **how I hid an hundred**

men of the LORD's **prophets** by fifty in a cave, and fed them with bread and water? 14. And now thou sayest, Go, tell thy lord, Behold, Elijah *is here:* and he shall slay me. 15. **And Elijah said, As the LORD of hosts liveth,** before whom I stand, **I will** surely **shew myself unto him to-day.** 16. **So Obadiah went to meet Ahab, and told him: and Ahab went to meet Elijah.** 17. **And** it came to pass, when Ahab saw Elijah, that **Ahab said** unto him, **Art thou he that troubleth Israel?** 18. **And he answered, I have not troubled Israel; but** thou, and thy father's house, in that **ye have** forsaken the commandments of the LORD, and thou hast **followed Baalim.** 19. **Now** therefore send, *and* **gather** to me **all Israel unto mount Carmel, and the prophets of Baal** four hundred and fifty, **and the prophets of the groves** four hundred, which eat at Jezebel's table. 20. **So Ahab** sent unto all the children of Israel, and **gathered the prophets** together **unto mount Carmel.** 21. **And Elijah came unto** all **the people, and said, How long halt ye between two opinions? if the LORD be God, follow him: but if Baal, then follow him. And the people answered** him **not a word.** 22. **Then said Elijah** unto the people, I, *even* **I only, remain a prophet** of the LORD; but Baal's prophets are four hundred and fifty men.

23. Let them therefore give us two bullocks; and let them choose one bullock for themselves, and cut it in pieces, and lay it on wood, and put no fire under: and I will dress the other bullock, and lay *it* on wood, and put no fire under:

24. And call ye on the name of your gods, and I will call on the name of the LORD: and the God that answereth by fire, let him be God. And all the people answered and said, It is well spoken.

25. And Elijah said unto the prophets of Baal, Choose you one bullock for yourselves, and dress *it* first; for ye *are* many; and call on the name of your gods, but put no fire *under*.

26. And they took the bullock which was given them, and they dressed *it*, and called on the name of Baal from morning even until noon, saying, O Baal, hear us. But there was no voice, nor any that answered. And they leaped upon the altar which was made.

27. And it came to pass at noon, that Elijah mocked them, and said, Cry aloud: for he is a god; either he is talking, or he is pursuing, or he is in a journey, or peradventure he sleepeth, and must be awaked.

28. And they cried aloud, and cut themselves after their manner with knives and lancets, till the blood gushed out upon them.

29. And it came to pass, when midday was past, and they prophesied until the *time* of the offering of the evening sacrifice, that there was neither voice, nor any to answer, nor any that regarded.

30. And Elijah said unto all the people, Come near unto me. And all the people came near unto him. And he repaired the altar of the LORD *that was* broken down.

31. And Elijah took twelve stones, according to the number of the tribes of the sons of Jacob, unto whom the word of the LORD came, saying, Israel shall be thy name:

32. And with the stones he built an altar in the name of the LORD: and he made a trench about the altar, as great as would contain two measures of seed.

33. And he put the wood in order, and cut the bullock in pieces, and laid him on the wood, and said, Fill four barrels with water, and pour it on the burnt sacrifice, and on the wood.

34. And he said, Do it the second time. And they did *it* the second time. And he said, Do it the third time. And they did *it* the third time.

35. And the water ran round about the altar; and he filled the trench also with water.

36. And it came to pass at *the time of* the offering of the *evening* sacrifice, that Elijah the prophet came near, and said, LORD God of Abraham, Isaac, and of Israel, let it be known this day that thou art God in Israel, and that I am thy servant,

and that I have done all
these things at thy word.

37. Hear me, O LORD, hear me,
that this people may know
that thou art the LORD
God, and *that* thou hast turned their
heart back again.

38. **Then the fire of the LORD
fell, and consumed the** burnt
sacrifice, and
the wood, and
the stones, and
**the dust, and licked
up the water** that *was*
in the trench.

39. **And** when all
the people saw *it,* they
fell on their faces: and they
said, The LORD, he is the
God; the LORD, he *is* the God.

40. **And Elijah said** unto them,
Take the prophets of Baal;
let not one of them escape.
And they took them: and
Elijah brought them down
**to the brook Kishon,
and slew them** there.

41. **And Elijah said
unto Ahab,** Get thee up,
**eat and drink; for there
is a sound of** abundance of
rain.

42. So Ahab went up
to eat and to drink.
And Elijah went up
to the top of
Carmel; and he
cast himself down
upon the earth,
**and put his face
between his knees,**

43. **And said to his**
servant, Go up now,
**look toward the sea.
And he** went up, and
**looked, and said, There
is nothing. And he said,
Go again seven times.**

44. **And** it came to pass at
the seventh time,
that he said, Behold,
there ariseth a little cloud
out of the sea, like a man's hand.

And he said, Go up,
say unto Ahab,
Prepare *thy chariot,* and
**get thee down that the
rain stop thee not.**

45. **And** it came to pass in the
mean while, that the heaven was
black with clouds and wind, and
**there was a great rain.
And Ahab** rode, and
went to Jezreel.

46. **And** the hand of
the LORD was on
Elijah; and he girded
up his loins, and
**ran before Ahab to the
entrance of Jezreel.**

CHAPTER 19

1. **And Ahab told
Jezebel all** that
Elijah had done,
and withal how he had slain
all the prophets with the sword.

2. **Then Jezebel sent a
messenger unto Elijah,
saying, So let the gods
do to me,** and more also,
**if I make not thy life
as** the life of
**one of them by
to-morrow** about this time.

3. **And** when he saw *that,*
**he arose, and went for
his life,** and came to Beer-
sheba, which *belongeth* to Judah,
and left his servant there.

4. But he himself went a day's journey
**into the wilderness,
and** came and
sat down
under a juniper tree: and he
requested for himself
that he might die;
and said, It is enough; now,
O LORD, take away my life;
for I *am* not better than my fathers.

5. **And as he** lay and
slept under a juniper
tree, behold, then
**an angel touched
him, and said** unto him,
Arise and eat.

6. **And** he looked, and, **behold, there was a cake** baken on the coals, **and** a cruse of **water** at his head. **And he did eat and drink, and laid him down again.** 7. **And the angel** of the LORD **came again** the second time, and touched him, **and said, Arise and eat; because the journey is too great for thee.** 8. **And he** arose, and did eat and drink, and **went in the strength of that meat forty days and forty nights unto Horeb** the mount of God. 9. **And he came** thither **unto a cave, and lodged there; and,** behold, the word of **the LORD** came to him, and he **said** unto him, **What doest thou here, Elijah?** 10. **And he said,** I have been very jealous for the LORD God of hosts: for **the children of Israel have forsaken thy covenant,** thrown down thine altars, **and slain thy prophets** with the sword; **and I,** even I **only, am left; and they seek my life,** to take it away. 11. **And he said, Go** forth, and **stand upon the mount before the LORD. And,** behold, the LORD passed **by, and a** great and strong **wind rent the mountains, and brake** in pieces **the rocks** before the LORD; **but the LORD was not in the wind: and after the wind an earthquake; but the LORD was not in the earthquake:** 12. **And after the earthquake a fire; but the LORD was not in the fire: and after the fire a still small voice.** 13. **And** it was so, **when Elijah heard it,** that **he** wrapped his face in his mantle, and went out, and **stood in the entering in of the cave. And,** behold, **there came a voice** unto him, **and said, What doest thou here, Elijah?** 14. **And he said,** I have been very jealous for the LORD God of hosts: because **the children of Israel have forsaken thy covenant,** thrown down thine altars, and slain thy prophets with the sword; **and I,** even I **only, am left;** and they seek my life, to take it away. 15. **And the LORD said** unto him, **Go,** return on thy way **to** the wilderness of **Damascus: and** when thou comest, **anoint Hazael** to be **king over Syria:** 16. **And Jehu** the son of Nimshi **shalt thou anoint** to be **king over Israel: and Elisha** the son of Shaphat of Abel-meholah **shalt thou anoint to be prophet in thy room.** 17. **And** it shall come to pass, that **him that escapeth** the sword of **Hazael shall Jehu slay: and him that escapeth** from the sword of **Jehu shall Elisha slay.** 18. **Yet I have** left me **seven thousand in Israel,** all the knees **which have not bowed unto Baal,** and every mouth which hath not kissed him. 19. **So he departed** thence, **and found Elisha** the son of Shaphat, who was plowing with twelve yoke of oxen before him, and he with the twelfth: **and** Elijah passed by him, and **cast his mantle upon him.**

20. **And he** left the oxen, and **ran after Elijah, and said, Let me,** I pray thee, **kiss my father and** my **mother, and then I will follow thee. And he said** unto him, **Go back again:** for what have I done to thee? 21. **And he returned** back from him, **and took** a yoke of **oxen, and slew them, and boiled their flesh** with the instruments of the oxen, **and gave unto the people, and they did eat. Then he** arose, and **went after Elijah,** and ministered unto him.

CHAPTER 20

1. **And Ben-hadad the king of Syria** gathered all his host together: and *there were* thirty and two kings with him, and horses, and chariots; and he **went up and besieged Samaria,** and warred against it. 2. **And he sent messengers to Ahab** king of Israel into the city, **and said** unto him, **Thus saith Ben-hadad,** 3. **Thy silver and** thy **gold is mine; thy wives** also **and** thy **children,** *even* the goodliest, **are mine.** 4. **And the king of Israel** answered and **said,** My lord, **O king,** according to thy saying, **I am thine, and all that I have.** 5. **And the messengers came again, and said, Thus speaketh Ben-hadad,** saying, Although I have sent unto thee, saying, Thou shalt deliver me thy silver, and thy gold, and thy wives, and thy children; 6. **Yet I will send my**

servants unto thee **to-morrow** about this time, **and they shall search thine house, and the houses of thy servants; and** it shall be, *that* **whatsoever is pleasant** in thine eyes, **they shall** put *it* in their hand, and **take it** away. 7. **Then the king of Israel called** all **the elders** of the land, **and said,** Mark, I pray you, and see how **this man seeketh mischief: for he sent** unto me **for my wives,** and for **my children,** and for **my silver, and** for **my gold; and I denied him not.** 8. **And all the elders** and all the people **said** unto him, **Hearken not unto him,** nor consent. 9. **Wherefore he said unto the messengers of Ben-hadad, Tell** my lord **the king, All that thou didst send for** to thy servant **at** the **first I will do: but this** thing **I may not do.** And the messengers departed, and brought him word again. 10. **And Ben-hadad** sent unto him, and **said,** The gods do so unto me, and more also, if **the dust of Samaria shall suffice for handfuls for** all **the people that follow me.** 11. **And the king of Israel** answered and **said, Tell him, Let not him** that girdeth on *his harness* **boast himself** as he that putteth it off. 12. And it came to pass, **when Ben-hadad heard** this message, as he *was* drinking, he and

the kings in the pavilions, that
he said unto his servants,
Set yourselves in array. And
they set *themselves in array*
against the city.
13. And, behold,
there came a prophet
unto Ahab king of Israel,
saying, Thus saith
the LORD, Hast thou seen
all this great multitude?
behold, I will deliver it
into thine hand this day;
and thou shalt know
that I am the LORD.
14. And Ahab said, By
whom? And he said,
Thus saith the LORD,
Even by the young
men of the princes
of the provinces. Then
he said, Who shall order
the battle? And he
answered, Thou.
15. Then he numbered
the young men of the princes
of the provinces, and they
were two hundred and
thirty two: and
after them he numbered
all the people,
even all the children of Israel,
being seven thousand.
16. And they went out
at noon. But
Ben-hadad was
drinking himself
drunk in the pavilions,
he and the kings, the thirty and two
kings that helped him.
17. And the young men
of the princes of the provinces
went out first; and
Ben-hadad sent out, and
they told him, saying,
There are men come
out of Samaria.
18. And he said, Whether
they be come out for
peace, take them alive;
or whether they be come out for
war, take them alive.
19. So these young men

of the princes of the provinces
came out of the city,
and the army which
followed them.
20. And they slew every one
his man: and the Syrians
fled; and Israel pursued them:
and Ben-hadad
the king of Syria
escaped on an horse
with the horsemen.
21. And the king of Israel went out,
and smote the horses and chariots,
and slew the Syrians with a great
slaughter.
22. And the prophet came
to the king of Israel,
and said unto him, Go,
strengthen thyself, and mark,
and see what thou doest:
for at the return of the year
the king of Syria will come
up against thee.
23. And the servants of the
king of Syria said unto him,
Their gods are gods
of the hills; therefore they
were stronger than we; but
let us fight against them
in the plain, and surely
we shall be stronger
than they.
24. And do this thing, Take the kings
away, every man out of his place, and
put captains in their rooms:
25. And number thee an
army, like the army that thou
hast lost, horse for horse, and
chariot for chariot:
and we will fight against them
in the plain, *and* surely we shall
be stronger than they.
And he hearkened
unto their voice,
and did so.
26. And it came to pass
at the return of the year, that
Ben-hadad
numbered the Syrians, and
went up to Aphek,
to fight against Israel.
27. And the children of
Israel were numbered,

and were all present, and
went against them: and the
children of Israel pitched before them
like two little flocks of
kids; but the Syrians
filled the country.
28. And there came
a man of God, and spake
unto the king of Israel, and
said, Thus saith the LORD,
Because the Syrians have
said, The LORD is God of
the hills, but he is
not God
of the valleys, therefore
will I deliver all
this great
multitude into thine hand,
and ye shall know that
I am the LORD.
29. And they pitched one over
against the other seven days. And so
it was, that in the seventh day the
battle was joined: and the children of
Israel slew of the Syrians an
hundred thousand footmen
in one day.
30. But the rest fled
to Aphek, into the city;
and there
a wall fell upon twenty and
seven thousand of the
men that were left.
And Ben-hadad fled,
and came
into the city,
into an inner chamber.
31. And his servants said
unto him, Behold now,
we have heard that
the kings of the house of
Israel are merciful kings:
let us, I pray thee, put
sackcloth on our loins, and
ropes upon our heads, and
go out
to the king of Israel:
peradventure he
will save thy life.
32. So they girded sackcloth
on their loins, and put ropes on
their heads, and
came to the king of Israel,

and said, Thy servant
Ben-hadad saith, I pray thee,
let me live. And he said,
Is he yet alive? he is
my brother.
33. Now the men did diligently
observe whether any thing would
come from him, and did hastily catch
it: and they said, Thy brother
Ben-hadad. Then he said,
Go ye, bring him. Then
Ben-hadad came forth
to him; and he caused him to
come up into the chariot.
34. And Ben-hadad
said unto him,
The cities, which my father
took from thy father, I will
restore; and thou shalt make
streets for thee in Damascus, as my
father made in Samaria.
Then said Ahab, I will send
thee away with this
covenant. So he made a
covenant with him, and
sent him away.
35. And a certain
man of the sons
of the prophets said unto
his neighbour in the word
of the LORD, Smite
me, I pray thee.
And the man
refused to smite him.
36. Then said he unto him,
Because thou hast not
obeyed the voice of the
LORD, behold, as soon as
thou art departed from me,
a lion shall slay thee. And as
soon as he was departed from him,
a lion found him, and
slew him.
37. Then he found another
man, and said,
Smite me, I pray thee.
And the man smote him,
so that in smiting
he wounded him.
38. So the prophet
departed, and
waited for the king by the way,
and disguised himself with

■ **ashes** upon his face.
■ 39. **And as the king passed**
by, he cried unto the king: and
■ **he said, Thy**
■ **servant went** out
■ **into** the midst of
■ **the battle; and,** behold,
■ **a man** turned aside, and
■ **brought a man unto me,**
■ **and said, Keep this man:**
■ **if** by any means
■ **he be missing, then shall**
■ **thy life be for his life,**
■ **or else thou shalt pay**
■ **a talent of silver.**
■ 40. **And as thy servant**
■ **was busy** here and there,
■ **he was gone.**
■ **And the king** of Israel
■ **said** unto him,
■ **So shall thy judgment be;**
■ **thyself hast decided it.**
■ 41. **And he** hasted, and
■ **took the ashes away**
from his face;
■ **and the king** of Israel
■ **discerned** him that
■ **he was of the prophets.**
■ 42. **And he said** unto him,
■ **Thus saith the LORD,**
■ **Because thou hast**
■ **let go** out of *thy* hand
■ **a man** whom I
■ **appointed to** utter
■ **destruction, therefore thy**
■ **life shall go for his life, and**
■ **thy people for his people.**
■ 43. **And the king** of Israel
■ **went to his house**
■ **heavy and displeased,**
and came to Samaria.

CHAPTER 21

■ 1. **And** it came to pass
after these things, *that*
■ **Naboth** the Jezreelite
■ **had a vineyard,**
which *was* in Jezrel, hard
■ **by the palace of Ahab**
king of Samaria.
■ 2. **And Ahab spake unto**
■ **Naboth, saying,**
■ **Give me thy vineyard,** that I

may have it for a garden of herbs,
because it *is* near unto my house:
■ **and I will give thee** for it
■ **a better vineyard** than it;
■ **or,** if it seem good to thee, I
will give thee the worth of it in
■ **money.**
■ 3. **And Naboth said** to Ahab,
■ **The LORD forbid** it me,
■ **that I should give the**
■ **inheritance of my**
■ **fathers** unto thee.
■ 4. **And Ahab came**
into his house
■ **heavy and displeased**
because of the word which Naboth
the Jezreelite had spoken to him: for
he had said, I will not give thee the
inheritance of my fathers.
■ **And** he
■ **laid** him
■ **down** upon his bed, and
turned away his face,
■ **and would eat no bread.**
■ 5. **But Jezebel** his wife
came to him, and
■ **said** unto him,
■ **Why is thy spirit so sad,**
that thou eatest no bread?
■ 6. **And he said** unto her,
■ **Because I spake unto**
■ **Naboth** the Jezreelite,
■ **and said** unto him,
■ **Give me thy vineyard** for
money; or else, if it please thee, I will
give thee *another* vineyard for it:
■ **and he answered, I will not**
■ **give thee my vineyard.**
■ 7. **And Jezebel** his wife
■ **said** unto him,
■ **Dost thou** now
■ **govern** the kingdom of
■ **Israel?** arise, *and* eat bread, and
■ **let thine heart be merry: I**
■ **will give thee the vineyard**
of Naboth the Jezreelite.
■ 8. **So she wrote letters in**
■ **Ahab's name,** and sealed *them*
with his seal, and sent the letters
■ **unto the elders and** to the
■ **nobles** that *were*
■ **in his city,** dwelling with Naboth.
■ 9. And she wrote in the letters,

saying, Proclaim a fast,
and set Naboth on high
among the people:
10. And set two
men, sons of Belial,
before him, to bear
witness against him,
saying, Thou didst
blaspheme God and the king.
And then carry him out, and
stone him, that he may die.
11. And the men of his city,
even the elders and the nobles who
were the inhabitants in his city,
did as Jezebel had
sent unto them, and as
it was written in the letters
which she had sent unto them.
12. They proclaimed a fast, and
set Naboth on high
among the people.
13. And there came in
two men, children of Belial, and
sat before him: and the men of Belial
witnessed against him,
even against Naboth, in the
presence of the people,
saying, Naboth did
blaspheme God and the king.
Then they carried him
forth out of the city, and
stoned him
with stones, that he died.
14. Then they sent
to Jezebel, saying,
Naboth is stoned, and is
dead.
15. And it came to pass, when
Jezebel heard that Naboth was
stoned, and was dead, that
Jezebel said to Ahab, Arise,
take possession of the
vineyard of Naboth the Jezreelite,
which he refused to give thee
for money: for Naboth is not
alive, but dead.
16. And it came to pass, when
Ahab heard that Naboth was dead,
that Ahab rose up to go down
to the vineyard of Naboth the
Jezreelite, to take possession of it.
17. And the word of the
LORD came to Elijah

the Tishbite, saying,
18. Arise, go down
to meet Ahab king of Israel,
which is in Samaria: behold, he is in
the vineyard of Naboth, whither he is
gone down to possess it.
19. And thou shalt
speak unto him,
saying, Thus saith the LORD,
Hast thou killed, and also
taken possession? And thou
shalt speak unto him, saying,
Thus saith the LORD,
In the place where
dogs licked the blood
of Naboth shall dogs
lick thy blood, even thine.
20. And Ahab said to Elijah,
Hast thou found me, O
mine enemy? And he
answered, I have found
thee; because thou hast
sold thyself to work evil in the
sight of the LORD.
21. Behold, I will bring evil
upon thee, and will take away thy
posterity, and will cut off from Ahab
him that pisseth against the wall, and
him that is shut up and left in Israel,
22. And will make thine
house like the house of
Jeroboam the son of Nebat,
and like the house of Baasha the
son of Ahijah,
for the provocation wherewith
thou hast provoked me
to anger, and made
Israel to sin.
23. And of Jezebel also
spake the LORD, saying,
The dogs shall eat Jezebel
by the wall of Jezreel.
24. Him that dieth of Ahab in
the city the dogs shall eat; and
him that dieth in the field shall the
fowls of the air eat.
25. But there was none like
unto Ahab, which did sell himself
to work wickedness
in the sight of the LORD,
whom Jezebel his wife
stirred up.
26. And he did very

abominably in following
idols, according to all *things* as did
the Amorites, whom the LORD cast
out before the children of Israel.
27. And it came to pass,
when Ahab heard
those words, that
he rent his clothes, and
put sackcloth upon
his flesh, and
fasted, and lay in sackcloth,
and went softly.
28. And the word
of the LORD came
to Elijah the Tishbite,
saying,
29. Seest thou how
Ahab humbleth himself
before me? because he
humbleth himself before me,
I will not bring the evil in his
days: but in his son's days will I
bring the evil upon his house.

CHAPTER 22

1. And they continued
three years without war
between Syria and Israel.
2. And it came to pass
in the third year, that
Jehoshaphat the
king of Judah came down
to the king of Israel.
3. And the king of Israel
said unto his servants,
Know ye that Ramoth
in Gilead is ours,
and we *be* still, *and* take it not out of
the hand of the king of Syria?
4. And he said unto
Jehoshaphat, Wilt thou
go with me to battle
to Ramoth-gilead?
And Jehoshaphat
said to the king of Israel,
I am as thou art, my people as
thy people, my horses as thy horses.
5. And Jehoshaphat said
unto the king of Israel,
Inquire, I pray thee, at the
word of the LORD to-day.
6. Then the king of Israel
gathered the prophets

together, about four hundred men,
and said unto them,
Shall I go against
Ramoth-gilead
to battle, or shall I forbear?
And they said, Go up; for the
LORD shall deliver *it* into the hand of
the king.
7. And Jehoshaphat said, Is
there not here a prophet of
the LORD besides,
that we might inquire of him?
8. And the king of Israel
said unto Jehoshaphat,
There is yet one man,
Micaiah the son of Imlah, by whom
we may inquire of the LORD:
but I hate him; for he doth
not prophesy good
concerning me, but evil.
And Jehoshaphat said, Let not
the king say so.
9. Then the king of Israel
called an officer, and said,
Hasten hither Micaiah
the son of Imlah.
10. And the king of Israel
and Jehoshaphat
the king of Judah sat each
on his throne, having put on their
robes, in a void place in the entrance
of the gate of Samaria;
and all the prophets
prophesied before them.
11. And Zedekiah
the son of Chenaanah
made him
horns of iron: and he
said, Thus saith the LORD,
With these shalt thou push
the Syrians, until thou have
consumed them.
12. And all the prophets
prophesied so,
saying, Go up to
Ramoth-gilead, and prosper:
for the LORD shall deliver it
into the king's hand.
13. And the messenger that
was gone to call Micaiah
spake unto him, saying,
Behold now,
the words of the prophets

declare good
unto the king with one mouth:

let thy word, I pray thee, be
like the word of one of them, and
speak that which is good.

14. And Micaiah said,
As the LORD liveth,
what the LORD saith unto me,
that will I speak.

15. So he came to the king.
And the king said unto him,
Micaiah, shall we go
against Ramoth-gilead
to battle, or shall we forbear?
And he answered
him, Go, and prosper:
for the LORD shall deliver
it into the hand of the king.

16. And the king said
unto him, How many times
shall I adjure thee that thou
tell me nothing but
that which is true
in the name of the LORD?

17. And he said, I saw all
Israel scattered upon the hills,
as sheep that have not a
shepherd: and the LORD said,
These have no master:let them return
every man to his house in peace.

18. And the king of Israel
said unto Jehoshaphat,
Did I not tell thee that he
would prophesy
no good concerning me, but
evil?

19. And he said, Hear thou
therefore the word of the LORD:
I saw the LORD sitting on
his throne, and all the host of
heaven standing by him on his
right hand and on his left.

20. And the LORD said,
Who shall persuade Ahab,
that he may go up and
fall at Ramoth-gilead?
And one said on this manner, and
another said on that manner.

21. And there came forth a
spirit, and stood before the LORD,
and said, I will
persuade him.

22. And the LORD said unto him,
Wherewith? And he said, I will go
forth, and I will be a lying spirit in the
mouth of all his prophets. And he
said, Thou shalt persude *him,* and
prevail also: go forth, and do so.

23. Now therefore, behold,
the LORD hath put a lying
spirit in the mouth of all these
thy prophets, and the LORD hath
spoken evil concerning thee.

24. But Zedekiah the son of
Chenaanah went near, and
smote Micaiah on the
cheek, and said, Which
way went the spirit of the
LORD from me to speak unto thee?

25. And Micaiah said, Behold,
thou shalt see in that day,
when thou shalt go
into an inner chamber
to hide thyself.

26. And the king
of Israel said, Take
Micaiah, and carry him
back unto Amon the
governor of the city, and
to Joash the king's son;

27. And say, Thus saith the
king, Put this fellow in the
prison, and feed him with bread of
affliction and with water of affliction,
until I come in peace.

28. And Micaiah said, If
thou return at all in peace,
the LORD hath not spoken
by me. And he said, Hearken, O
people, every one of you.

29. So the king of
Israel and Jehoshaphat
the king of Judah went up
to Ramoth-gilead.

30. And the king of Israel
said unto Jehoshaphat,
I will disguise myself,
and enter into the
battle; but put thou
on thy robes. And the
king of Israel disguised
himself, and went into the battle.

31. But the king of Syria
commanded his thirty and
two captains that had
rule over his chariots,

saying, Fight neither with small nor great, save only with the king of Israel. 32. And it came to pass, when the captains of the chariots saw Jehoshaphat, that they said, Surely it is the king of Israel. And they turned aside to fight against him: and Jehoshaphat cried out. 33. And it came to pass, when the captains of the chariots perceived that it was not the king of Israel, that they turned back from pursuing him. 34. And a certain man drew a bow at a venture, and smote the king of Israel between the joints of the harness: wherefore he said unto the driver of his chariot, Turn thine hand, and carry me out of the host; for I am wounded. 35. And the battle increased that day: and the king was stayed up in his chariot against the Syrians, and died at even: and the blood ran out of the wound into the midst of the chariot. 36. And there went a proclamation throughout the host about the going down of the sun, saying, Every man to his city, and every man to his own country. 37. So the king died, and was brought to Samaria; and they buried the king in Samaria. 38. And one washed the chariot in the pool of Samaria; and the dogs licked up his blood; and they washed his armour; according unto the word of the LORD which he spake.

39. Now the rest of the acts of Ahab, and all that he did, and the ivory house which he made, and all the cities that he built, are they not written in the book of the chronicles of the kings of Israel? 40. So Ahab slept with his fathers; and Ahaziah his son reigned in his stead.

41. And Jehoshaphat the son of Asa began to reign over Judah in the fourth year of Ahab king of Israel. 42. Jehoshaphat was thirty and five years old when he began to reign; and he reigned twenty and five years in Jerusalem. And his mother's name was Azubah the daughter of Shilhi. 43. And he walked in all the ways of Asa his father; he turned not aside from it, doing that which was right in the eyes of the LORD: nevertheless the high places were not taken away; for the people offered and burnt incense yet in the high places. 44. And Jehoshaphat made peace with the king of Israel.

45. Now the rest of the acts of Jehoshaphat, and his might that he shewed, and how he warred, are they not written in the book of the chronicles of the kings of Judah? 46. And the remnant of the sodomites, which remained in the days of his father Asa, he took out of the land. 47. There was then no king in Edom: a deputy was king. 48. Jehoshaphat made ships of Tharshish to go to Ophir for gold: but they went not; for the ships were broken at Ezion-geber. 49. Then said Ahaziah the son of Ahab unto Jehoshaphat, Let my servants go with thy servants in the ships. But

■ Jehoshaphat would not.
■ 50. **And Jehosaphat slept** with his fathers,
■ **and was buried** with his fathers
■ **in the city of David** his father:
■ **and Jehoram his son**
■ **reigned** in his stead.
■ 51. **Ahaziah** the son of Ahab
■ **began to reign over**
■ **Israel in** Samaria
■ **the seventeenth year of**
■ **Jehoshaphat** king of Judah,

■ **and reigned two years** over Israel.
■ 52. **And he did evil** in the sight of the LORD, and walked in the way of his father and in the way of his mother, and in the way of Jeroboam the son of Nebat who made Israel to sin:
■ 53. **For he served Baal,**
■ **and worshipped him,**
■ **and provoked to anger**
■ **the LORD** God of Israel, according to all that his father had done.

ELIJAH AND ELISHA:

PROPHETS IN ISRAEL

- Israel, *the northern kingdom,*
- and Judah,
  the southern kingdom,
- were both in the
- throes of death.
- After *the reigns of*
- Kings David and Solomon,
- the deterioration
- came rapidly. *The children of*
- Israel, *miraculously delivered*
  from slavery and brought by God
  into The Promised Land,
- had turned from the Lord
- and His commandments.
- They had
  forsaken temple worship and
- joined themselves
- to *the*
- idolatrous practices
  of neighboring nations and made
  unholy alliances with them.
- The *official*
- priesthood was
- corrupted *by materialism*
  and a quest for power.
- Kings were *rising and*
- falling in the matter
- of weeks *and months.*

- All *social, commercial, and*
  governmental
- institutions were
- in disarray.
- Amidst the chaos stood two
- mighty prophets of God,
- Elijah and *his successor,*
- Elisha.
- Both were fearless,
- denouncing sin
- and corruption
  in both high and low places.
- Students of I and II Kings
- may grow weary of the
- incessant bent toward
- evil seen in the Kings
  of Israel and Judah.
- The stories of Elijah and
- Elisha, however, form some
- of the most exciting drama
- in the Bible *as well as* s
- howing how a man
- committed to God
  and His truth and couragous
  enough to stand, speak, and act,
- can often
  be used by the Holy Spirit to
- turn defeat into victory.

THE BOOK OF SECOND KINGS

BACKGROUND INFORMATION

Author: Unknown although some scholars have designated Jeremiah as the author

Date Written: Between 562 — 536 B.C.

Number of:
Verses–719
Chapters—25
Total Words— 23,532
Scan Words—10,477
Scan Words Represent Approximately 44% of Total Words

Theme: The History of the Divided kingdom from Ahaziah until the Babylonian Captivity

OUTLINE OF THE BOOK

I. **The Final Acts of** the Prophet **Elijah**
1:1 — 2:11

II. **The Ministry of the** Prophet **Elisha**
2:12 — 8:15

III. **The History of Israel to the Fall of Samaria**
8:16 — 17:41

IV. **The History of Hezekiah to the Captivity of Judah**
18:1 — 25:30

CHAPTER 1

1. Then Moab rebelled against Israel after the death of Ahab.

2. And Ahaziah fell down through a lattice in his upper chamber that *was* in Samaria, and was sick: and he sent messengers, and said unto them, Go, inquire of Baal-zebub the god of Ekron whether I shall recover of this disease.

3. But the angel of the LORD said to Elijah the Tishbite, Arise, go up to meet the messengers of the king of Samaria, and say unto them, Is it not because there is not a God in Israel, that ye go to inquire of Baal-zebub the god of Ekron?

4. Now therefore thus saith the LORD, Thou shalt not come down from that bed on which thou art gone up, but shalt surely die. And Elijah departed.

5. And when the messengers turned back unto him, he said unto them, Why are ye now turned back?

6. And they said unto him, There came a man up to meet us, and said unto us, Go, turn again unto the king that sent you, and say unto him, Thus saith the LORD, *Is it* not because *there is* not a God in Israel, *that* thou sendest to inquire of Baal-zebub the god of Ekron? therefore thou shalt not come down from that bed on which thou art gone up, but shalt surely die.

7. And he said unto them, What manner of man *was he* which came up to meet you, and told you these words?

8. And they answered him, *He was* an hairy man, and girt with a girdle of leather about his loins. And he said, It is Elijah the Tishbite.

9. Then the king sent unto him a captain of fifty with his fifty. And he went up to him: and, behold, he sat on the top of an hill. And he spake unto him, Thou man of God, the king hath said, Come down.

10. And Elijah answered and said to the captain of fifty, If I be a man of God, then let fire come down from heaven, and consume thee and thy fifty. And there came down fire from heaven, and consumed him and his fifty.

11. Again also he sent unto him another captain of fifty with his fifty. And he answered and said unto him, O man of God, thus hath the king said, Come down quickly.

12. And Elijah answered and said unto them, If I *be* a man of God, let fire come down from heaven, and consume thee and thy fifty. And the fire of God came down from heaven, and consumed him and his fifty.

13. And he sent again a captain of the third fifty with his fifty. And the third captain of fifty went up, and came and fell on his knees before Elijah, and besought him, and said unto him, O man of God, I pray thee, let my life, and the life of these fifty thy servants, be precious in thy sight.

14. **Behold,** there came **fire** down **from heaven, and burnt up the two captains** of the former fifties with their fifties: therefore let my life now be precious in thy sight. 15. **And the angel** of the LORD **said unto Elijah, Go down** with him: be not afraid of him. **And he** arose, and **went** down with him **unto the king.** 16. **And** he **said** unto him, Thus saith the LORD, **Forasmuch as thou hast sent messengers to inquire of Baal-zebub** the god of Ekron, *is it* not because *there is* no God in Israel to inquire of his word? therefore **thou** shalt not come down off that bed on which thou art gone up, but **shalt surely die.** 17. **So he died according to the word of the LORD** which Elijah had spoken. **And Jehoram reigned** in his stead in the second year of Jehoram the son of Jehoshaphat king of Judah; because he had no son. 18. **Now the rest of the acts of Ahaziah** which he did, **are** they not **written in the book of the chronicles** of the kings of Israel?

CHAPTER 2

1. **And** it came to pass, **when the LORD would take up Elijah into heaven by a whirlwind,** that **Elijah went with Elisha from Gilgal.** 2. **And Elijah said unto Elisha, Tarry here,** I pray thee; **for the LORD hath sent me to Beth-el. And Elisha said** unto him, As the LORD liveth, and *as* thy soul liveth, **I will not leave thee.** So they went down to Beth-el. 3. **And the sons of the prophets** that *were* **at Beth-el came** forth **to Elisha, and said** unto him, **Knowest thou that the LORD will take away thy master** from thy head **to-day? And he said,** Yea, **I know it;** hold ye your peace. 4. **And Elijah said unto him, Elisha, tarry here,** I pray thee; **for the LORD hath sent me to Jericho. And he said, As the LORD liveth,** and *as* thy soul liveth, **I will not leave thee. So they came to Jericho.** 5. **And** the sons of **the prophets** that *were* **at Jericho came to Elisha, and said** unto him, **Knowest thou that the LORD will take away thy master** from thy head **to-day? And he answered,** Yea, **I know** *it*; hold ye your peace. 6. **And Elijah said** unto him, **Tarry,** I pray thee, **here; for the LORD** hath **sent me to Jordan. And he said, As** the LORD liveth, and *as* thy soul liveth, **I will not leave thee. And they** two **went on.** 7. **And fifty** men of the sons of the **prophets** went, and stood to view afar off: and they two **stood by Jordan.** 8. **And Elijah took his mantle,** and wrapped *it* together, **and smote the waters, and they** were **divided** hither **and** thither, so that **they** two **went over on dry ground.** 9. **And** it came to pass, when they were gone over, that **Elijah said unto Elisha, Ask what I shall do for**

thee, before I be
taken away from thee.
And Elisha said, I pray thee,
let a double portion of
thy spirit be upon me.
10. And he said, Thou
hast asked a hard thing:
nevertheless, if thou see me
when I am taken from thee,
it shall be so unto thee;
but if not, it shall not be *so.*
11. And it came to pass,
as they still went on, and
talked, that, behold,
there appeared
a chariot of fire,
and horses of fire, and
parted them both asunder;
and Elijah went up by a
whirlwind into heaven.
12. And Elisha saw it, and he
cried, My father, my father,
the chariot of Israel,
and the horsemen thereof.
And he saw him no more:
and he took hold of his own clothes,
and rent them in two pieces.
13. He took up also the
mantle of Elijah that fell from
him, and went back, and stood
by the bank of Jordan;
14. And he took the
mantle of Elijah
that fell from him,
and smote the waters,
and said, Where is the LORD
God of Elijah? and
when he also had smitten
the waters, they
parted hither and thither:
and Elisha went over.
15. And when the sons of the
prophets which *were* to
view at Jericho
saw him, they said,
The spirit of Elijah
doth rest on Elisha.
And they came to meet him,
and bowed
themselves to the ground
before him.
16. And they
said unto him, Behold now,

there be with thy servants
fifty strong
men; let them go,
we pray thee, and
seek thy master: lest
peradventure the spirit of the LORD
hath taken him up, and cast him upon
some mountain, or into some valley.
And he said, Ye
shall not send.
17. And when they
urged him till he was ashamed,
he said, Send. They
sent therefore fifty men;
and they sought three
days, but found him not.
18. And when they
came again to him,
(for he tarried at Jericho,)
he said unto them,
Did I not say unto you,
Go not?
19. And the men of the city
said unto Elisha, Behold, I
pray thee, the situation of
this city is pleasant,
as my lord seeth:
but the water is nought,
and the ground barren.
20. And he said,
Bring me a new
cruse, and put salt therein.
And they brought *it* to him.
21. And he went forth
unto the spring of the waters,
and cast the salt in there,
and said, Thus saith the
LORD, I have healed these
waters; there shall not be from
thence any more death or barren*land.*
22. So the waters were
healed unto this day, according to
the saying of Elisha which he spake.
23. And he went up from thence
unto Beth-el: and as he
was going up by the way,
there came forth little
children out of the city, and
mocked him, and said unto him,
Go up, thou bald
head; go up, thou bald head.
24. And he turned back,
and looked on them, and

cursed them in the
name of the LORD.
And there came forth
two she bears out of the wood,
and tare forty and
two children of them.
25. And he went from thence
to mount
Carmel, and from thence he
returned to Samaria.

CHAPTER 3

1. Now Jehoram the son of
Ahab began to reign over Israel in
Samaria the eighteenth year of
Jehoshaphat king of Judah, and
reigned twelve years.
2. And he
wrought evil in the sight
of the LORD; but not
like his father, and like his
mother: for he put
away the image of Baal
that his father had made.
3. Nevertheless he cleaved
unto the sins of Jeroboam
the son of Nebat, which made Israel
to sin; he departed not therefrom.
4. And Mesha king of Moab was a
sheepmaster, and rendered unto
the king of Israel an hundred
thousand lambs, and an hundred
thousand rams, with the wool.
5. But it came to pass,
when Ahab was
dead, that the king of
Moab rebelled
against the king of
Israel.
6. And king
Jehoram went out of Samaria the
same time, and numbered all Israel.
7. And he went and
sent to Jehoshaphat the
king of Judah,
saying, The king of
Moab hath
rebelled against me:
wilt thou go with me
against Moab to battle?
And he said, I will go up: I
am as thou *art,* my people as thy
people, *and* my horses as thy horses.

8. And he said, Which
way shall we go up?
And he answered, The way
through the wilderness
of Edom.
9. So the king of
Israel went, and the king of
Judah, and the king of
Edom: and they
fetched a compass of
seven days' journey:
and there was no
water for the host, and for
the cattle that followed them.
10. And the king of
Israel said, Alas! that
the LORD hath called
these three kings together,
to deliver them into the
hand of Moab!
11. But Jehoshaphat
said, Is there not here
a prophet of the LORD,
that we may inquire
of the LORD by him?
And one of the king of Israel's
servants answered and said,
Here is Elisha the son of Shaphat,
which poured water
on the hands of Elijah.
12. And Jehoshaphat
said, The word of
the LORD is with him. So the
king of Israel and Jehoshaphat and
the king of Edom went down to him.
13. And Elisha said
unto the king of Israel,
What have I to do with
thee? get thee to the
prophets of thy father, and
to the prophets of thy mother.
And the king of Israel
said unto him,
Nay: for the LORD hath
called these
three kings together,
to deliver them into
the hand of Moab.
14. And Elisha said,
As the LORD of hosts liveth,
before whom I stand, surely,
were it not that I regard
the presence of

Jehoshaphat the king of Judah, **I would not** look toward thee, nor **see thee.** 15. **But** now **bring me a minstrel. And** it came to pass, **when the minstrel played,** that **the hand of the LORD came upon him.** 16. **And he said,** Thus saith the LORD, **Make this valley full of ditches.** 17. For thus saith the LORD, **Ye shall not see** wind, neither shall ye see **rain; yet that valley shall be filled with water,** that ye may drink, both ye, and your cattle, and your beasts. 18. **And** this is *but* a light thing in the sight of **the LORD:** he **will deliver the Moabites** also **into your hand.** 19. **And ye shall smite every** fenced **city,** and every choice city, **and** shall **fell every** good **tree,** and stop all wells of water, **and mar every** good **piece of land** with stones. 20. **And** it came to pass **in the morning,** when the meat offering was offered, that, behold, there came water by the way of Edom, and **the country was filled with water.** 21. **And when** all **the Moabites heard** that **the kings were come** up to fight **against them, they** gathered all that were able to **put on armour, and** upward, and **stood in the border.** 22. **And** they rose up early **in the morning,** and

the sun shone upon the water, and the Moabites saw the water on the other side *as* red **as blood:** 23. **And they said, This is blood: the kings** are surely slain, and they **have smitten one another:** now therefore, Moab, to the spoil. 24. **And when they came to the camp of Israel, the Israelites** rose up and **smote the Moabites, so that they fled** before them: but they went forward smiting the Moabites, even in *their* country. 25. **And they beat down the cities, and** on every good piece of land cast every man his stone, and filled it; and they **stopped** all **the wells** of water, **and felled** all **the** good **trees:** only in Kir–haraseth left they the stones thereof; howbeit the slingers went about *it*, and smote it. 26. **And when the king of Moab saw** that **the battle was too sore for him,** he took with him seven hundred men that drew swords, to break through *even* unto the king of Edom: but they could not. 27. **Then he took his eldest son** that should have reigned in his stead, **and offered him for a burnt offering** upon the wall. **And there was great indignation against Israel: and they** departed from him, and **returned to their own land.**

CHAPTER 4

1. **Now there cried a** certain **woman** of the wives of the sons of the prophets **unto Elisha,** saying, **Thy servant my husband is dead;** and thou knowest that thy servant did fear the LORD:

and the creditor is
come to take unto him
my two sons to
be bondmen.
2. And Elisha said unto her,
What shall I do for thee? tell me,
what hast thou in the
house? And she said,
Thine handmaid hath
not any thing in the house,
save a pot of oil.
3. Then he said, Go,
borrow thee vessels abroad
of all thy neighbours, *even*
empty vessels;
borrow not a few.
4. And when thou art
come in, thou shalt shut the
door upon thee and upon thy sons,
and shalt
pour out
into all
those vessels, and thou shalt
set aside that which is full.
5. So she went from him, and shut
the door upon her and upon her
sons, who brought *the vessels*
to her; and she poured out.
6. And it came to pass,
when the vessels
were full, that
she said unto her son,
Bring me yet a vessel.
And he said unto her,
There is not a vessel
more. And the oil stayed.
7. Then she came and
told the man of God.
And he said, Go,
sell the oil, and pay
thy debt, and live thou
and thy children of the rest.
8. And it fell on a day, that
Elisha passed to Shunem,
where was a great woman;
and she constrained him to eat
bread. And *so* it was, *that* as
oft as he passed by,
he turned in thither
to eat bread.
9. And she said unto
her husband, Behold now,
I perceive that

this is an holy man of God,
which passeth by us continually.
10. Let us make a little
chamber, I pray thee, on the wall;
and let us
set for him there a bed, and
a table, and
a stool, and a candlestick:
and it shall be,
when he cometh to us, that
he shall turn in thither.
11. And it fell on a day, that
he came thither,
and he
turned into the chamber,
and lay there.
12. And he said to Gehazi
his servant, Call this
Shunammite. And when he had
called her, she stood before him.
13. And he said unto him,
Say now unto her, Behold,
thou hast been careful
for us with all this care;
what is to be done for
thee? wouldest thou be spoken
for to the king, or to the captain
of the host? And she answered,
I dwell among mine own people.
14. And he said, What then
is to be done for her?
And Gehazi answered, Verily
she hath no child, and
her husband is old.
15. And he said, Call
her. And when he had called
her, she stood in the door.
16. And he said, About this
season, according to the time of life,
thou shalt embrace a
son. And she said, Nay,
my lord, *thou* man of God,
do not lie unto
thine handmaid.
17. And the woman
conceived, and
bare a son at that season
that Elisha had said unto her,
according to the time of life.
18. And when the child
was grown, it fell on a day, that
he went out
to his father to the reapers.

19. **And** he **said** unto his father, **My head, my head. And he said** to a lad, **Carry him to his mother.** 20. **And** when he had taken him, and brought him to his mother, **he sat on her knees till noon, and** then **died.** 21. **And she** went up, and **laid him on the bed of the man of God,** and shut *the door* upon him, and went out. 22. **And** she **called** unto **her husband, and said, Send me,** I pray thee, one of the young men, and one of the asses, **that I may run to the man of God,** and come again. 23. **And he said,** Wherefore **wilt thou go** to him **to-day? it is neither new moon, nor sabbath.** And she said, *It shall be* well. 24. Then she saddled an ass, and said to her servant, Drive, and go forward; slack not *thy* riding for me, except I bid thee. 25. **So she went** and came **unto the man of God** to mount Carmel. **And** it came to pass, **when the man of God saw her** afar off, that **he said to Gehazi** his servant, Behold, **yonder is that Shunammite:** 26. **Run** now, I pray thee, **to meet her, and say** unto her, **Is it well with thee?** *is it* well with thy husband? *is it* well with the child? **And she answered, It is well:** 27. **And when she came** to the man of God to the hill, **she caught him by the feet: but Gehazi** came near to **thrust her away. And the man of God said, Let her**

alone; for her soul *is* vexed within her: and the LORD hath hid *it* from me, and hath not told me. 28. **Then she said, Did I desire a son of my lord?** did I not say, Do not deceive me? 29. **Then he said to Gehazi,** Gird up thy loins, and take my staff in thine hand, and **go** thy way: if thou meet any man, salute him not; and if any salute thee, answer him not again: **and lay my staff upon the face of the child.** 30. **And the mother** of the child **said,** *As* the LORD liveth, and *as* thy soul liveth, **I will not leave thee.** And he arose, and followed her. 31. **And Gehazi** passed on before them, and **laid the staff upon** the face of **the child; but there was neither voice, nor hearing. Wherefore he went** again **to meet him,** and told him, **saying, The child is not awaked.** 32. **And when Elisha was come** into the house, behold, **the child was dead, and** laid upon his bed. 33. **He went in** therefore, and shut the door upon them twain, **and prayed** unto the LORD. 34. **And he** went up, and **lay upon the child,** and put his mouth upon his mouth, and his eyes upon his eyes, and his hands upon his hands: and stretched himself upon the child; **and the flesh of the child waxed warm.** 35. **Then he returned, and walked** in the house **to and fro; and** went up, and **stretched himself upon him: and the child sneezed seven times, and** the child **opened his eyes.** 36. **And he** called Gehazi, and **said, Call this**

Shunammite. So he called her. **And** when she was comein untohim, he said, Take up thy son. 37. **Then she** went in, and **fell at his feet,** and bowed herself to the ground, **and took up her son, and went out.** 38. **And Elisha came** again **to Gilgal: and there was a dearth in the land;** and the sons of the prophets *were* sitting before him: **and he said unto his servant, Set on the great pot, and seethe pottage** for the sons of the prophets. 39. **And one went** out into the field **to gather herbs, and** found a wild vine, and gathered thereof **wild gourds** his lap full, and came **and shred them into the** pot of **pottage:** for they knew *them* not. 40. **So they poured** out **for the men to eat. And** it came to pass, **as they were eating** of the pottage, that **they cried** out, and said, O *thou* **man of God, there is death in the pot.** And they could not eat *thereof.* 41. **But he said,** Then **bring meal. And** he **cast it into the pot; and** he **said, Pour out for the people,** that they may eat. **And there was no harm in the pot.** 42. **And there came a man from Baal–shalisha, and brought the man of God bread of the firstfruits,** twenty loaves of barley, and full ears of corn in the husk thereof. **And** he **said, Give unto the people,** that they may eat. 43. **And his servitor said,** What, **should I set this before**

an hundred men? He **said again, Give the people, that they may eat:** for thus saith the LORD, They shall eat, and shall leave *thereof.* 44. **So he set it before them, and they did eat,** and left *thereof,* according to the word of the LORD.

CHAPTER 5

1. **Now Naaman, captain** of the host of the king **of Syria, was a great man** with his master, and honourable, **because by him the LORD had given deliverance unto Syria:** he was also a mighty man in valour, **but he was a leper.** 2. **And the Syrians** had gone out by companies, and **had brought** away **captive out of** the land of **Israel a little maid; and she waited on Naaman's wife.** 3. **And she said unto her mistress, Would God my lord were with the prophet** that *is* **in Samaria! for he would recover** him of his leprosy. 4. And *one* went in, and told his lord, saying, Thus and thus said the maid that *is* of the land of Israel. 5. **And the king** of Syria **said, Go** to, go, **and I will send a letter unto the king of Israel. And he** departed, and **took** with him **ten talents of silver, and six thousand pieces of gold, and ten changes of raiment.** 6. **And he brought the letter** to the king of Israel, **saying,** Now when this letter is come unto thee, behold, **I have** therewith **sent Naaman** my servant to thee, **that thou mayest recover him of his leprosy.**

Naaman Seeks Elisha's Help

7. **And** it came to pass, **when the king** of Israel had **read the letter,** that **he rent his clothes, and said, Am I God,** to kill and to make alive, that this man doth send unto me **to recover a man of** his **leprosy?** wherefore consider, I pray you, and see how **he seeketh a quarrel against me.** 8. And it was *so,* **when Elisha** the man of God had **heard** that the king of Israel had rent his clothes, that **he sent to the king, saying,** Wherefore hast thou rent thy clothes? **let him come** now **to me, and he shall know** that **there is a prophet in Israel.** 9. **So Naaman came** with his horses and with his chariot, **and stood at** the door of **the house of Elisha.** 10. **And Elisha sent a messenger** unto him, **saying, Go** and **wash in Jordan seven times,** and thy flesh shall come again to thee, **and thou shalt be clean.** 11. **But Naaman was wroth,** and went away, **and said,** Behold, **I thought, He will** surely **come out** to me, and stand, **and call on the** name of the **LORD** his God, **and strike his hand** over the place, **and recover the leper.** 12. **Are not Abana and Pharpar, rivers of Damascus, better than** all **the waters of Israel? may I not wash in them,** and be clean? **So he** turned and **went away** in a rage. 13. **And his servants** came near, and spake unto him, and

said, My father, **if the prophet had bid thee do some great thing, wouldest thou not have done it? how much rather then,** when he saith to thee, **Wash, and be clean?** 14. **Then went he** down, **and dipped himself seven times in Jordan,** according to the saying of the man of God: and his flesh came again like unto the flesh of a little child, **and he was clean.** 15. **And he returned to the man of God,** he and all his company, and came, and stood before him: **and** he **said,** Behold, now **I know** that **there is no God** in all the earth, **but in Israel:** now therefore, I pray thee, **take a blessing of thy servant.** 16. **But he said,** *As* the LORD liveth, before whom I stand, **I will receive none.** And he urged him to take *it*; but he refused. 17. **And Naaman said, Shall there not** then, I pray thee, **be given** to thy servant **two mules' burden of earth?** for **thy servant will henceforth offer neither burnt offering nor sacrifice unto other gods,** but unto the LORD. 18. **In this** thing **the LORD pardon thy servant,** *that* **when my master goeth into** the house of **Rimmon to worship** there, and he leaneth on my hand, and I bow myself in the house of Rimmon: when I bow down myself in the house of Rimmon, **the LORD pardon** thy servant in **this thing.** 19. **And he said** unto him, **Go in peace. So he**

departed from him a little way.

20. **But Gehazi,** the servant of Elisha the man of God, **said,** Behold, **my master** hath **spared Naaman** this Syrian, **in not receiving** at his hands **that which he brought: but,** as the LORD liveth, **I will run after him, and take somewhat of him.**

21. **So Gehazi followed after Naaman.** And when Naaman saw *him* running after him, he lighted down from the chariot to meet him, and said, *Is* all well?

22. **And** he **said,** All *is* well. **My master** hath **sent me, saying,** Behold, even now **there** be **come** to me **from** mount **Ephraim two** young **men** of the sons of the prophets: **give them,** I pray thee, **a talent of silver, and two changes of garments.**

23. **And Naaman said,** Be content, take two talents. **And he** urged him, and **bound two talents of silver** in two bags, **with two changes of garments,** and laid *them* upon two of his servants; and they bare *them* before him.

24. And when he came to the tower, he took *them* from their hand, and bestowed *them* in the house: and he let the men go, and they departed.

25. **But he went in, and stood before his master,** And Elisha said unto him, **Whence comest thou,** Gehazi? **And he said, Thy servant went no whither.**

26. **And he said** unto him, **Went not mine heart with thee,** when the man turned again from his chariot to meet thee? **Is it a time to receive money, and** to receive **garments,** and oliveyards, and vineyards, and sheep, and oxen, and menservants, and maidservants?

27. **The leprosy therefore of Naaman shall cleave unto thee,** and unto thy seed for ever. **And he went out** from his presence **a leper** *as white* as snow.

CHAPTER 6

1. **And** the sons of **the prophets said unto Elisha,** Behold now, the place where we dwell with thee is too strait for us.

2. **Let us go,** we pray thee, **unto Jordan,** and take thence every man a beam, **and** let us **make** us **a place there, where we may dwell. And he** answered, Go ye.

3. **And one said,** Be content, I pray thee, and **go with thy servants.** And he answered, I will go.

4. **So he went with them. And when they came to Jordan, they cut** down **wood.**

5. **But as one was felling a beam, the axe head fell into the water: and he cried,** and said, Alas, master! for **it was borrowed.**

6. **And the man of God said, Where fell it?** And he shewed him the place. **And he cut** down **a stick, and cast it in** thither; **and the iron did swim.**

7. **Therefore said he, Take it** up to thee. And he put out his hand, and took it.

8. **Then the king of Syria warred against Israel, and took counsel** with his servants, **saying, In** such and **such a place shall be my camp.**

573

Chariots of Fire

9. **And the man of God sent unto the king of Israel, saying,** Beware that thou **pass not such a place; for** thither **the Syrians are come** down.

10. **And the king of Israel** sent to the place which the man of God told him and warned him of, and **saved himself** there, **not once nor twice.**

11. **Therefore** the heart of **the king of Syria was** sore **troubled** for this thing; **and** he **called his servants, and said** unto them, Will ye not **shew me which of us is for the king of Israel?**

12. **And** one of **his servants said, None, my lord,** O king: **but Elisha,** the prophet that *is* in Israel, **telleth the king of Israel the words** that **thou speakest** in thy bedchamber.

13. **And he said, Go and spy where he is, that I may** send and **fetch him. And it was** told him, **saying,** Behold, **he is in Dothan.**

14. **Therefore sent he** thither horses, and chariots, and **a great host:** and they came by night, **and compassed the city** about.

15. **And when the servant of the man of God was risen** early, and gone forth, behold, **an host compassed the city** both with horses and chariots. **And his servant said** unto him, **Alas,** my master! **how shall we do?**

16. **And he answered, Fear not: for they** that *be* **with us are more than they that be with them.**

17. **And Elisha prayed,** and said, **LORD,** I pray thee, **open his eyes,** that he may see. **And** the LORD opened the eyes of **the young man;** and he **saw;** and, behold, **the mountain** *was* **full of horses and chariots of fire round about Elisha.**

18. **And when they came down** to him, **Elisha prayed** unto the LORD, and said, **Smite this people,** I pray thee, **with blindness. And he smote them** with blindness according to the word of Elisha.

19. **And Elisha said** unto them, **This is not the way,** neither *is* this the city: **follow me, and I will bring you to the man whom ye seek.** But he led them to Samaria.

20. **And** it came to pass, **when they were come into Samaria,** that **Elisha said, LORD, open the eyes of these men,** that they may see. And the LORD opened their eyes, **and they saw;** and, behold, **they were in the midst of Samaria.**

21. **And the king of Israel said unto Elisha,** when he saw them, My father, **shall I smite them?** shall I smite *them*?

22. **And he answered, Thou shalt not smite them:** wouldest thou smite those whom thou hast taken captive with thy sword and with thy bow? **set bread and water before them, that they may** eat and drink, and **go to their master.**

23. And he prepared great provision for them: and when they had eaten and drunk, he sent them away, and they went to their master. **So the bands of Syria**

came no more into the land of
Israel.
24. And it came to pass
after this, that
Ben-hadad king of
Syria gathered all his host,
and went up, and
besieged Samaria.
25. And there was a great
famine in Samaria: and, behold,
they besieged it, until an ass's head
was *sold* for fourscore *pieces* of
silver, and the fourth part of a cab of
dove's dung for five *pieces* of silver.
26. And as the king of Israel
was passing by upon
the wall, there cried
a woman unto him,
saying, Help, my lord,
O king.
27. And he said, If the LORD
do not help thee, whence shall
I help thee? out of the barnfloor,
or out of the winepress?
28. And the king
said unto her,
What aileth thee?
And she answered,
This woman said unto me,
Give thy son, that we may
eat him to-day, and we
will eat my son tomorrow.
29. So we boiled my son, and
did eat him: and
I said unto her on
the next day, Give thy
son, that we may eat him:
and she hath
hid her son.
30. And it came to pass,
when the king
heard the words of
the woman, that
he rent his clothes; and he
passed by upon the wall, and the
people looked, and, behold, *he had*
sackcloth within upon his flesh.
31. Then he said, God
do so and more also
to me, if the head of
Elisha the son of Shaphat
shall stand on
him this day.

32. But Elisha sat in his
house, and the elders sat
with him; and the king
sent a man from before him:
but ere the
messenger came to him,
he said to the
elders, See ye how
this son of a murderer
hath sent to take away
mine head? look,
when the messenger cometh, shut
the door, and hold him fast at the
door: *is* not the sound of his master's
feet behind him?
33. And while he yet
talked with them, behold,
the messenger came down
unto him: and he said, Behold, this
evil *is* of the LORD; what should I
wait for the LORD any longer?

CHAPTER 7

1. Then Elisha said, Hear ye
the word of the
LORD; Thus saith the LORD,
To-morrow about this time
shall a measure of fine
flour be sold for a shekel,
and two measures of barley for a
shekel, in the gate of Samaria.
2. Then a lord on whose
hand the king leaned
answered the man of
God, and said, Behold,
if the LORD would
make windows in
heaven, might this thing
be? And he said, Behold,
thou shalt see it with thine eyes,
but shalt not eat thereof.
3. And there were
four leprous
men at the entering
in of
the gate: and they
said one to another,
Why sit we here
until we die?
4. If we say,
We will enter into
the city, then the
famine *is* in the city, and

we shall die there: and if we sit still here, we die also. Now **therefore** come, and **let us fall unto** the host of **the Syrians: if they save us** alive, **we shall live; and if they kill us, we shall but die.** 5. And they rose up in the twilight, to go unto the camp of the Syrians: **and when they were come to** the uttermost part of **the camp** of Syria, behold, **there was no man there.** 6. **For the LORD** had **made** the host of **the Syrians** to **hear a noise of chariots,** and a noise of horses, *even* the noise of a great host: **and they said** one to another, Lo, the king of **Israel hath hired** against us the kings of **the Hittites, and** the kings of the **Egyptians,** to come upon us. 7. **Wherefore they** arose and **fled** in the twilight, **and left their tents, and** their **horses,** and their asses, even the camp as it *was*, and fled for their life. 8. **And when these lepers came** to the uttermost part of the camp, **they** went into one tent, and **did eat and drink, and carried** thence **silver,** and **gold, and raiment,** and went **and hid it;** and came again, and entered into another tent, and carried thence *also*, and went and hid *it*. 9. **Then they said one to another,** We do not well: **this** day **is a day of good tidings,** and we hold our peace: if we tarry till the morning light, some mischief will come upon us: now therefore **come, that we may** go and **tell the king's household.** 10. **So they** came and **called** unto

the porter of the city: **and** they **told them,** saying, We came to the camp of the Syrians, and, behold, *there was* no man there, neither voice of man, but horses tied, and asses tied, and the tents as they *were*. 11. **And** he called **the porters;** and they **told it to the king's house** within. 12. **And the king arose** in the night, **and said** unto his servants, **I will now shew you what the Syrians have done** to us. **They know** that **we be hungry; therefore are they gone** out of the camp **to hide themselves** in the field, **saying, When they come out** of the city, **we shall catch them** alive, and get into the city. 13. **And one of his servants answered** and said, **Let some take,** I pray thee, five of the **horses** that remain, which are left in the city, (behold, they *are* as all the multitude of Israel that are left in it: behold, *I say*, they *are* even as all the multitude of the Israelites that are consumed:) **and let us** send and **see.** 14. **They took** therefore **two chariot horses;** and the king sent after the host of the Syrians, saying, Go and see. 15. **And** they **went** after them **unto Jordan:** and, lo, all **the way was full of garments and vessels, which the Syrians had cast away** in their haste. **And the messengers returned, and told the king.** 16. **And the people** went out, and **spoiled the tents of the Syrians. So**

a measure of fine
flour was sold for
a shekel, and
two measures
of barley for
a shekel, according to
the word of the LORD.
17. And the king appointed
the lord on whose hand
he leaned to have the
charge of the gate:
and the people trode
upon him in the gate,
and he died, as the man
of God had said, who spake
when the king came down to him.
18. And it came to pass
as the man of God had
spoken to the king, saying, Two
measures of barley for a shekel,
and a measure of fine flour for a
shekel, shall be to—morrow about
this time in the gate of Samaria:
19. And that lord answered the man
of God, and said, Now, behold, *if* the
LORD should make windows in
heaven, might such a thing be?
And he said, Behold, thou shalt
see it with thine eyes, but
shalt not eat thereof.
20. And so it fell out unto him:
for the people trode upon him
in the gate, and he died.

CHAPTER 8

1. Then spake Elisha
unto the woman,
whose son he had
restored to
life, saying, Arise, and
go thou and thine household, and
sojourn wheresoever
thou canst sojourn:
for the LORD hath called for
a famine; and it shall also
come upon the land
seven years.
2. And the woman arose,
and did after the saying of
the man of God: and she
went with her household,
and sojourned in the land
of the Philistines seven years.

3. And it came to pass
at the seven years' end, that
the woman returned out
of the land of the Philistines:
and she went forth to
cry unto the king for
her house and for her
land.
4. And the king talked
with Gehazi the servant
of the man of God,
saying, Tell me, I pray thee, all
the great things that
Elisha hath done.
5. And it came to pass,
as he was telling the
king how he had
restored a dead body
to life, that, behold,
the woman, whose son
he had restored to life,
cried to the king for
her house and for her land.
And Gehazi said,
My lord, O king,
this is the woman, and this *is*
her son, whom Elisha
restored to life.
6. And when the king
asked the woman, she
told him. So the king
appointed unto her
a certain officer, saying,
Restore all that was
hers, and all the fruits of
the field since the day that
she left the land, even until now.
7. And Elisha came to
Damascus; and
Ben—hadad the king of Syria
was sick; and it was
told him, saying, The man of God
is come hither.
8. And the king
said unto Hazael,
Take a present in thine hand,
and go, meet the man of
God, and inquire of the
LORD by him, saying,
Shall I recover of this disease?
9. So Hazael went to meet
him, and took a present with
him, even of every good thing of

Damascus, forty camels' burden, and came and stood before him, **and said**, Thy son **Ben-hadad** king of Syria **hath sent me** to thee, **saying, Shall I recover** of this disease? 10. **And Elisha said** unto him, Go, **say unto him, Thou mayest** certainly **recover: howbeit** the LORD hath **shewed me** that **he shall** surely **die.** 11. And he settled his countenance stedfastly, until he was ashamed: **and the man of God wept.** 12. **And Hazael said, Why weepeth** my lord? **And he answered, Because I know the evil** that **thou wilt do unto** the children of **Israel:** their strong holds wilt thou set on fire, and their young men wilt thou slay with the sword, and wilt dash their children, and rip up their women with child. 13. **And Hazael said,** But what, **is thy servant a dog, that he should do this** great **thing? And Elisha answered, The LORD** hath **shewed me that thou shalt be king over Syria.** 14. **So he** departed from Elisha, and **came to his master;** who said to him, **What said Elisha** to thee? **And he answered,** He told me *that* **thou shouldest** surely **recover.** 15. **And** it came to pass **on the morrow,** that **he took a** thick **cloth,** and **dipped it in water, and spread it on his face, so** that **he died: and Hazael reigned** in his stead. 16. **And in the fifth year**

of Joram the son of Ahab king of Israel, Jehoshaphat *being* then king of Judah, **Jehoram** the son of Jehoshaphat king **of Judah began to reign.** 17. Thirty and two years old was he when he began to reign; **and he reigned eight years** in Jerusalem. 18. And he walked in the way of the kings of Israel, as did the house of Ahab: for the daughter of Ahab was his wife: **and he did evil in the sight of the LORD.** 19. **Yet the LORD would not destroy Judah** for David his servant's sake, as he promised him to give him alway a light, *and* to his children. 20. **In his days Edom revolted from** under the hand of **Judah, and made a king over themselves.** 21. **So Joram went** over **to Zair,** and all the chariots with him: and he rose by night, **and smote the Edomites** which compassed him about, and the captains of the chariots: and the people fled into their tents. 22. Yet Edom revolted from under the hand of Judah unto this day. **Then Libnah revolted at the same time.** 23. And the rest of the acts of Joram, and all that he did, *are* they not written in the book of the chronicles of the kings of Judah? 24. **And Joram slept** with his fathers, **and was buried** with his fathers **in the city of David: and Ahaziah** his son **reigned** in his stead. 25. **In the twelfth year of Joram** the son of Ahab **King of Israel** did **Ahaziah** the son of Jehoram king **of Judah begin to reign.** 26. Two and twenty years old *was* Ahaziah when he began to reign;

and he reigned one year in Jerusalem. And his mother's name *was* Athaliah, the daughter of Omri king of Israel. 27. And he walked in the way of the house of Ahab, **and did evil in the sight of the LORD,** as *did* the house of Ahab: for he *was* the son in law of the house of Ahab. 28. **And he went with Joram** the son of Ahab **to the war against Hazael king of Syria** in Ramoth–gilead; **and the Syrians wounded Joram.** 29. **And** king **Joram went** back **to be healed in Jezreel** of the wounds which the Syrians had given him at Ramah, when he fought against Hazael king of Syria. **And Ahaziah the son** of Jehoram king of Judah **went** down **to see Joram** the son of Ahab **in Jezreel,** because he was sick.

CHAPTER 9

1. **And Elisha** the prophet **called one** of the children **of the prophets, and said** unto him, Gird up thy loins, and **take this** box of **oil** in thine hand, and go **to Ramoth-gilead:** 2. **And** when thou comest thither, **look out there Jehu** the son of Jehoshaphat the son of Nimshi, and go in, and make him arise up from among his brethren, and carry him to an inner chamber; 3. **Then take the** box of **oil, and pour it on his head, and say,** Thus saith the LORD, **I have anointed thee king over Israel. Then open the door, and flee**, and tarry not. 4. **So** the young man, *even* the young man **the prophet, went to Ramoth-gilead.** 5. And when he came, behold, the

captains of the host *were* sitting; **and** he **said, I have an errand** to thee, O captain. **And Jehu said, Unto which of** all **us? And he said, To thee,** O captain. 6. **And he** arose, and **went** into the house; **and** he **poured the oil on his head, and said** unto him, **Thus saith the LORD** God of Israel, **I have anointed thee king** over the people of the LORD, *even* **over Israel.** 7. **And thou shalt smite the house of Ahab** thy master, **that I may avenge the blood of** my servants **the prophets,** and the blood of all the servants of the LORD, **at the hand of Jezebel.** 8. **For the whole house of Ahab shall perish:** and I will cut off from Ahab him that pisseth against the wall, and him that is shut up and left in Israel: 9. And I will make the house of Ahab like the house of Jeroboam the son of Nebat, and like the house of Baasha the son of Ahijah: 10. **And the dogs shall eat Jezebel** in the portion of Jezreel, **and there shall be none to bury her. And** he opened the door, and **fled.** 11. **Then Jehu came forth to the servants of his lord: and one said** unto him, **Is all well?** wherefore came this mad *fellow* to thee? **And he said unto them, Ye know the man, and his communication.** 12. **And they said, It is false;** tell us now. **And he said,** Thus and thus **spake he to me, saying,**

Thus saith the LORD, I have
anointed thee king over Israel.
13. Then they hasted, and took
every man his garment, and put *it*
under him on the top of the stairs, and
blew with
trumpets, saying,
Jehu is king.
14. So Jehu the son of
Jehoshaphat the son of Nimshi
conspired against Joram.
(Now Joram had kept
Ramoth–gilead, he and all Israel,
because of Hazael king of Syria.
15. But king Joram was returned to be
healed in Jezreel of the wounds which
the Syrians had given him, when he
fought with Hazael king of Syria.)
And Jehu
said, If it be your minds, *then*
let none go forth *nor*
escape out of the city to go
to tell it in Jezreel.
16. So Jehu rode
in a chariot, and went
to Jezreel; for Joram lay there.
And Ahaziah king of Judah
was come down
to see Joram.
17. And there stood
a watchman on the tower
in Jezreel, and he
spied the company of
Jehu as he came, and
said, I see a company.
And Joram said,
Take an horseman, and
send to meet them,
and let him
say, *Is it* peace?
18. So there went one on
horseback to meet him, and
said, Thus saith the king,
Is it peace? And Jehu said,
What hast thou to do with
peace? turn thee behind
me. And the watchman told,
saying, The messenger came
to them, but he cometh not again.
19. Then he sent out
a second on
horseback, which came
to them, and said,

Thus saith the king,
Is it peace? And Jehu
answered, What hast thou
to do with peace? turn thee
behind me.
20. And the watchman
told, saying, He came even
unto them, and
cometh not again: and the
driving *is*
like the driving of
Jehu the son of Nimshi;
for he driveth furiously.
21. And Joram said,
Make ready. And
his chariot was made ready.
And Joram king of Israel
and Ahaziah king of Judah went
out, each in his chariot, and they
went out against Jehu,
and met him in the portion
of Naboth the Jezreelite.
22. And it came to pass,
when Joram saw Jehu, that
he said, Is it peace,
Jehu? And he answered,
What peace, so long as the
whoredoms of thy mother
Jezebel and her
witchcrafts are so many?
23. And Joram
turned his hands, and
fled, and said to Ahaziah,
There is treachery, O Ahaziah.
24. And Jehu drew a
bow with his full strength,
and smote Jehoram
between his arms, and the
arrow went out at his heart,
and he sunk down in his chariot.
25. Then said Jehu to
Bidkar his captain, Take up, *and*
cast him in the portion of the
field of Naboth the
Jezreelite: for
remember how that,
when I and thou rode
together after Ahab his father,
the LORD laid this
burden upon him;
26. Surely I have seen yesterday
the blood of Naboth, and the
blood of his sons, saith the

LORD; and I will requite thee in this plat, saith the LORD.

Now therefore take *and* **cast him into the plat of ground, according to the word of the LORD.** 27. **But when Ahaziah** the king of Judah **saw this, he fled** by the way of the garden house. **And Jehu followed** after **him, and said, Smite him also** in the chariot. **And they did so** at the going up to Gur, which *is* by Ibleam. **And he fled to Megiddo, and died there.** 28. **And his servants carried him** in a chariot **to Jerusalem, and buried him** in his sepulchre **with his fathers** in the city of David.

29. And in the eleventh year of Joram the son of Ahab began Ahaziah the son of Ahab to reign over Judah.

30. **And when** Jehu was come to Jezreel, **Jezebel heard** *of* **it;** and **she painted her face,** and tired her head, **and looked out** at **a window.** 31. **And as Jehu entered** in at the gate, **she said, Had Zimri peace, who slew his master?** 32. **And he lifted up his face to the window, and said, Who is on my side?** who? **And there looked out** to him **two or three eunuchs.** 33. **And he said, Throw her down. So they threw her down: and** *some* of **her blood was sprinkled on the wall,** and on the horses: **and he trode her under foot.** 34. **And** when he was come in, **he did eat and drink, and said, Go, see** now

this cursed woman, and bury her: for she *is* a king's daughter. 35. **And they went to bury her: but** they **found no more** of her **than the skull,** and the **feet, and the palms of her hands.** 36. **Wherefore they** came again, and **told him. And he said, This is the word of the LORD,** which he **spake by** his servant **Elijah** the Tishbite, **saying,** In the portion of Jezreel shall **dogs eat the flesh of Jezebel:** 37. And the carcase of Jezebel shall be as dung upon the face of the field in the portion of Jezreel; *so* that they shall not say, This *is* Jezebel.

CHAPTER 10

1. **And Ahab had seventy sons** in Samaria. **And Jehu** wrote letters, and **sent to Samaria, unto** the rulers of Jezreel, to **the elders, and** to **them that brought** up **Ahab's children, saying,** 2. Now as soon as this letter cometh to you, seeing your master's sons *are* with you, and *there are* with you chariots and horses, a fenced city also, and armour; 3. **Look** even **out the best** and meetest **of your master's sons, and set him on his father's throne, and fight for your master's house.** 4. **But they were** exceedingly **afraid, and said,** Behold, **two kings stood not before him: how** then **shall we stand?** 5. And he that *was* over the house, and he that *was* over the city, the elders also, and the bringers up *of*

the children, sent to Jehu, saying, **We** *are* thy servants, and **will do all that thou** shalt **bid us;** we will not make any king: do thou *that which is* good in thine eyes. 6. **Then he wrote** a letter **the second time to them, saying, If ye be mine,** and *if* ye will hearken unto my voice, **take** ye **the heads of** the men **your master's sons, and come to me** to Jezreel by **to-morrow** this time. **Now the king's sons,** *being* seventy persons, **were with the great men of the city,** which brought them up. 7. **And** it came to pass, **when the letter came** to them, that **they took the king's sons, and slew seventy persons, and put their heads in baskets, and sent** him **them to Jezreel.** 8. **And** there came **a messenger,** and **told him, saying, They have brought the heads of the king's sons. And he said, Lay ye them in two heaps at** the entering in of **the gate until the morning.** 9. **And** it came to pass **in the morning,** that **he** went out, and stood, and **said to** all **the people,** Ye *be* righteous: behold, **I conspired against my master, and slew him:** **but who slew all these?** 10. **Know** now **that there shall fall** unto the earth **nothing of the word** of the LORD, **which the LORD spake concerning** the house of **Ahab:** for the LORD hath done *that*

which he spake by his servant Elijah. 11. **So Jehu slew all that remained of the house of Ahab** in Jezreel, and all his great men, and his kinsfolks, and his priests, until he left him none remaining. 12. **And he** arose and departed, and **came to Samaria. And** as he *was* at the shearing house in the way, 13. **Jehu met with the brethren of Ahaziah king of Judah, and said, Who are ye? And they answered, We are the brethren of Ahaziah**; and we go down to salute the children of the king and the children of the queen. 14. **And he said, Take them alive. And they** took them alive, and **slew them at the pit of the shearing house,** *even* **two and forty men;** neither left he any of them. 15. **And when he** was **departed** thence, **he lighted on Jehonadab** the son of Rechab *coming* to meet him: and he saluted him, **and said** to him, **Is thine heart right,** as my heart *is* with thy heart? **And Jehonadab answered, It is.** If it be, give *me* thine hand. And he gave *him* his hand; **and he took him** up to him **into the chariot.** 16. **And** he **said, Come** with me, and **see my zeal for the LORD.** So they made him ride in his chariot. 17. **And when he came to Samaria, he slew all that remained unto Ahab** in Samaria, till he had destroyed him, according to the saying of the LORD, which he spake to Elijah. 18. **And Jehu** gathered all the people together, and **said** unto them, **Ahab served Baal a** little; but Jehu shall serve him much.

19. **Now** therefore **call** unto me all **the prophets of Baal,** all his servants, and all his priests; let none be wanting: **for I have a great sacrifice** to do **to Baal;** whosoever shall be wanting, he shall not live. **But Jehu did it in subtilty,** to the intent that he might destroy the worshippers of Baal.

20. **And Jehu said, Proclaim a solemn assembly for Baal.** And they proclaimed *it.*

21. And Jehu sent through all Israel: **and all the worshippers of Baal came,** so that there was not a man left that came not. And they came into the house of Baal; **and the house of Baal was full** from one end to another.

22. **And he said** unto him that *was* over the vestry, **Bring** forth **vestments for all the worshippers of Baal.** And he brought them forth vestments.

23. **And Jehu went,** and Jehonadab the son of Rechab, **into the house of Baal, and said** unto the worshippers of Baal, Search, and **look that there be** here with you **none of the servants of the LORD, but** the **worshippers of Baal only.**

24. **And when they went in to offer sacrifices** and burnt offerings, **Jehu appointed fourscore men** without, **and said, If any** of the men whom I have brought into your hands **escape, he that letteth him go, his life shall be for the life of him.**

25. **And** it came to pass, as soon **as he had made an end of offering** the burnt offering, that **Jehu said** to the guard and to the captains, **Go** in, *and* **slay them;** let none come forth. **And they smote them** with the edge of the sword; and the guard and the captains cast *them* out, and went to the city of the house of Baal.

26. **And** they **brought** forth **the images out** of the house of Baal, **and burned them.**

27. And they brake down the image of Baal, and brake down the house of Baal, and made it a draught house unto this day.

28. Thus Jehu destroyed Baal out of Israel.

29. **Howbeit** *from* the sins of Jeroboam the son of Nebat, who made Israel to sin, **Jehu departed not from** after them, *to wit,* **the golden calves** that *were* **in Bethel, and** that *were* in **Dan.**

30. **And the LORD said** unto Jehu, **Because thou hast done well in executing** *that which is* **right** in mine eyes, *and* hast done **unto the house of Ahab** according to all that *was* in mine heart, **thy children** of the fourth *generation* **shall sit on the throne of Israel.**

31. But Jehu took no heed **to walk in the law of the LORD** God of Israel with all his heart: for he departed not from the sins of Jeroboam, which made Israel to sin.

32. **In those days the LORD began to cut Israel short: and Hazael smote them** in all the coasts of Israel;

33. From Jordan eastward, all the land of Gilead, the Gadites, and the Reubenites, and the Manassites, from Aroer, which *is* by the river

Arnon, even Gilead and Bashan.

34. Now the rest of the acts of Jehu, and all that he did, and all his might, *are* they not written in the book of the chronicles of the kings of Israel?

35. **And Jehu slept** with his fathers: **and they buried him in Samaria. And Jehoahaz his son reigned** in his stead.

36. And the time that Jehu reigned over Israel in Samaria *was* twenty and eight years.

CHAPTER 11

1. **And when Athaliah** the **mother of Ahaziah saw that her son was dead, she** arose and **destroyed all the seed royal.**

2. **But Jehosheba, the daughter of king Joram,** sister of Ahaziah, **took Joash the son of Ahaziah, and** stole him from among the king's sons *which were* slain; and they **hid him,** *even* him and his nurse, in the bedchamber from Athaliah, so that he was not slain.

3. **And he was** with her **hid** in the house of the LORD **six years. And Athaliah did reign** over the land.

4. **And the seventh year Jehoiada** sent and **fetched the rulers** over hundreds, with the captains and the guard, **and brought them** to him **into the house of the LORD, and made a covenant with them,** and took an oath of them in the house of the LORD, **and shewed them the king's son.**

5. **And he commanded them, saying, This** *is* the thing that **ye shall do; A third part** of you that enter in on the sabbath **shall** even

be keepers of the watch of the king's house;

6. **And a third** part **shall be at the gate of Sur; and a third** part **at the gate behind the guard:** so shall ye keep the watch of the house, that it be not broken down.

7. **And two parts of** all **you** that go forth **on the sabbath,** even they **shall keep the watch of the house of the LORD** about the king.

8. **And ye shall compass the king** round about, every man with his weapons in his hand: **and he that cometh within the ranges, let him be slain:** and be ye with the king as he goeth out and as he cometh in.

9. And the captains over the hundreds did according to all *things* that Jehoiada the priest commanded: and they took every man his men that were to come in on the sabbath, with them that should go out on the sabbath, and came to Jehoiada the priest.

10. And to the captains over hundreds did the priest give king David's spears and shields, that *were* in the temple of the LORD.

11. And the guard stood, every man with his weapons in his hand, round about the king, from the right corner of the temple to the left corner of the temple, *along* by the altar and the temple.

12. **And he brought forth the king's son, and put the crown upon him,** and *gave him* the testimony; **and** they **made him king,** and anointed him; **and they** clapped their hands, and **said, God save the king.**

13. **And when Athaliah heard the noise** of the guard *and* of the people, **she came** to the people

into the temple of the LORD.

14. **And** when she looked, behold, **the king stood by a pillar,** as the manner *was,* and the princes and the trumpeters by the king, and all the people of the land rejoiced, and blew with trumpets: **and Athaliah rent her clothes, and cried, Treason,** Treason.

15. **But Jehoiada** the priest **commanded the captains** of the hundreds, the officers of the host, and said unto them, Have her forth without the ranges: and him that followeth her kill with the sword. For the priest had said, **Let her not be slain in the house of the LORD.**

16. **And** they laid hands on her; and **she went by the way** by the which **the horses came** into the king's house: **and there was she slain.**

17. **And Jehoiada made a covenant between the LORD** and the king and the people, **that they should be the LORD'S people;** between the king also and the people.

18. **And** all **the people** of the land **went into the house of Baal, and brake it down;** his altars and his images brake they in pieces thoroughly, **and slew Mattan the priest of Baal** before the altars. And the priest appointed officers over the house of the LORD.

19. And he took the rulers over hundreds, and the captains, and the guard, and all the people of the land; **and they brought** down **the king from the house of the LORD,** and came by the way of the gate of the guard to the king's house. **And he sat on the throne** of the kings.

20. **And** all **the people** of the land

rejoiced, and the city was in quiet: and they slew Athaliah with the sword *beside* the king's house.

21. **Seven years old was Jehoash when he began to reign.**

CHAPTER 12

1. In the seventh year of Jehu Jehoash began to reign; **and forty years reigned he in Jerusalem.** And his mother's name *was* Zibiah of Beer–sheba.

2. **And Jehoash did** *that which was* **right in the sight of the LORD** all his days wherein Jehoiada the priest instructed him.

3. **But the high places were not taken away:** the people still sacrificed and burnt incense in the high places.

4. **And Jehoash said to the priests,** All the money of the dedicated things that is brought into the house of the LORD, *even* the money of every one that passeth *the account,* the money that every man is set at, *and* **all the money that cometh into any man's heart to bring into the house of the LORD,**

5. **Let the priests take it** to them, every man of his acquaintance: **and** let them **repair the breaches of the house,** wheresoever any breach shall be found.

6. **But** it was *so, that* **in the three and twentieth year** of king Jehoash **the priests had not repaired the breaches** of the house.

7. **Then** king **Jehoash called** for Jehoiada the priest, and **the** *other* **priests, and said** unto them, **Why repair ye not** the breaches of **the house? now** therefore

receive no more money of your acquaintance, but deliver it for the breaches of the house.

8. And the priests consented to receive no *more* money of the people, neither to repair the breaches of the house.

9. But Jehoiada the priest took a chest, and bored a hole in the lid of it, and set it beside the altar, on the right side as one cometh into the house of the LORD: and the priests that kept the door put therein all the money *that was* brought into the house of the LORD.

10. And it was *so,* when they saw that there was much money in the chest, that the king's scribe and the high priest came up, and they put up in bags, and told the money that was found in the house of the LORD.

11. And they gave the money, being told, into the hands of them that did the work, that had the oversight of the house of the LORD: and they laid it out to the carpenters and builders, that wrought upon the house of the LORD,

12. And to masons, and hewers of stone, and to buy timber and hewed stone to repair the breaches of the house of the LORD, and for all that was laid out for the house to repair *it.*

13. Howbeit there were not made for the house of the LORD bowls of silver, snuffers, basons, trumpets, any vessels of gold, or vessels of silver, of the money *that was* brought into the house of the LORD:

14. But they gave that to the workmen, and repaired therewith the house of the LORD.

15. Moreover they reckoned not with the men, into whose hand they delivered the money to be bestowed on workmen: for they dealt faithfully.

16. The trespass money and sin money was not brought into the house of the LORD: it was the priests'.

17. Then Hazael king of Syria went up, and fought against Gath, and took it: and Hazael set his face to go up to Jerusalem.

18. And Jehoash king of Judah took all the hallowed things that Jehosha-phat, and Jehoram, and Ahaziah, his fathers, kings of Judah, had de-dicated, and his own hallowed things, and all the gold *that was* found in the treasures of the house of the LORD, and in the king's house, and sent it to Hazael king of Syria: and he went away from Jerusalem.

19. And the rest of the acts of Joash, and all that he did, are they not written in the book of the chronicles of the kings of Judah?

20. And his servants arose, and made a conspiracy, and slew Joash in the house of Millo, which goeth down to Silla.

21. For Jozachar the son of Shimeath, and Jehozabad the son of Shomer, his servants, smote him, and he died; and they buried him with his fathers in the city of David: and Amaziah his son reigned in his stead.

CHAPTER 13

1. In the three and twentieth year of Joash the son of Ahaziah king of Judah Jehoahaz the son of Jehu

began to reign over Israel in Samaria, and reigned seventeen years.

2. **And he did** *that which was* **evil in the sight of the LORD,** and followed the sins of Jeroboam the son of Nebat, which made Israel to sin; he departed not therefrom.

3. **And the anger of the LORD was kindled against Israel, and he delivered them into the hand of** Hazael king of **Syria,** and into the hand of Ben–hadad the son of Hazael, all *their* days.

4. **And Jehoahaz besought the LORD, and the LORD hearkened unto him:** for he saw the oppression of Israel, because the king of Syria oppressed them.

5. **(And** the LORD **gave Israel a saviour, so** that **they went out from under** the hand of **the Syrians: and** the children of Israel **dwelt in their tents, as beforetime.**

6. **Nevertheless they departed not from the sins of** the house of **Jeroboam,** who made Israel sin, *but* walked therein: and there remained the grove also in Samaria.)

7. Neither did he leave of the people to Jehoahaz but fifty horsemen, and ten chariots, and ten thousand footmen; for the king of Syria had destroyed them, and had made them like the dust by threshing.

8. **Now** the rest of **the acts of Jehoahaz,** and all that he did, and his might, **are** they not **written in** the book of **the chronicles** of the kings of Israel?

9. **And Jehoahaz slept** with his fathers; and they buried him in Samaria: **and Joash** his son

reigned in his stead.

10. In the thirty and seventh year of **Joash** king of Judah began Jehoash the son of Jehoahaz to reign over Israel in Samaria, *and* reigned sixteen years.

11. And he **did** *that which was* **evil in the sight of the LORD;** he departed not from all the sins of Jeroboam the son of Nebat, who made Israel sin: *but* he walked therein.

12. **And the rest** of **the acts of Joash,** and all that he did, and his might wherewith he fought against Amaziah king of Judah, **are** they not **written in** the book of **the chronicles** of the kings of Israel?

13. **And Joash slept with his fathers; and Jeroboam sat upon his throne:** and Joash was buried in Samaria with the kings of Israel.

14. **Now Elisha was** fallen **sick** of his sickness whereof he died. **And Joash** the king of Israel **came down unto him, and wept over his face, and said, O my father,** my father, **the chariot of Israel,** and the horsemen thereof.

15. **And Elisha said** unto him, **Take bow and arrows.** And he took unto him bow and arrows.

16. **And** he said to the king of Israel, **Put thine hand upon the bow.** And he put his hand *upon it:* **and Elisha put his hands upon the king's hands.**

17. **And he said, Open the window eastward.** And he opened *it.* **Then Elisha said, Shoot.** And he shot. **And he said, The arrow of the LORD'S deliverance,** and the arrow of deliverance from Syria:

for thou shalt smite the
Syrians in Aphek, till thou
have consumed *them*.
18. And he said, Take the
arrows. And he took *them*.
And he said unto the king of Israel,
Smite upon
the ground. And he smote
thrice, and stayed.
19. And the man of God
was wroth with him,
and said, Thou shouldest
have smitten five or six
times; then hadst thou
smitten Syria
till thou hadst consumed *it:*
whereas now thou shalt
smite Syria but thrice.
20. And Elisha
died, and they buried him.
And the bands of the
Moabites invaded the
land at the coming in of the year.
21. And it came to pass,
as they were burying
a man, that, behold,
they spied a band of
men; and they cast the
man into the sepulchre
of Elisha: and when the
man was let down, and
touched the bones of
Elisha, he revived,
and stood up on his feet.
22. But Hazael king of Syria
oppressed Israel all
the days of Jehoahaz.
23. And the LORD
was gracious unto them, and
had compassion on
them, and had respect unto them,
because of his covenant with
Abraham, Isaac, and Jacob,
and would not destroy
them, neither cast he them
from his presence as yet.
24. So Hazael king of Syria
died; and Ben-hadad
his son
reigned in his stead.
25. And Jehoash
the son of Jehoahaz
took again out of the hand

of Ben-hadad the son of Hazael
the cities, which he had
taken out of the hand
of Jehoahaz his
father by war.
Three times did
Joash beat him, and
recovered the cities
of Israel.

CHAPTER 14

1. In the second year
of Joash son
of Jehoahaz king
of Israel reigned Amaziah
the son of Joash king
of Judah.
2. He was twenty and five years
old when he began to reign, and
reigned twenty and nine years in
Jerusalem. And his mother's name
was Jehoaddan of Jerusalem.
3. And he did *that which was*
right in the sight of the
LORD, yet not like David his
father: he did according to all
things as Joash his father did.
4. Howbeit the high places
were not taken away: as yet
the people did sacrifice and burnt
incense on the high places.
5. And it came to pass,
as soon as the kingdom
was confirmed in his hand, that
he slew his servants
which had slain the king
his father.
6. But the
children of the murderers
he slew not: according unto
that which is
written in the book of
the law of Moses, wherein
the LORD commanded, saying,
The fathers shall not be put to
death for the children, nor the
children be put to death for the
fathers; but every man shall
be put to death for his own sin.
7. He slew of
Edom in the valley of salt
ten thousand, and
took Selah by war,

and called the name of it Joktheel unto this day.

8. Then Amaziah sent messengers to Jehoash, the son of Jehoahaz son of Jehu, king of Israel, saying, Come, let us look one another in the face.

9. And Jehoash the king of Israel sent to Amaziah king of Judah, saying, The thistle that *was* in Lebanon sent to the cedar that *was* in Lebanon, saying, Give thy daughter to my son to wife: and there passed by a wild beast that *was* in Lebanon, and trode down the thistle.

10. Thou hast indeed smitten Edom, and thine heart hath lifted thee up: glory *of this*, and tarry at home: for why shouldest thou meddle to thy hurt, that thou shouldest fall, *even* thou, and Judah with thee?

11. But Amaziah would not hear. Therefore Jehoash king of Israel went up; and he and Amaziah king of Judah looked one another in the face at Beth–shemesh, which *belongeth* to Judah.

12. And Judah was put to the worse before Israel; and they fled every man to their tents.

13. And Jehoash king of Israel took Amaziah king of Judah, the son of Jehoash the son of Ahaziah, at Beth–shemesh, and came to Jerusalem, and brake down the wall of Jerusalem from the gate of Ephraim unto the corner gate, four hundred cubits.

14. And he took all the gold and silver, and all the vessels that were found in the house of the LORD, and in the treasures of the king's house, and hostages, and returned to Samaria.

15. Now the rest of the acts of Jehoash which he did, and his might, and how he fought with Amaziah king of Judah, are they not written in the book of the chronicles of the kings of Israel?

16. And Jehoash slept with his fathers, and was buried in Samaria with the kings of Israel; and Jeroboam his son reigned in his stead.

17. And Amaziah the son of Joash king of Judah lived after the death of Jehoash son of Jehoahaz king of Israel fifteen years.

18. And the rest of the acts of Amaziah, are they not written in the book of the chronicles of the kings of Judah?

19. Now they made a conspiracy against him in Jerusalem: and he fled to Lachish; but they sent after him to Lachish, and slew him there.

20. And they brought him on horses: and he was buried at Jerusalem with his fathers in the city of David.

21. And all the people of Judah took Azariah, which was sixteen years old, and made him king instead of his father Amaziah.

22. He built Elath, and restored it to Judah, after that the king slept with his fathers.

23. In the fifteenth year of Amaziah the son of Joash king of Judah Jeroboam the son of Joash king

of Israel began to reign
in Samaria, *and reigned*
forty and one years.
24. **And he did** *that which was*
evil in the sight of the LORD:
he departed not from all the sins of
Jeroboam the son of Nebat,
who made Israel to sin.
25. **He restored the coast of**
Israel from the entering of
Hamath unto the sea of the plain,
according to the word of the LORD
God of Israel, which he spake by
the hand of his servant Jonah, the
son of Amittai, the prophet, which
was of Gath–hepher.
26. **For the LORD saw the**
affliction of Israel, *that it*
was very bitter: for *there was* not
any shut up, nor any left, nor
any helper for Israel.
27. **And the LORD said**
not that he would blot
out the name of Israel
from under heaven:
but he saved them by the
hand of Jeroboam the son of Joash.
28. **Now** the rest of
the acts of Jeroboam, and
all that he did, and his might, how
he warred, and how he recovered
Damascus, and Hamath, *which*
belonged to Judah, for Israel,
are they not
written in the book of
the chronicles of
the kings of Israel?
29. **And Jeroboam**
slept with his fathers,
even with the kings of Israel;
and Zachariah his son
reigned in his stead.

CHAPTER 15

1. In the twenty and seventh
year of Jeroboam king of
Israel began Azariah son of
Amaziah king of
Judah to reign.
2. Sixteen years old was he when he
began to reign, and he reigned
two and fifty years in Jerusalem.
And his mother's name *was*

Jecholiah of Jerusalem.
3. **And he did** *that which was*
right in the sight of the
LORD, according to all that
his father Amaziah had done;
4. **Save that the high**
places were not removed:
the people sacrificed and burnt
incense still on the high places.
5. **And the LORD smote**
the king, so that he was
a leper unto the day of
his death, and dwelt
in a several house.
And Jotham the king's son
was over the house,
judging the people of the land.
6. **And** the rest of
the acts of
Azariah, and all that he did,
are they not
written in the book of
the chronicles of the
kings of Judah?
7. **So Azariah**
slept with his fathers;
and they buried
him with his fathers
in the city of David:
and Jotham his son
reigned in his stead.
8. **In the thirty** and
eighth year of
Azariah king of Judah
did Zachariah
the son of Jeroboam
reign over Israel in Samaria **six**
months.
9. **And he did** *that which was*
evil in the sight of the LORD,
as his fathers had done: he departed
not from the sins of Jeroboam the son
of Nebat, who made Israel to sin.
10. **And Shallum**
the son of Jabesh
conspired against him,
and smote him before the people,
and slew him, and
reigned in his stead.
11. **And the rest of the acts**
of Zachariah, behold, they
are written in the book of
the chronicles of the

kings of Israel.

12. **This was the word of the LORD which he spake unto Jehu, saying, Thy sons shall sit on the throne of Israel unto the fourth generation.** And so it came to pass.

13. **Shallum** the son of Jabesh **began to reign in the nine and thirtieth year of Uzziah** king of Judah; **and he reigned a full month** in Samaria.

14. **For Menahem the** son of Gadi went up from Tirzah, and came to Samaria, and **smote Shallum** the son of Jabesh in Samaria, and slew him, **and reigned in his stead.**

15. **And the** rest of the **acts of Shallum, and his conspiracy** which he made, behold, they **are written in** the book of **the chronicles** of the kings of Israel.

16. **Then Menahem smote Tiphsah, and all** that *were* therein, and **the coasts** thereof **from Tirzah: because they opened not to him,** therefore he smote *it;* **and all the women** therein that were **with child he ripped up.**

17. **In the nine and thirtieth year** of Azariah king of Judah **began Menahem** the son of Gadi **to reign over Israel,** *and reigned* ten years in Samaria.

18. **And he did** *that which was* **evil in the sight of the LORD:** he departed not all his days from the sins of Jeroboam the son of Nebat, who made Israel to sin.

19. **And Pul** the king **of Assyria came against the land: and Menahem gave Pul a thousand talents of silver,** that his hand might be with him to confirm the kingdom in his hand.

20. **And Menahem exacted the money of Israel,** *even* of all the mighty men of wealth, of each man fifty shekels of silver, **to give** to the king of Assyria. **So the king of Assyria turned back,** and stayed not there in the land.

21. **And** the rest of **the acts of Menahem,** and all that he did, **are** they not **written in** the book of **the chronicles** of the kings of Israel?

22. **And Menahem slept** with his fathers; **and Pekahiah** his son **reigned in his stead.**

23. In the fiftieth year of Azariah king of Judah Pekahiah the son of Menahem began to reign over Israel in Samaria, *and reigned* two years.

24. **And he did** *that which was* **evil in the sight of the LORD:** he departed not from the sins of Jeroboam the son of Nebat, who made Israel to sin.

25. **But Pekah** the son of Remaliah, **a captain of his,** conspired against him, and smote him in Samaria, in the palace of the king's house, with Argob and Arieh, and with him fifty men of the Gileadites: and he **killed him, and reigned in his room.**

26. **And** the rest of **the acts of Pekahiah,** and all that he did, behold, they **are written in** the book of **the chronicles** of the kings of Israel.

27. In the two and fiftieth year of Azariah king of Judah **Pekah** the son of Remaliah began to reign over Israel in Samaria, *and*

reigned twenty years.

28. And he
- did *that which was*
- evil in the sight of the LORD:
he departed not from the sins of
Jeroboam the son of Nebat, who
made Israel to sin.

29. In the days of
- Pekah king of Israel
- came Tiglath-pileser king
- of Assyria, and took Ijon,
- and Abel-beth-
- maachah, and
- Janoah, and
- Kedesh, and
- Hazor, and
- Gilead, and
- Galilee, all the land
- of Naphtali, and carried
- them captive to Assyria.

30. And Hoshea the son of Elah
- made a conspiracy against
- Pekah the son
of Remaliah, and smote him,
- and slew him, and reigned
- in his stead, in the twentieth
year of Jotham the son of Uzziah.

31. And the rest of the
- acts of Pekah, and all
that he did, behold, they
- are written in the book of
- the chronicles of the
kings of Israel.

32. In the second
- year of Pekah the
son of Remaliah king of Israel
- began Jotham the
son of Uzziah king
- of Judah to reign.

33. Five and twenty years
old was he when he began
to reign, and he reigned
sixteen years in Jerusalem.
And his mother's name *was*
Jerusha, the daughter of Zadok.

34. And he
- did *that which was*
- right in the sight of the
- LORD: he did according to all
that his father Uzziah had done.

35. Howbeit the high places
- were not removed: the
people sacrificed and burned

incense still in the high places.
- He built the higher gate of
- the house of the LORD.

36. Now the rest of the
- acts of Jotham,
and all that he did,
- are they not
- written in the book of
- the chronicles of
the kings of Judah?

37. In those days the
- LORD began to send
- against Judah Rezin
- the king of Syria,
and Pekah the son of Remaliah.

38. And Jotham
- slept with his fathers,
and was buried with his fathers
in the city of David his father:
- and Ahaz his son
- reigned in his stead.

CHAPTER 16

1. In the seventeenth
- year of Pekah
the son of Remaliah
- Ahaz the son of
Jotham king of Judah
- began to reign.

2. Twenty years old *was*
- Ahaz when he began to
reign, and reigned sixteen
years in Jerusalem, and
- did not that which was right
- in the sight of the LORD his
God, like David his father.

3. But he walked in the way
of the kings of Israel, yea, and
- made his son to pass
- through the fire, according
to the abominations of the heathen,
whom the LORD cast out from
before the children of Israel.

4. And he
- sacrificed and burnt incense
- in the high places, and on the
hills, and under every green tree.

5. Then Rezin king of
- Syria and Pekah son
of Remaliah king
- of Israel came up
- to Jerusalem to
- war: and they

besieged Ahaz, but
could not overcome him.
6. **At that time Rezin king of
Syria recovered Elath** to Syria,
and drave the Jews from Elath:
and the Syrians came to Elath, and
dwelt there unto this day.
7. **So Ahaz sent messengers
to
Tiglath-pileser king of
Assyria, saying, I am
thy servant** and thy son:
come up,
**and save me out of
the hand of** the king of
Syria, and out of the
hand of the king of
Israel, which rise up against me.
8. **And Ahaz took the
silver and gold** that was found
**in the house of the
LORD, and** in the treasures of
**the king's house, and sent
it for a present to** the king of
Assyria.
9. **And the king of
Assyria** hearkened unto
him: for the king of Assyria
went up against Damascus,
and took it,
**and carried the
people** of it
**captive to Kir,
and slew Rezin.**
10. **And** king
Ahaz went to Damascus
**to meet
Tiglath-pileser** king of Assyria,
and saw an altar that *was*
at Damascus: and king Ahaz
sent to
Urijah the priest the
fashion of the altar, and
the pattern of it, according
to all the workmanship thereof.
11. **And Urijah** the priest
**built an altar according
to all that king Ahaz
had sent** from Damascus: so
Urijah the priest made *it* against king
Ahaz came from Damascus.
12. **And when the king** was
come from Damascus, the king

saw the altar: and the
king approached to the altar,
and offered thereon.
13. And
**he burnt his burnt
offering and** his
**meat offering, and poured
his drink offering,** and sprinkled
the blood of his peace offerings,
upon the altar.
14. **And** he
**brought also the
brasen altar,** which
was before the LORD, from
the forefront of the house,
**from between the altar and
the house of the LORD,** and
put it on the north side of the altar.
15. **And king
Ahaz commanded
Urijah** the priest,
**saying, Upon the great altar
burn the morning burnt
offering, and** the
**evening meat offering,
and the king's** burnt
sacrifice, and his meat
offering, with the burnt offering
of all the people of the land, and
their meat offering, and their drink
offerings; and sprinkle upon it
all the blood of the burnt offering,
and all the blood of the sacrifice: and
**the brasen altar shall be for
me to inquire by.**
16. Thus did Urijah the
priest, according to all that
king Ahaz commanded.
17. **And** king
Ahaz cut off the borders
of the bases, and
removed the laver from off
them; and took down the sea from off
the brasen oxen that *were* under it,
**and put it upon a
pavement of stones.**
18. **And** the covert for the sabbath
that they had built in the house,
and the king's entry without,
turned he
**from the house
of the LORD for the
king of Assyria.**

19. **Now** the rest of **the acts of Ahaz** which he did, **are** they not **written in** the book of **the chronicles of** the kings of Judah? 20. **And Ahaz slept** with his fathers, and wasburied with his fathers in the city of David: **and Hezekiah** his son **reigned** in his stead.

CHAPTER 17

1. **In the twelfth year of Ahaz** king of Judah **began Hoshea** the son of Elah **to reign** in Samaria **over Israel** nine years. 2. **And he did** *that which was* **evil in the sight of the LORD, but not as the kings** of Israel that were **before him.** 3. **Against him came** up **Shalmaneser king of Assyria; and Hoshea became his servant,** and gave him presents. 4. **And the king of Assyria found conspiracy in Hoshea: for he had sent messengers to** So king of **Egypt,** and brought no present to the king of Assyria, as *he had done* year by year: **therefore the king** of Assyria shut him up, and **bound him in prison.** 5. **Then the king of Assyria came** up **throughout** all **the land,** and went up to Samaria, **and besieged it three years.** 6. **In the ninth year of Hoshea** the king of **Assyria took Samaria, and carried Israel away into Assyria,** and placed them in Halah and in Habor *by* the river of Gozan, and in the cities of the Medes. 7. **For** *so* it was, that the children of **Israel had sinned against**

the LORD their God, which had brought them up out of the land of Egypt, from under the hand of Pharaoh king of Egypt, and had feared other gods, 8. **And walked in the statutes of the heathen,** whom the LORD cast out from before the children of Israel, and of the kings of Israel, which they had made. 9. **And** the children of Israel **did secretly those things that were not right against the LORD** their God, **and** they **built** them **high places** in all their cities, from the tower of the watchmen to the fenced city. 10. **And** they **set** them **up images and groves** in every high hill, and under every green tree: 11. **And there they burnt incense in all the high places,** as *did* the heathen whom the LORD carried away before them; **and wrought wicked things to provoke the LORD to anger:** 12. **For they served idols,** whereof the LORD had said unto them, Ye shall not do this thing. 13. **Yet the LORD testified against Israel, and** against **Judah, by all the prophets,** *and by* all the seers, **saying, Turn** ye **from** your **evil** ways, **and keep my commandments** *and* my statutes, according to all the law which I commanded your fathers, and which I sent to you by my servants the prophets. 14. **Notwithstanding they would not** hear, but hardened their necks, like to the neck of their fathers, that did not believe in the LORD their God. 15. **And they rejected his**

statutes, and his covenant
that he made with their fathers,
and his testimonies which he
testified against them;
and they
followed vanity,
and became vain,
**and went after the
heathen** that *were* round
about them, *concerning* whom
the LORD had charged them,
that they should not do like them.
16. **And** they
**left all the commandments
of the LORD** their God,
and made them
molten images, *even*
two calves, and made a grove,
and worshipped all the
host of heaven, and served
Baal.
17. **And they caused
their sons and** their
**daughters to pass
through the fire, and
used divination and
enchantments, and
sold themselves to
do evil** in the sight of the
LORD, to provoke him to anger.
18. **Therefore the LORD**
was very angry with Israel, and
**removed them out of
his sight: there was
none left but** the tribe of
Judah only.
19. **Also Judah kept not
the commandments of
the LORD** their God,
**but walked in the statutes
of Israel** which they made.
20. **And the LORD rejected
all the seed of Israel,** and
afflicted them, and delivered them
into the hand of spoilers, until he
had cast them out of his sight.
21. **For he rent Israel from
the house of David;** and they
made Jeroboam the son of Nebat
king: and Jeroboam drave Israel
from following the LORD, and
made them sin a great sin.
22. For the children of Israel walked

in all the sins of Jeroboam which he
did; they departed not from them;
23. Until the LORD removed Israel
out of his sight, as he had said by all
his servants the prophets.
So was Israel carried away
out of their own land
to Assyria unto this day.
24. **And the king of
Assyria brought men
from Babylon,** and from
Cuthah, and from
Ava, and from
Hamath, and from
**Sepharvaim, and
placed them in** the cities of
**Samaria instead
of** the children of
Israel: and they possessed
Samaria, and dwelt in the
cities thereof.
25. **And** *so* it was
**at the beginning of
their dwelling there,** *that*
**they feared not the
LORD: therefore the LORD
sent lions** among them,
which slew some of them.
26. **Wherefore they spake
to the king of Assyria,
saying, The nations** which
thou hast removed, and
placed in the cities of **Samaria,
know
not the** manner of the
**God of the land:
therefore he** hath
**sent lions among them,
and,** behold, they
slay them, because they know not
the manner of the God of the land.
27. **Then the king** of Assyria
**commanded, saying,
Carry** thither
one of the priests whom
ye brought from thence;
and let them go and
dwell there, and let him
teach them
the manner of the
God of the land.
28. **Then one of the
priests** whom they had

■ carried away from Samaria
■ **came** and dwelt in Beth–el,
■ **and taught them how they**
■ **should fear the LORD.**
■ 29. **Howbeit every nation**
■ **made gods of their own,**
and put *them* in the houses of the
high places which the Samaritans
had made, every nation in their
cities wherein they dwelt.
30. And the men of Babylon
made Succoth–benoth, and the
men of Cuth made Nergal, and
the men of Hamath made Ashima,
31. And the Avites made Nibhaz
and Tartak, and the Sepharvites
burnt their children in fire to
Adrammelech and Anammelech,
the gods of Sepharvaim.
32. So they feared the LORD,
■ **and made unto themselves**
of the lowest of them
■ **priests of the high places,**
which sacrificed for them in the
houses of the high places.
33. They feared the LORD,
■ **and served their own gods,**
after the manner of the nations whom
they carried away from thence.
34. **Unto this day** they do
after the former manners:
■ **they fear not the LORD,**
■ **neither do they** after their
statutes, or after their
ordinances, or after
■ **the law** and commandment
■ **which the LORD**
■ **commanded** the children
of Jacob, whom he named
■ **Israel;**
35. With whom the LORD had made
a covenant, and charged them,
■ **saying, Ye shall not fear**
■ **other gods,** nor bow
yourselves to them, nor serve
them, nor sacrifice to them:
36. **But the LORD,** who
brought you up out of the land
of Egypt with great power
and a stretched out arm, him
■ **shall ye fear, and** him shall ye
■ **worship,** and to him shall
ye do sacrifice.

37. And the statutes, and the
ordinances, and the law, and the
commandment, which he wrote
for you, ye shall observe to do
for evermore; and ye shall not
fear other gods.
38. **And the covenant**
that I have made with you
■ **ye shall not forget;** neither shall
ye fear other gods.
39. **But the LORD** your God
■ **ye shall fear; and he**
■ **shall deliver you** out of
the hand of all your enemies.
40. **Howbeit they did**
■ **not hearken,** but they
did after their former manner.
41. **So these nations**
feared the Lord, and
■ **served their graven images,**
both their children, and their children's
children: as did their fathers, so do
they unto this day.

CHAPTER 18

■ 1. **Now** it came to pass
■ **in the third year of**
■ **Hoshea** son of Elah king
■ **of Israel,** *that*
■ **Hezekiah** the son of Ahaz king
■ **of Judah began to reign.**
2. Twenty and five years old
was he when he began to reign;
and he reigned twenty and nine
years in Jerusalem. His mother's
name also *was* Abi,
the daughter of Zachariah.
3. **And he did** *that which was*
■ **right in the sight of the**
■ **LORD,** according to all
that David his father did.
4. **He removed the high**
■ **places, and brake the**
■ **images,** and cut down the groves,
■ **and brake** in pieces
■ **the brasen serpent** that
■ **Moses** had
■ **made: for** unto those
days the children of
■ **Israel did burn incense**
■ **to it:** and he called it Nehushtan.
5. **He trusted in the**
■ **LORD** God of Israel;

596

so that after him
was none like him
among all the kings of Judah,
nor any that were
before him.
6. For he clave to the LORD,
and departed not from
following him, but kept
his commandments, which the
LORD commanded Moses.
7. And the LORD was with
him; and he prospered
whithersoever he went forth:
and he rebelled
against the king of
Assyria, and
served him not.
8. He smote the Philistines,
even unto Gaza, and the
borders thereof, from the tower of
the watchmen to the fenced city.
9. And it came to pass
in the fourth year of king
Hezekiah, which was the
seventh year of Hoshea
son of Elah king of Israel, that
Shalmaneser king of
Assyria came up
against Samaria,
and besieged it.
10. And at the end of
three years they
took it: even in the sixth
year of Hezekiah, that is the
ninth year of Hoshea king of
Israel, Samaria was taken.
11. And the king of
Assyria did carry
away Israel unto Assyria,
and put them in Halah and in
Habor by the river of Gozan,
and in the cities of the Medes:
12. Because they
obeyed not the voice of
the LORD their God, but
transgressed his covenant,
and all that Moses the servant
of the LORD commanded, and
would not hear them, nor do them.
13. Now in the
fourteenth year of king
Hezekiah did
Sennacherib king of

Assyria come up
against all the fenced cities of
Judah, and took them.
14. And Hezekiah king of Judah
sent to the king of
Assyria to Lachish,
saying, I have offended;
return from me: that which
thou puttest on me will I
bear. And the king of
Assyria appointed unto
Hezekiah king of Judah
three hundred talents
of silver and thirty
talents of gold.
15. And Hezekiah
gave him all
the silver that was
found in the house
of the LORD, and in the
treasures of the king's house.
16. At that time did
Hezekiah cut off
the gold from the doors
of the temple of the LORD,
and from the pillars which
Hezekiah king of Judah had overlaid,
and gave it to the king of
Assyria.
17. And the king of
Assyria sent
Tartan and Rabsaris and
Rab-shakeh
from Lachish to king Hezekiah
with a great host against
Jerusalem. And they went up
and came to Jerusalem. And when
they were come up, they came
and stood by the conduit of the
upper pool, which is in the
highway of the fuller's field.
18. And when they
had called to the king,
there came out to them
Eliakim the son of Hilkiah,
which was over the
household, and Shebna the
scribe, and Joah the
son of Asaph the recorder.
19. And Rab-shakeh
said unto them,
Speak ye now
to Hezekiah, Thus

■ **saith the** great king, the
■ **king of Assyria, What**
■ **confidence is this**
■ **wherein thou trustest?**
■ 20. **Thou sayest,** (but
they are but vain words) ,
■ **I have counsel and strength**
■ **for the war.** Now
on whom dost thou trust, that
thou rebellest against me?
21. Now, behold,
thou trustest upon the
staff of this bruised reed, *even*
upon Egypt, on which if a man lean,
it will go into his hand, and
pierce it: so *is* Pharaoh king of
Egypt unto all that trust on him.
■ 22. **But if ye say** unto me,
■ **We trust in the LORD** our God:
■ **is not that he, whose**
■ **high places and** whose
■ **altars Hezekiah hath**
■ **taken away, and** hath
■ **said** to Judah and Jerusalem,
■ **Ye shall worship**
before this altar
■ **in Jerusalem?**
■ 23. **Now** therefore, I pray thee,
■ **give pledges to** my lord
■ **the king of Assyria,**
■ **and I will deliver** thee
■ **two thousand horses,**
■ **if thou be able** on thy part
■ **to set riders upon them.**
■ 24. **How then wilt thou** turn
away the face of one captain of the
least of my master's servants, and
■ **put thy trust on Egypt for**
■ **chariots** and for horsemen?
■ 25. **Am I now come** up
■ **without the LORD against**
■ **this place** to destroy it?
■ **The LORD said** to me,
■ **Go** up against this land,
■ **and destroy it.**
■ 26. **Then said Eliakim**
the son of Hilkiah, and Shebna,
and Joah, unto Rab–shakeh,
■ **Speak,** I pray thee,
■ **to thy servants in the Syrian**
■ **language;** for we understand *it.*
■ **and** talk
■ **not** with us

■ **in the Jews' language**
■ **in the ears of the**
■ **people** that *are* on the wall.
■ 27. **But Rab–shakeh**
said unto them,
■ **Hath my master sent**
■ **me** to thy master, and to thee,
■ **to speak these words? hath**
■ **he not sent me**
■ **to the men** which sit
■ **on the wall,** that they
may eat their own dung, and
drink their own piss with you?
■ 28. **Then Rab–shakeh**
stood and
■ **cried with a loud**
■ **voice in the Jews'**
■ **language,** and spake,
■ **saying, Hear** the
word of the great king,
■ **the king of Assyria:**
29. Thus saith the king,
■ **Let not Hezekiah deceive**
■ **you:** for he shall not be able
to deliver you out of his hand:
■ 30. **Neither let Hezekiah**
■ **make you trust in the LORD,**
saying, The LORD will surely deliver
us, and this city shall not be delivered
into the hand of the king of Assyria.
31. Hearken not to Hezekiah: for
thus saith the king of Assyria,
■ **Make an agreement**
■ **with me** by a present,
■ **and come** out
■ **to me, and then eat** ye
■ **every man of his own vine,**
■ **and** every one of his fig tree, and
■ **drink** ye every one
■ **the waters of his cistern:**
32. **Until I** come and
■ **take you** away
■ **to a land like your**
■ **own** land, a land of corn and
wine, a land of bread and vineyards,
a land of oil olive and of honey,
■ **that ye may live,** and not die:
■ **and hearken not**
■ **unto Hezekiah,** when
he persuadeth you,
■ **saying, The LORD**
■ **will deliver us.**
33. **Hath** any of

the gods of the
nations delivered at all
his land out of the
hand of the king of
Assyria?

34. Where *are* the gods of Hamath,
and of Arpad? where *are* the gods
of Sepharvaim, Hena, and Ivah?
have they delivered Samaria
out of mine hand?

35. **Who are they** among
all the gods of the countries,
that have delivered their
country out of mine hand,
that the LORD should deliver
Jerusalem out of mine hand?

36. **But the people**
held their peace, and
answered him not a word:
for the king's commandment was,
saying, Answer him not.

37. **Then came Eliakim**
the son of Hilkiah, which *was*
over the household, and
Shebna the scribe,
and Joah the son of
Asaph the recorder,
to Hezekiah with
their clothes rent,
and told him the
words of Rab–shakeh.

CHAPTER 19

1. **And** it came to pass,
when king
Hezekiah heard it, that
he rent his clothes, and
covered himself with
sackcloth, and went into
the house of the LORD.

2. **And** he
sent Eliakim, which *was* over the
household, and Shebna the scribe,
and the elders of the
priests, covered with sackcloth,
to Isaiah the prophet
the son of Amoz.

3. **And they**
said unto him,
Thus saith Hezekiah,
This day is a day of trouble,
and of rebuke, and
blasphemy; for the children

are come to the birth, and *there*
is not strength to bring forth.

4. **It may be the LORD** thy God
will hear all the words of
Rab–shakeh, whom the king
of Assyria his master hath sent
to reproach the living God;
and will reprove the
words which the LORD thy
God hath heard: wherefore
lift up thy prayer for the
remnant that are left.

5. **So the**
servants of king Hezekiah
came to Isaiah.

6. **And Isaiah said**
unto them, Thus shall ye
say to your master,
Thus saith the LORD,
Be not afraid of the words
which thou hast heard, with
which the servants of
the king of Assyria
have blasphemed me.

7. **Behold, I will send**
a blast upon him, and
he shall hear a
rumour, and shall
return to his own land;
and I will cause him to
fall by the sword
in his own land.

8. **So Rab–shakeh returned,**
and found the king of
Assyria warring against
Libnah: for he
had heard that he was
departed from Lachish.

9. **And when he heard**
say of Tirhakah king of
Ethiopia, Behold, he
is come out
to fight against thee: he
sent messengers again
unto Hezekiah, saying,

10. Thus shall ye speak to
Hezekiah king of Judah, saying,
Let not thy God in
whom thou trustest
deceive thee, saying,
Jerusalem shall not be delivered
into the hand of the king of Assyria.

11. Behold, thou hast heard what

the kings of Assyria have done to all lands, by destroying them utterly: and shalt thou be delivered? **12. Have the gods of the nations delivered them** which my fathers have destroyed; *as* Gozan, and Haran, and Rezeph, and the children of Eden which *were* in Thelasar? 13. Where *is* the king of Hamath, and the king of Arpad, and the king of the city of Sepharvaim, of Hena, and Ivah? **14. And Hezekiah received the letter** of the hand of the messengers, **and** read it: and Hezekiah **went up** into the house of the LORD, **and spread it before the LORD. 15. And Hezekiah prayed** before the LORD, and said, O LORD God of Israel, which dwellest *between* the cherubims, thou art the God, *even* thou alone, of all the kingdoms of the earth; thou hast made heaven and earth. **16. LORD, bow down thine ear,** and hear: **open,** LORD, **thine eyes, and see: and hear the words of Sennacherib, which hath sent him to reproach the living God. 17. Of a truth,** LORD, the kings of **Assyria** have **destroyed the nations** and their lands, 18. **And** have **cast their gods into the fire:** for they *were* no gods, but the work of men's hands, wood and stone: therefore they have destroyed them. 19. **Now** therefore, **O LORD** our God, I beseech thee, **save thou us out of his hand, that all the kingdoms of the earth may know** that **thou art** the LORD **God,** *even* thou only.

20. Then Isaiah the son of Amoz **sent to Hezekiah, saying, Thus saith the LORD** God of Israel, **That which thou hast prayed** to me **against Sennacherib** king of Assyria **I have heard.** 21. **This** *is* the word that **the LORD hath spoken concerning him; The virgin** the daughter **of Zion hath despised thee,** *and* laughed thee to scorn; the daughter of Jerusalem hath shaken her head at thee. **22. Whom hast thou reproached and blasphemed?** and against whom hast thou exalted *thy* voice, and lifted up thine eyes on high? **even** against **the Holy One of Israel.** 23. By thy messengers **thou hast reproached the LORD, and** hast **said, With the multitude** of my chariots **I am come up to the height of the mountains,** to the sides of Lebanon, **and will cut down the tall cedar trees** thereof, *and* the choice fir trees thereof: **and I will enter into the lodgings** of his borders, **and** *into* **the forest of** his **Carmel.** 24. **I have digged** and drunk **strange waters,** and with the sole of my feet have I dried up all the rivers of besieged places. **25. Hast thou not heard** long ago **how I have done it,** *and* of ancient times that I have formed it? **now have I brought it to pass, that thou shouldest** be to **lay waste fenced cities** *into* ruinous heaps.

26. **Therefore their inhabitants** were of small power, they **were dismayed and confounded;** they were *as* the grass of the field, and *as* the green herb, *as* the grass on the house tops, and *as corn* blasted before it be grown up.

27. **But I know thy abode,** and thy going out, and thy coming in, **and thy rage against me.**

28. Because thy rage against me and thy tumult is come up into mine ears, **therefore I will put my hook in thy nose,** and my bridle in thy lips, **and** I will **turn thee back** by **the way** by which **thou camest.**

29. **And this shall be a sign** unto thee, **Ye shall eat this year such things as grow of themselves,** and in the second year that which springeth of the same; and in the third year sow ye, and reap, and plant vineyards, and eat the fruits thereof.

30. **And the remnant** that is escaped of the house **of Judah shall** yet **again take root** downward, and bear fruit upward.

31. **For out of Jerusalem shall go forth a remnant, and** they that escape out of mount Zion: the zeal of **the LORD** *of hosts* **shall do this.**

32. **Therefore** thus saith the LORD **concerning the king of Assyria, He shall not come into this city,** nor shoot an arrow there, nor come before it with shield, nor cast a bank against it.

33. **By the way** that **he came,** by the same **shall he return,** and shall not come into this city, saith the LORD.

34. **For I will defend this city,** to save it, for mine own sake, and for my servant David's sake.

35. **And** it came to pass **that night,** that **the angel of the LORD** went out, and **smote** in the camp of **the Assyrians** an hundred fourscore and five thousand: **and** when they arose early **in the morning,** behold, **they were all dead** corpses.

36. **So Sennacherib** king of Assyria **departed,** and went and returned, and dwelt at Nineveh.

37. **And** it came to pass, **as he was worshipping in the house of Nisroch his god,** that Adrammelech and Sharezer **his sons smote him with the sword:** and they escaped into the land of Armenia. **And Esarhaddon** his son **reigned in his stead.**

CHAPTER 20

1. **In those days was Hezekiah sick unto death. And** the prophet **Isaiah** the son of Amoz **came** to him, **and said** unto him, Thus saith the LORD, **Set thine house in order; for thou shalt die,** and not live.

2. **Then he** turned his face to the wall, and **prayed unto the LORD,** saying,

3. **I beseech thee,** O LORD, remember now how **I have walked** before thee **in truth and with a perfect heart,** and have done *that which is* good in thy sight. **And Hezekiah wept** sore.

4. **And** it came to pass, **afore Isaiah was gone** out into the middle court, that **the word of the LORD came to him, saying,**

5. Turn again, and **tell Hezekiah** the captain of my people, Thus saith the LORD, the God of David thy father, **I have heard thy prayer, I have seen thy tears:** behold, **I will heal thee: on the third day** thou shalt go up unto the house of the LORD. 6. **And I will add unto thy days fifteen years; and I will deliver** thee and **this city out of the hand** of the king **of Assyria;** and I will defend this city for mine own sake, and for my servant David's sake. 7. **And Isaiah said, Take a lump of figs. And they** took and **laid it on the boil, and he recovered.** 8. **And Hezekiah said** unto Isaiah, **What shall be the sign** that the LORD will heal me, and **that I shall go** up **into the house of the LORD the third day?** 9. **And Isaiah said,** This sign shalt thou have of the LORD, that **the LORD will do the thing that he hath spoken: shall the shadow go forward ten degrees, or go back ten degrees?** 10. **And Hezekiah answered,** It is a light thing for the shadow to go down ten degrees: nay, but **let the shadow return backward ten degrees.** 11. **And** Isaiah the prophet cried unto **the LORD: and he brought the shadow ten degrees backward,** by which it had gone down in the dial of Ahaz. 12. **At that time Berodach–baladan,** the son of Baladan, **king of Babylon, sent letters and a present**

unto Hezekiah: for he had heard that Hezekiah had been sick. 13. **And Hezekiah** hearkened unto them, and **shewed them all** the house of **his precious things, the silver,** and the **gold,** and the **spices,** and the **precious ointment,** and *all* the house of **his armour, and all** that was found in **his treasures:** there was nothing in his house, nor in all his dominion, that Hezekiah shewed them not. 14. **Then came Isaiah** the prophet **unto** king **Hezekiah, and said** unto him, **What said these men?** and **from whence came they** unto thee? **And Hezekiah said,** They are come from a far country, *even* **from Babylon.** 15. **And he said, What have they seen** in thine house? **And Hezekiah answered, All the things** that *are* **in mine house** have they seen: there is nothing among my treasures that I have not shewed them. 16. **And Isaiah said** unto Hezekiah, **Hear the word of the LORD.** 17. **Behold, the days come, that all that is in thine house,** and that which thy fathers have laid up in store unto this day, **shall be carried into Babylon:** nothing shall be left, saith the LORD. 18. **And of thy sons** that shall issue from thee, which thou shalt beget, **shall they take away; and they shall be eunuchs in the palace of** the king of **Babylon.** 19. **Then said Hezekiah** unto Isaiah,

■ **Good is the word of**
■ **the LORD** which thou hast
spoken. And he said,
■ **Is it not good, if peace**
■ **and truth be in my days?**
20. And the rest of the acts of
Hezekiah, and all his might, and
how he made a pool, and a conduit,
and brought water into the city,
are they not written in the book of
the chronicles of the kings of Judah?
■ 21. **And Hezekiah**
■ **slept** with his fathers:
■ **and Manasseh** his son
■ **reigned in his stead.**

CHAPTER 21

■ 1. **Manasseh** *was* twelve years
old when he began to reign, and
■ **reigned fifty** and
■ **five years** in Jerusalem. And
his mother's name *was* Hephzibah.
■ 2. **And he did** *that which was*
■ **evil in the sight of the LORD,**
after the abominations of the
heathen, whom the LORD cast
out before the children of Israel.
■ 3. **For he built** up
■ **again the high places**
■ **which Hezekiah** his father
■ **had destroyed; and he**
■ **reared up altars for**
■ **Baal,** and made a grove,
as did Ahab king of Israel;
and worshipped all the host
of heaven, and served them.
■ 4. **And he built altars in**
■ **the house of the LORD,**
of which the LORD said, In
Jerusalem will I put my name.
5. And he built altars
■ **for** all
■ **the host of heaven** in the two
courts of the house of the LORD.
■ 6. **And** he
■ **made his son pass**
■ **through the fire,** and observed
times, and used enchantments,
■ **and dealt with familiar**
■ **spirits and wizards:**
he wrought much wickedness
in the sight of the LORD, to
provoke *him* to anger.

■ 7. **And he set a**
■ **graven image** of the
grove that he had made
■ **in the house,** of which the LORD
said to David, and to Solomon his
son, In this house, and
■ **in Jerusalem,** which I have
chosen out of all tribes of Israel,
will I put my name for ever:
8. Neither will I make the feet of
Israel move any more out of the land
which I gave their fathers; only if they
will observe to do according to all that
I have commanded them, and
according to all the law that my
servant Moses commanded them.
9. But they hearkened not:
■ **and Manasseh**
■ **seduced them to do**
■ **more evil than** did
■ **the nations whom the**
■ **LORD destroyed** before
the children of Israel.
■ 10. **And the LORD**
■ **spake by** his servants
■ **the prophets, saying,**
■ 11. **Because Manasseh**
■ **king of Judah**
■ **hath done** these
■ **abominations,** *and*
hath done wickedly
■ **above all that the Amorites**
did, which *were* before him,
■ **and** hath
■ **made Judah** also
■ **to sin with his idols:**
■ 12. **Therefore** thus saith
the LORD God of Israel, Behold,
■ **I am bringing such evil**
■ **upon Jerusalem and Judah,**
■ **that whosoever heareth of**
■ **it,** both
■ **his ears shall tingle.**
■ 13. **And I will** stretch over
Jerusalem the line of Samaria,
and the plummet of the house
of Ahab: and I will
■ **wipe Jerusalem as a man**
■ **wipeth a dish,** wiping *it,* and
turning *it* upside down.
■ 14. **And I will**
■ **forsake** the remnant of
■ **mine inheritance, and**

deliver them into the
hand of their enemies;
and they shall become a prey and
a spoil to all their enemies;

15. **Because they
have done** *that which was*
**evil in my sight, and have
provoked me to anger,**
since the day their fathers came forth
out of Egypt, even unto this day.

16. **Moreover Manasseh
shed innocent blood**
very much,

till he had filled Jerusalem
from one end to another; beside his
sin wherewith he made Judah to sin,
in doing *that which was* evil in
the sight of the LORD.

17. Now the rest of the acts of
Manasseh, and all that he
did, and his sin that he sinned,
are they not written in the book
of the chronicles of the
kings of Judah?

18. **And Manasseh
slept** with his fathers,
**and was buried in the
garden of his own
house,** in the garden of Uzza:
and Amon his son
reigned in his stead.

19. **Amon** *was* twenty and
two years old when he began
to reign, and he
reigned two years
in Jerusalem. And his mother's
name *was* Meshullemeth, the
daughter of Haruz of Jotbah.

20. **And he did** *that which was*
evil in the sight of the LORD,
as his father Manasseh did.

21. **And** he
walked in all
**the way that his father
walked** in, and served the
idols that his father served,
and worshipped them:

22. **And he forsook the
LORD** God of his fathers, and
walked not in the way of the LORD.

23. **And the servants
of Amon conspired
against him, and slew**

the king in his own house.

24. **And the people** of the land
slew all
them that had
**conspired against king
Amon;** and the people of the land
made Josiah his son king in his stead.

25. Now the rest of the acts of
Amon which he did, *are* they not
written in the book of the chronicles of
the kings of Judah?

26. And he
was buried in his sepulchre
in the garden of Uzza:
and Josiah his son
reigned in his stead.

CHAPTER 22

1. **Josiah was eight years
old when he began to
reign,** and he reigned thirty and
one years in Jerusalem. And
his mother's name *was* Jedidah,
the daughter of Adaiah of Boscath.

2. **And he did** *that which was*
**right in the sight of the
LORD,** and walked in all the way of
David his father, and turned not aside
to the right hand or to the left.

3. **And** it came to pass
**in the eighteenth
year** of king Josiah, *that*
**the king sent
Shaphan** the son of Azaliah,
the son of Meshullam, the scribe,
**to the house of the
LORD, saying,**

4. **Go up to Hilkiah the high
priest, that he may sum the
silver which is brought into
the house of the LORD,**
which the keepers of the door
have gathered of the people:

5. **And let them deliver it
into the hand of the doers of
the work,** that have the oversight
of the house of the LORD:
and let them give it to the
doers of the work which *is* in the
house of the LORD, to
**repair the breaches
of the house,**

6. Unto carpenters, and builders,

and masons, and to buy timber and hewn stone to repair the house.

7. **Howbeit there was no reckoning made** with them **of the money** that was delivered into their hand, **because they dealt faithfully.**

8. **And Hilkiah the high priest said unto Shaphan** the scribe, **I have found the book of the law in the house of the LORD. And Hilkiah gave the book to Shaphan, and he read it.**

9. **And Shaphan the** scribe came to the king, and **brought the king word** again, and said, **Thy servants have gathered the money** that was found in the house, **and have delivered it into the hand of them that do the work,** that have the oversight of the house of the LORD.

10. **And** Shaphan the scribe shewed the king, saying, **Hilkiah** the priest **hath delivered me a book. And Shaphan read it before the king.**

11. **And** it came to pass, **when the king** had **heard the words** of the book of the law, that **he rent his clothes.**

12. **And** the king **commanded Hilkiah the** priest, and Ahikam the son of Shaphan, and Achbor the son of Michaiah, and Shaphan the scribe, and Asahiah a servant of the king's, saying,

13. **Go ye, inquire of the LORD for me,** and for the people, and for all Judah, **concerning** the words of **this book** that is found: **for great is the wrath of the LORD** that is

kindled against us, **because our fathers have not hearkened unto the** words of this **book,** to do according unto all that which is written concerning us.

14. **So Hilkiah** the priest, and Ahikam, and Achbor, and Shaphan, and Asahiah, **went unto Huldah the prophetess,** the wife of Shallum the son of Tikvah, the son of Harhas, keeper of the wardrobe; (now she dwelt in Jerusalem in the college;) **and** they **communed with her.**

15. **And she said** unto them, **Thus saith the LORD** God of Israel, **Tell the man that sent you** to me,

16. **Thus saith the LORD,** Behold, **I will bring evil upon this place, and** upon **the inhabitants** thereof, *even* all the words of the book which the king of Judah hath read:

17. **Because they have forsaken me,** and have burned incense unto other gods, that they might provoke me to anger with all the works of their hands; **therefore my wrath shall be kindled** against this place, **and shall not be quenched.**

18. **But to the king of Judah** which sent you to inquire of the LORD, **thus shall ye say to him,** Thus saith the LORD God of Israel, **As touching the words which thou hast heard;**

19. **Because thine heart was tender, and thou hast humbled thyself before the LORD,** when thou heardest what I spake against this place, and against the inhabitants thereof, that they should become a desolation and a curse, and hast rent thy clothes, and wept before me; **I also**

have heard thee, saith the LORD.

20. Behold therefore, I will gather thee unto thy fathers, and thou shalt be gathered into thy grave in peace; and thine eyes shall not see all the evil which I will bring upon this place. And they brought the king word again.

CHAPTER 23

1. And the king sent, and they gathered unto him all the elders of Judah and of Jerusalem.

2. And the king went up into the house of the LORD, and all the men of Judah and all the inhabitants of Jerusalem with him, and the priests, and the prophets,and all the people, both small and great: and he read in their ears all the words of the book of the covenant which was found in the house of the LORD.

3. And the king stood by a pillar, and made a covenant before the LORD, to walk after the LORD, and to keep his commandments and his testimonies and his statutes with all *their* heart and all *their* soul, to perform the words of this covenant that were written in this book. And all the people stood to the covenant.

4. And the king commanded Hilkiah the high priest, and the priests of the second order, and the keepers of the door, to bring forth out of the temple of the LORD all the vessels that were made for Baal, and for the grove, and for all the host of heaven: and he burned them without Jerusalem in the fields of Kidron, and carried the ashes of them unto Beth–el.

5. And he put down the idolatrous priests, whom the kings of Judah had ordained to burn incense in the high places in the cities of Judah, and in the places round about Jerusalem; them also that burned incense unto Baal, to the sun, and to the moon, and to the planets, and to all the host of heaven.

6. And he brought out the grove from the house of the LORD, without Jerusalem, unto the brook Kidron, and burned it at the brook Kidron, and stamped it small to powder, and cast the powder thereof upon the graves o f the children of the people.

7. And he brake down the houses of the sodomites, that *were* by the house of the LORD, where the women wove hangings for the grove.

8. And he brought all the priests out of the cities of Judah, and defiled the high places where the priests had burned incense, from Geba to Beer–sheba, and brake down the high places of the gates that *were* in the entering in of the gate of Joshua the governor of the city, which *were* on a man's left hand at the gate of the city.

9. Nevertheless the priests of the high places came not up to the altar of the LORD in Jerusalem, but they did eat of the unleavened bread among their brethren.

10. And he defiled Topheth, which *is* in the valley of the children of Hinnom, that no man might make

■ **his son or** his
■ **daughter** to
■ **pass through the**
■ **fire to Molech.**
■ 11. **And he took**
■ **away the horses** that
■ **the kings of Judah had**
■ **given to the sun,** at the
entering in of the house of the
LORD, by the chamber of
Nathan–melech the chamberlain,
which *was* in the suburbs,
■ **and burned the**
■ **chariots** of the sun with fire.
■ 12. **And the altars** that *were* on
the top of the upper chamber of Ahaz,
■ **which the kings**
■ **of Judah** had
■ **made, and the altars** which
■ **Manasseh** had
■ **made in the** two
■ **courts of the house**
■ **of the LORD, did the**
■ **king** beat down, and
■ **brake** *them* down from thence,
■ **and cast the dust of them**
■ **into the brook Kidron.**
■ 13. **And the high**
■ **places** that *were*
■ **before Jerusalem,**
which *were* on the right hand
of the mount of corruption,
■ **which Solomon**
the king of Israel had
■ **builded for Ashtoreth** the
abomination of the Zidonians, and for
■ **Chemosh** the abomination
of the Moabites,
■ **and** for
■ **Milcom** the abomination
of the children of Ammon,
■ **did the king defile.**
■ 14. **And he brake** in pieces
■ **the images, and cut**
■ **down the groves, and**
■ **filled their places with**
■ **the bones of men.**
■ 15. **Moreover the**
■ **altar** that *was*
■ **at Beth–el, and the high**
■ **place which Jeroboam**
the son of Nebat, who
■ **made** Israel to sin, had made, both

that altar and the high place
■ **he brake** down,
■ **and burned the high**
■ **place,** *and* stamped *it* small to
powder, and burned the grove.
■ 16. **And** as
■ **Josiah** turned himself, he
■ **spied the sepulchres**
■ **that were there in**
■ **the mount,** and sent,
■ **and took the bones**
■ **out** of the sepulchres,
■ **and burned them upon**
■ **the altar, and polluted it,**
according to the word of the LORD
which the man of God proclaimed,
who proclaimed these words.
■ 17. **Then he said, What**
■ **title is that** that I see?
■ **And the men** of the city
■ **told him, It is the sepulchre**
■ **of the man of God, which**
■ **came from Judah, and**
■ **proclaimed these**
■ **things** that thou hast done
against the altar of Beth–el.
■ 18. **And he said, Let him**
■ **alone; let no man move**
■ **his bones.** So they let his bones
alone, with the bones of the prophet
that came out of Samaria.
■ 19. **And all the houses** also
■ **of the high places** that *were* in
the cities of Samaria, which the
kings of Israel had made to
provoke *the Lord* to anger,
■ **Josiah took away,** and
did to them according to all the
acts that he had done in Beth–el.
■ 20. **And he slew all the**
■ **priests of the high places**
that *were* there upon the altars,
■ **and burned men's**
■ **bones upon them,**
and returned to Jerusalem.
■ 21. **And the king**
■ **commanded** all
■ **the people, saying,**
■ **Keep the passover**
unto the LORD your God,
■ **as it is written in the**
■ **book** of this covenant.
■ 22. **Surely there**

was not holden such a passover from the days of the judges that judged Israel, nor in all the days of the kings of Israel, nor of the kings of Judah; 23. But in the eighteenth year of king Josiah, *wherein* this passover was holden to the LORD in Jerusalem. 24. Moreover the workers with familiar spirits, and the wizards, and the images, and the idols, and all the abominations that were spied in the land of Judah and in Jerusalem, did Josiah put away, that he might perform the words of the law which were written in the book that Hilkiah the priest found in the house of theLORD. 25. And like unto him was there no king before him, that turned to the LORD with all his heart, and with all his soul, and with all his might, according to all the law of Moses; neither after him arose there *any* like him. 26. Notwithstanding the LORD turned not from the fierceness of his great wrath, wherewith his anger was kindled against Judah, because of all the provocations that Manasseh had provoked him withal. 27. And the LORD said, I will remove Judah also out of my sight, as I have removed Israel, and will cast off this city Jerusalem which I have chosen, and the house of which I said, My name shall be there. 28. Now the rest of the acts of Josiah, and all that he did, *are* they not written in the book of the chronicles of the kings of Judah?

29. In his days Pharaoh-nechoh king of Egypt went up against the king of Assyria to the river Euphrates: and king Josiah went against him; and he slew him at Megiddo, when he had seen him. 30. And his servants carried him in a chariot dead from Megiddo, and brought him to Jerusalem, and buried him in his own sepulchre. And the people of the land took Jehoahaz the son of Josiah, and anointed him, and made him king in his father's stead. 31. Jehoahaz *was* twenty and three years old when he began to reign; and he reigned three months in Jerusalem. And his mother's name *was* Hamutal, the daughter of Jeremiah of Libnah. 32. And he did *that which was* evil in the sight of the LORD, according to all that his fathers had done. 33. And Pharaoh-nechoh put him in bands at Riblah in the land of Hamath, that he might not reign in Jerusalem; and put the land to a tribute of an hundred talents of silver, and a talent of gold. 34. And Pharaoh-nechoh made Eliakim the son of Josiah king in the room of Josiah his father, and turned his name to Jehoiakim, and took Jehoahaz away: and he came to Egypt, and died there. 35. And Jehoiakim gave the silver and the gold to Pharaoh; but he taxed the land to give the money according to the

commandment of Pharaoh: he exacted the silver and the gold of the people of the land, of every one according to his taxation, to give *it* unto Pharaoh–nechoh.

36. **Jehoiakim** *was* twenty and five years old when he began to reign; and he reigned eleven years in Jerusalem. And his mother's name *was* Zebudah, the daughter of Pedaiah of Rumah.

37. And he **did** *that which was* **evil in the sight of the LORD,** according to all that his fathers had done.

CHAPTER 24

1. **In his days Nebuchadnezzar king of Babylon came up, and Jehoiakim became his servant three years: then** he turned and **rebelled against him.**

2. **And the LORD sent against him** bands of **the Chaldees, and** bands of the **Syrians,** and bands of **the Moabites, and** bands of **the children of Ammon, and sent them against Judah to destroy it**, according to the word of the LORD, which he spake by his servants the prophets.

3. Surely at the commandment of the LORD came *this* upon Judah, **to remove them out of his sight, for the sins of Manasseh,** according to all that he did;

4. And also for the innocent blood that he shed: **for he filled Jerusalem with innocent blood; which the LORD would not pardon.**

5. Now the rest of the acts of Jehoiakim, and all that he did, *are* they not written in the book of the chronicles of the kings of Judah?

6. **So Jehoiakim slept** with his fathers:

and Jehoiachin his son **reigned in his stead.**

7. **And the king of Egypt came not again** any more out of his land: **for the king of Babylon had taken from the river of Egypt unto the** river **Euphrates all that pertained to** the king of **Egypt.**

8. **Jehoiachin was eighteen** years old **when he began to reign,** and he reigned in Jerusalem three months. And his mother's name *was* Nehushta, the daughter of Elnathan of Jerusalem.

9. **And he did** *that which was* **evil in the sight of the LORD,** according to all that his father had done.

10. **At that time the servants of Nebuchadnezzar king of Babylon came** up **against Jerusalem, and the city was besieged.**

11. And Nebuchadnezzar king of Babylon came against the city, and his servants did besiege it.

12. **And Jehoiachin** the king of Judah **went out to the king of Babylon,** he, and his mother, and his servants, and his princes, and his officers: **and the king of Babylon took him** in the eighth year of his reign.

13. **And** he **carried out thence all the treasures of the house of the LORD, and** the treasures of **the king's house,** and cut in pieces all the vessels of gold **which Solomon** king of Israel had **made** in the temple of the LORD, as the LORD had said.

14. **And he carried away all Jerusalem, and** all the princes, and all the

mighty men of valour,
■ **even ten thousand** captives,
■ **and** all the craftsmen and smiths:
■ **none remained, save the**
■ **poorest** sort of the people
■ **of the land.**
15. And he carried away Jehoiachin
to Babylon, and the king's mother,
and the king's wives, and his officers,
and the mighty of the land, *those*
carried he into captivity from
Jerusalem to Babylon.
■ 16. **And all the men of**
■ **might,** *even* seven thousand,
■ **and craftsmen and**
■ **smiths** a thousand, all *that*
■ **were** strong *and* apt for war,
even them the king of Babylon
■ **brought captive**
■ **to Babylon.**
■ 17. **And the king**
■ **of Babylon made**
■ **Mattaniah his father's**
■ **brother king** in his stead,
■ **and changed his**
■ **name to Zedekiah.**
18. Zedekiah *was* twenty and one
years old when he began to reign,
and he reigned eleven years in
Jerusalem. And his mother's name
was Hamutal, the daughter of
Jeremiah of Libnah.
■ 19. **And he did** *that which was*
■ **evil in the sight of the**
■ **LORD**, according to all that
Jehoiakim had done.
■ 20. **For through the anger**
■ **of the LORD it came to pass**
in Jerusalem and Judah, until he had
cast them out from his presence,
■ **that Zedekiah rebelled**
■ **against the king**
■ **of Babylon.**

CHAPTER 25

■ 1. **And** it came to pass
■ **in the ninth year of his**
■ **reign,** in the tenth month, in
the tenth *day* of the month, *that*
■ **Nebuchadnezzar**
king of Babylon
■ **came,** he, and all his host,
■ **against Jerusalem,**

and pitched against it:
■ **and** they
■ **built forts against**
■ **it** round about.
■ 2. **And the city was**
■ **besieged unto the**
■ **eleventh year of**
■ **king Zedekiah.**
■ 3. **And** on the ninth
day of the *fourth* month the
■ **famine prevailed** in the city,
■ **and there was no bread**
for the people of the land.
■ 4. **And the city was broken**
■ **up, and all the men** of war
■ **fled by night** by the way of the
gate between two walls, which *is* by
the king's garden: (now the Chaldees
were against the city round about:)
■ **and the king went** the way
■ **toward the plain.**
■ 5. **And** the army of
■ **the Chaldees pursued** after
■ **the king, and overtook**
■ **him in** the plains of
■ **Jericho: and** all
■ **his army** were
■ **scattered** from him.
■ 6. **So they took the**
■ **king,** and brought him up
■ **to the king of**
■ **Babylon** to Riblah;
■ **and** they
■ **gave judgment upon him.**
■ 7. **And they slew the sons of**
■ **Zedekiah before his eyes,**
■ **and put out the eyes of**
■ **Zedekiah, and bound**
■ **him** with fetters of brass,
■ **and carried him**
■ **to Babylon.**
■ 8. **And in** the fifth month, on the
seventh *day* of the month, which *is*
■ **the nineteenth year of** king
■ **Nebuchadnezzar**
king of Babylon,
■ **came Nebuzar-adan,**
■ **captain of the guard,** a
servant of the king of Babylon,
■ **unto Jerusalem:**
■ 9. **And he burnt the**
■ **house of the LORD,**
■ **and the king's house,**

■ **and all the houses of**
■ **Jerusalem,** and every great *man's*
house burnt he with fire.
■ 10. **And** all the army
of the Chaldees, that *were*
with the captain of the guard,
■ **brake down the walls**
■ **of Jerusalem** round about.
■ 11. **Now the rest of**
■ **the people** *that were*
■ **left in the city,** and the fugitives
that fell away to the king of Babylon,
with the remnant of the multitude,
■ **did Nebuzar-adan**
the captain of the guard
■ **carry away.**
■ 12. **But the captain** of the guard
■ **left** of
■ **the poor** of the land
■ **to be vinedressers**
■ **and husbandmen.**
■ 13. **And the** pillars of
■ **brass** that *were*
■ **in the house of the LORD,**
and the bases, and the brasen sea
that *was* in the house of the LORD,
■ **did the Chaldees**
■ **break in pieces, and**
■ **carried** the brass of them
■ **to Babylon.**
14. And the pots, and the shovels,
and the snuffers, and the spoons, and
all the vessels of brass wherewith
they ministered, took they away.
■ 15. **And** the firepans,
and the bowls, *and*
■ **such things** as *were*
■ **of gold,** *in* gold,
■ **and** of
■ **silver,** *in* silver,
■ **the captain of the**
■ **guard took away.**
16. The two pillars, one sea,
and the bases which Solomon
had made for the house of the
LORD; the brass of all these
vessels was without weight.
17. The height of the one pillar *was*
eighteen cubits, and the chapiter
upon it *was* brass: and the height of
the chapiter three cubits; and the
wreathen work, and pomegranates
upon the chapiter round about, all of

brass: and like unto these had the
second pillar with wreathen work.
■ 18. **And the**
■ **captain** of the guard
■ **took Seraiah the chief**
■ **priest, and Zephaniah**
the second priest,
■ **and the three keepers**
■ **of the door:**
■ 19. **And** out of the city he took
an officer that was set over the
men of war, and five men of
■ **them that were in the**
■ **king's presence,** which
were found in the city,
■ **and the** principal
■ **scribe** of the host,
■ **which mustered the**
■ **people** of the land,
■ **and threescore men**
of the people of the land *that were*
■ **found in the city:**
■ 20. **And Nebuzar-adan**
captain of the guard took these, and
■ **brought them to the king**
■ **of Babylon** to Riblah:
■ 21. **And the king** of
Babylon smote them, and
■ **slew them** at Riblah in
the land of Hamath.
■ **So Judah was carried away**
■ **out of their land.**
■ 22. **And as for the people**
■ **that remained** in the land of
Judah, whom Nebuchadnezzar
king of Babylon had left, even
■ **over them he made**
■ **Gedaliah** the son of
Ahikam, the son of Shaphan,
■ **ruler.**
■ 23. **And when** all
■ **the captains** of the
armies, they and their men,
■ **heard** that
■ **the king of Babylon** had
■ **made Gedaliah governor,**
■ **there came to**
■ **Gedaliah** to Mizpah, even
■ **Ishmael** the son of Nethaniah, and
Johanan the son of Careah, and
■ **Seraiah** the son of Tanhumeth
the Netophathite, and
■ **Jaazaniah** the son

of a Maachathite, they
■ **and their men.**
■ 24. **And Gedaliah**
■ **sware to them,** and to
their men, and said unto them,
■ **Fear not to be** the
■ **servants of the Chaldees:**
■ **dwell in the land, and serve**
■ **the king of Babylon; and**
■ **it shall be well with you.**
■ 25. **But** it came to pass in the
seventh month, that
■ **Ishmael** the son of Nethaniah,
the son of Elishama,
■ **of the seed royal,**
■ **came,** and ten men with him,
■ **and smote**
■ **Gedaliah,** that he died,
■ **and the Jews and** the
■ **Chaldees** that were
■ **with him** at Mizpah.
■ 26. **And** all
■ **the people,** both small
and great, and the captains
of the armies, arose, and
■ **came to Egypt: for**
■ **they were afraid**
■ **of the Chaldees.**
■ 27. **And** it came to pass

■ **in the seven and**
■ **thirtieth year of the**
■ **captivity of Jehoiachin**
king of Judah, in thetwelfth
month, on the seven and twentieth
day of the month, *that*
■ **Evil-merodach king of**
■ **Babylon** in the year that
he began to reign
■ **did lift up** the head of
■ **Jehoiachin** king of Judah
■ **out of prison;**
■ 28. **And he spake kindly**
■ **to him, and set his throne**
■ **above the throne of the**
■ **kings** that *were* with him
■ **in Babylon;**
■ 29. **And changed his**
■ **prison garments: and**
■ **he did eat bread**
■ **continually before**
■ **him** all the days of
■ **his life.**
■ 30. **And his allowance**
■ **was** a continual allowance
■ **given him of the**
■ **king,** a daily rate for
■ **every day,** all the days
■ **of his life.**

THE BOOK OF FIRST CHRONICLES

BACKGROUND INFORMATION

Author: Unknown
Date Written: Between 538 — 420 B.C.

Number of:
Verses—942
Chapters—29
Total Words—20,369
Scan Words—6,039
Scan Words Represent
Approximately 29% of
Total Words

Theme: The History of Israel from Saul's Death to the Babylonian Captivity

OUTLINE OF THE BOOK

I. **The Genealogies** of Israel's Twelve Tribes
1:1 — 9:44

II. **The Last Acts of** King **Saul**
10:1 — 14

III. **A Review of** the Reign of **King David**
11:1 — 29:30

CHAPTER 1

■ 1. **Adam, Sheth, Enosh,**
2. Kenan, Mahalaleel, Jered,
3. Henoch, Methuselah, Lamech,
■ 4. **Noah, Shem, Ham,**
■ **and Japheth.**
■ 5. **The sons of Japheth;**
■ **Gomer, and Magog,**
and Madai, and Javan, and
Tubal, and Meshech, and Tiras.
■ 6. **And the sons of**
■ **Gomer; Ashchenaz,**
and Riphath, and Togarmah.
7. And the sons of Javan; Elishah,
and Tarshish, Kittim, and Dodanim.
■ 8. **The sons of Ham; Cush,**
and Mizraim, Put, and Canaan.
9. And the sons of Cush; Seba,
and Havilah, and Sabta, and
Raamah, and Sabtecha. And the
sons of Raamah; Sheba, and Dedan.
■ 10. **And Cush begat**
■ **Nimrod:** he began to be
mighty upon the earth.
11. And Mizraim begat Ludim,
and Anamim, and Lehabim,
and Naphtuhim,
■ 12. **And** Pathrusim, and
■ **Casluhim, (of whom**
■ **came the Philistines,)**
and Caphthorim.
■ 13. **And Canaan begat**
Zidon his firstborn, and Heth,
■ 14. **The Jebusite** also, and
■ **the Amorite, and**
■ **the Girgashite,**
15. And the Hivite, and the
Arkite, and the Sinite,
16. And the Arvadite, and the
Zemarite, and the Hamathite.
■ 17. **The sons of Shem;**
Elam, and Asshur, and
■ **Arphaxad, and**
Lud, and Aram, and
■ **Uz,** and Hul, and Gether,
and Meshech.
■ 18. **And Arphaxad**
■ **begat Shelah, and**
■ **Shelah begat Eber.**
■ 19. **And unto Eber were born**
two sons: the name of the one *was*
■ **Peleg; because in his days**
■ **the earth was divided: and**

■ **his brother's name**
■ **was Joktan.**
20. And Joktan begat
Almodad, and Sheleph, and
Hazarmaveth, and Jerah,
21. Hadoram also, and
Uzal, and Diklah,
22. And Ebal, and
Abimael, and Sheba,
23. And Ophir, and Havilah,
and Jobab. All these *were*
the sons of Joktan.
■ 24. **Shem, Arphaxad,**
■ **Shelah,**
■ 25. **Eber, Peleg, Reu,**
■ 26. **Serug, Nahor, Terah,**
■ 27. **Abram; the same**
■ **is Abraham.**
■ 28. **The sons of Abraham;**
■ **Isaac, and Ishmael.**
■ 29. **These are their**
■ **generations:** The firstborn
of Ishmael, Nebaioth; then
Kedar, and Adbeel, and Mibsam,
30. Mishma, and Dumah,
Massa, Hadad, and Tema,
31. Jetur, Naphish, and Kedemah.
These are the sons of Ishmael.
32. Now the sons of Keturah,
Abraham's concubine: she bare
Zimran, and Jokshan, and Medan,
and Midian, and Ishbak, and
Shuah. And the sons of Jokshan;
Sheba, and Dedan.
33. And the sons of Midian;
Ephah, and Epher, and Henoch,
and Abida, and Eldaah. All
these *are* the sons of Keturah.
34. And Abraham begat Isaac.
■ **The sons of Isaac;**
■ **Esau and Israel.**
35. The sons of Esau; Eliphaz,Reuel,
and Jeush, and Jaalam, and Korah.
36. The sons of Eliphaz; Teman,
and Omar, Zephi, and Gatam,
Kenaz, and Timna, and Amalek.
37. The sons of Reuel; Nahath,
Zerah, Shammah, and Mizzah.
38. And the sons of Seir; Lotan, and
Shobal, and Zibeon, and Anah, and
Dishon, and Ezar, and Dishan.
39. And the sons of Lotan; Hori,
and Homam: and Timna *was*

Lotan's sister.

40. The sons of Shobal; Alian, and Manahath, and Ebal, Shephi, and Onam. and the sons of Zibeon; Aiah, and Anah.

41. The sons of Anah; Dishon. And the sons of Dishon; Amram, and Eshban, and Ithran, and Cheran.

42. The sons of Ezer; Bilhan, and Zavan, *and* Jakan. The sons of Dishan; Uz, and Aran.

43. Now these *are* the kings that reigned in the land of Edom before *any* king reigned over the children of Israel; Bela the son of Beor: and the name of his city *was* Dinhabah.

44. And when Bela was dead, Jobab the son of Zerah of Bozrah reigned in his stead.

45. And when Jobab was dead, Husham of the land of the Temanites reigned in his stead.

46. And when Husham was dead, Hadad the son of Bedad, which smote Midian in the field of Moab, reigned in his stead: and the name of his city *was* Avith.

47. And when Hadad was dead, Samlah of Masrekah reigned in his stead.

48. And when Samlah was dead, Shaul of Rehoboth by the river reigned in his stead.

49. And when Shaul was dead, Baal–hanan the son of Achbor reigned in his stead.

50. And when Baal–hanan was dead, Hadad reigned in his stead: and the name of his city *was* Pai; and his wife's name *was* Mehetabel, the daughter of Matred, the daughter of Mezahab.

51. Hadad died also. And the dukes of Edom were; duke Timnah, duke Aliah, duke Jetheth,

52. Duke Aholibamah, duke Elah, duke Pinon,

53. Duke Kenaz, duke Teman, duke Mibzar,

54. Duke Magdiel, duke Iram. These *are* the dukes of Edom.

CHAPTER 2

1. **These are the sons of Israel; Reuben, Simeon, Levi, and Judah, Issachar, and Zebulun,**

2. **Dan, Joseph, and Benjamin, Naphtali, Gad, and Asher.**

3. The sons of Judah; Er, and Onan, and Shelah: *which* three were born unto him of the daughter of Shua the Canaanitess. And Er, the firstborn of Judah, was evil in the sight of the LORD; and he slew him.

4. And Tamar his daughter in law bore him Pharez and Zerah.

All the sons of Judah were five.

5. The sons of **Pharez;** Hezron, and Hamul.

6. And the sons of **Zerah;** Zimri, and Ethan, and Heman, and Calcol, and Dara: five of them in all.

7. And the sons of **Carmi;** Achar, the troubler of Israel, who transgressed in the thing accursed.

8. And the sons of **Ethan;** Azariah.

9. **The sons also of Hezron,** that *were* born unto him; **Jerahmeel,** and **Ram, and Chelubai.**

10. **And Ram begat Amminadab; and Amminadab begat Nahshon,** prince of the children of Judah;

11. **And Nahshon begat Salma, and Salma begat Boaz,**

12. **And Boaz begat Obed, and Obed begat Jesse,**

13. **And Jesse begat** his firstborn Eliab, and Abinadab the second, and Shimma the third,

14. Nethaneel the fourth, Raddai the fifth,

15. Ozem the sixth, **David** the seventh:

16. Whose sisters *were* Zeruiah,

and Abigail. And the sons of Zeruiah;
Abishai, and Joab, and Asahel, three.
17. And Abigail bare Amasa: and
the father of Amasa *was* Jether
the Ishmeelite.
18. And Caleb the son of Hezron
begat *children* of Azubah *his* wife,
and of Jerioth: her sons *are* these;
Jesher, and Shobab, and Ardon.
19. And when Azubah was
dead, Caleb took unto him Ephrath,
which bare him Hur.
20. And Hur begat Uri, and Uri
begat Bezaleel.
21. And afterward Hezron
went in to the daughter of
Machir the father of Gilead, whom he
married when he *was* threescore
years old; and she bare him Segub.
22. And Segub begat Jair, who had
three and twenty cities in the
land of Gilead.
23. And he took Geshur, and Aram,
with the towns of Jair, from them,
with Kenath, and the
towns thereof, *even*
threescore cities. All
these *belonged* to the sons of
Machir the father of Gilead.
24. And after that Hezron was
dead in Caleb–ephratah, then
Abiah Hezron's wife bare him
Ashur the father of Tekoa.
25. And the sons of Jerahmeel
the firstborn of Hezron were, Ram
the firstborn, and Bunah, and
Oren, and Ozem, *and* Ahijah.
26. Jerahmeel had also another
wife, whose name *was* Atarah;
she *was* the mother of Onam.
27. And the sons of Ram the
firstborn of Jerahmeel were,
Maaz, and Jamin, and Eker.
28. And the sons of Onam were,
Shammai, and Jada. And the sons
of Shammai; Nadab and Abishur.
29. And the name of the wife of
Abishur *was* Abihail, and she bare
him Ahban, and Molid.
30. And the sons of Nadab;
Seled, and Appaim: but Seled
died without children.
31. And the sons of Appaim; Ishi.

And the sons of Ishi; Sheshan.
And the children of Sheshan; Ahlai.
32. And the sons of Jada the brother
of Shammai; Jether, and Jonathan:
and Jether died without children.
33. And the sons of Jonathan;
Peleth, and Zaza. These were the
sons of Jerahmeel.
34. Now Sheshan had no sons,
but daughters. And Sheshan
had a servant, an Egyptian,
whose name *was* Jarha.
35. And Sheshan gave his
daughter to Jarha his servant
to wife; and she bare him Attai.
36. And Attai begat Nathan,
and Nathan begat Zabad,
37. And Zabad begat Ephlal,
and Ephlal begat Obed,
38. And Obed begat Jehu,
and Jehu begat Azariah,
39. And Azariah begat Helez,
and Helez begat Eleasah,
40. And Eleasah begat Sisamai,
and Sisamai begat Shallum,
41. And Shallum begat Jekamiah,
and Jekamiah begat Elishama.
42. Now the sons of Caleb the
brother of Jerahmeel *were,* Mesha his
firstborn, which was the father of
Ziph; and the sons of Mareshah
the father of Hebron.
43. And the sons of Hebron;
Korah, and Tappuah, and
Rekem, and Shema.
44. And Shema begat Raham,
the father of Jorkoam: and
Rekem begat Shammai.
45. And the son of Shammai
was Maon: and Maon *was*
the father of Beth–zur.
46. And Ephah, Caleb's concubine,
bare Haran, and Moza, and Gazez:
and Haran begat Gazez.
47. And the sons of Jahdai; Regem,
and Jotham, and Gesham, and
Pelet, and Ephah, and Shaaph.
48. Maachah, Caleb's concubine,
bare Sheber, and Tirhanah.
49. She bare also Shaaph the father
of Madmannah, Sheva the father of
Machbenah, and the father of Gibea:
and the daughter ofCaleb *was* Achsa.

50. These were the sons of Caleb the son of Hur, the firstborn of Ephratah; Shobal the father of Kirjath–jearim.
51. Salma the father of Beth–lehem, Hareph the father of Beth–gader.
52. And Shobal the father of Kirjath–jearim had sons; Haroeh, *and* half of the Manahethites.
53. And the families of Kirjath–jearim; the Ithrites, and the Puhites, and the Shumathites, and the Mishraites; of them came the Zareathites, and the Eshtaulites,
54. The sons of Salma; Bethlehem, and the Netophathites, Ataroth, the house of Joab, and half of the Manahethites, the Zorites.
55. And the families of the scribes which dwelt at Jabez; the Tirathites, the Shimeathites, *and* Suchathites. These *are* the Kenites that came of Hemath, the father of the house of Rechab.

CHAPTER 3

1. **Now these were the sons of David,** which were **born** unto him **in Hebron;** the firstborn **Amnon,** of Ahinoam the Jezreelitess; the second **Daniel,** of Abigail the Carmelitess:
2. The third, **Absalom** the son of Maachah the daughter of Talmai king of Geshur: the fourth, **Adonijah** the son of Haggith:
3. The fifth, **Shephatiah** of Abital: the sixth, **Ithream** by Eglah his wife.
4. *These* six were born unto him in Hebron; and there he reigned seven years and six months: and in Jerusalem he reigned thirty and three years.
5. **And these were born** unto him **in Jerusalem; Shimea, and Shobab, and Nathan, and Solomon,** four, of Bath–shua the daughter of Ammiel:
6. Ibhar also, and Elishama, and Eliphelet,
7. And Nogah, and Nepheg, and Japhia,
8. And Elishama, and Eliada, and Eliphelet, nine.
9. *These were* all the sons of David, beside the sons of the concubines, and Tamar their sister.
10. **And Solomon's son was Rehoboam,** Abia his son, Asa his son, Jehoshaphat his son,
11. Joram his son, Ahaziah his son, Joash his son,
12. Amaziah his son, Azariah his son, Jotham his son,
13. Ahaz his son, Hezekiah his son, Manasseh his son,
14. Amon his son, Josiah his son.
15. And the sons of Josiah *were,* the firstborn Johanan, the second Jehoiakim, the third Zedekiah, the fourth Shallum.
16. And the sons of Jehoiakim: Jeconiah his son, Zedekiah his son.
17. And the sons of Jeconiah; Assir, Salathiel his son,
18. Malchiram also, and Pedaiah, and Shenazar, Jecamiah, Hoshama, and Nedabiah.
19. And the sons of Pedaiah *were,* Zerubbabel, and Shimei: and the sons of Zerubbabel; Meshullam, and Hananiah, and Shelomith their sister:
20. And Hashubah, and Ohel, and Berechiah, and Hasadiah, Jushab–hesed, five.
21. And the sons of Hananiah; Pelatiah, and Jesaiah: the sons of Rephaiah, the sons of Arnan, the sons of Obadiah, the sons of Shechaniah.
22. And the sons of Shechaniah; Shemaiah:and the sons of Shemaiah; Hattush, and Igeal, and Bariah, and Neariah, and Shaphat, six.
23. And the sons of Neariah;Elioenai, and Hezekiah, and Azrikam, three.
24. And the sons of Elioenai *were,* Hodaiah, and Eliashib, and Pelaiah, and Akkub, and Johanan, and Dalaiah, and Anani, seven.

CHAPTER 4

1. **The sons of Judah;**

■ **Pharez, Hezron, and Carmi,**
■ **and Hur, and Shobal.**

2. And Reaiah the son of Shobal
begat Jahath; and Jahath begat
Ahumai, and Lahad. These *are*
the families of the Zorathites.
3. And these *were* of the father of
Etam; Jezreel, and Ishma, and
Idbash: and the name of their
sister *was* Hazelelponi:
4. And Penuel the father of Gedor,
and Ezer the father of Hushah. These
are the sons of Hur, the firstborn of
Ephratah, the father of Beth–lehem.
5. And Ashur the father of Tekoa had
two wives, Helah and Naarah.
6. And Naarah bare him Ahuzam,
and Hepher, and Temeni, and
Haahashtari. These *were* the
sons of Naarah.
7. And the sons of Helah *were,*
Zereth, and Jezoar, and Ethnan.
8. And Coz begat Anub, and
Zobebah, and the families of
Aharhel the son of Harum.
9. And Jabez was more honourable
than his brethren: and his mother
called his name Jabez, saying,
Because I bare him with sorrow.
10. And Jabez called on the God of
Israel, saying, Oh that thou wouldest
bless me indeed, and enlarge my
coast, and that thine hand might be
with me, and that thou wouldest keep
me from evil, that it may not grieve
me! And God granted him that
which he requested.
11. And Chelub the brother of
Shuah begat Mehir, which was
the father of Eshton.
12. And Eshton begat Beth–rapha,
and Paseah, and Tehinnah the
father of Ir–nahash. These
are the men of Rechah.
13. And the sons of Kenaz;
Othniel, and Seraiah: and the
sons of Othniel; Hathath.
14. And Meonothai begat Ophrah:
and Seraiah begat Joab, the father
of the valley of Charashim; for
they were craftsmen.
15. And the sons of Caleb the son
of Jephunneh; Iru, Elah, and Naam:

and the sons of Elah, even Kenaz.
16. And the sons of Jehaleleel; Ziph,
and Ziphah, Tiria, and Asareel.
17. And the sons of Ezra *were,*
Jether, and Mered, and Epher,
and Jalon: and she bare Miriam,
and Shammai, and Ishbah the
father of Eshtemoa.
18. And his wife Jehudijah bare
Jered the father of Gedor, and Heber
the father of Socho, and Jekuthiel the
father of Zanoah. And these *are*
the sons of Bithiah the daughter
of Pharaoh, which Mered took.
19. And the sons of *his* wife Hodiah
the sister of Naham, the father of
Keilah the Garmite, and Eshtemoa
the Maachathite.
20. And the sons of Shimon *were,*
Amnon, and Rinnah, Ben–hanan,
and Tilon. And the sons of Ishi
were, Zoheth, and Ben–zoheth.
21. The sons of Shelah the son of
Judah *were,* Er the father of Lecah,
and Laadah the father of Mareshah,
and the families of the house of
them that wrought fine linen, of
the house of Ashbea,
22. And Jokim, and the men of
Chozeba, and Joash, and Saraph,
who had the dominion in Moab,
and Jashubi–lehem. And *these*
are ancient things.
23. These *were* the potters, and
those that dwelt among plants
and hedges: there they dwelt
with the king for his work.
24. The sons of Simeon *were,*
Nemuel, and Jamin, Jarib,
Zerah, *and* Shaul:
25. Shallum his son, Mibsam
his son, Mishma his son.
26. And the sons of Mishma;
Hamuel his son, Zacchur his
son, Shimei his son.
27. And Shimei had sixteen sons
and six daughters: but his brethren
had not many children, neither did
all their family multiply, like to the
children of Judah.
28. And they dwelt at Beer–sheba,
and Moladah, and Hazar–shual,
29. And at Bilhah, and at Ezem,

and at Tolad,

30. And at Bethuel, and at Hormah, and at Ziklag,

31. And at Beth–marcaboth, and Hazar–susim, and at Beth–birei, and at Shaaraim. These *were* their cities unto the reign of David.

32. And their villages *were,* Etam, and Ain, Rimmon, and Tochen, and Ashan, five cities:

33. And all their villages that *were* round about the same cities, unto Baal. These *were* their habitations, and their genealogy.

34. And Meshobab, and Jamlech, and Joshah, the son of Amaziah,

35. And Joel, and Jehu the son of Josibiah, the son of Seraiah, the son of Asiel,

36. And Elioenai, and Jaakobah, and Jeshohaiah, and Asaiah, and Adiel, and Jesimiel, and Benaiah,

37. And Ziza the son of Shiphi, the son of Allon, the son of Jedaiah, the son of Shimri, the son of Shemaiah;

38. **These mentioned by their names were princes in their families: and the house of their fathers increased greatly.**

39. And they went to the entrance of Gedor, *even* unto the east side of the valley, to seek pasture for their flocks.

40. **And they found fat pasture** and good, **and the land was** wide, and **quiet, and peaceable;** for *they* of **Ham had dwelt there of old.**

41. **And these written by name came in the days of Hezekiah king of Judah, and smote** their tents, and **the habitations** that were found there, **and destroyed them** utterly unto this day, and dwelt in their rooms: **because there was pasture there** for their flocks.

42. **And** *some* of them, *even of* **the sons of Simeon, five hundred men, went to mount Seir,** having for their captains Pelatiah, and Neariah, and Rephaiah, and Uzziel, the sons of Ishi.

43. **And** they **smote** the rest of **the Amalekites** that were escaped, and dwelt there unto this day.

CHAPTER 5

1. **Now** the sons of **Reuben** the firstborn of Israel, (for he **was the firstborn; but** forasmuch **as he defiled his father's bed, his birthright was given unto the sons of Joseph** the son of Israel: and the genealogy is not to be reckoned after the birthright.

2. **For Judah prevailed above his brethren, and of him came the chief ruler; but the birthright was Joseph's:)**

3. **The sons,** I *say,* **of Reuben** the firstborn of Israel *were,* Hanoch, and Pallu, Hezron, and Carmi.

4. The sons of Joel; Shemaiah his son, Gog his son, Shimei his son,

5. Micah his son, Reaia his son, Baal his son,

6. Beerah his son, whom Tilgath–pilneser king of Assyria carried away *captive:* he *was* prince of the Reubenites.

7. And his brethren by their families, when the genealogy of their generations was reckoned, *were* the chief, Jeiel, and Zechariah,

8. And Bela the son of Azaz, the son of Shema, the son of Joel, who dwelt in Aroer, even unto Nebo and Baal–meon:

9. And eastward he **inhabited** unto the entering in of **the wilderness** from the river Euphrates: because their

cattle were multiplied
■ **in the land of Gilead.**
■ 10. **And in the days of Saul**
■ **they made war with the**
■ **Hagarites,** who fell by their
hand: and they dwelt in their tents
throughout all the east *land* of Gilead.
■ 11. **And the children of Gad**
■ **dwelt over against them,**
in the land of Bashan unto Salcah:
12. Joel the chief, and Shapham
the next, and Jaanai, and Shaphat
in Bashan.
13. And their brethren of the house
of their fathers *were*, Michael, and
Meshullam, and Sheba, and Jorai,and
Jachan, and Zia, and Heber, seven.
14. These *are* the children of Abihail
the son of Huri, the son of Jaroah,
the son of Gilead, the son of
Michael, the son of Jeshishai, the
son of Jahdo, the son of Buz;
15. Ahi the son of Abdiel, the
son of Guni, chief of the house
of their fathers.
16. And they dwelt in Gilead in
Bashan, and in her towns, and in
all the suburbs of Sharon, upon
their borders.
17. All these were reckoned by
genealogies in the days of Jotham
king of Judah, and in the days of
Jeroboam king of Israel.
■ 18. **The sons of Reuben,** and
■ **the Gadites, and half the**
■ **tribe of Manasseh, of**
■ **valiant men, men able to**
■ **bear buckler and sword,**
■ **and to shoot with bow, and**
■ **skilful in war, were four and**
■ **forty thousand seven**
■ **hundred and threescore,**
that went out to the war.
■ 19. **And they made war**
■ **with the Hagarites,** with
■ **Jetur, and**
■ **Nephish,** and
■ **Nodab.**
20. And they were
helped against them,
■ **and the Hagarites were**
■ **delivered into their hand,**
and all that *were* with them:

■ **for they cried to**
■ **God** in the battle,
■ **and he** was
■ **intreated** of
■ **them; because they**
■ **put their trust in him.**
■ 21. **And they took**
■ **away their cattle;** of
■ **their camels** fifty
thousand, and of
■ **sheep** two hundred
and fifty thousand,
■ **and** of
■ **asses** two thousand,
■ **and of men an**
■ **hundred thousand.**
■ 22. **For there fell** down
■ **many slain, because the**
■ **war was of God.** And they dwelt
in their steads until the captivity.
■ 23. **And** the children of
■ **the half tribe of Manasseh**
■ **dwelt in the land:** they
increased from Bashan unto
Baal–hermon and Senir, and
unto mount Hermon.
24. And these *were* the heads of the
house of their fathers, even Epher,
and Ishi, and Eliel, and Azriel, and
Jeremiah, and Hodaviah, and
Jahdiel, mighty men of valour,
famous men, *and* heads of the
house of their fathers.
■ 25. **And they transgressed**
■ **against** the
■ **God** of their fathers,
■ **and went a whoring after**
■ **the gods of the people**
■ **of the land,** whom God
destroyed before them.
■ 26. **And** the
■ **God** of Israel
■ **stirred up the spirit**
■ **of Pul** king of Assyria,
■ **and** the spirit of
■ **Tilgath–pilneser** king
■ **of Assyria, and** he
■ **carried** them
■ **away,** even
■ **the Reubenites,** and
■ **the Gadites, and the**
■ **half tribe of Manasseh,**
■ **and brought them**

■ **unto Halah,** and
■ **Habor,** and
■ **Hara, and to the river**
■ **Gozan,** unto this day.

CHAPTER 6

■ 1. **The sons of Levi;**
Gershon, Kohath, and Merari.
2. And the sons of Kohath; Amram,
Izhar, and Hebron, and Uzziel.
3. And the children of Amram; Aaron,
and Moses, and Miriam. The sons
also of Aaron; Nadab, and Abihu,
Eleazar, and Ithamar.
4. Eleazar begat Phinehas,
Phinehas begat Abishua,
5. And Abishua begat Bukki,
and Bukki begat Uzzi,
6. And Uzzi begat Zerahiah,
and Zerahiah begat Meraioth,
7. Meraioth begat Amariah,
and Amariah begat Ahitub,
8. And Ahitub begat Zadok,
and Zadok begat Ahimaaz,
9. And Ahimaaz begat Azariah,
and Azariah begat Johanan,
10. And Johanan begat
Azariah, (he *it is* that
■ **executed the priest's office**
■ **in the temple that Solomon**
■ **built in Jerusalem:)**
11. And Azariah begat Amariah,
and Amariah begat Ahitub,
12. And Ahitub begat Zadok,
and Zadok begat Shallum,
13. And Shallum begat Hilkiah,
and Hilkiah begat Azariah,
14. And Azariah begat Seraiah,
and Seraiah begat Jehozadak,
■ 15. **And Jehozadak went**
■ **into captivity, when the**
■ **LORD carried away Judah**
■ **and Jerusalem by the hand**
■ **of Nebuchadnezzar.**
16. The sons of Levi; Gershom,
Kohath, and Merari.
17. And these *be* the names of the
sons of Gershom; Libni, and Shimei.
18. And the sons of Kohath
were, Amram, and Izhar, and
Hebron, and Uzziel.
19. The sons of Merari; Mahli, and
Mushi. And these *are* the families of

the Levites according to their fathers.
20. Of Gershom; Libni his son,
Jahath his son, Zimmah his son,
21. Joah his son, Iddo his son,
Zerah his son, Jeaterai his son.
22. The sons of Kohath; Amminadab
his son, Korah his son, Assir his son,
23. Elkanah his son, and Ebiasaph
his son, and Assir his son,
24. Tahath his son, Uriel his son,
Uzziah his son, and Shaul his son.
25. And the sons of Elkanah;
Amasai, and Ahimoth.
26. *As for* Elkanah: the sons of
Elkanah; Zophai his son, and
Nahath his son,
27. Eliab his son, Jeroham his
son, Elkanah his son.
28. And the sons of Samuel; the
firstborn Vashni, and Abiah.
29. The sons of Merari; Mahli, Libni
his son, Shimei his son, Uzza his son,
30. Shimea his son, Haggiah his
son, Asaiah his son.
31. And these *are they* whom
David set over the service of
song in the house of the LORD,
after that the ark had rest.
32. And they ministered before the
dwelling place of the tabernacle of
the congregation with singing, until
Solomon had built the house of the
LORD in Jerusalem: and *then* they
waited on their office according to
their order.
33. And these *are* they that waited
with their children. Of the sons of
the Kohathites: Heman a singer,
the son of Joel, the son of Shemuel,
34. The son of Elkanah, the son of
Jeroham, the son of Eliel, the son
of Toah,
35. The son of Zuph, the son
of Elkanah, the son of Mahath,
the son of Amasai,
36. The son of Elkanah, the son of
Joel, the son of Azariah, the son
of Zephaniah,
37. The son of Tahath, the son
of Assir, the son of Ebiasaph,
the son of Korah,
38. The son of Izhar, the son
of Kohath, the son of Levi, the

son of Israel.

39. And his brother Asaph, who stood on his right hand, *even* Asaph the son of Berachiah, the son of Shimea,

40. The son of Michael, the son of Baaseiah, the son of Malchiah,

41. The son of Ethni, the son of Zerah, the son of Adaiah,

42. The son of Ethan, the son of Zimmah, the son of Shimei,

43. The son of Jahath, the son of Gershom, the son of Levi.

44. And their brethren the sons of Merari *stood* on the left hand: Ethan the son of Kishi, the son of Abdi, the son of Malluch,

45. The son of Hashabiah, the son of Amaziah, the son of Hilkiah,

46. The son of Amzi, the son of Bani, the son of Shamer,

47. The son of Mahli, the son of Mushi, the son of Merari, the son of Levi.

48. Their brethren also **the Levites were appointed unto** all manner of **service of** the tabernacle of **the house of God.**

49. **But Aaron and his sons offered** upon the altar of the **burnt offering, and** on the altar of incense, *and* **were appointed** for all **the work of the place most holy, and to make an atonement for Israel, according to all that Moses the servant of God had commanded.**

50. And these *are* the sons of Aaron; Eleazar his son, Phinehas his son, Abishua his son,

51. Bukki his son, Uzzi his son, Zerahiah his son,

52. Meraioth his son, Amariah his son, Ahitub his son,

53. Zadok his son, Ahimaaz his son.

54. **Now these are their dwelling places** throughout their castles in their coasts, of the sons of Aaron, **of the families of the Kohathites:** for theirs was the lot.

55. **And they gave them Hebron in** the land of **Judah, and the suburbs thereof** round about it.

56. **But the fields** of the city, **and the villages** thereof, **they gave to Caleb** the son of Jephunneh.

57. And to the sons of Aaron they gave the cities of Judah, *namely,* Hebron, *the city* of refuge, and Libnah with her suburbs, and Jattir, and Eshtemoa, with their suburbs,

58. And Hilen with her suburbs, Debir with her suburbs,

59. And Ashan with her suburbs, and Beth–shemesh with her suburbs:

60. **And** out **of the tribe of Benjamin;** Geba with her suburbs, and Alemeth with her suburbs, and Anathoth with her suburbs. All their cities throughout their families **were thirteen cities.**

61. **And unto the sons of Kohath, which were left** of the family of that tribe, **were** *cities* **given** out of the half tribe, *namely, out of* the half *tribe* of Manasseh, by lot, **ten cities.**

62. **And to the sons of Gershom** throughout their families out of the tribe of Issachar, and out of the tribe of Asher, and out of the tribe of Naphtali, and out of the tribe of Manasseh in Bashan, **thirteen cities.**

63. **Unto the sons of Merari were given** by lot, throughout their families, out of the tribe of Reuben, and out of the tribe of Gad, and out of the tribe of Zebulun, **twelve cities.**

64. **And** the children of **Israel gave to the Levites** *these* cities with their suburbs.

65. And they gave by lot out of the tribe of the children of Judah, and out of the tribe of the children of Simeon, and out of the tribe of the children of Benjamin, these cities, which are

called by *their* names.

66. And *the residue* of the families of the sons of Kohath had cities of their coasts out of the tribe of Ephraim.

67. And they gave unto them, *of* **the cities of refuge,** Shechem in mount Ephraim with her suburbs; *they gave* also Gezer with her suburbs,

68. And Jokmeam with her suburbs, and Beth–horon with her suburbs,

69. And Aijalon with her suburbs, and Gath–rimmon with her suburbs:

70. **And out of the half tribe of Manasseh; Aner** with her suburbs, **and Bileam** with her suburbs, **for the** family of the **remnant of the sons of Kohath.**

71. **Unto the sons of Gershom were given out of** the family of the half tribe of **Manasseh, Golan** in Bashan with her suburbs, **and Ashtaroth** with her suburbs:

72. **And out of the tribe of Issachar; Kedesh** with her suburbs, **Daberath** with her suburbs,

73. And **Ramoth** with her suburbs, and **Anem** with her suburbs:

74. And out of the tribe of Asher; **Mashal** with her suburbs, and **Abdon** with her suburbs,

75. And **Hukok** with her suburbs, and **Rehob** with her suburbs:

76. **And out of the tribe of Naphtali; Kedesh in Galilee** with her suburbs, and **Hammon** with her suburbs, and **Kirjathaim** with her suburbs.

77. **Unto the rest** of the children **of Merari were given out of the tribe of Zebulun, Rimmon** with her suburbs, **Tabor** with her suburbs:

78. **And** on the other side Jordan by Jericho, **on the east side of Jordan, were given** them **out of the tribe of Reuben,**

Bezer in the wilderness with her suburbs, and **Jahzah** with her suburbs,

79. **Kedemoth** also with her suburbs, and **Mephaath** with her suburbs:

80. And out of the tribe of Gad; **Ramoth** in Gilead with her suburbs, and **Mahanaim** with her suburbs,

81. And **Heshbon** with her suburbs, **and Jazer** with her suburbs.

CHAPTER 7

1. **Now the sons of Issachar were, Tola,** and **Puah, Jashub, and Shimrom,** four.

2. **And the sons of Tola;** Uzzi, and Rephaiah, and Jeriel, and Jahmai, and Jibsam, and Shemuel, heads of their father's house, *to wit*, of Tola: *they* **were valiant men** of might in their generations; **whose number was in the days of David two and twenty thousand and six hundred.**

3. And the sons of Uzzi; Izrahiah: and the sons of Izrahiah; Michael, and Obadiah, and Joel, Ishiah, five: all of them chief men.

4. **And with them,** by their generations, after the house of their fathers, *were* **bands of soldiers for war, six and thirty thousand men:** for they had many wives and sons.

5. **And** their brethren among all the families **of Issachar were** valiant men of might, reckoned in all by their genealogies **fourscore and seven thousand.**

6. **The sons of Benjamin; Bela, and Becher, and Jediael,** three.

7. And the sons of Bela; Ezbon, and Uzzi, and Uzziel, and Jerimoth,

and Iri, five; heads of
■ **the** house of *their* fathers,
■ **mighty men of valour;** and
■ **were** reckoned by their genealogies
■ **twenty** and
■ **two thousand and thirty** and
■ **four.**
■ 8. **And** the sons
■ **of Becher;** Zemira, and Joash,
and Eliezer, and Elioenai, and
Omri, and Jerimoth, and Abiah, and
Anathoth, and Alameth. All these
are the sons of Becher.
9. And the number of them, after
their genealogy by their generations,
heads of the house of their fathers,
mighty men of valour,
■ **was twenty thousand** and
■ **two hundred.**
10. The sons also of Jediael; Bilhan:
and the sons of Bilhan; Jeush, and
Benjamin, and Ehud, and
Chenaanah, and Zethan, and
Tharshish, and Ahishahar.
■ 11. **All** these
■ **the sons of Jediael,** by
the heads of their fathers, mighty
■ **men of valour, were**
■ **seventeen thousand** and **two**
■ **hundred soldiers,** fit
to go out for war *and* battle.
12. Shuppim also, and Huppim,
the children of Ir, and Hushim,
the sons of Aher.
13. The sons of Naphtali; Jahziel,
and Guni, and Jezer, and Shallum,
the sons of Bilhah.
14. The sons of Manasseh; Ashriel,
whom she bare: *(but* his concubine
the Aramitess bare Machir the
father of Gilead:
15. And Machir took to wife *the sister*
of Huppim and Shuppim, whose
sister's name *was* Maachah;) and the
name of the second *was* Zelophehad:
and Zelophehad had daughters.
16. And Maachah the wife of Machir
bare a son, and she called his name
Peresh; and the name of his brother
was Sheresh; and his sons *were*
Ulam and Rakem.
17. And the sons of Ulam; Bedan.
These *were* the sons of Gilead, the

son of Machir, the son of Manasseh.
18. And his sister Hammoleketh bare
Ishod, and Abiezer, and Mahalah.
19. And the sons of Shemidah
were, Ahian, and Shechem, and
Likhi, and Aniam.
■ 20. **And the sons of**
■ **Ephraim;** Shuthelah, and Bered
his son, and Tahath his son, and
Eladah his son, and Tahath his son,
21. And Zabad his son,
and Shuthelah his son,
and Ezer, and Elead,
■ **whom the men of Gath**
that were born in *that* land
■ **slew, because**
■ **they came** down
■ **to take** away
■ **their cattle.**
■ 22. **And Ephraim** their father
■ **mourned many days,**
■ **and his brethren came**
■ **to comfort him.**
■ 23. **And** when he went in to
■ **his wife,** she
■ **conceived, and bare a**
■ **son, and he called his**
■ **name Beriah, because**
■ **it went evil with his house.**
24. (And his daughter *was* Sherah,
who built Beth–horon the nether, and
the upper, and Uzzen–sherah.)
25. And Rephah *was* his son, also
Resheph, and Telah his son,
and Tahan his son.
26. Laadan his son, Ammihud
his son, Elishama his son.
27. Non his son, Jehoshua his son.
28. And their possessions and
habitations *were,* Beth–el and the
towns thereof, and eastward Naaran,
and westward Gezer, with the towns
thereof; Shechem also and the
towns thereof, unto Gaza and
the towns thereof:
29. And by the borders of the children
of Manasseh, Beth–shean and her
towns, Taanach and her towns,
Megiddo and her towns, Dor and her
towns. In these dwelt the children
of Joseph the son of Israel.
■ 30. **The sons of Asher;** Imnah,
and Isuah, and Ishuai, and Beriah,

and Serah their sister.

31. And the sons of Beriah; Heber, and Malchiel, who *is* the father of Birzavith.

32. And Heber begat Japhlet, and Shomer, and Hotham, and Shua their sister.

33. And the sons of Japhlet; Pasach, and Bimhal, and Ashvath. These *are* the children of Japhlet.

34. And the sons of Shamer; Ahi, and Rohgah, Jehubbah, and Aram.

35. And the sons of his brother Helem; Zophah, and Imna, and Shelesh, and Amal.

36. The sons of Zophah; Suah, and Harnepher, and Shual, and Beri, and Imrah,

37. Bezer, and Hod, and Shamma, and Shilshah, and Ithran, and Beera.

38. And the sons of Jether; Jephunneh, and Pispah, and Ara.

39. And the sons of Ulla; Arah, and Haniel, and Rezia.

40. All these **were** the children of Asher, heads of *their* father's house, choice *and* mighty **men of valour,** chief of the princes. **And the number** throughout the genealogy **of them** that were apt to the war *and* to battle **was twenty** and **six thousand men.**

CHAPTER 8

1. **Now Benjamin begat Bela** his firstborn, **Ashbel** the second, and **Aharah** the third,

2. **Nohah** the fourth, **and Rapha** the fifth.

3. **And** the sons of Bela **were**, Addar, and Gera, and Abihud,

4. And Abishua, and Naaman, and Ahoah,

5. And Gera, and Shephuphan, and Huram.

6. And these *are* the sons of Ehud: these are the heads of the fathers of **the inhabitants of Geba,**

and they removed them to Manahath:

7. And Naaman, and Ahiah, and Gera, he removed them, and begat Uzza, and Ahihud.

8. And Shaharaim begat *children* in the country of **Moab,** after he had sent them away; Hushim and Baara *were* his wives.

9. And he begat of Hodesh his wife, Jobab, and Zibia, and Mesha, and Malcham,

10. And Jeuz, and Shachia, and Mirma. These *were* his sons, heads of the fathers.

11. And of Hushim he begat Abitub, and Elpaal.

12. The sons of Elpaal; Eber, and Misham, **and** Shamed, who **built Ono, and Lod,** with the towns thereof:

13. **Beriah also, and Shema, who were heads of the fathers of the inhabitants of Aijalon, who drove away the inhabitants of Gath:**

14. And Ahio, Shashak, and Jeremoth,

15. And Zebadiah, and Arad, and Ader,

16. And Michael, and Ispah, and Joha, the sons of Beriah;

17. And Zebadiah, and Meshullam, and Hezeki, and Heber,

18. Ishmerai also, and Jezliah, and Jobab, the sons of Elpaal;

19. And Jakim, and Zichri, and Zabdi,

20. And Elienai, and Zilthai, and Eliel,

21. And Adaiah, and Beraiah, and Shimrath, the sons of Shimhi;

22. And Ishpan, and Heber, and Eliel,

23. And Abdon, and Zichri, and Hanan,

24. And Hananiah, and Elam, and Antothijah,

25. And Iphedeiah, and Penuel, the sons of Shashak;

26. And Shamsherai, and Shehariah, and Athaliah,

27. **And Jaresiah,** and

Eliah, and Zichri, the sons of Jeroham.

28. These *were* heads of the fathers, by their generations, chief *men.* These dwelt in Jerusalem.

29. And at Gibeon dwelt the father of Gibeon; whose wife's name *was* Maachah:

30. And his firstborn son Abdon, and Zur, and Kish, and Baal, and Nadab,

31. And Gedor, and Ahio, and Zacher.

32. And Mikloth begat Shimeah. And these also dwelt with their brethren in Jerusalem, over against them.

33. And Ner begat Kish, and Kish begat Saul, and Saul begat Jonathan, and Malchi–shua, and Abinadab, and Esh–baal.

34. And the son of Jonathan *was* Merib–baal; and Meribbaal begat Micah.

35. And the sons of Micah *were,* Pithon, and Melech, and Tarea, and Ahaz.

36. And Ahaz begat Jehoadah; and Jehoadah begat Alemeth, and Azmaveth, and Zimri; and Zimri begat Moza,

37. And Moza begat Binea: Rapha *was* his son, Eleasah his son, Azel his son:

38. And Azel had six sons, whose names *are* these, Azrikam, Bocheru, and Ishmael, and Sheariah, and Obadiah, and Hanan. All these *were* the sons of Azel.

39. And the sons of Eshek his brother *were,* Ulam his firstborn, Jehush the second, and Eliphelet the third.

40. And the sons of Ulam were mighty men of valour, archers, and had many sons, and sons' sons, an hundred and fifty. All these *are* of the sons of Benjamin.

CHAPTER 9

1. So all Israel were reckoned by genealogies; and, behold, they were written in the book of the kings of Israel and Judah, who were carried away to Babylon for their transgression.

2. Now the first inhabitants that *dwelt* in their possessions in their cities were, the Israelites, the priests, Levites, and the Nethinims.

3. And in Jerusalem dwelt of the children of Judah, and of the children of Benjamin, and of the children of Ephraim, and Manasseh;

4. Uthai the son of Ammihud, the son of Omri, the son of Imri, the son of Bani, of the children of Pharez the son of Judah.

5. And of the Shilonites; Asaiah the firstborn, and his sons.

6. And of the sons of Zerah; Jeuel, and their brethren, six hundred and ninety.

7. And of the sons of Benjamin; Sallu the son of Meshullam, the son of Hodaviah, the son of Hasenuah,

8. And Ibneiah the son of Jeroham, and Elah the son of Uzzi, the son of Michri, and Meshullam the son of Shephathiah, the son of Reuel, the son of Ibnijah;

9. And their brethren, according to their generations, nine hundred and fifty and six. All these men were chief of the fathers in the house of their fathers.

10. And of the priests; Jedaiah, and Jehoiarib, and Jachin,

11. And Azariah the son of Hilkiah, the son of Meshullam, the son of Zadok, the son of Meraioth, the son of Ahitub, the ruler of the house of God;

12. And Adaiah the son of Jeroham, the son of Pashur, the son of Malchijah, and Maasiai the son of Adiel, the son of Jahzerah, the son of Meshullam, the son of Meshillemith, the son of Immer;

13. And their brethren, heads of the house of their fathers, a thousand and seven hundred and

- **threescore;** very able men
- **for the work** of the service
- **of the house of God.**
- 14. **And of the Levites;**

Shemaiah the son of Hasshub, the son of Azrikam, the son of Hashabiah, of the sons of Merari; 15. And Bakbakkar, Heresh, and Galal, and Mattaniah the son of Micah, the son of Zichri, the son of Asaph; 16. And Obadiah the son of Shemaiah, the son of Galal, the son of Jeduthun, and Berechiah the son of Asa, the son of Elkanah, that dwelt in the villages of the Netophathites.

- 17. **And the porters** *were,*

Shallum, and Akkub, and Talmon, and Ahiman, and their brethren: Shallum *was* the chief; 18. Who hitherto *waited* in the king's gate eastward: they *were* porters in the companies of the children of Levi. 19. And Shallum the son of Kore, the son of Ebiasaph, the son of Korah, and his brethren, of the house of his father, the Korahites,

- **were over the work of the**
- **service, keepers of the**
- **gates of the tabernacle:** and

their fathers, *being* over the host of the LORD, *were* keepers of the entry. 20. And Phinehas the son of Eleazar was the ruler over them in time past, *and* the LORD *was* with him. 21. *And* Zechariah the son of Meshelemiah *was* porter of the door of the tabernacle of the congregation.

- 22. **All these** *which were*
- **chosen to be**
- **porters** in the gates
- **were two hundred and**
- **twelve.** These were reckoned by

their genealogy in their villages, whom David and Samuel the seer did ordain in their set office. 23. So they and their children *had* the oversight of the gates of the house of the LORD, *namely,* the house of the tabernacle, by wards. 24. In four quarters were the porters, toward the east, west, north, and south.

25. And their brethren, *which were* in their villages, *were* to come after seven days from time to time with them.

- 26. **For these Levites, the**
- **four chief porters, were**
- **in their set office, and**
- **were over the chambers**
- **and treasuries of the**
- **house of God.**
- 27. **And they lodged**
- **round** about
- **the house of God,** because

the charge *was* upon them, and the

- **opening thereof every**
- **morning** pertained to them.
- 28. **And** *certain* of them
- **had the**
- **charge of the ministering**
- **vessels,** that they should

bring them in and out by tale.

- 29. **Some** of them also
- **were appointed to**
- **oversee the vessels,**
- **and** all the
- **instruments of**
- **the sanctuary,** and
- **the** fine
- **flour,** and the
- **wine,** and the
- **oil,** and the
- **frankincense,**
- **and the spices.**
- 30. **And some**

of the sons of the priests

- **made the ointment**
- **of the spices.**
- 31. **And Mattithiah,**
- **one of the Levites,** who *was*

the firstborn of Shallum the Korahite,

- **had the** set
- **office over the**
- **things** that were
- **made in** the
- **pans.**
- 32. **And** *other* of their

brethren, of the sons of

- **the Kohathites, were over**
- **the shewbread, to prepare**
- **it every sabbath.**
- 33. **And** these *are*
- **the singers,** chief of the

fathers of the Levites, who

■ **remaining in the**
■ **chambers** *were* free: for they
■ **were employed in that**
■ **work day and night.**

34. These chief fathers of the
Levites *were* chief throughout
their generations; these
dwelt at Jerusalem.

35. And in Gibeon dwelt the father
of Gibeon, Jehiel, whose wife's
name *was* Maachah:

36. And his firstborn son Abdon,
then Zur, and Kish, and Baal,
and Ner, and Nadab.

37. And Gedor, and Ahio, and
Zechariah, and Mikloth.

38. And Mikloth begat Shimeam.
And they also dwelt with their
brethren at Jerusalem, over
against their brethren.

39. And Ner begat Kish; and Kish
begat Saul; and Saul begat
Jonathan, and Malchishua, and
Abinadab, and Eshbaal.

40. And the son of Jonathan
was Merib–baal: and Meribbaal
begat Micah.

41. And the sons of Micah *were,*
Pithon, and Melech, and Tahrea,
and Ahaz.

42. And Ahaz begat Jarah; and Jarah
begat Alemeth, and Azmaveth, and
Zimri; and Zimri begat Moza;

43. And Moza begat Binea; and
Rephaiah his son, Eleasah his
son, Azel his son.

44. And Azel had six sons, whose
names *are* these, Azrikam, Bocheru,
and Ishmael, and Sheariah, and
Obadiah, and Hanan: these *were*
the sons of Azel.

CHAPTER 10

■ 1. **Now the Philistines**
■ **fought against Israel;**
■ **and** the men of
■ **Israel fled** from
before the Philistines,
■ **and fell** down
■ **slain in mount Gilboa.**
■ 2. **And the Philistines**
followed hard after Saul, and after
his sons; and the Philistines

■ **slew Jonathan, and**
Abinadab, and Malchi–shua,
■ **the sons of Saul.**
■ 3. **And** the battle went sore against
■ **Saul,** and the archers hit him, and he
■ **was wounded**
■ **of the archers.**
■ 4. **Then said Saul to his**
■ **armourbearer, Draw thy**
■ **sword, and thrust me**
■ **through therewith; lest**
■ **these uncircumcised**
come and
■ **abuse me. But his**
■ **armourbearer would**
■ **not;** for he was sore afraid.
■ **So Saul took a sword,**
■ **and fell upon it.**
■ 5. **And when his**
■ **armourbearer saw**
■ **that Saul was dead,**
■ **he fell likewise on the**
■ **sword, and died.**
6. So Saul died, and his three sons,
and all his house died together.
■ 7. **And when** all the men of
■ **Israel** that *were* in the valley
■ **saw that** they fled, and that
■ **Saul and his sons**
■ **were dead,** then
■ **they forsook their**
■ **cities,** and fled:
■ **and the Philistines** came and
■ **dwelt in them.**
8. **And** it came to pass
■ **on the morrow,** when
■ **the Philistines** came to
strip the slain, that they
■ **found Saul and his**
■ **sons** fallen in mount Gilboa.
■ 9. **And** when they had
■ **stripped him,** they
■ **took his head, and his**
■ **armour, and sent** into the land
of the Philistines round about, to carry
■ **tidings unto their**
■ **idols, and** to
■ **the people.**
10. **And** they
■ **put his armour in the**
■ **house of their gods,**
■ **and fastened his head**
■ **in the temple of Dagon.**

11. **And when all Jabesh-gilead heard** all that the Philistines had done to Saul,

12. **They arose,** all the valiant men, **and took** away **the body of Saul, and** the bodies of **his sons,** and brought them to Jabesh, **and buried their bones** under the oak in Jabesh, **and fasted seven days.**

13. **So Saul died for his transgression** which he committed against the LORD, *even* **against the word of the LORD,** which he kept not, and also **for asking counsel of** *one that had* **a familiar spirit,** to enquire *of it;*

14. **And enquired not of the LORD: therefore he slew him, and turned the kingdom unto David the son of Jesse.**

CHAPTER 11

1. **Then all Israel gathered themselves to David** unto Hebron, **saying,** Behold, we *are* thy bone and thy flesh.

2. And moreover in time past, even **when Saul was king, thou** *wast* he that **leddest out and broughtest in Israel: and** the LORD thy **God said** unto thee, Thou shalt feed my people Israel, and **thou shalt be ruler over** my people **Israel.**

3. **Therefore** came all **the elders of Israel** to the king to Hebron; and David made a covenant with them in Hebron before the LORD; and they **anointed David king** over Israel, according to the word of the LORD by Samuel.

4. **And David and all Israel went to Jerusalem,** which *is* Jebus; where the Jebusites *were,* the inhabitants of the land.

5. **And the inhabitants** of Jebus **said to David, Thou shalt not come hither. Nevertheless David took** the castle of **Zion,** which is **the city of David.**

6. **And** David **said, Whosoever smiteth the Jebusites first shall be** chief and **captain. So Joab** the son of Zeruiah **went first** up, **and was chief.**

7. And David dwelt in the castle; therefore they called it the city of David.

8. And he built the city round about, even from Millo round about: and Joab repaired the rest of the city.

9. **So David waxed greater** and greater: **for the LORD** of hosts **was with him.**

10. These also *are* the chief of the mighty men whom David had, who strengthened themselves with him in his kingdom, *and* with all Israel, to make him king, according to the word of the LORD concerning Israel.

11. **And** this *is* the number **of the mighty men whom David had; Jashobeam,** an Hachmonite, the chief of the captains: he **lifted up his spear against three hundred slain by him at one time.**

12. **And** after him *was* **Eleazar** the son of Dodo, the Ahohite, who **was one of the three mighties.**

13. **He was with David at Pas-dammim, and** there **the Philistines were gathered** together **to battle,** where was a parcel

629

of ground full of barley;
and the people fled from
before the Philistines.
14. **And they** set themselves
in the midst of *that* parcel,
and delivered it, and
**slew the Philistines; and
the LORD saved them**
by a great deliverance.
15. **Now three of the** thirty
**captains went
down** to the rock
**to David, into the cave
of Adullam; and** the host of
**the Philistines encamped
in the valley** of Rephaim.
16. And David *was* then in the hold,
and the Philistines' garrison *was*
then at Beth–lehem.
17. **And David** longed, and
**said, Oh that one would
give me drink** of the water
of the well of Beth–lehem,
that *is* at the gate!
18. **And the three brake
through** the host of
**the Philistines, and
drew water out of the
well** of Beth–lehem, that
was by the gate, and took *it*,
**and brought it to David: but
David** would not drink *of* it, but
poured it out to the LORD.
19. **And said,** My
God forbid it me,
**that I should do this
thing: shall I drink the blood
of these** men
**that have put their lives in
jeopardy?** for with *the jeopardy of*
their lives they brought it. Therefore
he would not drink it. These things
did these three mightiest.
20. **And Abishai**
the brother of Joab, he
was chief of the three: for
**lifting up his spear
against three hundred,
he slew them,** and had
a name among the three.
21. **Of the three, he was
more honourable** than the two;
for he was their captain: howbeit he

attained not to the *first* three.
22. **Benaiah** the son of Jehoiada,
the son of a valiant man of Kabzeel,
who had done many acts; he
**slew two lionlike men
of Moab: also he went
down and slew a lion**
in a pit in a snowy day.
23. **And he slew an
Egyptian,** a man of *great* stature,
**five cubits high; and in the
Egyptian's hand was a
spear like a weaver's
beam; and he** went down
to him with a staff, and
**plucked the spear out
of the Egyptian's hand,
and slew him with
his own spear.**
24. These *things* did Benaiah the
son of Jehoiada, and had the
name among the three mighties.
25. **Behold, he was
honourable** among the thirty,
but attained not to the *first* three:
**and David set him
over his guard.**
26. Also the valiant men of the
armies *were*, Asahel the brother
of Joab, Elhanan the son of
Dodo of Beth–lehem,
27. Shammoth the Harorite,
Helez the Pelonite,
28. Ira the son of Ikkesh the
Tekoite, Abiezer the Antothite,
29. Sibbecai the Hushathite,
Ilai the Ahohite,
30. Maharai the Netophathite, Heled
the son of Baanah the Netophathite,
31. Ithai the son of Ribai of Gibeah,
that pertained to the children of
Benjamin, Benaiah the Pirathonite,
32. Hurai of the brooks of Gaash,
Abiel the Arbathite,
33. Azmaveth the Baharumite,
Eliahba the Shaalbonite,
34. The sons of Hashem the
Gizonite, Jonathan the son
of Shage the Hararite,
35. Ahiam the son of Sacar the
Hararite, Eliphal the son of Ur,
36. Hepher the Mecherathite,
Ahijah the Pelonite,

37. Hezro the Carmelite,
Naarai the son of Ezbai,
38. Joel the brother of Nathan,
Mibhar the son of Haggeri,
39. Zelek the Ammonite, Naharai
the Berothite, the armourbearer
of Joab the son of Zeruiah,
40. Ira the Ithrite, Gareb the Ithrite,
41. Uriah the Hittite, Zabad
the son of Ahlai,
42. Adina the son of Shiza the
Reubenite, a captain of the
Reubenites, and thirty with him,
43. Hanan the son of Maachah,
and Joshaphat the Mithnite,
44. Uzzia the Ashterathite,
Shama and Jehiel the sons of
Hothan the Aroerite,
45. Jediael the son of Shimri, and
Joha his brother, the Tizite,
46. Eliel the Mahavite, and Jeribai,
and Joshaviah, the sons of Elnaam,
and Ithmah the Moabite,
47. Eliel, and Obed, and
Jasiel the Mesobaite.

CHAPTER 12

1. **Now these** *are* they that
came to David to Ziklag,
while he yet
**kept himself close because
of Saul** the son of Kish: and they
were among the
mighty men, helpers of the war.
2. **They were armed with
bows, and could use both
the right hand and the left
in hurling stones and
shooting arrows** out of a bow,
even of Saul's brethren of Benjamin.
3. The chief *was* Ahiezer, then Joash,
the sons of Shemaah the Gibeathite;
and Jeziel, and Pelet, the sons of
Azmaveth; and Berachah, and
Jehu the Antothite.
4. And Ismaiah the Gibeonite, a
mighty man among the thirty, and
over the thirty; and Jeremiah, and
Jahaziel, and Johanan, and
Josabad the Gederathite,
5. Eluzai, and Jerimoth, and Bealiah,
and Shemariah, and Shephatiah
the Haruphite,

6. Elkanah, and Jesiah, and
Azareel, and Joezer, and
Jashobeam, the Korhites,
7. And Joelah, and Zebadiah,
the sons of Jeroham of Gedor.
8. And of
the Gadites there
**separated themselves
unto David** into the hold to the
wilderness men of might, *and*
men of war *fit* for the battle, that
could handle shield and buckler,
**whose faces were
like** the faces of
**lions, and were as swift
as the roes** upon the mountains;
9. Ezer the first, Obadiah the
second, Eliab the third,
10. Mishmannah the fourth,
Jeremiah the fifth,
11. Attai the sixth, Eliel the seventh,
12. Johanan the eighth, Elzabad
the ninth,
13. Jeremiah the tenth,
Machbanai the eleventh.
14. These *were* of
the sons of Gad,
captains of the host: one of the least
was over an hundred, and the
greatest over a thousand.
15. These *are* they that
**went over Jordan in the
first month, when it had
overflown** all his banks;
and they
**put to flight all them of
the valleys,** *both* toward the
east, and toward the west.
16. **And there came** of
**the children of
Benjamin and Judah**
to the hold unto David.
17. **And David went** out
to meet them, and answered
and said unto them,
If ye be
come peaceably unto me
**to help me, mine heart
shall be knit unto you:
but if ye** be come to
betray me to mine
enemies, seeing *there is*
no wrong in mine hands, the

God of our fathers look *thereon,* and rebuke it.

18. **Then** the spirit came upon **Amasai,** *who was* chief of the captains, *and he* said, **Thine are we, David,** and on thy side, thou son of Jesse: peace, peace *be* unto thee, and peace *be* to thine helpers; **for thy God helpeth thee. Then David received them,** and made them captains of the band.

19. **And there fell some of Manasseh to David, when he came with the Philistines against Saul** to battle: **but they helped them not: for** the lords of **the Philistines** upon advisement **sent him away, saying,** **He will fall to** his master **Saul** to *the jeopardy of* our heads.

20. **As he went to Ziklag, there fell to him of Manasseh,** Adnah, and Jozabad, and Jediael, and Michael, and Jozabad, and Elihu, and Zilthai, **captains of the thousands** that *were* of Manasseh.

21. **And they helped David against the band of** *the* **rovers:** for they *were* all mighty men of valour, and were captains in the host.

22. **For** at *that* time **day by day there came to David** to help him, until *it was* **a great host, like the host of God.**

23. **And these are the numbers** of the bands **that** *were* ready armed to the war, *and* **came to David to Hebron,** to turn the kingdom of Saul to him, according to the word of the LORD.

24. **The children of Judah** that bare shield and spear *were* **six thousand** and **eight hundred,** ready armed to the war.

25. **Of the children of Simeon,** mighty men of valour for the war, **seven thousand** and **one hundred.**

26. Of the children **of Levi four thousand** and **six hundred.**

27. **And** Jehoiada *was* **the leader of the Aaronites, and** with him were **three thousand** and **seven hundred;**

28. **And Zadok, a** young man mighty of valour, **and** of his father's house **twenty** and **two captains.**

29. **And of the children of Benjamin,** the kindred of Saul, **three thousand:** for hitherto the greatest part of them had kept the ward of the house of Saul.

30. **And of the children of Ephraim twenty thousand** and **eight hundred,** mighty men of valour, famous throughout the house of their fathers.

31. **And of the half tribe of Manasseh eighteen thousand,** which were expressed by name, to come and make David king.

32. **And of the children of Issachar,** *which were* men that had understanding of the times, to know what Israel ought to do; **the heads of them were two hundred; and all their brethren were at their commandment.**

33. **Of Zebulun,** such as went forth to battle, expert in war, with all instruments of war, **fifty thousand,** which could keep rank: *they were* not of double heart.

34. **And of Naphtali a thousand captains, and with them** with shield and spear **thirty** and **seven thousand.**

35. **And of the**

■ **Danites** expert in war
■ **twenty** and
■ **eight thousand** and
■ **six hundred.**
■ 36. **And of Asher,** such as
went forth to battle, expert in war,
■ **forty thousand.**
37. And on the other side of Jordan,
■ **of the Reubenites, and**
■ **the Gadites, and** of
■ **the half tribe of Manasseh,**
with all manner of instruments
of war for the battle,
■ **an hundred** and
■ **twenty thousand.**
38. All these men of war, that
could keep rank, came with a
perfect heart to Hebron, to
make David king over all Israel:
■ **and all the rest** also
■ **of Israel were of one heart**
■ **to make David king.**
39. **And** there
■ **they were with David**
■ **three days, eating**
■ **and drinking:** for their
brethren had prepared for them.
40. **Moreover they** that were
nigh them, *even* unto Issachar
and Zebulun and Naphtali,
■ **brought bread** on asses, and on
camels, and on mules, and on oxen,
■ **and meat,** meal,
■ **cakes of figs,** and bunches of
■ **raisins, and**
■ **wine, and**
■ **oil, and oxen, and sheep**
■ **abundantly: for there**
■ **was joy in Israel.**

CHAPTER 13

■ 1. **And David consulted**
with the captains of thousands
and hundreds, *and*
■ **with every leader.**
■ 2. **And David said** unto
all the congregation of Israel, If *it*
seem good unto you, and *that it*
be of the LORD our God,
■ **let us send** abroad
■ **unto our brethren**
every where, *that are*
■ **left in** all the land of

■ **Israel, and** with them
■ **also** to
■ **the priests and Levites**
which are in their cities *and* suburbs,
■ **that they** may
■ **gather** themselves
■ **unto us:**
3. **And let us bring** again
■ **the ark of** our
■ **God** to us: for we inquired
not at it in the days of Saul.
■ 4. **And** all
■ **the congregation said**
that they would do so: for
■ **the thing was right** in
the eyes of all the people.
5. So David gathered all Israel
together, from Shihor of Egypt even
unto the entering of Hemath, to bring
the ark of God from Kirjath–jearim.
■ 6. **And David went** up,
and all Israel, to Baalah, *that is,*
■ **to Kirjath–jearim,** which
belonged to Judah,
■ **to bring** up thence
■ **the ark** of God the LORD, that
dwelleth *between* the cherubims,
whose name is called *on it.*
■ 7. **And they carried**
■ **the ark** of God
■ **in a new cart out of the**
■ **house of Abinadab:**
■ **and Uzza and Ahio**
■ **drave the cart.**
■ 8. **And David and all**
■ **Israel played before**
■ **God** with all *their* might, and
■ **with singing, and with**
■ **harps,** and with psalteries,
and with timbrels, and with
cymbals, and with trumpets.
■ 9. **And** when
■ **they came unto the**
■ **threshingfloor of Chidon,**
■ **Uzza put forth his hand**
■ **to hold the ark; for the**
■ **oxen stumbled.**
■ 10. **And the anger of the**
■ **LORD was kindled against**
■ **Uzza, and he smote him,**
■ **because he put his hand**
■ **to the ark:** and there he
died before God.

11. And David was displeased, because the LORD had made a breach upon Uzza: wherefore that place is called Perez-uzza to this day.

12. **And David was afraid of God** that day, **saying, How shall I bring the ark** of God **home** to me?

13. **So David** brought not the ark *home* to himself to the city of David, but **carried it** aside **into the house of Obed-edom** the Gittite.

14. **And the ark** of God **remained** with the family of Obed-edom **in his house three months. And the LORD blessed** the house of **Obed-edom, and all that he had.**

CHAPTER 14

1. **Now Hiram king of Tyre sent messengers to David, and timber** of cedars, **with masons** and carpenters, **to build him an house.**

2. **And David perceived** that **the LORD had confirmed him king** over Israel, for his kingdom was lifted up on high, because of his people Israel.

3. **And David took more wives** at Jerusalem: **and** David **begat** more **sons and daughters.**

4. Now these *are* the names of *his* children which he had in Jerusalem; Shammua, and Shobab, Nathan, and Solomon,

5. And Ibhar, and Elishua, and Elpalet,

6. And Nogah, and Nepheg, and Japhia,

7. And Elishama, and Beeliada, and Eliphalet.

8. **And when the Philistines heard that David was anointed king** over all Israel, all **the Philistines went up to seek David.** And David heard *of it*, and went out against them.

9. And the Philistines came and spread themselves in the valley of Rephaim.

10. **And David inquired of God, saying, Shall I go** up **against the Philistines?** And wilt thou deliver them into mine hand? **And the LORD said** unto him, **Go** up; for **I will deliver them** into thine hand.

11. So they came up to Baal-perazim; **and David smote them** there. Then David said, God hath broken **in** upon mine enemies by mine hand like the breaking forth of waters: therefore they called the name of that place **Baal-perazim.**

12. **And when they had left their gods there, David gave a commandment, and they were burned** with fire.

13. **And the Philistines** yet **again spread themselves** abroad **in the valley.**

14. **Therefore David inquired again of God; and God said** unto him, **Go not up after** them; turn away from them, **and come upon them over against the mulberry trees.**

15. **And** it shall be, **when thou shalt hear a sound** of going **in the tops of the** mulberry **trees,** *that* then **thou shalt go** out **to battle:** for God is gone forth before thee to smite the host of the Philistines.

16. **David** therefore

did as God commanded him: and they **smote the** host of the **Philistines** from Gibeon even to Gazer.

17. And the fame of David went out into all lands; and the LORD brought the fear of him upon all nations.

CHAPTER 15

1. And David made him houses in the city of David, and prepared a place for the ark of God, and pitched for it a tent.

2. Then David said, None ought to carry the ark of God **but the Levites:** for them hath the LORD chosen to carry the ark of God, and to minister unto him for ever.

3. And David gathered all Israel together to Jerusalem, **to bring up the ark** of the LORD **unto his place,** which he had prepared for it.

4. And David assembled the children of Aaron, and the Levites:

5. Of the sons of Kohath; Uriel the chief, and his brethren an hundred and twenty:

6. Of the sons of Merari; Asaiah the chief, and his brethren two hundred and twenty:

7. Of the sons of Gershom; Joel the chief and his brethren an hundred and thirty:

8. Of the sons of Elizaphan; Shemaiah the chief, and his brethren two hundred:

9. Of the sons of Hebron; Eliel the chief, and his brethren fourscore:

10. Of the sons of Uzziel;Amminadab the chief, and his brethren an hundred and twelve.

11. And David called for Zadok and Abiathar the priests, and for the Levites, for Uriel, Asaiah, and Joel, Shemaiah, and Eliel,and Amminadab,

12. And said unto them, Ye are the chief of the fathers of the **Levites: sanctify yourselves,** *both* ye and your brethren, **that ye may bring up the ark** of the LORD God of Israel **unto the place that I have prepared** for it.

13. For because ye did it not at the first, the LORD our **God made a breach upon us,** for that we sought him not after the due order.

14. So the priests and the Levites sanctified themselves to bring up the ark of the LORD God of Israel.

15. And the children of the Levites **bare the ark** of God **upon their shoulders with the staves** thereon, **as Moses commanded** according to the word of the LORD.

16. And David spake to the chief of the **Levites to appoint** their brethren *to be the* **singers with instruments of music,** psalteries and harps and cymbals, sounding, by lifting up the voice with joy.

17. So the Levites appointed Heman the son of Joel; **and of his brethren,** Asaph the son of Berechiah; and of the sons of Merari their brethren, Ethan the son of Kushaiah;

18. And with them their brethren of the second degree, Zechariah, Ben, and Jaaziel, and Shemiramoth, and Jehiel, and Unni, Eliab, and Benaiah, and Maaseiah, and Mattithiah, and Elipheleh, and Mikneiah, and Obed–edom, and Jeiel, the porters.

19. So the singers, Heman, Asaph, and Ethan, *were appointed* to sound with cymbals of brass;

20. And Zechariah, and Aziel, and Shemiramoth, and Jehiel, and Unni, and Eliab, and Maaseiah, and Benaiah, with psalteries on Alamoth;

21. And Mattithiah, and Elipheleh, and Mikneiah, and Obed–edom, and Jeiel, and Azaziah, with harps on the Sheminith to excel.

22. **And Chenaniah,** chief of the Levites, *was* for song: he **instructed about the song,** because he *was* skilful.

23. **And Berechiah and Elkanah were doorkeepers for the ark.**

24. **And Shebaniah,** and **Jehoshaphat,** and **Nethaneel,** and **Amasai,** and **Zechariah,** and **Benaiah, and Eliezer,** the priests, **did blow with the trumpets** before the ark of God: **and Obed–edom and Jehiah were doorkeepers for the ark.**

25. **So David, and the elders** of Israel, and the captains over thousands, **went to bring** up **the ark** of the covenant of the LORD **out of the house of Obed–edom** with joy.

26. **And** it came to pass, when **God helped the Levites that bare the ark** of the covenant of the LORD, that they offered seven bullocks and seven rams.

27. **And David was clothed with a robe of** fine **linen, and** all **the Levites** that bare the ark, **and** the **singers, and** Chenaniah the master of the song with the singers: **David also had upon him an ephod of linen.**

28. **Thus all Israel brought up the ark** of the covenant of the LORD **with shouting, and with sound of the cornet,** and with **trumpets, and** with **cymbals,** making a noise with psalteries and harps.

29. **And** it came to pass, **as the ark** of the covenant of the LORD **came to the city** of David, that **Michal, the daughter of Saul** looking out at a window **saw** king **David dancing** and playing: **and she despised him in her heart.**

CHAPTER 16

1. **So they brought the ark** of God, **and set it in the** midst of the **tent that David had pitched** for it: **and** they **offered burnt sacrifices and peace offerings** before God.

2. **And** when **David** had made an end of offering the burnt offerings and the peace offerings, he **blessed the people in the name of the LORD.**

3. **And he dealt to every one of Israel,** both man and woman, to every one **a loaf of bread, and a** good **piece of flesh, and a flagon of wine.**

4. **And he appointed** *certain* of the **Levites to minister before the ark** of the LORD, and **to record, and to thank and praise the LORD** God of Israel:

5. Asaph the chief, and next to him Zechariah, Jeiel, and Shemiramoth, and Jehiel, and Mattithiah, and Eliab, and Benaiah, and Obed–edom: and Jeiel with psalteries and with harps; but Asaph made a sound with cymbals;

6. Benaiah also and Jahaziel the priests with trumpets continually before the ark of the covenant of God.

7. **Then** on that day **David delivered first this**

psalm to thank the LORD into the hand of Asaph and his brethren.

8. Give thanks unto the LORD, call upon his name, make known his deeds among the people.

9. Sing unto him, sing psalms unto him, talk ye of all his wondrous works.

10. Glory ye in his holy name: let the heart of them rejoice that seek the LORD.

11. Seek the LORD and his strength, seek his face continually.

12. Remember his marvellous works that he hath done, his wonders, and the judgments of his mouth;

13. O ye seed of Israel his servant, ye children of Jacob, his chosen ones.

14. He is the LORD our God; his judgments are in all the earth.

15. Be ye mindful always of his covenant; the word *which* he commanded to a thousand generations;

16. *Even of the covenant* which he made with Abraham, and of his oath unto Isaac;

17. And hath confirmed the same to Jacob for a law, *and* to Israel for an everlasting covenant,

18. Saying, Unto thee will I give the land of Canaan, the lot of your inheritance;

19. When ye were but few, even a few, and strangers in it.

20. And *when* they went from nation to nation, and from *one* kingdom to another people;

21. He suffered no man to do them wrong: yea, he reproved kings for their sakes,

22. *Saying,* Touch not mine anointed, and do my prophets no harm.

23. Sing unto the LORD, all the earth; shew forth from day to day his salvation.

24. Declare his glory among the heathen; his marvellous works among all nations.

25. For great is the LORD, and greatly to be praised: he also *is* to be feared above all gods.

26. For all the gods of the people are idols: but the LORD made the heavens.

27. Glory and honour *are* in his presence; strength and gladness *are* in his place.

28. Give unto the LORD, ye kindreds of the people, give unto the LORD glory and strength.

29. Give unto the LORD the glory due unto his name: bring an offering, and come before him: worship the LORD in the beauty of holiness.

30. Fear before him, all the earth: the world also shall be stable, that it be not moved.

31. Let the heavens be glad, and let the earth rejoice: and let *men* say among the nations, The LORD reigneth.

32. Let the sea roar, and the fulness thereof: let the fields rejoice, and all that *is* therein.

33. Then shall the trees of the wood sing out at the presence of the LORD, because he cometh to judge the earth.

34. O give thanks unto the LORD; for he is good; for his mercy endureth for ever.

35. And say ye, Save us, O God of our salvation, and gather us together, and deliver us from the heathen, that we may give thanks to thy holy name, *and* glory in thy praise.

36. Blessed *be* the LORD God

of Israel for ever and ever.
**And all the people said,
Amen,** and praised the LORD.
37. **So he left** there before the
ark of the covenant of the LORD
**Asaph and his brethren,
to minister before the
ark continually,** as
every day's work required:
38. **And Obed-edom with
their brethren,** threescore and
eight; Obed–edom also the son of
Jeduthun and Hosah *to be* porters:
39. And Zadok the priest, and his
brethren the priests, before the
tabernacle of the LORD in the high
place that *was* at Gibeon,
40. **To offer burnt offerings
unto the LORD** upon the altar
of the burnt offering continually
morning and evening,
and to do according to
**all that is written in the
law of the LORD,** which
he commanded Israel;
41. And with them
Heman and Jeduthun,
**and the rest that
were chosen,** who
were expressed by name,
to give thanks to the LORD,
because his mercy *endureth* for ever;
42. And with them Heman and
Jeduthun with trumpets and
cymbals for those that should
make a sound, and with musical
instruments of God. And the
sons of Jeduthun *were* porters.
43. **And all the people
departed** every man
to his house: and David
returned to bless his house.

CHAPTER 17

1. **Now** it came to pass, as
David sat in his house, that
**David said to Nathan the
prophet, Lo, I dwell in an
house of cedars, but the
ark** of the covenant of the LORD
remaineth under curtains.
2. **Then Nathan
said** unto David,

**Do all that is in thine heart;
for God is with thee.**
3. **And** it came to pass
the same night, that
**the word of God came
to Nathan, saying,**
4. Go and
tell David my servant,
Thus saith the LORD,
**Thou shalt not build me
an house** to dwell in:
5. **For I have not dwelt in
an house** since the day that
I brought up Israel unto this day;
but have gone from
tent to tent, and
**from one tabernacle
to another.**
6. **Wheresoever** I
have walked with all Israel,
spake I a word
to any of
the judges of Israel,
whom I commanded to
feed my people, saying,
**Why have ye not built
me an house** of cedars?
7. **Now therefore** thus shalt thou
say unto my servant
David, Thus saith the
LORD of hosts,
**I took thee from the
sheepcote,** even from
following the sheep,
**that thou shouldest
be ruler over** my people
Israel:
8. **And I have been with
thee** whithersoever thou hast
walked, and have cut off all
thine enemies from before thee,
and have
made thee a name like
the name of the great men
that *are* in the earth.
9. **Also I will ordain
a place for** my people
Israel, and will plant them,
and they shall dwell
in their place, and
shall be moved no more;
neither shall the children of
wickedness waste them any more,

as at the beginning,

10. And since the time that I commanded judges *to be* over my people Israel. Moreover

I will subdue all thine enemies.

Furthermore I tell thee that the LORD will build thee an house.

11. **And** it shall come to pass, **when thy days be expired** that thou must go *to be* with thy fathers, that **I will raise up thy seed** after thee, which shall be of thy sons; **and I will establish his kingdom.**

12. **He shall build me an house, and I will stablish his throne for ever.**

13. I will be his father, and he shall be my son: **and I will not take my mercy away from him,** as I took *it* from *him* that was before thee:

14. But I will settle him in mine house and in my kingdom for ever: **and his throne shall be established for evermore.**

15. According to all these words, and according to all this vision, so did Nathan speak unto David.

16. **And David** the king came and sat before the LORD, and **said, Who am I, O LORD** God, and what *is* mine house, **that thou hast brought me hitherto?**

17. And *yet* this was a small thing in thine eyes, O God; for thou hast *also* spoken of thy servant's house for a great while to come, and hast regarded me according to the estate of a man of high degree, O LORD God.

18. What can David *speak* more to thee for the honour of thy servant? for thou knowest thy servant.

19. **O LORD,** for thy servant's sake, and **according to thine own heart, hast thou done all this greatness,** in making known all *these* great things.

20. **O LORD, there is none like thee,** neither *is there any* God beside thee, according to all that we have heard with our ears.

21. **And what** one **nation** in the earth **is like** thy people **Israel, whom God went to redeem to be his own** people, to make thee a name of greatness and terribleness, by driving out nations from before thy people whom thou hast redeemed out of Egypt?

22. For thy people Israel didst thou make thine own people for ever; and thou, LORD, becamest their God.

23. **Therefore** now, **LORD, let the thing** that thou hast **spoken concerning thy servant and** concerning **his house be established** for ever, and do as thou hast said.

24. Let it even be established, **that thy name may be magnified for ever, saying, The LORD of hosts is the God of Israel,** *even* a God to Israel: and *let* the house of David thy servant *be* established before thee.

25. For thou, O my God, hast told thy servant that thou wilt build him an house: therefore thy servant hath found *in his heart* to pray before thee.

26. And now, LORD, thou art God, and hast promised this goodness unto thy servant:

27. **Now** therefore let it please thee to **bless the house of thy servant,** that it may be before thee for ever: for thou blessest, O LORD, **and it shall be blessed for ever.**

CHAPTER 18

1. **Now after this** it came to pass, that **David smote the Philistines, and subdued them,** and took Gath and her towns out of the hand of the Philistines.

2. **And** he smote Moab; and **the Moabites became**

639

David's servants, *and* brought gifts.

3. And David smote Hadarezer king of Zobah unto Hamath, as he went to stablish his dominion by the river Euphrates.

4. And David took from him a thousand chariots, and seven thousand horsemen, and twenty thousand footmen: David also houghed all the chariot horses, but reserved of them an hundred chariots.

5. And when the Syrians of Damascus came to help Hadarezer king of Zobah, David slew of the Syrians two and twenty thousand men.

6. Then David put *garrisons* in Syria–damascus; *and* the Syrians became David's servants, and brought gifts. Thus the LORD preserved David whithersoever he went.

7. And David took the shields of gold that were on the servants of Hadarezer, and brought them to Jerusalem.

8. Likewise from Tibhath, and from Chun, cities of Hadarezer, brought David very much brass, wherewith Solomon made the brasen sea, and the pillars, and the vessels of brass.

9. Now when Tou king of Hamath heard how David had smitten all the host of Hadarezer king of Zobah;

10. He sent Hadoram his son to king David, to inquire of his welfare, and to congratulate him, because he had fought against Hadarezer, and smitten him; (for Hadarezer had war with Tou;)

and with him all manner of vessels of gold and silver and brass.

11. Them also king David dedicated unto the LORD, with the silver and the gold that he brought from all these nations; from Edom, and from Moab, and from the children of Ammon, and from the Philistines, and from Amalek.

12. Moreover Abishai the son of Zeruiah slew of the Edomites in the valley of salt eighteen thousand.

13. And he put garrisons in Edom; and all the Edomites became David's servants. Thus the LORD preserved David whithersoever he went.

14. So David reigned over all Israel, and executed judgment and justice among all his people.

15. And Joab the son of Zeruiah *was* over the host; and Jehoshaphat the son of Ahilud, recorder.

16. And Zadok the son of Ahitub, and Abimelech the son of Abiathar, *were* the priests; and Shavsha was scribe;

17. And Benaiah the son of Jehoiada *was* over the Cherethites and the Pelethites; and the sons of David *were* chief about the king.

CHAPTER 19

1. Now it came to pass after this, that Nahash the king of the children of Ammon died, and his son reigned in his stead.

2. And David said, I will shew kindness unto Hanun the son of Nahash, because his father shewed kindness to me. And David sent messengers to comfort him concerning his father. So the servants of David came into the land

of the children of Ammon to Hanun, to comfort him.

3. **But the princes** of the children **of Ammon said** to Hanun, **Thinkest thou that David doth honour thy father,** that he hath sent comforters unto thee? **are not his servants come** unto thee for to search, and to overthrow, and **to spy out the land?**

4. **Wherefore Hanun took David's servants, and shaved them, and cut off their garments** in the midst hard by their buttocks, **and sent them away.**

5. **Then** there went *certain*, and told **David** how the men were served. And he **sent to meet them: for the men were** greatly **ashamed. And** the king said, Tarry at Jericho **until your beards be grown,** and *then* return.

6. **And when** the children of **Ammon saw** that **they had made themselves odious to David, Hanun** and the children of Ammon **sent a thousand talents of silver to hire** them **chariots and horsemen out of Mesopotamia, and** out of **Syria–maachah, and** out of **Zobah.**

7. **So they** hired thirty and two thousand chariots, and the king of Maachah and his people; who came and pitched before Medeba. And the children of Ammon gathered themselves together from their cities, and **came to battle.**

8. **And when David heard** *of it,* **he sent Joab, and all** the host of **the mighty men.**

9. And the children of Ammon came out, and put the battle in array before the gate of the city: and the kings that were come *were* by themselves in the field.

10. **Now when Joab saw** that **the battle was** set **against him** before and behind, **he chose** out of all **the choice of Israel, and put them in array against the Syrians.**

11. **And the rest** of the people he delivered unto the hand of Abishai his brother, and they set *themselves* in array **against** the children of **Ammon.**

12. **And he said, If the Syrians be too strong for me,** then thou shalt **help me: but if** the children of **Ammon be too strong for thee, then I will help thee.**

13. **Be of good courage,** and let us behave ourselves valiantly for our people, and for the cities of our God: and **let the LORD do that which is good in his sight.**

14. **So Joab** and the people that *were* with him **drew nigh before the Syrians** unto the battle; **and they fled before him.**

15. **And when** the children of **Ammon saw that the Syrians** were **fled, they likewise fled** before Abishai his brother, and entered into the city. Then Joab came to Jerusalem.

16. **And** when the Syrians saw that they were put to the worse before Israel, they **sent messengers, and drew forth the Syrians** that *were* **beyond the river:** and Shophach the captain of the host of Hadarezer *went* before them.

17. **And** it was told **David;** and he **gathered** all **Israel, and passed over Jordan,** and came upon them, **and set the battle in array**

against them. So when David had put *the battle* in array against the Syrians, they fought with him.

18. But the Syrians fled before Israel; and David slew of the Syrians seven thousand men *which fought* in chariots, and forty thousand footmen, and killed Shophach the captain of the host.

19. And when the servants of Hadarezer saw that they were put to the worse before Israel, they made peace with David, and became his servants: neither would the Syrians help the children of Ammon any more.

CHAPTER 20

1. And it came to pass, that after the year was expired, at the time that kings go out to battle, Joab led forth the power of the army, and wasted the country of the children of Ammon, and came and besieged Rabbah. But David tarried at Jerusalem. And Joab smote Rabbah, and destroyed it.

2. And David took the crown of their king from off his head, and found it to weigh a talent of gold, and there were precious stones in it; and it was set upon David's head: and he brought also exceeding much spoil out of the city.

3. And he brought out the people that *were* in it, and cut them with saws, and with harrows of iron, and with axes. Even so dealt David with all the cities of the children of Ammon. And David and all the people returned to Jerusalem.

4. And it came to pass after this, that there arose war at Gezer with the Philistines; at which time Sibbechai the Hushathite slew Sippai, *that was* of the children of the giant: and they were subdued.

5. And there was war again with the Philistines; and Elhanan the son of Jair slew Lahmi the brother of Goliath the Gittite, whose spear staff *was* like a weaver's beam.

6. And yet again there was war at Gath, where was a man of great stature, whose fingers and toes were four and twenty, six on each hand, and six *on each* foot and he also was the son of the giant.

7. But when he defied Israel, Jonathan the son of Shimea David's brother slew him.

8. These were born unto the giant in Gath; and they fell by the hand of David, and by the hand of his servants.

CHAPTER 21

1. And Satan stood up against Israel, and provoked David to number Israel.

2. And David said to Joab and to the rulers of the people, Go, number Israel from Beer–sheba even to Dan; and bring the number of them to me, that I may know *it*.

3. And Joab answered, The LORD make his people an hundred times so many more as they *be*: but, my lord the king, *are* they not all my lord's servants? why then doth my lord require this thing? why will he be a cause of trespass to Israel?

4. Nevertheless the king's word prevailed against

Joab. Wherefore Joab departed, and went throughout all Israel, and came to Jerusalem.

5. **And Joab gave** the sum of **the number of the people unto David. And all they of Israel were a thousand thousand and an hundred thousand men** that drew sword: **and Judah was four hundred threescore and ten thousand** men that drew sword.

6. **But Levi and Benjamin counted he not** among them: **for the king's word was abominable to Joab.**

7. **And God was displeased with this thing; therefore he smote Israel.**

8. **And David said unto God, I have sinned** greatly, because I have done this thing: **but** now, I beseech thee, **do away the iniquity** of thy servant; **for I have done** very **foolishly.**

9. **And the LORD spake unto Gad, David's seer, saying,**

10. Go and **tell David,** saying, Thus saith the LORD, **I offer** thee **three things: choose** thee **one** of them, **that I may do it unto thee.**

11. **So Gad came** to David, **and said** unto him, Thus saith the LORD, **Choose** thee

12. **Either three years' famine; or three months to be destroyed before** thy foes, while that the sword of **thine enemies** overtaketh *thee;* **or else three days** the sword **of** the LORD, even the **pestilence, in the land,** and the angel of the LORD destroying throughout all the coasts **of Israel.** Now therefore advise thyself what word I shall bring

again to him that sent me.

13. **And David said** unto Gad, I am in a great strait: **let me fall now into the hand of the LORD; for** very **great are his mercies: but let me not fall into the hand of man.**

14. **So the LORD sent pestilence upon Israel:** and there fell of Israel seventy thousand men.

15. **And God sent an angel unto Jerusalem to destroy it: and as he was destroying, the LORD** beheld, and he **repented** him of the evil, **and said to the angel** that destroyed, **It is enough,** stay now thine hand. **And the angel** of the LORD **stood by the threshingfloor of Ornan** the Jebusite.

16. **And David** lifted up his eyes, and **saw the angel** of the LORD stand between the earth and the heaven, **having a drawn sword** in his hand **stretched out over Jerusalem. Then David and the elders** of Israel, who *were* clothed in sackcloth, **fell upon their faces.**

17. **And David said** unto God, *Is it* not **I that commanded the people to be numbered?** even I it is that **have sinned** and done evil indeed; **but** *as for* these sheep, **what have they done? let thine hand,** I pray thee, O LORD my God, **be on me,** and on my father's house; but not on thy people, that they should be plagued.

18. **Then the angel** of the LORD **commanded** Gad to say to David, **that David** should go up, and

set up an altar unto the LORD
in the threshingfloor of
Ornan the Jebusite.
19. And David went up at the
saying of Gad, which he spake
in the name of the LORD.
20. And Ornan turned back, and
saw the angel; and his
four sons with him
hid themselves.
Now Ornan was threshing wheat.
21. And as David came to Ornan,
Ornan looked and
saw David, and went out of
the threshingfloor, and bowed himself
to David with his face
to the ground.
22. Then David said to
Ornan, Grant me the place of
this threshingfloor, that I
may build an altar therein
unto the LORD: thou shalt grant
it me for the full price:
that the plague may be
stayed from the people.
23. And Ornan said unto David,
Take *it* to thee, and let
my lord the king do *that which
is* good in his eyes: lo,
I give thee the oxen also for
burnt offerings, and the
threshing instruments for
wood, and the wheat for
the meat offering; I give it all.
24. And king
David said to Ornan,
Nay; but I will verily
buy it for the full price:
for I will not take
that which is thine for
the LORD, nor offer burnt
offerings without cost.
25. So David gave to
Ornan for the place
six hundred shekels
of gold by weight.
26. And David
built there
an altar unto the LORD,
and offered
burnt offerings and peace
offerings, and called upon
the LORD; and he answered

him from heaven
by fire upon the altar
of burnt offering.
27. And the LORD commanded the
angel; and he
put up his sword again
into the sheath thereof.
28. At that time
when David saw that the
LORD had answered
him in the threshingfloor of
Ornan the Jebusite,
then he sacrificed there.
29. For the tabernacle
of the LORD, which Moses
made in the wilderness,
and the altar of
the burnt offering,
were at that season
in the high place at
Gibeon.
30. But David could
not go before it
to inquire of God: for he
was afraid because of the sword
of the angel of the LORD.

CHAPTER 22

1. Then David said, This *is* the house
of the LORD God, and this *is* the altar
of the burnt offering for Israel.
2. And David commanded
to gather together the strangers that
were in the land of Israel; and he set
masons to hew wrought
stones to build the
house of God.
3. And David prepared
iron in abundance
for the
nails for the doors of the
gates, and for the joinings;
and brass in
abundance without weight;
4. Also cedar trees in
abundance: for the Zidonians
and they of Tyre brought much
cedar wood to David.
5. And David
said, Solomon my son
is young and tender,
and the house *that is*
to be builded for the LORD

644

■ **must be exceeding**
■ **magnifical,** of fame and of
glory throughout all countries:
■ **I will therefore** now
■ **make preparation** for it.
So David prepared abundantly
before his death.
■ 6. **Then he called** for
■ **Solomon** his son,
■ **and charged him to**
■ **build an house for**
■ **the LORD** God of Israel.
■ 7. **And David said** to
Solomon, My son, as for me,
■ **it was in my mind to build**
■ **an house unto the** name of the
■ **LORD** my God:
■ 8. **But the word of**
■ **the LORD came** to me,
■ **saying, Thou hast shed**
■ **blood abundantly,**
and hast made great wars:
■ **thou shalt not build an**
■ **house unto my name,**
because thou hast shed much
blood upon the earth in my sight.
■ 9. **Behold, a son**
■ **shall be born** to thee,
■ **who shall be a man of**
■ **rest;** and I will give him rest from
all his enemies round about: for
■ **his name shall be Solomon,**
■ and I will give peace and quietness
unto Israel in his days.
■ 10. **He shall build an house**
■ **for my name;** and he shall be
my son, and I *will be* his father;
and I will establish the throne of
his kingdom over Israel for ever.
■ 11. **Now, my son, the**
■ **LORD be with thee;**
and prosper thou, and
■ **build the house of the LORD**
thy God, as he hath said of thee.
■ 12. **Only the LORD give**
■ **thee wisdom and**
■ **understanding,** and give
thee charge concerning Israel,
■ **that thou mayest keep**
■ **the law** of the LORD thy God.
■ 13. **Then shalt thou prosper,**
if thou takest heed to fulfil the statutes
and judgments which the LORD

charged Moses with concerning
Israel: be strong, and of good
courage; dread not, nor be dismayed.
14. Now, behold, in my trouble
■ **I have prepared for the**
■ **house of the LORD** an hundred
thousand talents of gold, and a
thousand thousand talents of
silver; and of brass and iron without
weight; for it is in abundance: timber
also and stone have I prepared;
■ **and thou mayest**
■ **add thereto.**
■ 15. **Moreover there are**
■ **workmen with thee**
in abundance, hewers and workers
of stone and timber, and
all manner of cunning men
for every manner of work.
16. Of the gold, the silver,
and the brass, and the iron,
there is no number.
■ **Arise** *therefore,*
■ **and be doing, and**
■ **the LORD be with thee.**
■ 17. **David also**
■ **commanded all the**
■ **princes of Israel to**
■ **help Solomon** his son,
■ **saying,**
18. *Is* not the LORD your God with
you? and hath he *not* given you rest
on every side? for he hath given the
inhabitants of the land into mine hand;
and the land is subdued before the
LORD, and before his people.
■ 19. **Now set your heart**
and your soul
■ **to seek the LORD** your God;
■ **arise** therefore,
■ **and build ye the sanctuary**
■ **of the LORD** God,
■ **to bring the ark**
of the covenant of the LORD,
■ **and the holy vessels** of God,
■ **into the house that is to**
■ **be built** to the name of the LORD.

CHAPTER 23

■ 1. **So when David**
■ **was old** and full of days,
■ **he made Solomon** his son
■ **king** over Israel.

■ 2. **And he gathered** together all
■ **the princes** of Israel,
■ **with the priests and** the
■ **Levites.**
■ 3. **Now the**
■ **Levites** were numbered
■ **from** the age of
■ **thirty years and upward:**
and their number by their polls,
■ **man by man, was thirty** and
■ **eight thousand.**
■ 4. **Of which, twenty** and
■ **four thousand were to**
■ **set forward the work of**
■ **the house of the LORD;**
■ **and six thousand were**
■ **officers and judges:**
■ 5. **Moreover four thousand**
■ **were porters; and four**
■ **thousand praised the LORD**
with the instruments which I made,
said David, to praise *therewith*.
■ 6. **And David divided**
them into courses among
the sons of Levi, *namely,* Gershon,
Kohath, and Merari.
7. Of the Gershonites *were,*
Laadan, and Shimei.
8. The sons of Laadan; the chief *was*
Jehiel, and Zetham, and Joel, three.
9. The sons of Shimei; Shelomith, and
Haziel, and Haran, three. These *were*
the chief of the fathers of Laadan.
10. And the sons of Shimei *were,*
Jahath, Zina, and Jeush, and Beriah.
These four *were* the sons of Shimei.
11. And Jahath was the chief, and
Zizah the second: but Jeush and
Beriah had not many sons; therefore
they were in one reckoning,
according to *their* father's house.
12. The sons of Kohath; Amram,
Izhar, Hebron, and Uzziel, four.
13. The sons of Amram; Aaron and
Moses: and Aaron was separated,
that he should sanctify the most holy
things, he and his sons for ever, to
burn incense before the LORD, to
minister unto him, and to bless in
his name for ever.
14. Now *concerning* Moses the
man of God, his sons were named
of the tribe of Levi.

15. The sons of Moses
were, Gershom, and Eliezer.
16. Of the sons of Gershom,
Shebuel *was* the chief.
17. And the sons of Eliezer *were,*
Rehabiah the chief. And Eliezer
had none other sons; but the sons
of Rehabiah were very many.
18. Of the sons of Izhar;
Shelomith the chief.
19. Of the sons of Hebron; Jeriah the
first, Amariah the second, Jahaziel
the third, and Jekameam the fourth.
20. Of the sons of Uzziel; Micah the
first and Jesiah the second.
21. The sons of Merari; Mahli,
and Mushi. The sons of Mahli;
Eleazar, and Kish.
22. And Eleazar died, and had
no sons, but daughters: and their
brethren the sons of Kish took them.
23. The sons of Mushi; Mahli,
and Eder, and Jeremoth, three.
24. These *were*
■ **the sons of Levi** after the
house of their fathers; *even* the
chief of the fathers, as they were
counted by number of names by
their polls, that did the work
■ **for the service of the house**
■ **of the LORD, from** the age of
■ **twenty years and upward.**
■ 25. **For David said,**
■ **The LORD** God of Israel
■ **hath given rest unto his**
■ **people,** that they may dwell
in Jerusalem for ever:
■ 26. **And** also unto
■ **the Levites;** they
■ **shall no more carry the**
■ **tabernacle,** nor any vessels
of it for the service thereof.
27. For by the last words of David
the Levites *were* numbered from
twenty years old and above:
■ 28. **Because their office**
■ **was to wait on the sons**
■ **of Aaron for the service**
■ **of the house of the LORD,**
in the courts, and in the chambers,
■ **and in** the
■ **purifying** of all
■ **holy things,** and the work of

the service of the house of God;

29. **Both for the shewbread, and** for the fine flour for **meat offering, and** for the **unleavened cakes,** and for *that which is baked in* the pan, and for that which is fried, and for all manner of measure and size;

30. **And to stand every morning to thank and praise the LORD, and likewise at even:**

31. **And to offer all burnt sacrifices unto the LORD** in the sabbaths, in the new moons, and on the set feasts, by number, according to the order commanded unto them, continually before the LORD:

32. **And that they should keep** the **charge of the tabernacle** of the congregation, **and** the charge of **the holy place, and** the charge **of the sons of Aaron** their brethren, **in the service** of the house **of the LORD.**

CHAPTER 24

1. **Now these are the divisions of the sons of Aaron. The sons of** Aaron; Nadab, and Abihu, Eleazar, and Ithamar.

2. But Nadab and Abihu died before their father, and had no children: therefore **Eleazar and Ithamar executed the priest's office.**

3. And David distributed them, both Zadok of the sons of Eleazar, and Ahimelech of the sons of Ithamar, according to their offices in their service.

4. And there were more chief men found of the sons of Eleazar than of the sons of Ithamar, and *thus* were they divided. **Among the sons of Eleazar there were sixteen chief men** of the house of *their* fathers, **and eight among the sons of Ithamar** according to the house of their fathers.

5. **Thus were they divided by lot,** one sort with another; **for the governors of the sanctuary,** and governors *of the house* of God, were of the sons of Eleazar, and of the sons of Ithamar.

6. And Shemaiah the son of Nethaneel the scribe, *one* of the Levites, wrote them before the king, and the princes, and Zadok the priest, and Ahimelech the son of Abiathar, and *before* the chief of the fathers of the priests and Levites: one principal household being taken for Eleazar, and *one* taken for Ithamar.

7. Now the first lot came forth to Jehoiarib, the second to Jedaiah,

8. The third to Harim, the fourth to Seorim,

9. The fifth to Malchijah, the sixth to Mijamin,

10. The seventh to Hakkoz, the eighth to Abijah,

11. The ninth to Jeshuah, the tenth to Shecaniah,

12. The eleventh to Eliashib, the twelfth to Jakim,

13. The thirteenth to Huppah, the fourteenth to Jeshebeab,

14. The fifteenth to Bilgah, the sixteenth to Immer,

15. The seventeenth to Hezir, the eighteenth to Aphses,

16. The nineteenth to Pethahiah, the twentieth to Jehezekel,

17. The one and twentieth to Jachin, the two and twentieth to Gamul,

18. The three and twentieth to Delaiah, the four and twentieth to Maaziah.

19. These *were* the orderings of them in their service to come into the house of the LORD, according to their manner, under Aaron their father, as the LORD God of Israel had commanded him.

20. And the rest of the sons of Levi *were these*: Of the sons of Amram; Shubael: of the sons of Shubael;

Jehdeiah.

21. Concerning Rehabiah: of the sons of Rehabiah, the first was Isshiah.

22. Of the Izharites; Shelomoth: of the sons of Shelomoth; Jahath.

23. And the sons *of Hebron*; Jeriah *the first*, Amariah the second, Jahaziel the third, Jekameam the fourth.

24. *Of* the sons of Uzziel; Michah: of the sons of Michah; Shamir.

25. The brother of Michah *was* Isshiah: of the sons of Isshiah; Zechariah.

26. The sons of Merari *were* Mahli and Mushi: the sons of Jaaziah; Beno.

27. The sons of Merari by Jaaziah; Beno, and Shoham, and Zaccur, and Ibri.

28. Of Mahli *came* Eleazar, who had no sons.

29. Concerning Kish: the son of Kish *was* Jerahmeel.

30. The sons also of Mushi; Mahli, and Eder, and Jerimoth. These *were* the sons of the Levites after the house of their fathers.

31. These likewise cast lots over against their brethren the sons of Aaron in the presence of David the king, and Zadok, and Ahimelech, and the chief of the fathers of the priests and Levites, even the principal fathers over against their younger brethren.

CHAPTER 25

1. **Moreover David and the captains** of the host **separated to the service of the sons of Asaph,** and of Heman, and of Jeduthun, **who should prophesy with harps,** with **psalteries, and** with **cymbals: and the number of the workmen** according to their service **was:**

2. Of the sons of Asaph; Zaccur, and Joseph, and Nethaniah, and Asarelah, the sons of Asaph under the hands of Asaph, which prophesied according to the order of the king.

3. Of Jeduthun: the sons of Jeduthun; Gedaliah, and Zeri, and Jeshaiah, Hashabiah, and Mattithiah, six, under the hands of their father Jeduthun, who prophesied with a harp, to give thanks and to praise the LORD.

4. Of Heman: the sons of Heman: Bukkiah, Mattaniah, Uzziel, Shebuel, and Jerimoth, Hananiah, Hanani, Eliathah, Giddalti, and Romamtiezer, Joshbekashah, Mallothi, Hothir, *and* Mahazioth:

5. All these *were* the sons of Heman the king's seer in the words of God, to lift up the horn. And God gave to Heman fourteen sons and three daughters.

6. All these *were* under the hands of their father for song *in* the house of the LORD, with cymbals, psalteries, and harps, for the service of the house of God, according to the king's order to Asaph, Jeduthun, and Heman.

7. So the number of them, with their brethren that were instructed in the songs of the LORD, *even* all that were cunning, was **two hundred fourscore and eight.**

8. **And they cast lots, ward against ward, as well the small as the great,** the teacher as the scholar.

9. Now the first lot came forth for Asaph to Joseph: the second to Gedaliah, who with his brethren and sons *were* twelve:

10. The third to Zaccur, *he*, his sons, and his brethren, *were* twelve:

11. The fourth to Izri, *he*, his sons, and his brethren, *were* twelve:

12. The fifth to Nethaniah, *he*, his sons, and his brethren, *were* twelve:

13. The sixth to Bukkiah, *he*, his sons, and his brethren, *were* twelve:

14. The seventh to Jesharelah, *he*, his sons, and his brethren, *were* twelve:

15. The eighth to Jeshaiah, *he*, his sons, and his brethren, *were* twelve:

16. The ninth to Mattaniah, *he*, his sons, and his brethren, *were* twelve:
17. The tenth to Shimei, *he*, his sons, and his brethren, *were* twelve:
18. The eleventh to Azareel, *he*, his sons, and his brethren, *were* twelve:
19. The twelfth to Hashabiah, *he*, his sons, and his brethren, *were* twelve:
20. The thirteenth to Shubael, *he*, his sons, and his brethren, *were* twelve:
21. The fourteenth to Mattithiah, *he*, his sons, and his brethren, *were* twelve:
22. The fifteenth to Jeremoth, *he*, his sons, and his brethren, *were* twelve:
23. The sixteenth to Hananiah, *he*, his sons, and his brethren, *were* twelve:
24. The seventeenth to Joshbekashah, *he*, his sons, and his brethren, *were* twelve:
25. The eighteenth to Hanani, *he*, his sons, and his brethren, *were* twelve:
26. The nineteenth to Mallothi, *he*, his sons, and his brethren, *were* twelve:
27. The twentieth to Eliathah, *he*, his sons, and his brethren, *were* twelve:
28. The one and twentieth to Hothir, *he*, his sons, and his brethren, *were* twelve:
29. The two and twentieth to Giddalti, *he*, his sons, and his brethren, *were* twelve:
30. The three and twentieth to Mahazioth, *he*, his sons, and his brethren, *were* twelve:
31. The four and twentieth to Romamtiezer, *he*, his sons, and his brethren, *were* twelve.

CHAPTER 26

1. **Concerning the divisions of the porters: Of the Korhites** *was* Meshelemiah the son of Kore, of the sons of Asaph.
2. And the sons of Meshelemiah *were*, Zechariah the firstborn, Jediael the second, Zebadiah the third, Jathniel the fourth,
3. Elam the fifth, Jehohanan the sixth, Elioenai the seventh.
4. Moreover the sons of Obed–edom *were*, Shemaiah the firstborn, Jehozabad the second, Joah the third, and Sacar the fourth, and Nethaneel the fifth.
5. Ammiel the sixth, Issachar the seventh, Peulthai the eighth: for God blessed him.
6. Also unto Shemaiah his son were sons born, that ruled throughout the house of their father: for they *were* mighty men of valour.
7. The sons of Shemaiah; Othni, and Rephael, and Obed, Elzabad, whose brethren *were* strong men, Elihu, and Semachiah.
8. All these of the sons of Obed–edom: they and their sons and their brethren, able men for strength for the service, *were* threescore and two of Obed–edom.
9. And Meshelemiah had sons and brethren, strong men, eighteen.
10. Also Hosah, of the children of Merari, had sons; Simri the chief, (for *though* he was not the firstborn, yet his father made him the chief;)
11. Hilkiah the second, Tebaliah the third, Zechariah the fourth: all the sons and brethren of Hosah *were* thirteen.
12. **Among these were the** divisions of the **porters,** *even* among the chief men, *having* wards one against another, **to minister in the house of the LORD.**
13. **And they cast lots,** as well the small as the great, according to the house of their fathers, **for every gate.**
14. **And** the lot eastward fell to Shelemiah. Then for Zechariah his son, a wise counsellor, they cast lots; and his lot came out northward.
15. To Obed–edom southward; and to his sons the house of Asuppim.
16. To Shuppim and Hosah *the lot came forth* westward, with the gate Shallecheth, by the causeway of the going up, ward against ward.
17. Eastward *were* six Levites, northward four a day, southward four a day, and toward Asuppim two *and* two.

18. At Parbar westward, four at the causeway, *and* two at Parbar.

19. These *are* the divisions of the porters among the sons of Kore, and among the sons of Merari.

20. And of the Levites, Ahijah *was* over the treasures of the house of God, and over the treasures of the dedicated things.

21. *As concerning* the sons of Laadan; the sons of the Gershonite Laadan, chief fathers, *even* of Laadan the Gershonite, *were* Jehieli.

22. The sons of Jehieli; Zetham, and Joel his brother, *which were* over the treasures of the house of the LORD.

23. Of the Amramites, *and* the Izharites, the Hebronites, *and* the Uzzielites:

24. And Shebuel the son of Gershom, the son of Moses, *was* ruler of the treasures.

25. And his brethren by Eliezer; Rehabiah his son, and Jeshaiah his son, and Joram his son, and Zichri his son, and Shelomith his son.

26. Which **Shelomith and his brethren were over** all **the treasures of the dedicated things, which David** the king, and the chief fathers, the captains over thousands and hundreds, and the captains of the host, **had dedicated.**

27. **Out of the spoils won in battles** did they dedicate **to maintain the house of the LORD.**

28. And all that Samuel the seer, *and* Saul the son of Kish, and Abner the son of Ner, and Joab the son of Zeruiah, had dedicated; *and* whosoever had dedicated *any thing, it was* under the hand of Shelomith, and of his brethren.

29. **Of the Izharites, Chenaniah and his sons were for the outward business over Israel,** for officers and judges.

30. **And of the Hebronites,**

Hashabiah and his brethren, men of valour, a thousand and seven hundred, **were officers** among them of Israel **on this side Jordan westward in all the business of the LORD, and** in the service **of the king.**

31. Among the Hebronites *was* Jerijah the chief, *even* among the Hebronites, according to the generations of his fathers. **In the fortieth year of the reign of David** they were sought for, and **there were found** among them mighty men of valour at Jazer of Gilead.

32. And his brethren, men of valour, *were* **two thousand and seven hundred chief fathers, whom king David made rulers over the Reubenites, the Gadites, and the half tribe of Manasseh, for** every matter pertaining to God, and affairs of the king.

CHAPTER 27

1. **Now** the children of Israel after their number, *to wit,* **the chief fathers** and captains of thousands and hundreds, **and their officers that served the king** in any matter of the courses, which came in and went out month by month throughout all the months of the year, of every course **were twenty and four thousand.**

2. Over the first course for the first month *was* Jashobeam the son of Zabdiel: and in his course *were* twenty and four thousand.

3. Of the children of Perez *was* the chief of all the captains of the host\for the first month.

4. And over the course of the second month *was* Dodai an Ahohite, and of

his course *was* Mikloth also the ruler: in his course likewise *were* twenty and four thousand.

5. The third captain of the host for the third month *was* Benaiah the son of Jehoiada, a chief priest: and in his course *were* twenty and four thousand.

6. This *is that* Benaiah, *who was* mighty *among* the thirty, and above the thirty: and in his course *was* Ammizabad his son.

7. The fourth *captain* for the fourth month *was* Asahel the brother of Joab, and Zebadiah his son after him: and in his course *were* twenty and four thousand.

8. The fifth captain for the fifth month *was* Shamhuth the Izrahite: and in his course *were* twenty and four thousand.

9. The sixth *captain* for the sixth month *was* Ira the son of Ikkesh the Tekoite: and in his course *were* twenty and four thousand.

10. The seventh *captain* for the seventh month *was* Helez the Pelonite, of the children of Ephraim: and in his course *were* twenty and four thousand.

11. The eighth *captain* for the eighth month *was* Sibbecai the Hushathite, of the Zarhites: and in his course *were* twenty and four thousand.

12. The ninth *captain* for the ninth month *was* Abiezer the Anetothite, of the Benjamites: and in his course *were* twenty and four thousand.

13. The tenth *captain* for the tenth month *was* Maharai the Netophathite, of the Zarhites: and in his course *were* twenty and four thousand.

14. The eleventh *captain* for the eleventh month *was* Benaiah the Pirathonite, of the children of Ephraim: and in his course *were* twenty and four thousand.

15. The twelfth *captain* for the twelfth month *was* Heldai the Netophathite, of Othniel: and in his course *were* twenty and four thousand.

16. Furthermore over the tribes of Israel: the ruler of the Reubenites

was Eliezer the son of Zichri: of the Simeonites, Shephatiah the son of Maachah:

17. Of the Levites, Hashabiah the son of Kemuel: of the Aaronites, Zadok:

18. Of Judah, Elihu, *one* of the brethren of David: of Issachar, Omri the son of Michael:

19. Of Zebulun, Ishmaiah the son of Obadiah: of Naphtali, Jerimoth the son of Azriel:

20. Of the children of Ephraim, Hoshea the son of Azaziah: of the half tribe of Manasseh, Joel the son of Pedaiah:

21. Of the half *tribe* of Manasseh in Gilead, Iddo the son of Zechariah: of Benjamin, Jaasiel the son of Abner:

22. Of Dan, Azareel the son of Jeroham. These *were* the princes of the tribes of Israel.

23. **But David took not the number of themfrom twenty years old and under: because the LORD had said he would increase Israel like to the stars** of the heavens.

24. **Joab** the son of Zeruiah **began to number, but he finished not, because there fell wrath for it against Israel;** neither was the number put in the account of the chronicles of king David.

25. **And over the king's treasures was Azmaveth** the son of Adiel: **and over the storehouses** in the fields, in the cities, and in the villages, and in the castles, **was Jehonathan** the son of Uzziah:

26. **And over them that did the work of the field** for till age of the ground **was Ezri** the son of Chelub:

27. **And over the vineyards was Shimei** the Ramathite: **over** the increase of the vineyards for the wine cellars was Zabdi

the Shiphmite:

28. **And over the olive** trees **and** the **sycomore trees** that *were* in the low plains **was Baal-hanan** the Gederite: **and over the cellars of oil was Joash:**

29. **And over the herds** that fed **in Sharon was Shitrai** the Sharonite: **and** over the herds *that were* **in the valleys was Shaphat** the son of Adlai:

30. **Over the camels** also **was Obil** the Ishmaelite: **and** over **the asses** *was* **Jehdeiah** the Meronothite:

31. **And over the flocks was Jaziz** the Hagerite. All these *were* the rulers of the substance which *was* king David's.

32. **Also Jonathan David's uncle was a counsellor,** a wise man, and a scribe: **and Jehiel** the son of Hachmoni **was with the king's sons:**

33. **And Ahithophel was the king's counsellor: and Hushai** the Archite **was the king's companion:**

34. And after Ahithophel *was* Jehoiada the son of Benaiah, and Abiathar: **and the general of the king's army was Joab.**

CHAPTER 28

1. **And David assembled all the princes of Israel,** the princes of the tribes, and the captains of the companies that ministered to the king by course, and the captains over the thousands, and captains over the hundreds, and the stewards over all the substance and possession of the king, and of his sons, with the officers, and with the mighty men, and with all the valiant men, **unto Jerusalem.**

2. Then David the king stood up upon his feet, **and said,** Hear me, my brethren, and my people: *As for me,* **I had in mine heart to build an house of rest for the ark** of the covenant of the LORD, and for the footstool of our God, **and had made ready for the building:**

3. **But God said** unto me, **Thou shalt not build an house for my name, because thou hast been a man of war,** and hast shed blood.

4. **Howbeit the LORD** God of Israel **chose me** before all the house of my father **to be king over Israel** for ever: for he hath chosen Judah *to be* the ruler; and of the house of Judah, the house of my father; and among the sons of my father he liked *me* to make *me* king over all Israel:

5. **And of all my sons,** (for **the LORD hath** given me many sons,) he hath **chosen Solomon** my son **to sit upon the throne** of the kingdom of the LORD over Israel.

6. **And he said** unto me, **Solomon** thy son, he **shall build my house** and my courts: for I have chosen him *to be* my son, and I will be his father.

7. **Moreover I will establish his kingdom for ever,** if he be constant to do my commandments and my judgments, as at this day.

8. **Now therefore** in the sight of all Israel the congregation of the LORD, and in the audience of our God, **keep and seek for all the commandments of the LORD** your God: **that ye may possess this good land,** and leave *it* for an inheritance for your children after you for ever.

9. **And thou, Solomon my**

son, know thou the God of thy father, and serve him with a perfect heart and with a willing mind: for the LORD searcheth all hearts, and understandeth all the imaginations of the thoughts: if thou seek him, he will be found of thee; but if thou forsake him, he will cast thee off for ever. 10. Take heed now; for the LORD hath chosen thee to build an house for the sanctuary: be strong, and do it. 11. Then David gave to Solomon his son the pattern of the porch, and of the houses thereof, and of the treasuries thereof, and of the upper chambers thereof, and of the inner parlours thereof, and of the place of themercy seat, 12. And the pattern of all that he had by the spirit, of the courts of the house of the LORD, and of all the chambers round about, of the treasuries of the house of God, and of the treasuries of the dedicated things: 13. Also for the courses of the priests and the Levites, and for all the work of the service of the house of the LORD, and for all the vessels of service in the house of the LORD. 14. He gave of gold by weight for *things* of gold, for all instruments of all manner of service; *silver* also for all instruments of silver by weight, for all instruments of every kind of service: 15. Even the weight for the candlesticks of gold, and for their lamps of gold, by weight for every candlestick, and for the

lamps thereof: and for the candlesticks of silver by weight, *both* for the candlestick, and *also* for the lamps thereof, according to the use of every candlestick. 16. And by weight *he gave* gold for the tables of shewbread, for every table; and *likewise* silver for the tables of silver: 17. Also pure gold for the fleshhooks, and the bowls, and the cups: and for the golden basins *he gave gold* by weight for every bason; and *likewise silver* by weight for every basin of silver: 18. And for the altar of incense refined gold by weight; and gold for the pattern of the chariot of the cherubims, that spread out their wings, and covered the ark of the covenant of the LORD. 19. All this, said David, the LORD made me understand in writing byhis hand upon me, *even* all the works of this pattern. 20. And David said to Solomon his son, Be strong and of good courage, and do *it*. fear not, nor be dismayed: for the LORD God, *even* my God, will be with thee; he will not fail thee, nor forsake thee, until thou hast finished all the work for the service of the house of the LORD. 21. And, behold, the courses of the priests and the Levites, *even they shall be* with *thee* for all the service of the house of God: and *there shall be* with thee for all manner of workmanship every willing skilful man, for any manner of service: also the princes and all the people will be wholly at

|■| thy commandment.

CHAPTER 29

■ 1. **Furthermore David** the king
■ **said unto all the**
■ **congregation,**
■ **Solomon** my son,
■ **whom** alone
■ **God hath chosen, is** *yet*
■ **young** and tender,
■ **and the work is great:**
for the palace *is* not for man,
but for the LORD God.
■ 2. **Now I have**
■ **prepared** with all my might
■ **for the house of** my
■ **God the gold** for
things to be made of
gold, and the
■ **silver** for *things* of silver, and the
■ **brass** for *things* of brass, the
■ **iron** for *things* of iron, and
■ **wood** for *things* of wood;
onyx stones, and *stones* to
be set, glistering stones,
and of divers colours,
■ **and all manner of**
■ **precious stones, and**
■ **marble** stones in abundance.
■ 3. **Moreover,** because
I have set my affection to
the house of my God, I have
■ **of mine own** proper good, of
■ **gold and silver,** *which*
■ **I have given**
to the house of my God,
■ **over and above all**
■ **that I have prepared**
■ **for the holy house.**
■ 4. **Even three**
■ **thousand talents**
■ **of gold,** of the gold of Ophir,
■ **and seven thousand talents**
■ **of refined silver,** to overlay the
walls of the houses *withal*:
5. The gold for *things* of gold, and
the silver for *things* of silver,
and for all manner of work *to be
made* by the hands of artificers. And
■ **who then is**
■ **willing to consecrate**
■ **his service** this day
■ **unto the LORD?**

■ 6. **Then the chief** of the
■ **fathers and**
■ **princes** of the tribes
■ **of Israel** and the captains of
thousands and of hundreds,
with the rulers of the king's work,
■ **offered willingly,**
■ 7. **And gave** for the service
of the house of God of
■ **gold** five thousand talents
and ten thousand drams, and of
■ **silver** ten thousand talents, and of
■ **brass** eighteen thousand talents,
■ **and** one hundred
thousand talents of
■ **iron.**
■ 8. **And** they with whom
■ **precious stones**
were found gave *them*
■ **to the treasure of the**
■ **house of the LORD,**
by the hand of Jehiel the Gershonite.
■ 9. **Then the people** rejoiced,
for that they offered willingly,
because with perfect heart they
offered willingly to the LORD:
■ **and David** the king also
■ **rejoiced** with great joy.
■ 10. **Wherefore David**
■ **blessed the LORD** before all
the congregation: and David said,
Blessed *be* thou, LORD God of
Israel our father, for ever and ever.
■ 11. **Thine, O LORD is**
■ **the greatness,** and the
■ **power,** and the
■ **glory,** and the
■ **victory, and** the
■ **majesty: for all that is**
■ **in the heaven and** in the
■ **earth is thine;** thine *is* the
kingdom, O LORD, and thou
art exalted as head above all.
■ 12. **Both riches and honour**
■ **come of thee, and thou**
■ **reignest over all; and in**
■ **thine hand is power and**
■ **might; and** in thine hand *it is*
■ **to make great, and** to
■ **give strength unto all.**
■ 13. **Now** therefore, our God,
■ **we thank thee,** and
praise thy glorious name.

14. **But who am I, and** what *is*
my people, that we
should be able to
offer so willingly
after this sort?
for all things *come* of thee, and
of thine own have
we given thee.
15. **For we are strangers**
before thee, and sojourners,
as *were* all our fathers:
our days on the earth
are as a shadow,
and *there is* none abiding.
16. **O LORD** our God, all
this store that we have
prepared to build thee
an house for thine holy name
cometh of thine
hand, and *is* all thine own.
17. **I know also,** my God, that
thou triest the heart,
and hast pleasure in
uprightness. As for me,
in the uprightness of mine heart
I have willingly offered all
these things:
and now have I seen with joy
thy people, which
are present here, to
offer willingly unto thee.
18. **O LORD** God of Abraham,
Isaac, and of Israel, our fathers,
keep this for ever in the
imagination of the thoughts of
the heart of thy people,
and prepare their heart unto thee:
19. **And give** unto
Solomon my son
a perfect heart, to
keep thy commandments,
thy testimonies, and thy statutes,
and to do all *these things*, and to
build the palace, *for* the
which I have made provision.
20. **And David said**
to all the congregation, Now
bless the LORD your God.
And all
the congregation blessed the
LORD God of their fathers, and
bowed down
their heads, and

worshipped the
LORD, and the king.
21. **And** they
sacrificed sacrifices unto
the LORD, and offered
burnt offerings unto
the LORD, on the morrow after
that day, *even* a thousand bullocks,
a thousand rams, *and* a thousand
lambs, with their drink offerings, and
sacrifices in abundance for all Israel:
22. **And did eat and**
drink before the LORD on
that day with great
gladness. And they made
Solomon the son of David
king the second time,
and anointed him unto
the LORD to be the chief
governor, and Zadok
to be priest.
23. **Then Solomon sat**
on the throne of the LORD
as king instead of David
his father, and prospered;
and all Israel obeyed him.
24. And all the princes, and the
mighty men, and all the sons likewise
of king David, submitted themselves
unto Solomon the king.
25. **And the LORD magnified**
Solomon exceedingly
in the sight of all Israel,
and bestowed upon him
such royal
majesty as had not been
on any king before him in Israel.
26. **Thus David** the son of Jesse
reigned over all
Israel.
27. And the time that he
reigned over Israel *was*
forty years; seven
years reigned he
in Hebron, and thirty and
three years reigned
he in Jerusalem.
28. **And he died** in a good old
age, full of days, riches, and honour:
and Solomon his son
reigned in his stead.
29. **Now the acts of David**
the king, first and last, behold, they

I CHRONICLES 29

- **are written in the book**
- **of Samuel** the seer,
- **and in the book of Nathan**
- **the prophet, and in the**
- **book of Gad the seer,**

30. With all his reign and his might, and the times that went over him, and over Israel, and over all the kingdoms of the countries.

THE BOOK OF SECOND CHRONICLES

BACKGROUND INFORMATION

Author: Unknown
Date Written: Between 538 — 420 B.C.

Number of:
Verses—822
Chapters—36
Total Words—26,074
Scan Words—10,748
Scan Words Represent
Approximately 41% of
Total Words

Theme: The Building of Solomon's Temple Revival under king **Hezekiah, and the Destruction of Jerusalem**

OUTLINE OF THE BOOK

I. **The Building of the Temple** During the Reign of Solomon
   1:1 — 9:31

II. **The** History of the **reign of Rehoboam and the Destruction of Jerusalem**
   10:1 — 36:23

1. **And Solomon** the son of David **was strengthened** in his kingdom, **and** the LORD his **God was with him,** and magnified him exceedingly.

2. Then Solomon spake unto all Israel, to the captains of thousands and of hundreds, and to the judges, and to every governor in all Israel, the chief of the fathers.

3. **So Solomon, and all the congregation** with him, **went to** the high place that *was* at **Gibeon; for there was the tabernacle** of the congregation of God, which Moses the servant of the LORD had made in the wilderness.

4. **But the ark** of God **had David brought** up from Kirjath–jearim **to** *the place which* David had prepared for it: for he had pitched a tent for it at **Jerusalem.**

5. Moreover the brasen altar, that Bezaleel the son of Uri, the son of Hur, had made, he put before the tabernacle of theLORD: and Solomon and the congregation sought unto it.

6. **And Solomon went** up thither **to the brasen altar** before the LORD, which *was* at the tabernacle of the congregation, **and offered a thousand burnt offerings** upon it.

7. **In that night did God appear unto Solomon, and said** unto him, **Ask what I shall give thee.**

8. **And Solomon said** unto God, Thou hast shewed great mercy unto David my father, and hast made me to reign in his stead.

9. Now, O LORD God, **let thy promise unto David** my father **be established;** for thou hast made me king over a people like the dust of the earth in multitude.

10. **Give me** now **wisdom and knowledge, that I may** go out and come in before this people: for who can **judge this** thy **people,** *that is so* great?

11. **And God said** to Solomon, Because this was in thine heart, and **thou hast not asked riches,** wealth, or honour, **nor** the life of thine enemies, neither yet hast asked **long life;** but hast asked wisdom and knowledge for thyself, that thou mayest judge my people, over whom I have made thee king:

12. **Wisdom and knowledge is granted** unto thee; **and I will give thee riches, and** wealth, and honour, such as **none** of the kings have had that *have been* **before thee, neither shall** there **any after theehave the like.**

13. **Then Solomon came** *from his journey* to the high place that *was* at Gibeon **to Jerusalem,** from before the tabernacle of the congregation, **and reigned over Israel.**

14. **And Solomon** gathered chariots and horsemen: and he **had** a thousand and four hundred **chariots, and** twelve thousand **horsemen,** which he **placed in the chariot cities, and** with the king **at Jerusalem.**

15. And the king made silver and gold at Jerusalem *as plenteous* as stones, and cedar trees made he as the sycomore trees that *are* in the vale for abundance.

16. And Solomon had horses brought out of Egypt, and linen yarn: the king's merchants received the linen yarn at a price.

17. And they fetched up, and brought forth out of Egypt a chariot for six hundred *shekels* of silver, and an horse for an hundred and fifty: and so brought they out *horses* for all

the kings of the Hittites, and for the kings of Syria, by their means.

CHAPTER 2

1. **And Solomon determined to build an house for** the name of **the LORD,** and an house for his kingdom.

2. And Solomon told out threescore and ten thousand men to bear burdens, and fourscore thousand to hew in the mountain, and three thousand and six hundred to oversee them.

3. **And Solomon sent to Huram the king of Tyre, saying,** As thou didst deal with David my father, and didst send him cedars to build him an house to dwell therein, *even so deal with me.*

4. **Behold, I build an house to** the name of **the LORD** my God, to dedicate *it* to him, *and* to burn before him sweet incense, and for the continual shewbread, and for the burnt offerings morning and evening, on the sabbaths, and on the new moons, and on the solemn feasts of the LORD our God. This *is an ordinance* for ever to Israel.

5. And the house which I build *is* great: **for great is our God** above all gods.

6. **But who is able to build him an house, seeing** the **heaven** and heaven of heavens **cannot contain him? who am I then, that I should build him an house, save only to burn sacrifice before him?**

7. **Send me** now therefore **a man cunning to work in gold,** and in **silver,** and in **brass,** and in **iron, and in purple, and crimson,** and blue, and that can skill to grave with the

cunning men that *are* with me in Judah and in Jerusalem, whom David my father did provide.

8. **Send me also** cedar **trees,** fir trees, and algum trees, **out of Lebanon:** for I know that thy servants can skill to cut timber in Lebanon; and, behold, my servants *shall be* with thy servants,

9. Even to prepare me timber **in abundance: for the house** which I am about to build **shall be** wonderful **great.**

10. **And,** behold, **I will give** to thy servants, **the hewers** that cut timber, twenty thousand measures of beaten **wheat, and** twenty thousand measures of **barley,** and twenty thousand baths of **wine, and** twenty thousand baths of **oil.**

11. **Then Huram the king of Tyre answered in writing,** which he sent to Solomon, Because the LORD hath loved his people, he hath made thee king over them.

12. Huram said moreover, Blessed *be* the LORD God of Israel, that made heaven and earth, who hath given to David the king a wise son, endued with prudence and understanding, that might build an house for the LORD, and an house for his kingdom.

13. And now **I have sent a** cunning **man, endued with understanding, of** Huram my father's,

14. The son of a woman of the daughters of Dan, and his father *was* a man of Tyre, **skilful to work in gold,** and in **silver,** in **brass,** in **iron,** in stone, and in **timber,** in purple, in blue, **and in fine linen,** and in crimson; also to grave any manner of graving, and to find out every device which

shall be put to him, with thy cunning men, and with the cunning men of my lord David thy father.

■ 15. **Now** therefore
■ **the wheat,** and the
■ **barley,** the
■ **oil, and** the
■ **wine, which my lord hath**
■ **spoken of, let him send**
■ **unto his servants:**
■ 16. **And we will cut**
■ **wood** out of Lebanon, as much as thou shalt need:
■ **and** we will
■ **bring it** to thee in floats by sea to Joppa;
■ **and thou shalt carry it**
■ **up to Jerusalem.**

17. And Solomon numbered all the strangers that *were* in the land of Israel, after the numbering wherewith David his father had numbered them; and they were found an hundred and fifty thousand and three thousand and six hundred.

18. And he set threescore and ten thousand of them *to be* bearers of burdens, and fourscore thousand *to be* hewers in the mountain, and three thousand and six hundred overseers to set the people a work.

CHAPTER 3

■ 1. **Then Solomon began to**
■ **build the house of the LORD**
■ **at Jerusalem in mount**
■ **Moriah,** where *the Lord* appeared unto David his father, in the place that David had prepared in the threshingfloor of Ornan the Jebusite.

2. And he began to build
■ **in the** second *day* of the second month, in the
■ **fourth year of his reign.**

3. **Now** these *are the things wherein*
■ **Solomon was**
■ **instructed for** the
■ **building** of
■ **the house of God.**
■ **The length** by cubits after the first measure *was*
■ **threescore cubits, and the**
■ **breadth twenty cubits.**

■ 4. **And the porch** that *was* in the front *of the house*, the length *of it*
■ **was** according to the breadth of the house,
■ **twenty cubits, and**
■ **the height** *was*
■ **an hundred and**
■ **twenty:** and he
■ **overlaid** it
■ **within with** pure
■ **gold.**

5. **And the greater house he**
■ **cieled with fir** tree, which he
■ **overlaid with** fine
■ **gold,** and set thereon palm trees and chains.

6. And he
■ **garnished** the house
■ **with precious stones** for beauty: and the gold *was* gold of Parvaim.

7. He overlaid also the house, the beams, the posts, and the walls thereof, and the doors thereof,
■ **with** gold; and
■ **graved cherubims**
■ **on the walls.**

8. **And he made the**
■ **most holy house, the length** whereof *was* according to the breadth of the house, twenty cubits,
■ **and the breadth thereof**
■ **twenty cubits:** and he
■ **overlaid** it
■ **with** fine
■ **gold, amounting to**
■ **six hundred talents.**

9. **And** the weight of
■ **the nails** *was*
■ **fifty shekels of gold.** And he overlaid the upper chambers with gold.

10. **And** in the most holy house
■ **he made two cherubims** of image work, and
■ **overlaid** them
■ **with gold.**

11. And the wings of the cherubims *were*
■ **twenty cubits long:** one wing *of the one cherub was* five cubits, reaching to the wall of the house: and the other wing *was likewise*

five cubits, reaching to the wing of the other cherub.

12. And *one* wing of the other cherub *was* five cubits, reaching to the wall of the house: and the other wing *was* five cubits *also*, joining to the wing of the other cherub.

13. The wings of these cherubims spread themselves forth twenty cubits: and they stood on their feet,

and their faces were inward.

14. **And he made the vail of** blue, and purple, and crimson, and **fine linen, and wrought cherubims thereon.**

15. **Also he made** before the house **two pillars** of **thirty** and **five cubits high,** and the chapiter that *was* on the top of each of them *was* five cubits.

16. **And he made chains,** *as* in the oracle, and put *them* **on the heads of the pillars; and** made **an hundred pomegranates,** and put *them* **on the chains.**

17. **And he reared** up the **pillars before the temple,** one on the right hand, and the other on the left; **and called the name of that on the right hand Jachin, and** the name of that on **the left Boaz.**

CHAPTER 4

1. **Moreover he made an altar of brass, twenty cubits the length** thereof, **and** twenty cubits the **breadth** thereof, **and ten cubits the height** thereof.

2. **Also he made a molten sea of ten cubits from brim to brim,** round in compass, **and five cubits the height** thereof; and a line of thirty cubits did compass it round about.

3. **And under it was the similitude of** oxen, which did compass it round about: ten in a cubit, compassing the sea round about. Two rows of oxen *were* cast, when it was cast.

4. It stood upon **twelve oxen,** three looking toward the north, and three looking toward the west, and three looking toward the south, and three looking toward the east: and the sea *was set* above upon them, and **all their hinder parts were inward.**

5. **And the thickness** of it **was an handbreadth, and the brim** of it **like** the work of the brim of **a cup, with flowers** of lilies; **and it** received and **held three thousand baths.**

6. **He made also ten lavers,** and put five on the right hand, and five on the left, **to wash** in them: such **things as they offered for the burnt offering** they washed in them; **but the sea was for the priests to wash in.**

7. **And he made ten candlesticks of gold** according to their form, and set *them* in the temple, five on the right hand, and five on the left.

8. He made **also ten tables,** and placed *them* in the temple, five on the right side, and five on the left. **And** he made **an hundred basons of gold.**

9. **Furthermore he made the court of the priests, and the great court, and doors** for the court, and **overlaid** the doors of them **with brass.**

10. And he set the sea on the right side of the east end,

over against the south.

■ 11. **And Huram made** the
■ **pots,** and the
■ **shovels, and** the
■ **basins. And Huram**
■ **finished** the work that he was
to make for king Solomon for
■ **the house of God;**
12. *To wit*, the two pillars, and the
pommels, and the chapiters *which
were* on the top of the two pillars, and
the two wreaths to cover the two
pommels of the chapiters which
were on the top of the pillars;
13. And four hundred pomegranates
on the two wreaths; two rows of
pomegranates on each wreath, to
cover the two pommels of the
chapiters which *were* upon the pillars.
14. He made also bases, and lavers
made he upon the bases;
15. One sea, and
twelve oxen under it.
16. The pots also, and the shovels,
and the fleshhooks, and all their
instruments, did Huram his father
make to king Solomon for the house
of the LORD of bright brass.
17. In the plain of Jordan did the king
cast them, in the clay ground between
Succoth and Zeredathah.
■ 18. **Thus Solomon**
■ **made** all these
■ **vessels in great**
■ **abundance:** for
■ **the weight of the brass**
■ **could not be found out.**
■ 19. **And Solomon**
■ **made** all the
■ **vessels** that *were*
■ **for the house**
■ **of God, the** golden
■ **altar** also,
■ **and the tables whereon**
■ **the shewbread was set;**
■ 20. **Moreover the**
■ **candlesticks** with their lamps,
that they should burn after the manner
before the oracle, of pure gold;
■ 21. **And** the
■ **flowers, and** the
■ **lamps,** and
■ **the tongs,** *made he of*

gold, and that perfect gold;
22. And the
■ **snuffers,** and
■ **the basins,** and the
■ **spoons, and** the
■ **censers,** *of* pure gold: and the
entry of the house, the inner doors
thereof for the most holy *place*,
■ **and the doors of the house**
■ **of the temple, were of gold.**

CHAPTER 5

■ 1. **Thus** all the work
that Solomon made for
■ **the house of the LORD**
■ **was finished: and**
■ **Solomon brought** in *all*
■ **the things** that
■ **David** his father
■ **had dedicated; and**
■ **the silver, and** the
■ **gold, and all the**
■ **instruments, put he**
■ **among the treasures**
of the house of God.
■ 2. **Then Solomon**
■ **assembled** the
elders of Israel, and
■ **all** the heads of the tribes, the chief
of the fathers of the children of
■ **Israel, unto Jerusalem,**
■ **to bring up the ark** of
the covenant of the LORD
■ **out of** the city of David, which *is*
■ **Zion.**
3. Wherefore all the men of Israel
assembled themselves unto the
king in the feast which *was* in
the seventh month.
4. And all the elders of Israel came;
and the Levites took up the ark.
5. And they brought up the ark, and
the tabernacle of the congregation,
and all the holy vessels that *were* in
the tabernacle, these did the priests
and the Levites bring up.
6. Also king Solomon**,**
■ **and** all the congregation of
■ **Israel** that were assembled
unto him before the ark,
■ **sacrificed sheep and**
■ **oxen, which could**
■ **not be** told nor

numbered for multitude.

7. And the priests brought in
the ark of the covenant of the
LORD unto his place, to the
oracle of the house,
into the most holy
place, *even*
under the wings
of the cherubims:

8. For the cherubims spread forth
their wings over the place of the ark,
and the cherubims covered the
ark and the staves thereof above.

9. And they drew out the staves *of*
the ark, that the ends of the staves
were seen from the ark before the
oracle; but they were not seen
without. And there it is unto this day.

10. There was nothing
in the ark save
the two tables which
Moses put therein at
Horeb, when the LORD made *a*
covenant with the children of Israel,
when they came
out of Egypt.

11. And it came to pass,
when the priests were
come out of the holy place:
(for all the priests *that were* present
were sanctified, *and* did not
then wait by course:

12. Also the Levites *which were* the
singers, all of them of Asaph, of
Heman, of Jeduthun, with their
sons and their brethren,
being arrayed in white
linen, having cymbals
and psalteries and harps,
stood at the east end of the
altar, and with them an
hundred and twenty priests
sounding with trumpets:)

13. It came even to pass, as the
trumpeters and singers *were* as one,
to make one sound to be heard in
praising and thanking the
LORD; and when they lifted up *their*
voice with the trumpets and
cymbals and instruments of music,
and praised the LORD, *saying*,
For *he is* good; for his mercy
endureth for ever: that

then the house was filled
with a cloud, *even* the
house of the LORD;

14. So that the priests
could not stand to
minister by reason of the cloud:
for the glory of the LORD
had filled the house of God.

CHAPTER 6

1. Then said Solomon,
The LORD hath said that
he would dwell in the thick
darkness.

2. But I have built an house
of habitation for thee, and a place
for thy dwelling for ever.

3. And the king turned his face,
and blessed the whole congregation
of Israel: and all the congregation
of Israel stood.

4. And he said,
Blessed be the LORD
God of Israel, who
hath with his hands
fulfilled that which
he spake with his mouth
to my father
David, saying,

5. Since the day that
I brought forth
my people out of the land of
Egypt I chose no city
among all the tribes of Israel
to build an house in,
that my name might be there;
neither chose I any man to be
a ruler over my people
Israel:

6. But I have chosen Jerusalem,
that my name might be there;
and have chosen David to be
over my people Israel.

7. Now it was in the
heart of David my father
to build an house
for the name of
the LORD God of Israel.

8. But the LORD said to
David my father, Forasmuch as it
was in thine heart to build an house
for my name, thou didst well in
that it was in thine heart:

9. Notwithstanding **thou shalt not build the house; but thy son** which shall come forth out of thy loins, he **shall** build the house for my name. 10. **The LORD** therefore **hath performed his word** that he hath spoken: **for I** am risen up in the room of David my father, and am set on the throne of Israel, as the LORD promised, and **have built the house for** the name of **the LORD** God of Israel. 11. **And in it have I put the ark,** wherein *is* the covenant of the LORD, that he made with the children of Israel. 12. **And** he stood before the altar of the LORD in the presence of all the congregation of Israel, and spread forth his hands: 13. For **Solomon** had **made a brasen scaffold,** of five cubits long, and five cubits broad, and three cubits high, **and** had **set it in** the midst of **the court:** and upon it he stood, **and kneeled** down upon his knees **before** all **the congregation** of Israel, **and spread** forth **his hands toward heaven.** 14. **And said, O LORD** God of Israel, **there is no God like thee** in the heaven, nor in the earth; **which keepest covenant, and shewest mercy unto thy servants, that walk before thee with all their hearts:** 15. Thou which hast kept with thy servant David my father that which thou hast promised him; and spakest with thy mouth, and hast fulfilled *it* with thine hand, as *it is* this day. 16. **Now** therefore, **O LORD** God of Israel, **keep with** thy servant

David my father **that which thou hast promised** him, **saying, There shall not fail** thee **a man** in my sight to sit **upon the throne of Israel; yet so that thy children take heed to** their way to walk in **my law,** as thou hast walked before me. 17. Now then, O LORD God of Israel, **let thy word be verified,** which thou hast spoken unto thy servant David. 18. **But will God** in very deed **dwell with men on the earth?** behold, heaven and the **heaven** of heavens **cannot contain thee;** how **much less this house** which I have built! 19. **Have respect therefore to the prayer of thy servant,** and to his supplication, O LORD my God, to hearken unto the cry and the prayer which thy servant prayeth before thee: 20. **That thine eyes may be** open **upon this house day and night,** upon the place whereof thou hast said that thou wouldest put thy name there; to hearken unto the prayer which thy servant prayeth toward this place. 21. **Hearken** therefore **unto the supplications of** thy servant, and of thy people **Israel,** which they shall make toward this place: **hear thou from thy dwelling place,** *even* from heaven; **and** when thou hearest, **forgive.** 22. **If a man sin** against his neighbour, and an oath be laid upon him to make him swear, **and** the oath **come before thine altar in this house;** 23. **Then hear thou**

from heaven, and do, and judge thy servants, **by requiting the wicked,** by recompensing his way upon his own head; **and** by **justifying the righteous,** by giving him according to his righteousness.

24. **And if** thy people **Israel be put to the worse before the enemy, because they have sinned** against thee; **and shall return** and confess thy name, and pray **and make supplication** before thee in this house;

25. **Then hear** thou from the heavens, **and forgive the sin** of thy people Israel, **and bring them again unto the land** which thou gavest to them and to their fathers.

26. **When** the heaven is shut up, and **there is no rain, because they have sinned** against thee; **yet if they** pray toward this place, and **confess** thy name, **and turn from their sin,** when thou dost afflict them;

27. **Then** hear thou from heaven, and **forgive the sin** of thy servants, and of thy people Israel, when thou hast taught them the good way, wherein they should walk; **and send rain** upon thy land, which thou hast given unto thy people for an inheritance.

28. **If there be dearth** in the land, if there be **pestilence,** if there be **blasting, or mildew, locusts, or caterpillers; if their enemies besiege** them in the cities of **their land;** whatsoever sore or whatsoever sickness *there be:*

29. **Then** what prayer *or* what **supplication** soever **shall be made** of any man, or of all thy people Israel, when every one shall know his own sore and his own grief, and shall spread forth his hands **in this house:**

30. **Then hear thou from heaven** thy dwelling place, **and forgive,** and render unto every man according unto all his ways, whose heart thou knowest; (for thou only knowest the hearts of the children of men:)

31. **That they may fear thee,** to walk in thy ways, so long as they live in the land which thou gavest unto our fathers.

32. **Moreover** concerning **the stranger,** which is not of thy people Israel, but is come **from a far country** for thy great name's sake, and thy mighty hand, and thy stretched out arm; **if they come and pray in this house;**

33. **Then hear** thou from the heavens, *even* from thy dwelling place, **and do according to all that the stranger calleth to thee** for; **that all people of the earth may know** thy name, **and fear thee,** as *doth* thy people Israel, and may know that this house which I have built is called by thy name.

34. **If thy people go** out **to war** against their enemies by the way that thou shalt send them, **and they pray** unto thee **toward this city** which thou hast chosen, and the house which I have built for thy name;

35. **Then hear** thou from the heavens **their prayer** and their supplication, **and maintain their cause.**

36. **If they sin** against thee, **(for** *there is* **no man** which **sinneth not,) and thou** be

angry with them, and

deliver them over before

their enemies, and they carry them away captives unto a land far off or near;

37. **Yet if they** bethink themselves in the land whither they are carried captive, and

turn and pray unto thee in the land of their captivity, saying, We have sinned, we have done amiss, and have dealt wickedly;

38. **If they return to thee with all their heart and** with all their **soul** in the land of their captivity, whither they have carried them captives, and pray *toward* their land, which thou gavest unto their fathers, and toward the city which thou hast chosen, and toward the house which I have built for thy name:

39. **Then hear** thou from the heavens, *even* from thy dwelling place,

their prayer and their supplications, and maintain their cause,

and forgive thy people which have sinned against thee.

40. **Now, my God,** let, I beseech thee, thine eyes be open, and *let* thine ears *be*

attent unto the prayer *that is* **made in this place.**

41. **Now** therefore

arise, O LORD God,

into thy resting place,

thou, and the ark of thy strength: let thy priests, O LORD God, be clothed with salvation,

and let thy saints

rejoice in goodness.

42. **O LORD** God,

turn not away the face of thine anointed: remember the mercies of David thy servant.

CHAPTER 7

1. **Now when Solomon had made an end of praying,** the **fire came down from heaven, and consumed the**

burnt offering and the sacrifices;

and the glory of the LORD

filled the house.

2. And the priests could not enter into the house of the LORD, because the glory of the LORD had filled the LORD's house.

3. **And when** all the children of **Israel saw** how **the fire** came down, **and the glory of the LORD** upon the house, **they bowed** themselves with their faces to the ground upon the pavement,

and worshipped, and praised the LORD, *saying,* For *he is* good; for his mercy *endureth* for ever.

4. Then the king and all the people offered sacrifices before the LORD.

5. **And** king **Solomon offered a sacrifice of twenty** and **two thousand oxen, and an hundred and twenty thousand sheep:** so the king and all the people dedicated the house of God.

6. **And the priests waited on their offices: the Levites also with instruments of music** of the LORD, **which David** the king had **made to praise the LORD,** because his mercy *endureth* for ever, when David praised by their ministry; and the priests sounded trumpets before them, and all Israel stood.

7. **Moreover Solomon hallowed the middle** of the **court** that *was* before the house of the LORD: for **there he offered burnt offerings,** and the fat of the peace offerings, **because the brasen altar** which Solomon had made **was not able to receive the burnt offerings,** and the meat offerings, and the fat.

8. Also at the same time **Solomon kept the feast**

seven days, and all Israel with him, a very great congregation, from the entering in of Hamath unto the river of Egypt.

9. **And in the eighth day they made a solemn assembly:** for they kept the dedication of the altar seven days, and the feast seven days.

10. **And on the three and twentieth day of the seventh month he sent the people** away **into their tents,** glad and merry in heart for the goodness that the LORD had shewed unto David, and to Solomon, and to Israel his people.

11. **Thus Solomon finished the house of the LORD, and the king's house:** and all that came into Solomon's heart to make in the house of the LORD, and in his own house, he prosperously effected.

12. **And the LORD appeared to Solomon** by night, **and said** unto him, **I have heard thy prayer, and have chosen this place** to myself f **or an house of sacrifice.**

13. **If I shut up heaven that there be no rain, or** if I **command the locusts to devour the land, or** if I **send pestilence** among my people;

14. **If my people, which are called by my name, shall humble themselves, and pray,** and seek my face, **and turn from their wicked ways; then will I** hear from heaven, and will **forgive their sin, and will heal their land.**

15. Now mine eyes shall be open, and mine ears attent unto the prayer *that is made* in this place.

16. **For** now have **I** chosen and **sanctified this house, that my name may be there for ever:** and mine eyes and mine

heart shall be there perpetually.

17. **And as for thee, if thou wilt walk before me,** as David thy father walked, and do according to all that I have commanded thee, and shalt observe my statutes and my judgments;

18. **Then will I stablish the throne of thy kingdom,** according as I have covenanted with David thy father, saying, There shall not fail thee a man *to be* ruler inIsrael.

19. **But if ye turn away,** and forsake my statutes and my commandments, which I have set before you, **and** shall go and **serve other gods,** and worship them;

20. **Then will I pluck them** up by the roots **out of my land** which I have given them; **and this house,** which I have sanctified for my name, **will I cast out of my sight,** and will make it *to be* a proverb and a byword among all nations.

21. **And this house,** which is high, **shall be an astonishment to every one** that passeth by it; **so** that **he shall say, Why hath the LORD done thus** unto this land, and unto this house?

22. **And it shall be answered, Because they forsook the LORD** God of their fathers, which brought them forth out of the land of Egypt, **and laid hold on other gods,** and worshipped them, and served them: therefore hath he brought all this evil upon them.

CHAPTER 8

1. **And** it came to pass **at the end of twenty years,** wherein Solomon had built the house of the LORD, and his own house,

2. That **the cities which Huram** had

restored to Solomon, Solomon built them, and caused the children of Israel to dwell there. 3. And Solomon went to Hamath-zobah, and prevailed against it. 4. And he built Tadmor in the wilderness, and all the store cities, which he built in Hamath. 5. Also he built Beth-horon the upper, and Beth-horon the nether, fenced cities, with walls, gates, and bars; 6. And Baalath, and all the store cities that Solomon had, and all the chariot cities, and the cities of the horsemen, and all that Solomon desired to build in Jerusalem, and in Lebanon, and throughout all the land of his dominion. 7. As for all the people *that were* left of the Hittites, and the Amorites, and the Perizzites, and the Hivites, and the Jebusites, which *were* not of Israel, 8. *But* of their children, who were left after them in the land, whom the children of Israel consumed not, them did Solomon make to pay tribute until this day. 9. But of the children of Israel did Solomon make no servants for his work; but they were men of war, and chief of his captains, and captains of his chariots and horsemen. 10. And these *were* the chief of king Solomon's officers, even two hundred and fifty, that bare rule over the people. 11. And Solomon brought up the daughter of Pharaoh out of the city of David unto the house

that he had built for her: for he said, My wife shall not dwell in the house of David king of Israel, because the places are holy, whereunto the ark of the LORD hath come. 12. Then Solomon offered burnt offerings unto the LORD on the altar of the LORD, which he had built before the porch, 13. Even after a certain rate every day, offering according to the commandment of Moses, on the sabbaths, and on the new moons, and on the solemn feasts, three times in the year, *even* in the feast of unleavened bread, and in the feast of weeks, and in the feast of tabernacles. 14. And he appointed, according to the order of David his father, the courses of the priests to their service, and the Levites to their charges, to praise and minister before the priests, as the duty of every day required: the porters also by their courses at every gate: for so had David the man of God commanded. 15. And they departed not from the commandment of the king unto the priests and Levites concerning any matter, or concerning the treasures. 16. Now all the work of Solomon was prepared unto the day of the foundation of the house of the LORD, and until it was finished. So the house of the LORD was perfected. 17. Then went Solomon to Ezion-geber, and to Eloth, at the sea side in the land of Edom. 18. And Huram sent him by the hands of his servants ships, and servants that had knowledge of the sea; and they went with the servants of Solomon to Ophir, and took thence four hundred and fifty talents of gold, and brought *them* to king Solomon.

CHAPTER 9

1. And when the queen of Sheba heard of the fame of Solomon, she came to prove Solomon with hard questions at Jerusalem, with a very great company, and camels that bare spices, and gold in abundance, and precious stones: and when she was come to Solomon, she communed with him of all that was in her heart.

2. And Solomon told her all her questions: and there was nothing hid from Solomon which he told her not.

3. And when the queen of Sheba had seen the wisdom of Solomon, and the house that he had built,

4. And the meat of his table, and the sitting of his servants, and the attendance of his ministers, and their apparel; his cupbearers also, and their apparel; and his ascent by which he went up into the house of the LORD; there was no more spirit in her.

5. And she said to the king, It was a true report which I heard in mine own land of thine acts, and of thy wisdom:

6. Howbeit I believed not their words, until I came, and mine eyes had seen *it*: and, behold, the one half of the greatness of thy wisdom was not told me: for thou exceedest the fame that I heard.

7. Happy *are* thy men, and happy *are* these thy servants, which stand continually before thee, and hear thy wisdom.

8. Blessed be the LORD thy God, which delighted in thee to set thee on his throne, *to be* king for the LORD thy God: because thy God loved Israel, to establish them for ever, therefore made he thee king over them, to do judgment and justice.

9. And she gave the king an hundred and twenty talents of gold, and of spices great abundance, and precious stones: neither was there any such spice as the queen of Sheba gave king Solomon.

10. And the servants also of Huram, and the servants of Solomon, which brought gold from Ophir, brought algum trees and precious stones.

11. And the king made *of* the algum trees terraces to the house of the LORD, and to the king's palace, and harps and psalteries for singers: and there were none such seen before in the land of Judah.

12. And king Solomon gave to the queen of Sheba all her desire, whatsoever she asked, beside *that* which she had brought unto the king. So she turned, and went away to her own land, she and her servants.

13. Now the weight of gold that came to Solomon in one year was six hundred and threescore and six talents of gold;

14. Beside that which chapmen and merchants brought. And all the kings of Arabia and governors of the country

brought gold and silver to Solomon.

15. And king Solomon made two hundred targets *of* beaten gold: six hundred *shekels* of beaten gold went to one target.

16. And three hundred shields *made he* of beaten gold: three hundred *shekels* of gold went to one shield. And the king put them in the house of the forest of Lebanon.

17. Moreover the king made a great throne of ivory, and overlaid it with pure gold.

18. And there were six steps to the throne, with a footstool of gold, *which were* fastened to the throne, and stays on each side of the sitting place, and two lions standing by the stays:

19. And twelve lions stood there on the one side and on theother upon the six steps. There was not the like made in any kingdom.

20. And all the drinking vessels of king Solomon *were of* gold, and all the vessels of the house of the forest of Lebanon were of pure gold: none *were of* silver; it *was not* any thing accounted of in the days of Solomon.

21. For the king's ships went to Tarshish with the servants of Huram: every three years once came the ships of Tarshish bringing gold, and silver, ivory, and apes, and peacocks.

22. And king Solomon passed all the kings of the earth in riches and wisdom.

23. And all the kings of the earth sought the presence of Solomon, to hear his wisdom, that God had put in his heart.

24. And they brought every man his present, vessels of silver, and vessels of gold, and raiment, harness, and spices, horses, and mules, a rate year by year.

25. And Solomon had four thousand stalls for horses and chariots, and twelve thousand horsemen; whom he bestowed in the chariot cities, and with the king at Jerusalem.

26. And he reigned over all the kings from the river even unto the land of the Philistines, and to the border of Egypt.

27. And the king made silver in Jerusalem as stones, and cedar trees made he as the sycomore trees that *are* in the low plains inabundance.

28. And they brought unto Solomon horses out of Egypt, and out of all lands.

29. Now the rest of the acts of Solomon, first and last, are they not written in the book of Nathan the prophet, and in the prophecy of Ahijah the Shilonite, and in the visions of Iddo the seer against Jeroboam the son of Nebat?

30. And Solomon reigned in Jerusalem over all Israel forty years.

31. And Solomon slept with his fathers, and he was buried in the city of David his father: and Rehoboam his son reigned in his stead.

CHAPTER 10

1. And Rehoboam went to Shechem: for to Shechem were all Israel come to make him king.

2. And it came to pass,

■ **when Jeroboam**
the son of Nebat,
■ **who was in Egypt,**
whither he fled from the presence
of Solomon the king,
■ **heard it,** that
■ **Jeroboam returned**
■ **out of Egypt.**
■ 3. **And** they sent and called him. So
Jeroboam and all Israel came and
■ **spake to Rehoboam,**
■ **saying,**
■ 4. **Thy father made our**
■ **yoke grievous: now** therefore
■ **ease** thou somewhat
■ **the** grievous
■ **servitude** of thy father, and his
heavy yoke that he put upon us, **and**
■ **we will serve thee.**
■ 5. **And he said** unto them,
■ **Come again** unto me
■ **after three days.** And
the people departed.
■ 6. **And** king
■ **Rehoboam took counsel**
■ **with the old men that had**
■ **stood before Solomon** his
father while he yet lived, saying,
What counsel give ye *me* to
return answer to this people?
■ 7. **And they**
■ **spake** unto him,
■ **saying,** If thou
■ **be kind to this people,**
■ **and** please them, and
speak good words to them,
■ **they will be thy**
■ **servants** for ever.
■ 8. **But he forsook the**
■ **counsel which the old**
■ **men gave** him,
■ **and took counsel with the**
■ **young men** that were brought
up with him, that stood before him.
9. And he said unto them, What
advice give ye that we may return
answer to this people, which have
spoken to me, saying, Ease
somewhat the yoke that thy
father did put upon us?
■ 10. **And the young men**
that were brought up with him
■ **spake** unto him,

■ **saying, Thus shalt thou**
■ **answer** the people that spake unto
thee, saying, Thy father made our
yoke heavy, but make thou *it*
somewhat lighter for us; thus shalt
thou say unto them, My little *finger*
shall be thicker than my father's loins.
11. For whereas my father put
a heavy yoke upon you,
■ **I will put more to your yoke:**
my father chastised you with whips,
but *I will chastise you* with scorpions.
■ 12. **So Jeroboam** and
all the people
■ **came to Rehoboam** on
■ **the third day,** as the king
bade, saying, Come again to
me on the third day.
■ 13. **And the king answered**
■ **them roughly;** and king
Rehoboam forsook the counsel
of the old men,
14. And answered them
■ **after the advice of the**
■ **young men,** saying, My father
made your yoke heavy, but I will
add thereto: my father chastised
you with whips, but *I will chastise*
you with scorpions.
15. So the king hearkened
not unto the people:
■ **for the cause was of God,**
■ **that the LORD might**
■ **perform his word,**
which he spake by the hand
of Ahijah the Shilonite to
Jeroboam the son of Nebat.
■ 16. **And when** all
■ **Israel saw that the king**
■ **would not hearken** unto them,
■ **the people**
■ **answered** the king,
■ **saying, What portion have**
■ **we in David?** and *we have* none
inheritance in the son of Jesse:
■ **every man to your**
■ **tents,** O Israel: *and* now,
David, see to thine own house.
So all Israel went to their tents.
17. **But** *as for* the children
of Israel that dwelt in
■ **the cities of Judah,**
■ **Rehoboam reigned**

over them.

18. **Then** king **Rehoboam sent Hadoram that was over the tribute; and** the children of **Israel stoned him with** stones, that he died. But king **Rehoboam made speed** to get him up to *his* chariot, **to flee to Jerusalem.**

19. **And Israel rebelled against the house of David** unto this day.

CHAPTER 11

1. **And when Rehoboam was come to Jerusalem, he gathered** of the house **of Judah and Benjamin an hundred** and **fourscore thousand** chosen *men*, which were **warriors, to fight against Israel,** that he might bring the kingdom again to Rehoboam.

2. **But the word of the LORD came to Shemaiah the man of God, saying,**

3. **Speak unto Rehoboam** the son of Solomon, king of Judah, and to all Israel in Judah and Benjamin, saying,

4. Thus saith the LORD, **Ye shall not** go up, nor **fight against your brethren:** return every man to his house: for this thing is done of me. **And they obeyed** the words of the LORD, and returned from going against Jeroboam.

5. **And Rehoboam dwelt in Jerusalem, and built cities for defence in Judah.**

6. **He built** even **Beth–lehem, and Etam,** and **Tekoa,**

7. And **Beth–zur, and Shoco,** and **Adullam,**

8. And **Gath, and Mareshah, and Ziph,**

9. And **Adoraim, and Lachish, and Azekah,**

10. And **Zorah,** and **Aijalon, and Hebron,** which *are* in Judah and in Benjamin fenced cities.

11. And he fortified the strong holds, and put captains in them, and store of victual, and of oil and wine.

12. And in every several city *he put* shields and spears, and made them exceeding strong, having Judah and Benjamin on his side.

13. **And the priests and** the **Levites** that **were** in all Israel **resorted to him** out of all their coasts.

14. **For the Levites left their suburbs** and their possession, **and came to Judah** and Jerusalem: **for Jeroboam** and his sons **had cast them off from executing the priest's office unto the LORD:**

15. **And he ordained** him **priests for the high places, and** for the **devils, and** for the **calves which he** had **made.**

16. **And** after them out of all the tribes of Israel **such as set their hearts to seek the LORD** God of Israel **came to Jerusalem, to sacrifice unto the LORD** God of their fathers.

17. **So they strengthened** the kingdom of **Judah, and made Rehoboam** the son of Solomon **strong,** three years: for three years they walked in the way of David and Solomon.

18. **And Rehoboam took** him **Mahalath** the daughter of

Jerimoth the son of David
to wife, and Abihail the
daughter of Eliab the son of Jesse;
19. Which bare him
children; Jeush, and
Shamariah, and Zaham.
20. And after her
he took Maachah the
daughter of Absalom;
which bare him Abijah, and
Attai, and Ziza, and Shelomith.
21. And Rehoboam
loved Maachah the
daughter of Absalom
above all his wives
and his concubines:
(for he took eighteen wives,
and threescore concubines;
and begat twenty and
eight sons, and
threescore daughters.)
22. And Rehoboam
made Abijah
the son of Maachah the chief,
to be ruler among his
brethren: for he thought
to make him king.
23. And he dealt wisely, and
dispersed of all his children
throughout all the countries of
Judah and Benjamin, unto every
fenced city: and he gave them
victual in abundance. And he
desired many wives.

CHAPTER 12

1. And it came to pass,
when Rehoboam had
established the kingdom,
and had strengthened himself,
he forsook the law of the
LORD, and all Israel with him.
2. And it came to pass, *that*
in the fifth year of king
Rehoboam Shishak king
of Egypt came up against
Jerusalem, because
they had transgressed
against the LORD,
3. With twelve hundred chariots,
and threescore thousand horsemen:
and the people *were* without number
that came with him out of Egypt;

the Lubims, the Sukkiims,
and the Ethiopians.
4. And he took the fenced
cities which *pertained* to Judah,
and came to Jerusalem.
5. Then came Shemaiah
the prophet to Rehoboam,
and to the princes of Judah,
that were gathered together to
Jerusalem because of Shishak,
and said unto them,
Thus saith the LORD, Ye
have forsaken me, and
therefore have I also
left you in the hand
of Shishak.
6. Whereupon the
princes of Israel
and the king humbled
themselves; and they said,
The LORD *is* righteous.
7. And when the LORD
saw that they humbled
themselves, the word of the
LORD came to Shemaiah,
saying, They have humbled
themselves; *therefore*
I will not destroy them, but I
will grant them some deliverance; and
my wrath shall not be poured outupon
Jerusalem by the hand of Shishak.
8. Nevertheless they shall
be his servants; that they may
know my service, and the service of
the kingdoms of the countries.
9. So Shishak king of Egypt
came up
against Jerusalem,
and took away
the treasures of the
house of the LORD,
and the treasures of
the king's house; he
took all: he carried away
also the shields of gold which
Solomon had made.
10. Instead of which king
Rehoboam made shields of brass,
and committed *them* to the hands
of the chief of the guard, that kept
the entrance of the king's house.
11. And when
the king entered into

the house of the LORD, the guard came and fetched them, and brought them again into the guard chamber.

12. **And when he humbled himself, the wrath of the LORD turned from him, that he would not destroy him** altogether: **and** also in Judah things went well.

13. So king Rehoboam strengthened himself in Jerusalem, and reigned: for **Rehoboam was one and forty years old when he began to reign, and he reigned seventeen years** in Jerusalem, the city which the LORD had chosen out of all the tribes of Israel, to put his name there. And his mother's name *was* Naamah an Ammonitess.

14. **And he did evil, because he prepared not his heart to seek the LORD.**

15. Now the acts of Rehoboam, first and last, *are* they not written in the book of Shemaiah the prophet, and of Iddo the seer concerning genealogies? **And there were wars between Rehoboam and Jeroboam continually.**

16. **And Rehoboam** slept with his fathers, and **was buried in the city of David: and Abijah** his son **reigned** in his stead.

CHAPTER 13

1. **Now in the eighteenth year of** king **Jeroboam began Abijah to reign over Judah.**

2. **He reigned three years** in Jerusalem. His mother's name also *was* Michaiah the daughter of Uriel of Gibeah. **And therewas war between Abijah and Jeroboam.**

3. **And Abijah set the battle** in array **with an army of** valiant men of war, *even*

four hundred thousand chosen men: Jeroboam also set the battle in array against him **with eight hundred thousand chosen men,** *being* mighty men of valour.

4. **And Abijah stood** up **upon** mount Zemaraim, which *is* in **mount Ephraim, and said, Hear me,** thou Jeroboam, and all **Israel;**

5. Ought ye not to know that the LORD **God** of Israel **gave the kingdom over Israel to David for ever,** *even* to him and to his sons by a covenant of salt?

6. **Yet Jeroboam** the son of Nebat, the servant of Solomon the son of David, is risen up, and **hath rebelled against his lord.**

7. **And** there are gathered unto him vain men, **the children of Belial, and have strengthened themselves against Rehoboam** the son of Solomon, when Rehoboam was young and tenderhearted, and could not withstand them.

8. **And now ye think to withstand the kingdom of the LORD** in the hand of the sons of David; **and ye be a great multitude,** and *there are* **with your golden calves,** which Jeroboam made you **for gods.**

9. **Have ye not cast out the priests of the LORD,** the sons of Aaron, and the Levites, and have made you priests after the manner of the nations of *other* lands? **so** that **whosoever cometh** to consecrate himself with a young bullock and seven rams, *the same* **may be a priest of** them *that are*

no gods.

10. **But** as for us, **the LORD is our God, and we have not forsaken him;** and the priests, which minister unto the LORD, *are* the sons of Aaron, and the Levites *wait* upon *their* business: 11. And they burn unto the LORD every morning and every evening burnt sacrifices and sweet incense: the shewbread also *set they in order* upon the pure table; and the candlestick of gold with the lamps thereof, to burn every evening: for we keep the charge of theLORD our God; **but ye have forsaken him.** 12. **And**, behold, **God** himself **is with us** for *our* captain, **and his priests** with sounding trumpets to **cry** alarm **against you.** O children of Israel, fight ye not against the LORD God of your fathers; for ye shall not prosper. 13. **But Jeroboam caused an ambushment** to come about **behind them:** so they were before Judah, and the ambushment *was* behind them. 14. **And when Judah looked back, behold, the battle was before and behind: and they cried unto the LORD,** and the priests sounded with the trumpets. 15. **Then the men of Judah gave a shout: and** as the men of Judah shouted, it came to pass, that **God smote Jeroboam and all Israel** before Abijah and Judah. 16. **And** the children of **Israel fled before Judah: and God delivered them** into their hand. 17. **And Abijah and his people slew them** with a great slaughter: **so there fell** down slain of Israel **five hundred thousand chosen men.** 18. **Thus** the children of

Israel were brought under at that time, and the children of **Judah prevailed, because they relied upon the LORD** God of their fathers. 19. **And Abijah** pursued after Jeroboam, and **took** cities from him, **Beth-el** with the towns thereof, and **Jeshanah** with the towns thereof, **and Ephraim** with the towns thereof. 20. **Neither did Jeroboam recover strength** again in the days of Abijah: and **the LORD struck him, and he died.** 21. But Abijah waxed mighty, and married fourteen wives, and begat twenty and two sons, and sixteen daughters. 22. **And the rest of the acts of Abijah,** and his ways, and his sayings, **are written in the story of** the prophet **Iddo.**

CHAPTER 14

1. **So Abijah slept** with his fathers, and they buried him in the city of David: **and Asa his son reigned in his stead.** In his days the land was quiet ten years. 2. **And Asa did that which was** good and **right in the eyes of the LORD** his God: 3. **For he took away the altars of the strange gods,** and the high places, **and brake down the images,** and cut down the groves: 4. **And commanded Judah to seek the LORD** God of their fathers, and to do the law and the commandment. 5. Also he took away out of all the cities of Judah the high places and the images: and the kingdom was quiet before him. 6. **And he built fenced**

■ **cities in Judah:** for the land had
rest,and he hadno war in those years;
■ **because the LORD**
■ **had given him rest.**
7. Therefore he said unto Judah, Let
us build these cities, and make about
them walls, and towers, gates, and
bars, *while* the land *is* yet before us;
because we have sought the LORD
our God, we have sought *him,* and he
hath given us rest on every side.
■ **So they built and**
■ **prospered.**
■ 8. **And Asa had an army** *of*
men that bare targets and spears,
■ **out of Judah three hundred**
■ **thousand; and out of**
■ **Benjamin,** that bare shields
and drew bows,
■ **two hundred** and
■ **fourscore thousand:** all
these *were* mighty men of valour.
■ 9. **And there came out**
■ **against them Zerah the**
■ **Ethiopian with** an host of
■ **a thousand thousand,** and
■ **three hundred chariots;**
and came unto Mareshah.
10. Then Asa went out against him,
■ **and they set the**
■ **battle** in array
■ **in the valley of**
■ **Zephathah** at Mareshah.
■ 11. **And Asa cried unto**
■ **the LORD** his God, and said,
LORD, *it is* nothing with thee to
help, whether with many, or
with them that have no power:
■ **help us, O LORD** our God;
■ **for we rest on thee,** and in
thy name we go against this
multitude. O LORD, thou *art* our God;
■ **let no man prevail**
■ **against thee.**
■ 12. **So the LORD smote**
■ **the Ethiopians** before
Asa, and before Judah;
and the Ethiopians fled.
■ 13. **And Asa** and the
people that *were* with him
■ **pursued them** unto Gerar:
■ **and the Ethiopians** were
overthrown, that they could not

recover themselves; for they
■ **were destroyed before**
■ **the LORD,** and before his host;
■ **and they carried away**
■ **very much spoil.**
14. And they smote all the cities
round about Gerar; for the fear of the
LORD came upon them: and they
spoiled all the cities; for there was
exceeding much spoil in them.
15. They smote also the tents of
cattle, and carried away sheep
and camels in abundance,
■ **and returned to Jerusalem.**

CHAPTER 15

■ 1. **And the Spirit of God**
■ **came upon Azariah**
the son of Oded:
■ 2. **And he went** out
■ **to meet Asa, and said**
unto him, Hear ye me, Asa, and
all Judah and Benjamin;
■ **The LORD is with you, while**
■ **ye be with him;** and if ye seek
him, he will be found of you; but if ye
forsake him, he will forsake you.
■ 3. **Now for a long season**
■ **Israel hath been without**
■ **the true God,** and without a
teaching priest, and without law.
■ 4. **But when they**
in their trouble
■ **did turn unto the LORD**
God of Israel, and sought him,
■ **he was found of them.**
■ 5. **And in those times there**
■ **was no peace** to him that went
out, nor to him that came in, but great
vexations *were* upon all the
inhabitants of the countries.
■ 6. **And nation** was
■ **destroyed** of
■ **nation,** and city of city:
■ **for God did vex them with** all
■ **adversity.**
■ 7. **Be ye strong** therefore,
and let not your hands be weak:
■ **for your work shall**
■ **be rewarded.**
■ 8. **And when Asa heard**
■ **these words,** and the
prophecy of Oded the prophet,

676

he took courage, and put away the abominable idols out of all the land of Judah and Benjamin, and out of the cities which he had taken from mount Ephraim.

and renewed the altar of the LORD, that *was* before the porch of the LORD.

9. And he gathered all Judah and Benjamin, and the strangers with them out of Ephraim and Manasseh, and out of Simeon: for they fell to him out of Israel in abundance, when they saw that the LORD his God was with him.

10. So they gathered themselves together at Jerusalem in the third month, in the fifteenth year of the reign of Asa.

11. And they offered unto the LORD the same time, of the spoil *which* they had brought, seven hundred oxen and seven thousand sheep.

12. And they entered into a covenant to seek the LORD God of their fathers with all their heart and with all their soul;

13. That whosoever would not seek the LORD God of Israel should be put to death, whether small or great, whether man or woman.

14. And they sware unto the LORD with a loud voice, and with shouting, and with trumpets, and with cornets.

15. And all Judah rejoiced at the oath: for they had sworn with all their heart, and sought him with their whole desire; and he was found of them: and the LORD gave them rest round about.

16. And also concerning Maachah the mother of Asa the king, he removed her from being queen, because she had made an idol in a grove: and Asa cut down her idol, and stamped *it*, and burnt *it* at the brook Kidron.

17. But the high places were not taken away out of Israel: nevertheless the heart of Asa was perfect all his days.

18. And he brought into the house of God the things that his father had dedicated, and that he himself had dedicated, silver, and gold, and vessels.

19. And there was no more war unto the five and thirtieth year of the reign of Asa.

CHAPTER 16

1. In the six and thirtieth year of the reign of Asa Baasha king of Israel came up against Judah, and built Ramah, to the intent that he might let none go out or come in to Asa king of Judah.

2. Then Asa brought out silver and gold out of the treasures of the house of the LORD and of the king's house, and sent to Ben-hadad king of Syria, that dwelt at Damascus, saying,

3. *There is* a league between me and thee, as *there was* between my father and thy father: behold, I have sent thee silver and gold; go, break thy league with Baasha king of Israel, that he may depart from me.

4. And Ben-hadad hearkened unto king Asa, and sent the captains of his armies against the cities of Israel; and they smote Ijon, and Dan, and Abel-maim, and all the store cities of Naphtali.

5. And it came to pass, when Baasha heard *it*, that

■ he left off building of
■ Ramah, and let his work cease.
■ 6. Then Asa the king
took all Judah; and they
■ carried away the stones
■ of Ramah, and the
■ timber thereof, wherewith
Baasha was building;
■ and he
■ built therewith
■ Geba and Mizpah.
■ 7. And at that time
■ Hanani the seer came
■ to Asa king of Judah,
■ and said unto him,
■ Because thou hast
■ relied on the king of
■ Syria, and not relied
■ on the LORD thy God, therefore is
■ the host of the king of
■ Syria escaped out
■ of thine hand.
■ 8. Were not the
■ Ethiopians and the Lubims
■ a huge host, with very
many chariots and horsemen?
■ yet, because thou didst rely on
■ the LORD, he
■ delivered them
■ into thine hand.
■ 9. For the eyes of the
■ LORD run to and fro
■ throughout the whole
■ earth, to shew himself
■ strong in the
■ behalf of them whose
■ heart is perfect toward
■ him. Herein thou hast done foolishly:
■ therefore from henceforth
■ thou shalt have wars.
■ 10. Then Asa was wroth with
■ the seer, and put him in a
■ prison house; for *he was* in a
rage with him because of this
thing. And Asa oppressed *some*
of the people the same time.
11. And, behold, the acts of Asa, first
and last, lo, they *are* written in the
book of the kings of Judah and Israel.
■ 12. And Asa in the thirty
and ninth year of his reign
■ was diseased in his feet, until
his disease *was* exceeding *great*.

■ yet in his disease
■ he sought not to the
■ LORD, but to
■ the physicians.
■ 13. And Asa slept
with his fathers, and
■ died in the one and
■ fortieth year of his reign.
14. And they buried him in his own
sepulchres, which he had made for
himself in the city of David, and laid
him in the bed which was filled with
sweet odours and divers kinds *of*
spices prepared by the apothecaries'
art: and they made a very
great burning for him.

CHAPTER 17

■ 1. And Jehoshaphat his
■ son reigned in his stead,
■ and strengthened
■ himself against Israel.
■ 2. And he placed forces
■ in all the fenced cities of
■ Judah, and set garrisons
in the land of Judah,
■ and in the cities of
■ Ephraim, which Asa
his father had taken.
■ 3. And the LORD was with
■ Jehoshaphat, because he
walked in the first ways of his father
David, and sought not unto Baalim;
4. But
■ sought to
■ the Lord God of his father,
■ and walked in his
■ commandments, and not
after the doings of Israel.
■ 5. Therefore the LORD
■ stablished the
■ kingdom in his hand;
■ and all Judah
■ brought to Jehoshaphat
■ presents; and he had
■ riches and honour
in abundance.
■ 6. And his heart was lifted
■ up in the ways of the LORD:
■ moreover he took away
■ the high places and groves
out of Judah.
■ 7. Also in the third year of

his reign he sent to
his princes, *even* to Ben-hail,
and to Obadiah, and to Zechariah,
and to Nethaneel, and to Michaiah,
to teach in the cities
of Judah.
8. **And** with them
he sent Levites, *even*
Shemaiah, and Nethaniah,
and Zebadiah, and Asahel, and
Shemiramoth, and Jehonathan,
and Adonijah, and Tobijah, and
Tob-adonijah, Levites; and with them
Elishama and Jehoram, priests.
9. **And they taught** in Judah,
and *had* the book of
the law of the LORD with
them, and went about throughout
all the cities of Judah, and
taught the people.
10. **And the fear of the LORD**
fell upon all the kingdoms
of the lands that *were*
round about
Judah, so that
they made no war
against Jehoshaphat.
11. **Also** *some* of
the Philistines brought
Jehoshaphat
presents, and tribute silver;
and the Arabians
brought him
flocks, seven thousand and seven
hundred rams, and seven thousand
and seven hundred he goats.
12. **And Jehoshaphat**
waxed great exceedingly;
and he
built in Judah
castles, and cities of store.
13. And he had much business
in the cities of Judah: and the
men of war, mighty men of
valour, *were* in Jerusalem.
14. **And these are the**
numbers of them according
to the house of their fathers:
Of Judah, the
captains of thousands;
Adnah the chief, and
with him mighty men of valour
three hundred thousand.

15. And next to him *was*
Jehohanan the captain, and
with him
two hundred and
fourscore thousand.
16. And next him *was*
Amasiah the son of Zichri,
who willingly offered himself
unto the LORD; and
with him
two hundred
thousand mighty men of valour.
17. **And of Benjamin; Eliada**
a mighty man of valour, and
with him armed men
with bow and shield
two hundred thousand.
18. **And** next him *was*
Jehozabad, and
with him
an hundred and
fourscore thousand
ready prepared for the war.
19. **These waited on**
the king, beside those
whom the king put
in the fenced cities
throughout all
Judah.

CHAPTER 18

1. Now Jehoshaphat
had riches and
honour in abundance,
and joined affinity
with Ahab.
2. **And** after *certain* years
he went down to Ahab to
Samaria. And Ahab killed
sheep and oxen
for him in abundance, and
for the people that *he had*
with him, and persuaded
him to go up
with him to Ramoth-gilead.
3. **And Ahab king of Israel**
said unto Jehoshaphat
king of Judah,
Wilt thou go with me
to Ramoth-gilead?
And he answered him, I
am as thou *art*,
and my people

as thy people; and *we* will be with thee in the war.

4. And Jehoshaphat said unto the king of Israel, Inquire, I pray thee, at the word of the LORD to day.

5. Therefore the king of Israel gathered together of prophets four hundred men, and said unto them, Shall we go to Ramoth-gilead to battle, or shall I forbear? And they said, Go up; for God will deliver it into the king's hand.

6. But Jehoshaphat said, Is there not here a prophet of the LORD besides, that we might inquire of him?

7. And the king of Israel said unto Jehoshaphat, There is yet one man, by whom we may inquire of the LORD: but I hate him; for he never prophesied good unto me, but always evil: the same is Micaiah the son of Imla. And Jehoshaphat said, Let not the king say so.

8. And the king of Israel called for one *of his* officers, and said, Fetch quickly Micaiah the son of Imla.

9. And the king of Israel and Jehoshaphat king of Judah sat either of them on his throne, clothed in *their* robes, and they sat in a void place at the entering in of the gate of Samaria; and all the prophets prophesied before them.

10. And Zedekiah the son of Chenaanah had made him horns of iron, and said, Thus saith the LORD, With these thou shalt push Syria until they be consumed.

11. And all the prophets prophesied so, saying, Go up to Ramoth-gilead, and prosper: for the LORD shall deliver *it* into the hand of the king.

12. And the messenger that went to call Micaiah spake to him, saying, Behold, the words of the prophets declare good to the king with one assent; let thy word therefore, I pray thee, be like one of their's, and speak thou good.

13. And Micaiah said, *As* the LORD liveth, even what my God saith, that will I speak.

14. And when he was come to the king, the king said unto him, Micaiah, shall we go to Ramoth-gilead to battle, or shall I forbear? And he said, Go ye up, and prosper, and they shall be delivered into your hand.

15. And the king said to him, How many times shall I adjure thee that thou say nothing but the truth to me in the name of the LORD?

16. Then he said, I did see all Israel scattered upon the mountains, as sheep that have no shepherd: and the LORD said, These have no master; let them return therefore every man to his house in peace.

17. And the king of Israel said to Jehoshaphat, Did I not tell thee *that* he would not prophesy good unto me, but evil?

18. Again he said, Therefore hear the word of the LORD; I saw the LORD sitting upon his throne, and all the host of heaven standing on his right hand and *on* his left.

19. And the LORD said, Who shall entice

Ahab king of Israel, that he may go up and fall at Ramoth-gilead? And one spake saying after this manner, and another saying after that manner.

20. **Then there came out a spirit,** and stood before the LORD, **and said, I will entice him.** And the LORD said unto him, Wherewith?

21. And he said, **I will** go out, and **be a lying spirit in the mouth of** all **his prophets. And the Lord said,** Thou shalt entice *him*, and thou shalt also prevail: **go out, and do** *even* **so.**

22. **Now** therefore, behold, **the LORD hath put a lying spirit in the mouth of** these **thy prophets,** and the LORD hath spoken evil against thee.

23. **Then Zedekiah** the son of Chenaanah came near, and **smote Micaiah upon the cheek, and said, Which way went the Spirit of the LORD from me to speak unto thee?**

24. **And Micaiah said,** Behold, **thou shalt see** on that day **when thou shalt go into an inner chamber to hide thyself.**

25. **Then the king of Israel said, Take** ye **Micaiah,** and carry him **back to Amon** the governor of the city, and **to** Joash the king's son;

26. And say, Thus saith the king, Put this *fellow* in the **prison, and feed him** with **bread** of affliction **and** with **water** of affliction, **until I return in peace.**

27. **And Micaiah said, If thou** certainly **return in peace, then hath** **not the LORD spoken by me.** And he said, Hearken, all ye people.

28. **So the king of Israel and Jehoshaphat** the king **of Judah went up to Ramoth-gilead.**

29. **And the king of Israel said unto Jehoshaphat, I will disguise myself,** and I will go to the battle; **but put thou on thy robes.** So the king of Israel disguised himself; and they went to the battle.

30. **Now the king of Syria had commanded the captains** of the chariots that *were* with him, **saying, Fight** ye not with small or great, save **only with the king of Israel.**

31. **And** it came to pass, **when the captains** of the chariots **saw Jehoshaphat,** that they said, It is the king of Israel. Therefore **they compassed about him** to fight: **but Jehoshaphat cried out, and the LORD helped him; and** God moved them *to depart* from him.

32. For it came to pass, that, when **the captains** of the chariots perceived that it was not the king of Israel, they **turned back** again **from pursuing him.**

33. **And a certain man drew a bow at a venture, and smote the king of Israel** between the joints of the harness: **therefore he said to his chariot man,** Turn thine hand, that thou mayest **carry me out of the host; for I am wounded.**

34. And the battle increased that day: **howbeit the king of Israel** stayed himself up in his chariot against the Syrians until the even: and about the time of the sun

going down he
died.

CHAPTER 19

1. **And Jehoshaphat**
the king of Judah
returned to his house
in peace to Jerusalem.
2. **And Jehu the son of**
Hanani the seer went out
to meet him, and
said to king Jehoshaphat,
Shouldest thou
help the ungodly,
and love them that hate
the LORD? therefore is
wrath upon thee from before
the LORD.
3. **Nevertheless** there
are good things found in thee, in that
thou hast taken away
the groves out of the land,
and has
prepared thine
heart to seek God.
4. **And Jehoshaphat**
dwelt at Jerusalem: and he
went out again
through the people
from Beer-sheba to mount Ephraim,
and brought them
back unto the LORD
God of their fathers.
5. **And he set judges**
in the land throughout all the
fenced cities of
Judah, city by city,
6. **And said** to the judges,
Take heed what ye do:
for ye judge not for man, but
for the LORD, who *is* with
you in the judgment.
7. **Wherefore** now
let the fear of the LORD
be upon you; take heed
and do it: for *there is*
no iniquity with the LORD
our God, nor respect of
persons, nor taking of gifts.
8. **Moreover in**
Jerusalem did
Jehoshaphat set of the
Levites, and *of* the

priests, and of the chief
of the fathers of Israel,
for the judgment
of the LORD, and for
controversies, when
they returned to Jerusalem.
9. **And he charged**
them, saying,
Thus shall ye do in the
fear of the LORD, faithfully,
and with a perfect heart.
10. **And what cause** soever
shall come to you of your
brethren that dwell in your cities,
between blood and blood,
between law and commandment,
statutes and judgments,
ye shall even
warn them that they
trespass not against the
LORD, and *so* wrath come upon
you, and upon your brethren:
this do, and ye shall not trespass.
11. And, behold, Amariah the chief
priest *is* over you in all matters of
the LORD; and Zebadiah the son
of Ishmael, the ruler of the
house of Judah, for all the king's
matters: also the Levites *shall*
be officers before you.
Deal courageously,
and the LORD shall
be with the good.

CHAPTER 20

1. It came to pass
after this also, *that*
the children of
Moab, and the children of
Ammon, and with them *other*
beside the Ammonites,
came against Jehoshaphat
to battle.
2. **Then there came some**
that told Jehoshaphat,
saying, There cometh a great
multitude against thee from
beyond the sea on this side
Syria; and, behold, they *be* in
Hazazon–tamar, which *is* En–gedi.
3. **And Jehoshaphat**
feared, and set himself
to seek the LORD,

and proclaimed a
fast throughout all
Judah.
4. And Judah
gathered themselves
together, to ask *help* of
the LORD: even out of all the
cities of Judah they came
to seek the LORD.
5. And Jehoshaphat
stood in the congregation
of Judah and Jerusalem,
in the house of the
LORD, before the new court,
6. And said, O LORD
God of our fathers, *art* not
thou God in heaven? and
rulest *not* thou
over all the kingdoms of the
heathen? and in thine hand *is
there not* power and might, so that
none is able to
withstand thee?
7. *Art* not
thou our God,
who didst drive out
the inhabitants of this
land before thy people Israel,
and gavest it to the
seed of Abraham thy
friend for ever?
8. And they dwelt
therein, and have
built thee a
sanctuary therein for thy name,
saying,
9. If, when evil cometh
upon us, *as* the sword, judgment,
or pestilence, or famine,
we stand before
this house, and in
thy presence, (for thy
name *is* in this house,)
and cry unto
thee in our affliction,
then thou wilt
hear and help.
10. And now,
behold, the children of
Ammon and Moab
and mount Seir,
whom thou wouldest
not let Israel invade,

when they came out of the land
of Egypt, but they turned from
them, and destroyed them not;
11. Behold, *I say, how*
they reward us, to
come to cast us out of
thy possession, which
thou hast given us to inherit.
12. O our God,
wilt thou not judge them?
for we have no might
against this great
company that cometh against
us; neither know we what to do:
but our eyes are upon thee.
13. And all Judah stood
before the LORD, with their little
ones, their wives, and their children.
14. Then upon Jahaziel the
son of Zechariah, the son of Benaiah,
the son of Jeiel, the son of Mattaniah,
a Levite of the sons of Asaph,
came the Spirit of the LORD
in the midst of the congregation;
15. And he said, Hearken
ye, all Judah, and ye inhabitants
of Jerusalem, and thou
king Jehoshaphat,
Thus saith the LORD unto you,
Be not afraid nor dismayed
by reason of this great multitude;
for the battle is not
yours, but God's.
16. To morrow go ye
down against them: behold,
they come up by the cliff of Ziz;
and ye shall find them at the
end of the brook, before the
wilderness of Jeruel.
17. Ye shall not need to
fight in this *battle*: set yourselves,
stand ye still, and see the
salvation of the LORD with
you, O Judah and Jerusalem: fear
not, nor be dismayed; to morrow
go out against them: for the
LORD *will be* with you.
18. And Jehoshaphat
bowed his head with
his face to the ground:
and all Judah and the
inhabitants of Jerusalem
fell before the LORD,

worshipping the LORD.

19. And the Levites, of the children of the Kohathites, and of the children of the Korhites, **stood up to praise the LORD** God of Israel with a loud voice on high.

20. **And they** rose early in the morning, and **went forth into** the wilderness of **Tekoa: and** as they went forth, **Jehoshaphat** stood and **said,** Hear me, O Judah, and ye inhabitants of Jerusalem; **Believe in the LORD** your God, **so shall ye be established; believe his prophets, so shall ye prosper.**

21. **And** when he had consulted with the people, **he appointed singers** unto the LORD, **and** that should praise the beauty of holiness, as **they went out before the army,** and **to say, Praise the LORD;** for his mercy *endureth* for ever.

22. **And when they began to sing and** to **praise, the LORD set ambushments against** the children of **Ammon, Moab, and mount Seir,** which were come against Judah; **and they were smitten.**

23. **For** the children of **Ammon and Moab stood up against the inhabitants of mount Seir,** utterly **to** slay and **destroy them: and** when **they** had **made an end of** the inhabitants of **Seir, every one helped to destroy another.**

24. **And** when **Judah** came toward the watch tower in the wilderness, they **looked** unto the multitude, **and, behold, they were dead bodies fallen to the earth,** and none escaped.

25. **And when Jehoshaphat** and his people **came to take** away **the spoil** of them, **they found** among them in abundance both **riches** with the dead bodies, and precious jewels, which they stripped off for themselves, **more than they could carry away:** and **they were three days in gathering of the spoil,** it was so much.

26. **And on the fourth day they assembled** themselves **in the valley of Berachah;** for **there they blessed the LORD:** therefore the name of the same place was called, The valley of Berachah, unto this day.

27. **Then they returned,** every man of Judah and Jerusalem, and Jehoshaphat in the forefront of them, to go again **to Jerusalem** with joy; for the LORD had made them to rejoice over their enemies.

28. And they came to Jerusalem **with psalteries and harps and trumpets unto the house of the LORD.**

29. **And the fear of God was on all the kingdoms** of *those* countries, **when they** had **heard** that **the LORD fought** against **the enemies of Israel.**

30. **So the realm of Jehoshaphat was quiet:** for his God gave him rest round about.

31. **And Jehoshaphat reigned over Judah:** *he was* thirty and five years old when he began to reign, and he reigned **twenty** and **five years** in Jerusalem. And his mother's name *was* Azubah the daughter of Shilhi.

32. **And he walked in**

the way of Asa his father, and departed not from it, doing *that which was* right in the sight of the LORD. 33. Howbeit the high places were not taken away: for as yet the people had not prepared their hearts unto the God of their fathers.

34. Now the rest of the acts of Jehoshaphat, first and last, behold, they *are* written in the book of Jehu the son of Hanani, who is mentioned in the book of the kings of Israel.

35. And after this did Jehoshaphat king of Judah join himself with Ahaziah king of Israel, who did very wickedly:

36. And he joined himself with him to make ships to go to Tarshish: and they made the ships in Ezion–gaber.

37. Then Eliezer the son of Dodavah of Mareshah prophesied against Jehoshaphat, saying, Because thou hast joined thyself with Ahaziah, the LORD hath broken thy works. And the ships were broken, that they were not able to go to Tarshish.

CHAPTER 21

1. Now Jehoshaphat slept with his fathers, and was buried with his fathers in the city of David. And Jehoram his son reigned in his stead.

2. And he had brethren the sons of Jehoshaphat, Azariah, and Jehiel, and Zechariah, and Azariah, and Michael, and Shephatiah: all these *were* the sons of Jehoshaphat king of Israel.

3. And their father gave them great gifts of silver, and of gold, and of precious things, with fenced cities in Judah: but the kingdom gave he to Jehoram; because he *was* the firstborn.

4. Now when Jehoram was risen up to the kingdom of his father, he strengthened himself, and slew all his brethren with the sword, and divers also of the princes of Israel.

5. Jehoram was thirty and two years old when he began to reign, and he reigned eight years in Jerusalem.

6. And he walked in the way of the kings of Israel, like as did the house of Ahab: for he had the daughter of Ahab to wife: and he wrought that which was evil in the eyes of the LORD.

7. Howbeit the LORD would not destroy the house of David, because of the covenant that he had made with David, and as he promised to give a light to him and to his sons for ever.

8. In his days the Edomites revolted from under the dominion of Judah, and made themselves a king.

9. Then Jehoram went forth with his princes, and all his chariots with him: and he rose up by night, and smote the Edomites which compassed him in, and the captains of the chariots.

10. So the Edomites revolted from under the hand of Judah unto this day. The same time also did Libnah revolt from under his hand; because he had forsaken the LORD God of his fathers.

11. Moreover he made high places in the mountains of Judah and caused the inhabitants of Jerusalem to commit fornication, and compelled Judah *thereto.*

12. And there came a writing to him from Elijah the prophet, saying, Thus saith the LORD God of David thy father, Because thou hast not walked in the ways of Jehoshaphat thy father, nor in the ways of Asa king of Judah,

13. But hast walked in the way of the kings of Israel, and hast made Judah and the inhabitants of Jerusalem to go a whoring, like to the whoredoms of the house of Ahab, and also hast slain thy brethren of thy father's house, which were better than thyself:

14. Behold, with a great plague will the LORD smite thy people, and thy children, and thy wives, and all thy goods:

15. And thou shalt have great sickness by disease of thy bowels, until thy bowels fall out by reason of the sickness day by day.

16. Moreover the LORD stirred up against Jehoram the spirit of the Philistines, and of the Arabians, that *were* near the Ethiopians:

17. And they came up into Judah, and brake into it, and carried away all the substance that was found in the king's house, and his sons also, and his wives; so that there was never a son left him, save Jehoahaz, the youngest of his sons.

18. And after all this the LORD smote him in his bowels with an incurable disease.

19. And it came to pass, that in process of time, after the end of two years, his bowels fell out by reason of his sickness: so he died of sore diseases. And his people made no burning for him, like the burning of his fathers.

20. Thirty and two years old was he when he began to reign, and he reigned in Jerusalem eight years, and departed without being desired. Howbeit they buried him in the city of David, but not in the sepulchres of the kings.

CHAPTER 22

1. And the inhabitants of Jerusalem made Ahaziah his youngest son king in his stead: for the band of men that came with the Arabians to the camp had slain all the eldest. So Ahaziah the son of Jehoram king of Judah reigned.

2. Forty and two years old was Ahaziah when he began to reign, and he reigned one year in Jerusalem. His mother's name also *was* Athaliah the daughter of Omri.

3. He also walked in the ways of the house of Ahab: for his mother was his counsellor to do wickedly.

4. Wherefore he did evil in the sight of the LORD like the house of Ahab: for they were his counsellors after the death of his father to his destruction.

5. He walked also after their counsel, and went with Jehoram the son of Ahab king of Israel to war

686

against Hazael king of Syria at Ramoth–gilead: and the Syrians smote Joram. 6. And he returned to be healed in Jezreel because of the wounds which were given him at Ramah, when he fought with Hazael king of Syria. And Azariah the son of Jehoram king of Judah went down to see Jehoram the son of Ahab at Jezreel, because he was sick. 7. And the destruction of Ahaziah was of God by coming to Joram: for when he was come, he went out with Jehoram against Jehu the son of Nimshi, whom the LORD had anointed to cut off the house of Ahab. 8. And it came to pass, that, when Jehu was executing judgment upon the house of Ahab, and found the princes of Judah, and the sons of the brethren of Ahaziah, that ministered to Ahaziah, he slew them. 9. And he sought Ahaziah: and they caught him, (for he was hid in Samaria,) and brought him to Jehu: and when they had slain him, they buried him: Because, said they, he is the son of Jehoshaphat, who sought the LORD with all his heart. So the house of Ahaziah had no power to keep still the kingdom. 10. But when Athaliah the mother of Ahaziah saw that her son was dead, she arose and destroyed all the seed royal of the house of Judah. 11. But Jehoshabeath, the daughter of the king,

took Joash the son of Ahaziah, and stole him from among the king's sons that were slain, and put him and his nurse in a bedchamber. So Jehoshabeath, the daughter of king Jehoram, the wife of Jehoiada the priest, (for she was the sister of Ahaziah,) hid him from Athaliah, so that she slew him not. 12. And he was with them hid in the house of God six years: and Athaliah reigned over the land.

CHAPTER 23

1. And in the seventh year Jehoiada strengthened himself, and took the captains of hundreds, Azariah the son of Jeroham, and Ishmael the son of Jehohanan, and Azariah the son of Obed, and Maaseiah the son of Adaiah, and Elishaphat the son of Zichri, into covenant with him. 2. And they went about in Judah, and gathered the Levites out of all the cities of Judah, and the chief of the fathers of Israel, and they came to Jerusalem. 3. And all the congregation made a covenant with the king in the house of God. And he said unto them, Behold, the king's son shall reign, as the LORD hath said of the sons of David. 4. This is the thing that ye shall do; A third part of you entering on the sabbath, of the priests and of the Levites, shall be porters of the doors; 5. And a third part shall be at the king's house; and a third part at the gate of the foundation: and all the people shall be in the courts of the house of the LORD. 6. But let none come into

the house of the LORD, save
the priests, and they that minister
of the Levites; they shall go in, for
they *are* holy: but all the people shall
keep the watch of the LORD.

7. And the Levites shall
compass the king
round about, every man with
his weapons in his hand;
and whosoever *else*
cometh into the house, he
shall be put to death: but
be ye with the king when he
cometh in, and when he goeth out.

8. So the Levites and all Judah
did according to
all things that
Jehoiada the priest had
commanded, and took every
man his men that were to come in on
the sabbath, with them that were to
go *out* on the sabbath: for Jehoiada
the priest dismissed not the courses.

9. Moreover
Jehoiada the priest
delivered to the
captains of hundreds
spears, and bucklers,
and shields, that *had been*
king David's, which *were* in
the house of God.

10. And he set all
the people,
every man having his weapon
in his hand, from the right side of the
temple to the left side of the
temple, along by the altar and
the temple, by the king
round about.

11. Then they brought
out the king's son, and put
upon him the crown, and
gave him the testimony,
and made him king. And
Jehoiada and his sons anointed him,
and said, God save the king.

12. Now when Athaliah
heard the noise of the people
running and praising the king,
she came to the people
into the house of the LORD:

13. And she looked, and, and, behold,
the king stood at his pillar at
the entering in, and the princes
and the trumpets by the king:
and all the people of the land
rejoiced, and sounded with
trumpets, also the singers with
instruments of music, and such
as taught to sing praise.

Then Athaliah rent
her clothes, and said,
Treason, Treason.

14. Then Jehoiada the priest
brought out the captains of
hundreds that were set over the host,
and said unto them, Have
her forth of the ranges: and
whoso followeth her, let
him be slain with the sword.
For the priest said, Slay
her not in the house
of the LORD.

15. So they laid hands on her; and
when she was come
to the entering of
the horse gate
by the king's house,
they slew her there.

16. And Jehoiada made
a covenant between
him, and between all
the people, and between the
king, that they should be
the LORD's people.

17. Then all the people went
to the house of Baal, and
brake it down, and brake
his altars and his images in pieces,
and slew Mattan
the priest of Baal
before the altars.

18. Also Jehoiada
appointed the offices of the
house of the LORD by the hand
of the priests the Levites, whom David
had distributed in the house of the
LORD, to offer the burnt offerings of
the LORD, as *it is* written in the law of
Moses, with rejoicing and withsinging,
as it was ordained
by David.

19. And he set the
porters at the gates
of the house of the LORD,
that none which was

unclean in any thing **should enter** in. 20. **And he** took the captains of hundreds, and the nobles, and the governors of the people, and all the people of the land, and **brought** down **the king from the house of the LORD:** and they came through the high gate into the king's house, **and set the king upon the throne** of the kingdom. 21. **And all the people** of the land **rejoiced:** and the city was quiet, after that they had slain Athaliah with the sword.

CHAPTER 24

1. **Joash was seven years old when he began to reign, and he reigned forty years** in Jerusalem. His mother's name also *was* Zibiah of Beer-sheba. 2. **And Joash did that which was right in the sight of the LORD** all the days of Jehoiada the priest. 3. And Jehoiada took for him two wives; and he begat sons and daughters. 4. **And** it came to pass after this, *that* **Joash was minded to repair the house of the LORD.** 5. **And he gathered** together **the priests and** the **Levites, and said** to them, Go out unto the cities of Judah, and **gather** of all Israel **money to repair the house of your God** from year to year, **and** see that ye **hasten the matter. Howbeit the Levites hastened it not.** 6. **And the king called for Jehoiada** the chief, **and said** unto him, **Why hast thou not required** of **the Levites to bring in** out of Judah and out of Jerusalem **the collection, according to the commandment of Moses** the servant of the LORD, and of the congregation of Israel, for the tabernacle of witness? 7. **For the sons of Athaliah,** that wicked woman, **had broken up the house of God; and** also all **the dedicated things** of the house of the LORD **did they bestow upon Baalim.** 8. **And at the king's commandment they made a chest, and set it** without **at the gate of the house of the LORD.** 9. And they made a proclamation through Judah and Jerusalem, **to bring** in **to the LORD the collection** *that* Moses the servant of God *laid* upon Israel in the wilderness. 10. **And** all the princes and all **the people rejoiced, and brought in, and cast into the chest,** until they had made an end. 11. **Now** it came to pass, that at what time **the chest was brought unto the king's office** by the hand of the Levites, **and** when they saw that *there was* much money, **the king's scribe and the high priest's officer** came and **emptied** the chest, and took **it, and carried it to his place again. Thus they did day by day,** and gathered money in abundance. 12. **And the king and Jehoiada** gave it to such as did the work of the service of the house of the LORD, and **hired masons and carpenters to repair the house of the LORD,** and also such as wrought iron and brass to mend the house of the LORD.

13. So the workmen wrought, and the work was perfected by them, and they set the house of God in his state, and strengthened it.

14. And when they had finished it, they brought the rest of the money before the king and Jehoiada, whereof were made vessels for the house of the LORD, even vessels to minister, and to offer withal, and spoons, and vessels of gold and silver. And they offered burnt offerings in the house of the LORD continually all the days of Jehoiada.

15. But Jehoiada waxed old, and was full of days when he died; an hundred and thirty years old was he when he died.

16. And they buried him in the city of David among the kings, because he had done good in Israel, both toward God, and toward his house.

17. Now after the death of Jehoiada came the princes of Judah, and made obeisance to the king. Then the king hearkened unto them.

18. And they left the house of the LORD God of their fathers, and served groves and idols: and wrath came upon Judah and Jerusalem for this their trespass.

19. Yet he sent prophets to them, to bring them again unto the LORD; and they testified against them: but they would not give ear.

20. And the Spirit of God came upon Zechariah the son of Jehoiada the priest, which stood above the people, and said unto them, Thus saith God, Why transgress ye the commandments of the LORD, that ye cannot prosper? because ye have forsaken the LORD, he hath also forsaken you.

21. And they conspired against him, and stoned him with stones at the commandment of the king in the court of the house of the LORD.

22. Thus Joash the king remembered not the kindness which Jehoiada his father had done to him, but slew his son. And when he died, he said, The LORD look upon it, and require it.

23. And it came to pass at the end of the year, that the host of Syria came up against him: and they came to Judah and Jerusalem, and destroyed all the princes of the people from among the people, and sent all the spoil of them unto the king of Damascus.

24. For the army of the Syrians came with a small company of men, and the LORD delivered a very great host into their hand, because they had forsaken the LORD God of their fathers. So they executed judgment against Joash.

25. And when they were departed from him, (for they left him in great diseases,) his own servants conspired against him for the blood of the sons of Jehoiada the priest, and slew him on his bed, and he died: and they buried him in the city of David, but they buried him not in the sepulchres of the kings.

26. And these are they that conspired against him; Zabad the son of

690

Shimeath an Ammonitess, and Jehozabad the son of Shimrith a Moabitess.

27. Now *concerning* his sons, and the greatness of the burdens *laid* upon him,and therepairing of the house of God, behold, they *are* written in the story of the book of the kings. **And Amaziah his son reigned in his stead.**

CHAPTER 25

1. **Amaziah** *was* twenty and five years old *when* he began to reign, and he **reigned twenty** and **nine years in Jerusalem.** And his mother's name *was* Jehoaddan of Jerusalem.

2. **And he did** *that which was* **right in the sight of the LORD, but not with a perfect heart.**

3. Now it came to pass, when the kingdom was established to him, that **he slew his servants that had killed** the king **his father.**

4. **But** he slew **not their children, but did as** *it is* written in the law in the book of **Moses,** where the LORD **commanded,** saying, The fathers shall not die for the children, neither shall the children die for the fathers, but **every man shall die for his own sin.**

5. **Moreover Amaziah gathered Judah together,** and made them captains over thousands, and captains over hundreds, according to the houses of *their* fathers, throughout all Judah and Benjamin: **and** he **numbered them** from twenty years old and above, **and found them three hundred thousand** choice *men, able* to go forth to war, **that could handle**

spear and shield.

6. **He hired also an hundred thousand mighty men** of valour **out of Israel** for an hundred talents of silver.

7. **But there came a man of God** to him, **saying,** O king, **let not** the army of **Israel go with thee; for the LORD is not with Israel,** *to wit, with* all the children of Ephraim.

8. **But if thou** wilt go, **do it;** be strong for the battle: **God shall make thee fall before the enemy:** for God hath power to help, and to cast down.

9. **And Amaziah said** to the man of God, But what shall we do for the hundred talents which I have given to the army of Israel? And the man of God answered, The LORD is able to give thee much more than this.

10. **Then Amaziah separated** them, *to wit,* **the army** that was come to him **out of Ephraim, to go home again: wherefore their anger was** greatly **kindled against Judah,** and they returned home in great anger.

11. **And Amaziah** strengthened himself, and led forth his people, and **went to the valley of salt, and smote of the children of Seir ten thousand.**

12. **And other ten thousand** *left* alive **did** the children of **Judah carry away captive,** and brought them **unto the top of the rock, and cast them down** from the top of the rock, that they all were broken in pieces.

13. **But the soldiers** of the army **which Amaziah sent back,** that they should

not go with him to battle,
fell upon the cities of
Judah, from Samaria
even unto Beth-horon,
and smote three
thousand of them,
and took much
spoil.
14. Now it came to pass,
after that
Amaziah was come
from the slaughter
of the Edomites, that
he brought the
gods of the children
of Seir, and set them up
to be his gods, and bowed
down himself before them,
and burned incense unto them.
15. **Wherefore** the anger of
the LORD was kindled
against Amaziah, and he
sent unto him
a prophet, which
said unto him,
Why hast thou sought after
the gods of the people,
which could not deliver
their own people out
of thine hand?
16. **And** it came to pass,
as he talked with him, that
the king said unto him,
Art thou made of
the king's counsel? forbear;
why shouldest thou be smitten?
Then the prophet forbare, and
said, I know that God hath
determined to destroy
thee, because thou hast
done this, and hast not hear
kened unto my counsel.
17. **Then Amaziah** king of Judah
took advice, and sent
to Joash, the son of
Jehoahaz, the son of Jehu,
king of Israel, saying,
Come, let us see one
another in the face.
18. **And Joash king of Israel**
sent to Amaziah king of
Judah, saying, The
thistle that *was*

in Lebanon sent to the
cedar that *was* in Lebanon,
saying, Give thy daughter
to my son to wife:
and there passed by
a wild beast that
was in Lebanon, and
trode down the thistle.
19. Thou sayest, Lo,
thou hast smitten
the Edomites; and thine
heart lifteth thee up to boast:
abide now at home;
why shouldest thou
meddle to thine hurt,
that thou shouldest fall,
even thou, and Judah with thee?
20. **But Amaziah would not**
hear; for it *came* of God, that he
might deliver them into the hand
of their enemies, because they
sought after the gods of Edom.
21. **So Joash** the king
of Israel went up; and
they saw one another
in the face, *both* he and Amaziah
king of Judah, at Beth–shemesh,
which *belongeth* to Judah.
22. **And Judah was put**
to the worse before
Israel, and they
fled every man to his tent.
23. **And Joash** the king
of Israel took Amaziah king
of Judah, the son of Joash, the
son of Jehoahaz, at Beth–shemesh,
and brought him to
Jerusalem, and brake
down the wall of Jerusalem
from the gate of Ephraim to the
corner gate, four hundred cubits.
24. **And he took all the**
gold and the silver, and all
the vessels that were
found in the house
of God with Obed–edom,
and the treasures of the
king's house, the hostages also,
and returned to Samaria.
25. **And Amaziah** the
son of Joash king of Judah
lived after the
death of Joash son

of Jehoahaz king of Israel
fifteen years.
26. Now the rest of the acts of Amaziah, first and last, behold, *are* they not written in the book of the kings of Judah and Israel?
27. **Now after the time that Amaziah did turn away from following the LORD they made a conspiracy against him** in Jerusalem; **and he fled to Lachish: but they sent to Lachish** after him, **and slew him** there.
28. **And** they brought him upon horses, and **buried him** with his fathers **in the city of Judah.**

CHAPTER 26

1. **Then** all **the people** of Judah **took Uzziah, who was sixteen years old, and made him king** in the room of his father Amaziah.
2. He built Eloth, and restored it to Judah, after that the king slept with his fathers.
3. Sixteen years old *was* Uzziah when he began to reign, **and he reigned fifty** and **two years** in Jerusalem. His mother's name also *was* Jecoliah of Jerusalem.
4. **And he did that which was right in the sight of the LORD,** according to all that his father Amaziah did.
5. **And he sought God in the days of Zechariah,** who had understanding in the visions of God: **and** as long ashe sought the LORD, **God made him to prosper.**
6. **And he** went forth and **warred against the Philistines, and brake down the wall of Gath, and** the wall of **Jabneh, and** the wall of **Ashdod, and built cities** about Ashdod, and

among the Philistines.
7. **And God helped him against the Philistines, and** against **the Arabians** that dwelt in Gur–baal, and the Mehunims.
8. **And the Ammonites gave gifts to Uzziah: and his name spread abroad** *even* to the entering in of Egypt; for he strengthened *himself* exceedingly.
9. **Moreover Uzziah built towers in Jerusalem** at the corner gate, **and** at the valley gate, and at the turning *of the wall*, and fortified them.
10. Also he built towers **in the desert, and digged many wells: for he had much cattle,** both in the low country, **and** in the plains: **husbandmen** *also,* and vine dressers in the mountains, and in Carmel: **for he loved husbandry.**
11. **Moreover Uzziah had an host of fighting men,** that went out to war by bands, according to the number of their account by the hand of Jeiel the scribe and Maaseiah the ruler, under the hand of Hananiah, *one* of the king's captains.
12. **The** whole **number of the chief** of the **fathers** of the mighty men of valour **were two thousand** and **six hundred.**
13. **And under their hand was an army, three hundred** thousand and **seven thousand** and **five hundred,** that made war with mighty power, to help the king against the enemy.
14. **And Uzziah prepared** for them throughout all the host **shields,** and **spears,** and **helmets,** and **habergeons,** and **bows, and slings to cast stones.**

15. **And he made** in Jerusalem **engines, invented by cunning men,** to be **on the towers** and upon the bulwarks, **to shoot arrows and great stones** withal. And his name spread far abroad; for he was marvellously helped, till he was strong.

16. **But when he was strong, his heart was lifted up to his destruction: for he transgressed against the LORD** his God, **and went into the temple of the LORD to burn incense** upon the altar of incense.

17. **And Azariah** the priest **went in after him, and with** him **fourscore priests** of the LORD, *that were* valiant men:

18. **And they withstood Uzziah** the king, **and said** unto him, **It appertaineth not unto thee,** Uzziah, **to burn incense** unto the LORD, **but** to **the priests** the sons of Aaron, **that are consecrated to burn incense: go out of the sanctuary; for thou hast trespassed;** neither *shall it be* for thine honour from the LORD God.

19. **Then Uzziah was wroth,** and *had* a censer in his hand to burn incense: **and** while he was wroth with the priests, the **leprosy** even **rose up in his forehead** before the priests in the house of the LORD, from beside the incense altar.

20. **And** Azariah the chief priest, and all **the priests,** looked upon him, and, behold, he *was* leprous in his forehead, and they **thrust him out** from thence; yea, himself hasted also to go out, because the LORD had smitten him.

21. **And Uzziah** the king **was a leper unto the day of his death,** and dwelt in a several house, *being* a leper; for he was cut off from the house of the LORD: **and Jotham his son was over the king's house,** judging the people of the land.

22. **Now the rest of the acts of Uzziah,** first and last, **did Isaiah** the prophet, the son of Amoz, **write.**

23. **So Uzziah slept** with his fathers, and they buried him with his fathers in the field of the burial which *belonged* to the kings; for they said, He *is* a leper: **and Jotham** his son **reigned in his stead.**

CHAPTER 27

1. **Jotham was twenty** and **five** years old when he began to reign, **and he reigned sixteen years** in Jerusalem. His mother's name also *was* Jerushah, the daughter of Zadok.

2. **And** he **did** *that which was* **right in the sight of the LORD,** according to all that his father Uzziah did: **howbeit he entered not into the temple of the LORD. And the people did** yet **corruptly.**

3. **He built the high gate of the house of the LORD,** and on the wall of Ophel he built much.

4. **Moreover he built cities** in the mountains of Judah, **and** in the forests he built **castles and towers.**

5. **He fought** also **with** the king of **the Ammonites, and prevailed against them. And** the children of **Ammon gave him** the same year an hundred talents of

silver, and ten thousand measures of

wheat, and ten thousand of barley. So much did the children of Ammon pay unto him, both the second year, and the third.

6. **So Jotham became mighty,** because he prepared his ways before the LORD his God.

7. **Now the rest of the acts of Jotham,** and all his wars, and his ways, lo, they **are written in the book of the kings** of Israel and Judah.

8. He was five and twenty years old when he began to reign, and reigned sixteen years in Jerusalem.

9. **And Jotham slept** with his fathers, and they buried him in the city of David: **and Ahaz his son reigned** in his stead.

CHAPTER 28

1. **Ahaz was twenty years old when he began to reign, and** he **reigned sixteen years** in Jerusalem: **but he did not that which was right in the sight of the LORD,** like David his father:

2. **For he** walked in the ways of the kings of Israel, and **made** also molten **images for Baalim.**

3. **Moreover he burnt incense** in the valley of the son of Hinnom, **and burnt his children in the fire, after the abominations of the heathen** whom the LORD had cast out before the children of Israel.

4. He sacrificed also and burnt incense in the high places, and on the hills, and under every green tree.

5. **Wherefore the LORD** his God **delivered him into the hand** of the king **of Syria; and they smote him, and carried away a** great **multitude** of them captives, and brought *them* **to Damascus.** And **he was also delivered into the hand of the king of Israel, who** smote him with a great slaughter.

6. For Pekah the son of Remaliah **slew in Judah an hundred and twenty thousand in one day,** *which were* all valiant men; **because they had forsaken the LORD** God of their fathers.

7. And Zichri, a mighty man of Ephraim, slew Maaseiah the king's son, and Azrikam the governor of the house, and Elkanah *that was* next to the king.

8. **And the children of Israel carried away captive of their brethren two hundred thousand, women, sons, and daughters, and took** also away much spoil from them, and brought **the spoil to Samaria.**

9. **But a prophet** of the LORD was there, **whose name was Oded:** and he **went out before the host** that came to Samaria, **and said** unto them, Behold, **because the LORD** God of your fathers **was wroth with Judah, he** hath **delivered them into your hand, and ye have slain them** in a rage *that* reacheth up unto heaven.

10. **And now ye purpose to keep** under **the children of** Judah and Jerusalem **for bondmen** and bondwomen unto you: **but are there not with you,** even with you, **sins against the**

LORD your God?

11. **Now** hear me therefore, and **deliver the captives** again, which ye have taken captive **of your brethren: for the fierce wrath of the LORD is upon you.**

12. **Then certain** of the heads of the children **of Ephraim,** Azariah the son of Johanan, Berechiah the son of Meshillemoth, and Jehizkiah the son of Shallum, and Amasa the son of Hadlai, **stood up against them that came from the war,**

13. **And said** unto them, **Ye shall not bring** in **the captives** hither: **for** whereas **we have offended** against **the LORD already, ye intend to add more to our sins** and to our trespass: for our trespass is great, and *there is* fierce wrath against Israel.

14. **So the armed men left the captives and the spoil before the princes** and all the congregation.

15. **And the men** which were expressed by name rose up, and **took the captives, and** with the spoil **clothed** all that were naked among **them,** and arrayed them, and shod them, **and gave them to eat and to drink,** and anointed them, and carried all the feeble of them upon asses, **and brought them to Jericho,** the city of palm trees, **to their brethren:** then they returned to Samaria.

16. **At that time** did king **Ahaz send unto** the kings of **Assyria to help him.**

17. **For** again **the Edomites had** come and **smitten Judah,** and carried away captives.

18. **The Philistines also** **had invaded** the cities of the low country, and of **the south of Judah,** and had taken Beth–shemesh, and Ajalon, and Gederoth, and Shocho with the villages thereof, and Timnah with the villages thereof, Gimzo also and the villages thereof: and they dwelt there.

19. **For the LORD brought Judah low because of Ahaz** king of Israel; **for he made Judah naked, and transgressed** sore **against the LORD.**

20. **And Tilgathpilneser king of Assyria came** unto him, **and distressed him, but** strengthened him not.

21. **For Ahaz took** away **a portion out of the house of the LORD, and** *out* of the house of the king, and of the princes, and **gave it unto the king of Assyria: but he helped him not.**

22. **And in the time of his distress did he trespass yet more against the LORD:** this *is that* king Ahaz.

23. **For he sacrificed unto the gods of Damascus,** which smote him: **and** he said, Because the gods of the kings of Syria help them, *therefore* will I sacrifice to them, that they may help me. But **they were the ruin of him, and of all Israel.**

24. **And Ahaz** gathered together the vessels of the house of God, and **cut in pieces the vessels of the house of God, and shut up the doors** of the house of the LORD, **and** he made him **altars in** every corner of **Jerusalem.**

25. **And in every** several **city of Judah he made high places** to burn incense **unto other gods, and** provoked to anger the

■ **LORD** God of his fathers.
■ 26. **Now the rest of his**
■ **acts** and of all his ways, first
and last, behold, they
■ **are written in the book of**
■ **the kings** of Judah and Israel.
■ 27. **And Ahaz slept**
with his fathers,
■ **and they buried him**
in the city, *even* in Jerusalem: but
they brought him not into the
sepulchres of the kings of Israel:
■ **and Hezekiah his son**
■ **reigned** in his stead.

CHAPTER 29

■ 1. **Hezekiah began to reign**
■ **when he was five and**
■ **twenty years old, and he**
■ **reigned nine and twenty**
■ **years** in Jerusalem. And his
mother's name *was* Abijah, the
daughter of Zechariah.
■ 2. **And** he
■ **did** *that which was*
■ **right in the sight of the**
■ **LORD,** according to all that
David his father had done.
■ 3. **He** in the first year of his
reign, in the first month,
■ **opened the doors of**
■ **the house of the LORD,**
and repaired them.
■ 4. **And** he
■ **brought in the**
■ **priests and** the
■ **Levites,** and gathered them
together into the east street,
■ 5. **And said** unto them,
Hear me, ye Levites,
■ **sanctify** now
■ **yourselves, and** sanctify
■ **the house of the**
■ **LORD** God of your fathers,
■ **and carry** forth
■ **the filthiness out of**
■ **the holy place.**
■ 6. **For our fathers have**
■ **trespassed, and** done
that which was evil in the eyes
of the LORD our God, and
have forsaken him, and have
■ **turned away** their faces

■ **from** the habitation of
■ **the LORD,** and turned *their* backs.
7. Also they have shut up the doors
of the porch, and put out the lamps,
and have not burned incense nor
offered burnt offerings in the holy
place unto the God of Israel.
■ 8. **Wherefore the wrath**
■ **of the LORD was upon**
■ **Judah** and Jerusalem,
■ **and he** hath
■ **delivered them to trouble,**
to astonishment, and to hissing,
■ **as ye see** with your eyes.
■ 9. **For,** lo,
■ **our fathers have fallen**
■ **by the sword, and our**
■ **sons and** our
■ **daughters and** our
■ **wives are in captivity**
■ **for this.**
■ 10. **Now it is in mine heart**
■ **to make a covenant**
■ **with the LORD** God of Israel,
■ **that his** fierce
■ **wrath may turn**
■ **away from us.**
11. My sons,
■ **be not** now
■ **negligent:** for
■ **the LORD hath chosen**
■ **you to stand before him,**
to serve him, and that ye should
minister unto him, and burn incense.
■ 12. **Then the Levites arose,**
Mahath the son of Amasai, and Joel
the son of Azariah, of the sons of
the Kohathites: and of the sons of
Merari, Kish the son of Abdi, and
Azariah the son of Jehalelel: and of
the Gershonites; Joah the son of
Zimmah, and Eden the son of Joah:
13. And of the sons of Elizaphan;
Shimri, and Jeiel: and of the sons of
Asaph; Zechariah, and Mattaniah:
14. And of the sons of Heman;
Jehiel, and Shimei: and of the sons of
Jeduthun; Shemaiah, and Uzziel.
■ 15. **And** they gathered
their brethren, and
■ **sanctified themselves,**
■ **and came,** according to the
commandment of the king,

by the words of the LORD,

to cleanse the house of the LORD.

16. **And the priests went into** the inner part of **the house** of the LORD, to cleanse *it,* **and brought out** all **the uncleanness** that they found in the temple of the LORD into the court of the house of the LORD. And the Levites took *it,* to carry *it* out abroad into the brook Kidron.

17. **Now they began on the first day of the first month to sanctify,** and on the eighth day of the month came they to the porch of the LORD: so they sanctified **the house of the LORD** in eight days; **and in the sixteenth day of the first month they made an end.**

18. **Then they went** in **to Hezekiah** the king, **and said, We have cleansed** all **the house of the LORD, and the altar** of burnt offering, **with all the vessels** thereof, and the shewbread table, with all the vessels thereof.

19. **Moreover all the vessels, which** king **Ahaz** in his reign did **cast away** in his transgression, have **we** prepared and **sanctified, and,** behold, **they are before the altar of the LORD.**

20. **Then Hezekiah** the king rose early, and **gathered the rulers** of the city, **and went up to the house of the LORD.**

21. **And they brought seven bullocks,** and **seven rams,** and **seven lambs, and seven he goats, for a sin offering** for the kingdom, and for the sanctuary, and for Judah.

And he commanded the priests the sons of Aaron to offer *them* on the altar of the LORD.

22. So they killed the bullocks, and the priests received the blood, and sprinkled *it* on the altar: likewise, when they had killed the rams, they sprinkled the blood upon the altar: they killed also the lambs, and they sprinkled the blood upon the altar.

23. And they brought forth the he goats *for* the sin offering before the king and the congregation; and they laid their hands upon them:

24. **And the priests killed them, and** they **made reconciliation with** their **blood upon the altar, to make an atonement for all Israel:** for the king commanded *that* the burnt offering and the sin offering *should be made* for all Israel.

25. **And he set** the **Levites** in the house of the LORD **with cymbals, with psalteries, and** with **harps, according to the commandment of David, and of Gad** the king's seer, **and Nathan the prophet:** for *so was* the commandment of the LORD by his prophets.

26. **And the Levites stood with the instruments** of David, **and the priests with** the **trumpets.**

27. **And Hezekiah commanded to offer the burnt offering** upon the altar. **And** when the burnt offering began, **the song** of the LORD **began also** with the trumpets, and with the instruments *ordained* by David king of Israel.

28. **And all the congregation** worshipped, and the singers sang, and the trumpeters sounded: *and* all *this continued* until the burnt offering was finished.

29. And when they had made an

end of offering, the king and all that were present with him bowed themselves, and worshipped.

30. Moreover Hezekiah the king and the princes commanded the Levites to sing praise unto the LORD with the words of David, and of Asaph the seer. And they **sang praises with gladness, and** they **bowed their heads and worshipped.**

31. **Then Hezekiah** answered and **said, Now** ye have consecrated yourselves unto the **LORD, come near and bring sacrifices and thank offerings** into the house of the LORD. And the congregation brought in sacrifices and thank offerings; and as many as were of a free heart burnt offerings.

32. **And the number of the burnt offerings,** which the congregation brought, **was threescore and ten bullocks, an hundred rams, and two hundred lambs:** all these *were* for a burnt offering to the LORD.

33. **And the consecrated things were six hundred oxen and three thousand sheep.**

34. **But the priests were too few,** so that they could not flay all the burnt offerings: **wherefore** their brethren **the Levites did help** them, **till the work was ended, and** until the **other priests had sanctified themselves:** for the Levites were **more upright** in heart to sanctify themselves **than the priests.**

35. And also the burnt offerings *were* in abundance, with the fat of the peace offerings, and the drink offerings for *every* burnt offering.

So the service of the house **of the LORD was set in order.**

36. And Hezekiah rejoiced, and all the people, that God had prepared the people: for the thing was *done* suddenly.

CHAPTER 30

1. **And Hezekiah sent to all Israel and Judah,** and wrote **letters** also to Ephraim and Manasseh, **that they should** come to the house of the LORD at Jerusalem, to **keep the passover** unto the LORD God of Israel.

2. For the king had taken counsel, and his princes, and all the congregation in Jerusalem, to keep the passover **in the second month.**

3. **For they could not keep it at that time, because the priests had not sanctified themselves** sufficiently, neither had the people gathered themselves together to Jerusalem.

4. And the thing pleased the king and all the congregation.

5. **So they established a decree** to make proclamation throughout all Israel, from Beer-sheba even to Dan, **that they should come to keep the passover** unto the LORD God of Israel **at Jerusalem:** for they had not done *it* of a long *time in such sort* as it was written.

6. **So** the posts **went** with the **letters** from the king and his princes **throughout all Israel and Judah,** and according to the commandment of the king, **saying, Ye children of Israel, turn again unto the LORD** God of Abraham, Isaac, and Israel, **and he will return**

to the remnant of you, that are escaped out of the hand of the kings of Assyria. 7. And be not ye like your fathers, and like your brethren, which trespassed against the LORD God of their fathers, who therefore gave them up to desolation, as ye see. 8. Now be ye not stiffnecked, as your fathers were, but yield yourselves unto the LORD, and enter into his sanctuary, which he hath sanctified for ever: and serve the LORD your God, that the fierceness of his wrath may turn away from you. 9. For if ye turn again unto the LORD, your brethren and your children shall find compassion before them that lead them captive, so that they shall come again into this land: for the LORD your God is gracious and merciful, and will not turn away his face from you, if ye return unto him. 10. So the posts passed from city to city through the country of Ephraim and Manasseh even unto Zebulun: but they laughed them to scorn, and mocked them. 11. Nevertheless divers of Asher and Manasseh and of Zebulun humbled themselves, and came to Jerusalem. 12. Also in Judah the hand of God was to give them one heart to do the commandment of the king and of the princes, by the word of the LORD. 13. And there assembled at Jerusalem much people to keep the feast of unleavened bread in the second month, a very great congregation. 14. And they arose and took away the altars that were in Jerusalem, and all the altars for incense took they away, and cast them into the brook Kidron. 15. Then they killed the passover on the fourteenth day of the second month: and the priests and the Levites were ashamed, and sanctified themselves, and brought in the burnt offerings into the house of the LORD. 16. And they stood in their place after their manner, according to the law of Moses the man of God: the priests sprinkled the blood, which they received of the hand of the Levites. 17. For there were many in the congregation that were not sanctified: therefore the Levites had the charge of the killing of the passovers for every one that was not clean, to sanctify them unto the LORD. 18. For a multitude of the people, even many of Ephraim, and Manasseh, Issachar, and Zebulun, had not cleansed themselves, yet did they eat the passover otherwise than it was written. But Hezekiah prayed for them, saying, The good LORD pardon every one 19. That prepareth his heart to seek God, the LORD God of his fathers, though he be not cleansed according to the purification of the sanctuary. 20. And the LORD hearkened to Hezekiah, and healed the people. 21. And the children of Israel that were present at Jerusalem kept the feast of unleavened bread seven days with great gladness: and the

Levites and the priests praised the LORD day by day, *singing* with loud instruments unto the LORD.

22. **And Hezekiah spake comfortably unto all the Levites that taught the good knowledge of the LORD: and they did eat** throughout **the feast seven days,** offering peace offerings, and making confession to the LORD God of their fathers.

23. **And the whole assembly** took counsel to keep other seven days: and they **kept other seven days with gladness.**

24. **For Hezekiah** king of Judah **did give** to the congregation **a thousand bullocks and seven thousand sheep; and the princes gave** to the congregation **a thousand bullocks and ten thousand sheep:** and a great number of priests sanctified themselves.

25. **And all** the congregation of Judah, with the priests and the Levites, and all the congregation that came out of Israel, and the strangers that came out of the land of Israel, and **that dwelt in Judah, rejoiced.**

26. **So there was great joy** in Jerusalem: **for since the time of Solomon** the son of David king of Israel **there was not the like in Jerusalem.**

27. Then the priests the Levites arose and blessed the people: and their voice was heard, and their prayer came *up* to his holy dwelling place, *even* unto heaven.

CHAPTER 31

1. **Now when** all **this was finished,** all **Israel** that were present **went out** to the cities of Judah,

and brake the images in pieces, **and cut down the groves, and threw down the high places and** the **altars out of all Judah** and **Benjamin,** in **Ephraim** also **and Manasseh,** until they had utterly destroyed them all. Then all the children of Israel returned, every man to his possession, into their own cities.

2. **And Hezekiah appointed** the courses of the **priests and the Levites** after their courses, every man according to his service, the priests and Levites for burnt offerings and for peace offerings, **to minister, and to give thanks, and to praise in the** gates of the **tents of the LORD.**

3. **He appointed** also **the king's portion** of his substance **for the burnt offerings,** *to wit,* for the morning and evening burnt offerings, and the burnt offerings for the sabbaths, and for the new moons, and for the set feasts, **as it is written in the law** of the LORD.

4. **Moreover he commanded the people** that dwelt **in Jerusalem to** give the portion of the priests and the Levites, that they might **be encouraged in the law of the LORD.**

5. **And** as soon as the commandment came abroad, the children of **Israel brought in abundance** the firstfruits of corn, wine, and oil, and honey, and **of all the increase of the field; and the tithe of all things** brought they in abundantly.

6. And *concerning* the children of Israel and Judah, that

dwelt in the cities of Judah,
■ **they** also
■ **brought** in the tithe of
■ **oxen** and
■ **sheep, and** the tithe of
■ **holy things**
which were consecrated
■ **unto the LORD** their God,
■ **and laid them by heaps.**
7. In the third month they began to
lay the foundation of the heaps, and
finished *them* in the seventh month.
■ 8. **And when Hezekiah**
■ **and the princes** came and
■ **saw the heaps, they**
■ **blessed the LORD,**
and his people Israel.
9. Then Hezekiah questioned
with the priests and the Levites
concerning the heaps.
■ 10. **And Azariah the**
■ **chief priest** of the house
of Zadok answered him, and
■ **said, Since the people**
■ **began to bring the offerings**
into the house of the LORD,
■ **we havehad enough to eat,**
■ **and have left plenty:** for the
LORD hath blessed his people; and
that which is left *is* this great store.
■ 11. **Then Hezekiah**
■ **commanded to prepare**
■ **chambers** in the house of the
LORD; and they prepared *them,*
■ 12. **And brought** in
■ **the offerings and** the
■ **tithes and** the
■ **dedicated things**
faithfully:
■ **over which Cononiah**
■ **the Levite was ruler,** and
Shimei his brother *was* the next.
13. And Jehiel, and Azaziah, and
Nahath, and Asahel, and Jerimoth,
and Jozabad, and Eliel, and
Ismachiah, and Mahath, and Benaiah,
were overseers under the hand of
Cononiah and Shimei his brother,
at the commandment of Hezekiah
the king, and Azariah the ruler
of the house of God.
■ 14. **And Kore** the son
of Imnah the Levite,

■ **the porter** toward the east,
■ **was over the freewill**
■ **offerings** of God,
■ **to distribute the**
■ **oblations** of the LORD,
■ **and the most holy things.**
15. **And next** him
■ **were** Eden, and Miniamin, and
Jeshua, and Shemaiah, Amariah, and
Shecaniah, in the cities of
■ **the priests,** in *their* set office, to
give to *their* brethren by courses, as
well to the great as to the small:
16. Beside their genealogy of males,
from three years old and upward,
even unto every one that entereth into
the house of the LORD, his daily
portion for their service in their
charges according to their courses;
17. Both to the genealogy of the
priests by the house of their fathers,
and the Levites from twenty years
old and upward, in their charges
by their courses;
18. And to the genealogy of all
their little ones, their wives, and
their sons, and their daughters,
through all the congregation:
■ **for** in their set office
■ **they sanctified**
■ **themselves in holiness:**
19. Also of the sons of Aaron the
priests, *which were* in the fields of the
suburbs of their cities, in every
several city, the men that were
expressed by name, to give
portions to all the males among
the priests, and to all that were
reckoned by genealogies
among the Levites.
■ 20. **And thus did**
■ **Hezekiah throughout**
■ **all Judah, and wrought**
■ **that which was good**
■ **and right and truth**
■ **before the LORD** his God.
■ 21. **And in every work** that
■ **he began in the service**
of the house of God, and in
the law, and in the commandments,
■ **to seek** his
■ **God, he did it with all**
■ **his heart,** and prospered.

CHAPTER 32

1. **After these things**, and the establishment thereof, **Sennacherib king of Assyria came,** and entered **into Judah, and encamped against the fenced cities,** and thought to win them for himself. 2. **And when Hezekiah saw that Sennacherib was** come, and that he was **purposed to fight against Jerusalem,** 3. **He took counsel** with his princes and his mighty men **to stop the waters of the fountains which were without the city:** and they did help him. 4. **So there** was **gathered much people** together, **who stopped all the fountains, and the brook that ran through** the midst of **the land, saying, Why should the kings of Assyria** come, and **find** much **water?** 5. **Also he** strengthened himself, and **built up** all **the wall that was broken,** and raised *it* up to the towers, and another wall without, and repaired Millo *in* the city of David, **and made darts and shields in abundance.** 6. **And he** set captains of war over the people, and gathered them together to him in the street of the gate of the city, and **spake comfortably to them, saying,** 7. **Be strong and courageous, be not afraid nor dismayed for the king of Assyria,** nor for all the multitude that *is* with him: for *there be* more with us than with him: 8. **With him is an arm of flesh; but with us is the LORD** our God to help us, and to fight our battles. **And** the people rested themselves upon the words of Hezekiah king of Judah.

9. **After this did Sennacherib** king of Assyria **send his servants to Jerusalem,** (but he *himself laid* siege against Lachish, and all his power with him,) unto Hezekiah king of Judah, and unto all Judah that *were* at Jerusalem, **saying,** 10. **Thus saith Sennacherib** king of Assyria, **Whereon do ye trust, that ye abide in the siege in Jerusalem?** 11. **Doth not Hezekiah persuade you** to give over yourselves **to die** by famine and by thirst, **saying,** The LORD our **God shall deliver us** out of the hand of the king of Assyria? 12. **Hath not** the same **Hezekiah taken away his high places** and his altars, **and commanded** Judah and Jerusalem, **saying, Ye shall worship before one altar,** and burn incense upon it? 13. **Know ye not what I** and my fathers **have done unto** all the people of **other lands? were the gods** of the nations **of those lands** any ways **able to deliver their lands out of mine hand?** 14. **Who** *was there* **among** all **the gods** of those nations that my fathers utterly destroyed, that **could deliver his people out of mine hand,** that your God should be able to deliver you out of mine hand? 15. **Now** therefore **let not Hezekiah deceive you,** nor persuade you on this

manner, neither yet believe him: for
no god of any nation or kingdom
was able to deliver his
people out of mine hand, and
out of the hand of my fathers:
how much less shall
your God deliver you
out of mine hand?
16. **And his servants**
spake yet *more*
against the LORD God,
and against his servant
Hezekiah.
17. **He wrote also letters to**
rail on the LORD God of Israel,
and to speak against him, saying,
As the gods of the nations of *other*
lands have not delivered their
people out of mine hand, so shall
not the God of Hezekiah deliver
his people out of mine hand.
18. **Then they**
cried with a loud voice
in the Jews' speech
unto the people of Jerusalem
that *were* on the wall,
to affright them, and to trouble
them; that they might take the city.
19. **And** they
spake against the God of
Jerusalem, as against the gods of
the people of the earth, *which were*
the work of the hands of man.
20. **And** for this *cause*
Hezekiah the king,
and the prophet
Isaiah the son of Amoz,
prayed and cried to heaven.
21. **And the LORD sent an**
angel, which cut off all
the mighty men of valour,
and the leaders and captains **in**
the camp of the king of
Assyria. So he returned with
shame of face
to his own land. And when
he was come into the
house of his god, they
that came forth of his own bowels
slew him there with the sword.
22. **Thus the LORD saved**
Hezekiah and the inhabitants of
Jerusalem from the

hand of Sennacherib the king of
Assyria, and from the hand of all
other, and guided them on every side.
23. **And many brought**
gifts unto the LORD
to Jerusalem,
and presents to
Hezekiah king of Judah:
so that he was magnified
in the sight of all
nations from thenceforth.
24. **In those days Hezekiah**
was sick to the death,
and prayed unto the LORD:
and he spake unto him, and
he gave him a sign.
25. **But Hezekiah**
rendered not again
according to the benefit
done unto him; for his
heart was lifted up:
therefore there was
wrath upon him, and upon
Judah and Jerusalem.
26. **Notwithstanding**
Hezekiah humbled
himself for the pride of his heart,
both he and the
inhabitants of Jerusalem,
so that the wrath of the
LORD came not upon them
in the days of Hezekiah.
27. **And Hezekiah**
had exceeding much
riches and honour:
and he made himself
treasuries for silver, and for gold,
and for precious stones, and for
spices, and for shields, and for
all manner of pleasant jewels;
28. **Storehouses** also for the
increase of corn, and wine, and
oil; and stalls for all manner of
beasts, and cotes for flocks.
29. **Moreover he**
provided him
cities, and possessions
of flocks and herds
in abundance: for God
had given him substance
very much.
30. This same
Hezekiah also

stopped the upper
watercourse of Gihon,
and brought it straight down
to the west side
of the city of David.
And Hezekiah prospered
in all his works.
31. Howbeit in *the business of*
the ambassadors
of the princes
of Babylon, who
sent unto him
to inquire of the
wonder that was *done*
in the land, God left
him, to try him, that he
might know all *that was* in
his heart.
32. Now the rest of the
acts of Hezekiah, and
his goodness, behold, they
are written in the
vision of Isaiah the
prophet, the son of Amoz,
and in
the book of the
kings of Judah and Israel.
33. And Hezekiah
slept with his fathers, and
they buried him in the chiefest
of the sepulchres of the sons of
David: and all Judah and the
inhabitants of Jerusalem did
him honour at his death.
And Manasseh his son
reigned in his stead.

CHAPTER 33

1. Manasseh was
twelve years old
when he began to reign,
and he reigned fifty and
five years in Jerusalem:
2. But did *that which was*
evil in the sight of the LORD,
like unto the abominations of the
heathen, whom the LORD had cast
out before the children of Israel.
3. For he built again the
high places which
Hezekiah his father
had broken down, and he
reared up altars for

Baalim, and made groves, and
worshipped all the host of heaven,
and served them.
4. Also he built altars in the
house of the LORD, whereof
the LORD had said, In Jerusalem
shall my name be for ever.
5. And he built altars
for all
the host of heaven in the two
courts of the house of the LORD.
6. And he
caused his children
to pass through the
fire in the valley of
the son of Hinnom:
also he observed times, and
used enchantments, and used
witchcraft, and dealt with
a familiar spirit, and with
wizards: he wrought much
evil in the sight of the LORD,
to provoke him to anger.
7. And he set a carved
image, the idol which he had made,
in the house of God, of which
God had said to David and to
Solomon his son, In this house, and
in Jerusalem, which I have chosen
before all the tribes of Israel, will
I put my name for ever:
8. Neither will I any more remove the
foot of Israel from out of the land
which I have appointed for your
fathers; so that they will take heed
to do all that I have commanded
them, according to the whole law
and the statutes and the ordinances
by the hand of Moses.
9. So Manasseh made
Judah and the inhabitants of
Jerusalem to
err, *and* to do
worse than the heathen,
whom the LORD had destroyed
before the children of Israel.
10. And the LORD spake
to Manasseh, and to his people:
but they would
not hearken.
11. Wherefore the
LORD brought upon
them the captains of

the host of the king of
Assyria, which took
Manasseh among the thorns,
and bound him with fetters,
and carried him
to Babylon.
12. And when he was
in affliction, he besought
the LORD his God, and
humbled himself greatly
before the
God of his fathers,
13. And prayed unto him:
and he was entreated of him, and
heard his supplication, and
brought him again to
Jerusalem into his kingdom.
Then Manasseh knew
that the LORD he
was God.
14. Now after this he built
a wall without the city of David,
on the west side of Gihon,
in the valley, even to the
entering in at the fish gate,
and compassed about Ophel,
and raised it up a very
great height, and put captains of
war in all the fenced cities of Judah.
15. And he took away the
strange gods, and the idol
out of the house of the LORD,
and all the altars that he
had built in the mount of the house
of the LORD, and in Jerusalem,
and cast them out
of the city.
16. And he repaired
the altar of the LORD,
and sacrificed thereon peace
offerings and thank
offerings, and commanded
Judah to serve the
LORD God of Israel.
17. Nevertheless the
people did sacrifice still
in the high places, yet
unto the LORD their God
only.
18. Now the rest of the acts
of Manasseh, and his prayer unto
his God, and the words of the seers
that spake to him in the name of the

LORD God of Israel, behold, they
are written in the book
of the kings of Israel.
19. His prayer also, and *how God* was
entreated of him, and all his sins, and
his trespass, and the places wherein
he built high places, and set up
groves and graven images, before he
was humbled: behold, they *are* written
among the sayings of the seers.
20. So Manasseh slept
with his fathers, and they buried
him in his own house:
and Amon his son
reigned in his stead.
21. Amon was two
and twenty years old
when he began to
reign, and reigned
two years in Jerusalem.
22. But he did *that which was*
evil in the sight of the LORD,
as did Manasseh his father:
for Amon sacrificed
unto all the
carved images which
Manasseh his father had
made, and served them;
23. And humbled not
himself before the LORD,
as Manasseh his father had
humbled himself; but Amon
trespassed more and more.
24. And his servants
conspired against him,
and slew him in his own house.
25. But the people of the land
slew all them that had
conspired against king
Amon; and the
people of the land
made Josiah his son
king in his stead.

CHAPTER 34

1. Josiah was eight
years old when he
began to reign, and he
reigned in Jerusalem
one and thirty years.
2. And he did *that which was*
right in the sight of the
LORD, and walked in the ways of

David his father, and declined *neither* to the right hand, nor to the left.

3. **For in the eighth year of his reign,** while he was yet young, **he began to seek** after the **God** of David his father: **and in the twelfth year he began to purge Judah** and Jerusalem **from the high places,** and the **groves,** and the **carved** images, **and** the **molten images.**

4. **And they brake down the altars of Baalim** in his presence; and the images, that *were* on high above them, he cut down; and the groves, and the carved images, and the molten images, he brake in pieces, and made dust *of them,* and strowed *it* upon the graves of them that had sacrificed unto them.

5. And he burnt the bones of the priests upon their altars, and cleansed Judah and Jerusalem.

6. And *so did he* in the cities of Manasseh, and Ephraim, and Simeon, even unto Naphtali, with their mattocks round about.

7. **And when he had broken down the altars** and the groves, and had beaten the graven images into powder,and cut down all the idols **throughout all the land of Israel, he returned to Jerusalem.**

8. **Now in the eighteenth year of his reign,** when he had purged the land, and the house, **he sent Shaphan the son of Azaliah, and** Maaseiah **the governor of the city, and Joah** the son of Joahaz the recorder, **to repair the house of the LORD** his God.

9. **And** when they came to Hilkiah the high priest, **they delivered the money** that was brought into the house of God, which the Levites that kept the doors had gathered of the hand of Manasseh and Ephraim, and of all the remnant of Israel, and of all Judah and Benjamin; and they returned to Jerusalem.

10. And they put *it* in the hand of the workmen that had the oversight of the house of the LORD, and they gave it **to the workmen that wrought in the house of the LORD, to repair and amend the house:**

11. Even to the artificers and builders gave they *it,* to buy hewn stone, and timber for couplings, and to floor the houses **which the kings of Judah had destroyed.**

12. **And the men did the work faithfully:** and the overseers of them *were* Jahath and Obadiah, the Levites, of the sons of Merari; and Zechariah and Meshullam, of the sons of the Kohathites, to set *it* forward; and *other of* the Levites, all that could skill of instruments of music.

13. Also *they were* over the bearers of burdens, and *were* overseers of all that wrought the work in any manner of service: and of the Levites *there were* scribes, and officers, and porters.

14. **And** when they brought out the money that was brought into the house of the LORD, **Hilkiah the priest found a book of the law** of the LORD **given by Moses.**

15. And Hilkiah answered and said to Shaphan the scribe, I have found the book of the law in the house of the LORD. **And** Hilkiah **delivered the book to Shaphan.**

16. **And Shaphan carried the book to the king,** and brought the king word back again, saying, All that was committed to thy servants, they do *it.*

17. And they have gathered together the money that was found in the house of the LORD, and

have delivered it into the hand
of the overseers, and to the
hand of the workmen.
18. Then Shaphan the
scribe told the king,
saying, Hilkiah
**the priest hath given
me a book. And Shaphan
read it** before the king.
19. **And** it came to pass,
when the king had
heard the words of
the law, that
he rent his clothes.
20. **And** the king
commanded Hilkiah, and
Ahikam the son of Shaphan,
and Abdon the son of Micah, and
Shaphan the scribe, and Asaiah
a servant of the king's,
saying,
21. **Go, inquire of the
LORD** for me, and for them that
are left in Israel and in Judah,
concerning the words of the
book that is found:
**for great is the wrath of the
LORD** that is poured out upon us,
**because our fathers have
not kept the word of the
LORD,** to do after all that is
written in this book.
22. **And Hilkiah**, and *they*
that the king *had appointed*,
**went to Huldah the
prophetess, the wife of
Shallum** the son of Tikvath, the son
of Hasrah, keeper of the wardrobe;
(now she dwelt in Jerusalem in the
college:)
and they
spake to her to that *effect*.
23. **And she answered** them,
**Thus saith the
LORD** God of Israel,
Tell ye
the man that sent you to me,
24. **Thus saith the LORD,
Behold, I will bring evil
upon this place**, and upon
the inhabitants thereof,
even all the curses that are
written in the book which they

have read before the king of Judah:
25. **Because they have
forsaken me,** and have burned
incense unto other gods, that they
might provoke me to anger with all
the works of their hands; therefore my
wrath shall be poured out upon this
place, and shall not be quenched.
26. **And as for the king** of
Judah, who sent you to inquire of
the LORD, so shall ye say unto him,
Thus saith the LORD
God of Israel *concerning* the
words which thou hast heard;
27. **Because thine heart was
tender, and thou didst
humble thyself** before God,
when thou heardest his words
against this place, and against
the inhabitants thereof, and
humbledst thyself before me, and
didst rend thy clothes, and weep
before me; I have even
heard thee also, saith the LORD.
28. Behold, I will gather
thee to thy fathers, and
**thou shalt be gathered to
thy grave in peace, neither
shall thine eyes see** all
**the evil that
I will bring upon this place,**
and upon the inhabitants of the same.
So they brought the king word again.
29. **Then the king** sent and
gathered together all
**the elders of Judah
and Jerusalem.**
30. **And** the king
**went up into the house
of the LORD,** and all the
men of Judah, and the
inhabitants of Jerusalem,
and the priests, and the Levites,
and all the people,
great and small:
and he read in their ears all
the words of the book
of the covenant that was found
in the house of the LORD.
31. **And the king**
stood in his place, and
**made a covenant
before the LORD,** to

walk after the LORD, and
■ **to keep his**
■ **commandments,** and his
testimonies, and his statutes, with
all his heart, and with all his soul, to
perform the words of the covenant
which are written in this book.

■ 32. **And he caused all**
■ **that were present** in
Jerusalem and Benjamin
■ **to stand to it.** And the
inhabitants of Jerusalem did
according to the covenant of
God, the God of their fathers.

■ 33. **And Josiah took away**
■ **all the abominations out**
■ **of all the countries** that
pertained to the children of Israel,
■ **and made all** that
were present in
■ **Israel** to serve, *even* to
■ **serve the LORD** their God.
■ **And all his days they**
■ **departed not from**
■ **following the LORD,**
the God of their fathers.

CHAPTER 35

■ 1. **Moreover Josiah kept**
■ **a passover unto the**
■ **LORD** in Jerusalem: and they killed
the passover on the fourteenth *day*
of the first month.
■ 2. **And he set the priests in**
■ **their charges,** and encouraged
them to the service of the house
of the LORD,
■ 3. **And said unto the**
■ **Levites** that taught all Israel,
which were holy unto the LORD,
■ **Put the holy ark in the**
■ **house which Solomon**
the son of David king of Israel
■ **did build;** *it shall* not *be* a
burden upon *your* shoulders:
serve now the LORD your
God, and his people Israel,
■ 4. **And prepare yourselves**
by the houses of your fathers, after
your courses, according to the writing
of David king of Israel, and according
to the writing of Solomon his son.
■ 5. **And stand in the holy**

■ **place** according to the divisions
of the families of the fathers of your
brethren the people, and *after* the
division of the families of the Levites.
■ 6. **So kill the passover, and**
■ **sanctify yourselves,** and
prepare your brethren, that *they*
may do according to the word of the
LORD by the hand of Moses.
7. And Josiah gave to the people, of
the flock, lambs and kids, all
for the passover offerings, for all that
were present, to the number of
thirty thousand, and three thousand
bullocks: these *were* of the king's
substance.
8. And his princes gave willingly unto
the people, to the priests, and to the
Levites: Hilkiah and Zechariah and
Jehiel, rulers of the house of God,
gave unto the priests for the passover
offerings two thousand and six
hundred *small cattle* and three
hundred oxen.
9. Conaniah also, and Shemaiah and
Nethaneel, his brethren, and
Hashabiah and Jeiel and Jozabad,
chief of the Levites, gave unto the
Levites for passover offerings
five thousand *small cattle*,
and five hundred oxen.
■ 10. **So the service was**
■ **prepared,** and the priests
stood in their place, and the
Levites in their courses, according
to the king's commandment.
■ 11. **And they killed**
■ **the passover, and**
■ **the priests sprinkled**
■ **the blood** from their hands,
■ **and the Levites**
■ **flayed them.**
12. And they removed the burnt
offerings, that they might give
according to the divisions of the
families of the people, to offer unto
the LORD, as *it is* written in the book of
Moses. And so *did they* with the oxen.
■ 13. **And they roasted**
■ **the passover** with fire
according to the ordinance:
■ **but the other holy**
■ **offerings sod they in pots,**

and in caldrons, and in pans,
and divided *them* speedily
among all
the people.
14. **And** afterward
they made ready for
themselves, and for
the priests: because
the priests the sons of Aaron
were busied in offering of
burnt offerings and the fat until
night; therefore the Levites prepared
for themselves, and for the priests
the sons of Aaron.
15. **And the singers**
the sons of Asaph
were in their place, according
to the commandment of David, and
Asaph, and Heman, and Jeduthun the
king's seer; and the porters *waited* at
every gate; they might not depart
from their service; for their brethren
the Levites prepared for them.
16. So all the service of the LORD
was prepared the same day, to keep
the passover, and to offer burnt
offerings upon the altar of the
LORD, according to the
commandment of king Josiah.
17. And the children of Israel that
were present kept the passover
at that time, and the feast of
unleavened bread seven days.
18. **And there was no**
passover like to that kept in
Israel from the days of
Samuel the prophet; neither did
all the kings of Israel keep such a
passover as Josiah kept, and the
priests, and the Levites, and all
Judah and Israel that were present,
and the inhabitants of Jerusalem.
19. In the eighteenth year of the reign
of Josiah was this passover kept.
20. **After all this,** when
Josiah had prepared the temple,
Necho king of Egypt
came up to fight against
Charchemish by Euphrates:
and Josiah went
out against him.
21. **But he sent**
ambassadors to him,

saying, What have I
to do with thee,
thou king of Judah? I come
not against thee this day,
but against the house
wherewith I have war:
for God commanded
me to make haste: because
thee from *meddling with* God,
who *is* with me, that he
destroy thee not.
22. **Nevertheless Josiah**
would not turn his face
from him, but disguised
himself, that he might
fight with him, and hearkened
not unto the words of Necho
from the mouth of God,
and came to fight in
the valley of Megiddo.
23. **And the archers shot**
at king Josiah; and the
king said to his servants,
Have me away; for
I am sore
wounded.
24. **His servants** therefore
took him out of that chariot, and
put him in the second
chariot that he had;
and they
brought him to Jerusalem,
and he died, and was
buried in one of the
sepulchres of his fathers.
And all Judah and Jerusalem
mourned for Josiah.
25. **And Jeremiah lamented**
for Josiah: and all the
singing men and the singing
women spake of Josiah
in their lamentations to
this day, and made them an
ordinance in Israel: and, behold,
they *are* written in the lamentations.
26. **Now the rest of the acts**
of Josiah, and his goodness,
according to *that which was* written
in the law of the LORD,
27. And his deeds, first
and last, behold, they
are written in the book of
the kings of Israel and Judah.

CHAPTER 36

1. **Then the people** of the land **took Jehoahaz** the son of Josiah, **and made him king** in his father's stead in Jerusalem.

2. **Jehoahaz was twenty** and **three** years old **when he began to reign, and** he **reigned three months** in Jerusalem.

3. **And the king of Egypt put him down** at Jerusalem, and condemned the land in an hundred talents of silver and a talent of gold.

4. **And** the king of Egypt **made Eliakim his brother king** over Judah and Jerusalem, **and turned his name to Jehoiakim. And Necho took Jehoahaz** his brother, and carried him **to Egypt.**

5. **Jehoiakim was twenty** and **five** years old when he began to reign, **and he reigned eleven years** in Jerusalem: **and** he **did** *that which was* **evil in the sight of the LORD** his God.

6. **Against him came** up **Nebuchadnezzar king of Babylon, and bound him** in fetters, **to carry him to Babylon.**

7. **Nebuchadnezzar also carried** of **the vessels of the house of the LORD** to Babylon, **and put them in his temple at Babylon.**

8. **Now the rest of the acts of Jehoiakim,** and his abominations which he did, and that which was found in him, behold, they **are written in the book of the kings** of Israel and Judah: **and Jehoiachin** his son **reigned in his stead.**

9. **Jehoiachin was eight years old when he began to reign, and he reigned three months and ten days** in Jerusalem: **and** he **did** *that which was* **evil in the sight of the LORD.**

10. **And** when the year was expired, king **Nebuchadnezzar** sent, and **brought him to Babylon, with the** goodly **vessels of the house of the LORD, and made Zedekiah** his brother **king** over Judah and Jerusalem.

11. **Zedekiah was one and twenty years old** when he began to reign, **and reigned eleven years** in Jerusalem.

12. **And** he **did** *that which was* **evil in the sight of the LORD** his God, **and humbled not himself before Jeremiah the prophet** *speaking* from the mouth of the LORD.

13. **And** he **also rebelled against** king **Nebuchadnezzar,** who had made him swear by God: but he stiffened his neck, and hardened his heart from turning unto the LORD God of Israel.

14. **Moreover** all **the chief** of the **priests, and the people, transgressed** very much after all the abominations of the heathen; **and polluted the house of the LORD** which he had hallowed in Jerusalem.

15. **And the LORD** God of their fathers **sent** to them by **his messengers,** rising up betimes, and sending; **because he had compassion on his people,** and on his dwelling place:

16. **But they mocked the**

■ ■ messengers of God, and
despised his words,
and misused his prophets,
■ until the wrath of the
■ LORD arose against his
■ people, till *there was* no remedy.
17. **Therefore** he
brought upon them
■ the king of the
■ Chaldees, who
■ slew their young
■ men with the sword
■ in the house of
■ their sanctuary, and
■ had no compassion upon
young man or maiden, old man, or
him that stooped for age: he gave
them all into his hand.
■ 18. **And all the vessels of the**
■ **house of God,** great and small,
and the treasures of the house of the
LORD, and the treasures of
the king, and of his princes; all *these*
■ he brought to Babylon.
■ 19. **And they burnt the**
■ **house of God, and** brake down
the wall of Jerusalem, and burnt all
■ the palaces thereof with fire,
■ and destroyed all
■ the goodly vessels thereof.
■ 20. **And them that** had
■ escaped from the sword
■ carried he away to
■ Babylon; where they were
■ servants to him and his sons

■ until the reign of the kingdom of
■ Persia:
■ 21. **To fulfil the word of**
■ the LORD by the mouth of
■ Jeremiah, until the land had
enjoyed her sabbaths:
■ for as long as
■ she lay desolate
she kept sabbath, to fulfil
■ threescore and ten years.
22. **Now in the first year of**
Cyrus king of Persia, that
the word of the LORD *spoken*
by the mouth of
Jeremiah might be
accomplished, the
LORD stirred up the spirit of
■ Cyrus king of Persia, that he
■ made a proclamation
throughout all his kingdom,
and *put it* also in writing,
■ saying,
23. Thus saith Cyrus king of Persia,
■ All the kingdoms of
■ the earth hath the
■ LORD God of heaven
■ given me; and he hath
■ charged me to build him
■ an house in Jerusalem, which
is in Judah.
■ Who is there among you
■ of all his people?
The LORD his
■ God be with him,
■ and let him go up.

THE BOOK OF EZRA

BACKGROUND INFORMATION

Author: Ezra
Date Written: Between 456 — 444 B.C.

Number of:
Verses—280
Chapters—10
Total Words—7441
Scan Words—2,914
Scan Words Represent
Approximately 39% of
Total Words

Theme: The Rebuilding of the Temple in Jerusalem

OUTLINE OF THE BOOK

I. **The Return** from Captivity **and** the **Rebuilding** of **the Temple**
1:1 — 6:22

II. **The Ministry of Ezra**
7:1 — 10:44

CHAPTER 1

■ 1. **Now in the first year**
■ **of Cyrus king of Persia,**
■ **that the word of the**
■ **LORD by** the mouth of
■ **Jeremiah might be fulfilled,**
■ **the LORD stirred up** the spirit of
■ **Cyrus** king of Persia,
■ **that he made a**
■ **proclamation** throughout
all his kingdom,
and *put it* also in writing,
■ **saying,**
■ 2. **Thus saith**
■ **Cyrus** king of Persia,
■ **The LORD** God of heaven
hath given me all the
kingdoms of the earth; and he
■ **hath charged me to**
■ **build him an house at**
■ **Jerusalem,** which *is* in Judah.
■ 3. **Who** *is there*
■ **among you** of all his people? his
■ **God be with him,**
■ **and let him go** up
■ **to Jerusalem,** which *is* in Judah,
■ **and build the house**
■ **of** the LORD
■ **God** of Israel, (he *is* the
God,) which *is* in Jerusalem.
■ 4. **And whosoever**
■ **remaineth** in any place
where he sojourneth,
■ **let the men** of his place
■ **help him with silver, and** with
■ **gold, and** with
■ **goods,** and with beasts,
■ **beside the freewill**
■ **offering for the house**
■ **of God** that *is* in Jerusalem.
■ 5. **Then rose up** the chief of the
fathers of Judah and Benjamin, and
the priests, and the Levites, with
■ **all them whose spirit**
■ **God had raised,** to go up
to build the house of the LORD
which *is* in Jerusalem.
■ 6. **And** all
■ **they** that
■ **were** about them
■ **strengthened** their hands with
vessels of silver, with gold, with
goods, and with beasts, and

■ **with precious things,**
■ **beside all that was**
■ **willingly offered.**
■ 7. **Also Cyrus** the king
■ **brought** forth
■ **the vessels of the house**
■ **of the LORD, which**
■ **Nebuchadnezzar** had
■ **brought forth out of**
■ **Jerusalem, and** had
■ **put** them
■ **in the house of his gods;**
8. Even those did Cyrus king of
Persia bring forth by the hand of
Mithredath the treasurer, and
numbered them unto Sheshbazzar,
the prince of Judah.
9. And this *is* the number
of them: thirty chargers of
gold, a thousand chargers of
silver, nine and twenty knives,
10. Thirty basins of gold, silver
basins of a second *sort* four
hundred and ten, *and* other
vessels a thousand.
■ 11. **All the vessels**
■ **of gold and** of
■ **silver were**
■ **five thousand and**
■ **four hundred. All these**
■ **did Sheshbazzar**
■ **bring** up with *them of* the
captivity that were brought up
■ **from Babylon unto**
■ **Jerusalem.**

CHAPTER 2

■ 1. **Now these** *are* the
children of the province that
■ **went up out of the**
■ **captivity, of** those which
had been carried away, whom
Nebuchadnezzar the king of
Babylon had carried away unto
■ **Babylon, and came** again
unto Jerusalem and Judah,
every one unto his city;
2. Which came
■ **with Zerubbabel:** Jeshua,
Nehemiah, Seraiah, Reelaiah,
Mordecai, Bilshan, Mizpar, Bigvai,
Rehum, Baanah. The number of the
men of the people of Israel:

■ 3. **The children of**
■ **Parosh,** two thousand an
hundred seventy and two.
4. The children of
■ **Shephatiah,** three
hundred seventy and two.
5. The children of
■ **Arah,** seven hundred
seventy and five.
6. The children of
■ **Pahath-moab,**
of the children of
■ **Jeshua and Joab,** two
thousand eight hundred and twelve.
7. The children of
■ **Elam,** a thousand two
hundred fifty and four.
8. The children of
■ **Zattu,** nine hundred forty and five.
9. The children of
■ **Zaccai,** seven hundred
and threescore.
10. The children of
■ **Bani,** six hundred forty and two.
11. The children of
■ **Bebai,** six hundred
twenty and three.
12. **The children of**
■ **Azgad,** a thousand two
hundred twenty and two.
13. The children of
■ **Adonikam,** six
hundred sixty and six.
14. The children of
■ **Bigvai,** two thousand fifty and six.
15. The children of
■ **Adin,** four hundred fifty and four.
16. The children of
■ **Ater** of Hezekiah, ninety and eight.
17. The children of
■ **Bezai,** three hundred
twenty and three.
18. The children of
■ **Jorah,** an hundred and twelve.
19. The children of
■ **Hashum,** two hundred
twenty and three.
20. The children of
■ **Gibbar,** ninety and five.
21. The children of
■ **Beth-lehem,** an hundred
twenty and three.
22. **The men of**

■ **Netophah,** fifty and six.
23. The men of
■ **Anathoth,** an hundred
twenty and eight.
24. **The children of**
■ **Azmaveth,** forty and two.
25. The children of
■ **Kirjath-arim, Chephirah,**
■ **and Beeroth,** seven hundred
and forty and three.
26. The children of
■ **Ramah and Gaba,** six
hundred twenty and one.
27. **The men of Michmas,**
an hundred twenty and two.
28. The men of
■ **Beth-el and Ai,** two
hundred twenty and three.
29. **The children of**
■ **Nebo,** fifty and two.
30. The children of
■ **Magbish,** an hundred fifty and six.
31. The children of the other
■ **Elam,** a thousand two
hundred fifty and four.
32. The children of
■ **Harim,** three hundred and twenty.
33. The children of
■ **Lod, Hadid, and Ono,**
seven hundred twenty and five.
34. **The children of Jericho,**
three hundred forty and five.
35. The children of
■ **Senaah,** three thousand
and six hundred and thirty.
36. **The priests: the**
■ **children of Jedaiah,**
of the house of Jeshua, nine
hundred seventy and three.
37. The children of
■ **Immer,** a thousand fifty and two.
38. The children of
■ **Pashur,** a thousand two
hundred forty and seven.
39. The children of
■ **Harim,** a thousand and seventeen.
40. **The Levites:** the children of
Jeshua and Kadmiel, of the children
of Hodaviah, seventy and four.
■ 41. **The singers:** the children of
Asaph, an hundred twenty and eight.
■ 42. **The children of the**
porters: the children of Shallum, the

children of Ater, the children of Talmon, the children of Akkub, the children of Hatita, the children of Shobai, *in* all an hundred thirty and nine.

43. **The Nethinims:** the children of Ziha, the children of Hasupha, the children of Tabbaoth,

44. The children of Keros, the children of Siaha, the children of Padon,

45. The children of Lebanah, the children of Hagabah, the children of Akkub,

46. The children of Hagab, the children of Shalmai, the children of Hanan,

47. The children of Giddel, the children of Gahar, the children of Reaiah,

48. The children of Rezin, the children of Nekoda, the children of Gazzam,

49. The children of Uzza, the children of Paseah, the children of Besai,

50. The children of Asnah, the children of Mehunim, the children of Nephusim,

51. The children of Bakbuk, the children of Hakupha, the children of Harhur,

52. The children of Bazluth, the children of Mehida, the children of Harsha,

53. The children of Barkos, the children of Sisera, the children of Thamah,

54. The children of Neziah, the children of Hatipha.

55. The children of Solomon's servants: the children of Sotai, the children of Sophereth, the children of Peruda,

56. The children of Jaalah, the children of Darkon, the children of Giddel,

57. The children of Shephatiah, the children of Hattil, the children of Pochereth of Zebaim, the children of Ami.

58. **All the Nethinims, and the children of Solomon's servants,** were three hundred ninety and two.

59. **And** these *were* **they which** went up from Tel–melah, Tel–harsa, Cherub, Addan, *and* Immer: but they **could not shew their father's house,** and their seed, **whether they were of Israel:**

60. The children of Delaiah, the children of Tobiah, the children of Nekoda, six hundred fifty and two.

61. **And of the children of the priests:** the children of **Habaiah,** the children of **Koz,** the children of **Barzillai; which took a wife of the daughters of** Barzillai the **Gileadite,** and was called after their name:

62. **These sought their register** *among* those that were reckoned by genealogy, **but they were not found: therefore were they,** as polluted, **put from the priesthood.**

63. **And the Tirshatha said** unto them, that **they should not eat of the most holy things, till there stood up a priest with Urim and** with **Thummim.**

64. **The whole congregation** together **was forty** and **two thousand three hundred and threescore,**

65. **Beside their servants** and their maids, of whom *there were* **seven thousand three hundred thirty** and **seven:** and *there were* **among them two hundred singing men and** singing **women.**

66. Their horses *were* seven hundred thirty and six; their mules, two hundred forty and five;

67. Their camels, four hundred thirty and five; *their* asses, six thousand seven hundred and twenty.

68. **And** *some of* **the chief** of the **fathers,** when they **came to the house of the LORD** which *is* **at Jerusalem, offered freely for the house of God** to set it up in his place: 69. **They gave** after their ability unto the treasure of the work **threescore and one thousand drams of gold, and five thousand pound of silver, and one hundred priests' garments.** 70. **So** the priests, and the Levites, and *some of* **the people,** and the singers, and the porters, and the Nethinims, **dwelt in their cities, and** all **Israel in their cities.**

CHAPTER 3

1. **And** when **the seventh month** was come, and the children of Israel *were* in the cities, **the people gathered** themselves together as one man **to Jerusalem.** 2. **Then stood up Jeshua** the son of Jozadak, **and** his brethren **the priests, and Zerubbabel** the son of Shealtiel, **and his brethren, and builded the altar of** the God of Israel, **to offer burnt offerings** thereon, as *it is* written in the law of Moses the man of God. 3. **And** they set the altar upon his bases; for **fear was upon them because of the people of those countries: and they offered burnt offerings** thereon **unto the LORD,** *even* burnt offerings **morning and evening.** 4. **They kept also the feast of tabernacles,** as *it is* written, and *offered* the **daily** burnt offerings by number, according to the custom, **as** the duty of every day **required;** 5. **And** afterward *offered* **the continual burnt offering, both of the new moons, and** of all the **set feasts of the LORD** that were consecrated, **and** of **every one** that willingly **offered a freewill offering unto the LORD.** 6. **From** the first day of **the seventh month** began **they** to **offer burnt offerings** unto the LORD. **But the foundation of the temple** of the LORD **was not yet laid.** 7. **They gave money** also **unto the masons, and** to the **carpenters; and meat, and drink,** and oil, **unto** them of **Zidon, and** to them of **Tyre, to bring cedar trees from Lebanon** to the sea of Joppa, according to the grant that they had of Cyrus king of Persia. 8. **Now in the second year** of their coming unto the house of God at Jerusalem, in the second month, **began** Zerubbabel the son of Shealtiel, and Jeshua the son of Jozadak, and the remnant of their brethren **the priests and** the **Levites, and all** they **that were come** out of the captivity **unto Jerusalem;** and appointed the Levites, from twenty years old and upward, **to set forward the work of the house of the LORD.** 9. Then stood Jeshua *with* his sons and his brethren, Kadmiel and his sons, the sons of Judah, together, to set forward the workmen in

the house of God: the sons of Henadad, *with* their sons and their brethren the Levites.

10. **And when the builders laid the foundation of the temple** of the LORD, **they set the priests in their apparel** with trumpets, and the Levites the sons of Asaph with cymbals, **to praise the LORD,** after the ordinance of David king of Israel.

11. **And they sang together** by course in **praising and giving thanks unto the LORD; because he is good,** for his mercy *endureth* for ever toward Israel. And all the people shouted with a great shout, when they praised the LORD, because the foundation of the house of the LORD was laid.

12. **But many of the** priests and Levites and chief of the fathers, *who were* **ancient men, that had seen the first house,** when the foundation of this house was laid before their eyes, **wept** with a loud voice; **and** many **shouted** aloud **for joy:**

13. **So that the people could not discern the noise of the** shout of **joy from the** noise of the **weeping** of the people: for the people shouted with a loud shout, **and the noise was heard afar off.**

CHAPTER 4

1. **Now when the adversaries of Judah and Benjamin heard** that the children **of the** captivity builded the **temple** unto the LORD God of Israel;

2. **Then they came** to Zerubbabel, and to the chief of the fathers, **and said** unto them, **Let us build with you: for we seek your God**, as ye *do*; **and we** do **sacrifice unto him** since the days of Esar–haddon king of Assur, which brought us up hither.

3. **But** Zerubbabel, and Jeshua, and the rest of **the chief of the fathers of Israel, said** unto them, **Ye have nothing to do with us** to build an house unto our God; but **we** ourselves together **will build** unto the LORD God of Israel, **as king Cyrus** the king of Persia **hath commanded us.**

4. **Then the people of the land** weakened the hands of the people of Judah, and **troubled them in building,**

5. And hired counsellors against them, **to frustrate their purpose, all the days of Cyrus** king of Persia, even **until the reign of Darius** king of Persia.

6. **And in the reign of Ahasuerus,** in the beginning of his reign, **wrote they** *unto him* **an accusation against** the inhabitants of **Judah and Jerusalem.**

7. And in the days of Artaxerxes wrote Bishlam, Mithredath, Tabeel, and the rest of their companions, unto Artaxerxes king of Persia; and the writing of the letter *was* written in the Syrian tongue, and interpreted in the Syrian tongue.

8. Rehum the chancellor and Shimshai the scribe wrote a letter against Jerusalem to Artaxerxes the king in this sort:

9. Then *wrote* Rehum the chancellor, and Shimshai the scribe, and the rest of their companions; the Dinaites, the Apharsathchites, the Tarpelites, the Apharsites, the Archevites, the

Babylonians, the Susanchites, the Dehavites, *and* the Elamites, 10. And the rest of the nations whom the great and noble Asnapper brought over, and set in the cities of Samaria, and the rest *that are* on this side the river, and at such a time. 11. **This is the copy of the letter that they sent** unto him, *even* unto Artaxerxes the king; Thy servants the men on this side the river, and at such a time.

12. **Be it known** unto the king, **that the Jews** which came up from thee to us **are** come unto Jerusalem, building the **rebellious** and the bad city, **and have set up the walls** *thereof*, **and** joined the **foundations.** 13. **Be it known** now unto the king, that, **if this city be builded,** and the walls set up *again,* **then will they not pay toll, tribute, and custom, and so** thou shalt **endamage the revenue of the kings.** 14. **Now** because we have maintenance from *the king's* palace, and it was not meet for us to see the king's dishonour, **therefore** have we sent and certified the king; 15. That **search** may be made in the book of **the records** of thy fathers: so shalt thou find in the book of the records, **and know** that **this** city **is a rebellious city, and** hurtful unto kings and provinces, and that **they have moved sedition** within the same of old time: **for which cause was this city destroyed.** 16. **We certify** the king **that, if this city be builded**

again, and the walls thereof set up, by this means **thou shalt have no portion on this side the river.** 17. **Then sent the king an answer unto** Rehum the chancellor, and *to* Shimshai the scribe, and *to* the rest of their companions that dwell in **Samaria,** and *unto* the rest beyond the river, Peace, and at such a time. 18. **The letter which ye sent** unto us **hath been plainly read before me.** 19. **And I** commanded, and search hath been made, and it is **found that this city of old** time hath **made insurrection against kings,** and *that* rebellion and sedition have been made therein. 20. There have been mighty kings also over Jerusalem, which have ruled over all *countries* beyond the river; and toll, tribute, and custom, was paid unto them. 21. **Give** ye now **commandment** to cause these men to cease, and **that this city be not builded,** until *another* commandment shall be given from me. 22. Take heed now that ye fail not to do this: why should damage grow to the hurt of the kings? 23. **Now when the** copy of king Artaxerxes' **letter was read** before Rehum, and Shimshai the scribe, and their companions, **they went up** in haste **to Jerusalem** unto the Jews, **and made them to cease by force and power.** 24. **Then ceased the work** of the house of God which *is* at Jerusalem. So it ceased **unto the second year of the reign of Darius king of Persia.**

719

CHAPTER 5

■ 1. **Then the prophets,**
■ **Haggai** the prophet,
■ **and Zechariah** the son of Iddo,
■ **prophesied unto the Jews**
that *were* in Judah and Jerusalem
■ **in the name of the God**
■ **of Israel,** *even* unto them.
■ 2. **Then rose up Zerubbabel**
the son of Shealtiel,
■ **and Jeshua** the son of Jozadak,
■ **and began to build**
■ **the house of God**
which is at Jerusalem: and
■ **with** them *were*
■ **the prophets of**
■ **God helping them.**
■ 3. **At the same time**
■ **came** to them
■ **Tatnai, governor on**
■ **this side the river,**
and Shethar–boznai and
their companions,
■ **and said** thus unto them,
■ **Who hath commanded**
■ **you to build this house,**
■ **and** to make up
■ **this wall?**
■ 4. Then said we unto
them after this manner,
■ **What are the names**
■ **of the men that make**
■ **this building?**
■ 5. **But the eye of their**
■ **God was upon** the elders of
■ **the Jews, that they**
■ **could not** cause them to
■ **cease, till the matter**
■ **came to Darius:** and
then they returned answer by
letter concerning this *matter.*
■ 6. **The copy of the letter that**
■ **Tatnai,** governor on this side the
river, and Shethar–boznai and his
companions the Apharsachites,
which *were* on this side the river,
■ **sent unto Darius the king:**
■ 7. They sent a letter
unto him, wherein
■ **was written thus;**
Unto Darius the king, all peace.
■ 8. **Be it known unto the**
■ **king, that we went into**

the province of
■ **Judea, to the**
■ **house of** the great
■ **God,** which is builded with great
stones, and timber is laid in the walls,
■ **and this work goeth fast**
on, and prospereth in their hands.
■ 9. **Then asked we those**
■ **elders,** *and* said unto them thus,
■ **Who commanded you**
■ **to build this house,**
and to make up these walls?
■ 10. **We asked their names**
■ **also,** to certify thee, that we
might write the names of the
men that *were* the chief of them.
■ 11. **And** thus
■ **they returned us answer,**
■ **saying, We are the**
■ **servants of the God of**
■ **heaven and earth,** and build
■ **the house** that
■ **was builded** these
■ **many years ago, which**
■ **a great king of Israel**
■ **builded** and set up.
■ 12. **But** after that
■ **our fathers** had
■ **provoked the God of**
■ **heaven** unto wrath, he
gave them into the hand of
■ **Nebuchadnezzar the king**
■ **of Babylon,** the Chaldean, who
■ **destroyed this house,**
■ **and carried the people**
■ **away into Babylon.**
■ 13. **But** in the first year of
■ **Cyrus** the
■ **king of Babylon** *the*
same king Cyrus
■ **made a decree to build**
■ **this house of God.**
■ 14. **And the vessels** also
of gold and silver of the house of God,
■ **which Nebuchadnezzar**
■ **took out of the temple** that
was in Jerusalem, and brought them
into the temple of Babylon, those
■ **did Cyrus** the king
■ **take out of the temple**
■ **of Babylon, and** they were
■ **delivered unto** *one,*
whose name *was*

Sheshbazzar, whom he
had made governor;

15. And said unto him, Take these
vessels, go, carry them into the
temple that *is* in Jerusalem, and let the
house of God be builded in his place.

16. **Then came** the same
**Sheshbazzar, and laid
the foundation** of the house
of God which *is* in Jerusalem:
and since that time
even until now
**hath it been in
building, and** *yet* it
is not finished.

17. **Now** therefore, if *it seem*
good to the king, let there be
search made in
the king's treasure house,
which *is* there at Babylon,
whether it be *so,* that
**a decree was made
of Cyrus** the king to build this
house of God at Jerusalem,
**and let the king send
his pleasure to us
concerning this matter.**

CHAPTER 6

1. **Then Darius** the king
made a decree, and
search was made
**in the house of the
rolls,** where the treasures
were laid up in Babylon.

2. **And there was found
at Achmetha, in** the palace
that *is* in the province of the Medes,
a roll, and therein *was* a record
thus written:

3. **In the first year of
Cyrus** the king *the same* Cyrus
**the king made a decree
concerning the house
of God** at Jerusalem,
Let the house be builded,
the place where they offered
sacrifices, and let the foundations
thereof be strongly laid;
the height thereof
threescore cubits,
and the breadth thereof
threescore cubits;

4. **With** three rows of
great stones, and a row of
**new timber: and let the
expenses be given out
of the king's house:**

5. **And also let the**
golden and silver
vessels of the house of God,
**which Nebuchadnezzar
took** forth
out of the temple which *is* at
Jerusalem, and brought unto Babylon,
**be restored,
and brought** again
unto the temple which *is*
at Jerusalem, *every one*
to his place, and place *them*
in the house of God.

6. **Now therefore, Tatnai,**
governor beyond the river,
Shethar–boznai, and your
companions the Apharsachites,
which *are* beyond the river,
be ye far from thence:

7. **Let the work**
of this house of God
alone; let the governor of
the Jews and the elders of the
**Jews build this house
of God** in his place.

8. **Moreover I make a
decree** what ye shall do to
the elders of these Jews for the
building of this house of God:
that of the king's goods, *even* of the
tribute beyond the river, forthwith
**expenses be given unto
these men, that they be
not hindered.**

9. **And that which they** have
need of, both young bullocks,
and rams, and lambs,
for the burnt offerings of the
God of heaven, wheat, salt, wine, and
oil, according to the appointment of
the priests which *are* at Jerusalem,
**let it be given them day
by day without fail:**

10. **That they may offer
sacrifices** of sweet savours
unto the
God of heaven,
and pray for the life of

721

the king, and of his sons.

11. **Also** I have made a decree, that **whosoever shall alter this word,** let timber be pulled down from his house, and being set up, **let him be hanged** thereon; and let his house be made a dunghill for this.

12. **And the God that** hath caused his name to **dwell there destroy all kings and people, that shall** put to their hand to alter *and* to **destroy this house** of God which *is* at Jerusalem. **I Darius have made a decree; let it be done** with speed.

13. Then Tatnai, governor on this side the river, Shethar–boznai, and their companions, according to that which Darius the king had sent, so they did speedily.

14. **And** the elders of **the Jews builded, and** they prospered through the prophesying of Haggai the prophet and Zechariah the son of Iddo. And they builded, and **finished it, according to the commandment of** the **God** of Israel, **and** according to **the** commandment of Cyrus, and Darius, and Artaxerxes **king of Persia.**

15. **And this house was finished** on the third day of the month Adar, which was **in the sixth year of the reign of Darius** the king.

16. **And the children of Israel,** the priests, and the Levites, and the rest of the children of the captivity, **kept the dedication of this house of God with joy.**

17. **And offered** at the dedication of this house of God **an hundred bullocks, two hundred rams, four hundred lambs; and for a sin offering** for all Israel, **twelve he goats,** according to the number of **the tribes of Israel.**

18. **And they set the priests** in their divisions, **and** the **Levites** in their courses, **for the service of God,** which *is* at Jerusalem; **as it is written in the book of Moses.**

19. **And** the children of the captivity **kept the passover** upon **the fourteenth day of the first month.**

20. For the priests and the Levites were purified together, all of them *were* pure, and killed the passover for all the children of the captivity, and for their brethren the priests, and for themselves.

21. **And the children of Israel,** which were come again out of captivity, and all such as had **separated themselves** unto them **from the filthiness of the heathen of the land, to seek the LORD** God of Israel, did eat,

22. And kept the feast **of unleavened bread seven days** with joy: **for the LORD had** made them joyful, and **turned the heart of the king of Assyria unto them, to strengthen their hands in the work of the house of God,** the God of Israel.

CHAPTER 7

1. **Now after these things, in the reign of Artaxerxes king of Persia, Ezra** the son of Seraiah, the son of Azariah, the son of Hilkiah,

2. The son of Shallum, the son of Zadok, the son of Ahitub,

3. The son of Amariah, the son of Azariah, the son of Meraioth,

4. The son of Zerahiah, the son of Uzzi, the son of Bukki,

5. The son of Abishua, the son

of Phinehas, the son of Eleazar,
the son of Aaron the chief priest:

6. This Ezra **went up from Babylon; and he was a ready scribe in the law of Moses,** which the LORD God of Israel had given: and the king granted him all his request, according to the hand of the LORD his God upon him.

7. And there went up *some* of the children of Israel, and of the priests, and the Levites, and the singers, and the porters, and the Nethinims, unto Jerusalem, in the seventh year of Artaxerxes the king.

8. **And he came to Jerusalem in the fifth month,** which *was in* **the seventh year of the king.**

9. For upon the first *day* of the first month began he to go up from Babylon, and on the first *day* of the fifth month came he to Jerusalem, according to the good hand of his God upon him.

10. **For Ezra had prepared his heart to seek the law of the LORD,** and to do *it*, **and to teach in Israel** statutes and judgments.

11. **Now this is** the copy of **the letter that the king Artaxerxes gave unto Ezra** the priest, the scribe, *even* a scribe of the words of the commandments of the LORD, and of his statutes to Israel.

12. Artaxerxes, king of kings, unto Ezra the priest, a scribe of the law of the God of heaven, perfect *peace*, and at such a time.

13. **I make a decree, that all** they of the people of **Israel,** and *of* his priests and Levites, in my realm, which are minded of their own freewill to go up to Jerusalem, **go with thee.**

14. **Forasmuch as thou art sent of the king,** and of his seven counsellors,

to inquire concerning **Judah and Jerusalem, according to the law of** thy **God** which *is* in thine hand;

15. **And to carry the silver and gold, which the king and his counsellors have freely offered** unto the God of Israel, whose habitation *is* in Jerusalem,

16. And all the silver and gold that thou canst find in all the province of Babylon, **with the freewill offering of the people,** and of the priests, offering willingly **for the house of their God** which *is* in Jerusalem:

17. **That thou mayest buy** speedily with this money **bullocks, rams, lambs,** with their meat offerings and their drink offerings, **and offer them upon the altar of** the house of your **God** which *is* in Jerusalem.

18. **And** whatsoever shall seem good to thee, and to thy brethren, to **do with the rest of the silver and the gold,** that do **after the will of your God.**

19. **The vessels** also that are given thee **for the service of the house of thy God,** *those* **deliver thou before** the **God** of Jerusalem.

20. **And whatsoever more shall be needful** for the house of thy God, which thou shalt have occasion to bestow, **bestow it out of the king's treasure house.**

21. **And** I, *even* I Artaxerxes the king, do make a decree to all the treasurers which *are* beyond the river, that **whatsoever Ezra the** priest, the scribe of the law of the God of heaven, **shall require of you, it be done speedily,**

22. Unto an hundred talents of silver,

and to an hundredmeasures of wheat, and to an hundred baths of wine, and to an hundred baths of oil, and salt without prescribing *how much.*

23. **Whatsoever is commanded by** the **God** of heaven, **let it be** diligently **done** for the house of the God of heaven: for **why should there be wrath against the realm of the king and his sons?**

24. **Also we certify you, that touching** any of **the priests and Levites, singers, porters, Nethinims, or ministers of** this house of **God, it shall not be lawful to impose toll, tribute, or custom,** upon them.

25. **And thou, Ezra,** after the wisdom of thy God, that *is* in thine hand, **set magistrates and judges,** which may judge all the people that *are* beyond the river, all such as know the laws of thy God; and teach ye them that know *them* not.

26. **And whosoever will not do the law of thy God, and the** law of the **king, let judgment be executed speedily upon him, whether** *it be* unto **death,** or to **banishment,** or to **confiscation of goods, or** to **imprisonment.**

27. **Blessed be the LORD** God of our fathers, **which hath put** *such a thing* as **this in the king's heart, to beautify the house of the LORD** which *is* in Jerusalem:

28. **And hath extended mercy unto me before the king, and his** counsellors, and before all the king's mighty **princes. And I was strengthened as the hand of the LORD** my God **was upon me, and I gathered** together out of Israel **chief men togo up with me.**

CHAPTER 8

1. **These** *are* now the chief of their fathers, and *this is* the genealogy of them that **went up with me from Babylon,** in the reign of Artaxerxes the king.

2. Of the sons of Phinehas; **Gershom:** of the sons of Ithamar; **Daniel:** of the sons of David; **Hattush.**

3. Of the sons of Shechaniah, of the sons of Pharosh; **Zechariah: and with him** were reckoned by genealogy of the males **an hundred and fifty.**

4. Of the sons of Pahath–moab; **Elihoenai** the son of Zerahiah, **and with him two hundred males.**

5. Of the sons of **Shechaniah;** the son of Jahaziel, **and with him three hundred males.**

6. Of the sons also of Adin; **Ebed the son of Jonathan, and** with him **fifty males.**

7. **And** of the sons of Elam; **Jeshaiah** the son of Athaliah, **and** with him **seventy males.**

8. **And** of the sons of Shephatiah; **Zebadiah** the son of Michael, **and with him fourscore males.**

9. Of the sons of Joab; **Obadiah** the son of Jehiel, **and** with him **two hundred and eighteen males.**

10. **And** of the sons of **Shelomith;** the son of Josiphiah, **and with him an hundred and threescore males.**

11. And of the sons of Bebai;

724

Zechariah the son of Bebai, **and** with him **twenty** and **eight males.** 12. **And** of the sons of Azgad; **Johanan** the son of Hakkatan, **and** with him **an hundred and ten males.** 13. **And** of the last sons of Adonikam, whose names *are* these, **Eliphelet, Jeiel, and Shemaiah, and with them threescore males.** 14. Of the sons also of Bigvai; **Uthai, and Zabbud, and** with them **seventy males.** 15. **And I gathered them together** to the river that runneth to Ahava; and there abode we in tents **three days: and I viewed the people, and** the priests, and **found** there **none of the sons of Levi.** 16. **Then sent I** for Eliezer, for Ariel, for Shemaiah, and for Elnathan, and for Jarib, and for Elnathan, and for Nathan, and for Zechariah, and for Meshullam, **chief men;** also for Joiarib, **and** for Elnathan, **men of understanding.** 17. And I sent them with commandment **unto Iddo** the chief at the place Casiphia, and I told them what they should say unto Iddo, **and** to **his brethren** the Nethinims, at the place Casiphia, **that they should bring** unto us **ministers for the house of our God.** 18. **And** by the good hand of our God upon us **they brought us a man of understanding,** of the sons of Mahli, the son of Levi, the son of Israel; and **Sherebiah, with his sons and his brethren,** eighteen; 19. **And Hashabiah,**

and with him **Jeshaiah** of the sons of Merari, his brethren and their sons, twenty; 20. **Also** of the Nethinims, whom David and the princes had appointed for the service of the Levites, **two hundred and twenty Nethinims:** all of them were expressed by name. 21. **Then I proclaimed a fast** there, **at the river of Ahava,** that we might afflict ourselves before our God, **to seek** of him **a right way for us,** and for our little ones, **and for all our substance.** 22. **For I was ashamed to require of the king** a band of **soldiers** and horsemen **to help us against the enemy in the way:** because we had spoken unto the king, **saying, The hand of our God is upon all them** for good **that seek him;** but his power and his wrath *is* against all them that forsake him. 23. **So we fasted and besought our God for this:** and he was intreated of us. 24. **Then I separated twelve of the chief of the priests, Sherebiah, Hashabiah, and ten of their brethren** with them, 25. **And weighed unto them the silver, and the gold,** and the vessels, *even* the offering of the house of our God, **which the king,** and his counsellors, **and his lords,** and all Israel *there* present, **had offered:** 26. I even weighed unto their hand six hundred and fifty talents of silver, and silver vessels an hundred talents, *and* of gold an hundred talents; 27. Also twenty basons of gold, of a thousand drams; and two vessels of fine copper, precious as gold.

28. **And I said** unto them, **Ye are holy unto the LORD; the vessels are holy also; and the silver and** the **gold** *are* a freewill offering unto the LORD God of your fathers.

29. **Watch** ye, **and keep them, until ye weigh them** before the chief of the priests and the Levites, and chief of the fathers of Israel, at Jerusalem, **in the chambers of the house of the LORD.**

30. So took the priests and the Levites the weight of the silver, and the gold, and the vessels, to bring *them* to Jerusalem unto the house of our God.

31. **Then we departed** from the river of Ahava on **the twelfthday** of the first month, **to go unto Jerusalem: and the hand of** our **God** was upon us, and he **delivered us from** the hand of **the enemy,** and of such as lay in wait by the way.

32. **And we came to Jerusalem, and abode there three days.**

33. **Now on the fourth day was the silver and the gold and the vessels weighed in the house of our God** by the hand of Meremoth the son of Uriah the priest; and with him *was* Eleazar the son of Phinehas; and with them *was* Jozabad the son of Jeshua, and Noadiah the son of Binnui, Levites;

34. **By number and by weight** of every one: **and all the weight was written** at that time.

35. **Also the children of those** that had been carried away, **which were come out of the captivity, offered** burnt offerings unto the God of Israel, **twelve bullocks** for all Israel, **ninety** and **six rams, seventy** and **seven lambs, twelve he goats for a sin offering: all this was a burnt offering unto the LORD.**

36. **And they delivered the king's commissions unto the king's lieutenants, and** to the **governors** on this side the river: **and they furthered the people, and the house of God.**

CHAPTER 9

1. **Now when these things were done, the princes came** to me, **saying, The people of Israel, and the** priests, and the Levites, **have not separated themselves from the people of the lands,** *doing* according to their abominations, *even* of the Canaanites, the Hittites, the Perizzites, the Jebusites, the Ammonites, the Moabites, the Egyptians, and the Amorites.

2. **For they have taken of their daughters** for themselves, and for their sons: **so that the holy seed have mingled** themselves **with the people of those lands:** yea, the hand of the princes and rulers hath been chief in this trespass.

3. **And when I heard this** thing, **I rent my garment** and my mantle, and plucked off the hair of my head and of my beard, **and sat down astonied.**

4. **Then were assembled unto me every one that trembled** at the words of the God of Israel, **because of the transgression** of those that had been carried away; and I sat astonied until the evening sacrifice.

5. **And at the evening sacrifice** I arose up from my heaviness; and having rent my

garment and my mantle,
I fell upon my knees,
and spread out my hands
unto the LORD my God,

6. **And said, O my God,
I am ashamed** and blush to
lift up my face to thee, my God:
**for our iniquities are
increased over our head,**
and our trespass is grown
up unto the heavens.

7. **Since the days of our
fathers have we been in a
great trespass** unto this day;
**and for our iniquities have
we,** our kings, *and* our priests,
been delivered into the
hand of the kings of the lands,
**to the sword, to
captivity,** and to a spoil,
**and to confusion
of face,** as *it is* this day.

8. **And now** for a little space
**grace hath been shewed
from the LORD** our God,
**to leave us a remnant to
escape,** and to give us a nail in
his holy place, that our God may
lighten our eyes, and give us a
little reviving in our bondage.

9. **For we were bondmen;
yet our God hath** not forsaken
us in our bondage, but hath
**extended mercy unto us
in the sight of the kings
of Persia,** to give us a reviving,
**to set up the house
of our God,** and to repair the
desolations thereof, and to give us
a wall in Judah and in Jerusalem.

10. **And now, O** our
**God, what shall
we say** after this?
**for we have forsaken
thy commandments,**

11. **Which thou hast
commanded by** thy servants
**the prophets, saying,
The land,** unto which
ye go to possess it,
is an
unclean land
with the filthiness of the
people of the lands, with their
abominations, which have filled
it from one end to another with
their uncleanness.

12. **Now therefore give not
your daughters unto their
sons, neither take their
daughters** unto your sons,
nor seek their peace or their
wealth for ever: that ye
may be strong, and eat the good
of the land, and leave *it* for an
inheritance to your children for ever.

13. **And after all** that is
come upon us for
our evil deeds,
and for our great trespass,
seeing that thou our
**God hast punished us less
than our iniquities deserve,
and hast given us such
deliverance** as this;

14. **Should we again break
thy commandments,
and join** in affinity
with the people of
these abominations?
**wouldest not thou be angry
with us till thou hadst
consumed us,** so that *there
should be* no remnant nor escaping?

15. **O LORD** God of Israel,
**thou art righteous: for we
remain yet escaped,** as *it is*
this day: behold, we *are* before thee
in our trespasses: for
**we cannot stand before
thee** because of this.

CHAPTER 10

1. **Now when Ezra had
prayed, and** when he had
confessed, weeping and
casting himself down before
the house of God,
there assembled
unto him out of Israel
a very great congregation
of men and women and children:
for the people wept very sore.

2. **And Shechaniah** the
son of Jehiel, *one* of the sons
of Elam, answered and

said unto Ezra, **We have trespassed against** our **God, and have taken strange wives** of the people of the land: yet now there is hope in Israel concerning this thing.

3. **Now therefore let us make a covenant with our God to put away** all **the wives, and such as are born of them,** according to the counsel of my lord, and of those that tremble at the commandment of our God; **and let it be done according to the law.**

4. **Arise; for** *this* **matter** *belongeth* **unto thee: we** also **will be with thee:** be of good courage, and do *it.*

5. **Then arose Ezra, and made** the chief priests, the Levites, and all **Israel,** to **swear that they should do according to this word.** And they sware.

6. **Then Ezra** rose up from before the house of God, and went into the chamber of Johanan the son of Eliashib: and *when* he came thither, he did eat no bread, nor drink water: for he **mourned because of the transgression** of them that had been carried away.

7. **And they made proclamation throughout Judah and Jerusalem** unto all the children of the captivity, **that they should gather** themselves together **unto Jerusalem;**

8. **And that whosoever would not come within three days,** according to the counsel of the princes and the elders, **all his substance should be forfeited, and himself separated from the congregation** of those that had been carried away.

9. Then all the men of Judah and Benjamin gathered themselves together unto Jerusalem within three days. **It was the ninth month, on the twentieth day** of the month; **and all the people sat in** the street of the house of God, **trembling because of this matter,** and for the great rain.

10. **And Ezra** the priest stood up, and **said** unto them, **Ye have transgressed, and have taken strange wives,** to increase the trespass of Israel.

11. **Now therefore make confession unto the LORD** God of your fathers, **and do his pleasure: and separate yourselves** from the people of the land, and from the strange wives.

12. **Then all the congregation answered** and said with a loud voice, **As thou hast said, so must we do.**

13. **But the people are many,** and *it is* a time of much rain, and we are not able to stand without, **neither is this a work of one day or two:** for we are many that have transgressed in this thing.

14. **Let now our rulers** of all the congregation **stand, and let all them which have taken strange wives** in our cities **come at appointed times, and with them the elders** of every city, **and the judges** thereof, **until the fierce wrath of** our **God** for this matter **be turned from us.**

15. **Only Jonathan** the son of Asahel **and Jahaziah** the son of Tikvah **were employed about this matter: and Meshullam**

■ **and Shabbethai** the Levite
■ **helped them.**
16. And the children of the
captivity did so.
■ **And Ezra** the priest,
■ **with certain chief of the**
■ **fathers,** after the house of their
fathers, and all of them by *their*
names, were separated, and
■ **sat down** in the first day
of the tenth month
■ **to examine the matter.**
■ 17. **And they made an**
■ **end with all the men**
■ **that had taken strange**
■ **wives by the first day**
■ **of the first month.**
18. And among the sons of the
priests there were found that had
taken strange wives: *namely,* of the
sons of Jeshua the son of Jozadak,
and his brethren; Maaseiah, and
Eliezer, and Jarib, and Gedaliah.
■ 19. **And they** gave their
hands that they would
■ **put away their wives;**
■ **and being guilty, they**
■ **offered a ram** of the flock
■ **for their trespass.**
20. And of the sons of Immer;
Hanani, and Zebadiah.
21. And of the sons of Harim;
Maaseiah, and Elijah, and
Shemaiah, and Jehiel, and Uzziah.
22. And of the sons of Pashur;
Elioenai, Maaseiah, Ishmael,
Nethaneel, Jozabad, and Elasah.
23. Also of the Levites; Jozabad,
and Shimei, and Kelaiah, (the
same *is* Kelita,) Pethahiah,
Judah, and Eliezer.
24. Of the singers also; Eliashib:
and of the porters; Shallum,
and Telem, and Uri.
25. Moreover of Israel: of the sons of

Parosh; Ramiah, and Jeziah, and
Malchiah, and Miamin, and Eleazar,
and Malchijah, and Benaiah.
26. And of the sons of Elam;
Mattaniah, Zechariah, and Jehiel,
and Abdi, and Jeremoth, and Eliah.
27. And of the sons of Zattu; Elioenai,
Eliashib, Mattaniah, and Jeremoth,
and Zabad, and Aziza.
28. Of the sons also of Bebai;
Jehohanan, Hananiah, Zabbai,
and Athlai.
29. And of the sons of Bani;
Meshullam, Malluch, and Adaiah,
Jashub, and Sheal, and Ramoth.
30. And of the sons of Pahath–moab;
Adna, and Chelal, Benaiah,Maaseiah,
Mattaniah, Bezaleel, and Binnui,
and Manasseh.
31. And *of* the sons of Harim;
Eliezer, Ishijah, Malchiah,
Shemaiah, Shimeon,
32. Benjamin, Malluch,
and Shemariah.
33. Of the sons of Hashum; Mattenai,
Mattathah, Zabad, Eliphelet, Jeremai,
Manasseh, *and* Shimei.
34. Of the sons of Bani;
Maadai, Amram, and Uel,
35. Benaiah, Bedeiah, Chelluh,
36. Vaniah, Meremoth, Eliashib,
37. Mattaniah, Mattenai, and Jaasau,
38. And Bani, and Binnui, Shimei,
39. And Shelemiah, and
Nathan, and Adaiah,
40. Machnadebai, Shashai, Sharai,
41. Azareel, and Shelemiah,
Shemariah,
42. Shallum, Amariah, *and* Joseph.
43. Of the sons of Nebo; Jeiel,
Mattithiah, Zabad, Zebina, Jadau,
and Joel, Benaiah.
44. All these had taken strange
wives: and *some* of them had wives
by whom they had children.

NEHEMIAH:

In contemporary Christian circles
a person who is
a believer and, yet,
has not received a specific
calling to be a pastor, a
teacher, an evangelist, etc.
is designated as
a "Layman."
Although the term is not a
Biblical one used to describe
any Christian or his vocation,
it is widely used
and recognized.
Nehemiah was a
"Layman." He did not claim to be
called into the priesthood. Nor did he
possess the gifts of a prophet.
He was merely a man
who loved God, His law, and
the Institution He had established.
Much of the book of Nehemiah is
written in the first person and can be
described as memoirs. Nehemiah
was a man of action with the right
motivation. Lacking priestly
ordination or the gifts of a prophet,

he saw a deplorable
situation which demanded
action. He did not go to his
formal religious leaders and
urge them to do something.
At the time he was in
captivity. He had risen to become
Cup-bearer to king Artaxerxes.
His brother returned
from Jerusalem to tell
of the terrible conditions
in the city. The walls were broken
down. The city was in shambles.
Nehemiah was
heartbroken over the report.
He prayed. He fasted.
But he did more.
He acted.
With the permission of the king
he returned to
Jerusalem and against
constant opposition and living
under the threat of death,
he organized the people,
rebuilt the walls, and
restored Jerusalem.

THE BOOK OF NEHEMIAH

BACKGROUND INFORMATION

Author: Nehemiah
Date Written: Between 423 — 404 B.C.

Number of:
Verses—406
Chapters—13
Total Words—10,483
Scan Words—4,081
Scan Words Represent
Approximately 38% of
Total Words

Theme: The Rebuilding of the walls of Jerusalem

OUTLINE OF THE BOOK

I. **Nehemiah's Visit to Jerusalem**
   1:1 — 2:8
II. **The Rebuilding of the Walls** of Jerusalem
   2:9 — 7:73
III. **The Revival** Under Ezra
   8:1 — 10:39
IV. **The Conditions of the Remnant** of Israel
   11:1 — 13:31

CHAPTER 1

1. **The words of Nehemiah** the son of Hachaliah. **And it came to pass** in the month Chisleu, in the twentieth year, **as I was in Shushan the palace,** 2. **That Hanani,** one of my brethren, **came, he and certain men** of Judah; **and I asked them concerning the Jews** that had escaped, which were left of the captivity, **and** concerning **Jerusalem,** 3. **And they said** unto me, **The remnant** that are left of the captivity there in the province **are in great affliction and reproach: the wall of Jerusalem also is broken down,** and the gates thereof are burned with fire. 4. And it came to pass, **when I heard** these words, that **I** sat down and wept, and **mourned** *certain* days, **and fasted, and prayed** before the God of heaven, 5. And said, I beseech thee, **O LORD** God of heaven, the great and terrible God, that keepeth covenant and mercy for them that love him and observe his commandments: 6. **Let thine ear** now be attentive, and thine eyes open, that thou mayest **hear the prayer of thy servant, which I pray** before thee now, **day and night, for** the children of **Israel** thy servants, **and confess the sins** of the children of Israel, **which we have sinned against thee:** both I and my father's house have sinned. 7. **We have** dealt very corruptly against thee, and have

not kept the **commandments, nor** the **statutes, nor** the **judgments, which thou commandedst** thy servant **Moses.** 8. **Remember,** I beseech thee, **the word that thou commandedst** thy servant **Moses,** saying, **If ye transgress, I will scatter you** abroad among the nations: 9. **But if ye** turn unto me, and **keep my commandments,** and do them; though there were of you cast out unto the uttermost part of the heaven, *yet* will **I** gather them from thence, and **will bring them unto the place that I have chosen to set my name** there. 10. **Now these are** thy servants and **thy people, whom thou hast redeemed** by thy great power, and by thy strong hand. 11. **O LORD,** I beseech thee, let now thine ear **be attentive to the** prayer of thy servant, and to the **prayer of thy servants, who desire to fear thy name:** and prosper, I pray thee, thy servant this day, **and grant him mercy in the sight of this man. For I was the king's cupbearer.**

CHAPTER 2

1. **And it came to pass** in the month Nisan, in the twentieth year of Artaxerxes the king, **that** wine *was* before him: and **I took up the wine,** and gave it **unto the king. Now I had not been beforetime sad in his presence.** 2. **Wherefore the king said** unto me, **Why is thy countenance sad,** seeing thou *art* not sick? this is nothing *else* but sorrow of heart.

732

Then I was very sore
afraid,
3. **And said** unto the king, Let
the king live for ever: why should
not my countenance be sad, when
the city, the place
of my fathers' sepulchres,
lieth waste, and the gates
thereof are consumed with fire?
4. **Then the king said** unto me,
For what dost thou make
request? So I prayed
to the God of heaven.
5. **And I**
said unto the king,
If it please the king, and if
thy servant have found favour in
thy sight, that thou wouldest
send me unto Judah,
unto the city of my
fathers' sepulchres,
that I may build it.
6. And the king said unto me, (the
queen also sitting by him,) For how
long shall thy journey be? and
when wilt thou return?
So it pleased the king
to send me; and I set him a time.
7. **Moreover I said** unto
the king, If it please the king,
let letters be given me to
the governors beyond
the river, that they may convey
me over till I come into Judah;
8. **And** a letter
unto Asaph the keeper
of the king's forest,
that he may give me
timber to make beams
for the gates of the palace
which *appertained* to the house,
and for
the wall of the city, and for
the house that I shall enter into.
And the king granted
me, according to the good
hand of my God upon me.
9. Then I came to the
governors beyond the river,
and gave them the king's
letters. Now the king had
sent captains of the army
and horsemen with me.

10. **When Sanballat**
the Horonite,
and Tobiah the
servant, the Ammonite,
heard of it, it grieved
them exceedingly
that there was come
a man to seek the
welfare of the children of
Israel.
11. **So I came to Jerusalem,**
and was there three days.
12. And I arose in the night, I
and some few men with me;
neither told I any man what
my God had put in my
heart to do at Jerusalem: neither
was there any beast with me,
save the beast that I rode upon.
13. **And I went out by night**
by the gate of the valley, even before
the dragon well, and to the dung port,
and viewed the walls of
Jerusalem, which were
broken down, and the gates
thereof were consumed with fire.
14. Then I went on to the gate of
the fountain, and to the king's pool:
but *there was* no place for the
beast *that was* under me to pass.
15. Then went I up in the night by
the brook, and viewed the wall,
and turned back, and entered
by the gate of the valley,
and so returned.
16. **And the rulers knew**
not whither I went, or what
I did; neither had I as yet
told *it* to
the Jews, nor to
the priests, nor to the nobles,
nor to the rulers, nor to the
rest that did the work.
17. **Then said I unto them,**
Ye see the distress that we
are in, how Jerusalem lieth
waste, and the gates thereof
are burned with fire: come, and
let us build up the wall
of Jerusalem, that we
be no more a reproach.
18. **Then I told them of**
the hand of my

God which was good
upon me; as
also the king's words
that he had spoken unto me.
And they said, Let us
rise up and build. So they
strengthened their hands
for *this* good *work.*
19. **But when**
Sanballat the Horonite,
and Tobiah the
servant, the Ammonite,
and Geshem the Arabian,
heard it, they laughed
us to scorn, and despised us,
and said, What is this
thing that ye do?
will ye rebel against
the king?
20. **Then** answered
I them, and
said unto them, The
God of heaven, he
will prosper us;
therefore we his servants
will arise and build: but
ye have no portion,
nor right, nor memorial,
in Jerusalem.

CHAPTER 3

1. **Then** Eliashib the high priest
rose up with his brethren
the priests, and they
builded the sheep gate;
they sanctified it, and set up the
doors of it; even unto the tower
of Meah they sanctified it, unto
the tower of Hananeel.
2. **And next unto him**
builded the men of Jericho.
And next to them builded
Zaccur the son of Imri.
3. **But the fish gate did the**
sons of Hassenaah build,
who *also* laid the beams thereof, and
set up the doors thereof, the locks
thereof, and the bars thereof.
4. **And next unto them**
repaired Meremoth the son of
Urijah, the son of Koz.
And next unto them repaired
Meshullam the son of Berechiah,

the son of Meshezabeel.
And next unto them repaired
Zadok the son of Baana.
5. **And next unto them the**
Tekoites repaired; but their nobles
put not their necks to the
work of their LORD.
6. **Moreover the old gate**
repaired Jehoiada the son of
Paseah, and Meshullam the son of
Besodeiah; they laid the beams
thereof, and set up the doors
thereof, and the locks thereof,
and the bars thereof.
7. **And next unto**
them repaired
Melatiah the Gibeonite,
and Jadon the Meronothite,
the men of Gibeon, and of
Mizpah, unto the throne of the
governor on this side the river.
8. **Next unto him repaired**
Uzziel the son of Harhaiah,
of the goldsmiths. Next
unto him also repaired
Hananiah the son of *one of* the
apothecaries, and they fortified
Jerusalem unto the broad wall.
9. **And next unto them** repaired
Rephaiah the son of Hur,
the ruler of the half part
of Jerusalem.
10. **And next unto**
them repaired
Jedaiah the son of Harumaph,
even over against his house.
And next unto him repaired
Hattush the son of Hashabniah.
11. **Malchijah** the son of Harim,
and Hashub the
son of Pahath–moab,
repaired the other piece, and
the tower of the furnaces.
12. **And next unto him**
repaired Shallum
the son of Halohesh,
the ruler of the
half part
of Jerusalem, he
and his daughters.
13. **The valley gate repaired**
Hanun, and the inhabitants
of Zanoah; they built it, and

734

set up the doors thereof, the locks thereof, and the bars thereof, and **a thousand cubits on the wall unto the dung gate.** 14. **But the dung gate repaired Malchiah** the son of Rechab, the ruler of part of Beth–haccerem; he built it, and set up the doors thereof, the locks thereof, and the bars thereof.

15. **But the gate of the fountain repaired Shallun** the son of Col–hozeh, the ruler of part of Mizpah; he built it, and covered it, and set up the doors thereof, the locks thereof, and the bars thereof, **and the wall of the pool of Siloah by the king's garden, and unto the stairs that go down from the city of David.** 16. **After him repaired Nehemiah** the son of Azbuk, the ruler of the half part of Beth–zur, unto *the place* over against the sepulchres of David, and to the pool that was made, and unto the house of the mighty.

17. **After him** repaired the Levites, **Rehum** the son of Bani. **Next unto him** repaired **Hashabiah,** the ruler of the half part of Keilah, in his part. 18. **After him** repaired **their brethren, Bavai** the son of Henadad, the ruler of the half part of Keilah. 19. **And next to him repaired Ezer** the son of Jeshua, the ruler of Mizpah, another piece over against the going up **to the** armoury at the **turning of the wall.** 20. **After him Baruch** the son of Zabbai earnestly repaired the other piece, **from the turning of the wall unto the door of the house of Eliashib the high priest.** 21. **After him repaired Meremoth** the son of Urijah the son of Koz another piece, from the door of the house of Eliashib even to the end of the house of Eliashib.

22. **And after him repaired the priests, the men of the plain.** 23. **After him repaired Benjamin and Hashub** over against their house. **After him** repaired **Azariah** the son of Maaseiah the son of Ananiah by his house. 24. **After him** repaired **Binnui** the son of Henadad another piece, from the house of Azariah unto the turning *of the wall*, even unto the corner. 25. **Palal** the son of Uzai, over against the turning *of the wall*, and the tower which lieth out from the king's high house, that *was* by the court of the prison. **After him Pedaiah** the son of Parosh.

26. Moreover **the Nethinims** dwelt in Ophel, unto *the place* over against the water gate toward the east, and the tower that lieth out.

27. **After them the Tekoites** repaired another piece, over against the great tower that lieth out, even unto the wall of Ophel.

28. From above the horse gate repaired the priests, every one over against his house. 29. **After them** repaired **Zadok** the son of Immer over against his house. **After him repaired** also **Shemaiah** the son of Shechaniah, **the keeper of the east gate.** 30. **After him** repaired **Hananiah** the son of Shelemiah, **and Hanun** the sixth son of Zalaph, another piece. **After him** repaired **Meshullam** the son of Berechiah over against his chamber. 31. **After him** repaired **Malchiah** the goldsmith's son unto the place of the Nethinims, and of the merchants, over against the gate Miphkad, and to the going up of the corner.

32. **And between** the going up of **the corner unto the sheep gate repaired the goldsmiths and the merchants.**

CHAPTER 4

1. **But** it came to pass, that **when Sanballat heard that we builded the wall, he was wroth,** and took great indignation, **and mocked the Jews.**

2. And he spake before his brethren and the army of Samaria, and said, **What do these feeble Jews? will they fortify themselves?** will they sacrifice? will they make an end in a day? **will they revive the stones out** of the heaps **of the rubbish** which are burned?

3. **Now Tobiah** the Ammonite *was* by him, and he **said,** Even that which they build, **if a fox go up, he shall** even **break down their stone wall.**

4. **Hear, O** our **God; for we are despised:** and turn their reproach upon their own head, and give them for a prey in the land of captivity:

5. And cover not their iniquity, and **let not their sin be blotted out** from before *thee*: **for they have provoked thee to anger** before thebuilders.

6. **So built we the wall;** and all the wall was joined together unto the half thereof: **for the people had a mind to work.**

7. **But** it came to pass, *that* **when Sanballat, and Tobiah,** and the Arabians, and the Ammonites, and the Ashdodites, **heard that the walls** of Jerusalem **were made up,** *and* that the breaches began to be stopped, then **they were** very **wroth,**

8. **And conspired** all of them together to come *and* to fight **against Jerusalem,** and **to hinder it.**

9. **Nevertheless we made our prayer** unto our God, **and set a watch** against them day and night, because of them.

10. And Judah said, The strength of the bearers of burdens is decayed, and *there is* much rubbish; so that we are not able to build the wall.

11. **And our adversaries said, They shall not know,** neither see, **till we come** in the midst among them, **and slay them,** and cause the work to cease.

12. **And** it came to pass, that **when the Jews which dwelt by them came, they said** unto us ten times, **From all places** whence ye shall return unto us **they will be upon you.**

13. **Therefore set I in the lower places** behind the wall, **and on the higher places,** I even set the **people** after their families **with their swords,** their spears, and their bows.

14. **And I** looked, and rose up, and **said** unto the nobles, and to the rulers, and to the rest of the people, **Be not** ye **afraid** of them: **remember the LORD,** *which is* great and terrible, **and fight for your brethren,** your sons, and your daughters, your wives, **and your houses.**

15. **And** it came to pass, **when our enemies heard that** it was known unto us, and **God had brought their counsel to nought,** that **we returned** all of us to the wall, **every one unto his work.**

16. **And** it came to pass **from that time** forth, *that* the **half** of my servants

wrought in the work,
and the other half of them
held both
the spears, the
shields, and the
bows, and the habergeons;
and the rulers *were* behind
all the house of Judah.

17. They which builded on the wall,
and they that bare burdens, with
those that laded, *every one* with one
of his hands wrought in the work, and
with the other *hand* held a weapon.

18. For the builders,
every one had
his sword girded
by his side, and
so builded. And he that
sounded the trumpet
was by me.

19. And I said unto the
nobles, and to the rulers,
and to the rest of the people,
The work is great and large,
and we are separated
upon the wall,
one far from another.

20. In what place *therefore*
ye hear the sound of the
trumpet, resort ye
thither unto us: our
God shall fight for us.

21. So we laboured in the work:
and half of them held the spears
from the rising of
the morning till the
stars appeared.

22. Likewise at the same
time said I unto the people, Let
every one with his
servant lodge within
Jerusalem, that in
the night they
may be a
guard to us,
and labour on the day.

23. So neither I, nor
my brethren, nor my servants, nor the
men of the guard which followed me,
none of us
put off our clothes, saving
that every one put them off
for washing.

CHAPTER 5

1. And there was a great cry
of the people and of their wives
against their brethren
the Jews.

2. For there were that said, We,
our sons, and our
daughters, are many:
therefore we take
up corn *for them*,
that we may eat, and live.

3. *Some* also there were that said,
We have mortgaged our
lands, vineyards, and houses,
that we might buy corn,
because of the dearth.

4. There were also that said,
We have borrowed money
for the king's tribute, *and*
that upon our lands and vineyards.

5. Yet now our flesh is as the
flesh of our brethren, our children
as their children: and, lo,
we bring into bondage
our sons and our
daughters to be servants,
and *some* of our daughters are
brought unto bondage *already*:
neither is it in our power to
redeem them; for other men
have our lands and vineyards.

6. And I was very
angry when I heard
their cry and these
words.

7. Then I consulted with myself, and
I rebuked the nobles,
and the rulers,
and said unto them,
Ye exact usury, every
one of his brother. And I set
a great assembly against them.

8. And I said unto them,
We after our ability
have redeemed our
brethren the Jews,
which were sold
unto the heathen; and
will ye even sell your
brethren? or shall they
be sold unto us? Then held
they their peace, and
found nothing to answer.

9. **Also I said,** It is not good that ye do: ought ye not to **walk in the fear of our God** because of the reproach of the heathen our enemies? 10. I likewise, *and* my brethren, and my servants, might exact of them money and corn: I pray you, **let us leave off this usury.** 11. **Restore,** I pray you, to them, even this day, **their lands,** their vineyards, their oliveyards, **and their houses, also the hundredth part of the money,** and of the corn, the wine, and the oil, **that ye exact of them.** 12. **Then said they, We will restore them,** and will require nothing of them; so will we do as thou sayest. **Then I called the priests, and took an oath** of them, **that they should do according to this promise.** 13. **Also I shook my lap, and said, So God shake out every man** from his house, and from his labour, **that performeth not this promise,** even thus be he shaken out, and emptied. And all the congregation said, Amen, and praised the LORD. And the people did according to this promise. 14. **Moreover from the time that I was appointed** to be their **governor** in the land **of Judah,** from the twentieth year even unto the two and thirtieth year of Artaxerxes the king, *that is,* **twelve years, I and my brethren have not eaten the bread of the governor.** 15. **But the former governors** that *had been* before me were chargeable unto the people, and **had taken of them bread and wine, beside forty shekels of silver;** yea, **even their servants bare rule over the people: but** so did **not I, because of the fear of God.** 16. **Yea, also I** continued in the work of this wall, neither bought we any land: **and all my servants were gathered** thither **unto the work.** 17. **Moreover there were at my table an hundred and fifty** of the **Jews and rulers, beside those that came** unto us **from among the heathen** that *are* about us. 18. Now *that* which was prepared *for me* daily *was* one ox *and* six choice sheep; also fowls were prepared for me, and once in ten days store of all sorts of wine: **yet** for all this **required not I the bread of the governor,** because the bondage was heavy upon this people. 19. **Think upon me, my God, for good,** *according* to all that I have done for this people.

CHAPTER 6

1. **Now it came to pass when Sanballat,** and **Tobiah, and Geshem** the Arabian, and the rest of our enemies, **heard that I had builded the wall,** and *that* there was no breach left therein; (though at that time I had not set up the doors upon the gates;) 2. **That Sanballat** and Geshem **sent unto me, saying, Come, let us meet together** in *some one of* the villages in the plain of Ono. **But they thought to do me mischief.** 3. **And I sent messengers** unto them, **saying,** I *am* doing a

great work, so that
**I cannot come down: why
should the work cease,
whilst I** leave it, and
come down to you?
4. Yet they sent unto me four times
after this sort; and I answered them
after the same manner.
5. **Then sent Sanballat**
his servant unto me in like
manner the fifth time with
an open letter in his hand;
6. **Wherein was written,
It is reported** among the
heathen, and Gashmu saith *it,*
that thou and
the Jews think to rebel: for
which cause thou buildest the wall,
**that thou mayest be their
king,** according to these words.
7. **And** thou
hast also
**appointed prophets
to preach of thee at
Jerusalem,** saying, *There is*
a king in Judah: and now shall
it be reported to the king
according to these words.
Come now therefore, and
**let us take counsel
together.**
8. **Then I sent**
unto him, saying,
**There are no such
things done** as thou sayest,
**but thou feignest them
out of thine own heart.**
9. **For they all made us
afraid, saying, Their hands
shall be weakened
from the work,** that it be
not done. Now therefore,
**O God, strengthen
my hands.**
10. **Afterward I came
unto** the house of
Shemaiah the son of Delaiah the
son of Mehetabeel, who *was* shut up;
and he said, Let us meet
together in the house of God,
**within the temple, and let
us shut the doors** of the temple:
for they will come to

slay thee; yea,
in the night will they
come to slay thee.
11. **And I said,
Should** such a man as
I flee? and who *is there,* that,
being as I *am,* would go into
the temple to save his life?
I will not go in.
12. **And,** lo,
**I perceived that God
had not sent him;**
but that he pronounced
this prophecy against me: for
**Tobiah and Sanballat
had hired him.**
13. Therefore *was* he hired,
**that I should be
afraid,** and do so,
and sin, and that they might
have matter for an evil report,
that they might reproach me.
14. My God, think thou upon Tobiah
and Sanballat according to these their
works, and on the prophetess
Noadiah, and the rest of the prophets,
that would have put me in fear.
15. **So the wall was
finished** in the twenty
and fifth *day* of *the month* Elul,
in fifty and
two days.
16. **And** it came to pass, that
**when all our enemies
heard** *thereof,* and all the heathen
that *were* about us saw *these things,*
**they were much cast down
in their own eyes: for
they perceived** that
this work was wrought
of our
God.
17. **Moreover** in those days
**the nobles of Judah
sent many letters unto
Tobiah,** and *the letters* of
Tobiah came unto them.
18. **For there were many in
Judah sworn unto him,**
because he *was* the son in
law of Shechaniah the son of
Arah; and his son Johanan had
taken the daughter of Meshullam

the son of Berechiah.

19. Also they reported his good deeds before me, and uttered my words to him.

■ ■ **And Tobiah sent letters to put me in fear.**

CHAPTER 7

■ 1. **Now** it came to pass,
■ **when the wall was built,**
■ **and I had set up the doors,**
■ **and the porters and** the
■ **singers and** the
■ **Levites were appointed,**
■ 2. **That I gave my brother**
■ **Hanani,** and Hananiah the ruler of the palace,
■ **charge over Jerusalem:**
■ **for he was a faithful man,**
■ **and feared God** above many.
■ 3. **And I said** unto them,
■ **Let not the gates** of Jerusalem
■ **be opened until the sun be**
■ **hot;** and while they stand by, let them shut the doors, and bar *them*:
■ **and appoint watches** of the inhabitants of Jerusalem, every one in his watch, and every one *to be* over against his house.
■ 4. **Now the city**
■ **was large** and great:
■ **but the people**
■ **were few** therein,
■ **and the houses**
■ **were not builded.**
■ 5. **And my God put into**
■ **mine heart to gather** together the nobles, and the rulers, and
■ **the people, that they**
■ **might be reckoned by**
■ **genealogy. And I found a**
■ **register of the genealogy of**
■ **them which came up** at the
■ **first,** and found written therein,
■ 6. **These are the children**
of the province, that went up out of the captivity,
■ **of those that had been**
■ **carried away,** whom Nebuchadnezzar the king of Babylon had carried away,
■ **and came again to**
■ **Jerusalem and** to

■ **Judah,** every one unto his city;

7. Who came with Zerubbabel, Jeshua, Nehemiah, Azariah, Raamiah, Nahamani, Mordecai, Bilshan, Mispereth, Bigvai, Nehum, Baanah. The number, I say, of the men of the people of Israel *was this;*

■ 8. **The children of Parosh,** two thousand an hundred seventy and two.

9. The children of
■ **Shephatiah,** three hundred seventy and two.

10. The children of
■ **Arah,** six hundred fifty and two.

11. The children of
■ **Pahath–moab,** of the children of
■ **Jeshua and Joab,** two thousand and eight hundred *and* eighteen.

12. The children of
■ **Elam,** a thousand two hundred fifty and four.

13. The children of
■ **Zattu,** eight hundred forty and five.

14. The children of
■ **Zaccai,** seven hundred and threescore.

15. The children of
■ **Binnui,** six hundred forty and eight.

16. The children of
■ **Bebai,** six hundred twenty and eight.

17. The children of
■ **Azgad,** two thousand three hundred twenty and two.

18. The children of
■ **Adonikam,** six hundred threescore and seven.

19. The children of
■ **Bigvai,** two thousand threescore and seven.

20. The children of
■ **Adin,** six hundred fifty and five.

21. The children of
■ **Ater of Hezekiah,** ninety and eight.

22. The children of
■ **Hashum,** three hundred twenty and eight.

23. The children of
■ **Bezai,** three hundred

twenty and four.

24. The children of **Hariph,** an hundred and twelve.

25. The children of **Gibeon,** ninety and five.

26. **The men of Beth-lehem and Netophah,** an hundred fourscore and eight.

27. The men of **Anathoth,** an hundred twenty and eight.

28. The men of **Beth-azmaveth,** forty and two.

29. The men of **Kirjath-jearim, Chephirah, and Beeroth,** seven hundred forty and three.

30. The men of **Ramah and Gaba,** six hundred twenty and one.

31. The men of **Michmas,** an hundred and twenty and two.

32. The men of **Beth-el and Ai,** an hundred twenty and three.

33. The men of the other **Nebo,** fifty and two.

34. The children of the other **Elam,** a thousand two hundred fifty and four.

35. The children of **Harim,** three hundred and twenty.

36. The children of **Jericho,** three hundred forty and five.

37. The children of **Lod, Hadid, and Ono,** seven hundred twenty and one.

38. And the children of **Senaah,** three thousand nine hundred and thirty.

39. **The priests: the children of Jedaiah,** of the house of Jeshua, nine hundred seventy and three.

40. The children of **Immer,** a thousand fifty and two.

41. The children of **Pashur,** a thousand two hundred forty and seven.

42. The children of **Harim,** a thousand and seventeen.

43. **The Levites: the children of Jeshua,** of **Kadmiel, and** of the children of **Hodevah,** seventy and four.

44. **The singers: the children of Asaph,** an hundred forty and eight.

45. **The porters: the children of Shallum,** the children of **Ater,** the children of **Talmon,** the children of **Akkub,** the children of **Hatita,** the children of **Shobai,** an hundred thirty and eight.

46. **The Nethinims: the children of Ziha,** the children of **Hashupha,** the children of **Tabbaoth,**

47. The children of **Keros,** the children of **Sia,** the children of **Padon,**

48. The children of **Lebana,** the children of **Hagaba,** the children of **Shalmai,**

49. The children of **Hanan,** the children of **Giddel,** the children of **Gahar,**

50. The children of **Reaiah,** the children of **Rezin,** the children of **Nekoda,**

51. The children of **Gazzam,** the children of **Uzza,** the children of **Phaseah,**

52. The children of **Besai,** the children of **Meunim,** the children of **Nephishesim,**

53. The children of **Bakbuk,** the children of **Hakupha,** the children of **Harhur,**

54. The children of **Bazlith,** the children of **Mehida,** the children of **Harsha,**

55. The children of **Barkos,** the children of

■ **Sisera,** the children of
■ **Tamah,**
56. The children of
■ **Neziah,** the children of
■ **Hatipha.**
■ 57. **The children**
■ **of Solomon's**
■ **servants:** the children of
■ **Sotai,** the children of
■ **Sophereth,** the children of
■ **Perida,**
58. The children of
■ **Jaala,** the children of
■ **Darkon,** the children of
■ **Giddel,**
59. The children of
■ **Shephatiah,** the children of
■ **Hattil,** the children of
■ **Pochereth** of
■ **Zebaim,** the children of
■ **Amon,**
60. All the Nethinims, and the
children of Solomon's servants,
were three hundred ninety and two.
■ 61. **And these were**
■ **they which** went up *also* from
Tel–melah, Telharesha, Cherub,
Addon, and Immer: but they
■ **could not shew** their
father's house, nor their seed,
■ **whether they were**
■ **of Israel.**
■ 62. **The children of**
■ **Delaiah,** the children of
■ **Tobiah,** the children of
■ **Nekoda,** six hundred
forty and two.
■ 63. **And of the priests:**
■ **the children of**
■ **Habaiah,** the children of
■ **Koz,** the children of
■ **Barzillai, which took** *one* of
■ **the daughters of**
■ **Barzillai** the Gileadite
■ **to wife,** and was called
after their name.
64. These sought their register
among those that were reckoned by
genealogy, but it was not found:
■ **therefore were they,**
■ **as polluted, put from**
■ **the priesthood.**
65. And the Tirshatha said unto

them, that they should not eat of the
most holy things, till there stood
up a priest with Urim and Thummim.
■ 66. **The whole**
■ **congregation** together
■ **was forty** and
■ **two thousand three**
■ **hundred and threescore,**
■ 67. **Beside their**
■ **manservants and** their
■ **maidservants, of**
■ **whom there were**
■ **seven thousand three**
■ **hundred thirty** and
■ **seven: and they had**
■ **two hundred forty** and
■ **five singing men and** singing
■ **women.**
68. Their horses, seven
hundred thirty and six: their
mules, two hundred forty and five:
69. *Their* camels, four hundred
thirty and five: six thousand seven
hundred and twenty asses.
■ 70. **And** some of
■ **the chief** of the
■ **fathers gave** unto the work.
The Tirshatha gave
■ **to the treasure a thousand**
■ **drams of gold, fifty basons,**
■ **five hundred and thirty**
■ **priests' garments.**
■ 71. **And some** of the
chief of the fathers
■ **gave** to the treasure of the work
■ **twenty thousand drams of**
■ **gold, and two thousand** and
■ **two hundred pound**
■ **of silver.**
■ 72. **And** *that* which
■ **the rest of the**
■ **people gave** *was*
■ **twenty thousand drams**
■ **of gold, and two thousand**
■ **pound of silver, and**
■ **threescore and seven**
■ **priests' garments.**
■ 73. **So** the priests, and the Levites,
and the porters, and the singers,
and *some* of the people, and the
Nethinims, and all Israel, dwelt
■ **in** their cities; and when
■ **the seventh month** came,

the children of Israel were in their cities.

CHAPTER 8

1. **And all the people gathered** themselves together as one man **into the street** that *was* **before the water gate; and they spake unto Ezra the scribe to bring the book** of the law **of Moses,** which the LORD had commanded to Israel.

2. **And Ezra** the priest **brought the law** before the congregation both of men and women, and all that could hear with understanding, upon the first day of the seventh month.

3. **And he read** therein before the street that *was* before the water gate **from the morning until midday,** before the men **and** the women, and those that could understand; and the ears of **all the people were attentive** unto the book of the law.

4. **And Ezra** the scribe **stood upon a pulpit of wood,** which they had made for the purpose; and beside him stood Mattithiah, and Shema, and Anaiah, and Urijah, and Hilkiah, andMaaseiah, on his right hand; and on his left hand, Pedaiah, and Mishael, and Malchiah, and Hashum, and Hashbadana, Zechariah, *and* Meshullam.

5. **And** Ezra **opened the book** in the sight of all the people; (for he was above all the people;) **and** when he opened it, **all the people stood up:**

6. **And Ezra blessed the LORD,** the great God. **And** all **the people answered, Amen, Amen, with lifting up their hands: and they bowed their heads, and worshipped** the LORD with *their* faces to the ground.

7. Also Jeshua, and Bani, and Sherebiah, Jamin, Akkub, Shabbethai, Hodijah, Maaseiah, Kelita, Azariah, Jozabad, Hanan, Pelaiah, and the Levites, caused the people to understand the law: and the people stood in their place.

8. **So they read** in the book **in the law of God distinctly, and gave the sense, and caused them to understand the reading.**

9. **And Nehemiah,** which *is* the Tirshatha, **and Ezra** the priest the scribe, **and the Levites that taught the people, said** unto all the people, **This day is holy unto the LORD** your God; **mourn not, nor weep. For** all **the people wept,when they heard the words of the law.**

10. **Then he said** unto them, **Go** your way, **eat** the fat, **and drink** the sweet, **and send portions unto them for whom nothing is prepared:** for *this* day *is* holy unto our LORD: **neither be** ye **sorry; for the joy of the LORD is your strength.**

11. So the Levites stilled all the people, saying, Hold your peace, for the day *is* holy; neither be ye grieved.

12. **And all the people went their way** to eat, and to drink, and to send portions, and to make great mirth, because they had understood the words that were declared unto them.

13. **And on the second day** were **gathered** together **the chief** of the **fathers** of all the people, **the priests, and** the **Levites, unto Ezra** the scribe, even **to understand the**

words of the law.

14. **And they found** written in the law which the LORD had commanded by Moses, **that** the children of **Israel should dwell in booths in the feast of the seventh month:**

15. **And that they should publish** and proclaim **in all their cities,** and in Jerusalem, **saying, Go forth** unto the mount, **and fetch** olive **branches,** and pine branches, and myrtle branches, and palm branches, and branches of thick trees, **to make booths,** as *it is* written.

16. **So the people** went forth, and brought *them*, and **made** themselves **booths,** every one upon the roof of his house, and in their courts, and in the courts of the house of God, and in the street of the water gate, and in the street of the gate of Ephraim.

17. And all the congregation of them that were come again out of the captivity made booths, **and sat under the booths: for since the days of Jeshua the** son of Nun unto that day **had not the children of Israel done so. And there was** very great **gladness.**

18. **Also day by day,** from the first day unto the last day, **he read in the book of the law of God. And they kept the feast seven days; and on the eighth day was a solemn assembly,** according unto the manner.

CHAPTER 9

1. **Now in the twenty and fourth day of this month the children of Israel were assembled**

with fasting, and with sackclothes, and earth upon them.

2. **And** the seed of Israel **separated themselves from** all **strangers, and** stood and **confessed their sins,** and the iniquities of their fathers.

3. **And they** stood up in their place, and **read in the book of the law** of the LORD their God **one fourth** part **of the day; and another fourth** part **they confessed, and worshipped the LORD** their God.

4. **Then stood up** upon the stairs, of **the Levites, Jeshua, and Bani,** Kadmiel, Shebaniah, Bunni, Sherebiah, Bani, *and* Chenani, **and cried** with a loud voice **unto the LORD** their God.

5. Then the Levites, Jeshua, and Kadmiel, Bani, Hashabniah, Sherebiah, Hodijah, Shebaniah, **and** Pethahiah, **said, Stand up and bless the LORD** your God for ever and ever: and blessed be thy glorious name, **which is exalted** above all blessing and praise.

6. **Thou,** *even* thou, **art LORD alone; thou hast made heaven,** the heaven of heavens, with all their host, **the earth, and all things** that *are* **therein, the seas,** and all that *is* therein, **and** thou **preservest them all;** and the host of heaven **worshippeth thee.**

7. **Thou** *art* the LORD the God, who **didst choose Abram,** and broughtest him forth out of Ur of the Chaldees, and gavest him the name of Abraham;

8. **And foundest his heart faithful** before thee, **and madest a covenant with him to give the land** of the Canaanites, the Hittites, the Amorites, and the Perizzites, and the Jebusites, and the Girgashites, to give *it, I say*, **to his seed,** and hast performed thy words; for thou *art* righteous:

9. **And didst see the affliction of our fathers in Egypt, and** heardest their cry **by the Red sea;**

10. **And shewedst signs and wonders upon Pharaoh,** and on all his servants, **and** on all **the people of his land:** for thou knewest that they dealt proudly against them. So; didst thou get thee a name, as *it is* this day.

11. **And thou didst divide the sea** before them, **so** that **they went through** the midst of the sea **on** the **dry land;** and their persecutors thou threwest into the deeps, as a stone into the mighty waters.

12. **Moreover thou leddest them** in the day **by a cloudy pillar; and** in the night by **a pillar of fire,** to give them light in the way wherein they should go.

13. **Thou camest down also upon mount Sinai,** and spakest with them from heaven, and gavest them right judgments, and true laws, good statutes and commandments:

14. **And madest known unto** them thy holy sabbath, and commandedst **them precepts, statutes, and laws, by** the hand of **Moses** thy servant:

15. **And gavest them bread from heaven** for their hunger, **and** broughtest forth **water** for them **out of the rock** for their thirst,

and promisedst them that they should go in to possess the land which thou hadst sworn to give them.

16. **But they** and our fathers dealt proudly, and hardened their necks, and **hearkened not to thy commandments,**

17. And refused to obey, neither were mindful of thy wonders that thou didst among them; but hardened their necks, **and in their rebellion appointed a captain to return to their bondage: but thou art** a God ready to pardon, gracious and **merciful,** slow to anger, and of great kindness, **and forsookest them not.**

18. **Yea, when they** had **made** them **a molten calf, and** said, This *is* thy God that brought thee up out of Egypt, and had **wrought great provocations;**

19. **Yet thou** in thy manifold mercies **forsookest them not** in the wilderness: the pillar of the cloud departed not from them by day, to lead them in the way; neither the pillar of fire by night, to shew them light, and the way wherein they should go.

20. **Thou gavest** also **thy** good **spirit to instruct them, and withheldest not thy manna** from their mouth, **and** gavest them **water** for their thirst.

21. **Yea, forty years didst thou sustain them** in the wilderness, *so that* they lacked nothing; their clothes waxed not old, and their feet swelled not.

22. **Moreover thou gavest them kingdoms and nations,** and didst divide them into corners: so they possessed the land of Sihon, and the land of the king of Heshbon, and the land

of Og king of Bashan.

23. **Their children also multipliedst** thou **as the stars of heaven,** and broughtest them into the land, concerning which thou hadst promised to their fathers, that they should go in to possess *it*.

24. **So the children went in and possessed the land, and thou subduedst** before them **the inhabitants** of the land, the Canaanites, and gavest them into their hands, with their kings, and the people of the land, that they might do with them as they would.

25. **And they took strong cities,** and a fat land, **and possessed** houses full of all **goods,** wells digged, vineyards, and oliveyards, and fruit trees **in abundance:** so they did eat, and were filled, and became fat, **and delighted themselves in thy** great **goodness.**

26. **Nevertheless they** were disobedient, and **rebelled against thee,** and cast thy law behind their backs, **and slew thy prophets** which testified against them to turn them to thee, **and** they **wrought great provocations.**

27. **Therefore thou deliveredst them into the hand of their enemies,** who vexed them: **and** in the time of their trouble, **when they cried unto thee, thou heardest them** from heaven; **and** according to thy manifold mercies thou **gavest them saviours,** who saved them out of the hand of their enemies.

28. **But after** they had **rest, they did evil again** before thee: **therefore leftest thou** them in the land of **their enemies, so that they had** the **dominion over them: yet when they** returned, and **cried unto thee,** thou heardest *them* from heaven; and **many times didst thou deliver them according to thy mercies;**

29. And testifiedst against them, that thou mightest bring them again unto thy law: **yet they** dealt proudly, and hearkened not unto thy commandments, but **sinned against thy judgments,** (which if a man do, he shall live in them;) and withdrew the shoulder, and hardened their neck, and would not hear.

30. Yet many years didst thou forbear them, and testifiedst against them by thy spirit in thy prophets: yet would they not give ear: **therefore gavest thou them into the hand of the people of the lands.**

31. **Nevertheless for** thy great mercies' sake **thou didst not** utterly **consume** them, **nor forsake them; for thou art a** gracious and **merciful God.**

32. **Now therefore, our God,** the great, the mighty, and the terrible God, who keepest covenant and mercy, let not all **the trouble** seem little before thee, **that hath come upon us,** on our kings, on our princes, and on our priests, and on our prophets, and on our fathers, and on all thy people, **since the time of the kings of Assyria unto this day.**

33. **Howbeit thou art just in all that is brought upon us; for** thou hast done right, but **we have done wickedly: **

34. **Neither have**

our kings, our
princes, our
priests, nor our fathers,
kept thy law, nor hearkened
unto thy commandments
and thy testimonies,
wherewith thou didst
testify against them.
35. For they have not
served thee in their kingdom,
and in thy great goodness that
thou gavest them, and
in the large and fat land
which thou gavest before
them, neither turned they from
their wicked works.
36. Behold, we *are* servants this day,
and *for* the land that thou gavest
unto our fathers to eat the
fruit thereof and the good thereof,
behold, we *are* servants in it:
37. And it yieldeth much
increase unto the kings
whom thou hast
set over us because of
our sins: also
they have dominion
over our bodies, and
over our cattle, at their pleasure,
and we are in
great distress.
38. And because of all
this we make a sure
covenant, and write *it*;
and our princes, Levites,
and priests, seal unto it.

CHAPTER 10

1. Now those that sealed
were, Nehemiah, the
Tirshatha, the son of
Hachaliah, and Zidkijah,
2. Seraiah, Azariah, Jeremiah,
3. Pashur, Amariah, Malchijah,
4. Hattush, Shebaniah, Malluch,
5. Harim, Meremoth, Obadiah,
6. Daniel, Ginnethon, Baruch,
7. Meshullam, Abijah, Mijamin,
8. Maaziah, Bilgai, Shemaiah:
these *were* the priests.
9. And the Levites: both Jeshua
the son of Azaniah, Binnui of the
sons of Henadad, Kadmiel;

10. And their brethren, Shebaniah,
Hodijah, Kelita, Pelaiah, Hanan,
11. Micha, Rehob, Hashabiah,
12. Zaccur, Sherebiah, Shebaniah,
13. Hodijah, Bani, Beninu.
14. The chief of the people; Parosh,
Pahath-moab, Elam, Zatthu, Bani,
15. Bunni, Azgad, Bebai,
16. Adonijah, Bigvai, Adin,
17. Ater, Hizkijah, Azzur,
18. Hodijah, Hashum, Bezai,
19. Hariph, Anathoth, Nebai,
20. Magpiash, Meshullam, Hezir,
21. Meshezabeel, Zadok, Jaddua,
22. Pelatiah, Hanan, Anaiah,
23. Hoshea, Hananiah, Hashub,
24. Hallohesh, Pileha, Shobek,
25. Rehum, Hashabnah, Maaseiah,
26. And Ahijah, Hanan, Anan,
27. Malluch, Harim, Baanah.
28. And the rest of
the people, the priests,
the Levites, the porters, the
singers, the Nethinims, and
all they that had separated
themselves from the people
of the lands unto the law of
God, their wives,
their sons, and their daughters,
every one having knowledge,
and having understanding;
29. They clave to their
brethren, their nobles, and
entered into a curse, and into
an oath, to walk in
God's law, which was
given by Moses the
servant of God, and to observe
and do all the
commandments of
the LORD our Lord, and his
judgments and his statutes;
30. And that we would
not give our daughters
unto the people of the
land, not take their
daughters for our sons:
31. And *if* the people of the
land bring ware or any victuals
on the sabbath day to sell, *that*
we would not buy it of them
on the sabbath, or on the
holy day: and *that* we would

■ leave the seventh year,
■ and the exaction of
■ every debt.
■ 32. **Also** we made
ordinances for us,
■ **to charge ourselves**
■ **yearly with the third part**
■ **of a shekel for** the service
of the house of our God;
33. For the shewbread, and for the
continual meat offering, and for the
continual burnt offering, of the
sabbaths, of the new moons, for the
set feasts, and for the holy *things*,
and for the sin offerings to make an
atonement for Israel, and *for*
■ **all the work of the**
■ **house of our God.**
■ 34. **And we cast the**
■ **lots among** the priests,
the Levites, and
■ **the people,**
■ **for the wood offering, to**
■ **bring it** into the house of our God,
after the houses of our fathers,
■ **at times appointed**
year by year,
■ **to burn upon the altar**
of the LORD our God, as *it is*
written in the law:
■ 35. **And to bring the**
■ **firstfruits** of our ground, and
the firstfruits of all fruit of all trees,
■ **year by year, unto the**
■ **house of the LORD:**
■ 36. **Also the firstborn of**
■ **our sons, and** of our
■ **cattle,** as *it is* written in
the law, and the firstlings of
our herds and of our flocks,
■ **to bring to** the house
of our God, unto
■ **the priests that minister**
■ **in the house of our God:**
■ 37. **And that we should**
■ **bring** the firstfruits of
our dough, and
■ **our offerings,** and the fruit of all
manner of trees, of wine and of oil,
■ **unto the priests,** to the
chambers of the house of our God;
■ **and the tithes** of our ground
■ **unto the Levites,** that the same

Levites might have the tithes
in all the cities of our tillage.
38. And the priest the son of
Aaron shall be with the Levites,
when the Levites take tithes:
■ **and the Levites shall**
■ **bring up the tithe of the**
■ **tithes unto the house**
■ **of our God,** to the chambers,
■ **into the treasure house.**
■ 39. **For** the children of Israel and the
children of Levi shall bring the offering
of the corn, of the new wine, and the
oil, unto the chambers, where *are* the
vessels of the sanctuary, and
the priests that minister, and the
porters, and the singers: and
■ **we will not forsake the**
■ **house of our God.**

CHAPTER 11

■ 1. **And the rulers** of the people
■ **dwelt at Jerusalem: the**
■ **rest of the people also**
■ **cast lots, to bring one**
■ **of ten to** dwell in Jerusalem
■ **the holy city,** and nine
parts *to dwell* in *other* cities.
■ 2. **And the people**
■ **blessed all** the men,
■ **that willingly** offered
themselves to
■ **dwell at Jerusalem.**
■ 3. **Now these are the chief**
■ **of the province that dwelt**
■ **in Jerusalem:** but in the
cities of Judah dwelt every
one in his possession in
their cities, *to wit,* Israel,
■ **the priests, and**
■ **the Levites, and**
■ **the Nethinims,**
■ **and the children of**
■ **Solomon's servants.**
■ 4. **And** at Jerusalem dwelt
■ **certain of the children of**
■ **Judah, and** of the children of
■ **Benjamin. Of the children**
■ **of Judah;** Athaiah the son
of Uzziah, the son of Zechariah,
the son of Amariah, the son of
Shephatiah, the son of Mahalaleel,
of the children of Perez;

5. And Maaseiah the son of Baruch, the son of Col–hozeh, the son of Hazaiah, the son of Adaiah, the son of Joiarib, the son of Zechariah, the son of Shiloni.

6. All the sons of Perez that dwelt at Jerusalem **were four hundred threescore and eight valiant men.**

7. **And** these *are* **the sons of Benjamin;** Sallu the son of Meshullam, the son of Joed, the son of Pedaiah, the son of Kolaiah, the son of Maaseiah, the son of Ithiel, the son of Jesaiah.

8. And after him Gabbai, Sallai, **nine hundred twenty and eight.**

9. **And Joel** the son of Zichri **was their overseer: and Judah** the son of Senuah **was second over the city.**

10. **Of the priests:** Jedaiah the son of Joiarib, Jachin.

11. Seraiah the son of Hilkiah, the son of Meshullam, the son of Zadok, the son of Meraioth, the son of Ahitub, *was* the ruler of the house of God.

12. And their brethren that did the work of the house **were eight hundred twenty and two:** and Adaiah the son of Jeroham, the son of Pelaliah, the son of Amzi, the son of Zechariah, the son of Pashur, the son of Malchiah.

13. And his brethren, chief of the fathers, **two hundred forty and two: and** Amashai the son of Azareel, the son of Ahasai, the son of Meshillemoth, the son of Immer,

14. And their brethren, mighty men of valour, **an hundred twenty and eight: and their overseer was Zabdiel,** the son of *one* of the great men.

15. **Also of the Levites:** Shemaiah the son of Hashub, the son of Azrikam, the son of Hashabiah, the son of Bunni;

16. And Shabbethai and Jozabad, of the chief of the Levites, *had* the oversight of the outward business of the house of God.

17. And Mattaniah the son of Micha, the son of Zabdi, the son of Asaph, *was* the principal to begin the thanksgiving in prayer: and Bakbukiah the second among his brethren, and Abda the son of Shammua, the son of Galal, the son of Jeduthun.

18. All the Levites in the holy city **were two hundred fourscore and four.**

19. **Moreover the porters,** Akkub, Talmon, and their brethren that kept the gates, **were an hundred seventy and two.**

20. **And the residue of** Israel, of the **priests, and** the **Levites, were in all the cities of Judah,** every one in his inheritance.

21. **But the Nethinims dwelt in Ophel:** and Ziha and Gispa *were* over the Nethinims.

22. **The overseer** also **of the Levites at Jerusalem was Uzzi** the son of Bani, the son of Hashabiah, the son of Mattaniah, the son of Micha. Of the sons of Asaph, **the singers were over the business of the house of God.**

23. **For it was the king's commandment** concerning them, **that a certain portion should be for the singers,** due for **every day.**

24. **And Pethahiah** the son of Meshezabeel, of the children of Zerah the son of Judah, **was at the king's hand in all matters concerning the people.**

25. And for the villages, with their fields, *some* of the children of Judah

dwelt at Kirjath–arba, and *in* the villages thereof, and at Dibon, and *in* the villages thereof, and at Jekabzeel, and *in* the villages thereof,

26. And at Jeshua, and at Moladah, and at Beth–phelet,

27. And at Hazar–shual, and at Beer–sheba, and *in* the villages thereof,

28. And at Ziklag, and at Mekonah, and in the villages thereof,

29. And at En–rimmon, and at Zareah, and at Jarmuth,

30. Zanoah, Adullam, and *in* their villages, at Lachish, and the fields thereof, at Azekah, and *in* the villages thereof. And they dwelt from Beer–sheba unto the valley of Hinnom.

31. The children also of Benjamin from Geba *dwelt* at Michmash, and Aija, and Beth–el, and *in* their villages.

32. *And* at Anathoth, Nob, Ananiah,

33. Hazor, Ramah, Gittaim,

34. Hadid, Zeboim, Neballat,

35. Lod, and Ono, the valley of craftsmen.

36. And of the Levites *were* divisions *in* Judah, *and* in Benjamin.

CHAPTER 12

1. Now these *are* the priests and the Levites that went up with Zerubbabel the son of Shealtiel, and Jeshua: Seraiah, Jeremiah, Ezra,

2. Amariah, Malluch, Hattush,

3. Shechaniah, Rehum, Meremoth,

4. Iddo, Ginnetho, Abijah,

5. Miamin, Maadiah, Bilgah,

6. Shemaiah, and Joiarib, Jedaiah,

7. Sallu, Amok, Hilkiah, Jedaiah. These *were* the chief of the priests and of their brethren in the days of Jeshua.

8. Moreover the Levites: Jeshua, Binnui, Kadmiel, Sherebiah, Judah, and Mattaniah, *which was* over the thanksgiving, he and his brethren.

9. Also Bakbukiah and Unni, their brethren, *were* over against them in the watches.

10. And Jeshua begat Joiakim, Joiakim also begat Eliashib,

and Eliashib begat Joiada,

11. And Joiada begat Jonathan, and Jonathan begat Jaddua.

12. And in the days of Joiakim were priests, the chief of the fathers: of Seraiah, Meraiah; of Jeremiah, Hananiah;

13. Of Ezra, Meshullam; of Amariah, Jehohanan;

14. Of Melicu, Jonathan; of Shebaniah, Joseph;

15. Of Harim, Adna; of Meraioth, Helkai;

16. Of Iddo, Zechariah; of Ginnethon, Meshullam;

17. Of Abijah, Zichri; of Miniamin, of Moadiah, Piltai:

18. Of Bilgah, Shammua; of Shemaiah, Jehonathan;

19. And of Joiarib, Mattenai; of Jedaiah, Uzzi;

20. Of Sallai, Kallai; of Amok, Eber;

21. Of Hilkiah, Hashabiah; of Jedaiah, Nethaneel.

22. The Levites in the days of Eliashib, Joiada, and Johanan, and Jaddua, *were* recorded chief of the fathers: also the priests, to the reign of Darius the Persian.

23. The sons of Levi, the chief of the fathers, *were* written in the book of the chronicles, even until the days of Johanan the son of Eliashib.

24. And the chief of the Levites: Hashabiah, Sherebiah, and Jeshua the son of Kadmiel, with their brethren over against them, to praise *and* to give thanks, according to the commandment of David the man of God, ward over against ward.

25. Mattaniah, and Bakbukiah, Obadiah, Meshullam, Talmon, Akkub, *were* porters keeping the ward at the thresholds of the gates.

26. These *were* in the days of Joiakim the son of Jeshua, the son of Jozadak, and in the days of Nehemiah the governor, and of Ezra the priest, the scribe.

27. **And at the dedication of the wall of Jerusalem they sought the Levites out of all their places,**

to bring them to Jerusalem, to keep the dedication with gladness, both with thanksgivings, and with singing, with cymbals, psalteries, and with harps.

28. And the sons of the singers gathered themselves together, both out of the plain country round about Jerusalem, and from the villages of Netophathi;

29. Also from the house of Gilgal, and out of the fields of Geba and Azmaveth: for the singers had builded them villages round about Jerusalem.

30. And the priests and the Levites purified themselves, and purified the people, and the gates, and the wall.

31. Then I brought up the princes of Judah upon the wall, and appointed two great companies of them that gave thanks, whereof one went on the right hand upon the wall toward the dung gate:

32. And after them went Hoshaiah, and half of the princes of Judah,

33. And Azariah, Ezra, and Meshullam,

34. Judah, and Benjamin, and Shemaiah, and Jeremiah,

35. And certain of the priests' sons with trumpets; namely, Zechariah the son of Jonathan, the son of Shemaiah, the son of Mattaniah, the son of Michaiah, the son of Zaccur, the son of Asaph:

36. And his brethren, Shemaiah, and Azarael, Milalai, Gilalai, Maai, Nethaneel, and Judah, Hanani, with the musical instruments of David the man of God, and Ezra the scribe before them.

37. And at the fountain gate, which was over against them, they went up by the stairs of the city of David, at the going up of the wall, above the house of David, even unto the water gate eastward.

38. And the other company of them that gave thanks went over against them, and I after them, and the half of the people upon the wall, frombeyond the tower of the furnaces even unto the broad wall;

39. And from above the gate of Ephraim, and above the old gate, and above the fish gate, and the tower of Hananeel, and the tower of Meah, even unto the sheep gate: and they stood still in the prison gate.

40. So stood the two companies of them that gave thanks in the house of God, and I, and the half of the rulers with me:

41. And the priests; Eliakim, Maaseiah, Miniamin, Michaiah, Elioenai, Zechariah, and Hananiah, with trumpets;

42. And Maaseiah, and Shemaiah, and Eleazar, and Uzzi, and Jehohanan, and Malchijah, and Elam, and Ezer. And the singers sang loud, with Jezrahiah their overseer.

43. Also that day they offered great sacrifices, and rejoiced: for God had made them rejoice with great joy: the wives also and the children rejoiced: so that the joy of Jerusalem was heard even afar off.

44. And at that time were some appointed over the chambers for the treasures, for the offerings, for the firstfruits, and for the tithes, to gather into them out of the fields of the cities the portions of the law for the priests and Levites: for Judah rejoiced for the priests and for the

Levites that waited.

45. **And** both **the singers and** the **porters kept the ward of their God, and** the ward of the **purification, according to the commandment of David,** *and* of Solomon his son.

46. For in the days of David and Asaph of old *there were* chief of the singers, and songs of praise and thanksgiving unto God.

47. **And all Israel** in the days of Zerubbabel, and in the days of Nehemiah, **gave the portions of the singers and the porters, every day his portion: and** they **sanctified holy things unto the Levites;** and the Levites sanctified *them* unto **the children of Aaron.**

CHAPTER 13

1. **On that day they read in the book of Moses** in the audience of the people; and **therein was found written, that the Ammonite and the Moabite should not come into the congregation of God** for ever;

2. **Because they met not** the children of **Israel with bread and** with **water, but hired Balaam** against them, **that he should curse them: howbeit** our **God turned the curse into a blessing.**

3. **Now** it came to pass, **when they** had **heard the law,** that **they separated from Israel all the mixed multitude.**

4. **And** before this, **Eliashib the priest, having the oversight of the chamber of the house of our God, was** allied unto Tobiah:

5. **And he had prepared for him a great chamber, where aforetime they laid the** meat **offerings,** the frankincense, and **the vessels, and the tithes** of the corn, the new wine, and the oil, which was commanded **to be given to the Levites, and the singers,** and **the porters; and** the offerings of **the priests.**

6. **But in all this time was not I at Jerusalem:** for in the two and thirtieth year of Artaxerxes king of Babylon came I unto the king, **and after certain days obtained I leave of the king:**

7. **And I came to Jerusalem, and understood of the evil that Eliashib did for Tobiah,** in preparing him a chamber in the courts of the house of God.

8. **And** it grieved me sore: therefore **I cast forth all the household stuff of Tobiah** out of the chamber.

9. Then I commanded, **and they cleansed the chambers: and** thither **brought** I again **the vessels of the house of God,** with the meat offering and the frankincense.

10. **And I perceived that the portions of the Levites had not been given them:** for the Levites and the singers, that did the work, were fled every one to his field.

11. **Then contended I with the rulers, and said, Why is the house of God forsaken? And I** gathered them together, and **set them in their place.**

12. **Then brought all Judah the tithe of the corn** and the new **wine and the oil unto the treasuries.**

13. **And I made treasurers over the treasuries,** Shelemiah the priest, and Zadok the scribe, and of the Levites, Pedaiah: and next to them *was* Hanan the son of Zaccur, the son of Mattaniah: for they were counted faithful, and their office *was* to distribute unto their brethren.

14. Remember me, O my God, concerning this, and wipe not out my good deeds that I have done for the house of my God, and for the offices thereof.

15. **In those days saw I** in Judah **some treading wine presses** on the sabbath, **and bringing** in **sheaves, and lading asses;** as also wine, grapes, and figs, and all manner of burdens, which they brought into Jerusalem **on the sabbath day: and I testified against them** in the day wherein they sold victuals.

16. **There dwelt men of Tyre** also therein, **which brought fish, and all manner of ware, and sold on the sabbath** unto the children of Judah, and in Jerusalem.

17. **Then I contended with the nobles** of Judah, **and said** unto them, **What evil thing is this** that ye do, and profane the sabbath day?

18. Did not your fathers thus, and did not our God bring all this evil upon us, and upon this city? yet **ye bring more wrath upon Israel by profaning the sabbath.**

19. And it came to pass, that when the gates of Jerusalem began to be dark before the sabbath, **I commanded that the gates** should **be shut, and** charged that they should **not be opened till after the sabbath:** and *some* of my servants set I at the gates, *that* there should no burden be brought in on the sabbath day.

20. **So the merchants and sellers** of all kind of ware **lodged without Jerusalem once or twice.**

21. **Then I** testified against them, and **said unto them, Why lodge ye about the wall? if ye do so again, I will lay hands on you. From that time** forth **came they no more on the sabbath.**

22. **And I commanded the Levites that they** should **cleanse themselves, and** that they should come and keep the gates, to **sanctify the sabbath day.** Remember me, O my God, *concerning* this also, and spare me according to the greatness of thy mercy.

23. **In those days also saw I Jews that** had **married wives of Ashdod,** of **Ammon, and** of **Moab:**

24. **And their children** spake half in the speech of Ashdod, and **could not speak in the Jews' language,** but according to the language of each people.

25. **And I contended with them,** and cursed them, and smote certain of them, and plucked off their hair, and made them swear by God, **saying, Ye shall not give your daughters unto their sons, nor take their daughters unto your sons,** or for yourselves.

26. **Did not Solomon** king of Israel **sin by these things?** yet among many nations **was there no king like him, who was beloved of** his **God,** and God made him king over all Israel: nevertheless even him did outlandish women cause to sin.

27. **Shall we** then hearken unto you to

■ do all
■ this great evil, to
transgress against our God
■ in marrying strange wives?
■ 28. And one of the sons of Joiada,
■ the son of Eliashib
■ the high priest,
■ was son in law to Sanballat
■ the Horonite: therefore I
■ chased him from me.
■ 29. Remember them,
■ O my
■ God, because they have
■ defiled the priesthood,

and the covenant of the
priesthood, and of the Levites.
■ 30. Thus cleansed I
■ them from all strangers,
■ and appointed
the wards of
■ the priests and the
■ Levites, every one
■ in his business;
31. And for the wood offering,
at times appointed, and
for the firstfruits.
■ Remember me, O
■ my God, for good.

THE BOOK OF ESTHER

BACKGROUND
INFORMATION

Author: Unknown
Date Written: Between
486 — 465 B.C.

Number of:
Verses—167
Chapters—10
Total Words—5,637
Scan Words—2,479
Scan Words Represent
Approximately 43% of
Total Words

Theme: The Salvation of the
Jewish Exiles through Esther,
the Queen of Persia

OUTLINE OF
THE BOOK

I. **Esther is Chosen Queen**
1:1 — 2:18
II. **The Deliverance** of the
Jews Through Esther
2:19 — 7:10
III. **The Revenge** of the Jews
8:1 — 10:3

CHAPTER 1

1. **Now** it came to pass in the days of **Ahasuerus,** (this *is* Ahasuerus which **reigned,** from India even unto Ethiopia, **over an hundred** and **seven and twenty provinces:**) 2. *That* in those days, when the king Ahasuerus sat on **the throne of his kingdom,** which **was in Shushan** the palace, 3. **In the third year of his reign, he made a feast unto all his princes and** his **servants; the power of Persia and Media,** the nobles and princes of the provinces, **being before him:** 4. When he shewed the riches of his glorious kingdom and the honour of his excellent majesty many days, *even* an hundred and fourscore days. 5. **And when these days were expired, the king made a feast unto all the people** that were present **in Shushan** the palace, both unto great and small, seven days, in the court of the garden of the king's palace; 6. *Where were* white, green, and blue, *hangings,* fastened with cords of fine linen and purple to silver rings and pillars of marble: the beds *were of* gold and silver, upon a pavement of red, and blue, and white, and black, marble. 7. And they gave *them* drink in vessels of gold, (the vessels being diverse one from another,) and royal wine in abundance, according to the state of the king. 8. And the drinking *was* according to the law; none did compel: for so the king had appointed to all the officers of his house, that they should do according to every man's pleasure. 9. **Also Vashti the queen made a feast for the women** *in* the royal house which *belonged* to king Ahasuerus.

10. **On the seventh day,** when the heart of **the king** was merry with wine, he **commanded** Mehuman, Biztha, Harbona, Bigtha, and Abagtha, Zethar, and Carcas**, the seven chamberlains** that served in the presence of Ahasuerus the king, 11. **To bring Vashti** the queen **before the king** with the crown royal, **to shew the people** and the princes **her beauty:** for she *was* fair to look on. 12. **But the queen Vashti refused to come** at the king's commandment by *his* chamberlains: **therefore was the king very wroth,** and his anger burned in him. 13. **Then the king said to the wise men,** which knew the times, (for so *was* the king's manner toward all that knew law and judgment: 14. And the next unto him *was* Carshena, Shethar, Admatha, Tarshish, Meres, Marsena, *and* Memucan, the seven princes of Persia and Media, which saw the king's face, *and* which sat the first in the kingdom;) 15. **What shall we do unto the queen** Vashti according to law, **because she hath not performed the commandment of the king** Ahasuerus by the chamberlains? 16. **And Memucan answered** before the king and the princes, **Vashti** the queen **hath not done wrong to the king only, but** also to all the princes, and **to all the people** that *are* in all the provinces of the king Ahasuerus. 17. **For** *this* deed of the queen shall come abroad unto **all women,** *so* that they

shall despise their
husbands in their eyes,
when it shall be reported, The king
Ahasuerus commanded Vashti the
queen to be brought in before him,
but she came not.

18. **Likewise shall the ladies
of Persia and Media** say this
day unto all the king's princes,
**which have heard of the
deed of the queen. Thus
shall there arise** too much
contempt and wrath.
19. **If it please the
king, let** there go
a royal commandment
from him, and let it
be written among
the laws of the Persians and the
Medes, that it be not altered,
**That Vashti come no
more before king
Ahasuerus; and** let the king
**give her royal estate unto
another** that is better than she.
20. **And when the king's
decree** which he shall make
shall be published throughout
all his empire, (for it is great,)
**all the wives shall give to
their husbands honour,**
both to great and small.
21. **And the saying pleased
the king** and the princes; and
the king did according to the
word of Memucan:
22. **For he sent letters into all
the king's provinces,**
into every province according to
the writing thereof, and to every
people after their language,
**that every man should bear
rule in his own
house,** and that it should
be published according to the
language of every people.

CHAPTER 2

1. **After** these things,
when the wrath of king
**Ahasuerus was appeased,
he remembered Vashti,**
and what she had done, and what

was decreed against her.
2. **Then said the king's
servants** that ministered unto him,
**Let there be fair young
virgins sought for the king:**
3. And let the king appoint officers
in all the provinces of his kingdom,
that they may gather
together all the fair young virgins
unto Shushan the palace,
to the house of the women,
unto the custody of Hege the king's
chamberlain, keeper of the women;
and let their
**things for purification
be given them:**
4. **And let the maiden
which pleaseth the king be
queen instead of Vashti.
And the thing pleased
the king;** and he did so.
5. **Now in Shushan** the palace
there was a certain
**Jew, whose name was
Mordecai,** the son of Jair,
the son of Shimei, the son of Kish,
a Benjamite;
6. **Who had been carried
away from Jerusalem with
the captivity** which had been
carried away with Jeconiah king
of Judah, whom
Nebuchadnezzar the
king of Babylon had
carried away.
7. **And he brought
up** Hadassah, that is
**Esther, his uncle's
daughter:** for she had neither
father nor mother, and the
maid was fair and beautiful;
whom Mordecai, when
her father and mother were dead,
took for his own daughter.
8. **So** it came to pass,
**when the king's
commandment** and his decree
was heard, and when many
maidens were gathered together
unto Shushan the palace, to the
custody of Hegai, that
**Esther was brought also
unto the king's house, to**

the custody of Hegai,
keeper of the women.
9. **And the maiden**
pleased him, and she
obtained kindness of him;
and he speedily
gave her her
things for purification,
with such things as belonged to her,
and seven maidens,
which were meet to be given
her, out of the king's house:
and he preferred her and
her maids unto
the best place of
the house of the women.
10. Esther had not shewed her
people nor her kindred: for
Mordecai had charged her
that she should not shew *it*.
11. And Mordecai walked every day
before the court of the women's
house, to know how Esther did, and
what should become of her.
12. **Now when every maid's**
turn was come to go in
to king Ahasuerus,
after that she had been
twelve months, according
to the manner of the women,
(for so were the days
of their purifications
accomplished, *to wit*,
six months with oil of myrrh,
and six months with sweet
odours, and with *other* things for
the purifying of the women;)
13. **Then thus came every**
maiden unto the king;
whatsoever she desired
was given her to go with her
out of the house of the women
unto the king's house.
14. **In the evening she went,**
and on the morrow she
returned into the second
house of the women,
to the custody of Shaashgaz,
the king's chamberlain, which
kept the concubines:
she came in unto the king
no more, except the king
delighted in her, and that

she were called by name.
15. **Now when the turn of**
Esther, the daughter of Abihail
the uncle of Mordecai, who had
taken her for his daughter,
was come to go in unto
the king, she required
nothing but what
Hegai the king's chamberlain,
the keeper of the women,
appointed. And Esther
obtained favour in the sight
of all them
that looked upon her.
16. So Esther was taken unto king
Ahasuerus into his house royal in
the tenth month, which is the
month Tebeth, in the seventh
year of his reign.
17. **And the king loved**
Esther above all the
women, and she obtained
grace and favour in his sight
more than all the virgins;
so that he set the royal
crown upon her head,
and made her queen
instead of Vashti.
18. **Then the king made**
a great feast unto all his
princes and his servants,
even Esther's feast; and
he made a release to the
provinces, and gave gifts,
according to the state of the king.
19. And when the virgins were
gathered together the second time,
then Mordecai sat in the king's gate.
20. **Esther had not yet**
shewed her kindred
nor her people;
as Mordecai had charged
her: for Esther did the
commandment of Mordecai, like as
when she was brought up with him.
21. **In those days, while**
Mordecai sat in the king's
gate, two of the king's
chamberlains, Bigthan
and Teresh, of those which kept
the door, were wroth, and
sought to lay hands
on the king Ahasuerus.

22. **And** the thing was known to **Mordecai,** who **told it unto Esther** the queen; **and Esther certified the king thereof in Mordecai's name.** 23. **And when** inquisition was made of **the matter,** it **was found out;** therefore **they were both hanged** on a tree: and it was written in the book of the chronicles before the king.

CHAPTER 3

1. **After these things did king Ahasuerus promote Haman** the son of Hammedatha **the Agagite,** and advanced him, and set his seat **above all the princes** that *were* with him. 2. **And all the king's servants,** that *were* in the king's gate, **bowed, and reverenced Haman: for the king had so commanded** concerning him. **But Mordecai bowed not, nor did him reverence.** 3. Then the king's servants, which *were* in the king's gate, said unto Mordecai, Why transgressest thou the king's commandment? 4. Now it came to pass, when they spake daily unto him, and he hearkened not unto them, that they told Haman, to see whether Mordecai's matters would stand: for he had told them that he *was* a Jew. 5. **And when Haman saw that Mordecai bowed not,** nor did him reverence, then was Haman full of wrath. 6. And **he thought** scorn **to lay hands on Mordecai** alone; for they had shewed him the people of Mordecai: **wherefore Haman sought to destroy all the Jews** that *were* throughout the whole kingdom of Ahasuerus, *even*

the people of Mordecai. 7. In the first month, that *is,* the month Nisan, in the twelfth year of king Ahasuerus, they cast Pur, that *is,* the lot, before Haman from day to day, and from month to month, *to* the twelfth *month,* that *is,* the month Adar. 8. **And Haman said unto king Ahasuerus, There is a certain people** scattered abroad and dispersed among the people in all the provinces **of thy kingdom; and their laws are diverse** from all people; **neither keep they the king's laws: therefore** it *is* not for the king's profit to suffer them. 9. **If it please the king, let it be written that they may be destroyed: and I will pay ten thousand talents of silver to** the hands of **those that have** the **charge** of the business, to bring *it* into the king's treasuries. 10. And the king took **his ring** from his hand, **and gave it unto Haman** the son of Hammedatha the Agagite, **the Jews' enemy.** 11. **And the king said** unto Haman, **The silver is given to thee, the people also, to do with them as it seemeth good to thee.** 12. **Then were the king's scribes called** on the thirteenth day of the first month, **and there was written according to all that Haman had commanded** unto the king's lieutenants, and to the governors that *were* over every province, and to the rulers of every people of every province according to the writing thereof, and *to* every people after their language; in the name of king Ahasuerus was it written, and sealed with the king's ring. 13. **And the letters were**

■ sent by posts into all the
■ king's provinces, to destroy,
to kill, and to cause to perish,
■ all Jews, both young and old, little
children and women, in one day,
■ even upon the thirteenth
■ day of the twelfth month,
which *is* the month Adar, and *to*
take the spoil of them for a prey.
■ 14. The copy of the writing
for a commandment to be
given in every provice
■ was published unto all
■ people, that they should be
■ ready against that day.
15. The posts went out, being
hastened by the king's
commandment, and the decree
was given in Shushan the palace.
■ And the king and Haman
■ sat down to drink; but
■ the city Shushan was
■ perplexed.

CHAPTER 4

■ 1. When Mordecai
■ perceived all that was
■ done, Mordecai
rent his clothes, and
■ put on sackcloth with
■ ashes, and went out into
■ the midst of the city, and
■ cried with a loud and a bitter cry;
2. And came even before the king's
gate: for none *might* enter into the
king's gate clothed with sackcloth.
■ 3. And in every province,
whithersoever the king's
commandment and his decree came,
■ there was great mourning
■ among the Jews,
■ and fasting, and
■ weeping, and wailing;
■ and many lay in
■ sackcloth and ashes.
■ 4. So Esther's maids
and her chamberlains
■ came and told *it*
■ her. Then was the queen
exceedingly grieved; and she sent
raiment to clothe Mordecai, and
to take away his sackcloth
from him: but he received *it* not.

■ 5. Then called Esther for
■ Hatach, one of the king's
■ chamberlains, whom he had
appointed to attend upon her,
■ and gave him a
■ commandment to
■ Mordecai, to know what
■ it was, and why it *was*.
6. So Hatach went forth to Mordecai
unto the street of the city, which
was before the king's gate.
■ 7. And Mordecai told
■ him of all that had
■ happened unto him,
■ and of the sum of
■ the money that Haman had
■ promised to pay to the
■ king's treasuries for the
■ Jews, to destroy them.
■ 8. Also he gave him the
■ copy of the writing of
■ the decree that was given
at Shushan to destroy them,
■ to shew *it* unto
■ Esther, and to declare *it*
unto her, and to charge her
■ that she should go in
■ unto the king, to make
■ supplication unto him,
and to make request before him
■ for her people.
■ 9. And Hatach came and
■ told Esther the words
■ of Mordecai.
■ 10. Again Esther spake
■ unto Hatach, and gave
■ him commandment
■ unto Mordecai;
■ 11. All the king's
■ servants, and the people
of the king's provinces, do
■ know, that whosoever,
whether man or women,
■ shall come unto the
■ king into the inner court,
■ who is not called,
■ there is one law of his
■ to put him to death,
■ except such to whom
■ the king shall hold out the
■ golden sceptre, that he
■ may live: but I have not been
called to come in unto the king

these thirty days.

12. And they told to Mordecai Esther's words.

13. **Then Mordecai commanded to answer Esther, Think not with thyself that thou shalt escape** in the king's house, more than all the Jews.

14. **For if thou** altogether **holdest thy peace** at this time, *then* **shall** there enlargement and **deliverance arise to the Jews from another** place; but thou and thy father's house shall be destroyed: **and who knoweth whether thou art come to the kingdom for such a time as this?**

15. **Then Esther bade them return Mordecai this answer,**

16. **Go, gather** together all **the Jews that are present in Shushan, and fast** ye for me, and neither eat nor drink **three days,** night or day: I also and my maidens will fast likewise; **and so will I go in unto the king,** which *is* not according to the law: **and if I perish, I perish.**

17. **So Mordecai** went his way, and **did according to all that Esther had commanded him.**

CHAPTER 5

1. **Now** it came to pass **on the third day**, that **Esther put on her royal apparel, and stood in the inner court** of the king's house, over against the king's house: **and the king sat upon his** royal **throne** in the royal house, over against the gate of the house.

2. **And** it was so, **when the king saw Esther** the

queen standing in the court, *that* **she obtained favour** in his sight: **and the king held out** to Esther **the golden sceptre** that *was* in his hand. **So Esther drew near, and touched** the top of **the sceptre.**

3. **Then said the king** unto her, What wilt thou, queen Esther? and **what is thy request**? it shall be even given thee to the half of the kingdom.

4. **And Esther answered,** If *it seem* good unto the king, **let the king and Haman come this day unto the banquet that I have prepared** for him.

5. Then the king said, Cause Haman to make haste, that he may do as Esther hath said. **So the king and Haman came to the banquet** that Esther had prepared.

6. **And the king said** unto Esther **at the banquet** of wine, **What is thy petition? and it shall be granted** thee: and what *is* thy request? **even to the half of the kingdom** it shall be performed.

7. **Then answered Esther**, and said, My petition and my request *is*;

8. **If I have found favour** in the sight of the king, and if it please the king to grant my petition, and to perform my request, **let the king and Haman come to the banquet that I shall prepare for them, and I will do to morrow as the king hath said.**

9. **Then went Haman** forth that day joyful and **with a glad heart: but when Haman saw Mordecai** in the king's gate, that he stood not up, nor moved for him,

he was full of indignation against Mordecai. 10. Nevertheless Haman refrained himself: and when he came home, he sent and called for his friends, and Zeresh his wife. 11. And Haman told them of the glory of his riches, and the multitude of his children, and all *the things* wherein the king had promoted him, and how he had advanced him above the princes and servants of the king. 12. Haman said moreover, Yea, Esther the queen did let no man come in with the king unto the banquet that she had prepared but myself; and to morrow am I invited unto her also with the king. 13. Yet all this availeth me nothing, so long as I see Mordecai the Jew sitting at the king's gate. 14. Then said Zeresh his wife and all his friends unto him, Let a gallows be made of fifty cubits high, and to morrow speak thou unto the king that Mordecai may be hanged thereon: then go thou in merrily with the king unto the banquet. And the thing pleased Haman; and he caused the gallows to be made.

CHAPTER 6

1. On that night could not the king sleep, and he commanded to bring the book of records of the chronicles; and they were read before the king. 2. And it was found written, that Mordecai had told of Bigthana and Teresh, two of the king's chamberlains,

the keepers of the door, who sought to lay hand on the king Ahasuerus. 3. And the king said, What honour and dignity hath been done to Mordecai for this? Then said the king's servants that ministered unto him, There is nothing done for him. 4. And the king said, Who is in the court? Now Haman was come into the outward court of the king's house, to speak unto the king to hang Mordecai on the gallows that he had prepared for him. 5. And the king's servants said unto him, Behold, Haman standeth in the court. And the king said, Let him come in. 6. So Haman came in. And the king said unto him, What shall be done unto the man whom the king delighteth to honour? Now Haman thought in his heart, To whom would the king delight to do honour more than to myself? 7. And Haman answered the king, For the man whom the king delighteth to honour, 8. Let the royal apparel be brought which the king *useth* to wear, and the horse that the king rideth upon, and the crown royal which is set upon his head: 9. And let this apparel and horse be delivered to the hand of one of the king's most noble princes, that they may array the man *withal* whom the king delighteth to honour, and bring him on horseback through the street of the city, and proclaim before him, Thus shall it be done to the man whom the king delighteth to honour.

10. **Then the king said to Haman,** Make haste, *and* **take the apparel and the horse,** as thou hast said, **and do** even so **to Mordecai** the Jew, that sitteth at the king's gate: let nothing fail of **all that thou hast spoken.**

11. **Then** took **Haman** the apparel and the horse, and **arrayed Mordecai, and brought him on horseback through** the street of **the city, and proclaimed** before him, **Thus shall it be done unto the man whom the king delighteth to honour.**

12. And Mordecai came again to the king's gate. But Haman hasted to his house mourning, and having his head covered.

13. **And Haman told** Zeresh **his wife and** all his **friends every thing** that had befallen him. **Then said his wise men and** Zeresh his **wife** unto him, **If Mordecai be of the seed of the Jews,** before whom thou hast begun to fall, **thou shalt not prevail** against him, **but shalt surely fall before him.**

14. **And while they were** yet **talking** with him, came **the king's chamberlains,** and **hasted to bring Haman unto the banquet** that **Esther had prepared.**

CHAPTER 7

1. **So the king and Haman came to banquet with Esther** the queen.

2. **And the king said** again unto Esther on the second day at the banquet of wine,
What is thy petition, queen Esther? and it shall be granted thee: and what *is* thy request? and it shall be performed, *even* to the half of the kingdom.

3. **Then Esther** the queen **answered** and said, If I have found favour in thy sight, O king, and **if it please the king, let my life be given me** at my petition, **and my people** at my request:

4. **For we are sold,** I and my people, **to be destroyed,** to be slain, and to perish. But if we had been sold for bondmen and bondwomen, I had held my tongue, although the enemy could not countervail the king's damage.

5. **Then the king** Ahasuerus **answered** and said unto Esther the queen, **Who is he,** and where is he, **that durst presume** in his heart **to do so?**

6. **And Esther said, The adversary and enemy is this wicked Haman. Then Haman was afraid** before the king and the queen.

7. **And the king arising** from the banquet of wine **in his wrath went into the palace garden: and Haman stood up to make request for his life to Esther** the queen; for he saw that there was evil determined against him by the king.

8. **Then the king returned** out of the palace garden into the place of the banquet of wine; **and Haman was fallen upon the bed whereon Esther was. Then said the king, Will he force the queen also before me** in the house? As the word went out of king's mouth, they covered Haman's face.

9. **And Harbonah, one of the chamberlains, said** before the king, Behold also,

the gallows fifty cubits high,
which Haman had
made for Mordecai, who
had spoken good for the king,
standeth in the house of
Haman. Then the king said,
Hang him thereon.
10. So they hanged Haman
on the gallows that he had
prepared for Mordecai.
Then was the king's wrath pacified.

ESTHER 8

1. On that day did
the king Ahasuerus
give the house of
Haman the Jews' enemy
unto Esther the queen.
And Mordecai came before
the king; for Esther had told
what he *was* unto her.
2. And the king took off
his ring, which he had taken
from Haman, and gave it
unto Mordecai. And Esther set
Mordecai over the house of Haman.
3. And Esther spake yet again
before the king,
and fell down at his feet,
and besought him with
tears to put away the
mischief of Haman
the Agagite, and his device
that he had devised
against the Jews.
4. Then the king held out
the golden sceptre toward
Esther. So Esther arose, and
stood before the king,
5. And said, If it please the
king, and if I have favour in his
sight, and the thing *seem* right
before the king, and
I be pleasing in his eyes, let
it be written to reverse the
letters devised by Haman
the son of Hammedatha the Agagite,
which he wrote to destroy the Jews
which *are* in all the king's provinces:
6. For how can I endure
to see the evil that shall come unto
my people? or how can I endure
to see the destruction

of my kindred?
7. Then the king Ahasuerus
said unto Esther the queen
and to
Mordecai the Jew, Behold, I have
given Esther the house of Haman,
and him they have hanged upon
the gallows, because he laid
his hand upon the Jews.
8. Write ye also
for the Jews, as it liketh you,
in the king's name, and
seal it with the king's ring:
for the writing which is written in
the king's name, and
sealed with the king's ring,
may no man reverse.
9. Then were the king's
scribes called at that time
in the third month, that *is,* the
month Sivan, on the three and
twentieth *day* thereof;
and it was written
according to all that
Mordecai commanded unto
the Jews, and to the lieutenants,
and the deputies and rulers of the
provinces which *are* from India unto
Ethiopia, an hundred twenty and
seven provinces, unto every province
according to the writing thereof, and
unto every people after their
language, and to the Jews according
to their writing, and according
to their language.
10. And he wrote in the
king Ahasuerus' name,
and sealed *it* with the king's ring,
and sent letters by posts on
horseback, *and* riders on mules,
camels, *and* young dromedaries:
11. Wherein the king
granted the Jews which
were in every city to gather
themselves together, and
to stand for their life,
to destroy, to slay and
to cause to perish,
all the power of the
people and province
that would assault them,
both little ones and women, and *to*
take the spoil of them for a prey,

12. Upon one day in all the provinces of king Ahasuerus, *namely,* upon the thirteenth *day* of the twelfth month, which *is* the month Adar.

13. **The copy of the writing** for a commandment to be given in every province **was published unto all people, and that the Jews should be ready** against that day **to avenge themselves on their enemies.**

14. *So* the posts that rode upon mules *and* camels went out, being hastened and pressed on by the king's commandment. And the decree was given at Shushan the palace.

15. **And Mordecai went out from the presence of the king in royal apparel** of blue and white, and with a great crown of gold, and with a garment of fine linen and purple: **and the city of Shushan rejoiced** and was glad.

16. The Jews had light, and gladness, and joy, and honour.

17. **And in every province,** and in every city, whithersoever the king's commandment and his decree came, **the Jews had joy and gladness,** a feast and a good day. **And many of the people** of the land **became Jews; for the fear of the Jews fell upon them.**

CHAPTER 9

1. **Now in the twelfth month,** that *is,* the month Adar, on **the thirteenth day** of the same, **when the king's commandment** and his decree **drew near to be put in execution,** in the day that the enemies of the Jews hoped to have power over them, (though it was turned to the contrary, that the Jews had rule over them that hated them;)

2. **The Jews gathered** themselves **together** in their cities throughout all the provinces of the king Ahasuerus, **to lay hand on such as sought their hurt: and no man could withstand them;** for the fear of them fell upon all people.

3. **And all the rulers** of the provinces, and the lieutenants, and the deputies, **and officers of the king, helped the Jews; because the fear of Mordecai fell upon them.**

4. **For Mordecai** *was* great in the king's house, and his fame went out throughout all the provinces: for this man Mordecai **waxed greater and greater.**

5. **Thus the Jews smote all their enemies** with the stroke of the sword, and slaughter, and destruction, **and did what they would unto those that hated them.**

6. **And in Shushan** the palace **the Jews** slew and **destroyed five hundred men.**

7. And Parshandatha, and Dalphon, and Aspatha,

8. And Poratha, and Adalia, and Aridatha,

9. And Parmashta, and Arisai, and Aridai, and Vajezatha,

10. The ten sons of Haman the son of Hammedatha, the enemy of the Jews, slew they; but on the spoil laid they not their hand.

11. On that day the number of those that were slain in Shushan the palace was brought before the king.

12. **And the king said unto Esther** the queen, **The Jews have** slain and **destroyed five hundred men in Shushan** the palace, **and the ten sons of Haman; what have they done** in the rest of the king's provinces? **now what is thy petition?** and

it shall be granted thee: or what *is* thy request further? and it shall be done. 13. **Then said Esther, If it please the king, let it be granted** to the Jews which *are* in Shushan to do **to-morrow** also according unto this day's decree, **and let Haman's ten sons be hanged upon the gallows.** 14. And the king commanded it so to be done: **and the decree was given** at Shushan; **and they hanged Haman's ten sons.** 15. **For the Jews** that *were* **in Shushan** gathered themselves together on the fourteenth day also of the month Adar, and **slew three hundred men** at Shushan; **but on the prey they laid not their hand.** 16. **But the other Jews** that *were* **in the king's provinces** gathered themselves together, and stood for their lives, and had rest from their enemies, and **slew of their foes seventy and five thousand, but they laid not their hands on the prey,** 17. On the thirteenth day of the month Adar; and on the fourteenth day of the same rested they, and made it a day of feasting and gladness. 18. **But the Jews** that *were* **at Shushan assembled** together **on the thirteenth day** thereof, **and on the fourteenth** thereof; and **on the fifteenth day** of the same **they rested, and made it a day of feasting and gladness.** 19. **Therefore the Jews of the villages,** that dwelt in the unwalled towns, **made the fourteenth day** of the month Adar **a day of gladness and feasting,** and a good day, and of sending portions one to another. 20. **And Mordecai** wrote these things, and **sent letters unto all the Jews** that *were* **in all the provinces of the king Ahasuerus,** *both* nigh and far, 21. To stablish *this* among them, **that they should keep the fourteenth** day of the month Adar, **and** the **fifteenth day** of the same, **yearly,** 22. **As the days wherein the Jews rested from their enemies,** and the month which was turned unto them from sorrow to joy, and from mourning into a good day: **that they should make them days of feasting and joy, and of sending** portions one to another, and **gifts** to the poor. 23. **And the Jews undertook to do as** they had begun, and as **Mordecai had written** unto them; 24. **Because Haman** the son of Hammedatha, the Agagite, the enemy of all the Jews, **had devised** against the Jews **to destroy them,** and had cast Pur, that *is,* the lot, to consume them, and to destroy them; 25. **But when Esther came before the king, he commanded by letters that his wicked device,** which he devised against the Jews, **should return upon his own head,** and that he and his sons should be hanged on the gallows. 26. Wherefore they called these days Purim after the name of Pur. Therefore for all the words of this letter, and *of that* which they had seen concerning this matter, and which had come unto them,

■ 27. **The Jews ordained,**
and took upon them, and upon
their seed, and upon all such as
joined themselves unto them, so
as it should not fail,

■ **that they would keep**
■ **these two days** according
to their writing, and

■ **according to their**
■ **appointed time every year;**
■ 28. **And that these days**
■ **should be remembered**
■ **and kept throughout every**
■ **generation,** every family, every
province, and every city; and *that*
these days of Purim should not
fail from among the Jews, nor the
memorial of them perish from
their seed.

■ 29. **Then Esther** the queen,
the daughter of Abihail,

■ **and Mordecai** the Jew,
■ **wrote with all authority,** to
confirm this second letter of Purim.

■ 30. **And** he
■ **sent the letters unto all**
■ **the Jews,** to the hundred
twenty and seven provinces of
the kingdom of Ahasuerus,

■ **with words of peace**
■ **and truth,**
■ 31. **To confirm these**

■ **days** of Purim
■ **in their times appointed,**
according as Mordecai the Jew and
Esther the queen had enjoined them,
and as they had decreed for
themselves and for their seed, the
matters of the fastings and their cry.
32. And the decree of Esther
confirmed these matters of Purim;

■ **and it was written in**
■ **the book.**

CHAPTER 10

1. And the king Ahasuerus laid a
tribute upon the land, and *upon*
the isles of the sea.

■ 2. **And all the acts** of his power
■ **and** of his might,
and the declaration of

■ **the greatness of Mordecai,**
whereunto the king advanced him,

■ **are** they not
■ **written in the book of**
■ **the chronicles** of the
kings of Media and Persia?

3. **For Mordecai** the Jew
■ **was** next unto king Ahasuerus, and
■ **great** among the Jews, and
accepted of the multitude of
his brethren,

■ **seeking the wealth of his**
■ **people, and speaking**
■ **peace to all his seed.**

JOB:

SUFFERING AND GOD'S ANSWER

Many Bible Scholars conclude that Job may be the oldest book in the Bible.

- **The book,** of course, **is named after its protagonist.** The content of the book, along with its artistic structure and elegant style, place it among the literary masterpieces of all time.
- **The book treats the problem of the suffering of the innocent.**
- **Job, pious,** upright, **and prosperous,** suddenly **suffers a reversal** of fortune.
- **He loses** his **children,** his **property, and his body is afflicted with** a horrible, life-threatening and extremely painful **disease.**
- **Job did not complain against God.**
- **Friends visited** him **and he defended his** personal **integrity and lamented that he could not understand** why he had been so severely afflicted.
- **He** cursed the day he was born and **cried out to die** to end the suffering.
- **His friends** chided him, and **sought to prove** to him **that his plight could only be punishment for wrong doing** on his part.
- **Job** vehemently **rejected their claim and asserted that an answer** as to why he was suffering **could only come from God.** Job and his friends debated back and fourth.
- **Finally God answered. He did not justify Himself** nor what He had allowed to happen to Job.
- **He pointed to His omniscience and power. The answer satisfied Job.** He was now willing to humbly trust God in all things, even in the trauma of loss and severe pain.
- **He came to understand that man's finite mind could not fathom the works of God** and that **man must trust in God's righteousness and justice.**
- **Upon** these realizations and **Job's submission** to God, **he was restored.**

THE BOOK OF JOB

BACKGROUND INFORMATION

Author: Unknown
Date Written: Actual date unknown, but many scholars believe it is **the oldest book of the Old Testament**

Number of:
Verses—1,070
Chapters—42
Total Words—18,143
Scan Words—8,315
Scan Words Represent Approximately 45% of Total Words

Theme: How Job, a Man of Faith, **Suffered** at the Hands of Satan **and Endured to Trust in God**

OUTLINE OF THE BOOK

I. **The Prologue** to the Suffering of Job
   1:1 — 2:11
II. **Job Contends with his Friends** in this Suffering
   3:1 — 37:24
III. **Job Receives the Wisdom of God**
   38:1 —41:34
IV. **Job Responds to God**
   42:1 — 6
V. **The Restoration** of Job
   42:7 — 17

CHAPTER 1

1. There was a man in the land of Uz, whose name *was* **Job;** and that man **was perfect and upright, and** one that **feared God,** and eschewed evil. 2. **And there were born unto him seven sons and three daughters.** 3. **His substance** also **was seven thousand sheep,** and **three thousand camels,** and **five hundred yoke of oxen, and five hundred** she **asses,** and a very great household; so that **this man was the greatest** of all the men **of the east.** 4. **And his sons** went and **feasted in their houses,** every one his day; and sent **and** called for **their three sisters** to eat and to drink with them. 5. And it was so, when the days of *their* feasting were gone about, that **Job** sent and **sanctified them,** and rose up early in the morning, **and offered burnt offerings** *according* to the number of them all: **for Job said, It may be that my sons have sinned, and cursed God in their hearts.** Thus did Job continually. 6. Now there was a day when **the sons of God came to** present themselves before **the LORD, and Satan came** also among them. 7. **And the LORD said unto Satan, Whence comest thou?** Then **Satan** answered the LORD, and **said, From going to and fro in the earth,** and from walking up and down in it. 8. **And the LORD said** unto Satan, **Hast thou considered**

my servant Job, that *there is* none like him in the earth, **a perfect and an upright man,** one that feareth God, and escheweth evil? 9. **Then Satan** answered the LORD, and **said, Doth Job fear God for nought?** 10. **Hast not thou made an hedge about him,** and about his house, and about all that he hath on every side? **thou hast blessed the work of his hands,** and his substance is increased in the land. 11. **But** put forth thine hand now, and **touch all that he hath, and he will curse thee** to thy face. 12. **And the LORD said unto Satan,** Behold, **all that he hath is in thy power; only upon himself put not forth thine hand. So Satan went** forth from the presence of the LORD. 13. And there was a day when his sons and his daughters *were* eating and drinking wine in their eldest brother's house: 14. **And there came a messenger unto Job, and said,** The oxen were plowing, and the asses feeding beside them: 15. And **the Sabeans** fell *upon them,* and took them away; yea, they **have slain the servants** with the edge of the sword; and I only am escaped alone to tell thee. 16. While he *was* yet speaking, there came also another, and said, **The fire of God is fallen from heaven, and hath burned up the sheep, and the servants,** and consumed them; and I only am escaped alone to tell thee. 17. While he *was* yet speaking, there came also another, and said, **The Chaldeans** made out three bands, and **fell upon the camels,** and have carried them away, yea, and slain the servants with the edge of the sword; and I only am escaped alone to tell thee.

18. While he *was* yet speaking, there came also another, and said, **Thy sons and thy daughters were eating and drinking wine** in their eldest brother's house:

19. **And,** behold, there came **a great wind** from the wilderness, and **smote the four corners of the house, and it fell** upon the young men, **and they are dead;** and I only am escaped alone to tell thee.

20. **Then Job arose,** and **rent his mantle,** and **shaved his head, and fell down** upon the ground, **and worshipped,**

21. **And said, Naked came I out of my mother's womb, and naked shall I return** thither: **the LORD gave, and the LORD hath taken away; blessed be the name of the LORD.**

22. **In all this Job sinned not,** nor charged God foolishly.

CHAPTER 2

1. **Again** there was a day when **the sons of God came** to present themselves **before the LORD, and Satan came also** among them to present himself before the LORD.

2. **And the LORD said unto Satan, From whence comest thou? And Satan** answered the LORD, and **said, From going to and fro in the earth,** and from walking up and down in it.

3. **And the LORD said unto Satan, Hast thou considered my servant Job,** that *there is* none like him in the earth,

a perfect and an upright man, one that feareth God, and escheweth evil? and still **he holdeth fast his integrity, although thou movedst me** against him, **to destroy him without cause.**

4. **And Satan** answered the LORD, and **said,** Skin for skin, yea, **all that a man hath will he give for his life.**

5. But put forth thine hand now, and **touch his bone and his flesh, and he will curse thee** to thy face.

6. **And the LORD said** unto Satan, Behold, **he is in thine hand; but save his life.**

7. **So** went **Satan** forth from the presence of the LORD, and **smote Job with sore boils** from the sole of his foot unto his crown.

8. **And he took him a potsherd to scrape himself** withal; and he sat down among the ashes.

9. **Then said his wife** unto him, Dost thou still retain thine integrity? **curse God, and die.**

10. **But he said** unto her, **Thou speakest as one of the foolish women** speaketh. What? **shall we receive good at the hand of God, and** shall we **not receive evil? In all this did not Job sin** with his lips.

11. Now when **Job's three friends** heard of all this evil that was come upon him, they came every one from his own place; **Eliphaz** the Temanite, and **Bildad** the Shuhite, **and Zophar** the Naamathite: for they had **made an appointment** together to come

771

to mourn with him
and to comfort him.
12. **And when they
lifted up their eyes afar
off, and knew him not,
they** lifted up their voice, and
wept; and they
**rent every one his mantle,
and sprinkled dust upon
their heads** toward heaven.
13. **So they sat** down
with him upon the ground
**seven days and seven
nights, and none spake**
a word unto him: for they saw
that *his* grief was very great.

CHAPTER 3

1. **After this** opened
Job his mouth, and
cursed his day.
2. And Job spake,
and said,
3. **Let the day perish
wherein I was born,** and
the night in which it was said,
There is a man child conceived.
4. Let that day be darkness;
**let not God
regard it** from above, neither
let the light shine upon it.
5. **Let darkness**
and the shadow of death
stain it; let a cloud dwell upon it;
let the blackness of the day terrify it.
6. As for that night, let darkness
seize upon it;
**let it not be joined unto the
days of the year,** let it not come
into the number of the months.
7. **Lo, let that night be
solitary,** let no joyful
voice come therein.
8. Let them curse it that
curse the day, who are
ready to raise up their mourning.
9. Let the stars of the
twilight thereof be dark;
**let it look for light, but
have none;** neither let it
see the dawning of the day:
10. **Because it shut
not up the doors of**

my mother's womb,
nor hid sorrow from mine eyes.
11. **Why died I not from the
womb?** *why* did I not give up the
ghost when I came out of the belly?
12. Why did the knees prevent me?
or why the breasts that I should suck?
13. For now should I have lain still
and been quiet, I should have slept:
then had I been at rest,
14. With kings and counsellors
of the earth, which build desolate
places for themselves;
15. Or with princes that had gold,
who filled their houses with silver:
16. Or as an hidden untimely
birth I had not been;
**as infants which
never saw light.**
17. **There the wicked
cease from troubling;**
and there the weary be at rest.
18. **There the prisoners
rest** together;
they hear not the voice of
the oppressor.
19. **The small and great are
there; and the servant is
free from his master.**
20. **Wherefore is
light given** to
him that is in misery,
and life unto the bitter *in* soul;
21. **Which long for death,**
but it *cometh* not; and dig for it more
than for hid treasures;
22. Which rejoice exceedingly,
**and are glad, when they
can find the grave?**
23. **Why is light given to
a man** whose way is hid, and
**whom God hath
hedged in?**
24. For my sighing cometh before
I eat, and my roarings are poured
out like the waters.
25. **For the thing which I
greatly feared is come
upon me,** and that which I
was afraid of is come unto me.
26. I was not in safety, neither
had I rest, neither was I quiet;
yet trouble came.

CHAPTER 4

■ 1. **Then Eliphaz** the Temanite answered and ■ **said,**

2. If we assay to commune with thee, wilt thou be grieved? but ■ **who can withhold** himself ■ **from speaking?**

3. Behold, ■ **thou hast instructed** ■ **many,** and ■ **thou hast strengthened** ■ **the weak** hands.

4. Thy words have upholden him that was falling, ■ **and** thou hast strengthened ■ **the feeble** knees.

5. ■ **But now it is come upon** ■ **thee, and thou faintest;** it toucheth thee, and thou art troubled.

6. Is not *this* thy fear, thy confidence, thy hope, and the uprightness of thy ways?

7. Remember, I pray thee, ■ **who ever perished,** ■ **being innocent?** or where were the righteous cut off?

8. Even as I have seen, ■ **they that** plow iniquity, and ■ **sow wickedness,** ■ **reap the same.**

9. ■ **By the blast of God** ■ **they perish,** and by the breath of his nostrils are they consumed.

10. The roaring of the lion, and the voice of the fierce lion, and the teeth of the young lions, are broken.

11. The old lion perisheth for lack of prey, and the stout lion's whelps are scattered abroad.

12. Now a thing was secretly brought to me, and mine ear received a little thereof.

13. ■ **In thoughts** from the visions of the night, ■ **when deep sleep** ■ **falleth on men,**

14. ■ **Fear came upon** ■ **me,** and trembling, which made all my bones to shake.

15. Then ■ **a spirit passed before my** ■ **face; the hair of my flesh**

■ **stood up:**

16. It stood still, but I could not discern the form thereof: an image *was* before mine eyes, *there was* silence, and ■ **I heard a voice, saying,**

17. ■ **Shall mortal man be** ■ **more just than God?** ■ **shall a man be more** ■ **pure than his maker?**

18. Behold, he put no trust in his servants; and his angels he charged with folly:

19. How much less *in* them that dwell in houses of clay, whose foundation is in the dust, *which* are crushed before the moth?

20. They are destroyed from morning to evening: they perish for ever without any regarding *it.*

21. Doth not their excellency which is in them go away? ■ **they die, even** ■ **without wisdom.**

CHAPTER 5

■ 1. **Call now, if** there be ■ **any** that ■ **will answer** thee; ■ **and to which of the** ■ **saints wilt thou turn?**

2. For wrath killeth the foolish man, and envy slayeth the silly one.

3. ■ **I have seen the foolish** ■ **taking root:** but suddenly I cursed his habitation.

4. ■ **His children are** ■ **far from safety,** and they are crushed in the gate, ■ **neither is there any to** ■ **deliver them.**

5. ■ **Whose harvest the** ■ **hungry eateth** up, and taketh it even out of the thorns, ■ **and the robber** ■ **swalloweth** up ■ **their substance.**

6. ■ **Although affliction** ■ **cometh not** forth ■ **of** the ■ **dust, neither doth trouble** ■ **spring out of the ground;**

7. ■ **Yet man is born unto**

trouble, as the sparks
fly upward.
8. **I would seek unto
God, and** unto God would I
commit my cause:
9. **Which doeth** great
things and unsearchable;
marvellous things
without number:
10. **Who** giveth rain
upon the earth, and
**sendeth waters
upon the fields:**
11. **To set** up
**on high those that
be low;** that those which
mourn may be exalted to safety.
12. **He disappointeth**
the devices of
the crafty, so that
**their hands cannot
perform** *their* enterprise.
13. He taketh the wise in
their own craftiness:
**and the counsel
of the froward is
carried headlong.**
14. **They meet** with
**darkness in the day time,
and grope in the noonday
as in the night.**
15. **But he saveth the poor**
from the sword, from their mouth,
and from the hand of the mighty.
16. **So the poor hath hope,**
and iniquity stoppeth her mouth.
17. **Behold, happy is
the man whom God
correcteth: therefore
despise not thou the
chastening of the Almighty:**
18. For
**he maketh sore,
and bindeth up: he
woundeth, and his
hands make whole.**
19. **He shall deliver
thee in six troubles:** yea,
**in seven there shall
no evil touch thee.**
20. **In famine he shall
redeem thee** from death:
and in war from the

power of the sword.
21. Thou shalt be hid from the
scourge of the tongue: neither
shalt thou be afraid of destruction
when it cometh.
22. **At destruction and
famine thou shalt laugh:**
neither shalt thou be afraid
of the beasts of the earth.
23. For thou shalt be in league
with the stones of the field:
**and the beasts of the field
shall be at peace with thee.**
24. **And** thou shalt know that
**thy tabernacle shall be
in peace; and thou** shalt
visit thy habitation, and
shalt not sin.
25. Thou shalt know also that
thy seed shall be great,
and thine offspring as the
grass of the earth.
26. **Thou shalt come
to thy grave in a full
age,** like as a shock of
corn cometh in in his season.
27. Lo
**this, we have
searched** it, so it is;
hear it,
and know thou
it for thy good.

CHAPTER 6

1. **But Job** answered and
said,
2. **Oh that my grief were
throughly weighed, and
my calamity laid in the
balances together!**
3. For now
**it would be heavier than
the sand of the sea:** therefore
my words are swallowed up.
4. **For the arrows of the
Almighty are within me,** the
poison whereof drinketh up my spirit:
the terrors of God do
set themselves in array
against me.
5. Doth the wild ass bray when
he hath grass? or loweth the
ox over his fodder?

774

6. Can that which is unsavoury be eaten without salt? or is there *any* taste in the white of an egg?

7. **The things that my soul refused to touch are as my sorrowful meat.**

8. **Oh that I might have my request; and that God would grant** *me* **the thing that I long for!**

9. Even **that** it would please **God** to **destroy me; that he would** let loose his hand, and **cut me off!**

10. Then should I yet have comfort; yea, **I would harden myself in sorrow: let him not spare; for I have not concealed the words of the Holy One.**

11. What *is* my strength, that I should hope? and **what is mine end, that I should prolong my life?**

12. *Is* my strength the strength of stones? or *is* my flesh of brass?

13. *Is* not my help in me? and is wisdom driven quite from me?

14. **To him that is afflicted pity should be shewed from his friend;** but he forsaketh the fear of the Almighty.

15. **My brethren have dealt deceitfully as a brook, and as the** stream of **brooks they pass away;**

16. Which are blackish by reason of the ice, *and* wherein the snow is hid:

17. What time they wax warm, they vanish: when it is hot, they are consumed out of their place.

18. **The paths of their way are turned aside; they** go to nothing, and **perish.**

19. The troops of Tema looked, the companies of Sheba waited for them.

20. **They were confounded because they had hoped;** they came thither, and were ashamed.

21. **For now ye are nothing;** ye see *my* casting down, **and are afraid.**

22. **Did I say,** Bring unto me? or, **Give a reward for me** of your substance?

23. **Or, Deliver me from the enemy's hand? or, Redeem me** from the hand of the mighty?

24. **Teach me, and I will hold my tongue:** and cause me to understand wherein I have erred.

25. **How forcible are right words!** but what doth your arguing reprove?

26. Do ye imagine to reprove words, and **the speeches of one that is desperate,** *which* **are as wind?**

27. Yea, ye overwhelm the fatherless, and ye dig a *pit* for your friend.

28. **Now** therefore **be content,** look upon me; for **it is evident** unto you **if I lie.**

29. Return, I pray you, let it not be iniquity; yea, return again, my righteousness *is* in it.

30. **Is there iniquity in my tongue?** cannot my taste discern perverse things?

CHAPTER 7

1. **Is there not an appointed time to man upon earth?** are not his days also like the days of an hireling?

2. As a servant earnestly desireth the shadow, and **as an hireling looketh for the reward of his work:**

3. So am **I** made to **possess months of vanity, and wearisome nights** are appointed to me.

4. **When I lie down,** I say, When shall I arise, and the night be gone? and **I am full of tossings to**

and fro unto the
dawning of the day.
5. **My flesh is clothed
with worms and** clods of
dust; my skin is
broken, and become
loathsome.
6. **My days** are swifter
than a weaver's shuttle, and
are spent without hope.
7. O remember that
my life is wind: mine
eye shall no more see good.
8. **The eye of him**
that hath seen me
**shall see me no
more:** thine eyes are upon me,
and I am not.
9. **As the cloud** is consumed and
**vanisheth away:
so he that goeth** down
**to the grave shall
come up no more.**
10. **He shall return no more
to his house,** neither shall
his place know him any more.
11. **Therefore I will
not refrain** my mouth;
I will speak in the
anguish of my spirit;
I will complain in the
bitterness of my soul.
12. **Am I a sea,** or a whale,
**that thou settest a
watch over me?**
13. When I say, My bed shall
comfort me, my couch shall
ease my complaints;
14. Then thou scarest me with
dreams, and terrifiest me
through visions:
15. **So that my soul
chooseth** strangling, *and*
death rather than my life.
16. **I loathe it;** I would not
live alway: let me alone;
for my days are vanity.
17. **What is man, that thou
shouldest magnify him?
and** that thou shouldest
set thine heart upon him?
18. **And** *that* thou shouldest
visit him every morning,

and try him every moment?
19. How long wilt thou not depart
from me, nor let me alone till I
swallow down my spittle?
20. **I have sinned;
what shall I do** unto thee,
O thou preserver of men?
why hast thou set me as a
mark against thee, so that I
am a burden to myself?
21. And
why dost thou not
pardon my transgression, and
take away my iniquity?
for now shall I sleep in the dust; and
**thou shalt seek me in the
morning, but I shall not be.**

CHAPTER 8

1. **Then answered Bildad**
the Shuhite, and said,
2. **How long wilt thou
speak these things?**
and *how long shall* the words of
thy mouth be like a strong wind?
3. **Doth God pervert
judgment?** or doth the
Almighty pervert justice?
4. **If thy children have
sinned against him, and
he have cast them away**
for their transgression;
5. If thou wouldest seek unto
God betimes, and make thy
supplication to the Almighty;
6. **If thou wert pure**
and upright; surely now
**he would awake for thee,
and make the habitation
of thy righteousness
prosperous.**
7. **Though thy beginning
was small,** yet
thy latter end should greatly
increase.
8. For
inquire, I pray thee,
of the former age, and prepare
thyself to the search of their fathers:
9. **(For we** *are but* of yesterday,
and **know nothing, because
our days upon earth
are a shadow:)**

10. Shall not they teach thee, *and* tell thee, and utter words out of their heart?

11. Can the rush grow up without mire? **can the flag grow without water?**

12. **Whilst it is yet in his greenness,** *and* not cut down, **it withereth before any other herb.**

13. **So are the paths of all that forget God;** and **the hypocrite's hope shall perish:**

14. Whose hope shall be cut off, and **whose trust shall be a spider's web.**

15. **He shall lean upon his house, but it shall not stand:** he shall hold it fast, but it shall not endure.

16. **He is green before the sun,** and his branch shooteth forth in his garden.

17. **His roots are wrapped about the heap,** *and* seeth the place of stones.

18. If he destroy him from his place, then *it* shall deny him, *saying,* I have not seen thee.

19. Behold, this *is* the joy of his way, and out of the earth shall others grow.

20. Behold, **God will not cast away a perfect man, neither** will he **help the evil doers:**

21. Till he fill thy mouth with laughing, and thy lips with rejoicing.

22. **They that hate thee shall be clothed with shame; and the dwelling place of the wicked shall come to nought.**

CHAPTER 9

1. **Then Job** answered and **said,**

2. **I know it is so** of a truth: **but how should man be just with God?**

3. If he will contend with him, he cannot answer him one of a thousand.

4. **He is wise in heart, and** mighty in **strength: who hath hardened himself against him, and** hath **prospered?**

5. Which removeth the mountains, and they know not: which overturneth them in his anger.

6. **Which shaketh the earth out of her place,** and the pillars thereof tremble.

7. **Which commandeth the sun, and it riseth not;** and sealeth up the stars.

8. **Which alone spreadeth out the heavens,** and treadeth upon the waves of the sea.

9. Which maketh Arcturus, Orion, and Pleiades, and the chambers of the south.

10. **Which doeth** great things past finding out; yea, and **wonders without number.**

11. **Lo, he goeth by me, and I see him not:** he passeth on also, but I perceive him not.

12. Behold, he taketh away, who can hinder him? **who will say unto him, What doest thou?**

13. **If God will not withdraw his anger,** the proud helpers do stoop under him.

14. How much less **shall I** answer him, *and* **choose out my words to reason with him?**

15. Whom, though I were righteous, *yet* would I not answer, *but* I would make supplication to my judge.

16. **If I had called, and he had answered me; yet would I not believe** that he had hearkened unto my voice.

17. **For he** breaketh me with a tempest, and **multiplieth my wounds without cause.**

18. **He** will not suffer me to take my breath, but **filleth me with bitterness.**

19. If I *speak* of strength, lo, he is

strong: and if of judgment, who shall set me a time *to plead?*

20. **If I justify myself, mine own mouth shall condemn me:** if I say, I am perfect, **it shall also prove me perverse.**

21. *Though* I *were* perfect, *yet* would I not know my soul: I would despise my life.

22. This is one thing, therefore I said *it,* **He destroyeth the perfect and the wicked.**

23. If the scourge slay suddenly, he will laugh at the trial of the innocent.

24. **The earth is given into the hand of the wicked:** he covereth the faces of the judges thereof; if not, where, *and* who *is* he?

25. Now **my days** are swifter than a post: they **flee away,** they see no good.

26. **They are passed away as the swift ships:** as the eagle *that* hasteth to the prey.

27. **If I say, I will** forget my complaint, I will leave off my heaviness, and **comfort myself:**

28. I am afraid of all my sorrows, I know that **thou wilt not hold me innocent.**

29. **If I be wicked, why then labour I in vain?**

30. **If I wash myself** with snow water, and make my hands never **so clean;**

31. **Yet shalt thou plunge me in the ditch,** and mine own clothes shall abhor me.

32. **For he is not a man, as I am, that I should answer him,** and we should come together in judgment.

33. Neither is there any daysman betwixt us, *that* might lay his hand upon us both.

34. **Let him take his rod away from me,** and let not his fear terrify me:

35. **Then would I speak, and not fear him;** but it is not so with me.

CHAPTER 10

1. **My soul is weary of my life;** I will leave my complaint upon myself; I will speak in the bitterness of my soul.

2. **I will say unto God, Do not condemn me;** shew me wherefore thou contendest with me.

3. **Is it good unto thee that thou** shouldest oppress, that thou shouldest **despise the work of thine hands,** and shine upon the counsel of the wicked?

4. Hast thou eyes of flesh? or **seest thou as man seeth?**

5. *Are* thy days as the days of man? *are* thy years as man's days,

6. That thou enquirest after mine iniquity, and searchest after my sin?

7. **Thou knowest that I am not wicked;** and *there is* none that can deliver out of thine hand.

8. **Thine hands have made me and fashioned me together** round about; **yet thou dost destroy me.**

9. **Remember,** I beseech thee, **that thou hast made me as the clay; and wilt thou bring me into dust again?**

10. Hast thou not poured me out as milk, and curdled me like cheese?

11. **Thou hast clothed me with skin and flesh, and hast fenced me with bones and sinews.**

12. **Thou hast granted me life** and favour, **and thy visitation hath preserved my spirit.**

13. And these *things* hast thou hid in thine heart: I know that this *is* with thee.

14. **If I sin,** then thou markest me, and **thou wilt not acquit me from mine iniquity.**

15. **If I be wicked,
woe unto me;** and
**if I be righteous, yet will
I not lift up my head. I
am full of confusion;**
therefore see thou mine affliction;
16. For it increaseth.
**Thou huntest me as
a fierce lion:** and again thou
shewest thyself marvellous upon me.
17. **Thou renewest thy
witnesses against me,** and
increasest thine indignation upon me;
changes and war *are* against me.
18. Wherefore then hast thou
brought me forth out of the womb?
Oh that I had given up the ghost,
and no eye had seen me!
19. I should have been as
though I had not been;
**I should have been
carried from the
womb to the grave.**
20. **Are not my days few?**
cease *then, and* let me alone,
that I may take comfort a little,
21. Before
**I go whence I
shall not return,** even
**to the land of darkness and
the shadow of death;**
22. A land of darkness, as darkness
itself; and of the shadow of death,
without any order, and
**where the light
is as darkness.**

CHAPTER 11

1. **Then answered Zophar**
the Naamathite, and said,
2. Should not the multitude
of words be answered? and
**should a man full of
talk be justified?**
3. **Should thy lies make
men hold their peace?**
and when thou mockest, shall
no man make thee ashamed?
4. For
**thou hast said, My doctrine
is pure, and
I am clean in thine eyes.**
5. **But oh that God would**

speak, and open his lips
against thee;
6. **And** that he would
**shew thee the secrets
of wisdom,** that *they are*
double to that which is!
Know therefore
**that God exacteth
of thee less than thine
iniquity deserveth.**
7. **Canst thou by searching
find out God?** canst thou find
out the Almighty unto perfection?
8. It is as high as heaven; what
canst thou do? deeper than hell;
what canst thou know?
9. The measure thereof *is* longer than
the earth, and broader than the sea.
10. **If he cut off, and shut
up,** or gather together, then
who can hinder him?
11. For
**he knoweth vain men: he
seeth wickedness also;**
will he not then consider *it?*
12. For vain men would be
wise, though man be born
like a wild ass's colt.
13. If thou prepare thine heart, and
stretch out thine hands toward him;
14. **If iniquity be in thine
hand, put it far away, and
let not wickedness dwell
in thy tabernacles.**
15. For
then shalt thou lift up
**thy face without
spot;** yea, thou
**shalt be stedfast,
and shalt not fear:**
16. Because thou shalt forget
thy misery, *and* remember *it* as
waters *that* pass away:
17. And *thine* age shall be
clearer than the noonday:
**thou shalt shine forth, thou
shalt be as the morning.**
18. And
**thou shalt be secure,
because there is hope;** yea,
thou shalt dig *about thee, and* thou
shalt take thy rest in safety.
19. **Also thou shalt lie down,**

and none shall make
thee afraid; yea,
many shall make suit unto thee.
20. But the eyes of the
wicked shall fail,
and they shall not escape,
and their hope shall be as
the giving up of the ghost.

CHAPTER 12

1. And Job
answered and said,
2. No doubt but
ye are the people, and
wisdom shall die with you.
3. But I have understanding
as well as you; I am not
inferior to you: yea, who knoweth
not such things as these?
4. I am as one
mocked of his neighbour,
who calleth upon
God, and he answereth
him: the just upright *man is*
laughed to scorn.
5. He that is ready to slip with *his* feet
is as a lamp despised in the thought
of him that is at ease.
6. The tabernacles of
robbers prosper, and
they that provoke God
are secure; into whose
hand God bringeth *abundantly*.
7. But ask now
the beasts, and they shall
teach thee; and the fowls
of the air, and they shall
tell thee:
8. Or speak to
the earth, and it
shall teach thee: and
the fishes of the sea
shall declare unto thee.
9. Who knoweth not in all these
that the hand of
the LORD hath wrought this?
10. In whose hand is the
soul of every living thing,
and the breath of all
mankind.
11. Doth not the ear try words?
and the mouth taste his meat?
12. With the ancient is wisdom; and

in length of days understanding.
13. With him is wisdom
and strength, he hath
counsel and
understanding.
14. Behold,
he breaketh down, and it
cannot be built again: he
shutteth up a man, and
there can be no opening.
15. Behold,
he withholdeth the waters,
and they dry up: also he
sendeth them out, and they
overturn the earth.
16. With him is strength and
wisdom: the deceived and
the deceiver are his.
17. He leadeth counsellors
away spoiled,
and maketh the
judges fools.
18. He looseth the bond of kings,
and girdeth their loins with a girdle.
19. He leadeth princes
away spoiled, and
overthroweth the mighty.
20. He removeth away the speech
of the trusty, and taketh away the
understanding of the aged.
21. He poureth contempt
upon princes, and
weakeneth the strength of
the mighty.
22. He discovereth deep
things out of darkness, and
bringeth out to light
the shadow of death.
23. He increaseth the nations, and
destroyeth them: he enlargeth the
nations, and straiteneth them *again*.
24. He taketh away the
heart of the chief of the
people of the earth,
and causeth them to
wander in a wilderness
where there is no way.
25. They grope in the dark
without light, and he maketh
them to stagger like *a* drunken *man*.

CHAPTER 13

1. Lo, mine eye hath seen

all this, mine ear hath heard
and understood it.

2. **What ye know**, *the same* do
**I know also: I am
not inferior unto you.**

3. Surely I would speak
to the Almighty, and
**I desire to reason
with God**.

4. **But ye are forgers of lies**,
ye *are* all physicians of no value.

5. **O that ye would** altogether
**hold your peace! and it
should be your wisdom**.

6. **Hear** now
**my reasoning,
and hearken** to the
pleadings of my lips.

7. **Will ye speak wickedly
for God?** and talk
deceitfully for him?

8. **Will ye accept** his
person? will ye contend for
God?

9. Is it good that he should
search you out? or as one
man mocketh another,
do ye *so*
mock him?

10. **He will surely
reprove you**, if ye
do secretly accept persons.

11. Shall not his excellency make you
afraid? and his dread fall upon you?

12. **Your remembrances
are like** unto
ashes, your bodies
to bodies of clay.

13. Hold your peace, that
let me alone, that
I may speak, and
let come on me what will.

14. Wherefore do I take my flesh
in my teeth, and put my life in
mine hand?

15. **Though he slay me, yet
will I trust in him**: but I will
maintain mine own ways before him.

16. **He** also
shall be my salvation: for an
hypocrite shall not come before him.

17. **Hear** diligently
my speech, and my declaration

with your ears.

18. Behold now, I have
ordered *my* cause;
**I know that I shall
be justified**.

19. Who *is* he *that* will
plead with me? for now,
**if I hold my tongue, I
shall give up the ghost**.

20. **Only do not two things
unto me**: then will I not
hide myself from thee.

21. **Withdraw thine hand** far
**from me: and let not thy
dread make me afraid**.

22. **Then call** thou,
and I will answer: or let
me speak, and answer thou me.

23. **How many are
mine** iniquities and
sins? make me to know
my transgression and
my sin.

24. Wherefore hidest thou thy face,
and holdest me for thine enemy?

25. Wilt thou break a leaf driven
to and fro? and wilt thou pursue
the dry stubble?

26. For
**thou writest bitter
things against me, and
makest me to possess
the iniquities of my youth**.

27. **Thou** puttest my feet
also in the stocks, and
**lookest narrowly unto
all my paths**; thou settest
a print upon the heels of my feet.

28. **And he**, as a rotten thing,
consumeth, as a garment
that is moth eaten.

CHAPTER 14

1. **Man that is born of a
woman is of few days
and full of trouble**.

2. **He cometh forth like
a flower, and is cut
down**: he fleeth also as
a shadow, and continueth not.

3. And doth thou open thine eyes
upon such an one, and bringest
me into judgment with thee?

4. **Who can bring a clean thing out of an unclean? not one**.

5. Seeing **his days are determined**, the number of his months are with thee, **thou hast appointed his bounds** that he cannot pass;

6. Turn from him, that he may rest, till he shall accomplish, as an hireling, his day.

7. For **there is hope of a tree,** if it be **cut down**, that **it will sprout again**, and that the tender branch thereof will not cease.

8. **Though the root** thereof **wax old in the earth, and the stock** thereof **die in the ground**;

9. **Yet through the scent of water it will bud, and bring forth boughs** like a plant.

10. **But man dieth**, and wasteth away: yea, man giveth up the ghost, **and where is he?**

11. **As the waters** fail from the sea, and the flood decayeth and **drieth up**:

12. **So man lieth down, and** riseth not: till the heavens *be* no more, they **shall not** awake, nor **be raised out of their sleep**.

13. **O that thou wouldest hide me in the grave, that thou wouldest keep me secret**, until thy wrath be past, that thou wouldest **appoint me a set time, and remember me!**

14. **If a man die, shall he live again?** all the days of my appointed time **will I wait**, till my change come.

15. **Thou shalt call, and I will answer thee**: thou wilt have a desire to the work of thine hands.

16. **For now thou numberest my steps**: dost thou not watch over my sin?

17. **My transgression is sealed** up in a bag, **and** thou sewest up **mine iniquity**.

18. And **surely the mountain falling cometh to nought,** and therock is removed out ofhis place.

19. **The waters wear the stones**: thou washest away the things which grow *out* of the dust of the earth; **and thou destroyest the hope of man**.

20. **Thou prevailest** for ever **against him, and he passeth**: thou changest his countenance, and sendest him away.

21. **His sons come to honour**, and he knoweth it not; **and they are brought low, but he perceiveth it not** of them.

22. But his flesh upon him shall have pain, and his soul within him shall mourn.

CHAPTER 15

1. Then answered **Eliphaz** the Temanite, and **said**,

2. **Should a wise man utter vain knowledge, and** fill his belly with the east wind?

3. Should he **reason with unprofitable talk?** or with speeches wherewith he can do no good?

4. Yea, **thou castest off fear, and restrainest prayer before God**.

5. For **thy mouth uttereth** thine **iniquity, and** thou choosest the tongue of the crafty.

6. **Thine own mouth condemneth thee**, and not I: yea, thine own lips testify against thee.

7. **Art thou the first man that was born?** or wast

thou made before the hills?

8. Hast thou heard the secret of God? **and dost thou restrain wisdom to thyself?**

9. **What knowest thou, that we know not?** *what* understandest thou, which *is* not in us?

10. With us *are* both the grayheaded and very aged men, much elder than thy father.

11. **Are the consolations of God small** with thee? **is there any secret thing with thee?**

12. **Why doth thine heart carry thee away?** and what do thy eyes wink at,

13. **That thou turnest** thy spirit **against God, and lettest such words go out of thy mouth?**

14. What is man, that he should be clean? and *he which is* born of a woman, that he should be righteous?

15. Behold, **he putteth no trust in his saints**; yea, **the heavens are not clean in his sight**.

16. **How much more** abominable and **filthy is man, which drinketh iniquity like water?**

17. **I will shew thee**, hear me; and that *which* I have seen I will declare;

18. **Which wise men have told from their fathers**, and have not hid *it*:

19. Unto whom alone the earth was given, and no stranger passed among them.

20. **The wicked man travaileth with pain all his days**, and the number of years is hidden to the oppressor.

21. A dreadful sound is in his ears: **in prosperity the destroyer shall come upon him**.

22. **He believeth not that he shall return out of darkness**, and he is waited

for of the sword.

23. He wandereth abroad for bread, *saying*, Where *is it*? **he knoweth that the day of darkness is ready at his hand.**

24. **Trouble** and anguish **shall make him afraid**; they shall prevail against him, as a king ready to the battle.

25. For **he stretcheth out his hand against God, and strengtheneth himself against the Almighty.**

26. He runneth upon him, *even* on *his* neck, upon the thick bosses of his bucklers:

27. Because **he covereth his face with his fatness**, and maketh collops of fat on *his* flanks.

28. **And he dwelleth in desolate cities, and** in **houses** which no man inhabiteth, **which are ready to become heaps.**

29. **He shall not be rich, neither shall his substance continue**, neither shall he prolong the perfection thereof upon the earth.

30. **He shall not depart out of darkness**; the flame shall dry up his branches, **and by** the breath of **his mouth shall he go away.**

31. **Let not him that is deceived trust in vanity: for vanity shall be his recompence.**

32. **It shall be accomplished before his time**, and his branch shall not be green.

33. He shall shake off his unripe grape as the vine, and shall cast off his flower as the olive.

34. **For the congregation of hypocrites shall be desolate**, and fire shall consume the tabernacles of bribery.

35. **They conceive mischief, and** bring forth vanity, and their belly prepareth **deceit.**

CHAPTER 16

1. **Then Job** answered and **said,**

2. I have heard many such things: **miserable comforters are ye all.**

3. **Shall vain words have an end?** or what emboldeneth thee that thou answerest?

4. I also **could speak as ye do: if your soul were in my soul's stead, I could** heap up words against you, and **shake mine head at you.**

5. **But I would strengthen you with my mouth, and** the moving of my lips should **assuage your grief.**

6. Though I speak, my grief is not assuaged: and *though* I forbear, what am I eased?

7. **But** now he hath made me weary: **thou hast made desolate all my company.**

8. **And** thou hast **filled me with wrinkles, which is a witness against me**: and my leanness rising up in me beareth witness to my face.

9. **He teareth me in his wrath,** who hateth me: **he gnasheth** upon **me with his teeth**; mine enemy sharpeneth his eyes upon me.

10. They have gaped upon me with their mouth; they have smitten me upon the cheek reproachfully; **they have gathered** themselves together **against me.**

11. **God hath** delivered me to the ungodly, and **turned me over into the hands of the wicked.**

12. **I was at ease, but he** **hath broken me** asunder: he hath also taken *me* by my neck, and shaken me to pieces, **and set me up for his mark.**

13. **His archers compass me** round about, he cleaveth my reins asunder, **and** doth not spare; he **poureth out my gall upon the ground.**

14. He breaketh me with breach upon breach, he runneth upon me like a giant.

15. **I have sewed sackcloth upon my skin,** and defiled my horn in the dust.

16. My face is foul with weeping, **and on my eyelids is the shadow of death;**

17. **Not for any injustice in mine hands: also my prayer is pure.**

18. O earth, cover not thou my blood, and let my cry have no place.

19. Also now, behold, **my witness is in heaven, and my record** *is* on high.

20. **My friends scorn me:** but mine eye poureth **out tears** unto God.

21. **O that one might plead for a man with God, as a man pleadeth for his neighbour!**

22. When a few years are come, then I shall go the way whence I shall not return.

CHAPTER 17

1. **My breath is corrupt,** my days are extinct, **the graves are ready for me.**

2. *Are there* not mockers with me? and doth not mine eye continue in their provocation?

3. Lay down now, put me in a surety with thee; who *is* he *that* will strike hands with me?

4. For thou hast hid their heart from understanding: therefore shalt thou not exalt them.

5. He that speaketh flattery to his

friends, even the eyes
of his children shall fail.

6. **He hath made me** also
a byword of the people; and
aforetime I was as a tabret.

7. **Mine eye** also
is dim by reason of sorrow,
and all my members *are* as a shadow.

8. **Upright men shall
be astonied** at this,
**and the innocent
shall stir** up himself
against the hypocrite.

9. **The righteous** also shall
hold on his way, and he that
hath clean hands
shall be stronger and stronger.

10. **But as for you** all, do ye
return, and come now: for
**I cannot find one wise
man among you**.

11. My days are past, my
purposes are broken off,
even the thoughts of my heart.

12. They change the night into day:
the light *is* short because of darkness.

13. If I wait, the grave *is* mine house:
I have made my bed in the darkness.

14. **I have said to
corruption, Thou art my
father: to the worm, Thou
art my mother**, and my sister.

15. And
where is now
my hope? as for my
hope, who shall see it?

16. They shall go down to the
bars of the pit, when *our* rest
together *is* in the dust.

CHAPTER 18

1. **Then** answered
Bildad the Shuhite, and
said,

2. **How long will it be ere ye
make an end of words?**
mark, and afterwards we will speak.

3. **Wherefore are we**
counted as beasts, *and*
reputed vile in your sight?

4. **He teareth himself
in his anger**: shall the earth be
forsaken for thee? and shall the rock

be removed out of his place?

5. **Yea, the light of the
wicked shall be put out**, and
the spark of his fire shall not shine.

6. The light shall be dark in his
tabernacle, and his candle
shall be put out with him.

7. The steps of his strength shall
be straitened, and his own counsel
shall cast him down.

8. For he is cast into a net
by his own feet, and he
walketh upon a snare.

9. The gin shall take *him* by
the heel, *and* the robber shall
prevail against him.

10. **The snare is laid
for him** in the ground, and
a trap for him in the way.

11. **Terrors shall make
him afraid** on every side,
and shall drive him to his feet.

12. His strength shall be
hungerbitten, and
destruction shall be ready
at his side.

13. **It shall devour the
strength of his skin**:
even the firstborn of death
shall devour his strength.

14. **His confidence shall be
rooted out** of his tabernacle, and
it shall bring him to the king of terrors.

15. It shall dwell in his tabernacle,
because *it is* none of his: brimstone
shall be scattered upon his
habitation.

16. **His roots shall
be dried** up beneath, **and** above shall
his branch be
cut off.

17. **His remembrance
shall perish** from the earth, and
he shall have no name in the street.

18. **He shall be** driven from
light into darkness, and
chased out of the world.

19. **He shall neither have
son nor nephew**
among his people, nor any
remaining in his dwellings.

20. They that come after *him* shall be

astonied at his day, as they that went before were affrighted.

21. Surely such *are* the dwellings of the wicked, and **this is the place of him that knoweth not God.**

CHAPTER 19

1. **Then Job** answered and **said,**

2. **How long will ye** vex my soul, and **break me** in pieces **with words?**

3. These **ten times have ye reproached me: ye are not ashamed** *that* ye make yourselves strange to me.

4. **And be it indeed that I have erred,** mine error remaineth with myself.

5. If indeed ye will magnify *yourselves* against me, and plead against me my reproach:

6. **Know now that God hath overthrown me,** and hath compassed me with his net.

7. Behold, **I cry out of wrong, but I am not heard: I cry aloud, but there is no judgment.**

8. He hath fenced up my way that I cannot pass, and he hath set darkness in my paths.

9. **He hath stripped me of my glory,** and taken the crown *from* my head.

10. **He hath destroyed me** on every side, and I am gone: **and mine hope hath he removed** like a tree.

11. **He hath** also **kindled his wrath** against me, **and** he **counteth me** unto him **as one of his enemies.**

12. **His troops** come together, and raise up their way against me, and **encamp round** about **my tabernacle.**

13. He hath put **my brethren** far from me,

and mine acquaintance are verily **estranged from me.**

14. My kinsfolk have failed, and **my** familiar **friends have forgotten me.**

15. They that dwell in mine house, and **my maids, count me** for **a stranger: I am an alien** in their sight.

16. **I called my servant, and he gave me no answer;** I entreated him with my mouth.

17. **My breath is strange to my wife,** though I entreated for the children's *sake* of mine own body.

18. Yea, **young children despised me;** I arose, and they spake against me.

19. **All my** inward **friends abhorred me:** and they whom I loved are turned against me.

20. My bone cleaveth to my skin and to my flesh, and **I am escaped with the skin of my teeth.**

21. **Have pity upon me,** have pity upon me, O ye my friends; **for the hand of God hath touched me.**

22. **Why do ye persecute me** as God, and are not satisfied with my flesh?

23. **Oh that my words** were now written! oh that they **were printed in a book!**

24. That they were graven with an iron pen and lead in the rock for ever!

25. **For I know that my redeemer liveth, and** *that* **he shall stand at the latter day upon the earth:**

26. **And though** after my skin **worms destroy this body, yet in my flesh shall I see God:**

27. **Whom** I shall see for myself, and **mine eyes shall behold, and not another;** *though* my

786

reins be consumed within me.

28. But ye should say, Why persecute we him, seeing the root of the matter is found in me?

29. Be ye afraid of the sword: for **wrath bringeth the punishments of the sword, that ye may know there is a judgment**.

CHAPTER 20

1. Then answered **Zophar** the Naamathite, and **said**,

2. Therefore do my thoughts cause me to answer, and for *this* I make haste.

3. I have heard the check of my reproach, and **the spirit of my understanding causeth me to answer**.

4. **Knowest thou not this** of old, since man was placed upon earth,

5. **That the triumphing of the wicked is short**, and the joy of the hypocrite *but* for a moment?

6. **Though his** excellency mount up to the heavens, and his **head reach unto the clouds**;

7. **Yet he shall perish** for ever like his own dung: they which have seen him shall say, Where is he?

8. **He shall fly away as a dream**, and shall not be found: yea, he shall be chased away as a vision of the night.

9. **The eye** also **which saw him shall see him no more**; neither shall his place any more behold him.

10. **His children shall seek to please the poor**, and his hands shall restore their goods.

11. **His bones are full of the sin of his youth**, which shall lie down with him in the dust.

12. **Though wickedness be sweet in his mouth**, *though* he hide it under his tongue;

13. **Though he** spare it, and forsake it not; but **keep it still within his mouth**:

14. **Yet his meat in his bowels** is turned, *it* **is the gall of asps within him**.

15. **He hath swallowed** down **riches**, and he shall vomit them up again: **God shall cast them out of his belly**.

16. He shall suck the poison of asps: **the viper's tongue shall slay him**.

17. **He shall not see the rivers**, the floods, the brooks **of honey and butter**.

18. **That which he laboured for shall he restore**, and shall not swallow *it* down: **according to his substance shall the restitution be**, and he shall not rejoice *therein*.

19. **Because** he hath oppressed *and* hath forsaken the poor; *because* **he hath** violently **taken away an house which he builded not**;

20. Surely he shall not feel quietness in his belly, he shall not save of that which he desired.

21. **There shall none of his meat be left**; therefore shall no man look for his goods.

22. In the fulness of his sufficiency he shall be in straits: **every hand of the wicked shall come upon him**.

23. *When* he is about to fill his belly, **God shall cast the fury of his wrath upon him**, and shall rain it upon him while he is eating.

24. **He shall flee from the iron weapon, and** the bow of steel shall strike him through.

25. It is drawn, and cometh out of the body; yea, **the glittering sword cometh out of his gall**: terrors *are* upon him.

26. All darkness *shall* be hid in his

secret places: a fire not blown shall consume him; it shall go ill with him that is left in his tabernacle.

27. **The heaven shall reveal his iniquity**; and the earth shall rise up against him.

28. **The increase of his house shall depart**, *and his goods* shall flow away in the day of his wrath.

29. **This is the portion of a wicked man from God**, and the heritage appointed unto him by God.

CHAPTER 21

1. **But Job** answered and **said,**

2. **Hear diligently my speech**, and let this be your consolations.

3. Suffer me that I may speak; **and after** that **I have spoken, mock on.**

4. As for me, **is my complaint to man? and if** *it were* **so, why should not my spirit be troubled?**

5. Mark me, and be astonished, and lay *your* hand upon *your* mouth.

6. **Even when I remember** I am afraid, **and trembling taketh hold on my flesh.**

7. **Wherefore do the wicked live**, become old, **yea, are mighty in power?**

8. **Their seed is established** in their sight with them, and their offspring before their eyes.

9. **Their houses are safe** from fear, neither *is* the rod of God upon them.

10. **Their bull gendereth**, and faileth not; **their cow calveth**, and casteth not her calf.

11. They send forth their little ones like a flock, **and their children dance.**

12. They take the timbrel and harp, **and rejoice at the sound of the organ.**

13. **They spend their days in wealth**, and in a moment go down to the grave.

14. **Therefore they say unto God, Depart from us**; for **we desire not the knowledge of thy ways.**

15. **What is the Almighty, that we should serve him? and what profit should we have, if we pray unto him?**

16. Lo, their good *is* not in their hand: **the counsel of the wicked is far from me.**

17. **How oft is the candle of the wicked put out! and** *how oft* **cometh their destruction** upon them! God distributeth sorrows in his anger.

18. **They are as stubble before the wind**, and as chaff that the storm carrieth away.

19. **God** layeth up his iniquity for his children: he **rewardeth him, and he shall know it.**

20. His eyes shall see his destruction, and **he shall drink of the wrath of the Almighty.**

21. For **what pleasure hath he** in his house after him, **when the number of his months is cut off** in the midst?

22. **Shall any teach God knowledge? seeing he judgeth those that are high.**

23. **One dieth in his full strength**, being wholly at ease and quiet.

24. **His breasts are full** of milk, **and his bones are moistened with marrow.**

25. **And another dieth** in the bitterness of his soul, **and never eateth with pleasure.**

26. **They shall lie down alike in the dust**, and the worms shall cover them.

27. **Behold, I know** your thoughts, and **the devices which ye wrongfully imagine against me**.

28. **For ye say**, Where is the house of the prince? and **where are the dwelling places of the wicked?**

29. Have ye not asked them that go by the way? **and do ye not know** their tokens,

30. **That the wicked is reserved to the day of destruction?** they shall be brought forth to the day of wrath.

31. Who shall declare his way to his face? and **who shall repay him what he hath done?**

32. **Yet shall he be brought to the grave, and shall remain in the tomb**.

33. The clods of the valley shall be sweet unto him, and every man shall draw after him, as *there are* innumerable before him.

34. **How then comfort ye me** in vain, **seeing in your answers there remaineth falsehood?**

CHAPTER 22

1. **Then Eliphaz** the Temanite answered and **said**,

2. **Can a man be profitable unto God**, as he that is wise may be profitable unto himself?

3. **Is it any pleasure to the Almighty, that thou art righteous?** or *is it* gain to *him*, that thou makest thy ways perfect?

4. **Will he reprove thee for fear of thee?** will he enter with thee into judgment?

5. **Is not thy wickedness great?** and thine iniquities infinite?

6. **For thou hast** taken a pledge from thy brother for nought, and **stripped the naked**

of their clothing.

7. **Thou hast not given water to the weary to drink**, and thou hast withholden bread from the hungry.

8. But *as for* the mighty man, he had the earth; and the honourable man dwelt in it.

9. **Thou hast sent widows away empty**, and the arms of the fatherless have been broken.

10. **Therefore** snares are round about thee, and **sudden fear troubleth thee;**

11. **Or darkness**, *that* thou canst not see; and abundance of waters **cover thee**.

12. **Is not God in the height of heaven?** and behold the height of the stars, how high they are!

13. And thou sayest, How doth God know? **can he judge through the dark cloud?**

14. **Thick clouds are a covering to him, that he seeth not**; and he walketh in the circuit of heaven.

15. **Hast thou marked the old way which wicked men have trodden?**

16. Which were cut down out of time, whose foundation was overflown with a flood:

17. **Which said unto God, Depart from us**: and **what can the Almighty do for them?**

18. **Yet he filled their houses with good things**: but the counsel of the wicked is far from me.

19. **The righteous see it, and are glad**: and the innocent laugh them to scorn.

20. **Whereas our substance is not cut down**, but the remnant of them the fire consumeth.

21. **Acquaint now thyself with him**, and be at peace: **thereby good shall come unto thee**.

22. **Receive**, I pray thee, **the law from his mouth**,

■ and lay up his
■ words in thine heart.
■ 23. If thou return to the
■ Almighty, thou shalt
■ be built up, thou shalt put away
iniquity far from thy tabernacles.
■ 24. Then shalt thou lay up
■ gold as dust, and the *gold* of
Ophir as the stones of the brooks.
■ 25. Yea, the Almighty shall
■ be thy defence, and thou
shalt have plenty of silver.
■ 26. For then shalt thou have
■ thy delight in the Almighty,
■ and shalt lift up thy face
■ unto God.
■ 27. Thou shalt make
■ thy prayer unto him,
■ and he shall hear thee,
and thou shalt pay thy vows.
■ 28. Thou shalt also decree
■ a thing, and it shall be
■ established unto thee: and the
light shall shine upon thy ways.
■ 29. When men are cast
■ down, then thou shalt say,
■ There is lifting up; and he
shall save the humble person.
■ 30. He shall deliver the
■ island of the innocent:
and it is delivered by the
pureness of thine hands.

CHAPTER 23

■ 1. Then Job answered and
■ said,
■ 2. Even to day is my
■ complaint bitter: my stroke
is heavier than my groaning.
■ 3. Oh that I knew where
■ I might find him! *that* I
might come *even* to his seat!
■ 4. I would order my
cause before him, and
■ fill my mouth with
■ arguments.
■ 5. I would know the words
which he would answer me, and
■ understand what he
■ would say unto me.
6. Will he plead against me
with *his* great power? No; but
■ he would put

■ strength in me.
■ 7. There the righteous might
■ dispute with him; so should I be
delivered for ever from my judge.
8. Behold,
■ I go forward, but he *is not there*;
■ and backward, but
I cannot perceive him:
■ 9. On the left hand,
where he doth work,
■ but I cannot behold
■ him: he hideth himself
on the right hand,
■ that I cannot see him:
■ 10. But he knoweth
the way that I take:
■ when he hath tried me, I
■ shall come forth as gold.
11. My foot hath held his steps,
■ his way have I kept,
and not declined.
12. Neither have I gone back
from the commandment of his lips;
■ I have esteemed the words
■ of his mouth more than my
■ necessary food.
■ 13. But he is in one mind,
■ and who can turn him?
and *what* his soul desireth,
even *that* he doeth.
■ 14. For he performeth
■ the thing that is appointed
■ for me: and many such
things are with him.
15. Therefore am I troubled at
his presence: when I consider,
■ I am afraid of him.
■ 16. For God maketh
■ my heart soft, and the
Almighty troubleth me:
■ 17. Because I was
■ not cut off before the darkness,
■ neither hath he covered the
■ darkness from my face.

CHAPTER 24

■ 1. Why, seeing times are
not hidden from the Almighty,
■ do they that know him
■ not see his days?
■ 2. Some remove the
landmarks; they violently
■ take away flocks,

790

and feed thereof.

3. They drive away the ass of the fatherless,

they take the widow's ox for a pledge.

4. **They turn the needy out of the way**: the poor of the earth hide themselves together.

5. Behold,

as wild asses in the desert, **go they forth to their work**; rising betimes for a prey: the wilderness *yieldeth* food for them *and* for *their* children.

6. **They reap** every one his corn in the field: **and they gather the vintage of the wicked.**

7. **They cause the naked to** lodge without clothing, that *they* **have no covering in the cold.**

8. **They are wet** with the showers of the mountains, **and embrace the rock for** want of **a shelter.**

9. **They pluck the fatherless from the breast**, and take a pledge of the poor.

10. **They cause him to go naked** without clothing, **and they take** away the sheaf **from the hungry**;

11. **Which make oil within their walls, and tread their wine presses**, and suffer thirst.

12. Men groan from out of the city, and the soul of the wounded crieth out: **yet God layeth not folly to them.**

13. **They are of those that** rebel against the light; they **know not the ways** thereof, **nor abide in the paths thereof.**

14. **The murderer** rising with the light **killeth the poor and needy**, and in the night is as a thief.

15. The eye also of **the adulterer waiteth for** the twilight, saying, **No eye shall see me**: and disguiseth his face.

16. **In the dark they dig through houses, which they had marked** for themselves **in the daytime**: they know not the light.

17. **For the morning is to them** even **as the shadow of death**: if *one* know *them, they are in* the terrors of the shadow of death.

18. He *is* swift as the waters; **their portion is cursed in the earth**: he beholdeth not the way of the vineyards.

19. Drought and heat consume the snow waters: *so doth* the grave *those which* have sinned.

20. The womb shall forget him; **the worm shall feed sweetly on him; he shall be no more remembered**; and wickedness shall be broken as a tree.

21. **He** evil entreateth the barren *that* beareth not: and **doeth not good to the widow.**

22. He draweth also the mighty with his power: **he riseth up, and no man is sure of life.**

23. **Though** it be given him to be in safety, whereon **he resteth; yet his eyes are upon their ways.**

24. **They are exalted for a little while, but are gone and brought low**; they are taken out of the way as all *other*, and cut off as the tops of the ears of corn.

25. **And if it be not so now, who will make me a liar**, and make my speech nothing worth?

CHAPTER 25

1. **Then answered Bildad** the Shuhite, and said,

2. **Dominion and fear are with him,** he maketh peace in his high places.

3. Is there any number of his armies?

and upon whom doth
not his light arise?
4. **How** then
**can man be justified
with God?** or
**how can he be
clean that is born
of a woman?**
5. **Behold** even to the
moon, and it shineth not; yea,
**the stars are not
pure in his sight**.
6. **How much less man,
that is a worm?** and the
son of man, *which is* a worm?

CHAPTER 26

1. **But Job answered** and said,
2. **How hast thou
helped him** *that is* without
power? *how* savest thou the arm
that hath no strength?
3. **How hast thou
counselled him that hath no
wisdom?** and *how* hast thou
plentifully declared the thing as it is?
4. To whom hast thou uttered words?
and whose spirit came from thee?
5. Dead *things* are formed from
under the waters, and the
inhabitants thereof.
6. **Hell is naked before him**,
and destruction hath no covering.
7. **He stretcheth out the
north over the empty
place, and hangeth the
earth upon nothing**.
8. **He bindeth up the waters
in his thick clouds**; and the
cloud is not rent under them.
9. **He holdeth back the
face of his throne,** *and*
spreadeth his cloud upon it.
10. He hath compassed the
waters with bounds, until the
day and night come to an end.
11. **The pillars of heaven
tremble** and are
astonished at his reproof.
12. **He divideth the sea
with his power**, and by his
understanding he smiteth
through the proud.

13. **By his spirit he hath
garnished the heavens**;
his hand hath formed the
crooked serpent.
14. **Lo, these are parts of his
ways: but how little a
portion is heard of him?
but** the thunder of
**his power who
can understand?**

CHAPTER 27

1. **Moreover Job**
continued his parable, and
said,
2. **As God liveth, who hath
taken away my judgment**;
and the Almighty, *who* hath
vexed my soul;
3. All the while my breath is in me, and
**the spirit of God
is in my nostrils**;
4. **My lips shall not
speak wickedness**,
nor my tongue utter deceit.
5. God forbid that I should justify you:
**till I die I will not remove
mine integrity from me.**
6. **My righteousness I hold
fast**, and will not let it go: my heart
shall not reproach *me* so long as I live.
7. **Let mine enemy be as
the wicked**, and he that riseth
up against me as the unrighteous.
8. **For what is the hope
of the hypocrite**, though
he hath gained,
**when God taketh
away his soul?**
9. **Will God hear his cry
when trouble cometh
upon him?**
10. Will he delight himself
in the Almighty?
**will he always call
upon God?**
11. I will teach you by the
hand of God: *that* which *is* with
the Almighty will I not conceal.
12. Behold,
**all ye yourselves have seen
it; why then are ye
thus altogether vain?**

13. **This is the portion of a wicked man** with God, and the heritage of oppressors, *which* they shall receive of the Almighty.

14. **If his children be multiplied, it is for the sword**: and his offspring shall not be satisfied with bread.

15. **Those that remain** of him **shall be buried in death**: and his widows shall not weep.

16. **Though he heap up silver as the dust,** and prepare raiment as the clay;

17. He may prepare *it*, but the just shall put *it* on, **and the innocent shall divide the silver**.

18. He buildeth his house as a moth, and as a booth *that* the keeper maketh.

19. **The rich man shall lie down**, but he shall not be gathered: **he openeth his eyes, and he is not**.

20. **Terrors take hold on him** as waters, a tempest stealeth him away in the night.

21. The east wind carrieth him away, and he departeth: and as **a storm hurleth him** out of his place.

22. **For God shall cast upon him**, and not spare: he would fain flee out of his hand.

23. **Men shall** clap their hands at him, and shall **hiss him out of his place**.

CHAPTER 28

1. Surely there is a vein for the silver, and a place for gold *where* they fine *it*.

2. Iron is taken out of the earth, and brass *is* molten *out of* the stone.

3. **He setteth an end to darkness, and searcheth out** all **perfection**: the stones of darkness, and the shadow of death.

4. The flood breaketh out from the inhabitant; *even the waters* forgotten of the foot: they are dried up, they are

gone away from men.

5. **As for the earth, out of it cometh bread**: and under it is turned up as it were fire.

6. **The stones of it are the place of sapphires**: and it hath dust of gold.

7. **There is a path which no fowl knoweth**, and which the vulture's eye hath not seen:

8. **The lion's whelps have not trodden it**, nor the fierce lion passed by it.

9. **He putteth forth his hand** upon the rock; **he overturneth the mountains by the roots**.

10. He cutteth out rivers among the rocks; and **his eye seeth every precious thing**.

11. He bindeth the floods from overflowing; *and* **the thing that is hid bringeth he forth to light**.

12. **But where shall wisdom be found? and** where *is* the place of **understanding?**

13. **Man knoweth not the price thereof;** neither is it found in the land of the living.

14. **The depth** saith, It *is* not in me: **and the sea saith, It is not with me**.

15. **It cannot be gotten for gold, neither** shall **silver** be weighed for the price thereof.

16. **It cannot be valued with the gold of Ophir,** with the precious **onyx, or the sapphire**.

17. **The gold and** the **crystal cannot equal it**: and the exchange of it *shall* **not** be for **jewels of fine gold**.

18. No mention shall be made of coral, or of pearls: for **the price of wisdom is above rubies**.

19. **The topaz of Ethiopia shall not equal it**, neither shall it be valued with pure gold. 20. Whence then cometh wisdom? and where *is* the place of understanding? 21. Seeing **it is hid from the eyes of all living,** and kept close from the fowls of the air. 22. Destruction and death say, We have heard the fame thereof with our ears. 23. **God understandeth** the way thereof, **and he knoweth** the place thereof. 24. **For he looketh to the ends of the earth, and seeth** under **the whole heaven**; 25. **To make the weight for the winds**; and he weigheth the waters by measure. 26. **When he made a decree for the rain, and** a way for the lightning of **the thunder**: 27. **Then did he see it,** and **declare it**; he **prepared it**, yea, **and searched it out.** 28. And unto man he said, **Behold, the fear of the LORD, that is wisdom; and to depart from evil is understanding**.

CHAPTER 29

1. **Moreover Job continued** his parable, and said, 2. **Oh that I were** as *in* months past, **as in the days when God preserved me**; 3. **When his candle shined upon my head,** *and when* by his light I walked *through* darkness; 4. As I was in the days of my youth, **when the secret of God was upon my tabernacle**; 5. **When the Almighty was yet with me, when my** children were about me; 6. **When** I washed my steps with butter, and **the rock poured me out rivers of oil**; 7. **When I went out to the gate through the city**, when I prepared my seat in the street! 8. **The young men** saw me, and **hid themselves: and the aged** arose, *and* **stood up**. 9. **The princes refrained talking**, and laid their hand on *their* mouth. 10. **The nobles held their peace**, and their tongue cleaved to the roof of their mouth. 11. **When the ear heard me**, then it blessed me; **and when the eye saw me, it gave witness to me**: 12. **Because I delivered the poor** that cried, and the fatherless, and *him that had* none to help him. 13. **The blessing of him that was ready to perish came upon me: and I caused the widow's heart to sing for joy.** 14. **I put on righteousness**, and it clothed me: my judgment *was* as a robe and a diadem. 15. **I was eyes to the blind, and feet** *was* I **to the lame**. 16. **I was a father to the poor**: and the cause *which* I knew not I searched out. 17. **And I brake the jaws of the wicked**, and plucked the spoil out of his teeth. 18. Then I said, I shall die in my nest, and I shall multiply *my* days as the sand. 19. **My root was spread out by the waters, and the dew lay all night upon my branch**. 20. My glory *was* fresh in me, and my bow was renewed in my hand. 21. **Unto me men gave ear**,

and waited, and kept silence at my counsel.
22. **After my words they spake not again**; and my speech dropped upon them.
23. **And they waited for me** as for the rain; and they opened their mouth wide *as* for the latter rain.
24. *If* I laughed on them, they believed *it* not; and the light of my countenance they cast not down.
25. **I chose out their way**, and sat chief, **and dwelt as a king** in the army, as one *that* comforteth the mourners.

CHAPTER 30

1. **But now they that are younger than I have me in derision, whose fathers I would have disdained to have** set **with the dogs of my flock**.
2. Yea, whereto *might* the strength of their hands *profit* me, in whom old age was perished?
3. **For want and famine they were solitary**; fleeing into the wilderness in former time desolate and waste.
4. **Who cut up** mallows by the bushes, and **juniper roots for their meat**.
5. **They were driven forth** from among *men,* (they cried after them **as** *after* **a thief**;)
6. **To dwell in the cliffs** of the valleys, **in caves** of the earth, **and in the rocks**.
7. Among the bushes they brayed; under the nettles they were gathered together.
8. **They were children of fools**, yea, children of base men: they were **viler than the earth**.
9. **And now** am I their song, yea, **I am their byword**.
10. **They abhor me**,

they flee far from me, **and spare not to spit in my face**.
11. **Because he hath** loosed my cord, and **afflicted me**, they have also let loose the bridle before me.
12. Upon *my* right *hand* rise **the youth**; they push away my feet, and they **raise up against me** the ways of their destruction.
13. They mar my path, **they set forward my calamity**, they have no helper.
14. **They came upon me** as a wide breaking in *of waters*: in the desolation they rolled themselves *upon me.*
15. **Terrors are turned upon me: they pursue my soul as the wind**: and my welfare passeth away as a cloud.
16. And now my soul is poured out upon me; **the days of affliction have taken hold** upon me.
17. My bones are pierced in me in the night season: **and my sinews take no rest**.
18. By the great force *of my disease* is my garment changed: it bindeth me about as the collar of my coat.
19. **He hath cast me into the mire**, and I am become like dust and ashes.
20. **I cry unto thee, and thou dost not hear me**: I stand up, and thou regardest me *not.*
21. **Thou art become cruel to me**: with thy strong hand thou opposest thyself against me.
22. **Thou liftest me up to the wind**; thou causest me to ride *upon it,* and dissolvest my substance.
23. For **I know that thou wilt bring me to death**, and to the house appointed for all living.
24. Howbeit he will not stretch out

his hand to the grave, though they cry in his destruction.

25. Did not I weep for him that was in trouble?
was not my soul grieved for the poor?

26. **When I looked for good, then evil came unto me: and when I waited for light, there came darkness**.

27. My bowels boiled, and rested not: the days of affliction prevented me.

28. I went mourning without the sun: I stood up, *and* I cried in the congregation.

29. **I am** a brother to dragons, and **a companion to owls**.

30. My skin is black upon me, and **my bones are burned with heat**.

31. **My harp also is turned to mourning**, and my organ into the voice of them that weep.

CHAPTER 31

1. **I made a covenant with mine eyes; why then should I think upon a maid?**

2. **For what portion of God is there from above?** and *what* inheritance of the Almighty from on high?

3. **Is not destruction to the wicked?** and a strange *punishment* to the workers of iniquity?

4. **Doth not he see my ways**, and count all my steps?

5. **If I have walked with vanity, or** if my foot hath hasted to **deceit**;

6. **Let me be weighed** in an even balance **that God may know mine integrity**.

7. **If my step hath turned out of the way**, and mine heart walked after mine eyes, and if any blot hath cleaved to mine hands;

8. **Then let me sow, and let another eat**; yea, let my offspring be rooted out.

9. **If mine heart have been deceived by a woman**, or if I

have laid wait at my neighbour's door;

10. **Then let my wife grind unto another**, and let others bow down upon her.

11. **For this is an heinous crime**; yea, it *is* an iniquity to be *punished by* the judges.

12. For it *is* a fire that consumeth to destruction, **and would root out all mine increase**.

13. **If I did despise the cause of my manservant or** of my **maidservant, when they contended with me**;

14. **What then shall I do when God riseth up?** and when he visiteth, what shall I answer him?

15. **Did not he that made me in the womb make him?** and did not one fashion us in the womb?

16. **If I** have withheld the poor from *their* desire, or **have caused the eyes of the widow to fail**;

17. **Or have eaten my morsel** myself **alone**, and the fatherless hath not eaten thereof;

18. (For from my youth he was brought up with me, as *with* a father, and I have guided her from my mother's womb;)

19. **If I have seen any perish for want of clothing**, or any poor without covering;

20. If his loins have not blessed me, **and if he were not warmed with the fleece of mysheep**;

21. **If I have lifted up my hand against the fatherless**, when I saw my help in the gate:

22. **Then let mine arm fall** from my shoulder blade, and mine arm **be broken from the bone**.

23. For destruction *from* God *was* a terror to me, and by reason of his highness I could not endure.

24. **If I have made gold my hope**, or have said to the fine

gold, *Thou art* my confidence;

25. **If I rejoice because my wealth was great**, and because mine hand had gotten much;

26. **If I beheld the sun when it shined**, or the moon walking *in* brightness;

27. **And my heart hath been secretly enticed**, or my mouth hath kissed my hand:

28. This also *were* an iniquity to *be punished* by the judge: **for I should have denied the God that is above**.

29. **If I rejoice at the destruction of him that hated me**, or lifted up myself when evil found him:

30. **Neither have I suffered my mouth to sin by wishing a curse to his soul**.

31. If the men of my tabernacle said not, Oh that we had of his flesh! we cannot be satisfied.

32. The stranger did not lodge in the street: **but I opened my doors to the traveller**.

33. **If I covered my** transgressions as Adam, by hiding mine **iniquity in my bosom**:

34. Did I fear a great multitude, or did the contempt of families terrify me, that I kept silence, *and* went not out of the door?

35. **Oh that one would hear me!** behold, my desire *is,* **that the Almighty would answer me**, and *that* mine adversary had written a book.

36. Surely I would take it upon my shoulder, *and* bind it as a crown to me.

37. **I would declare unto him the number of my steps**; as a prince would I go near unto him.

38. If my land cry against me, or that the furrows likewise thereof complain;

39. If I have eaten the fruits thereof without money, or have caused the owners thereof to lose their life:

40. **Let thistles grow instead of wheat**, and cockle instead of barley. **The words of Job are ended**.

CHAPTER 32

1. **So these three men ceased to answer Job, because he was righteous in his own eyes**.

2. **Then was kindled the wrath of Elihu** the son of Barachel the Buzite, of the kindred of Ram: **against Job was his** wrath kindled, **because he justified himself rather than God**.

3. **Also against his three friends** was his wrath kindled, **because they** had **found no answer, and yet** had **condemned Job**.

4. **Now Elihu** had **waited till Job had spoken**, because they *were* elder than he.

5. When Elihu saw that *there was* no answer in the mouth of *these* three men, then his wrath was kindled.

6. **And Elihu** the son of Barachel the Buzite answered and **said, I am young, and ye are** very **old; wherefore I** was afraid, and **durst not shew you mine opinion**.

7. I said, Days should speak, and multitude of years should teach wisdom.

8. **But there is a spirit in man: and the inspiration of the Almighty giveth them understanding**.

9. **Great men are not always wise**: neither do the aged understand judgment.

10. **Therefore I said**, Hearken to me; **I also will shew mine opinion**.

11. **Behold, I waited** for your words;

■ **I gave ear to your reasons**,
whilst ye searched out what to say.
12. Yea, I attended unto you,
■ **and,** behold,
■ **there was none of you**
■ **that convinced Job,**
or that answered his words:
13. Lest ye should say, We
have found out wisdom: God
thrusteth him down, not man.
■ 14. **Now he hath not**
■ **directed his words against**
■ **me: neither will I answer**
■ **him with your speeches**.
■ 15. **They were amazed,**
■ **they answered no more**:
they left off speaking.
16. When I had waited, (for they
spake not, but stood still, *and*
answered no more;)
■ 17. **I said, I will answer** also
my part, I also will shew mine opinion.
18. For I am full of matter,
■ **the spirit within me**
■ **constraineth me**.
■ 19. **Behold, my belly** *is*
as wine *which* hath no vent; it
■ **is ready to burst**
■ **like new bottles**.
20. I will speak, that I
may be refreshed: I will
open my lips and answer.
■ 21. **Let me not**, I pray you, accept
any man's person, neither let me
■ **give flattering titles**
■ **unto man**.
22. For I know not to
give flattering titles;
■ **in so doing my maker**
■ **would soon take me away**.

CHAPTER 33

■ 1. **Wherefore, Job**, I pray
thee, hear my speeches, and
■ **hearken to all my words**.
2. Behold, now I have opened
my mouth, my tongue hath
spoken in my mouth.
3. My words *shall be of* the
uprightness of my heart: and
■ **my lips shall utter**
■ **knowledge clearly**.
4. The spirit of

■ **God hath made me,**
■ **and** the breath of the Almighty
■ **hath given me life.**
5. If thou canst answer me, set *thy*
words in order before me, stand up.
6. Behold, I *am* according to
thy wish in God's stead:
■ **I also am formed**
■ **out of the clay**.
■ 7. **Behold, my terror shall**
■ **not make thee afraid**,
neither shall my hand be
heavy upon thee.
8. Surely thou hast spoken
in mine hearing, and
■ **I have heard** the voice of
■ **thy words, saying,**
9. I am clean without transgression,
■ **I am innocent**; neither
is there iniquity in me.
10. Behold, he findeth
occasions against me,
■ **he counteth me**
■ **for his enemy**,
11. He putteth my feet in the stocks,
■ **he marketh all my paths**.
■ 12. **Behold, in this thou**
■ **art not just: I will answer**
■ **thee, that God is**
■ **greater than man.**
13. Why dost thou strive against
him? for he giveth not account
of any of his matters.
■ 14. **For God**
■ **speaketh** once, yea
■ **twice, yet man**
■ **perceiveth it not**.
15. In a dream, in a
vision of the night,
■ **when deep sleep**
■ **falleth upon men**, in
slumberings upon the bed;
■ 16. **Then he openeth**
■ **the ears** of men,
■ **and sealeth their**
■ **instruction**,
17. That he may withdraw man *from*
his purpose, and hide pride from man.
■ 18. **He keepeth back his**
■ **soul from the pit**, and his life
from perishing by the sword.
■ 19. **He is chastened also**
■ **with pain** upon his bed, and

the multitude of his bones with strong *pain:*

20. So that his life abhorreth bread, and his soul dainty meat.

21. **His flesh is consumed** away, that it cannot be seen; **and his bones** *that* were not seen **stick out.**

22. Yea, **his soul draweth near** unto **the grave**, and his life to the destroyers.

23. **If there be** a messenger with him, an interpreter, **one among a thousand, to shew unto man his uprightness:**

24. **Then he** is gracious unto him, and **saith, Deliver him from going down to the pit:** I have found a ransom.

25. His flesh shall be fresher than a child's: he shall return to the days of his youth:

26. **He shall pray unto God,** and he will be favourable unto him: **and he shall see his face with joy:** for he will render unto man his righteousness.

27. **He looketh upon men, and if any say, I have sinned,** and perverted that *which was* right, and it profited me not;

28. **He will deliver his soul from going into the pit,** and his life shall see the light.

29. **Lo, all these things worketh God** oftentimes **with man,**

30. **To bring back his soul from the pit,** to be enlightened with the light of the living.

31. Mark well, **O Job,** hearken unto me: **hold thy peace, and I will speak.**

32. **If thou hast anything to say,** answer me: **speak,** for I desire to justify thee.

33. **If not,** hearken unto me:

hold thy peace, and I shall teach thee wisdom.

CHAPTER 34

1. **Furthermore Elihu** answered and said,

2. **Hear my words, O ye wise men;** and give ear unto me, ye that have knowledge.

3. **For the ear trieth words, as the mouth tasteth meat.**

4. Let us choose to us judgment: **let us know among ourselves what is good.**

5. For **Job hath said, I am righteous:** and God hath taken away my judgment.

6. Should I lie against my right? my wound *is* incurable without transgression.

7. **What man is like Job, who drinketh up scorning like water?**

8. **Which** goeth in company with the workers of iniquity, and **walketh with wicked men.**

9. **For he** hath **said, It profiteth a man nothing that he should delight himself with God.**

10. **Therefore hearken unto me** ye men of understanding: **far be it from God, that he should do wickedness;** and from the Almighty, **that he should commit iniquity.**

11. For **the work of a man shall he render unto him,** and cause every man to find according to *his* ways.

12. **Yea, surely God will not do wickedly, neither** will the Almighty **pervert judgment.**

13. **Who hath given him a charge over the earth?** or who hath disposed the whole world?

14. If he set his heart upon man, **if he gather unto himself**

his spirit and his breath;

15. **All flesh shall perish** together, **and** man shall **turn** again **unto dust**.

16. **If** now **thou hast understanding, hear this**: hearken to the voice of my words.

17. Shall even he that hateth right govern? and **wilt thou condemn him that is most just?**

18. **Is it fit to say to a king, Thou art wicked?** *and* to princes, **Ye are ungodly?**

19. *How much less* **to him that accepteth not** the persons of **princes, nor regardeth the rich more than the poor?** for they all *are* the work of his hands.

20. **In a moment** shall **they die**, and the people shall be troubled at midnight, and pass away: and the mighty shall be taken away without hand.

21. For **his eyes are upon** the ways of **man, and** he seeth all **his goings.**

22. **There is no darkness**, nor shadow of death, **where** the **workers of iniquity may hide** themselves.

23. For he will not lay upon man more *than right;* that he should enter into judgment with God.

24. **He shall break** in pieces **mighty men** without number, **and set others in their stead**.

25. Therefore he knoweth their works, and he overturneth *them* in the night, so that **they are destroyed.**

26. He striketh them as wicked men **in** the **open sight of others;**

27. **Because they turned back from him**, and would not consider any of his ways:

28. So that they cause the cry of the poor to come unto him, and he heareth the cry of the afflicted.

29. When he giveth quietness, who then can make trouble? and **when he hideth his face, who** then **can behold him? whether** *it be* **done against a nation, or** against **a man only**:

30. That the hypocrite reign not, **lest the people be ensnared.**

31. **Surely it is meet to be said unto God**, I have borne *chastisement*, I will not offend *any more*:

32. *That which* I see not teach thou me: **if I have done iniquity, I will do no more**.

33. *Should it* be according to thy mind? he will recompense it, whether thou refuse, or whether thou choose; and not I: therefore speak what thou knowest.

34. Let men of understanding tell me, and let a wise man hearken unto me.

35. **Job hath spoken** without knowledge, and his words *were* **without wisdom.**

36. **My desire is that Job may be tried unto the end** because of his answers for wicked men.

37. **For he addeth rebellion unto his sin**, he clappeth *his hands* among us, **and multiplieth his words against God.**

CHAPTER 35

1. **Elihu** spake moreover, and **said,**

2. **Thinkest** thou **this to be right, that thou saidst, My righteousness is**

more than God's?

CHAPTER 36

3. For thou saidst, What advantage will it be unto thee? *and,* **What profit shall I have, if I be cleansed from my sin?**

4. **I will answer thee, and thy companions** with thee.

5. Look unto the heavens, and see; and behold the clouds *which* are higher than thou.

6. **If thou sinnest**, what doest thou against him? or *if* thy transgressions be multiplied, **what doest thou unto him?**

7. If thou be righteous, what givest thou him? **or what receiveth he** of thine hand?

8. **Thy wickedness may hurt a man as thou art;** and thy righteousness *may profit* the son of man.

9. By reason of the multitude of oppressions they make **the oppressed** to cry: they **cry out by reason of the arm of the mighty**.

10. **But none saith, Where is God** my maker, **who giveth songs** in the night;

11. **Who teacheth us** more than the beasts of the earth, **and maketh us wiser** than the fowls of heaven?

12. There they cry, but none giveth answer, because of the pride of evil men.

13. Surely **God will not hear vanity, neither** will the Almighty **regard it**.

14. Although thou sayest thou shalt not see him, **yet judgment is before him; therefore trust thou in him**.

15. But now, because *it is* not so, he hath visited in his anger; yet he knoweth *it* not in great extremity:

16. Therefore doth **Job** open his mouth in vain; he **multiplieth words without knowledge**.

1. **Elihu** also proceeded, and **said**,

2. Suffer me a little, and **I will shew thee that I have yet to speak on God's behalf**.

3. **I will** fetch my knowledge from afar, and will **ascribe righteousness to my Maker**.

4. For truly my words *shall not be* false: **he that is perfect** in knowledge **is with thee**.

5. Behold, **God is mighty**, and despiseth *not any: he* is mighty **in strength and wisdom**.

6. **He** preserveth not the life of the wicked: but **giveth right to the poor**.

7. **He withdraweth not his eyes from the righteous**: but with kings *are they* on the throne; yea, he doth establish them for ever, and they are exalted.

8. **And if they be bound in fetters**, *and* be holden in cords of affliction;

9. **Then he sheweth them** their work, and **their transgressions** that they have exceeded.

10. He openeth also their ear to discipline, **and commandeth that they return from iniquity**.

11. **If they obey and serve him, they** shall **spend their days in prosperity, and** their years in **pleasures**.

12. But **if they obey not**, they shall perish by the sword, and **they shall die without knowledge**.

13. **But the hypocrites** in heart heap up wrath: they **cry not when he bindeth them**.

14. **They die in youth, and**

their life *is* among the
unclean.
15. He delivereth the
poor in his affliction, and
openeth their ears in oppression.
16. Even so
would he
have removed thee out
of the strait into a broad
place, where *there is* no straitness;
and that which should be set on thy
table *should be* full of fatness.
17. But thou hast fulfilled the
judgment of the wicked:
judgment and justice
take hold on thee.
18. Because there is wrath,
beware lest he take thee
away with his stroke: then a great
ransom cannot deliver thee.
19. Will he esteem thy riches? *no,*
not gold, nor all the forces of strength.
20. Desire not the night, when
people are cut off in their place.
21. Take heed, regard
not iniquity: for this hast
thou chosen rather than affliction.
22. Behold, God exalteth by
his power: who teacheth like him?
23. Who hath enjoined
him his way? or
who can say, Thou
hast wrought iniquity?
24. Remember that
thou magnify his work,
which men behold.
25. Every man may
see it; man may behold *it*
afar off.
26. Behold,
God is great, and we
know him not, neither can the
number of his years be searched out.
27. For
he maketh small the drops
of water: they pour down
rain according to
the vapour thereof:
28. Which the
clouds do drop *and*
distil upon man abundantly.
29. Also can any
understand the spreadings of
the clouds, *or* the noise
of his tabernacle?
30. Behold, he spreadeth
his light upon it, and
covereth the bottom of
the sea.
31. For by them judgeth he the
people; he giveth meat in abundance.
32. With clouds he covereth
the light; and commandeth
it not to shine by *the cloud*
that cometh betwixt.
33. The noise thereof
sheweth concerning it,
the cattle also concerning
the vapour.

CHAPTER 37

1. At this also
my heart trembleth,
and is moved out of his place.
2. Hear attentively the noise
of his voice, and the sound *that*
goeth out of his mouth.
3. He directeth it under
the whole heaven, and
his lightning unto the
ends of the earth.
4. After it a voice roareth: he
thundereth with the voice of his
excellency; and he will not stay
them when his voice is heard.
5. God thundereth marvellously
with his voice;
great things doeth he,
which we cannot
comprehend.
6. For
he saith to the snow, Be thou
on the earth; likewise
to the small rain,
and to
the great rain of his strength.
7. He sealeth up
the hand of every
man; that all men
may know his work.
8. Then the beasts go into
dens, and remain in their places.
9. Out of the south cometh the
whirlwind: and cold out of the north.
10. By the breath of God
frost is given: and the breadth of

the waters is straitened.

■ 11. **Also by watering**
he weareith the thick cloud:
■ **he scattereth his** bright
■ **cloud:**
12. **And** it is turned round about
by his counsels: that they may
do whatsoever he commandeth
them upon the face of the
world in the earth.
■ 13. **He causeth it** to come,
■ **whether for correction, or**
■ **for his land, or for mercy**.
14. Hearken unto this, O
■ **Job: stand still, and**
■ **consider the wondrous**
■ **works of God**.
■ 15. **Dost thou know when**
■ **God** disposed them, and
■ **caused the light** of his cloud
■ **to shine?**
■ 16. **Dost thou know** the
balancings of the clouds,
■ **the wondrous works of him**
■ **which is perfect** in knowledge?
■ 17. **How thy garments are**
■ **warm**, when he quieteth the earth
■ **by the south wind?**
■ 18. **Hast thou** with him
■ **spread out the sky**,
which is strong, *and*
■ **as a** molten
■ **looking glass?**
■ 19. **Teach us what we shall**
■ **say unto him**; *for* we cannot order
our speech by reason of darkness.
20. Shall it be told him
that I speak? if a man
speak, surely he shall
be swallowed up.
21. And now *men* see not
the bright light which *is* in the
clouds: but the wind passeth,
and cleanseth them.
22. Fair weather cometh out of the
north: with God *is* terrible majesty.
■ 23. **Touching the Almighty,**
■ **we cannot** find him out:
■ **he is excellent in**
■ **power, and** in
■ **judgment, and** in plenty of
■ **justice**: he will not afflict.
■ 24. **Men do** therefore

■ **fear him:** he respecteth
not any *that are* wise of heart.

CHAPTER 38

1. Then
■ **the LORD answered Job out**
■ **of the whirlwind,** and said,
■ 2. **Who is this that darkeneth**
■ **counsel** by words
■ **without knowledge?**
3. Gird up now thy loins like a man;
for I will demand of thee, and
■ **answer thou me**.
■ 4. **Where wast thou when**
■ **I laid the foundations of**
■ **the earth?** declare, if thou
hast understanding.
■ 5. **Who** hath
■ **laid the measures**
thereof, if thou knowest? or
■ **who** hath
■ **stretched the line** upon it?
6. Whereupon are the foundations
thereof fastened? or
■ **who laid the corner**
■ **stone** thereof;
■ 7. **When the morning**
■ **stars sang** together, and all
the sons of God shouted for joy?
■ 8. **Or who shut up the sea**
with doors, when it brake forth, *as*
if it had issued out of the womb?
■ 9. **When I made the cloud**
the garment thereof, and thick
darkness a swaddlingband for it,
■ 10. **And** brake up
■ **for it** my decreed *place,* and
■ **set bars and doors,**
■ 11. **And said,** Hitherto
■ **shalt thou come, but no**
■ **further: and here shall thy**
■ **proud waves be stayed?**
12. **Hast thou commanded**
■ **the morning** since thy days;
and caused the dayspring to
know his place;
13. That it might take hold
of the ends of the earth,
■ **that the wicked might**
■ **be shaken out of it?**
14. It is turned as clay *to* the seal;
and they stand as a garment.
15. And from the wicked their light is

withholden, and the high arm shall be broken.

■ 16. **Hast thou entered into**
■ **the springs of the sea?**
or hast thou walked in the search of the depth?

■ 17. **Have the gates of death**
■ **been opened unto thee?**
or hast thou seen the doors of the shadow of death?

■ 18. **Hast thou perceived**
■ **the breadth of the**
■ **earth? declare if**
■ **thou knowest it all**.

19. Where *is* the way
■ **where light dwelleth?**
■ **and** *as for*
■ **darkness**, where
is the place thereof,

20. That thou shouldest take it to the bound thereof, and that thou shouldest know the paths to the house thereof?

■ 21. **Knowest thou it**, because
thou wast then born? or

■ **because the number**
■ **of thy days is great?**

22. Hast thou entered into the treasures of the snow? or hast thou seen the treasures of the hail,

23. Which I have reserved against the time of trouble, against the day of battle and war?

■ 24. **By what way is the**
■ **light parted**, *which* scattereth
the east wind upon the earth?

■ 25. **Who hath divided a**
■ **watercourse for**
the overflowing of

■ **waters, or** *a* way
■ **for the lightning** of thunder;

■ 26. **To cause it to**
■ **rain** on the earth,

■ **where no man is**; on the
wilderness, wherein *there is* no man;

27. To satisfy the desolate and waste *ground*; and

■ **to cause the bud of the**
■ **tender herb to spring forth?**

28. Hath the rain a father? or

■ **who hath begotten**
■ **the drops of dew?**

29. Out of whose womb came

■ **the ice? and** the hoary
■ **frost of heaven**,
who hath gendered it?

30. The waters are hid as *with* a stone, and the face of the deep is frozen.

■ 31. **Canst thou bind**
the sweet influences of

■ **Pleiades, or**
■ **loose** the bands of
■ **Orion?**

■ 32. **Canst thou bring forth**
■ **Mazzaroth** in his season?
■ **or** canst thou
■ **guide Arcturus** with his sons?

■ 33. **Knowest thou the**
■ **ordinances of heaven?**
canst thou set the dominion thereof in the earth?

■ 34. **Canst thou lift up**
■ **thy voice to the clouds**,
that abundance of waters may cover thee?

■ 35. **Canst thou send**
■ **lightnings**, that they may go
and say unto thee, Here we *are?*

■ 36. **Who hath put**
■ **wisdom** in the inward parts?
■ **or** who hath given
■ **understanding**
■ **to the heart?**

■ 37. **Who can number**
■ **the clouds** in wisdom?
■ **or** who can
■ **stay the bottles of heaven,**

38. When the dust groweth into hardness, and the clods cleave fast together?

■ 39. **Wilt thou hunt the**
■ **prey for the lion?** or fill
the appetite of the young lions,

■ 40. **When they couch**
■ **in their dens**, *and* abide
in the covert to lie in wait?

■ 41. **Who provideth**
■ **for the raven** his food?
■ **when his young ones**
■ **cry unto God**, they
wander for lack of meat.

CHAPTER 39

■■ 1. **Knowest thou** the time
■■ **when the wild goats**

of the rock

■ **bring forth? or** canst thou mark
■ **when the hinds do calve?**

2. Canst thou number the months *that* they fulfil? or knowest thou the time when they bring forth?

3. They bow themselves, they bring forth their young ones, the y cast out their sorrows.

4. Their young ones are in good liking, they grow up with corn; they go forth, and return not unto them.

■ 5. **Who hath sent out the**
■ **wild ass free?** or who hath loosed the bands of the wild ass?

6. **Whose house I have**
■ **made the wilderness, and**
■ **the barren land** his dwellings.

7. **He scorneth the**
■ **multitude of the city**, neither regardeth he the crying of the driver.

■ 8. **The range of the**
■ **mountains is his pasture,**
and he searcheth after every green thing.

■ 9. **Will the unicorn be**
■ **willing to serve thee,**
or abide by thy crib?

10. Canst thou bind the unicorn with his band in the furrow? or
■ **will he harrow the**
■ **valleys after thee?**

■ 11. **Wilt thou trust him,**
■ **because his strength**
■ **is great?** or wilt thou leave thy labour to him?

■ 12. **Wilt thou believe him,**
■ **that he will bring home thy**
■ **seed,** and gather *it into* thy barn?

■ 13. **Gavest thou the**
■ **goodly wings unto**
■ **the peacocks?** or wings
■ **and** feathers unto
■ **the ostrich?**

■ 14. **Which leaveth her eggs** in the earth, and warmeth them in dust,

■ 15. **And forgetteth** that the foot may crush them, or that
■ **the wild beast may**
■ **break them.**

■ 16. **She is hardened** against her young ones,
■ **as though they were**

■ **not her's:** her labour is in vain without fear;

■ 17. **Because God hath**
■ **deprived her of wisdom,**
■ **neither** hath he imparted to her
■ **understanding.**

18. What time she lifteth up herself on high,
■ **she scorneth the**
■ **horse and his rider.**

■ 19. **Hast thou given the**
■ **horse strength?** hast thou clothed his neck with thunder?

20. **Canst thou make**
■ **him afraid** as a grasshopper? the glory of his nostrils *is* terrible.

21. **He** paweth in the valley, and
■ **rejoiceth in his**
■ **strength: he goeth** on
■ **to meet the armed men.**

22. **He mocketh at fear,**
and is not affrighted;
■ **neither turneth he**
■ **back from the sword.**

23. The quiver rattleth against him, the glittering spear and the shield.

■ 24. **He swalloweth the**
■ **ground with fierceness**
■ **and rage:** neither believeth he that *it is* the sound of the trumpet.

25. He saith among the trumpets, Ha, ha; and he smelleth the battle afar off, the thunder of the captains, and the shouting.

■ 26. **Doth the hawk fly**
■ **by thy wisdom,** *and* stretch her wings toward the south?

■ 27. **Doth the eagle mount**
■ **up at thy command,**
and make her nest on high?

■ 28. **She dwelleth and**
■ **abideth on the rock,** upon the crag of the rock, and the strong place.

■ 29. **From thence she**
■ **seeketh the prey,** *and* her eyes behold afar off.

30. Her young ones also suck up blood: and where the slain *are,* there *is* she.

CHAPTER 40

■| 1. **Moreover the LORD**
■| **answered Job,** and said,

2. **Shall he that contendeth with the Almighty instruct him?** he that reproveth God, let him answer it.

3. **Then Job answered** the LORD, and said,

4. **Behold, I am vile**; what shall I answer thee? I will lay mine hand upon my mouth.

5. **Once have I spoken**; but I will not answer: **yea, twice; but I will proceed no further**.

6. **Then answered the LORD unto Job out of the whirlwind**, and said,

7. **Gird up thy loins now like a man:** I will demand of thee, and declare thou unto me.

8. Wilt thou also disannul my judgment? **wilt thou condemn me, that thou mayest be righteous?**

9. **Hast thou an arm like God?** or canst thou thunder with a voice like him?

10. **Deck thyself now with majesty and excellency**; and array thyself **with glory and beauty**.

11. **Cast abroad the rage of thy wrath**: and behold every one *that is* proud, and abase him.

12. Look on **every one that is proud, and bring him low**; and tread down the wicked in their place.

13. **Hide them in the dust** together; *and* bind their faces in secret.

14. **Then will I also confess unto thee that thine own right hand can save thee**.

15. **Behold** now **behemoth**, which I made with thee; **he eateth grass as an ox**.

16. Lo now, **his strength is in his loins**, and his force *is* in the navel of his belly.

17. **He moveth his tail like a cedar**: the sinews of his stones are wrapped together.

18. **His bones are as strong pieces of brass**; his bones *are* like bars of iron.

19. **He is the chief of the ways of God**: he that made him can make his sword to approach *unto him.*

20. Surely **the mountains bring him forth food**, where all the beasts of the field play.

21. He lieth under the shady trees, in the covert of the reed, and fens.

22. **The shady trees cover him with their shadow**; the willows of the brook compass him about.

23. Behold, he drinketh up a river, *and* hasteth not: **he trusteth that hecan draw up Jordan into his mouth**.

24. **He taketh it with his eyes**: his nose pierceth through snares.

CHAPTER 41

1. **Canst thou draw out leviathan with an hook?** or his tongue with a cord *which* thou lettest down?

2. **Canst thou put an hook into his nose?** or bore his jaw through with a thorn?

3. Will he make many supplications unto thee? **will he speak soft words unto thee?**

4. **Will he make a covenant with thee?** wilt thou take him for a servant for ever?

5. **Wilt thou play with him as with a bird?** or wilt thou bind him for thy maidens?

6. Shall the companions make a banquet of him? shall they part him among the merchants?

7. **Canst thou fill his skin with barbed irons?** or his head with fish spears?

8. **Lay thine hand upon him**, remember the battle, **do no more.**

9. Behold, the hope of him is in vain: shall not *one* be cast down even at the sight of him?

10. **None is so fierce that dare stir him up: who then is able to stand before me?**

11. Who hath prevented me, that I should repay *him*? **whatsoever is under the whole heaven is mine**.

12. **I will not conceal** his parts, nor **his power**, nor his comely proportion.

13. Who can discover the face of his garment? *or* **who can come to him with his double bridle?**

14. Who can open the doors of his face? **his teeth are terrible** round about.

15. **His scales are his pride**, shut up together as *with* a close seal.

16. **One is so near to another, that no air can come between** them.

17. They are joined one to another, they stick together, that they cannot be sundered.

18. By his neesings a light doth shine, and his eyes *are* like the eyelids of the morning.

19. **Out of his mouth go burning lamps**, *and* sparks of fire leap out.

20. **Out of his nostrils goeth smoke**, as *out* of a seething pot or caldron.

21. **His breath kindleth coals**, and a flame goeth out of his mouth.

22. In his neck remaineth strength, **and sorrow is turned into joy before him**.

23. The flakes of his flesh are joined together: they are firm in themselves; they cannot be moved.

24. **His heart is as firm as a stone**; yea, as hard as a piece of the nether *millstone*.

25. **When he raiseth up himself, the mighty are afraid**: by reason of breakings they purify themselves.

26. **The sword** of him **that layeth at him cannot hold: the spear, the dart, nor the habergeon**.

27. He esteemeth iron as straw, *and* brass as rotten wood.

28. **The arrow cannot make him flee**: slingstones are turned with him into stubble.

29. **Darts are counted as stubble**: he laugheth at the shaking of a spear.

30. Sharp stones *are* under him: he spreadeth sharp pointed things upon the mire.

31. **He maketh the deep to boil like a pot**: he maketh the sea like a pot of ointment.

32. He maketh a path to shine after him; *one* would think the deep to be hoary.

33. **Upon earth there is not his like**, who is made without fear.

34. He beholdeth all high *things*: **he is a king over all the children of pride**.

CHAPTER 42

1. **Then Job answered the LORD**, and said,

2. **I know that thou canst do every thing, and** *that* **no thought can be withholden from thee**.

3. Who *is* he that hideth counsel without knowledge? therefore have I uttered that I understood not; things too wonderful for me, which I knew not.

4. Hear, I beseech thee, and I will speak: I will demand of thee, and declare thou unto me.

5. **I have heard of thee** by the hearing of the ear: **but now mine eye seeth thee**.

6. **Wherefore I** abhor *myself*, and **repent in dust and ashes**.

7. And it was so, that **after the LORD had**

spoken these words
unto Job, the LORD said
to Eliphaz the Temanite,
My wrath is kindled
against thee, and against
thy two friends: for ye
have not spoken of me
the thing that is right,
as my servant Job hath.
8. Therefore take unto you now
seven bullocks and
seven rams, and go
to my servant Job, and
offer up for yourselves
a burnt offering; and my
servant Job shall pray for
you: for him will I accept:
lest I deal with you *after your* folly,
in that ye have not spoken of me
the thing which is right, like my
servant Job.
9. So Eliphaz the Temanite *and*
Bildad the Shuhite
and Zophar
the Naamathite went, and
did according as the
LORD commanded them:
the LORD also accepted Job.
10 And the LORD turned
the captivity of Job, when
he prayed for his friends:
also the LORD gave
Job twice as much
as he had before.
11. Then came there unto him
all his brethren, and all his
sisters, and all
they that had been

of his acquaintance
before, and did eat
bread with him in his house:
and they
bemoaned him, and
comforted him over all
the evil that the LORD had
brought upon him: every man
also gave him a piece of money, and
every one an earring of gold.
12. So the LORD blessed
the latter end of Job more
than his beginning: for he
had fourteen thousand
sheep, and six thousand
camels, and a thousand yoke of
oxen, and a thousand
she asses.
13. He had also
seven sons and
three daughters.
14. And he called the name
of the first, Jemima; and the
name of the second, Kezia;
and the name of the third,
Keren–happuch.
15. And in all the land were
no women found *so* fair as
the daughters of Job: and
their father gave them inheritance
among their brethren.
16. After this lived Job
an hundred and forty
years, and saw his sons,
and his sons' sons, *even*
four generations.
17. So Job died,
being old and full of days.

THE BOOK OF PSALMS

BACKGROUND INFORMATION

Author: Numerous writers
Date Written: Over
a period of
several years

Number of:
Verses—2,461
Chapters—150
Total Words—43,743
Scan Words—21,796
Scan Words Represent
Approximately 49% of
Total Words

Theme: Songs and
Psalms of Thanksgiving,
Praise, and Prophecies of
the Coming Savior

OUTLINE OF THE PSALMS

I. **Songs of Blessedness, of**
   Falling, and Recovering
   1:1 — 41:13
II. **Songs of** the
   Ruin and Redemption
   of Israel.
   42:1 — 72:20
III. **Songs of the**
   Congregation
   73:1 — 89:50
IV. **Songs of Trials and**
   Protection
   90:1 — 106:48
V. **Songs of Perfection**
   and Praise
   107:1 — 150:6

PSALM 1

1. **Blessed is the man
that walketh not in the
counsel of the ungodly,
nor standeth in the way
of sinners, nor sitteth in
the seat of the scornful.**
2. **But his delight is** in
the law of the LORD; and in his
law doth he meditate day and night.
3. **And he shall be like a
tree planted by** the
rivers of water,
that bringeth forth his
fruit in his season; his leaf
also shall not wither; and
**whatsoever he doeth
shall prosper.**
4. **The ungodly**
are not so: but
**are like the chaff which
the wind driveth away.**
5. **Therefore the ungodly
shall not stand in the
judgment, nor sinners
in the congregation
of the righteous.**
6. **For the LORD
knoweth the** way of the
righteous: but the way of the
ungodly shall perish.

PSALM 2

1. **Why do the heathen
rage, and** the people
imagine a vain thing?
2. **The kings** of the
earth set themselves,
and the
rulers take counsel together,
**against the LORD,
and** against
his anointed, saying,
3. **Let us break
their bands** asunder,
and cast away
their cords from us.
4. **He that sitteth in the
heavens shall laugh:**
the LORD shall have them in derision.
5. **Then shall he speak
unto them in his wrath,**
and vex them in his sore displeasure.

6. **Yet have I set
my king upon** my holy hill of
Zion.
7. I will declare the decree:
the LORD hath said unto me,
**Thou art my Son; this day
have I begotten thee.**
8. **Ask of me, and I shall
give thee the heathen**
for thine inheritance,
**and the uttermost parts
of the earth** *for* thy possession.
9. **Thou shalt break them**
with a rod of iron; thou
shalt dash them in pieces
like a potter's vessel.
10. **Be wise** now therefore, O
ye kings: be instructed,
ye judges of the earth.
11. **Serve the LORD
with fear, and** rejoice with
trembling.
12. **Kiss the Son, lest he
be angry, and ye perish**
from the way, when his wrath is
kindled but a little.
Blessed are all
they that put their
trust in him.

PSALM 3

1. **LORD, how are they
increased that trouble me!**
many *are* they that rise up against me.
2. **Many** *there be* which
say of my soul,
There is no help for him
in God. Selah.
3. **But thou, O LORD, art
a shield** for me; my glory,
**and the lifter up
of mine head.**
4. **I cried unto the
LORD** with my voice,
and he heard me
out of his holy hill. Selah.
5. I laid me down and
slept; I awaked; for
the LORD sustained me.
6. **I will not be afraid of ten
thousands** of people, that have
set *themselves*
against me round about.

7. **Arise, O LORD; save me,** O my God: for **thou hast smitten** all **mine enemies** *upon* the cheek bone; thou hast broken the teeth of the ungodly. 8. **Salvation belongeth unto the LORD**: thy blessing *is* upon thy people. Selah.

PSALM 4

1. **Hear me** when I call, **O God of my righteousness**: thou hast enlarged me *when I was* in distress; **have mercy upon me, and hear my prayer.** 2. **O ye sons of men, how long will ye turn my glory into shame? how long will ye love vanity,** *and* seek after leasing? Selah. 3. But know that **the LORD hath set apart him that is godly for himself: the LORD will hear when I call** unto him. 4. **Stand in awe, and sin not**: commune with your own heart upon your bed, and be still. Selah. 5. **Offer the sacrifices of righteousness, and** put your **trust in the LORD.** 6. *There be* **many** that **say, Who will shew us** *any* **good? LORD, lift** thou **up the light of thy countenance** upon us. 7. **Thou hast put gladness in my heart,** more than in the time *that* their corn and their wine increased. 8. **I will** both **lay** me **down in peace,** and sleep: **for thou, LORD,** only **makest me dwell in safety.**

PSALM 5

1. **Give ear to my words, O LORD,** consider my meditation. 2. Hearken unto the voice of my cry,

my King, and my God: **for unto thee will I pray.** 3. **My voice shalt thou hear in the morning,** O LORD; in the morning will I direct *my prayer* unto thee, and will look up. 4. **For thou art not a God that hath pleasure in wickedness**: neither shall evil dwell with thee. 5. **The foolish shall not stand in thy sight**: thou hatest all workers of iniquity. 6. **Thou shalt destroy them that speak leasing:** the LORD will abhor the bloody and deceitful man. 7. **But** as for me, **I will come into** thy house in **the multitude of thy mercy: and in** thy **fear will I worship** toward thy holy temple. 8. **Lead me, O LORD, in thy righteousness because of mine enemies;** make thy way straight before my face. 9. **For there is no faithfulness in their mouth;** their inward part *is* very wickedness; their throat *is* an open sepulchre; **they flatter with their tongue.** 10. **Destroy** thou **them,** O God; **let them fall by their own counsels;** cast them out in the multitude of their transgressions; **for they have rebelled against thee.** 11. **But let all those that put their trust in thee rejoice:** let them ever shout for joy, **because thou defendest them:** let them also that love thy name be joyful in thee. 12. **For thou,** LORD, **wilt bless the righteous;** with favour wilt thou compass him as *with* a shield.

PSALM 6

■ 1. **O LORD, rebuke**
■ **me not in** thine
■ **anger**, neither chasten
me in thy hot displeasure.
■ 2. **Have mercy**
■ **upon me,** O LORD;
■ **for I am weak**: O LORD,
■ **heal me; for my**
■ **bones are vexed.**
■ 3. **My soul is also** sore
■ **vexed**: but thou,
■ **O LORD, how long?**
■ 4. **Return,** O LORD,
■ **deliver my soul:**
oh save me for thy mercies' sake.
■ 5. **For in death there**
■ **is no remembrance**
■ **of thee:** in the grave
■ **who shall give**
■ **thee thanks?**
■ 6. **I am weary** with my groaning;
■ **all the night make I my**
■ **bed to swim**; I water my couch
■ **with my tears.**
■ 7. **Mine eye is**
■ **consumed because**
■ **of grief**; it waxeth old
because of all mine enemies.
■ 8. **Depart** from me, all
■ **ye workers of iniquity;**
■ **for the LORD hath**
■ **heard** the voice of
■ **my weeping.**
9. The LORD hath heard
my supplication;
■ **the LORD will receive**
■ **my prayer.**
■ 10. **Let all mine enemies**
■ **be** ashamed and sore
■ **vexed**: let them return
■ **and** be
■ **ashamed** suddenly.

PSALM 7

■ 1. **O LORD** my God,
■ **in thee do I put my**
■ **trust: save me** from
all them that persecute me,
■ **and deliver me:**
■ 2. **Lest he tear my**
■ **soul** like a lion, rending it
■ **in pieces,**

while *there is* none to deliver.
■ 3. **O LORD** my God,
If I have done this;
■ **if there be iniquity**
■ **in my hands;**
■ 4. **If I have rewarded evil**
■ **unto him that was at peace**
■ **with me**; (yea, I have delivered him
that without cause is mine enemy:)
■ 5. **Let the enemy persecute**
■ **my soul**, and take *it*; yea,
■ **let him tread down my life**
upon the earth, and lay mine
honour in the dust. Selah.
■ 6. **Arise, O LORD, in**
■ **thine anger,** lift up thyself
■ **because of** the rage of
■ **mine enemies**: and
■ **awake** for me
■ **to the judgment** *that*
■ **thou hast commanded.**
7. So shall the congregation of the
people compass thee about: for their
sakes therefore return thou on high.
8. The LORD shall judge the people:
■ **judge me, O LORD,**
■ **according to my**
■ **righteousness**, and according
to mine integrity *that is* in me.
■ 9. **Oh let** the
■ **wickedness** of the wicked
■ **come to an end; but**
■ **establish the just:**
■ **for** the righteous
■ **God trieth the**
■ **hearts and reins.**
■ 10. **My defence is of God,**
which saveth the upright in heart.
■ 11. **God judgeth** the righteous,
■ **and** God
■ **is angry with the**
■ **wicked** every day.
■ 12. **If he turn not, he will**
■ **whet his sword**; he hath
bent his bow, and made it ready.
■ 13. **He hath** also
■ **prepared** for him
■ **the instruments of**
■ **death;** he ordaineth his
arrows against the persecutors.
■ 14. **Behold, he travaileth**
■ **with iniquity**, and hath
conceived mischief,

and brought forth falsehood.

15. He made a pit, and digged it, and *is* fallen into the ditch *which* he made.

16. **His mischief** shall return upon his own head, **and his violent dealing shall come down upon his own pate.**

17. **I will praise the LORD according to his righteousness:** and will sing praise to the name of the LORD most high.

PSALM 8

1. **O LORD**, our Lord, **how excellent is thy name** in all the earth! who hast set thy glory above the heavens.

2. **Out of the mouth of babes** and sucklings **hast thou ordained strength** because of thine enemies, **that thou mightest still the enemy** and the avenger.

3. **When I consider** thy heavens, **the work of thy fingers, the moon and the stars**, which thou hast ordained;

4. **What is man, that thou art mindful of him? and** the son of man, **that thou visitest him?**

5. **For thou** hast **made him a little lower than the angels, and** hast **crowned him with glory** and honour.

6. **Thou madest him to have dominion over** the works of thy hands; thou hast put **all things** under his feet:

7. **All** sheep and oxen, yea, and **the beasts of the field;**

8. **The fowl of the air, and the fish** of the sea, **and whatsoever passeth through** the paths of **the seas.**

9. **O LORD** our Lord, **how excellent is thy name** in all the earth!

PSALM 9

1. **I will praise thee,** O LORD, **with my whole heart**; I will shew forth all thy marvellous works.

2. **I will** be glad and **rejoice in thee:** I will sing praise to thy name, O thou most High.

3. **When mine enemies are turned back, they** shall fall and **perish at thy presence.**

4. **For thou hast maintained** my right and **my cause**; thou satest in the throne judging right.

5. **Thou hast rebuked the heathen**, thou hast destroyed the wicked, thou hast put out their name for ever and ever.

6. **O thou enemy**, destructions are come to a perpetual end: and **thou hast destroyed cities;** their memorial is perished with them.

7. **But the LORD shall endure for ever**: he hath prepared his throne for judgment.

8. **And he shall judge the world** in righteousness, he shall minister judgment to the people in uprightness.

9. **The LORD** also **will be a refuge for the oppressed,** a refuge in times of trouble.

10. And they that know thy name will put their trust in thee: for **thou, LORD, hast not forsaken them that seek thee.**

11. **Sing praises to the LORD**, which dwelleth in Zion: declare among the people his doings.

12. When he maketh inquisition for blood, he remembereth them: **he forgetteth not the cry of the humble.**

13. **Have mercy upon me, O LORD; consider my trouble which I suffer of them that hate me**, thou that liftest me up from the gates of death:

14. That I may shew forth all thy praise in the gates of the daughter of Zion:

PSALM 10

I will rejoice in thy salvation.

15. The heathen are sunk down in the pit that they made: in the net which they hid is their own foot taken.

16. The LORD is known by the judgment which he executeth: the wicked is snared in the work of his own hands. Higgaion. Selah.

17. The wicked shall be turned into hell, and all the nations that forget God.

18. For the needy shall not alway be forgotten: the expectation of the poor shall not perish for ever.

19. Arise, O LORD; let not man prevail: let the heathen be judged in thy sight.

20. Put them in fear, O LORD: that the nations may know themselves to be but men. Selah.

PSALM 10

1. Why standest thou afar off, O LORD? why hidest thou thyself in times of trouble?

2. The wicked in his pride doth persecute the poor: let them be taken in the devices that they have imagined.

3. For the wicked boasteth of his heart's desire, and blesseth the covetous, whom the LORD abhorreth.

4. The wicked, through the pride of his countenance, will not seek after God: God is not in all his thoughts.

5. His ways are always grievous; thy judgments are far above out of his sight: as for all his enemies, he puffeth at them.

6. He hath said in his heart, I shall not be moved: for I shall never be in adversity.

7. His mouth is full of cursing and deceit and fraud: under his tongue is mischief and vanity.

8. He sitteth in the lurking places of the villages: in the secret places doth he murder the innocent: his eyes are privily set against the poor.

9. He lieth in wait secretly as a lion in his den: he lieth in wait to catch the poor: he doth catch the poor, when he draweth him into his net.

10. He croucheth, and humbleth himself, that the poor may fall by his strong ones.

11. He hath said in his heart, God hath forgotten: he hideth his face; he will never see it.

12. Arise, O LORD; O God, lift up thine hand: forget not the humble.

13. Wherefore doth the wicked contemn God? he hath said in his heart, Thou wilt not require it.

14. Thou hast seen it; for thou beholdest mischief and spite, to requite it with thy hand: the poor committeth himself unto thee; thou art the helper of the fatherless.

15. Break thou the arm of the wicked and the evil man: seek out his wickedness till thou find none.

16. The LORD is King for ever and ever: the heathen are perished out of his land.

17. LORD, thou hast heard the desire of the humble: thou wilt prepare their heart, thou wilt cause thine ear to hear:

18. To judge the fatherless and the oppressed, that the man of the earth may no more oppress.

PSALM 11

1. **In the LORD put I my trust: how say ye** to my soul, **Flee as a bird** to your mountain? 2. **For, lo, the wicked** bend *their* bow, they **make ready their arrow** upon the string, that they may privily shoot at the upright in heart. 3. **If the foundations be destroyed, what can the righteous do?** 4. **The LORD is in his holy temple,** the LORD'S throne *is* in heaven: **his eyes behold,** his eyelids try, **the children of men.** 5. **The LORD trieth the righteous: but the wicked** and him that loveth violence **his soul hateth.** 6. **Upon the wicked he shall rain snares,** fire and brimstone, and an horrible tempest: **this shall be** the portion of **their cup.** 7. **For the righteous LORD loveth righteousness;** his countenance doth behold the upright.

PSALM 12

1. **Help, LORD;** for the godly man ceaseth; **for the faithful fail** from **among the children of men.** 2. **They speak vanity** every one with his neighbour: **with** flattering lips *and* with **a double heart** do they speak. 3. **The LORD shall cut off** all **flattering lips,** *and* the tongue that speaketh proud things: 4. **Who have said, With our tongue will we prevail;** our lips *are* our own: **who is lord over us?** 5. **For the oppression of the poor,** for the sighing of the needy, **now will I arise, saith the LORD; I will set him in safety** from him that puffeth at him. 6. **The words of the LORD are pure** words: **as silver tried in a furnace** of earth, purified seven times. 7. Thou shalt keep them, **O LORD, thou shalt preserve them** from this generation for ever. 8. **The wicked walk on every side, when the vilest** men **are exalted.**

PSALM 13

1. **How long wilt thou forget me, O LORD?** for ever? how long wilt thou hide thy face from me? 2. **How long shall I take counsel** in my soul, **having sorrow in my heart** daily? **how long shall mine enemy be exalted over me?** 3. Consider *and* **hear me, O LORD** my God: **lighten mine eyes, lest I sleep the sleep of death;** 4. **Lest mine enemy say, I have prevailed against him;** *and* those that trouble me rejoice when I am moved. 5. **But I have trusted** in **thy mercy;** my heart shall rejoice in thy salvation. 6. **I will sing unto the LORD, because he hath dealt bountifully with me.**

PSALM 14

1. **The fool hath said in his heart, There is no God. They are corrupt,** they have done abominable works, *there is* none that doeth good. 2. **The LORD looked down** from heaven upon the children of men, **to see if there were any that did understand, and seek God.** 3. **They are all** gone aside, they are *all* together **become filthy: there is** none that doeth good,

■ no, not one.
■ 4. Have all the workers of
■ iniquity no knowledge?
who eat up my people *as* they eat
bread, and call not upon the LORD.
5. There were they in great fear:
for God *is* in the generation of
the righteous.
■ 6. Ye have shamed the
■ counsel of the poor,
because the LORD *is* his refuge.
■ 7. Oh that the salvation
■ of Israel were come out
■ of Zion! when the LORD
■ bringeth back the captivity
■ of his people, Jacob shall
rejoice, *and* Israel shall be glad.

PSALM 15

■ 1. LORD, who shall abide
■ in thy tabernacle?
who shall dwell in thy holy hill?
■ 2. He that walketh
■ uprightly, and worketh
righteousness, and speaketh
the truth in his heart.
■ 3. He that backbiteth
■ not with his tongue,
■ nor doeth evil to his
■ neighbour, nor taketh up a
reproach against his neighbour.
■ 4. In whose eyes a vile
■ person is contemned;
but he honoureth them that fear
the LORD. *He that* sweareth to
his own hurt, and changeth not.
■ 5. He that putteth not out
■ his money to usury, nor
■ taketh reward against
■ the innocent. He
that doeth these *things*
■ shall never be moved.

PSALM 16

■ 1. Preserve me, O God:
■ for in thee do I put my
■ trust.
■ 2. O my soul, thou
■ hast said unto the LORD,
■ Thou art my Lord:
■ my goodness extendeth
■ not to thee;
■ 3. But to the saints that *are* in

the earth, and *to* the excellent,
■ in whom is all my delight.
■ 4. Their sorrows shall be
■ multiplied that hasten after
■ another god: their drink offerings
of blood will I not offer, nor take up
their names into my lips.
■ 5. The LORD is the portion
■ of mine inheritance and of
my cup: thou maintainest my lot.
6. The lines are fallen unto me in
pleasant *places;*
■ yea, I have a
■ goodly heritage.
■ 7. I will bless the LORD, who
■ hath given me counsel:
my reins also instruct
me in the night seasons.
■ 8. I have set the LORD
■ always before me:
because *he is* at my right
hand, I shall not be moved.
■ 9. Therefore my heart
■ is glad, and my glory rejoiceth:
my flesh also shall rest in hope.
■ 10. For thou wilt not leave
■ my soul in hell; neither wilt
■ thou suffer thine Holy One
■ to see corruption.
■ 11. Thou wilt shew
■ me the path of life:
in thy presence *is* fulness of joy;
■ at thy right hand there are
■ pleasures for evermore.

PSALM 17

■ 1. Hear the right, O LORD,
attend unto my cry,
■ give ear unto my prayer,
that goeth not out of feigned lips.
2. Let my sentence come forth from
thy presence; let thine eyes behold
the things that are equal.
■ 3. Thou hast proved
■ mine heart; thou hast
■ visited me in the night;
■ thou hast tried me,
and shalt find nothing;
■ I am purposed that my
■ mouth shall not transgress.
4. Concerning the works of
men, by the word of thy lips
■ I have kept me from the

■ paths of the destroyer.

5. Hold up my goings in thy paths, *that* my footsteps slip not.

■ 6. **I have called upon**
■ **thee,** for thou wilt hear me,
■ **O God: incline thine ear**
■ **unto me,** *and hear* my speech.
■ 7. **Shew thy** marvellous
■ **lovingkindness,** O thou that savest by thy right hand them which put their trust *in thee* from those that rise up *against them*.
■ 8. **Keep me as the apple**
■ **of the eye, hide me** under the shadow of thy wings,
■ 9. **From the wicked that**
■ **oppress me,** *from* my deadly enemies, *who* compass me about.
■ 10. **They are enclosed in**
■ **their own fat:** with their mouth
■ **they speak proudly.**

11. They have now compassed us in our steps: they have set their eyes bowing down to the earth;

12. Like as a lion *that* is greedy of his prey, and as it were a young lion lurking in secret places.

■ 13. **Arise, O LORD,**
disappoint him, cast him down:
■ **deliver my soul from**
■ **the wicked,** *which is* thy sword:

14. From men *which are* thy hand, O LORD, from men of the world, *which have* their portion in *this* life, and whose belly thou fillest with thy hid *treasure:* they are full of children, and leave the rest of their *substance* to their babes.

■ 15. **As for me, I will behold**
■ **thy face in righteousness:**
■ **I shall be satisfied,**
when I awake,
■ **with thy likeness.**

PSALM 18

■ 1. **I will love thee,**
■ **O LORD, my strength.**
■ 2. **The LORD is my rock,**
■ **and my fortress,** and my deliverer; my God, my strength,
■ **in whom I will trust;**
my buckler, and the horn of my salvation, *and* my high tower.

■ 3. **I will call upon the**
■ **LORD, who is worthy**
■ **to be praised:** so shall I be saved from mine enemies.
■ 4. **The sorrows of death**
■ **compassed me,** and
■ **the floods of ungodly**
■ **men made me afraid.**

5. The sorrows of hell compassed me about: the snares of death prevented me.

6. In my distress
■ **I called upon the LORD,**
and cried unto my God:
■ **he heard my voice**
out of his temple, and my cry came before him, *even* into his ears.

■ 7. **Then the earth**
■ **shook** and trembled;
■ **the foundations** also of the hills
■ **moved** and were shaken, because he was wroth.
■ 8. **There went** up a
smoke out of his nostrils, and
■ **fire out of his**
■ **mouth** devoured:
coals were kindled by it.
■ 9. **He** bowed the heavens also, and
■ **came down:** and darkness
was under his feet.
■ 10. **And he rode**
■ **upon a cherub,**
■ **and did fly:** yea, he did fly
■ **upon** the wings of
■ **the wind.**
■ 11. **He made darkness**
■ **his secret place;** his pavilion round about him *were* dark waters *and* thick clouds of the skies.

12. At the brightness *that was* before him his thick clouds passed, hail *stones* and coals of fire.

■ 13. **The LORD** also
■ **thundered in the heavens,**
and the Highest gave his voice; hail *stones* and coals of fire.
■ 14. **Yea, he sent out his**
■ **arrows,** and scattered them;
■ **and** he
■ **shot** out
■ **lightnings,** and discomfited them.

15. **Then** the channels of waters were seen, and

the foundations of the
world were discovered
at thy rebuke, O LORD, at the
blast of the breath of thy nostrils.
16. He sent from above,
he took me, he
drew me out
of many waters.
17. He delivered me
from my strong enemy, and from
them which hated me: for they
were too strong for me.
18. They prevented me in
the day of my calamity: but
the LORD was my stay.
19. He brought me forth also into
a large place; he delivered me,
because he delighted in me.
20. The LORD rewarded
me according to my
righteousness; according
to the cleanness of my hands
hath he recompensed me.
21. For I have kept the ways
of the LORD, and have not
wickedly departed from my God.
22. For all his judgments
were before me, and
I did not put away
his statutes from me.
23. I was also upright
before him, and I kept
myself from mine iniquity.
24. Therefore hath the LORD
recompensed me according
to my righteousness, according
to the cleanness of my hands
in his eyesight.
25. With the merciful thou
wilt shew thyself merciful;
with an upright man thou
wilt shew thyself upright;
26. With the pure thou wilt
shew thyself pure; and with the
froward thou wilt shew thyself froward.
27. For thou wilt save
the afflicted people; but
wilt bring down high looks.
28. For thou wilt light my candle:
the LORD my God will enlighten
my darkness.
29. For by thee I have
run through a troop;

and by my God
have I
leaped over a wall.
30. As for God, his way
is perfect: the word of the
LORD is tried:
he is a buckler to all
those that trust in him.
31. For who is God save
the LORD? or who is a
rock save our God?
32. It is God that girdeth me
with strength, and maketh
my way perfect.
33. He maketh my
feet like hinds' feet,
and setteth me upon my high places.
34. He teacheth my hands to war,
so that a bow of steel is broken by
mine arms.
35. Thou hast also given me
the shield of thy salvation:
and thy right hand hath holden me up,
and thy gentleness hath
made me great.
36. Thou hast enlarged my steps
under me, that my feet did not slip.
37. I have pursued mine
enemies, and overtaken
them: neither did I turn again
till they were consumed.
38. I have wounded them that
they were not able to rise:
they are fallen under my feet.
39. For thou hast girded me
with strength unto the battle: thou
hast subdued under me those that
rose up against me.
40. Thou hast also
given me the necks of
mine enemies; that I might
destroy them that hate me.
41. They cried, but there
was none to save them:
even unto the LORD, but he
answered them not.
42. Then did I beat them small as the
dust before the wind: I did cast them
out as the dirt in the streets.
43. Thou hast delivered me
from the strivings of the
people; and thou hast
made me the head of

the heathen: a people *whom* I have not known shall serve me.

44. As soon as they hear of me, they shall obey me: the strangers shall submit themselves unto me.

45. The strangers shall fade away, and be afraid out of their close places.

46. **The LORD liveth; and blessed be my rock; and let the God of my salvation be exalted.**

47. *It is* God that avengeth me, and subdueth the people under me.

48. **He delivereth me from mine enemies:** yea, thou liftest me up above those that rise up against me: thou hast delivered me from the violent man.

49. **Therefore will I give thanks** unto thee, **O LORD,** among the heathen, **and sing praises unto thy name.**

50. **Great deliverance giveth he** to his king; and sheweth mercy to his anointed, to David, and **to his seed for evermore.**

PSALM 19

1. **The heavens declare the glory of God; and the firmament sheweth his handiwork.**

2. **Day unto day uttereth speech, and night unto night sheweth knowledge.**

3. **There is no** speech nor **language, where their voice is not heard.**

4. Their line is gone out through all the earth, and their words to the end of the world. **In them hath he set a tabernacle for the sun,**

5. **Which is as a bridegroom** coming out of his chamber, **and rejoiceth as a strong man to run a race.**

6. **His going forth is from the end of the heaven, and his** circuit unto the ends of it: and there is nothing hid from the heat thereof.

7. **The law of the LORD is perfect, converting the soul: the testimony of the LORD is sure, making wise the simple.**

8. **The statutes of the LORD are right, rejoicing the heart: the commandment of the LORD is pure, enlightening the eyes.**

9. **The fear of the LORD is clean, enduring for ever: the judgments of the LORD are true** *and* righteous altogether.

10. **More to be desired are they than gold,** yea, than much fine gold: **sweeter also than honey** and the honeycomb.

11. Moreover by them is thy servant warned: **and in keeping** of **them there is great reward.**

12. **Who can understand his errors?** cleanse thou me from secret *faults.*

13. **Keep back thy servant also from presumptuous sins;** let them not have dominion over me: **then shall I be upright,** and I shall be innocent from the great transgression.

14. **Let the words of my mouth, and the meditation of my heart, be acceptable in thy sight, O LORD, my strength, and** my **redeemer.**

PSALM 20

1. **The LORD hear thee in the day of trouble;** the name of the God of Jacob defend thee;

2. **Send thee help** from the sanctuary, **and strengthen thee** out of Zion;

3. **Remember all thy offerings,** and accept thy

burnt sacrifice; Selah.

■ 4. **Grant thee according**
■ **to thine own heart,**
and fulfil all thy counsel.

■ 5. **We will rejoice in thy**
■ **salvation,** and in the name of
our God we will set up *our* banners:
the LORD fulfil all thy petitions.

6. Now know I that
the LORD saveth
■ **his anointed;** he will hear him
from his holy heaven with the saving
strength of his right hand.

■ 7. **Some trust in chariots,**
■ **and some in horses: but we**
■ **will remember** the name of
■ **the LORD** our God.

■ 8. **They are brought**
■ **down** and fallen:
■ **but we are risen,**
and stand upright.

■ 9. **Save, LORD: let the king**
■ **hear us when we call.**

PSALM 21

■ 1. **The king shall joy in thy**
■ **strength, O LORD;** and in thy
salvation how greatly shall he rejoice!

■ 2. **Thou hast given him**
■ **his heart's desire,** and
hast not withholden the request
of his lips. Selah.

■ 3. **For thou preventest**
■ **him with** the
■ **blessings**
of goodness: thou settest a crown
of pure gold on his head.

■ 4. **He asked life of thee,**
■ **and thou gavest it him,** *even*
length of days for ever and ever.

■ 5. **His glory is great in thy**
■ **salvation:** honour and majesty
hast thou laid upon him.

■ 6. **For thou hast made him**
■ **most blessed for ever:**
thou hast made him exceeding
glad with thy countenance.

■ 7. **For the king trusteth in the**
■ **LORD, and through the**
■ **mercy of the most High he**
■ **shall not be moved.**

■ 8. **Thine hand shall find out**
■ **all thine enemies:** thy right

hand shall find out those
that hate thee.

■ 9. **Thou shalt** make them as a
fiery oven in the time of thine anger:
the LORD shall
■ **swallow them up** in his wrath,
and the fire shall devour them.

■ 10. **Their fruit shalt thou**
■ **destroy** from the earth,
■ **and their seed**
from among the children of men.

■ 11. **For they intended evil**
■ **against thee:** they imagined a
mischievous device, *which* they are
not able *to perform.*

12. Therefore shalt thou make them
turn their back, *when* thou shalt make
ready *thine arrows* upon thy strings
against the face of them.

■ 13. **Be thou exalted, LORD,** in
thine own strength:
■ **so will we sing and**
■ **praise thy power.**

PSALM 22

■ 1. **My God, my God,**
■ **why hast thou**
■ **forsaken me?**
why art thou so far from helping me,
and from the words of my roaring?

2. O my God,
■ **I cry in the day time, but**
■ **thou hearest not;** and in the
night season, and am not silent.

■ 3. **But thou art holy,** *O thou* that
inhabitest the praises of Israel.

■ 4. **Our fathers trusted**
■ **in thee:** they trusted, and
thou didst deliver them.

■ 5. **They cried unto thee, and**
■ **were delivered:** they trusted in
thee, and were not confounded.

■ 6. **But I am a worm,** and
no man; a reproach of men, and
■ **despised of the people.**

■ 7. **All they that see me**
■ **laugh** me to scorn: they shoot out
the lip, they shake the head,
■ **saying,**

■ 8. **He trusted on the LORD**
that he would deliver him:
■ **let him deliver him, seeing**
■ **he delighted in him.**

9. **But thou art he that took me out of the womb:** thou didst make me hope *when I was* upon my mother's breasts.

10. **I was cast upon thee from the womb:** thou *art* my God from my mother's belly.

11. **Be not far from me; for trouble is near;** for *there is* none to help.

12. **Many** bulls have compassed me: strong *bulls* of Bashan **have beset me** round.

13. They gaped upon me *with* their mouths, **as** a ravening and **a roaring lion.**

14. **I am poured out like water,** and all my bones are out of joint: **my heart is like wax;** it is melted in the midst of my bowels.

15. **My strength is dried up like a potsherd;** and **my tongue cleaveth to my jaws;** and thou hast brought me into the dust of death.

16. **For dogs have compassed me:** the assembly of the wicked have enclosed me: **they pierced my hands and** my **feet.**

17. I may tell all my bones: they look *and* stare upon me.

18. **They part my garments** among them, **and cast lots upon my vesture.**

19. But be not thou far from me, O LORD: O my strength, haste thee to help me.

20. **Deliver my soul** from the sword; my darling from the power of the dog.

21. **Save me from the lion's mouth:** for thou hast heard me from the horns of the unicorns.

22. **I will declare thy name** unto my brethren: **in the midst of the congregation will I praise thee.**

23. **Ye that fear the LORD, praise him;** all ye the seed of Jacob, glorify him; and fear him, all ye the seed of Israel.

24. **For he hath not despised** nor abhorred the affliction of **the afflicted; neither hath he hid his face** from him; but when he cried unto him, he heard.

25. **My praise shall be of thee in the great congregation:** I will pay my vows before them that fear him.

26. **The meek shall eat and be satisfied:** they shall praise the LORD that seek him: your heart shall live for ever.

27. **All the ends of the world shall remember and turn unto the LORD: and all the** kindreds of the **nations shall worship** before **thee.**

28. For the kingdom *is* the LORD'S: and he *is* the governor among the nations.

29. **All they that be fat** upon earth **shall eat and worship: all they that go down to the dust shall bow before him:** and none can keep alive his own soul.

30. A seed shall serve him; it shall be accounted to the Lord for a generation.

31. **They shall come, and** shall **declare his righteousness unto a people that shall be born,** that he hath done *this*.

PSALM 23

1. **The LORD is my shepherd; I shall not want.**

2. **He maketh me to lie down in green pastures: he leadeth me beside the still waters.**

3. **He restoreth my soul: he leadeth me in the paths of righteousness for his**

name's sake.

4. Yea, though I walk through the valley of the shadow of death, I will fear no evil: for thou art with me; thy rod and thy staff they comfort me.

5. Thou preparest a table before me in the presence of mine enemies: thou anointest my head with oil; my cup runneth over.

6. Surely goodness and mercy shall follow me all the days of my life: and I will dwell in the house of the LORD for ever.

PSALM 24

1. The earth is the LORD'S, and the fulness thereof; the world, and they that dwell therein.

2. For he hath founded it upon the seas, and established it upon the floods.

3. Who shall ascend into the hill of the LORD? or who shall stand in his holy place?

4. He that hath clean hands, and a pure heart; who hath not lifted up his soul unto vanity, nor sworn deceitfully.

5. He shall receive the blessing from the LORD, and righteousness from the God of his salvation.

6. This is the generation of them that seek him, that seek thy face, O Jacob. Selah.

7. Lift up your heads, O ye gates; and be ye lift up, ye everlasting doors;

and the King of glory shall come in.

8. Who is this King of glory? The LORD strong and mighty, the LORD mighty in battle.

9. Lift up your heads, O ye gates; even lift them up, ye everlasting doors;

and the King of glory shall come in.

10. Who is this King of glory?

The LORD of hosts, he is the King of glory. Selah.

PSALM 25

1. Unto thee, O LORD, do I lift up my soul.

2. O my God, I trust in thee: let me not be ashamed, let not mine enemies triumph over me.

3. Yea, let none that wait on thee be ashamed: let them be ashamed which transgress without cause.

4. Shew me thy ways, O LORD; teach me thy paths.

5. Lead me in thy truth, and teach me: for thou art the God of my salvation; on thee do I wait all the day.

6. Remember, O LORD, thy tender mercies and thy loving kindnesses; for they have been ever of old.

7. Remember not the sins of my youth, nor my transgressions: according to thy mercy remember thou me for thy goodness' sake, O LORD.

8. Good and upright is the LORD: therefore will he teach sinners in the way.

9. The meek will he guide in judgment: and the meek will he teach his way.

10. All the paths of the LORD are mercy and truth unto such as keep his covenant and his testimonies.

11. For thy name's sake, O LORD, pardon mine iniquity; for it is great.

12. What man is he that feareth the LORD? him shall he teach in the way that he shall choose.

13. His soul shall dwell at ease; and his seed shall inherit the earth.

14. The secret of the LORD

■ *is* with them that fear him; and he
■ will shew them
■ his covenant.
■ 15. Mine eyes are ever
■ toward the LORD; for he
shall pluck my feet out of the net.
■ 16. Turn thee
■ unto me,and have mercy uponme;
■ for I am desolate and afflicted.
17. The troubles of my
heart are enlarged:
■ O bring thou me out
■ of my distresses.
18. Look upon mine affliction
and my pain; and
■ forgive all my sins.
■ 19. Consider mine enemies;
■ for they are many; and
■ they hate me with cruel hatred.
20. O keep my soul, and
■ deliver me:
let me not be ashamed;
■ for I put my trust in thee.
■ 21. Let integrity and
■ uprightness preserve
■ me; for I wait on thee.
■ 22. Redeem Israel, O God,
■ out of all his troubles.

PSALM 26

■ 1. Judge me, O LORD; for I
■ have walked in mine
■ integrity: I have trusted also
■ in the LORD; *therefore*
■ I shall not slide.
■ 2. Examine me, O LORD, and
prove me; try my reins and my heart.
■ 3. For thy lovingkindness
■ is before mine eyes: and
I have walked in thy truth.
■ 4. I have not sat with
■ vain persons, neither
will I go in with dissemblers.
5. I have hated the congregation
of evildoers; and will not sit with
■ the wicked.
6. I will wash mine hands in
innocency: so will I compass
thine altar, O LORD:
■ 7. That I may publish with
the voice of thanksgiving, and
■ tell of all thy
■ wondrous works.

■ 8. LORD, I have loved the
■ habitation of thy house,
and the place where thine
honour dwelleth.
■ 9. Gather not my
■ soul with sinners,
nor my life with bloody men:
10. In whose hands is mischief,
and their right hand is full of bribes.
11. But as for me, I will
walk in mine integrity:
■ redeem me, and be
■ merciful unto me.
12. My foot standeth in an
even place: in the congregations
will I bless the LORD.

PSALM 27

■ 1. The LORD is my
■ light and my
■ salvation; whom shall
■ I fear? the LORD is the
■ strength of my life; of
■ whom shall I be afraid?
■ 2. When the wicked, *even*
■ mine enemies and my foes,
■ came upon me
■ to eat up my flesh,
■ they stumbled and
■ fell.
■ 3. Though an host should
■ encamp against me, my
■ heart shall not fear:
though war should rise against me,
■ in this will I be confident.
■ 4. One thing
have I desired of the LORD, that
■ will I seek after; that I
■ may dwell in the house of
■ the LORD all the days of
■ my life, to behold the beauty of the
LORD, and to inquire in his temple.
■ 5. For in the time of trouble
■ he shall hide me in his pavilion:
in the secret of his tabernacle shall
he hide me;
■ he shall set me
■ up upon a rock.
■ 6. And now shall mine
■ head be lifted up above
■ mine enemies round about me:
therefore will I offer in his tabernacle
sacrifices of joy; I will sing, yea, I will

sing praises unto the LORD.

7. Hear, O LORD, **when I cry** with my voice: **have mercy** also upon me, and answer me.

8. **When thou saidst, Seek ye my face; my heart said** unto thee, **Thy face, LORD, will I seek.**

9. Hide not thy face *far* from me; put not thy servant away in anger: thou hast been my help; **leave me not,** neither forsake me, **O God of my salvation.**

10. **When my father and my mother forsake me, then the LORD will take me up.**

11. Teach me thy way, O LORD, and lead me in a plain path, because of mine enemies.

12. **Deliver me not over unto** the will of **mine enemies:** for false witnesses are risen up against me, and such as breathe out cruelty.

13. **I had fainted, unless I had believed to see the goodness of the LORD** in the land of the living.

14. **Wait on the LORD:** be of good courage, **and he shall strengthen thine heart:** wait, I say, on the LORD.

PSALM 28

1. **Unto thee will I cry, O LORD my rock;** be not silent to me: lest, *if* thou be silent to me, I become like them that go down into the pit.

2. **Hear the voice of my supplications,** when I cry unto thee, when I lift up my hands toward thy holy oracle.

3. **Draw me not away with the wicked,** and with the workers of iniquity, **which speak peace** to their neighbours, **but mischief is in their hearts.**

4. Give them according to their deeds, and according to the wickedness of their endeavours: give them after the work of their hands; **render to them their desert.**

5. **Because they regard not the works of the LORD,** nor the operation of his hands, **he shall destroy them,** and not build them up.

6. **Blessed be the LORD, because he hath heard** the voice of **my supplications.**

7. **The LORD is my strength and my shield; my heart trusted in him,** and I am helped: therefore my heart greatly rejoiceth; and with my song will I praise him.

8. **The LORD is** their strength, **and** he *is* **the saving strength of his anointed.**

9. **Save thy people,** and bless thine inheritance: feed them also, **and lift them up** for ever.

PSALM 29

1. **Give unto the LORD, O ye mighty,** give unto the LORD glory and strength.

2. **Give unto the LORD the glory due** unto **his name; worship the LORD in the beauty of holiness.**

3. **The voice of the LORD is upon the waters:** the God of glory thundereth: the LORD *is* upon many waters.

4. **The voice of the LORD is powerful;** the voice of the LORD *is* full of majesty.

5. **The voice of the LORD breaketh the cedars;** yea, the LORD breaketh the cedars of Lebanon.

6. He maketh them also to skip like a calf; Lebanon and Sirion like a young unicorn.

7. The voice of the LORD **divideth the flames of fire.**

8. The voice of the LORD

shaketh the wilderness;
the LORD shaketh the wilderness
of Kadesh.
9. The voice of the LORD
maketh the hinds to
calve, and discovereth the
forests: and in his temple doth
every one speak of *his* glory.
10. The LORD sitteth upon
the flood; yea, the LORD
sitteth King for ever.
11. The LORD will give strength
unto his people; the LORD will
bless his people
with peace.

PSALM 30

1. I will extol thee,
O LORD; for thou hast lifted
me up, and hast not made my
foes to rejoice over me.
2. O LORD my God,
I cried unto thee, and
thou hast healed me.
3. O LORD,
thou hast brought up
my soul from the grave:
thou hast kept me alive, that
I should not go down to
the pit.
4. Sing unto the LORD,
O ye saints
of his, and give thanks at the
remembrance of his holiness.
5. For his anger endureth
but a moment;
in his favour *is* life:
weeping may endure for
a night, but joy cometh
in the morning.
6. And in my prosperity
I said, I shall never
be moved.
7. LORD, by thy favour thou
hast made my mountain to stand
strong: thou didst hide thy face,
and I was troubled.
8. I cried to thee, O
LORD; and unto the LORD
I made supplication.
9. What profit is there in my
blood, when I go down to the pit?
Shall the dust praise thee?

shall it declare thy truth?
10. Hear, O LORD, and
have mercy upon me:
LORD, be thou my helper.
11. Thou hast turned for me
my mourning into dancing:
thou hast put off my sackcloth,
and girded me with gladness;
12. To the end that *my* glory may
sing praise to thee, and not be silent.
O LORD my God, I will give
thanks unto thee for ever.

PSALM 31

1. In thee, O LORD, do I put
my trust; let me never beashamed:
deliver me in thy righteousness.
2. Bow down thine ear to me;
deliver me speedily: be
thou my strong rock,
for an house of defence to save me.
3. For thou art my rock
and my fortress; therefore
for thy name's sake lead me, and
guide me.
4. Pull me out of the net that
they have laid privily for me: for
thou *art* my strength.
5. Into thine hand I commit
my spirit: thou hast redeemed me,
O LORD God of truth.
6. I have hated them that
regard lying vanities:
but I trust in the LORD.
7. I will be glad and rejoice
in thy mercy: for thou hast
considered my trouble;
thou hast known my
soul in adversities;
8. And hast not shut me up
into the hand of the enemy:
thou hast set my feet in a large room.
9. Have mercy upon me,
O LORD, for I am in trouble:
mine eye is consumed with grief,
yea, my soul and my belly.
10. For my life is spent with
grief, and my years with sighing:
my strength faileth because
of mine iniquity, and my bones
are consumed.
11. I was a reproach
among all mine enemies,

PSALM 32

- but especially among
- my neighbours, and a fear
to mine acquaintance: they that
did see me without fled from me.
- 12. I am forgotten as
- a dead man out of mind:
- I am like a broken vessel.
13. For I have heard the slander of
- many:
fear *was* on every side: while they
- took counsel together
- against me, they devised
- to take away
- my life.
- 14. But I trusted in
- thee, O LORD: I said,
- Thou art my God.
15. My times *are* in thy hand: deliver
me from the hand of mine enemies,
and from them that persecute me.
- 16. Make thy face to shine
- upon thy servant: save
- me for thy mercies' sake.
17. Let me not be ashamed, O
LORD; for I have called upon thee: let
the wicked be ashamed, *and* let them
be silent in the grave.
- 18. Let the lying lips be put
- to silence; which speak grievous
things proudly and contemptuously
against the righteous.
- 19. Oh how great is thy
- goodness, which thou hast
laid up for them that fear thee;
- which thou hast wrought
- for them that trust in thee
before the sons of men!
- 20. Thou shalt hide
- them in the secret of
- thy presence from the
- pride of man: thou shalt
keep them secretly in a pavilion
from the strife of tongues.
- 21. Blessed be the LORD:
for he hath shewed me his marvellous
kindness in a strong city.
- 22. For I said in my haste, I
- am cut off from before thine eyes:
- nevertheless thou heardest
the voice of my supplications
- when I cried unto thee.
23. O love the LORD,
all ye his saints: *for*

- the LORD preserveth
- the faithful, and plentifully
rewardeth the proud doer.
- 24. Be of good courage,
and he shall strengthen your heart,
- all ye that hope
- in the LORD.

PSALM 32

- 1. Blessed is he whose
- transgression is forgiven,
whose sin *is* covered.
- 2. Blessed is the man unto
- whom the LORD imputeth
- not iniquity, and in whose
spirit *there is* no guile.
- 3. When I kept silence,
my bones waxed old through
my roaring all the day long.
4. For day and night
- thy hand was heavy upon
- me: my moisture is turned into the
drought of summer. Selah.
- 5. I acknowledge
- my sin unto thee,
- and mine iniquity have I not hid. I
- said, I will confess my
- transgressions unto
- the LORD; and thou
- forgavest the iniquity of
- my sin. Selah.
- 6. For this shall every one
- that is godly pray unto thee
in a time when thou mayest be found:
surely in the floods of great waters
they shall not come nigh unto him.
- 7. Thou art my hiding
- place; thou shalt preserve
- me from trouble; thou shalt
compass me about with songs
of deliverance. Selah.
- 8. I will instruct thee
- and teach thee in
- the way which
- thou shalt go:
I will guide thee with mine eye.
- 9. Be ye not as the
- horse, *or* as the mule,
- which have no
- understanding: whose
- mouth must be held
- in with bit and bridle,
lest they come near unto thee.

10. **Many sorrows shall be to the wicked: but he that trusteth in the LORD, mercy shall compass him** about.

11. Be glad in the LORD, and rejoice, ye righteous: and shout for joy, all *ye that are* upright in heart.

PSALM 33

1. **Rejoice in the LORD, O ye righteous:** *for* praise is comely for the upright.

2. **Praise the LORD with harp:** sing unto him **with the psaltery and an instrument of ten strings.**

3. **Sing** unto him **a new song;** play skilfully with a loud noise.

4. **For the word of the LORD is right;** and all his works *are done* in truth.

5. **He loveth righteousness and judgment:** the earth is full of the goodness of the LORD.

6. **By the word of the LORD were the heavens made;** and all the host of them by the breath of his mouth.

7. He gathereth the waters of the sea together as an heap: he layeth up the depth in storehouses.

8. **Let all the earth fear the LORD:** let all the inhabitants of the world stand in awe of him.

9. **For he spake, and it was done;** he commanded, and it stood fast.

10. The LORD bringeth the counsel of the heathen to nought: **he maketh the devices of the people of none effect.**

11. **The counsel of the LORD standeth for ever,** the thoughts of his heart to all generations.

12. **Blessed is the nation whose God is the LORD;** *and* the people *whom* he hath chosen for his own inheritance.

13. **The LORD looketh** from heaven; he beholdeth all the sons of men.

14. From the place of his habitation he looketh **upon all the inhabitants of the earth.**

15. **He fashioneth their hearts alike; he considereth all their works.**

16. There is no king saved by the multitude of an host: a mighty man is not delivered by much strength.

17. An horse *is* a vain thing for safety: neither shall he deliver *any* by his great strength.

18. **Behold, the eye of the LORD is upon them that fear him,** upon them that hope in his mercy;

19. **To deliver their soul** from death, **and to keep them alive in famine.**

20. **Our soul waiteth for the LORD:** he *is* our help and our shield.

21. **For our heart shall rejoice in him,** because we have **trusted in his** holy **name.**

22. **Let thy mercy, O LORD, be upon us,** according as we hope in thee.

PSALM 34

1. **I will bless the LORD at all times: his praise shall continually be in my mouth.**

2. My soul shall make her boast in the LORD: the humble shall hear *thereof,* and be glad.

3. **O magnify the LORD with me, and** let us **exalt his name** together.

4. **I sought the LORD, and he** heard me, and **delivered me from all my fears.**

5. They looked unto him, and were lightened: and their faces were not ashamed.

6. **This poor man cried, and the LORD heard him, and saved him** out of all his troubles.

7. **The angel of the LORD encampeth** round

about them that fear him, and delivereth them.

8. O taste and see that the LORD is good: blessed *is* the man *that* trusteth in him.

9. O fear the LORD, ye his saints: for *there is* no want to them that fear him.

10. The young lions do lack, and suffer hunger: but they that seek the LORD shall not want any good thing.

11. Come, ye children, hearken unto me: I will teach you the fear of the LORD.

12. What man *is he that* desireth life, *and* loveth *many* days, that he may see good?

13. Keep thy tongue from evil, and thy lips from speaking guile.

14. Depart from evil, and do good; seek peace, and pursue it.

15. The eyes of the LORD *are* upon the righteous, and his ears *are open* unto their cry.

16. The face of the LORD is against them that do evil, to cut off the remembrance of them from the earth.

17. *The righteous* cry, and the LORD heareth, and delivereth them out of all their troubles.

18. The LORD *is* nigh unto them that are of a broken heart; and saveth such as be of a contrite spirit.

19. Many are the afflictions of the righteous: but the LORD delivereth him out of them all.

20. He keepeth all his bones: not one of them is broken.

21. Evil shall slay the wicked: and they that hate the righteous shall be desolate.

22. The LORD redeemeth the soul of his servants: and none of them that trust in him shall be desolate.

PSALM 35

1. Plead my cause, O LORD, with them that strive with me: fight against them that fight against me.

2. Take hold of shield and buckler, and stand up for mine help.

3. Draw out also the spear, and stop *the way* against them that persecute me: say unto my soul, I am thy salvation.

4. Let them be confounded and put to shame that seek after my soul: let them be turned back and brought to confusion that devise my hurt.

5. Let them be as chaff before the wind: and let the angel of the LORD chase them.

6. Let their way be dark and slippery: and let the angel of the LORD persecute them.

7. For without cause have they hid for me their net *in* a pit, *which* without cause they have digged for my soul.

8. Let destruction come upon him at unawares; and let his net that he hath hid catch himself: into that very destruction let him fall.

9. And my soul shall be joyful in the LORD: it shall rejoice in his salvation.

10. All my bones shall say, LORD, who is like unto thee, which deliverest the poor from him that is too strong for him, yea, the poor and the needy from him that spoileth him?

11. False witnesses did rise up; they laid to my charge things that I knew not.

12. They rewarded me evil for good *to* the spoiling of my soul.

13. But as for me, when they were sick, my clothing *was* sackcloth:

I humbled my soul
with fasting; and my prayer
returned into mine own bosom.
14. I behaved myself
as though he had been
my friend or brother: I bowed
down heavily, as one that
mourneth for his mother.
15. But in mine adversity
they rejoiced, and gathered
themselves together: yea, the
abjects gathered themselves
together against me, and I knew it
not; they did tear me, and ceased not:
16. With hypocritical mockers in
feasts, they gnashed upon me
with their teeth.
17. Lord, how long
wilt thou look on?
rescue my soul
from their destructions,
my darling from the lions.
18. I will give thee
thanks in the great congregation:
I will praise thee
among much people.
19. Let not them that are
mine enemies wrongfully
rejoice over me:
neither let them wink with the eye
that hate me without a cause.
20. For they speak
not peace: but they devise
deceitful matters against them that
are quiet in the land.
21. Yea, they opened their mouth
wide against me, and said, Aha,
aha, our eye hath seen it.
22. This thou hast seen,
O LORD: keep not silence:
O Lord, be not far from me.
23. Stir up thyself, and
awake to my judgment, even
unto my cause, my God and my Lord.
24. Judge me, O LORD my God,
according to thy
righteousness;
and let them not rejoice over me.
25. Let them not say in their hearts,
Ah, so would we have it: let them not
say, We have swallowed him up.
26. Let them be ashamed
and brought to confusion together

that rejoice at mine hurt:
let them be clothed with shame
and dishonour that magnify
themselves against me.
27. Let them shout
for joy, and be glad,
that favour my righteous
cause: yea, let them say
continually, Let the LORD be
magnified, which hath pleasure in
the prosperity of his servant.
28. And my tongue shall
speak of thy righteousness and
of thy praise all the day long.

PSALM 36

1. The transgression of the
wicked saith within my
heart, that there is no fear
of God before his eyes.
2. For he flattereth himself
in his own eyes, until his iniquity
be found to be hateful.
3. The words of his
mouth are iniquity and
deceit: he hath left
off to be wise, and to do good.
4. He deviseth mischief upon
his bed; he setteth himself in
a way that is not good;
he abhorreth not evil.
5. Thy mercy,
O LORD, is in the heavens; and thy
faithfulness reacheth unto the clouds.
6. Thy righteousness
is like the great
mountains; thy judgments
are a great deep: O LORD,
thou preservest man and beast.
7. How excellent is thy
lovingkindness, O God!
therefore the children of men put their
trust under the shadow of thy wings.
8. They shall be abundantly satisfied
with the fatness of thy house; and
thou shalt make them drink of
the river of thy pleasures.
9. For with thee is the
fountain of life: in thy
light shall we see light.
10. O continue thy
lovingkindness unto
them that know thee; and thy

righteousness to
- **the upright in heart.**
11. Let not the foot of pride
come against me, and let not
the hand of the wicked remove me.
12. There are
- **the workers of**
- **iniquity** fallen: they
- **are cast down,**
- **and shall not** be able to
- **rise.**

- 1. **Fret not** thyself
- **because of evildoers,**
neither be thou envious against
the workers of iniquity.
- 2. **For they shall** soon
- **be cut down** like the grass,
and wither as the green herb.
- 3. **Trust in the LORD, and do**
- **good;** so shalt thou dwell in the
land, and verily thou shalt be fed.
- 4. **Delight thyself also**
- **in the LORD: and he**
- **shall give thee the**
- **desires of thine heart.**
- 5. **Commit thy way unto**
- **the LORD;** trust also in him; and
- **he shall bring it to pass.**
- 6. **And he shall bring forth**
- **thy righteousness as**
- **the light,** and thy judgment
as the noonday.
- 7. **Rest in the LORD,**
- **and wait patiently**
- **for him: fret not** thyself
- **because of** him who prospereth
in his way, because of
- **the man who bringeth**
- **wicked devices** to pass.
8. Cease from anger,
and forsake wrath: fret not
thyself in any wise to do evil.
- 9. **For evildoers shall be**
- **cut off: but those that**
- **wait upon the LORD, they**
- **shall inherit the earth.**
10. For yet a little while, and the
wicked shall not be: yea, thou shalt
diligently consider his place,
and it shall not be.
11. But the meek shall

inherit the earth; and
shall delight themselves
in the abundance of peace.
- 12. **The wicked plotteth**
- **against the just,** and gnasheth
upon him with his teeth.
- 13. **The LORD shall laugh**
- **at him:** for he seeth that
his day is coming.
- 14. **The wicked have**
- **drawn out the sword,**
and have bent their bow, to
cast down the poor and needy, and
- **to slay such as be of**
- **upright conversation.**
- 15. **Their sword shall enter**
- **into their own heart,** and their
bows shall be broken.
- 16. **A little that a righteous**
- **man hath is better than the**
- **riches of many wicked.**
17. For the arms of the wicked
shall be broken: but the LORD
upholdeth the righteous.
- 18. **The LORD knoweth**
the days of
- **the upright:** and their
inheritance shall be for ever.
- 19. **They shall not be**
- **ashamed** in the evil time:
and in the days of famine
- **they shall be satisfied.**
- 20. **But the wicked shall**
- **perish,** and the enemies of the
LORD shall be as the fat of lambs:
they shall consume; into smoke
shall they consume away.
- 21. **The wicked borroweth,**
- **and payeth not** again:
- **but the righteous**
sheweth mercy, and
- **giveth.**
- 22. **For such as be blessed**
- **of him shall inherit the**
- **earth;** and they that be cursed
of him shall be cut off.
- 23. **The steps of a good**
- **man are ordered by the**
- **LORD:** and he delighteth in his way.
- 24. **Though he fall, he**
- **shall not be** utterly
- **cast down: for the LORD**
- **upholdeth him** with his hand.

25. I have been young, and *now* am old; yet have I not seen the righteous forsaken, nor his seed begging bread. 26. He is ever merciful, and lendeth; and his seed *is* blessed. 27. Depart from evil, and do good; and dwell for evermore. 28. For the LORD loveth judgment, and forsaketh not his saints; they are preserved for ever: but the seed of the wicked shall be cut off. 29. The righteous shall inherit the land, and dwell therein for ever. 30. The mouth of the righteous speaketh wisdom, and his tongue talketh of judgment. 31. The law of his God is in his heart; none of his steps shall slide. 32. The wicked watcheth the righteous, and seeketh to slay him. 33. The LORD will not leave him in his hand, nor condemn him when he is judged. 34. Wait on the LORD, and keep his way, and he shall exalt thee to inherit the land: when the wicked are cut off, thou shalt see *it*. 35. I have seen the wicked in great power, and spreading himself like a green bay tree. 36. Yet he passed away, and, lo, he *was* not: yea, I sought him, but he could not be found. 37. Mark the perfect man, and behold the upright: for the end of that man is peace. 38. But the transgressors shall be destroyed together: the end of the wicked shall be cut off. 39. But the salvation of the righteous is of the LORD: he is their strength in the time of trouble. 40. And the LORD shall help them, and deliver them: he shall deliver them from the wicked, and save them,

because they trust in him.

PSALM 38

1. O LORD, rebuke me not in thy wrath: neither chasten me in thy hot displeasure. 2. For thine arrows stick fast in me, and thy hand presseth me sore. 3. *There is* no soundness in my flesh because of thine anger; neither is there any rest in my bones because of my sin. 4. For mine iniquities are gone over mine head: as an heavy burden they are too heavy for me. 5. My wounds stink *and* are corrupt because of my foolishness. 6. I am troubled; I am bowed down greatly; I go mourning all the day long. 7. For my loins are filled with a loathsome *disease:* and *there is* no soundness in my flesh. 8. I am feeble and sore broken: I have roared by reason of the disquietness of my heart. 9. Lord, all my desire is before thee; and my groaning is not hid from thee. 10. My heart panteth, my strength faileth me: as for the light of mine eyes, it also is gone from me. 11. My lovers and my friends stand aloof from my sore; and my kinsmen stand afar off. 12. They also that seek after my life lay snares for me: and they that seek my hurt speak mischievous things, and imagine deceits all the day long. 13. But I, as a deaf *man,* heard not; and *I was* as a dumb man *that* openeth not his mouth. 14. Thus I was as a man that heareth not, and in whose mouth *are* no reproofs.

15. **For in thee, O LORD, do I hope:** thou wilt hear, O Lord my God.

16. **For I said, Hear me, lest otherwise they should rejoice over me:** when my foot slippeth, they magnify *themselves* against me.

17. **For I am ready to halt,** and my sorrow *is* continually before me.

18. For I will declare mine iniquity; **I will be sorry for my sin.**

19. **But mine enemies** *are* lively, *and* they **are strong:** and **they** that **hate me** wrongfully are multiplied.

20. They also that render evil for good are mine adversaries; **because I follow the thing that good is.**

21. Forsake me not, O LORD: O my God, be not far from me.

22. **Make haste to help me, O LORD my salvation.**

PSALM 39

1. **I said, I will take heed** to my ways, **that I sin not with my tongue: I will keep my mouth with a bridle,** while the wicked is before me.

2. **I was dumb with silence, I held my peace,** *even* from good; and my sorrow was stirred.

3. **My heart was hot** within me, while I was musing the fire burned: **then spake I** with my tongue,

4. **LORD, make me to know** mine end, and the measure of my days, what it *is: that* I may know **how frail I am.**

5. **Behold,** thou hast made **my** days *as* an handbreadth; and mine **age is as nothing before thee: verily every man at his best state is altogether vanity.** Selah.

6. Surely every man walketh in a vain shew: surely they are disquieted in vain: he heapeth up *riches,* and knoweth not who shall gather them.

7. **And now, Lord,** what wait I for? **my hope is in thee.**

8. **Deliver me from** all **my transgressions:** make me not the reproach of the foolish.

9. **I was dumb, I opened not my mouth; because thou didst it.**

10. Remove thy stroke away from me: **I am consumed by the blow of thine hand.**

11. **When thou** with rebukes **dost correct man for iniquity, thou makest his beauty to consume away** like a moth: surely every man *is* vanity. Selah.

12. **Hear my prayer,** O LORD, and give ear unto my cry; hold not thy peace at my tears: **for I am a stranger with thee,** *and* a sojourner, as all my fathers *were.*

13. **O spare me,** that I may recover strength, **before I go hence, and be no more.**

PSALM 40

1. **I waited patiently for the LORD; and he** inclined unto me, and **heard my cry.**

2. **He brought me** up also out of an horrible pit, **out of the miry clay, and set my feet upon a rock,** *and* established my goings.

3. **And he hath put a new song in my mouth, even praise unto our God:** many shall see *it,* and fear, and shall trust in the LORD.

4. **Blessed is that man that maketh the LORD his trust, and respecteth not the proud,** nor such as turn aside to lies.

5. **Many, O LORD** my God, **are thy wonderful works**

which thou hast done, and thy thoughts *which are* to us-ward: they cannot be reckoned up in order unto thee: *if*

I would declare and speak *of* them, they are more than can be numbered. 6. Sacrifice and offering thou didst not desire; mine ears hast thou opened: burnt offering and sin offering hast thou not required. 7. Then said I, Lo, I come: in the volume of the book it is written of me, 8. I delight to do thy will, O my God: yea, thy law is within my heart. 9. I have preached righteousness in the great congregation: lo, I have not refrained my lips, O LORD, thou knowest. 10. I have not hid thy righteousness within my heart;

I have declared thy faithfulness and thy salvation: I have not concealed thy lovingkindness and thy truth from the great congregation. 11. Withhold not thou thy tender mercies from me, O LORD: let thy lovingkindness and thy truth continually preserve me. 12. For innumerable evils have compassed me about: mine iniquities have taken hold upon me, so that I am not able to look up; they are more than the hairs of mine head: therefore my heart faileth me. 13. Be pleased, O LORD, to deliver me: O LORD, make haste to help me. 14. Let them be ashamed and confounded together that seek after my soul to destroy it; let them be driven backward and put to shame that wish me evil. 15. Let them be desolate for a reward of their shame that say

unto me, Aha, aha. 16. Let all those that seek thee rejoice and be glad in thee: let such as love thy salvation say continually, The LORD be magnified. 17. But I am poor and needy; yet the Lord thinketh upon me: thou art my help and my deliverer; make no tarrying, O my God.

PSALM 41

1. Blessed is he that considereth the poor: the LORD will deliver him in time of trouble. 2. The LORD will preserve him, and keep him alive; and he shall be blessed upon the earth: and thou wilt not deliver him unto the will of his enemies. 3. The LORD will strengthen him upon the bed of languishing: thou wilt make all his bed in his sickness. 4. I said, LORD, be merciful unto me: heal my soul; for I have sinned against thee. 5. Mine enemies speak evil of me, When shall he die, and his name perish? 6. And if he come to see *me,* he speaketh vanity: his heart gathereth iniquity to itself; *when* he goeth abroad, he telleth *it.* 7. All that hate me whisper together against me: against me do they devise my hurt. 8. An evil disease, *say they,* cleaveth fast unto him: and *now* that he lieth he shall rise up no more. 9. Yea, mine own familiar friend, in whom I trusted, which did eat of my bread, hath lifted up his heel against me. 10. But thou, O LORD, be merciful unto me, and raise me up, that I may requite them.

11. **By this I know that thou favourest me, because mine enemy doth not triumph** over me. 12. And as for me, thou upholdest me in mine integrity, and settest me before thy face for ever. 13. **Blessed be the LORD God of Israel** from everlasting, and to everlasting. **Amen,** and Amen.

PSALM 42

1. **As the hart panteth after the water brooks, so panteth my soul after thee, O God.** 2. **My soul thirsteth for** God, **for the living God:** when shall I come and appear before God? 3. **My tears have been my meat day and night,** while **they continually say** unto me, **Where is thy God?** 4. When I remember these *things,* I pour out my soul in me: for **I had gone with the multitude,** I went with them **to the house of God, with** the voice of **joy and praise,** with a multitude that kept holyday. 5. **Why art thou cast down, O my soul?** and *why* art thou disquieted in me? **hope thou in God:** for I shall yet praise him *for* the help of his countenance. 6. O my God, my soul is cast down within me: therefore will I remember thee from the land of Jordan, and of the Hermonites, from the hill Mizar. 7. **Deep calleth unto deep** at the noise of thy waterspouts: **all thy waves and thy billows are gone over me.** 8. **Yet** the LORD will command his lovingkindness in the day time, and **in the night his song shall be with me,** *and* my prayer unto the God of my life. 9. **I will say unto God my rock, Why hast thou forgotten me?** why go I mourning because of the oppression of the enemy? 10. *As* with a sword in my bones, mine enemies reproach me; while they say daily unto me, Where *is* thy God? 11. **Why art thou cast down, O my soul?** and why art thou disquieted within me? **hope thou in God: for I shall yet praise him,** *who is* the health of my countenance, and my God.

PSALM 43

1. **Judge me, O God, and plead my cause against an ungodly nation:** O deliver me from the deceitful and unjust man. 2. **For thou art the God of my strength: why dost thou cast me off?** why go I mourning because of the oppression of the enemy? 3. **O send out thy light and** thy truth: let them **lead me;** let them bring me **unto thy holy hill,** and to thy tabernacles. 4. **Then will I go unto the altar of God,** unto God my exceeding joy: yea, **upon the harp will I praise thee,** O God my God. 5. Why art thou cast down, O my soul? and why art thou disquieted within me? **hope in God: for I shall yet praise him,** *who is* the health of my countenance, and my God.

PSALM 44

1. We have heard with our ears, **O God, our fathers have told us, what work thou didst in** their days, in the **times of old.** 2. **How thou didst drive out the heathen** with thy hand, **and** plantedst them; *how* thou **didst afflict the people, and cast them out.** 3. **For they got** not

the land in possession
by their own sword, neither
did their own arm save them: but
thy right hand, and thine
arm, and the light of thy
countenance, because thou
hadst a favour unto them.

4. Thou art my King, O God:
command deliverances for Jacob.

5. Through thee will we push
down our enemies: through
thy name will we tread them under
that rise up against us.

6. For I will not trust in
my bow, neither shall
my sword save me.

7. But thou hast saved us from
our enemies, and hast put them
to shame that hated us.

8. In God we boast
all the day long,
and praise thy
name for ever. Selah.

9. But thou hast cast off,
and put us to shame; and
goest not forth
with our armies.

10. Thou makest us to turn back
from the enemy: and they which
hate us spoil for themselves.

11. Thou hast given us like
sheep appointed for meat; and hast
scattered us among
the heathen.

12. Thou sellest thy people for
nought, and dost not increase
thy wealth by their price.

13. Thou makest us
a reproach to our
neighbours, a scorn and
a derision to them that are
round about us.

14. Thou makest us a
byword among the
heathen, a shaking of the
head among the people.

15. My confusion is
continually before me,
and the shame of my face
hath covered me,

16. For the voice of him that
reproacheth and blasphemeth; by
reason of the enemy and avenger.

17. All this is come upon us;
yet have we not forgotten
thee, neither have we dealt falsely
in thy covenant.

18. Our heart is not
turned back, neither
have our steps declined
from thy way;

19. Though thou hast sore broken us
in the place of dragons, and covered
us with the shadow of death.

20. If we have forgotten the
name of our God, or stretched
out our hands to a strange god;

21. Shall not God search
this out? for he knoweth
the secrets of the heart.

22. Yea, for thy sake are
we killed all the day long;
we are counted as sheep
for the slaughter.

23. Awake, why sleepest
thou, O Lord? arise,
cast us not off for ever.

24. Wherefore hidest thou thy
face, and forgettest our affliction
and our oppression?

25. For our soul is
bowed down to the
dust: our belly cleaveth unto
the earth.

26. Arise for our help,
and redeem us
for thy mercies' sake.

PSALM 45

1. My heart is inditing
a good matter: I speak
of the things which I have
made touching the king:
my tongue is the pen
of a ready writer.

2. Thou art fairer than the
children of men: grace is
poured into thy lips: therefore
God hath blessed thee for ever.

3. Gird thy sword upon thy thigh,
O most mighty, with thy glory
and thy majesty.

4. And in thy majesty ride
prosperously because of
truth and meekness and
righteousness; and thy right

hand shall teach thee terrible things.

5. **Thine arrows are sharp** in the heart of the king's enemies; *whereby* the people fall under thee.

6. **Thy throne, O God, is for ever** and ever: the sceptre of thy kingdom *is* a right sceptre.

7. **Thou lovest righteousness, and hatest wickedness:** therefore God, thy God, hath anointed thee with the oil of gladness above thy fellows.

8. **All thy garments smell of myrrh, and aloes, and cassia,** out of the ivory palaces, whereby they have made thee glad.

9. **Kings' daughters were among thy honourable women:** upon thy right hand did stand the queen in gold of Ophir.

10. **Hearken, O daughter, and consider,** and incline thine ear; **forget** also **thine own people, and thy father's house;**

11. **So shall the king greatly desire thy beauty: for he is thy Lord;** and worship thou him.

12. And the daughter of Tyre *shall be there* with a gift; *even* the rich among the people shall intreat thy favour.

13. **The king's daughter is all glorious within:** her clothing is of wrought gold.

14. **She shall be brought unto the king in raiment of needlework:** the virgins her companions that follow her shall be brought unto thee.

15. **With gladness and rejoicing shall they be brought:** they shall enter into the king's palace.

16. Instead of thy fathers shall be thy children, whom thou mayest make princes in all the earth.

17. **I will make thy name to be remembered in all generations: therefore shall the people praise thee for ever** and ever.

PSALM 46

1. **God is our refuge and strength, a very present help in trouble.**

2. **Therefore will not we fear, though the earth be removed, and though the mountains be carried into the midst of the sea;**

3. *Though* the waters thereof roar *and* be troubled, *though* the mountains shake with the swelling thereof. Selah.

4. **There is a river, the streams whereof shall make glad the city of God,** the holy *place* of the tabernacles of the most High.

5. **God is in the midst of her;** she shall not be moved: **God shall help her,** *and that* right early.

6. **The heathen raged,** the kingdoms were moved: **he uttered his voice, the earth melted.**

7. **The LORD of hosts is with us;** the God of Jacob *is* our refuge. Selah.

8. **Come, behold the works of the LORD,** what desolations he hath made in the earth.

9. **He maketh wars to cease** unto the end of the earth; he breaketh the bow, and cutteth the spear in sunder; **he burneth the chariot** in the fire.

10. **Be still, and know that I am God: I will be exalted among the heathen, I will be exalted in the earth.**

11. The LORD of hosts *is* with us; the God of Jacob *is* our refuge. Selah.

PSALM 47

1. **O clap your hands,** all ye people; **shout unto God with the voice of triumph.**

2. **For the LORD** most high *is* terrible; *he* **is** a great

King over all the earth.

3. **He shall subdue the people** under us, and the nations **under our feet.**

4. He shall choose our inheritance for us, the excellency of Jacob whom he loved. Selah.

5. **God is gone up with** a shout, the LORD with **the sound of a trumpet.**

6. **Sing praises to God,** sing praises: sing praises unto our King, sing praises.

7. **For God is the King of all the earth:** sing ye praises with understanding.

8. **God reigneth over the heathen: God sitteth upon the throne of his holiness.**

9. The princes of the people are gathered together, *even* the people of the God of Abraham: for the shields of the earth *belong* unto God: **he is greatly exalted.**

PSALM 48

1. **Great is the LORD, and greatly to be praised in the city of our God, in the mountain of his holiness.**

2. **Beautiful for situation, the joy of the whole earth, is mount Zion, on the sides of the north, the city of the great King.**

3. God is known in her palaces for a refuge.

4. **For, lo, the kings** were assembled, they passed by together.

5. They saw *it, and* so they marvelled; they **were troubled, and hasted away.**

6. Fear took hold upon them there, *and* pain, as of a woman in travail.

7. Thou breakest the ships of Tarshish with an east wind.

8. As we have heard, **so have we seen in the city of the LORD** of hosts, in the city of our God: **God will establish it for ever.** Selah.

9. **We have thought of thy lovingkindness, O God,** in the midst of thy temple.

10. According to thy name, O God, so *is* thy praise unto the ends of the earth: **thy right hand is full of righteousness.**

11. **Let mount Zion rejoice,** let the daughters of Judah be glad, because of thy judgments.

12. **Walk about Zion,** and go round about her: tell the towers thereof.

13. Mark ye well her bulwarks, **consider her palaces;** that ye may tell *it* to the generation following.

14. **For this God is our God for ever** and ever: **he will be our guide even unto death.**

PSALM 49

1. **Hear this, all ye people;** give ear, all *ye* inhabitants of the world:

2. **Both** low and high, **rich and poor,** together.

3. **My mouth shall speak of wisdom;** and the meditation of my heart *shall be* of understanding.

4. I will incline mine ear to a parable: I will open my dark saying upon the harp.

5. **Wherefore should I fear** in the days of **evil,** *when* the iniquity of my heels shall compass me about?

6. **They that trust in their wealth,** and boast themselves in the multitude of their riches;

7. **None** *of them* **can by any means redeem his brother,** nor give to God a ransom for him:

8. (For the redemption of their soul *is* precious, and it ceaseth for ever:)

9. **That he should still live for ever, and not see corruption.**

10. For he seeth that wise men die, likewise the fool

- and the brutish person
- perish, and leave their
wealth to others.
- 11. **Their inward thought is,**
- **that their houses shall**
- **continue for ever,** and their
dwelling places to all generations;
- **they call their lands after**
- **their own names.**
- 12. **Nevertheless man**
being in honour
- **abideth not:** he is like
the beasts *that* perish.
- 13. **This** their way
- **is their folly:** yet their posterity
approve their sayings. Selah.
- 14. Like sheep they are
laid in the grave;
- **death shall feed on them;**
- **and the upright shall have**
- **dominion over them**
in the morning; and their
beauty shall consume
in the grave from their dwelling.
- 15. **But God will redeem**
- **my soul from the power**
- **of the grave:** for he shall
receive me. Selah.
- 16. **Be not thou afraid when**
- **one is made rich,** when the
glory of his house is increased;
- 17. **For when he dieth he**
- **shall carry nothing away:** his
glory shall not descend after him.
- 18. Though while he lived he blessed
his soul: and *men* will praise thee,
when thou doest well to thyself.
- 19. He shall go to
the generation of
his fathers;
they shall never see light.
- 20. **Man that is in honour,**
- **and understandeth not, is**
- **like the beasts that perish.**

PSALM 50

- 1. **The mighty God,** *even*
the LORD, hath spoken, and
- **called the earth from the**
- **rising of the sun unto the**
- **going down thereof.**
- 2. **Out of Zion,** the
perfection of beauty,

- God hath shined.
- 3. **Our God shall come,** and
shall not keep silence: a fire shall
devour before him, and it shall be
very tempestuous round about him.
- 4. **He shall call to the**
- **heavens** from above,
- **and to the earth, that he**
- **may judge his people.**
- 5. **Gather my saints**
together unto me; those
- **that have made a covenant**
- **with me by sacrifice.**
- 6. And the heavens shall declare
his righteousness: for God *is*
judge himself. Selah.
- 7. **Hear, O my people,**
and I will speak; O Israel, and
- **I will testify against thee:**
- **I am God,** *even* thy God.
- 8. **I will not reprove thee**
- **for thy sacrifices** or thy
burnt offerings, *to have been*
continually before me.
- 9. I will take no bullock out of thy
house, *nor* he goats out of thy folds.
- 10. **For every beast of**
- **the forest is mine, and**
- **the cattle upon a**
- **thousand hills.**
- 11. **I know all the**
- **fowls** of the mountains:
- **and the wild**
- **beasts** of the field
- **are mine.**
- 12. If I were hungry, I
would not tell thee: for
- **the world is mine, and**
- **the fulness thereof.**
- 13. **Will I eat the flesh**
- **of bulls, or drink the**
- **blood of goats?**
- 14. **Offer unto God**
- **thanksgiving;** and pay
thy vows unto the most High:
- 15. **And call upon**
- **me** in the day of trouble:
- **I will deliver thee, and**
- **thou shalt glorify me.**
- 16. **But unto the wicked God**
- **saith, What hast thou to do**
- **to declare my statutes,**
or *that* thou shouldest take my

covenant in thy mouth?

17. **Seeing thou hatest instruction,** and casteth
my words behind thee.

18. **When thou sawest a thief, then thou consentedst with him,** and hast been partaker
with adulterers.

19. **Thou givest thy mouth to evil,** and thy tongue frameth deceit.

20. Thou sittest *and* speakest against
thy brother; thou slanderest thine own
mother's son.

21. **These things hast thou done, and I kept silence;**
thou thoughtest that I was altogether
such an one as thyself:

but I will reprove thee, and
set *them* in order before thine eyes.

22. **Now consider this, ye that forget God, lest I tear you in pieces,** and
there be none to deliver.

23. **Whoso offereth praise glorifieth me: and to him**
that ordereth *his* conversation *aright*
will I shew the salvation of God.

PSALM 51

1. **Have mercy** upon me,
O God, according to thy
lovingkindness:
according unto the multitude of thy tender mercies blot out my transgressions.

2. **Wash me throughly**
from mine iniquity,
and cleanse me from my sin.

3. For I acknowledge my
transgressions: and
my sin is ever before me.

4. **Against thee,** thee only,
have I sinned, and done this evil in thy sight: that
thou mightest be justified when
thou speakest, *and* be clear
when thou judgest.

5. **Behold, I was shapen in iniquity, and in sin did my mother conceive me.**

6. **Behold, thou desirest truth** in the inward parts:
and in the hidden *part* thou
shalt make me to know wisdom.

7. Purge me with hyssop,
and I shall be clean:
wash me, and I shall be whiter than snow.

8. Make me to hear joy and
gladness; *that* the bones *which*
thou hast broken may rejoice.

9. Hide thy face from my sins,
and blot out all mine iniquities.

10. **Create in me a clean heart, O God; and renew a right spirit within me.**

11. Cast me not away from
thy presence; and
take not thy holy spirit from me.

12. **Restore unto me the joy of thy salvation;** and uphold
me *with thy* free spirit.

13. **Then will I teach transgressors thy ways; and sinners shall be converted** unto thee.

14. **Deliver me from bloodguiltiness, O God,** thou God
of my salvation: *and* my tongue
shall sing aloud of thy righteousness.

15. **O Lord, open thou my lips; and my mouth shall shew forth thy praise.**

16. **For thou desirest not sacrifice;** else would I give *it:*
thou delightest not in burnt offering.

17. **The sacrifices of God are a broken spirit: a broken and a contrite heart,** O God, thou wilt not despise.

18. **Do good in thy good pleasure unto Zion:**
build thou the walls of Jerusalem.

19. **Then shalt thou be pleased with the sacrifices of righteousness,**
with burnt offering and whole
burnt offering: then shall they
offer bullocks upon thine altar.

PSALM 52

1. **Why boastest thou thyself** in mischief, **O mighty man?** the goodness of God *endureth* continually.

2. **The tongue deviseth mischiefs; like a sharp razor,** working deceitfully.

3. **Thou lovest evil** more than good; **and lying** rather than to speak righteousness. Selah.

4. **Thou lovest all devouring words,** O *thou* deceitful tongue.

5. **God shall likewise destroy thee** for ever, he shall take thee away, and pluck thee out of *thy* dwelling place, **and root thee out of the land of the living.** Selah.

6. **The righteous also shall see, and fear, and** shall **laugh at him:**

7. **Lo, this is the man that made not God his strength; but trusted in** the abundance of **his riches,** *and* strengthened himself in his wickedness.

8. **But I am like a green olive tree in the house of God: I trust in the mercy of God** for ever and ever.

9. **I will praise thee for ever,** because thou hast done *it:* **and** I will **wait on thy name;** for *it is* good before thy saints.

PSALM 53

1. **The fool hath said in his heart, There is no God. Corrupt are they,** and have done abominable iniquity: *there is* none that doeth good.

2. **God looked down from heaven** upon the children of men, **to see if there were any that did understand, that did seek God.**

3. Every one of them is gone back: they are altogether become filthy; **there is none that doeth good, no, not one.**

4. Have the workers of iniquity no knowledge? who eat up my people *as* they eat bread: they have not called upon God.

5. **There were they in great fear, where no fear was: for God** hath **scattered** the bones of **him that encampeth against thee:** thou hast put *them* to shame, because God hath despised them.

6. **Oh that the salvation of Israel were come out of Zion!** When **God bringeth back the captivity of his people,** Jacob shall rejoice, **and Israel shall be glad.**

PSALM 54

1. **Save me, O God,** by thy name, and judge me by thy strength.

2. **Hear my prayer,** O God; give ear to the words of my mouth.

3. **For strangers are risen up against me,** and oppressors seek after my soul: they have not set God before them. Selah.

4. **Behold, God is mine helper:** the Lord *is* with them that uphold my soul.

5. **He shall reward evil unto mine enemies:** cut them off in thy truth.

6. **I will freely sacrifice unto thee:** I will praise thy name, O LORD; for *it is* good.

7. **For he hath delivered me** out of all trouble: **and mine eye hath seen his desire upon mine enemies.**

PSALM 55

1. **Give ear to my prayer, O God;** and hide not thyself from my supplication.

2. **Attend unto me,** and hear me: I mourn in my complaint, and make a noise;

3. **Because** of the voice of the enemy, because of the oppression of **the wicked:** for they cast iniquity

upon me, and in wrath they **hate me.**

4. **My heart is sore** pained **within me: and the terrors of death are** fallen **upon me.**

5. Fearfulness and trembling are come upon me, and **horror hath overwhelmed me.**

6. **And I said, Oh that I had wings like a dove! for then would I fly away,** and be at rest.

7. Lo, *then* would I wander far off, *and* remain in the wilderness. Selah.

8. **I would** hasten my **escape from the** windy storm *and* **tempest.**

9. **Destroy, O Lord, and divide their tongues:** for I have seen violence and strife in the city.

10. **Day and night they go about** it upon the walls thereof: **mischief** also and sorrow *are* in the midst of it.

11. Wickedness *is* in the midst thereof: deceit and guile depart not from her streets.

12. **For it was not an enemy that reproached me;** then I could have borne *it:* **neither was it he that hated me** *that* did magnify *himself* against me; then I would have hid myself from him:

13. **But it was** thou, a man **mine equal,** my guide, **and mine acquaintance.**

14. **We took sweet counsel together,** *and* walked unto the house of God in company.

15. **Let death seize upon them, and let them go** down quick **into hell:** for wickedness *is* in their dwellings, *and* among them.

16. **As for me, I will call upon God;** and the LORD shall save me.

17. **Evening, and morning, and at noon, will I pray, and** cry aloud: and he shall hear my voice.

18. He hath delivered my soul in peace from the battle *that was* against me: for there were many with me.

19. **God shall hear,** and afflict them, even he that abideth of old. Selah. Because they have no changes, therefore they fear not God.

20. **He hath put forth his hands against such as be at peace** with him: he hath broken his covenant.

21. **The words of his mouth were smoother than butter, but war was in his heart:** his words were softer than oil, yet *were* they drawn swords.

22. **Cast thy burden upon the LORD, and he shall sustain thee:** he shall never suffer the righteous to be moved.

23. **But thou, O God, shalt bring them down into the pit of destruction:** bloody and deceitful men shall not live out half their days; **but I will trust in thee.**

PSALM 56

1. **Be merciful unto me, O God:** for man would swallow me up; he fighting daily oppresseth me.

2. **Mine enemies would daily swallow me up:** for *they be* many that fight against me, O thou most High.

3. **What time I am afraid, I will trust in thee.**

4. In God I will praise his word, in God I have put my trust; **I will not fear what flesh can do unto me.**

5. Every day they wrest my words: all their thoughts *are* against me for evil.

6. They gather themselves together, they hide themselves, they mark my steps, when they wait for my soul.

7. **Shall they escape by iniquity?** in *thine* anger cast down the people, O God.

8. **Thou tellest my**

■ wanderings: put thou
■ my tears into thy bottle:
are they not in thy book?
■ 9. When I cry unto thee,
■ then shall mine enemies
■ turn back: this I know;
■ for God is for me.
■ 10. In God will I praise
■ his word: in the LORD will
I praise his word.
■ 11. In God have I put my
■ trust: I will not be afraid
what man can do unto me.
12. Thy vows are upon me, O God:
I will render praises unto thee.
■ 13. For thou hast delivered
my soul from death:
■ wilt not thou
■ deliver my feet from
■ falling, that I may
■ walk before God
in the light of the living?

PSALM 57

■ 1. Be merciful unto me,
■ O God, be merciful unto me:
for my soul trusteth in thee: yea,
■ in the shadow of thy
■ wings will I make my
■ refuge, until these
■ calamities be overpast.
2. I will cry unto God most high; unto
God that performeth all things for me.
3. He shall send from heaven, and
save me from the reproach of him
that would swallow me up. Selah.
■ God shall send forth his
■ mercy and his truth.
■ 4. My soul is among lions:
and I lie even among them that areset
on fire, even the sons of men, whose
teeth are spears and arrows, and
their tongue a sharp sword.
5. Be thou exalted,
■ O God, above the heavens;
■ let thy glory be above
■ all the earth.
■ 6. They have prepared a
■ net for my steps; my soul is
bowed down: they have digged a pit
before me, into the midst whereof
they are fallen themselves. Selah.
■ 7. My heart is fixed, O God,

my heart is fixed:
■ I will sing and
■ give praise.
8. Awake up, my glory;
awake, psaltery and harp:
■ I myself will awake early.
■ 9. I will praise thee,
O Lord, among the people:
■ I will sing unto thee
■ among the nations.
■ 10. For thy mercy is great
unto the heavens, and thy
truth unto the clouds.
■ 11. Be thou exalted, O
■ God, above the heavens: let
thy glory be above all the earth.

PSALM 58

■ 1. Do ye indeed speak
■ righteousness, O
■ congregation? do ye judge
uprightly, O ye sons of men?
■ 2. Yea, in heart ye work
■ wickedness; ye weigh the
violence of your hands in the earth.
■ 3. The wicked are
■ estranged from the womb:
■ they go astray as soon as
■ they be born, speaking lies.
■ 4. Their poison is like the
■ poison of a serpent:
they are like the deaf adder
that stoppeth her ear;
5. Which will not hearken
to the voice of charmers,
charming never so wisely.
■ 6. Break their teeth, O God,
in their mouth: break out the great
teeth of the young lions, O LORD.
■ 7. Let them melt away as
waters which run continually: when he
bendeth his bow to shoot his arrows,
let them be as cut in pieces.
■ 8. As a snail which melteth,
let every one of them pass away: like
the untimely birth of a woman, that
they may not see the sun.
9. Before your pots can feel
the thorns, he shall take them
away as with a whirlwind,
both living, and in his wrath.
■ 10. The righteous shall
rejoice when he seeth

the vengeance: he shall
wash his feet in the
blood of the wicked.
11. **So that a man shall**
say, Verily there is a
reward for the righteous:
verily he is a God that
judgeth in the earth.

PSALM 59

1. **Deliver me from mine**
enemies, O my God: defend
me from them that rise up against me.
2. Deliver me from the workers
of iniquity, and
save me from bloody men.
3. **For, lo, they lie in wait**
for my soul: the mighty are
gathered against me;
not for my transgression, nor *for*
my sin, O LORD.
4. **They** run and
prepare themselves
without my fault:
awake to help me, and behold.
5. **Thou therefore, O LORD**
God of hosts, the God of Israel,
awake to visit all
the heathen: be not
merciful to any wicked
transgressors. Selah.
6. They return at evening:
they make a noise like a dog,
and go round about the city.
7. **Behold, they belch** out
with their mouth: swords
are in their lips: for who, *say*
they, doth hear?
8. **But thou, O LORD,**
shalt laugh at them;
thou shalt have all the
heathen in derision.
9. *Because of* his strength
will I wait upon thee: for
God is my defence.
10. The God of my mercy
shall prevent me:
God shall let me see my
desire upon mine enemies.
11. **Slay them not, lest my**
people forget: scatter
them by thy power;
and bring them down,

O Lord our shield.
12. **For the sin of their**
mouth *and* the words of their lips
let them even
be taken in their pride:
and for cursing and lying
which they speak.
13. **Consume them in wrath,**
consume *them,* that they *may* not *be:*
and let them know that
God ruleth in Jacob unto the ends
of the earth. Selah.
14. And at evening let them return;
and let them make a noise like a dog,
and go round about the city.
15. **Let them wander up**
and down for meat,
and grudge if they
be not satisfied.
16. **But I will sing of**
thy power; yea, I will sing aloud
of thy mercy in the morning: for
thou hast been my defence
and refuge in the day of my trouble.
17. **Unto thee, O my**
strength, will I sing:
for God *is* my defence, *and*
the God of my mercy.

PSALM 60

1. **O GOD,** thou hast cast us off,
thou hast scattered us,
thou hast been
displeased; O turn
thyself to us again.
2. **Thou hast made the**
earth to tremble; thou hast
broken it: heal the breaches
thereof; for it shaketh.
3. Thou hast shewed thy
people hard things:
thou hast made us to drink
the wine of astonishment.
4. **Thou hast given a banner**
to them that fear thee,
that it may be displayed because
of the truth. Selah.
5. **That thy beloved may**
be delivered; save *with* thy
right hand, and hear me.
6. **God hath spoken in his**
holiness; I will rejoice, I will
divide Shechem, and mete

out the valley of Succoth.

7. **Gilead** is mine,
**and Manasseh is
mine; Ephraim also**
is the strength of mine head;
Judah is my lawgiver;
8. **Moab is my washpot;
over Edom will I cast out
my shoe:** Philistia, triumph
thou because of me.
9. Who will bring me into the strong
city? who will lead me into Edom?
10. Wilt not thou, O God, which hadst
cast us off? and thou, O God, which
didst not go out with our armies?
11. **Give us help from
trouble: for vain is
the help of man.**
12. **Through God we shall
do valiantly: for he** it is that
**shall tread down
our enemies.**

PSALMS 61

1. **Hear my cry, O God;
attend unto my prayer.**
2. **From the end of the earth
will I cry unto thee,** when my
heart is overwhelmed: lead me to
the rock that is higher than I.
3. For thou hast been a
shelter for me, and a strong
tower from the enemy.
4. I will abide in thy
tabernacle for ever:
**I will trust in the covert
of thy wings.** Selah.
5. **For thou, O God,
hast heard my vows:**
thou hast given me the heritage
of those that fear thy name.
6. **Thou wilt prolong the
king's life: and** his years
as many generations.
7. **He shall abide before
God for ever:** O prepare mercy
and truth, which may preserve him.
8. So will I sing praise unto thy
name for ever, that I may daily
perform my vows.

PSALMS 62

1. **Truly my soul waiteth**
upon God: from him
cometh my salvation.
2. **He only is my rock**
and my salvation; he is my defence;
I shall not be greatly
moved.
3. **How long will ye imagine
mischief against a man?
ye shall be slain**
all of you: as a bowing wall shall
ye be, and as a tottering fence.
4. **They only consult to cast
him down** from his excellency:
they delight in lies:
they bless with their mouth, but
they curse inwardly. Selah.
5. **My soul, wait thou
only upon God;** for my
expectation is from him.
6. **He only is my rock**
and my salvation: he is my defence;
I shall not be moved.
7. **In God is my salvation
and my glory:** the rock of my
strength, and my refuge, is in God.
8. **Trust in him at all times;**
ye people, pour out your
heart before him:
God is a refuge for us. Selah.
9. **Surely men** of low degree are
vanity, and men of high degree are a
lie: to be laid in the balance, they
**are altogether lighter
than vanity.**
10. **Trust not in oppression,
and** become not vain in
**robbery: if riches increase,
set not your heart
upon them.**
11. **God hath spoken** once;
twice have I heard this; that
**power belongeth
unto God.**
12. **Also unto thee, O Lord,
belongeth mercy: for thou
renderest to every man
according to his work.**

PSALMS 63

1. **O GOD,** thou art my God;
**early will I seek thee: my
soul thirsteth for thee,**
my flesh longeth for thee

in a dry and thirsty

land, where no water is;

2. To see thy power and thy glory, so as I have seen thee in the sanctuary.

3. Because thy lovingkindness is better than life, my lips shall praise thee.

4. Thus will I bless thee while I live: I will lift up my hands in thy name.

5. My soul shall be satisfied as with marrow and fatness; and my mouth shall praise thee with joyful lips:

6. When I remember thee upon my bed, and meditate on thee in the night watches.

7. Because thou hast been my help, therefore in the shadow of thy wings will I rejoice.

8. My soul followeth hard after thee: thy right hand upholdeth me.

9. But those that seek my soul, to destroy it, shall go into the lower parts of the earth.

10. They shall fall by the sword: they shall be a portion for foxes.

11. But the king shall rejoice in God; every one that sweareth by him shall glory: but the mouth of them that speak lies shall be stopped.

PSALMS 64

1. Hear my voice, O God, in my prayer: preserve my life from fear of the enemy.

2. Hide me from the secret counsel of the wicked; from the insurrection of the workers of iniquity:

3. Who whet their tongue like a sword, and bend their bows to shoot their arrows, even bitter words:

4. That they may shoot in secret at the perfect: suddenly do they shoot at him, and fear not.

5. They encourage themselves in an evil matter: they commune of laying snares privily; they say, Who shall see them?

6. They search out iniquities; they accomplish a diligent search: both the inward thought of every one of them, and the heart, is deep.

7. But God shall shoot at them with an arrow; suddenly shall they be wounded.

8. So they shall make their own tongue to fall upon themselves: all that see them shall flee away.

9. And all men shall fear, and shall declare the work of God; for they shall wisely consider of his doing.

10. The righteous shall be glad in the LORD, and shall trust in him; and all the upright in heart shall glory.

PSALMS 65

1. Praise waiteth for thee, O God, in Sion: and unto thee shall the vow be performed.

2. O thou that hearest prayer, unto thee shall all flesh come.

3. Iniquities prevail against me: as for our transgressions, thou shalt purge them away.

4. Blessed is the man whom thou choosest, and causest to approach unto thee, that he may dwell in thy courts: we shall be satisfied with the goodness of thy house, even of thy holy temple.

5. By terrible things in righteousness wilt thou answer us, O God of our salvation; who art the

confidence of all the ends of
the earth, and of them that
are afar off *upon* the sea:
6. Which by his strength
setteth fast the mountains;
being girded with power:
7. Which stilleth the
noise of the seas,
the noise of their waves,
and the tumult of the people.
8. They also that dwell in the
uttermost parts are afraid at
thy tokens: thou
makest the outgoings
of the morning and
evening to rejoice.
9. Thou visitest the earth,
and waterest it: thou greatly
enrichest it with the river of God,
which is full of water:
thou preparest them corn,
when thou hast so provided for it.
10. Thou waterest the ridges
thereof abundantly: thou settlest
the furrows thereof: thou makest it
soft with showers: thou blessest the
springing thereof.
11. Thou crownest the
year with thy goodness;
and thy paths drop fatness.
12. They drop *upon* the pastures
of the wilderness: and the little
hills rejoice on every side.
13. The pastures are
clothed with flocks;
the valleys also are
covered over
with corn; they shout
for joy, they also sing.

PSALMS 66

1. Make a joyful noise
unto God, all ye lands:
2. Sing forth the honour of his
name: make his praise glorious.
3. Say unto God, How
terrible art thou in thy
works! through the greatness of
thy power shall
thine enemies
submit themselves
unto thee.
4. All the earth shall
worship thee,
and shall
sing unto thee;
they shall sing *to* thy name. Selah.
5. Come and see the works
of God: *he is* terrible *in his* doing
toward the children of men.
6. He turned the sea into
dry land: they went through
the flood on foot:
there did we rejoice in him.
7. He ruleth by his power for ever;
his eyes behold the
nations: let not the
rebellious exalt
themselves. Selah.
8. O bless our God,
ye people, and make the voice
of his praise to be heard:
9. Which holdeth
our soul in life, and suffereth
not our feet to be moved.
10. For thou, O God,
hast proved us: thou
hast tried us,
as silver is tried.
11. Thou broughtest us into the net;
thou laidst affliction
upon our loins.
12. Thou hast caused men
to ride over our heads; we
went through fire and through
water: but thou broughtest
us out into a wealthy place.
13. I will go into thy house
with burnt offerings:
I will pay thee my vows,
14. Which my lips have uttered,
and my mouth hath spoken,
when I was in trouble.
15. I will offer unto thee
burnt sacrifices of fatlings,
with the incense of rams; I will offer
bullocks with goats. Selah.
16. Come and hear, all ye
that fear God, and I will
declare what he hath
done for my soul.
17. I cried unto
him with my mouth,
and he was extolled
with my tongue.
18. If I regard iniquity

in my heart, the Lord
will not hear me:
19. **But verily God
hath heard me;** he hath
attended to the voice of my prayer.
20. **Blessed be God,
which hath not turned**
away my prayer, nor
his mercy from me.

PSALMS 67

1. **GOD be merciful
unto us,** and bless us;
**and cause his face
to shine upon us;** Selah.
2. **That thy way
may be known**
upon earth, thy saving health
among all nations.
3. **Let the people
praise thee,** O God; let
all the people praise thee.
4. **O let the nations
be glad** and sing for joy:
**for thou shalt judge
the people** righteously,
and govern the nations
upon earth. Selah.
5. Let the people praise thee, O
God; let all the people praise thee.
6. **Then shall the earth
yield her increase;
and God,** even our own God,
shall bless us.
7. God shall bless us;
and all the ends of the
earth shall fear him.

PSALMS 68

1. **Let God arise, let his
enemies** be scattered: let
them also that hate him
flee before him.
2. As smoke is driven away,
so drive them away:
**as wax melteth before
the fire, so let the wicked
perish at the presence
of God.**
3. **But let the
righteous** be glad; let them
rejoice before God: yea,
let them exceedingly rejoice.

4. **Sing unto God,**
sing praises to his name:
extol him
that rideth upon the heavens
**by his name JAH,
and rejoice before him.**
5. **A father of the fatherless,
and a judge of the widows,**
is God in his holy habitation.
6. **God setteth the solitary
in families: he bringeth out
those which are bound
with chains:** but the rebellious
dwell in a dry land.
7. **O God, when
thou wentest** forth
before thy people,
when thou didst march through
the wilderness; Selah:
8. **The earth shook,**
the heavens also dropped
at the presence of God:
**even Sinai itself was
moved** at the presence
of God, the God of Israel.
9. **Thou,** O God,
didst send a plentiful rain,
whereby thou didst confirm thine
inheritance, when it was weary.
10. Thy congregation
hath dwelt therein:
**thou, O God, hast
prepared of
thy goodness for the poor.**
11. **The Lord gave the word:
great was the company of
those that published it.**
12. **Kings of armies did
flee** apace: and she that tarried
at home divided the spoil.
13. Though ye have lien among the
pots, yet shall ye be as the wings of
a dove covered with silver, and her
feathers with yellow gold.
14. When the Almighty
scattered kings in it, it was
white as snow in Salmon.
15. The hill of God is as the
hill of Bashan; an high hill
as the hill of Bashan.
16. Why leap ye, ye high hills? this is
the hill which God desireth to dwell in;
yea, the LORD will dwell in it for ever.

■ 17. **The chariots of God**
■ **are** twenty thousand, even
■ **thousands of angels:**
■ **the Lord is among**
■ **them,** *as in* Sinai,
■ **in the holy place.**
■ 18. **Thou hast ascended**
■ **on high, thou hast led**
■ **captivity captive:**
thou hast received gifts for men;
yea, *for* the rebellious also,
■ **that** the LORD
■ **God might dwell**
■ **among them.**
■ 19. **Blessed be the Lord,**
■ **who daily loadeth us**
■ **with benefits,** *even* the
God of our salvation. Selah.
■ 20. **He** *that is* our God
■ **is the God of salvation;**
and unto GOD the Lord *belong*
the issues from death.
■ 21. **But God shall**
■ **wound** the head of
■ **his enemies,** *and* the hairy
scalp of such an one as goeth
on still in his trespasses.
■ 22. **The Lord said,**
I will bring again from Bashan,
■ **I will bring my people**
■ **again from the**
■ **depths** of the sea:
■ 23. **That thy foot may be**
■ **dipped in the blood of**
■ **thine enemies,** *and* the
tongue of thy dogs in the same.
■ 24. **They have seen thy**
■ **goings, O God;** *even* the goings
of my God, my King, in the sanctuary.
■ 25. **The singers went**
■ **before, the** players on
■ **instruments followed** after;
■ **among them were the**
■ **damsels playing** with
■ **timbrels.**
■ 26. **Bless** ye
■ **God** in the congregations,
even the Lord,
■ **from the fountain of Israel.**
27. There *is* little
Benjamin *with* their ruler,
the princes of Judah *and*
their council, the princes of

Zebulun, and the princes of Naphtali.
28. Thy God hath commanded
thy strength:
■ **strengthen,** O God,
■ **that which thou**
■ **hast wrought for us.**
29. Because of thy temple at
Jerusalem shall kings bring
presents unto thee.
■ 30. **Rebuke**
the company of spearmen,
■ **the multitude** of the bulls,
with the calves of the people,
■ **till every one submit**
■ **himself with** pieces of
■ **silver: scatter** thou
■ **the people that**
■ **delight in war.**
■ 31. **Princes shall come out**
■ **of Egypt;** Ethiopia shall soon
stretch out her hands unto God.
■ 32. **Sing unto God,**
ye kingdoms of the earth;
■ **O sing praises**
unto the Lord; Selah:
■ 33. **To him that rideth**
■ **upon the heavens**
of heavens, *which were* of old; lo,
■ **he doth send out his**
■ **voice,** *and that* a mighty voice.
34. Ascribe ye strength unto God:
■ **his excellency is**
■ **over Israel,** and his
strength *is* in the clouds.
35. O God, *thou art* terrible
out of thy holy places: the
■ **God** of Israel *is* he that
■ **giveth strength and**
■ **power unto his people.**
■ **Blessed be God.**

PSALMS 69

■ 1. **Save me, O God;**
for the waters are
come in unto *my* soul.
■ 2. **I sink in deep mire,**
where *there is* no standing:
■ **I am come into**
■ **deep waters,**
where the floods overflow me.
■ 3. **I am weary of my**
■ **crying:** my throat is dried:
■ **mine eyes fail while I**

wait for my God.

4. **They that hate me without a cause are more than the hairs of mine head:** they that would destroy me, *being* mine enemies wrongfully, are mighty: then I restored *that* which I took not away.

5. O God, **thou knowest my foolishness; and my sins** are not hid from thee.

6. **Let not them that wait on thee,** O Lord GOD of hosts, **be ashamed for my sake:** let not those that seek thee be confounded for my sake, O God of Israel.

7. **Because for thy sake I have borne reproach;** shame hath covered my face.

8. **I am** become **a stranger unto my brethren,** and an alien unto my mother's children.

9. **For the zeal of thine house hath eaten me up; and the reproaches of them** that reproached thee **are fallen upon me.**

10. When I wept, *and chastened* my soul with fasting, that was to my reproach.

11. I made sackcloth also my garment; and **I became a proverb to them.**

12. **They** that sit in the gate **speak against me;** and I *was* the song of the drunkards.

13. **But** as for me, **my prayer is unto thee, O LORD,** *in* an acceptable time: O God, **in the multitude of thy mercy hear me,** in the truth of thy salvation.

14. **Deliver me out of the mire,** and let me not sink: **let me be delivered** from them that hate me, and **out of the deep waters.**

15. Let not the waterflood overflow me, neither let the deep swallow me up, and let not the pit shut her mouth upon me.

16. **Hear me, O LORD; for thy lovingkindness is good:** turn unto me according to the multitude of thy tender mercies.

17. **And hide not thy face** from thy servant; **for I am in trouble:** hear me speedily.

18. **Draw nigh unto my soul, and redeem it:** deliver me because of mine enemies.

19. **Thou hast known my reproach, and** my **shame, and my dishonour:** mine adversaries *are* all before thee.

20. **Reproach hath broken my heart;** and I am full of heaviness: and **I looked for some to take pity,** but *there was* none; and for comforters, **but I found none.**

21. **They gave me** also **gall for** my **meat; and** in my thirst they gave me **vinegar to drink.**

22. **Let their table become a snare** before them: **and** *that which should have been* for *their* welfare, *let it become* **a trap.**

23. **Let their eyes be darkened,** that they see not; **and make their loins** continually to **shake.**

24. **Pour out thine indignation upon them,** and let thy wrathful anger take hold of them.

25. **Let their habitation be desolate;** *and* let none dwell in their tents.

26. **For they persecute** *him* whom thou hast smitten; and they talk to the grief of **those whom thou hast wounded.**

27. Add iniquity unto

their iniquity: and
**let them not come
into thy righteousness.**
28. **Let them be blotted out
of the book of the living,**
and not be written with the righteous.
29. But I *am* poor and sorrowful:
let thy salvation, O God, set me
up on high.
30. **I will praise** the
name of God with a song,
and will
**magnify him with
thanksgiving.**
31. *This* also shall please the LORD
better than an ox *or* bullock that
hath horns and hoofs.
32. **The humble shall see** *this,*
**and be glad: and your
heart shall live that
seek God.**
33. **For the LORD heareth
the poor, and despiseth
not his prisoners.**
34. **Let the heaven and
earth praise him,** the seas, and
every thing that moveth therein.
35. **For God will save Zion,**
and will build the cities of Judah:
that they may dwell there,
and have it in possession.
36. The seed also of his
servants shall inherit it:
**and they that love his
name shall dwell therein.**

PSALMS 70

1. **MAKE haste,** O GOD,
to deliver me;
make haste to help me,
O LORD.
2. **Let them be
ashamed** and confounded
that seek after
my soul: let them be turned
backward, and put to confusion,
that desire my hurt.
3. **Let them be turned
back for** a reward of their
shame that say, Aha, aha.
4. **Let** all
**those that seek thee rejoice
and** be glad in thee: and let such as

love thy salvation say continually,
Let God be magnified.
5. But I *am* poor and needy:
make haste unto me, O God:
thou *art* my help and my deliverer;
O LORD, make no tarrying.

PSALMS 71

1. **In thee, O LORD,
do I put my trust:** let me
never be put to confusion.
2. **Deliver me in thy
righteousness,** and cause me to
escape: incline thine ear unto me,
and save me.
3. **Be thou my** strong
habitation, whereunto I may
continually resort: thou hast given
commandment to save me;
for thou art my rock and my
fortress.
4. **Deliver me,** O my God,
**out of the hand of the
wicked,** out of the hand of the
unrighteous and cruel man.
5. **For thou art my
hope,** O Lord GOD:
thou art my trust from my youth.
6. By thee have I been holden
up from the womb:
thou art he that
**took me out of my
mother's bowels: my
praise shall be** continually
of thee.
7. I am as a wonder unto many;
but thou *art* my strong refuge.
8. Let my mouth be filled *with* thy
praise *and with* thy honour all the day.
9. **Cast me not off in** the time of
old age; forsake me not when
my strength faileth.
10. **For mine enemies**
speak against me; and they that
lay wait for my soul
take counsel together,
11. **Saying, God hath
forsaken him:**
persecute and take him; for
**there is none to
deliver him.**
12. O God, be not far from me: O
my God, make haste for my help.

13. **Let them be confounded
and consumed** that are
adversaries to my soul; let them be
covered *with* reproach and dishonour
that seek my hurt.
14. **But I will**
hope continually, and will yet
**praise thee more
and more.**
15. **My mouth shall shew
forth** thy righteousness *and*
thy salvation all the day; for I
know not the numbers *thereof.*
16. **I will go in the strength
of the Lord** GOD: I will make
mention of thy righteousness,
even of thine only.
17. **O God, thou hast taught
me from my youth:**and hitherto
have I declared thy wondrous works.
18. **Now** also
when I am old
and greyheaded, O God,
**forsake me not; until I
have shewed** thy strength
unto *this* generation, *and*
**thy power to every
one that is to come.**
19. Thy righteousness also, O God,
is very high, who hast done great
things: O God, who *is* like unto thee!
20. **Thou, which hast
shewed me great and
sore troubles,** shalt
quicken me again, and shalt
bring me up again
from the depths of the earth.
21. **Thou shalt increase
my greatness,**
and comfort me on every side.
22. **I will also praise thee**
with the psaltery, *even* thy truth,
O my God: unto thee will I sing
with the harp,
O thou Holy One of Israel.
23. **My lips shall greatly
rejoice** when I sing unto thee;
and my soul, which
thou hast redeemed.
24. **My tongue** also
**shall talk of thy
righteousness** all the day long:
for they are confounded,

for they are brought unto shame,
that seek my hurt.

PSALMS 72

1. **Give the king thy
judgments,** O God,
and thy
**righteousness unto
the king's son.**
2. **He shall judge thy
people with righteousness,**
and thy poor with judgment.
3. The mountains shall bring peace
to the people, and the little hills,
by righteousness.
4. **He shall judge the
poor** of the people, he shall
save the children of
the needy, and shall
break in pieces
the oppressor.
5. They shall fear thee as long
as the sun and moon endure,
throughout all generations.
6. **He shall come down**
like rain upon the mown grass:
**as showers that
water the earth.**
7. **In his days shall
the righteous flourish;**
and abundance of peace so
long as the moon endureth.
8. He shall have dominion also from
sea to sea, and from the river unto
the ends of the earth.
9. They that dwell in the wilderness
shall bow before him;
**and his enemies
shall lick the dust.**
10. **The kings**
of Tarshish and of the isles
shall bring presents:
the kings of Sheba and Seba
shall offer gifts.
11. **Yea, all kings shall
fall down before him: all
nations shall serve him.**
12. **For he shall deliver
the needy** when he crieth;
the poor also,
**and him that hath
no helper.**
13. He shall spare the poor

and needy, and shall save
the souls of the needy.

14. **He shall redeem their soul** from deceit and violence: **and precious shall their blood be in his sight.**

15. **And he shall live, and** to him shall be given of the gold of Sheba: **prayer** also **shall be made for him continually; and daily shall he be praised.**

16. There shall be an handful of corn in the earth upon the top of the mountains; the fruit thereof shall shake like Lebanon: and *they* of the city shall flourish like grass of the earth.

17. **His name shall endure for ever:** his name shall be continued as long as the sun: **and men shall be blessed in him:** all nations shall call him blessed.

18. **Blessed be the LORD** God, the God of Israel, **who only doeth wondrous things.**

19. **And blessed be his** glorious **name** for ever: and **let the whole earth be filled with his glory; Amen,** and Amen.

20. The prayers of David the son of Jesse are ended.

PSALMS 73

1. **Truly God is good** to Israel, *even* **to such as are of a clean heart.**

2. **But as for me,** my feet were almost gone; **my steps had well nigh slipped.**

3. **For I was envious** at the foolish, *when* I saw the prosperity **of the wicked.**

4. For *there are* no bands in their death: but their strength *is* firm.

5. **They are not in trouble** *as other* men; **neither are they plagued like other men.**

6. **Therefore pride** compasseth them about as a chain; violence **covereth them** *as* a garment.

7. Their eyes stand out with fatness: **they have more than heart could wish.**

8. **They are corrupt, and** speak wickedly *concerning* oppression: they **speak loftily.**

9. **They set their mouth against the heavens,** and their tongue walketh through the earth.

10. Therefore his people return hither: and waters of a full *cup* are wrung out to them.

11. **And they say, How doth God know?** and is there knowledge in the most High?

12. **Behold, these are the ungodly, who prosper** in the world; they increase *in* riches.

13. **Verily I have cleansed my heart in vain,** and washed my hands in innocency.

14. **For all the day long have I been plagued, and chastened** every morning.

15. **If I** say, I will **speak thus; behold, I** should **offend** *against* the generation of **thy children.**

16. **When I thought to know this, it was too painful** for me;

17. **Until I went into the sanctuary of God; then understood I their end.**

18. **Surely** thou didst set them in slippery places: **thou castedst them down into destruction.**

19. How are they *brought* into desolation, as in a moment! **they are utterly consumed** with terrors.

20. As a dream when *one* awaketh; *so,* O Lord, when thou awakest, thou shalt despise their image.

21. **Thus my heart was**

grieved, and I was
pricked in my reins.
22. So foolish was I,
and ignorant: I was as a
beast before thee.
23. Nevertheless
I *am* continually with thee:
thou hast holden me
by my right hand.
24. Thou shalt guide me with
thy counsel, and afterward
receive me to glory.
25. Whom have I in
heaven *but thee?*
and *there is* none upon
earth that I desire
beside thee.
26. My flesh and my heart
faileth: but God is
the strength of my heart, and
my portion for ever.
27. For, lo,
they that are far from thee
shall perish: thou hast destroyed
all them that go a whoring from thee.
28. But *it is* good for me
to draw near to God:
I have put my trust
in the Lord GOD,
that I may declare
all thy works.

PSALMS 74

1. O GOD, why
hast thou cast us off for
ever? *why* doth thine anger smoke
against the sheep of thy pasture?
2. Remember thy
congregation, which
thou hast purchased
of old; the rod of thine inheritance,
which thou hast redeemed;
this mount Zion, wherein
thou hast dwelt.
3. Lift up thy feet
unto the perpetual
desolations; *even* all
that the enemy hath done
wickedly in the sanctuary.
4. Thine enemies roar in the
midst of thy congregations; they
set up their ensigns
for signs.

5. *A man* was famous according
as he had lifted up axes upon
the thick trees.
6. But now they break down
the carved work thereof at
once with axes and hammers.
7. They have
cast fire into thy
sanctuary, they have
defiled *by casting down*
the dwelling place
of thy name to the ground.
8. They said in their hearts,
Let us destroy them together:
they have
burned up
all the synagogues
of God in the land.
9. We see not our signs:
there is no more any
prophet: neither *is there* among
us any that knoweth how long.
10. O God, how long
shall the adversary
reproach? shall the enemy
blaspheme thy
name for ever?
11. Why withdrawest thou
thy hand, even thy right hand?
pluck *it* out of thy bosom.
12. For God is my King of old,
working salvation in the
midst of the earth.
13. Thou didst divide
the sea by thy strength:
thou brakest the heads of
the dragons in the waters.
14. Thou brakest the
heads of leviathan in pieces,
and gavest him *to be*
meat to the people
inhabiting the wilderness.
15. Thou didst cleave the
fountain and the flood: thou
driedst up mighty rivers.
16. The day is thine,
the night also *is* thine:
thou hast
prepared the light and
the sun.
17. Thou hast
set all
the borders of the earth:

thou hast made
summer and winter.
18. Remember this, *that* the
enemy hath reproached,
O LORD, and *that* the
foolish people have
blasphemed thy name.
19. O deliver not the
soul of thy turtledove
unto the multitude of
the wicked: forget not the
congregation of thy poor for ever.
20. Have respect unto the covenant:
for the dark places of the earth are
full of the habitations of cruelty.
21. O let not the oppressed
return ashamed: let the
poor and needy praise
thy name.
22. Arise, O God,
plead thine own cause:
remember how
the foolish man
reproacheth thee daily.
23. Forget not the voice of
thine enemies: the tumult
of those that rise up against thee
increaseth continually.

PSALMS 75

1. Unto thee, O God,
do we give thanks,
unto thee do we give thanks:
for *that* thy name is near
thy wondrous works declare.
2. When I shall
receive the congregation
I will judge uprightly.
3. The earth and all the inhabitants
thereof are dissolved: I bear up
the pillars of it. Selah.
4. I said unto the
fools, Deal not foolishly:
and to
the wicked, Lift not up the horn:
5. Lift not up your horn on high:
speak not with a stiff neck.
6. For promotion cometh
neither from the east,
nor from the
west, nor from
the south.
7. But God *is* the judge: he

putteth down one, and
setteth up another.
8. For in the hand of the LORD *there*
is a cup, and the wine is red; it is full
of mixture; and he poureth out of the
same: but the dregs thereof, all the
wicked of the earth shall wring *them*
out, *and* drink *them*.
9. But I will declare for ever; I will
sing praises to the
God of Jacob.
10. All the horns of the wicked also
will I cut off; *but* the horns of the
righteous shall be exalted.

PSALMS 76

1. In Judah is God known:
his name is great in Israel.
2. In Salem also
is his tabernacle,
and his dwelling place
in Zion.
3. There brake he the arrows of
the bow, the shield, and the
sword, and the battle. Selah.
4. Thou art more
glorious and excellent
than the mountains of prey.
5. The stout-hearted are spoiled, they
have slept their sleep: and none of the
men of might have found their hands.
6. At thy rebuke,
O God of Jacob, both
the chariot and horse are
cast into a dead sleep.
7. Thou, *even* thou,
art to be feared: and
who may stand in thy sight
when once
thou art angry?
8. Thou didst cause
judgment to be heard
from heaven; the earth
feared, and was still.
9. When God arose to
judgment, to save all
the meek of the earth. Selah.
10. Surely the wrath of man
shall praise thee: the remainder
of wrath shalt thou restrain.
11. Vow, and pay unto
the LORD your God:
let all that be round

about him bring presents
unto him that ought to be feared.
12. He shall cut off the spirit
of princes: *he is* terrible to the
kings of the earth.

PSALMS 77

1. **I cried unto God** with my
voice, *even* unto God with my voice;
and he gave ear unto me.
2. **In** the day of
my trouble I sought
the Lord: my sore ran in
the night, and ceased not:
my soul refused
to be comforted.
3. **I remembered God,**
and was troubled: I complained,
and my spirit was
overwhelmed. Selah.
4. Thou holdest mine eyes waking:
I am so troubled that
I cannot speak.
5. I have considered the days of
old, the years of ancient times.
6. I call to remembrance my
song in the night:
I commune with mine own
heart: and my spirit
made diligent search.
7. **Will the Lord**
cast off for ever? and will he
be favourable no more?
8. **Is his mercy** clean
gone for ever? doth his
promise fail for evermore?
9. **Hath God forgotten to**
be gracious? hath he in
anger shut up his tender
mercies? Selah.
10. And I said, This *is* my infirmity:
but I will remember the years of the
right hand of the most High.
11. **I will remember the**
works of the LORD: surely
I will remember thy wonders of old.
12. I will meditate also of all thy work,
and talk of thy doings.
13. **Thy way,** O God,
is in the sanctuary:
who is so great a God
as our God?
14. **Thou** *art* the God that

doest wonders: thou hast
declared thy strength
among the people.
15. **Thou hast** with *thine* arm
redeemed thy people, the
sons of Jacob and Joseph. Selah.
16. **The waters saw thee,**
O God, the waters saw thee;
they were afraid:
the depths also were troubled.
17. **The clouds poured out**
water: the skies sent out a sound:
thine arrows also went abroad.
18. The voice of thy
thunder was in
the heaven: the
lightnings lightened
the world: the earth
trembled and shook.
19. Thy way *is* in the sea, and thy
path in the great waters, and
thy footsteps
are not known.
20. **Thou leddest thy**
people like a flock
by the hand of Moses
and Aaron.

PSALMS 78

1. **Give ear,** O my people,
to my law: incline your ears
to the words of my mouth.
2. **I will open my mouth**
in a parable:
I will utter dark sayings of old:
3. **Which we have**
heard and known,
and our fathers have told us.
4. **We will not hide**
them from their children,
shewing to the
generation to come the
praises of the LORD,
and his strength,
and his wonderful
works that he hath done.
5. **For he established**
a testimony
in Jacob, and appointed a
law in Israel, which he
commanded our fathers,
that they should make
them known to their children:

6. **That the generation to come might know them,** *even* the children *which* should be born; *who* should arise and declare *them* to their children:

7. **That they might set their hope in God,** and not forget the works of God, but keep his commandments:

8. **And might not be as their fathers, a stubborn and rebellious generation;** a generation *that* set not their heart aright, and whose spirit was not stedfast with God.

9. **The children of Ephraim,** *being* armed, *and* carrying bows, **turned back in the day of battle.**

10. **They kept not the covenant of God,** and refused to walk in his law;

11. And forgat his works, and his wonders that he had shewed them.

12. **Marvellous things did he in the sight of their fathers, in** the land of **Egypt,** *in* the field of Zoan.

13. **He divided the sea, and caused them to pass through;** and he made the waters to stand as an heap.

14. In the daytime also **he led them with a cloud, and** all the night with **a** light of **fire.**

15. He clave the rocks in the wilderness, and gave *them* drink as *out of* the great depths.

16. **He brought streams also out of the rock,** and caused waters to run down like rivers.

17. **And they sinned yet more against him** by provoking the most High in the wilderness.

18. **And they tempted God** in their heart **by asking meat for their lust.**

19. **Yea, they spake against God;** they said, Can God furnish a table in the wilderness?

20. Behold, he smote the rock, that the waters gushed out, and the streams overflowed; can he give bread also? can he provide flesh for his people?

21. **Therefore the LORD heard this, and was wroth:** so a fire was kindled against Jacob, and anger also came up against Israel;

22. **Because they believed not in God, and trusted not in his salvation:**

23. **Though he** had commanded the clouds from above, and **opened the doors of heaven,**

24. **And** had **rained** down **manna upon them** to eat, and had given them of the corn of heaven.

25. **Man did eat angels' food:** he sent them meat to the full.

26. He caused an east wind to blow in the heaven: and by his power he brought in the south wind.

27. **He rained flesh also upon them** as dust, and feathered fowls like as the sand of the sea:

28. And he let *it* fall in the midst of their camp, round about their habitations.

29. So they did eat, and were well filled: **for he gave them their** own **desire;**

30. They were not estranged from their lust.

But while their meat was yet in their mouths,

31. **The wrath of God came upon them, and slew the fattest of them, and** smote down **the chosen men of Israel.**

32. **For** all this **they sinned still, and believed not** for **his wondrous works.**

33. Therefore their days did he consume in vanity, and their years in trouble.

34. **When he slew them,**

then they sought him: and
**they returned
and inquired** early
after God.
35. **And they
remembered** that
**God was their rock,
and** the high God their
redeemer.
36. **Nevertheless** they did
flatter him with their mouth, and
they lied unto him
with their tongues.
37. **For their heart was not
right with him,** neither were
they stedfast in his covenant.
38. **But he, being full of
compassion, forgave their
iniquity,** and destroyed *them* not:
yea, many a time turned he his anger
away, and did not stir up all his wrath.
39. **For he remembered
that they were but flesh;**
a wind that passeth away,
and cometh not again.
40. **How oft did they
provoke him in the
wilderness,**
and grieve him in the desert!
41. Yea, they turned back and
tempted God, and limited the
Holy One of Israel.
42. **They remembered
not** his hand, *nor*
the day when
**he delivered them
from the enemy.**
43. **How he** had
wrought his
signs in Egypt, and his
wonders in the field of Zoan.
44. **And** had
**turned their rivers into
blood;** and their floods,
that they could not drink.
45. **He sent** divers sorts of
flies among them,
which devoured them;
and frogs, which destroyed them.
46. **He gave**
also their increase unto
the caterpiller, and
their labour unto the

locust.
47. **He destroyed their vines
with hail, and their** sycomore
trees with frost.
48. He gave up their cattle also
to the hail, and their flocks to hot
thunderbolts.
49. **He cast upon them the
fierceness of his anger,**
wrath, and indignation, and trouble,
**by sending evil angels
among them.**
50. He made a way to his anger; he
spared not their soul from death, but
gave their life over to the pestilence;
51. **And smote all the
firstborn in Egypt;**
the chief of *their* strength in
the tabernacles of Ham:
52. **But made his
own people** to
go forth like sheep,
and guided them
**in the wilderness
like a flock.**
53. **And he led them** on safely,
so that
they feared not: but the sea
overwhelmed their enemies.
54. **And he brought them** to
the border of his sanctuary, *even*
to this mountain, *which*
his right hand had purchased.
55. **He cast out
the heathen** also
before them, and divided
them an inheritance by line,
and made the tribes of
Israel to dwell in their tents.
56. **Yet they tempted**
and provoked the most high
**God, and kept not
his testimonies:**
57. But turned back, and dealt
unfaithfully like their fathers: they
were turned aside like a deceitful bow.
58. **For they provoked
him** to anger
with their high places, and
moved him to jealousy with their
graven images.
59. When God heard *this,* he was
wroth, and greatly abhorred Israel:

■ 60. **So** that
■ **he forsook the tabernacle**
■ **of Shiloh,**
the tent *which* he placed among men;
■ 61. **And delivered his**
■ **strength** into captivity,
■ **and** his
■ **glory into**
■ **the enemy's hand.**
■ 62. **He** gave his people over
also unto the sword; and
■ **was wroth with**
■ **his inheritance.**
■ 63. **The fire consumed their**
■ **young men;** and their maidens
were not given to marriage.
■ 64. **Their priests fell by**
■ **the sword;** and their widows
made no lamentation.
■ 65. **Then the LORD awaked**
■ **as one out of sleep,**
and like a mighty man that
shouteth by reason of wine.
■ 66. **And he smote his**
■ **enemies** in the hinder parts: he
put them to a perpetual reproach.
■ 67. **Moreover he** refused
the tabernacle of Joseph, and
■ **chose not the tribe**
■ **of Ephraim:**
■ 68. **But** chose the tribe of
■ **Judah,** the mount Zion
■ **which he loved.**
■ 69. **And he built**
■ **his sanctuary** like high
palaces, like the earth which
he hath established for ever.
■ 70. **He chose David**
also his servant, and took him
■ **from the sheepfolds:**
71. From following the
ewes great with young
■ **he brought him to feed** Jacob
■ **his people,**
and Israel his inheritance.
■ 72. **So he fed them** according
to the integrity of his heart;
■ **and guided them by**
the skilfulness of
■ **his hands.**

PSALMS 79

I■I 1. **O GOD, the heathen**

■ **are come into thine**
■ **inheritance; thy holy**
■ **temple have they defiled;**
they have laid Jerusalem on heaps.
2. The dead bodies of thy servants
have they given *to be* meat unto the
fowls of the heaven, the flesh of thy
saints unto the beasts of the earth.
3. Their blood have they shed like
water round about Jerusalem; and
there was none to bury *them.*
■ 4. **We are** become
■ **a reproach to our**
■ **neighbours,** a scorn and derision
to them that are round about us.
■ 5. **How long, LORD? wilt**
■ **thou be angry** for ever? shall
thy jealousy burn like fire?
■ 6. **Pour out thy wrath upon**
■ **the heathen that have not**
■ **known thee,** and upon the
kingdoms that have not
called upon thy name.
7. For they have devoured Jacob,
and laid waste his dwelling place.
■ 8. **O remember not against**
■ **us former iniquities:** let thy
tender mercies speedily prevent
us: for we are brought very low.
■ 9. **Help us, O God of our**
■ **salvation, for the glory of**
■ **thy name:** and deliver us, and
■ **purge away our sins,**
■ **for thy name's sake.**
■ 10. **Wherefore should the**
■ **heathen say, Where is their**
■ **God? let him be known**
■ **among the heathen** in oursight
■ **by the revenging of the**
■ **blood of thy servants**
which is shed.
11. Let the sighing of the prisoner
come before thee; according to
the greatness of thy power
■ **preserve** thou
■ **those** that are
■ **appointed to die;**
■ 12. **And render unto**
■ **our neighbours**
sevenfold into their bosom
■ **their reproach, wherewith**
■ **they have reproached**
■ **thee, O Lord.**

13. **So we thy people** and sheep of thy pasture **will give thee thanks for ever:** we will shew forth thy praise to all generations.

PSALMS 80

1. **Give ear, O Shepherd** of Israel, thou **that leadest Joseph like a flock;** thou that dwellest *between* the cherubims, shine forth.
2. Before Ephraim and Benjamin and Manasseh stir up thy strength, and come *and* save us.
3. **Turn us again, O God,** and cause thy face to shine; **and we shall be saved.**
4. **O LORD** God of hosts, **how long wilt thou be angry** against the prayer of thy people?
5. **Thou feedest them with the bread of tears;** and givest them tears to drink in great measure.
6. **Thou makest us** a **strife unto** our neighbours: and **our enemies** laugh among themselves.
7. Turn us again, O God of hosts, and cause thy face to shine; and we shall be saved.
8. **Thou hast brought a vine out of Egypt: thou hast cast out the heathen, and planted it.**
9. **Thou** preparedst *room* before it, and **didst cause it to take deep root, and it filled the land.**
10. The hills were covered with the shadow of it, and the boughs thereof *were like* the goodly cedars.
11. She sent out her boughs unto the sea, and her branches unto the river.
12. **Why hast thou** *then* **broken** down **her hedges,** so that all they which pass by the way do pluck her?
13. The boar out of the wood doth waste it, and the wild beast of the field doth devour it.
14. **Return,** we beseech thee, **O God** of hosts:

look down from heaven, and behold, **and visit this vine;**
15. **And the vineyard** which thy right hand hath planted, and the branch *that* thou madest strong for thyself.
16. *It* **is burned** with fire, *it is* cut down: **they perish at the rebuke of thy countenance.**
17. **Let thy hand be upon the man of thy right hand,** upon the son of man **whom thou madest strong for thyself.**
18. **So** will not we go back from thee: quicken us, and **we will call upon thy name.**
19. **Turn us again, O LORD** God of hosts, **cause thy face to shine; and we shall be saved.**

PSALMS 81

1. **Sing** aloud **unto God** our strength: **make a joyful noise** unto the God of Jacob.
2. Take a psalm, and **bring** hither **the timbrel,** the pleasant harp **with the psaltery.**
3. **Blow** up **the trumpet in the** new moon, in the time appointed, on our solemn **feast day.**
4. **For this was** a statute for Israel, *and* **a law of** the **God** of Jacob.
5. **This he ordained** in Joseph **for a testimony, when he went** out **through** the land of **Egypt:** *where* I heard a language *that* I understood not.
6. I removed his shoulder from the burden: his hands were delivered from the pots.
7. Thou calledst in trouble, and I delivered thee; I answered thee in the secret place of thunder: I proved thee

at the waters of Meribah. Selah.

8. **Hear, O my people, and I will testify unto thee:** O Israel, **if thou wilt hearken unto me;**

9. **There shall no strange god be in thee;** neither shalt thou worship any strange god.

10. **I am the LORD** thy God, **which brought thee out of** the land of **Egypt: open thy mouth** wide, **and I will fill it.**

11. **But my people would not hearken** to my voice; and Israel would none of me.

12. **So I gave them up unto their own** hearts' **lust:** *and* they walked in their own counsels.

13. **Oh that** my people had hearkened unto me, *and* **Israel had walked in my ways!**

14. **I should soon have subdued their enemies,** and turned my hand against their adversaries.

15. The haters of the LORD should have submitted themselves unto him: but their time should have endured for ever.

16. **He should have fed them** also with **the finest** of the **wheat: and** with **honey out of the rock** should I have satisfied thee.

PSALMS 82

1. **GOD standeth in the congregation** of the mighty; **he judgeth** among **the gods.**

2. **How long will ye** judge unjustly, and **accept** the persons of **the wicked?** Selah.

3. **Defend the poor and fatherless:** do justice to the afflicted and needy.

4. **Deliver** the poor and needy: rid **them out of the hand** of the wicked.

5. They know not, neither will they understand; they walk on in darkness: all the foundations of the earth are out of course.

6. **I have said, Ye are gods; and** all of you *are* **children of the most High.**

7. **But ye shall die** like men, **and fall like** one of **the princes.**

8. **Arise, O God, judge the earth: for thou shalt inherit all nations.**

PSALMS 83

1. **Keep not thou silence, O God:** hold not thy peace, and be not still, O God.

2. **For,** lo, **thine enemies make a tumult:** and they that hate thee have lifted up the head.

3. **They have taken** crafty **counsel against thy people,** and consulted against thy hidden ones.

4. **They have said,** Come, and **let us cut them off** from *being* a nation; **that the name of Israel may be no more** in remembrance.

5. **For they have consulted together** with one consent: they are confederate **against thee:**

6. The tabernacles of Edom, and the Ishmaelites; of Moab, and the Hagarenes;

7. Gebal, and Ammon, and Amalek; the Philistines with the inhabitants of Tyre;

8. Assur also is joined with them: they have holpen the children of Lot. Selah.

9. **Do unto them as unto the Midianites;** as *to* Sisera, as *to* Jabin, at the brook of Kison:

10. **Which perished at En-dor:** they became *as* dung for the earth.

11. Make their nobles like Oreb, and

like Zeeb: yea, all their princes as Zebah, and as Zalmunna:

12. Who said, Let us take to ourselves the houses of God in possession.

13. O my God, make them like a wheel; as the stubble before the wind.

14. As the fire burneth a wood, and as the flame setteth the mountains on fire;

15. So persecute them with thy tempest, and make them afraid with thy storm.

16. Fill their faces with shame; that they may seek thy name, O LORD.

17. Let them be confounded and troubled for ever; yea, let them be put to shame, and perish:

18. That men may know that thou, whose name alone is JEHOVAH, art the most high over all the earth.

PSALMS 84

1. How amiable are thy tabernacles, O LORD of hosts!

2. My soul longeth, yea, even fainteth for the courts of the LORD: my heart and my flesh crieth out for the living God.

3. Yea, the sparrow hath found an house, and the swallow a nest for herself, where she may lay her young, even thine altars, O LORD of hosts, my King, and my God.

4. Blessed are they that dwell in thy house: they will be still praising thee. Selah.

5. Blessed is the man whose strength is in thee; in whose heart are the ways of them.

6. Who passing through the valley of Baca make it a well; the rain also filleth the pools.

7. They go from strength to strength, every one of them in Zion appeareth before God.

8. O LORD God of hosts, hear my prayer: give ear, O God of Jacob. Selah.

9. Behold, O God our shield, and look upon the face of thine anointed.

10. For a day in thy courts is better than a thousand. I had rather be a doorkeeper in the house of my God, than to dwell in the tents of wickedness.

11. For the LORD God is a sun and shield: the LORD will give grace and glory: no good thing will he withhold from them that walk uprightly.

12. O LORD of hosts, blessed is the man that trusteth in thee.

PSALMS 85

1. LORD, thou hast been favourable unto thy land: thou hast brought back the captivity of Jacob.

2. Thou hast forgiven the iniquity of thy people, thou hast covered all their sin. Selah.

3. Thou hast taken away all thy wrath: thou hast turned thyself from the fierceness of thine anger.

4. Turn us, O God of our salvation, and cause thine anger toward us to cease.

5. Wilt thou be angry with us for ever? wilt thou draw out thine anger to all generations?

6. Wilt thou not revive us again: that thy people may rejoice in thee?

7. Shew us thy mercy, O LORD, and grant us thy salvation.

8. I will hear what God the LORD will speak: for he will speak peace unto his people, and to his saints: but let them not turn again to folly.

9. Surely his salvation is nigh them that fear him;

that glory may dwell in our land.

10. **Mercy and truth are met together;** righteousness and peace have kissed *each other*.

11. **Truth** shall spring out of the earth; **and righteousness shall look down from heaven.**

12. **Yea, the LORD shall give that which is good;** and our land shall yield her increase.

13. **Righteousness** shall go before him; and **shall set us in the way of his steps.**

PSALMS 86

1. Bow down thine ear, **O LORD, hear me: for I am poor and needy.**

2. Preserve my soul; for I *am* holy: O thou my God, **save thy servant that trusteth in thee.**

3. **Be merciful** unto me, **O Lord: for I cry unto thee daily.**

4. Rejoice the soul of thy servant: for unto thee, O Lord, do I lift up my soul.

5. **For thou,** Lord, **art good, and ready to forgive;** and plenteous in mercy unto all **them that call upon thee.**

6. **Give ear,** O LORD, **unto my prayer;** and attend to the voice of my supplications.

7. **In** the day of **my trouble I will call upon thee: for thou wilt answer me.**

8. Among the gods **there is none like** unto **thee, O Lord;** neither *are there any works* like unto thy works.

9. **All nations** whom thou hast made **shall** come and **worship before thee,** O Lord; **and shall glorify thy name.**

10. **For thou art great,** and doest wondrous things:

thou *art* God alone.

11. **Teach me thy way, O LORD;** I will walk in thy truth: **unite my heart to fear thy name.**

12. **I will praise thee,** O Lord my God, **with all my heart: and I will glorify thy name for evermore.**

13. For great *is* thy mercy toward me: and **thou hast delivered my soul from** the lowest **hell.**

14. **O God,** the **proud** are risen against me, **and** the assemblies of **violent men have sought** after **my soul;** and have not set thee before them.

15. **But thou,** O Lord, **art** a God **full of compassion,** and **gracious, long suffering, and plenteous in mercy and truth.**

16. O turn unto me, and have mercy upon me; **give thy strength** unto thy servant, **and save the son of thine handmaid.**

17. **Shew me** a token for **good; that they which hate me may see** *it,* **and be ashamed: because thou,** LORD, **hast holpen** me, **and comforted me.**

PSALMS 87

1. **His foundation is in the holy mountains.**

2. **The LORD loveth** the gates of **Zion** more than all the dwellings of Jacob.

3. **Glorious things are spoken of thee, O city of God.** Selah.

4. **I will make mention** of Rahab and Babylon to them

that know me: behold Philistia, and Tyre, with Ethiopia; **this man was born there.**

5. And of Zion it shall be said, This and that man was born in her: **and the highest** himself **shall establish her.**

6. **The LORD** shall count, when he **writeth** up the people, **that this man was born there.** Selah.

7. As well **the singers** as the players on instruments **shall be there: all my springs are in thee.**

PSALMS 88

1. **O LORD** God of my salvation, I have cried day *and* night before thee:

2. Let my prayer come before thee: **incline thine ear unto my cry;**

3. **For my soul is full of troubles: and my life draweth nigh unto the grave.**

4. **I am counted with them that go down into the pit:** I am as a man *that hath* no strength:

5. Free among the dead, like the slain that lie in the grave, **whom thou rememberest no more:** and they are cut off from thy hand.

6. Thou hast laid me in the lowest pit, in darkness, in the deeps.

7. **Thy wrath** lieth hard upon me, and thou **hast afflicted me** with all thy waves. Selah.

8. Thou hast put away mine acquaintance far from me; **thou hast made me an abomination** unto them: *I am* shut up, and I cannot come forth.

9. **Mine eye mourneth by reason of affliction: LORD, I have called daily upon thee,** I have stretched out my hands unto thee.

10. Wilt thou shew wonders to the dead? **shall the dead arise and praise thee?** Selah.

11. **Shall thy lovingkindness be declared in the grave?** *or* thy faithfulness in destruction?

12. **Shall thy wonders be known** in the dark? and thy righteousness **in the land of forgetfulness?**

13. **But unto thee have I cried, O LORD;** and in the morning shall my prayer prevent thee.

14. LORD, why castest thou off my soul? **why hidest thou thy face from me?**

15. **I am afflicted and ready to die** from *my* youth up: *while* I suffer thy terrors I am distracted.

16. **Thy** fierce **wrath goeth over me;** thy terrors have cut me off.

17. **They came** round **about me** daily **like water;** they compassed me about together.

18. **Lover and friend hast thou put far from me,** *and* mine acquaintance into darkness.

PSALMS 89

1. **I will sing of the mercies of the LORD for ever: with my mouth will I make known thy faithfulness** to all generations.

2. For I have said, Mercy shall be built up for ever: thy faithfulness shalt thou establish in the very heavens.

3. **I have made a covenant with** my chosen, I have sworn unto **David my servant,**

4. **Thy seed will I establish for ever,** and build up thy throne to all generations. Selah.

5. **And the heavens shall praise thy wonders,** O LORD: thy faithfulness also in the congregation of the saints.

6. **For who** in the heaven **can be compared unto the LORD?** *who* among the sons of the mighty can be likened unto the LORD? 7. **God is greatly to be feared** in the assembly of the saints, **and to be had in reverence** of all *them that are* about him. 8. **O LORD** God of hosts, **who is** a **strong LORD like** unto **thee?** or to thy faithfulness round about thee? 9. **Thou rulest** the raging of **the sea:** when the waves thereof arise, thou stillest them. 10. **Thou hast broken Rahab** in pieces, **as one** that is **slain; thou hast scattered thine enemies** with thy strong arm. 11. The heavens *are* thine, the earth also *is* thine: **as for the world and the fulness thereof, thou hast founded them.** 12. The north and the south thou hast created them: Tabor and Hermon shall rejoice in thy name. 13. **Thou hast a mighty arm:** strong is thy hand, *and* high is thy right hand. 14. **Justice and judgment are the habitation of thy throne: mercy and truth** shall **go before thy face.** 15. **Blessed is the people that** know the joyful sound: they shall **walk,** O LORD, **in the light of thy countenance.** 16. **In thy name shall they rejoice** all the day: **and in thy righteousness shall they be exalted.** 17. For thou art the glory of their strength: and in thy favour our horn shall be exalted. 18. **For the LORD is our defence; and the Holy One of Israel is our king.** 19. **Then thou spakest** in vision to thy holy one, **and saidst, I** have laid **help** upon **one that is mighty; I** have **exalted one chosen** out **of the people.** 20. **I have found David** my servant; **with my holy oil** have **I anointed him:** 21. With whom my hand shall be established: mine arm also shall strengthen him. 22. **The enemy shall not** exact upon him; nor the son of wickedness **afflict him.** 23. **And I will beat down** his foes before his face, **and plague them that hate him.** 24. **But my faithfulness and** my **mercy shall be with him:** and in my name shall his horn be exalted. 25. I will set his hand also in the sea, and his right hand in the rivers. 26. **He shall cry unto me, Thou art my father, my God, and the rock of my salvation.** 27. **Also I will make** him **my firstborn, higher than** the **kings** of the earth. 28. **My mercy** will I keep for him for evermore, **and my covenant shall stand fast with him.** 29. **His seed also will I make to endure for ever,** and his throne as the days of heaven. 30. **If his children forsake my law,** and walk not in my judgments; 31. If they break my statutes, and keep not my commandments; 32. **Then will I visit their transgression with the rod,** and their iniquity with stripes.

33. **Nevertheless my lovingkindness will I not utterly take from him,** nor suffer my faithfulness to fail.
34. **My covenant will I not break,** nor alter the thing that is gone out of my lips.
35. Once have I sworn by my holiness that **I will not lie unto David.**
36. His seed shall endure for ever, and **his throne** as the sun before me.
37. **It shall be established for ever** as the moon, and **as a faithful witness in heaven.** Selah.
38. **But thou hast** cast off and **abhorred,** thou hast been wroth with **thine anointed.**
39. **Thou hast made void the covenant** of thy servant: thou hast profaned his crown *by casting it* to the ground.
40. Thou hast broken down all his hedges; **thou hast brought his strong holds to ruin.**
41. All that pass by the way spoil him: he is a reproach to his neighbours.
42. Thou hast set up the right hand of his adversaries; **thou hast made all his enemies to rejoice.**
43. **Thou hast** also **turned** the edge of **his sword,** and hast not made him to stand in the battle.
44. **Thou hast made his glory to cease, and cast his throne down** to the ground.
45. The days of his youth hast thou shortened: **thou hast covered him with shame.** Selah.
46. **How long, LORD?** wilt thou hide thyself for ever? **shall thy wrath burn** like fire?
47. **Remember how short my time is:** wherefore **hast thou made** all **men in vain?**
48. **What man** *is he that* liveth, and shall not see death? **shall he deliver** his soul **from** the hand of the **grave?** Selah.
49. **Lord, where are thy** former **lovingkindnesses,** *which* thou swarest unto David in thy truth?
50. Remember, Lord, the reproach of thy servants; *how* I do bear in my bosom *the reproach of* all the mighty people;
51. **Wherewith thine enemies** have reproached, O LORD; wherewith they **have reproached the footsteps of thine anointed.**
52. **Blessed be the LORD for evermore. Amen,** and Amen.

PSALM 90

1. **LORD, thou hast been our dwelling place** in all generations.
2. **Before** the mountains were brought forth, or ever **thou** hadst **formed the earth and the world, even from everlasting** to everlasting, **thou art God.**
3. **Thou turnest man to destruction; and sayest, Return, ye** children of **men.**
4. **For a thousand years in thy sight are but** as yesterday when it is past, and *as* **a watch in the night.**
5. **Thou carriest them away** as with a flood; they are *as* a sleep: in the morning **they are like grass** *which* groweth up.
6. **In the morning it** flourisheth, and **groweth** up; **in the evening it is cut down,** and withereth.
7. **For we are consumed by thine anger,**

and by thy wrath are we troubled.

8. Thou hast set our iniquities before thee, **our secret sins in the light of thy countenance.**

9. For all **our days are passed away in thy wrath:** we spend our years as a tale *that is told.*

10. The days of our years are threescore years and ten; and if by reason of strength *they be* fourscore years, yet *is* their strength labour and sorrow; for it is soon **cut off, and we fly away.**

11. Who knoweth the power of thine anger? even according to thy fear, *so is* thy wrath.

12. So teach us to number our days, that we may apply our hearts unto wisdom.

13. Return, O LORD, how long? and let it repent thee concerning thy servants.

14. O satisfy us early with thy mercy; that we may rejoice and be glad **all our days.**

15. Make us glad according to the days **wherein thou hast afflicted us,** *and* the years *wherein* we have seen evil.

16. Let thy work appear unto thy servants, **and thy glory** unto their children.

17. And let the beauty of the LORD our God **be upon us: and establish** thou **the work of our hands** upon us; yea, the work of our hands establish thou it.

PSALM 91

1. He that dwelleth in the secret place of the most High shall abide under the shadow of the Almighty.

2. I will say of the LORD, He is my refuge and **my fortress: my God; in him will I trust.**

3. Surely he shall deliver thee from the snare of the fowler, **and** from the noisome **pestilence.**

4. He shall cover thee with his feathers, and **under his wings shalt thou trust:** his truth *shall be thy* shield and buckler.

5. Thou shalt not be afraid for the terror by night; nor for the arrow *that* flieth **by day;**

6. *Nor* for the pestilence *that* walketh in darkness; *nor* for the destruction *that* wasteth at noonday.

7. A thousand shall fall at thy side, and ten thousand at thy right hand; but it shall not come nigh thee.

8. Only with thine eyes shalt thou behold and see the reward of the wicked.

9. Because thou hast made the LORD, *which is* my refuge, *even* the most High, **thy habitation;**

10. There shall no evil befall thee, neither shall any plague come nigh thy dwelling.

11. For he shall give his angels charge over thee, to keep thee in all thy ways.

12. They shall bear thee up in *their* hands, **lest thou dash thy foot against a stone.**

13. Thou shalt tread upon the lion and adder: the young lion and the dragon shalt thou trample under feet.

14. Because he hath set his love upon me, therefore will I deliver him: I will set him on high, because he hath known my name.

15. He shall call upon me, and I will answer him: I *will be* with him in trouble; **I will deliver him, and honour him.**

■ 16. With long life will I satisfy him,
■ **and shew him my**
■ **salvation.**

PSALM 92

■ 1. **IT is a good thing to give**
■ **thanks unto the LORD, and**
■ **to sing praises unto thy**
■ **name,** O most High
■ 2. **To shew** forth
■ **thy lovingkindness**
in the morning,
■ **and** thy
■ **faithfulness** every night,
3. Upon an instrument of ten strings,
and upon the psaltery; upon the
harp with a solemn sound.
■ 4. **For thou, LORD, hast**
■ **made me glad through**
■ **thy work:**
I will triumph in the works
of thy hands.
5. O LORD, how
■ **great are thy works!**
■ **and thy thoughts**
are very deep.
■ 6. **A brutish man knoweth**
■ **not; neither doth a fool**
understand this.
■ 7. **When the wicked**
spring as the grass, and when
all the workers of iniquity do
■ **flourish;** *it is* that
■ **they shall be**
■ **destroyed** for ever:
■ 8. **But thou, LORD,**
■ **art most high** for evermore.
9. For, lo, thine enemies,
O LORD, for, lo,
■ **thine enemies shall perish;**
■ **all the workers of iniquity**
■ **shall be scattered.**
■ 10. **But my horn shalt thou**
■ **exalt** like *the horn of* an unicorn:
■ **I shall be anointed**
■ **with fresh oil.**
11. Mine eye also shall see *my*
desire on mine enemies, *and* mine
ears shall hear *my desire* of the
wicked that rise up against me.
■ 12. **The righteous shall**
■ **flourish** like the palm tree: he
shall grow like a cedar in Lebanon.

■ 13. Those that be planted in the
house of the LORD shall flourish
■ **in the courts of our God.**
■ 14. **They shall still bring**
■ **forth fruit in old age;**
they shall be fat and flourishing;
15. To shew that
■ **the LORD is upright:**
■ **he is my rock,** and
■ **there is no unrighteousness**
■ **in him.**

PSALM 93

■ 1. **The LORD reigneth,** he is
clothed with majesty; the LORD is
clothed with strength, *wherewith* he
hath girded himself: the world also is
stablished, that it cannot be moved.
■ 2. **Thy throne is**
■ **established** of old:
■ **thou art** from
■ **everlasting.**
3. The floods have lifted up, O LORD,
■ **the floods have lifted**
■ **up their voice;**
the floods lift up their waves.
■ 4. **The LORD** on high
■ **is mightier than the**
■ **noise of** many waters, *yea, than*
■ **the mighty waves**
of the sea.
■ 5. **Thy testimonies are** very
■ **sure: holiness becometh**
■ **thine house, O LORD,**
■ **for ever.**

PSALM 94

■ 1. **O Lord God,** to whom
vengeance belongeth; O God, to
whom vengeance belongeth,
■ **shew thyself.**
■ 2. **Lift up thyself,**
thou judge of the earth:
■ **render a reward**
■ **to the proud.**
■ 3. **LORD, how long shall the**
■ **wicked,** how long shall the wicked
■ **triumph?**
■ 4. **How long shall** they utter
and speak hard things? *and* all
■ **the workers of iniquity**
■ **boast** themselves?
■ 5. **They break**

in pieces thy people, O LORD,
and afflict thine heritage.
6. **They slay the widow and
the** stranger, and murder the
fatherless.
7. **Yet they say, The LORD
shall not see, neither**
shall the God of Jacob
regard it.
8. Understand, ye brutish
among the people: and *ye*
fools, when will ye be wise?
9. **He that planted the
ear, shall he not hear?
he that formed the eye,
shall he not see?**
10. **He that chastiseth the
heathen, shall not he
correct? he that teacheth
man knowledge, shall
not he know?**
11. **The LORD knoweth the
thoughts of man,** that they
are vanity.
12. **Blessed is the man
whom thou chastenest,
O LORD,**
and teachest him out of thy law;
13. **That thou mayest give
him rest from** the days of
**adversity, until the pit be
digged for the wicked.**
14. **For the LORD will not
cast off his people,** neither
will he forsake his inheritance.
15. **But judgment shall return
unto righteousness:** and all the
upright in heart
shall follow it.
16. **Who will rise up** for me
against the evildoers? *or* who
will stand up for me against
the workers of iniquity?
17. **Unless the LORD
had been my help,
my soul had** almost
dwelt in silence.
18. **When** I said,
**My foot slippeth; thy
mercy, O LORD,
held me up.**
19. In the multitude of my
thoughts within me thy

comforts delight my soul.
20. **Shall** the throne of
**iniquity have fellowship
with thee,** which frameth
mischief by a law?
21. **They gather**
themselves together
against the soul of
**the righteous,
and condemn** the
innocent blood.
22. **But the LORD is
my defence;** and my
God *is* the rock of my refuge.
23. **And he shall bring upon
them their own iniquity,
and shall cut them off**
in their own wickedness; *yea,* the
LORD our God shall cut them off.

PSALM 95

1. **O come, let us sing
unto the LORD:**
let us make a joyful noise to
the rock of our salvation.
2. **Let us come before
his presence with
thanksgiving,** and make a
joyful noise unto him with psalms.
3. **For the LORD is** a
great God, and a great
King above all gods.
4. **In his hand are the deep
places of the earth: the
strength of the hills** *is* his also.
5. **The sea is his,** and he made it:
and his hands formed the dry *land.*
6. **O come, let us worship**
and bow down: let us kneel before
the LORD our maker.
7. **For he is our God;
and we are the** people
of his pasture, and the
**sheep of his hand.
To day if ye will hear
his voice,**
8. **Harden not your heart,
as in** the provocation, *and* as *in*
the day of temptation
in the wilderness:
9. **When your fathers
tempted me, proved me,
and saw my work.**

10. **Forty years** long **was I grieved** with *this* generation, **and said,** It *is* a people that do err in their heart, and **they have not known my ways:** 11. **Unto whom I sware** in my wrath **that they should not enter** into **my rest.**

PSALM 96

1. **O sing unto the LORD a new song:** sing unto the LORD, all the earth. 2. Sing unto the LORD, **bless his name; shew forth his salvation** from day to day. 3. **Declare his glory** among the heathen, his wonders among all people. 4. **For the LORD is great, and greatly to be praised:** he *is* to be feared above all gods. 5. For all the gods of the nations *are* idols: but the LORD made the heavens. 6. **Honour and majesty** *are* before him: **strength and beauty are in his sanctuary.** 7. **Give** unto **the LORD,** O ye kindreds of the people, give unto the LORD **glory and strength.** 8. Give unto the LORD the glory *due unto* his name: **bring an offering,** and come **into his courts.** 9. **O worship the LORD in the beauty of holiness:** fear before him, all the earth. 10. **Say among the heathen that the LORD reigneth:** the world also shall be established that it shall not be moved: **he shall judge the people righteously.** 11. **Let the heavens** rejoice, **and** let the **earth be glad;** let the sea roar,

and the fulness thereof. 12. Let the field be joyful, and all that is therein: then shall all the trees of the wood rejoice 13. Before the LORD: for he cometh, **for** he cometh to judge the earth: **he shall judge** the world **with righteousness, and** the people with his **truth.**

PSALM 97

1. **The LORD reigneth;** let the earth rejoice; let the multitude of isles be glad *thereof.* 2. Clouds and darkness *are* round about him: **righteousness and judgment are the habitation of his throne.** 3. **A fire goeth before him, and burneth up his enemies** round about. 4. His lightnings enlightened the world: the earth saw, and trembled. 5. **The hills melted** like wax **at the presence of the LORD,** at the presence of the Lord of the whole earth. 6. **The heavens declare his righteousness, and** all the people see **his glory.** 7. **Confounded be** all **they that serve** graven images, that boast themselves of **idols:** worship him, all *ye* gods. 8. **Zion** heard, **and** was glad; and the daughters of **Judah rejoiced because of thy judgments, O LORD.** 9. **For thou, LORD,** *art* high above all the earth: thou **art exalted** far **above all gods.** 10. **Ye that love the LORD, hate evil:** he preserveth the souls of his saints; he delivereth them out of the hand of the wicked. 11. Light is sown for the righteous, and gladness for the upright in heart. 12. **Rejoice in the LORD,**

ye righteous;
and give thanks at the
remembrance of his holiness.

PSALM 98

1. **O sing unto the
LORD** a new song;
**for he hath done
marvellous things:** his
right hand, and his holy arm,
hath gotten him the victory.
2. **The LORD hath made
known his salvation:**
his righteousness hath he openly
shewed in the sight of the heathen.
3. **He hath remembered
his mercy** and his truth
toward the house of
Israel: all the ends of the earth
have seen the salvation of our God.
4. **Make a joyful noise
unto the LORD,** all the earth:
make a loud noise, and rejoice,
and sing praise.
5. **Sing** unto the LORD
with the harp; with the harp, and
the voice of a psalm.
6. **With trumpets and sound
of cornet make a joyful
noise** before the LORD, the King.
7. **Let the sea**
roar, and the fulness thereof;
the world, and they that dwell
therein.
8. **Let the floods
clap** their hands:
**let the hills be
joyful together**
9. **Before the LORD; for he
cometh to judge the earth:
with righteousness**
shall he judge the world,
and the people with
equity.

PSALM 99

1. **The LORD reigneth; let
the people tremble:**
he sitteth between the cherubims;
let the earth be moved.
2. **The LORD**
is great in Zion; and he
is high above

all the people.
3. **Let them praise
thy** great and terrible
name; for it is holy.
4. The king's strength also loveth
judgment; thou dost establish equity,
thou executest judgment and
righteousness in Jacob.
5. **Exalt** ye
the LORD our God,
**and worship at his
footstool;** for he is holy.
6. **Moses and Aaron**
among his priests,
and Samuel among them
that call upon his name; they
**called upon the LORD,
and he answered them.**
7. **He spake unto them in
the cloudy pillar: they
kept** his testimonies, and
the ordinance that
he gave them.
8. Thou answeredst them, O LORD
our God: thou wast a God that
forgavest them, though thou tookest
vengeance of their inventions.
9. **Exalt the LORD** our God,
and worship at his holy hill;
for the LORD our God
is holy.

PSALM 100

1. **Make a joyful noise
unto the LORD,** all ye lands.
2. **Serve the LORD with
gladness: come before
his presence with singing.**
3. Know ye that
the LORD he
is God: it is
he that hath
made us, and not we ourselves;
we are his people, and
the sheep of his pasture.
4. **Enter into his gates with
thanksgiving, and into his
courts with praise: be
thankful unto him,
and bless his name.**
5. **For the LORD is good;
his mercy is everlasting;
and his truth endureth**

|■| to all generations.

PSALM 101

■ 1. **I will sing of mercy**
■ **and judgment:**
unto thee, O LORD, will I sing.
■ 2. **I will behave** myself
■ **wisely** in a perfect way.
O when wilt thou come unto me?
I will walk within my house
■ **with a perfect heart.**
■ 3. **I will set no wicked thing**
■ **before mine eyes:** I hate the
work of them that turn aside;
it shall not cleave to me.
■ 4. **A froward heart shall**
■ **depart from me:** I will
not know a wicked *person.*
■ 5. **Whoso** privily
■ **slandereth**
■ **his neighbour,** him
■ **will I cut off:** him that hath an high
look and a proud heart will not I suffer.
6. Mine eyes *shall be* upon the
faithful of the land, that they
may dwell with me:
■ **he that walketh in**
■ **a perfect way,** he
■ **shall serve me.**
■ 7. **He that worketh deceit**
■ **shall not dwell within**
■ **my house:**
he that telleth lies shall
not tarry in my sight.
8. I will early destroy all the wicked of
the land; that I may cut off all wicked
doers from the city of the LORD.

PSALM 102

■ 1. **Hear my prayer, O LORD,**
and let my cry come unto thee.
■ 2. **Hide not thy face from me**
in the day *when* I am in trouble;
incline thine ear unto me: in the day
■ **when I call answer**
■ **me speedily.**
■ 3. **For my days are**
■ **consumed** like smoke, and my
bones are burned as an hearth.
■ 4. **My heart is smitten,**
and withered like grass; so that
I forget to eat my bread.
5. By reason of the voice of my

groaning my bones cleave to my skin.
6. I am like a pelican of the
wilderness: I am like an
owl of the desert.
7. I watch, and am as a sparrow
alone upon the house top.
■ 8. **Mine enemies reproach**
■ **me** all the day; *and* they that are
mad against me are sworn against me.
9. For I have eaten ashes like bread,
and mingled my drink with weeping.
■ 10. **Because of thine**
■ **indignation and thy**
■ **wrath:** for thou hast lifted
me up, and cast me down.
11. My days *are* like a shadow
that declineth; and
■ **I am withered like grass.**
■ 12. **But thou, O LORD, shalt**
■ **endure for ever;** and thy
remembrance unto all generations.
■ 13. **Thou shalt** arise, *and*
■ **have mercy upon Zion:**
for the time to favour her, yea,
the set time, is come.
■ 14. **For thy servants take**
■ **pleasure in her stones,**
and favour the dust thereof.
■ 15. **So the heathen**
■ **shall fear the** name of the
■ **LORD,** and all the kings
of the earth thy glory.
■ 16. **When the LORD shall**
■ **build up Zion, he shall**
■ **appear in his glory.**
■ 17. **He will regard the**
■ **prayer of the destitute,**
and not despise their prayer.
18. This shall be written for
the generation to come:
■ **and the people**
which shall be created
■ **shall praise the LORD.**
■ 19. **For he hath looked**
■ **down** from the height
of his sanctuary;
■ **from heaven**
did the LORD behold the earth;
■ 20. **To hear the groaning**
■ **of the prisoner; to**
■ **loose those** that are
■ **appointed to death;**
■ 21. **To declare the name**

of the LORD in Zion,
and his praise in Jerusalem;
22. **When the people** are
gathered
together, and the kingdoms,
to serve the LORD.
23. **He weakened**
my strength in the way;
he shortened my days.
24. **I said, O my God, take**
me not away in the midst
of my days: thy years *are*
throughout all generations.
25. Of old hast
thou laid the foundation of
the earth: and the heavens
are the work of thy hands.
26. **They shall perish,**
but thou shalt endure: yea, all of them
shall wax old like a garment; as a
vesture shalt thou change them,
and they shall be changed:
27. **But thou art the same,**
and thy years shall
have no end.
28. **The children of**
thy servants shall
continue, and their seed
shall be established
before thee.

PSALM 103

1. **Bless the LORD, O my**
soul: and all that is within
me, bless his holy name.
2. Bless the LORD, O my soul, and
forget not all his benefits:
3. **Who forgiveth** all
thine iniquities; who healeth
all thy diseases;
4. **Who redeemeth thy**
life from destruction;
who crowneth thee with
lovingkindness and
tender mercies;
5. **Who satisfieth thy**
mouth with good things;
so that thy youth is
renewed like the eagle's.
6. **The LORD executeth**
righteousness and
judgment for all that
are oppressed.

7. **He made known his**
ways unto Moses, his acts unto
the children of Israel.
8. **The LORD is merciful and**
gracious, slow to anger,
and plenteous in mercy.
9. **He will not always**
chide: neither will he
keep his anger for ever.
10. **He hath not**
dealt with us after our sins; nor
rewarded us according
to our iniquities.
11. **For as the heaven is**
high above the earth,
so great is his mercy
toward them that fear him.
12. **As far as the east is**
from the west, so far
hath he removed our
transgressions from us.
13. **Like as a father pitieth**
his children, so the LORD
pitieth them that fear him.
14. **For he knoweth** our
frame; he remembereth that
we are dust.
15. **As for man,**
his days *are* as grass:
as a flower of the field, so
he flourisheth.
16. For the wind passeth over it,
and it
is gone; and the place thereof
shall know it no more.
17. **But the mercy of**
the LORD is from
everlasting to everlasting
upon them that fear him,
and his righteousness
unto children's children;
18. To such as keep his covenant,
and to those that remember his
commandments to do them.
19. **The LORD** hath
prepared his throne in
the heavens; and his
kingdom ruleth over all.
20. **Bless the LORD,**
ye his angels, that excel in strength,
that do his commandments,
hearkening unto the voice of
his word.

21. **Bless** ye **the LORD,** all *ye* his hosts; **ye ministers** of his, **that do his pleasure.** 22. **Bless the LORD, all his works** in all places of his dominion: **bless the LORD, O my soul.**

PSALM 104

1. Bless the LORD, O my soul. **O LORD** my God, **thou art** very **great;** thou art **clothed with honour and majesty.** 2. **Who coverest thyself with light** as *with* a garment: **who stretchest out the heavens** like a curtain: 3. Who layeth the beams of his chambers in the waters: **who maketh the clouds his chariot: who walketh upon** the wings of **the wind:** 4. **Who maketh his angels spirits; his ministers a flaming fire:** 5. **Who laid the foundations of the earth,** *that* it should not be removed for ever. 6. **Thou coveredst it with** the deep as *with* **a garment: the waters stood above the mountains.** 7. **At thy rebuke they fled;** at the voice of thy thunder they hasted away. 8. **They go** up by the mountains; they go down by the valleys **unto the place** which **thou** hast **founded for them.** 9. **Thou hast set a bound that they may not pass** over; **that they turn not again to cover the earth.** 10. **He sendeth the springs into the valleys,** *which* run among the hills. 11. **They give drink to every beast** of the field: the wild asses quench their thirst. 12. **By them shall the fowls** of the heaven **have their habitation,** *which* sing among the branches. 13. **He watereth the hills from his chambers: the earth is satisfied with the fruit of thy works.** 14. **He causeth the grass to grow for the cattle, and herb for** the service of **man:** that he may bring forth food out of the earth; 15. **And wine that maketh glad the heart of man, and oil to make his face** to **shine, and bread which strengtheneth man's heart.** 16. **The trees** of the LORD **are full of sap;** the cedars of Lebanon, which he hath planted; 17. Where the birds make their nests: *as for* the stork, the fir trees *are* her house. 18. The high hills *are* a refuge for the wild goats; *and* the rocks for the conies. 19. **He appointed the moon for seasons: the sun knoweth his going down.** 20. **Thou makest darkness,** and it is night: **wherein** all **the beasts of the forest** do **creep forth.** 21. **The young lions** roar after their prey, and **seek their meat from God.** 22. **The sun ariseth,** they gather themselves together, and lay them down in their dens. 23. **Man goeth** forth **unto his work** and to his labour **until the evening.** 24. **O LORD, how manifold are thy works! in wisdom hast thou made them** all: **the earth is full of thy riches.** 25. **So is this great** and wide **sea, wherein are things** creeping innumerable,

873

both small and great beasts.
26. There go the ships: *there is* that leviathan, *whom* thou hast made to play therein.
27. **These wait all upon thee; that thou mayest give them** their **meat** in due season.
28. *That* thou givest them they gather: thou openest thine hand, **they are filled with good.**
29. **Thou hidest thy face, they are troubled: thou takest away their breath, they die,** and return to their dust.
30. **Thou sendest** forth **thy spirit, they are created:** and thou renewest the face of the earth.
31. **The glory of the LORD shall endure for ever: the LORD shall rejoice in his works.**
32. He looketh on the earth, and it trembleth: he toucheth the hills, and they smoke.
33. **I will sing unto the LORD as long as I live:** I will sing praise to my God while I have my being.
34. **My meditation** of him **shall be sweet:** I will be glad in the LORD.
35. **Let** the **sinners be consumed** out of the earth, and let the wicked be no more. **Bless** thou **the LORD, O my soul. Praise** ye **the LORD.**

1. **O give thanks unto the LORD;** call upon his name: **make known his deeds** among the people.
2. Sing unto him, **sing psalms unto him: talk** ye **of all his wondrous works.**
3. **Glory** ye **in his holy name:** let the heart of them rejoice that seek the LORD.
4. **Seek the LORD,** and his strength: seek his face evermore.
5. **Remember his marvellous works** that he hath done; his wonders, and the judgments of his mouth;
6. O ye seed of Abraham his servant, ye children of Jacob his chosen.
7. **He is the LORD our God:** his judgments *are* in all the earth.
8. **He hath remembered his covenant** for ever, the word *which* he commanded to a thousand generations.
9. **Which** *covenant* **he made with Abraham,** and his oath unto Isaac;
10. **And confirmed** the same **unto** Jacob for a law, *and* to **Israel** *for* an everlasting covenant:
11. **Saying, Unto thee will I give** the land of **Canaan, the lot of your inheritance:**
12. **When they were** *but* a **few** men **in number;** yea, very few, and strangers in it.
13. When they went from one nation to another, from *one* kingdom to another people;
14. **He suffered no man to do them wrong:** yea, he reproved kings for their sakes;
15. **Saying, Touch not mine anointed,** and do my prophets no harm.
16. **Moreover he called for a famine** upon the land: he brake the whole staff of bread.
17. **He sent a man before them, even Joseph,** *who* was sold for a servant:
18. Whose feet they hurt with fetters: he was laid in iron:
19. **Until the time** that **his word came:** the word of the LORD tried him.
20. **The king** sent and **loosed him;** *even* the ruler of the people, and let him go free.
21. **He made him lord**

of his house,
and ruler of all his substance:
22. To bind his princes at his
pleasure; and teach his
senators wisdom.
23. **Israel** also
came into Egypt; and Jacob
sojourned in the land of Ham.
24. **And he increased his
people** greatly; and made them
stronger than their enemies.
25. **He turned their heart
to hate his people,**
to deal subtilly with his servants.
26. **He sent Moses** his servant;
**and Aaron whom
he had chosen.**
27. **They shewed his
signs among them,**
and wonders in the land of Ham.
28. **He sent darkness,**
and made it dark; and they
rebelled not against his word.
29. **He turned their waters
into blood, and slew
their fish.**
30. **Their land brought
forth frogs** in abundance,
in the chambers of their kings.
31. **He spake, and there
came** divers sorts of
flies, and lice in all their coasts.
32. **He gave them hail** for rain,
and flaming fire in their land.
33. **He smote their vines** also
and their
fig trees; and brake
the trees of their coasts.
34. **He spake, and** the
**locusts came, and
caterpillers,** and that
without number,
35. And did eat up all the herbs
in their land, and devoured the
fruit of their ground.
36. **He smote** also
all the firstborn in their land,
the chief of all their strength.
37. **He brought them forth
also with silver and gold:
and there was not one
feeble person among
their tribes.**

38. **Egypt was glad when
they departed:** for the fear
of them fell upon them.
39. **He spread a cloud for
a covering; and fire to
give light in the night.**
40. *The people* asked, and
**he brought quails, and
satisfied them with the
bread of heaven.**
41. **He opened
the rock, and** the
**waters gushed
out;** they ran in the
dry places *like* a river.
42. **For he remembered
his holy promise,**
and Abraham his servant.
43. **And** he
**brought forth his
people with joy,**
and his chosen with gladness:
44. **And gave them the
lands of the heathen:** and they
inherited the labour of the people;
45. **That they might observe
his statutes, and keep his
laws. Praise ye the LORD.**

PSALM 106

1. Praise ye the LORD.
**O give thanks unto the
LORD; for he is good:** for
**his mercy endureth
for ever.**
2. **Who can utter the mighty
acts of the LORD?** *who* can
shew forth all his praise?
3. **Blessed are they that
keep judgment, and** he that
doeth righteousness
at all times.
4. **Remember me, O
LORD,** with the favour *that thou
bearest unto* thy people: O
visit me with thy salvation;
5. **That I may see the good
of thy chosen, that I may
rejoice** in the gladness of
thy nation, that I may glory
with thine inheritance.
6. **We have sinned** with our
fathers, we have committed iniquity,

we have done wickedly.

7. Our fathers understood not thy wonders in Egypt; they remembered not the multitude of thy mercies; but provoked *him* at the sea, *even* at the Red sea.

8. Nevertheless he saved them for his name's sake, that he might make his mighty power to be known.

9. He rebuked the Red sea also, and it was dried up: so he led them through the depths, as through the wilderness.

10. And he saved them from the hand of him that hated them, and redeemed them from the hand of the enemy.

11. And the waters covered their enemies: there was not one of them left.

12. Then believed they his words; they sang his praise.

13. They soon forgat his works; they waited not for his counsel:

14. But lusted exceedingly in the wilderness, and tempted God in the desert.

15. And he gave them their request; but sent leanness into their soul.

16. They envied Moses also in the camp, and Aaron the saint of the LORD.

17. The earth opened and swallowed up Dathan and covered the company of Abiram.

18. And a fire was kindled in their company; the flame burned up the wicked.

19. They made a calf in Horeb and worshipped the molten image.

20. Thus they changed their glory into the similitude of an ox that eateth grass.

21. They forgat God their saviour, which had done great things in Egypt;

22. Wondrous works in the land of Ham, *and* terrible things by the Red sea.

23. Therefore he said that he would destroy them, had not Moses his chosen stood before him in the breach, to turn away his wrath, lest he should destroy *them.*

24. Yea, they despised the pleasant land, they believed not his word:

25. But murmured in their tents, *and* hearkened not unto the voice of the LORD.

26. Therefore he lifted up his hand against them, to overthrow them in the wilderness:

27. To overthrow their seed also among the nations, and to scatter them in the lands.

28. They joined themselves also unto Baal-peor, and ate the sacrifices of the dead.

29. Thus they provoked him to anger with their inventions: and the plague brake in upon them.

30. Then stood up Phinehas, and executed judgment: and *so* the plague was stayed.

31. And that was counted unto him for righteousness unto all generations for evermore.

32. They angered him also at the waters of strife, so that it went ill with Moses for their sakes:

33. Because they provoked his spirit, so that he spake unadvisedly with his lips.

34. They did not destroy the nations, concerning whom the LORD commanded them:

35. But were

mingled among the
heathen, and learned their works.
36. And they
served their idols:
which were a snare unto them.
37. Yea, they sacrificed
their sons and their
daughters unto devils,
38. And shed innocent blood, *even*
the blood of their sons and of their
daughters, whom they sacrificed
unto the idols of Canaan:
and the land was
polluted with blood.
39. Thus were they
defiled with their own works,
and went a whoring with
their own inventions.
40. Therefore was the wrath
of the LORD kindled against
his people, insomuch that he
abhorred his own inheritance.
41. And he gave them into
the hand of the heathen; and
they that hated them ruled over them.
42. Their enemies also
oppressed them, and
they were brought into subjection
under their hand.
43. Many times did he
deliver them; but they
provoked him with their
counsel, and were brought low for
their iniquity.
44. Nevertheless he
regarded their affliction,
when he heard their cry:
45. And he
remembered for them
his covenant, and
repented according to the
multitude of his mercies.
46. He made them
also to be pitied
of all those that carried
them captives.
47. Save us, O LORD
our God, and gather us
from among
the heathen, to give thanks
unto thy holy name,
and to triumph in thy praise.
48. Blessed be the LORD

God of Israel from
everlasting to everlasting:
and let all the people say,
Amen. Praise ye the LORD.

PSALM 107

1. O give thanks unto
the LORD, for *he is* good:
for his mercy endureth
for ever.
2. Let the redeemed
of the LORD say so,
whom he hath redeemed
from the hand of the enemy;
3. And gathered them out of the
lands, from the east, and from
the west, from the north,
and from the south.
4. They wandered in the
wilderness in a solitary way;
they found no city to dwell in.
5. Hungry and thirsty,
their soul fainted in them.
6. Then they cried unto
the LORD in their trouble,
and he delivered them
out of their distresses.
7. And he
led them forth
by the right way, that they
might go to a city of habitation.
8. Oh that men would
praise the LORD *for* his
goodness, and *for* his wonderful
works to the children of men!
9. For he satisfieth the
longing soul, and filleth the
hungry soul with goodness.
10. Such as sit in darkness and
in the shadow of death, *being*
bound in affliction and iron;
11. Because they rebelled
against the words of
God, and contemned the
counsel of the most High:
12. Therefore he brought
down their heart with
labour; they fell down,
and *there was* none to help.
13. Then they cried
unto the LORD
in their trouble, and
he saved them

out of their distresses.

14. He brought them out of darkness and **the shadow of death, and brake their bands in sunder.**

15. Oh that men would praise the LORD for his goodness, and for his wonderful works to the children of men!

16. For he hath broken the gates of brass, and cut the bars of iron in sunder.

17. Fools because of their transgression, and because **of their iniquities, are afflicted.**

18. Their soul abhorreth all manner of meat; and **they draw near unto the gates of death.**

19. Then they cry unto the LORD in their trouble, **and he saveth them** out of their distresses.

20. He sent his word, and healed them, and delivered them from their destructions.

21. Oh that men would praise the LORD for his goodness, and for his wonderful works to the children of men!

22. And let them sacrifice the sacrifices of thanksgiving, and declare his works with rejoicing.

23. They that go down to the sea in ships, that do business in great waters;

24. These see the works of the LORD, and his wonders in the deep.

25. For he commandeth, and raiseth **the stormy wind,** which lifteth up the waves thereof.

26. They mount up to the heaven, they go down again to the depths: their soul is melted because of trouble.

27. They reel to and fro, and stagger **like a drunken man, and** are at their wit's end.

28. Then they cry unto the LORD in their trouble, and he bringeth them out of their distresses.

29. He maketh the storm a calm, so that the waves thereof are still.

30. Then are they glad because they be quiet; so he bringeth them unto their desired haven.

31. Oh that men would praise the LORD for his goodness, and for his wonderful works to the children of men!

32. Let them exalt him also in the congregation of the people, and praise him in the assembly of the elders.

33. He turneth rivers into a wilderness, and the watersprings into dry ground;

34. A fruitful land into barrenness, for the wickedness of them that dwell therein.

35. He turneth the wilderness into a standing water, and **dry ground into watersprings.**

36. And there he **maketh the hungry to dwell,** that they may prepare a city for habitation;

37. And sow the fields, and plant vineyards, which may yield fruits of increase.

38. He blesseth them also, so that they are multiplied greatly; and suffereth not their cattle to decrease.

39. Again, they are minished and **brought low through oppression, affliction, and sorrow.**

40. He poureth contempt upon princes, and **causeth them to wander in the wilderness,** where there is no way.

41. Yet setteth he the poor on high from affliction,

and maketh *him* families like a flock.

42. **The righteous shall see it, and rejoice:** and all iniquity shall stop her mouth.

43. **Whoso is wise,** and will observe these *things,* even they **shall understand the lovingkindness of the LORD.**

PSALM 108

1. **O GOD, my heart is fixed; I will sing and give praise,** even with my glory.

2. Awake, psaltery and harp: I *myself* will awake early.

3. **I will praise thee, O LORD, among the people:** and I will sing praises unto thee among the nations.

4. **For thy mercy is great** above the heavens: and thy truth *reacheth* unto the clouds.

5. **Be thou exalted, O God,** above the heavens: and thy glory above all the earth;

6. **That thy beloved may be delivered:** save *with* thy right hand, and answer me.

7. **God hath spoken in his holiness; I will rejoice,** I will divide Shechem, and mete out the valley of Succoth.

8. **Gilead is mine; Manasseh is mine; Ephraim also** *is* the strength of mine head; **Judah is my lawgiver;**

9. Moab *is* my washpot; over Edom will I cast out my shoe; over Philistia will I triumph.

10. **Who will bring me into the strong city?** who will lead me into Edom?

11. **Wilt not thou, O God, who hast cast us off?** and wilt not thou, O God, go forth with our hosts?

12. **Give us help** from trouble: **for vain is the help of man.**

13. **Through God we shall do valiantly: for he** *it is that* **shall tread down our enemies.**

PSALM 109

1. **Hold not thy peace, O God of my praise;**

2. **For the mouth of the wicked** and the mouth of the deceitful **are opened against me:** they have spoken against me with a lying tongue.

3. **They compassed me** about also **with words of hatred;** and fought against me **without a cause.**

4. For my love **they are my adversaries: but I give myself unto prayer.**

5. **And they have rewarded me evil for good,** and hatred for my love.

6. **Set thou a wicked man over him: and let Satan stand at his right hand.**

7. **When he shall be judged, let him be condemned: and let his prayer become sin.**

8. **Let his days be few;** *and* let another take his office.

9. **Let his children be fatherless, and** his wife a widow.

10. Let his children be continually **vagabonds, and** beg: **let them seek their bread** also **out of their desolate places.**

11. **Let the extortioner catch all that he hath;** and let the strangers spoil his labour.

12. **Let there be none to extend mercy** unto him: neither let there be any to favour his fatherless children.

13. **Let his posterity be cut off; and** in the generation following let **their name be blotted out.**

14. **Let the iniquity of his fathers be remembered with the LORD;** and let not the

sin of his mother be blotted out.

15. **Let them be before the LORD** continually, **that he may cut off the memory of them** from the earth.

16. **Because that he remembered not to shew mercy,** but persecuted the poor and needy man, that he might even slay the broken in heart.

17. **As he loved cursing, so let it come unto him: as he delighted not in blessing, so let it be far from him.**

18. As he clothed himself with cursing like as with his garment, so let it come into his bowels like water, and like oil into his bones.

19. Let it be unto him as the garment which covereth him, and for a girdle wherewith he is girded continually.

20. **Let this be the reward of mine adversaries** from the LORD, **and** of **them that speak evil against my soul.**

21. **But do** thou **for me, O GOD** the Lord, **for thy name's sake: because thy mercy is good,** deliver thou me.

22. **For I am poor and needy,** and my heart is wounded within me.

23. **I am gone like the shadow** when it declineth: I am tossed up and down as the locust.

24. **My knees are weak through fasting;** and my flesh faileth of fatness.

25. **I became** also **a reproach** unto them: when they looked upon me they shaked their heads.

26. **Help me, O LORD** my God: O **save me according to thy mercy:**

27. **That they may know** that this is thy hand; **that thou, LORD, hast done it.**

28. **Let them curse,** but bless thou: when they arise, let them be ashamed; **but let thy servant rejoice.**

29. **Let mine adversaries be clothed with shame, and** let them cover themselves **with their own confusion,** as with a mantle.

30. **I will greatly praise the LORD** with my mouth; yea, I will praise him **among the multitude.**

31. **For he shall stand at the right hand of the poor,** to save him from those that condemn his soul.

PSALM 110

1. **The LORD said unto my Lord, Sit thou at my right hand, until I make thine enemies thy footstool.**

2. **The LORD shall send** the rod of thy **strength out of Zion:** rule thou in the midst of thine enemies.

3. **Thy people shall be willing in the day of thy power,** in the beauties of holiness from the womb of the morning: thou hast the dew of thy youth.

4. **The LORD hath sworn,** and will not repent, **Thou art a priest for ever after the order of Melchizedek.**

5. **The Lord** at thy right hand **shall strike through kings in the day of his wrath.**

6. **He shall judge** among **the heathen,** he shall fill the places with the dead bodies; **he shall wound the heads over many countries.**

7. He shall drink of the brook in the way: therefore shall he lift up the head.

PSALM 111

1. Praise ye the LORD. I will praise the LORD with my whole heart,

in the assembly of the upright,
and *in* the congregation.

2. **The works of the
LORD are** great,
sought out
**of all them that have
pleasure therein.**

3. **His work is honourable
and** glorious: and
**his righteousness
endureth for ever.**

4. **He hath made his** wonderful
**works to
be remembered: the
LORD is gracious and
full of compassion.**

5. He hath given meat
unto them that fear him:
**he will ever be mindful
of his covenant.**

6. **He hath shewed his
people** the power of
his works, that he may give
them the heritage of the heathen.

7. **The works of his hands
are verity and judgment;
all his commandments
are sure.**

8. **They stand** fast
for ever and ever,
**and are done in truth
and uprightness.**

9. **He sent redemption unto
his people:** he hath commanded
his covenant for ever:
**holy and reverend
is his name.**

10. **The fear of the LORD is
the beginning of wisdom:**
a good understanding have all they
that do *his commandments:* his
praise endureth for ever.

PSALM 112

1. Praise ye the LORD.
**Blessed is the man
that feareth the LORD,**
that delighteth greatly in
his commandments.

2. **His seed shall be mighty
upon earth:** the generation
of the upright shall be blessed.

3. **Wealth and riches shall**

be in his house: and his
righteousness endureth for ever.

4. **Unto the upright there
ariseth light in the
darkness: he is
gracious, and full of
compassion,** and righteous.

5. A good man sheweth
favour, and lendeth:
**he will guide his
affairs with discretion.**

6. **Surely he shall not
be moved** for ever:
the righteous shall
be in everlasting remembrance.

7. He shall
not be afraid of evil tidings:
his heart is fixed,
trusting in the LORD.

8. His heart *is* established, he
shall not be afraid, until he see
his desire upon his enemies.

9. He hath dispersed,
**he hath given to the poor;
his righteousness endureth
for ever; his horn shall
be exalted** with honour.

10. **The wicked shall see
it, and be grieved;**
he shall gnash with his teeth,
and melt away: the desire
of the wicked shall perish.

PSALM 113

1. Praise ye the LORD. Praise,
O ye servants of the LORD,
**praise the name
of the LORD.**

2. Blessed be the name of the
LORD from this time forth and
for evermore.

3. **From the rising of
the sun unto the going
down** of the same
**the LORD's name is
to be praised.**

4. **The LORD is high above
all nations, and his glory
above the heavens.**

5. **Who is like unto the LORD**
our God, who dwelleth on high,

6. **Who humbleth himself to
behold the things** that are

in heaven, and in the
earth!

7. **He raiseth** up
the poor out of the dust,
and lifteth the
needy out of the dunghill;

8. **That he may set**
him with princes,
even with the princes of his people.

9. **He maketh the barren**
woman to keep house, *and to be*
a joyful mother of children.
Praise ye the LORD.

PSALM 114

1. **When Israel went out**
of Egypt, the house of Jacob
from a people of strange language;

2. Judah was his sanctuary,
and Israel his dominion.

3. **The sea** saw *it,* and
fled: Jordan was
driven back.

4. **The mountains**
skipped like rams,
and the little hills like lambs.

5. **What ailed thee,**
O thou sea, that thou fleddest?
thou Jordan,
that thou wast driven back?

6. **Ye mountains,** *that* ye
skipped like rams; and ye
little hills, like lambs?

7. **Tremble, thou earth,**
at the presence of the Lord,
at the presence of the God of Jacob;

8. **Which turned**
the rock into a standing
water, the flint into
a fountain of waters.

PSALM 115

1. Not unto us,
O LORD, not unto us, but
unto thy name give glory,
for thy mercy, and for thy
truth's sake.

2. **Wherefore should the**
heathen say, Where is now
their God?

3. **But our God is in the**
heavens: he hath done
whatsoever he hath

---

pleased.

4. **Their idols are**
silver and gold,
the work of men's hands.

5. **They have mouths, but**
they speak not: eyes
have they,
but they see not:

6. They have
ears, but they
hear not: noses have they,
but they
smell not:

7. **They have hands, but** they
handle not: feet have they,
but they walk not: neither
speak they through their throat.

8. **They that make**
them are like unto
them; *so is* every one
that trusteth in them.

9. **O Israel, trust** thou
in the LORD:
he *is* their help and their shield.

10. O house of Aaron, trust in
the LORD: he *is* their help
and their shield.

11. **Ye that fear the LORD,**
trust in the LORD: he is
their help and their
shield.

12. **The LORD**
hath been mindful of us: he
will bless us; he will bless
the house of Israel; he will bless
the house of Aaron.

13. **He will bless**
them that fear the LORD,
both small and great.

14. **The LORD shall**
increase you more and
more, you and your children.

15. **Ye are blessed**
of the LORD
which made heaven and earth.

16. **The** heaven, *even* the
heavens, are the LORD's:
but the earth hath he given
to the children of men.

17. **The dead praise not**
the LORD, neither any that
go down into silence.

18. **But we will bless the**

LORD from this time forth and for evermore. Praise the LORD.

PSALM 116

1. **I love the LORD, because he** hath **heard my** voice and my **supplications.**

2. Because he hath inclined his ear unto me, **therefore will I call upon him as long as I live.**

3. **The sorrows of death compassed me, and** the pains of **hell gat hold upon me:** I found trouble and sorrow.

4. **Then called I upon** the name of **the LORD;** O LORD, **I beseech thee, deliver my soul.**

5. **Gracious is the LORD,** and righteous; **yea, our God is merciful.**

6. **The LORD preserveth the simple: I was brought low, and he helped me.**

7. **Return unto thy rest, O my soul; for the LORD hath dealt bountifully with thee.**

8. **For thou hast delivered my soul from death,** mine eyes from tears, and my feet from falling.

9. **I will walk before the LORD in the land of the living.**

10. **I believed, therefore have I spoken:** I was greatly afflicted:

11. **I said in my haste, All men are liars.**

12. **What shall I render unto the LORD for all his benefits toward me?**

13. **I will take the cup of salvation, and call upon** the name of **the LORD.**

14. I will pay my vows unto the LORD now in the presence of all his people.

15. **Precious in the sight of the LORD is the death of his saints.**

16. **O LORD,** truly I am thy servant; **I am thy servant,** and the son of thine handmaid: **thou hast loosed my bonds.**

17. **I will offer** to thee **the sacrifice of thanksgiving, and** will **call upon** the name of **the LORD.**

18. **I will pay my vows unto the LORD** now **in the presence of** all **his people.**

19. In the courts of the LORD's house, in the midst of thee, O Jerusalem. Praise ye the LORD.

PSALM 117

1. **O praise the LORD,** all ye nations: praise him, **all ye people.**

2. **For his merciful kindness** is great toward us: **and** the **truth** of the LORD **endureth for ever. Praise ye the LORD.**

PSALM 118

1. O give thanks unto the LORD; for he is good: because his mercy endureth for ever.

2. **Let Israel** now say, that his mercy endureth for ever.

3. **Let the house of Aaron** now say, that his mercy endureth for ever.

4. **Let them** now **that fear the LORD say,** that **his mercy endureth for ever.**

5. I called upon the LORD in distress: the LORD answered me, and set me in a large place.

6. **The LORD is on my side;** I will not fear: **what can man do unto me?**

7. The LORD taketh my part with them that help me: therefore shall I see my desire upon them that hate me.

8. **It is better to trust** in **the LORD than to put confidence in man.**

9. *It is* better to trust in the LORD than to put confidence in princes.

10. **All nations compassed me** about: **but in the name of the LORD will I destroy them.**

11. They compassed me about; yea, they compassed me about: but in the name of the LORD I will destroy them.

12. They compassed me about like bees: they are quenched as the fire of thorns: for in the name of the LORD I will destroy them.

13. **Thou hast thrust sore at me that I might fall: but the LORD helped me.**

14. **The LORD is my strength and** song, and is become **my salvation.**

15. The voice of **rejoicing and salvation is in the tabernacles of the righteous:** the right hand of the LORD doeth valiantly.

16. **The right hand of the LORD is exalted:** the right hand of the LORD doeth valiantly.

17. **I shall** not die, but live, and **declare the works of the LORD.**

18. **The LORD hath chastened me** sore: **but** he hath **not** given me over **unto death.**

19. **Open** to me **the gates of righteousness: I will go into them, and** I will **praise the LORD:**

20. This gate of the LORD, into which the righteous shall enter.

21. I will praise thee: for thou hast heard me, and art become my salvation.

22. **The stone which the builders refused is become the head stone of the corner.**

23. **This is the LORD'S doing; it is marvellous in our eyes.**

24. **This is the day which the LORD hath made; we will rejoice and be glad in it.**

25. **Save now,** I beseech thee, O LORD: **O LORD,** I beseech thee, **send** now **prosperity.**

26. **Blessed be he that cometh in the name of the LORD:** we have blessed you out of the house of the LORD.

27. God *is* the LORD, **which hath shewed us light:** bind the sacrifice with cords, *even* unto the horns of the altar.

28. **Thou art my God, and I will praise thee:** *thou art* my God, I will exalt thee.

29. **O give thanks unto the LORD;** for *he is* good: **for his mercy endureth for ever.**

PSALM 119

1. **Blessed are the undefiled** in the way, **who walk in the law of the LORD.**

2. Blessed *are* they **that keep his testimonies, and that seek him with the whole heart.**

3. They also do no iniquity: **they walk in his ways.**

4. **Thou hast commanded us to keep thy precepts** diligently.

5. O that my ways were directed to keep thy statutes!

6. **Then shall I not be ashamed,** when I have respect unto all thy commandments.

7. **I will praise thee with uprightness of heart,** when I shall have learned thy righteous judgments.

8. **I will keep thy statutes:** O forsake me not utterly.

9. **Wherewithal shall a**

young man cleanse his way? by taking heed *thereto* according to thy word.

10. **With my whole heart have I sought thee:** O let me not wander from thy commandments.

11. **Thy word have I hid in mine heart, that I might not sin against thee.**

12. Blessed *art* thou, **O LORD: teach me thy statutes.**

13. With my lips have I declared all the judgments of thy mouth.

14. **I have rejoiced in** the way of **thy testimonies,** as *much as* in all riches.

15. **I will meditate in thy precepts,** and have respect unto thy ways.

16. I will delight myself in thy statutes: I will not forget thy word.

17. **Deal bountifully with thy servant, that I may** live, and **keep thy word.**

18. **Open** thou **mine eyes, that I may behold wondrous things out of thy law.**

19. **I am a stranger in the earth: hide not thy commandments from me.**

20. My soul breaketh for the longing *that it hath* unto thy judgments at all times.

21. **Thou hast rebuked the proud** *that are* cursed, **which do err from thy commandments.**

22. **Remove from me reproach and contempt;** for I have kept thy testimonies.

23. **Princes** also did sit *and* **speak against me: but** thy servant did meditate in thy statutes.

24. **Thy testimonies** also **are my delight** *and* my counsellors.

25. My soul cleaveth unto the dust: **quicken** thou **me according to thy word.**

26. I have declared my ways, and thou heardest me: **teach me thy statutes.**

27. **Make me to understand** the way of **thy precepts: so shall I talk of thy wondrous works.**

28. My soul melteth for heaviness: **strengthen** thou **me according unto thy word.**

29. Remove from me the way of lying: and grant me thy law graciously.

30. **I have chosen the way of truth:** thy judgments have I laid *before me.*

31. **I have stuck unto thy testimonies:** O LORD, put me not to shame.

32. **I will run the way of thy commandments, when thou shalt enlarge my heart.**

33. **Teach me, O LORD,** the way of **thy statutes;** and I shall keep it *unto* the end.

34. **Give me understanding,** and I shall keep thy law; yea, I shall observe it with *my* whole heart.

35. **Make me to go in the path of thy commandments;** for therein do I delight.

36. **Incline my heart unto thy testimonies, and not to covetousness.**

37. **Turn** away **mine eyes from beholding vanity;** *and* quicken thou me in thy way.

38. **Stablish thy word unto thy servant,** who *is devoted* to thy fear.

39. **Turn away my reproach** which I fear: **for thy judgments are good.**

40. Behold, **I have longed after thy precepts:** quicken me in thy righteousness.

885

41. **Let thy mercies come**
also unto me, O LORD,
even thy salvation,
according to thy word.
42. **So shall I** have wherewith to
answer him that
reproacheth me: for
I trust in thy word.
43. **And take not the** word of
truth utterly
out of my mouth;
for I have hoped in thy judgments.
44. **So shall I keep**
thy law continually
for ever and ever.
45. And I will walk at liberty:
for I seek thy precepts.
46. **I will speak of thy**
testimonies also before
kings, and will not be ashamed.
47. **And I will delight myself**
in thy commandments,
which I have loved.
48. My hands also will I lift up unto thy
commandments, which I have loved;
and I will meditate
in thy statutes.
49. **Remember the**
word unto thy servant,
upon which thou hast
caused me to hope.
50. **This is my comfort**
in my affliction:
for thy word hath
quickened me.
51. **The proud have** had
me greatly
in derision: yet have I not
declined from thy law.
52. **I remembered thy**
judgments of old, O LORD;
and have
comforted myself.
53. **Horror hath taken hold**
upon me because of
the wicked that
forsake thy law.
54. Thy statutes have been my songs
in the house of my pilgrimage.
55. **I have**
remembered thy name,
O LORD, in the night,
and have kept thy law.

56. This I had, because
I kept thy precepts.
57. **Thou art my portion,**
O LORD: I have
said that
I would keep thy words.
58. **I entreated thy favour**
with *my* whole heart:
be merciful unto me
according to thy word.
59. **I** thought on my ways, and
turned my feet unto
thy testimonies.
60. **I made haste,**
and delayed not
to keep thy
commandments.
61. **The** bands of the
wicked have robbed me:
but I have not forgotten
thy law.
62. At midnight
I will rise to
give thanks unto
thee because of thy
righteous judgments.
63. **I am a companion of** all
them that fear thee,
and of them that keep thy precepts.
64. **The earth, O LORD,**
is full of thy mercy:
teach me thy statutes.
65. Thou hast dealt well with
thy servant, O LORD, according
unto thy word.
66. **Teach me good**
judgment and
knowledge: for I have
believed thy commandments.
67. **Before I was afflicted**
I went astray: but now
have I kept thy word.
68. Thou *art* good, and doest
good; teach me thy statutes.
69. **The proud have forged**
a lie against me: but I will
keep thy precepts
with *my* whole heart.
70. Their heart is as fat as grease;
but I delight in thy law.
71. **It is good** for me
that I have been afflicted;
that I might learn

thy statutes.

72. **The law of thy mouth is better** unto me **than thousands of gold and silver.**

73. **Thy hands have** made me and **fashioned me: give me understanding, that I may learn thy commandments.**

74. **They that fear thee will be glad** when they see me; **because I have hoped in thy word.**

75. **I know, O LORD,** that thy judgments *are* right, and **that thou in faithfulness hast afflicted me.**

76. **Let,** I pray thee, **thy merciful kindness be** for **my comfort,** according to thy word unto thy servant.

77. **Let thy tender mercies come unto me,** that I may live: **for thy law is my delight.**

78. **Let the proud be ashamed; for they dealt perversely with me without a cause: but I will meditate in thy precepts.**

79. Let those that fear thee turn unto me, and those that have known thy testimonies.

80. **Let my heart be sound in thy statutes; that I be not ashamed.**

81. **My soul fainteth for thy salvation: but I hope in thy word.**

82. **Mine eyes fail for thy word, saying, When wilt thou comfort me?**

83. For I am become like a bottle in the smoke; *yet* do I not forget thy statutes.

84. **How many are the days of thy servant?** when wilt thou **execute judgment on them that persecute me?**

85. **The proud have digged pits for me, which are not after thy law.**

86. All thy commandments *are* faithful: they persecute me wrongfully; help thou me.

87. **They had almost consumed me** upon earth; **but I forsook not thy precepts.**

88. **Quicken me** after thy lovingkindness; **so shall I keep the testimony** of thy mouth.

89. **For ever, O LORD, thy word is settled in heaven.**

90. **Thy faithfulness is unto all generations:** thou hast established the earth, and it abideth.

91. **They continue** this day **according to thine ordinances:** for all *are* thy servants.

92. **Unless thy law had been my delights, I should** then **have perished** in mine affliction.

93. **I will never forget thy precepts:** for with them thou hast quickened me.

94. **I am thine,** save me: **for I** have **sought thy precepts.**

95. **The wicked** have **waited** for me **to destroy me: but I will consider thy testimonies.**

96. **I have seen an end of all perfection: but thy commandment is exceeding broad.**

97. O how I love **thy law!** it **is my meditation all** the **day.**

98. **Thou through thy commandments hast made me wiser than mine enemies:** for they *are* ever with me.

99. **I have more understanding than** all **my teachers:** for thy testimonies *are* my meditation.

100. I understand more than the ancients, **because I keep thy precepts.**

101. I have
refrained my feet from every
evil way,
that I might keep thy word.
102. I have not departed
from thy judgments: for
thou hast taught me.
103. How sweet are thy
words unto my taste!
yea, sweeter than
honey to my mouth!
104. Through thy precepts
I get understanding:
therefore I hate every false way.
105. Thy word is a lamp
unto my feet, and a
light unto my path.
106. I have sworn,
and I will perform *it*,
that I will keep thy
righteous judgments.
107. I am afflicted very much:
quicken me, O LORD,
according unto thy word.
108. Accept, I beseech thee,
the freewill
offerings of my mouth,
O LORD, and teach me
thy judgments.
109. My soul *is* continually in my
hand: yet do I not forget thy law.
110. The wicked have laid
a snare for me: yet I erred
not from thy precepts.
111. Thy testimonies have I
taken as an heritage for ever:
for they are the rejoicing
of my heart.
112. I have inclined
mine heart to perform
thy statutes alway,
even unto the end.
113. I hate vain thoughts:
but thy law do I love.
114. Thou art my hiding place and
my shield: I hope
in thy word.
115. Depart from me, ye
evildoers: for I will keep
the commandments
of my God.
116. Uphold me according
unto thy word, that I may live:

and let me not be
ashamed of my hope.
117. Hold thou
me up, and I shall
be safe: and I will have
respect unto
thy statutes continually.
118. Thou hast trodden
down all
them that err
from thy statutes:
for their deceit *is* falsehood.
119. Thou puttest away all
the wicked of the earth
like dross: therefore
I love thy testimonies.
120. My flesh trembleth for
fear of thee; and I am afraid
of thy judgments.
121. I have done
judgment and justice:
leave me not to mine oppressors.
122. Be surety for thy
servant for good:
let not the proud
oppress me.
123. Mine eyes fail for
thy salvation, and for
the word of thy
righteousness.
124. Deal with thy servant
according unto thy mercy,
and teach me thy statutes.
125. I *am* thy servant;
give me understanding,
that I may know thy
testimonies.
126. It is time for thee, LORD,
to work: for they have
made void thy law.
127. Therefore I love thy
commandments above
gold; yea, above fine gold.
128. Therefore
I esteem all
thy precepts concerning all things
to be right; and I hate
every false way.
129. Thy testimonies
are wonderful:
therefore doth my soul keep them.
130. The entrance of thy
words giveth light; it giveth

understanding unto the simple.

131. I opened my mouth,
and panted: for
I longed for thy
commandments.

132. Look thou upon me, and
be merciful unto
me, as thou usest
to do unto
those that love thy name.

133. Order my steps in
thy word: and let not any
iniquity have
dominion over me.

134. Deliver me from the
oppression of man: so
will I keep thy precepts.

135. Make thy face to shine
upon thy servant; and
teach me thy statutes.

136. Rivers of waters run
down mine eyes, because
they keep not thy law.

137. Righteous art thou, O LORD,
and upright are thy
judgments.

138. Thy testimonies
that thou hast commanded
are righteous and very
faithful.

139. My zeal hath
consumed me, because
mine enemies have
forgotten thy words.

140. Thy word is very pure:
therefore thy servant
loveth it.

141. I am small
and despised: yet
do not I forget thy precepts.

142. Thy righteousness is an
everlasting righteousness,
and thy law is the truth.

143. Trouble and anguish
have taken hold on me:
yet thy commandments
are my delights.

144. The righteousness
of thy testimonies
is everlasting:
give me understanding,
and I shall live.

145. I cried with my whole
heart; hear me, O LORD:
I will keep thy statutes.

146. I cried unto thee; save me,
and I shall keep
thy testimonies.

147. I prevented the dawning
of the morning, and cried:
I hoped in thy word.

148. Mine eyes prevent the
night watches, that I might
meditate in thy word.

149. Hear my voice according unto
thy lovingkindness: O LORD, quicken
me according to thy judgment.

150. They draw nigh that
follow after mischief: they
are far from thy law.

151. Thou art near,
O LORD; and all
thy commandments
are truth.

152. Concerning thy
testimonies,
I have known of old that
thou hast founded
them for ever.

153. Consider mine
affliction, and deliver
me: for I do not forget thy law.

154. Plead my cause, and
deliver me: quicken me
according to thy word.

155. Salvation is far from
the wicked: for they seek
not thy statutes.

156. Great are thy tender
mercies, O LORD: quicken
me according to thy judgments.

157. Many are my
persecutors and mine enemies;
yet do I not decline
from thy testimonies.

158. I beheld the
transgressors, and was
grieved; because they
kept not thy word.

159. Consider how I love thy
precepts: quicken me, O
LORD, according to thy
lovingkindness.

160. Thy word is true
from the beginning:
and every one of

thy righteous judgments endureth for ever.

161. **Princes have persecuted me** without a cause: **but my heart standeth in awe of thy word.**

162. **I rejoice at thy word,** as one that findeth great spoil.

163. **I hate** and abhor **lying: but thy law do I love.**

164. **Seven times a day do I praise thee because of thy righteous judgments.**

165. **Great peace have they which love thy law:** and nothing shall offend them.

166. LORD, I have hoped for thy salvation, and done thy commandments.

167. **My soul hath kept thy testimonies; and I love them exceedingly.**

168. **I have kept thy precepts** and thy testimonies: **for all my ways are before thee.**

169. **Let my cry come** near **before thee, O LORD: give me understanding according to thy word.**

170. **Let my supplication come before thee: deliver me according to thy word.**

171. **My lips shall utter praise,** when thou hast taught me thy statutes.

172. **My tongue shall speak of thy word:** for all thy commandments *are* righteousness.

173. **Let thine hand help me; for I have chosen thy precepts.**

174. **I have longed for thy salvation, O LORD;** and **thy law is my delight.**

175. **Let my soul live, and it shall praise thee;** and let thy judgments help me.

176. **I have gone astray like a lost sheep; seek thy servant; for I do not forget thy commandments.**

PSALM 120

1. **In my distress I cried unto the LORD, and he heard me.**

2. **Deliver my soul, O LORD,** from lying lips, *and* **from a deceitful tongue.**

3. **What shall be** given unto thee? or what shall be **done unto thee, thou false tongue?**

4. **Sharp arrows** of the mighty, **with coals of juniper.**

5. **Woe is me,** that I sojourn in Mesech, *that* I dwell in the tents of Kedar!

6. **My soul hath** long **dwelt with him that hateth peace.**

7. **I am for peace: but when I speak, they are for war.**

PSALM 121

1. **I will lift up mine eyes unto the hills, from whence cometh my help.**

2. **My help cometh from the LORD, which made heaven and earth.**

3. **He will not suffer thy foot to be moved:** he that keepeth thee will not slumber.

4. **Behold, he that keepeth Israel shall neither slumber nor sleep.**

5. The LORD *is* thy keeper: the LORD *is* thy shade upon thy right hand.

6. **The sun shall not smite thee by day, nor the moon by night.**

7. **The LORD shall preserve thee from** all **evil:** he shall preserve thy soul.

8. **The LORD shall preserve thy going out and thy coming in** from this time forth, and even for evermore.

PSALM 122

1. **I was glad when they said unto me, Let us go into the house of the LORD.**

2. **Our feet shall stand within**

thy gates,
O Jerusalem.
3. Jerusalem is builded as a city that is compact together:
4. Whither the tribes go up, the tribes of the LORD, unto the testimony of Israel, to give thanks unto the name of the LORD.
5. For there are set thrones of judgment, the thrones of the house of David.
6. Pray for the peace of Jerusalem: they shall prosper that love thee.
7. Peace be within thy walls, and prosperity within thy palaces.
8. For my brethren and companions' sakes, I will now say, Peace be within thee.
9. Because of the house of the LORD our God I will seek thy good.

PSALM 123

1. Unto thee lift I up mine eyes, O thou that dwellest in the heavens.
2. Behold, as the eyes of servants look unto the hand of their masters, and as the eyes of a maiden unto the hand of her mistress; so our eyes wait upon the LORD our God, until that he have mercy upon us.
3. Have mercy upon us, O LORD, have mercy upon us: for we are exceedingly filled with contempt.
4. Our soul is exceedingly filled with the scorning of those that are at ease, and with the contempt of the proud.

PSALM 124

1. If it had not been the LORD who was on our side, now may Israel say;

2. If it had not been the LORD who was on our side, when men rose up against us:
3. Then they had swallowed us up quick, when their wrath was kindled against us:
4. Then the waters had overwhelmed us, the stream had gone over our soul:
5. Then the proud waters had gone over our soul.
6. Blessed be the LORD, who hath not given us as a prey to their teeth.
7. Our soul is escaped as a bird out of the snare of the fowlers: the snare is broken, and we are escaped.
8. Our help is in the name of the LORD, who made heaven and earth.

PSALM 125

1. They that trust in the LORD shall be as mount Zion, which cannot be removed, but abideth for ever.
2. As the mountains are round about Jerusalem, so the LORD is round about his people from henceforth even for ever.
3. For the rod of the wicked shall not rest upon the lot of the righteous; lest the righteous put forth their hands unto iniquity.
4. Do good, O LORD, unto those that be good, and to them that are upright in their hearts.
5. As for such as turn aside unto their crooked ways, the LORD shall lead them forth with the workers of iniquity: but peace shall be upon Israel.

PSALM 126

1. **When the LORD turned again the captivity of Zion,** we were like them that dream.
2. **Then was our mouth filled with laughter, and our tongue with singing: then said they among the heathen,** The LORD hath done great things for them.
3. **The LORD hath done great things for us;** *whereof* we are glad.
4. Turn again our captivity, O LORD, as the streams in the south.
5. **They that sow in tears shall reap in joy.**
6. **He that goeth forth and weepeth, bearing precious seed, shall** doubtless **come again** with rejoicing, **bringing his sheaves with him.**

PSALM 127

1. **Except the LORD build the house, they labour in vain** that build it: **except the LORD keep the city, the watchman waketh** but **in vain.**
2. **It is vain for you to rise up early, to sit up late, to eat the bread of sorrows: for so he giveth his beloved sleep.**
3. **Lo, children are an heritage of the LORD:** **and** the fruit of the womb *is* **his reward.**
4. **As arrows are in the hand of a mighty man; so are children of the youth.**
5. **Happy is the man that hath his quiver full of them:** they shall not be ashamed, but they shall speak with the enemies in the gate.

PSALM 128

1. **Blessed is every one that feareth the LORD;** that walketh in his ways.
2. **For thou shalt eat the labour of thine hands: happy shalt thou be, and it shall be well with thee.**
3. **Thy wife shall be as a fruitful vine** by the sides of thine house: **thy children like olive plants** round about thy table.
4. Behold, that **thus shall the man be blessed that feareth the LORD.**
5. **The LORD shall bless** thee out of **Zion: and thou shalt see the good of Jerusalem all** the days of **thy life.**
6. **Yea, thou shalt see thy children's children, and peace upon Israel.**

PSALM 129

1. **Many a time have they afflicted me** from my youth, may Israel now say:
2. Many a time have they afflicted me from my youth: **yet they have not prevailed** against me.
3. **The plowers plowed upon my back:** they made long their furrows.
4. **The LORD** *is* righteous: he **hath cut asunder the cords of the wicked.**
5. **Let them** all **be confounded** and turned back **that hate Zion.**
6. **Let them be as the grass** *upon* the housetops, **which withereth** afore it groweth up:
7. Wherewith the mower filleth not his hand; nor he that bindeth sheaves his bosom.
8. **Neither do they** which go by **say, The blessing of the LORD be upon you:** we bless you in the name of the LORD.

PSALM 130

1. Out of the depths have I cried unto thee, O LORD.

2. Lord, hear my voice: let thine ears be attentive to the voice of my supplications.

3. If thou, LORD, shouldest mark iniquities, O Lord, who shall stand?

4. But there is forgiveness with thee, that thou mayest be feared.

5. I wait for the LORD, my soul doth wait, and in his word do I hope.

6. My soul waiteth for the Lord more than they that watch for the morning: I say, more than they that watch for the morning.

7. Let Israel hope in the LORD: for with the LORD there is mercy, and with him is plenteous redemption.

8. And he shall redeem Israel from all his iniquities.

PSALM 131

1. Lord, my heart is not haughty, nor mine eyes lofty: neither do I exercise myself in great matters, or in things too high for me.

2. Surely I have behaved and quieted myself, as a child that is weaned of his mother: my soul is even as a weaned child.

3. Let Israel hope in the LORD from henceforth and for ever.

PSALM 132

1. LORD, remember David, and all his afflictions:

2. How he sware unto the LORD, and vowed unto the mighty God of Jacob;

3. Surely I will not come into the tabernacle of my house, nor go up into my bed;

4. I will not give sleep to mine eyes, or slumber to mine eyelids,

5. Until I find out a place for the LORD, an habitation for the mighty God of Jacob.

6. Lo, we heard of it at Ephratah: we found it in the fields of the wood.

7. We will go into his tabernacles: we will worship at his footstool.

8. Arise, O LORD, into thy rest; thou, and the ark of thy strength.

9. Let thy priests be clothed with righteousness; and let thy saints shout for joy.

10. For thy servant David's sake turn not away the face of thine anointed.

11. The LORD hath sworn in truth unto David; he will not turn from it; Of the fruit of thy body will I set upon thy throne.

12. If thy children will keep my covenant and my testimony that I shall teach them, their children shall also sit upon thy throne for evermore.

13. For the LORD hath chosen Zion; he hath desired it for his habitation.

14. This is my rest for ever: here will I dwell; for I have desired it.

15. I will abundantly bless her provision: I will satisfy her poor with bread.

16. I will also clothe her priests with salvation: and her saints shall shout aloud for joy.

17. There will I make the horn of David to bud: I have ordained a lamp for mine anointed.

18. His enemies will I clothe with shame: but upon himself shall his crown flourish.

PSALM 133

1. **Behold, how good** and how pleasant **it is for brethren to dwell** together **in unity!** 2. **It is like the precious ointment upon the head, that ran down upon** the beard, *even* **Aaron's beard:** that went down **to the skirts of his garments;** 3. As the dew of Hermon, **and as the dew** that descended **upon the mountains of Zion: for there the LORD commanded** the blessing, *even* **life for evermore.**

PSALM 134

1. Behold, **bless ye the LORD,** all **ye servants** of the LORD, **which** by night **stand in the house of the LORD.** 2. **Lift up your hands** in the sanctuary, **and bless the LORD.** 3. **The LORD** that made heaven and earth **bless thee out of Zion.**

PSALM 135

1. Praise ye the LORD. Praise ye the name of the LORD; praise *him,* O ye servants of the LORD. 2. **Ye that stand in the house of the LORD,** in the courts of the house of our God. 3. **Praise the LORD; for the LORD is good: sing praises unto his name;** for *it is* pleasant. 4. **For the LORD hath chosen** Jacob unto himself, *and* **Israel for his peculiar treasure.** 5. **For** I know that **the LORD is great,** and *that* our Lord *is* above all gods. 6. **Whatsoever the LORD** **pleased, that did** he in heaven, **and** in **earth,** in the seas, and all deep places. 7. **He causeth the vapours to ascend** from the ends of the earth; **he maketh lightnings for the rain; he bringeth the wind out of his treasuries.** 8. **Who smote the firstborn of Egypt,** both of man and beast. 9. **Who sent** tokens and **wonders into the midst of** thee, O **Egypt,** upon Pharaoh, and upon all his servants. 10. **Who smote great nations,** and slew mighty kings; 11. Sihon king of the Amorites, and Og king of Bashan, and all the kingdoms of Canaan: 12. **And gave their land for an heritage,** an heritage **unto Israel** his people. 13. **Thy name, O LORD, endureth for ever;** *and* thy memorial, O LORD, throughout all generations. 14. **For the LORD will judge his people,** and he will repent himself concerning his servants. 15. **The idols of the heathen are** silver and gold, **the work of men's hands.** 16. They have mouths, but **they speak not;** eyes have they, but they see not; 17. They have ears, but **they hear not; neither is there any breath in their mouths.** 18. **They that make them are like** unto **them: so is every one that trusteth in them.** 19. Bless the LORD, O house of Israel: bless the LORD, O house of Aaron: 20. **Bless the LORD,** O house of Levi: **ye that fear the LORD,** bless the LORD.

21. Blessed be the LORD out of Zion, which dwelleth at Jerusalem. Praise ye the LORD.

PSALM 136

1. **O give thanks unto** the LORD; for *he is* good: for his mercy *endureth* for ever.
2. O give thanks unto the God of gods: for his mercy *endureth* for ever.
3. O give thanks to **the Lord of lords: for his mercy endureth for ever.**
4. **To him who alone doeth great wonders:** for his mercy *endureth* for ever.
5. To him **that by wisdom made the heavens:** for his mercy *endureth* for ever.
6. To him **that stretched** out **the earth above the waters:** for his mercy *endureth* for ever.
7. To him **that made great lights:** for his mercy *endureth* for ever:
8. **The sun to rule by day:** for his mercy *endureth* for ever:
9. **The moon and stars to rule by night:** for his mercy *endureth* for ever.
10. **To him that smote Egypt in their firstborn:** for his mercy *endureth* for ever:
11. **And brought out Israel from among them:** for his mercy *endureth* for ever:
12. With a strong hand, and with a stretched out arm: for his mercy *endureth* for ever.
13. To him **which divided the Red sea** into parts: for his mercy *endureth* for ever:
14. **And made Israel** to **pass through the midst** of it: for his mercy *endureth* for ever:
15. **But overthrew Pharaoh and his host in the Red sea:** for his mercy *endureth* for ever.
16. **To him which led his people through the wilderness:** for his mercy *endureth* for ever.
17. To him **which smote great kings:** for his mercy *endureth* for ever:
18. And slew famous kings: for his mercy *endureth* for ever:
19. Sihon king of the Amorites: for his mercy *endureth* for ever:
20. And Og the king of Bashan: for his mercy *endureth* for ever:
21. **And gave their land for an heritage:** for his mercy *endureth* for ever:
22. *Even* an heritage **unto Israel** his servant: for his mercy *endureth* for ever.
23. **Who remembered us in our low estate:** for his mercy *endureth* for ever:
24. **And** hath **redeemed us from our enemies:** for his mercy *endureth* for ever.
25. **Who giveth food to all flesh:** for his mercy *endureth* for ever.
26. **O give thanks unto the God of heaven: for his mercy endureth for ever.**

PSALM 137

1. **By the rivers of Babylon,** there we sat down, yea, **we wept, when we remembered Zion.**
2. **We hanged our harps upon the willows** in the midst thereof.
3. **For there they that carried us away captive required** of us **a song;** and they that wasted us *required of us* mirth, **saying, Sing us one of the songs of Zion.**
4. **How shall we sing the LORD's song in a strange land?**
5. **If I forget thee, O Jerusalem, let my right hand forget her cunning.**
6. If I do not remember thee,

let my tongue cleave to the
roof of my mouth; if I prefer
not Jerusalem above my chief joy.
7. Remember, O LORD, the
children of Edom in the day
of Jerusalem; who said,
Rase it, rase *it, even*
to the foundation thereof.
8. O daughter of
Babylon, who art
to be destroyed; happy
shall he be, that rewardeth thee
as thou hast served us.
9. Happy shall he be,
that taketh and dasheth
thy little ones against
the stones.

PSALM 138

1. I will praise thee with my
whole heart: before the gods
will I sing praise unto thee.
2. I will worship toward thy
holy temple, and praise
thy name for thy
lovingkindness and for thy
truth: for thou hast
magnified thy word
above all thy name.
3. In the day when
I cried thou answeredst
me, and strengthenedst
me *with* strength in
my soul.
4. All the kings of the earth
shall praise thee, O LORD,
when they hear the words
of thy mouth.
5. Yea, they shall sing in the ways
of the LORD: for great *is* the glory
of the LORD.
6. Though the LORD be high,
yet hath he respect unto
the lowly: but the proud he
knoweth afar off.
7. Though I walk in the midst of
trouble, thou wilt revive me:
thou shalt stretch forth thine
hand against the wrath of
mine enemies,
and thy right hand
shall save me.
8. The LORD will perfect that

which concerneth me:
thy mercy, O LORD,
endureth for ever: forsake
not the works of thine own hands.

PSALM 139

1. O LORD, thou hast
searched me, and
known me.
2. Thou knowest my
downsitting and mine
uprising, thou
understandest
my thought afar off.
3. Thou compassest
my path and my lying down,
and art acquainted
with all my ways.
4. For there is not a word in
my tongue, but, lo, O LORD,
thou knowest it altogether.
5. Thou hast beset me
behind and before, and
laid thine hand upon me.
6. Such knowledge is too
wonderful for me; it is high,
I cannot attain unto it.
7. Whither shall I go from
thy spirit? or whither shall I flee from
thy presence?
8. If I ascend up
into heaven, thou art
there: if I make my
bed in hell, behold,
thou art there.
9. If I take the wings
of the morning, *and*
dwell in the uttermost
parts of the sea;
10. Even there shall
thy hand lead me,
and thy right hand shall hold me.
11. If I say, Surely the
darkness shall cover me;
even the night shall be light about me.
12. Yea, the darkness hideth
not from thee;
but the night shineth as the day:
the darkness and the light
are both alike to thee.
13. For thou hast possessed my
reins: thou hast covered me in
my mother's womb.

14. **I will praise thee;** for **I am fearfully and wonderfully made: marvellous are thy works;** and *that* my soul knoweth right well.

15. **My substance was not hid from thee, when I was made in secret,** *and* curiously wrought in the lowest parts of the earth.

16. **Thine eyes did see my substance,** yet being unperfect; **and in thy book all my members were written, which in continuance were fashioned,** when *as yet there was* none of them.

17. **How precious** also **are thy thoughts unto me,** O God! how great is the sum of them!

18. *If* I should count them, **they are more in number than the sand:** when I awake, I am still with thee.

19. **Surely thou wilt slay the wicked,** O God: depart from me therefore, ye bloody men.

20. **For they** speak against thee wickedly, *and* thine enemies **take thy name in vain.**

21. **Do not I hate them, O LORD, that hate thee?** and am not I grieved with those that rise up against thee?

22. I hate them with perfect hatred: I count them mine enemies.

23. **Search me, O God, and know my heart: try me, and know my thoughts:**

24. **And see if there be any wicked way in me, and lead me in the way everlasting.**

PSALM 140

1. **Deliver me,** O LORD, **from the evil man:** preserve me from the violent man;

2. **Which imagine mischiefs** in *their* heart; **continually** are they gathered together *for* war.

3. They have sharpened their tongues like a serpent; **adders' poison is under their lips.** Selah.

4. **Keep me, O LORD, from the hands of the wicked;** preserve me from the violent man; **who have purposed to overthrow my goings.**

5. **The proud have hid a snare for me,** and cords; they have spread a net by the wayside; they have set gins for me. Selah.

6. **I said unto the LORD, Thou art my God: hear** the voice of **my supplications, O LORD.**

7. **O GOD** the Lord, **the strength of my salvation,** thou hast covered my head in the day of battle.

8. **Grant not,** O LORD, **the desires of the wicked:** further not his wicked device; **lest they exalt themselves.** Selah.

9. **As for** the head of **those that compass me** about, **let the mischief of their own lips cover them.**

10. Let burning coals fall upon them: **let them be cast into the fire; into deep pits, that they rise not** up **again.**

11. **Let not an evil speaker be established** in the earth: **evil shall hunt the violent man to overthrow him.**

12. **I know that the LORD will maintain the cause of the afflicted, and** the right of **the poor.**

13. **Surely the righteous shall give thanks unto thy name: the upright shall dwell in thy presence.**

PSALM 141

1. **LORD, I cry unto thee:** make haste unto me; give ear unto

my voice, when I cry unto thee.

2. **Let my prayer be**
set forth before thee
**as incense; and the lifting
up of my hands as the
evening sacrifice.**
3. **Set a watch,** O LORD,
before my mouth;
keep the door of my lips.
4. **Incline not my heart to** *any*
evil thing,
to practise wicked works
with men that work iniquity: and
let me not eat of their dainties.
5. **Let the righteous** smite me;
it shall be a kindness: and let him
**reprove me; it shall be
an excellent oil,** *which* shall not
break my head: for yet my prayer
also *shall be* in their calamities.
6. **When their judges are
overthrown** in stony places,
**they shall hear my words;
for they are sweet.**
7. Our bones are scattered at the
grave's mouth, as when one cutteth
and cleaveth *wood* upon the earth.
8. **But mine eyes are unto
thee,** O GOD the Lord:
in thee is my trust;
leave not my soul destitute.
9. **Keep me from the
snares** *which* they have
laid for me, and the gins
of the workers of iniquity.
10. **Let the wicked fall into
their own nets, whilst** that
I withal
escape.

PSALM 142

1. **I cried unto the LORD**
with my voice; with my voice unto the
LORD did I make my supplication.
2. **I poured out my
complaint before him;**
I shewed before him my trouble.
3. **When my spirit was
overwhelmed** within me,
then thou knewest my path.
In the way wherein I walked have
they privily laid a snare for me.
4. **I looked** on *my* right hand,

and beheld, but
there was no man that would
know me: refuge failed me;
no man cared for my soul.
5. **I cried unto thee,**
O LORD: I said,
Thou art my refuge
and my portion in the
land of the living.
6. Attend unto my cry; for
I am brought very low:
**deliver me from my
persecutors; for they
are stronger than I.**
7. **Bring my soul out of
prison, that I may praise**
thy name: the righteous
shall compass me about;
**for thou shalt deal
bountifully with me.**

PSALM 143

1. **Hear my prayer, O LORD,**
give ear to my supplications:
**in thy faithfulness answer
me,** *and* in thy righteousness.
2. **And enter not into
judgment** with thy servant:
**for in thy sight
shall no man** living
be justified.
3. **For the enemy hath
persecuted my soul;** he hath
smitten my life down to the ground;
he hath made me to
dwell in darkness, as
those that have been long dead.
4. **Therefore is my spirit
overwhelmed** within me;
my heart within me
is desolate.
5. **I remember** the days
of old; I meditate on all
thy works; I muse on
the work of thy hands.
6. I stretch forth my hands unto thee:
**my soul thirsteth after
thee,** as a thirsty land. Selah.
7. **Hear me** speedily,
**O LORD: my spirit faileth:
hide not thy face from
me, lest I be like** unto
them that go down

into the pit.

8. **Cause me to hear thy lovingkindness** in the morning; **for in thee do I trust: cause me to know the way wherein I should walk;** for I lift up my soul unto thee.

9. **Deliver me,** O LORD, **from mine enemies: I flee unto thee to hide me.**

10. Teach me to do thy will; for thou *art* my God: thy spirit *is* good; **lead me into the land of uprightness.**

11. **Quicken me, O LORD, for thy name's sake:** for thy righteousness' sake bring my soul out of trouble.

12. And of thy mercy cut off mine enemies, **and destroy** all **them that afflict my soul: for I am thy servant.**

PSALM 144

1. **Blessed be the LORD my strength** which teacheth my hands to war, *and* my fingers to fight:

2. My goodness, and my fortress; my high tower, **and my deliverer; my shield, and he in whom I trust;** who subdueth my people under me.

3. **LORD, what is man, that thou takest knowledge of him!** *or* the son of man, that thou makest account of him!

4. **Man is like to vanity: his days are as a shadow that passeth away.**

5. Bow thy heavens, **O LORD, and come down:** touch the mountains, and they shall smoke.

6. Cast forth lightning, and scatter them: shoot out thine arrows, and destroy them.

7. **Send thine hand from above;** rid me, **and deliver me** out of great waters, **from the hand of**

strange children;

8. **Whose mouth speaketh** vanity, and their right hand *is* a right hand of **falsehood.**

9. **I will sing a new song unto thee, O God:** upon a psaltery *and* an instrument of ten strings will I sing praises unto thee.

10. **It is he that giveth salvation** unto kings: **who delivereth David** his servant **from the** hurtful **sword.**

11. Rid me, and **deliver me from the** hand of **strange children,** whose mouth speaketh vanity, and their right hand *is* a right hand of falsehood:

12. **That our sons may be as plants grown up** in their youth; *that* **our daughters** *may be* **as corner stones,** polished after the **similitude of a palace:**

13. **That our garners may be full,** affording all manner of store: **that our sheep may bring forth** thousands and **ten thousands** in our streets:

14. **That our oxen may be strong to labour;** *that there be* no breaking in, nor going out; that *there be* no complaining in our streets.

15. **Happy is that people,** that is in such a case: *yea,* happy *is that* people, **whose God is the LORD.**

PSALM 145

1. **I will extol thee, my God,** O king; and **I will bless thy name for ever** and ever.

2. **Every day will I bless thee; and** I will **praise thy name** for ever and ever.

3. **Great is the LORD, and**

PSALM 146

greatly to be praised; and
his greatness is
unsearchable.
4. One generation shall
praise thy works to another,
and shall
declare thy mighty acts.
5. I will speak
of the glorious honour
of thy majesty, and of
thy wondrous works.
6. And *men* shall speak of
the might of thy terrible acts:
and I will declare
thy greatness.
7. They shall abundantly
utter the memory of thy
great goodness, and shall
sing of thy righteousness.
8. The LORD is gracious,
and full of compassion;
slow to anger, and of
great mercy.
9. The LORD *is* good to all: and his
tender mercies *are* over all his works.
10. All thy works shall
praise thee, O LORD;
and thy saints shall bless thee.
11. They shall speak of
the glory of thy kingdom,
and talk of thy power;
12. To make known
to the sons of
men his mighty acts, and
the glorious majesty
of his kingdom.
13. Thy kingdom is an
everlasting kingdom,
and thy dominion endureth
throughout all generations.
14. The LORD upholdeth
all that fall, and raiseth up
all *those that be* bowed down.
15. The eyes of all wait
upon thee; and thou
givest them their
meat in due season.
16. Thou openest thine hand,
and satisfiest the desire of
every living thing.
17. The LORD is
righteous in all his ways,
and holy in all his works.

18. The LORD is nigh unto all
them that call upon
him, to all that call upon him
in truth.
19. He will fulfil the desire of
them that fear him: he also
will hear their cry, and
will save them.
20. The LORD preserveth all
them that love him: but all
the wicked will he destroy.
21. My mouth shall speak
the praise of the LORD:
and let all flesh bless his holy
name for ever and ever.

PSALM 146

1. Praise ye the LORD.
Praise the LORD,
O my soul.
2. While I live will I praise the LORD:
I will sing praises unto
my God while I have
any being.
3. Put not your trust
in princes, *nor*
in the son of man, in
whom there is no help.
4. His breath goeth forth,
he returneth to his earth;
in that very day his
thoughts perish.
5. Happy is he that hath the
God of Jacob
for his help, whose hope
is in the LORD his God:
6. Which made heaven,
and earth, the sea,
and all that therein is:
which keepeth truth for ever:
7. Which executeth
judgment for the
oppressed: which
giveth food to the hungry.
The LORD looseth
the prisoners:
8. The LORD openeth the
eyes of the blind: the LORD
raiseth them that are
bowed down: the LORD
loveth the righteous:
9. The LORD preserveth the
strangers; he relieveth the

fatherless and widow: but the way of the wicked he turneth upside down.

10. The LORD shall reign for ever, *even* thy God, O Zion, unto all generations. Praise ye the LORD.

PSALM 147

1. Praise ye the LORD: for it is good to sing praises unto our God; for it is pleasant; *and* praise is comely.
2. The LORD doth build up Jerusalem: he gathereth together the outcasts of Israel.
3. He healeth the broken in heart, and bindeth up their wounds.
4. He telleth the number of the stars; he calleth them all by their names.
5. Great is our Lord, and of great power: his understanding is infinite.
6. The LORD lifteth up the meek: he casteth the wicked down to the ground.
7. Sing unto the LORD with thanksgiving; sing praise upon the harp unto our God:
8. Who covereth the heaven with clouds, who prepareth rain for the earth, who maketh grass to grow upon the mountains.
9. He giveth to the beast his food, *and* to the young ravens which cry.
10. He delighteth not in the strength of the horse: he taketh not pleasure in the legs of a man.
11. The LORD taketh pleasure in them that fear him, in those that hope in his mercy.
12. Praise the LORD, O Jerusalem; praise thy God, O Zion.

13. For he hath strengthened the bars of thy gates; he hath blessed thy children within thee.
14. He maketh peace *in* thy borders, *and* filleth thee with the finest of the wheat.
15. He sendeth forth his commandment upon earth: his word runneth very swiftly.
16. He giveth snow like wool: he scattereth the hoarfrost like ashes.
17. He casteth forth his ice like morsels: who can stand before his cold?
18. He sendeth out his word, and melteth them: he causeth his wind to blow, and the waters flow.
19. He sheweth his word unto Jacob, his statutes and his judgments unto Israel.
20. He hath not dealt so with any nation: and *as for his* judgments, they have not known them. Praise ye the LORD.

PSALM 148

1. Praise ye the LORD. Praise ye the LORD from the heavens: praise him in the heights.
2. Praise ye him, all his angels: praise ye him, all his hosts.
3. Praise ye him, sun and moon: praise him, all ye stars of light.
4. Praise him, ye heavens of heavens, and ye waters that *be* above the heavens.
5. Let them praise the name of the LORD: for he commanded, and they were created.
6. He hath also stablished them

for ever and ever:
he hath made a decree
which shall not pass.
7. **Praise the LORD**
from the earth,
ye dragons, and all
deeps:
8. **Fire,** and
hail; snow, and
vapours; stormy wind
fulfilling his word:
9. **Mountains,** and all
hills; fruitful
trees, and all cedars:
10 **Beasts,** and all cattle;
creeping things, and flying
fowl:
11. **Kings** of the earth, and all
people; princes, and all
judges of the earth
12 Both
young men, and
maidens; old men,
and children:
13 **Let them praise the**
name of the LORD: for his
name alone is excellent; his
glory *is* above the earth and heaven.
14 **He** also
exalteth the horn of his
people, the praise of all
his saints; *even* of the children
of Israel, a people near unto him.
Praise ye the LORD.

PSALM 149

1. Praise ye the LORD.
Sing unto the LORD
a new song, *and* his praise
in the congregation of saints.
2. **Let Israel rejoice in him**
that made him: let the children
of Zion be joyful in their King.
3. **Let them praise his**
name in the dance:
let them sing praises unto him
with the timbrel and harp.

4. **For the LORD taketh**
pleasure in his people:
he will beautify the
meek with salvation.
5. **Let the saints be**
joyful in glory: let them
sing aloud upon their beds.
6. **Let the high praises**
of God be in their
mouth, and a two-edged
sword in their hand;
7. **To execute vengeance**
upon the heathen, *and*
punishments upon the people;
8. To bind their kings with chains,
and their nobles with fetters of iron;
9. **To execute upon them**
the judgment written: this
honour have all his saints.
Praise ye the LORD.

PSALM 150

1. Praise ye the LORD.
Praise God in his
sanctuary: praise him
in the firmament
of his power.
2. **Praise him for**
his mighty acts: praise him
according to his
excellent greatness.
3. **Praise him with the**
sound of the trumpet:
praise him with the
psaltery and harp.
4. **Praise him with**
the timbrel and
dance: praise him with
stringed instruments and
organs.
5. Praise him upon the
loud cymbals: praise him upon
the high sounding
cymbals.
6. **Let every thing that hath**
breath praise the LORD.
Praise ye the LORD.

THE BOOK OF PROVERBS

BACKGROUND INFORMATION

Author: Solomon and possibly **other people of wisdom**
Date Written:
Approximately 400 B.C.

Number of:
Verses—915
Chapters—31
Total Words—15,043
Scan Words—11,302
Scan Words Represent
Approximately 75% of
Total Words

Theme: Advice and Wisdom **Concerning the** Proper **Way People Should Conduct Their Lives**

OUTLINE OF THE PROVERBS

I.   The Contrast Between **Wisdom and Folly**
    1:1 — 9:18
II. **The Special Proverbs Attributed to Solomon**
    10:1 — 24:34
III. **The Proverbs Attributed to Hezekiah**
    25:1 — 29:27
IV. **The Oracle of Agur**
    30:1 — 33
V.   **The Oracle of Lemuel**
    31:1 — 31

(Since the verses which form Proverbs are usually self-contained units, they, for the most part, must be presented in their entirety and therefore the SCAN percentage is much higher.)

PROVERBS 1

CHAPTER 1

■ 1. **The proverbs of Solomon**
the son of David, king of Israel;
■ 2. **To know** wisdom
■ **and** instruction; to perceive
the words of understanding;
■ 3. **To receive the instruction**
■ **of wisdom, justice,** and
■ **judgment, and equity;**
■ 4. **To give subtilty** to
the simple, to the young man
■ **knowledge and discretion.**
■ 5. **A wise man** will hear, and
■ **will increase learning;** and
■ **a man of understanding**
■ **shall attain** unto wise
■ **counsels:**
■ 6. **To understand a**
■ **proverb, and the**
■ **interpretation;** the words of
the wise, and their dark sayings.
■ 7. **The fear of the LORD**
■ **is the beginning of**
■ **knowledge: but**
■ **fools despise**
■ **wisdom** and instruction.
■ 8. **My son, hear** the
■ **instruction** of thy father,
■ **and forsake not the**
■ **law of thy mother:**
■ 9. **For they shall be**
■ **an ornament of grace**
unto thy head, and chains
■ **about thy neck.**
10. My son,
■ **if sinners entice**
■ **thee, consent** thou
■ **not.**
■ 11. **If they say, Come** with us,
■ **let us lay wait** for
blood, let us lurk privily
■ **for the innocent** without cause:
■ 12. **Let us swallow them** up
alive as the grave; and whole,
■ **as those that go** down
■ **into the pit:**
■ 13. **We shall** find all
precious substance, we shall
■ **fill our houses with spoil:**
14. Cast in thy lot among us;
■ **let us** all
■ **have one purse:**
15. My son,

■ **walk not** thou in the way
■ **with them; refrain** thy foot
■ **from their path:**
■ 16. **For their feet**
■ **run** to evil, and make haste
■ **to shed blood.**
17. Surely in vain the net is
spread in the sight of any bird.
18. And they lay wait
for their *own* blood;
■ **they lurk privily**
■ **for their own lives.**
■ 19. **So are the** ways
of every one that is
■ **greedy** of gain;
■ **which taketh** away
■ **the life of the**
■ **owners** thereof.
■ 20. **Wisdom** crieth without; she
■ **uttereth her voice**
■ **in the streets:**
■ 21. **She crieth** in the chief
place of concourse, in the
openings of the gates: in the
city she uttereth her words,
■ **saying,**
■ 22. **How long,** ye simple ones,
■ **will ye love simplicity?**
■ **and** the scorners
■ **delight in** their
■ **scorning,** and
■ **fools hate knowledge?**
23. **Turn** you
■ **at my reproof:** behold,
I will pour out my spirit unto you,
■ **I will make known**
■ **my words unto you.**
■ 24. **Because I** have
■ **called,** and ye refused;
I have stretched out my hand,
■ **and no man regarded;**
25. **But ye** have
■ **set at nought** all
■ **my counsel, and would**
none of my reproof:
26. **I** also
■ **will laugh at your calamity;** I
will mock when your fear cometh;
■ 27. **When your fear**
cometh as desolation,
■ **and** your
■ **destruction cometh**
as a whirlwind;

904

when distress and anguish cometh upon you. 28. **Then shall they call upon me, but I will not answer;** they shall seek me early, but they shall not find me: 29. **For** that **they hated knowledge,** and did not choose the fear of the LORD: 30. They would none of my counsel: **they despised all my reproof.** 31. **Therefore shall they** eat of the fruit of their own way, and **be filled with their own devices.** 32. **For the turning away of the simple shall slay them, and** the prosperity of fools **shall destroy them.** 33. **But whoso hearkeneth unto me shall dwell safely,** and shall be quiet from fear of evil.

CHAPTER 2

1. **My son,** if thou wilt **receive my words, and** hide my **commandments** with thee; 2. **So** that thou **incline** thine ear **unto wisdom, and** apply thine heart to **understanding;** 3. Yea, if thou criest after knowledge, *and* liftest up thy voice for understanding; 4. **If thou seekest her as silver, and** searchest for her as *for* **hid treasures;** 5. **Then shalt thou** understand the **fear** of **the LORD, and find** the **knowledge of God.** 6. **For the LORD giveth wisdom:** out of his mouth *cometh* **knowledge and understanding.** 7. He layeth up sound wisdom for the righteous: *he is* a buckler

to them that walk uprightly. 8. **He** keepeth the paths of judgment, and **preserveth the way of his saints.** 9. **Then shalt thou understand righteousness, and judgment**, and equity; *yea*, every good path. 10. When wisdom entereth into thine heart, and knowledge is pleasant unto thy soul; 11. **Discretion** shall preserve thee, **understanding shall keep thee:** 12. **To deliver thee from** the way of the **evil man,** from the man that speaketh froward things; 13. **Who** leave the paths of uprightness, to **walk in the ways of darkness;** 14. **Who rejoice** to do evil, **and delight in the** frowardness of the **wicked;** 15. Whose ways *are* crooked, **and** *they* froward in their paths: 16. To deliver thee **from the strange woman**, *even* from the stranger *which* flattereth with her words; 17. **Which** forsaketh the guide of her youth, and **forgetteth** the covenant of her **God.** 18. **For her house inclineth unto death,** and her paths unto the dead. 19. **None that go unto her return** again, **neither take** they **hold of** the paths of **life.** 20. That thou mayest **walk** in **the way of good men, and keep** the paths of the **righteous.** 21. **For the upright shall**

■ dwell in the land, and the perfect shall remain in it.

■ 22. But the wicked shall be cut off from the earth, and the transgressors ■ shall be rooted out of it.

CHAPTER 3

■ 1. My son, forget not ■ my law; but let thine heart keep my commandments:

■ 2. For length of days, and ■ long life, and peace, ■ shall they add to thee.

■ 3. Let not mercy and ■ truth forsake thee: bind them about thy neck; write them upon the table of thine heart:

■ 4. So shalt thou find ■ favour and good understanding ■ in the sight of God and man.

■ 5. Trust in the LORD with all thine heart; and ■ lean not unto thine ■ own understanding.

6. In all thy ways ■ acknowledge him, and ■ he shall direct thy paths.

■ 7. Be not wise in thine ■ own eyes: fear the LORD, ■ and depart from evil.

8. It shall be health to thy navel, and marrow to thy bones.

■ 9. Honour the LORD with ■ thy substance, and with the firstfruits of all thine increase:

■ 10. So shall thy barns be ■ filled with plenty, and thy presses shall burst out with new wine.

■ 11. My son, despise not the ■ chastening of the LORD; neither be weary of his correction:

■ 12. For whom the LORD ■ loveth he correcteth; even as a father the son in whom hedelighteth.

■ 13. Happy is the man ■ that findeth wisdom, ■ and the man that ■ getteth understanding.

14. For the merchandise of ■ it is better than the merchandise of ■ silver, and the gain

■ thereof than fine ■ gold.

15. She is more precious than rubies: and all the things thou canst desire are not to be compared unto her.

■ 16. Length of days is in her ■ right hand; and in her left ■ hand riches and honour.

■ 17. Her ways are ways of ■ pleasantness, ■ and all her paths are ■ peace.

■ 18. She is a tree of life to them that lay hold upon her: and happy is every one that retaineth her.

■ 19. The LORD by wisdom hath ■ founded the earth; by ■ understanding hath he ■ established the heavens.

20. By his knowledge the depths are broken up, and the clouds drop down the dew.

■ 21. My son, let not them depart from thine eyes: ■ keep sound wisdom ■ and discretion:

■ 22. So shall they be life unto ■ thy soul, and grace to thy neck.

■ 23. Then shalt thou ■ walk in thy way safely, ■ and thy foot shall ■ not stumble.

■ 24. When thou liest ■ down, thou shalt not be afraid: yea, thou shalt lie down, and ■ thy sleep shall be sweet.

■ 25. Be not afraid of sudden fear, neither ■ of the ■ desolation of the wicked, when it cometh.

■ 26. For the LORD shall be ■ thy confidence, and shall keep thy foot from being taken.

■ 27. Withhold not good from them to whom it is due, ■ when it is in the power ■ of thine hand to do it.

28. Say not unto thy neighbour, Go, and come again, and ■ tomorrow I will give; ■ when thou hast it by thee.

29. Devise not evil against

thy neighbour, seeing he dwelleth securely by thee.

30. **Strive not** with a man **without cause**, if he have done thee no harm.

31. **Envy** thou **not the oppressor,** and choose none of his ways.

32. **For the froward is abomination** to the LORD: but his secret *is* with the righteous.

33. **The curse of the LORD is in the house of the wicked: but he blesseth the habitation of the just.**

34. **Surely he** scorneth the scorners: but he **giveth grace unto the lowly.**

35. **The wise shall inherit glory: but shame shall be the promotion of fools.**

CHAPTER 4

1. **Hear,** ye children, **the instruction of a father,** and attend to know understanding.

2. For I give you good doctrine, **forsake ye not my law.**

3. For I was my father's son, tender and only *beloved* in the sight of my mother.

4. **He taught me also,** and said unto me, **Let thine heart retain** my words: keep **my commandments,** and live.

5. **Get wisdom, get understanding:** forget *it* not; neither decline from the words of my mouth.

6. Forsake her not, and she shall preserve thee: love her, and she shall keep thee.

7. **Wisdom is the principal thing;** *therefore* get wisdom: and with all thy getting get understanding.

8. **Exalt her, and she shall** promote thee: she shall **bring thee to honour,** when thou dost embrace her.

9. **She shall give to thine head** an ornament of grace: **a crown of glory** shall she deliver to thee.

10. **Hear,** O my son, and receive **my sayings; and the years of thy life shall be many.**

11. **I have taught thee** in the way of **wisdom;** I have led thee in right paths.

12. When thou goest, **thy steps shall not be straitened; and** when thou runnest, **thou shalt not stumble.**

13. **Take** fast **hold of instruction;** let *her* not go: keep her; **for she is thy life.**

14. **Enter not** into **the path of the wicked,** and go not in the way of evil *men*.

15. **Avoid it,** pass not by it, turn from it, and pass away.

16. **For they sleep not,** except they have done mischief; and their sleep is taken away, **unless they cause some to fall.**

17. **For they eat** the bread of **wickedness, and drink** the wine of **violence.**

18. **But the path of the just is as the shining light,** that shineth more and more unto the perfect day.

19. **The way of the wicked is as darkness:** they know not at what they stumble.

20. **My son,** attend to my words; **incline** thine ear **unto my sayings.**

21. Let them not depart from thine eyes; **keep them in** the midst of **thine heart.**

22. **For they are life** unto those that find them, **and health** to all their flesh.

23. **Keep thy heart** with all diligence; **for out of it are the issues of life.**

24. **Put away** from

thee a froward mouth, and
perverse lips put far from thee.
25. Let thine eyes look
right on, and let thine eyelids
look straight before thee.
26. Ponder the path of
thy feet, and let all thy
ways be established.
27. Turn not to the
right hand
nor to the
left: remove thy
foot from evil.

CHAPTER 5

1. My son, attend unto my
wisdom, and bow thine ear to my
understanding:
2. That thou mayest
regard discretion,
and that thy lips may
keep knowledge.
3. For the lips of a
strange woman drop
as an honeycomb, and
hermouth is smoother than oil:
4. But her end is bitter
as wormwood, sharp as a
two-edged sword.
5. Her feet go down to
death; her steps take hold on
hell.
6. Lest thou shouldest
ponder the path of
life, her ways are
moveable, that thou
canst not know them.
7. Hear me now
therefore, O ye children,
and depart not from the
words of my mouth.
8. Remove thy way
far from her, and come not
nigh the door of her house:
9. Lest thou give thine
honour unto others, and
thy years unto the cruel:
10. Lest strangers be
filled with thy wealth;
and thy labours be
in the house of a stranger;
11. And thou mourn at the last,
when thy flesh and thy

body are consumed,
12. And say, How have
I hated instruction,
and my heart despised
reproof;
13. And have not
obeyed the voice of
my teachers, nor inclined mine
ear to them that instructed me!
14. I was almost in all evil in the midst
of the congregation and assembly.
15. Drink waters out of
thine own cistern, and
running waters out of thine own
well.
16. Let thy fountains
be dispersed abroad,
and rivers of waters in the streets.
17. Let them be only
thine own, and not
strangers' with thee.
18. Let thy fountain be
blessed: and rejoice
with the wife of thy youth.
19. Let her be as the loving hind
and pleasant roe; let her breasts
satisfy thee at all times; and be
thou ravished always with her love.
20. And why
wilt thou, my son,
be ravished with a
strange woman, and
embrace the bosom of a stranger?
21. For the ways of man
are before the eyes of
the LORD, and he pondereth
all his goings.
22. His own iniquities shall take
the wicked himself, and he
shall be holden with
the cords of his sins.
23. He shall die without
instruction; and in the greatness of
his folly he shall go astray.

CHAPTER 6

1. My son, if thou
be surety for thy friend,
if thou hast stricken thy
hand with a stranger,
2. Thou art snared with the
words of thy mouth, thou art
taken with the words of thy mouth.

3. Do this now, my son, and **deliver thyself**, when thou art come into the hand of thy friend; go, **humble thyself,** and make sure thy friend. 4. **Give not sleep to thine eyes,** nor slumber to thine eyelids. 5. **Deliver thyself** as a roe from the hand *of the hunter*, and **as a bird from the hand of the fowler.** 6. **Go to the ant**, thou sluggard; **consider her ways,** and be wise: 7. **Which having no** guide, overseer, or **ruler,** 8. **Provideth** her meat in the summer, *and* gathereth **her food in the harvest.** 9. **How long wilt thou sleep,** O sluggard? when wilt thou arise out of thy sleep? 10. *Yet* a little sleep, a little slumber, **a little folding of the hands to sleep:** 11. **So shall** thy **poverty come** as one that travelleth, and thy want as an armed man. 12. A naughty person, **a wicked man, walketh with a froward mouth.** 13. **He winketh** with his eyes, **he speaketh with his feet, he teacheth with his fingers;** 14. Frowardness *is* in his heart, **he deviseth mischief continually;** he soweth discord. 15. **Therefore shall his calamity come** suddenly; suddenly shall he be broken **without remedy.** 16. **These six things doth the LORD hate: yea, seven are an abomination** unto him: 17. **A proud look, a lying tongue, and** hands that shed **innocent blood,** 18. **An heart that deviseth wicked imaginations,**

feet that be swift in **running to mischief,** 19. **A false witness** *that* speaketh lies, **and he that soweth discord among brethren.** 20. **My son, keep thy father's commandment, and forsake not the law of thy mother:** 21. **Bind them** continually **upon thine heart**, *and* tie them about thy neck. 22. When thou goest, **it shall lead thee**; when thou sleepest, it shall keep thee; and *when* thou awakest, it shall talk with thee. 23. **For the commandment is a lamp; and the law is light; and reproofs** of instruction *are* **the way of life:** 24. **To keep thee** from the evil woman, **from the flattery of the tongue** of a strange woman. 25. **Lust not** after her beauty **in thine heart**; neither let her take thee with her eyelids. 26. **For by** means of **a whorish woman** *a* **man is brought to a piece of bread:** and the adultress will hunt for the precious life. 27. **Can a man take fire** in his bosom, **and** his clothes **not be burned?** 28. **Can one go upon hot coals, and his feet not be burned?** 29. **So he that goeth in to his neighbour's wife;** whosoever toucheth her **shall not be innocent.** 30. **Men do not despise a thief, if he steal to** satisfy his soul **when he is hungry;** 31. **But** *if* he be found, **he shall restore sevenfold**; he shall give all the substance of his house.

32. **But whoso committeth adultery** with a woman lacketh understanding: he *that* doeth it **destroyeth his own soul**.

33. **A wound and dishonour shall he get; and his reproach shall not be wiped away.**

34. **For jealousy is the rage of a man:** therefore **he will not spare in the day of vengeance.**

35. **He will not regard any ransom; neither** will he rest content, though thou givest **many gifts.**

CHAPTER 7

1. **My son,** keep my words, and lay up my commandments with thee.

2. **Keep my commandments,** and live; and my law **as the apple of thine eye.**

3. Bind them upon thy fingers, **write them upon the table of thine heart.**

4. **Say unto wisdom, Thou art my sister; and call understanding thy kinswoman:**

5. **That they may keep thee** from the strange woman, **from the stranger which flattereth with her words.**

6. **For at the window** of my house **I looked** through my casement,

7. **And beheld** among the simple ones, I discerned among the youths, **a young man void of understanding,**

8. **Passing** through the street near **her corner;** and he went the way **to her house,**

9. In the twilight, **in the evening,** in the black and dark night:

10. **And,** behold, there **met** him a woman *with* the attire of **an harlot,** and subtil of heart.

11. (She *is* loud and stubborn; her feet abide not in her house:

12. Now *is* she without, now in the streets, and lieth in wait at every corner.)

13. **So she** caught him, and **kissed him, and** with an impudent face **said** unto him,

14. *I have* peace offerings with me; **this day have I payed my vows.**

15. **Therefore** came I forth to meet thee, diligently to seek thy face, and **I have found thee.**

16. **I have decked my bed** with coverings of tapestry, with carved *works*, with fine linen of Egypt.

17. I have perfumed my bed with myrrh, aloes, and cinnamon.

18. **Come, let us take our fill of love** until the morning: let us solace ourselves with loves.

19. **For the goodman** *is* not at home, he **is gone** a long journey:

20. He hath taken a bag of money with him, *and* will come home at the day appointed.

21. With her much fair speech **she caused him to yield, with the flattering of her lips** she forced him.

22. **He goeth after her** straightway, **as an ox** goeth **to the slaughter,** or as a fool to the correction of the stocks;

23. Till a dart strike through his liver; as a bird hasteth to the snare, and knoweth not that it *is* for his life.

24. **Hearken unto me** now therefore, O ye children, and attend to the words of my mouth.

25. **Let not thine heart decline to her ways,** go not astray in her paths.

26. **For** she hath cast down many wounded: yea, **many strong men have been slain by her.**

27. **Her house is the way to hell,** going down

to the chambers of death.

CHAPTER 8

1. **Doth not wisdom cry? and understanding put forth her voice?**
2. **She standeth in** the top of high places, by the way in the places of **the paths.**
3. **She crieth at the gates,** at the entry of the city, at the coming in at the doors.
4. **Unto you,** O men, **I call;** and my voice *is* to the sons of man.
5. **O ye** simple, understand wisdom: and, ye **fools, be ye of an understanding heart.**
6. **Hear;** for I will speak of excellent things; and the opening of my lips *shall be* right things.
7. **For my mouth shall speak truth; and wickedness is an abomination** to my lips.
8. **All the words of my mouth are in righteousness;** *there is* nothing froward or perverse in them.
9. **They are** all **plain to him that understandeth,** and right to them that find knowledge.
10. **Receive my instruction,** and not silver; **and knowledge** rather than choice gold.
11. **For wisdom is better than rubies;** and all the things that may be desired are not to be compared to it.
12. I wisdom dwell with prudence, and find out knowledge of witty inventions.
13. **The fear of the LORD is to hate evil:** pride, and arrogancy, and the evil way, and the froward mouth, do I hate.
14. **Counsel is mine, and sound wisdom: I am understanding;**

I have strength.
15. **By me kings reign, and** princes decree justice.
16. By me **princes rule,** and nobles, **even** all the **judges** of the earth.
17. **I love them that love me;** and **those that seek me early shall find me.**
18. **Riches and honour are with me;** *yea,* durable riches and righteousness.
19. **My fruit is better than gold,** yea, than fine gold; and my revenue than choice silver.
20. **I lead in the way of righteousness,** in the midst of the paths of judgment:
21. **That I may cause those that love me to inherit substance;** and I will fill their treasures.
22. **The LORD possessed me** in the beginning of his way, before his works of old.
23. I was set up from everlasting, **from the beginning,** or ever the earth was.
24. **When there were no depths,** I was brought forth; **when there were no fountains** abounding with water.
25. **Before the mountains** were settled, **before the hills was I brought forth:**
26. While as yet he had not made the earth, nor the fields, nor the highest part of the dust of the world.
27. **When he prepared the heavens, I was there:** when he set a compass upon the face of the depth:
28. **When he established the clouds** above: when he strengthened the fountains of the deep:
29. **When he gave to the sea his decree,** that the waters should not pass his commandment: when he appointed

the foundations of the earth:

30. **Then I was by him**, *as* one brought up *with him*: **and I was** daily **his delight, rejoicing** always **before him;**

31. Rejoicing in the habitable part of his earth; and my delights *were* with the sons of men.

32. Now therefore **hearken unto me,** O ye children: **for blessed are they that keep my ways.**

33. **Hear instruction, and be wise**, and refuse it not.

34. Blessed *is* the man that heareth me, watching daily at my gates, waiting at the posts of my doors.

35. **For whoso findeth me findeth life**, **and** shall obtain **favour of the LORD.**

36. **But he that sinneth** against me **wrongeth his own soul:** all they that hate me love death.

CHAPTER 9

1. **Wisdom hath builded her house,** she hath hewn out her seven pillars:

2. She hath killed her beasts; she hath mingled her wine; **she hath** also **furnished her table.**

3. **She hath sent forth her maidens**: she crieth upon the highest places of the city,

4. **Whoso is simple, let him turn in** hither: **as for him that wanteth understanding,** she saith to him,

5. **Come, eat** of my bread, **and drink** of the wine *which* I have mingled.

6. **Forsake the foolish**, and live; **and go in the way of understanding.**

7. He that reproveth a scorner getteth to himself shame: and

he that rebuketh a wicked *man* getteth himself a blot.

8. **Reprove not a scorner, lest he hate thee: rebuke a wise man, and he will love thee.**

9. **Give instruction to a wise man, and he will be** yet **wiser: teach a just man, and he will increase in learning.**

10. **The fear of the LORD is the beginning of wisdom: and the knowledge of the holy is understanding.**

11. **For by me thy** days shall be multiplied, and the **years** of thy life **shall be increased.**

12. If thou be wise, thou shalt be wise for thyself: but *if* thou scornest, thou alone shalt bear *it*.

13. **A foolish woman is clamorous**: *she is* simple, **and knoweth nothing.**

14. For she sitteth at the door of her house, on a seat in the high places of the city,

15. To call passengers who go right on their ways:

16. **Whoso is simple**, let him turn in hither: **and** *as for* him that **wanteth understanding, she saith to him,**

17. **Stolen waters are sweet, and bread eaten in secret is pleasant.**

18. **But** he knoweth not that the dead *are* there; *and that* **her guests are in the depths of hell.**

CHAPTER 10

1. **The proverbs of Solomon. A wise son maketh a glad father: but a foolish son is the heaviness of his mother.**

2. **Treasures of wickedness profit nothing**: but righteousness delivereth from death.

3. **The LORD will not suffer**

the soul of the righteous to famish: but he casteth away the substance of the wicked.

4. He becometh poor that dealeth with a slack hand: but the hand of the diligent maketh rich.

5. He that gathereth in summer is a wise son: *but* he that sleepeth in harvest *is* a son that causeth shame.

6. Blessings are upon the head of the just: but violence covereth the mouth of the wicked.

7. The memory of the just is blessed: but the name of the wicked shall rot.

8. The wise in heart will receive commandments: but a prating fool shall fall.

9. He that walketh uprightly walketh surely: but he that perverteth his ways shall be known.

10. He that winketh with the eye causeth sorrow: but a prating fool shall fall.

11. The mouth of a righteous man is a well of life: but violence covereth the mouth of the wicked.

12. Hatred stirreth up strifes: but love covereth all sins.

13. In the lips of him that hath understanding wisdom is found: but a rod is for the back of him that is void of understanding.

14. Wise men lay up knowledge: but the mouth of the foolish is near destruction.

15. The rich man's wealth is his strong city: the destruction of the poor is their poverty.

16. The labour of the righteous tendeth to life: the fruit of the wicked to sin.

17. He is in the way of life that keepeth instruction: but he that refuseth reproof erreth.

18. He that hideth hatred with lying lips, and he that uttereth a slander, is a fool.

19. In the multitude of words there wanteth not sin: but he that refraineth his lips is wise.

20. The tongue of the just is as choice silver: the heart of the wicked is little worth.

21. The lips of the righteous feed many: but fools die for want of wisdom.

22. The blessing of the LORD, it maketh rich, and he addeth no sorrow with it.

23. It is as sport to a fool to do mischief: but a man of understanding hath wisdom.

24. The fear of the wicked, it shall come upon him: but the desire of the righteous shall be granted.

25. As the whirlwind passeth, so is the wicked no *more*: but the righteous is an everlasting foundation.

26. As vinegar to the teeth, and as smoke to the eyes, so is the sluggard to them that send him.

27. The fear of the LORD prolongeth days: but the years of the wicked shall be shortened.

28. The hope of the righteous shall be gladness: but the expectation of the wicked shall perish.

29. The way of the LORD is strength to the upright: but destruction *shall be*

to the workers of iniquity.

30. **The righteous shall never be removed: but the wicked shall not inhabit the earth.**

31. **The mouth of the just bringeth** forth **wisdom: but the froward tongue shall be cut out.**

32. **The lips of the righteous know what is acceptable: but the mouth of the wicked speaketh frowardness.**

CHAPTER 11

1. **A false balance is abomination** to the LORD: **but a just weight is his delight.**

2. *When* **pride cometh, then** cometh **shame: but with the lowly is wisdom.**

3. **The integrity of the upright shall guide them: but the perverseness of transgressors shall destroy them.**

4. **Riches profit not in the day of wrath: but righteousness delivereth from death.**

5. **The righteousness of the perfect shall direct his way: but the wicked shall fall by his** own **wickedness.**

6. The righteousness of the upright shall deliver them: but transgressors shall be taken in *their own* naughtiness.

7. **When a wicked man dieth, his expectation** shall perish: **and** the **hope** of unjust *men* **perisheth.**

8. **The righteous is delivered out of trouble**, and the wicked cometh in his stead.

9. **An hypocrite with his mouth destroyeth his neighbour: but through** knowledge shall the **just be delivered.**

10. When it goeth well with the righteous, the city rejoiceth: and when the wicked perish, *there is* shouting.

11. **By the blessing of the upright the city is exalted: but it is overthrown by the mouth of the wicked.**

12. **He that is void of wisdom despiseth his neighbour: but a man of understanding holdeth his peace.**

13. **A talebearer revealeth secrets: but he** that is **of a faithful spirit concealeth the matter.**

14. **Where no counsel is, the people fall: but in the multitude of counsellors there is safety.**

15. He that is surety for a stranger shall smart *for it*: and he that hateth suretyship is sure.

16. **A gracious woman retaineth honour: and strong men** retain **riches.**

17. **The merciful man doeth good to his** own **soul: but he that is cruel troubleth his** own **flesh.**

18. **The wicked worketh a deceitful work: but to him that soweth righteousness shall be a sure reward.**

19. As righteousness *tendeth* to life: so he that pursueth evil *pursueth it* to his own death.

20. **They** that *are* **of a froward heart are abomination** to the LORD: **but such as are upright** in *their* way **are his delight.**

21. *Though* hand *join* in hand, **the wicked shall not be unpunished: but** the seed of **the righteous shall be delivered.**

22. **As a jewel** of gold

in a swine's snout, so is a fair woman which is without discretion.

23. The desire of the righteous is only good: but the expectation of the wicked is wrath.

24. There is that scattereth, and yet increaseth; and there is that withholdeth more than is meet, but it tendeth to poverty.

25. The liberal soul shall be made fat: and he that watereth shall be watered also himself.

26. He that withholdeth corn, the people shall curse him: but blessing shall be upon the head of him that selleth it.

27. He that diligently seeketh good procureth favour: but he that seeketh mischief, it shall come unto him.

28. He that trusteth in his riches shall fall; but the righteous shall flourish as a branch.

29. He that troubleth his own house shall inherit the wind: and the fool shall be servant to the wise of heart.

30. The fruit of the righteous is a tree of life; and he that winneth souls is wise.

31. Behold, the righteous shall be recompensed in the earth: much more the wicked and the sinner.

CHAPTER 12

1. Whoso loveth instruction loveth knowledge: but he that hateth reproof is brutish.

2. A good man obtaineth favour of the LORD: but a man of wicked devices will he condemn.

3. A man shall not be established by wickedness: but the root of the righteous shall not be moved.

4. A virtuous woman is a crown to her husband: but she that maketh ashamed is as rottenness in his bones.

5. The thoughts of the righteous are right: but the counsels of the wicked are deceit.

6. The words of the wicked are to lie in wait for blood: but the mouth of the upright shall deliver them.

7. The wicked are overthrown, and are not: but the house of the righteous shall stand.

8. A man shall be commended according to his wisdom: but he that is of a perverse heart shall be despised.

9. He that is despised, and hath a servant, is better than he that honoureth himself, and lacketh bread.

10. A righteous man regardeth the life of his beast: but the tender mercies of the wicked are cruel.

11. He that tilleth his land shall be satisfied with bread: but he that followeth vain persons is void of understanding.

12. The wicked desireth the net of evil men: but the root of the righteous yieldeth fruit.

13. The wicked is snared by the transgression of his lips: but the just shall come out of trouble.

14. A man shall be satisfied with good by the fruit of his mouth: and the recompence of a man's hands shall be rendered unto him.

15. **The way of a fool is right in his own eyes: but he that hearkeneth unto counsel is wise.**

16. **A fool's wrath is** presently **known: but a prudent man covereth shame.**

17. **He that speaketh truth sheweth forth righteousness:** but a false witness deceit.

18. There is that speaketh like the piercings of a sword: but the tongue of the wise *is* health.

19. **The lip of truth shall be established for ever: but a lying tongue is but for a moment.**

20. **Deceit is in the heart of them that imagine evil: but to the counsellors of peace is joy.**

21. **There shall no evil happen to the just: but the wicked shall be filled with mischief.**

22. **Lying lips are abomination to the LORD: but they that deal truly are his delight.**

23. **A prudent man concealeth knowledge: but** the heart of **fools proclaimeth foolishness.**

24. **The hand of the diligent shall bear rule: but the slothful shall be under tribute.**

25. **Heaviness in the heart** of man **maketh it stoop: but a good word maketh it glad.**

26. **The righteous is more excellent than his neighbour: but** the way of **the wicked seduceth them.**

27. **The slothful man roasteth not that which he took in hunting: but the substance of a diligent man is precious.**

28. **In the way of**

righteousness is life: and *in* the pathway *thereof there is* no death.

CHAPTER 13

1. **A wise son heareth his father's instruction: but a scorner heareth not rebuke.**

2. **A man shall eat good by the fruit of his mouth: but** the soul of **the transgressors shall eat violence**.

3. **He that keepeth his mouth keepeth his life: but he that openeth wide his lips shall have destruction.**

4. **The soul of the sluggard** desireth, and **hath nothing: but the soul of the diligent shall be made fat.**

5. **A righteous man hateth lying: but a wicked man** is loathsome, and **cometh to shame.**

6. **Righteousness keepeth him that is upright in the way: but wickedness overthroweth the sinner.**

7. **There is that maketh himself rich, yet hath nothing: there is that maketh himself poor, yet hath great riches.**

8. **The ransom of a man's life are his riches: but the poor heareth not rebuke.**

9. **The light of the righteous rejoiceth: but the lamp of the wicked shall be put out.**

10. **Only by pride cometh contention: but with the well advised is wisdom.**

11. **Wealth gotten by vanity shall be diminished: but he that gathereth by labour shall increase.**

12. **Hope deferred maketh the heart sick: but when the desire cometh, it is a tree of life.**

13. Whoso despiseth the word shall be destroyed: but he that feareth the commandment shall be rewarded.

14. The law of the wise is a fountain of life, to depart from the snares of death.

15. Good understanding giveth favour: but the way of transgressors is hard.

16. Every prudent man dealeth with knowledge: but a fool layeth open his folly.

17. A wicked messenger falleth into mischief: but a faithful ambassador is health.

18. Poverty and shame shall be to him that refuseth instruction: but he that regardeth reproof shall be honoured.

19. The desire accomplished is sweet to the soul: but it is abomination to fools to depart from evil.

20. He that walketh with wise men shall be wise: but a companion of fools shall be destroyed.

21. Evil pursueth sinners: but to the righteous good shall be repayed.

22. A good man leaveth an inheritance to his children's children: and the wealth of the sinner is laid up for the just.

23. Much food is in the tillage of the poor: but there is that is destroyed for want of judgment.

24. He that spareth his rod hateth his son: but he that loveth him chasteneth him betimes.

25. The righteous eateth to the satisfying of his soul: but the belly of the wicked shall want.

CHAPTER 14

1. Every wise woman buildeth her house: but the foolish plucketh it down with her hands.

2. He that walketh in his uprightness feareth the LORD: but he that is perverse in his ways despiseth him.

3. In the mouth of the foolish is a rod of pride: but the lips of the wise shall preserve them.

4. Where no oxen are, the crib is clean: but much increase is by the strength of the ox.

5. A faithful witness will not lie: but a false witness will utter lies.

6. A scorner seeketh wisdom, and findeth it not: but knowledge is easy unto him that understandeth.

7. Go from the presence of a foolish man, when thou perceivest not in him the lips of knowledge.

8. The wisdom of the prudent is to understand his way: but the folly of fools is deceit.

9. Fools make a mock at sin: but among the righteous there is favour.

10. The heart knoweth his own bitterness; and a stranger doth not intermeddle with his joy.

11. The house of the wicked shall be overthrown: but the tabernacle of the upright shall flourish.

12. There is a way which seemeth right unto a man, but the end thereof are the ways of death.

13. Even in laughter the heart is sorrowful; and

917

the end of that mirth is heaviness.

14. The backslider in heart shall be filled with his own ways: and a good man shall be satisfied from himself.

15. The simple believeth every word: but the prudent man looketh well to his going.

16. A wise man feareth, and departeth from evil: but the fool rageth, and is confident.

17. He that is soon angry dealeth foolishly: and a man of wicked devices is hated.

18. The simple inherit folly: but the prudent are crowned with knowledge.

19. The evil bow before the good; and the wicked at the gates of the righteous.

20. The poor is hated even of his own neighbour: but the rich hath many friends.

21. He that despiseth his neighbour sinneth: but he that hath mercy on the poor, happy is he.

22. Do they not err that devise evil? but mercy and truth shall be to them that devise good.

23. In all labour there is profit: but the talk of the lips tendeth only to penury.

24. The crown of the wise is their riches: but the foolishness of fools is folly.

25. A true witness delivereth souls: but a deceitful witness speaketh lies.

26. In the fear of the LORD is strong confidence: and his children shall have a place of refuge.

27. The fear of the LORD is a fountain of life, to depart from the snares of death.

28. In the multitude of people is the king's honour: but in the want of people is the destruction of the prince.

29. He that is slow to wrath is of great understanding: but he that is hasty of spirit exalteth folly.

30. A sound heart is the life of the flesh: but envy the rottenness of the bones.

31. He that oppresseth the poor reproacheth his Maker: but he that honoureth him hath mercy on the poor.

32. The wicked is driven away in his wickedness: but the righteous hath hope in his death.

33. Wisdom resteth in the heart of him that hath understanding: but that which is in the midst of fools is made known.

34. Righteousness exalteth a nation: but sin is a reproach to any people.

35. The king's favour is toward a wise servant: but his wrath is against him that causeth shame.

CHAPTER 15

1. A soft answer turneth away wrath: but grievous words stir up anger.

2. The tongue of the wise useth knowledge aright: but the mouth of fools poureth out foolishness.

3. The eyes of the LORD are in every place, beholding the evil and the good.

4. A wholesome tongue is a tree of life: but perverseness therein is a breach in the spirit.

5. A fool despiseth his

father's instruction: but he that regardeth reproof is prudent.

6. In the house of the righteous is much treasure: but in the revenues of the wicked is trouble.

7. The lips of the wise disperse knowledge: but the heart of the foolish doeth not so.

8. The sacrifice of the wicked is an abomination to the LORD: but the prayer of the upright is his delight.

9. The way of the wicked is an abomination unto the LORD: but he loveth him that followeth after righteousness.

10. Correction is grievous unto him that forsaketh the way: and he that hateth reproof shall die.

11. Hell and destruction are before the LORD: how much more then the hearts of the children of men?

12. A scorner loveth not one that reproveth him: neither will he go unto the wise.

13. A merry heart maketh a cheerful countenance: but by sorrow of the heart the spirit is broken.

14. The heart of him that hath understanding seeketh knowledge: but the mouth of fools feedeth on foolishness.

15. All the days of the afflicted are evil: but he that is of a merry heart hath a continual feast.

16. Better is little with the fear of the LORD than great treasure and trouble therewith.

17. Better is a dinner of herbs where love is, than a stalled ox

and hatred therewith.

18. A wrathful man stirreth up strife: but he that is slow to anger appeaseth strife.

19. The way of the slothful man is as an hedge of thorns: but the way of the righteous is made plain.

20. A wise son maketh a glad father: but a foolish man despiseth his mother.

21. Folly is joy to him that is destitute of wisdom: but a man of understanding walketh uprightly.

22. Without counsel purposes are disappointed: but in the multitude of counsellors they are established.

23. A man hath joy by the answer of his mouth: and a word spoken in due season, how good is it!

24. The way of life is above to the wise, that he may depart from hell beneath.

25. The LORD will destroy the house of the proud: but he will establish the border of the widow.

26. The thoughts of the wicked are an abomination to the LORD: but the words of the pure are pleasant words.

27. He that is greedy of gain troubleth his own house; but he that hateth gifts shall live.

28. The heart of the righteous studieth to answer: but the mouth of the wicked poureth out evil things.

29. The LORD is far from the wicked: but he heareth the prayer of the righteous.

30. The light of the eyes rejoiceth the heart: and a good report maketh the bones fat.

31. The ear that heareth

the reproof of life
abideth among the wise.
32. He that refuseth
instruction despiseth his
own soul: but he that
heareth reproof getteth
understanding.
33. The fear of the LORD
is the instruction of
wisdom; and before
honour is humility.

CHAPTER 16

1. The preparations
of the heart in man,
and the answer of the
tongue, is from the LORD.
2. All the ways of a man
are clean in his own
eyes; but the LORD
weigheth the spirits.
3. Commit thy works unto
the LORD, and thy thoughts
shall be established.
4. The LORD hath made
all things for himself: yea,
even the wicked for the
day of evil.
5. Every one that is proud
in heart is an abomination
to the LORD: though hand
join in hand, he shall not
be unpunished.
6. By mercy and truth
iniquity is purged: and by
the fear of the LORD men
depart from evil.
7. When a man's ways
please the LORD, he
maketh even his enemies
to be at peace with him.
8. Better is a little with
righteousness than great
revenues without right.
9. A man's heart deviseth
his way: but the LORD
directeth his steps.
10. A divine sentence is
in the lips of the king: his
mouth transgresseth
not in judgment.
11. A just weight and
balance are the LORD's:
all the weights of the
bag are his work.
12. It is an abomination
to kings to commit
wickedness: for the
throne is established
by righteousness.
13. Righteous lips are
the delight of kings; and
they love him that
speaketh right.
14. The wrath of a king is as
messengers of death: but
a wise man will pacify it.
15. In the light of the king's
countenance is life; and
his favour is as a cloud of
the latter rain.
16. How much better is it
to get wisdom than gold!
and to get understanding
rather to be chosen
than silver!
17. The highway of the
upright is to depart from
evil: he that keepeth his
way preserveth his soul.
18. Pride goeth before
destruction, and an
haughty spirit before a fall.
19. Better it
is to be of
an humble spirit with the
lowly, than to divide the
spoil with the proud.
20. He that handleth a
matter wisely shall find
good: and whoso trusteth
in the LORD, happy is he.
21. The wise in heart shall
be called prudent: and
the sweetness of the lips
increaseth learning.
22. Understanding
is a wellspring of
life unto him that hath it:
but the instruction
of fools is folly.
23. The heart of the wise
teacheth his mouth, and
addeth learning to his lips.
24. Pleasant words are
as an honeycomb,

sweet to the soul, and
health to the bones.
25. There is a way that
seemeth right unto a
man, but the end thereof
are the ways of death.
26. He that laboureth
laboureth for himself; for
his mouth craveth it of him.
27. An ungodly man diggeth
up evil: and in his lips
there is as a burning fire.
28. A froward man
soweth strife: and
a whisperer separateth
chief friends.
29. A violent man enticeth
his neighbour, and
leadeth him into the
way that is not good.
30. He shutteth his eyes
to devise froward things:
moving his lips he
bringeth evil to pass.
31. The hoary head is
a crown of glory, if it
be found in the way
of righteousness.
32. He that is slow to anger
is better than the mighty;
and he that ruleth his spirit
than he that taketh a city.
33. The lot is cast into
the lap; but the whole
disposing thereof
is of the LORD.

CHAPTER 17

1. Better is a dry morsel,
and quietness therewith,
than an house full of
sacrifices with strife.
2. A wise servant shall have
rule over a son that causeth
shame, and shall have part
of the inheritance among
the brethren.
3. The fining pot is for
silver, and the furnace
for gold: but the LORD
trieth the hearts.
4. A wicked doer giveth
heed to false lips; and

a liar giveth ear to a
naughty tongue.
5. Whoso mocketh the
poor reproacheth his
Maker: and he that is
glad at calamities shall
not be unpunished.
6. Children's children
are the crown of old
men; and the glory of
children are their fathers.
7. Excellent speech
becometh not a fool: much
less do lying lips a prince.
8. A gift is as a precious
stone in the eyes of him that
hath it: whithersoever it
turneth, it prospereth.
9. He that covereth a
transgression seeketh
love; but he that repeateth
a matter separateth very
friends.
10. A reproof entereth more
into a wise man than an
hundred stripes into a fool.
11. An evil man seeketh
only rebellion: therefore
a cruel messenger shall
be sent against him.
12. Let a bear robbed of her
whelps meet a man, rather
than a fool in his folly.
13. Whoso rewardeth evil
for good, evil shall not
depart from his house.
14. The beginning of strife
is as when one letteth out
water: therefore leave
off contention, before
it be meddled with.
15. He that justifieth the
wicked, and he that
condemneth the just, even
they both are abomination
to the LORD.
16. Wherefore is there a
price in the hand of a fool
to get wisdom, seeing he
hath no heart to it?
17. A friend loveth at all
times, and a brother is
born for adversity.

18. A man void of understanding striketh hands, and becometh surety in the presence of his friend.

19. He loveth transgression that loveth strife: and he that exalteth his gate seeketh destruction.

20. He that hath a froward heart findeth no good: and he that hath a perverse tongue falleth into mischief.

21. He that begetteth a fool doeth it to his sorrow: and the father of a fool hath no joy.

22. A merry heart doeth good like a medicine: but a broken spirit drieth the bones.

23. A wicked man taketh a gift out of the bosom to pervert the ways of judgment.

24. Wisdom is before him that hath understanding; but the eyes of a fool are in the ends of the earth.

25. A foolish son is a grief to his father, and bitterness to her that bare him.

26. Also to punish the just is not good, nor to strike princes for equity.

27. He that hath knowledge spareth his words: and a man of understanding is of an excellent spirit.

28. Even a fool, when he holdeth his peace, is counted wise: and he that shutteth his lips is esteemed a man of understanding.

CHAPTER 18

1. Through desire a man, having separated himself, seeketh and intermeddleth with all wisdom.

2. A fool hath no delight in understanding, but that his heart may discover itself.

3. When the wicked cometh, then cometh also contempt, and with ignominy reproach.

4. The words of a man's mouth are as deep waters, and the wellspring of wisdom as a flowing brook.

5. It is not good to accept the person of the wicked, to overthrow the righteous in judgment.

6. A fool's lips enter into contention, and his mouth calleth for strokes.

7. A fool's mouth is his destruction, and his lips are the snare of his soul.

8. The words of a talebearer are as wounds, and they go down into the innermost parts of the belly.

9. He also that is slothful in his work is brother to him that is a great waster.

10. The name of the LORD is a strong tower: the righteous runneth into it, and is safe.

11. The rich man's wealth is his strong city, and as an high wall in his own conceit.

12. Before destruction the heart of man is haughty, and before honour is humility.

13. He that answereth a matter before he heareth it, it is folly and shame unto him.

14. The spirit of a man will sustain his infirmity; but a wounded spirit who can bear?

15. The heart of the prudent getteth knowledge; and the ear of the wise

seeketh knowledge.

16. **A man's gift maketh room for him,** and bringeth him **before great men.**

17. **He that is first in his own cause seemeth just; but his neighbour** cometh and **searcheth him.**

18. **The lot causeth contentions to cease,** and parteth between the mighty.

19. **A brother offended is harder to be won than a strong city: and their contentions are like the bars of a castle.**

20. **A man's belly shall be satisfied with the fruit of his mouth; and with the increase of his lips shall he be filled.**

21. **Death and life are in the power of the tongue: and they that love it shall eat the fruit thereof.**

22. **Whoso findeth a wife findeth a good thing, and** obtaineth **favour of the LORD.**

23. **The poor useth entreaties; but the rich answereth roughly.**

24. **A man that hath friends must shew himself friendly: and there is a friend that sticketh closer than a brother.**

CHAPTER 19

1. **Better is the poor that walketh in his integrity, than he that is perverse in his lips,** and is a fool.

2. **Also**, that **the soul** be **without knowledge,** it **is not good; and he that hasteth with his feet sinneth.**

3. **The foolishness of man perverteth his way: and his heart fretteth against** the LORD.

4. **Wealth maketh many friends; but the poor is separated from his neighbour.**

5. A false witness shall not be unpunished, and he that speaketh lies shall not escape.

6. **Many will entreat the favour of the prince: and every man is a friend to him that giveth gifts.**

7. **All the brethren of the poor do hate him: how much more do his friends go far from him? he pursueth them with words, yet they are wanting to him.**

8. **He that getteth wisdom loveth his own soul: he that keepeth understanding shall find good.**

9. **A false witness shall not be unpunished, and he that speaketh lies shall perish.**

10. **Delight is not seemly for a fool; much less for a servant to have rule over princes.**

11. **The discretion of a man deferreth his anger; and it is his glory to pass over a transgression.**

12. **The king's wrath is as the roaring of a lion; but his favour is as dew upon the grass.**

13. **A foolish son is the calamity of his father: and the contentions of a wife are a continual dropping.**

14. **House and riches are the inheritance of fathers: and a prudent wife is from the LORD.**

15. **Slothfulness casteth into a deep sleep; and an idle soul shall suffer hunger.**

16. **He that keepeth the commandment keepeth his own soul; but he that despiseth his ways**

shall die.

17. He that hath pity upon the poor lendeth unto the LORD; and that which he hath given will he pay him again.

18. Chasten thy son while there is hope, and let not thy soul spare for his crying.

19. A man of great wrath shall suffer punishment: for if thou deliver him, yet thou must do it again.

20. Hear counsel, and receive instruction, that thou mayest be wise in thy latter end.

21. There are many devices in a man's heart; nevertheless the counsel of the LORD, that shall stand.

22. The desire of a man is his kindness: and a poor man is better than a liar.

23. The fear of the LORD tendeth to life: and he that hath it shall abide satisfied; he shall not be visited with evil.

24. A slothful man hideth his hand in his bosom, and will not so much as bring it to his mouth again.

25. Smite a scorner, and the simple will beware: and reprove one that hath understanding, and he will understand knowledge.

26. He that wasteth his father, and chaseth away his mother, is a son that causeth shame, and bringeth reproach.

27. Cease, my son, to hear the instruction that causeth to err from the words of knowledge.

28. An ungodly witness scorneth judgment: and the mouth of the wicked devoureth iniquity.

29. Judgments are prepared for scorners, and stripes for the back of fools.

CHAPTER 20

1. Wine is a mocker, strong drink is raging: and whosoever is deceived thereby is not wise.

2. The fear of a king is as the roaring of a lion: whoso provoketh him to anger sinneth against his own soul.

3. It is an honour for a man to cease from strife: but every fool will be meddling.

4. The sluggard will not plow by reason of the cold; therefore shall he beg in harvest, and have nothing.

5. Counsel in the heart of man is like deep water; but a man of understanding will draw it out.

6. Most men will proclaim every one his own goodness: but a faithful man who can find?

7. The just man walketh in his integrity: his children are blessed after him.

8. A king that sitteth in the throne of judgment scattereth away all evil with his eyes.

9. Who can say, I have made my heart clean, I am pure from my sin?

10. Divers weights, and divers measures, both of them are alike abomination to the LORD.

11. Even a child is known by his doings, whether his work be pure, and whether it be right.

12. The hearing ear, and the seeing eye, the LORD hath made even both of them.

13. Love not sleep, lest thou

come to poverty; open thine eyes, and thou shalt be satisfied with bread.

14. It is nought, *it is* nought, saith the buyer: but when he is gone his way, then he boasteth.

15. There is gold, and a multitude of rubies: but the lips of knowledge are a precious jewel.

16. Take his garment that is surety for a stranger: and take a pledge of him for a strange woman.

17. Bread of deceit is sweet to a man; but afterwards his mouth shall be filled with gravel.

18. Every purpose is established by counsel: and with good advice make war.

19. He that goeth about as a talebearer revealeth secrets: therefore meddle not with him that flattereth with his lips.

20. Whoso curseth his father or his mother, his lamp shall be put out in obscure darkness.

21. An inheritance may be gotten hastily at the beginning; but the end thereof shall not be blessed.

22. Say not thou, I will recompense evil; but wait on the LORD, and he shall save thee.

23. Divers weights are an abomination unto the LORD; and a false balance is not good.

24. Man's goings are of the LORD; how can a man then understand his own way?

25. It is a snare to the man who devoureth that which is holy, and after vows to make inquiry.

26. A wise king scattereth the wicked, and bringeth the wheel over them.

27. The spirit of man is the candle of the LORD, searching all the inward parts of the belly.

28. Mercy and truth preserve the king: and his throne is upholden by mercy.

29. The glory of young men is their strength: and the beauty of old men is the grey head.

30. The blueness of a wound cleanseth away evil: so do stripes the inward parts of the belly.

CHAPTER 21

1. The king's heart is in the hand of the LORD, *as* the rivers of water: he turneth it whithersoever he will.

2. Every way of a man is right in his own eyes: but the LORD pondereth the hearts.

3. To do justice and judgment is more acceptable to the LORD than sacrifice.

4. An high look, and a proud heart, *and the* plowing of the wicked, is sin.

5. The thoughts of the diligent tend only to plenteousness; but of every one that is hasty only to want.

6. The getting of treasures by a lying tongue is a vanity tossed to and fro of them that seek death.

7. The robbery of the wicked shall destroy them; because they refuse to do judgment.

8. The way of man is froward and strange:

925

■ but as for the pure,
■ his work is right.
■ 9. It is better to dwell in a
■ corner of the housetop,
■ than with a brawling
■ woman in a wide house.
■ 10. The soul of the
■ wicked desireth evil: his
■ neighbour findeth no
■ favour in his eyes.
■ 11. When the scorner is
■ punished, the simple is
■ made wise: and when
■ the wise is instructed, he
■ receiveth knowledge.
■ 12. The righteous *man* wisely
■ considereth the house
■ of the wicked: but God
■ overthroweth the
■ wicked for *their* wickedness.
■ 13. Whoso stoppeth
■ his ears at the cry
■ of the poor, he also
■ shall cry himself, but
■ shall not be heard.
■ 14. A gift in secret pacifieth
■ anger: and a reward in
■ the bosom strong wrath.
■ 15. It is joy to the just to
■ do judgment: but
■ destruction shall be to
■ the workers of iniquity.
■ 16. The man that wandereth
■ out of the way of
■ understanding shall remain
■ in the congregation of the
■ dead.
■ 17. He that loveth pleasure
■ shall be a poor man:
■ he that loveth wine
■ and oil shall not be rich.
■ 18. The wicked shall be a
■ ransom for the righteous,
■ and the transgressor
■ for the upright.
■ 19. It is better to dwell in
■ the wilderness, than with
■ a contentious and an
■ angry woman.
■ 20. There is treasure to
■ be desired and oil in the
■ dwelling of the wise; but a
■ foolish man spendeth it up.

■ 21. He that followeth after
■ righteousness and mercy
■ findeth life, righteousness,
■ and honour.
■ 22. A wise man scaleth the
■ city of the mighty, and
■ casteth down the strength of
■ the confidence thereof.
■ 23. Whoso keepeth his
■ mouth and his tongue
■ keepeth his soul
■ from troubles.
■ 24. Proud and haughty
■ scorner is his name, who
■ dealeth in proud wrath.
■ 25. The desire of the slothful
■ killeth him; for his hands
■ refuse to labour.
■ 26. He coveteth greedily
■ all the day long: but the
■ righteous giveth and
■ spareth not.
■ 27. The sacrifice of the
■ wicked is abomination:
■ how much more, when
■ he bringeth it with a
■ wicked mind?
■ 28. A false witness
■ shall perish: but the
■ man that heareth
■ speaketh constantly.
■ 29. A wicked man
■ hardeneth his face: but *as for*
■ the upright, he
■ directeth his way.
■ 30. There is no wisdom nor
■ understanding nor counsel
■ against the LORD.
■ 31. The horse *is* prepared against
■ the day of battle: but
■ safety is of the LORD.

CHAPTER 22

■ 1. A GOOD name is rather
■ to be chosen than great
■ riches, and loving favour
■ rather than silver and gold.
■ 2. The rich and poor meet
■ together: the LORD is the
■ maker of them all.
■ 3. A prudent man foreseeth
■ the evil, and hideth himself:
■ but the simple pass on,

and are punished.

4. By humility and the fear of the LORD are riches, and honour, and life.

5. Thorns and snares are in the way of the froward: he that doth keep his soul shall be far from them.

6. Train up a child in the way he should go: and when he is old, he will not depart from it.

7. The rich ruleth over the poor, and the borrower is servant to the lender.

8. He that soweth iniquity shall reap vanity: and the rod of his anger shall fail.

9. He that hath a bountiful eye shall be blessed; for he giveth of his bread to the poor.

10. Cast out the scorner, and contention shall go out; yea, strife and reproach shall cease.

11. He that loveth pureness of heart, for the grace of his lips the king shall be his friend.

12. The eyes of the LORD preserve knowledge, and he overthroweth the words of the transgressor.

13. The slothful man saith, There is a lion without, I shall be slain in the streets.

14. The mouth of strange women is a deep pit: he that is abhorred of the LORD shall fall therein.

15. Foolishness is bound in the heart of a child; but the rod of correction shall drive it far from him.

16. He that oppresseth the poor to increase his riches, and he that giveth to the rich, shall surely come to want.

17. Bow down thine ear, and hear the words of the wise, and apply thine heart unto my knowledge.

18. For it is a pleasant thing if thou keep them within thee; they shall withal be fitted in thy lips.

19. That thy trust may be in the LORD, I have made known to thee this day, even to thee.

20. Have not I written to thee excellent things in counsels and knowledge,

21. That I might make thee know the certainty of the words of truth; that thou mightest answer the words of truth to them that send unto thee?

22. Rob not the poor, because he is poor: neither oppress the afflicted in the gate:

23. For the LORD will plead their cause, and spoil the soul of those that spoiled them.

24. Make no friendship with an angry man; and with a furious man thou shalt not go:

25. Lest thou learn his ways, and get a snare to thy soul.

26. Be not thou one of them that strike hands, or of them that are sureties for debts.

27. If thou hast nothing to pay, why should he take away thy bed from under thee?

28. Remove not the ancient landmark, which thy fathers have set.

29. Seest thou a man diligent in his business? he shall stand before kings; he shall not stand before mean men.

CHAPTER 23

1. When thou sittest to eat with a ruler, consider diligently what is before thee:

2. **And put a knife to thy throat, if thou be** a man **given to appetite.**

3. **Be not desirous of his dainties: for they are deceitful meat.**

4. Labour **not to be rich: cease from thine own wisdom.**

5. **Wilt thou set thine eyes upon that which is not? for riches** certainly **make themselves wings; they fly away as an eagle** toward heaven.

6. **Eat** thou **not the bread of him that hath an evil eye,** neither desire thou his dainty meats:

7. **For as he thinketh in his heart, so is he: Eat and drink, saith he to thee; but his heart is not with thee.**

8. **The morsel which thou hast eaten shalt thou vomit up,** and lose thy sweet words.

9. **Speak not in the ears of a fool: for he will despise the wisdom of thy words.**

10. **Remove not the old landmark; and enter not** into **the fields of the fatherless:**

11. **For their redeemer is mighty; he shall plead their cause** with thee.

12. **Apply thine heart unto instruction, and thine ears to** the words of **knowledge.**

13. **Withhold not correction from the child: for if thou beatest him with the rod, he shall not die.**

14. **Thou shalt** beat him with the rod, and shalt **deliver his soul from hell.**

15. **My son, if thine heart be wise, my heart shall rejoice,** even mine.

16. **Yea, my reins shall rejoice, when thy lips speak right things.**

17. **Let not thine heart envy sinners: but** be thou in the **fear of the LORD** all the day long.

18. **For surely there is an end; and thine expectation shall not be cut off.**

19. **Hear** thou, my son, **and be wise, and guide thine heart in the way.**

20. **Be not among winebibbers; among riotous eaters of flesh:**

21. **For the drunkard and the glutton shall come to poverty**: and drowsiness shall clothe a man with rags.

22. **Hearken unto thy father** that begat thee, **and despise not thy mother when she is old.**

23. **Buy the truth, and sell it not; also wisdom, and instruction, and understanding.**

24. **The father of the righteous shall** greatly **rejoice: and he that begetteth a wise child shall have joy of him.**

25. **Thy father and thy mother shall be glad,** and she that bare thee shall rejoice.

26. **My son, give me thine heart, and let thine eyes observe my ways.**

27. **For a whore is a deep ditch**; and a strange woman is a narrow pit.

28. **She** also **lieth in wait as for a prey, and increaseth the transgressors** among men.

29. **Who hath woe**? who hath **sorrow**? who hath **contentions?** who hath **babbling?** who hath **wounds without cause?** who hath **redness of eyes?**

30. **They that tarry long at the wine;** they that go

to seek mixed wine.

31. **Look not** thou **upon the wine when it is red**, when it giveth his colour in the cup, *when* it moveth itself aright.

32. **At the last it biteth** like a serpent, **and stingeth** like an adder.

33. **Thine eyes shall behold strange women, and thine heart shall utter perverse things.**

34. **Yea, thou shalt be as he that lieth down in** the midst of **the sea, or** as he that lieth **upon the top of a mast.**

35. **They have stricken me,** *shalt thou say,* **and I was not sick; they have beaten me, and I felt it not: when shall I awake? I will seek it** yet **again.**

CHAPTER 24

1. **Be not** thou **envious against evil men, neither desire to be with them.**

2. **For their heart studieth destruction, and their lips talk of mischief.**

3. **Through wisdom is an house builded; and by understanding it is established:**

4. **And by knowledge shall the chambers be filled with** all precious and pleasant **riches.**

5. **A wise man is strong**; yea, **a man of knowledge increaseth strength.**

6. **For by wise counsel** thou shalt **make thy war:** and **in multitude of counsellors there is safety.**

7. **Wisdom is too high for a fool: he openeth not his mouth** in the gate.

8. **He that deviseth** to do **evil shall be called a mischievous person**.

9. **The thought of foolishness is sin: and the scorner is an abomination** to men.

10. **If thou faint in the day of adversity, thy strength is small.**

11. **If thou forbear to deliver them that are drawn unto death, and those** *that are* **ready to be slain;**

12. **If thou sayest,** Behold, **we knew it not; doth not he that pondereth the heart consider it? and he that keepeth thy soul,** doth *not* he **know it? and shall** *not* he **render to every man according to his works?**

13. **My son, eat** thou **honey,** because *it is* good; **and the honeycomb, which is sweet** to thy taste:

14. **So shall the knowledge of wisdom be** unto thy soul: **when thou hast found it, then there shall be a reward, and thy expectation shall not be cut off.**

15. **Lay not wait, O wicked man, against** the dwelling of **the righteous; spoil not his** resting **place**:

16. **For a just man falleth seven times, and riseth** up **again: but the wicked shall fall into mischief.**

17. **Rejoice not when thine enemy falleth, and** let not thine heart be glad **when he stumbleth:**

18. **Lest the LORD see it, and it displease him, and** he turn away his wrath from him.

19. **Fret not** thyself **because of evil men, neither be** thou **envious** at the wicked:

20. **For there shall be no reward to the evil man**; the

candle of the wicked shall be put out.

21. My son, fear thou the LORD and the king: and meddle not with them that are given to change:

22. For their calamity shall rise suddenly; and who knoweth the ruin of them both?

23. These things also belong to the wise. It is not good to have respect of persons in judgment.

24. He that saith unto the wicked, Thou art righteous; him shall the people curse, nations shall abhor him:

25. But to them that rebuke him shall be delight, and a good blessing shall come upon them.

26. Every man shall kiss his lips that giveth a right answer.

27. Prepare thy work without, and make it fit for thyself in the field; and afterwards build thine house.

28. Be not a witness against thy neighbour without cause; and deceive not with thy lips.

29. Say not, I will do so to him as he hath done to me: I will render to the man according to his work.

30. I went by the field of the slothful, and by the vineyard of the man void of understanding;

31. And, lo, it was all grown over with thorns, and nettles had covered the face thereof, and the stone wall thereof was broken down.

32. Then I saw, and considered it well: I looked upon it, and received instruction.

33. Yet a little sleep, a little slumber, a little folding of the hands to sleep:

34. So shall thy poverty come as one that travelleth; and thy want as an armed man.

CHAPTER 25

1. These are also proverbs of Solomon, which the men of Hezekiah king of Judah copied out.

2. It is the glory of God to conceal a thing: but the honour of kings is to search out a matter.

3. The heaven for height, and the earth for depth, and the heart of kings is unsearchable.

4. Take away the dross from the silver, and there shall come forth a vessel for the finer.

5. Take away the wicked from before the king, and his throne shall be established in righteousness.

6. Put not forth thyself in the presence of the king, and stand not in the place of great men:

7. For better it is that it be said unto thee, Come up hither; than that thou shouldest be put lower in the presence of the prince whom thine eyes have seen.

8. Go not forth hastily to strive, lest thou know not what to do in the end thereof, when thy neighbour hath put thee to shame.

9. Debate thy cause with thy neighbour himself; and discover not a secret to another:

10. Lest he that heareth it put thee to shame, and thine infamy turn not away.

11. **A word fitly spoken is like** apples of **gold** in pictures of silver.

12. **As** an earring of **gold**, and an ornament of fine gold, **so is a wise reprover upon an obedient ear.**

13. **As the cold of snow in the time of harvest, so is a faithful messenger** to them that send him: for he refresheth the soul of his masters.

14. **Whoso boasteth** himself **of a false gift is like clouds** and wind **without rain.**

15. **By long forbearing is a prince persuaded, and a soft tongue breaketh the bone.**

16. **Hast thou found honey? eat so much as is sufficient** for thee, **lest thou** be filled therewith, and **vomit it.**

17. **Withdraw** thy foot **from thy neighbour's house; lest he be weary of thee,** and so hate thee.

18. **A man that beareth false witness** against his neighbour **is a maul, and a sword,** and a sharp arrow.

19. **Confidence in an unfaithful man** in time of trouble **is like a broken tooth,** and a foot out of joint.

20. **As he that taketh away a garment in cold weather,** and as vinegar upon nitre, **so is he that singeth** songs **to an heavy heart.**

21. **If thine enemy be hungry, give him bread** to eat; **and if he be thirsty, give him water** to drink:

22. **For thou shalt heap coals of fire upon his head, and the LORD shall reward thee.**

23. **The north wind driveth away rain: so doth an angry countenance a backbiting tongue.**

24. It is better to dwell in the corner of the housetop, than with a brawling woman and in a wide house.

25. **As cold waters to a thirsty soul, so is good news from a far country.**

26. **A righteous man falling down before the wicked is as a troubled fountain,** and a corrupt spring.

27. It is not good to eat much honey: so **for men to search their own glory is not glory.**

28. **He that hath no rule over his own spirit is like a city** that is broken down, and **without walls.**

CHAPTER 26

1. **As snow in summer, and as rain in harvest, so honour is not seemly for a fool.**

2. **As the bird by wandering, as the swallow by flying, so the curse causeless shall not come.**

3. A whip for the horse, a bridle for the ass, and a rod for the fool's back.

4. **Answer not a fool according to his folly, lest thou** also **be like** unto **him.**

5. **Answer a fool according to his folly, lest he be wise in his own conceit.**

6. **He that sendeth a message by the hand of a fool cutteth off the feet,** and drinketh damage.

7. **The legs of the lame are not equal: so is a parable in the mouth of fools.**

8. **As he that bindeth a stone in a sling, so is he that giveth honour to a fool.**

9. **As a thorn goeth** up **into the hand of a**

931

drunkard, so is a parable in the mouths of fools.

10. The great God that formed allthings both rewardeth the fool, and rewardeth transgressors.

11. As a dog returneth to his vomit, so a fool returneth to his folly.

12. Seest thou a man wise in his own conceit? there is more hope of a fool than of him.

13. The slothful man saith, There is a lion in the way; a lion is in the streets.

14. As the door turneth upon his hinges, so doth the slothful upon his bed.

15. The slothful hideth his hand in his bosom; it grieveth him to bring it again to his mouth.

16. The sluggard is wiser in his own conceit than seven men that can render a reason.

17. He that passeth by, and meddleth with strife belonging not to him, is like one that taketh a dog by the ears.

18. As a mad man who casteth firebrands, arrows, and death,

19. So is the man that deceiveth his neighbour, and saith, Am not I in sport?

20. Where no wood is, there the fire goeth out: so where there is no talebearer, the strife ceaseth.

21. As coals are to burning coals, and wood to fire; so is a contentious man to kindle strife.

22. The words of a talebearer are as wounds, and they go down into the innermost parts of the belly.

23. Burning lips and a wicked heart are like a potsherd covered with silver dross.

24. He that hateth dissembleth with his lips, and layeth up deceit within him;

25. When he speaketh fair, believe him not: for there are seven abominations in his heart.

26. Whose hatred is covered by deceit, his wickedness shall be shewed before the whole congregation.

27. Whoso diggeth a pit shall fall therein: and he that rolleth a stone, it will return upon him.

28. A lying tongue hateth those that are afflicted by it; and a flattering mouth worketh ruin.

CHAPTER 27

1. Boast not thyself of tomorrow; for thou knowest not what a day may bring forth.

2. Let another man praise thee, and not thine own mouth; a stranger, and not thine own lips.

3. A stone is heavy, and the sand weighty; but a fool's wrath is heavier than them both.

4. Wrath is cruel, and anger is outrageous; but who is able to stand before envy?

5. Open rebuke is better than secret love.

6. Faithful are the wounds of a friend; but the kisses of an enemy are deceitful.

7. The full soul loatheth an honeycomb; but to the hungry soul every bitter thing is sweet.

8. As a bird that wandereth from her nest, so is a man that wandereth from his place.

9. Ointment and perfume rejoice the heart: so doth the sweetness of a man's friend by hearty counsel.

10. Thine own friend, and thy father's friend, forsake not; neither go into thy brother's house in the day of thy calamity: for better is a neighbour that is near than a brother far off.

11. My son, be wise, and make my heart glad, that I may answer him that reproacheth me.

12. A prudent man foreseeth the evil, and hideth himself; but the simple pass on, and are punished.

13. Take his garment that is surety for a stranger, and take a pledge of him for a strange woman.

14. He that blesseth his friend with a loud voice, rising early in the morning, it shall be counted a curse to him.

15. A continual dropping in a very rainy day and a contentious woman are alike.

16. Whosoever hideth her hideth the wind, and the ointment of his right hand, which bewrayeth itself.

17. Iron sharpeneth iron; so a man sharpeneth the countenance of his friend.

18. Whoso keepeth the fig tree shall eat the fruit thereof: so he that waiteth on his master shall be honoured.

19. As in water face answereth to face, so the heart of man to man.

20. Hell and destruction are never full; so the eyes of man are never satisfied.

21. As the fining pot for silver, and the furnace for gold; so is a man to his praise.

22. Though thou shouldest bray a fool in a mortar among wheat with a pestle, yet will not his foolishness depart from him.

23. Be thou diligent to know the state of thy flocks, and look well to thy herds.

24. For riches are not for ever: and doth the crown endure to every generation?

25. The hay appeareth, and the tender grass sheweth itself, and herbs of the mountains are gathered.

26. The lambs are for thy clothing, and the goats are the price of the field.

27. And thou shalt have goats' milk enough for thy food, for the food of thy household, and for the maintenance for thy maidens.

CHAPTER 28

1. The wicked flee when no man pursueth: but the righteous are bold as a lion.

2. For the transgression of a land many are the princes thereof: but by a man of understanding and knowledge the state thereof shall be prolonged.

3. A poor man that oppresseth the poor is like a sweeping rain which leaveth no food.

4. They that forsake the law praise the wicked: but such as keep the law contend with them.

5. Evil men understand not judgment: but they that seek the LORD understand all things.

6. Better is the poor that walketh in his

uprightness, than he that is perverse *in his* ways, though he be rich. 7. Whoso keepeth the law is a wise son: but he that *is* a companion of riotous men shameth his father. 8. He that by usury and unjust gain increaseth his substance, he shall gather it for him that will pity the poor. 9. He that turneth away his ear from hearing the law, even his prayer shall be abomination. 10. Whoso causeth the righteous to go astray in an evil way, he shall fall himself into his own pit: but the upright shall have good things in possession. 11. The rich man is wise in his own conceit; but the poor that hath understanding searcheth him out. 12. When righteous men do rejoice, there is great glory: but when the wicked rise, a man is hidden. 13. He that covereth his sins shall not prosper: but whoso confesseth and forsaketh them shall have mercy. 14. Happy is the man that feareth alway: but he that hardeneth his heart shall fall into mischief. 15. As a roaring lion, and a ranging bear; so is a wicked ruler over the poor people. 16. The prince that wanteth understanding is also a great oppressor: but he that hateth covetousness shall prolong his days. 17. A man that doeth violence to the blood of *any* person

shall flee to the pit; let no man stay him. 18. Whoso walketh uprightly shall be saved: but he that is perverse *in his* ways shall fall at once. 19. He that tilleth his land shall have plenty of bread: but he that followeth after vain persons shall have poverty enough. 20. A faithful man shall abound with blessings: but he that maketh haste to be rich shall not be innocent. 21. To have respect of persons is not good: for a piece of bread that man will transgress. 22. He that hasteth to be rich hath an evil eye, and considereth not that poverty shall come upon him. 23. He that rebuketh a man afterwards shall find more favour than he that flattereth with the tongue. 24. Whoso robbeth his father or his mother, and saith, It is no transgression; the same is the companion of a destroyer. 25. He that is of a proud heart stirreth up strife: but he that putteth his trust in the LORD shall be made fat. 26. He that trusteth in his own heart is a fool: but whoso walketh wisely, he shall be delivered. 27. He that giveth unto the poor shall not lack: but he that hideth his eyes shall have many a curse. 28. When the wicked rise, men hide themselves: but when they perish, the righteous increase.

1. He, that being often reproved hardeneth his neck, shall suddenly be destroyed, and that without remedy.

2. When the righteous are in authority, the people rejoice: but when the wicked beareth rule, the people mourn.

3. Whoso loveth wisdom rejoiceth his father: but he that keepeth company with harlots spendeth his substance.

4. The king by judgment establisheth the land: but he that receiveth gifts overthroweth it.

5. A man that flattereth his neighbour spreadeth a net for his feet.

6. In the transgression of an evil man there is a snare: but the righteous doth sing and rejoice.

7. The righteous considereth the cause of the poor: but the wicked regardeth not to know it.

8. Scornful men bring a city into a snare: but wise men turn away wrath.

9. If a wise man contendeth with a foolish man, whether he rage or laugh, there is no rest.

10. The bloodthirsty hate the upright: but the just seek his soul.

11. A fool uttereth all his mind: but a wise man keepeth it in till afterwards.

12. If a ruler hearken to lies, all his servants are wicked.

13. The poor and the deceitful man meet together: the LORD lighteneth both their eyes.

14. The king that faithfully judgeth the poor, his throne shall be established for ever.

15. The rod and reproof give wisdom: but a child left to himself bringeth his mother to shame.

16. When the wicked are multiplied, transgression increaseth: but the righteous shall see their fall.

17. Correct thy son, and he shall give thee rest; yea, he shall give delight unto thy soul.

18. Where there is no vision, the people perish: but he that keepeth the law, happy is he.

19. A servant will not be corrected by words: for though he understand he will not answer.

20. Seest thou a man that is hasty in his words? there is more hope of a fool than of him.

21. He that delicately bringeth up his servant from a child shall have him become his son at the length.

22. An angry man stirreth up strife, and a furious man aboundeth in transgression.

23. A man's pride shall bring him low: but honour shall uphold the humble in spirit.

24. Whoso is partner with a thief hateth his own soul: he heareth cursing, and bewrayeth it not.

25. The fear of man bringeth a snare: but whoso putteth his trust in the LORD shall be safe.

26. Many seek the ruler's favour; but every man's judgment cometh from the LORD.

27. An unjust man is

■ an abomination to
■ the just: and he that
■ is upright in the way
■ is abomination to
■ the wicked.

CHAPTER 30

■ 1. **The words of Agur** the
son of Jakeh, *even* the prophecy:
the man spake unto Ithiel, even
■ **unto Ithiel and Ucal,**
■ 2. **Surely I am** more
■ **brutish** than *any* man,
■ **and have not** the
■ **understanding** of a man.
■ 3. **I neither learned**
■ **wisdom, nor have** the
■ **knowledge** of the holy.
■ 4. **Who hath ascended** up
■ **into heaven, or**
■ **descended? who hath**
■ **gathered the wind in his**
■ **fists? who hath bound**
■ **the waters** in a garment?
■ **who hath**
■ **established** all the ends of
■ **the earth? what is his**
■ **name, and** what *is*
■ **his son's name,** if
thou canst tell?
■ 5. **Every word of**
■ **God is pure: he is a**
■ **shield unto them that**
■ **put their trust in him.**
■ 6. **Add thou not unto his**
■ **words, lest he reprove**
■ **thee,** and thou be found a liar.
■ 7. **Two things have I**
■ **required of thee;** deny
me *them* not before I die:
■ 8. **Remove** far
■ **from me vanity and lies:**
■ **give me neither poverty nor**
■ **riches; feed me with food**
■ **convenient for me:**
■ 9. **Lest I be full, and deny**
■ **thee,** and say, Who *is* the LORD?
■ **or lest I be poor, and steal,**
■ **and take the name of my**
■ **God in vain.**
■ 10. **Accuse not a**
■ **servant** unto his master,
■ **lest he curse thee, and**

■ **thou be found guilty.**
■ 11. **There is a generation**
■ **that curseth their father,**
■ **and** doth not bless their mother.
■ 12. *There is* a generation *that*
■ **are pure in their own**
■ **eyes**, and *yet* is not washed
from their filthiness.
■ 13. There is a generation, O
■ **how lofty are their eyes!**
and their eyelids are lifted up.
■ 14. *There is* a generation,
■ **whose teeth are as swords,**
■ **and their jaw teeth as**
■ **knives, to devour the poor**
from off the earth, and the needy
from *among* men.
■ 15. **The horseleach hath**
■ **two daughters, crying,**
■ **Give, give.** There are
■ **three things** *that*
■ **are never satisfied,**
■ **yea, four things say**
■ **not, It is enough:**
■ 16. **The grave**; and
■ **the barren womb; the**
■ **earth that is not filled with**
■ **water; and the fire that saith**
■ **not, It is enough.**
■ 17. **The eye that**
■ **mocketh at his father,**
■ **and despiseth** to obey
■ **his mother,** the ravens of the
valley shall pick it out, and the
young eagles shall eat it.
■ 18. **There be three**
■ **things which are too**
■ **wonderful** for me,
■ **yea, four which I know not:**
■ 19. **The way of an eagle**
■ **in the air; the** way of a
■ **serpent upon a**
■ **rock; the** way of a
■ **ship in the** midst of the
■ **sea; and** the way of
■ **a man with a maid.**
■ 20. **Such is the way of an**
■ **adulterous woman; she**
■ **eateth,** and wipeth her mouth,
■ **and saith, I have done**
■ **no wickedness.**
■ 21. **For three things the**
■ **earth is disquieted,** and for

four which it cannot bear:

22. For a servant when he reigneth; and a fool when he is filled with meat;

23. For an odious woman when she is married; and an handmaid that is heir to her mistress.

24. There be four things which are little upon the earth, but they are exceeding wise:

25. The ants are a people not strong, yet they prepare their meat in the summer;

26. The conies are but a feeble folk, yet make they their houses in the rocks;

27. The locusts have no king, yet go they forth all of them by bands;

28. The spider taketh hold with her hands, and is in kings' palaces.

29. There be three things which go well, yea, four are comely in going:

30. A lion which is strongest among beasts, and turneth not away for any;

31. A greyhound; an he goat also; and a king, against whom there is no rising up.

32. If thou hast done foolishly in lifting up thyself, or if thou hast thought evil, lay thine hand upon thy mouth.

33. Surely the churning of milk bringeth forth butter, and the wringing of the nose bringeth forth blood: so the forcing of wrath bringeth forth strife.

CHAPTER 31

1. The words of king Lemuel, the prophecy that his mother taught him.

2. What, my son? and what, the son of my womb? and what, the son of my vows?

3. Give not thy strength unto women, nor thy ways to that which destroyeth kings.

4. It is not for kings, O Lemuel, it is not for kings to drink wine; nor for princes strong drink:

5. Lest they drink, and forget the law, and pervert the judgment of any of the afflicted.

6. Give strong drink unto him that is ready to perish, and wine unto those that be of heavy hearts.

7. Let him drink, and forget his poverty, and remember his misery no more.

8. Open thy mouth for the dumb in the cause of all such as are appointed to destruction.

9. Open thy mouth, judge righteously, and plead the cause of the poor and needy.

10. Who can find a virtuous woman? for her price is far above rubies.

11. The heart of her husband doth safely trust in her, so that he shall have no need of spoil.

12. She will do him good and not evil all the days of her life.

13. She seeketh wool, and flax, and worketh willingly with her hands.

14. She is like the merchants' ships; she bringeth her food from afar.

15. She riseth also while it is yet night, and giveth meat to her household, and

a portion to her maidens.

16. **She considereth a field, and buyeth it: with** the fruit of **her hands she planteth a vineyard.**

17. **She girdeth her loins with strength,** and strengtheneth her arms.

18. **She perceiveth that her merchandise is good: her candle goeth not out by night.**

19. **She layeth her hands to the spindle, and** her hands hold **the distaff.**

20. **She stretcheth out her hand to the poor; yea,** she reacheth forth her hands to **the needy.**

21. **She is not afraid of the snow** for her household: **for** all **her household are clothed with scarlet.**

22. **She maketh herself coverings of tapestry; her clothing is silk and purple.**

23. **Her husband is known in the gates,** when he sitteth among the elders of the land.

24. **She maketh fine linen,** and selleth *it,* **and delivereth girdles unto the merchant.**

25. **Strength and honour are her clothing;** and she shall rejoice in time to come.

26. **She openeth her mouth with wisdom; and in her tongue is the law of kindness.**

27. **She looketh well to the ways of her household, and eateth not the bread of idleness.**

28. **Her children arise up, and call her blessed; her husband** *also,* and he **praiseth her.**

29. **Many daughters have done virtuously, but thou excellest them all.**

30. **Favour is deceitful, and beauty** *is* **vain: but a woman that feareth the LORD**, she **shall be praised.**

31. **Give her of the fruit of her hands; and let her** own **works praise her in the gates.**

THE BOOK OF ECCLESIASTES

BACKGROUND INFORMATION

Author: Primarily Solomon
Date Written: The exact date is **Unknown**

Number of:
Verses—222
Chapters—12
Total Words—5,584
Scan Words—2,510
Scan Words Represent
Approximately 44% of
Total Words

Theme: The Folly of Living a Materialistic Life

OUTLINE OF THE BOOK

I. **The Basic Problems** of the Materialistic Life are Developed
1:1 — 1:3

II. **Experimentations with Life** are Discussed
1:4 — 12:12

III. **The Results** are Examined **and Conclusions** are Drawn
12:13 — 14

CHAPTER 1

1. **The words of the Preacher** the son of David, king in Jerusalem.
2. **Vanity of vanities,** saith the Preacher, vanity of vanities; **all is vanity.**
3. **What profit hath a man of** all **his labour** which he taketh under the sun?
4. **One generation passeth** away, **and another** generation **cometh: but the earth abideth for ever.**
5. **The sun also ariseth, and** the sun **goeth down,** and hasteth to his place where he arose.
6. **The wind goeth toward the south, and** turneth about unto the north; it **whirleth about** continually, **and** the wind **returneth** again according to his circuits.
7. **All the rivers run into the sea; yet the sea is not full;** unto the place from whence the rivers come, thither they return again.
8. **All things are full of labour;** man cannot utter *it:* the eye is not satisfied with seeing, nor the ear filled with hearing.
9. **The thing that hath been, it** is that which **shall be;** and that which is done *is* that which shall be done: **and there is no new thing under the sun.**
10. **Is there any thing** whereof it may be said, See, this is **new?** it hath been already of old time, which was before us.
11. There is no remembrance of former things; neither shall there be any remembrance of things that are to come with those that shall come after.
12. **I** the Preacher **was king over Israel** in Jerusalem.
13. **And I gave my heart** **to seek** and search out by **wisdom** concerning all *things* that are done under heaven: this sore travail hath God given to the sons of man to be exercised therewith.
14. **I have seen all** the works that are **done under the sun; and,** behold, **all is vanity and vexation** of spirit.
15. **That which is crooked cannot be made straight:** and that which is wanting cannot be numbered.
16. **I communed** with mine own heart, **saying, Lo, I am come to great estate,** and have gotten more wisdom than all *they* that have been before me in Jerusalem: yea, my heart had great experience of wisdom and knowledge.
17. **And I gave my heart to know wisdom, and** to know **madness and folly:** I perceived that **this also is vexation of spirit.**
18. **For in much wisdom is much grief:** and he that increaseth knowledge increaseth sorrow.

CHAPTER 2

1. **I said** in mine heart, Go to now, **I will** prove thee with mirth, therefore **enjoy pleasure:** and, behold, **this also is vanity.**
2. I said of **laughter, It is mad:** and of mirth, What doeth it?
3. **I sought** in mine heart **to give myself unto wine,** yet acquainting mine heart with wisdom; **and to** lay hold on **folly,** till I might see what was that good for the sons of men, which they should do under the heaven all the days of their life.
4. I made me great works; **I builded** me **houses; I planted** me

vineyards:

5. I made me **gardens** and **orchards, and** I planted **trees** in them of all kind of fruits:

6. **I made** me **pools** of water, **to water** therewith the wood that bringeth forth **trees:**

7. **I got** me **servants and maidens, and** had servants born in my house; also I **had great possessions** of great and small cattle **above all** that were **in Jerusalem before me:**

8. **I gathered** me also **silver** and **gold, and the** peculiar **treasure of kings** and of the provinces: **I gat me men** singers **and women singers,** and the delights of the sons of men, as musical instruments, and that of all sorts.

9. **So I** was great, and **increased more than all** that were before me **in Jerusalem: also my wisdom remained** with me.

10. And whatsoever mine eyes desired I kept not from them, **I withheld not** my heart **from any joy;** for my heart rejoiced in all my labour: and this was my portion of all my labour.

11. **Then I looked on all the works that my hands had wrought,** and on the labour that I had laboured to do: **and, behold, all was vanity** and vexation of spirit, **and there was no profit under the sun.**

12. **And I turned** myself **to** behold **wisdom,** and **madness, and folly:** for what can the man *do* that cometh after the king? *even* that which

hath been already done.

13. **Then I saw that wisdom excelleth folly,** as far as light excelleth darkness.

14. The wise man's eyes are in his head; but **the fool walketh in darkness: and I** myself **perceived** also **that** one event happeneth to them all.

15. Then said I in my heart, **As it happeneth to the fool, so it happeneth even to me; and why was I then more wise?** Then I said in my heart, that this also is vanity.

16. For there is no remembrance of the wise more thanof the fool for ever; seeing that which now is in the days to come shall all be forgotten. And **how dieth the wise man? as the fool.**

17. **Therefore I hated life;** because the work that is wrought under the sun is grievous unto me: **for all is** vanity and **vexation of spirit.**

18. **Yea, I hated** all my **labour** which I had taken under the sun: **because I should leave it unto the man** that shall be **after me.**

19. **And who knoweth whether he shall be a wise man or a fool?** yet shall he have rule over all my labour wherein I have laboured, and wherein I have shewed myself wise under the sun. This is also vanity.

20. Therefore I went about to cause my heart to despair of all the labour which I took under the sun.

21. **For there is a man whose labour is in wisdom,** and in knowledge, and in equity **yet to a man that hath not laboured** therein **shall he leave it** *for* his portion. **This** also **is vanity and** a great **evil.**

22. **For what hath man of all his labour,** and of the vexation of his heart, wherein he hath laboured under the sun? 23. **For all his days are sorrows, and** his travail **grief; yea, his heart taketh not rest** in the night. This is also vanity. 24. There is nothing better for **a man,** than that he **should eat and drink, and** that he should **make his soul enjoy good in his labour. This also** I saw, that it **was from the hand of God.** 25. For who can eat, or who else can hasten hereunto, more than I? 26. **For God giveth** to a man that is good in his sight **wisdom, and knowledge, and joy: but to the sinner he giveth travail,** to gather and to heap up, that he may give to him that is good before God. **This also is vanity** and vexation of spirit.

CHAPTER 3

1. **To every thing there is a season, and a time to every purpose** under the heaven: 2. **A time to be born, and** a time to **die;** a time **to plant, and** a time to **pluck up** that which is planted; 3. A time **to kill, and** a time to **heal;** a time **to break down, and** a time to **build up;** 4. A time **to weep, and** a time to **laugh;** a time **to mourn, and** a time to **dance;** 5. A time **to cast away stones, and** a time to **gather stones** together; a time **to embrace, and** a time **to refrain from embracing;** 6. A time **to get, and** a time to **lose;** a time **to keep, and** a time to **cast away;** 7. A time **to rend, and** a time **to sew;** a time **to keep silence, and** a time to **speak;** 8. A time **to love, and** a time to **hate; a time of war, and a time of peace.** 9. What profit hath he that worketh in that wherein he laboureth? 10. **I have seen the travail, which God hath given** to the sons of men to be exercised in it. 11. **He hath made every thing beautiful in his time: also he hath set the world in their heart,** so that no man can find out the work that God maketh from the beginning to the end. 12. **I know that there is no good** in them, **but for a man to rejoice, and to do good** in his life. 13. And also that **every man should eat** and **drink, and enjoy the good of all his labour, it is the gift of God.** 14. I know that, **whatsoever God doeth, it shall be for ever: nothing can be** put to it, nor any thing **taken from it: and God doeth it, that men should fear before him.** 15. **That which hath been is now;** and that which is to be hath already been; and God requireth that which is past. 16. **And moreover I saw** under the sun **the place of judgment,** that

wickedness was there;
and the place of
righteousness,
that iniquity was there.
17. I said in mine heart
God shall judge the
righteous and the wicked:
for there is a time there for every
purpose and for every work.
18. I said in mine heart
concerning the estate
of the sons of men, that
God might manifest them,
and that they might see
that they themselves
are beasts.
19. For that which befalleth
the sons of men befalleth
beasts; even one thing befalleth
them: as the one dieth, so dieth the
other; yea they have all one breath
so that a man hath no
preeminence above
a beast: for all is vanity.
20. All go unto one place;
all are of the dust, and
all turn to dust again.
21. Who knoweth the spirit
of man that goeth upward
and the spirit of the
beast that goeth
downward to the earth?
22. Wherefore I perceive that
there is nothing belter,
than that a man should
rejoice in his own works;
for that is his portion;
for who shall bring him
to see what shall be
after him?

CHAPTER 4

1. So I returned, and
considered all the
oppressions that are done
under the sun: and behold the
tears of such as were oppressed,
and they had no comforter
and on the side of their
oppressors there was
power; but they had no comforter.
2. Wherefore I praised the
dead which are already dead

more than the living
which are yet alive.
3. Yea, better is he
than both they,
which hath not yet been,
who hath not seen the
evil work that is done under the sun.
4. Again, I considered
all travail, and
every right work, that for this
a man is envied of his neighbour.
This is also vanity
and vexation of spirit.
5. The fool foldeth
his hands together,
and eateth his own flesh.
6. Better is an handful with
quietness, than both the
hands full with travail
and vexation of spirit.
7. Then I returned, and I
saw vanity under the sun.
8. There is one alone,
and there is not a second
yea, he hath neither child
nor brother: yet is there
no end of all his labour
neither is his eye satisfied
with riches;
neither saith he, For whom do I
labour, and bereave my soul of good?
This is also vanity,
yea, it is a sore travail.
9. Two are better than one;
because they have a good
reward for their labour.
10. For if they fall. the one
will lift up his fellow:
but woe to him that
is alone when he falleth;
for he hath not another
to help him up.
11. Again, if two
lie together, then
they have heat:
but how can one be warm alone?
12. And if one prevail against him, two
shall withstand him; and a threefold
cord is not quickly broken.
13. Better is a poor and
a wise child than an
old and foolish king,
who will no more be admonished.

14. For out of prison
he cometh to reign;
whereas also he that is born
in his kingdom becometh poor.
15. I considered all the living which
walk under the sun, with the second
child that shall stand up in his stead.
16. There is no end of all
the people, even of all that
have been before them:
they also that come after
shall not rejoice in him.
Surely this also
is vanity and vexation of spirit.

CHAPTER 5

1. Keep thy foot
when thou goest to
the house of God, and
be more ready to hear,
than to give the sacrifice
of fools: for they consider
not that they do evil.
2. Be not rash with thy
mouth, and let not thine heart be
hasty to utter any thing before God:
for God is in heaven, and
thou upon earth: therefore
let thy words be few.
3. For a dream cometh through
the multitude of business; and
a fool's voice is known
by multitude of words.
4. When thou vowest a vow
unto God, defer not to pay it;
for he hath no pleasure in fools:
pay that which
thou hast vowed.
5. Better is itthat thou shouldest
not vow, than that thou shouldest
vow and not pay.
6. Suffer not thy mouth to
cause thy flesh to sin;
neither say thou before the angel,
that it was an error: wherefore should
God be angry at thy voice, and
destroy the work of thine hands?
7. For in the multitude
of dreams and
many words there
are also divers
vanities: but fear thou God.
8. If thou seest the

oppression of the poor, and violent
perverting of judgment
and justice in a province,
marvel not at the matter:
for he that is higher than
the highest regardeth;
and there be higher than they.
9. Moreover the profit
of the earth is for all:
the king himself is served by the field.
10. He that loveth silver
shall not be satisfied with
silver; nor he that loveth abundance
with increase: this is also vanity.
11. When goods increase, they
are increased that eat them: and
what good is there to the owners
thereof, saving the beholding of
them with their eyes?
12. The sleep of a labouring
man is sweet, whether he eat
little or much: but the abundance of
the rich will not suffer him to sleep.
13. There is a sore evil
which I have seen under the sun
namely, riches kept for the
owners thereof to their hurt.
14. But those riches perish
by evil travail: and he begetteth a son,
and there is nothing in his hand.
15. As he came forth of his
mother's womb, naked
shall he return to go as he came,
and shall take nothing
of his labour, which he may carry
away in his hand.
16. And this also is a sore
evil, that in all points
as he came, so shall he go:
and what profit hath he that
hath laboured for the wind?
17. All his days also
he eateth in darkness
and he hath much
sorrow and wrath
with his sickness.
18. Behold that which I have seen:
it is good and comely
for one to eat and to drink,
and to enjoy the good of all
his labour that he taketh under
the sun all the days of his life,
which God giveth him:

for it is his portion.

19. **Every man also to whom God hath given riches** and wealth, and hath given him power to eat thereof, and to take his portion, and to rejoice in his labour; this **is the gift of God.**

20. For he shall not much remember the days of his life; because God answereth him in the joy of his heart.

CHAPTER 6

1. **There is an evil which I have seen** under the sun, and it is common among men:

2. **A man to whom God hath given riches,** wealth, **and honour, so that he wanteth nothing** for his soul of all that he desireth, **yet God giveth him not power to eat thereof,** but a stranger eateth it: **this** is vanity, and it **is an evil disease.**

3. **If a man** beget an hundred children, and **live many years,** so that the days of his years be many, **and his soul be not filled with good,** and also that he have no burial; **I say, that an untimely birth is better than he.**

4. **For** he cometh in with vanity, and departeth in darkness, and **his name shall be covered with darkness.**

5. Moreover he hath not seen the sun, nor known any thing: this hath more rest than the other.

6. Yea, though he live a thousand years twice told, yet hath he seen no good: do not all go to one place?

7. **All the labour of man is for his mouth, and yet the appetite is not filled.**

8. **For what hath the wise more than the fool?** what hath the poor, that knoweth to walk before the living?

9. Better is the sight of the eyes than the wandering of the desire: this is also vanity and vexation of spirit.

10. That which hath been is named already, and it is known that it is man: neither may he contend with him that is mightier than he.

11. Seeing there be many things that increase vanity, what is man the better?

12. **For who knoweth what is good for man** in this life, **all the days of his vain life which he spendeth as a shadow?** for who can tell a man what shall be after him under the sun?

CHAPTER 7

1. **A good name is better than precious ointment;** and the day of death than the day of one's birth.

2. **It is better to go to the house of mourning, than to go to the house of feasting:** for that is the end of all men; and the living will lay itto his heart.

3. **Sorrow is better than laughter: for by the sadness of the countenance the heart is made better.**

4. The heart of the wise is in the house of mourning; but **the heart of fools is in the house of mirth.**

5. **It is better to hear the rebuke of the wise, than** for a man **to hear the song of fools.**

6. For as the crackling of thorns under a pot, so is the laughter of the fool: this also is vanity.

7. **Surely oppression maketh a wise man mad;** and a gift destroyeth the heart.

8. **Better is the end** of a thing **than the beginning** thereof: **and the patient in spirit is better than the proud** in spirit.

9. **Be not** hasty in thy spirit to be **angry: for anger resteth in the bosom of fools.**

10. Say not thou, What is the cause that the former days were better than

these? for thou dost not enquire wisely concerning this.

11. **Wisdom is good** with an inheritance: and by it there is profit to them that see the sun.

12. **For wisdom is a defence,** and money is a defence: but the excellency of knowledge is, that **wisdom giveth life to them that have it.**

13. **Consider the work of God: for who can make that straight, which he hath made crooked?**

14. In the day of prosperity be joyful, but in the day of adversity consider: God also hath set the one over against the other, to the end that man should find nothing after him.

15. **All things have I seen** in the days of my vanity: **there is a just man that perisheth** in his righteousness, **and there is a wicked man that prolongeth his life** in his wickedness.

16. Be not righteous over much; neither make thyself over wise: why shouldest thou destroy thyself?

17. **Be not** over much **wicked, neither be** thou **foolish: why shouldest thou die before thy time?**

18. *It* is good that thou shouldest take hold of this; yea, also from this withdraw not thine hand: for **he that feareth God shall come forth of them all.**

19. **Wisdom strengtheneth** the wise **more than ten mighty men** which are in the city.

20. **For there is not a just man** upon earth, **that** doeth good, and **sinneth not.**

21. Also take no heed unto all words that are spoken; lest thou hear thy servant curse thee:

22. For oftentimes also thine own heart knoweth that thou thyself likewise hast cursed others.

23. All this have I proved by wisdom: **I said, I will be wise; but it was far from me.**

24. That which is far off, and exceeding deep, who can find it out?

25. **I applied mine heart** to know, and to search, and **to seek** out **wisdom, and the reason of things,** and to know the wickedness of folly, even of foolishness and madness:

26. **And I find more bitter than death the woman,** whose heart is snares and nets, and her hands as bands: **whoso pleaseth God shall escape from her; but the sinner shall be taken by her.**

27. Behold, this have I found, saith the preacher, counting one by one, to find out the account:

28. Which yet my soul seeketh, but I find not: **one man among a thousand have I found; but a woman among all those have I not found.**

29. **Lo**, this only have I found, that **God hath made man upright; but they have sought** out **many inventions.**

CHAPTER 8

1. Who is as the wise man? and who knoweth the interpretation of a thing? **a man's wisdom maketh his face to shine,** and the boldness of his face shall be changed.

2. **I counsel thee to keep the king's commandment,** and that in regard of the oath of God.

3. Be not hasty to go out of his sight: stand not in an evil thing; for he doeth whatsoever pleaseth him.

4. **Where the word of a king is, there is power:** and who may say unto him, What doest thou?

5. **Whoso keepeth the commandment shall feel**

■ no evil thing: and a wise man's heart
discerneth both time and judgment.

■ 6. **Because to every purpose**
■ **there is time**
■ **and judgment, therefore**
■ **the misery of man is**
■ **great upon him.**
7. For he knoweth not that
which shall be: for who can
tell him when it shall be?

■ 8. **There is no man that**
■ **hath power** over the spirit
■ **to retain the spirit, neither**
■ **hath he power in** the day of
■ **death:**
and there is no discharge in that war;
■ **neither shall wickedness**
■ **deliver those that**
■ **are given to it.**
9. All this have I seen, and applied
my heart unto every work that is
done under the sun: there is
a time wherein one man ruleth
over another to his own hurt.

■ 10. **And so I saw the wicked**
■ **buried,** who had come and
gone from the place of the holy,
■ **and they were forgotten**
in the city where they had so
done: this is also vanity.

■ 11. **Because sentence**
■ **against** an
■ **evil** work
■ **is not executed**
■ **speedily, therefore**
■ **the heart** of the sons of men
■ **is** fully
■ **set** in them
■ **to do evil.**
■ 12. **Though a sinner**
■ **do evil** an hundred times,
■ **and his days be**
■ **prolonged, yet**
surely I know that
■ **it shall be well with**
■ **them that fear God,**
which fear before him:

■ 13. **But it shall not be**
■ **well with the wicked,**
neither shall he prolong his
days, which are as a shadow;
■ **because he**
■ **feareth not** before

■ **God.**
14. There is a vanity which is done
upon the earth; that there be just
men, unto whom it happeneth
according to the work of the
wicked; again, there be wicked men,
to whom it happeneth according
to the work of the righteous:
I said that this also is vanity.

■ 15. **Then I commended**
■ **mirth,** because a man hath no better
thing under the sun, than to eat,
■ **and to drink, and to be**
■ **merry: for that shall abide**
■ **with him** of his labour
■ **the days of his life,**
which God giveth him under the sun.
16. When I applied mine heart to
know wisdom, and to see the
business that is done upon the earth
(for also there is that neither day nor
night seeth sleep with his eyes):

■ 17. **Then I beheld all the**
■ **work of God, that a man**
■ **cannot find out** the work
that is done under the sun:
■ **because though a man**
■ **labour to seek it out, yet he**
■ **shall not find it; yea** farther
■ **though a wise man think**
■ **to know it, yet shall he**
■ **not be able to find it.**

CHAPTER 9

1. For all this I considered in my
heart even to declare all this, that
■ **the righteous, and the**
■ **wise, and their works,**
■ **are in the hand of God:**
no man knoweth either love or
hatred by all that is before them.

■ 2. **All things come alike**
■ **to all:** there is one event
■ **to the righteous, and to the**
■ **wicked;** to the good and to the
clean, and to the unclean; to him
that sacrificeth, and to him that
sacrificeth not: as *is* the good,
so *is* the sinner; and he that
sweareth, as *he* that feareth an oath.
3. This is an evil among all *things* that
are done under the sun, that
■ **there is one event unto all:**

■ yea, also the heart
■ of the sons of
■ men is full of evil,
and madness is in their heart
while they live, and after
that they go to the dead.
4. For to him that is joined to all
the living there is hope: for a living
dog is better than a dead lion.
■ 5. For the living know that
■ they shall die: but the dead
■ know not any thing, neither
have they any more a reward;
■ for the memory of them
■ is forgotten.
■ 6. Also their love, and
■ their hatred, and their
■ envy, is now perished;
neither have they any more a portion
for ever in any *thing* that is done
under the sun.
■ 7. Go thy way, eat thy bread
■ with joy, and drink
thy wine with a merry heart;
■ for God now
■ accepteth thy works.
8. Let thy garments be always white;
and let thy head lack no ointment.
■ 9. Live joyfully with the wife
■ whom thou lovest all the
days of the life of thy vanity, which
he hath given thee under the sun,
all the days of thy vanity:
■ for that is thy portion
in this life, and in thy labour which
thou takest under the sun.
■ 10. Whatsoever thy hand
■ findeth to do, do it with
■ thy might; for there is
■ no work, nor device, nor
knowledge, nor wisdom,
■ in the grave, whither thou goest.
■ 11. I returned, and
■ saw under the sun,
■ that the race is not to the
■ swift, nor the battle to the
■ strong, neither yet bread
■ to the wise, nor yet riches
to men of understanding,
■ nor yet favour to men of
■ skill; but time and chance
■ happeneth to them all.
■ 12. For man also

■ knoweth not his time:
as the fishes that are taken
in an evil net, and
■ as the birds that are
■ caught in the snare;
■ so are the sons of
■ men snared
in an evil time, when it falleth
■ suddenly upon them.
13. This wisdom have I seen
also under the sun, and it
seemed great unto me:
■ 14. There was a little
■ city, and few men within it;
■ and there came a great
■ king against it, and
■ besieged it, and built
great bulwarks against it:
■ 15. Now there was found in it
■ a poor wise man, and
■ he by his wisdom
■ delivered the city; yet
■ no man remembered
that same poor man.
16. Then said I, Wisdom is better
than strength: nevertheless
■ the poor man's
■ wisdom is despised,
and his words are not heard.
17. The words of wise men are
heard in quiet more than the cry
of him that ruleth among fools.
■ 18. Wisdom is better
■ than weapons of war:
■ but one sinner destroyeth
■ much good.

CHAPTER 10

■ 1. Dead flies cause the
■ ointment of the apothecary
■ to send forth a stinking
■ savour: so doth a little
■ folly him that is in reputation
for wisdom and honour.
2. A wise man's heart is at his right
hand; but a fool's heart at his left.
3. Yea also, when he that is a fool
walketh by the way, his wisdom
faileth him, and he saith to
every one that he is a fool.
■ 4. If the spirit of the
■ ruler rise up
■ against thee, leave

not thy place, for yielding
pacifieth great offences.
5. **There is an evil** which I have
seen under the sun, as an error
which proceedeth
from the ruler:
6. **Folly is set in great**
dignity, and the rich
sit in low place.
7. **I have seen servants**
upon horses, and
princes walking
as servants upon the earth.
8. **He that diggeth a pit shall**
fall into it; and whoso breaketh an
hedge, a serpent shall bite him.
9. **Whoso removeth stones**
shall be hurt therewith;
and he that cleaveth wood shall
be endangered thereby.
10. **If the iron be blunt,**
and he do not whet the edge,
then must he put to more
strength: but wisdom is
profitable to direct.
11. **Surely the serpent will**
bite without enchantment;
and a babbler is no better.
12. **The words of a wise**
man's mouth are gracious;
but the lips of a fool will
swallow up himself.
13. The beginning of the words of his
mouth is foolishness: and the end of
his talk is mischievous madness.
14. **A fool** also
is full of words: a man cannot
tell what shall be; and what shall
be after him, who can tell him?
15. **The labour of the foolish**
wearieth every one
of them, because he knoweth
not how to go to the city.
16. **Woe to thee, O land,**
when thy king is a child,
and thy princes eat in
the morning!
17. **Blessed art thou, O**
land, when thy king is
the son of nobles, and
thy princes eat in due
season, for strength,
and not for drunkenness!

18. **By much slothfulness**
the building decayeth;
and through idleness of the hands
the house droppeth through.
19. A feast is made for laughter, and
wine maketh merry:
but money answereth
all things.
20. **Curse not the king,**
no not in thy thought; and curse
not the rich in thy bedchamber:
for a bird of the air shall
carry the voice, and
that which hath wings shall
tell the matter.

CHAPTER 11

1. **Cast thy bread upon the**
waters: for thou shalt find
it after many days.
2. Give a portion to seven, and
also to eight; for thou knowest not
what evil shall be upon the earth.
3. **If the clouds be full of**
rain, they empty themselves
upon the earth: and if the
tree fall toward the south,
or toward the north, in
the place where the tree
falleth, there it shall be.
4. He that observeth the wind shall
not sow; and he that regardeth
the clouds shall not reap.
5. **As thou knowest not**
what is the way of the
spirit, nor how the bones do
grow in the womb
of her that is with child:
even so thou knowest
not the works of God
who maketh all.
6. In the morning sow thy seed, and in
the evening withhold not thine hand:
for thou knowest not whether shall
prosper, either this or that, or whether
they both shall be alike good.
7. **Truly the light is sweet,**
and a pleasant thing
it is for the eyes to behold the sun:
8. **But if a man live many**
years, and rejoice in them all; yet
let him remember the days
of darkness; for they shall be

many. All that cometh is vanity.

9. **Rejoice,** O young man,

in thy youth; and let thy heart cheer thee in the days of thy youth, and walk in the ways of thine heart, and in the sight of thine eyes:

but know thou,

that for

all these

things God will bring thee **into judgment.**

10. **Therefore remove sorrow** from thy heart, **and put away evil** from thy flesh: **for childhood and youth are vanity.**

CHAPTER 12

1. **Remember now thy Creator in the days of thy youth, while the evil days come not,** nor the years draw nigh **when thou shalt say, I have no pleasure in them;**

2. **While the sun,** or the light, or the moon, or the stars, **be not darkened,** nor the clouds return after the rain:

3. **In the day when the keepers of the house shall tremble,** and **the strong** men **shall bow** themselves, **and the grinders cease** because they are few, and those that look out of the windows be darkened,

4. **And the doors shall be shut** in the streets, when the sound of the grinding is low, and he shall rise up at the voice of the bird **and all the daughters of music shall be brought low;**

5. Also when they shall be afraid of that which is high, **and fears shall be in the way,** and the almond tree shall flourish, and the

grasshopper shall be a burden, **and desire shall fail:** because man goeth to his long home, **and the mourners go about the streets:**

6. Or ever the silver cord be loosed, **or the golden bowl** be broken, **or the pitcher be broken** at the fountain, or the wheel broken at the cistern.

7. **Then** shall the dust return to the earth as it was: and **the spirit shall return unto God who gave it.**

8. **Vanity of vanities,** saith the preacher; **all is vanity.**

9. **And** moreover, because **the preacher** was wise, he still **taught the people knowledge;** yea, he gave good heed, and sought out, **and set in order many proverbs.**

10. **The preacher sought to find out acceptable words:** and that which was written was upright, **even words of truth.**

11. **The words of the wise are** as goads, and **as nails fastened by the masters** of assemblies, which are given from one shepherd.

12. **And** further, by these, my son, be admonished: of **making many books there is no end; and much study is a weariness** of the flesh.

13. **Let us hear the conclusion** of the whole matter: **Fear God, and keep his commandments: for this is the whole duty of man.**

14. **For God shall bring every work into judgment, with every secret thing, whether it be good, or whether it be evil.**

THE SONG OF SOLOMON

BACKGROUND INFORMATION

Author: Probably Solomon
Date Written: Unknown

Number of:
Verses—117
Chapters—8
Total Words—2,661
Scan Words—1,266
Scan Words Represent
Approximately 47% of
Total Words

Theme: A story of love
Between a Man and a
Woman which Points
Toward a Deeper Love

OUTLINE OF THE BOOK

I. **Mutual Love and**
    Affection
    1:1 — 2:7
II. **The Bride Dreams of her**
    Bridegroom
    2:8 — 3:5
III. **The Bridal Procession**
     and a Second Dream
     3:6 — 6:3
IV. **The Bridegroom Praises**
    his Bride
    6:4 — 8:4
V. **The Expressions of Love.**
    8:5 — 14

CHAPTER 1

1 . **The song** of songs, **which is Solomon's.**

2. **Let him kiss me** with the kisses of his mouth: **for thy love is better than wine.** 3. Because of the savour of thy good ointments **thy name is as ointment** poured forth, **therefore do the virgins love thee.** 4. Draw me, we will run after thee: **the king** hath **brought me into his chambers: we will be glad and rejoice** in thee, we will remember thy love more than wine: the upright love thee.

5. **I am black, but comely,** O ye daughters of Jerusalem, **as the tents of Kedar, as the curtains of Solomon.** 6. **Look not upon me,** because I *am* black, because the sun hath looked upon me: **my mother's children** were angry with me; they **made me the keeper of the vineyards; but mine own vineyard have I not kept.** 7. **Tell me, O thou whom my soul loveth,** where thou feedest, where thou makest thy *flock* to rest at noon: for **why should I be as one that turneth aside** by the flocks of thy companions? 8. **If thou know not, O thou fairest among women,** go thy way forth by the footsteps of the flock, and feed thy kids beside the shepherds' tents.

9. **I have compared thee,** O my love **to a company of horses in Pharaoh's chariots.** 10. **Thy cheeks are comely** with rows of *jewels* **thy neck with chains of gold.** 11. **We will make thee borders of gold with studs of silver.**

12. **While the king sitteth** at his table, **my spikenard sendeth forth the smell** thereof. 13. **A bundle of myrrh is my wellbeloved** unto me; **he shall lie** all night **betwixt my breasts.** 14. **My beloved is** unto me **as a cluster of camphire** in the vineyards of En-gedi. 15. **Behold, thou art fair,** my love, behold, thou *art* fair; **thou hast doves' eyes.** 16. **Behold, thou art** fair, my beloved, yea, **pleasant:** also our bed *is* green. 17. The beams of our house are cedar, *and* our rafters of fir.

CHAPTER 2

1. **I am the rose of Sharon, and the lily of the valleys.** 2. As the lily among thorns, so *is* my love among the daughters. 3. **As the apple tree among the trees** of the wood, **so is my beloved among the sons.** I sat down under his shadow with great delight, **and his fruit was sweet to my taste.** 4. He brought me to the banqueting house, **and his banner over me was love.** 5. Stay me with flagons, **comfort me with apples: for I am sick of love.** 6. **His left hand is under my head, and his right hand doth embrace me.** 7. **I charge you,** O ye daughters of Jerusalem, by the roes, and by the hinds of the field, that ye **stir not** up, **nor awake my love, till he please.** 8. The voice of my beloved! behold, **he cometh leaping upon the mountains, skipping**

upon the hills.

9. **My beloved is like a**
roe or a young hart:
behold, hestandeth behind our wall,
he looketh fonh at the windows,
shewing himself
through the lattice.
10. **My beloved** spake, and
said unto me.
Rise up, my love, my fair one,
and come away.
11. **For, lo, the winter is**
past, the rain is over and gone;
12. **The flowers**
appear on the eanh;
the time of the singing of
birds is come, and the voice
of the turtle is heard in our land;
13. **The fig tree**
putteth forth her green
figs, and the vines with the
tender grape give a
goodsmell. Arise, my love,
my fair one, and come away.
14. **O my dove,** that *art* in
the clefts of the rock, in the
secret *places* of the stairs,
let me see thycountenance,
let me hear thy voice;
for sweet is thy voice, and
thy countenance is comely
15. Take us the foxes, the
little foxes, that spoil the vines:
for our vines *have* tender grapes.
16. **My beloved**
is mine, and I *am* his: he
feedeth among the lilies.
17. **Until the day break,**
and the shadows flee
away, turn, my beloved, and be
thou like a roe or a young han
upon the mountains of Bether.

CHAPTER 3

1. **By night** on my bed
I sought him whom my
soul loveth: I sought him,
but I found him not.
2. I will rise now, and go about the city
in the streets, and in the broad ways
I will seek him whom
my soul loveth: I sought
him, but I found him not.

3. **The watchmen**
that go about the city
found me: to whom
I said, Saw ye him
whom my soul loveth?
4. I*t was* but a little that
I passed from them, but I
found him whom my soul loveth:
I held him, and would
not let him go, until I
had brought him
into my mother's house, and
into the chamber
of her that conceived me.
5. I charge you, O ye daughters of
Jerusalem, by the roes, and by the
hinds of the field, that ye stir not up,
nor awake *my* love, till he please.
6. **Who is this that cometh**
out of the wilderness
like pillars of smoke
perfumed with myrrh
and frankincense, with all
powders of the merchant?
7. **Behold his bed,**
which is Solomon's;
threescore valiant men are
about it, of the valiant of Israel.
8. They all hold swords, being expert
in war: every man hath his swordupon
his thigh because of fear in the night.
9. **King Solomon made**
himself a chariot
of the wood of Lebanon.
10. **He made the**
pillars thereof
of silver the bottom thereof
of gold, the covering of it
of purple, the midst thereof
being paved with love,
for the daughters of Jerusalem.
11. **Go forth, O ye**
daughters of Zion, and
behold king Solomon with
the crown wherewith his mother
crowned him in the day of his
espousals, and in the day of the
gladness of his heart.

CHAPTER 4

1. **Behold, thou art fair,**
my love; behold, thou *art* fair;
thou hast doves' eyes

within thy locks:
■ **thy hair is as a**
■ **flock of goats,**
that appear from mount Gilead.
■ 2. **Thy teeth are like a flock**
■ **of sheep** that are even shorn,
which came up from the washing;
whereof every one bear twins, and
none is barren among them.
■ 3. **Thy lips are like** a thread of
■ **scarlet, and thy speech** *is*
■ **comely: thy temples are**
■ **like a piece of a**
■ **pomegranate** within thy locks.
■ 4. **Thy neck is like the tower**
■ **of David** builded for an armoury,
whereon there hang a thousand
bucklers, all shields of mighty men.
■ 5. **Thy two breasts are like**
■ **two young roes** that are
twins,which feed among the lilies.
6. Until the day break, and the
shadows flee away, I will get me
to the mountain of myrrh, and to
the hill of frankincense.
7. Thou art all fair,
■ **my love; there is**
■ **no spot in thee.**
■ 8. **Come with me** from Lebanon,
■ **my spouse,** with me from
Lebanon: look from the top of
Amana, from the top of Shenir
and Hermon, from the lions' dens,
from the mountains of the leopards.
■ 9. **Thou hast ravished my**
■ **heart,** my sister, *my* spouse;
thou hast ravished my hean
■ **with one of thine eyes,**
■ **with one chain of thy neck.**
10. How fair is thy love,
my sister, my spouse!
■ **how much better is thy**
■ **love than wine!** and the smell
of thine ointments than all spices!
■ 11. **Thy lips,** O *my* spouse,
■ **drop as the honeycomb:**
■ **honey and milk are under**
■ **thy tongue;** and the smell of thy
garments *is* like the smell of Lebanon.
12. A garden enclosed *is* my
sister, *my* spouse; a spring
shut up, a fountain sealed.
■ 13. **Thy plants are an**

■ **orchard** of pomegranates,
■ **with pleasant fruits;**
camphire,with spikenard,
14. Spikenard and saffron; calamus
and cinnamon, with all trees of
frankincense; myrrh and aloes,
with all the chief spices:
■ 15. **A fountain of gardens, a**
■ **well of living waters, and**
■ **streams from Lebanon.**
16. **Awake, O** north
■ **wind; and** come, thou south;
■ **blow upon my garden,**
■ **that the spices** thereof
■ **may flow** out.
■ **Let my beloved come**
■ **into his garden, and**
■ **eat his pleasant fruits.**

CHAPTER 5
■ 1. **I am come into my**
■ **garden,** my sister, *my*
spouse: I have gathered my
myrrh with my spice;
■ **I have eaten** my honeycomb with
■ **my honey; I have drunk**
■ **my wine** with my milk: eat,
O friends; drink, yea, drink
abundantly, O beloved.
■ 2. **I sleep, but my heart**
■ **waketh: it is** the voice of
■ **my beloved that knocketh,**
saying, Open to me, my sister,
■ **my love,** my dove,
■ **my undefiled:** for my head
is filled with dew, and my locks
with the drops of the night.
■ 3. **I have put off my**
■ **coat;** how shall I put it on?
■ **I have washed my feet;**
how shall I defile them?
4. My beloved put in his hand
by the hole of the door, and
my bowels were moved for him.
■ 5. **I rose up to**
■ **open** to my beloved;
■ **and my hands dropped**
■ **with myrrh,** and my fingers
with sweet smelling myrrh,
upon the handles of the lock.
■ 6. **I opened** to my beloved;
■ **but my beloved** had
withdrawn himself, and

was gone: my soul failed when he spake: I sought him, but
I could not find him; I called him, but he gave me no answer.

7. The watchmen that went about the city found me, they smote me, they wounded me; the keepers of the walls took away my veil from me.

8. I charge you, O daughters of Jerusalem, if ye find my beloved, that ye tell him, that I am sick of love.

9. What *is* thy beloved more than another beloved, O thou fairest among women? what is thy beloved more than another beloved, that thou dost so charge us?

10. My beloved is white and ruddy, the chiefest among ten thousand.

11. His head is as the most fine gold, his locks are bushy, and black as a raven.

12. His eyes are as the eyes of doves by the rivers of waters, washed with milk, and fitly set.

13. His cheeks are as a bed of spices, as sweet flowers: his lips like lilies, dropping sweet smelling myrrh.

14. His hands are as gold rings set with the beryl: his belly is as bright ivory overlaid with sapphires.

15. His legs are as pillars of marble, set upon sockets of fine gold: his countenance *is* as Lebanon, excellent as the cedars.

16. His mouth *is* most sweet: yea, he is altogether lovely. This *is* my beloved, and this is my friend, O daughters of Jerusalem.

CHAPTER 6

1. Whither is thy beloved gone, O thou fairest among women? whither is thy beloved turned aside? that we may seek him with thee.

2. My beloved is gone down into his garden, to the beds of spices, to feed in the gardens, and to gather lilies.

3. I am my beloved's, and my beloved is mine: he feedeth among the lilies.

4. Thou art beautiful, O my love, as Tirzah, comely as Jerusalem, terrible as an army with banners.

5. Turn away thine eyes from me, for they have overcome me: thy hair *is* as a flock of goats that appear from Gilead.

6. Thy teeth *are* as a flock of sheep which go up from the washing, whereof every one beareth twins, and *there* is not one barren among them.

7. As a piece of a pomegranate are thy temples within thy locks.

8. There are threescore queens, and fourscore concubines, and virgins without number.

9. My dove, my undefiled is *but* one; she is the only one of her mother, she *is* the choice one of her that bare her. The daughters saw her, and blessed her yea, the queens and the concubines, and they praised her.

10. Who is she that looketh forth as the morning, fair as the moon, clear as the sun, and terrible as an army with banners?

11. I went down into the garden of nuts to see the fruits of the valley, and

to see whether the
vine flourished, *and* the
pomegranates budded.
12. Or ever I was aware,
my soul made me *like* the
chariots of Amminadib.
13. **Return,** return, O
Shulamite; return, return,
**that we may look upon
thee.** What will ye see in the
Shulamite? As it were the
company of two armies.

CHAPTER 7

1. **How beautiful are thy
feet with shoes, O prince's
daughter! the joints of
thy thighs are like jewels,**
the work of the hands
of a cunning workman.
2. **Thy navel is like a round
goblet,** which wanteth not liquor:
**thy belly is
like an heap of
wheat** set about with lilies.
3. **Thy** two
**breasts are like two
young roes** that are twins.
4. **Thy neck is as a tower of
ivory; thine eyes like the
fishpools in Heshbon,**
by the gate of Bath-rabbim:
**thy nose is as the
tower of Lebanon**
which looketh toward Damascus.
5. **Thine head** upon thee
**is like Carmel, and the hair
of thine head like purple;**
the king *is* held in the galleries.
6. How fair and
**how pleasant art
thou,** O love, for delights!
7. **This thy stature is like to a
palm tree, and thy breasts
to clusters of grapes.**
8. I said, I will go up to the palm tree,
I will take hold of the boughs thereof:
**now also thy breasts shall
be as clusters of the vine,**
and the smell of thy nose like apples;
9. **And the roof of thy
mouth like the best
wine** for my beloved,

**that goeth down
sweetly,** causing the lips of
those that are asleep to speak.
10. **I am my beloved's, and
his desire is toward me.**
11. **Come, my beloved,**
let us go forth into the field; let
us lodge in the villages.
12. **Let us get up early
to the vineyards;**
let us see if the vine flourish,
**whether the tender
grape appear, and**
the pomegranates bud forth:
**there will I give
thee my loves.**
13. The mandrakes give a
smell, and at our gates are
all manner of
pleasant fruits,
new and old, *which*
**I have laid up for
thee, O my beloved.**

CHAPTER 8

1. O that thou *wert* as my brother, that
sucked the breasts of my mother!
**when I should find thee
without, I would kiss thee;**
yea, I should not be despised.
2. **I would** lead thee, and
**bring thee into my mother's
house,** who would instruct me:
**I would cause thee to
drink of spiced wine**
of the juice of my pomegranate.
3. His left hand *should* be
under my head, and his right
hand should embrace me.
4. I charge you, O daughters of
Jerusalem, that ye stir not up, nor
awake *my* love, until he please.
5. **Who is this that
cometh** up from the wilderness,
leaning upon her beloved?
I raised thee up under the apple
tree: there thy mother brought
thee forth: there she brought
thee forth that bare thee.
6. **Set me as a seal
upon thine heart,**
as a seal upon thine arm:
for love is strong as

death; jealousy is
cruel as the grave:
the coals thereof are coals of fire,
which hath a most vehement flame.
7. Many waters
cannot quench love,
neither can the floods drown it:
if a man would give
all the substance of
his house for love,
it would utterly be
contemned.
8. We have a little sister,
and she hath no breasts:
what shall we do for
our sister in the day
when she shall
be spoken for?
9. If she be a wall,
we will build upon
her a palace of silver:
and if she be
a door, we will enclose
her with boards of cedar.
10. I am a wall, and

my breasts like towers:
then was I in his eyes as
one that found favour.
11. Solomon
had a vineyard at Baal-hamon; he
let out the vineyard
unto keepers; every
one for the fruit
thereof was to
bring a thousand
pieces of silver.
12. My vineyard,
which is mine, is before me: thou,
O Solomon, must have
a thousand and those
that keep the fruit thereof
two hundred.
13. Thou that dwellest in the
gardens, the companions hearken
to thy voice: cause me to hear it.
14. Make haste, my
beloved, and be
thou like to a roe or to
a young hart upon the
mountains of spices.

ISAIAH:
Prince of Prophets

During the second half of the eighth century B.C. **The Northern Kingdom, Israel, fell to the Assyrians and** *before the end of the century,* **probably in 701 B.C., Sennacherib came** *with a mighty army* **to** *surround and* **lay siege to Jerusalem. The times could not have been more critical.** *The Northern Kingdom was on the verge of collapse.* **As is often the case in times of** *extreme* **crisis, God raised up a special man,** *isaiah. Bible scholars have* **called Isaiah "The Prince of the Prophets." Isaiah's vision** *of the Lord in the temple recorded in chapter six of the book,* **presents a** *magnificent* **description of God in his holiness and glory. Upon this vision** *of God,* **Isaiah saw** *himself and* **all mankind. He understood the** *enormous* **abyss between God's** *sovereign* **holiness and man's** *utter* **sinfulness.** *He was overwhelmed.*

Only *a purifying act by* **God** *himself* **could cleanse him and prepare him for service. After** *he had received* **a** *divine* **vision, a cleansing** *of his sins,* **and a** *direct* **call** *from God,* **Isaiah went forth to prophesy**, *to expose the moral decay of Judah and its capital, Jerusalem. Later,* **he became an adviser to King Ahaz. He** *passionately* **urged the king to come to God in faith, and with courage to resist** *the Assyrian* **invasion. Ahaz rejected** *both pleas* **and Judah fell. But Isaiah** *never stepped back,* **never compromised.** *He called God's people to repentance and* **upon seeing Judah's** *inevitable* **destruction, he foretold of** *the coming messiah,* **a suffering servant, who would redeem mankind and establish the Kingdom of God** *among man.*

THE BOOK OF ISAIAH

BACKGROUND INFORMATION

Author: Isaiah
Date written: Approximately **740 B.C.**

Number of:
Versus—1292
Chapters—66
Total Words—37,044
Scan Words—15,208
Scan Words Represent
Approximately 41% of
Total Words.

Theme: Prophecies Concerning the Rebellion of Israel, its Consequences, **and of** a Coming **Redemption** and Restoration **Through** Gods Suffering Servant, **The Messiah**

OUTLINE OF THE BOOK

I. **Judgement Presented** in Poetry
   1:1 — 35:10
II. Prophetic Picture of **Israel in the Last Days**
   36:1 — 39:8
III. **Salvation** of Jehovah **Through the Suffering Servant**
   40:1 — 66:24

CHAPTER 1

1. **The vision of Isaiah** the son of Amoz, which he saw **concerning Judah and Jerusalem** in the days of Uzziah, Jotham, Ahaz, *and* Hezekiah, kings of Judah. 2. **Hear, O heavens, and** give ear, O **earth: for the LORD hath spoken, I** have **nourished and brought up children, and they** have **rebelled against me.** 3. **The ox knoweth his owner,** and the ass his master's crib: **but Israel doth not know,** my people doth not consider. 4. **Ah sinful nation,** a people **laden with iniquity,** a seed of evildoers, children that are corrupters: **they have forsaken the LORD,** they have provoked the Holy One of Israel unto anger, **they are gone** away **backward.** 5. **Why** should ye **be stricken** any more? **ye** will **revolt more and more: the** whole **head is sick, and the** whole **heart faint.** 6. From the sole of the foot even unto the head *there is* no soundness in it; *but* wounds, and bruises, and putrefying sores: they have not been closed, neither bound up, neither mollified with ointment. 7. **Your country is desolate,** your cities *are* burned with fire: your land, strangers devour it in your presence, and *it is* desolate, as overthrown by strangers. 8. **And the daughter of Zion is left** as a cottage in a vineyard, as a lodge in a garden of cucumbers, **as a besieged city.** 9. **Except the LORD** of hosts **had left** unto us **a** very small

remnant, **we should have been as Sodom, and** we should have been like unto **Gomorrah.** 10. **Hear the word of the LORD,** ye rulers of Sodom; give ear unto the law of our God, ye people of Gomorrah. 11. **To what purpose is** the multitude of **your sacrifices** unto me? saith the LORD: I am full of the burnt offerings of rams, and the fat of fed beasts; and **I delight not in the blood of bullocks, or** of **lambs,** or of he goats. 12. When ye come to appear before me, **who hath required this** at your hand, **to tread my courts?** 13. **Bring no more vain oblations;** incense is an abomination unto me; the new moons and sabbaths, the calling of assemblies, I cannot away with; *it is* iniquity, even the solemn meeting. 14. **Your new moons and** your **appointed feasts my soul hateth:** they are a trouble unto me; I am weary to bear *them.* 15. And when ye spread forth your hands, I will hide mine eyes from you: yea, **when ye make many prayers, I will not hear: your hands are full of blood.** 16. **Wash** you, **make you clean;** put away the evil of your doings from before mine eyes; **cease to do evil;** 17. **Learn to do well;** seek judgment, relieve the oppressed, judge the fatherless, plead for the widow. 18. **Come now,** and **let us reason together, saith the LORD: though**

your sins be as scarlet,
they shall be as white
as snow; though they be
red like crimson, they
shall be as wool.
19. If ye be willing and
obedient, ye shall
eat the good
of the land:
20. But if ye refuse and
rebel, ye shall be
devoured with the sword:
for the mouth of
the LORD hath spoken it.
21. How is the faithful city become
an harlot! it was full of judgment;
righteousness lodged in it; but
now murderers.
22. Thy silver is become dross,
thy wine mixed with water:
23. Thy princes are rebellious,
and companions of thieves:
every one loveth gifts,
and followeth after
rewards: they judge not the
fatherless, neither doth the cause
of the widow come unto them.
24. Therefore saith the
LORD, the LORD of hosts,
the mighty One of Israel, Ah,
I will ease me of mine
adversaries, and
avenge me of
mine enemies:
25. And I will turn my
hand upon thee, and purely
purge away thy
dross, and take away
all thy tin:
26. And I will restore
thy judges as at the first,
and thy
counsellors as at the beginning:
afterward thou shalt be
called, The city of
righteousness, the faithful city.
27. Zion shall be redeemed
with judgment, and her converts
with righteousness.
28. And the destruction
of the transgressors and of
the sinners shall be together,
and they that forsake the

LORD shall be consumed.
29. For they shall be
ashamed of the oaks which
ye have desired, and ye shall
be confounded for the gardens
that ye have chosen.
30. For ye shall be
as an oak whose leaf
fadeth, and as a garden
that hath no water.
31. And the strong
shall be as tow, and
the maker of it as a
spark, and they shall
both burn together,
and none
shall quench them.

CHAPTER 2

1. The word that Isaiah the
son of Amoz saw concerning
Judah and Jerusalem.
2. And it shall come to pass
in the last days,
that the mountain of
the LORD's house
shall be established
in the top of the mountains,
and shall be
exalted above the hills;
and all nations
shall flow unto it.
3. And many
people shall go and
say, Come ye, and
let us go up to the
mountain of the LORD,
to the house of the
God of Jacob;
and he will teach
us of his ways,
and we will walk in
his paths: for out of Zion
shall go forth the law, and the word
of the LORD from Jerusalem.
4. And he shall
judge among the
nations, and shall
rebuke many people:
and they shall beat their
swords into plowshares,
and their spears into
pruninghooks: nation

961

shall not lift up sword against nation,
neither shall they learn
war any more.
5. **O** house of
Jacob, come ye, and
let us walk in the light
of the LORD.
6. **Therefore thou hast**
forsaken thy people
the house of Jacob,
because they be replenished
from the east, and *are* soothsayers
like the Philistines, and they
please themselves in the children
of strangers.
7. Their land also is full of silver
and gold, neither *is there any* end
of their treasures; their land is
also full of horses, neither *is there*
any end of their chariots:
8. **Their land** also
is full of idols;
they worship the work of
their own hands, that which
their own fingers have made:
9. And the mean man boweth
down, and the great man humbleth
himself: therefore forgive them not.
10. **Enter into the rock,**
and hide thee in the dust,
for fear of the LORD, and
for the glory of his majesty.
11. **The lofty** looks of man
shall be humbled,
and the haughtiness of men
shall be bowed down, and
the LORD alone shall
be exalted in that day.
12. **For** the day of
the LORD of hosts
shall be upon every one that
is proud and lofty, and upon every *one*
that is lifted up; and he shall
be brought low:
13. And upon all the cedars of
Lebanon, *that are* high and lifted up,
and upon all the oaks of Bashan,
14. And upon all the high mountains,
and upon all the hills *that are* lifted up,
15. And upon every high tower, and
upon every fenced wall,
16. And upon all the ships
of Tarshish, and upon all
pleasant pictures.
17. **And the loftiness**
of man shall be bowed down,
and the haughtiness of
men shall be made low:
and the LORD alone shall
be exalted in that day.
18. **And the idols**
he shall utterly
abolish.
19. And they shall go into the holes of
the rocks, and into the caves of the
earth, for fear of the LORD, and for
the glory of his majesty, when he
ariseth to shake terribly the earth.
20. **In that day a man shall**
cast his idols of silver, and
his idols of gold, which they made
each one for himself to worship,
to the moles and
to the bats;
21. **To go into the clefts**
of the rocks, and into the
tops of the ragged rocks,
for fear of the LORD, and
for the glory of his majesty,
when he ariseth to shake
terribly the earth.
22. Cease ye
from man, whose breath
is in his nostrils:
for wherein is he to
be accounted of ?

CHAPTER 3

1. **For,** behold,
the Lord, the LORD of hosts,
doth take away from
Jerusalem and from
Judah the stay and the
staff, the whole stay of
bread, and the whole stay of
water.
2. **The mighty man,**
and the man of war,
the judge, and the
prophet, and the prudent,
and the ancient,
3. **The captain** of fifty,
and the honourable man,
and the counsellor,
and the cunning artificer,
and the eloquent orator.

■ 4. **And I will give children**
■ **to be their princes,**
and babes shall rule over them.
■ 5. **And the people shall**
■ **be oppressed,**
every one by another, and
■ **every one by his**
■ **neighbour: the child**
shall behave himself proudly
■ **against the ancient,**
■ **and the base against**
■ **the honourable.**
■ 6. **When a man shall**
■ **take hold of his brother**
of the house of his father,
■ **saying, Thou hast**
■ **clothing, be** thou
■ **our ruler, and let this**
■ **ruin be under thy hand:**
■ 7. **In that day shall**
■ **he swear,** saying,
■ **I will not be an healer; for**
■ **in my house is neither**
■ **bread nor clothing: make**
■ **me not a ruler** of the people.
■ 8. **For Jerusalem** is ruined,
■ **and Judah is fallen:**
■ **because their** tongue and their
■ **doings are against**
■ **the LORD,** to provoke the
eyes of his glory.
■ 9. **The shew of their**
■ **countenance doth**
witness against them; and they
■ **declare their sin** as Sodom,
■ **they hide it not.** Woe
unto their soul! for
■ **they have rewarded**
■ **evil unto themselves.**
■ 10. **Say** ye
■ **to the righteous,** that
■ **it shall be well with him:** for
they shall eat the fruit of their doings.
■ 11. **Woe unto the wicked!**
it shall be ill *with him:*
■ **for the reward of his hands**
■ **shall be given him.**
■ 12. **As for my people,**
■ **children are their**
■ **oppressors, and women**
■ **rule over them.** O my people,
they which lead thee cause *thee* to
err, and destroy the way of thy paths.

■ 13. **The LORD standeth up**
■ **to plead, and** standeth to
■ **judge the people.**
14. The LORD will enter nto judgment
with the ancients of his people, and
the princes thereof: for ye have
eaten up the vineyard; the spoil
of the poor *is* in your houses.
■ 15. **What mean ye that ye**
■ **beat my people to pieces,**
and grind the faces of the poor?
■ **saith the Lord** GOD of hosts.
16. Moreover the LORD saith,
■ **Because the daughters of**
■ **Zion are haughty, and walk**
■ **with stretched forth necks**
■ **and wanton eyes, walking**
■ **and mincing as they go,**
and making a tinkling with their feet:
■ 17. **Therefore the LORD**
■ **will smite** with a scab the
crown of the head of
■ **the daughters of Zion,**
■ **and** the LORD will
■ **discover their secret parts.**
18. **In that day the Lord**
■ **will take away** the bravery of
■ **their** tinkling
■ **ornaments** *about their feet,*
■ **and** *their* cauls, and *their* round
tires like the moon,
■ 19. **The chains, and** the
■ **bracelets,** and the mufflers,
20. The bonnets, and the ornaments
of the legs, and the headbands, and
the tablets, and the earrings,
21. The rings, and nose jewels,
■ 22. **The changeable suits**
■ **of apparel,** and the mantles, and
the wimples, and the crisping pins,
■ 23. **The glasses, and** the
■ **fine linen,** and the hoods,
and the vails.
24. **And** it shall come to pass, *that*
■ **instead of sweet smell**
■ **there shall be stink;**
and instead of a girdle a rent;
■ **and instead of** well set
■ **hair baldness;** and instead of a
stomacher a girding of sackcloth;
■ **and burning instead**
■ **of beauty.**
■ 25. **Thy men shall fall by**

■ the sword, and thy mighty
■ in the
■ war.
■ 26. And her gates
■ shall lament and
■ mourn; and she
■ being desolate shall
■ sit upon the ground.

CHAPTER 4

■ 1. And in that day seven
■ women shall take hold of
■ one man, saying, We will
eat our own bread, and wear
our own apparel: only
■ let us be called by thy
■ name, to take away
■ our reproach.
■ 2. In that day shall the
■ branch of the LORD be
■ beautiful and glorious, and
the fruit of the earth *shall be*
excellent and comely for them
that are escaped of Israel.
3. And it shall come to pass, *that*
■ he that is left in Zion,
■ and *he that* remaineth in
■ Jerusalem, shall be called
■ holy, *even* every one that is written
among the living in Jerusalem:
■ 4. When the Lord shall
■ have washed away the
■ filth of the daughters of
■ Zion, and shall have
purged the blood of
■ Jerusalem from the midst thereof
■ by the spirit of judgment,
■ and by the spirit of
■ burning.
■ 5. And the LORD will create
■ upon every dwelling place
■ of mount Zion, and upon
■ her assemblies, a cloud
■ and smoke by day, and
■ the shining of a flaming
■ fire by night: for
upon all the glory *shall be*
■ a defence.
■ 6. And there shall be
■ a tabernacle for a
shadow in the day time
■ from the heat, and for
■ a place of refuge,

■ and for a covert
■ from storm and from rain.

CHAPTER 5

■ 1. Now will I sing
to my wellbeloved
■ a song of my beloved
■ touching his vineyard.
My wellbeloved hath a vineyard
■ in a very fruitful hill:
■ 2. And he fenced it, and
gathered out the stones thereof,
■ and planted it with
■ the choicest vine, and
■ built a tower in the midst of it,
■ and also made
■ a winepress therein:
and he looked that it should
bring forth grapes,
■ and it brought forth
■ wild grapes.
■ 3. And now, O inhabitants
■ of Jerusalem, and men of
■ Judah, judge, I pray you,
■ betwixt me and
■ my vineyard.
■ 4. What could have been
■ done more to my vineyard,
■ that I have not done in it?
wherefore, when I looked that it
should bring forth grapes, brought
it forth wild grapes?
■ 5. And now go to;
■ I will tell you what I will
■ do to my vineyard: I
■ will take away the hedge
thereof, and it shall be eaten up;
■ and break down the
■ wall thereof,
■ and it shall
■ be trodden down:
6. And I will lay it waste: it shall
not be pruned, nor digged; but
■ there shall come up
■ briers and thorns: I will also
command the clouds that
they rain no rain upon it.
■ 7. For the vineyard
of the LORD of hosts
■ is the house of Israel,
■ and the men of
■ Judah his pleasant
■ plant: and he looked for

judgment, but behold oppression; for **righteousness, but behold a cry.**

8. Woe unto them that join house to house, *that* lay **field to field, till there be no place, that they may be placed alone in the** midst of the **earth!**

9. In mine ears *said* the LORD of hosts, Of a truth **many houses shall be desolate,** *even* great and fair, without inhabitant.

10. Yea, ten acres of vineyard shall yield one bath, and the seed of an homer shall yield an ephah.

11. **Woe unto them that** rise up early in the morning, that they may **follow strong drink;** that continue until night, **till wine inflame them!**

12. **And the harp,** and the viol, the tabret, **and pipe, and wine, are in their feasts: but they regard not the work of the LORD,** neither consider the operation of his hands.

13. **Therefore my people are gone into captivity, because they have no knowledge:** and their honourable men *are* famished, and their multitude dried up with thirst.

14. **Therefore hell hath enlarged herself,** and opened her mouth without measure: and their glory, **and their multitude,** and their pomp, and he that rejoiceth, **shall descend into it.**

15. **And the mean man** shall be brought down, **and the mighty man** shall be humbled, **and the** eyes of the **lofty shall be humbled:**

16. **But the LORD** of hosts **shall be exalted in judgment, and** God that is holy shall be **sanctified in righteousness.**

17. **Then shall the lambs feed** after their manner, **and the waste places of the fat ones shall strangers eat.**

18. **Woe unto them that draw iniquity with cords of vanity,** and sin as it were with a cart rope:

19. **That say, Let him** make speed, *and* **hasten his work, that we may see it: and let the counsel of the Holy One** of Israel **draw nigh** and come, **that we may know it!**

20. **Woe unto them that call evil good, and good evil;** that put darkness for light, **and** light for darkness; that put bitter for sweet, and sweet for bitter!

21. Woe unto **them that are wise in their own eyes, and** prudent in their own sight!

22. Woe unto **them that** *are* mighty to **drink wine, and** men of strength to mingle **strong drink:**

23. **Which justify the wicked for reward,** and take away the righteousness of the righteous from him!

24. **Therefore as the fire devoureth the stubble,** and the flame consumeth the chaff, **so their root shall be as rottenness, and their blossom shall go up as dust: because they** have cast away the law of the LORD of hosts, and **despised the word of the Holy One** of Israel.

25. **Therefore is the anger of the LORD kindled against his people, and he hath** stretched forth his hand against them, and hath

smitten them:
and the hills did tremble,
and their carcases
were torn in the midst of the
streets. For all this his anger
is not turned away, but his hand
is stretched out still.
26. And he will lift up
an ensign to the
nations from far,
and will hiss unto
them from the end of the earth:
and, behold,
they shall come with speed
swiftly:
27. None shall be weary
nor stumble among them;
none shall slumber
nor sleep; neither shall
the girdle of their loins
be loosed, nor the
latchet of their shoes be
broken:
28. Whose arrows are
sharp, and all their bows bent,
their horses' hoofs shall be
counted like flint,
and their wheels
like a whirlwind:
29. Their roaring shall be
like a lion, they shall roar like
young lions: yea, they shall roar, and
lay hold of the prey,
and shall carry it away safe,
and none shall deliver it.
30. And in that day they shall roar
against them like the roaring of the
sea: and if *one* look unto the land,
behold darkness and sorrow,
and the light is darkened in
the heavens thereof.

CHAPTER 6

1. In the year that
king Uzziah died I saw also
the LORD sitting upon a
throne, high and lifted
up, and his train filled
the temple.
2. Above it stood the
seraphims: each one
had six wings; with twain
he covered his face,
and with twain he covered
his feet, and with
twain he did fly.
3. And one cried unto
another, and said,
Holy, holy, holy,
is the LORD of hosts:
the whole
earth is full of his glory.
4. And the posts of the door moved
at the voice of him that cried, and
the house was filled with smoke.
5. Then said I, Woe is me! for
I am undone; because I am
a man of unclean lips, and I
dwell in the midst of a
people of unclean lips:
for mine eyes
have seen the King,
the LORD of hosts.
6. Then flew one of the
seraphims unto me,
having a live coal in his hand,
which he had taken with the tongs
from off the altar:
7. And he laid it upon my
mouth, and said, Lo,
this hath touched thy lips; and
thine iniquity is taken
away, and thy sin purged.
8. Also I heard the voice
of the Lord, saying,
Whom shall I send, and
who will go for us?
Then said I, Here
am I; send me.
9. And he said, Go,
and tell this people,
Hear ye indeed, but
understand not;
and see ye indeed, but
perceive not.
10. Make the heart of
this people fat, and make
their ears heavy, and
shut their eyes; lest
they see with their eyes,
and hear with their ears,
and understand
with their heart,
and convert,
and be healed.
11. Then said I, Lord,

how long? And he
answered, Until the
cities be wasted
without inhabitant,
and the houses without man,
and the land be utterly
desolate,
12. And the LORD have removed
men far away, and *there be* a great
forsaking in the midst of the land.
13. But yet in it shall be a
tenth, and it shall return,
and shall be eaten: as a teil tree, and
as an oak, whose substance *is* in
them, when they cast *their leaves*:
so the holy seed *shall be* the
substance thereof.

CHAPTER 7

1. And it came to pass
in the days of Ahaz the
son of Jotham, the son of Uzziah,
king of Judah, *that*
Rezin the king of Syria,
and Pekah the son of Remaliah,
king of Israel, went up
toward Jerusalem to
war against it, but
could not prevail against it.
2. And it was told the house of
David, saying, Syria is confederate
with Ephraim. And his heart was
moved, and the heart of his people,
as the trees of the wood are
moved with the wind.
3. Then said the LORD
unto Isaiah, Go forth now to
meet Ahaz, thou, and
Shear-jashub thy son, at the end
of the conduit of the upper pool in
the highway of the fuller's field;
4. And say unto him,
Take heed, and be quiet;
fear not, neither be fainthearted
for the two tails of these smoking
firebrands, for the fierce anger
of Rezin with Syria, and of the
son of Remaliah.
5. Because Syria, Ephraim,
and the son of Remaliah,
have taken evil counsel
against thee, saying,
6. Let us go up against Judah, and

vex it, and let us make a breach
therein for us, and set a king in the
midst of it, *even* the son of Tabeal:
7. Thus saith the Lord GOD,
It shall not stand, neither shall it
come to pass.
8. For the head of Syria *is*
Damascus, and the head of
Damascus *is* Rezin; and
within threescore and
five years shall Ephraim be
broken, that it be not a people.
9. And the head of
Ephraim *is* Samaria, and
the head of Samaria *is*
Remaliah's son.
If ye will not believe, surely ye shall
not be established.
10. Moreover the
LORD spake again
unto Ahaz, saying,
11. Ask thee a sign of the
LORD thy God; ask it either in the
depth, or in the height above.
12. But Ahaz said, I
will not ask, neither will I
tempt the LORD.
13. And he said, Hear ye now,
O house of David; *Is it* a
small thing for you to weary men,
but will ye weary my God also?
14. Therefore the Lord himself
shall give you a sign; Behold,
a virgin shall conceive, and
bear a son, and shall call
his name Immanuel.
15. Butter and honey shall he eat,
that he may know to refuse the evil,
and choose the good.
16. For
before the child shall
know to refuse the
evil, and choose the
good, the land
that thou abhorrest
shall be forsaken of
both her kings.
17. The LORD shall bring
upon thee, and upon thy people,
and upon thy father's house, days
that have not come, from the day that
Ephraim departed from Judah; *even*
the king of Assyria.

18. **And** it shall come to pass in that day, *that* **the LORD shall hiss for the fly** that *is* in the uttermost part of the rivers of Egypt, **and** for **the bee that is in** the land of **Assyria.** 19. **And they shall come, and** shall **rest** all of them **in the desolate valleys, and in the** holes of the **rocks, and upon** all **thorns, and** upon all **bushes.** 20. **In the same day shall the Lord shave** with a razor that is hired, *namely,* by **them** beyond the river, **by the king of Assyria, the head,** and **the hair of the feet: and** it shall also consume **the beard.** 21. **And** it shall come to pass **in that day,** *that* **a man shall nourish a young cow, and two sheep;** 22. **And** it shall come to pass, for the abundance of milk *that* they shall give he shall eat butter: for **butter and honey shall every one eat that is left in the land.** 23. **And** it shall come to pass in that day, *that* every place shall be, **where there were** a thousand **vines** at a thousand silverlings, it **shall** *even* **be** for **briers and thorns.** 24. **With arrows and with bows shall men come** thither; because all the land shall become briers and thorns. 25. **And** *on* all hills that shall be digged with the mattock, there shall not come thither the fear of briers and

thorns: but it shall be for the sending forth of oxen, and for the treading of lesser cattle.

CHAPTER 8

1. **Moreover the LORD said** unto me, **Take** thee **a** great **roll, and write** in it with a man's pen concerning Maher-shalalhash-baz. 2. **And I took** unto me faithful **witnesses** to record, Uriah the priest, and Zechariah the son of Jeberechiah. 3. **And I went unto the prophetess; and she conceived, and bare a son. Then said the LORD** to me, **Call his name Maher-shalalhash-baz.** 4. **For before the child shall** have knowledge to **cry,** My **father, and** my **mother, the riches of Damascus and** the spoil of **Samaria shall be taken away** before the king of Assyria. 5. The LORD spake also unto me again, saying, 6. **Forasmuch as this people refuseth the waters of Shiloah** that go softly, **and rejoice in** Rezin and **Remaliah's son;** 7. **Now therefore,** behold, **the Lord bringeth** up **upon them** the waters of the river, strong and many, *even* **the king of Assyria, and** all his glory: and he shall come up over all his channels, and go over all his banks: 8. **And he shall pass through Judah;** he shall overflow and go over, he shall reach *even* to the neck; **and the stretching out of his**

wings shall fill the breadth
of thy land, O Immanuel.
9. Associate yourselves,
O ye people, and ye shall be broken
in pieces; and give ear, all ye of far
countries: gird yourselves, and
ye shall be broken in pieces;
gird yourselves, and ye shall
be broken in pieces.
10. Take counsel together,
and it shall come to nought;
speak the word, and
it shall not stand:
for God is with us.
11. For the LORD spake
thus to me with a strong hand,
and instructed me
that I should not walk in the
way of this people, saying,
12. Say ye not, A confederacy, to all
them to whom this people shall say,
A confederacy; neither fear ye
their fear, nor be afraid.
13. Sanctify the
LORD of hosts himself;
and let him be your
fear, and *let* him *be* your
dread.
14. And he shall be for
a sanctuary; but for
a stone of stumbling and for
a rock of offence to
both the houses of
Israel, for a gin
and for a snare to the inhabitants of
Jerusalem.
15. And many among them
shall stumble, and fall,
and be broken, and be snared,
and be taken.
16. Bind up
the testimony, seal the law
among my disciples.
17. And I will
wait upon the LORD, that
hideth his face from the house of
Jacob, and I will look for him.
18. Behold, I and the
children whom the LORD
hath given me are for
signs and for
wonders in Israel from
the LORD of hosts, which

dwelleth in mount Zion.
19. And when they
shall say unto you,
Seek unto
them that have
familiar spirits,
and unto
wizards that peep, and
that mutter:
should not a
people seek unto their
God? for the living to
the dead?
20. To the law and to the testimony:
if they speak not according
to this word, *it is* because
there is no light in them.
21. And they shall pass through
it, hardly bestead and hungry:
and it shall come to pass, that
when they shall be hungry,
they shall fret themselves, and
curse their king and their
God, and look upward.
22. And they shall look
unto the earth; and
behold trouble and
darkness, dimness of anguish;
and *they shall be* driven to
darkness.

CHAPTER 9

1. Nevertheless the
dimness *shall* not *be* such as *was*
in her vexation, when at the first
he lightly afflicted the land
of Zebulun and the land of
Naphtali, and afterward
did more grievously
afflict her *by* the way of the sea,
beyond Jordan,
in Galilee of the nations.
2. The people
that walked in darkness
have seen a great light:
they that dwell in the land of the
shadow of death, upon them
hath the light shined.
3. Thou hast multiplied the
nation, and not increased the joy:
they joy before thee according to the
joy in harvest, *and as men* rejoice
when they divide the spoil.

4. For thou hast **broken the yoke of his burden,** and the staff of his shoulder, the rod of his oppressor, as in the day of Midian.

5. **For every battle** of the warrior **is with confused noise,** and garments rolled in blood; but *this* shall be with burning *and* fuel of fire.

6. **For unto us a child is born, unto us a son is given: and the government shall be upon his shoulder: and his name shall be** called **Wonderful, Counsellor, The mighty God,** The everlasting Father, **The Prince of Peace.**

7. **Of the increase of his government and peace there shall be no end, upon the throne of David,** and upon his kingdom, to order it, and **to establish it with judgment and** with **justice** from henceforth even **for ever. The** zeal of the **LORD** of hosts **will perform this.**

8. **The Lord sent a word into Jacob, and** it hath lighted upon **Israel**.

9. **And all the people shall know**, *even* Ephraim and the inhabitant of Samaria, **that say in** the **pride** and stoutness of heart,

10. **The bricks are fallen** down, **but we will build with hewn stones:** the sycomores are cut down, but we will change *them into* cedars.

11. **Therefore the LORD shall** set up the adversaries of Rezin against him, and **join his enemies together;**

12. The Syrians before, and the Philistines behind; **and they shall devour Israel** with open mouth. **For all this his anger is not turned away,** but h is hand *is* stretched out still.

13. **For the people turneth not unto** him that smiteth them, neither do they seek **the LORD** of hosts.

14. **Therefore the LORD will cut off from Israel head and tail,** branch and rush, in one day.

15. **The ancient** and honourable, he **is the head; and the prophet that teacheth lies, he is the tail.**

16. **For the leaders** of this people **cause them to err;** and *they that are* led of them *are* destroyed.

17. Therefore the LORD shall have no joy in their young men, neither shall have mercy on their fatherless and widows: for **every one is an hypocrite and an evildoer,** and every mouth speaketh folly. For all this his anger is not turned away, but his hand *is* stretched out still.

18. **For wickedness burneth as the fire:** it shall devour the briers and thorns, and shall kindle in the thickets of the forest, and they shall mount up *like* the lifting up of smoke.

19. Through the wrath of the LORD of hosts is the land darkened, **and the people shall be as the fuel of the fire:** no man shall spare his brother.

20. **And he shall** snatch on the right hand, and **be hungry; and he shall eat** on the left hand, **and** they shall **not be satisfied: they shall eat** every man **the flesh of his own arm:**

21. **Manasseh, Ephraim;** and Ephraim, Manasseh: *and* they together **shall be against Judah.**

■ ■ ■ For all this his anger is not turned away, but his hand is stretched out still.

CHAPTER 10

■ 1. **Woe unto them** that decree unrighteous decrees, and ■ **that write grievousness** ■ **which they** have ■ **prescribed;** ■ 2. **To turn aside the** ■ **needy** from judgment, and ■ **to take away** the right ■ **from the poor** of my people, ■ **that widows may be their** ■ **prey, and that they may rob** ■ **the fatherless!** ■ 3. **And what will ye do in** ■ **the day of visitation,** and in the desolation *which* shall come from far? ■ **to whom will ye flee** ■ **for help?** and where will ye leave your glory? ■ 4. **Without me they shall** ■ **bow down under the** ■ **prisoners, and** they shall ■ **fall under the slain.** For all this his anger *is* not turned away, but his hand is stretched out still. ■ 5. **O Assyrian, the** ■ **rod of mine anger,** and the staff in their hand is mine indignation. ■ 6. **I will send him against** ■ **an hypocritical nation,** and against the people of my wrath will I give him a charge, ■ **to take** the ■ **spoil, and** to take the ■ **prey, and to tread** ■ **them down** like the mire of the streets. ■ 7. **Howbeit** he meaneth not so, neither doth his heart think so; but ■ **it is in his heart to** ■ **destroy** and cut off ■ **nations** not a few. ■ 8. **For he saith,** *Are* not my princes altogether kings? 9. *Is* not Calno as Carchemish? *is* not Hamath as Arpad? *is* not Samaria as Damascus? 10. As my hand hath found the

kingdoms of the idols, and whose graven images did excel them of Jerusalem and of Samaria;

■ ■ ■ 11. **Shall I not, as I have done unto Samaria and her idols, so do to Jerusalem** and her idols? ■ 12. **Wherefore** it shall come to pass, *that* ■ **when the Lord hath** ■ **performed his** whole ■ **work upon** mount ■ **Zion and** on ■ **Jerusalem, I will** ■ **punish** the fruit of ■ **the stout heart** ■ **of the king of Assyria,** and the glory of his high looks. ■ 13. **For he saith,** ■ **By** the strength of ■ **my hand I have done it,** and by my wisdom; for I am prudent: and I have removed the bounds of the people, and have robbed their treasures, and I have put down the inhabitants like a valiant *man:* 14. And my hand hath found as a nest the riches of the people: and as one gathereth eggs *that are* left, have I gathered all the earth; and there was none that moved the wing, or opened the mouth, or peeped. ■ 15. **Shall the axe boast itself** ■ **against him that heweth** ■ **therewith?** *or* shall the saw magnify itself against him that shaketh it? as if the rod should shake *itself* against them that lift it up, *or* as if the staff should lift up *itself, as if it were* no wood. ■ 16. **Therefore shall** ■ **the Lord,** the Lord of hosts, ■ **send** among his fat ones ■ **leanness;** and under his glory he shall kindle a burning like the burning of a fire. ■ 17. **And the light of Israel** ■ **shall be for a fire,** and his Holy One for a flame: ■ **and it shall** burn and ■ **devour his thorns and** his ■ **briers** in one day;

18. **And shall consume**
the glory of his forest, and
of his fruitful field,
both soul and body:
and they shall be as when
a standard-bearer fainteth.
19. And the rest of the trees
of his forest shall be few, that
a child may write them.
20. **And** it shall come to pass
in that day, *that*
the remnant of Israel, and
such as are escaped of the house of
Jacob, shall no more again
stay upon him that smote them;
but shall stay upon the LORD,
the Holy One of Israel, in truth.
21. The remnant
shall return, *even* the
remnant of Jacob,
unto the mighty God.
22. **For though** thy people
Israel be as the sand of the
sea, yet a remnant of them
shall return:
the consumption decreed shall
overflow with righteousness.
23. For the Lord GOD of hosts
shall make a consumption,
even determined, in the
midst of all the land.
24. **Therefore thus saith**
the Lord GOD of hosts, O my
people that dwellest in Zion,
be not afraid of the
Assyrian: he shall smite
thee with a rod, and shall
lift up
his staff against thee,
after the manner of Egypt.
25. **For yet**
a very little
while, and the indignation
shall cease, and mine anger
in their destruction.
26. **And the LORD** of hosts
shall stir up a scourge for him
according to the slaughter
of Midian at the rock of Oreb:
and as his rod was upon
the sea, so shall he lift it up
after the manner of Egypt.
27. **And** it shall come to pass

in that day, *that*
his burden shall be taken
away from off thy shoulder, and
his yoke from off thy neck, and
the yoke shall be destroyed
because of the anointing.
28. He is come to Aiath, he is passed
to Migron; at Michmash he hath
laid up his carriages:
29. They are gone over the passage:
they have taken up their lodging
at Geba; Ramah
is afraid; Gibeah of Saul is fled.
30. Lift up thy voice, O daughter
of Gallim: cause it to be heard
unto Laish, O poor Anathoth.
31. Madmenah is removed;
the inhabitants of Gebim
gather themselves to flee.
32. As yet shall he remain at Nob
that day: he shall shake his hand
against the mount of the daughter
of Zion, the hill of Jerusalem.
33. **Behold, the Lord,**
the LORD of hosts,
shall lop the bough with
terror: and the high ones of
stature *shall be* hewn down, and
the haughty shall
be humbled.
34. And he shall cut down the
thickets of the forest with iron,
and Lebanon shall fall
by a mighty one.

CHAPTER 11

1. **And** there shall come forth a rod
out of the stem of
Jesse, and
a Branch shall grow
out of his roots:
2. **And the spirit of the LORD**
shall rest upon him, the spirit of
wisdom and understanding, the spirit
of counsel and might, the
spirit of knowledge and of the
fear of the LORD;
3. And shall make him of
quick understanding in
the fear of the LORD:
and he shall not judge
after the sight of his eyes,
neither reprove after

972

the hearing of his ears:

4. **But with righteousness shall he judge** the poor, **and reprove** with equity for the meek of the earth: and he shall smite **the earth:** with the rod of his mouth, and with the breath of his lips shall he slay the wicked.

5. **And righteousness shall be the girdle of his loins,** and faithfulness the girdle of his reins.

6. **The wolf** also **shall dwell with the lamb, and the leopard** shall lie down **with the kid;** and the calf and the young lion and the fatling together; **and a little child shall lead them.**

7. **And the cow and the bear shall feed;** their young ones shall lie down together: **and the lion shall eat straw** like the ox.

8. **And the sucking child shall play on the hole of the asp, and** the weaned child shall put his hand on the cockatrice' den.

9. **They shall not** hurt nor **destroy in all my holy mountain: for the earth shall be full of the knowledge of the LORD,** as the waters cover the sea.

10. **And** in that day there shall be **a root of Jesse,** which **shall stand for an ensign** of the people; **to it shall the Gentiles seek: and his rest shall be glorious.**

11. **And** it shall come to pass **in that day,** *that* **the Lord shall** set his hand again the second time to **recover the remnant of his people,** which shall be left, from Assyria, and from Egypt, and from Pathros, and from Cush, and from Elam, and from Shinar, and from Hamath, and from the islands of the sea.

12. **And he shall set up an ensign for the nations,** **and shall assemble** the outcasts of **Israel, and** gather together the dispersed of **Judah from the four corners of the earth.**

13. The envy also of Ephraim shall depart, and the adversaries of Judah shall be cut off: **Ephraim** shall not envy Judah, **and Judah** shall not vex Ephraim.

14. But they **shall fly upon the shoulders of the Philistines** toward the west; **they shall spoil them of the east together:** they shall lay their hand upon **Edom** and **Moab; and** the children of **Ammon shall obey them.**

15. **And the LORD shall** utterly **destroy the** tongue of the **Egyptian sea; and** with his mighty wind shall he shake his hand over the river, and shall smite it in **the seven streams,** and make *men* go over dryshod.

16. **And there shall be an highway for** the remnant of **his people,** which shall be left, from Assyria; like **as it was to Israel in the day** that **he came** up **out of** the land of **Egypt.**

CHAPTER 12

1. **And in that day thou shalt say, O LORD, I will praise thee:** though thou wast angry with me, **thine anger is turned away,** and thou comfortedst me.

2. **Behold, God is my salvation;** I will trust, and not be afraid: for **the LORD JEHOVAH is my strength** and *my* song; he also is become my salvation.

3. **Therefore with joy** shall ye draw water out of the

973

wells of salvation.

4. And in that day **shall ye** say, Praise the LORD, **call upon his name,** declare his doings among the people, make mention that his name is exalted.

5. **Sing unto the LORD; for he hath done excellent things:** this *is* known in all the earth.

6. **Cry out and shout,** thou inhabitant of Zion: **for great is the Holy One of Israel** in the midst of thee.

CHAPTER 13

1. **The burden of Babylon, which Isaiah** the son of Amoz **did see.**

2. **Lift ye up a banner** upon the high mountain, exalt the voice unto them, shake the hand, that they may go into the gates of the nobles.

3. **I have commanded** my sanctified ones, I have also called **my mighty ones for** mine anger, *even* them that rejoice in my highness.

4. The noise of a multitude in the mountains, like as of a great people; a tumultuous noise of the kingdoms of nations gathered together: the LORD of hosts mustereth the host of **the battle.**

5. **They come from a far country,** from the end of heaven, **even the LORD, and the weapons of his indignation, to destroy the whole land.**

6. **Howl ye; for the day of the LORD is at hand;** it shall come as a destruction from the Almighty.

7. Therefore shall all hands be faint, and every man's heart shall melt:

8. And they shall be afraid: pangs and sorrows shall take hold of them; they shall be in pain as a woman that travaileth: they shall be amazed one at another; their faces *shall be as* flames.

9. **Behold, the day of the LORD cometh,** cruel **both with wrath and** fierce **anger, to lay the land desolate: and** he shall **destroy the sinners** thereof out of it.

10. **For the stars** of heaven and the constellations thereof **shall not give their light: the sun shall be darkened** in his going forth, **and the moon shall not** cause her light to **shine.**

11. **And I will punish** the world for *their* evil, and **the wicked** for their iniquity; **and I will cause the arrogancy of the proud to cease,** and will lay low the haughtiness of the terrible.

12. **I will make a man more precious than** fine **gold;** even a man than the golden wedge of Ophir.

13. **Therefore I will shake the heavens, and the earth shall remove out of her place, in the wrath of the LORD** of hosts, and in the day of his fierce anger.

14. **And it shall be as the chased roe,** and as a sheep that no man taketh up: they shall every man turn to his own people, and flee every one into his own land.

15. **Every one that is found shall** be thrust through; and every one that is joined *unto them* shall **fall by the sword.**

16. **Their children also shall be dashed to pieces** before their eyes; their houses shall be spoiled, **and their wives ravished.**

17. **Behold, I will stir up the Medes against them,** which shall not regard silver; and *as for* gold, they shall not delight in it.

18. *Their* bows also shall dash the young men to pieces; and they shall have no pity on the fruit of the womb; their eyes shall not spare children.

19. **And Babylon,** the glory of kingdoms, the beauty of the Chaldees' excellency,

shall be as when God overthrew **Sodom and Gomorrah.**
20. **It shall never be inhabited,** neither shall it be dwelt in from generation to generation: neither shall the Arabian pitch tent there; neither shall the shepherds make their fold there.
21. **But wild beasts of the desert shall lie there;** and their houses shall be full of doleful creatures; and owls shall dwell there, and satyrs shall dance there.
22. And the wild beasts of the islands shall cry in their desolate houses, and dragons in *their* pleasant palaces: and **her time is near** to come, **and** her days **shall not be prolonged.**

CHAPTER 14

1. **For the LORD will have mercy on Jacob, and** will yet choose **Israel, and set them in their own land:** and the strangers shall be joined with them, and they shall cleave to the house of Jacob.
2. **And** the people shall take them, and bring them to their place: and the house of **Israel** shall possess them in the land of the LORD for servants and handmaids: and they **shall take** them **captives, whose captives they were; and they shall rule over their oppressors.**
3. **And** it shall come to pass **in the day** that **the LORD shall give thee rest** from thy sorrow, and from thy fear, and from the hard bondage wherein thou wast made to serve,
4. That thou shalt **take up this proverb against** the king of **Babylon, and say, How hath the oppressor ceased!** the golden city ceased!

5. **The LORD** hath broken the staff of the wicked, *and* the sceptre of the rulers.
6. He who **smote the people** in wrath with a continual stroke, he that ruled the nations **in anger,** is persecuted, *and* none hindereth.
7. **The whole earth is at rest, and is** quiet: they break forth into **singing.**
8. Yea, the fir trees rejoice at thee, *and* the cedars of Lebanon, *saying,* Since thou art laid down, no feller is come up against us.
9. **Hell** from beneath **is moved** for thee **to meet thee at thy coming:** it stirreth up the dead for thee, **even** all **the chief ones of the earth;** it hath raised up from their thrones all the kings of the nations.
10. **All they shall speak** and say unto thee, **Art thou** also **become weak** as we? art thou become **like** unto **us?**
11. **Thy pomp is brought down** to the grave, *and* the noise of thy viols: the worm is spread under thee, and the worms cover thee.
12. **How art thou fallen from heaven, O Lucifer,** son of the morning! *how* art thou cut down to the ground, which didst weaken the nations!
13. **For thou hast said** in thine heart, **I will** ascend into heaven, I will **exalt my throne above** the stars of **God:** I will sit also upon the mount of the congregation, in the sides of the north:
14. I will ascend above the heights of the clouds; **I will be like the most High.**
15. **Yet thou shalt be brought down to hell,**

to the sides of the pit.

16. **They that see thee shall narrowly look** upon thee, **and consider thee, saying, Is this the man that made the earth to tremble,** that did shake kingdoms;

17. *That* made the world as a wilderness, and destroyed the cities thereof; *that* opened not the house of his prisoners?

18. **All the kings** of the nations, *even* all of them, **lie in** glory, every one in **his own house.**

19. **But thou art cast out of thy grave like an abominable branch,** *and as* the raiment of those that are slain, thrust through with a sword, that go down to the stones of the pit; *as a* carcase trodden under feet.

20. **Thou shalt not be joined with them in burial, because** thou hast destroyed thy land, *and* slain thy people: **the seed of evildoers shall never be renowned.**

21. Prepare slaughter for his children for the iniquity of their fathers; that they do not rise, nor possess the land, nor fill the face of the world with cities.

22. **For I will rise up against** them, saith the LORD of hosts, and cut off from **Babylon** the name, and remnant, and son, and nephew, **saith the LORD.**

23. I will also make it a possession for the bittern, and pools of water: and I will sweep it with the besom of destruction, saith the LORD of hosts.

24. **The LORD** of hosts **hath sworn, saying,** Surely as I have thought, *so* shall it come to pass; and as **I have purposed,** so shall it stand:

25. **That I will break the Assyrian in my land,** and upon my mountains tread him under foot:

then shall his yoke depart from off them, and his burden depart from off their shoulders.

26. This *is* the purpose that is purposed upon the whole earth: and this *is* the hand that is stretched out upon all the nations.

27. For the LORD of hosts hath purposed, and who shall disannul *it*? and his hand *is* stretched out, and who shall turn it back?

28. In the year that king Ahaz died was this burden.

29. **Rejoice not** thou, whole **Palestina, because the rod of him that smote thee is broken: for out of the serpent's root shall come** forth a cockatrice, and his fruit *shall be* **a fiery flying serpent.**

30. And the firstborn of the poor shall feed, and the needy shall lie down in safety: **and I will kill thy root with famine,** and he shall slay thy remnant.

31. **Howl,** O gate; cry, O city; thou, whole **Palestina,** *art* dissolved: **for there shall come from the north a smoke,** and none *shall be* alone in his appointed times.

32. **What shall one** then **answer the messengers of the nation? That the LORD hath founded Zion, and** the poor of **his people shall trust in it.**

CHAPTER 15

1. **The burden of Moab. Because in the night** Ar of **Moab is laid waste,** *and* brought to silence; because in the night Kir of Moab is laid waste, *and* brought to silence;

2. He is gone up to Bajith, and to Dibon, the high places, to weep: Moab shall howl over Nebo, and over Medeba: on all their heads *shall be*

baldness, *and* every beard cut off.

3. **In their streets they shall gird themselves with sackcloth:** on the tops of their houses, and in their streets, **every one** shall howl, **weeping** abundantly.

4. And Heshbon shall cry, and Elealeh: their voice shall be heard *even* unto Jahaz: therefore **the** armed **soldiers of Moab shall cry out;** his life shall be grievous unto him.

5. My heart shall cry out for Moab; his fugitives *shall flee* unto Zoar, an heifer of three years old: for by the mounting up of Luhith with weeping shall they go it up; for in the way of Horonaim **they shall raise up a cry of destruction.**

6. **For the waters of Nimrim shall be desolate:** for the hay is withered away, the grass faileth, there is no green thing.

7. **Therefore the abundance they have gotten,** and that which they have laid up, **shall they carry away** to the brook of the willows.

8. **For the cry is gone round** about **the borders of Moab;** the howling thereof unto Eglaim, and the howling thereof unto Beerelim.

9. **For the waters of Dimon shall be full of blood:** for **I will bring more** upon Dimon, **lions upon him that escapeth** of Moab, and upon the remnant of the land.

CHAPTER 16

1. **Send ye the lamb to the ruler** of the land from Sela to the wilderness, unto the mount of the daughter **of Zion.**

2. **For** it shall be, *that,* **as a wandering bird** cast out of the nest,

so the daughters of Moab shall be at the fords of Arnon.

3. **Take counsel,** execute judgment; make thy shadow as the night in the midst of the noonday; hide the outcasts; bewray not him that wandereth.

4. **Let mine outcasts dwell with thee, Moab; be** thou **a covert to them** from the face of the spoiler: for the extortioner is at an end, the spoiler ceaseth, the oppressors are consumed out of the land.

5. **And in mercy shall the throne be established: and he shall sit upon it in truth** in the tabernacle of David, **judging,** and seeking judgment, **and hasting righteousness.**

6. We have heard of the pride of **Moab;** *he* **is very proud:** *even* of his haughtiness, and his pride, and his wrath: *but* his lies *shall* not *be* so.

7. **Therefore shall Moab howl for** Moab, every one shall howl: for the foundations of Kir-hareseth shall ye mourn; surely **they are stricken.**

8. For the fields of Heshbon languish, *and* the vine of Sibmah: the lords of the heathen have broken down the principal plants thereof, they are come *even* unto Jazer, they wandered *through* the wilderness: her branches are stretched out, they are gone over the sea.

9. **Therefore** I will bewail **with the weeping of Jazer** the vine of Sibmah: **I will water thee with my tears,** O Heshbon, and Elealeh: for the shouting **for thy** summer fruits and for thy **harvest is fallen.**

10. **And gladness is taken** away, and joy **out of the plentiful field;** and in the vineyards there shall

be no singing, neither shall there be shouting: the treaders shall tread out no wine in *their* presses; ■ **I have made their** vintage ■ **shouting to cease.**

11. Wherefore my bowels shall sound like an harp for Moab, and mine inward parts for Kir-haresh.

■ 12. **And** it shall come to pass, ■ **when** it is seen that ■ **Moab is weary on** the high place, that ■ **he shall come to his** ■ **sanctuary to pray; but** ■ **he shall not prevail.**

13. This *is* the word that the LORD hath spoken concerning Moab since that time.

14. But now the LORD hath spoken, saying, ■ **Within three years, as** the years of an hireling, and ■ **the glory of Moab** ■ **shall be** contemned, with all that great multitude; and the remnant *shall be* very ■ **small and feeble.**

CHAPTER 17

■ 1. **The burden of Damascus.** ■ **Behold, Damascus is taken** away from *being* a city, and it ■ **shall be a ruinous heap.** ■ 2. **The cities of Aroer are** ■ **forsaken:** they shall be for flocks, which shall lie down, and none shall make *them* afraid. ■ 3. **The fortress also shall** ■ **cease from Ephraim,** ■ **and the kingdom from** Damascus, and the remnant of ■ **Syria:** they ■ **shall be as the** ■ **glory** of the children ■ **of Israel, saith the** ■ **LORD** of hosts. ■ 4. **And** in that day it shall come to pass, *that* ■ **the glory of Jacob shall be** ■ **made thin, and** the fatness of ■ **his flesh** shall wax ■ **lean.** ■ 5. **And** it shall be as

■ **when the harvestman** ■ **gathereth the corn,** and reapeth the ears with his arm; ■ **and it shall be as** he that gathereth ears ■ **in the valley of Rephaim.** ■ 6. **Yet gleaning grapes** ■ **shall be left** in it, as the shaking of an olive tree, two *or* three berries in the top of the uppermost bough, four *or* five in the outmost fruitful branches thereof, saith the LORD God of Israel. ■ 7. **At that day shall a** ■ **man** look to his Maker, and his eyes shall ■ **have respect** to the Holy One of Israel. ■ 8. **And he shall not look to** the altars, the work of his hands, neither shall respect *that* which his fingers have made, either the groves, or the ■ **images.** ■ 9. **In that day shall** ■ **his strong cities be** as a ■ **forsaken** bough, and an uppermost branch, which they left because of the children of Israel: and there shall be desolation. ■ 10. **Because thou hast** ■ **forgotten the God of** ■ **thy salvation,** and hast not been mindful of the rock of thy strength, therefore shalt thou plant pleasant plants, and shalt set it with strange slips: ■ 11. **In the day shalt** ■ **thou** make thy ■ **plant** to grow, and in the morning shalt thou make thy seed to flourish: ■ **but the harvest shall** ■ **be a heap** in the day of grief and of desperate sorrow. ■ 12. **Woe to the** multitude of many ■ **people,** *which* make a noise like the noise of the seas; ■ **and** to the rushing of ■ **nations,** *that* make a rushing like the rushing of mighty waters!

■ 13. **The nations shall rush**
like the rushing of many waters:

■ **but God shall rebuke them**,
■ **and they** shall flee far off, and
■ **shall be chased as** the
■ **chaff** of the mountains
■ **before the wind,** and like a
rolling thing before the whirlwind.
14. And behold at eveningtide
trouble; *and* before the
morning he *is* not.

■ **This is the portion of**
■ **them that spoil** us,
■ **and** the lot of them that
■ **rob us**.

CHAPTER 18

■ 1. **Woe to the land**
■ **shadowing with wings,** which
is beyond the rivers of Ethiopia:

■ 2. **That sendeth**
■ **ambassadors by the**
■ **sea,** even in vessels of
bulrushes upon the waters,

■ **saying, Go,** ye swift messengers,
■ **to a nation scattered** and
peeled, to a people terrible from their
beginning hitherto; a nation meted out

■ **and trodden down,**
■ **whose land the rivers**
■ **have spoiled!**
■ 3. **All ye** inhabitants
of the world, and

■ **dwellers on the**
■ **earth, see** ye,
■ **when he lifteth up an**
■ **ensign** on the mountains;
■ **and** when he
■ **bloweth a trumpet,** hear ye.
■ 4. **For so the LORD**
■ **said** unto me,
■ **I will take my rest,**
and I will consider in my dwelling
place like a clear heat upon
herbs, *and* like a cloud of dew
in the heat of harvest.

■ 5. **For afore the harvest,**
■ **when the bud is perfect**,
and the sour grape is
ripening in the flower,

■ **he shall** both
■ **cut off the sprigs** with

pruning hooks, and
take away *and* cut
down the branches.

■ 6. **They shall be left** together
■ **unto the fowls** of the mountains,
■ **and** to the
■ **beasts** of the earth: and
the fowls shall summer upon them,
and all the beasts of the earth
shall winter upon them.

■ 7. **In that time shall the**
■ **present be brought**
■ **unto the LORD** of hosts
■ **of a people scattered**
and peeled, and from a people
terrible from their beginning
hitherto; a nation meted out
and trodden under foot, whose
land the rivers have spoiled,

■ **to the place of the** name of the
■ **LORD of hosts, the**
■ **mount Zion.**

CHAPTER 19

■ 1. **The burden of Egypt.**
Behold, the LORD rideth upon a swift
cloud, and shall come into Egypt: and

■ **the idols of Egypt shall be**
■ **moved at his presence,**
■ **and the heart of Egypt**
■ **shall melt** in the midst of it.
■ 2. **And** I will set
■ **the Egyptians** against
the Egyptians: and they

■ **shall fight every one**
■ **against his brother,**
■ **and** every one against
■ **his neighbour;** city against
city, *and* kingdom against kingdom.

■ 3. **And the spirit of Egypt**
■ **shall fail** in the midst thereof;
■ **and I will destroy**
■ **the counsel** thereof:
■ **and they shall seek** to the
■ **idols,** and to the
■ **charmers,** and to
■ **them that have familiar**
■ **spirits, and** to
■ **the wizards.**
■ 4. **And the Egyptians**
■ **will I give** over
■ **into the hand of a**
■ **cruel** lord;

and a
fierce king shall rule
over them, saith the Lord,
the LORD of hosts.
5. **And the waters shall** fail
from the sea, and the river shall
be wasted and dried up.
6. And they shall turn the rivers far
away; *and* the brooks of defence
shall be emptied and dried up:
the reeds and flags shall wither.
7. The paper reeds by the brooks,
by the mouth of the brooks,
and every thing sown
by the brooks,
shall wither, be driven
away, and be no *more.*
8. **The fishers also** shall
mourn, and all they that cast angle
into the brooks shall lament, and they
that spread nets upon the waters
shall languish.
9. **Moreover they that**
work in fine flax, and
they that weave networks,
shall be confounded.
10. And they shall be broken in the
purposes thereof, all that make
sluices *and* ponds for fish.
11. **Surely the princes**
of Zoan are fools, the
counsel of the wise
counsellors of Pharaoh
is become brutish: how say ye
unto Pharaoh, I *am* the son of the
wise, the son of ancient kings?
12. **Where are** they? where *are*
thy wise men? and
let them tell thee now, and
let them know what
the LORD of hosts
hath purposed upon Egypt.
13. **The princes** of Zoan are
become fools, the princes of Noph
are deceived; they
have also
seduced Egypt, *even they that*
are the stay of the tribes thereof.
14. **The LORD hath mingled**
a perverse spirit in
the midst thereof: and
they have caused Egypt
to err in every work thereof,

as a drunken man
staggereth in his vomit.
15. **Neither shall there be**
any work for Egypt, which the
head or tail, branch or rush, may do.
16. In that day shall
Egypt be like unto women: and *it*
shall be afraid and fear
because of the shaking
of the hand of the LORD
of hosts, which he shaketh over it.
17. **And** the land of
Judah shall be a terror
unto Egypt, every one that
maketh mention thereof shall
be afraid in himself,
because of the counsel
of the LORD of hosts,
which he hath
determined against it.
18. In that day shall five cities in the
land of Egypt speak the language
of Canaan, and swear to the LORD
of hosts; one shall be called, The
city of destruction.
19. **In that day shall there**
be an altar to the LORD
in the midst of the land of
Egypt, and a pillar
at the border thereof
to the LORD.
20. **And it shall be**
for a sign and for a witness
unto the LORD of hosts
in the land of Egypt:
for they shall cry unto
the LORD because of
the oppressors, and
he shall send them
a saviour, and
a great one, and he shall
deliver them.
21. And the LORD shall
be known to Egypt,
and the Egyptians shall
know the LORD in that day,
and shall do sacrifice
and oblation; yea,
they shall vow a vow unto
the LORD, and perform *it.*
22. **And the LORD shall**
smite Egypt: he shall
smite and heal *it:*

and they shall return *even*
to the LORD, and he shall
be intreated of them, and
shall heal them.
23. In that day shall there be a
highway out of Egypt to Assyria, and
the Assyrian shall
come into Egypt,
and the Egyptian into Assyria,
and the Egyptians shall
serve with the Assyrians.
24. In that day shall
Israel be the third
with Egypt and with
Assyria, *even* a blessing in
the midst of the land:
25. Whom the LORD of hosts
shall bless, saying,
Blessed be
Egypt my people, and
Assyria
the work of my hands,
and Israel mine inheritance.

CHAPTER 20

1. In the year that Tartan
came unto Ashdod
(when Sargon the king of Assyria sent
him), and fought against Ashdod,
and took it;
2. At the same time
spake the LORD by
Isaiah the son of Amoz,
saying, Go and loose
the sackcloth from off
thy loins, and put off
thy shoe from thy foot.
And he did so, walking
naked and barefoot.
3. And the LORD
said, Like as my servant
Isaiah hath
walked naked and
barefoot three years
for a sign and wonder
upon Egypt and upon
Ethiopia;
4. So shall the king of
Assyria lead away the
Egyptians prisoners,
and the Ethiopians captives,
young and old,
naked and barefoot,

even with *their* buttocks uncovered,
to the shame of Egypt.
5. And they shall be
afraid and ashamed of Ethiopia their
expectation, and of Egypt their glory.
6. And the inhabitant of this isle shall
say in that day, Behold, such *is*
our expectation, whither we flee for
help to be delivered from the king of
Assyria: and how shall we escape?

CHAPTER 21

1. The burden of the
desert of the sea.
As whirlwinds in the
south pass through; *so* it
cometh from the desert,
from a terrible land.
2. A grievous vision
is declared unto
me; the treacherous
dealer dealeth treacherously,
and the spoiler spoileth.
Go up, O Elam: besiege,
O Media; all the sighing
thereof have I made
to cease.
3. Therefore are my loins
filled with pain: pangs have
taken hold upon me, as the pangs of
a woman that travaileth: I was bowed
down at the hearing *of it*; I was
dismayed at the seeing *of it.*
4. My heart panted,
fearfulness affrighted me: the night of
my pleasure hath he
turned into fear unto me.
5. Prepare the table, watch in the
watchtower, eat, drink: arise, ye
princes, *and* anoint the shield.
6. For thus hath
the LORD said unto me,
Go, set a watchman,
let him declare
what he seeth.
7. And he saw a
chariot with a couple of
horsemen, a chariot
of asses, and a
chariot of camels;
and he hearkened diligently
with much heed:
8. And he cried, A lion: My

lord, I stand continually upon the watchtower in the daytime, and I am set in my ward whole nights:

9. **And, behold, here cometh a chariot of men**, *with* a couple of horsemen. **And he** answered and **said, Babylon is fallen,** is fallen; **and all the graven images** of her gods **he hath broken unto the ground.**

10. O my threshing, and the corn of my floor: that which I have heard of the LORD of hosts, the God of Israel, have I declared unto you.

11. **The burden of Dumah. He calleth** to me **out of Seir, Watchman, what of the night?** Watchman, what of the night?

12. **The watchman said, The morning cometh,** and also the night: if ye will enquire, enquire ye: return, come.

13. **The burden upon Arabia. In the forest in Arabia shall ye lodge, O ye travelling companies of Dedanim.**

14. The inhabitants of the land of **Tema brought water to him** that was thirsty, **they prevented with their bread him that fled.**

15. **For they fled** from the swords, from the drawn sword, and from the bent bow, and **from the** grievousness of **war.**

16. **For** thus hath **the LORD said** unto me, **Within a year,** according to the years of an hireling, and all **the glory of Kedar shall fail:**

17. **And the** residue of the number of archers, the **mighty men** of the children **of Kedar, shall be diminished:** for the LORD God of Israel hath spoken *it*.

CHAPTER 22

1. **The burden of the valley of vision. What aileth thee now,** that thou art wholly gone up to the housetops?

2. **Thou** that **art** full of stirs, **a tumultuous city,** joyous city: thy slain *men are* not slain with the sword, nor dead in battle.

3. **All thy rulers are fled** together, they are bound by the archers: all that are found in thee are bound together, *which* have fled from far.

4. **Therefore said I,** Look away from me; I will weep bitterly, **labour not to comfort me, because of the spoiling of** the daughter of **my people.**

5. **For it is a day of trouble, and of treading down,** and of perplexity **by the Lord** GOD of hosts **in the valley of vision,** breaking down the walls, and of crying to the mountains.

6. And Elam bare the quiver with chariots of men *and* horsemen, and Kir uncovered the shield.

7. And it shall come to pass, *that* thy choicest valleys shall be full of chariots, and the horsemen shall set themselves in array at the gate.

8. And he discovered the covering of Judah, and thou didst look in that day to the armour of the house of the forest.

9. Ye have seen also the breaches of the city of David, that they are many: and ye gathered together the waters of the lower pool.

10. And ye have numbered the houses of Jerusalem, and the houses have ye broken down to fortify the wall.

11. Ye made also a ditch between

the two walls for the water of the old pool: but ye have not looked unto the maker thereof, neither had respect unto him that fashioned it long ago.

■ 12. **And in that day did**
■ **the Lord** GOD of hosts
■ **call to weeping,** and to mourning, and to baldness, and to girding

■ **with sackcloth:**
■ 13. **And behold joy**
■ **and gladness,** slaying oxen, and killing sheep,
■ **eating** flesh,
■ **and drinking** wine: let us eat and drink;
■ **for to morrow we shall die.**
■ 14. **And it was**
■ **revealed** in mine ears
■ **by the LORD** of hosts, Surely
■ **this iniquity shall not**
■ **be purged** from you
■ **till ye die,** saith the Lord GOD of hosts.

15. Thus saith the Lord GOD of hosts, Go, get thee unto this treasurer, *even* unto Shebna, which *is* over the house, *and say,*
16. What hast thou here? and whom hast thou here, that thou hast hewed thee out a sepulchre here, *as* he that heweth him out a sepulchre on high, *and* that graveth an habitation for himself in a rock?

■ 17. **Behold, the LORD will**
■ **carry thee away** with a mighty captivity, and will surely cover thee.
■ 18. **He will** surely
■ **violently** turn and
■ **toss thee like a ball** into a large country:
■ **there shalt thou die**, and there the chariots of thy glory *shall be* the shame of thy lord's house.

19. And I will drive thee from thy station, and from thy state shall he pull thee down.

■ 20. **And it shall come**
■ **to pass** in that day,
■ **that I will call my servant**
■ **Eliakim** the son of Hilkiah:
■ 21. **And I will clothe him**
■ **with thy robe, and**

■ **strengthen him** with thy girdle,
■ **and** I will
■ **commit thy government**
■ **into his hand: and he shall**
■ **be a father to** the inhabitants of
■ **Jerusalem, and** to the house of
■ **Judah.**
■ 22. **And the key of the house**
■ **of David will I lay upon his**
■ **shoulder;** so he shall open, and none shall shut; and he shall shut, and none shall open.
■ 23. **And I will fasten him**
■ **as a nail in a sure place;** and he shall be for a glorious throne to his father's house.

24. And they shall hang upon him all the glory of his father's house, the offspring and the issue, all vessels of small quantity, from the vessels of cups, even to all the vessels of flagons.

■ 25. **In that day,** saith the LORD of hosts,
■ **shall the nail** that is fastened in the sure place be removed, and be cut down, and
■ **fall; and the burden that**
■ **was upon it shall be cut off:**
■ **for the LORD hath spoken it.**

CHAPTER 23

■ 1. **The burden of Tyre. Howl,**
■ **ye ships of Tarshish; for it is**
■ **laid waste,** so that there is no house, no entering in: from the land of Chittim it is revealed to them.

2. Be still, ye inhabitants of the isle; thou whom the merchants of Zidon, that pass over the sea, have replenished.
3. And by great waters the seed of Sihor, the harvest of the river, is her revenue; and she is a mart of nations.

■ 4. **Be thou ashamed,**
■ **O Zidon:** for the sea hath spoken, *even* the strength of the sea, saying, I travail not, nor bring forth children, neither do I nourish up young men, *nor* bring up virgins.

5. As

■ **at the report concerning** Egypt, *so* shall they be sorely pained at the report of

Tyre.

6. Pass ye over to Tarshish; howl, ye inhabitants of the isle.

7. *Is* this your joyous *city*, whose antiquity *is* of ancient days? her own feet shall carry her afar off to sojourn.

8. **Who hath taken this counsel against Tyre,** the crowning *city,* whose merchants *are* princes, whose traffickers *are* the honourable of the earth?

9. **The LORD** of hosts **hath purposed it, to stain the pride** of all glory, **and to bring into contempt all the honourable of the earth.**

10. Pass through thy land as a river, O daughter of Tarshish: *there is* no more strength.

11. He stretched out his hand over the sea, he shook the kingdoms: **the LORD hath given a commandment against the merchant city, to destroy the strong holds** thereof.

12. And he said, Thou shalt no more rejoice, O thou oppressed virgin, daughter of Zidon: arise, pass over to Chittim; there also shalt thou have no rest.

13. Behold the land of the Chaldeans; this people was not, *till* the Assyrian founded it for them that dwell in the wilderness: they set up the towers thereof, they raised up the palaces thereof; *and* he brought it to ruin.

14. **Howl, ye ships of Tarshish: for your strength is laid waste.**

15. And it shall come to pass in that day, that **Tyre shall be forgotten seventy years,** according to the days of one king: after the end of seventy years shall Tyre sing as an harlot.

16. Take an harp, go about the city, thou harlot that hast been forgotten; make sweet melody, sing many songs, that thou mayest be remembered.

17. **And** it shall come to pass **after the** end of **seventy years, that the LORD will visit Tyre,** and **she shall** turn to her hire, and shall **commit fornication with all the kingdoms of the world** upon the face of the earth.

18. **And her merchandise** and her hire **shall be** holiness to the LORD: it shall not be treasured nor laid up; for her merchandise shall be **for them that dwell before the LORD, to eat sufficiently, and for durable clothing.**

CHAPTER 24

1. **Behold, the LORD maketh the earth** empty, and maketh it **waste, and** turneth it upside down, and **scattereth** abroad **the inhabitants thereof.**

2. And it shall be, as with the people, so with the priest; as with the servant, so with his master; as with the maid, so with her mistress; as with the buyer, so with the seller; as with the lender, so with the borrower; as with the taker of usury, so with the giver of usury to him.

3. **The land shall be** utterly **emptied, and** utterly **spoiled:** for the LORD hath spoken this word.

4. The earth mourneth *and* fadeth away, the world languisheth *and* fadeth away, the haughty people of the earth do languish.

5. **The earth** also **is defiled under the inhabitants** thereof; **because they have transgressed the laws,** changed the ordinance, broken the everlasting covenant.

6. **Therefore hath the curse**

devoured the earth, and
they that dwell therein are desolate:
**therefore the
inhabitants** of the earth
**are burned, and
few men left.**
7. The new wine mourneth, the
vine languisheth, all the merry
hearted do sigh.
8. The mirth of tabrets ceaseth,
the noise of them that rejoice
endeth, the joy of the harp ceaseth.
9. They shall not drink wine with
a song; strong drink shall be
bitter to them that drink it.
10. The city of confusion is broken
down: every house is shut up, that
no man may come in.
11. *There is* a crying for wine in the
streets; all joy is darkened, the
mirth of the land is gone.
12. **In the city is left
desolation,** and the gate
is smitten with destruction.
13. **When thus it shall
be** in the midst of the land
among the people,
there shall be as the shaking of an
olive tree, *and* as the gleaning
grapes when the vintage is done.
14. **They shall** lift up their
voice, they shall
**sing for the majesty
of the LORD,** they shall
cry aloud from the sea.
15. **Wherefore glorify** ye
the LORD in the fires, *even*
the name of the LORD God of
Israel in the isles of the sea.
16. **From the uttermost
part of the earth** have
**we heard songs, even
glory to the righteous.
But I said, My leanness,**
my leanness,
woe unto me! the treacherous
dealers have dealt treacherously; yea,
the treacherous dealers
have dealt very treacherously.
17. **Fear, and the pit,**
and the snare,
**are upon thee, O
inhabitant of the earth.**

18. **And** it shall come to pass, *that*
**he who fleeth from the
noise of the fear shall fall
into the pit;** and he that cometh
up out of the midst of the pit shall be
taken in the snare: for the windows
from on high are open, and the
foundations of the earth do shake.
19. The earth is utterly broken down,
the earth is clean dissolved, the
earth is moved exceedingly.
20. **The earth shall reel to
and fro like a drunkard,**
and shall be removed like a
cottage; and the transgression thereof
shall be heavy upon it;
**and it shall fall, and
not rise again.**
21. **And** it shall come to pass
in that day, *that*
**the LORD shall
punish** the host of
the high ones *that*
are on high, and the kings
of the earth upon the earth.
22. **And they shall
be gathered** together,
as prisoners are gathered
in the pit, and shall be shut
up in the prison,
**and after many days
shall they be visited.**
23. **Then** the moon shall be
confounded, and the
sun ashamed, when
the LORD of hosts
shall reign in mount Zion, and in
Jerusalem, and before his ancients
gloriously.

CHAPTER 25

1. **O Lord,** thou *art* my God;
I will exalt thee,
I will praise thy name; for
**thou hast done wonderful
things;** *thy* counsels
of old *are* faithfulness *and* truth.
2. **For thou hast made**
of a city an heap; *of*
a defenced city a ruin:
a palace of strangers to be
no city; it shall never be built.
3. **Therefore shall the strong**

■ **people glorify thee,** the city of
the terrible nations shall fear thee.
■ 4. **For thou hast been**
■ **a strength to the**
■ **poor,** a strength to
■ **the needy** in his distress,
■ **a refuge from the storm,**
a shadow from the heat, when the
blast of the terrible ones *is* as a
storm *against* the wall.
5. Thou shalt bring down the noise
of strangers, as the heat in a dry
place; *even* the heat with the shadow
of a cloud: the branch of the terrible
ones shall be brought low.
■ 6. **And in this mountain**
■ **shall the LORD** of hosts
■ **make** unto all people
■ **a feast** of fat things, a feast of
wines on the lees, of fat things full
of marrow, of wines on the
lees well refined.
■ 7. **And he will destroy**
in this mountain the face of
■ **the covering cast over**
■ **all people,** and the
veil that is spread over all nations.
■ 8. **He will swallow up death**
■ **in victory; and the Lord** GOD
■ **will wipe away tears**
from off all faces;
■ **and the rebuke of his**
■ **people shall he take away**
from off all the earth:
for the LORD hath spoken *it.*
■ 9. **And it shall be said**
■ **in that day,** Lo, this *is* our
God; we have waited for him,
and he will save us:
■ **this is the LORD;**
■ **we have waited for him,**
■ **we will be glad and**
■ **rejoice in his salvation.**
■ 10. **For in this mountain shall**
■ **the hand of the LORD rest,**
■ **and Moab** shall be trodden down
under him, even as straw is trodden
down for the dunghill.
11. And he shall spread forth his
hands in the midst of them, as
he that swimmeth spreadeth
forth *his hands* to swim: and
■ **he shall bring down**

their pride together with
the spoils of their hands.
12. And the fortress of the
high fort of thy walls shall he
bring down, lay low, *and* bring
to the ground, *even*
■ **to the dust.**

CHAPTER 26

■ 1. **In that day shall this**
■ **song be sung in** the land of
■ **Judah; We have a strong**
■ **city;** salvation will *God* appoint
for walls and bulwarks.
■ 2. **Open ye the gates,**
■ **that the righteous nation**
which keepeth the truth
■ **may enter** in.
■ 3. **Thou wilt keep him in**
■ **perfect peace, whose mind**
is stayed *on thee*: because he
■ **trusteth in thee.**
■ 4. **Trust** ye
■ **in the LORD** for ever:
■ **for in the LORD JEHOVAH**
■ **is everlasting strength:**
■ 5. **For** he bringeth down
them that dwell on high;
■ **the lofty city,**
■ **he layeth it low;**
he layeth it low, *even* to the
ground; he bringeth it
even to the dust.
6. The foot shall tread it down,
even the feet of the poor,
and the steps of the needy.
■ 7. **The way of the just is**
■ **uprightness:** thou, most upright,
dost weigh the path of the just.
8. Yea, in the way of thy judgments,
O LORD, have we waited for thee;
■ **the desire of our soul is**
to thy name, and to the
■ **remembrance of thee.**
9. With my soul have I desired thee
in the night; yea, with my spirit
within me will I seek thee early: for
■ **when thy judgments**
■ **are in the earth, the**
■ **inhabitants** of the world will
■ **learn righteousness.**
■ 10. **Let favour be shewed to**
■ **the wicked, yet will he not**

■ **learn righteousness:**
in the land of uprightness will he
deal unjustly, and will not behold
the majesty of the LORD.
11. LORD, *when* thy hand is lifted
up, they will not see: *but* they shall
see, and be ashamed for *their* envy
at the people; yea, the fire of
thine enemies shall devour them.
■ 12. **LORD, thou wilt**
■ **ordain peace** for us:
■ **for thou** also
■ **hast wrought all**
■ **our works in us.**
13. O LORD our God,
■ **other lords** beside thee
■ **have had dominion**
■ **over us:** *but* by thee only will
we make mention of thy name.
■ 14. **They are dead,**
they shall not live; *they are*
deceased, they shall not rise:
■ **therefore hast thou** visited and
■ **destroyed them,**
■ **and made** all
■ **their memory to perish.**
■ 15. **Thou hast increased**
■ **the nation,** O LORD,
thou hast increased the nation:
■ **thou art glorified:**
thou hadst removed *it* far
unto all the ends of the earth.
16. LORD, in trouble
have they visited thee,
■ **they poured out a prayer**
■ **when thy chastening**
■ **was upon them.**
■ 17. **Like as a woman with**
■ **child,** *that* draweth near the time
of her delivery, is in pain, *and*
■ **crieth out in her pangs;**
■ **so have we been in**
■ **thy sight,** O LORD.
18. We have been with child, we
have been in pain, we have as it were
brought forth wind; we have not
wrought any deliverance in the
earth; neither have the inhabitants
of the world fallen.
■ 19. **Thy dead** *men* shall live,
■ **together with my**
■ **dead body shall** they
■ **arise. Awake and sing,**

ye that dwell in dust: for thy dew
is as the dew of herbs, and the
earth shall cast out the dead.
■ 20. **Come,** my people, enter thou
■ **into thy chambers,**
and shut thy doors about thee:
■ **hide thyself** as it were
■ **for a** little
■ **moment, until the**
■ **indignation be overpast.**
■ 21. **For,** behold,
■ **the LORD cometh**
out of his place
■ **to punish the inhabitants**
■ **of the earth for their**
■ **iniquity:** the earth also shall
disclose her blood, and shall
no more cover her slain.

CHAPTER 27

■ 1. **In that day the LORD** with
his sore and great and strong sword
■ **shall punish leviathan**
■ **the** piercing
■ **serpent,** even leviathan
that crooked serpent; and
■ **he shall slay the dragon**
that *is* in the sea.
■ 2. **In that day sing ye**
■ **unto her, A vineyard**
■ **of red wine.**
■ 3. **I the LORD do keep it;**
I will water it every moment:
lest *any* hurt it,
I will keep it night and day.
■ 4. **Fury is not in me:** who would
set the briers *and* thorns against me
in battle? I would go through them,
I would burn them together.
5. Or let him
■ **take hold of my strength,**
that he may make peace with me;
■ **and** he shall
■ **make peace with me.**
■ 6. **He shall cause**
them that come of
■ **Jacob to take root: Israel**
■ **shall blossom and bud, and**
■ **fill** the face of
■ **the world with fruit.**
■ 7. **Hath he smitten him,**
as he smote those that smote him?
■ **or is he slain** according to

the slaughter of them
that are slain by him?
8. In measure,

■ **when it shooteth**
■ **forth, thou wilt**
■ **debate with it**:
he stayeth his rough wind
in the day of the east wind.
■■ 9. **By this** therefore
■ **shall the iniquity of Jacob**
■ **be purged;** and this *is* all the
fruit to take away his sin; when
he maketh all
■ **the stones of the altar**
as chalkstones that are
beaten in sunder, the groves
■ **and images shall**
■ **not stand up.**
■ 10. **Yet the defenced city**
■ **shall be desolate,** *and* the
habitation forsaken, and left like a
wilderness: there shall the calf feed,
and there shall he lie down, and
consume the branches thereof.
11. When the boughs thereof are
withered, they shall be broken off: the
women come, *and* set them on fire:
for it *is* a people of no understanding:
therefore he that made them will not
have mercy on them, and he that
formed them will shew themno favour.
■ 12. **And** it shall come to pass
■ **in that day**, *that* the
LORD shall beat off
from the channel of the river unto
the stream of Egypt, and
ye shall be gathered one by one,
O ye children of Israel.
■ 13. **And** it shall come
to pass in *that* day, that the great
trumpet shall be blown, and
■ **they** shall come
■ **which were ready**
■ **to perish in** the land of
■ **Assyria, and** the outcasts
in the land of
■ **Egypt,** and
■ **shall worship the**
■ **LORD in** the holy mount at
■ **Jerusalem.**

CHAPTER 28

I■I 1. **Woe** to the crown of pride,

■ **to the drunkards of**
■ **Ephraim,** whose glorious
beauty is a fading flower,
which *are* on the head of the
fat valleys of them that are
overcome with wine!
2. Behold, the Lord hath a mighty
and strong one, *which* as a tempest
of hail *and* a destroying storm,
as a flood of mighty waters
overflowing, shall cast down
to the earth with the hand.
3. The crown of pride, the
drunkards of
■ **Ephraim, shall be**
■ **trodden under feet:**
■ 4. **And the glorious beauty,**
which *is* on the head of the fat valley,
■ **shall be a fading flower**,
and as the hasty fruit before the
summer; which *when* he that
looketh upon it seeth, while it
is yet in his hand he eateth it up.
■ 5. **In that day shall**
■ **the LORD** of hosts
■ **be for a crown** of glory,
and for a diadem of beauty,
■ **unto the residue**
■ **of his people,**
6. And for
■ **a spirit of judgment**
to him that sitteth in judgment,
■ **and** for
■ **strength** to them
that turn the battle to the gate.
■ 7. **But they** also
■ **have erred** through wine,
and through strong drink are
out of the way; the priest and
the prophet have erred through
strong drink, they are swallowed
up of wine, they are out of the way
through strong drink; they err in
vision, they stumble *in* judgment.
8. For all tables are full of vomit
and filthiness, *so that there*
is no place *clean*.
■ 9. **Whom shall he teach**
■ **knowledge? and**
whom shall he
■ **make to understand**
■ **doctrine? them that are**
■ **weaned from the milk,**

and drawn from the breasts.

10. **For precept must be upon precept,** precept upon precept;

line upon line, line upon line; **here a little, and there a little**:

11. **For with stammering lips** and another tongue **will he speak to this people.**

12. **To whom he said, This is the rest** wherewith ye may cause the weary to rest; **and** this *is* the **refreshing: yet they would not hear.**

13. **But the word** of the LORD **was** unto them precept upon precept, precept upon precept; line upon line, line upon line; **here a little, and there a little; that they might** go, and fall backward, and **be broken**, and snared, **and taken**.

14. **Wherefore hear the word** of the LORD, **ye scornful men, that rule** this people which *is* **in Jerusalem.**

15. **Because ye** have **said, We have made a covenant with death, and** with **hell** are we at agreement; **when the** overflowing **scourge shall pass** through, **it shall not come unto us: for** we have made lies our refuge, and **under falsehood have we hid ourselves:**

16. **Therefore thus saith the Lord** GOD, Behold, **I lay in Zion** for **a foundation** a **stone,** a tried stone, a precious corner *stone*, a sure foundation: **he that believeth shall not make haste.**

17. Judgment also will I lay to the line, and righteousness to the

plummet: and the hail shall sweep away the refuge of lies, and the waters shall overflow the hiding place.

18. **And your covenant with death shall be disannulled, and** your agreement with hell shall not stand; **when the** overflowing **scourge shall pass** through, then **ye shall be trodden down by it.**

19. From the time that it goeth forth it shall take you: for morning by morning shall it pass over, by day and by night: **and it shall be a vexation** only *to* understand the report.

20. For the bed is shorter than that *a man* can stretch himself *on it*: and the covering narrower than that he can wrap himself *in it*.

21. **For the LORD shall** rise up as *in* mount Perazim, he shall be wroth as *in* the valley of Gibeon, that he may do his work, his strange work; and **bring to pass his act,** his strange act.

22. **Now therefore be ye not mockers,** lest your bands be made strong: **for I have heard from the Lord** GOD **of** hosts **a consumption,** even **determined upon the whole earth.**

23. **Give ye ear, and hear my voice;** hearken, and hear my speech.

24. **Doth the plowman plow** all day to sow? doth he open and break the clods of **his ground?**

25. When he hath made plain the face thereof, **doth he not cast abroad** the fitches, and scatter the cummin, and cast in the principal wheat and the appointed barley and the rie in their place?

989

26. **For his God** doth instruct him to discretion, *and* **doth teach him.**

27. For the fitches are not threshed with a threshing instrument, neither is a cart wheel turned about upon the cummin; but the fitches are beaten out with a staff, and the cummin with a rod.

28. Bread *corn* is bruised; because he will not ever be threshing it, nor break *it with* the wheel of his cart, nor bruise it *with* his horsemen.

29. **This also cometh** forth **from the LORD** of hosts, **which is wonderful in counsel, and excellent in working.**

CHAPTER 29

1. **Woe to Ariel,** to Ariel, **the city where David dwelt!** add ye year to year; let them kill sacrifices.

2. **Yet I will distress Ariel,** and there shall be heaviness and sorrow: and it shall be unto me as Ariel.

3. **And** I will camp against thee round about, and will **lay siege against thee** with a mount, and I will raise forts against thee.

4. **And thou shalt be brought down,** *and* shalt speak out of the ground, and thy speech shall be low out of the dust, and thy voice shall be, as of one that hath a familiar spirit, out of the ground, and thy speech shall whisper out of the dust.

5. **Moreover** the multitude of thy strangers shall be like small dust, and the multitude of the terrible ones *shall be* as chaff that passeth away: yea, **it shall be** at an instant **suddenly.**

6. **Thou shalt be visited** of the LORD of hosts

with thunder, and with **earthquake,** and great noise, with storm and tempest, **and the flame of** devouring **fire.**

7. **And** the multitude of **all** the nations **that fight against Ariel,** even all that fight against her and her munition, and that distress her, **shall be as a dream of a night vision.**

8. **It shall even be as when an hungry man dreameth, and,** behold, **he eateth;** but he awaketh, and his soul is empty: **or as when a thirsty man dreameth, and,** behold, **he drinketh; but he awaketh,** and, behold, **he is faint, and his soul hath appetite: so shall the** multitude of all the **nations be, that fight against mount Zion.**

9. Stay yourselves, and wonder; **cry ye out**, and cry: they are drunken, but not with wine; they stagger, but not with strong drink.

10. **For the LORD hath poured out upon you** the spirit of deep **sleep**, and hath closed your eyes: the prophets and your rulers, the seers hath he covered.

11. **And the vision** of all **is become** unto you **as** the words of **a book that is sealed,** which *men* deliver to one that is learned, saying, Read this, I pray thee: and he saith, I cannot; for it *is* sealed:

12. And the book is delivered to him that is not learned, saying, Read this, I pray thee: and he saith, I am not learned.

13. **Wherefore the Lord said,** Forasmuch as **this people** draw near *me* with their mouth, and **with their lips do honour**

me, but have removed
their heart far from me,
and their fear toward me is
taught by the precept of men:
14. **Therefore,** behold, I will
proceed to do a marvellous work
among this people, *even* a
marvellous work and a wonder: for
the wisdom of their wise
men shall perish, and the
understanding of their
prudent men shall be hid.
15. **Woe unto them**
that seek deep
to hide their counsel
from the LORD, and
their works are in the dark,
and they
say, Who seeth us?
and who knoweth us?
16. **Surely your turning of
things upside down shall be
esteemed as the potter's
clay: for shall the work say
of him that made it, He
made me not?** or shall the thing
framed say of him that framed it, He
had no understanding?
17. *Is* it not yet a very little while, and
**Lebanon shall be turned
into a fruitful field,**
and the fruitful field shall
be esteemed as a forest?
18. **And** in that day shall
**the deaf hear the
words of the book,**
and the eyes of the
blind shall see
out of obscurity, and out of darkness.
19. **The meek** also shall
increase *their* joy in the LORD,
and the poor among men
shall rejoice in the
Holy One of Israel.
20. **For the terrible**
one is brought to nought, and
the scorner is consumed,
**and all that watch for
iniquity are cut off:**
21. That make a man an offender for
a word, and lay a snare for him that
reproveth in the gate, and turn aside
the just for a thing of nought.

22. **Therefore thus saith the
LORD,** who redeemed Abraham,
concerning the house of Jacob,
**Jacob shall not now be
ashamed,** neither shall his
face now wax pale.
23. **But** when he seeth his
children, the work of mine
hands, in the midst of him,
they shall sanctify my name, and
**sanctify the Holy One
of Jacob, and** shall
fear the God of Israel.
24. **They** also
that erred in spirit
**shall come to
understanding, and
they that murmured
shall learn doctrine.**

CHAPTER 30

1. **Woe to the rebellious
children,** saith the LORD,
that take counsel, but not of
me; and that cover with a
covering, but not of my spirit,
that they may
add sin to sin:
2. **That** walk to go down into Egypt,
and have not asked at my mouth;
to strengthen themselves in the
strength of Pharaoh, and to
trust in the shadow of
Egypt!
3. **Therefore shall**
the strength of
**Pharaoh be your
shame,** and the
trust in the shadow of
Egypt *your* confusion.
4. For his princes were at Zoan, and
his ambassadors came to Hanes.
5. **They were all ashamed
of a people that could
not profit them,**
nor be an help nor profit, but
a shame, and also a reproach.
6. The burden of the beasts of
the south: into the land
of trouble and anguish,
from whence *come* the young
and old lion, the viper and fiery
flying serpent, they will carry their

riches upon the shoulders of young asses, and their treasures upon the bunches of camels, to a people *that* shall not profit *them*.

■ 7. **For the Egyptians shall**
■ **help in vain,** and to no purpose: therefore have I cried concerning this, Their strength *is* to sit still.

■ 8. **Now go, write it** before them in a table, and note it
■ **in a book,** that it may be for the time to come for ever and ever:

■ 9. **That this is a rebellious**
■ **people,** lying children, children
■ **that will not hear the**
■ **law of the LORD:**
■ 10. **Which say to**
■ **the seers,** See not;
■ **and** to
■ **the prophets,** Prophesy not unto us right things,
■ **speak unto us smooth**
■ **things,** prophesy deceits:
11. Get you out of the way, turn aside out of the path,
■ **cause the Holy**
■ **One of Israel to cease**
■ **from before us.**
■ 12. **Wherefore thus saith**
■ **the Holy One of Israel,**
■ **Because ye despise**
■ **this word,** and trust in oppression and perverseness, and stay thereon:

■ 13. **Therefore this iniquity**
■ **shall be to you as a**
■ **breach ready to fall,** swelling out in a high wall,
■ **whose breaking cometh**
■ **suddenly** at an instant.
■ 14. **And he shall break**
■ **it as** the breaking of
■ **the potters' vessel** that
■ **is broken in pieces;** he shall not spare: so that there shall not be found in the bursting of it a sherd to take fire from the hearth, or to take water *withal* out of the pit.
■ 15. **For thus saith the**
■ **Lord** GOD, the Holy One of Israel;
■ **In returning** and rest
■ **shall ye be saved;**

in quietness and in confidence shall be your strength: and ye would not.

■ 16. **But ye said, No;** for
■ **we will flee upon horses;** therefore shall ye flee: and, We will ride upon the swift; therefore shall they that pursue you be swift.

■ 17. **One thousand shall flee**
■ **at the rebuke of one;** at the rebuke of five shall ye flee: till ye be left as a beacon upon the top of a mountain, and as an ensign on an hill.

■ 18. **And therefore will the**
■ **LORD wait,** that he may be gracious unto you, and therefore will he be exalted,
■ **that he may have mercy** upon you: for the LORD *is* a God of judgment: blessed *are* all they that wait for him.

■ 19. **For the people shall**
■ **dwell in Zion** at Jerusalem: thou shalt weep no more:
■ **he will be** very
■ **gracious unto**
■ **thee at** the voice of
■ **thy cry;** when he shall hear it, he will answer thee.

■ 20. **And though the**
■ **Lord give you** the bread of
■ **adversity, and** the water of
■ **affliction, yet shall not thy**
■ **teachers be removed** into a corner any more,
■ **but thine eyes shall**
■ **see thy teachers:**
■ 21. **And thine ears shall**
■ **hear** a word behind thee, saying,
■ **This is the way, walk ye**
■ **in it,** when ye turn to the right hand, and when ye turn to the left.
■ 22. **Ye shall defile** also the covering of
■ **thy graven images** of silver, and the ornament of thy molten images of gold:
■ **thou shalt cast them**
■ **away** as a menstruous cloth; thou shalt say unto it, Get thee hence.
■ 23. **Then shall he give the**
■ **rain of thy seed,** that thou shalt sow the ground withal;

and bread of the increase of **the earth,** and it **shall be** fat and **plenteous:** in that day shall thy cattle feed in large pastures. 24. The oxen likewise and the young asses that ear the ground shall eat clean provender, which hath been winnowed with the shovel and with the fan. 25. **And there shall be** upon every high mountain, and upon every high hill, **rivers and streams of waters** in the day of the great slaughter, when the towers fall. 26. Moreover the light of the moon shall be as the light of the sun, and the light of the sun shall be sevenfold, as the light of seven days, **in the day that the LORD bindeth up the breach of his people, and healeth** the stroke of **their wound.** 27. **Behold, the name of the LORD cometh** from far, **burning with his anger,** and the burden *thereof is* heavy: his lips are full of indignation, and his tongue as a devouring fire: 28. And his breath, as an overflowing stream, shall reach to the midst of the neck, **to sift the nations** with the sieve of vanity: and *there shall be* a bridle in the jaws of the people, causing *them* to err. 29. **Ye shall have a song,** as in the night *when* a holy solemnity is kept; **and gladness of heart,** as *when* one goeth with a pipe to come into the mountain of the LORD, to the mighty One of Israel. 30. **And the LORD shall cause his** glorious **voice to be heard,** and shall shew the lighting down of his arm, with the indignation of *his* anger, and *with* the flame of a devouring fire, *with* scattering, and tempest, and hailstones. 31. **For through the voice of the LORD shall the Assyrian be beaten down,** which smote with a rod. 32. **And in every place where the** grounded **staff shall pass, which the LORD shall lay upon him, it shall be with tabrets and harps:** and in battles of shaking will he fight with it. 33. **For Tophet is ordained of old;** yea, **for the king** it is prepared; he **hath made** *it* deep *and* large: **the pile** thereof *is* fire and much **wood; the breath of the LORD,** like a stream of brimstone, **doth kindle it.**

CHAPTER 31

1. **Woe to them that go** down **to Egypt for help;** and stay on horses, and trust in chariots, because *they are* many; and in horsemen, because they are very strong; **but** they **look not unto the** Holy One of Israel, neither seek the **LORD!** 2. **Yet he** also *is* wise, and **will bring evil,** and will not call back his words: but will arise **against** the house of the evildoers, and against the help of **them that work iniquity.** 3. **Now the Egyptians are men, and not God;** and their horses flesh, and not spirit. **When the LORD shall stretch out his hand, both he that helpeth** shall fall, **and he that is holpen shall fall** down, and they all shall fail together. 4. For thus hath the LORD spoken unto me, Like as the lion and the

young lion roaring on his prey, when a multitude of shepherds is called forth against him, *he* will not be afraid of their voice, nor abase himself for the noise of them: so shall the LORD of hosts come down to fight for mount Zion, and for the hill thereof.

5. **As birds flying, so will the LORD** of hosts **defend Jerusalem;** defending also he will deliver *it*, **and** passing over he will **preserve it.**

6. **Turn ye unto him** *from* whom the children of Israel have deeply revolted.

7. **For in that day every man shall cast away his idols** of silver, and his idols of gold, which your own hands have made unto you *for* a sin.

8. **Then shall the Assyrian fall with the sword, not of a mighty man**; and the sword, not of a mean man, shall devour him: **but he shall flee** from the sword, and his young men shall be discomfited.

9. **And he shall** pass over to his strong hold for **fear,** and his princes shall be afraid of the ensign, **saith the LORD, whose fire is in Zion**, and his furnace in Jerusalem.

CHAPTER 32

1. **Behold, a king shall reign in righteousness, and princes** shall rule **in judgment.**

2. **And a man shall be as an hiding place** from the wind, and a covert from the tempest; as rivers of water in a dry place, as the shadow of a great rock in a weary land.

3. And the eyes of them that see shall not be dim, and the ears of them that hear shall hearken.

4. **The heart** also of the rash **shall understand knowledge, and the** tongue of the **stammerers shall** be ready to **speak plainly.**

5. **The vile person** shall be no more called liberal, nor the churl said *to be* bountiful.

6. For the vile person **will speak villany, and his heart will work iniquity,** to practise hypocrisy, and to utter error against the LORD, to make empty the soul of the hungry, and he will cause the drink of the thirsty to fail.

7. **The instruments** also **of the churl are evil: he deviseth wicked devices to destroy the poor with lying words,** even when the needy speaketh right.

8. **But the liberal deviseth liberal things;** and by liberal things shall he stand.

9. **Rise up, ye women that are at ease;** hear my voice, ye careless daughters; give ear unto my speech.

10. **Many days** and years **shall ye be troubled,** ye careless women: **for the vintage shall fail,** the gathering shall not come.

11. Tremble, ye women that are at ease; be troubled, ye careless ones: strip you, and make you bare, and gird *sackcloth* upon *your* loins.

12. They shall lament for the teats, for the pleasant fields, for the fruitful vine.

13. **Upon the land of my people shall come up thorns and briers;** yea, upon all the houses of joy *in* the joyous city:

14. **Because the palaces shall be forsaken;** the multitude of the city shall be left; the forts and towers shall be for dens for ever, a joy of wild asses, a pasture of flocks;

15. **Until the spirit be poured upon us from on high,** and the wilderness be a

fruitful field, and the fruitful field be counted for a forest.

16. **Then judgment shall dwell in the wilderness, and righteousness remain in the fruitful field.**

17. **And the work of righteousness shall be peace; and the effect of righteousness quietness and assurance for ever.**

18. **And my people shall dwell** in a peaceable habitation, and in sure dwellings, and **in quiet resting places;**

19. When it shall hail, coming down on the forest; and the city shall be low in a low place.

20. Blessed *are* ye that sow beside all waters, that send forth *thither* the feet of the ox and the ass.

CHAPTER 33

1. **Woe to thee that spoilest,** and thou *wast* not spoiled; **and dealest treacherously,** and they dealt not treacherously with thee! **when thou shalt cease to spoil, thou shalt be spoiled; and when thou** shalt **make an end to deal treacherously, they shall deal treacherously with thee.**

2. **O LORD, be gracious unto us;** we have waited for thee: **be** thou their arm every morning, **our salvation** also **in the time of trouble.**

3. **At the noise of the tumult the people** fled; at the lifting up of thyself the nations **were scattered.**

4. And your spoil shall be gathered *like* the gathering of the caterpillar: as the running to and fro of locusts shall he run upon them.

5. **The LORD is exalted;** for he dwelleth on high:

he hath filled Zion with judgment and righteousness.

6. **And wisdom and knowledge shall be the stability of thy times, and strength of salvation: the fear of the LORD is his treasure.**

7. Behold, their valiant ones shall cry without: the ambassadors of peace shall weep bitterly.

8. The highways lie waste, the wayfaring man ceaseth: he hath broken the covenant, **he hath despised the cities, he regardeth no man.**

9. **The earth mourneth and languisheth:** Lebanon is ashamed *and* hewn down: Sharon is like a wilderness; and Bashan and Carmel shake off *their fruits.*

10. **Now will I rise, saith the LORD; now will I be exalted;** now will I lift up myself.

11. **Ye shall conceive chaff, ye shall bring forth stubble: your breath, as fire, shall devour you.**

12. And the people shall be *as* the burnings of lime: *as* thorns cut up shall they be burned in the fire.

13. **Hear,** ye *that are* far off, **what I have done;** and, ye *that are* near, **acknowledge my might.**

14. **The sinners in Zion are afraid;** fearfulness hath surprised the hypocrites. Who among us shall dwell with the devouring fire? **who among us shall dwell with everlasting burnings?**

15. **He that walketh righteously, and speaketh uprightly;** he that despiseth the gain of oppressions, that shaketh his hands from holding of bribes, that stoppeth his ears from hearing of blood, and shutteth his eyes from seeing evil;

16. **He shall dwell on**

high: his place of defence *shall be* the munitions of rocks: **bread shall be given him; his waters shall be sure.** 17. **Thine eyes shall see the king in his beauty: they shall behold the land** that is very **far off.** 18. Thine heart shall meditate terror. Where *is* the scribe? where *is* the receiver? where *is* he that counted the towers? 19. Thou shalt not see a fierce people, a people of a deeper speech than thou canst perceive; of a stammering tongue, *that thou canst* not understand. 20. **Look upon Zion,** the city of our solemnities: thine eyes shall see Jerusalem **a quiet habitation, a tabernacle that shall not be taken down;** not one of the stakes thereof shall ever be removed, neither shall any of the cords thereof be broken. 21. **But there the glorious LORD will be unto us a place of broad rivers and streams;** wherein shall go no galley with oars, neither shall gallant ship pass thereby. 22. **For the LORD is our judge,** the LORD *is* **our lawgiver,** the LORD *is* **our king; he will save us.** 23. Thy tacklings are loosed; they could not well strengthen their mast, they could not spread the sail: then is the prey of a great spoil divided; the lame take the prey. 24. **And the inhabitant** shall not say, I am sick: the people that dwell therein **shall be forgiven their iniquity.**

CHAPTER 34

1. **Come near,** ye nations, **to hear;** and hearken, ye people: let the earth hear, and all that is therein; the world, and all things that come forth of it. 2. **For the indignation of the LORD is upon all nations,** and *his* fury upon all their armies: **he hath utterly destroyed them,** he hath delivered them to the slaughter. 3. Their slain also shall be cast out, and their stink shall come up out of their carcases, and the mountains shall be melted with their blood. 4. **And all the host of heaven shall be dissolved, and the heavens shall be rolled together as a scroll:** and all their host shall fall down, as the leaf falleth off from the vine, and as a falling *fig* from the fig tree. 5. **For my sword shall be bathed in heaven:** behold, **it shall come down** upon Idumea, and **upon the people of my curse, to judgment.** 6. The sword of the LORD is filled with blood, it is made fat with fatness, *and* with the blood of lambs and goats, with the fat of the kidneys of rams: for the LORD hath a sacrifice in Bozrah, and a great slaughter in the land of Idumea. 7. And the unicorns shall come down with them, and the bullocks with the bulls; **and their land shall be soaked with blood,** and their dust made fat with fatness. 8. **For it is the day of the LORD's vengeance,** *and* the year of recompences for the controversy of Zion. 9. **And the streams** thereof **shall be turned into pitch,** and the dust thereof into brimstone, **and the land** thereof **shall become burning pitch.** 10. **It shall not be quenched** night nor day; **the smoke** thereof

shall go up for ever:
from generation to generation
it shall lie waste;
none shall pass through it
for ever and ever.

11. But the cormorant and the bittern
shall possess it; the owl also and the
raven shall dwell in it: and he shall
stretch out upon it the line of
confusion, and the stones
of emptiness.

12. **They shall call**
the nobles thereof
to the kingdom, but none
shall be there, and all her
princes shall be nothing.

13. **And thorns shall come**
up in her palaces, nettles and
brambles in the fortresses thereof:
and it shall be an habitation of
dragons, *and* a court for owls.

14. **The wild beasts of the**
desert shall also meet with the
wild beasts of the island, and
the satyr shall cry to his fellow;
the screech owl also
shall rest there, and find
for herself a place of rest.

15. There shall the great owl make
her nest, and lay, and hatch,
and gather under her shadow:
there shall the vultures
also be gathered,
every one with her mate.

16. **Seek** ye
out of
the book of the
LORD, and read:
no one of these shall
fail, none shall want her mate:
for my mouth it hath
commanded, and
his spirit it
hath gathered them.

17. **And he hath cast the**
lot for them, and his hand hath
divided it unto them by line:
they shall possess it
for ever, from generation to
generation shall they dwell therein.

CHAPTER 35

1. **The wilderness** and the
solitary place shall be glad for them;
and the desert shall
rejoice, and blossom
as the rose.

2. It shall blossom abundantly, and
rejoice even with joy and singing:
the glory of Lebanon shall
be given unto it, the excellency of
Carmel and Sharon, they
shall see the
glory of the LORD, *and*
the excellency
of our God.

3. **Strengthen** ye
the weak hands,
and confirm the
feeble knees.

4. Say to them *that*
are of a fearful heart,
Be strong, fear not: behold, your
God will come with
vengeance, *even* God
with a recompence;
he will come and
save you.

5. **Then the eyes of the**
blind shall be opened,
and the ears of the deaf
shall be unstopped.

6. **Then shall the lame**
man leap as an hart,
and the tongue of the
dumb sing: for in the wilderness
shall waters break out, and
streams in the desert.

7. **And the parched ground**
shall become a pool, and the
thirsty land springs of water: in the
habitation of dragons, where each lay,
shall be grass with reeds and rushes.

8. **And an highway shall be**
there, and a way, and it *shall be*
called The way of holiness;
the unclean shall not pass
over it; but it *shall be* for those:
the wayfaring men, though fools,
shall not err *therein*.

9. No lion shall be there, nor
any ravenous beast shall go up
thereon, it shall not be found there;
but the redeemed
shall walk there:

10. **And the ransomed**

of the LORD shall return, and come to Zion

with songs and everlasting

joy upon their heads: they shall obtain joy and gladness, and sorrow and sighing shall flee away.

CHAPTER 36

1. Now it came to pass
in the fourteenth year
of king Hezekiah, *that*
Sennacherib king of
Assyria came up
against all the defenced cities of
Judah, and took them.
2. And the king of Assyria
sent Rabshakeh from Lachish
to Jerusalem unto king Hezekiah
with a great army. And he
stood by the conduit of the upper pool
in the highway of the fuller's field.
3. Then came forth unto him Eliakim,
Hilkiah's son, which was over the
house, and Shebna the scribe, and
Joah, Asaph's son, the recorder.
4. And Rabshakeh said
unto them, Say ye now
to Hezekiah, Thus saith the
great king, the king of Assyria,
What confidence is this wherein
thou trustest?
5. I say, *sayest thou,* (but
they are but vain words)
I have counsel and
strength for war: now
on whom dost thou trust,
that thou rebellest against me?
6. Lo, thou trustest in
the staff of this broken reed, on
Egypt; whereon if a man lean,
it will go into his hand, and pierce
it: so *is* Pharaoh king of Egypt
to all that trust in him.
7. But if thou say to me,
We trust in the LORD our God:
is it not he, whose high places and
whose altars Hezekiah hath
taken away, and
said to Judah and to
Jerusalem, Ye shall worship
before this altar?
8. Now therefore
give pledges, I pray thee,

to my master
the king of Assyria, and I
will give thee two thousand
horses, if thou be
able on thy part
to set riders upon them.
9. How then wilt thou
turn away the face of
one captain of the least of
my master's servants, and
put thy trust on Egypt
for chariots and for horsemen?
10. And am I now come up
without the LORD against
this land to destroy it?
the LORD said unto me,
Go up against this
land, and destroy it.
11. Then said Eliakim and
Shebna and Joah unto
Rabshakeh, Speak,
I pray thee,
unto thy servants
in the Syrian language; for
we understand it: and speak not
to us in the Jews' language, in the
ears of the people that are on the wall.
12. But Rabshakeh said, Hath
my master sent me to thy master
and to thee to speak these words?
hath he not *sent me* to the men
that sit upon the wall, that they
may eat their own dung, and
drink their own piss with you?
13. Then Rabshakeh stood,
and cried with a loud voice
in the Jews'
language, and said,
Hear ye
the words of the great king, the
king of Assyria.
14. Thus saith the king,
Let not Hezekiah deceive
you: for he shall not be
able to deliver you.
15. Neither let Hezekiah
make you trust in the LORD,
saying, The LORD will surely
deliver us: this city shall not
be delivered into the hand of
the king of Assyria.
16. Hearken not to Hezekiah:
for thus saith the king of Assyria,

Make an agreement with me *by* a present, and come out to me: and eat ye every one of his vine, and every one of his fig tree, and drink ye every one the waters of his own cistern;

17. **Until I come and take you** away **to a land like your own** land, a land of corn and wine, a land of bread and vineyards.

18. *Beware* lest Hezekiah persuade you, saying, the LORD will deliver us. **Hath any of the gods** of the nations **delivered his land out of the hand of the king of Assyria?**

19. Where *are* the gods of Hamath and Arphad? where *are* the gods of Sepharvaim? and have they delivered Samaria out of my hand?

20. Who *are* they among all the gods of these lands, that have delivered their land out of my hand, that the LORD should deliver Jerusalem out of my hand?

21. **But they held their peace,** and answered him not a word: **for the king's commandment was,** saying, **Answer him not.**

22. **Then came Eliakim,** the son of Hilkiah, that *was* over the household, and Shebna the scribe, and Joah, the son of Asaph, the recorder, **to Hezekiah with** *their* clothes rent, **and told him the words of Rabshakeh.**

CHAPTER 37

1. **And** it came to pass, **when king Hezekiah heard it,** that **he** rent his clothes, and **covered himself with sackcloth, and went into** **the house of the LORD.**

2. **And he sent Eliakim, who** *was* over the household, and Shebna the scribe, and the elders of the priests covered with sackcloth, **unto Isaiah the prophet** the son of Amoz.

3. **And** they **said** unto him, **Thus saith Hezekiah, This** day **is a day of trouble,** and of rebuke, and of blasphemy: for the children are come to the birth, and *there is* not strength to bring forth.

4. **It may be the LORD** thy God **will hear** the words of **Rabshakeh,** whom the king of Assyria his master hath sent to reproach the living God, and will reprove the words which the LORD thy God hath heard: wherefore lift up *thy* prayer for the remnant that is left.

5. **So the servants of king Hezekiah came to Isaiah.**

6. **And Isaiah said** unto them, Thus shall ye say unto your master, **Thus saith the LORD, Be not afraid** of the words that thou hast heard, wherewith the servants of the king of Assyria have blasphemed me.

7. **Behold,** I will send a blast upon him, and **he shall hear a rumour, and return to his own land;** and I will cause him to fall by the sword in his own land.

8. **So Rabshakeh returned, and found** the king of **Assyria warring against Libnah:** for he had heard that he was departed from Lachish.

9. **And he heard say** concerning Tirhakah king of **Ethiopia, He is come forth to make war** with thee. **And** when he heard *it,* **he sent messengers to Hezekiah,** saying,

10. Thus shall ye speak to Hezekiah king of Judah, saying, **Let not thy God,**

in whom thou trustest,
deceive thee, saying,
Jerusalem shall not
be given into the
hand of the king of
Assyria.
11. Behold, thou hast heard what the
kings of Assyria have done to all
lands by destroying them utterly;
and shalt thou be delivered?
12. Have the gods of the nations
delivered them which my fathers
have destroyed, *as* Gozan, and
Haran, and Rezeph, and the children
of Eden which *were* in Telassar?
13. Where *is* the king of Hamath, and
the king of Arphad, and the king of the
city of Sepharvaim, Hena, and Ivah?
14. **And Hezekiah received**
the letter from the hand of
the messengers, and read it:
and Hezekiah
went up unto the house
of the LORD, and spread
it before the LORD.
15. **And Hezekiah prayed**
unto the LORD, saying,
16. **O LORD** of hosts, God
of Israel, that dwellest
between the cherubims,
thou art the
God, *even* thou alone,
of all the kingdoms
of the earth: thou hast
made heaven and earth.
17. Incline thine ear, O LORD,
and hear; open thine eyes,
O LORD, and see: and
hear all
the words of
Sennacherib, which hath
sent to reproach
the living God.
18. **Of a truth, LORD, the**
kings of Assyria have
laid waste all the
nations, and their countries,
19. And have cast their gods into the
fire: for they *were* no gods, but the
work of men's hands, wood and stone:
therefore they have destroyed them.
20. **Now** therefore,
O LORD our God,

save us from his hand,
that all
the kingdoms of the earth
may know that thou art
the LORD, *even* thou only.
21. **Then Isaiah** the son of Amoz
sent unto Hezekiah,
saying, Thus saith the
LORD God of Israel,
Whereas thou hast prayed
to me against Sennacherib
king of Assyria:
22. **This is the word which**
the LORD hath spoken
concerning him;
The virgin, the daughter of
Zion, hath despised thee, *and*
laughed thee to scorn;
the daughter of
Jerusalem hath shaken
her head at thee.
23. Whom hast thou reproached
and blasphemed? and
against whom hast thou
exalted thy voice,
and lifted up thine eyes on high?
even against the
Holy One of Israel.
24. By thy servants hast
thou reproached the Lord,
and hast said, By the
multitude of my chariots am
I come up to the height of the
mountains, to the sides of Lebanon;
and I will cut down the tall cedars
thereof, *and* the choice fir trees
thereof: and I will enter into the
height of his border, *and* the
forest of his Carmel.
25. I have digged, and drunk water;
and with the sole of my feet have
I dried up all the rivers of the
besieged places.
26. Hast thou not heard long ago,
how I have done it; *and* of ancient
times, that I have formed it? now have
I brought it to pass, that thou
shouldest be to lay waste defenced
cities *into* ruinous heaps.
27. Therefore their inhabitants *were* of
small power, they were dismayed and
confounded: they were *as* the grass of
the field, and *as* the green herb, as

the grass on the housetops, and *as corn* blasted before it be grown up.

28. **But I know thy** abode, and thy going out, and thy coming in, and thy **rage against me.**

29. Because thy rage against me, and thy tumult, is come up into mine ears, **therefore will I put my hook in thy nose, and my bridle in thy lips, and I will turn thee back** by **the way** by which **thou camest.**

30. **And this shall be a sign** unto thee, Ye shall eat *this* year such as groweth of itself; and the second year that which springeth of the same: and **in the third year** sow ye, and reap, and plant vineyards, and eat the fruit thereof.

31. And **the remnant that** is escaped of the house **of Judah shall again take root** downward, and bear fruit upward:

32. For out of Jerusalem shall go forth a remnant, and **they that escape out of mount Zion:** the zeal of **the LORD** of hosts **shall do this.**

33. **Therefore thus saith the LORD concerning the king of Assyria, He shall not come into this city,** nor shoot an arrow there,nor come before it with shields, nor cast a bank against it.

34. By the way that he came, by the same shall he return, and shall not come into this city, saith the LORD.

35. **For I will defend this city** to save it **for mine own sake,** and for my servant David's sake.

36. **Then the angel of the LORD went forth, and smote** in **the camp of the Assyrians** a hundred and fourscore

and five thousand: **and when they arose early in the morning, behold, they were all dead** corpses.

37. **So Sennacherib king of Assyria** departed, and **went** and returned, **and dwelt at Nineveh.**

38. **And** it came to pass, **as he was worshipping** in the house of **Nisroch his god,** that Adrammelech and Sharezer **his sons smote him with the sword;** and they escaped into the land of Armenia: **and Esarhaddon his son reigned in his stead.**

CHAPTER 38

1. **In those days was Hezekiah sick unto death. And Isaiah** the prophet the son of Amoz **came unto him, and said** unto him, **Thus saith the LORD, Set thine house in order: for thou shalt die,** and not live.

2. **Then Hezekiah** turned his face toward the wall, and **prayed** unto the LORD,

3. **And said, Remember now, O LORD,** I beseech thee, **how I have walked before thee in truth** and with a perfect heart, and have done *that which is* good in thy sight. **And Hezekiah wept** sore.

4. **Then came the word of the LORD to Isaiah, saying,**

5. **Go, and say to Hezekiah,** Thus saith the LORD, the God of David thy father, **I have heard thy prayer,** I have seen thy tears: behold, **I will add unto thy days fifteen years.**

6. **And I will deliver thee** and this city **out of the hand of** the king of **Assyria:** and I will defend this city.

7. **And this shall be a sign** unto thee from the LORD, that the LORD will do this thing that he hath spoken;

8. **Behold, I will bring** again the shadow of the degrees, which is gone down in **the sun dial** of Ahaz, **ten degrees backward. So the sun returned ten degrees,** by which degrees it was gone down.

9. **The writing of Hezekiah** king of Judah, **when he** had been sick, and was **recovered of his sickness:**

10. **I said in the cutting off of my days,** I shall go to the gates of the grave: I am deprived of the residue of my years.

11. I said, **I shall not see the LORD,** *even* the LORD, **in the land of the living:** I shall behold man no more with the inhabitants of the world.

12. **Mine age is departed,** and is removed from me as a shepherd's tent: I have cut off like a weaver my life: he will cut me off with pining sickness: from day *even* to night wilt thou make an end of me.

13. I reckoned till morning, *that,* as a lion, so will he break all my bones: from day *even* to night wilt thou make an end of me.

14. Like a crane *or* a swallow, so did I chatter: I did mourn as a dove: mine eyes fail *with looking* upward: **O LORD, I am oppressed; undertake for me.**

15. **What shall I say?** **he hath** both spoken unto me, and himself hath **done it:** I shall go softly all my years in the bitterness of my soul.

16. **O LORD,** by these *things* men live, and in all these *things is* the life of my spirit: so wilt thou recover me, and **make me to live.**

17. Behold, for peace I had great bitterness: but thou hast in love to my soul delivered it from the pit of corruption: for thou hast cast all my sins behind thy back.

18. For the grave cannot praise thee, death can *not* celebrate thee: **they that go down into the pit cannot hope for thy truth.**

19. **The living,** the living, he **shall praise thee, as I do this day:** the father to the children shall make known thy truth.

20. **The LORD was ready to save me:** therefore we will sing my songs to the stringed instruments all the days of our life in the house of the LORD.

21. **For Isaiah had said,** Let them **take a lump of figs,** and lay *it* **for a plaster upon the boil, and he shall recover.**

22. Hezekiah also had said, What *is* the sign that I shall go up to the house of the LORD?

CHAPTER 39

1. **At that time Merodach-baladan,** the son of Baladan, **king of Babylon, sent letters** and a present **to Hezekiah: for he** had **heard that he had been sick, and** was **recovered.**

2. **And Hezekiah was glad** of them, **and shewed them** the house of **his precious things,** the silver, and the gold, and the spices, and the precious ointment, and all the house of his armour, and all that was found in his treasures: there was nothing in his house, nor in all his dominion, that Hezekiah shewed them not.

3. **Then came Isaiah** the prophet unto king Hezekiah, **and said** unto him, **What said these men? and**

from whence came they
unto thee? And Hezekiah said,
They are come from a
far country unto me, *even*
from Babylon.
4. Then said he,
What have they seen
in thine house?
And Hezekiah answered,
All that *is* in mine house have
they seen: there is nothing among
my treasures that
I have not shewed them.
5. Then said Isaiah
to Hezekiah,
Hear the word of
the LORD of hosts:
6. Behold, the days come,
that all that is in thine
house, and *that* which thy fathers
have laid up in store until this day,
shall be carried to
Babylon: nothing shall
be left, saith the LORD.
7. And of
thy sons that shall issue from
thee, which thou shalt beget,
shall they take away;
and they shall be eunuchs
in the palace of the king of Babylon.
8. Then said
Hezekiah to Isaiah,
Good is the word of
the LORD which thou hast
spoken. He said moreover,
For there shall be
peace and truth
in my days.

CHAPTER 40

1. Comfort ye, comfort ye
my people, saith your God.
2. Speak ye comfortably to
Jerusalem, and cry unto her,
that her warfare is accomplished,
that her iniquity is
pardoned: for she hath
received of the LORD's hand
double for all her sins.
3. The voice of him that
crieth in the wilderness,
Prepare ye the way of
the LORD, make straight
in the desert
a highway for our God.
4. Every valley shall be exalted, and
every mountain and hill shall be made
low: and the crooked shall be made
straight, and the rough places plain:
5. And the glory of the LORD
shall be revealed, and all flesh
shall see *it* together: for the mouth
of the LORD hath spoken *it*.
6. The voice said, Cry.
And he said, What shall I cry?
All flesh is grass, and
all the goodliness thereof
is as the flower of the field:
7. The grass withereth,
the flower fadeth: because the
spirit of the LORD bloweth upon
it: surely the people *is* grass.
8. The grass withereth,
the flower fadeth:
but the word of our God
shall stand for ever.
9. O Zion, that bringest good tidings,
get thee up into the high mountain; O
Jerusalem, that bringest good tidings,
lift up thy voice with strength; lift *it* up,
be not afraid; say unto the cities of
Judah, Behold your God!
10. Behold, the Lord GOD
will come with strong *hand*,
and his arm shall rule
for him: behold,
his reward is with him,
and his work before him.
11. He shall feed his flock
like a shepherd: he shall
gather the lambs with his arm,
and carry *them* in his bosom,
and shall gently lead
those that are with young.
12. Who hath measured
the waters in the hollow of
his hand,
and meted out
heaven with the span,
and comprehended
the dust of the earth
in a measure, and weighed
the mountains in scales, and
the hills in a balance?
13. Who hath directed the
Spirit of the LORD, or *being*

14. **With whom took he counsel**, and *who* instructed him, and taught him in the path of judgment, and taught him knowledge, and shewed to him the way of understanding?

15. **Behold, the nations are as a drop of a bucket,** and are counted as the small dust of the balance: behold, he taketh up the isles as a very little thing.

16. And Lebanon *is* not sufficient to burn, nor the beasts thereof sufficient for a burnt offering.

17. **All nations before him are as nothing;** and they are counted to him less than nothing, and vanity.

18. **To whom** then **will ye liken God? or** what likeness will ye **compare unto him?**

19. The workman melteth a graven image, and the goldsmith spreadeth it over with gold, and casteth silver chains.

20. He that *is* so impoverished that he hath no oblation chooseth a tree *that* will not rot; he seeketh unto him a cunning workman to prepare a graven image, *that* shall not be moved.

21. **Have ye not known?** have ye not heard? hath it not been told you from the beginning? have ye not understood from the foundations of the earth?

22. **It is he that sitteth upon the circle of the earth, and the inhabitants thereof are as grasshoppers;** that stretcheth out the heavens as a curtain, and spreadeth them out as a tent to dwell in:

23. **That bringeth** the **princes to nothing;** he maketh the judges of the earth as vanity.

24. Yea, they shall not be planted; yea, they shall not be sown: yea, their stock shall not take root in the earth: and he shall also blow upon them, and they shall wither, and the whirlwind shall take them away as stubble.

25. **To whom then will ye liken me, or shall I be equal? saith the Holy One.**

26. **Lift up your eyes on high,** and behold who hath created these things, that bringeth out their host by number: he calleth them all by names by the greatness of his might, for that *he is* strong in power; **not one faileth.**

27. **Why sayest thou, O Jacob,** and speakest, O Israel, **My way is hid from the LORD,** and my judgment is passed over from my God?

28. **Hast thou not known?** hast thou not heard, **that the everlasting God,** the LORD, the Creator of the ends of the earth, **fainteth not, neither is weary? there is no searching of his understanding.**

29. **He giveth power to the faint;** and to *them that have* no might he increaseth strength.

30. **Even the youths shall faint and be weary,** and the young men shall utterly fall:

31. **But they that wait upon the LORD shall renew their strength; they shall mount up** with wings **as eagles; they shall run, and not be weary; and they shall walk, and not faint.**

CHAPTER 41

1. **Keep silence** before me, O islands; **and let the people renew their strength:** let them come near; then let them speak: **let us come near together to judgment.**

2. **Who raised up the righteous** man **from the east,** called him to his

foot, gave the nations before him,

■ **and made him rule**
■ **over kings?** he gave *them* as the
dust to his sword, *and* as
driven stubble to his bow.
3. He pursued them, *and* passed
safely; *even* by the way *that* he
had not gone with his feet.
4. Who hath wrought and
done *it*, calling the generations
from the beginning?
■ **I the LORD,** the first,
and with the last; I
■ **am he.**
■ 5. **The isles saw it, and**
■ **feared;** the ends of the earth
were afraid, drew near, and came.
■ 6. **They helped every**
■ **one his neighbour;**
and every one said to his
brother, Be of good courage.
7. So the carpenter encouraged the
goldsmith, *and* he that smootheth *with*
the hammer him that smote the anvil,
saying, It *is* ready for the soldering:
and he fastened it with nails, *that* it
should not be moved.
■ 8. **But thou, Israel, art**
■ **my servant,** Jacob,
■ **whom I have chosen,**
■ **the seed of Abraham**
■ **my friend.**
9. *Thou* whom I have taken from the
ends of the earth, and called thee
from the chief men thereof, and said
unto thee, Thou *art* my servant; I have
chosen thee, and not cast thee away.
■ 10. **Fear** thou
■ **not; for I am with thee:**
be not dismayed; for
■ **I am thy God: I will**
■ **strengthen thee;** yea,
I will help thee; yea,
■ **I will uphold thee**
■ **with** the right hand of
■ **my righteousness.**
■ 11. **Behold, all they that**
■ **were incensed against**
■ **thee shall be ashamed**
and confounded:
■ **they shall be as nothing;** and
they that strive with thee shall perish.
■ 12. **Thou shalt seek**

■ **them, and** shalt
■ **not find them,** *even*
them that contended with thee:
■ **they that war against**
■ **thee shall be as nothing,**
and as a thing of nought.
■ 13. **For I the LORD**
thy God will hold thy right hand,
saying unto thee, Fear not; I
■ **will help thee.**
■ 14. **Fear not,** thou worm
■ **Jacob, and** ye men of
■ **Israel; I will help thee,**
■ **saith** the LORD, and
■ **thy redeemer, the**
■ **Holy One of Israel.**
15. **Behold, I will make**
■ **thee a** new sharp
■ **threshing instrument**
■ **having teeth: thou shalt**
■ **thresh the mountains,**
■ **and beat them** small,
and shalt make the hills
■ **as chaff.**
16. Thou shalt fan them,
■ **and the wind shall** carry
them away, and the whirlwind shall
■ **scatter them: and thou**
■ **shalt rejoice in the**
■ **LORD,** *and* shalt glory in
the Holy One of Israel.
■ 17. **When the poor** and needy
■ **seek water, and there**
■ **is none,** *and* their tongue
faileth for thirst, I
■ **the LORD will hear them,** *I* the
God of Israel will not forsake them.
■ 18. **I will open rivers**
in high places,
■ **and** fountains
in the midst of the valleys: I will
■ **make the wilderness**
■ **a pool of water,** and the
dry land springs of water.
■ 19. **I will plant** in
■ **the wilderness** the cedar,
the shittah tree, and the myrtle,
and the oil tree; I will set in the
desert the fir tree, *and* the pine,
and the box tree together:
■ 20. **That they may see,**
and know, and consider,
and understand together,

that the hand of the LORD
hath done this, and the Holy
One of Israel hath created it.

21. **Produce your cause,
saith the LORD;**
bring forth your strong *reasons*,
saith the King of Jacob.

22. **Let them** bring *them* forth, and
**shew us what shall
happen**: let them shew the
former things, what they *be*,
that we may consider them,
and know the latter end of them; or
declare us things for to come.

23. **Shew the things that
are to come** hereafter,
**that we may know that ye
are gods**: yea, do good, or do
evil, that we may be dismayed,
and behold *it* together.

24. **Behold, ye are** of
nothing, and your work of nought:
**an abomination is he
that chooseth you.**

25. **I have raised up one
from the north, and he
shall** come: from the
rising of the sun shall he
call upon my name:
and he shall come upon princes
as *upon* morter, and as the
potter treadeth clay.

26. **Who hath declared from
the beginning, that we may
know?** and beforetime, that we
may say, *He is* righteous? yea,
there is none that sheweth, yea,
**there is none that
declareth, yea,** *there is*
**none that heareth
your words.**

27. The first *shall say* to Zion,
Behold, behold them: and
**I will give to Jerusalem one
that bringeth good tidings.**

28. For I beheld, and
there was no man; even
among them, and
there was no counsellor,
that, when I asked of them,
could answer a word.

29. Behold, they *are* all vanity;
their works are nothing:

their molten
images are wind and
confusion.

CHAPTER 42

1. **Behold my servant,**
whom I uphold;
**mine elect, in whom my
soul delighteth;** I have
put my spirit upon him:
**he shall bring forth
judgment to the Gentiles.**

2. **He shall not cry,**
nor lift up, nor cause his voice to
be heard in the street.

3. **A bruised reed shall he
not break,** and the smoking flax
shall he not quench: he shall bring
forth judgment unto truth.

4. **He shall not fail**
nor be discouraged,
**till he have set judgment
in the earth:** and the isles
shall wait for his law.

5. **Thus saith** God
the LORD, he that created the
heavens, and stretched them out;
**he that spread forth
the earth, and** that which
cometh out of it; he that
**giveth breath unto the
people upon it,** and spirit
to them that walk therein:

6. **I the LORD have called
thee in righteousness,**
and will hold thine hand,
**and will keep thee,
and give thee for a
covenant** of the people,
for a light of the Gentiles;

7. To open the blind eyes, to bring
out the prisoners from the prison,
and them that sit in darkness out
of the prison house.

8. **I am the LORD:**
that *is* my name:
**and my glory will I not give
to another, neither my
praise** to graven images.

9. **Behold,** the former things
are come to pass, and
new things do I declare:
before they spring forth

I tell you of them.

■ 10. **Sing unto the**
■ **LORD a new song**,
and his praise from the end
of the earth, ye that go down to the
sea, and all that is therein; the isles,
and the inhabitants thereof.
11. Let the wilderness and the cities
thereof lift up *their voice*, the villages
that Kedar doth inhabit: let the
inhabitants of the rock sing, let them
shout from the top of the mountains.
■ 12. **Let them give glory**
■ **unto the LORD,** and declare
his praise in the islands.
■ 13. **The LORD shall**
■ **go forth** as a mighty man,
he shall stir up jealousy
■ **like a man of war:**
he shall cry, yea, roar;
■ **he shall prevail against**
■ **his enemies.**
■ 14. **I have long time holden**
■ **my peace;** I have been still,
and refrained myself:
■ **now will I cry** like
a travailing woman;
■ **I will destroy and**
■ **devour at once.**
15. I will make waste mountains
and hills, and dry up all their herbs;
and I will make the rivers islands,
and I will dry up the pools.
■ 16. **And I will bring the**
■ **blind** by a way *that* they knew
not; I will lead them
■ **in paths that they have**
■ **not known: I will make**
■ **darkness light before them,**
and crooked things straight.
These things will
I do unto them,
and not forsake them.
■ 17. **They shall be** turned
back, they shall be greatly
■ **ashamed, that trust in**
■ **graven images,** that say to the
molten images, Ye *are* our gods.
18. Hear, ye deaf; and look,
ye blind, that ye may see.
19. Who *is* blind, but my servant?
or deaf, as my messenger *that* I
sent? who is blind as *he that is*

perfect, and blind
as the LORD's servant?
20. Seeing many things,
but thou observest not; opening the
ears, but he heareth not.
■ 21. **The LORD is well**
■ **pleased for his**
■ **righteousness' sake;**
■ **he will magnify the law,**
■ **and make it honourable.**
■ 22. **But this is a people**
■ **robbed and spoiled;**
they are all of them snared in
holes, and they are hid in prison
houses: they are for a prey,
■ **and none delivereth;** for a
spoil, and none saith, Restore.
23. Who among you will
give ear to this?
■ **who will hearken and**
■ **hear for the time to come?**
■ 24. **Who gave**
■ **Jacob** for a spoil,
■ **and Israel to the robbers?**
■ **did not the LORD,**
he against whom we have sinned?
■ **for they would not walk**
■ **in his ways,** neither were
they obedient unto his law.
■ 25. **Therefore he** hath
■ **poured upon him** the fury of
■ **his anger,** and the strength of
battle: and it hath set him on fire
round about, yet he knew not; and it
burned him, yet he laid *it* not to heart.

CHAPTER 43

■ 1. **But now** thus
■ **saith the LORD** that created
thee, O Jacob, and he that
formed thee, O Israel,
■ **Fear not:** for I have redeemed thee,
I have called *thee* by thy name;
■ **thou art mine.**
2. When thou passest
through the waters,
■ **I will be with thee;**
and through the rivers, they
shall not overflow thee:
■ **when thou walkest**
■ **through the fire, thou**
■ **shalt not be burned**; neither
shall the flame kindle upon thee.

3. **For I am the LORD** thy God, the Holy One of Israel, **thy Saviour:** I gave Egypt *for* thy ransom, Ethiopia and Seba for thee. 4. **Since thou wast precious in my sight,** thou hast been honourable, and **I have loved thee: therefore will I give** men for thee, and **people for thy life.** 5. **Fear not: for I am with thee: I will bring thy seed from the east, and** gather thee from the **west;** 6. **I will** say to the north, Give up; and to the south, Keep not back: **bring my sons** from far, **and** my **daughters from the ends of the earth;** 7. *Even* every one that is called by my name: for I have created him for my glory, I have formed him; yea, I have made him. 8. Bring forth the blind people that have eyes, and the deaf that have ears. 9. **Let all the nations** be gathered together, **and** let **the people be assembled: who among them can declare this, and shew us former things?** let them bring forth their witnesses, that they may be justified: or let them hear, and say, *It is* truth. 10. **Ye are my witnesses, saith the LORD,** and my servant **whom I have chosen: that ye may know and believe me,** and understand that I *am* he: **before me there was no God** formed, **neither shall there be after me.** 11. I, *even* I, *am* the LORD; **and beside me there is no saviour.** 12. I have declared, and have saved, and I have shewed, when *there was* no strange *god* among you:

therefore ye are my **witnesses, saith the LORD, that I am God.** 13. **Yea, before the day was I am he; and there is none that can deliver out of my hand:** I will work, and who shall let it? 14. **Thus saith the LORD,** your redeemer, the Holy One of Israel; **For your sake I** have sent to Babylon, and have **brought down** all their nobles, and **the Chaldeans,** whose cry *is* in the ships. 15. I *am* the LORD, your Holy One, the creator of Israel, your King. 16. Thus saith the LORD, which maketh a way in the sea, and a path in the mighty waters; 17. Which bringeth forth the chariot and horse, the army and the power; they shall lie down together, they shall not rise: they are extinct, they are quenched as tow. 18. **Remember ye not the former things,** neither consider the things of old. 19. **Behold, I will do a new thing;** now it shall spring forth; shall ye not know it? **I will even make a way in the wilderness,** *and* rivers in the desert. 20. **The beast** of the field **shall honour me,** the dragons and the owls: **because I give waters in the wilderness,** *and* rivers in the desert, to give drink **to my people,** my chosen. 21. **This people** have I formed for myself; they **shall shew forth my praise.** 22. **But thou hast not called upon me, O Jacob; but thou hast been weary of me, O Israel.** 23. **Thou hast not brought me** the small cattle of **thy burnt offerings; neither** hast thou honoured me with

■ **thy sacrifices.** I have not caused thee to serve with an offering, nor wearied thee with incense.

24. Thou hast bought me no sweet cane with money, neither hast thou filled me with the fat of thy sacrifices: ■ **but thou hast** made me to serve with thy sins, thou hast ■ **wearied me with** ■ **thine iniquities.**

25. **I,** *even* I, *am* he that ■ **blotteth out thy** ■ **transgressions** ■ **for mine own sake,** ■ **and will not remember** ■ **thy sins.**

26. Put me in remembrance: let us plead together: declare thou, that thou mayest be justified.

27. ■ **Thy** first ■ **father** hath sinned, ■ **and** thy ■ **teachers have transgressed** ■ **against me.**

28. **Therefore I** have profaned the princes of the sanctuary, and ■ **have given Jacob** to the curse, ■ **and Israel to reproaches.**

CHAPTER 44

■ 1. **Yet now hear,** O ■ **Jacob** my servant; ■ **and Israel, whom** ■ **I have chosen:**

2. Thus saith the LORD that made thee, and formed thee from the womb, *which* will help thee; Fear not, O Jacob, my servant; and thou, Jesurun, whom I have chosen.

3. ■ **For I will pour water upon** ■ **him that is thirsty, and** floods upon the dry ground: I will pour ■ **my spirit upon thy seed,** and my blessing upon thine offspring:

4. ■ **And they shall spring up** as among the grass, as willows by the water courses.

5. ■ **One shall say, I am the** ■ **LORD's; and another shall** ■ **call himself by the name** ■ **of Jacob; and another** shall subscribe *with* his hand

unto the LORD, and surname *himself* by the name of ■ **Israel.**

■ 6. **Thus saith the** ■ **LORD** the King of Israel, and his redeemer the LORD of hosts; ■ **I am the first, and** I *am* ■ **the last;** and ■ **beside me there is no God.**

7. **And who,** as I, shall call, and ■ **shall declare it,** and set it in order ■ **for me,** since I appointed the ancient people? and ■ **the things that are** ■ **coming,** and ■ **shall come,** let them shew unto them.

8. **Fear** ye ■ **not,** neither be afraid: have not I told thee from that time, and have declared *it*? ■ **ye are** even ■ **my witnesses.** Is there a God beside me? yea, *there is* no God; I know not *any*.

■ 9. **They that make a graven** ■ **image** *are* all of them vanity; and their delectable things ■ **shall not profit;** and they *are* their own witnesses; they see not, nor know; that they may be ashamed.

10. Who hath formed a god, or molten a graven image *that* is profitable for nothing?

11. Behold, all his fellows shall be ashamed: and the workmen, they *are* of men: let them all be gathered together, let them stand up; *yet* they shall fear, *and* they shall be ashamed together.

■ 12. **The smith** with the tongs both ■ **worketh in the coals, and** ■ **fashioneth it with hammers,** and worketh it with the strength of his arms: yea, he is hungry, and his strength faileth: he drinketh no water, and is faint.

■ 13. **The carpenter** stretcheth out *his* rule; he marketh it out with a line; he ■ **fitteth it with planes,**

■ **and** he marketh it out with
■ **the compass,** and maketh it
■ **after the figure of a man,**
according to the beauty of a man;
that it may remain in the house.
■ 14. **He heweth him down**
■ **cedars,** and taketh the
■ **cypress and** the
■ **oak,** which he strengtheneth for
himself among the trees of the
forest: he planteth an ash,
and the rain doth nourish *it*.
15. Then shall it be for a man to burn:
for he will take thereof, and warm
himself; yea, he kindleth *it*, and
baketh bread; yea, he maketh a god,
and worshippeth *it*; he maketh
it a graven image, and falleth
down thereto.
■ 16. **He burneth part thereof**
■ **in the fire;** with part thereof he
eateth flesh; he roasteth roast,
and is satisfied: yea,
■ **he warmeth himself,** and saith,
Aha, I am warm, I have seen the fire:
■ 17. **And the residue thereof**
■ **he maketh a god,** *even* his
graven image: he falleth down
unto it, and worshippeth *it*,
■ **and prayeth unto it,**
■ **and saith, Deliver me;**
■ **for thou art my god.**
18. They have not
known nor understood:
■ **for he hath shut their eyes,**
■ **that they cannot see**; *and* their
hearts, that they cannot understand.
19. And none considereth
in his heart,
neither *is there* knowledge
nor understanding to say,
I have burned part of it
in the fire; yea, also I have baked
bread upon the coals thereof; I
have roasted flesh, and eaten *it*:
and shall I make the residue
thereof an abomination? shall I
fall down to the stock of a tree?
20. He feedeth on ashes:
■ **a deceived heart hath**
■ **turned him aside, that he**
■ **cannot deliver his soul,** nor
say, *Is there* not a lie in my right hand?

■ 21. **Remember these,**
■ **O Jacob and Israel;**
for thou *art* my servant:
■ **I have formed thee;**
thou *art* my servant: O Israel,
thou shalt not be forgotten of me.
■ 22. **I have blotted out,**
as a thick cloud, thy
transgressions, and, as a cloud,
■ **thy sins: return unto me;**
■ **for I have redeemed thee.**
■ 23. **Sing, O ye heavens;**
for the LORD hath done *it*: shout,
ye lower parts of the earth: break
forth into singing, ye mountains,
O forest, and every tree therein:
■ **for the LORD hath**
■ **redeemed Jacob,**
■ **and** glorified himself in
■ **Israel.**
24. **Thus saith the**
■ **LORD,** thy redeemer, and
■ **he that formed thee from**
■ **the womb, I am the LORD**
■ **that maketh all things;**
that stretcheth forth the
heavens alone; that spreadeth
abroad the earth by myself;
25. That frustrateth the tokens of
the liars, and maketh diviners mad;
that turneth wise *men* backward,
and maketh their knowledge foolish;
■ 26. **That confirmeth the**
■ **word of his servant,**
and performeth the counsel
of his messengers;
■ **that saith to Jerusalem,**
■ **Thou shalt be inhabited;**
and to the cities of Judah, Ye
shall be built, and I will raise
up the decayed places thereof:
■ 27. **That saith to the**
■ **deep, Be dry,** and I
will dry up thy rivers:
■ 28. **That saith of Cyrus,**
■ **He** *is* my shepherd, and
■ **shall perform all**
■ **my pleasure: even**
■ **saying to Jerusalem,**
■ **Thou shalt be built;**
■ **and to the temple,**
■ **Thy foundation**
■ **shall be laid.**

CHAPTER 45

■ 1. **Thus saith the LORD to his**
■ **anointed, to Cyrus**, whose right
hand I have holden, to subdue
nations before him; and I will loose
the loins of kings, to open before
him the two leaved gates; and
the gates shall not be shut;

■ 2. **I will go before thee,** and
make the crooked places straight: I
will break in pieces the gates of brass,
and cut in sunder the bars of iron:

■ 3. **And I will give thee** the
treasures of darkness, and
■ **hidden riches of secret**
■ **places, that thou mayest**
■ **know that I,** the LORD,
which call *thee* by thy name,
■ **am the God of Israel.**
■ 4. **For Jacob my servant's**
■ **sake, and Israel mine**
■ **elect, I have even called**
■ **thee by thy name:** I have
surnamed thee,
■ **though thou hast**
■ **not known me.**
5. I *am* the LORD, and *there is*
none else, *there is* no God beside me:
■ **I girded thee,** though
thou hast not known me:
6. That they may know from the
rising of the sun, and from the
west, that *there is* none beside me.
I *am* the LORD, and
there is none else.
7. I form the light,
and create darkness:
I make peace, and create
evil: I the LORD do all these *things*.
8. Drop down, ye
heavens, from above, and
let the skies pour down
righteousness: let the
earth open, and let them
bring forth salvation, and
let righteousness spring up together;
I the LORD have created it.
9. Woe unto him that striveth
with his Maker!
Let the potsherd *strive* with
the potsherds of the earth.
Shall the clay say to him that
fashioneth it, What makest

thou? or thy work,
He hath no hands?
10. Woe unto him that saith unto *his*
father, What begettest thou? or to the
woman, What hast thou brought forth?
11. Thus saith the LORD, the Holy
One of Israel, and his Maker,
Ask me of things to
come concerning my
sons, and concerning
the work of my hands
command ye me.
■ 12. **I have made the earth,**
■ **and created man** upon it:
I, *even* my hands, have
stretched out the
heavens, and all their
host have I commanded.
13. I have raised him up
in righteousness,
■ **and I**
■ **will direct all his ways:**
■ **he shall build my**
■ **city, and** he
■ **shall let go my captives, not**
■ **for price nor reward,** saith the
LORD of hosts.
■ 14. **Thus saith the LORD,**
The labour of
■ **Egypt,**
and merchandise of
■ **Ethiopia and** of
■ **the Sabeans**,
men of stature, shall come
over unto thee, and they
■ **shall be thine:** they
shall come after thee; in
chains they shall come over,
■ **and they shall fall down**
■ **unto thee, they shall make**
■ **supplication unto thee,**
■ **saying, Surely God is in**
■ **thee**; and *there is* none else,
there is no God.
■ 15. **Verily thou art a God**
■ **that hidest thyself,**
O God of Israel, the Saviour.
■ 16. **They shall be**
■ **ashamed, and also**
■ **confounded, all of them**: they
shall go to confusion together
■ **that are makers of idols.**
■ 17. **But Israel shall be**

saved in the LORD with an everlasting salvation: ye shall not be ashamed nor confounded world without end.

18. For thus saith the LORD that created the heavens; God himself that formed the earth and made it; he hath established it, he created it not in vain, he formed it to be inhabited: I *am* the LORD; and *there is* none else.

19. I have not spoken in secret, in a dark place of the earth: I said not unto the seed of Jacob, Seek ye me in vain: I the LORD speak righteousness, I declare things that are right.

20. Assemble yourselves and come; draw near together, ye that are escaped of the nations: they have no knowledge that set up the wood of their graven image, and pray unto a god that cannot save.

21. Tell ye, and bring *them* near; yea, let them take counsel together: *who* hath declared this from ancient time? who hath told it from that time? *have* not I the LORD? and *there is* no God else beside me; a just God and a Saviour; *there is* none beside me.

22. Look unto me, and be ye saved, all the ends of the earth: for I am God, and *there is* none else.

23. I have sworn by myself, the word is gone out of my mouth *in* righteousness, and shall not return, That unto me every knee shall bow, every tongue shall swear.

24. Surely, shall *one* say, in the LORD have I righteousness and strength: *even* to him shall *men* come; and all that are incensed against him shall be ashamed.

25. In the LORD shall all the seed of Israel be justified, and shall glory.

CHAPTER 46

1. Bel boweth down, Nebo stoopeth, their idols were upon the beasts, and upon the cattle: your carriages *were* heavy loaden; they are a burden to the weary beast.

2. They stoop, they bow down together; they could not deliver the burden, but themselves are gone into captivity.

3. Hearken unto me, O house of Jacob, and all the remnant of the house of Israel, which are borne *by me* from the belly, which are carried from the womb:

4. And *even* to *your* old age I *am* he; and *even* to hoar hairs will I carry *you:* I have made, and I will bear; even I will carry, and will deliver you.

5. To whom will ye liken me, and make *me* equal, and compare me, that we may be like?

6. They lavish gold out of the bag, and weigh silver in the balance, and hire a goldsmith; and he maketh it a god: they fall down, yea, they worship.

7. They bear him upon the shoulder, they carry him, and set him in his place, and he standeth; from his place shall he not remove: yea, one shall cry unto him, yet can he not answer, nor save him out of his trouble.

8. Remember this, and shew yourselves men: bring *it* again to mind, O ye transgressors.

9. Remember the former things of old: for I am God, and *there is* none else; *I am* God, and there is none like me,

10. Declaring the end from the beginning, and from ancient times *the things* that are not *yet* done, saying, My counsel shall stand, and I will do all my

pleasure:

11. Calling a ravenous bird from the east, the man that executeth my counsel from a far country: yea, I have spoken *it,* I will also bring it to pass; I have purposed *it,* I will also do it.

12. **Hearken unto me, ye** stouthearted, **that are far from righteousness:**

13. **I bring near my righteousness;** it shall not be far off, and my salvation shall not tarry: **and I will place salvation in Zion for Israel my glory.**

CHAPTER 47

1. **Come down, and sit in the dust, O virgin daughter of Babylon,** sit on the ground: **there is no throne, O daughter of the Chaldeans:** for **thou shalt no more be** called tender and **delicate.**

2. Take the millstones, and **grind meal:** uncover thy locks, **make bare the leg,** uncover the thigh, pass over the rivers.

3. **Thy nakedness shall be uncovered,** yea, **thy shame shall be seen:** I will take vengeance, and **I will not meet thee as a man.**

4. **As for our redeemer, the LORD** of hosts **is his name,** the Holy One of Israel.

5. **Sit thou silent,** and get thee into darkness, **O daughter of the Chaldeans: for thou shalt no more be called, The lady of kingdoms.**

6. **I was wroth with my people, I have** polluted mine inheritance, and **given them into thine hand:** thou didst shew them no

mercy; upon the ancient hast thou very heavily laid thy yoke.

7. And thou saidst, I shall be a lady for ever: *so* that thou didst not lay these *things* to thy heart, neither didst remember the latter end of it.

8. **Therefore hear now this, thou** *that art* given to pleasures, that dwellest carelessly, **that sayest in thine heart,** I *am,* and none else beside me; **I shall not sit as a widow, neither shall I know the loss of children.**

9. **But these two things shall come to thee in** a moment in **one day, the loss of children, and widowhood:** they shall come upon thee in their perfection for the multitude of thy sorceries, *and* for the great abundance of thine enchantments.

10. **For thou hast trusted in thy wickedness:** thou hast said, None seeth me. Thy wisdom and thy knowledge, it hath perverted thee; and thou hast said in thine heart, I *am,* and none else beside me.

11. **Therefore** shall evil come upon thee; thou shalt not know from whence it riseth: and **mischief shall fall upon thee;** thou shalt not be able to put it off: **and desolation shall come upon thee suddenly,** which thou shalt not know.

12. **Stand** now **with thine enchantments, and** with the multitude of **thy sorceries,** wherein thou hast laboured from thy youth; **if so be thou shalt be able to** profit, if so be thou mayest **prevail.**

13. **Thou art wearied in** the multitude of **thy counsels. Let now the astrologers, the stargazers, the monthly prognosticators**, stand up, and

■ **save thee from these things**
that shall come upon thee.

■ 14. **Behold,** they shall be as
stubble; the fire shall burn them;

■ **they shall not deliver**

■ **themselves** from the power of
the flame: *there shall* not *be* a coal
to warm at, *nor* fire to sit before it.

15. Thus shall they be unto thee with
whom thou hast laboured, *even* thy
merchants, from thy youth: they shall
wander every one to his quarter;

■ **none shall save thee.**

CHAPTER 48

■ 1. **Hear** ye

■ **this, O** house of

■ **Jacob,** which are called by the
name of Israel, and are come forth
out of the waters of Judah,

■ **which swear by the name**

■ **of the LORD,** and make
mention of the God of Israel,

■ **but not in truth, nor**

■ **in righteousness.**
2. For they call themselves of the
holy city, and stay themselves
upon the God of Israel;
The LORD of hosts *is* his name.

■ 3. **I have declared the**

■ **former things** from the
beginning; and they went forth
out of my mouth, and I shewed
them; I did *them* suddenly,

■ **and they came to pass.**

■ 4. **Because I knew that**

■ **thou art obstinate, and**

■ **thy neck is an iron sinew,**
and thy brow brass;

■ 5. **I have** even from the beginning

■ **declared it to thee; before it**

■ **came to pass** I shewed *it* thee:

■ **lest thou shouldest say,**

■ **Mine idol hath done them,**
and my graven image, and my molten
image, hath commanded them.
6. Thou hast heard, see all this;
and will not ye declare *it?*

■ **I have shewed thee**
new things from
this time, even

■ **hidden things,**
and thou didst not know them.

7. They are created now, and not
from the beginning; even before
the day when thou heardest them
not; lest thou shouldest say,
Behold, I knew them.
8. Yea, thou heardest not; yea, thou
knewest not; yea, from that time *that*
thine ear was not opened: for I knew
that thou wouldest deal very
treacherously, and wast called a
transgressor from the womb.

■ 9. **For my name's sake**

■ **will I defer mine anger,**
and for my praise will I refrain for
thee, that I cut thee not off.

■ 10. **Behold, I have**

■ **refined thee,** but not with
silver; I have chosen thee

■ **in the furnace of affliction.**

■ 11. **For mine own sake,**
even for mine own sake,

■ **will I do it:** for how should
my name be polluted? and

■ **I will not give my glory**

■ **unto another.**

■ 12. **Hearken unto me,** O
Jacob and Israel, my called; I *am* he;

■ **I am the first, I**

■ **also** *am*

■ **the last.**

■ 13. **Mine hand** also hath

■ **laid the foundation of the**

■ **earth, and** my right hand hath

■ **spanned the heavens:**

■ **when I call** unto them,

■ **they stand up together.**
14. All ye, assemble
yourselves, and hear;

■ **which among them hath**

■ **declared these things?**

■ **The LORD** hath loved him: he

■ **will do his pleasure on**

■ **Babylon,** and his arm *shall*
be on the Chaldeans.

15. **I,** *even* I,

■ **have spoken;** yea,

■ **I have called him:**
I have brought him,

■ **and** he

■ **shall make his way**

■ **prosperous.**
16. Come ye near unto
me, hear ye this;

I have not spoken
in secret from the beginning;
from the time that it was,
there *am* I: and now the Lord
GOD, and his Spirit, hath sent me.
17. **Thus saith the LORD,** thy
Redeemer, the Holy One of Israel;
I am the LORD thy God
which teacheth thee to profit, which
leadeth thee by the way
that thou shouldest go.
18. O that thou hadst
hearkened to my
commandments! then
had thy peace been as
a river, and thy righteousness
as the waves of the sea:
19. Thy seed also had been
as the sand, and the offspring
of thy bowels like the gravel thereof;
his name should not have been cut
off nor destroyed from before me.
20. Go ye
forth of Babylon, flee ye
from the Chaldeans,
with a voice of singing
declare ye, tell
this, utter it *even* to the
end of the earth; say ye,
The LORD hath
redeemed his servant
Jacob.
21. And they thirsted not
when he led them through
the deserts: he caused the
waters to flow out of the
rock for them: he clave the rock
also, and the waters gushed out.
22. There is no peace, saith
the LORD, unto the wicked.

CHAPTER 49

1. Listen, O isles,
unto me; and hearken, ye
people, from far;
The LORD hath called
me from the womb;
from the bowels of my mother hath
he made mention of my name.
2. And he hath made my
mouth like a sharp sword; in
the shadow of his
hand hath he hid me,
and made me a polished shaft;
in his quiver hath he hid me;
3. And said unto me,
Thou art my servant,
O Israel, in whom I
will be glorified.
4. Then I said, I have
laboured in vain, I have spent
my strength for nought, and in vain:
yet surely my judgment
is with the LORD,
and my work with my God.
5. And now, saith the LORD that
formed me from the womb *to be* his
servant, to bring Jacob again to him,
Though Israel be not
gathered, yet shall I be
glorious in the eyes of
the LORD, and my God
shall be my strength.
6. And he said, It is a
light thing that thou
shouldest be my servant to
raise up the tribes
of Jacob, and to restore
the preserved of Israel:
I will also give thee for
a light to the Gentiles,
that thou mayest be
my salvation unto the
end of the earth.
7. Thus saith the LORD,
the Redeemer of Israel,
and his Holy One, to him
whom man despiseth,
to him whom the nation abhorreth,
to a servant of rulers,
Kings shall see
and arise,
princes also
shall worship, because of
the LORD that is faithful, *and*
the Holy One of Israel, and he
shall choose thee.
8. Thus saith the LORD, In
an acceptable time have
I heard thee, and in a
day of salvation have I
helped thee: and I will
preserve thee, and give
thee for a covenant
of the people,
to establish the

earth, to cause to inherit the desolate heritages;

9. **That thou mayest say to** the prisoners, Go forth; to **them** that *are* **in darkness, Shew yourselves.** They shall feed in the ways, and their pastures *shall be* in all high places.

10. **They shall not hunger nor thirst;** neither shall the heat nor sun smite them: **for he that hath mercy on them shall lead them,** even by the springs of water shall he guide them.

11. And I will make all my mountains a way, and my highways shall be exalted.

12. **Behold, these shall come from far:** and, lo, these from the north and from the west; and these from the land of Sinim.

13. **Sing, O heavens; and be joyful, O earth;** and break forth into singing, O mountains: **for the LORD** hath comforted his people, and **will have mercy upon his afflicted.**

14. **But Zion said, The LORD hath** forsaken me, and my Lord hath **forgotten me.**

15. **Can a woman forget her sucking child,** that she should not have compassion on the son of her womb? **yea, they may forget, yet will I not forget thee.**

16. **Behold, I have graven thee upon the palms of my hands;** thy walls *are* continually before me.

17. Thy children shall make haste; thy destroyers and they that made thee waste shall go forth of thee.

18. **Lift up thine eyes** round about, **and behold: all these gather themselves together, and come to thee.** *As* I live, saith the LORD,

thou shalt surely clothe thee with them all, **as with an ornament,** and bind them *on thee,* as a bride *doeth.*

19. **For thy** waste and thy desolate places, and the **land** of thy destruction, **shall even now be too narrow by reason of the inhabitants,** and they that swallowed thee up shall be far away.

20. **The children which thou shalt have, after thou hast lost the other, shall say** again in thine ears, **The place is too strait** for me: **give place to me that I may dwell.**

21. **Then shalt thou say** in thine heart, **Who hath begotten** me **these, seeing I** have **lost my children, and** am desolate, a captive, and removing to and fro? and **who hath brought up these?** Behold, I was left alone; these, where *had* they *been?*

22. **Thus saith the** Lord GOD, Behold, **I will lift up mine hand to the Gentiles,** and set up my standard to the people: **and they shall bring** thy **sons** in *their* arms, **and** thy **daughters** shall be carried upon *their* shoulders.

23. **And kings** shall be thy nursing fathers, **and their queens** thy nursing mothers: they **shall bow down to thee** with *their* face toward the earth, and lick up the dust of thy feet; **and thou shalt know that I am the LORD: for they shall not be ashamed that wait for me.**

24. Shall the prey be taken from the mighty, or the lawful captive delivered?

25. But thus saith the LORD,
Even the captives of
the mighty shall be
taken away, and the prey
of the terrible shall be delivered:
for I will contend with him
that contendeth with thee,
and I will save thy children.
26. **And I will feed them that**
oppress thee with their own
flesh; and they shall be drunken with
their own blood, as with sweet wine:
and all flesh shall know that
I the LORD am thy Saviour
and thy Redeemer,
the mighty One of Jacob.

CHAPTER 50

1. **Thus saith the LORD,**
Where is the bill of your
mother's divorcement,
whom I have put away?
or which of
my creditors *is it*
to whom I have
sold you? Behold,
for your iniquities have
ye sold yourselves,
and for your transgressions is
your mother put away.
2. **Wherefore,** when I
came, *was there* no man?
when I called, was
there none to
answer? Is my hand
shortened at all,
that it cannot redeem?
or have I no power to deliver?
behold, at my rebuke I
dry up the sea, I make the
rivers a wilderness: their fish
stinketh, because *there is* no
water, and dieth for thirst.
3. **I clothe the heavens**
with blackness, and I
make sackcloth their covering.
4. **The Lord GOD hath**
given me the tongue of the
learned, that I should know how
to speak a word in season
to him that is weary: he
wakeneth morning by morning,
he wakeneth mine ear to hear

as the learned.
5. **The Lord** GOD hath
opened mine ear, and
I was not rebellious,
neither turned away back.
6. **I gave my back to the**
smiters, and my cheeks to
them that plucked off the
hair: I hid not my face from
shame and spitting.
7. **For the Lord GOD will**
help me; therefore shall I not
be confounded: therefore have
I set my face like a flint,
and I know that I shall
not be ashamed.
8. **He is near that justifieth**
me; who will contend with me?
let us stand together: who *is* mine
adversary? let him come near to me.
9. Behold, the Lord GOD will help
me; who *is* he *that* shall condemn
me? lo, they all shall wax old
as a garment; the moth
shall eat them up.
10. **Who is**
among you that
feareth the LORD, that obeyeth
the voice of his servant, that walketh
in darkness, and hath no light?
let him trust in the name of the
LORD, and stay upon his God.
11. Behold, all ye that kindle a fire,
that compass *yourselves* about with
sparks: walk in the light of your fire,
and in the sparks *that* ye have
kindled. This shall ye have of mine
hand; ye shall lie down in sorrow.

CHAPTER 51

1. **Hearken to me, ye that**
follow after righteousness, ye
that seek the LORD: look unto the
rock *whence* ye are hewn, and to the
hole of the pit *whence* ye are digged.
2. **Look unto Abraham**
your father,
and unto Sarah *that* bare you:
for I called him alone, and
blessed him, and increased him.
3. **For the LORD shall**
comfort Zion:
he will comfort all her waste places;

and he
will make her wilderness
like Eden, and her desert
like the garden of the LORD;
joy and gladness shall
be found therein, thanksgiving,
and the voice of melody.
4. Hearken unto me,
my people; and give ear
unto me, O my nation:
for a law shall proceed from
me, and I will make
my judgment to rest
for a light of the people.
5. My righteousness is near;
my salvation is gone forth,
and mine arms shall judge the people;
the isles shall
wait upon me,
and on mine arm shall they trust.
6. Lift up your eyes
to the heavens, and look
upon the earth beneath:
for the heavens shall
vanish away like smoke,
and the earth shall wax old
like a garment, and they that dwell
therein shall die in like manner:
but my salvation shall be
for ever, and my righteousness
shall not be abolished.
7. Hearken unto me, ye
that know righteousness, the
people in whose heart is
my law; fear ye not the
reproach of men,
neither be ye afraid of their revilings.
8. For the moth shall eat
them up like a garment, and the
worm shall eat them like wool:
but my righteousness shall
be for ever, and my salvation from
generation to generation.
9. Awake, awake, put on strength,
O arm of the LORD; awake,
as in the ancient
days, in the generations
of old. Art thou not it that
hath cut Rahab,
and wounded the dragon?
10. Art thou not it which
hath dried the sea,
the waters of the great deep;

that hath
made the depths of the sea
a way for the ransomed
to pass over?
11. Therefore the redeemed
of the LORD shall return,
and come with singing unto Zion;
and everlasting joy shall
be upon their head:
they shall obtain gladness and joy;
and sorrow and mourning shall flee
away.
12. I, even I,
am he that comforteth you:
who art thou, that thou
shouldest be afraid of a
man that shall die, and of the son of
man which shall be made as grass;
13. And forgettest the LORD
thy maker, that hath
stretched forth the heavens,
and laid the foundations of
the earth;
and hast feared continually every
day because of the fury of
the oppressor, as if he were
ready to destroy? and where
is the fury of the oppressor?
14. The captive exile
hasteneth that he
may be loosed,
and that he should not die in the
pit, nor that his bread should fail.
15. But I am the LORD
thy God, that divided the sea,
whose waves roared: The LORD
of hosts is his name.
16. And I have put my
words in thy mouth, and I
have covered thee in the
shadow of mine hand, that I may plant
the heavens, and lay the foundations
of the earth, and say unto Zion,
Thou art my people.
17. Awake, awake, stand up,
O Jerusalem,
which hast drunk at the
hand of the LORD the cup
of his fury; thou hast drunken
the dregs of the cup of trembling,
and wrung them out.
18. There is none to guide her
among all the sons whom she hath

brought forth; neither is *there any*

■ **that taketh her by the**

■ **hand** of all the sons *that*

she hath brought up.

■ 19. **These two things**

■ **are come unto thee;**

who shall be sorry for thee?

■ **desolation, and**

■ **destruction,** and the

■ **famine, and the sword:** by

■ **whom shall I comfort thee?**

20. **Thy sons have fainted,**

they lie at the head of all the

streets, as a wild bull in a net:

■ **they are full of**

the fury of the LORD,

■ **the rebuke of** thy

■ **God.**

■ 21. **Therefore hear now**

■ **this, thou afflicted**,

and drunken, but

not with wine:

22. Thus saith thy Lord the

LORD, and thy God *that* pleadeth

the cause of his people,

■ **Behold, I have taken out**

■ **of thine hand the cup of**

■ **trembling,** *even* the dregs

of the cup of my fury;

■ **thou shalt no more**

■ **drink it again:**

■ 23. **But I will put it into the**

■ **hand of them that afflict**

■ **thee;** which have said to thy

soul, Bow down, that we may go

over: and thou hast laid thy

body as the ground, and as the street,

to them that went over.

CHAPTER 52

■ 1. **Awake,** awake;

■ **put on thy strength, O Zion;**

put on thy beautiful garments,

O Jerusalem, the holy city:

■ **for henceforth there shall**

■ **no more come into thee**

■ **the uncircumcised**

■ **and the unclean.**

■ 2. **Shake thyself from**

■ **the dust;** arise,

■ **and** sit down, O Jerusalem:

■ **loose thyself** from the

bands of thy neck,

■ **O captive** daughter of Zion.

3. For thus saith the LORD,

■ **Ye have sold yourselves for**

■ **nought; and ye shall be**

■ **redeemed without money.**

4. For thus saith the Lord GOD,

■ **My people went** down aforetime

■ **into Egypt** to sojourn there;

■ **and the Assyrian**

■ **oppressed them**

■ **without cause.**

5. **Now** therefore,

■ **what have I here,**

■ **saith the LORD,** that

■ **my people is taken**

■ **away for nought?**

they that rule over them make

them to howl, saith the LORD;

■ **and my name**

continually every day

■ **is blasphemed.**

6. **Therefore my people**

■ **shall know my name:**

therefore *they shall know* in

that day that I *am* he that doth

speak: behold, *it is* I.

■ 7. **How beautiful**

upon the mountains

■ **are the feet of him that**

■ **bringeth good tidings,**

that publisheth peace; that

bringeth good tidings of good,

■ **that publisheth salvation;**

■ **that saith** unto Zion,

■ **Thy God reigneth!**

8. **Thy watchmen shall**

■ **lift up the voice;** with the

voice together shall they sing:

for they shall see eye to eye,

■ **when the LORD shall**

■ **bring again Zion.**

9. **Break forth into joy,**

■ **sing** together,

■ **ye waste places of**

■ **Jerusalem:** for the LORD

hath comforted his people, he

■ **hath redeemed Jerusalem.**

10. **The LORD hath made**

■ **bare his holy arm** in the

eyes of all the nations;

■ **and all** the ends of

■ **the earth shall see the**

■ **salvation of our God.**

11. **Depart ye,** depart ye, go ye out from thence, **touch no unclean thing;** go ye out of the midst of her; **be ye clean, that bear the vessels of the LORD.** 12. **For ye shall not go out with haste,** nor go by flight: **for the LORD will go before you; and** the God of Israel *will* **be your rereward.** 13. **Behold, my servant** shall deal prudently, he **shall be exalted** and extolled, and be very high. 14. **As many were astonied** at thee; **his visage was** so **marred more than any man**, and his form more than the sons of men: 15. **So shall he sprinkle many nations; the kings shall shut their mouths** at him: **for that which had not been told them shall they see;** and *that* which they had not heard shall they consider.

CHAPTER 53

1. **Who hath believed our report? and to whom is the arm of the LORD revealed?** 2. **For he shall grow up** before him **as a tender plant,** and as a root **out of a dry ground: he hath no** form nor **comeliness;** and when we shall see him, *there is* no beauty **that we should desire him.** 3. **He is** despised and **rejected of men;** a man of sorrows, and **acquainted with grief: and we hid** as it were *our* faces **from him;** he was despised, **and** we **esteemed him not.** 4. **Surely he hath borne our griefs, and** carried our **sorrows: yet we did**

esteem him stricken, smitten **of God, and afflicted.** 5. **But he was wounded for our transgressions,** **he was bruised for our iniquities: the chastisement of our peace was** **upon him; and with his stripes we are healed.** 6. **All we like sheep have gone astray; we have turned every one to his own way; and the LORD hath laid on him the iniquity of us all.** 7. **He was oppressed, and** he was **afflicted, yet he opened not his mouth:** he is brought as a lamb to the slaughter, and as a sheep before her shearers is dumb, so he openeth not his mouth. 8. **He was taken from prison and from judgment:** and who shall declare his generation? **for he was cut off out of the land of the living: for the transgression of my people** was he stricken. 9. **And he made his grave with the wicked, and with the rich in his death;** because **he had done no violence, neither was any deceit in his mouth.** 10. **Yet it pleased the LORD to** bruise him; he hath put *him* to grief: when thou shalt **make his soul an offering for sin,** he shall see *his* seed, he shall prolong *his* days, and the pleasure of the LORD shall prosper in his hand. 11. **He shall see of the travail** of his soul, **and shall be satisfied: by his knowledge shall my righteous servant justify many; for he shall bear their iniquities.** 12. **Therefore will I divide him a portion with the**

great, and he shall divide the spoil with the strong; because he hath poured out his soul unto death: and he was numbered with the transgressors; and he bare the sin of many, and made intercession for the transgressors.

CHAPTER 54

1. **Sing,** O barren, thou *that* didst not bear; break forth into singing, and cry aloud, **thou that didst not travail with child:** for more *are* the children of the desolate than the children of the married wife, saith the LORD.

2. **Enlarge the place of thy tent,** and let them stretch forth the curtains of thine habitations: spare not, lengthen thy cords, and strengthen thy stakes;

3. **For thou shalt break forth** on the right hand and on the left; **and thy seed shall inherit the Gentiles, and make the desolate cities to be inhabited.**

4. **Fear not; for thou** shalt not be ashamed: neither be thou confounded; for thou shalt not be put to shame: for thou shalt forget the shame of thy youth, and **shalt not remember the reproach of thy widowhood** any more.

5. **For thy Maker is thine husband;** the LORD of hosts *is* his name; **and thy Redeemer** the Holy One of Israel; **The God of the whole earth** shall he be called.

6. **For the LORD hath called thee as a woman** forsaken and grieved in spirit, **and a wife** of youth, when thou wast refused, saith thy God.

7. **For a** small **moment have I forsaken**

thee; but with great mercies will I gather thee.

8. In a little wrath I hid my face from thee for a moment; but with everlasting kindness will I have mercy on thee, saith the LORD thy Redeemer.

9. For this *is as* the waters of Noah unto me: **for as I have sworn that the waters of Noah should no more go over the earth; so have I sworn that I would not be wroth with thee,** nor rebuke thee.

10. **For the mountains shall depart,** and the hills be removed; **but my kindness shall not depart** from thee, neither shall the covenant of my peace be removed, **saith the LORD** that hath mercy on thee.

11. **O thou afflicted,** tossed with tempest, *and* not comforted, behold, **I will lay** thy stones with fair colours, and lay **thy foundations with sapphires.**

12. **And** I will make **thy windows of agates, and thy gates of carbuncles, and all thy borders of pleasant stones.**

13. **And all thy children shall be taught of the LORD;** and great *shall be* the peace of thy children.

14. In righteousness shalt thou be established: thou shalt be far from oppression; for thou shalt not fear: and from terror; for it shall not come near thee.

15. Behold, they shall surely gather together, *but* not by me: **whosoever shall gather** together **against thee shall fall for thy sake.**

16. Behold, I have created the smith that bloweth the coals in the fire, and that bringeth forth an

instrument for his work; and I have created the waster to destroy.

17. **No weapon that is formed against thee shall prosper; and every tongue that shall rise against thee in judgment thou shalt condemn.** This *is* the heritage of the servants of the LORD, and their righteousness *is* of me, saith the LORD.

CHAPTER 55

1. **Ho, every one that thirsteth, come** ye **to the waters, and he that hath no money; come** ye, buy, **and eat;** yea, come, buy wine and milk **without money** and without price.

2. **Wherefore do ye spend money** for *that which is* not bread? and your labour **for that which satisfieth not? hearken** diligently **unto me, and eat ye that which is good**, and let your soul delight itself in fatness.

3. **Incline your ear,** and come **unto me:** hear, **and your soul shall live; and I will make an everlasting covenant with you,** *even* the sure mercies of David.

4. **Behold, I have given him for a witness** to the people, **a leader and commander** to the people.

5. **Behold**, thou shalt call a nation *that* thou knowest not, and **nations that knew not thee shall run unto thee because of the LORD** thy God, and for the Holy One of Israel; **for he hath glorified thee.**

6. **Seek** ye **the LORD while he may be found, call** ye **upon him while he is near:**

7. **Let the wicked forsake his way, and the unrighteous** man **his thoughts: and** let him **return unto the LORD,** and he will have mercy upon him; **and** to our **God,** for he **will abundantly pardon.**

8. **For my thoughts** *are* not your thoughts, neither *are* your ways **my ways,** saith the LORD.

9. For *as* the heavens **are higher** than the earth, so are my ways higher **than your ways, and** my thoughts than **your thoughts.**

10. **For as the rain cometh down, and** the snow from heaven, and returneth not thither, but **watereth the earth, and maketh it** bring forth and **bud, that it may give seed** to the sower, **and bread** to the eater:

11. **So shall my word** be that goeth forth out of my mouth: it shall **not return** unto me **void, but it shall accomplish that which I please,** and it shall prosper *in the thing* whereto I sent it.

12. **For ye shall go out with joy, and be led forth with peace: the mountains and the hills shall break forth** before you **into singing, and** all **the trees** of the field **shall clap their hands.**

13. Instead of the thorn shall come up the fir tree, and instead of the brier shall come up the myrtle tree: and it shall be to the LORD for a name, for an everlasting sign *that* shall not be cut off.

CHAPTER 56

1. **Thus saith the LORD,** Keep ye judgment, and do justice: for **my salvation is near** to come, **and my righteousness**

to be revealed.

2. **Blessed is the man that** doeth this, and the son of man *that* layeth hold on it; that keepeth the sabbath from polluting it, and **keepeth his hand from** doing any **evil.**

3. **Neither let** the son of **the stranger, that hath joined himself to the LORD, speak, saying, The LORD hath** utterly **separated me from his people:** neither let the eunuch say, Behold, I *am* a dry tree.

4. **For thus saith the LORD** unto the eunuchs that keep my sabbaths, and choose *the things* that please me, and take hold of my covenant;

5. **Even unto them will I give** in mine house and within my walls **a place and a name better than of** sons and of **daughters: I will give them an everlasting name,** that shall not be cut off.

6. **Also** the sons of **the stranger, that join themselves to the LORD, to serve** him, **and** to **love** the name of **the LORD,** to be his servants, every one that keepeth the sabbath from polluting it, and taketh hold of my covenant;

7. Even them **will I** bring to my holy mountain, and **make** them **joyful in my house of prayer:** their burnt offerings and their sacrifices *shall be* accepted upon mine altar; **for mine house shall be called an house of prayer for all people.**

8. **The Lord** GOD, which gathereth the outcasts of Israel **saith, Yet will I gather others to him,** beside those that are gathered unto him.

9. All ye beasts of the field, come to devour, *yea,* all ye beasts in the forest.

10. **His watchmen are blind:** they are all ignorant, they *are* all dumb dogs, they cannot bark; sleeping, lying down, **loving to slumber.**

11. **Yea, they are greedy dogs which can never have enough,** and they are shepherds *that* cannot understand: **they all look to their own way, every one for his gain,** from his quarter.

12. **Come ye, say they,** I will fetch wine, and **we will fill ourselves with strong drink; and to morrow shall be** as this day, *and* much **more abundant.**

CHAPTER 57

1. **The righteous perisheth,** and no man layeth *it* to heart: **and merciful men are taken away,** none considering that the righteous is taken away **from the evil to come.**

2. **He shall enter into peace:** they shall rest in their beds, *each one* walking *in* his uprightness.

3. **But draw near** hither, **ye** sons of the **sorceress,** the seed of **the adulterer and the whore.**

4. **Against whom do ye sport yourselves?** against whom make ye a wide mouth, *and* draw out the tongue? *are* ye not children of transgression, a seed of falsehood.

5. **Enflaming yourselves with idols** under every green tree, **slaying the children in the valleys** under the clifts of the rocks?

6. Among the smooth *stones* of the stream *is* thy portion; they, they *are* thy lot: even to them hast thou poured a drink offering, thou

hast offered a meat offering.
Should I receive
comfort in these?
7. **Upon a** lofty and
high mountain hast thou
set thy bed: even thither
wentest thou up to offer sacrifice.
8. **Behind the doors**
also and the posts
hast thou set up
thy remembrance:
for thou hast
discovered thyself
to another than me,
and art gone up; thou hast
enlarged thy bed,
and made thee
a covenant with them; thou
lovedst their bed where thou sawest *it.*
9. **And thou wentest**
to the king
with ointment, and didst increase
thy perfumes, and didst send
thy messengers far off,
and didst debase
thyself even unto hell.
10. Thou art wearied in
the greatness of thy
way; *yet* saidst thou
not, There is no hope: thou hast found
the life of thine hand; therefore thou
wast not grieved.
11. **And of whom hast**
thou been afraid or
feared, that thou
hast lied, and hast
not remembered me,
nor laid *it* to thy heart?
have not I held my
peace even of old,
and thou fearest me not?
12. I will declare
thy righteousness, and thy
works; for they
shall not profit thee.
13. **When thou criest, let**
thy companies deliver thee;
but the wind shall
carry them all away;
vanity shall take them: but
he that putteth his trust in
me shall possess the land, and
shall inherit my holy

mountain;
14. And shall say, Cast ye up,
cast ye up, prepare the way,
take up the stumblingblock
out of the way of my people.
15. **For thus saith the**
high and lofty One that
inhabiteth eternity,
whose name *is* Holy;
I dwell in the high and
holy place, with him also
that is of a contrite and
humble spirit, to revive
the spirit of the
humble, and to
revive the heart of
the contrite ones.
16. **For I will not contend for**
ever, neither will I be always
wroth: for the spirit should
fail before me, and the souls
which I have made.
17. **For the iniquity of his**
covetousness was I wroth,
and smote him: I hid me,
and was wroth,
and he went on frowardly
in the way of his heart.
18. I have seen his ways, and
will heal him: I will lead him also,
and restore comforts unto him
and to his mourners.
19. **I create the fruit of the**
lips; Peace, peace to *him that*
is far off, and to *him that is* near,
saith the LORD; and
I will heal him.
20. **But the wicked are**
like the troubled sea,
when it cannot rest, whose
waters cast up mire and dirt.
21. **There is no peace, saith**
my God, to the wicked.

CHAPTER 58

1. **Cry aloud,** spare not, lift
up thy voice like a trumpet, and
shew my people their
transgression, and the
house of Jacob their sins.
2. **Yet they seek me daily,**
and delight to know my ways,
as a nation that did

righteousness, and forsook not the ordinance of their God: they ask of me the ordinances of justice; **they take delight in approaching to God.** 3. **Wherefore have we fasted, say they, and** thou seest not? *wherefore* have we **afflicted our soul, and thou takest no knowledge?** Behold, in the day of your fast ye find pleasure, and exact all your labours. 4. **Behold, ye fast for strife and debate, and** to **smite with the fist of wickedness: ye shall not fast as ye do** this day, **to make your voice to be heard on high.** 5. **Is it such a fast that I have chosen?** a day for a man to afflict his soul? *is it* **to bow down his head** as a bulrush, **and** to **spread sackcloth and ashes under him?** wilt thou call this a fast, and an acceptable day to the LORD? 6. **Is not this the fast that I have chosen? to loose the bands of wickedness,** to undo the heavy burdens, **and to let the oppressed go free,** and that ye break every yoke? 7. *Is it* not **to deal thy bread to the hungry, and** that thou **bring the poor** that are cast out **to thy house? when thou seest the naked, that thou cover him;** and that thou hide not thyself from thine own flesh? 8. **Then** shall thy light break forth as the morning, and thine health shall spring forth speedily: and **thy righteousness shall go before thee; the glory of the LORD shall be thy rereward.** 9. **Then shalt thou call, and**

the LORD shall answer; thou shalt cry, and he shall say, Here I *am*. If thou take away from the midst of thee the yoke, the putting forth of the finger, and speaking vanity; 10. **And if thou draw out thy soul to the hungry, and satisfy the afflicted** soul; **then shall thy light rise in obscurity,** and thy darkness *be* as the noon day: 11. **And the LORD shall guide thee continually, and satisfy thy soul** in drought, and make fat thy bones: **and thou shalt be like a** watered garden, and like a **spring of water, whose waters fail not.** 12. And *they that shall be* of thee shall build the old waste places: thou shalt raise up the foundations of many generations; **and thou shalt be called, The repairer of the breach,** The restorer of paths to dwell in. 13. **If thou turn away** thy foot from the sabbath, **from doing thy pleasure on my holy day;** and call the sabbath a delight, the holy of the LORD, honourable; **and shalt honour him, not doing thine own** ways, nor finding thine own **pleasure,** nor speaking *thine own* words: 14. **Then shalt thou delight thyself in the LORD; and I will cause thee to ride upon the high places** of the earth, **and feed thee with the heritage of Jacob** thy father: **for** the mouth of **the LORD hath spoken it.**

CHAPTER 59

1. **Behold, the LORD's hand is not shortened, that it cannot save; neither his ear heavy, that it cannot hear:**

2. **But your iniquities have separated between you and** your **God, and your sins have hid his face** from you, **that he will not hear.** 3. **For your hands are defiled** with blood, **and** your fingers with iniquity; **your lips have spoken lies,** your tongue hath muttered perverseness. 4. **None** calleth for justice, nor *any* **pleadeth for truth:** they trust in vanity, and speak lies; they conceive mischief, and bring forth iniquity. 5. They hatch cockatrice' eggs, and weave the spider's web: he that eateth of their eggs dieth, and that which is crushed breaketh out into a viper. 6. Their webs shall not become garments, neither shall they cover themselves with their works: **their works are works of iniquity,** and the act of violence *is* in their hands. 7. **Their feet run to evil, and they** make haste to **shed innocent blood:** their thoughts *are* thoughts of iniquity; **wasting and destruction are in their paths.** 8. The way of peace they know not; and **there is no judgment in their** goings: they have made them crooked **paths:** whosoever goeth therein shall not know peace. 9. **Therefore is judgment far from us,** neither doth justice overtake us: **we wait for light, but behold obscurity;** for brightness, *but* we walk in darkness. 10. **We grope** for the wall **like the blind,** and we grope as if *we had* no eyes: we stumble at noon day as in the night; **we are in desolate places as dead men.**

11. We roar all like bears, and mourn sore like doves: **we look** for judgment, but *there is* none; **for salvation, but it is far off from us.** 12. **For our transgressions** are multiplied before thee, **and our sins testify against us:** for our transgressions *are* with us; and *as for* our iniquities, we know them; 13. **In** transgressing and **lying against the LORD,** and departing away from our God, speaking oppression and revolt, **conceiving** and uttering **from the heart words of falsehood.** 14. **And** judgment is turned away backward, and **justice standeth afar off:** for truth is fallen in the street, and equity cannot enter. 15. **Yea, truth faileth;** and he *that* departeth from evil maketh himself a prey: **and the LORD saw it, and it displeased him that there was no judgment.** 16. **And he saw that** *there was* no man, and wondered that **there was no intercessor: therefore** his arm brought salvation unto him; and **his righteousness,** it **sustained him.** 17. **For he put on righteousness as a breastplate,** and **an helmet of salvation** upon his head; and he put on the garments of **vengeance for clothing, and** was clad with **zeal as a cloak.** 18. **According to their deeds,** accordingly **he will repay,** fury to **his adversaries,** recompence to his enemies; to the islands he will

repay recompence.

19. So shall they fear the name of the LORD from the west, and his glory from the rising of the sun.

When the enemy shall come in like a flood, **the Spirit of the LORD shall lift up a standard against him.**

20. **And the Redeemer shall come to** Zion, and unto **them that turn from transgression in** Jacob, saith the LORD.

21. As for me, **this is my covenant with them, saith the LORD; My spirit** that *is* upon thee, **and my words** which I have put in thy mouth, **shall not depart out of thy mouth,** nor out of the mouth of thy seed, nor out of the mouth of thy seed's seed, saith the LORD, from **henceforth and for ever.**

CHAPTER 60

1. **Arise, shine; for thy light is come, and the glory of the LORD is risen upon thee.**

2. **For,** behold, the **darkness shall cover the earth,** and gross darkness the people: **but the LORD shall arise** upon thee, **and his glory shall be seen upon thee.**

3. **And the Gentiles shall come to thy light,** and kings to the brightness of thy rising.

4. Lift up thine eyes round about, and see: all they gather themselves together, they come to thee: thy sons shall come from far, and thy daughters shall be nursed at *thy* side.

5. **Then thou shalt see,** and flow together, **and thine heart shall fear,** and be enlarged;

because the abundance of the sea shall be converted unto thee, the forces of **the Gentiles shall come** unto thee.

6. The multitude of camels shall cover thee, the dromedaries of Midian and Ephah; all they from Sheba shall come: **they shall bring gold and incense; and** they **shall shew forth the praises of the LORD.**

7. **All the flocks of Kedar** shall be gathered together unto thee, **the rams of Nebaioth shall minister unto thee:** they shall come up with acceptance **on mine altar, and I will glorify the house of my glory.**

8. Who *are* these *that* fly as a cloud, and as the doves to their windows?

9. **Surely the isles shall wait for me, and the** ships of Tarshish first, **to bring thy sons** from far, their silver and their gold with them, unto the name of the LORD thy God, and **to the Holy One of Israel, because he hath glorified thee.**

10. **And** the sons of **strangers shall build** up **thy walls, and** their kings **shall minister unto thee: for in my wrath I smote thee, but in my favour have I had mercy on thee.**

11. **Therefore thy gates shall be open continually;** they shall not be shut day nor night; **that men may bring** unto thee **the forces of the Gentiles,** and *that* their kings *may be* brought.

12. **For the nation** and kingdom **that will not serve thee shall perish;** yea, *those* nations shall be utterly wasted.

13. **The glory of Lebanon shall come** unto thee, the fir tree, the pine tree, and the box together, **to beautify** the place of

my sanctuary; and
I will make the place
of my feet glorious.

14. **The sons also of them that afflicted thee**
shall come bending unto thee;
and all they that
despised thee shall bow themselves down at the soles of
thy feet; and they shall call thee; The city of the LORD,
The Zion of the Holy One of Israel.

15. Whereas thou has been forsaken and hated, so that no man went through *thee,*
I will make thee an eternal excellency,
a joy of many generations.

16. Thou shalt also suck the milk of the Gentiles, and shalt suck the breast of kings: and
thou shalt know that I the LORD am thy Saviour and thy Redeemer, the mighty One of Jacob.

17. **For brass I will bring gold, and for iron** I will bring **silver,** and for wood brass, and for stones iron:
I will also
make thy officers peace, and thine exactors righteousness.

18. **Violence shall no more be heard in thy land,** wasting nor destruction within thy borders;
but thou shalt call thy walls Salvation, and thy gates Praise.

19. **The sun shall be no more thy light** by day;
neither for brightness shall the moon give light unto thee:
but the LORD shall be unto thee
an everlasting light,
and thy God thy glory.

20. Thy sun shall no more go down; neither shall thy moon withdraw itself: for the LORD shall be thine everlasting light,
and the days of thy mourning shall be ended.

21. **Thy people also shall be all righteous:**
they shall inherit the land for ever, the branch of my planting, the work of my hands, that I may be glorified.

22. **A little one shall become** a thousand, and a small one
a strong nation: I the LORD will hasten it in his time.

CHAPTER 61

1. **The Spirit of the Lord GOD is upon me; because the LORD hath anointed me to preach good tidings unto the meek;** he hath sent me **to bind up the brokenhearted, to proclaim liberty to the captives, and the opening of the prison** to *them that are* bound;

2. **To proclaim the acceptable year** of the LORD, **and the day of vengeance of our God; to comfort** all that mourn;

3. To appoint unto them that mourn in Zion, **to give** unto them **beauty for ashes,** the oil of **joy for mourning,** the garment of **praise for** the spirit of **heaviness; that they might be called trees of righteousness,** the planting of the LORD, **that he might be glorified.**

4. And they shall build the old wastes, they shall raise up the former desolations, **and they shall repair the waste cities, the** desolations of many generations.

5. And strangers shall stand and feed your flocks, and the sons of the alien *shall be* your plowmen and your vinedressers.

6. **But ye shall be named the Priests of the LORD:**

men shall call you the
Ministers of our God: ye
shall eat the riches
of the Gentiles, and in their
glory shall ye boast yourselves.
7. **For your shame ye**
shall have double;
and *for* confusion they
shall rejoice in their
portion: therefore in their land
they shall possess the double:
everlasting joy shall
be unto them.
8. **For I the LORD love**
judgment, I hate robbery
for burnt offering; and
I will direct their work in truth,
and I will
make an everlasting
covenant with them.
9. **And their seed shall be**
known among the Gentiles,
and their offspring among
the people: all that see them
shall acknowledge them,
that they are the
seed which the LORD
hath blessed.
10. **I will greatly rejoice**
in the LORD, my soul shall
be joyful in my God;
for he hath clothed
me with the garments of
salvation, he hath
covered me with the robe of
righteousness, as a
bridegroom decketh *himself*
with ornaments, and as a bride
adorneth *herself* with her jewels.
11. **For as the earth bringeth**
forth her bud, and as the
garden causeth the things that
are sown in it to spring forth;
so the Lord GOD
will cause righteousness
and praise to spring forth
before all the nations.

CHAPTER 62

1. **For Zion's sake** will I not hold
my peace, and for Jerusalem's sake
I will not rest, until the
righteousness thereof

go forth as brightness,
and the salvation thereof
as a lamp *that* burneth.
2. **And the Gentiles shall**
see thy righteousness,
and all kings thy glory:
and thou shalt be
called by a new name,
which the mouth of
the LORD shall name.
3. **Thou shalt** also
be a crown of glory in
the hand of the LORD,
and a royal diadem in
the hand of thy God.
4. **Thou shalt no**
more be termed
Forsaken; neither shall
thy land any more be termed
Desolate: but thou shalt be called
Hephzibah, and thy land Beulah:
for the LORD delighteth in
thee, and thy land shall be married.
5. For *as* a young man marrieth
a virgin, *so* shall thy sons marry
thee: and
as the bridegroom
rejoiceth over the bride,
so shall thy God rejoice
over thee.
6. **I have set watchmen**
upon thy walls, O Jerusalem,
which shall never hold
their peace day nor night:
ye that make mention of the
LORD, keep not silence,
7. And give him no rest,
till he establish, and till he
make Jerusalem a
praise in the earth.
8. The LORD hath sworn
by his right hand, and by the
arm of his strength, Surely
I will no more give thy
corn *to be* meat for
thine enemies;
and the sons of the
stranger shall not drink
thy wine, for the
which thou hast laboured:
9. But they that have gathered it shall
eat it, and praise the LORD; and they
that have brought it together shall

drink it in the courts of my holiness.

10. **Go through,** go through **the gates;** prepare ye the way of the people; cast up, cast up the highway; **gather out the stones; lift up a standard for the people.** 11. **Behold, the LORD hath proclaimed unto** the end of **the world,** Say ye to the daughter of Zion, Behold, **thy salvation cometh; behold,** his **reward is with him,** and his work before him. 12. **And they shall call them,** The holy people, **The redeemed of the LORD:** and thou shalt be called, Sought out, A city not forsaken.

CHAPTER 63

1. **Who is this that cometh from Edom,** with dyed garments from Bozrah? this *that is* glorious in his apparel, travelling **in the greatness of his strength? I that speak in righteousness, mighty to save.** 2. **Wherefore art** *thou* red in thine apparel, and **thy garments like him that treadeth in the winefat?** 3. **I have trodden the winepress** alone; and of the people *there was* none with me: for I will tread them **in mine anger,** and trample them in my fury; **and their blood shall be sprinkled upon my garments,** and I will stain all my raiment. 4. **For the day of vengeance is in mine heart, and the year of my redeemed is come.** 5. **And** I looked, and **there was none to help;** and I wondered that *there was* none to uphold: **therefore mine own arm**

brought salvation unto me; and my fury, it upheld me. 6. **And I will tread down the people in mine anger,** and make them drunk in my fury, and I will bring down their strength to the earth. 7. **I will mention the lovingkindnesses** of the LORD, **and the praises of the LORD,** according to all that the LORD hath **bestowed on us, and the** great **goodness toward** the house of **Israel,** which he hath **bestowed on them according to his mercies,** and according to the multitude of his lovingkindnesses. 8. **For** he said, Surely **they are my people,** children *that* will not lie: **so he was their Saviour.** 9. **In all their affliction he was afflicted,** and the angel of his presence saved them: **in his love** and in his pity **he redeemed them;** and he bare them, and carried them all the days of old. 10. **But they rebelled,** and vexed his holy Spirit: therefore he was turned to be their enemy, **and he fought against them.** 11. **Then he remembered** the days of old, **Moses,** *and* his people, **saying, Where is he that brought them up out of the sea** with the shepherd of his flock? **where is he that put his holy Spirit within him?** 12. That led *them* by the right hand of Moses with his glorious arm, dividing the water before them, to make himself an everlasting name? 13. **That led them through the** deep, as an horse in the **wilderness,** *that* they should not stumble?

14. As a beast goeth down into the valley, the Spirit of the LORD caused him to rest:
so didst thou lead thy people, to make thyself a glorious name.
15. **Look down from heaven,** and behold from the habitation of thy holiness and of thy glory: **where is thy zeal** and thy strength, the sounding of thy bowels **and** of **thy mercies toward me? are they restrained?**
16. **Doubtless thou art our father,** though Abraham be ignorant of us, and Israel acknowledge us not: thou, O LORD, *art* our father, **our redeemer; thy name is from everlasting.**
17. **O LORD, why hast thou made us to err** from thy ways, **and hardened our heart** from thy fear? Return for thy servants' sake, the tribes of thine inheritance.
18. The people of thy holiness have possessed *it* but a little while: **our adversaries have trodden down thy sanctuary.**
19. **We are thine:** thou never barest rule over them; **they were not called by thy name.**

CHAPTER 64

1. **Oh that thou wouldest** rend the heavens, that thou wouldest **come down,** that the mountains might flow down at thy presence,
2. As *when* the melting fire burneth, the fire causeth the waters to boil, **to make thy name known to thine adversaries, that the nations may tremble at thy presence!**
3. When thou didst terrible things *which* we looked not for, thou camest down, the mountains flowed down at thy presence.
4. **For since the beginning of the world men have**

not heard, nor **perceived** by the ear, neither hath the eye seen, O God, beside thee, **what he hath prepared for him that waiteth for him.**
5. Thou meetest him that rejoiceth and worketh righteousness, *those that* remember thee in thy ways: **behold,** thou art wroth; for **we have sinned:** in those is continuance, and we shall be saved.
6. But we are all as an unclean *thing,* and **all our righteousnesses are as filthy rags;** and we all do fade as a leaf; **and our iniquities,** like the wind, **have taken us away.**
7. **And there is none that calleth upon thy name,** that stirreth up himself to take hold of thee: **for thou hast hid thy face from us,** and hast consumed us, **because of our iniquities.**
8. **But now, O LORD,** thou *art* our father; **we are the clay, and thou our potter;** and we all *are* the work of thy hand.
9. **Be not wroth** very sore, O LORD, **neither remember iniquity for ever:** behold, see, we beseech thee, **we are** all **thy people.**
10. Thy holy cities are a wilderness, Zion is a wilderness, Jerusalem a desolation.
11. **Our holy** and our beautiful **house,** where our fathers praised thee, **is burned up with fire:** and all our pleasant things are laid waste.
12. **Wilt thou refrain thyself for these things, O LORD?** wilt thou hold thy peace, and afflict us very sore?

CHAPTER 65

1. **I am sought of them that**

asked not for me; I am found of *them that* sought me not:

I said, Behold me, behold me, unto a nation that was not called by my name.

2. I have spread out my hands all the day unto a rebellious people, which walketh in a way *that was* not good,

after their own thoughts;

3. A people that provoketh me to anger continually to my face; that sacrificeth in gardens, and burneth incense upon altars of brick;

4. Which remain among the graves, and lodge in the monuments, which eat swine's flesh, and broth of abominable *things is in* their vessels;

5. Which say, Stand by thyself, come not near to me; for I am holier than thou. These *are* a smoke in my nose, a fire that burneth all the day.

6. Behold, *it is* written before me: I will not keep silence, but will recompense, even recompense into their bosom,

7. Your iniquities, and the iniquities of your fathers together, saith the LORD, which have burned incense upon the mountains, and blasphemed me upon the hills: therefore will I measure their former work into their bosom.

8. Thus saith the LORD, As the new wine is found in the cluster, and *one* saith, Destroy it not; for a blessing *is* in it: so will I do for my servants' sakes, that I may not destroy them all.

9. And I will bring forth a seed out of Jacob, and out of Judah an inheritor of my mountains: and mine elect shall inherit it, and my servants shall dwell there.

10. And Sharon shall be a fold of flocks, and the valley of Achor a place for the herds to lie down in, for my people that have sought me.

11. But ye are they that forsake the LORD, that forget my holy mountain, that prepare a table for that troop, and that furnish the drink offering unto that number.

12. Therefore will I number you to the sword, and ye shall all bow down to the slaughter: because when I called, ye did not answer; when I spake, ye did not hear; but did evil before mine eyes, and did choose *that* wherein I delighted not.

13. Therefore thus saith the Lord GOD, Behold, my servants shall eat, but ye shall be hungry: behold, my servants shall drink, but ye shall be thirsty: behold, my servants shall rejoice, but ye shall be ashamed:

14. Behold, my servants shall sing for joy of heart, but ye shall cry for sorrow of heart, and shall howl for vexation of spirit.

15. And ye shall leave your name for a curse unto my chosen: for the Lord GOD shall slay thee, and call his servants by another name:

16. That he who blesseth himself in the earth shall bless himself in the God of truth; and he that sweareth in the earth shall swear by the God of truth; because the former troubles are forgotten, and because they are hid from mine eyes.

17. For, behold, I create new heavens and a new earth: and the former shall not be remembered, nor come into mind.

18. But be ye glad and rejoice for ever in that which I create: for, behold, I create Jerusalem a rejoicing, and her people a joy.

19. **And I will rejoice in Jerusalem,** and joy in my people: **and the voice of weeping shall be no more heard** in her, nor the voice of crying. 20. **There shall be no more** thence **an infant of days, nor an old man that hath not filled his days**: for the child shall die an hundred years old; **but the sinner being an hundred years old shall be accursed.** 21. **And they shall build houses, and** inhabit *them*; and they shall **plant vineyards,** and eat the fruit of them. 22. They shall not build, and another inhabit; they shall not plant, and another eat: for as the days of a tree *are* the days of my people, **and mine elect shall long enjoy the work of their hands.** 23. **They shall not labour in vain**, nor bring forth for trouble; **for they are the seed** of the blessed **of the LORD,** and their offspring with them. 24. **And it shall come to pass, that before they call, I will answer;** and while they are yet speaking, I will hear. 25. **The wolf and the lamb shall feed together, and the lion shall eat straw** like the bullock: and dust *shall be* the serpent's meat. They shall not hurt nor destroy in all my holy mountain, saith the LORD.

CHAPTER 66

1. **Thus saith the LORD, The heaven is my throne, and the earth is my footstool: where is the house that ye build** unto me? **and** where *is* **the place of my rest?** 2. **For all those things hath mine hand made,** and all those *things* have been, saith the LORD: **but** to this *man* will **I look,** *even* **to him that is poor and of a contrite spirit, and trembleth at my word.** 3. He that killeth an ox *is as if* he slew a man; **he that sacrificeth a lamb, as if he cut off a dog's neck;** he that offereth an oblation, *as if he offered* swine's blood; he that burneth incense, *as if* he blessed an idol. **Yea, they have chosen their own ways, and their soul delighteth in their abominations.** 4. **I also will choose their delusions, and will** bring their fears upon them; **because** when I called, none did answer; when I spake, they did not hear: but **they did evil before mine eyes,** and chose *that* in which I delighted not. 5. Hear the word of the LORD, ye that tremble at his word; **Your brethren** that hated you, **that cast you out for my name's sake, said, Let the LORD be glorified: but he shall appear to your joy, and they shall be ashamed.** 6. A voice of noise from the city, a voice from the temple, a voice of the LORD that rendereth recompence to his enemies. 7. Before she travailed, she brought forth; before her pain came, she was delivered of a man child. 8. Who hath heard such a thing? who hath seen such things? Shall the earth be made to bring forth in one day? *or* shall a nation be born at once? for as soon as Zion travailed, she brought forth her children. 9. Shall I bring to the birth, and not

cause to bring forth? saith the LORD:
shall I cause to bring forth, and
shut *the womb*? saith thy God.

10. **Rejoice ye with Jerusalem,** and be glad with her,
all ye that love her: rejoice for joy
with her, all ye that mourn for her:

11. That ye may suck, and be
satisfied with the breasts of
her consolations; that ye
may milk out, and **be delighted with the abundance of her glory.**

12. **For** thus saith the LORD,Behold,
I will extend peace to her
like a river, and the glory of the
Gentiles like a flowing stream:
then shall ye suck, ye shall be
borne upon *her* sides, and be
dandled upon *her* knees.

13. **As one whom his mother comforteth, so will I comfort you;** and ye
shall be comforted in Jerusalem.

14. **And** when ye see *this*,
your heart shall rejoice, and
your bones shall flourish like an herb:
and the hand of the
LORD shall be known toward his servants, and his indignation toward his enemies.

15. **For,** behold,
the LORD will come with fire,
and with his chariots like a whirlwind,
to render his anger with fury,
and his rebuke with flames of fire.

16. **For by fire and by his sword will the LORD plead with all flesh:** and the slain
of the LORD shall be many.

17. **They that sanctify themselves,** and purify
themselves in the gardens behind
one *tree* in the midst,
eating swine's flesh, and the abomination,
and the mouse,
shall be consumed
together, saith the LORD.

18. For I *know* their
works and their thoughts:

it shall come, that
I will gather all nations and tongues;
and they shall come, and
see my glory.

19. **And I will set a sign among them, and I will send those that escape of them unto the nations,** *to*
Tarshish, Pul, and Lud, that draw the
bow, *to* Tubal, and Javan, *to* the isles
afar off, that have not heard my
fame, neither have seen my glory;
and they shall declare my glory among the Gentiles.

20. **And they shall bring all your brethren** *for* an
offering unto the LORD out of all
nations upon horses, and in
chariots, and in litters, and upon
mules, and upon swift beasts,
to my holy mountain Jerusalem, saith the LORD,
as the children of Israel bring
an offering in a clean vessel
into the house of the LORD.

21. **And I will** also
take of them for priests and for
Levites, saith the LORD.

22. **For** as
the new heavens and the new earth, which I will make,
shall remain before me, saith the LORD,
so shall your seed
and your name
remain.

23. And it shall come to pass, *that*
from one new moon to another,
and from one sabbath to another, shall all flesh come to worship before me, saith the LORD.

24. **And they shall** go forth, and
look upon the carcases of the men that have transgressed against me: for their worm shall not die, neither shall their fire be quenched; and they shall be an abhorring unto all flesh.

THE BOOK OF JEREMIAH

BACKGROUND INFORMATION

Author: Jeremiah
Date Written: Approximately **604 B.C.**

Number of:
Verses—1,364
Chapters—52
Total Words—42,659
Scan Words—16,453
Scan Words Represent
Approximately 38% of
Total Words

Theme: Prophecies Concerning Judah and Surrounding Nations

OUTLINE OF THE BOOK

I.   **The Call** of Jeremiah
     1:1 — 19:15
II. **Prophecies** of Judah and
     Jerusalem
     Before the Reign of
     Zedekiah
     20:1 — 18
III. **Prophecies During the
     Reign of Zedekiah**
     21:1 — 29:32
IV. **Future Prophecies of
     Judah and Jerusalem**
     30:1 — 39:18
V.   **Prophecies of the
     Remnant**
     40:1 — 42:22
VI. **Jeremiah's Last Days**
     43:1 — 51:64
VII. **Destruction of
     Jerusalem**
     52:1 — 34

CHAPTER 1

1. The words of **Jeremiah** the son of Hilkiah, of the priests that *were* in Anathoth in the land of Benjamin:

2. **To whom the word of the LORD came** in the days of Josiah the son of Amon king of Judah, in the thirteenth year of his reign.

3. It came also in the days of Jehoiakim the son of Josiah king of Judah, unto the end of the eleventh year of Zedekiah the son of Josiah king of Judah, unto the carrying away of Jerusalem captive in the fifth month.

4. Then the word of the LORD came unto me, **saying,**

5. **Before I formed thee in** the belly I knew thee; and before thou camest forth out of **the womb I sanctified thee, and** I **ordained thee a prophet** unto the nations.

6. **Then said I,** Ah, **Lord** GOD! behold, **I cannot speak: for I am a child.**

7. **But the LORD said** unto me, **Say not, I am a child: for** thou shalt go to all that **I shall send thee, and** whatsoever I command thee **thou shalt speak.**

8. **Be not afraid** of their faces: for **I am with thee** to deliver thee, saith the LORD.

9. **Then the LORD** put forth his hand, and **touched my mouth. And** the LORD **said** unto me, **Behold, I have put my words in thy mouth.**

10. **See, I have** this day **set thee over the nations and** over the **kingdoms, to root out, and** to pull down, and to **destroy,** and to throw down, **to build, and** to **plant.**

11. **Moreover** the word of **the LORD came** unto me, **saying,** Jeremiah, **what seest thou? And I said,** I see **a rod of an almond tree.**

12. **Then said the LORD** unto me, Thou hast well seen: for **I will hasten my word to perform it.**

13. **And the word** of the LORD **came** unto me **the second time, saying, What seest thou? And I said,** I see **a seething pot;** and **the face thereof is toward the north.**

14. **Then the LORD said** unto me, Out of the north an evil shall break forth upon all the inhabitants of the land.

15. For, lo, **I will call** all **the families** of the kingdoms **of the north,** saith the LORD; **and they shall come, and** they shall **set** every one **his throne at** the entering of **the gates of Jerusalem,** and against all the walls thereof round about, **and** against all the cities of **Judah.**

16. **And I will utter my judgments against them** touching all their wickedness, **who have forsaken me,** and have burned incense unto other gods, and worshipped the works of their own hands.

17. **Thou therefore** gird up thy loins, and **arise, and speak unto them** all that I command thee: **be not dismayed** at their faces, lest I confound thee before them.

18. For, behold, **I have made thee** this day **a defenced city,** and an iron

pillar, and brasen walls against the whole land, against the kings of Judah, against the princes thereof, against the priests thereof, and against the people of the land.

19. **And they shall fight against thee; but** they shall not prevail against thee; for **I am with thee,** saith the LORD, **to deliver thee.**

CHAPTER 2

1. **Moreover** the word of **the LORD came to me, saying,**

2. **Go** and **cry in the ears of Jerusalem, saying,** Thus saith the LORD; **I remember** thee, the kindness of thy youth, the love of thine espousals, **when thou wentest after me in the wilderness, in** a land that *was* not sown.

3. **Israel was holiness unto the LORD, and the firstfruits of his increase:** all that devour him shall offend; evil shall come upon them, saith the LORD.

4. Hear ye the word of the LORD, O house of Jacob, and all the families of the house of Israel:

5. Thus saith the LORD, **What iniquity have your fathers found in me, that they are gone** far **from me,** and have walked after vanity, **and** are **become vain?**

6. **Neither said they, Where is the LORD that brought us** up **out of** the land of **Egypt,** that led us through the wilderness, through a land of deserts and of pits, through a land of drought, and of the shadow of death, through a land that no man passed through, and where no man dwelt?

7. **And I brought you into a plentiful country,** to eat the fruit thereof **and** the goodness thereof; but when ye entered, **ye defiled my land, and made mine heritage an abomination.**

8. The priests said not, Where *is* the LORD? and they that handle the law knew me not: **the pastors** also **transgressed against me, and** the prophets prophesied by Baal, and **walked after things that do not profit.**

9. **Wherefore I** will yet **plead with you,** saith the LORD, and with your children's children will I plead.

10. For pass over the isles of Chittim, and see; and send unto Kedar, and consider diligently, and see if there be such a thing.

11. Hath a nation changed *their* gods, which *are* yet no gods? but **my people have changed their glory for that which doth not profit.**

12. **Be astonished,** O ye heavens, at this, **and** be horribly **afraid,** be ye very desolate, **saith the LORD.**

13. **For my people** have committed two evils; they **have forsaken me** the fountain of living waters, **and hewed** them **out** cisterns, broken **cisterns, that** can **hold no water.**

14. **Is Israel a servant?** *is* he a homeborn *slave?* why is he spoiled?

15. The young lions roared upon him, *and* yelled, and **they made his land waste: his cities are burned** without inhabitant.

16. Also the children of Noph and Tahapanes have broken the crown of thy head.

17. Hast thou not procured this unto thyself, in that thou hast forsaken the

LORD thy God, when he led thee by the way?

18. **And now** what hast thou to do in the way of Egypt, to drink the waters of Sihor? or what hast thou to do in the way of Assyria, to drink the waters of the river?

19. **Thine own wickedness shall correct thee,** and thy backslidings shall reprove thee: know therefore and see that **it is an evil thing** and bitter, **that thou hast forsaken the LORD** thy God, and that **my fear is not in thee,** saith the Lord GOD of hosts.

20. **For** of old time I have broken thy yoke, *and* burst thy bands; and thou saidst, I will not transgress; when **upon every** high **hill and under every** green **tree thou wanderest, playing the harlot.**

21. **Yet I** had **planted** thee **a noble vine,** wholly a right seed: **how** then **art thou turned into** the degenerate plant of **a strange vine** unto me?

22. **For though thou wash** thee **with** nitre, and take thee much **soap, yet thine iniquity is** marked **before me, saith the Lord** GOD.

23. **How canst thou say,** I am not polluted, **I have not gone after Baalim? see thy way** in the valley, **know what thou hast done:** *thou art* a swift dromedary traversing her ways;

24. A wild ass used to the wilderness, *that* snuffeth up the wind at her pleasure; in her occasion who can turn her away? all they that seek her will not weary themselves; in her month they shall find her.

25. Withhold thy foot from being unshod, and thy throat from thirst: but thou saidst, There is no hope: no; for I have loved strangers, and after them will I go.

26. **As the thief is ashamed when he is found, so is** the house of **Israel ashamed;** they, their kings, their princes, and their priests, and their prophets.

27. Saying to a stock, Thou *art* my father; and to a stone, Thou hast brought me forth: for **they have turned their back unto me,** and not *their* face **but in the time of** their **trouble they will say, Arise, and save us.**

28. **But where are thy gods that thou hast made** thee? **let them arise, if they can save thee** in the time of thy trouble: for *according to* the number of thy cities are thy gods, O Judah.

29. Wherefore will ye plead with me? **ye** all **have transgressed against me,** saith the LORD.

30. **In vain have I smitten your children; they received no correction:** your own sword hath devoured your prophets, like a destroying lion.

31. O generation, see ye the word of the LORD. Have I been a wilderness unto Israel? a land of darkness? wherefore say my people, We are lords;we will come no more untothee?

32. Can a maid forget her ornaments, *or* a bride her attire? **yet my people have forgotten me** days without number.

33. Why trimmest thou thy way to seek love? therefore hast thou also taught the wicked ones thy ways.

34. **Also in thy skirts is found the blood of the souls of the** poor **innocents:** I have not found it by secret search, but upon all these.

35. **Yet thou sayest,** Because **I am innocent,** surely his anger shall turn from me. Behold, I will plead

with thee, because thou sayest,

I have not sinned.

36. **Why gaddest thou about** so much **to change thy way?** thou also shalt be ashamed of Egypt, as thou wast ashamed of Assyria.

37. **Yea, thou shalt go forth** from him, and thine hands upon thine head: for the LORD hath rejected thy confidences, **and thou shalt not prosper** in them.

CHAPTER 3

1. **They say,**

If a man put away his wife, and she go from him, and **become another man's, shall he return unto her** again? **shall not that land be** greatly **polluted? but thou hast played the harlot** with many lovers; **yet return again to me,** saith the LORD.

2. **Lift up thine eyes** unto the high places, **and see where thou** hast not been lien with. In the ways hast thou sat for them, as the Arabian in the wilderness; and thou **hast polluted the land with** thy **whoredoms and** with thy **wickedness.**

3. **Therefore the showers have been withholden, and there hath been no latter rain; and** thou hadst a whore's forehead, **thou refusedst to be ashamed.**

4. **Wilt thou not** from this time **cry unto me,** My father, thou *art* the guide of my youth?

5. **Will he reserve his anger for ever?** will he keep it to the end? Behold, thou hast spoken and done evil things as thou couldest.

6. **The LORD said** also unto me in the days of Josiah the king,

Hast thou seen that which backsliding Israel hath done? she is gone up upon every high mountain and under every green tree, and there **hath played the harlot.**

7. **And** I said after she had done all these *things,* Turn thou unto me. But **she returned not.** And her treacherous sister Judah saw *it.*

8. **And** I saw, **when** for all the causes whereby **backsliding Israel committed adultery I had** put her away, and **given her a bill of divorce**; yet **her treacherous sister Judah feared not,** but went **and played the harlot also.**

9. And it came to pass through the lightness of her whoredom, that she defiled the land, and committed adultery with stones and with stocks.

10. **And yet** for all this her treacherous sister **Judah hath not turned unto me** with her whole heart, but feignedly, saith the LORD.

11. **And** the LORD said unto me, The **backsliding Israel hath justified herself more than** treacherous **Judah.**

12. **Go and proclaim these words** toward the north, **and** say, **Return,** thou backsliding Israel, saith the LORD; **and I will not cause mine anger to fall upon you: for I am merciful,** saith the LORD, *and* I will not keep *anger* for ever.

13. Only **acknowledge** thine iniquity, **that** thou hast transgressed against the LORD thy God, and hast scattered thy ways to the strangers under every green tree, and **ye have not obeyed my voice,** saith the LORD.

14. **Turn**, O backsliding children, **saith the LORD**; for **I am married unto you:** and I will take you one of a city, and two of a family, and I will bring you to Zion:

15. **And I will give you pastors** according to mine heart, **which shall feed you with knowledge and understanding.**

16. **And** it shall come to pass, when ye be multiplied and increased in the land, in those days, saith the LORD, **they shall say no more, The ark of the covenant** of the LORD: neither shall it come to mind: **neither shall they remember it;** neither shall they visit *it;* neither shall *that* be done **any more.**

17. At that time **they shall call Jerusalem the throne** of the LORD; **and** all **the nations shall be gathered unto it,** to the name of the LORD, to Jerusalem: neither shall they walk any more after the imagination of their evil heart.

18. In those days the house of **Judah shall walk with** the house of **Israel, and they shall come** together **out of** the land of **the north to the land that I have given** for an inheritance **unto your fathers.**

19. But I said, How shall I put thee among the children, and give thee a pleasant land, a goodly heritage of the hosts of nations? and I said, **Thou shalt call me,** My **father; and shalt not turn away** from me.

20. **Surely** *as* a wife treacherously departeth from her husband, so have **ye dealt treacherously with me, O** house of **Israel,** saith the LORD.

21. **A voice was heard** upon the high places, **weeping**

and supplications of the children of **Israel:** for they have **perverted their way, and they have forgotten the LORD** their God.

22. **Return,** ye backsliding children, **and I will heal your backslidings.** Behold, we come unto thee; for thou art the LORD our God.

23. Truly in vain *is salvation hoped for* from the hills, *and from* the multitude of mountains: truly in **the LORD** our God **is the salvation of Israel.**

24. For shame hath devoured the labour of our fathers from our youth; their flocks and their herds, their sons and their daughters.

25. **We lie** down **in** our **shame, and** our **confusion** covereth us: **for we have sinned against the LORD** our God, we and our fathers, from our youth even unto this day, and have not obeyed the voice of the LORD our God.

CHAPTER 4

1. **If thou wilt return, O Israel,** saith the LORD, return unto me: **and** if thou wilt **put away thine abominations** out of my sight, **then shalt thou not remove.**

2. And thou shalt swear, The LORD liveth, in truth, in judgment, and in righteousness; and the nations shall bless themselves in him, and in him shall they glory.

3. **For thus saith the LORD** to the men of Judah and Jerusalem, **Break up your fallow ground, and sow not among thorns.**

4. **Circumcise yourselves** to the LORD, **and take away the foreskins of your heart,** ye men of Judah and inhabitants of Jerusalem:

lest my fury come
forth like fire, and burn that
none can quench *it*, because of
the evil of your doings.

5. **Declare ye in**
Judah, and publish in
Jerusalem; and say,
Blow ye the trumpet in the
land: cry, gather together,
and say, Assemble
yourselves, and let us
go into the defenced cities.
6. **Set up the standard**
toward Zion: retire,
stay not: for I will bring
evil from the north, and
a great destruction.
7. The lion is come up from his
thicket, and
the destroyer of the Gentiles
is on his way;
he is gone forth from his place
to make thy land desolate;
and thy cities shall be laid waste,
without an inhabitant.
8. For this
gird you with sackcloth,
lament and howl:
for the fierce
anger of the LORD is not
turned back from us.
9. And it shall come to pass at that
day, saith the LORD, *that* the heart of
the king shall perish, and the heart of
the princes; and the priests shall be
astonished, and the prophets shall
wonder.
10. **Then said I,** Ah,
Lord GOD!
surely thou hast greatly
deceived this people and
Jerusalem, saying, Ye shall
have peace; whereas the sword
reacheth unto the soul.
11. **At that time shall it**
be said to this people and to
Jerusalem, A dry wind
of the high places in the wilderness
toward the daughter of my people,
not to fan, nor to cleanse,
12. *Even* a full wind from those *places*
shall come unto me:
now also

will I give sentence
against them.
13. **Behold, he shall come** up
as clouds, and his
chariots *shall be* as
a whirlwind: his horses
are swifter than eagles.
Woe unto us! for we are spoiled.
14. **O Jerusalem, wash**
thine heart from
wickedness, that thou
mayest be saved.
How long shall thy vain thoughts
lodge within thee?
15. **For a voice declareth**
from Dan, and publisheth
affliction from mount Ephraim.
16. Make ye mention to the nations;
behold, publish against Jerusalem,
that watchers come from a far
country, and give out their voice
against the cities of Judah.
17. As keepers of a field, are they
against her round about;
because she hath been
rebellious against me,
saith the LORD.
18. Thy way and thy doings have
procured these *things* unto thee;
this is thy wickedness, because it
is bitter, because it reacheth unto
thine heart.
19. My bowels, my bowels!
I am pained at my very heart;
my heart maketh a
noise in me;
I cannot hold my peace, because
thou hast heard,
O my soul, the sound of the trumpet,
the alarm of war.
20. **Destruction** upon destruction
is cried; for the whole land is
spoiled: suddenly are my tents
spoiled, *and* my curtains in a moment.
21. **How long shall I**
see the standard, *and*
hear the sound of
the trumpet?
22. **For my people**
is foolish, they
have not known me;
they *are* sottish children, and
they have none understanding:

■ they are wise to do evil,
■ but to do good they have
■ no knowledge.
23. I beheld the earth,
and, lo, *it was*
■ without form, and void;
■ and the heavens, and they
■ had no light.
24. I beheld
■ the mountains, and, lo, they
■ trembled, and all
■ the hills moved lightly.
25. I beheld, and, lo, *there was*
■ no man, and all the
■ birds of the heavens were
■ fled.
26. I beheld, and, lo,
■ the fruitful
■ place was a
■ wilderness, and all
■ the cities thereof
■ were broken down at the
■ presence of the LORD,
■ and by his fierce anger.
27. For thus hath
■ the LORD said, The whole
■ land shall be desolate;
yet will I not make a full end.
28. For this shall the earth mourn,
and the heavens above be black;
because I have spoken *it,*
■ I have purposed *it,* and
■ will not repent, neither will I
■ turn back from it.
29. The whole city shall flee
for the noise of the horsemen and
bowmen; they shall go
■ into thickets,
and climb up upon the rocks:
every city *shall be* forsaken,
■ and not a man
■ dwell therein.
30. And *when* thou *art* spoiled, what
wilt thou do? Though thou clothest
thyself with crimson, though thou
deckest thee with ornaments of gold,
though thou rentest thy face with
painting, in vain shalt thou make
thyself fair; *thy* lovers will despise
thee, they will seek thy life.
31. For I have heard a voice
■ as of a woman in travail, *and*
the anguish as of her that bringeth

forth her first child,
■ the voice of the daughter
■ of Zion, *that* bewaileth herself, *that*
spreadeth her hands, *saying,*
■ Woe is me now! for
■ my soul is wearied
■ because of murderers.

CHAPTER 5

■ 1. Run ye to and fro
■ through the streets of
■ Jerusalem, and see
now, and know, and seek in
the broad places thereof,
■ if ye can find a man,
if there be *any*
■ that executeth judgment,
■ that seeketh the truth; and
■ I will pardon it.
2. And though they say, The LORD
liveth; surely they swear falsely.
■ 3. O LORD,
are not thine eyes upon the truth?
■ thou hast stricken them, but
■ they have not grieved;
thou hast consumed them, *but*
they have refused to receive
correction: they have made
their faces harder than a rock;
■ they have refused to return.
■ 4. Therefore I said,
Surely these *are* poor;
■ they are foolish: for
■ they know not the way of
■ the LORD, *nor* the judgment
of their God.
5. I will get me unto
■ the great men,
and will speak unto them; for they
■ have known the way
■ of the LORD,
and the judgment of their God:
■ but these have altogether
■ broken the yoke, *and* burst the
■ bonds.
6. Wherefore a lion
out of the forest
■ shall slay them, *and* a wolf of the
evenings shall spoil them, a leopard
shall watch over their cities: every one
that goeth out thence shall be torn in
pieces: because
■ their transgressions

■ are many, and their
■ backslidings are
■ increased.
7. How shall I pardon thee for this? thy children have forsaken me, and sworn by *them that are* no gods: when I had fed them to the full,
■ they then
■ committed adultery, and
■ assembled themselves by troops
■ in the harlots' houses.
8. They were *as* fed horses in the morning:
■ every one neighed after
■ his neighbour's wife.
■ 9. Shall I not
visit for these *things?* saith the LORD: and shall not my soul
■ be avenged on such
■ a nation as this?
10. Go ye up
■ upon her walls, and
destroy; but make not a full end:
■ take away her battlements;
for they *are* not the LORD'S.
11. For the house of
■ Israel and the house of
■ Judah have dealt very
■ treacherously against
■ me, saith the LORD.
■ 12. They have
belied the LORD, and
■ said, It is not he; neither
■ shall evil come upon us;
neither shall we seesword nor famine:
13. And the prophets shall become wind,
■ and the word is not in them:
thus shall it be done unto them.
14. Wherefore thus saith the LORD God of hosts, Because ye speak this word,
■ behold, I will make my
■ words in thy mouth
■ fire, and this people
■ wood, and it shall
■ devour them.
■ 15. Lo, I will bring a nation
■ upon you from far, O house of
Israel, saith the LORD: it *is*
■ a mighty nation, it *is* an ancient
nation, a nation whose language thou knowest not, neither understandest

what they say.
16. Their quiver *is* as an open sepulchre, they *are* all mighty men.
■ 17. And they shall eat up
■ thine harvest, and thy bread,
which thy sons and thy daughters should eat: they shall eat up thy flocks and thine herds: they shall eat up thy vines and thy fig trees:
■ they shall impoverish
■ thy fenced
■ cities, wherein thou trustedst,
■ with the sword.
■ 18. Nevertheless
in those days, saith the LORD,
■ I will not make a full
■ end with you.
19. And it shall come to pass, when
■ ye shall say, Wherefore
■ doeth the LORD our God all
■ these things unto us? then
shalt thou answer them, Like
■ as ye have forsaken me, and
■ served strange gods in your
■ land, so shall ye serve
■ strangers in a land
■ that is not yours.
■ 20. Declare this in
the house of Jacob, and publish it in
■ Judah, saying,
■ 21. Hear now this,
■ O foolish people,
and without understanding;
■ which have eyes, and
■ see not; which have ears,
■ and hear not:
■ 22. Fear ye not me?
saith the LORD:
■ will ye not tremble at
■ my presence, which have placed
the sand *for* the bound of the sea by a perpetual decree, that it cannot pass it: and though the waves thereof toss themselves, yet can they not prevail; though they roar, yet can they not pass over it?
■ 23. But this people hath
■ a revolting and
■ a rebellious heart;
they are revolted and gone.
■ 24. Neither say they
in their heart,
■ Let us now

fear the LORD our God, **that giveth** rain, both the former and the latter, in his season: he reserveth unto us the appointed weeks of **the harvest.**

25. **Your** iniquities have turned away these *things,* and your **sins have withholden good things from you.**

26. **For among my people are found wicked men:** they lay wait, as he that setteth snares; they set a trap, they catch men.

27. As a cage is full of birds, so *are* their houses **full of deceit:** therefore **they are become** great, and waxen **rich.**

28. They are waxen fat, they shine: yea, they overpass the deeds of the wicked: they judge not the cause, the cause of the fatherless, yet they prosper; and the right of the needy do they not judge.

29. Shall I not visit for these *things?* saith the LORD: **shall not my soul be avenged on such a nation as this?**

30. **A** wonderful and **horrible thing is committed** in the land;

31. **The prophets prophesy falsely, and the priests bear rule** by their means; **and my people love** *to have* **it** *so:* and what will ye do in the end thereof?

CHAPTER 6

1. **O ye children** of Benjamin, **gather yourselves** to flee **out** of the midst **of Jerusalem,** and blow the trumpet in Tekoa, and set up a sign of fire in Beth–haccerem: **for evil appeareth out of the north,** and great destruction.

2. **I have likened** the daughter of **Zion to a** comely and **delicate woman.**

3. **The shepherds** with their flocks **shall come unto her;** they shall pitch *their* tents against her round about; they shall feed every one in his place.

4. **Prepare ye war against her;** arise, and let us go up at noon. Woe unto us! for the day goeth away, for the shadows of the evening are stretched out.

5. Arise, and let us go by night, and **let us destroy her palaces.**

6. For thus hath the LORD of hosts said, Hew ye down trees, and cast a mount against Jerusalem: this *is* the city to be visited; she *is* wholly oppression in the midst of her.

7. **As a fountain** casteth out her waters, so **she casteth out her wickedness: violence and spoil is** heard **in her;** before me continually *is* grief and wounds.

8. **Be thou instructed, O Jerusalem,** lest my soul depart from thee; **lest I make thee desolate,** a land not inhabited.

9. Thus saith the LORD of hosts, **They shall** throughly **glean** the remnant of **Israel as a vine:** turn back thine hand as a grapegatherer into the baskets.

10. **To whom shall I** speak, and **give warning,** that they may hear? behold, their ear *is* uncircumcised, and they cannot hearken: behold, **the word of the LORD is unto them a reproach; they have no delight in it.**

11. **Therefore I am full of** the **fury** of the LORD; I am weary with holding in: **I will pour it out upon** the children abroad, and upon **the assembly** of young men together: for even the husband with the wife shall be taken, the aged with *him that is* full of days.

12. And their houses shall be turned unto others, *with their* fields and wives together: for

■ **I will stretch out my hand**
■ **upon the inhabitants of**
■ **the land,** saith the LORD.

13. For from the least of them even unto the greatest of them

■ **every one is given to**
■ **covetousness; and**

from the prophet even unto the priest every one

■ **dealeth falsely.**
■ 14. **They have healed also**
■ **the hurt** *of the daughter*
■ **of my people slightly,**
■ **saying, Peace,** peace;
■ **when there is no peace.**
■ 15. **Were they ashamed**
■ **when they** had
■ **committed abomination?**
■ **nay, they were not** at all
■ **ashamed,**

neither could they blush:

■ **therefore** they shall fall

among them that fall: at the time *that* I visit them

■ **they shall be cast down,**

saith the LORD.

■ 16. **Thus saith the LORD,** Stand

ye in the ways, and see, and

■ **ask** for the old paths,
■ **where is the good way,** and
■ **walk therein, and** ye shall
■ **find rest for your souls.** But

they said, We will not walk *therein.*

17. Also I set watchmen over you, *saying,* Hearken to the sound of the trumpet.

■ **But they said, We will**
■ **not hearken.**

18. **Therefore** hear, ye nations, and know, O congregation, what *is* among them.

19. Hear, O earth: behold,

■ **I will bring evil**
■ **upon this people,**

even the fruit of their thoughts,

■ **because they have**
■ **not hearkened unto**

my words, nor to

■ **my law,** but rejected it.

20. To what purpose cometh there to me incense from Sheba, and the sweet cane from a far country?

■ **your burnt offerings**
■ **are not acceptable,**

nor your sacrifices sweet unto me.

21. Therefore thus saith the LORD, Behold,

■ **I will lay stumblingblocks**
■ **before this people,**

and the fathers and the sons together shall fall upon them; the neighbour and his friend shall perish.

22. Thus saith the LORD,

■ **Behold,** a people cometh

from the north country, and

■ **a great nation shall be**
■ **raised** from the sides of the earth.

23. **They shall** lay hold on bow and spear; they *are* cruel, and have no mercy; their voice roareth like the sea; and they ride upon horses, set in array as men for

■ **war against thee,**
■ **O daughter of Zion.**

24. We have heard the fame thereof: our hands wax feeble: anguish hath taken hold of us, *and* pain, as of a woman in travail.

■ 25. **Go not** forth
■ **into the field, nor** walk
■ **by the way; for**

the sword of the enemy *and*

■ **fear is on every side.**

26. O daughter of my people,

■ **gird thee with sackcloth,**
■ **and** wallow thyself in
■ **ashes:** make thee mourning, *as for*

an only son, most bitter lamentation:

■ **for the spoiler shall**
■ **suddenly come upon us.**

27. I have set thee *for* a tower *and* a fortress among my people, that thou mayest know and try their way.

■ 28. **They are all**
■ **grievous revolters,**

walking with slanders: *they are* brass and iron; they *are* all corrupters.

29. The bellows are burned, the lead is consumed of the fire; the founder melteth in vain: for the wicked are not plucked away.

■ 30. **Reprobate silver shall**
■ **men call them, because the**

|■| LORD hath rejected them.

CHAPTER 7

■ 1. **The word** that
■ **came to Jeremiah**
from the LORD,
■ **saying,**
■ 2. **Stand in the gate**
of the LORD'S house,
■ **and proclaim** there
■ **this word,** and say,
■ **Hear the word** of the LORD,
■ **all ye of Judah,** that enter in at
these gates to worship the LORD.
3. Thus saith the LORD of hosts, the
God of Israel,
■ **Amend your ways and**
■ **your doings,** and I will cause
you to dwell in this place.
■ 4. **Trust ye not in lying**
■ **words,** saying, The temple of the
LORD, The temple of the LORD, The
temple of the LORD, *are* these.
■ 5. **For if ye** throughly
■ **amend your ways and**
your doings; if ye throughly
execute judgment between
a man and his neighbour;
6. *If* ye oppress not the stranger,
the fatherless, and the widow,
and shed not innocent blood in
this place, neither walk after
other gods to your hurt:
■ 7. **Then will I cause you to**
■ **dwell in this place,** in the land
■ **that I gave to your fathers,**
■ **for ever and ever.**
8. Behold, ye trust in lying
words, that cannot profit.
■ 9. **Will ye steal, murder,**
■ **and commit adultery,**
and swear falsely, and burn
incense unto Baal, and walk after
other gods whom ye know not;
■ 10. **And** come and
■ **stand before me** in this house,
which is called by my name,
■ **and say, We are**
■ **delivered to do all**
■ **these abominations?**
■ 11. **Is this house,**
which is
■ **called by my name,**

■ **become a den of robbers**
in your eyes? Behold, even I have
seen *it,* saith the LORD.
■ 12. **But go** ye now
■ **unto** my place which *was* in
■ **Shiloh,** where I set my
name at the first,
■ **and see what I did to it** for the
wickedness of my people Israel.
■ 13. **And now,** because
■ **ye have done** all
■ **these works,** saith the LORD, and
I spake unto you, rising up early and
speaking, but ye heard not; and
■ **I called you, but ye**
■ **answered not;**
■ 14. **Therefore will I do unto**
this house, which is called by my
name, wherein ye trust, and unto
the place which I gave to
■ **you** and to your fathers,
■ **as I have done to Shiloh.**
■ 15. **And I will cast you out**
■ **of my sight,** as I have cast
out all your brethren, *even* the
whole seed of Ephraim.
16. Therefore
■ **pray not** thou
■ **for this people,**
neither lift up cry nor prayer for them,
neither make intercession to me:
■ **for I will not hear thee.**
■ 17. **Seest thou not what they**
■ **do in the cities of Judah**
and in the streets of Jerusalem?
■ 18. **The children**
gather wood, and
■ **the fathers** kindle the fire,
■ **and the women** knead *their*
dough, to make cakes to the
queen of heaven, and to
■ **pour out** drink
■ **offerings unto other gods,**
that they may provoke me to anger.
■ 19. **Do they provoke**
■ **me to anger?** saith the LORD:
do they not *provoke* themselves to
the confusion of their own faces?
20. Therefore thus
saith the Lord GOD;
■ **Behold, mine anger and my**
■ **fury shall be poured out**
■ **upon this place,** upon man, and

upon beast, and upon the trees of the field, and upon the fruit of the ground;
■ **and it shall burn, and**
■ **shall not be quenched.**
21. Thus saith the LORD of hosts, the God of Israel; Put your burnt offerings unto your sacrifices, and eat flesh.
■ 22. **For I spake** not
■ **unto your fathers,**
nor commanded them in the day that I brought them out of the land of Egypt, concerning burnt offerings or sacrifices:
23. But this thing commanded I them,
■ **saying, Obey my voice,**
and I will be your God, and ye shall be my people:
■ **and walk ye in all the ways**
■ **that I have commanded**
you, that it may be well unto you.
■ 24. **But they hearkened not,**
nor inclined their ear, but walked in the counsels *and* in the imagination of their evil heart, and went backward, and not forward.
■ 25. **Since** the day that
■ **your fathers came** forth
■ **out of** the land of
■ **Egypt** unto this day
■ **I have** even
■ **sent unto you** all my servants
■ **the prophets,** daily rising up early and sending *them:*
■ 26. **Yet they hearkened not**
unto me, nor inclined their ear,
■ **but** hardened their neck: they
■ **did worse than**
■ **their fathers.**
■ 27. **Therefore** thou shalt
■ **speak** all
■ **these words unto them;**
but they will not hearken to thee: thou shalt also call unto them; but they will not answer thee.
28. But thou shalt say unto them,
■ **This is a nation that**
■ **obeyeth not** the voice
of the LORD their God,
■ **nor receiveth correction:**
truth is perished, and is cut off from their mouth.
■ 29. **Cut off thine hair, O**
■ **Jerusalem,** and cast *it* away, and

■ **take up a lamentation**
on high places;
■ **for the LORD hath** rejected and
■ **forsaken the generation**
■ **of his wrath.**
30. For the children of
■ **Judah have done evil**
■ **in my sight,** saith the LORD:
■ **they have set** their
■ **abominations in the**
■ **house which is called**
■ **by my name,** to pollute it.
■ 31. **And** they
■ **have built the high places**
■ **of Tophet,** which *is* in the
valley of the son of Hinnom,
■ **to burn their sons and** their
■ **daughters**
in the fire; which I commanded *them* not, neither came it into my heart.
■ 32. **Therefore,** behold, the days come, saith the LORD, that
■ **it shall** no more
■ **be called** Tophet, nor the
valley of the son of Hinnom, but
■ **the valley of slaughter:**
for they shall bury in Tophet, till there be no place.
■ 33. **And the carcases**
of this people
■ **shall be meat for**
■ **the fowls** of the heaven,
■ **and** for the
■ **beasts** of the earth;
■ **and none shall**
■ **fray them away.**
34. Then will I cause to cease from the cities of Judah,
■ **and** from the streets of
Jerusalem, the voice of mirth, and the voice of gladness, the voice of the bridegroom, and the voice of the bride: for
■ **the land shall**
■ **be desolate.**

CHAPTER 8
1. At that time, saith the LORD,
■ **they shall bring** out
■ **the bones** of the kings of Judah, and the bones of his princes, and the bones of the priests, and the bones of the prophets, and the bones

of the inhabitants of Jerusalem, out of their graves: 2. **And** they shall **spread them before the sun, and** the **moon, and all the host of heaven,** whom they have loved, and whom they have served, and after whom they have walked, and whom they have sought, and **whom they have worshipped:** they shall not be gathered, nor be buried; **they shall be for dung upon the face of the earth.** 3. **And death shall be chosen** rather than life **by** all the residue of **them that remain** of this evil family, which remain in all the places whither I have driven them, saith the LORD of hosts. 4. **Moreover** thou shalt **say unto them,** Thus saith the LORD; Shall they fall, and not arise? shall he turn away, and not return? 5. **Why** then **is** this people of **Jerusalem slidden back** by a perpetual backsliding? they hold fast deceit, **they refuse to return.** 6. **I hearkened** and heard, **but** they spake not aright: **no man repented** him **of his wickedness,** saying, What have I done? every one turned to his course, as the horse rusheth into the battle. 7. **Yea, the stork in the heaven knoweth her appointed times;** and the turtle and the crane and the swallow observe the time of their coming; **but my people know not the judgment of the LORD.** 8. **How do ye say, We are wise,** and the law of the LORD is with us? Lo, certainly in vain made he *it;* the pen of the scribes *is* in vain. 9. **The wise men** are ashamed, they are dismayed and taken: lo, they **have rejected the word of the LORD;** and **what wisdom is in them?** 10. Therefore will I give their wives unto others, *and* their fields to them that shall inherit *them:* for every one from the least even unto the greatest is given to covetousness, **from the prophet even unto the priest every one dealeth falsely.** 11. **For they have healed the hurt** of the daughter **of my people** slightly, **saying, Peace,** peace; **when there is no peace.** 12. **Were they ashamed when they** had **committed abomination? nay,** they were not at all ashamed, neither could they blush: **therefore** shall they fall among them that fall: in the time of their visitation **they shall be cast down, saith the LORD.** 13. **I will surely consume them,** saith the LORD: *there shall be* no grapes on the vine, nor figs on the fig tree, and the leaf shall fade; **and the things that I have given them shall pass away** from them. 14. Why do we sit still? **assemble yourselves,** and let us enter into the defenced cities, and let us be silent there: **for the LORD** our God **hath put us to silence,** and given us water of gall to drink, **because we have sinned** against the LORD. 15. **We looked for peace,** but no good *came;* **and** for a time of **health, and behold trouble!** 16. **The** snorting of his horses was heard from Dan: the whole land trembled at the sound of the neighing of his **strong** ones; for they **are come, and have**

- devoured the land,
- and all that is in it; the

city, and those that dwell therein.

17. For, behold,

- I will send serpents,

cockatrices, among you,
which *will* not *be* charmed,

- and they shall bite you,

saith the LORD.

18. *When* I would comfort myself
against sorrow, my heart*is* faint in me.

- 19. Behold the voice of
- the cry of the daughter
- of my people because of them

that dwell in a far country:

- Is not the LORD in Zion?

is not her king in her?

- Why have they provoked
- me to anger with their graven

images, *and* with strange vanities?

- 20. The harvest is past,
- the summer is ended,
- and we are not saved.

21. For the hurt of
the daughter of

- my people am I hurt;

I am black; astonishment
hath taken hold on me.

- 22. Is there no balm in
- Gilead; *is there* no physician there?
- why then
- is not the health
- of the daughter of
- my people recovered?

CHAPTER 9

- 1. Oh that my head
- were waters, and mine eyes
- a fountain of tears, that I
- might weep day
- and night for

the slain of the daughter of

- my people!
- 2. Oh that I had in the wilderness
- a lodging place

of wayfaring men;

- that I might leave my
- people, and go from them!
- for they be all adulterers,
- an assembly of
- treacherous men.

3. And they bend their
tongues *like* their bow *for* lies: but

they are not valiant for the truth
upon the earth; for they

- proceed from evil
- to evil, and they
- know not me, saith the LORD.
- 4. Take ye
- heed every one of his neighbour,
- and trust ye
- not in any brother: for every

brother will utterly supplant, and every
neighbour will walk with slanders.

5. And they will deceive every
one his neighbour, and will not
speak the truth:

- they have taught their tongue to
- speak lies, and

weary themselves to

- commit iniquity.

6. Thine habitation *is*
in the midst of deceit;

- through deceit they refuse
- to know me, saith the LORD.

7. Therefore thus saith
the LORD of hosts, Behold,

- I will melt them, and
- try them; for how shall I do

for the daughter of my people?

8. Their tongue *is as* an arrow
shot out; it speaketh deceit:

- one speaketh peaceably

to his neighbour with his mouth,

- but in heart he
- layeth his wait.
- 9. Shall I not visit them for
- these things? saith the LORD:
- shall not my soul be
- avenged on such a nation as this?
- 10. For the mountains will I
- takeup a weeping and wailing, and

for the habitations of the wilderness a

- lamentation, because they
- are burned up, so that none can

pass through *them;* neither can *men*
hear the voice of the cattle; both the
fowl of the heavens and the beast
are fled; they are gone.

- 11. And I will make
- Jerusalem heaps,
- and a den of dragons;

and I will make

- the cities of Judah
- desolate, without an inhabitant.
- 12. Who *is* the wise man, that

■ **may understand this?**
■ **and who** *is he* to whom the mouth of the LORD hath spoken, that he
■ **may declare it,** for what the land perisheth *and* is burned up like a wilderness, that none passeth through?
■ 13. **And the LORD saith,**
■ **Because they have**
■ **forsaken my law** which I set before them,
■ **and** have not obeyed my voice, neither
■ **walked** therein;
14. But have walked after the imagination of their own heart, and
■ **after Baalim,** which their fathers taught them:
15. Therefore thus saith the LORD of hosts, the God of Israel; Behold,
■ **I will feed them,** *even* this people,
■ **with wormwood,**
■ **and give them** water of
■ **gall to drink.**
16. **I will scatter them also**
■ **among the heathen,** whom neither they nor their fathers have known:
■ **and** I will
■ **send a sword after them, till**
■ **I have consumed them.**
17. Thus saith the LORD of hosts, Consider ye, and
■ **call for the mourning**
■ **women,** that they may come; and send for cunning *women,*
■ **that they may** come:
18. And let them make haste, and
■ **take up a wailing** for us,
■ **that our eyes may run** down
■ **with tears,** and our eyelids gush out with waters.
19. **For a voice of wailing**
■ **is heard out of Zion,** How are we spoiled!
■ **we are greatly**
■ **confounded,** because we have forsaken the land, because our dwellings have cast *us* out.
20. Yet hear the word of the LORD,
■ **O ye women,** and let your ear
■ **receive the word** of his mouth,

■ **and teach your daughters**
■ **wailing, and** every one her neighbour
■ **lamentation.**
■ 21. **For death is come** up into our windows, *and* is entered
■ **into our palaces,** to cut off the children from without, *and* the young men from the streets.
22. Speak, Thus saith the LORD, Even the carcases of men shall fall as dung upon the open field, and as the handful after the harvestman, and none shall gather *them.*
23. Thus saith the LORD,
■ **Let not the wise man glory**
■ **in his wisdom, neither** let
■ **the mighty** *man* glory
■ **in his might,** let not the rich *man* glory in his riches:
■ 24. **But let him that glorieth**
■ **glory in this, that he**
■ **understandeth and**
■ **knoweth me, that I am**
■ **the LORD which exercise**
■ **lovingkindness, judgment,**
■ **and righteousness,** in the earth:
■ **for in these things I**
■ **delight,** saith the LORD.
■ 25. **Behold, the days**
■ **come,** saith the LORD,
■ **that I will punish** all
■ **them which are**
■ **circumcised with the**
■ **uncircumcised;**
■ 26. **Egypt,** and
■ **Judah,** and
■ **Edom,** and the children of
■ **Ammon,** and
■ **Moab, and all that are in**
■ **the utmost corners,** that dwell in the wilderness: for all
■ **these nations are**
■ **uncircumcised, and all**
■ **the house of Israel are**
■ **uncircumcised in the heart.**

CHAPTER 10

■ 1. **Hear ye** the word which the LORD speaketh unto you,
■ **O house of**

Israel:

2. Thus saith the LORD,

Learn not the way of the heathen, and be not dismayed at the signs of heaven; for **the heathen** are dismayed at them.

3. For the **customs** of the people **are vain:** for *one* cutteth a tree out of the forest, the work of the hands of the workman, with the axe.

4. They deck it with silver and with gold; they fasten it with nails and with hammers, that it move not.

5. They *are* upright as the palm tree, but speak not: they must needs be borne, because they cannot go. **Be not afraid of them; for they cannot do evil, neither** also **is it in them to do good.**

6. **Forasmuch as there is none like unto thee, O LORD; thou art great,** and thy name *is* great in might.

7. **Who would not fear thee, O King** of nations? for to thee doth it appertain: forasmuch as **among all the wise men** of the nations, **and** in all their **kingdoms, there is none like unto thee.**

8. **But they are** altogether brutish and **foolish:** the stock *is* a doctrine of vanities.

9. Silver spread into plates is brought from Tarshish, and gold from Uphaz, the work of the workman, **and** of the hands of the founder: blue and purple *is* their clothing: they *are* all the work of **cunning men.**

10. **But the LORD is the true** God, he *is* the **living God, and an everlasting king:** at his wrath **the earth shall tremble, and** the nations **shall not be able to**

abide his indignation.

11. Thus shall ye say unto them, The gods that have not made the heavens and the earth, *even* they shall perish from the earth, and from under these heavens.

12. **He hath made the earth by his power,** he hath established the world by his wisdom, **and** hath stretched out **the heavens by his discretion.**

13. **When he uttereth his voice,** *there is* a multitude of waters in the heavens, and he causeth the vapours to ascend from the ends of the earth; **he maketh** lightnings with **rain, and** bringeth forth the **wind** out of his treasures.

14. **Every man is brutish in his knowledge:** every founder is confounded by the graven image: for **his molten image is falsehood,** and *there is* no breath in them.

15. They *are* vanity, *and* the work of errors: in the time of their visitation **they shall perish.**

16. The portion of Jacob *is* not like them: for he *is* the former of all *things;* and **Israel is the rod of his inheritance: The LORD of hosts is his name.**

17. Gather up thy wares out of the land, O inhabitant of the fortress.

18. **For** thus saith the LORD, **Behold, I will sling out the inhabitants of the land** at this once, and will distress them, that they may find *it so.*

19. Woe is me for my hurt! **my wound is grievous;** but I said, Truly this *is* a grief, and I must bear it.

20. **My tabernacle is spoiled,** and all my cords are broken: my children are gone forth of me, and they *are* not: **there is none to stretch forth my tent** any more, **and to set up my curtains.**

21. **For the pastors** are become brutish, and **have not sought the LORD: therefore they shall not prosper, and** all their flocks **shall be scattered.**

22. Behold, the noise of the bruit is come, and a great commotion out of the north country, to make the cities of Judah desolate, *and* a den of dragons.

23. **O LORD,** I know that the way of man *is* not in himself: **it is not in man** that walketh **to direct his steps.**

24. O LORD, **correct me, but with judgment; not** in thine **anger,** lest thou bring me to nothing.

25. **Pour out thy fury upon the heathen that know thee not, and** upon the families **that call not on thy name:** for they have eaten up Jacob, and devoured him, and consumed him, and have made his habitation desolate.

CHAPTER 11

1. **The word that came to Jeremiah from the LORD saying,**

2. **Hear ye the words of this covenant, and speak unto** the men of **Judah,** and to the inhabitants of Jerusalem;

3. And say thou unto them, **Thus saith the LORD** God of Israel; **Cursed be the man that obeyeth not the words of this covenant,**

4. **Which I commanded your fathers in the day** *that* **I brought them** forth **out of** the land of **Egypt,** from the iron furnace, saying, **Obey** my voice, **and do** them, according to **all** which **I command you:** so shall ye be my people, and I will be your God:

5. **That I may** perform the oath which I have sworn unto your fathers, to **give them a land flowing with milk and honey,** as *it is* this day. **Then answered I,** and said, **So be it,** O LORD.

6. **Then the LORD said** unto me, **Proclaim** all these words **in the cities of Judah,** and in the streets of Jerusalem, **saying, Hear ye the words of this covenant,** and do them.

7. For I earnestly protested unto **your fathers** in the day *that* I brought them up out of the land of Egypt, *even* unto this day, rising early and protesting, saying, Obey my voice.

8. Yet they **obeyed not,** nor inclined their ear, but walked every one in the imagination of their evil heart: therefore I will bring upon them all **the words of this covenant,** which I commanded *them* to do: but they did *them* not.

9. **And** the LORD said unto me, **A conspiracy is found among** the men of **Judah, and** among the inhabitants of **Jerusalem.**

10. **They** are turned back to the iniquities of their forefathers, which refused to hear my words; and they went after other gods to serve them: the house of Israel and the house of Judah **have broken my covenant which I made with their fathers.**

11. **Therefore** thus saith the LORD, Behold, **I will bring evil upon them, which they shall not be**

able to escape;
and though they shall cry unto me,
I will not hearken unto them.

12. Then shall the cities of
Judah and inhabitants of
Jerusalem go, and
cry unto the gods
unto whom they offer
incense: but they shall
not save them at all
in the time of their
trouble.

13. For *according to* the number of
thy cities were thy gods, O Judah; and
according to the number of the streets
of Jerusalem have ye set up altars to
that shameful thing, *even* altars to
burn incense unto Baal.

14. Therefore pray not thou
for this people, neither lift up a
cry or prayer for them:
for I will not hear them
in the time that they cry unto
me for their trouble.

15. What hath my beloved to
do in mine house, *seeing*
she hath wrought lewdness
with many, and the holy flesh is
passed from thee?
when thou doest evil,
then thou rejoicest.

16. The LORD called thy name, A
green olive tree, fair, *and* of goodly
fruit: with the noise of a great tumult
he hath kindled fire upon it, and the
branches of it are broken.

17. For the LORD of hosts,
that planted thee,
hath pronounced evil
against thee, for the
evil of the house of
Israel and of the house of Judah,
which they have done
against themselves to
provoke me to anger in
offering incense unto Baal.

18. And the LORD hath
given me knowledge *of it,*
and I know *it:* then thou
shewedst me their doings.

19. But I *was* like a lamb *or* an ox *that*
is brought to the slaughter; and
I knew not that they had

devised devices
against me, saying, Let us
destroy the tree with the fruit
thereof, and let us cut
him off from the land of the living,
that his name may be
no more remembered.

20. But, O LORD
of hosts, that judgest righteously, that
triest the reins and the heart,
let me see thy vengeance
on them: for unto thee have I
revealed my cause.

21. Therefore thus saith the
LORD of the men of Anathoth,
that seek thy life, saying,
Prophesy not
in the name of the LORD,
that thou die not
by our hand:

22. Therefore thus
saith the LORD of hosts, Behold, I
will punish them:
the young men shall die by the sword;
their sons and their daughters shall
die by famine:

23. And there shall be no
remnant of them: for I will bring
evil upon the men of Anathoth, *even*
the year of their visitation.

CHAPTER 12

1. Righteous art thou, O
LORD, when I plead with thee: yet
let me talk with thee of
thy judgments: Wherefore
doth the way of
the wicked prosper?
wherefore are all
they happy that deal very
treacherously?

2. Thou hast planted them,
yea, they have taken root:
they grow, yea, they bring
forth fruit: thou *art* near in their
mouth, and far from their reins.

3. But thou, O LORD,
knowest me: thou hast
seen me, and
tried mine heart toward thee:
pull them out like sheep
for the slaughter, and prepare
them for the day of slaughter.

4. **How long shall the land mourn,** and the herbs of every field wither, **for the wickedness of them that dwell therein?** the beasts are consumed, and the birds; because they said, He shall not see our last end.

5. **If thou hast run with** the **footmen, and they have wearied thee,** then **how canst thou contend with horses? and if in** the land of **peace,** *wherein* thou trustedst, **they wearied thee,** then **how wilt thou do in the swelling of Jordan?**

6. **For even thy brethren,** and the house of thy father, even they **have dealt treacherously with thee;** yea, they have called a multitude after thee: **believe them not,** though they speak fair words unto thee.

7. **I have forsaken mine house,** I have left mine heritage; I have given the dearly beloved of my soul into the hand of her enemies.

8. **Mine heritage** is unto me as a lion in the forest; it **crieth out against me:** therefore have I hated it.

9. Mine heritage *is* unto me *as a* speckled bird, the birds round about *are* against her; come ye, assemble all the beasts of the field, come to devour.

10. **Many pastors have destroyed my vineyard,** they have trodden my portion under foot, they have made my pleasant portion a desolate wilderness.

11. They have made it desolate, *and* being desolate it mourneth unto me; **the whole land is made desolate,** because no man layeth *it* to heart.

12. The spoilers are come upon all high places through the wilderness: for **the sword of the LORD shall devour** from the *one* end of **the land** even to the *other* end of the land: **no flesh shall have peace.**

13. **They have sown wheat, but shall reap thorns:** they have put themselves to pain, *but* shall not profit: and they shall be ashamed of your revenues because of the fierce anger of the LORD.

14. **Thus saith the LORD** against **all** mine **evil neighbours, that touch the inheritance which** I have caused **my people** Israel to **inherit;** Behold, **I will pluck them out of their land,** and pluck out the house of Judah from among them.

15. **And** it shall come to pass, **after that I** have plucked them out I will return, and have compassion on them, and **will bring them again,** every man to his heritage, and **every man to his land.**

16. **And** it shall come to pass, **if they will** diligently learn the ways of my people, to **swear** by my name, **The LORD liveth;** as they taught my people to swear by Baal; **then shall they be** built in the midst of **my people.**

17. **But if** they will **not** obey, **I will** utterly pluck up and **destroy that nation,** saith the LORD.

CHAPTER 13

1. **Thus saith the LORD** unto me, Go and **get** thee **a linen girdle, and put it upon thy loins,** and put it not in water.

2. So I got a girdle according to the word of the LORD, and **put it on** my loins.

3. **And the word of the LORD came unto me the second time, saying,** 4. **Take the girdle** that thou hast got, **which is upon thy loins, and** arise, **go to Euphrates, and hide it** there in a hole of the rock. 5. **So I** went, and **hid it** by Euphrates, as the LORD commanded me. 6. **And** it came to pass **after many days, that the LORD said unto me,** Arise, **go to Euphrates, and take the girdle** from thence, which I commanded thee to hide there. 7. **Then I went** to Euphrates, **and digged,** and took the girdle from the place where I had hid it: **and, behold, the girdle was marred,** it was profitable for nothing. 8. **Then** the word of **the LORD** came unto me, saying, 9. Thus **saith** the LORD, After this manner will I mar the pride of Judah, and the great pride of Jerusalem. 10. **This evil people, which** refuse to hear my words, which walk in the imagination of their heart, and **walk after other gods,** to serve them, **and** to **worship them, shall** even **be as this girdle, which is good for nothing.** 11. **For as the girdle cleaveth to** the loins of **a man, so have I caused to cleave unto me** the whole house of **Israel** and the whole house of Judah, saith the LORD; **that they might be unto me** for **a people,** and for a name, and for a praise, and for a glory: **but they would not hear.** 12. **Therefore** thou shalt speak unto them this word; Thus saith the LORD God of Israel, **Every bottle shall be filled with wine:** and they shall say unto thee, Do we not certainly know that every bottle shall be filled with wine? 13. Then shalt thou say unto them, Thus saith the LORD, **Behold, I will fill** all the inhabitants of **this land,** even the kings that sit upon David's throne, and the priests, and the prophets, and all the inhabitants of Jerusalem, **with drunkenness.** 14. **And I will dash them one against another,** even the fathers and the sons together, saith the LORD: **I will** not pity, nor spare, nor have mercy, but **destroy them.** 15. Hear ye, and **give ear;** be not proud: **for the LORD hath spoken.** 16. **Give glory to the LORD** your God, before he cause darkness, and **before your feet stumble** upon the dark mountains, and, while ye look for light, he turn it **into** the shadow of death, *and* make *it* gross **darkness.** 17. **But if ye will not hear it,** my soul shall weep in secret places for *your* pride; and **mine eye shall weep** sore, and run down with tears, **because the LORD'S flock is carried away captive.** 18. Say unto the king and to the queen, **Humble yourselves,** sit down: **for your principalities shall come down,** *even* the crown of your glory. 19. **The cities** of the south **shall be shut up, and** none shall open *them:* **Judah shall be carried away captive** all of it, it shall be wholly carried away captive.

20. Lift up your eyes, and behold them that come from the north: where *is* the flock *that* was given thee, thy beautiful flock?

21. **What wilt thou say when he shall punish thee?** for thou hast taught them *to be* captains, *and* as chief over thee: **shall not sorrows take thee,** as a woman in travail?

22. **And if thou say** in thine heart, **Wherefore come these things upon me? For** the greatness of **thine iniquity** are thy skirts discovered, *and* thy heels made bare.

23. Can the Ethiopian change his skin, or the leopard his spots? *then* may ye also do good, that are accustomed to do evil.

24. Therefore **will I scatter them** as the stubble that passeth away by the wind of the wilderness.

25. **This is thy lot,** the portion of thy measures from me, **saith the LORD; because thou hast forgotten me,** and trusted in falsehood.

26. Therefore will I discover thy skirts upon thy face, that thy shame may appear.

27. **I have seen thine** adulteries, and thy neighings, the lewdness of thy whoredom, *and* thine **abominations** on the hills in the fields. **Woe unto thee, O Jerusalem!** wilt thou not be made clean? when *shall it* once *be?*

CHAPTER 14

1. **The word of the LORD** that came to Jeremiah **concerning the dearth.**

2. **Judah mourneth,** and the gates thereof languish; they are black unto the ground; and the cry of Jerusalem is gone up.

3. **And their nobles have sent their little ones to the** waters: they came to the pits, and found no water; they returned with their vessels empty; they were ashamed and confounded, and covered their heads.

4. Because the ground is chapt, **for there was no rain in the earth,** the plowmen were ashamed, they covered their heads.

5. Yea, the hind also calved in the field, and forsook *it,* because there was no grass.

6. And the wild asses did stand in the high places, they snuffed up the wind like dragons; their eyes did fail, because there was no grass.

7. **O LORD,** though our iniquities testify against us, do thou *it* for thy name's sake: for **our backslidings are many; we have sinned against thee.**

8. O the hope of Israel, the saviour thereof in time of trouble, **why shouldest thou be** as **a stranger** in the land, and as a wayfaring man *that* turneth aside to tarry for a night?

9. Why shouldest thou be as a man astonied, as a mighty man *that* cannot save? yet **thou,** O LORD, **art in the midst of us, and we are called by thy name;** leave us not.

10. Thus saith the LORD unto this people, Thus have they loved to wander, they have not refrained their feet, therefore the LORD doth not accept them; he will now remember their iniquity, and visit their sins.

11. **Then said the LORD** unto me, **Pray not for this people** for *their* good.

12. **When they fast, I will not hear their cry; and** when they offer burnt offering and an oblation, **I will not accept them:** but **I will consume them by the sword, and** by the **famine,** and by the pestilence.

13. **Then said I,** Ah,

■ **Lord** GOD! behold,
■ **the prophets say** unto them,
■ **Ye shall not see the sword,**
■ **neither** shall ye have
■ **famine;** but I will give you
assured peace in this place.
■ 14. **Then the LORD said**
unto me, The prophets prophesy lies
in my name: I sent them not, neither
have I commanded them, neither
spake unto them:
■ **they prophesy** unto you
■ **a false vision** and divination,
and a thing of nought, and the
deceit of their heart.
■ 15. **Therefore** thus saith the LORD
concerning the prophets that
prophesy in my name, and I sent
them not, yet they say, Sword and
famine shall not be in this land;
■ **By sword and famine**
■ **shall those prophets**
■ **be consumed.**
■ 16. **And the people**
to whom they prophesy
■ **shall be cast out**
in the streets of Jerusalem because
of the famine and the sword;
■ **and** they shall have none to bury
them, them, their wives, nor their
sons, nor their daughters: for
■ **I will pour their wickedness**
■ **upon them.**
17. Therefore thou shalt
■ **say this word unto them;**
■ **Let mine eyes run** down
■ **with tears night and day,**
■ **and** let them
■ **not cease: for**
the virgin daughter of
■ **my people is broken**
with a great breach, with
a very grievous blow.
18. If I go forth into the field, then
behold the slain with the sword! and if
I enter into the city, then behold them
that are sick with famine! yea, both
the prophet and the priest go about
into a land that they know not.
■ 19. **Hast thou utterly**
■ **rejected Judah?**
hath thy soul lothed Zion?
■ **why hast thou smitten us,**

and *there is* no healing for us?
■ **we looked for peace,**
and *there is* no good; and
for the time of healing,
■ **and behold trouble!**
■ 20. **We acknowledge,**
O LORD,
■ **our wickedness,**
and the iniquity of our fathers:
■ **for we have sinned**
■ **against thee.**
■ 21. **Do not abhor us,** for thy
name's sake, do not disgrace the
throne of thy glory: remember,
■ **break not thy**
■ **covenant with us.**
■ 22. **Are there any**
■ **among the** vanities of the
■ **Gentiles that can**
■ **cause rain?** or
■ **can the heavens**
■ **give showers?** *art* not thou he,
■ **O LORD** our God? therefore
■ **we will wait upon thee:**
for thou hast made all these *things.*

CHAPTER 15
■ 1. **Then said the LORD**
unto me, Though Moses and Samuel
stood before me, *yet* my mind *could*
not *be* toward this people:
■ **cast them out of my**
■ **sight,** and let them go forth.
■ 2. **And** it shall come to pass,
■ **if they say** unto thee,
■ **Whither shall we go**
forth? then thou shalt
■ **tell them,** Thus saith the
LORD; Such as *are* for death,
■ **to death;**
and such as *are* for the sword,
■ **to the sword;**
and such as are for the famine,
■ **to the famine; and**
such as *are* for the captivity,
■ **to the**
■ **captivity.**
■ 3. **And I will appoint** over them
■ **four kinds,** saith the LORD:
■ **the sword to slay,** and
■ **the dogs to tear,** and
■ **the fowls** of the heaven,
■ **and the beasts** of the earth,

to devour and destroy.
4. And I will cause them to be removed into all kingdoms of the earth, because of Manasseh the son of Hezekiah king of Judah, for *that* which he did in Jerusalem.
5. For who shall have pity upon thee, O Jerusalem? or who shall bemoan thee? or who shall go aside to ask how thou doest?
6. Thou hast forsaken me, saith the LORD, thou art gone backward: therefore will I stretch out my hand against thee, and destroy thee; I am weary with repenting.
7. And I will fan them with a fan in the gates of the land; I will bereave *them* of children, I will destroy my people since they return not from their ways.
8. Their widows are increased to me above the sand of the seas: I have brought upon them against the mother of the young men a spoiler at noonday: I have caused *him* to fall upon it suddenly, and terrors upon the city.
9. She that hath borne seven languisheth: she hath given up the ghost; her sun is gone down while *it was* yet day: she hath been ashamed and confounded: and the residue of them will I deliver to the sword before their enemies, saith the LORD.
10. Woe is me, my mother, that thou hast borne me a man of strife and a man of contention to the whole earth! I have neither lent on usury, nor men have lent to me on usury; *yet* every one of them doth curse me.
11. The LORD said, Verily it shall be well with thy remnant; verily I will cause the enemy to entreat thee well in the time of evil and in the time of affliction.
12. Shall iron break the northern iron and the steel?
13. Thy substance and thy treasures will I give to the spoil without price, and *that* for all thy sins, even in all thy borders.
14. And I will make thee to pass with thine enemies into a land which thou knowest not: for a fire is kindled in mine anger, *which* shall burn upon you.
15. O LORD, thou knowest: remember me, and visit me, and revenge me of my persecutors; take me not away in thy longsuffering: know that for thy sake I have suffered rebuke.
16. Thy words were found, and I did eat them; and thy word was unto me the joy and rejoicing of mine heart: for I am called by thy name, O LORD God of hosts.
17. I sat not in the assembly of the mockers, nor rejoiced; I sat alone because of thy hand: for thou hast filled me with indignation.
18. Why is my pain perpetual, and my wound incurable, *which* refuseth to be healed? wilt thou be altogether unto me as a liar, *and as* waters *that* fail?
19. Therefore thus saith the LORD, If thou return, then will I bring thee again, *and* thou shalt stand before me: and if thou take forth the precious from the vile, thou shalt be as my mouth: let them return unto thee; but return not thou unto them.
20. And I will make thee unto this people a fenced brasen wall: and they shall fight against thee, but they shall not prevail against thee:

■ **for I am with thee**
■ **to save** thee
■ **and** to
■ **deliver thee,** saith the LORD.
■ 21. **And I will deliver**
■ **thee out of the hand**
■ **of the wicked,** and I will redeem
thee out of the hand of the terrible.

CHAPTER 16

■ 1. **The word of the LORD**
■ **came** also unto me,
■ **saying,**
■ 2. **Thou shalt not take** thee
■ **a wife, neither** shalt thou
■ **have sons or daughters**
■ **in this place.**
■ 3. **For** thus saith the
LORD concerning
■ **the sons and** concerning the
■ **daughters** that are
■ **born in this place,**
■ **and** concerning
■ **their mothers** that bare them,
■ **and** concerning their
■ **fathers** that begat
them in this land;
4. They
■ **shall die** of grievous deaths;
■ **they shall not be lamented;**
■ **neither** shall they be
■ **buried;** *but* they shall be as dung
upon the face of the earth: and
they shall be consumed by the
sword, and by famine; and
■ **their carcases shall be**
■ **meat for the fowls** of heaven,
■ **and** for
■ **the beasts** of the earth.
5. For thus saith the LORD,
■ **Enter not into** the house of
■ **mourning,** neither go to
lament nor bemoan them:
■ **for I have taken away my**
■ **peace from this people,**
saith the LORD,
■ **even lovingkindness**
■ **and mercies.**
■ 6. **Both the great and** the
■ **small shall die** in this land: they
shall not be buried, neither shall *men*
lament for them, nor cut themselves,
nor make themselves bald for them:

7. Neither shall *men* tear *themselves*
for them in mourning, to comfort them
for the dead; neither shall *men* give
them the cup of consolation to drink
for their father or for their mother.
■ 8. **Thou shalt not**
also go into the house of feasting, to
■ **sit with them to eat and** to
■ **drink.**
9. **For** thus saith the LORD of
hosts, the God of Israel; Behold,
■ **I will cause to cease**
out of this place in your
eyes, and in your days,
■ **the voice of mirth,**
■ **and** the voice of
■ **gladness,**
the voice of the bridegroom,
and the voice of the bride.
■ 10. **And** it shall come to pass,
■ **when thou** shalt
■ **shew this people** all
■ **these words, and they** shall
■ **say** unto thee,
■ **Wherefore hath the LORD**
■ **pronounced** all this great
■ **evil against us?**
or what *is* our iniquity?
■ **or what is our sin**
that we have committed against
the LORD our God?
■ 11. **Then shalt**
■ **thou say** unto them,
■ **Because your fathers**
■ **have forsaken** me, saith
■ **the LORD, and** have
■ **walked after other gods,**
and have served them, and
have worshipped them, and
have forsaken me, and
■ **and have not kept my law;**
■ 12. **And ye have done**
■ **worse than your fathers;**
for, behold, ye walk every one after
the imagination of his evil heart, that
they may not hearken unto me:
■ 13. **Therefore will I cast you**
■ **out of this land into a land**
■ **that ye know not,**
neither ye nor your fathers;
■ **and** there shall ye serve o
ther gods day and night; where
■ **I will not shew you favour.**

14. Therefore, behold,
■ **the days come,** saith the LORD,
■ **that it shall** no more
■ **be said,** The LORD liveth,
that brought up the children
of Israel out of the land of Egypt;
15. But,
■ **The LORD liveth,**
■ **that brought** up the children of
■ **Israel** from the land of the north, and
from all the lands whither he had
driven them: and I will bring them
■ **again into their land**
that I gave unto their fathers.
16. Behold,
■ **I will send for** many
■ **fishers,** saith the LORD,
■ **and they shall fish them;**
■ **and** after will I send for many
■ **hunters, and they shall**
■ **hunt them** from every mountain,
and from every hill, and out
of the holes of the rocks.
■ 17. **For** mine eyes *are*
upon all their ways:
■ **they are not hid from my**
■ **face, neither is their iniquity**
■ **hid from mine eyes.**
18. And first
■ **I will recompense their**
■ **iniquity** and their sin
■ **double; because**
they have defiled my land,
■ **they have filled mine**
■ **inheritance with**
the carcases of their detestable and
■ **abominable things.**
■ 19. **O LORD,**
my strength, and my fortress,
and my refuge in the day of affliction,
■ **the Gentiles shall**
■ **come unto thee**
from the ends of the earth,
■ **and** shall
■ **say,** Surely
■ **our fathers have inherited**
lies, vanity, and
■ **things wherein**
■ **there is no profit.**
20. Shall a man make gods unto
himself, and they *are* no gods?
■ 21. **Therefore,** behold, I will
his once cause them to know, I

will cause them to know mine
hand and my might; and
■ **they shall know that**
■ **my name is The LORD.**

CHAPTER 17

■ 1. **The sin of Judah**
■ **is written with a pen**
■ **of iron,** *and* with the point
of a diamond: *it is* graven upon
the table of their heart, and
■ **upon** the horns of
■ **your altars;**
■ 2. **Whilst their children**
■ **remember their**
■ **altars and** their
■ **groves** by the green
trees upon the high hills.
3. O my mountain in the field,
■ **I will give** thy substance *and* all
■ **thy treasures to the spoil,**
and thy high places for sin,
throughout all thy borders.
■ 4. **And thou,** even thyself,
■ **shalt** discontinue from thine
heritage that I gave thee;
and I will cause thee to
■ **serve thine enemies in the**
■ **land which thou knowest**
■ **not:** for ye have kindled a fire in
mine anger, *which* shall burn for ever.
5. Thus saith the LORD;
■ **Cursed be the man that**
■ **trusteth in man,** and maketh
flesh his arm, and whose heart
departeth from the LORD.
■ 6. **For he shall** be like the heath
in the desert, and shall not see
when good cometh; but shall
■ **inhabit the parched**
■ **places** in the wilderness,
■ **in a salt land** and not inhabited.
■ 7. **Blessed is the man that**
■ **trusteth in the LORD,**
and whose hope the LORD is.
■ 8. **For he shall be as a tree**
■ **planted by the waters,**
and *that* spreadeth out her
roots by the river,
■ **and** shall not see
■ **when heat cometh,** but
■ **her leaf shall be green;**
and shall not be careful in

the year of drought,

neither shall cease from yielding fruit.

9. **The heart is deceitful above all things, and desperately wicked: who can know it?**

10. **I the LORD search the heart,** *I* try the reins, even **to give every man according to his ways, and** according **to the fruit of his doings.**

11. *As* the partridge sitteth *on eggs,* and hatcheth *them* not; *so* **he that getteth riches,** and **not by right, shall leave them** in the midst of his days, **and at his end shall be a fool.**

12. A glorious high throne from the beginning *is* the place of our sanctuary.

13. **O LORD,** the hope of Israel, **all that forsake thee shall be ashamed,** *and* they that depart from me shall be written in the earth, because they have forsaken the LORD, the fountain of living waters.

14. **Heal me,** O LORD, **and I shall be healed; save me, and I shall be saved: for thou art my praise.**

15. Behold, they say unto me, Where *is* the word of the LORD? let it come now.

16. As for me, **I have not hastened from being a pastor to follow thee:** neither have I desired the woeful day; **thou knowest: that which came out of my lips was right before thee.**

17. **Be** not a terror unto me: thou *art* **my hope in the day of evil.**

18. **Let them be confounded that persecute me,** but let not me be confounded: let them be dismayed, but let not me be dismayed: bring upon them the day of evil,

and destroy them with double destruction.

19. **Thus said the LORD** unto me; **Go and stand in the gate** of the children of the people, whereby the kings of Judah come in, and by the which they go out, and in all the gates **of Jerusalem;**

20. **And say unto them, Hear ye** the word of **the LORD, ye** kings of Judah, and all Judah, and all the **inhabitants of Jerusalem,** that enter in by these gates:

21. Thus saith the LORD; **Take heed to yourselves,** and **bear no burden on the sabbath day,** nor bring *it* in by the gates of Jerusalem;

22. Neither carry forth a burden out of your houses on the sabbath day, **neither do ye any work, but hallow ye the sabbath day,** as I commanded your fathers.

23. But they obeyed not, neither inclined their ear, but made their neck stiff, that they might not hear, nor receive instruction.

24. And it shall come to pass, **if ye** diligently **hearken unto me,** saith the LORD, to bring in no burden through the gates of this city on the sabbath day, but hallow the sabbath day, to do no work therein;

25. **Then** shall there enter into the gates of this city kings and princes sitting upon the throne of David, riding in chariots and on horses, they, and their princes, the men of Judah, and the inhabitants of Jerusalem: and **this city shall remain for ever.**

26. **And they shall come from the cities of Judah, and** from the places about **Jerusalem,** and from the land of Benjamin, and from the plain, and from the mountains, and from the south, bringing burnt offerings, and

sacrifices, and meat offerings,
and incense, and
■ **bringing sacrifices**
■ **of praise, unto** the house of
■ **the LORD.**
■ 27. **But if ye will not hearken**
■ **unto me to hallow the**
■ **sabbath day, and not to**
■ **bear a burden,** even entering
in at the gates of Jerusalem
■ **on the sabbath day; then**
■ **will I kindle a fire**
in the gates thereof,
■ **and it shall devour**
the palaces of
■ **Jerusalem,** and it
shall not be quenched.

CHAPTER 18

■ | 1. **The word** which
■ | **came to Jeremiah**
from the LORD,
■ **saying,**
■ 2. **Arise, and go down to**
■ **the potter's house,** and there
I will cause thee to hear my words.
■ 3. **Then I went** down
■ **to the potter's house,**
■ **and,** behold,
■ **he wrought a work**
■ **on the wheels.**
■ 4. **And the vessel**
■ **that he made** of clay
■ **was marred** in the
hand of the potter:
■ **so he made it again**
another vessel, as seemed
good to the potter to make *it.*
■ 5. **Then the word of the**
■ **LORD came to me, saying,**
6. O house of
■ **Israel, cannot I do with**
■ **you as this potter?**
saith the LORD. Behold,
■ **as the clay is in the potter's**
■ **hand, so are ye in mine**
■ **hand,** O house of Israel.
7. *At what* instant I shall speak
concerning a nation, and concerning
a kingdom, to pluck up, and to pull
down, and to destroy *it;*
■ 8. **If that nation,**
against whom I have pronounced,

■ **turn from their evil, I will**
■ **repent of the evil that I**
■ **thought to do unto them.**
■ 9. **And** *at what* instant I shall speak
concerning a nation, and concerning
a kingdom, to build and to plant *it;*
■ 10. **If it do evil**
in my sight, that it obey not my voice,
■ **then I will repent of the**
■ **good,** wherewith I said
I would benefit them.
11. Now therefore go to,
■ **speak to** the men of Judah,
and to the inhabitants of
■ **Jerusalem, saying,** Thus saith
the LORD; Behold, I frame evil against
you, and devise a device against you:
■ **return** ye now
■ **every one from his**
■ **evil way,** and make your ways
and your doings good.
■ 12. **And they said,**
There is no hope: but
■ **we will walk after our own**
■ **devices,** and we will every one
do the imagination of his evil heart.
■ 13. **Therefore** thus
■ **saith the LORD; Ask** ye now
■ **among the heathen, who**
■ **hath heard such things:**
the virgin of
■ **Israel hath done a** very
■ **horrible thing.**
14. Will *a man* leave the snow of
Lebanon *which cometh* from the
rock of the field? *or* shall the cold
flowing waters that come from
another place be forsaken?
■ 15. **Because my people**
■ **hath forgotten me,** they have
burned incense to vanity, and they
have caused them to stumble in their
ways *from* the ancient paths, to walk
in paths, *in* a way not cast up;
16. To make their land desolate,
and a perpetual hissing; every one
that passeth thereby shall be
astonished, and wag his head.
■ 17. **I will scatter them**
as with an east wind
■ **before the enemy;** I will
shew them the back, and not the
face, in the day of their calamity.

18. **Then said they,**
Come and
let us devise devices
against Jeremiah; for
the law shall not perish
from the priest,
nor counsel from the wise,
nor the word
from the prophet. Come, and
let us smite him with the
tongue, and let us
not give heed to any
of his words.
19. **Give heed to me, O**
LORD, and hearken to the voice
of them that contend with me.
20. Shall evil be recompensed
for good? for they have digged
a pit for my soul.
Remember that I stood
before thee to speak
good for them, and to
turn away thy wrath
from them.
21. **Therefore deliver** up
their children to the
famine, and pour out their *blood*
by the force of the sword; and let their
wives be bereaved of their children,
and *be* widows; and
let their men be put to
death; *let* their young men *be* slain
by the sword in battle.
22. Let a cry be heard from their
houses, when thou shalt bring a
troop suddenly upon them: for
they have digged a pit to take
me, and hid snares for my feet.
23. **Yet,** LORD,
thou knowest all their
counsel against me
to slay me:
forgive not their iniquity, neither blot
out their sin from thy sight, but
let them be overthrown
before thee; deal *thus* with them
in the time of thine anger.

CHAPTER 19

1. **Thus saith the LORD, Go**
and get a potter's earthen
bottle, and *take* of the
ancients of the people, and

of the ancients of the priests;
2. **And go** forth
unto the valley of the son of
Hinnom, which *is* by the entry of
the east gate, and proclaim there
the words that I shall tell thee,
3. **And say, Hear ye the**
word of the LORD,
O kings of Judah, and inhabitants of
Jerusalem; Thus saith the LORD of
hosts, the God of Israel; Behold,
I will bring evil upon
this place, the which whosoever
heareth, his ears shall tingle.
4. **Because they have**
forsaken me, and have estranged
this place, and have
burned incense in it
unto other gods, whom neither
they nor their fathers have known,
nor the kings of Judah,
and have
filled this place with the
blood of innocents;
5. **They have** built also
the high places of Baal, to
burn their sons with fire
for burnt offerings unto
Baal, which I commanded not, nor
spake *it,* neither came *it* into my mind:
6. **Therefore,** behold, the days
come, saith the LORD, that
this place shall no more
be called Tophet, nor The
valley of the son of Hinnom, but
The valley of slaughter.
7. And I will make void the
counsel of Judah and Jerusalem
in this place; and
I will cause them to fall by
the sword before their
enemies, and by the hands of
them that seek their lives: and their
carcases will I give to be meat for
the fowls of the heaven, and for
the beasts of the earth.
8. **And I will make this city**
desolate, and an hissing;
every one that
passeth thereby
shall be astonished
and hiss because of
all the plagues thereof.

9. **And I will cause them to eat the flesh of their sons and** the flesh of their **daughters,** and they shall eat every one the flesh of his friend in the siege and straitness, wherewith their enemies, and they that seek their lives, shall straiten them.

10. **Then shalt thou break the bottle in the sight of the men that go with thee,**

11. **And shalt say unto them,** Thus saith the LORD of hosts; **Even so will I break this people** and this city, **as one breaketh a potter's vessel,** that cannot be made whole again: **and they shall bury them in Tophet, till there be no place to bury.**

12. Thus will I do unto this place, saith the LORD, and to the inhabitants thereof, and *even* make this city as Tophet:

13. And the houses of Jerusalem, and the houses of the kings of Judah, shall be defiled as the place of Tophet, because of all the houses upon whose roofs they have burned incense unto all the host of heaven, and have poured out drink offerings unto other gods.

14. **Then came Jeremiah from Tophet, whither the LORD had sent him to prophesy; and he stood in the court of the LORD's house; and said** to all the people,

15. **Thus saith the LORD of hosts,** the God of Israel; **Behold, I will bring upon this city** and upon all her towns **all the evil that I have pronounced against it, because they have hardened their necks, that they might not hear**

my words

CHAPTER 20

1. **Now Pashur** the son of Immer the priest, **who was** also chief **governor in the house of the LORD, heard that Jeremiah** prophesied these things.

2. **Then Pashur smote Jeremiah** the prophet, **and put him in the stocks** that *were* in the high gate of Benjamin, which *was* **by the house of the LORD.**

3. **And** it came to pass **on the morrow, that Pashur brought** forth **Jeremiah out of the stocks. Then said Jeremiah** unto him, **The LORD hath** not **called thy name** Pashur, but **Magor-missabib.**

4. **For** thus saith the LORD, **Behold, I will make thee a terror to thyself, and** to all **thy friends: and they shall fall by the sword** of their enemies, **and thine eyes shall behold it:** and I will give all Judah into the hand of the king of Babylon, and he shall carry them captive into Babylon, and shall slay them with the sword.

5. **Moreover I will deliver all the strength of this city,** and all the labours thereof, and all the precious things thereof, and all the treasures of the kings of Judah will I give **into the hand of their enemies, which shall** spoil them, and take them, and **carry them to Babylon.**

6. **And thou, Pashur,** and all that dwell in thine house **shall go into captivity:** and thou shalt come to Babylon, **and there thou shalt die,** and shalt be buried there, thou, and all thy friends, to whom

thou hast prophesied lies.

7. **O LORD,**
thou hast deceived
me, and I was deceived;
thou art stronger than I,
and hast prevailed:
I am in derision daily,
every one mocketh me.
8. **For** since I spake, I cried out,
I cried violence and spoil;
because the word of the
LORD was made a
reproach unto me,
and a derision, daily.
9. **Then I said, I will not**
make mention of him, nor
speak any more in his
name. But his word was
in mine heart
as a burning fire shut
up in my bones,
and I was weary with forbearing,
and I could not stay.
10. For I heard the defaming of
many, fear on every side. Report,
say they, and we will report it.
All my familiars watched
for my halting, saying,
Peradventure he will be enticed, and
we shall prevail against him, and
we shall take our
revenge on him.
11. **But the LORD is with**
me as a mighty terrible one:
therefore my persecutors
shall stumble, and they shall
not prevail: they shall be greatly
ashamed; for they shall not prosper:
their everlasting confusion shall
never be forgotten.
12. But,
O LORD of hosts, that
triest the righteous, *and*
seest the reins and the heart,
let me see thy vengeance
on them: for unto thee have
I opened my cause.
13. Sing unto the LORD,
praise ye the LORD: for he
hath delivered the soul of
the poor from the hand
of evildoers.
14. **Cursed be the day** wherein

I was born: let not the
day wherein my mother
bare me be blessed.
15. **Cursed be** the man
who brought tidings to
my father, saying, A man child is
born unto thee; making him very glad.
16. And let that man be as the cities
which the LORD overthrew, and
repented not: and let him hear
the cry in the morning, and the
shouting at noontide;
17. **Because he slew me**
not from the womb;
or that my mother might have
been my grave, and her womb
to be always great *with me.*
18. **Wherefore came I**
forth out of the womb
to see labour and sorrow,
that my days should be
consumed with shame?

CHAPTER 21

1. The word which came unto
Jeremiah from the LORD,
when king Zedekiah
sent unto him Pashur
the son of Melchiah,
and Zephaniah
the son of Maaseiah
the priest, saying,
2. **Inquire,** I pray thee,
of the LORD for us; for
Nebuchadrezzar
king of Babylon
maketh war against us;
if so be that the LORD will deal with
us according to all his wondrous
works, that he may go up from us.
3. **Then said Jeremiah** unto
them, Thus shall ye say to Zedekiah:
4. **Thus saith the LORD**
God of Israel; Behold,
I will turn back the weapons
of war that are
in your hands, wherewith ye fight
against the king of Babylon,
and *against* the Chaldeans, which
besiege you without the walls,
and I will assemble them into
the midst of this city.
5. **And I myself will fight**

■ **against you** with an outstretched hand and with a strong arm, even in anger, and in fury, and
■ **in great wrath.**
■ 6. **And I will smite** the inhabitants of this city,
■ **both man and beast:** they shall die of a great pestilence.
■ 7. **And afterward,** saith the LORD,
■ **I will deliver Zedekiah**
■ **king of Judah,** and his servants, and the people,
■ **and such as are left** in this city from the pestilence, from the sword, and from the famine,
■ **into the hand of**
■ **Nebuchadrezzar** king of Babylon, and into the hand of their enemies, and into the hand of those that seek their life:
■ **and he shall smite**
■ **them with** the edge of
■ **the sword;** he shall not spare them, neither have pity, nor have mercy.
8. And unto this people thou shalt say, Thus saith the LORD;
■ **Behold, I set before you the**
■ **way of life, and** the way of
■ **death.**
■ 9. **He that abideth in this**
■ **city shall die** by the sword, and by the famine, and by the pestilence:
■ **but he that** goeth out, and
■ **falleth to the Chaldeans** that besiege you, he
■ **shall live,** and his life shall be unto him for a prey.
■ 10. **For I have set my face**
■ **against this city for evil,** and not for good, saith the LORD:
■ **it shall be given into the**
■ **hand of the king of**
■ **Babylon, and he shall**
■ **burn it with fire.**
11. And touching the house of the king of Judah, *say,*
■ **Hear ye the word**
■ **of the LORD;**
■ 12. **O house of David,** thus saith the LORD;
■ **Execute judgment**

in the morning,
■ **and deliver him that is**
■ **spoiled out of the hand**
■ **of the oppressor,** lest my fury go out like fire, and burn that none can quench *it,* because of the evil of your doings.
■ 13. **Behold, I am against**
■ **thee,** O inhabitant of the valley, *and* rock of the plain, saith the LORD; which say, Who shall come down against us? or who shall enter into our habitations?
14. But
■ **I will punish you according**
■ **to the fruit of your doings,** saith the LORD: and I will kindle a fire in the forest thereof, and it shall devour all things round about it.

CHAPTER 22

1. Thus saith the LORD;
■ **Go down to** the house of
■ **the king of Judah,** and speak there this word,
■ 2. **And say, Hear the word**
■ **of the LORD,** O king of Judah, that sittest upon the throne of David, thou, and thy servants, and thy people that enter in by these gates:
3. Thus saith the LORD;
■ **Execute ye judgment and**
■ **righteousness,** and deliver the spoiled out of the hand of the oppressor: and
■ **do no wrong, do no**
■ **violence** to the stranger, the fatherless, nor the widow,
■ **neither shed innocent**
■ **blood in this place.**
4. For if ye do this thing indeed, then shall there enter in by the gates of this house kings sitting upon the throne of David, riding in chariots and on horses, he, and his servants, and his people.
■ 5. **But if ye will not hear**
■ **these words,** I swear by myself, saith the LORD, that
■ **this house shall become**
■ **a desolation.**
6. For thus saith the LORD unto the king's house of Judah; Thou *art*

Gilead unto me, *and* the head of Lebanon: *yet* surely

I will make thee a wilderness, *and* cities *which* are not inhabited.

7. **And I will prepare destroyers against thee,** every one with his weapons: and they shall cut down thy choice cedars, and cast *them* into the fire.

8. **And** many **nations shall pass** by this city, **and** they shall **say** every man to his neighbour, **Wherefore hath the LORD done thus unto this great city?**

9. **Then they shall answer, Because they have forsaken the covenant of the LORD** their God, and worshipped other gods, and served them.

10. **Weep ye not for the dead,** neither bemoan him: **but weep** sore **for him that goeth away: for he shall return no more, nor see his native country.**

11. **For thus saith the LORD** touching **Shallum the son of Josiah king of Judah,** which reigned instead of Josiah his father, which went forth out of this place; He **shall not return** thither any more:

12. **But he shall die** in the place whither they have led him captive, **and shall see this land no more.**

13. **Woe unto him that buildeth his house by unrighteousness, and** his chambers by wrong; *that* **useth his neighbour's service without wages,** and giveth him not for his work;

14. That saith, I will build me a wide house and large chambers, and cutteth him out windows; and *it is* cieled with cedar, and painted with vermilion.

15. Shalt thou reign, because thou closest *thyself* in cedar? **did not thy father eat and drink, and do judgment and justice, and** then *it was* well with him?

16. He judged the cause of the poor and needy; then **it was well with him:** *was* not this to know me? saith the LORD.

17. **But thine eyes and** thine **heart are not but for thy covetousness, and** for **to shed innocent blood,** and for oppression, and for violence, to do *it.*

18. **Therefore** thus saith the LORD concerning Jehoiakim the son of Josiah king of Judah; **They shall not lament for him,** *saying,* Ah my brother! or, Ah sister! they shall not lament for him, *saying,* Ah lord! or, Ah his glory!

19. **He shall be** buried with the burial of an ass, **drawn and cast forth beyond the gates of Jerusalem.**

20. Go up to Lebanon, and cry; and lift up thy voice in Bashan, and cry from the passages: for all thy lovers are destroyed.

21. **I spake unto thee in thy prosperity; but thou saidst, I will not hear.** This *hath been* thy manner **from thy youth, that thou obeyedst not my voice.**

22. The wind shall eat up all thy pastors, and thy lovers shall go into captivity: surely then shalt thou be ashamed and confounded for all thy wickedness.

23. **O** inhabitant of **Lebanon,** that makest thy nest in the cedars, how gracious shalt thou be when pangs come upon thee, the pain as of a woman in travail!

24. *As* I live, saith the LORD, though Coniah the son of Jehoiakim king of Judah were the signet upon my right hand, yet would I pluck thee thence;

25. And
**I will give thee into the
hand of them that seek
thy life, and** into the hand of *them*
whose face thou fearest,
even into the hand of Nebuchadrezzar
king of Babylon, and into the hand
of the Chaldeans.
26. **And I will cast thee out,**
and thy mother that bare thee,
into another country,
where ye were not born;
and there shall ye die.
27. But to the land whereunto
they desire to return, thither
shall they not return.
28. *Is* this man Coniah a despised
broken idol? *is he* a vessel wherein *is*
no pleasure? wherefore are they cast
out, he and his seed, and are cast
into a land which they know not?
29. **O earth,** earth, earth,
hear the word of the LORD.
30. Thus saith the LORD, Write ye
this man childless, a man *that*
shall not prosper
in his days: for no man of his
seed shall prosper, sitting
upon the throne of David,
and ruling any more in Judah.

CHAPTER 23

1. **Woe be unto the pastors
that destroy and scatter
the sheep of my pasture!**
saith the LORD.
2. Therefore thus saith the
LORD God of Israel against the
pastors that feed my people;
**Ye have scattered
my flock,** and driven them away,
and have not visited them: behold,
**I will visit upon you the evil
of your doings,** saith the LORD.
3. **And I will gather**
the remnant of
my flock out of all countries
whither I have driven them,
and will
bring them again
**to their folds; and
they shall** be fruitful and
increase.

4. **And I will set** up
**shepherds over them which
shall feed them: and they
shall fear no more,** nor be
dismayed, neither shall they be
lacking, saith the LORD.
5. **Behold, the days
come,** saith the LORD,
that I will raise unto David a
righteous Branch, and
**a King shall reign and
prosper, and shall
execute judgment
and justice in the earth.**
6. In his days Judah shall
be saved, and Israel shall
dwell safely: and this *is* his
name whereby
**he shall be called,
THE LORD OUR
RIGHTEOUSNESS.**
7. **Therefore,** behold, the
days come, saith the LORD, that
**they shall no more say,
The LORD liveth, which
brought up** the children of
Israel out of the land of
Egypt;
8. **But, The LORD liveth,
which** brought up and which
led the seed of the house of
Israel out of the north
country, and from all countries
whither I had driven them;
**and they shall dwell
in their own land.**
9. **Mine heart** within me
**is broken because of the
prophets;** all my bones shake;
I am like a drunken man, and
like a man whom wine hath overcome,
**because of the LORD,
and** because of
the words of his holiness.
10. For the land is full of adulterers;
for because of swearing the land
mourneth; the pleasant places
of the wilderness are dried up,
and their course is evil, and
their force *is* not right.
11. **For both prophet and
priest are profane; yea,
in my house have I found**

**their wickedness,
saith the LORD.**
12. Wherefore their way shall be unto them as slippery *ways* in the darkness: they shall be driven on, and fall therein: for
I will bring evil upon them, *even* the year of their visitation, saith the LORD.
13. And I have seen folly in
the prophets of Samaria;
they prophesied in Baal, and
caused my people Israel to err.
14. I have seen also in
the prophets of Jerusalem
an horrible thing: they
commit adultery, and walk in lies:
they strengthen also the hands of evildoers, that none doth return from his wickedness;
they are all of them
unto me as Sodom, and
the inhabitants thereof as
Gomorrah.
15. Therefore thus saith the LORD of hosts concerning the prophets; Behold, I will feed them with wormwood, and make them drink the water of gall: for from the prophets of Jerusalem is profaneness gone forth into all the land.
16. Thus saith the LORD of hosts,
Hearken not unto the words of
the prophets that prophesy unto you: they make you vain:
they speak a vision of their own heart, and not out of the mouth of the LORD.
17. **They say** still unto them that despise me, The LORD hath said,
Ye shall have peace; and
they say unto every one that walketh after the imagination of his own heart,
No evil shall come upon you.
18. For who hath stood in the counsel of the LORD, and hath perceived and heard his word? who hath marked his word, and heard *it?*
19. **Behold, a whirlwind of the LORD is gone forth**

in fury, even a grievous whirlwind:
it shall fall grievously
upon the head of the wicked.
20. The anger of the LORD shall not return, until he have executed, and till he have performed the thoughts of his heart: in the latter days ye shall consider it perfectly.
21. **I have not sent these prophets,** yet they ran:
I have not spoken to them, yet they prophesied.
22. But if they had stood in my counsel, and had caused my people to hear my words, then they should have turned them from their evil way, and from the evil of their doings.
23. *Am* I a God at hand, saith the LORD, and not a God afar off?
24. Can any hide himself in secret places that I shall not see him? saith the LORD. Do not I fill heaven and earth? saith the LORD.
25. I have heard what the prophets said, that prophesy lies
in my name, saying, I have dreamed, I have dreamed.
26. How long shall *this* be in the heart of the prophets that prophesy lies? yea,
they are prophets of the deceit of their own heart;
27. **Which** think to
cause my people to forget my name by their dreams which they tell every man to his neighbour,
as their fathers have forgotten my name for Baal.
28. **The prophet** that hath a dream, let him tell a dream; and he
that hath my word, let him speak my word faithfully.
What *is* the chaff to the wheat? saith the LORD.
29. **Is not my word like as a fire?** saith the LORD;
and like a hammer that
breaketh the rock in pieces?
30. **Therefore,** behold,
I am against the prophets, saith the LORD,

■ **that steal my words**
every one from his neighbour.
31. Behold, I *am* against the
prophets, saith the LORD, that use
their tongues, and say, He saith.
32. Behold, I *am* against them
■ **that prophesy false**
■ **dreams,** saith the LORD,
and do tell them,
■ **and cause my people**
■ **to err** by their lies, and by
their lightness; yet
■ **I sent them not,**
nor commanded them:
■ **therefore they shall not**
■ **profit this people at all,**
saith the LORD.
■ 33. **And when this people,**
or the prophet, or a priest,
■ **shall ask thee,** saying,
■ **What is the burden of**
■ **the LORD?** thou shalt then
■ **say** unto them,
■ **What burden? I will even**
■ **forsake you,** saith the LORD.
■ 34. **And as for**
■ **the prophet,** and the
■ **priest, and the people,**
■ **that shall say, The burden**
■ **of the LORD, I will** even
■ **punish that man** and his house.
35. Thus shall ye say every one to
his neighbour, and every one to his
brother, What hath the LORD
answered? and, What hath the
LORD spoken?
■ 36. **And the burden of**
■ **the LORD shall ye mention**
■ **no more:** for every man's
word shall be his burden;
■ **for ye have perverted the**
■ **words of the living God,**
of the LORD of hosts our God.
37. Thus shalt thou say to the
prophet, What hath the LORD
answered thee? and, What hath the
LORD spoken?
■ 38. **But since ye say, The**
■ **burden of the LORD;**
therefore thus saith the LORD;
Because ye say this word, The
burden of the LORD, and I have sent
unto you, saying, Ye shall not say,

The burden of the LORD;
■ 39. **Therefore,** behold, I, even
■ **I, will** utterly forget you, and I will
forsake you, and the city that I gave
you and your fathers, *and*
■ **cast you out of**
■ **my presence:**
■ 40. **And I will bring an**
■ **everlasting reproach**
■ **upon you,** and a perpetual
shame, which shall not be forgotten.

CHAPTER 24

■ 1. **The LORD shewed**
■ **me,** and, behold,
■ **two baskets of figs** *were*
■ **set before the temple**
of the LORD,
■ **after** that
■ **Nebuchadrezzar**
king of Babylon had
■ **carried away captive**
■ **Jeconiah** the son of
Jehoiakim king of Judah,
■ **and the princes of Judah,**
with the carpenters and smiths, from
Jerusalem, and had brought them
■ **to Babylon.**
■ 2. **One basket had** very
■ **good figs,** *even* like the
figs *that are* first ripe:
■ **and the other basket**
■ **had** very naughty
■ **figs, which could**
■ **not be eaten,** they were so bad.
■ 3. **Then said the**
■ **LORD** unto me,
■ **What seest thou,** Jeremiah?
■ **And I said, Figs;** the
■ **good figs,** very good;
■ **and** the
■ **evil,** very evil, that cannot
be eaten, they are so evil.
■ 4. **Again the word of**
■ **the LORD came unto**
■ **me, saying,**
5. Thus saith the LORD, the
God of Israel;
■ **Like these good figs, so will I**
■ **acknowledge them that** are
carried away captive of Judah, whom
■ **I have**
■ **sent out of this** place into the

■ **land** of the Chaldeans
■ **for their good.**
■ 6. **For** I will set mine eyes
upon them for good, and
■ **I will bring them again to**
■ **this land:** and I will build them, and
not pull *them* down; and I will plant
them, and not pluck *them* up.
■ 7. **And I will give them**
■ **an heart to know me,**
that I *am* the LORD:
■ **and they shall be my**
■ **people, and I will be**
■ **their God:** for they shall return
unto me with their whole heart.
■ 8. **And** as
■ **the evil figs,** which cannot
be eaten, they are so evil; surely
thus saith the LORD, So will I give
Zedekiah the king of Judah,
and his princes, and the residue
of Jerusalem, that remain in this
land, and them that dwell in
the land of Egypt:
9. **And**
■ **I will deliver** them
■ **to be removed into all**
■ **the kingdoms of the**
■ **earth** for *their* hurt,
■ **to be a reproach**
and a proverb, a taunt and a curse,
■ **in all places whither**
■ **I shall drive them.**
10. And I will send the sword,
the famine, and the pestilence,
among them,
■ **till they be consumed**
from off the land that I gave unto
them and to their fathers.

CHAPTER 25

■ 1. **The word that came**
■ **to Jeremiah**
concerning all the people of Judah
■ **in the fourth year of**
■ **Jehoiakim** the son of Josiah king
of Judah, that *was* the first year of
Nebuchadrezzar king of Babylon;
2. The which
■ **Jeremiah** the prophet
■ **spake unto all the**
■ **people of Judah,** and to all
the inhabitants of Jerusalem,

■ **saying,**
3. From the thirteenth year of Josiah
the son of Amon king of Judah, even
unto this day, that *is* the three and
twentieth year, the word of the LORD
hath come unto me, and
■ **I have spoken unto you,**
rising early and speaking; but
ye have not hearkened.
■ 4. **And the LORD hath sent**
■ **unto you** all his servants
■ **the prophets,**
rising early and sending *them;*
but ye have not hearkened, nor
inclined your ear to hear.
■ 5. **They said, Turn** ye again now
■ **every one from his evil way,**
and from the evil of your doings, and
dwell in the land that the LORD hath
given unto you and to
your fathers for ever and ever:
6. And go not after other gods to
serve them, and to worship them,
and provoke me not to anger with
the works of your hands; and I will
do you no hurt.
■ 7. **Yet ye have not**
■ **hearkened unto me, saith**
■ **the LORD;** that ye might provoke
me to anger with the works of your
hands to your own hurt.
■ 8. **Therefore**
thus saith the LORD of
hosts; Because ye have
not heard my words,
9. Behold,
■ **I will send** and take all the families
of the north, saith the LORD, and
■ **Nebuchadrezzar**
the king of Babylon, my
servant, and will bring them
■ **against this land,**
■ **and** against
■ **the inhabitants thereof,** and
against all these nations round about,
■ **and will** utterly
■ **destroy them,** and make them
an astonishment, and an hissing,
and perpetual desolations.
■ 10. **Moreover I will take**
■ **from them the voice**
of mirth, and the voice
■ **of gladness,** the voice of the

bridegroom, and the voice of the bride, the sound of the millstones, and the light of the candle.

11. **And this whole land shall** be a desolation, *and an* astonishment; and these nations shall **serve the king of Babylon seventy years.**

12. **And** it shall come to pass, **when seventy years are accomplished,** *that* **I will punish the king of Babylon, and that nation,** saith the LORD, **for their iniquity,** and the land of the Chaldeans, and will make it perpetual desolations.

13. **And I will bring** upon that land **all my words** which I have pronounced against it, *even* all that is **written in this book, which Jeremiah hath prophesied against all the nations.**

14. For many nations and great kings shall serve themselves of them also: **and I will recompense them according to their deeds,** and according to the works of their own hands.

15. **For thus saith the LORD** God of Israel unto me; **Take the wine cup of this fury at my hand, and cause all the nations, to whom I send thee, to drink it.**

16. **And they shall** drink, and **be moved,** and be mad, because of the sword that I will send among them.

17. **Then took I the cup** at the LORD'S hand, and made all the nations to drink, **unto whom the LORD had sent me:**

18. **To wit, Jerusalem, and** the cities of **Judah,** and the kings thereof, and the princes thereof, to make them a desolation, an astonishment, an hissing, and a curse; as *it is* this day;

19. Pharaoh king of **Egypt,** and his servants, and his princes, and all his people;

20. And all the mingled people, and all the kings of the land of **Uz,** and all the kings of the land of **the Philistines,** and Ashkelon, and Azzah, and Ekron, and the remnant of Ashdod,

21. Edom, and Moab, and the children of Ammon,

22. And all the kings of **Tyrus, and** all the kings of **Zidon,** and the kings of the isles which *are* beyond the sea,

23. Dedan, and Tema, and Buz, and all *that are* in the utmost corners,

24. And all the kings of **Arabia,** and all the kings of the mingled people that dwell in the desert,

25. And all the kings of Zimri, and all the kings of Elam, and all the kings of the Medes,

26. And all **the kings of the north,** far and near, one with another, **and all the kingdoms of the world,** which are upon the face of the earth: and the king of Sheshach **shall drink after them.**

27. **Therefore thou shalt say unto them,** Thus saith the LORD of hosts, the God of Israel; **Drink ye, and be drunken,** and spue, **and fall, and rise no more,** because of the sword which I will send among you.

28. **And** it shall be, **if they refuse to take the cup** at thine hand **to drink, then** shalt thou **say unto them,** Thus saith the LORD of hosts; **Ye shall certainly drink.**

29. **For,** lo, **I** begin to **bring evil on the city which is called by my name,** and should ye be utterly unpunished? Ye shall not be unpunished: for **I will call for a sword upon all the inhabitants of the earth,** saith the LORD of hosts.

30. Therefore prophesy thou against them all these words, **and say unto them, The LORD shall roar** from on high, **and utter his voice** from his holy habitation; he shall mightily roar upon his habitation; he shall give a shout, as they that tread *the grapes,* **against all the inhabitants of the earth.**

31. A noise shall come *even* to the ends of the earth; for the LORD hath a controversy with the nations, **he will plead with all flesh;** he will give them *that are* wicked to the sword, saith the LORD.

32. Thus saith the LORD of hosts, Behold, evil shall go forth from nation to nation, and a great whirlwind shall be raised up from the coasts of the earth.

33. **And the slain** of the LORD **shall be** at that day **from one end of the earth** even **unto the other** end of the earth: **they shall not be lamented,** neither gathered, **nor buried;** they shall be dung upon the ground.

34. Howl, ye shepherds, and cry; and wallow yourselves *in the ashes,* ye principal of the flock: for the days of your slaughter and of your dispersions are accomplished; and ye shall fall like a pleasant vessel.

35. And the shepherds shall have no way to flee, nor the principal of the flock to escape.

36. A voice of **the cry of the shepherds,** and an howling of the principal of the flock, **shall be heard:** for the LORD hath spoiled their pasture.

37. **And the peaceable habitations are cut down** because of the fierce anger of the LORD.

38. He hath forsaken his covert, as the lion: for their land is desolate because of the fierceness of the oppressor, and **because of his fierce anger.**

CHAPTER 26

1. **In the** beginning of the **reign of Jehoiakim** the son of Josiah king of Judah **came this word from the LORD, saying,**

2. Thus saith the LORD; Stand in the court of the LORD's house, and **speak unto all the cities of Judah,** which come to worship in the LORD's house, all the words that I command thee to speak unto them; diminish not a word:

3. **If** so be **they will hearken, and turn** every man **from his evil** way, that **I may repent** me **of the evil, which I purpose to do unto them** because of the evil of their doings.

4. **And** thou shalt say unto them, Thus saith the LORD; **If ye will not hearken to me,** to walk in my law, which I have set before you,

5. To hearken to the words of my servants the prophets, whom I sent unto you, both rising up early, and sending *them,* but ye have not hearkened;

6. **Then will I make this** house like Shiloh, and will make this **city a curse** to all the nations of the earth.

7. **So** the priests and the prophets and **all the people heard Jeremiah speaking these words in the house of the LORD.**

8. **Now** it came to pass, **when Jeremiah had made an end of speaking all that the LORD had commanded him** to speak unto all the people, that the priests and the prophets and all **the people took him, saying, Thou shalt**

surely die.

9. Why hast thou prophesied in the name of the LORD, saying, This house shall be like Shiloh, and this city shall be desolate without an inhabitant? And all the people were gathered against Jeremiah in the house of the LORD.

10. When the princes of Judah heard these things, then they came up from the king's house unto the house of the LORD, and sat down in the entry of the new gate of the LORD's house.

11. Then spake the priests and the prophets unto the princes and to all the people, saying, This man is worthy to die; for he hath prophesied against this city, as ye have heard with your ears.

12. Then spake Jeremiah unto all the princes and to all the people, saying, The LORD sent me to prophesy against this house and against this city all the words that ye have heard.

13. Therefore now amend your ways and your doings, and obey the voice of the LORD your God; and the LORD will repent him of the evil that he hath pronounced against you.

14. As for me, behold, I am in your hand: do with me as seemeth good and meet unto you.

15. But know ye for certain, that if ye put me to death, ye shall surely bring innocent blood upon yourselves, and upon this city, and upon the inhabitants thereof: for of a truth the LORD hath sent me unto you to speak all these words in your ears.

16. Then said the princes and all the people unto the priests and to the prophets; This man is not worthy to die: for he hath spoken to us in the name of the LORD our God.

17. Then rose up certain of the elders of the land, and spake to all the assembly of the people, saying,

18. Micah the Morasthite prophesied in the days of Hezekiah king of Judah, and spake to all the people of Judah, saying, Thus saith the LORD of hosts; Zion shall be plowed like a field, and Jerusalem shall become heaps, and the mountain of the house as the high places of a forest.

19. Did Hezekiah king of Judah and all Judah put him at all to death? did he not fear the LORD, and besought the LORD, and the LORD repented him of the evil which he had pronounced against them? Thus might we procure great evil against our souls.

20. And there was also a man that prophesied in the name of the LORD, Urijah the son of Shemaiah of Kirjath-jearim, who prophesied against this city and against this land according to all the words of Jeremiah.

21. And when Jehoiakim the king, with all his mighty men, and all the princes, heard his words, the king sought to put him

to death: but when **Urijah** heard it, he was afraid, and **fled,** and went **into Egypt;**

22. And Jehoiakim the king sent men into Egypt, *namely,* Elnathan the son of Achbor, and *certain* men with him into Egypt.

23. **And they fetched** forth **Urijah out of Egypt, and** brought him unto Jehoiakim **the king;** who **slew him with the sword,** and cast his dead body into the graves of the common people.

24. **Nevertheless** the hand of **Ahikam** the son of Shaphan **was with Jeremiah, that they should not** give him into the hand of the people to **put him to death.**

CHAPTER 27

1. **In the beginning of the reign of Jehoiakim** the son of Josiah king of Judah **came this word unto Jeremiah from the LORD, saying,**

2. Thus saith the LORD to me; **Make thee bonds and yokes,** and put them upon thy neck,

3. **And send them to the king** of Edom, and to the king **of Moab, and** to the king of **the Ammonites,** and to the king of **Tyrus, and to the king of Zidon, by** the hand of the **messengers** which come to Jerusalem unto Zedekiah king of Judah;

4. **And command them to say unto their masters,** Thus saith the LORD of hosts, the God of Israel; Thus shall ye say unto your masters;

5. **I have made the earth, the man and the beast** that *are* upon the ground, **by my great power** and by my outstretched arm, and have given it

unto whom it seemed meet unto me.

6. **And now have I given all these lands into the hand of Nebuchadnezzar** the king of Babylon, my servant; and the beasts of the field have I given him also to serve him.

7. **And all nations shall serve him,** and his son, and his son's son, until the very time of his land come: and then many nations and great kings shall serve themselves of him.

8. **And** it shall come to pass, *that* **the nation** and kingdom **which will not serve** the same **Nebuchadnezzar** the king of Babylon, and that will not put their neck under the yoke of the king of Babylon, that nation **will I punish,** saith the LORD, with the sword, and with the famine, and with the pestilence, until I have consumed them by his hand.

9. **Therefore hearken not** ye **to your prophets,** nor to your diviners, nor to your dreamers, nor to your enchanters, nor to your sorcerers, which speak unto you, saying, Ye shall not serve the king of Babylon:

10. **For they prophesy a lie unto you,** to remove you far from your land; and that I should drive you out, and ye should perish.

11. **But the nations that bring their neck under the yoke of the king of Babylon, and serve him,** those **will** I let **remain** still **in their own land,** saith the LORD; and they shall till it, and dwell therein.

12. **I spake also to Zedekiah** king of Judah according to all these words, **saying, Bring your necks under the yoke of the king of Babylon, and serve him and his people, and live.**

13. Why will ye die, thou and thy

people, by the sword, by the famine, and by the pestilence, as the LORD hath spoken against the nation that will not serve the king of Babylon?

14. **Therefore hearken not unto** the words of **the prophets that speak** unto you, **saying, Ye shall not serve the king of Babylon: for they prophesy a lie** unto you.

15. **For I have not sent them,** saith the LORD, yet they prophesy a lie in my name; that I might drive you out, and that ye might perish, ye, and the prophets that prophesy unto you.

16. **Also I spake to the priests** and to all this people, **saying,** Thus saith the LORD; **Hearken not to** the words of **your prophets** that prophesy unto you, saying, Behold, the vessels of the LORD'S house shall now shortly be brought again from Babylon: for they prophesy a lie unto you.

17. **Hearken not unto them; serve the king of Babylon, and live:** wherefore should this city be laid waste?

18. **But if they be prophets, and if the word of the LORD be with them, let them** now **make intercession** to the LORD of hosts, **that the vessels which are left in** the house of the LORD, and *in* the house of the king of **Judah, and at Jerusalem, go not to Babylon.**

19. **For** thus saith the LORD of hosts concerning the pillars, and concerning the sea, and concerning the bases, and concerning the residue of the vessels that remain in this city.

20. Which Nebuchadnezzar king of Babylon took not, when he carried away captive Jeconiah the son of Jehoiakim king of Judah from Jerusalem to Babylon, and all the nobles of Judah and Jerusalem;

21. Yea, thus saith the LORD of hosts, the God of Israel, concerning **the vessels that remain in the house of the LORD, and in** the house of the king of **Judah and of Jerusalem;**

22. They **shall be carried to Babylon, and there shall they be until the day that I** visit them, saith the LORD; then will I bring them up, and **restore them to this place.**

CHAPTER 28

1. **And it came to pass the same year,** in the beginning of the reign of Zedekiah king of Judah, in the fourth year, *and* **in the fifth month, that Hananiah** the son of Azur the prophet, which *was* **of Gibeon, spake unto me in the house of the LORD, in the presence of the priests** and of all the people, **saying,**

2. **Thus speaketh the LORD of hosts,** the God of Israel, **saying, I have broken the yoke of the king of Babylon.**

3. **Within two full years will I bring again into this place all the vessels of the LORD's house, that Nebuchadnezzar** king of Babylon **took away from this place,** and carried them to Babylon:

4. **And I will bring** again to this place **Jeconiah** the son of Jehoiakim king of Judah, **with all the captives of Judah,** that went into Babylon, saith the LORD: **for I will break the yoke of the king of Babylon.**

5. **Then** the prophet **Jeremiah said unto** the prophet **Hananiah** in the presence of the priests, and in the presence of

1076

all the people that stood in the house of the LORD,

6. Even the prophet Jeremiah said, **Amen: the LORD do so: the LORD perform thy words which thou hast prophesied, to bring** again the vessels of the LORD'S house, and **all that is carried away captive, from Babylon into this place.**

7. **Nevertheless hear** thou **now this word that I speak** in thine ears, and in the ears of all the people;

8. **The prophets** that have been before me and before thee **of old prophesied both against many countries, and against great kingdoms,** of war, and of evil, and of pestilence.

9. The prophet which prophesieth of peace, **when the word of the prophet shall come to pass, then shall the prophet be known, that the LORD hath truly sent him.**

10. **Then Hananiah** the prophet **took the yoke from** off the prophet **Jeremiah's neck, and brake it.**

11. And Hananiah spake in the presence of all the people, **saying, Thus saith the LORD; Even so will I break the yoke of Nebuchadnezzar** king of Babylon **from the neck of all nations within the space of two full years.** And the prophet Jeremiah went his way.

12. **Then the word of the LORD came unto Jeremiah** *the prophet,* **after** that **Hananiah** the prophet **had broken the yoke from** off **the neck of** the prophet

Jeremiah, saying,

13. **Go and tell Hananiah, saying,** Thus saith the LORD; **Thou hast broken the yokes of wood; but thou shalt make for them yokes of iron.**

14. **For** thus saith the LORD of hosts, the God of Israel; **I have put a yoke of iron upon the neck of all these nations, that they may serve Nebuchadnezzar** king of Babylon; **and they shall serve him:** and I have given him the beasts of the field also.

15. **Then said** the prophet **Jeremiah unto Hananiah** the prophet, **Hear now,** Hananiah; **The LORD hath not sent thee; but thou makest this people to trust in a lie.**

16. **Therefore thus saith the LORD;** Behold, I will cast thee from off the face of the earth: **this year thou shalt die, because thou hast taught rebellion against the LORD.**

17. **So Hananiah the prophet died the same year** in the seventh month.

CHAPTER 29

1. **Now these are the words of the letter that Jeremiah** the prophet **sent from Jerusalem** unto the residue of the elders which were carried away captives, and to the priests, and to the prophets, and **to all the people whom Nebuchadnezzar had carried away captive from Jerusalem to Babylon;**

2. (After that Jeconiah the king, and the queen, and the eunuchs, the princes of Judah and Jerusalem, and the carpenters, and the smiths, were departed from Jerusalem;)

3. By the hand of Elasah the son of Shaphan, and Gemariah the son of

Hilkiah, (whom Zedekiah king of Judah sent unto Babylon to Nebuchadnezzar king of Babylon) saying,

4. Thus saith the LORD of hosts, the God of Israel, unto all that are carried away captives, whom I have caused to be carried away from Jerusalem unto Babylon;

5. **Build** ye **houses, and dwell in them;** and **plant gardens, and eat** the fruit **of them;**

6. **Take ye wives, and beget sons and daughters;** and take wives for your sons, and give your daughters to husbands, that they may bear sons and daughters; **that ye may be increased** there, and not diminished.

7. **And seek the peace of the city whither I have caused you to be carried away** captives, and pray unto the LORD for it: **for in the peace thereof shall ye have peace.**

8. **For thus saith the LORD of hosts,** the God of Israel; **Let not your prophets** and your diviners, that *be* in the midst of you, **deceive you,** neither hearken to your dreams which ye cause to be dreamed.

9. **For they prophesy falsely unto you in my name:I have not sent them,** saith the LORD.

10. For thus saith the LORD, That **after seventy years be accomplished at Babylon I will visit you, and perform my good word toward you, in causing you to return to this place.**

11. **For** I know **the thoughts** that **I think toward you,** saith the LORD, **thoughts of peace,** and **not** of **evil, to** give you an expected end.

12. **Then** shall ye call upon me, and **ye shall go and pray unto me, and I will hearken unto you.**

13. **And ye shall** seek me, and **find me, when ye** shall **search for me with all your heart.**

14. And I will be found of you, saith the LORD: **and I will turn away your captivity, and** I will **gather** you from **all the nations,** and from all the places whither I have driven you, saith the LORD; **and I will bring you** again **into the place whence I caused you to be carried away captive.**

15. **Because ye have said, The LORD hath raised us up prophets in Babylon;**

16. *Know* that thus saith the LORD of the king that sitteth upon the throne of David, and of all the people that dwelleth in this city, *and* of your brethren that are not gone forth with you into captivity;

17. Thus saith the LORD of hosts; Behold, **I will send upon them the sword, the famine, and the pestilence, and will make them like vile figs, that cannot be eaten, they are so evil.**

18. **And I will persecute them** with the sword, with the famine, and with the pestilence, **and** will **deliver them** to be removed **to all the kingdoms of the earth, to be** a curse, and an astonishment, and an hissing, and **a reproach,** among all the nations whither I have driven them:

19. **Because they have not hearkened to my words,** saith the LORD, which I sent unto them by my servants the prophets,

rising up early and sending *them;* but ye would not hear, saith the LORD.

20. Hear ye therefore the word of the LORD, all ye of the captivity, whom I have sent from Jerusalem to Babylon:

21. **Thus saith the LORD** of hosts, the God of Israel, **of Ahab** the son of Kolaiah, **and of Zedekiah** the son of Maaseiah, which prophesy a lie unto you in my name; Behold, **I will deliver them into the hand of Nebuchadrezzar king of Babylon; and he shall slay them** before your eyes;

22. And of them shall be taken up a curse by all the captivity of Judah which *are* in Babylon, saying, The LORD make thee like Zedekiah and like Ahab, whom the king of Babylon roasted in the fire;

23. **Because they have committed villany in Israel, and have committed adultery** with their neighbours' wives, **and have spoken lying words** in my name, which I have not commanded them; even **I** know, and **am a witness, saith the LORD.**

24. *Thus* shalt thou **also speak to Shemaiah** the Nehelamite, **saying,**

25. Thus speaketh the LORD of hosts, the God of Israel, saying, **Because thou hast sent letters in thy name unto all the people** that *are* **at Jerusalem, and to Zephaniah** the son of Maaseiah the priest, **and** to all **the priests, saying,**

26. **The LORD hath made thee priest in the stead of Jehoiada** the priest, **that ye should be officers in the house of the LORD, for every man that** *is* mad, and **maketh himself a prophet,** that thou shouldest **put** him **in prison,** and in the stocks.

27. Now therefore **why hast thou not reproved Jeremiah** of Anathoth, which maketh himself a prophet to you?

28. **For** therefore **he sent unto us in Babylon, saying, This captivity is long: build** ye **houses, and dwell in them;** and plant gardens, and eat the fruit of them.

29. **And Zephaniah the priest read this letter in the ears of Jeremiah the prophet.**

30. **Then came the word of the LORD unto Jeremiah, saying,**

31. Send to all them of the captivity, saying, Thus saith the LORD concerning Shemaiah the Nehelamite; **Because that Shemaiah hath prophesied unto you, and I sent him not, and he caused you to trust in a lie:**

32. Therefore thus saith the LORD; Behold, **I will punish Shemaiah** the Nehelamite, **and his seed:** he **shall not have a man** to dwell among this people; neither shall he behold the good that I will do for my people, saith the LORD; **because he hath taught rebellion against the LORD.**

CHAPTER 30

1. **The word that came to Jeremiah** from the LORD, **saying,**

2. Thus speaketh the LORD God of Israel, saying, **Write** thee all **the words that I have spoken unto thee in a book.**

3. **For,** lo,
the days come, saith the LORD,
that I will bring again
the captivity of my people
Israel and Judah, saith the
LORD: and I will cause them to return
to the land that I gave
to their fathers,
and they shall possess it.
4. And these *are* the words that
the LORD spake concerning
Israel and concerning Judah.
5. **For thus saith the LORD;**
We have heard a voice
of trembling, of fear,
and not of peace.
6. Ask ye now, and see whether a
man doth travail with child?
wherefore do I see every
man with his hands on his loins,
as a woman in
travail, and all
faces are
turned into paleness?
7. Alas! for
that day is great, so that
none *is* like it: it *is* even
the time of Jacob's
trouble, but he shall
be saved out of it.
8. **For it shall come to**
pass in that day,
saith the LORD of hosts,
that I will break his yoke
from off thy neck, and will burst
thy bonds, and strangers shall no
more serve themselves of him:
9. **But they shall serve**
the LORD their God, and
David their king, whom
I will raise up unto them.
10. Therefore
fear thou
not, O my servant
Jacob, saith the LORD;
neither be dismayed,
O Israel:
for, lo,
I will save thee from
afar, and thy seed from the
land of their captivity; and
Jacob shall return,
and shall be in rest, and be quiet,
and none shall
make him afraid.
11. **For I am with**
thee, saith the LORD,
to save thee: though I make
a full end of all nations whither
I have scattered thee,
yet I will not make a full
end of thee: but I will
correct thee in measure, and will
not leave thee altogether
unpunished.
12. For thus saith the LORD,
Thy bruise is incurable, and
thy wound is grievous.
13. *There is* none to plead thy cause,
that thou mayest be bound up:
thou hast no healing
medicines.
14. **All thy lovers**
have forgotten thee; they
seek thee not; for I have
wounded thee with the wound
of an enemy, with the chastisement
of a cruel one, for the multitude of
thine iniquity; *because* thy sins
were increased.
15. **Why criest thou**
for thine affliction? thy
sorrow *is* incurable for the
multitude of thine iniquity:
because thy sins were
increased, I have done
these things unto thee.
16. Therefore all
they that devour thee shall
be devoured; and all thine
adversaries, every one of them, shall
go into captivity; and they that spoil
thee shall be a spoil, and all that prey
upon thee will I give for a prey.
17. **For I will restore health**
unto thee, and I will
heal thee of thy wounds, saith
the LORD; because they called
thee an Outcast, *saying,* This *is*
Zion, whom no man seeketh after.
18. Thus saith the LORD; Behold,
I will bring again the
captivity of Jacob's tents,
and have mercy on his
dwellingplaces;
and the city shall be

■ **builded** upon her own heap,
■ **and the palace shall**
■ **remain** after the manner thereof.
■ 19. **And out of them shall**
■ **proceed thanksgiving** and
the voice of them that make merry:
■ **and I will multiply them,** and
they shall not be few; I will also glorify
them, and they shall not be small.
20. Their children also shall be
as aforetime, and
■ **their congregation shall**
■ **be established before me,**
■ **and I will punish all that**
■ **oppress them.**
21. And their nobles shall be of
themselves, and their governor shall
proceed from the midst of them; and I
will cause him to draw near, and he
shall approach unto me: for who *is*
this that engaged his heart to
approach unto me? saith the LORD.
■ 22. **And ye shall be my**
■ **people, and I will be**
■ **your God.**
■ 23. **Behold, the whirlwind**
■ **of the LORD** goeth forth with
fury, a continuing whirlwind: it
■ **shall fall with pain**
■ **upon the** head of the
■ **wicked.**
■ 24. **The fierce anger of the**
■ **LORD shall not return,**
until he hath done *it,* and
■ **until he have performed**
■ **the intents of his heart:**
in the latter days ye shall consider it.

CHAPTER 31

■ 1. **At the same time,**
saith the LORD,
■ **will I be the God**
of all the families
■ **of Israel, and they shall**
■ **be my people.**
2. Thus saith the LORD, The people
which were left of the sword found
grace in the wilderness; *even* Israel,
when I went to cause him to rest.
3. The LORD hath appeared of
old unto me, *saying,* Yea, I have
loved thee with an everlasting
love: therefore with lovingkindness

have I drawn thee.
■ 4. **Again I will build thee,**
and thou shalt be built,
■ **O virgin of Israel:** thou shalt
again be adorned with thy tabrets,
and shalt go forth in the dances
of them that make merry.
■ 5. **Thou shalt** yet
■ **plant vines upon the**
■ **mountains** of Samaria:
the planters shall plant,
■ **and shall eat them**
as common things.
■ 6. **For there shall be a**
■ **day, that the watchmen**
upon the mount Ephraim
■ **shall cry, Arise ye, and**
■ **let us go up to Zion unto**
■ **the LORD our God.**
7. For thus saith the LORD;
■ **Sing** with gladness for Jacob,
■ **and shout** among the chief
of the nations: publish ye,
■ **praise ye, and say, O**
■ **LORD, save thy people,**
the remnant of Israel.
8. Behold,
■ **I will bring them from the**
■ **north country, and** gather them
■ **from the coasts** of the earth, *and*
with them the blind and the lame, the
woman with child and her that
travaileth with child together:
■ **a great company**
■ **shall return thither.**
■ 9. **They shall come**
■ **with weeping, and** with
■ **supplications** will I lead them:
I will cause them to walk by the
rivers of waters in a straight way,
wherein they shall not stumble:
■ **for I am a father to**
■ **Israel, and Ephraim**
■ **is my firstborn.**
■ 10. **Hear** the word of
■ **the LORD,** O ye nations,
■ **and declare it** in the isles
■ **afar off,** and
■ **say, He that scattered**
■ **Israel will gather**
■ **him,** and keep him,
■ **as a shepherd**
■ **doth his flock.**

■ 11. **For the LORD hath**
■ **redeemed Jacob,** and
ransomed him from the hand of
him that was stronger than he.
12. **Therefore they**
■ **shall** come and
■ **sing** in the height of Zion, and shall
flow together to the goodness of the
LORD, for wheat, and for wine, and
for oil, and for the young of the flock
and of the herd: and their soul shall
be as a watered garden; and they
shall not sorrow any more at all.
13. Then shall the virgin rejoice
in the dance, both young men
and old together:
■ **for I will turn their mourning**
■ **into joy, and will comfort**
■ **them, and make them**
■ **rejoice** from their sorrow.
14. And I will satiate the soul
of the priests with fatness,
■ **and my people shall**
■ **be satisfied with my**
■ **goodness,** saith the LORD.
■ 15. **Thus saith the LORD;**
■ **A voice was heard**
■ **in Ramah,** lamentation,
and bitter weeping;
■ **Rahel weeping for**
■ **her children** refused to be
comforted for her children,
because they *were* not.
16. Thus saith the LORD;
■ **Refrain thy voice**
■ **from weeping,**
and thine eyes from tears: for
■ **thy work shall be**
■ **rewarded,** saith the LORD;
and they shall come again from
the land of the enemy.
17. **And** there is hope in thine
end, saith the LORD, that
■ **thy children shall come**
■ **again to their own border.**
18. **I** have surely
■ **heard Ephraim**
■ **bemoaning** himself
■ **thus; Thou hast chastised**
■ **me,** and I was chastised,
■ **as a bullock**
■ **unaccustomed to**
■ **the yoke: turn** thou

■ **me, and I shall be turned;**
■ **for thou art** the LORD
■ **my God.**
■ 19. **Surely** after that I was turned,
■ **I repented; and** after that I
■ **was instructed,**
I smote upon *my* thigh:
■ **I was ashamed,**
yea, even confounded,
■ **because I did bear the**
■ **reproach of my youth.**
20. **Is Ephraim my** dear
■ **son?** *is he* a pleasant child?
for since I spake against him,
■ **I** do earnestly
■ **remember him still:** therefore
my bowels are troubled for him;
■ **I will** surely
■ **have mercy upon**
■ **him,** saith the LORD.
21. Set thee up waymarks,
make thee high heaps:
■ **set thine heart toward**
the highway, *even*
■ **the way which**
■ **thou wentest:**
turn again, O virgin of Israel,
■ **turn again to** these
■ **thy cities.**
22. How long wilt thou go about, O
thou backsliding daughter? for the
LORD hath created a new thing in the
earth, A woman shall compass a man.
23. Thus saith the LORD of hosts,
the God of Israel; As yet
■ **they shall use this speech**
■ **in the land of Judah**
and in the cities thereof,
■ **when I** shall
■ **bring again their captivity;**
The LORD bless thee, O habitation of
justice, *and* mountain of holiness.
24. **And there shall dwell**
■ **in** Judah itself, and in all
■ **the cities** thereof together,
■ **husbandmen, and they**
■ **that go forth with flocks.**
25. **For I have satiated the**
■ **weary soul, and** I have
■ **replenished every**
■ **sorrowful soul.**
26. Upon this I awaked, and beheld;
and my sleep was sweet unto me.

27. Behold, the days come, saith the LORD, that I will sow the house of Israel and the house of Judah with the seed of man, and with the seed of beast.

28. **And it shall come to pass, that** like as I have watched over them, to pluck up, and to break down, and to throw down, and to destroy, and to afflict; so **will** I **watch over them,** to build, and to plant, saith the LORD.

29. In those days they shall say no more, The fathers have eaten a sour grape, and the children's teeth are set on edge.

30. **But every one shall die for his own iniquity:** every man that eateth the sour grape, his teeth shall be set on edge.

31. **Behold, the days come,** saith the LORD, **that I will make a new covenant with the house of Israel,** and with the house of Judah

32. **Not** according to **the covenant that I made with their fathers** in the day *that* I took them by the hand to bring them out of the land of Egypt; **which** my covenant **they brake,** although I was an husband unto them, saith the LORD:

33. But this *shall be* the covenant that I will make with the house of Israel; After those days, saith the LORD, **I will put my law in their inward parts, and write it in their hearts; and** will be their God, and they shall be my people.

34. And they shall teach no more every man his neighbour, and every man his brother, saying, Know the LORD: for **they shall all know me,** from the least of them unto the greatest of them, saith the LORD: **for I will forgive their iniquity, and I will remember their sin no more.**

35. Thus saith the LORD, which giveth the sun for a light by day, *and* the ordinances of the moon and of the stars for a light by night, which divideth the sea when the waves thereof roar; The LORD of hosts *is* his name:

36. **If those ordinances depart from before me,** saith the LORD, **then the seed of Israel also shall cease from being a nation before me for ever.**

37. Thus saith the LORD; **If heaven** above **can be measured, and the foundations of the earth searched out beneath, I will** also **cast off all the seed of Israel for all that they have done,** saith the LORD.

38. **Behold, the days come,** saith the LORD, **that the city shall be built** to the LORD from the tower of Hananeel unto the gate of the corner.

39. **And the measuring line shall** yet **go forth** over against it **upon the hill Gareb, and** shall **compass about** to **Goath.**

40. **And the** whole **valley** of the dead bodies, and of the ashes, **and** all the **fields** unto the brook **of Kidron,** unto the corner of the horse gate toward the east, **shall be holy unto the LORD; it shall not be** plucked up, nor **thrown down any more for ever.**

CHAPTER 32

1. **The word that came to Jeremiah** from the LORD **in the tenth year of Zedekiah king of Judah,** which *was* the eighteenth year of

Nebuchadrezzar.

2. For then the king of Babylon's army besieged Jerusalem:

■ **and Jeremiah** the prophet
■ **was** shut up
■ **in** the court of the
■ **prison,** which *was* in the king of Judah's house.

■ 3. **For Zedekiah** king of Judah
■ **had shut him up, saying,**
■ **Wherefore dost thou**
■ **prophesy, and say, Thus**
■ **saith the LORD,** Behold,
■ **I will give this city into the**
■ **hand of the king of**
■ **Babylon,** and he shall take it;
■ 4. **And Zedekiah** king of Judah
■ **shall not escape** out of the hand of the Chaldeans,
■ **but shall** surely
■ **be delivered into the hand**
■ **of the king** of Babylon, and shall speak with him mouth to mouth, and his eyes shall behold his eyes;
■ 5. **And he shall lead**
■ **Zedekiah to Babylon,** and there shall he be until I visit him, saith the LORD: though ye fight with the Chaldeans, ye shall not prosper.
■ 6. **And Jeremiah said, The**
■ **word of the LORD came**
■ **unto me, saying,**
■ 7. **Behold, Hanameel** the son of Shallum thine uncle
■ **shall come unto thee**
■ **saying, Buy** thee
■ **my field** that *is*
■ **in Anathoth:** for the right of redemption *is* thine to buy *it.*
■ 8. **So Hanameel** mine uncle's son
■ **came to me in** the court of the
■ **prison** according to the word of the LORD, and said unto me, Buy my field, I pray thee, that *is* in Anathoth, which *is* in the country of Benjamin: for the right of inheritance *is* thine, and the redemption *is* thine; buy *it* for thyself.
■ **Then I knew that this was**
■ **the word of the LORD.**
■ 9. **And I bought the field** of Hanameel my uncle's son, that *was*

in Anathoth,

■ **and weighed him** the money, *even*
■ **seventeen shekels**
■ **of silver.**
■ 10. **And I subscribed the**
■ **evidence, and sealed it,**
■ **and took witnesses, and**
■ **weighed him the money** in the balances.
■ 11. **So I took the evidence**
■ **of the purchase, both that**
■ **which was sealed**
■ **according to the law** and custom,
■ **and that which was open:**
■ 12. **And** I
■ **gave the evidence** of the purchase
■ **unto Baruch** the son of Neriah, the son of Maaseiah,
■ **in the sight of Hanameel** mine uncle's *son,*
■ **and** in the presence of
■ **the witnesses** that subscribed the book of the purchase, before all the Jews that sat in the court of the prison.
■ 13. **And I charged Baruch**
■ **before them, saying,**
14. Thus saith the LORD of hosts, the God of Israel;
■ **Take** these evidences,
■ **this evidence of** the
■ **purchase,** both which is sealed, and this evidence which is open;
■ **and put them in**
■ **an earthen vessel,** that they may continue many days.
15. For thus saith the LORD of hosts, the God of Israel; Houses and fields and vineyards shall be possessed again in this land.
■ 16. **Now when I had**
■ **delivered the evidence**
■ **of the purchase unto**
■ **Baruch** the son of Neriah,
■ **I prayed unto the**
■ **LORD, saying,**
17. **Ah Lord GOD!** behold,
■ **thou hast made** the
■ **heaven and** the
■ **earth** by thy great power and

stretched out arm,
**and there is nothing
too hard for thee:**
18. **Thou shewest
lovingkindness**
unto thousands,
and recompensest the
iniquity of the fathers into the
bosom of their children after them: the
Great, the Mighty God, the LORD of
hosts, is his name,
19. **Great in counsel,
and mighty in work:** for
thine eyes are open
upon all
the ways of the sons
of men: to give every one
according to his ways, and according
to the fruit of his doings:
20. Which hast set signs and
wonders in the land of Egypt, *even*
unto this day, and in Israel, and
among *other* men; and hast made
thee a name, as at this day;
21. **And hast brought** forth
thy people Israel
out of the land of
Egypt with signs, and with wonders,
and with a strong hand, and with
a stretched out arm, and with
great terror;
22. **And hast given them this
land,** which thou didst swear to their
fathers to give them, a land flowing
with milk and honey;
23. **And they came in,
and possessed it; but** they
obeyed not thy voice,
neither walked in thy law;
they have done nothing of
all **that thou commandedst
them to do: therefore thou
hast caused all this evil to
come upon them:**
24. Behold the mounts, they are
come unto the city to take it; and the
city is given into the hand of the
Chaldeans, that fight against it,
because of the sword, and of the
famine, and of the pestilence:
**and what thou hast spoken
is come to pass;**
and, behold, thou seest *it.*

25. **And thou hast said
unto me,** O Lord GOD,
**Buy thee the field
for money, and take
witnesses;** for the city is given
into the hand of the Chaldeans.
26. **Then came the
word of the LORD unto
Jeremiah, saying,**
27. **Behold, I am the
LORD,** the God of all flesh:
**is there any thing too
hard for me?**
28. **Therefore**
thus saith the LORD; Behold,
I will give this city into the
hand of the Chaldeans, and
**into the hand of
Nebuchadrezzar**
king of Babylon,
and he shall take it:
29. **And the Chaldeans,**
that fight against this city,
**shall come and set fire
on this city,** and burn it with the
houses, upon whose roofs they have
offered incense unto Baal, and
poured out drink offerings unto other
gods, to provoke me to anger.
30. **For the children of Israel**
and the children of Judah have only
done evil before me from their youth:
for the children of Israel
have only
provoked me to anger
with the work of their hands,
saith the LORD.
31. **For this city hath
been to me** *as*
a provocation of mine
anger and of my fury
from the day that
they built it even unto
this day; that I should remove
it from before my face,
32. **Because of all the
evil** of the children of Israel and
of the children of Judah,
**which they have done to
provoke me to anger,**
they, their kings, their princes,
their priests, and their prophets,
and the men of Judah, and the

inhabitants of Jerusalem.

33. And they have turned unto me the back, and not the face: though I taught them, rising up early and teaching *them,* **yet they have not hearkened to receive instruction.**

34. **But** they **set their abominations in the house,** which is **called by my name,** to defile it.

35. **And** they **built** the **high places of Baal,** which *are* in the valley of the son of Hinnom, to cause their sons and their daughters to pass through *the fire* unto Molech; which I commanded them not, neither came it into my mind, that they should do this abomination, to cause Judah to sin.

36. **And now** therefore thus saith the LORD, the God of Israel, concerning this city, whereof ye say, **It shall be delivered into the hand of the king of Babylon** by the sword, and by the famine, and by the pestilence;

37. **Behold, I will gather them out of all countries, whither I have driven them** in mine anger, and in my fury, and in great wrath; **and I will bring them again unto this place,** and I will cause them to dwell safely:

38. **And they shall be my people, and I will be their God:**

39. **And I will give them one heart,** and one way, **that they may fear me for ever,** for the good of them, and of their children after them:

40. **And I will make an everlasting covenant with them,** that I will not turn away from them, to do them good; but I will put my fear in their hearts, that they shall not depart from me.

41. **Yea, I will rejoice over them** to do them good, and I will plant them in this land assuredly with my whole heart and with my whole soul.

42. **For** thus saith the LORD; Like as I have brought all this great evil upon this people, so will **I bring upon them all the good that I have promised them.**

43. And fields shall be bought in this land, whereof ye say, *It is* desolate without man or beast; it is given into the hand of the Chaldeans.

44. **Men shall buy fields** for money, and subscribe evidences, and seal *them,* and take witnesses **in the land of Benjamin, and** in the places about **Jerusalem, and** in the cities of **Judah,** and in the cities of the mountains, and in the cities of the valley, and in the cities of the south: **for I will cause their captivity to return, saith the LORD.**

CHAPTER 33

1. **Moreover the word of the LORD came unto Jeremiah the second time, while he was** yet shut up **in** the court of the **prison, saying,**

2. Thus saith the LORD the maker thereof, the LORD that formed it, to establish it; the LORD *is* his name;

3. **Call unto me, and I will** answer thee, and **shew thee great and mighty things, which thou knowest not.**

4. **For** thus saith the LORD, the God of Israel, **concerning** the houses of **this city, and** concerning **the houses** of the kings **of Judah, which are thrown down** by the mounts, and by the sword;

5. They come to fight with the Chaldeans, but *it is* to fill them with the dead bodies of men, whom I have

slain in mine anger and in my fury, and for all whose wickedness I have hid my face from this city.

6. **Behold,** I will bring it health and cure, and **I will cure them,** and will reveal unto them the abundance of peace and truth.

7. And I will cause the captivity of Judah and the captivity of Israel to return, **and will build them, as at the first.**

8. **And I will cleanse them** from all their iniquity, whereby they have sinned against me; **and I will pardon all their iniquities,** whereby they have sinned, and whereby they have transgressed against me.

9. **And it shall be to me a name of joy, a praise and an honour before all the nations of the earth,** which shall hear all the good that I do unto them: and they shall fear and tremble for all the goodness and for all the prosperity that I procure unto it.

10. Thus saith the LORD; **Again there shall be heard** in this place, which ye say *shall be* desolate without man and without beast, *even* in the cities of Judah, and in the streets of Jerusalem, that are desolate, without man, and without inhabitant, and without beast,

11. **The voice of** joy, and the voice of gladness, the voice of the bridegroom, and the voice of the bride, the voice of **them that shall say, Praise the LORD of hosts: for the LORD is good; for his mercy endureth for ever:**and of them that shall bring the sacrifice of praise into the house of the LORD. For I will cause to return the captivity of the land, as at the first, saith the LORD.

12. Thus saith the LORD of hosts; Again in this place, which is desolate without man and without beast,

and in all **the cities** thereof, **shall be** an habitation of **shepherds causing their flocks to lie down.**

13. In the cities of the mountains, in the cities of the vale, and in the cities of the south, and in the land of Benjamin, and in the places about Jerusalem, and in the cities of Judah, shall the flocks pass again under the hands of him that telleth *them,* saith the LORD.

14. **Behold, the days come,** saith the LORD, **that I will perform that good thing which I have promised unto** the house of **Israel and** to the house of **Judah.**

15. **In those days,** and at that time, **will I cause the Branch of righteousness to grow** up unto David; **and he shall execute judgment and righteousness in the land.**

16. In those days shall **Judah** be saved, **and Jerusalem shall dwell safely: and** this *is the name* wherewith **she shall be called, The LORD our righteousness.**

17. For thus saith the LORD; **David shall never want a man to sit upon the throne** of the house of Israel;

18. **Neither shall the priests** the Levites **want a man** before me to offer burnt offerings, and to kindle meat offerings, and **to do sacrifice continually.**

19. **And** the word of the LORD came unto Jeremiah, saying,

20. Thus saith the LORD; **If ye** can **break my covenant** of the day, and my covenant of the night, and that there should not be day and night in their season;

■ 21. **Then may also my**
■ **covenant be broken**
■ **with David** my servant,
that he should not have a
son to reign upon his throne;
■ **and** with the Levites
■ **the priests,** my ministers.
■ 22. **As the host of heaven**
■ **cannot be numbered,** neither
the sand of the sea measured:
■ **so will I multiply the**
■ **seed of David** my servant,
■ **and the Levites**
that minister unto me.
23. Moreover the word of the LORD
came to Jeremiah, saying,
■ 24. **Considerest thou not**
■ **what this people have**
■ **spoken, saying, The two**
■ **families which the LORD**
■ **hath chosen, he hath even**
■ **cast them off?** thus they have
despised my people, that they should
be no more a nation before them.
25. Thus saith the LORD;
If my covenant be not with
day and night, and
■ **if I have not appointed**
■ **the ordinances of heaven**
■ **and earth;**
■ 26. **Then will I cast away the**
■ **seed of Jacob,** and David my
servant, so that I will not take any of
his seed to be rulers over the seed of
Abraham, Isaac, and Jacob: for I will
cause their captivity to return, and
have mercy on them.

CHAPTER 34

■ 1. **The word which came**
■ **unto Jeremiah** from the LORD,
■ **when Nebuchadnezzar** king
of Babylon, and all his army, and all
the kingdoms of the earth of his
dominion, and all the people,
■ **fought against Jerusalem,**
and against all the cities thereof,
■ **saying,**
2. Thus saith the LORD,
the God of Israel; Go and
■ **speak to Zedekiah**
king of Judah,
■ **and tell him,**

Thus saith the LORD; Behold,
■ **I will give this city into**
■ **the hand of the king of**
■ **Babylon, and he shall**
■ **burn it** with fire:
■ 3. **And thou shalt not**
■ **escape** out of his hand,
■ **but shalt surely be** taken, and
■ **delivered into his hand;**
and thine eyes shall behold the eyes
of the king of Babylon, and he shall
speak with thee mouth to mouth,
and thou shalt go to Babylon.
4. Yet hear the word of the LORD,
O Zedekiah king of Judah; Thus
saith the LORD of thee,
■ **Thou shalt not die**
■ **by the sword:**
■ 5. **But thou shalt die in**
■ **peace:** and with the burnings of
thy fathers, the former kings which
were before thee, so shall they
burn odours for thee; and they
will lament thee, saying, Ah lord!
for I have pronounced the word,
saith the LORD.
■ 6. **Then Jeremiah** the prophet
■ **spake all these words unto**
■ **Zedekiah king of Judah**
■ **in Jerusalem,**
7. When the king of Babylon's army
fought against Jerusalem, and against
all the cities of Judah that were left,
against Lachish, and against Azekah:
for these defenced cities remained of
the cities of Judah.
8. This is the word that came unto
Jeremiah from the LORD,
■ **after** that the king
■ **Zedekiah had made a**
■ **covenant with all the**
■ **people which were at**
■ **Jerusalem, to proclaim**
■ **liberty unto them;**
■ 9. **That every man should**
■ **let his manservant,**
■ **and** every man
■ **his maidservant, being an**
■ **Hebrew or an Hebrewess,**
■ **go free;** that none should
serve himself of them, to wit,
of a Jew his brother.
■ 10. **Now when**

- all the princes, and all
- **the people,** which had
entered into the covenant,
- **heard that every one**
- **should let his manservant,**
- **and** every one his
- **maidservant, go free,**
that none should serve themselves
of them any more,
- **then they obeyed,**
- **and let them go.**
- 11. **But afterward**
- **they** turned, and
- **caused the**
- **servants and** the
- **handmaids,**
whom they had let go free,
- **to return, and brought**
- **them into subjection**
for servants and for handmaids.
- 12. **Therefore** the word of
- **the LORD came to**
- **Jeremiah** from the LORD,
- **saying,**
13. Thus saith the LORD,
the God of Israel;
- **I made a covenant with**
- **your fathers in the day** that
- **I brought them** forth
- **out of** the land of
- **Egypt,** out of the house of bondmen,
- **saying,**
14. At the end of seven
- **years let ye go every man**
- **his brother an Hebrew,**
- **which hath been sold**
- **unto thee;** and when he hath
served thee six years, thou shalt
let him go free from thee:
- **but your fathers**
- **hearkened not unto me,**
neither inclined their ear.
- 15. **And ye** were now
- **turned, and had**
- **done right** in my sight,
- **in proclaiming liberty**
- **every man to his**
- **neighbour; and ye had**
- **made a covenant before**
- **me** in the house which is
called by my name:
- 16. **But ye turned and**
- **polluted my name,**

and caused every man his servant,
and every man his handmaid, whom
he had set at liberty at their pleasure,
to return, and brought them into
subjection, to be unto you for
servants and for handmaids.

- 17. **Therefore**
thus saith the LORD;
- **Ye have not hearkened**
- **unto me,** in proclaiming liberty,
every one to his brother, and
every man to his neighbour:
- **behold,** I proclaim a liberty for you,
saith the LORD, to the sword, to the
pestilence, and to the famine; and
- **I will make you to be**
- **removed into all the**
- **kingdoms of the earth.**
- 18. **And I will give the men**
- **that have transgressed my**
- **covenant,** which have not
performed the words of the covenant
which they had made before me,
when they cut the calf in twain, and
passed between the parts thereof,
19. The princes of Judah, and the
princes of Jerusalem, the eunuchs,
and the priests, and all the people
of the land, which passed between
the parts of the calf;
20. I will even give them
- **into the hand of their**
- **enemies,** and into the hand of
them that seek their life: and their
dead bodies shall be for meat unto
the fowls of the heaven, and to
the beasts of the earth.
- 21. **And Zedekiah** king of Judah
- **and his princes will I give**
- **into the hand** of their enemies,
and into the hand of them that seek
their life, and into the hand
- **of the king of Babylon's**
- **army,** which are gone up from you.
- 22. **Behold, I will**
command, saith the LORD, and
- **cause them to return**
- **to this city; and they**
- **shall fight against it,**
- **and take it, and burn it**
with fire: and I will make the
cities of Judah a desolation
without an inhabitant.

CHAPTER 35

■ 1. **The word** which
■ **came unto Jeremiah** from the
LORD in the days of Jehoiakim the
son of Josiah king of Judah,
■ **saying,**
■ 2. **Go unto the house**
■ **of the Rechabites,**
and speak unto them,
■ **and bring them into the**
■ **house of the LORD,**
into one of the chambers,
■ **and give them wine**
■ **to drink.**
■ 3. **Then I took Jaazaniah**
the son of Jeremiah, the son of
Habaziniah, and his brethren,
and all his sons,
■ **and the** whole
■ **house of the Rechabites;**
■ 4. **And I brought them into**
■ **the house of the LORD,**
into the chamber of the sons of
Hanan, the son of Igdaliah, a man of
God, which *was* by the chamber of
the princes, which *was* above the
chamber of Maaseiah the son of
Shallum, the keeper of the door:
■ 5. **And I set before**
the sons of the house of
■ **the Rechabites pots**
■ **full of wine,** and cups,
■ **and I said unto them,**
■ **Drink** ye wine.
■ 6. **But they said, We**
■ **will drink no wine:** for
Jonadab the son of Rechab
■ **our father commanded**
■ **us, saying, Ye shall**
■ **drink no wine,**
neither ye, nor your sons for ever:
■ 7. **Neither shall ye**
build house, nor sow seed, nor
■ **plant vineyard,** nor have *any:*
■ **but** all your days
■ **ye shall dwell in tents;**
■ **that ye may live many**
■ **days in the land where**
■ **ye be strangers.**
■ 8. **Thus have we obeyed** the
voice of Jonadab the son of Rechab
■ **our father in all that he hath**
■ **charged us,** to drink no

■ **wine** all our days, we, our wives,
our sons, nor our daughters;
■ 9. **Nor to build houses**
for us to dwell in: neither have we
vineyard, nor field, nor seed:
■ 10. **But we have dwelt in**
■ **tents, and have obeyed,**
and done according to all that
Jonadab our father commanded us.
■ 11. **But it came to pass,**
when Nebuchadrezzar king of
Babylon came up into the land,
■ **that we said,** Come, and
■ **let us go to Jerusalem for**
■ **fear of the army of the**
■ **Chaldeans, and**
for fear of the army of the
■ **Syrians: so we dwell**
■ **at Jerusalem.**
■ 12. **Then** came the word of
■ **the LORD** unto Jeremiah, saying,
13. Thus
■ **saith** the LORD of hosts,
the God of Israel;
■ **Go and tell the men**
■ **of Judah**
and the inhabitants of Jerusalem,
■ **Will ye not** receive instruction to
■ **hearken to my words?**
saith the LORD.
■ 14. **The words of Jonadab**
the son of Rechab, that he
commanded his sons
not to drink wine,
■ **are performed; for unto**
■ **this day they drink none,**
■ **but obey their father's**
■ **commandment:**
notwithstanding I have spoken unto
you, rising early and speaking;
but ye hearkened not unto me.
■ 15. **I have sent also**
unto you all my servants
■ **the prophets,** rising
up early and sending *them,*
■ **saying, Return** ye now
■ **every man from his evil**
■ **way,** and amend your doings, and
■ **go not after other**
■ **gods** to serve them,
■ **and ye shall dwell in the**
■ **land which I have given**
■ **to you** and to your fathers:

but ye have not inclined your ear, nor hearkened unto me. 16. **Because the sons of Jonadab** the son of Rechab **have performed the commandment of their father,** which he commanded them; **but this people hath not hearkened unto me:** 17. Therefore thus saith the LORD God of hosts, the God of Israel; Behold, **I will bring upon Judah and** upon all **the inhabitants of Jerusalem all the evil that I have pronounced against them:** because I have spoken unto them, but they have not heard; and I have called unto them, but they have not answered. 18. **And Jeremiah said unto the house of the Rechabites,** Thus saith the LORD of hosts, the God of Israel; **Because ye have obeyed** the commandment of Jonadab **your father, and kept all his precepts,** and done according unto all that he hath commanded you: 19. Therefore thus saith the LORD of hosts, the God of Israel; **Jonadab** the son of Rechab **shall not want a man to stand before me for ever.**

CHAPTER 36

1. **And** it came to pass **in the fourth year of Jehoiakim** the son of Josiah king of Judah, *that* **this word came unto Jeremiah from the LORD, saying,** 2. **Take** thee a roll of **a book, and write** therein **all the words that I have spoken unto thee against Israel,** and against **Judah, and** against **all the nations, from the** day I spake unto thee, from the days of Josiah, even **unto this day.** 3. It may be that the house of **Judah will hear all the evil which I purpose to do unto them; that they** may **return** every man **from his evil way; that I may forgive** their iniquity and **their sin.** 4. **Then Jeremiah called Baruch** the son of Neriah: **and Baruch wrote** from the mouth of Jeremiah all **the words of the LORD, which he had spoken** unto him, upon a roll of a book. 5. **And Jeremiah commanded Baruch, saying,** I *am* shut up; **I cannot go into the house of the LORD:** 6. **Therefore go** thou, **and read** in the roll, which thou hast written from my mouth, **the words of the LORD** in the ears of the people in the LORD'S house upon the fasting day: and also thou shalt read them in the ears of all Judah that come out of their cities. 7. **It may be they will present their supplication before the LORD, and** will **return every one from his evil way:** for great is the anger and the fury that the LORD hath pronounced against this people. 8. **And Baruch** the son of Neriah **did according to all that Jeremiah** the prophet **commanded him,** reading in the book the words of the LORD in the LORD'S house. 9. **And** it came to pass **in the fifth year of Jehoiakim** the son of Josiah king of Judah, in **the ninth month,** *that* **they proclaimed a fast** before the LORD to all the people in Jerusalem, and to all the people

that came from the cities of Judah unto Jerusalem.

■ 10. **Then read Baruch** in the book ■ **the words of Jeremiah in** ■ **the house of the LORD,** in the chamber of Gemariah the son of Shaphan the scribe, in the higher court, at the entry of the new gate of the LORD'S house, in the ears of all the people.

■ 11. **When Michaiah** the son of Gemariah, the son of Shaphan, had ■ **heard** out of the book all ■ **the words of the LORD,**

■ 12. **Then he went** down ■ **into the king's house,** into the scribe's chamber: and, lo, all the princes sat there, *even* Elishama the scribe, and Delaiah the son of Shemaiah, and Elnathan the son of Achbor, and Gemariah the son of Shaphan, and Zedekiah the son of Hananiah, ■ **and** all the princes.

13. Then Michaiah ■ **declared** unto them all ■ **the words that he** had ■ **heard,** when Baruch read the book in the ears of the people.

■ 14. **Therefore all the princes** ■ **sent** Jehudi the son of Nethaniah, the son of Shelemiah, the son of Cushi, ■ **unto Baruch, saying,** ■ **Take** in thine hand ■ **the roll** wherein thou hast read in the ears of the people, ■ **and come.** So Baruch the son of Neriah took the roll in his hand, and came unto them.

15. And they said unto him, Sit down now, ■ **and read it in our ears.** So Baruch read *it* in their ears.

■ 16. **Now** it came to pass, ■ **when they had heard** ■ **all the words, they were** ■ **afraid** both one and other, and said unto Baruch, We will surely tell the king of all these words.

■ 17. **And they asked** ■ **Baruch,** saying, Tell us now,

■ **How didst thou write** ■ **all these words** at his mouth?

■ 18. **Then Baruch** ■ **answered** them, ■ **He pronounced** all ■ **these words** unto me ■ **with his mouth, and** ■ **I wrote them** with ink ■ **in the book.**

■ 19. **Then said the** ■ **princes** unto Baruch, ■ **Go, hide thee,** thou ■ **and Jeremiah;** and let no man know where ye be.

20. And they went in to the king into the court, ■ **but they laid up the roll** in the chamber of Elishama the scribe, ■ **and told** all ■ **the words in the** ■ **ears of the king.**

■ 21. **So the king sent** Jehudi ■ **to fetch the roll:** and he took it out of Elishama the scribe's chamber. ■ **And Jehudi read it** in the ears of the king, and in the ears of all the princes which stood beside the king.

22. Now the king sat in the winterhouse in the ninth month: and *there was a fire* on the hearth burning before him.

■ 23. **And** it came to pass, *that* ■ **when Jehudi had read** ■ **three or four leaves, he** ■ **cut it** with the penknife, ■ **and cast it into the fire** that *was* on the hearth, ■ **until all the roll** ■ **was consumed** in the fire that *was* on the hearth.

■ 24. **Yet they were not afraid,** nor rent their garments, *neither* the king, nor any of his servants that heard all these words.

■ 25. **Nevertheless Elnathan** and Delaiah and Gemariah had ■ **made intercession to** ■ **the king that he would** ■ **not burn the roll:** but he would not hear them.

■ 26. **But the king** ■ **commanded** Jerahmeel the

son of Hammelech, and Seraiah
the son of Azriel, and Shelemiah
the son of Abdeel,

■ **to take Baruch** the scribe
■ **and Jeremiah** the prophet:
■ **but the LORD hid them.**
■ 27. **Then the word of the**
■ **LORD came to Jeremiah,**
after that the king had burned the roll,
and the words which Baruch wrote at
the mouth of Jeremiah, saying,

■ 28. **Take** thee again
■ **another roll, and write** in it all
■ **the** former
■ **words that were in the**
■ **first roll,** which Jehoiakim
the king of Judah hath burned.

■ 29. **And** thou shalt
■ **say to Jehoiakim**
king of Judah, Thus saith the LORD;
■ **Thou hast burned this**
■ **roll,** saying, Why hast thou
written therein, saying,
■ **The king of Babylon**
■ **shall** certainly
■ **come and destroy**
■ **this land,** and shall cause to cease
from thence man and beast?

■ 30. **Therefore thus saith the**
■ **LORD of Jehoiakim**
king of Judah;
■ **He shall have none to sit**
■ **upon the throne of David:**
and his dead body shall be cast
out in the day to the heat, and in
the night to the frost.

■ 31. **And I will punish him**
and his seed and his servants
for their iniquity;
■ **and I will bring upon them,**
and upon the inhabitants
of Jerusalem, and upon
the men of Judah,
■ **all the evil that I have**
■ **pronounced against them;**
but they hearkened not.

■ 32. **Then took Jeremiah**
■ **another roll, and gave**
■ **it to Baruch** the scribe,
the son of Neriah;
■ **who wrote** therein from
the mouth of Jeremiah
■ **all the words of the book**

■ **which Jehoiakim** king of Judah
■ **had burned** in the fire:
■ **and there were added**
besides unto them
■ **many like words.**

CHAPTER 37

■ 1. **And** king
■ **Zedekiah** the son of Josiah
■ **reigned instead**
of Coniah the son
■ **of Jehoiakim, whom**
■ **Nebuchadrezzar**
king of Babylon
■ **made king** in the land of Judah.

■ 2. **But neither he,**
nor his servants,
■ **nor the people** of the land,
■ **did hearken unto the**
■ **words of the LORD,** which he
spake by the prophet Jeremiah.

■ 3. **And Zedekiah the king**
■ **sent** Jehucal the son of Shelemiah
and Zephaniah the son of Maaseiah
■ **the priest to** the prophet
■ **Jeremiah, saying, Pray**
now unto the LORD our God
■ **for us.**

■ 4. **Now Jeremiah came** in
■ **and went** out among the people:
■ **for they had not put**
■ **him into prison.**

■ 5. **Then Pharaoh's**
■ **army was come** forth
■ **out of Egypt: and when the**
■ **Chaldeans that besieged**
■ **Jerusalem heard**
tidings of them,
■ **they departed** from Jerusalem.

■ 6. **Then came the word of**
■ **the LORD unto** the prophet
■ **Jeremiah saying,**
7. Thus saith the LORD,
the God of Israel;
■ **Thus shall ye say to the**
■ **king of Judah,** that sent you
unto me to inquire of me; Behold,
■ **Pharaoh's army,**
■ **which is come** forth
■ **to help you, shall**
■ **return to** Egypt into
■ **their own land.**
8. **And the Chaldeans shall**

■ **come again, and fight**
■ **against this city,** and take it,
■ **and burn it** with fire.

9. Thus saith the LORD; Deceive not yourselves, saying, The Chaldeans shall surely depart from us: for they shall not depart.

10. For though ye had smitten the wholearmy of the Chaldeans that fight against you, and there remained *but* wounded men among them,*yet* should they rise up every man in his tent, and burn this city with fire.

■ 11. **And** it came to pass, that
■ **when the army of the**
■ **Chaldeans was broken**
■ **up** from Jerusalem
■ **for fear of Pharaoh's army,**
■ 12. **Then Jeremiah went**
forth out of Jerusalem to go
■ **into the land of Benjamin,**
■ **to separate himself** thence
in the midst of the people.
■ 13. **And** when he was in the
gate of Benjamin,
■ **a captain of the ward**
was there, whose name *was*
■ **Irijah,** the son of Shelemiah,
the son of Hananiah; and he
■ **took Jeremiah** the prophet,
■ **saying, Thou fallest away**
■ **to the Chaldeans.**
■ 14. **Then said Jeremiah,**
■ **It is false;** I fall not away
to the Chaldeans.
■ **But** he hearkened not to him: so
■ **Irijah took Jeremiah, and**
■ **brought him to the princes.**
■ 15. **Wherefore the princes**
■ **were wroth with Jeremiah,**
■ **and smote him, and put him**
■ **in prison** in the house of
Jonathan the scribe: for they
had made that the prison.

16. When Jeremiah was entered into the dungeon, and into the cabins,
■ **and Jeremiah** had
■ **remained there**
■ **many days;**
■ 17. **Then Zedekiah**
the king sent, and
■ **took him out: and** the king
■ **asked him secretly**

in his house, and said,
■ **Is there any word from the**
■ **LORD? And Jeremiah said,**
■ **There is:** for, said he,
■ **thou shalt be delivered**
■ **into the hand of the**
■ **king of Babylon.**
18. Moreover Jeremiah said unto king Zedekiah,
■ **What have I offended**
■ **against thee,** or against thy
servants, or against this people,
■ **that ye have put**
■ **me in prison?**
■ 19. **Where are now**
■ **your prophets which**
■ **prophesied** unto you,
■ **saying, The king of Babylon**
■ **shall not come** against you,
nor against this land?
■ 20. **Therefore hear now,**
I pray thee, O my lord the king:
■ **let my supplication,**
I pray thee,
■ **be accepted** before thee;
that thou cause me not to return to the house of Jonathan the scribe, lest I die there.
■ 21. **Then Zedekiah** the king
■ **commanded that they** should
■ **commit Jeremiah into**
the court of the
■ **prison, and** that they should
■ **give him daily a piece**
■ **of bread** out of the bakers'
street, until all the bread in the city were spent. Thus Jeremiah remained in the court of the prison.

CHAPTER 38

■ 1. **Then Shephatiah**
the son of Mattan, and
■ **Gedaliah** the son of Pashur, and
■ **Jucal** the son of Shelemiah,
■ **and Pashur** the son of Malchiah,
■ **heard the words that**
■ **Jeremiah had spoken**
unto all the people,
■ **saying,**
2. Thus saith the LORD,
■ **He that remaineth in this**
■ **city shall die** by the sword, by
the famine, and by the pestilence:

but he that goeth forth
to the Chaldeans shall
live; for he shall have his life
for a prey, and shall live.
3. Thus saith the LORD, This city
shall surely be given into the hand
of the king of Babylon's army,
which shall take it.
4. **Therefore the princes
said unto the king,**
We beseech thee,
let this man be put
to death: for thus
he weakeneth the hands of
the men of war that remain in this
city, and the hands of all the people,
in speaking such words unto
them: for this man seeketh not the
welfare of this people, but the hurt.
5. **Then Zedekiah** the king
said, Behold,
he is in your hand:
for the king *is* not *he that* can
do *any* thing against you.
6. **Then took they
Jeremiah,** and
cast him into the dungeon
of Malchiah the son of Hammelech,
that *was* in the court of the prison:
and they let down
Jeremiah with cords.
And in the dungeon
there was no water, but
mire: so Jeremiah sunk
in the mire.
7. **Now when Ebed–melech**
the Ethiopian, one of the eunuchs
which was in the king's house,
heard that they had put
Jeremiah in the dungeon;
the king then sitting in the
gate of Benjamin;
8. **Ebed–melech went**
forth out of the king's house,
and spake to the king saying,
9. My lord the king,
these men have done evil
in all that they have done
to Jeremiah the prophet, whom
they have cast into the dungeon;
and he is like to die
for hunger in the place where he is:
for there is no more bread

in the city.
10. **Then the king
commanded** Ebed–melech
the Ethiopian, saying,
Take from hence thirty men
with thee, and take up
Jeremiah the prophet
out of the dungeon,
before he die.
11. **So Ebed–melech** took
the men with him, and went into the
house of the king under the treasury,
and took thence old cast clouts
and old rotten rags, and
let them
down by
cords into the dungeon
to Jeremiah.
12. **And Ebed–melech**
the Ethiopian
said unto Jeremiah, Put now
these old cast
clouts and rotten
rags under thine armholes
under the cords.
And Jeremiah did so.
13. **So they drew up
Jeremiah** with cords, and took
him up out of the dungeon:
and Jeremiah remained
in the court of the prison.
14. **Then Zedekiah**
the king sent, and
took Jeremiah
the prophet unto him
into the third entry that *is* in
the house of the
LORD: and the king
said unto Jeremiah,
I will ask thee a thing;
hide nothing from me.
15. **Then Jeremiah**
said unto Zedekiah,
If I declare it unto thee,
wilt thou not surely
put me to death? and
if I give thee counsel,
wilt thou not
hearken unto me?
16. **So Zedekiah** the king
sware secretly unto Jeremiah,
saying, *As* the LORD liveth,
that made us this soul,

I will not put thee to death, neither will I give thee into the hand of these men that seek thy life. 17. Then said Jeremiah unto Zedekiah, Thus saith the LORD, the God of hosts, the God of Israel; If thou wilt assuredly go forth unto the king of Babylon's princes, then thy soul shall live, and this city shall not be burned with fire; and thou shalt live, and thine house: 18. But if thou wilt not go forth to the king of Babylon's princes, then shall this city be given into the hand of the Chaldeans, and they shall burn it with fire, and thou shalt not escape out of their hand. 19. And Zedekiah the king said unto Jeremiah, I am afraid of the Jews that are fallen to the Chaldeans, lest they deliver me into their hand, and they mock me. 20. But Jeremiah said, They shall not deliver thee. Obey, I beseech thee, the voice of the LORD, which I speak unto thee: so it shall be well unto thee, and thy soul shall live. 21. But if thou refuse to go forth, this is the word that the LORD hath shewed me: 22. And, behold, all the women that are left in the king of Judah's house shall be brought forth to the king of Babylon's princes, and those women shall say, Thy friends have set thee on, and have prevailed against thee: thy feet are sunk in the mire, and they are turned away back. 23. So they shall bring out all thy wives and thy children to the Chaldeans: and thou shalt not escape out of their hand, but shalt be taken by the hand of the king of Babylon: and thou shalt cause this city to be burned with fire. 24. Then said Zedekiah unto Jeremiah, Let no man know of these words, and thou shalt not die. 25. But if the princes hear that I have talked with thee, and they come unto thee, and say unto thee, Declare unto us now what thou hast said unto the king, hide it not from us, and we will not put thee to death; also what the king said unto thee: 26. Then thou shalt say unto them, I presented my supplication before the king, that he would not cause me to return to Jonathan's house, to die there. 27. Then came all the princes unto Jeremiah, and asked him: and he told them according to all these words that the king had commanded. So they left off speaking with him; for the matter was not perceived. 28. So Jeremiah abode in the court of the prison until the day that Jerusalem was taken: and he was there when Jerusalem was taken.

CHAPTER 39

1. In the ninth year of Zedekiah king of Judah, in the tenth month, came Nebuchadnezzar king of Babylon and all his army against Jerusalem, and they besieged it. 2. And in the eleventh year of Zedekiah, in the fourth month, the ninth day of the month,

the city was broken up.

3. And all the princes of the king of Babylon came in, and sat in the middle gate, *even* Nergal–sharezer, Samgar–nebo, Sarsechim, Rab–saris, Nergal–sharezer, Rab–mag, with all the residue of the princes of the king of Babylon.

4. And it came to pass, *that* when Zedekiah the king of Judah saw them, and all the men of war, then they fled, and went forth out of the city by night, by the way of the king's garden, by the gate betwixt the two walls: and he went out the way of the plain.

5. But the Chaldeans' army pursued after them, and overtook Zedekiah in the plains of Jericho: and when they had taken him, they brought him up to Nebuchadnezzar king of Babylon to Riblah in the land of Hamath, where he gave judgment upon him.

6. Then the king of Babylon slew the sons of Zedekiah in Riblah before his eyes: also the king of Babylon slew all the nobles of Judah.

7. Moreover he put out Zedekiah's eyes, and bound him with chains, to carry him to Babylon.

8. And the Chaldeans burned the king's house, and the houses of the people, with fire, and brake down the walls of Jerusalem.

9. Then Nebuzar–adan the captain of the guard carried away captive into Babylon the remnant of the people that remained in the city, and those that fell away, that fell to him, with the rest of the people that remained.

10. But Nebuzar–adan the captain of the guard left of the poor of the people, which had nothing, in the land of Judah, and gave them vineyards and fields at the same time.

11. Now Nebuchadnezzar king of Babylon gave charge concerning Jeremiah to Nebuzaradan the captain of the guard, saying,

12. Take him, and look well to him, and do him no harm; but do unto him even as he shall say unto thee.

13. So Nebuzaradan the captain of the guard sent, and Nebushasban, Rabsaris, and Nergalsharezer, Rabmag, and all the king of Babylon's princes;

14. Even they sent, and took Jeremiah out of the court of the prison, and committed him unto Gedaliah the son of Ahikam the son of Shaphan, that he should carry him home: so he dwelt among the people.

15. Now the word of the LORD came unto Jeremiah, while he was shut up in the court of the prison, saying,

16. Go and speak to Ebed-melech the Ethiopian, saying, Thus saith the LORD of hosts, the God of Israel; Behold, I will bring my words upon this city for evil, and not for good; and they shall be accomplished in that day before thee.

17. But I will deliver thee in that day, saith the LORD: and thou shalt not be given into the hand of the

men of whom thou *art* afraid.

18. For I will surely deliver thee, **and** thou shalt not fall by the sword, but **thy life shall be for a prey unto thee: because thou hast put thy trust in me,** saith the LORD.

CHAPTER 40

1. The word that came to Jeremiah from the LORD, **after** that **Nebuzar-adan** the captain of the guard had let him go from Ramah, **when he had** taken him being bound in chains among all that were **carried away captive** of **Jerusalem and Judah,** which were carried away captive **unto Babylon.**

2. **And the captain** of the guard **took Jeremiah, and said** unto him, **The LORD** thy God **hath pronounced this evil upon this place.**

3. Now the LORD hath brought *it,* and done according as he hath said: **because ye have sinned** against the LORD, and have not obeyed his voice, therefore this thing is come upon you.

4. **And now,** behold, **I loose thee** this day **from the chains** which *were* upon thine hand. **If it seem good** unto thee **to come with me into Babylon, come; and I will look well unto thee: but if it seem ill** unto thee to come with me into Babylon, **forbear:** behold, all the land *is* before thee: whither it seemeth good and convenient for thee to go, thither go.

5. Now while he was not yet gone back, *he said,* **Go back** also **to Gedaliah** the son of Ahikam the son of Shaphan, whom **the** king of Babylon hath made **governor over** the cities of **Judah, and dwell with him** among the people: or go wheresoever it seemeth convenient unto thee to go. **So the captain of the guard** gave him victuals and a reward, and **let him go.**

6. **Then went Jeremiah** unto Gedaliah the son of Ahikam to Mizpah; **and dwelt** with him **among the people** that were **left in the land.**

7. **Now when all the captains** of the forces which *were* **in the fields,** even they and their men, **heard that the king** of Babylon **had made Gedaliah** the son of Ahikam **governor in the land,** and had committed unto him men, and women, and children, and of the poor of the land, of them that were not carried away captive to Babylon;

8. **Then they came to Gedaliah** to Mizpah, even Ishmael the son of Nethaniah, and Johanan and Jonathan the sons of Kareah, and Seraiah the son of Tanhumeth, and the sons of Ephai the Netophathite, and Jezaniah the son of a Maachathite, they and their men.

9. **And Gedaliah** the son of Ahikam the son of Shaphan **sware unto them** and to their men, **saying, Fear not to serve the Chaldeans: dwell in the land,** and serve the king of Babylon, **and it shall be well with you.**

10. **As for me,** behold, **I will dwell at Mizpah, to serve the Chaldeans,** which will come unto us: **but ye,** gather ye wine, and summer fruits, and oil, and put *them* in your vessels, and **dwell in your cities that ye have taken.**

11. Likewise when all the Jews that were in Moab, and among the Ammonites, and in Edom, and that were in all the countries, heard that the king of Babylon had left a remnant of Judah, and that he had set over them Gedaliah the son of Ahikam the son of Shaphan;

12. Even all the Jews returned out of all places whither they were driven, and came to the land of Judah, to Gedaliah, unto Mizpah, and gathered wine and summer fruits very much.

13. Moreover Johanan the son of Kareah, and all the captains of the forces that were in the fields, came to Gedaliah to Mizpah,

14. And said unto him, Dost thou certainly know that Baalis the king of the Ammonites hath sent Ishmael the son of Nethaniah to slay thee? But Gedaliah the son of Ahikam believed them not.

15. Then Johanan the son of Kareah spake to Gedaliah in Mizpah secretly saying, Let me go, I pray thee, and I will slay Ishmael the son of Nethaniah, and no man shall know it: wherefore should he slay thee, that all the Jews which are gathered unto thee should be scattered, and the remnant in Judah perish?

16. But Gedaliah the son of Ahikam said unto Johanan the son of Kareah, Thou shalt not do this thing: for thou speakest falsely of Ishmael.

CHAPTER 41

1. Now it came to pass in the seventh month, that Ishmael the son of Nethaniah the son of Elishama, of the seed royal, and the princes of the king, even ten men with him, came unto Gedaliah the son of Ahikam to Mizpah; and there they did eat bread together in Mizpah.

2. Then arose Ishmael the son of Nethaniah, and the ten men that were with him, and smote Gedaliah the son of Ahikam the son of Shaphan with the sword, and slew him, whom the king of Babylon had made governor over the land.

3. Ishmael also slew all the Jews that were with him, even with Gedaliah, at Mizpah, and the Chaldeans that were found there, and the men of war.

4. And it came to pass the second day after he had slain Gedaliah, and no man knew it,

5. That there came certain from Shechem, from Shiloh, and from Samaria, even fourscore men, having their beards shaven, and their clothes rent, and having cut themselves, with offerings and incense in their hand, to bring them to the house of the LORD.

6. And Ishmael the son of Nethaniah went forth from Mizpah to meet them, weeping all along as he went: and it came to pass, as he met them, he said unto them, Come to Gedaliah the son of Ahikam.

7. And it was so, when they came into the midst of the city, that Ishmael the son of Nethaniah

■ slew them, *and cast them* into the midst of the pit, he, and the men that *were* with him.

■ 8. But ten men were found ■ among them that ■ said unto Ishmael, ■ Slay us not: for we ■ have treasures in the field, ■ of wheat, and of ■ barley, and of ■ oil, and of ■ honey. So he forbare, and slew them not among their brethren.

■ 9. Now the pit wherein Ishmael had cast all the dead bodies of the men, whom he had slain because of Gedaliah, *was* it ■ which Asa the king ■ had made for fear of Baasha king of Israel: *and* ■ Ishmael the son of Nethaniah ■ filled it with them ■ that were slain.

■ 10. Then Ishmael carried ■ away captive all the ■ residue of the people that *were* in Mizpah, *even* the king's daughters, and all the people that remained in Mizpah, whom Nebuzar–adan the captain of the guard had committed to Gedaliah the son of Ahikam: and Ishmael the son of Nethaniah carried them away ■ captive, and departed to go over ■ to the Ammonites.

■ 11. But when Johanan the son of Kareah, ■ and all the captains ■ of the forces that *were* with him, ■ heard of all the evil that ■ Ishmael the son of Nethaniah ■ had done, ■ 12. Then they took all the men, and ■ went to fight with Ishmael the son of Nethaniah, ■ and found him by the ■ great waters that *are* ■ in Gibeon.

■ 13. Now it came to pass, *that* ■ when all the people which *were* ■ with Ishmael saw Johanan the son of Kareah, ■ and all the captains of ■ the forces that *were* ■ with him, then ■ they were glad.

■ 14. So all the people ■ that Ishmael had ■ carried away captive from Mizpah cast about and ■ returned, and went unto ■ Johanan the son of Kareah.

■ 15. But Ishmael the son of Nethaniah ■ escaped from Johanan ■ with eight men, and went ■ to the Ammonites.

■ 16. Then took Johanan the son of Kareah, ■ and all the captains of ■ the forces that *were* ■ with him, all the ■ remnant of the people ■ whom he had recovered ■ from Ishmael the son of Nethaniah, from Mizpah, after *that* he had slain Gedaliah the son of Ahikam, *even* mighty men of war, and the women, and the children, and the eunuchs, ■ whom he had brought ■ again from Gibeon:

■ 17. And they departed, and dwelt in the habitation of Chimham, which is by Beth–lehem, ■ to go to enter into ■ Egypt,

■ 18. Because of ■ the Chaldeans: for they ■ were afraid of them, because Ishmael the son of Nethaniah had slain Gedaliah the son of Ahikam, whom the king of Babylon made governor in the land.

CHAPTER 42

■ 1. Then all the captains of the forces, and Johanan the son of Kareah, and Jezaniah the son of Hoshaiah, and ■ all the people from the least even unto the greatest, ■ came near, ■ 2. And said unto Jeremiah the prophet, Let, we beseech thee, our supplication be accepted before thee, and **pray for us unto the LORD** thy God, *even* for all this remnant; **(for we are left but a few of many,** as thine eyes do behold us:) 3. **That the LORD thy God may shew us the way wherein we may walk,** and the thing that we may do. 4. **Then Jeremiah** the prophet **said** unto them, I have heard *you;* behold, **I will pray** unto the LORD your God according to your words; **and** it shall come to pass, *that* **whatsoever thing the LORD shall answer** you, **I will declare it unto you;** I will keep nothing back from you. 5. **Then they said** to Jeremiah, **The LORD be a true and faithful witness between us,** **if we do not** even according to **all things** for the **which the LORD** thy God **shall send** thee **to us.** 6. **Whether** *it be* **good, or** whether *it be* **evil, we will obey** the voice of the LORD our God, to whom we send thee; **that it may be well with us,** when we obey the voice of the LORD our God. 7. **And** it came to pass **after ten days, that** **the word of the LORD came unto Jeremiah.** 8. **Then called he Johanan** the son of Kareah, **and** all **the captains of the forces** which *were* with him, and all the people from the least even to the greatest, 9. **And said** unto them, **Thus saith the LORD,** the God of Israel, unto whom ye sent me to present your supplication before him; 10. **If ye will still abide in this land, then will I build you,**

and not pull you down, and I will plant you, and not pluck *you* up: for I repent me of the evil that I have done unto you. 11. **Be not afraid of the king of Babylon,** of whom ye are afraid; be not afraid of him, saith the LORD: **for I am with you** to save you, and **to deliver you from his hand.** 12. **And I will shew mercies unto you,** that he may have mercy upon you, and cause you to return to your own land. 13. **But if ye say, We will not** dwell in this land, neither **obey the voice of the LORD** your God, 14. Saying, No; **but we will go into** the land of **Egypt, where we shall see no war,** nor hear the sound of the trumpet, **nor have hunger** of bread; and there will we dwell: 15. And now therefore hear the word of the LORD, ye remnant of Judah; Thus saith the LORD of hosts, the God of Israel; If ye wholly set your faces to enter into Egypt, and go to sojourn there; 16. **Then it shall come to pass, that the sword,** which ye feared, **shall overtake you** there **in** the land of **Egypt, and the famine,** whereof ye were afraid, **shall follow** close after **you** there in Egypt; **and there ye shall die.** 17. So shall it be with all the men that set their faces to go into Egypt to sojourn there; they shall die by the sword, by the famine, and by the pestilence: **and none** of them **shall** remain or **escape from the evil that I will bring upon them.** 18. **For thus saith the LORD** of hosts, the God of Israel;

■ **As mine anger** and my fury
■ **hath been poured forth**
■ **upon** the inhabitants of
■ **Jerusalem; so shall my**
■ **fury be poured forth**
■ **upon you, when ye** shall
■ **enter** into
■ **Egypt:** and ye shall be an
execration, and an astonishment,
and a curse, and a reproach;
■ **and ye shall see this**
■ **place no more.**
■ 19. **The LORD hath said**
■ **concerning you, O ye**
■ **remnant of Judah;**
Go ye not into Egypt:
■ **know certainly that I have**
■ **admonished you this day.**
■ 20. **For ye dissembled in**
■ **your hearts, when ye sent**
■ **me unto the LORD** your God,
■ **saying, Pray for us**
unto the LORD our God;
■ **and according unto**
■ **all that the LORD** our God
■ **shall say, so**
declare unto us, and
■ **we will do it.**
21. And *now* I have this
day declared *it* to you;
■ **but ye have not**
■ **obeyed** the voice of
■ **the LORD** your God, nor
any *thing* for the which he
hath sent me unto you.
■ 22. **Now** therefore
■ **know certainly that ye shall**
■ **die** by the sword, by the famine, and
by the pestilence, in the place whither
ye desire to go *and* to sojourn.

CHAPTER 43

■ 1. **And** it came to pass, *that*
■ **when Jeremiah had made**
■ **an end of speaking**
unto all the people all the words of
the LORD their God, for which the
LORD their God had sent him to
them, *even* all these words,
■ 2. **Then spake Azariah**
the son of Hoshaiah, and Johanan
the son of Kareah,

■ **and all the proud men,**
■ **saying** unto Jeremiah,
■ **Thou speakest falsely:**
■ **the LORD** our God
■ **hath not sent thee to**
■ **say, Go not into Egypt**
to sojourn there:
■ 3. **But Baruch** the son of Neriah
■ **setteth thee** on
■ **against us, for**
■ **to deliver us into the**
■ **hand of the Chaldeans,**
that they might put us to death,
■ **and carry us away**
■ **captives into Babylon.**
■ 4. **So** Johanan the son of Kareah,
and all the captains of the forces, and
■ **all the people, obeyed not**
■ **the voice of the LORD,**
to dwell in the land of Judah.
■ 5. **But** Johanan the son
of Kareah, and all the captains
of the forces, took
■ **all the remnant of Judah,**
that were returned from all nations,
whither they had been driven, to
dwell in the land of Judah;
6. *Even* men, and women, a
nd children, and the king's
daughters, and
■ **every person that**
■ **Nebuzar-adan**
the captain of the guard
■ **had left with Gedaliah** the
son of Ahikam the son of Shaphan,
■ **and Jeremiah** the prophet,
■ **and Baruch** the son of Neriah.
7. So they
■ **came into the land of**
■ **Egypt: for they obeyed not**
■ **the voice of the LORD:** thus
came they *even* to Tahpanhes.
■ 8. **Then came the word of**
■ **the LORD unto Jeremiah**
in Tahpanhes, saying,
■ 9. **Take** great
■ **stones** in thine hand,
■ **and hide them in the clay**
■ **in the brickkiln, which** *is*
■ **at the entry of Pharaoh's**
■ **house** in Tahpanhes, in the
sight of the men of Judah;
■ 10. **And say** unto them,

Thus saith the LORD of hosts, the God of Israel; Behold, **I will send** and take **Nebuchadrezzar** the king of Babylon, **my servant, and** will **set his throne upon these stones** that I have hid; and he shall spread his royal pavilion over them.

11. **And** when he cometh, **he shall smite the land of Egypt, and deliver such** *as are* for death **to death; and such** *as are* for captivity **to captivity;** and such *as are* for the sword to the sword.

12. **And** I will kindle a fire in the houses of **the gods of Egypt;** and **he shall burn** them, and carry them away captives: **and** he **shall array himself with the land of Egypt,** as a shepherd putteth on his garment; **and he shall go forth** from thence **in peace.**

13. He shall break also the images of Beth–shemesh, that *is* in the land of Egypt; and the houses of the gods of the Egyptians shall he burn with fire.

CHAPTER 44

1. **The word that came to Jeremiah concerning all the Jews** which dwell **in** the land of **Egypt,** which dwell at Migdol, and at Tahpanhes, and at Noph, and in the country of Pathros, **saying,**

2. **Thus saith the LORD** of hosts, the God of Israel; **Ye have seen** all **the evil** that **I have brought upon Jerusalem, and** upon all the cities of **Judah;** and, behold, this day they *are* a desolation, and no man dwelleth therein,

3. **Because of their wickedness** which they have committed to provoke me to anger, **in that they went to** burn incense, *and* to **serve other gods,** whom they knew not, *neither* they, ye, nor your fathers.

4. **Howbeit I sent** unto you all my servants **the prophets,** rising early and sending *them,* **saying,** Oh, **do not this abominable thing** that I hate.

5. **But they hearkened not,** nor inclined their ear to turn from their wickedness, to burn no incense unto other gods.

6. **Wherefore my** fury and mine **anger was poured forth,** and was kindled **in the cities of Judah and** in the streets of **Jerusalem; and they are** wasted *and* **desolate,** as at this day.

7. **Therefore now thus saith the LORD,** the God of hosts, the God of Israel; **Wherefore commit ye this great evil** against your souls, to cut off from you man and woman, child and suckling, out of Judah, to leave you none to remain;

8. In that ye provoke me unto wrath with the works of your hands, burning incense unto other gods in the land of Egypt, whither ye be gone to dwell, that **ye** might **cut yourselves off,** and **that ye might be a curse and a reproach among all the nations of the earth?**

9. **Have ye forgotten the wickedness of your fathers, and** the wickedness of **the kings of Judah,** and the wickedness of their wives, and **your own wickedness,** and the wickedness of your wives, which they have committed in the

land of Judah, and in the streets of Jerusalem?

10. **They are not humbled** *even* unto this day, **neither have they feared,** nor walked in **my law,** nor in my statutes, that I set before you and before your fathers.

11. **Therefore** thus saith the LORD of hosts, the God of Israel; Behold, **I will set my face against you for evil,** and to cut off all Judah.

12. **And** I will take **the remnant of Judah, that** have set their faces to **go into** the land of **Egypt** to sojourn there, and they **shall all be consumed,** *and* fall in the land of Egypt; they shall *even* be consumed by the sword *and* by the famine: they shall die, from the least even unto the greatest, by the sword and by the famine: and they shall be an execration, and an astonishment, *and* a curse, and a reproach.

13. For I will punish them that dwell in the land of Egypt, as I have punished Jerusalem, by the sword, by the famine, and by the pestilence:

14. **So that none** of the remnant of Judah, which are gone into the land of Egypt to sojourn there, **shall escape** or remain, **that they should return into the land of Judah,** to the which they have a desire to return to dwell there: for none shall return but such as shall escape.

15. **Then all the men which knew that their wives had burned incense unto other gods,** and all the women that stood by, a great multitude, even all the people that dwelt in the land of Egypt, in Pathros, **answered Jeremiah,** saying,

16. *As for* the word that thou hast spoken unto us in the name of the LORD, **we will not hearken unto thee.**

17. **But we will** certainly do whatsoever thing goeth forth out of our own mouth, to **burn incense unto the queen of heaven,** and to pour out drink offerings unto her, **as we have done,** we, and our fathers, our kings, and our princes, in the cities of Judah, and in the streets of Jerusalem: **for then had we plenty of victuals,** and were well, **and saw no evil.**

18. **But since we left** off to burn incense to **the queen of heaven,** and to pour out drink offerings unto her, **we have wanted all things, and have been consumed by the sword** and by the famine.

19. And when we burned incense to the queen of heaven, and poured out drink offerings unto her, did we make her cakes to worship her, and pour out drink offerings unto her, without our men?

20. **Then Jeremiah said** unto all the people, to the men, and to the women, and to all the people which had given him *that* answer, saying,

21. **The incense that ye burned in** the cities of **Judah, and** in the streets of **Jerusalem,** ye, and your fathers, your kings, and your princes, and the people of the land, **did not the LORD remember** them, and came it *not* into his mind?

22. **So that the LORD could no longer bear,** because of **the evil** of your doings, *and* because of the abominations which ye have committed; **therefore is your land a desolation,** and an astonishment, and a curse, without an inhabitant, as at this day.

23. **Because ye** have burned incense, and because ye have sinned against the LORD, and **have not obeyed** the voice of **the LORD,** nor walked in his law,

nor in his statutes, nor
in his testimonies;

■ **therefore this evil is**
■ **happened unto you,**
as at this day.

■ 24. **Moreover Jeremiah**
■ **said** unto all the people,
and to all the women,

■ **Hear the word of the LORD,**
all Judah that *are* in the land of Egypt:
25. Thus saith the LORD of hosts,
the God of Israel, saying; Ye and your
wives have both spoken with your
mouths, and fulfilled with your hand,
saying, We will surely perform our
vows that we have vowed, to burn
incense to the queen of heaven, and
to pour out drink offerings unto her:
ye will surely accomplish your vows,
and surely perform your vows.
26. Therefore hear ye the word
of the LORD, all Judah that
dwell in the land of Egypt;

■ **Behold, I have sworn** by my
great name, saith the LORD,

■ **that my name shall no**
■ **more be named in the**
■ **mouth of any man of**
■ **Judah in all** the land of
■ **Egypt,** saying, The LORD
GOD liveth.
27. Behold, I will watch over
them for evil, and not for good:

■ **and all the men of Judah**
■ **that are in** the land of
■ **Egypt shall be consumed**
by the sword and by the famine,
until there be an end of them:

■ 28. **Yet a small number** that
escape the sword

■ **shall return out** of the land
■ **of Egypt into the land of**
■ **Judah, and all** the remnant of
■ **Judah,** that are gone into the
land of Egypt to sojourn there,

■ **shall know whose words**
■ **shall stand, mine, or theirs.**
■ 29. **And this shall be a sign**
■ **unto you,** saith the LORD, that I
will punish you in this place, that ye
may know that my words shall surely
stand against you for evil:
30. Thus saith the LORD; Behold,

■ **I will give Pharaoh–hophra**
■ **king of Egypt into the hand**
■ **of his enemies,** and into the
hand of them that seek his life;

■ **as I gave Zedekiah**
king of Judah

■ **into the hand of**
■ **Nebuchadrezzar** king
of Babylon, his enemy, and
that sought his life.

CHAPTER 45

■ 1. **The word that**
■ **Jeremiah** the prophet
■ **spake unto Baruch**
the son of Neriah,

■ **when he had written**
■ **these words in a book**
at the mouth of Jeremiah,

■ **in the fourth year of**
■ **Jehoiakim** the son of
Josiah king of Judah, saying,

■ 2. **Thus saith the LORD,**
the God of Israel,

■ **unto thee, O Baruch:**
3. Thou didst say, Woe is me now! for

■ **the LORD hath added**
■ **grief to my sorrow;**
I fainted in my sighing,

■ **and I find no rest.**
4. Thus shalt thou say unto him,

■ **The LORD saith** thus; Behold,
■ **that which I have built will I**
■ **break down,** and that which I
have planted I will pluck up,

■ **even this whole land.**
5. **And** seekest thou

■ **great things** for thyself?
■ **seek** them
■ **not: for,** behold,
■ **I will bring evil upon**
■ **all flesh,** saith the LORD:
■ **but thy life will I give** unto
■ **thee for a prey** in all places
whither thou goest.

CHAPTER 46

■ 1. **The word** of the LORD
■ **which came to**
■ **Jeremiah** the prophet
■ **against the Gentiles;**
■ 2. **Against Egypt, against**
■ **the army** of Pharaoh–necho king

1105

of Egypt, which was by the river Euphrates in Carchemish, which Nebuchadrezzar king of Babylon smote in the fourth year of Jehoiakim the son of Josiah king of Judah. 3. Order ye the buckler and shield, and draw near to battle.

4. Harness the horses; and get up, ye horsemen, and stand forth with *your* helmets; furbish the spears, *and* put on the brigandines.

5. Wherefore have I seen them dismayed *and* turned away back? and their mighty ones are beaten down, and are fled apace, and look not back: *for* fear *was* round about, saith the LORD.

6. Let not the swift flee away, nor the mighty man escape; they shall stumble, and fall toward the north by the river Euphrates.

7. Who is this that cometh up as a flood, whose waters are moved as the rivers?

8. Egypt riseth up like a flood, and *his* waters are moved like the rivers; and he saith, I will go up, *and* will cover the earth; I will destroy the city and the inhabitants thereof.

9. Come up, ye horses; and rage, ye chariots; and let the mighty men come forth; the Ethiopians and the Libyans, that handle the shield; and the Lydians, that handle *and* bend the bow.

10. For this is the day of the Lord GOD of hosts, a day of vengeance, that he may avenge him of his adversaries: and the sword shall devour, and it shall be satiate and made drunk with their blood: for the Lord GOD of hosts hath a sacrifice in the north country by the river Euphrates.

11. Go up into Gilead, and take balm, O virgin, the daughter of Egypt: in vain shalt thou use many medicines; for thou shalt not be cured.

12. The nations have heard of thy shame, and thy cry hath filled the land: for the mighty man hath stumbled against the mighty, *and* they are fallen both together.

13. The word that the LORD spake to Jeremiah the prophet, how Nebuchadrezzar king of Babylon should come and smite the land of Egypt.

14. Declare ye in Egypt, and publish in Migdol, and publish in Noph and in Tahpanhes: say ye, Stand fast, and prepare thee; for the sword shall devour round about thee.

15. Why are thy valiant men swept away? they stood not, because the LORD did drive them.

16. He made many to fall, yea, one fell upon another: and they said, Arise, and let us go again to our own people, and to the land of our nativity, from the oppressing sword.

17. They did cry there, Pharaoh king of Egypt is but a noise; he hath passed the time appointed.

18. As I live, saith the King, whose name is the LORD of hosts, Surely as Tabor is among the mountains, and as Carmel by the sea, so shall he come.

19. O thou daughter dwelling in Egypt, furnish thyself to go into captivity: for Noph shall be waste and desolate without an inhabitant.

20. Egypt *is like* a very fair heifer, *but* **destruction cometh;** it cometh **out of the north.**

21. Also her hired men *are* in the midst of her like fatted bullocks; for they also are turned back, *and* are fled away together: they did not stand, because the day of their calamity was come upon them, *and* the time of their visitation.

22. The voice thereof shall go like a serpent; for they shall march with an army, and come against her with axes, as hewers of wood.

23. They shall cut down her forest, saith the LORD, though it cannot be searched; because they are more than the grasshoppers, and *are* innumerable.

24. **The daughter of Egypt shall** be confounded; she shall **be delivered into the hand of the people of the north.**

25. **The LORD** of hosts, the God of Israel, **saith;** Behold, **I will punish the** multitude of No, and **Pharaoh, and Egypt, with their gods,** and their kings; even Pharaoh, **and all them that trust in him:**

26. **And I will deliver them into the hand of** those that seek their lives, and into the hand of **Nebuchadrezzar king of Babylon,** and into the hand of his servants: and afterward it shall be inhabited, as in the days of old, saith the LORD.

27. **But fear not** thou, O my servant Jacob, and be not dismayed, **O Israel: for,** behold, **I will save thee** from afar off, **and thy seed** from the land of their captivity; **and Jacob shall return, and be in rest** and at ease, and none shall make *him* afraid.

28. Fear thou not, O Jacob my servant, saith the LORD: **for I am with thee;** for

I will make a full end of all the nations whither I have driven thee: but I will not make a full end of thee, but correct thee in measure; yet will I not leave thee wholly **unpunished.**

CHAPTER 47

1. **The word of the LORD that came to Jeremiah** the prophet **against the Philistines,** before that Pharaoh smote Gaza.

2. Thus saith the LORD; **Behold, waters rise up out of the north,** and shall be an overflowing flood, **and shall overflow the land,** and all that is therein; the city, **and** them that dwell therein: then **the men shall cry,** and all the inhabitants of the land shall howl.

3. **At the noise of** the stamping of the hoofs of his strong *horses,* at the rushing of his **chariots, and** *at the* rumbling of his wheels, **the fathers shall not look back to their children for feebleness of hands;**

4. **Because** of **the day** that **cometh to spoil** all **the Philistines,** *and* to cut off from Tyrus and Zidon every helper that remaineth: for the LORD will spoil the Philistines, the remnant of the country of Caphtor.

5. Baldness is come upon Gaza; Ashkelon is cut off *with* the remnant of their valley: how long wilt thou cut thyself?

6. **O thou sword of the LORD,** how long *will it be* ere thou be quiet? **put up thyself into thy scabbard, rest, and be still.**

7. **How can it be quiet,** seeing the LORD hath **given it a charge against Ashkelon, and** against **the sea shore?**

I I there hath he appointed it.

CHAPTER 48

1. **Against Moab thus saith the LORD** of hosts, the God of Israel; Woe unto Nebo! for it is spoiled: Kiriathaim is confounded *and* taken: Misgab is confounded and dismayed.

2. **There shall be no more praise of Moab:** in Heshbon they have devised evil against it; come, and **let us cut it off from being a nation.** Also thou shalt be cut down, O Madmen; **the sword shall pursue thee.**

3. A voice of crying *shall be* from Horonaim, spoiling and great destruction.

4. **Moab is destroyed;** her little ones have caused a cry to be heard.

5. For in the going up of Luhith continual weeping shall go up; for in the going down of Horonaim the enemies have heard a cry of destruction.

6. **Flee,** save your lives, and be like the heath **in the wilderness.**

7. For because **thou hast trusted in thy works and** in thy **treasures, thou shalt also be taken:** and Chemosh shall go forth **into captivity** with his priests and his princes together.

8. **And the spoiler shall come** upon every city, **and no city shall escape:** the valley also shall perish, and the plain shall be destroyed, **as the LORD hath spoken.**

9. Give wings unto Moab, that it may flee and get away: for the cities thereof shall be desolate, without any to dwell therein.

10. **Cursed be he that doeth the work of the LORD deceitfully,** and cursed *be* he that keepeth back his sword from blood.

11. **Moab hath been at ease** from his youth, and he hath settled on his lees, **and hath not been emptied from vessel to vessel, neither hath he gone into captivity:** therefore his taste remained in him, and his scent is not changed.

12. **Therefore,** behold, the days come, saith the LORD, that **I will** send unto him wanderers, that shall **cause him to wander, and shall empty his vessels,** and break their bottles.

13. **And Moab shall be ashamed** of Chemosh, **as** the house of **Israel was ashamed** of Beth–el their confidence.

14. **How say ye, We are mighty** and strong men for the war?

15. **Moab is spoiled,** and gone up *out of* her cities, **and his** chosen **young men are gone** down **to the slaughter, saith** the King, whose name *is* **the LORD** of hosts.

16. The calamity of Moab *is* near to come, and his affliction hasteth fast.

17. **All ye** that are **about him, bemoan him;** and all ye that know his name, say, How is the strong staff broken, *and* the beautiful rod!

18. Thou daughter that dost inhabit Dibon, come down from *thy* glory, and sit in thirst; for **the spoiler of Moab shall come upon thee, and** he shall **destroy thy strong holds.**

19. O inhabitant of Aroer, stand by the way, and espy; ask him that fleeth, and her that escapeth, *and* say, What is done?

20. **Moab** is confounded; for it **is broken down:** howl and cry; tell ye it in Arnon, that Moab is spoiled,

21. **And judgment is come**

upon the plain country;
upon Holon, and upon Jahazah,
and upon Mephaath,
22. And upon Dibon, and upon
Nebo, and upon Beth–diblathaim,
23. And upon Kiriathaim, and upon
Beth–gamul, and upon Beth–meon,
24. And upon Kerioth, and upon
Bozrah, and upon all the cities
of the land of Moab, far or near.
25. **The horn of Moab
is cut off,** and his arm is
broken, saith the LORD.
26. Make ye him drunken:
**for he magnified himself
against the LORD:** Moab
also shall wallow in his vomit,
and he also shall be in derision.
27. **For was not Israel a
derision unto thee? was he
found among thieves?** for
since thou spakest of him, thou
skippedst for joy.
28. **O ye that dwell in Moab,
leave the cities, and dwell
in the rock,** and be like the
dove *that* maketh her nest in the
sides of the hole's mouth.
29. **We have heard the
pride of Moab, (he is
exceeding proud)** his loftiness,
and his arrogancy, and his pride, and
the haughtiness of his heart.
30. **I know his wrath, saith
the LORD;** but *it shall* not *be* so;
**his lies shall not
so effect it.**
31. Therefore will I howl for Moab, and
I will cry out for all Moab; *mine heart*
shall mourn for the men of Kir–heres.
32. O vine of Sibmah, I will weep for
thee with the weeping of Jazer: thy
plants are gone over the sea, they
reach *even* to the sea of Jazer: the
spoiler is fallen upon thy summer
fruits and upon thy vintage.
33. **And joy and gladness
is taken from** the plentiful
field, and from
**the land of Moab, and
I have caused wine to fail
from the winepresses:** none
shall tread with shouting; *their*

shouting *shall be* no shouting.
34. From the cry of Heshbon *even*
unto Elealeh, *and even* unto Jahaz,
have they uttered their voice, from
Zoar *even* unto Horonaim, as an
heifer of three years old: for
the waters also
**of Nimrim shall be
desolate.**
35. **Moreover I will cause to
cease** in Moab, saith the LORD,
**him that offereth in the
high places, and him
that burneth incense
to his gods.**
36. **Therefore mine heart
shall sound** for Moab
like pipes, and mine heart shall
sound like pipes for the men of
Kir–heres:
**because the riches that he
hath gotten are perished.**
37. **For every head shall
be bald, and every beard
clipped:** upon all the hands
shall be cuttings,
**and upon the loins
sackcloth.**
38. **There shall be
lamentation** generally upon
all the housetops of Moab, and
in the streets thereof:
**for I have broken Moab
like a vessel** wherein *is* no
pleasure, saith the LORD.
39. They shall howl, *saying,* How is
it broken down! how hath Moab
turned the back with shame! so
shall Moab be a derision and a
dismaying to all them about him.
40. **For thus saith the LORD;
Behold, he shall fly as an
eagle,** and shall spread his wings
over Moab.
41. Kerioth is taken, and the
strong holds are surprised, and
the mighty men's hearts
in Moab at that day
**shall be as the heart of
a woman in her pangs.**
42. **And Moab shall be
destroyed** from *being* a people,
because he hath magnified

■ himself against the LORD.
■ 43. **Fear, and the pit, and**
■ **the snare, shall be upon**
■ **thee,** O inhabitant of Moab,
■ **saith the LORD.**
44. He that fleeth from the fear shall fall into the pit; and he that getteth up out of the pit shall be taken in the snare:
■ **for I will bring upon**
■ **it,** *even* upon Moab,
■ **the year of their visitation,** saith the LORD.
45. They that fled stood under the shadow of Heshbon because of the force: but a fire shall come forth out of Heshbon, and a flame from the midst of Sihon, and shall devour the corner of Moab, and the crown of the head of the tumultuous ones.
46. Woe be unto thee, O Moab! the people of Chemosh perisheth: for thy sons are taken captives, and thy daughters captives.
■ 47. **Yet will I bring again the**
■ **captivity of Moab in the**
■ **latter days,** saith the LORD.
Thus far *is* the judgment of Moab.

CHAPTER 49

■ 1. **Concerning the**
■ **Ammonites,** thus saith the LORD;
■ **Hath Israel** no sons? hath he
■ **no heir? why then doth**
■ **their king inherit Gad,**
and his people dwell in his cities?
■ 2. **Therefore,** behold, the days come, saith the LORD, that
■ **I will cause** an alarm of
■ **war** to be heard
■ **in Rabbah of the**
■ **Ammonites; and** it shall be a desolate heap, and her daughters shall be burned with fire: then shall Israel be heir unto them that were his heirs, saith the LORD.
3. Howl, O Heshbon, for Ai is spoiled: cry, ye daughters of Rabbah, gird you with sackcloth; lament, and r un to and fro by the hedges; for
■ **their king shall go into**
■ **captivity,** *and* his priests and his princes together.

4. Wherefore gloriest thou in the valleys, thy flowing valley,
■ **O backsliding daughter?**
■ **that trusted in her**
■ **treasures,** *saying,* Who shall come unto me?
■ 5. **Behold, I will**
■ **bring a fear** upon thee, saith the Lord GOD of hosts,
■ **from** all
■ **those** that be
■ **about thee; and ye shall**
■ **be driven out** every man right forth; and none shall gather up him that wandereth.
■ 6. **And afterward I will**
■ **bring again the**
■ **captivity** of the children
■ **of Ammon,** saith the LORD.
■ 7. **Concerning Edom, thus**
■ **saith the LORD** of hosts; *Is* wisdom no more in Teman? is counsel perished from the prudent? is their wisdom vanished?
8. Flee ye, turn back, dwell deep, O inhabitants of Dedan; for
■ **I will bring the calamity**
■ **of Esau upon him,** the time *that* I will visit him.
9. If grapegatherers come to thee, would they not leave *some* gleaning grapes? if thieves by night, they will destroy till they have enough.
10. But I have made Esau bare,
■ **I have uncovered his**
■ **secret places, and he**
■ **shall not** be able to
■ **hide** himself:
■ .his seed is spoiled, and his brethren, and his neighbours,
■ **and he is not.**
11. Leave
■ **thy** fatherless
■ **children, I will**
■ **preserve** *them* alive;
■ **and let thy widows**
■ **trust in me.**
■ 12. **For thus saith the LORD;**
■ **Behold,** they whose judgment *was* not to drink of the cup have assuredly drunken; and *art* thou he *that* shall altogether go unpunished?
■ **thou shalt not go**

unpunished, but thou shalt surely drink *of it.*

13. **For I have sworn by myself, saith the LORD,** that **Bozrah shall become a** desolation, a reproach, a waste, and a curse; and all the cities thereof shall be **perpetual wastes.**

14. **I have heard** a rumour from the LORD, and **an ambassador is sent unto the heathen, saying,** Gather ye together, and **come against her,** and rise up **to the battle.**

15. For, lo, I will make thee small among the heathen, *and* despised among men.

16. **Thy terribleness hath deceived thee, and the pride of thine heart,** O thou that dwellest in the clefts of the rock, that holdest the height of the hill: though thou shouldest make thy nest as high as the eagle, **I will bring thee down** from thence, **saith the LORD.**

17. **Also Edom shall be a desolation: every one that goeth by it shall be astonished,** and shall hiss **at all the plagues thereof.**

18. As in the overthrow of Sodom and Gomorrah and the neighbour *cities* thereof, saith the LORD, no man shall abide there, neither shall a son of man dwell in it.

19. Behold, he shall come up like a lion from the swelling of Jordan against the habitation of the strong: but I will suddenly make him run away from her: and who *is* a chosen *man,* that I may appoint over her? for who *is* like me? and who will appoint me the time? and who *is* that shepherd that will stand before me?

20. **Therefore hear the counsel of the LORD, that he hath taken against Edom;** and his purposes, that he hath purposed against the inhabitants of Teman: Surely the least of the flock shall draw them out: **surely he shall make their habitations desolate** with them.

21. The earth is moved at the noise of their fall, at the cry the noise thereof was heard in the Red sea.

22. Behold, he shall come up and fly as the eagle, and spread his wings over Bozrah: and at that day shall the heart of the mighty men of Edom be as the heart of a woman in her pangs.

23. **Concerning Damascus.** Hamath is confounded, and Arpad:for **they have heard evil tidings: they are fainthearted;** *there is* sorrow on the sea; it cannot be quiet.

24. **Damascus is waxed feeble, and turneth** herself **to flee,** and fear hath seized on *her:* anguish and sorrows have taken her, as a woman in travail.

25. **How is the city of praise not left, the city of my joy!**

26. **Therefore** her young men shall fall in her streets, and all **the men of war shall be cut off** in that day, **saith the LORD** of hosts.

27. **And** I will kindle a **fire** in the wall of Damascus, and it **shall consume the palaces of Ben–hadad.**

28. **Concerning Kedar, and** concerning the kingdoms of **Hazor, which Nebuchadrezzar** king of Babylon **shall smite,** thus saith the LORD; Arise ye, go up to Kedar, and spoil the men of the east.

29. **Their tents and their flocks shall they take** away: they shall take to themselves their curtains, and all their vessels, and their camels; and they shall cry unto them, Fear *is* on every side.

30. Flee, get you far off, dwell deep, O ye inhabitants of Hazor, saith the LORD; for Nebuchadrezzar king of Babylon hath taken counsel

against you, and hath conceived a purpose against you.

31. Arise, get you up unto the wealthy nation, that dwelleth without care, saith the LORD, which have neither gates nor bars, *which* dwell alone.

32. And their camels shall be a booty, and the multitude of their cattle a spoil: and I will scatter into all winds them *that are* in the utmost corners; and I will bring their calamity from all sides thereof, saith the LORD.

33. **And Hazor shall be** a dwelling for dragons, *and* **a desolation for ever:** there shall no man abide there, nor *any* son of man dwell in it.

34. **The word of the LORD** that came to Jeremiah the prophet **against Elam in the beginning of the reign of Zedekiah king of Judah, saying,**

35. **Thus saith the LORD** of hosts; Behold, **I will break the bow of Elam,** the chief of their might.

36. **And** upon Elam **will I bring the four winds** from the four quarters of heaven, **and** will **scatter them toward all those winds;** and there shall be no nation whither the outcasts of Elam shall not come.

37. For I will cause Elam to be dismayed before their enemies, and before them that seek their life: and I will bring evil upon them, *even* my fierce anger, saith the LORD; **and I will send the sword after them, till I have consumed them:**

38. **And I will set my throne in Elam,** and will destroy from thence the king and the princes, **saith the LORD.**

39. **But** it shall come to pass **in the latter days,** *that* **I will bring again the captivity of Elam,** saith the LORD.

CHAPTER 50

1. **The word that the LORD spake against Babylon** *and* against the land of the Chaldeans **by Jeremiah** the prophet.

2. **Declare ye among the nations,** and publish, and set up a standard; publish, *and* conceal not: say, **Babylon is taken,** Bel is confounded, Merodach is broken in pieces; **her idols** are confounded, her images **are broken in pieces.**

3. **For out of the north** there **cometh** up **a nation** against her, **which shall make her** land **desolate,** and none shall dwell therein: they shall remove, they shall depart, both man and beast.

4. **In those days,** and in that time, saith the LORD, the children of **Israel shall come, they and** the children of **Judah together,** going and weeping: they **shall** go, and **seek the LORD** their God.

5. **They shall ask the way to Zion** with their faces thitherward, **saying,** Come, and **let us join ourselves to the LORD in a perpetual covenant** *that* shall not be forgotten.

6. **My people hath been lost sheep: their shepherds have caused them to go astray,** they have turned them away on the mountains: they have gone from mountain to hill: **they have forgotten their restingplace.**

7. All that found them have devoured them: and **their adversaries said, We offend not, because they have sinned against the LORD,** the habitation of justice, even the LORD, the hope of their fathers.

8. **Remove out of** the midst of **Babylon,** and go forth out of the land of the Chaldeans, and be as the he goats before the flocks.

9. **For,** lo, **I will raise** and cause to come up **against Babylon an assembly of great nations from the north** country: **and** they shall set themselves in array against her; from thence **she shall be taken:** their arrows *shall be* as of a mighty expert man; none shall return in vain.

10. **And Chaldea shall be a spoil: all that spoil her shall be satisfied,** saith the LORD.

11. Because ye were glad, because ye rejoiced, O ye destroyers of mine heritage, because ye are grown fat as the heifer at grass, and bellow as bulls;

12. Your mother shall be sore confounded; she that bare you *shall be* ashamed: behold, the hindermost of the nations shall be a wilderness, a dry land, and a desert.

13. **Because of the wrath of the LORD it shall** not be inhabited, but it shall **be wholly desolate: every one that goeth by Babylon shall be astonished,** and hiss **at all her plagues.**

14. Put yourselves in array against Babylon round about: all ye that bend the bow, shoot at her, spare no arrows: **for she hath sinned against the LORD.**

15. Shout against her round about: she hath given her hand: her foundations are fallen, her walls are thrown down: for it *is* the vengeance of the LORD: take vengeance upon her; as she hath done, do unto her.

16. Cut off the sower from Babylon, and him that handleth the sickle in the time of harvest: for fear of the oppressing sword they shall turn every one to his people, and they shall flee every one to his own land.

17. **Israel is a scattered sheep;** the lions have driven *him* away: **first** the king of **Assyria** hath **devoured him; and** last this **Nebuchadrezzar** king of Babylon **hath broken his bones.**

18. **Therefore thus saith the LORD** of hosts, the God of Israel; Behold, **I will punish** the king of **Babylon and** his land, as I have punished the king of **Assyria.**

19. **And I will bring Israel again to his habitation,** and he shall feed on Carmel and Bashan, **and his soul shall be satisfied** upon mount Ephraim and Gilead.

20. **In those days,** and in that time, saith the LORD, **the iniquity of Israel** shall be sought for, and *there shall be* none; **and** the sins of **Judah,** and they **shall not be found: for I will pardon them** whom I reserve.

21. **Go up against** the land of **Merathaim,** *even* against it, **and** against the inhabitants of **Pekod:** waste **and utterly destroy** after **them, saith the LORD,** and do according to all that I have commanded thee.

22. A sound of battle *is* in the land, and of great destruction.

23. How is the hammer of the whole earth cut asunder and broken! **how is Babylon become a desolation** among the nations!

24. I have laid a snare for thee, and thou art also taken, O Babylon, and thou wast not aware: thou art found, and also caught, **because thou hast striven against the LORD.**

25. **The LORD hath** opened his armoury, and hath **brought** forth the weapons of

■ **his indignation:** for this *is* the work of the Lord GOD of hosts
■ **in the land of the**
■ **Chaldeans.**
■ 26. **Come against her from**
■ **the utmost border,** open her storehouses: çast her up as heaps,
■ **and destroy her** utterly: let nothing of her be left.

27. Slay all her bullocks; let them go down to the slaughter: woe unto them! for their day is come, the time of their visitation.

28. The voice of them that flee and escape out of the land of Babylon, to declare in Zion the vengeance of the LORD our God, the vengeance of his temple.

29. Call together the archers against Babylon: all ye that bend the bow, camp against it round about; let none thereof escape: recompense her according to her work; according to all that she hath done, do unto her: for she hath been proud against the LORD, against the Holy One of Israel.

30. Therefore shall her young men fall in the streets, and all her men of war shall be cut off in that day, saith the LORD.

31. Behold, I *am* against thee, *O thou* most proud, saith the Lord GOD of hosts: for thy day is come, the time *that* I will visit thee.

32. And the most proud shall stumble and fall, and none shall raise him up: and I will kindle a fire in his cities, and it shall devour all round about him.

■ 33. **Thus saith the LORD** of hosts; The children of
■ **Israel and** the children of
■ **Judah were oppressed**
■ **together: and all that**
■ **took them captives** held them fast; they
■ **refused to let them go.**
■ 34. **Their Redeemer is strong;**
■ **the LORD of hosts is his**
■ **name: he shall** throughly
■ **plead their cause, that he**
■ **may give rest to the land,**
■ **and disquiet** the inhabitants of
■ **Babylon.**

■ 35. **A sword is upon the**
■ **Chaldeans,** saith the LORD,
■ **and upon** the inhabitants of
■ **Babylon,** and upon her princes, and upon her wise *men.*

36. A sword *is* upon the liars; and they shall dote: a sword is upon her mighty men; and they shall be dismayed.

37. A sword is upon their horses, and upon their chariots, and upon all the mingled people that *are* in the midst of her; and they shall become as women: a sword is upon her treasures; and they shall be robbed.

38. A drought *is* upon her waters; and they shall be dried up: for it *is* the land of graven images, and they are mad upon *their* idols.

39. Therefore the wild beasts of the desert with the wild beasts of the islands shall dwell *there,* and the owls shall dwell therein:
■ **and it shall be no more**
■ **inhabited for ever;** neither shall it be dwelt in from generation to generation.

40. As God overthrew Sodom and Gomorrah and the neighbour *cities* thereof, saith the LORD; so shall no man abide there, neither shall any son of man dwell therein.

■ 41. **Behold, a people**
■ **shall come from the**
■ **north,** and a great nation, and many kings shall be raised up from the coasts of the earth.

42. They shall hold the bow and the lance:
■ **they are cruel, and**
■ **will not shew mercy:** their voice shall roar like the sea, and they shall ride upon horses,
■ **every one** put
■ **in array,** like a man to the battle,
■ **against thee, O** daughter of
■ **Babylon.**
■ 43. **The king of Babylon** hath heard the report of them, and his hands waxed feeble: anguish took hold of him, *and* pangs as of a woman in travail.

44. Behold, he

shall come up like a lion
from the swelling of Jordan
unto the habitation
of the strong: but I will
make them suddenly
run away from her: and
who is a chosen man, that
I may appoint over her?
for who *is* like me? and who will
appoint me the time? and
who is that shepherd that
will stand before me?
45. **Therefore hear** ye
the counsel of the LORD,
that he hath taken
against Babylon; and his
purposes, that he hath purposed
against the land of
the Chaldeans: Surely the least
of the flock shall draw them out:
surely he shall make *their*
habitation desolate with them.
46. At the noise of the taking of
Babylon the earth is moved, and the
cry is heard among the nations.

CHAPTER 51
1. **Thus saith the LORD;**
Behold, I will raise up
against Babylon, and against
them that dwell in the midst of them
that rise up against me,
a destroying wind;
2. **And will send** unto Babylon
fanners, that shall fan her, and
shall empty her land: for in
the day of trouble they shall be
against her round about.
3. Against *him that* bendeth let the
archer bend his bow, and against
him that lifteth himself up in
his brigandine:
and spare ye not her young men;
destroy ye utterly all
her host.
4. Thus the slain shall fall in the land
of the Chaldeans, and *they that are*
thrust through in her streets.
5. **For Israel hath not been**
forsaken, nor Judah
of his God, of the LORD of hosts;
though their land was filled
with sin against the Holy

One of Israel.
6. **Flee out of** the midst of
Babylon, and deliver
every man his soul:
be not cut off in her iniquity;
for this is the time of the
LORD's vengeance; he will
render unto her a recompence.
7. **Babylon hath been a**
golden cup in the LORD's
hand, that made all the earth
drunken: the nations have drunken
of her wine; therefore the nations
are mad.
8. **Babylon is suddenly**
fallen and destroyed:
howl for her; take balm for her pain,
if so be she may be healed.
9. We would have healed Babylon,
but she is not healed:
forsake her, and let us
go every one into his
own country: for her judgment
reacheth unto heaven, and is lifted
up *even* to the skies.
10. **The LORD hath brought**
forth our righteousness:
come, and
let us declare in Zion the
work of the LORD our God.
11. Make bright the arrows; gather
the shields: the LORD hath raised up
the spirit of the kings of the Medes:
for his device *is* against Babylon, to
destroy it; because it *is* the
vengeance of the LORD, the
vengeance of his temple.
12. Set up the standard upon the
walls of Babylon, make the watch
strong, set up the watchmen,
prepare the ambushes: for
the LORD hath both
devised and done
that which he spake
against the inhabitants of
Babylon.
13. O thou that dwellest upon
many waters, abundant in
treasures, thine end is come, *and*
the measure of thy covetousness.
14. **The LORD** of hosts
hath sworn by himself,
saying, Surely

I will fill thee with men, as with caterpillers; and they shall lift up a shout against thee. 15. He hath made the earth by his power, he hath established the world by his wisdom, and hath stretched out the heaven by his understanding.

16. When he uttereth *his* voice, *there is* a multitude of waters in the heavens; and he causeth the vapours to ascend from the ends of the earth: he maketh lightnings with rain, and bringeth forth the wind out of his treasures.

17. Every man is brutish by his knowledge; every founder is confounded by the graven image: for his molten image *is* falsehood, and *there is* no breath in them.

18. They are vanity, the work of errors: in the time of their visitation they shall perish.

19. The portion of Jacob is not like them; for he *is* the former of all things: and Israel is the rod of his inheritance: the LORD of hosts is his name.

20. Thou art my battle axe *and* weapons of war: for with thee will I break in pieces the nations, and with thee will I destroy kingdoms;

21. And with thee will I break in pieces the horse and his rider; and with thee will I break in pieces the chariot and his rider;

22. With thee also will I break in pieces man and woman; and with thee will I break in pieces old and young; and with thee will I break in pieces the young man and the maid;

23. I will also break in pieces with thee the shepherd and his flock; and with thee will I break in pieces the husbandman and his yoke of oxen; and with thee will I break in pieces captains and rulers.

24. And I will render unto Babylon and to all the inhabitants of Chaldea all their evil that they have done in Zion in your sight, saith the LORD.

25. Behold, I am against thee, O destroying mountain, saith the LORD, which destroyest all the earth: and I will stretch out mine hand upon thee, and roll thee down from the rocks, and will make thee a burnt mountain.

26. And they shall not take of thee a stone for a corner, nor a stone for foundations; but thou shalt be desolate for ever, saith the LORD.

27. Set ye up a standard in the land, blow the trumpet among the nations, prepare the nations against her, call together against her the kingdoms of Ararat, Minni, and Ashchenaz; appoint a captain against her; cause the horses to come up as the rough caterpillars.

28. Prepare against her the nations with the kings of the Medes, the captains thereof, and all the rulers thereof, and all the land of his dominion.

29. And the land shall tremble and sorrow: for every purpose of the LORD shall be performed against Babylon, to make the land of Babylon a desolation without an inhabitant.

30. The mighty men of Babylon have forborn to fight, they have remained in *their* holds: their might hath failed; they became as women: they have burned her dwellingplaces;

her bars are broken.

31. One post shall run to meet another, and one messenger to meet another, to shew the king of Babylon that his city is taken at *one* end,

32. And that the passages are stopped, and the reeds they have burned with fire, and the men of war are affrighted.

33. **For thus saith the LORD** of hosts, the God of Israel; The daughter of **Babylon is like a threshingfloor,** *it is* time to thresh her: yet a little while, **and the time of her harvest shall come.**

34. Nebuchadrezzar the king of **Babylon hath devoured me,** he hath crushed me, he hath made me an empty vessel, he hath swallowed me up like a dragon, he hath filled his belly with my delicates, **he hath cast me out.**

35. **The violence done to me** and to my flesh **be upon Babylon,** shall the inhabitant of Zion say; and my blood upon the inhabitants of C haldea, shall Jerusalem say.

36. **Therefore thus saith the LORD;** Behold, **I will plead thy cause, and take vengeance for thee;** and I will dry up her sea, and make her springs dry.

37. **And Babylon shall become heaps,** a dwellingplace for dragons, an astonishment, and an hissing, without an inhabitant.

38. They shall roar together like lions: they shall yell as lions' whelps.

39. In their heat I will make their feasts, and I will make them drunken, that they may rejoice, and sleep a perpetual sleep, and not wake, saith the LORD.

40. I will bring them down like lambs to the slaughter, like rams with he goats.

41. **How is Sheshach taken! and** how is the praise of the whole earth surprised!

how is Babylon become an astonishment among the nations!

42. The sea is come up upon Babylon: she is covered with the multitude of the waves thereof.

43. Her cities are a desolation, a dry land, and a wilderness, a land wherein no man dwelleth, neither doth *any* son of man pass thereby.

44. And I will punish Bel in Babylon, and I will bring forth out of his mouth that which he hath swallowed up: and the nations shall not flow together any more unto him: yea, **the wall of Babylon shall fall.**

45. **My people, go** ye out of the midst of her, and **deliver ye every man his soul from the fierce anger of the LORD.**

46. And lest your heart faint, and ye fear for the rumour that shall be heard in the land; a rumour shall both come *one* year, and after that in *another* year *shall* come a rumour, and violence in the land, ruler against ruler.

47. **Therefore,** behold, the days come, that **I will do judgment upon the graven images of Babylon:** and her whole land shall be confounded, and all her slain shall fall in the midst of her.

48. **Then the heaven and the earth,** and all that *is* therein, **shall sing for Babylon:** for the spoilers shall come unto her from the north, saith the LORD.

49. **As Babylon hath caused the slain of Israel to fall, so at Babylon shall fall the slain of all the earth.**

50. **Ye that have escaped** the sword, go away, stand not still: **remember the LORD afar off, and let Jerusalem come into your mind.**

51. We are confounded, because we have heard reproach: **shame hath covered our**

■ faces: for strangers are
■ come into the sanctuaries
■ of the LORD's house.

52. Wherefore, behold, the days come, saith the LORD, that I will do judgment upon her graven images: and through all her land the wounded shall groan.

53. Though Babylon should mount up to heaven, and though she should fortify the height of her strength, *yet* from me shall spoilers come unto her, saith the LORD.

■ 54. **A sound of a cry**
■ **cometh from Babylon,** and great destruction from the land of the Chaldeans:

55. Because the LORD hath spoiled Babylon, and destroyed out of her the great voice; when her waves do roar like great waters, a noise of their voice is uttered:

■ 56. **Because the spoiler is**
■ **come** upon her, *even* upon Babylon, and her mighty men are taken, every one of their bows is broken: for the LORD God of recompences shall surely requite.

57. And I will make drunk her princes, and her wise *men*, her captains, and her rulers, and her mighty men: and they shall sleep a perpetual sleep, and not wake, saith the King, whose name *is* the LORD of hosts.

58. Thus saith the LORD of hosts;
■ **The** broad
■ **walls** of Babylon
■ **shall be** utterly
■ **broken, and her** high
■ **gates** shall be
■ **burned** with fire;
■ **and the people shall labour**
■ **in vain,** and the folk in the fire, and they shall be weary.

59. The word which Jeremiah the prophet commanded Seraiah the son of Neriah, the son of Maaseiah, when he went with Zedekiah the king of Judah into Babylon in the fourth year of his reign. And *this* Seraiah *was* a quiet prince.

■ 60. **So Jeremiah wrote in**
■ **a book all the evil that**

■ should come upon
■ **Babylon,** *even* all these words that are written against Babylon.

■ 61. **And Jeremiah said**
■ **to Seraiah, When thou**
■ **comest to Babylon,**
■ **and shalt see, and** shalt
■ **read** all
■ **these words;**

■ 62. **Then shalt thou say,**
■ **O LORD, thou hast spoken**
■ **against this place,** to cut it off, that none shall remain in it, neither man nor beast, but that it shall be desolate for ever.

■ 63. **And** it shall be,
■ **when thou hast made an**
■ **end of reading this book,**
■ **that thou shalt bind a stone**
■ **to it, and cast it into the**
■ **midst of Euphrates:**

■ 64. **And** thou
■ **shalt say, Thus shall**
■ **Babylon sink,** and shall not rise from the evil that I will bring upon her: and they shall be weary.
■ **Thus far are the words**
■ **of Jeremiah.**

CHAPTER 52

■ 1. **Zedekiah**
was one and twenty years old when he began to reign, and he
■ **reigned eleven years**
■ **in Jerusalem. And his**
■ **mother's name was**
■ **Hamutal the daughter**
■ **of Jeremiah of Libnah.**
■ 2. **And he did that which**
■ **was evil in the eyes of the**
■ **LORD,** according to all that Jehoiakim had done.

3. For through the anger of the LORD it came to pass in Jerusalem and Judah, till he had cast them out from his presence, that Zedekiah rebelled against the king of Babylon.

■ 4. **And** it came to pass
■ **in the ninth year of his**
■ **reign,** in the tenth month, in the tenth *day* of the month, *that*
■ **Nebuchadrezzar**
king of Babylon

came, he and all his army,
against Jerusalem, and pitched against it, and built forts against it round about.

5. So the city was besieged unto the eleventh year of king Zedekiah.

6. And in the fourth month, in the ninth *day* of the month, the famine was sore in the city, so that there was no bread for the people of the land.

7. Then the city was broken up, and all the men of war fled, and went forth out of the city by night by the way of the gate between the two walls, which was by the king's garden;(now the Chaldeans *were* by the city round about:) and they went by the way of the plain.

8. But the army of the Chaldeans pursued after the king, and overtook Zedekiah in the plains of Jericho; and all his army was scattered from him.

9. Then they took the king, and carried him up unto the king of Babylon to Riblah in the land of Hamath; where he gave judgment upon him.

10. And the king of Babylon slew the sons of Zedekiah before his eyes: he slew also all the princes of Judah in Riblah.

11. Then he put out the eyes of Zedekiah; and the king of Babylon bound him in chains, and carried him to Babylon, and put him in prison till the day of his death.

12. Now in the fifth month, in the tenth *day* of the month, which *was* the nineteenth year of Nebuchadrezzar king of Babylon, came Nebuzar-adan, captain of the guard, which

served the king of Babylon, into Jerusalem,

13. And burned the house of the LORD, and the king's house; and all the houses of Jerusalem, and all the houses of the great *men,* burned he with fire:

14. And all the army of the Chaldeans, that *were* with the captain of the guard, brake down all the walls of Jerusalem round about.

15. Then Nebuzar-adan the captain of the guard carried away captive certain of the poor of the people, and the residue of the people that remained in the city, and those that fell away, that fell to the king of Babylon, and the rest of the multitude.

16. But Nebuzar-adan the captain of the guard left certain of the poor of the land for vinedressers and for husbandmen.

17. Also the pillars of brass that *were* in the house of the LORD, and the bases, and the brasen sea that was in the house of the LORD, the Chaldeans brake, and carried all the brass of them to Babylon.

18. The caldrons also, and the shovels, and the snuffers, and the bowls, and the spoons, and all the vessels of brass wherewith they ministered, took they away.

19. And the basons, and the firepans, and the bowls, and the caldrons, and the candlesticks, and the spoons, and the cups; that which was of gold *in* gold, and *that* which *was* of silver *in* silver, took the captain of the guard away.

20. The two pillars, one sea, and twelve brasen bulls that

were under the bases, **which king Solomon had made in the house of the LORD:** the brass of all these vessels was without weight.

21. And *concerning* the pillars, the height of one pillar *was* eighteen cubits; and a fillet of twelve cubits did compass it; and the thickness thereof *was* four fingers: *it was* hollow.

22. And a chapiter of brass *was* upon it; and the height of one chapiter *was* five cubits, with network and pomegranates upon the chapiters round about, all *of* brass. The second pillar also and the pomegranates *were* like unto these.

23. And there were ninety and six pomegranates on a side; *and* all the pomegranates upon the network *were* an hundred round about.

24. **And the captain of the guard took** Seraiah **the** chief **priest,** and Zephaniah the second priest, **and the three keepers of the door:**

25. **He took also** out of the city an eunuch, which had the charge of the men of war; and seven men of **them that were near the king's person,** which were found in the city; and the principal scribe of the host, who mustered the people of the land; **and threescore men** of the people of the land, that were **found in the midst of the city.**

26. **So Nebuzar-adan the** captain of the guard took them, and **brought them to the king of Babylon** to Riblah.

27. **And the king of Babylon smote them,** and put them **to death** in Riblah in the land of Hamath.

Thus Judah was carried away captive out of his own land.

28. This is the people whom **Nebuchadrezzar carried away captive:** in the seventh year three thousand Jews and three and twenty:

29. In the eighteenth year of Nebuchadrezzar he carried away captive from Jerusalem eight hundred thirty and two persons:

30. In the three and twentieth year of Nebuchadrezzar Nebuzar-adan the captain of the guard carried away captive of the Jews seven hundred forty and five persons: all the persons *were* **four thousand and six hundred.**

31. **And** it came to pass **in the seven and thirtieth year of the captivity of Jehoiachin king of Judah,** in the twelfth month, in the five and twentieth *day* of the month, *that* **Evil-merodach king of Babylon in the first year of his reign lifted up the head of Jehoiachin king of Judah, and brought him** forth **out of prison.**

32. **And** spake kindly unto him, and **set his throne above** the throne of **the kings** that *were* with him **in Babylon,**

33. **And** changed his prison garments: and **he did** continually **eat bread before** him all the days of his life.

34. And *for* his diet, there was a continual diet given him of **the king of Babylon,** every day a portion **until the day of his death,** all the days of his life.

THE BOOK OF LAMENTATIONS

BACKGROUND INFORMATION

Author: Jeremiah
Date Written:
629 — 586 B.C.

Number of:
Verses—154
Chapters—5
Total Words—3,415
Scan Words—1,678
Scan Words Represent
Approximately 49% of
Total Words

Theme: Five Poems of Grief Over the Condition of **Jerusalem**

OUTLINE OF THE BOOK

I. **The Destruction of** Jerusalem
   1:1 — 22

II. **The Judgement of** God **on the Remnant**
   2:1 — 22

III. **The Mercy of God for** Jerusalem
   3:1 — 66

IV. **The Former Prosperity and Present Poverty** of Jerusalem
   4:1 — 22

V. **The Prayer for Jerusalem**
   5:1 — 22

CHAPTER 1

1. How doth the city sit solitary, that was full of people! how is she become as a widow! she that was great among the nations, and princess among the provinces, how is she become tributary! 2. She weepeth sore in the night, and her tears are on her cheeks: among all her lovers she hath none to comfort her: all her friends have dealt treacherously with her, they are become her enemies. 3. Judah is gone into captivity because of affliction, and because of great servitude: she dwelleth among the heathen, she findeth no rest: all her persecutors overtook her between the straits. 4. The ways of Zion do mourn, because none come to the solemn feasts: all her gates are desolate: her priests sigh, her virgins are afflicted, and she is in bitterness. 5. Her adversaries are the chief, her enemies prosper; for the LORD hath afflicted her for the multitude of her transgressions: her children are gone into captivity before the enemy. 6. And from the daughter of Zion all her beauty is departed: her princes are become like harts that find no pasture, and they are gone without strength before the pursuer. 7. Jerusalem remembered in the days of her affliction and of her miseries all her pleasant things that she had in the days of old, when her people fell into the hand of the enemy, and none did help her: the adversaries saw her, and did mock at her sabbaths. 8. Jerusalem hath grievously sinned; therefore she is removed: all that honoured her despise her, because they have seen her nakedness: yea, she sigheth, and turneth backward. 9. Her filthiness is in her skirts; she remembereth not her last end; therefore she came down wonderfully: she had no comforter. O LORD, behold my affliction: for the enemy hath magnified himself. 10. The adversary hath spread out his hand upon all her pleasant things: for she hath seen that the heathen entered into her sanctuary, whom thou didst command that they should not enter into thy congregation. 11. All her people sigh, they seek bread; they have given their pleasant things for meat to relieve the soul: see, O LORD, and consider; for I am become vile. 12. Is it nothing to you, all ye that pass by? behold, and see if there be any sorrow like unto my sorrow, which is done unto me, wherewith the LORD hath afflicted me in the day of his fierce anger. 13. From above hath he sent fire into my bones, and it prevaileth against them: he hath spread a net for my

feet, he hath turned me back:
■ **he** hath
■ **made me desolate**
and faint all the day.
■ 14. **The yoke of my**
■ **transgressions is bound by**
■ **his hand:** they are wreathed, *and*
come up upon my neck: he
hath made my strength to fall,
■ **the LORD** hath
■ **delivered me into**
■ **their hands,** *from whom*
I am not able to rise up.
■ 15. **The LORD hath**
■ **trodden under foot** all
■ **my mighty men** in
the midst of me:
■ **he hath called an**
■ **assembly against**
■ **me** to crush my young men:
■ **the LORD hath trodden**
the virgin, the daughter of
■ **Judah, as in a winepress.**
16. For these *things*
■ **I weep;** mine eye, mine eye
runneth down with water,
■ **because the comforter**
that should relieve my soul
■ **is far from me:** my
children are desolate, because
the enemy prevailed.
■ 17. **Zion spreadeth** forth
■ **her hands,** *and*
■ **there is none to comfort**
■ **her: the LORD** hath
■ **commanded** concerning
■ **Jacob, that his**
■ **adversaries should**
■ **be** round
■ **about him: Jerusalem**
■ **is as a menstruous**
■ **woman** among them.
■ 18. **The LORD is righteous;**
■ **for I have rebelled against**
■ **his commandment:** hear,
I pray you, all people, and
■ **behold my sorrow:**
■ **my virgins and** my
■ **young men are gone**
■ **into captivity.**
19. I called for
■ **my lovers,** *but* they
■ **deceived me:** my

■ **priests and** mine
■ **elders gave up the**
■ **ghost** in the city, while
■ **they sought** their
■ **meat to relieve their souls.**
20. Behold, O LORD; for
■ **I am in distress:** my
bowels are troubled; mine
heart is turned within me;
■ **for I have** grievously
■ **rebelled:** abroad the sword
bereaveth, at home *there is* as death.
21. They have heard that I sigh:
■ **there is none to**
■ **comfort me:** all
■ **mine enemies have heard** of
■ **my trouble; they are glad**
that thou hast done *it*: thou wilt
bring the day *that* thou hast called,
and they shall be like unto me.
■ 22. **Let all their wickedness**
■ **come before thee; and do**
■ **unto them, as thou hast**
■ **done unto me** for all my
transgressions: for my sighs
are many, and my heart *is* faint.

CHAPTER 2

1. How hath
■ **the LORD covered**
the daughter of
■ **Zion with a cloud in**
■ **his anger, and cast**
down from heaven
■ **unto the earth the beauty**
■ **of Israel,** and remembered not h
is footstool in the day of his anger!
2. **The LORD hath**
■ **swallowed** up all
■ **the habitations of Jacob,**
■ **and** hath not pitied: he hath
thrown down in his wrath
■ **the strong holds** of thedaughter
■ **of Judah;** he hath brought
them down to the ground:
■ **he hath polluted the**
■ **kingdom** and the princes thereof.
3. **He hath cut off** in *his*
fierce anger all the horn of
■ **Israel: he hath drawn back**
■ **his right hand from before**
■ **the enemy,** and he burned
against Jacob like a flaming fire,

which devoureth round about.

4. **He hath bent his bow like an enemy:** he stood with his right hand as an adversary, and slew all *that were* pleasant to the eye in the tabernacle of the daughter of Zion: **he poured out his fury like fire.**

5. **The LORD was as an enemy: he** hath **swallowed up Israel,** he hath swallowed up all her palaces: **he** hath **destroyed his strong holds, and** hath **increased** in **the** daughter of Judah **mourning and lamentation.**

6. **And he hath** violently **taken away his tabernacle**, as *if it were of* a garden: he hath destroyed his places of theassembly: **the LORD** hath **caused the** solemn **feasts and sabbaths to be forgotten** in Zion, and hath despised in the indignation of his anger the king and the priest.

7. **The LORD hath cast off his altar, he** hath **abhorred his sanctuary, he hath given** up into the hand of **the enemy the walls of her palaces;** they have made a noise in the house of the LORD, as in the day of a solemn feast.

8. **The LORD hath purposed to destroy the wall** of the daughter **of Zion**: he hath stretched out a line, he hath not withdrawn his hand from destroying: therefore **he made the rampart and the wall to lament;** they languished together.

9. **Her gates are sunk into the ground;** he hath destroyed and broken her bars: **her king and** her **princes are among the Gentiles: the law is no more; her prophets** also **find no vision from the LORD.**

10. **The elders** of the daughter of Zion **sit upon the ground, and** keep silence: they have **cast** up **dust upon their heads; they have girded themselves with sackcloth:** the virgins of Jerusalem hang down their heads to the ground.

11. **Mine eyes** do **fail with tears,** my bowels are troubled, my liver is poured upon the earth, **for the destruction** of the daughter of my people; **because the children** and the sucklings swoon in the streets of the city.

12. They say to their mothers, Where *is* corn and wine? when they **swooned as the wounded in the streets** of the city, **when their soul was poured out into their mothers' bosom.**

13. **What** thing **shall I** take to **witness for thee? what** thing shall I liken to thee, **O** daughter of **Jerusalem? what shall I equal to thee, that I may comfort thee,** O virgin daughter of Zion? **for thy breach is great** like the sea: **who can heal thee?**

14. **Thy prophets have seen vain and foolish things** for thee: **and** they **have not discovered thine iniquity, to turn away thy captivity;** but have seen for thee false burdens and causes of banishment.

15. **All that pass by clap their hands at thee; they hiss and wag their head** at the daughter of Jerusalem, **saying, Is this the city that**

men call The perfection
of beauty, The joy of
the whole earth?
16. **All thine enemies
have opened their
mouth against thee**:
they hiss and gnash the teeth:
**they say, We have
swallowed her up:** certainly
this *is* the day that we looked for;
we have found, we have seen *it*.
17. **The LORD** hath done
that which he had devised; he
hath fulfilled his word that
he had commanded in the days
of old: he hath thrown down, and
hath not pitied: and
he hath
**caused thine enemy to
rejoice over thee,** he hath set
up the horn of thine adversaries.
18. **Their heart
cried** unto the LORD,
O wall of the daughter
**of Zion, let tears run
down like a river** day and
night: give thyself no rest;
**let not the apple of
thine eye cease.**
19. **Arise, cry** out
in the night: in the
beginning of the watches
pour out thine heart like water
before the face of
the LORD: lift up
thy hands toward him for the
life of thy young children, that faint for
hunger in the top of every street.
20. **Behold, O LORD, and
consider to whom thou
hast done this. Shall** the
women eat their fruit, *and*
children of a span long?
shall the priest and the
**prophet be slain in the
sanctuary** of the Lord?
21. **The young and** the
old lie on the ground in the streets:
my virgins and my young men
**are fallen by the
sword; thou hast
slain them in** the day of
thine anger; thou hast killed,

and not pitied.
22. Thou hast called as in a solemn
day my terrors round about,
so that in the day
of the LORD's anger
**none escaped nor
remained:** those that I have
swaddled and brought up hath
mine enemy consumed.

CHAPTER 3

1. **I AM the man that
hath seen affliction**
by the rod of his wrath.
2. **He hath** led me, and
**brought me into
darkness,** but not *into* light.
3. **Surely** against me is he turned;
**he turneth his hand
against me** all the day.
4. **My flesh** and my skin
hath he made old; he
hath broken my bones.
5. **He hath** builded against me,
**and compassed me with
gall and travail.**
6. **He hath set me in dark
places, as they that
be dead** of old.
7. **He hath hedged me
about,** that I cannot get out:
**he hath made my
chain heavy.**
8. **Also when I cry** and shout,
he shutteth out my prayer.
9. He hath enclosed my ways
with hewn stone, he hath
made my paths crooked.
10. **He was** unto me
as a bear lying in wait,
and *as* a
lion in secret places.
11. **He hath** turned
aside my ways, and
pulled me in pieces: he hath
made me desolate.
12. **He hath bent his
bow, and set me as
a mark** for the arrow.
13. He hath caused the arrows
of his quiver to enter into my reins
14. **I was a derision to** all
my people; *and* their

song all the day.

15. He hath filled me with bitterness, he hath made me drunken with wormwood.

16. He hath also broken my teeth with gravel stones, he hath covered me with ashes.

17. And thou hast removed my soul far off **from peace:** I forgat prosperity.

18. And I said, **My strength** and my hope **is perished from the LORD:**

19. Remembering mine affliction and my **misery,** the wormwood and the gall.

20. My soul hath *them* still in remembrance, and **is humbled in me.**

21. This I recall to my mind, **therefore have I hope.**

22. It is of the LORD's mercies that we are not consumed, because his compassions fail not.

23. They are new every morning: great is thy faithfulness.

24. The LORD is my portion, saith my soul; **therefore will I hope in him.**

25. The LORD is good unto them that wait for him, to the soul **that seeketh him.**

26. It is good that a man should both hope and quietly **wait for the salvation of the LORD.**

27. *It is* good for a man **that he bear the yoke of his youth.**

28. He sitteth alone and keepeth silence, because he hath borne *it* upon him.

29. He putteth his mouth in the dust; if so be there may be hope.

30. He giveth his cheek to him that smiteth him: he is filled full with reproach.

31. For the LORD will not cast off for ever:

32. But though he cause grief, yet **will** he

have compassion according to the multitude of **his mercies.**

33. For he doth not afflict willingly nor grieve the children of men.

34. To crush under his feet all the prisoners of the earth.

35. To turn aside the right of a man before the face of the most High,

36. To subvert a man in his cause, the LORD approveth not.

37. Who *is* he *that* **saith, and it cometh to pass, when the Lord commandeth it not?**

38. Out of the mouth of the most High proceedeth not evil and good?

39. Wherefore doth a living **man complain,** a man **for the punishment of his sins?**

40. Let us search and try our ways, and **turn again to the LORD.**

41. Let us lift up our heart with *our* hands unto God in the heavens.

42. We have transgressed and have rebelled: **thou hast not pardoned.**

43. Thou hast covered with **anger, and persecuted us:** thou hast slain, **thou hast not pitied.**

44. Thou hast covered thyself with a cloud, **that our prayer should not pass through.**

45. Thou hast made us *as* the offscouring and refuse in the midst of the people.

46. All our enemies have opened their mouths against us.

47. Fear and a snare is come upon us, desolation and destruction.

48. Mine eye runneth down **with** rivers of **water for the destruction** of the daughter **of my people.**

49. Mine eye trickleth

down, and ceaseth not,
without any intermission.

■ 50. **Till the LORD look**
■ **down,** and behold
■ **from heaven.**

51. Mine eye affecteth mine
heart because of all the
daughters of my city.

■ 52. **Mine enemies**
■ **chased me** sore, like a bird,
■ **without cause.**

■ 53. **They have cut off**
■ **my life in the dungeon,**
and cast a stone upon me.

54. Waters flowed over mine
head; *then* I said, I am cut off.

■ 55. **I called** upon thy name,
■ **O LORD, out of the**
■ **low dungeon.**

■ 56. **Thou hast heard**
■ **my voice:** hide not thine
ear at my breathing, at my cry.

■ 57. **Thou drewest**
■ **near in the day** *that*
■ **I called** upon thee:
■ **thou saidst, Fear not.**

■ 58. **O LORD,** thou hast
pleaded the causes of my soul;
■ **thou hast redeemed**
■ **my life.**

59. O LORD,
■ **thou hast seen my**
■ **wrong: judge** thou
■ **my cause.**

60. Thou hast seen all their
vengeance *and* all their
imaginations against me.

■ 61. **Thou hast heard**
■ **their reproach,** O LORD,
and all their imaginations
■ **against me;**

62. The lips of those that
rose up against me, and their
device against me all the day.

63. Behold their sitting down, and
their rising up; I *am* their musick.

■ 64. **Render** unto them a
■ **recompence,** O LORD,
■ **according to the work**
■ **of their hands.**

65. Give them sorrow of
heart, thy curse unto them.

66. Persecute and

■ **destroy them** in anger from
■ **under the**
■ **heavens** of the LORD.

CHAPTER 4

■ 1. **How is the gold**
■ **become dim!** *how* is
the most fine gold changed!
■ **the stones of the sanctuary**
■ **are poured out in** the top of
■ **every street.**

2. **The** precious
■ **sons of Zion,**
■ **comparable to** fine
■ **gold, how are they**
■ **esteemed as**
■ **earthen pitchers,** the
work of the hands of the potter!

3. **Even the sea monsters**
draw out the breast, they
■ **give suck to their young**
■ **ones:** the daughter of
■ **my people is become**
■ **cruel,** like the ostriches
in the wilderness.

4. **The tongue of the**
■ **sucking child cleaveth to**
■ **the roof of his mouth for**
■ **thirst:** the young children ask bread,
and no
man breaketh *it* unto them.

5. **They that did feed**
■ **delicately are**
■ **desolate** in the streets:
■ **they that were brought**
■ **up in scarlet embrace**
■ **dunghills.**

6. **For the punishment of**
■ **the iniquity** of the daughter
■ **of my people is greater**
■ **than** the punishment of the sin of
■ **Sodom,** that was
overthrown as in a moment,
and no hands stayed on her.

7. **Her Nazarites were**
■ **purer than snow,** they were
whiter than milk, they were more
ruddy in body than rubies, their
polishing *was* of sapphire:

8. **Their visage is blacker**
■ **than a coal;** they are not
known in the streets: their skin
cleaveth to their bones; it is

withered, it is become like a stick.

9. **They that be slain with the sword are better than they that be slain with hunger: for these pine away,** stricken through for *want* of the fruits of the field.

10. **The** hands of the pitiful **women have sodden their own children: they were their meat** in the destruction of the daughter of my people.

11. **The LORD hath accomplished his fury;** he hath poured out his fierce anger, and hath kindled a fire in Zion, and it hath devoured the foundations thereof.

12. **The kings of the earth, and all** the inhabitants of **the world, would not have believed that** the adversary and **the enemy should have entered** into the gates of **Jerusalem.**

13. **For the sins of her prophets, and** the iniquities of her **priests, that have shed the blood of the just** in the midst of her,

14. They have wandered as blind *men* in the streets, **they have polluted themselves with blood, so** that **men could not touch their garments.**

15. **They cried** unto them, **Depart ye; it is unclean;** depart, depart, touch not: **when they fled** away **and wandered,** they said **among the heathen,** They shall no more sojourn *there.*

16. **The anger of the LORD hath divided them;** he will no more regard them: **they respected not** the persons of **the priests,** they favoured not the elders.

17. **As for us,** our eyes as yet failed for our vain help: in ourwatching

we have **watched for a nation that could not save us.**

18. **They hunt our steps,** that we cannot go in our streets: **our end is near,** our days are fulfilled; for our end is come.

19. **Our persecutors are swifter than the eagles** of the heaven: they pursued us upon the mountains, they laid wait for us in the wilderness.

20. The breath of our nostrils, **the anointed of the LORD, was taken in their pits,** of whom we said, **Under his shadow we shall live among the heathen.**

21. **Rejoice** and be glad, **O daughter of Edom, that dwellest in the land of Uz;** the cup also shall pass through unto thee: **thou shalt be drunken, and** shalt **make thyself naked.**

22. **The punishment of thine iniquity is accomplished,** O daughter of **Zion; he will no more carry thee** away **into captivity:** he will visit thine iniquity, O daughter of Edom; **he will discover thy sins.**

CHAPTER 5

1. **Remember, O LORD,** what is come upon us: consider, and behold **our reproach.**

2. **Our inheritance is turned to strangers,** our houses to aliens.

3. **We are** orphans and **fatherless, our** mothers *are* as widows.

4. **We have drunken our water for money; our wood is sold unto us.**

5. **Our necks are under persecution:** we labour, *and* have no rest.

6. We have given the hand *to* the Egyptians, *and to* the Assyrians, to be satisfied with bread.

■ 7. **Our fathers have**
■ **sinned**, *and are* not;
■ **and we have**
■ **borne their iniquities.**

8. Servants have ruled over us: *there is* none that doth deliver us out of their hand.

■ 9. **We gat our bread with**
■ **the peril of our lives** because of the sword of the wilderness.

■ 10. **Our skin was**
■ **black like an oven**
■ **because of** the terrible
■ **famine.**

■ 11. **They ravished the**
■ **women in Zion,** *and* the maids in the cities of Judah.

■ 12. **Princes are**
■ **hanged** up by their hand:
■ **the** faces of
■ **elders were not honoured.**

13. **They took the**
■ **young men to grind,**
■ **and the children fell**
■ **under the wood.**

14. The elders have ceased from the gate, the young men from their musick.

■ 15. **The joy of our heart**
■ **is ceased; our dance is**
■ **turned into mourning.**

16. The crown is fallen *from* our head: woe unto us, that we have sinned!

17. For this
■ **our heart is**
■ **faint**; for these *things*
■ **our eyes are dim.**

■ 18. **Because** of the mountain of
■ **Zion,** which
■ **is desolate,** the foxes walk upon it.

■ 19. **Thou, O LORD,**
■ **remainest for ever;** thy throne from generation to generation.

■ 20. **Wherefore dost**
■ **thou forget us** for ever,
and forsake us so long time?

■ 21. **Turn thou us unto thee, O**
■ **LORD**, and we shall be turned; renew our days as of old.

■ 22. **But thou hast**
■ **utterly rejected us;**
■ **thou art** very
■ **wroth against us.**

EZEKIEL:
The Prophet Priest

Unlike Elijah and Elisha, and like Jeremiah, **Ezekiel was a priest at the time God called him to be a prophet.** *Like Daniel* **he received his call** *in a foreign land while his people were* **in captivity.** *In the first part of his prophecy* **he predicted that a final act of Judgement was coming to the land of promise. He was vindicated in his prediction** *when,* **in 597 B.C., Nebuchadnezzar destroyed** *The Holy City,* **Jerusalem. After this prophesy** *of destruction,* **Ezekiel's message changed. He spoke of a coming salvation and a new covenant** *that God would establish with his people.* ***T**he **concluding eight chapters** *of the Book of Ezekiel* **form** *some of the most* **intriguing reading** *in The Bible.* **He spoke of a** *future time* **when the Lord would redeem his people,** **re-establish Israel, and** *firmly and* **directly rule.** *The famous episode of the* **dry bones taking on flesh** *and new life* **was a** *clean* **prophecy** *of a day* **of resurrection** *and restoration.* **He also spoke** *in graphic language* **about God's ultimate triumph over all** *nations, forces, and people* **in opposition to his** *perfect* **will. Perhaps no other prophet** *has* **expressed the** *absolute* **majesty of God as did Ezekiel.** *His message, based on visions from God, was that* **whatever God does to man or for man, was an expression of his seal, for his** *own* **name and holiness. The new heart and** *new* **covenant** *that would come into being* **in the future could only be the work of God** *who acts in grace.*

THE BOOK OF EZEKIEL

BACKGROUND INFORMATION

Author: Ezekiel
Date Written:
597 — 573 B.C.

Number of:
Versus—1,273
Chapters—48
Total Words—39,407
Scan Words—17,229
Scan Words Represent
Approximately 44% of
Total Words

Theme: Ezekiel's Call
to be a Watchman,
and His
Prophetic Proclamations
of the Glory and Triumph of
God

OUTLINE OF THE BOOK

I. **Ezekiel's Commission**
    1:1 — 7:27
II. **Captivity of Jerusalem and Judah**
    8:1 — 24:27
III. **The Judgement of the Nations**
    25:1 — 32:32
IV. **The Coming Kingdom**
    33:1 — 48:35

CHAPTER 1

1. Now it came to pass in the thirtieth year, in the fourth *month,* in the fifth *day* of the month, as I was among the captives by the river of Chebar, *that* the heavens were opened, and I saw visions of God.

2. In the fifth *day* of the month, which *was* the fifth year of king Jehoiachin's captivity,

3. The word of the LORD came expressly unto Ezekiel the priest, the son of Buzi, in the land of the Chaldeans by the river Chebar; and the hand of the LORD was there upon him.

4. And I looked, and, behold, a whirlwind came out of the north, a great cloud, and a fire infolding itself, and a brightness *was* about it, and out of the midst thereof as the colour of amber, out of the midst of the fire.

5. Also out of the midst thereof *came* the likeness of four living creatures. And this *was* their appearance; they had the likeness of a man.

6. And every one had four faces, and every one had four wings.

7. And their feet were straight feet; and the sole of their feet *was* like the sole of a calf's foot: and they sparkled like the colour of burnished brass.

8. And they had the hands of a man under their wings on their four sides; and they four had their faces and their wings.

9. Their wings were joined one to another; they turned not when they went; they went every one straight forward.

10. As for the likeness of their faces, they four had the face of a man, and the face of a lion, on the right side: and they four had the face of an ox on the left side; they four also had the face of an eagle.

11. Thus *were* their faces: and their wings *were* stretched upward; two *wings* of every one *were* joined one to another, and two covered their bodies.

12. And they went every one straight forward: whither the spirit was to go, they went; *and* they turned not when they went.

13. As for the likeness of the living creatures, their appearance was like burning coals of fire, and like the appearance of lamps: it went up and down among the living creatures; and the fire was bright, and out of the fire went forth lightning.

14. And the living creatures ran and returned as the appearance of a flash of lightning.

15. Now as I beheld the living creatures, behold one wheel upon the earth by the living creatures, with his four faces.

16. The appearance of the wheels and their work was like unto the colour of a beryl: and they four had one likeness: and their appearance and their work was as it were a wheel in the middle of a wheel.

17. When they went, **they went upon their four sides: and they turned not** when they went. 18. As for **their rings,** they were so high that they **were dreadful; and** their rings were **full of eyes** round about them four. 19. **And when the living creatures went, the wheels went** by them: **and when the** living **creatures were lifted up** from the earth, **the wheels were lifted up.** 20. Whithersoever the spirit was to go, they went, thither *was their* spirit to go; and the wheels were lifted up over against them: **for the spirit of the** living **creature was in the wheels.** 21. When those went, *these* went; and when those stood, *these* stood; and when those were lifted up from the earth, the wheels were lifted up over against them: for the spirit of the living creature *was* in the wheels. 22. **And the likeness of the firmament upon the heads of the** living **creature was as** the colour of the terrible **crystal, stretched forth over their heads** above. 23. **And under the firmament were their wings** straight, the one toward the other: every one had two, which covered on this side, and every one had two, which covered on that side, their bodies. 24. **And when they went, I heard the noise of their wings, like the noise of** great **waters, as the voice of the Almighty,** the voice of speech, as the noise of an host: when they stood, they let down their wings. 25. **And there was a voice from the firmament** that *was* **over their heads,** when they stood, *and* had let down their wings. 26. **And above the firmament** that *was* over their heads **was the likeness of a throne,** as the appearance of a sapphire stone: **and upon the** likeness of the **throne was** the likeness as **the appearance of a man** above upon it. 27. **And I saw** as the colour of amber, as the appearance of **fire** round about within it, **from** the appearance of **his loins** even **upward, and** from the appearance of his loins even **downward,** I saw as it were the appearance of fire, **and it had brightness round about.** 28. **As the appearance of the bow** that is **in the cloud in the day of rain,** so *was* the appearance of the brightness round about. **This was the appearance of the likeness of the glory of the LORD. And** when I saw *it,* **I fell upon my face, and I heard a voice of one that spake.**

CHAPTER 2

1. **And he said** unto me, Son of man, **stand** upon thy feet, **and I will speak unto thee.** 2. **And the spirit** entered into me when he spake unto me, and **set me upon my feet,** that I heard him that spake unto me. 3. **And he said** unto me, Son of man, I send **thee to** the children of **Israel, to a rebellious nation** that hath rebelled against me: they and their fathers have transgressed against me, *even* unto this very day. 4. **For they are**

■ **impudent** children
■ **and stiffhearted.**
I do send thee unto them;
■ **and thou shalt say** unto them,
■ **Thus saith the Lord** GOD.
■ 5. **And** they,
■ **whether they** will
■ **hear, or** whether they will
■ **forbear,** (for
■ **they** *are* a rebellious house,) yet
■ **shall know** that
■ **there hath been a**
■ **prophet among them.**
■ 6. **And** thou, son of man,
■ **be not afraid of them,**
neither be afraid of their words,
though briers and thorns *be* with
thee, and thou dost
dwell among scorpions: be not
afraid of their words, nor be
dismayed at their looks, though
they *be* a rebellious house.
7. And thou shalt
■ **speak my words** unto
them, whether they will hear, or
whether they will forbear: for
they *are* most rebellious.
■ 8. **But** thou, son of man,
hear what I say unto thee;
■ **Be not thou**
■ **rebellious** like that
rebellious house:
■ **open thy mouth, and**
■ **eat that I give thee.**
■ 9. **And when I**
■ **looked, behold,**
■ **an hand** *was* sent unto me;
■ **and,** lo,
■ **a roll of a book** *was* therein;
10. And he spread it before me;
■ **and it was written within**
■ **and without: and**
■ **there was written therein**
■ **lamentations,** and
■ **mourning, and woe.**

CHAPTER 3

■ 1. **Moreover** he said unto
me, Son of man, eat that thou
findest; eat this roll, and go
speak unto the house of Israel.
2. So I opened my mouth, and
■ **he caused me to**

■ **eat that roll.**
3. And he said unto me, Son of
man, cause thy belly to eat, and
fill thy bowels with this roll that
I give thee. Then did I eat *it*;
■ **and it was in my mouth**
■ **as honey** for sweetness.
■ 4. **And he said** unto
me, Son of man,
■ **go,** get thee
■ **unto** the house of
■ **Israel, and speak** with
■ **my words** unto them.
■ 5. **For thou art not sent**
■ **to a people of a**
■ **strange speech**
and of an hard language,
■ **but to** the house of
■ **Israel;**
6. Not to many people of a
strange speech and of an hard
language, whose words thou
canst not understand.
Surely, had I sent thee to them, they
would have hearkened unto thee.
■ 7. **But** the house of
■ **Israel will not hearken**
■ **unto thee; for they will**
■ **not hearken unto**
■ **me:** for all the house of Israel
are impudent and hardhearted.
8. Behold, I have made thy
face strong against their faces,
and thy forehead strong
against their foreheads.
9. As an adamant harder than
flint have I made thy forehead:
■ **fear them not,** neither
be dismayed at their looks,
■ **though they be a**
■ **rebellious house.**
■ 10. **Moreover** he
said unto me, Son of man,
■ **all** my words
■ **that I shall speak** unto thee
■ **receive in thine heart,**
and hear with thine ears.
■ 11. **And go,** get thee
■ **to them** of the captivity,
unto the children of thy people,
and speak unto them,
■ **and tell them,** Thus
saith the Lord GOD;

whether they will
hear, or whether they will
forbear.
12. **Then** the spirit took me up, and
I **heard** behind me
a voice of a great
rushing, saying,
Blessed be the glory of
the LORD from his place.
13. I **heard** also
the noise of the
wings of the living creatures
that touched one another,
and the noise of the
wheels over against them,
and a noise of a great rushing.
14. **So the spirit lifted
me up,** and took me away,
and I went in bitterness,
in the heat of my spirit;
but the hand of the LORD
was strong upon me.
15. Then I came to
them of the captivity at
Tel-abib, that dwelt by the river of
Chebar; and I sat where they sat,
and remained there astonished
among them seven days.
16. **And** it came to pass at
the end of seven days, that
the word of the LORD
came unto me, saying,
17. Son of man,
I have made thee a
watchman unto the house of
Israel: therefore hear the
word at my mouth, and
give them warning from me.
18. When I say unto the
wicked, Thou shalt surely
die; and thou
givest him not warning, nor
speakest to warn the wicked from
his wicked way, to save his life;
the same
wicked man
shall die in his iniquity;
but his blood will I
require at thine hand.
19. Yet if thou warn the
wicked, and he turn not
from his wickedness, nor from
his wicked way, he shall

die in his iniquity; but thou
hast delivered thy soul.
20. **Again, When a righteous
man doth** turn from
his righteousness, and
commit iniquity, and I
lay a stumblingblock before him,
he shall die: because
thou hast not given him
warning, he shall die in his sin,
and his righteousness
which he hath done
shall not be remembered;
but his blood will I
require at thine hand.
21. **Nevertheless if thou
warn the righteous man,**
that the righteous sin not,
and he doth not sin,
he shall surely
live, because he is warned;
also thou hast
delivered thy soul.
22. **And** the hand of
the LORD was there
upon me; and he
said unto me, Arise,
go forth
into the plain, and
I will there talk with thee.
23. **Then I** arose, and
went forth into the plain:
and, behold,
the glory of the LORD
stood there, as the glory which
I saw by the river of Chebar:
and I fell on my face.
24. **Then the spirit entered
into me, and set me upon
my feet, and** spake with me, and
said unto me,
Go, shut thyself
within thine house.
25. But thou, O son of man, behold,
they shall put bands
upon thee, and shall
bind thee with them,
and thou shalt not
go out among them:
26. **And** I will make thy tongue
cleave to the roof of thy mouth, that
thou shalt be dumb,
and shalt not be to them

a reprover: for they
are a rebellious house.
27. **But** when I speak with thee,
**I will open thy mouth, and
thou shalt say** unto them,
Thus saith the Lord GOD;
**He that heareth, let
him hear; and he that
forbeareth, let him
forbear: for they are** a
rebellious house.

CHAPTER 4

1. **Thou also,** son of man,
take thee
**a tile, and
lay it before thee, and
portray upon it** the city, *even*
Jerusalem:
2. **And lay siege against it,**
and build a fort against it, and cast a
mount against it; set the camp
also against it, and set *battering*
rams against it round about.
3. **Moreover take**
thou unto thee
**an iron pan, and
set it** *for* a wall of iron
**between thee and the
city:** and set thy face against
it, and it shall be besieged, and
thou shalt lay siege against it.
**This shall be a sign
to** the house of
Israel.
4. **Lie** thou also
**upon thy left side, and
lay the iniquity** of the house
of Israel upon it: *according*
to the number of the days that
thou shalt lie upon it thou
shalt bear their iniquity.
5. For I have laid upon thee the
years of their iniquity, according
to the number of the days,
**three hundred and
ninety days:** so
**shalt thou bear the
iniquity** of the house
of Israel.
6. **And** when thou hast
accomplished them,
lie again on thy right side,

and thou shalt
bear the iniquity of the house
of Judah forty days:
I have appointed thee
each day for a year.
7. Therefore thou shalt set thy face
toward the siege of Jerusalem, and
thine arm *shall be* uncovered, and
thou shalt prophesy against it.
8. **And,** behold,
**I will lay bands
upon thee,** and
thou shalt not turn thee
from one side to another,
**till thou hast ended
the days of thy siege.**
9. **Take** thou also unto thee
wheat, and
barley, and
beans, and
lentiles, and
millet, and fitches,
and put them in one vessel,
and make thee
bread thereof,
according to the number of
the days that
**thou shalt lie upon thy side,
three hundred and ninety
days** shalt thou eat thereof.
10. **And thy meat**
which thou shalt eat
shall be by weight,
twenty shekels a day: from
time to time shalt thou eat it.
11. **Thou shalt drink** also
water by measure,
the sixth part of an hin:
from time to time shalt thou drink.
12. **And thou shalt eat it
as barley cakes,
and** thou shalt
**bake it with dung
that cometh out
of man, in their sight.**
13. **And** the LORD said, Even
thus shall the children of
Israel eat their
**defiled bread among the
Gentiles,** whither I will drive them.
14. **Then said I,** Ah
Lord GOD! behold,
my soul hath not been

■ **polluted: for from my**
■ **youth** up even till now
■ **have I not eaten** of that
which dieth of itself, or is torn in
pieces; neither came there
■ **abominable flesh**
into my mouth.
■ 15. **Then he said** unto me, Lo,
■ **I have given thee**
■ **cow's dung for**
■ **man's** dung, and thou shalt
■ **prepare thy bread**
■ **therewith.**
16. Moreover he said
unto me, Son of man, behold,
■ **I will break the staff of**
■ **bread in Jerusalem:** and
■ **they shall eat bread**
■ **by weight, and** with
care; and they shall
■ **drink water by measure,**
and with astonishment:
17. That they may want bread
and water, and be astonied
one with another, and consume
away for their iniquity.

CHAPTER 5

1. And thou, son of man,
take thee a sharp knife,
■ **take** thee
■ **a barber's razor, and**
■ **cause it to pass upon**
■ **thine head and** upon thy
■ **beard: then** take thee balances to
■ **weigh, and divide the hair.**
2. Thou shalt
■ **burn** with fire
■ **a third part in** the midst of
■ **the city, when the**
■ **days of** the
■ **siege are fulfilled:**
■ **and** thou shalt
■ **take a third** part,
■ **and smite about it**
■ **with a knife: and**
■ **a third** part thou shalt
■ **scatter in the wind;** and I
will draw out a sword after them.
3. Thou shalt
■ **also take** thereof
■ **a few** in number,
■ ■ **and bind them in thy skirts.**

■ 4. **Then** take of them again, and
■ **cast them into** the midst of
■ **the fire**, and burn them in the fire;
■ **for thereof shall a**
■ **fire come** forth
■ **into** all the house of
■ **Israel.**
5. **Thus saith the**
Lord GOD;
This is Jerusalem:
I have set it
in the midst of the
nations and countries
that are round about her.
■ 6. **And she hath changed**
■ **my judgments into**
■ **wickedness** more than the
nations, and my statutes more than
the countries that *are* round about
her: for they have refused my
judgments and my statutes,
they have not walked in them.
7. Therefore thus saith the Lord GOD;
Because ye multiplied more than the
nations that *are* round about you,
and have not walked in my statutes,
neither have kept my judgments,
neither have done according to
the judgments of the nations
that *are* round about you;
■ 8. **Therefore** thus saith
the Lord GOD; Behold, I, even
■ **I, am against thee,**
■ **and will execute**
■ **judgments in the midst of**
■ **thee** in the sight of the nations.
■ 9. **And I will do** in thee
■ **that which I have not**
■ **done, and** whereunto I
■ **will not do any more**
■ **the like, because of** all
■ **thine abominations.**
■ 10. **Therefore the fathers**
■ **shall eat the sons** in
the midst of thee,
■ **and the sons** shall eat
■ **their fathers; and I will**
■ **execute judgments** in thee,
■ **and the** whole
■ **remnant** of thee
■ **will I scatter** into all the winds.
11. Wherefore, *as* I live, saith
the Lord GOD; Surely,

because thou hast defiled my sanctuary with all thy detestable things, and with all thine abominations, therefore will I also diminish thee; neither shall mine eye spare, neither will I have any pity.

12. A third part of thee shall die with the pestilence, and with famine shall they be consumed in the midst of thee: and a third part shall fall by the sword round about thee; and I will scatter a third part into all the winds, and I will draw out a sword after them.

13. Thus shall mine anger be accomplished, and I will cause my fury to rest upon them, and I will be comforted: and they shall know that I the LORD have spoken it in my zeal, when I have accomplished my fury in them.

14. Moreover I will make thee waste, and a reproach among the nations that are round about thee, in the sight of all that pass by.

15. So it shall be a reproach and a taunt, an instruction and an astonishment unto the nations that are round about thee, when I shall execute judgments in thee in anger and in fury and in furious rebukes. I the LORD have spoken it.

16. When I shall send upon them the evil arrows of famine, which shall be for their destruction, and which I will send to destroy you: and I will increase the famine upon you, and will break your staff of bread:

17. So will I send upon you famine and evil beasts, and they shall bereave thee: and pestilence and blood shall pass through thee; and I will bring the sword upon thee. I the LORD have spoken it.

CHAPTER 6

1. And the word of the LORD came unto me, saying,

2. Son of man, set thy face toward the mountains of Israel, and prophesy against them,

3. And say, Ye mountains of Israel, hear the word of the Lord GOD; Thus saith the Lord GOD to the mountains, and to the hills, to the rivers, and to the valleys; Behold, I, even I, will bring a sword upon you, and I will destroy your high places.

4. And your altars shall be desolate, and your images shall be broken: and I will cast down your slain men before your idols.

5. And I will lay the dead carcases of the children of Israel before their idols; and I will scatter your bones round about your altars.

6. In all your dwellingplaces the cities shall be laid waste, and the high places shall be desolate; that your altars may be laid waste and made desolate, and your idols may be broken and cease, and your images may be cut down, and your works may be abolished.

7. And the slain shall fall in the midst of you, and ye shall know that I am the LORD.

8. Yet will I leave a remnant, that ye may have some that shall escape the sword among the nations, when ye shall be scattered through the countries.

9. And they that escape of you shall remember me among the nations whither they shall be carried captives, because I am broken with their whorish heart, which hath departed from me, and with their eyes, which go

a–whoring after their idols:
and they shall lothe
themselves for
the evils which
they have committed
in all their abominations.
10. **And they shall know**
that I am the LORD, and
that I have not said in vain
that I would do this
evil unto them.
11. Thus saith the Lord GOD;
Smite with thine hand, and
stamp with thy foot,
and say, Alas for all
the evil
abominations of the house
of Israel! for they shall
fall by the sword, by the
famine, and by the
pestilence.
12. He that is far off shall die of the
pestilence; and he that is near
shall fall by the sword; and he
that remaineth and is besieged
shall die by the famine:
thus will I accomplish
my fury upon them.
13. **Then shall ye know** that
I am the
LORD, when their slain *men*
shall be among their
idols round about their altars,
upon every high hill, in
all the tops of the mountains,
and under every green tree,
and under every thick oak, the place
where they did
offer sweet savour to all
their idols.
14. So will I stretch out my hand
upon them, and make the land
desolate, yea, more desolate
than the wilderness toward Diblath,
in all their habitations: and they
shall know that I *am* the LORD.

CHAPTER 7

1. **Moreover the word**
of the LORD came
unto me, saying,
2. Also, thou son of man, thus saith
the Lord GOD unto the land of Israel;

An end, the end
is come upon the four corners of
the land.
3. Now *is* the end *come* upon thee,
and **I will send mine anger**
upon thee, and will
judge thee according to
thy ways, and will recompense
upon thee all thine abominations.
4. **And mine eye shall**
not spare thee,
neither will I have pity: but
I will recompense thy ways
upon thee, and thine abominations
shall be in the midst of thee: and
ye shall know that I
am the LORD.
5. **Thus saith the Lord GOD;**
An evil, an only evil, behold,
is come.
6. An end is come, the end is come:
it watcheth for thee;
behold, it is come.
7. The morning is come unto thee, O
thou that dwellest in
the land: the time is come,
the day of trouble is
near, and not the sounding
again of the mountains.
8. **Now will I shortly pour**
out my fury upon thee,
and accomplish mine anger
upon thee: and I will judge
thee according to thy ways,
and will recompense thee
for all thine abominations.
9. And mine eye shall not spare,
neither will I have pity: I will
recompense thee according to thy
ways and thine abominations *that* are
in the midst of thee; and ye shall know
that I *am* the LORD that smiteth.
10. Behold the day, behold, it is
come: the morning is gone forth;
the rod hath blossomed,
pride hath budded.
11. **Violence is risen**
up into a rod of wickedness:
none of them
shall remain, nor of their
multitude, nor of any of their's:
neither shall there
be wailing for them.

12. The time is come, the day draweth near: let not the buyer rejoice, nor the seller mourn: **for wrath is upon all the multitude** thereof.

13. For the seller shall not return to that which is sold, although they were yet alive: for the vision *is* touching the whole multitude thereof, *which* shall not return; **neither shall any strengthen himself** in the iniquity of his life.

14. **They have blown the trumpet,** even to make all ready; **but none goeth to the battle**: for my wrath *is* upon all the multitude thereof.

15. The sword *is* without, and the pestilence and the famine within: he that *is* in the field shall die with the sword; and he that *is* in the city, famine and pestilence shall devour him.

16. **But they that escape** of them shall escape, and **shall be on the mountains** like doves of the valleys, all of them **mourning,** every one **for his iniquity.**

17. **All hands** shall be feeble, **and** all **knees shall be weak** *as* water.

18. **They shall** also **gird themselves with sackcloth**, and horror shall cover them; and **shame shall be upon all faces, and baldness upon** all **their heads.**

19. They shall cast their silver in the streets, and their gold shall be removed: **their silver and** their **gold shall not** be able to **deliver them in the day of the wrath of the LORD**: they shall not satisfy their souls, neither fill their bowels: **because it is the stumblingblock of their iniquity.**

20. **As for the beauty of his ornament,** he set it in majesty: but **they made** the **images** of their abominations *and* of their detestable things therein: therefore have I set it far from them.

21. **And I will give it into the hands of** the **strangers** for a prey, and to the wicked of the earth **for a spoil;** and they shall pollute it.

22. **My face will I turn** also **from them, and they shall pollute my secret place:** for the robbers shall enter into it, and defile it.

23. Make a chain: for the land is full of bloody crimes, and the city is full of violence.

24. **Wherefore** I will bring the worst of **the heathen, and they shall possess their houses:** I will also make the pomp of the strong to cease; **and their holy places shall be defiled.**

25. **Destruction cometh;** and **they** shall **seek peace, and there shall be none.**

26. Mischief shall come upon mischief, and rumour shall be upon rumour; **then shall they seek a vision of the prophet; but the law shall perish from the priest,** and counsel from the ancients.

27. **The king shall mourn, and** the prince shall be clothed with desolation, and the hands of **the people** of the land **shall be troubled: I will do** unto them after their way, and **according to their deserts** will I judge them; **and they shall know that I am the LORD.**

CHAPTER 8

1. **And it came to pass** in

the sixth year, in the sixth *month,*
in the fifth *day* of the month,
as I sat in mine house,
and the elders of Judah
sat before me, that
the hand of the Lord GOD
fell there
upon me.
2. Then I beheld,
and lo a likeness as the
appearance of fire:
from the appearance of
his loins even downward, fire;
and from his loins even upward, as
the appearance of
brightness, as the colour
of amber.
3. And he put forth the
form of an hand, and
took me by a lock of
mine head; and the spirit
lifted me up between
the earth and the heaven,
and brought me in the
visions of God
to Jerusalem, to the door of
the inner gate that
looketh toward the north;
where was the seat of
the image of jealousy,
which provoketh to jealousy.
4. And, behold,
the glory of the
God of Israel
was there, according to
the vision that I saw in the plain.
5. Then said he
unto me, Son of man,
lift up thine eyes now the way
toward the north. So I lifted up
mine eyes the way toward the north,
and behold northward at
the gate of the altar this
image of jealousy in the entry.
6. He said furthermore
unto me, Son of man,
seest thou
what they do?
even the great
abominations
that the house of
Israel committeth here,
that I should go far off

from my sanctuary?
but turn thee yet again, *and*
thou shalt see
greater abominations.
7. And he brought me to
the door of the court;
and when I looked, behold
a hole in the wall.
8. Then said he
unto me, Son of man,
dig now
in the wall: and when
I had digged in the wall,
behold a door.
9. And he said unto me,
Go in, and behold the wicked
abominations that
they do here.
10. So I went in and
saw; and behold
every form of creeping
things, and abominable
beasts, and all
the idols of the house of Israel,
pourtrayed upon
the wall round about.
11. And there
stood before them
seventy men of the ancients of
the house of Israel, and
in the midst of them stood
Jaazaniah the son of Shaphan,
with every man his
censer in his hand;
and a thick cloud of
incense went up.
12. Then said he unto me, Son of
man, hast thou seen what the
ancients of the house of
Israel do in the dark, every man
in the chambers of his imagery?
for they say, the LORD
seeth us not; the LORD
hath forsaken the earth.
13. He said also unto
me, Turn thee yet
again, *and*
thou shalt see greater
abominations that they do.
14. Then he brought
me to the door of the
gate of the LORD'S house
which *was* toward the north;

■ **and,** behold,
■ **there sat women**
■ **weeping for Tammuz.**
15. Then said he unto me, Hast thou seen *this*, O son of man? turn thee yet again, *and* thou shalt see greater abominations than these.
■ 16. **And he brought**
■ **me into the inner**
■ **court** of the LORD'S house,
■ **and, behold, at the door**
■ **of the temple** of the LORD,
between the porch and the altar,
■ **were** about
■ **five and twenty men,**
■ **with their backs**
■ **toward** the temple of
■ **the LORD,** and their
faces toward the east;
■ **and they worshipped**
■ **the sun** toward the east.
■ 17. **Then he said** unto me, Hast thou seen *this,* O son of man?
■ **Is it a light thing to** the house of
■ **Judah that they commit** the
■ **abominations** which they
commit here? for they have filled the land with violence,
■ **and** have returned to
■ **provoke me to anger:** and, lo, they put the branch to their nose.
■ 18. **Therefore will I** also
deal in fury: mine eye shall
■ **not** spare, neither will I
■ **have pity: and though they**
■ **cry** in mine ears with a loud voice,
■ **yet will I not hear them.**

CHAPTER 9

■ 1. **He cried also** in mine
ears with a loud voice, saying,
■ **Cause them that have**
■ **charge over the city to**
■ **draw near,** even every man *with*
his destroying weapon in his hand.
■ 2. **And,** behold,
■ **six men came from** the way of
the higher gate, which lieth toward
■ **the north, and every**
■ **man a** slaughter
■ **weapon** in his hand;
■ **and one** man among them
■ **was clothed with linen, with**

■ **a writer's inkhorn by**
■ **his side: and they went**
■ **in, and stood beside**
■ **the brasen altar.**
■ 3. **And the glory of** the
■ **God** of Israel
■ **was gone** up
■ **from the cherub,** whereupon he
was, to the threshold of the house.
■ **And he called** to
■ **the man** clothed with linen,
■ **which had the writer's**
■ **inkhorn** by his side;
■ 4. **And the LORD said unto**
■ **him, Go through** the midst of
■ **the city,** through the
midst of Jerusalem,
■ **and set a mark upon**
■ **the foreheads of** the
■ **men that** sigh and that
■ **cry for** all
■ **the abominations** that
be done in the midst thereof.
■ 5. **And to the others he**
■ **said** in mine hearing,
■ **Go ye** after him through the city,
■ **and** smite: let not your eye
spare, neither have ye pity:
■ 6. **Slay** utterly
■ **old and young,** both
maids, and little
■ **children, and women: but**
■ **come not near any man**
■ **upon whom is the mark;**
■ **and begin at my sanctuary.**
Then they began at the ancient
men which *were* before the house.
■ 7. **And** he said unto them,
■ **Defile the house, and fill**
■ **the courts with the slain:**
go ye forth. And they went forth, and slew in the city.
■ 8. **And** it came to pass,
■ **while they were slaying**
■ **them,** and I was left, that
■ **I fell upon my face,**
■ **and cried,** and said, Ah
■ **Lord** GOD!
■ **wilt thou destroy all the**
■ **residue of Israel** in thy pouring
out of thy fury upon Jerusalem?
■ 9. **Then said he** unto me,
■ **The iniquity** of the house

of Israel and
Judah is exceeding
great, and the land is full of blood,
and the city full of perverseness:
for they say, The LORD hath
forsaken the earth, and
the LORD seeth not.
10. **And** as for me also,
mine eye shall not spare,
neither will I have pity,
but I will recompense their
way upon their head.
11. **And**, behold,
the man clothed with linen,
which *had* the inkhorn by his side,
reported the matter, saying,
I have done as thou hast
commanded me.

CHAPTER 10

1. **Then I looked, and**, behold,
in the firmament that was
above the head of
the cherubims there
appeared over them as it were
a sapphire
stone, as the appearance of
the likeness of a throne.
2. **And he spake unto**
the man clothed
with linen, and said,
Go in
between the wheels,
even under the cherub,
and fill thine hand
with coals of fire
from between the cherubims,
and scatter them over the
city. And he went in in my sight.
3. **Now the cherubims**
stood on the right
side of the house,
when the man went in; and
the cloud filled the inner court.
4. **Then the glory of the**
LORD went up from the cherub, *and*
stood over the
threshold of the house;
and the house was
filled with the cloud, and
the court was full of
the brightness of
the LORD'S glory.

5. **And the sound of the**
cherubims' wings was
heard *even* to the outer court,
as the voice of the Almighty
God when he speaketh.
6. **And it came**
to pass, that
when he had
commanded the man
clothed with linen,
saying, Take fire from
between the wheels, from
between **the cherubims;**
then he went in, and
stood beside the wheels.
7. **And one cherub**
stretched forth his hand
from between the cherubims
unto the fire that *was*
between the cherubims,
and took thereof, and put it
into the hands of him *that was*
clothed with linen: who took *it,*
and went out.
8. **And there appeared**
in the cherubims the form of
a man's hand under their wings.
9. **And** when I looked, behold the
four wheels by the
cherubims, one wheel by
one cherub, and another wheel
by another cherub: and the
appearance of the wheels
was as the colour of a beryl stone.
10. And *as for* their
appearances,
they four had one
likeness, as if a wheel
had been in the
midst of a wheel.
11. **When they went,**
they went upon their four sides;
they turned not as they went,
but to the place whither the head
looked they followed it; they
turned not as they went.
12. **And their** whole
body, and their
backs, and their
hands, and their
wings, and the wheels,
were full of eyes round about,
even the wheels that they four had.

13. As for the wheels, it was cried unto them in my hearing, O wheel.

14. **And every one had four faces:** the first face *was* **the face of a cherub,** and the second face *was* **the face of a man,** and the third **the face of a lion, and** the fourth **the face of an eagle.**

15. **And the cherubims were lifted up.** This *is* the living creature that I saw by the river of Chebar.

16. **And** when the cherubims went, **the wheels went by them: and** when the cherubims lifted up their wings to mount up from the earth, the same wheels also **turned not from beside them.**

17. When they stood, *these* stood; and when they were lifted up, *these* lifted up themselves *also*: **for the spirit of the living creature was in them.**

18. **Then the glory of the LORD departed from** off **the threshold** of the house, **and stood over the cherubims.**

19. **And the cherubims lifted up** their wings, and mounted up **from the earth** in my sight: when they went out, **the wheels also were beside them, and every one stood at the door** of the east gate **of the LORD'S house; and the glory of** the **God** of Israel **was over them** above.

20. **This is the living creature** that **I saw** under the God of Israel by the river of Chebar; **and I knew** that **they were** the **cherubims.**

21. **Every one had four faces** apiece, **and** every one **four wings; and**

the likeness of the **hands** of a man *was* **under their wings.**

22. And the likeness of their faces *was* the same faces which I saw by the river of Chebar, their appearances and themselves: they went every one straight forward.

CHAPTER 11

1. **Moreover the spirit lifted me up, and brought me unto** the east gate of **the LORD'S house,** which looketh eastward: **and behold** at the door of the gate **five and twenty men; among whom I saw Jaazaniah** the son of Azur, **and Pelatiah** the son of Benaiah, princes of the people.

2. **Then said he unto me,** Son of man, **these are the men that devise mischief,** and give wicked counsel in this city:

3. **Which say,** *It is* not near; **let us build houses: this city is the caldron, and we be the flesh.**

4. **Therefore prophesy against them,** prophesy, O son of man.

5. **And the Spirit** of the LORD **fell upon me, and said** unto me, Speak; **Thus saith the LORD;** Thus have ye said, O house of Israel: for **I know the things that come into your mind,** *every one of* them.

6. Ye have multiplied your slain in this city, and **ye have filled the streets** thereof **with the slain.**

7. **Therefore** thus saith the Lord GOD; **Your slain** whom ye have laid in the midst of it, they **are the flesh, and this**

city is the caldron: but
I will bring you forth
out of the midst
of it.

8. Ye have feared the sword;
and I
will bring a sword
upon you, saith the Lord GOD.
9. And I will bring you out
of the midst thereof,

and deliver you into the
hands of strangers, and
will execute judgments
among you.

10. Ye shall fall by the sword; I will
judge you in the border of Israel;
and ye shall know
that I am the LORD.

11. This city shall not be
your caldron, neither
shall ye be the
flesh in the midst thereof;
but I will judge you
in the border of Israel:

12. And ye shall know
that I am the LORD:
for ye have not
walked in my statutes, neither
executed my judgments, but have
done after the manners of the
heathen that are round about you.

13. And it came to pass,
when I prophesied, that
Pelatiah the son of Benaiah
died. Then fell I down
upon my face, and cried
with a loud voice, and said, Ah
Lord GOD! wilt thou
make a full end of the
remnant of Israel?

14. Again the word of
the LORD came unto me,
saying,

15. Son of man,
thy brethren, even thy brethren,
the men of thy kindred, and all the
house of Israel wholly, are they unto
whom the inhabitants of Jerusalem
have said, Get you
far from the LORD: unto us
is this land given in possession.

16. Therefore say,
Thus saith the Lord GOD;

Although I have
cast them far off
among the heathen,
and although I have
scattered them among the
countries, yet will I be to
them as a little sanctuary in
the countries where they shall come.

17. Therefore say, Thus
saith the Lord GOD;
I will even
gather you from the
people, and assemble
you out of the countries
where ye have been
scattered, and I
will give you the
land of Israel.

18. And they shall come thither,
and they shall take away all
the detestable things thereof
and all
the abominations
thereof from thence.

19. And I will give them
one heart, and I will put
a new spirit within you; and I will
take the stony heart out of their flesh,
and will give them an heart of flesh:

20. That they may walk in
my statutes, and keep mine
ordinances, and do them:
and they shall be
my people, and I
will be their God.

21. But as for
them whose heart
walketh after the heart of their
detestable things and
their abominations, I will
recompense their way upon their
own heads, saith the Lord GOD.

22. Then did the cherubims
lift up their wings, and the
wheels beside them; and
the glory of the God of Israel
was over them above.

23. And the glory of the LORD
went up from the midst of the city,
and stood upon the mountain
which is on the east side of the city.

24. Afterwards the
spirit took me up, and

■ **brought me in a**
■ **vision** by the Spirit of God
■ **into Chaldea, to them**
■ **of the captivity.** So the vision
that I had seen went up from me.
■ 25. **Then I spake unto**
■ **them of** the captivity all
■ **the things** that
■ **the LORD** had
■ **shewed me.**

CHAPTER 12

■ 1. **The word of the LORD** also
■ **came unto me, saying,**
2. Son of man,
■ **thou dwellest in** the midst of
■ **a rebellious house,** which have
eyes to see, and see not; they have
ears to hear, and hear not: for they
are a rebellious house.
■ 3. **Therefore**, thou son of man,
prepare thee stuff for removing, and
remove by day in their sight; and
■ **thou shalt**
■ **remove** from thy place
■ **to another place** in their sight:
■ **it may be they will**
■ **consider,** though they
be a rebellious house.
■ 4. **Then** shalt thou
■ **bring** forth
■ **thy stuff** by day in their sight, as
stuff for removing:
■ **and** thou shalt
■ **go** forth at even in their sight,
■ **as they that go** forth
■ **into captivity.**
■ 5. **Dig** thou
■ **through the**
■ **wall** in their sight,
■ **and carry** out thereby.
6. In their sight shalt thou bear
■ **it upon thy**
■ **shoulders, and** carry *it* forth
■ **in the twilight**: thou shalt
■ **cover thy face,** that
thou see not the ground:
■ **for I have set thee for**
■ **a sign unto** the house of
■ **Israel**.
■ 7. **And I did so** as I was
commanded: I brought forth my
stuff by day, as stuff for captivity,

■ **and** in the even I digged
through the wall with mine hand;
■ **I brought it forth** in the twilight,
and I bare *it* upon *my* shoulder
■ **in their sight.**
■ 8. **And in the morning came**
■ **the word of the LORD** unto me,
■ **saying,**
9. Son of man,
■ **hath not** the house of
■ **Israel,** the rebellious house,
■ **said** unto thee,
■ **What doest thou?**
■ 10. **Say thou unto them,**
■ **Thus saith the Lord** GOD;
■ **This burden concerneth**
the prince in Jerusalem, and
■ **all** the house of
■ **Israel** that *are* among them.
■ 11. **Say, I am your sign**: like
■ **as I have done, so shall**
■ **it be done unto them:** they
shall remove *and* go into captivity.
■ 12. **And the prince**
that *is* among them
■ **shall bear upon his**
■ **shoulder in the twilight,**
■ **and** shall go forth: they
■ **shall dig through the**
■ **wall** to carry out thereby:
■ **he shall cover his face,**
■ **that he see not** the
ground with *his* eyes.
■ 13. **My net also will I**
■ **spread upon him,** and
he shall be taken in my snare:
■ **and I will bring him**
■ **to Babylon** *to* the land
of the Chaldeans;
■ **yet shall he not see**
■ **it, though he** shall
■ **die there.**
■ 14. **And I will**
■ **scatter** toward every wind
■ **all that are about him** to
help him, and all his bands; and
I will draw out the sword after them.
■ 15. **And they shall know** that
■ **I am the LORD,** when I shall
scatter them among the nations,
and disperse them in the countries.
■ 16. **But I will leave a few** men
of them from the sword, from the

famine, and from the pestilence;
that they may declare all
their abominations among
the heathen whither they
come; and they shall know
that I *am* the LORD.

17. **Moreover the word**
of the LORD came
to me, saying,
18. Son of man, eat thy bread with
quaking, and drink thy water with
trembling and with carefulness;
19. And say unto the people of
the land, Thus saith the Lord
GOD of the inhabitants of
Jerusalem, *and* of the land of Israel;
They shall eat their
bread with carefulness,
and drink their water
with astonishment, that
her land may be desolate
from all that is therein,
because of the
violence of all them that dwell
therein.
20. **And the cities**
that are inhabited
shall be laid waste, and
the land shall be desolate; and ye
shall know that I *am* the LORD.
21. **And the word of the**
LORD came unto me,
saying,
22. Son of man,
what is that
proverb *that* ye have
in the land of
Israel, saying, The
days are prolonged,
and every vision faileth?
23. **Tell them** therefore,
Thus saith the Lord GOD;
I will make this proverb
to cease, and they shall no
more use it as a proverb in Israel;
but say unto them,
The days are at hand,
and the effect of every vision.
24. **For there shall be no**
more any vain vision
nor flattering divination
within the house of
Israel.

25. **For** I *am* the
LORD: I will speak, and
the word that
I shall
speak shall come to pass; it
shall be no more prolonged: for
in your days, O rebellious house,
will I say the word, and will
perform it, saith the Lord GOD.
26. Again the word of the
LORD came to me, saying.
27. Son of man, behold,
they of the house of
Israel say, The
vision that he seeth
is for many days to come,
and he prophesieth
of the times *that are*
far off.
28. **Therefore** say unto them,
Thus saith the Lord GOD;
There shall none of my
words be prolonged
any more, but the word which
I have spoken shall be done,
saith the Lord GOD.

CHAPTER 13

1. **And the word of the**
LORD came unto me,
saying,
2. Son of man,
prophesy against the
prophets of Israel that
prophesy, and say thou unto
them that prophesy out
of their own hearts, Hear
ye the word of the LORD;
3. **Thus saith the Lord** GOD;
Woe unto the foolish
prophets, that follow
their own spirit, and
have seen nothing!
4. **O Israel, thy**
prophets are like the
foxes in the deserts.
5. **Ye have not gone** up
into the gaps, neither made
up the hedge for the house of
Israel to stand in the
battle in the day
of the LORD.
6. **They have seen vanity**

■ **and lying divination,**
■ **saying,** The LORD saith: and
the LORD hath not sent them:
and they have made *others* to hope
that they would confirm the word.
7. Have ye not seen a vain vision,
and have ye not spoken a lying
divination, whereas ye say,
■ **The LORD saith it; albeit**
■ **I have not spoken?**
■ 8. **Therefore** thus saith
the Lord GOD; Because ye
have spoken vanity, and
seen lies, therefore, behold,
■ **I am against you,**
saith the Lord GOD.
■ 9. **And mine hand shall**
■ **be upon the prophets** that see
vanity, and that divine lies:
■ **they shall not be in the**
■ **assembly** of my people,
■ **neither shall they be written**
■ **in the writing of** the house of
■ **Israel, neither shall**
■ **they enter** into
■ **the land of Israel;** and ye
shall know that I *am* the Lord GOD.
10. Because, even
■ **because they** have
■ **seduced my people,** saying,
Peace; and *there was* no peace; and
■ **one built** up
■ **a wall, and,** lo,
■ **others daubed it with**
■ **untempered morter:**
■ 11. **Say unto them which**
■ **daub** *it* with untempered *morter,*
■ **that it shall fall:** there shall
be an overflowing shower; and ye,
O great hailstones, shall fall;
and a stormy wind shall rend *it.*
12. Lo, when the wall is fallen, shall
it not be said unto you, Where *is* the
daubing wherewith ye have daubed*it?*
13. Therefore thus
saith the Lord GOD;
■ **I will even rend it with** a stormy
■ **wind** in my fury;
■ **and** there shall be
■ **an overflowing**
■ **shower** in mine anger,
■ **and great hailstones**
■ **in my fury** to consume *it.*

14. So will I break down the wall that
ye have daubed with untempered
morter, and bring it down to the
ground,
■ **so that the foundation**
thereof shall be discovered, and it
■ **shall fall, and ye shall be**
■ **consumed in the midst**
■ **thereof**: and ye shall know
that I *am* the LORD.
■ 15. **Thus will I accomplish**
■ **my wrath** upon the wall,
and upon them that have daubed
it with untempered *morter,*
■ **and will say** unto you,
■ **The wall is no more,**
■ **neither they that daubed it;**
16. *To wit,* the prophets of Israel
which prophesy concerning
Jerusalem, and which see visions
of peace for her, and *there is* no
peace, saith the Lord GOD.
17. **Likewise,** thou son of man,
■ **set thy face against the**
■ **daughters** of thy people,
■ **which prophesy out of their**
■ **own heart;** and prophesy
thou against them,
■ 18. **And say, Thus**
■ **saith the Lord** GOD;
■ **Woe to the women that sew**
■ **pillows to all armholes, and**
■ **make kerchiefs**
■ **upon the head of every**
■ **stature to hunt souls!** Will ye
hunt the souls of my people, and
■ **will ye save the souls**
■ **alive that come unto you?**
■ 19. **And will ye pollute me**
■ **among my people for**
handfuls of barley and for pieces of
■ **bread**, to slay the souls that should
not die, and to save the souls alive
that should not live, by your lying to
my people that hear *your* lies?
20. Wherefore thus saith the Lord
GOD; Behold,
■ **I am against your pillows,**
wherewith ye there hunt the souls
to make *them* fly, and I will tear
them from your arms, and will let
the souls go, *even* the souls
that ye hunt to make *them* fly.

21. **Your kerchiefs also will I tear, and deliver my people out of your hand, and they shall be no more** in your hand to be **hunted**; and ye shall know that I *am* the LORD. 22. **Because with lies ye** have **made** the heart of **the righteous sad,** whom I have not made sad; **and strengthened the** hands of the **wicked,** that he should not return from his wicked way, **by promising him life:** 23. **Therefore** ye shall see no more vanity, nor divine divinations: for **I will deliver my people out of your hand:** and ye shall know that I *am* the LORD.

CHAPTER 14

1. **Then came** certain of **the elders of Israel unto me,** and sat before me. 2. **And the word of the LORD came unto me, saying,** 3. Son of man, **these men** have **set up** their **idols** in their heart, and put the stumblingblock of their iniquity before their face: **should I be inquired of** at all **by them?** 4. **Therefore** speak unto them, and say unto them, Thus saith the Lord GOD; **Every man** of the house of Israel **that setteth up** his **idols** in his heart, and putteth the stumblingblock of his iniquity before his face, **and cometh to the prophet; I the LORD will answer him** that cometh according to the multitude of his idols; 5. **That I may take** the house of **Israel in their own heart, because they are** all **estranged from me through their idols.**

6. **Therefore** say unto the house of Israel, Thus saith the Lord GOD; **Repent, and turn** *yourselves* **from your idols**; and turn away your faces from all your abominations. 7. **For every one** of the house of Israel, or of the stranger **that** sojourneth in Israel, which **separateth himself from me, and setteth up his idols in his heart,** and putteth the stumblingblock of his iniquity before his face, **and cometh to a prophet to inquire of** him concerning **me; I** the LORD will answer him by myself: 8. And I **will set my face against that man, and will make him** a sign and **a proverb, and** I will **cut him off from** the midst of **my people;** and ye shall know that I *am* the LORD. 9. **And if the prophet be deceived** when he hath spoken a thing, **I the LORD have deceived that prophet, and I** will stretch out my hand upon him, and **will destroy him** from the midst of my people Israel. 10. And they shall bear the punishment of their iniquity: the punishment of the prophet shall be even as the punishment of him that seeketh *unto him;* 11. **That** the house of **Israel may go no more astray** from me, neither be polluted any more with all their transgressions; **but that they may be my people, and I** may be **their God,** saith the Lord GOD. 12. **The word of the LORD came** again to me, **saying,** 13. Son of man, **when the land sinneth against me** by trespassing grievously,

■ **then will I** stretch out mine hand
upon it, and will break the staff
of the bread thereof, and will
■ **send famine upon it,**
■ **and will cut off man**
■ **and beast from it:**
14. **Though** these three men,
Noah, Daniel, and Job,
were in it, they should
deliver but their own souls
by their righteousness,
saith the Lord GOD.
■ 15. **If I cause** noisome
■ **beasts to** pass through
the land, and they
■ **spoil it, so that it be**
■ **desolate,** that no man may pass
through because of the beasts:
16. *Though* these three men *were* in
it, *as* I live, saith the Lord GOD,
they shall deliver neither sons
nor daughters; they only shall
be delivered, but the land shall
be desolate.
■ 17. **Or if I bring a**
■ **sword** upon that land,
■ **and say,** Sword,
■ **go through the land;** so that
I cut off man and beast from it:
18. Though these three men *were* in
it, *as* I live, saith the Lord GOD, they
shall deliver neither sons nor
daughters, but they only shall
be delivered themselves.
■ 19. **Or if I send a**
■ **pestilence** into that land,
■ **and pour out my fury**
■ **upon it** in blood, to cut off
from it man and beast:
■ 20. **Though Noah, Daniel,**
■ **and Job were in it,**
as I live, saith the Lord GOD,
■ **they shall deliver neither**
■ **son nor daughter;** they shall
■ **but** deliver
■ **their own souls**
by their righteousness.
■ 21. **For thus saith**
■ **the Lord** GOD;
■ **How much more when**
■ **I send my** four sore
■ **judgments upon**
■ **Jerusalem**, the sword,

and the famine, and the
noisome beast, and the pestilence,
■ **to cut off** from it
■ **man and beast?**
■ 22. **Yet**, behold,
■ **therein shall be left**
■ **a remnant** that shall be
brought forth, *both* sons
and daughters: behold,
■ **they shall come**
■ **forth** unto you,
■ **and ye shall see their way**
■ **and** their doings: and ye shall
■ **be comforted concerning**
■ **the evil** that I have brought
■ **upon Jerusalem,**
even concerning all that
I have brought upon it.
23. And they shall comfort you,
when ye see their ways and their
doings: and ye shall know that
I have not done without cause all that
I have done in it, saith the Lord GOD.

CHAPTER 15

■ 1. **And the word of the LORD**
■ **came unto me, saying,**
2. Son of man,
■ **what is the vine** tree
more than any tree,
■ **or** *than*
■ **a branch** which is
■ **among the trees**
■ **of the forest?**
■ 3. **Shall wood** be taken thereof to
■ **do any work? or will**
■ **men** take a pin of it to
■ **hang any**
■ **vessel thereon?**
■ 4. **Behold, it is cast into the**
■ **fire for fuel;** the fire devoureth both
the ends of it, and the midst of it is
burned. Is it meet for *any* work?
5. Behold,
■ **when it was whole, it**
■ **was meet for no**
■ **work: how much less**
shall it be meet yet for *any* work,
■ **when** the fire hath devoured it, and
■ **it is burned?**
6. Therefore thus saith the Lord GOD;
■ **As the vine tree**
■ **among the trees** of the forest,

which I have given to the fire
for fuel, so will I give the
inhabitants of Jerusalem.
7. And I will set my face
against them; they shall go
out from *one* fire, and *another* fire
shall devour them; and ye shall
know that I *am* the LORD, when
I set my face against them.
8. And I will
make the land desolate,
because they have
committed a trespass,
saith the Lord GOD.

CHAPTER 16

1. Again the word
of the LORD came
unto me, saying,
2. Son of man,
cause Jerusalem to know
her abominations,
3. And say, Thus saith
the Lord GOD unto Jerusalem;
Thy birth and thy nativity
is of the land of
Canaan; thy father *was* an
Amorite, and thy mother an Hittite.
4. And *as for* thy nativity,
in the day thou wast born
thy navel was not cut,
neither wast thou
washed in water to supple *thee;*
thou wast not salted at all,
nor swaddled at all.
5. None eye
pitied thee, to do
any of these unto thee,
to have compassion upon thee;
but thou wast cast
out in the open field,
to the lothing of thy person,
in the day that thou wast born.
6. And when
I passed by thee,
and saw thee polluted in
thine own blood, I said unto thee
when thou wast in thy blood, Live;
yea, I said unto thee
when thou wast in thy blood,
Live.
7. I have caused thee to
multiply as the bud of the field, and

thou hast increased and waxen great,
and thou art come to
excellent ornaments:
thy breasts are fashioned,
and thine hair is grown,
whereas thou
wast naked and bare.
8. Now when I
passed by thee, and
looked upon thee, behold, thy time
was the time of love; and
I spread my skirt over
thee, and covered thy
nakedness: yea,
I sware unto thee, and
entered into a covenant
with thee, saith the Lord GOD,
and thou becamest mine.
9. Then washed I thee
with water; yea, I throughly
washed away thy blood from thee,
and I anointed
thee with oil.
10. I clothed thee also with
broidered work, and shod thee with
badgers' skin, and I girded thee about
with fine linen,
and I covered thee with
silk.
11. I decked thee also
with ornaments, and I put
bracelets upon thy hands, and
a chain on thy neck.
12. And I put a jewel on thy
forehead, and earrings in
thine ears, and a beautiful
crown upon thine head.
13. Thus wast thou decked with
gold and silver; and thy raiment
was of fine linen, and silk, and
broidered work; thou didst eat
fine flour, and honey, and oil:
and thou wast exceeding
beautiful, and thou
didst prosper into a kingdom.
14. And thy renown went forth
among the heathen for thy beauty:
for it *was* perfect through my
comeliness, which I had put
upon thee, saith the Lord GOD.
15. But thou didst trust
in thine own beauty,
and playedst the

■ **harlot** because of thy renown,
■ **and pouredst out thy**
■ **fornications on every**
■ **one** that passed by; his it was.
16. And of thy garments
thou didst take,
■ **and deckedst thy high**
■ **places with divers colours,**
and playedst the harlot
thereupon: *the like things* shall
not come, neither shall it be *so.*
■ 17. **Thou hast** also
■ **taken thy** fair
■ **jewels** of my gold and of
my silver, which I had given thee,
■ **and madest** to thyself
■ **images of men, and**
■ **didst commit**
■ **whoredom with them,**
■ 18. **And tookest thy**
■ **broidered garments,**
■ **and coveredst them:**
and thou hast set mine oil
and mine incense before them.
■ 19. **My meat** also
■ **which I gave thee,**
fine flour, and oil, and
honey, *wherewith* I fed thee,
■ **thou hast** even
■ **set it before them for**
■ **a sweet savour:** and
thus it was, saith the Lord GOD.
■ 20. **Moreover thou hast**
■ **taken thy sons and** thy
■ **daughters,** whom
thou hast borne unto me,
■ **and** these hast thou
■ **sacrificed** unto
■ **them** to be devoured. *Is this* of
thy whoredoms a small matter,
21. That thou hast slain my children,
■ **and delivered**
■ **them** to cause them
■ **to pass through**
■ **the fire** for them?
■ 22. **And in all thine**
■ **abominations**
and thy whoredoms
■ **thou hast not**
■ **remembered** the days of
■ **thy youth, when thou**
■ **wast naked** and bare,
■ **and** wast

■ **polluted** in thy blood.
■ 23. **And it came to pass** after
all thy wickedness, (woe, woe unto
thee! saith the LORD GOD;)
■ 24. **That thou** hast also
built unto thee an eminent
place, and hast
■ **made** thee
■ **an high place**
■ **in every street.**
■ 25. **Thou** hast built thy high place
at every head of the way, and
■ **hast made thy beauty to**
■ **be abhorred, and hast**
opened thy feet to every one
that passed by, and
■ **multiplied thy whoredoms.**
■ 26. **Thou hast** also
■ **committed fornication with**
■ **the Egyptians** thy neighbours,
great of flesh; and hast increased thy
whoredoms, to provoke me to anger.
27. Behold,
■ **therefore I have** stretched
out my hand over thee, and have
diminished thine ordinary *food,* and
■ **delivered thee unto the will**
■ **of them that hate thee,** the
daughters of the Philistines, which
are ashamed of thy lewd way.
■ 28. **Thou hast played the**
■ **whore also with the**
■ **Assyrians, because thou**
■ **wast unsatiable;** yea, thou hast
played the harlot with them,
and yet couldest not be satisfied.
■ 29. **Thou hast** moreover
■ **multiplied thy fornication**
in the land of Canaan
■ **unto Chaldea; and yet** thou
■ **wast not satisfied** therewith.
30. How weak is thine heart, saith
the LORD GOD, seeing thou doest
all these *things,* the work of
an imperious whorish woman;
31. In that thou buildest thine eminent
place in the head of every way, and
makest thine high place in every
street; and hast not been as an
harlot, in that thou scornest hire;
■ 32. **But as a wife that**
committeth adultery, *which*
■ **taketh strangers instead**

of her husband!

33. **They give gifts to all whores: but thou givest** thy **gifts to** all **thy lovers, and hirest them,** that they may come unto thee on every side for thy whoredom.

34. **And the contrary is in thee from other women in thy whoredoms, whereas none followeth thee** to commit whoredoms: **and** in that **thou givest a reward, and no reward is given unto thee,** therefore thou art contrary.

35. **Wherefore, O harlot, hear the word of the LORD:**

36. Thus saith the Lord GOD; **Because thy filthiness was poured out, and thy nakedness discovered** through thy whoredoms with thy lovers, and **with** all the **idols** of thy abominations, **and** by **the blood of thy children, which thou didst give** unto **them;**

37. Behold, **therefore I will gather** all **thy lovers,** with whom thou hast taken pleasure, and all *them* that thou hast loved, with all *them* that thou hast hated; I will even gather them round about **against thee**, and will discover thy nakedness unto them, **that they may see all thy nakedness.**

38. **And I will judge thee, as women that break wedlock** and shed blood **are judged**; and I will give thee blood in fury and jealousy.

39. **And I will** also **give thee into their hand, and they shall throw down thine** eminent place, and shall break down thy **high places: they shall strip thee** also of thy

clothes, and shall take thy fair jewels, and leave thee naked and bare.

40. **They shall** also **bring** up **a company against thee, and** they shall **stone thee** with stones, and thrust thee through with their swords.

41. **And they shall burn thine houses** with fire, and execute judgments upon thee in the sight of many women: **and I will cause thee to cease from playing the harlot,** and thou also shalt give no hire any more.

42. **So will I make my fury** toward thee **to rest,** and my jealousy shall depart from thee, **and I will be** quiet, and will be **no more angry.**

43. **Because thou hast not remembered the days of thy youth,** but hast fretted me in all these *things*; behold, **therefore I** also **will recompense thy way** upon *thine* head, saith the Lord GOD: **and thou shalt not commit this lewdness** above all thine abominations.

44. **Behold, every one** that useth proverbs **shall use this proverb against thee, saying, As is the mother, so is her daughter.**

45. **Thou art thy mother's daughter, that lotheth her husband and** her **children**; and thou *art* the sister of thy sisters, which loathed their husbands and their children: **your mother was an Hittite, and your father an Amorite.**

46. **And thine elder sister is Samaria,** she and her daughters that dwell at thy left hand: **and thy younger sister,** that dwelleth at thy right hand,

is Sodom and her daughters.

47. **Yet hast thou not**
walked after their ways, nor
done after
their abominations: but,
as *if that were* a very little *thing*,
thou wast corrupted
more than they in
all thy ways.

48. *As* I live, saith the Lord GOD,
Sodom thy sister hath not done,
she nor her daughters, as thou
hast done, thou and thy daughters.

49. **Behold, this was**
the iniquity of thy sister
Sodom, pride, fulness of
bread, and abundance
of idleness was in her
and in her daughters,
neither did she strengthen
the hand of the poor
and needy.

50. **And they were**
haughty, and committed
abomination before me:
therefore I took them
away as I saw *good.*

51. **Neither hath Samaria**
committed half of thy sins;
but thou hast multiplied thine
abominations more than they, and
hast justified thy sisters in all thine
abominations which thou hast done.

52. **Thou also, which hast**
judged thy sisters, bear
thine own shame for thy
sins that thou hast committed
more abominable than they:
they are more righteous
than thou: yea, be thou
confounded also, and bear
thy shame, in that thou hast
justified thy sisters.

53. **When I shall bring**
again their captivity,
the captivity of
Sodom and her daughters,
and the captivity of
Samaria and her daughters,
then will I bring
again the captivity of
thy captives in the
midst of them:

54. **That thou mayest**
bear thine own shame,
and mayest
be confounded in all that
thou hast done, in that thou art
a comfort unto them.

55. **When** thy sisters,
Sodom and her daughters,
shall return to their former estate,
and Samaria and her daughters
shall return to their
former estate, then
thou and thy daughters
shall return to your
former estate.

56. For thy sister Sodom was
not mentioned by thy mouth
in the day of thy pride,

57. Before thy wickedness was
discovered, as at the time of *thy*
reproach of the daughters of Syria,
and all *that are* round about her, the
daughters of the Philistines, which
despise thee round about.

58. **Thou hast borne thy**
lewdness and thine
abominations, saith the LORD.

59. **For** thus saith the Lord GOD;
I will even
deal with thee
as thou hast done,
which hast despised
the oath in breaking
the covenant.

60. **Nevertheless I will**
remember my covenant
with thee in the days of thy youth,
and I will establish unto thee
an everlasting covenant.

61. **Then thou shalt**
remember thy ways, and
be ashamed, when thou shalt
receive thy sisters, thine elder
and thy younger: and I will give
them unto thee for daughters,
but not by thy covenant.

62. And I will establish my
covenant with thee;
and thou shalt know
that I am the LORD:

63. **That thou mayest**
remember, and be confounded,
and never open thy

■ **mouth** any more
■ **because of thy shame,**
■ **when I am pacified toward**
■ **thee for all that thou hast**
■ **done,** saith the Lord GOD.

CHAPTER 17

■ 1. **And the word of the LORD**
■ **came unto me, saying,**
2. Son of man, put forth a riddle, and
■ **speak a parable**
■ **unto** the house of
■ **Israel;**
■ 3. **And say,** Thus saith
the Lord GOD;
■ **A great eagle** with great wings,
longwinged, full of feathers,
■ **which had divers colours,**
■ **came unto Lebanon,**
■ **and took the highest**
■ **branch of the cedar:**
■ 4. **He cropped off**
■ **the top** of his
■ **young twigs, and carried**
■ **it into** a land of traffic; he set it in
■ **a city** of merchants.
■ 5. **He took also of**
■ **the seed** of the land,
■ **and planted it in a** fruitful
■ **field;** he placed *it*
■ **by great waters,** *and* set
it *as* a willow tree.
■ 6. **And it grew, and**
■ **became a** spreading
■ **vine** of low stature,
■ **whose branches**
■ **turned toward him,**
■ **and the roots** thereof
■ **were under him:** so it became
a vine, and brought forth
branches, and shot forth sprigs.
■ 7. **There was** also
■ **another great**
■ **eagle** with great wings
■ **and** many feathers: and, behold,
■ **this vine did bend**
■ **her roots** toward him,
■ **and** shot forth her
■ **branches toward him,**
■ **that he might water it**
by the furrows of her plantation.
■ 8. **It was planted in a**
■ **good soil by great**

■ **waters,** that it might
bring forth branches, and
■ **that it might bear fruit,**
that it might be a goodly vine.
■ 9. **Say thou, Thus**
■ **saith the Lord** GOD;
■ **Shall it prosper? shall he**
■ **not pull up the roots** thereof,
■ **and cut off the fruit** thereof,
■ **that it wither?** it shall wither in
all the leaves of her spring, even
without great power or many people
to pluck it up by the roots thereof.
10. Yea, behold, *being* planted,
shall it prosper? shall it not utterly
wither, when the east wind toucheth
it? it shall wither in the furrows
where it grew.
11. Moreover the word of the
LORD came unto me, saying,
■ 12. **Say now to the**
■ **rebellious house,** Know ye not
what these *things mean*? tell *them,*
■ **Behold, the king of Babylon**
■ **is come to Jerusalem, and**
■ **hath taken the king** thereof,
■ **and the princes** thereof,
■ **and led them** with him
■ **to Babylon;**
■ 13. **And hath taken** of
■ **the king's seed, and made**
■ **a covenant with him,** and
hath taken an oath of him: he hath
also taken the mighty of the land:
■ 14. **That the kingdom**
■ **might** be base, that it might
■ **not lift itself up,** *but* that
by keeping of his covenant
it might stand.
15. **But he rebelled** against him
■ **in sending** his
■ **ambassadors into Egypt,**
■ **that they might give him**
■ **horses and much people.**
Shall he prosper? shall he escape
that doeth such *things*? or
■ **shall he break the**
■ **covenant, and**
■ **be delivered?**
16. **As I live,** saith the Lord GOD,
■ **surely** in the place
■ **where the king dwelleth**
■ **that made him king,**

■ **whose oath he despised**,
and whose covenant he brake,
■ **even with him** in the
midst of Babylon
■ **he shall die**.
■ 17. **Neither shall**
■ **Pharaoh** with *his* mighty
army and great company
■ **make for him** in the
■ **war,** by casting up
mounts, and building forts,
■ **to cut off many persons:**
■ 18. **Seeing he despised**
■ **the oath by breaking the**
■ **covenant,** when, lo, he
had given his hand, and hath
done all these *things*,
■ **he shall not escape.**
■ 19. **Therefore** thus saith the
Lord GOD; *As* I live, surely mine
oath that he hath despised, and
■ **my covenant that he**
■ **hath broken,** even it
■ **will I recompense**
■ **upon his own head.**
■ 20. **And I will spread**
■ **my net upon him,** and he
shall be taken in my snare,
■ **and** I will
■ **bring him to Babylon, and**
■ **will plead with him there**
■ **for his trespass** that he
hath trespassed against me.
■ 21. **And** all
■ **his fugitives** with all his bands
■ **shall fall by the sword, and**
■ **they that remain shall be**
■ **scattered** toward all winds:
and ye shall know that I
the LORD have spoken *it*.
22. Thus saith the Lord GOD;
■ **I will also take** of
■ **the highest branch**
■ **of the** high
■ **cedar, and** will set *it;* I
■ **will crop off from**
■ **the top** of his young
■ **twigs** a tender one,
■ **and** will
■ **plant it upon an high**
■ **mountain** and eminent:
23. In the mountain of the
height of Israel will I plant it:

■ **and it shall bring forth**
■ **boughs, and bear fruit,**
and be a goodly cedar: and
under it shall dwell all fowl of
every wing; in the shadow of the
branches thereof shall they dwell.
■ 24. **And all the trees** of the field
■ **shall know that I** the LORD
■ **have brought down the**
■ **high tree, have exalted the**
■ **low tree,** have dried up the green tree,
■ **and** have
■ **made the dry tree** to
■ **flourish**: I the LORD have
spoken and have done *it.*

CHAPTER 18

■ 1. **The word of the**
■ **LORD came** unto me
■ **again, saying,**
■ 2. **What mean ye**, that ye use
■ **this proverb**
■ **concerning** the land of
■ **Israel, saying, The fathers**
■ **have eaten sour grapes,**
■ **and the children's teeth**
■ **are set on edge?**
3. *As* I live, saith the Lord GOD,
■ **ye shall not** have
occasion any more to
■ **use this proverb in Israel.**
■ 4. **Behold, all souls are**
■ **mine**; as the soul of the father,
so also the soul of the son is mine:
■ **the soul that sinneth,**
■ **it shall die.**
■ 5. **But if a man be just,**
■ **and do** that which is lawful and
■ **right,**
6. *And* hath not eaten upon the
mountains, neither hath lifted up
his eyes to the idols of the house
of Israel, neither hath defiled his
neighbour's wife, neither hath come
near to a menstruous woman,
7. And hath not oppressed any,
but hath restored to the debtor his
pledge, hath spoiled none by
violence, hath given his bread to
the hungry, and hath covered the
naked with a garment;
8. He *that* hath not given forth upon
usury, neither hath taken any

increase, *that* hath withdrawn his hand from iniquity, hath executed true judgment between man and man,

9. Hath walked in my statutes,

■ **and hath kept my**
■ **judgments**, to deal truly; he *is* just,
■ **he shall surely live**,
saith the Lord GOD.

10. **If he beget a son that**
■ **is a robber, a shedder of**
■ **blood, and** *that* doeth the
like to *any* one of these *things,*

11. And that doeth not any of those *duties*, but even hath eaten upon the mountains, and defiled his neighbour's wife,

12. Hath oppressed the poor and needy, hath spoiled by violence, hath not restored the pledge, and hath lifted up his eyes to the idols,

■ **hath committed**
■ **abomination,**

13. Hath given forth upon usury, and hath taken increase: shall he then live? he shall not live: he hath done all these abominations;

■ **he shall surely die**; his
blood shall be upon him.

14. ■ **Now**, lo,
■ **if he beget a son,**
■ **that seeth** all
■ **his father's sins** which he
hath done, and considereth,
■ **and doeth not such** like,

15. *That* hath not eaten upon the mountains, neither hath lifted up his eyes to the idols of the house of Israel, hath not defiled his neighbour's wife,

16. Neither hath oppressed any, hath not withholden the pledge, neither hath spoiled by violence, *but* hath given his bread to the hungry, and hath covered the naked with a garment,

17. *That* hath taken off his hand from the poor, *that* hath not received usury nor increase, hath executed my judgments, hath walked in my statutes;

■ **he shall not die for the**
■ **iniquity of his father,**
he shall surely live.

18. *As for* his father, because he cruelly oppressed, spoiled his brother by violence, and did *that* which *is* not good among his people, lo, even he shall die in his iniquity.

19. ■ **Yet say ye**, Why?
■ **doth not the son bear the**
■ **iniquity of the father?**
■ **When the son hath done**
that which is lawful and
■ **right**, and hath kept all my statutes, *and* hath done them,
■ **he shall surely live.**

20. ■ **The soul that sinneth,**
■ **it shall die.** The son shall not bear the iniquity of the father, neither shall the father bear the iniquity of the son: the righteousness of
■ **the righteous shall be**
■ **upon him, and the**
■ **wickedness of the**
■ **wicked shall be upon him.**

21. ■ **But if the wicked**
■ **will turn from** all
■ **his sins** that he hath committed, and keep all my statutes,
■ **and do that which**
■ **is** lawful and
■ **right**, he shall surely live,
■ **he shall not die.**

22. ■ **All his transgressions**
that he hath committed, they
■ **shall not be**
■ **mentioned unto him:**
■ **in his righteousness**
that he hath done
■ **he shall live.**

23. ■ **Have I any pleasure** at all
■ **that the wicked should**
■ **die?** saith the Lord GOD:
■ **and not that he should**
■ **return from his ways,**
■ **and live?**

24. ■ **But when the**
■ **righteous** turneth away
from his righteousness, and
■ **committeth iniquity,** *and* doeth according to all the abominations that the wicked *man* doeth,
■ **shall he live? All his**
■ **righteousness** that he hath done
■ **shall not be mentioned:** in his trespass that he hath trespassed,

■ **and in his sin** that he
hath sinned, in them
■ **shall he die.**
■ 25. **Yet ye say, The way**
■ **of the LORD is not equal.**
■ **Hear now, O** house of
■ **Israel;** Is not my way equal?
are not your ways unequal?
■ 26. **When a righteous**
■ **man** turneth away from his
righteousness, and
■ **committeth**
■ **iniquity,** and dieth in them;
■ **for his iniquity** that he hath done
■ **shall he die.**
■ 27. **Again, when the wicked**
■ **man turneth away**
■ **from his wickedness**
that he hath committed,
■ **and doeth that**
■ **which is** lawful and
■ **right, he shall save**
■ **his soul alive.**
28. Because he considereth, and
turneth away from all his
transgressions that he hath
committed, he shall surely
live, he shall not die.
29. Yet saith the house of Israel, The
way of the LORD is not equal. O
house of Israel, are not my ways
equal? are not your ways unequal?
■ 30. **Therefore I will**
■ **judge** you, O house of Israel,
■ **every one according to**
■ **his ways**, saith the Lord GOD.
■ **Repent,** and turn *yourselves* from
all your transgressions;
■ **so iniquity shall not**
■ **be your ruin.**
■ 31. **Cast away** from you all
■ **your transgressions,**
whereby ye have transgressed;
■ **and make you a new**
■ **heart and** a new
■ **spirit: for why will ye**
■ **die**, O house of Israel?
■ 32. **For I have no**
■ **pleasure in** the
■ **death** of him that dieth,
saith the Lord GOD:
■ **wherefore turn** *yourselves*,
■ **and live** ye.

CHAPTER 19

■ 1. **Moreover take** thou up
■ **a lamentation for the**
■ **princes of Israel,**
■ 2. **And say, What is**
■ **thy mother? A lioness:**
■ **she lay down among**
■ **lions,** she nourished her
whelps among young lions.
■ 3. **And she brought up one**
of her whelps: it became a young lion,
■ **and it** learned to catch the prey; it
■ **devoured men.**
■ 4. **The nations** also
■ **heard of him;** he
was taken in their pit,
■ **and they brought him**
■ **with chains unto** the land of
■ **Egypt.**
■ 5. **Now when** she saw
that she had waited, *and*
■ **her hope was lost,** then
■ **she took another** of her whelps,
■ **and made him**
■ **a young lion.**
■ 6. **And he** went up and down among
the lions, he became a young lion, and
■ **learned to catch** the prey,
■ **and devoured men.**
■ 7. **And he** knew their
desolate palaces, and he
■ **laid waste their cities;**
■ **and the land was desolate,**
and the fulness thereof,
■ **by the noise of his roaring.**
■ 8. **Then the nations set**
■ **against him** on every
side from the provinces,
■ **and spread their net over**
■ **him:** he was taken in their pit.
■ 9. **And they put him in** ward in
■ **chains, and brought**
■ **him to** the king of
■ **Babylon:** they brought him
into holds, that his voice should
no more be heard upon the
mountains of Israel.
■ 10. **Thy mother is**
■ **like a vine** in thy blood,
■ **planted by** the
■ **waters: she was fruitful**
■ **and full of branches**
by reason of many waters.

11. And she had strong rods for the sceptres of them that bare rule, and her stature was exalted among the thick branches, and she appeared in her height with the multitude of her branches.

12. **But she was plucked up in fury, she was cast** down **to the ground, and the** east **wind dried** up **her fruit: her** strong **rods were broken and** withered; the **fire consumed them.**

13. **And now she is planted in the wilderness, in a dry and thirsty ground.**

14. And fire is gone out of a rod of her branches, *which* hath devoured her fruit, so that she hath no strong rod *to be* a sceptre to rule. **This** *is* a lamentation, and **shall be for a lamentation.**

CHAPTER 20

1. **And it came to pass** in the seventh year, in the fifth *month*, the tenth *day* of the month, **that certain** of the **elders of Israel came to inquire of the LORD**, and sat before me.

2. **Then came the word of the LORD unto me, saying,**

3. Son of man, **speak unto the elders** of Israel, **and say** unto them, Thus saith the Lord GOD; Are ye come to inquire of me? *As* I live, saith the Lord GOD, **I will not be inquired of by you.**

4. Wilt thou judge them, son of man, wilt thou judge *them*? **cause them to know the abominations of their fathers:**

5. **And say** unto them, Thus saith the Lord GOD; **In the day when I chose Israel,** and lifted up mine hand unto the seed of the house of Jacob, **and made myself known unto them in the land of Egypt,** when I lifted up mine hand unto them, **saying, I am** the LORD **your God;**

6. In the day *that* **I lifted up mine hand** unto them, **to bring them forth** of the land of Egypt **into a land that I had espied for them, flowing with milk and honey,** which *is* the glory of all lands:

7. **Then said I** unto them, **Cast ye away** every man **the abominations of** *his* eyes, and defile not yourselves with the idols of Egypt: I *am* the LORD your God.

8. **But they rebelled** against me, and would not hearken unto me: they did not every man cast away the abominations of their eyes, neither did they forsake the idols of Egypt: **then I said, I will pour out my fury upon them, to** accomplish my anger against them in the midst of the land of Egypt.

9. **But I wrought for my name's sake, that it should not be polluted before the heathen, among whom** they *were*, in whose sight **I made myself known** unto them, **in bringing them** forth **out of** the land of **Egypt.**

10. **Wherefore I** caused them to go forth out of the land of Egypt, and **brought them into the wilderness.**

11. **And** I **gave them my statutes, and** shewed them my judgments, which *if* a man do, he shall even live in them.

12. Moreover also I gave them **my sabbaths, to be a sign between me and them,** that they might know that I *am* the LORD that sanctify them.

13. **But** the house of **Israel rebelled** against me in the wilderness: they walked not in my statutes, **and** they **despised my judgments,** which *if* a man do, he shall even live in them; **and my sabbaths they** greatly **polluted: then I said, I would** pour out my fury upon them in the wilderness, to **consume them.**

14. **But** I wrought **for my name's sake,** that it should not be polluted before the heathen, in whose sight **I brought them out.**

15. **Yet** also I lifted up my hand unto them in the wilderness, that **I would not bring them into the land** which I had given *them,* **flowing with milk and honey,** which *is* the glory of all lands;

16. **Because they despised my judgments,** and walked not in my statutes, but polluted my sabbaths: for their heart went after their idols.

17. **Nevertheless mine eye spared** them **from destroying them,** neither did I make an end of them in the wilderness.

18. **But I said unto their children** in the wilderness, **Walk** ye **not in the statutes of your fathers,** neither observe their judgments, **nor defile yourselves with their idols:**

19. I *am* the LORD your God; walk in my statutes, and **keep my judgments,** and do them;

20. **And hallow my sabbaths; and** they shall be a sign between me and you, that ye **may know that I am the LORD** your God.

21. **Notwithstanding the children rebelled** against me: they walked not in my statutes, neither kept my judgments to do them, which *if* a man do, he shall even live in them; they polluted my sabbaths: **then I said, I would pour out my fury upon them,** to accomplish my anger against them **in the wilderness.**

22. **Nevertheless** I withdrew mine hand, and wrought **for my name's sake,** that it should not be polluted in the sight of the heathen, in whose sight **I brought them forth.**

23. **I lifted up mine hand** unto them also **in the wilderness, that I would scatter them among the heathen,** and disperse them through the countries;

24. **Because they** had not executed my judgments, but had **despised my statutes,** and had polluted my sabbaths, and their eyes were after their fathers' idols.

25. Wherefore I gave them also statutes *that were* not good, and judgments whereby they should not live;

26. **And I polluted them** in their own gifts, in that they caused to pass through *the fire* all that openeth the womb, **that I might make them desolate,** to the end **that they might know that I am the LORD.**

27. **Therefore,** son of man, **speak unto** the house of **Israel, and say** unto them, Thus saith the Lord GOD; Yet **in this your fathers** have **blasphemed me,** in that they have committed a trespass against me.

28. **For when I had brought them into the land,** *for* the which I lifted up mine hand to give it to them, then **they saw every high hill,** and all the

■ **thick trees, and they**
■ **offered** there their
■ **sacrifices,** and there they
presented the provocation of
their offering: there also they
made their sweet savour, and poured
out there their drink offerings.
■ 29. **Then I said** unto them,
■ **What is the high place**
■ **whereunto ye go?** And
the name whereof is called
Bamah unto this day.
30. Wherefore say unto
the house of Israel,
■ **Thus saith the Lord** GOD;
■ **Are ye polluted after**
■ **the manner of your**
■ **fathers? and commit** ye
■ **whoredom** after their
abominations?
■ 31. **For when ye offer**
■ **your gifts, when ye**
■ **make your sons** to
■ **pass through** the
■ **fire, ye pollute**
■ **yourselves with** all your
■ **idols,** even unto this day:
and shall I be inquired of by
you, O house of Israel?
■ **As I live, saith the Lord** GOD,
■ **I will not be inquired**
■ **of by you.**
32. And that which cometh into
your mind shall not be at all, that
■ **ye say, We will be as** the
■ **heathen,** as the
families of the countries,
■ **to serve wood and stone.**
■ 33. **As I live, saith the Lord**
GOD, surely with a mighty hand,
and with a stretched out arm, and
■ **with fury** poured out,
■ **will I rule over you:**
■ 34. **And I will bring**
■ **you out** from the people,
and will gather you out
■ **of the countries wherein ye**
■ **are scattered,** with a mighty
hand, and with a stretched out arm,
and with fury poured out.
■ 35. **And I will bring you into**
■ **the wilderness** of the people,
■ **and** there will I

■ **plead with you**
■ **face to face.**
■ 36. **Like** as
■ **I pleaded with your**
■ **fathers** in the wilderness of
the land of Egypt, so will I plead
with you, saith the Lord GOD.
■ 37. **And I will cause you**
■ **to pass under the rod,**
and I will bring you into the
bond of the covenant:
■ 38. **And** I will
■ **purge out from among**
■ **you the rebels,** and them
that transgress against me: I
will bring them forth out of the
country where they sojourn, and
■ **they shall not**
■ **enter into** the land of
■ **Israel:** and ye shall know
that I *am* the LORD.
■ 39. **As for you, O** house of
■ **Israel,** thus saith the Lord GOD;
■ **Go** ye,
■ **serve** ye every one his
■ **idols,** and hereafter *also*,
■ **if ye will not hearken**
■ **unto me: but pollute** ye
■ **my holy name no more** with
your gifts, and with your idols.
■ 40. **For in mine holy**
■ **mountain,** in the mountain of the
height of Israel, saith the Lord GOD,
■ **there shall** all the house of
■ **Israel,** all of them in the land,
■ **serve me**: there will I accept them,
■ **and there will I require your**
■ **offerings, and** the firstfruits of
■ **your oblations,** with
all your holy things.
■ 41. **I will accept you**
with your sweet savour,
■ **when I bring you out from**
■ **the people,** and gather you
out of the countries wherein
ye have been scattered;
■ **and I will be sanctified in**
■ **you before the heathen.**
■ 42. **And ye shall know that**
■ **I am the LORD, when I**
■ **shall bring you into the**
■ **land of Israel,** into the
country *for* the which I lifted up mine

hand to give it to your fathers.

■ 43. **And there shall ye**
■ **remember your ways,**
■ **and** all your doings, wherein
ye have been defiled; and ye
■ **shall lothe yourselves**
in your own sight
■ **for all your evils** that
ye have committed.
■ 44. **And ye shall know that**
■ **I am the LORD when I**
■ **have wrought with you**
■ **for my name's sake, not**
■ **according to your wicked**
■ **ways,** nor according to your
corrupt doings, O ye house of
Israel, saith the Lord GOD.
■ 45. **Moreover the word**
■ **of the LORD came**
■ **unto me, saying,**
46. Son of man,
■ **set thy face toward the**
■ **south,** and drop *thy word*
toward the south,
■ **and prophesy against**
■ **the forest** of the south field;
47. And say to the forest of the south,
Hear the word of the LORD; Thus
saith the Lord GOD; Behold,
■ **I will kindle a fire**
■ **in thee, and** it shall
■ **devour** every green tree in
■ **thee,** and every dry tree:
■ **the** flaming
■ **flame shall not be**
■ **quenched, and all** faces
from the south to the north
shall be burned therein.
48. And all
■ **flesh shall see that I** the LORD
■ **have kindled it**: it shall
not be quenched.
■ 49. **Then said I,** Ah
■ **Lord** GOD!
■ **they say** of me,
■ **Doth he not**
■ **speak parables?**

CHAPTER 21

■ 1. **And the word of the LORD**
■ **came unto me, saying,**
2. Son of man,
■ **set thy face toward**

■ **Jerusalem,** and drop *thy word*
toward the holy places,
■ **and prophesy** against
the land of Israel,
■ 3. **And say to the**
■ **land of Israel, Thus**
■ **saith the LORD**; Behold,
■ **I am against thee, and** will
draw forth my sword out of his
sheath, and will cut off from thee
the righteous and the wicked.
4. Seeing then that
■ **I will cut off from thee the**
■ **righteous and the wicked,**
therefore shall my sword go forth
out of his sheath against all flesh
from the south to the north:
■ 5. **That all** flesh
■ **may know** that
■ **I** the LORD
■ **have drawn** forth
■ **my sword** out of his sheath:
it shall not return any more.
■ 6. **Sigh therefore,** thou
son of man, with the breaking
of *thy* loins; and
■ **with bitterness** sigh
before their eyes.
■ 7. **And** it shall be,
■ **when they say** unto thee,
■ **Wherefore sighest**
■ **thou?** that thou shalt
■ **answer,** For the tidings;
■ **because it cometh: and**
■ **every heart shall melt,** and all
■ **hands** shall be feeble,
■ **and** every spirit shall faint, and all
■ **knees shall be weak**
■ **as water:** behold,
■ **it cometh,** and shall
be brought to pass,
■ **saith the Lord** GOD.
■ 8. **Again** the word of the
LORD came unto me, saying,
9. Son of man,
■ **prophesy, and say,** Thus saith
the LORD; Say, A sword,
■ **a sword is**
■ **sharpened, and** also
■ **furbished:**
10. It is sharpened to make a
sore slaughter; it is furbished that
it may glitter: should we then

make mirth? it contemneth the
rod of my son, *as* every tree.

11. And he hath given it to be
furbished, that it may be handled:
this sword is sharpened,
and it is furbished, to
**give it into the hand
of the slayer.**

12. **Cry and howl,** son of
man: for it *shall be* upon my
people, it shall be upon all the
princes of Israel: terrors
**by reason of the
sword** shall be
upon my people:
smite therefore upon *thy* thigh.

13. Because it is a trial, and what
if *the sword* contemn even the rod? it
shall be no *more,* saith the Lord GOD.

14. Thou therefore, son of
man, prophesy,
**and smite thine hands
together. and let the sword
be doubled the third time,**
the sword of the slain: it *is* the sword
of the great *men that are* slain, which
entereth into their privy chambers.

15. **I have set the point
of the sword against** all
**their gates, that their heart
may faint,** and *their* ruins be
multiplied: ah! *it is* made bright,
**it is wrapped up
for the slaughter.**

16. Go thee one way or other, *either*
on the right hand, *or* on the left,
whithersoever thy face *is* set.

17. **I will also smite mine
hands together, and** I will
cause my fury to rest:
I the LORD have said *it.*

18. The word of the LORD
came unto me again, saying,

19. **Also, thou son of man,
appoint thee two ways,
that the sword of** the king of
**Babylon may
come: both** twain
shall come forth
out of one land: and
choose thou
a place, choose *it*
at the head of the

way to the city.

20. **Appoint a way, that
the sword may come to
Rabbath** of the Ammonites,
and to
Judah in Jerusalem the defenced.

21. **For** the king of
Babylon stood at
the parting of the way,
at the head of the
**two ways, to use
divination:** he made
his arrows bright,
**he consulted with
images,** he looked in the liver.

22. **At his right hand was the
divination for Jerusalem,**
to appoint captains, to open the
mouth in the slaughter, to lift up the
voice with shouting, to appoint
battering rams against the gates, to
cast a mount, *and* to build a fort.

23. **And it shall be** unto them
**as a false divination in their
sight,** to them that
have sworn oaths: but
**he will call to
remembrance the
iniquity,** that they may be taken.

24. **Therefore** thus
saith the Lord GOD;
Because ye have made your
iniquity to be remembered, in that
**your transgressions are
discovered,** so that in all
your doings your sins do appear;
because, *I say,* that ye are
come to remembrance,
ye shall be taken
with the hand.

25. **And thou,** profane
wicked prince of Israel,
whose day is come, when iniquity
shall have an end,

26. Thus saith the Lord GOD;
Remove the diadem, and
take off the crown: this *shall* not
be the same: exalt *him that is*
low, and abase *him that is* high.

27. I will overturn,
overturn, overturn, it: and
**it shall be no more, until he
come whose right it is; and I**

■ will give it him.
■ 28. **And** thou, son of man,
■ **prophesy** and say,
Thus saith the Lord GOD
■ **concerning the**
■ **Ammonites, and** concerning
■ **their reproach**; even
say thou, The sword,
■ **the sword is drawn**: for
the slaughter *it is* furbished, to
consume because of the glittering:
■ 29. **Whiles they**
■ **see vanity** unto thee,
■ **whiles they divine a lie**
■ **unto thee, to bring thee**
■ **upon the** necks of *them that are*
■ **slain**, of the wicked,
whose day is come,
■ **when their iniquity**
■ **shall have an end.**
30. Shall I cause *it* to return into
his sheath? I will judge thee in the
place where thou wast created,
in the land of thy nativity.
■ 31. **And I will pour out**
■ **mine indignation upon**
■ **thee,** I will blow against thee
in the fire of my wrath,
■ **and deliver thee into the**
■ **hand of brutish men,**
and skilful to destroy.
■ 32. **Thou shalt be for**
■ **fuel to the fire;** thy blood
shall be in the midst of the land;
■ **thou shalt be no more**
■ **remembered:** for I
the LORD have spoken *it.*

CHAPTER 22

■ 1. **Moreover** the word of the
LORD came unto me, saying,
2. Now, thou son of man, wilt thou
■ **judge**, wilt thou judge
■ **the bloody city?** yea, thou shalt
■ **shew her all her**
■ **abominations.**
■ 3. **Then say** thou,
Thus saith the Lord GOD,
■ **The city sheddeth**
■ **blood** in the midst of it,
that her time may come,
■ **and maketh idols against**
■ **herself** to defile herself.

■ 4. **Thou art** become
■ **guilty in** thy
■ **blood that**
■ **thou hast shed; and hast**
■ **defiled thyself in** thine
■ **idols** which thou hast made;
and thou hast caused thy
days to draw near, and art
come *even* unto thy years:
■ **therefore have I made**
■ **thee a reproach unto**
■ **the heathen,** and a
mocking to all countries.
■ 5. **Those** *that be*
■ **near, and** *those that be*
■ **far** from thee,
■ **shall mock thee**, *which art*
infamous *and* much vexed.
■ 6. **Behold, the princes**
■ **of Israel,** every one
■ **were in thee to their**
■ **power to shed blood.**
■ 7. **In thee have they** set
light by father and mother: in
the midst of thee have they
■ **dealt by oppression**
with the stranger: in thee have
■ **they vexed the**
■ **fatherless and** the
■ **widow.**
■ 8. **Thou hast despised**
■ **mine holy things, and** hast
■ **profaned my sabbaths.**
■ 9. **In thee** are
■ **men** that carry tales to
■ **shed blood: and** in thee
they eat upon the mountains:
in the midst of thee they
■ **commit lewdness.**
■ 10. **In thee** have
■ **they discovered**
■ **their fathers'**
■ **nakedness:** in thee have
■ **they humbled her that was**
■ **set apart for pollution.**
■ 11. **And** one hath
■ **committed abomination**
■ **with his neighbour's**
■ **wife; and** another hath
■ **lewdly defiled his daughter**
■ **in law; and** another in thee hath
■ **humbled his sister,** his
father's daughter.

12. In thee have they taken gifts to shed blood; **thou hast taken** usury and increase, **and** thou hast greedily **gained** of thy neighbours **by extortion, and hast forgotten me, saith the Lord** GOD.

13. Behold, **therefore I have smitten mine hand at thy dishonest gain** which thou hast made, **and at thy blood** which hath been **in the midst of thee.**

14. **Can thine heart endure,** or can thine hands be strong, **in the days that I shall deal with thee?** I the LORD have spoken *it,* and will do *it.*

15. **And I will scatter thee among the heathen,** and disperse thee in the countries, **and will consume thy filthiness** out of thee.

16. And thou shalt take thine inheritance in thyself in the sight of the heathen, **and thou shalt know that I am the LORD.**

17. **And the word of the LORD came unto me, saying,**

18. Son of man, the house of **Israel is** to me **become dross**: all they *are* brass, and tin, and iron, and lead, in the midst of the furnace; they are *even* the dross of silver.

19. **Therefore** thus saith the Lord GOD; Because ye are all become dross, behold, therefore **I will gather you into the midst of Jerusalem.**

20. **As they gather silver,** and brass, and iron, and lead, and tin, **into** the midst of **the furnace,** to blow the fire upon it, **to melt it;** so will I gather *you* in mine anger and in my fury, **and I will leave you there,** and melt you.

21. **Yea, I will gather you, and blow upon you in the fire of my wrath,** and ye shall be melted in the midst therof.

22. **As silver is melted in** the midst of **the furnace, so shall ye be** melted in the midst thereof; **and ye shall know that I the LORD have poured out my fury upon you.**

23. And the word of the LORD came unto me, saying,

24. Son of man, say unto her, **Thou art the land that is not cleansed,** nor rained upon in the day of indignation.

25. **There is a conspiracy of her prophets** in the midst thereof, **like a** roaring **lion ravening the prey; they have devoured souls;** they have taken the treasure and precious things; they have made her many widows in the midst thereof.

26. **Her priests have violated my law, and have profaned mine holy things:** they have put no *difference* between the holy and profane, neither have they shewed difference between the unclean and the clean, and have hid their eyes from my sabbaths, **and I am profaned among them.**

27. **Her princes** in the midst thereof **are like wolves** ravening the prey, **to shed blood, and to** destroy souls, to **get dishonest gain.**

28. And her prophets **have daubed them with untempered morter, seeing vanity, and** divining **lies** unto them, **saying, Thus saith the Lord** GOD, **when the LORD hath not spoken.**

29. **The people** of the land **have used oppression,** and exercised robbery, and have vexed the poor and needy: yea, they have oppressed the stranger wrongfully.

30. **And I sought for a man among them, that should make up the hedge, and stand in the gap before me for the land,** **that I should not destroy it: but I found none.**

31. **Therefore** have **I poured out mine indignation** upon them; **I** have **consumed them with** the **fire of my wrath: their own way have I recompensed upon their heads,** saith the Lord GOD.

CHAPTER 23

1. **The word of the LORD came again** unto me, **saying,**

2. Son of man, **there were two women,** the daughters of one mother:

3. **And they committed whoredoms in Egypt;** they committed whoredoms in their youth: there were their breasts pressed, **and** there they **bruised the teats of their virginity.**

4. **And the names** of them **were Aholah** the elder, **and Aholibah her sister:** and they were mine, **and they bare sons and daughters.** Thus *were* their names; **Samaria is Aholah, and Jerusalem Aholibah.**

5. **And Aholah played the harlot when she was mine; and she doted on her lovers,** on **the Assyrians** *her* neighbours,

6. *Which were* clothed with blue, captains and rulers, all of them desirable young men, horsemen riding upon horses.

7. **Thus she committed** her **whoredoms with them,** with all them *that were* the chosen men of Assyria, and with all on whom she doted: with all their idols she defiled herself.

8. **Neither left she her whoredoms brought from Egypt: for in her youth they** lay with her, and they bruised the breasts of her virginity, and **poured their whoredom upon her.**

9. **Wherefore I have delivered her into the hand** of her lovers, into the hand **of the Assyrians,** upon whom she doted.

10. These discovered her nakedness: **they took her sons and** her **daughters, and slew her with the sword:** and she became famous among women; for they had executed judgment upon her.

11. **And when** her sister **Aholibah saw this, she was more corrupt** in her inordinate love than she, and in her whoredoms more **than her sister** in her whoredoms.

12. **She doted upon the Assyrians** *her* neighbours, captains and rulers clothed most gorgeously, horsemen riding upon horses, all of them desirable young men.

13. Then I saw that she was defiled, *that* they *took* both one way,

14. **And** *that* **she increased her whoredoms: for when she saw men portrayed upon the wall,** the images of the Chaldeans portrayed with vermilion,

15. Girded with girdles upon their loins, exceeding in dyed attire upon their heads, all of them princes to look to,

after the manner of the
Babylonians of Chaldea,
the land of their nativity:

16. **And** as soon as she saw
them with her eyes,
**she doted upon them,
and sent messengers
unto them** into Chaldea.

17. **And the Babylonians
came** to her into the bed of love,
and they
**defiled her with their
whoredom,** and
she was polluted with them,
**and her mind was
alienated** from them.

18. **So she discovered
her whoredoms,
and** discovered her
**nakedness: then my mind
was alienated from her,** like
as my mind was alienated
from her sister.

19. **Yet she multiplied her
whoredoms,** in calling to
remembrance the days of her
youth, wherein she had played
the harlot in the land of Egypt.

20. **For she doted upon their
paramours,** whose flesh *is*
**as the flesh of asses,
and** whose issue *is like*
the issue of horses.

21. **Thus thou calledst to
remembrance the lewdness
of thy youth,** in bruising thy teats
by the Egyptians
for the paps of thy youth.

22. **Therefore, O Aholibah**,
thus saith the Lord GOD; Behold,
**I will raise up thy lovers
against thee,** from whom thy
mind is alienated, and I will bring them
against thee on every side;

23. **The Babylonians,
and** all the Chaldeans, Pekod,
and Shoa, and Koa, *and* all
the Assyrians with them: all of
them desirable young men, captains
and rulers, great lords and renowned,
all of them
riding upon horses.

24. **And they shall**

come against thee
**with chariots, wagons,
and** wheels, and with
an assembly of people, *which*
shall set against thee buckler and
shield and helmet round about:
and I will set judgment before them,
**and they shall judge
thee according to
their judgments.**

25. **And I will set my
jealousy against thee, and
they shall deal furiously with
thee:** they shall take away thy nose
and thine ears; and thy remnant shall
fall by the sword: they shall take thy
sons and thy daughters;
**and thy residue shall
be devoured by the fire**.

26. **They shall also
strip thee** out of thy clothes,
and take away
thy fair
jewels.

27. **Thus will I make thy
lewdness to cease** from thee,
and thy whoredom *brought* from the
land of Egypt: so that thou shalt not lift
up thine eyes unto them, nor
remember Egypt any more.

28. **For** thus saith the
Lord GOD; Behold,
**I will deliver thee into the
hand of them whom thou
hatest,** into the hand *of them* from
whom thy mind is alienated:

29. **And they shall deal
with thee hatefully, and**
shall take away all thy labour, and
shall leave thee naked and bare:
and the nakedness of
**thy whoredoms shall
be discovered,** both thy
lewdness and thy whoredoms.

30. **I will do these things
unto thee, because thou
hast gone a whoring after
the heathen, and** because
**thou art polluted with
their idols.**

31. Thou hast walked in the
way of thy sister; therefore will
I give her cup into thine hand.

32. Thus saith the Lord GOD;
Thou shalt drink of thy sister's
cup deep and large:
■ **thou shalt be laughed**
■ **to scorn and** had in
derision; it containeth much.
33. Thou shalt be
■ **filled with drunkenness**
■ **and sorrow, with** the cup of
■ **astonishment and**
■ **desolation, with the cup**
■ **of thy sister Samaria.**
■ 34. **Thou shalt even drink it**
■ **and suck it out, and** thou shalt
■ **break the sherds thereof**, and
pluck off thine own
breasts: for I have spoken *it*,
saith the Lord GOD.
■ 35. **Therefore thus**
■ **saith the Lord** GOD;
■ **Because thou hast forgotten**
■ **me**, and cast me behind thy back,
therefore bear thou also thy lewdness
and thy whoredoms.
36. The LORD said moreover
unto me; Son of man,
■ **wilt thou judge Aholah and**
■ **Aholibah? yea, declare**
unto them their abominations;
■ 37. **That they have**
■ **committed adultery,**
and blood *is* in their hands, and
■ **with their idols** have
they committed adultery,
■ **and have** also
■ **caused their sons**,
whom they bare unto me,
■ **to pass** for them
■ **through the fire**, to devour *them*.
■ 38. **Moreover** this
they have done unto me:
■ **they have defiled my**
■ **sanctuary** in the same day,
■ **and** have
■ **profaned my sabbaths.**
■ 39. **For when they had slain**
■ **their children to their idols,**
■ **then they came** the same day
■ **into my sanctuary to**
■ **profane it**; and,
lo, thus have they done in the
midst of mine house.
■ 40. **And** furthermore, that

■ **ye have sent for men**
■ **to come from far,** unto
whom a messenger *was* sent;
and, lo, they came:
■ **for whom thou didst**
■ **wash thyself, paintedst**
■ **thy eyes, and deckedst**
■ **thyself with ornaments,**
■ 41. **And satest upon a**
■ **stately bed,** and a table
prepared before it, whereupon thou
hast set mine incense and mine oil.
■ 42. **And a voice of a**
■ **multitude** being at ease
■ **was with her:** and
■ **with the men of the**
■ **common sort were brought**
■ **Sabeans from the**
■ **wilderness,** which put bracelets
upon their hands, and beautiful
crowns upon their heads.
■ 43. **Then said I** unto *her*
that was old in adulteries,
■ **Will they now commit**
■ **whoredoms with her,**
and she *with them*?
■ 44. **Yet they went in** unto her,
as they go in unto a woman that
playeth the harlot: so went they in
■ **unto Aholah and unto**
■ **Aholibah, the lewd women.**
■ 45. **And the**
■ **righteous** men, they
■ **shall judge them** after the
manner of adulteresses, and after the
manner of women that shed blood;
■ **because they are**
■ **adulteresses, and blood**
■ **is in their hands.**
46. For thus saith the Lord GOD;
I will bring up a company upon
them, and will give them to be
removed and spoiled.
■ 47. **And the company**
■ **shall stone them** with stones,
■ **and dispatch them with** their
■ **swords; they shall slay their**
■ **sons and** their
■ **daughters, and burn**
■ **up their houses** with fire.
■ 48. **Thus will I cause**
■ **lewdness to**
■ **cease** out of the land,

that all women may be taught not to do after your lewdness.

49. **And they shall recompense your lewdness** upon you, **and ye shall bear the sins of your idols: and** ye shall **know that I am the Lord GOD.**

CHAPTER 24

1. **Again** in the ninth year, in the tenth month, in the tenth *day* of the month, **the word of the LORD came unto me, saying,**

2. Son of man, **write** thee **the name of the day,** *even* of this same day: **the king of Babylon set himself against Jerusalem** this same day.

3. **And utter a parable unto the rebellious house, and say** unto them, Thus saith the Lord GOD; **Set** on **a pot,** set *it* on, **and** also **pour water into it:**

4. **Gather the pieces** thereof **into it**, *even* every good piece, **the thigh, and** the **shoulder; fill it with** the **choice bones.**

5. **Take the choice of the flock, and burn** also **the bones under it, and make it boil** well, **and** let them **seethe the bones** of it **therein.**

6. **Wherefore thus saith the Lord** GOD; **Woe to the bloody city, to the pot whose scum is therein**, and whose scum *is* not gone out of it! **bring it out piece by piece;** let no lot fall upon it.

7. **For her blood** is in the midst of her;

she set it upon the top of **a rock; she poured it not upon the ground, to cover it** with dust;

8. **That it might cause** fury to come up to take **vengeance; I have set her blood upon** the top of **a rock, that it should not be covered.**

9. **Therefore** thus saith the Lord GOD; **Woe to the bloody city! I will** even **make the** pile for **fire great.**

10. Heap on wood, kindle the fire, **consume the flesh, and** spice it well, and **let the bones be burned.**

11. **Then set it empty upon the coals** thereof, **that the brass** of it may be hot, and may burn, and *that* the filthiness of it **may be molten** in it, **that the scum** of it **may be consumed.**

12. She hath wearied *herself* with lies, and her great scum went not forth out of her: her scum *shall be* in the fire.

13. **In thy filthiness is lewdness**: because I have purged thee, and thou wast not purged, **thou shalt not be purged from thy filthiness** any more, **till I have caused my fury to rest upon thee.**

14. **I the LORD have spoken** *it.* it shall come to pass, and I will do *it*; **I will not** go back, neither will I spare, neither will I **repent;** according to thy ways, and according to thy doings, shall they judge thee, saith the Lord GOD.

15. **Also the word of the LORD came unto me, saying,**

16. Son of man, behold, **I take away** from thee **the desire of thine eyes with a stroke:** yet neither shalt thou mourn nor weep, neither

shall thy tears run down.

17. Forbear to cry, **make no mourning for the dead,** bind the tire of thine head upon thee, and put on thy shoes upon thy feet, and cover not *thy* lips, **and eat not** the **bread** of men.

18. **So I spake unto the people** in the morning: **and at even my wife died; and I did** in the morning **as I was commanded.**

19. **And the people said** unto me, **Wilt thou not tell us what** these *things are* to us, that **thou doest** *so*?

20. **Then I answered** them, The word of the LORD came unto me, **saying,**

21. Speak unto the house of Israel, **Thus saith the Lord** GOD; Behold, **I will profane my sanctuary,** the excellency of **your strength,** the desire of your eyes, and that which your soul pitieth; **and your sons and your daughters** whom ye have left **shall fall by the sword.**

22. **And** ye shall do as I have done: **ye shall not cover your lips, nor eat** the **bread** of men.

23. And your tires *shall be* upon your heads, and your shoes upon your feet: ye shall not mourn nor weep; **but ye shall pine away for your iniquities, and mourn one toward another.**

24. **Thus Ezekiel is** unto you **a sign:** according to **all that he hath done shall ye do: and** when this cometh, **ye shall know** that **I am the Lord** GOD.

25. **Also,** thou son of man, **shall it not be** in the day **when I take from them their strength,** the joy of their glory, the desire of their eyes, **and** that whereupon they set their minds, **their sons and** their **daughters,**

26. **That he that escapeth** in that day **shall come unto thee, to cause thee to hear** *it* with *thine* ears?

27. **In that day shall thy mouth be opened** to him which is escaped, and thou shalt speak, and be no more dumb: **and thou shalt be a sign unto them; and they shall know** that **I am the LORD.**

CHAPTER 25

1. **The word of the LORD came again** unto me, **saying,**

2. Son of man, **set thy face against the Ammonites,** and prophesy against them;

3. **And say** unto the Ammonites, Hear the word of the Lord GOD; **Thus saith the Lord** GOD; **Because thou saidst, Aha, against my sanctuary,** when it was profaned; **and against** the land of **Israel,** when it was desolate; **and** against the house of **Judah,** when they went into captivity;

4. **Behold,** therefore **I will deliver thee to the men of the east** for a possession, **and they shall** set their palaces in thee, and **make their dwellings in thee: they shall eat thy fruit, and** they shall **drink thy milk.**

5. **And I will make Rabbah a stable for camels, and the Ammonites a couchingplace for flocks:** and ye shall know that I *am* theLORD.

6. For thus saith the Lord GOD;

■ **Because thou hast**
clapped *thine* hands, and
stamped with the feet, and
■ **rejoiced** in heart with
all thy despite
■ **against** the land of
■ **Israel;**
7. Behold, therefore
■ **I will stretch out mine**
■ **hand upon thee, and** will
■ **deliver thee** for a spoil
■ **to the heathen; and** I will cut
thee off from the people, and I will
■ **cause thee to perish** out of the
countries: I will destroy thee; and thou
shalt know that I *am* the LORD.
8. Thus saith the Lord GOD;
■ **Because** that
■ **Moab and Seir** do
■ **say,** Behold,
■ **the house of Judah is**
■ **like unto all the heathen;**
9. Therefore, behold,
■ **I will open the side of**
■ **Moab** from the cities, from his cities
which are on his frontiers, the glory of
the country, Beth–jeshimoth,
Baal–meon, and Kiriathaim,
■ 10. **Unto the men of the**
■ **east** with the Ammonites,
■ **and** will
■ **give them in possession,**
■ **that the Ammonites**
■ **may not be remembered**
among the nations.
■ 11. **And I will execute**
■ **judgments upon Moab;** and
they shall know that I *am* the LORD.
12. Thus saith the Lord GOD;
■ **Because** that
■ **Edom hath dealt**
■ **against** the house of
■ **Judah by taking**
■ **vengeance,** and hath
greatly offended, and revenged
himself upon them;
■ 13. **Therefore** thus
saith the Lord GOD;
■ **I will** also
■ **stretch out mine hand**
■ **upon Edom, and** will
■ **cut off man and beast**
■ **from it**; and I will make it

desolate from Teman; and they
of Dedan shall fall by the sword.
■ 14. **And I will lay my**
■ **vengeance upon Edom**
■ **by the hand of** my people
■ **Israel:** and they shall do in Edom
according to mine anger and
according to my fury;
■ **and they shall know my**
■ **vengeance,** saith the Lord GOD.
15. Thus saith the Lord GOD;
■ **Because the Philistines**
■ **have** dealt by revenge, and have
■ **taken vengeance with**
■ **a despiteful heart,** to
destroy *it* for the old hatred;
16. Therefore thus saith
the Lord GOD; Behold,
■ **I will stretch out mine hand**
■ **upon the Philistines,** and
I will cut off the Cherethims,
■ **and destroy the remnant**
■ **of the sea coast.**
17. **And** I will
■ **execute great vengeance**
■ **upon them** with furious rebukes;
■ **and they shall know that**
■ **I am the LORD,** when I shall
lay my vengeance upon them.

CHAPTER 26

■ 1. **And** it came to pass in
the eleventh year, in the first
day of the month, *that*
■ **the word of the LORD**
■ **came unto me, saying,**
2. Son of man,
■ **because** that
■ **Tyrus hath said against**
■ **Jerusalem, Aha, she**
■ **is broken** *that was* the gates
of the people: she is turned unto
me: I shall be replenished, *now*
■ **she is laid waste:**
3. **Therefore** thus
saith the Lord GOD; Behold,
■ **I am against thee, O Tyrus,**
■ **and will cause many**
■ **nations to come** up
■ **against thee,** as the
sea causeth his waves to come up.
■ 4. **And they shall destroy**
■ **the walls of Tyrus,** and

break down her towers:
■ **I will also scrape**
■ **her dust** from her,
■ **and make her like** the top of
■ **a rock.**
5. It shall be *a place for* the spreading
of nets in the midst of the sea: for I
have spoken *it*, saith the Lord GOD:
■ **and it shall become a**
■ **spoil to the nations.**
■ **6. And her**
■ **daughters** which *are* in the field
■ **shall be slain** by the sword;
■ **and they shall know** that
■ **I am the LORD.**
7. For thus saith the
Lord GOD; Behold,
■ **I will bring upon Tyrus**
■ **Nebuchadrezzar king**
■ **of Babylon**, a king of kings, from
the north, with horses, and with
chariots, and with horsemen, and
companies, and much people.
■ 8. **He shall slay** with the sword
■ **thy daughters** in the field: and he
shall make a fort against thee, and
cast a mount against thee, and lift
up the buckler against thee.
■ 9. **And he shall set engines**
■ **of war against thy walls,**
■ **and** with his axes he shall
■ **break down thy towers.**
10. By reason of the abundance of
his horses their dust shall cover thee:
thy walls shall shake at the noise of
the horsemen, and of the wheels, and
of the chariots, when he shall enter
into thy gates, as men enter into
a city wherein is made a breach.
11. With the hoofs of his horses
shall he tread down all thy streets:
■ **he shall slay thy people** by
the sword, and thy strong garrisons
shall go down to the ground.
■ 12. **And** they
■ **shall make a spoil of thy**
■ **riches, and** make a prey of thy
merchandise: and they shall break
down thy walls, and destroy thy
pleasant houses: and they
■ **shall lay thy stones and** thy
■ **timber** and thy dust
■ **in the midst of the water.**

■ 13. **And I will cause** the noise of
■ **thy songs to cease;**
■ **and** the sound of
■ **thy harps shall be**
■ **no more heard.**
14. And I will make thee like the top
of a rock: thou shalt be *a place* to
spread nets upon; thou shalt be
built no more: for I the LORD have
spoken *it*, saith the Lord GOD.
■ 15. **Thus saith the Lord** GOD
■ **to Tyrus; Shall not the**
■ **isles shake at the sound**
■ **of thy fall,** when the wounded
cry, when the slaughter is made
in the midst of thee?
■ 16. **Then all the princes**
■ **of the sea shall come**
■ **down** from their thrones,
■ **and lay away their robes,**
■ **and** put off their broidered garments:
they shall clothe themselves with
trembling; they
■ **shall sit upon the**
■ **ground, and** shall
■ **tremble** at *every* moment,
and be astonished at thee.
■ 17. **And they shall take up a**
■ **lamentation for thee,** and say
to thee, How art thou destroyed, *that*
wast inhabited of seafaring men,
the renowned city, which wast
strong in the sea, she and her
inhabitants, which cause their
terror *to be* on all that haunt it!
18. Now shall the isles tremble in the
day of thy fall; yea, the isles
that *are* in the sea shall be
troubled at thy departure.
19. For thus saith the Lord GOD;
■ **When I shall make thee** a
■ **desolate** city, like the cities
that are not inhabited; when
■ **I shall bring up the**
■ **deep** upon thee,
■ **and great waters**
■ **shall cover thee;**
■ 20. **When I shall bring thee**
■ **down** with them that descend
■ **into the pit,** with the
people of old time,
■ **and** shall
■ **set thee in the low parts of**

■ **the earth**, in places desolate of old,
with them that go down to the pit,
■ **that thou be not inhabited;**
■ **and I shall set glory in**
■ **the land of the living;**
■ 21. **I will make thee a**
■ **terror, and thou shalt be no**
■ **more:** though thou be sought for,
yet shalt thou never be found again,
saith the Lord GOD.

CHAPTER 27

■ 1. **The word of the LORD**
■ **came again** unto me,
■ **saying,**
2. Now, thou son of man,
■ **take up a lamentation**
■ **for Tyrus;**
■ 3. **And say** unto Tyrus, O
■ **thou that art situate at the**
■ **entry of the sea,** which art a
merchant of the people for many
isles, Thus saith the Lord GOD;
■ **O Tyrus, thou hast said,**
■ **I am of perfect beauty.**
4. Thy borders are in the midst
of the seas,
■ **thy builders have**
■ **perfected thy beauty.**
■ 5. **They have made** all thy
■ **ship boards of fir**
■ **trees** of Senir:
■ **they have taken**
■ **cedars** from Lebanon
■ **to make masts** for thee.
■ 6. **Of the oaks** of Bashan have
■ **they made** thine
■ **oars;** the company of the
Ashurites have made
■ **thy benches of ivory,**
■ **brought out of** the isles of
■ **Chittim.**
■ 7. **Fine linen** with broidered work
■ **from Egypt** was that
which thou spreadest forth
■ **to be thy sail;** blue and
purple from the isles of Elishah
was that which covered thee.
■ 8. **The inhabitants of Zidon**
■ **and Arvad were thy**
■ **mariners: thy wise men,**
O Tyrus, that were in thee,
■ **were thy pilots.**

9. The ancients of Gebal and the wise
men thereof were in thee thy calkers:
■ **all the ships of the**
■ **sea** with their mariners
■ **were in thee to occupy**
■ **thy merchandise.**
10. **They of Persia** and of
■ **Lud and** of
■ **Phut were in thine army,**
thy men of war: they hanged the
shield and helmet in thee;
they set forth thy comeliness.
■ 11. **The men of Arvad** with
thine army were upon thy walls
round about, and the Gammadims
■ **were in thy towers:** they
hanged their shields upon thy
walls round about; they have
made thy beauty perfect.
■ 12. **Tarshish was thy**
■ **merchant by**
■ **reason** of the multitude
■ **of all kind of riches;**
with silver, iron, tin, and lead,
they traded in thy fairs.
■ 13. **Javan, Tubal,**
■ **and Meshech,** they
were thy merchants: they
■ **traded** the persons of
■ **men and vessels** of brass
■ **in thy market.**
■ 14. **They** of the house
■ **of Togarmah**
■ **traded** in thy fairs with
■ **horses and horsemen**
■ **and mules.**
15. **The men of Dedan** were
thy merchants; many isles were the
merchandise of thine hand: they
■ **brought** thee for a present
■ **horns of ivory and ebony.**
■ 16. **Syria was thy**
■ **merchant by reason**
■ **of the multitude of** the
■ **wares** of thy making: they
occupied in thy fairs with emeralds,
purple, and broidered work, and
fine linen, and coral, and agate.
■ 17. **Judah, and** the land of
■ **Israel,** they were thy
merchants: they
■ **traded** in thy market
■ **wheat** of Minnith,

■ and Pannag, and
■ honey, and
■ oil, and balm.
■ 18. **Damascus was thy**
■ **merchant** in the multitude
of the wares of thy making,
for the multitude of all riches;
■ in the
■ **wine** of Helbon,
■ **and white wool.**
■ 19. **Dan** also
■ **and Javan** going to and fro
■ **occupied** in
■ **thy fairs: bright iron,**
■ **cassia, and calamus,**
■ **were in thy market.**
■ 20. **Dedan was thy**
■ **merchant in precious**
■ **clothes for chariots.**
■ 21. **Arabia,** and all
the princes of Kedar, they
■ **occupied with thee**
■ **in lambs,** and
■ **rams, and goats:** in
these *were they* thy merchants.
■ 22. **The merchants of**
■ **Sheba and Raamah,** they
were thy merchants: they
■ **occupied** in
■ **thy fairs with** chief of all
■ **spices,** and with all
■ **precious stones, and gold.**
■ 23. **Haran,** and
■ **Canneh, and Eden,**
the merchants of Sheba,
Asshur, *and* Chilmad,
■ **were thy merchants.**
24. These *were* thy
merchants in all sorts *of things,*
■ **in blue clothes,** and
■ **broidered work, and** in
■ **chests of rich apparel,**
bound with cords, and made of
cedar, among thy merchandise.
■ 25. **The ships of Tarshish**
■ **did sing of thee in thy**
■ **market: and thou**
■ **wast** replenished, and
■ **made** very
■ **glorious in the**
■ **midst of the seas.**
26. Thy rowers have brought
thee into great waters:

■ the east wind hath
■ broken thee in the
■ midst of the seas.
■ 27. **Thy riches,**
■ **and** thy fairs, thy
■ **merchandise,** thy mariners, and
thy pilots, thy calkers, and the
occupiers of thy merchandise, and
all thy men of war, that *are* in thee,
■ **and** in
■ **all thy company**
which *is* in the midst of thee,
■ **shall fall into the** midst of the
■ **seas in the day of thy ruin.**
■ 28. **The suburbs**
■ **shall shake** at the sound
of the cry of thy pilots.
■ 29. **And** all that handle the oar,
■ **the mariners, and** all the
■ **pilots of the sea, shall** come
down from their ships, they shall
■ **stand upon the land;**
30. **And shall cause their**
■ **voice to be heard against**
■ **thee,** and shall cry bitterly, and shall
cast up dust upon their heads, they
shall wallow themselves in the ashes:
■ 31. **And** they shall
■ **make themselves** utterly
■ **bald for thee,** and gird them
■ **with sackcloth,** and
■ **they shall weep** for thee
■ **with** bitterness of heart *and*
■ **bitter wailing.**
■ 32. **And** in their wailing
■ **they shall take up**
■ **a lamentation for**
■ **thee,** and lament over thee,
■ **saying, What city**
■ **is like Tyrus,** like the
■ **destroyed in** the midst of
■ **the sea?**
33. When thy wares went forth out of
the seas, thou filledst many people;
■ **thou didst enrich the kings**
■ **of the earth with** the multitude of
■ **thy riches** and of thy
merchandise.
34. In the time *when* thou shalt
be broken by the seas in the
depths of the waters thy
merchandise and all thy company
in the midst of thee shall fall.

35. **All the inhabitants of the isles shall be astonished** at thee, **and their kings shall be** sore **afraid,** they shall be troubled in *their* countenance. 36. **The merchants among the people shall hiss at thee;** thou shalt be a terror, **and never shalt be any more.**

CHAPTER 28

1. **The word of the LORD came again** unto me, **saying,** 2. Son of man, **say unto the prince of Tyrus,** Thus saith the Lord GOD; **Because thine heart is lifted up, and thou hast said, I am a God,** I sit *in* the seat of God, in the midst of the seas; **yet thou art a man,** and not God, though thou set thine heart as the heart of God: 3. **Behold, thou art wiser than Daniel;** there is **no secret** that they **can hide from thee:** 4. **With thy wisdom and** with thine **understanding thou hast gotten** thee **riches,** and hast gotten gold and silver into thy treasures: 5. By thy great wisdom *and* by thy traffic hast thou increased thy riches, **and thine heart is lifted up because of thy riches:** 6. **Therefore** thus saith the Lord GOD; **Because thou hast set thine heart as** the heart of **God;** 7. Behold, therefore **I will bring strangers upon thee,** the terrible of the nations: **and they shall draw their swords** against the beauty of thy wisdom,

and they shall **defile thy brightness.** 8. **They shall bring thee down to the pit, and thou shalt die the deaths of them** *that are* **slain in** the midst of **the seas.** 9. **Wilt thou yet say** before him that slayeth thee, **I am God?** but thou *shalt be* a man, and no God, in the hand of him that slayeth thee. 10. **Thou shalt die** the deaths of the uncircumcised **by the hand of strangers:** for I have spoken *it,* saith the Lord GOD. 11. Moreover the word of the LORD came unto me, saying, 12. **Son of man, take up a lamentation upon the king of Tyrus, and say** unto him, Thus saith the Lord GOD; **Thou sealest up the sum, full of wisdom, and** perfect in **beauty.** 13. **Thou hast been in Eden** the garden of God; **every precious stone was thy covering,** the sardius, topaz, and the diamond, the beryl, the onyx, and the jasper, the sapphire, the emerald, and the carbuncle, and gold: the workmanship of thy tabrets and of thy pipes was prepared in thee in the day that thou wast created. 14. **Thou art the anointed cherub** that covereth; and I have set thee *so:* **thou wast upon the holy mountain of God;** thou hast walked up and down in the midst of the stones of fire. 15. **Thou wast perfect** in thy ways from the day that thou wast created, **till iniquity was found in thee.** 16. By the multitude of thy merchandise **they have filled** the midst of **thee with violence, and thou hast sinned: therefore I**

will cast thee as profane out of the mountain of God: and I will destroy thee, O covering cherub, from the midst of the stones of fire.

17. **Thine heart was lifted up because of thy beauty,** thou hast corrupted thy wisdom by reason of thy brightness: **I will cast thee to the ground,** I will lay thee before kings, that they may behold thee.

18. **Thou hast defiled thy sanctuaries by** the multitude of **thine iniquities,** by the iniquity of thy traffic; **therefore will I bring forth a fire from the midst of thee, it shall devour thee, and I will bring thee to ashes** upon the earth in the sight of all them that behold thee.

19. All they that know thee among the people shall be astonished at thee: thou shalt be a terror, **and never shalt thou be any more.**

20. **Again the word of the LORD came** unto me, **saying,**

21. Son of man, **set thy face against Zidon, and prophesy** against it,

22. **And say,** Thus saith the Lord GOD; Behold, **I am against thee, O Zidon; and I will be glorified in** the midst of **thee:** and they shall know that I *am* the LORD, **when I** shall **have executed judgments in her,** and shall be sanctified in her.

23. **For I will send into her pestilence, and blood into her streets;** and the wounded shall be judged in the midst of her by the sword upon her on every side; **and they shall know** that **I am the LORD.**

24. **And there shall be no more a pricking brier unto** the house of **Israel,** nor *any* grieving thorn of all *that are* round about them, that despised them; and they shall know that I *am* the Lord GOD.

25. Thus saith the Lord GOD; **When I** shall **have gathered** the house of **Israel from the people among whom they are scattered, and shall be sanctified in them** in the sight of the heathen, **then shall they dwell in their land** that I have given to my servant Jacob.

26. **And they shall dwell safely** therein, **and** shall build houses, and plant vineyards; yea, they shall dwell **with confidence, when I have executed judgments upon** all **those that despise them** round about them; **and they shall know** that **I am the LORD** their God.

CHAPTER 29

1. **In the tenth year,** in the tenth *month,* in the twelfth *day* of the month, **the word of the LORD came** unto me, **saying,**

2. Son of man, **set thy face against Pharaoh king of Egypt, and prophesy** against him, and against all Egypt:

3. Speak, and say, **Thus saith the Lord** GOD; Behold, **I am against thee, Pharaoh** king of Egypt, the great dragon that lieth in the midst of his rivers, **which hath said, My river is mine own,** and **I have made it for myself.**

4. **But I will put hooks in thy jaws, and** I will cause the fish of thy rivers to

■ **will bring thee up**
■ **out of** the midst of
■ **thy rivers, and** all
■ **the fish** of thy rivers
■ **shall stick unto thy scales.**
■ 5. **And I will leave thee**
thrown into the wilderness, thee
■ **and** all
■ **the fish of thy rivers:**
■ **thou shalt fall upon the** open
■ **fields;** thou shalt not be
brought together, nor gathered:
■ **I have given thee for meat**
■ **to the beasts** of the field
■ **and** to the
■ **fowls** of the heaven.
■ 6. **And all** the inhabitants of
■ **Egypt shall know that I**
■ **am the LORD, because**
■ **they have been a staff**
■ **of reed to** the house of
■ **Israel.**
7. When they took hold of thee by thy
hand, thou didst break, and rend all
their shoulder: and when they leaned
upon thee, thou brakest, and madest
all their loins to be at a stand.
■ 8. **Therefore** thus saith
the Lord GOD; Behold,
■ **I will bring a sword**
■ **upon thee,** and cut off
man and beast out of thee.
■ 9. **And** the land of
■ **Egypt shall be desolate**
■ **and waste;** and they
shall know that I *am* the LORD:
■ **because** he hath said,
■ **The river is mine,** and
■ **I have made it.**
10. Behold, therefore I *am* against
thee, and against thy rivers, and I will
make the land of Egypt utterly waste
and desolate, from the tower of Syene
even unto the border of Ethiopia.
■ 11. **No foot** of man
■ **shall pass through it,** nor
foot of beast shall pass through it,
■ **neither shall it be**
■ **inhabited forty years.**
12. And I will make the land of Egypt
desolate in the midst of the countries
that are desolate, and her cities

among the cities *that are* laid waste
shall be desolate forty years:
■ **and I will scatter the**
■ **Egyptians among the**
■ **nations,** and will disperse
them through the countries.
■ 13. **Yet** thus saith the Lord GOD;
■ **At the end of forty years**
■ **will I gather the**
■ **Egyptians** from the people
whither they were scattered:
14. And I will bring again
the captivity of Egypt,
■ **and will cause them to**
■ **return** *into* the land of Pathros,
■ **into the land of their**
■ **habitation;** and they shall
be there a base kingdom.
■ 15. **It shall be the**
■ **basest of** the
■ **kingdoms;** neither
shall it exalt itself any more
above the nations: for I will
diminish them, that they shall
no more rule over the nations.
■ 16. **And** it
■ **shall be no more the**
■ **confidence of** the house of
■ **Israel, which bringeth** *their*
■ **iniquity to remembrance**,
when they shall look after
them: but they shall know
that I *am* the Lord GOD.
■ 17. **And** it came to pass
in the seven and twentieth year,
in the first *month,* in the first *day*
of the month, the word of
■ **the LORD came** unto me,
■ **saying,**
■ 18. **Son of man,**
■ **Nebuchadrezzar king of**
■ **Babylon caused his army**
■ **to serve** a great service
■ **against Tyrus:** every
head *was* made bald, and
every shoulder *was* peeled:
■ **yet had he no wages,** nor his
army, for Tyrus, for the service that he
had served against it:
■ 19. **Therefore** thus
saith the Lord GOD; Behold,
■ **I will give** the land of
■ **Egypt unto**

■ **Nebuchadrezzar**
king of Babylon;
■ **and he shall take her**
■ **multitude, and** take
■ **her spoil,** and take her prey;
■ **and it shall be the**
■ **wages for his army.**
20. I have given him the
land of Egypt *for* his labour
wherewith he served against it,
■ **because they wrought for**
■ **me, saith the Lord** GOD.
21. **In that day will I**
■ **cause** the horn of the house of
■ **Israel to bud** forth, and I will
give thee the opening of the
mouth in the midst of them;
■ **and they shall know**
■ **that I am the LORD.**

CHAPTER 30

■ 1. **The word of the LORD**
■ **came again** unto me,
■ **saying,**
2. Son of man, prophesy and
say, Thus saith the Lord GOD;
Howl ye, Woe worth the day!
■ 3. **For the day** *is*
near, even the day
■ **of the LORD is**
■ **near,** a cloudy day;
■ **it shall be the time**
■ **of the heathen.**
■ 4. **And the sword**
shall come upon Egypt,
■ **and great pain shall be**
■ **in Ethiopia,** when the slain
shall fall in Egypt, and they shall take
away her multitude, and her
foundations shall be broken down.
5. Ethiopia, and Libya, and Lydia,
and all the mingled people, and Chub,
■ **and the men of the land**
■ **that is in league, shall fall**
■ **with them by the sword.**
6. Thus saith the LORD;
■ **They also that uphold Egypt**
■ **shall fall**; and the pride of her
power shall come down: from the
tower of Syene shall they fall in it
by the sword, saith the Lord GOD.
■ 7. **And they shall be**
■ **desolate** in the midst of the

countries *that are* desolate,
■ **and her cities** shall be in the
midst of the cities *that are*
■ **wasted.**
8. And they shall know
that I *am* the LORD, when I have set
a fire in Egypt, and *when* all her
helpers shall be destroyed.
■ 9. **In that day shall**
■ **messengers go** forth from me
■ **in ships to make the** careless
■ **Ethiopians afraid**, and great pain
shall come upon them, as in
the day of Egypt: for, lo, it cometh.
10. Thus saith the Lord GOD;
■ **I will also make the**
■ **multitude of Egypt to**
■ **cease by** the hand of
■ **Nebuchadrezzar**
king of Babylon.
■ 11. **He** and his people with
him, the terrible of the nations,
■ **shall** be brought to
■ **destroy the land:** and they
shall draw their swords against Egypt,
and fill the land with the slain.
■ 12. **And I will make the**
■ **rivers dry, and sell the**
■ **land into the hand of**
■ **the wicked: and** I will
■ **make the land waste,** and all
that is therein, by the hand of
strangers: I the LORD have spoken *it*.
13. Thus saith the Lord GOD;
■ **I will also destroy the**
■ **idols,** and I will cause
their images to cease out of Noph;
■ **and there shall be no**
■ **more a prince** of the land
■ **of Egypt:** and
■ **I will put a fear in the**
■ **land** of Egypt.
14. And I will make Pathros desolate,
and will set fire in Zoan, and will
execute judgments in No.
15. And I will pour my fury upon Sin,
the strength of Egypt; and I will
cut off the multitude of No.
■ 16. **And I will set fire in**
■ **Egypt**: Sin shall have great pain,
and No shall be rent asunder, and
Noph *shall have* distresses daily.
17. **The young men**

■ **shall fall by the sword:** and these *cities* shall go into captivity.
18. At Tehaphnehes also the day shall be darkened, when
■ **I shall break** there
■ **the yokes of Egypt:**
■ **and** the pomp of
■ **her strength shall**
■ **cease** in her: as for her,
■ **a cloud shall cover**
■ **her, and her daughters**
■ **shall go into captivity.**
19. Thus will I execute judgments in Egypt:
■ **and they shall know**
■ **that I am the LORD.**
20. And it came to pass in the eleventh year, in the first *month*, in the seventh *day* of the month, *that* the word of the LORD came unto me, saying,
21. ■ **Son of man, I have**
■ **broken the arm of**
■ **Pharaoh** king of Egypt;
■ **and,** lo,
■ **it shall not be** bound up to be
■ **healed,** to put a roller to bind it, to make it strong to hold the sword.
22. Therefore thus saith the Lord GOD; Behold,
■ **I am against**
■ **Pharaoh** king of Egypt,
■ **and will break**
■ **his arms,** the strong, and that which was broken;
■ **and I will cause the sword**
■ **to fall out of his hand.**
23. ■ **And I will scatter the**
■ **Egyptians among the**
■ **nations,** and will disperse them through the countries.
24. ■ **And I will strengthen** the arms of the king of
■ **Babylon, and put my sword**
■ **in his hand:** but I will break Pharaoh's arms, and he shall groan before him with the groanings of a deadly wounded *man.*
25. But I will strengthen the arms of the king of Babylon, and the arms of Pharaoh shall fall down; and they shall know that I *am* the LORD, when

I shall put my sword into the hand of the king of Babylon,
■ **and he shall stretch it**
■ **out upon** the land of
■ **Egypt.**
26. And I will scatter the Egyptians among the nations, and disperse them among the countries; and they shall know that I *am* the LORD.

CHAPTER 31

1. And it came to pass in the eleventh year, in the third *month,* in the first *day* of the month, *that* the word of the LORD came unto me, saying,
2. ■ **Son of man, speak**
■ **unto Pharaoh** king of Egypt,
■ **and to his multitude;**
■ **Whom art thou like in** thy
■ **greatness**?
3. ■ **Behold, the Assyrian was**
■ **a cedar in Lebanon** with fair branches, and with a shadowing shroud, and of an high stature; and his top was among the thick boughs.
4. ■ **The waters made him**
■ **great,** the deep set him up on high with her rivers running round about his plants, and sent her little rivers unto all the trees of the field.
5. Therefore
■ **his height was exalted**
■ **above all the trees** of the field, and his boughs were multiplied, and his branches became long because of the multitude of waters, when he shot forth.
6. ■ **All the fowls of heaven**
■ **made their nests in**
■ **his boughs,** and under his branches did all the beasts of the field bring forth their young,
■ **and under his shadow**
■ **dwelt all great nations.**
7. ■ **Thus was he fair** in his greatness, in the length of his branches:
■ **for his root was**
■ **by great waters.**
8. The cedars in the garden of God could not hide him: the fir trees were not like his boughs, and the chestnut trees were not like his branches; nor

1179

any tree in the garden of God was like unto him in his beauty.

9. I have made him fair by the multitude of his branches: so that all the trees of Eden, that *were* in the garden of God, envied him.

10. **Therefore thus saith the Lord** GOD; **Because thou hast lifted up thyself** in height, and he hath shot up his top among the thick boughs, and his heart is lifted up in his height;

11. **I have** therefore **delivered him into the hand** of the mighty one **of the heathen;** he shall surely deal with him: **I have driven him out for his wickedness.**

12. **And strangers,** the terrible of the nations, **have cut him off,** and have left him: upon the mountains and in all the valleys **his branches** are fallen, **and his boughs are broken** by all the rivers of the land; **and all the people of the earth are gone** down **from his shadow, and** have **left him.**

13. **Upon his ruin shall** all **the fowls** of the heaven **remain,** and all the beasts of the field shall be upon his branches:

14. **To the end that none** of all the trees by the waters **exalt themselves** for their height, neither shoot up their top among the thick boughs, neither their trees stand up in their height, all that drink water: **for they are all delivered unto death,** to the nether parts of the earth, in the midst of the children of men, **with them that go down to the pit.**

15. **Thus saith the Lord** GOD; In the day **when he went down to the grave I caused a mourning:**

I covered the deep for him, **and** I **restrained the floods** thereof, and the great waters were stayed: **and** I **caused Lebanon to mourn for him,** and all the trees of the field fainted for him.

16. **I made the nations to shake** at the sound of his fall, **when I cast him down to hell** with them that descend into the pit: **and** all **the trees of Eden,** the choice and best of Lebanon, all that drink water, **shall be comforted** in the nether parts of the earth.

17. **They also went down into hell** with him unto *them that be* slain with the sword; and *they that were* his arm, **that dwelt under his shadow** in the midst of the heathen.

18. **To whom art thou** thus **like in glory** and in greatness among the trees of Eden? **yet shalt thou be brought down** with the trees of Eden **unto the nether parts of the earth:** thou shalt lie in the midst of the uncircumcised with *them that be* slain by the sword. **This is Pharaoh and all his multitude, saith the Lord** GOD.

CHAPTER 32

1. And it came to pass in the twelfth year, in the twelfth month, in the first *day* of the month, *that* the word of the LORD came unto me, saying,

2. **Son of man, take up a lamentation for Pharaoh** king of Egypt, **and say** unto him, **Thou art like a young lion** of the nations, **and** thou art **as a whale** in the seas: and **thou camest**

forth with thy rivers,
and troubledst the waters
with thy feet, and fouledst their rivers.
3. Thus saith the Lord GOD;
I will therefore spread out
my net over thee with a
company of many people;
and they shall bring thee
up in my net.
4. Then will I leave
thee upon the land,
I will cast thee forth upon
the open field, and will
cause all
the fowls of the heaven
to remain upon
thee, and I will fill
the beasts of the whole earth
with thee.
5. **And I will lay thy flesh**
upon the mountains, and
fill the valleys with thy height.
6. **I will also water with thy**
blood the land wherein thou
swimmest, *even* to the mountains;
and the rivers shall be full of thee.
7. **And when I shall**
put thee out, I will
cover the heaven, and make
the stars thereof dark; I will cover
the sun with a cloud,
and the moon shall
not give her light.
8. All the bright lights of heaven
will I make dark over thee,
and set darkness upon thy land,
saith the Lord GOD.
9. **I will also vex the hearts**
of many people, when I shall
bring thy destruction
among the nations, into the countries
which thou hast not known.
10. **Yea,** I will make many
people amazed at thee, and
their kings shall be
horribly afraid for thee, when
I shall brandish my sword before
them; and they shall tremble at *every*
moment, every man for his own life,
in the day of thy fall.
11. For thus saith the Lord GOD;
The sword of the king
of Babylon shall come

upon thee.
12. By the swords of the mighty will
I cause thy multitude to fall, the
terrible of the nations, all of them: and
they shall spoil the pomp of
Egypt, and all the multitude
thereof shall be destroyed.
13. **I will destroy also** all
the beasts thereof from
beside the great
waters; neither
shall the foot of
man trouble them any more,
nor the hoofs of
beasts trouble them.
14. **Then will I make their**
waters deep, and cause
their rivers to run like oil,
saith the Lord GOD.
15. **When I** shall
make the land of
Egypt desolate, and the
country shall be destitute of that
whereof it was full, when I shall
smite all them that dwell therein,
then shall they know that
I am the LORD.
16. **This is the lamentation**
wherewith they shall lament
her: the daughters of
the nations shall lament
her: they shall lament for her, *even*
for Egypt, and for all her multitude,
saith the Lord GOD.
17. It came to pass also in the
twelfth year, in the fifteenth
day of the month, *that* the word of
the LORD came unto me, saying,
18. **Son of man,**
wail for the multitude of
Egypt, and cast them
down, *even* her, and the
daughters of the famous nations,
unto the nether parts of the earth,
with them that go
down into the pit.
19. **Whom dost thou**
pass in beauty?
go down, and be thou laid
with the uncircumcised.
20. **They shall fall** in
the midst of *them that are* slain
by the sword: she is

delivered to the sword: draw her and all her multitudes.

21. **The strong** among the mighty **shall speak** to him **out of** the midst of **hell with them that help him:** they are gone down, they lie uncircumcised, slain by the sword.

22. **Asshur is there** and all her company: his graves *are* about him: all of them slain, fallen by the sword:

23. Whose graves are set in the sides of the pit, and her company is round about her grave: all of them slain, fallen by the sword, **which caused terror in the land of the living.**

24. **There is Elam** and all her multitude round about her grave, all of them slain, fallen by the sword, **which are gone down uncircumcised into the nether parts of the earth, which caused their terror** in the land of the living; **yet have they borne their shame** with them that go down to the pit.

25. **They have set her a bed in the midst of the slain** with all her multitude: her graves *are* round about him: all of them uncircumcised, slain by the sword: though their terror was caused in the land of the living, yet have they borne their shame with them that go down to the pit: he is put in the midst of *them that be* slain.

26. **There is Meshech, Tubal, and** all **her multitude:** her graves *are* round about him: all of them uncircumcised, slain by the sword, though **they caused their terror** in the land of the living.

27. **And they shall not lie with the mighty that are fallen of the uncircumcised, which are gone down to hell** with their weapons of war: and they have laid their swords under their heads, but **their iniquities shall be upon their bones,** though *they were* the terror of the mighty in the land of the living.

28. **Yea, thou shalt be broken in the midst of the uncircumcised,** and shalt lie with *them that are* slain with the sword.

29. **There is Edom,** her kings, and all her princes, which with their might are laid by *them that were* **slain by the sword: they shall** lie with the uncircumcised, and with them that **go down to the pit.**

30. There *be* **the princes of the north,** all of them, **and** all **the Zidonians,** which are gone down with the slain; with their terror they **are ashamed of their might; and they** lie uncircumcised with *them that be* slain by the sword, and **bear their shame with them that go down to the pit.**

31. **Pharaoh shall see them, and shall be comforted** over all his multitude, *even* Pharaoh and all his army slain by the sword, saith the Lord GOD.

32. **For I have caused my terror in the land of the living:** and he shall be laid in the midst of the uncircumcised with *them that are* slain with the sword, *even* Pharaoh and all his multitude, saith the Lord GOD.

CHAPTER 33

1. **Again the word of the LORD came** unto me, **saying,**

2. Son of man, **speak to** the children of **thy people**, and say unto them, **When I bring the sword upon a land, if the**

people of the land
take a man of their coasts,
and set him for
their watchman:
3. **If when he seeth the**
sword come upon the land,
he blow the trumpet,
and warn the people;
4. **Then whosoever**
heareth the sound of
the trumpet, and
taketh not warning; if the
sword come, and take him away,
his blood shall be
upon his own head.
5. He heard the sound of the
trumpet, and took not warning;
his blood shall be upon him.
But he that taketh warning
shall deliver his soul.
6. **But if the watchman**
see the sword come, and
blow not the trumpet, and
the people be not warned;
if the sword come, and take *any*
person from among them,
he is taken away in his
iniquity; but his blood
will I require at the
watchman's hand.
7. **So** thou, O son of man,
I have set thee a
watchman unto the house of
Israel; therefore thou shalt
hear the word at my mouth,
and warn them from me.
8. **When I say unto the**
wicked, O wicked *man,*
thou shalt surely die;
if thou dost not speak to
warn the wicked from his way,
that wicked
man shall die in his iniquity;
but his blood will
I require at thine hand.
9. **Nevertheless, if thou**
warn the wicked
of his way to turn from it;
if he do not turn from his
way, he shall die in his
iniquity; but thou hast
delivered thy soul.
10. **Therefore, O**

thou son of man, speak
unto the house of
Israel; Thus ye speak, saying,
If our transgressions
and our
sins be upon us,
and we pine away in them,
how should we then
live?
11. **Say unto them,** *As*
I live, saith the Lord GOD,
I have no pleasure in the
death of the wicked;
but that the wicked turn
from his way and live: turn ye,
turn ye from your evil ways; for
why will ye die, O house of Israel?
12. **Therefore,**
thou son of man,
say unto the children
of thy people,
The righteousness of
the righteous shall not
deliver him in the day of
his transgression:
as for the wickedness of
the wicked, he shall
not fall thereby in
the day that
he turneth from his
wickedness; neither shall
the righteous be able to
live for his *righteousness*
in the day that he sinneth.
13. **When I** shall
say to
the righteous, *that* he
shall surely
live; if he trust to
his own
righteousness, and
commit iniquity, all
his righteousnesses
shall not be
remembered; but for his
iniquity that he hath committed,
he shall die for it.
14. **Again, when I say**
unto the wicked,
Thou shalt surely
die; if he turn from
his sin, and do that
which is lawful and

■ **right;**

15. *If* the wicked restore the
pledge, give again that he had
robbed, walk in the statutes of
life, without committing iniquity;

■ **he shall surely live,**
he shall not die.

■ 16. **None of his sins**
that he hath committed

■ **shall be mentioned** unto
him: he hath done that which is
lawful and right; he shall surely live.

■ 17. **Yet** the children of

■ **thy people say, The way**

■ **of the Lord is not equal:**

■ **but as for them, their**

■ **way is not equal.**

■ 18. **When the righteous**
turneth from his righteousness, and

■ **committeth iniquity,**

■ **he shall** even

■ **die** thereby.

■ 19. **But if the wicked turn**

■ **from his wickedness,** and
do that which is lawful and right,

■ **he shall live** thereby.

20. Yet ye say, The way of the Lord
is not equal. O ye house of Israel,

■ **I will judge** you

■ **every one after his ways.**

■ 21. **And it came to pass**

■ **in the twelfth year of our**

■ **captivity,** in the tenth *month*,
in the fifth *day* of the month, *that*

■ **one that had**

■ **escaped out of**

■ **Jerusalem came** unto me,

■ **saying, The city is smitten**.

22. Now the hand of the LORD
was upon me in the evening, afore he
that was escaped came; and had
opened my mouth, until he came to
me in the morning; and my mouth was
opened, and I was no more dumb.

■ 23. **Then the word of the**

■ **LORD came** unto me,

■ **saying,**

24. Son of man,

■ **they that inhabit**
those wastes of the land of

■ **Israel speak, saying,**
Abraham was one, and he
inherited the land: but

■ **we are many; the land is**

■ **given us for inheritance.**

■ 25. **Wherefore say unto**

■ **them,** Thus saith the Lord GOD;

■ **Ye eat with** the

■ **blood, and lift** up

■ **your eyes toward** your

■ **idols,** and shed blood: and

■ **shall ye possess the land?**

26. Ye stand upon your sword,

■ **ye work**

■ **abomination, and** ye

■ **defile every one his**

■ **neighbour's wife:** and

■ **shall ye possess the land?**

27. Say thou thus unto them,

■ **Thus saith the**

■ **Lord** GOD; *As* I live, surely

■ **they** that *are* in the wastes

■ **shall fall by the sword,**

■ **and him** that *is*

■ **in the open field will I give**

■ **to the beasts to be**

■ **devoured, and they** that *be*

■ **in the forts and** in the

■ **caves shall die**

■ **of the pestilence.**

■ 28. **For I will lay the land**
most desolate, and the pomp
of her strength shall cease;

■ **and the mountains**

■ **of Israel** shall be

■ **desolate,** that none
shall pass through.

29. Then shall they know
that I *am* the LORD, when I have
laid the land most desolate

■ **because of** all

■ **their abominations**
which they have committed.

■ 30. **Also,** thou son
of man, the children of

■ **thy people still are**

■ **talking against thee**
by the walls and in the doors of
the houses, and speak one to
another, every one to his brother,

■ **saying, Come,** I pray you,

■ **and hear what is the**

■ **word** that cometh forth

■ **from the LORD.**

31. And they come unto
thee as the people cometh,

and they sit before
thee *as* my people,
and they
hear thy words, but
they will not do them: for
with their mouth
they shew much
love, but their heart
goeth after their
covetousness.
32. And, lo,
thou art unto them
as a very
lovely song of one that
hath a pleasant voice, and
can play well on an instrument:
for they hear thy
words, but they
do them not.
33. And when this cometh
to pass, (lo, it will come,)
then shall they know
that a prophet hath
been among them.

CHAPTER 34

1. And the word of the LORD
came unto me, saying,
2. Son of man, prophesy
against the shepherds of
Israel, prophesy,
and say unto them, Thus saith
the Lord GOD unto the shepherds;
Woe be to the shepherds
of Israel that do feed
themselves! should not the shepherds
feed the flocks?
3. Ye eat the fat, and ye clothe you
with the wool, ye kill them that are fed:
but ye feed not the flock.
4. The diseased have ye not
strengthened, neither have ye
healed *that which was* sick, neither
have ye bound up that which was
broken, neither have ye brought again
that which was driven away,
neither have ye sought
that which was lost;
but with force and with
cruelty have ye ruled them.
5. And they were scattered,
because there is no
shepherd: and they became

meat to all the beasts of the field,
when they were scattered.
6. My sheep wandered
through all the mountains,
and upon every high
hill: yea, my flock
was scattered upon all
the face of the earth, and
none did search or seek
after them.
7. Therefore, ye shepherds,
hear the word of the LORD;
8. As I live, saith the
Lord GOD, surely
because my flock
became a prey, and
my flock became meat to
every beast of the field,
because there was
no shepherd,
neither did my shepherds
search for my flock, but the shepherds
fed themselves,
and fed not my flock;
9. Therefore, O ye shepherds,
hear the word of the LORD;
10. Thus saith the Lord GOD; Behold,
I am against the
shepherds; and
I will require my flock
at their hand, and
cause them to cease from
feeding the flock; neither
shall the shepherds feed
themselves any more;
for I will deliver my
flock from their mouth, that
they may not be meat for them.
11. For thus saith the
Lord GOD; Behold, I, *even*
I, will both
search my sheep,
and seek them out.
12. As a shepherd
seeketh out
his flock in the day that he is
among his sheep *that are* scattered;
so will I seek out my
sheep, and will
deliver them out of all
places where they
have been scattered
in the cloudy and dark day.

13. **And I will** bring them out from the people, and gather them from the countries, and will **bring them to their own land, and** feed them upon the mountains of Israel by the rivers, and in all the inhabited places of the country.

14. I will feed them in a good pasture, and **upon the** high **mountains of Israel shall their fold be:** there shall they lie in a good fold, and *in* a fat pasture shall they feed upon the mountains of Israel.

15. **I will feed my flock, and I will cause them to lie down, saith the Lord** GOD.

16. **I will seek that which was lost,** and bring again that which was driven away, and will bind up *that which was* broken, and will strengthen that which was sick: **but I will destroy the fat and the strong;** I will feed them with judgment.

17. **And as for you, O my flock,** thus saith the Lord GOD; Behold, **I judge between cattle and cattle, between** the **rams and** the he **goats.**

18. **Seemeth it a small thing** unto you **to have eaten** up **the good pasture, but ye must tread down** with your feet **the residue** of your pastures? **and to have drunk of the deep waters, but ye must foul the residue** with your feet?

19. **And** *as for* **my flock,** they **eat that which ye have trodden** with your feet; **and they drink that which ye have fouled** with your feet.

20. **Therefore** thus saith the Lord GOD unto them; Behold, I, *even* **I, will judge between the fat** cattle **and** between the **lean** cattle.

21. **Because ye have** thrust with side and with shoulder, and **pushed** all **the diseased** with your horns, **till ye have scattered them** abroad;

22. **Therefore will I save my flock,** and they shall no more be a prey; and I will judge between cattle and cattle.

23. **And I will set up one shepherd over them,** and he shall feed them, **even my servant David;** he **shall feed them,** and he shall be their shepherd.

24. **And I** the LORD **will be their God, and** my servant **David a prince among them;** I the LORD have spoken *it*.

25. **And I will make** with them **a covenant of peace,** and will cause the evil beasts to cease out of the land: and **they shall dwell safely in the wilderness, and** sleep in the woods.

26. **And I will make them** and the places round about my hill **a blessing**; and I will cause the shower to come down in his season; there shall be showers of blessing.

27. **And** the tree of the field shall yield her fruit, and **the earth shall yield her increase, and they shall** be safe in their land, and shall **know** that I *am* the LORD, when **I have** broken the bands of their yoke, and **delivered them** out of the hand of those that served themselves of them.

28. **And they shall no more be a prey to the heathen,** neither shall the beast of the land devour them; **but they shall dwell safely, and none shall make them afraid.**

■ 29. **And I will raise up** for them
■ **a plant of renown, and**
■ **they shall** be
■ **no more** consumed with
■ **hunger** in the land,
■ **neither bear** the
■ **shame** of the heathen any more.
■ 30. **Thus shall they know** that
■ I the LORD their God
■ **am with them,** and *that* they,
even the house of Israel, *are* my
people, saith the Lord GOD.
■ 31. **And ye** my flock,
■ **the flock of my pasture,**
■ **are men, and I am your**
■ **God**, saith the Lord GOD.

CHAPTER 35

■ 1. **Moreover** the word of the
LORD came unto me, saying,
■ 2. **Son of man, set thy**
■ **face against mount**
■ **Seir,** and prophesy against it,
■ 3. **And say** unto it, Thus saith the
Lord GOD; Behold, O mount Seir,
■ **I am against thee,** and I will
stretch out mine hand against thee,
■ **and I will make thee** most
■ **desolate.**
■ 4. **I will lay thy cities waste,**
and thou shalt be desolate, and thou
shalt know that I *am* the LORD.
■ 5. **Because thou hast** had
■ **a perpetual hatred,** and
hast shed *the blood of* the children
■ **of Israel** by the force of the sword
■ **in** the time of
■ **their calamity,** in the time
that their iniquity *had* an end:
■ 6. **Therefore,** *as* I live,
saith the Lord GOD,
■ **I will prepare thee**
■ **unto blood, and**
■ **blood shall pursue**
■ **thee:** sith thou hast not hated
blood, even blood shall pursue thee.
■ 7. **Thus will I make**
■ **mount Seir** most
■ **desolate,** and cut off from
it him that passeth out and
him that returneth.
■ 8. **And** I will
■ **fill his mountains with his**

■ **slain** *men*: in thy hills, and in thy
valleys, and in all thy rivers, shall they
fall that are slain with the sword.
■ 9. I will make thee perpetual
desolations, and thy cities
shall not return: and ye shall
know that I *am* the LORD.
■ 10. **Because thou hast**
■ **said, These two nations**
and these two countries
■ **shall be mine,** and we
will possess it; whereas the
LORD was there:
■ 11. **Therefore,** *as* I live,
■ **saith the Lord** GOD,
I will even do according to thine
anger, and according to thine envy
which thou hast used out of thy
hatred against them; and
■ **I will make myself**
■ **known among them,**
■ **when I have judged thee.**
■ 12. And thou shalt know that
I *am* the LORD, *and that*
■ **I have heard** all
■ **thy blasphemies**
which thou hast spoken
■ **against** the mountains of
■ **Israel, saying, They are** laid
■ **desolate, they are**
■ **given us to consume.**
■ 13. **Thus** with your mouth
■ **ye have boasted against**
■ **me,** and have multiplied your words
against me: I have heard *them*.
■ 14. Thus saith the Lord GOD;
■ **When the whole earth**
■ **rejoiceth, I will make**
■ **thee desolate.**
■ 15. **As thou didst**
■ **rejoice at** the
inheritance of the house of
■ **Israel, because it was**
■ **desolate, so** will I do unto thee:
■ **thou shalt be desolate**,
O mount Seir, and all Idumea,
even all of it: and they shall
know that I *am* the LORD.

CHAPTER 36

■ 1. **Also,** thou son of man,
■ **prophesy unto the**
■ **mountains of Israel,**

■ **and say,** Ye mountains of Israel, hear the word of the LORD:

■ 2. **Thus saith the Lord** GOD; **Because the enemy hath said against you, Aha, even the** ancient **high places are ours** in possession:

3. Therefore prophesy and say, Thus saith the Lord GOD; **Because they have made you desolate,** and swallowed you up on every side, **that ye might be a possession** unto the residue **of the heathen,** and ye are taken up in the lips of talkers, and *are* an infamy of the people:

4. Therefore, ye mountains of Israel, hear the word of the Lord GOD; Thus saith the Lord GOD to the mountains, and to the hills, to the rivers, and to the valleys, to the desolate wastes, and to the cities that are forsaken, which became a prey and derision to the residue of the heathen that *are* round about;

5. **Therefore thus saith the Lord** GOD; Surely **in the fire of my jealousy have I spoken against the** residue of the **heathen,** and against all Idumea, **which** have **appointed my land** into **their possession** with the joy of all *their* heart, with despiteful minds, to cast it out for a prey.

6. **Prophesy** therefore **concerning** the land of **Israel, and say** unto the mountains, and to the hills, to the rivers, and to the valleys, Thus saith the Lord GOD; Behold, I have spoken in my jealousy and in my fury, **because ye have borne the shame of the heathen:**

7. Therefore thus saith the Lord GOD; **I have lifted up mine hand, Surely the heathen that** *are* about you, they **shall bear their shame.**

■ 8. **But ye, O** mountains of **Israel,** ye **shall shoot forth your branches, and yield** your **fruit to my people** of Israel; for they are at hand to come.

■ 9. **For,** behold, I *am* for you, and I will turn unto you, and **ye shall be tilled and sown:**

■ 10. **And I will multiply men upon you,** all the house of Israel, *even* all of it: **and the cities shall be inhabited, and the wastes** shall be **builded:**

■ 11. **And I will** multiply upon you man and beast; and they shall increase and bring fruit: and I will settle you after your old estates, and will **do better unto you than at your beginnings:** and ye shall know that I *am* the LORD.

■ 12. **Yea, I will cause men to walk upon you,** *even* my people Israel; **and** they shall **possess thee, and** thou shalt be their inheritance, and thou shalt no more henceforth bereave them *of men.*

13. Thus saith the Lord GOD; **Because they say** unto you, **Thou land devourest** up **men, and** hast **bereaved** thy **nations:**

14. **Therefore thou shalt devour men no more, neither bereave** thy **nations** any more, **saith the Lord** GOD.

15. **Neither will** I cause **men to hear in thee the shame of the heathen** any more, **neither shalt thou bear** the **reproach** of the people **any more, neither shalt thou cause** thy **nations to fall** any more,

saith the Lord GOD.

16. Moreover the word of the LORD came unto me, saying,

17. Son of man, **when** the house of **Israel dwelt in their own land, they defiled it** by their own way and by their doings: their way was before me as the uncleanness of a removed woman.

18. **Wherefore I poured my fury upon them for the blood** that **they** had **shed** upon the land, **and for their idols** *wherewith* they had polluted it:

19. **And I scattered them among the heathen, and** they were dispersed through the countries: according to their way and **according to their doings I judged them.**

20. **And when they entered unto the heathen,** whither they went, **they profaned my holy name,** when they said to them, These are the people of the LORD, and *are* gone forth out of his land.

21. **But I had pity** for mine holy name, which the house of Israel had profaned among the heathen, whither they went.

22. **Therefore say unto** the house of **Israel,** thus saith the Lord GOD; **I do not this for your sakes**, O house of Israel, **but for mine holy name's sake,** which ye have profaned among the heathen, whither ye went.

23. **And I will sanctify my** great **name,** which was profaned among the heathen, which ye have profaned in the midst of them; **and the heathen shall know** that **I am the LORD,** saith the Lord GOD, **when I shall be sanctified** in you

before their eyes. 24. **For I will take you from among the heathen,** and gather you out of all countries, **and will bring you into your own land.**

25. **Then will I sprinkle clean water upon you, and ye shall be clean: from** all **your filthiness, and** from all **your idols,** will I cleanse you.

26. **A new heart** also **will I give you, and a new spirit will I put within you:** and I will take away the stony heart out of your flesh, and I will give you an heart of flesh.

27. **And I will** put my spirit within you, and **cause you to walk in my statutes,** and ye shall keep my judgments, and do *them*.

28. **And ye shall dwell in the land** that **I gave** to **your fathers; and ye shall be my people, and I will be your God.**

29. I will also save you from all your uncleannesses: and **I will** call for the corn, and will increase it, and **lay no famine upon you.**

30. **And I will multiply the fruit of the** tree, and the increase of the **field,** that ye shall receive no more reproach of famine among the heathen.

31. **Then shall ye remember your** own **evil ways,** and your doings that *were* not good, **and shall lothe yourselves** in your own sight for your iniquities and for your abominations.

32. Not for your sakes do I *this*, saith the Lord GOD, be it known unto you: be ashamed and confounded for your own ways, O house of Israel.

33. **Thus saith the Lord** GOD; **In the day that I** shall

■ have cleansed you
from all your iniquities
■ I will also
■ cause you to dwell
■ in the cities, and the
wastes shall be builded.
■ 34. And the desolate
■ land shall be tilled,
whereas it lay desolate in the
sight of all that passed by.
■ 35. And they shall say,
■ This land that was
■ desolate is become
■ like the garden of Eden;
■ and the waste and desolate and
■ ruined cities are
■ become fenced, *and* are
■ inhabited.
■ 36. Then the heathen
that are left round about you
■ shall know that I the LORD
build the ruined *places, and*
plant that that was desolate: I
■ the LORD have spoken *it*, and I
■ will do it.
■ 37. Thus saith the Lord GOD;
■ I will yet *for* this
■ be inquired of by the house of
■ Israel, to do *it* for them;
■ I will increase them
with men like a flock.
■ 38. As the holy flock, as
the flock of Jerusalem in her
solemn feasts; so shall the waste
cities be filled with flocks of men:
■ and they shall know
■ that I am the LORD.

CHAPTER 37

■ 1. The hand of the
■ LORD was upon me, and
■ carried me out
■ in the spirit of the LORD,
■ and set me down
■ in the midst of the
■ valley which was
■ full of bones,
2. And caused me to pass by them
round about: and, behold, *there*
were very many in the open valley;
■ and, lo,
■ they were very dry.
■ 3. And he said unto me,

■ Son of man, can these
■ bones live? And I
■ answered, O Lord GOD,
■ thou knowest.
■ 4. Again he said unto me,
■ Prophesy upon these
■ bones, and say unto them,
■ O ye dry bones, hear
■ the word of the LORD.
■ 5. Thus saith the Lord GOD
unto these bones; Behold,
■ I will cause breath
■ to enter into
■ you, and ye shall live:
■ 6. And I will lay sinews
■ upon you, and will
■ bring up
■ flesh upon you, and cover
■ you with skin, and put
■ breath in you, and ye shall live;
and ye shall know that I *am* the LORD.
■ 7. So I prophesied
as I was commanded:
■ and as I prophesied,
■ there was a noise,
■ and behold
■ a shaking, and the
■ bones came together,
bone to his bone.
■ 8. And when I beheld, lo,
■ the sinews and the
■ flesh came up
■ upon them, and the
■ skin covered them above:
■ but there was no
■ breath in them.
■ 9. Then said he unto
■ me, Prophesy unto
■ the wind, prophesy, son of man,
■ and say to the wind,
Thus saith the Lord GOD; Come
from the four winds, O breath, and
■ breathe upon these
■ slain, that they may live.
■ 10. So I prophesied
as he commanded me,
■ and the breath came
■ into them, and they lived,
■ and stood up upon their feet,
■ an exceeding great army.
■ 11. Then he said
unto me, Son of man,
■ these bones are the whole

house of Israel: behold,
they say, Our bones are dried, and
our hope is lost:
we are cut off for our parts.
12. **Therefore prophesy**
and say unto them, Thus saith the
Lord GOD; Behold, O my people,
I will open your
graves, and cause you to
come up out of your graves,
and bring you into
the land of Israel.
13. **And ye shall know** that
I am the LORD, when I
have opened your graves,
O my people, and brought
you up out of your graves,
14. And shall
put my spirit in you, and ye
shall live, and I shall place you in
your own land: then shall ye know
that I the LORD have spoken *it,*
and performed *it,* saith the LORD.
15. **The word of the LORD**
came again unto me,
saying,
16. Moreover, thou son of man,
take thee
one stick, and write
upon it, For Judah,
and for the children of
Israel his companions:
then take another
stick, and write upon it,
For Joseph, the stick of
Ephraim and *for* all the house of
Israel his companions:
17. **And join them** one to another
into one stick; and they
shall become
one in thine hand.
18. **And** when the children of
thy people shall
speak unto thee,
saying, Wilt thou not shew us
what thou
meanest by
these?
19. **Say unto them,**
Thus saith the Lord
GOD; Behold,
I will take the stick of
Joseph, which *is* in the

hand of Ephraim, and the
tribes of Israel his fellows,
and will put them with him,
even with the stick of
Judah, and make them
one stick, and they shall be one
in mine hand.
20. And the sticks whereon
thou writest shall be in thine
hand before their eyes.
21. And say unto them,
Thus saith the Lord GOD; Behold,
I will take the children of
Israel from among the
heathen, whither they be gone,
and will gather them on every side,
and bring them into
their own land:
22. **And I will make them**
one nation in the land
upon the mountains of Israel;
and one king shall
be king to them all:
and they shall be no more
two nations, neither shall they be
divided into two kingdoms
any more at all.
23. **Neither shall they**
defile themselves any more
with their
idols, nor with their
detestable things, nor with
any of their transgressions:
but I will save them out
of all their dwellingplaces,
wherein they have sinned,
and will cleanse them: so
shall they be my people,
and I will be their God.
24. **And David** my servant
shall be king over
them; and they all shall
have one shepherd: they
shall also
walk in my judgments,
and observe my
statutes, and do them.
25. **And they shall dwell in**
the land that I have given
unto Jacob my servant, wherein
your fathers have dwelt; and
they shall dwell therein, *even* they,
and their children, and their

children's children for ever:
■ **and** my servant
■ **David shall be**
■ **their prince for ever.**
26. **Moreover I will make**
■ **a covenant of peace**
■ **with them;** it shall be
■ **an everlasting**
■ **covenant** with them:
■ **and I will** place them, and
■ **multiply them, and** will
■ **set my sanctuary in the**
■ **midst of them for evermore.**
27. My tabernacle also shall be
with them: yea, I will be their God,
and they shall be my people.
■ 28. **And the heathen**
■ **shall know that I the**
■ **LORD do sanctify Israel,** when
my sanctuary shall be in
the midst of them for evermore.

CHAPTER 38

■ 1. **And the word of the LORD**
■ **came unto me, saying,**
2. Son of man,
■ **set thy face against**
■ **Gog,** the land of Magog,
the chief prince of Meshech
■ **and Tubal,** and
prophesy against him,
■ 3. **And say, Thus saith**
■ **the Lord** GOD; Behold,
■ **I am against thee, O**
■ **Gog,** the chief prince of
Meshech and Tubal:
■ 4. **And I will turn thee**
■ **back, and put hooks**
■ **into thy jaws, and** I will
■ **bring thee forth,** and all thine
army, horses and horsemen, all of
them clothed with all sorts *of*
armour, even a great company
with bucklers and shields, all
of them handling swords:
■ 5. **Persia, Ethiopia, and**
■ **Libya with them;** all of
them with shield and helmet:
■ 6. **Gomer, and** all his
bands; the house of
■ **Togarmah of the north**
quarters, and all his bands:
and many people with thee.

■ 7. **Be thou prepared,** and
prepare for thyself, thou, and
all thy company that are
assembled unto thee, and
be thou a guard unto them.
■ 8. **After many days**
■ **thou shalt be visited: in**
■ **the latter years thou**
■ **shalt come into the**
■ **land** *that is* brought back from
the sword, *and is* gathered out of
many people, against the mountains
of Israel, which have been
always waste: but it is brought
forth out of the nations,
■ **and** they shall
■ **dwell safely** all of them.
■ 9. **Thou shalt**
■ **ascend** and come
■ **like a storm,** thou shalt
be like a cloud to cover the
land, thou, and all thy bands,
and many people with thee.
10. Thus saith the Lord GOD;
It shall also come to pass, *that*
■ **at the same time** shall
things come into thy mind, and
■ **thou shalt think an**
■ **evil thought:**
11. **And** thou
■ **shalt say, I will go** up
■ **to the land of unwalled**
■ **villages;** I will go to them that
are at rest, that dwell safely, all of
them dwelling without walls, and
having neither bars nor gates,
■ 12. **To take a spoil,**
■ **and** to take a prey;
■ **to turn thine hand upon** the
■ **desolate places**
that are now inhabited,
■ **and** upon
■ **the people** *that are*
■ **gathered out of the nations,**
which have gotten cattle and goods,
that dwell in the midst of the land.
■ 13. **Sheba, and Dedan, and**
■ **the merchants of Tarshish,**
with all the young lions thereof,
■ **shall say** unto thee,
■ **Art thou come to take**
■ **a spoil?** hast thou gathered
thy company to take a prey? to

carry away silver and gold, to take away cattle and goods, to take a great spoil?

14. **Therefore,** son of man, **prophesy and say unto Gog,** Thus saith the Lord GOD; In that day **when** my people of **Israel dwelleth safely, shalt thou not know it ?**

15. **And thou shalt come** from thy place **out of the north** parts, thou, and many people **with** thee, all of them riding upon horses, a great company, and **a mighty army:**

16. **And thou shalt come** up **against** my people of **Israel,** as a cloud to cover the land; it shall be in the latter days, **and I will bring thee against my land, that the heathen may know me**, when I shall be sanctified in thee, O Gog, before their eyes.

17. Thus saith the Lord GOD; **Art thou he of whom** I have spoken in old time by my servants **the prophets** of Israel, which **prophesied** in those days *many* years that I would bring thee against them?

18. **And** it shall come to pass at the same time **when Gog shall come against** the land of **Israel,** saith the Lord GOD, *that* **my fury shall come up in my face.**

19. **For in my jealousy and** in the fire of my **wrath** have I spoken, Surely in that day **there shall be a great shaking in** the land of **Israel;**

20. **So that** the fishes of the sea, and the fowls of the heaven, and the beasts of the field, and all creeping things that creep upon the earth, and **all** the men **that are upon** the face of

the earth, shall shake at my presence, and the mountains shall be thrown down, and the steep places shall fall, and every wall shall fall to the ground.

21. **And** I will call for a sword against him throughout all my mountains, saith the Lord GOD: **every man's sword shall be against his brother.**

22. **And I will plead against him with pestilence and** with **blood; and I will rain upon him**, and upon his bands, and upon the many people that *are* with him, an overflowing rain, and **great hailstones, fire, and brimstone.**

23. **Thus will I magnify myself, and sanctify myself;** and I will be known in the eyes of many nations, **and they shall know that I am the LORD.**

CHAPTER 39

1. **Therefore,** thou son of man, **prophesy against Gog, and say, Thus saith the Lord** GOD; Behold, **I am against thee,** O Gog, the chief prince of Meshech and Tubal:

2. **And I will turn thee back, and leave but the sixth part of thee,** and will cause thee to come up from the north parts, **and will bring thee upon the mountains of Israel:**

3. And I will smite thy bow out of thy left hand, and will cause thine arrows to fall out of thy right hand.

4. **Thou shalt fall** upon the mountains of Israel, thou, **and all thy** bands, and the **people** that *is* **with thee: I will give thee unto the** ravenous **birds** of every sort, **and** *to* **the beasts** of the field **to be devoured.**

5. Thou shalt fall upon the open

field: for I have spoken *it,* saith the Lord GOD.

6. **And I will send a fire on Magog,** and among them that dwell carelessly in the isles: and they shall know that I *am* the LORD.

7. **So will I make my holy name known in** the midst of my people **Israel; and I will not let them pollute my holy name any more: and the heathen shall know** that **I am the LORD,** the Holy One in Israel.

8. **Behold,** it is come, and it is done, saith the Lord GOD; **this** *is* the **day** whereof I have spoken.

9. And they that dwell in the cities of **Israel** shall go forth, and **shall set on fire** and burn **the weapons,** both the shields and the bucklers, the bows and the arrows, and the handstaves, and the spears, **and they shall burn them** with fire **seven years:**

10. So that **they shall take no wood** out of the field, neither cut down *any* **out of the forests; for they shall burn the weapons** with fire: **and they shall spoil** those that spoiled them, **and rob those that robbed them, saith the Lord** GOD.

11. **And** it shall come to pass in that day, *that* **I will give unto Gog** a place there of **graves in Israel,** the valley of the passengers on the east of the sea: and it shall stop the *noses* of the passengers: **and there shall they bury Gog and all his multitude:** and they shall call *it* The valley of Hamon–gog.

12. **And seven months shall** the house of

Israel be burying of **them, that they may cleanse the land.**

13. Yea, all the people of the land shall bury *them*; and it shall be to them a renown the day **that I shall be glorified, saith the Lord** GOD.

14. **And they shall sever out men of continual employment, passing through the land to bury** with the passengers **those that remain** upon the face of the earth, to cleanse it: **after the** end of **seven months** shall they search.

15. And the passengers *that* pass through the land, **when any seeth a man's bone, then shall he set up a sign** by it, **till the buriers have buried it** in the valley of Hamon–gog.

16. And also the name of the city *shall be* Hamonah. Thus shall they cleanse the land.

17. **And, thou son of man,** thus saith the Lord GOD; **Speak unto every feathered fowl, and** to **every beast** of the field, **Assemble yourselves,** and come; gather yourselves on every side **to my sacrifice** that I do sacrifice for you, *even* a great sacrifice upon the mountains of Israel, **that ye may eat flesh, and drink blood.**

18. Ye shall eat the flesh of the mighty, and drink the blood of the princes of the earth, of rams, of lambs, and of goats, of bullocks, all of them fatlings of Bashan.

19. **And ye shall eat** fat **till ye be full, and drink** blood **till ye be drunken,** of my sacrifice which I have sacrificed for you.

20. Thus ye shall be filled at my table with horses and chariots,

with mighty men, and with all men of war, saith the Lord GOD.

21. **And I will set my glory among the heathen, and** all **the heathen shall see my judgment** that I have executed, and my hand that I have laid upon them.

22. **So** the house of **Israel shall know** that **I am the LORD** their God from that day and forward.

23. **And the heathen shall know that** the house of **Israel went into captivity for their iniquity:** because they trespassed against me, therefore hid I my face from them, and gave them into the hand of their enemies: so fell they all by the sword.

24. According to their uncleanness and according to their transgressions have I done unto them, and hid my face from them.

25. **Therefore** thus saith the Lord GOD; **Now will I bring again the captivity of Jacob, and have mercy upon** the whole house of **Israel, and will be jealous for my holy name;**

26. **After that they have borne their shame, and** all their trespasses whereby they have trespassed against me, **when they dwelt safely in their land, and none made them afraid.**

27. **When I** have brought them again from the people, and **gathered them out of their enemies' lands, and am sanctified in them** in the sight of many nations;

28. **Then shall they know** that **I am the LORD** their God, which caused them to be led into captivity among the heathen: but I have gathered them unto their own land, and have left none of them any more there.

29. Neither will I hide my face any more from them: **for I have poured out my spirit upon** the house of **Israel,** saith the Lord GOD.

CHAPTER 40

1. **In the five and twentieth year of our captivity,** in the beginning of the year, in the tenth *day* of the month, in the fourteenth year after that the city was smitten, in the selfsame day **the hand of the LORD was upon me, and brought me** thither.

2. **In** the **visions of** God brought he me **into** the land of **Israel, and set me upon a** very high **mountain,** by which *was* as the frame of a city on the south.

3. **And** he brought me thither, and, behold, **there was a man, whose appearance was like** the appearance of **brass, with a line** of flax **in his hand, and a measuring reed;** and he stood in the gate.

4. **And the man said** unto me, Son of man, behold with thine eyes, and hear with thine ears, and **set thine heart upon all that I shall shew thee;** for to the intent **that** I might shew *them* unto thee *art* **thou** brought hither: **declare all that thou seest to** the house of **Israel.**

5. **And behold a wall on the outside of the house** round about, **and in the man's hand a measuring reed of six cubits long** by the cubit and an hand breadth: **so he measured the breadth of the building, one reed; and the**

height, one reed.

6. **Then** came

he unto the gate which looketh toward the east, and went up the stairs thereof, and **measured the threshold of the gate, which was one reed broad;** and the other threshold *of the gate, which was* one reed broad.

7. **And every little chamber was one reed long, and one reed broad; and between the** little **chambers were five cubits; and** the threshold of the gate by the porch of the gate within *was* one reed.

8. He measured also **the porch of the gate within, one reed.**

9. Then measured he **the porch of the gate, eight cubits; and the posts** thereof, **two cubits;** and the porch of the gate *was* inward.

10. **And the** little **chambers** of the gate eastward **were three on this side, and** three on **that side;** they three *were* of one measure: and the posts had one measure on this side and on that side.

11. **And he measured the** breadth of the **entry** of the **gate, ten cubits; and the length** of the gate, **thirteen cubits.**

12. **The space** also **before the** little **chambers was one cubit** *on this side,* **and the** space *was* one cubit on that side: and the little **chambers were six cubits on this side, and** six cubits on **that side.**

13. He measured then **the gate from the roof of one** little **chamber to** the roof of **another:** the breadth **was five and twenty**

cubits, door against door.

14. **He made** also **posts** of **threescore cubits, even** unto the post of the court round about the gate.

15. **And from** the face of the gate of **the entrance unto** the face of **the porch of the inner gate were fifty cubits.**

16. **And there were** narrow **windows to the** little **chambers, and** to their **posts within the gate** round about, and likewise to the arches: and windows *were* round about inward: **and upon each post were palm trees.**

17. **Then brought he me into the outward court, and, lo, there were** chambers, and a pavement made for the court round about: **thirty chambers** *were* **upon the pavement.**

18. **And the pavement** by the side of the gates over against the length of the gates *was* the lower pavement.

19. Then he measured the breadth **from the forefront of the lower gate unto the** forefront of the **inner court** without, **an hundred cubits** eastward and northward.

20. **And the gate** of the outward court that looked **toward the north, he measured the length** thereof, **and** the **breadth** thereof.

21. **And the little chambers** thereof *were* three on this side and three on that side; and the posts thereof and the arches thereof **were** after the measure of the first gate: the length thereof *was* **fifty cubits, and the breadth five and twenty cubits.**

22. And their windows, and their

arches, and their palm trees, *were* after the measure of the gate that looketh toward the east; and they went up unto it by seven steps; and the arches thereof *were* before them.

23. **And the gate of the inner court** *was* over against the gate toward the **north, and** toward the **east**; and **he measured from gate to gate an hundred cubits.**

24. **After that he brought me toward** the south, and behold **a gate** toward the **south: and he measured the posts** thereof **and the arches** thereof according to these measures.

25. **And there were windows** in it and in the arches thereof round about, like those windows: the length *was* fifty cubits, and the breadth five and twenty cubits.

26. **And there were seven steps** to go up to it, **and** the **arches** thereof *were* **before them: and** it had **palm trees,** one on this side, and another on that side, **upon the posts** thereof.

27. **And there was a gate in the inner court toward the south: and he measured from gate to gate** toward the south an hundred cubits.

28. **And** he brought me to the inner court by the south gate: and **he measured the south gate** according to these measures;

29. **And the** little **chambers thereof, and the posts** thereof, **and** the **arches** thereof, according to these measures: **and** *there were* **windows** in it and in the arches thereof round about: *it was* fifty cubits long, and five

and twenty cubits broad.

30. And the arches round about *were* five and twenty cubits long, and five cubits broad.

31. **And the arches** thereof **were toward the utter court; and palm trees were upon the posts** thereof: and the going up to it *had* eight steps.

32. **And** he brought me into **the inner court** toward the **east: and he measured the gate** according to these measures.

33. **And the** little **chambers** thereof, and the **posts** thereof, **and** the **arches thereof,** *were* according to these measures: **and there were windows therein and** in the **arches** thereof **round about:** *it was* fifty cubits long, and five and twenty cubits broad.

34. **And the arches** thereof **were toward the outward court;** and palm trees *were* upon the posts thereof, on this side, and on that side: and the going up to it *had* eight steps.

35. **And he brought me to the north gate, and measured it** according to these measures;

36. **The** little **chambers** thereof, the **posts** thereof, and the **arches** thereof, **and the windows** to it round about: **the length was fifty cubits, and the breadth five and twenty cubits.**

37. And the posts thereof *were* toward the utter court; and palm trees *were* upon the posts thereof, on this side, and on that side: and the going up to it *had* eight steps.

38. **And the chambers and the entries** thereof

■ were by the posts of the
■ gates, where they washed
■ the burnt offering.
■ 39. And in the porch of the gate
■ were two
■ tables on this side, and
two tables on that side,
■ to slay thereon
■ the burnt offering and the
■ sin offering and the
■ trespass offering.
■ 40. And at the side
without, as one goeth up to
■ the entry of the
■ north gate, were two
■ tables; and on the other
side, which *was* at the porch
of the gate, *were* two tables.
41. Four tables *were* on this side,
and four tables on that side, by
the side of the gate; eight tables,
■ whereupon they slew
■ their sacrifices.
■ 42. And the four
■ tables were of hewn
■ stone for the burnt offering, of
■ a cubit and an half long,
■ and a cubit and an half
■ broad, and one cubit high:
whereupon also they laid the
instruments wherewith they slew
the burnt offering and the sacrifice.
43. And within *were* hooks, an
hand broad, fastened round
about: and upon the tables
was the flesh of the offering.
■ 44. And without the inner
■ gate were the chambers
■ of the singers in the inner
court, which *was* at the side of
the north gate; and their prospect
was toward the south: one at the
side of the east gate *having* the
prospect toward the north.
■ 45. And he said unto me,
■ This chamber, whose prospect *is*
■ toward the south, is
■ for the priests, the
■ keepers of the charge of
■ the house.
■ 46. And the chamber
whose prospect *is*
■ toward the north is

■ for the priests, the
■ keepers of the charge of
■ the altar: these *are* the sons
of Zadok among the sons of
Levi, which come near to the
LORD to minister unto him.
■ 47. So he measured the
■ court, an hundred cubits
■ long, and an hundred
■ cubits broad, foursquare;
■ and the altar *that*
■ was before the house.
■ 48. And he brought me
■ to the porch of the house,
■ and measured
■ each post of the porch, five cubits
on this side, and five
cubits on that side:
■ and the breadth of
■ the gate
was three cubits on this side,
■ and three cubits on that side.
49. The length of
■ the porch *was* twenty cubits,
and the breadth eleven cubits,
■ and *he brought me*
■ by the steps whereby
they went up to it: and
■ there were pillars by
the posts, one on this side,
and another on that side.

CHAPTER 41

■ 1. Afterward he brought
■ me to the temple, and
■ measured the posts,
■ six cubits broad on the
■ one side,
■ and six cubits broad on
■ the other side,
■ which was the breadth
■ of the tabernacle.
■ 2. And the breadth of the
■ door was ten cubits; and
■ the sides of the door *were*
■ five cubits on the one side,
and five cubits on the other side:
■ and he measured
■ the length thereof,
■ forty cubits: and the
■ breadth, twenty cubits.
■ 3. Then went
■ he inward, and

■ **measured the post**
■ **of the door,** two cubits;
■ **and the door,** six cubits; and
the breadth of the door, seven cubits.
■ 4. **So** he measured
■ **the length** thereof, twenty cubits;
■ **and the breadth, twenty**
■ **cubits,** before the temple:
■ **and he said** unto me,
■ **This is the most holy place.**
■ 5. **After he measured the**
■ **wall** of the house, six cubits;
■ **and** the breadth of
■ **every** side
■ **chamber,** four cubits,
■ **round** about
■ **the house on every side.**
■ 6. **And the side chambers**
■ **were three, one over**
■ **another,** and
■ **thirty in** order; and they entered into
■ **the wall** which *was*
■ **of the house** for the side
chambers round about, that they
might have hold, but they had not
hold in the wall of the house.
■ 7. **And there**
■ **was** an enlarging, and
■ **a winding** about still
■ **upward to the side**
■ **chambers**: for the winding
about of the house went still
upward round about the house:
■ **therefore the breadth of the**
■ **house** *was still* upward, and so
■ **increased from the**
■ **lowest chamber to the**
■ **highest** by the midst.
■ 8. I saw also the height of
the house round about:
■ **the foundations of the side**
■ **chambers were** a full reed of
■ **six** great
■ **cubits.**
■ 9. **The thickness of**
■ **the wall,** which *was* for the
side chamber without,
■ **was five cubits**: and *that* which
was left *was* the place of the side
chambers that *were* within.
■ 10. **And between the**
■ **chambers was the**
■ **wideness of twenty cubits**

round about the
house on every side.
11. And the doors of the side
chambers *were* toward *the place that*
was left, one door toward the north,
and another door toward the south:
■ **and the breadth** of
the place that was left *was*
■ **five cubits** round about.
12. **Now the building** that *was*
before the separate place at the end
■ **toward the west was**
■ **seventy cubits broad;**
■ **and the wall** of the building
■ **was five cubits**
■ **thick** round about,
■ **and the length** thereof
■ **ninety cubits.**
13. **So he measured the**
■ **house,** an hundred cubits long;
■ **and the separate**
■ **place, and** the building, with
■ **the walls** thereof, an
hundred cubits long;
14. Also the breadth of the face of the
house, and of the separate place
toward the east, an hundred cubits.
15. **And he**
■ **measured** the length of
■ **the building over**
■ **against the separate**
■ **place** which *was* behind it,
■ **and the galleries** thereof on the
one side and on the other side, an
hundred cubits, with the inner temple,
■ **and the porches** of the court;
16. **The door**
■ **posts,** and the narrow
■ **windows, and the**
■ **galleries round** about on
■ **their three stories,**
over against the door,
■ **cieled with wood**
round about, and
■ **from the ground** up
■ **to the windows, and the**
■ **windows were covered;**
17. To that above the door, even
unto the inner house, and without,
and by all the wall round about
within and without, by measure.
18. **And it was made with**
■ **cherubims and palm**

- **trees,** so that a palm tree *was* between a cherub and a cherub;
- **and every cherub**
- **had two faces;**
- 19. So that
- **the face of a man** *was* toward the palm tree on the one side,
- **and** the face of
- **a** young
- **lion** toward the palm tree on the other side: *it was* made through all the house round about.
- 20. From the ground unto above the door *were* cherubims and palm trees made, and *on* the wall of the temple.
- 21. **The posts** of the temple
- **were squared,** *and* the face of the sanctuary; the appearance *of the one* as the appearance *of the other.*
- 22. **The altar of wood**
- **was three cubits high,**
- **and the length** thereof
- **two cubits;** and the corners thereof, and the length thereof,
- **and the walls** thereof,
- **were of wood:**
- **and he said** unto me,
- **This is the table** that *is*
- **before the LORD.**
- 23. And the temple
- **and the sanctuary**
- **had two doors.**
- 24. **And the doors had**
- **two leaves** *apiece,* two turning *leaves;* two leaves for the one door, and two leaves for the other *door.*
- 25. **And there were** made on them,
- **on the doors** of the temple,
- **cherubims and palm trees,** like as *were* made upon the walls;
- **and** *there were* thick
- **planks upon** the face of
- **the porch without.**
- 26. **And** *there were*
- **narrow windows and**
- **palm trees** on the one side and
- **on the** other side, on the
- **sides of the porch,** and *upon* the side chambers of the house, and thick planks.

CHAPTER 42

- 1. **Then he brought me** forth
- **into the utter court,** the way toward the north: and he brought me
- **into the chamber** that *was* over
- **against the separate**
- **place,** and which *was* before the building toward the north.
- 2. **Before the length of an**
- **hundred cubits was the**
- **north door, and the**
- **breadth was fifty cubits.**
- 3. **Over against** the twenty *cubits* which *were* for
- **the inner court,**
- **and** over against
- **the pavement** which
- **was** for
- **the utter court,** *was*
- **gallery against gallery**
- **in three stories.**
- 4. And before the chambers *was* a walk to ten cubits breadth inward, a way of one cubit; and their doors toward the north.
- 5. **Now the upper chambers**
- **were shorter: for the**
- **galleries were higher** than these, than the lower, and than the middlemost of the building.
- 6. For they *were* in three *stories,* but had not pillars as the pillars of the courts:
- **therefore the building**
- **was straitened more** than the lowest and the middlemost
- **from the ground.**
- 7. **And the wall** that *was*
- **without** over against the chambers, toward
- **the utter court** on the forepart of the chambers, the length thereof
- **was fifty cubits.**
- 8. **For the length**
- **of the chambers** that *were* in the otter court
- **was fifty cubits: and,** lo,
- **before the temple were**
- **an hundred cubits.**
- 9. **And** from
- **under these chambers**
- **was the entry** on the east side, as one goeth into them

■ from the utter court.
■ 10. **The chambers were**
■ **in the** thickness of the
■ **wall of the court toward the**
■ **east,** over against the separate
place, and over against the building.
11. And the way before them *was*
like the appearance of the
chambers which *were* toward the
north, as long as they, *and* as
broad as they: and all their goings out
were both according to their fashions,
and according to their doors.
12. And according to the doors of
the chambers that *were* toward the
south *was* a door in the head of the
way, *even* the way directly before
the wall toward the east, as one
entereth into them.
■ 13. **Then said he unto**
■ **me, The north** chambers
■ **and the**
■ **south chambers,** which
■ **are** before the
separate place, they *be*
■ **holy chambers,**
■ **where the priests**
that approach unto the LORD
■ **shall eat the most holy**
■ **things:** there shall they lay the most
holy things, and the meat offering,
and the sin offering, and the trespass
offering; for the place *is* holy.
■ 14. **When the priests**
■ **enter therein,** then shall they
not go out of the holy *place* into
the utter court, but there
■ **they shall lay their**
■ **garments wherein they**
■ **minister; for they are**
■ **holy; and shall put on**
■ **other garments, and**
■ **shall approach** to
those things which *are* for
■ **the people.**
■ 15. **Now when he**
■ **had made an end of**
■ **measuring the inner house,**
■ **he brought me** forth
■ **toward the gate whose**
■ **prospect is** toward the
■ **east, and measured**
■ **it** round about.

■ 16. **He measured**
■ **the east side** with
the measuring reed,
■ **five hundred reeds,** with
the measuring reed round about.
17. He measured
■ **the north side, five**
■ **hundred reeds,** with the
measuring reed round about.
18. He measured
■ **the south side, five**
■ **hundred reeds,** with
the measuring reed.
19. He turned about to
■ **the west side,** *and* measured
■ **five hundred reeds** with
the measuring reed.
20. **He measured** it by
■ **the** four sides: it had a
■ **wall** round about,
■ **five hundred reeds long,**
■ **and five hundred broad,**
■ **to make a separation**
■ **between the sanctuary**
■ **and the profane place.**

CHAPTER 43

■ 1. **Afterward he brought**
■ **me to the gate,** *even* the gate
■ **that looketh toward**
■ **the east:**
■ 2. **And,** behold,
■ **the glory of** the
■ **God** of Israel
■ **came from** the way of
■ **the east:** and
■ **his voice was like** a noise of
■ **many waters: and the**
■ **earth shined with his glory.**
■ 3. **And it was** according
to the appearance of
■ **the vision** which I saw, *even*
according to the vision that
■ **I saw when I came to**
■ **destroy the city:** and the
visions *were* like the vision that I saw
■ **by the river Chebar;**
■ **and I fell upon my face.**
■ 4. **And the glory of the**
■ **LORD came into the house**
by the way of the gate whose
prospect *is* toward the east.
■ 5. **So the spirit took**

me up, and brought me
into the inner
court; and, behold,
the glory of the LORD
filled the house.
6. And I heard him
speaking unto
me out of the house;
and the man stood by me.
7. And he said
unto me, Son of man,
the place of my throne, and
the place of the soles of my feet,
where I will dwell in the
midst of the children of
Israel for ever, and my
holy name, shall the house of
Israel no more defile, *neither*
they, nor their kings, by their
whoredom, nor by the carcases of
their kings in their high places.
8. In their setting of their
threshold by my thresholds,
and their post by my posts,
and the wall between me and
them, they have even defiled
my holy name by their abominations
that they have committed: wherefore I
have consumed them in mine anger.
9. Now let them put away
their whoredom, and the
carcases of their kings, far from me,
and I will dwell in the
midst of them for ever.
10. Thou son of man,
shew the house to the house of
Israel, that they may be
ashamed of their iniquities:
and let them measure the pattern.
11. And if they be ashamed
of all that they have done,
shew them the form
of the house, and the fashion
thereof, and the goings out thereof,
and the comings in thereof, and
all the forms thereof, and all
the ordinances thereof,
and all the forms thereof, and
all the laws thereof: and
write it in their sight,
that they may keep the
whole form thereof, and all the
ordinances thereof, and do

them.
12. This is the
law of the house; Upon
the top of the mountain
the whole limit thereof
round about shall be
most holy. Behold, this *is*
the law of the house.
13. And these are the
measures of the altar
after the cubits: The cubit *is* a
cubit and an hand breadth; even
the bottom shall be a cubit,
and the breadth a cubit,
and the border thereof by
the edge thereof round about
shall be a span: and
this shall be the higher
place of the altar.
14. And from the bottom *upon*
the ground *even*
to the lower settle shall
be two cubits, and the
breadth one cubit; and
from the lesser settle *even*
to the greater settle *shall be*
four cubits, and the
breadth one cubit.
15. So the altar *shall be* four cubits;
and from the altar and
upward shall be
four horns.
16. And the altar shall be
twelve *cubits* long, twelve broad,
square in the four squares thereof.
17. And the settle *shall be*
fourteen cubits long
and fourteen broad in the
four squares thereof;
and the border about it *shall be*
half a cubit; and the
bottom thereof *shall be*
a cubit about;
and his stairs shall
look toward the east.
18. And he said unto me, Son
of man, thus saith the Lord GOD;
These are the ordinances of
the altar in the day when
they shall make it, to offer
burnt offerings thereon, and
to sprinkle blood thereon.
19. And thou shalt give to

the priests the Levites
that be of the seed of Zadok,
which approach unto me, to
minister unto me,
saith the Lord GOD,
a young bullock
for a sin offering.
20. **And** thou shalt
take of
the blood thereof,
and put it on the four
horns of it,
and on
the four
corners of the
settle, and upon
the border round about:
thus shalt thou cleanse
and purge it.
21. **Thou shalt**
take the bullock also of
the sin offering, and he shall
burn it in the appointed
place of the house,
without the sanctuary.
22. **And on the**
second day thou shalt
offer a kid of the goats
without blemish for a
sin offering; and they shall
cleanse the altar, as they did
cleanse *it* with the bullock.
23. **When thou hast**
made an end of
cleansing it, thou shalt
offer a young
bullock without blemish,
and a ram out of the flock
without blemish.
24. And thou shalt offer
them before the LORD,
and the priests shall cast
salt upon them, and they shall
offer them up
for a burnt
offering unto the LORD.
25. **Seven days** shalt thou
prepare every day
a goat for a sin
offering: they shall
also prepare a
young bullock,
and a ram out of the flock,

without blemish.
26. **Seven days shall**
they purge the altar
and purify it; and they shall
consecrate themselves.
27. And when these days
are expired, it shall be, *that*
upon the eighth
day, and *so* forward,
the priests shall make your
burnt offerings upon
the altar, and your
peace offerings; and
I will accept you,
saith the Lord GOD.

CHAPTER 44

1. **Then he brought me**
back the way of the
gate of the outward sanctuary
which looketh toward the
east; and it was shut.
2. **Then said the**
LORD unto me;
This gate shall be
shut, it shall not be opened,
and no man shall enter in
by it; because the
LORD, the God of Israel,
hath entered in
by it, therefore it shall be shut.
3. *It is* for the prince;
the prince, he
shall sit in it to eat bread
before the LORD; he shall
enter by the way of the
porch of *that* gate, and shall
go out by the way of the same.
4. **Then brought he me**
the way of the north
gate before the house:
and I looked, and, behold,
the glory of the LORD filled
the house of the LORD:
and I fell upon my face.
5. **And the LORD**
said unto me, Son of man,
mark well, and behold with thine
eyes, and hear with thine ears
all that I say unto thee
concerning all
the ordinances of the
house of the LORD, and all the

laws thereof; and mark well the
■ **entering in of the house,**
■ **with every going forth**
■ **of the sanctuary.**
■ 6. **And** thou shalt
■ **say to the rebellious,**
even to the house
■ **of Israel,** Thus saith
the Lord GOD; O ye house of Israel,
■ **let it suffice you of all**
■ **your abominations,**
7. In that
■ **ye have brought into my**
■ **sanctuary strangers,**
uncircumcised in heart, and
uncircumcised in flesh, to
be in my sanctuary,
■ **to pollute it,** *even* my
house, when ye offer my bread,
the fat and the blood,
■ **and they have broken**
■ **my covenant** because
of all your abominations.
■ 8. **And ye have not**
■ **kept** the charge of
■ **mine holy things**: but ye have
set keepers of my charge in my
sanctuary for yourselves.
9. Thus saith the Lord GOD;
■ **No stranger,** uncircumcised in
heart, nor uncircumcised in flesh,
■ **shall enter** into
■ **my sanctuary,** of any stranger
that *is* among the children of Israel.
■ 10. **And the Levites that**
■ **are gone away** far
■ **from me, when Israel went**
■ **astray,** which went astray away
from me after their idols; they
■ **shall** even
■ **bear their iniquity.**
■ 11. **Yet they shall be**
■ **ministers in my sanctuary,**
having charge at the gates of the
house, and ministering to the house:
■ **they shall slay the burnt**
■ **offering** and the sacrifice
for the people, and they shall
stand before them to
minister unto them.
■ 12. **Because they**
■ **ministered**
■ **unto** them before their

■ **idols, and**
■ **caused** the house of
■ **Israel to fall into**
■ **iniquity;** therefore have
■ **I lifted up mine hand**
against them, saith the Lord GOD,
■ **and they shall**
■ **bear their iniquity.**
■ 13. **And they shall**
■ **not come near** unto
■ **me, to do the office**
■ **of a priest** unto me, nor to come
near to any of my holy things, in the
most holy *place*: but they shall bear
their shame, and their abominations
which they have committed.
■ 14. **But I will make them**
■ **keepers** of the charge
■ **of the house, for** all
■ **the service thereof,** and
for all that shall be done therein.
■ 15. **But the priests** the Levites,
■ **the sons of Zadok,**
■ **that kept** the charge of
■ **my sanctuary**
■ **when** the children of
■ **Israel went astray** from me,
■ **they shall come near** to me
■ **to minister unto me, and** they
■ **shall** stand before me to
■ **offer** unto me
■ **the fat and the blood,**
saith the Lord GOD:
■ 16. **They shall enter** into
■ **my sanctuary,** and they
shall come near to my table,
■ **to minister unto me,**
and they shall keep my charge.
■ 17. **And** it shall come to pass, *that*
■ **when they enter** in
at the gates of
■ **the inner court, they shall**
■ **be clothed with linen**
■ **garments;** and no wool shall come
upon them, whiles they minister in the
gates of the inner court, and within.
■ 18. **They shall have linen**
■ **bonnets** upon their heads,
■ **and** shall have linen
■ **breeches** upon their loins;
■ **they shall not gird**
■ **themselves with any thing**
■ **that causeth sweat.**

19. **And when they go** forth **into the utter court,** *even* into the utter court to the people, **they shall put off their garments** wherein they ministered, **and lay them in the holy chambers, and** they shall **put on other garments;** and they shall not sanctify the people with their garments.

20. **Neither shall they shave their heads, nor suffer their locks to grow long;** they shall only poll their heads.

21. **Neither shall any priest drink wine, when they enter** into **the inner court.**

22. **Neither shall they take for their wives a widow, nor her that is put away: but** they shall take **maidens** of the seed of the house **of Israel, or a widow that had a priest before.**

23. **And they shall teach** my people **the difference between** the **holy and profane, and** cause them to discern between the unclean and the clean.

24. **And in controversy they shall stand in judgment;** *and* they shall judge it according to my judgments: **and** they **shall keep my laws and** my statutes in all mine assemblies; and they shall **hallow my sabbaths.**

25. **And they shall come at no dead person** to defile themselves: **but for father,** or for **mother,** or for **son,** or for **daughter,** for **brother, or for sister that hath had no husband, they may defile themselves.**

26. **And after he is cleansed,** they shall reckon unto him

seven days.

27. **And** in the day that he **goeth into the sanctuary,** unto the inner court, **to minister** in the sanctuary, **he shall offer his sin offering,** saith the Lord GOD.

28. **And it shall be unto them for an inheritance:** I *am* their inheritance: and **ye shall give them no possession in Israel:** I *am* their possession.

29. **They shall eat the meat offering, and the sin offering, and the trespass offering: and every dedicated thing in Israel shall be theirs.**

30. **And the first of all the firstfruits** of all *things,* **and** every **oblation** of all, of every *sort* of your oblations, **shall be the priest's:** ye shall also give unto the priest the first of your dough, **that he may cause the blessing to rest in thine house.**

31. **The priests shall not eat** of **any thing** that is **dead of itself, or torn,** whether it be fowl or beast.

CHAPTER 45

1. **Moreover, when ye** shall **divide** by lot **the land** for inheritance, ye shall **offer** an oblation unto **the LORD, an holy portion** of the land: the length *shall be* **the length** of **five and twenty thousand reeds, and the breadth** *shall be* **ten thousand.** This *shall be* holy in all the borders thereof round about.

2. **Of this there shall be for the sanctuary five hundred** *in length,* with five hundred *in breadth,* **square** round about;

■ and fifty cubits round about
■ for the suburbs thereof.
■ 3. And of this measure
shalt thou measure
■ the length of five and twenty
■ thousand, and the breadth
■ of ten thousand: and in it
■ shall be the
■ sanctuary and the
■ most holy place.
■ 4. The holy portion of the land
■ shall be for the priests the
ministers of the sanctuary, which shall
come near to minister unto
the LORD: and it shall be a place
■ for their houses,
■ and an holy place for
■ the sanctuary.
■ 5. And the five and twenty
thousand of length, and the
ten thousand of breadth
■ shall also the Levites,
the ministers of the house,
■ have for themselves,
for a possession for
■ twenty chambers.
■ 6. And ye shall appoint
■ the possession of the
city five thousand broad, and five
and twenty thousand long, over
■ against the oblation of the
■ holy portion: it shall be for
■ the whole house of Israel.
■ 7. And a portion shall be
for the prince on the one side and
on the other side of the oblation
■ of the holy portion, and of the
possession of the city, before the
oblation of the holy*portion,* and before
the possession of the city, from the
west side westward,and from the east
side eastward: and the length *shall be*
over against one of the portions, from
the west border unto the east border.
■ 8. In the land shall be his
possession in Israel: and
■ my princes shall no more
■ oppress my people; and
■ the rest of the land shall
■ they give to the house of
■ Israel according
■ to their tribes.
■ 9. Thus saith the Lord

GOD; Let it suffice you,
■ O princes of Israel:
■ remove violence and spoil,
■ and execute judgment and
■ justice,
take away your exactions from
my people, saith the Lord GOD.
■ 10. Ye shall have just
■ balances, and
■ a just ephah,
■ and a just bath.
11. The ephah and the bath shall
be of one measure, that the bath
may contain the tenth part of an
homer, and the ephah the tenth
part of an homer: the measure
thereof shall be after the homer.
12. And the shekel *shall be* twenty
gerahs: twenty shekels, five and
twenty shekels, fifteen shekels,
shall be your maneh.
■ 13. This is the oblation that
■ ye shall offer; the sixth
■ part of an ephah of an homer
■ of wheat, and ye shall give the
sixth part of an ephah of an homer of
■ barley:
■ 14. Concerning the
■ ordinance of oil, the bath of oil,
■ ye shall offer the tenth part
■ of a bath out of the cor,
which is an homer of ten baths;
for ten baths *are* an homer:
■ 15. And one lamb
out of the flock,
■ out of two hundred, out
of the fat pastures of Israel;
■ for a meat offering, and for
a burnt offering, and for peace
■ offerings, to make reconciliation for
them, saith the Lord GOD.
■ 16. All the people of the land
■ shall give this oblation
■ for the prince in Israel.
■ 17. And it shall be the
■ prince's part to give
burnt offerings, and meat
offerings, and drink
■ offerings, in the
■ feasts, and in the
■ new moons, and in the
■ sabbaths, in all solemnities
of the house of Israel:

he shall prepare the sin offering, and the meat offering, and the burnt offering, and the peace offerings, to make reconciliation for the house of Israel.

18. Thus saith the Lord GOD; In the first month, in the first *day* of the month, thou shalt take a young bullock without blemish, and cleanse the sanctuary:

19. And the priest shall take of the blood of the sin offering, and put it upon the posts of the house, and upon the four corners of the settle of the altar, and upon the posts of the gate of the inner court.

20. And so thou shalt do the seventh day of the month for every one that erreth, and for him that is simple: so shall ye reconcile the house.

21. In the first month, in the fourteenth day of the month, ye shall have the passover, a feast of seven days; unleavened bread shall be eaten.

22. And upon that day shall the prince prepare for himself and for all the people of the land a bullock for a sin offering.

23. And seven days of the feast he shall prepare a burnt offering to the LORD, seven bullocks and seven rams without blemish daily the seven days; and a kid of the goats daily for a sin offering.

24. And he shall prepare a meat offering of an ephah for a bullock, and an ephah for a ram, and an hin of oil for an ephah.

25. In the seventh month, in the fifteenth day of the month, shall he do the like in the feast of the seven days,

according to the sin offering, according to the burnt offering, and according to the meat offering, and according to the oil.

CHAPTER 46

1. Thus saith the Lord GOD; The gate of the inner court that looketh toward the east shall be shut the six working days; but on the sabbath it shall be opened, and in the day of the new moon it shall be opened.

2. And the prince shall enter by the way of the porch of that gate without, and shall stand by the post of the gate, and the priests shall prepare his burnt offering and his peace offerings, and he shall worship at the threshold of the gate: then he shall go forth; but the gate shall not be shut until the evening.

3. Likewise the people of the land shall worship at the door of this gate before the LORD in the sabbaths and in the new moons.

4. And the burnt offering that the prince shall offer unto the LORD in the sabbath day shall be six lambs without blemish, and a ram without blemish.

5. And the meat offering shall be an ephah for a ram, and the meat offering for the lambs as he shall be able to give, and an hin of oil to an ephah.

6. And in the day of the new moon it shall be a young bullock without blemish, and six lambs, and a ram: they shall be without blemish.

7. And he shall prepare a meat offering, an ephah for a bullock, and an ephah for a ram, and for the lambs according as his hand shall attain unto, and an hin of oil to an ephah. 8. **And** when **the prince shall enter,** he shall go in **by the** way of the **porch of that gate**, and he shall go forth by the way thereof. 9. **But** when **the people** of the land **shall come before the LORD** in the solemn feasts, **he that entereth** in **by the** way of the **north gate** to worship **shall go out by** the way of **the south gate; and he that entereth by the** way of the **south gate shall go** forth **by the** way of the **north gate**: he shall not return by the way of the gate whereby he came in, but shall go forth over against it. 10. **And the prince** in the midst of them, when they go in, **shall go** in; and **when they go** forth, shall go forth. 11. And in the feasts and in the solemnities the meat offering shall be an ephah to a bullock, and an ephah to a ram, and to the lambs as he is able to give, and an hin of oil to an ephah. 12. **Now when the prince shall prepare a voluntary** burnt **offering** or peace offerings, voluntarily unto the LORD, **one shall** then **open** him **the gate** that looketh **toward the east, and he shall prepare his** burnt **offering** and his peace offerings, **as he did on the sabbath day: then he shall go** forth; **and** after his going forth **one shall shut the gate.** 13. **Thou shalt daily prepare a burnt offering** unto the LORD **of a lamb of the first year without blemish**: thou shalt prepare it every morning. 14. **And thou shalt prepare a meat offering** for it **every morning**, the sixth part of an ephah, and the third part of an hin of oil, to temper with the fine flour; a meat offering **continually** by a perpetual ordinance **unto the LORD**. 15. Thus shall they prepare the lamb, and the meat offering, and the oil, every morning *for* a continual burnt offering. 16. Thus saith the Lord GOD; **If the prince give a gift unto** any of **his sons, the inheritance** thereof **shall be his sons'**; it shall be their possession by inheritance. 17. **But if he give** a gift **of his inheritance to one of his servants,** then **it shall be his to the year of liberty;** after it shall return to the prince: **but his inheritance shall be his sons'** for them. 18. **Moreover the prince shall not take** of **the people's inheritance by oppression,** to thrust them out of their possession; **but** he **shall give his sons inheritance out of his own possession:** that my people be not scattered every man from his possession. 19. **After he brought me through the entry,** which *was* at the side of the gate, **into the holy chambers** of the priests, which looked toward the north: and, behold, there *was* a place on the two sides westward. 20. **Then said he** unto me, **This is** the place

where the priests shall
boil the trespass
offering and the
sin offering, where they
shall bake the meat
offering; that they bear
them not out into the utter court,
to sanctify the people.
21. **Then he brought me** forth
into the utter court,
and caused me to pass by
the four corners of the court;
**and, behold, in every
corner** of the court
there was a court.
22. In the four corners of the court
there were courts joined of forty *cubits*
long and thirty broad: these four
corners *were* of one measure.
23. **And** *there was*
a row of building
round about in them,
round about them
four, and *it was*
made with boiling places
under the rows round about.
24. **Then said he** unto me,
**These are the
places** of them that boil,
**where the
ministers** of the house
**shall boil the
sacrifice** of the people.

CHAPTER 47

1. **Afterward he
brought me** again
unto the door of the house;
and, behold,
**waters issued out
from under the threshold** of
the house eastward: for the forefront
of the house *stood toward* the east,
and the waters came down
from under from
**the right side of the
house, at the south
side of the altar.**
2. **Then** brought
he me out of the way of
the gate northward, and
led me about the way without
unto the utter gate by the way

that looketh eastward;
and, behold,
**there ran out
waters** on the right side.
3. **And when the
man** that had the line in his hand
went forth
**eastward, he measured
a thousand cubits, and** he
**brought me through the
waters;** the waters *were*
to the ankles.
4. **Again he measured a
thousand, and brought
me through the
waters;** the waters *were*
**to the knees. Again he
measured** a thousand,
and brought me through;
the waters *were*
to the loins.
5. **Afterward** he
measured a thousand; *and*
**it was a river that I could not
pass over:** for the waters were
risen, waters to swim in, a river that
could not be passed over.
6. And he said unto me, Son
of man, hast thou seen *this?*
Then he brought me, and
**caused me to
return to** the brink of
the river.
7. Now when I had returned, behold,
at the bank of the river
were very
many trees on the one side and
on the other.
8. **Then said he** unto me,
**These waters issue out
toward the east** country,
and go down
into the desert, and go into
**the sea: which being
brought** forth
**into the sea, the waters
shall be healed.**
9. And it shall come to pass,
that every thing that liveth,
which moveth, whithersoever
the rivers shall come, shall live:
and there shall be a very
great multitude of fish,

because these waters shall come thither: for they shall be healed; **and every thing shall live whither the river cometh.** 10. **And** it shall come to pass, *that* **the fishers shall** stand upon it from En–gedi even unto Eneglaim; they shall be a *place* to **spread forth nets; their fish shall be** according to their kinds, as the fish of the great sea, **exceeding many.** 11. **But the miry places** thereof **and the marishes** thereof shall not be healed; they **shall be** given to **salt.** 12. **And by the river** upon the bank thereof, on this side and on that side, **shall grow** all **trees** for meat, **whose leaf shall not fade, neither shall the fruit** thereof **be consumed: it shall bring forth new fruit according to his months**, because their waters they issued out of the sanctuary: **and the fruit** thereof **shall be** for **meat, and the leaf** thereof for **medicine.** 13. Thus saith the Lord GOD; **This** *shall be* the border, whereby **ye shall inherit** the land **according to the twelve tribes** of Israel: Joseph *shall have two* portions. 14. And ye shall inherit it, one as well as another: *concerning* the which I lifted up mine hand to give it unto your fathers: and this land shall fall unto you for inheritance. 15. **And this shall be the border** of the land **toward the north** side, **from the great sea**, the way of Hethlon, as men go to Zedad; 16. Hamath, Berothah, Sibraim, which *is* **between the border of Damascus and** the border of **Hamath;** Hazar–hatticon,

which *is* by the coast of Hauran. 17. And the border from the sea shall be Hazar–enan, the border of Damascus, and the north northward, and the border of Hamath. And *this is* the north side. 18. **And the east side** ye shall measure **from Hauran, and** from **Damascus, and from Gilead,** and from the land of Israel **by Jordan,** from the border **unto the east sea.** And *this is* the east side. 19. **And the south side** southward, **from Tamar** *even* **to the waters** of strife **in Kadesh, the river to the great sea.** And *this is* the south side southward. 20. **The west side** also **shall be the great sea** from the border, till a man come **over against Hamath.** This *is* the west side. 21. **So shall ye divide this land** unto you **according to the tribes of Israel.** 22. **And** it shall come to pass, *that* **ye shall divide it** by lot **for an inheritance** unto you, **and to the strangers** that sojourn **among you, which** shall **beget children among you**: and they shall be unto you as born in the country among the children of Israel; **they shall have inheritance with you** among the tribes of Israel. 23. And it shall come to pass, *that* in what tribe the stranger sojourneth, there shall ye give *him* his inheritance, saith the Lord GOD.

CHAPTER 48

1. **Now these are the names of the tribes. From the north end to the coast** of the way of

Hethlon, as one goeth to Hamath, Hazar–enan, the border of Damascus northward, to the coast of Hamath; for these are his sides east *and* west;

■ **a portion for Dan.**
■ 2. **And by the border**
■ **of Dan,** from the east side unto the west side,
■ **a portion for Asher.**
■ 3. **And by the border**
■ **of Asher,** from the east side even unto the west side,
■ **a portion for Naphtali.**
■ 4. **And by the border**
■ **of Naphtali,** from the east side unto the west side,
■ **a portion for Manasseh.**
■ 5. **And by the border of**
■ **Manasseh,** from the east side unto the west side,
■ **a portion for Ephraim.**
■ 6. **And by the border of**
■ **Ephraim,** from the east side even unto the west side,
■ **a portion for Reuben.**
■ 7. **And by the border**
■ **of Reuben,** from the east side unto the west side,
■ **a portion for Judah.**
■ 8. **And by the border of**
■ **Judah,** from the east side unto the west side, shall be the offering which
■ **ye shall offer** of
■ **five and twenty thousand**
■ **reeds in breadth, and** *in*
■ **length** as one of the *other* parts, from the east side unto the west side:
■ **and the sanctuary**
■ **shall be in the midst of it.**
9. The oblation that ye shall offer unto the LORD *shall be* of five and twenty thousand in length, and of ten thousand in breadth.
■ 10. **And** for them, *even*
■ **for the priests, shall be this**
■ **holy oblation;** toward the north
■ **five and twenty thousand**
■ **in length, and** toward the west
■ **ten thousand in breadth,** and toward the east ten thousand in breadth, and toward the south five and twenty thousand in length:
■ **and the sanctuary**

of the LORD shall be
■ **in the midst** thereof.
■ 11. **It shall be for the priests** that are sanctified of the sons of Zadok; which have kept my charge,
■ **which went not astray** when the children of Israel went astray, as the Levites went astray.
■ 12. **And this oblation**
■ **of the land** that is offered
■ **shall be unto them** a
■ **thing most holy** by the border of the Levites.
■ 13. **And over against**
■ **the border** of the priests
■ **the Levites shall have five**
■ **and twenty thousand in**
■ **length, and ten thousand**
■ **in breadth:** all the length *shall be* five and twenty thousand, and the breadth ten thousand.
■ 14. **And they shall not sell** of
■ **it,** neither exchange, nor alienate the firstfruits of the land:
■ **for it is holy** unto the LORD.
■ 15. **And the five**
■ **thousand,** that are
■ **left in the breadth** over against the five and twenty thousand,
■ **shall be a profane place**
■ **for the city, for dwelling,**
■ **and for suburbs:** and the city shall be in the midst thereof.
16. And these *shall be* the measures thereof; the north side four thousand and five hundred, and the south side four thousand and five hundred, and on the east side four thousand and five hundred, and the west side four thousand and five hundred.
17. And the suburbs of the city shall be toward the north two hundred and fifty, and toward the south two hundred and fifty, and toward the east two hundred and fifty, and toward the west two hundred and fifty.
18. And the residue in length over against the oblation of the holy *portion shall be* ten thousand eastward, and ten thousand westward: and it shall

be over against the oblation of the holy *portion;* and the increase thereof shall be for food unto them that serve the city.

19. **And they that serve the city shall serve it out of all the tribes of Israel.**

20. All the oblation *shall be* five and twenty thousand by five and twenty thousand: ye shall offer the holy oblation foursquare, with the possession of the city.

21. And the residue *shall be* for the prince, on the one side and on the other of the holy oblation, and of the possession of the city, over against the five and twenty thousand of the oblation toward the east border, and westward over against the five and twenty thousand toward the west border, over against the portions for the prince: and it shall be the holy oblation; **and the sanctuary** of the house **shall be in the midst** thereof.

22. **Moreover from the possession of the Levites, and** from the possession of **the city,** *being* **in the midst of** *that* which is **the prince's, between** the border of **Judah and** the border of **Benjamin, shall be for the prince.**

23. **As for the rest of the tribes,** from the east side unto the west side, **Benjamin shall have a portion.**

24. **And by the border of Benjamin,** from the east side unto the west side, **Simeon shall have a portion.**

25. **And by the border of Simeon**, from the east side unto the west side, **Issachar a portion.**

26. **And by the border of Issachar,** from the east side unto the west side,

Zebulun a portion.

27. **And by the border of Zebulun,** from the east side unto the west side, **Gad a portion.**

28. **And by the border of Gad,** at the south side southward, the border shall be even **from Tamar unto** the waters of strife *in* **Kadesh,** *and* **to the river toward the great sea.**

29. This *is* the land which **ye shall divide by lot unto the tribes of Israel** for inheritance, and these *are* their portions, saith the Lord GOD.

30. And these *are* the goings out of the city on the north side, four thousand and five hundred measures.

31. **And the gates of the city shall be after the names of the tribes of Israel: three gates northward;** one gate **of Reuben,** one gate of **Judah,** one gate **of Levi.**

32. **And** at the **east** side four thousand and five hundred: and **three gates;** and one gate **of Joseph,** one gate of **Benjamin,** one gate of **Dan.**

33. **And at the south** side four thousand and five hundred measures: and **three gates;** one gate **of Simeon,** one gate of **Issachar**, one gate of **Zebulun.**

34. **At the west** side four thousand and five hundred, *with* their **three gates;** one gate **of Gad,** one gate of **Asher,** one gate of **Naphtali.**

35. *It was* round about eighteen thousand *measures*: **and the name of the city from that day shall be, The LORD is there.**

THE BOOK OF DANIEL

**BACKGROUND
INFORMATION**

**Author: Daniel
Date Written
597—573 B.C.**

Number of:
Verses—357
Chapters—12
Total Words—11,606
Scan Words—5,204
Scan Words Represent
Total Words

**Theme: The Exile of
Daniel,** His Faith in God,
**and His Visions Concerning
Future
World Events**

**OUTLINE OF
THE BOOK**

I.   Daniel and
     **the Reign of King
     Nebuchadnezzar**
     1:1 — 4:37
II. Daniel and
     the Reign of Belshazzar
     5:1 — 8:27
III. Daniel and
     The Reign of Cyrus
     9:1 — 12:13

CHAPTER 1

1. **In** the third year of **the reign of Jehoiakim king of Judah came Nebuchadnezzar king of Babylon unto Jerusalem, and besieged it.** 2. **And the Lord gave** Jehoiakim king of **Judah into his hand, with part of the vessels of the house of God:** which he carried into the land of Shinar to the house of his god; and he brought the vessels into the treasure house of his god. 3. **And the king spake unto** Ashpenaz **the master of his eunuchs, that he should bring certain of the children of Israel,** and of the king's seed, and of the princes; 4. **Children in whom was no blemish, but** well **favoured, and skilful** in all wisdom, and **cunning** in knowledge, **and understanding science,** and such as *had* ability in them to stand in the king's palace, and **whom they might teach the learning and the tongue of the Chaldeans.** 5. **And the king appointed them** a daily provision of the king's **meat,** and of the wine which he drank: **so nourishing them three years, that** at the end thereof **they might stand before the king.** 6. **Now among these were** of the children of Judah, **Daniel, Hananiah, Mishael, and Azariah:** 7. **Unto whom** the prince of **the eunuchs gave names:** for he gave unto Daniel *the name* **of Belteshazzar;** and to Hananiah, of **Shadrach;** and to Mishael, of **Meshach; and** to Azariah, of **Abed-nego.**

8. **But Daniel** purposed in his heart that he **would not defile himself with the** portion of the **king's meat,** nor with the wine which he drank: therefore he requested of the prince of the eunuchs that he might not defile himself. 9. **Now God had brought Daniel into favour** and tender love **with the prince of the eunuchs.** 10. **And the prince** of the eunuchs **said** unto Daniel, **I fear** my lord **the king, who hath appointed your meat** and your drink: **for why should he see your faces worse** liking than the children which *are* of your sort? **then shall ye** make *me* **endanger my head** to the king. 11. **Then said Daniel** to Melzar, whom the prince of the eunuchs had set over Daniel, Hananiah, Mishael, and Azariah, 12. **Prove thy servants,** I beseech thee, **ten days; and let them give us pulse** to eat, **and water** to drink. 13. Then let our countenances be looked upon before thee, and the countenance of the children that eat of the portion of the king's meat: **and as thou seest, deal with thy servants.** 14. **So he consented** to them in this matter, **and proved them ten days.** 15. **And at the end** of ten days **their countenances appeared fairer** and fatter in flesh **than all the children which did eat the** portion of the **king's meat.** 16. **Thus Melzar** took away the

portion of their meat, and the wine that they should drink; and

gave them pulse.

17. As for these four children, God gave them knowledge and skill in all learning and wisdom:

and Daniel had understanding in all visions and dreams.

18. Now at the end of the days that the king had said he should bring them in, then

the prince of the eunuchs brought them in before Nebuchadnezzar.

19. And the king communed with them; and

among them all was found none like Daniel, Hananiah, Mishael, and Azariah: therefore stood they before the king.

20. And in all matters of wisdom and understanding, that the king inquired of them, he found them ten times better than all the magicians and astrologers that *were* in all his realm.

21. And Daniel continued *even* unto the first year of king Cyrus.

CHAPTER 2

1. And in the second year of the reign of Nebuchadnezzar, Nebuchadnezzar dreamed dreams, wherewith his spirit was troubled, and his sleep brake from him.

2. Then the king commanded to call the magicians, and the astrologers, and the sorcerers, and the Chaldeans, for to shew the king his dreams. So they came and stood before the king.

3. And the king said unto them, I have dreamed a dream,

and my spirit was troubled to know the dream.

4. Then spake the Chaldeans to the king in Syriac, O king, live for ever: tell thy servants the dream, and we will shew the interpretation.

5. The king answered and said to the Chaldeans, The thing is gone from me: if ye will not make known unto me the dream, with the interpretation thereof, ye shall be cut in pieces, and your houses shall be made a dunghill.

6. But if ye shew the dream, and the interpretation thereof, ye shall receive of me gifts and rewards and great honour: therefore shew me the dream, and the interpretation thereof.

7. They answered again and said, Let the king tell his servants the dream, and we will shew the interpretation of it.

8. The king answered and said, I know of certainty that ye would gain the time, because ye see the thing is gone from me.

9. But if ye will not make known unto me the dream, *there is but* one decree for you: for ye have prepared lying and corrupt words to speak before me, till the time be changed: therefore tell me the dream, and I shall know that ye can shew me the interpretation thereof.

10. The Chaldeans answered before the king, and said, There is not a man upon the earth that can shew the king's matter: therefore *there is* no

king, lord, nor ruler, *that* asked such things at any magician, or astrologer, or Chaldean.

11. And *it is* a rare thing that the king requireth, and there is **none** other that **can shew it** before the king, **except the gods,** whose dwelling is not with flesh.

12. For this cause **the king was** angry and very **furious, and commanded to destroy all the wise men of Babylon.**

13. And the decree went forth that the wise *men* should be slain; **and they sought Daniel and his fellows to be slain.**

14. **Then Daniel answered** with counsel and wisdom to **Arioch the captain of the king's guard,** which was gone forth to slay the wise *men* of Babylon:

15. He answered and said to Arioch the king's captain, **Why is the decree so hasty from the king?** Then Arioch made the thing known to Daniel.

16. **Then Daniel** went in, and **desired of the king that he would give him time, and that he would shew** the king **the interpretation.**

17. **Then Daniel** went to his house, and **made the thing known to** Hananiah, Mishael, and Azariah, **his companions:**

18. **That they would desire mercies of the God** of heaven **concerning this secret; that Daniel and his fellows should not perish** with the rest of the wise *men* of Babylon.

19. **Then was the secret revealed unto Daniel in a night vision.** Then Daniel blessed the God of heaven.

20. **Daniel** answered and **said, Blessed be the name of God** for ever and ever: **for wisdom and might are his:**

21. **And** he changeth the times and the seasons: he removeth kings, and setteth up kings: **he giveth wisdom unto the wise, and knowledge to them that know understanding:**

22. **He revealeth the** deep and **secret things:** he knoweth what *is* in the darkness, **and the light dwelleth with him.**

23. **I thank thee,** and praise thee, **O** thou **God** of my fathers, **who hast given me wisdom** and might, **and** hast **made known unto me** now what we desired of thee: for thou hast *now* made known unto us **the king's matter.**

24. **Therefore Daniel went in unto Arioch,** whom the king had ordained to destroy the wise *men* of Babylon: he went **and said** thus unto him, **Destroy not the wise men** of Babylon: bring me in before the king, and **I will shew** unto the king **the interpretation.**

25. **Then Arioch brought** in **Daniel before the king** in haste, **and said** thus unto him, **I have found a man** of the captives of Judah, **that will make known** unto the king **the interpretation.**

26. **The king** answered and **said to Daniel,** whose name *was* Belteshazzar, **Art thou able to make known** unto me **the dream** which I have seen, **and the interpretation** thereof?

27. **Daniel answered** in the presence of the king, and said, The secret which the king hath

demanded cannot the wise *men,* the astrologers, the magicians, the soothsayers, shew unto the king;

28. But there is a

■ **God in heaven** that revealeth secrets, and

■ **maketh known** to the king Nebuchadnezzar

■ **what shall be in the latter**
■ **days. Thy dream, and** the
■ **visions** of thy head upon thy bed,
■ **are these;**

29. As for thee, O king, thy thoughts came *into thy mind* upon thy bed, what should come to pass hereafter: and he that revealeth secrets maketh known to thee what shall come to pass.

30. But as for me, this secret is not revealed to me for *any* wisdom that I have more than any living, but for *their* sakes that shall make known the interpretation to the king, and that thou mightest know the thoughts of thy heart.

■ 31. **Thou, O king,**
■ **sawest,** and behold
■ **a great image.** This great image,
■ **whose brightness was**
■ **excellent,** stood before thee;
■ **and the form** thereof *was*
■ **terrible.**

■ 32. **This image's head**
■ **was of fine gold, his**
■ **breast and** his
■ **arms of silver, his**
■ **belly and** his
■ **thighs of brass,**

■ 33. **His legs of iron,**
■ **his feet part** of
■ **iron and** part of
■ **clay.**

34. Thou sawest till that

■ **a stone was cut out without**
■ **hands, which smote the**
■ **image upon his feet**
that were of iron and clay,

■ **and brake them to pieces.**
■ 35. **Then was the iron,** the
■ **clay,** the
■ **brass,** the
■ **silver, and** the
■ **gold, broken** to pieces together,

■ **and became like the chaff**
of the summer threshingfloors; and the wind carried them away, that no place was found for them:

■ **and the stone**
that smote the image

■ **became a great mountain,**
■ **and filled the** whole
■ **earth.**

■ 36. **This is**
the dream; and we will tell

■ **the interpretation**
thereof before the king.

■ 37. **Thou, O king, art**
■ **a king of kings:** for the
■ **God** of heaven
■ **hath given thee** a kingdom,
■ **power,** and
■ **strength, and glory.**

■ 38. **And wheresoever the**
■ **children of men dwell,**
the beasts of the field and the fowls of the heaven hath

■ **he** given into thine hand, and
■ **hath made thee**
■ **ruler over them** all.
■ **Thou art this head of gold.**

■ 39. **And after thee shall**
■ **arise another kingdom**
■ **inferior to thee, and**
■ **another** third kingdom
■ **of brass,** which shall bear
rule over all the earth.

■ 40. **And the fourth** kingdom
■ **shall be strong as iron:**
forasmuch as iron breaketh in pieces and subdueth all *things:*

■ **and as iron**
that breaketh all these,

■ **shall it break in**
■ **pieces and bruise.**

■ 41. **And** whereas thou sawest
■ **the feet and toes,** part
■ **of potters' clay, and** part of
■ **iron, the kingdom**
■ **shall be divided;** but there shall
be in it of the strength of the iron, forasmuch as thou sawest the iron mixed with miry clay.

■ 42. **And** *as* the toes of the
feet *were* part of iron, and part of clay, *so* the kingdom

■ **shall be partly strong,**

■ and partly broken.

■ 43. **And** whereas thou sawest
iron mixed with miry clay,

■ **they shall mingle** themselves

■ **with the seed of men:**

■ **but** they

■ **shall not cleave**

■ **one to another,**
even as iron is not mixed with clay.

■ 44. **And in the days of**

■ **these kings shall** the

■ **God** of heaven

■ **set up a kingdom, which**

■ **shall** never be destroyed: and the
kingdom shall not be left to other
people, *but* it shall break in pieces and

■ **consume all these**

■ **kingdoms, and it**

■ **shall stand for ever.**

■ 45. **Forasmuch as**
thou sawest that

■ **the stone** was cut out of the
mountain without hands, and that it

■ **brake in pieces the iron,** the

■ **brass,** the

■ **clay,** the

■ **silver, and the gold;** the great

■ **God hath made known**
to the king

■ **what shall come** to pass
hereafter: and the dream *is* certain,
and the interpretation thereof sure.

■ 46. **Then** the king

■ **Nebuchadnezzar fell upon**

■ **his face, and worshipped**

■ **Daniel,** and commanded that they
should offer an oblation and sweet
odours unto him.

■ 47. **The king answered** unto

■ **Daniel,**
and said, Of a truth *it is,* that

■ **your God is** a God of gods, and a
Lord of kings, and

■ **a revealer of secrets,** seeing
thou couldest reveal this secret.

■ 48. **Then the king made**

■ **Daniel** a great man, and gave him
many great gifts, and made him

■ **ruler over** the whole province of

■ **Babylon, and chief of**

■ **the governors over all**

■ **the wise men** of Babylon.

■ 49. Then Daniel requested

of the king,

■ **and he set Shadrach,**

■ **Meshach, and Abed-nego,**

■ **over the affairs of**
the province of

■ **Babylon:** but Daniel *sat* in
the gate of the king.

CHAPTER 3

■ 1. **Nebuchadnezzar** the king

■ **made an image of gold,**
whose height *was* threescore cubits,

■ **and** the breadth
thereof six cubits: he

■ **set it up in the plain of Dura,**
in the province of Babylon.

■ 2. **Then** Nebuchadnezzar

■ **the king sent to gather**

■ **together the princes,** the

■ **governors,** and the

■ **captains,** the

■ **judges,** the

■ **treasurers,** the

■ **counsellors,** the

■ **sheriffs, and all the rulers**
of the provinces, to come

■ **to the dedication of**

■ **the image** which Nebuchadnezzar
the king had set up.

3. Then the princes, the governors,
and captains, the judges, the
treasurers, the counsellors, the
sheriffs, and all the rulers of the
provinces, were gathered together
unto the dedication of the image that
Nebuchadnezzar the king had set up;
and they stood before the image that
Nebuchadnezzar had set up.

■ 4. **Then an herald**

■ **cried aloud,**
To you it is commanded,

■ **O people,**
nations, and languages,

■ 5. **That at what time ye hear**

■ **the sound of** the cornet, flute,
harp, sackbut, psaltery, dulcimer, and

■ **all kinds of music, ye fall**

■ **down and worship the**

■ **golden image** that
Nebuchadnezzar
the king hath set up:

■ 6. **And whoso falleth not**

■ **down and worshippeth**

■ **shall** the same hour
■ **be cast into** the midst of
■ **a** burning
■ **fiery furnace.**

7. Therefore at that time, when all the people heard the sound of the cornet, flute, harp, sackbut, psaltery, and all kinds of music, all the people, the nations, and the languages, fell down *and* worshipped the golden image that Nebuchadnezzar the king had set up.

■ 8. **Wherefore** at that time
■ **certain Chaldeans**

came near, and

■ **accused the Jews.**
■ 9. **They** spake and
■ **said to the king**

Nebuchadnezzar, O king, live for ever.

10. Thou, O king, hast made a decree, that every man that shall hear the sound of the cornet, flute, harp, sackbut, psaltery, and dulcimer, and all kinds of music, shall fall down and worship the golden image:

11. And whoso falleth not down and worshippeth, *that* he should be cast into the midst of a burning fiery furnace.

■ 12. **There are certain Jews**
■ **whom thou hast set over the**
■ **affairs of the province**

of Babylon,

■ **Shadrach, Meshach, and**
■ **Abed–nego; these men,** O

king, have not regarded thee: they

■ **serve not thy gods, nor**
■ **worship the golden image**

which thou hast set up.

■ 13. **Then Nebuchadnezzar**
■ **in his rage** and fury
■ **commanded to bring**

Shadrach, Meshach, and Abed–nego. Then they brought

■ **these men** before the king.
■ 14. **Nebuchadnezzar**

spake and

■ **said** unto them, *Is it* true, O

Shadrach, Meshach, and Abed–nego, do not ye serve my gods, nor worship the golden mage which I have set up?

■ 15. **Now if ye** be ready that at what time ye hear the sound of the cornet,

flute, harp, sackbut, psaltery, and dulcimer, and all kinds of music, ye

■ **fall down and worship the**
■ **image** which I have made;
■ **well: but if ye worship not,**
■ **ye shall be cast** the same hour
■ **into the** midst of a burning
■ **fiery furnace; and who is**
■ **that God that shall deliver**
■ **you** out of my hands?
■ 16. **Shadrach, Meshach,**
■ **and Abed–nego,**
■ **answered** and said to the king,

O Nebuchadnezzar, we *are* not careful to answer thee in this matter.

■ 17. **If it be so, our God**

whom we serve

■ **is able to deliver us** from the

burning fiery furnace, and he will deliver *us* out of thine hand, O king.

■ 18. **But if not, be it**
■ **known** unto thee, O king,
■ **that we will not serve**
■ **thy gods, nor worship**
■ **the golden image**

which thou hast set up.

■ 19. **Then** was
■ **Nebuchadnezzar**
■ **full of fury,** and the form of his

visage was changed against Shadrach, Meshach, and Abed–nego: *therefore* he spake, and

■ **commanded that they**
■ **should heat the furnace** one
■ **seven times more**

than it was wont to be heated.

■ 20. **And he commanded**

the most

■ **mighty men** that *were* in his army
■ **to bind Shadrach,**
■ **Meshach, and Abed–nego,**
■ **and to cast them into the**

burning fiery

■ **furnace.**
■ 21. **Then these men** were bound

in their coats, their hosen, and their hats, and their *other* garments, and

■ **were cast into** the midst of
■ **the** burning fiery
■ **furnace.**
■ 22. **Therefore because the**
■ **king's commandment was**
■ **urgent, and the furnace**

exceeding hot,

the flame of the fire

slew those men that took

up Shadrach, Meshach,

and Abed-nego.

23. **And** these three men,

Shadrach, Meshach, and

Abed-nego, fell down bound

into the midst of the burning fiery

furnace.

24. **Then Nebuchadnezzar** the king

was astonied, and

rose up in haste, *and* spake,

and said unto his counsellors,

Did not we cast

three men bound

into the midst of

the fire? They answered and said unto the king, True, O king.

25. He answered and said,

Lo, I see four men loose,

walking in the midst of the

fire, and they have no hurt;

and the form of

the fourth is like the

Son of God.

26. **Then Nebuchadnezzar**

came near to

the mouth of the burning fiery

furnace, and spake, and

said, Shadrach, Meshach, and Abed-nego,

ye servants of the most

high God, come forth,

and come *hither.*

Then Shadrach, Meshach,

and Abed-nego, came

forth of the midst of the fire.

27. And the princes, governors, and captains, and the king's counsellors, being gathered together, saw these men,

upon whose bodies the fire

had no power, nor was an

hair of their head singed,

neither were their coats changed, nor the smell of fire had passed on them.

28. **Then Nebuchadnezzar** spake, and

said, Blessed be the God

of Shadrach, Meshach,

and Abed-nego, who

hath sent his angel, and

delivered his servants

that trusted in him,

and have changed the king's word, and yielded their bodies, that they might not serve nor worship any god, except their own God.

29. **Therefore I make**

a decree, That every

people, nation, and language,

which speak any thing amiss

against the God of

Shadrach, Meshach, and

Abed-nego, shall be cut

in pieces, and their houses shall be made a dunghill:

because there is

no other

God that

can deliver after this sort.

30. **Then the king promoted**

Shadrach, Meshach,

and Abed-nego,

in the province of Babylon.

CHAPTER 4

1. **Nebuchadnezzar** the king,

unto all people, nations, and languages, that dwell in all the earth;

Peace be multiplied

unto you.

2. **I thought it good to**

shew the signs and

wonders that the high

God hath wrought

toward me.

3. **How great are his signs!** and how mighty *are* his wonders! his kingdom *is* an everlasting kingdom, and his dominion *is* from generation to generation.

4. **I** Nebuchadnezzar

was at rest in mine house, and

flourishing in my palace:

5. **I saw a dream which** made me afraid, and the thoughts upon my bed and the visions of my head

troubled me.

6. **Therefore made I a**

decree to bring in all the

wise men of Babylon before me, that they might make known unto me the interpretation of the dream.

7. Then came in the magicians, the astrologers, the Chaldeans, and the soothsayers:

■ **and** I told the dream before them; but

■ **they did not**
■ **make known** unto me
■ **the interpretation** thereof.

■ 8. **But at the last Daniel**
■ **came** in before me, whose name *was* Belteshazzar, according to the name of my God, and in whom *is* the spirit of the holy gods:

■ **and** before him
■ **I told the dream, saying,**
■ 9. **O Belteshazzar,** master of the magicians, because I know that the spirit of the holy gods *is* in thee, and no secret troubleth thee,

■ **tell me the visions of my**
■ **dream** that I have seen,
■ **and the interpretation** thereof.

■ 10. **Thus were the**
■ **visions of mine** head in my bed;
■ **I saw,** and behold
■ **a tree in the midst**
■ **of the earth,**

and the height thereof *was* great.

11. The tree grew, and was strong,

■ **and the height** thereof
■ **reached unto heaven,**

and the sight thereof to the end of all the earth:

■ 12. **The leaves** thereof
■ **were fair, and the fruit** thereof
■ **much,** and in it *was* meat for all: the beasts of the field had shadow under it, and the fowls of the heaven dwelt in the boughs thereof,

■ **and all flesh was fed of it.**
■ 13. **I saw in the visions** of my head upon my bed,

■ **and,** behold, a watcher and
■ **an holy one came**
■ **down from heaven;**
■ 14. **He cried** aloud, and said thus,
■ **Hew down the tree,** and cut off his branches, shake off his leaves, and scatter his fruit: let the beasts get away from under it, and the fowls from his branches:

■ 15. **Nevertheless leave the**

■ **stump** of his roots
■ **in the earth,** even with a band of iron and brass, in the tender grass of the field; and let it be wet with the dew of heaven, and *let* his portion *be* with the beasts in the grass of the earth:

16. Let his heart be changed from man's,

■ **and let a beast's heart**
■ **be given unto him; and**
■ **let seven times pass**
■ **over him.**
■ 17. **This matter is** by the decree of the watchers, and the demand by the word of the holy ones:

■ **to the intent that the living**
■ **may know that the most**
■ **High ruleth in the kingdom**
■ **of men, and giveth it to**
■ **whomsoever he will,** and setteth up over it the basest of men.

■ 18. **This dream I** king Nebuchadnezzar
■ **have seen. Now** thou, O
■ **Belteshazzar, declare**
■ **the interpretation** thereof, forasmuch as all the wise *men* of my kingdom are not able to make known unto me the interpretation: but thou *art* able;

■ **for the spirit of the**
■ **holy gods is in thee.**
■ 19. **Then Daniel,** whose name *was* Belteshazzar, was astonied for one hour, and his thoughts troubled him. The king spake, and said, Belteshazzar, let not the dream, or the interpretation thereof, trouble thee. Belteshazzar answered and

■ **said, My lord, the dream**
■ **be to them that hate thee,** and the interpretation thereof to thine enemies.

■ 20. **The tree that thou**
■ **sawest,** which grew, and was strong, whose height reached unto the heaven, and the sight thereof to all the earth;

21. Whose leaves *were* fair, and the fruit thereof much, and in it *was* meat for all; under which the beasts of the field dwelt, and upon whose branches the fowls of the heaven

had their habitation:

22. **It is thou,** O king, that art grown and become strong: for thy greatness is grown, and reacheth unto heaven, and thy dominion to the end of the earth.

23. And whereas the king saw a watcher and an holy one coming down from heaven, and saying, Hew the tree down, and destroy it; yet leave the stump of the roots thereof in the earth, even with a band of iron and brass, in the tender grass of the field; and let it be wet with the dew of heaven, and *let* his portion *be* with the beasts of the field, till seven times pass over him;

24. **This is the interpretation, O king,** and this *is* the decree of the most High, which is come upon my lord the king:

25. **That they shall drive thee from men, and thy dwelling shall be with the beasts** of the field, and they shall make thee to eat grass as oxen, and they shall wet thee with the dew of heaven, **and seven times shall pass over thee, till thou know that the most High ruleth in the kingdom of men,** and giveth it to whomsoever he will.

26. **And whereas they commanded to leave the stump** of the tree roots; **thy kingdom shall be sure unto thee,** after that thou shalt have known that the heavens do rule.

27. **Wherefore,** O king, let my counsel be acceptable unto thee, and **break off thy sins** by righteousness, **and thine iniquities** by shewing mercy to the poor; **if it may be a lengthening of thy tranquillity.**

28. **All this came upon the king** Nebuchadnezzar.

29. **At the end of twelve months** he walked in the palace of the kingdom of Babylon.

30. **The king** spake, and **said, Is not this great Babylon, that I have built** for the house of the kingdom **by** the might of **my power,** and for the honour of my majesty?

31. **While the word was in the king's mouth, there fell a voice from heaven, saying,** O king Nebuchadnezzar, to thee it is spoken; **The kingdom is departed from thee.**

32. And they shall drive thee from men, and thy dwelling *shall be* with the beasts of the field: they shall make thee to eat grass as oxen, and seven times shall pass over thee, until thou know that the most High ruleth in the kingdom of men, and giveth it to whomsoever he will.

33. **The same hour was the thing fulfilled upon Nebuchadnezzar: and he was driven from men, and did eat grass** as oxen, and his body was wet with the dew of heaven, till **his hairs were** grown **like eagles' feathers, and his nails like birds' claws.**

34. **And at the end of the days I Nebuchadnezzar lifted up mine eyes unto heaven, and mine understanding returned** unto me, **and I blessed the most High, and I praised and honoured him** that liveth for ever, whose dominion *is* an everlasting dominion, and his kingdom *is* from generation to generation:

35. And all the inhabitants of the earth *are* reputed as nothing: and he doeth according to his will in the army of heaven, and *among* the inhabitants of the earth: and none can stay his hand, or say unto him, What doest thou?

36. **At the same time my reason returned** unto me; and

for the glory of my kingdom, mine honour and brightness returned unto me; and my counsellors and my lords sought unto me;

and I was established in my kingdom, and excellent majesty was added unto me.

37. **Now I** Nebuchadnezzar **praise and extol and honour the King of heaven,** all whose works *are* truth, and his ways judgment: **and those that walk in pride he is able to abase.**

CHAPTER 5

1. **Belshazzar the king made a great feast to a thousand of his lords, and** drank wine before the thousand.
2. **Belshazzar, whiles he tasted the wine, commanded to bring the** golden and silver **vessels which his father Nebuchadnezzar had taken out of the temple** which *was* **in Jerusalem;** that the king, and his princes, his wives, and his concubines, might drink therein.
3. **Then they brought the** golden **vessels** that were taken out of the temple of the house of God which *was* at Jerusalem; and the king, and his princes, his wives, **and** his concubines, **drank in them.**
4. **They drank wine, and praised the gods of gold, and of silver,** of brass, of iron, of wood, and of stone.
5. **In the same hour came forth fingers of a man's hand, and wrote** over against the candlestick **upon the plaster of the wall** of the king's palace: **and the king saw** the part of **the hand** that wrote.
6. **Then the king's** countenance

was changed, and his thoughts troubled him, so that the joints of his loins were loosed, and his **knees smote one against another.**
7. **The king cried** aloud to **bring in the astrologers,** the Chaldeans, and the soothsayers. **And the king spake, and said to the wise men** of Babylon, **Whosoever shall read this writing, and shew me the interpretation** thereof, shall be clothed with scarlet, and *have* a chain of gold about his neck, and **shall be the third ruler in the kingdom.**
8. Then came in all the king's wise *men:* **but they could not read the writing,** nor make known to the king the interpretation thereof.
9. **Then was king Belshazzar greatly troubled,** and his countenance was changed in him, and his lords were astonied.
10. **Now the queen** by reason of the words of the king and his lords, **came into the banquet house: and** the queen spake and **said,** O king, live for ever: let not thy thoughts trouble thee, nor let thy countenance be changed:
11. **There is a man in thy kingdom,** in whom *is* the spirit of the holy gods; and in the days of thy father light and understanding and wisdom, like the wisdom of the gods, was found in him; **whom** the king **Nebuchadnezzar thy father,** the king, *I say,* thy father, **made master of the magicians, astrologers, Chaldeans, and soothsayers;**
12. **Forasmuch as an excellent spirit, and** knowledge, and understanding, **interpreting of dreams,** and shewing of hard sentences, and dissolving of doubts,

were found in the same
Daniel, whom the king
named Belteshazzar; now
let Daniel be called, and
he will shew the interpretation.
13. Then was Daniel
brought in before the king.
And the king spake and
said unto Daniel, *Art* thou that
Daniel, which *art* of the children of the
captivity of Judah, whom the king my
father brought out of Jewry?
14. I have even
heard of thee,
that the spirit of
the gods *is* in thee, and *that* light and
understanding and excellent
wisdom is found in thee.
15. And now the wise
men, the astrologers,
have been brought
in before me,
that they should read
this writing, and make
known unto me
the interpretation thereof:
but they could not shew the
interpretation of the thing:
16. And I have heard of thee, that
thou canst make interpretations, and
dissolve doubts:
now if thou canst read
the writing, and make
known to me
the interpretation thereof,
thou shalt be clothed with
scarlet, and *have* a chain of
gold about thy neck, and shalt
be the third ruler
in the kingdom.
17. Then Daniel answered and
said before the king,
Let thy gifts be to thyself,
and give thy rewards to another;
yet I will read the
writing unto the king,
and make known to him
the interpretation.
18. O thou king, the most high
God gave
Nebuchadnezzar thy father
a kingdom, and majesty,
and glory, and honour:

19. And for the majesty
that he gave him, all
people, nations, and languages,
trembled and feared
before him: whom he would he
slew; and whom he would he kept
alive; and whom he would he set up;
and whom he would he put down.
20. But when his heart was
lifted up, and his mind hardened
in pride, he was deposed
from his kingly throne,
and they took his glory from him:
21. And he was driven
from the sons of
men; and his heart was
made like the beasts, and his
dwelling *was* with the wild asses:
they fed him with
grass like oxen, and his body
was wet with the dew of heaven;
till he knew that the most high
God ruled in the kingdom
of men, and *that* he appointeth
over it whomsoever he will.
22. And thou
his son, O Belshazzar,
hast not humbled
thine heart, though
thou knewest all
this;
23. But hast lifted up thyself
against the Lord of heaven; and
they have brought the vessels of his
house before thee, and thou, and thy
lords, thy wives,
and thy concubines,
have drunk wine in them;
and thou hast
praised the gods of silver,
and gold, of brass, iron,
wood, and stone, which see
not, nor hear, nor know:
and the God in whose
hand thy breath is, and whose
are all thy ways,
hast thou not glorified:
24. Then was the part of the hand
sent from him; and this writing was
written.
25. And this is the writing
that was written,
MENE, MENE,

TEKEL, UPHARSIN.

26. **This is the interpretation** of the thing **MENE; God hath numbered thy kingdom, and finished it.**

27. **TEKEL; Thou art weighed** in the balances, **and art found wanting.**

28. **PERES; Thy kingdom is divided, and given to the Medes and Persians.**

29. **Then** commanded Belshazzar, and **they clothed Daniel with scarlet,** and *put* a chain of gold about his neck, **and made a proclamation** concerning him, **that he should be the third ruler in the kingdom.**

30. **In that night was Belshazzar** the king of the Chaldeans **slain.**

31. **And Darius the Median took the kingdom,** *being* about threescore and two years old.

CHAPTER 6

1. **It pleased Darius to set over the kingdom an hundred and twenty princes,** which should be over the whole kingdom;

2. **And over these three presidents; of whom Daniel was first:** that the princes might give accounts unto them, and the king should have no damage.

3. **Then** this **Daniel was preferred above the presidents and princes, because an excellent spirit was in him; and the king thought to set him over the whole realm.**

4. **Then the presidents and princes sought to find occasion against Daniel** concerning the kingdom; **but they could find none** occasion nor fault; forasmuch as he

was faithful, neither was there any error or fault found in him.

5. **Then said these men, We shall not find any occasion against** this **Daniel, except** we find *it* against him **concerning the law of his God.**

6. **Then** these presidents and princes assembled together to the king, and said thus unto him, King Darius, live for ever.

7. **All the presidents of the kingdom,** the governors, and the princes, the counsellors, and the captains, have **consulted together to establish a royal** statute, and to make a firm **decree, that whosoever shall ask a petition of any God or man for thirty days, save of thee, O king, he shall be cast into the den of lions.**

8. **Now, O king,** establish the decree, and **sign the writing, that it be not changed,** according to the law of the Medes and Persians, which altereth not.

9. **Wherefore king Darius signed the** writing and the **decree.**

10. **Now when Daniel knew that the writing was signed, he went into his house; and** his windows being open in his chamber toward Jerusalem, he **kneeled** upon his knees **three times a day,** and prayed, and gave thanks **before his God,** as he did aforetime.

11. **Then these men** assembled, and **found Daniel praying** and making supplication before his God.

12. Then they came near, **and spake before the king concerning the** king's **decree;** Hast thou not signed a

decree, that every man that shall ask *a petition* of any God or man within thirty days, save of thee, O king, shall be cast into the den of lions? The king answered and said, The thing *is* true, according to the law of the Medes and Persians, which altereth not.

13. **Then** answered **they** and **said** before the king, **That Daniel,** which *is* of the children of the captivity of Judah, **regardeth not** thee, O king, nor **the decree** that thou hast signed, **but maketh his petition three times a day.**

14. **Then the king,** when he heard *these* words, **was** sore **displeased with himself, and set his heart on Daniel to deliver him:** and he laboured till the going down of the sun to deliver him.

15. **Then these men** assembled unto the king, and **said unto the king,** Know, O king, that **the law of the Medes and Persians is, That no decree** nor statute which the king establisheth **may be changed.**

16. **Then** the king commanded, and **they brought Daniel, and cast him into the den of lions. Now the king** spake and **said unto Daniel, Thy God** whom thou servest continually, he **will deliver thee.**

17. **And a stone was** brought, and **laid upon the mouth of the den; and the king sealed it** with his own signet, and with the signet of his lords; that the purpose might not be changed concerning Daniel.

18. **Then the king went to his palace, and passed the night fasting:** neither were instruments of music brought before him:

and his sleep went from him.

19. **Then the king arose very early** in the morning, **and went** in haste **unto the den of lions.**

20. **And** when he came to the den, he **cried** with a lamentable voice **unto Daniel:** *and* the king spake and said to Daniel, **O Daniel,** servant of the living God, **is thy God,** whom thou servest continually, **able to deliver thee** from the lions?

21. **Then said Daniel** unto the king, O king, live for ever.

22. **My God** hath sent his angel, and **hath shut the lions' mouths,** that they have not hurt me: forasmuch as before him innocency was found in me; and also before thee, O king, have I done no hurt.

23. **Then was the king exceeding glad** for him, **and commanded that they** should **take Daniel** up out of the den. So Daniel was taken up **out of the den, and no manner of hurt was found upon him, because he believed in his God.**

24. **And the king commanded, and** they brought **those** men **which had accused Daniel, and they cast** *them* **into the den of lions,** them, **their children, and their wives; and the lions** had the mastery of them, and **brake all their bones** in pieces or ever they came at the bottom of the den.

25. **Then king Darius wrote unto all people,** nations, and languages, that dwell in all the earth;

Peace be multiplied unto you.

■ 26. **I make a decree, That** in every dominion of my kingdom **men** tremble and **fear** before **the God of Daniel: for he is the living God,** and stedfast for ever, and his kingdom *that* which shall not be destroyed, and his dominion *shall be even* unto the end.

27. He delivereth and rescueth, and he worketh signs and wonders in heaven and in earth, who hath delivered Daniel from the power of the lions.

■ 28. **So** this **Daniel prospered in the reign of Darius,** and in the reign of **Cyrus the Persian.**

CHAPTER 7

■ 1. **In the first year of Belshazzar** king of Babylon **Daniel had a dream** and visions of his head **upon his bed: then he wrote the dream,** *and* told the sum of the matters.

■ 2. **Daniel** spake and **said, I saw** in my vision by night, and, behold, **the four winds of the heaven strove upon the great sea.**

■ 3. **And four great beasts came up** from the sea, diverse one from another.

■ 4. **The first was like a lion, and had eagle's wings:** I beheld till **the wings** thereof **were plucked,** and it was lifted up from the earth, and made stand upon the feet as a man, **and a man's heart was given to it.**

■ 5. **And** behold **another beast,** a second, **like to a bear,** and it raised up itself on one side, and *it* **had three ribs** in the mouth of it

■ **between the teeth** of it: ■ **and they said** thus unto it, **Arise, devour much flesh.**

■ 6. **After this** I beheld, and lo **another, like a leopard, which had** upon the back of it **four wings** of a fowl; the beast had **also four heads; and dominion was given to it.**

■ 7. **After this I saw** in the night visions, and behold ■ **a fourth beast,** dreadful and terrible, and strong exceedingly; and ■ **it had great iron teeth:** it devoured and brake in pieces, and stamped the residue with the feet of it: and it *was* diverse from all the beasts that *were* before it; ■ **and it had ten horns.**

8. I considered the horns, ■ **and,** behold, ■ **there came up among them another little horn, before whom there were three** of the first ■ **horns plucked up** by the roots: ■ **and,** behold, ■ **in this horn were eyes** like the eyes of man, ■ **and a mouth speaking great things.**

■ 9. **I beheld till the thrones were cast down, and the Ancient of days did sit,** whose garment *was* white as snow, and the hair of his head like the pure wool: his throne *was like* the fiery flame, ■ **and** his wheels *as* burning fire.

10. **A fiery stream** issued and ■ **came forth from before him: thousand thousands ministered unto him, and ten thousand times ten thousand stood before him: the judgment was set, and the books were opened.**

11. I beheld then because of the voice of the great words which the horn spake: ■ **I beheld even till the beast was slain, and his body**

destroyed, and
- given to the burning flame.
12. As concerning
- the rest of the beasts, they
- had their dominion
- taken away: yet their lives
- were prolonged for a
season and
- time.
13. I saw in the night visions,
- and, behold, one like the
- Son of man came with
- the clouds of heaven, and came
- to the Ancient of days, and
they brought him near before him.
14. And there was given
- him dominion, and
- glory, and a kingdom,
- that all people,
nations, and languages,
- should serve him:
- his dominion is an
- everlasting dominion, which shall
not pass away, and his kingdom *that*
which shall not be destroyed.
15. I Daniel was grieved
in my spirit in the midst of *my* body,
- and the visions of my head
- troubled me.
16. I came near unto one
of them that stood by, and
- asked him
- the truth of all this.
- So he told me, and made me
know the interpretation of the things.
17. These great
- beasts, which are four,
- are four kings,
- which shall arise
out of the earth.
18. But the saints
of the most High
- shall take the kingdom, and
- possess the kingdom for
- ever, even for ever and ever.
19. Then I would know
the truth
- of the fourth beast, which
was diverse from all the others,
exceeding dreadful,
- whose teeth were of iron,
and his nails *of* brass; *which*
devoured, brake in pieces, and

stamped the residue with his feet;
- 20. And of the ten horns
that *were* in his head,
- and *of*
- the other which came up,
and before whom three fell; even *of*
that horn that had eyes, and a mouth
that spake very great things, whose
look *was* more stout than his fellows.
- 21. I beheld, and the same
- horn made war with the
- saints, and prevailed
against them;
- 22. Until the Ancient of days
- came, and judgment was
- given to the saints
of the most High;
- and the time came that
- the saints possessed
- the kingdom.
23. Thus he said, The fourth
- beast shall be the fourth
- kingdom upon earth, which
shall be diverse from all kingdoms,
- and shall devour the whole
- earth, and shall tread it down, and
break it in pieces.
24. And the ten horns
out of this kingdom
- are ten kings *that* shall arise:
- and another shall rise
after them; and he shall be
diverse from the first,
- and he shall subdue
- three kings.
25. And he shall speak
great words
- against the most High,
- and shall wear out
- the saints
of the most High, and think to change
times and laws: and they
- shall be given into his hand
- until a time and times and
- the dividing of time.
26. But the
- judgment shall sit, and they
- shall take away his
- dominion, to consume
- and to
- destroy it unto the end.
27. And the kingdom
and dominion, and the greatness of

the kingdom under the whole heaven,
shall be given to the people of
the saints of the most High,
whose kingdom is an
everlasting kingdom,
and all dominions
shall serve and obey him.
28. Hitherto is the end of the matter.
As for me Daniel,
my cogitations much troubled
me, and my countenance
changed in me: but
I kept the matter
in my heart.

CHAPTER 8

1. **In the third year**
of the reign of king
Belshazzar a vision
appeared unto me,
even unto me
Daniel, after that which
appeared unto me at the first.
2. And I saw in a vision; and it came
to pass, when I saw, that I *was* at
Shushan *in* the palace, which *is* in the
province of Elam;
and I saw in a vision, and
I was by the river of Ulai.
3. Then I lifted up mine eyes,
and saw,
and, behold,
there stood before the river
a ram which had
two horns:
and the *two* horns *were* high; but
one was higher than the
other, and the higher came up last.
4. **I saw the ram pushing**
westward, and
northward, and
southward; so that no
beasts might stand
before him, neither *was there any*
that could deliver out of his hand; but
he did according to his will, and
became great.
5. **And** as I was considering,
behold, an he goat
came from the west
on the face of the whole earth,
and touched not the
ground: and the goat

had a notable
horn between his eyes.
6. **And he came to the**
ram that had *two* horns, which
I had seen standing before the
river, and ran unto him
in the fury of his power.
7. **And** I saw him come close unto
the ram, and he was moved with
choler against him, and
smote the ram, and brake
his two horns: and there was no
power in the ram to stand before him,
but he cast him down to the ground,
and stamped upon him:
and there was none
that could deliver
the ram out of his hand.
8. **Therefore the he**
goat waxed very
great: and when he was strong,
the great horn was broken;
and for it came up four
notable ones toward the
four winds of heaven.
9. **And out of one** of them
came forth
a little horn, which waxed
exceeding great, toward the south,
and toward the east, and toward the
pleasant *land.*
10. **And it waxed great,**
even to the host of heaven;
and it cast down *some* of the host and
of the stars to the ground, and
stamped upon them.
11. **Yea, he magnified**
himself even to the prince
of the host, and by him the
daily sacrifice was taken
away, and the place of his
sanctuary was cast down.
12. And an host was given *him*
against the daily *sacrifice* by reason of
transgression, and it cast down the
truth to the ground; and it practised,
and prospered.
13. **Then I heard one saint**
speaking, and another saint said
unto that certain *saint* which spake,
How long shall be the
vision concerning the
daily sacrifice, and the

transgression of
desolation, to give both
the sanctuary and the host
to be trodden under foot?
14. **And he said** unto me, Unto
**two thousand and three
hundred days; then shall
the sanctuary be cleansed.**
15. **And** it came to pass,
when I, *even*
I Daniel, had seen the vision, and
**sought for the meaning,
then,** behold,
**there stood before
me** as the appearance of
a man.
16. **And I heard a man's
voice** between *the banks of* Ulai,
which called, and
**said, Gabriel, make
this man to understand
the vision.**
17. **So he came
near** where I stood:
and when he came,
**I was afraid, and fell upon
my face: but he said** unto me,
Understand, O son of man:
**for at the time of the end
shall be the vision.**
18. **Now as he was
speaking** with me,
I was in a deep sleep
on my face toward the ground:
but he touched me, and
set me upright.
19. **And he said,** Behold,
**I will make thee know what
shall be in the last end of
the indignation:** for at the time
appointed the end *shall be.*
20. **The ram** which thou sawest
**having two horns are the
kings of Media and Persia.**
21. **And the rough goat
is the king of Grecia:
and the great horn**
that *is* between his eyes
is the first king.
22. **Now that being broken,**
whereas four stood up for it,
**four kingdoms shall
stand up** out of the nation,

but not in his power.
23. **And in the latter time**
of their kingdom, when the
transgressors are come to the full,
**a king of fierce
countenance,**
and understanding dark sentences,
shall stand up.
24. **And his power shall
be mighty, but not by his
own power: and he shall
destroy** wonderfully, and shall
prosper, and practise, and shall
destroy
**the mighty and the
holy people.**
25. **And** through his policy also
**he shall cause craft to
prosper in his hand;** and he
shall magnify *himself* in his heart,
**and by peace shall destroy
many: he shall also stand
up against the Prince of
princes; but he shall be
broken** without hand.
26. **And the vision**
of the evening and the morning
which was told
is true: wherefore shut thou
**up the vision; for it shall
be for many days.**
27. **And I Daniel fainted,
and was sick**
certain days; afterward I rose up, and
did the king's business; and I was
astonished at the vision, but none
understood *it.*

CHAPTER 9

1. **In the first year of Darius**
the son of Ahasuerus, of the seed
of the Medes, which was made
king over the realm of the
Chaldeans;
2. In the first year of his reign
**I Daniel understood
by books the number
of the years,** whereof
**the word of the LORD came
to Jeremiah** the prophet,
**that he would accomplish
seventy years in the
desolations of Jerusalem.**

3. And I set my face unto the Lord God, to seek by prayer and supplications, with fasting, and sackcloth, and ashes:

4. **And I prayed unto the LORD** my God, **and made my confession, and said, O Lord,** the great and dreadful God, keeping the covenant and mercy to them that love him, and to them that keep his commandments;

5. **We have sinned,** and have committed iniquity, and have done wickedly, and have rebelled, even **by departing from thy precepts** and from thy judgments:

6. **Neither have we hearkened unto** thy servants **the prophets,** which spake in thy name to our kings, our princes, and our fathers, and to all the people of the land.

7. **O LORD, righteousness belongeth unto thee, but unto us confusion of faces,** as at this day; to the men of Judah, and to the inhabitants of Jerusalem, and unto all Israel, *that are* near, and *that are* far off, through all the countries whither thou hast driven them, **because of their trespass that** they have trespassed **against thee.**

8. O Lord, to us *belongeth* confusion of face, to our kings, to our princes, and to our fathers, because we have sinned against thee.

9. **To the Lord** our God **belong mercies and forgivenesses, though we have rebelled** against him;

10. Neither have we obeyed the voice of the LORD our God, to walk in his laws, which he set before us by his servants the prophets.

11. Yea, all Israel have transgressed thy law, even by departing, that they might not obey thy voice; **therefore the curse is poured upon us, and the oath that is written in the law of Moses**

the servant of God, because we have sinned against him.

12. **And he hath confirmed his words, which he spake against us,** and against our judges that judged us, **by bringing** upon us **a great evil:** for under the whole heaven hath not been done as hath been done **upon Jerusalem.**

13. As *it is* written in the law of Moses, **all this evil is come upon us: yet made we not our prayer before the LORD** our God, **that we might turn from our iniquities,** and understand thy truth.

14. Therefore hath the LORD watched upon the evil, and brought it upon us: for the LORD our God *is* righteous in all his works which he doeth: **for we obeyed not his voice.**

15. **And now,** O Lord our God, that hast brought thy people forth out of the land of Egypt with a mighty hand, and hast gotten thee renown, as at this day; we have sinned, we have done wickedly.

16. **O LORD,** according to all thy righteousness, **I beseech thee, let thine anger** and thy fury **be turned away from** thy city **Jerusalem,** thy holy mountain: **because for our sins,** and for the iniquities of our fathers, Jerusalem and thy people *are become* a reproach to all *that are* about us.

17. Now therefore, O our God, hear the prayer of thy servant, and his supplications, and cause thy face to shine upon thy sanctuary that is desolate, for the Lord's sake.

18. O my God, incline thine ear, and hear; open thine eyes, and behold our desolations, and the city which is called by thy name: for **we do not present our supplications before thee for our righteousnesses, but**

for thy great mercies.

19. O Lord, hear; O Lord, forgive; O Lord, hearken and do; defer not, for thine own sake, O my God: for thy city and thy people are called by thy name.

20. And whiles I *was* speaking, and praying, and confessing my sin and the sin of my people Israel, and presenting my supplication before the LORD my God for the holy mountain of my God;

21. Yea, whiles I was speaking in prayer, even the man Gabriel, whom I had seen in the vision at the beginning, being caused to fly swiftly, touched me about the time of the evening oblation.

22. And he informed *me*, and talked with me, and said, O Daniel, I am now come forth to give thee skill and understanding.

23. At the beginning of thy supplications the commandment came forth, and I am come to shew *thee*; for thou art greatly beloved: therefore understand the matter, and consider the vision.

24. Seventy weeks are determined upon thy people and upon thy holy city, to finish the transgression, and to make an end of sins, and to make reconciliation for iniquity, and to bring in everlasting righteousness, and to seal up the vision and prophecy, and to anoint the most Holy.

25. Know therefore and understand, that from the going forth of the commandment to restore and to build Jerusalem unto the Messiah the Prince

shall be seven weeks, and threescore and two weeks: the street shall be built again, and the wall, even in troublous times.

26. And after threescore and two weeks shall Messiah be cut off, but not for himself: and the people of the prince that shall come shall destroy the city and the sanctuary; and the end thereof *shall be* with a flood, and unto the end of the war desolations are determined.

27. And he shall confirm the covenant with many for one week: and in the midst of the week he shall cause the sacrifice and the oblation to cease, and for the overspreading of abominations he shall make it desolate, even until the consummation, and that determined shall be poured upon the desolate.

CHAPTER 10

1. In the third year of Cyrus king of Persia a thing was revealed unto Daniel, whose name was called Belteshazzar; and the thing *was* true, but the time appointed *was* long: and he understood the thing, and had understanding of the vision.

2. In those days I Daniel was mourning three full weeks.

3. I ate no pleasant bread, neither came flesh nor wine in my mouth, neither did I anoint myself at all, till three whole weeks were fulfilled.

4. And in the four and twentieth day of the first month, as I was by the side of the great river, which *is* Hiddekel;

5. Then I lifted up mine eyes, and looked, and behold a certain man clothed in linen, whose loins were girded with fine gold of Uphaz: 6. His body also was like the beryl, and his face as the appearance of lightning, and his eyes as lamps of fire, and his arms and his feet like in colour to polished brass, and the voice of his words like the voice of a multitude. 7. And I Daniel alone saw the vision: for the men that were with me saw not the vision; but a great quaking fell upon them, so that they fled to hide themselves. 8. Therefore I was left alone, and saw this great vision, and there remained no strength in me: for my comeliness was turned in me into corruption, and I retained no strength. 9. Yet heard I the voice of his words: and when I heard the voice of his words, then was I in a deep sleep on my face, and my face toward the ground. 10. And, behold, an hand touched me, which set me upon my knees and upon the palms of my hands. 11. And he said unto me, O Daniel, a man greatly beloved, understand the words that I speak unto thee, and stand upright: for unto thee am I now sent. And when he had spoken this word unto me, I stood trembling. 12. Then said he unto me, Fear not, Daniel: for from the first day that thou didst set thine heart to understand, and to chasten thyself before thy God, thy words were heard, and I am come for thy words. 13. But the prince of the kingdom of Persia withstood me one and twenty days: but, lo, Michael, one of the chief princes, came to help me; and I remained there with the kings of Persia. 14. Now I am come to make thee understand what shall befall thy people in the latter days: for yet the vision is for many days. 15. And when he had spoken such words unto me, I set my face toward the ground, and I became dumb. 16. And, behold, one like the similitude of the sons of men touched my lips: then I opened my mouth, and spake, and said unto him that stood before me, O my lord, by the vision my sorrows are turned upon me, and I have retained no strength. 17. For how can the servant of this my lord talk with this my lord? for as for me, straightway there remained no strength in me, neither is there breath left in me. 18. Then there came again and touched me one like the appearance of a man, and he strengthened me, 19. And said, O man greatly beloved, fear not: peace be unto thee, be strong, yea, be strong. And when he had spoken unto me, I was strengthened, and said, Let my lord speak; for thou hast strengthened me. 20. Then said he, Knowest thou wherefore

I come unto thee?
and now will I return to fight
with the prince of Persia:
and when I am gone forth, lo,
the prince of Grecia
shall come.
21. But I will shew thee
that which is noted
in the scripture of truth: and
there is none that holdeth
with me in these things, but
Michael your prince.

CHAPTER 11

1. Also I in the first year
of Darius the Mede, *even*
I, stood to confirm and
to strengthen him.
2. And now will I shew thee
the truth. Behold,
there shall stand up yet
three kings in Persia; and
the fourth shall be far richer
than they all: and by his strength
through his riches
he shall stir up all against
the realm of Grecia.
3. And a mighty king shall
stand up, that shall rule with great
dominion, and do according to his will.
4. And when he shall stand up,
his kingdom shall be broken, and
shall be divided toward
the four winds of heaven;
and not to his posterity,
nor according to his dominion
which he ruled: for
his kingdom shall
be plucked up,
even for others beside those.
5. And the king of the south
shall be strong, and one of
his princes; and he
shall be strong above him,
and have dominion; his
dominion *shall be* a great dominion.
6. And in the end of years
they shall join themselves
together; for the king's
daughter of the south
shall come to the king
of the north to make an
agreement: but she shall not

retain the power of the arm;
neither shall he
stand, nor his arm: but she shall be
given up, and they that brought her,
and he that begat her, and he that
strengthened her in *these* times.
7. But out of a branch of
her roots shall one
stand up in his estate,
which shall come with an
army, and shall enter into
the fortress of the king
of the north,
and shall deal against them,
and shall prevail:
8. And shall also
carry captives
into Egypt their gods, with
their princes, and with
their precious
vessels of silver and of gold;
and he shall continue *more* years
than the king of the north.
9. So the king of
the south shall come into
his kingdom, and shall
return into his own land.
10. But his sons shall
be stirred up, and shall
assemble a multitude of
great forces: and *one* shall
certainly come, and overflow, and
pass through: then shall he return,
and be stirred up, *even* to his fortress.
11. And the king of the south
shall be moved with choler, and
shall come forth
and fight with him, *even* with
the king of the north:
and he shall set forth a great
multitude; but the multitude shall be
given into his hand.
12. *And* when he hath taken away
the multitude, his heart shall be lifted
up; and he shall cast down *many* ten
thousands:
but he shall not be
strengthened by it.
13. For the king of the
north shall return,
and shall set forth a multitude greater
than the former, and shall certainly
come after certain years

with a great army and with much riches.

14. **And** in those times there **shall many stand up against the king of the south:** also the robbers of thy people shall exalt themselves to establish the vision; but they shall fall.

15. **So the king of the north shall come,** and cast up a mount, and take the most fenced cities: **and the arms of the south shall not withstand,** neither his chosen people, neither *shall there be any* strength to withstand.

16. But he that cometh against him shall do according to his own will, **and none shall stand before him:** and he shall stand in the glorious land, which by his hand shall be consumed.

17. He shall also set his face to enter with the strength of his whole kingdom, and upright ones with him; thus shall he do: and he shall give him the daughter of women, corrupting her: but she shall not stand *on his side,* neither be for him.

18. **After this shall he turn his face unto the isles, and shall take many: but a prince for his own behalf shall cause the reproach** offered by him **to cease;** without his own reproach he shall cause *it* to turn upon him.

19. **Then he shall turn** his face **toward** the fort of **his own land: but he shall** stumble and **fall, and not be found.**

20. **Then shall stand** up in his estate **a raiser of taxes** *in* the glory of the kingdom: **but within few days he shall be destroyed,** neither in anger, nor in battle.

21. **And** in his estate shall stand up **a vile person,** to whom they shall not give the honour of the kingdom: but he **shall come in peaceably,** and obtain the kingdom by flatteries.

22. And with the arms of a flood shall they be overflown from before him, and shall be broken; yea, also the prince of the covenant.

23. **And** after the league *made* with him **he shall work deceitfully:** for he shall come up, **and** shall **become strong with a small people.**

24. **He shall enter peaceably** even upon **the fattest places** of the province; and he shall do *that* which his fathers have not done, nor his fathers' fathers; **he shall scatter among them the prey,** and spoil, and riches: *yea,* **and he shall forecast his devices against the strong** holds, even for a time.

25. **And he shall stir up his power** and his courage **against the king of the south** with a great army; and the king of the south shall be stirred up to battle with a very great and mighty army; **but he shall not stand: for they shall forecast devices against him.**

26. Yea, they that feed of the portion of his meat shall destroy him, and his army shall overflow: and many shall fall down slain.

27. **And both these kings'** hearts *shall be* to do mischief, and they **shall speak lies at one table; but it shall not prosper: for** yet **the end shall be at the time appointed.**

28. **Then shall he return into his land with great riches; and his heart shall be against the holy covenant;** and he shall do *exploits,* and return to his own land.

29. **At the time appointed he shall return,** and come **toward the south;** but it shall not be as the former, or as the latter. 30. **For the ships of Chittim shall come against him:** therefore he shall be grieved, and return, and have indignation against the holy covenant: so shall he do; **he shall even return, and have intelligence with them that forsake the holy covenant.** 31. And arms shall stand on his part, and they shall pollute the sanctuary of strength, and shall take away the daily *sacrifice,* **and they shall place the abomination that maketh desolate.** 32. And such as do wickedly against the covenant shall he corrupt by flatteries: **but the people that** do **know** their **God shall be strong, and do exploits.** 33. **And they that understand** among the people **shall instruct many: yet they shall fall** by the sword, and by flame, by captivity, and by spoil, *many* days. 34. Now when they shall fall, they shall be holpen with a little help: but many shall cleave to them with flatteries. 35. And *some* of them of understanding shall fall, to try them, and to purge, and to make *them* white, *even* to the time of the end: because *it is* yet for a time appointed. 36. **And the king shall** do according to his will; and he shall **exalt himself,** and magnify himself **above every god, and shall speak** marvellous things **against** the **God** of gods, **and shall prosper till the indignation be accomplished:** for that that is determined shall be done. 37. Neither shall he regard the God of his fathers, nor the desire of women, nor regard any god: for he shall magnify himself above all. 38. **But in his estate shall he honour the God of forces: and a god whom his fathers knew not shall he honour with gold, and silver,** and with precious stones, and pleasant things. 39. Thus shall he do in the most strong holds with a strange god, whom he shall acknowledge *and* increase with glory: and he shall cause them to rule over many, and shall divide the land for gain. 40. **And at the time of the end shall the king of the south** push at him: **and the king of the north** shall **come against him** like a whirlwind, with chariots, and with horsemen, and with many ships; **and he shall enter into the countries,** and shall overflow and pass over. 41. He shall enter also into the glorious land, **and many** countries **shall be overthrown: but these shall escape** out of his hand, **even Edom,** and **Moab, and** the chief of the children of **Ammon.** 42. He shall stretch forth his hand also upon the countries: **and the land of Egypt shall not escape.** 43. But he shall have power over the treasures of gold and of silver, and over all the precious things of Egypt: **and the Libyans and the Ethiopians shall be at his steps.** 44. **But tidings out of the east and** out of the **north shall trouble him:** therefore he shall go forth **with great fury to destroy,**

and utterly to make away many.
45. And he shall plant the tabernacles of his palace between the seas in the glorious holy mountain; **yet he shall come to his end, and none shall help him.**

CHAPTER 12

1. **And at that time shall Michael stand up,** the great prince which standeth for the children of thy people: **and there shall be a time of trouble, such as never was since there was a nation** *even* to that same time: **and** at that time **thy people shall be delivered, every one** that shall be **found written in the book.** 2. **And** many of **them that sleep** in the dust of the earth **shall awake, some to everlasting life, and some to** shame *and* **everlasting contempt.** 3. **And they that be wise shall shine as the brightness of the firmament; and they that turn many to righteousness as the stars for ever** and ever. 4. **But** thou, O Daniel, shut up the words, and **seal the book, even to the time of the end:** many shall run to and fro, and knowledge shall be increased. 5. **Then I** Daniel **looked, and,** behold, **there stood other two,** the one on this side of the bank of the river, and the other on that side of the bank of the river. 6. **And one said** to the man

clothed in linen, which *was* upon the waters of the river, **How long shall it be to the end of these wonders?** 7. **And I heard the man** clothed in linen, which *was* upon the waters of the river, when he held up his right hand and his left hand unto heaven, and **sware by him that liveth for ever that it shall be for a time, times, and an half; and when he shall have accomplished to scatter the power of the holy people, all these things shall be finished.** 8. **And** I heard, but **I understood not:** then said I, O my Lord, what *shall be* the end of these *things?* 9. **And he said, Go thy way, Daniel: for the words are** closed up and **sealed till the time of the end.** 10. Many shall be purified, and made white, and tried; but the wicked shall do wickedly: and **none of the wicked shall understand; but the wise shall understand.** 11. **And from the time** *that* the daily *sacrifice* shall be taken away, and **the abomination that maketh desolate set up, there shall be a thousand two hundred and ninety days.** 12. **Blessed is he that waiteth,** and cometh to the thousand three hundred and five and thirty days. 13. **But go** thou thy way till the end *be:* **for thou shalt** rest, and **stand** in thy lot **at the end of the days.**

HOSEA:
Prophet of Love

The Book of
Hosea presents a
beautiful, moving, and
tender story which
illustrates God's
love for sinful man, *and the*
eleventh chapter of the book is a peak
in Old Testament theology, showing
God's compassion for His people, and
his unwillingness to give them up.
The prophecy centers in
the circumstances of
Hosea's *unfortunate*
marriage to a prostitute
by the name of Gomer.
After Hosea had made
Gomer his wife *and given*
to her his love, protection and care,
she left *home,*
broke her *marriage*
vows, and went back
into prostitution. Hosea
could not give up Gomer
forever, even in face of open adultery.
Just as Hosea
loved Gomer, and

could not denounce
her forever, so God,
Hosea states,
could not *completely*
forsake his unfaithful
people. God would
chastise, *but it would be the*
chastisement of a jealous lover.
God longed to bring
back his beloved *into the joy*
of their first love. Israel's infidelity was
in the form of idolatry and
ignoring the needs of the poor.
Israel's sin was so
deeply ingrained that
sacrifices *on altars*
could not atone *for them*
God would *have to*
strip her and brake
her and He would.
But *God*
stood ready to forgive
her for her transgressions
if only she would
forsake her evil and
return *unto Him.*

THE BOOK OF HOSEA

BACKGROUND INFORMATION

Author: Hosea
Date Written:
784 — 725 B.C.

Number of:
Verses—197
Chapters—14
Total Words—5,175
Scan Words—2,143
Scan Words Represent
Approximately 41% of
Total Words

**Theme: God's Love
Revealed** Through the
Prophet's Love for an
Unfaithful Wife

OUTLINE OF
THE BOOK

I.   **Hosea's** Faithfulness and
     Marriage
     1:1 — 3:5
II. **Israel's** Depravity and
     Apostasy
     4:1 — 7:16
III. **God's Judgement**
     8:1 — 10:15
IV. **God's Love and Mercy**
     11:1 — 14:9

CHAPTER 1

■ 1. **The word of the LORD** that
■ **came unto Hosea,** the son of
Beeri, in the days of Uzziah, Jotham,
Ahaz, *and* Hezekiah, kings of Judah,
and in the days of Jeroboam the son
of Joash, king of Israel.
2. The beginning of the word
of the LORD by Hosea. And the
LORD said to Hosea,
■ **Go, take** unto thee
■ **a wife of whoredoms**
and children of whoredoms:
■ **for the land hath committed**
■ **great whoredom, departing**
■ **from the LORD.**
■ 3. **So he** went and
■ **took Gomer** the
daughter of Diblaim;
■ **which** conceived, and
■ **bare him a son.**
■ 4. **And the LORD said** unto him,
■ **Call his name Jezreel;**
■ **for** yet a little *while,* and
■ **I will avenge the blood**
■ **of Jezreel upon** the house of
■ **Jehu,** and will cause to cease the
kingdom of the house of Israel.
5. **And** it shall come to
pass at that day, that
■ **I will break the bow**
■ **of Israel, in the valley**
■ **of Jezreel.**
■ 6. **And she conceived**
■ **again, and bare**
■ **a daughter.**
■ **And God said** unto him,
■ **Call her** name
■ **Lo-ruhamah: for I will**
■ **no more have mercy**
■ **upon** the house of
■ **Israel;** but I will
utterly take them away.
■ 7. **But I will have mercy**
■ **upon** the house of
■ **Judah,** and will save them by the
LORD their God, and will not save
them by bow, nor by sword, nor by
battle, by horses, nor by horsemen.
■ 8. **Now** when
she had weaned Lo-ruhamah,
■ **she conceived,**
■ **and bare a son.**

■ 9. **Then said God, Call**
■ **his name Lo-ammi: for**
ye *are* not my people, and
■ **I will not be your God.**
10. **Yet** the number of
■ **the children of Israel** shall
be as the sand of the sea, which
■ **cannot be** measured nor
■ **numbered; and** it
shall come to pass, *that* in the
place where it was said unto
them, Ye *are* not my people, *there*
■ **it shall be said** unto them,
■ **Ye are the sons of the**
■ **living God.**
11. **Then shall** the children of
■ **Judah and** the children of
■ **Israel** be gathered together, and
■ **appoint** themselves
■ **one head, and** they
■ **shall come up out of the**
■ **land: for great shall be**
■ **the day of Jezreel.**

CHAPTER 2

■ 1. **Say ye unto your**
■ **brethren, Ammi; and to**
■ **your sisters, Ruhamah.**
■ 2. **Plead with your mother,**
plead: for she *is* not my wife,
neither *am* I her husband:
■ **let her** therefore
■ **put away** her whoredoms
out of her sight, and
■ **her adulteries**
from between her breasts;
■ 3. **Lest I strip her** naked, and set
her as in the day that she was born,
■ **and make her as a**
■ **wilderness, and**
set her like a dry land,
■ **and slay her with thirst.**
■ 4. **And I will not have mercy**
■ **upon her children;** for they
be the children of whoredoms.
■ 5. **For** their mother
hath played the harlot:
■ **she** that conceived them
■ **hath done shamefully:**
■ **for she said, I will go after**
■ **my lovers,** that give *me* my
bread and my water, my wool
and my flax, mine oil and my drink.

6. **Therefore,** behold,
**I will hedge up thy way with
thorns,** and make a wall, that
**she shall not
find her paths.**
7. **And she shall follow** after
her lovers, but she
shall not overtake them;
and she shall seek them,
but shall not find *them:*
**then shall she say,
I will** go and
**return to my first husband;
for then was it better**
with me than now.
8. **For** she did not know that
**I gave her corn,
and wine,** and oil,
and multiplied her silver and
gold, *which* they prepared for Baal.
9. **Therefore will I** return, and
take away my corn
in the time thereof,
and my
wine in the season thereof, and
will recover my wool and my flax
given to cover her nakedness.
10. **And** now
will I
discover her lewdness
in the sight of her lovers,
**and none shall deliver
her** out of mine hand.
11. **I will** also
cause all her mirth
to cease, her feast days,
her new moons, and her sabbaths,
and all her solemn feasts.
12. **And I will destroy
her vines and** her
fig trees, whereof she hath
said, These *are* my rewards that
my lovers have given me: and
I will make them a forest, and
**the beasts of the
field shall eat them.**
13. **And I will visit upon
her the days of Baalim,
wherein she burned
incense to them,**
and she decked herself with
her earrings and her jewels,
and she went after her

**lovers, and forgat
me, saith the LORD.**
14. Therefore, behold,
I will allure her, and bring her
into the wilderness,
and speak comfortably unto her.
15. **And I will give her** her
vineyards from thence, and the
valley of Achor for a door of hope:
and **she shall sing** there,
as in the days of
her youth, and as in the day
when she came up
out of the land of
Egypt.
16. **And** it shall be at that
day, saith the LORD, *that*
thou shalt call me Ishi;
and shalt call me no more Baali.
17. **For I will take
away** the names of
Baalim out of her mouth,
**and they shall no more be
remembered** by their name.
18. **And in that day will I
make a covenant for them
with the beasts** of the field
and with the
fowls of heaven, and *with* the
creeping things of the ground:
**and I will break
the bow and the sword**
and the battle out of the earth,
and will
make them to
lie down safely.
19. **And I will betroth
thee unto me for ever;**
yea, I will betroth thee unto me
in righteousness, and in
judgment, and in lovingkindness,
and in mercies.
20. **I will even betroth thee
unto me in faithfulness:**
and thou shalt know the LORD.
21. **And** it shall come to pass
in that day, I will hear,
saith the LORD,
**I will hear the heavens,
and** they shall hear the
earth;
22. **And the earth shall
hear the corn, and** the

■ **wine,** and the oil;
■ **and they shall**
■ **hear Jezreel.**
23. And I will sow
her unto me in the earth;
■ **and I will have mercy** upon
her that had not obtained mercy;
■ **and I will say to them which**
■ **were not my people, Thou**
■ **art my people; and they**
■ **shall say, Thou art my God.**

CHAPTER 3

■ 1. **Then said the**
■ **LORD** unto me,
■ **Go** yet,
■ **love** a woman
beloved of *her* friend, yet
■ **an adulteress, according**
■ **to the love of the LORD**
■ **toward** the children of
■ **Israel, who look to other**
■ **gods,** and love flagons of wine.
2. So I bought her to me for fifteen
pieces of silver, and *for* an homer of
barley, and an half homer of barley:
■ 3. **And I said unto her,** Thou
shalt abide for me many days;
■ **thou shalt not play the**
■ **harlot,** and thou shalt not be for
another man: so *will* I also *be* for thee.
■ 4. **For** the children of
■ **Israel shall abide** many days
■ **without a king,**
and without a prince,
■ **and without a sacrifice,**
■ **and without an image,**
■ **and without an**
■ **ephod, and** *without*
■ **teraphim:**
■ 5. **Afterward shall**
the children of
■ **Israel** return, and
■ **seek** the LORD their
God, and David their king;
■ **and** shall
■ **fear the LORD** and his
goodness in the latter days.

CHAPTER 4

■ 1. **Hear the word of the**
■ **LORD,** ye children of Israel: for the
LORD hath a controversy with the

inhabitants of the land, because
■ **there is no truth,** nor mercy,
■ **nor knowledge of**
■ **God in the land.**
2. By swearing, and lying,
and killing, and stealing, and
committing adultery, they break
out, and blood toucheth blood.
■ 3. **Therefore shall the**
■ **land mourn, and every**
■ **one** that dwelleth therein
■ **shall languish,** with
■ **the beasts** of the field,
■ **and** with
■ **the fowls** of heaven;
■ **yea, the fishes** of the sea
■ **also shall be taken away.**
■ 4. **Yet let no man strive,**
nor reprove another:
■ **for thy people are as they**
■ **that strive with the priest.**
5. Therefore shalt thou fall in
the day, and the prophet also
shall fall with thee in the night,
and I will destroy thy mother.
■ 6. **My people are**
■ **destroyed for lack**
■ **of knowledge:**
■ **because thou** hast
■ **rejected** knowledge,
I will also reject thee, that
thou shalt be no priest to me:
seeing thou hast forgotten
■ **the law of** thy
■ **God,** I will also forget thy children.
7. As they were increased, so
■ **they sinned** against me:
■ **therefore will I change**
■ **their glory into shame.**
8. They eat up the sin of
my people, and they set
their heart on their iniquity.
9. And there shall be,
like people, like priest: and
■ **I will punish them**
■ **for their ways,**
and reward them their doings.
■ 10. **For they shall eat, and**
■ **not have enough: they** shall
■ **commit whoredom,**
■ **and shall not increase:**
■ **because they** have
■ **left** off to take heed to

■ the LORD.

11. Whoredom and wine and new wine take away the heart.

■ 12. **My people** ask counsel at their stocks, and their staff declareth unto them: for the spirit of whoredoms hath caused *them* to

■ **err,** and they have gone a-whoring
■ **from** under
■ **their God.**

13. They sacrifice upon the tops of the mountains, and burn incense upon the hills, under oaks and poplars and elms, because the shadow thereof *is* good: therefore

■ **your daughters** shall commit whoredom,

■ **and your spouses** shall commit adultery.

14. I will not punish your daughters when they

■ **commit whoredom,** nor your spouses when

■ **they** commit adultery: for themselves

■ **are separated** with whores,
■ **and** they
■ **sacrifice with harlots:** therefore the people *that* doth not understand shall fall.

■ 15. **Though** thou,
■ **Israel, play the harlot,** *yet*
■ **let not Judah offend;** and come not ye unto Gilgal, neither go ye up to Beth-aven, nor swear, The LORD liveth.

■ 16. **For Israel slideth back as**
■ **a backsliding heifer:** now the LORD will feed them as a lamb in a large place.

■ 17. **Ephraim is joined to**
■ **idols: let him alone.**

18. Their drink is sour: they have committed whoredom continually: her rulers *with* shame do love, Give ye.

19. The wind hath bound her up in her wings,

■ **and they shall be ashamed** because of their sacrifices.

CHAPTER 5

■| 1. **Hear** ye
■| **this, O priests; and** hearken,

■ ye house of Israel; and give ye ear, O house of the king; for

■ **judgment is toward**
■ **you, because ye have**
■ **been a snare on Mizpah,**
■ **and** a net spread upon
■ **Tabor.**

2. And the revolters are profound to make slaughter, though I *have been* a rebuker of them all.

■ 3. **I know Ephraim, and**
■ **Israel** is not hid from me: for now, O Ephraim, thou

■ **committest whoredom,** *and* Israel is defiled.

■ 4. **They will not** frame their doings to

■ **turn unto their God:** for the spirit of whoredoms *is* in the midst of them, and they have not known the LORD.

5. And the pride of Israel doth testify to his face:

■ **therefore shall Israel**
■ **and Ephraim fall in their**
■ **iniquity: Judah also** shall fall
■ **with them.**

■ 6. **They shall** go with their flocks and with their herds to

■ **seek the LORD; but**
■ **they shall not find him;** he hath withdrawn himself from them.

7. They have dealt treacherously against the LORD: for they have begotten strange children: now shall a month devour them with their portions.

■ 8. **Blow ye the**
■ **cornet** in Gibeah,
■ **and the trumpet** in Ramah:
■ **cry aloud** *at* Beth-aven,
■ **after thee, O Benjamin.**

■ 9. **Ephraim shall be**
■ **desolate in the day**
■ **of rebuke:** among the tribes of Israel have

■ **I made known that**
■ **which shall** surely
■ **be.**

■ 10. **The princes of Judah**
■ **were like them** that remove the bound:
■ **therefore I will pour out my**

■ **wrath upon them** like water.
11. Ephraim *is* oppressed
and broken in judgment,
because he willingly
walked after the commandment.
12. Therefore *will* I *be* unto
Ephraim as a moth, and to the house
of Judah as rottenness.
■ 13. **When Ephraim saw his**
■ **sickness, and Judah** *saw*
■ **his wound, then** went
■ **Ephraim** to the Assyrian, and
■ **sent to king Jareb: yet**
■ **could he not heal you,**
nor cure you of your wound.
14. **For** I *will be* unto Ephraim
■ **as a lion,** and as a young lion
to the house of Judah: I, *even*
■ **I, will tear and go**
■ **away;** I will take away,
■ **and none shall rescue him.**
15. **I will go** *and* return to my place,
■ **till they** acknowledge
their offence, and
■ **seek my face: in their**
■ **affliction they will**
■ **seek me early.**

CHAPTER 6

■ 1. **Come,** and let us
■ **return unto the LORD:**
■ **for** he hath torn, and
■ **he will heal us;** he hath smitten,
■ **and** he will
■ **bind us** up.
2. After two days will he revive us: in
the third day he will raise us up,
■ **and we shall live**
■ **in his sight.**
3. **Then shall we know,**
if we follow on to know
■ **the LORD:** his going forth is
prepared as the morning; and he shall
come unto us as the rain, as the latter
and former rain unto the earth.
■ 4. **O Ephraim,**
what shall I do unto thee?
■ **O Judah, what shall I**
■ **do unto thee? for your**
■ **goodness** *is* as a morning
cloud, and as the early dew it
■ **goeth away.**
■ 5. **Therefore have I** hewed

them by the prophets; I have
■ **slain them by the words of**
■ **my mouth:** and thy judgments
are as the light *that* goeth forth.
■ 6. **For I desired mercy, and**
■ **not sacrifice;** and the knowledge
of God more than burnt offerings.
■ 7. **But they** like men have
■ **transgressed the**
■ **covenant:** there have
■ **they dealt treacherously**
■ **against me.**
8. Gilead *is* a city of them that work
iniquity, *and is* polluted with blood.
■ 9. **And** as troops of
robbers wait for a man, *so*
■ **the** company of
■ **priests murder** in the way
■ **by consent: for they**
■ **commit lewdness.**
10. **I have seen an**
■ **horrible thing in** the house of
■ **Israel:** there *is* the whoredom
of Ephraim, Israel is defiled.
■ 11. **Also, O**
■ **Judah, he hath** set
an harvest for thee, when I
■ **returned the captivity**
■ **of my people.**

CHAPTER 7

■ 1. **When I would have**
■ **healed Israel,** then the iniquity of
Ephraim was discovered, and the
wickedness of Samaria: for
■ **they commit falsehood;** and
the thief cometh in, *and* the troop of
robbers spoileth without.
■ 2. **And they consider**
■ **not** in their hearts
■ **that I remember all their**
■ **wickedness:** now their own
doings have beset them about;
■ **they are before my face.**
3. They make the king
glad with their wickedness,
and the princes with their lies.
■ 4. **They are all adulterers,**
as an oven heated by the baker,
who ceaseth from raising after
he hath kneaded the dough,
until it be leavened.
5. In the day of our king the

princes have made *him* sick with bottles of wine; he stretched out his hand with scorners.

6. **For they have made ready their heart like an oven,** whiles they lie in wait: their baker sleepeth all the night; **in the morning it burneth as a flaming fire.**

7. They are all hot as an oven, **and** have **devoured their judges;** all their kings are fallen: **there is none among them that calleth unto me.**

8. **Ephraim,** he **hath mixed himself among the people;** Ephraim is a cake not turned.

9. **Strangers have devoured his strength, and he knoweth it not:** yea, gray hairs are here and there upon him, yet he knoweth not.

10. And the pride of Israel testifieth to his face: **and they do not return to the LORD** their God, **nor seek him** for all this.

11. Ephraim also is like a silly dove without heart: they call to Egypt, they go to Assyria.

12. When they shall go, I will spread my net upon them; **I will bring them down** as the fowls of the heaven; **I will chastise them,** as their congregation hath heard.

13. Woe unto them! **for they** have **fled from me:** destruction unto them! because **they have transgressed against me: though I have redeemed them,** yet they have spoken lies against me.

14. **And they have not cried unto me with their heart,** when they howled upon their beds: they assemble themselves for corn and wine, *and* **they rebel against me.**

15. **Though I** have bound *and* **strengthened their arms,** yet do **they imagine mischief** against me.

16. **They return,** *but* **not to the most High: they are** like a **deceitful** bow: **their princes shall fall by the sword** for the rage of their tongue: **this shall be their derision in** the land of **Egypt.**

CHAPTER 8

1. **Set the trumpet to thy mouth.** *He shall come* as an eagle against the house of the LORD, because **they have transgressed my covenant, and** trespassed against **my law.**

2. **Israel shall cry** unto me, **My God, we know thee.**

3. **Israel hath cast off the** *thing that is* **good:** the enemy shall pursue him.

4. **They have set up kings,** but not by me: they have made princes, and I knew *it* not: **of their silver and** their **gold** have **they made** them **idols,** that they may be cut off.

5. Thy calf, O Samaria, hath cast *thee* off; **mine anger is kindled against them:** how long *will it be* ere they attain to innocency?

6. **For** from Israel *was* it also: **the workman made** it; therefore it *is* not God: but **the calf of Samaria** shall be broken in pieces.

7. For they have sown the wind, and they shall reap the whirlwind: it hath no stalk; the bud shall yield no meal: if so be it yield, the strangers shall swallow it up.

8. **Israel** is swallowed up: now **shall** they

be among the Gentiles
as a vessel wherein
is no pleasure.
9. For they are gone
up to Assyria, a wild ass
alone by himself:
Ephraim hath hired lovers.
10. Yea, though they have
hired among the nations,
now will I gather them,
and they shall sorrow a little for
the burden of the king of princes.
11. Because Ephraim hath
made many altars to sin, altars
shall be unto him to sin.
12. I have written
to him the great things
of my law, but they were
counted as a strange thing.
13. They sacrifice flesh
for the sacrifices of
mine offerings, and eat it;
but the LORD accepteth
them not; now will he
remember their iniquity, and visit
their sins: they shall
return to Egypt.
14. For Israel hath forgotten
his Maker, and buildeth temples;
and Judah hath multiplied
fenced cities: but I will
send a fire upon his cities,
and it shall
devour the palaces
thereof.

CHAPTER 9

1. Rejoice not, O Israel,
for joy, as other people:
for thou hast gone
a whoring from thy God,
thou hast loved a reward
upon every cornfloor.
2. The floor and the
winepress shall not
feed them, and the new
wine shall fail in her.
3. They shall not dwell in
the LORD's land; but
Ephraim shall return
to Egypt, and they shall
eat unclean things
in Assyria.

4. They shall not
offer wine offerings
to the LORD, neither shall they
be pleasing unto him: their
sacrifices shall be unto them
as the bread of mourners; all
that eat thereof
shall be polluted: for
their bread for their soul shall
not come into the house of the LORD.
5. What will ye do in the
solemn day, and in the day
of the feast of the LORD?
6. For, lo, they are gone
because of destruction:
Egypt shall gather them
up, Memphis shall bury them: the
pleasant places for their silver,
nettles shall possess
them: thorns shall be
in their tabernacles.
7. The days of visitation
are come, the days of
recompence are come;
Israel shall know it:
the prophet is a fool, the spiritual
man is mad, for the multitude of thine
iniquity, and the great hatred.
8. The watchman of Ephraim
was with my
God: but the prophet
is a snare of a fowler
in all his ways, and hatred
in the house of his God.
9. They have deeply
corrupted themselves, as
in the days of Gibeah: therefore he
will remember their iniquity,
he will visit their sins.
10. I found Israel like grapes
in the wilderness;
I saw your fathers as the firstripe in
the fig tree at her first time:
but they went to Baal-peor, and
separated themselves
unto that
shame; and their
abominations
were according as
they loved.
11. As for Ephraim, their
glory shall fly away like a
bird, from the birth, and from the

womb, and from the conception.

12. **Though they bring up their children, yet** will I bereave them, *that there* **shall** not *be* a man *left:* yea, woe also to them when **I depart from them!**

13. **Ephraim,** as I saw Tyrus, *is* planted in a pleasant place: but Ephraim **shall bring** forth **his children to the murderer.**

14. **Give them, O LORD:** what wilt thou give? give them **a miscarrying womb** and dry breasts.

15. All their wickedness *is* in Gilgal: for there I hated them: for the wickedness of their doings I will drive them out of mine house, **I will love them no more:** all their princes *are* revolters.

16. **Ephraim is smitten,** their root is dried up, they shall bear no fruit: yea, though they bring forth, yet will I slay *even* the beloved *fruit* of their womb.

17. **My God will cast them away, because they did not hearken unto him:** and **they shall be wanderers** among the nations.

CHAPTER 10

1. **Israel** *is* an empty vine, he **bringeth forth fruit unto himself:** according to the multitude of his fruit **he hath increased** the altars; according to the goodness of **his** land they have made goodly **images.**

2. **Their heart is divided;** now shall they be found faulty: **he shall break down** their altars, he shall spoil **their images.**

3. **For** now **they** shall **say, We have no king, because we feared not the LORD;**

what then should a king do to us?

4. **They have spoken** words, swearing **falsely in making a covenant:** thus **judgment springeth up** as hemlock in the furrows of the field.

5. **The inhabitants** of Samaria shall **fear** because of **the calves of Beth-aven:** for **the people** thereof shall **mourn** over it, and the priests thereof *that* rejoiced on it, **for the glory thereof,** because it **is departed** from it.

6. **It shall be** also **carried unto Assyria for a present** to king Jareb: **Ephraim** shall receive shame, **and Israel shall be ashamed** of his own counsel.

7. *As for* Samaria, her king is cut off as the foam upon the water.

8. **The high places** also **of Aven,** the sin of Israel, **shall be destroyed:** the thorn and the thistle shall come up on their altars; **and they shall say to the mountains,** Cover us; **and** to the **hills, Fall on us.**

9. **O Israel, thou hast sinned from the days of Gibeah:** there they stood: **the battle in Gibeah** against the children of iniquity **did** not **overtake them.**

10. **It is in my desire that I** should **chastise them;** and the people shall be gathered against them, **when they** shall **bind themselves in their two furrows.**

11. And Ephraim *is as* an heifer *that is* taught, *and* loveth to tread out *the corn;* but I passed over upon her fair neck: I will make Ephraim to ride; Judah shall plow, *and* Jacob shall

break his clods.

12. **Sow** to yourselves **in righteousness, reap in mercy;** break up your fallow ground: for *it is* time to **seek the LORD, till he come and rain righteousness upon you.**

13. **Ye have plowed wickedness, ye have reaped iniquity;** ye have eaten the fruit of lies: **because thou didst trust in thy way,** in the multitude of thy mighty men.

14. **Therefore** shall a tumult arise among thy people, and all **thy fortresses shall be spoiled,** as Shalman spoiled Beth-arbel in the day of battle: the mother was dashed in pieces upon *her* children.

15. **So shall** Beth-el do unto you because of your great wickedness: in a morning shall **the king of Israel** utterly **be cut off.**

CHAPTER 11

1. **When Israel was a child,** then **I loved him, and called my son out of Egypt.**

2. **As they called** them, so **they** went from them: they **sacrificed unto Baalim, and** burned incense to **graven images.**

3. I taught **Ephraim also** to go, taking them by their arms; but they **knew not that I healed them.**

4. **I drew them with** cords of a man, with bands of **love:** and I was to them as they that take off the yoke on their jaws, **and I laid meat unto them.**

5. He shall not return into the land of Egypt, and **the Assyrian shall be his king,** because they refused to return.

6. **And the sword shall** abide on his cities, and shall consume his branches, and **devour them,** because of their own counsels.

7. **And my people are** bent to **backsliding from me:** though they called them to the most High, none at all would exalt *him.*

8. **How shall I give thee up,** Ephraim? *how* shall I deliver thee, Israel? how shall I make thee as Admah? *how* shall I set thee as Zeboim? **mine heart is turned within me,** my repentings are kindled together.

9. **I will not** execute the fierceness of mine anger, I will not return to **destroy Ephraim: for I am God,** and not man; **the Holy One in the midst of thee:** and I will not enter into the city.

10. **They shall walk after the LORD:** he shall roar like a lion: when he shall roar, then the children shall tremble from the west.

11. **They shall tremble** as a bird out of Egypt, and as a dove out of the land of Assyria: **and I will place them in their houses,** saith the LORD.

12. **Ephraim compasseth me** about **with lies, and** the house of **Israel with deceit: but Judah** yet ruleth with God, and **is faithful with the saints.**

CHAPTER 12

1. **Ephraim** feedeth on wind, and followeth after the east wind: he **daily increaseth lies and desolation;** and they do make a covenant with the Assyrians, and oil is carried into Egypt.

2. **The LORD hath** also **a controversy with Judah,** and will punish **Jacob** according to his ways; according to his doings

will he recompense him.

3. He
took his brother by the heel
in the womb, and by his strength
he had power with God:
4. Yea, he had power over the angel,
and prevailed: he wept, and made
supplication unto him: he found him *in*
Beth-el, and there he spake with us;
5. **Even the LORD**
God of hosts; the LORD
is his memorial.
6. **Therefore turn** thou
to thy God: keep mercy
and judgment and
wait on thy
God continually.
7. *He is* a merchant, the
balances of deceit *are* in his hand:
he loveth to oppress.
8. **And Ephraim said,** Yet
I am become
rich, I have found me out substance:
in all my labours
they shall find none
iniquity in me that *were* sin.
9. **And I** *that am*
the LORD thy God from
the land of Egypt
will yet make thee to
dwell in tabernacles,
as in the days of the solemn feast.
10. **I have** also
spoken by the prophets,
and I have multiplied
visions, and used similitudes,
by the ministry of the prophets.
11. **Is there iniquity in**
Gilead? surely they are vanity:
they sacrifice bullocks in Gilgal; yea,
their altars are as
heaps in the furrows of
the fields.
12. **And Jacob fled** into the
country of Syria, and Israel
served for a wife,
and for a wife he
kept sheep.
13. **And by a prophet**
the LORD brought
Israel out of Egypt,
and by a prophet
was he

preserved.
14. **Ephraim provoked him**
to anger most bitterly: therefore
shall he leave his blood upon him,
and his reproach shall his
LORD return unto him.

CHAPTER 13

1. **When Ephraim spake**
trembling, he exalted
himself in Israel;
but when he offended
in Baal, he died.
2. **And now they**
sin more and more,
and have made them molten
images of their silver, *and*
idols according to
their own understanding, all of
it the work of the craftsmen:
they say of them,
Let the men that sacrifice
kiss the calves.
3. **Therefore they shall be**
as the morning cloud and as the
early dew that passeth away,
as the chaff *that* is driven with the
whirlwind out of the floor, and
as the smoke out
of the chimney.
4. **Yet I am the LORD**
thy God from the land of Egypt,
and thou shalt know no
god but me: for there is
no saviour beside me.
5. I did know thee in the wilderness,
in the land of great drought.
6. According to their pasture,
so were they filled;
they were filled, and their
heart was exalted;
therefore have they
forgotten me.
7. Therefore I will be unto
them as a lion: as a leopard
by the way will I observe *them:*
8. **I will** meet them as a bear *that is*
bereaved *of her whelps,* and will rend
the caul of their heart, and there will I
devour them like a lion:
the wild beast shall tear them.
9. **O Israel, thou hast**
destroyed thyself; but

■ **in me is thine help.**
10. I will be thy king:
■ **where is any other that**
■ **may save thee** in all thy cities?
and thy judges of whom thou saidst,
Give me a king and princes?
■ 11. **I gave thee a king in**
■ **mine anger, and took**
■ **him away in my wrath.**
■ 12. **The iniquity of**
■ **Ephraim is** bound up; his sin is
■ **hid.**
■ 13. **The sorrows**
of a travailing woman
■ **shall come upon him:**
he *is* an unwise son; for he should
not stay long in *the place of* the
breaking forth of children.
■ 14. **I will ransom**
■ **them from the power**
■ **of the grave;**
I will redeem them from death:
O death, I will be thy plagues;
■ **O grave, I will be**
■ **thy destruction:** repentance
shall be hid from mine eyes.
■ 15. **Though he be fruitful**
among*his* brethren, an east wind shall
come, the wind of the LORD shall
come up from the wilderness, and
■ **his spring shall become**
■ **dry,** and his fountain shall be
dried up: he shall spoil the treasure
of all pleasant vessels.
■ 16. **Samaria shall become**
■ **desolate; for she** hath
■ **rebelled against** her
■ **God:** they shall fall by the sword:
their infants shall be dashed in
pieces, and their women with
child shall be ripped up.

CHAPTER 14

■ 1. **O israel, return unto**
■ **the LORD** thy God; for thou

hast fallen by thine iniquity.
■ 2. **Take with you words,**
■ **and** turn to the LORD:
■ **say** unto him,
■ **Take away all iniquity, and**
■ **receive us** graciously: so will we
render the calves of our lips.
3. Asshur shall not save us; we will
not ride upon horses: neither will we
say any more to the work of our
hands, *Ye are* our gods:
■ **for in thee the fatherless**
■ **findeth mercy.**
■ 4. **I will heal their**
■ **backsliding, I will**
■ **love them** freely:
■ **for mine anger is**
■ **turned away** from him.
■ 5. **I will be as the dew unto**
■ **Israel:** he shall grow as the lily, and
cast forth his roots as Lebanon.
■ 6. **His branches shall**
■ **spread,** and his beauty shall be
■ **as the olive tree,**
and his smell as Lebanon.
■ 7. **They that dwell under his**
■ **shadow shall return;** they shall
revive *as* the corn, and grow
as the vine: the scent thereof
shall be as the wine of Lebanon.
■ 8. **Ephraim shall say,**
■ **What have I to do** any more
■ **with idols?**
I have heard *him,* and observed
him: I *am* like a green fir tree.
From me is thy fruit found.
■ 9. **Who is wise, and** he
shall understand these *things?*
■ **prudent, and** he
■ **shall know** them? for
■ **the ways of the LORD** *are* right,
■ **and** the just
■ **shall walk in them:**
■ **but the transgressors**
■ **shall fall** therein.

THE BOOK OF JOEL

BACKGROUND INFORMATION

Author: Joel
Date Written:
835 — 796 B.C.

Number of:
Verses—73
Chapters—3
Total Words—2,034
Scan Words—872
Scan Words Represent
Approximately 42% of
Total Words

Theme: God's Judgement
Through a Plague of Locusts

OUTLINE OF THE BOOK

I. **The Plague** of Locusts
1:1 — 12

II. **Joel's Intercession**
1:13 — 20

III. **Joel's Warning**
2:1 — 17

IV. **God's Response**
2:18 — 32

V. **God's Judgement, His Restoration and The Promise Of The Spirit**
3:1 — 21

CHAPTER 1

■ 1. **The word** of the LORD that
■ **came to Joel** the son of Pethuel.
■ 2. **Hear this,** ye old men, and give ear, all ye
■ **inhabitants of the land.**
■ **Hath this been**
■ **in your days,** or even in the days of your fathers?
■ 3. **Tell** ye
■ **your children** of it, and *let* your children *tell* their children, and their children another generation.

4. That which the palmerworm hath left hath the locust eaten; and that which the locust hath left hath the cankerworm eaten; and that which the cankerworm hath left hath the caterpillar eaten.

■ 5. **Awake,** ye drunkards,
■ **and weep;** and howl, all ye drinkers of wine, because of the new wine, for it is cut off from your mouth.
■ 6. **For a nation is come** up
■ **upon my land, strong, and**
■ **without number,** whose teeth *are* the teeth of a lion, and he hath the cheek teeth of a great lion.
■ 7. **He hath laid my vine**
■ **waste, and barked my**
■ **fig tree:** he hath made it clean bare, and cast *it* away; the branches thereof are made white.
■ 8. **Lament** like a virgin
■ **girded with sackcloth** for the husband of her youth.
■ 9. **The meat** offering
■ **and** the
■ **drink offering is cut off** from the house of the LORD;
■ **the priests,** the LORD's ministers,
■ **mourn.**
■ 10. **The field is wasted,** the land mourneth; for the corn is wasted:
■ **the** new
■ **wine** is
■ **dried up,** the oil languisheth.
■ 11. **Be ye ashamed,** O
■ **ye husbandmen;** howl, O ye vinedressers, for the wheat and for the barley;

■ **because the harvest** of the field
■ **is perished.**

12. The vine is dried up, and the fig tree languisheth; the pomegranate tree, the palm tree also, and the apple tree,
■ **even** all
■ **the trees** of the field,
■ **are withered:** because joy is withered away from the sons of men.

13. Gird yourselves, and
■ **lament,** ye priests: howl,
■ **ye ministers**
■ **of the altar:** come,
■ **lie** all night
■ **in sackcloth,** ye ministers of my God: for the meat offering and the drink offering is withholden from the house of your God.

■ 14. **Sanctify** ye
■ **a fast,** call a solemn assembly,
■ **gather** the elders *and* all
■ **the inhabitants** of the land
■ **into the house of** the LORD
■ **your God, and cry**
■ **unto the LORD.**

15. Alas for the day!
■ **for the day of the LORD**
■ **is at hand, and** as a
■ **destruction** from the Almighty
■ **shall** it
■ **come.**

16. **Is not the meat cut off** before our eyes, *yea,* joy and gladness from the house of our God?

■ 17. **The seed is rotten** under their clods, the garners are laid desolate, the barns are broken down; for
■ **the corn is withered.**
■ 18. **How** do
■ **the beasts groan!** the herds of cattle are perplexed,
■ **because they have no**
■ **pasture;** yea, the flocks of sheep are made desolate.
■ 19. **O LORD, to thee will I**
■ **cry:** for the fire hath devoured the pastures of the wilderness, and the flame hath burned all the trees of the field.
■ 20. **The beasts** of the field

cry also unto thee:
for the rivers of waters
are dried up, and the
fire hath devoured
the pastures of the wilderness.

CHAPTER 2

1. **Blow ye the trumpet**
in Zion, and
sound an alarm
in my holy mountain:
let all the inhabitants
of the land
tremble: for the day of
the LORD cometh,
for *it is* nigh at hand;

2. **A day of darkness** and of
gloominess, a day of clouds and of
thick darkness, as the morning
spread upon the
mountains: a great
people and a strong;
there hath not been ever the
like, neither shall be
any more after it, *even* to the
years of many generations.

3. **A fire devoureth** before them;
and behind them a flame burneth:
the land *is* as the garden of Eden
before them, and behind them a
desolate wilderness; yea,
and nothing shall
escape them.

4. **The appearance of**
them is as the appearance
of horses; and as
horsemen, so shall
they run.

5. **Like the noise of chariots**
on the tops of mountains shall they
leap, like the noise of a flame of fire
that devoureth the stubble,
as a strong people
set in battle array.

6. Before their face
the people shall be
much pained:
all faces shall gather blackness.

7. **They shall run like mighty**
men; they shall climb the wall
like men of war; and they shall
march every one on his ways, and
they shall not break

their ranks:

8. Neither shall one thrust another;
they shall walk every one in his path:
and when they fall upon
the sword, they shall not
be wounded.

9. **They shall run to and fro**
in the city; they shall run upon the
wall, they shall climb up upon the
houses; they shall enter in at the
windows like a thief.

10. **The earth shall quake**
before them; the heavens shall
tremble: the sun and the moon shall
be dark, and the stars shall withdraw
their shining:

11. **And the LORD shall utter**
his voice before his army:
for his camp *is* very great: for *he is*
strong that executeth his word: for
the day of the LORD is great
and very terrible; and
who can abide it?

12. **Therefore** also now,
saith the LORD, turn ye *even*
to me with all your heart, and
with fasting, and with
weeping, and with mourning:

13. And rend your heart, and not
your garments, and turn unto the
LORD your God:
for he is gracious and
merciful, slow to anger,
and of great kindness,
and repenteth him
of the evil.

14. **Who knoweth if**
he will return and repent,
and leave a blessing behind
him; *even* a meat offering and a drink
offering unto the LORD your God?

15. **Blow the trumpet**
in Zion, sanctify a fast,
call a solemn assembly:

16. **Gather the people,**
sanctify the congregation,
assemble the elders, gather the
children, and those that suck
the breasts: let the bridegroom
go forth of his chamber, and the
bride out of her closet.

17. **Let** the priests,
the ministers of the

LORD, weep between the porch and the altar,

and let them

say, Spare thy people,

O LORD, and give not thine heritage to reproach,

that the heathen should rule over them: wherefore should they

say among the people,

Where is their God?

18. Then will the LORD

be jealous for his land,

and pity his people.

19. Yea, the LORD

will answer and say unto his people, Behold, I will

send you

corn, and wine, and oil,

and ye shall be

satisfied therewith:

and I will no more make

you a reproach among

the heathen:

20. But I will remove far off from you

the northern army, and

will drive him into a land barren and desolate, with his face

toward the east sea, and his hinder part toward the utmost sea, and his stink shall come up, and his ill savour shall come up,

because he hath

done great things.

21. Fear not, O land; be glad and rejoice:

for the LORD will

do great things.

22. Be not afraid, ye beasts of the field: for

the pastures of the wilderness

do spring, for

the tree beareth her fruit, the fig tree and the vine do yield their strength.

23. Be glad then, ye children of Zion,

and rejoice in the LORD your God:

for he hath given you the former rain moderately, and he will cause to come down for you the rain,

the former rain, and the

latter rain in the first month.

24. And the floors shall be

full of wheat, and the

vats shall overflow

with wine and oil.

25. And I will restore to you the years that the locust hath eaten, the cankerworm, and the caterpillar, and the palmerworm, my great army which I sent among you.

26. And ye shall eat in plenty, and

be satisfied, and

praise the name of

the LORD your God,

that hath dealt wondrously

with you: and my people shall never be ashamed.

27. And ye shall

know that

I am in the midst of Israel,

and that I am the LORD your God, and none else: and

my people shall

never be ashamed.

28. And it shall come to pass afterward, that

I will pour out my spirit

upon all flesh; and

your sons and your

daughters shall prophesy, your old men shall dream dreams, your young men shall see visions:

29. And also upon the servants and upon the handmaids in those days will I pour out my spirit.

30. And I will shew wonders

in the heavens and in the

earth, blood, and fire, and pillars of smoke.

31. The sun shall be

turned into darkness,

and the moon into

blood, before the great and the

terrible day of

the LORD come.

32. And it shall come to pass, that

whosoever shall

call on the name of the

LORD shall be delivered: for in mount Zion and in Jerusalem shall be deliverance, as the LORD

hath said, and in the remnant
whom the LORD shall call.

CHAPTER 3

1. **For,** behold,
in those days,
and in that time, when
I shall bring again the
captivity of Judah
and Jerusalem,
2. **I will** also
gather all nations,
and will bring them down
into the valley of
Jehoshaphat, and will
plead with them there
for my people
and *for* my heritage
Israel, whom they have
scattered among the
nations, and parted my land.
3. **And they have cast lots**
for my people; and have
given a boy for an harlot,
and sold a girl for wine,
that they might drink.
4. **Yea, and** what have ye to do
with me, O Tyre, and Zidon, and
all the coasts of Palestine? will ye
render me a recompence? and if
ye recompense me, swiftly *and*
speedily will I return your
recompence upon your own head;
5. Because ye have
taken my silver and my
gold, and have carried
into your temples
my goodly pleasant things:
6. **The children also of**
Judah and the children of
Jerusalem have ye
sold unto the Grecians,
that ye might remove them
far from their border.
7. **Behold, I will raise them**
out of the place whither ye
have sold them, and will return your
recompence upon your own head:
8. **And I will sell your**
sons and your
daughters into the hand of the
children of Judah, and they shall
sell them to the Sabeans,

to a people far off:
for the LORD hath spoken *it.*
9. **Proclaim ye this among**
the Gentiles; Prepare war,
wake up the mighty men,
let all the men of
war draw near; let them
come up:
10. **Beat your plowshares**
into swords and your
pruninghooks into spears:
let the weak say, I *am* strong.
11. **Assemble yourselves,**
and come, all ye heathen, and
gather yourselves together round
about: thither cause thy mighty
ones to come down, O LORD.
12. **Let the heathen**
be wakened, and
come up
to the valley of
Jehoshaphat: for
there will I sit to
judge all
the heathen round about.
13. **Put** ye
in the sickle, for the harvest
is ripe: come, get you down; for the
press is full, the fats overflow; for
their wickedness is great.
14. **Multitudes,** multitudes
in the valley of decision:
for the day of the LORD
is near in the valley of decision.
15. The sun and the moon shall
be darkened, and the stars shall
withdraw their shining.
16. **The LORD** also
shall roar out of Zion, and
utter his voice from Jerusalem;
and the heavens and the
earth shall shake:
but the LORD *will be* the hope
of his people, and the strength
of the children of Israel.
17. **So shall ye know that**
I am the LORD your God
dwelling in Zion, my holy mountain:
then shall Jerusalem
be holy, and there shall no
strangers pass through her any more.
18. **And** it shall come to pass
in that day, *that*

■ **the mountains**
■ **shall drop** down
■ **new wine, and the hills shall**
■ **flow with milk, and** all **the**
■ **rivers** of Judah shall flow
■ **with waters, and a**
■ **fountain** shall come forth
■ **of the house**
■ **of the LORD,** and
■ **shall water the**
■ **valley of Shittim.**
■ 19. **Egypt** shall be a desolation,
■ **and Edom shall be** a

■ **desolate** wilderness, for the
violence *against* the children of Judah,
■ **because they** have
■ **shed innocent**
■ **blood** in their land.
■ 20. **But Judah shall dwell**
■ **for ever, and Jerusalem**
from generation to generation.
■ 21. **For I will cleanse**
■ **their blood** *that*
I have not cleansed:
■ **for the LORD**
■ **dwelleth in Zion.**

THE BOOK OF AMOS

BACKGROUND INFORMATION

Author: Amos
Date Written: 808 B.C.

Number of:
Verses—146
Chapters— 9
Total Words—4,217
Scan Words—1,788
Scan Words Represent
Approximately 42% of
Total Words

Theme: God's Judgement and Prophecies Concerning the Coming Messiah, and Jewish Restoration

OUTLINE OF THE BOOK

I. **The Nation Denounced**
1:1 — 2:16

II. **The Condemnation of Israel, and** the Prophecies About a Future **Restoration Through the Messiah**
3:1 — 9:15

CHAPTER 1

■ 1. **The words of Amos,** who was among the herdmen of Tekoa, which he saw **concerning Israel in the days of Uzziah king of Judah, and** in the days of **Jeroboam** the son of Joash **king of Israel, two years before the earthquake.** 2. **And he said, The LORD will** roar from Zion, and **utter his voice** from Jerusalem; **and the** habitations of the **shepherds shall mourn,** and the top of Carmel shall wither. 3. **Thus saith the LORD; For three transgressions of Damascus, and for four, I will not turn away** *the* **punishment** thereof; **because they have threshed Gilead with** threshing **instruments of iron:**

4. But I will send a fire into the house of Hazael, which shall devour the palaces of Ben-hadad. 5. I will break also the bar of Damascus, and cut off the inhabitant from the plain of Aven, and him that holdeth the sceptre from the house of Eden: and the people of Syria shall go into captivity unto Kir, saith the LORD.

■ 6. **Thus saith the LORD; For three transgressions of Gaza, and for four, I will not turn away** *the* **punishment** thereof; **because they carried** away captive **the whole captivity,** to deliver them up **to Edom:**

7. But I will send a fire on the wall of Gaza, which shall devour the palaces thereof: 8. And I will cut off the inhabitant from Ashdod, and him that holdeth the sceptre from Ashkelon, and I will turn mine hand against Ekron: and the remnant of the Philistines shall perish saith the Lord GOD.

■ 9. **Thus saith the LORD; For three transgressions of Tyrus, and for four, I will not turn away the punishment** thereof; **because they delivered up the whole captivity to Edom, and remembered not the brotherly covenant:**

10. But I will send a fire on the wall of Tyrus, which shall devour the palaces thereof.

■ 11. **Thus saith the LORD; For three transgressions of Edom,** and for four, I will not **turn away** *the* **punishment** thereof **because he did pursue his brother with the sword,** and did cast off all pity, and his anger did tear perpetually, and he kept his wrath for ever:

12. But I will send a fire upon Teman, which shall devour the palaces of Bozrah .

■ 13. **Thus saith the LORD; For three transgressions** of the children **of Ammon, and for four, I will not turn away** *the* **punishment** thereof; **because they have ripped up the women with child of Gilead, that they might enlarge their border:**

14. But I will kindle a fire in the wall of Rabbah, and it shall devour the palaces thereof, with shouting in the day of battle, with a tempest in the day of the whirlwind: 15. And their king shall go into captivity, he and his princes together, saith the LORD.

CHAPTER 2

■ 1. **Thus saith the LORD; For three transgressions of Moab, and for four, I will not turn away** *the* **punishment** thereof;

■ **because he burned**
■ **the bones of the king**
■ **of Edom into lime.**
2. But I will send a fire upon Moab, and it shall devour the palaces of Kirioth: and Moab shall die with tumult, with shouting, *and* with the sound of the trumpet:
3. And I will cut off the judge from the midst thereof, and will slay all the princes thereof with him, saith the LORD.
■ 4. **Thus saith the LORD;**
■ **For three transgressions**
■ **of Judah,** and for four, I will not turn away *the punishment* thereof;
■ **because they have**
■ **despised the law of the**
■ **LORD, and have not kept**
■ **his commandments,**
and their lies caused them to err, after the which their fathers have walked:
5. But I will send a fire upon Judah, and it shall devour the palaces of Jerusalem.
6. Thus saith the LORD;
■ **For three transgressions**
■ **of Israel,** and for four, I will not turn away *the punishment* thereof;
■ **because they sold the**
■ **righteous for silver,** and the poor for a pair of shoes;
7. That pant after the dust of the earth on the head of the poor, and turn aside the way of the meek: and a man and his father
■ **will go in** unto the *same* maid,
■ **to profane my holy name:**
■ 8. **And they lay** *themselves* down
■ **upon clothes laid to**
■ **pledge by every altar,**
■ **and they drink** the
■ **wine** of the
■ **condemned in the**
■ **house of their god.**
■ 9. **Yet destroyed I the**
■ **Amorite** before them, whose height *was* like the height of the cedars, and he *was* strong as the oaks; yet I destroyed his fruit from above, and his roots from beneath.
■ 10. **Also I brought you**
■ **up from** the land of

■ **Egypt, and led you forty**
■ **years through the**
■ **wilderness,** to possess the land of the Amorite.
■ 11. **And I raised up of**
■ **your sons for prophets,**
■ **and** of your young men for
■ **Nazarites.** *Is it* not even thus, O ye children of Israel? saith the LORD.
■ 12. **But ye gave the**
■ **Nazarites wine** to drink;
■ **and commanded the**
■ **prophets, saying,**
■ **Prophesy not.**
13. Behold, I am pressed under you, as a cart is pressed *that is* full of sheaves.
14. Therefore the flight shall perish from the swift, and the strong shall not strengthen his force, neither shall the mighty deliver himself:
15. Neither shall he stand that handleth the bow; and *he that is* swift of foot shall not deliver *himself:* neither shall he that rideth the horse deliver himself.
16. And *he that is* courageous among the mighty shall flee away naked in that day, saith the LORD.

CHAPTER 3

1. Hear this word that
■ **the LORD hath spoken**
■ **against you,** O children of
■ **Israel,** against the whole family which I brought up from the land of Egypt, saying,
■ 2 **You only have I known**
of all the families of the earth:
■ **therefore I will punish you**
■ **for all your iniquities.**
■ 3. **Can two walk together**
■ **except they be agreed?**
■ 4. **Will a lion roar** in the forest,
■ **when he hath no prey?**
will a young lion cry out of his den, if he have taken nothing?
■ 5. **Can a bird fall**
■ **in a snare** upon the earth,
■ **where no gin is for him?**
shall *one* take up a snare from the earth, and have taken nothing at all?
■ 6. **Shall a trumpet**

■ **be blown** in the city,
■ **and the people not be**
■ **afraid?** shall there be evil in a city,
and the LORD hath not done *it?*
■ 7. **Surely the Lord**
GOD will do nothing, but he
■ **revealeth his secret**
■ **unto his** servants the
■ **prophets.**
8. The lion hath roared,
who will not fear?
■ **the Lord GOD hath spoken,**
■ **who can but prophesy?**
■ 9. **Publish in the palaces**
at Ashdod, and in the palaces
in the land of Egypt,
■ **and say, Assemble**
■ **yourselves** upon
the mountains of Samaria
■ **and behold the great**
■ **tumults** in the midst thereof,
■ **and the oppressed**
in the midst thereof.
■ 10. **For they know not to do**
■ **right,** saith the LORD, who store up
violence and robbery in their palaces
■ 11 . **Therefore**
thus saith the Lord GOD;
■ **An adversary** *there shall be*
even round about the land; and he
■ **shall bring down**
■ **thy strength** from thee,
■ **and thy palaces**
■ **shall be spoiled.**
12. Thus saith the LORD;
■ **As the shepherd taketh**
■ **out of the mouth of the lion**
two legs, or a piece of an ear;
■ **so shall** the children of
■ **Israel be taken out that**
■ **dwell in Samaria**
in the corner of a bed,
■ **and in Damascus** *in* a couch.
13. Hear ye, and testify in the
house of Jacob, saith the
Lord GOD, the God of hosts,
14. That in the day that
■ **I shall visit the**
■ **transgressions of**
■ **Israel** upon him I will also visit
■ **the altars of Beth-el: and**
■ **the horns of the altar shall**
■ **be cut off,** and fall to the ground.

■ 15. **And I will smite** the winter
house with the summer house; and
the houses of ivory shall perish, and
■ **the great houses**
shall have an end,
■ **saith the LORD.**

CHAPTER 4

■ 1. **Hear** this word,
■ **ye kine of Bashan,** that
are in the mountain of Samaria
■ **which oppress the poor,**
which crush the needy,
■ **which say to their**
■ **masters,** Bring, and
■ **let us drink.**
■ 2. **The Lord GOD hath**
■ **sworn** by his holiness, that, lo,
the days shall come upon you,
■ **that he will take you**
■ **away with hooks,** and
your posterity with fish hooks.
■ 3. **And ye shall go out** at
■ **the breaches, every cow**
at that which is before her; and
■ **ye shall cast** *them*
■ **into the palace,**
saith the LORD.
■ 4. **Come to Beth-el, and**
■ **transgress;** at Gilgal
multiply transgression;
■ **and bring your sacrifices**
every morning, *and* your tithes
after three years:
5. And offer a sacrifice
■ **of thanksgiving** with leaven,
■ **and proclaim** *and* publish
■ **the free offerings: for this**
■ **liketh** you, O ye children of Israel,
■ **saith the Lord** GOD.
6. And I also have given you
cleanness of teeth in all your cities,
and want of bread in all your places:
■ **yet have ye not returned**
■ **unto me,** saith the LORD.
■ 7. **And also I have**
■ **withholden the rain**
from you, when *there were* yet
three months to the harvest: and
■ **I caused it to rain upon one**
■ **city, and caused it not to**
■ **rain upon another city:** one
piece was rained upon, and the piece

whereupon it rained not withered.

8. **So two** *or* three

cities wandered unto one

city, to drink water; but

they were not satisfied:

yet have ye not returned unto me, saith the LORD.

9. **I have smitten you with**

blasting and mildew:

when your gardens and your vineyards and your fig trees and your olive trees increased, the palmerworm devoured *them:*

yet have ye not returned

unto me, saith the LORD.

10. **I have sent** among you

the pestilence after the manner

of Egypt: your young men have I slain with the sword, and have taken away your horses; and I have made the stink of your camps to come up unto your nostrils:

yet have ye not returned

unto me, saith the LORD.

11 . **I have overthrown some**

of you, as God overthrew

Sodom and Gomorrah, and

ye were as a firebrand

plucked out of the burning:

yet have ye not returned

unto me, saith the LORD.

12. **Therefore**

thus will I do unto thee, O

Israel: *and* because I will do this unto thee

prepare to meet

thy God, O Israel.

13. For, lo, he that formeth the mountains, and createth the wind, and declareth unto man what *is* his thought, that maketh the morning darkness, and treadeth upon the high places of the earth, The LORD, The God of hosts, *is* his name.

CHAPTER 5

1. **Hear ye this word**

which I take up against you,

even a lamentation,

O house of Israel.

2. **The virgin of Israel is**

fallen; she shall no more rise:

she is forsaken upon her land;

there *is* none to raise her up.

3. For thus saith the Lord GOD;

The city that went out by

a thousand shall leave

an hundred, and that which went forth *by* an hundred shall leave ten, to the house of Israel.

4. **For thus saith the LORD**

unto the house of Israel,

Seek ye me, and

ye shall live:

5. But seek not Beth-el, nor enter into Gilgal, and pass not to Beer-sheba: for Gilgal shall surely go into captivity, and Beth-el shall come to nought.

6. **Seek the LORD,**

and ye shall live;

lest he break out like fire

in the house of Joseph,

and devour it, and there be none to quench *it* in Beth-el.

7. **Ye who** turn judgment

to wormwood, and

leave off righteousness

in the earth

8. **Seek him that** maketh the

seven stars and O-rion, and

turneth the shadow of

death into the morning,

and maketh the day dark with night: that calleth for the waters of the sea, and poureth them out upon the face of the earth:

The LORD is his name:

9. That strengtheneth the spoiled against the strong, so that the spoiled shall come against the fortress.

10. They hate him that rebuketh in the gate, and they abhor him that speaketh uprightly.

11 . Forasmuch therefore as your treading *is* upon the poor, and ye take from him burdens of wheat:

ye have built houses of

hewn stone, but ye shall

not dwell in them;

ye have planted pleasant

vineyards, but ye shall

not drink wine of them.

12. **For I know your** manifold

transgressions, and your mighty

sins: they afflict the just,

they take a bribe, and they turn aside

the poor in the gate from their right.

13. **Therefore** the prudent shall **keep silence** in that time; **for it is an evil time.**

14. **Seek good, and not evil,** that ye may live: **and so the LORD,** the God of hosts, **shall be with you,** as ye have spoken.

15. **Hate** the **evil, and love** the **good,** and establish judgment in the gate: **it may be that the LORD** God of hosts **will be gracious** unto the remnant of Joseph.

16. **Therefore the LORD,** the God of hosts, the LORD, **saith** thus; **Wailing shall be in all streets;** and they shall say in all the highways, Alas! alas! **and** they shall **call the husbandman to mourning,** and such as are skilful of lamentation to wailing.

17. And in all vineyards *shall be* wailing: **for I will pass through thee,** saith the LORD.

18. **Woe unto you that desire the day of the LORD!** to what end is **it** for you? the day of the LORD **is darkness,** and not light.

19. **As if a man did flee** from a lion **and a bear met him; or** went into the house, and leaned his hand on the wall, and **a serpent bit him.**

20. **Shall not the day** of the LORD **be darkness,** and not light? even very dark, and no brightness in it?

21. I hate, **I despise** your feast days, and I will not smell in your solemn assemblies.

22. Though ye offer me burnt offerings and **your** meat **offerings, I will not accept them:** neither will I regard the peace offerings of your fat beasts.

23. **Take** thou **away** from me **the noise of thy songs;** for I will not hear the melody of thy viols.

24. **But let judgment run down as waters, and righteousness as a mighty stream.**

25. Have **ye offered** unto me **sacrifices and** offerings in the wilderness **forty years,** O house of Israel?

26. **But ye have borne** the tabernacle of your Moloch and Chiun **your images,** the star of your god, **which ye made to yourselves.**

27. **Therefore will I cause you to go into captivity** beyond Damascus **saith the LORD,** whose name *is* The God of hosts.

CHAPTER 6

1. **Woe to them that are at ease in Zion,** and trust in the mountain of Samaria, *which are* names chief of the nations, to whom the house of Israel came!

2. Pass ye unto Calneh, and see; and from thence go ye to Hamath the great: then go down to Gath of the Philistines: *be they* better than these kingdoms? or their border greater than your border?

3. Ye that put far away the evil day, and cause the seat of violence to come near;

4. **That lie upon beds of ivory, and stretch themselves upon** their **couches, and eat** the **lambs** out of the flock, **and the calves** out of the midst of the stall;

5. **That chant** to the sound of the viol,

and invent to themselves
instruments of music,
like David;
6. That drink wine in bowls,
and anoint themselves
with the chief
ointments: but they
are not grieved for the
affliction of Joseph.
7. Therefore now shall
they go captive
with the first that go captive,
and the banquet of them
that stretched themselves
shall be removed.
8. The Lord GOD
hath sworn by himself,
saith the LORD the God of hosts,
I abhor the excellency
of Jacob, and hate
his palaces: therefore
will I deliver up the city
with all that is therein.
9. And it shall come to pass,
if there remain ten
men in one house,
that they shall die.
10. And a man's uncle
shall take him up,
and he that burneth him,
to bring out the bones
out of the house
and shall say unto him that is
by the sides of the
house, Is there yet any with
thee? and he shall say,
No. Then shall he say,
Hold thy tongue: for
we may not make
mention of the name of
the LORD.
11. For, behold,
the LORD commandeth, and he
will smite the great
house with breaches
and the little
house with clefts.
12. Shall horses run upon the rock?
will *one* plow *there* with oxen?
for ye have turned
judgment into gall,
and the fruit of
righteousness into

hemlock:
13. Ye which rejoice in a thing of
nought, which say, Have we not taken
to us horns by our own strength?
14. But, behold
I will raise up against you
a nation, O house of Israel,
saith the LORD the God of hosts;
and they shall afflict
you from the entering in of
Hemath unto the river of
the wilderness.

CHAPTER 7

1 . Thus hath
the Lord GOD
shewed unto
me; and, behold, he
formed grasshoppers in the
beginning of the shooting up of
the latter growth; and, lo *it was*
the latter growth after
the king's mowings.
2. And it came to pass, *that*
when they had
made an end of eating
the grass of the land, then
I said, O Lord GOD,
forgive, I beseech thee:
by whom shall Jacob
arise? for he is small.
3. The LORD repented for this:
It shall not be, saith the LORD.
4. Thus hath
the Lord GOD
shewed unto
me: and, behold, the Lord GOD
called to contend
by fire, and it
devoured the great deep,
and did eat up a part.
5. Then said I, O Lord GOD,
cease, I beseech thee:
by whom shall Jacob
arise? for he is small.
6. The LORD repented for this:
This also shall not be,
saith the Lord GOD.
7. Thus he shewed me:
and, behold,
the LORD stood upon
a wall *made* by a plumbline,
with a plumbline in his hand.

8. **And** the LORD
said unto me,
Amos, what seest thou?
And I said, A plumbline.
Then said the LORD, Behold,
I will set a plumbline in
the midst of my people
Israel: I will not again
pass by them any more:
9. **And the high places** of
Isaac shall be desolate,
and the sanctuaries
of Israel shall be
laid waste; and I will
rise against the house of
Jeroboam with the sword.
10. **Then** Amaziah
the priest of Beth-el
sent to Jeroboam
king of Israel,
saying Amos hath
conspired against thee
in the midst of the house of Israel:
the land is not able to
bear all his words.
11. **For** thus
Amos saith, Jeroboam
shall die by the sword,
and Israel shall surely
be led away captive
out of their own land.
12. **Also Amaziah said**
unto Amos, O thou seer, go,
flee thee away
into the land of Judah,
and there eat bread, and
prophesy there:
13. **But prophesy**
not again any more
at Beth-el: for it *is* the king's
chapel, and it *is* the king's court.
14. **Then answered**
Amos, and said to Amaziah,
I was no prophet,
neither *was* I
a prophet's son; but
I was an herdman, and
a gatherer of sycomore fruit:
15. **And the LORD took**
me as I followed the flock,
and the LORD
said unto me,
Go, prophesy unto my people

Israel.
16. **Now** therefore
hear thou
the word of the LORD: Thou
sayest, Prophesy not
against Israel, and drop not *thy*
word against the house of Isaac.
17. **Therefore thus saith**
the LORD, Thy wife shall
be an harlot in the city,
and thy sons and thy
daughters shall fall by
the sword, and thy land
shall be divided by line
and thou shalt die in
a polluted land: and
Israel shall surely
go into captivity
forth of his land.

CHAPTER 8

1. **Thus** hath
the Lord GOD
shewed unto
me: and behold
a basket of summer
fruit.
2. And he said, Amos, what
seest thou? And I said, A
basket of summer fruit.
Then said the LORD unto me,
The end is come
upon my people of
Israel; I will not again
pass by them any more.
3. **And the songs of the**
temple shall be howlings
in that day, saith the Lord GOD:
there shall be many
dead bodies in
every place; they
shall cast them
forth with silence.
4. **Hear this, O ye that**
swallow up the needy, even
to make the poor of the land to fail,
5. Saying, When will the new
moon be gone, that we may
sell corn? and the sabbath,
that we may set forth wheat,
making the ephah small, and
the shekel great, and
falsifying the balances

by deceit?

6. That we may buy the poor for silver, and the needy for a pair of shoes; *yea,* and sell the refuse of the wheat?

7. **The LORD hath sworn** by the excellency of Jacob, Surely **I will never forget** any of **their works.**

8. **Shall not the land tremble** for this, **and every one mourn** that dwelleth therein? **and it shall rise** up wholly **as a flood, and** it shall **be cast out** and drowned, as *by* the flood of Egypt.

9. **And it shall come to pass** in that day, saith the Lord GOD, that **I will cause the sun to go down at noon,** and I will darken the earth in the clear day:

10 **And I will turn your feasts into mourning, and** all **your songs into lamentation;** and I will bring up sackcloth upon all loins, and baldness upon every head; **and I will make it** as the mourning of an only *son,* and the end thereof as **a bitter day.**

11. **Behold,** the days come, saith the Lord GOD, that **I will send a famine** in the land **not a famine of bread,** nor a thirst for water, **but of hearing the words of the LORD:**

12. **And they shall wander** from sea to sea, and from the north even to the east, they shall run **to and fro to seek the word of the LORD and shall not find it.**

13. In that day shall the fair virgins and young men faint for thirst.

14. **They** that swear by the sin of Samaria, and say, Thy god, O Dan, liveth; and, The manner of Beer-sheba liveth; even they **shall fall, and never**

rise up again.

CHAPTER 9

1. **I saw the LORD standing upon the altar: and he** said, Smite the lintel of **the door, that the posts may shake:** and cut them in the head, all of them; and **I will slay the last of them with the sword:** he that fleeth of them shall not flee away, and he that escapeth of them shall not be delivered.

2. **Though they dig into hell,** thence shall mine hand take them; **though they climb up to heaven,** thence will I bring them down:

3. **And though they hide themselves** in the top of Carmel **I will search and** take them out thence; and though they be hid from my sight in the bottom of the sea, thence will I **command the serpent, and he shall bite them:**

4. And though they go into captivity before their enemies, thence will I command the sword, and it shall slay them: and **I will set mine eyes upon them for evil,** and not for good.

5. **And the Lord** GOD of hosts *is* he that **toucheth the land, and it shall melt,** and all that dwell therein shall mourn: **and it shall rise** up wholly **like a flood, and** shall **be drowned,** as *by* the flood of Egypt.

6. *It is* he that buildeth his stories in the heaven, and hath founded his troop in the earth; he that calleth for the waters of the sea, and poureth them out upon the face of the earth: The LORD *is* his name.

7. **Are ye not as** children of **the Ethiopians unto me, O** children of **Israel?** saith the LORD. Have not **I brought** up

Israel to be Redeemed

Israel out of the land of
Egypt? and the Philistines from
Caphtor, and the Syrians from Kir?
8. Behold, the eyes
of the Lord GOD
are upon the sinful
kingdom, and I will destroy
it from off the face of the
earth; saving that I will
not utterly destroy
the house of Jacob,
saith the LORD.
9. For, lo
I will command, and I will
sift the house of Israel
among all nations,
like as corn is sifted
in a sieve, yet shall not the
least grain fall upon the earth.
10. All the sinners of my people
shall die by the sword,
which say, The
evil shall not overtake
nor prevent us.
11. In that day will I raise up
the tabernacle of David
that is fallen, and close up the
breaches thereof; and I will raise
up his ruins, and I will build it
as the days of old: name,

saith the LORD that doeth this.
12. That they may possess the
remnant of Edom, and of all the
heathen, which are called by my
name saith the LORD that doeth this.
13. Behold the days come, saith the
Lord, that the plowman shall overtake
thereaper, and the treader of grapes
him that soweth seed; and the
mountains shall drop sweet wine,
and all the hills shall melt.
14. And I will bring
again the captivity of
my people of Israel
and they shall build the waste
cities, and inhabit them;
and they shall plant vineyards,
and drink the wine thereof;
they shall also
make gardens, and
eat the fruit of them.
15. And I will plant them
upon their land,
and they shall no
more be pulled
up out of their
land which I have
given them, saith
the LORD
thy God.

THE BOOK OF OBADIAH

BACKGROUND INFORMATION

Author: Obadiah
Date Written:
588 — 583 B.C.

Number of:
Verses—21
Chapters—1
Total Words—670
Scan Words—255
Scan Words Represent
Approximately 38% of
Total Words

**Theme: The Edomites
Denounced and the**
Glorious **Deliverance of
Zion,** God's People

OUTLINE OF
THE BOOK

I. **Destruction of Edom**
    1:1 — 16
II. **Restoration of Israel**
    1:17 — 21

CHAPTER 1

1. **The vision of Obadiah.**
Thus saith the Lord GOD
concerning Edom; We have
heard a rumour
from the LORD, and an
ambassador is sent among
the heathen, Arise ye, and let
us rise up against her in battle.
2. Behold,
I have made thee small
among the heathen:
thou art greatly despised.
3. **The pride of thine heart**
hath deceived thee, thou
that dwellest in the clefts of the
rock, whose habitation *is* high;
that saith in his heart, Who shall
bring me down to the ground?
4. **Though thou exalt thyself**
as the eagle, and though
thou set thy nest among the stars,
thence will I bring thee
down, saith the LORD.
5. **If thieves came**
to thee, if robbers by night,
(how art thou cut off!)
would they not have stolen
till they had enough?
if the grapegatherers came to thee,
would they not leave *some* grapes?
6. **How are the things of**
Esau searched out! *how* are
his hidden things sought up!
7. All the men of thy confederacy
have brought thee *even* to the border:
the men that were at
peace with thee have
deceived thee, *and*
prevailed against thee;
that they eat thy bread have
laid a wound under thee: *there*
is none understanding in him.
8. **Shall I not** in that
day, saith the LORD, even
destroy the wise *men* out
of Edom, and
understanding out of
the mount of Esau?
9. **And thy mighty men,**
O Teman, shall be
dismayed, to the end that every
one of the mount of Esau may be
cut off by slaughter.
10. **For thy violence**
against thy brother
Jacob shame shall cover thee, and
thou shalt be cut off for ever.
11. **In the day that**
thou stoodest on the other side, in
the day that the strangers carried
away captive his forces, and
foreigners entered into
his gates, and cast lots
upon Jerusalem, even
thou wast as one of them.
12. **But thou shouldest not**
have looked on the day of thy brother
in the day that he became a stranger;
neither shouldest thou
have rejoiced
over the children of
Judah in the day of
their destruction; neither
shouldest thou have spoken
proudly in the day of distress.
13. **Thou shouldest not have**
entered into the gate of my
people in the day of
their calamity; yea, thou
shouldest not have looked on their
affliction in the day of their calamity,
nor have
laid hands on
their substance
in the day of their calamity;
14. **Neither shouldest thou**
have stood in the crossway, to
cut off those of his that
did escape; neither
shouldest thou have
delivered up those
of his that did remain
in the day of distress.
15. For the day of the LORD
is near upon all the heathen:
as thou hast done, it shall
be done unto thee: thy reward
shall return upon thine own head.
16. **For as ye have drunk**
upon my holy mountain,
so shall all
the heathen drink
continually, yea, they shall drink,
and they shall swallow down,
and they shall be as

■ **though they had not been.**
■ 17. **But upon mount Zion**
■ **shall be deliverance,**
■ **and** there shall be
■ **holiness;** and the house of
■ **Jacob shall possess**
■ **their possessions.**
■ 18. **And the house**
■ **of Jacob** shall be a fire,
■ **and** the house of
■ **Joseph** a flame,
and the house of Esau
for stubble, and they
■ **shall** kindle in them, and
■ **devour** them; and there
shall not be *any* remaining of
■ **the house of Esau;**
for the LORD hath spoken *it.*

19. And *they of* the south *shall possess* the mount of Esau; and *they of* the plain the Philistines: and they shall possess the fields of Ephraim, and the fields of Samaria: and Benjamin *shall possess* Gilead.
20. And the captivity of this host of the children of Israel *shall possess* that of the Canaanites, *even* unto Zarephath; and the captivity of Jerusalem, which *is* in Sepharad, shall possess the cities of the south.
21. And saviours shall come up on mount Zion to judge the mount of Esau;
■ **and the kingdom shall**
■ **be the LORD's.**

JONAH:
Missionary Evangelist

The story of Jonah is fascinating and if it were not for the serious import of its massage, It could be called entertaining.

- The story presents an
- important *theological*
- message: God is
- concerned for all
- people *and not just for the children of Israel.*
- Significantly, His
- concern existed
- in the Old Testament.

A shallow reading of the Old Testament may give one the idea that God was not interested in any people other then Israel. Indeed,

- the Jewish people had
- come to believe that the
- Lord was disinterested
- in people who were
- not Israelites. Jonah
- had such a view *and*
- when God called him
- to *leave home and go to*
- preach to *the heathen people of*
- Nineveh, he rebelled.

He boards a ship to escape the command of God.

- Jonah's experiences *at sea, the storm and the big fish,*
- are well known.

- In the *belly of the*
- fish, Jonah repents *of his rebellion and cries out for deliverance,*
- promising God that
- he will *fulfill his call to*
- be a missionary
- evangelist. *The fish vomits him up on shore.*
- Jonah *reluctanly*
- goes to Nineveh *and holds evangelistic services as he travels through the city.*
- He pronounces God's
- message. *In forty days God would destroy the city.*
- The people believed *the message.*
- They *placed sackcloth upon themselves and*
- repented. *When the people repented,*
- God spared the city.
- Jonah, *although delivering God's message,*
- was *angered and*
- displeased *at the outcome.*
- Jonah's attitude
- was *typical of*
- narrow religiosity,
- which fails to see
- God's love *and concern*
- for all people, *regardless of race, creed, or color.*

THE BOOK OF JONAH

BACKGROUND INFORMATION

Author: Jonah
Date Written:
800 — 750 B.C.

Number of:
Verses—48
Chapters—4
Total Words—1,321
Scan Words—606
Scan Words represent 45 %
of Total Words

Theme: Jonah's Call, His Rebellion, His Repentance, and the Revival of Nineveh

OUTLINE OF THE BOOK

I. **Jonah's Rebellion, and God's Judgement**
upon Him
1:1 — 2:10

II. **Jonah's Successful Mission** to Nineveh
3:1 — 4:11

CHAPTER 1

■ 1. **Now the word of the**
■ **LORD came unto**
■ **Jonah** the son of Amittai,
■ **saying,**
■ 2. **Arise, go to**
■ **Nineveh,** that great city,
■ **and cry against** it; for
■ **their wickedness**
is come up before me.
■ 3. **But Jonah rose up to flee**
■ **unto Tarshish** from the presence
of the LORD, and went down to Joppa;
■ **and he found a ship going**
to Tarshish: so he paid the fare
thereof, and went down into it,
to go with them
■ **unto Tarshish from the**
■ **presence of the LORD.**
■ 4. **But the LORD sent** out a great
wind into the sea, and there was
■ **a mighty tempest**
■ **in the sea,** so that the
ship was like to be broken.
■ 5. **Then the mariners**
were afraid, and
■ **cried every man**
■ **unto his god, and cast**
■ **forth the wares** that *were*
■ **in the ship** into the sea,
■ **to lighten it** of them.
■ **But Jonah was**
gone down into the sides of
the ship; and he lay, and was
■ **fast asleep.**
■ 6. **So the shipmaster**
came to him, and
■ **said unto him, What**
■ **meanest thou,**
■ **O sleeper**? arise,
■ **call upon thy God,**
if so be that God will think upon us,
■ **that we perish not.**
■ 7. **And they said** every one
to his fellow, Come, and
■ **let us cast lots, that we**
■ **may know for whose**
■ **cause this evil is upon us.**
So they cast lots,
■ **and the lot fell upon Jonah.**
■ 8. **Then said they** unto him,
■ **Tell us**, we pray thee,
■ **for whose cause this**

■ **evil is upon us**; What *is* thine
occupation? and whence comest
thou? what *is* thy country? and of
what people *art* thou?
■ 9. **And he said** unto them,
■ **I am an Hebrew; and**
■ **I fear the LORD,**
the God of heaven,
■ **which hath made**
■ **the sea** and the dry *land*.
■ 10. **Then were**
■ **the men** exceedingly
■ **afraid**, and said unto him,
Why hast thou done this?
■ **For the men knew that**
■ **he fled from** the presence of
■ **the LORD, because he** had
■ **told them.**
11. Then said they unto him,
■ **What shall we do** unto thee,
■ **that the sea may be calm**
unto us? for the sea wrought,
and was tempestuous.
■ 12. **And he said**
unto them, Take me up, and
■ **cast me forth into the sea;**
so shall the sea be calm unto you: for
■ **I know that for my**
■ **sake this** great
■ **tempest is upon you.**
13. **Nevertheless the men**
■ **rowed hard to bring it**
■ **to the land; but** they
■ **could not**: for the sea wrought,
and was tempestuous against them.
■ 14. **Wherefore they cried**
unto the LORD, and said,
■ **We beseech thee,**
■ **O LORD,** we beseech thee,
■ **let us not perish for this**
■ **man's life**, and lay not upon us
innocent blood: for thou, O LORD,
hast done as it pleased thee.
■ 15. **So they took up Jonah,**
■ **and cast him** forth
■ **into the sea: and the sea**
■ **ceased from her raging.**
16. **Then the men feared**
■ **the LORD** exceedingly,
■ **and offered a sacrifice**
unto the LORD, and made vows.
17. **Now the LORD** had
■ **prepared a great**

fish to swallow up
Jonah. And Jonah was
in the belly of the fish
three days and three
nights.

CHAPTER 2

1. **Then Jonah prayed**
unto the LORD his God
out of the fish's belly,
2. **And said, I cried by**
reason of mine affliction
unto the LORD, and he heard me;
out of the belly of hell cried I,
and thou heardest
my voice.
3. **For thou hadst cast me**
into the deep, in the midst of
the seas; and the floods
compassed me about: all thy billows
and thy waves passed over me.
4. Then I said, I am cast out of
thy sight; yet I will look again
toward thy holy temple.
5. **The waters compassed**
me about, *even* to the soul:
the depth closed me round
about, the weeds were
wrapped about my head.
6. I went down to the bottoms of the
mountains; the earth with her bars
was about me for ever:
yet hast thou brought up
my life from corruption,
O LORD my God.
7. **When my soul**
fainted within me
I remembered the
LORD: and my prayer
came in unto thee,
into thine holy temple.
8. They that observe lying vanities
forsake their own mercy.
9. But I will sacrifice unto thee
with the voice of
thanksgiving; I will pay
that that I have vowed.
Salvation *is* of the LORD.
10. **And** the LORD spake unto
the fish, and it
vomited out
Jonah upon the
dry land.

CHAPTER 3

1. **And the word** of the LORD
came unto Jonah the
second time, saying,
2. **Arise, go unto**
Nineveh, that great city,
and preach unto it the preaching
that I bid thee.
3. **So Jonah** arose, and
went unto Nineveh,
according to the word of
the LORD. Now Nineveh
was an exceeding great
city of three days' journey.
4. **And Jonah began**
to enter into the city
a day's journey,
and he cried, and said,
Yet forty days, and
Nineveh shall be
overthrown.
5. **So the people** of Nineveh
believed God, and
proclaimed a fast, and put
on sackcloth, from the greatest of
them even to the least of them.
6. For word came unto
the king of Nineveh, and he arose
from his throne, and he laid his robe
from him, and covered *him* with
sackcloth, and sat in ashes.
7. And he caused *it* to be
proclaimed and
published through Nineveh
by the
decree of the king and his nobles,
saying, Let neither man nor
beast, herd nor flock,
taste any thing: let them not
feed, nor drink water:
8. **But** let man and beast
be covered with sackcloth,
and cry mightily
unto God: yea, let them turn every
one from his evil way, and from the
violence that *is* in their hands.
9. Who can tell *if* God will turn and
repent, and turn away from his fierce
anger, that we perish not?
10. **And God saw**
their works, that they
turned from their evil way;
and God

■ repented of the evil, that
■ he had
■ said that
■ he would do unto
■ them; and he did *it* not.

CHAPTER 4

■ 1. But it displeased Jonah
exceedingly, and he was very angry.
■ 2. And he prayed unto the
LORD, and said, I pray thee, O LORD,
■ was not this my saying, when
I was yet in my country? Therefore I
fled before unto Tarshish: for
■ I knew that thou art a
■ gracious God, and merciful,
■ slow to anger,
and of great kindness,
■ and repentest thee
■ of the evil.
3. Therefore now, O LORD,
■ take, I beseech thee,
■ my life from me; for *it is* better
for me to die than to live.
■ 4. Then said the LORD,
■ Doest thou well to
■ be angry?
■ 5. So Jonah went out
■ of the city, and sat on the
east side of the city,
■ and there
■ made him
■ a booth, and sat under it
in the shadow, till he might see
what would become of the city.
■ 6. And the LORD God
■ prepared a gourd, and made *it*
■ to come up over Jonah, that it might

■ be a shadow over his
■ head, to deliver him from his grief.
■ So Jonah was exceeding
■ glad of the gourd.
■ 7. But God prepared
■ a worm when the morning
rose the next day,
■ and it smote the gourd
■ that it withered.
■ 8. And it came to pass,
■ when the sun did
■ arise, that God prepared
a vehement east wind;
■ and the sun
■ beat upon the head of
■ Jonah, that he fainted,
■ and wished in himself
■ to die, and said, *It is* better
for me to die than to live.
■ 9. And God said to Jonah,
Doest thou well to be angry for
the gourd? And he said, I do well
to be angry, *even* unto death.
10. Then said the LORD,
■ Thou hast had pity
■ on the gourd, for the
■ which thou hast not
■ laboured, neither madest it
grow; which came up in a night,
and perished in a night:
■ 11. And should not I spare
■ Nineveh, that great city,
■ wherein are more then
■ sixscore thousand
■ persons that cannot
discern between their right
hand and their left hand;
and *also* much cattle?

THE BOOK OF MICAH

BACKGROUND INFORMATION

Author: Micah
Date Written: Contemporary of Isaiah

Number of:
Verses—105
Chapters—7
Total Words—3,153
Scan Words—1,365
Scan Words Represent
Approximately 43% of
Total Words

Theme: Reproach and **the Threat of Punishment, Ending on a Note of Hope** and Promise

OUTLINE OF THE BOOK

I. **The Coming Judgement**
    1:1 — 3:12
II. **The Glory of Restored Zion**
    4:1 — 5:14
III. **The Case Against Israel**
    6:1 — 7:20

CHAPTER 1

1. **The word of the LORD** that **came to Micah** the Morasthite in the days of Jotham, Ahaz, *and* Hezekiah, kings of Judah, which he saw **concerning Samaria and Jerusalem.**

2. **Hear,** all ye people; hearken, **O earth,** and all that therein is: **and let the Lord** GOD **be witness against you,** the LORD from his holy temple.

3. **For,** behold, **the LORD cometh** forth out of his place, **and will** come down, and **tread upon the high places** of the earth.

4. **And the mountains shall be molten** under him, **and the valleys** shall be **cleft, as wax before the fire,** *and* as the waters *that are* poured down a steep place.

5. For the transgression of Jacob *is* all this, and for the sins of the house of Israel. **What is the transgression of Jacob? is it not Samaria? and what are the high places of Judah? are they not Jerusalem?**

6. **Therefore I will make Samaria as an heap** of the field, *and* as plantings of a vineyard: and I will pour down the stones thereof into the valley, and I will discover the foundations thereof.

7. **And all the graven images** thereof **shall be beaten to pieces, and** all **the hires** thereof shall be **burned** with the fire, **and** all **the idols** thereof **will I lay desolate: for she gathered it of the hire of an harlot,** and they shall return to the hire of an harlot.

8. **Therefore I will wail and howl,** I will go stripped and naked: I will make a wailing like the dragons, and mourning as the owls.

9. **For her wound is incurable;** for it is come unto Judah; he is come unto the gate of my people, *even* to Jerusalem.

10. **Declare ye it not at Gath, weep ye not at all: in** the house of **Aphrah roll thyself in the dust.**

11. **Pass ye away,** thou inhabitant of **Saphir,** having thy shame naked: the inhabitant of **Zaanan came not** forth in the **mourning of Beth-ezel;** he shall receive of you his standing.

12. For the inhabitant of **Maroth waited** carefully **for good: but evil came** down **from the LORD unto** the gate of **Jerusalem.**

13. **O** thou inhabitant of **Lachish, bind the chariot to the swift beast:** she *is* the beginning of the sin to the daughter of Zion: **for the transgressions of Israel were found in thee.**

14. **Therefore** shalt thou **give presents to Moresheth-gath:** the houses of **Achzib shall be a lie to** the kings of **Israel.**

15. **Yet will I bring an heir unto** thee, O inhabitant of **Mareshah:** he shall come unto Adullam the glory of Israel.

16. **Make** thee bald, and poll thee for thy delicate children; enlarge **thy baldness as the eagle; for they are gone into captivity from thee.**

CHAPTER 2

1. **Woe to them that** devise iniquity, and **work evil upon their beds!** when the morning is light, **they practise it, because it is in the power of**

■ their hand.

2. And they covet fields, and take *them* by violence; and houses, and take *them* away: so ■ they oppress a man and ■ his house, even a man and ■ his heritage.

■ 3. Therefore thus saith ■ the LORD; Behold, against this family do ■ I devise an evil, from which ye shall not remove your necks; neither shall ye go haughtily: for this time *is* evil.

■ 4. In that day shall one take up a parable against you, and lament with a doleful lamentation, *and* ■ say, We be utterly spoiled: he hath changed the portion of my people: how hath he removed *it* from me! turning away ■ he hath divided our fields.

■ 5. Therefore thou shalt have ■ none that ■ shall cast a cord by lot in ■ the congregation of the LORD.

■ 6. Prophesy ye ■ not, *say they to them that* prophesy: they shall not prophesy to them, ■ that they shall not ■ take shame.

■ 7. O *thou that art* named the houseof ■ Jacob, is the spirit of the LORD ■ straitened? *are* these his doings? ■ do not my words do ■ good to him that walketh uprightly?

■ 8. Even of late ■ my people is risen up ■ as an enemy: ye pull off the robe with the garment from them that pass by securely as men averse from war.

■ 9. The women of my people ■ have ye cast out from ■ their pleasant houses; ■ from their children have ■ ye taken away ■ my glory for ever.

10. Arise ye, and depart; for ■ this is not your rest: because ■ it is polluted, it shall destroy *you,* even with a sore destruction.

■ 11. If a man walking in the spirit and falsehood do ■ lie, saying, I will prophesy unto thee of wine and ■ of strong drink; he shall ■ even be the prophet ■ of this people.

12. I will surely ■ assemble, O Jacob, all of thee; I will surely gather ■ the remnant of Israel; I will put them together as the sheep of Bozrah, as the flock in the midst of their fold: they shall make great noise by reason of ■ the multitude of men.

13. The breaker is come up before them: ■ they have broken up, and have ■ passed through the gate, and are gone out by it: and ■ their king shall pass ■ before them, and the LORD ■ on the head of them.

CHAPTER 3

1. And I said, ■ Hear, I pray you, ■ O heads of Jacob, and ye ■ princes of the house of ■ Israel; Is it not for ■ you to know judgment?

2. Who hate the good, and ■ love the evil; who pluck off their skin from off them, and their flesh from off their bones;

■ 3. Who also eat the ■ flesh of my people, and flay their skin from off them; ■ and they ■ break their bones, and chop them in pieces, ■ as for the pot, and as flesh within the caldron.

■ 4. Then shall they cry unto ■ the LORD, but he will not ■ hear them: he will even hide his face from them at that time, as they have behaved themselves ill in their doings.

■ 5. Thus saith the LORD ■ concerning the prophets ■ that make my people err, ■ that bite with their teeth,

1277

and cry, Peace; and
he that putteth not into their
mouths, they even
prepare war against him.
6. Therefore
night shall be unto you, that ye shall
not have a vision; and
it shall be dark unto you,
that ye shall not divine;
and the sun shall go down over
the prophets, and the day shall
be dark over them.
7. Then shall
the seers be ashamed, and
the diviners confounded:
yea, they shall all cover their lips;
for there is no answer
of God.
8. But truly
I am full of power by
the spirit of the LORD,
and of judgment, and of might, to
declare unto
Jacob his transgression,
and to Israel his sin.
9. Hear this, I pray you,
ye heads of the house of
Jacob, and princes of the house of
Israel, that abhor judgment,
and pervert all equity.
10. They build up Zion with
blood, and Jerusalem
with iniquity.
11. The heads thereof
judge for reward,
and the priests thereof
teach for hire,
and the prophets thereof
divine for money: yet will
they lean upon the LORD, and
say, Is not the LORD
among us?
none evil can come upon us.
12. Therefore shall
Zion for your sake
be plowed as a field, and
Jerusalem shall become
heaps, and the mountain of
the house as the high places of
the forest.

CHAPTER 4

1. But in the last days

it shall come to pass,
that the mountain of
the house of the LORD
shall be established
in the top of the mountains,
and it shall be
exalted above the hills;
and people shall
flow unto it.
2. And many
nations shall come,
and say, Come, and let us go up to
the mountain of the LORD, and to
the house of the God of Jacob;
and he will teach us of his
ways, and we will walk in
his paths: for the law shall go
forth of Zion, and the word of
the LORD from Jerusalem.
3. And he shall
judge among many
people, and rebuke strong
nations afar off;
and they shall beat their
swords into plowshares,
and their spears into
pruninghooks: nation shall
not lift up a sword against
nation, neither shall they
learn war any more.
4. But they
shall sit every man
under his vine and under his fig
tree; and none shall
make *them* afraid:
for the mouth of
the LORD of hosts
hath spoken it.
5. For all people will walk
every one in the name of his god,
and we will walk
in the name of
the LORD our God
for ever and ever.
6. In that day, saith the LORD,
will I assemble her that
halteth, and I will gather her
that is driven out, and
her that I have
afflicted;
7. And I will make
her that halted
a remnant, and

her that was cast far off

■ **a strong nation: and**
■ **the LORD shall reign**
■ **over them** in mount Zion
from henceforth, even for ever.

■ 8. **And** thou, O tower of the flock,
the strong hold of the daughter of
Zion, unto thee shall it come, even
the first dominion;

■ **the kingdom shall come to**
■ **the daughter of Jerusalem.**
9. Now why dost thou cry out aloud?
is there no king in thee? is thy
counsellor perished? for pangs have
taken thee as a woman in travail.

■ 10. **Be in pain, and labour**
to bring forth, O daughter of Zion,
■ **like a woman in travail:**
■ **for now shalt thou** go forth
out of the city, and thou shalt
■ **dwell in the field, and**
thou shalt go *even* to
■ **Babylon;** there shalt thou
be delivered;
■ **there the LORD shall**
■ **redeem thee from** the hand of
■ **thine enemies.**
11. Now also many
■ **nations are gathered**
■ **against thee,**
that say, Let her be defiled, and let
our eye look upon Zion.
■ 12. **But they know not**
the thoughts of
■ **the LORD,** neither underst
and they his counsel:
■ **for he shall gather them**
as the sheaves into the floor.
■ 13. **Arise** and thresh, O
■ **daughter of Zion: for**
I will make thine horn iron, and
I will make thy hoofs brass: and
■ **thou shalt beat in pieces**
■ **many people: and** I will
■ **consecrate their**
■ **gain** unto the LORD,
■ **and** their
■ **substance unto the**
■ **Lord** of the whole earth.

CHAPTER 5

■ 1. **Now gather thyself**
■ **in troops**, O daughter of troops:

■ **he hath laid siege**
■ **against us: they**
■ **shall smite the judge**
of Israel with a rod upon the cheek.
■ 2. **But** thou,
■ **Beth-lehem Ephratah,**
though thou be little among the
thousands of Judah, *yet*
■ **out of thee shall he**
■ **come** forth unto me
■ **that is to be ruler in Israel;**
■ **whose goings forth have**
■ **been** from of old,
■ **from everlasting.**
3. **Therefore will he give**
■ **them up, until the time**
that she which travaileth
hath brought forth: then
■ **the remnant** of his brethren
■ **shall return unto** the children of
■ **Israel.**
4. **And he shall stand** and feed
■ **in the strength of the**
■ **LORD,** in the majesty of the
name of the LORD his God;
■ **and** they shall abide: for now
■ **shall** he
■ **be great unto the**
■ **ends of the earth.**
5. **And** this *man* shall be the peace,
■ **when the Assyrian**
■ **shall come** into our land:
■ **and** when he shall
■ **tread in our palaces, then**
■ **shall we raise against him**
seven shepherds, and
eight principal men.
■ 6. **And** they shall
■ **waste the land of**
■ **Assyria** with the sword,
■ **and** the land of
■ **Nimrod** in the
entrances thereof:
■ **thus shall he deliver**
■ **us from the Assyrian,**
when he cometh into our land, and
when he treadeth within our borders.
■ 7. **And the remnant of**
■ **Jacob shall be in the midst**
■ **of** many people as a dew from the
LORD, as the showers upon the
grass, that tarrieth not for man, nor
waiteth for the sons of men.

8. And the remnant of Jacob shall be among **the Gentiles** in the midst of many people **as a lion** among the beasts of the forest, as a young lion **among** the flocks of **sheep: who,** if he go through, both treadeth down, and **teareth in pieces,** **and none can deliver.**

9. Thine hand shall be lifted up upon thine adversaries, **and all thine enemies** **shall be cut off.**

10. **And** it shall come to pass in that day, saith the LORD, that I will cut off thy horses out of the midst of thee, and **I will destroy** thy chariots:

11. And I will cut off **the cities** of thy land, **and** throw down all **thy strong holds:**

12. **And I will cut off** **witchcrafts** out of thine hand; **and** thou shalt have no *more* **soothsayers:**

13. **Thy graven images** also **will I cut off,** and thy standing images out of the midst of thee; **and thou shalt no more** **worship the work of** **thine hands.**

14. And I will pluck up thy groves out of the midst of thee: so will I destroy thy cities.

15. **And I will execute** **vengeance** in anger and fury **upon the heathen, such** **as they have not heard.**

CHAPTER 6

1. **Hear** ye now **what the LORD saith**; Arise, contend thou before the mountains, and let the hills hear thy voice.

2. Hear ye, O mountains, the LORD's controversy, and ye strong foundations of the earth: for the LORD hath a controversy with his people, and he will plead with Israel.

3. O my people, **what have I done** **unto thee?** and wherein have I wearied thee? testify against me.

4. **For I brought thee** **up out of** the land of **Egypt, and redeemed thee** out of the house of servants; **and I sent** before thee **Moses,** Aaron, and Miriam.

5. O my people, remember now what Balak king of Moab consulted, and what Balaam the son of Beor answered him from Shittim unto Gilgal; that ye may know the righteousness of the LORD.

6. **Wherewith shall I come** **before the LORD,** *and* bow myself before the high God? shall I come before him **with burnt offerings,** with calves of a year old?

7. **Will the LORD be pleased** with thousands of rams, *or* with ten thousands of rivers of oil? **shall I give my firstborn** *for* my transgression, the fruit of my body **for the sin of my soul?**

8. **He hath shewed thee,** O man, what *is* good; and **what doth the LORD** **require of thee, but to** **do justly,** and to **love mercy, and** to **walk humbly with thy God?**

9. **The LORD's voice crieth** unto the city, and *the man of* wisdom shall see thy name: hear ye the rod, and who hath appointed it.

10. **Are there** yet the **treasures of wickedness** **in the house of the** **wicked,** and the scant measure *that is* abominable?

11. Shall I count *them* pure with the wicked balances, and with the bag of deceitful weights?

12. **For the rich men** thereof **are full of violence,** and the inhabitants thereof have spoken lies, **and their tongue is** **deceitful** in their mouth.

13. **Therefore** also

■ **will I make thee sick** in smiting thee, in making *thee* desolate
■ **because of thy sins.**
■ **14. Thou shalt eat, but not**
■ **be satisfied;** and thy casting down *shall be* in the midst of thee; and thou shalt take hold, but shalt not deliver; and *that* which thou deliverest will I give up to the sword.
■ **15. Thou shalt sow,**
■ **but** thou shalt
■ **not reap; thou shalt tread**
■ **the olives, but** thou
■ **shalt not anoint** thee
■ **with oil;** and sweet wine, but shalt not drink wine.
■ **16. For the statutes of**
■ **Omri are kept, and** all
■ **the works** of the house
■ **of Ahab, and ye walk in**
■ **their counsels;** that I should make thee a desolation, and the inhabitants thereof an hissing:
■ **therefore ye shall bear the**
■| **reproach of my people.**

CHAPTER 7

■| **1. Woe is me! for I** am as when they have gathered the summerfruits, as the grapegleanings of the vintage: *there is* no cluster to eat: my soul
■ **desired the firstripe fruit.**
■ **2. The good man is**
■ **perished** out of the earth:
■ **and there is none upright** among men: they all lie in wait for blood; they hunt every man his brother with a net.
3. That
■ **they** may
■ **do evil** with both hands earnestly, the prince asketh,
■ **and** the judge
■ **asketh for** a
■ **reward;** and the great *man,* he uttereth his mischievous desire: so they wrap it up.
■ **4. The best of them is as** a brier: the most upright *is sharper* than
■ **a thorn hedge:** the day of thy watchmen *and*
■ **thy visitation cometh; now**
■| **shall be their perplexity.**

■ **5. Trust ye not in a friend,** put ye not confidence in a guide: keep the doors of thy mouth from her that lieth in thy bosom.
■ **6. For** the son dishonoureth the father, the daughter riseth up against her mother, the daughter in law against her mother in law;
■ **a man's enemies are the**
■ **men of his own house.**
■ **7. Therefore** I will
■ **look unto the** LORD; I will wait for the
■ **God of my salvation:**
■ **my God will hear me.**
■ **8. Rejoice not** against me, O mine enemy:
■ **when I fall, I shall**
■ **arise;** when I sit
■ **in darkness, the LORD**
■ **shall be a light** unto me.
■ **9. I will bear the indignation**
■ **of the LORD, because I**
■ **have sinned** against him, until he plead my cause, and execute judgment for me:
■ **he will bring me** forth
■ **to** the light, *and* I shall behold
■ **his righteousness.**
■ **10. Then** she that is
■ **mine enemy shall see it,**
■ **and shame shall cover**
■ **her which said** unto me,
■ **Where is the LORD** thy God? mine eyes shall behold her:
■ **now shall she be**
■ **trodden down** as the mire of the streets.
11. *In* the day that thy walls are to be built, *in* that day shall the decree be far removed.
■ **12. In that day** also
■ **he shall come** even to thee from Assyria, and *from* the fortified cities, and from the fortress even to the river, and from sea to sea,
■ **and** *from* mountain to mountain.
13. Notwithstanding
■ **the land shall be**
■ **desolate because**
■ **of** them that dwell therein, for
■ **the fruit of their doings.**
■ **14. Feed thy people**

with thy rod, the flock **of thine heritage,** which dwell solitarily *in* the wood, in the midst of Carmel: let them feed *in* Bashan and Gilead, as in the days of old.

15. According to the days of thy coming out of the land of Egypt will I shew unto him marvellous *things.*

16. **The nations shall** see and **be confounded at** all **their might:** they shall lay *their* hand upon *their* mouth, their ears shall be deaf.

17. **They shall lick the dust** like a serpent, **they shall move** out of their holes **like worms** of the earth: **they shall be afraid of the LORD** our God, a nd shall fear because of thee.

18. **Who is a God like** unto **thee, that pardoneth iniquity,** and passeth by the transgression of the remnant of his heritage? **he retaineth not his anger for ever, because he delighteth in mercy.**

19. **He will** turn again, he will **have compassion upon us;** he will subdue our iniquities; **and** thou **wilt cast all their sins into the** depths of the **sea.**

20. **Thou wilt perform the truth** to Jacob, *and* the mercy to Abraham, **which thou hast sworn** unto our fathers **from the days of old.**

THE BOOK OF NAHUM

BACKGROUND INFORMATION

Author: Nahum
Date Written: Around 612 B.C.

Number of:
Verses—47
Chapters—3
Total Words—1,285
Scan Words—552
Scan Words Represent Approximately 42% of Total Words

Theme: Prophecies of **The Lord Coming in Judgement, and the Fall of Nineveh**

OUTLINE OF THE BOOK

CHAPTER 1

1. **The burden of Nineveh. The book of the vision of Nahum** the Elkoshite. 2. **God is jealous, and** the LORD revengeth; the LORD revengeth, and *is* furious; the LORD **will take vengeance on his adversaries,** and he reserveth *wrath* for his enemies. 3. **The LORD is slow to anger,** and great in power, **and will not** at all **acquit the wicked:** the LORD hath his way in the whirlwind and in the storm, and the clouds *are* the dust of his feet. 4. **He rebuketh the sea, and maketh it dry,** and drieth up all the rivers: Bashan languisheth, and Carmel, and the flower of Lebanon languisheth. 5. **The mountains quake** at him, and **the hills melt, and the earth is burned at his presence,** yea, the world, and all that dwell therein. 6. **Who can stand before his indignation?** and who can abide in the fierceness of his anger? his fury is poured out like fire, and the rocks are thrown down by him. 7. **The LORD is good,** a strong hold in the day of trouble; **and he knoweth them that trust in him.** 8. **But** with an overrunning flood he will make an utter end of the place thereof, and **darkness shall pursue his enemies.** 9. **What do ye imagine against the LORD?** he will make an utter end: affliction shall not rise up the second time. 10. For while *they be* folden together *as* thorns, and **while they are drunken** *as* drunkards, **they shall be devoured** as stubble fully dry. 11. **There is one** come out of thee, **that imagineth evil against the LORD,** a wicked counsellor. 12. **Thus saith the LORD; Though they be quiet,** and likewise many, **yet** thus shall **they be cut down,** when he shall pass through. **Though I have afflicted thee, I will afflict thee no more.** 13. **For** now will **I** break his yoke from off thee, and **will burst thy bonds** in sunder. 14. And the LORD hath given a commandment concerning thee, *that* no more of thy name be sown: out of the house of thy gods will I cut off the graven image and the molten image: I will make thy grave; for thou art vile. 15. **Behold** upon the mountains the feet of **him that bringeth good tidings,** that publisheth peace! O **Judah,** keep thy solemn feasts, **perform thy vows: for the wicked shall no more pass through thee; he is** utterly **cut off.**

CHAPTER 2

1. **He that dasheth in pieces is come** up before thy face: **keep the munition, watch the way,** make *thy* loins strong, **fortify thy power** mightily. 2. **For the LORD hath turned away the excellency of** Jacob, as the excellency of **Israel:** for the emptiers have emptied them out, and marred their vine branches. 3. **The shield of his mighty men is made red,** the valiant men *are* in scarlet: the chariots *shall be* with flaming torches **in the day of his preparation,** and the fir **trees shall be** terribly **shaken.** 4. **The chariots shall rage in**

the streets, they shall justle one
against another in the broad ways:
**they shall seem like
torches, they shall run
like the lightnings.**
5. **He shall recount his
worthies: they shall
stumble in their**
walk; they shall make
haste to the wall thereof,
**and the defence
shall be prepared.**
6. The gates of the rivers shall be
opened, and the palace shall be
dissolved.
7. **And Huzzab shall be
led away captive,** she shall be
brought up, and her maids shall lead
her as with the voice of doves,
tabering upon their breasts.
8. **But Nineveh** *is* of old
like a pool of
water: yet they
shall flee away.
Stand, stand, *shall they cry;*
but none shall look back.
9. **Take** ye
the spoil
of silver, take the spoil of gold:
**for there is none end
of the store** *and* glory out
of all the pleasant furniture.
10. **She is empty,** and void,
and waste: and the heart melteth,
and the knees smite together, and
much pain *is* in all loins, and the faces
of them all gather blackness.
11. **Where is the dwelling of
the lions,** and the feedingplace of
the young lions, where the lion, *even*
the old lion, walked, *and* the lion's
whelp, and none made *them* afraid?
12. **The lion did tear
in pieces** enough for his whelps,
and strangled for his lionesses,
**and filled his holes
with prey,** and his dens with ravin.
13. **Behold, I am against
thee, saith the LORD**
of hosts, and
**I will burn her
chariots** in the smoke,
and the sword shall

devour thy young lions: and
I will cut off thy prey from the earth,
and the voice of
**thy messengers shall
no more be heard.**

CHAPTER 3

1. **Woe to the
bloody city!** it *is* all
full of lies and robbery;
the prey departeth not;
2. **The noise of a whip,
and** the noise of the
rattling of the
wheels, and of the
**prancing horses,
and** of the jumping
chariots.
3. **The horseman
lifteth** up both
the bright
sword and the glittering
**spear: and there
is a multitude** of
slain, and a great number of
carcases; and *there is* none end of
their corpses; they stumble upon
their corpses:
4. **Because of** the multitude of the
whoredoms
of the wellfavoured harlot, the
mistress of witchcrafts, that selleth
nations through her whoredoms,
and families through her
witchcrafts.
5. **Behold, I am against
thee,** saith the LORD of hosts;
and I
will discover thy skirts
upon thy face, and I will
shew the
**nations thy nakedness,
and** the kingdoms thy
shame.
6. **And** I
will cast abominable
filth upon thee,
and make thee vile, and will set
thee as a gazingstock.
7. **And** it shall come to pass, *that*
all they that look upon thee
**shall flee from thee, and
say, Nineveh is laid waste:**

who will bemoan her? whence shall I
seek comforters for thee?

■ 8. **Art thou better than**
■ **populous No,** that was situate
among the rivers, *that had* the waters
round about it, whose rampart *was* the
sea, *and* her wall *was* from the sea?
■ 9. **Ethiopia and Egypt were**
■ **her strength,** and *it was* infinite;
■ **Put and Lubim were**
■ **thy helpers.**
■ 10. **Yet was she carried**
■ **away,** she went
■ **into captivity: her**
■ **young** children also
■ **were dashed in pieces**
at the top of all the streets:
■ **and they cast lots for her**
■ **honourable men,** and all her
great men were bound in chains.
11. Thou also shalt be drunken: thou
shalt be hid, thou also shalt seek
strength because of the enemy.
■ 12. **All thy strong holds**
■ **shall be like** fig trees with the
■ **firstripe figs: if they**
■ **be shaken, they shall** even
■ **fall** into the mouth of the eater.
■ 13. **Behold, thy people**
in the midst of thee
■ **are women: the gates**
of thy land shall be set wide
■ **open unto thine enemies:**
the fire shall devour thy bars.
■ 14. **Draw** thee
■ **waters for the siege,**

■ **fortify thy strong holds:**
go into clay, and tread the mortar,
make strong the brickkiln.
■ 15. **There shall the fire**
■ **devour thee; the sword**
■ **shall cut thee off,** it shall eat
thee up like the cankerworm: make
thyself many as the cankerworm,
make thyself many as the locusts.
■ 16. **Thou hast multiplied thy**
■ **merchants above the stars**
of heaven: the cankerworm spoileth,
and flieth away.
17. Thy crowned *are* as the locusts,
■ **and thy captains as the**
■ **great grasshoppers,** which
camp in the hedges in the cold day,
■ **but** when the sun ariseth
■ **they flee away,** and their
place is not known where they *are.*
■ 18. **Thy shepherds slumber,**
■ **O king of Assyria:** thy nobles
shall dwell *in the dust:*
■ **thy people is scattered**
upon the mountains, and no
man gathereth *them.*
■ 19. **There is no healing**
■ **of thy** bruise; thy
■ **wound** is grievous:
■ **all that hear** the bruit of thee
■ **shall clap**
the hands over thee:
■ **for upon whom**
■ **hath not thy**
■ **wickedness passed**
continually?

THE BOOK OF HABAKKUK

BACKGROUND INFORMATION

Author – Habakkuk
Date Written – 630 B.C.

Number of:
Verses–56
Chapters–3
Total Worlds–1,476
Scan Words–655
Scan Words Represent
Approximately 44% of Total
Words

Theme: Habakkuk, the Prophet of Faith

OUTLINE OF THE BOOK

I. **Why God Permits Evil**
    1:1 — 4

II. **The Chaldeans are Used of God**
    1:5 — 11

III. **Why the Wicked are Used by God**
    1:12 — 2:1

IV. **The Righteous Must Live by Faith**
    2:2 — 4

V. **God's Judgement of the Wicked**
    2:5 — 20

VI. **Habakkuk's Prayer**
    3:1— 19

CHAPTER 1

■ 1. **The burden which**
■ **Habakkuk** the prophet
■ **did see.**
■ 2. **O LORD, how long**
■ **shall I cry,** and thou wilt
not hear! *even* cry out unto thee
■ **of violence, and thou**
■ **wilt not save!**
■ 3. **Why dost thou shew me**
■ **iniquity, and cause**
me to behold
■ **grievance?**
for spoiling and violence *are*
■ **before me:** and
■ **there are** *that* raise up
■ **strife and contention.**
■ 4. **Therefore the law is**
■ **slacked, and** judgment
doth never go forth: for
■ **the wicked** doth
■ **compass** about
■ **the righteous; therefore**
■ **wrong judgment**
■ **proceedeth.**
■ 5. **Behold** ye among
the heathen, and regard,
and wonder marvellously: for
■ **I will work a work**
■ **in your days,** which ye will
not believe, though it be told *you.*
■ 6. **For, lo, I raise up**
■ **the Chaldeans,** *that* bitter
and hasty nation, which shall march
through the breadth of the land,
■ **to possess** the
■ **dwellingplaces that**
■ **are not theirs.**
■ 7. **They are** terrible and
■ **dreadful:** their judgment and their
dignity shall proceed of themselves.
■ 8. **Their horses** also
■ **are swifter than** the
■ **leopards, and** are
■ **more fierce than** the evening
■ **wolves: and their horsemen**
shall spread themselves,
and their horsemen
■ **shall come** from far; they
shall fly as the eagle
that hasteth to eat.
9. They shall come all
■ **for violence:** their faces shall sup

up *as* the east wind, and they shall
gather the captivity as the sand.
■ 10. **And** they
■ **shall scoff at** the
■ **kings, and** the
■ **princes** shall be a scorn
unto them: they shall deride
■ **every strong hold;** for
■ **they shall** heap dust, and
■ **take** it.
■ 11. **Then** shall *his* mind change, and
■ **he shall pass over,**
and offend,
■ **imputing** this
■ **his power unto his god.**
■ 12. **Art thou not** from
■ **everlasting, O LORD**
my God, mine Holy One?
■ **we shall not die.** O LORD,
■ **thou hast ordained them**
■ **for judgment; and,**
O mighty God, thou hast
established them for
■ **correction.**
■ 13. **Thou art of purer eyes**
■ **than to behold evil, and**
■ **canst not look on iniquity:**
wherefore lookest thou upon them
that deal treacherously,
■ **and holdest thy tongue**
■ **when the wicked**
■ **devoureth the** *man that is* more
■ **righteous** than he?
■ 14. **And makest men**
■ **as the fishes**
of the sea, as the creeping things,
■ **that have no ruler** over them?
■ 15. **They take** up all of
■ **them with**
the angle, they catch them in
■ **their net, and** gather them in
their drag: therefore they
■ **rejoice** and are glad.
■ 16. **Therefore they sacrifice**
■ **unto their net,**
and burn incense unto their drag;
■ **because by them their**
■ **portion is** fat, and their meat
■ **plenteous.**
■ 17. **Shall they therefore**
■ **empty their net, and**
not spare continually to
■ **slay the nations?**

CHAPTER 2

■ 1. **I will stand upon**
my watch, and set me upon
■ **the tower,** and will watch
■ **to see what he**
■ **will say** unto me,
■ **and what I shall**
■ **answer when I am**
■ **reproved.**
■ 2. **And the LORD**
answered me, and
■ **said, Write the vision,**
■ **and make**
■ **it plain** upon tables,
■ **that he may run**
■ **that readeth it.**
■ 3. **For the vision is** yet
■ **for an appointed time,**
but at the end it shall speak,
and not lie: though it tarry,
■ **wait for it; because**
■ **it will** surely
■ **come,** it will not tarry.
■ 4. **Behold, his soul which is**
■ **lifted up is not upright** in him:
■ **but the just shall live by** his
■ **faith.**
5. Yea also, because he
transgresseth by wine, *he is*
■ **a proud man,** neither
keepeth at home, who
■ **enlargeth his desire**
as hell, and *is* as death,
■ **and cannot be satisfied,**
■ **but gathereth** unto him all
■ **nations, and** heapeth unto him all
■ **people:**
■ 6. **Shall not** all
■ **these** take up a parable
against him, and a taunting
proverb against him, and
■ **say, Woe to him that**
■ **increaseth that which**
■ **is not his!** how long? and to him
that ladeth himself with thick clay!
■ 7. **Shall they not rise up**
suddenly that shall bite thee,
■ **and** awake that shall
■ **vex thee,** and thou shalt be for
booties unto them?
■ 8. **Because thou**
■ **hast spoiled** many
■ **nations,** all

■ **the remnant** of the people
■ **shall spoil thee;** because of
men's blood, and *for* the violence of
the land, of the city, and of all that
dwell therein.
■ 9. **Woe to him**
■ **that coveteth** an
■ **evil** covetousness to his house,
that he may set his nest on high,
■ **that he may be**
■ **delivered from** the power of
■ **evil!**
■ 10. **Thou hast** consulted
■ **shame** to thy house
■ **by cutting off** many
■ **people, and hast sinned**
against thy soul.
11. For the stone shall cry out of the
wall, and the beam out of the timber
shall answer it.
■ 12. **Woe to him**
■ **that buildeth** a town
■ **with blood, and**
stablisheth a city by
■ **iniquity!**
■ 13. **Behold, is it not**
■ **of the LORD** of hosts
■ **that** the
■ **people** shall
■ **labour** in the very fire,
■ **and** the people shall
■ **weary themselves for** very
■ **vanity?**
■ 14. **For the earth shall be**
■ **filled with the knowledge**
■ **of the glory of the LORD,**
as the waters cover the sea.
■ 15. **Woe unto him that**
■ **giveth his neighbour drink,**
that puttest thy bottle
■ **to** *him,* and makest *him* drunken
also, that thou mayest
■ **look on their nakedness!**
■ 16. **Thou art filled with**
■ **shame** for glory:
drink thou also,
■ **and** let thy foreskin be uncovered:
■ **the cup of the LORD's**
■ **right hand shall be**
■ **turned unto thee,**
and shameful spewing
shall be on thy glory.
17. For the violence of Lebanon shall

cover thee, and the spoil of beasts, *which* made them afraid, because of men's blood, and for the violence of the land, of the city, and of all that dwell therein.

■ 18. **What profiteth** the graven image that the maker thereof hath graven it; the molten image, and a teacher of lies, that

■ **the maker of** his work trusteth therein, to make dumb

■ **idols?**

19. Woe unto him that saith to the wood, Awake; to the dumb stone, Arise, it shall teach! Behold, it *is* laid over with gold and silver, and

■ **there is no breath** at all
■ **in** the midst of
■ **it.**
■ 20. **But the LORD is in his**
■ **holy temple: let** all
■ **the earth keep silence**
before him.

CHAPTER 3

■ 1. **A prayer of Habakkuk** the prophet upon Shigionoth.
■ 2. **O LORD, I have heard** thy speech,
■ **and was afraid:** O LORD,
■ **revive thy work**
in the midst of the years, in the midst of the years make known;

■ **in wrath remember mercy.**
■ 3. **God came from Teman,**
■ **and** the Holy One from
■ **mount Paran.** Selah.
■ **His glory covered the**
■ **heavens,** and the earth
was full of his praise.
■ 4. **And his brightness** was
■ **as** the
■ **light;** he had horns
■ **coming out of his hand:**
■ **and there was** the hiding of
■ **his power.**
■ 5. **Before him went the**
■ **pestilence,** and burning coals
went forth at his feet.
■ 6. **He stood, and**
measured the earth: he
■ **beheld, and** drove asunder
■ **the nations;** and the

everlasting mountains were
■ **scattered,**
the perpetual hills did bow:
■ **his ways are everlasting.**
■ 7. **I saw** the tents of
■ **Cushan in affliction:**
■ **and** the curtains of the land of
■ **Midian** did
■ **tremble.**
8. Was the LORD displeased against the rivers?
■ **was thine anger against**
■ **the rivers? was thy wrath**
■ **against the sea,**
■ **that thou didst ride** upon
■ **thine horses and** thy
■ **chariots of salvation?**
9. Thy bow was made quite naked, *according* to the oaths of the tribes, *even thy* word. Selah. Thou didst cleave the earth with rivers.
■ 10. **The mountains**
saw thee, *and* they
■ **trembled: the**
■ **overflowing** of the
■ **water passed by: the**
■ **deep uttered his voice,**
and lifted up his hands on high.
■ 11. **The sun and moon**
■ **stood still** in their habitation:
at the light of thine arrows
they went, *and* at the shining
of thy glittering spear.
■ 12. **Thou didst**
march through the land
■ **in indignation,** thou didst
■ **thresh the heathen** in anger.
■ 13. **Thou wentest** forth
■ **for the salvation of thy**
■ **people, even** for salvation with
■ **thine anointed; thou**
■ **woundedst**
the head out of the house of
■ **the wicked,** by discovering the
foundation unto the neck. Selah.
■ 14. **Thou didst strike** through
with his staves the head of
■ **his villages:** they came out as a
whirlwind to scatter me: their rejoicing
was as to devour the poor secretly.
■ 15. **Thou didst walk through**
■ **the sea** with thine horses,
through the heap of great waters.

16. **When I heard,
my belly trembled;
my lips quivered** at the
voice: rottenness entered into
my bones, and I
trembled in myself, that I
might rest in the day of trouble:
when he cometh
up unto the people,
**he will invade them
with his troops.**
17. **Although the fig tree
shall not blossom,** neither
shall fruit *be* in the vines; the
labour of the olive shall fail,
**and the fields shall
yield no meat;** the flock
shall be cut off from the fold, and
there shall be no herd in the stalls:
18. **Yet I will rejoice in
the LORD,** I will joy in the God
of my salvation.
19. **The LORD God is my
strength, and he will make
my feet like hinds' feet,** and
he will make me to walk upon mine
high places. To the chief singer on
my stringed instruments.

THE LORD OF MIGHT AND JOY

*The Lord Thy God
in the Midst of Thee
is Mighty; He Will
Save, He Will Rejoice
Over Thee With Joy;
He Will Rest in His
Love, He Will Joy
Over Thee With
Singing.*

Zephaniah 3:17

THE BOOK OF ZEPHANIAH

BACKGROUND INFORMATION

Author: Zephaniah
Date Written:
639 — 608 B.C.

Number of:
Verses—53
Chapters— 3
Total Worlds—1,617
Scan Words—726
Scan Words Represent
Approximately 44% of
Total Words

Theme: A Prophecy
Concerning
**God's Judgement of the
Nations, and the
Restoration of a Remnant**

OUTLINE OF THE BOOK

I.   **God's Warning to Judah**
     1:1 — 18
II. **God's Judgement**
     2:1 — 3:8
III. **A Remnant of Israel**
     Shall be Restored
     3:9 — 20

CHAPTER 1

1. **The word of the LORD** which came **unto Zephaniah** the son of Cushi, the son of Gedaliah, the son of Amariah, the son of Hizkiah, **in the days of Josiah** the son of Amon, **king of Judah.**

2. **I will** utterly **consume all things from off the land, saith the LORD.**

3. **I will consume man and beast;** I will consume **the fowls** of the heaven, and **the fishes** of the sea, **and the stumblingblocks with the wicked;** and I will cut off man from off the land, saith the LORD.

4. **I will also stretch out mine hand upon Judah, and** upon all the inhabitants of **Jerusalem;** and **I will cut off the remnant of Baal** from this place, **and the name of the Chemarims with the priests;**

5. **And them that worship the host of heaven** upon the housetops; and them that worship *and* that swear by the LORD, **and that swear by Malcham;**

6. **And them that** are **turned** back **from the LORD; and those that have not sought** the LORD, **nor inquired for him.**

7. **Hold thy peace** at the presence of the Lord GOD: **for the day of the LORD is at hand:** for **the LORD hath prepared a sacrifice, he hath bid his guests.**

8. **And** it shall come to pass in the day of the LORD's sacrifice, that **I will punish the princes, and the king's children, and** all **such as are clothed with strange apparel.**

9. **In the same day** also will I punish all **those** that leap on the threshold, **which fill their masters' houses with violence and deceit.**

10. **And** it shall come to pass in that day, saith the LORD, *that* **there shall be** the noise of **a cry** from the fish gate, and an howling from the second, **and** a great **crashing from the hills.**

11. Howl, ye inhabitants of Maktesh, **for** all **the merchant people are cut down;** all they that bear silver are cut off.

12. **And** it shall come to pass at that time, *that* **I will search Jerusalem** with candles, **and punish the men** that are settled on their lees: **that say** in their heart, **The LORD will not do good, neither** will he do **evil.**

13. Therefore their goods shall become a booty, and their houses a desolation: they shall also build houses, but not inhabit *them;* and they shall plant vineyards, but not drink the wine thereof.

14. **The** great **day of the LORD is near, it is** near, and hasteth greatly, *even* the voice of the day of the LORD: the mighty man shall cry there bitterly.

15. That day *is* **a day of wrath,** a day of **trouble and distress,** a day of wasteness and desolation, **a day of darkness and gloominess,** a day of clouds and thick darkness,

16. A day of the trumpet and alarm against the fenced cities, and against the high towers.

17. **And** I will bring distress upon **men,** that they

shall walk like blind men, because they have sinned against the LORD: and their blood shall be poured out as dust, and their flesh as the dung.

18. **Neither** their **silver nor** their **gold shall** be able to **deliver them** in the day of the LORD's wrath; **but the** whole land shall be devoured by the **fire of his jealousy:** for he **shall make** even a **speedy riddance of** all **them that dwell in the land.**

CHAPTER 2

1. **Gather yourselves together,** yea, gather together, **O nation not desired;**

2. Before the decree bring forth, *before* the day pass as the chaff, before the fierce anger of the LORD come upon you, **before the** day of the **LORD'S anger come upon you.**

3. **Seek** ye **the LORD,** all **ye meek** of the earth, which have wrought his judgment; **seek righteousness,** seek meekness: **it may be ye shall be hid in the day of the LORD'S anger.**

4. **For Gaza** shall be forsaken, **and Ashkelon** a desolation: they shall drive out Ashdod at the noon day, **and Ekron shall be rooted up.**

5. **Woe unto** the inhabitants of the sea coast, **the nation of the Cherethites! the** word of the **LORD is against you;** **O Canaan,** the land of the Philistines, **I will even destroy thee,** that there shall be no inhabitant.

6. And the sea coast shall be dwellings *and* cottages for shepherds, and folds for flocks.

7. **And the coast shall be for the remnant of** the house of **Judah;** they shall feed thereupon: in the houses of Ashkelon shall they lie down in the evening: **for the LORD** their God **shall visit them, and turn away their captivity.**

8. **I have heard the reproach of Moab, and** the revilings of the children of **Ammon,** whereby they have reproached my people, and magnified *themselves* against their border.

9. **Therefore as I live, saith the LORD** of hosts, the God of Israel, Surely **Moab shall be as Sodom, and** the children of **Ammon as Gomorrah,** *even* the breeding of nettles, and saltpits, and a perpetual desolation: the residue of my people shall spoil them, **and the remnant of my people shall possess them.**

10. This shall they have for their pride, **because they** have **reproached and magnified themselves against the people of the LORD** of hosts.

11. **The LORD** *will be* terrible unto them: for he **will famish all the gods of the earth; and men shall worship him,** every one from his place, **even all the isles of the heathen.**

12. **Ye Ethiopians** also, ye **shall be slain** by my sword.

13. **And he will stretch out his hand against** the north, and destroy **Assyria; and** will make **Nineveh** a desolation, *and* dry like a wilderness.

14. **And** flocks shall lie down in the midst of her, all **the beasts** of the nations: both the

1295

■ cormorant and the bittern
■ **shall lodge in the**
■ **upper lintels** of it; *their* voice shall
sing in the windows; desolation *shall
be* in the thresholds: for he shall
uncover the cedar work.
■ 15. **This is the rejoicing city**
■ **that dwelt carelessly, that**
■ **said** in her heart, I *am*, and
■ **there is none beside me:**
■ **how is she** become a desolation,
■ **a place for beasts**
to lie down in!
■ **every one that**
■ **passeth by** her
■ **shall hiss, and**
■ **wag his hand.**

CHAPTER 3

■ 1. **Woe to her that**
■ **is filthy** and polluted,
■ **to the oppressing city!**
■ 2. **She obeyed not**
the voice; she received not
correction; she trusted not in
■ **the LORD;**
she drew not near to her God.
■ 3. **Her princes** within her
■ **are roaring lions; her**
■ **judges** *are* evening
■ **wolves;** they gnaw not
the bones till the morrow.
■ 4. **Her prophets are** light *and*
■ **treacherous** persons:
■ **her priests have polluted**
■ **the sanctuary,**
they have done violence to the law.
■ 5. **The just LORD**
is in the midst thereof; he
■ **will** not do iniquity:
every morning doth he
■ **bring his judgment to light,**
he faileth not; but the unjust
knoweth no shame.
■ 6. **I have cut off the nations:**
their towers are desolate; I made their
streets waste, that none passeth by:
■ **their cities are destroyed,**
■ **so that there is no**
man, that there is none
■ **inhabitant.**
■ 7. **I said, Surely thou wilt**
■ **fear me,** thou wilt receive

instruction; so their dwelling
should not be cut off,
howsoever I punished them:
■ **but they rose** early,
■ **and corrupted all**
■ **their doings.**
■ 8. **Therefore wait ye upon**
■ **me, saith the LORD,** until the
day that I rise up to the prey:
■ **for my determination is to**
gather the nations, that I may
■ **assemble the kingdoms,**
■ **to pour upon them mine**
indignation, *even* all my fierce
■ **anger:** for all the earth shall be
devoured with the fire of my jealousy.
■ 9. **For then will** I turn to the
people a pure language, that
■ **they** may all
■ **call upon the** name of the
■ **LORD, to serve him**
■ **with one consent.**
10. From beyond the rivers of
Ethiopia my suppliants, *even* the
daughter of my dispersed, shall bring
mine offering.
■ 11. **In that day shalt**
■ **thou not be ashamed**
for all thy doings,
■ **wherein thou hast**
■ **transgressed**
■ **against me:** for then
■ **I will take away**
out of the midst of thee
■ **them that** rejoice in thy
pride, and thou shalt no more
■ **be haughty because**
■ **of my holy mountain.**
12. **I will also leave**
in the midst of thee
■ **an afflicted and poor**
■ **people, and they shall**
■ **trust in the** name of the
■ **LORD.**
13. **The remnant of Israel**
■ **shall not do iniquity,** nor speak
lies; neither shall a deceitful tongue
be found in their mouth: for they shall
feed and lie down,
■ **and none shall make**
■ **them afraid.**
14. **Sing,** O daughter of Zion; shout,
■ **O Israel;**

be glad and rejoice with all the heart,
O daughter of Jerusalem.

15. The LORD hath taken away thy judgments,

he hath cast out thine enemy:
the king of Israel, *even* the LORD,
is in the midst of thee:

thou shalt not see evil any more.

16. In that day

it shall be said to Jerusalem,

Fear thou **not:** *and to* Zion, Let not thine hands be slack.

17. The LORD

thy God in the midst of thee

is mighty; he will save, he will rejoice over thee

with joy; he will rest in his love,
he will joy over thee

with singing.

18. I will gather them

that are sorrowful for the solemn assembly,

who are of thee,

to whom the reproach of it was a burden.

19. Behold, at that time **I will undo all that afflict thee:** and I will save her that halteth, **and** gather her that was driven out; and I **will get them praise and fame** in every land **where they have been put to shame.**

20. At that time will I bring you *again,* even in the time that I **gather you: for I will make you a name** and a praise **among all** people of **the earth,** when I turn back your captivity before your eyes, **saith the LORD.**

WILL A MAN ROB GOD

Will a man rob God?
yet ye have robbed me.
But ye say, wherein
have we robbed thee?
In tithes and offerings.

ye are cursed
with a curse: for ye have
robbed me, even this
whole nation.

Bring ye all the tithes
into the storehouse...
and prove me now
herewith, saith the Lord
of host, if I will not
open the windows of
heaven, and pour.
You out a blessing,
that there shall not
be room enough to
receive it.

And I will rebuke the
devourer for your sakes...
saith the Lord of host.

Micah 4:8–11

THE BOOK OF HAGGAI

BACKGROUND INFORMATION

Author: Haggai
Date Written: 520 B.C.

Number of:
Verses—38
Chapters— 2
Total Words—1,131
Scan Words—511
Scan Words Represent
Approximately 45% of
Total Words

Theme: The building of the Temple under Zerubbabel

OUTLINE OF THE BOOK

I. **The People Challenged**
to Build the Temple
1:1 — 15

II. **The People Respond**
2:1 — 9

III. **The Lord's Encouragement**
received
2:10 — 19

IV. **God's Promise to Zerubbabel**
2:20 — 23

CHAPTER 1

■ 1. **In the second year of**
■ **Darius the king,** in the sixth
month, in the first day of the month,
■ **came the word of the**
■ **LORD by Haggai** the prophet
■ **unto Zerubbabel**
the son of Shealtiel,
■ **governor of Judah, and to**
■ **Joshua** the son of Josedech,
■ **the high priest,** saying,
■ 2. **Thus speaketh the LORD**
of hosts, saying, This people say,
■ **The time is** not
■ **come,** the time
■ **that the LORD'S house**
■ **should be built.**
3. Then came the word of the LORD
by Haggai the prophet, saying,
4. *Is it* time for you, O ye, to dwell in
your cieled houses, and this house *lie*
waste?
■ 5. **Now therefore** thus
saith the LORD of hosts;
■ **Consider your ways.**
■ 6. **Ye have sown much,**
■ **and bring in little; ye eat,**
but ye have not enough;
■ **ye drink, but ye are not**
■ **filled** with drink; ye clothe
you, but there is none warm;
■ **and he** that
■ **earneth wages** earneth wages
■ **to put** *it*
■ **into a bag with holes.**
7. Thus saith the LORD of hosts;
Consider your ways.
■ 8. **Go** up to the mountain,
and bring wood,
■ **and build the house; and**
■ **I will take pleasure in it,**
■ **and I will be glorified,**
■ **saith the LORD.**
■ 9. **Ye looked for much, and,**
■ **lo it came to little;** and when ye
brought it home, I did blow upon it.
Why? saith the LORD of hosts.
■ **Because of mine house that**
■ **is waste,** and ye run
every man unto his own house.
■ 10. **Therefore the**
■ **heaven** over you
■ **is stayed from dew,**

■ **and the earth** is stayed
■ **from her fruit.**
■ 11. **And I called for a**
■ **drought upon the land,** and
upon the mountains, and upon the
corn, and upon the new wine, and
upon the oil, and upon *that* which the
ground bringeth forth, and upon men,
and upon cattle,
■ **and upon** all
■ **the labour of the hands.**
■ 12. **Then Zerubbabel**
the son of Shealtiel,
■ **and Joshua** the son of
Josedech, the high priest,
■ **with all** the remnant of
■ **the people, obeyed**
■ **the** voice of the
■ **LORD** their God, and the words
of Haggai the prophet, as the
LORD their God had sent him,
■ **and** the people
■ **did fear** before
■ **the LORD.**
■ 13. **Then spake Haggai**
the LORD'S messenger in
■ **the LORD'S message unto**
■ **the people, saying,**
■ **I am with you,** saith the LORD.
■ 14. **And the LORD stirred up**
■ **the spirit of Zerubbabel** the
son of Shealtiel, governor
of Judah, and the spirit of
■ **Joshua** the son of
Josedech, the high priest,
■ **and** the spirit of
■ **all** the remnant of
■ **the people; and they came**
■ **and did work in the house**
■ **of the LORD** of hosts, their God,
15. In the four and twentieth day
of the sixth month, in the second
year of Darius the king.

CHAPTER 2

■ 1. **In the seventh month,** in
the one and twentieth *day* of the
■ month, **came the word**
■ **of the LORD by** the prophet
■ **Haggai, saying,**
■ 2. **Speak** now
■ **to Zerubbabel** the son of
Shealtiel, governor of Judah,

and to Joshua the son of Josedech, the high priest,

and to the residue of the people, saying,

3. Who is left among you that saw this house in her first glory? and how do ye see it now? is it not in your eyes in comparison of it as nothing?

4. Yet now be strong, O Zerubbabel, saith the LORD; and be strong, O Joshua, son of Josedech, the high priest; and be strong, all ye people of the land, saith the LORD, and work: for I am with you, saith the LORD of hosts:

5. According to the word that I covenanted with you when ye came out of Egypt, so my spirit remaineth among you: fear ye not.

6. For thus saith the LORD of hosts; Yet once, it is a little while, and I will shake the heavens, and the earth, and the sea, and the dry land;

7. And I will shake all nations, and the desire of all nations shall come: and I will fill this house with glory, saith the LORD of hosts.

8. The silver is mine, and the gold is mine, saith the LORD of hosts.

9. The glory of this latter house shall be greater than of the former, saith the LORD of hosts: and in this place will I give peace, saith the LORD of hosts.

10. In the four and twentieth day of the ninth month, in the second year of Darius, came the word of the LORD by Haggai the prophet, saying,

11. Thus saith the LORD of hosts; Ask now the priests concerning the law, saying,

12. If one bear holy flesh in the skirt of his garment, and with his skirt do touch bread, or pottage, or wine, or oil, or any meat, shall it be holy? And the priests answered and said, No.

13. Then said Haggai, If one that is unclean by a dead body touch any of these, shall it be unclean? And the priests answered and said, It shall be unclean.

14. Then answered Haggai, and said, So is this people, and so is this nation before me, saith the LORD; and so is every work of their hands; and that which they offer there is unclean.

15. And now, I pray you, consider from this day and upward, from before a stone was laid upon a stone in the temple of the LORD:

16. Since those days were, whenone came to an heap of twenty measures, there were but ten: when one came to the pressfat for to draw out fifty vessels out of the press, there were but twenty.

17. I smote you with blasting and with mildew and with hail in all the labours of your hands; yet ye turned not to me, saith the LORD.

18. Consider now from this day and upward, from the four and twentieth day of the ninth month, even from the day that the foundation of the LORD'S temple was laid, consider it.

19. Is the seed yet in the barn? yea, as yet the vine, and the fig tree, and the pomegranate, and the olive tree, hath not brought forth:

■ **from this day will I**
■ **bless you.**

20. And again the word of the LORD came unto Haggai in the four and twentieth *day* of the month, saying,

21. Speak to Zerubbabel, governor of Judah, saying, I will shake the heavens and the earth;

■ 22. **And I will overthrow**
■ **the throne of**
■ **kingdoms, and** I will

■ **destroy the strength** of the kingdoms
■ **of the heathen;** and I will overthrow the chariots, and those that ride in them; and the horses and their riders shall come down, every one by the sword of his brother.

■ 23. **In that day,** saith the LORD of hosts,
■ **will I take thee, O**
■ **Zerubbabel,** my servant, the son of Shealtiel, saith the LORD,
■ **and will make thee as a**
■ **signet: for I have chosen**
■ **thee,** saith the LORD of hosts.

THE BOOK OF ZECHARIAH

BACKGROUND INFORMATION

Author: Zechariah
Date Written: 520 B.C.

Number of:
Verses—211
Chapters—14
Total Words—6,444
Scan Words—2,861
Scan Words Represent
Approximately 44% of
Total Words

Theme: Eight Visions
to Zechariah
**and The Coming
Restoration of Jerusalem**

OUTLINE OF THE BOOK

I. **The Messianic and Millennial Visions**
   1:1 — 6:15
II. **Discussion on Fasting**
   1:1 — 8:23
III. **The Prophecies of the Coming King**
   9:1 — 14:21

CHAPTER 1

1. **In the** eighth month, in the **second year of Darius, came the word of the LORD unto Zechariah,** the son of Berechiah, the son of Iddo the prophet, **saying,** 2. **The LORD hath been** sore **displeased with your fathers.** 3. **Therefore** say thou unto them, Thus saith the LORD of hosts; **Turn ye unto me, saith the LORD** of hosts, **and I will turn unto you,** saith the LORD of hosts. 4. **Be ye not as your fathers, unto whom the** former **prophets** have **cried,** saying, Thus saith the LORD of hosts; **Turn** ye now **from your evil ways,** and *from* your evil doings: **but they did not hear,** nor hearken unto me, saith the LORD. 5. **Your fathers, where are they? and the prophets, do they live** for ever? 6. **But my words and** my **statutes,** which I commanded my servants the prophets, **did they not take hold of your fathers? and they returned and said,** Like as the LORD of hosts thought to do unto us, **according to our ways,** and according to our doings, so hath **he dealt with us.** 7. Upon the four and twentieth day of **the eleventh month,** which *is* the month Sebat, in **the second year of Darius, came the word of the LORD unto Zechariah,** the son of Berechiah, the son of Iddo the prophet, saying, 8. **I saw** by night, and behold **a man riding upon a red horse, and he stood among the myrtle trees** that *were* in the bottom; and behind him *were-there* red horses, speckled, and white. 9. **Then said I,** O my lord, **what are these?** And the angel that talked with me said unto me, I will shew thee what these *be.* 10. **And the man** that stood **among the myrtle trees answered** and said, **These** *are they* whom the LORD hath sent to **walk to and fro through the earth.** 11. **And they answered the angel** of the LORD **that stood among the myrtle trees,** and said, We have walked to and fro through the earth, and, behold, **all the earth sitteth still, and is at rest.** 12. **Then the angel** of the LORD answered and **said, O LORD** of hosts, **how long wilt thou not have mercy on Jerusalem** and on the cities of Judah, against which **thou hast had indignation** these **threescore and ten years?** 13. **And the LORD answered** the angel that talked with me *with* good words *and* comfortable words. 14. So the angel that communed with me said unto me, Cry thou, saying, Thus saith the LORD of hosts; **I am jealous for Jerusalem** and for Zion with a great jealousy. 15. **And** I **am very** sore **displeased with the heathen that are at ease:** for I was but a little displeased, and they helped forward the affliction. 16. **Therefore** thus saith the LORD; **I am returned to Jerusalem with mercies: my house shall be built in** it, saith the LORD of hosts, and a line shall be stretched forth upon **Jerusalem.** 17. Cry yet, saying, Thus

saith the LORD of hosts;
My cities through prosperity
shall yet
be spread abroad;
and the LORD shall yet
comfort Zion, and shall yet
choose Jerusalem.
18. **Then** lifted
I up mine eyes, and
saw, and behold
four horns.
19. **And I said unto the**
angel that talked with me,
What be these?
And he answered me,
These *are* the horns which
have scattered Judah,
Israel, and Jerusalem.
20. **And the LORD shewed**
me four carpenters.
21. **Then said I, What come**
these to do? And he spake,
saying, These *are* the horns which
have scattered Judah, so that
no man did lift up his head: but
these are come to fray them,
to cast out the horns of the
Gentiles, which lifted up
their horn over the land of
Judah to scatter it.

CHAPTER 2

1. **I** lifted up mine eyes again, and
looked, and behold
a man with a measuring
line in his hand.
2. **Then said I, Whither goest**
thou? And he said unto me,
To measure Jerusalem,
to see what *is*
the breadth thereof,
and what *is*
the length thereof.
3. **And,** behold,
the angel that talked with me
went forth, and another
angel went out
to meet him,
4. **And said** unto him, Run,
speak to this young man, saying,
Jerusalem shall be
inhabited as towns
without walls for the multitude

of men and cattle therein:
5. **For** I, saith
the LORD, will be unto
her a
wall of fire round about,
and will be
the glory in the midst of her.
6. Ho, ho, *come forth,* and
flee from the land of the
north, saith the LORD:
for I have spread you
abroad as the four winds
of the heaven, saith the LORD.
7. **Deliver thyself, O Zion,**
that dwellest *with* the
daughter of Babylon.
8. **For** thus saith the LORD
of hosts; After the glory hath
he sent me unto the nations
which spoiled you: for he
that toucheth you toucheth
the apple of his eye.
9. **For,** behold,
I will shake mine
hand upon them,
and they shall be a
spoil to their servants:
and ye shall know that the
LORD of hosts hath sent me.
10. **Sing and rejoice,**
O daughter of
Zion: for, lo, I come, and
I will dwell in the midst of
thee, saith the LORD.
11. **And many nations shall**
be joined to the LORD in
that day, and shall be my people:
and I will dwell in the midst of thee,
and thou shalt
know that the LORD of hosts
hath sent me unto thee.
12. **And** the LORD shall inherit
Judah his portion in the holy land, and
shall choose
Jerusalem again.
13. **Be silent,** O all flesh, before
the LORD: for he
is raised up
out of his holy habitation.

CHAPTER 3

1. **And he shewed me**
Joshua the high priest

standing before the
angel of the LORD,
and Satan standing
at his right hand to
resist him.
2. And the LORD said unto
Satan, The LORD rebuke
thee, O Satan; even the LORD that
hath chosen Jerusalem rebuke thee:
is not this a brand plucked
out of the fire?
3. Now Joshua was clothed
with filthy garments,
and stood before the angel.
4. And he answered and
spake unto those that stood
before him, saying,
Take away the filthy
garments from him. And
unto him he said, Behold,
I have caused thine iniquity
to pass from thee, and I will
clothe thee with change of raiment.
5. And I said, Let them set a
fair mitre upon his head.
So they set a fair mitre upon
his head, and clothed him
with garments. And the angel of
the LORD stood by.
6. And the angel of the LORD
protested unto
Joshua, saying,
7. Thus saith the LORD of hosts;
If thou wilt walk in my ways, and
if thou wilt keep my charge,
then thou shalt also
judge my house,
and shalt also
keep my courts, and I will
give thee places to walk
among these that stand by.
8. Hear now, O Joshua
the high priest, thou, and thy
fellows that sit before thee:
for they *are* men wondered at:
for, behold, I will bring forth
my servant the BRANCH.
9. For behold
the stone that I have laid
before Joshua; upon one stone
shall be seven eyes: behold,
I will engrave the graving
thereof, saith the LORD of hosts,

and I will
remove the iniquity of
that land in one day.
10. In that day, saith the
LORD of hosts,
shall ye call every man
his neighbour under
the vine and under the
fig tree.

CHAPTER 4

1. And the angel that
talked with me came again, and
waked me, as a man
that is wakened
out of his
sleep.
2. And said unto me,
What seest thou?
And I said, I have
looked, and behold
a candlestick all
of gold, with a bowl
upon the top of it,
and his
seven lamps thereon,
and seven pipes to the
seven lamps, which *are*
upon the top thereof:
3. And two olive trees by it,
one upon the right *side* of the
bowl, and the other upon the
left *side* thereof.
4. So I answered and spake to
the angel that talked with me, saying,
What are these, my lord?
5. Then the angel that talked
with me answered and said
unto me, Knowest thou not what
these be? And I said, No, my lord.
6. Then he answered and
spake unto me, saying,
This is the word of the LORD
unto Zerubbabel, saying,
Not by might, nor by
power, but by my spirit,
saith the LORD of hosts.
7. Who *art* thou, O great mountain?
before Zerubbabel *thou shalt become*
a plain: and he shall bring forth the
headstone *thereof with* shoutings,
crying, Grace, grace unto it.
8. Moreover the word of

the LORD came unto me, saying,

9. The hands of Zerubbabel have laid the foundation of this house; his hands shall also finish it; and thou shalt know that the LORD of hosts hath sent me unto you.

10. For who hath despised the day of small things? for they shall rejoice, and shall see the plummet in the hand of Zerubbabel with those seven; they are the eyes of the LORD, which run to and fro through the whole earth.

11. Then answered I, and said unto him, What are these two olive trees upon the right side of the candlestick and upon the left *side* thereof?

12. And I answered again, and said unto him, What *be* these two olive branches which through the two golden pipes empty the golden oil out of themselves?

13. And he answered me and said, Knowest thou not what these *be?* And I said, No, my lord.

14. Then said he, These are the two anointed ones, that stand by the LORD of the whole earth.

CHAPTER 5

1. Then I turned, and lifted up mine eyes, and looked, and behold a flying roll.

2. And he said unto me, What seest thou? And I answered, I see a flying roll; the length thereof is twenty cubits, and the breadth thereof ten cubits.

3. Then said he unto me, This is the curse that goeth forth over the face of the whole earth: for every one that stealeth shall be cut off *as* on this side according to it; and every one that sweareth shall be cut off *as* on that side according to it.

4. I will bring it forth, saith the LORD of hosts, and it shall enter into the house of the thief, and into the house of him that sweareth falsely by my name: and it shall remain in the midst of his house, and shall consume it with the timber thereof and the stones thereof.

5. Then the angel that talked with me went forth, and said unto me, Lift up now thine eyes, and see what is this that goeth forth.

6. And I said, What *is* it? And he said, This is an ephah that goeth forth. He said moreover, This *is* their resemblance through all the earth.

7. And, behold, there was lifted up a talent of lead: and this *is* a woman that sitteth in the midst of the ephah.

8. And he said, This is wickedness. And he cast it into the midst of the ephah; and he cast the weight of lead upon the mouth thereof.

9. Then lifted I up mine eyes, and looked, and, behold, there came out two women, and the wind *was* in their wings; for they had wings like the wings of a stork: and they lifted up the ephah between the earth and the heaven.

10. Then said I to the angel that talked with me,

■ Whither do these
■ bear the ephah?
■ 11. **And he said** unto me,
■ **To build it an house in**
the land of
■ **Shinar: and** it shall be
established, and set there
■ **upon her own base.**

CHAPTER 6

■ 1. **And I** turned, and I
ifted up mine eyes, and
■ **looked, and,** behold,
■ **there came four chariots** out
■ **from between two**
■ **mountains;** and the
mountains *were* mountains
■ **of brass.**
■ 2. **In the first chariot were**
■ **red horses; and in the**
■ **second** chariot
■ **black horses;**
■ 3. **And in the third** chariot
■ **white horses; and in the**
■ **fourth** chariot
■ **grisled and bay horses.**
4. Then I answered and said
unto the angel that talked with
me, What *are* these, my lord?
5. And the angel answered
and said unto me,
■ **These are the four spirits**
of the heavens, which go forth
■ **from** standing
■ **before the LORD** of all the earth.
■ 6. **The black horses**
which *are* therein
■ **go forth into the north** country;
■ **and the white** go forth
■ **after them; and the**
■ **grisled** go forth
■ **toward the south** country.
■ 7. **And the bay** went forth, and
■ **sought to** go that they might
■ **walk** to and fro
■ **through the earth:** and he said,
Get you hence, walk to and fro
through the earth. So they walked
to and fro through the earth.
■ 8. **Then** cried
■ **he** upon me, and
■ **spake unto me,** saying, Behold,
■ **these that go toward the**

■ **north country have**
■ **quieted my spirit in**
■ **the north country.**
9. And the word of the LORD
came unto me, saying,
■ 10. **Take of them of the**
■ **captivity,** *even* of Heldai, of
Tobijah, and of Jedaiah,
■ **which** are
■ **come from Babylon, and**
■ **come** thou the same day, and go
■ **into the house of Josiah**
the son of Zephaniah;
■ 11. **Then** take silver and gold, and
■ **make crowns, and set them**
■ **upon the head of Joshua** the
son of Josedech, the high priest;
12. And speak unto him, saying,
Thus speaketh the LORD of hosts,
■ **saying, Behold the man**
■ **whose name is The**
■ **BRANCH; and he** shall grow up
out of his place, and he
■ **shall build the temple**
■ **of the LORD:**
13. Even he shall build the
temple of the LORD;
■ **and he**
■ **shall bear the glory,**
■ **and shall** sit and
■ **rule** upon his throne;
■ **and** he shall
■ **be a priest** upon his throne:
and the counsel of peace shall
be between them both.
■ 14. **And the crowns shall be**
to Helem, and to Tobijah, and to
Jedaiah, and to Hen the son of
Zephaniah, for
■ **a memorial in the**
■ **temple of the LORD.**
■ 15. **And they that are far off**
■ **shall come and build in the**
■ **temple** of the LORD, and ye shall
know that the LORD of hosts hath
sent me unto you.
■ **And this shall come**
■ **to pass, if ye will** diligently
■ **obey the** voice of the
■ **LORD** your God.

CHAPTER 7

■■ 1. **And** it came to pass

in the fourth year of king
Darius, *that* the word of the LORD
came unto Zechariah in the fourth *day*
of the ninth month, *even* in Chisleu;
2. **When they** had
sent unto the house
of God Sherezer and
Regem-melech, and their men,
to pray before the LORD,
3. **And to speak unto**
the priests which *were* in the
house of the LORD of hosts,
and to the
prophets, saying, Should I
weep in the fifth month,
separating myself, as I
have done these
so many years?
4. **Then came the word**
of the LORD of hosts
unto me, saying,
5. **Speak unto all**
the people of the land,
and to
the priests, saying,
When ye fasted and mourned
in the fifth and seventh *month,* even
those seventy years, did
ye at all fast unto me,
even to me?
6. **And** when
ye did eat, and when ye did
drink, did not ye eat
for yourselves, and
drink *for yourselves?*
7. **Should ye not**
hear the words which
the LORD hath
cried by the former
prophets, when Jerusalem
was inhabited and
in prosperity, and the cities
thereof round about her, when *men*
inhabited the south and the plain?
8. **And the word of the**
LORD came unto
Zechariah, saying,
9. Thus speaketh the
LORD of hosts, saying,
Execute true judgment,
and shew mercy and
compassions every
man to his brother:

10. **And oppress not** the
widow, nor the fatherless, the
stranger, nor the poor;
and let none of you
imagine evil against
his brother in your heart.
11. **But they refused to**
hearken, and pulled away the
shoulder, and stopped their ears, that
they should not hear.
12. Yea, they made their hearts *as*
an adamant stone, lest they should
hear the law, and the words which the
LORD of hosts hath sent in his spirit
by the former prophets:
therefore came a great
wrath from the LORD of hosts.
13. Therefore it is come to pass, *that*
as he cried, and they would not hear;
so they cried, and I would not hear,
saith the LORD of hosts:
14. **But I scattered**
them with a whirlwind
among all the nations
whom they knew not. Thus
the land was desolate after
them, that no man passed through
nor returned: for they laid the
pleasant land desolate.

CHAPTER 8

1. **Again the word**
of the LORD of hosts
came *to me,*
saying,
2. Thus saith the LORD of hosts;
I was jealous for Zion
with great jealousy, and
I was jealous for her
with great fury.
3. Thus saith the LORD;
I am returned unto Zion,
and will dwell in the midst of
Jerusalem: and Jerusalem
shall be called a city of
truth; and the mountain of the
LORD of hosts the
holy mountain.
4. Thus saith the LORD of hosts;
There shall yet
old men and old
women dwell in the streets
of Jerusalem, and every man with his

staff in his hand for very age.

5. **And** the streets of the city shall be full of **boys and girls playing in the streets** thereof.

6. Thus saith the LORD of hosts; **If it be marvellous in the eyes of the remnant of this people** in these days, **should it also be** marvellous **in mine eyes? saith the LORD** of hosts.

7. Thus saith the LORD of hosts; Behold, **I will save my people from the east** country, **and** from the **west** country;

8. **And** I will **bring them, and they shall dwell in** the midst of **Jerusalem: and** they shall **be my people,** and I will be their God, in truth and in righteousness.

9. **Thus saith the LORD** of hosts; Let your hands **be strong,** ye that hear in these days **these words** by the mouth **of the prophets, which were in the day that the foundation of the house of the LORD of hosts was laid,** that the temple might be built.

10. **For before these days there was no hire** for an, nor any hire for beast; **neither** *was there* **any peace** to him that went out or came in **because** of the affliction: for **I set** all men **every one against his neighbour.**

11. **But now I will not be unto** the residue of **this people as in the former days,** saith the LORD of hosts.

12. **For the seed shall** *be* prosperous; the vine shall **give her fruit, and the ground** shall give **her increase,** and the heavens

shall give their dew; **and I will cause** the remnant of **this people to possess all these things.**

13. And it shall come to pass, *that* as **ye were a curse among the heathen,** O house of Judah, and house of Israel; **so will I save you, and ye shall be a blessing:** fear not, *but* let your hands be strong.

14. For thus saith the LORD of hosts; As I thought to punish you, when your fathers provoked me to wrath, saith the LORD of hosts, and I repented not:

15. **So again have I thought in these days to do well unto Jerusalem and** to the house of **Judah:** fear ye not.

16. **These** *are* the **things** that **ye shall do; Speak** ye every man **the truth** to his neighbour; **execute the judgment of truth and peace** in your gates:

17. **And let none** of you **imagine evil in your hearts** against his neighbour; **and love no false oath:** for all **these** *are* **things** that **I hate, saith the LORD.**

18. And the word of the LORD of hosts came unto me, saying,

19. Thus saith the LORD of hosts; **The fast of the fourth month,** and the fast of the **fifth,** and the fast of the **seventh, and** the fast of the **tenth, shall be** to the house **of** Judah **joy and gladness, and cheerful feasts;** therefore love the truth and peace.

20. Thus saith the LORD of hosts; *It shall yet come to pass,* that there shall come people, and the inhabitants of many cities:

21. **And the inhabitants of one city shall go to**

another, saying,
Let us go speedily to
pray before the LORD,
and to
seek the LORD
of hosts: I will go also.
22. Yea, many people
and strong nations
shall come to
seek the LORD of hosts
in Jerusalem, and to pray
before the LORD.
23. Thus saith the LORD of hosts;
In those days it shall
come to pass, that ten
men shall take hold
out of all languages
of the nations, even
shall take hold of
the skirt of him that is
a Jew, saying, We will go
with you: for we have heard that
God is with you.

CHAPTER 9

1. The burden of the word
of the LORD in the land of
Hadrach, and Damascus
shall be the rest thereof:
when the eyes of man, as
of all the tribes of
Israel, shall be
toward the LORD.
2. And Hamath also
shall border thereby;
Tyrus, and Zidon,
though it be very
wise.
3. And Tyrus did build herself a
strong hold, and heaped up silver as
the dust, and fine gold as the mire of
the streets.
4. Behold, the LORD
will cast her out, and he
will smite her power in the sea;
and she shall be
devoured with fire.
5. Ashkelon shall see it, and fear;
Gaza also shall see it,
and be very sorrowful,
and Ekron; for her expectation
shall be ashamed; and the king shall
perish from Gaza, and Ashkelon

shall not be inhabited.
6. And a bastard shall dwell in
Ashdod, and I will cut off the
pride of the Philistines.
7. And I will take away his blood out
of his mouth, and his abominations
from between his teeth:
but he that
remaineth, even he,
shall be for our God, and he
shall be as a governor in
Judah, and Ekron as a Jebusite.
8. And I will encamp about
mine house because of the army,
because of him that passeth by, and
because of him that returneth:
and no oppressor shall
pass through them any more:
for now have I seen with mine eyes.
9. Rejoice greatly, O
daughter of Zion; shout, O
daughter of Jerusalem: behold,
thy King cometh unto thee:
he is just, and
having salvation; lowly,
and riding upon an ass,
and upon a colt
the foal of an ass.
10. And I will cut off the chariot
from Ephraim, and the horse from
Jerusalem, and the battle
bow shall be cut off:
and he shall speak peace
unto the heathen: and his
dominion shall be from sea
even to sea, and from the river even
to the ends of the earth.
11. As for thee also, by the
blood of thy covenant I have
sent forth
thy prisoners out of the pit
wherein is no water.
12. Turn you
to the strong hold, ye prisoners
of hope: even to day do I declare that
I will render double
unto thee;
13. When I have bent Judah
for me, filled the bow with Ephraim,
and raised up
thy sons, O Zion,
against thy sons, O
Greece, and made

thee as the sword of a **mighty** man.

14. And the LORD shall be seen over them, and his arrow shall go forth as the lightning: and the LORD God shall blow the trumpet, and shall go with whirlwinds of the south.

15. **The LORD** of hosts **shall defend them;** and they shall devour, and subdue with sling stones; and they shall drink, *and* make a noise as through wine; and they shall be filled like bowls, *and* as the corners of the altar.

16. **And** the LORD their God shall **save them** in that day as the flock of his people: for **they shall be as the stones of a crown,** lifted up as **an ensign upon his land.**

17. **For how great is his goodness, and** how great *is* his **beauty!** corn shall make the young men cheerful, and new wine the maids.

CHAPTER 10

1. **Ask ye of the LORD rain** in the time of the latter rain; **so the LORD shall make** bright **clouds, and give them showers** of rain, to every one grass in the field.

2. **For the idols have spoken vanity, and the diviners** have seen a lie, and have told false dreams; they **comfort in vain: therefore they went their way as a flock,** they were troubled, **because there was no shepherd.**

3. Mine anger was kindled **against the shepherds,** and I punished the goats: **for the LORD** of hosts hath **visited** his flock the house of **Judah, and** hath **made them as his goodly horse** in the battle.

4. Out of him came forth the corner, out of him the nail, out of him the battle bow, out of him every oppressor together.

5. **And they shall** be as mighty *men,* which **tread down their enemies** in the mire of the streets in the battle: and they shall fight, **because the LORD is with them,** and the riders on horses shall be confounded.

6. **And I will strengthen** the house of **Judah, and** I will **save the house of Joseph,** and I will bring them again to place them; for I have mercy upon them: and they shall be as though I had not cast them off: **for I am the LORD** their God, **and will hear them.**

7. **And** *they* of **Ephraim shall be** like a **mighty** *man,* **and** their heart shall rejoice as through wine: yea, their children shall see *it,* and be glad; their heart **shall rejoice in the LORD.**

8. **I will** hiss for them, and **gather them; for I have redeemed them:** and they shall increase as they have increased.

9. And I will sow them among the people: **and they shall remember me in far countries; and** they shall live with their children, and **turn again.**

10. **I will bring them** again also out of the land of Egypt, and gather them out of Assyria; and I will bring them **into the land of Gilead and Lebanon;** and *place* shall not be found for them.

11. **And he shall pass through** the sea with **affliction,** and shall smite the waves in the sea, and all the deeps of the river shall dry up: **and** the pride of **Assyria shall be brought down,** and the sceptre of Egypt shall depart away.

12. **And I will strengthen them in the LORD;** and they shall walk up and down in his name, saith the LORD.

CHAPTER 11

1. **Open thy doors, O Lebanon, that the fire may devour thy cedars.**

2. **Howl,** fir tree; for the cedar is fallen; **because the mighty are spoiled:** howl, O ye oaks of Bashan; for the forest of the vintage is come down.

3. *There is* a voice of the howling of **the shepherds;** for their **glory is spoiled:** a voice of the roaring of young lions; for **the pride of Jordan is spoiled.**

4. Thus saith the LORD my God; **Feed the flock** of the slaughter;

5. **Whose possessors slay** them, and hold themselves not guilty: **and** they that sell them **say, Blessed be the LORD; for I am rich: and their own shepherds pity them not.**

6. **For** I will no more pity the inhabitants of the land, saith the LORD: but, lo, **I will deliver the men** every one **into his neighbour's hand,** and into the hand of his king: **and they shall smite the land,** and out of their hand **I will not deliver them.**

7. And I will feed the flock of slaughter, *even* you, O poor of the flock. **And I took** unto me **two staves;** the **one I called Beauty, and the other** I called **Bands;** and I fed the flock.

8. **Three shepherds** also **I cut off** in one month; and my soul lothed them, **and their soul** also **abhorred me.**

9. Then said I, I will not feed you:

that that dieth, let it die; and that that is to be cut off, let it be cut off; and let the rest eat every one the flesh of another.

10. **And I took my staff,** *even* **Beauty, and cut it asunder, that I might break my covenant** which I had made **with** all **the people.**

11. And it was broken in that day: **and so the poor of the flock** that waited upon me **knew that it was the word of the LORD.**

12. **And I said** unto them, If ye think good, **give me my price;** and if not, forbear. **So they weighed** for my price **thirty pieces of silver.**

13. And the LORD said unto me, Cast it unto the potter: a goodly price that I was prised at of them. **And I took the thirty pieces of silver, and cast them to the potter in the house of the LORD.**

14. **Then I cut** asunder **mine other staff, even Bands, that I might break the brotherhood between Judah and Israel.**

15. **And the LORD said** unto me, Take unto thee yet the instruments of a foolish shepherd.

16. **For, lo, I will raise up a shepherd** in the land, **which shall not visit those that be cut off,** neither shall seek the young one, nor heal that that is broken, nor feed that that standeth still: but he shall eat the flesh of the fat, and tear their claws in pieces.

17. **Woe to the idol shepherd that leaveth the flock!** the sword *shall be* upon his arm, and upon his right eye: **his arm shall be** clean **dried up, and his right eye** shall be utterly **darkened.**

CHAPTER 12

■ 1. **The burden of** the word of
■ **the LORD for Israel,** saith the
LORD, which stretcheth forth the
heavens, and layeth the foundation
of the earth, and formeth the spirit
of man within him.

■ 2. **Behold, I will make**
■ **Jerusalem a cup of**
■ **trembling** unto all the people
round about, when they shall be
in the siege both against Judah
and against Jerusalem.

■ 3. **And** in that day
will I make Jerusalem
■ **a burdensome stone for all**
■ **people:** all that burden themselves
with it shall be cut in pieces,
though all the people of
the earth be gathered
together against it.
4. In that day, saith the LORD,
■ **I will smite every horse**
with astonishment,
■ **and his rider** with madness: and I
will open mine eyes upon the house
of Judah, and will smite every horse
of the people with blindness.

■ 5. **And** the governors of
■ **Judah shall say** in their heart,
■ **The inhabitants of**
■ **Jerusalem shall be my**
■ **strength in the LORD**
of hosts their God.

■ 6. **In that day** will I
make the governors of
■ **Judah** like an hearth of fire
among the wood, and like a
torch of fire in a sheaf; and they
■ **shall devour all the people**
■ **round about,** on the
right hand and on the left:
■ **and Jerusalem shall**
■ **be inhabited again in**
■ **her own place,**
even in Jerusalem.

■ 7. **The LORD also**
■ **shall save** the tents of
■ **Judah** first, that the glory of the
house of David and the glory of the
inhabitants of Jerusalem do not
magnify *themselves* against Judah.
8. In that day shall the LORD defend

the inhabitants of Jerusalem; and he
that is feeble among them at that day
shall be as David; and the house of
David *shall be* as God, as the angel
of the LORD before them.

■ 9. **And** it shall come to
pass in that day, *that*
■ **I will** seek to
■ **destroy all the nations that**
■ **come against Jerusalem.**
10. **And I will pour upon the**
■ **house of David, and**
upon the inhabitants of
■ **Jerusalem, the spirit of**
■ **grace** and of supplications:
■ **and they shall look upon**
■ **me whom they have**
■ **pierced, and** they
■ **shall mourn** for him,
■ **as** one mourneth
■ **for his only son,** and shall be in
bitterness for him, as one that is in
bitterness for *his* firstborn.
11. In that day shall there be a great
mourning in Jerusalem, as the
mourning of Hadadrimmon in the
valley of Megiddon.

■ 12. **And the land shall**
■ **mourn, every family apart;**
the family of the house of David apart,
and their wives apart; the family of
the house of Nathan apart, and
their wives apart;
13. The family of the house of Levi
apart, and their wives apart; thefamily
of Shimei apart, and their wives apart;
■ 14. **All the families** that remain,
every family apart,
■ **and their wives apart.**

CHAPTER 13

■ 1. **In that day there shall be**
■ **a fountain opened** to the
house of David and to the
inhabitants of Jerusalem
■ **for sin and for**
■ **uncleanness.**
■ 2. **And** it shall come to
pass in that day, saith
the LORD of hosts, *that*
■ **I will cut off the names of**
■ **the idols out of the land,** and
they shall no more be remembered:

- and also I will cause
- the prophets and the
- unclean spirit to pass
out of the land.
- 3. And it shall come to pass, *that*
- when any shall yet
- prophesy, then
- his father and his
- mother that begat him
- shall say unto him,
- Thou shalt not live;
- for thou speakest lies
- in the name of the LORD:
and his father
- and his mother that begat him
- shall thrust him through
when he prophesieth.
- 4. And it shall come to pass in that
day, *that* the
- prophets shall be
- ashamed every one
- of his vision, when he hath
prophesied; neither shall they wear a
rough garment to deceive:
- 5. But he shall say, I am
- no prophet, I *am* an
husbandman; for man taught
me to keep cattle from my youth.
- 6. And one shall say unto him,
- What are these wounds in
- thine hands? Then he shall
- answer, *Those* with which
- I was wounded in the
- house of my friends.
- 7. Awake, O sword, against
- my shepherd, and against the
man *that is* my fellow,
- saith the LORD of hosts:
- smite the shepherd, and
- the sheep shall be
- scattered: and I will turn mine
hand upon the little ones.
- 8. And it shall come to pass, *that*
- in all the land, saith the LORD,
- two parts therein
- shall be cut off *and*
- die; but the third
- shall be left therein.
- 9. And I will bring the third
- part through the fire, and will
refine them as silver is refined, and
- will try them as gold is tried:
- they shall call on my name,

- and I will hear them:
I will say, It *is* my people:
- and they shall say,
- The LORD is my God.

CHAPTER 14

- 1. Behold, the day of the
- LORD cometh, and thy spoil
shall be divided in the midst of thee.
- 2. For I will gather all
- nations against Jerusalem
- to battle; and the city shall be
taken, and the houses rifled, and the
women ravished; and half of the city
shall go forth into captivity, and the
residue of the people shall not be cut
off from the city.
- 3. Then shall the
- LORD go forth, and
- fight against those nations,
as when he fought in the day of battle.
- 4. And his feet shall
- stand in that day
- upon the mount
- of Olives, which *is*
- before Jerusalem on the
- east, and the mount of Olives
- shall cleave in the
- midst thereof toward the
east and toward the west,
- and there shall be a very
- great valley; and half of the
mountain shall remove toward the
north, and half of it toward the south.
5. And ye shall flee *to* the valley of
the mountains; for the valley of the
mountains shall reach unto Azal: yea,
ye shall flee, like as ye fled from
before the earthquake in the days of
Uzziah king of Judah:
- and the LORD my God
- shall come, and all the
- saints with thee.
6. And it shall come to pass
in that day, *that* the light shall
not be clear, *nor* dark:
7. But it shall be one day which shall
be known to the LORD, not day, nor
night: but it shall come to pass,
that at evening time it shall be light.
- 8. And it shall be in that day, *that*
- living waters shall go out
- from Jerusalem; half of them

toward the former sea, and half of them toward the hinder sea: in summer and in winter shall it be.

9. And the LORD shall be king over all the earth: in that day shall there be one LORD, and his name one.

10. All the land shall be turned as a plain from Geba to Rimmon south of Jerusalem: **and it shall be lifted up,** and inhabited in her place, from Benjamin's gate unto the place of the first gate, unto the corner gate, and *from* the tower of Hananeel unto the king's winepresses.

11. And men shall dwell in it, and there shall be no more utter destruction; but Jerusalem shall be safely inhabited.

12. And this shall be the plague wherewith the LORD will smite all the people that have fought against Jerusalem; Their flesh shall consume away while they stand upon their feet, and **their eyes** shall consume away in their holes, **and their tongue shall consume away** in their mouth.

13. And it shall come to pass in that day, *that* **a great tumult from the LORD shall be among them; and** they shall lay hold **every one** on the hand of his neighbour, and his hand **shall rise up against** the hand of **his neighbour.**

14. And Judah also **shall fight at Jerusalem; and the wealth of all the heathen** round about **shall be gathered** together, gold, and silver, and apparel, **in great abundance.**

15. And so shall be the plague of the horse, of the mule, of the camel, and of the ass, and **of all the beasts** that shall be in these tents, **as this plague.**

16. And it shall come to pass, *that* **every one** that is **left of all the nations which came against Jerusalem shall** even go up from year to year to **worship the King, the LORD** of hosts, and to keep the feast of tabernacles.

17. And it shall be, *that* **whoso will not come up** of *all* the families of the earth unto Jerusalem to worship the King, the LORD of hosts, even **upon them shall be no rain.**

18. And if the family of Egypt go not up, and come not, that *have* no *rain;* **there shall be the plague,** wherewith the LORD will smite the heathen that come not up to keep the feast of tabernacles.

19. This shall be the punishment of Egypt, and the punishment **of all nations that come not up to keep the feast of tabernacles.**

20. In that day shall there be upon the bells of the horses, HOLINESS UNTO THE LORD; and the pots in the LORD's house shall be like the bowls before the altar.

21. Yea, every pot in Jerusalem and in Judah shall be holiness unto the LORD of hosts: **and all** they **that sacrifice** shall come and take of them, and **seethe** therein: and in that day **there shall be no more** the **Canaanite in the house of the LORD** of hosts.

THE BOOK OF MALACHI

BACKGROUND INFORMATION

Author: Malachi
Date Written:
430 — 420 B.C.

Number of:
Verses—55
Chapters—4
Total Words—1,782
Scan Words—864
Scan Words Represent
Approximately 46% of
Total Words.

Theme: Reproof of Evil
Practices,
**and Prophecies
Concerning John
the Baptist and the
Coming Messiah**

OUTLINE OF THE BOOK

I. **Disrespect of God**
and His Will
1:1 — 14

II. **The Priests and** the
People Rebuked
2:1 — 16

III. **The Requirements
of God**
2:17 — 3:15

IV. **The Destiny of the
Righteous and the
Wicked**
3:16 — 4:6

CHAPTER 1

1. **The** burden of the
word of the LORD to
Israel by Malachi.
2. **I have loved you,**
saith the LORD.
Yet ye say, Wherein hast
thou loved us? *Was* not Esau
Jacob's brother? saith the LORD: yet
I loved Jacob,
3. **And I hated Esau, and**
laid his mountains and his
heritage waste
for the dragons of the wilderness.
4. **Whereas Edom saith,**
We are impoverished, but
we will return and build the
desolate places; thus saith
the LORD of hosts,
They shall build, but I will
throw down; and they shall call
them, The border of wickedness, and,
The people against whom the LORD
hath indignation for ever.
5. **And** your eyes shall see, and
ye shall say, The LORD
will be magnified from
the border of
Israel.
6. **A son honoureth his**
father, and a servant his
master: if then I *be* a father,
where is mine honour?
and if I *be* a master, where *is*
my fear? saith the LORD
of hosts unto you,
O priests, that despise
my name. And ye say, Wherein
have we despised thy name?
7. **Ye offer polluted bread**
upon mine altar;
and ye say, Wherein have we
polluted thee? In that
ye say, The table of the
LORD is contemptible.
8. **And** if
ye offer the blind for
sacrifice, *is it* not evil?
and if ye offer
the lame and sick, is it not
evil? offer it now unto thy governor;
will he be pleased with thee, oraccept
thy person? saith the LORD of hosts.

9. **And now,** I pray you,
beseech God that he
will be gracious unto us:
this hath been by your means:
will he regard your persons?
saith the LORD of hosts.
10. Who *is there* even among
you that would shut the doors *for*
nought? neither do
ye kindle fire on mine
altar for nought. I have
no pleasure in you,
saith the LORD of hosts,
neither will I accept
an offering at your hand.
11. **For from the rising**
of the sun even unto the
going down of the same
my name shall be great
among the Gentiles; and in
every place incense *shall be* offered
unto my name, and a pure offering:
for my name *shall be* great among the
heathen, saith the LORD of hosts.
12. **But ye have**
profaned it, in that
ye say, The table of the
LORD is polluted; and
the fruit thereof,
even his meat, is
contemptible.
13. Ye said also, Behold, what a
weariness *is it!* and ye have snuffed
at it, saith the LORD of hosts;
and ye brought that
which was torn, and
the lame, and the
sick; thus ye brought an offering:
should I accept this
of your hand? saith the LORD.
14. **But cursed be the**
deceiver, which hath in
his flock a male, and voweth,
and sacrificeth unto the LORD
a corrupt thing:
for I *am* a great King,
saith the LORD of hosts, and my
name *is* dreadful among the heathen.

CHAPTER 2

1. **And now, O ye priests,** this
commandment *is* for you.
2. **If ye will not hear,**

and if ye will not lay *it* to heart, to **give glory unto my name**, saith the LORD of hosts, **I will** even **send a curse upon you,** and I will curse your blessings: yea, I have cursed them already, because ye do not lay *it* to heart. 3. **Behold, I will corrupt your seed,** and spread dung upon your faces, *even* the dung of your solemn feasts; and *one* shall take you away with it. 4. **And ye shall know that I have sent this commandment** unto you, **that my covenant might be with Levi,** saith the LORD of hosts. 5. **My covenant was with him** of life and peace; **and I gave them to him for** the fear wherewith **he feared me,** and was afraid before my name. 6. **The** law of **truth was in his mouth, and** iniquity was not found in his lips: **he walked with me in peace and** equity, and **did turn many away from iniquity.** 7. For the priest's lips should keep knowledge, and they should seek the law at his mouth: for **he is the messenger of the LORD** of hosts. 8. **But ye** are departed out of the way; ye **have caused many to stumble at the law;** ye have corrupted the covenant of Levi, saith the LORD of hosts. 9. **Therefore have I also made you contemptible** and base before all the people, according as ye have not kept my ways, but have been partial in the law. 10. Have we not all one father? hath not one God created us? **why do we deal treacherously** every man against his brother, **by profaning the covenant** of our fathers?

11. **Judah** hath dealt treacherously, and an abomination is committed in Israel and in Jerusalem; for Judah hath **profaned the holiness of the LORD which he loved, and** hath **married the daughter of a strange god.** 12. **The LORD will cut off the man that doeth this,** the master and the scholar, out of the tabernacles of Jacob, and him that offereth an offering unto the LORD of hosts. 13. **And** this have ye done again, **covering the altar** of the LORD **with tears,** with weeping, and with crying out, insomuch that **he regardeth not the offering** any more, or receiveth *it* with good will at your hand. 14. **Yet ye say,** Wherefore? **Because the LORD** hath been **witness between thee and the wife** of thy youth, **against whom thou hast dealt treacherously: yet is she thy companion,** and the wife of thy covenant. 15. **And did not he make one?** Yet had he the residue of the spirit. And wherefore one? **That he might seek a godly seed.** Therefore take heed to your spirit, and let none deal treacherously against the wife of his youth. 16. **For the LORD,** the God of Israel, **saith that he hateth putting away: for** *one* coObserveth violence with his garment, saith the LORD of hosts: **therefore take heed** to your spirit, **that ye deal not treacherously.** 17. **Ye have wearied the LORD** with your words. Yet ye say, Wherein have we wearied *him*?

When ye say, Every one that doeth evil is good in the sight of the LORD, and he delighteth in them; or, Where *is* the God of judgment?

CHAPTER 3

1. **Behold,** I will send **my messenger,** and he **shall prepare the way before me: and the LORD,** whom ye seek, **shall** suddenly **come to his temple,** even the messenger of the covenant, whom ye delight in: behold, he shall come, saith the LORD of hosts. 2. **But who may abide** the day of his coming? **and who shall stand when he appeareth?** for he *is* like a refiner's fire, and like fullers' soap: 3. **And he shall sit as a refiner** and purifier of silver: **and** he shall **purify the sons of Levi,** and purge them as gold and silver, **that they may offer** unto the LORD **an offering in righteousness.** 4. **Then shall the offering of Judah and Jerusalem be pleasant unto the LORD,** as in the days of old, and as in former years. 5. **And I will come near** to you to judgment; **and** I will be a swift **witness against the sorcerers,** and against the **adulterers,** and against **false swearers, and** against **those that oppress** the hireling in *his* wages, the widow, and the fatherless, and that turn aside the stranger *from his right,* **and fear not me, saith the LORD** of hosts. 6. **For I** *am* the LORD, I **change not;** therefore ye sons of Jacob are not consumed. 7. Even from the days of your fathers ye are gone away from mine ordinances, and have not kept *them.* **Return unto me, and I will return** unto you, saith the LORD of hosts. **But ye said, Wherein shall we return?** 8. **Will a man rob God?** Yet **ye have robbed me.** But ye say, Wherein have we robbed thee? **In tithes and offerings.** 9. **Ye are cursed** with a curse: **for ye have robbed me,** *even* this whole nation. 10. **Bring ye all the tithes into the storehouse, that there may be meat in mine house, and prove me** now herewith, saith the LORD of hosts, **if I will not open** you **the windows of heaven, and pour you out a blessing, that there shall not be room** enough **to receive it.** 11. **And I will rebuke the devourer** for your sakes, **and he shall not destroy the fruits of your ground; neither shall your vine cast her fruit before the time** in the field, saith the LORD of hosts. 12. **And all nations shall call you blessed:** for ye shall be a delightsome land, saith the LORD of hosts. 13. **Your words have been stout against me,** saith the LORD. Yet ye say, What have we spoken *so much* against thee? 14. **Ye have said, It is vain to serve God: and what profit is it** that we have kept his ordinance, and that we have walked mournfully before the LORD of hosts? 15. And now we call the proud happy; yea, **they that work wickedness** are set up; **yea, they that tempt God are** even **delivered.**

16. **Then they that feared the LORD spake** often one to another: **and the LORD hearkened,** and heard *it,* **and a book of remembrance was written** before him **for them** that feared the LORD, and that thought upon his name.

17. **And they shall be mine,** saith the LORD of hosts, **in that day when I make up my jewels; and I will spare them,** as a man spareth his own son that serveth him.

18. **Then shall ye** return, and **discern between the righteous and the wicked,** between him that serveth God and him that serveth him not.

CHAPTER 4

1. **For,** behold, **the day cometh, that** shall burn as an oven; and all the proud, yea, and **all that do wickedly, shall be stubble: and** the day that cometh **shall burn** them up, saith the LORD of hosts, that it shall leave them neither root nor branch.

2. **But unto you that fear my name shall the Sun of righteousness arise with healing in his wings;** and ye shall go forth, and grow up as calves of the stall.

3. **And ye shall tread down the wicked;** for they shall be ashes **under** the soles of **your feet** in the day that I shall do *this,* saith the LORD of hosts.

4. **Remember** ye **the law of Moses** my servant, which I commanded unto him in Horeb for all Israel, **with the statutes and judgments.**

5. **Behold, I will send** you **Elijah** the prophet **before the coming of the great and dreadful day of the LORD:**

6. **And he shall turn the heart of the fathers to the children, and** the heart of the **children to their fathers,** lest I come and smite the earth with a curse.

New Testament

THE GOSPEL ACCORDING TO MATTHEW

BACKGROUND INFORMATION

Author: Matthew, a tax collector who became **one of The Twelve Disciples** of Jesus
Date Written: probably **between 61** and **70** A.D.

Number of:
Verses   1,071
Chapters   28
Total Words   23,684
Scan Words 11,770
Scan Words represent
49 % of Total Words

Theme: showing that **Jesus Christ is the Fulfillment of** The Old Testament **prophecies** concerning the promised Messiah

OUTLINE OF THE GOSPEL

I. **The Birth and Childhood**
   of Jesus Christ
   Chapters 1:1 - 2:23

II. **The Beginning of the Ministry** of Jesus Christ
   Chapters 3:1 - 4:11

III. **The public Ministry** of Jesus Christ in Fulfillment of Old Testament Prophecy
   Chapters 4:12 - 25:46

IV. **The Passion** of Jesus Christ in Fulfillment of Old Testament Prophecy
   Chapters 26:1 - 27:66

V. **The Resurrection** of Jesus Christ
   Chapter 28:1 - 20

CHAPTER 1

■ 1. **The book** of the generation ■ of Jesus Christ, ■ the son of David, ■ the son of Abraham.

2. Abraham begat Isaac; and Isaac begat Jacob; and Jacob begat Judas and his brethren;

3. And Judas begat Phares and Zara of Thamar; and Phares begat Esrom; and Esrom begat Aram;

4. And Aram begat Aminadab; and Aminadab begat Naasson; and Naasson begat Salmon;

5. And Salmon begat Boaz of Rachab; and Boaz begat Obed of Ruth; and Obed begat Jesse;

6. And Jesse begat David the king; and David the king begat Solomon of her *that had been the wife* of Urias;

7. And Solomon begat Roboam; and and Roboam begat Abia; and Abia begat; Asa;

8. And Asa begat Josaphat; and Josaphat begat Joram; and Joram begat Ozias;

9. And Ozias begat Joatham; and Joatham begat Achaz; and Achaz begat Ezekias;

10. And Ezekias begat Manasses; and Manasses begat Amon; and Amon begat Josias;

11. And Josias begat Jechonias and his brethren, about the time they were carried away to Babylon:

12. And after they were sought to Babylon, Jechonias begat Salathiel; and Salathiel begat Zorobabel;

13. And Zorobabel begat Abiud; and Abiud begat Eliakim; and Eliakim begat Azor;

14. And Azor begat Sadoc; and Sadoc begat Achim; and Achim begat Eliud;

15. And Eliud begat Eleazar; and Eleazer begat Matthan; and Matthan begat Jacob;

16. And Jacob begat Joseph the husband of Mary, of whom was born Jesus, who is called Christ.

17. So all the generations ■ **from Abraham to David** ■ **are fourteen generations;** ■ **and from David until the** ■ **carrying away into** ■ **Babylon are fourteen** ■ **generations; and from** the carrying away into ■ **Babylon unto Christ are** ■ **fourteen generations.**

18. **Now** the birth of Jesus Christ was on this wise; ■ **When** as his mother ■ **Mary was espoused to** ■ **Joseph, before they came** ■ **together, she was found** ■ **with child of the** ■ **Holy Ghost.**

19. **Then Joseph** her husband, ■ **being a just man,** and not willing to make her a public example, ■ **was minded to put her** ■ **away** privily.

20. **But** while he thought on these things, behold, ■ **the angel of the LORD** ■ **appeared** unto him in a dream, ■ **saying, Joseph,** thou son of David, **fear not to take** unto thee ■ **Mary** thy wife: **for that which is conceived** **in her is of the Holy Ghost.**

21. **And she shall bring** ■ **forth a son, and** thou shalt ■ **call his name JESUS: for** ■ **he shall save his people** from their sins.

22. **Now all this** was done, that it might be fulfilled which ■ **was spoken** of the Lord ■ **by the prophet, saying,** ■ 23. **Behold, a virgin shall** be with child, and shall ■ **bring forth a son, and** ■ **they shall call his name** ■ **Emmanuel, which** being interpreted ■ **is, God with us.**

24. **Then Joseph** being raised from sleep did as the angel of the Lord has bidden him, and ■ **took unto him his wife:** ■ 25. **And knew her not till she** ■ **had brought forth** her firstborn son: and he called his name ■ **JESUS.**

CHAPTER 2

■ 1. **Now** when Jesus was born in Bethlehem of Judaea
■ **in the days of Herod** the king, behold,
■ **there came wise men**
■ **from the east** to Jerusalem,
■ 2. **Saying, Where is he** that is **born King of the Jews?**
■ **for we have seen**
■ **his star** in the east
■ **and are come to**
■ **worship him.**
■ 3. **When Herod** the king had **heard** *these things,*
■ **he was troubled,** and all Jerusalem with him.
■ 4. **And when he had**
■ **gathered all the chief**
■ **priests and scribes** of the people together,
■ **he demanded** of them
■ **where Christ should**
■ **be born.**
■ 5. **And they said** unto him,
■ **In Bethlehem** of Judaea:
■ **for thus it is written**
■ **by the prophet,**
6. And thou Bethlehem, *in* the land of Judah, art not the least among the princes of Judah, for out of thee shall come a Governor, that shall rule my people Israel.
■ 7. **Then Herod,** when he had privily called the wise men,
■ **inquired** of them diligently
■ **what time the**
■ **star had appeared.**
■ 8. **And he** sent them to Bethlehem, and
■ **said, Go and search** diligently
■ **for the young child;** and when ye found *him,* bring me word again,
■ **that I may** come and
■ **worship him** also.
9. When they had heard the king,
■ **they departed; and, lo, the**
■ **star,** which they saw in the east,
■ **went before them,** till it came
■ **and stood** over
■ **where the** young
■ **child was.**

10. When they saw the star, they rejoiced with exceeding great joy.
■ 11. **And** when they were come into the house,
■ **they saw the** young
■ **child** with Mary his mother, and fell down,
■ **and worshipped him:**
■ **and** when they had opened their treasures, they
■ **presented** unto him
■ **gifts of gold,** and
■ **frankincense, and myrrh.**
■ 12. **And being warned of**
■ **God in a dream that they**
■ **should not return to**
■ **Herod, they departed into**
■ **their own country** another way.
■ 13. **And** when they were departed, behold,
■ **the angel** of the Lord
■ **appeareth to Joseph in a**
■ **dream, saying,** Arise, and
■ **take the young child and**
■ **his mother, and flee into**
■ **Egypt,** and be thou there until I bring thee word:
■ **for Herod will seek** the young child
■ **to destroy him.**
14. When he arose,
■ **he took the young child** and his mother by night,
■ **and departed into Egypt:**
15. And was there until the death of Herod:
■ **that it might be fulfilled**
■ **which was spoken**
■ **of** the Lord by
■ **the prophet, saying, Out of**
■ **Egypt have I called my son.**
■ 16. **Then Herod,** when he saw that he was mocked of the wise men, was exceeding wroth, and sent forth, and
■ **slew all the children** that were
■ **in Bethlehem, and in all**
■ **the coast** thereof,
■ **from two years**
■ **old and under,** according to the time which he had diligently inquired of the wise men.
■ 17. **Then was fulfilled**
■ **that** which was

3

spoken by Jeremy
the prophet, saying,
18. **In Rama was** there a voice
heard, lamentation, and
weeping, and great
mourning, Rachel weeping
for her children, and would not
be comforted, because they are not.
19. **But when Herod**
was dead, behold,
an angel of the Lord
appeareth in a dream
to Joseph in Egypt.
20. **Saying,** Arise, and
take the young child
and his mother, and
go into the land of
Israel: for they are dead which
sought the young child's life.
21. And he arose, and took the
young child and his mother,
and came into the land of Israel.
22. **But when he heard**
that Archelaus did reign
in Judæa in the room of
his father Herod,
he was afraid
to go thither: notwithstanding,
being warned of
God in a dream,
he turned aside
into the parts of
Galilee:
23. And he came
and dwelt in a city called
Nazareth: that it
might be fullfilled
which was spoken by the prophets,
He shall be called a
Nazarene.

CHAPTER 3

1. **In those days came**
John the Baptist, preaching
in the wilderness of Judaea,
2. **And saying, Repent ye:**
for the kingdom of heaven
is at hand.
3. **For this is he** that was
spoken of by the prophet
Esaias, saying, The voice
of one crying in the
wilderness, Prepare ye

the way of the Lord,
make his paths straight.
4. And the same John had his
raiment of camel's hair, and a leathern
girdle about his loins; and his meat
was locusts and wild honey.
5. **Then went out to**
him Jerusalem, and all
Judaea, and all
the region round about
Jordan,
6. **And were baptized**
of him in Jordan,
confessing their sins.
7. **But when he saw** many of
the Pharisees and
Sadducess come to his baptism,
he said unto them,
O generation of vipers,
who hath warned you
to flee from the wrath
to come?
8. **Bring forth** therefore
fruits meet
for repentance:
9. **And think not**
to say within yourselves,
We have Abraham to our
father: for I say unto you, that
God is able of these
stones to raise up children
unto Abraham.
10. And now also the axe is laid unto
the root of the trees: therefore every
tree which bringeth not forth good fruit
is hewn down, and cast into the fire.
11. **I indeed baptize you**
with water unto repentance
but he that cometh after me
is mightier than I, whose
shoes I am not worthy to
bear: he shall baptize you
with the Holy Ghost, and with
fire:
12. Whose fan *is* in his hand, and he
will throughly purge his floor, and
gather his wheat into the garner; but
he will burn up the chaff with
the unquenchable fire.
13. **Then cometh Jesus**
from Galilee to Jordan
unto John, to be
baptized of him.

14. **But John forbad him,** saying, I have need to be baptized of thee, and comest thou to me?

15. **And Jesus** answering **said** unto him, **suffer it to be so** now: for thus it becometh us **to fulfill all righteousness.** Then he suffered him.

16. **And Jesus, when he was baptized, went** up straightway **out of the water: and, lo, the heavens** were **opened** unto him, **and he saw the Spirit of God descending like a dove, and lighting upon him:**

17. **And lo a voice from heaven, saying, This is my beloved Son, in whom I am well pleased.**

CHAPTER 4

1. **Then was Jesus** led up of the Spirit into the wilderness to be **tempted of the devil.**

2. **And when he had fasted forty days and** forty **nights, he was** afterward an **hungered.**

3. And when **the tempter** came to him, he **said, If thou be the Son of God, command that these stones be made bread.**

4. **But he answered** and said, **It is written, Man shall not live by bread alone, but by every word** that proceedeth out of the mouth **of God.**

5. **Then the devil** taketh him up into the holy city, and **setteth him on a pinnacle of the temple,**

6. **And saith** unto him, If thou be the Son of God, **cast thyself down: for it is written,** He shall give his **angels** charge concerning thee: and in *their* hands they **shall bear thee up,** lest at any time thou dash thy foot against a stone.

7. **Jesus said** unto him, **It is written again, Thou shalt not tempt** the Lord thy **God.**

8. **Again, the devil taketh him up into an** exceeding **high mountain, and sheweth him all the kingdoms of the world,** and the glory of them;

9. **And saith** unto him, **All these** things will **I give thee, if thou wilt** fall down and **worship me.**

10. **Then saith Jesus** unto him, **Get thee hence, Satan: for** it is written, Thou shalt **worship the Lord** thy God, **and him only** shalt thou serve.

11. **Then the devil leaveth him, and,** behold, **angels** came and **ministered unto him.**

12. **Now when Jesus had heard that John was cast into prison, he departed into Galilee;**

13. And leaving Nazareth, he came and dwelt in Capernaum, which is upon the sea coast, in the borders of Zabulon and Nephthalim:

14. That it might be fulfilled which was spoken by Esaias the prophet, saying,

15. The land of Zabulon, and the land of Nephthalim, by the way of the sea, beyond Jordan, Galilee of the Gentiles;

16. The people which sat in darkness saw great light; and to them which sat in the region and shadow of death light is sprung up.

17. **From that time Jesus began to preach,** and to say, **Repent: for the kingdom of heaven is at hand.**

18. **And Jesus,** walking by the sea of Galilee, **saw** two brethren, Simon called **Peter, and Andrew his**

brother, casting a net into the sea: for they were fishers.

19. And he saith unto them, Follow me, and I will make you fishers of men.

20. And they straightway left *their* nets, and followed him.

21. And going on from thence, he saw other two brethren, James *the son* of Zebedee, and John his brother, in a ship with Zebedee their father, mending their nets; and he called them.

22. And they immediately left their ship and their father, and followed him.

23. And Jesus went about all Galilee, teaching in their synagogues, and preaching the gospel of the kingdom, and healing all manner of sickness and all manner of disease among the people.

24. And his fame went throughout all Syria: and they brought unto him all sick people that were taken with divers diseases and torments, and those which were possesed with devils, and those which were lunatic, and those that had the palsy; and he healed them.

25. And there followed him great multitudes of people from Galilee, and *from* Decapolis, and *from* Jerusalem, and *from* Judaea, and *from* beyond Jordan.

CHAPTER 5

1. And seeing the multitudes, he went up into a mountain: and when he was set, his disciples came into him:

2. And he opened his mouth, and taught them, saying,

3. Blessed are the poor in spirit: for theirs is the kingdom of heaven.

4. Blessed are they that mourn: for they shall be comforted.

5. Blessed are the meek: for they shall inherit the earth.

6. Blessed are they which do hunger and thirst after righteousness: for they shall be filled.

7. Blessed are the merciful: for they shall obtain mercy.

8. Blessed are the pure in heart: for they shall see God.

9. Blessed are the peacemakers: for they shall be called the children of God.

10. Blessed are they which are persecuted for righteousness' sake: for theirs is the kingdom of heaven.

11. Blessed are ye, when men shall revile you, and persecute you, and shall say all manner of evil against you falsely, for my sake.

12. Rejoice, and be exceeding glad: for great is your reward in heaven: for so persecuted they the prophets which were before you.

13. Ye are the salt of the earth: but if the salt have lost his savour, wherewith shall it be salted? it is thenceforth good for nothing, but to be cast out, and to be trodden under foot of men.

14. Ye are the light of the world. A city that is set on an hill cannot be hid.

15. Neither do men light a candle, and put it under a bushel, but on a candlestick; and it giveth light unto all that are in the house.

16. Let your light so shine before men, that they may see your good works, and glorify your Father

which is in heaven.

17. **Think not that I am come to destroy the law or prophets;** I am not come to destroy, **but to fulfill.**

18. For verily I say unto you, **Till heaven and earth pass, one jot** or one tittle **shall in no wise pass** from the law, **till all be fulfilled.**

19. **Whosoever therefore shall break one of these least commandments, and shall teach men so, he shall be** called the **least in the kingdom** of heaven: **but whosoever shall do and teach them,** the same **shall be called great** in the kingdom of heaven.

20. For I say unto you, That **except your righteousness shall exceed the righteousness of the scribes and Pharisees, ye shall in no case enter into the kingdom** of heaven.

21. **Ye have heard** that it was said by them of old time, **Thou shall not kill;** and whosoever shall kill shall be in danger of the judgment:

22. **But I say** unto you, That **whosoever is angry with his brother without a cause shall be in danger of the judgment: and** whosoever shall say to his brother, Raca, shall be in danger of the council: but **whosoever shall say, Thou fool, shall be in danger of hell** fire.

23. **Therefore if thou bring thy gift to the altar, and** there **rememberest that thy brother hath aught against thee;**

24. **Leave there thy gift** before the altar, **and** go thy way; **first be reconciled to thy brother,** and come and offer thy gift.

25. **Agree with thine adversary quickly,** whiles thou art in the way with him; lest at any time the adversary deliver thee to the judge, and the judge deliver thee to the officer, and thou be cast into prison.

26. Verily I say unto thee, Thou shalt by no means come out thence, till thou has paid the uttermost farthing.

27. **Ye have heard** that it was said by them of old time, **Thou shalt not commit adultery:**

28. **But I say** unto you, That **whosoever looketh on a woman to lust** after her **hath commited adultery** with her already **in his heart.**

29. **And if thy right eye offend thee, pluck it out,** and cast *it* from thee: **for it is profitable for thee that one of thy members shall perish, and not that thy whole body should be cast unto hell.**

30. And if thy right hand offend thee, cut it off, and cast *it* from thee: for it is profitable for thee that one of thy members shall perish, and not *that* thy whole body should be cast unto hell.

31. It hath been said, Whosoever shall put away his wife, let him give her a writing of divorcement:

32. But I say unto you, That **whosoever shall put away his wife, saving for** the cause of **fornication, causeth her to commit adultery: and whosoever shall marry her** that is divorced **committeth adultery.**

33. **Again, ye have heard** that it hath been said by them of old time, **Thou shalt not forswear**

7

thyself, but shalt perform
unto the Lord thine oaths:
34. But I say unto you,
Swear not at all; neither by
heaven; for it is God's throne:
35. Nor by the earth; for it is his
footstool: neither by Jerusalem;
for it is the city of the great King.
36. Neither shalt thy swear by thy
head, because thou canst not make
one hair white or black.
37. But let your communication be, Yea, yea; Nay,
nay: for whatsoever is
more than these
cometh of evil.
38. Ye have heard
that it hath been said,
An eye for an eye,
and a tooth for a tooth:
39. But I say unto you,
That ye resist not evil: but
whosoever shall smite
thee on thy right cheek,
turn to him the other also.
40. And if any man
will sue thee at the law,
and take away thy coat,
let him have thy cloak also.
41. And whosoever shall
compel thee to go a mile,
go with him twain.
42. Give to him that asketh
thee, and from him that
borrow of thee
turn not thou away.
43. Ye have heard
that it hath been said,
Thou shalt love thy
neighbour, and hate
thine enemy.
44. But I say unto you,
Love your enemies,
bless them that curse you, do good
to them that hate you, and pray for
them which despitefully use you,
and persecute you;
45. That ye may be the
children of your Father
which is in heaven:
for he maketh his sun
to rise on evil and on the
good, and sendeth rain on

the just and on the unjust.
46. For if ye love them which
love you, what reward have ye?
do not even the publicans
the same?
47. And if ye salute your
brethren only, what do
ye more than others?
do not the publicans so?
48. Be ye therefore perfect,
even as your Father
which is in heaven
is perfect.

CHAPTER 6

1. Take heed that ye
do not your alms before
men, to be seen of them:
otherwise ye have
no reward of your Father
which is in heaven.
2. Therefore when thou doest *thine*
alms, do not sound a trumpet before
thee, as the hypocrites do in the
synagogues and in the streets, that
they may have glory of men. Verily I
say unto you, They have their reward.
3. But when thou doest
alms, let not thy left hand
know what thy right
hand doeth:
4. That thine alms may be in secret:
and thy Father which
seeth in secret himself
shall reward thee openly.
5. And when thou prayest,
thou shalt not be as the
hypocrites are: for they love to
pray standing in the synagogues and
in the corners of the streets, that they
may be seen of men. Verily I say unto
you, They have their reward.
6. But thou,
when thou prayest, enter
into thy closet,
and when thou hast shut thy door,
pray to thy Father which is
in secret; and thy Father
which seeth in secret
shall reward thee openly.
7. But when ye pray,
use not vain repetitions,
as the heathen *do:* for they think that

they shall be heard for their much speaking.

8. Be not ye therefore like unto them: for **your Father knoweth what** things **ye** have **need** of, before ye ask him.

9. **After this manner** therefore **pray ye: Our Father which art in heaven, Hallowed be Thy name.**

10. **Thy kingdom come, Thy will be done in earth, as it is in heaven.**

11. **Give us this day our daily bread.**

12. **And forgive us our debts, as we forgive our debtors.**

13. **And lead us not into temptation, but deliver us from evil: For thine is the kingdom, and the power, and the glory, for ever. Amen.**

14. **For if ye forgive men** their trespasses, **your heavenly Father will also forgive you:**

15. But if ye forgive not men their trespasses, neither will your Father forgive your trespasses.

16. **Moreover when ye fast, be not, as the hypocrites, of a sad countenance**: for they disfigure their faces, that they may appear unto men to fast. Verily I say unto you, They have their reward.

17. **But** thou, when thou fastest, **anoint thine head, and wash thy face;**

18. **That thou appear not unto men to fast,** but unto thy Father which is in secret: **and thy Father, which seeth in secret, shall reward thee openly.**

19. **Lay not up for yourselves treasures upon earth,** where moth and rust doth corrupt, and where thieves break through and steal:

20. **But lay up** for yourselves **treasures in heaven,** where neither moth nor rust doth corrupt, and where thieves do not break through nor steal:

21. **For where your treasure is, there will your heart be also.**

22. The light of the body is the eye: if therefore thine eye be single, thy whole body shall be full of light.

23. But if thine eye be evil, thy whole body shall be full of darkness. If therefore the light that is in thee be darkness, how great *is* that darkness!

24. **No man can serve two masters:** for either he will hate the one, and love the other; or else he will hold to the one, and despise the other. **Ye cannot serve God and mammon.**

25. **Therefore I say unto you, Take no thought for your life, what ye** shall **eat, or** what ye shall **drink; nor** yet for your body, **what ye** shall **put on.** Is not the life more than meat, and the body than raiment?

26. **Behold the fowls** of the air: for **they sow not, neither do they reap,** nor gather into barns; **yet your** heavenly **Father feedeth them. Are ye not much better than they?**

27. **Which of you by taking thought can add** one cubit **unto his stature?**

28. **And why take** ye **thought for raiment? Consider the lilies** of the field, how they grow; **they toil not,** neither do they spin:

29. **And yet** I say unto you, That even **Solomon** in all his glory **was not arrayed like one of these.**

30. **Wherefore, if God so clothe the grass** of the field, which today is, and tomorrow is cast

into the oven,

shall he not much more clothe you, O ye of little faith?

31. **Therefore take no thought, saying, What shall we eat? or,** What shall we **drink? or, Wherewithal shall we be clothed?**

32. (For after all these things do the Gentiles seek:) for **your** heavenly **Father knoweth** that **ye have need** of all these things.

33. **But seek ye first the kingdom of God, and his righteousness; and all these things shall be added** unto you.

34. **Take therefore no thought for the morrow:** for the morrow shall take thought for the things of itself. Sufficient unto the day is the evil thereof.

CHAPTER 7

1. **Judge not, that ye be not judged.**

2. For with what judgment ye judge, ye shall be judged; and with what measure ye mete, it shall be measured to you again.

3. **And why beholdest** thou **the mote** that is **in thy brother's eye, but considerest not the beam** that is **in thine own eye?**

4. Or how wilt thou say to thy brother, Let me pull out the mote out of thine eye; and, behold, a beam *is* in thine own eye?

5. **Thou hypocrite, first cast out the beam** out **of thine own eye; and then** shalt thou see clearly to **cast out the mote** out **of thy brother's eye.**

6. Give not that which is holy unto the dogs, neither cast ye your pearls before swine, lest they trample them under feet, and turn again and rend you.

7. **Ask, and it shall be given** you; **seek, and ye shall find; knock, and it shall be opened** unto you:

8. For every one that asketh receiveth; and he that seeketh findeth; and to him that knocketh it shall be opened.

9. **Or what man** is there of you, whom **if his son ask bread, will he give him a stone?**

10. Or if he ask a fish, will he give him a serpent?

11. **If ye then, being evil, know how to give good gifts** unto your children, **how much more shall your Father** which is in heaven **give good things to them that ask** him?

12. Therefore all things **whatsoever ye would that men should do to you, do** ye even so **to them:** for this is the law and the prophets.

13. **Enter ye in at the straight gate: for wide is the gate, and broad is the way, that leadeth to destruction,** and many there be which go in there at:

14. **Because straight is the gate, and narrow is the way, which leadeth unto life, and few** there be that **find it.**

15. **Beware of false prophets, which come** to you **in sheep's clothing, but** inwardly they **are** ravening **wolves.**

16. **Ye shall know them by their fruits.** Do men gather grapes of thorns, or figs of thistles?

17. Even so every good tree bringeth forth good fruit; but a corrupt tree bringeth forth evil fruit.

18. **A good tree cannot bring forth evil fruit,** neither *can* a corrupt tree bring forth good fruit.

10

19. Every tree that bringeth not forth good fruit is hewn down, and cast into the fire.

20. Wherefore by their fruits ye shall know them.

21. **Not every one that saith unto me, Lord, Lord, shall enter into the kingdom** of heaven; **but he that doeth the will of my Father** which is in heaven.

22. **Many will say** to me in that day, **Lord, Lord, have we not prophesied in thy name? and in thy name** have **cast out devils?** and in thy name done many wonderful works?

23. **And then will I profess unto them, I never knew you:** depart from me, ye that work iniquity.

24. **Therefore whosoever heareth these sayings** of mine, **and doeth them, I will liken** him **unto a wise man, which built his house upon a rock:**

25. **And the rain** descended, **and the floods** came, **and the winds** blew, and **beat upon that house; and it fell not:** for it was founded upon a rock.

26. **And every one that heareth these sayings** of mine, **and doeth them not, shall be liken unto a foolish man, which built his house upon the sand:**

27. **And the rain** descended **and the floods** came, **and the winds** blew, and **beat upon that house; and it fell: and great was the fall** of it.

28. **And** it came to pass, when Jesus had ended these sayings, **the people were astonished at his doctrine:** 29. **For he taught** them **as one having authority,** and not as the scribes.

CHAPTER 8

1. **When he was come down** from the mountains, great **multitudes followed him.**

2. **And,** behold, there came **a leper** and **worshipped him, saying,** Lord, if thou wilt, **thou canst make me clean.**

3. **And Jesus** put forth *his* hand, and **touched him, saying,** I will; **be thou clean. And** immediately **his leprosy was cleansed.**

4. **And Jesus saith** unto him, **See thou tell no man; but go** thy way, **shew thyself to the priest,** and offer the gift that Moses commanded, **for a testimony** unto them.

5. **And when Jesus** was **entered** into **Capernaum, there came** unto him **a centurion,** beseeching him, 6. And **saying, Lord, my servant lieth** at home **sick of the palsy,** grievously tormented.

7. **And Jesus saith** unto him, **I will come and heal him.**

8. **The centurion** answered and **said, Lord, I am not worthy that thou shouldest come under my roof: but speak the word only, and my servant shall be healed.**

9. For I am a man under authority, having soldiers under me: and I say to this *man,* Go, and he goeth; and to another, Come, and he cometh; and to my servant, Do this, and he doeth *it.*

11

10. **When Jesus heard it, he** marvelled, and **said** to them that followed, Verily I say unto you **I have not found so great faith, no, not in Israel.**

11. And I say unto you, That many shall come from the east and west, and shall sit down with Abraham, and Isaac, and Jacob, in the kingdom of heaven.

12. But the children of the kingdom shall be cast out into outer darkness: there shall be weeping and gnashing of teeth.

13. **And Jesus said unto the centurion,** Go thy way; and **as thou hast believed, so be it done** unto thee. **And his servant was healed** in the selfsame hour.

14. **And when Jesus was come into Peter's house, he saw his wife's mother** laid, and **sick of a fever.**

15. **And he touched her hand, and the fever left** her : and she arose, and ministered unto them.

16. When the even was come, they brought unto him many that were possesed with devils: **and he cast out the spirits with his word, and healed all** that were sick:

17. **That it might be fulfilled** which was spoken by Esaias the prophet, saying, **Himself took our infirmities,** and bare *our* sickness.

18. Now when Jesus saw great multitudes about him, he gave commandment to depart unto the other side.

19. **And a certain scribe** came, and **said** unto him, Master, **I will follow thee** whithersoever thou goest.

20. **And Jesus saith** unto him, The foxes have holes, and the birds of the air *have* nests; but **the Son of man hath not where to lay his head.**

21. **And another** of his disciples **said** unto him, Lord, suffer me first to go and bury my father.

22. **But Jesus said** unto him, Follow me; and **let the dead bury their dead.**

23. **And when he** was **entered** into **a ship, his disciples followed** him.

24. **And, behold, there arose a great tempest** in the sea, insomuch that the ship was covered with the waves: **but he was asleep.**

25. **And his disciples** came to *him*, and **awoke him, saying, Lord, save us:** we perish.

26. **And he saith** unto them, Why are ye fearful, **O ye of little faith? Then he** arose, and **rebuked the winds** and the sea; **and there was a great calm.**

27. **But the men marvelled, saying, What manner of man is this,** that **even the winds and the sea obey him!**

28. **And when he was come** to the other side **into the country of the Gergesenes, there met him two possessed with devils,** coming out of the tombs, exceeding fierce, so that no man might pass by that way.

29. **And, behold, they cried out, saying, What have we to do with thee, Jesus, thou Son of God? art thou come** hither **to torment us before the time?**

30. And there was a good way off from them an herd of many swine feeding.

12

31. So the devils besought him, saying, If thou cast us out, **suffer us to go away into the herd of swine.** 32. **And he said** unto them, **Go.And** when they were come out, **they went into the herd** of swine: **and,** behold, **the whole herd** of swine **ran violently** down a steep place **into the sea, and perished** in the waters. 33. **And they that kept them fled,** and went their ways into the city, **and told every thing,** and what was befallen to the possesed of the devils. 34. **And, behold, the whole city came** out to meet Jesus: **and** when they saw him, they **besought him that he would depart** out of their coasts.

CHAPTER 9

1. **And he** entered into a ship, and passed over, and **came into his own city.** 2. **And,** behold **they brought** to **him a man sick of** the **palsy,** living on a bed: **and Jesus seeing their faith said** unto the sick of the palsy; **Son,** be of good cheer; **thy sins be forgiven** thee. 3. **And, behold,** certain of **the scribes said within themselves, This man blasphemeth.** 4. **And Jesus knowing their thoughts said, Whereof think ye evil** in your hearts? 5. **For whether is easier,** to say, Thy sins be **forgiven** thee; **or** to say, **Arise, and walk?** 6. **But that ye may know** that **the Son** of man **hath power** on earth **to forgive sins, (then saith**

he to the sick of the palsy,) **Arise,** take up thy bed, and go unto thine house. 7. **And he arose,** and departed to his house. 8. But when the multitudes saw *it,* they marvelled, and glorified God, which had given such power unto men. 9. **And as Jesus passed** forth from thence, **he saw** a man, named **Matthew,** sitting at the receipt of custom: **and he saith** unto him, **Follow me. And he** arose, and **followed him.** 10. **And** it came to pass, **as Jesus sat at meat in the house,** behold, **many publicans and sinners** came and **sat down with him** and his disciples. 11. **And when the Pharisees saw it, they said** unto to his disciples, **Why eateth your Master with** publicans and **sinners?** 12. **But** when **Jesus** heard *that,* he **said** unto them, **They that be whole need not a physician,** but they that are sick. 13. But go ye and learn what *that* meaneth, I will have mercy, and not sacrifice: for **I am not come to call the righteous, but sinners to repentance.** 14. **Then came** to him **the disciples of John, saying, Why do we and the Pharisees fast** oft, **but thy disciples fast not?** 15. **And Jesus said** unto them, **Can the children of the bridechamber mourn, as long as the bridegroom is with them?** but the days will come, when the bridegroom shall be taken from them, and then shall they fast.

16. No man putteth a piece of new cloth unto an old garment, for that which is put in to fill it up taketh from the garment, and the rent is made worse.

17. Neither do men put new wine into old bottles: else the bottles break, and the wine runneth out, and the bottles perish: but they put new wine into new bottles, and both are preserved.

18. **While he spake** these things unto them, behold, **there came a certain ruler, and worshipped him, saying, My daughter is** even now **dead: but come** and lay thy hand upon her, **and she shall live.**

19. And Jesus, arose, and followed him, and *so did* his disciples.

20. **And, behold, a woman,** which was diseased **with an issue of blood** twelve years, came behind *him,* and **touched** the hem of **his garment:**

21. **For she said** within herself, **If I may but touch his garment, I shall be whole.**

22. **But Jesus turned** him about, **and** when he saw her, he **said, Daughter,** be of good comfort; **thy faith hath made thee whole.** And the woman was made whole from that hour.

23. **And when Jesus came into the ruler's house,** and saw the minstrels and the people making noise,

24. **He said** unto them, Give place: for **the maid is not dead, but sleepeth. And they laughed him to scorn.**

25. **But** when the people were put forth, **he** went in, and **took her by the hand, and the maid arose.**

26. And the fame hereof went abroad into all that land.

27. **And when Jesus departed** thence, **two blind men followed him,** crying, and saying, *Thou* son of David, have mercy on us.

28. And when he was come **into the house,** the blind men came to him: **and Jesus saith** unto them, **Believe ye that I am able to do this? They said** unto him, **Yea, Lord.**

29. **Then touched he their eyes, saying, According to your faith be it unto you.**

30. **And their eyes were opened;** and Jesus straitly charged them, saying, See *that* no man know it.

31. But they, when they were departed, spread abroad his fame in all that country.

32. **As they went out,** behold, **they brought** to him **a dumb man possessed with a devil.**

33. **And when the devil was cast out, the dumb spake:** and the multitudes marvelled, saying, It was never so seen in Israel.

34. **But the Pharisees said, He casteth out devils through the prince of the devils.**

35. **And Jesus went about** all the cities and villages, **teaching** in their synagogues, **and preaching** the gospel of the kingdom, **and healing** every sickness and every disease among the people.

36. **But when he saw the multitudes, he was moved with compassion** on them, **because they** fainted, and **were** scattered abroad, **as sheep having no shepherd.**

37. **Then saith he** unto his disciples, **The harvest truly is plenteous, but the**

■ **labourers are few;**
■ 38. **Pray ye** therefore
■ **the Lord** of the harvest,
■ **that he will send forth**
■ **labourers** into his harvest.

CHAPTER 10

■ 1. **And** when he called
■ **unto** *him*
■ **his twelve disciples,**
■ **he gave** them
■ **power against unclean**
■ **spirits,** to cast them out,
■ **and to heal all** manner of
■ **sickness** and all
manner of disease.
2. Now the names of the twelve
apostles are these; The first, Simon,
who is called Peter, and Andrew his
brother; James *the son* of Zebedee,
and John his brother;
3. Philip, and Bartholomew; Thomas,
and Matthew the publican; James *the*
son of Alphaeus, and Lebbaeus,
whose surname was Thaddaeus;
4. Simon the Canaanite, and Judas
Iscariot, who also betrayed him.
■ 5. **These twelve Jesus**
sent forth, and
■ **commanded** them,
■ **saying, Go not into** the way of
■ **the Gentiles, and into**
any city of
■ **the Samaritans** enter ye not:
■ 6. **But go rather to the**
■ **lost sheep** of the house
■ **of Israel.**
■ 7. **And** as ye go,
■ **preach, saying, The**
■ **kingdom of heaven**
■ **is at hand.**
■ 8. **Heal** the sick, cleanse the lepers,
■ **raise the dead, cast out**
■ **devils: freely ye have**
■ **received, freely give.**
■ 9. **Provide neither gold,**
■ **nor silver, nor brass in**
■ **your purses,**
10. Nor scrip for *your* journey,
■ **neither two coats, neither**
■ **shoes, nor yet staves: for**
■ **the workman is worthy of**
■ **his meat.**

■ 11. **And into whatsoever**
■ **city** or town
■ **ye shall enter,**
■ **inquire who** in it
■ **is worthy; and there**
■ **abide** till ye go thence.
12. And when ye come into
an house, salute it.
■ 13. **And if the house be**
■ **worthy, let your peace**
■ **come upon it:** but if it be not
worthy, let your peace return to you.
■ 14. **And whosoever shall**
■ **not receive you,**
nor hear your words,
■ **when ye depart**
out of that house or city,
■ **shake off the dust**
■ **of your feet.**
15. Verily I say unto you,
■ **It shall be more tolerable**
■ **for** the land of
■ **Sodom and Gomorrha in**
■ **the day of judgement, than**
■ **for that city.**
■ 16. **Behold, I send you forth**
■ **as sheep in the midst of**
■ **wolves: be** ye therefore
■ **wise as serpents, and**
■ **harmless as doves.**
■ 17. **But beware** of men: for
■ **they will** deliver you up to the
councils, and they will
■ **scourge you**
in their synagogues;
■ 18. **And ye shall be brought**
■ **before governors and**
■ **kings for my sake,**
■ **for a testimony**
against them and the Gentiles.
19. But when they deliver you up,
■ **take no thought** how or
■ **what ye shall speak:**
■ **for it shall be given you**
in that same hour what ye shall speak.
20. **For it is** not ye that speak, but
■ **the Spirit of your Father**
■ **which speaketh** in you.
■ 21. **And the brother**
■ **shall deliver** up the
■ **brother to death, and the**
■ **father the child: and the**
■ **children** shall rise up against

their parents, and cause
them to be put to death.
22. **And ye shall be
hated** of all *men*
**for my name's sake: but
he that endureth** to the end
shall be saved.

23. But when they persecute you in
this city, flee ye into another: for
verily I say unto you, Ye shall not
have gone over the cities of Israel, till
the Son of man be come.

24. The disciples is not above *his*
master, nor the servant
above his lord.

25. It is enough for the disciple that
he be as his master, and the servants
as his lord. If they have called the
master of the house Beelzebub,
how much more *shall they call*
them of his household?

26. **Fear them not therefore:
for there is nothing** covered,
that shall not be revealed;
and hid, that shall not be known.

27. **What I tell you in
darkness,** *that* speak ye in light:
and what ye hear in the ear,
**that preach ye upon
the housetops.**

28. **And fear not them which
kill the body,**
but are not able to kill the soul:
**but rather fear him which is
able to destroy both soul
and body in hell.**

29. **Are not two sparrows
sold for a farthing? and
one of them shall not fall**
on the ground
without your Father.

30. **But the very hairs of your
head are all numbered.**

31. **Fear ye not** therefore,
ye are of more value
than many sparrows.

32. **Whosoever** therefore
**shall confess me before
men, him I will I confess
also before my Father**
which is in heaven.

33. **But whosoever shall
deny me** before men,

him will I also deny before
my **Father** which is in heaven.

34. **Think not that I am
come to send peace**
on earth: I came not to send peace,
but a sword.

35. **For I am come to
set a man** at variance
against his father, and the
daughter against her
mother, and the daughter in law
against her mother in law.

36. And a man's foes *shall be*
they of his own household.

37. **He that loveth father or
mother more that me is not
worthy of me: and he that
loveth son or daughter
more than me is not
worthy** of me.

38. **And he that taketh not
his cross,** and followeth after me,
is not worthy of me.

39. He that findeth his life
shall lose it: and
**he that loseth his life for
my sake shall find it.**

40. **And he that receiveth you
receiveth me, and he that
receiveth me receiveth
him that sent me.**

41. He that receiveth a prophet in the
name of a prophet shall receive a
prophet's reward; and he that
receiveth a righteous man in the
name of a righteous man shall
receive a righteous man's reward.

42. And whosoever shall give to drink
unto one of these little ones a cup of
cold *water* only in the name of a
disciple, verily I say unto you, he shall
in no wise lose his reward.

CHAPTER 11

1. And it came to pass, when Jesus
had made and end of commandinghis
twelve disciples, he departed thence
to teach and to preach in their cities.

2. **Now when John had
heard** in the prison
**the works of Christ, he
sent two of his disciples,**

3. **And said** unto him,

Art thou he that should come, or do we look for another? 4. **Jesus answered** and said unto them, **Go and shew John again those things which ye do hear and see:** 5. The blind receive their sight, and the lame walk, the lepers are cleansed, and the deaf hear, the dead are raised up, and the poor have the gospel preached to them. 6. **And blessed is he, whosoever shall not be offended in me.** 7. **And** as they departed, **Jesus began to say unto the multitudes concerning John, What went ye** out into the wilderness **to see?** A reed shaken with the wind? 8. But what went ye out for to see? A man clothed in soft raiment? behold, they that wear soft *clothing* are in kings' houses. 9. But what went ye out for to see? **A prophet? yea,** I say unto you, **and more than a prophet.** 10. **For this is he, of whom it is written, Behold, I send my messenger** before thy face, **which shall prepare thy way** before thee. 11. Verily I say unto you, Among them that are born of women **there hath not risen a greater than John the Baptist: notwithstanding he that is least in the kingdom** of heaven **is greater** than he. 12. And from the days of John the Baptist until now the kingdom of heaven suffereth violence, and the violent take it by force. 13. For all the prophet and the law prophesied until John. 14. **And if ye will receive it, this is Elias, which was for to come.** 15. He that hath ears to hear, let him hear.

16. **But whereunto shall I liken this generation?** It is like unto children sitting in the markets, and calling unto their fellows, 17. And saying, We have piped unto you, and ye have not danced; we have mourned unto you, and ye have not lamented. 18. **For John came neither eating nor drinking, and they say, He hath a devil.** 19. **The Son of man came eating and drinking, and they say, Behold a man gluttonous, and** a winebibber, **a friend of** publicans and **sinners.** But wisdom is justified of her children. 20. Then began he to upbraid the cities wherein most of his mighty works were done, because they repented not: 21. **Woe unto thee, Chorazin! woe unto thee, Bethsaida!** for if the mighty works, which were done in you, had been done in Tyre and Sidon they would have repented long ago in sackcloth and ashes. 22. But I say unto you, **It shall be more tolerable for Tyre and Sidon at the** day of **judgment, than for you.** 23. **And thou, Capernaum,** which art exulted unto heaven, shalt be brought down to hell: for **if the mighty works, which have been done in thee, had been done in Sodom, it would have remained** until this day. 24. **But** I say unto you, That **it shall be more tolerable for** the land of **Sodom in** the day of **judgment, than for thee.** 25. **At that time Jesus** answered and **said, I thank thee, O Father,** Lord of heaven and earth, **because thou hast hid**

these things
from the wise
and prudent
and hast
revealed them unto babes.
26. Even so, Father: for so it
seemed good in thy sight.
27. All things are delivered
unto me of my Father:
and no man knoweth
the Son, but the Father;
neither knoweth any man
the Father, save the Son,
and he to whomsoever
the Son will reveal him.
28. Come unto me, all ye
that labour and are heavy laden,
and I will give you rest.
29. Take my yoke upon you,
and learn of me; for
I am meek and lowly in heart:
and ye shall find
rest unto your souls.
30. For my yoke *is* easy, and
my burden is light.

CHAPTER 12

1. At that time
Jesus went on the sabbath
day through the corn;
and his disciples
were an hungered, and
began to pluck the ears of
corn and to eat.
2. But when the Pharisees
saw it, they said
unto him, behold,
thy disciples do that
which is not lawful to do
upon the sabbath day.
3. But he said unto them,
Have ye not read what
David did, when he
was an hungered, and
they that were with him;
4. How he entered into
the house of God, and
did eat the shewbread,
which was not lawful for
him to eat, neither for them
which were with him, but only
for the priests?
5. Or have ye not read in the law,

how that on the sabbath days the
priests in the temple profane the
sabbath, and are blameless?
6. But I say unto you, That
in this place is one
greater than the temple.
7. But if ye had known what *this*
meaneth, I will have mercy, and not
sacrifice, ye would not have
condemned the guiltless.
8. For the Son of man
is Lord even
of the sabbath day.
9. And when he was departed thence,
he went into their synagogue:
10. And, behold, there
was a man which had
his hand withered.
And they asked him, saying,
Is it lawful to heal on the
sabbath days? that they
might accuse him.
11. And he said unto them,
What man shall there
be among you, that
shall have one
sheep, and if it
fall into a pit on
the sabbath day,
will he
not lay hold on it, and
lift it out?
12. How much then is a
man better than a sheep?
Wherefore it is lawful to do
well on the sabbath days.
13. Then saith he to the man,
Stretch forth thine hand.
And he stretched *it* forth;
and it was restored
whole, like as the other.
14. Then the Pharisees
went out, and
held a council against him,
how they might destroy
him.
15. But when Jesus knew *it,*
he withdrew himself from thence:
and great multitudes
followed him;
and he healed them all;
16. And charged them that
they should not make

him known:

17. **That it might be fulfilled which was spoken by Esaias** the prophet, saying,

18. **Behold my servant, whom I have chosen;** my beloved, in **whom** my soul is well pleased: **I will put my spirit upon** him, and he shall shew judgment to the Gentiles.

19. He shall not strive, nor cry; neither shall any man hear his voice in the streets.

20. A bruised reed shall he not break, and smoking flax shall he not quench, till he send forth judgment unto victory.

21. **And in his name shall the Gentiles trust.**

22. **Then was brought** unto him **one** possessed **with a devil, blind, and dumb: and he healed him,** insomuch that the blind and dumb both spake and saw.

23. And all the people were amazed, and said, Is not this the son of David?

24. **But when the Pharisees heard** it, **they said, This fellow doth not cast out devils, but by Beelzebub** the prince of the devils.

25. **And Jesus knew their thoughts, and said** unto them, Every kingdom divided against itself is brought to desolation; and every city or house divided against itself shall not stand;

26. **And if Satan cast out Satan, he is divided** against himself: **how shall then his kingdom stand?**

27. And if I by Beelzebub cast out devils, by whom do your children cast them out? therefore they shall be your judges.

28. **But if I cast out devils by the Spirit of God, then the kingdom of God is come** unto you.

29. Or else how can one enter into a strong man's house, and spoil his goods, except he first bind the strong man? and then he will spoil his house.

30. **He that is not with me is against me;** and he that gathereth not with me scattereth abroad.

31. Wherefore I say unto you, **All manner of sin and blasphemy shall be forgiven** unto men: **but the blasphemy against the Holy Ghost** shall not be forgiven unto men.

32. **And whosoever speaketh** a word **against the Son of man, it shall be forgiven** him: **but whosoever speaketh against the Holy Ghost, it shall not be forgiven** him, neither **in this world, neither in the world to come.**

33. Either make the tree good, and his fruit good; or else make the tree corrupt, and his fruit corrupt: for the tree is known by *his* fruit.

34. **O generation of vipers,** how **can ye, being evil, speak good** things? for out of the abundance of the heart the mouth speaketh.

35. A good man out of the good treasure of the heart bringeth forth good things: and an evil man out of the evil treasure bringeth forth evil things.

36. **But I say** unto you, **That every idle word that men** shall **speak, they shall give account** thereof in the day of judgment.

37. **For by thy words thou shalt be justified, and** by thy words thou shalt be **condemned.**

38. **Then certain** of the scribes and of the

Pharisees answered, saying, Master, we would see a sign from thee. 39. But he answered and said unto them, An evil and adulterous generation seeketh after a sign; and there shall no sign be given to it, but the sign of the prophet Jonas: 40. For as Jonas was three days and three nights in the whale's belly; so shall the Son of man be three days and three nights in the heart of the earth. 41. The men of Nineveh shall rise in judgment with this generation, and shall condemn it: because they repented at the preaching of Jonas; and, behold, a greater than Jonas is here. 42. The queen of the south shall rise up in the judgment with this generation, and shall condemn it: for she came from the uttermost parts of the earth to hear the wisdom of Solomon, and, behold, a greater than Solomon *is* here.

43. When the unclean spirit is gone out of a man, he walketh through dry places, seeking rest, and findeth none. 44. Then he saith, I will return into my house from whence I came out; from whence I came out; and when he is come, he findeth it empty, swept, and garnished. 45. Then goeth he, and taketh with himself seven other spirits more wicked than himself, and they enter in and dwell there; and the last state of that man is worse than the first. Even so shall it be also unto this wicked generation.

46. While he yet talked to the people, behold, *his* mother and his brethren stood without, desiring to speak with him. 47. Then one said unto him, Behold, thy mother and thy brethren stand without, desiring to speak with thee. 48. But he answered and said unto him that told him, Who is my mother? and who are my brethren? 49. And he stretched forth his hand toward his disciples, and said, Behold my mother and my brethren! 50. For whosoever shall do the will of my Father which is in heaven, the same is my brother, and sister, and mother.

CHAPTER 13

1. The same day went Jesus out of the house, and sat by the sea side. 2. And great multitudes were gathered together unto him, so that he went into a ship, and sat; and the whole multitude stood on the shore. 3. And he spake many things unto them in parables, saying, Behold, a sower went forth to sow; 4. And when he sowed, some seeds fell by the way side, and the fowls came and devoured them up: 5. Some fell upon stony places, where they had not much earth: and forthwith they sprung up, because they had no deepness of earth: 6. And when the sun was up, they were scorched; and because they had no root, they withered away. 7. And some fell among thorns; and the thorns sprung up, and

choked them:

8. But other fell into good ground, and brought forth fruit, some an hundredfold, some sixtyfold, some thirtyfold.

9. Who hath ears to hear, let him hear.

10. And the disciples came, and said unto him, Why speakest thou unto them in parables?

11. He answered and said unto them, Because it is given unto you to know the mysteries of the kingdom of heaven, but to them it is not given.

12. For whosoever hath, to him shall be given, and he shall have more abundance: but whosoever hath not from him shall be taken away even that he hath.

13. Therefore speak I to them in parables: because they seeing see not; and hearing they hear not, neither do they understand.

14. And in them is fulfilled the prophecy of Esaias, which saith, By hearing ye shall hear, and shall not understand; and seeing ye shall see, and shall not perceive:

15. For this people's heart is waxed gross, and their ears are dull of hearing, and their eyes they have closed; lest at any time they should see with *their* eyes, and hear with *their* ears, and should understand with *their* heart, and should be converted, and I should heal them.

16. But blessed are your eyes, for they see: and your ears, for they hear.

17. For verily I say unto you, That many prophets and righteous *men* have desired to see *those* things which ye see, and have not seen *them;* and to hear *those* things which ye hear and have not heard *them.*

18. Hear ye therefore the parable of the sower.

19. When any one heareth the word of the kingdom, and understandeth it not, then cometh the wicked one, and catcheth away that which was sown in his heart. This is he which received seed by the way side.

20. But he that received the seed into stony places, the same is he that heareth the word, and anon with joy receiveth it;

21. Yet hath he not root in himself, but dureth for a while: for when tribulation or persecution ariseth because of the word, by and by he is offended.

22. He also that received seed among the thorns is he that heareth the word; and the care of this world, and the deceitfulness of riches, choke the word, and he becometh unfruitful.

23. But he that received seed into the good ground is he that heareth the word, and understandeth *it;* which also beareth fruit, and bringeth forth, some an hundredfold, some sixty, some thirty.

24. Another parable put he forth unto them, saying, The kingdom of heaven is likened unto a man which sowed good seed in his field:

25. But while men slept, his enemy came and sowed tares among the wheat,

and went his way.

26. But when the blade was sprung up, and brought forth fruit, then appeared the tares also.

27. **So the servants** of the householder came and **said** unto him, **Sir, didst not thou sow good seed** in thy field? **from whence** then **hath it tares?**

28. **He said** unto them, **An enemy hath done this.** The servants said unto him, Wilt thou then that we go and gather them up?

29. But he said, Nay; lest while ye gather up the tares, ye root up also the wheat with them.

30. **Let both grow together until the harvest: and in** the time of **harvest I will say** to the reapers, **Gather ye** together **first the tares, and** bind them in bundles to **burn them: but gather the wheat into my barn.**

31. **Another parable put he forth** unto them, **saying, The kingdom** of heaven **is like** to **a** grain of **mustard seed, which a man** took, and **sowed in his field:**

32. **Which indeed is** the **least of all seeds: but when** it is **grown, it is** the **greatest among herbs, and becometh a tree,** so that the birds of the air come and lodge in the branches thereof.

33. Another parable spake he unto them;

The kingdom of heaven **is like** unto **leaven, which a woman** took, and **hid in three measures of meal, till the whole**

was leavened.

34. **All these things spake Jesus** unto the multitude in parables; and without a parable spake he not unto them:

35. **That it might be fufilled** which was spoken by the prophet, saying, **I will** open my mouth **in parables** I will **utter things which have been kept secret from the foundation of the world.**

36. Then Jesus sent the multitude away, and went into the house: and **his disciples came** unto him, **saying, Declare** unto us **the parable of the tares** of the field.

37. **He answered** and said unto them, **He that soweth** the good seed **is the Son of man;**

38. **The field is the world; the good seed are the children of the kingdom; but the tares are the children of the wicked one;**

39. **The enemy** that sowed them **is the devil; the harvest is the end** of the world; **and the reapers are the angels.**

40. **As therefore the tares are gathered and burned** in the fire; **so shall it be in the end of this world.**

41. **The Son of man shall send** forth **his angels, and they shall gather** out of his kingdom **all things** that offend, and them **which do iniquity;**

42. **And shall cast them into a furnace of fire:** there shall be wailing and gnashing of teeth.

43. **Then shall the righteous shine forth** as the sun in the kingdom of their Father. Who hath ears to hear, let him hear.

44. **Again, the kingdom** of heaven

is like unto treasure hid in a field; the which when a man hath found, he hideth, and for joy thereof goeth and **selleth all** that **he hath, and buyeth that field.**

45. **Again, the kingdom** of heaven **is like** unto **a merchant** man, **seeking** goodly **pearls:**

46. **Who,** when he had **found one pearl of great price**, went and **sold all** that **he had, and bought it.**

47. **Again, the kingdom** of heaven **is like unto a net,** that was **cast into the sea, and gathered of every kind:**

48. Which, when it was full, they drew to shore, and sat down, **and gathered the good** into vessels, **but cast the bad away.**

49. **So shall it be at the end** of the world: **the angels shall** come forth, and **sever the wicked from** among **the just,**

50. **And shall cast them into the** furnace of **fire:** there shall be wailing and gnashing of teeth.

51. Jesus saith unto them, Have ye understood all these things? They say unto him, Yea, Lord.

52. Then said he unto them, therefore every scribe *which is* instructed unto the kingdom of heaven is like unto a man *that* is an householder, which bringeth forth out of his treasure *things* new and old.

53. **And** it came to pass, *that* when **Jesus** had finished these parables, he **departed** thence.

54. **And when he was come into his own country, he taught** them in their synagogue, **insomuch that they were astonished, and said, Whence hath this man this wisdom, and** *these* mighty **works?**

55. **Is not this the carpenter's son?** is not his mother called Mary? and his brethren, James, and Joses, and Simon, and Judas?

56. And his sisters, are they not all with us? Whence then hath this *man* all these things?

57. **And they were offended** in him. **But Jesus said** unto them, **A prophet is not without honour, save in his own country,** and in his own house.

58. And he did not many mighty works there because of their unbelief.

CHAPTER 14

1. At that time **Herod the tetrarch heard of the fame of Jesus,**

2. **And said** unto his servants, **This is John the Baptist;** he is **risen** from the dead; and therefore mighty works do shew forth themselves in him.

3. **For Herod had** laid hold on John, and bound him, and **put him in prison for Herodias' sake, his brother Philip's wife.**

4. **For John said unto him, It is not lawful for thee to have her.**

5. And when he would have put him to death, he feared the multitude, because they counted him as a prophet.

6. **But when Herod's birthday was kept, the daughter of Herodias danced** before them, **and pleased Herod.**

7. **Whereupon he promised** with an oath to give **her whatsoever she would ask.**

8. **And she, being** before

instructed of her mother, said, Give me here John Baptist's head in a charger. 9. And the king was sorry: nevertheless for the oath's sake, and them which sat with him at meat, he commanded it to be given *her.* 10. And he sent, and beheaded John in the prison. 11. And his head was brought in a charger, and given to the damsel: and she brought *it* to her mother. 12. And his disciples came, and took up the body, and buried it, and went and told Jesus. 13. When Jesus heard *of it,* he departed thence by ship into a desert place apart: and when the people had heard *thereof,* they followed him on foot out of the cities. 14. And Jesus went forth, and saw a great multitude, and was moved with compassion toward them, and he healed their sick. 15. And when it was evening, his disciples came to him, saying, This is a desert place, and the time is now past; send the multitude away, that they may go into the villages, and buy themselves victuals. 16. But Jesus said unto them, They need not depart; give ye them to eat. 17. And they say unto him, We have here but five loaves, and two fishes. 18. He said, Bring them hither to me. 19. And he commanded the multitude to sit down on the grass, and took the five loaves, and the two fishes, and looking up to heaven, he blessed, and brake, and gave the loaves to his disciples, and the disciples to the multitude. 20. And they did all eat, and were filled: and they took up of the fragments that remained twelve baskets full. 21. And they that had eaten were about five thousand men, beside women and children. 22.And straightway Jesus constrained his disciples to get into a ship, and to go before him unto the other side, while he sent the multitudes away. 23. And when he had sent the multitudes away, he went up into a mountain apart to pray: and when the evening was come, he was there alone. 24. But the ship was now in the midst of the sea, tossed with waves: for the wind was contrary. 25. And in the fourth watch of the night Jesus went unto them, walking on the sea. 26. And when the disciples saw him walking on the sea, they were troubled, saying, It is a spirit; and they cried out for fear. 27. But straightway Jesus spake unto them, saying, Be of good cheer; it is I; be not afraid. 28. And Peter answered him and said, Lord, if it be thou, bid me come unto thee on the water. 29. And he said, Come. And when Peter was come down out of the ship, he walked on the water, to go to Jesus. 30. But when he saw

■ **the wind** boisterous,
■ **he was afraid; and**
■ **beginning to sink,**
■ **he cried,** saying,
■ **Lord, save me.**
■ 31. **And immediately Jesus** stretched forth *his* hand, and
■ **caught him, and**
■ **said** unto him,
■ **O thou of little faith,** wherefore didst thou doubt?
32. And when they were come into the ship, the wind ceased.
■ 33. **Then they** that were in the ship came and
■ **worshipped him,**
■ **saying,** Of a truth
■ **thou art the Son of God.**
34. **And** when they were gone over,
■ **they came into** the land of
■ **Gennesaret.**
■ 35. **And** when the men of that place had knowledge of him,
■ **they** sent out into all that country round about, and
■ **brought unto him all**
■ **that were diseased;**
■ 36. **And besought him**
■ **that they might only**
■ **touch** the hem of
■ **his garment;**
■ **and** as many as touched
■ **were made** perfectly
■ **whole.**

CHAPTER 15

■ 1. **Then came** to Jesus
■ **scribes and Pharisees,** which were of Jerusalem,
■ **saying,**
■ 2. **Why do thy disciples**
■ **transgress the tradition** of the elders? for they wash not their hands when they eat bread.
■ 3. **But he answered** and said unto them,
■ **Why do ye also transgress**
■ **the commandment of**
■ **God** by your tradition?
4. For God commanded, saying, Honour thy father and mother: and, He that curseth father or mother, let him die the death.

5. But ye say, Whosoever shall say to *his* father or *his* mother, *It is* a gift, by whatsoever thou mightest be profited by me;
6. And honour not his father or his mother, *he shall be free.* Thus have ye made the commandment of God of none effect by your tradition.
■ 7. **Ye hypocrites, well did**
■ **Esaias prophesy** of you,
■ **saying,**
■ 8. **This people** draweth nigh unto me with their mouth, and
■ **honoureth me with their**
■ **lips; but their heart is**
■ **far from me.**
9. But in vain they do worship me, teaching *for* doctrines the commandments of men.
■ 10. **And he called the**
■ **multitude, and said** unto them, Hear, and understand:
■ 11. **Not that which goeth**
■ **into** the mouth defileth a man;
■ **but that which cometh**
■ **out of the mouth,** this
■ **defileth a man.**
■ 12. **Then came his disciples,**
■ **and said** unto him, Knowest thou that
■ **the Pharisees were**
■ **offended,** after they heard this saying?
■ 13. **But he answered** and said,
■ **Every plant, which**
■ **my** heavenly
■ **Father hath not planted,**
■ **shall be rooted up.**
■ 14. **Let them alone: they**
■ **be blind** leaders of the blind.
■ **And if the blind lead**
■ **the blind, both shall**
■ **fall** into the ditch.
15. Then answered Peter and said unto him, Declare unto us this parable.
■ 16. **And Jesus said,** Are ye also yet without understanding?
17. Do not ye yet understand, that
■ **whatsoever entereth** in at
■ **the mouth** goeth into the belly,
■ **and is cast out into**
■ **the draught?**

25

18. **But those things which proceed out of the mouth come** forth **from the heart;** and they defile the man.
19. **For out of the heart proceed evil thoughts,** murders, adulteries, fornications, thefts, false witness, blasphemies:
20. These are *the things* **which defile** a man: **but to eat with unwashen hands defileth not** a man.
21. **Then Jesus went** hence, and departed **into** the coasts of **Tyre and Sidon.**
22. **And, behold, a woman of Canaan** came out of the same coasts, and **cried** unto him, saying, **Have mercy** on me, **O Lord,** *thou* son of David; **my daughter is** grievously **vexed with a devil.**
23. **But he answered her not** a word. **And his disciples** came and **besought him, saying, Send her away;** for she crieth after us.
24. **But he answered** and said, **I am not sent but unto** the lost sheep of the house of **Israel.**
25. **Then came she and worshipped him, saying, Lord, help me.**
26. **But he answered** and said, **It is not meet to take the children's bread, and to cast it to dogs.**
27. **And she said,** Truth, Lord: **yet the dogs eat of the crumbs** which fall from their masters' table.
28. **Then Jesus** answered and **said** unto her, O woman, **great is thy faith: be it** unto thee even **as thou wilt. And her daughter was made whole** from that very hour.

29. **And Jesus** departed from thence, and **came** nigh **unto** the sea of **Galilee; and went** up **into a mountain,** and sat down there.
30. **And great multitudes came** unto him, having with them *those that were* lame, blind, dumb, maimed, and many others, and cast them down at Jesus' feet; **and he healed them:**
31. Insomuch that the multitude wondered, when they saw the dumb to speak, the maimed to be whole, the lame to walk, and the blind to see: **and they glorified the God of Israel.**
32. **Then Jesus** called his disciples *unto him,* and **said, I have compassion on the multitude,** because they continue with me now three days, and have nothing to eat: **and I will not send them away fasting,** lest they faint in the way.
33. And his disciples say unto him, Whence should we have so much bread in the wilderness, as to fill so great a multitude?
34. And Jesus saith unto them, **How many loaves have ye? And they said, Seven, and a few** little **fishes.**
35. And he commanded the multitude to sit down on the ground.
36. **And he took the seven loaves and** the **fishes, and gave thanks,** and brake *them,* **and gave to his disciples, and the disciples to the multitude.**
37. **And they did all eat,** and were filled: **and they** took up of the broken *meat* that was **left seven baskets** full.
38. **And they that did eat were four thousand men,**

26

beside women
and children.
39. **And he** sent away the
multitude, and took ship, and
came into the coasts of
Magdala.

CHAPTER 16

1. **The Pharisees** also
with the Sadducees
came, and
tempting desired
him that he would
shew them a sign from heaven.
2. **He answered** and said unto
them, When it is evening, ye say, *It*
will be fair weather: for the sky is red.
3. And in the morning, *It will*
be foul weather today: for
the sky is red and lowering.
O ye hypocrites, ye can
discern the face of the
sky; but can ye
not *discern*
the signs of the times?
4. **A wicked** and adulterous
generation seeketh after
a sign; and there shall
no sign be given unto it,
but the sign of the prophet
Jonas. And he left them,
and departed.
5. **And when his disciples**
were come to the other side,
they had forgotten to take
bread.
6. **Then Jesus said**
unto them, Take heed and
beware of the leaven
of the Pharisees and of the
Sadducees.
7. **And they reasoned**
among themselves,
saying, It is because we
have taken no bread.
8. **Which when Jesus**
perceived, he said unto them,
O ye of little faith, why reason ye
among yourselves, because ye
have brought no bread?
9. Do ye not yet understand, neither
remember the five loaves of the
five thousand, and how many

baskets ye took up?
10. Neither the seven loaves
of the four thousand, and how
many baskets ye took up?
11. How is it that ye do
not understand that
I spake it not to you
concerning bread, that ye
should beware of the leaven of the
Pharisees and of the Sadducees?
12. **Then understood they** how
that he bade them not
beware of the leaven of bread, but
of the doctrine of the
Pharisees and of the
Sadducees.
13. **When Jesus came**
into the coasts of
Caesarea Philippi, he
asked his disciples, saying,
Whom do men say
that I the Son of man
am?
14. **And they said,**
Some say *that thou art*
John the Baptist:
some, Elias; and
others, Jeremias,
or one of the prophets.
15. **He saith** unto them,
but whom say ye that I am?
16. **And** Simon
Peter answered
and said, Thou art
the Christ, the Son
of the living God.
17. **And Jesus answered**
and said unto him,
Blessed art
thou, Simon Bar-jona:
for flesh and blood
hath not revealed it unto thee,
but my Father which is inheaven.
18. And I say also unto thee, that
thou art Peter, and upon this
rock I will build my church;
and the gates
of hell shall not prevail
against it.
19. **And I will give unto**
thee the keys of the
kingdom of heaven:
and whatsoever thou shalt

bind on earth shall be bound in heaven: and whatsoever thou shalt loose on earth shall be loosed in heaven.

20. Then charged he his disciples that they should tell no man that he was Jesus the Christ.

21. From that time forth began Jesus to shew unto his disciples, how that he must go unto Jerusalem, and suffer many things of the elders and chief priests and scribes, and be killed, and be raised again the third day.

22. Then Peter took him, and began to rebuke him, saying, Be it far from thee, Lord: this shall not be unto thee.

23. But he turned, and said unto Peter, Get thee behind me, Satan: thou art an offence unto me: for thou savourest not the things that be of God, but those that be of men.

24. Then said Jesus unto his disciples, If any man will come after me, let him deny himself, and take up his cross, and follow me.

25. For whosoever will save his life shall lose it: and whosoever will lose his life for my sake shall find it.

26. For what is a man profited, if he shall gain the whole world, and lose his own soul? or what shall a man give in exchange for his soul?

27. For the son of man shall come in the glory of his Father with his angels; and then he shall reward every man according to his works.

28. Verily I say unto you, There be some standing here, which shall not taste of death, till they see the Son of man coming in his kingdom.

CHAPTER 17

1. And after six days Jesus taketh Peter, James, and John his brother, and bringeth them up into an high mountain apart,

2. And was transfigured before them: and his face did shine as the sun, and his raiment was white as the light.

3. And, behold, there appeared unto them Moses and Elias talking with him.

4. Then answered Peter, and said unto Jesus, Lord, it is good for us to be here: if thou wilt, let us make here three tabernacles; one for thee, and one for Moses, and one for Elias.

5. While he yet spake, behold, a bright cloud overshadowed them: and behold a voice out of the cloud, which said, This is my beloved Son, in whom I am well pleased; hear ye him.

6. And when the disciples heard it, they fell on their face, and were sore afraid.

7. And Jesus came and touched them, and said, Arise, and be not afraid.

8. And when they had lifted up their eyes, they saw no man, save Jesus only.

9. And as they came down from the mountain, Jesus charged them, saying, Tell the vision to no man, until the Son of man be risen again from the dead.

10. And his disciples asked him, saying, Why then say the scribes that Elias must first come?

11. **And Jesus answered** and said unto them, Elias truly shall first come, and restore all things.

12. But I say unto you, That **Elias is come already,** and they knew him not, but have done unto him whatsoever they listed. Likewise shall also the Son of man suffer of them.

13. **Then the disciples understood** that **he spake** unto them **of John the Baptist.**

14. **And** when they were come to the multitude, **there came** to him **a** *certain* **man, kneeling** down to him, **and saying,**

15. **Lord, have mercy on my son: for he is lunatic,** and sore vexed: for ofttimes he falleth into the fire, and oft into the water,

16. **And I brought him to thy disciples, and they could not cure him.**

17. Then Jesus answered and said, O faithless and perverse generation, how long shall I be with you? how long shall I suffer you? bring him hither to me.

18. **And Jesus rebuked the devil;** and he departed out of him: **and the child was cured** from that very hour.

19. **Then came the disciples** to Jesus apart, **and said, Why could not we cast him out?**

20. **And Jesus said** unto them, **Because of your unbelief:** for verily I say unto you, **If ye have faith as a** grain of **mustard seed, ye shall say unto this mountain, Remove** hence to yonder place; **and it shall remove; and nothing shall be impossible** unto you.

21. **Howbeit this kind goeth** not out but **by prayer and fasting.**

22. **And while** they abode

in Galilee, Jesus **said** unto them, **The Son of man shall be betrayed** into the hands of men:

23. **And they shall kill him, and the third day he shall be raised** again. And they were exceeding sorry.

24. **And when they were come to Capernaum, they that received tribute money came to Peter, and said, doth not your master pay tribute?**

25. **He saith, Yes. And when he was come into the house, Jesus prevented him, saying, What thinkest thou, Simon: of whom do the kings of** the earth **take** custom or **tribute? of their** own **children, or** of **strangers?**

26. **Peter saith** unto him, **Of strangers. Jesus saith** unto him, **Then are the children free.**

27. **Notwithstanding, lest we should offend** them, **go** thou **to the sea, and cast** an hook, **and take** up **the fish that first cometh** up; **and when thou hast opened his mouth, thou shalt find** a piece of **money:** that **take, and give unto them** for me and thee.

CHAPTER 18

1. **At the same time came the disciples** unto Jesus, **saying, Who is the greatest in the kingdom** of heaven?

2. **And Jesus called a little child** unto him, and set him in the midst of them,

3. **And said,** Verily I say unto you, **Except ye be converted, and become as** little

29

children, ye shall not enter into the kingdom of heaven. 4. Whosoever therefore shall humble himself as this little child, the same is greatest in the kingdom of heaven. 5. And whoso shall receive one such little child in my name receiveth me. 6. But whoso shall offend one of these little ones which believe in me, it were better for him that a millstone were hanged about his neck, and that he were drowned in the depth of the sea. 7. Woe unto the world because of offences! for it must needs be that offences come; but woe to that man by whom the offence cometh! 8. Wherefore if thy hand or thy foot offend thee, cut them off, and cast them from thee: it is better for thee to enter into life halt or maimed, rather than having two hands or two feet to be cast into everlasting fire. 9. And if thine eye offend thee, pluck it out, and cast it from thee: it is better for thee to enter into life with one eye, rather than having two eyes to be cast into hell fire. 10. Take heed that ye despise not one of these little ones; for I say unto you, That in heaven their angels do always behold the face of my Father which is in heaven. 11. For the Son of man is come to save that which was lost. 12. How think ye? if a man have an hundred sheep, and one of them be gone astray, doth he not leave the ninety and nine, and goeth into the mountains, and seeketh that which is gone astray? 13. And if so be that he find it, verily I say unto you, he rejoiceth more of that sheep, than of the ninety and nine which went not astray. 14. Even so it is not the will of your Father which is in heaven that one of these little ones should perish. 15. Moreover if thy brother shall trespass against thee, go and tell him his fault between thee and him alone: if he shall hear thee, thou hast gained thy brother. 16. But if he will not hear thee, then take with thee one or two more, that in the mouth of two or three witnesses every word may be established. 17. And if he shall neglect to hear them, tell it unto the church: but if he neglect to hear the church, let him be unto thee as an heathen man and a publican. 18. Verily I say unto you, Whatsoever ye shall bind on earth shall be found in heaven: and whatsoever ye shall loose on earth shall be loosed in heaven. 19. Again I say unto you, That if two of you shall agree on earth as touching any thing that they shall ask, it shall be done for them of my Father which is in heaven. 20. For where two or three are gathered together in my name, there am I in the midst of them. 21. Then came Peter to him,

and said, Lord,
how oft shall my
brother sin against me,
and I forgive him? till
seven times?
22. **Jesus saith** unto him,
I say not unto thee, Until
seven times: but, Until
seventy times seven.
23. **Therefore is the**
kingdom of heaven
likened unto a certain
king, which would
take account of
his servants.
24. And when he had begun to reckon,
one was brought unto him, which
owed him ten
thousand talents.
25. But forasmuch as
he had not to pay,
his lord commanded
him to be sold, and his wife, and
children, and all that he had, and
payment to be made.
26. **The servant** therefore
fell down, and worshipped him,
saying, Lord,
have patience with me,
and I will pay thee all.
27. **Then the lord** of that servant
was moved with
compassion, and loosed him,
and forgave him
the debt.
28. **But the same**
servant went out, and
found one of his fellow-
servants, which owed
him an hundred pence:
and he laid hands on him, and
took him by the throat,
saying, Pay me that thou owest.
29. **And this fellow-servant**
fell down at his feet,
and besought him,
saying, Have
patience with me,
and I will pay thee all.
30. **And he would not:**
but went and
cast him into prison,
till he should pay the debt.

31. **So when his fellow-**
servants saw what was done,
they were very sorry, and came and
told unto
their lord all that was done.
32. **Then his lord,**
after that he had called him,
said unto him, O
thou wicked servant,
I forgave thee all that debt,
because thou desiredst me:
33. **Shouldest not thou also**
have had compassion
on thy fellow-servant,
even as I had pity on thee?
34. **And his lord** was wroth, and
delivered him to the
tormentors, till he should
pay all that was due unto him.
35. **So likewise**
shall my heavenly
Father do also unto you,
if ye from your heart
forgive not every one
his brother their trespasses.

CHAPTER 19

1. **And** it came to pass, *that* when
Jesus had finished these sayings, he
departed from Galilee, and
came into the coasts of
Judaea beyond Jordan:
2. And great multitudes followed him;
and he healed them there.
3. **The Pharisees also**
came unto him, tempting him, and
saying unto him,
Is it lawful for a man
to put away his wife
for every cause?
4. **And he answered**
and said unto them,
Have ye not read, that he
which made *them* at the beginning
made them male and female,
5. And
said, For this cause shall a man
leave father and mother, and
shall cleave to his wife: and
they twain shall
be one flesh?
6. **Wherefore** they are
no more twain, but one flesh.

What therefore **God hath joined** together, **let not man put asunder.** 7. **They say** unto him, **Why did Moses** then command to **give** a writing of **divorcement,** and to put her away? 8. **He saith** unto them, **Moses because of the hardness of your hearts suffered you to put away your wives: but** from the beginning it was not so. 9. And I say unto you, **Whosoever shall put away his wife, except** it be **for fornication, and** shall **marry another, committeth adultery:** and whoso marrieth her which is put away doth commit adultery. 10. **His disciples say** unto him, If the case of the man be so with *his* wife, **it is not good to marry.** 11. **But he said** unto them, **All men cannot receive this saying, save they to whom it is given.** 12. For there are some eunuchs, which were so born from *their* mother's womb: and there are eunuchs, Which were made eunuchs, of men: and there be eunuchs, which have made themselves eunuchs for the kingdom of heaven's sake. **He that is able** to receive *it*, **let him receive it.** 13. **Then were there brought** unto him **little children,** that he should put *his* hands on them, and pray: **and the disciples rebuked them.** 14. **But Jesus said, Suffer little children,** and forbid them not, **to come unto me: for of such is the kingdom** of heaven. 15. And he laid *his* hands on them, and departed thence. 16. **And, behold, one** came and **said** unto him, **Good Master, what good thing shall I do, that I may have eternal life?** 17. **And he said** unto him, **Why callest** thou **me good? there is none good but** one, *that is,* **God: but if thou wilt enter** into **life, keep the commandments.** 18. **He saith** unto him, **Which? Jesus said, Thou shalt do no murder,** Thou shalt **not commit adultery,** Thou shalt **not steal,** thou shalt **not bear false witness,** 19. **Honour thy father and** *thy* **mother: and,** thou shalt **love thy neighbour as thyself.** 20. **The young man saith** unto him, **All these** things **have I kept** from my youth up: **what lack I** yet? 21. **Jesus said** unto him, If thou wilt be perfect, **go and sell that thou hast, and give to the poor,** and thou shalt have treasure in heaven: **and come** and **follow me.** 22. **But when the young man heard** that saying, **he went away sorrowful: for he had great possessions.** 23. **Then said Jesus** unto his disciples, Verily I say unto you, that a rich man shall hardly enter into the kingdom of heaven. 24. And again I say unto you, **It is easier for a camel to go through the eye of a needle, than for a rich man to enter into the kingdom** of God.

25. When his disciples heard *it,* they were exceedingly amazed, saying, Who then can be saved?

26. But Jesus beheld *them,* and said unto them, With men this is impossible; but with God all things are possible.

27. Then answered Peter and said unto him, Behold, we have forsaken all, and followed thee; what shall we have therefore?

28. And Jesus said unto them, Verily I say unto you, that ye which have followed me, in the regeneration when the Son of man shall sit in the throne of his glory, ye also shall sit upon twelve thrones, judging the twelve tribes of Israel.

29. And every one that hath forsaken houses, or brethren, or sisters, or father, or mother, or wife, or children, or lands, for my name's sake, shall receive an hundredfold, and shall inherit everlasting life.

30. But many *that are* first shall be last; and the last *shall be* first.

CHAPTER 20

1. For the kingdom of heaven is like unto a man *that is* an householder, which went out early in the morning to hire labourers into his vineyard.

2. And when he had agreed with the labourers for a penny a day, he sent them into his vineyard.

3. And he went out about the third hour, and saw others standing idle in the marketplace,

4. And said unto them; Go ye also into the vineyard, and whatsoever is right I will give you. And they went their way.

5. Again he went out about the sixth and ninth hour, and did likewise.

6. And about the eleventh hour he went out, and found others standing idle, and saith unto them, Why stand ye here all the day idle?

7. They say unto him, Because no man hath hired us. He saith unto them, Go ye also into the vineyard; and whatsoever is right, that shall ye receive.

8. So when even was come, the lord of the vineyard saith unto his steward, Call the labourers, and give them their hire, beginning from the last unto the first.

9. And when they came that were hired about the eleventh hour, they received every man a penny.

10. But when the first came, they supposed that they should have received more, and they likewise received every man a penny.

11. And when they had received it, they murmured against the goodman of the house,

12. Saying, These last have wrought but one hour, and thou hast made them equal unto us, which have borne the burden and heat of the day.

13. But he answered one of them and said, Friend, I do thee no wrong: didst not thou agree with me for a penny?

14. Take *that* thine *is,* and go thy way: I will give unto this last,

even as unto thee.

15. **Is it not lawful** for me **to do what I will with mine own?** Is thine eye evil, because I am good?

16. **So the last shall be first,** and the first last: **for many be called, but few chosen.**

17. **And Jesus** going up to Jerusalem **took the twelve disciples apart** in the way, **and said** unto them,

18. **Behold, we go** up **to Jerusalem; and the Son** of man **shall be betrayed** unto the chief priests and unto the scribes, **and they shall condemn** him to death,

19. **And shall deliver him** to the Gentiles to mock, and to scourge, and **to crucify him: and** the third day **he shall rise again.**

20. **Then came** to him **the mother of Zebedee's children** with her sons, worshipping *him,* and desiring a certain thing of him.

21. **And** he said unto her, What wilt thou? **She saith** unto him, **Grant that** these **my two sons may sit, the one on thy right hand, and the other on the left, in thy kingdom.**

22. **But Jesus answered** and said, Ye know not what ye ask. **Are ye able to drink of the cup that I shall drink** of, and to be baptized with the baptism that I am baptized with? **They say** unto him, **We are able.**

23. **And he saith** unto them, **Ye shall drink indeed** of my cup, and be baptized with the baptism that I am baptized with; **but to sit on my right hand,** and on my left, is not mine to give, but *it shall be given to them* for whom it is prepared of my Father.

24. **And when the ten heard** *it,* **they were moved with indignation** against the two brethren.

25. **But Jesus** called them *unto him,* and **said,** Ye know that the princes of the Gentiles exercise dominion over them, and they that are great exercise authority upon them,

26. But it shall not be so among you: but **whosoever will be great among you, let him be your minister;**

27. And whosoever will be chief among you, let him be your servant:

28. **Even as the Son of man came not to be ministered unto, but to minister, and to give his life a ransom for many.**

29. And as they departed from Jericho, a great multitude followed him.

30. **And, behold, two blind men** sitting by the way side, when they heard that Jesus passed by , **cried** out, saying, **Have mercy on us,** O Lord, *thou* son of David.

31. **And the multitude rebuked them,** because they should hold their peace: **but they cried the more,** saying, Have mercy on us, O Lord, *thou* son of David.

32. **And Jesus** stood still, and called them, and **said, What will ye that I shall do** unto you?

33. **They say** unto him, Lord, **that our eyes may be opened.**

34. **So Jesus** had compassion *on them,* and **touched their eyes: and** immediately their eyes received sight,

| | and they followed him.

CHAPTER 21

1. **And when they** drew nigh unto Jerusalem, and **were come to Bethphage,** unto the mount of Olives, **then sent Jesus two disciples,** 2. **Saying** unto them, **Go** into the village over against you, **and** straightway **ye shall find an ass tied, and a colt** with her: loose *them*, and **bring them unto me.** 3. And if any *man* say aught unto you, ye shall say, The Lord hath need of them; and straightway he will send them. 4. **All this** was done, that it might be fulfilled which **was spoken by the prophet, saying,** 5. Tell ye the daughter of Sion, Behold, **thy King cometh** unto thee, meek, and **sitting upon an ass,** and a colt the foal of an ass. 6. **And the disciples went, and did as Jesus commanded** them, 7. **And brought the ass,** and the colt, and put on them their clothes, **and they set him thereon.** 8. **And a very great multitude spread** their **garments** in the way; **others cut** down **branches** from the trees, **and strawed them in the way.** 9. **And** the multitudes that went before, and that followed, **cried,** saying, **Hosanna** to the son of David; **Blessed is he that cometh in the name of the Lord;** Hosanna in the highest. 10. And when he was come into Jerusalem, all the city was moved,

saying, Who is this? 11. And the multitude said, This is Jesus the Prophet of Nazareth of Galilee. 12. **And Jesus went into the temple** of God, **and cast out all** them **that sold and bought** in the temple, **and overthrew the tables** of the moneychangers, and the seats of them that sold doves, 13. **And said** unto them, **It is written, My house shall be called the house of prayer; but ye have made it a den of thieves.** 14. **And the blind and the lame came** to him in the temple; **and he healed them.** 15. **And when the chief priests and scribes saw the** wonderful **things** that **he did, and the children crying** in the temple, and saying, **Hosanna** to the son of David; **they were** sore **displeased,** 16. **And said** unto him, **Hearest** thou **what these say?** And **Jesus saith** unto them, **Yea; have ye never read, Out of the mouth of babes** and sucklings **thou hast perfected praise?** 17. **And he left** them, **and went** out of the city **into Bethany; and** he **lodged** there. 18. **Now in the morning** as he returned into the city, **he hungered.** 19. **And when he saw a fig tree** in the way, he came to it, **and found nothing thereon,** but leaves only, **and said** unto it, **Let no fruit grow on thee** henceforward for ever. **And** presently

35

the fig tree withered away. 20. And when the disciples saw *it*, they marvelled, saying, How soon is the fig tree withered away! 21. Jesus answered and said unto them, Verily I say unto you, If ye have faith, and doubt not, ye shall not only do this *which is done* to the fig tree, but also if ye shall say unto this mountain, Be thou removed, and be thou cast into the sea; it shall be done. 22. And all things, whatsoever ye shall ask in prayer, believing, ye shall receive. 23. And when he was come into the temple, the chief priests and the elders of the people came unto him as he was teaching, and said, By what authority doest thou these things? and who gave thee this authority? 24. And Jesus answered and said unto them, I also will ask you one thing, which if ye tell me, I in like wise will tell you by what authority I do these things. 25 The baptism of John, whence was it? from heaven, or of men? And they reasoned with themselves, saying, If we shall say, From heaven; he will say unto us, Why did ye not then believe him? 26. But if we shall say, Of men; we fear the people; for all hold John as a prophet. 27. And they answered Jesus, and said, We cannot tell. And he said unto them, Neither tell I you by what authority I do these things,

28. But what think ye? A *certain* man had two sons; and he came to the first, and said, Son, go work today in my vineyard. 29. He answered and said, I will not: but afterward he repented, and went. 30. And he came to the second, and said likewise. And he answered and said, I go, sir: and went not. 31. Whether of them twain did the will of his father? They say unto him, The first. Jesus saith unto them Verily I say unto you, that the publicans and the harlots go into the kingdom of God before you. 32. For John came unto you in the way of righteousness, and ye believed him not: but the publicans and the harlots believed him: and ye, when ye had seen *it,* repented not afterward, that ye might believe him. 33. Hear another parable: There was a certain householder, which planted a vineyard, and hedged it round about, and digged a winepress in it, and built a tower, and let it out to husbandmen, and went into a far country: 34. And when the time of the fruit drew near, he sent his servants to the husbandmen, that they might receive the fruits of it. 35. And the husbandmen took his servants, and beat one, and killed another, and stoned another. 36. Again, he sent other servants more than the first: and they did unto them likewise.

37. **But last** of all **he sent** unto them **his son,** saying, They will reverence my son.

38. **But when the husbandmen saw the son, they** said among themselves, This is the heir; come, let us kill him, and let us seize on his inheritance.

39. And they caught him, and cast *him* out of the vineyard, and **slew him.**

40. **When the lord** therefore **of the vineyard cometh, what will he do** unto those husbandmen?

41. **They say** unto him, **He will** miserably **destroy those wicked men and will let out his vineyard unto other husbandmen,** which shall render him the fruits in their seasons.

42. **Jesus saith** unto them, **Did ye never read** in the scriptures, **The stone which the builders rejected** the same **is become the head of the corner:** this is the Lord's doing, and it is marvellous in our eyes?

43. **Therefore say I unto you, The kingdom** of God **shall be taken from you, and given to a nation bringing forth** the **fruits** thereof.

44. **And whosoever shall fall on this stone shall be broken:** but on whomsoever it shall fall, it will grind him to powder.

45. And when the chief priests and Pharisees had heard his parables, **they perceived that he spake of them.**

46. But when they sought to lay hands on him they feared the multitude, because they took him for a prophet.

CHAPTER 22

1. **And Jesus** answered and **spake** unto them **again by parables,** and said,

2. The kingdom of heaven is like unto **a** certain **king,** which **made a marriage for his son,**

3. **And sent** forth his **servants to call them** that were **bidden to the wedding: and they would not come.**

4. **Again, he sent forth** other **servants, saying, Tell them** which are bidden, Behold, **I have prepared my dinner:** my oxen and *my* fatlings *are* killed, **and all things are ready:** come unto the marriage.

5. **But they made light of it, and went their ways,** one to his farm, another to his merchandise:

6. **And the remnant took his servants,** and entreated *them* spitefully, **and slew them.**

7. But when the king heard *thereof,* he was wroth: and **he sent** forth **his armies, and destroyed those murderers,** and burned up their city.

8. **Then saith he to his servants, the wedding is ready,** but they which were bidden were not worthy.

9. **Go** ye therefore **into the highways, and as many as ye** shall **find, bid to the marriage.**

10. **So those servants** went out into the highways, and **gathered** together all **as many as they found,** both bad and good: **and the wedding was furnished with guests.**

11. **And when the king came** in to see the guests, **he saw** there **a man which had not on a wedding garment:**

12. **And he saith** unto him, Friend, **how camest thou in** hither **not having a wedding**

Rendering unto Caesar

garment? And he was speechless.

13. Then said the king to the servants, bind him hand and foot, and take him away, and cast him into outer darkness, there shall be weeping and gnashing of teeth.

14. For many are called, but few *are* chosen.

15. Then went the Pharisees, and took counsel how they might entangle him in *his* talk.

16. And they sent out unto him their disciples with the Herodians, saying, Master, we know that thou art true, and teachest the way of God in truth, neither carest thou for any *man:* for thou regardest not the person of men.

17. Tell us therefore, What thinkest thou? Is it lawful to give tribute unto Caesar, or not?

18. But Jesus perceived their wickedness, and said, Why tempt ye me, ye hypocrites?

19. Shew me the tribute money. And they brought unto him a penny.

20. And he saith unto them, Whose is this image and superscription?

21. They say unto him, Caesar's. Then saith he unto them, Render therefore unto Caesar the things which are Caesar's; and unto God the things that are God's.

22. When they had heard *these words,* they marvelled, and left him, and went their way.

23. The same day came to him the Sadducees, which say that there is no resurrection,

and asked him,

24. Saying, Master, Moses said, If a man die, having no children, his brother shall marry his wife, and raise up seed unto his brother,

25. Now there were with us seven brethren: and the first, when he had married a wife, deceased, and, having no issue, left his wife unto his brother:

26. Likewise the second also, and the third, unto the seventh.

27. And last of all the woman died also.

28. Therefore in the resurrection whose wife shall she be of the seven? for they all had her.

29. Jesus answered and said unto them, Ye do err, not knowing the scriptures, nor the power of God.

30. For in the resurrection they neither marry, nor are given in marriage, but are as the angels of God in heaven.

31. But as touching the resurrection of the dead, have ye not read that which was spoken unto you by God, saying,

32. I am the God of Abraham, and the God of Isaac, and the God of Jacob? God is not the God of the dead, but of the living.

33. And when the multitude heard *this,* they were astonished at his doctrine.

34. But when the Pharisees had heard that he had put the Sadducees to silence, they were gathered together.

35. Then one of them, *which was* a lawyer, asked him a question, tempting him, and saying,

36. Master, which is the great commandment

in the law?

37. **Jesus said** unto him,
Thou shalt love the Lord thy God with all thy heart, and with all thy soul, and with all thy mind.

38. This is the first and great commandment.

39. **And the second is** like unto it, **Thou shalt love thy neighbour as thyself.**

40. **On these** two commandments **hang all the law and the prophets.**

41. While the Pharisees were gathered together, **Jesus asked** them,

42. **Saying, What think ye of Christ? whose son is he? They say** unto him, **The son of David.**

43. **He saith** unto them, **How then doth David** in spirit **call him Lord,** saying,

44. The LORD said unto my Lord, Sit thou on my right hand, till I make thine enemies thy footstool?

45. **If David then call him Lord, how is he his son?**

46. **And no man was able to answer** him a word, neither durst any *man* from that day forth ask him any more *questions.*

CHAPTER 23

1. **Then spake Jesus** to the multitude, and to his disciples,

2. **Saying, The** scribes and the **Pharisees sit in Moses' seat:**

3. All therefore **whatsoever they bid you observe,** *that* observe and do; **but do not ye after their works:** for they say, and do not.

4. **For they bind heavy burdens** and grievous to be borne, **and lay them on men's shoulders; but they themselves will not move** them with **one of their fingers.**

5. But all their works **they do** for **to be seen** of men: they make broad their phylacteries, and enlarge the borders of their garments

6. **And love** the uppermost rooms at feasts, and the chief seats in the synagogues,

7. And greetings in the markets, and **to be called** of men, **Rabbi,** Rabbi.

8. **But be not ye called Rabbi:** for **one is your Master, even Christ;** and all ye are brethren.

9. **And call no man** your **father** upon the earth: **for** one is **your Father,** which **is in heaven.**

10. Neither be ye called masters: for one is your Master, *even* Christ.

11. **But he that is greatest** among you **shall be your servant.**

12. And whosoever shall exalt himself shall be abased; and he that shall humble himself shall be exalted.

13. **But woe unto you,** scribes and **Pharisees,** hypocrites! **for ye shut up the kingdom** of heaven **against men:** for ye neither go in *yourselves,* neither suffer ye them that are entering to go in.

14. Woe unto you, scribes and Pharisees, hypocrites! for **ye devour widows' houses, and** for a pretence **make long prayer: therefore ye shall receive the greater damnation.**

15. Woe unto you, scribes and Pharisees, hypocrites! for **ye** compass sea and land to **make one proselyte, and** when he is made, ye **make him twofold more the child of hell than yourselves.**

16. **Woe unto you,** *ye* blind guides, **which say, Whosoever**

shall swear by the temple,
it is nothing; but whosoever
shall swear by the
gold of the temple, he
is a debtor!
17. *Ye* fools and blind:
for whether is greater, the
gold, or the temple that
sanctifieth the gold?
18. And, Whosoever shall
swear by the altar, it is
nothing; but whosoever
sweareth by the gift that is
upon it, he
is guilty.
19. Ye fools and blind: for
whether *is* greater, the gifts, or the
altar that sanctifieth the gift?
20. Whoso therefore shall
swear by the altar,
sweareth by it, and by
all things thereon.
21. And whoso shall swear by the
temple, sweareth by it, and by
him that dwelleth therein.
22. And he that shall swear by
heaven, sweareth by the thone of
God, and by him that sitteth thereon.
23. Woe unto you,
scribes and Pharisees,
hypocrites! for ye pay tithe
of mint and anise and cummin,
and have omitted the
weightier *matters* of the law,
judgment, mercy, and faith:
these ought ye to have done, and
not to leave the other undone.
24. Ye blind guides, which
strain at a gnat, and
swallow a camel.
25. Woe unto you, scribes and
Pharisees, hypocrites! for
ye make clean the outside
of the cup and of the platter,
but within they are full of
extortion and excess.
26. *Thou* blind Pharisee,
cleanse first that *which is*
within the cup and platter,
that the outside of them
may be clean also.
27. Woe unto you, scribes and
Pharisees, hypocrites! for

ye are like unto
whited sepulchres,
which indeed appear beautiful
outward, but are within
full of dead men's bones,
and of all uncleanness.
28. Even so ye also outwardly appear
righteous unto men, but within
ye are full of hypocrisy
and iniquity.
29. Woe unto you, scribes and
Pharisees, hypocrites! because
ye build the tombs of
the prophets, and garnish the
sepulchres of the righteous,
30. And say, If we had been
in the days of our fathers,
we would not have
been partakers with them
in the blood of the
prophets.
31. Wherefore ye be witnesses
unto yourselves, that
ye are the children of them
which killed the prophets.
32. Fill ye up then the measure
of your fathers.
33. Ye serpents, *ye*
generation of vipers,
how can ye
escape the damnation of
hell?
34. Wherefore, behold, I
send unto you prophets, and
wise men, and scribes:
and some of them ye
shall kill and crucify;
and *some* of them shall ye
scourge in your synagogues,
and persecute *them*
from city to city:
35. That upon you may
come all the righteous
blood shed upon the earth,
from the blood of righteous Abel unto
the blood of Zacharias son of
Barachias, whom ye slew between
the temple and the altar.
36. Verily I say unto you,
All these things shall come
upon this generation.
37. O Jerusalem, Jerusalem,
thou that killest the

prophets, and stonest them which are sent unto thee,

how often would I have gathered thy children together, even as a hen gathereth her chickens under *her* wings, and ye would not!

38. Behold, your house is left unto you desolate.

39. For I say unto you, Ye shall not see me henceforth, till ye shall say, Blessed *is* he that cometh in the name of the Lord.

CHAPTER 24

1. And Jesus went out, and departed from the temple: and his disciples came to *him* for to shew him the buildings of the temple.

2. And Jesus said unto them, See ye not all these things? verily I say unto you, There shall not be left here one stone upon another, that shall not be thrown down.

3. And as he sat upon the mount of Olives, the disciples came unto him privately, saying, Tell us, when shall these things be? and what *shall be* the sign of thy coming, and of the end of the world?

4. And Jesus answered and said unto them, Take heed that no man deceive you.

5. For many shall come in my name, saying, I am Christ; and shall deceive many.

6. And ye shall hear of wars and rumours of wars: see that ye be not troubled: for all *these things* must come to pass, but the end is not yet.

7. For nation shall rise against nation, and kingdom against kingdom:

and there shall be famines, and pestilences, and earthquakes, in divers places.

8. All these are the beginning of sorrows.

9. Then shall they deliver you up to be afflicted, and shall kill you: and ye shall be hated of all nations for my name's sake.

10. And then shall many be offended, and shall betray one another, and shall hate one another.

11. And many false prophets shall rise, and shall deceive many.

12. And because iniquity shall abound the love of many shall wax cold.

13. But he that shall endure unto the end, the same shall be saved.

14. And this gospel of the kingdom shall be preached in all the world for a witness unto all nations; and then shall the end come.

15. When ye therefore shall see the abomination of desolation, spoken of by Daniel the prophet, stand in the holy place, (whoso readeth, let him understand:)

16. Then let them which be in Judaea flee into the mountains:

17. Let him which is on the housetop not come down to take any thing out of his house:

18. Neither let him which is in the field return back to take his clothes.

19. And woe unto them that are with child, and to them that give suck in those days!

20. But pray ye that your flight be not in the winter, neither on the sabbath day:

21. For then shall be great tribulation, such as was not since the beginning of the world to this time, no,

nor ever shall be.

■ 22. **And except those days**
■ **should be shortened, there**
■ **should no flesh be saved:**
but for the elect's sake those
days shall be shortened.
■ 23. **Then if any man** shall
■ **say** unto you,
■ **Lo, here is Christ,** or there;
■ **believe it not.**
■ 24. **For there shall**
■ **arise false Christs,**
and false prophets,
■ **and** shall
■ **shew** great
■ **signs** and wonders;
■ **insomuch that, if it were**
■ **possible, they shall**
■ **deceive the** very
■ **elect.**
25. Behold, I have told you before.
■ 26. **Wherefore if they** shall
■ **say** unto you,
■ **Behold, he is in the desert;**
go not forth: behold,
he is in the secret chambers;
■ **believe** *it*
■ **not.**
■ 27. **For as the lightning**
■ **cometh** out of the east, and
shineth even unto the west;
■ **so shall also the coming**
■ **of the Son** of man
■ **be.**
28. For wheresoever the
carcase is, there will the
eagles be gathered together.
■ 29. **Immediately after the**
■ **tribulation** of those days shall the
sun be darkened, and the moon shall
not give her light, and the stars shall
fall from heaven, and the powers of
the heavens shall be shaken:
30. And then shall appear the sign of
the Son of man in heaven: and then
shall all the tribes of the
earth mourn, and
■ **they shall see the Son of**
■ **man coming**
in the clouds of heaven
■ **with power and**
■ **great glory.**
■ 31. **And he shall send his**

■ **angels** with a great
sound of a trumphet,
■ **and they shall gather** together
■ **his elect** from the four winds, from
one end of heaven to the other.
■ 32. **Now learn** a parable
■ **of the fig tree; When**
■ **his branch is** yet
■ **tender, and putteth**
■ **forth leaves,**
ye know that
■ **summer is nigh:**
■ 33. **So likewise** ye,
■ **when ye shall see all these**
■ **things, know that it is near,**
even at the doors.
34. Verily I say unto you,
This generation shall not pass,
till all these things be fulfilled.
■ 35. **Heaven and earth**
■ **shall pass** away,
■ **but my words shall**
■ **not pass** away.
36. **But of that day** and hour
■ **knoweth no man,** no,
not the angels of heaven,
■ **but my Father only.**
■ 37. **But as the days of Noe**
■ **were, so shall also the**
■ **coming of the Son** of man
■ **be.**
38. For as in the days that were
■ **before the flood they**
■ **were eating and** drinking,
■ **marrying** and giving in marriage,
■ **until** the day that
■ **Noe entered into the ark,**
39. **And** knew not until
■ **the flood** came, and
■ **took them** all away;
■ **so shall also the coming**
■ **of the Son** of man
■ **be.**
40. **Then shall two be in the**
■ **field; the one shall be**
■ **taken, and the other left.**
41. Two *women shall be* grinding at
the mill; the one shall be taken, and
the other left.
■ 42. **Watch** therefore: for
■ **ye know not what hour**
■ **your Lord doth come.**
43. But know this, that if the goodman

of the house had known in whatwatch the thief would come, he would have watched, and would not have suffered his house to be broken up.

44. Therefore be ye also ready: **for in such an hour as ye think not the Son of man cometh.**

45. Who then is a faithfull and wise servant, whom his lord hath made ruler over his household, to give them meat in due season?

46. **Blessed is that servant, whom his lord when he cometh shall find** so **doing.**

47. Verily I say unto you, That **he shall make him ruler** over all his goods.

48. **But** and if **that evil servant shall say** in his heart, **My lord delayeth his coming;**

49. And shall begin to smite *his* fellow-servants, and to eat and drink with the drunken;

50. **The lord** of that servant **shall come** in a day **when he looketh not for him,** and in an hour that he is not aware of,

51. **And shall cut him asunder, and** appoint *him* his portion with the hypocrites: **there shall be weeping and gnashing of teeth.**

CHAPTER 25

1. Then shall the kingdom of heaven be likened unto **ten virgins,** which **took** their **lamps, and went forth to meet the bridegroom.**

2. **And five** of them **were wise, and five were foolish.**

3. **They that were foolish took** their lamps, and took **no oil** with them:

4. **But the wise took oil** in their vessels with their lamps.

5. **While the bridegroom tarried, they** all slumbered and **slept.**

6. **And at midnight there was a cry** made, **Behold, the bridegroom cometh;** go ye out to meet him.

7. **Then all those virgins** arose, and **trimmed** their **lamps.**

8. **And the foolish said unto the wise, Give us** of your **oil; for our lamps are** gone **out.**

9. **But the wise answered,** saying, **Not so;** lest there be not enough for us and you: **but go** ye rather to them that sell, **and buy for yourselves.**

10. **And while they went to buy, the bridegroom came; and they that were ready went with him** to the marriage: **and the door was shut.**

11. **Afterward came also the other virgins, saying, Lord** Lord, **open to us.**

12. **But he answered** and said, Verily I say unto you, **I know you not.**

13. **Watch therefore, for ye know neither the day nor the hour** wherein **the Son** of man **cometh.**

14. For *the kingdom of heaven is* as **a man traveling** into a far country, *who* **called his own servants,** and delivered unto them his goods.

15. **And unto one he gave five talents, to another two, and to another one;** to every man according to his several ability: **and** staightway **took his journey.**

16. **Then he that had received the five talents** went and traded with the same, and **made them other**

five talents.

17. **And likewise he that had received two,** he also **gained** other **two.**

18. **But he that had received one** went and **digged in the earth, and hid his lord's money.**

19. **After a** long **time the lord** of those servants **cometh, and reckoneth with them.**

20. **And so he that had received five talents** came and **brought the other five talents,** **saying** Lord, thou deliveredst unto me five talents: behold, **I have gained** beside them **five talents more.**

21. **His lord said** unto him, **Well done,** *thou* good and faithful servant: **thou hast been faithful over a few things, I will make thee ruler over many** things: enter thou into the joy of thy lord.

22. **He also that had received two talents came and said,** Lord thou deliveredst unto me two talents: behold **I have gained two other talents** besides them.

23. **His lord said** unto him, **Well done,** good and **faithful servant;** thou hast been faithful over a few things, I will make thee ruler over many things: enter thou into the joy of thy lord.

24. **Then he which had received the one talent came and said,** Lord, **I knew** thee that **thou art** an **hard** man, reaping where thou hast not sown, and gathering where thou hast not strawed:

25. **And I was afraid, and went and hid thy talent** in the earth: lo, *there* thou hast *that* is thine.

26. **His lord answered** and said unto him,

Thou wicked and slothful servant, thou knewest that I reap where I sowed not, and gather where I have not strawed:

27. **Thou oughtest therefore to have put my money to the exchangers, and then** at my coming **I should have received** mine own with **usury.**

28. **Take therefore the talent from him, and give it unto him which hath ten talents.**

29. **For unto every one that hath shall be given,** and he shall have abundance: **but from him that hath not shall be taken away** even that which he hath.

30. **And cast ye the unprofitable servant into outer darkness:** there shall be weeping and gnashing of teeth.

31. **When the Son** of man **shall come** in his glory, **and** all the holy angels with him, then shall he **sit upon the throne of his glory:**

32. **And before him shall be gathered all nations: and he shall separate them** one from another, **as** a shepherd divideth *his* **sheep from the goats:**

33. **And he shall set the sheep on his right hand, but the goats on the left.**

34. **Then shall the King say unto them on his right hand, Come,** ye blessed of my Father, **inherit the kingdom** prepared for you from the foundation of the world:

35. **For I was an hungered, and ye gave me meat: I was thirsty, and ye gave me drink:** I was a stranger, and ye took me in:

36. Naked, and ye clothed me: I was sick, and ye visited me: I was in

prison, and ye came unto me.

37. **Then shall the righteous answer** him, saying, Lord, **when saw we thee** an hungred, and fed *thee?* or thirsty, and gave *thee* drink?

38. When saw we thee a stranger, and took *thee* in? or naked, and clothed *thee?*

39. Or when saw we thee sick, or in prison, and came unto thee?

40. **And the King shall answer** and say unto them, Verily I say into you, **Inasmuch as ye have done it unto one of the least of these my brethern, ye have done it unto me.**

41. **Then shall he say also unto them on the left hand, Depart from me, ye cursed,** into everlasting fire, prepared for the devil and his angels:

42. **For I was an hungered, and ye gave me no meat: I was thirsty, and ye gave me no drink:**

43. I was a stranger, and ye took me not in: naked, and ye clothed me not: sick, and in prison, and ye visted me not.

44. Then shall they also answer him, saying, Lord, when saw we thee an hungered, or athirst, or a stranger, or naked, or sick, or in prison, and did not minister unto thee?

45. Then shall he answer them, saying, Verily I say unto you, Inasmuch as ye did *it* not to one of the least of these, ye did *it* not to me.

46. **And these shall go away into everlasting punishment:** but the righteous into life eternal.

CHAPTER 26

1. And it came to pass, **when Jesus had finished** all these saying, **he said** unto his disciples,

2. Ye know that **after two days** is *the* feast *of* the passover, and **the Son** of man **is betrayed to be crucified.**

3. **Then assembled together the chief priests,** and the **scribes, and** the **elders** of the people, **unto the palace of** the high priest, who was called **Caiaphas,**

4. **And consulted that they might take Jesus** by subtilty, **and kill him.**

5. But they said, Not on the feast *day,* lest there be an uproar among the people.

6. **Now when Jesus was in Bethany,** in the house of Simon the leper,

7. **There came** unto him **a woman having** an alabaster box of very precious **oinment, and poured it on his head,** as he sat *at meat.*

8. **But when the disciples saw** *it,* **they had indignation,** saying, To what purpose *is* this waste?

9. **For this ointment might have been sold** for much, **and given to the poor.**

10. **When Jesus understood** *it,* **he said** unto them, Why trouble ye the woman? for **she hath wrought a good work** upon me.

11. For ye have the poor always with you; but me ye have not always.

12. **For** in that **she hath poured this ointment on my body,** she did *it* **for my burial.**

13. Verily I say unto you, **Wheresoever this gospel shall be preached** in the whole world, **there shall also this, that this woman hath done, be told for a memorial of her.**

14. **Then** one of the twelve, called **Judas** Iscariot, **went unto the chief priests,**

15. **And said** *unto them,* **What will ye give** me, **and I will deliver** him unto you? **And they covenanted** with him **for thirty pieces of silver.**

16. And from that time he sought opportunity to betray him.

17. Now the first *day* of the *feast of* unleavened bread **the disciples came to Jesus, saying** unto him, **Where wilt thou that we prepare for** thee to eat **the passover?**

18. **And he said, Go into the city to** such **a man, and say** unto him, **The Master saith,** My time is at hand; **I will keep the passover at thy house** with my disciples.

19. And the disciples did as Jesus had appointed them; and they made ready the passover.

20. **Now** when the even was come, **he sat down with the twelve.**

21. **And** as they did eat, **he said,** Verily I say unto you, that **one of you shall betray me.**

22. **And they were** exceeding **sorrowful, and began** every one of them **to say** unto him, **Lord, is it I?**

23. **And he answered** and said, **He that dippeth** *his* hand **with me** in the dish, **the same shall betray me.**

24. The Son of man goeth as it is written of him: but woe unto that man by whom the Son of man is betrayed! it had been good for that man if he had not been born.

25. **Then Judas,** which betrayed him, answered and **said,** Master, **is it I? He said** unto him, **Thou hast said.**

26. And as they were eating, **Jesus took bread, and blessed** *it,* **and brake it, and** gave it to the disciples, and **said, Take, eat; this is my body.**

27. **And he took the cup, and gave thanks,** and gave *it* to them, **saying, Drink** ye all of **it;**

28. **For this is my blood** of the new testament, which is **shed for** many for **the remissions of sins.**

29. But I say unto you, I will not drink henceforth of this fruit of the vine, until that day when I drink it new with you in my Father's kingdom.

30. **And when they had sung** an hymn **they went out** into the mount of Olives.

31. **Then saith Jesus** unto them, **All ye shall be offended because of me this night:** for it is written, I will smite the shepherd, and the sheep of the flock shall be scattered abroad.

32. **But after I am risen again, I will go before you into Galilee.**

33. **Peter answered** and said unto him, **Though all** *men* shall **be offended** because of thee, **yet will I never be offended.**

34. **Jesus said** unto him, Verily I say unto thee, That this night, **before the cock crow, thou shall deny me thrice.**

35. Peter said unto him, Though I should die with thee, yet will I not deny thee. Likewise also said all the disciples.

36. **Then cometh Jesus with them unto** a place called **Gethsemane, and saith** unto the disciples, **Sit** ye here, **while I go and pray** yonder.

37. **And he took** with him **Peter and the two sons of Zebedee,** and began to be sorrowful and very heavy.

38. **Then saith he** unto them, **My soul is** exceeding **sorrowful, even unto death: tarry** ye here, **and watch with me.**
39. **And he went** a little **farther,** and fell on his face, **and prayed,** saying, O my **Father, if it be possible, let this cup pass** from me: **nevertheless not as I will, but as thou wilt.**
40. **And he cometh** unto the disciples, **and findeth them asleep, and said unto Peter,** What, **could ye not watch** with me **one hour?**
41. Watch and pray, that ye enter not into temptation: **the spirit** indeed **is willing, but the flesh is weak.**
42. **He went** away again **the second time, and prayed,** saying, O my Father, **if this cup may not pass** away from me. **except I drink** it, **thy will be done.**
43. **And he** came and **found them asleep again:** for their eyes were heavy.
44. **And he** left them, and went away again, and **prayed the third time,** saying **the same words.**
45. **Then cometh he to his disciples, and saith** unto them, **Sleep on now,** and take *your* rest: behold, the hour is at hand, and the Son of man is betrayed into the hands of sinners.
46. Rise, let us be going: behold, he is at hand that doth betray me.
47. **And while he yet spake,** lo, **Judas,** one of the twelve, **came, and with him a great multitude** with swords and staves, **from the chief priests** and elders of the people.
48. **Now he** that betrayed him **gave them a sign, saying, Whomsoever I shall kiss,** that same **is he:** hold him fast.
49. **And forthwith he** came to Jesus, and said, Hail, master; and **kissed him.**
50. And Jesus said unto him, Friend, wherefore art thou come? **Then** came **they,** and **laid hand on Jesus and took him.**
51. **And, behold, one** of them which were **with Jesus** stretched out *his* hand, and **drew his sword, and struck a sevant of the high priest's, and smote off his ear.**
52. **Then said Jesus** unto him, **Put up again thy sword** into his place: **for** all **they that take the sword shall perish with the sword.**
53. **Thinkest thou that I cannot now pray to my Father, and he shall** presently **give me** more than **twelve legions of angels?**
54. **But how then shall the scriptures be fulfilled, that thus it must be?**
55. In that same hour said Jesus to the multitudes, Are ye come out as against a thief with swords and staves for to take me? I sat daily with you teaching in the temple, and ye laid no hold on me.
56. But all this was done, that the scriptures of the prophets might be fulfilled. **Then all the disciples** forsook him, and **fled.**
57. **And they** that had laid hold on Jesus **led him** away **to Caiaphas the high**

■ **priest,** where the scribes and the elders were assembled.

■ 58. **But Peter followed** him

■ **afar off** unto the high priest's palace, and went in,

■ **and sat with the servants,** to see the end.

■ 59. **Now** the chief priests, and elders, and all

■ **the council, sought false**

■ **witness against Jesus,** to put him to death;

■ 60. **But found none:** yea, though many false witnesses came, *yet* found they none.

■ **At the last came two** false witnesses,

■ 61. **And said, This fellow**

■ **said, I am able to destroy**

■ **the temple** of God,

■ **and** to

■ **build it in three days.**

■ 62. **And the high priest** arose, and

■ **said unto him, Answerest**

■ **thou nothing?** what *is it which* these witness against thee?

■ 63. **But Jesus held his**

■ **peace, And the high priest** answered and

■ **said** unto him, I adjure thee by the living God, that thou

■ **tell us whether thou be the**

■ **Christ,** the Son of God.

■ 64. **Jesus saith** unto him, Thou hadst said: nevertheless I say unto you,

■ **Hereafter shall ye see the**

■ **Son** of man

■ **sitting on the right hand of**

■ **power, and coming in the**

■ **clouds** of heaven.

■ 65. **Then the high priest rent**

■ **his clothes, saying, He hath**

■ **spoken blasphemy;** what further need have we of witnesses? behold, now ye have heard his blasphemy.

■ 66. **What think ye?**

■ **They** answered and

■ **said, He is guilty of death.**

■ 67. **Then** did

■ **they spit in his face, and**

■ buffeted him; and others

■ **smote him** with the palms of their hands,

■ 68. **Saying, Prophesy unto**

■ **us, thou Christ, Who** is he that

■ **smote thee?**

■ 69. **Now Peter sat** without in the palace:

■ **and a damsel came** unto him,

■ **saying, Thou** also

■ **wast with Jesus** of Galilee.

■ 70.**But he denied** before *them* all, saying, I know not what thou sayest.

■ 71. **And** when he was gone out into the porch,

■ **another maid saw him, and**

■ **said** unto them that were there,

■ **This fellow was** also

■ **with Jesus** of Nazareth.

■ 72. **And again he denied** with an oath, I do not know the man.

■ 73. **And** after a while came unto *him*

■ **they that stood by,** and

■ **said** to Peter,

■ **Surely thou** also

■ **art one of them;** for thy speech bewrayeth thee.

■ 74. **Then began he to**

■ **curse and** to

■ **swear, saying, I know not**

■ **the man. And** immediately

■ **the cock crew.**

■ 75. **And Peter remembered**

■ **the word of Jesus,** which said unto him, before the cock crow, thou shalt deny me thrice.

■ **And he went out,**

■ **and wept bitterly.**

CHAPTER 27

1. When the morning was come, all

■ **the chief priests and**

■ **elders** of the people

■ **took counsel against**

■ **Jesus** to put him to death:

■ 2. **And** when they had bound him,

■ **they** led *him* away, and

■ **delivered him to** Pontius

■ **Pilate the governor.**

■ 3. **Then Judas,** which had betrayed him, when he saw that he was condemned,

■ **repented** himself,

48

and brought again the thirty pieces of silver to the chief priests and elders,

4. Saying, I have sinned in that I have betrayed the innocent blood. And they said, What is that to us? see thou *to that.*

5. And he cast down the pieces of silver in the temple, and departed, and went and hanged himself.

6. And the chief priests took the silver pieces, and said, It is not lawful for to put them into the treasury, because it is the price of blood.

7. And they took counsel, and bought with them the potter's field, to bury strangers in.

8. Wherefore that field was called, The field of blood, unto this day.

9. Then was fulfilled that which was spoken by Jeremy the prophet, saying, And they took the thirty pieces of silver, the price of him that was valued, whom they of the children of Israel did value;

10. And gave them for the potter's field, as the Lord appointed me.

11. And Jesus stood before the governor: and the governor asked him, saying, Art thou the King of the Jews? And Jesus said unto him, Thou sayest.

12. And when he was accused of the chief priests and elders, he answered nothing.

13. Then said Pilate unto him, Hearest thou not how many things they witness against thee?

14. And he answered him to never a word; insomuch that the governor marvelled greatly.

15. Now at that feast the governor was wont to release unto the people a prisoner, whom they would.

16. And they had them a notable prisoner, called Barabbas.

17. Therefore when they were gathered together, Pilate said unto them, Whom will ye that I release unto you? Barabbas, or Jesus which is called Christ?

18. For he knew that for envy they had delivered him.

19. When he was set down on the judgment seat, his wife sent unto him, saying, Have thou nothing to do with that just man: for I have suffered many things this day in a dream because of him.

20. But the chief priests and elders persuaded the multitude that they should ask Barabbas, and destroy Jesus.

21. The governor answered and said unto them, Whether of the twain will ye that I release unto you? They said, Barabbas.

22. Pilate saith unto them, What shall I do then with Jesus which is called Christ? They all say unto him, Let him be crucified.

23. And the governor said, Why, what evil hath he done? But they cried out the more, saying, Let him be crucified.

24. When Pilate saw that he could prevail nothing, but *that* rather a tumult was made, he took water, and washed his hands before the multitude, saying, I am innocent of the blood of this just person: see

25. **Then** answered all **the people, and** said, **His blood be on us, and** on **our children.**
26. Then released he Barabbas unto them: **and when he had scourged Jesus, he delivered him to be crucified.**
27. **Then the soldiers** of the governor **took Jesus** into the common hall, and gathered unto him the whole band *of soldiers.*
28. **And they stripped him, and put on him a scarlet robe.**
29. **And** when they had platted **a crown of thorns, they put** *it* **upon his head,** and a reed in his right hand: **and** they **bowed** the knee before him, **and mocked** him, **saying, Hail, King of the Jews!**
30. **And they spit upon him,** and took the reed, **and smote him** on the head.
31. **And after that** they had mocked him, **they** took the robe off from him, and **put his own raiment on him, and led him away to crucify him.**
32. **And** as they came out, they found **a man of Cyrene,** Simon by name: him **they compelled to bear his cross.**
33. **And when they were come unto** a place called **Golgotha,** that is to say, a place of a skull,
34. **They gave him vinegar** to drink mingled **with gall: and** when he had tasted *thereof,* **he would not drink.**
35. **And they crucified him,** **and parted his garments, casting lots: that it might be fulfilled which was spoken by the prophet,** They parted my garments among them, and upon my vesture did they cast lots.
36. And sitting down they watched him there;
37. **And set up over his head his accusation written, THIS IS JESUS THE KING OF THE JEWS.**
38. **Then were there two thieves crucified with him,** one on the right hand, and another on the left.
39. **And they that passed by reviled him,** wagging their heads,
40. **And saying,** thou that destroyest the temple, and buildest *it* in three days, save thyself. **If thou be the Son of God, come down from the cross.**
41. **Likewise also the chief priests mocking** *him,* with the scribes and elders, **said,**
42. He saved others; himself he cannot save. **If he be the King of Israel, let him now come down** from the cross, **and we will believe** him.
43. He trusted in God; let him deliver him now, if he will have him: for he said, I am the Son of God.
44. The thieves also, which were crucified with him, cast the same in his teeth.
45. Now from the sixth hour there was darkness over all the land unto the ninth hour.
46. **And about the ninth hour Jesus cried** with a loud voice, saying, Eli, Eli, lama sabachthani? that is to say, **My God, my God, why hast thou forsaken me?**
47. Some of them that stood there, when they heard *that,* said, This *man* calleth for Elias.
48. **And straightway one**

of them ran, and
took a sponge, and
filled *it*
with vinegar, and
put *it* on a reed, and
gave him to drink.
49. **The rest said,** Let be,
let us see whether
Elias will come to
save him.
50. **Jesus, when he**
had cried again
with a loud voice,
yielded up the ghost.
51. **And, behold, the veil**
of the temple was rent
in twain from the top to the bottom;
and the earth did quake,
and the rocks rent;
52. **And** the graves
were opened; and
many bodies of the
saints which slept
arose,
53. **And came out of the**
graves after his resurrection,
and went into the holy city,
and appeared unto many.
54. **Now when the centurion,**
and they that were
with him, watching Jesus,
saw the earthquake, and
those things that were done,
they feared greatly,
saying, Truly this was
the Son of God.
55. **And many women were**
there beholding afar off, which
followed Jesus from Galilee,
ministering unto him:
56. Among which was Mary
Magdalene, and Mary the mother of
James and Joses, and the mother of
Zebedees children.
57. When the even was
come, there came
a rich man of Arimathaea,
named Joseph, who also
himself was Jesus' disciple:
58. **He went to Pilate, and**
begged the body of Jesus.
Then Pilate commanded the
body to be delivered.

59. **And when Joseph had**
taken the body, he
wrapped it in a clean
linen cloth,
60. **And laid it in his own** new
tomb, which he had hewn
out in the rock:
and he rolled a great
stone to the door of the
sepulchre, and departed.
61. And there was Mary Magdalene,
and the other Mary, sitting over
against the sepulchre.
62. **Now the next day,** that
followed the day of the preparation,
the chief priests and
Pharisees came together
unto Pilate,
63. **Saying, Sir, we remem-**
ber that that deceiver said,
while he was yet alive,
After three days I will
rise again.
64. **Command therefore that**
the sepulchre be made
sure until the third day,
lest his disciples
come by night, and
steal him away, and say unto
the people, He is risen from the dead:
so the last error shall be worse
than the first.
65. **Pilate said** unto them,
Ye have a watch: go your way,
make it as sure as ye can.
66. **So they went,**
and made the sepulchre sure,
sealing the stone, and
setting a watch.

CHAPTER 28

1. In the end of the sabbath, as it
began to dawn toward
the first day of the week,
came Mary Magdalene
and the other Mary to see
the sepulchre.
2. **And, behold, there was a**
great earthquake: for the
angel of the Lord
descended
from heaven, and came
and rolled back the stone

51

from the door, and sat upon it.

3. His countenance was like lightning, and his raiment white as snow:

4. **And for fear** of him **the keepers did shake, and became as dead men.**

5. **And the angel** answered and **said unto the women, Fear not** ye: for I know that **ye seek Jesus,** which was crucified.

6. **He is not here: for he is risen,** as he said. Come, see the place where the Lord lay.

7. **And go quickly, and tell his disciples** that he is risen form the dead; **and, behold, he goeth before you into Galilee;** there shall ye see him: lo, I have told you.

8. **And they** departed quickly from the sepulchre with fear and great joy; and **did run to bring his disciples word.**

9. **And as they went** to tell his disciples, behold, **Jesus met them,** saying, All hail. **And they** came and held him by the feet, and **worshipped him.**

10. Then said Jesus unto them, Be not afraid: go tell my brethren that they go into Galilee, and there shall they see me.

11. **Now** when they were going, behold, **some of the watch came** into the city, **and shewed** unto **the chief priests** all

the things that were done.

12. **And** when they were assembled with **the** elders, and had taken **counsel,** they **gave** large **money unto the soldiers,**

13. **Saying, Say ye, His disciples** came by night, and **stole him** *away* **while we slept.**

14. And if this come to the governor's ears, we will persuade him, and secure you.

15. **So they** took the money, and **did as they were taught:** and this saying is commonly reported among the Jews until this day.

16. **Then the eleven** disciples **went away into Galilee,** into a mountain where Jesus had appointed them.

17. And when they saw him, they worshipped him: but some doubted.

18. **And Jesus came and spake** unto them, **saying, All power is given unto me** in heaven and in earth.

19. **Go** ye therefore, **and teach all nations, baptizing them** in the name of the Father, and of the Son, and of the Holy Ghost:

20. **Teaching them to observe** all things **whatsoever I have commanded** you: **and, lo, I am with you alway, even unto the end** of the world. **Amen.**

THE GOSPEL ACCORDING TO MARK

BACKGROUND INFORMATION

Author: Mark, a missionary
Date Written: probably
between 57 and **65** A.D.

Number of:
Verses   678
Chapters   16
Total Words 15,171
Scan Words 7,290
Scan Words represent
48 % of Total Words

**Theme: written to Christians
to inform them of the
ministry of Jesus on earth as
the Son of God**

OUTLINE OF THE GOSPEL

I.   **Christ's Early Ministry,**
     Baptism and Temptation,
     Including Healings,
     Conflicts with Pharisees
     and Early Travels
     Chapters 1 - 8
II. **Christ's Predictions of
     his Death,** Doctrine of
     Discipleship
     and Transfiguration
     Chapters 9 - 10
III. **Christ's** Entry into
     Jerusalem and
     Crucifixion
     Chapters 11 - 15
IV. **Christ's Resurrection** and
     Appearances to His
     Disciples
     Chapter 16

CHAPTER 1

1. **The beginning of the gospel of Jesus Christ,** the Son of God;

2. **As it is written** in the prophets, Behold, I send **my messenger** before thy face, which **shall prepare thy way** before thee.

3. **The voice of one crying in the wilderness, Prepare ye the way of the Lord,** make his paths straight.

4. **John did baptize** in the wilderness, **and preach** the baptism of **repentance** for the remission **of sins.**

5. **And there went out** unto him **all** the land of **Judaea, and** they of **Jerusalem, and were all baptized** of him in the river of Jordan, **confessing their sins.**

6. **And John was clothed with camel's hair,** and with a girdle of a skin about his loins; and he did eat locusts and wild honey;

7. **And preached, saying, There cometh one mightier** than I after me, the latchet of **whose shoes I am not worthy to** stoop down and **unloose.**

8. I indeed have baptized you with water: but **he shall baptize you with the Holy Ghost.**

9. **And** it came to pass in those days, that **Jesus** came from Nazareth of Galilee, and **was baptized of John** in Jordan.

10. **And straightway coming up out of the water, he saw** the heavens opened, and **the Spirit like a dove descending upon him:**

11. **And there came a voice** from heaven, **saying, Thou art my beloved Son,** in whom I am well pleased.

12. **And immediately the spirit driveth him into** the wilderness.

13. And he was there in **the wilderness forty days, tempted of Satan;** and was with the wild beasts; **and the angels ministered unto him.**

14. **Now after that John was put in prison, Jesus come** into Galilee, **preaching the gospel** of the kingdom of God,

15. **And saying,** The time is fulfilled, and the kingdom of God is at hand: **repent ye, and believe the gospel.**

16. **Now** as he walked by the sea of Galilee, he saw **Simon and Andrew** his brother casting a net into the sea: for they **were fishers.**

17. **And Jesus said** unto them, **Come** ye after me, **and I will make you** to become **fishers of men.**

18. **And straightway they** forsook their nets, and **followed him.**

19. **And** when he had gone a little farther thence, **he saw James** the *son* of Zebedee, **and John** his brother, who also were in the ship **mending their nets.**

20. **And straightway he called them: and they left** their father Zebedee in **the ship** with the hired servants, **and went after him.**

21. **And** they went into Capernaum; and straightway **on the sabbath day he entered into the synagogue, and taught.**

22. And they were astonished at

his doctrine: for he taught them **as one that had authority, and not as the scribes.** 23. And there was in their synagogue **a man with an unclean spirit;** and he **cried out,** 24. **Saying, Let us alone;** what have we to do with thee, **thou Jesus of Nazareth?** art thou come to destroy us? I know thee who thou art, the Holy One of God. 25. **And Jesus rebuked him saying,** Hold thy peace, and **come out of him.** 26. **And when the unclean spirit** had torn him, and **cried** with a loud voice, **he came out of him.** 27. **And they were all amazed,** insomuch that they questioned among themselves, **saying, What** thing is this? what **new doctrine is this?** for with authority commandeth he **even the unclean spirits,** and they do **obey him.** 28. **And immediately his fame spread abroad** throughout all the region round about Galilee. 29. **And** forthwith, when they were come out of the synagogue, **they entered into the house of Simon and Andrew,** with James and John, 30. **But Simon's wife's mother lay sick** of a fever, and anon they tell him of her. 31. **And he** came and took her by the hand, and **lifted her up; and** immediately **the fever left her,** and she ministered unto them. 32. **And** at even, when the sun did set, **they brought** unto him **all that were diseased, and** them that were **possessed with devils.** 33. And all the city was gathered together at the door. 34. **And he healed many** that were sick of divers diseases, and cast out many devils; and suffered not the devils to speak, because they knew him. 35. **And in the morning,** rising up a great while **before day, he went** out, and departed **into a solitary place, and there prayed.** 36. **And Simon and they that were with him followed** after him. 37. **And when they had found him, they said** unto him, **All men seek for thee.** 38. **And he said** unto them, **Let us go** into the next towns, **that I may preach** there also: for therefore came I forth. 39. **And he preached** in their synagogues **throughout all Galilee, and cast out devils.** 40. **And there came a leper** to him, beseeching him, and kneeling down to him, and **saying** unto him, If thou wilt, **thou canst make me clean.** 41. **And Jesus,** moved with compassion, put forth *his* hand, and **touched him, and saith** unto him, I will; **be thou clean.** 42. **And** as soon as he had spoken, **immediately** the leprosy departed from him, and **he was cleansed.** 43. **And he** straitly charged him, and forthwith **sent him away;** 44. **And saith** unto him, See thou **say nothing to any man: but go** thy way, shew thyself **to the priest, and offer** for thy cleansing **those things which Moses commanded, for a testimony** unto them. 45. **But he** went out, and **began** to publish *it* much, and to blaze abroad the matter, insomuch that Jesus could no more openly enter into the city, but was without in desert places; and they came to him from every quarter.

CHAPTER 2

1. And again he entered into Capernaum after *some* days: and it was noised that he was in the house. 2. And straightway many were gathered together, insomuch that there was no room to receive *them,* no, not so much as about the door: and he preached the word unto them. 3. And they come unto him, bringing one sick of the palsy, which was borne of four. 4. And when they could not come nigh unto him for the press, they uncovered the roof where he was: and when they had broken *it* up, they let down the bed wherein the sick of the palsy lay. 5. When Jesus saw their faith, he said, unto the sick of the palsy, Son, thy sins be forgiven thee. 6. But there was certain of the scribes sitting there, and reasoning in their hearts, 7. Why doth this *man* thus speak blasphemies? who can forgive sins but God only? 8. And immediately when Jesus perceived in his spirit that they so reasoned within themselves, he said unto them, Why reason ye these things in your hearts? 9. Whether is it easier to say to the sick of the palsy, Thy sins be forgiven thee; or to say, Arise, and take up thy bed, and walk? 10. But that ye may know that the Son of man hath power on earth to forgive sins, (he saith to the sick of the palsy,) 11. I say unto thee, Arise, and take up thy bed, and go thy way into thine house. 12. And immediately he arose, took up the bed, and went forth before them all; insomuch that they were all amazed, and glorified God, saying, We never saw it on this fashion. 13. And he went forth again by the sea side; and all the multitude resorted unto him, and he taught them. 14. And as he passed by, he saw Levi the *son* of Alphaeus sitting at the receipt of custom, and said unto him, Follow me. And he arose and followed him. 15. And it came to pass, that, as Jesus sat at meat in his house, many publicans and sinners sat also together with Jesus and his disciples: for there were many, and they followed him. 16. And when the scribes and Pharisees saw him eat with publicans and sinners, they said unto his disciples, How is it that he eateth and drinketh with publicans and sinners? 17. When Jesus heard *it,* he saith unto them, They that are whole have no need of the physician, but they that are sick: I came not to call the righteous, but sinners to repentance. 18. And the disciples of John and of the Pharisees used to fast: and

■ **they** come and
■ **say unto him,** Why do
the disciples of John and
of the Pharisees fast, but
■ **thy disciples fast not?**
■ 19. **And Jesus said**
unto them, Can the children of
the bridechamber fast, while
the bridegroom is with them?
■ **as long as they have**
■ **the bridegroom** with them,
■ **they cannot fast.**
■ 20. **But** the days will come,
■ **when the bridegroom shall**
■ **be taken away** from them, and
■ **then shall they fast**
in those days.
■ 21. **No man also**
■ **seweth** a piece of
■ **new cloth on an**
■ **old garment:** else
■ **the new** piece that filled it up
■ **taketh away from the old,**
and the rent is made worse.
■ 22. **And no man putteth new**
■ **wine into old bottles: else**
■ **the new wine doth burst the**
■ **bottles,** and the wine is spilled,
and the bottles will be marred:
■ **but new wine must be**
■ **put into new bottles.**
■ 23. **And** it came to pass, that
■ **he went through the corn**
■ **fields on the sabbath**
■ **day; and his disciples**
■ **began,** as they went,
■ **to pluck the** ears of
■ **corn.**
■ 24. **And the Pharisees**
■ **said** unto him, Behold,
■ **why do they** on the sabbath day
■ **that which is not lawful?**
■ 25. **And he said** unto them,
■ **Have ye never read**
■ **what David did, when**
■ **he** had need, and was an
■ **hungered,** he, and they
that were with him?
■ 26. **How he went into the**
■ **house of God** in the days
of Abiathar the high priest,
■ **and did eat the shewbread,**
■ **which is**

■ **not lawful** to eat but for
the priests, and gave also
to them which were with him?
27. And he said unto them, The
sabbath was made for man,
and not man for the sabbath:
28. Therefore
■ **the Son of man is Lord**
■ **also of the sabbath.**

CHAPTER 3

1. And lhe entered again
into the synagogue; and
■ **there was a man** there
■ **which had a withered**
■ **hand.**
■ 2. **And they watched him,**
■ **whether he would heal him**
■ **on the sabbath day;** that
they might accused him.
■ 3. **And he saith unto the**
■ **man** which had the withered hand,
■ **Stand forth.**
4. And he saith unto them,
■ **Is it lawful to do good on**
■ **the sabbath days, or** to do
■ **evil?** to save life, or to kill?
but they held their peace.
■ 5. **And** when he had
looked round about on them
■ **with anger, being grieved**
■ **for the hardness of their**
■ **hearts, he saith unto the**
■ **man, Stretch forth thine**
■ **hand.** And he stretched *it* out:
■ **and his hand was**
■ **restored** whole as the other.
■ 6. **And the Pharisees**
went forth, and straightway
■ **took counsel** with the
Herodians against him,
■ **how they might**
■ **destroy him.**
■ 7. **But Jesus withdrew**
himself with his
disciples to the sea:
■ **and** a great multitude from Galilee
followed him, and from Judaea,
8. And from Jerusalem, and from
Idumaea, and *from* beyond
Jordan; and they about Tyre
and Sidon, a great multitude,
■ **when they had heard**

what great things he
did, came unto him.
9. And he spake to his
disciples, that a small
ship should wait on him
because of the multitude,
lest they should throng him.
10. For he had healed many;
insomuch that they pressed upon
him for to touch him, as many as
had plagues.
11. And unclean spirits,
when they saw him,
fell down before
him, and cried,
saying, Thou art the
Son of God.
12. And he straitly charged
them that they should
not make him known.
13. And he goeth up
into a mountain, and
calleth *unto him* whom he
would: and they came unto him.
14. And he ordained twelve,
that they should be with
him, and that he might
send them forth to preach,
15. And to have power
to heal sicknesses,
and to cast out devils:
16. And Simon he surnamed Peter;
17. And James the *son* of Zebedee,
and John the brother of James; and
he surnamed them Boanerges,
which is, The sons of thunder;
18. And Andrew, and Philip, and
Bartholomew, and Matthew, and
Thomas, and James the *son* of
Alphaeus, and Thaddaeus, and
Simon the Canaanite,
19. And Judas Iscariot, which
also betrayed him: and they
went into an house.
20. And the multitude
cometh together
again, so that they could
not so much as eat bread.
21. And when
his friends heard *of it,* they
went out to lay hold
on him: for they said,
He is beside himself.

22. And the scribes which
came down from Jerusalem
said, He hath Beelzebub, and
by the prince of the devils
casteth he out devils.
23. And he called
them *unto him,* and
said unto them
in parables, How can Satan
cast out Satan?
24. And if a kingdom be
divided against itself, that
kingdom cannot stand.
25. And if a house be divided against
itself, that house cannot stand.
26. And if Satan rise
up against himself, and
be divided, he cannot
stand, but hath an end.
27. No man can enter into
a strong man's house,
and spoil his goods
except he will first
bind the strong man;
and then he will spoil his house.
28. Verily I say unto you,
All sins shall be forgiven unto
the sons of men, and blasphemies
wherewith
soever they shall blaspheme:
29. But he that shall
blaspheme against the
Holy Ghost hath never
forgiveness, but is in danger of
eternal damnation.
30. Because they said, He
hath an unclean spirit.
31. There came
then his brethren and his
mother, and, standing without,
sent unto him
calling him.
32. And the multitude
sat about him, and they
said unto him, Behold,
thy mother and
thy brethren without
seek for thee.
33. And he answered them, saying,
Who is my mother, or my brethren?
34. And he looked round about
on them which sat about
him, and said, Behold my

58

■ **mother and my brethren!**
■ 35. **For whosoever shall**
■ **do the will of God,** the same
■ **is my brother, and my sister,**
■ **and mother.**

CHAPTER 4

■ 1. **And he** began again to teach by
the sea side: and there was gathered
unto him a great multitude, so that he
■ **entered into a ship,**
and sat in the sea;
■ **and the** whole
■ **multitude was** by the sea
■ **on the land.**
■ 2. **And he taught**
■ **them** many things
■ **by parables, and**
■ **said** unto them in his doctrine,
3. Hearken; Behold,
■ **there went out a**
■ **sower to sow:**
■ 4.**And** it came to pass, as he sowed,
■ **some fell by the way side,**
■ **and the fowls** of the air came and
■ **devoured it** up.
■ 5. **And some fell on**
■ **stony ground,** where
it had not much earth;
■ **and** immediately it sprang up,
■ **because it had no**
■ **depth** of earth:
6. But when
■ **the sun** was up, it was
■ **scorched; and**
because it had no root,
■ **it withered away.**
■ 7. **And some fell among**
■ **thorns, and the**
■ **thorns** grew up, and
■ **choked it,** and it yielded no fruit.
■ 8. **And other fell on good**
■ **ground, and did yield fruit**
that sprang up and increased; and
brought forth, some thirty, and some
sixty, and some an hundred.
9. And he said unto them, He that
hath ears to hear, let him hear.
■ 10. **And when** he was
■ **alone, they** that were
about him with the twelve
■ **asked of him the parable.**
■ 11. **And he said** unto them,

■ **Unto you** it
■ **is given** to know
■ **the mystery of the kingdom**
■ **of God: but unto them**
that are without, all *these*
■ **things are done**
■ **in parables:**
12. **That seeing**
■ **they may** see, and
■ **not perceive; and**
■ **hearing** they may hear, and
■ **not understand;**
■ **lest** at any time
■ **they** should
■ **be converted,** and *their*
sins should be forgiven them.
13. And he said unto them,
■ **Know** ye not
■ **this parable?** and how then
will ye know all parables?
■ 14. **The sower**
■ **soweth the word.**
■ 15. **And these** are they
■ **by the way side,**
where the word is sown; but
■ **when they** have
■ **heard, Satan**
■ **cometh** immediately,
■ **and taketh away the word**
that was sown in their hearts.
■ 16. **And these** are they
likewise which are
■ **sown on stony ground;** who,
■ **when they have heard**
the word, immediately
■ **receive it with gladness;**
■ 17. **And have no**
■ **root** in themselves, and
■ **so** endure but for a time: afterward,
■ **when affliction or**
■ **persecution ariseth**
for the word's sake, immediately
■ **they are offended.**
■ 18. **And these** are they which are
■ **sown among thorns;** such as
■ **hear the word,**
■ 19. **And the cares** of this world,
■ **and** the deceitfulness of
■ **riches,** and the lusts of
other things entering in,
■ **choke the word,**
and it becometh unfruitful.
■ 20. **And these** are they which are

sown on good ground; such as hear the word, and receive it, and bring forth fruit, some thirtyfold, some sixty, and some an hundred. 21. And he said unto them, is a candle brought to be put under a bushel, or under a bed? and not to be set on a candlestick? 22. For there is nothing hid, which shall not be manifested; neither was any thing kept secret, but that it should come abroad. 23. If any man have ears to hear, let him hear. 24. And he said unto them, Take heed what ye hear: with what measure ye mete, it shall be measured to you: and unto you that hear shall more be given. 25. For he that hath, to him shall be given: and he that hath not, from him shall be taken even that which he hath. 26. And he said, So is the kingdom of God, as if a man should cast seed into the ground; 27. And should sleep, and rise night and day, and the seed should spring and grow up, he knoweth not how. 28. For the earth bringeth forth fruit of herself; first the blade, then the ear, after that the full corn in the ear. 29. But when the fruit is brought forth, immediately he putteth in the sickle, because the harvest is come. 30. And he said, Whereunto shall we liken the kingdom of God? or with what comparison shall we compare it? 31. It is like a grain of mustard seed, which, when it is sown in the earth, is less than all the seeds that be in the earth: 32. But when it is sown, it groweth up, and becometh greater than all herbs, and shooteth out great branches; so that the fowls of the air may lodge under the shadow of it. 33. And with many such parables spake he the word unto them, as they were able to hear it. 34. But without a parable spake he not unto them: and when they were alone, he expounded all things to his disciples. 35. And the same day, when the even was come, he saith unto them, Let us pass over unto the other side. 36. And when they had sent away the multitude, they took him even as he was in the ship. And there were also with him other little ships. 37. And there arose a great storm of wind, and the waves beat into the ship, so that it was now full. 38. And he was in the hinder part of the ship, asleep on a pillow: and they awake him, and say unto him, Master, carest thou not that we perish? 39. And he arose, and rebuked the wind, and said unto the sea, Peace, be still. And the wind ceased, and there was a great calm. 40. And he said unto them, Why are ye so fearful? how is it that ye have no faith? 41. And they feared exceedingly, and said one to another, What manner of man

is this, that even the wind
and the sea obey him?

CHAPTER 5

1. **And they came** over
unto the other side of the sea
**into the country of
the Gadarenes.**
2. **And** when he was come
out of the ship, immediately
**there met him out of the
tombs a man with an
unclean spirit,**
3. **Who** had *his* dwelling
among the tombs; and
no man could bind
him, no, not with chains:
4. Because that he had been often
bound with fetters and chains, and the
chains had been plucked asunder by
him, and the fetters broken in pieces:
**neither could any
man tame him.**
5. **And always,** night and
day, he was in the mountains,
and in the tombs,
**crying, and cutting
himself with stones.**
6. **But when he
saw Jesus** afar off,
**he ran and
worshipped him,**
7. And cried with a loud voice,
**and said, What have I
to do with thee, Jesus,
thou Son of** the most high
God? I adjure thee
by God, that thou
torment me not.
8. For he said unto him, Come out
of the man, *thou* unclean spirit.
9. **And he asked him, What
is thy name? And he
answered,** saying, My name *is*
Legion: for we are many.
10. **And he besought him**
much that he would
not send them away
out of the country.
11. **Now there was**
there nigh unto the mountains
**a great herd of
swine feeding.**

12. **And all the devils
besought him,** saying
Send us into the swine,
that we may enter into them.
13. And forthwith
Jesus gave them leave.
And the unclean spirits went out,
and entered into the swine:
**and the herd ran
violently** down a steep place
into the sea, (they were
about two thousand;)
and were choked in the sea.
14. **And they** that fed
the swine fled, and
told it in the city, and in the
**country. And they went out
to see** what it was that was done.
15. And they come to
Jesus, and see him that
was possessed with the devil, and
**had the legion,
sitting,** and clothed,
and in his right mind:
and they were afraid.
16. And they that saw *it* told them
how it befell to him that was
possessed with the devil, and *also*
concerning the swine.
17. **And they began** to pray him
to depart out of their coasts.
18. **And** when he was
come into the ship,
**he that had been
possessed** with the devil
**prayed him that he
might be with him.**
19. Howbeit
Jesus suffered him not, but
**saith unto him,
Go home** to thy friends,
**and tell them how great
things the Lord hath done**
for thee, and hath had
compassion on thee.
20. **And he** departed, and
began to publish in Decapolis
**how great things Jesus
had done** for him:
and all men did marvel.
21. **And** when
Jesus was
passed over again

■ **by ship unto the other side,**
much people gathered unto him:
and he was nigh unto the sea.
■ 22. **And,** behold, there cometh
■ **one of the rulers**
of the synagogue,
■ **Jairus** by name: and
when he saw him, he
■ **fell at his feet,**
23. And besought him greatly,
■ **saying, My little daughter**
■ **lieth at the point of**
■ **death:** *I pray thee,*
■ **come** and lay thy hands on her,
■ **that she may be**
■ **healed;** and she shall live.
■ 24. **And Jesus went with**
■ **him;** and much people followed
him, and thronged him.
■ 25. **And a certain woman,**
■ **which had an issue of**
■ **blood twelve years,**
■ 26. **And had suffered many**
■ **things** of many physicians, and had
spent all that she had, and was nothing bettered, but rather grew worse,
■ 27. **When she had heard of**
■ **Jesus, came** in the press behind,
■ **and touched his garment.**
28. For she said, If I may touch but his
clothes, I shall be whole.
■ 29. **And straightway** the
fountain of her blood was dried
up; and she felt in *her* body that
■ **she was healed** of that plague.
■ 30. **And Jesus,** immediately
■ **knowing** in himself
■ **that virtue had gone**
■ **out of him,** turned him
about in the press, and
■ **said, Who touched**
■ **my clothes?**
■ 31. **And his disciples**
■ **said** unto him,
■ **Thou seest the multitude**
■ **thronging thee,** and sayest
thou, Who touched me?
■ 32. **And he looked**
■ **round** about
■ **to see her** that had
done this thing.
■ 33. **But the woman fearing**
and trembling, knowing what

was done in her,
■ **came** and fell down before him,
■ **and told him all the truth.**
■ 34. **And he said**
unto her, Daughter,
■ **thy faith hath made thee**
■ **whole; go in peace,** and
be whole of thy plague.
■ 35. **While he yet spake, there**
■ **came from the ruler of the**
■ **synagogue's house certain**
■ **which said, Thy daughter**
■ **is dead:** why troublest thou
the Master any further?
■ 36. **As soon as Jesus**
■ **heard** the word that was spoken,
■ **he saith** unto the ruler
of the synagogue,
■ **Be not afraid, only believe.**
37. And he suffered no man to follow
him, and save Peter, and James, and
John the brother of James.
■ 38. **And he cometh to**
■ **the house** of the ruler of the
synagogue, and seeth the tumult, and
them that wept and wailed greatly,
■ 39. **And** when he was come in, he
■ **saith** unto them,
■ **Why** make ye this ado, and
■ **weep? the damsel is**
■ **not dead, but sleepeth.**
■ 40. **And they**
■ **laughed** him to scorn.
■ **But when he had put them**
■ **all out, he taketh the father**
■ **and the mother** of the damsel,
and them that were with him,
■ **and entereth in where**
■ **the damsel was lying.**
■ 41. **And he took the damsel**
■ **by the hand, and said**
unto her, Talitha cumi; which
is, being interpreted,
■ **Damsel, I say unto**
■ **thee, arise.**
■ 42. **And straightway the**
■ **damsel arose,** and walked; for
she was *of the age* of twelve years.
■ **And they were astonished**
with a great astonishment.
■ 43. **And he** charged them straitly
that no man should know it; and
■ **commanded that**

■ something should be
■ given her to eat.

CHAPTER 6

■ 1. **And he** went out from thence,and
■ **came into his own country;**
and his disciples follow him.

■ 2. **And** when the
sabbath day was come,
■ **he began to teach in the**
■ **synagogue: and many**
■ **hearing him were**
■ **astonished, saying,** From
whence hath this *man* these things?
and what wisdom *is* this which is
given unto him, that even such mighty
works are wrought by his hands?
■ 3. **Is not this the carpenter,**
■ **the son of Mary,** the brother
of James, and Moses, and of
Juda, and Simon? and are not
his sisters here with us?
■ **And they were**
■ **offended** at him.
■ 4. **But Jesus, said** unto them,
■ **A prophet is not without**
■ **honour, but in his own**
■ **country,** and among his
own kin, and in his own house.
■ 5. **And he could** there
■ **do no mighty work,**
■ **save** that he laid his hands
■ **upon a few sick folk,**
and healed *them.*
■ 6. **And he marvelled**
■ **because of their unbelief.**
And he went round about the
villages, teaching.
■ 7. **And he called** *unto him*
■ **the twelve, and began to**
■ **send them forth by two**
■ **and two; and gave them**
■ **power** over unclean spirits;
■ 8. **And commanded them**
■ **that they should take**
■ **nothing for their journey,**
save a staff only; no scrip, no
bread, no money in *their* purse:
9. But *be* shod with sandals;
and not put on two coats.
■ 10. **And he said** unto them,
In what place soever ye enter
into an house, there abide till

ye depart from that place.
■ 11. **And whosoever shall not**
■ **receive you,** nor hear
you, when ye depart thence,
■ **shake off the dust**
■ **under your feet for a**
■ **testimony against them.**
Verily I say unto you,
■ **It shall be more tolerable**
■ **for Sodom and Gomorrha in**
■ **the day of judgement, than**
■ **for that city.**
12. **And they** went out, and
■ **preached that men**
■ **should repent.**
13. **And they cast out many**
■ **devils, and anointed** with oil
■ **many** that were
■ **sick, and healed them.**
14. **And king Herod** heard
of him; (for his name was
spread abroad:) and he
■ **said, That John the Baptist**
■ **was risen** from the dead, and
therefore mighty works do shew
forth themselves in him.
■ 15. **Others said, That**
■ **it is Elias,** And others
said, That it is a prophet,
■ **or** as
■ **one of the prophets.**
16. **But** when
■ **Herod** heard *thereof,* he
■ **said, It is John, whom**
■ **I beheaded:** he is risen
from the dead.
■ 17. **For Herod himself**
■ **had** sent forth and laid
hold upon John, and
■ **bound him in prison for**
■ **Herodias' sake,** his brother
Philip's wife: for he had married her.
■ 18. **For John had**
■ **said** unto Herod,
■ **It is not lawful** for thee
■ **to have thy brother's wife.**
■ 19. **Therefore Herodias**
had a quarrel against him and
■ **would have killed him;**
■ **but she could not:**
■ 20. **For Herod feared John,**
knowing that he was a just man
and an holy, and observed him;

John the Baptist beheaded

and when he heard him, he did
many things, and heard him gladly.
21. **And** when a convenient
day was come, that
Herod on his birthday
made a supper to his
lords, high captains, and
chief *estates* of Galilee;
22. **And when the**
daughter of the said
Herodias came in, and
danced, and pleased
Herod and them that sat with him
the king said unto the damsel,
Ask of me
whatsoever thou wilt,
and I will give it thee.
23. And he sware unto her,
Whatsoever thou shalt ask
of me, I will give *it* thee,
unto the half of my kingdom.
24. **And she went** forth, and said
unto her mother, What
shall I ask? And she
said, The head of
John the Baptist.
25. **And she came** in
straightway with haste unto the king,
and asked, saying, I will that thou
give me by and by in a charger
the head of John
the Baptist.
26. **And the king was** exceeding
sorry; yet for his oath's
sake, and for their sakes
which sat with him,
he would not reject her.
27. **And** immediately the king sent
an executioner, and
commanded his head to
be brought: and he went and
beheaded him in the prison,
28. **And brought his head** in
a charger, and gave it to the damsel;
and the damsel gave
it to her mother.
29. And when his disciples heard
of it, they came and took up his
corpse, and laid it in a tomb.
30. **And the apostles**
gathered themselves together
unto Jesus, and told
him all things, both

what they had done,
and what they had taught.
31. **And he said** unto them,
Come ye yourselves
apart into a desert place,
and rest a while: for there were
many coming and going, and they
had no leisure so much as to eat.
32. **And they departed**
into a desert place
by ship privately.
33. **And the people saw**
them departing, and many knew him,
and ran afoot thither
out of all cities, and outwent
them, and came together
unto him.
34. **And Jesus,** when he
came out, saw much people, and
was moved with
compassion toward them,
because they were as
sheep not having a
shepherd: and he began
to teach them many things.
35. **And when the day**
was now far spent, his
disciples came unto him, and
said, This is a desert
place, and now the
time is far passed;
36. **Send them away, that**
they may go into the country
round about, and into the villages, and
buy themselves
bread: for they have
nothing to eat.
37. **He answered**
and said unto them,
Give ye them to eat.
And they say unto him,
Shall we go and buy
two hundred pennyworth of
bread, and give them to eat?
38. **He saith** unto them,
How many loaves
have ye? go and see.
And when they knew,
they say, Five,
and two fishes.
39. **And he commanded**
them to make all
sit down by companies

upon the green grass.

40. And they sat down **in ranks,** by hundreds, and by fifties.

41. **And when he had taken the five loaves and the two fishes, he** looked up to heaven, and **blessed,** and brake the loaves, **and gave** *them* **to** his disciples to set before **them;** and the two fishes divided he among them all.

42. **And they** did all eat, and **were filled.**

43. **And they took up twelve baskets full of the fragments,** and of the fishes.

44. **And they that did eat** of the loaves **were about five thousand men.**

45. **And straightway he constrained his disciples to get into the ship, and to go to** the other side before unto **Bethsaida,** while he sent away the people.

46. **And** when he had sent them away, **he departed into a mountain to pray.**

47. And when even was come, the ship was in the midst of the sea, and he alone on the land.

48. **And he saw them toiling in rowing; for the wind was contrary** unto them: **and** about the fourth watch of the night **he cometh** unto them, **walking upon the sea, and would have passed by** them.

49. **But** when they saw him walking upon the sea, **they** supposed it had been a spirit, and **cried out:**

50. For they all saw him, and were troubled. **And immediately he** talked with them, and

saith unto them, **Be of good cheer: it is I; be not afraid.**

51. **And he went** up unto them **into the ship; and the wind ceased: and they were sore amazed** in themselves beyond measure, and wondered.

52. For they considered not *the miracle* of the loaves: for their heart was hardened.

53. **And** when they had passed over, **they came into the land of Gennesaret,** and drew to the shore.

54. **And when they** were come out of the ship, straightway they knew him,

55. And ran through that whole region round about, and **began to carry about in beds those that were sick,** where they heard he was.

56. And whithersoever he entered, into villages, or cities, or country, **they laid the sick in the streets,** and besought him **that they might touch** if it were but the border of **his garment: and** as many as touched him **were made whole.**

CHAPTER 7

1. **Then came** together unto him **the Pharisees, and** certain of the **scribes,** which came from Jerusalem.

2. **And** when they **saw** some of **his disciples eat bread** with defiled, that is to say, **with unwashen hands,** they found fault.

3. **For the Pharisees,** and all the Jews, **except they wash** *their* hands oft, **eat not,** holding the tradition of the elders.

4. **And when they** *come* from the market, except they wash, they

eat not. And many other things there be, which they have received to hold, *as* the washing of cups, and pots, brasen vessels, and of tables.

5. Then the Pharisees and Scribes **asked him, Why walk not thy disciples according to the tradition** of the elders, **but eat bread with unwashen hands?**

6. **He answered** and said unto them. Well hath Esaias prophesied of **you hypocrites, as it is written, This people honoureth me with their lips, but their heart is far from me.**

7. **Howbeit in vain do they worship me,** teaching *for* doctrines the commandments of men.

8. **For** laying aside the commandment of God, ye hold the tradition of men, *as* the washing of pots and cups: and many other such like things ye do.

9. And he said unto them, full well **ye reject the commandment of God, that ye may keep your own tradition.**

10. **For Moses said, Honour thy father and thy mother;** and, Whoso curseth father or mother, let him die the death:

11. **But ye say,** If a man shall say to his father or mother, **It is** Corban, that is to say, **a gift,** by whatsoever **thou mightest be profited by me;** *he shall be free.*

12. **And** ye suffer him **no more to do aught for his father or his mother;**

13. **Making the word of God of none effect** through your tradition, which ye have delivered: and many such like things do ye.

14. **And when he had called all the people** *unto him,* **he said** unto them, **Hearken** unto me every one *of you,* **and understand:**

15. **There is nothing from without a man, that** entering into him **can defile him: but the things which come out of him,** those are they that **defile the man.**

16. If any man have ears to hear, let him hear.

17. And when he was entered into the house from the people, **his disciples asked him concerning the parable.**

18. **And he saith** unto them, Are ye so without understanding also? Do ye not perceive, that **whatsoever thing from without entereth** into the **man, it cannot defile him:**

19. **Because it entereth** not into his heart, but **into the belly, and goeth out into the draught,** purging all meats?

20. **And he said, That which cometh out of the man, that defileth the man.**

21. **For from within,** out of the heart of men, **proceed evil thoughts,** adulteries, fornications, murders,

22. Thefts, covetousness, wickedness, deceit, lasciviousness, an evil eye, blasphemy, pride, foolishness:

23. All these evil things come from with in, and defile the man.

24. **And** from thence **he** arose, and **went into** the borders of **Tyre and Sidon,** and entered into an house, **and would have no man know it: but he could not be hid.**

25. **For a certain woman,** whose young daughter had an unclean spirit, heard of him, and came and fell at his feet;

26. The woman was a Greek, **a Syrophenician** by nation; and she **besought him that he would cast forth the devil out of her daughter.**

27. **But Jesus said** unto her, Let

the children first be filled: for

it is not meet to take the children's bread, and to cast it unto the dogs.

28. **And she answered** and said unto him, yes, Lord; **yet the dogs** under the table **eat** of the children's **crumbs.**

29. **And he said** unto her, **For this saying** go thy way; **the devil is gone out of thy daughter.**

30. And when she was come to her house, she found the devil gone out, and her daughter laid upon the bed.

31. **And** again, departing from the coasts of Tyre and Sidon, **he came unto** the sea of Galilee, through the midst of the coasts of **Decapolis.**

32. **And they bring unto him one that was deaf, and had an impediment in his speech;** and they beseech him to put his hand upon him.

33. **And he took him aside** from the multitude, **and put his fingers into his ears, and he spit, and touched his tongue;**

34. And looking up to heaven, he sighed, **and saith** unto him, Ephphatha, that is, **Be opened.**

35. **And straightway his ears were opened,** and the string of his tongue was loosed, **and he spake** plain.

36. **And he charged them that they should tell no man: but** the more he charged them, so much the more a great deal **they published it;**

37. **And were** beyond measure **astonished, saying,** He hath done all things well: **He maketh** both **the deaf to hear, and the dumb to speak.**

CHAPTER 8

1. In those days the multitude being very great, and having nothing to eat, **Jesus called his disciples** unto him, **and saith** unto them,

2. I have compassion on **the multitude,** because they have now been with me three days, and **have nothing to eat:**

3. **And if I send them away fasting** to their own houses, **they will faint** by the way: for divers of them came from far.

4. **And his disciples answered** him, **From whence can a man satisfy these men with bread** here in the wilderness?

5. **And he asked** them, **How many loaves have ye? And they said, Seven.**

6. And he commanded the people to sit down on the ground: and **he took the seven loaves, and gave thanks, and brake,** and gave to his disciples to set before *them;* **and** they did **set them before the people.**

7. And they had a few small fishes: and he blessed, and commanded to set them also before *them.*

8. **So they** did eat, and **were filled: and** they took up of **the** broken **meat that was left seven baskets.**

9. **And they** that had eaten **were about four thousand:** and he sent them away.

10. **And** straightway **he entered** into **a ship** with his disciples, **and came into** the parts of **Dalmanutha.**

11. **And the Pharisees came** forth, and began **to question** with **him, seeking** of him **a sign** from heaven, **tempting him.**

12. **And he** sighed deeply in his spirit, and **saith,** Why doth this generation seek after a sign? verily I say unto you, **There shall no sign be given** unto this generation. 13. **And he** left them, and entering into the ship again **departed** to the other side. 14. **Now the disciples had forgotten to take bread,** neither had they in the ship with them more than one loaf. 15. **And he charged them,** saying, Take heed, **beware of the leaven of the Pharisees, and** of the leaven *of* **Herod.** 16. **And they reasoned** among themselves, saying, **It is because we have no bread.** 17. And when **Jesus** knew *it*, he **saith** unto them, **Why reason ye,** because ye have no bread? **perceive ye not yet, neither understand?** have ye your heart yet hardened? 18. Having eyes, see ye not? and having ears, hear ye not? and **do ye not remember?** 19. **When I brake the five loaves among five thousand,** how many baskets full of fragments took ye up? They say unto him Twelve. 20. **And** when the **seven among four thousand,** how many baskets full of fragments took ye up? And they said, Seven. 21. **And he said unto them, How is it that ye do not understand?** 22. **And he cometh to Bethsaida; and they bring a blind man unto him,** and besought him to touch him. 23. **And he** took the blind man by the hand, and led him out of the town; and when he had **spit on his eyes, and** put his hands upon him, he **asked** him **if he saw aught.** 24. **And he** looked up, and **said, I see men as trees, walking.** 25. **After that he put his hands again upon his eyes,** and made him look up: **and he** was restored, and **saw every man clearly.** 26. And he sent him away to his house, saying, Neither go into the town, nor tell *it* to any in the town. 27. **And Jesus** went out, and his disciples, into the towns of Caesarea Philippi: and by the way he **asked his disciples,** saying unto thlem, **Whom do men say that I am?** 28. And **they answered, John the Baptist; but some say, Elias; and others, One of the prophets.** 29. **And he saith** unto them, **But whom say ye that I am? And Peter answereth** and saith unto him, **Thou art the Christ.** 30. And he charged them that they should tell no man of him. 31. **And he began to teach them, that the Son of man must suffer** many things, and be rejected of the elders, and *of* the chief priests, and scribes, **and be killed, and after three days rise again.** 32. And he spake that saying openly. **And Peter** took him, and **begun to rebuke him.** 33. **But** when he had turned about and looked on his disciples, **he rebuked Peter, saying, Get thee behind me, Satan:** for thou savourest not the things that be of God, but the things that be of men. 34. **And when he had**

called the people *unto him* with his disciples also,

he said *unto them,*

Whosoever will come after me, let him deny himself, and take up his cross, and follow me.

35. For whosoever will save his life shall lose it; but whosoever shall lose his life for my sake and the gospel's, the same shall save it.

36. For what shall it profit a man, if he shall gain the whole world, and lose his own soul?

37. Or what shall a man give in exchange for his soul?

38. Whosoever therefore shall be ashamed of me and of my words in this adulterous and sinful generation; of him also shall the Son of man be ashamed, when he cometh in the glory of his Father with the holy angels.

CHAPTER 9

1. And he said *unto them,* Verily I say unto you, That there be some of them that stand here, which shall not taste of death, till they have seen the kingdom of God come *with power.*

2. And after six days Jesus taketh *with him* Peter, and James, and John, and leadeth them up into an high mountain apart *by themselves:* and he was transfigured *before them.*

3. And his raiment became *shining, exceeding* white as snow; *so as no* fuller on earth can white them.

4. And there appeared *unto them* Elias with Moses: *and they were* talking with Jesus.

5. And Peter answered and said to Jesus,

Master, *it is good for us to be here; and* let us make three tabernacles; *one for thee, and one for Moses, and one Elias.*

6. For he wist not what to say; for they were sore afraid.

7. And there was a cloud that overshadowed them: and a voice came *out of the cloud,* saying, This is my beloved Son: hear him.

8. And suddenly, *when they had looked round about,* they saw *no man any more, save* Jesus only *with themselves.*

9. And as they came *down from the mountain,* he charged them that they should tell no man *what things they had seen,* till the Son of man were risen *from the dead.*

10. And they kept that *saying with themselves,* questioning one with another what the rising from the dead should mean.

11. And they asked *him, saying,* Why say the scribes that Elias must first come?

12. And he answered *and told them,* Elias verily cometh first, *and restoreth all things;* and *how it is written of* the Son of man, *that he* must suffer many things, *and be set at nought.*

13. But I say *unto you, That* Elias is indeed come, and they have done *unto him* whatsoever they listed, *as it is written of him.*

14. And when he came to his disciples, he saw a *great multitude about them, and* the scribes questioning *with them.*

15. And straightway all the people, when they beheld him, were greatly amazed, and running to *him* saluted him.

16. **And he asked** the scribes, **What question ye** with them?

17. **And one** of the multitude **answered** and said, Master, **I have brought** unto thee **my son, which hath a dumb spirit;**

18. And wheresoever he taketh him, he teareth him: and he foameth, and gnasheth with his teeth, and pineth away: **and I spake to thy disciples that they should cast him out; and they could not.**

19. **He answereth** him, and saith, O faithless generation, how long shall I be with you? how long shall I suffer thou? **bring him unto me.**

20. And they brought him unto him: **and when he saw him,** straightway **the spirit tare him; and he fell** on the ground, **and wallowed foaming.**

21. **And he asked his father, How long** is it ago **since this came unto him? And he said, Of a child.**

22. And ofttimes it hath cast him into the fire, and into the waters, to destroy him: **but if thou canst do any thing,** have compassion on us, and **help us.**

23. **Jesus said** unto him, If thou canst believe, **all things are possible to him that believeth.**

24. And straightway **the father** of the child **cried** out, and said with tears, **Lord, I believe;** help thou mine unbelief.

25. **When Jesus saw** that **the people** came running together, **he rebuked the foul spirit, saying** unto him, **Thou dumb and deaf spirit,** I charge thee, **come out of him,** and enter no more into him.

26. **And the spirit** cried, and rent him sore, and **came out of him: and he was as one dead;** insomuch that many said, He is dead.

27. **But Jesus** took him by the hand and **lifted him up; and he arose.**

28. And when he was come into the house, **his disciples asked** him privately, **Why could not we cast him out?**

29. **And he said** unto them, **This kind can come forth by nothing, but by prayer and fasting.**

30. And they departed thence, and passed through Galilee; **and he would not that any man should know** *it.*

31. **For he taught his disciples,** and said unto them, **The Son of man is delivered into the hands of men, and they shall kill him; and** after that he is killed, **he shall rise the third day.**

32. But they understood not that saying, and were afraid to ask him.

33. **And he** came to Capernaum: and being in the house he **asked them, What was it that ye disputed among yourselves** by the way?

34. But they held their peace: for by the way **they had disputed** among themselves, **who should be the greatest.**

35. **And he** sat down, and called the twelve, and **saith unto them, If any man desire to be first, the same shall be** last of all and **servant of all.**

36. And he took a child, and set him in the midst of them:and when he had taken him in his arms, he **said** unto them,

37. Whosoever shall receive one of such children **in my name, receiveth me: and** whosoever shall receive me, receiveth not me, but **him that sent me.**

38. And John answered him saying, Master, **we saw one casting out devils in thy name,** and he followeth not us: **and we forbad him, because he followeth not us.**

39. But Jesus said, Forbid him not: for there is no man which shall do a miracle in my name, that can lightly speak evil of me.

40. For he that is not against us is on our part.

41. For whosoever shall give you a cup of **water** to drink **in my name,** because ye belong to Christ, verily I say unto you, he **shall not lose his reward.**

42. And whosoever shall offend one of **these little ones** that believe in me, **it is better** for him that a millstone were hanged about his neck, and **he were cast into the sea.**

43. And if thy hand offend thee, cut it off: it is better for thee **to enter into life maimed, than having two hands to go into hell,** into the fire that never shall be quenched:

44. Where their worm dieth not, and the fire is not quenched.

45. And if thy foot offend thee, cut it off: it is better for thee to enter halt into life, **than having two feet to be cast into hell,** into the fire that never shall be quenched:

46. Where their worm dieth not, and the fire is not quenched.

47. And if thine eye offend thee, pluck it out: it is better for thee to enter into the kindom of God with one eye, **than have two eyes to be cast into hell fire:**

48. Where their worm dieth not, and the fire is not quenched.

49. For every one shall be salted with fire, and every sacrifice shall be salted with salt.

50. Salt *is* good: but if the salt have lost his saltness, wherewith will ye season it? Have salt in yourselves, and have peace one with another.

CHAPTER 10

1. And he arose from thence, and cometh into the coasts of Judaea **by the** farther side of **Jordan:** and the people resort unto him again; and, as he was wont, **he taught** them again.

2. And the Pharisees came to him, and **asked him, Is it lawful for a man to put away his wife?** tempting him.

3. And he answered and said unto them, **What did Moses command you?**

4. And they said, Moses suffered **to write a bill of divorcement,** and to put *her* away.

5. And Jesus answered and said unto them, **For the hardness of your heart he wrote** you this precept.

6. But from the beginning of the creation **God made them male and female.**

7. For this cause shall a man leave his father and mother, and cleave to his wife;

8. And they twain shall be one flesh: so then they are no more twain, but one flesh.

9. **What therefore God hath joined together, let not man put asunder.** 10. And in the house his disciples asked him again of the same *matter.* 11. **And he saith** unto them, **Whosoever shall put away his wife, and marry another, committeth adultery** against her. 12. **And if a woman shall put away her husband, and be married to another, she committeth adultery.** 13. **And they brought young children** to him, that he should touch them; **and his disciples rebuked those that brought them.** 14. **But** when **Jesus** saw *it,* he was much displeased, and **said** unto them, **Suffer the little children to come unto me,** and forbid them not; **for of such is the kingdom** of God. 15. Verily I say unto you, **Whosoever shall not receive the kingdom** of God **as a little child, he shall not enter** therein. 16. **And he** took them up in his arms, put *his* hands upon them, and **blessed them.** 17. And when he was gone forth into the way, **there came one** running, and kneeled to him, **and asked him,** good Master, **what shall I do that I may inherit eternal life?** 18. **And Jesus said** unto him, Why callest thou me good? *there is* none good but one, *that is,* God. 19. Thou knowest the commandments, **Do not commit adultery,** Do not **kill,** do not **steal,** Do not **bear false witness, Defraud**

not, **Honour thy father and mother.** 20. **And he** answered and **said** unto him, **Master, all these have I observed** from my youth. 21. **Then Jesus** beholding him loved him, and **said** unto him, **One thing thou lackest:** go thy way, **sell whatsoever thou hast, and give to the poor,** and thou shalt have treasure in heaven: and come, take up the cross, **and follow me.** 22. **And he was sad** at that saying, and went away grieved; **for he had great possessions.** 23. **And Jesus** looked round about, and **saith** unto his disciples, How hardly shall they that have riches enter into the kingdom of God! 24. And the disciples were astonished at his words. But Jesus answereth again, and saith unto them, Children, **how hard is it for them that trust in riches to enter into the kingdom of God!** 25. It is easier for a camel to go through the eye of a needle, than for a rich man to enter into the kingdom of God. 26. **And they were astonished** out of measure, **saying** among themselves, **Who then can be saved?** 27. **And Jesus** looking upon them **saith, With men it is impossible, but** not with God: for **with God all things are possible.** 28. **Then Peter began to say** unto him, Lo, **we have left all, and have followed thee.** 29. **And Jesus answered** and said, Verily I say unto you, **There is no man that hath left house, or brethren,**

or sisters, or father, or mother,
or wife, or children,
or lands, for my sake ,
and the gospel's,
30. **But he shall receive an**
hundredfold now in this
time, house, and brethren
and sisters, and mothers,
and children, and lands,
with persecutions;
and in the world to
come eternal life.
31. But many *that are* first
shall be last; and the last first.
32. **And** they were
in the way going up
to Jerusalem; and Jesus
went before them: and they were
amazed; and as they followed,
they were afraid. And
he took again the twelve, and
began to tell them what
things should happen
unto him,
33. **Saying,** Behold, we
go up to Jerusalem; and
the son of man shall be
delivered unto the chief
priests, and unto the
scribes; and they shall
condemn him to death, and
shall deliver him to the Gentiles:
34. And they shall mock him, and
shall scourge him, and shall spit
upon him, and shall kill him:
and the third day he
shall rise again.
35. **And James and**
John, the sons of Zebedee,
come unto him, saying,
Master, we would
that thou shouldest
do for us whatsoever
we shall desire.
36. **And he said** unto them,
What would ye that
I should do for you?
37. **They said** unto him,
Grant unto us
that we may sit, one
on thy right hand,
and the other on thy
left hand, in thy glory.

38. **But Jesus said** unto
them, Ye know not what ye ask:
can ye drink of the cup that
I drink of? and be baptized with
the baptism that I am baptized with?
39. **And they said** unto him,
We can. And Jesus
said unto them,
ye shall indeed drink of the
cup that I drink of; and with the
baptism that I am baptized withall
shall ye be baptized:
40. **But to sit on my right** hand
and on my
left hand is not mine
to give; but it *shall be given*
to them for whom it
is prepared.
41. And when
the ten heard it, they
began to be much
displeased with
James and John.
42. **But Jesus** called
them to *him,* and
saith unto them, Ye know that they
which are accounted to rule over
the Gentiles exercise lordship
over them; and their great ones
exercise authority upon them.
43. But so shall it not
be among you: but
whosoever will be
great among you,
shall be your minister:
44. **And** whosoever of you will be
the chiefest, shall be
servant of all.
45. **For even the Son of man**
came not to be ministered unto, but
to minister, and to give his
life a ransom for many.
46. **And they came to**
Jericho: and as he went
out of Jericho with his disciples
and a great number of people,
blind Bartimaeus,
the son of Timaeus,
sat by the highway
side begging.
47. **And** when he heard
that it was Jesus of Nazareth,
he began to cry out, and say,

Jesus, *thou* son of David, **have mercy on me.** 48. And many charged him that he should hold his peace: but he cried the more a great deal, *Thou* son of David, have mercy on me. 49. **And Jesus** stood still, and **commanded him to be called.** And they call the blind man, saying unto him, Be of good comfort, rise; he calleth thee. 50. **And he,** casting away his garment, rose, and **came to Jesus.** 51. **And Jesus** answered and **said** unto hlim, **What wilt thou that I should do** unto thee? **The blind man said** unto him, **Lord, that I might receive my sight.** 52. **And Jesus said** unto him, go thy way; **thy faith hath made thee whole. And immediately he received his sight,** and followed Jesus in the way.

CHAPTER 11

1. **And when they came nigh to** Jerusalem, unto Bethphage and Bethany, at **the mount of Olives, he sendeth** forth **two** of his **disciples.** 2.**And saith** unto them, **Go** your way **into the village** over against you: **and** as soon as ye be entered into it, **ye shall find a colt tied,** whereon never man sat; **loose him, and bring him.** 3. And if any man say unto you, Why do ye this? say ye that the Lord hath need of him; and straightway he will send him hither. 4. **And they** went their way, and **found the colt** tied by the door without in a place where two ways met; **and they loose him.**

5. **And certain** of them **that stood there said** unto them, **What do ye,** loosing the colt? 6. **And they said** unto them **even as Jesus** had **commanded:** and they let them go. 7. **And they brought the colt to Jesus,** and cast their garments on him; **and he sat upon him.** 8. **And many spread their garments** in the way: **and** others cut down **branches off the trees,** and strawed *them* **in the way.** 9. **And they** that went before, and they that followed, **cried,** saying, **Hosanna; Blessed** *is* **he that cometh in the name of the Lord:** 10. Blessed *be* the kingdom of our father David, that cometh in the name of the Lord: Hosanna in the highest. 11. **And Jesus entered** into Jerusalem, and **into the temple: and** when he had **looked round** about upon all things, **and** now the eventide was come, he **went** out **unto Bethany** with the twelve. 12. **And on the morrow,** when they were come from Bethany, **he was hungry:** 13. **And seeing a fig tree** afar off having leaves, **he came,** if haply he might find any thing thereon; **and** when he came to it, he **found nothing but leaves;** for the time of figs was not *yet*. 14. **And Jesus** answered and **said unto it, No man eat fruit of thee hereafter** for ever. And his disciples heard *it*. 15. **And they come to Jerusalem: and Jesus** went into the temple, and

74

began to cast out them that
sold and bought in the
temple, and overthrew the tables
of the moneychangers, and the
seats of them that sold doves;
16. And would not suffer that
any man should carry *any*
vessel through the temple.
17. And he taught, saying
unto them, Is it not written,
My house shall be
called of all nations
the house of prayer?
but ye have made it
a den of thieves.
18. And the scribes and
chief priests heard *it,* and
sought how they might
destroy him: for they feared
him, because
all the people were astonished
at his doctrine.
19. And when even was come,
he went out of the city.
20. And in the morning,
as they passed by,
they saw the fig tree
dried up from the roots.
21. And Peter calling
to remembrance
saith unto him,
Master, behold,
the fig tree which thou
cursedst is withered away.
22. And Jesus answering
saith unto them,
Have faith in God.
23. For verily I say unto you, That
whosoever shall say
unto this mountain,
Be thou removed, and
be thou cast into the sea;
and shall not doubt in his
heart, but shall believe that
those things which he saith
shall come to pass; he
shall have whatsoever
he saith.
24. Therefore I say unto you,
What things soever ye
desire, when ye pray,
believe that ye receive *them,*
and ye shall have them.

25. And when ye stand
praying, forgive, if ye have
aught against any: that your
Father also which is in heaven
may forgive you your trespasses.
26. But if ye do not forgive,
neither will your Father
which is in heaven
forgive your trespasses.
27. And they come again
to Jerusalem: and as
he was walking in the temple,
there come to him
the chief priests, and the
scribes, and the elders,
28. And say unto him,
by what authority doest
thou these things? and
who gave thee this authority
to do these things?
29. And Jesus answered
and said unto them,
I will also ask of you one
question, and answer me,
and I will tell you by what
authority I do these things.
30. The baptism of John,
was it from heaven,
or of men? answer me.
31. And they reasoned
with themselves, saying,
If we shall say, From
heaven; he will say,
Why then did ye not
believe him?
32. But if we shall say, Of
men; they feared the people:
for all men counted
John, that he was
a prophet indeed.
33. And they answered
and said unto Jesus,
We cannot tell. And Jesus
answering saith unto them,
Neither do I tell you bywhat
authority I do these things.

CHAPTER 12

1. And he began
to speak unto them
by parables. A certain
man planted a vineyard,
and set an hedge about *it,*

and digged a *place for* the winevat and built a tower, and let it out to husbandmen, and went into a far country.

2. And at the season he sent to the husbandmen a servant, that he might receive from the husbandmen of the fruit of the vineyard.

3. And they caught *him,* and beat him, and sent him away empty.

4. And again he sent unto them another servant; and at *him* they cast stones, and wounded him in the head, and sent *him* away shamefully handled.

5. And again he sent another; and him they killed, and many others; beating some, and killing some.

6. Having let therefore one son, his well beloved, he sent him also last unto them, saying, They will reverence my son.

7. But those husbandmen said among themselves, This is the heir; come, let us kill him, and the inheritance shall be ours.

8. And they took him, and killed him, and cast *him* out of the vineyard.

9. What shall therefore the lord of the vineyard do? he will come and destroy the husbandmen, and will give the vineyard unto others.

10. And have ye not read this scripture; The stone which the builders rejected is become the head of the corner:

11. This was the Lord's doing, and it is marvellous in our eyes?

12. And they sought to lay hold on him, but feared the people: for they knew that he had spoken the parable against them: and they left him, and went their way.

13. And they send unto him certain of the Pharisees and of the Herodians, to catch him in his words.

14. And when they were come, they say unto him Master, we know that thou art true, and carest for no man: for thou regardest not the person of men, but teachest the way of God in truth: Is it lawful to give tribute to Caesar, or not?

15. Shall we give, or shall we not give? But he, knowing their hypocrisy, said unto them, Why tempt ye me? bring me a penny, that I may see *it.*

16. And they brought it. And he saith unto them, whose is this image and superscription? And they said unto him, Caesar's.

17. And Jesus answering said unto them, Render to Caesar the things that are Caesar's, and to God the things that are God's. And they marvelled at him.

18. Then come unto him the Sadducees, which say there is no resurrection; and they asked him, saying

19. Master, Moses wrote unto us, If a man's brother die, and leave his wife *behind him,* and leave no children, that his brother should take his wife, and raise up seed unto his brother,

20. Now there were seven brethren: and the first took a wife, and dying left no seed.

21. And the second took her, and died, neither left he any seed: and third likewise.

22. **And the seven had her, and left no seed:** last of all woman died also.
23. **In the resurrection** therefore, when they shall rise, **whose wife shall she be** of them? for the seven had her to wife.
24. **And Jesus answering said** unto them, do ye not therefore err, Because ye know not the scripture, neither the power of God?
25. For **when they shall rise** from the dead, **they neither marry, nor are given in marriage; but are as the angels** which are in heaven.
26. **And as touching the dead,** that they rise: **have ye not read** in the book of Moses, how in the bush God spake unto him, saying, I *am* the God of Abraham, and the God of Isaac, and the God of Jacob?
27. **He is not the God of the dead, but** the God **of the living:** ye therefore do greatly err.
28. **And one of the scribes** came, and having heard them reasoning together, and perceiving that he had answered them well, **asked him, Which is the first commandment** of all?
29. **And Jesus answered** him, The first of all the commandments *is,* Hear, O Israel: **The Lord our God is one Lord:**
30. **And thou shalt love the Lord thy God with all thy heart,** and with all thy **soul,** and with all thy **mind, and** with all thy **strength:** this is the first commandment.
31. **And the second is** like, *namely* this, **Thou shalt love thy neighbour as thyself.** There is none other commandment greater than these.

32. **And the scribe said** unto him, Well, Master, **thou hast said the truth: for there is one God;** and there is none other but he:
33. **And to love him** with all the heart, and with all the understanding, and with all the soul, and with all the strength, **and to love his neighbour** as himself, **is more than all whole burnt offerings** and sacrifices.
34. And when **Jesus** saw that he answered discreetly, he **said** unto him, **Thou art not far from the kingdom** of God. And no man after that durst ask him *any question.*
35. **And Jesus** answered and **said,** while he taught in the temple, **How say the scribes that Christ is the son of David?**
36. **For David** himself **said** by the Holy Ghost, **The LORD said to my Lord, Sit thou on my right hand,** till I make thine enemies thy footstool.
37. **David** therefore himself **calleth him Lord; and whence is he** *then* **his son?** And the common people heard him gladly.,
38. **And he said** unto them in his doctrine, **Beware of the scribes, which love** to go in long **clothing, and** *love* **salutations** in the marketplaces,
39. **And the chief seats** in the synagogues, **and the uppermost rooms at feasts:**
40. **Which devour widows' houses, and** for a pretence **make long prayers: these shall receive greater damnation.**
41. **And Jesus sat** over against the treasury, **and beheld how the people cast money into**

the treasury: and many that were rich cast in much. 42. And there came a certain poor widow, and she threw in two mites, which make a farthing. 43. And he called *unto him* his disciples, and saith unto them, Verily I say unto you, That this poor widow hath cast more in, than all they which have cast into the treasury: 44. For all they did cast in of their abundance; but she of her want did cast in all that she had, *even* all her living.

CHAPTER 13

1. And as he went out of the temple, one of his disciples saith unto him Master, see what manner of stones and what buildings *are here!* 2. And Jesus answering said unto him, Seest thou these great buildings? there shall not be left one stone upon another, that shall not be thrown down. 3. And as he sat upon the mount of Olives over against the temple, Peter and James and John and Andrew asked him privately, 4. Tell us, when shall these things be? and what *shall be* the sign when all these things shall be fulfilled? 5. And Jesus answering them began to say, Take heed lest any *man* deceive you: 6. For many shall come in my name, saying, I am *Christ;* and shall deceive many. 7. And when ye shall hear of wars and rumours of wars, be ye not troubled: for *such things* must needs be; but

the end shall not be yet. 8. For nation shall rise against nation, and kingdom against kingdom: and there shall be earthquakes in divers places, and there shall be famines and troubles: these are the beginnings of sorrows. 9. But take heed to yourselves: for they shall deliver you up to councils; and in the synagogues ye shall be beaten: and ye shall be brought before rulers and kings for my sake, for a testimony against them. 10. And the gospel must first be published among all nations. 11. But when they shall lead *you,* and deliver you up, take no thought beforehand what ye shall speak, neither do ye premeditate: but whatsoever shall be given you in that hour, that speak ye: for it is not ye that speak, but the Holy Ghost. 12. Now the brother shall betray the brother to death, and the father the son; and children shall rise up against their parents, and shall cause them to be put to death. 13. And ye shall be hated of all *men* for my name's sake: but he that shall endure unto the end, the same shall be saved. 14. But when ye shall see the abomination of desolation, spoken of by Daniel the prophet, standing where it ought not, (let him that readeth understand,) then let them that be in Judaea flee to the mountains: 15. And let him that is on the housetop not go down into the house, neither enter *therein,* to take any thing out of his house:

16. And let him that is in the field not turn back again for to take up **his garment.**

17. But woe to them that are **with child,** and to them that give suck in those days!

18. And pray ye that **your flight be not in the winter.**

19. For in those days shall be affliction, such as was not from the beginning of the creation which God created unto this time, neither shall be.

20. And except that the Lord had shortened those days, no flesh should be saved: but for the elect's sake, whom he hath chosen, he hath shortened the days.

21. And then **if any man** shall **say** to you, Lo, **here is Christ;** or, lo, *he is* there; **believe him not;**

22. For false Christs and false prophets **shall rise,** and shall shew signs and wonders, **to seduce, if it were possible, even the elect.**

23. But take ye heed: behold, **I have foretold you all things.**

24. But in those days, **after that tribulation, the sun shall be darkened,** and the moon shall not give her light,

25. And the stars of heaven **shall fall, and the** powers that are in **heaven** shall be **shaken.**

26. And then shall they see the Son of man coming in the clouds with great power and glory.

27. And then shall he send **his angels,** and **shall gather** together **his elect** from the four winds, from the uttermost part of the earth to the uttermost part of heaven.

28. Now learn a parable of the fig tree; When her branch is yet tender, and **putteth forth leaves,** ye know that **summer is near;**

29. So ye in like manner, when ye shall see these things come to pass, **know that it is nigh,** *even* at the doors.

30. Verily I say unto you, that **this generation shall not pass, till all these things be done.**

31. Heaven and earth shall pass away: but my words shall not pass away.

32. But of that day and *that* **hour knoweth no man,** no, not the angels which are in heaven, **neither the Son, but the Father.**

33. Take ye heed, watch and pray: for ye know not when the time is.

34. For the son of Man is as a man taking a far journey, who left his house, and **gave** authority to his servants, and **to every man his work,** and commanded the porter to watch.

35. Watch ye therefore: for ye know not when the master of the house **cometh,** at even, or at midnight, or at the cockcrowing, or in the morning:

36. Lest coming suddenly he find you sleeping.

37. And what I say unto you I say unto all, Watch.

CHAPTER 14

1. After two days was *the feast of* **the passover,** and of unleavened bread; **and the chief priests and the scribes sought how they might** take him by craft, and **put him to death.**

2. But they said, Not on the feast *day,* lest there be an uproar of the people.

3. And being in Bethany

in the house of Simon the
leper, as he sat at meat,
■ **there came a woman**
■ **having an** alabaster box of
■ **ointment of spikenard** very
precious; and she brake the box,
■ **and poured it on his head.**
4. And there were
■ **some that had indignation**
within themselves, and
■ **said, Why was this**
■ **waste** of the ointment made?
5. **For it might have**
■ **been sold** for more
than three hundred pence,
■ **and** have been
■ **given to the poor.**
And they murmured against her.
6. **And Jesus said,** let
her alone; why trouble ye her?
■ **she hath wrought a**
■ **good work on me.**
7. **For ye have the**
■ **poor** with you
■ **always,** and whensoever
ye will ye may do them good:
■ **but me ye have not always.**
8. She hath done what she could:
■ **she is come** aforehand
■ **to anoint my body**
■ **to the burying.**
9. **Verily I say** unto you,
■ **Wheresoever this gospel**
■ **shall be preached**
throughout the whole world,
■ **this** also that she hath done
■ **shall be spoken of**
■ **for a memorial of her.**
10. **And Judas Iscariot,**
one of the twelve,
■ **went unto the chief priests,**
■ **to betray him** unto them.
11. **And** when
■ **they** heard it, they were glad, and
■ **promised** to give
■ **him money.** And he sought how
he might conveniently betray him.
12. **And the** first day of
unleavened bread, when
they killed the passover, his
■ **disciples said** unto him,
■ **Where wilt thou**
■ **that we** go and

■ **prepare** that thou mayest eat
■ **the passover?**
■ 13. **And he sendeth forth**
■ **two of his disciples,**
■ **and saith** unto them,
■ **Go** ye into the city, and there shall
■ **meet** you
■ **a man bearing**
■ **a pitcher of water:**
■ **follow him.**
■ 14. **And** wheresoever he shall go in,
■ **say** ye to the goodman of
the house, The Master saith,
■ **Where is the**
■ **guestchamber, where I**
■ **shall eat the passover**
■ **with my disciples?**
■ 15. **And he will shew you**
■ **a large upper room**
furnished *and* prepared:
■ **there make ready** for us.
16. And his disciples went
forth, and came into the
city, and found as he had
said unto them: and they
made ready the passover.
■ 17. **And in the evening**
he cometh with the twelve.
18. And
■ **as they sat and did eat,**
■ **Jesus said,** Verily I say unto you,
■ **One of you** which eateth with me
■ **shall betray me.**
■ 19. **And they began**
to be sorrowful, and
■ **to say** unto him one by one,
■ **Is it I?** and another *said, Is* it I?
■ 20. **And he answered**
and said unto them,
■ **It is one** of the twelve,
■ **that dippeth with**
■ **me in the dish.**
21. The son of man indeed goeth,
as it is written of him: but
■ **woe to that man** by whom
the son of man is betrayed!
■ **good were it** for that man
■ **if he had never been born.**
■ 22. **And** as they did eat,
■ **Jesus took bread,**
■ **and blessed,** and brake
it, and gave to them,
■ **and said, Take, eat:**

this is my body.

23. **And he took the cup, and when he had given thanks,** he gave *it* to them: and **they all drank** of it.

24. **And he said** unto them, **This is my blood** of the new testament, **which is shed for many.**

25. **Verily** I say unto you, **I will drink no more** of the fruit of the vine, **until** that day that **I drink it new in the kingdom of God.**

26. **And when they had sung an hymn, they went out into the mount of Olives.**

27. **And Jesus saith** unto them, **All ye shall be offended because of me this night:** for it is written, I will smite the shepherd, and the sheep shall be scattered.

28. But after that I am risen, I will go before you into Galilee.

29. **But Peter said** unto him, **Although all shall be offended, yet will not I.**

30. **And Jesus saith** unto him, Verily I say unto thee, that this day, *even* in **this night, before the cock crow twice, thou shalt deny me thrice.**

31. But he spake the more vehemently, If I should die with thee, I will not deny thee in any wise. Likewise also said they all.

32. **And they came to** a place which was named **Gethsemane; and he saith** to his disciples, **Sit ye here, while I shall pray.**

33. **And he taketh** with him **Peter and James and John,** and began to be sore amazed, and to be very heavy;

34. **And saith** unto them, **My soul is exceeding sorrowful unto death: tarry ye here,** and watch.

35. **And he went forward** a little, **and fell on the ground, and prayed** that, if it were possible, the hour might pass from him.

36. And he said, Abba, **Father,** all things *are* possible unto thee; **take away this cup from me: nevertheless not what I will, but what thou wilt.**

37. **And he cometh, and findeth them sleeping, and saith** unto Peter, Simon, sleepest thou? **couldest not thou watch one hour?**

38. **Watch ye and pray,** lest ye enter into temptation. The spirit truly *is* ready, but the flesh *is* weak.

39. **And again he** went away, and **prayed,** and spake **the same words.**

40. **And when he returned, he found them asleep again,** (for their eyes were heavy,) neither wist they what to answer him.

41. **And he cometh the third time, and saith** unto them, **Sleep on now,** and take *your* rest: it is enough, **the hour is come;** behold, the Son of man is betrayed into the hands of sinners.

42. Rise up, let us go; lo, **he that betrayeth me is at hand.**

43. **And immediately,** while he yet spake, **cometh Judas,** one of the twelve, **and with him a** great **multitude** with swords and staves, from the chief priests and the scribes and the elders.

44. **And he** that betrayed him **had given them a token, saying Whomsoever I shall kiss,** that same is he; **take him,** and lead *him* away safely.

45. **And** as soon as he was come, **he goeth** straightway **to him and**

saith, Master, master; and

■ **kissed him.**

■ 46. **And they** laid
their hands on him, and

■ **took him.**

■ 47. **And one** of them that stood by

■ **drew a sword, and smote a**

■ **servant of the high priest,**

■ **and cut off his ear.**

■ 48. **And Jesus** answered and

■ **said** unto them,

■ **Are ye come out, as**

■ **against a thief,** with
swords and *with* staves

■ **to take me?**

■ 49. **I was daily** with you

■ **in the temple teaching,**
and ye took me not:

■ **but the scriptures**

■ **must be fulfilled.**

■ 50. **And they all** forsook him, and

■ **fled.**

51. And there followed him a certain
young man, having a linen cloth cast
about *his* naked *body;* and the young
men laid hold on him:

52. And he left the linen cloth,
and fled from them naked.

■ 53. **And they led Jesus away**

■ **to the high priest:**
and with him were assembled all
the chief priests and the elders
and the scribes.

■ 54. **And Peter followed**

■ **him afar off,** even into the
palace of the high priest:

■ **and he sat with the**

■ **servants, and warmed**

■ **himself at the fire.**

■ 55. **And the chief**

■ **priests** and all the council

■ **sought for witness against**

■ **Jesus** to put him to death;

■ **and found none.**

■ 56. **For many bare**

■ **false witness** against him,

■ **but their witness**

■ **agreed not** together.

■ 57. **And there arose certain,**
and bare false witness against him,

■ **saying,**

■ 58. **We heard him say, I**

■ **will destroy this temple**

that is made with hands,

■ **and within three days**

■ **I will build another made**

■ **without hands.**

59. But neither so did their
witness agree together.

■ 60. **And the high priest**
stood up in the midst, and

■ **asked Jesus,** saying,

■ **Answerest thou nothing?**
what *is it which* these witness
against thee?

■ 61. **But he held his peace,**
and answered nothing.

■ **Again the high priest**

■ **asked him,** and said unto him,

■ **Art thou the Christ,** the
son of the Blessed?

■ 62. **And Jesus said, I am:**

■ **and ye shall see the Son**

■ **of man sitting on the**

■ **right hand of power,**

■ **and coming in the**

■ **clouds** of heaven,

■ 63. **Then the high priest rent**

■ **his clothes, and saith,** What
need we any futher witnesses?

■ 64. **Ye have heard the**

■ **blasphemy:** what think ye?

■ **And they all condemned**

■ **him to** be guilty of

■ **death.**

■ 65. **And some began** to spit
on him, and to cover his face, and

■ **to** buffet him, and to say
unto him, Prophesy:
and the servants did

■ **strike him** with the
palms of their hands.

■ 66. **And** as Peter was beneath
in the palace, there cometh

■ **one of the maids of**

■ **the high priest:**
67. And when she

■ **saw Peter warming**

■ **himself,** she looked upon him,

■ **and said,** and

■ **thou** also

■ **wast with Jesus** of Nazareth.

■ 68. **But he denied,** saying,
I know not, neither understand
I what thou sayest. And he
went out into the porch;

and the cock crew.

69. **And a maid saw him again,** and began to say to them that stood by, **This is one of them.**

70. **And he denied it again.** and a little after, **they that stood by said again** to Peter, **Surely thou art one of them:** for thou art a Galilaean, and thy speech agreeth *thereto*.

71. **But he began to curse** and to swear, **saying, I know not this man** of whom ye speak.

72. **And the second time the cock crew. And Peter called to mind the word that Jesus said** unto him, Before the cock crow twice, thou shalt deny me thrice. **And** when he thought thereon, **he wept.**

CHAPTER 15

1. **And** straightway in the morning **the chief priests held** a consultation with the elders and scribes **and the whole council,** and **bound Jesus,** and carried *him* away, **and delivered him to Pilate.**

2. **And Pilate asked** him, **Art thou the King of the Jews? And he** answering **said** unto him, **Thou sayest it.**

3. **And the chief priests accused him of many things:** but he answered nothing.

4. And Pilate asked him again, saying, Answerest thou nothing? behold how many things they witness against thee.

5. **But Jesus** yet **answered nothing; so that Pilate marvelled.**

6. **Now at that feast he released** unto them **one prisoner,** whomsoever they desired.

7. **And there was one named Barabbas,** *which* lay bound with them that had made insurrection with him, **who had committed murder** in the insurrection

8. And the multitude crying aloud began to desire *him to do* as he had ever done unto them.

9. But **Pilate answered** them, saying, **Will ye that I release unto you the King of the Jews?**

10. For he knew that the chief priests had delivered him for envy.

11. **But the chief priests moved the people, that he should** rather **release Barabbas** unto them.

12. **And Pilate answered** and said again unto them, **What will ye them that I** shall **do unto** *him* whom ye call **the King of the Jews?**

13. **And they cried** out again, **Crucify him.**

14. **Then Pilate said** unto them, **Why, what evil hath he done? And they cried out** the more exceedingly, **Crucify him.**

15. **And so Pilate,** willing to content the people, **released Barabbas** unto them, **and delivered Jesus,** when he had scourged *him,* to be crucified.

16. **And the soldiers led him** away **into the hall, called Praetorium;** and they call together the whole band.

17. **And they clothed him with purple, and planted a crown of Thorns,** and put it **about his head,**

18. And began to salute him, Hail, King of the Jews!

19. And they smote him on the head with a reed, and did spit upon him and bowing *their* knees worshipped him.

20. And when they had mocked him, they took off the purple from him, and put his own clothes on him, and led him out to crucify him.

21. And they compel one Simon a Cyrenian, who passed by, coming out of the country, the father of Alexander of Rufus, to bear his cross.

22. And they bring him unto the place Golgotha, which is, being interpreted, the place of a skull.

23. And they gave him to drink wine mingled with myrrh: but he received it not.

24. And when they had crucified him, they parted his garments, casting lots upon them, what every man should take.

25. And it was the third hour, and they crucified him.

26. And the superscription of his accusation was written over, THE KING OF THE JEWS.

27. And with him they crucify two thieves; the one on his right hand, and the other on his left.

28. And the scripture was fulfilled, which saith, And he was numbered with the transgressors.

29. And they that passed by railed on him, wagging their heads, and saying, Ah, thou that destroyest the temple, and buildest it in three days,

30. Save thyself, and come down from the cross.

31. Likewise also the chief priests mocking said among themselves with the scribes, He saved others; himself he cannot save.

32. Let Christ the King of Israel descend now from the cross, that we may see and believe. And they that were crucified with him reviled him.

33. And when the sixth hour was come, there was darkness over the whole land until the ninth hour.

34. And at the ninth hour Jesus cried with a loud voice, saying, Eloi, Eloi, lama sabachthani? which is, being interpreted, My God, my God, why hast thou forsaken me?

35. And some of them that stood by, when they heard it, said, Behold, he calleth Elias.

36. And one ran and filled a sponge full of vinegar, and put it on a reed, and gave him to drink, saying, Let alone; let us see whether Elias will come to take him down.

37. And Jesus cried with a loud voice, and gave up the ghost.

38. And the veil of the temple was rent in twain from the top to the bottom.

39. And when the centurion, which stood over against him, saw that he so cried out, and gave up the ghost, he said, Truly this man was the Son of God.

40. There were also women looking on afar off: among whom was Mary Magdalene, and Mary the mother of James the less and of Joses, and Salome;

41. (Who also, when he was in Galilee, followed him, and ministered unto him;) and many other women which came up with him unto Jerusalem.

42. And now when the even was come, because it was the preparation, that is, the day before the sabbath,

43. Joseph of Arimathaea, as honourable counsellor, which also waited for the kingdom of God, came, and

- **went** in boldly
- **unto Pilate, and craved**
- **the body of Jesus.**
- **44. And Pilate** marvelled if he were already dead: and calling *unto him* the centurion, he asked him whether he had been any while dead. 45. And when he knew *it* of the centurion, he
- **gave the body to Joseph.**
- **46. And he bought fine**
- **linen,** and took him down,
- **and wrapped him** in the linen,
- **and laid him in a sepulchre** which was hewn out of a rock,
- **and rolled a stone unto**
- **the door** of the sepulchre. 47. And Mary Magdalene and Mary *the mother* of Joses beheld where he was laid.

CHAPTER 16

1. And when the sabbath was past,
- **Mary Magdalene, and**
- **Mary the mother of James,**
- **and Salome,** had bought sweet spices, that they might come and anoint him. 2. And very early in the morning the first *day* of the week, they
- **came unto the sepulchre** at the rising of the sun.
- **3. And they said** among themselves,
- **Who shall roll** us
- **away the stone** from the door of the sepulchre? 4. **And** when they looked,
- **they saw that the stone**
- **was rolled away:** for it was very great.
- **5. And entering** into the sepulchre,
- **they saw a young**
- **man** sitting on the right side,
- **clothed in a long white**
- **garment;** and they were affrighted.
- **6. And he saith** unto them, be not affrighted:
- **Ye seek Jesus** of Nazareth, which was crucified:
- **he is risen; he is not here:** behold the place where they laid him.

7. But go you way,
- **tell his disciples** and Peter
- **that he goeth** before you
- **into Galilee: there shall**
- **ye see him,** as he said unto you.
- **8. And they went out**
- **quickly,** and fled from the sepulchre; for they trembled and were amazed: neither said they any thing to any *man;*
- **for they were afraid.** 9. Now when
- **Jesus** was risen early the first *day* of the week, he
- **appeared first to Mary**
- **Magdalene,** out of whom he had cast seven devils.
- **10. And she** went and
- **told them that had**
- **been with him,** as they mourned and wept.
- **11. And they,** when they had heard that he was alive, and had been seen of her,
- **believed not.**
- **12. After that he appeared**
- **in another form unto**
- **two of them,** as they walked, and went into the country.
- **13. And they** went and
- **told** *it* unto
- **the residue: neither**
- **believed they** them.
- **14. Afterward he appeared**
- **unto the eleven** as they sat at meat,
- **and upbraided them** with their unbelief and hardness of heart,
- **because they believed**
- **not them which had**
- **seen him** after he was risen.
- **15. And he said** unto the,
- **Go ye into all the world,**
- **and preach the gospel**
- **to every creature.**
- **16. He that believeth** and is baptized
- **shall be saved;** but he that believeth not shall be damned. 17. And these
- **signs shall follow them that**
- **believe;** In my name shall they cast out devils; they shall speak

with new tongues;

18. They shall take up serpents; and it they drink any deadly thing, it shall not hurt them; they shall lay hands on the sick, and they shall recover.

■ 19. **So then after the Lord**
■ **had spoken** unto them,
■ **he was received**
■ **up** into heaven,

■ **and sat on the right**
■ **hand of God.**
■ 20. **And they**
■ **went forth, and**
■ **preached every where,**
■ **the Lord** working with *them,* and
■ **confirming the word**
■ **with signs** following.
■ **Amen.**

THE GOSPEL ACCORDING TO LUKE

BACKGROUND INFORMATION

Author: Luke, physician and Gentile companion of Paul
Date Written: probably **between 60** and **80** A.D.

Number of:
Verses   1,151
Chapters   24
Total Words   25,944
Scan Words   12,707
Scan Words represent 48 % of Total Words

Theme: written to reveal that Jesus is **The Son of God** in a way that would appeal **to the Gentile world**

OUTLINE OF THE GOSPEL

I. **Christ's Birth Narratives** and Early Years
    Chapters 1 - 2
II. **Christ's Preparation for his Ministry**
    Chapters 3 - 4
III. **Christ's Galilaean Ministry** Including Sermon at Nazareth
    Chapters 5 - 9
IV. **Christ's Journey to Jerusalem** Including Resurrection of Lazarus and Conversion of Zacchaeus
    Chapters 10 - 19
V. **Christ's Crucifixion, Resurrection, and Ascension**
    Chapters 20 - 24

CHAPTER 1

■ 1. **Forasmuch as many have** taken in hand to **set forth** in order **a declaration of those things** which are most surely **believed among us,**

■ 2. **Even** as they delivered **them** unto us, **which** from the beginning **were eyewitnesses, and ministers of the word;**

■ 3. **It seemed good** to me also, having had perfect understanding of all things from the very first, **to write unto thee** in order, **most excellent Theophilus,**

■ 4. **That thou mightest know the certainty of those things, wherein thou hast been instructed.**

■ 5. **There was** in the days of Herod, the king of Judaea, **a certain priest named Zacharias,** of the course of Abia: **and his wife** was of the daughters of Aaron, and her name was **Elisabeth.**

■ 6. **And they were both righteous** before God, walking in all the commandments and ordinances of the Lord blameless.

■ 7. **And** they had no child, because that **Elisabeth was barren, and** they both were now **well stricken in years.**

■ 8. **And** it came to pass, that **while he executed the priest's office** before God n the order of his course,

9. According to the custom of the priest's office, **his lot was to burn incense when he went into the temple** of the Lord.

■ 10. **And the whole multitude** of the people **were praying without** at the time of incense.

■ 11. **And there appeared** unto him **an angel** of the Lord standing on the right side of the altar of incense.

■ 12. **And when Zacharias saw him,** he was troubled, and **fear fell upon him.**

■ 13. **But the angel said** unto him, **Fear not,** Zacharias: for thy prayer is heard; and **thy wife Elisabeth shall bear thee a son, and thou shalt call his name John.**

■ 14. **And** thou shalt have joy and gladness; and **many shall rejoice at his birth.**

■ 15. **For he shall be great** in the sight of the Lord, and shall drink neither wine nor strong drink; **and** he shall be **filled with the Holy Ghost,** even from his mother's womb.

■ 16. **And many** of the children of Israel **shall he turn to the Lord** their God.

■ 17. **And he shall go before him in the spirit and power of Elias,** to turn the hearts of the fathers to the children, and the disobedient to the wisdom of the just; **to make ready a people prepared for the Lord.**

■ 18. **And Zacharias said** unto the angel, **Whereby shall I know this?** for I am an old man, and my wife well stricken in years.

■ 19. **And the angel** answering **said** unto him, **I am Gabriel,** that stand in the presence of God; **and am sent to speak** unto thee, and to shew thee **these glad tidings.**

■ 20. **And, behold, thou shalt be dumb,** and not able to speak, until the day that these things shall be performed, **because thou believest not my words,** which shall be fulfilled in their season.

■ 21. **And the people** waited for Zacharias, and **marvelled that he tarried so** long in the temple.

22. **And when he came out,** he could not speak unto them: and **they perceived that he had seen a vision** in the temple: **for he beckoned unto them, and remained speechless.**

23. And it came to pass, that, as soon as the days of his ministration were accomplished, he departed to his own house.

24. **And** after those days his wife **Elisabeth conceived, and hid herself five months,** saying,

25.Thus hath the Lord dealt with mein the days wherein he looked on *me*, to take away my reproach among men.

26. **And in the sixth month** the angel **Gabriel was sent** from God **unto** a city of Galilee, named **Nazareth,**

27. **To a virgin** espoused to a man **whose** name was Joseph, of the house of David; and the virgin's **name was Mary.**

28. **And the angel** came in unto her, and **said, Hail,** *thou that art* highly favoured, the Lord *is* with thee: **blessed art thou among women.**

29. **And** when she saw *him*, **she was troubled at his** saying, and cast in her mind what manner of **salutation** this should be.

30. **And the angel said** unto her, **Fear not, Mary: for thou hast found favour with God.**

31. **And,** behold, **thou shalt conceive** in thy womb, **and bring forth a son, and shalt call his name JESUS.**

32. **He shall be** great, and shall be **called the Son of the Highest:** and the Lord God shall give unto him the throne of his father David:

33. **And** he shall reign over the house of Jacob for ever; and **of his kingdom there shall be no end.**

34. **Then said Mary** unto the angel, **How shall this be, seeing I know not a man?**

35. **And the angel answered** and said unto her, **The Holy Ghost shall come upon thee,** and the power of the Highest shall overshadow thee: **therefore also that** holy thing **which shall be born of thee shall be called the Son of God.**

36. **And, behold, thy cousin Elisabeth,** she **hath also conceived** a son in her old age: and this is the sixth month with her, who was called barren.

37. For with God nothing shall be impossible.

38. **And Mary said,** Behold the handmaid of the Lord; **be it unto me according to thy word.** And the angel departed from her.

39. **And Mary arose** in those days, **and went into** the hill country with haste, into a city of **Juda;**

40. **And entered** into **the house of Zacharias,** and saluted Elisabeth.

41. **And** it came to pass, that, **when Elisabeth heard the salutation of Mary, the babe leaped in her womb;** and Elisabeth was filled with the Holy Ghost:

42. **And she spake** out with a loud voice, and said, **Blessed art thou among women,** and blessed *is* the fruit of thy womb.

43. **And whence is this to me, that the mother of my Lord should come to me?**

44. For, lo, as soon as the voice of thy salutation sounded in mine ears, the babe leaped in my womb for joy.

45. And blessed *is* she that believed: for there shall be a performance of those things which were told her from the Lord.

46. **And Mary said, My soul doth magnify the Lord,**

47. **And my spirit hath rejoiced in God my Saviour.**

48. For he hath regarded the low estate of his handmaiden: for, behold, **from henceforth all generations shall call me blessed.**

49. For he that is mighty hath done to me great things; and holy *is* his name.

50. **And his mercy is on them that fear him** from generation to generation.

51. He hath shewed strength with his arm; he hath scattered the proud in the imagination of their hearts.

52. **He hath** put down the mighty from *their* seats, and **exalted them of low degree.**

53. He hath filled the hungry with good things; **and the rich he hath sent empty away.**

54. He hath holpen his servant Israel, in remembrance of *his* mercy;

55. As he spake to our fathers, to Abraham, and to his seed for ever.

56. **And Mary abode with her about three months,** and returned to her own house.

57. **Now Elisabeth's full time came** that she should be delivered; **and she brought forth a son.**

58. **And her neighbours** and her cousins heard how the Lord had shewed great mercy upon her; and they **rejoiced with her.**

59. *And* it came to pass, that **on the eighth day they came to circumcise the child; and they** called him Zacharias, after the name of his father.

60. **And his mother** answered and **said, Not so; but he shall be called John.**

61. And they said unto her, There is none of thy kindred that is called by this name.

62. **And they made signs to his father, how he would have him called.**

63. **And he asked for a writing table, and wrote,** saying, **His name is John.** And they marvelled all.

64. **And his mouth was opened** immediately, and his tongue *loosed*, **and he spake, and praised God.**

65. **And** fear came on all that dwelt round about them: and all **these sayings were noised abroad throughout** all the hill country of **Judaea.**

66. And all they that heard *them* laid *them* up in their hearts, saying, **What manner of child shall this be!** And the hand of the Lord was with him.

67. **And** his father **Zacharias** was filled with the Holy Ghost, and **prophesied, saying,**

68. **Blessed be the Lord** God of Israel; **for he hath visited and redeemed his people,**

69. **And hath raised up an horn of salvation** for us in the house of his servant David;

70. **As he spake by** the mouth of **his holy prophets,** which have been since the world began:

71. **That we should be saved** from our enemies, and from the hand of all that hate us;

72. To perform the mercy *promised* to our fathers, **and to remember**

his holy covenant;

73. The oath which he sware
to our father Abraham,

74. That he would grant unto us,
that we being delivered out
of the hand of our enemies
**might serve him
without fear,**
75. **In holiness and
righteousness** before him,
all the days of our life.
76. **And thou, child,**
shalt be called the prophet
of the Highest: for thou
shalt go before the face of
**the Lord to prepare
his ways;**
77. **To give knowledge of
salvation** unto his people
**by the remission of
their sins,**
78. Through the tender mercy of
our God; whereby the dayspring
from on high hath visited us,
79. **To give light to them that
sit in darkness and**
in the shadow of death,
to guide our feet
into the way of peace.
80. **And the child grew, and
waxed strong in spirit, and
was in the deserts till**
the day of
his shewing unto Israel.

CHAPTER 2

1. **And** it came to pass
in those days, that
**there went out a decree
from Caesar Augustus
that all the world should
be taxed.**
2. (*And* this taxing was first
made when Cyrenius was
governor of Syria.)
3. **And all went to
be taxed,** every one
into his own city.
4. **And Joseph also went**
up from Galilee, out of the city
of Nazareth, into Judaea,
unto the city of
David, which is called

Bethlehem; (because he was of
the house and lineage of David:)
5. **To be taxed with Mary**
his espoused wife,
being great with child.
6. **And** so it was, that,
while they were
there, the days were
accomplished that
she should be delivered.
7. And she
**brought forth her
firstborn son,** and wrapped
him in swaddling clothes,
and laid him in a manger;
because there was no
room for them in the inn.
8. **And there were**
in the same country
shepherds abiding in the field,
**keeping watch over their
flock by night.**
9. **And, lo, the angel of the
Lord came upon them,**
and the glory of the Lord shone
round about them: and
they were sore afraid.
10. **And** the angel
said unto them,
Fear not: for, behold,
**I bring you good
tidings of great joy,**
which shall be to all people.
11. **For unto you is born**
this day in the city of David
a Saviour,
which is Christ the Lord.
12. **And** this *shall be* a sign unto you;
Ye shall find the babe
wrapped in swaddling clothes,
lying in a manger.
13. **And suddenly there was
with the angel a multitude
of the heavenly host
praising God, and saying,**
14. **Glory to God in the
highest, and on earth
peace, good
will toward men.**
15. **And** it came to pass,
as the angels were gone
away from them into heaven,
the shepherds said

one to another,

■ **Let us now go**
even unto Bethlehem,

■ **and see this thing**
which is come to pass,

■ **which the Lord hath**

■ **made known** unto us.

■ **16. And they came** with haste,

■ **and found** Mary, and Joseph, and

■ **the babe lying in a manger.**

■ **17. And** when they had seen *it,*

■ **they made known abroad**

■ **the saying** which was

■ **told them concerning**

■ **this child.**

■ **18. And all they that heard it**

■ **wondered** at those things which
were told them by the shepherds.

■ **19. But Mary kept all these**

■ **things,** and pondered *them*

■ **in her heart.**

■ **20. And the shepherds**

■ **returned,** glorifying and

■ **praising God** for all the
things that they had heard and
seen, as it was told unto them.

■ **21. And when eight days**

■ **were accomplished for**

■ **the circumcising** of the child,

■ **his name was called**

■ **JESUS,** which was so named
of the angel before he was
conceived in the womb.

■ **22. And** when the days of her
purification according to the law of
Moses were accomplished,

■ **they brought him to**

■ **Jerusalem, to present**

■ **him to the Lord;**
23. (As it is written in the law of the
LORD, Every male that openeth the
womb shall be called holy to the Lord;)

■ **24. And to offer a sacrifice**
according to that which
is said in the law

■ **of** the Lord,

■ **A pair of turtledoves, or two**

■ **young pigeons.**
25. **And, behold, there was a**

■ **man in Jerusalem, whose**

■ **name was Simeon;** and the
same man *was* just and devout,
waiting for the consolation of Israel:

and the Holy Ghost was upon him.
26. And it was revealed unto him
by the Holy Ghost, that he should
not see death, before he had seen
the Lord's Christ.

■ **27. And he came by the**

■ **Spirit into the temple: and**

■ **when the parents brought**

■ **in the child Jesus,** to do for
him after the custom of the law,

■ **28. Then took he him up in**

■ **his arms, and blessed God,**

■ **and said,**

■ **29. Lord, now lettest thou thy**

■ **servant depart in peace,**
according to thy word:

■ **30. For mine eyes have**

■ **seen thy salvation,**
31. Which thou hast prepared
before the face of all people;
32. A light to lighten the Gentiles,
and the glory of thy people Israel.

■ **33. And Joseph and his**

■ **mother marvelled at those**

■ **things** which were spoken of him.

■ 34. **And Simeon**
blessed them, and

■ **said unto Mary** his mother,

■ **Behold, this child is set for**

■ **the fall and rising again**

■ **of many** in Israel; and for a sign
which shall be spoken against;
35. (Yea, a sword shall pierce
through thy own soul also,)

■ **that the thoughts of many**

■ **hearts may be revealed.**

■ **36. And there was one Anna,**

■ **a prophetess,** the daughter
of Phanuel, of the tribe of Aser:
she was of a great age, and had
lived with an husband seven
years from her virginity;
37. And she *was* a widow of
about fourscore and four years,

■ **which departed not from**

■ **the temple, but served**

■ **God with fastings and**

■ **prayers night and day.**

■ **38. And she** coming in that instant

■ **gave thanks**
likewise unto the Lord,

■ **and spake of him to all**

■ **them that looked for**

redemption in Jerusalem.

39. **And** when they had performed all things according to the law of the Lord,

they returned into Galilee, **to their own city Nazareth.**

40. **And the child grew, and waxed strong in spirit, filled with wisdom: and the grace of God was upon him.**

41. Now his parents went to Jerusalem every year at the feast of the passover.

42. **And when he was twelve years old, they went up to Jerusalem** after the custom of the feast.

43. **And** when they had fulfilled the days, as they returned, the child **Jesus tarried behind** in Jerusalem; **and Joseph and his mother knew not of it.**

44. **But they,** supposing him to have been in the company, **went a day's journey; and** they **sought him** among *their* kinsfolk and acquaintance.

45. **And** when they **found him not,** they turned back again to Jerusalem, seeking him.

46. **And** it came to pass, that **after three days they found him in the temple, sitting in the midst of the doctors, both hearing** them, **and asking them questions.**

47. And all that heard him were astonished at his understanding and answers.

48. **And** when they saw him, **they were amazed: and his mother said** unto him, **Son,** why hast thou thus dealt with us? **behold, thy father and I have sought thee sorrowing.**

49. **And he said** unto them, **How is it that ye sought me?**

wist ye not that I must be about my Father's business?

50. **And they understood not** the saying which he spake unto them.

51. **And he went down** with them, and came **to Nazareth, and was subject unto them:** but his mother kept all these sayings in her heart.

52. **And Jesus increased in wisdom and stature, and in favour with God and man.**

CHAPTER 3

1. **Now in the fifteenth year of the reign of** Tiberius **Caesar,** Pontius Pilate being governor of Judaea, and Herod being tetrarch of Galilee, and his brother Philip tetrarch of Ituraea and of the region of Trachonitis, and Lysanias the tetrarch of Abilene,

2. Annas and Caiaphas being the high priests, **the word of God came unto John** the son of Zacharias **in the wilderness.**

3. **And he came** into all the country **about Jordan, preaching the baptism of repentance** for the remission of sins;

4. **As it is written** in the book of the words of Esaias the prophet, saying, **The voice of one crying in the wilderness, Prepare ye the way of the Lord,** make his paths straight.

5. Every valley shall be filled, and every mountain and hill shall be brought low; and the crooked shall be made straight, and the rough ways *shall be* made smooth;

6. **And all flesh shall see the salvation of God.**

7. **Then said he to the multitude that came** forth **to be baptized** of him, **O generation of vipers,** who hath warned you to flee

from the wrath to come?
8. **Bring forth** therefore
fruits worthy of repentance,
and begin not to say within
yourselves, We have Abraham
to *our* father:
for I say unto you, That God is
able of these stones to raise up
children unto Abraham.
9. And now also the axe is
laid unto the root of the trees:
**every tree therefore which
bringeth not forth good
fruit is hewn down, and cast
into the fire.**
10. **And the people
asked him,** saying,
What shall we do then?
11. **He answereth**
and saith unto them,
**He that hath
two coats,** let him
**impart to him that hath
none;** and he that hath meat,
let him do likewise.
12. **Then came also
publicans** to be baptized,
and said unto him,
Master, what shall we do?
13. **And he said** unto them,
**Exact no more than that
which is appointed you.**
14. **And the soldiers likewise
demanded**
of him, saying, And
what shall we do?
And he said unto them,
Do violence to no man,
neither accuse *any* falsely; and
be content with your wages.
15. **And as the people were
in expectation,** and all men
mused in their hearts of John,
**whether he were
the Christ, or not;**
16. **John answered,**
saying unto *them* all, I indeed
baptize you with water; but
**one mightier than
I cometh,** the latchet of
**whose shoes I am not
worthy to unloose: he shall
baptize you with the Holy**

Ghost and with fire:
17. Whose fan *is* in his hand,
and he will
throughly purge his floor, and will
**gather the wheat into his
garner; but the chaff he will
burn** with fire unquenchable.
18. And many other things
in his exhortation preached
he unto the people.
19. **But Herod** the tetrarch,
**being reproved by
him for** Herodias
**his brother Philip's
wife, and for** all the
**evils which Herod
had done,**
20. Added yet this above all, that he
shut up John in prison.
21. **Now** when all the
people were baptized,
**it came to pass, that
Jesus also being
baptized,** and praying, the
heaven was
opened,
22. **And the Holy Ghost
descended** in a bodily shape
**like a dove upon him, and
a voice** came from heaven, which
**said, Thou art my beloved
Son; in thee I am
well pleased.**
23. And Jesus himself began to be
about thirty years of age, being (as
was supposed) the son of Joseph,
which was *the son* of Heli,
24. Which was *the son* of Matthat,
which was *the son* of Levi, which was
the son of Melchi, which was *the son*
of Janna, which was *the son* of
Joseph,
25. Which was *the son* of Mattathias,
which was *the son* of Amos, whichwas
the son of Naum, which was *the son*
of Esli, which was *the son* of Nagge,
26. Which was *the son* of Maath,
which was *the son* of Mattathias,
which was *the son* of Semei, which
was *the son* of Joseph, which was
the son of Juda,
27. Which was *the son* of Joanna,
which was *the son* of Rhesa, which

was *the son* of Zorobabel, which was *the son* of Salathiel, which was *the son* of Neri,

28. Which was *the son* of Melchi, which was *the son* of Addi, which was *the son* of Cosam, which was *the son* of Elmodam, which was *the son* of Er,

29. Which was *the son* of Jose, which was *the son* of Eliezer, which was *the son* of Jorim, which was *the son* of Matthat, which was *the son* of Levi,

30. Which was *the son* of Simeon, which was *the son* of Juda, which was *the son* of Joseph, which was *the son* of Jonan, which was *the son* of Eliakim,

31. Which was *the son* of Melea, which was *the son* of Menan, which was *the son* of Mattatha, which was *the son* of Nathan, which was *the son* of David,

32. Which was *the son* of Jesse, which was *the son* of Obed, which was *the son* of Booz, which was *the son* of Salmon, which was *the son* of Naasson,

33. Which was *the son* of Aminadab, which was *the son* of Aram, which was *the son* of Esrom, which was *the son* of Phares, which was *the son* of Juda,

34. Which was *the son* of Jacob, which was *the son* of Isaac, which was *the son* of Abraham, which was *the son* of Thara, which was *the son* of Nachor,

35. Which was *the son* of Saruch, which was *the son* of Ragau, which was *the son* of Phalec, which was *the son* of Heber, which was *the son* of Sala,

36. Which was *the son* of Cainan, which was *the son* of Arphaxad, which was *the son* of Sem, which was *the son* of Noe, which was *the son* of Lamech,

37. Which was *the son* of Mathusala, which was *the son* of Enoch, which was *the son* of Jared, which was *the son* of Maleleel, which was *the son* of Cainan,

38. Which was *the son* of Enos, which was *the son* of Seth, which was *the son* of Adam, which was *the son* of God.

CHAPTER 4

■ 1. **And Jesus** being full of the Holy Ghost returned from Jordan, and **was led by the Spirit into the wilderness,**

■ 2. **Being forty days tempted of the devil. And** in those days he **did eat nothing: and** when they were ended, **he** afterward **hungered.**

■ 3. **And the devil said** unto him, **If thou be the Son of God, command this stone** that it **be made bread.**

■ 4. **And Jesus answered** him, saying, It is written, That **man shall not live by bread alone, but by every word of God.**

■ 5. **And the devil,** taking him up into an high mountain, **shewed** unto **him all the kingdoms of the world** in a moment of time.

■ 6. **And the devil said** unto him, **All this power will I give thee,** and the glory of them: for that is delivered unto me; and to whomsoever I will I give it.

■ 7. **If thou therefore wilt worship me,** all shall be thine.

■ 8. **And Jesus answered** and said unto him, **Get thee behind me, Satan: for** it is written, **Thou shalt worship the Lord thy God,** and him **only** shalt thou serve.

■ 9. **And he brought him to Jerusalem,** and set him **on a pinnacle of the temple, and said** unto him, **If thou be the Son of God, cast thyself down** from hence:

■ 10. **For** it is written, **He shall give his angels charge over thee** to keep thee:

■ 11. **And** in *their* hands **they shall bear thee up,** lest at any time thou dash thy foot against a stone.

12. **And Jesus** answering said unto him, It is **said, Thou shalt not tempt the Lord thy God.** 13. **And when the devil had ended all the temptation, he departed** from him for a season. 14. **And Jesus returned** in the power of the Spirit **into Galilee: and there went out a fame of him** through all the region round about. 15. And he taught in their synagogues, being glorified of all. 16. **And he came to Nazareth,** where he had been brought up: **and,** as his custom was, he **went into the synagogue on the sabbath day,** and stood up for to read. 17. **And there was delivered** unto him **the book of the prophet Esaias.** And when he had opened the book, he found the place **where it was written,** 18. **The Spirit of the Lord** *is* upon me, because he **hath anointed me to preach the gospel** to the poor; he hath sent me **to heal** the brokenhearted, to preach deliverance to the captives, **and recovering of sight to the blind, to set at liberty them that are bruised,** 19. To preach the acceptable year of the Lord. 20. **And he closed the book,** and he gave *it* again to the minister, **and sat down.** And the eyes of all them that were in the synagogue were fastened on him. 21. **And he began to say** unto them, **This day is this scripture fulfilled** in your ears. 22. **And all bare him witness, and wondered** at the gracious words which proceeded out of his

mouth. And they said, **Is not this Joseph's son?** 23. And he said unto them, Ye will surely say unto me this proverb, Physician, heal thyself: whatsoever we have heard done in Capernaum, do also here in thy country. 24. **And he said,** Verily I say unto you, **No prophet is accepted in his own country.** 25. **But** I tell you of a truth, **many widows were in Israel in the days of Elias,** when the heaven was shut up three years and six months, **when great famine was throughout all the land;** 26. **But unto none of them was Elias sent, save** unto Sarepta, *a city* of Sidon, unto **a woman** *that was* a widow. 27. **And many lepers were in Israel** in the time of Eliseus the prophet; **and none of them was cleansed, saving Naaman** the Syrian. 28. **And all they in the synagogue,** when they heard these things, **were filled with wrath,** 29. **And** rose up, and thrust him out of the city, and **led him unto the brow of the hill** whereon their city was built, **that they might cast him down** headlong. 30. **But he passing through the midst of them went his way,** 31. **And came** down **to** Capernaum, a city of **Galilee, and taught** them on the sabbath days. 32. **And they were astonished at his doctrine:** for his word was with power. 33. **And** in the synagogue there was **a man, which had** a spirit of **an unclean devil, and cried out** with a loud voice, 34. **Saying, Let us alone;**

96

what have we to do with thee, **thou** Jesus of Nazareth? art thou come to destroy us? I know thee who thou art; the **Holy One of God.** 35. **And Jesus rebuked him,** saying, **Hold thy peace, and come out of him. And** when the devil had thrown him in the midst, **he came out of him,** and hurt him not. 36. **And they were all amazed,** and spake among themselves, **saying, What a word is this! for** with authority and power **he commandeth the unclean spirits, and they come out.** 37. And the fame of him went out into every place of the country round about. 38. **And he** arose out of the synagogue, and **entered into Simon's house. And Simon's wife's mother was taken with a great fever;** and they besought him for her. 39. **And he** stood over her, and **rebuked the fever;** and it left her: **and immediately she arose and ministered unto them.** 40. **Now when the sun was setting, all they that had any sick** with divers diseases **brought them unto him; and he** laid his hands on every one of them, and **healed them.** 41. **And devils also came out of many, crying out,** and saying, **Thou art Christ** the Son of God. **And he** rebuking *them* **suffered them not to speak:** for they knew that he was Christ. 42. **And** when it was day, **he departed** and went **into a desert place: and**

the people sought him, and **came unto him, and stayed him, that he should not depart** from them. 43. **And he said** unto them, **I must preach** the kingdom of God **to other cities also: for therefore am I sent.** 44. And he preached in the synagogues of Galilee.

CHAPTER 5

1. **And** it came to pass, that, **as the people pressed upon him** to hear the word of God, **he stood by the lake** of Gennesaret, 2. **And saw two ships** standing by the lake: but the fishermen were gone out of them, and were washing *their* nets. 3. **And he entered** into one of the ships, which was **Simon's, and prayed him that he would thrust out** a little from the land. **And he** sat down, and **taught the people out of the ship.** 4. **Now when he had left speaking, he said unto Simon, Launch out** into the deep, **and let down your nets** for a draught. 5. **And Simon** answering **said** unto him, **Master, we have toiled all the night, and have taken nothing: nevertheless at thy word I will let down the net.** 6. **And** when they had this done, **they enclosed a great multitude of fishes:** and their net brake. 7. **And they beckoned** unto **their partners,** which were **in the other ship,** that they should come and help them. **And they** came, and **filled both the ships,** so that they began to sink.

8. **When Simon Peter saw** it, **he fell down at Jesus' knees, saying, Depart** from me; for **I am** a **sinful** man, O Lord.

9. **For he was astonished,** and all that were with him, at the draught of the fishes which they had taken:

10. **And so** was also James, and John, the sons of Zebedee, which **were partners with Simon. And Jesus said** unto Simon, **Fear not; from henceforth thou shalt catch men.**

11. **And** when they had brought their ships to land, **they forsook all, and followed him.**

12. **And** it came to pass, when he was in a certain city, behold **a man full of leprosy:** who **seeing Jesus** fell on *his* face, and **besought him, saying, Lord, if thou wilt,** thou canst **make me clean.**

13. **And he** put forth *his* hand, and **touched him, saying, I will: be thou clean. And** immediately **the leprosy departed** from him.

14. **And he charged him to tell no man: but go,** and shew thyself **to the priest, and offer** for thy cleansing, **according as Moses commanded, for a testimony** unto them.

15. But so much the more went there a fame abroad of him: **and great multitudes came together to hear, and to be healed by him** of their infirmities.

16. And he withdrew himself into the wilderness, and prayed.

17. And it came to pass on a certain day, as he was teaching, that there were Pharisees and doctors of the law sitting by, which were come out of every town of Galilee, and Judaea, and Jerusalem: and the power of the Lord was *present* to heal them.

18. **And, behold, men brought in a bed a man** which was taken **with a palsy: and they sought** *means* to bring him in, and to lay *him* before him.

19. And when they could not find **by what way they might bring him in because of the multitude, they went upon the housetop, and let him down through the tiling** with *his* couch into the midst **before Jesus.**

20. **And when he saw their faith, he said** unto him, **Man, thy sins are forgiven thee.**

21. **And the scribes and the Pharisees began to reason,** saying, Who is this which speaketh blasphemies? **Who can forgive sins, but God** alone?

22. **But when Jesus perceived** their thoughts, **he** answering **said** unto them, What reason ye in your hearts?

23. **Whether is easier, to say, Thy sins be forgiven thee; or** to say, **Rise up and walk?**

24. **But** that ye may **know that the Son of man hath power** upon earth **to forgive sins, (he said unto the sick of the palsy,)** I say unto thee, **Arise,** and take up thy couch, **and go into thine house.**

25. **And** immediately **he rose up** before them, and took up that whereon he lay, **and departed** to his own house, glorifying God.

26. **And they were all amazed,** and they glorified God, and were filled with fear, saying, We have seen strange things to-day.

27. **And** after these things **he went forth, and saw** a publican, named **Levi, sitting at the receipt of custom: and** he **said** unto him, **Follow me.** 28. **And he left all,** rose up, **and followed him.** 29. **And Levi made him a great feast** in his own house: **and** there was a great company of **publicans** and of others that **sat** down **with them.** 30. **But their scribes and Pharisees murmured** against his disciples, **saying, Why do ye eat** and drink **with** publicans and **sinners?** 31. **And Jesus** answering **said** unto them, They that are whole need not a physician; but they that are sick. 32. **I came not to call the righteous, but sinners to repentance.** 33. **And they said** unto him, **Why do the disciples of John fast** often, and make prayers, and likewise *the disciples* of the Pharisees; **but thine eat and drink?** 34. **And he said** unto them, **Can** ye make **the children of the bridechamber fast, while the bridegroom is with them?** 35. **But** the days will come, when **the bridegroom shall be taken away** from them, and **then shall they fast** in those days. 36. **And he spake also a parable** unto them; **No man putteth a piece of a new garment upon an old;** if otherwise, then both the new maketh a rent, and the piece that was *taken* out of **the new agreeth not with the old.** 37. **And no man putteth new wine into old bottles;** else the new wine will burst the bottles, and be spilled, and the bottles shall perish. 38. But new wine must be put into new bottles; and both are preserved. 39. **No man also having drunk old wine** straightway **desireth new:** for he saith, The old is better.

CHAPTER 6

1. **And** it came to pass on the second sabbath after the first, that **he went through the corn fields; and his disciples plucked** the ears of **corn, and did eat,** rubbing *them* in *their* hands. 2. **And** certain of **the Pharisees said** unto them, **Why do ye that which is not lawful** to do **on the sabbath** days? 3. **And Jesus answering** them said, **Have ye not read** so much as this, **what David did,** when himself was an hungred, and they which were with him; 4. **How he went into the house of God, and did take** and eat **the shewbread,** and gave also to them that were with him; **which it is not lawful to eat but for the priests** alone? 5. And he said unto them, That **the Son of man is Lord also of the sabbath.** 6. **And** it came to pass also on another sabbath, that he entered into the synagogue and taught: and **there was a man whose right hand was withered.** 7. **And the scribes and Pharisees watched him, whether he would heal on the sabbath day;** that they might find an accusation against him.

8. **But he** knew their thoughts, and **said to the man** which had the withered hand, **Rise up,** and stand forth in the midst. And he arose and stood forth. 9. **Then said Jesus unto them,** I will ask you one thing; **Is it lawful on the sabbath days to do good, or** to do **evil?** to save life, or to destroy *it*? 10. **And** looking round about upon them all, **he said unto the man, Stretch forth thy hand.** And he did so: **and his hand was restored** whole as the other. 11. **And they** were filled with madness; and **communed** one with another **what they might do to Jesus.** 12. **And** it came to pass in those days, that **he went out into a mountain** to pray, **and continued all night in prayer to God.** 13. **And when it was day, he called** *unto him* **his disciples: and** of them he **chose twelve, whom** also **he named apostles;** 14. **Simon,** (whom he also named Peter,) **and Andrew** his brother, **James and John, Philip and Bartholomew.** 15. **Matthew and Thomas, James** the *son* of Alphaeus, **and Simon** called Zelotes, 16. **And Judas the brother of James, and Judas Iscariot, which also was the traitor.** 17. **And** he came down **with** them, and stood in the plain, and the company of **his disciples,** and **a great multitude** of people out of all Judaea and Jerusalem, and from the sea coast of Tyre and Sidon, which **came to hear him, and to be healed** of their diseases; 18. And they that were vexed with unclean spirits: and they were healed. 19. **And the** whole **multitude sought to touch him: for there went virtue out of him, and healed them all.** 20. **And he** lifted up his eyes on his disciples, and **said, Blessed be ye poor: for yours is the kingdom of God.** 21. **Blessed are ye that hunger** now: **for ye shall be filled. Blessed are ye that weep** now: **for ye shall laugh.** 22. **Blessed are ye, when men** shall hate you, and when they shall separate you *from their company,* and **shall reproach you,** and cast out your name as evil, **for the Son of man's sake.** 23.**Rejoice** ye in that day, and leap **for** joy: for, behold, **your reward is great in heaven:** for in the like manner did their fathers unto the prophets. 24. **But woe unto you that are rich! for ye have** received **your consolation.** 25. **Woe unto you that are full! for ye shall hunger. Woe unto you that laugh now!** for **ye shall mourn** and weep. 26. **Woe unto you, when** all **men** shall **speak well of you! for so did their fathers to the false prophets.** 27. **But I say** unto you which hear, **Love your enemies,** do good to them which hate you, 28. **Bless** them that curse you, **and pray for them which despitefully use you.** 29. **And unto him that**

■ smiteth thee on the
■ one cheek offer also
■ the other; and him
■ that taketh away
■ thy cloak forbid not
■ to take thy coat also.
30. **Give to every man**
■ that asketh of thee; and
of him that taketh away thy
goods ask *them* not again.
■ 31. **And as ye would**
■ that men should
■ do to you, do ye
■ also to them likewise.
■ 32. **For if ye love them**
which love you, what thank
have ye? for sinners also
love those that love them.
■ 33. **And** if ye
■ do good to them which
■ do good to you, what
■ thank have ye?
for sinners also do even the same.
■ 34. **And if ye lend to them of**
■ whom ye hope to receive,
■ what thank have ye? for
■ sinners also lend to sinners,
■ to receive as much again.
■ 35. **But love ye your**
■ enemies, and do good, and lend,
■ hoping for nothing again;
■ and your reward shall be
■ great, and ye shall be the children
of the Highest: for he is kind unto
the unthankful and *to* the evil.
■ 36. **Be ye therefore merciful,**
■ as your Father also is merciful.
■ 37. **Judge not, and**
ye shall not be judged:
■ condemn not,
and ye shall not be condemned:
■ forgive, and ye shall
■ be forgiven:
■ 38. **Give, and it shall be**
■ given unto you; good
■ measure, pressed down,
and shaken together,
■ and running over,
shall men give into your bosom.
■ For with the same measure
■ that ye mete withal
■ it shall be measured
■ to you again.

■ 39. **And he spake a**
■ parable unto them,
■ Can the blind lead the
■ blind? shall they not
■ both fall into the ditch?
■ 40. **The disciple is not above**
■ his master:
but every one that is perfect
shall be as his master.
■ 41. **And why beholdest**
■ thou the mote that is in thy
■ brother's eye, but perceivest
■ not the beam that is
■ in thine own eye?
42. Either how canst thou say to thy
brother, Brother, let me pull out the
mote that is in thine eye, when thou
thyself beholdest not the beam that is
in thine own eye? Thou hypocrite,
■ cast out first
■ the beam out
■ of thine own eye, and
■ then shalt thou see
■ clearly to pull out the
■ mote that is
■ in thy brother's eye.
■ 43. **For a good tree** bringeth
not forth corrupt fruit; neither
■ doth a corrupt tree
■ bring forth good fruit.
■ 44. **For every tree is known**
■ by his own fruit. For of thorns
men do not gather figs, nor of a
bramble bush gather they grapes.
■ 45. **A good man**
out of the good treasure of his heart
■ bringeth forth that which
■ is good; and an evil man
out of the evil treasure of his
heart bringeth forth
■ that which is evil: for of
■ the abundance of the
■ heart his mouth speaketh.
46. And why call ye me, Lord, Lord,
and do not the things which I say?
■ 47. **Whosoever**
cometh to me, and
■ heareth my sayings,
■ and doeth them,
I will shew you to whom he is like:
■ 48. **He is like a man which**
■ built an house, and digged
deep, and laid the foundation

■ on a rock: and when
■ the flood arose, the stream beat
vehemently upon that house,
■ and could not shake it:
for it was founded upon a rock.
■ 49. But he that heareth,
■ and doeth not, is like a
■ man that without a foundation
■ built an house upon the
■ earth; against which
■ the stream did beat
■ vehemently, and immediately
■ it fell; and the ruin of that house
■ was great.

CHAPTER 7

■ 1. Now when he had ended all his
sayings in the audience of the people,
■ he entered into
■ Capernaum.
■ 2. And a certain centurion's
■ servant, who was dear unto him,
■ was sick, and ready to die.
■ 3. And when he heard of
■ Jesus, he sent
unto him the elders of the Jews,
■ beseeching him that
■ he would come and
■ heal his servant.
■ 4. And when they came to
■ Jesus, they besought him instantly,
saying, That he was worthy for whom
he should do this:
5. For he loveth our nation, and
he hath built us a synagogue.
6. Then Jesus went with them.
And when he
■ was now not far from
■ the house, the centurion
■ sent friends to him,
■ saying unto him, Lord,
■ trouble not thyself:
■ for I am not worthy that
■ thou shouldest enter
■ under my roof:
7. Wherefore neither thought
I myself worthy to come unto thee:
■ but say in a word, and my
■ servant shall be healed.
8. For I also am a man set under
authority, having under me soldiers,
and I say unto one, Go, and he goeth;
and to another, Come, and he

cometh; and to my servant,
■ Do this, and he doeth *it*.
■ 9. When Jesus
■ heard these things,
■ he marvelled
at him, and turned him about,
■ and said unto the people that
followed him, I say unto you,
■ I have not found so
■ great faith, no, not
■ in Israel.
■ 10. And they that were sent,
■ returning to the house,
■ found the servant whole
that had been sick.
■ 11. And it came to pass
■ the day after, that
■ he went into a city called
■ Nain; and many of his disciples
went with him, and much people.
■ 12. Now when he came nigh
■ to the gate of the city, behold,
■ there was a dead man
■ carried out, the only son
■ of his mother, and she was
■ a widow: and much people
of the city was with her.
■ 13. And when the Lord saw
■ her, he had compassion
■ on her, and said unto her,
■ Weep not.
■ 14. And he came and
■ touched the bier: and
they that bare *him* stood still.
■ And he
■ said, Young man,
I say unto thee,
■ Arise.
■ 15. And he that was dead
■ sat up, and began to
■ speak. And he delivered
him to his mother.
■ 16. And there came a fear on all: and
■ they glorified God, saying,
■ That a great prophet is risen
■ up among us; and,
That God hath visited his people.
■ 17. And this rumour
■ of him went forth
■ throughout all Judaea,
and throughout all
■ the region round about.
■ 18. And the disciples of John

■ shewed him of all
■ these things.
■ 19. And John calling *unto him*
■ two of his
■ disciples sent them to
■ Jesus, saying, Art thou he that
should come? or look we for another?
■ 20. When the men were
■ come unto him,
■ they said, John Baptist hath
sent us unto thee, saying,
■ Art thou he that should
■ come? or look
■ we for another?
■ 21. And in that same hour
■ he cured many of their
■ infirmities and plagues, and of
■ evil spirits; and unto many
■ that were blind he
■ gave sight.
■ 22. Then Jesus answering
■ said unto them,
■ Go your way, and
■ tell John what things
■ ye have seen and heard;
how that the blind see, the lame walk,
the lepers are cleansed, the deaf
hear, the dead are raised, to the
poor the gospel is preached.
23. And blessed is *he*, whosoever
shall not be offended in me.
■ 24. And when the
■ messengers of John were
■ departed, he began to
■ speak unto the people
■ concerning John, What
■ went ye out into the
■ wilderness for to see?
A reed shaken with the wind?
25. But what went ye out for to see?
■ A man clothed in soft
■ raiment? Behold, they
which are gorgeously apparelled,
and live delicately,
■ are in kings' courts.
26. But what went ye out for to see?
 A prophet? Yea, I say unto you, and
much more than a prophet.
27. This is *he*, of whom it is written,
■ Behold, I send my
■ messenger before thy face,
■ which shall prepare
■ thy way before thee.

28. For I say unto you,
■ Among those that are
■ born of women there is
■ not a greater prophet
■ than John the Baptist:
■ but he that is least in
■ the kingdom of God is
■ greater than he.
29. And all the people that
■ heard *him*, and the publicans,
■ justified God, being
■ baptized with the baptism
■ of John.
30. But the Pharisees
and lawyers
■ rejected the counsel
of God against themselves,
■ being not baptized of him.
■ 31. And the Lord said,
Whereunto then shall I liken the
men of this generation? and to
what are they like?
■ 32. They are like unto
■ children sitting
■ in the marketplace,
and calling one to another, and
■ saying, We have
■ piped unto you,
■ and ye have not
■ danced; we have
■ mourned to you,
■ and ye have not wept.
33. For John the Baptist
■ came neither eating bread
■ nor drinking wine; and ye
say, He hath a devil.
34. The Son of man is come
■ eating and drinking; and ye
say, Behold a gluttonous
■ man, and
■ a winebibber, a
■ friend of publicans and
■ sinners!
35. But wisdom is justified
of all her children.
■ 36. And one of the Pharisees
■ desired him that he would
■ eat with him. And he went
into the Pharisee's house,
and sat down to meat.
■ 37. And, behold,
■ a woman in the city,
■ which was a sinner,

when she knew that *Jesus* sat at meat in the Pharisee's house,
■ **brought** an alabaster box of
■ **ointment,**
■ 38. **And** stood at his feet behind *him*
■ **weeping,** and
■ **began to wash his feet**
■ **with tears, and** did
■ **wipe them with the**
■ **hairs of her head,**
■ **and kissed** his feet,
■ **and anointed**
■ **them** with the ointment.
■ 39. **Now when the Pharisee**
which had bidden him
■ **saw it, he spake**
■ **within** himself,
■ **saying, This man, if he were**
■ **a prophet, would have**
■ **known** who and what manner of
woman *this is* that toucheth him: for
■ **she is a sinner.**
■ 40. **And Jesus** answering
■ **said** unto him,
■ **Simon,** I have somewhat
to say unto thee. And he
saith, Master, say on.
■ 41. **There was a certain**
■ **creditor which had two**
■ **debtors: the one owed**
■ **five hundred pence,**
■ **and the other fifty.**
■ 42. **And** when they had
nothing to pay,
■ **he** frankly
■ **forgave them both.**
Tell me therefore,
■ **which of them will**
■ **love him most?**
■ 43. **Simon answered**
and said, I suppose that
■ **he, to whom he forgave**
■ **most. And he said** unto him,
■ **Thou hast rightly judged.**
■ 44. **And he**
turned to the woman, and
■ **said unto Simon, Seest**
■ **thou this woman?**
I entered into thine house,
■ **thou gavest me no water**
■ **for my feet: but she** hath
■ **washed my feet with tears,**
and wiped *them* with the

hairs of her head.
■ 45. **Thou gavest me no**
■ **kiss: but this woman**
since the time I came in
■ **hath not ceased**
■ **to kiss my feet.**
46. My head with oil thou didst not anoint: but this woman hath anointed my feet with ointment.
■ 47. **Wherefore** I say unto thee,
■ **Her sins, which are many,**
■ **are forgiven; for she loved**
■ **much:** but to whom little is forgiven,
the same loveth little.
48. And he said unto her, Thy sins are forgiven.
■ 49. **And they that sat**
■ **at meat** with him
■ **began to say** within themselves,
■ **Who is this that forgiveth**
■ **sins** also?
■ 50. **And he said to the**
■ **woman, Thy faith hath**
■ **saved thee;** go in peace.

CHAPTER 8

1. And it came to pass afterward, that he went throughout every city and village, preaching and shewing the glad tidings of the kingdom of God: and the twelve *were* with him,
2. And certain women, which had been healed of evil spirits and infirmities,
■ **Mary called Magdalene,**
out of whom went seven devils,
3. And Joanna the wife of Chuza Herod's steward, and Susanna,
■ **and** many
■ **others,** which
■ **ministered unto him of**
■ **their substance.**
■ 4. **And when much people**
■ **were gathered** together, and
were come to him out of every city,
■ **he spake by a parable:**
■ 5. **A sower went out**
■ **to sow** his seed:
■ **and** as he sowed,
■ **some fell by the way**
■ **side;** and it was trodden down,
■ **and the fowls** of the air
■ **devoured it.**
■ 6. **And some fell**

upon a rock; and
as soon as it was sprung up,
it withered away,
because it lacked
moisture.
7. And some fell among
thorns; and the thorns
sprang up with it, and
choked it.
8. And other fell on good
ground, and sprang up,
and bare fruit an
hundredfold. And when he
had said these things, he cried, He
that hath ears to hear, let him hear.
9. And his disciples
asked him, saying,
What might this
parable be?
10. And he said, Unto you it is
given to know the mysteries of the
kingdom of God: but to others in
parables; that seeing they might
not see, and hearing they might
not understand.
11. Now the parable is this:
The seed is the word of God.
12. Those by the way
side are they that
hear; then cometh
the devil, and
taketh away the word
out of their hearts, lest
they should
believe and be saved.
13. They on the rock
are they, which, when they hear,
receive the word with joy;
and these
have no root,
which for a while believe,
and in time of temptation
fall away.
14. And that which fell
among thorns are they, which,
when they have heard, go forth, and
are choked with cares and
riches and pleasures of this
life, and bring no
fruit to perfection.
15. But that on the good
ground are they, which in an
honest and good heart, having heard

the word, keep it, and
bring forth fruit
with patience.
16. No man, when he
hath lighted a candle,
covereth it with a vessel,
or putteth it under a bed;
but setteth it on a
candlestick, that they
which enter in
may see the light.
17. For nothing is secret,
that shall not be made manifest;
neither any thing
hid, that shall not
be known and come abroad.
18. Take heed therefore how ye hear:
for whosoever hath, to
him shall be given; and
whosoever hath not, from
him shall be taken even that
which he seemeth to have.
19. Then came to him
his mother and his
brethren, and could not
come at him for the press.
20. And it was told him
by certain which said,
Thy mother and thy
brethren stand without,
desiring to see thee.
21. And he answered
and said unto them,
My mother and my
brethren are these
which hear the word of God,
and do it.
22. Now it came to pass
on a certain day, that
he went into a ship
with his disciples:
and he
said unto them,
Let us go over
unto the other side
of the lake. And they launched forth.
23. But as they sailed
he fell asleep: and
there came down
a storm of wind on the lake;
and they were filled with
water, and were in jeopardy.
24. And they came to him,

and awoke him,
saying, Master, master,
we perish. Then he arose, and
rebuked the wind and the
raging of the water: and they ceased,
and there was a calm.
25. And he said unto them,
Where is your faith? And
they being afraid
wondered, saying
one to another,
What manner of man
is this! for he commandeth
even the winds
and water, and they
obey him.
26. And they arrived
at the country of
the Gadarenes,
which is over against Galilee.
27. And when he went forth to land,
there met him out of the city
a certain
man, which had
devils long time,
and ware no clothes, neither
abode in *any* house, but in
the tombs.
28. When he saw
Jesus, he cried out, and
fell down before him,
and with a loud voice
said, What have I to do with thee,
Jesus, thou Son of God
most high? I beseech thee,
torment me not.
29. (For he had commanded the
unclean spirit to come out of the man.
For oftentimes it had caught him: and
he was kept bound
with chains and in fetters;
and he brake the bands,
and was driven of the devil
into the wilderness.)
30. And Jesus
asked him, saying,
What is thy name? And he
said, Legion: because
many devils were
entered into him.
31. And they besought him
that he would not command
them to go out into the deep.

32. And there was
there an herd of many
swine feeding
on the mountain:
and they besought him
that he would suffer them
to enter into them.
And he suffered them.
33. Then went
the devils out of the man, and
entered into
the swine: and the herd
ran violently down a steep place
into the lake, and were choked.
34. When they that fed
them saw what was done,
they fled, and went
and told it in the
city and in the country.
35. Then they went out to
see what was done; and came to
Jesus, and found
the man, out of whom the
devils were departed,
sitting at the feet of Jesus,
clothed, and in his right
mind: and they were afraid.
36. They also which saw *it*
told them by what means
he that was possessed of the devils
was healed.
37. Then the whole multitude
of the country of the
Gadarenes round about
besought him to
depart from them;
for they were taken with
great fear: and he went up into
the ship, and returned back again.
38. Now the man out of
whom the devils were departed
besought him that he might
be with him: but Jesus sent
him away, saying,
39. Return to thine own
house, and shew how great
things God hath done unto thee.
And he went his way,
and published
throughout the whole city
how great things Jesus
had done unto him.
40. And it came to pass, that,

when Jesus was
returned, the people
gladly received him: for they
were all
waiting for him.
41. **And,** behold,
there came a man named
Jairus, and he was
a ruler of the synagogue:
and he fell down at Jesus' feet, and
besought him that he would
come into his house:
42. **For he had one** only
daughter,
about twelve years of age,
and she lay a dying. But
as he went the people thronged him.
43. **And a woman having
an issue of blood twelve
years,** which had spent all her
living upon physicians, neither
could be healed of any,
44. **Came behind him,
and touched** the border of
his garment: and
immediately her issue
of blood stanched.
45. **And Jesus said, Who
touched me?** When all denied,
Peter and they that were with him
said, Master, the multitude
throng thee and press *thee*,
and sayest thou, Who
touched me?
46. **And Jesus said,**
Somebody hath touched me: for
I perceive that virtue is
gone out of me.
47. **And when the
woman saw** that
she was not hid,
she came trembling,
and falling down before him, she
declared unto him
before all the people
for what cause she had
touched him, and how
she was healed immediately.
48. **And he said** unto her,
Daughter, be of good comfort:
thy faith hath made
thee whole; go in peace.
49. **While he yet spake,**

there cometh one from the
ruler of the synagogue's
house, saying to him,
Thy daughter is dead;
trouble not the Master.
50. **But when Jesus heard
it, he answered** him, saying,
Fear not: believe only, and
she shall be made whole.
51. **And when he came into
the house,** he suffered no man
to go in, save Peter, and James,
and John, and the father and the
mother of the maiden.
52. And all wept, and bewailed her: but
he said, Weep not;
she is not dead, but
sleepeth.
53. **And they laughed him to
scorn,** knowing that she was dead.
54. **And he** put them all out, and
took her by the
hand, and called,
saying, Maid, arise.
55. **And** her spirit came again, and
she arose straightway:
and he commanded to give her meat.
56. And her parents were astonished:
but he charged them that they should
tell no man what was done.

CHAPTER 9

1. **Then he called his
twelve disciples** together,
and gave them power
and authority over all devils,
and to cure diseases.
2. **And he sent them to
preach** the kingdom of God,
and to heal the sick.
3. **And he said** unto them,
Take nothing for your
journey, neither staves, nor
scrip, neither bread, neither money;
neither have two coats apiece.
4. **And whatsoever
house ye enter** into,
there abide, and thence depart.
5. **And whosoever
will not receive you,**
when ye go out of that city,
shake off the very
dust from your feet for a

■ testimony against them.
■ 6. **And they** departed, and
■ **went** through the towns,
preaching the gospel,
and healing every where.
■ 7. **Now Herod** the tetrarch heard
of all that was done by him: and he
■ was perplexed,
■ because that
■ it was said of some,
■ that John was risen
■ from the dead;
8. And of some, that Elias had
appeared; and of others, that one
of the old prophets was risen again.
■ 9. **And Herod said, John**
■ have I beheaded: but who
■ is this, of whom I hear such things?
■ And he desired to see him.
■ 10. **And the apostles,**
■ when they were
■ returned, told him
■ all that
■ they had done. And
■ he took them, and went aside
■ privately into a desert
■ place belonging to the
city called Bethsaida.
■ 11. **And the people,**
when they knew *it,*
■ followed him: and
■ he received them, and
■ spake unto them of the
■ kingdom of God, and
■ healed them
that had need of healing.
■ 12. **And** when the day
began to wear away,
■ then came the twelve,
■ and said unto him,
■ Send the multitude away,
■ that they may go into the
towns and country round about,
■ and lodge, and get
■ victuals: for we are
here in a desert place.
■ 13. **But he said** unto them,
■ Give ye them to eat. And
■ they said, We have no more
■ but five loaves and two
■ fishes; except we should go
and buy meat for all this people.
■ 14. **For they were about five**

■ thousand men. And
■ he said to his disciples,
■ Make them sit down
by fifties in a company.
15. And they did so, and made
them all sit down.
■ 16. **Then he took the five**
■ loaves and the two fishes,
■ and looking up to heaven, he
■ blessed them, and brake,
■ and gave to the disciples to
■ set before the multitude.
■ 17. **And they did eat,**
and were all filled:
■ and there
was taken up of fragments that
■ remained to them
■ twelve baskets.
18. **And** it came to pass,
■ as he was alone
■ praying, his disciples
■ were with him: and he
■ asked them, saying,
■ Whom say the people
■ that I am?
19. **They** answering
■ said, John the Baptist; but
■ some say, Elias;
■ and others *say,* that
■ one of the old
■ prophets is risen again.
20. **He said** unto them,
■ But whom say ye that I am?
Peter answering said,
■ The Christ of God.
21. **And he**
straitly charged them, and
■ commanded them to
■ tell no man that thing;
22. **Saying, The Son of man**
■ must suffer many things, and be
rejected of the elders and chief
priests and scribes,
■ and be slain, and be
■ raised the third day.
23. **And he said** to *them all,*
■ If any man will come after
■ me, let him deny himself, and
■ take up his cross daily,
■ and follow me.
24. For whosoever will save his life
shall lose it: but whosoever will lose
his life for my sake, the same

shall save it.

25. For what is a man advantaged, if he gain the whole world, and lose himself, or be cast away? **26. For whosoever shall be ashamed of me** and of my words, of him **shall the Son of man be ashamed, when he shall come in his own glory,** and *in* his Father's, and of the holy angels.

27. But I tell you of a truth, there be some standing here, which shall not taste of death, till they see the kingdom of God.

28. And it came to pass about an **eight days after** these sayings, **he took Peter and John and James,** and went up **into a mountain to pray. 29. And** as he prayed, **the fashion of his countenance was altered,** and his raiment *was* white *and* glistering. **30. And, behold, there talked with him** two men, which were **Moses and Elias: 31. Who** appeared in glory, and **spake of his decease which he should accomplish** at Jerusalem. **32. But Peter and they that were with him** were heavy with sleep: and when they were awake, they **saw his glory, and the two men that stood with him. 33. And** it came to pass, **as they departed** from him, **Peter said** unto Jesus, Master, it is good for us to be here: and **let us make three tabernacles; one for thee, and** one for **Moses, and** one for **Elias:** not knowing what he said. **34. While he thus spake,** there came **a cloud,** and **overshadowed them:**

and they feared as they entered into the cloud.

35. And there came a voice out of the cloud, **saying, This is my beloved Son: hear him.**

36. And when the voice was past, Jesus was found alone. **And they** kept *it* close, and **told no man** in those days **any of those things** which they had seen. **37. And** it came to pass, that on the next day, **when they were come down** from the hill, **much people met him.** 38. And, behold, a **man** of the company **cried out,** saying, **Master,** I beseech thee, **look upon my** son: for he is mine **only child. 39. And, lo, a spirit taketh him,** and he suddenly crieth out; **and it teareth him** that he foameth again, and **bruising him** hardly departeth from him. **40. And I besought thy disciples to cast him out; and they could not. 41. And Jesus** answering **said, O faithless** and perverse **generation,** how long shall I be with you, and suffer you? **Bring thy son hither.** **42. And** as he was yet a-coming, **the devil threw him down,** and tare *him.* **And Jesus rebuked the unclean spirit, and healed the child,** and delivered him again to his father. **43. And they were all amazed at the mighty power of God.**

But while they wondered every one at all things which **Jesus** did, he **said** unto his disciples, 44. Let these sayings sink

The cost of discipleship

down into your ears: for
the Son of man shall
be delivered into the
hands of men.
45. But they understood
not this saying, and it was hid from
them, that they perceived it not:
and they
feared to ask
him of that saying.
46. Then there arose a
reasoning among them,
which of them
should be greatest.
47. And Jesus, perceiving
the thought of their heart,
took a child, and set him by him,
48. And said unto them,
Whosoever shall receive
this child in my name
receiveth me:
and whosoever shall receive
me receiveth him that sent me:
for he that is least
among you all, the same
shall be great.
49. And John answered and
said, Master,
we saw one casting
out devils in thy name;
and we forbad him,
because he followeth not with us.
50. And Jesus said unto him,
Forbid him not: for he that
is not against us is for us.
51. And it came to pass,
when the time was come
that he should be received
up, he stedfastly
set his face to
go to Jerusalem,
52. And sent messengers
before his face: and they
went, and entered
into a village of the
Samaritans, to make
ready for him.
53. And they did not receive
him, because his face was as
though he would go to Jerusalem.
54. And when his
disciples James and John
saw this, they said, Lord,

wilt thou that we command
fire to come down
from heaven, and consume
them, even as Elias did?
55. But he turned, and
rebuked them, and
said, Ye know not what
manner of spirit ye are of.
56. For the Son of man is not
come to destroy men's
lives, but to save them.
And they went to another village.
57. And it came to pass,
that, as they went in the way,
a certain man said unto him,
Lord, I will follow thee
whithersoever thou goest.
58. And Jesus said
unto him, Foxes have holes, and
birds of the air *have* nests; but
the Son of man hath not
where to lay his head.
59. And he said unto
another, Follow me.
But he said, Lord, suffer
me first to go and
bury my father.
60. Jesus said unto him,
Let the dead bury their
dead: but go thou
and preach the kingdom of God.
61. And another also
said, Lord, I will follow thee;
but let me first go
bid them farewell,
which are at home
at my house.
62. And Jesus said unto him,
No man, having put his
hand to the plough, and
looking back, is fit for the
kingdom of God.

CHAPTER 10

1. After these things the
LORD appointed other
seventy also,
and sent them
two and two before his face
into every city and place,
whither he himself
would come.
2. Therefore said he unto them,

The harvest truly
**is great, but the labourers
are few: pray** ye therefore
the Lord of the harvest,
that he would
send forth labourers
into his harvest.
3. **Go** your ways: behold,
I send you forth
as lambs among wolves.
4. **Carry neither purse, nor
scrip,** nor shoes: and
salute no man by the way.
5. **And into whatsoever
house ye enter, first say,
Peace be to this house.**
6. And if the son of peace be there,
your peace shall rest upon it: if not,
it shall turn to you again.
7. **And** in the same house
**remain, eating and drinking
such things as they give:
for the labourer is worthy
of his hire.**
Go not from house to house.
8. **And into whatsoever city
ye enter,** and they receive you,
eat such
things as are
set before you:
9. **And heal the sick**
that are therein,
and say unto them,
**The kingdom of God is
come nigh unto you.**
10. **But into whatsoever city
ye enter, and they receive
you not,** go your ways out into
the streets of the same, and
say,
11. **Even the very dust of
your city,** which cleaveth on us,
we do
wipe off against you:
notwithstanding be ye sure of
this, that the kingdom of God is
come nigh unto you.
12. But I say unto you, that it
shall be more tolerable in that
day for Sodom, than for that city.
13. Woe unto thee, Chorazin!
woe unto thee, Bethsaida!
for if the mighty works had

**been done in Tyre and
Sidon, which have been
done in you, they had**
a great while ago
repented,
sitting in sackcloth and ashes.
14. **But it shall be more
tolerable for Tyre and
Sidon at the judgment,
than for you.**
15. And thou, Capernaum, which
art exalted to heaven, shalt be
thrust down to hell.
16. He that heareth you heareth me;
and he that despiseth you despiseth
me; and he that despiseth me
despiseth him that sent me.
17. **And the seventy
returned** again with joy,
**saying, Lord, even the
devils are subject unto
us through thy name.**
18. **And he said** unto them,
**I beheld Satan as lightning
fall from heaven.**
19. **Behold, I give unto you
power** to tread on serpents
and scorpions, and over all
the power of the enemy:
and nothing shall
by any means
hurt you.
20. Notwithstanding in this
**rejoice not, that the spirits
are subject unto you; but
rather** rejoice,
**because your names
are written in heaven.**
21. **In that hour Jesus**
rejoiced in spirit, and
said, I thank thee, O Father,
Lord of heaven and earth,
**that thou hast hid these
things from the wise and
prudent, and hast revealed
them unto babes:**
even so, Father; for so it
seemed good in thy sight.
22. **All things are delivered
to me of my Father:**
and no man knoweth who the
Son is, but the Father; and
who the Father is, but the Son,

and he to whom the Son will reveal *him*.

23. **And he turned** him **unto his disciples, and said** privately, **Blessed are the eyes which see the things that ye see:**

24. **For** I tell you, that many **prophets and kings have desired to see those things** which ye see, and have not seen *them*; and to hear those things which ye hear, and have not heard *them*.

25. **And, behold, a** certain **lawyer** stood up, and **tempted him, saying,** Master, **what shall I do to inherit eternal life?**

26. **He said** unto him, **What is written** in the law? how readest thou?

27. **And he** answering **said, Thou shalt love the Lord thy God with all thy heart,** and with all thy **soul,** and with all thy **strength, and** with all thy **mind; and thy neighbour as thyself.**

28. **And he said** unto him, **Thou hast answered right:** this do, and thou shalt live.

29. **But he, willing to justify himself, said** unto Jesus, And **who is my neighbour?**

30. **And Jesus answering** said, **A certain man went down from Jerusalem to Jericho, and fell among thieves, which stripped him** of his raiment, **and wounded him,** and departed, **leaving him half dead.**

31. And by chance there came down **a certain priest** that way: and **when he saw him,** he **passed by** on the other side.

32. **And likewise a Levite,** when he was at the place, came and looked *on him*, and **passed by** on the other side.

33. **But a certain Samaritan,** as he journeyed, came where he was: and when he **saw him,** he had compassion *on him*,

34. **And** went to *him*, and **bound** up **his wounds,** pouring in oil and wine, and set him on his own beast, **and brought him to an inn, and took care of him.**

35. **And on the morrow** when he departed, **he took out two pence,** and gave *them* to the host, **and said** unto him, **Take care of him; and whatsoever thou spendest more,** when I come again, **I will repay** thee.

36. **Which** now of these three, thinkest thou, **was neighbour unto him** that fell among the thieves?

37. **And he said, He that shewed mercy** on him. **Then said Jesus** unto him, **Go, and do** thou **likewise.**

38. **Now** it came to pass, as they went, that **he entered into a** certain **village:** and a certain woman named **Martha received him into her house.**

39. **And** she had a sister called **Mary,** which **also** sat at Jesus' feet, and **heard his word.**

40. **But Martha was** cumbered about much **serving,** and came to him, **and said, Lord,** dost thou not care that **my sister hath left me to serve alone? bid her** therefore that she **help me.**

41. **And Jesus answered** and said unto her, Martha, **Martha, thou art** careful and

■ troubled about
■ many things:
■ 42. But one thing is needful: and
■ Mary hath chosen that
■ good part, which shall not
■ be taken away from her.

CHAPTER 11

■ 1. And it came to pass, that,
■ as he was praying
in a certain place, when he ceased,
■ one of his disciples
■ said unto him,
■ Lord, teach us to pray,
as John also taught his disciples.
■ 2. And he said unto them,
■ When ye pray, say, Our
■ Father which art in heaven,
■ Hallowed be thy name.
■ Thy kingdom come.
■ Thy will be done, as
■ in heaven, so in earth.
■ 3. Give us day by day
■ our daily bread.
■ 4. And forgive us our sins; for
■ we also forgive
every one that is indebted to us.
■ And lead us not into
■ temptation; but deliver
■ us from evil.
■ 5. And he said unto them,
■ Which of you shall have a
■ friend, and shall go unto
■ him at midnight, and say
unto him, Friend,
■ lend me three loaves;
■ 6. For a friend of mine in his
journey is come to me, and I
have nothing to set before him?
■ 7. And he from within
■ shall answer and say,
■ Trouble me not: the door
is now shut, and my children
are with me in bed;
■ I cannot rise and give thee.
■ 8. I say unto you,
■ Though he will not
■ rise and give him,
■ because he is his friend, yet
■ because of his importunity
■ he will rise and
■ give him as many as he needeth.
■ 9. And I say unto you,

■ Ask, and it shall
■ be given you;
■ seek, and ye shall find;
■ knock, and it shall be
■ opened unto you.
■ 10. For every one that asketh
receiveth; and he that seeketh
findeth; and to him that knocketh
it shall be opened.
■ 11. If a son shall
■ ask bread of any of you that is
■ a father, will he give him
■ a stone? or if *he ask*
■ a fish, will he for a fish
■ give him
■ a serpent?
12. Or if he shall ask an egg,
will he offer him a scorpion?
■ 13. If ye then, being evil,
know how to
■ give good gifts
unto your children:
■ how much more
■ shall your heavenly
■ Father give the Holy Spirit
■ to them that ask him?
■ 14. And he was casting
■ out a devil, and it was
■ dumb. And it came to pass,
■ when the devil was gone
■ out, the dumb spake;
and the people wondered.
■ 15. But some of them
■ said, He casteth out devils
■ through Beelzebub
the chief of the devils.
■ 16. And others, tempting *him*,
■ sought of him
■ a sign from heaven.
■ 17. But he, knowing their thoughts,
■ said unto them,
■ Every kingdom divided
against itself is brought to desolation;
and a house *divided* against a house
■ falleth.
■ 18. If Satan also be
■ divided against himself,
■ how shall his kingdom
■ stand? because ye say that I cast
out devils through Beelzebub.
19. And if I by Beelzebub cast
out devils, by whom do your sons
cast *them* out? therefore shall

20. **But if I with the finger of God cast out devils, no doubt the kingdom of God is come** upon you. 21. **When a strong man** armed **keepeth his palace, his goods are in peace:** 22. **But when a stronger** than he shall come upon him, and **overcome him, he taketh** from him **all** his armour wherein he trusted, and divideth **his spoils.** 23. **He that is not with me is against me:** and he that gathereth not with me scattereth. 24. **When the unclean spirit is gone out of a man,** he walketh through dry places, **seeking rest;** and finding none, **he saith, I will return unto my house** whence I came out. 25. **And** when he cometh, **he findeth it swept and garnished.** 26. **Then goeth he, and taketh** to him **seven other spirits** more wicked than himself; and they enter in, and dwell there: **and the last state** of that man **is worse than the first.** 27. And it came to pass, **as he spake** these things, **a certain woman** of the company lifted up her voice, and **said** unto him, **Blessed is the womb that bare thee,** and the paps which thou hast sucked. 28. **But he said,** Yea **rather, blessed are they that hear the word** of God, **and keep it.** 29. And when the people were gathered thick together, he began to say, **This** is an **evil generation:** they **seek a sign; and** there shall **no sign be given it, but the sign of Jonas** the prophet. 30. **For as Jonas was a sign unto the Ninevites, so shall also the Son of man be** to this generation. 31. The queen of the south shall rise up in the judgment with the men of this generation, and condemn them: for she came from the utmost parts of the earth to hear the wisdom of Solomon; and, behold, a greater than Solomon *is* here. 32. **The men of Nineve** shall rise up in the judgment with this generation, and shall condemn it: for they **repented at the preaching of Jonas; and,** behold, **a greater than Jonas is here.** 33. **No man, when he hath lighted a candle, putteth it** in a secret place, neither **under a bushel, but on a candlestick, that they** which come in **may see the light.** 34. **The light of the body is the eye:** therefore **when thine eye is single, thy whole body** also is full of light; but when *thine eye* is evil, thy body also *is* full of darkness. 35. Take heed therefore that the light which is in thee be not darkness. 36. If thy whole body therefore *be* full of light,having no part dark, the whole **shall be full of light,** as when the bright shining of a candle doth give thee light. 37. **And** as he spake, **a certain Pharisee besought him to dine with him:** and he went in, and sat down to meat. 38. **And** when the Pharisee saw *it,* **he marvelled that he had not** first **washed** before dinner. 39. **And the Lord said** unto him, **Now do ye Pharisees make clean the outside**

of the cup and the platter;
**but your inward part
is full of** ravening and
wickedness.
40. **Ye fools, did not he
that made that which is
without make that which
is within also?**
41. But rather give alms of such
things as ye have; and, behold,
all things are clean unto you.
42. **But woe unto you,
Pharisees! for ye tithe**
mint and rue and all manner of herbs,
and pass over judgment and
the love of God:
these ought ye to have done,
and not to leave the other undone.
43. Woe unto you, Pharisees! for
**ye love the uppermost
seats in the synagogues,
and greetings in
the markets.**
44. **Woe unto you,**
scribes and Pharisees,
hypocrites! for ye are as graves
which appear not, and the men that
walk over *them* are not aware of *them*.
45. **Then answered one of
the lawyers,** and said unto him,
**Master, thus saying thou
reproachest us also.**
46. **And he said, Woe unto
you also,** *ye* lawyers!
**for ye lade men with
burdens** grievous to be borne,
and ye yourselves
**touch not the burdens
with** one of
your fingers.
47. Woe unto you! for
**ye build the sepulchres of
the prophets, and your
fathers killed them.**
48. Truly ye bear witness that
ye allow the deeds of your fathers:
for they indeed killed them,
and ye build their sepulchres.
49. Therefore also said the
wisdom of God,
**I will send them prophets
and apostles, and
some** of them

**they shall slay
and persecute:**
50. **That the blood of all the
prophets,** which was shed from
the foundation of the world,
**may be required of
this generation;**
51. From the blood of Abel unto the
blood of Zacharias which perished
between the altar and the temple:
verily I say unto you, It shall be
required of this generation.
52. **Woe unto you, lawyers!
for ye have taken away
the key of knowledge:**
ye entered not in yourselves,
and them that were entering
in ye hindered.
53. **And as he said
these things** unto them,
**the scribes and the
Pharisees began to urge
him** vehemently, and to provoke him
to speak of many things:
54. Laying wait for him, and
**seeking to catch
something** out of his mouth,
that they might accuse him.

CHAPTER 12

1. In the mean time, when there were
gathered together an innumerable
multitude of people, insomuch that
they trode one upon another,
**he began to say unto
his disciples** first of all,
**Beware ye of the leaven
of the Pharisees, which
is hypocrisy.**
2. **For there is nothing** covered,
that shall not be revealed; neither hid,
that shall not be known.
3. Therefore whatsoever ye have
spoken in darkness shall be heard in
the light; and that which ye have
spoken in the ear in closets shall be
proclaimed upon the housetops.
4. **And I say** unto you my friends,
**Be not afraid of them that
kill the body,** and after that
have no more that they can do.
5. **But** I will forewarn
you whom ye shall fear:

The Rich man's barns

Fear him, which after he hath killed hath power to cast into hell; yea, I say unto you, Fear him. 6. Are not five sparrows sold for two farthings, and not one of them is forgotten before God? 7. But even the very hairs of your head are all numbered. Fear not therefore: ye are of more value than many sparrows.

8. Also I say unto you, Whosoever shall confess me before men, him shall the Son of man also confess before the angels of God: 9. But he that denieth me before men shall be denied before the angels of God. 10. And whosoever shall speak a word against the Son of man, it shall be forgiven him: but unto him that blasphemeth against the Holy Ghost it shall not be forgiven. 11. And when they bring you unto the synagogues, and unto magistrates, and powers, take ye no thought how or what thing ye shall answer, or what ye shall say: 12. For the Holy Ghost shall teach you in the same hour what ye ought to say.

13. And one of the company said unto him, Master, speak to my brother, that he divide the inheritance with me. 14. And he said unto him, Man, who made me a judge or a divider over you? 15. And he said unto them, Take heed, and beware of covetousness: for a man's life consisteth not in the abundance of the things which he possesseth.

16. And he spake a parable unto them, saying, The ground of a certain rich man brought forth plentifully: 17. And he thought within himself, saying, What shall I do, because I have no room where to bestow my fruits? 18. And he said, This will I do: I will pull down my barns, and build greater; and there will I bestow all my fruits and my goods. 19. And I will say to my soul, Soul, thou hast much goods laid up for many years; take thine ease, eat, drink, and be merry. 20. But God said unto him, Thou fool, this night thy soul shall be required of thee: then whose shall those things be, which thou hast provided? 21. So is he that layeth up treasure for himself, and is not rich toward God.

22. And he said unto his disciples, Therefore I say unto you, Take no thought for your life, what ye shall eat; neither for the body, what ye shall put on. 23. The life is more than meat, and the body is more than raiment. 24. Consider the ravens: for they neither sow nor reap; which neither have storehouse nor barn; and God feedeth them: how much more are ye better than the fowls? 25. And which of you with taking thought can add to his stature one cubit? 26. If ye then be not able to do that

thing which is least, why take
ye thought for the rest?

27. **Consider the lilies how**
they grow: they toil not,
they spin not; and
yet I say unto you, that
Solomon in all his glory
was not arrayed like one of
these.

28. **If then God so clothe the**
grass, which is to day in the field,
and to-morrow is cast into the oven;
how much more will he
clothe you, O ye of little faith?

29. **And seek not ye what ye**
shall eat, or what ye shall
drink, neither be ye
of doubtful mind.

30. For all these things do the nations
of the world seek after: and
your Father knoweth that ye
have need of these things.

31. **But rather seek ye the**
kingdom of God; and
all these things
shall be added unto you.

32. **Fear not,** little flock; for
it is your Father's good
pleasure to give you the
kingdom.

33. **Sell that ye have,**
and give alms;
provide yourselves
bags which wax not old,
a treasure in the heavens
that faileth not,
where no thief approacheth,
neither moth corrupteth.

34. **For where your**
treasure is, there will
your heart be also.

35. Let your loins be girded
about, and *your* lights burning;

36. And ye yourselves like unto men
that wait for their lord, when he will
return from the wedding; that when
he cometh and knocketh, they may
open unto him immediately.

37. **Blessed are**
those servants,
whom the lord when he
cometh shall find watching:
verily I say unto you, that he shall gird

himself, and make them to sit
down to meat, and will come
forth and serve them.

38. And if he shall come in the
second watch, or come in the
third watch, and find *them* so,
blessed are those servants.

39. And this know, that if the goodman
of the house had known what hour the
thief would come, he would have
watched, and not have suffered his
house to be broken through.

40. **Be ye therefore**
ready also:
for the Son of man
cometh at an hour
when ye think not.

41. Then Peter said unto him, Lord,
speakest thou this parable unto
us, or even to all?

42. And the Lord said,
Who then
is that faithful and wise
steward, whom his lord shall
make ruler over his
household, to give *them their*
portion of meat in due season?

43. Blessed *is* that servant,
whom his lord when he cometh
shall find so doing.

44. Of a truth I say unto you,
that he will make him ruler
over all that he hath.

45. **But and if that**
servant say in his heart,
My lord delayeth his
coming; and shall begin
to beat the menservants
and maidens, and
to eat and drink,
and to be drunken;

46. **The lord** of that servant
will come in a day when helooketh
not for *him,* and at an hour when he is
not aware, and will cut him in sunder,
and will appoint him his
portion with the
unbelievers.

47. **And that servant, which**
knew his lord's will, and
prepared not *himself,* neither did
according to his will,
shall be beaten

with many stripes.
48. But he that knew
not, and did commit
things worthy of stripes,
shall be beaten with
few stripes. For unto
whomsoever much
is given, of him
shall be much required:
and to whom men have committed
much, of him they will ask the more.
49. I am come to send fire on the
earth; and what will I, if it be
already kindled?
50. But I have a baptism to be
baptized with; and how am I
straitened till it be accomplished!
51. Suppose ye that I am
come to give peace
on earth? I tell you,
Nay; but rather division:
52. For from henceforth there shall
be five in one house divided, three
against two, and two against three.
53. The father shall be
divided against the son,
and the son against the father;
the mother against the
daughter, and the daughter
against the mother; the mother
in law against her daughter in
law, and the daughter in law
against her mother in law.
54. And he said
also to the people,
When ye see a cloud rise
out of the west, straightway
ye say, There cometh
a shower; and so it is.
55. And when *ye see* the south
wind blow, ye say, There will be
heat; and it cometh to pass.
56. *Ye* hypocrites,
ye can discern the face of the
sky and of the
earth; but how is it that
ye do not discern
this time?
57. Yea, and why even of yourselves
judge ye not what is right?
58. When thou goest
with thine adversary
to the magistrate,

as thou art in the way,
give diligence
that thou mayest
be delivered from him;
lest he hale thee to the judge,
and the judge deliver thee to
the officer, and the officer
cast thee into prison.
59. I tell thee, thou shalt
not depart thence,
till thou hast paid
the very last mite.

CHAPTER 13

1. There were
present at that season
some that told him of the
Galilaeans, whose blood
Pilate had mingled with
their sacrifices.
2. And Jesus answering
said unto them,
Suppose ye that these
Galilaeans were sinners
above all the Galilaeans,
because they suffered
such things?
3. I tell you, Nay: but, except ye
repent, ye shall all likewise perish.
4. Or those eighteen,
upon whom the tower
in Siloam fell,
and slew them, think ye
that they were sinners
above all men
that dwelt in Jerusalem?
5. I tell you, Nay: but,
except ye repent, ye
shall all likewise perish.
6. He spake also this
parable; A certain
man had a fig tree
planted in his vineyard;
and he came and
sought fruit thereon,
and found none.
7. Then said he unto the
dresser of his vineyard, Behold,
these three years I come seeking fruit
on this fig tree, and find none:
cut it down;
why cumbereth it the ground?
8. And he answering

said unto him,

Lord, let it alone

this year also,

till I shall dig about it, and

dung it:

9. And if it bear fruit, well: and

if not, then after that thou shalt

cut it down.

10. And he was teaching

in one of the synagogues

on the sabbath.

11. And, behold, there was

a woman which had

a spirit of infirmity

eighteen years,

and was bowed together,

and could in no wise lift up *herself*.

12. And when Jesus saw her,

he called *her to him*, and

said unto her,

Woman, thou art loosed

from thine infirmity.

13. And he laid *his* hands

on her: and immediately

she was made straight, and

glorified God.

14. And the ruler

of the synagogue

answered with indignation,

because that

Jesus had

healed on the sabbath day,

and said unto the people,

There are six days in which

men ought to work: in them

therefore come and be healed, and

not on the sabbath day.

15. The Lord then

answered him, and said,

Thou hypocrite, doth not

each one of you on the

sabbath loose his ox

or his ass from the stall,

and lead him away

to watering?

16. And ought not this

woman, being a daughter

of Abraham, whom Satan hath

bound, lo, these eighteen years,

be loosed from this

bond on the sabbath day?

17. And when he

had said these things,

all his adversaries were

ashamed: and all the people

rejoiced for all the glorious things

that were done by him.

18. Then said he, Unto what

is the kingdom of God like?

and whereunto shall I resemble it?

19. It is like a grain of

mustard seed, which

a man took, and

cast into his garden; and it

grew, and waxed a great

tree; and the fowls of the air lodged

in the branches of it.

20. And again he said, Whereunto

shall I liken the kingdom of God?

21. It is like leaven,

which a woman took and

hid in three measures of

meal, till the whole

was leavened.

22. And he went through the

cities and villages, teaching,

and journeying toward Jerusalem.

23. Then said one

unto him, Lord,

are there few that

be saved? And

he said unto them,

24. Strive to enter in at

the strait gate: for

many, I say unto you,

will seek to enter in,

and shall not be able.

25. When once the master

of the house is risen up, and

hath shut to

the door, and ye

begin to stand without, and to

knock at the door,

saying, Lord,

Lord, open unto us; and he

shall answer and say unto you,

I know you not whence ye are:

26. Then shall ye begin to

say, We have eaten and

drunk in thy presence,

and thou hast taught in our streets.

27. But he shall say, I tell you,

I know you not whence ye are;

depart from me, all

ye workers of iniquity.

28. There shall be weeping

■ ■ and gnashing of
■ teeth, when ye shall see
Abraham, and Isaac, and
Jacob, and all the prophets,
in the kingdom of God, and
you yourselves thrust out.
■ 29. And they shall come
■ from the east, and *from* the
■ west, and from the
■ north, and *from* the
■ south, and shall sit down
■ in the kingdom of God.
30. And, behold, there are last
which shall be first, and there
are first which shall be last.
■ 31. The same day there
■ came certain of
■ the Pharisees, saying
unto him, Get thee out, and
■ depart hence:
■ for Herod will kill thee.
■ 32. And he said unto them,
■ Go ye, and
■ tell that fox, Behold,
■ I cast out devils, and I do
■ cures today and tomorrow,
■ and the third day I
■ shall be perfected.
■ 33. Nevertheless I must walk
■ to-day, and to-morrow, and
the *day* following:
■ for it cannot be that
■ a prophet perish out
■ of Jerusalem.
■ 34. O Jerusalem, Jerusalem,
which killest the prophets, and
stonest them that are sent unto thee;
■ how often would I have
■ gathered thy children
■ together, as a hen *doth gather*
her brood under *her* wings,
■ and ye would not !
■ 35. Behold, your house
■ is left unto you
■ desolate: and
verily I say unto you,
■ Ye shall not see me,
■ until *the time* come when
■ ye shall
■ say, Blessed is
■ he that cometh
■ in the name of
■ the Lord.

CHAPTER 14

■ 1. And it came to pass, as
■ he went into the house of
■ one of the chief Pharisees
■ to eat bread
■ on the sabbath
day, that they watched him.
■ 2. And, behold,
■ there was a certain
■ man before him
■ which had the dropsy.
■ 3. And Jesus answering
■ spake unto the lawyers and
Pharisees, saying,
■ Is it lawful to heal
■ on the sabbath day?
■ 4. And they held their
■ peace. And he took *him*, and
■ healed him, and let him go;
5. And answered them, saying, Which
of you shall have an ass or an ox
fallen into a pit, and will not
straightway pull him out on
the sabbath day?
6. And they could not answer
him again to these things.
■ 7. And he put forth
■ a parable to those
which were bidden,
■ when he marked
■ how they chose out
■ the chief rooms;
saying unto them.
■ 8. When thou art
■ bidden of any *man*
■ to a wedding, sit not
■ down in the highest room;
■ lest a more honourable
■ man than thou
■ be bidden of him;
■ 9. And he that bade thee and him
■ come and say to thee,
■ Give this man place; and
■ thou begin with shame to
■ take the lowest room.
10. But when thou art bidden,
■ go and sit down
■ in the lowest room; that
when he that bade thee cometh,
■ he may say unto thee,
■ Friend, go up higher:
■ then shalt thou have
■ worship in the presence

■ **of them** that sit at meat
■ **with thee.**
11. For whosoever exalteth
himself shall be abased; and
■ **he that humbleth himself**
■ **shall be exalted.**
■ 12. **Then said he**
also to him that bade him,
■ **When thou makest**
■ **a dinner** or a supper,
■ **call not thy friends,** nor *thy*
brethren, neither thy kinsmen,
■ **nor** *thy*
■ **rich neighbours; lest**
they also bid thee again, and
■ **a recompence**
■ **be made** thee.
13. **But** when thou makest a feast,
■ **call the poor, the maimed,**
■ **the lame, the blind:**
14. **And thou shalt be**
■ **blessed;** for they cannot
recompense thee:
■ **for thou shalt be**
■ **recompensed at the**
■ **resurrection** of the just.
15. And when one of them that sat at
meat with him heard these things, he
said unto him, Blessed *is* he that shall
eat bread in the kingdom of God.
■ 16. **Then said he** unto him,
■ **A** certain
■ **man made a great supper,**
■ **and bade many:**
■ 17. **And sent his**
■ **servant** at supper time
■ **to say** to them that were bidden,
■ **Come; for all things**
■ **are now ready.**
18. **And they** all with one *consent*
■ **began to make excuse.**
The first said unto him, I have
bought a piece of ground, and
I must needs go and see it: I
pray thee have me excused.
19. And another said, I have bought
five yoke of oxen, and I go to prove
them: I pray thee have me excused.
20. And another said, I have married
a wife, and therefore I cannot come.
■ 21. **So that servant** came, and
■ **shewed his lord these**
■ **things. Then the master**

of the house
■ **being angry**
■ **said** to his servant,
■ **Go** out quickly
■ **into the streets**
■ **and lanes** of the city,
■ **and bring** in hither
■ **the poor, and the maimed,**
■ **and the halt, and the blind.**
22. **And the servant**
■ **said,** Lord,
■ **it is done** as thou
hast commanded, and
■ **yet there is room.**
23. **And the lord**
■ **said** unto the servant,
■ **Go out into the highways**
■ **and hedges, and compel**
■ **them to come** in, that my
house may be filled.
24. **For I say** unto you,
■ **That none of those**
men which were
■ **bidden shall taste**
■ **of my supper.**
25. And there went great multitudes
with him: and he turned, and said
unto them,
26. If any *man* come to me, and hate
not his father, and mother, and wife,
and children, and brethren, and
sisters, yea, and his own life also,
he cannot be my disciple.
27. **And whosoever doth not**
■ **bear his cross, and come**
■ **after me, cannot be**
■ **my disciple.**
28. **For which of you,**
■ **intending to build a**
■ **tower,** sitteth not down
■ **first,** and
■ **counteth the cost,** whether
he have *sufficient* to finish *it.*
29. **Lest haply,** after
■ **he** hath laid the foundation, and
■ **is not able to finish it,**
all that behold *it* begin to mock him,
30. Saying, This man began to
build, and was not able to finish.
■ 31. **Or what king,**
■ **going to** make
■ **war** against another
king, sitteth not down

first, and
consulteth whether he
be able with ten thousand
to meet him that
cometh against him
with twenty thousand?
32. Or else, while the
other is yet a great way off,
he sendeth an ambassage,
and desireth conditions of
peace.
33. So likewise, whosoever
he be of you
that forsaketh not
all that he hath, he
cannot be my disciple.
34. Salt is good: but if the salt
have lost his savour, wherewith
shall it be seasoned?
35. It is neither fit for the land, nor
yet for the dunghill; *but* men
cast it
out. He that hath ears
to hear, let him hear.

CHAPTER 15

1. Then drew near unto him all
the publicans and
sinners for to hear him.
2. And the Pharisees and
scribes murmured, saying,
This man receiveth sinners,
and eateth with them.
3. And he spake this
parable unto them, saying,
4. What man of you,
having an hundred sheep,
if he lose one of them,
doth not leave the ninety
and nine in the wilderness, and
go after that which
is lost, until he find it?
5. And when he hath found *it*, he
layeth it on his
shoulders, rejoicing.
6. And when he cometh home, he
calleth together his friends and
neighbours, saying unto them,
Rejoice with me; for I
have found my sheep
which was lost.
7. I say unto you, that likewise
joy shall be in heaven over

one sinner that repenteth,
more than over ninety and nine just
persons, which need no repentance.
8. Either what woman
having ten pieces of
silver, if she lose one piece,
doth not light a candle, and sweep
the house, and
seek diligently till
she find it?
9. And when she hath found *it*,
she calleth *her* friends and *her*
neighbours together, saying,
Rejoice with me; for I have
found the piece which I had lost.
10. Likewise, I say unto you,
there is joy in the
presence of the angels of
God over one sinner
that repenteth.
11. And he said, A certain
man had two sons:
12. And the younger of them
said to *his* father,
Father, give me the portion
of goods that falleth to me.
And he divided unto them *his* living.
13. And not many days after
the younger son
gathered all together, and
took his journey into a far
country, and there wasted
his substance with
riotous living.
14. And when he had spent all,
there arose a mighty
famine in that land;
and he began to
be in want.
15. And he went
and joined himself
to a citizen of that country;
and he sent him into his fields
to feed swine.
16. And he would fain have
filled his belly with the husks
that the swine
did eat: and no man
gave unto him.
17. And when he came to
himself, he said, How many
hired servants of my father's have
bread enough and to spare, and

I perish with hunger!

18. I will arise and go to my father, and will say unto him, Father, I have sinned against heaven, and before thee,

19. And am no more worthy to be called thy son: make me as one of thy hired servants.

20. And he arose, and came to his father. But when he was yet a great way off, his father saw him, and had compassion, and ran, and fell on his neck, and kissed him.

21. And the son said unto him, Father, I have sinned against heaven, and in thy sight, and am no more worthy to be called thy son.

22. But the father said to his servants, Bring forth the best robe, and put it on him; and put a ring on his hand, and shoes on his feet:

23. And bring hither the fatted calf, and kill it; and let us eat, and be merry:

24. For this my son was dead, and is alive again; he was lost, and is found. And they began to be merry.

25. Now his elder son was in the field: and as he came and drew nigh to the house, he heard music and dancing.

26. And he called one of the servants, and asked what these things meant.

27. And he said unto him, Thy brother is come; and thy father hath killed the fatted calf, because he hath received him safe and sound.

28. And he was angry, and would not go in: therefore came his father out, and entreated him.

29. And he answering said to his father, Lo, these many years do I serve thee, neither transgressed I at any time thy commandment: and yet thou never gavest me a kid, that I might make merry with my friends:

30. But as soon as this thy son was come, which hath devoured thy living with harlots, thou hast killed for him the fatted calf.

31. And he said unto him, Son, thou art ever with me, and all that I have is thine.

32. It was meet that we should make merry, and be glad: for this thy brother was dead, and is alive again; and was lost, and is found.

CHAPTER 16

1. And he said also unto his disciples, There was a certain rich man, which had a steward; and the same was accused unto him that he had wasted his goods.

2. And he called him, and said unto him, How is it that I hear this of thee? give an account of thy stewardship; for thou mayest be no longer steward.

3. Then the steward said within himself, What shall I do? for my lord taketh away from me the stewardship: I cannot dig; to beg I am ashamed.

4. I am resolved what to do, that, when I am put out of the stewardship, they may receive me into their houses.

5. So he called every one of his lord's debtors unto him,

and said unto the first,
How much owest thou unto
my lord?
6. And he said, An hundred
measures of oil. And he
said unto him,
Take thy bill,
and sit down quickly,
and write fifty.
7. Then said he
to another, And
how much owest
thou? And he said,
An hundred measures of
wheat. And he said unto him,
Take thy bill, and
write fourscore.
8. And the lord commended
the unjust steward,
because he had done wisely:
for the children of this
world are in their generation
wiser than the children
of light.
9. And I say unto you,
Make to yourselves
friends of the mammon of
unrighteousness;
that, when ye fail,
they may receive you
into everlasting habitations.
10. He that is faithful in
that which is least is faithful
also in much: and he that
is unjust in the least is unjust
also in much.
11. If therefore ye have
not been faithful
in the unrighteous mammon,
who will commit to your
trust the true riches?
12. And if ye have not been faithful in
that which is another man's, who shall
give you that which is your own?
13. No servant can serve
two masters: for either he will
hate the one, and love the other;
or else he will hold to the one,
and despise the other.
Ye cannot serve God
and mammon.
14. And the Pharisees
also, who were covetous,

heard all these things:
and they
derided him.
15. And he said unto them,
Ye are they which justify yourselves
before men; but
God knoweth your hearts:
for that which is highly
esteemed among men
is abomination in the
sight of God.
16. The law and the
prophets were until John:
since that time the kingdom
of God is preached,
and every man presseth into it.
17. And it is easier for
heaven and earth to
pass, than one tittle
of the law to fail.
18. Whosoever putteth
away his wife, and
marrieth another,
committeth adultery:
and whosoever
marrieth her that
is put away from her husband
committeth adultery.
19. There was a certain
rich man, which was clothed in
purple and fine linen, and fared
sumptuously every day:
20. And there was
a certain
beggar named
Lazarus, which was
laid at his gate, full of sores,
21. And desiring to be fed
with the crumbs which fell
from the rich man's
table: moreover the dogs
came and licked his sores.
22. And it came to pass, that
the beggar died, and
was carried by the angels
into Abraham's bosom:
the rich man also died,
and was buried;
23. And in hell he lift
up his eyes, being
in torments, and seeth
Abraham afar off,
and Lazarus in his bosom.

24. **And he cried** and said, **Father Abraham,** have mercy on me, and **send Lazarus, that he may dip** the tip of **his finger in water, and cool my tongue; for I am tormented in this flame.** 25. **But Abraham said,** Son, remember that **thou in thy lifetime receivedst thy good things, and** likewise **Lazarus evil things: but now he is comforted, and thou art tormented.** 26. **And beside** all this, **between us** and you **there is a great gulf fixed: so that** they which would pass from hence to **you cannot;** neither can they **pass** to us, that *would come* from thence. 27. **Then he said,** I pray thee therefore, father, that thou wouldest **send him to my father's house:** 28. **For I have five brethren;** that he may testify unto them, **lest they also come into this place** of torment. 29. **Abraham saith** unto him, **They have Moses and the prophets;** let them hear them. 30. **And he said,** Nay, father Abraham: but **if one went** unto them **from the dead, they will repent.** 31. **And he said** unto him, **If they hear not Moses and the prophets, neither will they be persuaded, though one rose from the dead.**

CHAPTER 17

1. **Then said he unto the disciples,** It is impossible but that **offences will come: but woe unto him, through whom they come!** 2. **It were better** for him **that** a millstone were hanged about his neck, and **he cast into the sea, than** that he should **offend one of these little ones.** 3. Take heed to yourselves: **If thy brother trespass** against thee, **rebuke him; and if he repent, forgive him.** 4. **And if he trespass** against thee **seven times in a day, and** seven times in a day turn again to thee, saying, I **repent;** thou shalt **forgive him.** 5. **And the apostles said** unto the Lord, **Increase our faith.** 6. **And the Lord said, If ye had faith as a** grain of **mustard seed, ye might say unto this** sycamine **tree, Be** thou plucked up by the root, and be **thou planted in the sea; and it should obey you.** 7. But which of you, having a servant plowing or feeding cattle, will say unto him by and by, when he is come from the field, Go and sit down to meat? 8. And will not rather say unto him, Make ready wherewith I may sup, and gird thyself, and serve me, till I have eaten and drunken; and afterward thou shalt eat and drink? 9. Doth he thank that servant because he did the things that were commanded him? I trow not. 10. So likewise ye, when ye shall have done all those things which are commanded you, say, We are unprofitable servants: we have done that which was our duty to do. 11. **And** it came to pass, **as he went to Jerusalem,** that he passed **through** the midst of **Samaria and Galilee.** 12. And as he entered into a certain village,

there met him ten men that were
lepers, which stood afar off:
13. And they
lifted up *their* voices, and
said, Jesus, Master,
have mercy on us.
14. And when he saw *them*,
he said unto them,
Go shew yourselves
unto the priests. And
it came to pass, that,
as they went, they
were cleansed.
15. And one of them,
when he saw that he was healed,
turned back, and
with a loud voice
glorified God,
16. And fell down on *his* face
at his feet, giving him
thanks: and he was a Samaritan.
17. And Jesus answering
said, Were there not ten
cleansed? but
where are the nine?
18. There are not found that
returned to give glory to God,
save this stranger.
19. And he said unto him,
Arise, go thy way:
thy faith hath made
thee whole.
20. And when he was
demanded of the
Pharisees, when the
kingdom of God
should come, he answered
them and said, The kingdom of
God cometh not with observation:
21. Neither shall they say, Lo
here! or, lo there! for, behold
the kingdom of
God is within you.
22. And he said unto the
disciples, The days will
come, when ye shall
desire to see one of the days of
the Son of man,
and ye shall not see *it*.
23. And they shall say to you,
See here; or, see there: go not
after *them*, nor follow *them*.
24. For as the lightning, that

lighteneth out of the
one *part* under heaven,
shineth unto the
other *part* under heaven;
so shall also
the Son of man be
in his day.
25. But first must
he suffer many things,
and be rejected
of this generation.
26. And as it was
in the days of Noe,
so shall it be also
in the days of the Son of man.
27. They did eat, they
drank, they
married wives,
they were given in marriage,
until the day that
Noe entered into
the ark, and the
flood came, and
destroyed them all.
28. Likewise also as it was
in the days of Lot; they did eat, they
drank, they bought, they sold,
they planted, they builded;
29. But the same day that
Lot went out of Sodom it
rained fire and brimstone
from heaven, and
destroyed them all.
30. Even thus shall
it be in the day
when the Son of man
is revealed.
31. In that day, he
which shall be upon
the housetop,
and his stuff in the house,
let him not come down
to take it away: and he that is in the
field, let him likewise not return back.
32. Remember Lot's wife.
33. Whosoever shall seek to save
his life shall lose it; and whosoever
shall lose his life shall preserve it.
34. I tell you, in that night
there shall be two
men in one bed; the
one shall be taken,
and the other shall be

left.

35. Two *women* shall be grinding together; the one shall be taken, and the other left.

36. Two *men* shall be in the field; the one shall be taken, and the other left.

37. **And they** answered and **said** unto him, **Where, Lord? And he said** unto them, **Wheresoever the body is, thither will the eagles be gathered** together.

CHAPTER 18

1. **And he spake a parable** unto them to *this* end, **that men ought always to pray, and not to faint;**

2. **Saying, There was** in a city **a judge, which feared not God,** neither regarded man:

3. **And** there was **a widow** in that city; and she **came unto him, saying, Avenge me of mine adversary.**

4. **And he would not** for a while: **but** afterward he **said within himself,** Though I fear not God, nor regard man;

5. Yet because this widow *troubleth* me, **I will avenge her, lest by her continual coming she weary me.**

6. **And the Lord said,** Hear what the unjust judge saith.

7. **And shall not God avenge his own elect, which cry** day and night **unto him,** though he bear long with them?

8. I tell you that he will avenge them speedily. Nevertheless when the Son of man cometh, shall he find faith on the earth?

9. **And he spake this parable unto certain which trusted in themselves** that they were righteous, **and despised others:**

10. **Two men went** up into the temple **to pray;** the one **a Pharisee, and** the other **a publican.**

11. **The Pharisee** stood and **prayed** thus with himself, **God, I thank thee, that I am not as other men** *are,* extortioners, unjust, adulterers, or even as this publican.

12. **I fast** twice in the week, **I give tithes** of all that I possess.

13. **And the publican,** standing afar off, **would not lift up** so much as **his eyes** unto heaven, but smote upon his breast, **saying, God be merciful to me a sinner.**

14. I tell you, **this man went** down **to his house justified** *rather* than the other: for every one that exalteth himself shall be abased; and **he that humbleth himself shall be exalted.**

15. **And they brought** unto him also **infants, that he would touch them: but** when **his disciples** saw *it,* they **rebuked them.**

16. **But Jesus** called them *unto him,* and **said, Suffer little children to come unto me,** and forbid them not: **for of such is the kingdom** of God.

17. Verily I say unto you, **Whosoever shall not receive the kingdom** of God **as a** little **child shall in no wise enter** therein.

18. **And a certain ruler asked** him, saying, Good Master, **what shall I do to inherit eternal life?**

19. **And Jesus said** unto him, Why callest thou me good? none *is* good, save one, *that is,* God.

20. Thou knowest the

commandments,

Do not commit adultery, Do not **kill,** Do not **steal,** Do not **bear false witness, Honour thy father and thy mother.** 21. **And he said, All these have I kept** from my youth up. 22. **Now when Jesus heard** these things, **he said** unto him, Yet lackest thou one thing: **sell all that thou hast, and distribute unto the poor, and thou shalt have treasure in heaven: and come, follow me.** 23. **And** when he heard this, **he was** very **sorrowful: for he was very rich.** 24. **And when Jesus saw** that he was very sorrowful, **he said, How hardly shall they that have riches enter into the kingdom** of God! 25. **For it is easier for a camel to go through a needle's eye,** than for a rich man to enter into the kingdom of God. 26. **And they that heard it said, Who then can be saved?** 27. **And he said, The things** which are **impossible with men are possible with God.** 28. **Then Peter said,** Lo, **we have left all, and followed thee.** 29. **And he said** unto them, Verily I say unto you, **There is no man that hath left house, or parents, or brethren, or wife, or children, for the kingdom** of God's sake, 30. **Who shall not receive manifold more** in this present time, **and** in the world to come **life everlasting.**

31. **Then he took** unto him **the twelve, and said** unto them, Behold, **we go up to Jerusalem, and all things** that are **written by the prophets** concerning the Son of man **shall be accomplished.** 32. **For he shall be delivered unto the Gentiles,** and shall be mocked, and spitefully entreated, and spitted on: 33. **And they shall** scourge *him*, and **put him to death: and the third day he shall rise** again. 34. And they understood none of these things: and this saying was hid from them, neither knew they the things which were spoken. 35. **And** it came to pass, that **as he was come** nigh **unto Jericho, a** certain **blind man sat** by the way side **begging:** 36. And hearing the multitude pass by, he asked what it meant. 37. And they told him, that Jesus of Nazareth passeth by. 38. **And he cried,** saying, **Jesus,** *thou* son of David, **have mercy on me.** 39. **And they** which went before **rebuked him,** that he should hold his peace: but he cried so much the more, *Thou* son of David, have mercy on me. 40. **And Jesus** stood, and **commanded him to be brought** unto him: and when he was come near, he asked him, 41. **Saying, What wilt thou that I shall do** unto thee? **And he said, Lord, that I may receive my sight.** 42. **And Jesus said** unto him, **Receive thy sight: thy faith hath saved thee.** 43. **And immediately he received his sight,** and followed him, glorifying God: and all the people, when they *saw it*, gave praise unto God.

CHAPTER 19

1. And *Jesus* entered and passed through Jericho.

2. And, behold, *there was* a man named Zacchaeus, which was the chief among the publicans, and he was rich.

3. And he sought to see Jesus who he was; and could not for the press, because he was little of stature.

4. And he ran before, and climbed up into a sycomore tree to see him: for he was to pass that *way*.

5. And when Jesus came to the place, he looked up, and saw him, and said unto him, Zacchaeus, make haste, and come down; for to day I must abide at thy house.

6. And he made haste, and came down, and received him joyfully.

7. And when they saw it, they all murmured, saying, That he was gone to be guest with a man that is a sinner.

8. And Zacchaeus stood, and said unto the Lord: Behold, Lord, the half of my goods I give to the poor; and if I have taken any thing from any man by false accusation, I restore him fourfold.

9. And Jesus said unto him, This day is salvation come to this house, forsomuch as he also is a son of Abraham.

10. For the Son of man is come to seek and to save that which was lost.

11. And as they heard these things, he added and spake a parable, because he was nigh to Jerusalem, and because they thought that the kingdom of God should immediately appear.

12. He said therefore, A certain nobleman went into a far country to receive for himself a kingdom, and to return.

13. And he called his ten servants, and delivered them ten pounds, and said unto them, Occupy till I come.

14. But his citizens hated him, and sent a message after him, saying, We will nothave this *man* to reign over us.

15. And it came to pass, that when he was returned, having received the kingdom, then he commanded these servants to be called unto him,to whom he had given themoney, that he might know how much every man had gained by trading.

16. Then came the first, saying, Lord, thy pound hath gained ten pounds.

17. And he said unto him, Well, thou good servant: because thou hast been faithful in a very little, have thou authority over ten cities.

18. And the second came, saying, Lord, thy pound hath gained five pounds.

19. And he said likewise to him, Be thou also over five cities.

20. And another came, saying, Lord, behold, here is thy pound, which I have kept laid up in a napkin:

21. For I feared thee, because thou art an austere man: thou takest up that thou layedst not down, and reapest that thou didst not sow.

22. And he saith unto him, Out of thine own mouth will I judge thee, thou wicked servant. Thou knewest that I was an austere man,

taking up that I laid not down,
and reaping that I did not sow:

23. **Wherefore then gavest not thou my money into the bank, that** at my coming **I might have** required mine own with **usury?**

24. And he said unto them that stood by, **Take** from him **the pound, and give it to him that hath ten pounds.**

25. (And they said unto him, Lord, he hath ten pounds.)

26. **For I say** unto you, **That unto every one which hath shall be given;** and from him that hath not, even that he hath shall be taken away from him.

27. **But those mine enemies,** which would not that I should reign over them, **bring hither, and slay them** before me.

28. And when he had thus spoken, he went before, ascending up to Jerusalem.

29. **And** it came to pass, **when he was come** nigh **to** Bethphage and Bethany, at the mount called **the mount of Olives, he sent two** of his **disciples,**

30. **Saying, Go ye into the village** over against *you*; in the which at your entering **ye shall find a colt tied,** whereon yet never man sat: loose him, and **bring him hither.**

31. **And if any man ask** you, **Why do ye loose him?** thus shall ye **say** unto him, Because **the Lord hath need of him.**

32. And they that were sent went their way, and found even as he had said unto them.

33. And as they were loosing the colt, the owners thereof said unto them, Why loose ye the colt?

34. And they said, The Lord hath need of him.

35. **And they brought him** to Jesus: **and** they **cast their garments upon the colt, and they set Jesus thereon.**

36. **And** as he went, they **spread their clothes in the way.**

37. **And** when he was come nigh, even now at the descent of the mount of Olives, **the whole multitude** of the disciples **began to** rejoice and **praise God** with a loud voice **for all the mighty works that they had seen;**

38. Saying, Blessed *be* the King that cometh in the name of the Lord:peace in heaven, and glory in the highest.

39. **And some of the Pharisees** from among the multitude **said** unto him, Master, **rebuke thy disciples.**

40. **And he answered** and said unto them, I tell you that, **if these should hold their peace, the stones would** immediately **cry out.**

41. **And** when he was come near, **he beheld the city, and wept over it,**

42. **Saying, If thou hadstknown,** even thou, at least in this thy day, **the things which belong unto thy peace! but now they are hid** from thine eyes.

43. **For** the days shall come upon thee, that **thine enemies shall** cast a trench about thee, and **compass thee round,** and keep thee in on every side,

44. **And shall lay thee even with the ground,** and thy children within thee; **and they shall**

not leave in thee
one stone upon another;
because thou knewest
not the time of
thy visitation.
45. And he went into the
temple, and began to cast
out them that sold therein,
and them that
bought;
46. Saying unto them,
It is written, My house is
the house of prayer: but
ye have made it a den
of thieves.
47. And he taught daily
in the temple. But
the chief priests and the
scribes and the chief of the people
sought to destroy him,
48. And could not find what they
might do: for all the people were
very attentive to hear him.

CHAPTER 20

1. And it came to pass, *that* on one
of those days, as he taught the
people in the temple,
and preached the gospel,
the chief priests and the
scribes came
upon *him* with the elders,
2. And spake unto him,
saying, Tell us, by what
authority doest thou these
things? or who is he that gave thee
this authority?
3. And he answered and
said unto them, I will also ask
you one thing; and answer me:
4. The baptism of John, was
it from heaven, or of men?
5. And they reasoned
with themselves,
saying, If we shall say, From
heaven; he will
say, Why then believed
ye him not?
6. But and if we
say, Of men; all
the people will stone
us: for they be persuaded
that John was a prophet.

7. And they answered,
that they could not
tell whence *it was.*
8. And Jesus said unto them,
Neither tell I you by what
authority I do these things.
9. Then began he to speak
to the people
this parable; A certain
man planted a vineyard,
and let it forth
to husbandmen, and
went into a far country
for a long time.
10. And at the season
he sent a servant
to the husbandmen,
that they should give him
of the fruit of the vineyard:
but the husbandmen beat
him, and sent *him* away empty.
11. And again he sent
another servant:
and they beat him also,
and entreated *him* shamefully,
and sent *him* away empty.
12. And again he sent a
third: and they wounded
him also, and cast *him* out.
13. Then said the lord
of the vineyard, What shall I do?
I will send my beloved
son: it may be they will reverence
him when they see him.
14. But when the
husbandmen saw him,
they reasoned
among themselves, saying,
This is the heir: come,
let us kill him, that the
inheritance may be ours.
15. So they cast him out of the
vineyard, and killed *him.*
What therefore shall
the lord of the vineyard
do unto them?
16. He shall come and
destroy these husbandmen,
and shall
give the vineyard to
others. And when they
heard *it,* they said, God forbid.
17. And he beheld them, and

■ **said,** What is this
then that is written,
■ **The stone which the**
■ **builders rejected,** the same
■ **is become the head of**
■ **the corner?**
18. Whosoever shall fall upon that
stone shall be broken; but on
whomsoever it shall fall, it will
grind him to powder.
■ 19. **And the** chief
■ **priests and the scribes**
the same hour sought to lay
hands on him; and they feared
the people: for they
■ **perceived that he**
■ **had spoken** this parable
■ **against them.**
■ 20. **And they watched**
him, and sent forth spies, which
should feign themselves just men,
■ **that they might take hold**
■ **of his words,** that
■ **so they might deliver him**
■ **unto** the power and authority of
■ **the governor.**
■ 21. **And they asked**
■ **him,** saying,
■ **Master, we know that thou**
sayest and teachest rightly, neither
acceptest thou the person *of any,* but
■ **teachest the way of**
■ **God truly:**
■ 22. **Is it lawful** for us
■ **to give tribute unto**
■ **Caesar,** or no?
■ 23. **But he** perceived
their craftiness, and
■ **said** unto them,
■ **Why tempt ye me?**
■ 24. **Shew me a penny.**
■ **Whose image** and superscription
■ **hath it? They**
■ **answered** and said,
■ **Caesar's.**
■ 25. **And he said** unto them,
■ **Render** therefore
■ **unto Caesar the things**
■ **which be Caesar's, and**
■ **unto God the things**
■ **which be God's.**
■ 26. **And they** could not take hold of
his words before the people: and they

■ **marvelled at his answer,** and
held their peace.
■ 27. **Then came** to him certain of
■ **the Sadducees, which**
■ **deny** that there is
■ **any resurrection;**
and they asked him,
■ 28. **Saying, Master,**
■ **Moses wrote** unto us,
■ **If any man's brother die,**
■ **having a wife,** and he die
■ **without children, that**
■ **his brother should take**
■ **his wife, and raise up**
■ **seed** unto his brother.
■ 29. **There were** therefore
■ **seven brethren: and the first**
■ **took a wife, and**
■ **died without children.**
30. And the second took her
to wife, and he died childless.
■ 31. **And** the third took her; and
■ **in like manner the seven**
■ **also:** and they
■ **left no children,** and died.
■ 32. **Last of all the woman**
■ **died** also.
■ 33. **Therefore in the**
■ **resurrection whose**
■ **wife** of them
■ **is she?** for seven had her to wife.
■ 34. **And Jesus answering**
■ **said** unto them,
The children of this world marry,
and are given in marriage:
■ 35. **But they which shall**
be accounted worthy to
■ **obtain** that world, and
■ **the resurrection** from the dead,
■ **neither marry, nor are given**
■ **in marriage:**
■ 36. **Neither can they die**
any more: for they are
equal unto the angels;
■ **and are the children**
■ **of God,** being the children
of the resurrection.
37. Now that the dead are raised,
even Moses shewed at the bush,
when he calleth the Lord the God
of Abraham, and the God of Isaac,
and the God of Jacob.
■ 38. **For he is not a God of**

the dead, but of the
living: for all live unto him.
39. Then certain of
the scribes answering
said, Master,
thou hast well said.
40. And after that they durst
not ask him any *question at all*.
41. And he said unto them,
How say they that
Christ is David's son?
42. And David himself
saith in the book of Psalms,
The Lord said unto
my Lord, Sit thou
on my right hand,
43. Till I make thine
enemies thy footstool.
44. David therefore
calleth him Lord, how
is he then his son?
45. Then in the audience
of all the people
he said unto his disciples,
46. Beware of the scribes,
which desire to walk in long robes,
and love greetings in the markets, and
the highest seats in the synagogues,
and the chief rooms at feasts;
47. Which devour widows'
houses, and for a shew
make long prayers: the
same shall receive
greater damnation.

CHAPTER 21

1. And he looked up, and
saw the rich men casting
their gifts into the treasury.
2. And he saw also
a certain
poor widow casting in thither
two mites.
3. And he said, Of a truth
I say unto you, that
this poor widow hath
cast in more than they all:
4. For all these have of their
abundance cast in
unto the offerings of God:
but she of her penury
hath cast in all the
living that she had.

5. And as some spake of
the temple, how it was adorned
with goodly stones and gifts,
he said,
6. *As for* these things which
ye behold, the days will come,
in the which
there shall not be left one
stone upon another,
that shall not be thrown down.
7. And they asked him,
saying, Master, but when shall
these things be? and
what sign will there be when
these things shall come to pass?
8. And he said, Take heed
that ye be not deceived: for
many shall come in my
name, saying, I am Christ;
and the time draweth near:
go ye
not therefore
after them.
9. But when ye shall hear
of wars and commotions,
be not terrified: for these things
must first come to pass;
but the end is not by and by.
10. Then said he unto them,
Nation shall rise
against nation, and
kingdom against kingdom:
11. And great earthquakes
shall be in divers places,
and famines,
and pestilences; and fearful sights
and great signs shall
there be from heaven.
12. But before all these, they
shall lay their hands on you, and
persecute you, delivering *you* up
to the synagogues, and into prisons,
being brought before kings and rulers
for my name's sake.
13. And it shall turn to
you for a testimony.
14. Settle it therefore in your hearts,
not to meditate before
what ye shall answer:
15. For I will give
you a mouth and
wisdom, which all your
adversaries shall not be able to

gainsay nor resist.

16. And ye shall be betrayed both by parents, and brethren, and kinsfolks, and friends; **and some** of you **shall** they cause to **be put to death. 17. And ye shall be hated** of all *men* **for my name's sake. 18. But there shall not an hair of your head perish.**

19. In your patience possess ye your souls.

20. And when ye shall see Jerusalem compassed with armies, then know that the desolation thereof **is nigh. 21. Then let them** which are **in Judaea flee** to the mountains; and let them which are in the midst of it depart out; and let not them that are in the countries enter thereinto. **22. For these be the days of vengeance, that all** things which are written **may be fulfilled.**

23. But woe unto them that are with child, and to them that give suck, in those days! for **there shall be great distress** in the land, and wrath upon this people.

24. And they shall fall by the edge of the sword, and shall be led away captive into all nations: **and Jerusalem shall be trodden down** of the Gentiles, **until the times of the Gentiles be fulfilled. 25. And there shall be signs in the sun,** and in the **moon, and** in the **stars; and upon the earth distress of nations,** with perplexity; the sea and the waves roaring; **26. Men's hearts failing them for fear,** and for looking after those things which are coming on the earth: for the powers of heaven shall be shaken.

27. And then shall they see the Son of man coming in a cloud with power and great glory. **28. And when these things** begin to **come to pass, then look up,** and lift up your heads; **for your redemption draweth nigh. 29. And he spake** to them **a parable; Behold the fig tree,** and all the trees; **30. When they now shoot forth, ye** see and **know** of your own selves **that summer is** now **nigh** at hand. **31. So likewise ye, when ye see these things** come to pass, **know** ye **that the kingdom of God is** nigh **at hand.**

32. Verily I say unto you, **This generation shall not pass away, till all be fulfilled. 33. Heaven and earth shall pass away: but my words shall not** pass away. **34. And take heed** to yourselves, **lest** at any time **your hearts be overcharged with** surfeiting, and drunkenness, and **cares of this life, and so that day come upon you unawares.**

35. For as a snare shall it come on all them that dwell on the face of the whole earth. **36. Watch** ye therefore, **and pray** always, **that ye may be accounted worthy** to escape all these things that shall come to pass, and **to stand before the Son** of man.

37. And in the day time he was teaching in the temple; and at night he went out, and abode in the mount that is called *the mount* of Olives.

134

38. And all the people came early in the morning to him in the temple, for to hear him.

CHAPTER 22

1. **Now the feast of unleavened bread drew nigh,** which is called the Passover. 2. **And the** chief **priests and scribes sought how they might kill him;** for they feared the people. 3. **Then entered Satan into Judas** surnamed Iscariot, being of the number of the twelve. 4. **And he went** his way, **and communed with the chief priests** and captains, **how he might betray him unto them.** 5. **And they** were glad, and **covenanted to give him money.** 6. **And he** promised, and **sought opportunity to betray him** unto them in the absence of the multitude. 7. **Then came the day of** unleavened bread, when **the passover** must be killed. 8. **And he sent Peter and John, saying, Go and prepare us the passover,** that we may eat. 9. And they said unto him, Where wilt thou that we prepare? 10. And he said unto them, Behold, when ye are entered into the city, there shall a man meet you, bearing a pitcher of water; follow him into the house where he entereth in. 11. And ye shall say unto the goodman of the house, The Master saith unto thee, Where is the guestchamber, where I shall eat the passover with my disciples? 12. And he shall shew you a large upper room furnished: there make ready. 13. **And they went, and** found as he had said unto them: and they **made ready the passover.** 14. **And** when the hour was come,

he sat down, and the **twelve apostles with him.** 15. **And he said** unto them, With desire **I have desired to eat this passover with you before I suffer:** 16. **For** I say unto you, **I will not any more eat** thereof, **until it be fulfilled in the kingdom** of God. 17. **And he took the cup, and gave thanks, and said, Take this,** and divide *it* among yourselves: 18. **For** I say unto you, **I will not drink of the fruit** of the vine, **until the kingdom of God shall come.** 19. **And he took bread,** and **gave thanks, and brake it,** and gave unto them, **saying, This is my body** which is **given for you: this do in remembrance of me.** 20. **Likewise also the cup** after supper, **saying, This cup is the new testament in my blood, which is shed for you.** 21. **But,** behold, the hand of **him that betrayeth me is with me on the table.** 22. **And truly the Son of man goeth,** as it was determined: **but woe unto that man by whom he is betrayed!** 23. **And they began to inquire** among themselves, **which of them** it was that **should do this thing.** 24. **And there was also a strife among them, which** of them **should be** accounted **the greatest.** 25. **And he said** unto them, The kings of the Gentiles exercise lordship over them; and they that exercise authority upon them are called benefactors.

26. But ye *shall* not *be* so: but **he that is greatest** among you, **let him** be as the younger; and he that is chief, as he that doth **serve.**

27. For whether *is* greater, he that sitteth at meat, or he that serveth? *is* not he that sitteth at meat? but **I am among you as he that serveth.**

28. **Ye** are they which **have continued with me** in my temptations.

29. **And I appoint** unto **you a kingdom,** as my Father hath appointed unto me;

30. **That ye may eat** and drink **at my table** in my kingdom, **and sit** on thrones **judging the twelve tribes of Israel.**

31. **And the Lord said, Simon,** Simon, behold, **Satan hath desired to have you,** that he may sift *you* as wheat:

32. **But I have prayed** for thee, **that thy faith fail not:** and when thou art converted, strengthen thy brethren.

33. **And he said** unto him, **Lord, I am ready to go with thee, both into prison, and to death.**

34. **And he said,** I tell thee, **Peter, the cock shall not crow** this day, **before that thou shalt thrice deny** that thou knowest **me.**

35. And he said unto them, When I sent you without purse, and scrip, and shoes, lacked ye any thing? And they said, Nothing.

36. Then said he unto them, But now, he that hath a purse, let him take *it,* and likewise *his* scrip: and he that hath no sword, let him sell his garment, and buy one.

37. For I say unto you, that this that is written must yet be accomplished in me, And he was reckoned among the transgressors: for the things

concerning me have an end.

38. And they said, Lord, behold, here *are* two swords. And he said unto them, It is enough.

39. **And he came** out, and went, as he was wont, **to the mount of Olives; and his disciples also followed** him.

40. And when he was at the place, he said unto them, Pray that ye enter not into temptation.

41. **And he was withdrawn from them** about a stone's cast, **and kneeled down, and prayed,**

42. **Saying, Father,** if thou be willing, **remove this cup from me: nevertheless not my will, but thine, be done.**

43. **And there appeared an angel** unto him **from heaven, strengthening him.**

44. **And being in an agony** he prayed more earnestly: and **his sweat was as it were great drops of blood falling** down **to the ground.**

45. **And when he** rose up from prayer, and **was come to his disciples, he found them sleeping** for sorrow,

46. **And said** unto them, Why sleep ye? **rise and pray, lest ye enter into temptation.**

47. **And** while he yet spake, **behold a multitude, and** he that was called **Judas,** one of the twelve, **went before them, and drew near** unto **Jesus to kiss him.**

48. **But Jesus said** unto him, **Judas, betrayest thou the Son** of man **with a kiss?**

49. When they which were about him saw what would follow, they said unto

him, Lord, shall we smite with the sword?

50. And one of them **smote the servant of the high priest, and cut off his right ear.**

51. And Jesus answered and said, Suffer ye thus far. And he **touched his ear, and healed him.**

52. Then Jesus said unto the chief priests, and captains of the temple, and the elders, which were come to him, **Be ye come** out, **as against a thief, with swords** and staves?

53. When I was daily with you in the temple, ye stretched forth no hands against me: but this is your hour, and the power of darkness.

54. Then took they him, and led *him*, **and brought him into the high priest's house. And Peter followed** afar off.

55. And when they had kindled a fire in the midst of the hall, and were set down together, **Peter sat** down **among them.**

56. But a certain maid beheld him as he sat by the fire, and earnestly looked upon him, **and said, This man was also with him.**

57. And he denied him, saying, Woman, I know him not.

58. And after a little while **another** saw him, and **said, Thou art also of them. And Peter said,** Man, **I am not.**

59. And about the space of one hour after **another** confidently **affirmed,** saying, Of a truth **this fellow** also **was with him:** for he is a Galilaean.

60. And Peter said, Man, **I know not what thou sayest. And immediately,**

while he yet spake, **the cock crew.**

61. And the Lord turned, and **looked upon Peter.** And Peter remembered the word of the Lord, how he had said unto him, Before the cock crow, thou shalt deny me thrice.

62. And Peter went out, and wept bitterly.

63. And the men that held Jesus mocked him, and smote *him*.

64. And when they had blindfolded him, they struck him on the face, and asked him, **saying, Prophesy, who** is that **smote thee?**

65. And many other things **blasphemously spake** they **against him.**

66. And as soon as it was day, **the elders** of the people and the chief priests and the scribes came together, and **led him into their council, saying,**

67. Art thou the Christ? tell us. **And he said** unto them, **If I tell you, ye will not believe:**

68. And if I also ask *you*, ye will not answer me, nor let *me* go.

69. Hereafter shall the Son of man sit on the right hand of the power of God.

70. Then said they all, **Art thou then the Son of God? And he said** unto them, **Ye say that I am.**

71. And they said, What need we any further witness? for we ourselves **have heard of his own mouth.**

CHAPTER 23

1. And the whole multitude of them arose, and **led him unto Pilate.**

2. And they began to accuse him, **saying, We found this**

137

fellow perverting the nation, and **forbidding to give tribute to Caesar, saying** that **he** himself **is Christ a King.** 3. **And Pilate asked** him, saying, **Art thou the King of the Jews? And he** answered him and **said, Thou sayest it.** 4. **Then said Pilate** to the chief priests and *to* the people, **I find no fault in this man.** 5. **And they were the more fierce, saying, He stirreth up the people,** teaching throughout all Jewry, beginning **from Galilee to this place.** 6. **When Pilate heard** of Galilee, he asked whether the man were a Galilaean. 7. And as soon as he knew **that he belonged unto Herod's jurisdiction, he sent him to Herod,** who himself also was at Jerusalem at that time. 8. **And when Herod saw Jesus, he was exceeding glad:** for he was desirous to see him of a long *season*, **because he had heard many things** of him; **and** he **hoped to have seen some miracle** done by him. 9. **Then he questioned** with **him** in many words; **but he answered** him **nothing.** 10. **And the chief priests and scribes** stood and **vehemently accused him.** 11. **And Herod** with his men of war set him at nought, and mocked *him*, and arrayed him in a gorgeous robe, and **sent him again to Pilate.** 12. And the same day Pilate and Herod were made friends together: for before they were at enmity between themselves. 13. **And Pilate,** when he had **called** together

the chief priests and the rulers and the people, 14. **Said** unto them, **Ye have brought this man** unto me, **as one that perverteth the people: and,** behold, **I,** having examined *him* before you, **have found no fault in** this man touching those things whereof ye accuse **him:** 15. No, nor yet Herod: for I sent you to him; and, lo, nothing worthy of death is done unto him. 16. **I will therefore chastise him, and release him.** 17. **(For** of necessity **he must release one** unto them **at the feast.)** 18. **And they cried** out all at once, saying, Away with this *man*, and **release** unto us **Barabbas:** 19. **(Who for** a certain **sedition** made in the city, **and** for **murder, was cast into prison.)** 20. **Pilate** therefore, **willing to release Jesus, spake again** to them. 21. **But they cried,** saying, Crucify *him*, **crucify him.** 22. **And he said** unto them **the third time, Why, what evil hath he done?** I have found no cause of death in him: I will therefore chastise him, and let *him* go. 23. **And they** were instant **with loud voices,** requiring that he might be crucified. And the voices of them and of the chief priests **prevailed.** 24. **And Pilate gave sentence** that it should be **as they required.** 25. **And** he released unto them him that for sedition and murder was cast into prison, whom they had desired; but he

delivered Jesus
to their will.
26. **And** as they led
him away, they laid hold
upon one
Simon, a Cyrenian, coming
out of the country, and on him
they laid the cross, that
he might bear *it* after Jesus.
27. **And** there followed him
a great company
of people, and of women,
which also bewailed and
lamented him.
28. **But Jesus** turning unto them
said, Daughters of Jerusalem,
weep not for me, but weep
for yourselves,
and for your children.
29. **For, behold, the days
are coming, in** the
**which they shall say,
Blessed are the barren,** and
the wombs that never bare, and the
paps which never gave suck.
30. **Then shall they** begin to
**say to the mountains,
Fall on us; and** to the hills,
Cover us.
31. For if they do these things
in a green tree, what shall be
done in the dry?
32. **And there were
also two** other,
malefactors, led with him
to be put to death.
33. **And when they were
come to** the place, which is called
Calvary, there
**they crucified him, and
the malefactors,** one
on the right hand,
and the other on
the left.
34. Then said Jesus, Father,
forgive them; for they
know not what they do.
And they parted his
raiment, and cast lots.
35. **And the people**
stood beholding. And the
rulers also with them
derided him, saying,

**He saved others; let
him save himself,** if he
be Christ, the chosen of God.
36. **And the soldiers also
mocked him,** coming to him, and
offering him vinegar,
37. And saying, If thou be the
king of the Jews, save thyself.
38. **And a superscription** also
was written over him in letters
of Greek, and Latin, and Hebrew,
**THIS IS THE KING
OF THE JEWS.**
39. **And one of the
malefactors** which were hanged
railed on him,
**saying, If thou be Christ,
save thyself and us.**
40. **But the other** answering
**rebuked him, saying, Dost
not thou fear God,** seeing
thou art in the same condemnation?
41. And we indeed justly; for
**we receive the due reward
of our deeds: but this man
hath done nothing** amiss.
42. **And he said** unto Jesus,
**Lord, remember me
when thou comest
into thy kingdom.**
43. **And Jesus said**
unto him, Verily I say unto thee,
**Today shalt thou be
with me in paradise.**
44. **And** it was about
the sixth hour, and
there was a darkness
over all the earth
until the ninth hour.
45. And the sun was darkened,
**and the veil of the temple
was rent** in the midst.
46. **And when Jesus had
cried** with a loud voice, he said,
**Father, into thy hands
I commend my spirit:**
and having said thus,
he gave up the ghost.
47. **Now when the centurion
saw** what was done,
**he glorified God,
saying,** Certainly
this was a righteous man.

48. And all the people that came together to that sight, beholding the things which were done, smote their breasts, and returned.

49. And all his acquaintance, and the women that followed him from Galilee, stood afar off, beholding these things.

50. **And,** behold, *there was* a man named **Joseph,** a counsellor; *and he was* a good man, and a just:

51. (The same had not consented to the counsel and deed of them); *he was* **of Arimathaea,** a city of the Jews: who also himself waited for the kingdom of God.

52. This *man* went unto Pilate, and **begged the body of Jesus.**

53. **And he** took it down, and **wrapped it in linen, and laid it in a sepulchre** that was hewn in stone, wherein never man before was laid.

54. And that day was the preparation, and the sabbath drew on.

55. **And the women** also, which came with him from Galilee, followed after, and beheld the sepulchre, and how his body was laid.

56. And they returned, and **prepared spices and ointments;** and rested the sabbath day according to the commandment.

CHAPTER 24

1. **Now upon the first day of the week,** very early in the morning, **they came unto the sepulchre, bringing the spices** which they had prepared, and certain *others* with them.

2. **And they found the stone rolled away** from the sepulchre.

3. **And they** entered in, and **found not the body of the Lord Jesus.**

4. **And** it came to pass, as they were much perplexed thereabout, behold, **two men stood by them in shining garments:**

5. **And** as they were afraid, and bowed down *their* faces to the earth, they **said** unto them, **Why seek ye the living among the dead?**

6. **He is not here, but is risen: remember how he spake** unto you when he was yet in Galilee,

7. **Saying, The Son of man must be** delivered into the hands of sinful men, and be **crucified, and the third day rise again.**

8. **And they remembered** his words,

9. **And returned** from the sepulchre, **and told** all these things unto **the eleven,** and to all the rest.

10. It was Mary Magdalene and Joanna, and Mary *the mother* of James, and other *women that were* with them, which told these things unto the apostles.

11. **And their words seemed** to them **as idle tales, and they believed them not.**

12. **Then arose Peter, and ran unto the sepulchre; and** stooping down, he **beheld the linen clothes laid by themselves,** and departed, wondering in himself at that which was come to pass.

13. **And, behold, two of them went** that same day **to** a village called **Emmaus,** which was from Jerusalem *about* threescore furlongs.

14. **And they talked** together **of** all **these things which had happened.**

15. **And** it came to pass, that, while they communed *together* and reasoned, **Jesus himself drew near,** and went with them.

16. **But their eyes were holden that they should**

not know him.

17. **And he said** unto them, **What** manner of **communications are these that ye have** one to another, as ye walk, and are sad?

18. **And the one** of them, **whose name was Cleopas,** answering **said** unto him, **Art thou only a stranger** in Jerusalem, **and hast not known the things which are come to pass** there in these days?

19. **And he said** unto them, **What things? And they said** unto him, **Concerning Jesus** of Nazareth, which was **a prophet mighty in deed and word** before God and all the people:

20. **And how the chief priests and our rulers delivered him to be** condemned to death, and have **crucified** him.

21. **But we trusted** that it had been **he** which **should have redeemed Israel:** and beside all this, today is the third day since these things were done.

22. **Yea, and certain women** also of our company made us astonished, which were early at the sepulchre;

23. And when they **found not his body,** they came, **saying, that they had** also **seen a vision of angels, which said that he was alive.**

24. And certain of them which were with us went to the sepulchre, and found *it* even so as the women had said: but him they saw not.

25. **Then he said** unto them, **O fools, and slow** of heart **to believe** all that

the prophets have spoken:

26. **Ought not Christ to have suffered** these things, **and** to **enter into his glory?**

27. **And beginning at Moses** and all the prophets, **he expounded** unto them in all **the scriptures** the things **concerning himself.**

28. And they drew nigh unto the village, whither they went: and he made as though he would have gone further.

29. But they constrained him, saying, Abide with us: for it is toward evening, and the day is far spent. And he went in to tarry with them.

30. **And** it came to pass, **as he sat at meat with them, he took bread, and blessed it,** and brake, **and gave to them.**

31. **And their eyes** were **opened, and they knew him; and he vanished** out of their sight.

32. **And they said** one to another, **Did not our heart burn within us,** while he talked with us by the way, and **while he opened to us the scriptures?**

33. **And they** rose up the same hour, and **returned to Jerusalem, and found the eleven** gathered together, and them that were with them,

34. Saying, The Lord is risen indeed, and hath appeared to Simon.

35. **And they told** what things *were done* in the way, and **how he was known of them in breaking of bread.**

36. **And** as they thus spake, **Jesus** himself **stood in the midst of them, and saith** unto them, **Peace be unto you.**

37. **But they were terrified** and affrighted,

and supposed that they had seen a spirit. 38. **And he said** unto them, **Why are ye troubled?** and why do thoughts arise in your hearts? 39. **Behold** my hands and my feet, that **it is I** myself: **handle me, and see; for a spirit hath not flesh and bones,** as ye see me have. 40. **And** when he had thus spoken, **he shewed** them **his hands and** *his* **feet**. 41. **And while they yet believed not for joy,** and wondered, **he said** unto them, **Have ye here any meat?** 42. **And they gave him** a piece of a broiled **fish, and** of an **honeycomb.** 43. And he took *it*, and did eat before them. 44. **And he said** unto them, **These are the words which I spake** unto you, while I was yet with you, **that all** things must **be fulfilled,** which were written in the law of Moses, and *in* the prophets, and *in* the psalms, **concerning me.** 45. **Then opened he their understanding,** that they might

understand the scriptures, 46. **And said** unto them, **Thus it is written, and** thus **it behoved Christ to suffer, and to rise** from the dead **the third day:** 47. **And that repentance** and remission of sins **should be preached in his name** among all nations, beginning at Jerusalem. 48. **And ye are witnesses** of these things. 49. **And, behold, I send the promise of my Father** upon you: **but tarry ye in** the city of **Jerusalem, until ye be endued with power** from on high. 50. **And he led them out** as far as **to Bethany, and** he lifted up his hands, and **blessed them.** 51. **And** it came to pass, while he blessed them, he **was** parted from them, and **carried up into heaven.** 52. **And they worshipped him,** and returned to Jerusalem with great joy: 53. And were continually in the temple, **praising and blessing God. Amen.**

THE GOSPEL ACCORDING TO JOHN

BACKGROUND INFORMATION

Author: John, one of The Twelve Disciples of Jesus
Date written: probably **between 70** and **85** A.D.

Number of:
Versus 879
Chapters 21
Total Words 19,099
Scan Words 9,115
Scan Words represent 47 % of Total Words

Theme: The Eternal Word of God who **became a human** being in order **that we might have** the gift of **eternal life** through Him

OUTLINE OF THE GOSPEL

I. **The Introduction**
Chapter 1
II. **Christ's Glory and Power** Revealed
Chapters 2 - 6
III. **Christ's Conflicts** as He Taught and Continued to Perform Miracles
Chapter 7 - 12
IV. **Christ's Special Revelations** to His Disciples
Chapters 13 - 17
V. **Christ's Arrest, Trial, Crucifixion and Resurrection**
Chapters 18 - 20
VI. **Christ's Appearance to His Disciples**
Chapter 21

CHAPTER 1

1. **In the beginning was the Word, and the Word was with God, and** the Word **was God.**

2. The same was in the beginning with God.

3. **All things were made by him; and** without him was not any thing made that was made.

4. **In him was life; and** the life was **the light of men.**

5. **And the light shineth** in darkness; **and the darkness comprehended it not.**

6. There was a man sent from God, whose name *was* **John.**

7. The same came for a witness, to bear witness of the Light, that all *men* through him might believe.

8. He was not that Light, but **was sent to bear witness of** that Light.

9. *That* was **the true Light,** which lighteth every man that cometh into the world.

10. **He was in the world,** and the world was made by him, **and the world knew him not.**

11. He came unto his own, **and his own received him not.**

12. **But as many as received him, to them gave he power to become the sons of God, even to them that believe on his name:**

13. **Which were born, not of blood,** nor of the will of the flesh, nor of the will of man, **but of God.**

14. **And the Word was made flesh, and dwelt among us,** (and we beheld his glory, the glory as of the only begotten of the Father,) **full of grace and truth.**

15. **John bare witness** of him, and cried, **saying, This was he** of whom I spake, He that cometh after me is **preferred before me:** for he was before me.

16. And of his fulness have all we received, and grace for grace.

17. For the law was given by Moses, *but* grace and truth came by Jesus Christ.

18. **No man hath seen God** at any time; **the only begotten Son,** which is in the bosom of the Father, he **hath declared him.**

19. **And this is the record of John, when the Jews** sent priests and Levites from Jerusalem to **ask him, Who art thou?**

20. **And he confessed,** and denied not; but confessed, **I am not the Christ.**

21. **And they asked** him, What then? Art thou Elias? And he saith, I am not. **Art thou that prophet? And he answered, No.**

22. **Then said they** unto him, **Who art thou?** that we may give an answer to them that sent us. What sayest thou of thyself?

23. **He said, I am the voice of one crying in the wilderness, Make straight the way of the Lord,** as said the prophet Esaias.

24. And they which were sent were of the Pharisees.

25. **And they asked him,** and said unto him, **Why baptizest thou then,** if thou be not that Christ, nor Elias, neither that prophet?

26. **John answered** them, saying, **I baptize with water: but there standeth one among you,** whom ye know not;

27. He it is, who coming after me is **preferred before me, whose shoe's latchet I am not worthy to unloose.**

28. These things were done in

Bethabara beyond Jordan, where John was baptizing.

29. **The next day John seeth Jesus coming** unto him, **and saith, Behold the Lamb of God, which taketh away the sin of the world.**

30. **This is he** of whom I said, After me cometh a man which is **preferred before me:** for he was before me.

31. And I knew him not: but that he should be made manifest to Israel, therefore am I come baptizing with water.

32. **And John bare record, saying, I saw the Spirit descending** from heaven **like a dove, and it abode upon him.**

33. And I knew him not: but **he that sent me to** baptize with water, the same **said** unto me, **Upon whom thou shalt see the Spirit descending, and remaining** on him **the same** is he which **baptizeth with the Holy Ghost.**

34. And I saw, and bare record that this is the Son of God.

35. **Again the next day after John stood, and two of his disciples;**

36. **And looking upon Jesus** as he walked, **he saith, Behold the Lamb of God!**

37. **And the two disciples** heard him speak, and they **followed Jesus.**

38. **Then Jesus** turned, and saw them following, and **saith unto them, What seek ye? They said** unto him, Rabbi, (which is to say, being interpreted, Master,) **where dwellest thou?**

39. **He saith** unto them, **Come and see. They came** and saw where he dwelt, **and abode with him that**

day: for it was about the tenth hour.

40. **One of the two** which heard John *speak,* and followed him, **was Andrew,** Simon Peter's brother.

41. **He first findeth his own brother Simon, and saith** unto him, **We have found the Messias,** which is, being interpreted, the Christ.

42. **And he brought him to Jesus.** And when **Jesus** beheld him, he **said,** Thou art Simon the son of Jona: **thou shalt be called Cephas,** which is by interpretation, **A stone.**

43. **The day following Jesus** would go forth into Galilee, and **findeth Philip, and saith** unto him, **Follow me.**

44. Now Philip was of Bethsaida, the city of Andrew and Peter.

45. **Philip findeth Nathanael, and saith** unto him, **We have found him, of whom Moses** in the law, **and the prophets, did write,** Jesus of Nazareth, the son of Joseph.

46. **And Nathanael said** unto him, **Can there be any good thing come out of Nazareth? Philip saith** unto him, **Come and see.**

47. **Jesus saw Nathanael** coming to him, **and saith** of him, Behold **an Israelite** indeed, **in whom is no guile!**

48. **Nathanael saith** unto him, **Whence knowest thou me? Jesus answered** and said unto him, Before that Philip called thee, **when thou wast under the fig tree, I saw thee.**

49. **Nathanael answered** and saith unto him,

■ ■ **Rabbi, thou art the Son of God;** thou art the King of Israel.

■ 50. **Jesus answered** and said unto him,

■ **Because** I said unto thee, ■ **I saw thee under the fig tree, believest thou? thou shalt see greater things than these.**

51. And he saith unto him, Verily verily, I say unto you,

■ **Hereafter ye shall see heaven open, and the angels of God ascending and descending upon the Son of man.**

CHAPTER 2

1. And the third day ■ **there was a marriage** ■ **in Cana** of Galilee; ■ **and** the mother of Jesus was there:

2. And both Jesus was called, and his disciples, to the marriage.

3. And when they wanted wine, ■ **the mother of Jesus** ■ **saith unto him, They** ■ **have no wine.**

4. Jesus saith unto her, Woman, what have I to do with thee? mine hour is not yet come.

■ 5. **His mother saith unto** ■ **the servants, Whatsoever** ■ **he saith** unto you, ■ **do it.**

■ 6. **And there were** set there ■ **six waterpots** of stone, after the manner of the purifying of the Jews, containing two or three firkins apiece.

■ 7. **Jesus saith** unto them, ■ **Fill the waterpots** ■ **with water.** And they filled them up to the brim.

■ 8. **And** he saith unto them, ■ **Draw out now, and bear** ■ **unto the governor** of the feast. And they bare *it.*

■ 9. **When the ruler** of the feast had **tasted the water** that was made wine, and knew not whence it was: (but the servants which drew the water knew;) ■ **the governor** of the feast

■ **called the bridegroom,**

■ 10. **And saith** unto him, ■ **Every man at the beginning** ■ **doth set forth good wine;** and when men have well drunk, then that which is worse: ■ **but thou hast kept the** ■ **good wine until now.**

■ 11. **This beginning of** ■ **miracles did Jesus in** ■ **Cana of Galilee,** and manifested forth his glory; and his disciples believed on him.

12. After this he went down to Capernaum, he, and his mother, and his brethren, and his disciples: and they continued there not many days.

■ 13. **And the Jews' passover** ■ **was at hand, and Jesus** ■ **went up to Jerusalem.**

■ 14. **And found in the** ■ **temple those that sold** oxen and sheep and doves, ■ **and the changers** ■ **of money** sitting:

■ 15. **And when he had** ■ **made a scourge** of small cords, ■ **he drove them all out** of the temple, and the sheep, and the oxen; and poured out the changers' money, ■ **and overthrew the tables;**

■ 16. **And said** unto them that sold doves, Take these things hence; ■ **make not my Father's** ■ **house an house of** ■ **merchandise.**

17. And his disciples remembered that it was written, The zeal of thine house hath eaten me up.

■ 18. **Then answered the** ■ **Jews** and said unto him, ■ **What sign shewest** thou unto us, ■ **seeing that thou doest** ■ **these things?**

■ 19. **Jesus answered** and said unto them, ■ **Destroy this temple, and in** ■ **three days I will raise it up.**

20. Then said the Jews, Forty and six years was this temple in building, and

wilt thou rear it up in three days?

■ 21. **But he spake of the**
■ **temple of his body.**
■ 22. **When therefore**
■ **he was risen** from the dead,
■ **his disciples remembered**
that he had said this unto them;
■ **and they believed** the
scripture, and the word which
Jesus had said.
■ 23. **Now** when he was in Jerusalem
■ **at the passover,**
in the feast *day,*
■ **many believed** in his name,
■ **when they saw the**
■ **miracles which he did.**
■ 24. **But Jesus did not commit**
■ **himself unto them,**
■ **because** he knew all *men,*
25. And needed not that any
should testify of man: for
■■ **he knew what was in man.**

CHAPTER 3

1. There was a man of
the Pharisees, named
■ **Nicodemus, a**
■ **ruler** of the Jews:
2. The same
■ **came to Jesus by**
■ **night, and said** unto him,
Rabbi, we know that
■ **thou art a teacher come**
■ **from God: for no man**
■ **can do these miracles**
that thou doest,
■ **except God be with him.**
■ 3. **Jesus** answered and
■ **said unto him,** Verily,
verily, I say unto thee,
■ **Except a man be born**
■ **again, he cannot see**
■ **the kingdom of God.**
■ 4. **Nicodemus saith** unto him,
■ **How can a man be born**
when he is old? can he enter
■ **the second time** into his
mother's womb, and be born?
■ 5. **Jesus answered,**
Verily, verily, I say unto thee,
■ **Except a man be born of**
■ **water and of the Spirit,**
■■ **he cannot enter into the**

■ **kingdom** of God.
■ 6. **That which is born**
■ **of the flesh is flesh;**
■ **and that** which is
■ **born of the Spirit is spirit.**
■ 7. **Marvel not that**
I said unto thee,
■ **Ye must be born again.**
■ 8. **The wind bloweth**
where it listeth,
■ **and thou** hearest
the sound thereof, but
■ **canst not tell whence**
■ **it cometh, and** whither it
■ **goeth: so is every**
■ **one** that is
■ **born of the Spirit.**
■ 9. **Nicodemus answered**
and said unto him,
■ **How can these things be?**
■ 10. **Jesus answered** and said
unto him, Art thou a master of Israel,
and knowest not these things?
11. Verily, verily, I say unto thee,
■ **We speak that we do know,**
and testify that we have seen; and
ye receive not our witness.
12. If I have told you earthly things,
■ **and ye believe not,**
how shall ye believe, if I tell
you *of* heavenly things?
13. And no man hath ascended
up to heaven, but he that came
down from heaven, *even* the
Son of man which is in heaven.
■ 14. **And as Moses lifted**
■ **up the serpent in the**
■ **wilderness, even so must**
■ **the Son of man be lifted up:**
■ 15. **That whosoever**
■ **believeth in him should**
■ **not perish,** but have eternal life.
■ 16. **For God so loved the**
■ **world, that he gave his**
■ **only begotten Son, that**
■ **whosoever believeth in**
■ **him should not perish,**
■ **but have everlasting life.**
■ 17. **For God sent not**
■ **his Son** into the world
■ **to condemn the world;**
■ **but that the world through**
■ **him might be saved.**

18. He that believeth on him is not condemned:

but he that believeth not is condemned already, because he hath not believed in the name of the only begotten Son of God. 19. And this is the condemnation, that light is come into the world, **and men loved darkness** rather than light, **because their deeds were evil.**

20. For every one that doeth evil hateth the light, neither cometh to the light, lest his deeds should be reproved.

21. **But he that doeth truth cometh to the light,** that his deeds may be made manifest, that they are wrought in God.

22. **After these things came Jesus** and his disciples **into** the land of **Judaea;** and there he tarried with them, and baptized.

23. **And John also was baptizing in Aenon** near to Salim, because there was much water there: and they came, and were baptized.

24. For John was not yet cast into prison.

25. **Then there arose a question** between *some* of John's disciples and the Jews **about purifying.**

26. **And they came unto John, and said** unto him, Rabbi, **he that was with thee** beyond Jordan, **to whom thou barest witness, behold,** the same baptizeth, and **all men come to him.**

27. **John answered** and said, A man can receive nothing, except it be given him from heaven.

28. Ye yourselves bear me witness, that I said, **I am not the Christ,** but that I am sent before him.

29. **He that hath the bride is the bridegroom: but the friend of the bridegroom,** which standeth and heareth him, **rejoiceth greatly** because of the bridegroom's voice: this **my joy therefore is fulfilled.**

30. **He must increase, but I must decrease.**

31. **He that cometh from above is above all:** he that is of the earth is earthly, and speaketh of the earth: he that cometh from heaven is above all.

32. And what he hath seen and heard, that he testifieth; and no manreceiveth his testimony.

33. **He that hath received his testimony hath set to his seal that God is true.**

34. For he whom God hath sent speaketh the words of God: for God giveth not the Spirit by measure *unto him.*

35. **The Father loveth the Son, and hath given all things into his hand.**

36. **He that believeth on the Son hath everlasting life: and he that believeth not** the Son shall not see life; but **the wrath of God abideth on him.**

CHAPTER 4

1. When therefore the LORD knew how the Pharisees had heard that **Jesus** made and baptized more disciples than John,

2. (Though Jesus himself baptized not, but his disciples,)

3. He left Judaea, and **departed again into Galilee.**

4. And he must needs go **through Samaria.**

5. **Then cometh he to a city** of Samaria, which is **called Sychar,** near to the parcel of ground that Jacob gave to his son Joseph.

6. **Now Jacob's well was there. Jesus** therefore, being

wearied with *his* journey,
■ **sat thus on the well: and**
it was about the sixth hour.
■ 7. **There cometh a**
■ **woman** of Samaria
■ **to draw water:**
■ **Jesus saith** unto her,
■ **Give me to drink.**
8. (For his disciples were gone
away unto the city to buy meat.)
■ 9. **Then saith the woman**
of Samaria unto him,
■ **How is it that** thou, being
■ **a Jew, askest drink**
■ **of** me, which am
■ **a woman of Samaria?**
for the Jews have no dealings
with the Samaritans.
■ 10. **Jesus answered**
and said unto her,
■ **If thou knewest**
the gift of God, and
■ **who it is that saith** to thee,
■ **Give me to drink; thou**
■ **wouldest have asked of**
■ **him, and he would have**
■ **given thee living water.**
■ 11. **The woman saith**
unto him, Sir,
■ **thou hast nothing to**
■ **draw with,** and the well is
deep: from whence then hast
thou that living water?
12. Art thou greater than our father
Jacob, which gave us the well, and
drank thereof himself, and his
children, and his cattle?
■ 13. **Jesus answered**
and said unto her,
■ **Whosoever drinketh of this**
■ **water shall thirst again:**
■ 14. **But whosoever drinketh**
■ **of the water that I**
■ **shall give** him
■ **shall never thirst;**
but the water that
■ **I shall give him** shall be in him
■ **a well of water springing**
■ **up into everlasting life.**
■ 15. **The woman saith** unto him,
■ **Sir, give me this water,** that I
thirst not, neither come hither to draw.
■ 16. **Jesus saith** unto her, Go,

■ **call thy husband,**
and come hither.
■ 17. **The woman** answered and
■ **said, I have no husband.**
■ **Jesus said** unto her,
■ **Thou hast well said,**
I have no husband:
■ 18. **For thou hast had five**
■ **husbands;** and he whom thou
now hast is not thy husband: in
that saidst thou truly.
■ 19. **The woman saith**
unto him, Sir, I perceive that
■ **thou art a prophet.**
■ 20. **Our fathers worshipped**
■ **in this mountain; and ye**
■ **say, that in Jerusalem is the**
■ **place** where men ought
■ **to worship.**
■ 21. **Jesus saith** unto her, Woman,
believe me, the hour cometh, whenye
shall neither in this mountain, nor yet
at Jerusalem, worship the Father.
■ 22. **Ye worship ye know not**
■ **what:** we know what we worship:
for salvation is of the Jews.
■ 23. **But the hour** cometh, and
■ **now is, when the true**
■ **worshippers shall worship**
■ **the Father in spirit and in**
■ **truth:** for the Father seeketh
such to worship him.
■ 24. **God is a Spirit: and**
■ **they that worship him**
■ **must worship him in**
■ **spirit and in truth.**
■ 25. **The woman saith** unto him,
■ **I know that Messias**
cometh, which is called Christ:
■ **when he is come,** he
■ **will tell us all things.**
■ 26. **Jesus saith** unto her,
■ **I** that speak unto thee
■ **am he.**
27. An upon this came his disciples,
and marvelled that he talked with
the woman: yet no man said, What
seekest thou? or, Why talkest
thou with her?
■ 28. **The woman**
then left her waterpot, and
■ **went** her way
■ **into the city, and**

■ **saith** to the men,

■ 29. **Come, see a man, which**
■ **told me all** things that ever
■ **I did: is not this the Christ?**

30. Then they went out of the
city, and came unto him.

■ 31. **In the mean while his**
■ **disciples prayed him,**
■ **saying, Master, eat.**

■ 32. **But he said** unto them,
■ **I have meat to eat**
■ **that ye know not of.**

33. Therefore said the
disciples one to another,
Hath any man brought
him*aught* to eat?

34. Jesus saith unto them,
■ **My meat is to do the will**
■ **of him that sent me,**
and to finish his work.

■ 35. **Say not ye, There are**
■ **yet four months, and**
■ **then cometh harvest?**
behold, I say unto you,
■ **Lift up your eyes,** and look on
■ **the fields;** for they
■ **are white already**
■ **to harvest.**

■ 36. **And he that reapeth**
receiveth wages, and
■ **gathereth fruit unto life**
■ **eternal:** that both he that
soweth and he that reapeth
may rejoice together.

37. And herein is that saying true,
One soweth, and another reapeth.

38. I sent you to reap that whereon
ye bestowed no labour: other men
laboured, and ye are entered
into their labours.

■ 39. **And many of the**
■ **Samaritans** of that city
■ **believed** on him
■ **for the saying of the**
■ **woman,** which testified,
He told me all that ever I did.

40. So when
■ **the Samaritans**
were come unto him, they
■ **besought him that he**
■ **would tarry** with them:
■ **and he abode**
■ **there two days.**

■ 41. **And many**
■ **more believed**
because of his own word;

■ 42. **And said unto the**
■ **woman, Now we believe,**
not because of thy saying:
■ **for we have heard him**
■ **ourselves, and know that**
■ **this is indeed the Christ,**
the Saviour of the world.

■ 43. **Now** after two days
■ **he** departed thence, and
■ **went into Galilee.**

■ 44. **For Jesus himself**
■ **testified, that a prophet**
■ **hath no honour in**
■ **his own country.**

■ 45. **Then** when he
was come into Galilee,
■ **the Galilaeans received**
■ **him, having seen all the**
■ **things that he did at**
■ **Jerusalem** at the feast:
for they also went unto the feast.

46. **So Jesus came**
■ **again into Cana**
of Galilee, where he
made the water wine.

■ **And** there was
■ **a certain nobleman,** whose
son was sick at Capernaum.

47. When he heard that Jesus was
come out of Judaea into Galilee,
he went unto him, and
■ **besought him that**
■ **he would** come down, and
■ **heal his son:** for he was
■ **at the point of death.**

48. Then said Jesus unto him,
Except ye see signs and wonders,
ye will not believe.

■ 49. **The nobleman saith**
unto him,
■ **Sir, come down**
■ **ere my child die.**

■ 50. **Jesus saith**
unto him, Go thy way;
■ **thy son liveth. And the**
■ **man believed** the word
that Jesus had spoken unto
him, and he went his way.

■ 51. **And** as he was now going down,
■ **his servants met him,**

and told *him,*

saying, Thy son liveth.

52. Then inquired he of them the hour when he began to amend. And they said unto him, Yesterday at the seventh hour the fever left him. 53. So the father knew that *it was* at the same hour, in the which Jesus said unto him, Thy son liveth: and himself believed, and his whole house.

54. **This is again the second miracle that Jesus did,** when he was come out of Judaea into Galilee.

CHAPTER 5

1. **After this** there was a feast of the Jews; and **Jesus went up to Jerusalem.** 2. Now there is at Jerusalem **by** the sheep *market* **a pool,** which is **called** in the Hebrew tongue **Bethesda, having five porches.** 3. **In these lay** a great multitude of **impotent folk,** of blind, halt, withered, **waiting for the moving of the water.** 4. **For an angel went down** at a certain season **into the pool, and troubled the water: whosoever then first after the troubling of the water stepped in was made whole** of whatsoever disease he had. 5. **And a certain man** was there, which **had an infirmity thirty and eight years.** 6. **When Jesus saw him** lie, and knew that he had been now a long time *in that case,* **he saith** unto him, **Wilt thou be made whole?** 7. **The impotent man answered** him, Sir, **I have no man,** when the water is troubled,

to put me into the pool: but while I am coming, another steppeth down before me. 8. **Jesus saith** unto him, **Rise, take up thy bed, and walk.** 9. **And immediately the man was made whole,** and took up his bed, and walked: and on the same day was the sabbath.

10. **The Jews therefore said unto him** that was cured, **It is the sabbath day: it is not lawful for thee to carry thy bed.** 11. **He answered** them, **He that made me whole,** the same **said** unto me, **Take up thy bed,** and walk. 12. **Then asked they him, What man** is that which said unto thee, Take up thy bed, and walk? 13. **And he** that was healed **wist not who it was:** for Jesus had conveyed himself away, a multitude being in *that* place. 14. **Afterward Jesus findeth him** in the temple, **and said** unto him, Behold, **thou art made whole: sin no more,** lest a worse thing come unto thee. 15. **The man** departed, and **told the Jews that it was Jesus,** which had made him whole. 16. **And** therefore did **the Jews** persecute Jesus, and **sought to slay him, because he had done these things on the sabbath day.** 17. **But Jesus answered** them, **My Father worketh** hitherto, **and I work.** 18. **Therefore the Jews sought the more to kill him, because he** not only had broken the sabbath, but **said** also that **God was his Father,** making himself equal with God. 19. **Then answered Jesus** and

said unto them, Verily, verily, I say unto you,

The Son can do nothing of himself, but what he seeth the Father do: for what things soever he doeth, these also doeth the Son likewise.

20. **For the Father loveth the Son, and sheweth him all things that himself doeth:** and he will shew him greater works than these, that ye may marvel.

21. **For as the Father raiseth up the dead,** and quickeneth *them;* **even so the Son quickeneth whom he will.**

22. **For the Father** judgeth no man, but **hath committed all judgment unto the Son:**

23. That all *men* should honour the Son, even as they honour the Father. **He that honoureth not the Son honoureth not the Father** which hath sent him.

24. Verily, verily, I say unto you, **He that heareth my word, and believeth** on him that sent me, **hath everlasting life, and** shall not come into condemnation; but **is passed from death unto life.**

25. Verily, verily, I say unto you, **The hour** is coming, and **now is, when the dead shall hear the voice of the Son** of God: **and they that hear shall live.**

26. For as the Father hath life in himself; so hath he given to the Son to have life in himself;

27. And hath given him authority to execute judgment also, because he is the Son of man.

28. Marvel not at this: for **the hour is coming, in the which all that are in the graves shall hear his voice,**

29. **And shall come forth;** they that have done good, **unto the resurrection of life; and** they that have done evil, unto the resurrection of **damnation.**

30. **I can** of mine own self **do nothing: as I hear, I judge:** and my judgment is just; because I seek not mine own will, but the will of the Father which hath sent me.

31. **If I bear witness of myself, my witness is not true.**

32. **There is another that beareth witness of me;** and I know that the witness which he witnesseth of me is true.

33. **Ye sent unto John, and he bare witness** unto the truth.

34. But I receive not testimony from man: but these things I say, that ye might be saved.

35. **He was** a burning and **a shining light:** and ye were willing for a season to rejoice in his light.

36. **But I have greater witness than** *that* of **John:** for the works which the Father hath given me to finish, **the same works that I do, bear witness of me, that the Father hath sent me.**

37. **And the Father** himself, which hath sent me, **hath borne witness of me.** Ye have neither heard his voice at any time, nor seen his shape.

38. **And ye have not his word** abiding in you: **for whom he hath sent, him ye believe not.**

39. **Search the scriptures; for** in them ye think ye have eternal life: and **they** are they which **testify of me.**

40. And ye will not come to me, that ye might have life.

41. I receive not honour from men.

42. **But** I know you, that **ye have not the love of God** in you. 43. **I am come in my Father's name, and ye receive me not:** if another shall come in his own name, him ye will receive. 44.How can ye believe, which receive honour one of another, and seek not the honour that *cometh* from God only? 45. **Do not think that I will accuse you** to the Father: **there is one that accuseth you, even Moses,** in whom ye trust. 46. For had ye believed **Moses,** ye would have believed me: for he **wrote of me.** 47. **But if ye believe not his writings, how shall ye believe my words?**

CHAPTER 6

1. After these things **Jesus went over the sea of Galilee,** which is *the sea* of Tiberias. 2. **And a great multitude followed him, because they saw his miracles** which he did on them that were diseased. 3. **And Jesus went up into a mountain,** and there he sat with his disciples. 4. And the passover, a feast of the Jews, was nigh. 5. **When Jesus** then lifted up *his* eyes, and **saw a great company come** unto him, **he saith unto Philip, Whence shall we buy bread,** that these may eat? 6. **And this he said to prove him:** for he himself knew what he would do. 7. **Philip answered him, Two hundred pennyworth of bread is not sufficient** for them, that every one of them

may take a little. 8. One of his disciples, **Andrew,** Simon Peter's brother, **saith** unto him, 9. There is **a lad** here, which **hath five barley loaves, and two small fishes:** but what are they among so many? 10. **And Jesus said, Make the men sit down.** Now there was much grass in the place. So the men sat down, **in number about five thousand.** 11. **And Jesus took the loaves; and when he had given thanks, he distributed** to the disciples, and the disciples to them that were set down; **and likewise of the fishes** as much as they would. 12. **When they were filled, he said** unto his disciples, **Gather up** the fragments that remain, **that nothing be lost.** 13. **Therefore they gathered** *them* together, and filled **twelve baskets with the fragments** of the five barley loaves, **which remained** over and above unto them that had eaten. 14. **Then those men, when they had seen the miracle** that Jesus did, **said, This** is of a truth **that prophet that should come** into the world. 15. **When Jesus** therefore **perceived that they would** come and take him by force, to **make him a king, he departed** again into a mountain himself alone. 16. **And** when even was *now* come, **his disciples went** down unto the sea, 17. **And entered into a ship, and went** over the sea **toward Capernaum.** And it was now dark, and Jesus was not come to them.

18. **And the sea arose** by reason **of a great wind** that blew. 19. **So when they had rowed about** five and twenty or **thirty furlongs, they see Jesus walking on the sea,** and drawing nigh unto the ship: **and they were afraid.** 20. **But he saith** unto them, **It is I; be not afraid.** 21. **Then they willingly received him** into the ship: **and immediately the ship was at the land** whither they went.

22. The day following, when the people which stood on the other side of the sea saw that there was none other boat there, save that one whereinto his disciples were entered, and that Jesus went not with his disciples into the boat, but *that* his disciples were gone away alone;

23. (Howbeit there came other boats from Tiberias nigh unto the place where they did eat bread, after that the Lord had given thanks:)

24. **When the people** therefore **saw that Jesus was not there,** neither his disciples, **they** also took shipping, and **came to Capernaum,** seeking for Jesus. 25. **And when they had found him** on the other side of the sea, **they said** unto him, Rabbi, **when camest thou hither?** 26. **Jesus answered** them and said, Verily, verily, I say unto you, **Ye seek me,** not because ye saw the miracles, but **because ye did eat of the loaves,** and were filled. 27. **Labour** not for the meat which perisheth, but **for that meat which endureth unto everlasting life, which the Son** of man **shall give** unto you: for him hath

God the Father sealed. 28. **Then said they** unto him, **What shall we do,** that we might work the works of God? 29. **Jesus answered** and said unto them, **This is the work of God, that ye believe on him whom he hath sent.** 30. **They said** therefore unto him, **What sign shewest thou** then, that we may see, and believe thee? **what dost thou work?** 31. **Our fathers did eat manna** in the desert; **as it is written, He gave them bread from heaven** to eat. 32. **Then Jesus said** unto them, Verily, verily, I say unto you, **Moses gave you not that bread from heaven;** but my Father giveth you the true bread from heaven. 33. **For the bread of God is he which cometh down** from heaven, **and giveth life** unto the world. 34. **Then said they** unto him, Lord, evermore **give us this bread.** 35. **And Jesus said** unto them, **I am the bread of life:** he that cometh to me shall never hunger; and he that believeth on me shall never thirst. 36. **But** I said unto you, That **ye** also have seen me, and **believe not.** 37. **All that the Father giveth** me shall **come to me;** and him that cometh to me I will in no wise cast out. 38. **For I came** down from heaven, **not to do mine own will, but the will of him that sent me.** 39. And this is the Father's will which hath sent me, that of all which he hath given me I should lose nothing, but should raise it up again at the last day. 40. **And** this is the will of him that sent me, that every one which seeth the Son, and believeth on him, may have everlasting life: and I will raise him up at the last day.

41. **The Jews then murmured** at him, **because he said, I am the bread** which came down **from heaven.**

42. **And they said, Is not this Jesus, the son of Joseph,** whose father and mother we know? **how is it** then that **he saith, I came down from heaven?**

43. **Jesus therefore answered** and said unto them, Murmur not among yourselves.

44. **No man can come to me, except the Father** which hath sent me draw him: and I will raise him up at the last day.

45. It is written in the prophets, And they shall be all taught of God. **Every man therefore that** hath heard, and **hath learned of the Father, cometh unto me.**

46. Not that any man hath seen the Father, save he which is of God, he hath seen the Father.

47. Verily, verily, I say unto you, **He that believeth on me hath everlasting life.**

48. **I am that bread of life.**

49. **Your fathers did eat manna** in the wilderness, **and are dead.**

50. This is the bread which cometh down from heaven, that a man may eat thereof, and not die.

51. **I am the living bread** which came down from heaven: **if any man eat** of this bread, **he shall live for ever: and the bread that I will give is my flesh,** which I will give for the life of the world.

52. **The Jews therefore strove** among themselves, **saying, How can this man give us his flesh to eat?**

53. **Then Jesus said** unto them, Verily, verily, I say unto you, **Except ye eat the flesh of the Son of man, and drink his blood, ye have no life** in you.

54. **Whoso eateth my flesh, and drinketh my blood, hath eternal life; and** I will raise him up at the last day.

55. For my flesh is meat indeed, and my blood is drink indeed.

56. He that eateth my flesh, and drinketh my blood, **dwelleth in me, and I in him.**

57. As the living Father hath sent me, and **I live by the Father: so he that eateth me,** even he **shall live by me.**

58. This is that bread which came down from heaven: not as your fathers did eat manna, and are dead: **he that eateth of this bread shall live for ever.**

59. These things said he in the synagogue, as he taught in Capernaum.

60. **Many therefore of his disciples,** when they had heard *this,* **said, This is an hard saying;** who can hear it?

61. **When Jesus knew** in himself that **his disciples murmured** at it, **he said** unto them, **Doth this offend you?**

62. *What* and if ye shall see the Son of man ascend up where he was before?

63. **It is the spirit that quickeneth;** the flesh profiteth nothing: **the words that I speak** unto you, *they* **are spirit, and** *they* are **life.**

64. **But** there are **some** of you that **believe not. For Jesus knew** from the beginning **who** they were that **believed not, and who**

155

■ **should betray him.**

65. **And he said,** Therefore said I unto you, that **no man can come unto me, except it were given unto him of my Father.** 66. **From that time many of his disciples** went back, and **walked no more with him.** 67. **Then said Jesus unto the twelve, Will ye also go away?**

68. Then Simon **Peter answered him, Lord, to whom shall we go? thou hast the words of eternal life.** 69. **And we believe** and are sure **that thou art** that Christ, **the Son of the living God.** 70. **Jesus answered** them, Have not I chosen you twelve, and **one of you is a devil?** 71. **He spake of Judas Iscariot** *the son* of Simon: for he it was that should betray him, being one of the twelve.

CHAPTER 7

1. After these things **Jesus walked in Galilee:** for he would not walk in Jewry, **because the Jews sought to kill him.** 2. Now the Jew's feast of tabernacles was at hand. 3. **His brethren therefore said** unto him, Depart hence, and **go into Judaea,** that thy disciples also may see the works that thou doest. 4. **For there is no man that doeth any thing in secret,** and he himself seeketh to be known openly. If thou do these things, **shew thyself to the world.** 5. For neither did his brethren believe in him. 6. **Then Jesus said** unto them, **My time is not yet come:** but your time is alway ready. 7. The world cannot hate you; but me it hateth, because I testify of it, that

the works thereof are evil.

8. **Go ye up unto this feast: I go not up yet** unto this feast; for my time is not yet full come. 9. **When he had said these words** unto them, **he abode still in Galilee.** 10. **But** when his brethren were gone up, **then went he also up** unto the feast, not openly, but as it were **in secret.** 11. **Then the Jews** sought him at the feast, and **said, Where is he?** 12. **And there was much murmuring** among the people concerning him: for **some said, He is a good man: others said, Nay;** but he deceiveth the people. 13. **Howbeit no man spake openly** of him **for fear** of the Jews. 14. **Now** about the midst of the feast **Jesus went up into the temple, and taught.** 15. **And the Jews marvelled, saying, How knoweth this man letters, having never learned?** 16. **Jesus answered** them, and said, **My doctrine is** not mine, but **his that sent me.** 17. **If any man will do his will, he shall know** of the doctrine, **whether it be of God,** or *whether* I speak of myself. 18. He that speaketh of himself seeketh his own glory: but he that seeketh his glory that sent him, the same is true, and no unrighteousness is in him. 19. **Did not Moses give you the law, and yet none** of you **keepeth the law? Why go ye about to kill me?** 20. **The people answered** and said, **Thou hast a devil:** who goeth about to kill thee?

21. **Jesus answered** and said unto them, **I have done one work,** and ye all marvel.
22. Moses therefore gave unto you circumcision; (not because it is of Moses, but of the fathers;) **and** ye on the sabbath day circumcise a man.
23. **If a man on the sabbath day receive circumcision, that the law** of Moses **should not be broken; are ye angry at me, because I have made a man** every whit **whole on the sabbath day?**
24. Judge not according to the appearance, but judge righteous judgment.
25. **Then said some** of them of Jerusalem, **Is not this he, whom they seek to kill?**
26. **But, lo,** he speaketh boldly, and **they say nothing** unto him. **Do the rulers know** indeed that **this is** the very **Christ?**
27. Howbeit we know this man whence he is: but when Christ cometh, no man knoweth whence he is.
28. **Then cried Jesus in the temple** as he taught, saying, Ye both know me, and ye know whence I am: and **I am not come of myself, but he that sent me is true, whom ye know not.**
29. **But I know him:** for I am from him, **and he hath sent me.**
30. **Then they sought to take him: but no man laid hands on him,** because his hour was not yet come.
31. **And many** of the people **believed** on him, **and said, When Christ cometh, will he do more miracles than these** which this *man* hath done?
32. The Pharisees heard that the people murmured such things concerning him; and **the Pharisees and the chief priests sent officers to take him.**
33. **Then said Jesus** unto them, Yet a little while am I with you, and *then* I go unto him that sent me.
34. **Ye shall seek me, and shall not find me: and where I am,** *thither* **ye cannot come.**
35. **Then said the Jews** among themselves, **Whither will he go,** that we shall not find him? will he go unto the dispersed among the Gentiles, and teach the Gentiles?
36. What *manner of* saying is this that he said, Ye shall seek me, and shall not find *me*: and where I am, *thither ye* cannot come?
37. **In the last day, that great day of the feast, Jesus** stood and **cried, saying, If any man thirst, let him come unto me, and drink.**
38. **He that believeth on me,** as the scripture hath said, **out of his belly shall flow rivers of living water.**
39. **(But this spake he of the Spirit,** which they that believe on him should receive: for the Holy Ghost was not yet *given*; because that Jesus was not yet glorified.)
40. **Many of the people** therefore, when they heard this saying, **said,** Of a truth **this is the Prophet.**
41. **Others said, This is the Christ. But some said, Shall Christ come out of Galilee?**
42. **Hath not the scripture said, That Christ cometh** of the seed of David, and **out of the town of Bethlehem, where David was?**
43. **So there was a division among the people**

because of him.

44. And some of them would have taken him; but no man laid hands on him.

45. **Then came the officers to the chief priests** and Pharisees; and **they said** unto them, **Why have ye not brought him?**

46. **The officers answered, Never man spake like this man.**

47. **Then answered them the Pharisees, Are ye also deceived?**

48. Have any of the rulers or of the Pharisees believed on him?

49. But this people who knoweth not the law are cursed.

50. **Nicodemus saith** unto them, (he that came to Jesus by night, being one of them,)

51. **Doth our law judge** *any* man, **before it hear him,** and know what he doeth?

52. **They answered** and said unto him, Art thou also of Galilee? **Search,** and look: **for out of Galilee ariseth no prophet.**

53. And every man went unto his own house.

CHAPTER 8

1. Jesus went unto the mount of Olives.

2. **And early in the morning he came again into the temple, and all the people came** unto him; **and he** sat down, and **taught them.**

3. **And the scribes and Pharisees brought** unto him **a woman taken in adultery;** and when they had set her in the midst,

4. **They say** unto him, **Master, this woman was taken in adultery,** in the very act.

5. Now Moses in **the law commanded us, that such should be stoned: but what sayest thou?**

6. This they said, tempting him, that they might have to accuse him. But **Jesus stooped down, and with his finger wrote on the ground,** *as though he heard them not.*

7. **So when they continued asking him, he** lifted up himself, and **said** unto them, **He that is without sin** among you, **let him first cast a stone at her.**

8. **And again he** stooped down, and **wrote on the ground.**

9. **And they** which heard *it,* **being convicted** by *their own* conscience, **went out** one by one, beginning at the eldest, *even* unto the last: **and Jesus was left alone, and the woman** standing in the midst.

10. When Jesus had lifted up himself, and saw none but the woman, **he said unto her, Woman, where are those thine accusers? hath no man condemned thee?**

11. **She said, No man, Lord. And Jesus said** unto her, **Neither do I** condemn thee: **go, and sin no more.**

12. **Then spake Jesus** again unto them, **saying, I am the light of the world:** he that followeth me shall not walk in darkness, but shall have the light of life.

13. **The Pharisees therefore said** unto him, **Thou bearest record of thyself; thy record is not true.**

14. **Jesus answered** and said unto them,

Though I bear
record of myself,
yet my record is true:
for I know whence I came,
and whither I go;
but ye cannot tell whence
I come, and whither I go.
15. Ye judge after the flesh;
I judge no man.
16. And yet if I judge, my
judgment is true: for I am
not alone, but I and the Father
that sent me.
17. It is also written in your law,
that the testimony of two
men is true.
18. I am one that
bear witness of myself,
and the Father that sent
me beareth witness of me.
19. Then said they unto him,
Where is thy Father?
Jesus answered, Ye
neither know me, nor my Father:
if ye had known me,
ye should have known
my Father also.
20. These words spake Jesus in the
treasury, as he taught in the temple:
and no man laid hands on him; for
his hour was not yet come.
21. Then said Jesus again
unto them, I go my way, and
ye shall seek me, and shall
die in your sins: whither I
go, ye cannot come.
22. Then said the Jews, Will
he kill himself? because he
saith, Whither I go, ye cannot come.
23. And he said unto them, Ye
are from beneath; I am from above:
ye are of this world; I
am not of this world.
24. I said therefore unto you,
that ye shall die in your sins: for
if ye believe not that
I am he, ye shall die
in your sins.
25. Then said they unto him,
Who art thou? And
Jesus saith unto them,
Even the same
that I said unto you

from the beginning.
26. I have many things to
say and to judge of you: but
he that sent me is true;
and I speak to the world
those things which I have
heard of him.
27. They understood not
that he spake to them of the Father.
28. Then said Jesus unto them,
When ye have lifted up the
Son of man,
then shall ye know that I
am he, and that I do nothing of
myself; but as my Father hath
taught me, I speak these things.
29. And he that sent me is with me:
the Father hath not left
me alone; for I
do always those things that
please him.
30. As he spake these words,
many believed on him.
31. Then said Jesus to those
Jews which believed on him,
If ye continue in my
word, then are ye
my disciples indeed;
32. And ye shall know the
truth, and the truth shall
make you free.
33. They answered him,
We be Abraham's seed, and
were never in
bondage to any man:
how sayest thou, Ye
shall be made free?
34. Jesus answered
them, Verily, verily, I say unto you,
Whosoever committeth
sin is the servant of sin.
35. And the servant abideth not
in the house for ever: but the
Son abideth ever.
36. If the Son therefore shall
make you free, ye shall
be free indeed.
37. I know that ye are Abraham's
seed; but ye seek to kill me, because
my word hath no place in you.
38. I speak that which I
have seen with my Father:
and ye do that which ye

■ have seen with your father.

■ 39. **They answered** and said unto him,

■ **Abraham is our father.**

■ **Jesus saith** unto them,

■ **If ye were Abraham's**

■ **children, ye would do**

■ **the works of Abraham.**

■ 40. **But now ye seek to kill**

■ **me,** a man that hath told you the truth, which I have heard of God:

■ **this did not Abraham.**

41. Ye do the deeds of your father.

■ **Then said they** to him, We be not born of fornication;

■ **we have one Father,**

■ **even God.**

■ 42. **Jesus said** unto them,

■ **If God were your Father,**

■ **ye would love me: for I** proceeded forth and

■ **came from God;** neither came I of myself, but he sent me.

43. Why do ye not understand my speech? *even* because ye cannot hear my word.

■ 44. **Ye are of your father**

■ **the devil,** and the lusts of your father ye will do.

■ **He was a murderer** from the beginning,

■ **and abode not in the**

■ **truth,** because there is no truth in him. When he speaketh a lie, he speaketh of his own:

■ **for he is a liar, and**

■ **the father of it.**

45. And because I tell *you* the truth, ye believe me not.

46. Which of you convinceth me of sin? And if I say the truth, why do ye not believe me?

■ 47. **He that is of God heareth**

■ **God's words:** ye therefore hear *them* not, because

■ **ye are not of God.**

■ 48. **Then answered**

■ **the Jews,** and said unto him, Say we not well that

■ **thou** art a Samaritan, and

■ **hast a devil?**

■ 49. **Jesus answered, I have**

■ **not a devil; but I honour my**

■ **Father,** and ye do dishonour me.

50. And I seek not mine own glory: there is one that seeketh and judgeth.

51. Verily, verily, I say unto you,

■ **If a man keep my saying,**

■ **he shall never see death.**

■ 52. **Then said the Jews** unto him, Now we know that thou hast a devil.

■ **Abraham is dead,** and the prophets; and thou sayest, If a man keep my saying, he shall never taste of death.

■ 53. **Art thou greater**

■ **than** our father

■ **Abraham,** which is dead? and the prophets are dead:

■ **whom makest thou thyself?**

■ 54. **Jesus answered,** If I honour myself, my honour is nothing:

■ **it is my Father that**

■ **honoureth me;** of whom ye say, that he is your God:

■ 55. **Yet ye have not known**

■ **him;** but I know him: and if I should say, I know him not, I shall be a liar like unto you:

■ **but I know him, and**

■ **keep his saying.**

■ 56. **Your father Abraham**

■ **rejoiced to see my day:** and he saw *it,* and was glad.

■ 57. **Then said the**

■ **Jews** unto him,

■ **Thou art not yet fifty** years old,

■ **and hast thou**

■ **seen Abraham?**

■ 58. **Jesus said** unto them, Verily, verily, I say unto you,

■ **Before Abraham was, I am.**

■ 59. **Then took they up stones**

■ **to cast at him: but Jesus** hid himself, and went out of the temple, going through the midst of them, and so

■ **passed by.**

CHAPTER 9

1. And as *Jesus* passed by,

■ **he saw a man** which was

■ **blind from his birth.**

■ 2. **And his disciples**

■ **asked** him, saying, Master,

who did sin, this man,
or his parents,
that he was born blind?
3. **Jesus answered, Neither**
hath this man sinned, nor his parents:
but that the works of
God should be made
manifest in him.
4. **I must work** the works of him
that sent me, while it is day:
the night cometh, when
no man can work.
5. As long as I am in the world,
I am the light of the world.
6. **When he had thus**
spoken, he spat on the
ground, and made clay of
the spittle, and he anointed
the eyes of the blind man
with the clay,
7. **And said** unto him,
Go, wash in the
pool of Siloam,
(which is by interpretation, Sent.)
He went his way therefore,
and washed,
and came seeing.
8. **The neighbours** therefore, and
they which before had seen
him that he was blind,
said, Is not this he that
sat and begged?
9. Some said, This is he: others
said, He is like him: *but*
he said, I am he.
10. **Therefore said**
they unto him,
How were thine
eyes opened?
11. **He answered**
and said, A man that is called
Jesus made clay, and
anointed mine eyes,
and said unto me,
Go to the pool of
Siloam, and wash:
and I went and washed,
and I received sight.
12. Then said they unto him,
Where is he? He said, I know not.
13. They brought to the Pharisees
him that aforetime was blind.
14. **And it was the sabbath**

day when Jesus made the
clay, and opened his eyes.
15. Then again
the Pharisees also asked
him how he had received
his sight. He said unto them,
He put clay upon mine eyes,
and I washed, and do see.
16. **Therefore said some**
of the Pharisees, This man
is not of God, because he
keepeth not the sabbath
day. Others said, How
can a man that is
a sinner do such miracles?
And there was a division amongthem.
17. They say unto the blind man
again, What sayest thou of him,
that he hath opened thine eyes?
He said, He is a prophet.
18. **But the Jews did not**
believe concerning him,
that he had been blind,
and received his sight, until they
called the parents of him
that had received his sight.
19. **And they asked**
them, saying,
Is this your son,
who ye say was born blind?
how then doth he now see?
20. **His parents answered**
them and said, We know that
this is our son,
and that he was born blind:
21. **But by what means**
he now seeth, we know
not; or who hath opened
his eyes, we know not:
he is of age; ask him:
e shall speak for himself.
22. These *words* spake his parents,
because they feared the Jews: for
the Jews had agreed already, that
if any man did confess that he
was Christ, he should be put
out of the synagogue.
23. Therefore said his parents,
He is of age; ask him.
24. **Then again called**
they the man that was
blind, and said
unto him, Give God the praise:

we know that this
man is a sinner.
25. **He answered** and said,
Whether he be a sinner *or no,*
I know not: one thing I
know, that, whereas
I was blind, now I see.
26. **Then said they** to him
again, What did he to thee?
how opened he thine eyes?
27. **He answered them, I**
have told you already,
and ye did not hear: wherefore
would ye hear *it* again?
will ye also be his
disciples?
28. **Then they reviled**
him, and said,
Thou art his disciple; but
we are Moses' disciples.
29. We know that God
spake unto Moses:
as for this fellow, we know
not from whence he is.
30. **The man answered**
and said unto them, Why herein
is a marvellous thing, that
ye know not from whence he is,
and yet he hath opened
mine eyes.
31. **Now we know that God**
heareth not sinners: but if any
man be a worshipper of God, and
doeth his will, him he heareth.
32. Since the world began was it not
heard that any man opened the eyes
of one that was born blind.
33. **If this man were not of**
God, he could do nothing.
34. **They answered**
and said unto him,
Thou wast altogether born
in sins, and dost thou teach us?
And they cast him out.
35. **Jesus heard**
that they had cast him out;
and when he had found
him, he said unto him,
Dost thou believe
on the Son of God?
36. **He answered** and said,
Who is he, Lord, that
I might believe on him?

37. **And Jesus said** unto him,
Thou hast both seen him, and
it is he that talketh
with thee.
38. **And he said, Lord,**
I believe. And he
worshipped him.
39. **And Jesus said,**
For judgment I am
come into this world,
that they which see not
might see; and that they
which see might
be made blind.
40. **And some of the**
Pharisees which were with
him heard these words, and
said unto him,
Are we blind also?
41. **Jesus said** unto them,
If ye were blind, ye should
have no sin: but now ye
say, We see; therefore
your sin remaineth.

CHAPTER 10

1. Verily, verily, I say unto you,
He that entereth not by the
door into the sheepfold, but
climbeth up some other way
the same is a
thief and a robber.
2. **But he that entereth**
in by the door is the
shepherd of the sheep.
3. To him the porter openeth;
and the sheep hear his
voice; and he calleth his own sheep
by name, and leadeth them out.
4. And when he putteth forth his
own sheep, he goeth before them,
and the sheep follow
him: for they know his voice.
5. **And a stranger will**
they not follow, but will flee
from him: for they know not the
voice of strangers.
6. This parable spake Jesus unto
them: but they understood not what
things they were which he
spake unto them.
7. **Then said Jesus** unto them
again, Verily, verily, I say unto you,

I am the door of the sheep.
8. All that ever came before me are thieves and robbers: but the sheep did not hear them.
9. I am the door: **by me if any man enter in, he shall be saved,** and shall go in and out, and find pasture.
10. **The thief cometh** not, but for **to steal, and to kill, and to destroy: I am come that they might have life,** and that they might have *it* **more abundantly.**
11. **I am the good shepherd:** the good shepherd giveth his life for the sheep.
12. **But he that is an hireling,** and not the shepherd, whose own the sheep are not, **seeth the wolf coming, and leaveth** the sheep, and fleeth: **and the wolf catcheth them, and scattereth the sheep.**
13. The hireling fleeth, because he is an hireling, and careth not for the sheep.
14. **I am the good shepherd, and know my sheep, and am known of mine.**
15. As the Father knoweth me, even so know I the Father: **and I lay down my life for the sheep.**
16. **And other sheep I have,** which are **not of this fold:** them also I must bring, and they shall hear my voice; **and there shall be one fold, and one shepherd.**
17. Therefore doth my Father love me, because **I lay down my life,** that I might take it again.
18. **No man taketh it** from me, but I lay it down of myself. I have power to lay it down, and **I have power to take it again.** This commandment have I received of my Father.
19. There was a division therefore again among the Jews for these sayings.

20. **And many** of them **said, He hath a devil,** and is mad; why hear ye him?
21. **Others said,** These are not the words of him that hath a devil. **Can a devil open the eyes of the blind?**
22. And it was at Jerusalem the feast of the dedication, and it was winter.
23. **And Jesus walked** in the temple **in Solomon's porch.**
24. **Then came the Jews** round about him, **and said** unto him, How long dost thou make us to doubt? **If thou be the Christ, tell us plainly.**
25. **Jesus answered** them, **I told you, and ye believed not:** the works that I do in my Father's name, they bear witness of me.
26. But ye believe not, because ye are not of my sheep, as I said unto you.
27. **My sheep hear my voice,** and I know them, and they follow me:
28. **And I give unto them eternal life; and they shall never perish, neither shall any man pluck them out of my hand.**
29. My Father, which gave *them* me, is greater than all; **and no man is able to pluck them out of my Father's hand.**
30. **I and my Father are one.**
31. **Then the Jews took up stones** again to stone him.
32. **Jesus answered** them, **Many good works have I shewed** you from my Father; **for which** of those works **do ye stone me?**
33. **The Jews answered** him, saying, For a good work **we stone thee** not; but **for blasphemy; and because that thou,** being a man,

■ makest thyself God.
■ 34. **Jesus answered** them,
■ **Is it not written** in your law, I said,
■ **Ye are gods?**
35. If he called them gods, unto
whom the word of God came, and
the scripture cannot be broken;
■ 36. **Say ye of him,** whom
the Father hath sanctified,
and sent into the world,
■ **Thou blasphemest;**
■ **because I said, I am**
■ **the Son of God?**
■ 37. **If I do not the works of**
■ **my Father, believe me not.**
38. But if I do, though ye believe
not me, believe the works: that ye
may know, and believe, that the
Father *is* in me, and I in him.
■ 39. **Therefore they sought**
■ **again to take him: but he**
■ **escaped** out of their hand,
40. And went away again
■ **beyond Jordan** into the place
■ **where John** at first
■ **baptized;** and there he abode.
■ 41. **And many**
resorted unto him, and
■ **said,** John did no miracle: but
■ **all things that John spake of**
■ **this man were true.**
■ 42. **And many**
■ **believed** on him there.

CHAPTER 11
■ 1. **Now a certain man was**
■ **sick, named Lazarus,**
of Bethany, the town of Mary
and her sister Martha.
2. (It was *that* Mary which anointed
the Lord with ointment, and wiped
his feet with her hair, whose
brother Lazarus was sick.)
■ 3. **Therefore his sisters**
■ **sent unto him, saying,**
■ **Lord, behold, he whom**
■ **thou lovest is sick.**
4. When Jesus heard *that,*
■ **he said, This sickness is not**
■ **unto death,** but for the
glory of God, that the Son of God
might be glorified thereby.
■ 5. **Now Jesus loved Martha,**

■ **and her sister,**
■ **and Lazarus.**
■ 6. **When he had**
■ **heard** therefore that
■ **he was sick, he abode**
■ **two days still in the**
■ **same place** where he was.
■ 7. **Then** after that
■ **saith he** to *his* disciples,
■ **Let us go into Judaea** again.
■ 8. **His disciples say**
unto him, Master,
■ **the Jews of late sought**
■ **to stone thee;**
and goest thou thither again?
9. Jesus answered, Are there
not twelve hours in the day? I
f any man walk in the day, he
stumbleth not, because he
seeth the light of this world.
10. But if a man walk in the
night, he stumbleth, because
there is no light in him.
11. These things said he: and
■ **after that he saith** unto them,
■ **Our friend Lazarus sleepeth;**
■ **but I go, that I may awake**
■ **him** out of sleep.
■ 12. **Then said his disciples,**
■ **Lord, if he sleep, he**
■ **shall do well.**
13. Howbeit Jesus spake of his death:
but they thought that he had spoken
of taking of rest in sleep.
■ 14. **Then said Jesus** unto them
■ **plainly, Lazarus is dead.**
15. And I am glad for your sakes
that I was not there, to the intent
ye may believe; nevertheless
let us go unto him.
16. Then said Thomas, which is called
Didymus, unto his fellow disciples, Let
us also go, that we may die with him.
■ 17. **Then when Jesus came,**
■ **he found that he had lain in**
■ **the grave four days** already.
18. Now Bethany was nigh unto
Jerusalem, about fifteen furlongs off:
19. And many of the Jews came to
Martha and Mary, to comfort them
concerning their brother.
■ 20. **Then Martha,** as soon as
she heard that Jesus was coming,

■ **went and met him:**
but Mary sat *still* in the house.

■ 21. **Then said**
■ **Martha** unto Jesus,
■ **Lord, if thou hadst**
■ **been here, my brother**
■ **had not died.**
■ 22. **But** I know, that even now,
■ **whatsoever thou**
■ **wilt ask** of God,
■ **God will give** *it* thee.
■ 23. **Jesus saith** unto her,
■ **Thy brother shall rise** again.
■ 24. **Martha saith** unto him,
■ **I know that he shall rise**
■ **again in the resurrection**
at the last day.
■ 25. **Jesus said** unto her,
■ **I am the resurrection, and**
■ **the life: he that believeth**
■ **in me, though he were**
■ **dead, yet shall he live:**
■ 26. **And whosoever liveth**
■ **and believeth in me shall**
■ **never die. Believest**
■ **thou this?**
■ 27. **She saith** unto him,
■ **Yea, Lord: I believe** that thou
art the Christ, the Son of God, which
should come into the world.
28. And when she had so said,
■ **she went her way, and**
■ **called Mary** her sister secretly,
■ **saying, The**
■ **Master** is come, and
■ **calleth for thee.**
29. As soon as she heard *that,*
■ **she arose quickly, and**
■ **came unto him.**
30. Now Jesus was not yet come
into the town, but was in that
place where Martha met him.
■ 31. **The Jews** then which were with
her in the house, and comforted her,
■ **when they saw Mary,** that
she rose up hastily and went out,
■ **followed her,** saying, She
goeth unto the grave to weep there.
■ 32. **Then when Mary** was
come where Jesus was, and
■ **saw him, she fell down**
■ **at his feet, saying** unto him,
■ **Lord, if thou hadst been**

■ **here, my brother**
■ **had not died.**
■ 33. **When Jesus therefore**
■ **saw her weeping,** and the Jews
also weeping which came with her,
■ **he groaned** in the spirit,
■ **and was troubled.**
■ 34. **And said, Where h**
■ **ave ye laid him? They**
■ **said** unto him, Lord,
■ **come and see.**
35. **Jesus wept.**
■ 36. **Then said the Jews,**
■ **Behold how he loved him!**
37. And some of them said, Could not
this man, which opened the eyes of
the blind, have caused that even
this man should not have died?
■ 38. **Jesus therefore**
again groaning in himself
■ **cometh to the grave.**
It was a cave, and a stone lay upon it.
■ 39. **Jesus said, Take ye**
■ **away the stone. Martha,**
the sister of him that was dead,
■ **saith** unto him,
■ **Lord, by this time he**
■ **stinketh:** for he hath
been *dead* four days.
■ 40. **Jesus saith** unto her,
Said I not unto thee, that,
■ **if thou wouldest believe,**
■ **thou shouldest see the**
■ **glory of God?**
■ 41. **Then they took away**
■ **the stone** *from the place* where
the dead was laid.
■ **And Jesus** lifted up *his* eyes, and
■ **said, Father, I thank thee**
■ **that thou hast heard me.**
■ 42. **And I knew that thou**
■ **hearest** me always:
■ **but because of the**
■ **people** which stand by
■ **I said it,** that they may
believe that thou hast sent me.
■ 43. **And** when he thus had spoken,
■ **he cried with a loud voice,**
■ **Lazarus, come forth.**
■ 44. **And he that was**
■ **dead came forth,**
■ **bound** hand and foot
■ **with graveclothes:** and his face

was bound about with a napkin.

■ **Jesus saith** unto them,

■ **Loose him,** and let him go.

■ **45. Then many of the Jews**
which came to Mary, and had seen
the things which Jesus did,

■ **believed on him.**

46. **But some** of them

■ **went** their ways

■ **to the Pharisees, and told**

■ **them** what things Jesus had done.

47. **Then gathered** the chief
priests and the Pharisees

■ **a council, and said,**

■ **What do we?** for this man
doeth many miracles.

■ 48. **If we let him thus alone,**

■ **all men will believe** on him:
and the Romans shall come and take
away both our place and nation.

■ 49. **And** one of them, *named*

■ **Caiaphas, being the**

■ **high priest** that same year,

■ **said** unto them,
Ye know nothing at all,

50. Nor consider that

■ **it is expedient** for us,

■ **that one man should**

■ **die for the people,** and
that the whole nation perish not.

■ 51. **And this spake he not of**

■ **himself: but**
being high priest that year,

■ **he prophesied that Jesus**

■ **should die for that nation;**

52. And not for that nation only,

■ **but that also he should**

■ **gather together in one**

■ **the children of God**
that were scattered abroad.

■ 53. **Then** from that day forth

■ **they took counsel** together for

■ **to put him to death.**

54. **Jesus** therefore walked no
more openly among the Jews; but

■ **went** thence unto a country
near to the wilderness,

■ **into a city called**

■ **Ephraim,** and there
continued with his disciples.

■ 55. **And the Jews'**

■ **passover was nigh** at hand:

■ **and many went**

out of the country up

■ **to Jerusalem**
before the passover,

■ **to purify themselves.**

56. Then sought they for Jesus, and
spake among themselves, as they
stood in the temple, What think ye,
that he will not come to the feast?

57. Now both the chief priests and the
Pharisees had given a
commandment, that, if any man knew
where he were, he should shew *it*,
that they might take him.

CHAPTER 12

■ 1. **Then Jesus**
six days before the passover

■ **came to Bethany,** where
Lazarus was which had been dead,
whom he raised from the dead.

■ 2. **There they made him**

■ **a supper;** and Martha served:
but Lazarus was one of them that
sat at the table with him.

■ 3. **Then took Mary** a pound of

■ **ointment of spikenard,**
very costly,

■ **and anointed the feet of**

■ **Jesus, and wiped his feet**

■ **with her hair:** and the house was
filled with the odour of the ointment.

■ 4. **Then saith** one of his disciples,

■ **Judas** Iscariot, Simon's *son,*

■ **which should betray him,**

■ 5. **Why was not this ointment**

■ **sold** for three hundred pence,

■ **and given to the poor?**

6. This he said, not that he cared
for the poor; but because he was
a thief, and had the bag, and bare
what was put therein.

■ 7. **Then said Jesus, Let**

■ **her alone: against the**

■ **day of my burying**

■ **hath she kept this.**

■ 8. **For the poor**

■ **always ye have**
with you; but me ye have not always.

■ 9. **Much people**
of the Jews therefore

■ **knew that he was there:**

■ **and they came not for**

■ **Jesus' sake only, but that**

they might see Lazarus also, whom he had raised from the dead. 10. **But the chief priests consulted that they might put Lazarus also to death;** 11. **Because that by reason of him many** of the Jews went away, and **believed on Jesus.** 12. On the next day **much people** that were come to the feast, **when they heard that Jesus was coming to Jerusalem,** 13. **Took branches of palm trees, and went forth** to meet him, **and cried, Hosanna: Blessed is the King of Israel** that cometh in the name of the Lord. 14. **And Jesus,** when he had **found a young ass, sat thereon; as it is written,** 15. Fear not, daughter of Sion: behold, **thy King cometh, sitting on an ass's colt.** 16. These things understood not his disciples at the first: but when Jesus was glorified, then remembered they that these things were written of him, and *that* they had done these things unto him. 17. **The people therefore that was with him when he called Lazarus** out of his grave, **and raised him** from the dead, **bare record.** 18. **For this cause the people also met him,** for that they heard that he had done this miracle. 19. The Pharisees therefore said among themselves, Perceive ye how ye prevail nothing? behold, the world is gone after him. 20. **And** there were **certain Greeks** among them that **came up to worship at the feast:** 21. **The same came therefore to Philip,** which was of Bethsaida of Galilee,

and desired him, **saying, Sir, we would see Jesus.** 22. Philip cometh **and** telleth Andrew: and again **Andrew and Philip tell Jesus.** 23. **And Jesus answered** them, saying, **The hour is come, that the Son of man should be glorified.** 24. Verily, verily, I say unto you, **Except a corn of wheat fall into the ground and die, it abideth alone: but if it die, it bringeth forth much fruit.** 25. **He that loveth his life shall lose it;** and he that hateth his life in this world shall keep it unto life eternal. 26. **If any man serve me, let him follow me;** and where I am, there shall also my servant be: if any man serve me, him will *my* Father honour. 27. Now is my soul troubled; and **what shall I say? Father, save me from this hour: but for this cause came I unto this hour.** 28. **Father, glorify thy name. Then came there a voice from heaven, saying, I have** both **glorified it, and will glorify it again.** 29. **The people** therefore, **that** stood by, and **heard it, said that it thundered: others said, An angel spake** to him. 30. **Jesus answered** and said, **This voice came** not because of me, but **for your sakes.** 31. **Now is the judgment of this world: now shall the prince** of this world **be cast out.** 32. **And I, if I be lifted up** from the earth, **will draw all men unto me.**

33. This he said, signifying what death he should die.

34. **The people answered** him, We have heard out of the law that **Christ abideth for ever: and how sayest thou, The Son** of man **must be lifted up?** who is this Son of man?

35. **Then Jesus said** unto them, Yet a little while is the light with you. **Walk while ye have the light,** lest darkness come upon you: **for he that walketh in darkness knoweth not whither he goeth.**

36. While ye have light, **believe in the light, that ye may be the children of light.** These things spake Jesus, and departed, and did hide himself from them.

37. **But though he had done so many miracles** before them, **yet they believed not** on him:

38. **That** the saying of **Esaias** the prophet **might be fulfilled,** which he spake, **Lord, who hath believed our report?** and to whom hath the arm of the Lord been revealed?

39. Therefore they could not believe, because that **Esaias said again,**

40. **He hath blinded their eyes,** and hardened their heart; **that they should not see** with *their* eyes, **nor understand** with *their* heart, **and be converted,** and I should heal them.

41. These things said Esaias, when he saw his glory, and spake of him.

42. **Nevertheless among the chief rulers also many believed** on him; **but** because of the Pharisees they **did not confess him,** lest they should be put out of the synagogue:

43. **For they loved the praise of men** more than the praise of God.

44. **Jesus cried** and said, **He that believeth on me, believeth** not on me, but **on him that sent me.**

45. And he that seeth me seeth him that sent me.

46. **I am** come a **light** into the world, that **whosoever believeth on me should not abide in darkness.**

47. And if any man hear my words, and believe not, I judge him not: for **I came not to judge the world, but to save the world.**

48. **He that rejecteth me,** and receiveth not my words, **hath one that judgeth him: the word** that I have spoken, the same **shall judge him in the last day.**

49. **For I have not spoken of myself; but the Father** which sent me, he **gave me** a commandment, **what I should say,** and what I should speak.

50. And I know that his commandment is life everlasting: whatsoever I speak therefore, even as the Father said unto me, so I speak.

CHAPTER 13

1. **Now before the** feast of the **passover,** when Jesus knew that his hour was come that he should depart out of this world unto the Father, having loved his own which were in the world, he loved them unto the end.

2. **And supper being ended, the devil having now put into** the heart of **Judas** Iscariot, Simon's son, **to betray him;**

3. **Jesus** knowing that the Father had given all things into his hands, and that he was come from God, and went to God;

4. He riseth from supper, and laid aside his garments; and

took a towel, and
girded himself.
5. After that he
poureth water into a basin,
and began to wash the
disciples' feet, and to wipe
them with the towel wherewith
he was girded.
6. Then cometh he to
Simon Peter: and
Peter saith unto him,
Lord, dost thou
wash my feet?
7. Jesus answered and said unto
him, What I do thou knowest not
now; but thou shalt know hereafter.
8. Peter saith unto him, Thou shalt
never wash my feet.
Jesus answered him,
If I wash thee not, thou
hast no part with me.
9. **Simon Peter saith** unto him,
Lord, not my feet
only, but also
my hands and my head.
10. **Jesus saith** to him,
He that is washed needeth
not save to wash
his feet, but is clean every whit:
and ye are clean,
but not all.
11. **For he knew who should**
betray him; therefore said he,
Ye are not all clean.
12. So after he had washed their
feet, and had taken his garments,
and was set down again,
he said unto them,
Know ye what I have
done to you?
13. Ye call me Master and Lord:
and ye say well; for *so* I am.
14. **If** I then,
your Lord and Master,
have washed your feet; ye
also ought to wash one
another's feet.
15. **For** I have given
you an example, that
ye should do as
I have done to you.
16. Verily, verily, I say unto you,
The servant is not greater

than his lord; neither he that is
sent greater than he that sent him.
17. If ye know these things, happy are
ye if ye do them.
18. **I speak not of you all:**
I know whom I have chosen: but that
the scripture may be fulfilled,
He that eateth bread with
me hath lifted up his heel
against me.
19. Now I tell you before it come, that,
when it is come to pass, ye may
believe that I am *he.*
20. Verily, verily, I say unto you, He
that receiveth whomsoever I send
receiveth me; and he that receiveth
me receiveth him that sent me.
21. When Jesus had thus said,
he was troubled in spirit,
and testified, and said, Verily,
verily, I say unto you, that
one of you shall betray me.
22. Then the disciples looked one on
another, doubting of whom he spake.
23. **Now there was leaning**
on Jesus' bosom one of his
disciples, whom Jesus loved.
24. **Simon Peter** therefore
beckoned to him,
that he should
ask who it should be
of whom he spake.
25. **He** then lying on Jesus' breast
saith unto him,
Lord, who is it?
26. **Jesus answered, He it is,**
to whom I shall give a sop,
when I have dipped *it.*
And when he had dipped the sop,
he gave it to Judas
Iscariot, *the son* of Simon.
27. **And** after the sop
Satan entered into him.
Then said Jesus unto him,
That thou doest,
do quickly.
28. Now no man at the table knew for
what intent he spake this unto him.
29. For some *of them* thought,
because Judas had the bag, that
Jesus had said unto him, Buy *those*
things that we have need of against
the feast; or, that he should give

something to the poor.

30. **He** then having received the sop **went immediately** out: and it was night.

31. Therefore, when he was gone out, **Jesus said, Now is the Son of man glorified, and God is glorified in him.**

32. If God be glorified in him, God shall also glorify him in himself, and shall straightway glorify him.

33. Little children, yet a little while I am with you. Ye shall seek me: and as I said unto the Jews, Whither I go, ye cannot come; so now I say to you.

34. **A new commandment I give** unto you, **That ye love one another;** as I have loved you, that ye also love one another.

35. **By this shall all men know that ye are my disciples,** if ye have love one to another.

36. **Simon Peter said** unto him, **Lord, whither goest thou? Jesus answered** him, Whither I go, **thou canst not follow me now; but thou shalt follow me afterwards.**

37. **Peter said** unto him, Lord, why cannot I follow thee now? **I will lay down my life for thy sake.**

38. **Jesus answered** him, Wilt thou lay down thy life for my sake? Verily, verily, I say unto thee, **The cock shall not crow, till thou hast denied me thrice.**

CHAPTER 14

1. **Let not your heart be troubled: ye believe in God, believe also in me.**

2. **In my Father's house are many mansions:** if *it* *were* not *so,* I would have told you. **I go to prepare a place for you.**

3. **And if I go** and prepare a place for you, **I will come again, and receive you** unto myself; **that where I am, there ye may be also.**

4. And whither I go ye know, and the way ye know.

5. **Thomas saith** unto him, Lord, we know not whither thou goest; and **how can we know the way?**

6. **Jesus saith** unto him, **I am the way, the truth, and the life: no man cometh unto the Father, but by me.**

7. If ye had known me, ye should have known my Father also: and from henceforth ye know him, and have seen him.

8. **Philip saith** unto him, Lord, **shew us the Father,** and it sufficeth us.

9. **Jesus saith** unto him, Have I been so long time with you, and yet hast thou not known me, Philip? **he that hath seen me hath seen the Father;** and how sayest thou *then,* Shew us the Father?

10. **Believest thou not that I am in the Father, and the Father in me?** the words that I speak unto you **I speak not of myself: but the Father** that dwelleth **in me,** he **doeth the works.**

11. Believe me that I *am* in the Father, and the Father in me: or else believe me for the very works' sake.

12. Verily, verily, I say unto you, **He that believeth on me, the works that I do shall he do also; and greater works than these shall he do;** because I go unto my Father.

13. **And whatsoever ye shall ask in my name, that will I do,** that the Father may be glorified in the Son.

14. If ye shall ask any thing in my name, I will do *it.*

15. **If ye love me, keep my commandments.**

16. **And I will pray the Father, and he shall give you another Comforter,** that

he may abide with you for ever;

17. Even the Spirit of truth; whom the world cannot receive, because it seeth him not, neither knoweth him: but ye know him; for he dwelleth with you, and shall be in you. 18. I will not leave you comfortless: I will come to you.

19. Yet a little while, and the world seeth me no more; but ye see me: because I live, ye shall live also. 20. At that day ye shall know that I *am* in my Father, and ye in me, and I in you.

21. He that hath my commandments, and keepeth them, he it is that **loveth me: and** he that loveth me shall be loved of my Father, and **I will** love him, and will **manifest myself to him.**

22. Judas saith unto him, **not Iscariot,** Lord, **how is it that thou wilt manifest thyself** unto us, and not unto the world?

23. Jesus answered and said unto him, **If a man love me, he will keep my words: and my Father will love him, and we will** come unto him, and **make our abode with him.** 24. He that loveth me not keepeth not my sayings: and the word which ye hear is not mine, but the Father's which sent me.

25. These things have I spoken unto you, **being yet present** with you. 26. **But the** Comforter, *which is* the **Holy Ghost,** whom the Father will send in my name, he **shall teach you all things, and bring all things to your remembrance,** whatsoever I have said unto you.

27. **Peace I leave** with you, my **peace I give** unto you: not as the world giveth, give I unto you. **Let not your heart be troubled, neither**

let it be afraid. 28. Ye have heard how I said unto you, **I go away, and** come *again* unto you. **If ye loved me, ye would rejoice, because** I said, **I go unto the Father:** for my Father is greater than I. 29. And now I have told you before it come to pass, that, when it is come to pass, ye might believe.

30. **Hereafter I will not talk much** with you: **for the prince of this world cometh,** and hath nothing in me. 31. But that the world may know that I love the Father; and as the Father gave me commandment, even so I do. Arise, let us go hence.

CHAPTER 15

1. **I am the true vine, and my Father is the husbandman.** 2. **Every branch** in me **that beareth not fruit he taketh away: and every branch that beareth fruit, he purgeth it, that it may bring forth more fruit.** 3. **Now ye are clean through the word which I have spoken** unto you. 4. Abide in me, and I in you. As **the branch cannot bear fruit** of itself, **except** it abide **in the vine;** no more can ye, except ye abide in me. 5. **I am the vine,** ye *are* the branches: **He that abideth in me,** and I in him, the same **bringeth forth much fruit:** for without me ye can do nothing. 6. **If a man abide not in me, he is cast forth** as a branch, **and is** withered; and men gather them, and cast *them* into the fire, and they are **burned.** 7. **If ye abide in me, and my words abide in you,** ye shall

■ ■ **ask what ye will, and it
shall be done** unto you.
8. Herein is my Father glorified,
that ye bear much fruit; so
shall ye be my disciples.
9. **As the Father hath loved
me, so have I loved you:**
continue ye in my love.
10. If ye keep my commandments, ye
shall abide in my love; even as I have
kept my Father's commandments,
and abide in his love.
11. **These things have
I spoken** unto you,
**that my joy might remain
in you, and** *that* **your joy
might be full.**
12. **This is mycommand-
ment, That ye love one
another,** as I have loved you.
13. **Greater love hath
no man than** this, that
**a man lay down his
life for his friends.**
14. Ye are my friends, if ye do
whatsoever I command you.
15. **Henceforth I call you
not servants;** for the servant
knoweth not what his lord doeth:
but I have called you
friends; for all things
that I have heard of my Father
**I have made known
unto you.**
16. Ye have not chosen me, but
**I have chosen you, and
ordained you, that ye
should go and bring
forth fruit,** and *that* your
fruit should remain: that
**whatsoever ye shall ask
of the Father in my name,
he may give it you.**
17. These things I command you,
that ye love one another.
18. **If the world hate
you, ye know that it
hated me** before *it hated* you.
19. If ye were of the world, the world
would love his own: but because ye
are not of the world, but
**I have chosen you out
of the world,** therefore the

world hateth you.
20. Remember the word that
I said unto you, The servant
is not greater than his lord.
**If they have persecuted
me, they will also persecute
you;** if they have kept my saying,
they will keep yours also.
21. **But all these things will
they do unto you for my
name's sake,** because they
know not him that sent me.
22. **If I had not come**
and spoken unto them,
**they had not had sin:
but now they have no
cloak** for their sin.
23. **He that hateth me
hateth my Father also.**
24. If I had not done among them
the works which none other man
did, they had not had sin: but
now have they both seen and
hated both me and my Father.
25. **But** *this cometh to pass,*
**that the word might be
fulfilled** that is written in their law,
**They hated me
without a cause.**
26. **But when the Comforter
is come,** whom I will send unto
you from the Father, *even* the
Spirit of truth, which proceedeth
from the Father,
he shall testify of me:
27. **And ye also shall bear
witness,** because ye have been
with me from the beginning.

CHAPTER 16

1. These things have I spoken unto
you, that ye should not be offended.
2. **They shall put you out
of the synagogues: yea,
the time cometh, that
whosoever killeth you
will think that he doeth
God service.**
3. And these things will they do
unto you, because they have
not known the Father, nor me.
4. **But these things have
I told you, that when the**

■ **time shall come,**
■ **ye may remember** that I
told you of them. And these things
I said not unto you at the beginning,
because I was with you.
5. But now I go my way to him that
sent me; and none of you asketh
me, Whither goest thou?
■ 6. **But because I have**
■ **said these things** unto you,
■ **sorrow hath filled**
■ **your heart.**
7. Nevertheless I tell you the truth;
■ **It is expedient** for you
■ **that I go away:**
■ **for if I go not** away,
■ **the Comforter will not**
■ **come** unto you; but if I depart,
I will send him unto you.
■ 8. **And** when he is come,
■ **he will reprove the world of**
■ **sin, and of righteousness,**
■ **and of judgment:**
9. Of sin, because they
believe not on me;
10. Of righteousness, because I go to
my Father, and ye see me no more;
11. Of judgment, because the prince
of this world is judged.
■ 12. **I have yet many**
■ **things to say** unto you,
■ **but ye cannot bear**
■ **them now.**
13. Howbeit
■ **when** he,
■ **the Spirit of truth, is come,**
■ **he will guide you into all**
■ **truth:** for he shall not speak
of himself; but whatsoever he
shall hear, *that* shall he speak:
■ **and he will shew you**
■ **things to come.**
■ 14. **He shall glorify me:**
for he shall receive of mine,
and shall shew *it* unto you.
15. All things that the Father
hath are mine: therefore said
I, that he shall take of mine,
and shall shew *it* unto you.
■ 16. **A little while, and ye**
■ **shall not see me: and**
■ **again, a little while, and ye**
■ **shall see me, because I go**

■ **to the Father.**
■ 17. **Then said some of his**
■ **disciples** among themselves,
■ **What is this that he saith**
■ **unto us,** A little while, and ye shall
not see me: and again, a little while,
and ye shall see me: and, Because
I go to the Father?
18. They said therefore, What is
this that he saith, A little while?
■ **we cannot tell**
■ **what he saith.**
■ 19. **Now Jesus knew that**
■ **they were desirous to**
■ **ask him, and said**
unto them, Do ye inquire among
yourselves of that I said, A little while,
and ye shall not see me: and again, a
little while, and ye shall see me?
20. Verily, verily,
■ **I say unto you, That ye shall**
■ **weep and lament,**
but the world shall rejoice:
and ye shall be sorrowful,
■ **but your sorrow shall**
■ **be turned into joy.**
■ 21. **A woman** when she is
■ **in travail hath sorrow,**
because her hour is come:
■ **but as soon as she is**
■ **delivered of the child,**
■ **she remembereth no**
■ **more the anguish,** for joy
that a man is born into the world.
■ 22. **And ye now therefore**
■ **have sorrow: but I will**
■ **see you again,**
and your heart shall rejoice,
■ **and your joy no**
■ **man taketh** from you.
23. And in that day ye shall ask me
nothing. Verily, verily, I say unto you,
■ **Whatsoever ye shall ask the**
■ **Father in my name,**
■ **he will give it you.**
24. Hitherto have ye asked
nothing in my name:
■ **ask, and ye shall receive,**
■ **that your joy may be full.**
25. These things have I spoken unto
you in proverbs: but the time cometh,
when I shall no more speak unto you
in proverbs, but I shall shew you

plainly of the Father.

26. At that day ye shall ask in my name: and I say not unto you, that I will pray the Father for you:

27. **For the Father himself loveth you, because ye have loved me,** and have believed that I came out from God.

28. I came forth from the Father, and am come into the world: again, **I leave the world, and go to the Father.**

29. **His disciples said** unto him, Lo, **now speakest thou plainly,** and speakest no proverb.

30. Now are we sure that **thou knowest all things,** and needest not that any man should ask thee: **by this we believe that thou camest forth from God.**

31. **Jesus answered** them, Do ye now believe?

32. **Behold, the hour cometh,** yea, is now come, **that ye shall be scattered,** every man to his own, **and shall leave me alone:** and yet I am not alone, because the Father is with me.

33. **These things I have spoken** unto you, **that in me ye might have peace. In the world ye shall have tribulation: but be of good cheer; I have overcome the world.**

CHAPTER 17

1. These words spake **Jesus,** and lifted up his eyes to heaven, and **said, Father, the hour is come; glorify thy Son,** that thy Son also may glorify thee:

2. As thou hast given him power over all flesh, **that he should give eternal life to as many as thou hast given him.**

3. **And this is life eternal, that they might know thee** the only true God, **and Jesus Christ,** whom thou hast sent.

4. I have glorified thee on the earth: **I have finished the work which thou gavest me** to do.

5. **And now, O Father, glorify thou me with** thine own self with **the glory which I had with thee before the world was.**

6. I have manifested thy name unto the men which thou gavest me out of the world: thine they were, and thou gavest them me; and they have kept thy word.

7. Now they have known that all things whatsoever thou hast given me are of thee.

8. **For I have given unto them the words which thou gavest me;** and they have received *them,* and have known surely that I came out from thee, and they have believed that thou didst send me.

9. I pray for them: **I pray not for the world, but for them which thou hast given me;** for they are thine.

10. And all mine are thine, and thine are mine; and I am glorified in them.

11. And now I am no more in the world, but these are in the world, and I come to thee. **Holy Father, keep through thine own name those whom thou hast given me, that they may be one, as we are.**

12. While I was with them in the world, I kept them in thy name: those that thou gavest me I have kept, and none of them is lost, but the son of perdition; that the scripture might be fulfilled.

13. **And now come I to thee;** and these things I speak in the world, **that they might have my joy fulfilled** in themselves.

14. I have given them thy word; and the world hath hated them, because they are not of the world, even as I

am not of the world.

15. **I pray not that thou shouldest take them out of the world, but** that thou shouldest **keep them from the evil.**

16. They are not of the world, even as I am not of the world.

17. **Sanctify them through thy truth: thy word is truth.**

18. As thou hast sent me into the world, even so have I also sent them into the world.

19. And for their sakes I sanctify myself, that they also might be sanctified through the truth.

20. **Neither pray I for these alone, but for them also which shall believe on me through their word;**

21. **That they all may be one;** as thou, Father, *art* in me, **and** I in thee, **that they also may be one in us: that the world may believe that thou hast sent me.**

22. And the glory which thou gavest me I have given them; that they may be one, even as we are one:

23. **I in them, and thou in me, that they may be made perfect in one;** and that the world may know that thou hast sent me, and hast loved them, as thou hast loved me.

24. **Father, I will that** they also, whom thou hast given me, be with me where I am; that **they may behold my glory,** which thou hast given me: **for thou lovedst me before the foundation of the world.**

25. O righteous Father, the world hath not known thee: but I have known thee, and these have known that thou hast sent me.

26. **And I have declared unto them thy name,** and will declare *it:* that the love wherewith thou hast loved me may be in them, and I in them.

CHAPTER 18

1. When Jesus had spoken these words, **he went forth with his disciples** over the brook Cedron, **where was a garden,** into the which he entered, and his disciples.

2. And Judas also, which betrayed him, knew the place: for Jesus ofttimes resorted thither with his disciples.

3. **Judas then, having received a band of men and officers** from the chief priests and Pharisees, **cometh thither** with lanterns and torches and weapons.

4. **Jesus** therefore, **knowing all things** that should come upon him, went forth, and **said unto them, Whom seek ye?**

5. **They answered** him, **Jesus of Nazareth. Jesus saith** unto them, **I am he. And Judas** also, which betrayed him, **stood with them.**

6. **As soon then as he** had **said** unto them, **I am he, they** went backward, and **fell to the ground.**

7. **Then asked he them again, Whom seek ye? And they said, Jesus** of Nazareth.

8. **Jesus answered, I have told you that I am he: if therefore ye seek me, let these go their way:**

9. **That the saying might be fulfilled,** which he spake, **Of them** which thou gavest me have **I lost none.**

10. Then Simon **Peter having a sword** drew it, and **smote the high priest's servant, and cut off his right ear.** The servant's name was Malchus.

11. **Then said Jesus** unto Peter, **Put up thy sword**

into the sheath:
the cup which my Father hath given me, shall I not drink it?
12. **Then** the band and the captain and officers of **the Jews took Jesus,** and bound him,
13. **And led him away to Annas first; for he was father in law to Caiaphas,** which was the high priest that same year.
14. Now Caiaphas was he, which gave counsel to the Jews, that it was expedient that one man should die for the people.
15. **And Simon Peter followed Jesus, and so did another disciple:** that disciple was known unto the high priest, and went in with Jesus into the palace of the high priest.
16. But Peter stood at the door without. **Then went out that other disciple,** which was known unto the high priest, **and spake unto her that kept the door, and brought in Peter.**
17. **Then saith the damsel** that kept the door unto Peter, **Art not thou also one of this man's disciples? He saith, I am not.**
18. **And the servants and officers** stood there, who had **made a fire** of coals; for it was cold: **and they warmed themselves: and Peter** stood with them, and **warmed himself.**
19. **The high priest then asked Jesus** of his disciples, and **of his doctrine.**
20. **Jesus answered** him, **I spake openly** to the world; I ever taught in the synagogue, and in the temple, whither the Jews always resort;

and in secret have I said nothing.
21. Why askest thou me? **ask them which heard me, what I have said** unto them: behold, they know what I said.
22. **And** when he had thus spoken, **one of the officers** which stood by **struck Jesus** with the palm of his hand, **saying, Answerest thou the high priest so?**
23. **Jesus answered** him, If I have spoken evil, bear witness of the evil: but if well, **why smitest thou me?**
24. **Now Annas had sent him** bound **unto Caiaphas the high priest.**
25. **And Simon Peter** stood and **warmed himself. They said** therefore unto him, **Art not thou also one of his disciples? He** denied *it,* and **said, I am not.**
26. **One of the servants of the high priest,** being *his* kinsman whose ear Peter cut off, **saith, Did not I see thee in the garden** with him?
27. **Peter then denied again: and** immediately **the cock crew.**
28. Then led they Jesus from Caiaphas unto the hall of judgment: and it was early; and they themselves went not into the judgment hall, lest they should be defiled; but that they might eat the passover.
29. **Pilate then** went out unto them, and **said, What accusation bring ye against this man?**
30. **They answered** and said unto him, **If he were not a malefactor, we would not have delivered him** up unto thee.
31. **Then said Pilate** unto them, Take ye him, and

judge him according to
your law. The Jews therefore
said unto him,
It is not lawful for us to put
any man to death:
32. That the saying of Jesus might be
fulfilled, which he spake, signifying
what death he should die.
33. Then Pilate entered into
the judgment hall again, and
called Jesus, and
said unto him,
Art thou the King
of the Jews?
34. Jesus answered him,
Sayest thou this thing
of thyself,
or did others tell it thee of me?
35. Pilate answered, Am I a
Jew? Thine own nation and the chief
priests have delivered thee unto me:
what hast thou done?
36. Jesus answered,
My kingdom is not of this
world: if my kingdom were of this
world, then would my servants fight,
that I should not be delivered to the
Jews: but now is my kingdom not
from hence.
37. Pilate therefore
said unto him,
Art thou a king then? Jesus
answered, Thou sayest that
I am a king. To this
end was I born, and for this
cause came I into the world,
that I should bear witness
unto the truth. Every one that
is of the truth heareth my voice.
38. Pilate saith unto him,
What is truth? And
when he had said this,
he went out again unto the
Jews, and saith unto them,
I find in him no fault at all.
39. But ye have a custom,
that I should release unto you
one at the passover:
will ye therefore that
I release unto you
the King of the Jews?
40. Then cried they
all again, saying,

Not this man, but Barabbas.
Now Barabbas was
a robber.

CHAPTER 19

1. Then Pilate
therefore took Jesus, and
scourged him.
2. And the soldiers platted
a crown of thorns, and put it
on his head, and they put
on him a purple robe,
3. And said, Hail, King
of the Jews! and they
smote him with their hands.
4. Pilate therefore went forth
again, and saith unto them,
Behold, I bring him forth to you,
that ye may know that
I find no fault in him.
5. Then came Jesus forth,
wearing the crown of thorns,
and the purple robe.
And Pilate saith unto them,
Behold the man!
6. When the chief
priests therefore
and officers saw him,
they cried out, saying,
Crucify him, crucify him.
Pilate saith unto them,
Take ye him, and crucify
him: for I find no fault in him.
7. The Jews answered
him, We have a law, and by our law
he ought to die, because
he made himself the
Son of God.
8. When Pilate therefore
heard that saying,
he was the more
afraid;
9. And went again into
the judgment hall, and
saith unto Jesus, Whence
art thou? But Jesus gave
him no answer.
10. Then saith Pilate unto him,
Speakest thou not unto
me? knowest thou not that
I have power to
crucify thee, and
have power to release thee?

11. **Jesus answered, Thou couldest have no power** at all against me, **except it were given thee from above:** therefore he that delivered me unto thee hath the greater sin. 12. And from thenceforth **Pilate sought to release him: but the Jews cried** out, saying, **If thou let this man go, thou art not Caesar's friend:** whosoever maketh himself a king speaketh against Caesar. 13. **When Pilate** therefore **heard** that saying, **he brought Jesus forth,** and sat down in the judgment seat in a place that is called the Pavement, but in the Hebrew, Gabbatha. 14. And it was the preparation of the passover, and about the sixth hour: **and he saith** unto the Jews, **Behold your King!** 15. **But they cried** out, Away with *him,* **away with him, crucify him. Pilate saith** unto them, **Shall I crucify your King? The chief priests answered, We have no king but Caesar.** 16. **Then delivered he him** therefore unto them **to be crucified. And they took Jesus,** and led *him* away. 17. **And he bearing his cross went forth into a place** called *the place* of a skull, which is **called** in the Hebrew **Golgotha:** 18. **Where they crucified him, and two other with him,** on either side one, and Jesus in the midst. 19. **And Pilate wrote a title, and put it on the cross.** And the writing was, **JESUS OF NAZARETH THE KING OF THE JEWS.** 20. This title then read many of the Jews: for the place where Jesus was crucified was nigh to the city: and it was written in Hebrew, *and* Greek, *and* Latin. 21. **Then said the chief priests** of the Jews to Pilate, **Write not, The King of the Jews; but that he said, I am King of the Jews.** 22. **Pilate answered, What I have written I have written.** 23. **Then the soldiers,** when they had crucified Jesus, **took his garments,** and made four parts, to every soldier a part; **and also his coat:** now the coat was **without seam,** woven from the top throughout. 24. **They said** therefore among themselves, **Let us not rend it, but cast lots for it,** whose it shall be: **that the scripture might be fulfilled,** which saith, **They parted my raiment** among them, **and for my vesture they did cast lots.** These things therefore the soldiers did. 25. **Now there stood by the cross of Jesus his mother,** and his mother's sister, Mary the *wife* of Cleophas, and Mary Magdalene. 26. **When Jesus therefore saw his mother, and the disciple** standing by, **whom he loved, he saith** unto his mother, **Woman, behold thy son!** 27. **Then saith he to the disciple, Behold thy mother!** And from that hour that disciple took her unto his own *home.* 28. **After this, Jesus** knowing that all things were now accomplished, that the scripture might be fulfilled, **saith, I thirst.** 29. Now there was set a vessel full of vinegar: **and they filled a sponge with vinegar,**

and put *it* upon hyssop,

■ **and put it to his mouth.**

■ 30. **When Jesus** therefore had

■ **received the vinegar,**

■ **he said, It is finished:**

and he bowed his head,

■ **and gave up the ghost.**

■ 31. **The Jews** therefore, because it
was the preparation, that the bodies
should not remain upon the cross on
the sabbath day, (for that sabbath day
was an high day,)

■ **besought Pilate that their**

■ **legs might be broken,**

and *that* they might be taken away.

■ 32. **Then** came

■ **the soldiers,** and

■ **brake the legs of the first,**

■ **and of the other which**

■ **was crucified with him.**

■ 33. **But** when they came to

■ **Jesus,** and saw that he

■ **was dead already,**

■ **they brake not his legs:**

■ 34. **But one** of the
soldiers with a spear

■ **pierced his side, and**

■ **forthwith came** there out

■ **blood and water.**

35. And he that saw *it* bare record,
and his record is true: and he
knoweth that he saith true,
that ye might believe.

■ 36. **For these things were**

■ **done, that the scripture**

■ **should be fulfilled, A bone**

■ **of him shall not be broken.**

37. **And** again another
scripture saith,

■ **They shall look on him**

■ **whom they pierced.**

■ 38. **And** after this

■ **Joseph of Arimathaea,**

being a disciple of Jesus, but
secretly for fear of the Jews,

■ **besought Pilate that**

■ **he might take away**

■ **the body** of Jesus:

■ **and Pilate gave him leave.**

He came therefore,
and took the body of Jesus.

■ 39. **And there came also**

■ **Nicodemus,** which at the first

came to Jesus by night,

■ **and brought a mixture**

■ **of myrrh and aloes,**

about an hundred pound *weight*.

■ 40. **Then took they**

■ **the body** of Jesus,

■ **and wound it in linen** clothes

■ **with the spices,** as the manner
of the Jews is to bury.

■ 41. **Now** in the place
where he was crucified

■ **there was a garden;**

■ **and in the garden**

■ **a new sepulchre,**

wherein was never man yet laid.

■ 42. **There laid they Jesus**

therefore because of the Jews'
preparation *day*; for the sepulchre
was nigh at hand.

CHAPTER 20

■ 1. **The first day of the**

■ **week cometh Mary**

■ **Magdalene** early,

■ **when it was yet dark,**

unto the sepulchre,

■ **and seeth the stone taken**

■ **away** from the sepulchre.

■ 2. **Then she runneth,**

and cometh

■ **to Simon Peter, and to**

■ **the other disciple,**

whom Jesus loved,

■ **and saith** unto them,

■ **They have taken away the**

■ **LORD** out of the sepulchre, and we
know not where they have laid him.

■ 3. **Peter** therefore went forth,

■ **and that other disciple,** and

■ **came to the sepulchre.**

4. So they ran both together: and

■ **the other disciple did**

■ **outrun Peter,**

and came first to the sepulchre.

■ 5. **And he stooping**

■ **down,** *and looking in,*

■ **saw the linen clothes**

■ **lying,** yet went he not in.

■ 6. **Then cometh Simon**

■ **Peter** following him,

■ **and went into the**

■ **sepulchre, and seeth**

■ **the linen** clothes lie,

JOHN 20   *Jesus resurrected*

7. And the napkin, that was about his head, not lying with the linen clothes, but wrapped together in a place by itself.

8. Then went in also that other disciple, which came first to the sepulchre, and he saw, and believed.

9. For as yet they knew not the scripture, that he must rise again from the dead.

10. Then the disciples went away again unto their own home.

11. But Mary stood without at the sepulchre weeping: and as she wept, she stooped down, *and* looked into the sepulchre,

12. And seeth two angels in white sitting, the one at the head, and the other at the feet, where the body of Jesus had lain.

13. And they say unto her, Woman, why weepest thou? She saith unto them, Because they have taken away my LORD, and I know not where they have laid him.

14. And when she had thus said, she turned herself back, and saw Jesus standing, and knew not that it was Jesus.

15. Jesus saith unto her, Woman, why weepest thou? whom seekest thou? She, supposing him to be the gardener, saith unto him, Sir, if thou have borne him hence, tell me where thou hast laid him, and I will take him away.

16. Jesus saith unto her, Mary. She turned herself, and saith unto him, Rabboni; which is to say, Master.

17. Jesus saith unto her, Touch me not; for I am not yet ascended to my Father: but go to my brethren, and say unto them, I ascend unto my Father, and your Father; and *to* my God, and your God.

18. Mary Magdalene came and told the disciples that she had seen the LORD, and that he had spoken these things unto her.

19. Then the same day at evening, being the first *day* of the week, when the doors were shut where the disciples were assembled for fear of the Jews, came Jesus and stood in the midst, and saith unto them, Peace be unto you.

20. And when he had so said, he shewed unto them his hands and his side. Then were the disciples glad, when they saw the LORD.

21. Then said Jesus to them again, Peace be unto you: as my Father hath sent me, even so send I you.

22. And when he had said this, he breathed on them, and saith unto them, Receive ye the Holy Ghost:

23. Whose soever sins ye remit, they are remitted unto them; and whose soever sins ye retain, they are retained.

24. But Thomas, one of the twelve, called Didymus, was not with them when Jesus came.

25. The other disciples therefore said unto him, We have seen the LORD. But he said unto them, Except I shall see in his hands the print of the nails, and put my finger into the print of the nails, and thrust my hand into his side, I will not believe.

26. **And after eight days again** his disciples were within, and Thomas with them: *then* came **Jesus,** the doors being shut, and **stood in the midst,** and said, Peace *be* unto you.

27. **Then saith he to Thomas, Reach hither thy finger, and behold my hands;** and reach hither thy hand, and thrust *it* into my side: and be not faithless, but believing.

28. **And Thomas answered** and said unto him, **My LORD and my God.**

29. **Jesus saith** unto him, Thomas, **because thou hast seen** me, **thou** hast **believed: blessed are they that have not seen, and** *yet* **have believed.**

30. **And many other signs truly did Jesus** in the presence of his disciples, **which are not written in this book:**

31. **But these are written, that ye might believe that Jesus is the Christ,** the Son of God; and that believing ye might have life through his name.

CHAPTER 21

1. After these things Jesus shewed himself again to the disciples at the sea of Tiberias; and on this wise shewed he *himself.*

2. **There were together Simon Peter, and Thomas** called Didymus, **and Nathanael** of Cana in Galilee, **and the sons of Zebedee, and two other** of his **disciples.**

3. **Simon Peter saith** unto them, **I go a fishing. They say** unto him, **We also go** with thee. **They went forth,** and entered into a ship immediately; **and** that night they **caught nothing.**

4. **But when the morning was** now **come, Jesus stood on the shore:** but the disciples knew not that it was Jesus.

5. **Then Jesus saith** unto them, **Children, have ye any meat? They answered** him, **No.**

6. **And he said** unto them, **Cast** the net **on the right side** of the ship, and ye shall find. **They cast** therefore, **and** now they **were not able to draw** it for **the multitude of fishes.**

7. **Therefore that disciple whom Jesus loved saith** unto Peter, **It is the Lord. Now when** Simon **Peter heard that** it was the Lord, **he** girt *his* fisher's coat *unto him,* (for he was naked,) and did **cast himself into the sea.**

8. **And the other disciples came** in a little ship; (for they were not far from land, but as it were two hundred cubits,) **dragging the net with fishes.**

9. As soon then as they were come to land, **they saw a fire** of coals there, **and fish laid thereon, and bread.**

10. Jesus saith unto them, Bring of the fish which ye have now caught.

11. Simon Peter went up, and drew the net to land full of great fishes, an hundred and fifty and three: and for all there were so many, yet was not the net broken.

12. **Jesus saith** unto them, **Come and dine. And** none of the disciples durst ask him, Who art thou? knowing that it was the Lord.

13. **Jesus** then cometh, and **taketh bread, and giveth them, and fish** likewise.

14. This is now the third time that

Jesus shewed himself to his disciples, after that he was risen from the dead.

15. **So when they had dined, Jesus saith** to **Simon** Peter, Simon, *son* of Jonas, **lovest thou me more than these? He saith** unto him, **Yea, Lord;** thou knowest that I love thee. **He saith** unto him, **Feed my lambs.**

16. **He saith** to him again **the second time, Simon,** *son* of Jonas, **lovest thou me? He saith** unto him, **Yea, Lord;** thou knowest that I love thee. **He saith** unto him, **Feed my sheep.**

17. **He saith** unto him the **third time, Simon,** *son* of Jonas, **lovest thou me? Peter was grieved** because he said unto him the third time, Lovest thou me? **And he said** unto him, **Lord,** thou knowest all things; **thou knowest that I love thee. Jesus saith** unto him, **Feed my sheep.**

18. Verily, verily, I say unto thee, **When thou wast young, thou** girdest thyself, and **walkedst whither thou wouldest: but when** thou shalt be **old,** thou shalt stretch forth thy hands, and **another shall gird thee, and carry thee whither thou wouldest not.**

19. **This spake he, signifying by what death he should glorify God.** And when he had spoken this, he saith unto him, Follow me.

20. **Then Peter,** turning about, **seeth the disciple** whom **Jesus loved** following; which also leaned on his breast at supper, and said, Lord, which is he that betrayeth thee?

21. **Peter** seeing him **saith** to Jesus, **Lord,** and **what shall this man do?**

22. **Jesus saith** unto him, **If I will that he tarry till I come, what is that to thee? follow thou me.**

23. Then went this saying abroad among the brethren, that that disciple should not die: yet Jesus said not unto him, He shall not die; but, If I will that he tarry till I come, what *is that* to thee?

24. This is the disciple which testifieth of these things, and wrote these things: and we know that his testimony is true.

25. **And there are also many other things which Jesus did, the** which, **if they should be written every one,** I suppose that even **the world itself could not contain the books that should be written. Amen.**

THE ACTS OF THE APOSTLES

BACKGROUND INFORMATION

Author: **Luke,** physician and Gentile companion of Paul. Date Written probably **between 60** and **64** A.D.

Number of:
Verses   1,007
Chapters   28
Total Words 24,250
Scan Words 11,781
Scan Words represent 48 % of Total Words

Theme: the ministry of the Holy Spirit in the early church as the gospel was spread in fulfillment of the Great Commission

OUTLINE OF THE ACTS

I.   **Christ's Commission, the Promise of the Holy Spirit, and His Ascension**
Chapter 1

II. Activities of **Peter, John and the Church at Jerusalem**
Chapter 2 - 5

III. Activities of **"The Twelve" and** of **Stephen**
Chapters 6 - 8

IV. Activities of Philip, Paul, Peter and other Christians in **Taking the Gospel to the Gentiles**
Chapters 9 - 12

V.   **Activities of Paul,** Barnabas and Silas until Paul's imprisonment in Rome
Chapters 13 - 28

CHAPTER 1

■ 1.The former treatise
■ have I made, O Theophilus,
■ of all that
■ Jesus began both
■ to do and teach,
■ 2. Until the day in which
■ he was taken up, after
■ that he through the Holy Ghost
■ had given commandments
■ unto the apostles
whom he had chosen:
■ 3. To whom also he shewed
■ himself alive after his passion
■ by many infallible proofs,
being seen of them forty days, and
speaking of the things pertaining to
the kingdom of God:
■ 4. And, being assembled together
■ with them,
■ commanded them
■ that they should not deparl
■ from Jerusalem, but wait for
■ the promise of the Father,
which, *saith he,* ye have heard of me.
5. For John truly baptized with water:
but ye shall be baptized with
■ the Holy Ghost
not many days hence.
■ 6. When they therefore
■ were come
■ together, they
■ asked of him, saying
■ Lord, wilt thou at
■ this time restore again
■ the kingdom to Israel?
■ 7. And he said unto them
■ It is not for you to know
■ the times or the seasons,
■ which the Father hath
■ put in his own power.
■ 8. But ye shall receive
■ power, atter that the Holy
■ Ghost is come upon you:
■ and ye shall be witnesses
■ unto me both in Jerusalem, and in
all Judaea, and in Samaria, and
■ unto the uttermost
■ part of the earth.
■ 9. And when he had
spoken these things,
■ while they beheld,
he was taken up; and

■ a cloud received him
■ out of their sight.
■ 10. And while they
■ looked stedfastly toward
heaven as he went up, behold,
■ two men stood by them
■ in white apparel;
■ 11 . Which also said,
Ye men of Galilee,
■ why stand ye
■ gazing up
■ into heaven? this
■ same Jesus, which is taken
up from you into heaven,
■ shall so come in like manner
■ as ye have seen
■ him go into heaven.
■ 12. Then returned they
■ unto Jerusalem from the
mount called Olivet, which is from
Jerusalem a sabbath day's journey.
■ 13. And when they
were come in, they
■ went up
■ into an upper room,
where abode both Peter, and James,
and John, and Andrew, Philip, and
Thomas, Bartholomew, and Matthew,
James *the son* of Alphaeus, and
Simon Zelotes, and Judas *the
brother* of James.
■ 14. These all continued
■ with one accord in prayer
■ andsupplication, with the
women, and Mary the mother of
Jesus, and with his brethren.
■ 15. And in those days
■ Peter stood
up in the midst of the disciples,
■ and said, (the number
of names together were about
an hundred and twenty,)
16. Men *and* brethren,
■ this scripture must needs
■ have been fulfilled,
which the Holy Ghost by the
mouth of David spake before
■ concerning Judas, which
was guide to them that took Jesus.
17. For he was numbered with us,
and had obtained part of this ministry.
■ 18. Now this man
■ purchased a field with the

reward of iniquity; and
falling headlong, he
burst asunder in the midst,
and all his bowels
gushed out.
19. And it was known
unto all the dwellers at
Jerusalem; insomuch
as that field is called
in their proper tongue,
Aceldama, that is to say,
The field of blood.
20. For it is written
in the book of Psalms,
Let his habitation
be desolate,
and let no man dwell therein:
and his bishopric
let another take.
21. Wherefore of these men
which have companied
with us all the time that the Lord
Jesus went in and out among us,
22. Beginning from the baptism
of John, unto that same day
that he was taken up from us,
must one be ordained to be
a witness with us of his resurrection.
23. And they appointed
two, Joseph called Barsabas,
who was surnamed Justus,
and Matthias.
24. And they prayed,
and said, Thou,
Lord, which knowest
the hearts of all *men,*
shew whether of these
two thou hast chosen,
25. That he may take
part of this ministry and
apostleship, from
which Judas by transgression
fell, that he might go to
his own place.
26. And they gave forth their lots;
and the lot fell upon
Matthias; and he was numbered
with the eleven apostles.

CHAPTER 2

1 . And when the day of
Pentecost was fully
come, they were all with
one accord in one place.
2. And suddenly there
came a sound from heaven
as of a rushing mighty wind,
and it filled all the house
where they were sitting.
3. And there
appeared unto them
cloven tongues like as of
fire, and it sat upon each of
them.
4. And they were all filled
with the Holy Ghost, and
began to speak with other
tongues, as the Spirit gave
them utterance.
5. And there were dwelling
at Jerusalem
Jews, devout men
out ot every
nation under heaven.
6. Now when this was noised
abroad, the multitude
came together,
and were confounded,
because that every
man heard them speak
in his own language.
7. And they were all
amazed and marvelled,
saying one to another, Behold,
are not all these which speak
Galilaeans?
8. And how hear we every
man in our own tongue,
wherein we were born?
9. Parthians, and Medes, and
Elamites, and the dwellers in
Mesopotamia, and in Judaea, and
Cappadocia, in Pontus, and Asia,
10. Phrygia, and Pamphylia, in Egypt,
and in the parts of Libya about
Cyrene, and strangers of Rome,
Jews and proselytes,
11. Cretes and Arabians, we do
hear them speak in our tongues
the wonderful works of God.
12. And they were
all amazed, and were
in doubt, saying one to another
What meaneth this?
13. Others mocking said,
These men are full

of new wine. 14. **But Peter,** standing up with the eleven, **lifted up his voice, and said** unto them, Ye men of Judaea, and all *ye* that dwell at Jerusalem, be this known unto you, and **hearken to my words:** 15. **For these are not drunken,** as ye suppose, seeing it is *but* the third hour of the day. 16. **But this is that** which was **spoken by** the prophet **Joel;** 17. And it shall come to pass **in the last days saith God, I will pour out of my Spirit upon all flesh:** and your sons and your daughters shall prophesy, and your young men shall see visions, and your old men shall dream dreams 18. And on my servants and on my handmaidens I will pour out in those days of my Spirit; and they shall prophesy: 19. **And I will shew wonders** in heaven above **and signs** in ihe earth beneath; blood, and fire, and vapour of smoke: 20. The sun shall be turned into darkness, and the moon into blood, before the great and notable day of the Lord come: 21 . **And** it shall come to pass, *that* **whosoever shall call on the name of the Lord shall be saved.** 22. Ye men of Israel, **hear these words; Jesus** of Nazareth, **a man approved of God** among you **by miracles** and wonders and signs, **which God did by him** in the midst of you, **as ye** yourselves also **know:** 23. **Him,** being delivered by the determinate counsel and foreknowledge ot God, **ye have taken, and** by wicked hands have

crucified and slain: 24. **Whom God hath raised up,** having loosed the pains of death because it was not possible that he should be holden of it. 25. **For David speaketh concerning him,** I foresaw the Lord always before my face, for he is on my right hand, that I should not be moved: 26. Therefore did my heart rejoice, and my tongue was glad; moreover also my flesh shall rest in hope: 27. **Because thou wilt not leave my soul in hell, neither wilt thou suffer thine Holy One to see corruption.** 28. Thou hast made known to me the ways of life; thou shalt make me full of joy with thy countenance. 29 Men *and* brethren, let me freely speak unto you of the patriarch **David,** that he **is both dead and buried, and his sepulchre is with us** unto this day. 30. **Therefore being a prophet, and knowing that God had sworn** with an oath to him **that of the fruit of his loins,** according to the flesh, **he would raise up Christ** to sit on his throne 31 . **He** seeing this before **spake of the resurrection of Christ,** that his soul was not left in hell, neither his flesh did see corruption. 32. **This Jesus hath God raised up,** whereof we all are witnesses. 33. **Therefore being** by the right hand of God **exalted,** and having received of the Father the promise of the Holy Ghost **he hath shed forth this, which ye now see and hear.** 34. **For David is not ascended into the**

■ **heavens:** but he saith himself,
The Lord said unto my Lord,
Sit thou on my right hand,
35. Until I make thy foes thy footstool.
■ 36. **Therefore** let all the house of
Israel know assuredly, that
■ **God hath made the same**
■ **Jesus, whom ye have**
■ **crucified, both Lord**
■ **and Christ.**
■ 37. **Now when they**
■ **heard** *this*
■ **they were pricked**
in their heart,
■ **and said** unto Peter
and to the rest of the
apostles, Men *and* brethren
■ **what shall we do?**
■ 38. **Then Peter said** unto them,
■ **Repent, and be**
■ **baptized** every one of you
■ **in the name of Jesus**
■ **Christ for the remission**
■ **of sins, and ye shall**
■ **receive** the gift of
■ **the Holy Ghost.**
■ 39. **For the promise is**
■ **unto** you, and to your children,
and to all that are afar off, *even*
■ **as many as the LORD** our God
■ **shall call.**
40. And with many other words
did he testify and exhort, saying, Save
yourselves from this
untoward generation.
■ 41. **Then they that** gladly
■ **received his word were**
■ **baptized: and** the same day
■ **there were added unto**
■ **them about three**
■ **thousand souls.**
■ 42. **And they**
■ **continued** stedfastly
■ **in the apostles' doctrine** and
■ **fellowship,** and in
■ **breaking** of
■ **bread, and** in
■ **prayers.**
43. And fear came upon every soul:
■ **and many wonders** and signs
■ **were done by the apostles.**
■ 44. **And all that believed**
were together, and

■ **had all things common;**
■ 45. **And sold their**
■ **possessions** and goods,
■ **and parted them** to all *men,*
■ **as every man had need.**
■ 46. **And they continuing**
■ **daily with one accord**
in the temple, and breaking bread
from house to house, did eat
their meat with gladness and
singleness of heart,
47. Praising God, and having
favour with all the people.
■ **And the Lord added**
■ **to the church daily**
such as should be saved.

CHAPTER 3

■ 1. **Now Peter and John**
■ **went** up together
■ **into the temple at the hour**
■ **of prayer,** *being* the ninth *hour.*
■ 2. **And a certain man lame**
■ **from his mother's womb**
■ **was** carried, whom they
■ **laid daily at the gate**
of the temple which is called
■ **Beautiful, to ask alms**
of them that entered into the temple;
■ 3. **Who seeing Peter and**
■ **John** about to go into the temple
■ **asked an alms.**
■ 4. **And Peter,** fastening his eyes
upon him with John,
■ **said, Look on us.**
5. And he gave heed unto them, expecting to receive something of them.
6. Then Peter said,
■ **Silver and gold**
■ **have I none; but**
■ **such as I have give**
■ **I thee: In the name**
■ **of Jesus Christ** of Nazareth
■ **rise** up
■ **and walk.**
■ 7. **And he took him**
by the right hand,
■ **and lifted him up:**
and immediately his feet and ankle
bones received strength.
■ 8. **And he leaping up**
stood, and walked, and
■ **entered** with them into

187

the temple, walking, and
leaping, and praising God.
9. And all the people
saw him walking and praising God:
10. And they knew that it was he
which sat for alms at the Beautiful
gate of the temple: and they
were filled with wonder
and amazement
at that which had
happened unto him.
11. And as the lame man which was
healed held Peter and John, all
the people ran together
unto them in the porch that is called
Solomon's, greatly wondering.
12. And when Peter saw it,
he answered
unto the people, Ye men of Israel,
why marvel ye at this?
or why look ye so earnestly on us, as
though by our own power or holiness
we had made this man to walk?
13. The God of
Abraham, and of
Isaac, and of
Jacob, the God of our fathers,
hath glorified his Son Jesus;
whom ye delivered up, and
denied him in the
presence of Pilate, when he was
determined to let *him* go.
14. But ye denied the
Holy One and the Just,
and desired a murderer
to be granted unto you;
15. And killed the Prince
of life, whom God hath
raised from the dead;
whereof we are witnesses.
16. And his name through
faith in his name hath
made this man strong,
whom ye see and know: yea, the
faith which is by him hath given
him this perfect soundness
in the presence of you all.
17. And now, brethren
I wot that through
ignorance ye did it,
as *did* also your rulers.
18. But those things, which
God before had shewed

by the mouth of all
his prophets, that
Christ should suffer,
he hath so fulfilled.
19. Repent ye therefore,and
be converted, that your sins
may be blotted out,
when the times of refreshing shall
come from the presence of the Lord.
20. And he shall send
Jesus Christ,
which before was preached unto
you: 21. Whom the heaven must
receive until the times of restitution
of all things
which God hath spoken
by the mouth of all his holy
prophets since the
world began.
22. For Moses truly
said unto the fathers
A prophet shall the Lord
your God
raise up unto you of your
brethren, like unto me; him
shall ye hear in all things
whatsoever he shall say unto you.
23. And it shall come to
pass, that every soul,
which will not hear that
prophet, shall
be destroyed
from among the people.
24. Yea, and all the prophets from
Samuel and those that follow after,
as many as have spoken, have
likewise foretold of these days.
25. Ye are the children
of the prophets, and
of the covenant which God
made with our fathers, saying
unto Abraham, And in thy
seed shall all the kindreds of the
earth be blessed.
26. Unto you first God,
having raised up his Son
Jesus, sent him to bless
you, in turning away every
one of you from his iniquities.

CHAPTER 4

1. And as they spake
unto the people,

■ **the priests,**
and the captain of the temple,
■ **and** the
■ **Sadducees, came**
■ **upon them,**
■ 2. **Being grieved that they**
taught the people, and
■ **preached through Jesus**
■ **the resurrection** from the dead.
■ 3. **And they laid hands**
■ **on them, and put them**
■ **in hold** unto the next day:
for it was now eventide.
■ 4. **Howbeit many** of them
■ **which heard** the word
■ **believed; and the**
■ **number of** the
■ **men was about**
■ **five thousand.**
5. And it came to pass on the
morrow that their rulers, and
elders, and scribes
■ 6. **And Annas the**
■ **high priest,** and
■ **Caiaphas,** and
■ **John, and Alexander,**
and as many as were of the
kindred of the high priest,
■ **were gathered**
■ **together** at Jerusalem.
■ 7. **And when**
they had set them in the midst
■ **they ask By what**
■ **power, or** by what
■ **name, have ye done this?**
■ 8. **Then Peter, filled with the**
■ **Holy Ghost, said**
unto them, Ye rulers of the
people, and elders of Israel,
■ 9. **If we** this day
■ **be examined of the**
■ **good deed done to**
■ **the impotent man,**
by what means he is made whole;
■ 10. **Be it known unto**
you all, and to all the people of
■ **Israel, that by** the name of
■ **Jesus Christ** of Nazareth,
■ **whom ye crucified, whom**
■ **God raised from the dead**
■ **even by him doth this man**
■ **stand** here before you whole.
■ 11. **This is the stone** which was

set at nought of you builders,
■ **which is become the**
■ **head of the corner.**
■ 12. **Neither is there**
■ **salvation in any other: for**
■ **there is none other name**
under heaven given among men,
■ **whereby we must**
■ **be saved.**
■ 13. **Now when they saw**
■ **the boldness of Peter**
■ **and John,** and perceived
that they were unlearned
and ignorant men,
■ **they marvelled; and they**
■ **took knowledge** of them,
■ **that they had been**
■ **with Jesus.**
■ 14. **And beholding**
■ **the man** which was
■ **healed** standing with them,
■ **they could say**
■ **nothing** against it.
■ 15. **But** when they had commanded
them to go aside out of the council,
■ **they conferred among**
■ **themselves,**
■ 16. **Saying, What**
■ **shall we do** to these
men? for that indeed
■ **a** notable
■ **miracle hath been done**
by them *is* manifest to all them
that dwell in Jerusalem;
■ **and we cannot deny it.**
■ 17. **But that it spread no**
■ **further** among the people,
■ **let us** straitly
■ **threaten them,** that they speak
henceforth to no man in this name.
■ 18. **And they** called them, and
■ **commanded them**
■ **not to speak** at all
■ **nor teach in the**
■ **name of Jesus.**
■ 19. **But Peter and John**
■ **answered** and said unto them,
■ **Whether it be right**
in the sight of God
■ **to hearken unto you more**
■ **than unto God, judge ye.**
■ 20. **For we cannot but**
■ **speak**the things which we

have seen and heard.

21. **So when they** had **further threatened them, they let them go, finding nothing how they might punish them because of the people: for all** *men* **glorified God** for that which was done.

22. For the man was above forty years old, on whom this miracle of healing was shewed.

23. **And being let go, they went** to their own company, **and reported all that the chief priests and elders had said** unto them.

24. **And** when they heard that, **they lifted up their voice to God** with one accord, **and said, Lord, thou art God, which hast made** heaven, and earth, and the sea, and **all** that in them is:

25. Who by the mouth of thy servant David hast said, Why did the heathen rage, and the people imagine vain things?

26. The kings of the earth stood up, and the rulers were gathered together against the Lord, and against his Christ.

27. For of a truth against thy holy child Jesus, whom thou hast anointed, both Herod, and Pontius Pilate, with the Gentiles, and the people of Israel, were gathered together,

28. For to do whatsoever thy hand and thy counsel determined before to be done.

29. **And now, Lord, behold their threatenings: and grant** unto **thy servants, that with** all **boldness they may speak thy word,**

30. By stretching forth thine hand to heal; **and that signs and wonders may be done by the name of** thy holy child **Jesus.**

31. **And when they had prayed, the place was shaken** where they were assembled together; **and they were all filled with the Holy Ghost,** and they spake the word of God with boldness.

32. **And the multitude** of them **that believed were of one heart and** of one soul: neither said any *of them* that aught of the things which he possessed was his own; but they **had all things common.**

33. **And with great power gave the apostles witness of the resurrection** of the Lord Jesus: and great grace was upon them all.

34. **Neither was there any** among them **that lacked: for as many as were possessors of lands or houses sold them, and brought the prices** of the things that were sold,

35. **And laid them down at the apostles' feet: and distribution was made unto every man** according **as he had need.**

36. And Joses, who by the apostles was surnamed Barnabas, (which is, being interpreted, The son of consolation,) a Levite, *and* of the country of Cyprus,

37. Having land, sold *it,* and brought the money, and laid *it* at the apostles' feet.

CHAPTER 5

1. **But** a certain man named **Ananias, with Sapphira his wife, sold a possession,**

2. **And kep back part of the price,** his wife also being privy *to it,* **and brought** a certain **part, and laid it at the apostles' feet.**

3. **But Peter said, Ananias, why hath Satan filled thine heart to lie to the Holy Ghost, and to keep back part of the price** of the land?

190

4. Whiles it remained, was it not thine own? and after it was sold, was it not in thine own power? why hast thou conceived this thing in thine heart?

thou hast not lied unto men, but unto God.

5. **And Ananias hearing these words fell down, and gave up the ghost:** and great fear came on all them that heard these things.

6. **And the young men** arose, wound him up, and carried *him* out, and **buried him.**

7. **And** it was about the space of **three hours after,** when **his wife, not knowing what was done, came in.**

8. **And Peter answered unto her, Tell me whether ye sold the land for so much? And she said, Yea,** for so much.

9. **Then Peter said** unto her, **How is it that ye have agreed together to tempt the Spirit of the Lord?** behold, the feet of them which have buried thy husband *are* at the door, and shall carry thee out.

10. **Then fell she down** straightway at his feet, **and yielded up the ghost:** and the young men came in, and found her dead, and, carrying *her* forth, buried *her by* her husband.

11 . **And great fear came upon all the church,** and upon as many as heard these things.

12. **And by the hands of the apostles were many signs and wonders wrought** among the people; (and they were all with one accord in Solomon's porch. 13. And of the rest durst no man join himself to them: but the people magnified them.

14. **And believers were** the more **added to the Lord,** multitudes both of men and women.)

15. **Insomuch that they brought** forth **the sick into the streets,** and laid *them* on beds and couches **that at the least the shadow of Peter passing by might overshadow** some of **them.**

16. **There came** also **a multitude out of the cities** round about unto Jerusalem, **bringing sick** folks, **and them** which were vexed **with unclean spirits: and they were healed** every one.

17. **Then the high priest** rose up, **and all** they **that were with him,** (which is the sect of the Sadducees,) and **were filled with indignation,**

18. **And laid their hands on the apostles, and put them in** the common **prison .**

19. **But the angel of the Lord** by night **opened the prison doors,** and brought them forth, **and said,**

20. **Go, stand and speak in the temple** to the people all the words of this life.

21. **And** when they heard *that* **they entered** into **the temple** early in the morning, **and taught. But the high priest came,** and they that were with him **and called the council** together, and all the senate of the children of Israel, **and sent to the prison to have them brought.**

22. **But when the officers** came, and **found them not in the prison, they returned** and told,

23. **Saying, The prison** truly **found we shut with all safety,** and the keepers standing without before the doors: **but** when we had opened,

■ we found no man within.

24. Now when the high priest and the captain of the temple and the chief priests heard these things, they doubted of them whereunto this would grow.

■ 25. **Then came**
■ **one** and told them,
■ **saying,** Behold,
■ **the men** whom
■ **ye put in prison are**
standing in the temple, and
■ **teaching the people.**
■ 26. **Then went the**
■ **captain** with the officers,
■ **and brought them** without
violence: for they feared the people, lest they should have been stoned.
■ 27. **And** when they had brought them, they set *them* before the council: and
■ **the high priest asked them,**
■ 28. **Saying, Did not we** straitly
■ **command you that ye**
■ **should not teach in this**
■ **name?** and, behold, ye have filled Jerusalem with your doctrine, and intend to bring this man's blood upon us.
■ 29 **Then Peter and the other**
■ **apostles answered** and said,
■ **We ought to obey God**
■ **rather than men.**
■ 30. **The God of our fathers**
■ **raised up Jesus,**
whom ye slew and hanged on a tree.
■ 31. **Him hath God**
■ **exalted** with his right hand
■ **to be a Prince and a**
■ **Saviour,** for to give repentance to Israel, and forgiveness of sins.
■ 32. **And we are his**
■ **witnesses** of these things;
■ **and so is also the Holy**
■ **Ghost,** whom God hath given to them that obey him.
■ 33. **When they heard that,**
■ **they** were cut *to the heart,* and
■ **took counsel to slay them.**
■ 34. **Then stood**
there up one in the council,
■ **a Pharisee, named**
■ **Gamaliel, a doctor of**

■ **the law,** had
■ **in reputation among all**
■ **the people,** and commanded to put the apostles forth a little space;
■ 35. **And said unto**
■ **them,** Ye men of Israel,
■ **take heed to yourselves**
■ **what ye intend to do**
as touching these men.
■ 36. **For before these days**
■ **rose up Theudas,**
boasting himself to be somebody; to whom a number of men, about four hundred, joined themselves:
■ **who was slain; and all, as**
■ **many as obeyed him, were**
■ **scattered,** and brought to nought.
■ 37. **After this man rose** up
■ **Judas of Galilee**
in the days of the taxing, and drew away much people after him:
■ **he also perished;**
and all, *even* as many as obeyed him, were dispersed.
■ 38. **And now I say** unto you,
■ **Refrain from these men,**
and let them alone:
■ **for if** this counsel or
■ **this work be of men, it**
■ **will come to nought:**
■ 39. **But if it be of God, ye**
■ **cannot overthrow it; lest**
■ **haply ye** be found even to
■ **fight against God.**
■ 40. **And to him they agreed:**
■ **and when they had called**
■ **the apostles, and beaten**
■ **them, they commanded**
■ **that they should not**
■ **speak** in the name
■ **of Jesus, and let them go.**
■ 41. **And they departed**
from the presence of the council,
■ **rejoicing that they were**
■ **counted worthy to suffer**
■ **shame for his name.**
■ 42. **And daily in the temple,**
■ **and in every house, they**
■ **ceased not to teach and**
■ **preach Jesus Christ.**

CHAPTER 6

| | 1. And in those days, when the

number of the disciples was multiplied,

there arose a murmuring of the Grecians against the Hebrews, because their widows were neglected in the daily ministration.

2. Then the twelve called the multitude of the disciples *unto them,* and said, It is not reason that we should leave the word of God, and serve tables.

3. Wherefore, brethren, look ye out among you seven men of honest report, full of the Holy Ghost and wisdom, whom we may appoint over this business.

4. But we will give ourselves continually to prayer, and to the ministry of the word.

5. And the saying pleased the whole multitude: and they chose Stephen, a man full of faith and of the Holy Ghost, and Philip, and Prochorus, and Nicanor, and Timon, and Parmenas, and Nicolas a proselyte of Antioch:

6. Whom they set before the apostles: and when they had prayed, they laid their hands on them.

7. And the word of God increased; and the number of the disciples multiplied in Jerusalem greatly; and a great company of the priests were obedient to the faith.

8. And Stephen, full of faith and power, did great wonders and miracles among the people.

9. Then there arose certain of the synagogue, which is called the synagogue of the Libertines, and Cyrenians and Alexandrians, and of them of Cilicia and of Asia, disputing with Stephen.

10. And they were not able to resist the wisdom and the spirit by which he spake.

11. Then they suborned men, which said, We have heard him speak blasphemous words against Moses, and *against* God.

12. And they stirred up the people, and the elders, and the scribes, and came upon him, and caught *him* and brought him to the council,

13. And set up false witnesses, which said, This man ceaseth not to speak blasphemous words against this holy place, and the law:

14. For we have heard him say, that this Jesus of Nazareth shall destroy this place, and shall change the customs which Moses delivered us

15. And all that sat in the council, looking stedfastly on him, saw his face as it had been the face of an angel.

CHAPTER 7

1 Then said the high priest, Are these things so?

2. And he said, Men, brethren, and fathers, hearken The God of glory appeared unto our father Abraham, when he was in Mesopotamia, before he dwelt in Charran,

3. And said unto him, Get thee out of thy country, and from thy kindred, and come into the land which I shall shew thee.

4. **Then** came he out of the land of the Chaldaeans, and dwelt in Charran: and from thence, when his father was dead, **he removed him into this land, wherein ye now dwell.**

5. And he gave him none inheritance in it, no, not *so much as* to set his foot on: yet he promised that he would give it to him for a possession, and to his seed after him, when *as yet* he had no child.

6. **And God spake** on this wise, **That his seed should sojourn in a strange land and that they should bring them into bondage,** and entreat *them* evil four hundred years.

7. And the nation to whom they shall be in bondage will I judge, said God: **and after that shall they** come forth, and **serve me in this place.**

8. **And he gave him the covenant of circumcision: and so Abraham begat Isaac,** and circumcised him the eighth day; **and Isaac** *begat* **Jacob; and Jacob** *begat* **the twelve patriarchs.**

9. **And the patriarchs,** moved with envy, **sold Joseph into Egypt: but God** was with him,

10. And delivered him out of all his afflictions, and **gave him favour and** wisdom in the sight of **Pharaoh** king of Egypt; and he **made him governor over Egypt** and all his house.

11 . **Now there came a dearth** over all the land of Egypt and Chanaan, and great affliction: and our fathers found no sustenance.

12. **But when Jacob heard that there was corn in Egypt, he sent out our fathers first.**

13. And at the second *time* Joseph was made known to his brethren; and Joseph's kindred was made known unto Pharaoh.

14. **Then sent Joseph, and called his father Jacob to him, and all his kindred,** threescore and fifteen souls.

15. **So Jacob** went down into Egypt, and **died,** he, **and our fathers,**

16. **And were** carried over into Sychem, and **laid in the sepulchre that Abraham bought** for a sum of money of the sons of Emmor *the father* of Sychem.

17. **But when the time of the promise drew nigh,** which God had sworn to Abraham, **the people grew and multiplied in Egypt,**

18. **Till another king arose, which knew not Joseph.**

19. **The same dealt subtilly with our kindred,** and evil entreated our fathers, so that they cast out their young children, to the end they might not live.

20. **In which time Moses was born,** and was exceeding fair, and nourished up in his father's house three months:

21 . **And** when he was cast out, **Pharaoh's daughter** took him up, and **nourished him for her own son.**

22. **And Moses was learned in all the wisdom of the Egyptians,** and was mighty in words and in deeds.

23. **And when he was** full **forty** years old, **it came into his heart to visit his brethren** the children of Israel.

24. **And seeing one of them suffer wrong, he defended** him, and avenged him that was oppressed, **and smote the Egyptian:**

25. **For he supposed his brethren** would have

understood how that **God by his hand would deliver them: but they understood not.**

26. And the next day he shewed himself unto them as they strove, and would have set them at one again, saying, Sirs, ye are brethren; why do ye wrong one to another?

27. But he that did his neighbour wrong thrust him away, saying, Who made thee a ruler and a judge over us?

28. Wilt thou kill me, as thou diddest the Egyptian yesterday?

29 **Then fled Moses** at this saying, **and was a stranger in** the land of **Madian, where he begat two sons.**

30. **And when forty years**were **expired, there appeared to him in** the wilderness of **mount Sina an angel of the Lord in a flame of fire in a bush.**

31. **When Moses saw it,** he wondered at the sight: and as he drew near to behold *it*, **the voice of the LORD came** unto him

32. **Saying, I am the God of thy fathers,** the God of Abraham, and the God of Isaac, and the God of Jacob. Then Moses trembled, and durst not behold.

33. **Then said the Lord** to him, **Put off thy shoes** from thy feet: **for the place** where thou standest **is holy ground.**

34. I have seen, **I have seen the affliction of my people** which is **in Egypt,** and I have heard their groaning, and am come down to deliver them. **And** now come **I will send thee into Egypt.**

35. **This Moses** whom they refused, saying, Who made thee a ruler and a judge? the same **did God send** *to be* a ruler and a deliverer by the hand of the angel which appeared to him in the bush.

36. **He brought them out,** **after that he had shewed wonders and signs** in the land of Egypt, and in the Red sea, and in the wilderness forty years.

37. **This is that Moses, which said** unto the children of Israel, **A prophet shall the Lord your God raise up** unto you of your brethren **like unto me; him shall ye hear.**

38. **This is he,** that was in the church in the wilderness with the angel which spake to him in the mount Sina, and *with* our fathers: who received the lively oracles to give unto us:

39. **To whom our fathers would not obey,** but thrust *him* from them, **and** in their hearts **turned back again** into Egypt,

40. **Saying unto Aaron Make us gods to go before us:** for *as for* this Moses, which brought us out of the land of Egypt, we wot not what is become of him.

41. **And they made a calf** in those days **and offered sacrifice unto the idol,** and rejoiced in the works of their own hands.

42 **Then God** turned, and **gave them up to worship the host ot heaven;** as it is written in the book of the prophets, O ye house of Israel, have ye offered to me slain beasts and sacrifices *by the space* of forty years in the wilderness?

43 Yea, ye took up the tabernacle of Moloch, and the star of your god Remphan, figures which ye made to worship them: and I will carry you away beyond Babylon.

44 **Our fathers had the tabernacle of witness**

in the wilderness, as he had appointed, speaking unto Moses, that he should make it according to the fashion that he had seen.

45 Which also our fathers that came after brought in with Jesus into the possession of the Gentiles, whom God drave out before the face of our fathers, unto the days of

David;

46 Who found favour before God, and desired to find a tabernacle for the God of Jacob.

47 But Solomon built him an house.

48 Howbeit the most High dwelleth not in temples made with hands;

as saith the prophet

49 Heaven is my throne, and earth *is* my footstool: what house will ye build me? saith the Lord: or what *is* the place of my rest?

50 Hath not my hand made all these things?

51 Ye stiffnecked and uncircumcised in heart and ears ye do always resist the Holy Ghost: as your fathers did, so do ye.

52 Which of the prophets have not your fathers persecuted? and they have slain them which shewed before of the coming of the Just One; of whom ye have been now the betrayers and murderers:

53 Who have received the law by the disposition of angels, and have not kept *it*.

54 When they heard these things, they were cut to the heart, and they gnashed on him with *their* teeth.

55 But he, being full of the Holy Ghost, looked up stedfastly

into heaven, and saw the glory of God, and Jesus standing on the right hand of God

56 And said, Behold, I see the heavens opened, and the Son of man standing on the right hand of God.

57 Then they cried out with a loud voice, and stopped their ears, and ran upon him with one accord,

58 And cast him out of the city, and stoned him and the witnesses laid down their clothes at a young man's feet, whose name was Saul.

59 And they stoned Stephen, calling upon *God*, and saying, Lord Jesus, receive my spirit.

60 And he kneeled down, and cried with a loud voice Lord, lay not this sin to their charge. And when he had said this, he fell asleep.

CHAPTER 8

1. And Saul was consenting unto his death. And at that time there was a great persecution against the church which was at Jerusalem; and they were all scattered abroad throughout the regions of Judaea and Samaria, except the apostles.

2. And devout men carried Stephen to *his burial,* and made great lamentation over him.

3. As for Saul, he made havock of the church, entering into every house, and haling men and women committed them to prison.

4. Therefore they that were scattered abroad went every where preaching the word.

5. Then Philip went down to the city of Samaria, and preached

Christ unto them.
6. **And the people** with one accord **gave heed unto those things which Philip spake,** hearing and seeing the miracles which he did.
7. **For unclean spirits,** crying with loud voice, **came out of many** that were possessed *with them:* **and many** taken with palsies, and that were lame, **were healed.**
8. **And there was great joy in that city.**
9. **But** there was a certain man, called **Simon, which beforetime** in the same city used sorcery, and **bewitched the people of Samaria, giving out that himself was some great one:**
10. **To whom they all gave heed,** from the least to the greatest **saying, This man is the great power of God.**
11. And to him they had regard, because that of long time he had bewitched them with sorceries.
12. **But when they believed Philip** preaching the things **concerning the kingdom of God, and** the name of **Jesus Christ, they were baptized,** both men and women.
13. **Then Simon himself believed also: and when he was baptized, he continued with Philip,** and wondered, beholding the miracles and signs which were done.
14. **Now when the apostles** which were at Jerusalem **heard** that Samaria had received the word of God, **they sent unto them Peter and John:**
15. **Who,** when they were come down **prayed** for them,

that they might receive the Holy Ghost:
16. **(For as yet he was fallen upon none of them: only they were baptized** in the name of the Lord Jesus.)
17. **Then laid they their hands on them, and they received the Holy Ghost.**
18. **And when Simon saw** that through laying on of the apostles' hands the Holy Ghost was given, **he offered them money,**
19. **Saying, Give me also this power,** that on whomsoever I lay hands, he may receive the Holy Ghost.
20. **But Peter said** unto him, **Thy money perish with thee**, because thou hast thought that the gift of God may be purchased with money.
21. **Thou hast neither part nor lot in this matter: for thy heart is not right** in the sight of God.
22. **Repent therefore** of this thy wickedness, **and pray God, if** perhaps **the thought of thine heart may be forgiven thee.**
23. For I perceive that thou art in the gall of bitterness, and *in* the bond of iniquity.
24. **Then answered Simon,** and said, **Pray ye to the LORD** for me, **that none of these things** which ye have spoken **come upon me.**
25. **And they,** when they had testified and preached the word of the Lord, **returned** to Jerusalem, **and preached the gospel in many villages of the Samaritans.**
26. **And the angel of the Lord spake unto Philip, saying,** Arise, and **go** toward the south unto the way that goeth down from Jerusalem **unto Gaza,** which is desert.

27. And he arose and went: and, behold, a man of Ethiopia, an eunuch of great authority under Candace queen of the Ethiopians, who had the charge of all her treasure, and had come to Jerusalem for to worship,

28. Was returning, and sitting in his chariot read Esaias the prophet.

29 Then the Spirit said unto Philip, Go near, and join thyself to this chariot.

30. And Philip ran thither to *him,* and heard him read the prophet Esaias, and said, Understandest thou what thou readest?

31. And he said, How can I, except some man should guide me? And he desired Philip that he would come up and sit with him.

32. The place of the scripture which he read was this, He was led as a sheep to the slaughter; and like a lamb dumb before his shearer, so opened he not his mouth:

33. In his humiliation his judgment was taken away: and who shall declare his generation? for his life is taken from the earth.

34. And the eunuch answered Philip, and said, I pray thee, of whom speaketh the prophet this? of himself or of some other man?

35. Then Philip opened his mouth, and began at the same scripture, and preached unto him Jesus.

36. And as they went on *their* way, they came unto a certain water: and the eunuch said, See, here is water; what doth hinder me to be baptized?

37. And Philip said, If thou believest with all thine heart, thou mayest and he answered and said,

I believe that Jesus Christ is the Son of God.

38. And he commanded the chariot to stand still: and they went down both into the water, both Philip and the eunuch and he baptized him.

39. And when they were come up out of the water, the Spirit of the Lord caught away Philip, that the eunuch saw him no more: and he went on his way rejoicing.

40. But Philip was found at Azotus: and passing through he preached in all the cities till he came to Caesarea.

CHAPTER 9

1. And Saul, yet breathing out threatenings and slaughter against the disciples of the Lord, went unto the high priest,

2. And desired of him letters to Damascus to the synagogues that if he found any of this way, whether they were men or women, he might bring them bound unto Jerusalem.

3. And as he journeyed, he came near Damascus: and suddenly there shined round about him a light from heaven:

4. And he fell to the earth, and heard a voice saying unto him Saul, Saul, why persecutest thou me?

5. And he said, Who art thou, Lord? And the Lord said, I am Jesus whom thou persecutest: it is hard for thee to kick against the pricks.

6. And he trembling and astonished said, Lord, what wilt thou have me to do? And the Lord said unto him, Arise, and go into the city, and it shall be

told thee what thou must do.

7. And the men which journeyed with him stood speechless, hearing a voice, but seeing no man.

8. **And Saul arose** from the earth **and when his eyes were opened, he saw no man: but they led him** by the hand, and brought *him* **into Damascus.**

9. **And he was three days without sight, and neither did eat nor drink.**

10. **And there was a certain disciple** at Damascus **named Ananias; and to him said the Lord in a vision, Ananias.** And he said, Behold, I *am here,* Lord.

11. And the Lord *said* unto him **Arise, and go into the street** which is called Straight, **and inquire** in the house of Judas **for one called Saul,** of Tarsus **for,** behold, **he prayeth,**

12. **And hath seen in a vision a man named Ananias coming** in, and putting *his* hand on him **that he might receive his sight.**

13. **Then Ananias answered, Lord, I have heard** by many of this man, **how much evil he hath done** to thy saints at Jerusalem:

14. And here he hath authority from the chief priests to bind all that call on thy name.

15. **But the Lord said** unto him, Go thy way: for **he is a chosen vessel** unto me **to bear my name before the Gentiles, and kings, and** the children of **Israel:**

16. For I will shew him how great things he must suffer for my name's sake.

17. **And Ananias** went his way, and **entered** into **the house; and** putting his hands on him **said, Brother Saul, the Lord, even Jesus, that appeared unto thee** in the way as thou camest, **hath sent me, that thou mightest receive thy sight, and be filled with the Holy Ghost.**

18. **And immediately** there fell from his eyes as it had been scales: and **he received sight** forthwith, and arose, **and was baptized.**

19. And when he had received meat, he was strengthened. **Then was Saul certain days with the disciples** which were at Damascus.

20. **And** straightway **he preached Christ in the synagogues,** that he is the Son of God.

21. **But all** that heard *him* **were amazed, and said; Is not this he that destroyed them which called on this name** in Jerusalem, and came hither for that intent, that he might bring them bound unto the chief priests?

22. **But Saul increased** the more **in strength, and confounded the Jews** which dwelt at Damascus, **proving that this is very Christ.**

23. **And** after that many days were fulfilled **the Jews took counsel to kill him:**

24. But their laying await was known of Saul. And they watched the gates day and night to kill him.

25. **Then the disciples took him by night, and let him down** by **the wall in a basket.**

199

26 And when Saul was come to Jerusalem, he assayed to join himself to the disciples: but they were all afraid of him, and believed not that he was a disciple. 27 But Barnabas took him, and brought him to the apostles, and declared unto them how he had seen the Lord in the way, and that he had spoken to him, and how he had preached boldly at Damascus in the name of Jesus. 28. And he was with them coming in and going out at Jerusalem. 29. And he spake boldly in the name of the Lord Jesus, and disputed against the Grecians: but they went about to slay him. 30. Which when the brethren knew, they brought him down to Caesarea, and sent him forth to Tarsus. 31. Then had the churches rest throughout all Judaea and Galilee and Samaria, and were edified; and walking in the fear of the Lord, and in the comfort of the Holy Ghost were multiplied. 32 And it came to pass, as Peter passed throughout all quarters, he came down also to the saints which dwelt at Lydda. 33 And there he found a certain man named Aeneas, which had kept his bed eight years, and was sick of the palsy. 34. And Peter said unto him, Aeneas, Jesus Christ maketh thee whole: arise, and make thy bed. And he arose immediately. 35. And all that dwelt at Lydda and Saron saw him, and turned to the Lord. 36. Now there was at Joppa a certain disciple named Tabitha, which by interpretation is called Dorcas: this woman was full of good works and almsdeeds which she did. 37 And it came to pass in those days, that she was sick, and died: whom when they hadwashed, they laid her in an upper chamber. 38 And forasmuch as Lydda was nigh to Joppa, and the disciples had heard that Peter was there, they sent unto him two men, desiring him that he would not delay to come to them. 39 Then Peter arose and went with them. When he was come they brought him into the upper chamber: and all the widows stood by him weeping, and shewing the coats and garments which Dorcas made, while she was with them. 40. But Peter put them all forth,and kneeled down, and prayed; and turning him to the body said, Tabitha, arise. And she opened her eyes: and when she saw Peter, she sat up. 41 And he gave her his hand, and lifted her up, and when he had called the saints and widows, presented her alive. 42 And it was known throughout all Joppa; and many believed in the Lord. 43 And it came to pass, that he tarried many days in Joppa with one Simon a tanner.

CHAPTER 10

■ 1. **There was** a certain man ■ **in Caesarea** called ■ **Cornelius, a centurion** of the band called the Italian *band,*

■ 2. **A devout man, and one** ■ **that feared God** with all his house, which gave much alms to the people, and prayed to God alway.

■ 3. **He saw in a vision** evidently about the ninth hour of the day ■ **an angel** of God coming in to him, and ■ **saying** unto him, ■ **Cornelius.**

4. And when he looked on him, he was afraid, and said, What is it, Lord? And he said unto him,

■ **Thy prayers** and thine alms ■ **are come up for a** ■ **memorial before God.**

■ 5. **And now** send men to Joppa, and ■ **call for one Simon, whose** ■ **surname is Peter:**

6. He lodgeth with one Simon a tanner. whose house is by the sea side: ■ **he shall tell thee what** ■ **thou oughtest to do.**

■ 7. **And** when the angel which spake unto Cornelius was departed, ■ **he called two** of his household ■ **servants, and a devout** ■ **soldier** of them that waited on him continually;

■ 8. **And** when he had declared all *these* things unto them ■ **he sent them to Joppa.**

9. On the morrow, ■ **as they** went on their journey, and ■ **drew** nigh ■ **unto the city, Peter went up** ■ **upon the housetop to pray** about the sixth hour:

■ 10. **And** he became very hungry, and would have eaten: but while they made ready, ■ **he fell into a trance,**

■ 11. **And saw heaven** ■ **opened, and a** certain ■ **vessel descending** unto him, ■ **as it had been a great** ■ **sheet knit at the four**

■ **corners,** and let down to the earth:

■ 12. **Wherein were all** ■ **manner of** fourfooted ■ **beasts** of the earth, and wild beasts ■ **and creeping things,** ■ **and fowls** of the air.

■ 13. **And there came a** ■ **voice to him, Rise,** ■ **Peter; kill, and eat.**

■ 14. **But Peter said, Not** ■ **so, Lord; for I have** ■ **never eaten any thing** that is ■ **common or unclean.**

■ 15. **And the voice spake** unto him again the second time, ■ **What God hath** ■ **cleansed, that call not** thou ■ **common.**

16. This was done thrice: and the vessel was received up again into heaven.

■ 17. **Now while Peter** ■ **doubted** in himself ■ **what this vision** which he had seen ■ **should mean,** behold, ■ **the men** which were ■ **sent from Cornelius** had made inquiry for Simon's house, and stood before the gate,

18. And called, and ■ **asked whether** Simon, which was surnamed ■ **Peter, were lodged there.**

■ 19. **While Peter thought** ■ **on the vision, the** ■ **Spirlt said** unto him, Behold, ■ **three men seek thee.**

■ 20. **Arise** therefore, and get thee down, ■ **and go with them,** doubting nothing: ■ **for I have sent them.**

■ 21. **Then Peter** went down to the men which were sent unto him from Cornelius; and ■ **said, Behold, I am he** ■ **whom ye seek:** what is the cause wherefore ye are come?

■ 22. **And they said, Cornelius** ■ **the centurion,** a just man, and one that feareth God, and of good report among all the nation of the Jews,

was warned from God by an holy angel **to send for thee** into his house, **and to hear** words of **thee.**

23. Then called he them in, and lodged *them*. And on the morrow Peter went away with them, and certain brethren from Joppa accompanied him.

24. **And the morrow after they entered** into **Caesarea.** And Cornelius waited for them, and he had called together his kinsmen and near friends.

25. **And as Peter was coming** in, **Cornelius met him,** and fell down at his feet, **and worshipped him.**

26. **But Peter took him up, saying, Stand up; I myself also am a man.**

27. **And as he talked** with him, **he** went in, and **found many that were come together.**

28. **And he said** unto them, **Ye know how that it is** an **unlawful** thing **for** a man that is **a Jew to keep company, or come unto one of another nation; but God hath shewed me that I should not call any man common or unclean.**

29 **Therefore came I unto you** without gainsaying, as soon as I was sent for: I ask therefore for what intent ye have sent for me?

30. **And Cornelius said, Four days ago I was fasting** until this hour; and at the ninth hour I prayed in my house, **and, behold, a man stood before me** in bright clothing,

31. **And said, Cornelius, thy prayer is heard,** and thine alms are had in remembrance in the sight of God.

32. **Send therefore to Joppa, and call** hither Simon, whose surname is **Peter;** he is lodged in the house of *one* Simon a tanner by the sea side: **who,** when he cometh, **shall speak unto thee.**

33. Immediately therefore I sent to thee; and thou hast well done that thou art come. **Now therefore are we all here** present before God, **to hear all things that are commanded thee of God.**

34. **Then Peter** opened *his* mouth, and **said, Of a truth I perceive that God is no respecter of persons:**

35. **But in every nation he that feareth him, and worketh righteousness, is accepted** with him.

36. **The word which God sent unto the children of Israel,** preaching peace by Jesus Christ: (he is Lord of all:)

37. That word, *I say*, ye know, which was published throughout all Judaea, and began from Galilee, after the baptism which John preached;

38. **How God anointed Jesus** of Nazareth with the Holy Ghost and with power: who went about doing good, and healing all that were oppressed of the devil; for God was with him.

39. **And we are witnesses of all things which he did** both in the land of the Jews, and in Jerusalem; whom they slew and hanged on a tree:

40. **Him God raised up the third day,** and shewed him openly;

41. Not to all the people, but unto witnesses chosen before God, *even* to us, who did eat and drink with him after he rose from the dead.

42. **And he commanded us to preach unto the people, and to testify that it is he which was ordained of God to be the Judge of quick and dead.**

43. To him give all the prophets witness,

■ **that through his name**
■ **whosoever believeth** in him
■ **shall receive remission**
■ **of sins.**
■ 44. **While Peter yet**
■ **spake** these words,
■ **the Holy Ghost fell on**
■ **all** them which heard the word.
■ 45. **And they of the**
■ **circumcision** which believed
■ **were astonished,** as
many as came with Peter,
■ **because that on the**
■ **Gentiles also was**
■ **poured out the gift**
■ **of the Holy Ghost.**
■ 46. **For they heard them**
■ **speak with tongues,**
and magnify God.
■ **Then answered Peter,**
■ 47. **Can any man forbid**
■ **water, that these should not**
■ **be baptized, which have**
■ **received the**
■ **Holy Ghost** as well as we?
■ 48. **And he commanded**
■ **them to be baptized**
in the name of the Lord. Then prayed
they him to tarry certain days

CHAPTER 11

1. And the apostles and brethren
that were in Judaea heard that
the Gentiles had also received
the word of God.
■ 2. **And when Peter was**
■ **come up to Jerusalem,**
■ **they that were of the**
■ **circumcision contended**
■ **with him,**
■ 3. **Saying, Thou wentest in**
■ **to men uncircumcised, and**
■ **didst eat with them.**
■ 4. **But Peter rehearsed the**
■ **matter from the beginning,**
■ **and expounded it by order**
■ **unto them, saying,**
5. I was in the city of Joppa praying:
and in a trance I saw a vision, A
certain vessel descend, as it had
been a great sheet, let down from

heaven by four corners;
and it came even to me:
6. Upon the which when I had
fastened mine eyes, I considered, and
saw fourfooted beasts of the earth,
and wild beasts, and creeping things,
and fowls of the air.
7. And I heard a voice saying unto
me, Arise, Peter; slay and eat.
8. But I said, Not so, Lord: for nothing
common or unclean hath at any
time entered into my mouth.
9. But the voice answered me again
from heaven, What God hath
cleansed, *that* call not thou common.
10. And this was done three times:
and all were drawn up again
into heaven.
11. And, behold, immediately there
were three men already come unto
the house where I was, sent from
Caesarea unto me.
12. And the Spirit bade me go with
them, nothing doubting. Moreover
these six brethren accompanied me,
and we entered into the man's house:
13. And he shewed us how he had
seen an angel in his house, which
stood and said unto him, Send men to
Joppa, and call for Simon, whose
surname is Peter;
14. Who shall tell thee words,whereby
thou and all thy house shall be saved.
15. And as I began to speak, the Holy
Ghost fell on them, as on us at
the beginning.
16. Then remembered I the word ofthe
Lord, how that he said, John indeed
baptized with water; but ye shall be
baptized with the Holy Ghost.
■ 17. **Forasmuch then as God**
■ **gave them the like gift as**
■ **he did unto us, who**
■ **believed on the Lord Jesus**
■ **Christ; what was I, that I**
■ **could withstand God?**
■ 18. **When they heard these**
■ **things, they held their**
■ **peace,** and glorified God,
■ **saying, Then hath God also**
■ **to the Gentiles granted**
■ **repentance unto life.**
■ 19. **Now they** which

■ were scattered abroad upon
the persecution that arose about
Stephen travelled as far as Phenice,
and Cyprus, and Antioch,
■ preaching the word to
■ none but unto the Jews only.
■ 20. And some of them were
men of Cyprus and Cyrene, which,
when they were come to Antioch,
■ spake unto the Grecians,
■ preaching the LORD Jesus.
21. And the hand of the Lord
was with them:
■ and a great number
■ believed, and turned
unto the Lord.
■ 22. Then tidings of these things
■ came unto the ears of
■ the church which was
■ in Jerusalem: and
■ they sent forth
■ Barnabas, that he
should go as far as Antioch.
■ 23. Who, when he came, and had
seen the grace of God, was glad, and
■ exhorted them all, that with
■ purpose of heart they
■ would cleave
■ unto the Lord.
■ 24. For he was a good man,
■ and full of the Holy Ghost
■ and of faith: and much people
was added unto the Lord.
■ 25. Then departed Barnabas
■ to Tarsus, for
■ to seek Saul:
■ 26. And when he had found him,
■ he brought him unto
■ Antioch. And
it came to pass, that
■ a whole year they
■ assembled themselves with
■ the church, and
■ taught much people. And
■ the disciples were called
■ Christians first in Antioch.
■ 27. And in these days
■ came prophets from
■ Jerusalem unto Antioch.
■ 28. And there stood
■ up one of them
■ named Agabus, and
■ signified by the Spirit

■ that there should be great
■ dearth throughout all the
■ world: which came to pass in the
days of Claudius Caesar.
■ 29. Then the disciples,
every man according to his ability,
■ determined to send relief
■ unto the brethren which dwelt
■ in Judaea:
30. Which also they did,
and sent it to the elders
■ by the hands of
■ Barnabas and Saul.

CHAPTER 12

■ 1. Now about that time
■ Herod the king stretched
■ forth *his* hands
■ to vex certain of thechurch.
■ 2. And he killed James
the brother of John with the sword.
■ 3. And because he saw
■ it pleased the Jews, he
■ proceeded further
■ to take Peter also. (Then
were the days of unleavened bread.)
■ 4. And when he had
apprehended him,
■ he put him in prison, and
delivered *him* to four quaternions of
soldiers to keep him; intending after
Easter to bring him forth to thepeople.
■ 5. Peter therefore was kept
■ in prison: but prayer was
■ made without ceasing of
■ the church unto God
■ for him.
■ 6. And when Herod would
■ have brought him forth,
■ the same night Peter was
■ sleeping between two
■ soldiers, bound with two
■ chains: and the keepers before
the door kept the prison.
■ 7. And, behold, the angel
■ of the Lord came upon *him*,
and a light shined in the prison:
■ and he smote Peter
on the side,
■ and raised him up,
■ saying, Arise up quickly.
■ And his chains fell
■ off from *his* hands.

8. And the angel said unto him, Gird thyself, and bind on thy sandals. And so he did. And he **saith unto him,** Cast thy garment about thee, and **follow me.**

9. And he went out, and followed him; and wist not that it was true which was done by the angel; **but thought he saw a vision.**

10. When they were past the first and the second ward, they came unto the iron gate that leadeth unto the city; which opened to them of his own accord: **and they went out, and passed on through one street; and** forthwith **the angel departed** from him.

11. And when Peter was come to himself, he said, Now I know of a surety, **that the LORD hath** sent his angel, and hath **delivered me out of the hand of Herod,** and *from* all the expectation of the people of the Jews.

12. And when he had considered *the thing,* **he came to the house of Mary the mother of** John, whose surname was **Mark;** where many were gathered together praying.

13. And as Peter knocked at the door of the gate, **a damsel came** to hearken, **named Rhoda.**

14. And when she knew Peter's voice, she opened not the gate for gladness, but ran in, and **told how Peter stood before the gate.**

15. And they said unto her, Thou art mad. But she constantly affirmed that it was even so. Then said they, It is his angel.

16. But Peter continued knocking: and when they had **opened the door,** and saw him, **they were astonished.**

17. But he, beckoning unto them with the hand to hold their peace, **declared** unto them **how the Lord had brought him out of the prison. And he said, Go shew these things unto James,** and to the brethren. **And he departed,** and went into another place.

18. Now as soon as it was day, there was no small stir among the soldiers, what was become of Peter.

19. And when Herod had sought for him, and found him not, he examined the keepers, and commanded that they should **be put to death. And he went down from Judaea to Caesarea,** and *there* abode.

20. And Herod was highly displeased with them of Tyre and Sidon: but they came with one accord to him, and, having made Blastus the king's chamberlain their friend, desired peace; because their country was nourished by the king's *country.*

21. And upon a set day **Herod, arrayed in royal apparel,** sat upon his throne, and **made an oration unto them.**

22. And the people gave a shout, saying, It is the voice of a god, and not of a man.

23. And immediately the angel of the Lord smote him, because he gave not God the glory: and he was eaten of worms, and gave up the ghost.

24. But the word of God grew and multiplied.

25. And Barnabas and Saul returned from Jerusalem, when they had fulfilled *their* ministry, **and took with them** John, whose surname was

|■| Mark.

CHAPTER 13

■ 1. Now there were in
■ the church that was
■ at Antioch certain prophets
■ and teachers; as Barnabas,
■ and Simeon
that was called Niger,
■ and Lucius of Cyrene,
■ and Manaen, which had been
brought up with Herod the tetrarch,
■ and Saul.
■ 2. As they ministered
to the Lord, and fasted,
■ the Holy Ghost
■ said, Separate me
■ Barnabas and Saul
■ for the work whereunto
■ I have called them.
■ 3. And when they had
■ fasted and prayed,
and laid *their* hands on them,
■ they sent them away.
■ 4. So they, being sent forth
■ by the Holy Ghost, departed
unto Seleucia; and from thence they
■ sailed to Cyprus.
■ 5. And when they were at Salamis,
■ they preached
■ the word of God
■ in the synagogues of
■ the Jews: and they had
also John to *their* minister.
■ 6. And when they had gone
through the isle unto Paphos,
■ they found a certain
■ sorcerer, a false prophet, a
■ Jew, whose name
■ was Barjesus:
■ 7. Which was with the
■ deputy of the country,
■ Sergius Paulus,
a prudent man;
■ who called for
■ Barnabas and Saul,
■ and desired to hear
■ the word of God.
■ 8. But Elymas the sorcerer
■ (for so is his name by
■ interpretation) withstood
■ them, seeking to turn away
■ the deputy from the faith.

■ 9. Then Saul, (who also *is called*
Paul,) filled with the Holy Ghost,
■ set his eyes on him.
■ 10. And said,
O full of all subtilty and all mischief,
■ thou child of the devil,
thou enemy of all righteousness,
wilt thou not cease to pervert the
right ways of the Lord?
11. And now, behold, the hand
of the Lord *is* upon thee, and
■ thou shalt be blind,
not seeing the sun
■ for a season. And
■ immediately there
■ fell on him a mist and a
■ darkness;
and he went about seeking
some to lead him by the hand.
■ 12. Then the deputy,
when he saw what was done,
■ believed, being astonished
at the doctrine of the Lord.
■ 13. Now when Paul and
■ his company loosed
■ from Paphos, they came
to Perga in Pamphylia: and
■ John departing from them
■ returned to Jerusalem.
■ 14. But when they
departed from Perga,
■ they came to Antioch
■ in Pisidia, and went
■ into the synagogue
on the sabbath day, and sat down.
15. And after the reading of the law
■ and the prophets
■ the rulers of the synagogue
■ sent unto them, saying,
Ye men *and* brethren,
■ if ye have any
■ word of exhortation
■ for the people, say on.
■ 16. Then Paul stood up,
■ and beckoning with *his* hand
■ said, Men of Israel, and ye
that fear God, give audience.
■ 17. The God of this people
■ of Israel chose our fathers,
and exalted the people when they
dwelt as strangers in the land of
Egypt, and with an high arm
brought he them out of it.

18. **And about** the time of **forty years suffered he their manners in the wilderness.** 19. **And** when he had destroyed seven nations in the land of Chanaan, **he divided their land to them by lot.** 20. **And after that he gave** *unto* **them judges** about the space of four hundred and fifty years, **until Samuel the prophet.** 21. **And afterward they desired a king: and God gave unto them Saul** the son of Cis, a man of the tribe of Benjamin, by the space of forty years. 22. **And when he had removed him, he raised up** unto them **David to be their king;** to whom also he gave their testimony, and said, I have found David the *son* of Jesse, a man after mine own heart, which shall fulfil all my will. 23. **Of this man's seed hath God** according to *his* promise **raised unto Israel a Saviour, Jesus:** 24. When John had first preached before his coming the baptism of repentance to all the people of Israel. 25. **And as John fulfilled his course, he said, Whom think ye that I am? I am not he. But,** behold, **there cometh one after me,** whose shoes of *his* feet I am not worthy to loose. 26. **Men and brethren,** children of the stock of Abraham, and whosoever among you feareth God, **to you is the word of this salvation sent.** 27. **For they that dwell at Jerusalem,** and their rulers, **because they knew him not, nor yet the voices of the prophets** which are read every sabbath day, **they have fulfilled them in condemning him.**

28. **And though they found no cause of death in him, yet desired they Pilate that he should be slain.** 29. **And when they had fulfilled all that was written of him, they** took *him* down from the tree, and **laid him in a sepulchre.** 30. **But God raised him from the dead:** 31. And he was seen many days of them which came up with him from Galilee to Jerusalem, who are his witnesses unto the people. 32. **And we declare** unto you glad tidings, how **that the promise** which was **made unto the fathers,** 33. **God hath fulfilled** the same unto us their children, **in** that he hath raised up **Jesus** again; as it is also written in the second psalm, Thou art my Son, this day have I begotten thee. 34. **And as concerning that he raised him up** from the dead, **now no more to return to corruption,** he said on this wise, I will give you the sure mercies of David. 35. **Wherefore he saith** also **in another psalm, Thou shalt not suffer thine Holy One to see corruption.** 36. **For David,** after he had served his own generation by the will of God, fell on sleep, and was laid unto his fathers, and **saw corruption:** 37. **But he, whom God raised again, saw no corruption.** 38. **Be it known** unto you therefore, men *and* brethren, **that through this man is preached unto you the forgiveness of sins:** 39. And by him all that believe are justified from all things, from which ye could not be justified by the law of Moses. 40. **Beware** therefore,

lest that come upon you,
which is spoken of
in the prophets;
41. Behold, ye despisers, and wonder, and perish:
for I work a work in your days, a work
which ye shall in no wise believe, though
a man declare it unto you.
42. And when the Jews were gone out of the synagogue,
the Gentiles besought that these words might be preached to them the next sabbath.
43. Now when the congregation was broken up, many of the Jews and religious proselytes followed Paul and Barnabas: who, speaking to them, persuaded them to continue in the grace of God.
44. And the next sabbath day came almost the whole city together to hear the word of God.
45. But when the Jews saw the multitudes, they were filled with envy, and spake against those things which were spoken by Paul, contradicting and blaspheming.
46. Then Paul and Barnabas waxed bold, and said, It was necessary that the word of God should first have been spoken to you: but seeing ye put it from you, and judge yourselves unworthy of everlasting life, lo, we turn to the Gentiles.
47. For so hath the Lord commanded us, saying, I have set thee to be a light of the Gentiles, that thou shouldest be for salvation unto the ends of the earth.
48. And when the Gentiles heard this, they were glad,
and glorified the word of the Lord: and as many as were ordained to eternal life believed.
49. And the word of the Lord was published throughout all the region.
50. But the Jews stirred up the devout and honourable women, and the chief men of the city, and raised persecution against Paul and Barnabas, and expelled them out of their coasts.
51. But they shook off the dust of their feet against them, and came unto Iconium.
52. And the disciples were filled with joy, and with the Holy Ghost.

CHAPTER 14

1. And it came to pass in Iconium, that they went both together into the synagogue of the Jews, and so spake, that a great multitude both of the Jews and also of the Greeks believed.
2. But the unbelieving Jews stirred up the Gentiles, and made their minds evil affected against the brethren.
3. Long time therefore abode they speaking boldly in the Lord, which gave testimony unto the word of his grace, and granted signs and wonders to be done by their hands.
4. But the multitude of the city was divided: and part held with the Jews, and part with the apostles.
5. And when there was an assault made both of the Gentiles, and also of the Jews with their rulers, to use *them* despitefully, and to stone them,
6. They were ware of it, and fled unto Lystra and Derbe,

cities of Lycaonia, and unto the region that lieth round about: 7. And there they preached the gospel. 8. **And there sat a certain man at Lystra,** impotent in his feet, **being a cripple from his mother's womb,** who never had walked: 9. **The same heard Paul speak: who** stedfastly beholding him, and **perceiving that he had faith** to be healed, 10. **Said with a loud voice, Stand upright on thy feet. And he leaped and walked.** 11. **And when the people saw what Paul had done, they lifted** up their **voices, saying** in the speech of Lycaonia, **The gods are come down to us in the likeness of men.** 12. **And they called Barnabas, Jupiter; and Paul, Mercurius,** because he was the chief speaker. 13. Then the priest of Jupiter, which was before their city, brought oxen and garlands unto the gates, and would have done sacrifice with the people. 14. **Which when the apostles, Barnabas and Paul, heard of, they rent their clothes, and ran in among the people, crying out,** 15. And saying, **Sirs,** why do ye these things? **We also are men** of like passions with you, **and preach** unto you **that ye should turn** from these vanities **unto the living God,** which made heaven, and earth, and the sea, and all things that are therein: 16. **Who in times past suffered all nations to walk** in their own ways. 17. **Nevertheless he left not himself without witness,** in that he did good, **and gave us rain** from heaven, **and fruitful seasons,** filling our hearts with food and gladness. 18. And with these sayings scarce restrained they the people, that they had not done sacrifice unto them. 19. **And there came** thither **certain Jews from Antioch and Iconium,** who persuaded the people, **and having stoned Paul, drew him out of the city, supposing he had been dead.** 20. **Howbeit,** as the disciples stood round about him, **he rose up, and came into the city: and the next day he departed with Barnabas to Derbe.** 21. **And when they** had **preached the gospel** to that city, **and** had taught many, **they returned again to Lystra, and to Iconium, and Antioch,** 22. **Confirming** the souls of the disciples, **and exhorting them to continue in the faith, and that we must through much tribulation enter into the kingdom** of God. 23. **And when they had ordained them elders** in every church, and had prayed with fasting, **they commended them to the Lord,** on whom they believed. 24. And after they had passed throughout Pisidia, they came to Pamphylia. 25. And when they had preached the word in Perga, they went down into Attalia: 26. And thence sailed to Antioch, from whence they had been recommended to the grace of God for the work which

they fulfilled.
27. And when they were come, and had gathered the church together, they rehearsed all that God had done with them, and how he had opened the door of faith unto the Gentiles.
28. And there they abode long time with the disciples.

CHAPTER 15

1. **And certain men** which came down **from Judaea taught the brethren, and said, Except ye be circumcised** after the manner of Moses, **ye cannot be saved.**
2. **When therefore Paul and Barnabas had** no small dissension and **disputation with them, they determined that Paul and Barnabas,** and certain other of them, **should go** up to Jerusalem **unto the apostles** and elders **about this question.**
3. And being brought on their way by the church, they passed through Phenice and Samaria, declaring the conversion of the Gentiles: and they caused great joy unto all the brethren.
4. **And when they were come to Jerusalem, they were received of the church,** and *of* the apostles and elders, **and they declared all things that God had done** with them.
5. **But there rose up** certain of the sect of the **Pharisees which believed, saying, That it was needful to circumcise them,** and to command *them* to keep the law of Moses.
6. And the apostles and elders came together for to consider of this matter.
7. **And** when there had been much disputing, **Peter rose up, and said** unto them, Men *and* brethren, **ye know how** that a good while ago **God made choice** among us, **that the Gentiles by my mouth should hear the word** of the gospel, **and believe.**
8. **And God,** which knoweth the hearts, **bare them witness, giving them the Holy Ghost,** even as *he did* unto us;
9. **And put no difference between us and them,** purifying their hearts by faith.
10. **Now therefore why tempt ye God, to put a yoke upon the neck of the disciples,** which neither our fathers nor we were able to bear?
11. But we believe that through the grace of the LORD Jesus Christ we shall be saved, even as they.
12. **Then all the multitude** kept silence, and **gave audience to Barnabas and Paul,** declaring what miracles and wonders God had wrought among the Gentiles by them.
13. **And after** they had held their peace, **James answered,** saying, Men *and* brethren, hearken unto me:
14. **Simeon hath declared how God** at the first **did visit the Gentiles, to take out of them a people for his name.**
15. **And to this agree the words of the prophets;** as it is written,
16. **After this I** will return, and **will build again the tabernacle of David,** which is fallen down; and I will build again the ruins thereof, and I will set it up:
17. **That the residue of men might seek after the Lord, and all the Gentiles, upon whom my name is called,** saith the Lord, who doeth all these things.
18. Known unto God are all his works

from the beginning of the world.

19. **Wherefore my sentence is, that we trouble not them, which from among the Gentiles are turned to God:**

20. **But that we write** unto them, **that they abstain from pollutions** of idols, **and from fornication,** and *from* things strangled, **and from blood.**

21. For Moses of old time hath in every city them that preach him, being read in the synagogues e very sabbath day.

22. **Then pleased it the apostles** and elders with the whole church, **to send chosen men of their own company to Antioch with Paul and Barnabas;** *namely*, Judas surnamed Barsabas and Silas, chief men among the brethren:

23. **And they wrote letters by them after this manner;** The apostles and elders and brethren *send* greeting unto the brethren which are of the Gentiles in Antioch and Syria and Cilicia.

24. **Forasmuch as we have heard, that certain which went out from us have troubled you** with words, subverting your souls, **saying, Ye must be circumcised,** and keep the law: **to whom we gave no such commandment:**

25. **It seemed good unto us,** being assembled with one accord, **to send chosen men** unto you **with our beloved Barnabas and Paul,**

26. Men that have hazarded their lives for the name of our Lord Jesus Christ.

27. **We have sent therefore Judas and Silas,** who shall also tell *you* the same things by mouth.

28. **For it seemed good to the Holy Ghost,** and to us, **to lay upon you no greater burden than these**

necessary things;

29. **That ye abstain from meats offered to idols,** and **from blood,** and **from things strangled, and** from **fornication:** from which if ye keep yourselves, ye shall do well. Fare ye well.

30. **So when they were dismissed, they came to Antioch: and** when they had gathered the multitude together, they **delivered the epistle:**

31. **Which when they had read, they rejoiced** for the consolation.

32. And Judas and Silas, being prophets also themselves, exhorted the brethren with many words, and confirmed *them*.

33. **And after** they had tarried *there* **a space, they were let go** in peace from the brethren unto the apostles.

34. **Notwithstanding it pleased Silas to abide there still.**

35. **Paul also and Barnabas continued in Antioch,** teaching and preaching the word of the Lord, with many others also.

36. **And** some days after **Paul said unto Barnabas, Let us** go again and **visit** our brethren in **every city where we have preached the word** of the LORD, **and see how they do.**

37. **And Barnabas determined to take** with them John, whose surname was **Mark.**

38. **But Paul thought not good to take him** with them, **who departed from them from Pamphylia,** and went not with them to the work.

39. **And the contention was so sharp** between them, **that they departed** asunder **one from the other: and so**

- Barnabas took
- Mark, and sailed
- unto Cyprus;
- 40. And Paul chose Silas,
- and departed,

being recommended by the
brethren unto the grace of God.

- 41. And he went through
- Syria and Cilicia, confirming the

churches.

CHAPTER 16

- 1. Then came he
- to Derbe and Lystra:
- and, behold,
- a certain disciple was
- there, named Timotheus,

the son of a certain woman, which
was a Jewess, and believed;
but his father *was* a Greek:

- 2. Which was well reported
- of by the brethren

that were at Lystra and Iconium.

- 3. Him would Paul have
- to go forth with him; and
- took and circumcised
- him because of the
- Jews which were
- in those quarters: for they knew

all that his father was a Greek.

- 4. And as they went

through the cities,

- they delivered them
- the decrees for to keep,
- that were ordained of
- the apostles and elders

which were at Jerusalem.

- 5. And so were thechurches
- established in the faith,

and increased in number daily.
6. Now when they had gone
throughout Phrygia and the region
of Galatia, and were forbidden
of the Holy Ghost to preach
the word in Asia,
7. After they were come to Mysia,
they assayed to go into Bithynia: but
the Spirit suffered them not.

- 8. And they passing by Mysia
- came down to Troas.
- 9. And a vision appeared
- to Paul in the night;
- There stood a man of

- Macedonia, and prayed him,
- saying, Come over into
- Macedonia, and help us.
- 10. And after he had seen thevision,
- immediately we
- endeavoured to go

into Macedonia, assuredly
gathering that the Lord had
called us for to preach
the gospel unto them.

- 11. Therefore loosing
- from Troas, we came

with a straight course to Samothracia,
and the next day to Neapolis;
12. And from thence

- to Philippi, which is

the chief city of that

- part of Macedonia,

and a colony: and we were in
that city abiding certain days.

- 13. And on the sabbath
- we went out of the city

by a river side, where prayer was
wont to be made; and we sat down,
and spake unto the women which
resorted *thither*.

- 14. And a certain woman
- named Lydia, a seller of

purple, of the city of Thyatira,

- which worshipped God,
- heard us: whose heart the Lord

opened, that she attended unto the
things which were spoken of Paul.

- 15. And when she was
- baptized, and her household,
- she besought us, saying,

If ye have judged me to be
faithful to the Lord,

- come into my house,
- and abide *there*.

And she constrained us.

- 16. And it came to pass,

as we went to prayer,

- a certain damsel possessed
- with a spirit of divination
- met us, which brought her
- masters much
- gain by soothsaying:
- 17. The same followed
- Paul and us,
- and cried, saying,
- These men are the
- servants of the most high

God, which shew unto us the way of salvation.

18. **And this did she many days. But Paul,** being grieved, **turned and said to the spirit, I command thee in the name of Jesus** Christ **to come out** of her. **And he came out** the same hour.

19. **And when her masters saw that the hope of their gains was gone, they caught Paul and Silas,** and drew *them* into the marketplace unto the rulers,

20. **And brought them to the magistrates,** saying, These men, being Jews, do exceedingly trouble our city,

21. And teach customs, which are not lawful for us to receive, neither to observe, being Romans.

22. **And the multitude rose** up together **against them: and the magistrates** rent off their clothes, and **commanded to beat them.**

23. **And** when they had laid many stripes upon them, **they cast them into prison, charging the jailor to keep them safely:**

24. Who, having received such a charge, thrust them into the inner prison, and made their feet fast in the stocks.

25. **And at midnight Paul and Silas prayed, and sang praises unto God:** and the prisoners heard them.

26. **And suddenly there was a great earthquake,** so that the foundations of the prison were shaken: **and immediately all the doors were opened,** and every one's bands were loosed.

27. **And the keeper** of the prison awaking out of his sleep, and **seeing the** prison **doors open,** he

drew out **his sword, and would have killed himself,** supposing that **the prisoners had** been **fled.**

28. **But Paul cried** with a loud voice, saying, **Do thyself no harm: for we are all here.**

29. **Then he** called for a light, and sprang in, and came trembling, and **fell down before Paul and Silas,**

30. **And** brought them out, and **said, Sirs, what must I do to be saved?**

31. **And they said, Believe on the Lord Jesus Christ, and thou shalt be saved, and thy house.**

32. And they spake unto him the word of the Lord, and to all that were in his house.

33. **And he took them** the same hour of the night, **and washed their stripes; and was baptized,** he and all his, straightway.

34. **And when he had brought them into his house, he** set meat before them, and **rejoiced, believing in God** with all his house.

35. **And** when it was day, **the magistrates sent** the **sergeants, saying, Let those men go.**

36. **And the keeper** of the prison **told** this saying to **Paul,** The magistrates have sent **to** let you go: now therefore **depart,** and go **in peace.**

37. **But Paul said** unto them, **They have beaten us openly** uncondemned, **being Romans, and** have **cast us into prison; and now** do **they thrust us out privily? nay** verily;

but let them come
themselves and fetch us out.
38. And the sergeants
told these words unto
the magistrates: and they
feared, when they heard
that they were Romans.
39. And they came
and besought them,
and brought them out,
and desired them to
depart out of the city.
40. And they
went out of the prison, and
entered into the house
of Lydia: and when they
had seen the brethren,
they comforted them,
and departed.

CHAPTER 17

1. Now when they had passed
through Amphipolis and Apollonia,
they came to Thessalonica,
where
was a synagogue of the Jews:
2. And Paul, as his manner was,
went in unto them,
and three sabbath days
reasoned with them
out of the scriptures,
3. Opening and
alleging, that
Christ must needs
have suffered, and
risen again from the dead;
and that this
Jesus, whom I preach unto you,
is Christ.
4. And some of them
believed, and consorted
with Paul and Silas;
and of the devout Greeks a
great multitude, and of the
chief women not a few.
5. But the Jews which
believed not, moved with envy,
took unto them certain lewd fellows
of the baser sort, and gathered
a company, and
set all the city on an
uproar, and assaulted the
house of Jason, and sought to

bring them out to the people.
6. And when they found them not,
they drew Jason
and certain brethren
unto the rulers of the city,
crying, These that have
turned the world upside
down are come hither also;
7. Whom Jason hath
received: and these all
do contrary to the
decrees of Caesar,
saying that there is
another king, one Jesus.
8. And they troubled the people
and the rulers of the city, when
they heard these things.
9. And when they had taken
security of Jason, and of the
other, they let them go.
10. And the brethren
immediately sent
away Paul and Silas
by night unto Berea:
who coming thither
went into the synagogue
of the Jews.
11. These were more noble than
those in Thessalonica, in that they
received the word with all readiness
of mind, and searched the scriptures
daily, whether those things were so.
12. Therefore many of them
believed; also of honourable
women which were
Greeks, and of men, not a few.
13. But when the Jews of
Thessalonica had
knowledge that the word of
God was preached
of Paul at Berea,
they came thither
also, and stirred up the people.
14. And then immediately
the brethren sent away
Paul to go as it were to the sea:
but Silas and Timotheus
abode there still.
15. And they that conducted Paul
brought him unto
Athens: and
receiving a commandment
unto Silas and Timotheus for

to come to him with all speed, they departed.

16. **Now while Paul waited** for them at Athens, his spirit was stirred in him, when **he saw the city wholly given to idolatry.**

17. **Therefore disputed he** in the synagogue **with the Jews, and with** the **devout persons, and in the market** daily with them that met with him.

18. **Then certain philosophers of the Epicureans, and** of the **Stoics, encountered him. And** some **said, What will this babbler say?** other some, He seemeth to be a setter forth of strange gods: because he preached unto them Jesus, and the resurrection.

19. **And they took him,** and brought him **unto Areopagus, saying, May we know what this new doctrine,** whereof thou speakest, **is?**

20. For thou bringest certain strange things to our ears: we would know therefore what these things mean.

21. **(For all the Athenians** and strangers which were there **spent their time in nothing** else, **but either to tell, or to hear some new thing.)**

22. **Then Paul stood in the midst of Mars' hill, and said,** Ye men of Athens, I perceive that in all things **ye are too superstitious.**

23. **For** as I passed by, and beheld your devotions, **I found an altar with this inscription, TO THE UNKNOWN GOD.** Whom therefore ye ignorantly worship, **him declare I unto you.**

24. **God that made the world and all things therein,** seeing that **he** is Lord of heaven and earth, **dwelleth not in temples** made with hands;

25. **Neither is worshipped with** men's **hands, as though he needed any thing, seeing he giveth to all life,** and breath, and all things;

26. **And hath made** of one blood all nations of **men** for to dwell on all the face of the earth, and hath determined the times before appointed, and the bounds of their habitation;

27. **That they should seek the Lord,** if haply they might feel after him, and find him, **though he be not far from every one of us:**

28. **For in him we live, and move, and have our being;** as certain also of your own poets have said, For we are also his offspring.

29. Forasmuch then as we are the offspring of God, **we ought not to think that the Godhead is like** unto **gold, or silver, or stone,** graven by art and man's device.

30. **And the times of this ignorance God winked at; but now commandeth all men** everywhere **to repent:**

31. **Because** he hath appointed a day, in the which **he will judge the world in righteousness by that man whom he hath ordained;** whereof he hath given assurance unto all **men, in that he hath raised him from the dead.**

32. **And when they heard of the resurrection** of the dead, **some mocked: and others said, We will hear thee again** of this *matter.*

33. **So Paul departed from among them.**

34. Howbeit certain men clave unto

him, and believed: among the which *was* Dionysius the Areopagite, and a woman named Damaris, and others with them

CHAPTER 18

1. **After these things Paul departed from Athens, and came to Corinth;**
2. **And found a** certain **Jew named Aquila,** born in Pontus, lately come from Italy, **with his wife Priscilla;** (because that Claudius had commanded all Jews to depart from Rome:) and came unto them.
3. **And** because he was of the same craft, **he abode with them,** and wrought: **for by their occupation they were tentmakers.**
4. **And he reasoned in the synagogue** every sabbath, **and persuaded the Jews and the Greeks.**
5. **And when Silas and Timotheus were come** from Macedonia, **Paul** was pressed in the spirit, and **testified to the Jews that Jesus was Christ.**
6. **And when they opposed** themselves, **and blasphemed, he shook his raiment, and said** unto them, **Your blood be upon your own heads; I am clean; from henceforth I will go unto the Gentiles.**
7. **And he departed** thence, **and entered into a** certain **man's house, named Justus,** *one* that worshipped God, whose house joined hard to the synagogue.
8. **And Crispus, the chief ruler of the synagogue, believed on the Lord** with all his house; **and many of the Corinthians** hearing

believed, and were baptized.
9. **Then spake the Lord to Paul** in the night **by a vision, Be not afraid, but speak,** and hold not thy peace:
10. **For I am with thee, and no man shall** set on thee to **hurt thee:** for I have much people in this city.
11. **And he continued there a year and six months, teaching the word** of God among them.
12. **And when Gallio was the deputy** of Achaia, **the Jews made insurrection** with one accord **against Paul, and brought him to the judgment seat,**
13. **Saying, This fellow persuadeth men to worship God contrary to the law.**
14. **And** when Paul was now about to open *his* mouth, **Gallio said** unto the Jews, **If it were a matter of wrong** or wicked lewdness, O *ye* Jews, reason would that **I should bear with you:**
15. **But if it be** a question of words and names, and **of your law,** look ye *to it*; for **I will be no judge** of such *matters*.
16. **And he drave them from the judgment seat.**
17. **Then all the Greeks took** Sosthenes, **the chief ruler of the synagogue, and beat him** before the judgment seat. And Gallio cared for none of those things.
18. **And Paul** *after this* tarried *there* yet a good while, and then took his leave of the brethren, and **sailed thence into Syria,** and with him Priscilla and Aquila; having shorn *his* head in Cenchrea: for he had a vow
19. **And he came to**

Ephesus, and left them there: but he himself entered into the synagogue, and reasoned with the Jews.

20. When they desired him to tarry longer time with them, he consented not;

21. But bade them farewell, saying, I must by all means keep this feast that cometh in Jerusalem: but I will return again unto you, if God will. And he sailed from Ephesus.

22. And when he had landed at Caesarea, and gone up, and saluted the church, he went down to Antioch.

23. And after he had spent some time there, he departed, and went over all the country of Galatia and Phrygia in order, strengthening all the disciples.

24. And a certain Jew named Apollos, born at Alexandria, an eloquent man, and mighty in the scriptures, came to Ephesus.

25. This man was instructed in the way of the Lord; and being fervent in the spirit, he spake and taught diligently the things of the Lord, knowing only the baptism of John.

26. And he began to speak boldly in the synagogue: whom when Aquila and Priscilla had heard, they took him unto *them*, and expounded unto him the way of God more perfectly.

27. And when he was disposed to pass into Achaia, the brethren wrote, exhorting the disciples to receive him: who, when he was come, helped them much which had believed through grace:

28. For he mightily convinced the Jews, *and that* publicly, shewing by the scriptures that Jesus was Christ.

CHAPTER 19

1. And it came to pass, that, while Apollos was at Corinth, Paul having passed through the upper coasts came to Ephesus: and finding certain disciples,

2. He said unto them, Have ye received the Holy Ghost since ye believed? And they said unto him, We have not so much as heard whether there be any Holy Ghost.

3. And he said unto them, Unto what then were ye baptized? And they said, Unto John's baptism.

4. Then said Paul, John verily baptized with the baptism of repentance, saying unto the people, that they should believe on him which should come after him, that is, on Christ Jesus.

5. When they heard this, they were baptized in the name of the Lord Jesus.

6. And when Paul had laid his hands upon them, the Holy Ghost came on them; and they spake with tongues, and prophesied.

7. And all the men were about twelve.

8. And he went into the synagogue, and spake boldly for the space of three months, disputing and persuading the things concerning the kingdom of God.

9. But when divers were

■ **hardened,** and believed
not, but spake evil of that
way before the multitude,

■ **he departed** from them,
and separated the disciples,

■ **disputing daily** in the
school of one Tyrannus.

■ 10. **And this continued**
by the space of

■ **two years; so that**

■ **all** they which dwelt

■ **in Asia heard the word** of the
Lord Jesus, both Jews and Greeks.

■ 11. **And God wrought** special

■ **miracles by** the hands of

■ **Paul:**

■ 12. **So that from his body**

■ **were brought unto the sick**

■ **handkerchiefs** or aprons,

■ **and the diseases**

■ **departed** from them,

■ **and the evil spirits**

■ **went out** of them.

■ 13. **Then** certain of the

■ **vagabond Jews,** exorcists,

■ **took upon them to call**

■ **over them which had evil**

■ **spirits the name of** the LORD

■ **Jesus, saying, We adjure**

■ **you by Jesus whom**

■ **Paul preacheth.**

14. And there were seven sons
of *one* Sceva, a Jew, *and* chief
of the priests, which did so.

■ 15. **And the evil spirit**

■ **answered** and said,

■ **Jesus I know, and Paul**

■ **I know; but who are ye?**

■ 16. **And the man in whom**

■ **the evil spirit was leaped on**

■ **them,** and overcame them,

■ **and prevailed against**

■ **them, so that they fled**

■ **out of that house naked**

■ **and wounded.**

■ 17. **And this was**

■ **known to all** the

■ **Jews and Greeks** also dwelling

■ **at Ephesus;**

and fear fell on them all,

■ **and the name of the Lord**

■ **Jesus was magnified.**

■ 18. **And many that believed**

■ **came, and confessed,**
and shewed their deeds.

■ 19. **Many** of them also

■ **which used curious arts**

■ **brought their books** together,

■ **and burned them**
before all *men*: and they counted the
price of them, and found *it* fifty
thousand *pieces* of silver.

■ 20. **So mightily grew the**

■ **word** of God and prevailed.

■ 21. **After these things were**

■ **ended, Paul** purposed in the
spirit, when he had passed through
Macedonia and Achaia, to go to
Jerusalem, saying, After I have
been there, I must also see Rome.
22. So he sent into Macedonia two
of them that ministered unto him,
Timotheus and Erastus;
but he himself

■ **stayed in Asia**

■ **for a season.**
23. And the same time there arose
no small stir about that way.
24. For a certain *man*
named Demetrius,

■ **a silversmith, which made**

■ **silver shrines for Diana,**

■ **brought** no small

■ **gain unto the craftsmen;**

■ 25.**Whom hecalled together**
with the workmen of like occupation,

■ **and said, Sirs,** ye know that

■ **by this craft we have**

■ **our wealth.**

■ 26. **Moreover** ye see and hear,
that not alone at Ephesus, but
almost throughout all Asia, this

■ **Paul hath persuaded**
and turned away

■ **much people, saying that**

■ **they be no gods,** which are

■ **made with hands:**

■ 27. **So that not only this**

■ **our craft is in danger**
to be set at nought;

■ **but also** that

■ **the temple of** the great goddess

■ **Diana should be** despised,
and her magnificence should be

■ **destroyed,** whom all Asia
and the world worshippeth.

28. **And** when they heard *these sayings*, **they were full of wrath, and cried out, saying, Great is Diana** of the Ephesians.

29. And the whole city was filled with confusion: **and having caught Gaius and Aristarchus,** men of Macedonia, **Paul's companions** in travel, **they rushed** with one accord **into the theatre.**

30. **And when Paul would have entered** in unto the people, **the disciples suffered him not.**

31. **And certain of the chief of Asia,** which were his friends, **sent unto him, desiring him that he would not adventure** himself **into the theatre.**

32. Some therefore cried one thing, and some another: for the assembly was confused: and the more part knew not wherefore they were come together.

33. **And they drew Alexander out of the multitude,** the Jews putting him forward. **And Alexander** beckoned with the hand, and **would have made his defence** unto the people.

34. **But when they knew** that **he was a Jew, all with one voice about** the space of **two hours cried out, Great is Diana** of the Ephesians.

35. **And when the townclerk** had appeased the people, he **said,** *Ye* men of Ephesus, **what man** is there that **knoweth not** how **that the city** of the Ephesians **is a worshipper of** the great goddess **Diana,** and of the *image* which fell down from Jupiter?

36. **Seeing** then **that** these things **cannot be spoken against, ye ought to be quiet,** and to do nothing rashly.

37. **For** ye have brought hither **these men,** which **are neither robbers of churches, nor yet blasphemers** of your goddess.

38. **Wherefore if** Demetrius, and **the craftsmen** which are with him, **have a matter against any** man, **the law is open,** and there are deputies: **let them implead one another.**

39. But if ye inquire any thing concerning other matters, it shall be determined in a lawful assembly.

40. **For we are in danger to be called in question for this day's uproar,** there being no cause whereby we may give an account of this concourse.

41. **And** when he had thus spoken, **he dismissed the assembly.**

CHAPTER 20

1. **And after the uproar** was ceased, **Paul called** unto *him* **the disciples, and embraced them, and departed** for to go into Macedonia.

2. **And** when he had gone over those parts, and had given them much exhortation, **he came into Greece,**

3. **And there abode three months. And when the Jews laid wait for him,** as he was about to sail into Syria, **he purposed to return through Macedonia.**

4. And there accompanied him into Asia Sopater of Berea; and of the Thessalonians, Aristarchus and Secundus; and Gaius of Derbe, and

Timotheus; and of Asia, Tychicus and Trophimus.

5. These going before tarried for us at Troas.

6. **And we sailed away from Philippi** after the days of unleavened bread, **and came** unto them **to Troas** in five days; **where we abode seven days.**

7. **And upon the first day of the week,** when the disciples came together to break bread, **Paul preached unto them,** ready to depart on the morrow; **and continued his speech until midnight.**

8. And there were many lights in the upper chamber, where they were gathered together.

9. **And there sat in a window a** certain **young man named Eutychus, being fallen into a deep sleep:** and **as Paul was long preaching, he sunk down** with sleep, **and fell** down **from the third loft, and was taken up dead.**

10. **And Paul** went down, and fell on him, and **embracing him said, Trouble not yourselves; for his life is in him.**

11. When he therefore was come up again, and had broken bread, and eaten, and talked a long while, even till break of day, so he departed.

12. **And they brought the young man alive,** and were not a little comforted.

13. **And we went** before to ship, and sailed **unto Assos, there intending to take** in **Paul: for so had he appointed,** minding himself to go afoot.

14. **And** when he met with us at Assos,

we took him in, and came to Mitylene.

15. **And we sailed** thence, **and** came the next *day* over against Chios; and the next *day* we arrived at Samos, and tarried at Trogyllium; and the next *day* we came to Miletus.

16. **For Paul had determined** to sail by Ephesus, because he would not spend the time in Asia: for he hasted, if it were possible for him, **to be at Jerusalem the day of Pentecost.**

17. **And from Miletus he sent to Ephesus, and called the elders** of the church.

18. **And when they were come** to him, **he said** unto them, **Ye know,** from the first day that I came into Asia, after what manner **I have been with you at all seasons,**

19. **Serving the LORD** with all humility of mind, and **with many tears, and temptations,** which befell me **by** the lying in wait of **the Jews:**

20. **And how I** kept back nothing that was profitable *unto you,* but have shewed you, and **have taught** you publicly, and from house to house,

21. **Testifying both to the Jews, and** also to the **Greeks, repentance** toward God, **and faith toward our Lord Jesus Christ.**

22. **And now, behold, I go bound in the spirit unto Jerusalem, not knowing the things that shall befall me** there:

23. Save that the Holy Ghost witnesseth in every city, saying that bonds and afflictions abide me.

24. **But none of these things move me, neither count I my life dear** unto myself, **so that I might finish my course with joy,**

and the ministry, which I have received of the Lord Jesus, to testify the gospel of the grace of God.

25. **And now,** behold, **I know that ye** all, among whom I have gone preaching the kingdom of God, **shall see my face no more.** 26. **Wherefore I take you to record** this day, **that I am pure from the blood of all men.** 27. **For I have not shunned to declare** unto you **all the counsel of God.** 28. **Take heed therefore** unto yourselves, and to all the flock, over the which the Holy Ghost hath made you overseers, **to feed the church of God,** which he hath **purchased with his own blood.** 29. **For I know** this, that **after my departing shall** grievous **wolves enter in among you,** not sparing the flock. 30. **Also of your own selves shall men arise, speaking perverse things,** to draw away disciples after them. 31. **Therefore** watch, and **remember, that** by the space of three years **I ceased not to warn every one** night and day **with tears.** 32. **And now, brethren, I commend you to God, and to the word** of his grace, **which is able to build you** up, and to give you an inheritance among all them which are sanctified. 33. **I have coveted no man's** silver, or **gold,** or apparel. 34. Yea, ye yourselves know, that these hands have ministered unto my necessities, and to them that were with me. 35. I have shewed you all things, how that so labouring

ye ought to support the weak, and to remember the words of the Lord **Jesus, how he said, It is more blessed to give** than to receive. 36. **And** when he had thus spoken, **he kneeled** down, **and prayed with them** all. 37. **And they all wept** sore, **and fell on Paul's neck, and kissed him,** 38. Sorrowing most of all for the words which he spake, that they should see his face no more. And they accompanied him unto the ship.

CHAPTER 21

1. **And** it came to pass, that **after we were gotten from them,** and had launched, we came with a straight course unto Coos, and the *day* following unto Rhodes, and from thence unto Patara: 2. And finding a ship sailing over unto Phenicia, **we went aboard,** and set forth. 3. Now when we had discovered Cyprus, we left it on the left hand, **and sailed into Syria, and landed at Tyre:** for there the ship was to unlade her burden. 4. **And finding disciples, we tarried there seven days: who said to Paul through the Spirit, that he should not go up to Jerusalem.** 5. And when we had accomplished those days, we departed and went our way; and they all brought us on our way, with wives and children, till *we were* out of the city: and we kneeled down on the shore, and prayed. 6. And when we had taken our leave one of another, we took ship; and they returned home again. 7. **And** when we had finished *our* course from Tyre, **we came to Ptolemais, and saluted the brethren,** and abode with them one day. 8. **And the next day we** that were of Paul's company

■ departed, and came
■ unto Caesarea: and we
■ entered into the house of
■ Philip the evangelist, which
was *one* of the seven; and
abode with him.
9. And the same man had four
daughters, virgins, which
did prophesy.
■ 10. And as we tarried
there many days,
■ there came down from Judaea
■ a certain prophet,
■ named Agabus.
■ 11. And when he was come unto us,
■ he took Paul's girdle, and
■ bound his own hands and
■ feet, and said, Thus saith
■ the Holy Ghost, So shall
■ the Jews at Jerusalem
■ bind the man that owneth
■ this girdle, and shall
■ deliverhim into the
■ hands of the Gentiles.
■ 12. And when we
■ heard these things, both
■ we, and they of that place,
■ besought him not
■ to go up to Jerusalem.
■ 13. Then Paul answered,
■ What mean ye to weep
and to break mine heart?
■ for I am ready not to
■ be bound only, but
■ also to die at Jerusalem
■ for the name of
■ the Lord Jesus.
14. And when he would not be
persuaded, we ceased, saying,
The will of the Lord be done.
■ 15. And after those days
■ we took up our carriages, and
■ went up to Jerusalem.
16. There went with us also *certain* of
the disciples of Caesarea, and
brought with them one Mnason
of Cyprus, an old disciple, with
whom we should lodge.
■ 17. And when we were
come to Jerusalem,
■ the brethren received
■ us gladly.
■ 18. And the *day* following

■ Paul went in with us
■ unto James; and all
the elders were present.
■ 19. And when he had saluted them,
■ he declared particularly
■ what things God had
■ wrought among the
■ Gentiles by his ministry.
■ 20. And when they heard *it*,
■ they glorified the Lord,
■ and said unto him,
■ Thou seest, brother,
■ how many thousands
■ of Jews there are
■ which believe; and
they are all zealous of the law:
■ 21. And they are informed
■ of thee, that thou teachest
■ all the Jews which are
among the Gentiles
■ to forsake Moses,
■ saying that
■ they ought not to
■ circumcise *their* children,
neither to walk after the customs.
22. What is it therefore?
■ the multitude must needs
■ come together: for they will
■ hear that thou art come.
■ 23. Do therefore this
that we say to thee:
■ We have four men which
■ have a vow on them;
24. Them take, and
■ purify thyself with
■ them, and be at
■ charges with them,
that they may shave *their* heads:
■ and all may know that those
things, whereof they were informed
concerning thee, are nothing; but
■ that thou thyself
also walkest orderly, and
■ keepest the law
25. As touching the Gentiles which
believe, we have written *and*
concluded that they observe no such
thing, save only that they keep
themselves from *things* offered to
idols, and from blood, and from
strangled, and from fornication.
■ 26. Then Paul took the
men, and the next day

■ **purifying himself with them**
■ **entered into the temple, to**
■ **signify theaccomplish-**
■ **ment** of the days of purification,
until that an offering should be
offered for every one of them.
■ 27. **And** when the seven
days were almost ended,
■ **the Jews** which were
■ **of Asia, when they**
■ **saw him** in the temple,
■ **stirred up all the people,**
■ **and laid hands on him,**
■ 28. **Crying out,** Men of Israel,
■ **help: This is the man, that**
■ **teacheth** all *men* every where
■ **against** the people, and
■ **the law,** and this place:
■ **and further brought**
■ **Greeks** also
■ **into the temple, and hath**
■ **polluted this holy place.**
29. (For they had seen before with
him in the city Trophimus an
Ephesian, whom they supposed that
Paul had brought into the temple.)
■ 30. **And all the city**
■ **was moved,**
and the people ran together:
■ **and they took Paul, and**
■ **drew him out of the temple:**
and forthwith the doors were shut.
■ 31. **And as they went** about
■ **to kill him, tidings**
■ **came unto the chief**
■ **captain** of the band,
■ **that all Jerusalem**
■ **was in an uproar.**
■ 32. Who **immediately**
■ **took soldiers** and centurions,
■ **and ran** down
■ **unto them: and when they**
■ **saw** the chief captain and
■ **the soldiers, they left**
■ **beating of Paul.**
■ 33. **Then the chief captain**
came near, and took him, and
■ **commanded him to**
■ **be bound** with two chains;
■ **and demanded who**
■ **he was, and what he**
■ **had done.**
34. And some cried one thing, some

another, among the multitude:
■ **and when he could not**
■ **know the certainty for the**
■ **tumult, he commanded**
■ **him to be carried into**
■ **the castle.**
35. And when he came upon
the stairs, so it was, that he
was borne of the soldiers for
the violence of the people.
■ 36. **For the multitude**
of the people
■ **followed after, crying,**
■ **Away with him.**
■ 37. **And as Paul was** to be
■ **led** into the castle,
■ **he said unto the chief**
captain, May I speak unto thee? Who
said, Canst thou speak Greek?
38. Art not thou that Egyptian,
which before these days madest
anuproar, and leddest out into
the wilderness four thousand
men that were murderers?
39. But Paul said,
■ **I am** a man *which am*
■ **a Jew of Tarsus,** *a city* in
Cilicia, a citizen of no mean city: and,
■ **I beseech thee, suffer me**
■ **to speak unto the people.**
40. **And** when he had
given him licence,
■ **Paul stood on the**
■ **stairs,** and beckoned with
the hand unto the people.
■ **And when there**
■ **was** made a great
■ **silence, he spake** unto *them*
■ **in the Hebrew tongue,**
■ **saying,**

CHAPTER 22

1. Men, brethren, and fathers,
■ **hear ye my defence**
which I make now unto you.
■ 2. **(And when they**
■ **heard** that he spake in
■ **the Hebrew tongue** to them,
■ **they kept the more**
■ **silence:** and he saith,)
■ 3. **I am** verily a man *which am*
■ **a Jew, born in**
■ **Tarsus,** *a city* in Cilicia,

yet brought up in this city
at the feet of Gamaliel,
and taught according to
the perfect manner of the
law of the fathers, and was
zealous toward God,
as ye all are this day.
4. And I persecuted this
way unto the death,
binding and delivering into
prisons both men and women.
5. As also the high priest
doth bear me witness,
and all the estate of the elders:
from whom also
I received letters
unto the brethren,
and went to Damascus,
to bring them which were
there bound unto Jerusalem, for
to be punished.
6. And it came to pass, that,
as I made my journey,
and was come nigh unto
Damascus about noon,
suddenly there
shone from heaven
a great light round about me.
7. And I fell unto the
ground, and heard
a voice saying unto me,
Saul, Saul, why
persecutest thou me?
8. And I answered,
Who art thou, Lord?
And he said unto me,
I am Jesus of Nazareth,
whom thou persecutest.
9. And they that were with me saw
indeed the light, and were afraid;
but they heard not the voice of
him that spake to me.
10. And I said, What shall
I do, LORD? And the Lord
said unto me, Arise, and
go into Damascus; and there it
shall be told thee of all things
which are appointed for thee to do.
11. And when I could not see
for the glory of that light,
being led by the hand
of them that were with me,
I came into Damascus.

12. And one Ananias,
a devout man according to the
law, having a good report of all
the Jews which dwelt there,
13. Came unto me, and stood,
and said unto me,
Brother Saul, receive
thy sight. And the same
hour I looked up upon him.
14. And he said, The God of
our fathers hath chosen
thee, that thou shouldest
know his will, and see that
Just One, and shouldest
hear the voice of
his mouth.
15. For thou shalt be his
witness unto all men of what
thou hast seen and heard.
16. And now
why tarriest thou? arise, and
be baptized,
and wash away thy sins,
calling on the name
of the Lord.
17. And it came to pass, that, when
I was come again to Jerusalem,
even while I prayed in the temple,
I was in a trance;
18. And saw him saying
unto me, Make haste, and
get thee quickly
out of Jerusalem:
for they will not receive thy
testimony concerning me.
19. And I said, Lord, they
know that I imprisoned
and beat in every synagogue
them that believed on thee:
20. And when the blood
of thy martyr Stephen
was shed, I also
was standing by, and
consenting unto his
death, and kept the raiment
of them that slew him.
21. And he said unto me,
Depart: for I will send
thee far hence
unto the Gentiles.
22. And they gave him
audience unto this
word, and then

lifted up their voices, and **said, Away with such a fellow** from the earth: for **it is not fit that he should live.**

23. And as they cried out, and cast off *their* clothes, and threw dust into the air, 24. **The chief captain commanded** him to be brought into the castle, and bade that **he** should **be examined by scourging;** that he might know wherefore they cried so against him. 25. **And as they bound him** with thongs, **Paul said** unto the centurion that stood by, **Is it lawful for you to scourge** a man that is **a Roman,** and uncondemned? 26. **When the centurion heard** *that*, **he went and told the chief** captain, **saying, Take heed** what thou doest: **for this man is a Roman.** 27. **Then the chief captain** came, and **said unto him,** Tell me, **art thou a Roman? He said, Yea.** 28. **And the chief captain answered, With a great sum obtained I this freedom. And Paul said,** But **I was free born.** 29. **Then** straightway they departed from him which should have examined him: and **the chief captain also was afraid,** after he knew that he was a Roman, and **because he had bound him.** 30. **On the morrow,** because he would have known the certainty wherefore he was accused of the Jews, **he loosed him** from *his* bands, **and commanded the** chief

priests and all their council to appear, and brought Paul down, and set him **before them.**

CHAPTER 23

1. **And Paul,** earnestly beholding the council, **said,** Men *and* brethren, **I have lived in all good conscience before God** until this day. 2. **And the high priest Ananias commanded them** that stood by him **to smite him on the mouth.** 3. **Then said Paul unto him, God shall smite thee,** *thou* whited wall: **for sittest thou** to judge me **after the law, and commandest me to be smitten contrary to the law?** 4. **And they** that stood by **said, Revilest thou God's high priest?** 5. **Then said Paul, I wist not, brethren, that he was the high priest:** for it is written, Thou shalt not speak evil of the ruler of thy people. 6. **But when Paul perceived that the one part were Sadducees, and the other Pharisees, he cried out** in the council, Men *and* brethren, **I am a Pharisee,** the son of a Pharisee: **of the hope and resurrection of the dead am called in question.** 7. **And** when he had so said, **there arose a dissension between the Pharisees and** the **Sadducees:** and the multitude was divided. 8. **For the Sadducees say** that **there is no resurrection,** neither angel, nor spirit: **but the Pharisees**

225

confess both.

9. **And** there arose a great cry: and the scribes *that were* of **the Pharisees' part arose,** and strove, **saying, We find no evil in this man:** but if a spirit or an angel hath spoken to him, let us not fight against God.

10. **And** when there arose a great dissension, **the chief captain, fearing lest Paul should have been pulled in pieces** of them, **commanded the soldiers to** go down, and to **take him by force** from among them, **and** to **bring him into the castle.**

11. **And the night following the Lord stood by him, and said, Be of good cheer, Paul: for as thou hast testified of me in Jerusalem, so must thou bear witness** also **at Rome.**

12. **And** when it was day, **certain** of the **Jews banded together,** and bound themselves under a curse, saying that they would neither eat nor drink till they had killed Paul.

13. And they were more than forty which had made this conspiracy.

14. **And they came to the chief priests** and elders, **and said, We have bound ourselves** under a great curse, **that we will eat nothing until we have slain Paul.**

15. **Now therefore** ye with the council **signify to the chief captain that he bring him down** unto you to-morrow, as though ye would inquire something more perfectly concerning him: **and we,** or ever he come near, **are ready to kill him.**

16. **And when Paul's sister's son heard** of their lying in wait,

he went and entered into the castle, **and told Paul.**

17. **Then Paul called one of the centurions** unto *him,* **and said, Bring this young man unto the chief captain:** for he hath a certain thing to tell him.

18. So he took him, and brought *him* to the chief captain, and said, Paul the prisoner called me unto *him,* and prayed me to bring this young man unto thee, who hath something to say unto thee.

19. **Then the chief captain took him** by the hand, and went *with him* aside privately, **and asked** *him,* **What is that thou hast to tell** me?

20. **And he said, The Jews** have agreed to **desire** thee **that thou wouldest bring** down **Paul** to morrow **into the council,** as though they would inquire somewhat of him more perfectly.

21. **But do not** thou **yield unto them:for there lie in wait** for him of them more than **forty men,** which have **bound** themselves **with an oath, that they will neither eat nor drink till they have killed him:** and now are they ready, looking for a promise from thee.

22. **So the chief captain** then **let the young man depart,** and charged *him, See thou* tell no man that thou hast shewed these things to me.

23. **And he called** unto *him* **two centurions, saying, Make ready two hundred soldiers to go to Caesarea,** and horsemen threescore and ten, and spearmen two hundred, at the third hour of the night;

24. And provide *them* beasts,

that they may set Paul on, and bring him safe unto Felix the governor.
25. **And he wrote a letter** after this manner:
26. Claudius Lysias **unto** the most excellent governor **Felix** *sendeth* greeting.
27. This man was taken of the Jews, and should have been killed of them: then came I with an army, and rescued him, having understood that he was a Roman.
28. And when I would have known the cause wherefore they accused him, I brought him forth into their council:
29. Whom I perceived to be accused of questions of their law, but to have nothing laid to his charge worthy of death or of bonds.
30. And when it was told me how that the Jews laid wait for the man, I sent straightway to thee, and gave commandment to his accusers also to say before thee what *they had* against him. Farewell.
31. **Then the soldiers,** as it was commanded them, **took Paul,** and brought *him* by night to Antipatris.
32. On the morrow they left the horsemen to go with him, and returned to the castle:
33. Who, when they came **to Caesarea and** delivered the epistle **to the governor,** presented Paul also before him.
34. **And when the governor had read the letter, he asked of what province he was.** And when he understood that *he was* of Cilicia;
35. **I will hear thee, said he, when thine accusers** are also **come.** And he commanded him to be kept in Herod's judgment hall.

CHAPTER 24

1. **And after five days Ananias** the high priest **descended** with the elders, and **with a** certain **orator named Tertullus,** who informed the governor against Paul.
2. **And** when he was called forth, **Tertullus began to accuse him, saying,** Seeing that by thee we enjoy great quietness, and that **very worthy deeds are done unto this nation by thy providence,**
3. **We accept it always,** and in all places, **most noble Felix, with all thankfulness.**
4. Notwithstanding, that I be not further tedious unto thee, **I pray** thee **that thou wouldest hear us** of thy clemency a few words.
5. **For we have found this man** *a* pestilent *fellow,* and **a mover of sedition among** all the **Jews throughout the world, and a ringleader** of the sect **of the Nazarenes:**
6. Who also hath gone about to profane the temple: **whom we** took, and **would have judged** according to our law.
7. **But the chief captain Lysias** came *upon us,* and with great violence **took him away** out of our hands,
8. **Commanding his accusers to come unto thee:** by examining of whom thyself mayest take knowledge of all these things, whereof we accuse him.
9. And the Jews also assented, saying that these things were so.
10. **Then Paul,** after that the governor had beckoned unto him to speak, **answered, Forasmuch as I know that thou hast been of many years a judge unto this nation, I do** the more cheerfully **answer for myself:**
11. **Because that thou**

mayest understand,
that there are yet
but twelve days
since I went up
to Jerusalem for to worship.
12. And they neither
found me in the temple
disputing with any man,
neither raising up the people, neither
in the synagogues,
nor in the city:
13. Neither can they prove the things
whereof they now accuse me.
14. But this I confess unto thee,
that after the way which
they call heresy, so worship
I the God of
my fathers, believing
all things which are written
in the law and in
the prophets:
15. And have hope toward God,
which they themselves also allow,
that there shall be a
resurrection of the dead,
both of the just and unjust.
16. And herein do I exercise myself,
to have always a conscience void to
offence toward God, and *toward* men.
17. Now after many years
I came to bring alms
to my nation, and offerings.
18. Whereupon certain
Jews from Asia found
me purified in the temple,
neither with multitude, nor with tumult.
19. Who ought to have been
here before thee, and object,
if they had aught
against me.
20. Or else
let these same *here*
say, if they have found
any evil doing in me,
while I stood before the council,
21. Except it be for this one voice,
that I cried standing among them,
Touching the resurrection of
the dead I am called
in question by you this day.
22. And when Felix heard
these things, having more perfect
knowledge of *that* way,

he deferred them, and
said, When Lysias
the chief captain
shall come down,
I will know the uttermost
of your matter.
23. And he commanded
a centurion to keep
Paul, and to
let him have liberty, and
that he should forbid
none of his acquaintance
to minister or
come unto him.
24. And after certain
days, when Felix came
with his wife Drusilla,
which was a Jewess,
he sent for Paul, and heard
him concerning the faith in
Christ.
25. And as he reasoned
of righteousness,
temperance, and
judgment to come,
Felix trembled, and
answered, Go thy
way for this time;
when I have a
convenient season,
I will call for thee.
26. He hoped also that money should
have been given him of Paul, that he
might loose him: wherefore he sent
for him the oftener, and
communed with him.
27. But after two years Porcius
Festus came into Felix'
room: and Felix, willing to
shew the Jews a pleasure,
left Paul bound.

CHAPTER 25

1. Now when Festus was
come into the province, after three
days he ascended from Caesarea
to Jerusalem.
2. Then the high priest and the chief
of the Jews informed him
against Paul, and besought him,
3. And desired
favour against him,
that he would send for

him to Jerusalem,
laying wait in the way
to kill him.
4. But Festus answered, that
Paul should be kept at
Caesarea, and that he himself
would depart shortly *thither.*
5. Let them therefore, said he,
which among you are able,
go down with *me,*
and accuse this man, if there
be any wickedness in him.
6. And when he had tarried among
them more than ten days,
he went down unto Caesarea;
and the next day sitting
on the judgment seat
commanded Paul
to be brought.
7. And when he was come,
the Jews which came down from
Jerusalem stood round about, and
laid many and grievous
complaints against
Paul, which they
could not prove.
8. While he answered
for himself,
Neither against the law
of the Jews, neither against
the temple, nor yet against
Caesar, have I offended
any thing at all.
9. But Festus, willing
to do the Jews a
pleasure, answered Paul, and
said, Wilt thou go up
to Jerusalem, and there
be judged of these things
before me?
10. Then said Paul, I stand at
Caesar's judgment seat,
where I ought to be judged:
to the Jews have I done no wrong,
as thou very well
knowest.
11. For if I be an offender,
or have committed any thing
worthy of death,
I refuse not to die: but if
there be none of these
things whereof these
accuse me, no man may

deliver me unto them.
I appeal unto Caesar.
12. Then Festus, when he had
conferred with the council,
answered, Hast thou
appealed unto Caesar?
unto Caesar shalt thou go.
13. And after certain days
king Agrippa and Bernice
came unto Caesarea
to salute Festus.
14. And when they had
been there many days,
Festus declared Paul's
cause unto the king,
saying, There is a certain
man left in bonds by Felix:
15. About whom,
when I was at
Jerusalem, the chief
priests and the elders of
the Jews informed me,
desiring to have judgment
against him.
16. To whom I answered, It is not the
manner of the Romans to deliver
any man to die, before that he which
is accused have the accusers face to
face, and have licence to answer for
himself concerning the crime
laid against him.
17. Therefore,
when they were come
hither, without any
delay on the morrow
I sat on the judgment seat, and
commanded the man
to be brought forth.
18. Against whom
when the accusers stood
up, they brought none
accusation of such things
as I supposed:
19. But had certain
questions against him
of their own superstition,
and of one Jesus, which
was dead, whom Paul
affirmed to be alive.
20. And because I doubted
of such manner of questions,
I asked him whether he
would go to Jerusalem,

and there
be judged of these matters.
21. **But when Paul** had
appealed to be reserved
unto the hearing of
Augustus, I commanded
him to be kept till I might
send him to Caesar.
22. **Then Agrippa**
said unto Festus,
I would also hear the
man myself. To morrow,
said he, thou shalt hear him.
23. **And on the morrow,**
when Agrippa was come,
and Bernice, with great pomp,
and was entered into the place of
hearing, with the chief captains,
and principal men of the city,
at Festus' commandment
Paul was brought forth.
24. **And Festus said, King**
Agrippa, and all men which are
here present with us,
ye see this man,
about whom all the
multitude of the Jews
have dealt with me,
both at Jerusalem, and *also* here,
crying that he ought
not to live any longer.
25. But when I found that he had
committed nothing worthy of death,
and that he himself hath appealed
to Augustus, I have determined
to send him.
26. Of whom I have no certain
thing to write unto my lord.
Wherefore I have brought
him forth before you,
and specially before thee,
O king Agrippa, that, after
examination had, I might have
somewhat to write.
27. For it seemeth to me unreasonable
to send a prisoner, and not withal
to signify the crimes *laid* against him.

CHAPTER 26

1. **Then Agrippa said unto**
Paul, Thou art permitted
to speak for thyself.
Then Paul

stretched forth the hand, and
answered for himself:
2. **I think myself happy,**
king Agrippa, because
I shall answer for myself
this day before thee
touching all the things
whereof I am accused
of the Jews:
3. **Especially because I**
know thee to be expert in
all customs
and questions which are
among the Jews: wherefore I
beseech thee to hear me patiently.
4. **My manner of life from** my
youth, which was at the first among
mine own nation at Jerusalem,
know all the Jews;
5. Which knew me from the
beginning, if they would testify,
that after the most straitest
sect of our religion
I lived a Pharisee.
6. **And now I** stand and
am judged for the hope of
the promise made of God, unto
our fathers:
7. Unto which *promise* our twelve
tribes, instantly serving *God* day
and night, hope to come. For
which hope's sake, king Agrippa,
I am accused of the Jews.
8. **Why should it**
be thought a thing
incredible with you,
that God should
raise the dead?
9. **I verily thought** with myself,
that I ought to do many things
contrary to the name of
Jesus of Nazareth.
10. **Which thing I** also
did in Jerusalem:
and many of the
saints did I shut up
in prison, having received authority
from the chief priests;
and when they were put
to death, I gave my voice
against them.
11. And I punished them oft in every
synagogue, and compelled *them* to

blaspheme; and being exceedingly mad against them,

I persecuted them even unto strange cities. 12. **Whereupon as I went to Damascus** with authority and commission from the chief priests, 13. At midday, O king, **I saw** in the way **a light from heaven,** above the brightness of the sun, shining round about me and them which journeyed with me. 14. **And when we were all fallen** to the earth, **I heard a voice** speaking unto me, and **saying** in the Hebrew tongue, Saul, **Saul, why persecutest thou me?** *it is* hard for thee to kick against the pricks. 15. **And I said, Who art thou, Lord? And he said, I am Jesus whom thou persecutest** 16. But rise, and stand upon thy feet: for **I have appeared unto thee** for this purpose, **to make thee a minister** and a witness both of these things which thou hast seen, and of those things in the which I will appear unto thee; 17. Delivering thee from the people, and *from* the Gentiles, unto whom now I send thee, 18. To open their eyes, *and* **to turn them** from darkness to light, and **from the power of Satan unto God,** that they may receive forgiveness of sins, and inheritance among them which are sanctified by faith that is in me. 19. **Whereupon**, O king Agrippa, **I was not disobedient unto the** heavenly **vision:** 20. **But shewed first** unto **them of Damascus, and** at **Jerusalem, and throughout all the coasts of Judaea, and then to the**

Gentiles, that they should repent and turn to God, and do works meet for repentance. 21. **For these causes the Jews** caught me in the temple, and **went about to kill me.** 22. **Having therefore obtained help of God, I continue** unto this day, **witnessing both** to small and great, **saying none other things than those which the prophets and Moses did say** should come 23. **That Christ should suffer**, *and* that he should be the first that **should rise from the dead, and should shew light unto the people, and** to **the Gentiles.** 24. **And** as he thus spake for himself, **Festus said** with a loud voice, **Paul,** thou art beside thyself; **much learning doth make thee mad.** 25. **But he said, I am not mad,** most noble **Festus; but speak** forth the **words of truth** and soberness. 26. **For the king knoweth** of these things, before whom also I speak freely: for I am persuaded that none of these things are hidden from him; for **this thing was not done in a corner.** 27. **King Agrippa, believest** thou **the prophets? I know** that **thou believest.** 28. **Then Agrippa said** unto Paul, **Almost thou persuadest me to be a Christian** 29. **And Paul said, I would** to God, **that not only thou, but** also **all** that hear me this day, **were** both almost, and altogether such **as I am,** except these bonds.

30. And when he had thus spoken, the king rose up, and the governor, and Bernice, and they that sat with them: 31. And when they were gone aside, they talked between themselves, saying, This man doeth nothing worthy of death or of bonds. 32. **Then said Agrippa unto Festus, This man might have been set at liberty, if he had not appealed unto Caesar.**

CHAPTER 27

1. **And when it was determined that we should sail into Italy, they delivered Paul** and certain other prisoners **unto** *one* named **Julius, a centurion** of Augustus' band. 2. And entering into a ship of Adramyttium, we launched, meaning to sail by the coasts of Asia; *one* Aristarchus, a Macedonian of Thessalonica, being with us. 3. And the next *day* we touched at Sidon. And Julius courteously entreated Paul, and gave *him* liberty to go unto his friends to refresh himself. 4. And when we had launched from thence, we sailed under Cyprus, because the winds were contrary. 5. **And when we had sailed over the sea of Cilicia** and Pamphylia, **we came to Myra,** *a city* of Lycia. 6. **And there the centurion found a ship** of Alexandria **sailing into Italy; and he put us therein.** 7. And when we had sailed slowly many days, and scarce were come over against Cnidus, the wind not suffering us, we sailed under Crete, over again Salmone; 8. And, hardly passing it, came unto a place which is called The fair havens; nigh whereunto was the city of Lasea.

9. Now when much time was spent, **and when sailing was now dangerous, because the fast was** now **already past, Paul admonished them,** 10. **And said** unto them, Sirs, **I perceive that this voyage will be with hurt and** much **damage, not only of the** lading and **ship, but also** of **our lives.** 11. **Nevertheless the centurion believed the master** and the owner **of the ship, more than** those things which were spoken by **Paul.** 12. **And because the haven was not commodious to winter in, the more part advised to depart** thence also, if by any means they might attain to Phenice, *and there* to winter; *which is* an haven of Crete, and lieth toward the south-west and north-west. 13. **And when the south wind blew softly,** supposing that they had obtained *their* purpose, loosing *thence*, **they sailed close by Crete.** 14. **But** not long after **there arose** against it **a tempestuous wind,** called Euroclydon. 15. **And when the ship was caught,** and could not bear up into the wind, **we let her drive.** 16. **And running under a** certain **island** which is **called Clauda, we had much work** to come by the boat: 17. Which when they had taken up, they used helps, undergirding the ship; and, fearing lest they should fall into the quicksands, strake sail, and so were driven. 18. **And we being** exceedingly **tossed with a tempest, the**

next day they
lightened the ship;
19. And the third day we
cast out with our own hands
the tackling of the ship.
20. And when neither
sun nor stars in many days
appeared, and no small
tempest lay on *us*,
all hope that we should be saved
was then taken away.
21. But after long abstinence
Paul stood forth in
the midst of them,
and said, Sirs, ye should have
hearkened unto me, and not have
loosed from Crete, and to have
gained this harm and loss.
22. And now I exhort you to
be of good cheer: for there
shall be no loss of *any man's*
life among you, but
of the ship.
23. For there stood by me
this night the angel of God,
whose I am, and whom I serve,
24. Saying, Fear not,
Paul; thou must be brought
before Caesar: and, lo,
God hath given thee all
them that sail with thee.
25. Wherefore, sirs,
be of good cheer: for
I believe God, that it shall
be even as it was told me
26. Howbeit we must be
cast upon a certain island.
27. But when the fourteenth
night was come, as we
were driven up and down
in Adria, about midnight
the shipmen deemed
that they drew near
to some country;
28. And sounded, and
found it twenty fathoms:
and when they had gone
a little further, they sounded
again, and
found it fifteen fathoms.
29. Then fearing lest we
should have fallen upon
rocks, they cast four

anchors out of the stern,
and wished for the day.
30. And as the shipmen
were about to flee out of the
ship, when they had let down the
boat into the sea, under colour as
though they would have cast
anchors out of the foreship,
31. Paul said to
the centurion and to
the soldiers, Except
these abide in the ship,
ye cannot be saved.
32. Then the soldiers
cut off the ropes of the
boat, and let her fall off.
33. And while the
day was coming on,
Paul besought
them all to take meat,
saying, This day
is the fourteenth day
that ye have tarried and
continued fasting,
having taken nothing.
34. Wherefore I pray you to
take some meat: for this is
for your health: for there
shall not an hair fall
from the head of
any of you.
35. And when he had thus spoken,
he took bread, and
gave thanks to God
in presence of them all:
and when he had broken *it*, he
began to eat.
36. Then were they all of
good cheer, and they also
took some meat.
37. And we were in all in the
ship two hundred threescore
and sixteen souls.
38. And when they
had eaten enough,
they lightened the ship, and
cast out the wheat into the sea.
39. And when it was day,
they knew not the land: but
they discovered a certain
creek with a shore,
into the
which they were minded,

if it were possible,
to thrust in
the ship.
40. **And** when they had
taken up the anchors,
they committed themselves
unto the sea, and loosed the
rudder bands, and hoised up the
mainsail to the wind, and made
toward shore.
41. **And** falling into a
place where two seas met,
they ran the ship
aground; and the
forepart stuck fast,
and remained unmoveable,
but the hinder
part was broken
with the violence of the waves.
42. **And the soldiers'**
counsel was to kill the
prisoners, lest any of them should
swim out, and escape.
43. **But the centurion,**
willing to save Paul,
kept them from their
purpose; and commanded
that they which could swim
should cast *themselves*
first *into the sea*, and
get to land:
44. **And the rest,** some
on boards, and some on
broken pieces of the ship.
And so it came to pass, that they
escaped all safe
to land.

CHAPTER 28

1. **And** when they were
escaped, then they knew that
the island was
called Melita.
2. **And the barbarous**
people shewed us no little
kindness: for they
kindled a fire, and received
us every one,
because of the present
rain, and because of the
cold.
3. **And when Paul** had
gathered a bundle of

sticks, and laid them on
the fire, there came a
viper out of the heat,
and fastened on his hand.
4. **And when the barbarians**
saw the venomous beast
hang on his hand, they
said among themselves, No doubt
this man is a murderer,
whom, though he hath
escaped the sea, yet
vengeance suffereth
not to live.
5. **And he shook off**
the beast into the fire,
and felt no harm.
6. **Howbeit they looked** when
he should have swollen, or fallen
down dead suddenly: but after
they had looked a great while,
and saw no harm come to
him, they changed their minds,
and said that he was
a god.
7. In the same quarters
were possessions of
the chief man of the island,
whose name was Publius;
who received us, and
lodged us three
days courteously.
8. **And** it came to pass,
that the father of Publius lay
sick of a fever and of
a bloody flux: to whom Paul
entered in, and prayed,
and laid his
hands on him,
and healed him.
9. **So** when this was done,
others also,
which had
diseases in the island,
came, and were healed:
10. Who also honoured us with many
honours; and when we departed,
they laded *us* with such things
as were necessary.
11. **And after three months**
we departed in a ship of
Alexandria, which had wintered
in the isle, whose sign was
Castor and Pollux.

12. **And landing at Syracuse, we tarried there** three days.

13. **And from thence** we fetched a compass, and **came to Rhegium:** and after one day the south wind blew, **and** we came the **next** day **to Puteoli:**

14. **Where we found brethren, and** were **desired to tarry** with them **seven days: and so we went toward Rome.**

15. **And** from thence, **when the brethren heard of us, they came to meet us as far as Appii forum,** and The three taverns: whom when Paul saw, he thanked God, and took courage.

16. **And when we came to Rome, the centurion delivered** the prisoners to the captain of the guard: but **Paul** was suffered **to dwell by himself with a soldier** that kept him.

17. **And** it came to pass, that **after three days Paul called the chief of the Jews together: and** when they were come together, he **said unto them,** Men *and* brethren, **though I have committed nothing against the people,** or customs of our fathers, **yet was I delivered prisoner from Jerusalem into the hands of the Romans.**

18. **Who,** when they had examined me, **would have let me go,** because there was no cause of death in me.

19. **But** when **the Jews spake against it, I was constrained to appeal unto Caesar;** not that I had ought to accuse my nation of.

20. **For this cause** therefore have **I called for you,** to see *you*, and to speak with *you* : **because** that **for the hope of Israel I am bound** with this chain.

21. **And they said** unto him, **We neither received letters** out of Judaea concerning thee, **neither any of the brethren** that came shewed or **spake any harm of thee.**

22. **But we desire to hear** of thee **what thou thinkest:** for as concerning this sect, we know that every where it is spoken against.

23. **And** when they had appointed him a day, **there came many to** him into **his lodging; to whom he** expounded and **testified the kingdom of God, persuading them concerning Jesus, both out of the law of Moses, and** *out of* **the prophets,** from morning till evening.

24. **And some believed** the things which were spoken, **and some believed not.**

25. **And** when they agreed not among themselves, **they departed, after** that **Paul had spoken** one word, **Well spake the Holy Ghost by Esaias** the prophet unto our fathers,

26. **Saying, Go unto this people, and say, Hearing ye shall hear, and shall not understand;** and seeing ye shall see, and not perceive:

27. **For the heart of this people is waxed gross, and their ears are dull of hearing,** and their eyes have they closed; lest they should see with *their* eyes, and hear with *their* ears, and understand with *their* heart,

■ and should be converted,
■ and I should heal them.
■ 28. **Be it known**
■ **therefore** unto you,
■ **that the salvation of God**
■ **is sent unto the Gentiles,**
■ and *that* they will hear it.
■ 29. **And when he had said**
■ **these words, the Jews**
■ **departed,** and had great
reasoning among themselves.

■ 30. **And Paul dwelt two** whole
■ **years in his own hired**
■ **house, and received**
■ **all that came** in unto him,
■ 31. **Preaching the**
■ **kingdom** of God,
■ **and teaching**
those things which concern
■ **the Lord Jesus Christ,**
■ **with all confidence,**
no man forbidding him.

THE EPISTLE TO THE ROMANS

BACKGROUND INFORMATION

Author: **Paul,** an Apostle.
Date Written: probably **between 58** and **60** A.D.

Number of:
Verses   433
Chapters   16
Total Words 9,447
Scan Words 4,700
Scan Words represent
49 % of Total Words

Theme: the righteousness of God revealed and accomplished **in Jesus Christ** and how believers should live in light of God's righteousness

OUTLINE OF THE EPISTLE

Prologue
Chapter 1 - 1:15

I. The Righteousness of God Revealed in the **judgment of Sin**
Chapters 1 - 2

II. The Righteousness of God Revealed in **Justification by Faith**
Chapters 3 - 4

III. The Righteousness of God Revealed in **Salvation**
Chapters 5 - 8

IV. The Righteousness of God Revealed in **History**
Chapters 9 - 12

V. The Righteousness of God Revealed in **Christian Living**
Chapters 13 - 16.

CHAPTER 1

■ ■ 1. **Paul,** a servant of Jesus Christ,
■ **called to be an apostle,**
separated unto the gospel of God,
2. (Which he had promised afore by
his prophets in the holy scriptures,)
■ 3. **Concerning** his Son Jesus
■ **Christ** our Lord, which was
made of the seed of David
according to the flesh;
4. And declared *to be*
■ **the Son of God with power,**
according to the spirit of holiness,
■ **by the resurrection**
from the dead:
5. By whom we have received grace
and apostleship, for obedience to the
faith among all nations, for his name:
6. Among whom are ye also
the called of Jesus Christ:
■ 7. **To all that be in**
■ **Rome,** beloved of God,
■ **called to be saints:**
■ **Grace** to you and peace
■ **from God** our Father,
■ **and the Lord Jesus** Christ.
■ 8. **First, I thank my God**
through Jesus Christ for you all,
■ **that your faith is spoken**
■ **of throughout the**
■ **whole world.**
■ 9. **For God is my witness,**
whom I serve with my spirit in
the gospel of his Son, that
■ **without ceasing I make**
■ **mention of you** always
■ **in my prayers;**
10. Making request, if by any
means now at length I might
have a prosperous journey by
the will of God to come unto you.
■ 11. **For I long to see you,**
■ **that I may impart unto you**
■ **some spiritual gift,** to the
end ye may be established;
12. That is, that I may be comforted
together with you by the mutual faith
both of you and me.
13. Now I would not have you
ignorant, brethren, that oftentimes
I purposed to come unto you, (but
was let hitherto,) that I might
have some fruit among you also,

even as among other Gentiles.
■ 14. **I am debtor both to**
■ **the Greeks, and** to the
■ **Barbarians;** both to
the wise, and to the unwise.
15. **So,** as much as in me is,
■ **I am ready to preach**
■ **the gospel to you**
that are at Rome also.
■ 16. **For I am not ashamed**
■ **of the gospel of Christ:**
■ **for it is the power of**
■ **God unto salvation to every**
■ **one that believeth;** to the Jew
first, and also to the Greek.
■ 17. **For therein is the**
■ **righteousness of God**
■ **revealed** from faith to faith:
■ **as it is written, The just**
■ **shall live by faith.**
■ 18. **For the wrath of**
■ **God is** revealed from heaven
■ **against all** ungodliness and
unrighteousness of men,
■ **who hold the truth in**
■ **unrighteousness;**
19. Because that which may be
known of God is manifest in them;
for God hath shewed *it* unto them.
■ 20. **For the invisible**
■ **things of him from the**
■ **creation of the world**
■ **are clearly seen,**
being understood
■ **by the things** that are
■ **made, even his eternal**
■ **power and Godhead;**
■ **so that they are**
■ **without excuse:**
■ 21. **Because that, when**
■ **they knew God, they**
■ **glorified him not**
as God, neither were thankful;
■ **but became vain** in their
imaginations, and their foolish
heart was darkened.
■ 22. **Professing themselves to**
■ **be wise, they**
■ **became fools,**
■ 23. **And changed the glory**
■ **of the uncorruptible God**
■ **into an image** made
like to corruptible man, and to birds,

and fourfooted beasts, and creeping things.

24. **Wherefore God also gave them up to** uncleanness through the **lusts** of their own hearts, **to dishonour their own bodies between themselves:**

25. **Who changed the truth of God into a lie, and worshipped** and served **the creature more than the Creator,** who is blessed for ever. Amen.

26. For this cause God gave them up unto vile affections: **for even their women did change the natural use into that which is against nature:**

27. **And likewise also the men,** leaving the natural use of the woman, **burned in** their **lust one toward another;** men with men working that which is unseemly, and **receiving in themselves that recompence of their error** which was meet.

28. **And** even as they did not like to retain God in *their* knowledge, **God gave them over to a reprobate mind,** to do those things which are not convenient;

29. **Being filled with all unrighteousness,** fornication, wickedness, covetousness, maliciousness; full of envy, murder, debate, deceit, malignity; whisperers,

30. Backbiters, haters of God, despiteful, proud, boasters, inventors of evil things, disobedient to parents,

31. Without understanding, covenant breakers, without natural affection, implacable, unmerciful:

32. **Who knowing the judgment of God, that they which commit such things are worthy of death, not only do the same, but have pleasure in them** that do them.

CHAPTER 2

1. **Therefore thou art inexcusable, O man,** whosoever thou art that judgest: **for wherein thou judgest another, thou condemnest thyself;** for thou that judgest doest the same things.

2. **But** we are sure that **the judgment of God is according to truth** against them which commit such things.

3. **And thinkest thou** this, O man, **that judgest them which do such things, and doest the same, that thou shalt escape the judgment** ofGod?

4. **Or despisest thou** the riches of **his goodness** and forbearance and longsuffering; **not knowing that the goodness of God leadeth** thee **to repentance?**

5. **But after thy** hardness and **impenitent heart treasurest up** unto thyself **wrath against the day of** wrath and **revelation of the righteous judgment of God;**

6. **Who will render to every man according to his deeds:**

7. **To them who** by patient continuance in well-doing **seek for glory** and honour **and immortality, eternal life:**

8. **But unto them that** are contentious, and **do not obey the truth,** but obey unrighteousness, indignation and wrath,

9. **Tribulation and anguish,** upon every soul of man that doeth evil, of the Jew first, and also of the Gentile;

10. But glory, honour, and peace, to

every man that worketh good, to the Jew first, and also to the Gentile:

11. **For there is no respect of persons with God.**

12. **For as many as have sinned without law shall** also **perish without law: and as many as have sinned in the law shall be judged by the law;**

13. **(For not the hearers** of the law *are* just before God, **but the doers of the law shall be justified.**

14. **For when the Gentiles, which have not the law, do by nature** the **things** contained **in the law, these,** having not the law, **are a law unto themselves:**

15. **Which shew the work of the law written in their hearts,** their conscience also bearing witness, and *their* thoughts the mean while accusing or else excusing one another;)

16. **In the day when God shall judge the secrets of men by Jesus** Christ according to my gospel.

17. **Behold, thou art called a Jew, and** restest in the law, and makest thy boast of God,

18. And knowest *his* will, and approvest the things that are more excellent, being instructed out of the law;

19. And art confident that thou thyself art a guide of the blind, a light of them which are in darkness,

20. **An instructor** of the foolish, a teacher of babes, which hast the form of knowledge and of the truth **in the law.**

21. **Thou therefore which teachest another, teachest thou not thyself?** thou that preachest a man should not steal, dost thou steal?

22. **Thou that sayest a man should not commit adultery, dost thou commit**

adultery? thou that abhorrest idols, dost thou commit sacrilege?

23. Thou that makest thy boast of the law, through breaking the law dishonourest thou God?

24. For the name of God is blasphemed among the Gentiles through you, as it is written.

25. **For circumcision** verily **profiteth, if thou keep the law: but if thou be a breaker** of the law, **thy circumcision is made uncircumcision.**

26. **Therefore if the uncircumcision keep the** righteousness of the **law, shall not his uncircumcision be counted for circumcision?**

27. **And shall not uncircumcision which** is by nature, if it **fulfil the law, judge thee, who** by the letter and circumcision **dost transgress the law?**

28. **For he is not a Jew, which is one outwardly;** neither *is that* circumcision, which is outward in the flesh:

29. **But he is a Jew, which is one inwardly; and circumcision is** *that* of the heart, **in the spirit, and not in the letter;** whose praise *is* not of men, but of God.

CHAPTER 3

1. **What advantage then hath the Jew?** or what profit *is there* of circumcision?

2. **Much** every way: chiefly, **because** that **unto them were committed the oracles of God.**

3. **For what if some did not believe? shall their unbelief make the faith of God without effect?**

4. **God forbid:** yea, **let God be true, but every man a liar;** as it is written, That

thou mightest be justified in thy sayings, and mightest overcome when thou art judged.

5. **But if our unrighteousness commend the righteousness of God,** what shall we say? **Is God unrighteous who taketh vengeance?** (I speak as a man)

6. **God forbid: for then how shall God judge the world?**

7. **For if the truth** of God hath more **abounded through my lie unto his glory; why** yet **am I** also **judged as a sinner?**

8. And not *rather,* (as we be slanderously reported, and as some affirm that we say,) Let us do evil, that good may come? whose damnation is just.

9. **What then? are we better than they? No,** in no wise: for **we have** before **proved both Jews and Gentiles,** that they **are** all **under sin;**

10. **As it is written, There is none righteous,** no, not one:

11. **There is none** that understandeth, there is none **that seeketh after God.**

12. They are all gone out of the way, they are together become unprofitable; **there is none that doeth good,** no, not one.

13. Their throat *is* an open sepulchre; with their tongues they have used deceit; the poison of asps *is* under their lips:

14. Whose mouth *is* full of cursing and bitterness:

15. Their feet *are* swift to shed blood:

16. Destruction and misery *are* in their ways:

17. And the way of peace have they not known:

18. There is no fear of God before their eyes.

19. **Now we know that** what things soever

the law saith, it saith **to them** who are **under the law: that every mouth** may **be stopped, and all** the world **may become guilty before God.**

20. **Therefore by the** deeds of the **law** there **shall no flesh be justified** in his sight: for by the law is the **knowledge of sin.**

21. **But now the righteousness of God without the law is manifested,** being witnessed by the law and the prophets;

22. Even the righteousness of God **which is by faith of Jesus Christ unto all** and upon all them **that believe: for there is no difference:**

23. **For all have sinned, and come short of the glory of God;**

24. **Being justified** freely **by his grace through** the **redemption** that is **in Christ Jesus:**

25. **Whom God hath set forth to be a propitiation through faith in his blood, to** declare his righteousness for **the remission of sins** that are past, through the forbearance of God;

26. To declare, *I say,* at this time his righteousness: that he might be just, and the justifier of him which believeth in Jesus.

27. **Where is boasting then? It is excluded.** By what law? of works? Nay: but by the law of faith.

28. **Therefore we conclude that a man is justified by faith without the deeds of the law.**

29. *Is he* the God of the Jews only? *is he* not also of the Gentiles? Yes, of the Gentiles also:

30. **Seeing it is one God, which shall justify the**

circumcision by faith, and uncircumcision through faith. 31. **Do we then make void the law through faith? God forbid:** yea, we establish the law.

CHAPTER 4

1. **What shall we say** then **that Abraham** our father, as pertaining to the flesh, **hath found?** 2. **For if Abraham were justified by works, he hath whereof to glory; but** not before God. 3. For what saith the scripture? **Abraham believed God, and it was counted** unto him for **righteousness.** 4. **Now to him that worketh is the reward not** reckoned **of grace,** but of debt. 5. **But to him that worketh not, but believeth on him that justifieth the ungodly, his faith is counted** for **righteousness.** 6. **Even** as **David** also **describeth** the blessedness of the man, unto whom God imputeth righteousness without works, 7. **Saying, Blessed are they whose iniquities are forgiven,** and whose sins are covered. 8. Blessed *is* the man to whom the Lord will not impute sin. 9. **Cometh this blessedness then upon the circumcision only, or upon the uncircumcision also? for** we say that **faith was reckoned to Abraham for righteousness.** 10. **How was it then reckoned?** when he was in circumcision, or in uncircumcision? **Not in circumcision,**

but in uncircumcision. 11. And he received the sign of circumcision, a seal of the righteousness of the faith which *he had yet* being uncircumcised: **that he might be the father of all** them **that believe, though they be not circumcised;** that righteousness might be imputed unto them also: 12. **And the father of** circumcision to **them who** are not of the circumcision only, but who also **walk in** the steps of that **faith** of our father Abraham, which *he had* **being yet uncircumcised.** 13. **For the promise,** that he should be the heir of the world, **was not to Abraham,** or to his seed, **through the law, but through the righteousness of faith.** 14. **For if they** which are **of the law be heirs, faith is** made **void,** and the promise made of none effect: 15. Because the law worketh wrath: for where no law is, *there is* no transgression. 16. **Therefore it is of faith, that it might be by grace;** to the end the promise might be sure to all the seed; not to that only which is of the law, but to that also which is of the faith of **Abraham; who is the father of us all,** 17. (As it is written, I have made thee a father of many nations,) **before** him whom he believed, *even* **God, who quickeneth the dead, and calleth those things which be not as though they were.** 18. **Who against hope believed** in hope, **that he might become the father of many nations,**

242

according to that which was spoken, So shall thy seed be. 19. **And being not weak in faith,** he **considered not his own body** now dead, when he was about an hundred years old, **neither** yet **the deadness of Sarah's womb:** 20. **He staggered not at the promise of God** through unbelief; **but was strong in faith,** giving glory to God; 21. And being fully **persuaded that, what he had promised, he was able** also **to perform.** 22. **And therefore it was imputed to him for righteousness.** 23. **Now it was not written for his sake alone,** that it was imputed to him; 24. **But for us also, to whom it shall be imputed, if we believe on him that raised up Jesus** our Lord from the dead; 25. Who was delivered for our offences, and was raised again **for our justification.**

CHAPTER 5

1. **Therefore being justified by faith, we have peace with God through** our Lord Jesus **Christ:** 2. **By whom also we have access by faith** into this grace wherein we stand, and rejoice in hope of the glory of God. 3. And not only *so,* **but we glory in tribulations also: knowing that tribulation worketh patience;** 4. **And patience, experience; and experience, hope:** 5. **And hope maketh not ashamed; because the love of God is** shed abroad **in our hearts by the Holy Ghost** which is given unto us. 6. **For when we were** yet **without strength,** in due time **Christ died for the ungodly.** 7. For scarcely for a righteous man will one die: yet peradventure for a good man some would even dare to die. 8. **But God commendeth his love** toward us, **in that, while we were** yet **sinners, Christ died for us.** 9. Much more then, **being now justified by his blood, we shall be saved** from wrath through him. 10. **For if, when we were enemies, we were reconciled** to God **by the death of his Son, much more, being reconciled, we shall be saved by his life.** 11. And not only *so,* but **we also joy in God through** our Lord Jesus **Christ, by whom we** have now **received the atonement.** 12. **Wherefore, as by one man sin entered** into the world, **and death by sin; and so death passed upon all** men, for that all have sinned: 13. **(For until the law sin was in the world: but sin is not imputed when there is no law.)** 14. **Nevertheless death reigned from Adam to Moses,** even over them that had not sinned **after the similitude of Adam's transgression,** who is the figure of him that was to come. 15. But not as the offence, so also *is* the free gift. For if through the offence of one many be dead, much more the grace of God, and the gift by grace, *which is* by one man, Jesus Christ, hath abounded unto many.

16. And not as *it was* by one that sinned, *so is* the gift: for the judgment *was* by one to condemnation, but the free gift *is* of many offences unto justification.

17. For if by one man's offence death reigned by one; much more they which receive abundance of grace and of the gift of righteousness shall reign in life by one, Jesus Christ.)

18. **Therefore as by the offence of one judgment came** upon all men to condemnation; **even so by the righteousness of one the free gift came** upon all men unto justification of life.

19. **For as by one man's disobedience many were made sinners, so by the obedience of one shall many be made righteous.**

20. **Moreover the law entered, that the offence might abound. But where sin abounded, grace did much more abound:**

21. That as sin hath reigned unto death, even so might grace reign through righteousness unto eternal life by Jesus Christ our Lord.

CHAPTER 6

1. What shall we say then? **Shall we continue in sin, that grace may abound?**

2. **God forbid.** How shall we, that are dead to sin, live any longer therein?

3. **Know ye not, that so many of us as were baptized into Jesus Christ were baptized into his death?**

4. **Therefore we are buried with him by baptism into death: that** like **as Christ was raised** up from the dead by the glory of the Father, even **so we also should walk in newness of life.**

5. For if we have been planted together in the likeness of his death, we shall be also *in the likeness* of *his* resurrection:

6. Knowing this, that **our old man is crucified with him, that the body of sin might be destroyed, that** henceforth **we should not serve sin.**

7. For he that is dead is freed from sin.

8. **Now if we be dead with Christ,** we believe that **we shall also live with him:**

9. **Knowing that Christ** being raised from the dead **dieth no more;** death hath no more dominion over him.

10. **For** in that he died, **he died unto sin once: but** in that he liveth, **he liveth unto God.**

11. **Likewise reckon** ye also **yourselves to be dead** indeed **unto sin, but alive unto God through Jesus** Christ our Lord.

12. **Let not sin** therefore **reign in your mortal body,** that ye should obey it in the lusts thereof.

13. Neither yield ye your members *as* instruments of unrighteousness unto sin: **but yield yourselves unto God,** as those that are alive from the dead, **and your members as instruments of righteousness** unto God.

14. **For sin shall not have dominion over you:** for ye are not under the law, but under grace.

15. **What then? shall we sin, because we are** not under the law, but **under grace? God forbid.**

16. **Know ye not, that** to whom ye yield yourselves servants to obey, **his servants ye are to whom ye obey;** whether of sin unto death, or of obedience unto righteousness?

17. But God be thanked, that ye were the servants of sin, but ye have obeyed from the heart that form of doctrine which was delivered you.

18. **Being then made free from sin, ye became** the **servants of righteousness.**

19. I speak after the manner of men because of the infirmity of your flesh: for **as ye have yielded** your members servants **to uncleanness** and to iniquity unto iniquity; **even so now yield** your members servants **to righteousness unto holiness.**

20. For when ye were the servants of sin, ye were free from righteousness.

21. What fruit had ye then in those things whereof ye are now ashamed? for the end of those things *is* death.

22. **But now** being made **free from sin, and** become **servants to God, ye have your fruit unto holiness, and** the end **everlasting life.**

23. **For the wages of sin is death; but the gift of God is eternal life through Jesus Christ** our Lord.

CHAPTER 7

1. **Know ye not,** brethren, (for I speak to them that know the law,)how **that the law hath dominion over a man as long as he liveth?**

2. **For the woman** which hath an husband **is bound by the law to her husband so long as he liveth; but if the husband be dead, she is loosed** from the law of *her* husband.

3. So then if, while *her* husband liveth, she be married to another man, she shall be called an adulteress: but if her husband be dead, she is free from that law; so that she is no adulteress, though she be married to another man.

4. Wherefore, my brethren, **ye also are become dead to the law by** the body of **Christ; that ye should be married** to another, *even* **to him who is raised** from the dead, **that we should bring forth fruit** unto God.

5. For when we were in the flesh, the motions of sins, which were by the law, did work in our members to bring forth fruit unto death.

6. **But now we are delivered from the law,** that being dead wherein we were held; **that we should serve in newness of spirit,** and not *in* the oldness of the letter.

7. What shall we say then? **Is the law sin?** God forbid. **Nay, I had not known sin, but by the law:** for I had not known lust, except the law had said, Thou shalt not covet.

8. **But sin,** taking occasion **by the commandment, wrought** in me all manner of **concupiscence.** For without the law sin *was* dead.

9. **For I was alive without the law once: but when the commandment came, sin revived, and I died.**

10. **And the commandment, which was ordained to life, I found to be unto death.**

11. **For sin,** taking occasion **by the commandment,** deceived me, and by it **slew me.**

12. **Wherefore the law is holy,** and the commandment holy, and just, **and good.**

13. Was then that which is good made death unto me? God forbid. But sin, that itmight appear sin, working death in me by that which is good; that sin by the commandment might become exceeding sinful.

14. **For** we know that

the law is spiritual: but I am carnal, sold under sin. 15. **For that which I do I allow not: for what I would, that do I not; but what I hate, that do I.**

16. If then I do that which I would not, I consent unto the law that *it is* good.

17. Now then it is no more I that do it, but sin that dwelleth in me.

18. **For I know that** in me (that is, **in my flesh,) dwelleth no good thing:** for to will is present with me; but **how to perform that which is good I find not.**

19. **For the good that I would I do not: but the evil** which I would not, that **I do.**

20. **Now if I do that I would not, it is no more I** that do it, **but sin that dwelleth in me.**

21. I find then a law, that, when I would do good, evil is present with me.

22. **For I delight in the law of God after the inward man:**

23. **But I see another law** in my members, **warring against the law of my mind,** and bringing me into captivity to the law of sin which is in my members.

24. **O wretched man that I am! who shall deliver me from the body of this death?**

25. **I thank God through Jesus Christ** our Lord. So then with the mind Imyself serve the law of God; but with the flesh the law of sin.

CHAPTER 8

1. **There is therefore now no condemnation to them** which are **in Christ** Jesus, **who walk not after the flesh, but after the Spirit.**

2. **For the law of the Spirit** of life in Christ Jesus **hath made me free from the law of sin and death.**

3. **For what the law could not do,** in that it was weak through the flesh, **God sending his own Son in the likeness of sinful flesh,** and for sin, **condemned sin in the flesh:**

4. **That the righteousness of the law might be fulfilled in us,** who walk not after the flesh, but after the Spirit.

5. For they that are after the flesh do mind the things of the flesh; but they that are after the Spirit the things of the Spirit.

6. **For to be carnally minded is death; but to be spiritually minded is life** and peace.

7. **Because the carnal mind is enmity against God:** for it is not subject to the law of God, neither indeed can be.

8. **So then they that are in the flesh cannot please God.**

9. **But ye are** not in the flesh, but **in the Spirit,** if so be that the Spirit of God dwell in you. Now if any man have not the Spirit of Christ, he is none of his.

10. **And if Christ be in you, the body is dead because of sin; but the Spirit is life because of righteousness.**

11. **But if the Spirit** of him **that raised up Jesus** from the dead **dwell in you, he that raised up Christ** from the dead **shall also quicken your mortal bodies by his Spirit** that dwelleth in you.

12. Therefore, brethren, we are debtors, not to the flesh, to live after the flesh.

13. For if ye live after the flesh, ye shall die: but if ye through the Spirit do mortify the deeds of the body, ye shall live.

14. **For as many as are led by the Spirit of God, they are the sons of God.**

15. **For ye** have not received the spirit of bondage again to fear; but ye **have received the Spirit of adoption, whereby we cry, Abba, Father.** 16. **The Spirit itself beareth witness with our spirit, that we are the children of God:** 17. **And if children,** then heirs; **heirs of God, and joint-heirs with Christ; if so be that we suffer with him, that we may be also glorified together.** 18. **For** I reckon that **the sufferings of this present time are not** worthy **to be compared with the glory which shall be revealed** in us. 19. **For** the earnest expectation of **the creature waiteth for the manifestation of the sons of God.** 20. For the creature was made subject to vanity, not willingly, but by reason of him who hath subjected *the same* in hope, 21. **Because the creature itself also shall be delivered from** the bondage of **corruption into** the **glorious liberty** of the children of God. 22. **For we know that the whole creation groaneth and travaileth in pain** together until now. 23. **And** not only *they,* but **ourselves also,** which have the first fruits of the Spirit, even we ourselves **groan within** ourselves, **waiting for** the adoption, *to wit,* **the redemption of our body.** 24. **For we are saved by hope:** but hope that is seen is not hope: for what a man seeth, why doth he yet hope for? 25. **But if we hope for that we see not, then do we with**

patience wait for it. 26. **Likewise the Spirit** also **helpeth our infirmities: for we know not what we should pray** for as we ought: **but the Spirit itself maketh intercession for us** with groanings which cannot be uttered. 27. **And** he that searcheth the hearts knoweth what *is* the mind of **the Spirit,** because he **maketh intercession** for the saints **according to the will of God.** 28. **And we know that all things work together for good to them that love God, to them** who are the **called according to his purpose.** 29. **For whom he did foreknow, he** also **did predestinate to be conformed to the image of his Son,** that he might be the firstborn among many brethren. 30. Moreover whom he did predestinate, **them he also called:** and whom he called, **them he also justified:** and whom he justified, **them he also glorified.** 31. What shall we then say to these things? **If God be for us, who can be against us?** 32. **He that spared not his own Son,** but delivered him up for us all, how **shall he not with him** also **freely give us all things?** 33. **Who shall lay any thing to the charge of God's elect? It is God that justifieth.** 34. Who *is* he that condemneth? **It is Christ that died, yea** rather, **that is risen** again, who is even at the right hand of God, **who also maketh**

- intercession for us
- 35. **Who shall separate us.**
- **from the love of Christ?**
- **shall tribulation,**
  or distress, or persecution,
  or famine, or nakedness, or peril,
- **or sword?**
- 36. **As it is written, For thy**
- **sake we are killed all the**
- **day long;** we are accounted as
  sheep for the slaughter.
- 37. **Nay, in all these things**
- **we are more than**
- **conquerors through**
- **him that loved us.**
- 38. **For I am persuaded, that**
- **neither death, nor life, nor**
- **angels,** nor principalities, nor
  powers, nor things present,
  nor things to come,
  39. Nor height, nor depth,
- **nor any other creature,**
- **shall** be able to
- **separate us from the**
- **love of God,** which is
- **in Christ** Jesus our Lord.

CHAPTER 9
- 1. **I say the truth in Christ,**
  I lie not, my conscience also bearing
  me witness in the Holy Ghost,
- 2. **That I have**
  great heaviness and continual
- **sorrow in my heart.**
- 3. **For I could wish that**
- **myself were accursed from**
- **Christ for my brethren,**
  my kinsmen according to the flesh:
- 4. **Who are Israelites;**
  to whom *pertaineth* the adoption,
  and the glory, and the covenants,
  and the giving of the law, and the
  service *of God,* and the promises;
  5. Whose *are* the fathers,
- **and of whom as concern-**
- **ing the flesh Christ came,**
  who is over all, God blessed
  for ever. Amen.
- 6. **Not as though**
- **the word** of God
- **hath** taken
- **none effect. For they**
- **are not all Israel,**

- which are of Israel:
- 7. **Neither, because**
- **they are** the seed
- **of Abraham, are they**
- **all children:** but, In Isaac
  shall thy seed be called.
- 8. **That is, They**
  which are the children
- **of the flesh,** these
- **are not the children**
- **of God: but the**
- **children of the promise**
- **are counted** for the seed.
- 9. **For this is the word**
- **of promise,**
  At this time will I come, and
- **Sarah shall have a son.**
- 10. **And** not only *this*; but when
- **Rebecca also had**
- **conceived by**
  one, *even* by our father
- **Isaac;**
- 11. **(For the children being**
- **not yet born, neither having**
- **done any good or evil, that**
- **the purpose of God**
  according to election
- **might stand, not of works,**
- **but of him that calleth;)**
- 12. **It was said unto her,**
- **The elder shall serve**
- **the younger.**
- 13. **As it is written, Jacob**
- **have I loved, but Esau**
- **have I hated.**
- 14. **What shall we say then?**
- **Is there unrighteousness**
- **with God?** God forbid.
- 15. **For he saith to Moses,**
- **I will have mercy on**
- **whom I will** have mercy,
- **and I will have compassion**
- **on whom**
- **I will** have compassion.
- 16. **So then it is not**
- **of him that willeth,**
  nor of him that runneth,
- **but of God** that sheweth mercy.
  17. For the scripture saith unto
  Pharaoh, Even for this same purpose
  have I raised thee up, that I might
  shew my power in thee, and that
  my name might be declared

throughout all the earth.

18. Therefore hath he mercy on whom he will *have mercy,* **and whom he will he hardeneth.**

19. Thou wilt say then unto me, Why doth he yet find fault? For who hath resisted his will?

20. Nay but, O man, **who art thou that repliest against God? Shall the thing formed say to him that formed it, Why hast thou made me thus?**

21. Hath not the potter power over the clay, of the same lump to make one vessel unto honour, and another unto dishonour?

22. *What* if God, willing to shew *his* wrath, and to make his power known, endured with much longsuffering the vessels of wrath fitted to destruction:

23. And that he might make known the riches of his glory on the vessels of mercy, which he had afore prepared unto glory,

24. Even us, whom he hath called, not of the Jews only, but also of the Gentiles?

25. As he saith also in Osee, **I will call them my people, which were not my people;** and her beloved, which was not beloved.

26. And it shall come to pass, *that* in the place where it was said unto them, Ye *are* not my people; there shall they be called the children of the living God.

27. Esaias also crieth concerning Israel, Though the number of the children of Israel be as the sand of the sea, a remnant shall be saved:

28. For he will finish the work, and cut *it* short in righteousness: because a short work will the Lord make upon the earth.

29. And as Esaias said before, Except the Lord of Sabaoth had left us a seed, we had been as Sodoma, and been made like unto Gomorrha.

30. What shall we say then? **That the Gentiles, which followed not after righteousness, have attained** to righteousness, even **the righteousness** which is **of faith.**

31. But Israel, which followed after the law of righteousness, hath not attained to the law of **righteousness.**

32. Wherefore? Because they sought it not by faith, but as it were **by the works of the law.** For they stumbled at that stumblingstone;

33. As it is written, Behold, I lay in Sion a stumblingstone and rock of offence: and whosoever believeth on him shall not be ashamed.

CHAPTER 10

1. Brethren, my heart's desire and prayer to God **for Israel is, that they might be saved.**

2. For I bear them record that **they have a zeal of God, but not according to knowledge.**

3. For they being ignorant of God's righteousness, and going about to establish their own righteousness, have not submitted themselves **unto the righteousness of God.**

4. For Christ is the end of the law for righteousness to every one that believeth.

5. For Moses describeth the righteousness which is **of the law,** That the man which doeth those things shall live by them.

6. But the righteousness which is **of faith speaketh on this wise,** Say not in thine heart, Who shall ascend into heaven? (that is, to bring Christ down *from above:*)

7. Or, Who shall descend into the

deep? (that is, to bring up Christ again from the dead.)

8. But what saith it? The word is nigh thee, *even* in thy mouth, and in thy heart: that is, the word of faith, which we preach;

9. **That if thou shalt confess with thy mouth the Lord Jesus, and shalt believe in thine heart that God hath raised him from the dead, thou shalt be saved.** 10. **For with the heart man believeth unto righteousness; and with the mouth confession is made unto salvation.** 11. **For the scripture saith, Whosoever believeth on him shall not be ashamed.**

12. For there is no difference between the Jew and the Greek: for the same Lord over all is rich unto all that call upon him.

13. **For whosoever shall call upon the name of the Lord shall be saved.** 14. **How then shall they call on him** in **whom they have not believed? and how shall they believe in him of whom they have not heard? and how shall they hear without a preacher?** 15. **And how shall they preach, except they be sent? as it is written, How beautiful are the feet of them that preach the gospel** of peace, and bring glad tidings of good things!

16. But they have not all obeyed the gospel. For Esaias saith, Lord, who hath believed our report?

17. **So then faith cometh by hearing, and hearing by the word of God.**

18. But I say, Have they not heard? Yes verily, their sound went into all the earth, and their words unto the ends of the world.

19. **But I say, Did not Israel know? First Moses saith,** I will provoke you to jealousy by *them that are* no people, *and* **by a foolish nation I will anger you.** 20. **But Esaias** is very bold, and **saith, I was found of them that sought me not;** I was made manifest unto them that asked not after me. 21. **But to Israel he saith,** All day long **I have stretched** forth **my hands unto a disobedient** and gainsaying **people.**

CHAPTER 11

1. **I say then, Hath God cast away his people? God forbid. For I also am an Israelite,** of the seed of Abraham, *of* the tribe of Benjamin. 2. **God hath not cast away his people** which he foreknew. Wot ye not what **the scripture saith of Elias? how he maketh intercession** to God **against Israel saying,** 3. **Lord, they have killed thy prophets,** and digged down thine altars; and I am left alone, **and they seek my life.** 4. **But what saith** the answer of **God** unto him? **I have reserved** to myself **seven thousand men,** who have not bowed the knee to *the image* of Baal. 5. **Even so then at this present time also there is a remnant according to the election of grace.** 6. **And if by grace, then is it no more of works:** otherwise grace is no more grace. But if *it be* of works, then it is no more grace: otherwise work is no more work. 7. **What then? Israel hath not obtained that which he seeketh** for; **but the election hath**

250

■ **obtained it, and the**
■ **rest were blinded.**
8. (According as it is written, God
hath given them the spirit of slumber,
eyes that they should not see, and
ears that they should not hear;)
unto this day.
9. And David saith, Let their table
be made a snare, and a trap, and a
stumblingblock, and a recompence
unto them:
10. Let their eyes be darkened, that
they may not see, and bow down
their back alway.
■ 11. **I say then, Have they**
■ **stumbled that they should**
■ **fall? God forbid: but rather**
■ **through their fall salvation is**
■ **come unto the Gentiles,** for
to provoke them to jealousy.
12. Now if the fall of them *be* the
riches of the world, and the
diminishing of them the riches
of the Gentiles; how much more
their fulness?
■ 13. **For** I speak to
you Gentiles, inasmuch
■ **as I am the apostle of**
■ **the Gentiles, I magnify**
■ **mine office:**
■ 14. **If by any means I may**
■ **provoke to emulation them**
■ **which are my flesh, and**
■ **might save some of them.**
15. For if the casting away of them
be the reconciling of the world,
what *shall* the receiving *of them be*,
but life from the dead?
■ 16. **For if the firstfruit be**
■ **holy, the lump is** also
■ **holy: and if the**
■ **root be holy, so**
■ **are the branches.**
■ 17. **And if some** of the
■ **branches be broken off,**
■ **and thou, being a wild**
■ **olive tree, wert grafted in**
■ **among them, and** with them
■ **partakest of the root**
and fatness of the olive tree;
■ 18. **Boast not against the**
■ **branches.** But if thou boast,
■ **thou bearest not the root,**

■ **but the root thee.**
■ 19. **Thou wilt say** then,
■ **The branches were**
■ **broken** off,
■ **that I might be**
■ **grafted** in.
20. **Well; because of**
■ **unbelief they were**
■ **broken** off,
■ **and thou standest**
■ **by faith. Be not**
■ **highminded,** but fear:
■ 21. **For if God spared not**
■ **the natural branches,**
■ **take heed lest he also**
■ **spare not thee.**
22. **Behold therefore the**
■ **goodness and severity of**
■ **God: on them which fell,**
■ **severity; but toward thee,**
■ **goodness,** if thou continue
in *his* goodness: otherwise thou
also shalt be cut off.
■ 23. **And they also, if**
■ **they abide not** still
■ **in unbelief, shall be grafted**
■ **in:** for God is able to graft them in
■ **again.**
24. For if thou wert cut out of
the olive tree which is wild by
nature, and wert grafted contrary to
nature into a good olive tree: how
much more shall these, which be
the natural *branches*, be grafted
into their own olive tree?
■ 25. **For** I would not, brethren, that ye
should be ignorant of this mystery,
lest ye should be wise in your own
conceits; that
■ **blindness in part is**
■ **happened to Israel,**
■ **until the fulness of the**
■ **Gentiles** be come in.
■ 26. **And so all Israel shall be**
■ **saved: as it is written,** There
shall come out of Sion the Deliverer,
and shall turn away ungodliness from
Jacob:
■ 27. **For this is my**
■ **covenant** unto them, when
■ **I shall take away their sins.**
■ 28. **As concerning the**
■ **gospel, they are enemies**

■ **for your sakes: but as**
■ **touching the election,**
■ **they are beloved for**
■ **the father's sakes.**
29. For the gifts and calling
of God *are* without repentance.
■ 30. **For as ye** in times past have
not believed God, yet have now
■ **obtained mercy through**
■ **their unbelief:**
■ 31. **Even so** have these
also now not believed, that
■ **through your mercy**
■ **they also may**
■ **obtain mercy.**
32. For God hath concluded
them all in unbelief, that he
might have mercy upon all.
■ 33. **O the depth** of the riches
■ both **of the wisdom and**
■ **knowledge of God!**
■ **how unsearchable**
■ **are his judgments,**
and his ways past finding out!
■ 34. **For who hath known**
■ **the mind of the Lord?**
or who hath been his counsellor?
35. Or who hath first given to him,
and it shall be recompensed unto
him again?
■ 36. **For of him, and through**
■ **him, and to him, are all**
■ **things:** to whom *be* glory for ever.
Amen.

CHAPTER 12

■ 1. **I beseech you**
therefore, brethren,
■ **by the mercies of God, that**
■ **ye present your bodies a**
■ **living sacrifice, holy,**
■ **acceptable unto God,**
which is your reasonable service.
■ 2. **And be not conformed**
■ **to this world: but be ye**
■ **transformed by the**
■ **renewing of your mind,** that
ye may prove what *is* that good, and
acceptable, and perfect, will of God.
■ 3. **For I say,** through the
grace given unto me,
■ **to every man**
that is among you,

■ **not to think of himself more**
■ **highly than he ought** to think;
■ **but to think soberly,**
according as God hath dealt to
every man the measure of faith.
■ 4. **For as we have many**
■ **members in one body,** and all
members have not the same office:
■ 5. **So we, being many, are**
■ **one body in Christ,** and every
one members one of another.
■ 6. **Having then gifts differing**
■ **according to the grace** that
■ is **given to us,** whether prophecy,
let us prophesy according to the
proportion of faith;
7. Or ministry, *let us wait* on *our*
ministering: or he that teacheth,
on teaching;
8. Or he that exhorteth, on
exhortation: he that giveth, *let him do
it* with simplicity; he that ruleth, with
diligence; he that sheweth mercy,
with cheerfulness.
■ 9. **Let love be without**
■ **dissimulation. Abhor**
■ **that which is evil; cleave**
■ **to that which is good.**
■ 10. **Be kindly affectioned**
■ **one to another**
with brotherly love; in honour
■ **preferring one another;**
■ 11. **Not slothful in business;**
■ **fervent in spirit;**
serving the Lord;
■ 12. **Rejoicing in hope;**
■ **patient in tribulation;**
■ **continuing instant**
■ **in prayer;**
■ 13. **Distributing to the**
■ **necessity of saints;**
given to hospitality.
■ 14. **Bless them which**
■ **persecute you:**
bless, and curse not.
■ 15. **Rejoice with them that**
■ **do rejoice, and weep**
■ **with them that weep.**
16. *Be* of the same mind
one toward another.
■ **Mind not high things, but**
■ **condescend to men of low**
■ **estate. Be not wise in your**

■ own conceits.
■ 17. **Recompense to no man**
■ **evil for evil.** Provide things honest
in the sight of all men.
■ 18. **If it be possible,**
as much as lieth in you,
■ **live peaceably**
■ **with all men.**
■ 19. **Dearly beloved, avenge**
■ **not yourselves,**
but *rather* give place unto wrath:
■ **for it is written, Vengeance**
■ **is mine;** I will repay,
■ **saith the Lord.**
■ 20. **Therefore if thine enemy**
■ **hunger, feed him;**
if he thirst, give him drink: for
■ **in so doing thou shalt heap**
■ **coals of fire on his head.**
■ 21. **Be not overcome of**
■ **evil, but overcome evil**
■ **with good.**

CHAPTER 13

■ 1. **Let every soul be subject**
■ **unto the higher powers.**
■ **For there is no power**
■ **but** of God: the powers
■ **that be** are
■ **ordained of God.**
■ 2. **Whosoever therefore**
■ **resisteth the power,**
■ **resisteth** the ordinance of
■ **God: and** they that resist
■ **shall receive** to themselves
■ **damnation.**
■ 3. **For rulers are not a terror**
■ **to good works, but to the**
■ **evil.** Wilt thou then not be afraid of
the power? do that which is good, and
thou shalt have praise of the same:
■ 4. **For he is the minister**
■ **of God to thee for good.**
■ **But if thou do** that which is
■ **evil, be afraid;** for he beareth not
the sword in vain:
■ **for he is** the minister of God,
■ **a revenger to execute**
■ **wrath upon him that**
■ **doeth evil.**
■ 5. **Wherefore ye must needs**
■ **be subject,** not only for wrath,
but also for conscience sake.

6. For for this cause
■ **pay ye tribute also: for**
■ **they are God's ministers,**
attending continually upon
this very thing.
■ 7. **Render therefore to all**
■ **their dues:** tribute to whom tribute
is due; custom to whom custom; fear
to whom fear;honour to whomhonour.
■ 8. **Owe no man any thing,**
■ **but to love one another:**
■ **for he that loveth** another hath
■ **fulfilled the law.**
9. For this, Thou shalt not commit
adultery, Thou shalt not kill, Thou
shalt not steal, Thou shalt not
bear false witness, Thou
shalt not covet; and
■ **if there be any other**
■ **commandment, it is**
briefly comprehended
■ **in this saying,** namely,
■ **Thou shalt love thy**
■ **neighbour as thyself.**
10. Love worketh no ill to his
neighbour: therefore love
is the fulfilling of the law.
11. And that, knowing the time, that
now *it is* high time to awake out of
sleep: for now is our salvation
nearer than when we believed.
12. The night is far spent,
the day is at hand:
■ **let us** therefore
■ **cast off the works of**
■ **darkness, and** let us
■ **put on the armour of light.**
■ 13. **Let us walk honestly,**
as in the day; not in rioting and
drunkenness, not in chambering
and wantonness, not in strife
and envying.
■ 14. **But put ye on the Lord**
■ **Jesus Christ, and make**
■ **not provision for the**
■ **flesh,** to *fulfil* the lusts *there*of.

CHAPTER14

■ 1. **Him that is weak in**
■ **the faith receive** ye,
■ **but not to** doubtful
■ **disputations.**
■ 2. **For one believeth that he**

may eat all things: another, who is weak, eateth herbs.

3. Let not him that eateth despise him that eateth not; and let not him which eateth not judge him that eateth: for God hath received him.

4. Who art thou that judgest another man's servant? to his own master he standeth or falleth. Yea, he shall be holden up: for God is able to make him stand.

5. One man esteemeth one day above another: another esteemeth every day alike. Let every man be fully persuaded in his own mind.

6. He that regardeth the day, regardeth it unto the Lord; and he that regardeth not the day, to the Lord he doth not regard it.

He that eateth, eateth to the Lord, for he giveth God thanks; and he that eateth not, to the Lord he eateth not, and giveth God thanks.

7. For none of us liveth to himself, and no man dieth to himself.

8. For whether we live, we live unto the Lord; and whether we die, we die unto the Lord: whether we live therefore, or die, we are the Lord's.

9. For to this end Christ both died, and rose, and revived, that he might be Lord both of the dead and living.

10. But why dost thou judge thy brother? or why dost thou set at nought thy brother? for we shall all stand before the judgment seat of Christ.

11. For it is written, As I live, saith the Lord, every knee shall bow to me, and every tongue shall confess to God.

12. So then every one of us shall give account of himself to God.

13. Let us not therefore judge one another any more: but judge this rather, that no man put a stumblingblock or an occasion to fall in his brother's way.

14. I know, and am persuaded by the Lord Jesus, that there is nothing unclean of itself: but to him that esteemeth any thing to be unclean, to him it is unclean.

15. But if thy brother be grieved with thy meat, now walkest thou not charitably. Destroy not him with thy meat, for whom Christ died.

16. Let not then your good be evil spoken of:

17. For the kingdom of God is not meat and drink; but righteousness, and peace, and joy in the Holy Ghost.

18. For he that in these things serveth Christ is acceptable to God, and approved of men.

19. Let us therefore follow after the things which make for peace, and things wherewith one may edify another.

20. For meat destroy not the work of God. All things indeed are pure; but it is evil for that man who eateth with offence.

21. It is good neither to eat flesh, nor to drink wine, nor any thing whereby thy brother stumbleth, or is offended, or is made weak.

22. Hast thou faith? have it to thyself before God. Happy is he that condemneth not himself in that thing which he alloweth.

23. And he that doubteth is

damned if he eat, because *he eateth* not of faith:
for whatsoever is not of faith is sin.

CHAPTER 15

1. **We then that are strong ought to bear** the infirmities of **the weak, and not to please ourselves.**

2. Let every one of us please *his* neighbour for *his* good to edification.

3. **For even Christ pleased not himself;** but, as it is written, The reproaches of them that reproached thee fell on me.

4. **For whatsoever things were written aforetime were written for our learning, that we through** patience and comfort of **the scriptures might have hope.**

5. Now the God of patience and consolation grant you to be likeminded one toward another according to Christ Jesus:

6. **That ye may with one mind and one mouth glorify God,** even the Father of our Lord Jesus Christ.

7. Wherefore receive ye one another, as Christ also received us to the glory of God.

8. **Now I say that Jesus Christ was a minister** of the circumcision for the truth of God, **to confirm the promises made unto the fathers:**

9. **And that the Gentiles might glorify God for his mercy; as it is written,** For this cause **I will confess to thee among the Gentiles,** and sing unto thy name.

10. And again he saith, Rejoice, ye Gentiles, with his people.

11. **And again, Praise the Lord, all ye Gentiles;** and laud him, all ye people.

12. **And again, Esaias saith, There shall be a root of Jesse, and** he that shall rise to reign over the Gentiles; **in him shall the Gentiles trust.**

13. **Now the God of hope fill you with all joy** and peace **in believing,** that ye may abound in hope, **through** the power of **the Holy Ghost.**

14. **And I myself** also **am persuaded** of you, my brethren, **that ye also are full of goodness,** filled with all knowledge, **able also to admonish one another.**

15. **Nevertheless, brethren, I have written the more boldly** unto you in some sort, as putting you in mind, **because of the grace that is given to me** of God,

16. **That I should be the minister of Jesus Christ to the Gentiles,** ministering the gospel of God, that the offering up of the Gentiles might be acceptable, being sanctified by the Holy Ghost.

17. **I have therefore whereof I may glory through Jesus** Christ in those things which pertain to God.

18. **For I will not dare to speak of** any of those **things which Christ hath not wrought by me, to make the Gentiles obedient,** by word and deed,

19. **Through mighty signs and wonders, by the power of the Spirit of God; so** that from Jerusalem, and round about unto Illyricum, **I have fully preached the gospel** of Christ.

20. Yea, so have I strived to preach the gospel, **not where Christ was named,** lest I should build upon another man's foundation:

Contributions for the poor

21. **But as it is written, To whom he was not spoken of, they shall see:** and they that have not heard shall understand.

22. **For which cause** also **I have been much hindered from coming to you.**

23. **But** now having no more place in these parts, and **having a great desire** these many years **to come unto you;**

24. **Whensoever I take my journey into Spain, I will come to you:** for I trust to see you in my journey, and to be brought on my way thitherward by you, if first I be somewhatfilled with your *company*.

25. **But now I go unto Jerusalem** to minister unto the saints.

26. **For it hath pleased them of Macedonia and Achaia to make a certain contribution for the poor saints** which are **at Jerusalem.**

27. It hath pleased them verily; and their debtors they are. For if the Gentiles have been made partakers of their spiritual things, their duty is also to minister unto them in carnal things.

28. When therefore I have performed this, and have sealed to them this fruit, I will come by you into Spain.

29. And I am sure that, when I come unto you, I shall come in the fulness of the blessing of the gospel of Christ.

30. **Now I beseech you, brethren, for** the Lord Jesus **Christ's sake,** and for the love of the Spirit, **that ye strive together** with me **in your prayers to God for me;**

31. **That I may be delivered from them that do not believe in Judaea; and that my service** which *I have* **for Jerusalem may be accepted of the saints;**

32. That I may come unto you with joy by the will of God, and may with you be refreshed.

33. Now the God of peace *be* with you all. Amen.

CHAPTER 16

1. I commend unto you Phoebe our sister, which is a servant of the church which is at Cenchrea:

2. That ye receive her in the Lord, as becometh saints, and that ye assist her in whatsoever business she hath need of you: for she hath been a succourer of many, and of myself also.

3. Greet Priscilla and Aquila my helpers in Christ Jesus:

4. Who have for my life laid down their own necks: unto whom not only I give thanks, but also all the churches of the Gentiles.

5. Likewise *greet* the church that is in their house. Salute my well-beloved Epaenetus, who is the firstfruits of Achaia unto Christ.

6. Greet Mary, who bestowed much labour on us.

7. Salute Andronicus and Junia, my kinsmen, and my fellow-prisoners, who are of note among the apostles, who also were in Christ before me.

8. Greet Amplias my beloved in the Lord.

9. Salute Urbane, our helper in Christ, and Stachys my beloved.

10. Salute Apelles approved in Christ. Salute them which are of Aristobulus' *household.*

11. Salute Herodion my kinsman. Greet them that be of the *household* of Narcissus, which are in the Lord.

12. Salute Tryphena and Tryphosa, who labour in the Lord. Salute the beloved Persis, which laboured much in the Lord.

13. Salute Rufus chosen in the Lord, and his mother and mine.

14. Salute Asyncritus, Phlegon, Hermas, Patrobas, Hermes, and the brethren which are with them.

15. Salute Philologus, and Julia, Nereus, and his sister, and Olympas, and all the saintswhich are with them.

16. **Salute one another with an holy kiss.** The churches of Christ salute you.

17. **Now I beseech you, brethren, mark them which cause divisions** and offences contrary to the doctrine which ye have learned; **and avoid them.**

18. **For they** that are such **serve not our Lord** Jesus Christ, **but their own belly; and** by good words and fair speeches **deceive the hearts of the simple.**

19. For your obedience is come abroad unto all *men*. I am glad therefore on your behalf: but yet **I would have you wise unto that which is good,** and simple concerning evil.

20. **And the God of peace shall bruise Satan under your feet shortly.** The grace of our Lord Jesus Christ *be* with you. Amen.

21. Timotheus my workfellow, and Lucius, and Jason, and Sosipater, my kinsmen, salute you.

22. I Tertius, who wrote *this* epistle, salute you in the Lord.

23. Gaius mine host, and of the whole church, saluteth you. Erastus the chamberlain of the city saluteth you, and Quartus a brother.

24. The grace of our Lord Jesus Christ *be* with you all. Amen.

25. **Now to him that is of power to stablish you according to** my gospel, and the preaching of Jesus **Christ, according to the revelation of the mystery, which was** kept **secret since the world began,**

26. **But now is made manifest,** and **by the scriptures** of the prophets, **according to the commandment of** the everlasting **God,** made known to all nations **for the obedience of faith:**

27. **To God only wise, be glory through Jesus Christ** for ever. **Amen.**

THE EPISTLE TO THE ROMANS
The bridge between the Gospels, the Acts, and the rest of the New Testament

■ Paul's Epistle to the
■ **Romans is** recognized as
■ **one of the great**
■ **masterpieces of literature,**
both sacred
■ **and** secular. Addressed to
Christians living in Rome – the city
which was the center of the ancient
world – Romans
■ **is the only book in the New**
■ **Testament,** with the possible
exception of Hebrews,
■ **which was written as a**
■ **Theological Treatise**
rather than an encouraging or
correcting letter.
■ **In Romans, Paul** forcefully
■ **presents the entire scope**
■ **of Christian doctrine and**
provides an authoritative theology as
well as expresses the universality of
the Gospel. Romans
■ **gives a comprehensive**
■ **interpretation of the**
■ **Incarnation and the ministry**
■ **of Christ, showing** with
convincing logic and supported by
Old Testament scriptures,
■ **that God has made a**
■ **radical breakthrough**

■ into human history
■ **in the life, death, and**
■ **resurrection of His Son.**
■ **The** dilemma of the
■ **human condition,**
■ **sinfulness, is met with**
a profound solution –
■ **the righteousness of God**
■ **made real** for the individual
■ **by faith.** Many of the great revivals
began with a study of Romans.
■ **Augustine, Luther and**
■ **Wesley, credit Romans as**
■ **the source from which they**
■ **gained an understanding of**
■ **the Gospel.**
■ **Christian theology has**
■ **never had a higher**
■ **expression** than presented by
Paul in Romans under the inspiration
of the Holy Spirit.
■ **The Epistle has another**
■ **significance** for the student of the
Bible.
■ **It interprets the**
■ **life of Jesus as seen in the**
■ **Gospels, and** finally, it
■ **forms a bridge between the**
■ **Acts and the rest of the**
■ **New Testament.**

THE FIRST EPISTLE
TO THE CORINTHIANS

BACKGROUND
INFORMATION

Author: Paul, an Apostle.
Date Written: probably
between 55 and **60** A.D.

Number of:
Verses   437
Chapters   16
Total Words 9,489
Scan Words 4,543
Scan Words represent
47 % of Total Words

Theme: written to reveal
the new life believers
have in Christ, and
**how believers should
conduct themselves
individually and as
members of the Church**

OUTLINE OF
THE EPISTLE

I.   Paul Denounces Factions
     and Stresses
     **the Need for Church
     Discipline**
     Chapters 1 - 6
II. Paul Answers Questions
     **Concerning Marriage
     and** the Christian's
     Influence Upon Others
     Chapters 7 - 10
III. Paul Contrasts
     Disorderly Worship with
     the Way of Love and
     Explains
     the Meaning of the
     Resurrection
     Chapter 11 - 16

CHAPTER 1

■ 1. **Paul** called *to be* an apostle of Jesus Christ through the will of God,

■ **and Sosthenes** *our* brother,

■ 2. **Unto the church**

■ **of God** which is

■ **at Corinth,** to them that are sanctified in Christ Jesus, called *to be* saints, with all that in every place call upon the name of Jesus Christ our Lord, both theirs and ours:

■ 3. **Grace be unto you,** and peace, from God our Father, and *from* the Lord Jesus Christ.

■ 4. **I thank** my

■ **God** always on your behalf,

■ **for the grace** of God which is

■ **given you by Jesus Christ;**

■ 5. **That in every thing ye are**

■ **enriched by him,** in all utterance, and *in* all knowledge;

6. Even as the testimony of Christ was confirmed in you:

■ 7. **So that ye come behind**

■ **in no gift; waiting for the**

■ **coming of** our Lord Jesus

■ **Christ:**

■ 8. **Who shall also**

■ **confirm you** unto the end,

■ **that ye may be blameless** in the day of our Lord Jesus Christ.

9. God *is* faithful, by whom ye were called unto the fellowship of his Son Jesus Christ our Lord.

■ 10. **Now I beseech**

■ **you,** brethren,

■ **by** the name of

■ **our Lord** Jesus Christ, that ye all speak the same thing, and

■ **that there be no divisions**

■ **among you;** but *that* ye be perfectly joined together in the same mind and in the same judgment.

■ 11. **For it hath been**

■ **declared** unto me of you, my brethren, by them *which are of the house* of Chloe,

■ **that there are contentions**

■ **among you.**

12. Now this I say, that

■ **every one of you saith,**

■ **I am of Paul;** and

■ **I of Apollos;** and

■ **I of Cephas; and I of Christ.**

■ 13. **Is Christ divided? was**

■ **Paul crucified for you? or**

■ **were ye baptized in the**

■ **name of Paul?**

■ 14. **I thank God that I**

■ **baptized none of you,** but Crispus and Gaius;

■ 15. **Lest any should say**

■ **that I** had

■ **baptized in mine**

■ **own name.**

16. And I baptized also the household of Stephanas: besides, I know not whether I baptized any other.

■ 17. **For Christ sent me**

■ **not to baptize, but to**

■ **preach** the gospel:

■ **not with wisdom of words,**

■ **lest the cross** of Christ should

■ **be made of none effect.**

■ 18. **For** the preaching of

■ **the cross is to them that**

■ **perish foolishness; but unto**

■ **us which are saved**

■ **it is the power of God.**

■ 19. **For it is written, I will**

■ **destroy the wisdom of the**

■ **wise,** and will bring to nothing the understanding of the prudent.

20. Where *is* the wise? where *is* the scribe? where *is* the disputer of this world?

■ **hath not God made foolish**

■ **the wisdom of this world?**

■ 21. **For** after that in the wisdom of God

■ **the world by wisdom knew**

■ **not God, it pleased God**

■ **by the foolishness of**

■ **preaching to save them**

■ **that believe.**

■ 22. **For the Jews**

■ **require a sign, and**

■ **the Greeks** seek after

■ **wisdom:**

■ 23. **But we preach Christ**

■ **crucified,** unto the Jews a stumblingblock, and unto the Greeks foolishness;

24. But unto them which are called, both Jews and Greeks, Christ

the power of God, and
the wisdom of God.
25. **Because the foolishness
of God is wiser than men;**
and the weakness of God is
stronger than men.
26. For ye see your calling, brethren,
how that not many wise men after
the flesh, not many mighty, not
many noble, *are called:*
27. **But God hath chosen the
foolish** things of the world
to confound the wise;
and God hath chosen the weak
things of the world to confound
the things which are mighty;
28. **And base things** of the
world, and things which are despised,
hath God chosen, *yea*, and
things which are not, to bring to
nought things that are:
29. **That no flesh should glory
in his presence.**
30. **But** of him are ye
in Christ Jesus, who of
God is made unto us
wisdom, and
righteousness, and
**sanctification, and
redemption:**
31. That, according as it is written,
**He that glorieth, let him
glory in the Lord.**

CHAPTER 2

1. **And I,**
brethren, when I came to you,
**came not with excellency
of speech or** of
wisdom, declaring unto
you the testimony of God.
2. **For I determined not to
know any thing** among you,
save Jesus
Christ, and him crucified.
3. And I was with you in weakness,
and in fear, and in much trembling.
4. **And my speech**
and my preaching
was not with enticing words
**of man's wisdom, but in
demonstration of the
Spirit and of power:**

5. **That your faith should
not stand in the
wisdom of men,
but in the power of God.**
6. Howbeit we speak wisdom among
them that are perfect: yet not the
wisdom of this world, nor of the
princes of this world,
that come to nought:
7. **But we speak the wisdom
of God in a mystery,** *even*
the hidden *wisdom*, which God
**ordained before the
world unto our glory:**
8. Which none of the princes of this
world knew: for had they known *it*,
they would not have crucified the
Lord of glory.
9. **But as it is written,
Eye hath not seen,** nor
ear heard, neither have entered
into the heart of man,
**the things which God
hath prepared for them
that love him.**
10. **But God hath
revealed them** unto us
**by his Spirit: for the Spirit
searcheth all things, yea,
the deep things of God.**
11. For what man knoweth the
things of a man, save the spirit
of man which is in him? even so
the things of God knoweth no
man, but the Spirit of God.
12. **Now we have received,**
not the spirit of the world, but
the spirit which is of God;
**that we might know the
things** that are freely given to us
of God.
13. **Which things** also we speak,
not in the words which man's wisdom
teacheth, but which
the Holy Ghost teacheth;
comparing spiritual things
with spiritual.
14. **But the natural man
receiveth not the things of
the Spirit** of God: for they are
foolishness unto him:
**neither can he know them,
because they are**

spiritually discerned.

15. But he that is spiritual judgeth all things, yet he himself is judged of no man.

16. For who hath known the mind of the Lord, that he may instruct him? But we have the mind of Christ.

CHAPTER 3

1. And I, brethren, could not speak unto you as unto spiritual, but as unto carnal, *even* as unto babes in Christ.

2. I have fed you with milk, and not with meat: forhitherto ye were not able to bear it, neither yet now are ye able.

3. For ye are yet carnal: for whereas there is among you envying, and strife, and divisions, are ye not carnal, and walk as men?

4. For while one saith, I am of Paul; and another, I am of Apollos; are ye not carnal?

5. Who then is Paul, and who *is* Apollos, but ministers by whom ye believed, even as the Lord gave to every man?

6. I have planted, Apollos watered; but God gave the increase.

7. So then neither is he that planteth any thing, neither he that watereth; but God that giveth the increase.

8. Now he that planteth and he that watereth are one: and every man shall receive his own reward according to his own labour.

9. For we are labourers together with God: ye are God's husbandry, ye are God's building.

10. According to the grace of God which is given unto me, as a wise masterbuilder, I have laid the foundation, and another buildeth thereon. But let every man take heed how he buildeth thereupon.

11. For other foundation can no man lay than that is laid, which is Jesus Christ.

12. Now if any man build upon this foundation gold, silver, precious stones, wood, hay, stubble;

13. Every man's work shall be made manifest: for the day shall declare it, because it shall be revealed by fire; and the fire shall try every man's work of what sort it is.

14. If any man's work abide which he hath built thereupon, he shall receive a reward.

15. If any man's work shall be burned, he shall suffer loss: but he himself shall be saved; yet so as by fire.

16. Know ye not that ye are the temple of God, and that the Spirit of God dwelleth in you?

17. If any man defile the temple of God, him shall God destroy: for the temple of God is holy, which *temple* ye are.

18. Let no man deceive himself. If any man among you seemeth to be wise in this world, let him become a fool, that he may be wise

19. For the wisdom of this world is foolishness with God. For it is written, He taketh the wise in their own craftiness.

20. And again, The Lord knoweth the thoughts of the wise, that they are vain.

21. Therefore let no man glory in men. For all things are yours;

22. Whether Paul, or Apollos, or Cephas, or the world, or life, or death,or things present, or

things to come; all are yours;

23. **And ye are Christ's; and Christ is God's.**

CHAPTER 4

1. **Let a man so account** of **us, as** of the **ministers** of Christ, **and stewards** of the mysteries **of God.**

2. **Moreover it is required in stewards, that a man be** found **faithful.**

3. But with me **it is a very small thing that I** should **be judged** of you, or **of man's judgment:** yea, I judge not mine own self.

4. **For** I know nothing by myself; yet am I not hereby justified: but **he that judgeth me is the Lord.**

5. **Therefore judge nothing** before the time, **until the Lord come,** who both will bring to light the hidden things of darkness, and will make manifest the counsels of the hearts: and then shall every man have praise of God.

6. **And these things, brethren, I have in a figure transferred to myself and** to **Apollos** for your sakes; **that ye might learn** in us **not to think of men** above that which is written, that no one of you be puffed up for one against another.

7. For who maketh thee to differ *from another*? and what hast thou that thou didst not receive? now if thou didst receive *it*, why dost thou glory, as if thou hadst not received *it*?

8. Now ye are full, now ye are rich, **ye have reigned as kings without us: and I would to God ye did reign,** that we also might reign with you.

9. **For I think that God hath set forth** us **the apostles last,** as it were appointed to death: for we are made a spectacle unto the world, and to angels, and to men.

10. **We are fools for Christ's sake,** but ye *are* wise in Christ; we *are* weak, but ye *are* strong; ye *are* honourable, but we *are* despised.

11. **Even unto this** present **hour we** both **hunger,** and **thirst,** and are naked, and are buffeted, **and have no certain dwellingplace;**

12. **And labour,** working **with our own hands:** being reviled, we bless; being persecuted, we suffer it:

13. Being defamed, we entreat: **we are made as the filth of the world,** *and are* the off scouring of all things unto this day.

14. **I write not these things to shame you, but** as my beloved sons **I warn you.**

15. **For though ye have ten thousand instructors in Christ, yet have ye not many fathers:** for in Christ Jesus I have begotten you through the gospel.

16. **Wherefore** I beseech you, **be** ye **followers of me.**

17. **For this cause have I sent** unto you **Timotheus,** who is my beloved son, and faithful in the Lord, **who shall bring you into remembrance of my ways** which be **in Christ,** as I teach every where in every church.

18. **Now some are puffed up, as though I would not come** to you.

19. **But I will come** to you shortly, **if the Lord will,** and will know, not the speech of them which are puffed up, but the power.

20. For the kingdom of God *is*

not in word, but in power.

21. **What will ye?**
shall I come unto you
with a rod, or in love,
and *in* the spirit of meekness?

CHAPTER 5

1. **It is reported** commonly
that there is fornication
among you, and
such fornication as is not so much
as named among the Gentiles,
that one should have
his father's wife.
2. **And ye** are puffed up, and
have not rather
mourned, that he that hath
done this deed might be
taken away from among you.
3. **For I** verily, as absent in
body, but present in spirit,
have judged already,
as though I were present, *concerning*
him that hath so
done this deed,
4. In the name of our Lord Jesus
Christ, when ye are gathered
together, and my spirit, with the
power of our Lord Jesus Christ,
5. **To deliver such an**
one unto Satan for the
destruction of the flesh,
that the spirit may be
saved in the day of the
Lord Jesus.
6. Your glorying *is* not good.
Know ye not that a little
leaven leaveneth
the whole lump?
7. **Purge out therefore the**
old leaven, that ye may be a
new lump, as ye are unleavened.
For even Christ our passover is
sacrificed for us:
8. **Therefore let us keep the**
feast, not with old leaven,
neither with the
leaven of malice and wickedness;
but with the unleavened *bread* of
sincerity and truth.
9. **I wrote unto you** in an epistle
not to company
with fornicators:

10. **Yet not altogether with**
the fornicators of this
world, or with the covetous,
or extortioners, or with idolaters;
for then must ye needs
go out of the world.
11. **But now I have**
written unto you
not to keep company, if
any man that is called a
brother be a fornicator,
or covetous, or an idolater, or a railer,
or a drunkard, or an extortioner;
with such an one
no not to eat.
12. For what have I to do to judge
them also that are without? do not
ye judge them that are within?
13. But them that are
without God judgeth.
Therefore put away from
among yourselves that
wicked person.

CHAPTER 6

1. **Dare any** of you, having
a matter against another,
go to law before the unjust,
and not before the saints?
2. **Do ye not know that the**
saints shall judge the
world? and
if the world shall be judged by you,
are ye unworthy to judge
the smallest matters?
3. **Know ye not that we shall**
judge angels? how much more
things that pertain to this life?
4. **If then ye have judgments**
of things pertaining to this life,
set them to judge who
are least esteemed
in the church.
5. I speak to your shame.
Is it so, that there
is not a wise man among
you? no, not one that shall be
able to judge between his
brethren?
6. **But brother goeth to**
law with brother, and that
before the unbelievers.
7. Now therefore there is utterly a

fault among you, because ye go to law one with another.

■ **Why** do ye
■ **not rather take**
■ **wrong? why** do ye
■ **not rather** *suffer yourselves to*
■ **be defrauded?**

8. Nay, ye do wrong, and defraud, and that *your* brethren.

■ 9. **Know ye not that the**
■ **unrighteous shall not inherit**
■ **the kingdom** of God?
■ **Be not deceived: neither**
■ **fornicators,** nor
■ **idolaters,** nor
■ **adulterers,** nor
■ **effeminate,** nor
■ **abusers of themselves**
■ **with mankind,**
■ 10. **Nor thieves,** nor
■ **covetous,** nor
■ **drunkards,** nor
■ **revilers, nor**
■ **extortioners, shall**
■ **inherit the kingdom** of God
■ 11. **And such were some**
■ **of you:** but ye are washed,
  but ye are sanctified,
■ **but ye are justified**
■ **in the name of** the Lord
■ **Jesus, and by**
■ **the Spirit** of our God.
■ 12. **All things are**
■ **lawful** unto me,
■ **but all things are not**
■ **expedient:** all things are
  lawful for me, but I will not be
  brought under the power of any.
  13. Meats for the belly, and the belly
  for meats: but God shall destroy
  both it and them. Now
■ **the body is not for**
■ **fornication, but for the**
■ **Lord;** and the Lord for the body.
■ 14. **And God** hath both
■ **raised up the Lord, and**
■ **will also raise up us**
  by his own power.
■ 15. **Know ye not that your**
■ **bodies are the members**
■ **of Christ? shall I then**
  take the members of Christ, and
■ **make them the members of**

■ **an harlot?** God forbid.
16. What? know ye not that he which
is joined to an harlot is one body?
for two, saith he, shall be one flesh.
17. But he that is joined unto
the Lord is one spirit.
■ 18. **Flee fornication.** Every sin
that a man doeth is without the body;
but he that committeth fornication
sinneth against his own body.
■ 19. **What? know ye not**
■ **that your body is the**
■ **temple of the Holy Ghost**
which is in you, which ye have ofGod,
■ **and ye are not your own?**
■ 20. **For ye are bought with**
■ **a price: therefore glorify**
■ **God in your body,**
and in your spirit, which are God's.

CHAPTER 7

1. Now concerning the things
whereof ye wrote unto me:
■ **It is good for a man**
■ **not to touch a woman.**
■ 2. **Nevertheless, to avoid**
■ **fornication, let every man**
■ **have his own wife, and let**
■ **every woman have**
■ **her own husband.**
■ 3. **Let the husband**
■ **render** unto the wife
■ **due benevolence:**
■ **and likewise** also
■ **the wife** unto the husband.
■ 4. **The wife hath not power**
■ **of her own body,**
but the husband: and
■ **likewise also the husband**
■ **hath not power of his own**
■ **body,** but the wife.
■ 5. **Defraud ye not one**
■ **the other, except**
it be with consent for a time,
■ **that ye may give**
■ **yourselves to fasting and**
■ **prayer;** and come together
again,that Satan tempt you not
for your incontinency.
■ 6. **But I speak this by**
■ **permission, and not**
■ **of commandment.**
7. **For I would that all men**

were even **as I myself. But every man hath his proper gift of God,** one after this manner, and another after that. 8. **I say therefore to the unmarried and widows, It is good** for them **if they abide** even **as I.** 9. **But if they cannot contain, let them marry:** for it is better to marry than to burn. 10. **And unto the married I command, yet not I, but the Lord, Let not the wife depart from her husband:** 11. **But and if she depart, let her remain unmarried or be reconciled** to *her* husband: and **let not the husband put away his wife.** 12. But to the rest speak I, not the Lord: **If any brother hath a wife that believeth not, and she be pleased to dwell with him, let him not put her away.** 13. And the woman which hath an husband that believeth not, and if he be pleased to dwell with her, let her not leave him. 14. **For the unbelieving husband is sanctified by the wife, and the unbelieving wife** is sanctified **by the husband:** else were your children unclean; but now are they holy. 15. **But if the unbelieving depart, let him depart. A brother or a sister is not under bondage in such cases:** but God hath called us to peace. 16. **For** what **knowest thou,** O wife, **whether thou shalt save thy husband? or** how knowest thou, O man, whether thou shalt save **thy wife?** 17. **But** as God hath distributed to every man, **as the Lord hath called every one, so let him walk.** And so ordain I in all churches. 18. **Is any man called being circumcised? let him not become uncircumcised.** Is **any** called in **uncircumcision? let him not be circumcised.** 19. **Circumcision** is nothing, **and uncircumcision is nothing, but the keeping of the commandments of God.** 20. Let every man abide in the same calling wherein he was called. 21. Art thou called *being* a servant? care not for it: but if thou mayest be made free, use *it* rather. 22. **For he that is called** in the Lord, **being a servant, is the Lord's freeman: likewise** also **he that is called, being free, is Christ's servant.** 23. **Ye are bought with a price; be not ye the servants of men.** 24. Brethren, let every man, wherein he is called, therein abide with God. 25. **Now concerning virgins I have no commandment of the Lord: yet I give my judgment,** as one that hath obtained mercy of the Lord to be faithful. 26. **I suppose** therefore that this is good for the present distress, *I say,* **that it is good for a man so to be.** 27. Art thou bound unto a wife? seek not to be loosed. Art thou loosed from a wife? seek not a wife. 28. **But and if thou marry, thou hast not sinned;** and if a virgin marry, she hath not sinned. Nevertheless such shall have trouble in the flesh: but I spare you. 29. **But** this I say, **brethren, the time is short: it**

■ **remaineth, that** both
■ **they that have wives be**
■ **as though they had none;**
30. And they that weep, as though they wept not; and they that rejoice, as though they rejoiced not; and they that buy, as though they possessed not;
31. And they that use this world, as not abusing *it*: for the fashion of this world passeth away.
32. But I would have you without carefulness.
■ **He that is unmarried**
■ **careth for the things**
■ **that belong to the Lord,**
how he may please the Lord:
■ 33. **But he that is married**
■ **careth for the things**
■ **that are of the world,**
how he may please *his* wife.
34. **There is difference also**
■ **between a wife and a**
■ **virgin. The unmarried**
■ **woman careth for the**
■ **things of the Lord,** that she may be holy both in body and in spirit:
■ **but she that is married**
■ **careth for the things**
■ **of the world,**
how she may please *her* husband.
35. And this I speak for your own profit; not that I may cast a snare upon you, but for that which is comely, and that ye may attend upon the Lord without distraction.
■ 36. **But if any man** think that he
■ **behaveth himself**
■ **uncomely toward his**
■ **virgin, if she pass the**
■ **flower of her age,**
and need so require,
■ **let him do what he will, he**
■ **sinneth not: let them marry.**
37. Nevertheless he that standeth stedfast in his heart, having no necessity, but hath power over his own will, and hath so decreed in his heart that he will keep his virgin, doeth well.
■ 38. **So then he that giveth**
■ **her in marriage doeth**
■ **well; but he that giveth**

■ **her not** in marriage
■ **doeth better.**
39. **The wife** is bound by the law as long as her husband liveth; but
■ **if her husband be dead,** she
■ **is at liberty to be married**
to whom she will; only
■ **in the Lord.**
40. **But she is happier**
■ **if she so abide,**
after my judgment: and I think also that I have the Spirit of God.

CHAPTER 8

1. Now as touching things offered unto idols, we know that we all have knowledge. Knowledge puffeth up, but charity edifieth.
2. And if any man think that he knoweth any thing, he knoweth nothing yet as he ought to know.
3. But if any man love God, the same is known of him.
■ 4. **As concerning** therefore the
■ **eating** of those
■ **things** that are
■ **offered** in sacrifice
■ **unto idols, we know** that
■ **an idol is nothing** in the world,
■ **and** that
■ **there is none other**
■ **God but one.**
5. For though there be that are called gods, whether in heaven or in earth, (as there be gods many, and lords many,)
6. But to us *there is but* one God, the Father, of whom *are* all things, and we in him;
■ **and one Lord Jesus Christ,**by whom *are* all things, and we by him.
■ 7. **Howbeit there is not in**
■ **every man that knowledge:**
■ **for some** with conscience of the idol unto this hour
■ **eat it as a thing offered**
■ **unto an idol; and their**
■ **conscience** being weak
■ **is defiled.**
8. But meat commendeth us not to God:
■ **for neither, if we eat, are we**
■ **the better; neither, if we eat**

■ **not, are we the worse.**
■ 9. **But take heed lest**
by any means
■ **this liberty** of yours
■ **become a stumblingblock**
■ **to them that are weak.**
10. For if any man see thee which
hast knowledge sit at meat in the
idol's temple, shall not the conscience
of him which is weak
be emboldened to eat those things
which are offered to idols;
11. And through thy knowledge
shall the weak brother perish,
for whom Christ died?
12. But when ye sin so against the
brethren, and wound their weak
conscience, ye sin against Christ.
■ 13. **Wherefore, if meat**
■ **make my brother to**
■ **offend, I will eat no flesh**
while the world standeth, lest I
make my brother to offend.

CHAPTER 9

■ 1. **Am I not an apostle? am**
■ **I not free? have I not seen**
■ **Jesus Christ** our Lord?
are not ye my work in the Lord?
2. If I be not an apostle unto others,
yet doubtless I am to you: for the
seal of mine apostleship
are ye in the Lord.
■ 3. **Mine answer to them that**
■ **do examine me is this,**
■ 4. **Have we not power**
■ **to eat and to drink?**
■ 5. **Have we not power**
■ **to lead** about a sister,
■ **a wife, as well as other**
■ **apostles,** and *as* the brethren
of the Lord, and Cephas?
6. Or I only and Barnabas,
■ **have not we power to**
■ **forbear working?**
7. Who goeth a warfare any time
at his own charges? who planteth
a vineyard, and eateth not of the
fruit thereof? or
■ **who feedeth a flock,**
■ **and eateth not of the**
■ **milk of the flock?**
8. Say I these things as a man?

or saith not the law the same also?
9. For it is written in the law of Moses,
Thou shalt not muzzle the mouth of
the ox that treadeth out the corn. Doth
God take care for oxen?
10. Or saith he *it* altogether
for our sakes?
■ **For our sakes, no doubt,**
■ **this is written: that he that**
■ **ploweth should plow in**
■ **hope; and**
that he that thresheth in hope
■ **should be partaker**
■ **of his hope.**
■ 11. **If we have sown** unto you
■ **spiritual things, is it a great**
■ **thing if we shall reap your**
■ **carnal things?**
12. If others be partakers of *this*
power over you, *are* not we rather?
■ **Nevertheless we have not**
■ **used this power; but suffer**
■ **all things, lest we should**
■ **hinder the gospel** of Christ.
■ 13. **Do ye not know that they**
■ **which minister** about holy things
■ **live of the things of the**
■ **temple?** and they which wait at the
altar are partakers with the altar?
■ 14. **Even so hath the Lord**
■ **ordained that they which**
■ **preach** the gospel
■ **should live of the gospel.**
■ 15. **But I have used none**
■ **of these things:**
neither have I written these things,
that it should be so done unto me:
■ **for it were better for me to**
■ **die, than that any man**should
■ **make my glorying void.**
■ 16. **For though I**
■ **preach** the gospel,
■ **I have nothing to glory of:**
for necessity is laid upon me; yea,
■ **woe is unto me, if I preach**
■ **not the gospel!**
17. For if I do this thing willingly,
I have a reward: but if against my
will, a dispensation of *the gospel* is
committed unto me.
■ 18. **What is my reward then?**
■ **Verily that, when I preach**
the gospel, I may make the gospel of

Christ without charge,
that I abuse not my
power in the gospel.
19. **For though I be free**
from all *men*,
yet have I made myself
servant unto all,
that I might gain the more.
20. **And unto the Jews I**
became as a Jew, that I
might gain the Jews;
to them that are under the law,
as under the law, that I might gain
them that are under the law;
21. **To them that are without**
law, as without law,
(being not without law to God,
but under the law to Christ,)
that I might gain them
that are without law.
22. To the weak became I as weak,
that I might gain the weak:
I am made all things to
all men, that I might by
all means save some.
23. And this I do for the gospel's
sake, that I might be partaker
thereofwith *you*.
24. **Know ye not that they**
which run in a race run all,
but one receiveth the prize?
So run, that ye may obtain.
25. And every man that striveth
for the mastery is temperate in
all things. Now they *do it* to obtain
a corruptible crown;
but we an incorruptible.
26. **I therefore** so
run, not as uncertainly; so
fight I, not as one that beateth the air:
27. **But I keep under my**
body, and bring it into
subjection: lest
that by any means,
when I have
preached to others,
I myself should be
a castaway.

CHAPTER 10

1. **Moreover, brethren, I**
would not that ye should
be ignorant, how that all our

fathers were under the cloud,
and all passed through the sea;
2. And were all baptized unto Moses
in the cloud and in the sea;
3. And did all eat the
same spiritual meat;
4. And did all drink the same spiritual
drink: for they drank of that
spiritual Rock that followed them:
and that Rock was Christ.
5. But with many of them God was
not well pleased: for they were
overthrown in the wilderness.
6. Now these things were our
examples, to the intent
we should not lust after evil
things, as they also lusted.
7. **Neither be ye idolaters,** as
were some of them; as it is written,
The people sat down to eat and
drink, and rose up to play.
8. **Neither let us commit**
fornication, as some of them
committed, and fell in one day
three and twenty thousand.
9. **Neither let us tempt**
Christ, as some of them
also tempted, and were
destroyed of serpents.
10. **Neither murmur ye,** as
some of them also murmured, and
were destroyed of the destroyer.
11. Now all these things happened
unto them for ensamples: and they
are written for our admonition, upon
whom the ends of the world arecome.
12. **Wherefore let him that**
thinketh he standeth
take heed lest he fall.
13. **There hath no temptation**
taken you but such as
is common to man: but
God is faithful, who will not
suffer you to be tempted
above that ye are able;
but will with the temptation also
make a way to escape,
that ye may be able to bear *it*.
14. **Wherefore,**
my dearly beloved,
flee from idolatry.
15. I speak as to wise men;
judge ye what I say.

16. **The cup of blessing which we bless, is it not the communion of the blood of Christ? The bread** which we break, **is it not the communion of the body of Christ?**

17. **For we being many are** one bread, *and* **one body: for we are all partakers of that one bread.**

18. Behold Israel after the flesh: are not they which eat of the sacrifices partakers of the altar?

19. What say I then? that the idol is any thing, or that which is offered in sacrifice to idols is any thing?

20. But *I say*, that **the things which the Gentiles sacrifice, they sacrifice to devils,** and not to God: **and I would not that ye should have fellowship with devils.**

21. **Ye cannot drink the cup of the Lord, and** the cup **of devils:** ye cannot be partakers of the Lord's table, and of the table of devils.

22. Do we provoke the Lord to jealousy? are we stronger than he?

23. **All things are lawful for me, but all things are not expedient:** all things are lawful for me, but all things edify not.

24. **Let no man seek his own, but every man another's wealth.**

25. **Whatsoever is sold** in the shambles, **that eat, asking no question for conscience sake:**

26. **For the earth is the Lord's, and the fulness thereof.**

27. If **any** of them **that believe not bid you to a feast,** and ye be disposed to go; **whatsoever is set before**

you, eat, asking no question for conscience sake.

28. **But if any man say** unto you, **This is offered** in sacrifice **unto idols, eat not for his sake** that shewed it, **and for conscience sake:** for the earth *is* the Lord's, and the fulness thereof:

29. Conscience, I say, not thine own, but of the other: for why is my liberty judged of another *man's* conscience?

30. For if I by grace be a partaker, why am I evil spoken of for that for which I give thanks?

31. **Whether therefore ye eat, or drink, or whatsoever ye do, do all to the glory of God.**

32. **Give none offence,** neither to the Jews, nor to the Gentiles, nor to the church of God:

33. **Even as I please all men** in all *things*, **not seeking mine own profit, but the profit of many, that they may be saved.**

CHAPTER 11

1. Be ye followers of me, even as I also *am* of Christ.

2. Now I praise you, brethren, that ye remember me in all things, and keep the ordinances, as I delivered *them* to you.

3. **But I would have you know, that the head of every man is Christ; and the head of the woman is the man; and the head of Christ is God.**

4. **Every man** praying or prophesying, **having his head covered, dishonoureth his head.**

5. **But every woman that prayeth** or prophesieth **with her head uncovered dishonoureth her head:** for that is even all one as if she were shaven.

6. For if the woman be not covered, let her also be shorn: but if it be a shame for a woman to be shorn or shaven, let her be covered.

7. For a man indeed ought not to cover his head, forasmuch **as he is the image** and glory **of God: but the woman is the glory of the man.**

8. For the **man is not of** the **woman: but** the **woman of** the **man.**

9. Neither was the man created for the woman; but the woman for the man.

10. For this cause ought the woman to have power on *her* head because of the angels.

11. Nevertheless neither is the man without the woman, neither the woman without the man, in the Lord.

12. For as the woman is of the man, even so is the man also by the **woman; but all things of God.**

13. Judge in yourselves: is it comely that a woman pray unto God uncovered?

14. Doth not even nature itself **teach you, that, if a man have long hair, it is a shame** unto him?

15. But if a woman have long hair, it is a glory to her: for *her* hair is given her for a covering.

16. But if any man seem to be contentious, we have no such custom, neither the churches of God.

17. Now in this that I declare *unto you* **I praise you not, that ye come together not for the better, but** for **the worse.**

18. For first of all, **when ye come together in the church, I hear that there be divisions among**

you; and I partly believe it.

19. For there must be also heresies among you, that they which are approved may be made manifest among you.

20. When ye come together therefore into one place, **this is not to eat the Lord's supper.**

21. For in eating every one taketh before *other* his own supper: **and one is hungry, and another is drunken.**

22. What? have ye not houses to eat and to drink **in? or despise ye the church** of God, and shame them that have not? What shall I say to you? shall I praise you in this? I praise *you* not.

23. For I have received of the Lord that which also **I delivered unto you, That the Lord Jesus** the *same* night in which he was betrayed **took bread:**

24. And when he had given thanks, he brake it, and said, Take, eat: this is my body, which is **broken for you: this do in remembrance of me.**

25. After the same manner **also he took the cup,** when he had supped, **saying, This cup is the new testament in my blood: this do ye,** as oft as ye drink *it,* **in remembrance of me.**

26. For as often as **ye eat this bread, and drink this cup, ye do shew the Lord's death till he come.**

27. Wherefore whosoever shall eat this bread, and drink *this* cup of the Lord, unworthily, shall be guilty of the body and blood of the Lord.

28. But let a man examine himself, and so let him eat of *that* bread, and drink of *that* cup.

29. For he that eateth and drinketh unworthily, eateth

and drinketh damnation to himself, not discerning the Lord's body.

30. **For this cause many are** weak and **sickly** among you, **and many sleep.**

31. For if we would judge ourselves, we should not be judged.

32. But when we are judged, we are chastened of the Lord, that we should not be condemned with the world.

33. **Wherefore,** my brethren, **when ye** come together to **eat, tarry one for another.**

34. **And if any man hunger, let him eat at home; that ye come not** together **unto condemnation.** And the rest will I set in order when I come.

CHAPTER 12

1. **Now concerning spiritual gifts,** brethren, I would not have you ignorant.

2. Ye know that ye were Gentiles, carried away unto these dumb idols, even as ye were led.

3. Wherefore I give you to understand, that **no man speaking by the Spirit of God calleth Jesus accursed: and** that **no man can say** that **Jesus is the Lord, but by the Holy Ghost.**

4. **Now there are diversities of gifts, but the same Spirit.**

5. And there are differences of administrations, but the same Lord.

6. And there are diversities of operations, but it is the same God which worketh all in all.

7. But the manifestation of the Spirit is given to every man to profit withal.

8. **For to one is given by the Spirit the word of wisdom; to another the word of knowledge** by the same Spirit;

9. **To another faith** by the same Spirit; **to another the gifts of healing** by the same Spirit;

10. **To another** the working of **miracles; to another prophecy; to another discerning of spirits; to another divers** kinds of **tongues; to another the interpretation of tongues:**

11. **But all these worketh** that one and **the selfsame Spirit,** dividing to every man severally as he will.

12. For as the body is one, and hath many members, and all the members of that one body, being many, are one body: so also *is* Christ.

13. **For by one Spirit are we all baptized into one body,** whether *we be* Jews or Gentiles, whether *we be* bond or free; and have been all made to drink into one Spirit.

14. **For the body is not one member, but many.**

15. **If the foot shall say, Because I am not the hand, I am not of the body; is it therefore not of the body?**

16. And if the ear shall say, Because I am not the eye, I am not of the body; is it therefore not of the body?

17. **If the whole body were an eye, where were the hearing?** If the whole *were* hearing, where *were* the smelling?

18. But now hath God set the members every one of them in the body, as it hath pleased him.

19. And if they were all one member, where *were* the body?

20. **But now are they many members**, yet **but one body.**

21. And the eye cannot say unto the hand, I have no need of thee: nor again the head to the feet, I have no need of you.

22. Nay, much more **those members** of the body, **which seem** to be **more feeble, are necessary:**

23. **And those members** of the body, **which we think** to be

less honourable,
upon these we
bestow more abundant
honour; and our uncomely *parts*
have more abundant comeliness.
24. For our comely *parts*
have no need:
but God hath tempered
the body together,
having given more
abundant honour to
that part which lacked.
25. That there should be
no schism in the body; but
that the members should have
the same care one for another.
26. And whether one
member suffer, all the
members suffer with it;
or one member be honoured,
all the members rejoice with it.
27. Now ye are the body
of Christ, and members
in particular.
28. And God hath set
some in the church, first
apostles, secondarily
prophets, thirdly teachers,
after that miracles, then
gifts of healings,
helps, governments,
diversities of tongues.
29. Are all apostles? are
all prophets? *are* all teachers?
are all workers of miracles?
30. Have all the gifts of healing? doall
speak with tongues? do all interpret?
31. But covet earnestly
the best gifts:
and yet shew I unto you
a more excellent way.

CHAPTER 13

1. Though I speak with the
tongues of men and of
angels, and have not
charity, I am become
as sounding brass, or
a tinkling cymbal.
2. And though I have
the gift of prophecy,
and understand all
mysteries,and all

knowledge; and though I
have all faith, so
that I could remove
mountains, and have not
charity, I am nothing.
3. And though I
bestow all my goods to
feed the poor, and though I
give my body to be burned,
and have not charity, it
profiteth me nothing.
4. Charity suffereth long,
and is kind; charity envieth
not; charity vaunteth not itself,
is not puffed up,
5. Doth not behave itself
unseemly, seeketh not
her own, is not easily
provoked, thinketh no evil;
6. Rejoiceth not in iniquity, but
rejoiceth in the truth;
7. Beareth all things, believeth all things, hopeth all
things, endureth all things.
8. Charity never faileth:
but whether *there be*
prophecies, they
shall fail; whether *there be*
tongues, they
shall cease; whether *there be*
knowledge, it
shall vanish away.
9. For we know in part,
and we prophesy in part.
10. But when that which is
perfect is come, then
that which is
in part shall be
done away.
11. When I was a child,
I spake as a child,
I understood as a child,
I thought as a child: but
when I became a man, I
put away childish things.
12. For now we see through
a glass, darkly; but then
face to face: now I know
in part; but then shall I
know even as also
I am known.
13. And now abideth faith,
hope, charity, these three;

273

■ **but the greatest of**
■ **these is charity.**

CHAPTER 14

■ 1. **Follow after charity,**
and desire spiritual *gifts*, but
rather that ye may prophesy.
■ 2. **For he that speaketh** in
■ **an unknown tongue**
■ **speaketh** not unto men, but
■ **unto God: for no man**
■ **understandeth him;**
■ **howbeit** in the spirit
■ **he speaketh mysteries.**
■ 3. **But he that prophesieth**
■ **speaketh unto men**
■ **to edification,**
and exhortation, and comfort.
■ 4. **He that speaketh in an**
■ **unknown tongue edifieth**
■ **himself;** but he that
prophesieth edifieth the church.
■ 5. **I would that ye all spake**
■ **with tongues but rather that**
■ **ye prophesied:** for greater
is he that prophesieth than he that
speaketh with tongues, except he
interpret, that the church may
receive edifying.
■ 6. **Now, brethren, if**
■ **I come** unto you
■ **speaking with tongues,**
■ **what shall I profit you,**
■ **except I** shall
■ **speak** to you either
■ **by revelation, or by know-**
■ **ledge, or by prophesying,**
■ **or by doctrine?**
7. And even things without life giving
sound, whether pipe or harp,
except they give a distinction in
the sounds, how shall it be known
what is piped or harped?
8. For if the trumpet give an
uncertain sound, who shall
prepare himself to the battle?
9. So likewise ye,
■ **except ye utter by the**
■ **tongue words easy to be**
■ **understood, how shall it be**
■ **known what is spoken?**
for ye shall speak into the air.
10. There are, it may be, so many

kinds of voices in the world, and
none of them *is* without signification.
11. Therefore if I know not the
meaning of the voice, I shall be
unto him that speaketh a barbarian,
and he that speaketh *shall be* a
barbarian unto me.
12. Even so ye,
■ **forasmuch as ye are**
■ **zealous of spiritual gifts,**
■ **seek that ye may excel to**
■ **the edifying of the church.**
■ 13. **Wherefore let him that**
■ **speaketh in an unknown**
■ **tongue pray that he**
■ **may interpret.**
■ 14. **For if I pray in an**
■ **unknown tongue, my**
■ **spirit prayeth, but my**
■ **understanding is unfruitful.**
15. What is it then?
■ **I will pray with the**
■ **spirit, and** I will pray
■ **with the understanding** also: I
will sing with the spirit, and I will sing
with the understanding also.
16. Else when thou shalt bless with
the spirit, how shall he that occupieth
the room of the unlearned say Amen
at thy giving of thanks, seeing
he understandeth not what
thou sayest?
17. For thou verily givest thanks
well, but the other is not edified.
■ 18. **I thank my God, I**
■ **speak with tongues**
■ **more than ye all:**
■ 19. **Yet in the church**
■ **I had rather speak**
■ **five words with** my
■ **understanding,**
■ **that** by my voice
■ **I might teach others** also,
■ **than ten thousand words**
■ **in an unknown tongue.**
■ 20. **Brethren, be not**
■ **children** in understanding:
howbeit in malice be ye children,
■ **but** in understanding
■ **be men.**
21. In the law it is written, With *men*
of other tongues and other lips
will I speak unto this people; and yet

for all that will they not hear me, saith the LORD.

22. **Wherefore tongues are for a sign,** not to them that believe, but **to them that believe not: but prophesying** *serveth* not **for them that believe** not, but for them which believe.

23. **If therefore the** whole **church be come together** into one place, **and all speak with tongues, and there come** in **those that are unlearned, or unbelievers, will they not say** that **ye are mad?**

24. **But if all prophesy, and there come in one that believeth not,** or *one* unlearned, he is convinced of all, he is judged of all:

25. **And thus are the secrets of his heart made manifest;** and so falling down on *his* face **he will worship God,** and report that God is in you of a truth.

26. **How is it then,** brethren? **when ye come together, every one of you hath a psalm,** hath **a doctrine,** hath **a tongue,** hath **a revelation,** hath **an interpretation.** Let all things be done unto edifying.

27. **If any man speak in an unknown tongue,** *let it be* by two, or at the most *by* three, and *that* by course; and **let one interpret.**

28. **But if there be no interpreter, let him keep silence** in the church; and let him speak to himself, and to God.

29. **Let the prophets speak** two or three, **and let the other judge.**

30. **If any thing be revealed to another** that sitteth by, **let the first hold his peace.**

31. For ye may all prophesy one by one, that all may learn, and all may be comforted.

32. And the spirits of the prophets are subject to the prophets.

33. **For God is not the author of confusion, but of peace,** as in all churches of the saints.

34. **Let your women keep silence in the churches:** for it is not permitted unto them to speak; but *they are commanded* to be under obedience as also saith the law.

35. **And if they will learn any thing, let them ask their husbands at home:** for it is a shame for women to speak in the church.

36. What? came the word of God out from you? or came it unto you only?

37. **If any man think himself to be a prophet, or spiritual, let him acknowledge that the things that I write** unto you **are the commandments of the Lord.**

38. But if any man be ignorant, let him be ignorant.

39. Wherefore, brethren, **covet to prophesy, and forbid not to speak with tongues.**

40. **Let all things be done** decently and **in order.**

CHAPTER 15

1. Moreover, brethren, **I declare** unto you **the gospel** which I preached unto you, which also ye have received, and wherein ye stand;

2. **By which also ye are saved,** if ye keep in memory what I preached unto you, **unless ye have believed in vain.**

3. **For I delivered** unto you **first** of all that which I also received, how **that Christ died for our sins according to the scriptures;**

275

4. And that he was buried, and **that he rose again the third day** according to the scriptures:

5. **And that he was seen of Cephas, then of the twelve:**

6. **After that, he was seen of above five hundred** brethren at once; of whom the greater part remain unto this present, but some are fallen asleep.

7. **After that, he was seen of James; then of all the apostles.**

8. **And last** of all **he was seen of me** also, as of one born out of due time.

9. **For I am the least of the apostles,** that am not meet to be called an apostle, **because I persecuted the church** of God.

10. **But by the grace of God I am what I am: and his grace** which *was bestowed* upon me **was not in vain; but I laboured more abundantly than they all: yet not I, but the grace of God** which was **with me.**

11. Therefore whether *it were* I orthey, so we preach, and so ye believed.

12. **Now if Christ** be preached that he **rose from the dead, how say some** among you that **there is no resurrection** of the dead?

13. But if there be no resurrection of the dead, then is Christ not risen:

14. **And if Christ be not risen, then is our preaching vain,** and your faith *is* also vain.

15. **Yea, and we are** found **false witnesses of God; because we** have **testified of God that he raised** up **Christ:** whom he raised not up, if so be that the dead rise not.

16. For if the dead rise not, then is not Christ raised

17. **And if Christ be not raised, your faith is vain;** **ye are yet in your sins.**

18. Then they also which are fallen asleep in Christ are perished.

19. **If in this life only we have hope in Christ, we are of all men most miserable.**

20. **But now is Christ risen** from the dead, *and* become the firstfruits of them that slept.

21. **For since by man came death, by man came also the resurrection** of the dead.

22. **For as in Adam all die, even so in Christ shall all be made alive.**

23. But every man in his own order: Christ the firstfruits; afterward they that are Christ's at his coming.

24. **Then cometh the end,** when he shall have delivered up the kingdom to God, even the Father; **when he shall have put down all** rule and all **authority and power.**

25. **For he must reign, till he hath put all enemies under his feet.**

26. **The last enemy that shall be destroyed is death.**

27. For he hath put all things under his feet. But when he saith all things are put under *him, it is* manifest that he is excepted, which did put all things under him.

28. **And when all things shall be subdued unto him, then shall the Son also** himself **be subject unto him** that put all things under him, **that God may be all in all.**

29. **Else what shall they do which are baptized for the dead, if the dead rise not** at all? why are they then baptized for the dead?

30. **And why stand** we **in jeopardy every hour?**

31. I protest by your rejoicing which I have in Christ Jesus our LORD, I die daily.

32. **If after the manner of men I have fought with beasts** at Ephesus,

what advantageth it me, if the dead rise not? let us eat and drink; for to morrow we die.

33. Be not deceived: evil communications corrupt good manners.

34. Awake to righteousness, and sin not; for some have not the knowledge of God: I speak this to your shame.

35. But some man will say, How are the dead raised up? and with what body dothey come?

36. Thou fool, that which thou sowest is not quickened, except it die:

37. And that which thou sowest, thou sowest not that body that shall be, but bare grain, it may chance of wheat, or of some other grain:

38. But God giveth it a body as it hath pleased him, and to every seed his own body.

39. All flesh is not the same flesh: but there is one kind of flesh of men, another flesh of beasts, another of fishes, and another of birds.

40. There are also celestial bodies, and bodies terrestrial: but the glory of the celestial is one, and the glory of the terrestrial is another.

41. There is one glory of the sun, and another glory of the moon, and another glory of the stars: for one star differeth from another star in glory.

42. So also is the resurrection of the dead. It is sown in corruption; it is raised in incorruption:

43. It is sown in dishonour; it is raised in glory: it is sown in weakness; it is raised in power:

44. It is sown a natural body; it is raised a spiritual body. There is a natural body, and there is a spiritual body.

45. And so it is written, The first man Adam was made a living soul; the last Adam was made a quickening spirit.

46. Howbeit that was not first which is spiritual, but that which is natural; and afterward that which is spiritual.

47. The first man is of the earth, earthy; the second man is the Lord from heaven.

48. As is the earthy, such are they also that are earthy: and as is the heavenly, such are they also that are heavenly.

49. And as we have borne the image of the earthy, we shall also bear the image of the heavenly.

50. Now this I say, brethren, that flesh and blood cannot inherit the kingdom of God; neither doth corruption inherit incorruption.

51. Behold, I shew you a mystery; We shall not all sleep, but we shall all be changed,

52. In a moment, in the twinkling of an eye, at the last trump: for the trumpet shall sound, and the dead shall be raised incorruptible, and we shall be changed.

53. For this corruptible must put on incorruption, and this mortal must put on immortality.

54. So when this corruptible shall have put on incorruption, and this mortal shall have put on immortality, then shall be brought to pass the saying that is written, Death is swallowed up in victory.

55. O death, where is thy sting? O grave, where is thy victory?

56. The sting of death is sin; and the strength of sin is the law.

57. But thanks be to God, which giveth us the victory through our Lord Jesus

The receiving of offerings

■ **Christ.**
■ 58. **Therefore,**
my beloved brethren,
■ **be ye stedfast,**
unmoveable, always
abounding in the work ofthe Lord,
■ **forasmuch as ye know** that
■ **your labour is not in**
■ **vain in the Lord.**

CHAPTER 16

■ 1. **Now concerning the**
■ **collection for the saints,**
as I have given order to the churches
of Galatia, even so do ye.
■ 2. **Upon the first day of the**
■ **week let every one** of you
■ **lay by him in store, as God**
■ **hath prospered him,** that there
be no gatherings when I come.
3. And when I come,
■ **whomsoever ye** shall
■ **approve** by *your* letters,
■ **them will I send to bring**
■ **your liberality**
■ **unto Jerusalem.**
4. And if it be meet that I go
also, they shall go with me.
■ 5. **Now I will come unto you,**
when I shall pass through Macedonia:
for I do pass through Macedonia.
■ 6. **And it may be that**
■ **I will abide,** yea,
■ **and winter with you,**
that ye may bring me on my
journey whithersoever I go.
7. For I will not see you now
by the way; but
■ **I trust to tarry a while**
■ **with you,** if the Lord permit.
■ 8. **But I will tarry at Ephesus**
■ **until Pentecost.**
■ 9. **For a great door**
and effectual
■ **is opened unto me,**
■ **and there are**
■ **many adversaries.**
■ 10. **Now if Timotheus come,**
■ **see that he may be with**
■ **you without fear:** for he worketh
the work of the Lord, as I also *do.*

11. Let no man therefore despise him:
but conduct him forth in peace, that
he may come unto me: for I look for
him with the brethren.
■ 12. **As touching** *our* brother
■ **Apollos, I** greatly
■ **desired him to come**
■ **unto you** with the brethren:
■ **but his will was not** at all
■ **to come at this time;**
but he will come when he
shall have convenient time.
■ 13. **Watch ye, stand**
■ **fast in the faith,**
quit you like men, be strong.
■ 14. **Let all your things**
■ **be done with charity.**
15. I beseech you, brethren,
(ye know the house of
Stephanas, that it is the
firstfruits of Achaia, and *that*
they have addicted themselves
to the ministry of the saints,)
16. That ye submit yourselves unto
such, and to every one that helpeth
with *us,* and laboureth.
17. I am glad of the coming of
Stephanas and Fortunatus and
Achaicus: for that which was lacking
on your part they have supplied.
18. For they have refreshed my spirit
and yours: therefore acknowledge
ye them that are such.
19. The churches of Asia salute you.
Aquila and Priscilla salute you much
in the Lord, with the church that is in
their house.
■ 20. **All the brethren**
■ **greet you.** Greet ye one
another with an holy kiss.
21. The salutation of *me*
Paul with mine own hand.
■ 22. **If any man love**
■ **not the Lord Jesus** Christ,
■ **let him be Anathema**
■ **Maranatha.**
23. The grace of our Lord
Jesus Christ *be* with you.
24. My love *be* with you
all in Christ Jesus.
■ **Amen.**

THE SECOND EPISTLE TO THE CORINTHIANS

BACKGROUND INFORMATION

Author: **Paul,** an Apostle of Jesus Christ.
Date Written: probably **between 55** and **60** A.D.

Number of:
Verses   257
Chapters   13
Total Words   6,092
Scan Words   2,646
Scan Words represent
47 % of Total Words

Theme: written by Paul to recount his perils in the service of Christ **and to lay claim on the Corinthians as his children in Christ**

OUTLINE OF THE EPISTLE

I. **Paul's** Personal **Testimony**
Chapters 1:1 - 2:13

II. **Paul's** Account of his **Ministry**
Chapters 2:14 - 6:10

III. **Paul's Plea for** Reconciliation
Chapters 6:11 - 7:16

IV. **Paul's Appeal for** an Offering for **the Poor**
Chapters 8 - 9

V. **Paul's** Defense of his **Apostleship**
Chapters 10:1 - 13:10

VI. **Paul's Closing Words** to the Corinthian Church
Chapters 13:11 - 14

CHAPTER 1

■ 1. **Paul,** an apostle of
Jesus Christ by the will of God,
■ **and Timothy** *our* brother,
■ **unto the church** of God which is
■ **at Corinth,** with all the saints
which are in all Achaia.
■ 2. **Grace be to you and**
■ **peace from God** our Father,
■ **and from the**
■ **Lord Jesus** Christ.
■ 3. **Blessed be** God, even
■ **the Father of our Lord Jesus**
■ **Christ,** the Father of mercies, and
the God of all comfort;
■ 4. **Who comforteth**
■ **us** in all our tribulation,
■ **that we may** be able to
■ **comfort them** which are
■ **in** any
■ **trouble,** by the comfort wherewith
we ourselves are comforted of God.
5. For as the sufferings of Christ
abound in us, so our consolation
also aboundeth by Christ.
■ 6. **And whether we be**
■ **afflicted, it is for your**
■ **consolation and**
■ **salvation,** which is effectual in the
enduring of the same sufferings which
we also suffer: or whether we be
comforted, *it is* for your consolation
and salvation.
7. And our hope of you *is* stedfast,
■ **knowing, that as ye are**
■ **partakers of the sufferings,**
■ **so shall ye be** also
■ **of the consolation.**
■ 8. **For** we would not, brethren, have
you ignorant of our trouble which
came to us in Asia, that
■ **we were pressed out of**
■ **measure,** above strength,
■ **insomuch that we**
■ **despaired** even of life:
■ 9. **But we had the sentence**
■ **of death** in ourselves,
■ **that we should not trust in**
■ **ourselves, but in God which**
■ **raiseth the dead:**
■ 10. **Who delivered us**
from so great a death,
■ **and** doth deliver:

■ **in whom we trust**
that he will yet deliver *us*;
11. Ye also helping together byprayer
for us, that for the gift *bestowed*
upon us by the means of many
persons thanks may be given by
many on our behalf.
■ 12. **For our rejoicing is** this, the
testimony of our conscience, *that*
■ **in** simplicity and
■ **godly sincerity,** not with fleshly
wisdom, but by the grace of God,
we have had our conversation in
the world, and more abundantly
to you-ward.
13. For we write none other things
unto you, than what ye read or
acknowledge; and I trust ye shall
acknowledge even to the end;
■ 14. **As** also
■ **ye have acknowledged**
us in part,
■ **that we are your rejoicing,**
■ **even as ye** also
■ **are our's in the day**
■ **of the Lord** Jesus.
15. And in this confidence
■ **I was minded to come**
■ **unto you** before, that ye
might have a second benefit;
■ 16. **And to pass by you**
■ **into Macedonia,** and to come
again out of Macedonia unto you,
and of you to be brought on my
way toward Judaea.
17. When I therefore was thus
minded, did I use lightness? or the
things that I purpose, do I purpose
according to the flesh, that with me
there should be yea yea,
and nay nay?
18. But *as* God *is* true,
■ **our word toward you**
■ **was not yea and nay.**
■ 19. **For the Son of**
■ **God,** Jesus Christ,
■ **who was preached**
■ **among you** by us, *even* by
me and Silvanus and Timotheus,
■ **was not yea and**
■ **nay, but** in him was
■ **yea.**
20. **For all the**

■ **promises** of God
■ **in him are yea,** and in him
Amen, unto the glory of God by us.
■ 21. **Now he which**
■ **stablisheth us with you in**
■ **Christ,** and hath anointed us,
■ **is God;**
22. Who hath also sealed us,
and given the earnest of the
Spirit in our hearts.
23. Moreover I call God for a record
upon my soul, that to spare you I
came not as yet unto Corinth.
■ 24. **Not** for
■ **that we have dominion**
■ **over your faith,**
but are helpers of your joy:
■ **for by faith ye stand.**

CHAPTER 2

■ 1. **But** I determined
this with myself, that
■ **I would not come again**
■ **to you in heaviness.**
2. For if I make you sorry, who is he
then that maketh me glad, but the
same which is made sorry by me?
3. And I wrote this same unto you,
lest, when I came, I should have
sorrow from them of whom I ought to
rejoice; having confidence in you all,
that my joy is *the joy* of you all.
4. For out of much affliction and
anguish of heart I wrote unto you
withmany tears; not that ye should
be grieved, but that ye might know
the love which I have more
abundantly unto you.
■ 5. **But if any have caused**
■ **grief, he hath not grieved**
■ **me,** but in part: that I may not
overcharge you all.
■ 6. **Sufficient to such a man**
■ **is this punishment,** which
was inflicted of many.
7. So that contrariwise
■ **ye ought** rather
■ **to forgive him,** and comfort *him,*
■ **lest** perhaps
■ **such a one** should
■ **be swallowed** up
■ **with** overmuch
■ **sorrow.**

8. Wherefore I beseech
you that ye would
■ **confirm your love**
■ **toward him.**
9. For to this end also did I write,
that I might know the proof of you,
whether ye be obedient in all things.
■ 10. **To whom ye**
■ **forgive** any thing,
■ **I forgive** also: for if I forgave
anything, to whom I forgave *it,*
for your sakes *forgave I it* in
the person of Christ;
■ 11. **Lest Satan should**
■ **get an advantage** of us:
■ **for we are not ignorant**
■ **of his devices.**
■ 12. **Furthermore, when**
■ **I came to Troas**
to *preach* Christ's gospel, and
■ **a door was opened** unto me
■ **of the Lord,**
■ 13. **I had no rest** in my spirit,
■ **because I found not**
■ **Titus** my brother: but taking
my leave of them, I went from
thence into Macedonia.
■ 14. **Now thanks be unto**
■ **God, which** always
■ **causeth us to triumph**
■ **in Christ,** and maketh manifest
the savour of his knowledge
by us in every place.
■ 15. **For we are unto God a**
■ **sweet savour of Christ,**
in them that are saved, and in
them that perish:
■ 16. **To the one we are the**
■ **savour of death** unto death;
■ **and to the other the savour**
■ **of life** unto life. And who
is sufficient for these things?
■ 17. **For we are not as many,**
■ **which corrupt the word**
of God: but as of sincerity, but as
of God, in the sight of God speak
we in Christ.

CHAPTER 3

1. Do we begin again to
commend ourselves? or need
we, as some *others,* epistles of
commendation to you, or *letters*

of commendation from you?

■ 2. **Ye are our epistle**
written in our hearts,

■ **known and read of all** men:

3. *Forasmuch as ye are* manifestly
declared to be the epistle of Christ
ministered by us,

■ **written not with ink, but with**

■ **the Spirit** of the living God; not in
tables of stone, but in fleshy tables
of the heart.

■ 4. **And such trust have we**

■ **through Christ** to God-ward:

■ 5. **Not that we are sufficient**
of ourselves to think any thing
as of ourselves;

■ **but our sufficiency**

■ **is of God;**

■ 6. **Who also hath made us**

■ **able ministers** of the new
testament; not of the letter, but

■ **of the spirit: for the letter**

■ **killeth, but the spirit**

■ **giveth life.**

■ 7. **But if the ministration**
of death,

■ **written** *and* engraven

■ **in stones, was glorious,**
so that the children of Israel could not
stedfastly behold the face of Moses
for the glory of his countenance;
which *glory* was to be done away:

■ 8. **How shall not the**

■ **ministration of the spirit**

■ **be rather glorious?**

9. For if the ministration of
condemnation *be* glory, much more
doth the ministration of righteousness
exceed in glory.

10. For even that which was made
glorious had no glory in this respect,
by reason of the glory that excelleth.

■ 11. **For if that which is done**

■ **away was glorious, much**

■ **more that which remaineth**

■ **is glorious.**

■ 12. **Seeing then that we have**

■ **such hope, we use** great

■ **plainness of speech:**

■ 13. **And not as Moses,**

■ **which put a vail over his**

■ **face,** that the children of Israel
could not stedfastly look to the end of

that which is abolished:

14. But their minds were blinded:

■ **for until this day remaineth**

■ **the same vail** untaken away in
the reading of the old testament;

■ **which vail is done**

■ **away in Christ.**

■ 15. **But even unto this day,**

■ **when Moses is read, the**

■ **vail is upon their heart.**

16. Nevertheless when it shall turn to
the Lord, the vail shall be taken away.

■ 17. **Now the Lord is that**

■ **Spirit: and where the**

■ **Spirit** of the Lord

■ **is, there is liberty.**

■ 18. **But we all, with open**

■ **face beholding** as in a glass

■ **the glory of the Lord, are**

■ **changed into the same**

■ **image** from glory to glory, *even* as

■ **by the Spirit** of the LORD.

CHAPTER 4

■ 1. **Therefore** seeing we have this
ministry, as we have received mercy,

■ **we faint not;**

■ 2. **But have renounced**

■ **the hidden things of**

■ **dishonesty, not walking in**

■ **craftiness, nor handling**

■ **the word** of God

■ **deceitfully; but by**

■ **manifestation of the**

■ **truth** commending ourselves
to every man's conscience

■ **in the sight of God.**

■ 3. **But if our gospel be hid, it**

■ **is hid to them that are lost:**

■ 4. **In whom the god of this**

■ **world hath blinded the**

■ **minds of them which**

■ **believe not,** lest the light
of the glorious gospel of Christ,
who is the image of God, should
shine unto them.

5. For we preach not ourselves, but
Christ Jesus the Lord; and ourselves
your servants for Jesus' sake.

■ 6. **For God,** who commanded the
light to shine out of darkness,

■ **hath shined in our hearts, to**

■ **give the light**

of the knowledge
**of the glory of God in
the face of Jesus** Christ.
7. **But we have this treasure
in earthen vessels, that**
the excellency of
the power may
be of God, and not of us.
8. **We are troubled**
on every side,
yet not distressed; *we are*
perplexed, but not in despair;
9. Persecuted, but not forsaken;
**cast down,
but not destroyed;**
10. **Always bearing about in
the body the dying of** theLord
Jesus, that the life also
of Jesus might be made
manifest in our body.
11. For we which live are alway
delivered unto death for Jesus' sake,
that the life also of Jesus might be
made manifest in our mortal flesh.
12. So then death worketh
in us, but life in you.
13. **We having the same
spirit of faith, according
as it is written,** I believed,
and therefore have I spoken;
we also
**believe, and
therefore speak;**
14. **Knowing that he
which raised up** the Lord
Jesus shall raise up
us also
by Jesus,
and shall present *us* with you.
15. For all things *are* for your sakes,
that the abundant grace might
through the thanksgiving of many
redound to the glory of God.
16. For which cause
**we faint not; but though
our outward man perish,
yet the inward** *man*
is renewed day by day.
17. For our light affliction, which is
but for a moment, worketh for us
a far more exceeding *and*
eternal weight of glory;
18. **While we look not at** the

things which are
seen, but at the
things which are
not seen: for the
things which are
seen are temporal; but the
things which are
not seen are eternal.

CHAPTER 5

1. **For we know that if our
earthly** house of *this*
**tabernacle were
dissolved, we have a
building of God,** an house
not made with hands, eternal
in the heavens.
2. **For** in this
**we groan, earnestly
desiring** to be clothed upon with
our house which is
from heaven:
3. If so be that being clothed
we shall not be found naked.
4. For we that are in *this* tabernacle
do groan, being burdened: not for
that we would be unclothed, but
clothed upon, that mortality might
be swallowed up of life.
5. **Now he that hath wrought
us** for the selfsame thing
is God, who also
**hath given unto
us** the earnest of
the Spirit.
6. **Therefore**
we are always confident,
knowing that, whilst we are
**at home in the body, we
are absent from the Lord:**
7. (For we walk by faith, not by sight:)
8. **We are** confident, *I say*, and
**willing rather to be absent
from the body, and to be
present with the Lord.**
9. **Wherefore we labour,
that,** whether present or absent,
we may be accepted of him.
10. **For we must all appear
before the judgment seat
of Christ;** that every one may
receive the things *done* in *his* body,
according to that he hath done,

whether *it be* good or bad.

■ 11. **Knowing therefore**
■ **the terror of the Lord,**
■ **we persuade men;** but
we are made manifest unto
God; and I trust also are made
manifest in your consciences.
12. For we commend not ourselves
again unto you, but give you occasion
to glory on our behalf, that ye may
have somewhat to *answer* them which
glory in appearance, and not in heart.
13. For whether we be beside
ourselves, *it is* to God: or whether
we be sober, *it is* for your cause.
■ 14. **For the love of Christ**
constraineth us; because we thus
judge, that if one died for all, then
were all dead:
15. And *that* he died for all, that
■ **they which live**
■ **should not** henceforth
■ **live unto themselves, but**
■ **unto him which died** for them,
■ **and rose** again.
16. Wherefore henceforth know
we no man after the flesh: yea,
though we have known Christ after
the flesh, yet now henceforth
know we *him* no more.
■ 17. **Therefore if any man**
■ **be in Christ, he is a new**
■ **creature: old things are**
■ **passed away; behold, all**
■ **things are become new.**
■ 18. **And** all things *are* of
■ **God,** who
■ **hath reconciled us** to himself
■ **by Jesus** Christ,
■ **and** hath
■ **given** to
■ **us the ministry of**
■ **reconciliation;**
■ 19. **To wit, that God was**
■ **in Christ, reconciling the**
■ **world** unto himself, not imputing
their trespasses unto them;
■ **and hath committed**
■ **unto us the word of**
■ **reconciliation.**
■ 20. **Now then we are**
■ **ambassadors** for Christ, as
though God did beseech *you* by us:

we pray *you*
■ **in Christ's stead,**
be ye reconciled to God.
■ 21. **For he hath**
■ **made him** *to be*
■ **sin** for us,
■ **who knew no sin; that**
■ **we might be made the**
■ **righteousness of**
■ **God in him.**

CHAPTER 6
■ 1. **We** then, *as* workers
together *with him,*
■ **beseech you** also
■ **that ye receive not the**
■ **grace of God in vain.**
■ 2. **(For he saith,** I have heard thee
in a time accepted, and in the day of
salvation have I succoured thee:
■ **behold, now is the**
■ **accepted time;** behold,
■ **now is the day**
■ **of salvation.)**
■ 3. **Giving no**
■ **offence** in any thing,
■ **that the ministry be**
■ **not blamed:**
■ 4. **But** in all *things*
■ **approving ourselves as** the
■ **ministers** of God,
■ **in much patience,** in afflictions,
in necessities, in distresses,
■ 5. **In stripes, in**
■ **imprisonments,** in tumults,
in labours, in watchings,
■ **in fastings;**
■ 6. **By pureness, by**
■ **knowledge,** by
longsuffering, by kindness,
■ **by the Holy Ghost,**
by love unfeigned,
■ 7. **By the word** of truth,
■ **by the power of God,**
by the armour of righteousness
on the right hand and on the left,
8. By honour and dishonour,
by evil report and good report:
as deceivers, and *yet* true;
9. As unknown, and *yet* well known;
■ **as dying, and, behold, we**
■ **live;** as chastened, and not killed;
■ 10. **As sorrowful, yet**

alway rejoicing; as
poor, yet making many rich; as
having nothing, and yet
possessing all things.
11. O ye Corinthians,
our mouth is open unto you,
our heart is enlarged.
12. Ye are not straitened in us, but ye
are straitened in your own bowels.
13. Now for a recompence in the
same, (I speak as unto my children,)
be ye also enlarged.
14. Be ye not unequally
yoked together
with unbelievers: for what
fellowship hath righteousness
with unrighteousness? and
what communion hath
light with darkness?
15. And what concord
hath Christ with Belial?
or what part hath he that
believeth with an infidel?
16. And what agreement
hath the temple of God
with idols? for ye are
the temple of the living
God; as God hath said,
I will dwell in them,
and walk in *them*; and I will be their
God, and they shall be my people.
17. Wherefore come
out from among them,
and be ye
separate, saith the Lord, and
touch not the unclean *thing*;
and I will receive you.
18. And will be a Father unto
you, and ye shall be my sons and
daughters, saith the Lord Almighty.

CHAPTER 7

1. Having therefore these
promises, dearly beloved,
let us cleanse
ourselves from all
filthiness of the flesh and spirit,
perfecting holiness
in the fear of God.
2. Receive us; we have
wronged no man,
we have corrupted no man,
we have defrauded no man.

3. I speak not this to
condemn you: for
I have said before, that
ye are in our hearts
to die and live with *you*.
4. Great is my boldness of
speech toward you,
great *is* my glorying of you: I am filled
with comfort, I am exceeding joyful in
all our tribulation.
5. For, when we were come into
Macedonia, our flesh had no rest, but
we were troubled on every
side; without *were* fightings,
within *were* fears.
6. Nevertheless God, that
comforteth those that are cast down,
comforted us by the
coming of Titus;
7. And not by his coming only, but
by the consolation wherewith
he was comforted in you,
when he told us
your earnest desire, your mourning,
your fervent mind toward
me; so that I rejoiced the more.
8. For though I made you
sorry with a letter, I do
not repent, though I did repent:
for I perceive that the same epistle
hath made you sorry, though *it*
were but for a season.
9. Now I rejoice,
not that ye were made sorry, but
that ye sorrowed to
repentance: for ye were
made sorry after a godly manner,
that ye might receive damage
by us in nothing.
10. For godly sorrow
worketh repentance to
salvation not to be repented of:
but the sorrow of the
world worketh death.
11. For behold this self
same thing, that
ye sorrowed after a godly
sort, what carefulness it wrought in
you, yea, *what* clearing of yourselves,
yea, *what* indignation, yea, *what* fear,
yea, *what* vehement desire, yea, *what*
zeal, yea, *what* revenge!
In all things ye have

approved yourselves to be clear in this matter.

12. **Wherefore,** though I wrote unto you, *I did it* not for his cause that had done the wrong, nor for his cause that suffered wrong, but that our care for you in the sight of God might appear unto you.

13. **Therefore we were comforted in your comfort:** yea, and exceedingly the more joyed we for the joy of Titus, because his spirit was refreshed by you all.

14. **For** if I have boasted any thing to him of you, I am not ashamed; but as we spake all things to you in truth, even so our boasting, which *I made* before Titus, is found a truth.

15. **And his inward affection is more abundant toward you,** whilst he remembereth the obedience of you all, how with fear and trembling ye received him.

16. I rejoice therefore that I have confidence in you in all *things.*

CHAPTER 8

1. **Moreover,** brethren, we do you to wit of the grace of God bestowed on the churches of Macedonia;

2. How that in a great trial of affliction the abundance of their joy and their deep poverty abounded unto the riches of their liberality.

3. **For** to *their* power, I bear record, yea, and beyond *their* power they were willing of themselves;

4. **Praying** us with much entreaty that we would receive the gift, and *take upon us* the fellowship of the ministering to the saints.

5. And *this they did,* not as we hoped,

but first gave their own selves to the Lord, and unto us by the will of God.

6. **Insomuch that we desired Titus, that** as he had begun, so he would also finish in you the same grace also.

7. **Therefore, as ye abound in every thing,** *in* faith, and utterance, and knowledge, and *in* all diligence, and *in* your love to us, see that ye abound in this grace also.

8. I speak not by commandment, but by occasion of the forwardness of others, and to prove the sincerity of your love.

9. **For ye know the grace of our Lord** Jesus Christ, that, though he was rich, yet for your sakes he became poor, that ye through his poverty might be rich.

10. And herein I give *my* advice: for this is expedient for you, who have begun before, not only to do, but also to be forward a year ago.

11. **Now therefore perform the doing of it;** that as *there was* a readiness to will, so *there may be* a performance also out of that which ye have.

12. For if there be first a willing mind, it is accepted according to that a man hath, and not according to that he hath not.

13. **For I mean not that other men be eased, and ye burdened:**

14. **But by an equality, that** now at this time your abundance may be a supply for their want, that their abundance also may be a supply for your want: that there may be equality:

15. **As it is written, He that** *had* gathered much had nothing over; and he that *had* gathered little had no lack.

16. **But thanks be to God, which put the same earnest care into the heart of Titus for you.** 17. For indeed he accepted the exhortation; but being more forward, of his own accord he went unto you. 18. **And we have sent with him the brother, whose praise is in the gospel** throughout all the churches; 19. **And** not *that* only, but **who was** also **chosen of the churches to travel with us** with this grace, which is administered by us to the glory of the same Lord, and *declaration of* your ready mind: 20. Avoiding this, that no man should blame us in this abundance which is administered by us: 21. Providing for honest things, not only in the sight of the Lord, butalso in the sight of men. 22. **And we have sent** with them **our brother, whom we have oftentimes proved diligent** in many things, but now much more diligent, upon the great confidence which *I have* in you. 23. **Whether any do inquire of Titus, he is my partner and fellowhelper concerning you: or our brethren** be inquired of, **they are the messengers of the churches,** *and* the glory of Christ. 24. **Wherefore shew ye to them** and before the churches, **the proof of your love,** and of our boasting on your behalf.

CHAPTER 9

1. **For as touching the ministering to the saints, it is superfluous** for me **to write** to you: 2. **For I know the forwardness of your mind, for which I boast** of you to them of Macedonia, that Achaia was ready a year ago; **and your zeal hath provoked** very **many.** 3. **Yet have I sent the brethren, lest our boasting** of you should **be in vain** in this behalf; that, as I said, ye may be ready: 4. Lest haply if they of Macedonia come with me, and find you unprepared, we (that we say not, ye) should be ashamed in this same confident boasting. 5. **Therefore I thought it necessary to exhort the brethren, that they would go** before unto you, **and make up** beforehand **your bounty,** whereof ye had notice before, that the same might be ready, as *a matter of* bounty, and not as *of* covetousness. 6. **But this I say, He which soweth sparingly shall reap** also **sparingly; and he which soweth bountifully shall reap** also **bountifully.** 7. **Every man according as he purposeth in his heart, so let him give; not grudgingly,** or of necessity: **for God loveth a cheerful giver.** 8. **And God is able to make all grace abound toward you;** that ye, always having all sufficiency in all *things,* may abound to every good work: 9. **(As it is written,** He hath dispersed abroad; **he hath given to the poor: his righteousness remaineth** for ever. 10. **Now he that ministereth seed to the sower both minister bread for your food, and multiply your seed sown,** and increase the fruits of your righteousness;) 11. Being enriched in every thing to

all bountifulness, which causeth through us thanksgiving to God.

■ 12. **For** the administration of
■ **this service not only**
■ **supplieth** the want of
■ **the saints, but is**
■ **abundant also by** many
■ **thanksgivings unto God;**
■ 13. **Whiles** by the experiment of this ministration
■ **they glorify God**
■ **for your** professed
■ **subjection unto**
■ **the gospel** of Christ,
■ **and for your liberal**
■ **distribution** unto them, and
■ **unto all men;**
■ 14. **And by their prayer** for you, which long after you
■ **for the** exceeding
■ **grace of God in you.**
■ 15. **Thanks be unto God for**
■ **his unspeakable gift.**

CHAPTER 10

1. Now I Paul myself beseech you by the meekness and gentleness of Christ, who in presence *am* base among you, but being absent am bold toward you:
■ 2. **But I beseech you, that I**
■ **may not be bold when I am**
■ **present** with that confidence,
■ **wherewith I think to be bold**
■ **against some, which think**
■ **of us as if we walked**
■ **according to the flesh.**
3. For though we walk in the flesh,
■ **we do not war**
■ **after the flesh:**
■ 4. **(For the weapons of our**
■ **warfare are not carnal,**
■ **but mighty through God**
■ **to the pulling down of**
■ **strong holds;)**
■ 5. **Casting down**
■ **imaginations, and every**
■ **high thing** that exalteth itself
■ **against the knowledge of**
■ **God, and bringing into**
■ **captivity every thought**
■ **to the obedience of Christ;**
■ 6. **And having in a readiness**

■ **to revenge**
■ **all disobedience,**
when your obedience is fulfilled.
7. Do ye look on things after the outward appearance?
■ **If any man**
■ **trust** to himself
■ **that he is Christ's,**
let him of himself think this again, that, as he *is* Christ's,
■ **even so are we Christ's.**
■ 8. **For though I should**
■ **boast** somewhat more
■ **of** our
■ **authority, which**
■ **the Lord hath given** us
■ **for edification, and**
■ **not** for your
■ **destruction,**
I should not be ashamed:
■ 9. **That I may not**
■ **seem as if I** would
■ **terrify you by letters.**
■ 10. **For his letters, say they,**
■ **are weighty** and powerful;
■ **but his** bodily
■ **presence is weak, and his**
■ **speech contemptible.**
11. Let such an one think this, that, such
■ **as we are** in word
■ **by letters when** we are
■ **absent, such will we be** also
■ **in deed when** we are
■ **present.**
■ 12. **For we dare not**
make ourselves of the number, or
■ **compare ourselves**
■ **with some that commend**
■ **themselves:** but they measuring themselves by themselves, and
■ **comparing themselves**
■ **among themselves,**
are not wise.
■ 13. **But we will not**
■ **boast of** things without
■ **our measure, but**
■ **according to the**
■ **measure of** the rule which
■ **God** hath distributed to us,
■ **a measure to reach** even unto
■ **you.**
14. For we stretch not ourselves

beyond *our measure*, as though we reached not unto you: for we are come as far as to you also in *preaching* the gospel of Christ:

15. **Not boasting of** things without *our* measure, *that is*, of **other men's labours; but having hope,** when your faith is increased, **that we shall be enlarged by you** according to our rule abundantly, 16. To preach the gospel in the *regions* beyond you, **and not to boast in another man's line of things** made ready to our hand. 17. **But he that glorieth, let him glory in the Lord.** 18. **For not he that commendeth himself is approved, but whom the Lord commendeth.**

CHAPTER 11

1. Would to God ye could bear with me a little in *my* folly: and indeed bear with me.

2. **For I am jealous over you with godly jealousy: for I have espoused you** to one husband, that I may present *you* **as a** chaste **virgin to Christ.** 3. **But I fear,** lest by any means, **as the serpent beguiled Eve** through his subtilty, **so your minds should be corrupted from the simplicity** that is **in Christ.** 4. **For if he that cometh preacheth another Jesus,** whom we have not preached, or *if* ye receive another spirit, which ye have not received, **or another gospel,** which ye have not accepted, **ye might** well **bear with him.** 5. For I suppose **I was not** a whit **behind the** very

chiefest apostles.

6. **But though I be rude in speech,** yet not in knowledge; but we have been throughly made manifest among you in all things. 7. Have I committed an offence in abasing myself that ye might be exalted, because **I have preached** to you **the gospel** of God **freely?** 8. **I robbed other churches,** taking wages *of them*, **to do you service.** 9. **And when I was present with you,** and wanted, I was chargeable to no man: for that which was lacking to me the brethren which came from Macedonia supplied: and in all *things* I have **kept myself from being burdensome** unto you, and *so* will I keep *myself*.

10. **As the truth of Christ is in me, no man shall stop** me of **this boasting** in the regions of Achaia. 11. Wherefore? because I love you not? God knoweth. 12. But what I do, that I will do, **that I may cut off occasion from them which desire occasion;** that wherein they glory, they may be found even as we. 13. **For such are false apostles,** deceitful workers, **transforming themselves into the apostles of Christ.** 14. **And no marvel; for Satan** himself **is transformed into an angel of light.** 15. **Therefore it is no great thing if his ministers** also **be transformed** as the ministers of righteousness; whose end shall be according to their works. 16. **I say again, Let no man think me a fool;** if otherwise, yet as a fool receive me, that I may boast myself a little. 17. That which I speak, I speak *it* not

after the Lord, but as it were foolishly, in this confidence of boasting.

18. Seeing that many glory after the flesh, I will glory also.

19. For ye suffer fools gladly, seeing ye *yourselves* are wise.

20. For ye suffer, if a man bring you into bondage, if a man devour *you*, if a man take *of you*, if a man exalt himself, if a man smite you on the face.

21. I speak as concerning reproach, as though we had been weak. **Howbeit whereinsoever any is bold, (I speak foolishly,) I am bold also.**

22. **Are they Hebrews? so am I.** Are they Israelites? so am I. **Are they the seed of Abraham? so am I.**

23. **Are they ministers of Christ?** (I speak as a fool) **I am more;** in labours more abundant, in stripes above measure, **in prisons more frequent, in deaths oft.**

24. **Of the Jews five times received I forty stripes save one.**

25. **Thrice was I beaten with rods, once was I stoned, thrice I suffered shipwreck,** a night and a day **I have been in the deep;**

26. *In* journeyings often, *in* perils of waters, **in perils of robbers,** *in* perils by *mine own* countrymen, *in* perils by the heathen, *in* perils in the city, *in* perils in the wilderness, *in* perils in the sea, *in* perils among false brethren;

27. **In weariness and painfulness,** in watchings often, **in hunger** and thirst, **in fastings** often, **in cold and nakedness.**

28. Beside those things that are without, that which cometh upon me daily, the care of all the churches.

29. Who is weak, and I am not weak? who is offended, and I burn not?

30. **If I must needs glory, I will glory of** the things which concern

mine infirmities.

31. **The God and Father of our Lord** Jesus Christ, which is blessed for evermore, **knoweth that I lie not.**

32. **In Damascus the governor** under Aretas the king kept the city of the Damascenes with a garrison, **desirous to apprehend me:**

33. **And through a window** in a basket was **I** let down by the wall, and **escaped his hands.**

CHAPTER 12

1. It is not expedient for me doubtless to glory. **I will come to visions and revelations of the Lord.**

2. **I knew a man in Christ** above fourteen years ago, **(whether in the body, I cannot tell;** or whether out of the body, I cannot tell: **God knoweth;) such an one caught up to the third heaven.**

3. And I knew such a man, (whether in the body, or out of the body, I cannot tell: God knoweth;)

4. **How that he was caught up into paradise, and heard unspeakable words,** which it is **not lawful** for a man **to utter.**

5. **Of such an one will I glory:** yet of myself I will not glory, but in mine infirmities.

6. For though I would desire to glory, I shall not be a fool; for I will say the truth: but *now* I forbear, lest any man should think of me above that which he seeth me *to be*, or *that* he heareth of me.

7. **And lest I should be exalted** above measure **through** the abundance of **the revelations, there was given to me a thorn** in the flesh, **the messenger of Satan**

to buffet me, lest I should be exalted above measure.
8. For this thing **I besought the Lord thrice, that it might depart** from me.
9. **And he said** unto me, **My grace is sufficient** for thee: for my strength is made perfect in weakness. **Most gladly therefore will I** rather **glory in my infirmities, that the power of Christ may rest upon me.**
10. **Therefore I take pleasure in** infirmities, in reproaches, in necessities, in persecutions, in **distresses for Christ's sake: for when I am weak, then am I strong.**
11. I am become a fool in glorying; ye have compelled me: for I ought to have been commended of you: for **in nothing am I behind the** very **chiefest apostles,** though I be nothing.
12. **Truly the signs of an apostle were wrought among you** in all patience, in signs, and wonders, and mighty deeds.
13. For what is it wherein ye were inferior to other churches, except *it be* that I myself was not burdensome to you? forgive me this wrong.
14. **Behold, the third time I am ready to come to you; and I will not beburdensome** to you: for I seek not your's but you: for the children ought not to lay up for the parents, but the parents for the children.
15. **And I will very gladly spend and be spent for you;** though the more abundantly I love you, the less I be loved.
16. But be it so, I did not burden you: nevertheless, being crafty, I caught you with guile.
17. Did I make a gain of you by any of them whom I sent unto you?

18. I desired Titus, and with *him* I sent a brother. Did Titus make a gain of you? walked we not in the samespirit? *walked we* not in the same steps?
19. Again, think ye that we excuse ourselves unto you? we speak before God in Christ: but **we do all things,** dearly beloved, **for your edifying.**
20. **For I fear, lest, when I come,** I shall not find you such as I would, and *that* I shall be found unto you such as ye would not: lest **there be debates,** envyings, wraths, strifes, **backbitings, whisperings** swellings, tumults:
21. **And lest, when I come again,** my God will humble me among you, and *that* **I shall bewail many which have sinned** already, **and have not repented of the uncleanness and** fornication and lasciviousness **which they have committed.**

CHAPTER 13

1. This *is* the third *time* I am coming to you. In the mouth of two or three witnesses shall every word be established.
2. I told you before, and foretell you, as if I were present, the second time; and being absent now **I write to them which** heretofore **have sinned, and to all other, that, if I come again, I will not spare:**
3. **Since ye seek a proof of Christ speaking in me, which to you-ward is not weak, but is mighty in you.**
4. **For though he was crucified through weakness, yet he liveth by the power of God. For we** also **are weak in him, but we shall live with him by the power of God** toward you.

5. **Examine yourselves, whether ye be in the faith;** prove your own selves. Know ye not your own selves, how that Jesus Christ is in you, except ye be reprobates?

6. But I trust that ye shall know that we are not reprobates.

7. **Now I pray to God that ye do no evil;** not that we should appear approved, **but that ye should do that which is honest,** though we be as reprobates.

8. For we can do nothing against the truth, but for the truth.

9. For we are glad, when we are weak, and ye are strong: and this also we wish, *even* your perfection.

10. **Therefore I write** these things **being absent, lest being present I should use sharpness, according to the power which the Lord hath given me to edification,** and not to destruction.

11. **Finally,** brethren, farewell. **Be perfect,** be of good comfort, be of one mind, **live in peace; and** the **God** of love and peace **shall be with you.**

12. Greet one another with an holy kiss.

13. All the saints salute you.

14. **The grace of the Lord Jesus** Christ, **and the love of God, and the communion of the Holy Ghost, be with you all. Amen.**

THE EPISTLE TO THE GALATIANS

BACKGROUND INFORMATION

Author: Paul, an Apostle.
Date Written: probably
between 45 and **56** A.D.

Number of:
Verses   149
Chapters   6
Total Words 3,098
Scan Words 1,496
Scan Words represent 48 %
of Total Words

Theme: written to
show that we are
justified by God
through faith and not through
keeping laws

OUTLINE OF THE EPISTLE

I. **Paul's Vindication of his Apostleship**
    and of our Redemption
    through Christ
    Chapter 1

II. Paul's Rebuke
    of Peter, and
    Defense of Justification by Faith
    Chapters 2:1 - 3:9

III. Paul's Explanation of
    the Curse of the Law,
    and Christ's power
    to Redeem
    Chapters 3:9 - 3:29

IV. Paul's Exposition of Our
    Freedom and Benefits as Sons of God
    Chapters 4:1 - 5:14

V. Paul's teaching on
    Subjecting the Flesh to the Holy Spirit
    Chapters 5:15 - 6:18

CHAPTER 1

1. **Paul,** an apostle, (not of men, neither by man, but by Jesus Christ, and God the Father, who raised him from the dead;) 2. And all the brethren which are with me, **unto the churches of Galatia:** 3. **Grace be to you and peace from God the Father, and from our Lord Jesus Christ,** 4. **Who gave himself for our sins, that he might deliver us from this present evil world, according to the will of God** and our Father: 5. To whom *be* glory for ever and ever. Amen.

6. **I marvel that ye are so soon removed** from him that called you into the grace of Christ **unto another gospel:** 7. **Which is not another; but there be some that** trouble you, and would **pervert the gospel of Christ.** 8. **But though we, or an angel** from heaven, **preach any other gospel** unto you than that which we have preached unto you, **let him be accursed.** 9. As we said before, **so say I now again, if any man preach any other gospel** unto you than that ye have received, **let him be accursed.** 10. For do I now persuade men, or God? or do I seek to please men? for if I yet pleased men, I should not be the servant of Christ. 11. But I certify you, brethren, that **the gospel which was preached of me is not after man.** 12. For I neither received it of man, neither was I taught *it,* **but by the revelation of Jesus Christ.**

13. **For ye have heard** of my conversation in time past in the Jews' religion, **how that** beyond measure **I persecuted the church** of God, **and wasted it:** 14. **And profited in the Jews' religion** above many my equals in mine own nation, **being more** exceedingly **zealous of the traditions** of my fathers. 15. **But when it pleased God,** who separated me from my mother's womb, and called *me* by his grace, 16. **To reveal his Son in me,** that I might preach him among the heathen; **immediately I conferred not with flesh and blood:** 17. Neither went I up to Jerusalem to them which were apostles before me; **but I went into Arabia, and returned** again **unto Damascus.** 18. **Then after three years I went** up to Jerusalem **to see Peter, and** abode with him fifteen days. 19. **But other of the apostles saw I none, save James** the Lord's brother. 20. Now the things which I write unto you, behold, before God, I lie not. 21. **Afterwards I came into** the regions of **Syria and Cilicia;** 22. **And was unknown by face** unto the churches of Judaea which were in Christ: 23. **But they had heard only, That he which persecuted us** in times past **now preacheth the faith** which once he destroyed. 24. And they glorified God in me.

CHAPTER 2

1. **Then fourteen years after I went up again to Jerusalem** with Barnabas, and took Titus with *me* also.

2. And I went up **by revelation, and communicated** unto them **that gospel which I preach among the Gentiles,** but privately to them which were of reputation, lest by any means I should run, or had run, in vain. 3. **But neither Titus,** who was with me, **being a Greek, was compelled to be circumcised:** 4. **And** that because of **false brethren** unawares brought in, who **came in privily to spy out our liberty** which we have **in Christ Jesus, that they might bring us into bondage:** 5. **To whom we gave place** by subjection, no, **not for an hour; that the truth** of the gospel **might continue** with you. 6. But of these who seemed to be somewhat, (whatsoever they were, it maketh no matter to me: God accepteth no man's person:) for they who seemed *to be somewhat* in conference added nothing to me: 7. **But** contrariwise, when **they saw that the gospel of the uncircumcision was committed unto me, as** *the gospel* of **the circumcision was unto Peter;** 8. (For he that wrought effectually in Peter to the apostleship of the circumcision, the same was mighty in me toward the Gentiles:) 9. **And when James, Cephas, and John,** who seemed to be pillars, **perceived the grace** that was **given** unto **me, they gave to me and Barnabas the right hands of fellowship; that we should go unto the heathen,** and

they unto the circumcision. 10. Only *they would* that we should remember the poor; the same which I also was forward to do. 11. **But when Peter was come to Antioch, I withstood him to the face, because he was to be blamed.** 12. **For before** that certain came from James, **he did eat with the Gentiles: but** when they were come, **he** withdrew and **separated himself, fearing them** which were **of the circumcision.** 13. **And the other Jews dissembled likewise** with him; insomuch that **Barnabas also was carried away** with their dissimulation. 14. **But when I saw that they walked not** uprightly **according to** the truth of **the gospel, I said unto Peter** before *them* all, **If thou, being a Jew, livest after the manner of Gentiles, and not as** do the **Jews, why compellest** thou the **Gentiles to live as** do the **Jews?** 15. We *who are* Jews by nature, and not sinners of the Gentiles, 16. Knowing that a **man is not justified by the works of the law, but by the faith of Jesus Christ,** even we have believed in Jesus Christ, that we might be justified by the faith of Christ, and not by the works of the law: **for by the works of the law shall no flesh be justified.** 17. But if, while we seek to be justified by Christ, we ourselves also are found sinners, *is* therefore Christ the minister of sin? God forbid. 18. For if I build again the things

which I destroyed, I make
myself a transgressor.

19. **For I through the
law am dead** to the law,
that I might live unto God.

20. **I am crucified with Christ:
neverthless I live; yet not I,
but Christ liveth in me: and
the life which I now live in
the flesh I live by the faith of
the Son of God,
who loved me, and gave
himself for me.**

21. I do not frustrate
the grace of God: for
**if righteousness come
by the law, then Christ
is dead in vain.**

CHAPTER 3

1. **O foolish Galatians,
who hath bewitched you,**
that ye should not obey the truth,
before whose eyes Jesus Christ
hath been evidently set forth, crucified
among you?

2. This only would I learn of you,
Received ye the Spirit by the works
of the law, or by the hearing of faith?

3. **Are ye so foolish? having
begun in the Spirit, are ye
now made perfect by
the flesh?**

4. Have ye suffered so many
things in vain? if *it be* yet in vain.

5. **He therefore that
ministereth** to you
**the Spirit, and worketh
miracles** among you,
doeth he it by the works of
the law, or by the hearing of
faith?

6. **Even as Abraham
believed God, and it
was accounted** to him for
righteousness.

7. Know ye therefore that
they which are
of faith, the same
**are the children
of Abraham.**

8. **And the scripture,
foreseeing that God**
**would justify the heathen
through faith, preached
before** the gospel
**unto Abraham, saying,
In thee shall all nations
be blessed.**

9. So then they which be of faith
are blessed with faithful Abraham.

10. **For as many as
are of the** works of the
law are under the curse:
for it is written, Cursed *is* every one
that continueth not in all things
which are written in the book
of the law to do them.

11. **But that no man is
justified by the law**
in the sight of God, *it*
**is evident: for, The
just shall live by faith.**

12. And the law is not of faith: but, The
man that doeth them shall live in them.

13. **Christ hath redeemed us
from the curse of the law,
being made a curse for
us:** for it is written, Cursed *is*
every one that hangeth on a tree:

14. **That the blessing of
Abraham might come on
the Gentiles through Jesus
Christ;** that we might receive the
promise of the Spirit through faith.

15. Brethren, I speak after the manner
of men; Though *it be* but a man's
covenant, yet *if it be* confirmed, no
man disannulleth, or addeth thereto.

16. **Now to Abraham and his
seed were the promises
made. He saith not, And
to seeds,** as of many;
**but as of one, And to thy
seed, which is Christ.**

17. And this I say, *that* the covenant,
that was confirmed before of God in
Christ, the law, which was four
hundred and thirty years after,
cannotdisannul, that it should
make the promise of none effect.

18. For if the inheritance *be* of the
law, *it is* no more of promise: but
**God gave it to Abraham
by promise.**

19. **Wherefore then serveth**

the law? It was
added because of
transgressions, till the
seed should come to
whom the promise was
made; *and it was* ordained by
angels in the hand of a mediator.
20. Now a mediator is not a *mediator*
of one, but God is one.
21. **Is the law then against
the promises of God? God
forbid: for if** there had been
a law given which
could have given life, verily
**righteousness should
have been by the law.**
22. **But the scripture hath
concluded all under sin,
that the** promise by
**faith of Jesus Christ might
be given** to them that believe.
23. But before faith came, we were
kept under the law, shut up unto
the faith which should afterwards
be revealed.
24. **Wherefore the law
was our schoolmaster
to bring us unto Christ,**
that we might be justified by faith.
25. **But after** that
**faith is come, we
are no longer under
a schoolmaster.**
26. **For ye are all the
children of God by
faith in Christ Jesus.**
27. **For** as many of
you as have been
**baptized into Christ
have put on Christ.**
28. **There is neither Jew
nor Greek,** there is neither
bond nor free, there is
**neither male nor female:
for ye are all one in
Christ Jesus.**
29. And if ye *be* Christ's,
then are ye Abraham's seed,
**and heirs according
to the promise.**

CHAPTER 4

1. Now I say, *That*

the heir, as long as he is
a child, differeth nothing
from a servant,
though he be lord of all;
2. But is under tutors
and governors
until the time appointed
of the father.
3. Even so we, when we
were children, were in
bondage under the
elements of the world:
4. But when the fulness
of the time was come,
God sent forth
his Son, made of a woman,
made under the law,
5. To redeem them that were
under the law, that we might
receive the adoption of sons.
6. And because ye
are sons, God hath
sent forth
the Spirit of his Son into your
hearts, crying,
Abba, Father.
7. Wherefore thou art no
more a servant, but a
son; and if a son, then
an heir of God
through Christ.
8. Howbeit then, when ye knew
not God, ye did service unto them
which by nature are no gods.
9. But now, after that
ye have known God,
or rather are known of God,
how turn ye again
to the weak and beggarly elements,
whereunto ye desire again
to be in bondage?
10. Ye observe days, and
months, and times, and years.
11. I am afraid of you, lest
I have bestowed upon
you labour in vain.
12. Brethren, I beseech you, be
as I *am*; for I *am* as ye *are*: ye
have not injured me at all.
13. Ye know how
through infirmity of the
flesh I preached the
gospel unto you at the first.

14. **And** my temptation which was in my flesh **ye despised not, nor rejected; but received me** as an angel of God, *even* **as Christ Jesus.**

15. Where is then the blessedness ye spake of? for I bear you record, that, if *it had been* possible, **ye would have plucked out your own eyes, and have given them to me.**

16. **Am I therefore** become **your enemy, because I tell you the truth?**

17. They zealously affect you, *but* not well; yea, they would exclude you, that ye might affect them.

18. But *it is* good to be zealously affected always in *a good thing*, and not only when I am present with you.

19. **My little children, of whom I travail in birth** again **until Christ be formed in you,**

20. I desire to be present with you now, and to change my voice; for I stand in doubt of you.

21. Tell me, ye that desire to be under the law, **do ye not hear the law**

22. For it is written, that **Abraham had two sons, the one by a bondmaid, the other by a freewoman.**

23. **But he** *who was* **of the bondwoman was born after the flesh; but he of the freewoman was by promise.**

24. **Which things are an allegory: for** these are the **two covenants;** the **one** from the mount Sinai, which **gendereth to bondage, which is Agar.**

25. For this Agar is mount Sinai in Arabia, and answereth to Jerusalem which now is, and is in bondage with her children.

26. **But Jerusalem** which is above **is free, which is the mother of us all.**

27. For it is written, Rejoice, *thou* barren that bearest not; break forth and cry, thou that travailest not: for the desolate hath many more children than she which hath an husband.

28. **Now we,** brethren, **as Isaac** was, **are the children of promise.**

29. **But** as then **he that was born after the flesh persecuted him** *that was* **born after the Spirit,** even so *it is* now.

30. **Nevertheless what saith the scripture? Cast out the bondwoman and her son: for the son of the bondwoman shall not be heir** with the son of the freewoman.

31. So then, brethren, **we are** not **children** of the bondwoman, but **of the free.**

CHAPTER 5

1. **Stand fast** therefore in the liberty wherewith **Christ hath made us free, and be not entangled again with the yoke of bondage.**

2. Behold, I Paul say unto you, that **if ye be circumcised, Christ shall profit you nothing.**

3. For I testify again to **every man that is circumcised,** that he **is a debtor to do the whole law.**

4. Christ is become of no effect unto you, **whosoever of you are justified by the law; ye are fallen from grace.**

5. For we through the Spirit wait for the hope of righteousness by faith.

6. **For in Jesus Christ neither circumcision availeth any thing, nor uncircumcision; but faith which worketh by love.**

7. Ye did run well;
■ **who did hinder you that ye**
■ **should not obey the truth?**
■ 8. **This persuasion cometh**
■ **not of him that calleth you.**
9. A little leaven leaveneth
the whole lump.
■ 10. **I have confidence**
in you through the Lord,
that ye will be none
■ **otherwise minded: but he**
■ **that troubleth you shall**
■ **bear his judgment,**
whosoever he be.
11. And I, brethren, if I yet preach
circumcision, why do I yet suffer
persecution? then is the offence
of the cross ceased.
12. I would they were even
cut off which trouble you.
13. For, brethren,
■ **ye have been called**
■ **unto liberty; only use**
■ **not liberty** for an occasion
■ **to the flesh,**
but by love serve one another.
■ 14. **For all the law is fulfilled**
■ **in one word,** *even* in this;
■ **Thou shalt love thy**
■ **neighbour as thyself.**
15. But if ye bite and devour one
another, take heed that ye be not
consumed one of another.
16. *This* I say then,
■ **Walk in the Spirit, and**
■ **ye shall not fulfil the**
■ **lust of the flesh.**
■ 17. **For the flesh**
lusteth against the Spirit,
■ **and the Spirit**
against the flesh: and these
■ **are contrary the one to**
■ **the other:** so that ye cannot
do the things that ye would.
18. But if ye be led of the Spirit,
ye are not under the law.
■ 19. **Now the works of the**
■ **flesh are manifest, which**
■ **are these;** Adultery,
■ **fornication, uncleanness,**
■ **lasciviousness,**
■ 20. **Idolatry, witchcraft,**
■ **hatred, variance,**

■ **emulations, wrath, strife,**
■ **seditions, heresies,**
■ 21. **Envyings, murders,**
■ **drunkenness, revellings,** and
such like: of the which I tell
you before, as I have also told
you in time past, that
■ **they which do such things**
■ **shall not inherit the**
■ **kingdom** of God.
■ 22. **But the fruit of the Spirit**
■ **is love, joy, peace,**
■ **long-suffering, gentleness,**
■ **goodness, faith,**
■ 23. **Meekness, temperance:**
■ **against such there**
■ **is no law.**
24. And they that are Christ's
have crucified the flesh with
the affections and lusts.
■ 25. **If we live in the Spirit, let**
■ **us also walk in the Spirit.**
26. Let us not be desirous of vain
glory, provoking one another,
envying one another.

CHAPTER 6

■ 1. **Brethren, if a man be**
■ **overtaken in a fault,**
ye which are spiritual,
■ **restore such an one in**
■ **the spirit of meekness;**
considering thyself, lest thou
also be tempted.
■ 2. **Bear one another's**
■ **burdens,** and so fulfil
the law of Christ.
■ 3. **For if a man think himself**
■ **to be something, when**
■ **he is nothing, he**
■ **deceiveth himself.**
4. But let every man prove his own
work, and then shall he have rejoicing
in himself alone, and not in another.
5. For every man shall bear
his own burden.
6. Let him that is taught in the
word communicate unto him that
teacheth in all good things.
■ 7. **Be not deceived; God**
■ **is not mocked: for what-**
■ **soever a man soweth,**
■ **that shall he also reap.**

■ 8. **For he that soweth to**
■ **his flesh shall** of the flesh
■ **reap corruption;**
■ **but he that soweth to the**
■ **Spirit shall** of the Spirit
■ **reap life everlasting.**
9. And let us not be weary in well-
doing: for in due season we shall
reap, if we faint not.
■ 10. **As we have** therefore
■ **opportunity, let us do**
■ **good unto all men,**
especially unto them who are
of the household of faith.
11. Ye see how large a letter I have
written unto you with mine own hand.
12. As many as desire to
make a fair shew in the flesh,
they constrain you to
be circumcised; only lest they
should suffer persecution for
the cross of Christ.
■ 13. **For neither they**
■ **themselves who are**

■ circumcised keep the law;
■ but desire to have you
■ circumcised, that they
■ may glory in your flesh.
■ 14. **But God forbid that I**
■ **should glory, save in the**
■ **cross of our Lord**
■ **Jesus Christ,**
by whom the world is crucified
unto me, and I unto the world.
■ 15. **For in Christ Jesus**
■ **neither circumcision**
■ **availeth** any thing,
■ **nor uncircumcision,**
■ **but a new creature.**
16. And as many as walk according
to this rule, peace *be* on them, and
mercy, and upon the Israel of God.
17. From henceforth let no man
trouble me: for I bear in my body
the marks of the Lord Jesus.
18. Brethren, the grace of our Lord
Jesus Christ *be* with your spirit.
■ **Amen.**

THE EPISTLE TO THE EPHESIANS

BACKGROUND INFORMATION

Author: Paul, an Apostle.
Date Written: probably
between 60 and **65** A.D.

Number of:
Verses   155
Chapters   6
Total Words 3,039
Scan Words 1,486
Scan Words represent
48 % of Total Words

Theme: written to show that
**the Church is the Body of
Christ, and** the quality of
Christian conduct which
should follow

OUTLINE OF THE EPISTLE

I. **The Supremacy
    of Christ,**
    God's Gift of Salvation to
    Both Jew and Gentile and
    Paul's Mission to
    the Gentiles
    Chapters 1 - 3
II. **The Ministry of
    the Church** in God's Plan
    of Reconciliation Through
    Christ, the Unity of the
    Church Despite its
    Variety of Gifts and His
    Instructions to the Family
    Chapters 4 - 5
III. A Discourse to
    Christians on
    the Full Armor of Christ
    and the Responsibility of
    the Believer to the Church
    Chapter 6

CHAPTER 1

■ 1. **Paul,** an apostle of Jesus Christ by the will of God,

■ **to the saints** which are

■ **at Ephesus, and to the**
■ **faithful in Christ Jesus:**

2. Grace *be* to you, and peace, from God our Father, and *from* the Lord Jesus Christ.

■ 3. **Blessed be the God** and Father

■ **of** our Lord

■ **Jesus** Christ,

■ **who hath blessed us with** all
■ **spiritual blessings in**
■ **heavenly places in Christ:**

■ 4. **According as he hath**
■ **chosen us in him before the**
■ **foundation of the world,**

that we should be holy and without blame before him in love:

■ 5. **Having predestinated us**
■ **unto the adoption of**
■ **children by Jesus** Christ

to himself, according to the good pleasure of his will,

6. To the praise of the glory of his grace, wherein he hath made us accepted in the beloved.

■ 7. **In whom we have**
■ **redemption through his**
■ **blood, the forgiveness of**
■ **sins, according to**

the riches of

■ **his grace;**

■ 8. **Wherein he hath**
■ **abounded toward us in all**
■ **wisdom** and prudence;

■ 9. **Having made known unto**
■ **us the mystery of his will,**

according to his good pleasure which he hath purposed in himself:

■ 10. **That in** the dispensation of
■ **the fulness of times he**
■ **might gather together** in one
■ **all things in Christ,**
■ **both** which are
■ **in heaven, and** which are on
■ **earth;** *even* in him:

■ 11. **In whom also**
■ **we have** obtained
■ **an inheritance, being**

■ **predestinated**
■ **according to the purpose**
■ **of him who worketh all**
■ **things after** the counsel of
■ **his own will:**

■ 12. **That we should be to the**
■ **praise of his glory, who first**
■ **trusted in Christ.**

■ 13. **In whom** ye also *trusted*, after that ye heard the word of truth, the gospel of your salvation: in whom also after that ye believed,

■ **ye were sealed with that**
■ **holy Spirit of promise,**

■ 14. **Which is the earnest of**
■ **our inheritance until the**
■ **redemption of the**
■ **purchased possession,** unto the praise of his glory.

■ 15. **Wherefore I** also, after I heard of your faith in the Lord Jesus, and love unto all the saints,

■ 16. **Cease not to give thanks**
■ **for you, making mention of**
■ **you in my prayers;**

■ 17. **That the God of our Lord** Jesus Christ, the Father of glory,

■ **may give** unto
■ **you** the spirit of
■ **wisdom and revelation in**
■ **the knowledge of him:**

18. The eyes of your understanding being enlightened;

■ **that ye may know what**
■ **is the hope of his calling,**
■ **and** what the riches of
■ **the glory of his**
■ **inheritance in the saints,**

■ 19. **And what is the** exceeding
■ **greatness of his power to**
■ **us-ward who believe,**
■ **according to** the working of
■ **his** mighty
■ **power,**

20. Which he wrought
■ **in Christ, when he raised**
■ **him** from the dead,
■ **and set him at his** own
■ **right hand** in the heavenly *places*,

■ 21. **Far above all**
■ **principality, and power,** and might, and dominion, and every name that is named, not only in this world,

but also in that which is to come:

22. **And hath put all things under his feet, and gave him to be the head over all things to the church,**

23. **Which is his body,** the fulness of him that filleth all in all.

CHAPTER 2

1. **And you hath he quickened, who were dead in** trespasses and **sins;**

2. **Wherein in time past ye walked according to** the course of **this world, according to the prince of** the power of **the air,** the spirit that now worketh in the children of disobedience:

3. **Among whom also we all had our conversation** in times past **in the lusts of our flesh,** fulfilling the desires of the flesh and of the mind; and were by nature the children of wrath, even as others.

4. **But God, who is rich in mercy,** for his great love wherewith he loved us,

5. **Even when we were dead in sins, hath quickened us together with Christ,** (by grace ye are saved;)

6. **And hath raised us up together,** and made *us* sit together in heavenly *places* in Christ Jesus:

7. **That in the ages to come he might shew the exceeding riches of his grace** in *his* kindness toward us through Christ Jesus.

8. **For by grace are ye saved through faith; and** that **not of yourselves:** it is the gift of God:

9. **Not of works, lest any man should boast.**

10. **For we are his workmanship, created in Christ Jesus unto good works,** which God hath before

ordained that we should walk in them.

11. **Wherefore remember, that ye being** in time past **Gentiles in the flesh,** who are called Uncircumcision by that which is called the Circumcision in the flesh made by hands;

12. **That at that time ye were without Christ, being** aliens from the commonwealth of Israel, and **strangers from the covenants of promise,** having no hope, **and without God** in the world:

13. **But now in Christ Jesus ye** who sometimes were far off **are made nigh by the blood** of Christ.

14. **For he is our peace,** who hath made both one, **and hath broken down the middle wall of partition** *between us*;

15. Having abolished in his flesh the enmity, *even* the law of commandments *contained* in ordinances; for to make in himself of twain one new man, *so* making peace;

16. **And that he might reconcile both unto God in one body by the cross,** having slain the enmity thereby:

17. And came and preached peace to you which were afar off, and to them that were nigh.

18. **For through him we both have access by one Spirit unto the Father.**

19. **Now therefore ye are** no more strangers and foreigners, but **fellowcitizens with the saints,** and of the household of God;

20. **And are built upon the foundation of the apostles and prophets, Jesus Christ himself being the chief corner stone;**

21. In whom all the building fitly framed together groweth unto an holy temple in the Lord:

22. **In whom ye also are builded** together

■ **for an habitation of God**
through the Spirit.

CHAPTER 3

1. For this cause I Paul, the prisoner of Jesus Christ for you Gentiles,

■ 2. **If ye have heard of the**
■ **dispensation of the grace**
■ **of God which is given me**
■ **to you-ward:**
■ 3. **How that by revelation**
■ **he made known** unto me
■ **the mystery;**
(as I wrote afore in few words,
4. Whereby, when ye read, ye may understand my knowledge in the mystery of Christ)
5. Which in other ages was not made known unto the sons of men, as it is now revealed unto his holy apostles and prophets by the Spirit;

■ 6. **That the Gentiles should**
■ **be fellow heirs, and**
of the same body, and
■ **partakers of his promise in**
■ **Christ** by the gospel:
■ 7. **Whereof I was made a**
■ **minister,** according to the gift of the grace of God given unto me by the effectual working of his power.
8. Unto me, who am less than the least of all saints, is this
grace given,
■ **that I should preach among**
■ **the Gentiles**
the unsearchable riches of Christ;

■ 9. **And to make all men see**
■ **what is the fellowship of the**
■ **mystery, which**
from the beginning of the world
■ **hath been hid in God, who**
■ **created all things by**
■ **Jesus Christ:**
10. To the intent that now unto the principalities and powers in heavenly *places* might be known by the church the manifold wisdom of God,
11. According to the eternal purpose which he purposed in Christ Jesus our Lord:
■ 12. **In whom we have**
■ **boldness and access**
with confidence

■ **by the faith of him.**
■ 13. **Wherefore I desire that**
■ **ye faint not at my**
■ **tribulations for you,**
which is your glory
■ 14. **For this cause I bow**
my knees
■ **unto** the Father of
■ **our Lord Jesus Christ,**
15. Of whom the whole family in heaven and earth is named,
■ 16. **That he would grant you,**
according to the riches of his glory,
■ **to be strengthened with**
■ **might by his Spirit**
in the inner man;
■ 17. **That Christ may dwell in**
■ **your hearts by faith;** that ye,
being rooted and grounded in love,
18. May be able to comprehend with all saints what *is* the breadth, and length, and depth, and height;
■ 19. **And to know the love of**
■ **Christ,** which passeth knowledge,
that ye might be filled with all the fulness of God.
■ 20. **Now unto him that is**
■ **able to do** exceeding abundantly
■ **above all that we ask or**
■ **think,** according to the power that worketh in us,
■ 21. **Unto him be glory**
in the church by Christ Jesus
■ **throughout all ages,**
world without end. Amen.

CHAPTER 4

■ 1. **I therefore,**
the prisoner of the Lord,
■ **beseech you that ye walk**
■ **worthy of the vocation**
■ **wherewith ye are called,**
■ 2. **With all lowliness and**
meekness, with longsuffering,
■ **forbearing one another**
■ **in love;**
■ 3. **Endeavouring to keep the**
■ **unity of the Spirit**
in the bond of peace.
■ 4. **There is one body,**
and one Spirit, even as ye are called in one hope of your calling;
■ 5. **One Lord, one faith,**

■ **one baptism,**
■ 6. **One God and Father of**
■ **all,** who *is* above all, and through all, and in you all.
■ 7. **But unto every one of us is**
■ **given grace** according to the measure of the gift of Christ.
8. Wherefore he saith, When he ascended up on high, he led captivity captive, and gave gifts unto men.
9. (Now that he ascended, what is it but that he also descended first into the lower parts of the earth?
10. He that descended is the same also that ascended up far above all heavens, that he might fill all things.)
■ 11. **And he gave some,**
■ **apostles;** and
■ **some, prophets;** and
■ **some, evangelists;**
■ **and some, pastors**
■ **and teachers;**
■ 12. **For the perfecting of the**
■ **saints,** for the work of the ministry,
■ **for the edifying of the**
■ **body of Christ:**
■ 13. **Till we all come** in the unity of the faith, and of the knowledge of the Son of God, unto a perfect man,
■ **unto the measure**
■ **of the** stature of the
■ **fulness of Christ:**
■ 14. **That we henceforth**
■ **be no more children,**
tossed to and fro, and
■ **carried about with every**
■ **wind of doctrine,** by the sleight of men, *and* cunning craftiness, whereby they lie in wait to deceive;
■ 15. **But speaking the truth in**
■ **love,** may grow up into him in all things, which is the head, *even* Christ:
16. From whom the whole body fitly joined together and compacted by that which every joint supplieth, according to the effectual working in the measure of every part, maketh increase of the body unto the edifying of itself in love.
■ 17. **This I say therefore,**
and testify in the Lord, that ye henceforth
■ **walk not as**

■ **other Gentiles** walk,
■ **in the vanity of their mind,**
■ 18. **Having the**
■ **understanding darkened,**
being alienated from the life of God through the ignorance that is in them,
■ **because of the**
■ **blindness of**
■ **their heart:**
■ 19. **Who being past feeling**
■ **have given themselves**
■ **over unto lasciviousness,** to work all uncleanness with greediness.
■ 20. **But ye have not so**
■ **learned Christ;**
21. If so be that
■ **ye** have heard him, and
■ **have been taught** by him, as
■ **the truth is in Jesus:**
■ 22. **That ye put off**
■ **concerning the**
■ **former conversation**
■ **the old man,** which is corrupt according to the deceitful lusts;
■ 23. **And be renewed in**
■ **the spirit of your mind;**
■ 24. **And that ye put on**
■ **the new man,**
which after God is created in righteousness and true holiness.
■ 25. **Wherefore putting away**
■ **lying, speak** every man
■ **truth** with his neighbour:
for we are members one of another.
26. Be ye angry, and sin not:
■ **let not the sun go down**
■ **upon your wrath:**
■ 27. **Neither give place to**
■ **the devil.**
■ 28. **Let him that stole steal**
■ **no more: but rather let him**
■ **labour,** working with *his* hands the thing which is good, that he may have to give to him that needeth.
■ 29. **Let no corrupt**
■ **communication proceed**
■ **out of your mouth,**
but that which is good to the use of edifying, that it may minister grace unto the hearers.
■ 30. **And grieve not the holy**

Spirit of God, whereby ye are sealed unto the day of redemption.

31. Let all bitterness, and wrath, and anger, and clamour, and evil speaking, be put away from you, with all malice:

32. And be ye kind one to another, tenderhearted, forgiving one another, even as God for Christ's sake hath forgiven you.

CHAPTER 5

1. Be ye therefore followers of God, as dear children;

2. And walk in love, as Christ also hath loved us, and hath given himself for us an offering and a sacrifice to God for a sweet smelling savour.

3. But fornication, and all uncleanness, or covetousness, let it not be once named among you, as becometh saints;

4. Neither filthiness, nor foolish talking, nor jesting, which are not convenient: but rather giving of thanks.

5. For this ye know, that no whoremonger, nor unclean person, nor covetous man, who is an idolater, hath any inheritance in the kingdom of Christ and of God.

6. Let no man deceive you with vain words: for because of these things cometh the wrath of God upon the children of disobedience.

7. Be not ye therefore partakers with them.

8. For ye were sometimes darkness, but now are ye light in the Lord: walk as children of light:

9. (For the fruit of the Spirit *is* in all goodness and righteousness and truth;)

10. Proving what is acceptable unto the Lord.

11. And have no fellowship with the unfruitful works of darkness, but rather reprove them.

12. For it is a shame even to speak of those things which are done of them in secret.

13. But all things that are reproved are made manifest by the light: for whatsoever doth make manifest is light.

14. Wherefore he saith, Awake thou that sleepest, and arise from the dead, and Christ shall give thee light.

15. See then that ye walk circumspectly, not as fools, but as wise,

16. Redeeming the time, because the days are evil.

17. Wherefore be ye not unwise, but understanding what the will of the Lord is.

18. And be not drunk with wine, wherein is excess; but be filled with the Spirit;

19. Speaking to yourselves in psalms and hymns and spiritual songs, singing and making melody in your heart to the Lord;

20. Giving thanks always for all things unto God and the Father in the name of our Lord Jesus Christ;

21. Submitting yourselves one to another in the fear of God.

22. Wives, submit yourselves unto your own husbands, as unto the Lord.

23. For the husband is the head of the wife, even as Christ is the head of the church: and he is the saviour of the body.

24. Therefore as the church is subject unto Christ, so let the wives be to their own husbands in every thing.

25. Husbands, love your wives, even as Christ also loved the church, and gave himself for it;

26. That he might sanctify and

cleanse it with the washing of water by the word,

27. That he might present it to himself a glorious church, not having spot, or wrinkle, or any such thing; but that it should be holy and without blemish.

28. **So ought men to love their wives as their own bodies.** He that loveth his wife loveth himself.

29. **For no man ever yet hated his own flesh; but** nourisheth and **cherisheth it,** even as the Lord the church:

30. For we are members of his body, of his flesh, and of his bones.

31. **For this cause shall a man leave his father and mother, and shall be joined unto his wife, and they two shall be one flesh.**

32. **This is a great mystery: but I speak concerning** Christ and the church.

33. Nevertheless let every one of you in particular so love his wife even as himself; and the wife *see* that she reverence *her* husband.

CHAPTER 6

1. **Children, obey your parents** in the Lord: for this is right.

2. **Honour thy father and mother;** which is the first commandment with promise;

3. **That it may be well with thee, and thou mayest live long** on the earth.

4. **And, ye fathers, provoke not your children to wrath: but bring them up in the nurture and admonition of the Lord.**

5. **Servants, be obedient to** them that are **your masters** according to the flesh, with fear and trembling, in singleness of your heart, as unto Christ;

6. Not with eye service, as men pleasers; but as the servants of Christ, doing the will of God from the heart;

7. **With good will doing service, as to the Lord, and not to men:**

8. **Knowing that whatsoever good thing any man doeth, the same shall he receive of the Lord, whether** *he be* **bond or free.**

9. **And, ye masters, do the same** things unto them, forbearing threatening: knowing that your Master also is in heaven; neither is there respect of persons with him.

10. **Finally,** my brethren, **be strong in the Lord,** and in the power of his might.

11. **Put on the whole armour of God,** that ye may be able **to stand against the wiles of the devil.**

12. **For we wrestle not against flesh** and blood, **but against** principalities, against powers, against **the rulers of the darkness of this world, against spiritual wickedness in high places.**

13. Wherefore take unto you the whole armour of God, that ye may be able to withstand in the evil day, and having done all, to stand.

14. **Stand therefore, having your loins girt about with truth, and having on the breastplate of righteousness;**

15. **And your feet shod with the** preparation of the **gospel of peace;**

16. **Above all, taking the shield of faith,** wherewith ye shall be able **to quench all the fiery darts of the wicked.**

17. **And take the helmet of salvation, and the sword of the Spirit, which is the word of God:**

18. **Praying always with all prayer and supplication in**

■ **the Spirit,** and watching thereunto with all perseverance and supplication for all saints;

■ 19. **And for me,** that utterance may be given unto me,

■ **that I may open my mouth**
■ **boldly, to make known** the mystery of
■ **the gospel,**
■ 20. **For which I am an**
■ **ambassador in bonds:** that therein I may speak boldly, as I ought to speak.

21. But that ye also may know my affairs, *and* how I do, Tychicus, a beloved brother and faithful minister in the Lord, shall make known to you all things:

22. Whom I have sent unto you for the same purpose, that ye might know our affairs, and *that* he might comfort your hearts.

■ 23. **Peace** *be* to the brethren,
■ **and love with faith, from**
■ **God** the Father
■ **and the Lord Jesus** Christ.
■ 24. **Grace be with all them**
■ **that love our Lord** Jesus Christ
■ **in sincerity.**
■ **Amen.**

THE EPISTLE TO THE PHILIPPIANS

BACKGROUND INFORMATION

Author: **Paul**, an Apostle.
Date Written: probably **between 60** and **65** A.D.

Number of:
Verses   104
Chapters   4
Total Words   2,002
Scan Words 1,055
Scan Words represent
52 % of Total Words

Theme: written to show the **radiant joy** which the believer possesses even **in the** stresses and **storms of life**

OUTLINE OF THE EPISTLE

I. **Paul's Call to Live Worthy of the Gospel** and to Follow Christ's Example of Humility
    Chapters 1 - 3:2

II. **Paul's Warning Against the Judaizers** and His Appeal for Harmony and Joy
    Chapter 3:3 - 3:17

III. **Paul's Caution About Worldliness** and His Appeal for Steadfastness

    Chapters 3:18 - 4

CHAPTER 1

1. **Paul and Timotheus,** the servants of Jesus Christ, **to all the saints** in Christ Jesus which are **at Philippi,** with the bishops and deacons: 2. Grace *be* unto you, and peace, from God our Father, and *from* the Lord Jesus Christ.

3. **I thank** my **God upon** every **remembrance of you,** 4. **Always in** every **prayer** of mine for you all **making request** with joy, 5. **For your fellowship in the gospel** from the first day until now; 6. **Being confident** of this very thing, **that he which hath begun a good work in you will perform it** until the day of Jesus Christ:

7. Even as it is meet for me to think this of you all, because **I have you in my heart;** inasmuch as both **in my bonds, and in the defence** and confirmation **of the gospel, ye all are partakers of my grace.** 8. For God is my record, how greatly **I long** after you all in the bowels of Jesus Christ.

9. And this I pray, **that your love may abound** yet more and more **in knowledge and** *in* all **judgment;** 10. **That ye** may **approve things** that are **excellent; that ye** may **be sincere and without offence** till the day of Christ; 11. **Being filled with** the fruits of **righteousness,** which are **by Jesus Christ,** unto the glory and praise of God.

12. **But** I would ye should **understand,** brethren, **that the things which happened unto me have fallen** out rather **unto the furtherance of the gospel;** 13. **So that my bonds in Christ are manifest** in all the palace, and in all other *places;* 14. **And** many of **the brethren** in the Lord, **waxing confident by my bonds, are** much more **bold to speak the word** without fear.

15. **Some** indeed **preach Christ** even **of** envy and **strife; and some** also **of good will:** 16. **The one preach Christ** of contention, **not sincerely,** supposing to add affliction to my bonds: 17. **But the other of love,** knowing that I am set for the defence of the gospel.

18. **What then?** notwithstanding, every way, whether **in pretence, or in truth, Christ is preached; and I** therein do rejoice, yea, and will **rejoice.** 19. For I know that **this shall turn to my salvation through your prayer, and the supply of the Spirit** of Jesus Christ, 20. According to my earnest expectation and **my hope, that in nothing I shall be ashamed, but** *that* **with** all **boldness,** as always, *so* now also **Christ shall be magnified** in my body, whether *it be* **by life, or by death.** 21. **For to me to live is Christ, and to die is gain.** 22. But if I live in the flesh, this *is* the fruit of my labour: yet what I shall choose I wot not. 23. **For I am** in a strait **betwixt two, having a desire to depart, and to be with Christ;** which is far better:

24. **Nevertheless to abide** in the flesh **is** more **needful for you.**
25. And having this confidence, **I know** that **I shall abide** and continue **with you** all **for your furtherance** and joy **of faith;**
26. That your rejoicing may be more abundant in Jesus Christ for me by my coming to you again.
27. **Only let your conversation be** as it becometh the gospel **of Christ: that** whether I come and see you, or else be absent, **I may hear** of your affairs, **that ye stand** fast **in one spirit, with one mind** striving together **for the** faith of the **gospel;**
28. **And in nothing terrified by your adversaries:** which is to them an evident token of perdition, but to you of salvation, and that of God.
29. For unto you **it is given in the behalf of Christ, not only to believe on him, but also to suffer for his sake;**
30. Having the same conflict which ye saw in me, and now hear *to be* in me.

CHAPTER 2

1. **If there be** therefore **any consolation in Christ,** if any comfort of love, if any fellowship of the Spirit, if any bowels and mercies,
2. **Fulfil ye my joy,** that ye be like-minded, **having the same love, being** of one accord, **of one mind.**
3. **Let nothing be done through strife or vainglory;** but in lowliness of mind let each esteem other better than themselves.
4. **Look not every man on his own things, but** every man also **on the things of others.**
5. **Let this mind be in you, which was** also **in Christ Jesus:**
6. **Who, being in the form of God, thought it not robbery to be equal with God:**
7. **But** made himself of no reputation, and took upon him the form of a servant, and **was made in the likeness of men:**
8. **And** being found in fashion **as a man, he humbled himself, and became obedient unto death,** even the death of the cross.
9. **Wherefore God** also **hath** highly **exalted him, and given him a name** which is **above every name:**
10. **That at the name of Jesus every knee should bow**, of *things* in heaven, and *things* in earth, and *things* under the earth;
11. **And** *that* **every tongue** should **confess that Jesus Christ is Lord,** to the glory of God the Father.
12. **Wherefore,** my beloved, as ye have always obeyed, not as in my presence only, but now much more in my absence, **work out your own salvation with fear and trembling.**
13. **For it is God which worketh in you both to will and to do** of **his good pleasure.**
14. **Do all things without** murmurings and **disputings:**
15. **That ye may be blameless** and harmless, the sons of God, without rebuke, **in** the midst of **a** crooked and **perverse nation, among**

whom ye shine
as lights in the world;
16. Holding forth
the word of life;
that I may rejoice in the
day of Christ, that I have not run
in vain, neither laboured in vain.
17. Yea, and if I be offered upon the
sacrifice and service of your faith, I
joy, and rejoice with you all.
18. For the same cause also do ye
joy, and rejoice with me.
19. But I trust in the Lord
Jesus to send Timotheus
shortly unto you, that I also may be of
good comfort, when I know
your state.
20. For I have no man like minded,
who will naturally care for your state.
21. For all seek their own,
not the things which are
Jesus Christ's.
22. But ye know the proof
of him, that, as a son
with the father,
he hath served
with me in the gospel.
23. Him therefore I hope to send
presently, so soon as I shall see how
it will go with me.
24. But I trust in the Lord that
I also myself shall
come shortly.
25. Yet I supposed it necessary to
send to you
Epaphroditus, my brother,
and companion in labour,
and fellow-soldier, but
your messenger, and he
that ministered to my wants.
26. For he longed after you
all, and was full of heaviness,
because that
ye had heard that
he had been sick.
27. For indeed he
was sick nigh
unto death: but God
had mercy on him;
and not on him only, but
on me also, lest I should
have sorrow upon sorrow.
28. I sent him therefore

the more carefully,
that, when ye see him again,
ye may rejoice, and that
I may
be the
less sorrowful.
29. Receive him
therefore in the Lord
with all
gladness; and hold
such in reputation:
30. Because for the work of
Christ he was nigh
unto death, not regarding
his life, to supply your lack of
service toward me.

CHAPTER 3

1. Finally, my brethren,
rejoice in the Lord.
To write the same things
to you, to me indeed
is not grievous, but for you
it is safe.
2. Beware of dogs,
beware of evil workers,
beware of the concision.
3. For we are the
circumcision, which
worship God in the spirit,
and rejoice in Christ Jesus,
and have no confidence in
the flesh.
4. Though I might also have
confidence in the flesh.
If any other
man thinketh that
he hath whereof he might
trust in the flesh, I more:
5. Circumcised the eighth day,
of the stock of Israel, of the
tribe of Benjamin,
an Hebrew of the Hebrews;
as touching the law,
a Pharisee;
6. Concerning zeal, persecuting
the church; touching the
righteousness which is in
the law, blameless.
7. But what things were
gain to me, those I
counted loss for Christ
8. Yea doubtless, and

312

I count all things but
loss for the excellency of
the knowledge of
Christ Jesus my Lord:
for whom I have
suffered the loss of
all things, and do
count them but dung,
that I may win Christ,
9. And be found in him,
not having mine own
righteousness, which is
of the law, but that which is
through the faith of Christ,
the righteousness which is
of God by faith:
10. That I may know him,
and the power of his
resurrection, and
the fellowship of
his sufferings, being
made conformable
unto his death;
11. If by any means I might attain
unto the resurrection of the dead.
12. Not as though I
had already attained, either
were already
perfect: but I follow after, if
that I may apprehend
that for which also
I am apprehended
of Christ Jesus.
13. Brethren, I count not myself to
have apprehended: but
this one thing I do,
forgetting those things
which are
behind, and reaching forth
unto those things which are before,
14. I press toward
the mark for the prize of
the high calling of
God in Christ Jesus.
15. Let us therefore,
as many as be perfect,
be thus minded:
and if in any thing
ye be otherwise minded,
God shall reveal even
this unto you.
16. Nevertheless, where
to we have already

attained, let us walk by the
same rule,
let us mind the same thing.
17. Brethren, be followers together of
me, and mark them which walk so as
ye have us for an ensample.
18. (For many walk,
of whom I have told you often,
and now tell you even weeping,
that they
are the
enemies of the
cross of Christ:
19. Whose end
is destruction,
whose God *is their* belly, and
whose glory *is* in their shame,
who mind earthly things.)
20. For our conversation is in
heaven; from whence also
we look for the
Saviour, the Lord Jesus Christ:
21. Who shall change
our vile body, that it
may be fashioned
like unto
his glorious body,
according to the working whereby he
is able even to subdue all things
unto himself.

CHAPTER 4

1. Therefore, my brethren dearly
beloved and longed for, my joy and
crown, so stand fast in the Lord, *my*
dearly beloved.
2. I beseech Euodias, and beseech
Syntyche, that they be of the same
mind in the Lord.
3. And I entreat thee also, true yoke-
fellow, help those women which
laboured with me in the gospel, with
Clement also, and *with* other my
fellow-labourers, whose names *are* in
the book of life.
4. Rejoice in the Lord alway:
and again I say, Rejoice.
5. Let your moderation be
known unto all men.
The Lord is at hand.
6. Be careful for nothing; but
in every thing by prayer
and supplication with

thanksgiving let your requests be made known unto God. 7. And the peace of God, which passeth all understanding, shall keep your hearts and minds through Christ Jesus. 8. Finally, brethren, whatsoever things are true, whatsoever things *are* honest, whatsoever things *are* just, whatsoever things *are* pure, whatsoever things *are* lovely, whatsoever things *are* of good report; if there be any virtue, and if *there be* any praise, think on these things. 9. Those things, which ye have both learned, and received, and heard, and seen in me, do: and the God of peace shall be with you.

10. But I rejoiced in the Lord greatly, that now at the last your care of me hath flourished again; wherein ye were also careful, but ye lacked opportunity. 11. Not that I speak in respect of want: for I have learned, in whatsoever state I am, therewith to be content. 12. I know both how to be abased, and I know how to abound: every where and in all things I am instructed both to be full and to be hungry, both to abound and to suffer need. 13. I can do all things through Christ which strengtheneth me. 14. Notwithstanding ye have well done, that ye did communicate with my affliction. 15. Now ye Philippians know also, that in the beginning of the gospel, when I departed from Macedonia, no church communicated with me as concerning giving and receiving, but ye only. 16. For even in Thessalonica ye sent once and again unto my necessity. 17. Not because I desire a gift: but I desire fruit that may abound to your account. 18. But I have all, and abound: I am full, having received of Epaphroditus the things which were sent from you, an odour of a sweet smell, a sacrifice acceptable, wellpleasing to God. 19. But my God shall supply all your need according to his riches in glory by Christ Jesus.

20. Now unto God and our Father *be* glory for ever and ever. Amen. 21. Salute every saint in Christ Jesus. The brethren which are with me greet you. 22. All the saints salute you, chiefly they that are of Caesar's household. 23. The grace of our Lord Jesus Christ *be* with you all. Amen.

THE EPISTLE TO THE COLOSSIANS

BACKGROUND INFORMATION

Author: Paul, an Apostle.
Date Written: probably
between 60 and **65** A.D.

Number of:
Verses   95
Chapters   4
Total Words 1,998
Scan Words 844
Scan words represent
42 % of total words

Theme: written to show
the pre-eminence of Christ
over all competing systems,
and how believers should
conduct their lives

OUTLINE OF THE EPISTLE

I.   Paul Describes
     **the Pre-eminence of
     Christ,** our Reconciliation
     in Christ and His Own
     Service for Christ
     Chapters 1 - 2:3
II. Paul Warns Against False
     Teaching, Explains
     the New Life in Christ,
     Christian Virtues and
     Gives Advice for
     Domestic Life
     Chapters 2:4 - 4

CHAPTER 1

■ 1. **Paul,** an apostle of Jesus Christ by the will of God,

■ **and Timotheus** *our* brother,

■ 2. **To the saints** and faithful brethren in Christ which are

■ **at Colosse:** Grace *be* unto you, and peace, from God our Father and the Lord Jesus Christ.

■ 3. **We give thanks to God** and the Father of our Lord Jesus Christ, praying always for you,

■ 4. **Since we heard of your**
■ **faith in Christ Jesus, and of**
■ **the love which ye have to**
■ **all the saints,**

5.For the hope which is laid up foryou in heaven, whereof ye heard before in the word of the truth of the gospel;

6. Which is come unto you, as *it is* in all the world; and bringeth forth fruit, as *it doth* also in you, since the day ye heard *of it*, and knew the grace of God in truth:

7.As ye also learned of Epaphras our dear fellow-servant, who is for you a faithful minister of Christ;

8. Who also declared unto us your love in the Spirit.

■ 9. **For this cause we**
also, since the day we heard *it*,

■ **do not cease to pray for**
■ **you,** and to desire
■ **that ye might be filled with**
■ **the knowledge of his**
■ **will** in all wisdom
■ **and spiritual**
■ **understanding;**

■ 10. **That ye might walk**
■ **worthy of the Lord**
unto all pleasing,

■ **being fruitful** in every good work, and increasing in the knowledge of God;

■ 11. **Strengthened** with all might,
■ **according to his** glorious
■ **power, unto** all
■ **patience** and longsuffering
■ **with joyfulness;**

■ 12. **Giving thanks unto the**
■ **Father,** which hath made us meet
to be partakers of the inheritance of the saints in light:

■ 13. **Who hath delivered**
■ **us from** the power of
■ **darkness, and** hath
■ **translated u s into the**
■ **kingdom of his dear Son:**

■ 14. **In whom we have**
■ **redemption through**
■ **his blood,**
even the forgiveness of sins:

■ 15. **Who is the image of the**
■ **invisible God,**
the firstborn of every creature:

■ 16. **For by him were all**
■ **things created,** that are in
heaven, and that are in earth,

■ **visible and invisible,** whether
they be thrones, or dominions, or principalities, or powers: all things were created by him, and for him:

■ 17. **And he is before all**
■ **things, and by him all**
■ **things consist.**

■ 18. **And he is the**
■ **head of** the body,
■ **the church:**
who is the beginning,
the firstborn from the dead;

■ **that in all things he might**
■ **have the preeminence.**

■ 19. **For it pleased the Father**
■ **that in him should all**
■ **fulness dwell;**

■ 20. **And, having made**
■ **peace through the blood of**
■ **his cross, by him to**
■ **reconcile all things unto**
■ **himself;** by him, *I say*, whether *hey*
be things in earth, or things in heaven.

■ 21. **And you,** that were sometime
alienated and enemies in *your* mind by wicked works, yet now

■ **hath he reconciled**
22. **In** the body of
■ **his flesh through death, to**
■ **present you** holy and
■ **unblameable** and unreproveable
■ **in his sight:**

■ 23. **If ye continue in the f**
■ **aith** grounded and settled,
■ **and be not moved away**
■ **from** the hope of
■ **the gospel,** which ye have heard,
and which was preached to every

creature which is
under heaven; whereof

■ **I Paul** am made a minister;
■ 24. **Who now rejoice in my**
■ **sufferings for you,** and fill up
that which is behind of the afflictions
of Christ in my flesh for his body's
sake, which is the church:

■ 25. **Whereof I am made a**
■ **minister,** according to the
dispensation of God which is given to
me for you,

■ **to fulfil the word of God;**
■ 26. **Even the mystery which**
■ **hath been hid** from ages and
■ **from generations,** but now
■ **is made manifest**
■ **to his saints:**
27. To whom God would make known
what *is* the riches of the glory of this
mystery among the Gentiles; which is
■ **Christ** in you, the hope of glory:
■ 28. **Whom we preach,**
■ **warning** every man,
■ **and teaching every**
■ **man** in all wisdom;
■ **that we may present every**
■ **man perfect in Christ** Jesus:
29. Whereunto I also labour, striving
according to his working, which
worketh in me mightily.

CHAPTER 2

1. For I would that ye knew what great
conflict I have for you, and *for* them at
Laodicea, and *for* as many as have
not seen my face in the flesh;
2. That their hearts might be
comforted, being knit together in love,
and unto all riches of the full
assurance of understanding, to the
acknowledgement of the mystery of
God, and of the Father, and of Christ;
3. In whom are hid all the treasures of
wisdom and knowledge.
■ 4. **And this I say,**
■ **lest any** man should
■ **beguile you** with enticing words.
■ 5. **For though I be absent in**
■ **the flesh, yet am I with you**
■ **in the spirit,** joying and beholding
your order, and the stedfastness of
your faith in Christ.

■ 6. **As ye have** therefore
■ **received Christ** Jesus the Lord,
■ **s o walk ye in him:**
■ 7. **Rooted and built up in**
■ **him, and stablished in the**
■ **faith,** as ye have been taught,
abounding therein with thanksgiving.
■ 8. **Beware lest any man**
■ **spoil you through**
■ **philosophy** and vain deceit,
■ **after the tradition of men,**
after the rudiments of the world,
■ **and not after Christ.**
■ 9. **For in him dwelleth**
■ **all the fulness of the**
■ **Godhead bodily.**
■ 10. **And ye are complete in**
■ **him,** which is the head of all
principality and power:
■ 11. **In whom also ye are**
■ **circumcised** with the
circumcision made without hands,
■ **in putting off the body of** the
■ **s i n s** of the flesh
■ **by the circumcision**
■ **of Christ:**
■ 12. **Buried with him in**
■ **baptism, wherein also ye**
■ **are risen** with *him*
■ **through** the
■ **faith** of the operation of God, who
hath raised him from the dead.
■ 13. **And you, being**
■ **dead in** your
■ **s i n s** and the uncircumcision
of your flesh,
■ **hath he quickened**
together with him,
■ **having forgiven you**
all trespasses;
■ 14. **Blotting out** the handwriting of
■ **ordinances** that was
■ **against us,**
which was contrary to us,
■ **and** took it out of the way,
■ **nailing it to his cross;**
■ 15. **And having spoiled**
■ **principalities and powers,**
he made a shew of them openly,
■ **triumphing over them** in it.
■ 16. **Let no man therefore**
■ **judge you in meat, or in**
■ **drink, or in respect of an**

■ ■ ■ **holyday, or of the new moon, or of the sabbath days:**

17. Which are a shadow of things to come; but the body *is* of Christ.

■ 18. **Let no man beguile you** of your reward ■ **in a voluntary humility and** ■ **worshipping of angels,** intruding into those things which he hath not seen, ■ **vainly puffed up by his** ■ **fleshly mind,**

■ 19. **And not holding the** ■ **Head, from which all the** ■ **body by joints** and bands ■ **having nourishment** ministered, ■ **and knit together,** ■ **increaseth** with the increase of God.

■ 20. **Wherefore if ye be** ■ **dead with Christ** from the rudiments of the world, ■ **why, as though living in the** ■ **world, are ye subject** ■ **to** ordinances,

21. (Touch not; taste not; handle not;

22. Which all are to perish with the using;) after ■ **the** commandments and ■ **doctrines of men?**

■ 23. **Which things have** ■ **indeed a shew of wisdom** ■ **in** will worship, and humility, and ■ **neglecting** of ■ **the body; not in any** ■ **honour to the satisfying** ■ **of the flesh.**

CHAPTER 3

■ 1. **If ye then be risen with** ■ **Christ, seek** those ■ **things** which are ■ **above,** where Christ sitteth on the right hand of God.

2. Set your affection on things above, ■ **not** on ■ **things on the earth.**

3. For ye are dead, and your life is hid with Christ in God.

4. When Christ, *who is* our life, shall appear, then shall ye also appear with him in glory.

■ 5. **Mortify therefore your** ■ **members** which are ■ **upon the earth;** fornication, uncleanness, inordinate affection, evil concupiscence, and covetousness, which is idolatry:

6. For which things' sake the wrath of God cometh on the children of disobedience:

7. In the which ye also walked some time, when ye lived in them.

8. But now ye also put off all these; anger, wrath, malice, blasphemy, filthy communication out of your mouth.

■ 9. **Lie not one to another,** ■ **seeing that ye have put off** ■ **the old man with his deeds;**

■ 10. **And have put on the new** ■ **man,** which is renewed in knowledge ■ **after the image of him that** ■ **created him:**

■ 11. **Where there is neither** ■ **Greek nor Jew,** ■ **circumcision nor** ■ **uncircumcision,** Barbarian, Scythian, ■ **bond nor free: but Christ** ■ **i s all, and in all.**

■ 12. **Put on therefore, as** ■ **the elect of God,** holy and beloved, bowels of mercies, ■ **kindness, humbleness** ■ **of mind,** meekness, ■ **longsuffering;**

■ 13. **Forbearing** one another, ■ **and forgiving one another,** if any man have a quarrel against any: even as Christ forgave you, so also *do* ye.

■ 14. **And above all** these things ■ **put on charity, which is the** ■ **bond of perfectness**.

■ 15. **And let the peace of God** ■ **rule in your hearts,** to the which also ye are called in one body; ■ **and be ye thankful.**

■ 16. **Let the word of Christ** ■ **dwell in you** richly in all wisdom; ■ **teaching and admonishing** ■ **one another in psalms** and

■ hymns and spiritual songs,
■ singing with grace in your
■ hearts to the Lord.

■ 17. And whatsoever ye
■ do in word or deed, do
■ all in the name of the Lord
■ Jesus, giving thanks to God and
the Father by him.

■ 18. Wives, submit
■ yourselves unto your own
■ husbands, as it is fit in the Lord.

■ 19. Husbands, love your
■ wives, and be not bitter
against them.

■ 20. Children, obey your
■ parents in all things: for this is well
pleasing unto the Lord.

■ 21. Fathers, provoke not
■ your children to anger, lest
they be discouraged.

■ 22. Servants, obey in all things
■ your masters according to the
flesh; not with eye-service, as men
pleasers; but in singleness of heart,
fearing God:

■ 23. And whatsoever ye do,
■ do it heartily, as to the
■ Lord, and not unto men;
24. Knowing that of the Lord ye shall
receive the reward of the inheritance:
for ye serve the Lord Christ.
25. But he that doeth wrong shall
receive for the wrong which he hath
done: and there is no
respect of persons.

CHAPTER 4

■ 1. Masters, give unto
■ your servants that which
■ is just and equal; knowing that ye
also have a Master in heaven.

■ 2. Continue in prayer,
■ and watch in the same
■ with thanksgiving;

■ 3. Withal praying also for
■ us, that God would open
unto us
■ a door of utterance,
■ to speak the mystery
■ of Christ, for which
■ I am also in bonds:
4. That I may make it manifest, as I
ought to speak.

■ 5. Walk in wisdom toward
■ them that are without,
redeeming the time.

■ 6. Let your speech be alway
■ with grace, seasoned with salt,
that ye may know how ye ought to
answer every man.

■ 7. All my state shall
■ Tychicus declare unto you,
who is a beloved brother, and a
faithful minister and fellow-servant
in the Lord:
8. Whom I have sent unto you for the
same purpose, that he might know
your estate, and comfort your hearts;

■ 9. With Onesimus, a faithful and
beloved brother, who is *one* of you.
They shall make known unto you all
things which *are done* here.

■ 10. Aristarchus
my fellow prisoner
■ saluteth you, and Marcus,
■ sister's son to Barnabas,
(touching whom ye received
commandments: if he come unto you,
receive him;)

■ 11. And Jesus, which is called
■ Justus, who are of the
circumcision.
■ These only are my fellow-
■ workers unto the kingdom
of God, which have been a
comfort unto me.

■ 12. Epaphras, who is *one* of you,
a servant of Christ,
■ saluteth you, always
■ labouring fervently
■ for you in prayers,
that ye may stand perfect and
complete in all the will of God.
13. For I bear him record, that he hath
a great zeal for you, and them
that are in Laodicea, and
them in Hierapolis.

■ 14. Luke, the beloved
■ physician, and Demas,
■ greet you.
15. Salute the brethren which are in
Laodicea, and Nymphas, and the
church which is in his house.

■ 16. And when this epistle is
■ read among you,
■ cause that it be read also

319

■ **in the church** of the Laodiceans; and that ye likewise read the *epistle* from Laodicea.

17. And say to Archippus, Take heed to the ministry which thou hast received in the Lord, that thou fulfil it.

■ 18. **The salutation by the**
■ **hand of me Paul.**
■ **Remember my bonds.**
Grace *be* with you.
■ **Amen.**

THE FIRST EPISTLE
TO THE THESSALONIANS

BACKGROUND
INFORMATION

Author: Paul, an Apostle.
Date Written: probably
between 50 and 52 A.D.

Number of:
Verses   89
Chapters   5
Total Words 1,857
Scan Words 878
Scan Words represent
48 % of Total Words

Theme: written to instruct
the church in practical
Christian living, and
**how Christians should
respond to the Second
Coming**

OUTLINE OF
THE EPISTLE

I.   **Paul** Gives Thanks for the
      Thessalonian's Spiritual
      Progress and
      Defends His Message
      Chapters 1 - 2

II.   Paul Sends Timothy to
      the Thessalonians and
      Paul's Prayer for Them
      Chapter 3

III. Paul Outlines Christian
      Doctrine Concerning
      Morality,
      **the Second Coming
      and Church Life**
      Chapters 4 - 5

CHAPTER 1

1. **Paul,** and **Silvanus, and Timotheus, unto the church of the Thessalonians** *which is* in God the Father and *in* the Lord Jesus Christ: Grace *be* unto you, and peace, from God our Father, and the Lord Jesus Christ.

2. **We give thanks** to God always **for you** all, making mention of you **in our prayers;**

3. **Remembering** without ceasing **your** work of **faith,** and labour of **love, and patience** of hope **in our Lord** Jesus Christ, in the sight of God and our Father;

4. **Knowing,** brethren beloved, **your election** of God.

5. **For our gospel came not** unto you **in word only, but** also **in power,** and **in the Holy Ghost, and** in much **assurance;** as ye know what manner of men we were among you for your sake.

6. **And ye became followers of us, and** of **the Lord, having received the word in** much **affliction, with joy of the Holy Ghost:**

7. **So that ye were ensamples** to all that believe in Macedonia and Achaia.

8. **For from you sounded out the word** of the Lord **not only in Macedonia and Achaia, but also in every place your faith** to God-ward **is spread** abroad; so that we need not to speak any thing.

9. **For they themselves shew** of us what manner of entering in we had unto you, and **how ye turned** to God **from idols to serve the** living and **true God;**

10. **And to wait for his Son** from heaven, **whom he raised** from the dead, **even Jesus, which delivered us from the wrath to come.**

CHAPTER 2

1. For yourselves, brethren, know our entrance in unto you, that it was not in vain:

2. **But even after that we had suffered** before, and were shamefully entreated, as ye know, **at Philippi, we were bold** in our God **to speak** unto you **the gospel** of God with much contention.

3. For our exhortation *was* not of deceit, nor of uncleanness, nor in guile:

4. **But as we were** allowed of God to be **put in trust with the gospel,** even so **we speak; not as pleasing men, but God,** which trieth our hearts.

5. **For neither** at any time **used we flattering words,** as ye know, nor a cloak of covetousness; God *is* witness.

6. **Nor** of men **sought we glory,** neither of you, nor *yet* of others, when we might have been burdensome, as the apostles of Christ.

7. **But we were gentle among you,** even as a nurse cherisheth her children:

8. So being affectionately desirous of you, **we were willing to have imparted** unto you, **not the gospel** of God **only, but also our own souls,** because ye were dear unto us.

9. **For ye remember, brethren, our labour and travail:** for labouring night and day,

because we would not be chargeable unto any of you, we preached unto you the gospel of God.

10. Ye are witnesses, and God also, how holily and justly and unblameably we behaved ourselves among you that believe:

11. As ye know how we exhorted and comforted and charged every one of you, as a father *doth* his children,

12. That ye would walk worthy of God, who hath called you unto his kingdom and glory

13. For this cause also thank we God without ceasing, because, when ye received the word of God which ye heard of us, ye received it not as the word of men, but as it is in truth, the word of God, which effectually worketh also in you that believe.

14. For ye, brethren, became followers of the churches of God which in Judaea are in Christ Jesus: for ye also have suffered like things of your own countrymen, even as they *have* of the Jews:

15. Who both killed the Lord Jesus, and their own prophets, and have persecuted us; and they please not God, and are contrary to all men:

16. Forbidding us to speak to the Gentiles that they might be saved, to fill up their sins alway: for the wrath is come upon them to the uttermost.

17. But we, brethren, being taken from you for a short time in presence, not in heart, endeavoured the more abundantly to see your face with great desire.

18. Wherefore we would have come unto you, even I Paul, once and again; but Satan hindered us.

19. For what *is* our hope, or joy, or crown of rejoicing? *Are* not even ye in the presence of our Lord Jesus Christ at his coming?

20. For ye are our glory and joy.

CHAPTER 3

1. Wherefore when we could no longer forbear, we thought it good to be left at Athens alone;

2. And sent Timotheus, our brother, and minister of God, and our fellow-labourer in the gospel of Christ, to establish you, and to comfort you concerning your faith:

3. That no man should be moved by these afflictions: for yourselves know that we are appointed thereunto.

4. For verily, when we were with you, we told you before that we should suffer tribulation; even as it came to pass, and ye know.

5. For this cause, when I could no longer forbear, I sent to know your faith, lest by some means the tempter have tempted you, and our labour be in vain.

6. But now when Timotheus came from you unto us, and brought us good tidings of your faith and charity, and that ye have good remembrance of us always, desiring greatly to see us, as we also *to see* you:

7. Therefore, brethren, we were comforted over you in all our affliction and distress by your faith:

8. For now we live, if ye stand fast in the Lord.

9. For what thanks can we render to God again for you, for all the joy wherewith we joy for your sakes before our God;

10. **Night and day praying exceedingly that we might see your face,** and might perfect that which is lacking in your faith? 11. **Now God himself** and our Father, and our Lord Jesus Christ, **direct our way unto you.** 12. **And the Lord make you to increase and abound in love** one toward another, and toward all *men,* even as we *do* toward you: 13. **To the end he may stablish your hearts unblameable** in holiness before God, even our Father, **at the coming of** our Lord Jesus **Christ** with all his saints.

CHAPTER 4

1. **Furthermore then we beseech you,** brethren, and exhort *you* by the Lord Jesus, **that as ye have received of us** how **ye ought to** walk and to **please God,** *so* ye would abound **more** and more. 2. For ye know what commandments we gave you by the Lord Jesus. 3. **For this is the will of God, even your sanctification, that ye** should **abstain from fornication:** 4. **That every one of you** should **know how to possess his vessel in sanctification and honour;** 5. Not in the lust of concupiscence, even as the Gentiles which know not God: 6. **That no man** go beyond and **defraud his brother in any matter:** because that the Lord *is* the avenger of all such, as we also have forewarned you and testified. 7. **For God hath not called us unto uncleanness,** but unto holiness. 8. **He therefore that despiseth, despiseth not man, but God,** who hath also given unto us his holy Spirit

9. **But as touching brotherly love** ye need not that I write unto you: for **ye yourselves are taught of God to love one another.** 10. **And indeed ye do** it toward all the brethren which are in all Macedonia: **but we beseech you,** brethren, **that ye increase more** and more; 11. **And that ye study to be quiet, and to do your own business, and to work with your own hands,** as we commanded you; 12. **That ye may walk honestly** toward them that are without, **and** *that* ye may **have lack of nothing.** 13. **But I would not have you to be ignorant, brethren, concerning them which are asleep, that ye sorrow not,** even as others which have no hope. 14. **For** if we believe that Jesus died and rose again, even so **them** also **which sleep in Jesus will God bring with him.** 15. **For** this we say unto you by the word of the Lord, that **we which are alive** *and* remain **unto the coming of the Lord shall not prevent them** which are **asleep.** 16. **For the Lord himself shall descend from heaven with a shout, with the voice of the archangel, and with the trump of God: and the dead in Christ shall rise first:** 17. **Then we which** are alive *and* **remain shall be caught up** together **with them in the clouds, to meet the Lord** in the air: **and so shall we ever be with the Lord.** 18. **Wherefore comfort one**

|■| **another with these words.**

CHAPTER 5

|■| 1. **But of the times** and the seasons, brethren, **ye have no need that I write** unto you. 2. **For** yourselves know perfectly that **the day of the Lord so cometh as a thief in the night.** 3. **For when they shall say, Peace and safety; then sudden destruction cometh** upon them, as travail upon a woman with child; and they shall not escape. 4. **But ye, brethren, are not in darkness, that that day should overtake you** as a thief. 5. **Ye are all the children of light,** and the children of the day: we are not of the night, nor of darkness. 6. **Therefore** let us not sleep, as *do* others; but **let us watch and be sober.** 7. For they that sleep sleep in the night; and they that be drunken are drunken in the night. 8. But let us, who are of the day, be sober, **putting on the breastplate of faith and love; and for an helmet, the hope of salvation.** 9. **For God hath not appointed us to wrath, but to obtain salvation by** our Lord Jesus **Christ,** 10. **Who died for us, that, whether we wake or sleep, we should live** together **with him.** 11. Wherefore comfort yourselves together, and edify one another, even as also ye do. 12. And we beseech you, brethren, to know **them which labour among you, and are over you in the Lord,** and admonish you; 13. And to **esteem them** very highly **in love** for their work's sake. *And* be at peace among yourselves. 14. Now we exhort you, brethren, **warn them that are unruly,** comfort the feebleminded, **support the weak, be patient** toward all *men*. 15 . **Seeing that none render evil for evil** unto any *man*; but ever follow that which is good, both among yourselves, and to all *men*. 16. **Rejoice evermore.** 17. **Pray without ceasing.** 18. **In every thing give thanks: for this is the will of God** in Christ Jesus concerning you. 19. **Quench not the Spirit.** 20. **Despise not prophesyings.** 21. Prove all things; hold fast that which is good. 22. **Abstain from all appearance of evil.** 23. And the very God of peace sanctify you wholly; **and I pray God your whole spirit and soul and body be preserved blameless unto the coming of our Lord** Jesus Christ. 24. Faithful *is* he that calleth you, who also will do *it*. 25. Brethren, pray for us. 26. Greet all the brethren with an holy kiss. 27. I charge you by the Lord that this epistle be read unto all the holy brethren. 28. The grace of our Lord Jesus Christ *be* with you. |■| **Amen.**

THE SECOND EPISTLE TO THE THESSALONIANS

BACKGROUND INFORMATION

Author: Paul, an apostle.
Date Written: probably between 50 and **52** A.D.

Number of:
Verses   47
Chapters   3
Total Words 1,042
Scan Words 487
Scan Words represent
46 % of Total Words

Theme: written to instruct Christians in **practical conduct, and the** continued **need for industry in light of the Second Coming**

OUTLINE OF THE EPISTLE

I. Paul Offers **Encouragement in Persecution and Instruction** Concerning the Day of the Lord Chapters 1 - 2
II. Paul Gives Confession of Confidence and **Commandments to Work** Chapter 3

CHAPTER 1

1. **Paul, and Silvanus, and Timotheus, unto the church of the Thessalonians** in God our Father and the Lord Jesus Christ:

2. Grace unto you, and peace, from God our Father and the Lord Jesus Christ.

3. **We** are bound to **thank God** always for you, brethren, as it is meet, **because** that **your faith groweth** exceedingly, and the charity of every one of you all toward each other aboundeth;

4. **So that we** ourselves **glory in you** in the churches of God **for your patience** and faith **in** all your **persecutions** and tribulations that ye endure:

5. **Which is a manifest token of the righteous judgment of God, that ye may be counted worthy of the kingdom** of God, for which ye also suffer:

6. **Seeing it is a righteous thing with God to recompense tribulation to them that trouble you;**

7. And to you who are troubled rest with us, **when** the Lord **Jesus shall be revealed from heaven with his mighty angels,**

8. **In flaming fire taking vengeance on them that know not God, and that obey not the gospel** of our Lord Jesus Christ:

9. **Who shall be punished with everlasting destruction** from the presence of the Lord, and from the glory of his power;

10. **When he shall come to be glorified in his saints,** and to be admired in all them that believe (because our testimony among you was believed) in that day.

11. **Wherefore also we pray** always for you, **that** our **God** would **count you worthy of this calling,** and fulfil all the good pleasure of *his* goodness, and the work of faith with power:

12. **That** the name of our Lord **Jesus Christ may be glorified in you, and ye in him,** according to the grace of our God and the Lord Jesus Christ.

CHAPTER 2

1. **Now we beseech you,** brethren, by the coming of our Lord Jesus Christ, and *by* our gathering together unto him,

2. **That ye be not soon shaken in mind,** or be troubled, neither by spirit, nor by word, nor by letter as from us, as that the day of Christ is at hand.

3. **Let no man deceive you** by any means: **for that day shall not come, except there come a falling away first, and that man of sin be revealed,** the son of perdition;

4. **Who opposeth and exalteth himself above all that is called God,** or that is worshipped; so that he as God sitteth in the temple of God, **shewing himself that he is God.**

5. Remember ye not, that, when I was yet with you, I told you these things?

6. And now ye know what withholdeth that he might be revealed in his time.

7. **For the mystery of iniquity doth already work: only he who now letteth will let, until he be taken out of the way.**

8. **And then shall that Wicked be revealed, whom the Lord shall consume with the spirit of his mouth, and** shall destroy with the

327

brightness of

his coming:

9. **Even him, whose coming**

is after the working

of Satan with all power and

signs and lying wonders,

10. **And with all**

deceivableness

of unrighteousness

in them that perish;

because they received not

the love of

the truth, that they might be saved.

11. **And for this cause God**

shall send them strong

delusion, that they

should believe a lie:

12. **That they** all might

be damned who believed

not the truth, but had pleasure

in unrighteousness.

13. **But** we are bound to give thanks

alway to God for you, brethren

beloved of the Lord, because

God hath from the beginning

chosen you to salvation

through sanctification of the

Spirit and belief of the truth:

14. Whereunto he called you by our

gospel, to the obtaining of the glory

of our Lord Jesus Christ.

15. **Therefore, brethren,**

stand fast, and hold the traditions

which ye have been taught, whether

by word, or our epistle.

16. **Now our Lord** Jesus Christ

himself, and God, even our Father,

which hath loved us, and hath given

us everlasting consolation and good

hope through grace,

17. **Comfort your hearts, and**

stablish you in every good

word and work.

CHAPTER 3

1. **Finally, brethren, pray for**

us, that the word of the Lord

may have free course, and

be glorified, even as *it is* with you:

2. **And that we may be**

delivered from

unreasonable and wicked

men: for all *men* have not faith.

3. **But the Lord is faithful,**

who shall stablish you, and

keep you from evil.

4. **And we have confidence**

in the Lord touching you, that ye

both do and will do the things which

we command you.

5. **And the Lord direct your**

hearts into the love of God,

and into the patient waiting

for Christ.

6. Now we command you, brethren,

in the name of our Lord

Jesus Christ, that ye

withdraw yourselves from

every brother that walketh

disorderly, and not after the

tradition which he received of us.

7. **For yourselves know how**

ye ought to follow us: for

we behaved not ourselves disorderly

among you;

8. **Neither did we eat any**

man's bread for nought; but

wrought with labour

and travail night and day,

that we might not be

chargeable to any of you:

9. Not because we have

not power, but

to make ourselves an

ensample unto you to follow us.

10. **For** even when

we were with you, this

we commanded you, that if

any would not work, neither

should he eat.

11. **For we hear that** there are

some which

walk among you disorderly,

working not at all, but are

busybodies.

12. Now them that are such we

command and exhort by our Lord

Jesus Christ, that with quietness they

work, and eat their own bread.

13. **But ye, brethren, be not**

weary in well doing.

14. **And if any** man

obey not our word

by this epistle, note that man, and

have no company with him,

that he may be ashamed.

15. Yet count him not as an enemy, but admonish him as a brother.

16. Now the Lord of peace himself give you peace always by all means. The Lord *be* with you all.

17. The salutation of Paul with mine own hand, which is the token in every epistle: so I write.

18. The grace of our Lord Jesus Christ *be* with you all.

Amen.

THE FIRST EPISTLE TO TIMOTHY

BACKGROUND INFORMATION

Author: Paul, an Apostle.
Date Written: probably
between 60 and **65** A.D.

Number of:
Verses   113
Chapters   6
Total Words 2,269
Scan Words 1,059
Scan Words represent
46 % of Total Words

**Theme: written to
encourage a young
minister, and instruct him**
in the proper conduct of
his ministry

OUTLINE OF THE EPISTLE

I.   **Paul** Greets Timothy and
     **Warns About False
     Teachers**
     Chapter 1:1 - 1:11
II. **Paul Declares
     the Apostolic
     Commission**
     Chapter 1:12 - 20
III. **Paul Outlines
     Rules for Public Worship
     and
     Qualifications for
     Church Leaders**
     Chapters 2 - 3
IV. **Paul Gives Timothy
     Personal Advice**
     Chapters 4 - 6

CHAPTER 1

1. **Paul,** an apostle of Jesus Christ by the commandment of God our Saviour, and Lord Jesus Christ, *which is* our hope;

2. **Unto Timothy,** *my* own son in the faith: Grace, mercy, *and* peace, from God our Father and Jesus Christ our Lord.

3. **As I besought thee to abide still at Ephesus,** when I went into Macedonia, **that thou mightest charge some that they teach no other doctrine,**

4. **Neither give heed to fables and** endless **genealogies,** which minister questions, **rather than godly edifying** which is in faith: *so do.*

5. **Now the end of the commandment is charity out of a pure heart, and** *of* a good conscience, and **of faith unfeigned:**

6. **From which some** having swerved **have turned aside** unto vain jangling;

7. **Desiring to be teachers of the law;** understanding neither what they say, nor whereof they affirm.

8. But we know that **the law is good, if a man use it lawfully;**

9. **Knowing this, that the law is not made for a righteous man, but for the lawless** and disobedient, for the ungodly and for sinners, for unholy and profane, for murderers of fathers and murderers of mothers, for manslayers,

10. For whoremongers, for them that defile themselves with mankind, for menstealers, for liars, for perjured persons, and if there be any other thing that is contrary to sound doctrine;

11. According to the glorious gospel of the blessed God, which was committed to my trust.

12. **And I thank Christ** Jesus our Lord, who hath enabled me, **for** that he counted me faithful, **putting me into the ministry;**

13. **Who was before a blasphemer,** and a **persecutor, and injurious: but I obtained mercy, because I did it ignorantly in unbelief.**

14. And the grace of our Lord was exceeding abundant with faith and love which is in Christ Jesus.

15. **This is a faithful saying,** and worthy of all acceptation, **that Christ Jesus came into the world to save sinners; of whom I am chief.**

16. Howbeit for this cause **I obtained mercy, that in me** first Jesus **Christ might shew** forth all **longsuffering, for a pattern to them which should** hereafter **believe** on him to life everlasting.

17. Now unto the King eternal, immortal, invisible, the only wise God, *be* honour and glory for ever and ever. Amen.

18. **This charge I commit unto thee,** son Timothy, **according to the prophecies** which went before **on thee, that thou** by them **mightest war a good warfare;**

19. **Holding faith, and a good conscience;** which some having put away concerning faith have made shipwreck:

20. Of whom is Hymenaeus and Alexander; whom I have delivered unto Satan, that they may learn not to blaspheme.

CHAPTER 2

1. **I exhort therefore, that,** first of all, **supplications, prayers, intercessions, and giving of thanks, be made for all men;**

2. **For kings, and for all** that are **in authority; that we may lead a** quiet and **peaceable life** in all godliness and honesty.

3. **For this is good** and acceptable **in the sight of God our Saviour;**

4. **Who will have all men to be saved,** and to come unto the knowledge of the truth.

5. **For there is one God, and one mediator between God and men, the man Christ Jesus;**

6. **Who gave himself a ransom for all,** to be testified in due time.

7. **Whereunto I am** ordained a preacher, and **an apostle,** (I speak the truth in Christ, *and* lie not;) **a teacher of the Gentiles** in faith and verity.

8. **I will therefore that men pray** every where, **lifting up holy hands,** without wrath and doubting.

9. **In like manner also, that women adorn themselves in modest apparel, with** shamefacedness and **sobriety; not with** broided hair, or gold, or pearls, or **costly array;**

10. **But** (which becometh women professing godliness) **with good works.**

11. **Let the woman learn in silence** with all subjection.

12. **But I suffer not a woman** to teach, nor **to usurp authority over the man,** but to be in silence.

13. **For Adam was first formed,** then Eve.

14. **And Adam was not deceived, but the woman** being deceived was in the transgression.

15. Notwithstanding she shall be saved in childbearing, if they continue in faith and charity and holiness with sobriety.

CHAPTER 3

1. This *is* a true saying, **If a man desire the office of a bishop, he desireth a good work.**

2. **A bishop then must be blameless,** the husband of one wife, vigilant, sober, of good behaviour, given to hospitality, apt to teach;

3. Not given to wine, no striker, not greedy of filthy lucre; but patient, not a brawler, not covetous;

4. One that ruleth well his own house, having his children in subjection with all gravity;

5. (For if a man know not how to rule his own house, how shall he take care of the church of God?)

6. Not a novice, lest being lifted up with pride he fall into the condemnation of the devil.

7. **Moreover he must have a good report of them which are without;** lest he fall into reproach and the snare of the devil.

8. **Likewise must the deacons be grave, not double tongued,** not given to much wine, not greedy of filthy lucre;

9. Holding the mystery of the faith in a pure conscience.

10. **And let these also first be proved;** then let them use the office of a deacon, being *found* blameless.

11. **Even so must their wives be grave, not slanderers,** sober, faithful in all things.

12. **Let the deacons be the husbands of one wife,** ruling their children and their own houses well.

13. **For they that have used the office of a deacon well purchase** to themselves **a good degree,** and great boldness in the faith which is in Christ Jesus.

14. These things write I unto thee, hoping to come unto thee shortly:

15. **But if I tarry** long, that **thou mayest know how thou oughtest to behave** thyself **in the house of God,** which is the church of the living God, the pillar and ground of the truth.

16. And without controversy **great is the mystery of godliness: God was manifest in the flesh, justified in the Spirit, seen of angels, preached unto the Gentiles, believed on in the world, received up into glory.**

CHAPTER 4

1. **Now the Spirit speaketh** expressly, **that in the latter times some shall depart** from the faith, **giving heed to seducing spirits,** and doctrines of devils;

2. **Speaking lies in hypocrisy;** having their conscience seared with a hot iron;

3. **Forbidding to marry, and commanding to abstain from meats, which God hath created to be received with thanksgiving** of them which believe and know the truth.

4. **For every creature of God is good, and nothing to be refused,** if it be received with thanksgiving:

5. **For it is sanctified by the word of God and prayer.**

6. **If thou put the brethren in remembrance of these things, thou shalt be a good minister** of Jesus Christ, nourished up in the words of faith and of good doctrine, whereunto thou hast attained.

7. **But refuse** profane and **old wives' fables, and exercise thyself rather unto godliness.**

8. **For bodily exercise profiteth little: but godliness is profitable unto all things, having promise of the life that now is, and of that** which is **to come.**

9. This *is* a faithful saying and worthy of all acceptation.

10. For therefore **we** both **labour and suffer** reproach, **because we trust** in the living **God, who is the Saviour** of all men, specially of those that believe.

11. **These things command and teach.**

12. **Let no man despise thy youth; but be thou an example** of the believers, in word, in conversation, in charity, in spirit, in faith, in purity.

13. **Till I come, give attendance to reading, to exhortation, to doctrine.**

14. **Neglect not the gift** that is in thee, which was **given thee by prophecy, with the laying on of the hands** of the presbytery.

15. **Meditate upon these things; give thyself wholly to them;** that thy profiting may appear to all.

16. **Take heed unto thyself, and** unto **the doctrine;** continue in them: for in doing this thou shalt both save thyself, and them that hear thee.

CHAPTER 5

1. **Rebuke not an elder,** but **entreat** *him* as a father; *and* **the younger men as brethren;**

2. **The elder women as mothers; the younger as sisters,** with all purity.

3. **Honour widows** that are widows indeed.

4. **But if any widow have children** or nephews, **let them learn**

first to shew piety at home, and **to requite their parents:** for that is good and acceptable before God.

5. **Now she that is a widow** indeed, **and desolate, trusteth in God, and continueth in supplications and prayers** night and day.

6. **But she that liveth in pleasure is dead** while she liveth.

7. And these things give in charge, that they may be blameless.

8. **But if any provide not for his own,** and specially for those of his own house, **he** hath denied the faith, and **is worse than an infidel.**

9. **Let not a widow be taken into the number under threescore** years old, having been the wife of one man,

10. Well reported of for good works; if she have brought up children, if she have lodged strangers, if she have washed the saints' feet, if she have relieved the afflicted, if she have diligently followed every good work.

11. **But the younger widows refuse: for** when they have begun to wax wanton against Christ, **they will marry;**

12. Having damnation, because they have cast off their first faith.

13. **And withal they learn to be idle,** wandering about from house to house; **and** not only idle, but **tattlers also and busybodies,** speaking things which they ought not.

14. **I will therefore that the younger women marry,** bear children, guide the house, give none occasion to the adversary to speak reproachfully.

15. For some are already turned aside after Satan.

16. **If any man** or woman that believeth **have widows, let them** relieve them, **and let not the church be charged;** that it may relieve them that are widows indeed.

17. **Let the elders that rule well be counted worthy of double honour,** especially they who labour in the word and doctrine.

18. For the scripture saith, Thou shalt not muzzle the ox that treadeth out the corn. And, The labourer *is* worthy of his reward.

19. **Against an elder receive not an accusation, but before two or three witnesses.**

20. **Them that sin rebuke before all,** that others also may fear.

21. **I charge thee** before God, and the Lord Jesus Christ, and the elect angels, **that thou observe these things without preferring one before another,** doing nothing by partiality.

22. **Lay hands suddenly on no man,** neither be partaker of other men's sins: **keep thyself pure.**

23. **Drink no longer water, but** use a little **wine for thy stomach's sake** and thine often infirmities.

24. **Some men's sins are open** beforehand, going **before to judgment; and some** *men* they **follow** after.

25. **Likewise also the good works** *of some* are manifest beforehand; and they that are otherwise cannot be hid.

CHAPTER 6

1. **Let** as many **servants** as are under the yoke **count their own masters worthy of all honour,** that the name of God and *his* doctrine be not blasphemed.

2. **And** they that have believing masters, **let them not despise them,**

because they are brethren; but rather do *them* service, because they are faithful and beloved, partakers of the benefit. These things teach and exhort.

3. **If any man teach otherwise,** and consent not to wholesome words, *even* the words of our Lord Jesus Christ, and to the doctrine which is according to godliness;

4. **He is proud, knowing nothing,** but doting about questions and strifes of words, whereof cometh envy, strife, railings, evil surmisings,

5. Perverse disputings of men of corrupt minds, and destitute of the truth, supposing that gain is godliness: **from such withdraw** thyself.

6. **But godliness with contentment is great gain.**

7. **For we brought nothing into this world, and it is certain we can carry nothing out.**

8. **And having food and raiment let us be** therewith **content.**

9. **But they that will be rich fall into temptation** and a snare, **and into many** foolish and hurtful **lusts,** which drown men in destruction and perdition.

10. **For the love of money is the root of all evil:** which while some coveted after, they have erred from the faith, and pierced themselves through with many sorrows.

11. **But thou, O man of God, flee these things; and follow after righteousness,** godliness, faith, love, patience, meekness.

12. **Fight the good fight of faith, lay hold on eternal life,** whereunto thou art also called, and hast professed a good profession before many witnesses.

13. **I give thee charge** in the sight of God, who quickeneth all things, and *before* Christ Jesus, who before Pontius Pilate witnessed a good confession;

14. **That thou keep this commandment** without spot, unrebukable, **until the appearing of our Lord** Jesus Christ:

15. Which in his times he shall shew, **who is the blessed and only Potentate,** the King of kings, and Lord of lords;

16. **Who only hath immortality, dwelling in the light which no man can approach** unto; **whom no man hath seen,** nor can see: to whom *be* honour and power everlasting. Amen.

17. **Charge them that are rich** in this world, **that they be not highminded, nor trust in** uncertain **riches, but in the living God,** who giveth us richly all things to enjoy;

18. **That they** do good, that they **be rich in good works, ready to distribute,** willing to communicate;

19. **Laying up** in store **for themselves a good foundation** against the time to come, **that they may lay hold on eternal life.**

20. **O Timothy, keep that** which is **committed to thy trust, avoiding profane** *and* vain **babblings, and oppositions of science falsely so called:**

21. Which some professing have erred concerning the faith. Grace *be* with thee. **Amen.**

THE SECOND EPISTLE TO TIMOTHY

BACKGROUND INFORMATION

Author: **Paul,** an Apostle.
Date Written: probably **between 64** and **65** A.D.

Number of:
Verses   83
Chapters   4
Total Words 1,703
Scan Words 782
Scan Words represent
45 % of Total Words

Theme: written to challenge a young minister to **hold fast to the truths of the Gospel**

OUTLINE OF THE EPISTLE

I. **Paul Gives Thanks** for Timothy, Exhorts Him to Endurance, and Offers Advice on Personal Conduct and Relationships
Chapters 1 - 2

II. **Paul Speaks of the Coming Apostasy** and the Reliability of the Scriptures
Chapter 3

III. **Paul Charges Timothy to Preach** and Paul Presents his Own Last Testament
Chapter 4

CHAPTER 1

1. **Paul,** an apostle of Jesus Christ by the will of God, according to the promise of life which is in Christ Jesus,

2. **To Timothy,** *my* dearly beloved son: Grace, mercy, *and* peace, from God the Father and Christ Jesus our Lord.

3. I thank God, whom I serve from *my* forefathers with pure conscience, that without ceasing I have remembrance of thee in my prayers night and day;

4. Greatly desiring to see thee, being mindful of thy tears, that I may be filled with joy;

5. When I call to remembrance the unfeigned faith that is in thee, which dwelt first in thy grandmother Lois, and thy mother Eunice; and I am persuaded that in thee also.

6. Wherefore I put thee in remembrance that thou **stir up the gift of God,** which is **in thee by the putting on of my hands.**

7. **For God hath not given us the spirit of fear; but of power,** and of **love, and of a sound mind.**

8. **Be not** thou therefore **ashamed** of the testimony **of our Lord, nor of me** his prisoner: **but be thou partaker of the afflictions of the gospel according to the power of God;**

9. **Who hath saved us, and called us** with an holy calling, **not according to** our **works, but according to his own purpose and grace,** which was **given us in Christ** Jesus **before the world began,**

10. **But is now made manifest by** the appearing of our Saviour Jesus **Christ, who** hath **abolished death, and** hath **brought life** and immortality to light through the gospel:

11. Whereunto **I am appointed a preacher,** and an **apostle, and** a **teacher of the Gentiles.**

12. **For** the **which cause I** also **suffer** these things: **nevertheless I am not ashamed: for I know whom I have believed, and am persuaded that he is able to keep that which I have committed unto him against that day.**

13. **Hold fast the form of sound words,** which thou hast heard of me, in faith and love which is in Christ Jesus.

14. **That good thing which was committed unto thee keep by the Holy Ghost** which dwelleth in us.

15. **This thou knowest,** that **all** they which are **in Asia be turned away from me;** of whom are Phygellus and Hermogenes.

16. **The Lord give mercy unto the house of Onesiphorus; for he oft refreshed me,** and was not ashamed of my chain:

17. But, when he was in Rome, he sought me out very diligently, and found *me.*

18. The Lord grant unto him that he may find mercy of the Lord in that day: and in how many things he ministered unto me at Ephesus, thou knowest very well.

CHAPTER 2

1. **Thou therefore,** my son, **be strong in** the **grace** that is in Christ Jesus.

2. **And the things** that thou hast **heard of me among many witnesses, the same commit thou to faithful men,** who shall be able to teach others also.

3. Thou therefore

337

endure hardness, as a good soldier of Jesus Christ. 4. No man that warreth entangleth himself with the affairs of this life; that he may please him who hath chosen him to be a soldier. 5. And if a man also strive for masteries, yet is he not crowned, except he strive lawfully. 6. The husbandman that laboureth must be first partaker of the fruits. 7. Consider what I say; and the Lord give thee understanding in all things. 8. Remember that Jesus Christ of the seed of David was raised from the dead according to my gospel: 9. Wherein I suffer trouble, as an evildoer, even unto bonds; but the word of God is not bound. 10. Therefore I endure all things for the elect's sakes, that they may also obtain the salvation which is in Christ Jesus with eternal glory. 11. *It is* a faithful saying: For if we be dead with him, we shall also live with him: 12. If we suffer, we shall also reign with him: if we deny him, he also will deny us: 13. If we believe not, *yet* he abideth faithful: he cannot deny himself. 14. Of these things put *them* in remembrance, charging *them* before the Lord that they strive not about words to no profit, *but* to the subverting of the hearers. 15. Study to shew thyself approved unto God, a workman that needeth not to be ashamed, rightly dividing the word of truth. 16. But shun profane and vain babblings: for they will increase unto more ungodliness.

17. And their word will eat as doth a canker: of whom is Hymenaeus and Philetus; 18. Who concerning the truth have erred, saying that the resurrection is past already; and overthrow the faith of some. 19. Nevertheless the foundation of God standeth sure, having this seal, The Lord knoweth them that are his. And, Let every one that nameth the name of Christ depart from iniquity. 20. But in a great house there are not only vessels of gold and of silver, but also of wood and of earth; and some to honour, and some to dishonour. 21. If a man therefore purge himself from these, he shall be a vessel unto honour, sanctified, and meet for the master's use, *and* prepared unto every good work. 22. Flee also youthful lusts: but follow righteousness, faith, charity, peace, with them that call on the Lord out of a pure heart. 23. But foolish and unlearned questions avoid, knowing that they do gender strifes. 24. And the servant of the Lord must not strive; but be gentle unto all *men*, apt to teach, patient, 25. In meekness instructing those that oppose themselves; if God peradventure will give them repentance to the acknowledging of the truth; 26. And *that* they may recover themselves out of the snare of the devil, who are taken captive by him at his will.

CHAPTER 3

1. This know also, that in the

last days perilous times shall come.

2. **For men shall be lovers of their own selves, covetous, boasters, proud, blasphemers, disobedient to parents, unthankful, unholy,**

3. **Without natural affection, trucebreakers, false accusers, incontinent, fierce, despisers of those that are good,**

4. **Traitors,** heady, **highminded,** lovers of pleasures more than lovers of God;

5. **Having a form of godliness, but denying the power thereof: from such turn away.**

6. **For** of **this sort** are they which creep into houses, and **lead captive silly women laden with sins,** led away with divers lusts,

7. **Ever learning, and never able to come to** the knowledge of **the truth.**

8. Now as Jannes and Jambres withstood Moses, so do these also resist the truth: men of corrupt minds, reprobate concerning the faith.

9. **But they shall proceed no further: for their folly shall be manifest** unto all *men,* as theirs also was.

10. **But thou hast** fully **known my doctrine, manner of life, purpose, faith,** longsuffering, charity, patience,

11. **Persecutions,** afflictions, **which** came unto me at Antioch, at Iconium, at Lystra; what persecutions **I endured:** but out of *them* all the Lord delivered me.

12. **Yea, and all that will live godly in Christ** Jesus **shall suffer persecution.**

13. **But evil men** and seducers **shall wax worse** and worse,

deceiving, and being deceived.

14. **But continue** thou **in the things** which thou hast learned and hast been assured of, knowing of whom **thou hast learned** *them;*

15. And that **from a child thou hast known the holy scriptures, which** are able to **make thee wise** unto salvation through faith which is in Christ Jesus.

16. **All scripture is given by inspiration of God, and is profitable for doctrine, for reproof, for correction, for instruction in righteousness:**

17. **That the man of God may be perfect, throughly furnished unto all good works.**

CHAPTER 4

1. **I charge thee** therefore before God, and the Lord Jesus Christ, who shall judge the quick and the dead at his appearing and his kingdom;

2. **Preach the word; be instant in season; out of season; reprove, rebuke, exhort with all longsuffering** and doctrine.

3. **For the time will come when they will not endure** sound doctrine; but after their own lusts shall they heap to themselves teachers, having itching ears;

4. **And they shall turn away** *their* ears **from the truth,** and shall be turned unto fables.

5. **But watch thou in all things,** endure afflictions, do the work of an evangelist, make full proof of thy ministry.

6. **For I am now ready to be offered,** and the time of my departure is at hand.

7. **I have fought a good fight, I have finished my course,** I have kept the faith:

8. Henceforth there is laid

■ up for me a crown of
■ righteousness, which the
■ Lord, the righteous judge,
■ shall give me at that day:
■ and not to me only, but
■ unto all them also
■ that love his appearing.
9. Do thy diligence to
■ come shortly unto me:
10. For Demas hath forsaken
■ me, having loved this present world,
and is departed unto Thessalonica;
Crescens to Galatia, Titus unto
Dalmatia.
■ 11. Only Luke is with me.
■ Take Mark, and bring him
■ with thee: for he is profitable to me
for the ministry.
12. And Tychicus have I sent
to Ephesus.
13. The cloak that I left at Troas with
Carpus, when thou comest, bring
with thee, and the books, *but*
especially the parchments.
14. Alexander the coppersmith
did me much evil: the Lord
reward him according
to his works:
15. Of whom be thou ware also; for he

hath greatly withstood our words.
■ 16. At my first answer no
■ man stood with me, but all
men forsook me: *I pray God* that it
may not be laid to their charge.
■ 17. Notwithstanding the Lord
■ stood with me,
and strengthened me;
■ that by me the preaching might
be fully known, and *that* all
■ the Gentiles might hear:
and I was delivered out of the mouth
of the lion.
■ 18. And the Lord shall
■ deliver me from every evil
■ work, and will preserve *me* unto his
heavenly kingdom: to whom *be* glory
for ever and ever. Amen.
19. Salute Prisca and Aquila, and the
household of Onesiphorus.
20. Erastus abode at Corinth: but
Trophimus have I left at Miletum sick.
21. Do thy diligence to come before
winter. Eubulus greeteth thee, and
Pudens, and Linus, and Claudia, and
all the brethren.
22. The Lord Jesus Christ *be* with thy
spirit. Grace *be* with you.
■ Amen.

THE EPISTLE TO TITUS

BACKGROUND INFORMATION

Author: Paul, an Apostle.
Date Written: probably **between 62** and **65** A.D.

Number of:
Verses   46
Chapters   3
Total Words 921
Scan Words 466
Scan Words represent
50 % of Total Words

Theme: written **to instruct a** young **minister in the** proper **conduct and role of believers in the Church**

OUTLINE OF THE EPISTLE

I.   Paul Presents **the Qualifications of Elders and Bishops** and Warns Against False Teachers Chapter 1
II. Paul Describes **Domestic Regulations** and the Christian Life Chapter 2
III. Paul Tells Timothy the Bases of **Christian Ethics and** Advises Him on How to **Discipline** Factious Men Chapter 3

CHAPTER 1

1. **Paul,** a servant of God, and **an apostle** of Jesus Christ, according to the faith of God's elect, and the acknowledging of the truth which is after godliness;

2. **In hope of eternal life, which God,** that cannot lie, **promised before the world began;**

3. But hath in due times manifested his word through preaching, which is committed unto me according to the commandment of God our Saviour;

4. **To Titus, mine own son after the** common **faith:** Grace, mercy, *and* peace, from God the Father and the Lord Jesus Christ our Saviour.

5. **For this cause left I thee in Crete, that thou shouldest set in order the things that are wanting, and ordain elders** in every city, as I had appointed thee:

6. If any be blameless, the husband of one wife, having faithful children not accused of riot or unruly.

7. **For a bishop must be blameless,** as the steward of God; **not selfwilled, not soon angry, not given to wine,** no striker, not given to filthy lucre;

8. **But a lover of hospitality,** a lover **of good men, sober, just, holy, temperate;**

9. **Holding fast the faithful word** as he hath been taught, **that he may be able by sound doctrine both to exhort and to convince the gainsayers.**

10. **For there are many** unruly and **vain talkers and deceivers,** specially they of the circumcision:

11. **Whose mouths must be stopped, who subvert whole houses,** teaching things which they ought not, for filthy lucre's sake

12. **One of** themselves, *even* a prophet of **their own, said, The Cretians are alway liars, evil beasts,** slow bellies.

13. **This witness is true. Wherefore rebuke them sharply, that they may be sound in the faith;**

14. **Not giving heed to Jewish fables,** and commandments of men, that turn from the truth.

15. **Unto the pure all things are pure: but unto them that are defiled** and unbelieving **is nothing pure;** but even their mind and conscience is defiled.

16. **They profess that they know God; but in works they deny him,** being abominable, and disobedient, and unto every good work reprobate.

CHAPTER 2

1. **But speak thou the things which become sound doctrine:**

2. **That the aged men be sober, grave, temperate, sound in faith, in charity, in patience.**

3. **The aged women likewise,** that *they be* in behaviour as becometh holiness, not false accusers, not given to much wine, teachers of good things;

4. **That they may teach the young women to be sober, to love their husbands, to love their children,**

5. **To be discreet, chaste, keepers at home, good, obedient to their** own **husbands,** that the word of God be not blasphemed.

6. **Young men like wise** exhort to be **sober minded.**

7. **In all things she wing** thyself a pattern of **good works: in doctrine**

shewing uncorruptness, gravity, sincerity,

8. **Sound speech, that cannot be condemned;** that he that is of the contrary part may be ashamed, having no evil thing to say of you.

9. **Exhort servants to be obedient** unto their own masters, *and* to please *them* well in all *things;* not answering again;

10. **Not purloining, but shewing** all good **fidelity;** that they may adorn the doctrine of God our Saviour in all things.

11. **For the grace of God that bringeth salvation hath appeared to all men,**

12. **Teaching us that, denying ungodliness and** worldly **lusts, we should live soberly,** righteously, **and godly, in this** present **world;**

13. **Looking for** that blessed hope, and **the glorious appearing of** the great God and **our Saviour** Jesus Christ;

14. **Who gave himself** for us, **that he might redeem us from all iniquity, and purify** unto himself **a peculiar people, zealous of good works.**

15. **These things speak,** and exhort, and rebuke **with all authority. Let no man despise thee.**

CHAPTER 3

1. **Put them in mind to be subject to principalities and** powers, **to obey magistrates,** to be ready to every good work,

2. **To speak evil of no man,** to be no brawlers, *but* gentle, shewing all meekness unto all men.

3. **For we ourselves also were sometimes foolish,** disobedient, deceived, **serving divers lusts** and pleasures, living in malice and envy, hateful, **and hating one another.**

4. **But** after that **the** kindness and **love of God our Saviour** toward man **appeared,**

5. **Not by works of righteousness which we have done, but according to his mercy he saved us, by the washing of regeneration, and renewing of the Holy Ghost;**

6. Which he shed on us abundantly through Jesus Christ our Saviour;

7. **That being justified by his grace, we should be** made **heirs** according to the hope **of eternal life.**

8. **This is a faithful saying,** and these things I will that thou affirm constantly, **that they which have believed in God might be careful to maintain good works.** These things are good and profitable unto men.

9. **But avoid foolish questions,** and **genealogies,** and **contentions, and strivings about the law;** for they are unprofitable and vain.

10. **A man that is an heretic after the first and second admonition reject;**

11. Knowing that he that is such is subverted, and sinneth, being condemned of himself.

12. When I shall send Artemas unto thee, or Tychicus, be diligent to come unto me to Nicopolis: for I have determined there to winter.

13. Bring Zenas the lawyer and Apollos on their journey diligently, that nothing be wanting unto them.

14. And let ours also learn to maintain good works for necessary uses, that they be not unfruitful.

■ 15. **All that are with me**
■ **salute thee.** Greet them that love
us in the faith. Grace *be* with you all.
■ **Amen.**

THE EPISTLE TO PHILEMON

BACKGROUND INFORMATION

Author: Paul, an Apostle.
Date Written: probably **between 60** and **65** A.D.

Number of:
Verses   25
Chapters   1
Total Words 445
Scan Words 214
Scan Words represent
48 % of Total Words

Theme: written to show that **relationships** between people **take on a new dimension when** they become **Christians**

OUTLINE OF THE EPISTLE

I. **Paul's Greeting** to Philemon
    Verses 1 - 3
II. **Paul's** Offer of **Thanksgiving**
    Verses 4 - 7
III. **Paul's Appeal for Onesimus,** a Slave
    Verses 8 - 21
IV. **Paul's Conclusion**
    Verses 22 - 25

CHAPTER 1

1. **Paul, a prisoner of** Jesus **Christ,** and Timothy *our* brother, **unto Philemon** our dearly beloved, and fellow-labourer,

2. And to *our* beloved Apphia, and Archippus our fellow-soldier, and to the church in thy house:

3. Grace to you, and peace, from God our Father and the Lord Jesus Christ.

4. **I thank my God,** making mention of thee always in my prayers,

5. **Hearing of thy love and faith, which thou hast toward the Lord Jesus, and toward all saints;**

6. That the communication of thy faith may become effectual by the acknowledging of every good thing which is in you in Christ Jesus.

7. **For we have great joy** and consolation in thy love, **because** the bowels of **the saints are refreshed by thee,** brother.

8. **Wherefore, though I might be** much **bold in Christ** to enjoin thee that which is convenient,

9. **Yet for love's sake I rather beseech thee, being** such an one as **Paul the aged, and** now also **a prisoner of Jesus Christ.**

10. **I beseech thee for my son Onesimus, whom I have begotten in my bonds:**

11. **Which in time past was to thee unprofitable, but now profitable to thee and to me:**

12. **Whom I have sent again: thou therefore receive him,** that is, mine own bowels:

13. **Whom I would have** retained **with me,** that in thy stead he might have ministered unto me in the bonds of the gospel:

14. **But without thy mind would I do nothing;** that thy benefit should not be as it were of necessity, but willingly.

15. **For perhaps he** therefore **departed** for a season, **that thou shouldest receive him for ever;**

16. **Not now as a servant, but** above a servant, **a brother beloved,** specially to me, but how much more unto thee, both in the flesh, and in the Lord?

17. **If thou count me** therefore **a partner, receive him as myself.**

18. **If he hath wronged thee,** or oweth *thee* aught, **put that on mine account;**

19. **I Paul have written it** with mine own hand, **I will repay it:** albeit I do not say to thee how thou owest unto me even thine own self besides.

20. **Yea, brother, let me have joy of thee in the Lord:** refresh my bowels in the Lord.

21. **Having confidence in thy obedience I wrote** unto thee, **knowing that thou wilt** also **do more than I say.**

22. But withal **prepare me also a lodging: for I trust that through your prayers I shall be given unto you.**

23. There salute thee Epaphras, my fellow-prisoner in Christ Jesus;

24. Marcus, Aristarchus, Demas, Lucas, my fellow-labourers.

25. The grace of our Lord Jesus Christ *be* with your spirit. **Amen.**

THE EPISTLE
TO THE HEBREWS

BACKGROUND
INFORMATION

Author: Unknown
Date Written: probably
between 65 and **85** A.D.

Number of:
Versus   303
Chapters   13
Total Words 6,913
Scan Words 3,493
Scan Words represent
50 % of Total Words

Theme: written to
encourage believers,
especially Jewish believers,
to endure persecution and
remain faithful to the Lord,
showing the superiority
of Jesus Christ

OUTLINE OF
THE EPISTLE

I. **Christ as Superior**
   to Angels
   Chapters 1 - 2
II. **Christ as Superior to**
    Moses and Joshua
    Chapters 3 - 4
III. **Christ's Superiority**
     as the High Priest
     Chapters 5 - 10:18
IV. **Christ and**
    the Superiority of
    the New Covenant
    Chapters 10:19 - 13

CHAPTER 1

■ 1. **God,** who at sundry times and in divers manners spake in time past unto the fathers by the prophets,

■ 2. **Hath in these last days**
■ **spoken** unto us
■ **by his Son, whom he hath**
■ **appointed heir of all things,**
■ **by whom also he made**
■ **the worlds;**
■ 3. **Who being**
the brightness of *his* glory, and
■ **the** express
■ **image of his person,**
■ **and upholding all things**
■ **by the word of his power,**
■ **when he had** by himself
■ **purged our sins, sat down**
■ **on the right hand of the**
■ **Majesty** on high;
■ 4. **Being made** so much
■ **better than** the
■ **angels,** as
■ **he hath** by inheritance
■ **obtained a more**
■ **excellent name** than they.
■ 5. **For unto which of the**
■ **angels said he** at any time,
■ **Thou art my Son, this day**
■ **have I begotten thee?**
And again, I will be to him a Father, and he shall be to me a Son?
■ 6. **And again,** when he bringeth in the first begotten into the world,
■ **he saith,** And
■ **let all the angels** of God
■ **worship him.**
■ 7. **And of the angels he**
■ **saith, Who maketh his**
■ **angels spirits,**
and his ministers a flame of fire.
■ 8. **But unto the Son he saith,**
■ **Thy throne, O God,**
■ **is for ever**
and ever: a sceptre of righteousness *is* the sceptre of thy kingdom.
9. Thou hast loved righteousness, and hated iniquity;
therefore God, *even* thy God, hath anointed thee with the oil of gladness above thy fellows.
■ 10. **And, Thou,**
Lord, in the beginning

■ **hast laid the foundation**
■ **of the earth; and the**
■ **heavens are** the works
■ **of thine hands:**
■ 11. **They shall perish;**
but thou remainest; and they all shall wax old as doth a garment;
12. And as a vesture shalt thou fold them up, and they shall be changed:
■ **but thou art the same, and**
■ **thy years shall not fail.**
■ 13. **But to which of the**
■ **angels said he** at any time,
■ **Sit on my right hand,**
■ **until I make thine enemies**
■ **thy footstool?**
14. Are they not all ministering spirits, sent forth to minister for them who shall be heirs of salvation?

CHAPTER 2

■ 1. **Therefore** we ought to
■ **give** the more
■ **earnest heed to the**
■ **things** which we have
■ **heard, lest** at any time
■ **we should let them slip.**
■ 2. **For if the word spoken by**
■ **angels was stedfast, and**
■ **every transgression**
and disobedience
■ **received a just**
■ **recompence** of reward;
■ 3. **How shall we escape,**
■ **if we neglect** so great
■ **salvation;** which
at the first began to be
■ **spoken by the Lord, and**
was confirmed unto us by
■ **them that heard him;**
■ 4. **God also bearing**
■ **them witness,** both
■ **with signs** and
■ **wonders,** and with divers
■ **miracles, and gifts of the**
■ **Holy Ghost,**
according to his own will?
5. For unto the angels hath he not put in subjection the world to come, whereof we speak.
■ 6. **But one** in a certain place
■ **testified, saying,**
■ **What is man,**

348

that thou art
mindful of him?
or the son of man,
that thou visitest him?
7. **Thou madest him a little
lower than the angels;** thou
crownedst him with glory and honour,
and didst
**set him over the works
of thy hands:**
8. **Thou hast put all things**
in subjection
under his feet.
For in that he put all
in subjection under him, he left
nothing *that is* not put under him.
But now
we see not yet all things
put under him.
9. **But we see Jesus, who
was made a little lower
than** the
**angels for the suffering
of death,**
crowned with glory and honour;
that he by the
grace of God
**should taste death
for every man.**
10. **For it became him,**
for whom *are* all things, and by whom
are all things, in bringing many sons
unto glory,
to make the captain of their
**salvation perfect
through sufferings.**
11. **For both he
that sanctifieth
and they** who are
sanctified are all of
**one: for which cause
he is not ashamed to
call them brethren,**
12. Saying, I will declare thy
name unto my brethren,
in the midst of the church will
I sing praise unto thee.
13. And again, I will put my trust in
him. And again, Behold I and the
children which God hath given me.
14. **Forasmuch then as the
children are** partakers of
flesh and blood, he also

himself likewise
**took part of the same;
that through death he
might destroy** him that had
the power of death, that is,
the devil;
15. **And deliver them who**
through fear of death
were all their lifetime
subject to bondage.
16. For verily he took not on *him
the nature of* angels; but he took on
him the seed of Abraham.
17. Wherefore in all things
**it behoved him to be made
like unto his brethren, that
he might be a**
merciful and faithful
high priest
in things *pertaining* to God,
**to make reconciliation for
the sins of the people.**
18. For in that he himself
hath suffered being tempted, he is
able to succour them that
are tempted.

CHAPTER 3

1. **Wherefore,** holy brethren,
partakers of the heavenly calling,
consider the Apostle and High
Priest of our profession,
Christ Jesus;
2. Who was faithful to him that
appointed him, as also
Moses *was faithful* in all his house.
3. **For this man was** counted
**worthy of more glory than
Moses, inasmuch as
he who hath builded the
house hath more honour
than the house.**
4. For every house is builded
by some *man;* but
**he that built all
things is God.**
5. **And Moses verily
was faithful** in all his house,
as a servant,
for a testimony of those things which
were to be spoken after;
6. **But Christ as a son**
over his own house;

■ whose house are we, if we
■ hold fast the confidence and the
rejoicing of the hope firm
■ unto the end.
■ 7. Wherefore (as the Holy
■ Ghost saith, To day if ye will
■ hear his voice,
■ 8. Harden not your hearts,
as in the provocation, in the day of
temptation in the wilderness:
9. When your fathers tempted me,
proved me, and saw
my works forty years.
10. Wherefore I was grieved with that
generation, and said, They do alway
err in *their* heart; and they
have not known my ways.
11. So I sware in my wrath, They
shall not enter into my rest.)
■ 12. Take heed, brethren,
■ lest there be
in any of you an evil heart of
■ unbelief, in departing
from the living God.
■ 13. But exhort one another
daily, while it is called To day;
■ lest any of you
■ be hardened through the
■ deceitfulness of sin.
■ 14. For we are made
■ partakers of Christ, if we
■ hold the beginning of
our confidence
■ stedfast unto the end;
15. While it is said,
■ To day if ye will
■ hear his voice, harden not
■ your hearts,
as in the provocation.
■ 16. For some, when they
■ had heard, did provoke:
■ howbeit not all that
■ came out of Egypt by Moses.
17. But with whom was he grieved
forty years? *was it* not
with them that had sinned,
■ whose carcases fell
■ in the wilderness?
18. And to whom sware he that they
should not enter into his rest, but
to them that believed not?
19. So we see that
■ they could not enter in

■ because of unbelief.

CHAPTER 4

■ 1. Let us therefore fear, lest,
a promise being left *us* of
■ entering into his rest, any
of you should seem to
■ come short of it.
■ 2. For unto us was the gospel
preached, as well as unto them: but
■ the word preached
■ did not profit them, not
■ being mixed with faith
in them that heard *it*.
■ 3. For we which have
■ believed do enter into rest,
as he said, As I have sworn in my
wrath, if they shall enter into my rest:
■ although the works were
■ finished from the foundation
■ of the world.
■ 4. For he spake in a certain place of
the seventh *day* on this wise, And
■ God did rest the seventh
■ day from all his works.
5. And in this *place* again, If
they shall enter into my rest.
■ 6. Seeing therefore it remaineth
■ that some
must enter therein, and they
■ to whom it was first
■ preached entered not in
■ because of unbelief:
■ 7. Again, he limiteth a certain day,
■ saying in David, To day, after
so long a time; as it is said,
■ To day if ye will hear
■ his voice, harden
■ not your hearts.
■ 8. For if Jesus had given
■ them rest, then would he
■ not afterward have spoken
■ of another day.
■ 9. There remaineth therefore
■ a rest to the people of God.
10. For he that is entered into his rest,
he also hath ceased from his own
works, as God *did* from his.
■ 11. Let us labour therefore
■ to enter into that rest,
lest any man fall after the same
example of unbelief.
■ 12. For the word of God is

quick, and powerful, and
sharper than any two edged
sword, piercing
even to the dividing asunder
of soul and spirit,
and of the joints and marrow,
and is a discerner of the
thoughts and intents
of the heart.
13. Neither is there any creature
that is not manifest in his sight: but
all things are naked and
opened unto the eyes of
him with whom we have to do.
14. Seeing then that we
have a great high priest,
that is passed into the heavens,
Jesus the Son of God,
let us hold fast
our profession.
15. For we have not
an high priest which
cannot be touched
with the feeling of
our infirmities; but
was in all points
tempted like
as we are, yet without sin.
16. Let us therefore come
boldly unto the throne of
grace, that we may obtain
mercy, and find grace to
help in time of need.

CHAPTER 5

1. For every high priest
taken from among men
is ordained
for men in things *pertaining* to God,
that he may offer
both gifts and
sacrifices for sins:
2. Who can have
compassion
on the ignorant, and
on them that are out of the
way; for that
he himself
also is compassed
with infirmity.
3. And by reason hereof he ought, as
for the people, so also for himself,
to offer for sins.

4. And no man taketh
this honour unto himself,
but he that is called of God,
as was Aaron.
5. So also Christ glorified not
himself to be made an
high priest; but he that said
unto him, Thou art my Son,
to day have I begotten thee.
6. As he saith also in another *place*,
Thou art a priest for ever
after the order
of Melchisedec.
7. Who in the days of
his flesh, when he had
offered up prayers
and supplications
with strong crying and
tears unto him that
was able to save
him from death,
and was heard in that he feared;
8. Though he were
a Son, yet learned he
obedience by the
things which he suffered;
9. And being made perfect,
he became the author of
eternal salvation
unto all them that obey him;
10. Called of God an high priest after
the order of Melchisedec.
11. Of whom we have many
things to say, and hard to
be uttered, seeing ye are
dull of hearing.
12. For when for the time
ye ought to be teachers,
ye have need that one
teach you again which *be*
the first principles of the
oracles of God; and
are become such as
have need of milk,
and not of
strong meat.
13. For every one that
useth milk *is* unskilful in the word
of righteousness: for he
is a babe.
14. But strong meat
belongeth to them that are
of full age, even those who

by reason of use have
their senses exercised to
■ **discern both good**
■ **and evil.**

CHAPTER 6

■ 1. **Therefore** leaving the principles
of the doctrine of Christ,
■ **let us go on unto**
■ **perfection; not laying**
■ **again the foundation of**
■ **repentance** from dead works,
■ **and of faith** toward God,
■ 2. **Of** the doctrine of
■ **baptisms, and of laying**
■ **on of hands, and of**
■ **resurrection** of the dead,
■ **and of** eternal
■ **judgment**
3. And this will we do, if God permit.
■ 4. **For it is impossible for**
■ **those who were once**
■ **enlightened, and have**
■ **tasted of the heavenly gift,**
■ **and were made partakers**
■ **of the Holy Ghost,**
■ 5. **And have tasted the**
■ **good word** of God,
■ **and the powers** of the world
■ **to come,**
■ 6. **If they shall fall away, to**
■ **renew them** again
■ **unto repentance; seeing**
■ **they crucify** to themselves
■ **the Son of God afresh,**
and put *him* to an open shame.
7. For the earth which drinketh in the
rain that cometh oft upon it, and
bringeth forth herbs meet for them by
whom it is dressed, receiveth
blessing from God:
8. But that which beareth thorns and
briers *is* rejected, and *is* nigh unto
cursing; whose end *is* to be burned.
■ 9. **But, beloved, we are**
■ **persuaded better things**
■ **of you,**
and things that accompany salvation,
though we thus speak.
■ 10. **For God is not**
■ **unrighteous to forget**
■ **your** work and
■ **labour of love, which ye**

■ **have shewed** toward his name,
■ **in that ye have ministered**
■ **to the saints,** and do minister.
■ 11. **And** we desire that
every one of you do
■ **shew the same diligence**
to the full assurance of hope
■ **unto the end:**
12. That ye
■ **be not slothful, but**
followers of them who
■ **through faith and patience**
■ **inherit the promises.**
■ 13. **For when God made**
■ **promise to Abraham,** because
he could
swear by no greater,
■ **he sware by himself,**
■ 14. **Saying,** Surely blessing
■ **I will bless thee,**
and multiplying I will multiply thee.
■ 15. **And so, after he had**
■ **patiently endured,**
■ **he obtained** the promise.
16. For men verily swear by the
greater: and an oath for confirmation
is to them an end of all strife.
■ 17. **Wherein God,**
willing more abundantly
■ **to shew** unto the heirs of promise
■ **the immutability of his**
■ **counsel, confirmed it**
■ **by an oath:**
18. That by two immutable things,
■ **in which it was impossible**
■ **for God to lie,** we might have a
strong consolation, who have
fled for refuge to lay hold upon the
hope set before us:
■ 19. **Which hope we have**
■ **as an anchor** of the soul,
both sure and stedfast, and
■ **which entereth into** that within
■ **the veil;**
■ 20. **Whither the forerunner is**
for us entered, *even*
■ **Jesus, made an high**
■ **priest for ever after the**
■ **order of Melchisedec.**

CHAPTER 7

■ 1. **For this Melchisedec,**
king of Salem, priest of the

352

most high God, who
■ **met Abraham** returning
from the slaughter of the kings,
■ **and blessed him;**
■ 2. **To whom also Abraham**
■ **gave a tenth part of all; first**
■ **being by interpretation King**
■ **of righteousness,**
and after that also King of Salem,
which is, King of peace;
■ 3. **Without father,** without
mother, without descent,
■ **having neither**
■ **beginning** of days,
■ **nor end of life; but made**
■ **like unto the Son of God;**
■ **abideth a**
■ **priest continually.**
■ 4. **Now consider how great**
■ **this man was, unto whom**
even the patriarch
■ **Abraham gave**
■ **the tenth** of the spoils.
5. And verily they that are of
■ **the sons of Levi,** who receive
the office of the priesthood,
■ **have a commandment to**
■ **take tithes** of the people
according to the law, that is,
■ **of their brethren,** though they
come out of the loins of Abraham:
■ 6. **But he whose descent is**
■ **not counted from them**
■ **received tithes of**
■ **Abraham,** and blessed
him that had the promises.
■ 7. **And** without all contradiction
■ **the less is blessed**
■ **of the better.**
8. And here men that die receive
tithes; but there he *receiveth them*, of
whom it is witnessed that he liveth.
9. And as I may so say,
■ **Levi also, who receiveth**
■ **tithes, payed tithes**
■ **in Abraham.**
10. For he was yet in the loins of his
father, when Melchisedec met him.
■ 11. **If therefore**
■ **perfection were by the**
■ **Levitical priesthood,** (for under
it the people received the law,)
■ **what** further

■ **need was there that**
■ **another priest should rise**
■ **after the order of**
■ **Melchisedec,** and not be
called after the order of Aaron?
12. For the priesthood being
changed, there is made of necessity a
change also of the law.
■ 13. **For he of whom these**
■ **things are spoken**
■ **pertaineth to another**
■ **tribe,** of which no man gave
attendance at the altar.
■ 14. **For** *it is* evident that
■ **our Lord sprang out of**
■ **Juda; of which** tribe
■ **Moses spake nothing**
■ **concerning priesthood.**
■ 15. **And** it is yet
far more evident: for that
■ **after the similitude of**
■ **Melchisedec** there
■ **ariseth another priest,**
■ 16. **Who is made, not**
after the law
■ **of a carnal commandment,**
■ **but after the power of**
■ **an endless life.**
■ 17. **For he testifieth, Thou art**
■ **a priest for ever after the**
■ **order of Melchisedec.**
18. For there is verily a disannulling of
the commandment going before
for the weakness and
unprofitableness thereof.
■ 19. **For the law made**
■ **nothing perfect, but**
the bringing in of
■ **a better hope did; by**
■ **the which we draw nigh**
■ **unto God.**
■ 20. **And** inasmuch as
■ **not without an oath**
■ **he was made priest:**
21. (For those priests were made
without an oath; but this with an oath
by him that said unto him,
■ **The Lord sware**
and will not repent,
■ **Thou art a priest for**
■ **ever after the order**
■ **of Melchisedec:)**
22. By so much was

■ **Jesus made a surety of**
■ **a better testament.**
23. And they truly
were many priests, because they
were not suffered to continue
by reason of death:
24. But this *man*,
■ **because he** continueth ever,
■ **hath an unchangeable**
■ **priesthood.**
■ 25. **Wherefore he is able**
■ **also to save them**
to the uttermost
■ **that come unto God by**
■ **him, seeing he ever liveth**
■ **to make intercession** for them.
■ 26. **For such an high priest**
■ **became us, who is holy,**
harmless, undefiled,
■ **separate from sinners,**
■ **and** made
■ **higher than the heavens;**
■ 27. **Who needeth not daily,**
as those high priests,
■ **to offer up sacrifice,** first
■ **for his own sins, and** then for
■ **the people's: for this he did**
■ **once, when he offered**
■ **up himself.**
28. For the law maketh men high
priests which have infirmity; but the
word of the oath, which was since the
law, *maketh* the Son, who is
consecrated for evermore.

CHAPTER 8

■ 1. **Now** of the things which we have
spoken *this is* the sum:
■ **We have** such
■ **an high priest,** who is
■ **set on the right hand of the**
■ **throne of the Majesty**
in the heavens;
■ 2. **A minister of**
the sanctuary, and of
■ **the true tabernacle,** which
■ **the Lord pitched,**
■ **and not man.**
3. For every high priest is ordained to
offer gifts and sacrifices: wherefore *it
is* of necessity that this man have
somewhat also to offer.
■ 4. **For if he were on earth, he**

■ **should not be a priest,**
■ **seeing that there are**
■ **priests** that offer gifts
■ **according to the law:**
■ 5. **Who serve unto the**
■ **example** and shadow
■ **of heavenly things, as**
■ **Moses was admonished**
■ **of God** when he was about
■ **to** make the tabernacle:
for, See, saith he, *that* thou
■ **make all things**
■ **according to the**
■ **pattern shewed** to thee
■ **in the mount.**
■ 6. **But now hath he obtained**
■ **a more excellent ministry,**
by how much
■ **also he is the mediator of**
■ **a better covenant,** which was
established upon better promises.
■ 7. **For if that first covenant**
■ **had been faultless, then**
■ **should no place have been**
■ **sought for the second.**
■ 8. **For** finding fault with them,
■ **he saith,** Behold,
■ **the days come,** saith the Lord,
■ **when I will make a new**
■ **covenant with** the house of
■ **Israel and** with the house of
■ **Judah:**
9. Not according to the covenant that
I made with their fathers in the day
when I took them by the hand to lead
them out of the land of Egypt;
because they continued not in my
covenant, and I regarded them not,
saith the Lord.
■ 10. **For this is the covenant**
■ **that I will make**
with the house of Israel after those
days, saith the Lord;
■ **I will put my laws into their**
■ **mind, and write them in**
■ **their hearts: and I will be to**
■ **them a God, and they shall**
■ **be to me a people:**
11. And they shall not teach every
man his neighbour, and every man his
brother, saying, Know the Lord: for all
shall know me, from the
least to the greatest.

■ 12. **For I will be merciful** to their unrighteousness, **and their sins and** their **iniquities will I remember no more.**

13. In that he saith, A new *covenant*, he hath made the first old. Now that which decayeth and waxeth old *is* ready to vanish away.

CHAPTER 9

■ 1. **Then verily the first covenant had also ordinances** of divine service, **and a worldly sanctuary.** 2. **For there was a tabernacle made;** the first, wherein *was* the candlestick, and the table, and the shewbread; **which is called the sanctuary.** 3. **And after the second veil, the** tabernacle which is called the **Holiest of all;** 4. **Which had** the golden censer, and **the ark of the covenant** overlaid round about with gold, wherein *was* the golden pot that had manna, **and Aaron's rod** that budded, **and** the **tables of the covenant;** 5. **And over it the cherubims** of glory **shadowing the mercyseat;** of which we cannot now speak particularly. 6. **Now** when these things were thus ordained, **the priests went** always **into the first tabernacle, accomplishing the service of God.** 7. **But into the second went the high priest alone once every year, not without blood,** which he **offered for himself, and for the errors of the people:**

■ 8. **The Holy Ghost this signifying, that the way into the holiest** of all **was not yet** made **manifest, while** as **the first tabernacle was** yet **standing:** 9. Which *was* a figure for the time then present, in which were offered both gifts and sacrifices, that could not make him that did the service perfect, as pertaining to the conscience; 10. *Which stood* only in meats and drinks, and divers washings, and carnal ordinances, imposed *on them* until the time of reformation. 11. **But Christ being come an high priest** of good things to come, **by a** greater and more **perfect tabernacle, not made with hands,** that is to say, not of this building; 12. **Neither by the blood of goats and calves, but by his own blood he entered** in **once** into **the holy place, having obtained eternal redemption for us.** 13. **For if the blood of bulls and of goats,** and the ashes of an heifer sprinkling the unclean, **sanctifieth** to the purifying of **the flesh:** 14. **How much more shall the blood of Christ, who** through the eternal Spirit **offered himself without spot to God, purge your conscience** from dead works **to serve** the living **God?** 15. **And** for this cause **he is the mediator of the new testament,** that by means of death, for the redemption of the transgressions *that were* under the first testament, they which are called might receive the promise of eternal inheritance. 16. **For where a testament is,**

- there must also of necessity
- be the death of the testator.
- 17. For a testament is of
- force after men are dead:
  otherwise it is of no strength at all
  while the testator liveth.
- 18. Whereupon neither the
- first testament was
- dedicated without blood.
- 19. For when Moses had
- spoken every precept to all the
  people according to the law,
- he took the blood of calves
- and of goats, with water, and
  scarlet wool, and hyssop, and
  sprinkled both the book,
  and all the people,
- 20. Saying, This is the blood
- of the testament which God
- hath enjoined unto you.
- 21. Moreover he sprinkled
  with blood
- both the tabernacle,
- and all the vessels
- of the ministry.
- 22. And almost
- all things are by the law
- purged with blood;
  and without shedding of
  blood is no remission.
  23. *It was* therefore necessary that
  the patterns of things in the heavens
  should be purified with these; but the
  heavenly things themselves with
  better sacrifices than these.
- 24. For Christ is not
- entered into the holy places
  made with hands, *which are* the
  figures of the true; but into heaven
  itself, now to appear in
- the presence of God for us:
- 25. Nor yet that he should
  offer himself often,
- as the high priest entereth
- into the holy place every
- year with blood of others;
  26. For then must he often have
  suffered since the foundation
  of the world:
- but now
- once in the end of the world hath
- he appeared to put away
- sin by the sacrifice

- of himself.
- 27. And as it is appointed
- unto men once to die, but
- after this the judgment:
- 28. So Christ was once
- offered to bear the sins of
- many; and unto them
- that look for him shall he
- appear the second time
- without sin unto salvation.

CHAPTER 10

- 1. For the law having a shadow
  of good things to come, *and* not the
  very image of the things,
- can never with those
- sacrifices which they
- offered year by
- year continually
- make the comers
- thereunto perfect.
- 2. For then would they not
- have ceased to be offered?
- because that
  the worshippers once
- purged should have had no
- more conscience
- of sins.
- 3. But in those sacrifices
- there is a remembrance
  again *made*
- of sins every year.
- 4. For it is not possible that
- the blood of bulls and of
- goats should take
- away sins.
- 5. Wherefore when he
- cometh into the world,
- he saith, Sacrifice and
- offering thou wouldest not,
- but a body hast thou
- prepared me:
  6. In burnt offerings and *sacrifices* for
  sin thou hast had no pleasure.
  7. Then said I, Lo, I come (in the
  volume of the book it is written of
  me,) to do thy will, O God.
  8. Above when he said, Sacrifice and
  offering and burnt offerings and
  offering for sin thou wouldest not,
  neither hadst pleasure *therein;* which
  are offered by the law;
- 9. Then said he, Lo, I come

to do thy will, O God.

He taketh away the first, that he may establish the second.

10. **By the which will we are sanctified through the offering of the body of Jesus Christ once for all.**

11. And every priest standeth daily ministering and offering oftentimes the same sacrifices, which can never take away sins:

12. **But this man, after he had offered one sacrifice for sins** for ever, **sat down on the right hand of God;**

13. From henceforth expecting **till his enemies be made his footstool.**

14. **For by one offering he hath perfected** for ever **them that are sanctified.**

15. **Whereof the Holy Ghost** also **is a witness** to us: **for** after that **he had said before,**

16. **This is the covenant that I will make** with them after those days, saith the Lord, **I will put my laws into their hearts,** and in their minds will I write them;

17. **And their sins** and iniquities **will I remember no more.**

18. **Now where remission** of these **is, there is no more offering for sin.**

19. **Having therefore,** brethren, **boldness to enter into the holiest by the blood of Jesus,**

20. **By a new and living way,** which he hath consecrated for us, **through the veil, that is** to say, **his flesh;**

21. **And having an high priest** over the house of God;

22. **Let us draw near with a true heart** in full assurance **of faith,** having our hearts sprinkled

from an evil conscience, and our bodies washed with pure water.

23. **Let us hold fast the profession of our faith** without wavering;

(for he *is* faithful that promised;)

24. **And let us consider one another** to provoke unto love and to good works:

25. **Not forsaking the assembling of ourselves together,** as the manner of some *is;* but exhorting *one another:* and so much the more, as ye see the day approaching.

26. **For if we sin wilfully after** that **we have received the knowledge of the truth, there remaineth no more sacrifice for sins,**

27. **But a certain** fearful looking for of **judgment and fiery indignation,** which shall devour the adversaries.

28. **He that despised Moses' law died** without mercy **under two or three witnesses:**

29. **Of how much sorer punishment,** suppose ye, **shall he be** thought **worthy, who hath trodden under foot the Son** of God, **and hath counted the blood** of the covenant, wherewith he was sanctified, **an unholy thing, and hath done despite unto the Spirit of grace?**

30. **For we know him that** hath **said,** Vengeance *belongeth* unto me, **I will recompense,** saith the Lord. And again, The Lord shall judge his people.

31. **It is a fearful thing to fall into the hands of the living God.**

32. But call to remembrance the former days, in which, after ye were

illuminated, ye endured a great fight of afflictions;

33. Partly, whilst ye were made a gazingstock both by reproaches and afflictions; and partly, whilst ye became companions of them that were so used.

34. For ye had compassion of me in my bonds, and took joyfully the spoiling of your goods, knowing in yourselves that ye have in heaven a better and an enduring substance.

35. **Cast not away therefore your confidence,** which hath great recompence of reward.

36. **For** ye have need of patience, that, **after ye have done the will of God, ye might receive the promise.**

37. For yet a little while, and he that shall come will come, and will not tarry.

38. **Now the just shall live by faith: but if any man draw back, my soul shall have no pleasure** in him.

39. **But we are not of them** who draw back unto perdition; **but of them that believe to the saving of the soul.**

CHAPTER 11

1. **Now faith is the substance of things hoped for, the evidence of things not seen.**

2. For by it the elders obtained a good report.

3. **Through faith** we understand that **the worlds were framed by the word of God, so that things** which are **seen were not made of things which do appear.**

4. **By faith Abel offered** unto God **a more excellent sacrifice** than Cain, by which he obtained witness that he was righteous, God testifying of his gifts: and by it he being dead yet speaketh.

5. **By faith Enoch was translated** that he should not see death; and was not found, because God had translated him: **for before his translation** he had this testimony, that **he pleased God.**

6. **But without faith it is impossible to please** *him:* for he that cometh to **God** must believe that he is, and *that* he is a rewarder of them that diligently seek him.

7. **By faith Noah,** being warned of God of things not seen as yet, moved with fear, **prepared an ark to the saving of his house;** by the which he condemned the world, **and became heir of the righteousness** which is **by faith.**

8. **By faith Abraham,** when he was called to go out into a place which he should after receive for an inheritance, obeyed; and he **went out, not knowing whither he went.**

9. **By faith he sojourned in the land of promise,** as *in* a strange country, dwelling in tabernacles **with Isaac and Jacob, the heirs with him** of the same promise:

10. **For he looked for a city which hath foundations, whose builder** and maker **is God.**

11. **Through faith also Sara** herself **received strength to conceive** seed, and was delivered of a child **when she was past age,** because she judged him faithful who had promised.

12. **Therefore sprang** there even **of one,** and him **as good as dead, so many as the stars** of the sky in multitude,

- **and** as
- **the sand** which is
- **by the sea** shore innumerable.
- **13. These all died in faith,**
- **not having received the**
- **promises, but having seen**
- **them afar off,** and were
persuaded of *them*, and embraced *them*,
- **and confessed that they**
- **were strangers** and pilgrims on the earth.
- **14. For** they that say such things declare plainly that
- **they seek a country.**
15. And truly, if they had been mindful of that *country* from whence they came out, they might have had opportunity to have returned.
16. But now they desire a better *country*,
- **that is,** an
- **heavenly: wherefore God is**
- **not ashamed to be** called
- **their God: for he hath**
- **prepared for them a city.**
- 17. **By faith Abraham,** when he was tried,
- **offered up Isaac;** and he that had received the promises offered up his only begotten *son*,
- **18. Of whom it was said, That**
- **in Isaac shall thy**
- **seed be called:**
- **19. Accounting that God**
- **was able to raise him** up, even
- **from the dead;** from whence also he received him in a figure.
- **20. By faith Isaac blessed**
- **Jacob** and Esau concerning things to come.
- **21. By faith Jacob,** when he was a-dying,
- **blessed** both
- **the sons of Joseph;** and worshipped, *leaning* upon the top of his staff.
- **22. By faith Joseph,** when he died,
- **made mention of** the departing of the children of

- **Israel;** and gave commandment concerning his bones.
- **23. By faith Moses,** when he was born,
- **was hid three months of his**
- **parents,** because they saw *he was* a proper child; and they were not afraid of the king's commandment.
- **24. By faith Moses,** when he was come to years,
- **refused to be called the**
- **son of Pharaoh's daughter;**
- **25. Choosing rather to**
- **suffer affliction with the**
- **people of God, than to**
- **enjoy the pleasures of**
- **sin** for a season;
- **26. Esteeming the reproach**
- **of Christ greater** riches
- **than the treasures in Egypt:** for he had respect unto the recompence of the reward.
- **27. By faith he forsook**
- **Egypt,** not fearing the wrath of the king: for he endured, as
- **seeing him who**
- **is invisible.**
- **28. Through faith he kept the**
- **passover,** and the sprinkling of blood, lest he that destroyed the firstborn should touch them.
- **29. By faith they passed**
- **through the Red sea** as by dry *land:* which the Egyptians assaying to do were drowned.
- **30. By faith the walls of**
- **Jericho fell** down, after they were compassed about seven days.
- **31. By faith the harlot**
- **Rahab perished not** with them that believed not, when she had received the spies with peace.
- **32. And what shall I more**
- **say?** for the
- **time would fail me to**
- **tell of Gedeon,** and *of*
- **Barak,** and *of*
- **Samson,** and *of*
- **Jephthae;** *of*
- **David** also, and
- **Samuel, and** *of*
- **the prophets:**
- **33. Who through faith**

■ subdued kingdoms,
■ wrought righteousness,
■ obtained promises,
■ stopped the mouths
■ of lions.
■ 34. Quenched the violence of
■ fire, escaped the edge of the
■ sword, out of weakness were made
strong, waxed valiant in fight,
■ turned to flight the
■ armies of the aliens.
■ 35. Women received their
■ dead raised to life again:
■ and others were tortured,
not accepting deliverance;
■ that they might obtain a
■ better resurrection:
■ 36. And others had
■ trial of *cruel*
■ mockings and scourgings,
yea, moreover of bonds
■ and imprisonment:
37. They were stoned,
■ they were sawn asunder,
were tempted, were
■ slain with the sword: they wandered
about in sheepskins and
goatskins; being
■ destitute, afflicted,
■ tormented;
38. (Of whom the world was
■ not worthy:) they wandered in
deserts, and *in* mountains, and *in*
dens and caves of the earth.
■ 39. And these all, having
■ obtained a good report
■ through faith, received not
■ the promise:
■ 40. God having provided
■ some better thing for us,
■ that they without us should
■ not be made perfect.

CHAPTER 12

■ 1. Wherefore seeing we also
■ are compassed about with
■ so great a cloud of
■ witnesses, let us lay aside
■ every weight, and the
■ sin which doth so easily beset *us*,
■ and let us
■ run with patience
■ the race that is set

before us,
■ 2. Looking unto Jesus
■ the author and finisher
■ of our faith; who for the joy
that was set before him
■ endured the cross,
despising the shame,
■ and is set down at the
■ right hand of the throne of
■ God.
■ 3. For consider him that
■ endured such contradiction of
sinners against himself,
■ lest ye be wearied and
■ faint in your minds.
■ 4. Ye have not yet resisted
■ unto blood, striving against sin.
■ 5. And ye have forgotten
■ the exhortation which speaketh
unto you as unto children,
■ My son, despise not thou
■ the chastening of the Lord,
nor faint when thou art rebuked of him:
■ 6. For whom the Lord loveth
■ he chasteneth, and scourgeth
every son whom he receiveth.
■ 7. If ye endure chastening,
■ God dealeth with you as
■ with sons; for what son is he
whom the father chasteneth not?
■ 8. But if ye be without
■ chastisement,
whereof all are partakers,
■ then are ye bastards,
and not sons.
■ 9. Furthermore we have
■ had fathers of our flesh
■ which corrected us,
and we gave *them* reverence:
■ shall we not much rather
■ be in subjection unto the
■ Father of spirits, and live?
■ 10. For they verily for a few days
■ chastened us after their own
■ pleasure; but he for *our* profit,
■ that we might be partakers
■ of his holiness.
11. Now no chastening
for the present seemeth to be joyous,
but grievous: nevertheless afterward
it yieldeth the peaceable fruit of
righteousness unto them which
are exercised thereby.

12. **Wherefore lift up the hands which hang down,** and the feeble knees;

13. And make straight paths for your feet, lest that which is lame be turned out of the way; but let it rather be healed.

14. **Follow peace with all men, and holiness, without which no man shall see the Lord:**

15. **Looking diligently lest any man fail of the grace of God;** lest any root of bitterness springing up trouble *you*, and thereby many be defiled;

16. **Lest there be any fornicator, or profane person, as Esau, who** for one morsel of meat **sold his birthright.**

17. **For** ye know how that **afterward,** when he would have inherited the blessing, **he was rejected: for he found no place of repentance,** though he sought it carefully with tears.

18. **For ye are not come unto the mount that might be touched,** and that burned with fire, nor unto blackness, and darkness, and tempest,

19. And the sound of a trumpet, and the voice of words; which *voice* they that heard entreated that the word should not be spoken to them any more:

20. **(For they could not endure that which was commanded,** And if so much as a beast touch the mountain, it shall be stoned, or thrust through with a dart:

21. **And so terrible was the sight, that Moses said, I exceedingly fear** and quake:)

22. **But ye are come unto mount Sion,** and unto **the city of** the living **God, the heavenly Jerusalem, and to** an innumerable company of **angels,**

23. **To the** general assembly and **church of the firstborn, which are written in heaven, and to God the Judge** of all, **and to the spirits of just men** made perfect,

24. **And to Jesus the mediator of the new covenant, and to the blood** of sprinkling, **that speaketh better things** than *that of* Abel.

25. **See that ye refuse not** him that speaketh. **For if they escaped not who refused him that spake on earth, much more shall not we escape, if we turn** away **from him that speaketh from heaven:**

26. Whose voice then shook the earth: but now he hath promised, saying, Yet once more I shake not the earth only, but also heaven.

27. And this *word,* Yet once more, signifieth the removing of those things that are shaken, as of things that are made, that those things which cannot be shaken may remain.

28. **Wherefore we receiving a kingdom which cannot be moved, let us** have grace, whereby we may **serve God** acceptably **with** reverence and godly **fear:**

29. **For our God is a consuming fire.**

CHAPTER 13

1. **Let brotherly love continue.**

2. Be not forgetful to **entertain strangers: for thereby some have entertained angels unawares.**

3. **Remember them** that are **in bonds,** as bound with them; **and them which**

suffer adversity,
as being yourselves
also in the body.
4. **Marriage is
honourable** in all,
**and the bed undefiled:
but** whoremongers and
adulterers God will judge.
5. *Let your* conversation
be without covetousness;
**and be content with such
things as ye have:
for he** hath
said, I will never leave thee, nor
forsake thee.
6. **So that we may boldly
say, The Lord is my helper,**
and I will not fear what
man shall do unto me.
7. **Remember them which
have the rule over you,** who
have spoken unto you the word of
God: whose faith follow, considering
the end of *their* conversation.
8. **Jesus Christ the same
yesterday,** and
to-day, and for ever.
9. **Be not carried about with**
divers and
**strange doctrines. For it is a
good thing that the heart
be established with grace;
not with meats, which have
not profited** them that have been
occupied therein.
10. We have an altar,
whereof they have no right to eat
which serve the tabernacle.
11. **For the bodies of
those beasts, whose blood
is brought**
into the sanctuary
**by the high priest
for sin, are burned
without the camp.**
12. **Wherefore Jesus also,** that
he might sanctify the
people with his own blood,
suffered without the gate.
13. **Let us go** forth therefore
unto him without the camp,

bearing his reproach.
14. **For here have we no
continuing city, but we
seek one to come.**
15. **By him**
therefore let us
**offer the sacrifice of praise
to God continually,**
that is, the fruit of *our* lips
giving thanks to his name.
16. But to do good and to
communicate forget not:
**for with such sacrifices God
is well pleased.**
17. Obey them that have the rule over
you, and submit yourselves: for they
watch for your souls, as they that
must give account, that they may do
it with joy, and not with grief: for that
is unprofitable for you.
18. **Pray for us:** for we trust we
have a good conscience, in all things
willing to live honestly.
19. But I beseech *you* the rather to do
this, that I may be restored
to you the sooner.
20. **Now the God of peace,
that brought** again
**from the dead our Lord
Jesus, that great shepherd**
of the sheep,
**through the blood of the
everlasting covenant,**
21. **Make you perfect**
in every good work to do his will,
**working in you that which is
wellpleasing** in his sight,
through Jesus Christ; to whom
be glory for ever and ever. Amen.
22. And I beseech you, brethren,
suffer the word of exhortation:
for I have written a letter
unto you in few words.
23. Know ye that *our* brother Timothy
is set at liberty; with whom, if he
come shortly, I will see you.
24. Salute all them that have the
rule over you, and all the saints.
They of Italy salute you.
25. Grace *be* with you all.
Amen.

THE EPISTLE OF JAMES

BACKGROUND INFORMATION

Author: James, a pastor in Jerusalem.
Date Written: probably **between 45** and **60** A.D.

Number of:
Verses   108
Chapters   5
Total Words 2,309
Scan Words 1,129
Scan Words represent
48 % of Total Words

Theme: written to instruct believers of the necessity of **demonstrating faith through** the conduct of their lives, through practical **Christian living**

OUTLINE OF THE EPISTLE

I. James Instructs **Believers on Facing Trials, Hearing and Doing the Word,** Impartiality **and Faith That Works** Chapters 1 - 2

II. James Warns of **the Dangers of the Tongue,** True and **False Wisdom, Worldliness and** Pride, Inconsideration and **Unchristian Conduct** Chapters 3 - 4

III. James Exhorts the Believer to Have **Patience in Affliction and** to Save **an Erring Brother** Chapter 5

CHAPTER 1

1. **James,** a servant of God and of the Lord Jesus Christ, **to the twelve tribes** which are **scattered abroad,** greeting. 2. **My brethren, count it all joy when ye fall into divers temptations;** 3. **Knowing** *this,* **that the trying of your faith worketh patience.** 4. **But let patience** have *her* perfect **work, that ye may be perfect** and entire, wanting nothing. 5. **If any of you lack wisdom,** let him **ask of God,** that giveth to all *men* liberally, and upbraideth not; **and it shall be given** him. 6. **But let him ask in faith,** nothing wavering. **For he that wavereth** is like a wave of the sea driven with the wind and tossed. 7. For let not that man think that he shall receive any thing of the Lord. 8. A double-minded man **is unstable in all his ways.** 9. **Let the brother of low degree rejoice in that he is exalted:** 10. **But the rich,** in that he **is made low: because as the flower** of the grass **he shall pass away.** 11.For the sun is no sooner risen with a burning heat, but it withereth the grass, and the flower thereof falleth, and the grace of the fashion of it perisheth: so also shall the rich man fade away in his ways. 12. **Blessed is the man that endureth temptation: for** when he is tried, **he shall receive the crown of life,** which the Lord hath promised to them that love him. 13. **Let no man say** when he is tempted, **I am tempted of God:** for God cannot be tempted with evil, neither tempteth he any man:

14. **But every man is tempted,** when he is drawn away **of his own lust, and** enticed. 15. Then when **lust** hath conceived, it **bringeth forth sin: and sin,** when it is finished, **bringeth forth death.** 16. Do not err, my beloved brethren. 17. **Every good gift and every perfect gift is** from above, and cometh down **from the Father** of lights, **with whom is no variableness,** neither shadow of turning. 18. **Of his own will begat he us** with the word of truth, **that we should be a kind of firstfruits** of his creatures. 19. **Wherefore,** my beloved brethren, let every man **be swift to hear, slow to speak, slow to wrath:** 20. **For the wrath of man worketh not the righteousness of God.** 21. Wherefore lay apart all filthiness and superfluity of naughtiness, and **receive** with meekness **the engrafted word, which is able to save your souls.** 22. **But be ye doers of the word, and not hearers only,** deceiving your own selves. 23. **For** if any be **a hearer** of the word, and not a doer, he **is like** unto **a man beholding his** natural **face in a glass:** 24. For he beholdeth himself, **and goeth his way, and** straightway **forgetteth what manner of man he was.** 25. **But whoso looketh into the perfect law** of liberty, and continueth *therein,* he **being** not a forgetful hearer, but **a doer of the work,** this man

shall be blessed in his deed.

26. If any man among you seem to be religious, and bridleth not his tongue, but deceiveth his own heart, this man's religion is vain.

27. Pure religion and undefiled before God and the Father is this, To visit the fatherless and widows in their affliction, and to keep himself unspotted from the world.

CHAPTER 2

1. My brethren, have not the faith of our Lord Jesus Christ, *the Lord* of glory, with respect of persons.

2. For if there come unto your assembly a man with a gold ring, in goodly apparel, and there come in also a poor man in vile raiment;

3. And ye have respect to him that weareth the gay clothing, and say unto him, Sit thou here in a good place; and say to the poor, Stand thou there, or sit here under my footstool:

4. Are ye not then partial in yourselves, and are become judges of evil thoughts?

5. Hearken, my beloved brethren, Hath not God chosen the poor of this world rich in faith, and heirs of the kingdom which he hath promised to them that love him?

6. But ye have despised the poor. Do not rich men oppress you, and draw you before the judgment seats?

7. Do not they blaspheme that worthy name by the which ye are called?

8. If ye fulfil the royal law according to the scripture, Thou shalt love thy neighbour as thyself, ye do well:

9. But if ye have respect to persons, ye commit sin, and are convinced of the law as transgressors.

10. For whosoever shall keep the whole law, and yet offend in one point, he is guilty of all.

11. For he that said, Do not commit adultery, said also, Do not kill. Now if thou commit no adultery, yet if thou kill, thou art become a transgressor of the law.

12. So speak ye, and so do, as they that shall be judged by the law of liberty.

13. For he shall have judgment without mercy, that hath shewed no mercy; and mercy rejoiceth against judgment.

14. What doth it profit, my brethren, though a man say he hath faith, and have not works? can faith save him?

15. If a brother or sister be naked, and destitute of daily food,

16. And one of you say unto them, Depart in peace, be ye warmed and filled; notwithstanding ye give them not those things which are needful to the body; what doth it profit?

17. Even so faith, if it hath not works, is dead, being alone.

18. Yea, a man may say, Thou hast faith, and I have works: shew me thy faith without thy works, and I will shew thee my faith by my works.

19. Thou believest that there is one God; thou doest well: the devils also believe, and tremble.

20. But wilt thou know, O vain man, that faith without works is dead?

21. Was not Abraham our father

■ justified by works,
■ when he had
■ offered Isaac
his son upon the altar?
■ 22. Seest thou how faith wrought
■ with his works,
and by works
■ was faith made perfect?
23. And the scripture was fulfilled
which saith,
■ Abraham believed God,
and it was imputed unto him
■ for righteousness: and he
■ was called the Friend
■ of God.
24. Ye see then how that
■ by works a man is justified,
■ and not by faith only.
25. Likewise also was not Rahab the
harlot justified by works, when she
had received the messengers, and
had sent *them* out another way?
■ 26. For as the body without
■ the spirit is dead, so faith
■ without works is dead also.

CHAPTER 3

■ 1. My brethren, be not many
■ masters, knowing that we shall
receive the greater condemnation.
2. For in many things we offend all.
■ If any man offend not in
■ word, the same is
a perfect man, *and*
■ able also to bridle the
■ whole body.
■ 3. Behold, we put bits in the
■ horses' mouths,
that they may obey us;
■ and we turn about their
■ whole body.
■ 4. Behold also the ships,
which though *they be* so great, and
are driven of fierce winds, yet
■ are they
■ turned about with a very
■ small helm, whithersoever the
governor listeth.
■ 5. Even so the tongue is a
■ little member, and boasteth
great things. Behold, how great a
matter a little fire kindleth!
6. And the tongue *is* a fire, a world of

iniquity: so is the tongue among
our members, that
■ it defileth the whole body,
and setteth on fire the course
of nature;
■ and it is set on fire of hell.
■ 7. For every kind of beasts,
and of birds, and of serpents, and of
things in the sea, is tamed, and
■ hath been tamed
■ of mankind:
■ 8. But the tongue can no
■ man tame; *it is* an unruly evil,
full of deadly poison.
■ 9. Therewith bless
■ we God, even the Father;
■ and therewith
■ curse we
■ men, which are made after the
similitude of God.
■ 10. Out of the same mouth
■ proceedeth blessing and
■ cursing. My brethren, these things
ought not so to be.
■ 11. Doth a fountain send
■ forth at the same place sweet
water and bitter?
12. Can the fig tree, my brethren,
bear olive berries? either a vine, figs?
so *can* no fountain
■ both yield
■ salt water and fresh.
■ 13. Who is a wise man
and endued with knowledge
■ among you? let him shew
■ out of a good conversation
■ his works
with meekness of wisdom.
■ 14. But if ye have bitter
■ envying and strife in your
■ hearts, glory not, and lie not
against the truth.
15. This wisdom descendeth not from
above, but *is* earthly,
sensual, devilish.
16. For where envying and strife *is*,
■ there is confusion and
■ every evil work.
■ 17. But the wisdom that is
■ from above is first pure,
then peaceable, gentle, *and* easy to
be entreated,
■ full of mercy and good fruits,

■ **without partiality,**
■ **and** without
■ **hypocrisy.**
18. And the fruit of righteousness is
sown in peace of them that
make peace.

CHAPTER 4

■ 1. **From whence come wars**
■ **and fightings** among you?
■ **come they not hence,**
■ **even of your lusts**
that war in your members?
■ 2. **Ye lust,** and have not: ye kill,
and desire to have,
■ **and cannot obtain:**
ye fight and war,
■ **yet ye have not, because**
■ **ye ask not.**
■ 3. **Ye ask,** and receive not,
because ye ask
■ **amiss, that ye may**
■ **consume it upon**
■ **your lusts.**
4. Ye adulterers and adulteresses,
■ **know ye not that the**
■ **friendship** of the world is enmity
with God? whosoever therefore will
be a friend
■ **of the world is the enemy**
■ **of God.**
5. Do ye think that
■ **the scripture saith** in vain,
■ **The spirit that dwelleth**
■ **in us lusteth to envy?**
■ 6. **But he giveth more grace.**
Wherefore he saith, God resisteth the
proud, but giveth grace
■ **unto the humble.**
■ 7. **Submit yourselves**
■ **therefore to God. Resist the**
■ **devil, and he will flee**
from you.
■ 8. **Draw nigh to God, and he**
■ **will draw nigh to you.** Cleanse
your hands, *ye* sinners; and purify
your hearts, *ye* double-minded.
9. Be afflicted, and mourn, and weep:
let your laughter be turned to
mourning, and *your* joy to heaviness.
■ 10. **Humble yourselves**
in the sight of the Lord,
■ **and he shall lift you** up.

11. Speak not evil one of
another brethren.
■ **He that speaketh evil of**
■ **his brother, and judgeth**
his brother,
■ **speaketh evil of the law,**
and judgeth the law: but if thou judge
the law, thou art not a doer of the law,
but a judge.
■ 12. **There is one lawgiver,** who
is able to save and to destroy:
■ **who art thou that judgest**
another?
13. Go to now,
■ **ye that say, To-day or to-**
■ **morrow we will** go into such a
city, and continue there a year, and
■ **buy and sell, and get gain:**
■ 14. **Whereas ye know not**
■ **what shall be on the**
■ **morrow. For** what *is*
■ **your life**? It
■ **is even a vapour, that**
■ **appeareth** for a little time,
■ **and then vanisheth** away.
■ 15. **For that ye ought to say,**
■ **If the Lord will, we shall**
live, and
■ **do this, or that.**
16. But now ye rejoice in your
boastings: all such rejoicing is evil.
■ 17. **Therefore to him that**
■ **knoweth to do good, and**
■ **doeth it not, to him it is sin.**

CHAPTER 5

1. Go to now,
■ **ye rich men,**
weep and howl for your
miseries that shall come upon *you.*
■ 2. **Your riches are**
■ **corrupted,** and your
garments are motheaten.
3. Your gold and silver is cankered;
■ **and the rust of them shall**
■ **be a witness against you,**
and shall eat your flesh as it were fire.
■ **Ye have heaped treasure**
■ **together for the last days.**
4. Behold, the hire of the labourers
who have reaped down your fields,
which is of you kept back by fraud,
crieth: and the cries of them which

have reaped are entered into the ears of the Lord of sabaoth.

5. **Ye have lived in pleasure** on the earth,

and been wanton; ye have nourished your hearts, as in a day of slaughter.

6. **Ye have condemned and killed the just; and he doth not resist** you.

7. **Be patient** therefore, brethren, **unto the coming of the Lord.** Behold, **the husbandman waiteth for the precious fruit of the earth,** and hath long patience for it, until he receive the early and latter rain.

8. Be ye also patient; stablish your hearts: for **the coming of the Lord draweth nigh.**

9. **Grudge not one against another,** brethren, lest ye be condemned: behold, the judge standeth before the door.

10. **Take,** my brethren, **the prophets,** who have spoken in the name of the Lord, **for an example of suffering affliction,** and of patience.

11. **Behold, we count them happy which endure.** Ye have heard of the patience of Job, and have seen the end of the Lord; that the Lord is very pitiful, and of tender mercy.

12. **But above all things,** my brethren, **swear not,** neither by heaven, neither by the earth, neither by any other oath: **but let your yea be yea;**

and your nay, nay; lest ye fall into condemnation.

13. Is any among you afflicted? let him pray. Is any merry? let him sing psalms.

14. **Is any sick** among you? **let** him call for **the elders of** the church; and let them **pray** over him, **anointing him with oil in the name of the Lord:**

15. **And the prayer of faith shall save the sick, and the Lord shall raise him up;** and if he have committed sins, they shall be forgiven him.

16. **Confess your faults** one to another, **and pray one for another,** that ye may be healed. **The effectual fervent prayer of a righteous man availeth much.**

17. **Elias** was a man subject to like passions as we are, and he **prayed earnestly** that it might not rain: **and it rained not** on the earth **by the space of three years and six months.**

18. **And he prayed again, and the heaven gave rain,** and the earth brought forth her fruit.

19. **Brethren, if any** of you do **err** from the truth, **and one convert him;**

20. **Let him know, that he which converteth the sinner** from the error of his way, **shall save a soul from death,** and shall hide a multitude of sins.

THE FIRST EPISTLE OF PETER

BACKGROUND INFORMATION

Author: **Peter,** an Apostle.
Date Written: probably **between 60** and **70** A.D.

Number of:
Verses   105
Chapters   5
Total Words 2,482
Scan Words 1,201
Scan Words represent
48 % of Total Words

Theme: written to show believers that **in spite of persecution, there is** living hope and **ultimate triumph in Jesus Christ**

OUTLINE OF THE EPISTLE

I. **Peter Explains** that **Salvation** is Wrought by the Father, the Son and the Holy Spirit **and** he **Gives a Call for Christian Dedication** Chapters 1 - 2:10

II. **Peter Outlines** the Nature of **Christian** Social **Relationships,** Sufferings, Rewards, **and Explains the Ministry** of the Elders and the Flock Chapters 2:11 - 5

CHAPTER 1

1. **Peter,** an apostle of Jesus Christ, **to the strangers scattered throughout Pontus, Galatia, Cappadocia, Asia, and Bithynia,** 2. **Elect** according to the foreknowledge of God the Father, **through sanctification of the Spirit,** unto obedience **and** sprinkling of **the blood of Jesus Christ:** Grace unto you, and peace, be multiplied.

3. **Blessed be the God** and Father of our Lord Jesus Christ, **which according to his abundant mercy hath begotten us** again unto a lively hope **by the resurrection of Jesus Christ** from the dead,

4. **To an inheritance** incorruptible, and undefiled, and that fadeth not away, **reserved in heaven for you,**

5. **Who are kept by the power of God through faith unto salvation** ready to be revealed in the last time.

6. Wherein ye greatly rejoice, **though now for a season,** if need be, **ye are in heaviness through manifold temptations:**

7. **That the trial of your faith, being much more precious than** of **gold** that perisheth, though it be tried with fire, **might be found unto praise** and honour and glory **at the appearing of Jesus Christ:**

8. **Whom having not seen, ye love;** in whom, **though** now **ye see him not, yet believing, ye rejoice with joy unspeakable and full of glory:**

9. **Receiving the end of your faith, even the salvation of your souls.**

10. **Of which** salvation **the prophets** have **inquired** and searched diligently, who prophesied **of the grace that should come unto you:**

11. **Searching what,** or what manner of time **the Spirit** of Christ which was in them did signify, when it **testified beforehand the sufferings of Christ,** and the glory that should follow.

12. **Unto whom it was revealed,** that not unto themselves, but unto us they did minister the things, which are now reported unto you **by them that have preached the gospel** unto you with the Holy Ghost sent down from heaven; which things the angels desire to look into.

13. **Wherefore** gird up the loins of your mind, **be sober, and hope** to the end **for the grace** that is **to be brought unto you at the revelation of Jesus Christ;**

14. **As obedient children,** not fashioning yourselves according to the former lusts in your ignorance:

15. But as he which hath called you is holy, so **be ye holy in all manner of conversation;**

16. **Because it is written, Be ye holy; for I am holy.**

17. And if ye call on the Father, who without respect of persons judgeth according to every man's work, pass the time of your sojourning *here* in fear:

18. **Forasmuch as ye know that ye were not redeemed with corruptible things,** as silver and gold, from your vain conversation *received* by tradition

from your fathers;

19. **But with the precious blood of Christ,** as of a lamb without blemish and without spot:

20. **Who verily was foreordained before the foundation of the world,** but was manifest in these last times for you,

21. **Who** by him do believe in **God, that raised him up from the dead,** and gave him glory; **that your faith** and hope **might be in God.**

22. **Seeing ye have purified your souls** in obeying the truth **through the Spirit** unto unfeigned love of the brethren, *see that ye* **love one another** with a pure heart **fervently:**

23. **Being born again,** not of corruptible seed, but of incorruptible, **by the word of God, which liveth and abideth for ever.**

24. **For all flesh is as grass, and** all the glory of man as the flower of grass. The grass **withereth, and** the flower thereof **falleth away:**

25. **But the word of the Lord endureth for ever.** And this is the word which by the gospel is preached unto you.

CHAPTER 2

1. **Wherefore** laying aside all malice, and all guile, and hypocrisies, and envies, all evil speakings,

2. **As newborn babes, desire the sincere milk of the word, that ye may grow thereby:**

3. If so be ye have tasted that the Lord *is* gracious.

4. To whom coming, *as unto* a living stone, disallowed indeed of men, but chosen of God, *and* precious,

5. **Ye also,** as lively stones, are built up a spiritual house, an holy priesthood, to **offer up spiritual sacrifices, acceptable to God by Jesus Christ.**

6. **Wherefore also it is contained in the scripture,** Behold, **I lay in Sion a chief corner stone,** elect, precious: **and he that believeth on him shall not be confounded.**

7. Unto you therefore which believe *he is* precious: **but** unto them which be disobedient, **the stone which the builders disallowed,** the same **is made the head of the corner,**

8. **And a stone of stumbling,** and a rock of offence, *even* **to them which stumble at the word,** being disobedient: whereunto also they were appointed.

9. **But ye are a chosen generation, a royal priesthood, an holy nation, a peculiar people;** that ye should shew forth the praises of him who hath **called** you out of darkness **into his marvellous light:**

10. Which in time past *were* not a people, but *are* now the peopleofGod: which had not obtained mercy, but now have obtained mercy.

11. **Dearly beloved,** I beseech *you* as strangers and pilgrims, **abstain from fleshly lusts, which war against the soul;**

12. **Having yourconver- sation honest among the Gentiles: that,** whereas they speak against you as evildoers, **they may by your good works,** which they shall behold, **glorify God in the day of visitation.**

13. **Submit yourselves to every ordinance of man for the Lord's sake: whether it be to the king,** as supreme;

14. **Or unto governors, as** unto **them** that are **sent by him for the punishment of evildoers,** and for the praise of them that do well.

15. **For so is the will of God, that** with well doing **ye may put to silence the ignorance of foolish men:**

16. As free, and not using *your* liberty for a cloak of maliciousness, but as the servants of God.

17. **Honour all men.** Love the brotherhood. Fear God. Honour the king.

18. **Servants, be subject to your masters** with all fear; not only to the good and gentle, but also to the froward.

19. **For this is thankworthy, if a man for conscience toward God endure grief, suffering wrongfully.**

20. For what glory *is it*, if, when ye be buffeted for your faults, ye shall take it patiently? but if, when ye do well, and suffer *for it*, ye take it patiently, this *is* acceptable with God.

21. For even hereunto were ye called: because **Christ also suffered for us, leaving us an example,** that ye should follow his steps:

22. **Who did no sin,** neither was guile found in his mouth:

23. Who, when he was reviled, reviled not again; when he suffered, he threatened not; **but committed himself to him that judgeth righteously:**

24. **Who** his own self **bare our sins in his own body on the tree, that we,** being dead to sins, **should live unto righteousness: by whose stripes ye were healed.**

25. **For ye were as sheep going astray; but are now returned unto the Shepherd** and Bishop **of your souls.**

CHAPTER 3

1. **Likewise, ye wives, be in subjection to your own husbands; that,** if any obey not the word, **they also may** without the word **be won by** the conversation of the wives;

2. While they behold **your chaste conversation coupled with fear.**

3. **Whose adorning let it not be** that **outward** *adorning* of plaiting the hair, and of wearing of gold, or of putting on of apparel;

4. **But let it be the hidden man of the heart,** in that which is not corruptible, *even the ornament* of a meek and quiet spirit, which is in the sight of God of great price.

5. **For after this manner in the old time the holy women** also, who trusted in God, **adorned themselves, being in subjection unto their own husbands:**

6. **Even as Sara obeyed Abraham, calling him lord:** whose daughters ye are, as long as ye do well, and are not afraid with any amazement.

7. **Likewise, ye husbands,** dwell with *them* according to knowledge, giving **honour** unto **the wife, as** unto **the weaker vessel, and as being heirs together of the grace of life; that your prayers be not hindered.**

8. **Finally,** *be ye* all of one mind, **having compassion one of another,** love as brethren, *be* pitiful, *be* courteous:

9. Not rendering evil for evil, or railing for railing: but contrariwise blessing; **knowing that ye are thereunto called,**

that ye should inherit a blessing.

10. **For he that will love life,** and see good days, **let him refrain** his tongue **from evil,** and his lips that they speak no guile:

11. Let him eschew evil, and do good; let him seek peace, and ensue it.

12. **For the eyes of the Lord are over the righteous, and his ears are open unto their prayers:** but the face of the Lord *is* against them that do evil.

13. **And who is he that will harm you,** if ye be followers of that which is good?

14. **But and if ye suffer for righteousness' sake, happy are ye:** and be not afraid of their terror, neither be troubled;

15. **But sanctify the Lord God in your hearts: and be ready always to give an answer to every man that asketh you a reason of the hope that is in you** with meekness and fear:

16. Having a good conscience; **that,** whereas they speak evil of you, as of evildoers, **they may be ashamed that falsely accuse your good conversation in Christ.**

17. **For it is better,** if the will of God be so, **that ye suffer for well doing, than for evil doing.**

18. **For Christ also hath once suffered for sins,** the just for the unjust, **that he might bring us to God, being put to death** in the flesh, **but quickened by the Spirit:**

19. By which also **he went and preached unto the spirits in prison;**

20. **Which sometime were disobedient, when** once the longsuffering of **God waited in the days of Noah, while the ark was a-preparing, wherein** few, that is, **eight souls were saved by water.**

21. The like figure whereunto *even* **baptism doth also now save us** (not the putting away of the filth of the flesh, but the answer of a good conscience toward God,) **by the resurrection of Jesus Christ:**

22. **Who is gone into heaven, and is on the right hand of God; angels and authorities and powers being made subject unto him.**

CHAPTER 4

1. **Forasmuch then as Christ hath suffered for us** in the flesh, **arm yourselves** likewise **with the same mind: for he** that hath suffered in the flesh **hath ceased from sin;**

2. **That he** no longer **should live the rest of his time** in the flesh to the lusts of men, but **to the will of God.**

3. **For the time past** of *our* life may suffice us to have wrought the will of the Gentiles, when **we walked in lasciviousness,** lusts, excess of wine, revellings, banquetings, **and abominable idolatries:**

4. **Wherein they think it strange that ye run not with them to the same excess** of riot, speaking evil of *you:*

5. Who shall give account to him that is ready to judge the quick and the dead.

6. **For** for **this cause was the gospel preached also to them that are dead, that they might** be judged according to men in the flesh, but **live according to God in the spirit.**

7. **But the end** of all things **is at hand:** be ye therefore sober, and **watch unto prayer.** 8. **And above all things have fervent charity** among yourselves: **for charity shall cover the multitude of sins.** 9. Use hospitality one to another without grudging. 10. **As every man hath received the gift, even so minister** the same one to another, as good stewards of **the manifold grace of God.** 11. If any man speak, *let him speak* as the oracles of God; if any man minister, *let him do it* as of the ability which God giveth: **that God in all things may be glorified** through Jesus Christ, to whom be praise and dominion for ever and ever. Amen. 12. **Beloved, think it not strange concerning the fiery trial which is to try you,** as though some strange thing happened unto you: 13. **But rejoice, inasmuch as ye are partakers of Christ's sufferings;** that, when his glory shall be revealed, ye may be glad also with exceeding joy. 14. **If ye be reproached for the name of Christ, happy are ye; for the spirit** of glory and **of God resteth upon you:** on their part he is evil spoken of, but on your part he is glorified. 15. **But let none** of you **suffer as** a murderer, or *as* a thief, or *as* **an evildoer,** or as a busybody in other men's matters. 16. **Yet if any man suffer as a Christian,** let him not be ashamed; but **let him glorify God** on this behalf. 17. **For** the time *is come* that **judgment must begin at the house of God: and** if *it* first *begin* at us, **what shall the end be of them that obey not the gospel** of God? 18. And if the righteous scarcely be saved, where shall the ungodly and the sinner appear? 19. **Wherefore let them that suffer according to the will of God commit** the keeping of **their souls to him** in well doing, **as unto a faithful Creator.**

CHAPTER 5

1. **The elders** which are among you **I exhort,** who am also an elder, and a witness of the sufferings of Christ, and also a partaker of the glory that shall be revealed: 2. **Feed the flock of God** which is among you, taking the oversight *thereof,* **not by constraint, but willingly;** not for filthy lucre, but of a ready mind; 3. Neither as being lords over *God's* heritage, but **being ensamples to the flock.** 4. **And when the chief Shepherd shall appear, ye shall receive a crown of glory** that fadeth not away. 5. **Likewise, ye younger, submit** yourselves **unto the elder.** Yea, all *of you* be subject one to another, and be clothed with humility: **for God resisteth the proud, and giveth grace to the humble.** 6. **Humble yourselves therefore** under the mighty hand of God, **that he may exalt you** in due time: 7. **Casting all your care upon him; for he careth for you.** 8. **Be sober,** be vigilant; **because** your adversary

■ **the devil,** as a roaring lion,
■ **walketh about, seeking**
■ **whom he may devour:**
9. Whom resist stedfast in the faith, knowing that the same afflictions are accomplished in your brethren that are in the world.
■ 10. **But the God of all grace,** who hath called us unto his eternal glory by Christ Jesus, after that ye have suffered a while,
■ **make you perfect,** stablish, strengthen, settle *you.*

■ 11. **To him be glory** and dominion for ever and ever. Amen.
12. By Silvanus, a faithful brother unto you, as I suppose, I have written briefly, exhorting, and testifying that this is the true grace of God wherein ye stand.
13. The *church that is* at Babylon, elected together with *you,* saluteth you; and *so doth* Marcus my son.
14. Greet ye one another with a kiss of charity. Peace *be* with you all that are in Christ Jesus.
■ **Amen.**

THE SECOND EPISTLE OF PETER

BACKGROUND INFORMATION

Author: Peter, an Apostle.
Date Written: unknown.

Number of:
Verses   61
Chapters   3
Total Words 1,559
Scan Words 758
Scan Words represent
48 % of Total Words

Theme: written to urge believers to defeat false teachings by practicing Christian virtues,
and to
prepare for the coming of the Lord

OUTLINE OF THE EPISTLE

I. **Peter's Salutation,** Advice for Growing in Grace, and Being Grounded in the Truth
    Chapter 1
II. **Peter's Warning** About False Teachers
    Chapter 2
III. **Peter's Admonition** as to How Believers Must Live **in Hope of the Second Coming** of Christ
    Chapter 3

CHAPTER 1

1. **Simon Peter,** a servant and an apostle of Jesus Christ, **to them that have obtained** like precious **faith with us through the righteousness of God and our Saviour Jesus Christ:** 2. **Grace and peace be multiplied unto you through the knowledge of God,** and of Jesus our Lord, 3. **According as his divine power hath given unto us** all things that *pertain* unto life and godliness, through the **knowledge of him that hath called us to glory and virtue:** 4. Whereby are given unto us exceeding great and precious promises: **that** by these **ye might be partakers of the divine nature,** having escaped the corruption that is in the world through lust. 5. **And** beside this, giving all diligence, **add to your faith virtue; and** to virtue **knowledge;** 6. **And** to knowledge **temperance; and** to temperance **patience; and** to patience **godliness;** 7. **And** to godliness **brotherly kindness; and** to brotherly kindness **charity.** 8. **For if these things be in you,** and abound, they make *you that* **ye shall neither be barren nor unfruitful in the know- ledge of our Lord** Jesus Christ. 9. **But he that lacketh these things** is blind, and cannot see afar off, and **hath forgotten that he was purged from his old sins.** 10. **Wherefore** the rather, brethren, **give diligence to make your calling and election sure:** for if ye do these things, ye shall never fall:

11. For so an entrance shall be ministered unto you abundantly into the everlasting kingdom of our Lord and Saviour Jesus Christ.

12. Wherefore I will not be negligent to put you always in remembrance of these things, though ye know *them,* and be established in the present truth.

13. **Yea, I think it meet,** as long as I am in this tabernacle, **to stir you up by putting you in remembrance;** 14. **Knowing** that shortly **I must put off this** my **tabernacle,** even as our Lord Jesus Christ hath shewed me.

15. Moreover I will endeavour that ye may be able after my decease to have these things always in remembrance.

16. **For we have not followed** cunningly devised **fables, when we made known unto you the power and coming of our Lord Jesus Christ, but were eyewitnesses of his majesty.** 17. **For he received** from God the Father **honour and glory, when there came such a voice to him** from the excellent glory, **This is my beloved Son, in whom I am well pleased.** 18. **And this voice** which came from heaven **we heard,** when we were with him **in the holy mount.** 19. We have also a more **sure word of prophecy;** whereunto ye do well that ye take heed, as unto a light that shineth in a dark place, until the day dawn, and the day star arise in your hearts: 20. **Knowing** this first, **that no prophecy**

of the scripture
■ **is of** any
■ **private interpretation.**
■ 21. **For the prophecy came**
■ **not** in old time
■ **by the will of man: but holy**
■ **men of God spake as they**
■ **were moved by the**
■ **Holy Ghost.**

CHAPTER 2

■ 1. **But there were false**
■ **prophets** also among the people,
■ **even as there shall be**
■ **false teachers** among you,
■ **who** privily shall
■ **bring in damnable**
■ **heresies, even denying**
■ **the Lord** that bought them,
■ **and bring upon themselves**
■ **swift destruction.**
■ 2. **And many shall follow**
■ **their pernicious ways;**
by reason of whom the way of truth
shall be evil spoken of.
■ 3. **And through**
■ **covetousness shall they** with
feigned words
■ **make merchandise of you:**
■ **whose judgment**
now of a long time
■ **lingereth not,** and their
damnation slumbereth not.
■ 4. **For if God spared not the**
■ **angels that sinned, but cast**
■ **them down to hell,**
and delivered *them* into chains
of darkness, to be reserved
unto judgment;
■ 5. **And spared not the old**
■ **world, but saved Noah**
the eighth *person*, a preacher
of righteousness,
■ **bringing in the flood upon**
■ **the** world of the
■ **ungodly;**
■ 6. **And turning the cities of**
■ **Sodom and Gomorrha into**
■ **ashes** condemned
them with an overthrow,
■ **making them an ensample**
unto those that after
should live ungodly;

■ 7. **And delivered just Lot,**
vexed with the filthy conversation
of the wicked:
8. (For that righteous man dwelling
among them, in seeing and hearing,
vexed *his* righteous soul from day to
day with *their* unlawful deeds;)
■ 9. **The Lord knoweth how to**
■ **deliver the godly out of**
■ **temptations, and to**
■ **reserve the unjust unto the**
■ **day of judgment to**
■ **be punished:**
■ 10. **But chiefly them that**
■ **walk** after the flesh
■ **in** the lust of
■ **uncleanness, and despise**
■ **government.** Presumptuous *are*
they, self-willed, they are not afraid to
speak evil of dignities.
■ 11. **Whereas angels,**
which are greater in power and might,
■ **bring not railing accusation**
■ **against them before**
■ **the Lord.**
■ 12. **But these,**
as natural brute beasts, made to be
taken and destroyed,
■ **speak evil of the things that**
■ **they understand not;** and shall
utterly perish in their own corruption;
13. And shall receive the reward of
unrighteousness,
as they that count it pleasure to riot in
the day time. Spots *they are* and
blemishes, sporting themselves with
their own deceivings while
they feast with you;
■ 14. **Having eyes full of**
■ **adultery,** and that cannot cease
from sin; beguiling unstable souls: an
heart they have exercised with
covetous practices; cursed children:
■ 15. **Which have forsaken the**
■ **right way, and are gone**
astray, following
■ **the way of Balaam**
the son of Bosor,
■ **who loved** the wages of
■ **unrighteousness;**
■ 16. **But was rebuked**
for his iniquity:
■ **the dumb ass speaking**

■ with man's voice forbad the
madness of the prophet.

■ 17. **These are wells without**
■ **water,** clouds that are carried
with a tempest;

■ **to whom** the mist of
■ **darkness is reserved**
■ **for ever.**

18. For when they speak great
swelling *words* of vanity, they allure
through the lusts of the flesh, *through
much* wantonness, those that were
clean escaped from
them who live in error.

■ 19. **While they promise them**
■ **liberty, they themselves are**
■ **the servants of**
■ **corruption:** for of whom a man is
overcome, of the same is he brought
in bondage.

■ 20. **For if after they have**
■ **escaped** the pollutions of
■ **the world through the**
■ **knowledge of**
the Lord and Saviour Jesus
■ **Christ, they are again**
■ **entangled therein,**
and overcome,
■ **the latter end**
■ **is worse** with them
■ **than the beginning.**

■ 21. **For it had been better for**
■ **them not to have known**
■ **the way of righteousness,**
■ **than,** after they have known *it*,
■ **to turn from the holy**
■ **commandment**
delivered unto them.

■ 22. **But it is happened**
unto them
■ **according to the** true
■ **proverb, The dog is turned**
■ **to his own vomit**
again; and the sow that was washed
to her wallowing in the mire.

CHAPTER 3

■ 1. **This second epistle,** beloved,
■ **I now write** unto you; in *both*
which I stir up your pure minds by
way of remembrance:

■ 2. **That ye may be mindful**
■ **of the words** which were

■ **spoken** before
■ **by the holy prophets, and**
■ **of the commandment of us**
■ **the apostles**
of the Lord and Saviour:

■ 3. **Knowing** this first,
■ **that there shall come**
in the last days
■ **scoffers,** walking after their
own lusts,

■ 4. **And saying, Where is the**
■ **promise of his coming? for**
since the fathers fell asleep,
■ **all things continue as they**
■ **were from the beginning**
of the creation.

■ 5. **For** this they willingly are ignorant
of, that
■ **by the word of God the**
■ **heavens were of old,**
and the earth standing out of the
water and in the water:

■ 6. **Whereby the world**
that then was,
■ **being overflowed with**
■ **water, perished:**

■ 7. **But the heavens and the**
■ **earth,** which are now,
■ **by the same word are**
kept in store,
■ **reserved unto fire against**
■ **the day of judgment**
and perdition of ungodly men.

■ 8. **But,** beloved, be not ignorant of
this one thing, that one day *is* with
the Lord as a thousand years, and a
thousand years as one day.

■ 9. **The Lord** is not slack concerning
his promise, as some men count
slackness; but
■ **is longsuffering to us-ward,**
■ **not willing that any should**
■ **perish,** but that all should come to
repentance.

■ 10. **But** the day of
■ **the Lord will come as a thief**
■ **in the night;** in the which
■ **the heavens shall**
■ **pass away** with a great noise,
■ **and the elements shall**
■ **melt** with fervent heat,
■ **the earth also and the**
■ **works** that are

■ therein shall be burned up.
■ 11. **Seeing** then *that* all
■ **these things** shall be dissolved,
■ **what manner of persons**
■ **ought ye to be in all**
holy conversation and
■ **godliness,**
■ 12. **Looking for** and hasting unto
■ **the coming of the day of**
■ **God, wherein** the heavens being
on fire shall be dissolved, and
■ **the elements shall melt**
■ **with fervent heat?**
■ 13. **Nevertheless we,**
according to his promise,
■ **look for new heavens and a**
■ **new earth, wherein**
■ **dwelleth righteousness.**
■ 14. **Wherefore,** beloved, seeing
that ye look for such things,
■ **be diligent that ye may be**
■ **found** of him in peace,
■ **without spot,**
■ **and blameless.**
■ 15. **And account that the**
■ **longsuffering of**

■ **our Lord is salvation; even**
as our beloved brother
■ **Paul** also according to the
wisdom given unto him
■ **hath written** unto you;
16. As also in all *his* epistles,
speaking in them of these things; in
which are some
■ **things hard to be**
■ **understood,** which they that are
unlearned and unstable wrest, as
they do also the other scriptures, unto
their own destruction.
■ 17. **Ye therefore,** beloved,
seeing ye know *these things* before,
■ **beware lest ye also,**
being led away with the
error of the wicked,
■ **fall from your**
■ **own stedfastness.**
■ 18. **But grow in grace,**
■ **and in the knowledge of**
■ **our Lord** and Saviour Jesus Christ.
To him *be* glory both now and for
ever.
■ **Amen.**

THE FIRST EPISTLE OF JOHN

BACKGROUND INFORMATION

Author: John, one of the twelve disciples.

Date Written: probably **between 90** and **96** A.D.

Number of:
Verses   105
Chapters   5
Total Words 2,523
Scan Words 1,234
Scan Words represent
48 % of Total Words

Theme: written to show that **through** personal experience with **Jesus Christ,** The Word, **one has passed from death to life**

OUTLINE OF THE EPISTLE

I.   **John's Testimony Concerning Christ,** His Tests of Fellowship With God and His Declaration of the Importance of Love Chapters 1 - 2:17

II. **John's Warning Concerning Antichrists** and His Explanation of Righteousness and God's Children Chapter 2:18 - 3

III. **John's Teaching Concerning the Trying of Spirits,** the Nature of God and the Victory of Faith Chapters 4 - 5

CHAPTER 1

1. **That which was from the beginning, which we have heard, which we have seen** with our eyes, which we have looked upon,
and our hands have handled, of the Word of life;
2. **(For the life was manifested, and we** have seen *it*, and **bear witness,**
and shew unto you that eternal life, which was with the Father, and was manifested unto us;)
3. That which we have seen and heard declare we unto you,
that ye also may have fellowship with us: and truly our fellowship *is* **with the Father, and with his Son** Jesus Christ.
4. **And these things write we** unto you,
that your joy may be full.
5. **This then is the message which we** have heard of him, and **declare** unto you,
that God is light, and in him is no darkness at all.
6. **If we say that we have fellowship with him, and walk in darkness, we lie,** and do not the truth:
7. **But if we walk in the light,** as he is in the light,
we have fellowship one with another,
and the blood of Jesus Christ his Son **cleanseth us from all sin.**
8. If we say that we have no sin, we deceive ourselves, and the truth is not in us.
9. **If we confess our sins, he is faithful** and just **to forgive us** our **sins, and to cleanse us from all unrighteousness.**
10. **If we say that we have not sinned,**
we make him a liar, and **his word is not in us.**

CHAPTER 2

1. **My little children,**
these things write I unto you, that ye sin not. And
if any man sin, we have an advocate with the Father, Jesus Christ the righteous:
2. **And he is the propitiation** for our sins: and not for ours only, but also
for the sins of the whole world.
3. **And hereby** we do know that **we know him, if we keep his commandments.**
4. He that saith, I know him, and keepeth not his commandments, is a liar, and the truth is not in him.
5. **But whoso keepeth his word, in him** verily **is the love of God perfected:** hereby know we that we are in him.
6. **He that saith he abideth in him ought** himself also so **to walk, even as he walked.**
7. Brethren, I write no new commandment unto you, but an old commandment which ye had from the beginning. The old commandment is the word which ye have heard from the beginning.
8. **Again, a new commandment I write** unto you, which thing is true in him and in you:
because the darkness is past, and
the true light now shineth.
9. **He that saith he is in the light, and hateth his brother, is in darkness** even until now.
10. He that loveth his brother abideth in the light, and there is none occasion of stumbling in him.
11. But he that hateth his brother is in darkness, and walketh in darkness, and knoweth not whither he goeth, because that darkness hath blinded his eyes.
12. **I write unto you, little**

children, because your sins are forgiven you for his name's sake.

13. I write unto you, fathers, because ye have known him *that is* from the beginning. I write unto you, young men, because ye have overcome the wicked one. I write unto you, little children, because ye have known the Father.

14. I have written unto you, fathers, because ye have known him that is from the beginning. I have written unto you, young men, because ye are strong, and the word of God abideth in you, and ye have overcome the wicked one.

15. Love not the world, neither the things that are in the world. If any man love the world, the love of the Father is not in him.

16. For all that is in the world, the lust of the flesh, and the lust of the eyes, and the pride of life, is not of the Father, but is of the world.

17. And the world passeth away, and the lust thereof: but he that doeth the will of God abideth for ever.

18. Little children, it is the last time: and as ye have heard that antichrist shall come, even now are there many antichrists; whereby we know that it is the last time.

19. They went out from us, but they were not of us; for if they had been of us, they would *no doubt* have continued with us: but *they went out,* that they might be made manifest that they were not all of us.

20. But ye have an unction from the Holy One, and ye know all things.

21. I have not written unto you because ye know not the truth, but becaue ye know it, and that no lie is of the truth.

22. Who is a liar but he that denieth that Jesus is the Christ? He is antichrist, that denieth the Father and the Son.

23. Whosoever denieth the Son, the same hath not the Father: *he that acknowledgeth the Son hath the Father also.*

24. Let that therefore abide in you, which ye have heard from the beginning. If that which ye have heard from the beginning shall remain in you, ye also shall continue in the Son, and in the Father.

25. And this is the promise that he hath promised us, *even* eternal life.

26. These *things* have I written unto you concerning them that seduce you.

27. But the anointing which ye have received of him abideth in you, and ye need not that any man teach you: but as the same anointing teacheth you of all things, and is truth, and is no lie, and even as it hath taught you, ye shall abide in him.

28. And now, little children, abide in him; that, when he shall appear, we may have confidence, and not be ashamed before him at his coming.

29. If ye know that he is righteous, ye know that every one that doeth right-eousness is born of him.

CHAPTER 3

1. Behold, what manner of love the Father hath bestowed upon us, that we should be called the sons of God: therefore the world knoweth us not, because it knew him not.

2. Beloved, now are we the sons

of God,

and it doth not yet appear what we shall be: but **we know that, when he shall appear, we shall be like him;** for we shall see him as he is.

3. **And every man that hath this hope in him purifieth himself,** even as he is pure.

4. Whosoever committeth sin transgresseth also the law: for sin is the transgression of the law.

5. **And ye know that he was manifested to take away our sins;** and in him is no sin.

6. **Whosoever abideth in him sinneth not:** whosoever sinneth hath not seen him, neither known him.

7. Little children, let no man deceive you: **he that doeth righteousness is righteous,** even as he is righteous.

8. **He that committeth sin is of the devil;** for the devil sinneth from the beginning. **For** this purpose **the Son of God was manifested, that he might destroy the works of the devil.**

9. **Whosoever is born of God doth not commit sin; for his seed remaineth in him:** and he cannot sin, because he is born of God.

10. **In this the children of God are manifest,** and the children of the devil: **whosoever doeth not righteousness is not of God, neither** he that **loveth** not **his brother.**

11. **For this is the message that** ye heard from the beginning, that **we should love one another.**

12. **Not as Cain, who** was of that wicked one, and **slew his brother.** And wherefore slew he him? **Because his own works were evil,** and his brother's righteous.

13. Marvel not, my brethren, if the world hate you.

14. **We know that we have passed from death unto life, because we love the brethren.** He that loveth not *his* brother abideth in death.

15. **Whosoever hateth his brother is a murderer: and** ye know that **no murderer hath eternal life** abiding in him.

16. **Hereby perceive we the love of God, because he laid down his life for us: and we ought to lay down our lives for the brethren.**

17. **But whoso hath this world's good, and seeth his brother have need, and shutteth up his** bowels *of* **compassion from him, how dwelleth the love of God in him?**

18. **My little children, let us not love in word,** neither in tongue; **but in deed and in truth.**

19. And hereby we know that we are of the truth, and shall assure our hearts before him.

20. For if our heart condemn us, God is greater than our heart, and knoweth all things.

21. **Beloved, if our heart condemn us not, then have we confidence toward God.**

22. **And whatsoever we ask, we receive of him, because we** keep his commandments, and do those things that **are pleasing in his sight.**

23. **And this is his commandment, That we should believe on the name of his Son** Jesus Christ, **and love one another,** as he

gave us commandment.

24. And he that keepeth his commandments dwelleth in him, and he in him.

■ **And hereby we know that**
■ **he abideth in us, by the**
■ **Spirit** which he hath given us.

CHAPTER 4

■ 1. **Beloved, believe not**
■ **every spirit, but try the**
■ **spirits** whether they are of God: because many false prophets are gone out into the world.

2. Hereby know ye the Spirit of God:

■ **Every spirit that confesseth**
■ **that Jesus Christ is come in**
■ **the flesh is of God:**
■ 3. **And every spirit that**
■ **confesseth not** that Jesus Christ is come in the flesh is not of God: and this

■ **is that spirit of antichrist,**
whereof ye have heard that it should come;

■ **and even now already is it**
■ **in the world.**

■ 4. **Ye** are of God, little children, and
■ **have overcome** them:
■ **because greater is he that**
■ **is in you, than he that is in**
■ **the world.**

5. They are of the world: therefore speak they of the world, and the world heareth them.

■ 6. **We are of God: he that**
■ **knoweth God heareth us;**
he that is not of God heareth not us.

■ **Hereby know we the spirit**
■ **of truth, and** the spirit of
■ **error.**

7. **Beloved,** let us love one another: for

■ **love is of God;** and every one that loveth is born of God, and knoweth God.

8. He that loveth not knoweth not God; for God is love.

■ 9. **In this was manifested the**
■ **love of God toward us,**
because that

■ **God sent his only begotten**
■ **Son into the world,**

that we might live through him.

10. Herein is love, not that we loved God, but that he loved us, and sent his Son

■ **to be the propitiation for our**
■ **sins.**

11. Beloved, if God so loved us, we ought also to love one another.

12. No man hath seen God at any time.

■ **If we love one another, God**
■ **dwelleth in us,**
and his love is perfected in us.

13. Hereby know we that we dwell in him, and he in us, because he hath given us of his Spirit.

■ 14. **And we have seen and**
■ **do testify that the Father**
■ **sent the Son to be the**
■ **Saviour of the world.**
■ 15. **Whosoever shall**
■ **confess that Jesus is the**
■ **Son** of God,
■ **God dwelleth in him,**
and he in God.

■ 16. **And** we have known and believed the love that God hath to us. God is love; and

■ **he that dwelleth in love**
■ **dwelleth in God, and God**
■ **in him.**
■ 17. **Herein is our love made**
■ **perfect, that we may have**
■ **boldness in the day of**
■ **judgment:** because as he is, so are we in this world.

■ 18. **There is no fear in love;**
■ **but perfect love casteth out**
■ **fear:** because fear hath torment. He that feareth is not made perfect in love.

■ 19. **We love him, because**
■ **he first loved us.**
■ 20. **If a man** say, I love God, and hateth his brother, he is a liar: for he that

■ **loveth not his brother**
■ **whom he hath seen, how**
■ **can he love God whom he**
■ **hath not seen?**

21. And this commandment have we from him, That he who loveth Godlove his brother also.

CHAPTER 5

1. **Whosoever believeth that Jesus is the Christ is born of God:** and every one that loveth him that begat loveth him also that is begotten of him.

2. **By this we know that we love the children of God, when we love God, and keep his commandments.**

3. For this is the love of God, that we keep his commandments: **and his commandments are not grievous.**

4. **For whatsoever is born of God overcometh the world:** and this is the victory that overcometh the world, *even* our faith.

5. Who is he that overcometh the world, but **he that believeth that Jesus is the Son of God?**

6. **This is he that came by water and blood, even Jesus Christ;** not by water only, but by water and blood. **And** it is **the Spirit** that **beareth witness,** because the Spirit is truth.

7. **For there are three that bear record in heaven, the Father, the Word, and the Holy Ghost:** and these three are one.

8. **And there are three that bear witness in earth, the Spirit, and the water, and the blood:** and these three agree in one.

9. **If we receive the witness of men, the witness of God is greater:** for this is the witness of God which he hath testified of his Son.

10. He that believeth on the Son of God hath the witness in himself: he that believeth not God hath made him a liar; because he believeth not the record that God gave of his Son.

11. **And this is the record, that God hath given** to **us eternal life,** and this life is **in his Son.**

12. **He that hath the Son hath life;** *and* he that hath not the Son of God hath not life.

13. **These things have I written** unto you that believe on the name of the Son of God; **that ye may know that ye have eternal life,** and that ye may believe on the name of the Son of God.

14. **And this is the confidence that we have in him, that, if we ask any thing according to his will, he heareth us:**

15. **And** if we know that he hear us, whatsoever we ask, we know that **we have the petitions that we desired of him.**

16. **If any man see his brother sin a sin which is not unto death, he shall ask, and he shall give him life** for them that sin not unto death. **There is a sin unto death:** I do not say that he shall pray for it.

17. **All unrighteousness is sin:** and there is a sin not unto death.

18. We know that whosoever is born of God sinneth not; but he that is begotten of God keepeth himself, and that wicked one toucheth him not.

19. **And we know** that we are of God, and **the whole world lieth in wickedness.**

20. **And we know that the Son of God is come,** and hath given us an understanding, **that we may know him** that is true, **and we are in him** that is true, **even in his Son** Jesus Christ. This is the true God, and eternal life.

21. **Little children, keep** yourselves **from idols. Amen.**

THE SECOND EPISTLE OF JOHN

BACKGROUND INFORMATION

Author: John, one of the twelve disciples.
Date Written: probably **between 90** and **99** A.D.

Number of:
Verses   13
Chapters   1
Total Words 303
Scan Words 151
Scan Words represent
49 % of Total Words

Theme: written to show **the importance of** Christian **truth and** the necessity to practice Christian **love**

OUTLINE OF THE EPISTLE

I.   **John's Greeting**
     Verses 1 - 3
II. **John's Teachings on Love**
     Verses 4 - 6
III. **John's Warning Concerning Deceivers**
     Verses 7 - 11
IV. **John's Final Greeting**
     Verses 12, 13

CHAPTER 1

1. **The elder unto the elect lady and her children,** whom I love in the truth; and not I only, but also all they that have known the truth;

2. For the truth's sake, which dwelleth in us, and shall be with us for ever.

3. **Grace** be with you, **mercy, and peace, from God the Father, and** from **the Lord Jesus Christ,** the Son of the Father, in truth and love.

4. **I rejoiced greatly that I found** of **thy children walking in truth,** as we have received a commandment from the Father.

5. **And now I beseech thee, lady,** not as though I wrote a new commandment unto thee, but that which we had from the beginning, **that we love one another.**

6. **And this is love, that we walk after his command-ments.** This is the commandment, That, as ye have heard from the beginning, ye should walk in it.

7. **For many deceivers** are entered into the world, who **confess not that Jesus** **Christ is come in the flesh. This is** a deceiver and an **antichrist.**

8. **Look to yourselves, that we lose not those things which we have wrought, but that we receive a full reward.**

9. **Whosoever** transgresseth, and **abideth not in** the doctrine of **Christ, hath not God. He that abideth in the doctrine of Christ, he hath both the Father and the Son.**

10. **If** there come **any** unto you, and **bring not this doctrine, receive him not** into *your* house, **neither bid him God speed:**

11. **For he that biddeth him** God speed **is partaker of his evil deeds.**

12. Having many things to write unto you, I would not *write* with paper and ink: but **I trust to come unto you,** and speak face to face, **that our joy may be full.**

13. The children of thy elect sister greet thee. **Amen.**

THE THIRD EPISTLE OF JOHN

BACKGROUND INFORMATION

Author: John, one of the twelve disciples
Date Written: probably **between 90** and **99** A.D.

Number of:
Verses   14
Chapters   1
Total Words 299
Scan Words 154
Scan Words represent 51 % of Total Words

Theme: written to show that **error must be challenged to maintain Christian purity** and fellowship

OUTLINE OF THE EPISTLE

I.   **John Offers Greeting,** Tells Believers to Serve Others, and Rebukes Diotrephes
     Verses 1 - 10
II. **John Implores Believers to Have a Good Testimony**
     Verses 11 - 14

CHAPTER 1

■ 1. **The elder unto** the well-beloved

■ **Gaius,** whom I love in the truth.

■ 2. **Beloved, I wish** above all things

■ **that thou** mayest

■ **prosper and be in**

■ **health,** even

■ **as thy soul prospereth.**

■ 3. **For I rejoiced** greatly, when the brethren came and testified

■ **of the truth that is in thee,** even as thou walkest in the truth.

■ 4. **I have no greater joy**

■ **than to hear that my**

■ **children walk in truth.**

■ 5. **Beloved, thou doest**

■ **faithfully** whatsoever thou doest

■ **to the brethren, and** to

■ **strangers;**

■ 6. **Which have borne**

■ **witness of thy charity** before the church: whom if thou bring forward on their journey after a godly sort, thou shalt do well: 7. Because that for his name's sake they went forth, taking nothing of the Gentiles.

■ 8. **We therefore ought to**

■ **receive such, that we might**

■ **be fellow-helpers**

■ **to the truth.**

■ 9. **I wrote unto the church:**

■ **but Diotrephes, who loveth** to have the

■ **preeminence** among them,

■ **receiveth us not.** 10. Wherefore, if I come,

■ **I will remember his deeds** which he doeth, prating against us with malicious words: and not content therewith,

■ **neither doth he** himself

■ **receive the brethren,** and forbiddeth them that would,

■ **and casteth them out of**

■ **the church.**

■ 11. **Beloved, follow not** that which is

■ **evil,** but that which is good.

■ **He that doeth good is of**

■ **God: but he that doeth evil**

■ **hath not seen God.**

■ 12. **Demetrius hath good**

■ **report of all men,** and of the truth itself: yea, and we *also* bear record; and ye know that our record is true.

■ 13. **I had many things to**

■ **write,** but I will not with ink and pen write unto thee:

■ 14. **But I trust I shall shortly**

■ **see thee,** and we shall speak face to face.

■ **Peace be to thee.** *Our* friends salute thee.

■ **Greet the friends by name.**

THE GENERAL EPISTLE
OF JUDE

BACKGROUND
INFORMATION

Author: Jude, probably the brother of James]

Date Written: probably **between 70** and **100** A.D.

Number of:
Verses   25
Chapters   1
Total Words   613
Scan Words 288
Scan Words represent
46 % of Total Words

Theme: written to warn Christians **against false** teachers and their **doctrines**

OUTLINE OF
THE EPISTLE

I.   **Jude Offers** a
     Salutation and a
     Warning Against
     False Teachers
     Verses 1 - 15

II. **Jude Presents**
     Exhortations to Christians
     and a Benediction
     Verses 16 - 25

CHAPTER 1

■ 1. **Jude,** the servant of Jesus Christ, and brother of James,

■ **to them that are sanctified**
■ **by God** the Father,
■ **and preserved in Jesus**
■ **Christ,** *and* called:

2. Mercy unto you, and peace, and love, be multiplied.

■ 3. **Beloved,** when
■ **I** gave all diligence to
■ **write unto you**
■ **of the common salvation,**
it was needful for me to write unto you,
■ **and exhort you that ye**
should earnestly
■ **contend for the faith**
which was
■ **once delivered**
unto the saints.

■ 4. **For there are** certain men crept in unawares, who were before of old ordained to this condemnation,
■ **ungodly men, turning the**
■ **grace of our God into**
■ **lasciviousness, and denying**
the only Lord God, and
■ **our Lord Jesus Christ.**

5. I will therefore put you in remembrance, though
■ **ye once knew** this,
■ **how that the Lord,**
■ **having saved the**
■ **people out** of the land
■ **of Egypt, afterward**
■ **destroyed them that**
■ **believed not.**

6. And the angels which
■ **kept not their first estate,**
but left their own habitation,
■ **he hath reserved in** everlasting
■ **chains** under darkness
■ **unto the judgment**
of the great day.

■ 7. **Even as Sodom and**
■ **Gomorrha,** and the cities about
them in like manner, giving
themselves over to fornication, and
going after strange flesh,
■ **are set forth for an**
■ **example, suffering the**
■ **vengeance of eternal fire.**

8. Likewise also these *filthy* dreamers
defile the flesh, despise
dominion, and speak evil of dignities.

■ 9. **Yet Michael**
the archangel, when
■ **contending with the devil**
he disputed
■ **about the body of Moses,**
■ **durst not bring against him**
■ **a railing accusation,**
■ **but said, The Lord**
■ **rebuke thee.**

10. **But these speak evil of**
■ **those things which they**
■ **know not:** but what
they know naturally, as brute beasts,
in those things they
corrupt themselves.

■ 11. **Woe unto them! for they**
■ **have gone in the way of**
■ **Cain,** and ran greedily after the
error of Balaam for reward, and
perished in the gainsaying of Core.

■ 12. **These are spots in your**
■ **feasts of charity,**
when they feast with you, feeding
themselves without fear:
■ **clouds** *they are*
■ **without water,**
carried about of winds;
■ **trees** whose fruit withereth,
■ **without fruit,** twice dead,
■ **plucked up by the roots;**

13. **Raging waves** of the sea,
foaming out their own shame;
wandering stars,
■ **to whom is reserved**
the blackness of
■ **darkness for ever.**

14. And Enoch
also, the seventh from Adam,
■ **prophesied** of these, saying,
■ **Behold, the Lord cometh**
■ **with** ten thousands of
■ **his saints,**

15. **To execute judgment**
■ **upon all,** and to convince all that
are ungodly among them of all their
ungodly deeds which they have
ungodly committed, and of all their
hard *speeches* which
■ **ungodly sinners**
have spoken against him.

16. **These are**

■ murmurers, complainers,
■ **walking after their own**
■ **lusts;** and their mouth speaketh
great swelling *words*, having men's
persons in admiration
because of advantage.
■ 17. **But, beloved, remember**
ye the words which were spoken
before of the apostles of our Lord
Jesus Christ;
■ 18. **How that** they told you
■ **there should be mockers in**
■ **the last time,** who should walk
after their own ungodly lusts.
■ 19. **These be they** who separate
themselves, sensual,
■ **having not the Spirit.**
■ 20. **But ye,** beloved, building up
yourselves on your most holy faith,
■ **praying in the Holy Ghost,**
■ 21. **Keep yourselves in the**

■ **love of God, looking for**
the mercy of our Lord Jesus
■ **Christ unto eternal life.**
■ 22. **And of some**
■ **have compassion,**
making a difference:
■ 23. **And others save with**
■ **fear, pulling them out of the**
■ **fire;** hating even the garment spotted
by the flesh.
■ 24. **Now unto him that is**
■ **able to keep you from**
■ **falling, and to present**
■ **you faultless** before the presence
of his glory with
exceeding joy,
■ 25. **To** the only wise
■ **God our Saviour, be glory**
■ **and majesty,**
dominion and power,
■ **both now and ever. Amen.**

THE REVELATION OF JESUS CHRIST TO JOHN

BACKGROUND INFORMATION

Author: John, one of the twelve Apostles.
Date Written: probably **between 90** and **99** A.D.

Number of:
Verses   404
Chapters   22
Total Words 12,000
Scan Words 5,973
Scan Words represent
49 % of Total Words

Theme: written to reveal that in spite of adverse world events,
Jesus Christ will triumph over all the enemies of God

OUTLINE OF THE REVELATION

I.   The Revelation of the Son of Man, **the Letters to the Seven Churches** and the Open Door in Heaven Chapters 1 - 5

II. The Revelation of the **Seven Seals, the Seven Trumpets and the War in Heaven** Chapters 6 - 14

III. The Revelation of **the Seven Vials and the Fall of Babylon** Chapters 15 - 19

IV. The Revelation of **the Millennium and the Holy City** Chapters 20 - 22

THE REVELATION OF JESUS CHRIST TO JOHN
The Conclusion Of History

The first book of the Bible, **Genesis, is a revelation of the beginnings of history,** both the beginning of the created order, and human beings. The final book of the Bible, **Revelation, is a revelation of the conclusion of history** – the end of time, the created order as we know it today, and of man in his fallen state. **Revelation,** in essence, **shows what will occur when** God in **Christ concludes** human **history and ushers in a New Order.** For centuries now, Bible scholars have studied the Book of Revelation. There has been a wide variety of interpretations. **Some Bible students give a literal interpretation to the Revelation. At the other extreme,** there are **scholars** who **attempt to show that the Revelation is totally symbolic.** There is, of course, a great deal of symbolism in the book, **but for the** Bible **student** who is **committed to the Scripture as the** authoritative, written **word of God, the symbolism points to a deeper reality. That reality,** regardless of one's interpretations of specific verses or chapters in the Revelation, **is that** God in **Christ will** ultimately **triumph over all the enemies of the truth** – sin, satan, political systems, **and all** that stands **in opposition to the** purposes and **will of God. Evil will be defeated,** the saints of God will be sustained, **persecution** and tribulation **shall end, and a new creation,** a new heaven and a new earth – **without sorrows,** tears, suffering, heartache, **and death – shall be established by** a direct act of **God. The Eden** which was **lost** by the first Adam, **shall be restored** by the second Adam, Jesus Christ. **What seems plain** in the Revelation **is that man, through his own** ingenuity or **effort, cannot solve his problems,** he cannot save himself individually, socially, or politically. **But God in sheer grace, shall finish all that was accomplished in the death and resurrection of His Son, and in that new beginning, He,** the Alpha and Omega, **shall be All in All.**

CHAPTER 1

1. **The Revelation of Jesus Christ, which God gave** unto him, **to shew** unto his servants **things which must shortly come to pass; and** he **sent** and signified *it* by his angel **unto** his servant **John:**
2. Who bare record of the word of God, and of the testimony of Jesus Christ, and of all things that he saw.
3. **Blessed is he that readeth, and they that hear** the words of **this prophecy, and keep those things** which are **written therein:** for the time *is* at hand.
4. **John to the seven churches** which are **in Asia: Grace be unto you,** and peace, **from** him which is, and which was, and which is to come; and from theseven Spirits which are before his throne;
5. And from Jesus **Christ, who is the** faithful witness, *and* the first begotten of the dead, and the **prince** of the kings of the earth. Unto him **that loved us, and washed us from our sins in his own blood**
6. **And hath made us kings and priests** unto God and his Father; to him *be* glory and dominion for ever and ever. Amen.
7. **Behold, he cometh** with clouds; **and every eye shall see him,** and they *also* which pierced him: and all kindreds of the earth shall wail because of him. Even so, Amen.
8. **I am** Alpha and Omega, **the beginning and the ending, saith the Lord,** which is, and which was, and which is

to come, the Almighty.
9. **I John,** who also am your brother, and companion in tribulation, and in the kingdom and patience of Jesus Christ, **was in the isle** that is **called Patmos,** for the word of God, and for the testimony of Jesus Christ.
10. **I was in the Spirit on the Lord's day, and heard** behind me **a great voice,** as of a trumpet,
11. **Saying,** I am Alpha and Omega, the first and the last: and, **What thou seest, write** in a book, **and send it unto the seven churches** which are **in Asia;** unto Ephesus, and unto Smyrna, and unto Pergamos, and unto Thyatira, and unto Sardis, and unto Philadelphia, and unto Laodicea.
12. And I turned to see the voice that spake with me. **And** being turned, **I saw seven golden candlesticks;**
13. **And in the midst** of the seven candlesticks **one like unto the Son of man,** clothed with a garment down to the foot, and girt about the paps with a golden girdle.
14. His head and *his* hairs *were* white like wool, as white as snow; and his eyes *were* as a flame of fire;
15. And his feet like unto fine brass, as if they burned in a furnace; and his voice as the sound of many waters.
16. **And he had in his right hand seven stars:** and out of his mouth went a sharp two-edged sword: and his countenance *was* as the sun shineth in his strength.
17. **And when I saw him, I fell at his feet as dead. And he laid his right hand upon me, saying** unto me, **Fear not;** I am the first and the last:

18. **I am he that liveth, and was dead;** and, behold, **I am alive for evermore,** Amen; **and have the keys of hell** and of death. 19. **Write the things** which thou hast seen, and the things **which are, and** the things which **shall be** hereafter; 20. The mystery of the seven stars which thou sawest in my right hand, and the seven golden candlesticks. **The seven stars are the angels of the seven churches: and the seven candlesticks** which thou sawest **are the seven churches.**

CHAPTER 2

1. **Unto the angel of the church of Ephesus write;** These things saith he that holdeth the seven stars in his right hand, who walketh in the midst of the seven golden candlesticks; 2. **I know thy works,** and thy labour, and thy patience, **and how thou canst not bear them which are evil: and** thou **hast tried them which say they are apostles, and** are not, and hast **found them liars:** 3. **And** hast borne, and hast patience, and **for my name's sake** hast laboured, and **hast not fainted.** 4. **Nevertheless** I have *somewhat* against thee, because **thou hast left thy first love.** 5. Remember therefore from whence thou art fallen, and **repent,** and do the first works; **or else I will come** unto thee quickly, **and** will **remove thy candlestick** out of his place, except thou repent. 6. **But this thou hast, that thou hatest the deeds**

of the Nicolaitanes, which I also hate. 7. He that hath an ear, let him hear what **the Spirit saith unto the churches; To him that overcometh will I give to eat of the tree of life,** which is in the midst of the paradise of God. 8. **And unto the angel of the church in Smyrna write;** These things saith the first and the last, which was dead, and is alive; 9. **I know thy works, and tribulation,** and poverty, (but thou art rich) **and** *I know* **the blasphemy of them which say they are Jews,** and are not, **but are** the synagogue **of Satan.** 10. Fear none of those things which thou shalt suffer: behold, **the devil shall cast some of you into prison,** that ye may be tried; **and ye shall have tribulation ten days: be thou faithful** unto death, **and I will give thee a crown of life.** 11. He that hath an ear, let him hear what the Spirit saith unto the churches; **He that overcometh shall not be hurt of the second death.** 12. **And to the angel of the church in Pergamos write;** These things saith he which hath the sharp sword with two edges; 13. I know thy works, and where **thou dwellest, even where Satan's seat is: and thou holdest fast my name, and hast not denied my faith,** even in those days wherein Antipas *was* my faithful martyr, who was slain among you, where Satan dwelleth. 14. **But I have** a few **things against thee, because thou hast** there

them that hold the doctrine
of Balaam, who taught
Balac to cast a stumblingblock
before the children of
Israel, to eat things
sacrificed unto idols, and
to commit fornication.
15. So hast thou also them that hold
the doctrine of the Nicolaitanes,
which thing I hate.
16. **Repent; or else I will
come** unto thee quickly,
and will
fight against
**them with the sword
of my mouth.**
17. He that hath an ear,
let him hear what the Spirit saith
unto the churches;
**To him that overcometh
will I give** to eat of
**the hidden manna,
and** will give him
**a white stone, and in the
stone a new name written,**
which no man knoweth saving he
that receiveth *it*.
18. **And unto the angel of
the church in Thyatira write;**
These things saith the Son of God,
who hath his eyes like unto a flame of
fire, and his feet *are* like fine brass;
19. **I know thy works,**
and charity, and service,
and faith,
and thy patience, and thy works; and
the last *to be* more than the first.
20. **Notwithstanding
I have** a few
**things against thee,
because thou sufferest
that woman Jezebel,**
which calleth herself a prophetess,
to teach and
**to seduce my servants
to commit fornication,
and to eat things
sacrificed unto idols.**
21. And I gave her space to
repent of her fornication;
and she repented not.
22. **Behold, I will cast
her** into a bed,
**and them that commit
adultery with her into** great
**tribulation, except they
repent** of their deeds.
23. **And I will kill her
children** with death; and all
the churches shall know that
**I am he which searcheth
the** reins and
hearts: and I will
give unto every one of you
according to your
works.
24. **But** unto you I say, and
unto the rest in Thyatira,
**as many as have not this
doctrine,** and which have not
known the depths of Satan,
as they speak;
**I will put upon you
none other burden.**
25. But that which ye have *already*
hold fast till I come.
26. **And he that
overcometh,** and keepeth
my works unto the end, to him
**will I give power over
the nations:**
27. **And he shall rule** them with
a rod of iron; as the vessels of a
potter shall they be broken to shivers:
even as I received of my Father.
28. **And I will give him
the morning star.**
29. He that hath an ear,
let him hear what the Spirit
saith unto the churches.

CHAPTER 3

1. **And unto the angel of the
church in Sardis write;** These
things saith he that hath the seven
Spirits of God, and the seven stars; I
know thy works, that
**thou hast a name that
thou livest, and art dead.**
2. Be watchful, and
**strengthen the things
which remain, that are
ready to die: for I have
not found thy works
perfect before God.**
3. Remember therefore how thou hast

received and heard, and hold fast, **and repent. If** therefore **thou shalt not watch, I will come** on thee **as a thief, and thou shalt not know what hour** I will come upon thee. 4. **Thou hast a few** names even in Sardis **which have not defiled their garments; and they** shall **walk** with me **in white: for they are worthy.** 5. **He that overcometh,** the same shall be clothed in white raiment; and **I will not blot out his name out of the book of life, but I will confess his name before my Father,** and before his angels. 6. He that hath an ear, let him hear what the Spirit saith unto the churches. 7. **And to the angel of the church in Philadelphia write;** These things saith he that is holy, he that is true, he that hath the key of David, he that openeth, and no man shutteth; and shutteth, and no man openeth; 8. I know thy works: behold, **I have set before thee an open door,** and no man can shut it: **for thou hast a little strength,** and hast kept my word, **and hast not denied my name.** 9. Behold, I will make **them of the synagogue of Satan, which say they are Jews, and are not,** but do lie; behold, **I will make** them **to** come and **worship before thy feet,** and to know that I have loved thee. 10. **Because thou hast kept the word** of my patience, **I also will keep thee from the hour of temptation,**

which shall come upon all the world, to try them that dwell upon the earth. 11. Behold, I come quickly: **hold that fast** which thou hast, **that no man take thy crown.** 12. **Him that overcometh will I** make a pillar in the temple of my God, and he shall go no more out: and I will **write upon him** the name of my God, and the name of the city of my God, *which is* new Jerusalem, which cometh down out of heaven from my God: and *I will write upon him* **my new name.** 13. He that hath an ear, let him hear what the Spirit saith unto the churches. 14.**And unto the angel of the church of the Laodiceans write;** These things saith the Amen, the faithful and true witness, the beginning of the creation of God; 15. I know thy works, that **thou art neither cold nor hot:** I would thou wert cold or hot. 16. **So then because thou art lukewarm,** and neither cold nor hot, **I will spue thee out of my mouth.** 17. **Because thou sayest, I am rich,** and increased with goods, and have need of nothing; **and knowest not that thou art** wretched, and miserable, and **poor, and blind, and naked:** 18. **I counsel thee to buy of me gold tried in the fire, that thou mayest be rich; and** white raiment, that thou **mayest be clothed,** and *that* the shame of thy nakedness do not appear; **and anoint thine eyes with eye-salve, that thou mayest see.** 19. **As many as I love, I rebuke** and chasten: be zealous **therefore, and**

■ repent.
■ 20. **Behold, I stand at the**
■ **door, and knock:** if any
■ **man hear my voice, and**
■ **open the door,**
■ **I will come in** to him,
■ **and** will
■ **sup with him,** and he with me.
■ 21. **To him that overcometh**
■ **will I grant to sit with me in**
■ **my throne,** even as I also
overcame, and am set down with
my Father in his throne.
■ 22. **He that hath an ear, let**
■ **him hear** what the Spirit saith unto
the churches.

CHAPTER 4

■ 1. **After this** I looked, and, behold,
■ **a door was opened in**
■ **heaven: and the**
■ **first voice** which
■ **I heard** was as it were of a
trumpet talking with me; which
■ **said, Come** up hither,
■ **and I will shew thee things**
■ **which must be hereafter.**
■ 2. **And immediately I was in**
■ **the spirit; and,** behold,
■ **a throne was** set
■ **in heaven, and one**
■ **sat on the throne.**
3. And he that sat was to look upon
like a jasper and a sardine stone: and
there was a rainbow round about the
throne, in sight like unto an emerald.
■ 4. **And round about the**
■ **throne were four and**
■ **twenty seats: and**
upon the seats I saw
■ **four and twenty elders**
■ **sitting,** clothed in white raiment;
and they had on their heads
crowns of gold.
5. And out of the throne proceeded
lightnings and thunderings
and voices:
■ **and there were seven**
■ **lamps of fire burning before**
■ **the throne, which are the**
■ **seven Spirits**
■ **of God.**
6. And before the throne *there was* a

■ sea of glass like unto crystal:
■ **and** in the midst of the throne, and
■ **round about the throne,**
■ **were four beasts full of eyes**
before and behind.
■ 7. **And the first beast**
■ **was like a lion,** and
■ **the second** beast
■ **like a calf,** and
■ **the third** beast
■ **had a face as a man,**
■ **and the fourth** beast
■ **was like a flying eagle.**
8. And the four beasts had each of
them six wings about *him*; and *they
were* full of eyes within:
■ **and they rest not day and**
■ **night, saying, Holy, holy,**
■ **holy, LORD God Almighty,**
■ **which was,** and
■ **is, and is to come.**
9. And when those beasts give glory
and honour and thanks to him that sat
on the throne, who liveth
for ever and ever,
■ 10. **The four and twenty**
■ **elders fall down**
before him that sat on the throne,
■ **and worship him that liveth**
■ **for ever** and ever, and cast their
crowns before the throne,
■ **saying,**
■ 11. **Thou art worthy, O**
■ **Lord, to receive glory**
and honour and power:
■ **for thou hast created**
■ **all** things, and
■ **for thy pleasure**
they are and were created.

CHAPTER 5

■ 1. **And I saw in the**
■ **right hand of him**
that sat on the throne
■ **a book** written within and on the
backside, sealed
■ **with seven seals.**
■ 2. **And I saw a strong angel**
■ **proclaiming** with a loud voice,
■ **Who is worthy to**
■ **open the book,**
and to loose the seals thereof?
■ 3. **And no man in heaven,**

400

■ **nor in earth,**
neither under the earth,
■ **was able to open the book,**
neither to look thereon.
■ 4. **And I wept much,** because
no man was found worthy to open
and to read the book, neither to
look thereon.
■ 5. **And one of the elders**
■ **saith** unto me,
■ **Weep not: behold, the**
■ **Lion of the tribe of Juda,**
the Root of David,
■ **hath prevailed to**
■ **open the book,**
and to loose the seven seals thereof.
■ 6. **And** I beheld, and, lo,
■ **in the midst of the**
■ **throne** and of the four beasts,
and in the midst of the elders,
■ **stood a Lamb as it had**
■ **been slain,** having seven horns
and seven eyes, which are the seven
Spirits of God sent forth
into all the earth.
■ 7. **And he came and took**
■ **the book** out of the right hand of
him that sat upon the throne.
■ 8. **And** when he had taken the book,
■ **the four beasts and four**
■ **and twenty elders fell down**
■ **before the Lamb,** having every
one of them harps, and golden vials
full of odours, which are the
prayers of saints.
■ 9. **And they sung a new**
■ **song, saying, Thou art**
■ **worthy to take the book,**
and to open the seals thereof:
■ **for thou wast slain, and hast**
■ **redeemed us** to God
■ **by thy blood**
out of every kindred, and tongue,
and people, and nation;
■ 10. **And hast made us unto**
■ **our God kings and priests:**
■ **and we shall reign**
■ **on the earth.**
11. And I beheld,
■ **and I heard the**
■ **voice of** many
■ **angels** round about the
throne and the

■ **beasts and** the
■ **elders:** and the number of them was
ten thousand times ten thousand, and
thousands of thousands;
■ 12. **Saying with a loud**
■ **voice, Worthy is the**
■ **Lamb that was slain**
■ **to receive power,** and
■ **riches,** and
■ **wisdom,** and
■ **strength,** and
■ **honour,** and
■ **glory, and blessing.**
■ 13. **And every creature**
which is in heaven, and on the
earth, and under the earth, and
such as are in the sea, and all
that are in them, heard I
■ **saying, Blessing,**
and honour, and
■ **glory, and power, be** unto him
that sitteth upon the throne, and
■ **unto the Lamb** for ever and ever.
14. And the four beasts said, Amen.
And the four *and* twenty elders fell
down and worshipped him that liveth
for ever and ever.

CHAPTER 6

■ 1. **And** I saw when
■ **the Lamb opened one of**
■ **the seals, and I heard,**
as it were the noise of thunder,
■ **one of the** four
■ **beasts saying,**
■ **Come and see.**
■ 2. **And I saw,** and behold
■ **a white horse: and he that**
■ **sat on him** had a bow; and a
crown was given unto him: and he
■ **went forth conquering,**
and to conquer.
■ 3.**And when he had opened**
■ **the second seal,** I heard the
second beast say, Come and see.
■ 4. **And there went out**
■ **another horse that was red:**
■ **and power was given to**
■ **him** that sat thereon
■ **to take peace from the**
■ **earth, and that they should**
■ **kill one another:** and there was
given unto him a great sword.

■ 5.**And when he had opened**
■ **the third seal,** I heard the third
beast say, Come and see. And
■ **I beheld,** and lo
■ **a black horse; and**
■ **he that sat on him**
■ **had** a pair of
■ **balances** in his hand.
■ 6. **And I heard a voice**
in the midst of the four beasts
■ **say, A measure of wheat**
■ **for a penny, and three**
■ **measures of barley for a**
■ **penny; and** *see* thou
■ **hurt not the oil and** the
■ **wine.**
■ 7. **And when he** had
■ **opened the fourth seal,**
I heard the voice of the fourth
beast say, Come and see.
8. And I looked, and
■ **behold a pale horse: and**
■ **his name that sat on him**
■ **was Death, and Hell**
followed with him.
■ **And power was given** unto
■ **them over the fourth** part
■ **of the earth, to kill** with sword,
and with hunger, and with death, and
with the beasts of the earth.
■ 9. **And when he had**
■ **opened the fifth seal,**
■ **I saw** under the altar
■ **the souls** of them that were
■ **slain for the word of God,**
and for the testimony which they held:
■ 10. **And they cried**
with a loud voice, saying,
■ **How long, O Lord,**
holy and true,
■ **dost thou not** judge and
■ **avenge our blood**
on them that dwell on the earth?
■ 11. **And white robes were**
■ **given unto** every one of
■ **them; and**
it was said unto them, that
■ **they should rest**
yet for a little season,
■ **until their fellow servants** also
and their brethren, that
■ **should be killed** as they
were, should be fulfilled.

■ 12. And I beheld
■ **when he** had
■ **opened the**
■ **sixth seal,** and, lo,
■ **there was a great**
■ **earthquake; and the**
■ **sun became black**
as sackcloth of hair,
■ **and the moon**
■ **became as blood;**
■ 13. **And the stars** of heaven
■ **fell** unto the earth, even as a fig
tree casteth her untimely figs, when
she is shaken of a mighty wind.
■ 14. **And the heaven**
■ **departed** as a scroll
when it is rolled together;
■ **and every mountain and**
■ **island were moved**
out of their places.
■ 15. **And the kings**
of the earth, and the
■ **great men,** and the
■ **rich men,** and the
■ **chief captains,** and the
■ **mighty men,** and
■ **every bondman, and** every
■ **free man, hid** themselves
■ **in the dens and** in the
■ **rocks of** the
■ **mountains;**
■ 16. **And said to the**
■ **mountains and rocks, Fall**
■ **on us, and hide us** from the
face of him that sitteth on the throne,
and from the wrath of the Lamb:
■ 17. **For the great day of his**
■ **wrath is come; and who**
■ **shall be able to stand?**

CHAPTER 7

■ 1. **And** after these things
■ **I saw four angels** standing
on the four corners of the earth,
■ **holding the four winds**
of the earth,
■ **that the wind should not**
■ **blow on the earth,**
nor on the sea, nor on any tree.
■ 2. **And I saw another angel**
■ **ascending** from the east,
■ **having the seal of** the living
■ **God: and he cried**

with a loud voice **to the four angels,** to whom it was given to hurt the earth and the sea, 3. **Saying, Hurt not the earth,** neither the sea, nor the trees, **till we have sealed the servants of our God in their foreheads.** 4. And I heard the number of them which were sealed: **and there were sealed an hundred and forty and four thousand of** all **the tribes of** the children of **Israel.** 5. Of the tribe of Juda *were* sealed twelve thousand. Of the tribe of Reuben *were* sealed twelve thousand. Of the tribe of Gad *were* sealed twelve thousand. 6. Of the tribe of Aser *were* sealed twelve thousand. Of the tribe of Nephthalim *were* sealed twelve thousand. Of the tribe of Manasses *were* sealed twelve thousand. 7. Of the tribe of Simeon *were* sealed twelve thousand. Of the tribe of Levi *were* sealed twelve thousand. Of the tribe of Issachar *were* sealed twelve thousand. 8. Of the tribe of Zabulon *were* sealed twelve thousand. Of the tribe of Joseph *were* sealed twelve thousand. Of the tribe of Benjamin *were* sealed twelve thousand. 9. **After this** I beheld, and, lo, **a great multitude,** which no man could number, of all nations, and kindreds, and people, and tongues, **stood before the throne, and before the Lamb, clothed with white robes,** and palms in their hands; 10. **And cried** with a loud voice, saying, **Salvation to our God** which sitteth upon the throne, **and** unto **the Lamb.** 11. **And all the angels** stood round about the throne, and *about* the elder and the four beasts, and fell

before the throne on their faces, and **worshipped God,** 12. **Saying, Amen: Blessing,** and **glory,** and **wisdom,** and **thanksgiving,** and **honour,** and **power, and might, be unto our God for ever** and ever. Amen. 13. **And one of the elders answered,** saying unto me, **What are these** which are **arrayed in white robes?** and whence came they? 14. **And I said** unto him, **Sir, thou knowest. And he said** to me, **These** are they which **came out of great tribulation, and have washed their robes,** and made them white **in the blood of the Lamb.** 15. **Therefore are they before** the throne of **God,** and serve him day and night in his temple: **and he** that sitteth on the throne **shall dwell among them.** 16. They shall hunger no more, neither thirst any more; neither shall the sun light on them, nor any heat. 17. **For the Lamb** which is in the midst of the throne **shall feed them, and** shall **lead them unto living fountains** of waters: **and God shall wipe away all tears** from their eyes.

CHAPTER 8

1. **And when he had opened the seventh seal, there was silence** in heaven about the space of half an hour. 2. And I saw **the seven angels** which stood before God; and to them **were given seven trumpets.** 3. **And another angel** came and stood at the altar,

■ having a golden
■ censer; and there
■ was given unto him
■ much incense, that he
■ should offer it with the
■ prayers of all saints
upon the golden altar which was
before the throne.
■ 4. And the smoke of the
■ incense, *which came* with the
prayers of the saints,
■ ascended up before
■ God out of the angel's hand.
■ 5. And the angel
■ took the censer, and
■ filled it
■ with fire of the altar, and
■ cast it into the earth: and there
were voices, and thunderings, and
lightnings, and an earthquake.
■ 6. And the seven angels
■ which had the seven
■ trumpets prepared
themselves
■ to sound.
■ 7. The first angel sounded,
■ and there followed hail
■ and fire mingled
■ with blood, and they were cast
■ upon the earth: and the
■ third part of trees
was burnt up,
■ and all green
■ grass was burnt up.
■ 8. And the second angel
■ sounded, and as it were a great
mountain burning with fire was cast
into the sea:
■ and the third part of the
■ sea became blood;
■ 9. And the third part of
■ the creatures which were
■ in the sea, and had life,
■ died; and the third part of
■ the ships were destroyed.
■ 10. And the third angel
■ sounded, and there fell
■ a great star from heaven,
burning as it were a lamp, and it
■ fell upon the third part of
■ the rivers, and upon the
■ fountains of waters;
11. And the name of

■ the star is called
■ Wormwood: and the third part
of the waters became wormwood;
■ and many men died of the
■ waters, because they were
■ made bitter.
■ 12. And the fourth angel
■ sounded, and the third part
of the sun was smitten, and
the third part of
■ the moon, and the third part of
■ the stars; so as the third part of
them was darkened,
■ and the day shone not for a
■ third part of it, and the
■ night likewise.
13. And I beheld, and
■ heard an angel flying
■ through the midst of
■ heaven, saying
with a loud voice, Woe, woe,
■ woe, to the inhabiters of the
■ earth by reason of the
■ other voices of the trumpet of the
three angels, which are
■ yet to sound!

CHAPTER 9

■ 1. And the fifth angel
■ sounded, and I saw a star
■ fall from heaven
■ unto the
■ earth: and to him was given
■ the key of the
■ bottomless pit.
■ 2. And he opened the
bottomless
■ pit; and there arose a smoke out of
the pit, as the smoke of a great
furnace; and the sun and the air
were darkened by reason of the
smoke of the pit.
■ 3. And there came out
of the smoke
■ locusts upon the earth:
■ and unto them was given
■ power, as the scorpions
of the earth
■ have power.
■ 4. And it was commanded
them
■ that they should
■ not hurt the grass

of the earth, neither any green thing,
neither any tree;
but only those
men which have not
the seal of God in
their foreheads.
5. **And** to them it was given that
they should not kill them,
but that
they should be tormented
five months: and their torment
was as the torment of a scorpion,
when he striketh a man.
6. **And** in those days shall
men seek death,
and shall not find it; and
shall desire to die, and
death shall flee from them.
7. **And the shapes of the**
locusts were like unto **horses**
prepared unto
battle; and on their heads *were*
as it were crowns like gold, and
their faces *were*
as the faces of
men.
8. **And they had hair as**
the hair of
women, and their teeth were
as *the teeth* of
lions.
9. **And they had**
breastplates, as it were
breastplates of iron; and
the sound of their wings *was*
as the sound of
chariots of many horses
running to battle.
10. **And they had**
tails like unto
scorpions, and there were
stings in their tails:
and their
power *was*
to hurt men five months.
11. **And they had**
a king over them,
which is the angel
of the bottomless
pit, whose name in the
Hebrew tongue
is Abaddon, but in the
Greek tongue hath *his* name

Apollyon.
12. One woe is past; *and*, behold,
there come two woes more hereafter.
13. **And the sixth angel**
sounded, and I heard a
voice from the four horns of the
golden altar which is before God,
14. **Saying to the sixth angel**
which had the trumpet,
Loose the four angels
which are
bound in the great
river Euphrates.
15. **And the four angels were**
loosed, which were prepared for an
hour, and a day, and a month, and a
year, for
to slay the third part
of men.
16. And the number of
the army of the
horsemen were two
hundred thousand
thousand:
and I heard the number of them.
17. **And thus I saw the horses**
in the vision, and them that
sat on them,
having breastplates of fire, and of
jacinth, and brimstone:
and the heads of the horses
were
as the heads of lions; and
out of their mouths
issued fire and smoke
and brimstone.
18. **By these three was the**
third part of men killed,
by the fire, and by the smoke, and
by the brimstone, which issued
out of their mouths.
19. **For their power is in**
their mouth, and in their
tails: for their tails *were* like unto
serpents, and had heads, and with
them they do hurt.
20. **And the rest** of the men
which were not killed
by these plagues
yet repented not
of the works of their hands,
that they should not
worship devils, and idols

of gold, and silver, and brass, and stone, and of wood: which neither can see, nor hear, nor walk:

■ 21. **Neither repented they of**
■ **their murders,** nor of their
■ **sorceries,** nor of their
■ **fornication, nor** of their
■ **thefts.**

CHAPTER 10

■ 1. **And I saw another mighty**
■ **angel come** down from heaven, clothed with a cloud: and a rainbow *was* upon his head, and his face *was* as it were the sun, and his feet as pillars of fire:
■ 2. **And he had** in his hand
■ **a little book open:** and he set his right foot upon the sea, and *his* left *foot* on the earth,
3. And cried with a loud voice, as *when* a lion roareth:
■ **and when he** had
■ **cried, seven thunders**
■ **uttered their voices.**
4. **And** when the seven thunders had uttered their voices,
■ **I was about to write: and**
■ **I heard a voice** from heaven
■ **saying** unto me,
■ **Seal up those things** which the seven thunders
■ **uttered, and write** them
■ **not.**
■ 5. **And the angel which I saw** stand upon the sea and upon the earth
■ **lifted up his hand** to heaven,
■ 6. **And sware by him that**
■ **liveth for ever** and ever, who created heaven, and the things that therein are, and the earth, and the things that therein are, and the sea, and the things which are therein,
■ **that there should**
■ **be time no longer:**
■ 7. **But in the days of the**
■ **voice of the seventh angel,** when he shall begin to sound,
■ **the mystery of God should**
■ **be finished,** as he hath declared to his servants the prophets.
■ 8. **And the voice which I**

■ **heard** from heaven spake unto me again, and
■ **said,** Go *and*
■ **take the little book** which is open in the hand of the angel which standeth upon the sea and upon the earth.
■ 9. **And I went unto the**
■ **angel, and said** unto him,
■ **Give me the little book.**
■ **And he said** unto me,
■ **Take it, and eat it** up; and it shall make thy belly bitter, but it shall be in thy mouth sweet as honey.
■ 10. **And I** took the little book out of the angel's hand, and
■ **ate it** up;
■ **and it was in my mouth**
■ **sweet as honey: and** as soon as I had eaten it,
■ **my belly was bitter.**
■ 11. **And he said** unto me,
■ **Thou must prophesy** again before many peoples, and nations, and tongues, and kings.

CHAPTER 11

■ 1. **And there was**
■ **given me** a reed like unto
■ **a rod: and the angel stood,**
■ **saying, Rise, and measure**
■ **the temple** of God,
■ **and the altar, and them**
■ **that worship** therein.
■ 2. **But the court** which is without the temple leave out, and
■ **measure it not; for it is given**
■ **unto the Gentiles:** and the holy city shall they tread under foot forty *and* two months.
■ 3. **And I will give power unto**
■ **my two witnesses, and they**
■ **shall prophesy a thousand**
■ **two hundred** *and*
■ **threescore days,** clothed in sackcloth.
4. These are the two olive trees, and the two candlesticks standing before the God of the earth.
■ 5. **And if any man will hurt**
■ **them,** fire proceedeth out of their mouth, and devoureth their enemies: and if any man will hurt them,

he must in this manner
be killed.
6. **These have power to shut**
heaven, that it rain not
in the days of their prophecy:
and have power
over waters to turn them
to blood, and to smite
the earth with all
plagues, as often as
they will.
7. **And when they** shall
have finished their
testimony, the beast
that ascendeth
out of the bottomless
pit shall make war against
them, and shall overcome them,
and kill them.
8. **And their dead bodies**
shall lie in the street of
the great city, which spiritually
is called Sodom and Egypt,
where also our Lord
was crucified.
9. **And they of the people** and
kindreds and tongues and nations
shall see their dead
bodies three days and
an half, and shall not
suffer their dead
bodies to be put in graves.
10. **And they** that dwell
upon the earth shall rejoice
over them, and make merry, and
shall send gifts one to another;
because these two
prophets tormented them
that dwelt on the earth.
11. **And after three days and**
an half the Spirit of life from God
entered into
them, and they stood
upon their feet;
and great fear fell
upon them which saw them.
12. **And they heard a**
great voice from heaven
saying unto them,
Come up hither.
And they ascended up
to heaven in a cloud; and their
enemies beheld them.

13. **And the same hour was**
there a great earthquake,
and the tenth part of the city fell,
and in the earthquake
were slain of men
seven thousand: and
the remnant were
affrighted, and
gave glory to the
God of heaven.
14. The second woe is past;
and, behold, the third
woe cometh quickly.
15. **And the seventh**
angel sounded; and
there were great
voices in heaven,
saying, The kingdoms of
this world are become
the kingdoms of our Lord,
and of his Christ; and he
shall reign for ever and ever.
16. **And the four and twenty**
elders, which sat before God on
their seats, fell upon their faces, and
worshipped God,
17. **Saying, We give** thee
thanks, O LORD God Almighty,
which art, and
wast, and art to come;
because thou hast
taken to thee thy
great power, and
hast reigned.
18. And the nations were angry, and
thy wrath is come, and
the time of the dead, that
they should be judged, and
that thou shouldest give
reward unto thy servants the
prophets, and to the saints, and
them that fear thy
name, small and great;
and shouldest destroy them
which destroy
the earth.
19. **And the temple of God**
was opened in heaven,
and there was
seen in his temple
the ark of his testament:
and there were lightnings, and voices,
and thunderings, and an earthquake,

407

| | and great hail.

CHAPTER 12

1. **And there appeared** a great wonder **in heaven; a woman** clothed with the sun, and the moon under her feet, and upon her head a crown of twelve stars:
2. **And she being with child cried,** travailing in birth, and pained **to be delivered.**
3. **And there appeared** another wonder in heaven;and behold **a** great **red dragon,** having seven heads and ten horns, and seven crowns upon his heads.
4. And his tail drew the third part of the stars of heaven, and did cast them to the earth: **and the dragon stood before the woman** which was ready to be delivered, for **to devour her child as soon as it was born.**
5. **And she brought forth a man child, who was to rule all nations** with a rod of iron: **and her child was caught up unto God,** and *to* his throne.
6. **And the woman fled into** the wilderness, where she hath **a place prepared of God,** that they should feed her there a thousand two hundred *and* threescore days.
7. **And there was war in heaven: Michael and his angels fought against the dragon; and the dragon** fought and his angels,
8. And **prevailed not;** neither was their place found any more in heaven.
9. **And the great dragon** was cast out, that old serpent, **called** the Devil, and **Satan, which deceiveth the whole world:** he **was cast out** into the earth, **and his angels were cast out with him.**
10. **And I heard a loud voice saying** in heaven, **Now is come salvation,** and strength, and the kingdom of our God, and the power of his Christ: **for the accuser of our brethren is cast down,** which accused them before our God day and night.
11. **And they overcame him by the blood of the Lamb, and by** the word of **their testimony;** and they loved not their lives unto the death.
12. Therefore rejoice, *ye* heavens, and ye that dwell in them. **Woe to the inhabiters of** the **earth and** of the **sea! for the devil is come down** unto you, **having great wrath, because** he knoweth that **he hath but a short time.**
13. **And when the dragon** saw that he **was cast unto** the **earth, he persecuted the woman** which brought forth the man *child.*
14. **And to the woman were given two wings** of a great eagle, **that she might fly** into the wilderness, **into her place,** where she is nourished **for a time,** and times, and half a time, **from** the face of **the serpent.**
15. **And the serpent cast** out of his mouth **water as a flood** after the woman, **that he might cause her to be carried away** of the flood.
16. **And the earth** helped the woman, and the earth opened her mouth, and **swallowed up the flood** which the dragon cast out of his mouth.

408

17. **And the dragon** was wroth with the woman, and **went to** make **war with** the remnant of **her seed, which keep the commandments** of God, **and have the testimony of Jesus** Christ.

CHAPTER 13

1. **And I** stood upon the sand of the sea, and **saw a beast rise** up **out of the sea, having seven heads and ten horns,** and upon his horns ten crowns, **and upon his heads the name of blasphemy.**

2. And the beast which I saw was like unto a leopard, and his feet were as *the feet* of a bear, and his mouth as the mouth of a lion: and the dragon gave him his power, and his seat, and great authority.

3. **And I saw one of his heads** as it were **wounded to death; and his** deadly **wound was healed: and all the world wondered after the beast.**

4. **And they worshipped the dragon which gave power unto the beast: and they worshipped the beast, saying, Who is like unto the beast?** who is able to make war with him?

5. **And there was given** unto **him a mouth speaking great things and blasphemies; and power** was given unto him **to continue forty and two months.**

6. **And he opened his mouth** in blasphemy **against God, to blaspheme his name,** and his tabernacle, and them that dwell in heaven.

7. **And it was given** unto **him to make war with the saints, and** to **overcome them: and power** was given him **over all** kindreds, and tongues, and **nations.**

8. **And all** that dwell upon **the earth shall worship him, whose names are not** written **in the book of life of the Lamb slain from the foundation of the world.**

9. If any man have an ear, let him hear.

10. He that leadeth into captivity shall go into captivity: he that killeth with the sword must be killed with the sword. Here is the patience and the faith of the saints.

11. **And I beheld another beast** coming up out of the earth; **and he had two horns like a lamb, and he spake as a dragon.**

12. **And he** exerciseth all the power of the first beast before him, and **causeth the earth and them** which dwell **therein to worship the first beast, whose deadly wound was healed.**

13. **And he doeth great wonders,** so that he maketh fire come down from heaven on the earth in the sight of men,

14. **And deceiveth** them that dwell on the earth **by the means of** those **miracles** which he had power to do in the sight of the beast; **saying** to them that dwell on the earth, **that they should make an image to the beast, which had the wound** by a sword, **and did live.**

15. **And he had power to give life unto the image of the beast,** that the image of the beast should both speak,

and cause that as many
as would not worship the
image of the beast should
be killed.

16. And he causeth all,
both small and great, rich
and poor, free and bond,
to receive a mark in their
right hand, or in their
foreheads:

17. And that no man might
buy or sell, save he that
had the mark, or the
name of the beast,
or the number of his name.

18. Here is wisdom. Let him that
hath understanding
count the number of the
beast: for it is the number of a
man; and his number is
Six hundred threescore and
six.

CHAPTER 14

1. And I looked, and, lo,
a Lamb stood on the mount
Sion, and
with him
an hundred forty and
four thousand, having his
Father's name written in
their foreheads.

2. And I heard a voice from
heaven, as the voice of many
waters, and as the voice of a
great thunder:
and I heard the voice
of harpers harping
with their harps:

3. And they sung as it were
a new song before the throne,
and before the four beasts,
and the elders:
and no man could
learn that song but
the hundred and
forty and
four thousand, which were
redeemed from the earth.

4. These are they which were not
defiled with women;
for they are virgins.
These are they which

follow the Lamb whithersoever
he goeth. These were redeemed
from among men,
being the firstfruits unto
God and to the Lamb.

5. And in their mouth was found
no guile:
for they are without fault
before the throne of God.

6. And I saw another
angel fly in the midst of heaven,
having the everlasting
gospel to preach unto
them that dwell on the earth, and to
every nation, and
kindred, and
tongue, and people,

7. Saying with a loud voice,
Fear God, and give glory to him;
for the hour of
his judgment is come: and
worship him that made heaven,
and earth, and the sea, and the
fountains of waters.

8. And there followed
another angel, saying,
Babylon is fallen,
is fallen, that great city,
because she made
all nations drink of
the wine of the wrath of
her fornication.

9. And the third angel
followed them,
saying with a loud voice,
If any man worship the
beast and his image,
and receive his mark
in his forehead, or in his hand,

10. The same shall drink of
the wine of the wrath of
God, which is poured out without
mixture into the cup of his indignation;
and he shall be tormented
with fire and brimstone
in the presence of the holy
angels, and in the presence of
the Lamb:

11. And the smoke of their
torment ascendeth
up for ever and ever:
and they have no
rest day nor night,

■ who worship the beast
■ and his image, and whosoever
■ receiveth the mark
of his name.
12. Here is the patience of the
saints: here *are* they that keep
the commandments of God,
and the faith of Jesus.
■ 13. And I heard a
■ voice from heaven
■ saying unto me,
■ Write, Blessed are
■ the dead which die
■ in the Lord from henceforth:
■ Yea, saith the Spirit, that
■ they may rest from their labours;
■ and their works do
■ follow them.
■ 14. And I looked, and
■ behold a white cloud,
■ and upon the cloud
■ one sat like unto
■ the Son of man,
■ having on his head
■ a golden crown,
■ and in his hand
■ a sharp sickle.
■ 15. And another angel
■ came out of the temple,
■ crying with a loud voice
■ to him that sat on the cloud,
■ Thrust in
■ thy sickle, and reap: for the
time is come for thee to reap;
■ for the harvest of the earth
■ is ripe.
■ 16. And he that sat on the cloud
■ thrust in
■ his sickle on the earth;
■ and the earth was
■ reaped.
■ 17. And another angel
■ came out of the temple
which is in heaven, he also
■ having a sharp
■ sickle.
■ 18. And another angel
came out from the altar,
■ which had power over fire;
and
■ cried with a loud cry
■ to him that had the sharp
sickle, saying,

■ Thrust in thy sharp
■ sickle, and gather the
■ clusters of the vine
of the earth;
■ for her grapes are fully
■ ripe.
■ 19. And the angel thrust in his
sickle into the earth, and
■ gathered the vine of the earth,
■ and cast it into the great
■ winepress of the wrath
■ of God.
20. And the winepress was
trodden without the city,
■ and blood came out of the
■ winepress, even unto the horse
bridles, by the space of a thousand
and six hundred furlongs.

CHAPTER 15

■ 1. And I saw another sign in
heaven, great and marvellous,
■ seven angels having the
■ seven last plagues; for i
n them is filled up the wrath of God.
■ 2. And I saw as it were
■ a sea of glass mingled
■ with fire: and them that
■ had gotten the victory
■ over the beast, and over his
image, and over his mark, *and*
over the number of his name,
■ stand on the sea of glass,
having the harps of God.
■ 3. And they sing the song
■ of Moses the servant of God,
■ and the song of the Lamb,
■ saying, Great and marvellous
■ are thy works, Lord
God Almighty;
■ just and true are thy ways,
■ thou King of saints.
■ 4. Who shall not fear
thee, O Lord,
■ and glorify thy name? for
■ thou only art holy: for all
■ nations shall come and
■ worship before
■ thee; for thy judgments
are made manifest.
5. And after that I looked, and,
behold, the temple of the tabernacle
of the testimony in heaven

was opened:

6. **And the seven angels came out of the temple,** having the seven plagues, clothed in pure and white linen, and having their breasts girded with golden girdles.

7. **And one of the four beasts gave unto the** seven **angels seven golden vials full of the wrath of God,** who liveth for ever and ever.

8. And the temple was filled with smoke from the glory of God, and from his power; and no man was able to enter into the temple, till the seven plagues of the seven angels were fulfilled.

CHAPTER 16

1. **And I heard a great voice** out of the temple **saying to the** seven **angels,** Go your ways, and **pour out the vials of the wrath of God** upon the earth.

2. **And the first** went, and **poured out his vial upon** the **earth; and there fell a** noisome and **grievous sore upon** the **men which had the mark of the beast,** and *upon* them which worshipped his image.

3. **And the second** angel **poured out his vial upon the sea;** **and it became as** the **blood** of a dead *man;* **and every** living **soul died in the sea.**

4. **And the third** angel **poured out his vial upon** the **rivers and** fountains of **waters; and they became blood.**

5. **And I heard the angel of** the **waters say, Thou art righteous, O Lord,** which art, and wast, and shalt be, **because thou hast judged thus.**

6. **For they have shed the blood of saints** and prophets, and thou hast given them blood to drink; for they are worthy.

7. And I heard another out of the altar say, Even so, Lord God Almighty, true and righteous *are* thy judgments.

8. **And the fourth** angel **poured out his vial upon the sun; and** **power was given** unto **him to scorch** men **with fire.**

9. **And men were scorched** with great heat, **and blasphemed** the name of **God,** which hath power over these plagues: **and** they **repented not** to give him glory.

10. **And the fifth** angel **poured out his vial upon** the seat of **the beast; and his kingdom** was full of darkness; **and they gnawed their tongues for pain,**

11. **And blasphemed** the **God** of heaven **because of** their **pains and** their **sores, and repented not** of their deeds.

12. **And the sixth** angel **poured out his vial upon the** great river **Euphrates; and the water** thereof was **dried up, that the way of the kings of the east** might **be prepared.**

13. And I saw three unclean **spirits** like frogs **come out of the mouth of the dragon,** and out of the mouth of **the beast, and** out of the mouth of **the false prophet.**

14. **For they are the spirits of devils,** working miracles, **which go forth unto the kings of the earth** and of the whole world,

to gather them to the battle of that great day of God Almighty.

15. Behold, I come as a thief. Blessed *is* he that watcheth, and keepeth his garments, lest he walk naked, and they see his shame.

16. And he gathered them together into a place called in the Hebrew tongue Armageddon.

17. And the seventh angel poured out his vial into the air; and there came a great voice out of the temple of heaven, from the throne, saying, It is done.

18. And there were voices, and thunders,and lightnings; and there was a great earthquake, such as was not since men were upon the earth,so mighty an earthquake, *and* so great.

19. And the great city was divided into three parts, and the cities of the nations fell: and great Babylon came in remembrance before God, to give unto her the cup of the wine of the fierceness of his wrath.

20. And every island fled away, and the mountains were not found.

21. And there fell upon men a great hail out of heaven, *every stone* about the weight of a talent: and men blasphemed God because of the plague of the hail; for the plague thereof was exceeding great.

CHAPTER 17

1. And there came one of the seven angels which had the seven vials, and talked with me, saying unto me, Come hither; I will shew unto the judgment of the great whore that sitteth upon many waters:

2. With whom the kings of the earth have committed fornication, and the inhabitants of the earth have been made drunk with the wine of her fornication.

3. So he carried me away in the spirit into the wilderness: and I saw a woman sit upon a scarlet coloured beast, full of names of blasphemy, having seven heads and ten horns.

4. And the woman was arrayed in purple and scarlet colour, and decked with gold and precious stones and pearls, having a golden cup in her hand full of abominations and filthiness of her fornication

5. And upon her forehead was a name written, MYSTERY, BABYLON THE GREAT, THE MOTHER OF HARLOTS AND ABOMINATIONS OF THE EARTH.

6. And I saw the woman drunken with the blood of the saints, and with the blood of the martyrs of Jesus: and when I saw her, I wondered with great admiration.

7. And the angel said unto me, Wherefore didst thou marvel? I will tell thee the mystery of the woman, and of the beast that carrieth her, which hath the seven heads and ten horns.

8. The beast that thou sawest was, and is not; and shall ascend out of the bottomless pit, and go into perdition: and they that dwell on the earth shall wonder, whose names were not written in the book of life from the foundation of the world, when they behold the beast that was, and is not, and yet is.

9. And here *is* the mind which hath wisdom.

The seven heads are seven mountains, on which the woman sitteth.

10. **And there are seven kings: five are fallen,** and **one is, and the other is not yet come; and when he cometh, he must continue a short space.**

11. **And the beast** that was, and is not, even he is the eighth, and **is of the seven, and goeth into perdition.**

12. **And the ten horns** which thou sawest **are ten kings, which have received no kingdom as yet; but receive power** as kings **one hour with the beast.**

13. **These** have one mind, and **shall give their power** and strength **unto the beast.**

14. **These shall make war with the Lamb, and the Lamb shall overcome them: for he is Lord of lords, and King of kings:** and they that are with him *are* called, and chosen, and faithful.

15. **And he saith** unto me, **The waters** which thou sawest, **where the whore sitteth, are** peoples, and **multitudes, and nations,** and tongues.

16. **And the ten horns** which thou sawest upon the beast, these **shall hate the whore, and** shall **make her desolate** and naked, and shall eat her flesh, and burn her with fire.

17. **For God hath put in their hearts to fulfil his will,** and to agree, **and give their kingdom unto the beast,** until the words of God shall be fulfilled.

18. **And the woman** which thou sawest **is that great city, which reigneth** over the kings of the earth.

CHAPTER 18

1. **And** after these things **I saw another angel** come down from heaven, having great power; and the earth was lightened with his glory.

2. **And he cried** mightily with a strong voice, saying, **Babylon** the great **is fallen,** is fallen, **and is** become **the habitation of devils, and the hold of every foul spirit, and a cage of every unclean** and hateful **bird.**

3. **For all nations have drunk** of the wine of **the wrath of her fornication,** and the kings of the earth have committed fornication with her, **and the merchants** of the earth **are** waxed **rich through** the abundance of **her delicacies.**

4. **And I heard another voice from heaven, saying, Come out of her, my people,** that ye be not partakers of her sins, and that ye receive not of her plagues.

5. **For her sins have reached** unto **heaven, and God hath remembered her iniquities.**

6. **Reward her even as she rewarded you,** and double unto her double according to her works: in the cup which she hath filled fill to her double.

7. **How much she hath glorified herself,** and lived deliciously, so much **torment and sorrow give her: for she saith** in her heart, **I sit a queen,** and am no widow, and shall see no sorrow.

8. **Therefore shall her**

■ **plagues come in one day,**
death, and mourning, and famine;
■ **and she shall be utterly**
■ **burned with fire: for** strong *is*
■ **the Lord** God who
■ **judgeth her.**
■ 9. **And the kings** of the earth,
who have committed fornication
and lived deliciously with her,
■ **shall** bewail her, and
■ **lament for her,** when they
shall see the smoke of her burning,
10. Standing afar off for the fear
of her torment,
■ **saying, Alas,** alas that great city
■ **Babylon,** that mighty city! for
■ **in one hour is thy**
■ **judgment come.**
■ 11. **And the merchants**
of the earth
■ **shall weep** and mourn
■ **over her; for no man buyeth**
■ **their merchandise**
■ **any more:**
12. The merchandise of gold, and
silver, and precious stones, and of
pearls, and fine linen, and purple, and
silk, and scarlet, and all thyine wood,
and all manner vessels of ivory, and
all manner vessels of most precious
wood, and of brass, and iron,
and marble,
13. And cinnamon, and odours, and
ointments, and frankincense, and
wine, and oil, and fine flour, and
wheat, and beasts, and sheep, and
horses, and chariots, and slaves, and
souls of men.
■ 14. **And the fruits that thy**
■ **soul lusted after are**
■ **departed** from thee,
■ **and all things**
which were dainty and
■ **goodly are departed**
from thee, and thou shalt find
them no more at all.
■ 15. **The merchants**
of these things, which were
■ **made rich by her, shall**
■ **stand afar off for the fear of**
■ **her torment,**weeping and wailing,
■ 16. **And saying, Alas, alas**
■ **that great city,** that was clothed

in fine linen, and purple, and scarlet,
and decked with gold, and precious
stones, and pearls!
■ 17. **For in one hour so great**
■ **riches is come to nought.**
■ **And** every shipmaster, and
■ **all** the company in
■ **ships, and sailors,**
and as many as trade by sea,
■ **stood afar off,**
18. And cried when they saw the
smoke of her burning, saying, What
city is like unto this great city!
■ 19. **And they**
cast dust on their heads, and
■ **cried,** weeping and wailing,
■ **saying,** Alas, alas
■ **that great city, wherein**
■ **were made rich all that**
■ **had ships** in the sea by
reason of her costliness!
■ **for in one hour is she**
■ **made desolate.**
20. **Rejoice** over her,
thou heaven, and
■ **ye holy apostles and**
■ **prophets; for God hath**
■ **avenged you** on her.
21. **And a mighty angel took**
■ **up a stone** like a great millstone,
■ **and cast it into the sea,**
■ **saying,** Thus
■ **with violence shall that**
■ **great city** Babylon
■ **be thrown down, and** shall be
■ **found no more** at all.
22. And the voice of harpers, and
musicians, and of pipers, and
trumpeters, shall be heard no more at
all in thee; and no craftsman, of
whatsoever craft *he be,* shall be
found any more in thee; and the
sound of a millstone shall be heard no
more at all in thee;
23. And the light of a candle shall
shine no more at all in thee; and the
voice of the bridegroom and of the
bride shall be heard no more at all in
thee: for thy merchants were the
great men of the earth; for by thy
sorceries were all nations deceived.
■ 24. **And in her was found the**
■ **blood of prophets,** and of

■ saints, and of
■ all that were
■ slain upon the earth.

CHAPTER 19

1. And after these things
■ I heard a great voice
■ of much people in
■ heaven, saying,
■ Alleluia; Salvation, and
■ glory, and
■ honour, and power,
■ unto the Lord our God:
■ 2. For true and righteous
■ are his judgments: for he
■ hath judged the great
■ whore, which did corrupt
■ the earth with her fornication,
and hath avenged the blood
of his servants at her hand.
3. And again they said, Alleluia. And
her smoke rose up for ever and ever.
■ 4. And the four and twenty
■ elders and the four beasts
fell down and
■ worshipped God
that sat on the throne,
■ saying, Amen; Alleluia.
■ 5. And a voice came out
■ of the throne, saying,
■ Praise our God, all ye his
■ servants, and ye that fear him,
both small and great.
■ 6. And I heard as it were the
voice of a great multitude, and as the
■ voice of many waters, and
as the voice of mighty
■ thunderings, saying,
Alleluia: for
■ the Lord God
■ omnipotent reigneth.
■ 7. Let us be glad and
■ rejoice, and give honour to
■ him: for the marriage of the
■ Lamb is come, and his wife
■ hath made herself ready.
■ 8. And to her was granted
that she should be arrayed in
■ fine linen, clean and white:
■ for the fine linen is the
■ righteousness of saints.
■ 9. And he saith unto me,
■ Write, Blessed are

■ they which are
■ called unto the marriage
■ supper of the Lamb.
And he saith unto me, These
are the true sayings of God.
■ 10. And I fell at his feet
■ to worship him. And
■ he said unto me,
See thou do it not: I am
■ thy fellow servant,
and of thy brethren that have
the testimony of Jesus:
■ worship God: for the
■ testimony of Jesus is the
■ spirit of prophecy.
■ 11. And I saw heaven
■ opened, and behold a
■ white horse; and he that sat
■ upon him was called
■ Faithful and True, and in
■ righteousness he doth
■ judge and make war.
12. His eyes *were* as a flame of fire,
and on his head *were* many crowns;
and he had a name written, that no
man knew, but he himself.
■ 13. And he was clothed with
■ a vesture dipped in blood:
■ and his name is called The
■ Word of God.
■ 14. And the armies *which were*
■ in heaven followed him
upon white horses,
■ clothed in fine linen,
white and clean.
■ 15. And out of his mouth
■ goeth a sharp sword,
■ that with it he should
■ smite the nations:
■ and he shall rule them
■ with a rod of iron:
and he treadeth the winepress
of the fierceness and wrath
of Almighty God.
■ 16. And he hath
on *his* vesture and
■ on his thigh a name written,
■ KING OF KINGS, AND
■ LORD OF LORDS.
■ 17. And I saw an angel
standing in the sun;
■ and he cried
with a loud voice, saying

to all the fowls that fly
in the midst of heaven,
Come and gather
yourselves together
unto the supper of
the great God;
18. That ye may
eat the flesh of
kings, and the flesh of
captains, and the flesh of
mighty men, and the flesh of
horses, and of them
that sit on them,
and the flesh of all men,
both free and bond,
both small and great.
19. And I saw the beast, and
the kings of the earth,
and their armies,
gathered together
to make war against
him that sat
on the horse, and against
his army.
20. And the beast was
taken, and with him
the false prophet
that wrought miracles before him,
with which he deceived them that
had received the mark of the beast,
and them that worshipped
his image. These
both were cast alive
into a lake of fire
burning with brimstone.
21. And the remnant
were slain with the
sword of him that sat
upon the horse, which *sword*
proceeded out of his mouth:
and all the fowls were
filled with their flesh.

CHAPTER 20

1. And I saw an angel
come down from heaven,
having the key of the
bottomless pit and a great
chain in his hand.
2. And he laid hold on
the dragon, that old serpent,
which is the Devil, and
Satan, and bound him a

thousand years,
3. And cast him into the
bottomless pit, and shut him
up, and set a seal upon him,
that he should deceive the
nations no more, till the
thousand years should be
fulfilled: and after that he
must be loosed a
little season.
4. And I saw thrones, and they
sat upon them, and judgment
was given unto them:
and I saw the souls of
them that were beheaded
for the witness of
Jesus, and for
the word of God, and which
had not worshipped the beast,
neither his image, neither had
received *his* mark upon their
foreheads, or in their hands;
and they lived
and reigned with Christ
a thousand years.
5. But the rest of the dead
lived not again
until the thousand years
were finished. This is the
first resurrection.
6. Blessed and holy
is he that hath part in the
first resurrection: on such
the second death hath no
power, but they shall be
priests of God and of Christ,
and shall reign with him
a thousand years.
7. And when the thousand
years are expired, Satan
shall be loosed
out of his prison,
8. And shall go out to
deceive the nations
which are in the four quarters
of the earth, Gog, and Magog,
to gather them together
to battle: the number of
whom *is* as the sand of the sea.
9. And they went up on the
breadth of the earth, and
compassed the camp
of the saints

about, and the beloved city:

and fire came down
from God out of heaven,
and devoured them.

10. And the devil
that deceived them
was cast into the lake
of fire and brimstone,
where the beast and the
false prophet are, and
shall be tormented
day and night
for ever and ever.

11. And I saw a great white
throne, and him that sat
on it, from whose face the earth
and the heaven fled away; and
there was found no place for them.

12. And I saw the dead,
small and great,
stand before God; and the
books were opened: and
another book was opened,
which is the book of life:
and the dead were judged
out of those things which were
written in the books,
according to their works.

13. And the sea gave up
the dead which were in it;
and death and hell
delivered up the dead
which were in them:
and they were
judged every man
according to their works.

14. And death and hell were
cast into the lake of fire.
This is the second death.

15. And whosoever was not
found written in the book of
life was cast into the lake of
fire.

CHAPTER 21

1. And I saw a new heaven
and a new earth:
for the first heaven and the first
earth were passed away; and

there was no more sea.

2. And I John saw the holy
city, new Jerusalem,
coming down
from God out of heaven,
prepared as a bride adorned
for her husband.

3. And I heard a great
voice out of heaven
saying, Behold,
the tabernacle of God is
with men, and he will dwell with
them, and they shall be his people,
and God himself shall be
with them, and be
their God.

4. And God shall wipe
away all tears from their eyes;
and there shall be no more
death, neither sorrow, nor crying,
neither shall there be any more
pain: for the former things are
passed away.

5. And he that sat upon
the throne said, Behold,
I make all things new.
And he said unto me,
Write: for these words
are true and faithful.

6. And he said unto me,
It is done. I am Alpha and
Omega, the beginning and the end.
I will give unto him that is
athirst of the fountain of
the water of life freely.

7. He that overcometh shall
inherit all things; and I will be his
God, and he shall be my son.

8. But the fearful, and
unbelieving, and the abominable,
and murderers, and whoremongers,
and sorcerers, and idolaters,
and all liars,
shall have their part in
the lake which burneth
with fire and brimstone:
which is the second death.

9. And there came unto me
one of the seven angels
which had the seven vials full of the
seven last plagues, and
talked with me,
saying, Come hither,

I will shew thee the bride, the Lamb's wife. 10. And he carried me away in the spirit to a great and high mountain, and shewed me that great city, the holy Jerusalem, descending out of heaven from God, 11. Having the glory of God: and her light was like unto a stone most precious, even like a jasper stone, clear as crystal; 12. And had a wall great and high, and had twelve gates, and at the gates twelve angels, and names written thereon, which are the names of the twelve tribes of the children of Israel: 13. On the east three gates; on the north three gates; on the south three gates; and on the west three gates. 14. And the wall of the city had twelve foundations, and in them the names of the twelve apostles of the Lamb. 15. And he that talked with me had a golden reed to measure the city, and the gates thereof, and the wall thereof. 16. And the city lieth foursquare, and the length is as large as the breadth: and he measured the city with the reed, twelve thousand furlongs. The length and the breadth and the height of it are equal. 17. And he measured the wall thereof, an hundred and forty and four cubits, according to the measure of a man, that is, of the angel. 18. And the building of the wall of it was of jasper: and the city was pure gold, like unto clear glass. 19. And the foundations of the wall of the city were garnished with all manner of precious stones. The first foundation was jasper; the second, sapphire; the third, a chalcedony; the fourth, an emerald; 20. The fifth, sardonyx; the sixth, sardius; the seventh, chrysolyte; the eighth, beryl; the ninth, a topaz; the tenth, a chrysoprasus; the eleventh, a jacinth; the twelfth, an amethyst. 21. And the twelve gates were twelve pearls: every several gate was of one pearl: and the street of the city was pure gold, as it were transparent glass. 22. And I saw no temple therein: for the Lord God Almighty and the Lamb are the temple of it. 23. And the city had no need of the sun, neither of the moon, to shine in it: for the glory of God did lighten it, and the Lamb is the light thereof. 24. And the nations of them which are saved shall walk in the light of it: and the kings of the earth do bring their glory and honour into it. 25. And the gates of it shall not be shut at all by day: for there shall be no night there. 26. And they shall bring the glory and honour of the nations into it. 27. And there shall in no wise enter into it any thing that defileth, neither whatsoever worketh abomination, or maketh a lie: but they which are written in the Lamb's book of life.

CHAPTER 22

■ 1. **And he shewed me**
■ **a pure river of water**
■ **of life,** clear as crystal,
■ **proceeding out of**
■ **the throne of God**
■ **and of the Lamb.**
2. In the midst of the street of it,
■ **and on either side of**
■ **the river, was** *there*
■ **the tree of life,** which bare
twelve *manner of* fruits, *and* yielded
her fruit every month:
■ **and the leaves** of the tree
■ **were for the healing of**
■ **the nations.**
■ 3. **And there shall be no**
■ **more curse:** but the throne of
God and of the Lamb shall be in it;
■ **and his servants**
■ **shall serve him:**
■ 4. **And they shall see his**
■ **face; and his name shall**
■ **be in their foreheads.**
■ 5. **And there shall be no**
■ **night** there; and they need no
candle, neither light of the sun;
■ **for the Lord** God
■ **giveth** them
■ **light: and they shall**
■ **reign for ever** and ever.
6. **And he said** unto me,
■ **These sayings are** faithful and
■ **true:** and the Lord God of the holy
prophets sent his angel to shew unto
his servants the things which must
shortly be done.
■ 7. **Behold, I come**
■ **quickly: blessed is he**
■ **that keepeth** the sayings of
■ **the prophecy of this book.**
■ 8. **And I John** saw these things,
and heard *them*. And when I had
heard and seen, I
■ **fell down to worship**
before the feet of
■ **the angel**
which shewed me these things.
■ 9. **Then saith he** unto me,
■ **See thou do it not:** for I am thy
fellow servant, and of thy brethren
the prophets, and of them which
keep the sayings of this book:

■ **worship God.**
■ 10. **And he saith** unto me,
■ **Seal not** the sayings of
■ **the prophecy** of this book:
■ **for the time is at hand.**
■ 11. **He that is unjust, let him**
■ **be unjust still:** and he which is
filthy, let him be filthy still: and he that
is righteous, let him be righteous still:
■ **and he that is holy, let**
■ **him be holy still.**
■ 12. **And, behold, I come**
■ **quickly; and my reward is**
■ **with me,** to give every man
according as his work shall be.
■ 13. **I am Alpha and Omega,**
the beginning and the end, the
first and the last.
■ 14. **Blessed are they that**
■ **do his commandments,**
■ **that they** may have right to
the tree of life, and
■ **may enter** in through the gates
■ **into the city.**
15. For without *are* dogs, and
sorcerers, and whoremongers, and
murderers, and idolaters, and
whosoever loveth and maketh a lie.
■ 16. **I Jesus have sent mine**
■ **angel to testify** unto you
these things in the churches.
■ **I am the root** and the offspring
■ **of David, and the bright**
■ **and morning star.**
■ 17. **And the Spirit and the**
■ **bride say, Come.** And let him
that heareth say, Come. And let
him that is athirst come.
■ **And whosoever will, let him**
■ **take the water of life freely.**
■ 18. **For I testify** unto every man
■ **that** heareth the words of the
prophecy of this book,
■ **If any man shall add unto**
■ **these things, God shall add**
■ **unto him the plagues** that are
written
■ **in this book:**
■ 19. **And if any man**
■ **shall take away from**
the words of the book of
■ **this prophecy, God shall**
■ **take away his part out of**

■ the book of life, and out
■ of the holy city, and *from* the
things which are written in this book.
■ 20. **He** which testifieth these things
■ saith, Surely I come quickly.
■ Amen.
■ Even so, come, Lord Jesus.
21. The grace of our Lord Jesus
Christ *be* with you all.
■ Amen.